USEFUL SUBJECT INDEX TERMS

Administration
Agents
Financial operations
   Accounting
   Funding
   Payroll
   Taxes
Legal aspects
   Censorship
   Contracts
   Copyright
   Liabilities
   Regulations
Personnel
   Labor relations
Planning/operation
   Producing
Public relations
   Advertising
   Community relations
   Marketing

Audience
Audience composition
Audience-performer relationship
Audience reactions/comments

Basic theatrical documents
Choreographies
Film treatments
Librettos
Miscellaneous texts
Playtexts
Promptbooks
Scores

Design/technology
Costuming
Equipment
Lighting
Make-up
Masks
Projections
Properties
Puppets
Scenery
Sound
Technicians/crews
Wigs
   Special effects

Institutions
Institutions, associations
Institutions, producing
Institutions, research
Institutions, service
Institutions, social
Institutions, special
Institutions, training

Performance/production
Acting
Acrobatics
Aerialists
Aquatics
Animal acts
Choreography
Clowning
Dancing
Equestrian acts
Equilibrists
Instrumentalists
Juggling
Magic
Martial arts

Puppeteers
Singing
Staging
Ventriloquism

Performance spaces
Amphitheatres/arenas
Fairgrounds
Found spaces
Halls
Religious structures
Show boats
Theatres
   Auditorium
   Foyer
   Orchestra pit
   Stage,
      Adjustable
      Apron
      Arena
      Proscenium
   Support areas

Plays/librettos/scripts
Adaptations
Characters/roles
Dramatic structure
Editions
Language
Plot/subject/theme

Reference materials
Bibliographies
Catalogues
Collected Materials
Databanks
Descriptions of resources
Dictionaries
Directories
Discographies
Encyclopedias
Glossaries
Guides
Iconographies
Indexes
Lists
Videographies
Yearbooks

Relation to other fields
Anthropology
Economics
Education
Ethics
Literature
Figurative arts
Philosophy
Politics
Psychology
Religion
Sociology

Research/historiography
Methodology
Research tools

Theory/criticism
Aesthetics
Deconstruction
Dialectics
Phenomenology
Semiotics

Training
Apprenticeship
Teaching methods
   Train

INTERNATIONAL BIBLIOGRAPHY OF THEATRE: 1987

International Bibliography of Theatre: 1987

Published by the Theatre Research Data Center, Brooklyn College, City University of New York, NY 11210 USA.

© Theatre Research Data Center, 1992: ISBN 0-945419-02-3. All rights reserved.

This publication was made possible in part by grants from the National Endowment for the Humanities and the American Society for Theatre Research, by gifts from individual members of the Society and by in-kind support and services provided by Brooklyn College of the City University of New York.

The paper used in this book complies with the Permanent Paper Standard issued by the National Information Standards Organization (Z39.48-1984).

THE THEATRE RESEARCH DATA CENTER
Allen Kennedy, Assoc. Dir.

The Theatre Research Data Center at Brooklyn College houses, publishes and distributes the International Bibliography of Theatre. Inquiries about the bibliographies and the databank are welcome. Telephone (718) 780-5998; FAX (718) 951-7428; E-Mail RXWBC@CUNYVM on BITNET.

INTERNATIONAL BIBLIOGRAPHY OF THEATRE: 1987

Benito Ortolani, Editor

Catherine Hilton, Executive Editor   Margaret Loftus Ranald, Associate Editor

Rosabel Wang, Systems Analyst

Rose Bonczek, Coordinating Editor   Helen Huff, Online Editor

The University Consortium
for the
International Bibliography of Theatre

University of California
Santa Barbara

University of Guelph
Ontario

Florida State University
Tallahassee

University of Washington
Seattle

Brooklyn College
City University of New York

The International Bibliography of Theatre project is sponsored by the American Society for Theatre Research and the International Association of Libraries and Museums of the Performing Arts in cooperation with the International Federation for Theatre Research.

Theatre Research Data Center
New York 1992

QUICK ACCESS GUIDE

GENERAL

The Classed Entries are equivalent to library shelf arrangements.

The Indexes are equivalent to a library card catalogue.

SEARCH METHODS

By subject:

Look in the alphabetically arranged Subject Index for the relevant term(s), topic(s) or name(s): e.g., Staging; *Macbeth*; Shakespeare, William; etc.

Check the number at the end of each relevant précis.

Using that number, search the Classed Entries section to find full information.

By country:

Look in the Geographical-Chronological Index for the country related to the *content* of interest.

Note: Countries are arranged in alphabetical order and then subdivided chronologically.

Find the number at the end of each relevant précis.

Using that number, search the Classed Entries section to find full information.

By periods:

Determine the country of interest.

Look in the Geographical-Chronological Index, paying special attention to the chronological subdivisions.

Find the number at the end of each relevant précis.

Using that number, search the Classed Entries section to find full information.

By authors of listed books or articles:

Look in the alphabetically arranged Document Authors Index for the relevant names.

Using the number at the end of each Author Index entry, search the Classed Entries section to find full information.

SUGGESTIONS

Search a variety of possible subject headings.

Search the **most specific subject heading** first, e.g., if interested in acting in Ibsen plays, begin with Ibsen, Henrik, rather than the more generic Acting or Plays/librettos/scripts.

When dealing with large clusters of references under a single subject heading, note that items are listed in **alphabetical order of content geography** (Afghanistan to Zimbabwe). Under each country items are ordered alphabetically by author, following the same numerical sequence as that of the Classed Entries.

TABLE OF CONTENTS

PREFACE

With the advent of the IBT Consortium (five universities sharing the data collection and editing responsibilities), IBT coverage of contemporary theatre publications has broadened to include some new and other increased flows of materials from Czechoslovakia, Netherlands, Mexico, Cuba, Philippines, Korea, Japan, China and Ireland.

Editorial refinements for IBT:87 emphasize tighter control of the proliferation of subject heads and the reduction in the Classed Entries of single listings of each one of the plays in collected reviews of plays.

A finding list for periodical titles has been added to facilitate relating titles to acronyms. The finding list is simply an alphabetical listing of periodicals by title, each accompanied by its assigned acronym. Further information about a particular title will be found in the periodicals list.

ACKNOWLEDGMENTS

We are grateful to the many institutions and individuals who have helped us make this volume possible:

The participating officers, faculty and staff members of the University Consortium institutions:

> Brooklyn College: Provost Christoph Kimmich; Professor Benito Ortolani;

> Florida State University: Dean Gil Lazier, Professor John Degen;

> University of California, Santa Barbara: Professor Simon Williams, Graduate Assistant Victoria Gilbert;

> University of Guelph, Ontario: Vice President Leonard W. Conolly, Reference Librarian Helen Salmon;

> University of Washington, Seattle: Professor Barry Witham, Drama Librarian Liz Fugate, Graduate Assistant Charlotte Canning;

Other University Consortium associates:

> Professor Joseph Donohue, University of Massachusettes, Amherst, Chair, and the late Professor Emeritus Thomas F. Marshall, Kent State University, of the Consortium Council Board;

> Professor Emeritus Irving M. Brown, Brooklyn College, Consultant to the Consortium;

President Oscar Pausch and the International Bibliography Commission of SIBMAS:

> Heinrich Huesmann, Deutches Theatermuseum, Munich, Chair; Hedvig Belitska-Scholtz, National Széchényi Library, Budapest; Rainer Köppl, University of Vienna; Paul Ulrich, Berlin Public Library; and Gerhard Heldt, University of Munich;

President Wolfgang Greisenegger and the University Commission of FIRT;

Hedwig Belitska-Scholtz, National Széchényi Library, Budapest;

Stephen Butler, Alliance of Resident Theatres/New York, New York;

Marvin Carlson, Graduate Center, City University of New York;

Elaine Fadden, Kennedy School Library, Harvard University;

Arturo García Giménez, Institut del Teatre, Barcelona;

William Gargan, Brooklyn College Library, City University of New York;

Cécile Giteau, Bibliotèque Nationale, Paris;

Benjamin S. Klein and Pat Reber, CUNY/University Computer Center;

Tamara Il. Lapteva, Lenin State Library, Moscow;

Lindsay Newman, Univ. of Lancaster Library, and the SIBMAS of Great Britain;

Louis Rachow, International Theatre Institute, New York;

Jane Rosenberg, Division of Research Programs, National Endowment for the Humanities;

Jarmila Svobodová, Theatre Institute, Prague, Czechoslovakia;

Alessandro Tinterri, Museo Biblioteca dell'Attore di Genova;

Zbigniew Wilski, Polska Akademia Nauk, Warsaw.

And we thank our field bibliographers whose contributions have made this work a reality:

Jerry Bangham	Alcorn State Univ., Lorman, MS
Thomas L. Berger	St. Lawrence Univ., Canton, NY
Helen Bickerstaff	University of Sussex Library, UK
Magnus Blomkvist	Stockholm Univ. Bibliotek
Magdolna Both	National Széchényi Library, Budapest
David F. Cheshire	Middlesex Polytechnic Library, UK
Nancy Copeland	University of Toronto, ON
Clifford O. Davidson	Western Michigan Univ., Kalamazoo, MI
Linda Dolben	Central School of Speech and Drama, London
Angela M. Douglas	Central School of Speech and Drama, London
Angela Eder	Institute für Theaterwissenchaft, Vienna
Veronika Eger	National Széchényi Library, Budapest
Angela Escott	Royal College of Music Library, UK
Dorothy Faulkner	Dartington College of Arts, Devon
Mari Kathleen Fielder	Glenside, PA
Gabriele Fischborn	Theaterhochschule Hans Otto, Leipzig
Linda Fitzsimmons	Univ. of Bristol, UK
Marion J. Fordom	Library, Royal Scottish Academy, Music and Drama
David P. Gates	Univ. of Western Ontario, London, ON
Stephen H. Gale	Kentucky State University, KY
Donatella Giuliano	Civico Museo Biblioteca dell'Attore, Genoa
Carmen Sáez González	Institute del Teatre, Barcelona
Carol Goodger-Hill	Univ. of Guelph, ON
Temple Hauptfleisch	Univ. of Stellenbosch, Rep. of South Africa
Frank S. Hook	Lehigh Univ., Bethlehem, PA
Claire Hudson	Theatre Museum, London
Robert Jordan	Univ. of New South Wales, Australia
Rainer Maria Köppl	Institut für Theaterwissenschaft, Vienna
Danuta Kźnicka	Polska Akademia Nauk, Warsaw
Felicity Lander	Roehampton Institute of Higher Education, London
Nicole Leclercq	Archives et Musée de la Littérature ASBL
Ted Little	University of Guelph, ON
Tamotsu Matsuda	Nishogakusha Univ., Japan
Clair Myers	Elon College, Elon, NC
Bill Nelson	Carnegie-Mellon Univ., Pittsburgh
Lauren Nesbitt	Univ. of Guelph, ON
Andrea Nouryeh	St. Lawrence University, Canton, NY
Jennifer Preston	Hamilton, ON
Elizabeth Rae	Puslinch, ON
Margaret Loftus Ranald	Queens College, City Univ. of New York
Maarten A. Reilingh	McNeese State Univ., LA
Jörg Ryser	Schweizerische Theatersammlung, Bern
Marilyn Smith	Granby, MA
Rina Varley	Univ. of Guelph, ON
Daniel Watermeier	Univ. of Toledo, OH
David Whitton	Univ. of Lancaster, UK

and the many students in the graduate Theatre History and Research and Bibliography courses at Brooklyn College, CUNY.

A GUIDE FOR USERS

SCOPE OF THE BIBLIOGRAPHY

Materials Included

The *International Bibliography of Theatre: 1987* lists theatre books, book articles, dissertations, journal articles and miscellaneous other theatre documents published during 1987. It also includes items from prior years received too late for inclusion in earlier volumes. Published works (with the exceptions noted below) are included without restrictions on the internal organization, format, or purpose of those works. Materials selected for the Bibliography deal with any aspect of theatre significant to research, without historical, cultural or geographical limitations. Entries are drawn from theatre histories, essays, studies, surveys, conference papers and proceedings, catalogues of theatrical holdings of any type, portfolios, handbooks and guides, dictionaries, bibliographies, thesauruses and other reference works, records and production documents.

Materials Excluded

Reprints of previously published works are usually excluded unless they are major documents which have been unavailable for some time. In general only references to newly published works are included, though significantly revised editions of previously published works are treated as new works. Purely literary scholarship is generally excluded, since it is already listed in established bibliographical instruments. An exception is made for material published in journals completely indexed by *IBT*. Studies in theatre literature, textual studies, and dissertations are represented only when they contain significant components that examine or have relevance to theatrical performance.

Playtexts are excluded unless they are published with extensive or especially noteworthy introductory material, or when the text is the first translation or adaptation of a classic from especially rare language into a major language. Book reviews and reviews of performances are not included, except for those reviews of sufficient scope to constitute a review article, or clusters of reviews published under one title.

Language

There is no restriction on language in which theatre documents appear, but English is the primary vehicle for compiling and abstracting the materials. The Subject Index gives primary importance to titles in their original languages, transliterated into the Roman Alphabet where necessary. Original language titles also appear in Classed Entries that refer to plays in translation and in the précis of Subject Index items.

CLASSED ENTRIES

Content

The **Classed Entries** section contains one entry for each document analyzed and provides the user with complete information on all material indexed in this volume. It is the only place where publication citations may be found and where detailed abstracts are furnished. Users are advised to familiarize themselves with the elements and structure of the Taxonomy to simplify the process of locating items indexed in the **classed entries** section.

Organization

Entries follow the order provided in Columns I, II and III of the Taxonomy.

Column I classifies theatre into nine categories beginning with Theatre in General and thereafter listed alphabetically from "Dance" to "Puppetry." Column II divides most of the nine Column I categories into a number of subsidiary components. Column III headings relate any of the previously selected Column I and Column II categories to specific elements of the theatre. A list of Useful Subject Index Terms is also given (see frontpapers). These terms are also sub-components of the Column III headings.

Examples:

Items classified under "Theatre in General" appear in the Classed Entries before those classified under "Dance" in Column I, etc.

Items classified under the Column II heading of "Musical theatre" appear before those classified under the Column II heading of "Opera," etc.

Items further classified under the Column III heading of "Administration" appear before those classified under "Design/technology," etc.

Every group of entries under any of the divisions of the **Classed Entries** is printed in alphabetical order according to its content geography: e.g., a cluster of items concerned with plays related to Spain, classified under "Drama" (Column I) and "Plays/librettos/scripts" (Column III) would be printed together after items concerned with plays related to South Africa and before those related to Sweden. Within these country clusters, each group of entries is arranged alphabetically by author.

Relation to Subject Index

When in doubt concerning the appropriate Taxonomy category for a **Classed Entry** search, the user should refer to the **Subject Index** for direction. The **Subject Index** provides several points of access for each entry in the **Classed Entries** section. In most cases it is advisable to use the **Subject Index** as the first and main way to locate the information contained in the **Classed Entries**.

TAXONOMY TERMS

The following descriptions have been established to clarify the terminology used in classifying entries according to the Taxonomy. They are used for clarification only, as a searching tool for users of the Bibliography. In cases where clarification has been deemed unnecessary (as in the case of "Ballet", "*Kabuki*", "Film", etc.) no further description appears below. Throughout the Classed Entries, the term "General" distinguishes miscellaneous items that cannot be more specifically classified by the remaining terms in the Column II category. Sufficient subject headings enables users to locate items regardless of their taxonomical classification.

THEATRE IN GENERAL: Only for items which cannot be properly classified by categories "Dance" through "Puppetry," or for items related to more than one theatrical category.

DANCE: Only for items published in theatre journals that are indexed by *IBT*, or for dance items with relevance to theatre.

DANCE-DRAMA: Items related to dramatic genres where dance is the dominant artistic element. Used primarily for specific forms of non-Western theatre, e.g., *Kathakali, Nō.*

DRAMA: Items related to playtexts and performances where the spoken word is traditionally considered the dominant element. (i.e., all Western dramatic literature and all spoken drama everywhere). An article on acting as a discipline will also fall into this category, as well as books about directing, unless these endeavors are more closely related to musical theatre forms or other genres.

MEDIA: Only for media related-items published in theatre journals completely indexed by *IBT*, or for media items with relevance to theatre.

MIME: Items related to performances where mime is the dominant element. This category comprises all forms of mime from every epoch and/or country.

PANTOMIME: Both Roman Pantomime and the performance form epitomized in modern times by Étienne Decroux and Marcel Marceau. English pantomime is indexed under "Mixed Entertainment."

MIXED ENTERTAINMENT: Items related either 1) to performances consisting of a variety of performance elements among which none is considered dominant, or 2) to performances where the element of spectacle and the function of broad audience appeal are dominant. Because of the great variety of terminology in different circumstances, times, and countries for similar types of spectacle, such items as café-concert, quadrille réaliste, one-man-shows, night club acts, pleasure gardens, tavern concerts, night cellars, saloons, Spezialitätentheater, storytelling, divertissement, rivistina, etc., are classified under "General", "Variety acts", or "Cabaret", etc. depending on time period, circumstances, and/or country.

Variety acts: Items related to variety entertainment of mostly unconnected "numbers", including some forms of vaudeville, revue, petite revue, intimate revue, burlesque, etc.

PUPPETRY: Items related to all kinds of puppets, marionettes and mechanically operated figures.

N.B.: Notice that entries related to individuals are classified according to the Column III category describing the individual's primary field of activity: e.g., a manager under "Administration," a set designer under "Design/technology," an actor under "Performance/production," a playwright under "Plays/librettos/scripts," a teacher under "Training," etc.

CITATION FORMS

Basic bibliographical information

Each citation includes the standard bibliographical information: author(s), title, publisher, pages, and notes, preface, appendices, etc., when present. Journal titles are usually given in the form of an acronym, whose corresponding title may be found in the **List of Periodicals**. Pertinent publication information is also provided in this list.

Translation of original language

When the play title is not in English, a translation in parentheses follows the original title. Established English translations of play titles or names of institutions are used when they exist. Names of institutions, companies, buildings, etc., unless an English version is in common use, are as a rule left untranslated. Geographical names are given in standard English form as defined by *Webster's New Geographical Dictionary* (1984).

Time and place

An indication of the time and place to which a document pertains is included wherever appropriate and possible. The geographical information refers usually to a country, sometimes to a larger region such as Europe or English-speaking countries. The geographical designation is relative to the time of the content: Russia is used before 1917, USSR to 1991; East and West Germany 1945-1990; Roman Empire until its official demise, Italy thereafter. When appropriate, precise dates related to the content of the item are given. Otherwise the decade or century is indicated.

Abstract

Unless the content of a document is made sufficiently clear by the title, the classed entry provides a brief abstract. Titles of plays not in English are given in English translation in the abstract, except for most operas and titles that are widely known in their original language. If the original title does not appear in the document title, it is provided in the abstract.

Spelling

English form is used for transliterated personal names. In the **Subject Index** each English spelling refers the users to the international or transliterated spelling under which all relevant entries are listed.

Varia

Affiliation with a movement and influence by or on individuals or groups is indicated only when the document itself suggests such information.

When a document belongs to more than one Column I category of the Taxonomy, the other applicable Column I categories are cross-referenced in the **Subject Index**.

Document treatment

"Document treatment" indicates the type of scholarly approach used in the writing of the document. The following terms are used in the present bibliography:

Bibliographical studies treat as their primary subject bibliographic material.

Biographical studies are articles on part of the subject's life.

Biographies are book-length treatments of entire lives.

Critical studies present an evaluation resulting from the application of criteria.

Empirical research identifies studies that incorporate as part of their design an experiment or series of experiments.

Historical studies designate accounts of individual events, groups, movements, institutions, etc., whose primary purpose is to provide a historical record or evaluation.

Histories-general cover the whole spectrum of theatre—or most of it—over a period of time and typically appear in one or several volumes.

Histories-specific cover a particular genre, field, or component of theatre over a period of time and usually are published as a book.

Histories-sources designate source materials that provide an internal evaluation or account of the treated subject: e.g. interviews with theatre professionals.

Histories-reconstruction attempt to reconstruct some aspect of the theatre.

Instructional materials include textbooks, manuals, guides or any other publication to be used in teaching.

Reviews of performances examine one or several performances in the format of review articles, or clusters of several reviews published under one title.

Technical studies examine theatre from the point of view of the applied sciences or discuss particular theatrical techniques.

Textual studies examine the texts themselves for origins, accuracy, and publication data.

Example with diagram

Here follows an example (in this case a book article) of a **Classed Entries** item with explanation of its elements:

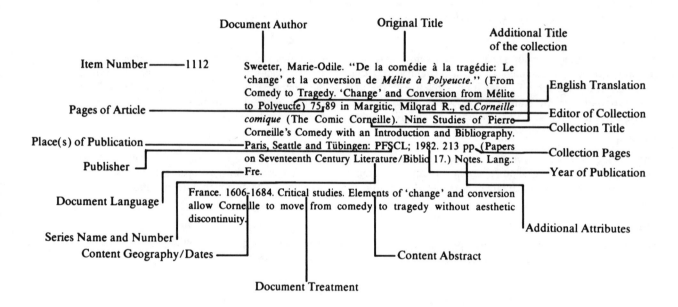

SUBJECT INDEX

Function

The **Subject Index** is a primary means of access to the major aspects of documents referenced by the **Classed Entries**.

Content

Each **Subject Index** item contains
- (a) subject headings, e.g., names of persons, names of institutions, forms and genres of theatre, elements of the theatre arts, titles of plays.
- (b) column III category indicating primary focus of the entry
- (c) short abstracts describing the items of the **Classed Entries** related to the subject heading
- (d) content country, city, time and language of document
- (e) the number of the **Classed Entry** from which each Subject Index item was generated.

Standards

Names of persons, including titles of address, are listed alphabetically by last names according to the standard established in *Anglo-American Cataloguing Rules* (Library of Congress, 2nd edition, 1978).

All names and terms originating in non-Roman alphabets, including Russian, Greek, Chinese and Japanese have been transliterated and are listed by the transliterated forms.

Geographical names are spelled according to *Webster's Geographical Dictionary* (1984).

"SEE" references direct users from common English spellings or titles to names or terms indexed in a less familiar manner.

Example:

Chekhov, Anton
SEE
Čechov, Anton Pavlovič

Individuals are listed in the Subject Index when:

- (a) they are the primary or secondary focus of the document;
- (b) the document addresses aspects of their lives and/or work in a primary or supporting manner;
- (c) they are the author of the document, but only when their life and/or work is also the document's primary focus;
- (d) their lives have influenced, or have been influenced by, the primary subject of the document or the writing of it, as evidenced by explicit statement in the document.

This Subject Index is particularly useful when a listed individual is the subject of numerous citations. In such cases a search should not be limited only to the main subject heading (e.g., Shakespeare). A more relevant one (e.g., *Hamlet*) could bring more specific results.

"SEE" References

Institutions, groups, and social or theatrical movements appear as subject headings, following the above criteria. Names of theatre companies, theatre buildings, etc. are given in their original languages or transliterated. "See" references are provided for the generally used or literally translated English terms;

Example: "Moscow Art Theatre" directs users to the company's original title:

Moscow Art Theatre
SEE
Moskovskij Chudožestvennyj Akedemičeskij Teat'r

No commonly used English term exists for "Comédie-Française," it therefore appears only under its title of origin. The same is true for *commedia dell'arte*, Burgtheater and other such terms.

Play titles appear in their original languages, with "SEE" references next to their English translations. Subject headings for plays in a third language may be provided if the translation in that language is of unusual importance.

Widely known opera titles are not translated.

Similar subject headings

Subject headings such as "Politics" and "Political theatre" are neither synonymous nor mutually exclusive. They aim to differentiate between a phenomenon and a theatrical genre. Likewise, such terms as "Feminism" refer to social and cultural movements and are not intended to be synonymous with "Women in theatre." The term "Ethnic theatre" is used to classify any type of theatrical literature or performance where the ethnicity of those concerned is of primary importance. Because of the number of items, and for reasons of accessibility, "Black theatre," "Native American theatre" and the theatre of certain other ethnic groups are given separate subject headings.

Groups/movements, periods, etc.

Generic subject headings such as "Victorian theatre," "Expressionism," etc., are only complementary to other more specific groupings and do not list all items in the bibliography related to that period or generic subject: e.g., the subject heading "Elizabethan theatre" does not list a duplicate of all items related to Shakespeare, which are to be found under "Shakespeare," but lists materials explicitly related to the actual physical conditions or style of presentation typical of the Elizabethan theatre. For a complete search according to periods, use the **Geographical-Chronological Index**, searching by country and by the years related to the period.

Subdivision of Subject Headings

Each subject heading is subdivided into Column III categories that identify the primary focus of the cited entry. These subcategories are intended to facilitate the user when searching under such broad terms as "Black theatre" or "*King Lear.*" The subcategory helps to identify the relevant cluster of entries. Thus, for instance, when the user is interested only in Black theatre companies, the subheading "Institutions" groups all the relevant items together. Similarly, the subheading "Performance/production" groups together all the items dealing with production aspects of *King Lear.* It is, however, important to remember that these subheadings (i.e. Column III categories) are not subcategories of the subject heading itself, but of the main subject matter treated in the entry.

Printing order

Short abstracts under each subject heading are listed according to Column III categories. These Column categories are organized alphabetically. Short abstracts within each cluster, on the other hand, are arranged sequentially according to the item number they refer to in the Classed Entries. This enables the frequent user to recognize immediately the location and classification of the entry. If the user cannot find one specific subject heading, a related term may suffice, e.g., for Church dramas, see Religion. In some cases, a "SEE" reference is provided.

Example with diagram

Here follows an example of a **Subject Index** entry with explanation of its elements:

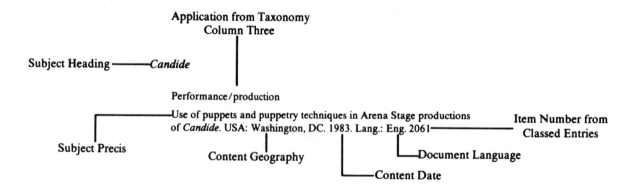

GEOGRAPHICAL-CHRONOLOGICAL INDEX

Organization

The **Geographical-Chronological Index** is arranged alphabetically by the country relevant to the subject or topic treated. The references under each country are then subdivided by date. References to articles with contents of the same date are then listed according to their category in the Taxonomy's Column III. The last item in each Geographical-Chronological Index listing is the number of the Classed Entry from which the listing was generated.

Example: For material on Drama in Italy between World Wars I and II, look under Italy, 1918-1939. In the example below, entries 2734, 2227 and 891 match this description.

Italy — cont'd		
1907-1984.	**Theory/criticism.**	
	Cruelty and sacredness in contemporary theatre poetics. Germany. France. Lang.: Ita.	2734
1914.	**Plays/librettos/scripts.**	
	Comparative study of *Francesca da Rimini* by Riccardo Zandonai and *Tristan und Isolde* by Richard Wagner. Lang.: Eng.	3441
1920-1936.	**Plays/librettos/scripts.**	
	Introductory analysis of twenty-one of Pirandello's plays Lang.: Eng.	2227
1923-1936.	**Institutions.**	
	History of Teatro degli Indipendenti. Rome. Lang.; Ita.	891
1940-1984.	**Performance/production.**	
	Italian tenor Giuseppe Giacomini speaks of his career and art. New York, NY. Lang.; Eng.	3324

Dates

Dates reflect the content period covered by the item, not the publication year. However, the publication year is used for theoretical writings and for assessments of old traditions, problems, etc. When precise dates cannot be established, the decade (e.g., 1970-1979) or the century (e.g., 1800-1899) is given.

Biographies and histories

In the case of biographies of people who are still alive, the year of birth of the subject and the year of publication of the biography are given. The same criterion is followed for histories of institutions such as theatres or companies which are still in existence. The founding date of beginning of such institutions and the date of publication of the entry are given - unless the entry explicitly covers only a specific period of the history of the institution.

Undatable content

No dates are given when the content is either theoretical or not meaningfully definable in time. Entries without date(s) print first.

DOCUMENT AUTHORS INDEX

The term "Document Author" means the author of the article or book cited in the **Classed Entries**. The author of the topic under discussion, e.g., Molière in an article about one of his plays, is *not* found in the **Document Authors Index**. (See Subject Index).

The **Document Authors Index** lists these authors alphabetically and in the Roman alphabet. The numbers given after each name direct the researcher to the full citations in the Classed Entries section.

N.B.: Users are urged to familiarize themselves with the Taxonomy and the indexes provided. The four-way access to research sources possible through consultation of the Classed Entries section, the Subject Index, the Geographical-Chronological Index and the Document Authors Index is intended to be sufficient to locate even the most highly specialized material.

CLASSED ENTRIES

THEATRE IN GENERAL

1   Cook, Philip. *How to Enjoy Theatre.* Loughton, Essex: Piatkus; 1983. 192 pp. Index. Notes. Gloss. Illus.: Photo. Dwg. Sketches. Diagram. Fr.Elev. Grd.Plan. 35. Lang.: Eng.
Europe. 500 B.C.-1983 A.D. Histories-general. ■Popular history of theatre from ancient Greece to contemporary stage. Analysis of components of theatre including roles of theatre artists, genres, production and playwriting.

Administration

2   Parsons, Philip, ed. *Shooting the Pianist: The Role of Government in the Arts.* Sydney: Currency; 1987. 152 pp. Lang.: Eng.
Australia. 1986. Histories-sources. ■Record of a one-day seminar held in response to, and protest of, the McLeay Report, a government paper on arts policy. Contains background essays, transcripts of speeches and debates, all concerned with the implications of the paper for the theatre, or with the broader issues of government and the arts.

3   Jaumain, Michel. "Le secteur théâtral de la Communauté Française de Belgique: Activité, audience, flux économique pour la saison 1985/1986." (The Theatrical Field in Belgium's French Community: Activity, Audience and the Financial Stream for the 1985/1986 Season.) 213-235 in *Annuaire du spectacle de la Communauté Française de Belgique 1985-1986.* Bruxelles: Archives et Musée de la Littérature; 1987. 258 pp. Illus.: Graphs. 31. Lang.: Fre.
Belgium. 1985-1986. Historical studies. ■Description of the theatre as a part of the economic sphere, with products, consumers and financial streams.

4   Nayer, André; Capiau, Suzanne. *Droit social et fiscal des artistes.* (Artists' Tax and Social Rights.) Brussels/Liège: Mardaga; 1987. 515 pp. (Création et communication.) Lang.: Fre.
Belgium. 1900-1987. Historical studies. ■An attempt to define the status of artists (writers, filmmakers, actors, dancers, musicians, etc.) with respect to the law: contracts, copyright, unemployment, taxation.

5   Toronto Theatre Alliance. "Preliminary Report on Toronto Small Theatres." *CTR.* 1987 Sum; 51: 41. Lang.: Eng.
Canada: Toronto, ON. 1987. Critical studies. ■Early census results outline the economic realities of the small theatre company. Report addresses issues such as budget and source financing, cost of production and actors' salaries.

6   Bouzek, Don. "In the Neighborhood of My Heart." *CTR.* 1987 Win; 53: 20-25. Illus.: Photo. Print. B&W. 5. [Meanwhile in Toronto.../1.] Lang.: Eng.
Canada: Toronto, ON. 1987. Historical studies. ■Ground Zero Theatre Company's thirteen-step account of their alternative theatre project for the homeless. A multi-media approach using live theatre and videotape. Related to Media: Mixed media.

7   Burgess, David. "When Cowboys Are Ranchers." *CTR.* 1987 Sum; 51: 36-41. Illus.: Photo. Print. B&W. 6. Lang.: Eng.
Canada: Toronto, ON. 1987. Critical studies. ■Critical analysis of the reasons behind the merger between CentreStage and Toronto Free Theatre. Mandate of the 'new and improved' company is examined in terms of theory and practice, with projected audience dominating the article.

8   Gerson, Mark. "Festival Lennoxville: A Victim of Circumstances." *PAC.* 1982 Fall; 19(3): 36-38. Illus.: Photo. Print. B&W. 4. Lang.: Eng.
Canada: Lennoxville, PQ. 1982. Historical studies. ■A discussion of the abrupt closing of Festival Lennoxville in the face of outstanding debts— a consideration of its successes and problems.

9   Hirsch, John. "Exit John Hirsch." *PAC.* 1985 Sep.; 22(3): 39-41, 64. Illus.: Photo. Print. B&W. 1. Lang.: Eng.
Canada: Stratford, ON. 1947-1985. Histories-sources. ■Excerpts from a speech delivered by John Hirsch during the lecture series at Stratford, presented to mark his departure from the Stratford Festival.

10   Macduff, Pierre. "Le projet de loi c-54 sur la pornographie: une menace potentielle pour les arts." (Draft Bill C-54 on Pornography: A Potential Threat to the Arts.) *JCT.* 1987; 45: 10-12. Illus.: Photo. Print. B&W. 1. Lang.: Fre.
Canada: Quebec, PQ. 1985-1988. Historical studies. ■The proposed federal censorship legislation could be a problem for theatre and for actors.

11   MacLean, Sally-Beth. "REED Present and Future." *REEDN.* 1987; 12(1): 1-2. Lang.: Eng.
Canada: Toronto, ON. 1987. Historical studies. ■Discusses the continuing need for and response to a request by Records of Early English Drama for letters of protest regarding a severe cutback in its funding by the Social Sciences and Humanities Research Council of Canada.

12   Paquet, Marion A.; Ralston, Rory; Cardinal, Donna. *A Handbook for Cultural Trustees.* Waterloo, ON: Univ. of Waterloo; 1987. 75 pp. Lang.: Eng.
Canada. Technical studies. ■Guide to the role, responsibilities and functions of boards of trustees of cultural organizations in Canada.

13   Patterson, Tom; Gould, Allan. *First Stage: The Making of the Stratford Festival.* Toronto, ON: McClelland Stewart; 1987. 224 pp. Illus.: Photo. Lang.: Eng.
Canada: Stratford, ON. 1952-1953. Histories-sources. ■Tom Patterson's reminiscences of the eighteen months preceding the opening of the first Stratford Festival in 1953.

14   Peterson, Michel. "Le bénévolat au théâtre: un concours obligé." (Volunteers in Theatre: A Necessary Cooperation.) *JCT.* 1987; 42: 135-139. 2. Lang.: Fre.
Canada: Montreal, PQ. 1987. Histories-sources. ■Interview with Madeleine Rivest and her role as coordinator of volunteers for the Maison Théâtre, which presents children's theatre.

15   Porter, Deborah. "The Grants Race: A Look at the Feedbag." *Theatrum.* 1987 Fall/Win; 8: 30-34. Illus.: Dwg. 1. Lang.: Eng.

CLASSED ENTRIES

THEATRE IN GENERAL: —Administration

Canada: Toronto, ON. 1987. Historical studies. ■Discusses the impact of project grants from various levels of government on Toronto's small theatre community.

16   Smith, Patricia Keeney. "John Hirsch at Stratford: Nurturing New Growth." *PAC*. 1982 Spr; 19(1): 39-42. Illus.: Photo. B&W. 1. Lang.: Eng.
Canada: Stratford, ON. 1982. Biographical studies. ■A profile of the new artistic director of the Stratford Festival and his plans for the 1982 season.

17   Smith, Patricia Keeney. "Theatre Boards and the Business of Art." *PAC*. 1982 Sum; 19(2): 22-26. B&W. 4. Lang.: Eng.
Canada: Toronto, ON, Halifax, NS. 1982. Histories-sources. ■A survey of the thoughts of various artistic directors, including John Neville of the Neptune Theatre (Halifax) and Marion André of Theatre Plus (Toronto), on the ideal composition of a board of directors.

18   Wachtel, Eleanor. "That's Entertainment." *BooksC*. 1984 Apr.; 13(4): 3-5. Lang.: Eng.
Canada: Vancouver, BC. 1983-1984. Historical studies. ■The Jesse Richardson Theatre Awards of 1983 served to reward local talent, especially the Arts Club Theatre. Perception that theatre in Vancouver lacks a sense of direction and a group of local drama critics.

19   Wallace, Robert. "Competition." *CTR*. 1987 Sum; 51: 3. Illus.: Photo. Print. B&W. 1. Lang.: Eng.
Canada. 1987. Critical studies. ■Critical analysis of the concept and practice of the Canadian theatre awards system suggests that awards institutionalize competition in Canadian theatre.

20   Wilson, Ann. "A Jury of Her Peers." *CTR*. 1987 Sum; 51: 4-8. Notes. Illus.: Photo. Print. B&W. 4. Lang.: Eng.
Canada. 1987. Critical studies. ■Analysis of the Canada Council, a Canadian government funding agency: its origins, strengths and weaknesses.

21   Burling, William J. "Theophilus Cibber and the Experimental Summer Season of 1723 at Drury Lane." *THSt*. 1987; 7: 3-11. Notes. Append. Lang.: Eng.
England: London. 1723. Historical studies. ■A highly innovative season: details about casting, production, play selection and summer theatrical practice in 18th century London theatre.

22   Milhous, Judith; Hume, Robert D. "Charles Killigrew's Petition about the Master of the Revels' Power as Censor (1715)." *TN*. 1987; 41(2): 74-79. Notes. Lang.: Eng.
England: London. 1662-1737. Historical studies. ■Role of the Master of the Revels as censor. Drury Lane Theatre's defiance of controls resulted in more oppressive licensing.

23   Sawyer, Paul. *Christopher Rich of Drury Lane: The Biography of a Theatre Manager.* Langham, MD: UP of America; 1986. 136 pp. Index. Notes. Biblio. Lang.: Eng.
England: London. 1647-1715. Biographies. ■Biography of English theatre manager Christopher Rich. Includes newly discovered information.

24   *Osobennosti social'no-ékonomičeskogo i pravovogo položenija artistov-ispolnitelej v razvityh kapitalističeskih stranah.* (Peculiarities of the Socioeconomic and Legal Situation of Performing Artists in Capitalist Countries.) Kul'tura i iskusstvo za rubežom. Moscow: Gosudarstvennaja Biblioteka im. V.I. Lenina; 1987. 20 pp. (Zreliščnije iskusstva: Express-informacija 2.) Lang.: Rus.
Europe. 1987. Historical studies.

25   Ginsburg, Jane C. "Reforms and Innovations Regarding Authors' and Performers' Rights in France: Commentary on the Law of July 3, 1985." *JAML*. 1985 Fall; 10(1): 83-117. Notes. Lang.: Eng.
France: Paris. 1957-1985. Histories-sources. ■Highlights and summary of new French law which introduces major reforms and additions to the copyright act of 1957. New provisions introduced for computer software, royalties for home videotaping, neighboring rights.

26   Dillenz, Walter. "What Is and to Which End Do We Engage in Copyright." *ColJL&A*. 1987 Fall; 12(1): 1-29. Notes. Lang.: Eng.

Germany. USA. 1930-1987. Historical studies. ■Copyright issues and international copyright conventions.

27   Megyeri, László. "A bűvös pénzmaradvány összetevői és manipulálása." (The Components and Manipulation of the Magic Money Cure.) *Sz*. 1987 Aug.; 20(8): 43-48. Tables. Illus.: Photo. B&W. 4. Lang.: Hun.
Hungary: Budapest. 1979-1987. Critical studies. ■Review of the economic conditions and economy, as well as the state subvention of the Hungarian theatres, on the basis of data from 13 Budapest theatres.

28   Papa, Velia. "La politique théâtrale des institutions publiques par rapport au développement d'un théâtre de recherche: Quelques notes à partir du cas italien." (Theatrical Policy of Public Institutions in Relation to the Development of Research Theatre: Some Remarks Concerning Italy.) 135-144 in Coca, Jordi, ed.; Conesa, Laura, comp. *Congrés Internacional de Teatre a Catalunya 1985. Actes. Volum III., Seccions 4, 5 i 6.* Barcelona: Institut del Teatre; 1987. 302 pp. [Section 5: Policy and Legislation.] Lang.: Fre.
Italy. 1970-1985. Historical studies. ■Theatre subsidies of the Italian government: at first quantity (of shows, audience, cities) was rewarded. In the 1970s companies without vertical hierarchy and regional government agencies appeared. The present policy is characterized by decentralization.

29   Ham, Gung-Heon; Yun, Cho-Pyeong; Lee, Yurina. "Kong Yeon Ye Sul ni Cheo Chak Kwan Peop Mun Che." (The Problem of Copyright Law in the Performing Arts.) *KTR*. 1987 June; 6(2): 12-21. Lang.: Kor.
Korea: Seoul. 1980-1987. Critical studies. ■Influence of copyright on the performing arts. Proposed solution to the problem.

30   Kim, Mido. "Tong-Yang Kuk Chang ui Seal Rip Kwa Un Yeong." (The Foundation and Management of Tong-Yang Theatre.) *KTR*. 1987 May; 5(2): 12-26. Lang.: Kor.
Korea: Seoul. 1935-1945. Historical studies. ■Management of Tong-Yang Kuk Chang, the first commercial theatre in Korea, and its resident companies.

31   Kwan, Yeong-Seong; Cho, Yo-Han; Yu, Chae-Chan; Park, Cho-Yeal; Ahu, Mim-Soo. "Pyohyean ui chayu, ku Jsang kwa Hankye." (The Ideal of Freedom of Expression and its Limitation.) *KTR*. 1987 Sep.(2): 14-32. Lang.: Kor.
Korea. 1987. Critical studies. ■Censorship and the freedom of artistic expression in terms of constitutional law, artistic philosophy and sociology.

32   Lee, Dan. "Ji'bang Yŏnguk ui Hyin'sil." (The Current State of Regional Theatre in Korea.) 173-176 in Seoul P'yongnon'ga Group, ed. *Han'guk Yŏnguk kwa Chŏlmon Üislk.* Mineum SA: Park. Maznegho; 1979. 262 pp. Notes. Lang.: Kor.
Korea. 1970-1979. Historical studies. ■Discussion of activation of local theatre.

33   Blokdijk, Tom. "Het verstikkende motief." (The Suffocating Motive.) *Toneel*. 1987 June; 6(4): 35-38. Illus.: Dwg. 5. Lang.: Dut.
Netherlands. 1987. Histories-sources. ■Review of mini-conference and Blokdijk's opening speech held by Instituut voor Theateronderzoek (Institute for Theatre Research) about funding for smaller and beginning theatre groups and the methods and difficulties of financing them.

34   Goesbloed, Loes. "Verslaafd aan Toneel." (Addicted to Theatre.) *Toneel*. 1987 Apr.; 4(4): 13. Illus.: Photo. B&W. 1. Lang.: Dut.
Netherlands. 1987. Histories-sources. ■Interview with Hans Kemna, first casting director to be associated with a repertory company. His casting work in film and TV. Related to Media: Video forms.

35   Jehoram, Herman Cohen. "Battles Over Agreements Concerning Simultaneous Cable Distribution of Broadcasting Programs in the Netherlands." *ColJL&A*. 1987 Spr; 11(3): 441-447. Notes. Lang.: Eng.

THEATRE IN GENERAL: —Administration

Netherlands. 1981-1987. Historical studies. ■History of conflict, government theory of double payment, analysis of court cases, model agreements.

36 Mielart, Alice. "Schouwburgen en theaterwerkplaatsen." (Presenting Organizations and Theatre Companies.) *Toneel.* 1987 May; 5(5): 18-22. Illus.: Photo. Dwg. B&W. 3. Lang.: Dut.

Netherlands. 1987. Critical studies. ■Comparative look at the large presenting organizations versus the smaller theatre groups that produce their own works. Differences in fare, funding and marketing.

37 Vos, Nico. "Crisisbeheersing of Toneel beleid?" (Crisis Management or Theatre Management?)*Toneel.* 1987 May; 5(4): 45-48 . Illus.: Photo. Dwg. 3. Lang.: Dut.

Netherlands. 1987. Historical studies. ■Government subsidy policies together with a list of currently available subsidies.

38 Raszewski, Zbigniew. "Warszawski afisz dzienny. Teatr Narodowy i jego kontynuacje (1765-1915)." (Playbill of the Day in Warsaw: Narodowy Theatre and its Continuations, 1765-1915.) *PaT.* 1987; 4: 491-542. Pref. Notes. Illus.: Photo. Print. B&W. 36. Lang.: Pol.

Poland: Warsaw. 1765-1915. Histories-sources. ■Analysis of form and content of Warsaw theatre playbills: classification into types and groups.

39 Sirera, Rodolf. "Les politiques teatrals: teatres institucionals." (Theatrical Policies: Institutional Theatres.) 145-162 in Coca, Jordi, ed.; Conesa, Laura, comp. *Congrés Internacional de Teatre a Catalunya 1985. Actes. Volum III., Seccions 4, 5 i 6.* Barcelona: Institut del Teatre; 1987. 302 pp. (Western Europe.) Notes. Tables. [Section 5: Policy and Legislation.] Lang.: Cat.

Spain. Europe. 1976-1985. Critical studies. ■Many Western European countries have theatrical structures that favor government adoption of formerly private functions, a museum attitude toward theatre and a dichotomy between centralization and decentralization. In Spain a coherent theatrical policy is beginning to develop.

40 Asplund, Carin. "Teaterprojeckt Bohuslän." (The Theatre Project Bohuslän.) *Teaterf.* 1987; 20(5): 12. Illus.: Photo. Lang.: Swe.

Sweden: Uddevalla. 1987. Historical studies. ■Cooperation between the county council and the association of theatres has introduced a special adviser for theatre at schools, information for audiences and amateur theatre.

41 Frieberg, Joakim. "Grassman: 'Låt inte lura er! Visst har vi råd med teater!'." (Grassman: 'Don't Be Cheated! To Be Sure We Can Afford Theatre!'.) *NT.* 1987; 36: 44-45. Illus.: Photo. Lang.: Swe.

Sweden. 1976-1987. Critical studies. ■Criticism of reduced government funding for the arts.

42 Karnell, Dr. Gunnar. "Extended Collective License Clauses and Agreements in Nordic Copyright." *JAML.* 1985 Fall; 10(1): 73-81. Notes. Lang.: Eng.

Sweden. 1984-1985. Histories-sources. ■Summary of extended collective license clauses in Nordic countries. Describes the extent and functioning of such systems and illustrates some of their problems.

43 Reck, Hans Ulrich. "Sponsoring, Public Relations: Dienst oder Einflussnahme?" (Sponsoring, Public Relations: Service or Exercise of Influence?)*Bulletin (SBV/UTS).* 1987 Mar.; 5(12): 12-14. Lang.: Ger.

Switzerland. 1987. Critical studies. ■Since the major part of the theatrical expense is covered by public means (taxpayers), the increasing interference of private sponsors raises a number of problems ranging from mere exercise of influence to downright censorship.

44 Strasser, Hannes. "Probleme der Einflussnahme durch den Sponsor." (Problems of Influence by the Sponsor.) *Bulletin (SBV/UTS).* 1987 Mar.; 5(12): 6-9. Illus.: Photo. B&W. Lang.: Ger.

Switzerland. 1987. Critical studies. ■Contrary to the situation in the Anglo-Saxon world, theatres in German-speaking Europe are mainly financed by public means (i.e. the tax-payers). Private sponsoring is

minor, but still sponsors try to influence theatre management as to program, artist selection and public relations.

45 "London's West End Fights off an Attack of the Glums." *Econ.* 1986 May 17; 299(7446): 101-104. Illus.: Photo. Graphs. B&W. 6. Lang.: Eng.

UK-England: London. 1983-1986. Historical studies. ■Financial profile of West End Theatre: drops in attendance, sale of theatres, investors, box office revenues, relationship between art and business.

46 "On a World Stage." *Econ.* 1986 July 15; 300(7453): 54. Lang.: Eng.

UK-England: London. 1986. Critical studies. ■Difference between commercial and subsidized theatre: rising costs driving producers to make deals with state funded theatre before risking investment.

47 "Alas, Poor Drama." *Econ.* 1986 Sept 27; 300(7465): 65. Lang.: Eng.

UK-England. 1985-1986. Critical studies. ■Findings of bankruptcy expert Kenneth Cork on the state of Britain's theatre: decrease in funding and companies, neglect of regional theatres.

48 "Funding." *Econ.* 1986 Nov 22; 301(7473): 61. Lang.: Eng.

UK-England: London. 1986. Historical studies. ■Arts minister Richard Luce releases spending figures for Arts Council and other arts institutions. Decreased funding, plans to increase private donorship.

49 *Phantom of the Opera* Exchange Assures Leading Roles for Americans in London, As Producers, British Union Accept Equity's Proposal." *EN.* 1987 Aug.; 72(8): 1. Lang.: Eng.

UK-England: London. USA: New York, NY. 1987. Historical studies. ■Agreement between AEA and British Equity to allow Sarah Brightman to recreate the role of Christine in *Phantom of the Opera.*

50 "AEA, British Equity Hold New Talks on Exchange, Reciprocity." *EN.* 1987 Mar.; 72(3): 1. Tables. Lang.: Eng.

UK-England. USA. 1981-1987. Critical studies. ■Meeting between officials of Actors' Equity and British Equity regarding exchanges between these unions.

51 "The Arts Have Their Politics." *Econ.* 1983 8 Jan.; 286: 43-44. Illus.: Photo. B&W. Lang.: Eng.

UK-England. 1983. Critical studies. ■Conservative shifts in government policies on financing the arts.

52 "Shooting the Pianists." *Econ.* 1987 14 Mar.; 302: 86-88. Illus.: Photo. B&W. 2. Lang.: Eng.

UK-England. France. USA. 1987. Critical studies. ■France, USA and Great Britain examine different ways of financing the arts. A look at each country's funding system.

53 Booth, Michael R. "Theatrical Business in the 1880s." *TN.* 1987; 41(2): 51-56. Notes. B&W. Lang.: Eng.

UK-England: London. 1885. Histories-sources. ■Six articles on theatrical business published in the *St. James Gazette*, January 10 and February 13, 1885.

54 Branagh, Kenneth. "Renaissance Man." *Drama.* 1987; 3(165): 9-10. Illus.: Photo. B&W. 2. Lang.: Eng.

UK-England: London. 1987. Critical studies. ■Interim report on the Renaissance Theatre Company.

55 Plouviez, Peter. "General Secretary, British Actors Equity Association." *EN.* 1982 Feb.; 67(2): 2. Lang.: Eng.

UK-England. Denmark: Copenhagen. 1982. Histories-sources. ■Issues that create division between unions in the international exchange of artists.

56 Vance, Charles. "Amateur or Professional?" *Drama.* 1987; 4(166): 17. Illus.: Photo. B&W. 1. Lang.: Eng.

UK-England. 1987. Histories-sources. ■Charles Vance, who recently took over the editorship of *Amateur Stage*, reflects on his first six months working in the amateur movement.

57 "Money Sings (Edinburgh Festival)." *Econ.* 1982 28 Aug.; 284: 42. Illus.: Photo. B&W. 1. Lang.: Eng.

UK-Scotland: Edinburgh. 1982. Critical studies. ■Methods of funding the 1.5M pound festival combining industrial monies and private patronage.

58 "Proof of U.S. Citizenship Is Needed Before You Can Be Hired." *EN.* 1987 Oct.; 72(10): 1. Lang.: Eng.

THEATRE IN GENERAL: —Administration

USA. 1987. Historical studies. ■A new immigration law which went into effect on June 1, 1987, requires every new employee to show proof of U.S. citizenship or legal residency prior to being hired.

59 "New Equity Program Helps Mature Members Prepare for Interim Jobs, Second Careers." *EN.* 1987 Sep.; 72(9): 1-2, 4. Illus.: Photo. B&W. 1. Lang.: Eng.

USA: New York, NY. 1986-1987. Historical studies. ■Discusses the Actors' Work Program, a training and re-education program created by AEA in 1986 to help actors find appropriate interim employment or meaningful second careers. Also an interview with the program's director Dr. Ronda Ormont.

60 "Law Protects New York Members in Rent Controlled Apartments." *EN.* 1987 Nov.; 72(11): 5. Lang.: Eng.

USA: New York, NY. 1987. Historical studies. ■The rights of actors who accept out-of-town employment to maintain their rent-regulated apartments under New York's rent control and rent stabilization laws. Definition of 'domicile', requirements of the law.

61 "Equity and British Equity Approve Equal Anglo-American Cast for *Carrie*." *EN.* 1987 Dec.; 72(12): 1. Lang.: Eng.

USA: New York, NY. UK-England: London. 1987. Historical studies. ■The first Anglo-American commercial production, the musical *Carrie*, will open on Broadway following performances in Stratford-upon-Avon and will include a cast evenly divided between British and American Equity members.

62 "LORT Pact in Jeopardy." *EN.* 1985 Sep.; 70(9): 1. Lang.: Eng.

USA: New York, NY. 1985. Critical studies. ■Potential for League of Resident Theatres strike.

63 "Sixteen Area Liaisons Attend Annual National Conference." *EN.* 1985 June; 70(4): 1. Illus.: Photo. B&W. 1. Lang.: Eng.

USA: New York, NY. 1985. Critical studies. ■12th annual national conference discusses job development, standardization of rules, filming and recording rights. Related to Media.

64 "Dramatists' Guild Urges Reconsideration of Equity's Conversion Rights Provisions." *EN.* 1985 June; 70(5): 1. Lang.: Eng.

USA: New York, NY. 1985. Critical studies. ■Letter from 10 important playwrights addressing showcase 'Letter of Agreement and Tiered Code'.

65 "Changes Effective in Welfare Eligibility." *EN.* 1985 June; 70(5): 1, 12. Lang.: Eng.

USA. 1985. Critical studies. ■Major revisions made in eligibility and insurance coverage rules for Equity League Welfare Fund.

66 "Equity Raises LORT Pact." *EN.* 1985 Oct.; 70(10): 1-2. Lang.: Eng.

USA: New York, NY. 1985. Critical studies. ■Significant gains for Equity members after Equity ratifies League of Resident Theatres pact.

67 "Major Changes Made in Welfare Benefits." *EN.* 1985 Dec.; 70(12): 1. Lang.: Eng.

USA: New York, NY. 1985. Critical studies. ■Equity League Welfare Trust Fund has eliminated and reduced benefits due to depletion of welfare funds.

68 "Colleen Dewhurst Represents Equity at Hearings of Pornography Commission." *EN.* 1986 Mar.; 71(3): 1, 6. Lang.: Eng.

USA: New York, NY. 1986. Historical studies. ■Presentation of censored and uncensored pornography in the theatre. Individual judgment regarding what is art and what is offensive material.

69 "How to Complete a Claim Form." *EN.* 1986 June; 71(6): 2. Lang.: Eng.

USA: New York, NY. 1986. Historical studies. ■Equity League pension and health trust funds office provides important information for expediting claims.

70 "New National Theatre Plan is Adopted." *EN.* 1986 July; 71(7): 1. Lang.: Eng.

USA: New York, NY. 1979-1986. Critical studies. ■Actors' Equity Council accepts a minority report of the National Theatre subcommittee and endorses plan that favors soliciting theatres to implement establishment of a national theatre in the US.

71 "Credit Union Marks 25th Anniversary: Adds Members, Computers, Services: How it All Began." *EN.* 1987 Apr.; 72(4): 7,8. Lang.: Eng.

USA: New York, NY. 1985-1987. Historical studies. ■How the Actors Federal Credit Union was formed out of the need to help actors in getting loans or credit, made possible by volunteer work of members.

72 "Equity Protests Immigration Rule Changes." *EN.* 1987 May; 72(5): 1. Lang.: Eng.

USA. 1987. Historical studies. ■Letter-writing campaign is mounted to protest the changes proposed by the Immigration and Naturalization Service in governing the importation of non-immigrant aliens to work in the US.

73 "Know Your Stock Employment Contracts." *EN.* 1987 May; 72(5): 6. Lang.: Eng.

USA. 1987. Historical studies. ■Rule books and employment contracts for summer stock: resident dramatic stock (CORST), resident musical stock (RMTA), non-resident indoor stock (COST), outdoor musical stock, outdoor drama.

74 "American Actors, Royal Shakespeare Company Exchange Views on British-American Exchange." *EN.* 1985 June; 70(6): 5. Lang.: Eng.

USA. UK-England. 1985. Historical studies. ■American Actors' Equity actors meet with the Royal Shakespeare Company to discuss British-American exchange.

75 "On Stage Coast to Coast—A Survey Spanning Two Decades of Equity Employment." *EN.* 1985 Mar.; 70(3): 3-7. Illus.: Diagram. Photo. Chart. 2. Lang.: Eng.

USA: New York, NY, Chicago, IL. 1961-1984. Critical studies. ■Detailed analysis of Actors' Equity Association. Examines employment, earnings and contract developments.

76 "Equity Representative in Washington for Talks with British Equity Leaders." *EN.* 1985 Jan.; 70(1): 1. Illus.: Photo. B&W. 1. Lang.: Eng.

USA: Washington, DC. UK-England. 1984. Critical studies. ■Actors' Equity and British Equity leaders gather to improve liaison work and communication.

77 "New Contract Developed to Assist Broadway's 'Endangered' Theatres." *EN.* 1987 July; 72(7): 1. Lang.: Eng.

USA: New York, NY. 1986-1987. Critical studies. ■'Endangered Theatres Production Contract' developed to stimulate activity in certain Broadway theatres which often go unused.

78 "Touring This Summer? Here are Two Ways to Go!" *EN.* 1987 May; 72(5): 7. Lang.: Eng.

USA. 1987. Historical studies. ■Two different summer stock contracts: consecutive stock jobbing or unit. Salary, *per diem*, work rules are compared.

79 "New Immigration Reform Law Requires Citizenship Proof for All Employees." *EN.* 1987 June; 72(6): 1. Lang.: Eng.

USA: New York, NY. 1987. Critical studies. ■New immigration law requires proof of citizenship or legal residency before hiring.

80 "P & H Trustees Reiterate Changes in the Second Surgical Opinion Program." *EN.* 1987 Aug.; 72(8): 2. Lang.: Eng.

USA: New York, NY. 1987. Critical studies. ■Questions and answers regarding changes made by Trustees of the Equity League Health Plan in the mandatory second surgical opinion program.

81 "Welfare Fund Enlarged: Review Underway by Trustees." *EN.* 1985 Jan.; 70(1): 1. Lang.: Eng.

USA. 1985. Historical studies. ■Audit by the Welfare Fund's accountants showed a $1.4 million deficit in Equity Welfare plan.

82 "Roundtable: Perspectives on Volunteers." *JAML.* 1987 Sum; 17(2): 83-106. Lang.: Eng.

USA. 1987. Histories-sources. ■Panel discussion on the importance of volunteers in the arts. Requirements of the volunteer coordinator.

83 "Dinner Theatre Contract Approved: Work Stoppage is Avoided." *EN.* 1985 Feb.; 70(2): 1 and 8. Lang.: Eng.

USA: New York, NY. 1985. Historical studies. ■A 3-year contract is implemented between Actors' Equity and the American Dinner Theatre Institute.

THEATRE IN GENERAL: —Administration

84 "Equity Producers Reach Landmark Agreement on Effort to Solve Problems of Alien Actors." *EN.* 1982 Feb.; 67(2): 1. Lang.: Eng.
USA: New York, NY. UK-England. 1982. Critical studies. ■Actors' Equity and League of New York Theatre and Producers' joint effort to achieve reciprocity in exchanging British and American actors.

85 "AEA Reps Visit LORT Companies: Liaison Cities Hold Meetings." *EN.* 1985 Mar.; 70(3): 1. Lang.: Eng.
USA: New York, NY, Chicago, IL. 1984. Critical studies. ■Actors' Equity staff members from all regional offices contact invited LORT members to negotiate and continue liaison work.

86 "Conversion Rights for *Mass Appeal* Denied." *EN.* 1982 Feb.; 67(2): 1. Lang.: Eng.
USA: New York, NY. 1982. Critical studies. ■Understudies and stage managers lose in arbitration of conversion rights dispute.

87 "AIDS Committee Offers Fundraising Ideas." *EN.* 1987 Oct.; 72(10): 3. Lang.: Eng.
USA: New York, NY. 1987. Critical studies. ■Equity Fights AIDS Committee has written letter to all Equity Area Liaisons, stage managers and deputies of working companies to let members know about their work and goals and to raise money during Thanksgiving week for AIDS support.

88 "Film, TV Procedures are Streamlined." *EN.* 1982 Feb.; 67(2): 3. Lang.: Eng.
USA: New York, NY. 1982. Critical studies. ■Creation of committee representing Actors' Equity, Screen Actors Guild and American Federation of Television and Radio Artists to expedite procedures for granting permission for filming and recording productions under Equity contracts.

89 "Tax Bill Keeps Deductibility of Expenses, Provides Help for Low Income Performers." *EN.* 1986 Nov.; 71(11): 1, 2. Lang.: Eng.
USA: New York, NY. 1986. Historical studies. ■Tax reform bill seen as a victory for Equity.

90 "Tax Help Office Opens." *EN.* 1982 Feb.; 67(2): 4. Lang.: Eng.
USA: New York, NY. 1982. Critical studies. ■Equity's Volunteer Income Tax Assistance Office to aid actors with free tax information.

91 "New Production Contract Features 97 Percent Increase in Health Contributions—Bus and Truck Provisions." *EN.* 1986 Oct.; 71(10): 1, 2. Lang.: Eng.
USA: New York, NY. 1986. Historical studies. ■A new 3-year agreement with the League of American Theatres & Producers: revitalizes Equity's health plan and provides theatres with needed relief. Created an experimental bus and truck contract for tours.

92 "Judge Rules for AEA: Merrick Loses Again." *EN.* 1982 May; 67(5): 1. Lang.: Eng.
USA: New York, NY. 1982. Critical studies. ■Equity successfully defends its 'just cause' provision in court battle with producer David Merrick after termination of a member from understudy position.

93 "New Equity Program Helps Mature Members Prepare for Interim Jobs, Second Careers." *EN.* 1987 Sep.; 72(9): 1, 2, 4. Lang.: Eng.
USA: New York, NY. 1987. Histories-sources. ■Interview with Ronda Ormont, director of the Actor's Work Program.

94 "Equity is Upheld in Whitelaw Arbitration." *EN.* 1982 May; 67(5): 1. Lang.: Eng.
USA: New York, NY. 1982. Critical studies. ■New York Shakespeare Festival's request to employ non-resident Billie Whitelaw denied by arbitrator.

95 "Visa Credit Cards Available Through Actors Credit Union." *EN.* 1987 Oct.; 72(10): 1, 2. Lang.: Eng.
USA: New York, NY. 1987. Critical studies. ■The implementation by the Actors Federal Credit Union of a Visa credit card program which includes low interest, cash services, travel benefits and payment assistance.

96 "Per Diem Is Increased 100 Percent in New Outdoor Musical Pact." *EN.* 1982 May; 67(5): 1. Lang.: Eng.
USA: New York, NY. 1982. Historical studies. ■Actors win 100 percent increase in per diem with Outdoor Musical Stock agreement.

97 "Health Fund Continues Improvement, Pension Fund Reserves Increase." *EN.* 1987 Nov.; 72(11): 1. Lang.: Eng.
USA: New York, NY. 1987. Histories-sources. ■Annual Report for fiscal year June 1, 1985-May 31, 1986 by the Equity-League Pension and Health Fund Trustees concerning improved benefits, cost containment measures, and the well funded pension fund.

98 "Bikel Installs Burstyn as Equity's First Woman President." *EN.* 1982 July; 67(7). Illus.: Photo. B&W. Lang.: Eng.
USA: New York, NY. 1982. Historical studies. ■Theodore Bikel steps down from presidency and officiates at inauguration of first female president, Ellen Burstyn.

99 "Chicago Actors Appear in Program Commemorating Labor's Struggle." *EN.* 1986 Aug.; 71(8): 1, 4. Illus.: Photo. 3. Lang.: Eng.
USA: Chicago, IL. 1986. Historical studies. ■Chicago Equity members took part in the 100th anniversary of labor's fight for the eight-hour day and the Chicago Haymarket Square tragedy. Actors interviewed on labor today.

100 "Eisenberg Describes Job Development and Commitment to Equal Opportunity." *EN.* 1982 July; 67(7): 1. Lang.: Eng.
USA: New York, NY. 1982. Historical studies. ■Executive secretary Alan Eisenberg reports to national membership committee on job development, contract administration, improvement of conditions, equal opportunity.

101 "Equity in Washington to Discuss Aliens." *EN.* 1982 July; 67(7): 4. Lang.: Eng.
USA: Washington, DC. 1982. Historical studies. ■Meeting between Actors' Equity and Labor Department officials in Washington regarding admission and employment of non-immigrant aliens.

102 "Win for *The First*." *EN.* 1982 Aug.; 67(8): 2. Lang.: Eng.
USA: New York, NY. 1982. Critical studies. ■Favorable ruling for Actors' Equity in dispute involving compensation for cast members of *The First*.

103 "Salary and Per Diem—They're Both Taxable." *EN.* 1982 Aug.; 67(8): 4. Lang.: Eng.
USA: New York, NY. 1982. Historical studies. ■Tax regulations regarding salary and per diem for performers working out of town.

104 "Constitutional Amendment Will Add Stage Managers to Council." *EN.* 1982 Sep.; 67(9): 1. Lang.: Eng.
USA: New York, NY. 1982. Critical studies. ■Constitutional amendment providing seats for stage managers on Actors' Equity Council.

105 "Artists Groups are Battered by Lawsuits." *EN.* 1982 Sep.; 67(9): 1. Lang.: Eng.
USA: New York, NY. 1982. Historical studies. ■Lawsuits brought against Screen Actors Guild and American Federation of Television and Radio Artists which may have impact on all labor unions.

106 "AEA Wins Arbitration with Dinner Theatre." *EN.* 1987 Sep.; 67(9): 1. Lang.: Eng.
USA: La Mesa, CA. 1987. Critical studies. ■Arbitrator upholds Equity's contention that the Lyric Dinner Theatre was not operating under its claimed contract.

107 "Handbook on the Way." *EN.* 1982 Sep.; 67(9): 1. Lang.: Eng.
USA: New York, NY. 1982. Historical studies. ■New Actors' Equity handbook published for membership.

108 "National Members Approve Amendment Adding 5 Stage Managers to Council." *EN.* 1982 Nov.; 67(11): 1. Illus.: Photo. B&W. 1. Lang.: Eng.
USA: New York, NY. 1982. Historical studies. ■Constitutional amendment approves addition of stage managers to Actors' Equity Council.

109 "Burstyn Says It Is Union's Job to Help Make Theatre Healthy." *EN.* 1982 Nov.; 67(11): 1. Lang.: Eng.
USA: New York, NY. 1982. Historical studies. ■Actors' Equity president Ellen Burstyn addresses employment for minorities and women.

110 "Equity Protests Casting of *Price of Genius*." *EN.* 1982 Nov.; 67(11): 2. Illus.: Photo. B&W. 1. Lang.: Eng.

THEATRE IN GENERAL: —Administration

USA: New York, NY. 1982. Historical studies. ■Equity members support strike by Hispanic Organization of Latin Americans due to inadequate casting of Hispanic actors.

111 "New York Members Reaffirm and Support National Theatre Plan." *EN*. 1982 Nov.; 67(11): 2. Lang.: Eng.
USA: New York, NY. 1982. Historical studies. ■Conference on Equity's plan to create a National Theatre in America.

112 *Sophisticated Ladies* Is Taped as Equity Members Protest Terms." *EN*. 1982 Dec.; 67(12): 1. Lang.: Eng.
USA: New York, NY. 1982. Historical studies. ■Broadway production of *Sophisticated Ladies* is taped for cable television amid heated controversy.

113 "Equity's National Conference Urges Greater Communication with Regions." *EN*. 1982 Dec.; 67(12): 1. Illus.: Photo. B&W. 1. Lang.: Eng.
USA: New York, NY. 1982. Historical studies. ■National Conference focuses on communication between national office and all other areas of the country.

114 "Equity and AFTRA Unite for Waiver Videotaping Contract." *EN*. 1982 Dec.; 67(12): 3. Lang.: Eng.
USA: New York, NY. 1982. Historical studies. ■Contract signed between Equity, American Federation of Television and Radio Artists and producer Clarence Ross for videotaping of '99-seat waiver' production for basic cable TV distribution.

115 "Illness of Star Rule Tested in *Camelot*." *EN*. 1983 Jan.; 68(1): 1. Lang.: Eng.
USA: New York, NY. 1983. Historical studies. ■Arbitration for payment of cast members between Equity and the *Camelot* Company and Dome productions when production's star Richard Harris became ill.

116 "Affirmative Action Makes Major Gains." *EN*. 1983 Jan.; 68(1): 1. Lang.: Eng.
USA: New York, NY. 1983. Historical studies. ■Circle Repertory Theatre's plan to increase membership of minorities and to seek out scripts with minority roles.

117 "Procedures Set Up for Chorus Calls." *EN*. 1983 Jan.; 68(1): 2. Lang.: Eng.
USA: New York, NY. 1983. Critical studies. ■Advisory Committee on Chorus Affairs and Equity devise procedures for official Equity chorus calls.

118 Abrash, Victoria. "The Act of Commission." *TT*. 1987 Apr.; 6(3): 6-7. Lang.: Eng.
USA: New York, NY. 1987. Historical studies. ■American theatre's view of the commissioning process: paying for a play which has yet to be written.

119 Allen, Kenn. "A New Competitive Edge: Volunteers from the Workplace." *FundM*. 1987 Jan.; 17(11): 40-47. Tables. Illus.: Graphs. 6. Lang.: Eng.
USA. 1983-1987. Historical studies. ■Volunteer programs help corporations sharpen employee skills, demonstrate moral leadership in the community and respond to employee concerns regarding quality of life.

120 Anthoine, Robert. "Charitable Contributions after 1986 Tax Act and Problems in Valuation of Appreciated Property." *ColJL&A*. 1987 Win; 11(2): 283-314. Notes. Lang.: Eng.
USA. 1986-1987. Critical studies. ■Basic structure of Charitable Contributions deduction law after 1986 and problems in valuation of appreciated property.

121 Archer, Lynn. "Summer Stock: Diagnosis and Prognosis." *EN*. 1985 May; 70(5): 3-5. Illus.: Photo. B&W. 6. Lang.: Eng.
USA. 1985. Critical studies. ■Current trends and future of summer stock companies.

122 Archer, Lynn. "Medical Coverage is Improved in New Three-Year COST Pact." *EN*. 1986 Mar.; 71(3): 1,2. Lang.: Eng.
USA: New York, NY. 1986. Historical studies. ■New COST contract and how it affects auditions, interviews, costumes, publicity, conversion rehearsals, housing, stage managers, termination and understudies.

123 Baker, Denys; Fait, Susan A.; Kawolsky, Christopher. "Shortcuts to Success?" *PerfM*. 1985 Win; 11(1): 2-4. Illus.: Photo. Sketches. B&W. 3. Lang.: Eng.
USA: New York, NY. 1985. Critical studies. ■Debate over value of having a degree in arts management as a road to success. Survey of graduates of Brooklyn College Arts Management program.

124 Ballantine, Frank. "Nonprofit Entrepreneurship: The Astoria Motion Picture and Television Center." *JAML*. 1982 Spr; 12(1): 5-25. Notes. Biblio. Lang.: Eng.
USA: New York, NY. 1920-1982. Historical studies. ■Astoria Studios: creation of nonprofit organization to manage facility and renovation coalition.

125 Barlett, Robin; Gord, Douglas. "Majority Report of the National Theatre Committee." *EN*. 1985 Nov.; 70(11): 4, 6. Lang.: Eng.
USA. 1985. Histories-sources. ■Actors' Equity plans National Theatre project: funding, employment and personnel.

126 Beck, Kirsten. *How to Run a Small Box Office*. New York, NY: Drama Book Specialists; 1980. 71 pp. Pref. Index. Illus.: Photo. Sketches. B&W. 27. Lang.: Eng.
USA: New York, NY. 1980. ■Comprehensive guide to establishing and running a box office for a small theatre, including blank box office forms, procedural checklist for operations and policy guidelines.

127 Biles, George E.; Morris, Valerie B. "Charitable Giving to the Arts: *Quo Vadis?*." *JAML*. 1982 Spr; 12(1): 59-67. Notes. Tables. Lang.: Eng.
USA. 1981. Critical studies. ■Impact of the 1981 Economic Recovery Tax Act on individual charitable giving. A recently completed Urban Institute econometric study of the issue.

128 Black, Mel. "AEA and LORT: The Equity Viewpoint." *PerfM*. 1987 Win; 13(1): 2-3. Lang.: Eng.
USA. 1987. Historical studies. ■Working relationship of League of Resident Theatres and Actors' Equity Association. Contracts, negotiations, management and labor's roles.

129 Borchard, William M. "Trademarks and the Arts." *A&L*. 1982; 7(1): 1-18. Lang.: Eng.
USA: New York, NY. 1970-1982. Technical studies. ■Overview of the highlights of Trademark Law. Reviews some areas in which trademark principles and precedents have been established as applied to the arts.

130 Breyer, Jane. "Mergers and Acquisitions: The Impact on Corporate Philanthropy." *PerfM*. 1987 Spr; 12(1): 6-8. Biblio. Illus.: Photo. B&W. 1. Lang.: Eng.
USA. 1985-1987. Historical studies. ■Influence of mergers and corporate takeovers on corporate giving. Impact on community, nonprofit organizations. Acquisition of RCA Corporation by General Electric explored as example.

131 Brustein, Robert. "In Need of Actors, Not Stars." *AmTh*. 1987 Oct.; 4(7): 80-81. Lang.: Eng.
USA: New York, NY. 1987. Critical studies. ■Examines recent Actors' Equity policy decisions on granting performing permission to actors from foreign countries based on their stature as stars.

132 Burstyn, Ellen. "Minority Report of the National Theatre Committee." *EN*. 1985 Nov.; 70(11): 5-6. Lang.: Eng.
USA. 1985. Histories-sources. ■U.S. theatre system is developed to promote better regional theatre and to diminish social, racial and economic discrimination in theatre.

133 Carney, Kay; Boyd, Julianne. "Directors and Designers Report on Sex Discrimination in the Theatre." *WPerf*. 1984 Win; 1(2): 46-54. Lang.: Eng.
USA: New York, NY. 1976-1984. Historical studies. ■Analysis of reports and interviews about how and why women are discriminated against in American theatres, specifically studies bias against women directors and designers.

134 Carrol, Nora. "Tracking the Itinerant Subscriber: Data Base in the Arts Industry." *JAML*. 1984 Spr; 14(1): 68-76. Notes. Biblio. Illus.: Plan. Chart. 1. Lang.: Eng.
USA. 1981-1983. Histories-sources. ■A guide to establishing a database for a consortium of arts organizations including examples of entry files and network configurations.

THEATRE IN GENERAL: —Administration

135 Caswell, Gordon M. "How to Market Planned Giving." *FundM.* 1987 Feb.; 17(12): 56-61. Illus.: Photo. Graphs. Print. B&W. 6. Lang.: Eng.

USA. 1987. Historical studies. ▪Sharing concepts in charitable estate planning can help prospects with their own estate planning and attract more dollars to charity.

136 Chamberlain, Oliver. "Pricing Management for the Performing Arts." *JAML.* 1986 Fall; 16(3): 49-60. Notes. Tables. 3. Lang.: Eng.

USA: Bowling Green, OH. 1986. Critical studies. ▪Pricing management for the performing arts: an essential element of marketing management and financial management.

137 Clubb, Pat. "An Analysis of the Instability of Arts Organizations." *JAML.* 1987 Spr; 17(1): 47-74. Notes. Illus.: Graphs. 13. Lang.: Eng.

USA. 1976-1987. Critical studies. ▪Crisis of financial survival in arts organizations, examining structure, funding systems, budgets.

138 Cok, Mary Van Someren; Dickey, Edward. "The National Information Systems Project." *JAML.* 1984 Spr; 14(1): 19-27. Notes. Lang.: Eng.

USA. 1977-1984. Histories-specific. ▪History of the development and implementation of a national standard and the National Information Systems Project (NISP) with goals and related activities.

139 Conover, Susan P. "Response Enhancement: A New Computerized Marketing Technique." *TT.* 1987 Jan/Feb.; 6(2): 11. Lang.: Eng.

USA: New York, NY. 1986. Critical studies. ▪Computer analysis of mailing lists and response enhancement.

140 Cooper, Lee G.; Jacobs, Daniel. "Market Information Systems for the Profession and Science of Arts Management." *JAML.* 1984 Spr; 14(1): 77-89. Notes. Illus.: Graphs. Lang.: Eng.

USA. 1984. Empirical research. ▪Review of assumptions underlying economic analyses of arts organizations and a description of some of the principles and specifics of evolving market information systems for arts organizations.

141 Cooper, Paul G. "The Office of the Borough President of Manhattan." *TT.* 1987 June/July; 6(5): 7, 14. Lang.: Eng.

USA: New York, NY. 1987. Historical studies. ▪Manhattan Borough President David Dinkins, his support of theatre in New York City. Board of Estimate and its role in working with the arts.

142 Cornwell, Terri Lynn. "Congressional Arts Caucus Legislative Summary 99th Congress." *JAML.* 1987 Spr; 17(1): 37-46. Illus.: Graphs. 4. Lang.: Eng.

USA. 1985-1987. Critical studies. ▪1986-87 US legislation pending and approved by Congress. Includes appropriations and tables showing tax changes.

143 Curry, David J. "Marketing Research and Management Decision." *JAML.* 1982; 12(1): 42-58. Notes. Lang.: Eng.

USA: Iowa City, IA. 1982. Critical studies. ▪Application of three marketing research methods on fundraising, decision structure analysis and competitive structure analysis.

144 Davis, Clinton Turner. "A Call to Action." *EN.* 1987 Jan.; 72(1): 2. Illus.: Photo. B&W. 1. Lang.: Eng.

USA: New York, NY. 1986-1987. Critical studies. ▪Reaction to the first national symposium on nontraditional casting and a call for actors, directors and agents to encourage multiracial casting.

145 Dobbs, Gigi. "The Art Museum Association of America Computer Software Project." *JAML.* 1984 Spr; 14(1): 34-38. Lang.: Eng.

USA. 1981-1983. Histories-specific. ▪History of the development and implementation of the Art Museum Association of America's Computer Software Project. Includes goals, organization names and evaluation.

146 Easter, Leonard D.; Kernochan, John M. "The Columbia-Volunteer Lawyers for the Arts Art Law Clinic: A New Kind of Law School Clinic." *A&L.* 1982; 7(1): 53-82. Lang.: Eng.

USA: New York, NY. 1969-1982. Historical studies. ▪Origins and development of a law clinic focused exclusively on the Arts. Traces the founding and development of Volunteer Lawyers for the Arts.

147 Eisenberg, Alan. "Welfare Fund Trustees Act to Cut Costs and Preserve Benefits." *EN.* 1985 June; 70(4): 1. Lang.: Eng.

USA. 1985. Critical studies. ▪Executive secretary Alan Eisenberg reports on approved program by Equity League Welfare Fund trustees.

148 Ellis, Susan J. "Evaluation of Volunteer Efforts." *JAML.* 1987 Sum; 17(2): 67-81. Lang.: Eng.

USA. 1987. Critical studies. ▪Evaluation of volunteers in an arts organization, includes guidelines.

149 Fabiani, Mario. "Report of Governmental Experts on Model Provisions for National Laws on Employed Authors." *ColJL&A.* 1987 Win; 11(2): 315-331. Lang.: Eng.

USA. 1986-1987. Historical studies. ▪Draft and annotated model provisions for national laws on employed authors.

150 Farber, Donald C. *Producing Theatre: A Comprehensive Legal and Business Guide.* New York, NY: Limelight; 1987. 472 pp. Notes. Index. Append. Lang.: Eng.

USA: New York, NY. 1987. Technical studies. ▪Complete guide to producing a play from obtaining a property through opening. Contracts, fundraising, options, Broadway and out of town licensing. Detailed appendices of contracts and agreements necessary for producing.

151 Fox, Judith A.; Carter, Richard. "Modems." *TT.* 1987 Apr.; 6(3): 13. Lang.: Eng.

USA: New York, NY. 1987. Technical studies. ▪Non-profit organizations benefit from use of computer modems in preparing programs, annual reports, newsletters and brochures.

152 Fox, Judith A.; Carter, Richard. "When Donated Equipment Lands at Your Door." *TT.* 1986 Nov.; 6(1): 9. Lang.: Eng.

USA: New York, NY. 1986. Technical studies. ▪How to computerize your non-profit organization.

153 Fox, Judith A. "The Tax Reform Act and Charitable Giving." *TT.* 1987 Jan/Feb.; 6(2): 14-15. Lang.: Eng.

USA. 1986. Historical studies. ▪Effects of the 1986 Tax Reform Act on non-profit organizations.

154 Gates, Tom. "Anna Sosenko: One of the Best Friends the Theater Ever Had." *TheaterW.* 1987 Nov 2; 1(12): 10-13. Illus.: Photo. B&W. 7. Lang.: Eng.

USA: New York, NY. 1930-1987. Histories-sources. ▪Manager, historian and producer Anna Sosenko: her career, private archives and collection of theatre memorabilia.

155 Gates, Tom. "Superagent Milton Goldman: Or, How a Stagestruck Kid from New Jersey Built a Stairway to the Stars." *TheaterW.* 1987 7-13 Sep.(4): 28-31. Illus.: Photo. B&W. 5. Lang.: Eng.

USA. 1930-1987. Biographical studies. ▪Career of theatrical agent Milton Goldman.

156 Gelblum, Seth. "Artists and Unions: Equity's Fight for Commercial Rights in Off-off Broadway." *JAML.* 1982; 12(1): 26-41 . Notes. Lang.: Eng.

USA: New York, NY. 1966-1982. Historical studies. ▪Problems of Actors' Equity union actors working without pay in Off-off Broadway shows: retroactive rights in future commercial productions and probable solutions.

157 Giulano, Mike. "Arnoult's Territory Spans the Globe." *AmTh.* 1987 Mar.; 3(12): 36-37. Illus.: Photo. B&W. 2. Lang.: Eng.

USA: Baltimore, MD. 1971-1987. Critical studies. ▪Philip Arnoult, founding director of the Baltimore Theatre Project, and his search for new works.

158 Godfrey, Marian. "Corporate Sponsorships: New Funding for the Theatre?" *TT.* 1987 June/July; 6(5): 10, 11, 15. Lang.: Eng.

USA: New York, NY. 1987. Histories-sources. ▪Interview with Karen Brookes Hopkins and Kate Busch regarding marketing focus on corporations and funding special projects for theatres.

159 Goodale, Toni K. "Teaching Volunteers the Arts of Asking." *FundM.* 1987 Jan.; 17(11): 32-38. Illus.: Photo. B&W. 1. Lang.: Eng.

THEATRE IN GENERAL: —Administration

USA. 1987. Historical studies. ■Role playing as a method to teach volunteers successful solicitation of gifts.

160   Gordon, Douglas. "National Theatre Committee Conference is Scheduled for October 4." *EN*. 1982 Aug.; 67(8): 4. Lang.: Eng.

USA: New York, NY. 1982. Critical studies. ■Committee meets to discuss establishment of a National Theatre of the United States.

161   Gravely, Edmund K., Jr. "Basic Hacking, From Data Base to Port." *JAML*. 1984 Spr; 14(1): 122-126. Lang.: Eng.

USA. 1981-1984. Critical studies. ■Computer glossary for new users.

162   Greco, Lisa. "The Performance Pirate and the Diva: Can Federal Law Come to the Rescue." *A&L*. 1982; 7(2): 177-192. Lang.: Eng.

USA: New York, NY. 1954-1982. Critical studies. ■Reasons for laws against music and performance piracy. Definition of piracy and laws governing it. Related to Media: Video forms.

163   Gross, Roger. "The Death of ATA." *TDR*. 1986 Win; 30(4): 148-155. Notes. Lang.: Eng.

USA. 1983-1986. Critical studies. ■Analysis of how American Theatre Association ceased to exist.

164   Gurin, Maurice G. "Is Marketing Dangerous for Fundraising." *FundM*. 1987 Jan.; 17(11): 72-76. Illus.: Photo. Print. B&W. 1. Lang.: Eng.

USA: New York, NY. 1980-1987. Critical studies. ■Veteran fundraiser discusses current concerns that slick marketing endangers non-profit fundraising.

165   Haft, Jonathan D. "Universal City Studios vs. Sony Corporation of America." *A&L*. 1982; 7(2): 85-124. Lang.: Eng.

USA: New York, NY. 1976-1982. Historical studies. ■Court ruling protecting the copyright of audio-visual works. Related to Media: Video forms.

166   Hanlon, Brendon. "Taxes: The Code is Dead! Long Live the Code!" *ThCr*. 1987 Mar.; 21(3): 12, 73-74. Lang.: Eng.

USA. 1987. Critical studies. ■Tax Reform Act of 1986 and how it affects theatre professionals.

167   Harding, Alfred. "Looking Back—Ziegfeld Loses 'The Follies'." *EN*. 1986 Mar.; 71(3): 7. Lang.: Eng.

USA: New York, NY. 1919. Historical studies. ■The Ziegfeld Follies strike. Performers Eddie Cantor, Johnny Dooley, Gus Van, Joe Schenck and Phil Dwyer walked out and were joined by chorus girls.

168   Harrow, Gustave. "Creativity and Control." *JAML*. 1986 Sum; 16(2): 47-76. Notes. Lang.: Eng.

USA: New York, NY. 1986. Histories-sources. ■Nature of creativity: artistic creation, freedom and control. Urges integration of creative process in society placing the artist in leadership position.

169   Havlicek, Franklin J.; Kelso, J. Clark. "The Rights of Composers and Lyricists: Before and After Bernstein." *JAML*. 1986 Sum; 16(2): 77-93. Notes. Lang.: Eng.

USA. 1984-1986. Histories-specific. ■Exploitation of artists' work in the marketplace: fair value for fair work, and representation for artists who are viewed as independent contractors.

170   Hirschhorn, Robert. "New Tax Law Helps Equity Members." *EN*. 1982 Feb.; 67(2): 3. Lang.: Eng.

USA: New York, NY. 1982. Critical studies. ■Changes in tax laws regarding Independent Retirement Accounts affect Actors' Equity members enrolled in League Pension fund.

171   Hoffman, Miles K.; Fitschner, Linda Marie. "Art and Art Audiences: Testing the Market." *JAML*. 1984 Sum; 14(4): 5-19. Tables. Biblio. Lang.: Eng.

USA. 1984. Critical studies. ■Limited arts survey done for a small city art center as an experiment in a 'people audit'. Demographic characteristics, consumer and service attributes.

172   Holley, Robert. "Theatre Communication Group's National Computer Project." *JAML*. 1984 Spr; 14(1): 28-33. Lang.: Eng.

USA. 1980-1983. Histories-specific. ■Theatre Communication Group's (TCG) National Computer Project for the Performing Arts. Development of the Arts Income Management System (AIMS) and related technical information.

173   Holley, Robert. "Theatre Facts '86." *AmTh*. 1987 Apr.; 4(1): 20-27. Illus.: Graphs. Dwg. Chart. 9. Lang.: Eng.

USA. 1986. Empirical research. ■Theatre Communication Group's annual survey of financial results for over 45 nonprofit theatres.

174   Holley, Robert. "'Keep Out' Is U.S. Visa Message." *AmTh*. 1987 Mar.; 3(12): 26-27. Illus.: Photo. Print. B&W. 1. Lang.: Eng.

USA: New York, NY. 1987. Critical studies. ■Potential effects of new immigration rules on performing arts organizations.

175   Holley, Robert. "Rocky Congress Ahead." *AmTh*. 1987 Jan.; 3(10): 28-29. Lang.: Eng.

USA. 1980-1987. Histories-sources. ■Government financing of nonprofit theatre and debate over the National Endowment for the Arts.

176   Horowitz, David H. "The Record Rental Amendment of 1984: A Case Study in the Effort to Adapt Copyright Law to New Technology." *ColJL&A*. 1987 Fall; 12(1): 31-71. Notes. Tables. Lang.: Eng.

USA. 1964-1987. Technical studies. ■Economic and legal issues of record rental as related to copyright infringement and the 1984 Record Rental Amendment. Related to Media: Audio forms.

177   Hull, Carolyn D. "The Board President." *PerfM*. 1987 Spr; 12(1): 1-3. Illus.: Photo. WB. 1. Lang.: Eng.

USA. 1987. Histories-sources. ■Conversation with John Friedman, Lewis C. Ross and Christina Sterner on the role of board presidents in nonprofit organizations: management, leadership, planning.

178   Huntsinger, Jerald E. "On Fundraising Letters: How to Use Self Hypnosis for Better Letters." *FundM*. 1987 Jan.; 17(11): 88, 91. Illus.: Photo. Print. B&W. 1. Lang.: Eng.

USA: Los Angeles, CA. 1986-1987. Historical studies. ■Use of self-hypnosis techniques for fundraiser to put himself into the funder's place and thereby learn to write better fundraising letters.

179   Istel, John. "Ad Team Turns TV Into Ally." *AmTh*. 1987 Mar.; 3(12): 40-41. Illus.: Poster. B&W. 2. Lang.: Eng.

USA: New York, NY. 1984-1987. Critical studies. ■Influence of TV ads on success of Broadway plays.

180   Jeffri, Joan. "Making Money: Real Estate Strategies for the Arts." *JAML*. 1982 Fall; 12(3): 32-50. Notes. [Reprint from *Arts Money*.] Lang.: Eng.

USA. 1982. Historical studies. ■Possible strategies in real estate for arts organizations. Air rights, local development corporations, public buildings and city space, amenity strategies.

181   Jeffri, Joan; Hosie, Joseph; Greenblatt, Robert. "The Artist Alone: Work Related, Human, and Social Needs—Selected Findings." *JAML*. 1987 Fall; 17(3): 4-22. Tables. 4. Lang.: Eng.

USA: New York, NY. 1987. Critical studies. ■Results of a survey conducted by the New York Foundation for the Arts recording the needs of artists.

182   Jochnowitz, Daniel M. "Proof of Harm: A Dangerous Prerequisite for Copyright Protection." *JAML*. 1985 Fall; 10(1): 153-168. Notes. Lang.: Eng.

USA. 1985. Histories-sources. ■Sets forth the development of the 'Proof of Harm' doctrine and demonstrates the inconsistencies with the principles of copyright law, the doctrine of fair use and the ramifications of a requisite.

183   Karas, Sandra. "VITA Answers Some Questions Frequently Asked about Taxes." *EN*. 1987 June; 72(6): 1, 2, 4. Lang.: Eng.

USA: New York, NY. 1986-1987. Critical studies. ■Questions and answers regarding tax returns in compliance with new laws.

184   Karas, Sandra. "Render unto Caesar or Is There Life After Tax Reform." *EN*. 1987 Nov.; 72(11): 3. Lang.: Eng.

USA. 1987. Historical studies. ■The pros and cons of tax reform from the actor's point of view. Article focuses on unemployment insurance, freelance income and the deductibility of actors' expenses.

185   Karas, Sandra. "Things to Know When You're on the Road." *EN*. 1986 Mar.; 71(3): 3. Lang.: Eng.

USA: New York, NY. 1986. Historical studies. ■Information on problems confronted by actors and stage managers with their taxes.

THEATRE IN GENERAL: —Administration

186 Karas, Sandra. "So, You're Being Audited." *EN*. 1987 Apr.; 72(4): 2, 8. Lang.: Eng.
USA: New York, NY. 1987. Critical studies. ■Suggestions and tips for getting through an IRS tax audit.

187 Karas, Sandra. "A Dependent by Any Other Name..." *EN*. 1987 Feb.; 72(2): 1. Lang.: Eng.
USA: New York, NY. 1987. Critical studies. ■Employees witholding Allowance Certificate (W-4 Form) and how it alters the actor's income tax return.

188 Karas, Sandra. "Income Tax: What You Pay and What You Deduct." *EN*. 1987 Mar.; 72(3): 2. Lang.: Eng.
USA: New York, NY. 1987. Historical studies. ■1987 tax law and its impact on actors. Emphasis on New York business tax, status of actors as independent contractors, deductibility and record keeping.

189 Karl, Matthew. "Dorothy Olim on the Commercial Theatre." *PerfM*. 1983 Dec.; 9(1): 3-4, 7. Tables. Illus.: Plan. 2. Lang.: Eng.
USA: New York, NY. 1983. Histories-sources. ■Lecture by Broadway and Off Broadway producer Dorothy Olim. Definitions of New York commercial theatre, relationship with artists unions, media.

190 Karlen, Peter H. "Fakes, Forgeries, and Expert Opinions." *JAML*. 1986 Fall; 16(3): 5-32. Notes. Lang.: Eng.
USA. 1986. Critical studies. ■Legal ramifications and remedies for artists whose work is fake or forged.

191 Katon, Lawrence. "Equity Reaffirms Fairness of Conversion Rights Provisions." *EN*. 1985 May; 70(5): 1, 12. Lang.: Eng.
USA: New York, NY. 1985. Critical studies. ■Effectiveness of the Showcase Code and playwrights who supported it.

192 Katz, Steven. "Museum Trusteeship: The Fiduciary Ethic Applied." *JAML*. 1987 Win; 17(4): 57-77. Notes. Lang.: Eng.
USA. 1987. Critical studies. ■Fiduciary responsibilities of the museum trustee and the development of systems and methods.

193 Kirkland, Lane. "Labor and the Arts." *EN*. 1982 Sep.; 67(9): 1. Illus.: Photo. B&W. 1. Lang.: Eng.
USA. 1982. Critical studies. ■Labor and the arts as advocates of social and cultural democracy.

194 Kramer, Tom. "From Rockefeller to Reagan: Do You Read Me?" *PerfM*. 1985 Spr; 10(2): 1-3. Lang.: Eng.
USA. 1965-1985. Historical studies. ■Reagan administration's attempts to cut arts funding through budget cuts to the National Endowment for the Arts. Examines original Rockefeller Panel report on the arts to explore consequences by such actions.

195 Kuyper, Joan. "Cultural Volunteer Program History in The United States: Where Does Your Organization Fit?" *JAML*. 1987 Sum; 17(2): 11-34. Notes. Lang.: Eng.
USA. 1700-1987. Historical studies. ■Volunteer programs, examples of kinds of organizations and their role in the cultural community.

196 Kwiatkowski, George; DeFee, Dallas. "Computers in Arts Organizations: Tool or Toll for Modern Times?" *JAML*. 1984 Spr; 14(1): 112-121. Lang.: Eng.
USA. 1980-1984. Critical studies. ■Effect of computers on not-for-profit arts organizations: management of changes, organizational problems, principles for successful implementation.

197 Lamb, Terry. "New Officers Outline Goals for SF/BAAC." *EN*. 1987 July; 72(7): 3. Illus.: Photo. B&W. 1. Lang.: Eng.
USA: San Francisco, CA. 1987. ■Goals of San Francisco/Bay Area Advisory Committee (SF/BAAC), a liaison group between bay area actors and AEA's Western Advisory Board which is based in Los Angeles.

198 Larkin, Christopher C. "Recent Developments in the Law of Parallel Imports: Nothing is Black and White in the Gray Market." *ColJL&A*. 1987 Sum; 11(4): 505-529. Notes. Lang.: Eng.
USA. 1986-1987. Technical studies. ■Recent legal decisions regarding customs regulations over imports of gray market items.

199 Lesnick, Howard. "Artists, Workers, and the Law of Work: Keynote Address." *JAML*. 1986 Sum; 16(2): 39-46. Lang.: Eng.
USA. 1986. Histories-sources. ■Speech on the consciousness of work, comparing literal and imaginative perceptions.

200 Levine, Mindy N. "Management Digest—Alternatives to Eight: Midday and Late-Night Programming." *TT*. 1986 Nov.; 6(1): 15. Lang.: Eng.
USA: New York, NY. 1986. Histories-sources. ■Alternative curtain times as a way to increase attendance.

201 Light, Jeffrey B. "The California Injunction Statute and the Music Industry: What Price Injunctive Relief." *A&L*. 1982; 7(2): 141-176. Lang.: Eng.
USA. 1958-1982. Critical studies. ■Effects of injunctions placed on small or medium sized record companies. Discusses the intentions of the law and how it has affected copyright fraud. Related to Media: Audio forms.

202 Linzy, Jerry A. "Involving Key Community Leaders In Your Program." *FundM*. 1987 Jan.; 17(11): 60-65. Illus.: Photo. Pntg. Color. B&W. 2. Lang.: Eng.
USA. 1987. Empirical research. ■Survey reveals what qualities volunteers look for in an organization and what gets them.

203 London, Todd. "Casting Across Color Lines: Imaginative Acts." *TT*. 1987 June/July; 6(5): 5-7. Illus.: Photo. B&W. 2. Lang.: Eng.
USA: New York, NY. 1987. Critical studies. ■Nontraditional casting: forms, purposes, and representative institutions, including The Nontraditional Casting Project.

204 London, Todd. "L.O.A.'s Come of Age." *TT*. 1987 May; 6(4): 6-7. Illus.: Photo. B&W. 3. Lang.: Eng.
USA: New York, NY. 1987. Historical studies. ■Diversity of Letter of Agreement theatres that operate in New York City.

205 Mai, Charles F. "Cultivating Major Gifts: Multiply Your Solicitation Efforts with Volunteers." *FundM*. 1987 Jan.; 17(11): 90-91. Illus.: Photo. Print. B&W. 1. Lang.: Eng.
USA. 1987. Historical studies. ■How to solicit and train volunteers to enhance efforts to obtain major gifts.

206 McCann, Joseph. "Videotape Recorders and Copyright Infringement: The Fair Use Doctrine on Instant Replay." *JAML*. 1984 Win; 13(4): 5-30. Notes. Lang.: Eng.
USA. 1984. Historical studies. ■Historical look at the Copyright Act and the 1984 Supreme Court case. Focus on sections of Copyright Act discussing problems and remedies for such infringement. Related to Media: Video forms.

207 McNamee, Thomas A. "Funding and Using Potential Volunteer Expertise." *FundM*. 1987 Jan.; 17(11): 66-68. Illus.: Photo. B&W. 1. Lang.: Eng.
USA: New York, NY. 1987. Historical studies. ■Preparing effective volunteer application forms: information-gathering techniques, recruitment materials.

208 Merlin, Joanna. "'Imagination or Baseball Caps?'." *EN*. 1986 Jan.; 72(1): 1, 2. Illus.: Photo. B&W. 1. Lang.: Eng.
USA: New York, NY. 1975-1987. Critical studies. ■Problems regarding nontraditional casting and the events that led to the formation of the first nontraditional casting symposium.

209 Meyer, David J. "Misapplication of the Misappropriation Doctrine to Merchandising." *ColJL&A*. 1987 Sum; 11(4): 601-634. Notes. Lang.: Eng.
USA. 1987. Technical studies. ■Language and legislative history of section 43(a) of the Copyright Act as related to trademark protection in merchandising properties.

210 Miller, Christopher. "Charles Ziff on Marketing the Arts." *PerfM*. 1983 Dec.; 9(1): 5, 7. Illus.: Photo. B&W. 1. Lang.: Eng.
USA: New York, NY. 1983. Histories-sources. ■Seminar given by marketing consultant Charles Ziff: analysis of marketing problems, marketing research.

211 Moore, John D. "The Independent Booking Office—'Linking Producers and Theatres'." *PerfM*. 1983 May; 8(2): 5. Lang.: Eng.

THEATRE IN GENERAL: —Administration

USA: New York, NY. 1983. Historical studies. ∎Profile of services and operations of Independent Booking Office, a scheduling agency for legit tours. Economic impact on touring industry.

212   Moore, Whitney McKendree. "Volunteers: A Changing Scene." *FundM.* 1987 Jan.; 17(11): 56-58. Illus.: Photo. B&W. 1. Lang.: Eng.

USA. 1987. Historical studies. ∎Attracting volunteers to non-profit organizations in spite of heavier workloads and busier schedules.

213   Mouchet, Dr. Carlos. "Problems of the 'Domaine Public Payant'." *A&L.* 1983; 8(2): 137-159. Lang.: Eng.

USA: New York, NY. 1983. Critical studies. ∎Aspects of paying for works in the public domain.

214   Mulcahy, Kevin V. "The Arts and Their Economic Impact: The Values of Utility." *JAML.* 1986 Fall; 16(3): 33-48. Notes. Lang.: Eng.

USA: Baton Rouge, LA. 1986. Empirical studies. ∎Impact of the arts on the economy, politics and society.

215   Newman, Harry. "Realization Is Not Enough." *EN.* 1987 Jan.; 72(1): 2. Illus.: Photo. B&W. 1. Lang.: Eng.

USA: New York, NY. 1986-1987. Critical studies. ∎The first national symposium on nontraditional casting from the point of its producer. How to continue work begun by symposium.

216   O'Quinn, Jim. "Voices in Congress Call Support of Arts Vital." *AmTh.* 1987 July/Aug.; 4(4): 28-30. Tables. Lang.: Eng.

USA: Washington, DC. 1987. Critical studies. ∎Report on a hearing of House Appropriations Committee on the Interior to evaluate proposed cuts by Reagan administration for the NEA and NEH.

217   Ossola, Charles D. "Work for Hire: A Judicial Quagmire and a Legislative Solution." *JAML.* 1987 Fall; 17(3): 23-63. Notes.

USA. 1987. Historical studies. ∎Copyright law regarding ownership of works for hire. Includes definitions of types of work for hire.

218   Pace, Guy; Viola, Tom. "Equity Employment: A Recent Update." *EN.* 1987 Feb.; 72(2): 1, 3, 4. Tables. Lang.: Eng.

USA. 1975-1985. Critical studies. ∎Survey of Actors' Equity membership employment from 1975-1985. Focus on statistics regarding work weeks and earnings.

219   Paran, Janice. "Money Tight for Music and Dance." *AmTh.* 1987 May; 4(2): 28-29. Notes. Illus.: Graphs. B&W. 1. Lang.: Eng.

USA. 1987. Critical studies. ∎Financial analysis of problems facing American theatre and how it may affect both artistry and audience attendance.

220   Patrinos, Sondra. "Arbitrator Rules for Equity in Midwest Just Cause Claim." *EN.* 1986 Mar.; 71(3): 4. Lang.: Eng.

USA: Chicago, IL. 1985-1986. Historical studies. ∎Actress Wysandria Woolsey received 5 weeks back salary after taking Firehouse Dinner Theatre to court for 'termination without just cause'.

221   Patrinos, Sondra. "Currie Takes Over Midwest Regional Office." *EN.* 1986 June; 71(6): 3. Lang.: Eng.

USA: Chicago, IL. 1986. Historical studies. ∎Tad Currie coordinates labor-sponsored conference for Chicago Actors' Equity members. Haymarket Theatre tragedy recalled with performance, new members initiated, blood donor participation and CPR training.

222   Phillips, Gary W. "How Key Volunteers Raised $143 Million." *FundM.* 1987 Jan.; 17(11): 28-30. Illus.: Photo. Print. B&W. Color. 6. Lang.: Eng.

USA: Los Angeles, CA. 1980-1986. Historical studies. ∎Organizational techniques and planning needed to raise large sums from individual donors for Orange County's Performing Arts Center.

223   Pollock, Karen D. "Pennsylvania Arts Information System For Local Arts Agencies." *JAML.* 1984 Spr; 14(1): 90-94. Lang.: Eng.

USA. 1982-1983. Historical studies. ∎Development and implementation of the Pennsylvania Arts Information Systems Project (PAIS) for major local arts agencies.

224   Rapson, David J. "Legislature Relief and the Betamax Problem." *A&L.* 1982; 7(2): 125-140. Lang.: Eng.

USA: Los Angeles, CA. 1980-1982. Critical studies. ∎Judicial and legislative remedies that can be used to deal with the problem of home video recording of copyrighted works. Related to Media: Video forms.

225   Recer, J. Dan. "How Planned Charitable Gifts Benefit Heirs." *FundM.* 1987 Feb.; 17(12): 38-43. Tables. Illus.: Photo. Print. B&W. 7. Lang.: Eng.

USA. 1985-1987. Critical studies. ∎How sound charitable estate plan can still leave heirs well-provided for.

226   Renick, Kyle. "The Greening of Magnolias: Commercial Transfers Come of Age." *TT.* 1987 Nov.; 7(1): 4-5. Illus.: Photo. B&W. 2. Lang.: Eng.

USA: New York, NY. 1987. Critical studies. ∎Artistic director of WPA Theatre discusses transferring *Steel Magnolias* to the Lucille Lortel Theatre as a commercial production.

227   Robinson, Alma. "Dispute Resolution for the Arts Community." *ColJL&A.* 1987 Win; 11(2): 333-345. Lang.: Eng.

USA: San Francisco, CA. 1980-1987. Critical studies. ∎Education for artists on legal problems and how to negotiate for themselves.

228   Schmoll, Herbert. "Acquiring Software, Hardware and Expertise." *JAML.* 1984 Spr; 14(1): 40-44. Lang.: Eng.

USA. 1983. Technical studies. ∎Beginner's guide includes definitions and explanations of technical terms and references for more advanced information.

229   Schooner, Steven L. "Obscene Parody: The Judicial Exception to Fair Use Analysis." *JAML.* 1984 Fall; 14(3): 69-94. Notes. Lang.: Eng.

USA. 1976-1984. Critical studies. ∎Fair use standards of the Copyright Act of 1976: difficulties encountered with obscene parodies, satire, burlesque and mimicry.

230   Schultz, A. Charles. "Four Steps to Closing a Major Planned Gift." *FundM.* 1987 Feb.; 17(12): 44-46, 54. Illus.: Photo. Graphs. Print. B&W. 6. Lang.: Eng.

USA. 1987. Historical studies. ∎Use of written word and graphics communicates concept of planned gifts and wins support of lawyers and accountants.

231   Schuster, J. Mark Davidson. "Issues in Supporting the Arts Through Tax Incentives." *JAML.* 1987 Win; 17(4): 31-50. Notes. Lang.: Eng.

USA. 1987. Critical studies. ∎Supporting the arts through government-instituted tax programs, comparison of methods.

232   Shewey, Don. "The Little Theatre That Could." *AmTh.* 1987 June; 4(3): 20-24, 45. Notes. Illus.: Photo. B&W. 3. Lang.: Eng.

USA: New York, NY. 1987. Critical studies. ∎Profile of Ensemble Studio Theatre describing structure and accomplishments.

233   Simon, Jules F. "The Collapse of Consensus: Effects of the Deregulation of Cable Television." *A&L.* 1982; 7(1): 19-52. Lang.: Eng.

USA: New York, NY. 1934-1982. Historical studies. ∎Problems associated with the deregulation of cable television. The role of the FCC, history of cable television. Related to Media: Video forms.

234   Skloot, Edward. "The Rules of the Game Have Changed." *AmTh.* 1987 Sep.; 4(6): 44-46. Lang.: Eng.

USA. 1984-1987. Historical studies. ∎Recent legislative changes and their impact on nonprofit theatre and their funding sources.

235   Stewart, William; Fichandler, Zelda; White, David R.; Dean, Laura; Bikel, Theodore. "Professional Standards and Managerial Realities." *JAML.* 1986 Sum; 16(2): 9-38. Lang.: Eng.

USA. 1986. Histories-sources. ∎Panel discussion on problems faced by regional theatres and dance companies using union labor and negotiating union contracts.

236   Strang, Judith; Strang, Roger A. "Implications of Information Systems for Performing Arts Management: A Case Study." *JAML.* 1984 Spr; 14(1): 105-111. Lang.: Eng.

USA. 1979-1983. Historical studies. ∎Experience of a major performing arts organization three years after the installation of a computer-based information system. Detailed description of benefits and current limitations, recommendations for other organizations.

THEATRE IN GENERAL: —Administration

237   Sullivan, Dan. "Are We Creating Splendid Structures for Starving Artists?" *AmTh*. 1987 Nov.; 4(8): 50. Illus.: Photo. B&W. 1. Lang.: Eng.
USA. 1987. Critical studies. ■Tendency for arts patrons to donate money for buildings for the arts versus sponsoring the artists themselves.

238   Swanson, Joann. "Contract Development at AEA: An Interview." *PerfM*. 1987 Win; 13(1): 3-5. Lang.: Eng.
USA. 1987. Histories-sources. ■Interview with Ron Aja of Actors' Equity Association discussing the Letter of Agreement and Small Professional Theatre contracts.

239   Szentgyorgi, Tom. "Is There a Life After the Life of One's Theatre Ends?" *TT*. 1987 Nov.; 7(1): 6-7. Illus.: Dwg. 7. Lang.: Eng.
USA. 1981-1987. Histories-sources. ■Margaret Booker, Bob Kulfin, Steve Robman, Norman Rene discuss their creation of theatre companies as well as their failure.

240   Tetrault, Helen. "Pension Deductions May Cut Unemployment Insurance." *EN*. 1982 Aug.; 67(8): 2. Lang.: Eng.
USA: New York, NY. 1982. Critical studies. ■Instructions for Actors' Equity members regarding new regulations in unemployment.

241   Truex, Duane P., III. "Decision Support Systems' Applications in Museum Management." *JAML*. 1984 Spr; 14(1): 95-103. Notes. Biblio. Lang.: Eng.
USA. 1983-1984. Technical studies. ■Decision Support Systems (DSS): its evolution, definition, purpose, service to the arts and the Museum Users Strategic Environmental Support System (MUSESS).

242   Urice, John K. "Information Systems and the Arts: An Overview." *JAML*. 1984 Spr; 14(1): 9-17. Notes. Lang.: Eng.
USA. 1977-1984. Histories-specific. ■Information systems used in arts organizations. Definition, history, fears and legitimate concerns.

243   Watkins, Clyde P. "Major Gift Volunteers: A Balanced View." *FundM*. 1987 Jan.; 17(11): 48-54. Lang.: Eng.
USA: Chicago, IL. 1987. Historical studies. ■Successful volunteers and their methods of fundraising.

244   Wehle, Philippa. "Foreign Artists, Stay Home!" *TT*. 1987 Apr.; 6(3): 9-10. Illus.: Photo. 2. Lang.: Eng.
USA. 1987. Critical studies. ■Legal difficulties facing producers who present foreign artists and dance troupes.

245   Weil, Stephen E. "Artists, Workers and the Law of Work: Introductory Comments." *JAML*. 1986 Sum; 16(2): 37-38. Lang.: Eng.
USA. 1986. Histories-sources. ■Introduction of speech on the working world and the legal terms we currently use to describe it.

246   Weinlein, Craig W. "Federal Taxation of Not-for-Profit Arts Organizations: A Primer for Arts Managers." *JAML*. 1982 Sum; 12(2): 33-50. Notes. Lang.: Eng.
USA. 1982. Historical studies. ■The requirements for obtaining and maintaining an exemption from federal income taxation for a not-for-profit arts organization. Attention is paid to Section 501(c)(3) of the Internal Revenue Code.

247   White, Douglas E. "Planned Giving and Computers." *FundM*. 1987 Feb.; 17(12): 24-26. Illus.: Photo. Print. B&W. 2. Lang.: Eng.
USA. 1987. Historical studies. ■How computers provide complex calculations necessary for donor prospects to make planned giving decision.

248   Williams, James J. "A Problem with Baumol and Bowen's 'Dilemma'." *PerfM*. 1985 Spr; 10(2): 7-8. Illus.: Photo. B&W. 1. Lang.: Eng.
USA. 1966-1985. Historical studies. ■Influence of William J. Baumol and William G. Bowen's report *Performing Arts—The Economic Dilemma* on the structure of financing the arts.

249   Wry, Brann J. "Recent Software Developments: A Roundtable." *JAML*. 1984 Spr; 14(1): 45-76. Pref. Lang.: Eng.
USA. 1983-1984. Histories-sources. ■Series of interviews with four professionals in the arts information systems industry posing the same questions to each participant. Recent developments and current services of computer vendors.

250   Wry, Brann J. "The Trustee: The Ultimate Volunteer." *JAML*. 1987 Sum; 17(2): 35-47. Notes. Illus.: Graphs. 1. Lang.: Eng.
USA. 1987. Technical studies. ■Board of directors, function of a board member: qualifications and recruitment.

251   Wyszomirski, Margaret Jane. "Philanthropy, The Arts, and Public Policy." *JAML*. 1987 Win; 17(4): 5-30. Notes. Tables. 3. Lang.: Eng.
USA. 1987. Critical studies. ■Relationship of philanthropy to the arts and public policy. Comparison of revenue to unearned revenue in non-profit organizations.

252   Youngstrom, Donn M. "The Board vs. the Artistic Director: A Case in Point." *PerfM*. 1987 Spr; 12(1): 3-4. Lang.: Eng.
USA. 1987. Historical studies. ■Responsibilities of a board of directors to a theatre, relationship to artistic and managing directors. Resignation of Christopher Martin from CSC Repertory after conflict with board is cited as case study.

253   Yurke, Alice F. "Copyright Issues Concerning the Publication of Samizdat Literature in the United States." *ColJL&A*. 1987 Spr; 11(3): 449-470. Notes. Lang.: Eng.
USA. USSR. 1973-1987. Historical studies. ■Publication of works by Soviet authors circumventing official publishing network. Soviet copyright law, US law and policy concerning foreign authors.

254   Zeisler, Peter. "A New Delicate Balance." *AmTh*. 1987 Aug.: 5. Lang.: Eng.
USA. 1987. Critical studies. ■Relation of government spending to non-profit organizations. Concepts of tithing and 'Give Five' campaign.

255   Zeisler, Peter. "Do-It-Yourself Patronage." *AmTh*. 1987 Nov.: 5. Lang.: Eng.
USA. 1987. Critical studies. ■Discusses the new trend toward production sharing among non-profit theatres in an effort to develop new works for theatre in a financially sound way. Relationships between commercial and non-profit theatre companies.

256   Zesch, Lindy. "Launching Challenge III." *AmTh*. 1987 Jan.; 3(10): 30-31. Lang.: Eng.
USA. 1977-1987. Historical studies. ■Debate over the National Endowment for the Arts' new guidelines. History of the NEA budget and funding.

257   Zimmerman, Jory Brad. "Exclusivity of Personal Services: The Viability and Enforceability of Contractual Rights." *JAML*. 1986 Fall; 16(3): 61-88. Notes. Lang.: Eng.
USA. 1986. Critical studies. ■Relationships between artists and producers regarding exclusivity of services and enforceability of contractual rights.

258   "Teatr i deti." (Theatre and Children.) *TeatrM*. 1987; 2: 95-135. Lang.: Rus.
USSR. 1986-1987. Histories-sources. ■Selection of articles by critics, directors, actors and teachers on the problems of children's theatres.

259   Altaev, A.; Tjutjunik, A. "Proverim algebru garmonij." (Let Us Verify the Algebra of Harmonies.) *TeatrM*. 1987; 1: 22-26 . Lang.: Rus.
USSR. 1986-1987. ■Economic questions of the theatrical experiment.

260   Begunov, V. "Est' ideja!" (The Idea Exists.) *TeatZ*. 1987; 9: 14-15. Lang.: Rus.
USSR. 1987. Critical studies. ■Problems of arts patronage, cooperation between theatres and businesses.

261   Borovskij, A.D. *Russkij teatral'nyj plakat: 1870-1970-e gody: Stanovlenie, osnovnye tendencii, sovremennaja problematika: Avtoref. dis. kand. iskusstvovedenija.* (The Russian Theatre Poster, 1870-1979: Establishment Basic Tendencies, Problems: Abstract of a Dissertation by a Candidate in Art Criticism.)
USSR. 1870-1979. Historical studies.

262   Dikich, A.L. "Éksperiment vozrodil naši nadeždy." (Experiment Revitalized Our Hopes.) *TeatZ*. 1987; 8: 13. Lang.: Rus.
USSR: Moscow. 1986-1987. Histories-sources. ■Director of Sovremennik Theatre on theatrical experimentation.

CLASSED ENTRIES

THEATRE IN GENERAL: —Administration

263 Focht-Babuškin, Ju. U.; Nel'gol'dberg, V. Ja.; Osokin, Ju. V. *Chudočestvennaja kul'tura i razvitie ličnosti: Problemy dolzosročnogo planirovanija.* (Artistic Culture and the Development of Personality: Problems of Long-Term Planning.) Moscow: VNII Iskusstvoznanija; 1987. Lang.: Rus.
USSR. 1987. Critical studies.

264 Klimontovič, N. "Beg v meške." (Running in a Sack.) *MK.* 1987; 7: 84-90. Lang.: Rus.
USSR: Moscow. 1986-1988. Critical studies. ■Difficulties of perestrojka in literature and art, especially Moscow professional studio theatres, reception of work by young playwrights.

265 Kogan, I.A. "Takoj éksperiment menja ne ustraivaet." (Such an Experiment Doesn't Suit Me.) *TeatZ.* 1987; 8: 12. Lang.: Rus.
USSR: Moscow. 1987. Histories-sources. ■Interview with director of Teat'r na Maloj Bronnoj.

266 Orenov, V. "Vedat' ili byt'." (To Manage or to Exit.) *SovD.* 1987; 1: 241-246. Lang.: Rus.
USSR. 1986-1988. Histories-sources. ■A critic's views of the status of the director of literary affairs in the theatre experiment.

267 Smeljanskij, A.M.; Svydkoj, M.E. *Teatr...vremja peremen: Sbornik statej.* (Theatre—A Time of Changes: A Collection of Essays.) Moscow: Iskusstvo; 1987. 223 pp. Lang.: Rus.
USSR. 1985-1987. Critical studies. ■Articles by leading playwrights, critics and economists on training for the theatrical experiment.

268 Solodovnikov, A. "U kolybeli 'Sovremennika'." (By the Cradle of the 'Sovremennik'.) *TeatrM.* 1987; 10: 58-69. Lang.: Rus.
USSR: Moscow. 1956-1957. Histories-sources. ■Former director on foundation of Sovremennik Studio theatre.

269 Starosel'skaja, N. "Kogda scena sovremenna zalu." (When the Stage is Contemporary with the House.) *DetLit.* 1987; 9: 46-50. Lang.: Rus.
USSR: Moscow. 1980-1987. Historical studies. ■Changes in children's theatre repertory, most significant recent performances.

270 Švedova, O. "'Ideal'nyj portret'." ('Ideal Portrait'.) *SovD.* 1987; 1: 247-249. Lang.: Rus.
USSR. 1980-1987. Critical studies. ■Problems of the enhancement of literary director's prestige.

271 Ul'janov, Michajl A.; Ščerbakov, K. "Pomoščnik, a ne sluga." (An Assistant, But Not a Servant.) *DruzNar.* 1987; 3: 198-205. Lang.: Rus.
USSR. 1986-1988. Historical studies. ■Perestrojka in the theatre business: the Union of Theatre Workers of the Russian SFSR.

272 Ul'janov, Michajl A. "I skaždogo iz nas sprositsja." (And It Will Be Asked of Each of Us.) *TeatZ.* 1987; 9: 3-5. Lang.: Rus.
USSR. 1986-1988. Histories-sources. ■Chairman of the board of the STD of the Russian Federated Republic on problems of theatre business.

273 Vaganova, N.K.; Dondošanskaja, A.I.; Sundstrem, L.G. *Nekotorye finansovo-ékonomičeskie problemy sovremennogo teatra.* (Some Financial-Economic Problems of the Contemporary Theatre.) Moscow: Gosudarstvennaja Biblioteka im V.I. Lenina; 1987. 36 pp. (Zreliščmije iskusstva. Obzornaja informacija 3.) Lang.: Rus.
USSR. 1986-1987. Historical studies.

274 Vergasova, I. "Poučitel'naja istorija." (An Instructive Story.) *TeatZ.* 1987; 7: 20-21. Lang.: Rus.
USSR. 1987. Critical studies. ■Work and problems of a children's theatre in an outlying district.

275 Židkov, V. "Pogovorim o modeljah." (Let's Speak of Models.) *TeatZ.* 1987; 16: 10-11. Lang.: Rus.
USSR. 1986-1987. Critical studies. ■Economic problems of the theatrical experiment.

Audience

276 Brown, Paul. "Making *Coal Town*." *Meanjin.* 1987; 46(4): 477-448. Lang.: Eng.

Australia: Collinsville. 1984-1985. Historical studies. ■A participant's impressionistic account of a Sydney-based theatre group, Death Defying Theatre, arriving in the isolated mining town of Collinsville to devise a play *Coal Town*, about the community and the miners.

277 Colbert, François. "Le loisir, le théâtre et le théâtre d'été." (Leisure, Theatre and Summer Theatre.) *JCT.* 1987; 42: 127-134. Illus.: Photo. Graphs. Print. B&W. 4. Lang.: Fre.
Canada. 1964-1984. Technical studies. ■Low demand for summer theatre contrasted with availability of other entertainments.

278 Foster, Deborah. "Toronto STARR: Teaching Responsible Sex." *CTR.* 1987 Win; 53: 76-78. Illus.: Photo. Print. B&W. 1. [Carte Blanche.] Lang.: Eng.
Canada: Toronto, ON. 1987. Critical studies. ■The practice of kids teaching kids through drama is explored through the STARR project. Public Health funded this experiment to serve the dual purpose of encouraging kids to alleviate fears by asking questions, and to posit possible answers together using accurate information.

279 Zhuang, Yi. "Lun xi ju de san du chuang zao." (The Three Dimensions in Drama.) *XYishu.* 1985 Sum; 30: 38-48. Notes. Lang.: Chi.
China, People's Republic of. 1985. Critical studies. ■Outlines the relationship between script, actors and audience.

280 Wolohojian, G. *George Colman the Elder and the Late Eighteenth-Century Theatre Audience.* Oxford: Univ. of Oxford; 1986. Notes. Biblio. [D.Phil. thesis, *Index to Theses,* 37-2150.] Lang.: Eng.
England: London. 1767-1774. Historical studies. ■Examines the influence of the audience on Colman's artistic choices. Studies the link between Colman's managerial policies and theatre economics.

281 "L'estat de la qüestió." (The Matter at Issue.) 9-17 in Coca, Jordi, ed.; Conesa, Laura, comp. *Congrés Internacional de Teatre a Catalunya 1985. Actes. Volum III. Seccions 7, 8 i 9.* Barcelona: Institut del Teatre; 1987. 350 pp. [Section 7: The New Technologies.] Lang.: Cat.
Europe. 1885-1985. Critical studies. ■Effects of film and television on theatrical practice: accentuation of tension between written text and the textuality of representation, alteration of audience-performer relationship. Related to Media: Film.

282 Müller-Kampel, Beatrix. "Vom Seelengenuss zum Sinnengenuss. Theater und Schauspiel in der zweiten Hälfte des 19. Jahrhunderts am Beispiel Berlins." (From Enjoyment of the Soul to Enjoyment of the Senses. Theatre and Spectacle in the Second Half of the Nineteenth Century.) *MuK.* 1986; 32(1-2): 115-128. Lang.: Ger.
Germany: Berlin. 1850-1900. Historical studies.

283 Eytan, Mina. "Theatron Yeladim Ve-Noahar Beahuoda Kehilatit." (Theatre for Children and Youth in Commercial Work.) *Bamah.* 1987; 22(108): 34-39. Lang.: Heb.
Israel. 1987. Critical studies. ■Importance of children's theatre and community theatre to the community.

284 DeMarinis, Marco. "Dramaturgy of the Spectator." *TDR.* 1987 Sum; 31(2): 100-114. Notes. Biblio. Illus.: Photo. Lang.: Eng.
Italy. 1987. Critical studies. ■Scientific and psychological study of the role of audience as dramaturgs.

285 Nishidō, Kōjin. "Butai to kyakuseki no aida." (Between Stage and Audience.) *Sg.* 1987 Feb; 407: 92-97. Illus.: Photo. B&W. 3. Lang.: Jap.
Japan: Tokyo. 1960-1986. Critical studies. ■Compares present relationship between Japanese performers and their audience with that of the 1960s, when interaction was considered appropriate. Traces the influence of contemporary culture, based on mass information, on theatrical performances, resulting in uniformity.

286 Jung, Jon Woo. "Yŏn'gŭk Ŭisik." (Difficult Time for Theatre.) 22-27 pp in Seoul P'yongnon'ga Group, ed. *Han'guk Yŏnguk kwa Chŏlmon Ŭislk.* Mineum SA: Park. Mazngho; 1979. 262 pp. Notes. Lang.: Kor.
Korea. 1970-1979. Historical studies. ■Lack of theatre consciousness in Korean audiences.

THEATRE IN GENERAL: —Audience

287   Lee, Sang-Il. "Moodaewa kwankaeksukui keunwonjeok jubchok." (The Fundamental Relation of Stage and Auditorium.) *DongukDA*. 1976 Dec.; 9: 122-129. Lang.: Kor.
Korea. 1976. Empirical research. ■Personal view of the relation between stage and audience.

288   Sŏ, Yŏn-ho. "Yŏngŭk Gong'yŏn Kwa Kwangak." (Theatre Performance and Audience.) 56-60 pp in Seoul P'yong-non'ga Group, ed. *Han'guk Yŏnguk kwa Chŏlmon Üislk*. Mineum SA: Park. Mazngho; 1979. 262 pp. Notes. Lang.: Kor.
Korea. 1900-1970. Historical studies. ■Definition of the role of theatre in society.

289   Becker, Maria. "Das Publikum." (The Audience.) *MuT*. 1987 June; 8(6): 8-12. Illus.: Photo. B&W. Lang.: Ger.
Switzerland. 1987. Critical studies. ■A number of hints as to the function of the audience. Due to the varying audience the individual performances are not alike: success of a performance seems to rely on a telepathic interaction between audience and actors.

290   Blau, Herbert. "Odd, Anonymous Needs: The Audience in a Dramatized Society." *PerAJ*. 1985 Sum/Fall; 9(26-27): 199-212. Lang.: Eng.
USA. 1985. Critical studies. ■The nature, needs and power of the theatre audience.

291   Daniels, Barry V., ed. "Letters of Joseph Chaikin." *TDR*. 1987 Spr; 31(1): 89-100. Pref. Illus.: Photo. Print. B&W. 5. Lang.: Eng.
USA: Washington, DC, New York, NY. 1974-1984. Histories-sources. ■Series of letters written by Joseph Chaikin to his cast of *The Dybbuk* and to Sam Shepard on actor-audience relationship and his illness.

292   Martin, Christopher. "Yogi's Out, Billy's In: The Great American Theatre Ballgame." *PerAJ*. 1985 Sum/Fall; 9(26-27): 91-98. Lang.: Eng.
USA. 1985. Critical studies. ■Need for American theatre creators to connect with contemporary audiences.

293   Salazar, Laura Gardner. "The Emergence of Children's Theatre, A Study in America's Changing Values and the Stage, 1900 to 1910." *THSt*. 1987; 7: 73-83. Notes. Lang.: Eng.
USA. 1900-1910. Historical studies. ■A matrix of unique social and aesthetic trends promoted the development of children's theatre in early twentieth-century America.

294   Ivčenko, V.N. *Sociologičeskie problemy teatra (teorija i praktika issledovanija): Avtoref. dis. kand. filos. nauk*. (Sociological Problems of the Theatre—The Theory and Practice of Research: Abstract of a Dissertation by a Candidate in Philosophy.) Minsk: In-t filosofii i prava; 1987. 19 pp. Lang.: Rus.
USSR. 1980-1987. Critical studies.

295   Kljavina, T. "Parad populjarnosti." (A Parade of Popularity.) *TeatZ*. 1987; 23: 12-13. Lang.: Rus.
USSR. 1980-1987. Empirical studies. ■Sociological study of the popularity of directors, dramatists and performances.

Basic theatrical documents

296   Alexander, Robert I. "Some Dramatic Records from Percy Household Accounts on Microfilm." *REEDN*. 1987; 12(2): 10-17. Notes. Lang.: Eng.
England. 1582-1639. Histories-sources. ■Selected records of the household accounts of the Percy family (Earls of Northumberland) and the use of such records in analyzing the Percy contribution to theatre.

297   Kluger, Garry Michael. *Original Audition Scenes for Actors: A Collection of Professional Level Short Scenes*. Colorado Springs, CO: Meriwether; 1987. 105 pp. Lang.: Eng.
USA. 1987. Instructional materials. ■Author has written a selection of short audition pieces: scenes and monologues for men and women.

298   Litvin, Je. Ju. "Iz pisem Michaila Bulgakova, 1924-1931." (From the Letters of Michajl Bulgakov, 1924-1931.) *Pamir*. 1987; 8: 92-100. Lang.: Rus.
USSR: Moscow. 1924-1931. Histories-sources. ■Moscow theatrical world, reception of his plays, articles on theatre and dramaturgy.

Design/technology

299   Piizzi, Paola. *Rito e mito della maschera. L'opera dei Sartori*. (The Ritual and Myth of Masks: The Work of the Sartoris.) Florence: Usher; 1987. 127 pp. Illus.: Handbill. Photo. Sketches. Print. Color. B&W. Lang.: Ita.
Historical studies. ■A panorama of the world of masks, their use in theatre and their evolution throughout the world, based on the research of Donato and Amleto Sartori.

300   Cannon, Cate; Figueroa, Lydia; Grossman, Laura. "Theatre Painting Seminar in Salzburg." *TD&T*. 1987; 22(4): 5-6. Illus.: Photo. B&W. 3. Lang.: Eng.
Austria: Salzburg. 1986. Histories-sources. ■Experiences of three students at the third international scene painting seminar conducted primarily by Othmar Schwarz at the Mozarteum.

301   Vanhaecke, Frank, ed.; Pausch, Oskar, gen. ed. *La garderobe du rêve/De garderobe van de droom: Costumes de théâtre viennois*. (The Wardrobe of Dreams: Viennese Theatre Costumes.) Brussels: Europalia/City of Brussels; 1987. 38 pp. Illus.: Photo. Color. B&W. 18. Lang.: Fre, Dut.
Austria: Vienna. 1888-1972. Histories-sources. ■Illustrated catalogue of an exhibit of Viennese costume past and present, from the theatre collections of the National Library of Austria and the Austrian Museum of Theatre.

302   Le Blanc, Danièle. "Live on T.V. You Can Watch Them Die." *JCT*. 1987; 44: 136-138. Illus.: Photo. Print. B&W. 2. Lang.: Fre.
Canada. 1900-1987. Histories-specific. ■Theatre in the twentieth century has been enriched by the use of technology, reducing the central importance of the spoken word in drama.

303   Ouaknine, Serge. "Le réel théâtral et le réel médiatique." (Theatrical Reality and Media Reality.) *JCT*. 1987; 44: 93-111. Illus.: Photo. Print. B&W. 14. Lang.: Fre.
Canada. 1977-1987. Histories-specific. ■Special effects have spread throughout the theatre and given us different interpretations of reality.

304   Hu, Miao-Sheng. "Wu tai she ji ABC." (Stage Design ABC.) *XYishu* 1985 Spr; 29: 100-109. Lang.: Chi.
China, People's Republic of. 1984-1985. Instructional materials. ■Everything about stage design.

305   Aronson, Arnold. "The Svoboda Dimension." *AmTh*. 1987 Oct.; 4(7): 24-25, 94-96. Illus.: Photo. B&W. 2. Lang.: Eng.
Czechoslovakia: Prague. 1940-1987. Biographical studies. ■Work of noted set designer and technological innovator Josef Svoboda: his earliest work and innovations with film and slide projections.

306   Bennett-Hunter, A.K. "Luddite Among the Lasers." *Sin*. 1987; 21(2): 23-24. Lang.: Eng.
Czechoslovakia: Prague. 1987. Technical studies. ■Report on the Prague Quadrennial design competition.

307   Bögel, József. "Prágai Quadriennálé '87." (The Prague Quadrennial '87.) *SFo*. 1987; 14(4): 11-15. Illus.: Photo. B&W. 9. Lang.: Hun.
Czechoslovakia: Prague. 1987. Histories-sources. ■Account by the national commissioner of the Hungarian exhibition.

308   Bolt, Jenny. "Divine Disasters." *Sin*. 1987; 21(2): 24-25. Illus.: Photo. Color. B&W. 4. Lang.: Eng.
Czechoslovakia: Prague. 1987. Technical studies. ■The contribution of Josef Svoboda to the 1987 Prague Quadrennial design competition exhibition.

309   Burian, Jarka M. "Svoboda and Vychodil." *ThCr*. 1987 Oct.. Illus.: Photo. Color. 13. Lang.: Eng.
Czechoslovakia: Prague. USA. 1950-1987. Historical studies. ■Czechoslovakia's two master scenographers and their work: Josef Svoboda and Ladislav Vychodil.

310   Bury, John. "Gentlemen of the Jury." *Sin*. 1987; 21(2): 15-17. Illus.: Photo. B&W. 2. Lang.: Eng.
Czechoslovakia: Prague. 1987. Histories-sources. ■Judge of Prague Quadrennial design competition describes jury's work.

311   Fielding, Eric. "The United States Prague Quadrennial." *ThCr*. 1987 Oct.. Illus.: Photo. B&W. 7. Lang.: Eng.

CLASSED ENTRIES

THEATRE IN GENERAL: —Design/technology

Czechoslovakia: Prague. USA. 1967-1987. Historical studies. ■First American participation in primarily Western European theatre design contest.

312 Nilsson, Nils-Gunnar. "PQ 87. Silvermedalj till Norrbottenteatern." (PQ 87: The Silver Medal to the Norrbottenteatern.) *ProScen.* 1987; 10(3): 12-18. Illus.: Photo. 12. Lang.: Swe.

Czechoslovakia: Prague. 1987. Histories-sources. ■A report from the Prague Quadrennial theatre design contest.

313 Ptáčková, Věra. "Osud a tvorba." (The Doom and the Production.) *ScenaP.* 1987; 12(10): 3. Lang.: Cze.

Czechoslovakia: Prague. 1911-1939. Biographical studies. ■About the stage-design production of Josef Čapek.

314 Smejkal, Frantisek. "Il Futurismo nell'opera di Jiři Kroha." (Futurism in the Work of Jiři Kroha.) *TeatrC.* 1987 ; 7(14): 163-168. Lang.: Ita.

Czechoslovakia. 1918-1923. Biographical studies. ■The influence of futurism in the scenographic work of Jiři Kroha. Grp/movt: Futurism.

315 Unruh, Delbert. "Action Design." *TD&T.* 1987; 23(1): 6-13. Illus.: Photo. B&W. 6. Lang.: Eng.

Czechoslovakia: Prague. 1980-1987. Historical studies. ■Identification and discussion of new theory of scenography emerging in Eastern Europe. Departure from school of design pioneered by Josef Svoboda and his generation of designers, Action Design is motivated both by economic and aesthetic concerns.

316 Astington, John H. "Counterweights in Elizabethan Stage Machinery." *TN.* 1987; 41(1): 18-24. Notes. B&W. Lang.: Eng.

England. 1433-1579. Critical studies. ■Presents evidence for the use of counterweights in England in support of speculations by W.J. Lawrence's published assertion, 1927.

317 Baugh, Christopher. "Philippe James de Loutherbourg and the Early Pictorial Theatre: Some Aspects of Its Cultural Context." *TID.* 1987; 9: 99-128. Notes. Append. Illus.: Photo. Dwg. B&W. 14. Lang.: Eng.

England. 1700-1800. Critical studies. ■De Loutherbourg's systematic use of scenic elements radically reconfigured English theatre in the eighteenth century. New language of the theatre later replaced by realism. Response to historical situation.

318 de Toro, Fernando. "Vers un théâtre multimédia." (Towards a Multimedia Theatre.) *JCT.* 1987; 44: 116-123. Illus.: Photo. Print. B&W. 6. Lang.: Fre.

Europe. 1900-1987. Historical studies. ■The traditional focus on the actor and on language has changed with the introduction of multimedia into theatre.

319 Gastambide, Ariane. "A Spadeful of Dead Leaves." *Sin.* 1987; 21(2): 18-22. Illus.: Photo. Dwg. Color. B&W. 10. Lang.: Eng.

Europe. 1987. Technical studies. ■Stage designer's review of Prague Quadrennial design competition.

320 Hopkins, Albert A.; Hector, David Stefan, transl. "Vetenskapen och teatern. Första kapitlet: Bakom kulisserna." (Science and the Theatre. First Chapter: Behind the Scenes.) *ProScen.* 1987; 10(1-2): 29-36. Illus.: Dwg. 14. Lang.: Swe.

Europe. USA. 1870-1900. Histories-sources. ■A description of typical 19th-century stage technology from the Swedish version of Albert A. Hopkins' *Magic, Stage Illusions and Scientific Diversion* (New York). Chapter 2 in *ProScen* 10:3 (1987), 34-44. Chapter 3, *ProScen* 10:4 (1987), 33-44.

321 Cooper, Douglas. *Picasso teatro.* (Picasso Theatre.) Milan: Jaca; 1987. 365 pp. (I contemporanei.) Pref. Biblio. Index. Illus.: Photo. Pntg. Dwg. Sketches. Print. B&W. Lang.: Ita.

France. Spain. 1917-1965. Historical studies. ■Translation of *Picasso et le théâtre* (Paris): Picasso's stage designs for theatre and ballet, his two plays.

322 Overy, Paul. "Theatrical Experiments: Artists in the Theatre, Hatton Gallery, Newcastle-upon-Tyne." *Studio International.* 1987; 200(1087): 52. Illus.: Design. B&W. 2. Lang.: Eng.

France. Critical studies. ■Exhibition of work by Fernand Léger, Jean Cocteau, Oskar Kokoschka and Wassily Kandinsky.

323 Gieling, Lia. "Zoeken naar verbanden." (Looking for Connections.) *Toneel.* 1987 Feb.; 2(4): 29-32. Illus.: Photo. Sketches. 12. Lang.: Dut.

Germany. 1888-1943. Biographical studies. ■The work of Oskar Schlemmer, German artist and theatre experimenter. Known as the 'refresher of the phenomenon theatre'. Relationship between space and man. His work in costuming and theatre.

324 "Szinpadgépészeti tapasztalatok." (Experiences Concerning the Stage Machinery of the Friedrichstadtpalast.) *SFo.* 1987; 14(1): 27-30. Illus.: Photo. B&W. Grd.Plan. 9. Lang.: Hun.

Germany, East: Berlin, East. 1984. Technical studies. ■Description and evaluation of the stage machinery in the new Friedrichstadtpalast.

325 Pálfí, Ferenc; Szabó-Jilek, Iván. "A modern szinháztechnika: a fejlődés helyzete, lehetőségek, korlátek." (Up-to-Date Theatre Technology: Development, Possibilities, Limits.) *SFo.* 1987; 14(1): 10-11. Lang.: Hun.

Germany, East: Berlin, East. 1986. Histories-sources. ■The text of the report of December 3, 1986 introducing the discussion at the East Berlin session of the Working Commission for the Development of Equipment and Products of Theatre Technology.

326 Rhinow, Karl. "Laser—das ungewöhnliche Licht." (Laser—the Unusual Light.) *TZ.* 1987; 42(11): 32-33. Illus.: Photo. B&W. 1. Lang.: Ger.

Germany, East: Berlin, East. 1983-1987. Technical studies. ■Application of lasers in stage design.

327 Kaiser, Gunter. "Szenografie. Die vieldeutige Welt des Interieurs und Exterieurs." (Scenography: The Ambiguous World of Interior and Exterior.) *TZ.* 1987; 42(4): 26-30. Illus.: Photo. 10. Lang.: Ger.

Germany, West. Germany, East. 1840-1986. Historical studies. ■On specific usage of interior and exterior scenic spaces, their dependence on different theatrical conceptions, their expressional possibilities.

328 Keller, Max. "Stage Lighting in Germany." *LDim.* 1982; 6(2): 46-47, 49-50. Illus.: Photo. Lighting. 8. Lang.: Eng.

Germany, West: Munich. 1982. Technical studies. ■Designer examines regulations and restrictions imposed on German theatre.

329 Szlávik, István. "A szcenográfus bizettság ülése. Friedrichshafen (NSZK), 1986. június 16-20." (Meeting of the Scenographers' Commission: Friedrichshafen, June 16-20, 1986.) *SFo.* 1987; 14(1): 6-7. Lang.: Hun.

Germany, West: Friedrichshafen. 1986. Histories-sources. ■Meeting of scenographers' committee of OISTAT.

330 "A Szegedi Nemzeti Szinház müszaki szervezete." (The Technical Organization of the National Theatre of Szeged.) *SFo.* 1987; 14(1): 9. Illus.: Photo. B&W. 1. Lang.: Hun.

Hungary: Szeged. 1987. Critical studies.

331 Bartha, Andrea. "Ki volt Kéméndy Jenő?" (Who Was Jenő Kéméndy.) *SFo.* 1987; 14(4): 25-28. Illus.: Photo. 3. [Part 1.] Lang.: Hun.

Hungary. 1860-1925. Historical studies. ■Jenő Kéméndy, a painter, was, between 1895 and 1925, Inspector General of stage-production at the Royal Opera House and the National Theatre of Budapest. He was the first to raise scene design to an artistic rank in Hungary.

332 Ézsiás, Erzsébet. "Hruby Mária: 'A szinész a ruháira emlékszik'." (Mária Hruby: 'The Actor Remembers his Clothes'.) *FSM.* 1987 Jan.; 31(1): 18-19. Illus.: Photo. Color. B&W. 7. Lang.: Hun.

Hungary. 1970-1987. Histories-sources. ■Mária Hruby, costume designer, speaks about her experiences during her career, the relation between actor, director and costume designer.

333 Grosser, Helmut. "Lehetőségek, elvárások, feladatok az elektronika alkalmazásának területén." (Possibilities, Expectations, Duties in the Domain of Electronics Applied in the Theatre.) *SFo.* 1987; 14(3): 10-12. Illus.: Photo. B&W. 1. Lang.: Hun.

THEATRE IN GENERAL: —Design/technology

Hungary: Szeged. 1987. Technical studies. ■Presented before Section for Theatre Technology, Hungarian Optical, Acoustical and Cinematographical Society.

334 Hajagos, Árpád. "A szinháztechnika helyzetének elemzése." (Analysis of the Situation of Theatre Technology.) *SFo.* 1987; 14(3): 7-10. Illus.: Photo. B&W. 2. Lang.: Hun.

Hungary: Szeged. 1987. Histories-sources. ■Presented to Section for Theatre Technology, Hungarian Optical, Acoustical and Cinematographical Society.

335 Kárpáti, Imre. "Vidám diszletek és kosztümök." (Merry Sceneries and Costumes.) *SFo.* 1987; 14(4) : 22-23. Illus.: Design. 3. Lang.: Hun.

Hungary: Budapest. 1927-1987. Critical studies. ■A one-man show has been mounted in the Vigadó Gallery, on the occasion of the 80th birthday of the scene and costume-designer and graphic artist Erik Vogel. All the important stages of the artist's sixty years of activity were put on show at the exhibition.

336 Kárpáti, Imre. "Térszinházi szcenika Zalaegerszegen." (Open Stage Scenery in Zalaegerszeg.) *SFo.* 1987; 14(1): 12-16. Illus.: Photo. B&W. 6. Lang.: Hun.

Hungary: Zalaegerszeg. 1982-1986. Critical studies. ■The particular technical and scenic solutions, ingenuities in scene design and realizations of Hevesi Sándor Theatre. Its novel decorations and interesting techniques have been developed with a particular view to studio performances.

337 Nagy, László. "Nagy László igazgató beszéde a megnyitón (részletek)." (Director László Nagy's Speech at the Opening of the Convention.) *SFo.* 1987; 14(3): 6-7. Illus.: Photo. B&W. 1. Lang.: Hun.

Hungary: Szeged. 1987. Histories-sources. ■Parts of the speech of the Director of the National Theatre of Szeged to Section for Theatre Technology, Hungarian Optical, Acoustical and Cinematographical Society.

338 Pálfi, Ferenc. "A szakmai nap." (The Exhibition.) *SFo.* 1987; 14(3): 16-19. Illus.: Photo. B&W. 14. Lang.: Hun.

Hungary: Szeged. 1987. Histories-sources. ■Report on exhibition at meeting of Section for Theatre Technology, Hungarian Optical, Acoustical and Cinematographical Society.

339 Répászky, Ernő. "8. Szinháztechnikai Napok. Szeged, 1987. június 4-6." (The 8th Convention for Theatre Technology Szeged, June 4-6, 1987.) *SFo.* 1987; 14(3): 5. Illus.: Photo. B&W. 1. Lang.: Hun.

Hungary: Szeged. 1987. Histories-sources. ■Secretary's summary of events of conference held by Section for Theatre Technology, Hungarian Optical, Acoustical and Cinematographical Society.

340 Tolnay, Pál. "Javaslat a Nemzeti Szinház szinpadvilágitásának korszerüsitésére." (Proposal for the Modernization of the Stage Lighting of the National Theatre.) *SFo.* 1987; 14(3): 33-36. Illus.: Sketches. 1. Lang.: Hun.

Hungary: Budapest. 1957. Technical studies. ■Tolnay's original plan for lighting renovation at National Theatre. As chief engineer at the theatre, he was considered a designer of stage techniques.

341 Tolnay, Pál. "Forgószinpad." (Revolving Stage.) *SFo.* 1987; 14(2): 9-10. Illus.: Photo. B&W. 4. Lang.: Hun.

Hungary: Budapest. 1930. Technical studies. ■A detailed description of the mobile revolving stage designed by the author. The 145 mm thick revolving platform could be moved with the scenery by two men manually.

342 Tolnay, Pál. "Javaslat a Nemzeti Szinház szinpadberendezésének korszerüsitésére." (Proposal for the Modernization of the Stage Installations of the National Theatre.) *SFo.* 1987; 14(2): 11-17. Illus.: Photo. Dwg. B&W. 10. [Part I.] Lang.: Hun.

Hungary: Budapest. 1957. Technical studies. ■Original plans include the mechanics of the revolving stage and modification of the forestage.

343 Várady, Gyula. "Utazó együttesek—A Magyar Állami Népi Együttes." (Touring Ensembles: The Hungarian State Folk Ensemble.) *SFo.* 1987; 14(1): 17-19. Illus.: Photo. B&W. 3. Lang.: Hun.

Hungary. 1951-1987. Historical studies. ■The heroic years of the Ensemble founded 36 years ago: the hard travelling, dressing, stage-conditions under which the 150 persons (with troup of dancers, choir and orchestra) started working.

344 Vychodil, Ladislav. "Szakmunkás képzés Pozsonyban." (Vocational Training in Bratislava.) *SFo.* 1987; 14(3): 14-15. Lang.: Hun.

Hungary: Szeged. Czechoslovakia: Bratislava. 1980-1987. Histories-sources. ■Address of professor of scene design (Academy of Performing Arts, Bratislava) before Section for Theatre Technology, Hungarian Optical, Acoustical and Cinematographical Society.

345 *Fortuny e Caramba: la moda a teatro. Costumi di scene 1906-1936.* (Fortuny and Caramba: Fashion at the Theatre, Stage Costumes 1905-1936.) Venezia: Marsilio; 1987. 149 pp. Index. Illus.: Photo. Dwg. Print. Color. Lang.: Ita.

Italy. 1906-1936. Histories-sources. ■Illustrated catalogue of the Venetian exhibition of the works of the costumers Fortuny and Caramba.

346 Anselmo, Stefano. *Il trucco: nella vita, nell'arte, nello spettacolo.* (Make-up: In Real Life, In Art and In Performance.) Milan: BCM; 1987. 282 pp. Index. Pref. Biblio. Illus.: Photo. Sketches. Print. Color. B&W. Lang.: Ita.

Italy. 1987. Instructional materials. ■Presentation and illustration of techniques, procedures, materials, use and application of make-up for stage and screen. Related to Media: Film.

347 Ault, C. Thomas. "Baroque Stage Machines for Venus and Mars From the Archivio di Stato, Parma." *ThS.* 1987 Nov.; 28(2): 27-40. Notes. Illus.: Dwg. 7. Lang.: Eng.

Italy: Parma. 1675-1700. Historical studies. ■Designs are characteristic of Baroque stage machines and illustrate use of sliding winches in grid.

348 Fossati, Silvia. "L'ingresso della prospettiva a Venezia e il fissarsi del topos scenico della Piazzetta." (The Coming of Perspective to Venice and the Establishment of the Scenic Topos of the Piazzetta.) *BiT.* 1987; 5/6: 115-132. Lang.: Ita.

Italy: Venice. 1500-1600. Historical studies. ■The fortune of perspective in 16th century Venice. The piazzetta as a perspective topos and the concept of limit as represented by the quay columns. Venice on stage.

349 Sorrentino, Letizia. "La scenografia dell'Inferno nel teatro religioso del Trecento." (The Scenography of Hell in the Religious Theatre of the 14th Century.) *BiT.* 1987; 8: 45-59. Lang.: Ita.

Italy. France. 1300-1399. Historical studies. ■The tower in the French *Mystères* and the mountain in the Italian *Laudi* are the two main scenic elements connected to the representation of Hell. Two types of play: the comic *diableries* and the tragic *laudi*.

350 Gotō, Hajime. *Chūsei kamen no rekishiteki Minzokugaku teki kenkyū.* (Historical and Anthropological Study of Medieval Masks.) Tokyo: Tōga shuppan; 1987. 1026 pp.. Pref. Notes. Biblio. Illus.: Photo. Print. B&W. 100. Lang.: Jap.

Japan. 110-1500. Historical studies. ■History of masks in popular entertainment.

351 Chang, June-Bo. "Hyundae yonkuke yeeseoseo jomyungui yeokhal." (The Role of Stage Lighting in the Modern Drama.) *DongukDA.* 1978 Apr.; 10-11: 29-36. Lang.: Kor.

Korea. 1978. Historical studies. ■Development of stage lighting instruments, general theory of lighting design.

352 Cho, Young-Rae. "Mudaemisului teukjingkwa pyohyunyangsik." (The Creative Style Character of Stage Setting.) *DongukDA.* 1976 Dec.; 9: 21-27. Lang.: Kor.

Korea. 1876. Technical studies. ■The theory of stage setting: a practical approach by a set designer.

353 Go, Sul-Bong. "Bunchanglon." (Theory of Make-up.) 78-86 in *The Development of Korean Modern Theatre in the First Half of the Twentieth Century.* Seoul: Shin Hyup Theatre Company; 1986. 105 pp. Lang.: Kor.

Korea. 1987. Technical studies. ■General theory of theatrical make-up in Korean theatre.

354 Kim, Heung-Woo. "Moonkan kim jung-whan yongu." (A Study of Kim Jung-Whan.) *DongukDA.* 1978 Apr.; 10-11: 44-56. Lang.: Kor.

THEATRE IN GENERAL: —Design/technology

Korea. 1978. Biographical studies. ▪Kim Jung-Whan, set designer.

355   Lee, Chang-Gu. "Moodaebunjanglon." (A View of Stage Make-up.) *DongukDA*. 1976 Dec.; 9: 80-92. Lang.: Kor.
Korea. 1976. Instructional materials. ▪The theory and application of make-up.

356   Blomqvist, Kurt. "OISTAT. Teaterteknisk kongress i Amsterdam 25-30 Augusti 1987." (OISTAT: Conference on Theatre Technology in Amsterdam, Aug. 25-30 1987.) *ProScen*. 1987; 10: 12-15. Illus.: Photo. 6. Lang.: Swe.
Netherlands: Amsterdam. 1987. Histories-sources. ▪Some impressions from the conference.

357   Gieling, Lia. "Je moet de gatterij steeds op blijven laden." (You Have to Keep Loading the Battery.) *Toneel*. 1987 May; 5(8): 26-33. Illus.: Photo. B&W. 11. Lang.: Dut.
Netherlands. 1987. Histories-sources. ▪Interview with costume designer Rien Bekkers. His influences, dreams, changes he would like to see in treatment of costume designers and training.

358   Vajda, Ferenc. "OISTAT találkozó a Holland Szinháztechnikai Kongresszus keretében. Amsterdam, 1987. augusztus 25-30." (OISTAT Meeting at the Dutch Convention for Theatre Technology: Amsterdam, August 25-30, 1987.) *SFo*. 1987; 14(4): 6-9. Illus.: Photo. B&W. 5. Lang.: Hun.
Netherlands: Amsterdam. 1987. Histories-sources. ▪Report on meeting of the Organization Internationale de Scénographes, Techniciens et Architectes de Théâtre (OISTAT).

359   Blomqvist, Kurt. "MODA system." (MODA-System.) *ProScen*. 1987; 10(1-2): 38. Illus.: Photo. Dwg. Lang.: Swe.
Norway: Trondheim. 1986. Technical studies. ▪A presentation of a transportable and flexible podium system.

360   Mitzner, Piotr. *Teatr światła i cienia*. (Theatre of Light and Shadow.) Warsaw: Państwowy Instytut Wydawniczy; 1987. 303 pp. Index. Notes. Illus.: Photo. Print. B&W. 55. Lang.: Pol.
Poland: Warsaw. Europe. 1258-1980. Histories-specific. ▪Stage lighting from the Middle Ages to the present, with emphasis on Warsaw.

361   "Utbildning i Teaterteknik. Första kullen ut från DI." (Education in Technical Theatre: The First Batch Out of DI.) *ProScen*. 1987; 10(1-2): 45-47. Illus.: Photo. Lang.: Swe.
Sweden: Stockholm. 1987. Biographical studies. ▪A presentation of the first twelve technicians graduated from Dramatiska Institutet.

362   Augustsson, Tinn; Hagman, Eva; Lindström, Peter; Rembe, Fredrik; Rönngren, Carita; Östensson, Mikael. "TT-elever på turné." (Pupils of TT on Tour.) *ProScen*. 1987; 10(1-2): 14-16. Illus.: Photo. 6. Lang.: Swe.
Sweden. 1986. Historical studies. ▪Impressions from a study tour to see how touring companies managed to build the sets at the local theatres.

363   Guillemaut, Alf. "Södrans scenteknik. Modern teknik i gammal teater." (The Stage Technology of Södran: Modern Technique in Old Theatre.) *ProScen*. 1987; 10(3): 28-32. Illus.: Photo. 7. Lang.: Swe.
Sweden: Stockholm. 1985-1987. Technical studies. ▪The system of fly facilities of the 130 year old Södra Teatern has been computerized.

364   Kull, Gustaf. "Alumbalken, ett alternativ till mycket." (Aluma-Girder, An Alternative to Many Things.) *ProScen*. 1987; 10(1-2): 40-41. Illus.: Photo. Dwg. Lang.: Swe.
Sweden. 1980-1986. Technical studies. ▪A presentation of the girder, made of aluminum combined with wood, which can be used for many purposes.

365   Luukkonen, Veija. "På scen—vi gör bilder av världen." (On Stage—We Create Images of the World.) *ProScen*. 1987; 10(3): 24-26. Illus.: Photo. Lang.: Swe.
Sweden: Gävle. 1987. Histories-sources. ▪About an exhibition of the craftmanship by the artisans behind the stage.

366   Nordqvist, Lasse. "'Elefanten' som löste problemet." ('The Elephant' That Solved the Problem.) *ProScen*. 1987; 10(1-2): 44. Illus.: Photo. Lang.: Swe.
Sweden: Uppsala. 1986. Technical studies. ▪A presentation of a transport advice for moving grand pianos, without any heaving.

367   Skönvall, Morgan. "Scenteknisk kurs i Göteborg. Fackman eller kuli?" (A Course of Stage Technics at Gothenburg: Professional or Coolie?)*ProScen*. 1987; 10(3): 9-10. Illus.: Photo. Lang.: Swe.
Sweden: Gothenburg. 1987. Histories-sources. ▪A report from a two-week course for theatre technicians.

368   Li, Wei. "Dang dai ying guo wu tai bu jing." (British Stage Design.) *XYishu*. 1985 Spr; 29: 129-139. Notes. Illus.: Design. B&W. 17. Lang.: Chi.
UK. USA: New York, NY. 1982-1985. Historical studies. ▪Introduction to seven stage designers in the UK and how they influenced designers on Broadway.

369   Morgan, Charles. "Out of the Box." *Sin*. 1987; 21(1): 15-17. Illus.: Photo. Plan. Diagram. B&W. 2. Lang.: Eng.
UK. 1984-1987. Technical studies. ▪Contribution of Modelbox Computer Aided Design.

370   Power, Ron. "Let's Hear It for the Loop." *Sin*. 1987; 21(2): 27-29. Tables. 2. Lang.: Eng.
UK. 1987. Technical studies. ▪RNID Technical Officer: advice on systems for hard of hearing in theatres.

371   Alberg, Ian. "Trade Winds of Change." *Sin*. 1987; 21(1): 37. Lang.: Eng.
UK-England: London. 1987. Histories-sources. ▪Managing director of theatre equipment manufacturer Donmar looks at the business as a whole.

372   Cummings, Valerie. "Ellen Terry: An Aesthetic Actress and her Costumes." *Costume*. 1987; 21: 60-66. Lang.: Eng.
UK-England: London. 1856-1902. Biographical studies. ▪Ellen Terry's choice of costumes, influenced by G.F. Watts and E.W. Goodwin and designed by Alice Comyns Carr were simple in design and allowed her freedom of movement.

373   Herbert, Ian. "Setting Out the Stall." *Sin*. 1987; 21(1): 18-21. Illus.: Photo. Dwg. B&W. 13. Lang.: Eng.
UK-England. 1983-1987. Histories-sources. ▪Review of the British Theatre Design 83-87 exhibition.

374   Offord, John. "Reflektorfényben a Silhouettek." (Spotlights on the Silhouettes.) *SFo*. 1987; 14(4): 28-31. Illus.: Photo. B&W. 4. Lang.: Hun.
UK-England. 1864-1987. Histories-sources. ▪Interview with Don Hindle, Managing Director, and Phil Rose, Technical Director of CCT Theatre Lighting Ltd., translated from *Lighting and Sound International* (1987 Mar).

375   Power, Ron. "Can You Hear Me at the Back." *Sin*. 1987; 21(1): 34-37. Tables. 2. Lang.: Eng.
UK-England: London. 1987. Technical studies. ▪Survey on the performance of induction hoop systems.

376   Schouvaloff, Alexander. *Set and Costume Design for Ballet and Theatre*. New York, NY: Vendome P; 1987. 268 pp. Biblio. Pref. Index. Illus.: Design. Sketches. Photo. Print. Color. B&W. 150. Lang.: Eng.
UK-England. 1902-1980. Histories-sources. ▪Catalogue designs of the Thyssen-Bornemisza collection in Gloucestershire, by the curator of the Theatre Museum in London. Designers include Léon Bakst, George Barbier, Alexandre Benois, Lucien Bertaux, Erté, Alexandra Exter and José de Zamora. Includes original design photos, original production information and photos of productions. Some films are included. Short biographical sketches of designers. Related to Dance: Ballet.

377   Willmore, David. "The Phantom's Heritage." *Sin*. 1987; 21(2): 10-11. Illus.: Diagram. Photo. B&W. 3. Lang.: Eng.
UK-England: London. 1890-1987. Technical studies. ▪Description of Victorian under-stage machinery at Her Majesty's Theatre, London.

378   Wirdnam, Ken. "The Dealer Shows His Hand." *Sin*. 1987; 21(2): 35-37. Lang.: Eng.
UK-England. 1987. Technical studies. ▪Managing director of Raxcrest Electrical reviews the trade as a whole.

379   Wyckham, John. "The Ninth Bright Shiner." *Sin*. 1987; 21(1): 23-25. Tables. Illus.: Photo. B&W. 2. Lang.: Eng.
UK-England: London. 1987. Histories-sources. ▪Review of the Association of British Theatre Technicians' Trade Show 1987.

THEATRE IN GENERAL: —Design/technology

380 Little, Kim. "Par for the Course." *Sin.* 1987; 21(2): 31-33. Illus.: Dwg. B&W. 1. Lang.: Eng.
UK-Scotland: Glasgow. 1987. Technical studies. ■Problems associated with setting up a training course in design.

381 Bottle, Ted. "Stage Machinery at the Grand Theatre Llandudno." *TN.* 1987; 41(1): 4-18. Notes. Illus.: Dwg. Photo. B&W. 10. Lang.: Eng.
UK-Wales: Llandudno. 1901-1987. Historical studies. ■Describes the theatre's stage machinery which is being preserved and restored. Compares other examples.

382 "Gelatin Molds." *TechB.* 1987 Oct.: 1. [TB 1179.] Lang.: Eng.
USA. 1987. Technical studies. ■Method for creating a flexible negative mold for use in making plaster or polyester resin castings.

383 "A Do-It-Yourself Lesson in Lighting." *LDim.* 1987 Jan/Feb.; 11(1): 58-59. Illus.: Dwg. 4. Lang.: Eng.
USA. 1987. Technical studies. ■Experiments with light, various effects that help analyze lighting conditions.

384 "USITT DMX512 and USITT AMX192." *TD&T.* 1987; 22(4): 22-27. Illus.: Diagram. Schematic. 5. Lang.: Eng.
USA. 1987. Technical studies. ■Two standards developed by the USITT Dimmer Standards Committee in the face of requests by distributors and users confronted with the difficulties of interfacing controllers and dimmers manufactured by different companies.

385 Aronson, Arnold. "Contemporary American Design: Carrie Robbins." *TD&T.* 1987; 22(4): 8-20. Illus.: Photo. Dwg. B&W. 16. Lang.: Eng.
USA. 1966-1986. Biographical studies. ■Work and career of costume designer Carrie Robbins from her work as a student at Yale to her designs for Broadway, regional theatre, and television, to her position as a full-time teacher at NYU School of the Arts. Includes chronology of her work.

386 Balk, Steven. "Two Devices for Simplifying Cable Tracing." *TechB.* 1987 Apr.: 1-2. [TB 1176.] Lang.: Eng.
USA. 1987. Technical studies. ■Description of inexpensive testing devices for cable tracing: how to use and where to buy them.

387 Billington, Ken. "The Power of Glory." *LDim.* 1984; 8(2): 42-49. Illus.: Photo. Lighting. Dwg. 14. Lang.: Eng.
USA. 1982. Technical studies. ■Design aspects of *The Glory of Easter*, a 'spectacular' written by church members and presented at the Crystal Cathedral. Lighting designer describes computerized lighting, lasers and pyrotechnics.

388 Birringer, Johannes. "Postmodern Performance and Technology." *PerAJ.* 1985 Sum/Fall; 9(2-3): 221-233. Lang.: Eng.
USA. 1985. Technical studies. ■Use of technology in post-modern theatre.

389 Blase, Linda. "Photographing Your Own Show." *LDim.* 1984; 8(2): 14-21. Illus.: Photo. 9. Lang.: Eng.
USA. 1982. Technical studies. ■Photographer and lighting designer Linda Blase describes equipment and procedures necessary to photograph a production.

390 Bliese, Thomas G. "Nylon Rollers Modified." *TechB.* 1986 Apr.: 1. Illus.: Dwg. B&W. [TB 1137 addendum.] Lang.: Eng.
USA. 1986. Technical studies. ■Change in axle-wielding results in a thinner furniture or prop pallet.

391 Blumenthal, Eileen. "There's a Message in Lee's Masks." *AmTh.* 1987 July/Aug.; 4(4): 22-23. Illus.: Photo. Print. B&W. 4. Lang.: Eng.
USA: New York, NY. 1960-1987. Technical studies. ■Artistry of maskmaker Ralph Lee. Introduction to his work, origins of his masks and their many applications in theatre. Related to Puppetry.

392 Borey, Susan. "Aural Fixation." *ThCr.* 1987 Oct.. Illus.: Photo. Diagram. B&W. Detail. Schematic. 5. Lang.: Eng.
USA: New York, NY. 1984-1987. Technical studies. ■Sound designer Guy Sherman's innovations in creating sound cues and their adaptation to theatre equipment and acoustics.

393 Boyle, Michael E.; Forton, Raymond P. "A Curved Handrail of Wep." *TechB.* 1985 Oct.: 1-3. Illus.: Dwg. 2. [TB 1157.] Lang.: Eng.
USA. 1985. Technical studies. ■Making a curved handrail out of Wep.

394 Brewczynski, James. "Mass Producing Styrofoam Balusters." *TechB.* 1985 Apr.: 1-3. Notes. Illus.: Dwg. 3. [TB 1154.] Lang.: Eng.
USA. 1985. Technical studies. ■Mass producing styrofoam balusters economically.

395 Brightman, Adam. "Fog...Foggier...Foggiest." *ThCr.* 1987 Mar.; 21(3): 28-29, 57-61. Tables. 1. Lang.: Eng.
USA. 1987. Technical studies. ■Manufacturers of theatrical fog machines: design standards, safety factors and usage.

396 Bush, Catherine. "Still Life in Motion." *ThCr.* 1987 Feb.; 21(2): 32-33, 54-58. Illus.: Photo. Color. 2. Lang.: Eng.
USA. 1986. Technical studies. ■Modern dance production of *Portraits in Reflection*, a collaboration between choreographer Lucinda Childs, photographer Robert Mapplethorpe and lighting designer Gregory Meeh. Related to Dance: Modern dance.

397 Campbell, Stancil. "How to Construct Contoured Hills." *ThCr.* 1985 Jan.; 19(1): 100, 102-103. Illus.: Diagram. 2. Lang.: Eng.
USA. 1985. Technical studies. ■Challenge of a designer to build a low budget contoured hill set.

398 Carlson, Jon. "Easily Concealed Low-Profile Lighting Fixtures." *TechB.* 1987 Jan.: 1-3. [TB 1171.] Lang.: Eng.
USA. 1987. Technical studies. ■Descriptions of Lumilines, Showcase Lamps and Stik-Ups: uses, availability, prices.

399 Dennstaedt, Jeff; Monsey, Steven E. "Pneumatic Door Stabilizer." *TechB.* 1987 Oct.: 1-3. Illus.: Diagram. B&W. Schematic. 1. [TB 1180.] Lang.: Eng.
USA. 1987. Technical studies. ■Installation and use of a pneumatic door stabilizer to prevent lightweight doors from bouncing open when slammed onstage.

400 Dolan, Jill. "The Play's the Thing: Kevin Rigdon's Set and Lighting Designs Strive for Simplicity." *ThCr.* 1987 Feb.; 21(2): 28-31, 76-81. Append. Illus.: Photo. Color. B&W. 8. Lang.: Eng.
USA. 1986. Technical studies. ■Work of set and lighting designer Kevin Rigdon, resident designer for Steppenwolf Theatre.

401 Dorn, Dennis; Keller, Jim; Richard, Terry. "Measuring the Deflection of Your Modular Staging: Predicted and Actual." *TD&T.* 1987; 23(2): 18-23. Illus.: Photo. Plan. B&W. Explod.Sect. 11. Lang.: Eng.
USA. 1987. Technical studies. ■Intended to increase the knowledge of the average theatre technician on the advantages and disadvantages of a metal/wood composite platform design. They apply elementary engineering techniques to quantify the response of common theatrical structures.

402 Dulanski, Gary. "Dimming: Another Side of Light Control." *L&DA.* 1987 Dec.; 17(12): 31-35. Illus.: Photo. Diagram. Chart. 5. Lang.: Eng.
USA. 1987. Technical studies. ■Dimmers can be used to save energy and to gain more control over a visual environment. Various types of dimmers can be used for different lighting types. Also a description of how solid-state dimmers work.

403 Eller, Claudia. "Unions: USA All the Way." *ThCr.* 1987 Mar.; 21(3): 14-15, 74-77. Lang.: Eng.
USA. 1987. Historical studies. ■Merger of the west, midwest and east coast locals of United Scenic Artists into one national union.

404 Eller, Claudia. "Lighting to Sculpt Shadows." *ThCr.* 1987 Mar.; 21(3): 26, 27, 68-70. Illus.: Photo. Color. 3. Lang.: Eng.
USA. 1987. Technical studies. ■The work of lighting designer Paulie Jenkins.

405 Fanjoy, Allan. "How to Create Laminated Curves." *ThCr.* 1985 Jan.; 19(1): 101, 104-105. Illus.: Diagram. Print. Color. 4. Lang.: Eng.
USA. 1985. Technical studies. ■Economic construction of laminated curves of vast size in stage scenery.

THEATRE IN GENERAL: —Design/technology

406 Fisher, Edmond B. "Comparing Four Plastics as Scenery Glides." *TechB.* 1986 Jan.: 1-3. Notes. Tables. Illus.: Dwg. B&W. [TB 1159.] Lang.: Eng.
USA. 1986. Technical studies. ■Ranking of Nylon, Delrin, Nylatron and Teflon in terms of cost, workability and friction.

407 Gavenas, Mary Lisa. "Flexibility & Fine Fabrics: Jess Goldstein's Costume Designs." *ThCr.* 1987 Feb.; 21(2): 18-21, 41-43. Illus.: Design. Photo. B&W. Color. 9. Lang.: Eng.
USA. 1967-1987. Technical studies. ■Designer Jess Goldstein: his background, methodology and attitudes toward design.

408 Gillette, J. Michael. *Theatrical Design and Production: An Introduction to Scene Design and Construction, Lighting, Sound, Costume and Make-Up.* Palo Alto, CA: Mayfield; 1987. 500 pp. Pref. Index. Biblio. Gloss. Illus.: Design. Photo. Graphs. Plan. Dwg. Sketches. Diagram. Lighting. B&W. Color. Architec. Grd.Plan. 300. Lang.: Eng.
USA. 1987. Instructional materials. ■Textbook organized as reference tool for students and instructors.

409 Ginsburg, Fred, C.A.S. "Missing Link: A Practical Guide to Wireless Mics." *ThCr.* 1987 Apr.; 21(4): 49-52. Illus.: Photo. B&W. 3. Lang.: Eng.
USA. 1987. Technical studies. ■Pros and cons of using wireless microphones.

410 Gleason, John. "Understanding Color." *LDim.* 1987 Sep/Oct.; 11(5): 32-37. Lang.: Eng.
USA. 1987. Technical studies. ■Definition of phenomena of light. Discusses terms such as chroma, hue, value regarding theatrical lighting.

411 Glerum, Jay O. *Stage Rigging Handbook.* Carbondale, IL: Southern Illinois UP; 1987. xi, 137 pp. Pref. Biblio. Append. Gloss. Illus.: Photo. Dwg. Sketches. Diagram. Detail. Blprnt. 113. Lang.: Eng.
USA. 1987. Technical studies. ■Care and safe use of stage rigging equipment: hemp rigging, counterweight rigging, motorized rigging, cutting and knotting rope, attaching loads, special problems.

412 Glerum, Jay O. "Retrofitting the Sixties: Rigging and Rigging Control." *ThCr.* 1987 Feb.; 21(2): 26-27, 50-54. Illus.: Photo. B&W. 2. Lang.: Eng.
USA. 1960-1987. Technical studies. ■Innovative rigging installations of the 1960s and how they compare to today's standards.

413 Green, Sara. "The Eyes and Ears Have It in D.C." *ThCr.* 1987 Apr.; 21(4): 41, 66-69. Lang.: Eng.
USA: Washington, DC. 1987. Technical studies. ■Washington, DC area theatres create access for hearing and visually impaired theatregoers.

414 Grubb, Kevin. "Rethinking a Set for Touring." *TheaterW.* 1987 Aug 17; 1: 24-26. Illus.: Photo. 4. Lang.: Eng.
USA. 1987. Technical studies. ■Four scenic designers, James Morgan, Michael Bottari, Joel Evans and Tony Walton discuss specific methods for duplicating the quality of Broadway designs for economy and durability on the road.

415 Gwinup, Martin. "Dancing Light." *TechB.* 1987 Oct.: 1. [TB 1182.] Lang.: Eng.
USA. 1987. Technical studies. ■Inexpensive way to create a lighting effect to work in rhythm with a music cue.

416 Gwinup, Martin. "Texture Techniques Using Paper and Flexible Glue." *TechB.* 1987 Jan.: 1-2. [TB 1172.] Lang.: Eng.
USA. 1987. Technical studies. ■Achieving believable relief textures on stage using paper products and flexible glue: application, suppliers, safety notes.

417 Hale, Alice M. "James LeBrecht." *ThCr.* 1987 Feb.; 21(2): 34-35, 58-64. 3. Lang.: Eng.
USA: Berkeley, CA. 1978-1987. Technical studies. ■Sound designer James LeBrecht, his approach and methodology.

418 Hale, Alice M. "The Speed of Lighting." *ThCr.* 1987 Apr.; 21(4): 34-39, 56-61. Illus.: Photo. Diagram. Color. B&W. 10. Lang.: Eng.
USA. 1980-1987. Technical studies. ■Lighting designer Paul Gallo: his approach and methodology.

419 Harman, Leonard. "Computer-Assisted Lighting Design: Using AutoCAD." *TD&T.* 1987; 23(1): 18-23. Illus.: Photo. Lighting. 5. Lang.: Eng.
USA. 1987. Technical studies. ■Discussion of what designers consider the best computer-aided drafting package for micro-computers. Describes set-up work needed to apply software to theatre lighting design.

420 Haye, Bethany. "Real Rep Comes to Broadway." *ThCr.* 1985 Jan.; 19(1): 38-41, 73-76. Illus.: Lighting. Print. Color. B&W. 4. Lang.: Eng.
USA: New York, NY. 1984. Technical studies. ■Gershwin Theatre's accommodation of The Royal Shakespeare Company's tour of *Cyrano de Bergerac* and *Much Ado About Nothing.*

421 Holder, Don. "A Simultaneous Travel-Fly Rig." *TechB.* 1985 Oct.: 1-3. Notes. Illus.: Diagram. 2. [TB 1158.] Lang.: Eng.
USA. 1985. Technical studies. ■Simple rigging system allowing both vertical and horizontal movement of scenery in simultaneous operations.

422 Hulser, Kathleen. "Electric Language." *AmTh.* 1987 June; 4(3): 10-16. Notes. Illus.: Photo. B&W. 5. Lang.: Eng.
USA. 1987. Histories-sources. ■Multimedia experts discuss the creation of special effects within plays. Examples of technique illustrated in productions at the Impossible Theatre.

423 Karl, Ruling. "An Inexpensive Monitor Microphone." *TechB.* 1987 Jan.: 1-2. Illus.: Dwg. B&W. 1. [TB 1174.] Lang.: Eng.
USA. 1987. Technical studies. ■Discussion of the inexpensive electret microphone element as a substitute for a higher quality dynamic microphone used as a pick-up mike.

424 Kaufman, David. "Electronic Ebony and Ivory: A New Sound for the Theatre." *TT.* 1987 Jan/Feb.; 6(2): 12-13. Illus.: Photo. B&W. 1. Lang.: Eng.
USA. 1986. Technical studies. ■The effect of computer synthesizers on theatrical composition.

425 Knox, Kerro. "A Simple Flush-Mount Hinge." *TechB.* 1986 Jan.: 1-2. Notes. Illus.: Dwg. B&W. [TB 1160.] Lang.: Eng.
USA. 1986. Technical studies. ■Construction of a concealed hinge joint.

426 Lagerquist, Jon. "An Improved Boom-Based Sandbag." *TechB.* 1985 Oct.: 1. Notes. [TB 1155.] Lang.: Eng.
USA. 1985. Technical studies. ■How to make boom-base sandbag out of auto or truck inner tubes.

427 LaRue, Michèle. "*Brighton Beach Memoirs*: Not So Simple Simon." *ThCr.* 1987 Feb.; 21(2): 22-25, 43-49. Illus.: Photo. Plan. Dwg. B&W. Color. Fr.Elev. Grd.Plan. 7. Lang.: Eng.
USA. 1983-1987. Technical studies. ■How several theatres have approached the casting and design problems inherent in Neil Simon's *Brighton Beach Memoirs.*

428 Levine, Mindy N. "An Interview with Dennis Parichy." *TT.* 1987 June/July; 6(5): 8-9. Illus.: Photo. B&W. 6. Lang.: Eng.
USA: New York, NY. 1986-1987. Histories-sources. ■Lighting designer Dennis Parichy discusses design, his training, career and relationships with directors and playwrights.

429 Levine, Mindy N. "Design and Vision—Edward Gianfrancesco." *TT.* 1987 Apr.; 6(3): 8. Illus.: Photo. B&W. 4. Lang.: Eng.
USA: New York, NY. 1987. Histories-sources. ■Interview with set designer Edward Gianfrancesco.

430 Levine, Mindy N. "Physicalizing the Imagination: An Interview with John Arnone." *TT.* 1987 May; 6(4): 8-10. Illus.: Photo. B&W. 5. Lang.: Eng.
USA: New York, NY. 1987. Histories-sources. ■Set designer John Arnone describes design as turning imagination into physical existence.

431 Levine, Mindy N. "Seeing the Light: An Interview with Jennifer Tipton." *TT.* 1987 Jan/Feb.; 6(2): 9-10. Pref. Illus.: Photo. B&W. 1. Lang.: Eng.
USA: New York, NY. 1986. Histories-sources. ■Interview with lighting designer Jennifer Tipton regarding the current state of theatrical lighting.

THEATRE IN GENERAL: —Design/technology

432 Lipp, Jonathan. "Look Ma, No Wires." *ThCr*. 1985 Jan.; 19(1): 45-62. Print. B&W. 1. Lang.: Eng.
USA. 1985. Technical studies. ■Pros and cons of wireless microphones as opposed to hard wired systems for stage.

433 Loeffler, Mark. "F. Mitchell Dana." *LDim*. 1987 July/Aug.; 11(4): 36-43, 62. Illus.: Photo. Lighting. 6. Lang.: Eng.
USA: New York, NY. 1987. Histories-sources. ■Interview with designer F. Mitchell Dana regarding his career, style and best-known works.

434 Long, Robert. "Scene Painting." *ThCr*. 1987 Oct.; 21(8): 44-54. Illus.: Pntg. Color. 4. Lang.: Eng.
USA. 1600-1987. Technical studies. ■Instruction in painting, professional and academic training.

435 Long, Robert. "Retrofitting the Sixties: Rethinking your Intercom System." *ThCr*. 1987 Dec.; 21(10): 84-87. Illus.: Photo. B&W. 1. Lang.: Eng.
USA. 1960-1987. Technical studies. ■Advances in theatre intercom systems and whether to upgrade or replace existing installations.

436 Lydecker, Garritt D. "How to Use a Side Drill." *ThCr*. 1985 Jan.; 19(1): 100, 103. Illus.: Diagram. Lang.: Eng.
USA. 1985. Technical studies. ■Tools that fasten to the work arbor through a center hole, exemplifying those jobs best for side drill arrangement and explaining a simple conversion into a drill press.

437 Maginnis, Tara. "Stereographs as an Educational Resource in Costume History." *TD&T*. 1987; 23(1): 25-29. Biblio. Illus.: Photo. 8. Lang.: Eng.
USA. 1987. Technical studies. ■Use of stereographs, a double set of photographs each one taken from a slightly different angle to be viewed through a stereoscope, for costume design in the theatre. Picture gives detail and depth on various subjects. Includes a list of sources for information and supplies.

438 McClintock, Bob. "Theatrical Hardware, Computer-Style." *ThCr*. 1985 Jan.; 19(1): 14-15, 81-84. Tables. Lang.: Eng.
USA. 1987. Instructional materials. ■Guidelines for purchasing a computer system for a theatre without having to hire an outside service.

439 McKenzie, M. Craig. "Laying Out Odd-Shaped Raked Decks." *TechB*. 1986 Jan.: 1-3. Notes. Illus.: Dwg. B&W. [TB 1161.] Lang.: Eng.
USA. 1986. Technical studies. ■Solution to minimize costs of building and installation.

440 Miller, James Hull. *Small Stage Sets on Tour: A Practical Guide to Portable Stage Sets*. Colorado Springs, CO: Meriwether; 1987. 100 pp. Pref. Illus.: Sketches. B&W. 55. Lang.: Eng.
USA. 1987. Instructional materials. ■A 'how-to' manual for freestanding scenery for touring groups. Practical guide to the most efficient use of portable stage sets and designs for small theatres based on touring experience of author.

441 Miller, James Hull. *Stage Lighting in the Boondocks*. Downers Grove, IL: Contemporary Drama Service; 1987. 71 pp. Illus.: Diagram. Print. B&W. Lang.: Eng.
USA. 1987. Instructional materials. ■Methods of lighting for theatre audiences. Written for beginners. Gives information on equipment, how to use it and some basic schematics.

442 Monsey, Steven E. "A Versatile Audio Power Meter." *TechB*. 1986 Jan.: 1-3. Notes. Tables. Illus.: Diagram. B&W. Schematic. [TB 1162.] Lang.: Eng.
USA. 1986. Technical studies. ■Construction of a unit to monitor the amplifier output levels of practicals whose speakers must be driven by the system amplifiers.

443 Neville, Tom. "Two Simple Lead Circuits." *TechB*. 1985 Oct.: 1-3. Illus.: Dwg. 4. [TB 1156.] Lang.: Eng.
USA. 1985. Technical studies. ■LED circuits and suggestions for possible theatrical applications.

444 Owen, Bobbi. *Costume Design on Broadway: Designers and Their Credits, 1915-1985*. New York, NY: Greenwood P; 1987. 254 pp. (Bibliographies and Indexes in the Performing Arts 5.) Pref. Index. Tables. Append. Illus.: Design. Photo. Print. B&W. 100. Lang.: Eng.
USA: New York, NY. 1915-1985. Bibliographical studies. ■Index of costume design on Broadway. Short bios on designers, including their credits, list of Tony award winning costume designers, photos of original costumes, sketches and index of plays.

445 Perlman, David C. "A Plasticene/Styrofoam Deck Plug." *TechB*. 1987 Apr.: 1-2. [TB 1177.] Lang.: Eng.
USA. 1987. Technical studies. ■Using plasticene in a styrofoam deck to plug holes that need to be masked for each performance.

446 Pollack, Steve; Burns, Bree; Loeffler, Mark. "1987 New Product Buyer's Guide." *ThCr*. 1987 Aug/Sep.; 21(7): 39-57. Illus.: Photo. B&W. 10. Lang.: Eng.
USA: Minneapolis/St. Paul, MN. 1987. Technical studies. ■1987 USITT convention showcasing technical theatre innovations.

447 Pollock, Steve. "AES Report." *ThCr*. 1987 Mar.; 21(3): 31-34. Lang.: Eng.
USA. 1987. Technical studies. ■Audio Engineering Society reports on use of digital and analog sound equipment, current technology.

448 Pollock, Steve. "Rock 'N Roll Lighting Control." *ThCr*. 1987 Apr.; 21(4): 44, 71-72, 74-82. Illus.: Photo. B&W. 1. Lang.: Eng.
USA. 1987. Technical studies. ■History of rock 'n roll lighting control boards, current models.

449 Rich, Frank; Aronson, Lisa. *The Theatre Art of Boris Aronson*. New York, NY: Knopf; 1987. 323 pp. Index. Biblio. Illus.: Design. Handbill. Photo. Pntg. Dwg. Sketches. Print. B&W. Color. Grd.Plan. 500. Lang.: Eng.
USA. 1925-1979. Historical studies. ■The theatre designs of Boris Aronson. Detailed photographs, designs of his Broadway career as well as other art venues in New York. Includes specific productions and discusses how set designer adds to production through his work. Includes a chronological list of all his work.

450 Richmond, Charlie. "Theatre Sound Leads Film Sound?" *TD&T*. 1987; 23(2): 41, 49-51. Lang.: Eng.
USA. 1987. Technical studies. ■Comparison of roles of sound designer in film and theatrical productions. Related to Media: Film.

451 Robbins, Aileen. "Restaurants as Theatre." *ThCr*. 1985 Jan.; 19(1): 28-31, 66-68. Illus.: Photo. Color. Grd.Plan. 6. Lang.: Eng.
USA. 1980-1985. Technical studies. ■Influence of theatrical lighting, scenery and technology on restaurant architecture and design.

452 Salzer, Beeb. "The Last Interview or Ask Me No Questions and I'll..." *LDim*. 1982; 6(3): 15, 17. Illus.: Photo. 1. Lang.: Eng.
USA. 1982. Histories-sources. ■Interview with designer Pericles McCohen.

453 Sanders, Kenneth. "A Fog Machine Silencer." *TechB*. 1987 Jan.: 1-2. Illus.: Dwg. B&W. 2. [TB 1173.] Lang.: Eng.
USA. 1987. Technical studies. ■Solving the problem of noisy fog machines using principles borrowed from the firearms industry: PVC pipe and styrofoam.

454 Schwartz, Bonnie S. "The Struggle for Identity at Parsons." *LDim*. 1987 May/June; 11(3): 103-107. Lang.: Eng.
USA: New York, NY. 1987. Technical studies. ■Description of MFA program in lighting design offered at Parsons School of Design, including list of courses.

455 Shapiro, Bruce G. "The Leo Kurtz Exhibition: The Harvard Acting Theatre Collection." *Gestus*. 1986 Win; 11(4): 257-264. Illus.: Sketches. Pntg. Architec. 6. Lang.: Eng.
USA: Cambridge, MA. 1986. Technical studies. ■Exhibition of the design renderings of designer Leo Kurtz who worked closely with Bertolt Brecht and Erwin Piscator.

456 Sisk, Douglass F. "Retrofitting the Sixties: Turntables, Lifts, and Other Stage Machinery." *ThCr*. 1987 Mar.; 21(3): 30, 70-73. Illus.: Photo. B&W. 1. Lang.: Eng.
USA. 1960-1987. Technical studies. ■Experimental stage machinery of the 1960s, comparison to today's standards.

457 Sisk, Douglass F. "Computers in Theatre." *ThCr*. 1987 Aug/Sep.; 21(7): 38, 89. Lang.: Eng.

THEATRE IN GENERAL: —Design/technology

USA. 1987. Technical studies. ■Available computer system technology for dimmer functions: retail guide included.

458 Sisk, Douglass F. "USITT Dimmer Standards." *ThCr.* 1987 Feb.; 21(2): 16, 81-91. Tables. Illus.: Diagram. 5. Lang.: Eng.

USA. 1986. Technical studies. ■Proposed digital and analog transmission protocol standards for dimmers developed by the United States Institute for Theatre Technology.

459 Sisk, Douglass F. "Computer-Assisted Lighting Controllers." *ThCr.* 1987 Feb.; 21(2): 36-41. Tables. 2. Lang.: Eng.

USA. 1987. Technical studies. ■Survey of current computer-assisted lighting controllers, comparing features and prices.

460 Sisk, Douglass F. "Hot Lights on Broadway." *LDim.* 1987 May/June; 11(3): 108-115. Illus.: Photo. 4. Lang.: Eng.

USA: New York, NY. 1987. Technical studies. ■Current Broadway shows and their lighting designers.

461 Sisk, Douglass F. "Sunlight on the Sand." *LDim.* 1987 Mar/Apr.; 11(2): 30-118. Illus.: Photo. Lighting. B&W. 2. Lang.: Eng.

USA: New York, NY. 1987. Technical studies. ■Analysis of the work of lighting designer Dennis Parichy, with special attention paid to his design for *Coastal Disturbances.*

462 Smith, Ronn. "A Company of Her Own." *LDim.* 1987 Mar/Apr.; 11(2): 72-75, 90-91. Illus.: Photo. Chart. 7. Lang.: Eng.

USA. 1987. Histories-sources. ■Interview with designer Marilyn Lowey who established her own business by using computers for lighting design.

463 Sommers, Michael. "*Les Liaisons Dangereuses.*" *ThCr.* 1987 Aug/Sep.; 21(7): 26-31, 84. Fr.Elev. Grd.Plan. 6. Lang.: Eng.

USA: New York, NY. UK-England: London. 1985-1987. Technical studies. ■Set designer Bob Crowley's work on *Les Liaisons Dangereuses* from its inception at Royal Shakespeare Company's experimental black box to Broadway's Music Box Theatre.

464 Sommers, Michael; Hale, Alice M. "Special Report: Touring." *ThCr.* 1987 Aug/Sep.; 21(7): 19-77. Illus.: Design. Photo. Dwg. Plan. Schematic. 8. Lang.: Eng.

USA. 1987. Technical studies. ■Comprehensive look at touring theatre.

465 Stern, Gary M. "Tony Walton at the Beaumont." *ThCr.* 1987 Mar.; 21(3): 16-21, 41-44. Illus.: Photo. Plan. Color. B&W. Grd.Plan. 7. Lang.: Eng.

USA: New York, NY. 1986-1987. Technical studies. ■Putting scenery on the stage of the Vivian Beaumont Theatre, Tony Walton's design solutions for 2 plays.

466 Stern, Lawrence. *Stage Management: A Guidebook of Practical Techniques.* 3d ed. Newton, MA: Allyn & Bacon; 1987. xviii, 324 pp. Pref. Index. Append. Gloss. Illus.: Handbill. Photo. Plan. Maps. Dwg. Sketches. Diagram. Lighting. B&W. Grd.Plan. Chart. 118. Lang.: Eng.

USA. 1987. Technical studies. ■Summary of principles and needs of stage management: scheduling, budgeting, rehearsal procedures, supervision. Practical information on getting a job.

467 Sword, David. "PVC and Steel Pipe Traveller System." *TechB.* 1987 Oct.: 1. Illus.: Dwg. B&W. 1. [TB 1181.] Lang.: Eng.

USA. 1987. Technical studies. ■Devising a traveller track system to move light scenery pieces across the stage.

468 Terry, Steve. "USITT Data Transmission Standards." *LDim.* 1987 Mar/Apr.; 11(2): 102-115. Illus.: Diagram. 4. Lang.: Eng.

USA. 1987. Technical studies. ■United Institute for Theater Technology (USITT) formally adopts two important new standards for dimmers and controllers.

469 Thomas, Richard K. "Sound: The Need for Union Representation for Sound Designers." *TD&T.* 1987; 23(3): 5-7. Lang.: Eng.

USA. 1985-1987. Technical studies. ■Effort to find appropriate union representation for theatrical sound designers with either International Alliance of Theatrical Stage Employees (IATSE) or United Scenic Artists (USA).

470 VanDyke, Michael. "A Television Lighting Effect." *TechB.* 1987 Apr.: 1-3. Illus.: Diagram. B&W. 2. [TB 1178.] Lang.: Eng.

USA. 1987. Technical studies. ■How to devise a circuit to simulate TV light on stage.

471 Warfel, William B. "Working with White Light." *LDim.* 1982; 6(6): 26-32. Illus.: Graphs. Maps. 6. Lang.: Eng.

USA. 1982. Technical studies. ■Idea and uses of white light: developing method of organizing and identifying color filters for predictable mixtures.

472 Watson, Lee. "Watson on the Performing Arts." *L&DA.* 1987 May; 17(5): 62-63. Lang.: Eng.

USA: New York, NY. 1987. Reviews of performances. ■Reviews of productions and their lighting for *Les Misérables, Starlight Express, Blithe Spirit* and *South Pacific.*

473 Watson, Lee. "Watson on the Performing Arts." *L&DA.* 1987 Apr.; 17(4): 58-59. Lang.: Eng.

USA: New York, NY. 1987. Reviews of performances. ■Reviews of productions and their lighting for *Sweet Sue, Wild Honey* and *Olympus on My Mind.*

474 Watson, Lee. "Watson on the Performing Arts." *L&DA.* 1987 Feb.; 17(2): 58-60. Lang.: Eng.

USA: New York, NY. 1987. Reviews of performances. ■Reviews of productions and their lighting for *Die Walküre, Parsifal, Me and My Girl, You Never Can Tell, Stepping Out, Front Page, Broadway Bound, CIVIL warS, Lady Day, Oh, Coward!* and *Alvin Ailey Dance Theatre.*

475 Watson, Lee. "Watson on the Performing Arts." *L&DA.* 1987 June; 17(6): 60-61. Lang.: Eng.

USA: New York, NY. 1987. Reviews of performances. ■Reviews of productions and their lighting for *Stardust, Sweet Charity, Death and the King's Horsemen, The Colored Museum, The Knife, The Nerd* and *Women Beware Women.*

476 Watson, Lee. "Watson on the Performing Arts." *L&DA.* 1987 Aug.; 17(8): 54. Lang.: Eng.

USA: New York, NY. 1987. Reviews of performances. ■Reviews of productions and their lighting for *Funny Feet, Sleeping Beauty, Staggerlee, Fences, The Musical Comedy Murders of 1940* and *Les Liaisons Dangereuses.*

477 Watson, Lee. "Watson on the Performing Arts." *L&DA.* 1987 Oct.; 17(10): 54-56. Lang.: Eng.

USA: New York, NY. 1987. Reviews of performances. ■Reviews of productions and their lighting for *Holy Ghosts, Coastal Disturbances, Dreamgirls, Magic Flute, Beehive* and *Moms.*

478 Watson, Lee. "Nicholas Nickleby:A Dickens of a Show." *LDim.* 1982; 6(2): 18-25. Illus.: Photo. Lighting. 15. Lang.: Eng.

USA: New York, NY. 1982. Technical studies. ■Instruments, focusing process, hook up sheets for production of Dickens' *Nicholas Nickleby.*

479 Watson, Lee. "Light's Labours Not Lost." *LDim.* 1984; 8(2): 23-27. Illus.: Photo. Lighting. 12. Lang.: Eng.

USA. 1982. Technical studies. ■Challenges of repertory lighting: equipment and dimmers to create appropriate effects but rapid changeovers from one production to the next.

480 Webb, Geoff. "A System for Duplicating Steel Tube Frames." *TechB.* 1987 Apr.: 1-2. Illus.: Dwg. B&W. 1. [TB 1175.] Lang.: Eng.

USA. 1987. Technical studies. ■How to make 'duplicating clamps' to be used when building identical units in scenery.

481 Webb, Michael. "New Life for Neon." *LDim.* 1982; 6(4): 26-27, 29-31. Illus.: Photo. 12. Lang.: Eng.

USA. 1982. Technical studies. ■Use of neon lights from film making to theatrical productions.

482 Weisang, Myriam. "Aiming for the Mind's Eye." *ThCr.* 1987 Apr.; 21(4): 42-43, 69-71. Illus.: Photo. Color. B&W. 2. Lang.: Eng.

USA. 1987. Technical studies. ■ShaSha Higby, her philosophy and approach to costume sculpture performance.

THEATRE IN GENERAL: —Design/technology

483 Welker, David Harold. *Stagecraft: A Handbook for Organization, Construction and Management.* Boston, MA: Allyn and Bacon; 1987. xviii, 492 pp. Pref. Index. Illus.: Photo. Plan. Dwg. Sketches. Diagram. B&W. Explod.Sect. Fr.Elev. Detail. R.Elev. Schematic. Grd.Plan. Chart. 141. [2d ed.] Lang.: Eng.
USA. 1987. Instructional materials. ■Comprehensive guide to basic stagecraft skills (technical drawings, equipment, construction, painting, setup and strike) with discussion of production staff's function and sceneshop management.

484 White, Michael. "Merging Two Disciplines." *LDim.* 1987 Jan/Feb.; ll(1): 56, 60-61. Lang.: Eng.
USA: New York, NY. 1987. Technical studies. ■Lighting designer Mark Stanley of New York City Opera discusses how principles of theatre lighting can be expanded into architectural lighting.

485 Williams, Mike. "A World of Light." *LDim.* 1987 Jan/Feb.; 11(1): 38-41, 52-54. Illus.: Photo. 4. Lang.: Eng.
USA: Boston, MA. 1987. Histories-sources. ■Interview with lighting designer Ishii Motoko, honored twice by the Illumination Engineering Society.

486 Wolff, Fred M. "Lights Have Starred on Broadway: Evolution of Theatrical Lighting Equipment." *L&DA.* 1987 Dec.; 17(12): 18-30. Biblio. Illus.: Photo. Dwg. Diagram. Schematic. 29. Lang.: Eng.
USA. 1700-1987. Historical studies. ■A very brief history of the development of lighting equipment, primarily in the United States. Discussion is given to lighting instruments as well as how they are controlled.

487 Anarina, N. "Vladimir Serebrovskij." *TeatrM.* 1987; 2: 173-176. Lang.: Rus.
USSR. Biographical studies. ■Portrait of theatre artist, designer and costumer.

488 Dobužinskij, M.V. *Vospominanija.* (Memoirs.) Moscow: Navka; 1987. 477 pp. Lang.: Rus.
USSR. 1875-1958. Histories-sources. ■Memoirs of theatre artist and designer M.V. Dobužinskij.

489 Fedosova, G. "Teatral'no-dekoracionnoe iskusstvo Moskvy i Leningrada 1920-30. Opyt sravnitel'nogo analiza." (The Ornamental Theatre Art of Moscow and Leningrad in the 1920's and 1930's: A Comparative Analysis.) *Iskusstvo.* 1987; 5: 34-41. Lang.: Rus.
USSR: Moscow, Leningrad. 1920-1939. Historical studies. ■Costume and scenery.

490 Frenkel, M.A. *Plastika sceniceskogo prostranstva: (Nekotorye voprosy teorii i praktiki scenografii).* (The Plastic Art of Stage Space: Some Questions on the Theory and Practice of Scene Design.) Kiev: Mistectvo; 1987. 180 pp. Lang.: Rus.
USSR. 1987. Critical studies.

491 Jakovleva, Je. "'Eto bylo sčastlivejšee vremja...'." ('It Was the Happiest Time'.) *Neva.* 1987; 8: 171-176. Lang.: Rus.
USSR. 1935-1939. Historical studies. ■Collaboration of V.E. Mejerchol'd with theatre artists A. Jakovlev and V. Suchaev.

492 Kancurašvili, K.S. *Brecht i gruzinskaja scenografija (tendencii razvitija gruzinskogo teatral'no-dekoracionnogo 60-80 godov): Avtoref.: dis. kand. iskusstvovedenija.* (Brecht and Georgian Scenography—Tendencies in the Development of Georgian Set Design from the Sixties through the Eighties: Abstract of a Dissertation by a Candidate in Art Criticism.) Tbilisi: In-t istorii gruzinskogo iskusstva; 1987. 21 pp. Lang.: Rus.
USSR. 1960-1987. Historical studies.

493 Kuman'kov, E. "Radost' krasoty." (The Joy of Beauty.) *TeatZ.* 1987; 7: 18-19. Lang.: Rus.
USSR: Moscow. 1985. Critical studies. ■Well-known theatre artist discusses V. Levental's scenery for Čechov's *Diadia Vania (Uncle Vanya)* performed by Moscow Art Theatre.

494 Kuznecov, Je. "Teatr Niko Pirosmanašvili." (The Theatre of Niko Pirosmanašvili.) *TeatrM.* 1987; 10: 129-132. Lang.: Rus.

USSR. Historical studies. ■Theatrical designs by artist Niko Pirosmanašvili.

495 Luckaja, E. "Nina Gaponova." *TeatrM.* 1987; 3: 145-148. Lang.: Rus.
USSR. 1986. Biographical studies. ■Portrait of designer Nina Gaponova.

496 Nikolaeva, G.V. *Jevoljucija principov scenografii dramatičeskogo spektaklja: Avtoref. diss. kand. iskusstvovedenija.* (The Evolution of the Principles of Scene Design for Dramatic Performances: Abstract of a Dissertation by a Candidate in Art Criticism.) Moscow: GITIS; 1987. 22 pp. Lang.: Rus.
USSR. 1987. Historical studies.

497 Ostrovskij, S. "Čelovek ot teatra, ili tri stula chudožnika Šejncisa." (A Man from the Theatre, or the Three Chairs of the Artist Šejncis.) *TeatZ.* 1987; 6: 10-13. Lang.: Rus.
USSR. 1987. Biographical studies. ■Work of theatre artist Oleg Šejncis.

498 Savickaja, O. *Kompozicija sceničeskogo prostranstva v spektakljah 70-80-h godov: Avtoref. dis. kand. iskusstvovedenija.* (The Composition of Stage Space in Performances of the Seventies and Eighties: Abstract of a Dissertation by a Candidate in Art Criticism.) Leningrad: LGIT-MiK; 1987. 17 pp. Lang.: Rus.
USSR. 1970-1987. Critical studies.

499 Savickaja, O. "Sreda obitanija na scene." (Habitational Milieu on the Stage.) *DekorIsk.* 1987; 7: 18-21. Lang.: Rus.
USSR. 1970-1987. ■Work of designer M. Kitaev and scenographer E. Kočergin, general problems of scene design.

500 Tkač, E. "Čto takoe krasota?" (What is Beauty?) *TeatZ.* 1987; 3: 14-15. Lang.: Rus.
USSR. 1987. Histories-sources. ■Interview with theatrical artist A.P. Vasiljëv.

Institutions

501 Perinetti, André-Louis. "Ni diffusion ni contrôle: solidarité. Le rôle d'une institution internationale." (Neither Diffusion nor Control: Solidarity. The Role of an International Institution.) 235-245 in Coca, Jordi, ed.; Conesa, Laura, comp. *Congrés Internacional de Teatre a Catalunya 1985. Actes. Volum III. Seccions 4, 5 i 6.* Barcelona: Institut del Teatre; 1987. 302 pp. Notes. [Section 6: International Cultural Institutions.] Lang.: Fre.
1927-1985. Historical studies. ■Evolution of International Theatre Institute, its antecedents, fundamental principles, major events and relations with UNESCO.

502 *Brisbane Arts Theatre, The First Fifty Years 1936-1986.* Brisbane: Brisbane Arts Theatre; 1987. 84 pp. Lang.: Eng.
Australia: Brisbane. 1936-1986. Historical studies. ■A history of Brisbane's leading amateur theatre companies which, until the emergence of subsidized professional theatre in the late 1950s, played a major part in maintaining quality theatre in Queensland's capital city.

503 Layne, Ronald. *Australian Studies in Theatre Arts and Drama.* Canberra: Committee to Review Australian Studies in Education; 1987. 95 pp. (Craste Paper 20.) Lang.: Eng.
Australia. 1987. Historical studies. ■Survey of contemporary liberal arts and professional training courses in Australian tertiary institutions, with special reference to the role of Australian studies in those courses.

504 *Cerfontaine et Soumoy, Dramatiques d'hier.* (Cerfontaine and Soumoy: Yesterday's Performances.) Cerfontaine: Musée de Cerfontaine; 1987. 63 pp. Pref. Lang.: Fre.
Belgium: Cerfontaine, Soumoy. 1912-1961. Histories-sources. ■Reproductions of forty amateur theatre programs from two rural Belgian villages.

505 Allen, Richard. "New Director in Charlottetown." *OC.* 1987 Sum; 28(2): 22-23. Illus.: Photo. B&W. 1. [Soundings.] Lang.: Eng.
Canada: Charlottetown, PE. 1965-1987. Historical studies. ■Briefly discusses the history of the Charlottetown Festival and its recent appointment of Walter Learning as artistic director.

CLASSED ENTRIES

THEATRE IN GENERAL: —Institutions

506 Brennan, Brian. "Alberta Theatre Wars." *CTR*. 1987 Sum; 51: 66-69. Illus.: Photo. Print. B&W. 5. [Carte Blanche.] Lang.: Eng.
Canada: Edmonton, AB, Calgary, AB. 1987. Historical studies. ■Overview of history of Alberta theatre companies, both mainstream and alternative.

507 Chusid, Harvey. "Calgary's Olympic Arts Festival Entertains the World." *OC*. 1987 Win; 28(4): 22-23. Illus.: Photo. B&W. 1. [Soundings.] Lang.: Eng.
Canada: Calgary, AB. 1987. Historical studies. ■The historical mandate of the Olympic Arts Festival and the scope of Calgary's 1988 showcase.

508 Filewod, Alan. *Collective Encounters: Documentary Theatre in English Canada*. Toronto, ON: U of Toronto P; 1987. 214 pp. Illus.: Photo. B&W. Lang.: Eng.
Canada. 1970-1986. Histories-specific. ■Examines the collective documentary tradition in English Canada. Analyzes plays produced by various alternative theatre companies.

509 Filewod, Alan. "The Hand that Feeds." *CTR*. 1987 Sum; 51: 9-16. Illus.: Photo. Plan. Print. B&W. 8. Lang.: Eng.
Canada. 1987. Critical studies. ■Critical analysis of the Governor General's Awards for Canadian playwriting. Issues under debate include jury selection, conditions of eligibility, text vs. performance.

510 Friedlander, Mira. "Toronto Free Theatre: Measuring up to the Mandate." *PAC*. 1984 Spr/Sum; 21(1): 18-21. Illus.: Photo. Print. 3. Lang.: Eng.
Canada: Toronto, ON. 1984. Critical studies. ■Traces the development of the Toronto Free Theatre from the 1970s, illustrating how its goals, ethics and artistic values developed through the theatre's productions.

511 Garebian, Keith. "English Drama Hits Hard Times in Quebec." *PAC*. 1982 Fall; 19(3): 47-50. Illus.: Photo. Print. B&W. 2. Lang.: Eng.
Canada: Montreal, PQ. 1982. Historical studies. ■The limited venues for English-language theatre on the occasion of the closing of the Saidye Bronfman Centre in Montreal.

512 Ghitan, John; Flaherty, Kathleen; Langner, Pat. "A Play on the Fringe: Or Three Albertans Sitting Around Talking." *Theatrum*. 1987 Fall/Win; 8: 9-15, 39. Lang.: Eng.
Canada: Edmonton, AB. 1987. Reviews of performances. ■Discusses the 1987 Edmonton Fringe Festival.

513 Hunt, Nigel. "...Lest Ye Be Judged." *CTR*. 1987 Sum; 51: 17-23. Illus.: Photo. Print. B&W. 6. Lang.: Eng.
Canada: Toronto, ON. 1987. Critical studies. ■Critical analysis of the Chalmers Awards, given by the Toronto Drama Bench. Questions the value of the award as well as what it symbolizes to theatre workers.

514 Knowles, Richard Paul. "Atlantic Canada." *JCNREC*. 1987 Spr; 22(1): 135-140. Lang.: Eng.
Canada. 1985-1986. Historical studies. ■Theatre companies in Atlantic Canada brought together in April 1985/86 to discuss professional concerns.

515 Lavoie, Pierre. "Le complexe de quichotte." (The Quixote Complex.) *JCT*. 1987; 44: 7-13. Illus.: Dwg. Sketches. Print. B&W. 7. Lang.: Fre.
Canada. 1986. Critical studies. ■The disappearance of theatrical organizations in Quebec, and the weakness of theatrical resources is a sign of apathy in the theatre world and in *Jeu*.

516 Leiren-Young, Mark. "Vancouver Entrances and Exits." *CTR*. 1987 Fall; 52: 91-94. Illus.: Photo. Print. B&W. 3. Lang.: Eng.
Canada: Vancouver, BC. 1987. Historical studies. ■Survey of Vancouver theatres based on press releases: changes in personnel, format and content.

517 Leiren-Young, Mark. "Definite Jesse Material." *CTR*. 1987 Sum; 51: 32-35. Illus.: Photo. Print. B&W. 5. [The Envelope Please.../2.] Lang.: Eng.
Canada: Vancouver, BC. 1983. Critical studies. ■Analysis of the Jesse Awards: debates the benefits and disadvantages of generating competition among theatre professionals. Are awards professional acknowledgement or popularity contests?.

518 MacPherson, Rod. "Saskatoon Reopening the Carleton Trail." *CTR*. 1987 Sum; 51: 70-72. Illus.: Photo. B&W. 3. [Carte Blanche.] Lang.: Eng.
Canada: Saskatoon, SK. 1987. Critical studies. ■Practical analysis of the policy of co-production, which entails swapping two shows between two companies in order to generate exposure. Shows are created and shared in the west, diffusing the necessity to send shows eastward.

519 MacSween, Donald. "National Theatre School Celebrates a Successful 25 Years with a Tour." *PAC*. 1986 Jan.; 22(4): 14-21. Notes. Illus.: Photo. Print. 4. Lang.: Eng.
Canada: Montreal, PQ. 1960-1985. Historical studies. ■Historical background of National Theatre School.

520 Neil, Boyd. "Theatre Plus Under André: A Decade of Direction." *PAC*. 1982 Fall; 19(3): 31-33. B&W. 4. Lang.: Eng.
Canada: Toronto, ON. 1972-1982. Historical studies. ■A profile of Theatre Plus, the only serious summer theatre in Toronto, on its 10th anniversary under the direction of Marion André.

521 Pettigrew, John; Portman, Jamie; Davies, Robertson, foreword. *Stratford: The First Thirty Years*. Toronto, ON: Macmillan; 1985. xx, 198 pp, 314 pp. [2 vols.] Lang.: Eng.
Canada: Stratford, ON. 1953-1982. Histories-specific. ■The first published attempt to provide a complete history of the Stratford Festival.

522 Selman, Jan. "Three Cultures, One Issue." *CTR*. 1987 Win; 53: 11-19. Notes. Illus.: Photo. Print. B&W. 9. [Popular Theatre in the Northwest Territories.] Lang.: Eng.
Canada. 1987. Historical studies. ■A personal account describing two popular theatre projects with natives of the Northwest territories. Issues discussed include cultural realities clashing with government content regulations. Excerpts from plays are provided, illustrating the relationships between community concerns and working for change.

523 Sherman, Jason. "Reclaiming the Doras: The Envelope Please.../1." *CTR*. 1987 Sum; 51: 24-31. Illus.: Photo. Print. B&W. 7. Lang.: Eng.
Canada: Toronto, ON. 1987. Critical studies. ■Critical analysis of the Dora Mavor Moore Awards reveals that the prime purpose is promotion and generating competition, rather than recognition of achievement. History of inception is provided.

524 Smith, Patricia Keeney. "For Young Audiences, a Magical Spring Fling." *PAC*. 1982 Spr; 19(1): 19-24. B&W. 8. Lang.: Eng.
Canada: Toronto, ON. 1982. Reviews of performances. ■A preview of the International Children's Festival at Toronto's Harbourfront, with background information on the theatre companies involved.

525 Thurlow, Ann. "Maritime Moods." *PAC*. 1985 Sum; 22(2): 33-35. Illus.: Photo. Print. B&W. 4. Lang.: Eng.
Canada: Charlottetown, PE. 1965-1985. Historical studies. ■A preview of the upcoming Charlottetown Festival and a brief review of its history, with reference to its most famous and longest-running production, *Anne of Green Gables*.

526 Dillon, John. "Bogota Behind Bullet-Proof Glass." *AmTh*. 1987 Oct.; 4(7): 74-76. Illus.: Photo. B&W. 1. Lang.: Eng.
Colombia: Bogotá. 1948-1987. Historical studies. ■Account of a recent trip that several regional theatre directors took to Latin American countries to foster new relationships with U.S. and Latin American artists.

527 Štěpán, Václav. "Národní muzeum v Praze—divadelní oddělení." (The National Museum in Prague—Theatre Department.) *Prog*. 1987; 59(2): 50-54. Illus.: Photo. Pntg. B&W. 8. Lang.: Cze.
Czechoslovakia: Prague. 1987. Histories-sources. ■History and present condition of theatre museums.

528 Jorgensen, Aage. "Touring the 1970's with the Solvognen in Denmark." *TDR*. 1982 Fall; 26(3): 15-28. Illus.: Photo. B&W. 3. Lang.: Eng.
Denmark. 1969-1982. Historical studies. ■The experimental theatre company Solvognen: influence of politics on their work. Productions, techniques, political street theatre, group's philosophy and their socialist beliefs.

THEATRE IN GENERAL: —Institutions

529 De Marinis, Marco. *Il nuovo teatro 1947-1970.* (The New Theatre, 1947-1970.) Milan: Bompiani; 1987. 310 pp. (Strumenti Bompiani.) Pref. Index. Notes. Biblio. Lang.: Ita.
Europe. North America. 1947-1970. Historical studies. ■Theatre companies and individuals that sought to oppose official, commercial and established theatre, including Living Theatre, Odin Teatret, Bread and Puppet Theatre, Laboratory Theatre.

530 Scott, Virginia. "Saved by the Magic Wand of *Circé.*" *ThS.* 1987 Nov.; 28(2): 1-16. Notes. Lang.: Eng.
France: Paris. 1673-1679. Historical studies. ■Financial, operational and artistic issues surrounding the survival of the Troupe of the Hôtel Guénégaud with reference to a spectacular production of *Circé* in 1675.

531 Freydank, Ruth. "Die Nationaltheateridee und das deutsche Kaiserreich, Der Weg zur Gründung des Deutschen Theaters." (The Idea of a National Theatre and the German Empire: The Way to the Foundation of Deutsches Theater.) *TZ.* 1987; 42(11): 14-18. Illus.: Photo. B&W. 8. Lang.: Ger.
Germany: Berlin. 1854-1883. Historical studies. ■On the special situation of German theatre and reform efforts, resulting in the founding of Deutsches Theater Berlin.

532 Martineau, Maureen. "De l'Autre Côté du Mur, la Face Cachée du Théâtre Allemand." (From the Other Side of the Wall, the Hidden Side of German Theatre.) *JCT.* 1987; 43: 61-71. 5. Lang.: Fre.
Germany, East. Canada. 1985. Historical studies. ■Discusses modern theatre in East Germany and compares it to Quebec theatre.

533 Huesmann, Heinrich. "New Theatre Documentation Technology at the Munich *Deutsches Theatermuseum.*" *THSt.* 1987; 7: 117-121. Illus.: Photo. Print. B&W. 33. Lang.: Eng.
Germany, West: Munich. 1987. Critical studies. ■Description of the Tandem database system used by the Deutsches Theatermuseum to catalog and retrieve information and documents in the collection.

534 Lavoie, Pierre; Pavlovic, Diane. "Allemagne: L'hellénisme Culturel. Entretien avec Wolfgang Kolneder." (Germany: Cultural Hellenism. Interview with Wolfgang Kolneder.) *JCT.* 1987; 43: 50-60. 4. Lang.: Fre.
Germany, West: Berlin, West. 1945-1986. Historical studies. ■Kolneder discusses the influence of the youth movement in theatre in Germany since World War II. Contemporary directors are re-exploring classical theatre.

535 Lich-Knight, L. *Reconstruction in the West German Theatre: From the* Stunde Null *to the Currency Reform.* Warwick: University of Warwick; 1986. Notes. Biblio. [Ph.D. thesis, *Index to Theses*, 37-4376.] Lang.: Eng.
Germany, West. 1945-1948. Historical studies. ■Examines types and numbers of theatres and reconstructs twenty repertoirs. Discusses theatre as a focus for re-establishing national and personal identity.

536 Földes, Anna. "A színház mint a népek saját és közös nyelve." (Theatre as the Own and Common Language of the People.) *Sz.* 1987 July; 20(7): 41-45. Lang.: Hun.
Hungary: Budapest. 1987. Critical studies. ■The International Association of Theatre Critics held its conference in March 1987 the subject of which was: 'The theatre as own and common language of people'.

537 Gápelné Tóth, Rózsa. "Rendet teremteni a színházban! Két évad között, egy évadzárás tanulságaiból." (Making Order in the Theatre! Between Two Seasons, from the Conclusions of Two Seasons' Closings.) *Napj.* 1987 Aug.; 26(8): 38-39. Lang.: Hun.
Hungary: Miskolc. 1986-1987. Histories-sources. ■Closing speech by Miskolc city official evaluates theatrical season.

538 Kerényi, Ferenc. "A nemzeti színházak alapításának történetéhez." (Additions to the History of the Foundation of National Theatres.) *Sz.* 1987 Dec.; 20(12): 3-7. Lang.: Hun.
Hungary. 1987. Historical studies. ■Text of a lecture given at Hungarian Theatre Institute conference on national theatres.

539 Koltai, Tamás. "A színház: a megismerés művészete. Beszélgetés Zsámbéki Gáborral." (Theatre—Art of Cognition: Interview with Gábor Zsámbéki.) *Krit.* 1987 Nov.(11):

8-9. Illus.: Photo. B&W. 3. [Close-Up of the Katona József Theatre II.] Lang.: Hun.
Hungary. 1968-1987. Histories-sources. ■Gábor Zsámbéki, artistic director of the Katona József Theatre speaks about his career, the theatre's situation and program policy.

540 Müller, Péter P. "Pécsi évadok. Az 1981/82-es szezontól máig." (Seasons in Pécs. From the 1981/82 Season up to Now.) *Sz.* 1987 Sep.; 20(9): 10-18. Illus.: Photo. B&W. 6. Lang.: Hun.
Hungary: Pécs. 1981-1987. Critical studies. ■Short review of six seasons, their analysis and evaluation: the place the National Theatre of Pécs takes in Hungarian theatre life.

541 Nánay, István. "'A Nemzeti Színház a nemzet iskolája'. Nemzetközi tanácskozás a Magyar Tudományos Akadémián." ('The National Theatre, School of the Nation'. International Conference at the Hungarian Academy of Sciences.) *Sz.* 1987 Dec.; 20(12): 1-2. Lang.: Hun.
Hungary: Budapest. 1987. Histories-sources. ■An international conference on 'The Idea and Practice of National Theatres in European Countries' was held at the Hungarian Academy of Sciences on the occasion of the 150th anniversary of the Hungarian National Theatre. Guests from seven countries attended the event.

542 Székely, Györky. "Gondolatok a Nemzeti Színházról." (Thoughts on the National Theatre.) *Sz.* 1987 Sep.; 20(9): 1-4. Lang.: Hun.
Hungary: Budapest. 1837-1987. Historical studies. ■Review of the most important events of the Hungarian National Theatre on the occasion of its 150th anniversary with special attention to the role of the National Theatre played in Hungarian culture.

543 Szűcs, Katalin. "'Debrecenbe kéne menni'." ('We Ought to Go to Debrecen'.) *Sz.* 1987 Sep.; 20(9): 28-32. Lang.: Hun.
Hungary: Debrecen. 1987. Histories-sources. ■Interview with Gyula Kertész, director of the Csokonai Theatre, chief stage manager István Pinczés and Károly Tar, head of section of the County Council, on the present and future of the theatre on the occasion of the change.

544 Vámos, László. "Kell-e Nemzeti Színház?" (Do We Need National Theatres?) *Sz.* 1987 Dec.; 20(12): 7-9. Lang.: Hun.
Hungary. 1987. Critical studies. ■The lecture of László Vámos, artistic director of the National Theatre in Budapest given at the two-day debate on national theatres.

545 Raftery, Mary. "Thoroughbreds or White Elephants?" *ThIr.* 1984 Dec-Mar.; 5: 65-70. Illus.: Graphs. B&W. 3. Lang.: Eng.
Ireland: Dublin, Cork. UK-Ireland: Belfast. 1965-1984. Historical studies. ■Funding and financial difficulties of the Cork Opera House, the Olympia Theatre, the Gaiety Theatre and the Belfast Grand Opera House. Performance space repair needs are also addressed.

546 Kaminer, Amira. "Horaahat Amanut Ahteatron Be-Emtzaut Thahlich Trom Ahfaka Ve Hafaka." (Teaching Theatre Through Pre-Production and Production Process.) *Bamah.* 1987; 22(109-110): 122-126. Lang.: Heb.
Israel: Tel Aviv. 1987. Historical studies. ■Creative teaching of theatre through Seminar Hakibuzim.

547 Ente Teatrale Italiano; Antonucci, Giovanni, ed. *Catalogo dei centri di documentazione teatrale.* (Catalogue of Theatrical Documentation Centres.) Rome: Il Ventaglio; 1987. 292 pp. (Documenti di teatro 5.) Lang.: Ita.
Italy. 1987. Bibliographical studies. ■A list of the Italian institutions committed to collecting and preserving theatrical documents and books.

548 Alberti, Carmelo. "Il ritorno dei Comici. Vicende del Teatro Vendramin di San Luca (1700-1733)." (The Return of the Comici: Ups and Downs of the Vendramin Theatre of San Luca, 1700-1733.) *BiT.* 1987; 5/6: 133-187. Lang.: Ita.
Italy: Venice. 1700-1733. Histories-sources. ■The story of San Luca theatre through the documents of the Vendramin archives. Letters, contracts and actors' engagements.

549 d'Amico, Alessandro; Tinterri, Alessandro. *Pirandello capocomico.* (Pirandello, Company Manager.) Palermo: Sellerio; 1987. 465 pp. Index. Append. Illus.: Design. Photo. Plan. Print. B&W. 234. Lang.: Ita.

THEATRE IN GENERAL: —Institutions

Italy. 1924-1928. Biographical studies. ■Pirandello's experiences as director of the Teatro d'Arte reconstructed through documentation of the performances.

550 Seragnoli, Daniele. *L'industria del teatro. Carlo Ritorni e lo spettacolo a Reggio Emilia nell'Ottocento.* (The Theatre Industry: Carlo Ritorni and the Theatre in Reggio Emilia in the Nineteenth-Century.) Bologna: Mulino; 1987. 400 pp. (Proscenio 4.) Index. Pref. Notes. Append. Lang.: Ita.
Italy: Reggio Emilia. 1800-1900. Critical studies. ■Based on the writings of Carlo Ritorni, an aristocrat and theatre expert, the work proposes a reading of performance in Reggio Emilia in the context of nineteenth-century theatre organization.

551 Kang, Gyu-Sik. "Han guk-ui keukdan." (Theatre Companies of Korea.) 30-48 in *The Development of Korean Modern Theatre in the First Half of the Twentieth Century.* Seoul: Shin Hyup Theatre Company; 1986. 105 pp. Lang.: Kor.
Korea. 1900-1950. Histories-specific. ■Development of Korean theatre in the twentieth century.

552 Kim, Mido. "Yonguk yu 1940s." (Plays of the 1940s.) *KTR.* 1987 Mar.; 3(1): 27-29. Illus.: Photo. B&W. 1. Lang.: Kor.
Korea: Seoul. 1940-1947. Historical studies. ■Closing of the Tong-Yang theatre due to a lack of money, personnel and scripts.

553 Houtman, Dirkje; Steyn, Robert. "Pragmatiek als ideaal." (Pragmatism as an Ideal.) *Toneel.* 1987 May; 5(4): 39-42. Illus.: Photo. B&W. 7. Lang.: Dut.
Netherlands: Amsterdam. 1987. Historical studies. ■Toneelgroep Amsterdam and its mission in the eighties. No more ideology, but a pragmatic approach to theatre. Discussion of plans and expectations with youngest members of company.

554 Ogden, Dunbar H. *Performance Dynamics and the Amsterdam Werkteater.* Berkeley, CA: Univ of California P; 1987. 261 pp. Append. Pref. Index. Illus.: Photo. Print. B&W. 45. Lang.: Eng.
Netherlands: Amsterdam. 1969-1985. Historical studies. ■The beginning and the growth of the Werkteater from the viewpoint of the actors. They created their work improvisationally. Analyzes the work through the productions.

555 Schiller, Leon. "Wydział Dramaturgiczny PIST. Program studiów." (Department of Drama of the Theatre Institute: Program of Studies.) *PaT.* 1987; 3: 341-368. Pref. Lang.: Pol.
Poland: Warsaw. 1943. Histories-sources. ■A director's vision of future drama department at the theatre institute, including courses for students in art history, theatre history, stage design, history of literature, acting, philosophy, theory of theatre.

556 Gergely, Géza. "Múló évek—feltörő emlékek. A romániai magyar szinművészeti oktatás negyven éve." (Passing Years—Arising Memories. Forty Years of Hungarian Dramatic Education in Romania.) *Sz.* 1987 Apr.; 20(4): 34-38. Lang.: Hun.
Romania: Tîrgu-Mures. Hungary. 1946-1986. Histories-sources. ■Author's memories of his student years in István Szentgyörgyi Dramatic Institute and of his career as professor in the same institute, of his contemporaries, of whom many are outstanding personalities of Hungarian theatre life in Romania.

557 Csillag, Ilona. "A Habima útja." (The Way of HaBimah.) *Nvilag.* 1987 Dec.; 32(12): 1865-1870. Lang.: Hun.
Russia: Moscow. Israel. 1912-1980. Historical studies. ■Brief history of Hebrew theatre group: from Moscow to the United States to Tel Aviv. Major productions, actors, directors.

558 Coca, Jordi, ed.; Capmany, Maria Aurèlia, intro.; Gallén, Enric; Schroeder, Juan-Germán; Manegat, Julio; Pérez de Olaguer, Gonzalo; Oliveda, Maria Lluísa; Melendres, Jaume; Bartomeus, Antoni; Benach, Joan Anton; Vilà i Folch, Joaquim. *Teatre Grec de Montjuíc. 1929-1986.* (The Teatre Grec of Montjuíc. 1929-1986.) Barcelona: Ajuntament de Barcelona. Area de Cultura; 1987. 220 pp. (Catàlegs d'Exposicions 66.) Pref. Index. Tables. Append. Illus.: Design. Photo. Print. Color. B&W. 261. Lang.: Cat.
Spain-Catalonia: Barcelona. 1929-1986. Historical studies. ■Catalogue of exhibit on Teatre Grec. Includes various texts on the theatre's history. Interviews.

559 Pérez Coterillo, Moisés. "Una propuesta para recoger y procesar la información teatral." (A Proposal for Gathering and Processing Theatrical Information.) 247-258 in Coca, Jordi, ed.; Conesa, Laura, comp. *Congrés Internacional de Teatre a Catalunya 1985. Actes. Volum III. Seccions 4, 5 i 6.* Barcelona: Institut del Teatre; 1987. 302 pp. Notes. [Section 6: International Cultural Institutions.] Lang.: Spa.
Spain-Catalonia. 1975-1985. Critical studies. ■Evolution of Catalan theatrical activity and its inadequate treatment by the Madrid press. Proposes creation of a theatrical data base with linked centers in each community.

560 Federació de Teatre Amateur de Catalunya. *Memòria del Primer Congrés de Teatre Amateur de Catalunya.* (Memoir of the First Congress of Catalan Amateur Theatre.) Barcelona: Department de Cultura de la Generalitat de Catalunya; 1987. 198 pp. Illus.: Photo. Print. B&W. 33. Lang.: Cat.
Spain-Catalonia. 1850-1685. Histories-sources. ■Documentation of the first conference on amateur theatre in Catalonia.

561 "Handlingsplan för de kommande tio åren." (Plan for the Next Ten Years.) *Teaterf.* 1987; 20(6): 14. Lang.: Swe.
Sweden. 1987. Histories-sources. ■The future tasks for the Amatörteaterns Riksförbund.

562 Torch, Chris. "Earthcirkus." *TDR.* 1982 Fall; 26(3): 97-104. Illus.: Photo. B&W. 4. Lang.: Eng.
Sweden: Stockholm. 1977-1982. Historical studies. ■Profile and history of theatre company Earthcirkus. Their forms of street theatre, audience interaction, content of performances, collective process and political activities.

563 Richard, Christine. "Autorenförderung in der Schweiz: Wo der Hund begraben liegt." (Playwright Promoting in Switzerland: Where's the Root of the Matter?)*DB.* 1987 Jan.; 58(1): 42-44. Illus.: Photo. B&W. Lang.: Ger.
Switzerland. 1982-1986. Critical studies. ■Analysis of reasons for the failure of the project to promote young Swiss playwrights launched in 1982: political conservatism, lack of themes, lack of talent, stubbornness of the established theatre elite.

564 "Enter the Theatre Museum." *Econ.* 1987 18 Apr.; 303: 90. Illus.: Sketches. 1. Lang.: Eng.
UK-England: London. Historical studies. ■Opening of National Theatre Museum in London, Britain's first permanent tribute to its theatre tradition.

565 Dongill, David. "The Theatre Museum." *Drama.* 1987; 3(165): 22-24. Notes. Illus.: Photo. 6. Lang.: Eng.
UK-England: London. 1924-1987. Historical studies. ■The Theatre Museum, Covent Garden, which opened on April 23, 1987.

566 Kruger, Loren. "'Our National House': The Ideology of the National Theatre in Great Britain." *TJ.* 1987 Mar.; 39(1): 35-50. Notes. Lang.: Eng.
UK-England. 1800-1987. Critical studies. ■Debate over value of a National Theatre in Great Britain. Examination of political and social function of national theatres and duty of government to support it.

567 Saunders, Kay. "An Interview with Elizabeth Clark." *Hecate.* 1987; 13(1): 114-122. Lang.: Eng.
UK-England. London. Caribbean. Histories-sources. ■Elizabeth Clark, director of Temba Theatre Company, discusses Caribbean theatre, black actors and performance groups in Britain and their relation to mainstream work. Focus on her adaptation of *The Tempest*.

568 Wolf, Matt. "Return of the National." *AmTh.* 1987 Sep.; 4(6): 38-39. Illus.: Photo. B&W. 1. Lang.: Eng.
UK-England: London. 1985-1987. Critical studies. ■Recent work by the National Theatre of Great Britain: plays, playwrights, actors and directors who have worked there.

THEATRE IN GENERAL: —Institutions

569 Spurr, Chris. "Going Down the Country." *ThIr.* 1987; 13: 23-25. Illus.: Photo. B&W. 3. Lang.: Eng.
UK-Ireland. 1974-1987. Historical studies. ■Discussion of the touring company Irish Theatre Company.

570 "Actors' Fund Services, Programs Are Discussed at Deputy Meeting." *EN.* 1987 Nov.; 72(11): 3. Lang.: Eng.
USA: New York, NY. 1987. Historical studies. ■The services and benefits that the Actors' Fund makes available to professionals in the entertainment industry. Includes financial assistance grants, substance abuse counseling and maintenance of the Actors' Fund home, a retirement home in Englewood, New Jersey.

571 "Bill Ross Receives Philip Loeb Award." *EN.* 1985 Sep.; 70(8): 1. Illus.: Photo. B&W. 1. Lang.: Eng.
USA: New York, NY. 1985. Historical studies. ■Philip Loeb Humanitarian Award given to Bill Ross after serving on the Equity Council for nearly two decades.

572 "Equity Celebrates Black History Month." *EN.* 1986 Apr.; 71(4): 2. Lang.: Eng.
USA: New York, NY. 1986. Historical studies. ■Reviewing activities for Black History Month with emphasis on theme 'Blacks in the American Theatre—Past, Present and Future'.

573 "The Actors Strike for Recognition." *EN.* 1986 Jan.; 71(1): 1, 3. Lang.: Eng.
USA: New York, NY. 1921-1925. Historical studies. ■Actors strike against the Producing Managers Association. Efforts of E.H. Sothern to resolve conflicts.

574 "Special Election Section—Nominees for Election to Council Submit Statements." *EN.* 1986 Apr.; 71(4): 3, 4, 5. Lang.: Eng.
USA: New York, NY. 1986. Critical studies. ■All nominees for Actors' Equity Association council present their electoral statements.

575 "Lena Horne Receives Paul Robeson Award." *EN.* 1985 Feb.; 70(2): 1. Illus.: Photo. B&W. 2. Lang.: Eng.
USA. 1985. Critical studies. ■Lena Horne is the 1984 recipient of the Kennedy Center Honors for Lifetime Achievement (Paul Robeson Award).

576 "Health Care Institute for Performers Is Created at St. Luke's-Roosevelt Hospital." *EN.* 1985 Feb.; 70(2): 5. Lang.: Eng.
USA: New York, NY. 1985. Historical studies. ■The Kathyrn and Gilbert Miller Health Care Institute for Performing Artists is first health care facility to focus exclusively on performers.

577 "99 Seat Waiver is Debated in Los Angeles." *EN.* 1986 Oct.; 71(10): 1, 3. Lang.: Eng.
USA: Los Angeles, CA. 1986. Historical studies. ■Protest against limiting rules, such as salary, rehearsal, space and time in 99 seat waiver theatres. The Western Advisory Board refused to meet with the waiver theatre producers.

578 "Papp Receives Robeson Award." *EN.* 1987 Nov.; 72(11): 1, 4. Lang.: Eng.
USA: New York, NY. 1987. Historical studies. ■Joseph Papp received the 14th Annual Paul Robeson Award from Actors' Equity for helping to establish lasting cultural traditions.

579 "Behind the Scenes: Developments on the OOB Circuit, Other News." *DGQ.* 1987; 24(1): 57-62. Illus.: Sketches. 1. Lang.: Eng.
USA: New York, NY. 1987. Histories-sources. ■News about various New York area theatres: changes of locations, planned equity showcases, American plays in Australia, preserving old theatres, building new ones. Gives contact phone numbers and addresses.

580 "The Dramatists' Diary, Mid-January to May." *DGQ.* 1987; 24(1): 71-88. Illus.: Sketches. 1. Lang.: Eng.
USA. 1987. Histories-sources. ■Activities in and news on regional theatres. Includes notes on Dramatists' Guild Council meetings, new members, plays produced around the USA, plays optioned by various theaters, plays published, new books by members of the Guild.

581 "The Council's Reception, June 17, 1987." *DGQ.* 1987; 24(2): 7-11. Illus.: Photo. B&W. 12. Lang.: Eng.
USA: New York, NY. 1987. Histories-sources. ■Photographs taken at the Dramatists' Guild Council's reception for dramatists whose plays and musicals were presented during the previous season. A record of the hosts, guests, awards presented.

582 "1987-88 Directory." *DGQ.* 1987; 24(2): 22-56. Illus.: Sketches. 4. Lang.: Eng.
USA. 1987-1988. ■A complete listing of Broadway and Off-Broadway producers, agents based primarily in New York City, dinner theatres interested in new plays, sources of support for dramatists including artists colonies, fellowships and grants, workshops and play contests.

583 "Behind the Scenes: Women's Three-Day Event, Outreach '88." Illus.: Sketches. 3. Lang.: Eng.
USA. 1987. Histories-sources. ■Dramatists' Guild Women's Committee conference, June 5-7: text of letter sent by committee to the Kennedy Center about lack of opportunities there for women, all awards given to Guild members.

584 "The Dramatists' Diary, August to November." *DGQ.* 1987; 24(3): 52-64. Illus.: Sketches. 1. Lang.: Eng.
USA: New York, NY. 1987. ■Notes from the Dramatists' Guild's Council meetings of the Steering Committee, the credit union, increase in membership dues. Plays being produced on Broadway, Off Broadway, Off-off Broadway regionally and abroad. Lists of new members.

585 "Behind the Scenes: Writer's Block, OOB Updates: Directory Addenda." *DGQ.* 1987; 24(3): 33-41. Illus.: Sketches. 2. Lang.: Eng.
USA: New York, NY. 1987. Histories-sources. ■Various activities of the Dramatists' Guild including workshop by Joan Minninger on the psychology of writer's block. Also notes on work of various theatres.

586 "FDG/CBS New Plays Conference: Highlights of the Conference Sessions." *DGQ.* 1987; 23(4): 26-31. Illus.: Sketches. 1. Lang.: Eng.
USA. 1987. Histories-sources. ■Excerpts from the summary session: working on new plays, helping playwrights, ramifications of play development, commissioning plays versus soliciting them, how to produce new plays.

587 Acker, Iris. "Burt Reynolds Institute Offers a Unique Apprentice Program." *EN.* 1987 July; 72(7): 3. Illus.: Photo. B&W. 1. Lang.: Eng.
USA: Miami, FL. 1987. Critical studies. ■Burt Reynolds Institute for Theatre Training provides a year long training program in all phases of live theatre to college graduates of Florida state university system.

588 Bowman, Ned A. "What If?" *TD&T.* 1987; 23(1): 5, 69-73. Lang.: Eng.
USA. 1986. Critical studies. ■Text of a past-president's annual fellows address at the 1986 USITT conference. He offers four suggestions for the future of the organization on the subject of future conferences, publishing data, creating consensus and the institute's stand on issues.

589 Christiansen, Richard. "Chicago Grows Its Own." *AmTh.* 1987 Oct.; 4(7): 50-54. Illus.: Photo. B&W. 4. Lang.: Eng.
USA: Chicago, IL. 1987. Historical studies. ■Analysis of the changing scene in Chicago's theatres: from the traditional Loop theatres playing host to New York touring productions to thriving Off-Loop theatres.

590 Cox, Bill J. "The Next Wave Festival at the Brooklyn Academy of Music." *PerfM.* 1984 May; 9(2): 4-5. Lang.: Eng.
USA: New York, NY. 1984. Historical studies. ■Profile of Brooklyn Academy of Music's Next Wave Festival: promotion of productions, companies featured.

591 Dasgupta, Gautam. "Squat: Nature Theatre of New York." 93-102 in Cardullo, Bert, ed. *Before His Eyes: Essays in Honor of Stanley Kauffmann.* Lanham, MD: UP of America; 1986. 185 pp. Pref. Notes. Biblio. Lang.: Eng.
USA: New York, NY. Hungary: Budapest. 1975-1986. Historical studies. ■Historical overview of Squat Theatre: its beginnings in Budapest and its continued history in New York City. Analyzes its anti-realistic doctrine and methodology.

592 Denmark, Leon. "Black Theatre: A Roundtable Discussion." *TT.* 1987 Apr.; 6(3): 4-5, 15-16. Illus.: Photo. B&W. 3. Lang.: Eng.
USA: New York, NY. 1987. Histories-sources. ■Roundtable discussion with members of the Negro Ensemble Company, New Federal Theatre and American Place Theatre exploring artistic agendas.

THEATRE IN GENERAL: —Institutions

593　Dent, Tom; Ward, Jerry W., Jr. "After the Free Southern Theatre." *TDR*. 1987 Fall; 31(3): 120-125. Notes. Biblio. Illus.: Photo. B&W. 1. Lang.: Eng.
USA. 1960-1987. Histories-sources. ■Dialogue on black community theatre of the 1960s and its decline in the 1970s.

594　Dunn, Thomas G. "Dramaturgs and Literary Managers: They Have a Base at New Dramatists and They Don't Bite." *DGQ*. 1987; 24(1): 13-14. Lang.: Eng.
USA: New York, NY. 1987. Critical studies. ■Founding Literary Managers and Dramaturgs of America. Confusion and debate over the two roles. Help for playwrights.

595　Durham, Weldon B. *American Theatre Companies, 1888-1930*. New York, NY: Greenwood P; 1987. 541 pp. Lang.: Eng.
USA. 1888-1930. Bibliographical studies. ■Bibliographical yearbook of American theatre companies, includes short historical sketch, personnel list, repertory production list and brief bibliography on each company.

596　Eisenberg, Alan. "Equity's National Role Expanded in 1985." *EN*. 1986 Feb.; 71(2): 1,2. [Also published in annual edition of *Variety*, Jan. 8 1986.] Lang.: Eng.
USA. 1985-1986. Historical studies. ■Actors' Equity, supported by AFL-CIO outreach to encourage new theatres around the country. Small Professional Theatre contract emphasis.

597　Guerra, Victor. "An Interview with Rodrigo Duarte of Teatro de la Esperanza." *Revista Chicano-Riquena*. 1983 Spr; 9(1): 112-120. Lang.: Eng.
USA: Santa Barbara, CA. 1971-1983. Histories-sources. ■Genesis of Teatro de la Esperanza (Theatre of Hope), process of creating a theatre company.

598　Hage, David. "A Community of Choice: Cherry Creek Theatre." *TDR*. 1983 Sum; 27(2): 36-43. Illus.: Sketches. Photo. B&W. 5. Lang.: Eng.
USA: St. Peter, MN. 1979-1983. Historical studies. ■Profile of Cherry Creek Theatre: development of new works, interaction with community and audience, collective process, philosophy and techniques. Artistic director David Matthew Olson discusses influences on company and their ambitions.

599　Hatfield, Sharon. "Tales of Appalachia: Roadside Theatre." *TDR*. 1983 Sum; 27(2): 44-49. Illus.: Photo. B&W. 3. Lang.: Eng.
USA. 1971-1983. Historical studies. ■Profile of Roadside Theatre. Story-telling, use of regional folklore as source material to enlighten the Appalachian experience.

600　Hill, Errol, ed. *The Theatre of Black Americans: A Collection of Critical Essays*. New York, NY: Applause; 1987. viii, 363 pp. Notes. Biblio. Lang.: Eng.
USA: New York, NY. 1915-1987. Histories-specific. ■Collection of essays examining Black theatre as an art and industry: an expression of culture and source of livelihood for artists and craftsmen, a medium of instruction and purveyor of entertainment.

601　Karl, Matthew. "The New York State Council on the Arts—Presenting Organizations Program." *PerfM*. 1983 May; 8(2): 1-2, 6 . Lang.: Eng.
USA: New York. 1960-1983. Historical studies. ■New York State Council on the Arts' (NYSCA) commitment to its Presenting Organizations Program: funding, economic impact on presenters.

602　Kramer, Tom. "Symphony Space." *PerfM*. 1984 May; 9(2): 6-7. Illus.: Photo. B&W. 2. Lang.: Eng.
USA: New York, NY. 1977-1984. Historical studies. ■Profile and history of Symphony Space: management, programming, audience, budget and fundraising.

603　LaRue, Michèle. "USITT Preview." *ThCr*. 1987 Apr.; 21(4): 18-22. Append. Illus.: Photo. Diagram. Color. B&W. Lang.: Eng.
USA: Minneapolis, MN. 1987. Technical studies. ■Events and programming for the 1987 United States Institute for Theatre Technology conference.

604　London, Todd. "Theatre Focus: Hudson Guild Theatre and Duma Ndlovu." *TT*. 1986 Nov.; 6(1): 10. Lang.: Eng.
USA: New York, NY. South Africa, Republic of. 1976-1986. Historical studies. ■Duma Ndlovu and the Woza Afrika Foundation: their connection to the Hudson Guild Theatre.

605　McCrohan, Donna. *The Second City: A Backstage History of Comedy's Hottest Troupe*. New York, NY: Perigee P; 1987. 272 pp. Index. Illus.: Photo. Print. B&W. 75. Lang.: Eng.
USA: Chicago, IL. Canada: Toronto, ON. 1959-1987. Historical studies. ■History of Second City, improvisational comedy troupe. Includes famous people who came out of the tradition. Related to Media: Video forms.

606　Miguelez, Armando. "El Teatro Carmen (1915-1923): Centro del Arte Escenico en Tucson." (El Teatro Carmen (1915-1923): Center of Dramatic Art in Tucson.) *Revista Chicano-Riquena*. 1983 Spr; 9(1): 52-67. Lang.: Spa.
USA: Tucson, AZ. 1915-1923. Historical studies. ■Development of theatre company El Teatro Carmen and its place in Arizona history.

607　Niles, Richard. "LORT and the Unions: A Manager's Viewpoint." *PerfM*. 1987 Win; 13(1): 1-2. Illus.: Photo. B&W. 1. Lang.: Eng.
USA. 1987. Historical studies. ■Discussion with executive director of the Roundabout Theatre, Todd Haimes, on LORT's relationship with unions, influence on contract and labor negotiations.

608　Pack, Alison. "Off Broadway Babes." *Drama*. 1987; 3(165): 25-26. Illus.: Photo. B&W. 2. Lang.: Eng.
USA: New York, NY. 1987. Historical studies. ■Contribution of non-commercial theatre to the New York community.

609　Patrinos, Sondra. "Chicago 'Concerned' About AIDS Patients." *EN*. 1987 Dec.; 72(12): 3. Lang.: Eng.
USA: Chicago, IL. 1987. Historical studies. ■Plans for *A Season of Concern*, a year-long fundraising effort involving Chicago's theatre community, Equity and The League of Chicago Theatres. Theatre benefits will be given throughout the year in the hopes of raising $250,000.

610　Patterson, Lindsay. "Does Black Theatre Exist?" *TheaterW*. 1987 Dec 21-27; 1(19): 27-30. 3. Lang.: Eng.
USA. 1987. Historical studies. ■Major Black voices in theatre debate whether Black theatre really exists.

611　Saxton, Lydia A. "Towards the Survival of Urban Ethnic Performing Arts: An Institutional Approach." *PerfM*. 1984 May; 9(2): 1-3. Lang.: Eng.
USA: New York, NY. 1966-1984. Historical studies. ■Profile of Ethnic Folk Arts Center: focuses on research, encouraging, presenting and preserving ethnic music and dance found in urban American communities. Origins, development, directors, productions.

612　Sheehy, Helen. "Six Theatres and How They Grew." *AmTh*. 1987 Oct.; 4(7): 62-64. Illus.: Design. B&W. 1. Lang.: Eng.
USA: Cleveland, OH, Los Angeles, CA, Houston, TX, Detroit, MI, Ashland, OR, Montgomery, AL. 1987. Historical studies. ■Discussion of six recent books, each one exploring the genesis, growth and development of a different American regional theatre.

613　Siegel, Fern. "Through the Looking Glass: Kids and Theaterworks." *TheaterW*. 1987 Nov 16; 1(14): 11-13. Illus.: Photo. B&W. 5. Lang.: Eng.
USA: New York, NY. 1961-1987. Historical studies. ■Theaterworks/ USA, the only national theatre for young people: its history, productions, relationship with audience.

614　Smith, Michael. "The Living Theatre at Cooper Union." *TDR*. 1987 Fall; 31(3): 103-119. Pref. Illus.: Photo. B&W. 9. Lang.: Eng.
USA: New York, NY. 1986. Histories-sources. ■Symposium on 'The Significance and Legacy of the Living Theatre' at Cooper Union, and impact it had on the speakers' lives.

615　Sommers, Michael. "Southeast Style: A Fair and Warmer Arts Climate." *ThCr*. 1987 Mar.; 21(3): 22, 23, 49-57. Illus.: Photo. Color. B&W. 7. Lang.: Eng.
USA. 1987. Critical studies. ■Growth of theatres in the southeastern region and some major producing organizations.

CLASSED ENTRIES

THEATRE IN GENERAL: —Institutions

616 Taylor, Bob. "Singing the Body Eclectic: The Theatre Collection of the Museum of the City of New York." *THSt.* 1987; 7: 135-147. Notes. Illus.: Photo. Print. B&W. 11. Lang.: Eng.
USA: New York, NY. 1987. Historical studies. ■Description of the theatre collection of the Museum of the City of New York.

617 Thompson, Daniel W. "Mabou Mines: A Theatre Collective." *PerfM.* 1987 Spr; 12(1): 4-5. Illus.: Photo. B&W. 1. Lang.: Eng.
USA: New York, NY. 1987. Historical studies. ■Profile of the artist-run theatre collective Mabou Mines. Conversation with founding member Ruth Maleczech discussing economic impact on company, board of directors and their responsibilities.

618 Timmerman, Dolph. "Colden Center for the Performing Arts." *PerfM.* 1984 May; 9(2): 5-6. Lang.: Eng.
USA: Flushing, NY. 1961-1984. Historical studies. ■Profile and history of Colden Center for the Performing Arts: seating, stage design, audience profile and marketing of events.

619 Tkatch, Peter Jack. "Equity Fights AIDS: A Beginning." *EN.* 1987 Dec.; 72(12): 3. Lang.: Eng.
USA: New York, NY. 1987. Historical studies. ■The work of the Equity Fights AIDS Committee of AEA and the coordination of fundraising and consciousness raising activities between this committee and representatives of Broadway and Off Broadway casts.

620 Trost, Maxine. "The Heart of the Family Business Papers." *PasShow.* 1986 Sum; 10(2): 3-5. Illus.: Photo. B&W. 3. Lang.: Eng.
USA: New York, NY. 1900-1953. Histories-sources. ■Family letters and business papers of the Shuberts.

621 Zeisler, Peter. "Inching up on Pangloss." *AmTh.* 1987 Oct.; 4(7): 7. Lang.: Eng.
USA. 1967-1987. Critical studies. ■Current trends in American theatre. Various regional non-profit companies and their resident artists.

622 Parchomenko, S. "Po sjužetnomu principu." (According to Plot Principle.) *TeatrM.* 1987; 3: 62-74. Lang.: Rus.
USSR. 1986. Histories-sources. ■A participant's account of the XV Congress, All-Russian Theatre Society October 1986.

623 Techeleth, Hayim. "Aual Anachnu Metzigim Mashehu Shehu Ahrbe Yoter Mishanachnu Atzmenu." (But We Represent Something Which Is Something More Than We Ourselves.) *Bamah.* 1987; 22(109-110): 9-26. Illus.: Photo. Dwg. B&W. 4. [Interviews with HaBimah Theatre People.] Lang.: Heb.
USSR: Moscow. Israel: Tel Aviv. 1913-1955. Histories-sources. ■Interview with Benjamin Zemach on the creation and history of the HaBimah Theatre and collaboration with Stanislavskij and Vachtangov to create a Hebrew language theatre.

624 Ul'janov, Michajl A. "Pod'jem v goru po nechožennym tropam." (Ascent up the Mountain on Untrodden Paths.) *Kommunist.* 1987; 5: 51-57. Lang.: Rus.
USSR. 1970-1987. Histories-sources. ■President of board of Union of Theatre Workers of the Russian Republic and actor in Vachtangov Theatre discusses social changes in the country, problems of developing theatre and film, stagnant features of past decade. Related to Media: Film.

Performance spaces

625 Forsyth, Michael. *Edifici per la musica. L'architetto, il musicista, il pubblico dal Seicento ad oggi.* (Buildings for Music: The Architect, the Musician, and the Listener from the Seventeenth Century to the Present Day.) Bologna: Zanichelli; 1987. 352 pp. Pref. Index. Notes. Biblio. Append. Illus.: Photo. Plan. Pntg. Dwg. Print. Color. B&W. Lang.: Ita.
1600-1985. Historical studies.

626 Rogers, Maurine. "Some Canberra Theatre History." *Canberra Historical Journal.* 1987 Mar.(19): 36-32. Lang.: Eng.
Australia: Canberra. 1925-1965. Historical studies. ■Describes the range of multi-purpose halls used in the newly established city, and the building of the Canberra Theatre Centre which largely replaced them.

The local amateur groups and professional touring organizations that used the spaces and influenced their development are discussed.

627 Marsolais, Gilles. "Dites-moi où l'on vous loge." (Tell Me Where You Stay.) *JCT.* 1987; 42: 9-18. Illus.: Photo. Print. B&W. 7. Lang.: Fre.
Canada: Montreal, PQ. 1900-1987. Historical studies. ■Theatre buildings meeting changing needs of modern productions. Spaces already built must be accessible to all groups.

628 Rooke, Don. "The Modern Acoustics of Thomson Hall: Clarity Before Warmth." *PAC.* 1983 Apr.; 20(1): 15-20. Notes. Illus.: Photo. Print. 6. Lang.: Eng.
Canada: Toronto, ON. 1982. Technical studies. ■Regarding the improved sound quality in the new Thomson Hall.

629 Stolk, Gini. "The Other Housing Crisis: Facilities for Small Theatres." *CTR.* 1987 Sum; 51: 31. Lang.: Eng.
Canada: Toronto, ON. 1987. Historical studies. ■A synopsis of the housing crisis faced by the Toronto theatre community. Due to economic conditions, theatre funding is not available.

630 "Czechs on the Restoration List." *Econ.* 1987 3 Jan.; 302: 68. Illus.: Photo. B&W. Lang.: Eng.
Czechoslovakia: Prague. 1987. Historical studies. ■Preservation and maintenance of cultural sites in Prague. Deterioration and financial allocations for reconstruction.

631 Howell, Mark A. "A Note on the Dimensions of the Bridges Street Theatre." *TN.* 1987; 41(2): 67-70. Notes. Illus.: Diagram. B&W. 2. Lang.: Eng.
England: London. 1663. Historical studies. ■Exeter house plan suggests that Richard Ryder used his first theatre as a dimensional plan for his second.

632 Orrell, John. *The Theatres of Inigo Jones and John Webb.* New York, NY: Cambridge UP; 1985. xiii, 240 pp. Index. Biblio. Lang.: Eng.
England. 1573-1672. Histories-general. ■Reconstruction and analysis of the theatre designs of Inigo Jones and John Webb. Claims that the work of Webb and Jones in the Jacobean and Caroline theatres laid the foundations for the elaborate scenic stage of the Restoration.

633 Bablet, Denis. "Problems of Contemporary Theatre Space." *TD&T.* 1987; 23(3): 8-17, 60. Illus.: Photo. Plan. Sketches. B&W. 10. Lang.: Eng.
France. Germany, West. 1875-1987. Histories-sources. ■Talk given on lecture tour of the USA discussing the concept of theatre space, particularly the space in which the play occurs and is experienced simultaneously by the performers and the audience.

634 Brown, John Russell. "More Problems of Contemporary Theatre Space." *TD&T.* 1987; 23(3): 9, 51-57. Lang.: Eng.
France. Germany, West. UK-England. 1987. Historical studies. ■Response to Denis Bablet's 'Problems of Contemporary Theatre Space' in same issue. Contests Bablet's interpretation of history of theatre space and advocates examining the creative needs of theatre artists as a way to design theatre spaces.

635 Scolnicov, Hanna. "Theatre Space, Theatrical Space, and the Theatrical Space Without." *TID.* 1987; 9: 11-26. Notes. Lang.: Eng.
Germany. England. Greece. 400 B.C.-1987 A.D. Critical studies. ■Theatrical space defined solely through performance, vs. 'theatre space', the architectural space that exists independently of performance.

636 "A Kelet-Berlini Német Állami Operaház rekon-strukciója (1983-1986)." (Reconstruction of the German State Opera-House in Berlin, 1983-1986.) *SFo.* 1987; 14(4): 32-35. Illus.: Photo. B&W. Fr.Elev. Schematic. 5. Lang.: Hun.
Germany, East: Berlin, East. 1742-1986. Technical studies. ■Abridged translation from *Podium* 1 (1987). East Germany's gold medal at Prague Quadrennial '87 for exhibition on theatre reconstruction.

637 "Az új berlini Friedrichstadtpalast." (The New Friedrichstadtpalast in Berlin.) *SFo.* 1987; 14(1): 26-27. Illus.: Photo. B&W. 4. Lang.: Hun.
Germany, East: Berlin, East. 1984. Technical studies. ■The most interesting technical equipment of the new building which replaces the famous variety theatre of the same name, sited on the bank of the Spree. (Based on articles published in *Bauten der Kultur* 86/1).

THEATRE IN GENERAL: —Performance spaces

638 "Jurta Szinház." (Jurta Theatre, Budapest.) *SFo.* 1987; 14(2): 2-3. Lang.: Hun.
Hungary: Budapest. 1987. Historical studies. ■Press selections about the new theatre built by the Hungarian Theatre in the form of small cooperative. A few days after the opening celebration the theatre was temporarily closed by the fire-service and basic shortcomings had to be corrected.

639 Borsos, Károly. "Az új Nemzeti Szinház." (The New National Theatre.) *SFo.* 1987; 14(2): 20-22. Illus.: Plan. Sketches. 2. Lang.: Hun.
Hungary: Budapest. 1987. Technical studies. ■The designer proposes to build the National Theatre on the Castle Hill of Buda and tries to compose the new complex into the historical environment.

640 Gergely, Gábor. "A József Attila Szinház felújitása." (The József Attila Theatre as Renovated.) *SFo.* 1987; 14(3): 21-22. Illus.: Photo. B&W. 3. Lang.: Hun.
Hungary: Budapest. 1985-1986. Technical studies. ■The interior architect's report of the design and construction processes involved in rebuilding a cultural hall from the 1950s.

641 Hofer, Miklós. "A Budavári elhelyezés tanulmányterve." (The Study of the Site in Buda Castle.) *SFo.* 1987; 14(2): 29-31. Illus.: Plan. 2. Lang.: Hun.
Hungary: Budapest. 1983. Technical studies. ■Comparison of the two most recent sites of the National Theatre: the older on Dózsa György Avenue, the new in Buda Castle.

642 Jókai, Mór. "A 150 éves Nemzeti Szinház. A hajdani Nemzeti Szinházról." (The 150 Year Old National Theatre in Budapest: About the Old-Time National Theatre.) *SFo.* 1987; 14(2): 6-8. Illus.: Photo. Dwg. B&W. 3. Lang.: Hun.
Hungary: Budapest. 1900. Histories-sources. ■Mór Jókai, the famous writer of the last century, wrote his remembrance in 1900: detailed description of the building of the first National Theatre, gas lighting installed for the first time in the city.

643 Nilsson, Nils-Gunnar. "OISTAT:s arkitekturkommission." (OISTAT's Commission for Architects.) *ProScen.* 1987; 10(1-2): 50 . Illus.: Photo. Lang.: Swe.
Hungary: Budapest. 1987. Histories-sources. ■A report from OISTAT's future plans for the next years.

644 Schandl, Gábor László. "Angyalföld szinháza." (The Theatre of Angyalföld.) *SFo.* 1987; 14(3): 24-27. Illus.: Photo. B&W. Grd.Plan. 7. Lang.: Hun.
Hungary: Budapest. 1985-1986. Technical studies. ■The technical director is giving full details of the experiences he made during the renovation carried out in the course of two summer holidays.

645 Schmidt, János. "A magyarországi szinházak helyzetéről." (The Situation of the Theatres in Hungary.) *SFo.* 1987; 14(3): 15-16. Lang.: Hun.
Hungary. 1980-1986. Histories-sources. ■Section for Theatre Technology, Hungarian Optical, Acoustical and Cinematographical Society.

646 Szabó-Jilek, Iván. "A pályázat után. Beszélgetés a Szinháztudományi Intézetben Virág Csabával—1966. március." (After the Competition: A Talk with Csaba Virág in the Institute of Theatre Sciences in March 1966.) *SFo.* 1987; 14(2): 23-25. Lang.: Hun.
Hungary: Budapest. 1966. Histories-sources. ■Interview with architect Csaba Virág, designer of the present National Theatre building.

647 *A teatro con i Lorena: feste, personaggi e luoghi scenici della Firenze granducale.* (At the Theatre with the Lorenas: Feasts, Characters, Stage Places of Grand-Ducal Florence.) Zambelli, Lucia: Medicea; 1987. 280 pp. Biblio. Index. Lang.: Ita.
Italy: Florence. 1700-1800. Historical studies. ■Theatrical life in eighteenth-century Florence seen through the history of its performance spaces.

648 *Il Teatro di San Carlo.* (The San Carlo Theatre.) Naples: Guida; 1987. 451 pp, 1020 pp. Index. Tables. Illus.: Pntg. Dwg. Sketches. [Two vols.] Lang.: Ita.
Italy: Naples. 1737-1987. Histories-specific. ■Collection of essays on the history and activities of the Teatro San Carlo: musicians, actors, impresari. In Volume II, chronology of performances.

649 Aggarbati, Fabrizio; Costacurta, Rino; Saggioro, Carla; Sennato, Marina. *L'architettura dei teatri di Roma 1513-1981.* (The Architecture of the Theatres of Rome 1513-1981.) Rome: Kappa; 1987. 167 pp. (Roma. Storia/Immagini/Progetti.) Lang.: Ita.
Italy: Rome. 1531-1981. Historical studies. ■Index of Roman theatres public and private, with photos, plans, and statistics. Also a census of performance spaces from 1951.

650 Attisani, Antonio. "Beyond Perspective: Scenic Space in New Italian Theatre." *PerAJ.* 1985 Spr; 9(25): 31-37. Illus.: Photo. B&W. 4. Lang.: Eng.
Italy. 1980. Critical studies. ■Recent trends in Italian theatre.

651 Ault, Thomas C. "Ground Plan and Elevation of the New Theatre in Bologna." *TD&T.* 1987; 23(3): 19-26. Notes. Illus.: Plan. Explod.Sect. Fr.Elev. 2. Lang.: Eng.
Italy: Bologna. 1763. Historical studies. ■Discussion and analysis of a volume containing comprehensive plans and detailed description of the New Theatre's machinery and stage to mark the opening of the theatre.

652 Brusatin, Manlio; Pavanello, Giuseppe. *Il teatro La Fenice. I progetti. L'architettura. Le decorazioni.* (La Fenice Theatre: Designs, Architecture, Decorations.) Venice: Albrizzi; 1987. 291 pp. Index. Biblio. Illus.: Photo. Design. Plan. Pntg. Dwg. Print. Color. Lang.: Ita.
Italy: Venice. 1787-1976. Historical studies. ■Reconstruction of the birth of Teatro La Fenice, history of its various restorations and renovations.

653 Cantone, Gaetana, ed.; Greco, Franco Carmelo, ed. *Il Teatro del Re. Il San Carlo da Napoli all'Europa.* (The King's Theatre: The San Carlo Theatre from Naples to Europe.) Naples: Edizioni Scientifiche Italiane; 1987. 255 pp. Index. Illus.: Photo. Plan. Pntg. Dwg. Print. Color. B&W. Lang.: Ita.
Italy: Naples. 1737-1987. Historical studies. ■Collection of essays on the Teatro San Carlo published on the occasion of its 250th anniversary.

654 Larson, Orville K. "Portrait of a Seventeenth-Century Playhouse: Il Teatro dei Comici, Mantova, 1688." *ThS.* 1987 Nov.; 28(2): 17-26. Notes. Illus.: Plan. 1. Lang.: Eng.
Italy: Mantua. 1688-1800. Historical studies. ■Description of theatre interior (including details of stage, scenery and auditorium) and operations based on contemporary documents.

655 Lucchini, Flaminio. *L'auditorium e i teatri per Roma: 1789-1957.* (The Auditorium and the Theatres for Rome: 1789-1957.) Rome: Officina; 1987. 95 pp. Illus.: Plan. Lang.: Ita.
Italy: Rome. 1789-1953. Historical studies. ■Architectural plans for unrealized auditorium and theatres.

656 Mancini, Franco; Cagli, Bruno, ed.; Ziino, Agostino, ed. *Il Teatro San Carlo 1737-1987.* (The San Carlo Theatre 1737-1987.) Naples: Electa; 1987. 180 pp., 344 pp., 214 pp. Illus.: Photo. Plan. Pntg. Dwg. Sketches. Print. Color. B&W. Architec. [3 vols.] Lang.: Ita.
Italy: Naples. 1737-1987. Histories-specific. ■History of San Carlo Theatre, essays on its structure, performances, scenery, costumes. Volume III lists scene designers, 1949-1987.

657 Muraro, Maria Teresa. "Il teatro Grimani a San Giovanni Grisostomo." (The Grimani Theatre at San Giovanni Grisostomo.) *BiT.* 1987; 5/6: 105-113. Lang.: Ita.
Italy: Venice. 1675-1750. Histories-sources. ■The Grimanis and the building of the San Giovanni Grisostomo, the most famous theatre of the 18th century. The descriptions of the hall and of the stage written by Chassebras de Cramailles and by Nicodemus Tessin at the end of the 17th century.

658 "Japán új Nemzeti Szinháza. A nemzetközi pályázat dijazett tervei." (The New National Theatre in Japan: Rewarded Designs of the International Competition.) *SFo.* 1987; 14(2): 3-4. Illus.: Plan. Dwg. Grd.Plan. 10. Lang.: Hun.
Japan. 1986. Technical studies. ■Note on the results of the theatrical design competition based on the periodical *Japanese Architect*.

659 Chang, Han-Gi. "Hanguk minsokkukui gongkan." (The Space of Korean Folk Play.) *DongukDA.* 1978 Apr.; 10-11: 92-108. Lang.: Kor.

THEATRE IN GENERAL: —Performance spaces

Korea. 57 B.C. Critical studies. ■Study of the performing space of Korean traditional drama.

660 Cho, Dong-Il. "Yonkuguloseoui tukjing." (The Characteristics of Korean Mask Theatre.) 109-182 in *History & Theory of Mask Theatre.* Seoul: Hongik-SA; 1987. 406 pp. Lang.: Kor.

Korea. 57 B.C.-1987 A.D. Historical studies. ■Original performing area of Korean mask theatre.

661 Kim, Mido. "Yonguk Guzo Hygok." (Construction of a Theatre Exclusively for Plays.) *KTR.* 1987 Mar.; 3(1): 14-21. Illus.: Photo. Plan. B&W. Lang.: Kor.

Korea: Seoul. 1930-1935. Historical studies. ■The first Korean theatre exclusively for drama: Tong-Yang Kuk Chang.

662 Kim, Se-Kŭn. "Gong-yon kwa Bepyong." (Performance and Criticism.) *KTR.* 1987 Mar.; 3(1): 44-47, 51. B&W. 1. Lang.: Kor.

Korea: Kwang-ju. 1986-1987. Critical studies. ■Criticism of the city's antiquated theatre facilities.

663 Kim, Woo-Suk. *Hanguk juntongyonkukkwa ken goyumoodae.* (Korean Traditional Theatre and Its Performing Place.) Seoul: Sungkyunkwan Univ; 1986. 209 pp. Lang.: Kor.

Korea. Japan. 57 B.C.-1986 A.D. Historical studies. ■Performance spaces and staging theory in the traditional Korean genres such as *pansori, changuk* and mask theatre. Related to Dance-Drama.

664 Kim, Woo-Taek. *Hankuk juntongyunkugkwa-keu-koyoumoodae.* (Korean Traditional Drama and Stage.) Seoul: Sungkyunkuan Univ Press; 1986. 209 pp. Lang.: Kor.

Korea. China. India. 57 B.C.-1987 A.D. Historical studies. ■Analysis of the stages of Indian, Chinese and Korean traditional theatre. Explanation of the development of Korean *changuk.* Related to Dance-Drama.

665 Carlson, Ebbe. "Två år i Moçambique." (Two Years in Mozambique.) *ProScen.* 1987; 10(4): 5-10. Illus.: Photo. 5. Lang.: Swe.

Mozambique: Maputo. 1986-1987. Historical studies. ■How Maputo's only theatre, Teatro Avenida, was restored to working order.

666 Losnegaar, Rolf. "*Splint* on the Theatreship *Innvik.*" *TDR.* 1983 Sum; 27(2): 97-98. Illus.: Photo. B&W. 1. Lang.: Eng.

Norway. 1982. Historical studies. ■Conversion of ferryboat into the Innvik Theatre: seating, layout. Description of production and the group of nomadic peoples of the culture it is based on.

667 Van der Waal, Gergard-Mark. "Voetligte in Johannesburg—Teaterbou Tydens die Stad se Eerste Halfeeu." (Footlights in Johannesburg—Theatre Building During the City's First Half-Century.) *SATJ.* 1987; 1(1): 17-44. Illus.: Photo. B&W. 12. Lang.: Afr.

South Africa, Republic of: Johannesburg. 1887-1940. Historical studies. ■Theatres built in Johannesburg in this period and influences on design.

668 Puigserver, Fabià. "Un teatre, un espai de somni." (A Theatre, a Space of Dream.) 26-32 in *Teatre Lliure 1976-1987.* Barcelona: Institut del Teatre; 1987. 297 pp. Lang.: Cat.

Spain-Catalonia: Barcelona. 1976-1987. Historical studies. ■Working conditions of the technicians of Teatre Lliure, importance of a stable technical team to proper functioning of the theatre.

669 Kull, Gustaf. "Härnösandsmodellen för uppsökande teater." (The Model of Härnösand for Touring Companies.) *ProScen.* 1987; 10(1-2): 39. Illus.: Photo. Lang.: Swe.

Sweden: Härnösand. 1980-1987. Technical studies. ■A presentation of the mobile performance space 'Södra Norrland', for constructing small theatres within big halls.

670 Cave, Richard Allen. "Paul Shelving, Stage Designer." *Sin.* 1987; 21(1): 11-14. Tables. Illus.: Photo. B&W. 2. Lang.: Eng.

UK-England. 1888-1968. Histories-sources. ■Paul Shelving's contribution to stage design exhibited by Birmingham Museum.

671 Leech, Michael. "The Call of the Mermaid." *DRAMA.* 1987; 3(165): 19-20. Illus.: Photo. B&W. 2. Lang.: Eng.

UK-England: London. 1959-1987. Historical studies. ■Assessment of the Mermaid Theatre, home of the Royal Shakespeare Company in London.

672 Maguire, Laurie E. "New Swan's First Season." *TN.* 1987; 41(3): 101-107. Notes. Illus.: Photo. B&W. 1. Lang.: Eng.

UK-England: Stratford. 1987. Critical studies. ■Design of theatre removes audience/performance division and recreates ambience of an Elizabethan playhouse.

673 Schempp, James I. "The Swan Theatre at the Royal Shakespeare Company: An Interview with Michael Dembowicz." *TD&T.* 1987; 23(2): 12-16. Illus.: Photo. B&W. 1. Lang.: Eng.

UK-England: Stratford. 1986. Histories-sources. ■Interview with the stage manager of the Royal Shakespeare Company about their newly opened theatre, a replica of an Elizabethan playhouse. Project cost, house size, seating arrangements, and budget.

674 "ELT Launches 45th Season in New York, Renovates Theatre, Plans Fundraiser." *EN.* 1987 Oct.; 72(10): 1-2, 4. Lang.: Eng.

USA: New York, NY. 1943-1987. Histories-sources. ■Interview with George Wojtasik, managing director of the Equity Library Theatre, New York's longest running professional showcase.

675 "Preservation Commission Adopts Landmark Guidelines for Theatres." *EN.* 1986 Jan.; 71(1): 1. Lang.: Eng.

USA: New York, NY. 1985-1986. Historical studies. ■City Landmarks Preservation Commission adopted guidelines which exclude production-related changes to theatre interiors and exteriors.

676 "Should Broadway Theatres be Landmarked?" *EN.* 1986 Apr.; 71(4): 7. Lang.: Eng.

USA: New York, NY. 1986. Historical studies. ■Opposing views on whether theatres should be landmarked. Gerald Schoenfeld, chairman of the board, Shubert Organization, and Jack Goldstein, director of Save the Theatres, are featured.

677 "The Morosco Comes Down." *EN.* 1982 May; 67(5): 1, 4. Lang.: Eng.

USA: New York, NY. 1982. Historical studies. ■Morosco Theatre torn down despite efforts by Actors' Equity to save it.

678 "Landmark Hearings Extended to October." *EN.* 1982 July; 67(7): 1. Lang.: Eng.

USA: New York, NY. 1982. Historical studies. ■Landmark Preservation Commission conducts hearings for granting landmark status to forty-five Broadway theatres.

679 "Theatre Architecture." *TD&T.* 1987; 23(1): 33-41. Illus.: Photo. Plan. B&W. Grd.Plan. 16. Lang.: Eng.

USA. 1987. Technical studies. ■Renovations made to five theatres: Scarsdale High School Auditorium in New York, Morganton Auditorium in North Carolina, Fine Arts Center at Lake Michigan College in Benton Harbor, MI, the Triplex of the Borough of Manhattan Community College in NY, and the Theater of the Arts in Sarasota, FL. Continued *TD&T* 22:4 (1987), pp. 30-32, with discussion of the Maguire Theatre at State University College in Old Westbury, New York, Experimental Media Facilities at MIT and the Walker Arts Center in Asheville, North Carolina.

680 Aronson, Arnold. "No More Theatre!" *TD&T.* 1987; 23(3): 9, 61-61. Lang.: Eng.

USA. 1987. Historical studies. ■Response to Denis Bablet's 'Problems of Contemporary Theatre Space' in same issue. Argues that poor theatre design and lack of understanding theatre's relation to society are responsible for the state of theatre today.

681 Bauschard, Jane. "Van Dijk Paints a Fair Face for Cleveland." *L&DA.* 1987 Jan.; 17(1): 14-16. Illus.: Photo. 5. Lang.: Eng.

USA: Cleveland, OH. 1964-1986. Historical studies. ■The Cleveland Playhouse Square Re-Development Project. Peter van Dijk, architect, speaks of visions for Cleveland relating to Playhouse Square. Brief summaries of Ohio, State and Palace Theatre restorations.

682 Burns, Bree. "Loeb Drama Center." *ThCr.* 1987 Dec.; 21(10): 40-41, 66-68. Notes. Illus.: Photo. Plan. Color. B&W. Grd.Plan. 4. Lang.: Eng.

THEATRE IN GENERAL: —Performance spaces

USA: Cambridge, MA. 1960-1987. Technical studies. ■Loeb Drama Center at Harvard and changes made since the arrival of the American Repertory Theatre.

683 Campbell, Donna. "Recapturing the Past, Designing for the Future." *PerfM.* 1984 Dec.; 10(1): 4-5. Illus.: Photo. B&W. 1. Lang.: Eng.

USA: New York, NY. 1984. Historical studies. ■Architect Roger Morgan discusses plans for restoring seven Broadway theatres to their 'legitimate' state.

684 Cowan, C. Lynn. "Second Homes: Multiple Bases for Performing Arts Organizations." *JAML.* 1987 Spr; 17(1): 23-35. Lang.: Eng.

USA. 1980-1986. Critical studies. ■Process of setting up a second performing space, includes guidelines.

685 Destro, Ronni. "The Rise and Decline of Times Square." *PerfM.* 1984 Dec.; 10(1): 1-3. Illus.: Plan. 1. Lang.: Eng.

USA: New York, NY. 1883-1984. Historical studies. ■History of theatres in the Times Square area: impact of economic and crime factors that led to its decline, projected attempts to revitalize district and performance spaces.

686 Dolan, Jill. "Born in the USA." *ThCr.* 1987 Aug/Sep.; 21(7): 32-37. Architec. 9. Lang.: Eng.

USA: Pittsburgh, PA. 1975-1987. Technical studies. ■History and technical data on Pittsburgh's Public Theatre.

687 Fisher, Jules; Marantz, Paul. "Hult Center." *L&DA.* 1987 July; 17(7): 15. Illus.: Photo. 1. Lang.: Eng.

USA: Eugene, OR. 1987. Technical studies. ■The use of lighting in Hult Center helps guide the audience in mood and focus from the moment they enter to the moment they exit.

688 French, William W. "Rich Joy of the Sixties: The Streets of New York City as Theatrical Space." *TID.* 1987; 9: 177-186. Notes. Lang.: Eng.

USA: New York, NY. 1960-1975. Critical studies. ■The streets of New York as the ultimate playing space and the final destination of avante-garde and experimental theatre invested in the community, breaking with tradition and reaching across class, race, social and economic barriers.

689 Frick, John W., ed.; Ward, Carlton, ed. *Directory of Historic American Theatres.* New York, NY: Greenwood P; 1987. 347 pp. Index. Illus.: Photo. B&W. 80. Lang.: Eng.

USA. 1809-1915. Historical studies. ■Data on extant theatres built in the U.S. before 1915: structural features, opening dates, productions and performers, seating, dimensions, degree of restoration.

690 Gerle, János. "Az Earl Carroll Szinház New Yorkban." (The Earl Carroll Theatre in New York.) *SFo.* 1987; 14(2): 35-36. Illus.: Dwg. Sketches. 3. Lang.: Hun.

USA: New York, NY. 1931-1933. Technical studies. ■The imposing theatre opened in 1931 had been functioning only for two years and was soon pulled down. As a business undertaking it failed, but from the architectural point of view it had great interest. The designer of its 'inner and outer decoration' was József Bábolnay.

691 Guither, Peter. "The Shuberts Vote 'Aye'." *PerfM.* 1984 Dec.; 10(1): 7-8. Lang.: Eng.

USA: New York, NY. 1984. Historical studies. ■Commitment of Shubert Organization to cleaning up Broadway theatre district.

692 Hagedorn, Curt. "More Broadway Theatres Landmarked: City Begins Active Role in Promotion of Theatre." *EN.* 1987 Dec.; 72 (12): 1, 4. Lang.: Eng.

USA: New York, NY. 1982. Historical studies. ■New York Landmark Preservation Commission designated Broadway theatres as city landmarks, recognizing architectural, cultural and historical significance of the Brooks Atkinson, Ethel Barrymore, Belasco, Booth, Broadhurst, Martin Beck and Biltmore theatres.

693 Hale, Alice M. "Retrofitting the Sixties: Making Your Theatre Accessible." *ThCr.* 1987 Apr.; 21(4): 40, 61-66. Illus.: Photo. B&W. 4. Lang.: Eng.

USA. 1987. Technical studies. ■Making existing theatres accessible to the physically handicapped.

694 Hale, Alice M. "La Jolla Playhouse." *ThCr.* 1987 Oct.. Illus.: Photo. Sketches. Color. Grd.Plan. Blprnt. 14. Lang.: Eng.

USA: La Jolla, CA. 1947-1987. Technical studies. ■Architecture of La Jolla Playhouse and challenges it presents for designers.

695 Houseman, John. "The Acting Company: New Home, Enduring Principles." *EN.* 1986 Nov.; 71(11): 3, 4. Lang.: Eng.

USA: New York, NY. 1972-1986. Histories-sources. ■John Houseman and Margot Harley founded the Acting Company with Houseman's acting students from Juilliard and they finally have a home in New York.

696 Kirby, Victoria. "The Oakland Ensemble Theatre." *TD&T.* 1987; 23(1): 14-17. Illus.: Photo. Plan. B&W. Explod.Sect. Grd.Plan. 7. Lang.: Eng.

USA: Oakland, CA. 1983-1987. Historical studies. ■Oakland Ensemble Theatre's search for a permanent home after being evicted in 1983. Discusses problems and processes of collaborating among city government, architects, and theatre consultants. Also describes the final product, the Alice Arts Center.

697 Kramer, Tom. "The New Apollo: Prophetic Failure?" *PerfM.* 1984 Dec.; 10(1): 5-7. Illus.: Photo. B&W. 2. Lang.: Eng.

USA: New York, NY. 1977-1984. Historical studies. ■Renovation and subsequent failure of the New Apollo Theatre: economic impact on Broadway theatre, production costs.

698 LaRue, Michèle. "Tampa Bay Performing Arts Center." *ThCr.* 1987 Dec.; 21(10): 38-39, 60-65. Notes. Illus.: Photo. Plan. Color. Grd.Plan. 5. Lang.: Eng.

USA: Tampa, FL. 1987. Technical studies. ■Tampa Bay Performing Arts Center, its specifications and process of planning its design.

699 LaRue, Michèle. "Omaha Community Playhouse." *ThCr.* 1987 Dec.; 21(10): 44-45, 81-83. Notes. Illus.: Photo. Plan. Color. B&W. Architec. 5. Lang.: Eng.

USA: Omaha, NE. 1984-1987. Technical studies. ■Major expansion of the facilities at the Omaha Community Playhouse.

700 Loeffler, Mark. "Bayfront Center." *ThCr.* 1987 Dec.; 21(10): 5-51, 75-77. Notes. Illus.: Photo. Plan. B&W. Architec. 3. Lang.: Eng.

USA: St. Petersburg, FL. 1960-1987. Technical studies. ■Renovations at the Bayfront Center.

701 Loeffler, Mark. "Wortham Theatre Center." *ThCr.* 1987 Dec.; 21(10): 42-43, 68-71. Notes. Illus.: Photo. Plan. Color. Architec. Grd.Plan. 6. Lang.: Eng.

USA: Houston, TX. 1987. Technical studies. ■Architecture of recently completed Wortham Theatre Center.

702 MacKay, Patricia. "Retrofitting the Sixties: Wear, Tear and the Way We Were." *ThCr.* 1987 Jan.; 21(1): 34-35, 39-41. Illus.: Diagram. B&W. Detail. 3. Lang.: Eng.

USA. 1960-1986. Technical studies. ■1960s theatres and the pros and cons of rebuilding them. Architectural design of that period.

703 MacKay, Patricia. "Architecture 87." *ThCr.* 1987 Dec.; 21(10): 37, 58-60. Illus.: Photo. Color. 4. Lang.: Eng.

USA. 1987. Technical studies. ■All performing arts centers covered in architecture 87 issue.

704 Mackintosh, Iain. "On Not Building for Posterity." *ThCr.* 1987 Dec.; 21(10): 51, 78-79. Lang.: Eng.

USA. UK. 1960-1987. Technical studies. ■Query as to whether theatre architects have learned from mistakes of the last 25 years.

705 Marchese, Karen. "Intiman Playhouse at Seattle Center." *ThCr.* 1987 Dec.; 21(10): 46-47, 83. Notes. Illus.: Photo. Plan. Color. B&W. Architec. 5. Lang.: Eng.

USA: Seattle, WA. 1983-1987. Technical studies. ■Renovation of the Seattle Center Playhouse into the new home of the Intiman Theatre.

706 Moy, James S. "Subverting/Alienating Performance Structures." *TID.* 1987; 9: 161-176. Notes. Illus.: Photo. Plan. Sketches. Poster. B&W. Explod.Sect. 9. Lang.: Eng.

USA. 1800-1910. Critical studies. ■The way performance structures, both architectural and scenic, can actively alienate the audience from the staged representation, subverting proscenium-type theatre.

THEATRE IN GENERAL: —Performance spaces

707 Roberts, Tony. "The Ambassador." *EN*. 1986 Mar.; 71(3): 6. Lang.: Eng.
USA: New York, NY. 1986. Historical studies. ■Theatres being threatened with replacement by bigger auditoriums creating adverse circumstances for writers and performers to enlighten and inform audiences in intimate settings.

708 Rottenbach, Jane. "A Great Hall Is Made Even Greater: Carnegie Hall Restored and Revitalized." *L&DA*. 1987 Feb.; 17(2): 4-7. Illus.: Photo. Diagram. Schematic. 5. Lang.: Eng.
USA: New York, NY. 1986. Technical studies. ■The restoration of Carnegie Hall included new lighting, as well as building design, changes. Modern techniques to light the hall, both internally and externally, are discussed.

709 Slar, Albert. "Old Globe Reopens." *EN*. 1982 May; 67(5): 2. Illus.: Photo. B&W. 1. Lang.: Eng.
USA: San Diego, CA. 1982. Historical studies. ■New Old Globe Theatre in Balboa Park, San Diego replaces the previous theatre destroyed by arson.

710 Sommers, Michael. "Krannert Center for the Performing Arts." *ThCr*. 1987 Dec.; 21(10): 48-49, 71-75. Notes. Illus.: Photo. Plan. Color. B&W. Grd.Plan. 7. Lang.: Eng.
USA: Urbana, IL. 1969-1987. Technical studies. ■One of the premier facilities built in the late 1960s and its current condition.

711 Sullivan, Dan. "Are We Creating Mausoleums Filled with Starving Artists?" *EN*. 1987 Aug.; 72(8): 3. Illus.: Photo. B&W. 1. Lang.: Eng.
USA: Los Angeles, CA. 1987. Historical studies. ■A reprint from a Los Angeles Times article questioning the wisdom of spending $50 million on a new concert hall. Instead the author suggests that the money be spent on artists.

712 Willis, Beverly. "Design of the San Francisco Ballet Association Building." *TD&T*. 1987; 23(2): 6-10. Illus.: Photo. Plan. B&W. Explod.Sect. Fr.Elev. 8. Lang.: Eng.
USA: San Francisco, CA. 1987. Technical studies. ■San Francisco Ballet Board of Directors' decision to build a new facility instead of renovating their existing space. Architect describes the process from start to finish with details about site considerations to decisions about the facade.

713 Yarnal, Thom. "The Theatres in the 42nd Street Redevelopment Project Area: An Overview." *PerfM*. 1984 Dec.; 10(1): 3-4. Lang.: Eng.
USA: New York, NY. 1984. Historical studies. ■Proposal for renovations of Broadway theatres: history of theatres and suggested structural changes.

Performance/production

714 Bono, Paola; Tessitore, Maria Vittoria. "Quando non fare è dire. L'enunciazione a teatro." (When Not To Do Is To Tell: Enunciation in the Theatre.) *BiT*. 1987; 7: 135-144. Lang.: Ita.
Critical studies. ■Theatre performance as an 'enunciative event'. If a subject is to be found in any enunciation, in a performance such a subject is not easily isolated. Examples of performances where self-referential markers are presented.

715 Gung, Suk-kee. *Dong seo yonkukui beekyo yongu.* (Comparative Study on the Eastern and Western Theatre.) Seoul: Koryo Univ.; 1987. 295 pp. Lang.: Kor.
Critical studies. ■Comparison of Eastern and Western theatre.

716 Jiang, Wei-Guo. "Duo yuan xi ju zhong biao yan de duo yuan xing." (The Pluralism of Theatre.) *XYishu*. 1987 Spr; 37: 19-28. Lang.: Chi.
500 B.C.-1987 A.D. Historical studies. ■The performing style in theatre from ancient Greece to the present.

717 Kirk, Kris; Heath, Ed. *Uomodonna. Il mondo dei travestiti in teatro.* (Man-Woman. The World of Transvestites in the Theatre.) Como: Lyra; 1987. 202 pp. (I sensi dell'amore 14.) Index. Biblio. Illus.: Photo. Print. B&W. Lang.: Ita.

1987. Critical studies. ■Transvestitism in the theatre.

718 Mango, Lorenzo. *La scena della perdita. Il teatro fra avanguardia e postavanguardia.* (Theatre of Loss: Between Avant-Garde and Post-Avant-Garde.) Rome: Kappa; 1987. 94 pp. (Teatro.) Pref. Lang.: Ita.
1900-1987. Critical studies. ■Avant-garde theatre: a new linguistic code that gives prominence to performance over text.

719 Rodriguez de Anca, Antonio. "La vanguardia teatral Argentina." (The Argentinian Avant-Garde Theatre.) *Cjo*. 1987 July-Sep.(73): 95-99. Illus.: Dwg. Explod.Sect. 1. Lang.: Spa.
Argentina. 1950-1983. Historical studies. ■The development of the avant-garde theatre in Argentina.

720 Yeo, Seok-Gi. "Asia Yeon-Geuk eui Seo-Sa-Seong gwa Yang-Shik-Seong." (Characteristics of Asian Theatre.) 15-54 in *Study on the Comparison of Eastern Theatre and Western Theatre.* Seoul: Korea Univ.; 1987. 295 pp. Lang.: Kor.
Asia. 1987. Critical studies. ■Characteristics of Asian theatre, in terms of stylization and the epic.

721 Blokdijk, Tom. "De Macht der Verbeelding." (The Power of the Imagination.) *Toneel*. 1987 July; 7(6): 16-21. Illus.: Photo. B&W. 6. Lang.: Dut.
Austria: Vienna. 1986-1987. Historical studies. ■Claus Peymann, new artistic director of Vienna's Burgtheater, searches to recapture the magic of the imagination so well loved by the Viennese. Also discusses his productions *Ritter, Dene, Vos* and *Der Theatermacher (The Theaterworker)* both by Thomas Bernhard.

722 Radnóti, Zsuzsa. "'Főleg politikai színházat csinálunk'. Interjú Bécsben 1987 júniusában." ('It is Mainly Political Theatre that We Make': Interview in Vienna, June 1987.) *Sz*. 1987 Oct.; 20(10): 44-46. Lang.: Hun.
Austria: Vienna. 1987. Histories-sources. ■Hungarian-born director George Tabori speaks about his motivation to lead a theatre in Vienna at his age of 73: characteristic difficulties and plans of present day theatre life.

723 Kerimov, Ingilab Salach ogly. *Problemy zaroždenija, stanovlenija i razvitija azerbajdžans-kogo teatra (konec XIX-nač. XX vekov). Avtoref. dis. kand. iskusstvovedenija.* (Problems of the Conception, Establishment and Development of Azerbaijani Theatre in the Late Nineteenth and Early Twentieth Centuries: Abstract of a Dissertation by a Candidate in Art Criticism.) Moscow: VNII Iskusstvoznanija; 1987. 47 pp. Lang.: Rus.
Azerbaijan. 1875-1925. Historical studies.

724 Schoor, Jaak van. "The Kaaitheater and Afterwards." *MuK*. 1987; 33(1-2): 101-104. Lang.: Eng.
Belgium. 1980-1987. Historical studies. ■History of Kaaitheater.

725 Blumenthal, Eileen. "West Meets East Meets West." *AmTh*. 1987 Jan.; 3(10): 11-16. Illus.: Photo. B&W. 6. Lang.: Eng.
Canada: Vancouver, BC. 1987. Critical studies. ■Influences of Asian theatre and art on Western artists. Theory, script, techniques.

726 Burns, Kevin. "Edmonton Peter Puck, Meet Peter Pork." *CTR*. 1987 Win; 53: 70-73. Illus.: Photo. B&W. 2. [Carte Blanche.] Lang.: Eng.
Canada: Edmonton, AB. 1987. Historical studies. ■Critical account of circumstances that generated popular theatre. Problems of working collectively, responding to a common crisis problematic when company members hold differing philosophies on the issue that presents itself.

727 Butt, Robyn-Marie. "Interview with Tanja Jacobs." *Theatrum*. 1987 Sum; 7: 13-16, 36. Illus.: Photo. B&W. 2. Lang.: Eng.
Canada: Toronto, ON. 1987. Histories-sources. ■Interview with Jacobs discussing Richard Rose, Necessary Angel Theatre Company and Howard Barker's script *The Castle*. Discusses actor's relationship to text.

728 Conian, Joanne. "The Directors' Colloquium at Calgary: From the Conceptual to the Concrete." *CTR*. 1987 Fall; 52: 18-21. Notes. Illus.: Photo. NP. B&W. 3. Lang.: Eng.

CLASSED ENTRIES

THEATRE IN GENERAL: —Performance/production

Canada: Calgary, AB. 1987. Historical studies. ▪Critical summary of various philosophies and techniques revealed over course of Directors' Colloqium, focusing on role of the director.

729 Daoust, Jean-Paul. "Un Star System au Québec?" (A Star System in Quebec?)*JCT*. 1987; 43: 47-49. Illus.: Photo. Print. B&W. 4. Lang.: Fre.
Canada. 1960-1987. Critical studies. ▪The theatre star system in Quebec is fragile and actors (especially in relation to hockey stars) are poorly paid.

730 Devine, Michael. "Toronto Director Training." *CTR*. 1987 Fall; 52: 82-88. Illus.: Photo. Print. B&W. 13. [Carte Blanche.] Lang.: Eng.
Canada: Toronto, ON. 1987. Histories-sources. ▪Several Toronto directors share educational and practical backgrounds highlighting philosophies and approaches to craft of directing.

731 Devine, Michael; Hunt, Nigel; Dubois, Jocelyne. "Glimpses." *Theatrum*. 1987 Sum; 7: 37-40. Illus.: Photo. B&W. 1. Lang.: Eng.
Canada: Toronto, ON, Montreal, PQ. 1987. Reviews of performances. ▪A collection of very brief reviews generally focusing on alternative companies in Toronto. Includes Montreal production of *Carmen*.

732 Devine, Michael; Hinton, Peter; Hunt, Nigel. "Glimpses." *Theatrum*. 1987 Fall/Win; 8: 35-37. Illus.: Photo. B&W. 2. Lang.: Eng.
Canada: Toronto, ON, Stratford, ON. 1987. Reviews of performances. ▪A collection of brief reviews of productions by several of Toronto's smaller theatre companies as well as five shows at Stratford.

733 Filewod, Alan. "Popular Theatre." *CTR*. 1987 Win; 53: 3. Illus.: Photo. Print. B&W. 1. Lang.: Eng.
Canada. Africa. Asia. 1987. Critical studies. ▪A brief summary of the history and mandate of popular theatre. Quotations from pioneers are used to evidence the greater acceptance and wider understanding of this theatrical form for social action and community development.

734 Gaines, Robert A. *John Neville Takes Command: The Story of the Stratford Shakespearean Festival in Production.* Stratford, ON: William Street P; 1987. 339 pp. Index. Illus.: Photo. Lang.: Eng.
Canada: Stratford, ON. 1986. Histories-sources. ▪John Neville's first season as artistic director at Stratford. A compilation and analysis of data on the production process based on interviews with directors, designers, actors, composers and attendance at rehearsals.

735 Garebian, Keith. "*Intimate Admiration*: Richard Epp." *Queen's Quarterly*. 1987 Fall; 94(3): 753-755. Lang.: Eng.
Canada: Stratford, ON. 1987. Reviews of performances. ▪Reviews the Stratford production of *Intimate Admiration* directed by John Wood with John Neville and Lucy Peacock, written by Richard Epp.

736 Garebian, Keith. "*Play Memory*: Joanna M. Glass." *Queen's Quarterly*. 1987 Fall; 94(3): 755-757. Lang.: Eng.
Canada: Toronto, ON. 1987. Reviews of performances. ▪Reviews the Theatre Plus production of Joanna Glass's *Play Memory* directed by Malcolm Black with Patricia Hamilton, Roland Hewgill and Graeme Campbell.

737 Garebian, Keith. "*Ma Rainey's Black Bottom*: August Wilson." *Queen's Quarterly*. 1987 Win; 94(4): 1074-1076. Lang.: Eng.
Canada: Toronto, ON. 1987. Reviews of performances. ▪Reviews August Wilson's play *Ma Rainey's Black Bottom* at Theatre Passe Muraille (Toronto) directed by Jon Michaelson.

738 Garebian, Keith. "The Rise and Fall of London's Grand Theatre." *PAC*. 1984 Fall; 21(2): 25-29. Illus.: Photo. Print. B&W. 3. Lang.: Eng.
Canada: London, ON. 1983-1984. Historical studies. ▪Reviews of productions and analysis of the attempt to establish a repertory theatre in London, Ontario, under the direction of Robin Phillips, former director of the Stratford Festival.

739 Hunt, Nigel. "Hillar Liitoja, Chaos and Control." *CTR*. 1987 Fall; 52: 45-49. Illus.: Photo. Print. B&W. 3. Lang.: Eng.
Canada. 1987. Critical studies. ▪Experimental approach combining poetry of Ezra Pound and unconventional images choreographed to create chaos.

740 Hunt, Nigel. "Theatre Festival of the Americas Report." *Theatrum*. 1987 Sum; 7: 17-20, 31-35. Illus.: Photo. B&W. 4. Lang.: Eng.
Canada: Montreal, PQ. 1987. Reviews of performances. ▪Briefly reviews ten of twenty-one productions. Brief assessment of festival trends.

741 Knowles, Richard Paul. "Robin Phillips, Text and Context." *CTR*. 1987 Fall; 52: 50-57. Notes. Illus.: Photo. Print. B&W. 8. Lang.: Eng.
Canada: Stratford, ON. 1987. Critical studies. ▪Analysis of rehearsal process created by wholistic directorial techniques discussed by Stratford actors.

742 Laberge, Marie. "Janine Angers va me manquer." (I am Going to Miss Janine Angers.) *JCT*. 1987; 45: 13. Illus.: Photo. Print. B&W. 1. Lang.: Fre.
Canada. 1987. Biographical studies. ▪Eulogy for actress Janine Angers.

743 Levine, Meredith. "The Director's Role." *CTR*. 1987 Fall; 52: 4-6. Illus.: Photo. Print. B&W. 2. [The Directors' Colloquium at Calgary:1/The Workshops: Transformations.] Lang.: Eng.
Canada: Calgary, AB. 1987. Critical studies. ▪Assessment of success of guest directors during colloquium. Emphasis on hesitancy to divulge individual techniques as a result of competition.

744 Liitoja, Hillar. "Liitoja Scores." *Theatrum*. 1987 Fall/Win; 8: 19-21. Illus.: Photo. B&W. 1. Lang.: Eng.
Canada: Toronto, ON. 1987. Histories-sources. ▪Liitoja's use of a system of notation akin to a musical score as a directorial aid. Provides an example from *Private Performances*.

745 Pavlovic, Diane; Gannon, Roger E.; Gill, Rosalind. "Gilles Maheu Corps à Corps." (Gilles Maheu: Face to Face.) *CTR*. 1987 Fall; 52: 22-29. Notes. Illus.: Photo. Print. B&W. 10. Lang.: Eng.
Canada. 1987. Critical studies. ▪Directorial approach of Gilles Maheu who uses language to provide mood rather than meaning. Multi-media theatre of the Carbon 14 Company is described.

746 Prosser, David. "Defining the New World: The Role of Festivals in Canadian Theatre." *MuK*. 1987; 33(1-2): 105-110. Lang.: Eng.
Canada. 1987. Historical studies.

747 Raby, Gyl. "The Role of the Director in New Play Development." *CTR*. 1987 Fall; 52: 7-13. Illus.: Photo. Print. B&W. 7. [The Directors Colloquium at Calgary: 2/Panel Session One: 16 May 1987.] Lang.: Eng.
Canada: Calgary, AB. 1987. Histories-sources. ▪Five directors discuss their views on director/playwright relationship and need to focus on development of playwright rather than on production of play.

748 Smith, Brian. "Actor Expectations." *CTR*. 1987 Fall; 52: 14-17. Illus.: Photo. Print. B&W. 4. [The Directors' Colloquium at Calgary:3/Panel Session Two: 23 May 1987.] Lang.: Eng.
Canada: Calgary, AB. 1987. Histories-sources. ▪Actors and directors discuss their various expectations and experiences.

749 Smith, Patricia Keeney. "Stratford's Festival of Sight and Sound." *PAC*. 1982 Fall; 19(3): 51-54. Illus.: Photo. Print. B&W. 3. Lang.: Eng.
Canada: Stratford, ON. 1982. Reviews of performances. ▪A review of the 1982 Stratford Festival under the direction of John Hirsch.

750 Wallace, Robert. "Directing." *CTR*. 1987 Fall; 52: 3. Illus.: Photo. Print. B&W. 1. Lang.: Eng.
Canada. 1987. Critical studies. ▪Status and recognition of the Canadian director and changing relationship between directors and playwrights as playwrights opt to direct their own work.

751 Warren, Roger. "Shakespeare's Late Plays at Stratford, Ontario." *ShS*. 1987; 40: 155-168. Illus.: Photo. B&W. 6. Lang.: Eng.

THEATRE IN GENERAL: —Performance/production

Canada: Stratford, ON. 1986. Critical studies. ■Analysis and review of the 1986 season at Stratford Festival during which Shakespeare's later plays (*Cymbeline*, *The Winter's Tale*, and *Pericles*) were performed.

752 Whittaker, Herbert. "The Brecht Legacy." *AmTh.* 1987 Feb.; 3(11): 18-19. Illus.: Photo. B&W. 1. Lang.: Eng.
Canada: Toronto, ON. USA. 1987. Critical studies. ■New performances of Brecht plays. Adaptation, staging, acting, analysis of relevancy of Brecht's plays today.

753 Whittaker, Herbert. "Changes at Stratford." *AmTh.* 1987 Nov.; 4(8): 52-53. Illus.: Photo. B&W. 2. Lang.: Eng.
Canada: Stratford, ON. 1953-1987. Critical studies. ■Changes in staff, policy and artistic direction of the Stratford Theatre Festival since the appointment of John Neville as artistic director.

754 Liu, Hui. "Lun wu shu fu." (The Discussion of Wu Shu-fu.) *XYishu.* 1987 Spr; 37: 108-117. Notes. Lang.: Chi.
China. 1657-1720. Biographical studies. ■Wu Shu-fu and his times.

755 Tang, Heng. "Song tsun fang lun." (Discussion of Song Tsun-fang.) *XYishu.* 1987 Sum; 38: 43-61. Notes. Lang.: Chi.
China. 1880-1930. Biographical studies. ■The biography of Song Tsun-fang.

756 "Shou tuu chju hsieng shang hsiao-yu tan ch'en pa sh wu chou ián chi nain ian ch'wu." (Memorial Performance of the Metropolitan Theatre for Shang Hsio-Yu's Eighty-fifth Birthday.) *XLunc.* 1984; 2: 117. Illus.: Photo. B&W. 1. Lang.: Chi.
China, People's Republic of. 1984. Historical studies. ■The Metropolitan Theatre stages a play by Shang Hsio Yu by a group of students, to memorialize Mr. Shang's contribution to the theatre and his 85th birthday.

757 Hu, Dao. "Dao yan ji qiao jiao xue." (Directing Class.) *XYishu.* 1985 Spr; 29: 110-125. Lang.: Chi.
China, People's Republic of. 1985. Histories-sources. ■Two-part article, continued in *XYishu* 30 (1985 Sum), 89-103. Part I: Theatre professionals as complex artists. Role of director. Part II: Influence of theatres, scripts, scenery and props on director's work.

758 Lee, Chuen Shi. "Shih Cheu Yean Yuann Dih Chyng Gann Tii Yeng." (Dramatic Actor's Sentient Experience.) *XYanj.* 1987; 8(19): 212-236. Lang.: Chi.
China, People's Republic of: Beijing. 1368-1986. Critical studies. ■How a Chinese actor transformed his life experiences into his character.

759 Licher, Edmund. "Brecht en Azië: Overtuigingskracht ontleend aan vrijheid." (Brecht and Asia: Power of Persuasion Drawn from Freedom.) *Toneel.* 1987 Apr.; 4(5): 4-8. Illus.: Handbill. 3. Lang.: Dut.
China, People's Republic of: Hong Kong. 1986. Historical studies. ■Review of International Brecht Festival in Hong Kong. Seventh International Symposium paralleled festival. Review of productions of various Brecht plays by Hong Kong Repertory Theatre, China Youth Art Theatre, Unity Theatre (Bengal), PETA (Philippines).

760 Suen, Mei. "Lun Shih Cheu Dih Teh Shu Yih Shuh Sheng Chaan Fang Shyh—Yean Chwan Toong Shih." (The Special Production Form of Chinese Drama—Performing the Traditional Drama.) *XYanj.* 1987; 8(19): 237-258. Lang.: Chi.
China, People's Republic of: Beijing. 1271-1986. Critical studies. ■Special nature of traditional Chinese drama: recreation and continuation, not just stage activity.

761 Sun Huizhu, William; Fei Chunfang, Faye. "*The Old B Hanging on the Wall* in the Changing Chinese Theatre." *TDR.* 1986 Win; 30(4): 84-105. Notes. Illus.: Photo. B&W. 8. Lang.: Eng.
China, People's Republic of. 1984-1986. Critical studies. ■Performance of *Old B Hanging on the Wall* represents innovations in Chinese theatre through influences of more accessible Western culture.

762 Wang, Bang-Xiong. "Dao yan ren han kong jian de dui hua." (The Dialogue Between Directing and Space in Theatre.) *XYishu.* 1987 Spr; 37: 54-70. Notes. Illus.: Dwg. Print. B&W. 11. Lang.: Chi.

China, People's Republic of. 1949-1987. Critical studies. ■Using space in the theatre to communicate abstract concepts.

763 Wang, Kun. "Yan yuan chuang zuo xin li dong li." (Outline of Creativity Motive in Acting.) *XYishu.* 1985 Sum; 30: 79-81. Lang.: Chi.
China, People's Republic of. 1985. Critical studies. ■The influence of the audience on the actor and his performance.

764 Wong, You-Yue. "Er tong ju te zheng chu tan." (The Characteristics of Children's Theatre.) *XYishu.* 1987 Sum; 38: 89-92. Lang.: Chi.
China, People's Republic of. 1975-1987. Historical studies. ■Improvisation and other forms in children's theatre.

765 "Divácký hit bez roucha." (The Audience Hits *Noises Off.*) *ScenaP.* 1987; 12(3): 4. Illus.: Photo. B&W. 7. Lang.: Cze.
Czechoslovakia: Prague. 1987. Reviews of performances. ■Michael Frayn's *Noises Off* directed by Jiří Menzel at Činoherní klub theatre.

766 Adamovič, I.I. *Slovackaja akterskaja škola: (Étapy formirovahija, harakternye čerty): Avtoref. dis. kand. iskusstvovedenija.* (The Slovak Acting School-Stages of Formation, Characteristic Features: Abstract of a Dissertation by a Candidate in Art Criticism.) Moscow: M-vo kultury RSFSR, GITIS; 1987. 19 pp. Lang.: Rus.
Czechoslovakia. 1830-1987. Historical studies.

767 Foll, Jan. "Vivisekce: zákrok bez umrtvení." (*Vivisection*: A Non-Fatal Operation.) *ScenaP.* 1987; 12(14): 4. Illus.: Photo. B&W. Lang.: Cze.
Czechoslovakia: Prague. 1987. Reviews of performances. ■*Vivisekce (Vivisection)* directed by the author Antonín Máša at Laterna magika, the Prague stage of the national theatre.

768 Hořínek, Zdeněk. "Ladislav Smoček (pokus o určení typu)." (Ladislav Smoček: The Attempt at Object of the Type.) *ScenaP.* 1987; 12(19): 3. Lang.: Cze.
Czechoslovakia: Prague. 1965-1987. Critical studies. ■Director and playwright Smoček's plays *Piknik (Picnic)*, *Podivné odpoledne doktora Zvonka Burkeho (Strange Afternoon of Doctor Zvonek Burke)*, *Bitva na kopci (A Battle on a Hill)* at Činoherní klub theatre.

769 Kiss Péntek, József. "Színház—őrhelyen. A csehszlovákiai Magyar Területi Színház." (Theatre—On Guard: Hungarian Regional Theatre in Czechoslovakia.) *Sz.* 1987 Sep.; 20(9): 45-47. Lang.: Hun.
Czechoslovakia: Kosice, Komarno. 1953-1987. Historical studies. ■Hungarian-language theatre in an ethnic Hungarian region of Czechoslovakia.

770 Königsmark, Václav. "Dobové tance konečně v Praze." (*Period Dances* at Last in Prague.) *ScenaP.* 1987; 12(19): 4. Lang.: Cze.
Czechoslovakia: Prague. 1987. Reviews of performances. ■Karel Steigerwald's *Dobové tance (Period Dances)*, directed by Miroslav Krobot at the Nejedlý Realistic Theatre.

771 Königsmark, Václav. "Dva Cyranové na Vinohradech." (Two Cyranos at the Vinohradské Theatre.) *ScenaP.* 1987; 12(1): 4. Illus.: Photo. B&W. 2. Lang.: Cze.
Czechoslovakia: Prague. 1986. Critical studies. ■Comparison of two interpretations of the title role in Rostand's *Cyrano de Bergerac* by actors Jaromír Hanzlík and Viktor Preiss, in a production directed by Jaroslav Dudek.

772 Shaan, Nava. "Lehayot Sachkanit Be-Terezenshtat." (On Being an Actress in Theresienstadt.) *Bamah.* 1987; 22(108): 5-16. Illus.: Photo. Poster. Print. B&W. 3. Lang.: Heb.
Czechoslovakia: Terezín. 1938-1968. Historical studies. ■Theatrical activity at the concentration camp Theresienstadt during World War II and the artists involved: puppet theatre, children's theatre.

773 Sinel'čenko, V.N. *Jaroslav Kvapil i stanovlenie česskoj professional'noj režissury na rubeže XIX-XX v. (1900-1918 gg.): Avtoref. dis. kand. iskusstvovedenija.* (Jaroslav Kvapil and the Formation of Professional Czech Directing at the Turn of the Century (1900-1918): Abstract of a Dissertation by a Candidate in Art Criticism.) Leningrad: M-vo kul'tury RSFSR, LGITMiK; 1987. 17 pp. Lang.: Rus.

THEATRE IN GENERAL: —Performance/production

Czechoslovakia. 1900-1918. Historical studies.

774 Štěpánek, Bohuš. "Nezapomínaj!" (They Don't Forget-!)*ScenaP.* 1987; 12(2): 3. Lang.: Cze.

Czechoslovakia: Prague. 1987. Reviews of performances. ∎*I dol'še veka dlitsja den'* (*A Day Lasts Longer than a Century*) by Čingiz Ajmatov, dramatized by Vjačelav Spesivcev and directed by Jaroslav Dudek at Vinohradské Theatre under the title *Den delší než století.*

775 Hibbard, G.R., ed. *The Elizabethan Theatre IX.* Port Credit, ON: P.D. Meany; 1986. xiv, 234 pp. [9th International Conference on Elizabethan Theatre (Univ. of Waterloo, 1981).] Lang.: Eng.

England. 1546-1616. Critical studies. ∎Collection of papers on 'The Staging of Plays in the Age of Shakespeare'.

776 Pederson, Steven I. *The Tournament Tradition and Staging The Castle of Perseverance.* Ann Arbor, MI: UMI Research P; 1987. 136 pp. (Theatre and Dramatic Studies 38.) Index. Notes. Tables. Biblio. Illus.: Photo. Plan. Print. B&W. 7. Lang.: Eng.

England. 1425. Historical studies. ∎Postulates staging based on the medieval tournament tradition, with the original staging plan sketch as evidence. Related to Mixed Entertainment: Court entertainment.

777 Pentzell, Raymond J. "Actor, *Maschera,* and Role: An Approach to Irony in Performance." *CompD.* 1982 Fall; 16(3): 201-226. Notes. Lang.: Eng.

England. 1575-1982. Historical studies. ∎Irony in *Gammer Gurton's Needle* and other plays of the Renaissance. Low humor of comedy, actors' maschera and role, relationship to audience.

778 Guccini, Gerardo. "Attori e comici nella prima metà del Settecento." (Actors and Comics in the First Half of the Eighteenth Century.) *QT.* 1987 Aug.; 10(37): 85-94. Lang.: Ita.

Europe. 1700-1750. Historical studies. ∎Relations between actors and comics—with reference to the performance of *Ifigenia (Iphigeneia)* by Luigi Riccoboni.

779 Lee, Chang-Gu. "Sosaekicho yonchulkalon." (Study of the Directors of the Early Twentieth Century.) *DongukDA.* 1983 Dec.; 14: 43-78. Lang.: Kor.

Europe. North America. 1900-1950. Historical studies. ∎Includes Antoine, Stanislavskij, Craig, Appia.

780 Merschmeier, Michael; Sjögren, Frederik, transl. "Inte de stora gesterna utan de små undanskymda ögonblicken." (Not the Big Gestures But the Small Secluded Glimpses.) *NT.* 1987; 39: 3-11. Illus.: Photo. 6. Lang.: Swe.

Europe. USA. 1968-1987. Histories-sources. ∎Peter Sellars speaks about the American theatre in general compared to the European attitude, and his own way to becoming a director.

781 Serpieri, Alessandro, ed.; Elam, Keir, ed. *Mettere in scena Shakespeare.* (To Stage Shakespeare.) Parma: Pratiche; 1987. 169 pp. (Sedicesimo 9.) Pref. MU. Discography. Illus.: Dwg. Lang.: Ita.

Europe. 1596-1987. Critical studies. ∎Essays on modern problems in directing Shakespeare.

782 Suchanova, T.N. *Chudožestvenno-estetičeskie koncepcii zapadnoevropejskoj režissury i sovremennaja sociokul'turnaja situacija.* (The Artistic-Esthetic Conception of Western European Directing and the Contemporary Sociocultural Situation.) Moscow: Gosudarstvennaja Biblioteka im. V.I. Lenina; 1987. 24 pp. (Zreliščnije iskusstva. Obzornaja informacija 2.) Lang.: Rus.

Europe. 1980-1987. Critical studies.

783 Vazzoler, Anna, ed. *Il teatro degli anni Venti.* (The Theatre of the Twenties.) Rome: Bulzoni; 1987. 268 pp. (Biblioteca Teatrale 48.) Index. Biblio. [Atti del Convegno Internazionale di Studi. Istituto Internazionale per la Ricerca Teatrale-Venezia 1986.] Lang.: Ita.

Europe. 1920-1930. Critical studies. ∎Collection of essays on European theatre between 1920 and 1930.

784 Banu, Georges; Deprats, Jean-Michel; Durand, Régis; Millon, Martine; Sallenave, Danièle. "Invisible mais partout présent: le metteur en scène." (Invisible But Present Everywhere: The Director.) *AdT.* 1987 Spr; 1(6): 11-24. Illus.: Dwg. 1. Lang.: Fre.

France. 1987. Critical studies. ∎Directing as something first relevant to the text: the mutation of the directing activity. No longer just making an interpretation, but guiding the actors and not letting subjectivity be a screen in front of the text.

785 Benhamou, Anne-Françoise. "La chair gobée du théâtre." (The Gobbled Flesh of Theatre.) *AdT.* 1987 Spr; 1 (6): 78-83. Notes. Lang.: Fre.

France. 1987. Critical studies. ∎The task of the director is not to create an envelope of things (actors, set) that exalts the actor's work, but to create a dimension that enhances the actor's desire.

786 Brasey, Georges. "Adolphe Appia: Qu'en est-il du théâtre dans l'oeuvre d'art vivant?" (Adolphe Appia: What Is the Role of Theatre in the Living Work of Art?)*Mimos.* 1987; 39(1): 8-9. Illus.: Photo. B&W. Lang.: Fre.

France. 1900-1987. Critical studies. ∎In taking up Appia's notion of the relation between text, actor and producer, Brasey concentrates in his very personal article on the function of the actor having changed through time.

787 Corvin, Michel. "Et si la mise en scène était une fonction sacrée?" (What if Directing Were a Sacred Office?) *AdT.* 1987 Spr; 1(6): 86-90. Lang.: Fre.

France. 1987. Critical studies. ∎Directing seen as an unveiling: the director's task is to make one see. Director Antoine Vitez is used as an example.

788 Deprats, Jean-Michel. "Glissements progressifs du discours." (The Progressive Sliding of Discourse.) *AdT.* 1987 Spr; 1 (6): 25-30. Notes. Lang.: Fre.

France. 1987. Critical studies. ∎Directing seen as an activity that no longer proceeds from a critical and ideological statement, but from the art of translation and thus, of variation.

789 Franǫn, Alain. "Les silences et la parole juste." (Silences and True Speech.) *AdT.* 1987 Spr; 1(6): 41-46. Illus.: Dwg. 1. Lang.: Fre.

France. 1987. Critical studies. ∎Directing defined as team work. The director determines a conception of the play but has to first listen and adapt to actors.

790 Gunthert, André. "La jeune mise en scène: essai d'identification." (The Young Directors: The Experiment of Identification.) *AdT.* 1987 Spr; 1(6): 70-72. Notes. Lang.: Fre.

France. 1987. Historical studies. ∎Directorial style of young directors such as Pascal Rambert and Dominique Pithoiset: an emphasis on concept, writing, work with actors and text rather than on theory.

791 Hyslop, Gabrielle. "Researching the Acting of French Melodrama, 1800-1830." *NCT.* 1987; 15(2): 85-114. Notes. Illus.: Dwg. Print. B&W. 4. Lang.: Eng.

France: Paris. 1800-1830. Historical studies. ∎Examination of the primary sources available about the acting of melodrama and the basic problems posed in analyzing the information they contain.

792 Isaev, S. "Otkrytoe prostranstvo teatra." (The Open Expanse of the Theatre.) *TeatZ.* 1987; 13: 28-29. Lang.: Rus.

France. 1980-1987. Critical studies. ∎Analysis of new productions by French directors Patrice Chéreau, Claude Régg, Ariane Mnouchkine. Comparison with work of Peter Brook.

793 Piemme, Jean-Marie. "Le sens du jeu." (The Sense of the Game.) *AdT.* 1987 Spr; 1(6): 75-77. Lang.: Fre.

France. 1987. Critical studies. ∎Directing seen as an activity that oscillates between deciphering and legibility, but more and more aware of its direction toward working with the actor.

794 Tanase, Virgil. "La subversion par la touche." (Subversion by Touch.) *AdT.* 1987 Spr; 1(6): 84-85. Lang.: Fre.

France. 1987. Critical studies. ∎What is revolutionary in any directing work (and in any form of art) is the manner and the touch, not the subject of the play. Questioning a policy or a habit is nothing compared to questioning the sake of theatre itself.

795 Tifft, Stephen. "Theatre in the Round: The Politics of Space in the Films of Jean Renoir." *TJ.* 1987 Oct.; 39(3): 328-346. Notes. Illus.: Photo. B&W. 7. Lang.: Eng.

CLASSED ENTRIES

THEATRE IN GENERAL: —Performance/production

France. 1987. Critical studies. ■Filmmaker Jean Renoir's techniques of using deep space and long takes and their influences on theatrical staging. Related to Media: Film.

796 Ubersfeld, Anne. "L'homme du jugement." (The Man of Judgment.) *AdT*. 1987 Spr; 1(6): 73-74. Lang.: Fre.

France. 1987. Critical studies. ■The task of directing today is to go against: against the imposed perception, against visual habits, against the media.

797 Bauer, Oswald G. "Festspiele zwischen Muster und Reform: Des Beispiel Bayreuth." (Festival Between Design and Reform: The Example of Bayreuth.) *MuK*. 1987; 33(1-2): 81-88. Lang.: Ger.

Germany: Bayreuth. 1876-1987. Critical studies.

798 Poljanova, N.B. *Fridrich Ljudvig Šreder.* (Friedrich Ludwig Schröder.) Moscow: Iskusstvo; 1987. 269 pp. Lang.: Rus.

Germany. 1744-1816. Biographical studies. ■Life and work of actor, director, theatrical figure of eighteenth-century Germany.

799 Hoffman, Ludwig; Siebig, Karl. *Ernst Busch. Eine Biographie in Texten, Bildern und Dokumenten.* (Ernst Busch: A Biography in Texts, Photographs and Documents.) East Berlin: Henschelverlag; 1987. 387 pp. Index. Append. Illus.: Photo. Print. B&W. 700. Lang.: Ger.

Germany, East: Berlin, East. 1900-1980. Biographies. ■Comprehensive representation of the actor-singer's life and work.

800 Neef, Sigrid. "Widerspruch ist Bewegung. Nachdenken über Ruth Berghause." (Contradiction as Movement: Reflections on Ruth Berghaus.) *TZ*. 1987; 42(6): 53-55. Illus.: Photo. B&W. 6. Lang.: Ger.

Germany, East: Berlin, East, Dresden. 1964-1987. Biographical studies. ■Artistic profile of opera director Ruth Berghaus.

801 Hamburger, Mark. "New Concepts of Staging *A Midsummer Night's Dream.*" *ShS*. 1987; 40: 51-61. Illus.: Photo. B&W. 5. Lang.: Eng.

Germany, West. 1970-1975. Critical studies. ■Comparative study of two German productions of *A Midsummer Night's Dream* during the early 1970s as well as some discussion of other German productions of the same play.

802 Ablonczy, László. "Találkozás Sík Ferenccel. A párbeszéd esélyéről." (Interview with Ferenc Sík: On the Chance of Dialogue.) *FSM*. 1987 May; 31(19): 8-9. Illus.: Photo. B&W. 1. Lang.: Hun.

Hungary. 1987. Histories-sources. ■Ferenc Sík speaks about the staging of László Németh's drama *Galilei*, the relation of theatre and contemporary literature, his plans.

803 Baló, Júlia. "Találkozás Garas Dezsővel. 'Maradok tisztelettel: színész'." (Interview with Dezső Garas. 'Yours Faithfully: the Actor'.) *FSM*. 1987 May; 31(19): 15-18. Illus.: Photo. Color. B&W. 8. Lang.: Hun.

Hungary. 1983-1987. Histories-sources. ■Dezső Garas speaks about his basic principles as an actor, his stagings, his plans to found a theatre.

804 Csizner, Ildikó. "Tablókép a Vas utcából. Horvai-tanítványok vizsgaelőadásai." (Group Photograph on Vas Street: Examination Performances of Students of Professor Horvai.) *Sz*. 1987 May; 20(5): 15-19. Illus.: Photo. B&W. 3. Lang.: Hun.

Hungary: Budapest. 1986-1987. Reviews of performances. ■Examination performances of the final class of the College of Theatre and Film Art (Students of István Horvai and Dezső Kapás).

805 Futaky, Hajna. "Színészportrék pécsi háttérrel 7. Turay Ida." (Portraits of Actors with a Background in Pécs 7: Ida Turay.) *Jelenkor*. 1987 Feb.; 30(2): 143-149. Lang.: Hun.

Hungary: Pécs. 1924-1986. Histories-sources. ■Life and career of the splendid actress Ida Turay.

806 Gábor, István. "A brettlitől a magánszámig." (From the Board to the Private Number.) *Sz*. 1987 Sep.; 20(9): 18-21. Illus.: Photo. B&W. 3. Lang.: Hun.

Hungary: Budapest. 1987. Critical studies. ■Short review and evaluation of the 1987 productions of the Gaiety Theatre and its Chamber Stage.

807 Kerényi, Ferenc, comp., transl.; Törzsök, Édua, transl.; Ziegler, Vilmos, transl. *A vándorszínészettől a Nemzeti*

Szinházig. (From Itinerant Acting to the National Theatre.) Budapest: Szépirod. Kvk.; 1987. 386 pp. (Magyar levelestár.) Notes. Index. 32. Lang.: Hun.

Hungary. 1790-1837. Histories-sources. ■Development of professional theatre in Hungary up to inauguration of the National Theatre seen through letters of theatre professionals.

808 Koltai, Tamás. "Kaposváron a helyzet változatlan. Széljegyzetek az évadról." (The Situation Is Unchanged in Kaposvár. Notes on the Season.) *Jelenkor*. 1987 July/Aug.; 30(7-8): 714-717. Lang.: Hun.

Hungary: Kaposvár. 1986-1987. Reviews of performances. ■Survey of the season's productions—plays, conceptions, directors and actors.

809 Koltai, Tamás. "Az állampolgári közérzetet kell kifejezni." (The Citizens' Disposition Has to Be Expressed: Interview with Gábor Székely.) *Krit*. 1987 Oct.(10): 9-10. Illus.: Photo. B&W. 2. [Close-Up of Katona József Theatre.] Lang.: Hun.

Hungary: Budapest. 1982-1987. Histories-sources. ■Gábor Székely, managing director and stage manager of the Katona József Theatre, speaks about the operation conditions, program policy and some success plays of the theatre.

810 Nánay, István. "Rendezőgondok." (Problems of Producers.) *Sz*. 1987 May; 20(5): 1-3. Lang.: Hun.

Hungary. 1986-1987. Critical studies. ■On the basis of the performances in 1986/87 the author reviews the employment, age and qualification of the Hungarian producers.

811 Ruszt, József. "A helyzetkép." (State of Affairs.) *Krit*. 1987 Sep.(9): 12-13. Illus.: Photo. B&W. 2. Lang.: Hun.

Hungary. 1986-1987. Critical studies. ■The author, a director himself, reviews the productions of the 6th National Theatre Meeting. According to him regional companies need development and protection as compared to the theatres in the capital.

812 Takács, István. "Pontos-e a tükörkép?" (Is the Image Reflected by the Mirror Precise?)*Krit*. 1987 Sep.(9): 15-16. Illus.: Photo. B&W. 3. Lang.: Hun.

Hungary. 1986-1987. Critical studies. ■The 22 plays performed on the 6th National Theatre meeting amount to about 10 of the rehearsals of 1986/87. How far can these performances be considered a cross section of the season.

813 George, David E.R. "Ritual Drama: Between Mysticism and Magic." *ATJ*. 1987 Fall; 4(2): 127-165. Notes. Biblio. Illus.: Photo. Diagram. B&W. 12. Lang.: Eng.

India. Japan. Sri Lanka. 1987. Historical studies. ■Origins of theatre and the spectator. Shamanism, ritual, nō and other Eastern ontology connecting origins of theatre to spiritual underpinnings.

814 Zarrilli, Phillip B. "'Where the Hand [Is]...'." *ATJ*. 1987 Fall; 4(2): 205-214. Notes. Biblio. Illus.: Photo. B&W. 8. Lang.: Eng.

India. 1987. Critical studies. ■Discussion of the *Abhinayadarpanam*, medieval text on classical Indian performance from performance versus scholarly point of view: includes passages of text.

815 "Sticking At It! What Does the Future Hold for Wet Paint?" *ThIr*. 1987; 12: 45-46. Illus.: Photo. B&W. 2. Lang.: Eng.

Ireland: Dublin. 1985. Historical studies. ■Discussion of Wet Paint, a young people's theatre.

816 "Dublin's Young at Art." *ThIr*. 1987; 12: 47-49. Illus.: Photo. B&W. 5. Lang.: Eng.

Ireland: Dublin. 1980-1987. Historical studies. ■Discussion of DYT (Dublin Youth Theatre), a theatre group for young people in Dublin.

817 Henderson, Lynda. "Another Brick in the Wall?" *ThIr*. 1987; 12: 43-44. Illus.: Photo. B&W. 2. Lang.: Eng.

Ireland: Cork. 1987. Historical studies. ■Discussion of the theatre group known as Graffiti which tours through schools in southern Ireland.

818 Wilcox, Angela. "Ireland's A-Team." *ThIr*. 1987; 12: 40-42. Illus.: Photo. B&W. 4. Lang.: Eng.

Ireland: Dublin. 1984-1987. Historical studies. ■Description of TEAM, an educational theatre company which tours schools throughout Ireland.

THEATRE IN GENERAL: —Performance/production

819 Amministrazione Provinciale di Pavia; Comitato Nazionale Italiano Musica (CIDIM). *Leggere lo spettacolo 1987: Catalogo dei libri di cinema, teatro-danza e musica pubblicati nel 1987.* (Reading Entertainment 1987: Catalogue of Books About Cinema, Theatre-Dance and Music Published in 1987.) Pavia: Editrice Bibliografica; 1987. 252 pp. (Cataloghi di Biblioteche 9.) Index. Lang.: Ita.

Italy. 1987. Bibliographical studies. ■Bibliography of Italian books on entertainment published in 1987.

820 Bellotto, Francesca. "Ars Veneta. Storia di una compagnia dialettale." (Ars Veneta: History of a Dialect Company.) *BiT.* 1987; 5/6: 287-305. Lang.: Ita.

Italy: Venice. 1921-1922. Histories-sources. ■A collection of letters illustrates the activities of a Venetian-dialect theatre company, Ars Veneta.

821 Castelli, Cristina. "Renato Simoni regista. *I giganti della montagna* di Pirandello." (Renato Simoni, Director: *The Giants of the Mountain* by Pirandello.) *QT.* 1987 May; 9(36): 148-163. Lang.: Ita.

Italy: Florence. 1937. Critical studies. ■Playwright and critic Renato Simoni as director, his staging of *I giganti della montagna (The Giants of the Mountain)* for the Maggio Musicale Fiorentino.

822 Cruciani, Fabrizio, ed.; Seragnoli, Daniele, ed. *Il teatro italiano nel Rinascimento.* (Italian Theatre during the Renaissance.) Bologna: Mulino; 1987. 768 pp. (Problemi e prospettive. Serie di musica e spettacolo.) Pref. Biblio. Illus.: Pntg. Dwg. 16. Lang.: Ita.

Italy. 1400-1500. Historical studies. ■Essays by various authors explore Italian Renaissance theatre from several angles.

823 Dasgupta, Gautam. "The Director as Thinker: Carmelo Bene's *Otello.*" *PerAJ.* 1985 Spr; 9(25): 12-16. Lang.: Eng.

Italy: Florence. 1985. Critical studies. ■Italian actor/dramatist/director Carmelo Bene, in particular his production of *Otello/Secondo.*

824 Dolan, Jill. "Teatro Viola's *Shoe-Show.*" *TDR.* 1982 Fall; 26(3): 111-114. Illus.: Photo. B&W. 1. [Theatre Reports.] Lang.: Eng.

Italy. 1982. Critical studies. ■Feminist theatre group Teatro Viola's production: description of production elements and action of play which was developed collectively. Company's focus on women's issues.

825 Esposito, Giovanni, ed.; Pollini, Franco, ed.; Righetti, Loretta, ed. *La maschera doppia. Materiali e percorsi di lettura. Stagione teatrale per ragazzi 1987.* (The Double Mask: Materials and Reading Guide. Children's Theatre Season, 1987.) Cesena: Comune di Cesena; 1987. (La maschera doppia 12.) Biblio. Illus.: Dwg. Lang.: Ita.

Italy: Cesena. 1987. Bibliographical studies. ■List of productions and bibliographical materials.

826 Fo, Dario; Hood, Stuart, transl. "Totò: The Violence of the Marionette and the Mask." *ThM.* 1987; 18(3): 6-12. Illus.: Photo. B&W. 4. Lang.: Eng.

Italy. 1898-1978. Histories-sources. ■Text taken from the compilation and transcription of several improvisations done by Dario Fo about the Italian clown/performer Totò, the naturalistic clown, who works with violence and sexuality as well as the more traditional subjects.

827 Fo, Dario. *Manuale minimo dell'attore.* (The Smallest Acting Manual.) Turin: Einaudi; 1987. 374 pp. (Gli Struzzi 315.) Biblio. Gloss. Illus.: Sketches. Lang.: Ita.

Italy. 1987. Instructional materials. ■Amid autobiographical digressions and concrete examples, the book is intended to address the concerns of those who aspire to 'tread the boards'. With a contribution by Franca Rame.

828 Gori, Gabriella. "I diari di Marino Sanuto." (The Diaries of Marino Sanuto.) *QT.* 1987 May; 9(36): 113-133. Lang.: Ita.

Italy. 1496-1533. Histories-sources. ■Private diaries shed light on the theatrical life of the Veneto in the late fifteenth and early sixteenth centuries.

829 Guarino, Raimondo. "Cherea o le commedie in città." (Cherea, or Theatre in the City.) *BiT.* 1987; 5/6: 29-52. Lang.: Ita.

Italy: Venice. 1500-1600. Historical studies. ■Under the Terentian nickname of Cherea, Francesco de' Nobili, from Lucca, brought court drama to Venice. This study goes through the source material about this Renaissance player, from the point of view of the relationships between acting and civic celebrations in early Cinquecento Venice.

830 Hecker, Kristine. "La visione dell'attore dal Cinque al Settecento." (The Vision of the Actor from the Sixteenth to the Eighteenth Centuries.) *QT.* 1987 Aug.; 10(37): 95-122. Lang.: Ita.

Italy. France. 1500-1700. Historical studies. ■Relation between dramatic text, staging and the actor.

831 Lapini, Lia. "Il teatro futurista italiano dalla teoria alla pratica." (Italian Futurist Theatre from Theory to Practice.) *QT.* 1987 Feb.; 9(35): 101-115. Lang.: Ita.

Italy. 1909. Critical studies. ■Problems of staging relative to the theoretical and literary ideas of the futurist theatre as a challenge to current theatrical norms.

832 Lapini, Lia, ed.; Rinaldi, Tamara; Sardelli, Alessandro; Poesio, Paolo Emilio; Innamorati, Isabella; Clementi, Enrica Benini; Nicolodi, Fiamma; De Angelis, Marcello. "Vita teatrale a Firenze tra Otto e Novecento." (Theatrical Life in Florence Between the Nineteenth and the Twentieth Centuries.) *QT.* 1987 May; 9(36): 5-112. Lang.: Ita.

Italy: Florence. 1800-1900. Histories-sources. ■Collection of articles on theatrical culture in Florence through representative characters and important events of the time.

833 Lucignani, Luciano, ed. *Anna Maria Guarnieri.* Rome: A. Curcio; 1987. Illus.: Photo. Print. B&W. Lang.: Ita.

Italy. 1954-1987. Histories-sources. ■Collection of testimonials on the career and personality of actress Guarnieri, on the award of the Armando Curcio Prize.

834 Mariotti, Arnaldo. *Spettacoli di prosa da una poltrona. Cronache del teatro di prosa.* (Performances from a Stall: Theatre Reviews.) Florence: Libreria Editrice Fiorentina; 1987. 161 pp. Illus.: Photo. Print. B&W. 1. [Vol. 2.] Lang.: Ita.

Italy. 1958-1982. Reviews of performances. ■Chronological collection of theatre reviews.

835 Menichi, Angela. "Virgilio Talli fra tradizione e avanguardia. L'incontro con Rosso di San Secondo." (Virgilio Talli Between Vanguard and Tradition: The Meeting with Rosso di San Secondo.) *QT.* 1987 Feb.; 9(35): 149-161. Lang.: Ita.

Italy. 1917-1920. Histories-reconstruction. ■The collaboration of Virgilio Talli, actor and director, with playwright Pier Maria Rosso di San Secondo on occasion of the staging of *Marionette che passione! (Marionettes, What Passion!)* and *La bella addormentata (Sleeping Beauty).*

836 Napolitano, Gian Gaspare. "Il teatro sperimentale degli Indipendenti." (The Experimental Theatre of the Independents.) *TeatrC.* 1987; 7(14): 189-193. Lang.: Ita.

Italy: Rome. 1911-1932. Histories-sources. ■Anton Giulio Bragaglia and the Theatre of the Independents as told by one of the exponents of the group.

837 Poesio, Paolo Emilio. *Maurizio Scaparro. L'utopia teatrale.* (Maurizio Scaparro: Theatrical Utopia.) Venice: Marsilio; 1987. 157 pp. Index. Illus.: Photo. Print. Color. B&W. Lang.: Ita.

Italy. 1964-1987. Historical studies. ■Maurizio Scaparro's artistic journey from theatre criticism to staging to administration. His work as artistic director.

838 Romano Rochira, Giuseppina. *Pirandello capocomico e regista nelle testimonianze e nella critica.* (Pirandello as Company Manager and Director: Testimony and Criticism.) Bari: Adriatica; 1987. 127 pp. (Biblioteca di Critica e Letteratura 26.) Pref. Append. Lang.: Ita.

Italy. 1915-1936. Critical studies. ■Contemporary critical reaction to plays staged by Pirandello, as well as interviews with Marta Abba and Sergio Tofano.

839 Santarelli, Cristina; Pulcini, Franco; Salotti, Marco; Rondolino, Gianni. *Storia sociale e culturale d'Italia. Lo spettacolo.*

THEATRE IN GENERAL: —Performance/production

(Social and Cultural History of Italy: Entertainment.) Busto Arsizio: Bramante; 1987. 493 pp. Biblio. Illus.: Pntg. Photo. Print. Color. B&W. [Vol. 3.] Lang.: Ita.
Italy. Histories-general. ■History of performance in Italy: music, theatre, film. Related to Media: Film.

840 Zappulla, Sarah; Zappulla, Enzo. *Musco immagini di un attore.* (Musco: Pictures of an Actor.) Catania: G. Maimone; 1987. 435 pp. Index. Illus.: Photo. Sketches. Print. B&W. 25. Lang.: Ita.
Italy: Catania. 1904-1937. Histories-sources. ■A collection of photographs, caricatures, letters and other documentary materials about the Sicilian actor Angelo Musco.

841 Zappulla, Sarah; Zappulla, Enzo. *Angelo Musco il gesto la mimica l'arte.* (Angelo Musco: His Gesture, Miming and Art.) Palermo: Novecento; 1987. (Grandi libri.) Biblio. Illus.: Handbill. Photo. Sketches. Print. B&W. Lang.: Ita.
Italy. 1872-1937. Biographies. ■The artistic life of the Sicilian actor Angelo Musco accompanied by a wide chronology of his performances from 1914 to 1937.

842 Eddison, Robert. "An Actor's Diary." *Drama.* 1987; 3(165): 52-54. Illus.: Photo. B&W. 1. Lang.: Eng.
Japan. 1979. Histories-sources. ■Robert Eddison's diary of a Far Eastern tour.

843 Savarese, Nicola. "Cronache di Kawakami e Sada Yacco." (Chronicle of Kawakami and Sada Yacco.) *TeatroS.* 1987; 2(1): 3-65. Biblio. Lang.: Ita.
Japan. 1899-1946. Biographical studies. ■Kawakami Otojirō (a *shimpa* actor) and his wife Sadayacco (a former geisha who became an actress) were active in the best Western and Oriental theatres around the turn of the twentieth century.

844 Shichiji, Eisuke. "86nen rainichi kōen o megutte." (On Foreign Performing Arts Tours in Japan during 1986.) *Sg.* 1987 Feb.; 407: 98-103. Illus.: Photo. B&W. 5. Lang.: Jap.
Japan: Tokyo. 1986. Critical studies. ■Includes Pina Bausch, Chinese opera, performance art, several Broadway musicals.

845 Dept. of Drama & Cinema, Dongguk Univ. "Yonkuksa jalyo/dongkyung haksaeng yesuljwapyun." (Material: Tokyo Has Theatre.) *DongukDA.* 1978 Apr.; 10-11: 109-118. Lang.: Kor.
Korea. Japan: Tokyo. 1910-1945. Histories-sources. ■Korean theatre in Tokyo: documentary essay by a Korean student on theatrical activity under Japanese domination.

846 Chang, Han-Gi. *Hanguk yonkuksa.* (History of Korean Theatre.) Seoul: Dongguk Univ.; 1986. 360 pp. Lang.: Kor.
Korea. 57 B.C.-1986 A.D. Histories-specific. ■General history of Korean theatre from ancient to modern.

847 Cho, Dong-Il. *Talchumui-youksawa-wonli.* (History and Theory of Mask Theatre.) Seoul: Hongik-SA; 1987. 406 pp. Lang.: Kor.
Korea. 57 B.C.-1987 A.D. Histories-specific. ■The development of Korean mask theatre.

848 Cho, Dong-Il. "Yonkugsajeok munjaejum." (The Development of Mask Theatre.) 11-108 in *History & Theory of Mask Theatre.* Seoul: Hongik-SA; 1987. 406 pp. Lang.: Kor.
Korea. 57 B.C.-1987 A.D. Historical studies. ■The development of Korean mask theatre and audience participation.

849 Kim, Gi-Duk. "Kukjeokchukmyunaeseoui moouibunsuk." (An Analysis of Necromancy from a Theatrical Viewpoint.) *DongukDA.* 1976 Dec.; 9: 93-121. Lang.: Kor.
Korea. 57 B.C.-935 A.D. Historical studies. ■The relation of traditional ritual to theatre.

850 Kim, Jae-Kil. *Chosun yonkuksa.* (History of Theatre in Chosun Dynasty.) Seoul: Minhaksa; 1974. 181 pp. Lang.: Kor.
Korea. 1392-1910. Histories-general. ■History of theatre under Chosun dynasty.

851 Lee, Jin-Soon. "Baewoosool." (On Acting.) *DongukDA.* 1987; 18: 149-174. Lang.: Kor.

Korea. 1987. Instructional materials. ■Advice for novice actors.

852 Lee, Mun-Hwan. "Che II Hoe Seould Yeonkukche Sang Pan Ki Kong Yeon ul Poko." (Theatre Review of the 11th Seoul Theatre Festival.) *KTR.* 1987 Oct.(8): 36-43. Lang.: Kor.
Korea: Seoul. 1987. Reviews of performances. ■Reviews of plays presented at the festival.

853 Lee, Sa-Hyun. *Hanguk yonkuksa.* (History of Korean Theatre.) Seoul: Hakyonsa; 1987. 374 pp. [2d ed.] Lang.: Kor.
Korea. 57 B.C.-1987 A.D. Histories-specific. ■General study on Korean theatre from ancient to modern.

854 Lee, See-chul. "Baewoo wa Kwan gak." (Actor and Audience.) *KTR.* 1987 Aug.; 8(1): 102-110. Illus.: Plan. B&W. 1. Lang.: Kor.
Korea: Seoul. 1987. Critical studies. ■Actors should portray their characters as clearly as possible. Audiences also have a responsibility to try to understand the characters.

855 Lee, Young-Taek. "Hanguk-lieollijum-yungukui-yangtae bunsuk." (Aspects of Korean Realism in Theatre.) *DongukDA.* 1987; 18: 24-82. Lang.: Kor.
Korea. 1980-1987. Historical studies. ■Trend toward realism in Korean theatre.

856 Lee, Yurina; Park, Chung-Yeong. "Che II Hoe Seoul Yeonkukche Chamka Yeon Chul Katul." (Directors in the 11th Seoul Theatre Festival.) *KTR.* 1987 Oct.(7): 30-34. Lang.: Kor.
Korea: Seoul. 1987. Histories-sources. ■Interviews with participating directors.

857 Park, Choen Yeal. "Mimsok Yesul KyeongYeon." (The Contest of the Folk Arts.) *KTR.* 1987 Dec.(8): 48-49. Lang.: Kor.
Korea. 1986-1987. Histories-general. ■The concept of the traditional folk arts and the problem of the contest of the folk arts.

858 Park, Jin-Tae. *Hanguk kamyunkuk yongu.* (Study of Korean Mask Theatre.) Seoul: Saemoonsa; 1985. 220 pp. Lang.: Kor.
Korea. 57 B.C.-1985 A.D. Histories-specific. ■Origins and theory of Korean traditional mask theatre. Related to Dance-Drama.

859 Kerr, David. "Unmasking the Spirits—Theatre in Malawi." *TDR.* 1987 Sum; 31(2): 115-125. Biblio. Illus.: Photo. Maps. B&W. 11. Lang.: Eng.
Malawi. 1987. Historical studies. ■Progression of Malawian theatre stressing its eclecticism of performance styles.

860 Pietzsch, Ingeborg. "Das Eigene und das Fremde." (The Own and the Alien.) *TZ.* 1987; 42(2): 45-48. Illus.: Photo. B&W. 5. Lang.: Ger.
Mongolia: Ulan-Bator. 1921-1986. Historical studies. ■Impressions of art, life and theatre in the Mongolian People's Republic: traditions and new trends.

861 Pályi, András. "Távolítás és közelítés. Két holland vendégjáték." (Departing and Approaching: Two Dutch Guest Plays.) *Sz.* 1987 Feb.; 20(2): 42-45. Illus.: Photo. B&W. 3. Lang.: Hun.
Netherlands. 1986. Reviews of performances. ■*Panic in Berlin* performed by the Dutch Orkater ensemble made of the libretto *Conflict* by Kurt Schwitters, and Jozef van den Berg's two plays *Amgo and the Fool* and *The Message of the One-Eyed Magician.*

862 Rutten, André. "Veertig Jaar Nederlands Toneel XIV." (Forty Years of Dutch Theatre, Part 14.) *Toneel.* 1987 Jan.; 1: 40-42. Lang.: Dut.
Netherlands. 1970-1985. Historical studies. ■History of Dutch theatre post-World War II: political theatre movement, theatre group 'Proloog', educational theatre, moving toward portrayals of everyday life.

863 Van Nispen, Maarten. "De fhiweten coupe van hetjengd-theatre." (The Velvet Coup of Children's Theatre.) *Toneel.* 1987 Feb.; 2: 40. Lang.: Dut.
Netherlands. 1987. Historical studies. ■Growth of children's theatre, financially, artistically, in audience. Festival in Den Bosch.

THEATRE IN GENERAL: —Performance/production

864 Allen, Deborah; Barthol, Bruce. "In the Face of Fear and Struggle, Art." *AmTh.* 1987 June; 4(3): 26-29. Notes. Illus.: Photo. B&W. 4. Lang.: Eng.
Nicaragua: Managua. Uganda. 1987. Historical studies. ■An American mime troupe at the National Theatre Festival in Managua, and the cultural exchange shared by teacher Deborah Allen and the National Theatre of Uganda.

865 Beik, Janet. *Hausa Theatre in Niger: A Contemporary Oral Art.* New York, NY: Garland; 1987. 327 pp. (Critical Studies on Black Life and Culture 16.) Index. Biblio. Append. Illus.: Photo. Maps. Print. B&W. 10. Lang.: Eng.
Niger, Republic of. 1876-1982. Histories-specific. ■Traditional Hausa theatre in the Niger. The long-standing traditional form of African theatre took Western flavor in the colonial period and from this Hausa theatre was formed. Includes synopses of scenes and character lists.

866 Okagbue, Osita. "Theatre on the Street: Two Nigerian Samples." *MuK.* 1987; 33(1-2): 159-164. Lang.: Eng.
Nigeria. 1900-1987. Historical studies.

867 Feldman, Peter. "Working with Actors on Textual Images." *Theatrum.* 1987 Fall/Win; 8: 17-18, 22-24, 38-39. Lang.: Eng.
North America. 1987. Histories-sources. ■Examples of Feldman's work with actors on textual images in relation to North American theatre.

868 Lyttkens, Ulla. "Rapport från Nordkalottfestivalen." (Report from the Festival of the Arctic Area of the Scandanavian Countries and the Kola Peninsula.) *Teaterf.* 1987; 20(4): 14. Lang.: Swe.
Norway: Hammerfest. 1987. Historical studies. ■Some impressions from the northernmost amateur theatre festival and a survey of the conditions for Norwegian amateur theatre.

869 Fernandez, Doreen G. "Philippine Theatre After Martial Law." *ATJ.* 1987 Spr; 4(1): 108-114. Notes. Illus.: Photo. B&W. 2. Lang.: Eng.
Philippines. 1972-1986. Critical studies. ■Protest in Philippine theatre during and after martial law, the survival of playwrights and theatre itself.

870 "Leon Šiller—Čelovek i ego delo." (Leon Schiller: A Man and His Work.) *TeatrM.* 1987; 12: 160-169. Lang.: Rus.
Poland. 1920-1939. Biographical studies. ■Prominent and innovative director.

871 Baniewicz, Elżbieta. "26th Festival of Contemporary Polish Plays in Wrocław." (26e Festival de pièces polonaises contemporaines de Wrocław.) *TP.* 1987 Nov-Dec.(11-12): 9-15. Illus.: Photo. Print. B&W. 6. Lang.: Eng, Fre.
Poland: Wrocław. 1987. Historical studies. ■Overview of the 1987 Festival of Polish Plays. Briefly describes plays presented with an emphasis on the difference between drama and theatre.

872 Grodzicki, August. "17th Warsaw Theatre Meetings." (17es Rencontres théâtrales de Varsovie.) *TP.* 1987 Jul-Aug. (7-8): 22-29. Illus.: Photo. Print. B&W. 6. Lang.: Eng, Fre.
Poland: Warsaw. 1987. Historical studies. ■The 17th Warsaw theatre conference was an exchange of the best productions between the theatres of Poland for 1987 and previous years. Included are brief synopses of plays presented, both classical and contemporary.

873 Grodzicki, August. "The 4th International Theatre Meetings Warsaw 1986." (4es Rencontres Internationales de théâtre Varsovie 1986.) *TP.* 1987 Apr-June(4-6): 3-12. Illus.: Photo. Print. B&W. 12. Lang.: Eng, Fre.
Poland: Warsaw. 1986. Historical studies. ■A short synopsis of the 4th International Theatre Meetings, who attended and their contributions.

874 Loney, Glenn. "Polished Polish Performances: Without Benefit of Translation." *SEEDTF.* 1987 Dec.; 7(2 & 3): 54-61. Lang.: Eng.
Poland: Warsaw, Cracow. 1987. Historical studies. ■Overview of the Polish theatre scene during a two-week period, taking into account productions of American musicals, new works, classics, children's theatre, puppet theatre, performance art and a popular production of *Play It Again, Sam.*

875 Michalik, Jan; Solarska-Zachuta, Anna; Hałabuda, Stanisław; Duniec, Krystyna. *Teatr polski w latach 1890-1918.*

Zabór austriacki i pruski. (Polish Theatre Between 1890 and 1918: Austrian and Prussian Sector.) Warsaw: Państwowe Wydawnictwo Naukowe; 1987. 495 pp. (Dzieje teatru polskiego.) Pref. Index. Notes. Illus.: Photo. Dwg. Poster. Print. B&W. 100. [Summary in French.] Lang.: Pol.
Poland. Austria-Hungary. Prussia. 1890-1918. Histories-specific. ■History of Polish theatre in the parts of Poland annexed by Austria-Hungary and Prussia including all its aspects: drama, opera, operetta, cabaret. Related to Music-Drama.

876 Miklaszewski, Krzysztof. "Tadeusz Kantor: Exegi monumentum... or *The Love and Death Machine.*" (Tadeusz Kantor: Exegi monumentum... ou *La Machine de l'amour et de la mort.*) *TP.* 1987 Nov-Dec.(11-12): 3-8. Illus.: Photo. Print. B&W. 4. Lang.: Eng, Fre.
Poland: Cracow. Germany, West: Kassel. Italy: Milan. Italy: Sicily. 1987. Histories-sources. ■Interview with Polish playwright Tadeusz Kantor on the world premieres in West Germany, Poland and Italy, of his newest production, a 'cricotage' entitled *The Love and Death Machine (Maszyna miłości i śmierci).*

877 Śmigielski, Wojciech, ed. *VIII International Meeting of Open Theatre Wroclaw 28.09-11.10.1987. Presentation, Integration, Cooperation.* Wrocław: Centre of the Open Theatre; 1987. 64 pp., 56 pp. Illus.: Photo. Maps. Print. B&W. 16. Lang.: Pol, Eng, Fre.
Poland: Wrocław. 1982-1987. Histories-sources. ■Information about all avant-garde performances presented during the meetings in 1987 as well as 1982.

878 Walaszek, Joanna. "Swinarski: Życie, myśli, prace." (Swinarski: His Life, Thoughts and Works.) *DialogW.* 1987; 6 : 125-134. Notes. Lang.: Pol.
Poland. 1929-1955. Biographical studies. ■Life and career of director Konrad Swinarski. Continued in: *DialogW* 7 (1987), 141-154. 8, 103-119. 9, 100-107. 10, 120-128.

879 Švydkoj, M. "Postskriptum." (Postscript.) *TeatrM.* 1987; 4: 127-129. Lang.: Rus.
Romania: Bucharest. 1980-1987. Historical studies. ■On Teatrul C.I. Nottara of Bucharest: its history, its Soviet tours.

880 *Brat'ja Adel'gejm: Rasskazy o zanjatijah, rabote i besedach s brat'jami. Vospominanija Rafaila Adel'gejma.* (The Brothers Adel'gejm: Stories of their Occupations and Work, Conversations with the Brothers, Reminiscences of Rafail Adel'gejm.) Moscow: STD RSFSR; 1987. 293 pp. Lang.: Rus.
Russia. 1860-1938. Biographies. ■Work of actor brothers who followed the 'German School': their influence on provincial culture in pre-revolutionary Russia.

881 Kneubuhl, Victoria N. "Traditional Performance in Samoan Culture: Two Forms." *ATJ.* 1987 Fall; 4(2): 166-176. Notes. Biblio. Illus.: Dwg. B&W. 2. Lang.: Eng.
Samoa. 1884-1980. Historical studies. ■Comparative study of Samoa's practice of fofo (patient healing) and fa'dluma (satirical village comedy). Theatrical and ritual/spiritual elements.

882 Eichbaum, Julius. "Scenaria—The First Decade." *Scenaria.* 1987 May; 76: 3-5. Lang.: Eng.
South Africa, Republic of. 1977-1987. Historical studies. ■Opera, ballet, theatre and music in South Africa, developments and areas for improvement.

883 Wakashe, T. Philemon. "*Pula*: An Example of Black Protest Theatre in South Africa." *TDR.* 1986 Win; 30(4): 36-47. Notes. Biblio. Illus.: Photo. B&W. 3. Lang.: Eng.
South Africa, Republic of: Soweto. 1969-1984. Critical studies. ■Performances of Matsemela Manaka's play *Pula* and its anti-apartheid expressions.

884 Watson, Ian. "Is the Third Theatre Dead?" *TDR.* 1987 Sum; 31(2): 31-32. Lang.: Eng.
South America. UK-Wales. 1960-1987. Historical studies. ■Theatre groups existing in small countries and communities.

885 Sagarra, Josep Maria de; Fàbregas, Xavier, ed., intro. *Crítiques de teatre La Publicitat, 1922-1927.* (Theatrical

CLASSED ENTRIES

THEATRE IN GENERAL: —Performance/production

Critiques from *La Publicitat, 1922-1927*.) Barcelona: Institut del Teatre; 1987. 518 pp. (Monografies de Teatre 21.) Index. Tables. [The prologue was originally published in 'Serra d'Or', 258, 1981 March.] Lang.: Cat.

Spain-Catalonia: Barcelona. 1922-1927. Critical studies. ■Collection of theatre reviews by Sagarra, published in *La Publicitat*. Five sections: Catalan, Spanish, contemporary foreign theatres, classic and non-dramatic genres.

886 Byttner, Cecilia. "Anarki? 'Regikurs för erfarna'." (Anarchy? 'Class in Directing for Veterans'.) *Teaterf.* 1987; 20 (6): 5-7. Illus.: Photo. Lang.: Swe.

Sweden. 1987. Historical studies. ■A different course at Dalslands Folkhögskola, where everyone tried to cultivate originality more through practical work than through theories.

887 Hägglund, Kent. "Grundläggande regi." (Basic Directing.) *Teaterf.* 1987; 20(4): 13. Illus.: Photo. Lang.: Swe.

Sweden: Katrineberg. 1987. Histories-sources. ■A class for amateur directors.

888 Lundin, Immi; Josefsson, Birgitta; Waaranperä, Ingegärd. "Ton av äkthet." (A Note of Genuineness.) *NT.* 1987 ; 38: 19-34. Illus.: Photo. Lang.: Swe.

Sweden: Gothenburg. 1987. Critical studies. ■Report from a children's theatre festival.

889 Lycksell, Sofie. "Lokalteatern i Kalmar spelar för dövblinda." (The Local Theatre of Kalmar Plays for Deaf and Blind People.) *Teaterf.* 1987; 20(5): 7-8. Illus.: Photo. Lang.: Swe.

Sweden: Kalmar. 1987. Historical studies. ■A report from a performance for deaf and blind people who, thanks to slow tempo and the interpreter, found it very exciting.

890 Samuelsson, Björn. "Sökande efter an hållning." (In Search of an Attitude.) *NT.* 1987; 38: 8-9. Lang.: Swe.

Sweden. 1977-1987. Critical studies. ■The first editor of *Nya Teatertidningen* compares early and present editorial policies.

891 Schwartz, Nils. "Från kampvilligt språkrör till glättad spegel?" (From Argumentative Mouthpiece to a Glossy Mirror?)*NT.* 1987; 38: 4-7. Illus.: Photo. Lang.: Swe.

Sweden. 1977-1987. Critical studies. ■A survey of *Nya Teatertidningen*'s first decade as an organ for the fringe theatre in Sweden.

892 Apothéloz, Anne-Lise, comp. *Szene Schweiz—Scène Suisse—Scena Svizzera: Eine Dokumentation des Theaterlebens in der Schweiz.* (Scene Switzerland: A Documentation of Theatrical Activity in Switzerland.) Bonstetten: Theaterkultur-Verlag; 1987. 218 pp. (SSSS 15.) Index. Biblio. Illus.: Photo. B&W. [v. 15.] Lang.: Fre, Ger, Ita.

Switzerland. 1987-1988. Historical studies. ■The series lists all places and productions of theatre (dramatic and musical) in Switzerland. It is accompanied by a detailed bibliography listing all items of interest concerning Swiss theatrical activities. Related to Music-Drama: Musical theatre.

893 Cahn, Roger. "Klosterdorf Einsiedeln: Nach fünf Jahren wieder Welttheater." (Einsiedeln Monastery: Another World Theatre After Five Years.) *MuT.* 1987 June; 8(6): 23-24. Illus.: Photo. B&W. Lang.: Ger.

Switzerland: Einsiedeln. 1987. Critical studies. ■Since 1924 Calderón's *El gran teatro del mundo (The Great Stage of the World)* has been put on stage with amateur actors in front of the baroque cathedral at Einsiedeln. The 1987 production by Dieter Bitterli tries to present life on earth not so much as mere suffering but as chance to live an indefinite number of possibilities.

894 Jauslin, Christian, ed. *Theater der Rätoromanen.* (Theatre of the Romansh.) Schweizerische Gesellschaft für Theaterkul. Zürich: Theaterkultur-Verlag; 1987. 47 pp. (Schriften 18.) Pref. Notes. Biblio. Illus.: Photo. B&W. Lang.: Ger.

Switzerland. 1984-1987. Histories-general. ■The first comprehensive survey in German of theatrical activities in the Romansh speaking part of Switzerland.

895 Schweizer, Regula. "Theaterszene Baden: Ein Rückblick auf die letzten zwanzig Jahre." (Theatre in Baden: Looking

Back Over the Past Twenty Years.) *Badener Neujahrsblätter.* 1987; 62: 26-32. Lang.: Ger.

Switzerland: Baden. 1967-1987. Histories-specific. ■Cultural and historical survey of Baden's theatrical activities: traditional summer festival by St. Gall theatre company, history of the Claque Theatre Group, other small companies.

896 Stadler, Edmund. "Die Schweiz als Ursprungsland des neuen Freilicht- und Festspieltheaters." (Switzerland as the Homeland of the New Open-Air and Festival Theatre.) *MuK.* 1987; 33(1-2): 89-100. Lang.: Ger.

Switzerland. 1987. Historical studies.

897 Özgü, Melahat. "Festivals in der Türkei: Wesen und Lage." (Festivals in Turkey: Nature and Status.) *MuK.* 1987; 33(1-2): 115-118. Lang.: Ger.

Turkey. 1900-1987. Historical studies.

898 Anikst, A. "Larri i sér Lorens." (Larry or Sir Laurence.) *TeatZ.* 1987; 3: 28-29. Lang.: Rus.

UK-England. 1907-1987. Biographical studies. ■Career of actor Lord Laurence Olivier.

899 Ashcroft, Peggy. "Playing Shakespeare." *ShS.* 1987; 40: 11-19. Illus.: Photo. B&W. 4. Lang.: Eng.

UK-England. 1935-1964. Histories-sources. ■Conversation with actress Dame Peggy Ashcroft regarding her experiences as a Shakespearean actress.

900 Bates, Brian. *The Way of the Actor: A Path to Knowledge and Power.* Boston, MA: Shambhala; 1987. 216 pp. Index. Notes. Biblio. Lang.: Eng.

UK-England: London. USA. 1977-1987. Historical studies. ■An exploration of how actors understand human nature from the viewpoint of shamanism and other ways of self-knowledge. Includes dialogues with actors. Part I: interviews with actors. Part II: how actors obtain self-knowledge and creative knowledge.

901 Berkowitz, Gerald M. "*The Lover* and *A Slight Ache.*" *PintR.* 1987; 1: 50-51. Lang.: Eng.

UK-England: London. 1987. Reviews of performances. ■Production review of staging of *The Lover* and *A Slight Ache* at the Young Vic Theatre in 1987.

902 Cadden, Michael. "A Woman of Abundance." *AmTh.* 1987 Nov.; 4(8): 38-39. Illus.: Photo. B&W. 1. Lang.: Eng.

UK-England: London. 1847-1928. Biographical studies. ■Life and work of English actress Ellen Terry. Discusses recent biography of her life and times by Nina Auerbach.

903 Carleton, Don. "South West: Triumphant Bull." *Drama.* 1987; 3(165): 38-39. Illus.: Photo. B&W. 1. Lang.: Eng.

UK-England: Bristol. 1987. Reviews of performances. ■Theatre productions in Southwest England.

904 Davies, Andrew. *Other Theatres: The Development of Alternative and Experimental Theatre in Britain.* London: Macmillan; 1987. 249 pp. Pref. Index. Biblio. Lang.: Eng.

UK-England. 1800-1987. Histories-specific. ■Begins with theatre history of the nineteenth century and traces the earliest development of alternative theatre.

905 Dessen, Alan C. "Modern Productions and the Elizabethan Scholar." *RenD.* 1987; 18: 205-223. Lang.: Eng.

UK-England. 1977-1987. Critical studies. ■Discussion of performance metholodology and differences between play scripts as literary texts and as performance texts.

906 Fenta, Rose. "Lift Together." *Drama.* 1987; 3(165): 27-30. Tables. Illus.: Photo. B&W. 7. Lang.: Eng.

UK-England: London. 1967-1987. Histories-specific. ■History of the London International Festival of Theatre.

907 Gale, Steven H. "Observations on Two Productions of Harold Pinter's *Old Times.*" *PintR.* 1987; 1: 40-43. Lang.: Eng.

UK-England: London. USA: New York, NY, St. Louis, MO. 1971-1985. Reviews of performances. ■Two productions of Pinter's *Old Times* demonstrate different approaches to the play: one intellectual, one emotional.

THEATRE IN GENERAL: —Performance/production

908 Janaczewska, Noëlle. "'Do We Want a Piece of the Cake, or Do We Want to Bake a Whole New One?' Feminist Theatre in Britain." *Hecate.* 1987; 13(1): 106-113. Lang.: Eng.
UK-England. 1970-1987. Historical studies. ■Briefly surveys the emergence of feminist theatre groups within the alternative theatre movement, the diversity of their performing styles, and some of the theoretical issues arising out of their work.

909 Jellicoe, Ann. "Community Theatre." *Drama.* 1987; 4(166): 15-16. Illus.: Photo. B&W. 2. Lang.: Eng.
UK-England. 1987. Historical studies. ■The process involved in staging community theatre.

910 Marklund, Björn; Öhrström, Anders. "Hos Shakespeare i Stratford." (At Shakespeare in Stratford.) *Teaterf.* 1987; 20(5): 9-11. Illus.: Photo. Lang.: Swe.
UK-England: Stratford. 1987. Historical studies. ■A report from the first European Youth Theatre Encounter.

911 Martin, Mick. "South: Powerful Work." *Drama.* 1987; 3(165): 39. Illus.: Photo. B&W. 1. Lang.: Eng.
UK-England: Salisbury. 1987. Reviews of performances. ■Review of theatre in the South of England.

912 Meewezen, Judy. "North: Problems of Rep." *Drama.* 1987; 3(165): 36-37. Illus.: Photo. B&W. 1. Lang.: Eng.
UK-England: Liverpool. 1987. Reviews of performances. ■Review of repertory theatre in Northern England.

913 Pigott-Smith, Tim. "Casting the Community Play." *Drama.* 1987; 4(166): 11-12. Illus.: Photo. B&W. 1. Lang.: Eng.
UK-England: Dorchester. 1987. Historical studies. ■A two-week workshop held to cast some of the parts that were already commissioned in a community play.

914 Ratcliffe, Michael. "London Slippery Slope." *Drama.* 1987; 3(165): 31-32. Illus.: Photo. B&W. 2. Lang.: Eng.
UK-England: London. 1987. Reviews of performances. ■Review of current theatre productions.

915 Russell, Barry. "Midlands: Evil in the Eighties." *Drama.* 1987; 3(165): 37. Illus.: Photo. B&W. 1. Lang.: Eng.
UK-England. 1987. Reviews of performances. ■Review of productions in the Midlands region.

916 Senelik, Laurence. "Melodramatic Gesture in Carte-de-Visite Photographs." *ThM.* 1987; 18(2): 5-13. Notes. Illus.: Photo. B&W. 22. Lang.: Eng.
UK-England. France. USA. 1850-1920. Critical studies. ■Carte-de-visites as the preservation of 19th-century acting styles: records of gestural styles organized under Delsartian headings: despondency, defiance, fear and revulsion, grotesques and naturalism.

917 Shrimpton, Nicholas. "Shakespeare Performances in London, Manchester, and Stratford-upon-Avon 1985-1986." *ShS.* 1987; 40 : 169-183. Illus.: Photo. B&W. 8. Lang.: Eng.
UK-England: London, Manchester, Stratford. 1985-1986. Critical studies. ■Analysis and review of the Shakespearean productions of the 1985-1986 season.

918 Wandor, Michelene. *Carry On, Understudies: Theatre and Sexual Politics.* New York, NY: Routledge & Kegan Paul; 1986. 210 pp. Pref. Notes. Biblio. Index. Append. Lang.: Eng.
UK-England. USA. 1969-1985. Historical studies. ■Alternative theatre movement gave new life to the social division of labor in theatre by developing collaborative work methods, developing new audiences and representing experiences and interests of oppressed and exploited people.

919 Weisfeld, Zelma H. "The British Theatre Museum." *TD&T.* 1987; 23(3): 28-32. Illus.: Photo. Sketches. B&W. 5. Lang.: Eng.
UK-England: London. 1987. Historical studies. ■Brief history and discussion of the new museum with details of exhibits, exhibition spaces, collection contents and memorabilia covering all areas of the theatre.

920 Worth, Katherine. "Theatre Museum." *TN.* 1987; 41(3): 99-101. Lang.: Eng.

UK-England: London. 1987. Critical studies. ■Description of scope and content of new museum in Covent Garden.

921 Brennan, Mary. "Scotland: Nancy Knows Box." *Drama.* 1987; 3(165): 35-36. Illus.: Photo. B&W. 2. Lang.: Eng.
UK-Scotland: Edinburgh. 1987. Reviews of performances. ■Review of Scottish theatre for the first 6 months of 1987.

922 Bassnett, Susan. "The Magdalena Experiment." *TDR.* 1987 Win; 31(4): 10-17. Illus.: Photo. Print. B&W. 7. Lang.: Eng.
UK-Wales: Cardiff. 1986-1987. Historical studies. ■'The Magdalena Experiment' of 1986, an experimental women's theatre workshop.

923 Nevolov, V.V. *Teatral'nyj process na Ukraine i kritika 70-ch godov: Avtoref. dis. kand. iskusstvovedenija.* (The Theatrical Process in the Ukraine, and Criticism of the Seventies: Abstract of a Dissertation by a Candidate in Art Criticism.) Moscow: GITIS; 1987. 22 pp. Lang.: Rus.
Ukraine. 1970-1979. Critical studies.

924 Staniševskij, Ju. *Teatr, roždennyj revoljuciej.* (Theatre, Born of Revolution.) Kiev: Mistectvo; 1987. 243 pp. Lang.: Ukr.
Ukraine. 1917-1987. Historical studies. ■Sketches of the history of Ukrainian Soviet theatrical culture.

925 "Council Adopts Definition of Non-Traditional Casting." *EN.* 1987 Aug.; 72(8): 1. Lang.: Eng.
USA: New York, NY. 1987. Historical studies. ■Discusses Equity Council's adoption of a definition for nontraditional casting which was recommended by the Ethnic Minorities Committee.

926 "Member Hails Exchange Program, Saying It's 'A Dream Come True'." *EN.* 1987 Apr.; 72(4): 1, 8. Lang.: Eng.
USA: New York, NY. UK-England: London. 1987. Histories-sources. ■Equity member Stephen Hanan praises and discusses the Equity exchange with British Equity in his role of Thenadier in *Les Misérables.*

927 "Couple Plays *I Do! I Do!* More than 5,500 Times." *EN.* 1986 Aug.; 71(8): 2. Illus.: Photo. 2. Lang.: Eng.
USA: Minneapolis, MN. 1971-1986. Historical studies. ■*I Do! I Do!* starring David Anders and Susan Groppinger opened in 1971 for a six week run and is now in its 16th year-giving it the national record as the longest running play in the U.S..

928 "Equity Applauds Non-Traditional Casting at the Eureka Theatre in San Francisco." *EN.* 1986 Sep.; 71(9): 4. Lang.: Eng.
USA: San Francisco, CA. 1986. Historical studies. ■Eureka Theatre follows Ethnic Minorities Committee recommendations for nontraditional casting in *Višnëvyj sad (The Cherry Orchard).*

929 "1987-1988 Season Listings." *TT.* 1987 Nov.; 7(1): 8-10. Illus.: Photo. Print. B&W. 6. Lang.: Eng.
USA: New York, NY. 1987. Histories-specific. ■Listing of the projected 1987-1988 theatre season in New York City for 69 theatres (excluding Broadway).

930 Berson, Misha. "Stages, A War Within." *AmTh.* 1987 May; 4(2): 4-5. Notes. Illus.: Photo. B&W. 2. Lang.: Eng.
USA: San Francisco, CA. 1987. Critical studies. ■Collaboration between Joseph Chaikin and Travelling Jewish Theatre on *A War Within.* Chaikin's personal battle with heart surgery and a stroke, and how it affected the rehearsal process and staging of the play.

931 Black, Lendley C. *Mikhail Chekhov as Actor, Director, and Teacher.* Ann Arbor, MI: UMI Research P; 1987. 116 pp. (Theater and Dramatic Studies, No. 43.) Index. Notes. Pref. Biblio. Lang.: Eng.
USA. USSR. 1891-1955. Historical studies. ■Actor, teacher and director Michajl Čechov's career from early beginnings in Russia to his career in the U.S. Includes detailed analysis of his teaching method.

932 Breslauer, Jan. "Man with a Press Camera." *ThM.* 1987; 18(2): 34-36. Lang.: Eng.
USA. 1987. Critical studies. ■Role of photograph in the process of mounting a production. Absence of artistic vision: photography not an integrated part of the production.

933 Butrova, T.V. *Social'naja i chudožestvennaja priroda 'Teatra protesta' USA (60-70-e gody): Avtoref. dis. kand. iskusstvovedenija.* (Social and Artistic Nature of the 'Theatre of Protest' in the United States in the Sixties and

THEATRE IN GENERAL: —Performance/production

Seventies: Abstract of a Dissertation by a Candidate in Art Criticism.) Moscow: VNII iskusstvoznanija; 1987. 24 pp. Lang.: Rus.
USA. 1960-1979. Historical studies.

934 Cooper, Roberta Krenska. *The American Shakespeare Theatre, Stratford, 1955-1985.* Stratford, CT: Folger/Assoc. Univ. Presses; 1987. 353 pp. Notes. Index. Biblio. Append. Lang.: Eng.
USA: Stratford, CT. 1955-1985. Historical studies. ■Organizational and production history of the American Shakespeare Festival.

935 Curtin, Kaier. *'We Can Always Call Them Bulgarians': The Emergence of Lesbians and Gay Men on the American Stage.* Boston, MA: Alyson; 1987. 342 pp. Index. Notes. Illus.: Photo. Print. B&W. 17. Lang.: Eng.
USA. 1896-1987. Historical studies. ■Gay and lesbian playwrights and actors. Homosexual relationships in drama. Includes criticism of performances.

936 Davis, Clinton Turner; Newman, Harry. "Statement of Need for a Nontraditional Casting Symposium." *EN.* 1986 Oct.; 71(10) : 1, 4. Lang.: Eng.
USA: New York, NY. 1986. Historical studies. ■Nontraditional casting issues: do not work because of race, many roles are stereotypes, casting practices for LORT theatres.

937 Filichia, Peter. "The Late, Lamented Out-of-Town Try-outs." *TheaterW.* 1987 Nov 9; 1(13): 16-19. Illus.: Photo. B&W. 6. Lang.: Eng.
USA: New York, NY. 1965-1987. Historical studies. ■The end of the out-of-town tryout system for plays slated for Broadway openings: financial and logistical reasons, impact on ability of creative teams to make changes before opening.

938 Gagnon, Pauline D. "The State of the Archives." *TT.* 1987 Nov.; 7(1): 8-9. Lang.: Eng.
USA: New York, NY. 1987. Critical studies. ■Maintaining theatre archives and designating a coordinator.

939 Garnett, Gale. "The Day Ethnic Minorities Showed Up." *EN.* 1986 Mar.; 71(3): 7. Lang.: Eng.
USA. 1986. Historical studies. ■Auditions for minorities only as celebration of Black History Month. Actors were permitted to audition with any material they desired.

940 Gates, Tom. "*La Cage aux Folles* Four Years Later. And They Said It Couldn't Be Done." *TheaterW.* 1987 Aug 31; 3: 7-9. Illus.: Photo. 7. Lang.: Eng.
USA: New York, NY. 1983-1987. Critical studies. ■Allan Carr's efforts in transforming *La Cage aux Folles* from a hit movie into an old-fashioned Broadway musical blockbuster written by Harvey Fierstein and Jerry Herman.

941 Gates, Tom. "*A Chorus Line*: 5000 Singular Sensations." *TheaterW.* 1987 Aug 24; 2: 8-13. Illus.: Photo. 7. Lang.: Eng.
USA: New York, NY. 1975-1987. Critical studies. ■Brief history of *A Chorus Line* from its inception to its gala 5000th performance. Description of conflict between author James Kirkwood and producer Joseph Papp.

942 Goodstein, Gerry. "Past, Present, Future Photography: An Essay and Photo Portfolio." *ThM.* 1987; 18(2): 22-33. Illus.: Photo. B&W. 8. Lang.: Eng.
USA. Histories-sources. ■Essay by an actor who is primarily a theatre photographer. His relationship as a performer to the representation of the photograph. The art of the photo call.

943 Hannis, Robert A. "African Retentions in American Vocal and Choral Music." *WJBS.* 1987; 9(3): 175-181. Lang.: Eng.
USA. 1600-1987. Historical studies. ■The influence of the music of Africa on Americans, especially African-Americans. Specifically mentions ragtime, spirituals, blues, gospel and jazz.

944 Hill, Holly. *Playing Joan: Actresses on the Challenge of Shaw's Saint Joan.* New York, NY: Theatre Communications Group; 1987. 253 pp. Illus.: Photo. Print. B&W. Lang.: Eng.

USA. Canada. UK-England. 1987. Histories-sources. ■Actresses discuss playing the role of Joan in Shaw's play *Saint Joan.*

945 Jang, Kyung-wook. "'Living Theatre' ui jakpum *Paradise Now* ae natanan kwankaekchamyoui yeelonkwa siljae." (The Theory and Practice of Audience Participation in *Paradise Now*: Living Theatre's Collective Creation.) *DongukDA.* 1987; 18: 83-148. Lang.: Kor.
USA: New York, NY. 1968. Critical studies. ■Living Theatre's collective piece *Paradise Now*: theory and practice of audience participation.

946 Kanellos, Nicolás. *Mexican American Theatre: Legacy and Reality.* Houston, TX: Arte Publico P; 1987. 126 pp. Lang.: Eng.
USA. Mexico. 1850-1987. Historical studies. ■Essays documenting Mexican-American theatre from the touring companies of the mid-nineteenth century up to today's Chicano theatre. Includes Los Angeles playwriting in the 1920s, the Mexican American Circus/tent show, folklore and popular culture in Chicano theatre and the work of Luis Valdez.

947 Katz, Leon. "In Memory—Charles Ludlam." *TDR.* 1987 Win; 31(4): 8-9. Illus.: Photo. B&W. 1. Lang.: Eng.
USA. 1973-1987. Biographical studies. ■Eulogy of actor Charles Ludlam discussing highlights of his career as a comic actor.

948 Kleb, William. "The San Francisco New Vaudeville Festival: Feats of Idiosyncracy." *ThM.* 1987; 18(3): 13-20. Illus.: Photo. B&W. 12. Lang.: Eng.
USA: San Francisco, CA. 1987. Critical studies. ■Description/analysis of the many performers and groups that appeared, assessment of the new vaudeville movement, connections to the Bay area. Grp/movt: New Vaudeville.

949 Kramer, Richard E. "Theatre of Nations—Baltimore 1986." *TDR.* 1987 Spr; 31(1): 102-116. Notes. Biblio. Illus.: Photo. Print. B&W. 11. Lang.: Eng.
USA: Baltimore, MD. 1981-1986. Historical studies. ■Evaluation of the Theatre of Nations which provided an opportunity for various countries to view each other's work.

950 Kueppers, Brigitte. "Interview with Kathryn Lynch, Part One: The Century Library." *PasShow.* 1986 Win; 10(1): 7-9. Illus.: Photo. B&W. 3. Lang.: Eng.
USA. 1945-1986. Histories-sources. ■Part one of interview with Kathryn Lynch, manager of Shubert's Century Library. Continued in *PasShow* 10:2 (1986 Sum), 8-9.

951 Leonard, William Torbert. *Once Was Enough.* Metuchen, NJ: Scarecrow P; 1986. 282 pp. Index. Lang.: Eng.
USA: New York, NY. 1923-1983. Historical studies. ■Index of Broadway productions which ran for one night only. Includes dates, theatres, casts, directors, producers and production staff, play synopses, excerpts from New York reviews, brief biographies of some actors associated with shows.

952 Leverett, James. "Charles Ludlam: 1943-1987." *AmTh.* 1987 July/Aug.; 4(4): 44. Illus.: Photo. B&W. 1. Lang.: Eng.
USA: New York, NY. 1967-1987. Biographical studies. ■Life and works of playwright, director, designer Charles Ludlam who died after a short bout with AIDS.

953 Levett, Karl. "New York: Imported and Domestic." *Drama.* 1987; 3(165): 40-41. Illus.: Photo. B&W. 1. Lang.: Eng.
USA: New York, NY. 1987. Reviews of performances. ■Review of several productions in New York.

954 London, Todd. "Profile—Andre Ernotte." *TT.* 1987 Apr.; 6(3): 19. Illus.: Photo. B&W. 1. Lang.: Eng.
USA: New York, NY. 1987. Histories-sources. ■Andre Ernotte's career as theatre and film director, producer and author.

955 London, Todd. "Theatre in the Year 2000." *TT.* 1987 Jan/Feb.; 6(2): 4-6. Pref. Lang.: Eng.
USA: New York, NY. 1970-1987. Historical studies. ■Ten essays on where theatre will be in the year 2000.

956 MacLean, David. "In and Out of the World of Dreams: Charles Ludlam Remembered." *Theatrum.* 1987 Fall/Win; 8: 25-29. Illus.: Photo. B&W. 2. Lang.: Eng.

THEATRE IN GENERAL: —Performance/production

USA: New York, NY. 1964-1987. Biographical studies. ■Eulogizes the life and work of Charles Ludlam. Discusses Ludlam's Ridiculous Theatre Company and its approach to comedy.

957 Martin, Carol. "Dance Marathons 'For No Good Reason'." *TDR.* 1987 Spr; 31(1): 48-63. Notes. Biblio. Illus.: Photo. Print. B&W. 11. Lang.: Eng.
USA. 1920-1987. Histories-specific. ■History of dance marathons from the 1920s and perceptions of them in retrospect.

958 Marx, Robert. "When the Center Does Not Hold—Regional Theatre, Decentralization, and Community." *PerAJ.* 1985 May-Sep.; 9(2-3): 99-105. Lang.: Eng.
USA. 1960-1980. Critical studies. ■Decentralization of theatre in America through the nationwide establishment of regional theatres.

959 McAnuff, Des. "The Reproduced Actor." *AmTh.* 1987 Oct.; 4(7): 20-21, 86-90. Illus.: Photo. B&W. 12. Lang.: Eng.
USA: Los Angeles, CA. 1987. Critical studies. ■Analysis of the differences in influence and impact of the electronic media as opposed to the live theatre experience. Content and concepts of each art form and current leaders. Related to Media.

960 McGaw, Charles; Clark, Larry D. *Acting is Believing: A Basic Method.* New York, NY: Holt, Rinehart & Winston; 1987. 262 pp. Pref. Index. Biblio. Append. Illus.: Photo. Diagram. Print. B&W. 50. [5th ed.] Lang.: Eng.
USA. 1987. Instructional materials. ■Acting teacher's text on acting. Functions as a beginning text for actors.

961 Morris, Steven. "Los Angeles." *Drama.* 1987; 3(165): 41-42. Illus.: Photo. B&W. 2. Lang.: Eng.
USA: Los Angeles, CA. 1987. Reviews of performances. ■Los Angeles theatre performances are reviewed.

962 Moscati, Italo. *Ridolini il re della risata.* (Larry Semon, the King of Laughs.) Genoa: Lo Vecchio; 1987. 143 pp. Notes. Biblio. Filmography. Print. B&W. Lang.: Ita.
USA. 1889-1928. Biographies. ■Amply illustrated biography of comedian Larry Semon.

963 Myers, Larry. "Bouncing Back: Ron Link Speaks Out." *TheaterW.* 1987 Nov 9; 1(13): 10-14. Illus.: Photo. B&W. 7. Lang.: Eng.
USA: New York, NY. 1987. Histories-sources. ■Interview with Ron Link, director of *Bouncers*: the production, his career, directorial methods, collaboration with playwrights.

964 Myers, Larry. "Lucille Lortel: The Queen of Off Broadway." *TheaterW.* 1987 7-13 Sep.(4): 10-12. Illus.: Photo. Dwg. B&W. 2. Lang.: Eng.
USA: Waterford, CT. 1987. Histories-sources. ■Lucille Lortel's career as an Off Broadway producer is discussed.

965 O'Brien, Linda P. "Lincoln Center Library: The Billy Rose Theatre Collection." *TheaterW.* 1987 31 Aug.-6 Sep.; 1(3): 28-31. Illus.: Photo. B&W. 5. Lang.: Eng.
USA: New York, NY. 1987. ■Resources of the Billy Rose Collection at Lincoln Center Performing Arts Library.

966 Paran, Janice. "LATC Festival Emphasizes Diversity." *AmTh.* 1987 May; 4(2): 41. Notes. Illus.: Photo. B&W. 1. Lang.: Eng.
USA: Los Angeles, CA. 1987. Historical studies. ■The Los Angeles Theatre Center Festival of 1987: plays produced, funding sources, audience response.

967 Rabkin, Gerald. "The Academy of Fashion." *PerAJ.* 1985 Spr; 9(25): 47-53. Illus.: Photo. Print. B&W. 4. Lang.: Eng.
USA: New York, NY. 1984. Historical studies. ■The 1984 Next Wave Season at BAM, whether the work presented was truly experimental, or in the mainstream of contemporary art.

968 Salinas, Mike. "Come to the Great White Way, Old Chum: *Cabaret* Returns to Broadway." *TheaterW.* 1987 Aug 24; 2: 14-19. Illus.: Photo. 6. Lang.: Eng.
USA: New York, NY. Germany. 1966-1987. Critical studies. ■The revived and rewritten *Cabaret* is discussed in terms of the four major actresses that played and will play the role of Sally Bowles: Jill Hayworth, Liza Minelli, Allison Reed and Helen Schneider.

969 Santiago, Chiori. "A Feast for the Eyes." *AmTh.* 1987 May; 4(2): 20-26. Notes. Illus.: Photo. B&W. 11. Lang.: Eng.
USA. 1987. Critical studies. ■West Coast artists explore new ways of interpreting scripts using audiovisual effects.

970 Schaeffer, Martin. "A Feeling for Ritual: A Conversation with Director A. J. Antoon." *TheaterW.* 1987 Aug 17; 1: 29-30. Illus.: Photo. 2. Lang.: Eng.
USA: New York, NY. 1987. Histories-sources. ■A.J. Antoon discusses his approach to the directing of *Sherlock's Last Case*, the use of live music to underscore the play and set its mood.

971 Schechter, Joel. "From Theatre to Paratheatre: An Introduction." *ThM.* 1987; 19(1): 4. Lang.: Eng.
USA. 1987. Critical studies. ■Introduction to a special issue on paratheatre, the translation of traditional theatre arts to popular and new locations. The illusions and representations that are essentially theatrical but exist outside the boundaries of traditional performance spaces.

972 Schechter, Joel. "Theatre and Photography: An Introduction." *ThM.* 1987; 18(2): 4. Illus.: Photo. B&W. 1. Lang.: Eng.
USA. 1987. Critical studies. ■Introduction to special issue about the relationship of theatre and photography. Art of the photograph in connection to rehearsal and performance. Staging images for media and politics. Picture frame as replacement for proscenium frame.

973 Schechter, Joel. "Turning Green: Confessions of an Actor Politician." *ThM.* 1987; 18(3): 54-62. Illus.: Photo. Sketches. B&W. 5. Lang.: Eng.
USA: New Haven, CT. 1983-1987. Historical studies. ■The formation of a Green Party that mixes political action and protest with experimental theatre. Improvisations and performance. Politics as performed satire. Accounts of specific issues around which the party/group is organized.

974 Shewey, Don. "The Prime of Robert Brustein." *AmTh.* 1987 May; 4(2): 12-18. Notes. Illus.: Photo. B&W. 5. Lang.: Eng.
USA: Cambridge, MA. 1987. Histories-sources. ■Interview with director Robert Brustein: his views on acting, American Repertory Theatre and his functions in the theatre.

975 Shewey, Don. "Getting Acquainted with Mr. Wright." *AmTh.* 1987 Nov.; 4(8): 22-28. Illus.: Photo. B&W. 7. Lang.: Eng.
USA. 1972-1987. Biographical studies. ■The directing career of Garland Wright from his early work at the American Shakespeare Festival to his Off Broadway plays. His tenure at the Guthrie as artistic director.

976 Siegel, Fern. "Letting Audiences in On the Process: A Profile of Mary Robinson." *TheaterW.* 1987 7-13 Dec.; 1(17): 18-19 . Illus.: Photo. B&W. 2. Lang.: Eng.
USA. 1976-1987. Biographical studies. ■Career of director Mary Robinson. Focus on her regional theatre experience and her belief in its significance.

977 Steele, Mike. "Jeune Lune Rising." *AmTh.* 1987 Apr.; 4(1): 29-31. Illus.: Photo. Print. B&W. 2. Lang.: Eng.
USA: Minneapolis, MN. France: Paris. 1980-1987. Critical studies. ■Théâtre de la Jeune Lune, its Parisian origins, *commedia dell'arte* influence, and unique interpretations of Shakespeare and Molière. Related to Mixed Entertainment: *Commedia dell'arte.*

978 Sumner, Mark R. "Outdoor Drama Pact Meets Special Problems." *EN.* 1985 May; 70(5): 4. Illus.: Photo. B&W. 4. Lang.: Eng.
USA. 1985. Critical studies. ■Open-air theatre and the Foundation for Extension and Development of the American Professional Theatre (FEDAPT).

979 Towsen, John. "With Your Brains and My Body: The Future Imperfect of Physical Theatre." *MimeJ.* 1987/88: 15-20. Lang.: Eng.
USA. 1987. Critical studies. ■Threat of extinction of live intimate performances: future performing artists need to broaden horizons.

980 Warren, Steve. "Exploring the Contradictions: A Profile of Tim Curry." *TheaterW.* 1987 Dec 14-20; 1(18): 16-18. Illus.: Photo. 2. Lang.: Eng.

THEATRE IN GENERAL: —Performance/production

USA. UK-England. 1987. Biographical studies. ■A sketch of Tim Curry's performance history, comparison to *The Rocky Horror Show.*

981 Weiner, Sally Dixon. "Black Eve and Oriental Adam? Yes, At Non-Traditional Casting Confab." *DGQ.* 1987; 23(4): 35-40. Illus.: Sketches. 1. Lang.: Eng.

USA. 1987. Histories-sources. ■Discussion of Actor's Equity symposium. Emphasis on ethnic minorities, not women or the disabled. Discussed different approaches based on specific productions.

982 *Teatral'nyj kalendar' 1988.* (Theatrical Calendar 1988.) Leningrad: Iskusstvo; 1987. 192 pp. Lang.: Rus.

USSR. 1988. Histories-sources.

983 "Nepredskazuemoe prostranstvo 86/87." (Unforetold Space 86/87.) *TeatrM.* 1987; 12: 63-70. Lang.: Rus.

USSR: Leningrad. 1986-1987. Histories-sources. ■Round-table discussion of Leningrad critics on the season.

984 "'Nutri' i 'snaruzi'." ('From Inside' and 'From Outside'.) *TeatZ.* 1987; 11: 4-6. Lang.: Rus.

USSR: Moscow. 1986-1987. Critical studies. ■Review of Moscow theatre season.

985 "Pamjat'." (Memory.) *TeatrM.* 1987; 5: 159-161. Lang.: Rus.

USSR. 1972-1987. Histories-sources. ■Poems by actor Vladimir Vysockij, a 1972 interview, notes on his work.

986 "My sozdaem geroičeskij teatr." (We Will Create an Heroic Theatre.) *TeatrM.* 1987; 8: 52-66. Lang.: Rus.

USSR. 1886-1937. Histories-sources. ■Collections of articles by leading theatre figures on the one hundredth anniversary of the birth of director Aleksand'r (Sandro) Achmeteli.

987 "Molodaja press-studija na Bol'šoj Nikitskoj." (Young Press-Studio on the Bol'šaja Nikitskaja.) *TeatrM.* 1987; 9: 115-139.

USSR: Moscow. 1980-1987. ■Articles on creative quests of young theatre people in the 1980s, including discussion of various Moscow studio theatres.

988 "Stanislavskij repetiruet *Kaina.*" (Stanislavskij Rehearses *Cain.*) *TeatrM.* 1987; 11: 37-53. Lang.: Rus.

USSR. 1920. Histories-sources. ■From the director's lectures and notes, with commentary by the editor.

989 "Vtoroe dychanie." (Second Breath.) *TeatZ.* 1987; 9: 4-7. Lang.: Rus.

USSR: Moscow. 1980-1987. Histories-sources. ■Round-table discussion of Soviet directors from the early 1980s V. Fokin, M. Levitin, Je. Lazarev, M. Rozovskij, G. Tovstonogov, B. Morozov.

990 "Vybiraju Šekspira." (I Choose Shakespeare.) *TeatZ.* 1987; 10: 8-9. Lang.: Rus.

USSR: Moscow. 1926-1987. Biographical studies. ■Portrait of actor Eugenij Leonov, Moscow Komsomol Theatre.

991 "Teatry dlja detej: problemy i perspektivy." (Theatres for Children: Problems and Prospects.) *TeatZ.* 1987; 10: 18-19. Lang.: Rus.

USSR. 1987. Histories-sources. ■Exchange of opinions by Soviet directors of children's theatres.

992 "Portrat teatra." (Portrait of the Theatre.) *TeatZ.* 1987; 12: 3-19. Lang.: Rus.

USSR: Moscow. 1980-1987. Historical studies. ■Moscow Children's Theatre.

993 "Kak vy sebja čuvstvuete v uslovijah glasnosti?" (How Do You Feel Under the Conditions of Glasnost?) *TeatZ.* 1987; 14 : 16-18. Lang.: Rus.

USSR: Moscow. 1987. Histories-sources. ■Roundtable of Moscow actors (V. Lanaroj, V. Solomin, G. Burkov, M. Zudina, V. Ledogorov) on contemporary theatrical process.

994 "Sprint v Ermitaže." (Sprint in the Hermitage.) *TeatZ.* 1987; 24: 4-21. Lang.: Rus.

USSR: Moscow. 1980-1987. Historical studies. ■Performances, dramaturgy, directing and acting at Theatre of Miniatures under Michajl Levitin.

995 "'Bol' smešnoj ne byvaet...' Novye štrichi k portretu Sergeja Jurskogo." ('Pain Is Not Funny': New Strokes for a Portrait of Sergej Jurskij.) *LO.* 1987; 8: 83-88. Lang.: Rus.

USSR: Moscow. 1970-1980. Biographical studies. ■Work of actor, director of Mossovet Theatre.

996 "Sud'by teatral'nych professij: akter." (The Fortunes of Theatrical Professions: The Actor.) *TeatrM.* 1987; 11: 77-96. Lang.: Eng.

USSR. 1987. Histories-sources. ■Actors discuss their profession: N. Annenkov, Je. Lebeder, R. Pljatt, Je. Vasiljěva, O. Tabakov, I. Kostolevskij, T. Dogileva, S. Jurskij.

997 Achmedžanova, T. "Perestrojku načat' s aktera." (Begin Perestrojka With the Actor.) *TeatrM.* 1987; 12: 145-146. Lang.: Rus.

USSR. 1987. Critical studies. ■Problems of raising standards in the professional actor's craft.

998 Ajchenval'd, Ju. A. *Aleksandr Ivanovič Sumbatov Južin.* Moscow: Iskusstvo; 1987. 303 pp. (Žizn' v iskusstve.) Lang.: Rus.

USSR: Moscow. 1857-1927. ■Life of actor and dramatist of the Malyj Theatre, A.I. Južin (real name Sumbatov).

999 Akimova, B.; Terent'eva, O. "V. Vysockij: Épizody tvorčeskoj sud'by." (V. Vysockij: Episodes of His Creative Fortune.) *StudM.* 1987; 10: 40-46. Lang.: Rus.

USSR: Moscow. 1938-1980. Biographical studies. ■Career of poet and actor of the Taganka Theatre.

1000 Bagdasarjan, N., ed. *Babken Nersisjan.* Erevan: ATO; 1987. 233 pp. Lang.: Rus.

USSR. 1917-1987. Biographical studies. ■Collection of articles on Soviet Armenian folk artist, Babken Nersisjan.

1001 Balašova, N. "Tabakov, 'Echo' i drugie." (Tabakov, 'Echo' and Others.) *Sobesednik.* 1987; 3: 55-59. Lang.: Rus.

USSR. 1980-1987. Historical studies. ■On the creation of the experimental theatre group 'Echo'.

1002 Bermont, A. "Artističeskie stranstvija." (Artistic Wanderings.) *TeatZ.* 1987; 23: 23-25. Lang.: Rus.

USSR: Moscow. 1980-1987. Biographical studies. ■Portrait of actor Jevgenij Gerčakov of the Theatre of Miniatures.

1003 Bondarenko, V. "Neuspokoennost'." (Disquiet.) *TeatZ.* 1987; 22: 10-18. Lang.: Rus.

USSR: Yakutsk. 1980-1987. Biographical studies. ■Work of Andrej Borisov, principal director of Jakutskij Drama Theatre.

1004 Burjakov, V. "Byl teatr..." (There Was a Theatre.) *TeatrM.* 1987; 3: 110-118. Lang.: Rus.

USSR: Moscow. 1960-1980. Critical studies. ■History of the student theatre at Moscow State University and the problems of its current development.

1005 Caune, C. *Lidija Frejmane: Bibliografičeskij ukazatel'.* (Lidija Frejmane: Bibliographic Index.) Riga: Gos. baka LatvSSR im. Bilisa Lacisa; 1987. 108 pp. Lang.: Rus.

USSR. 1987. Bibliographical studies. ■Actors of Soviet Latvia, folk artists of the Soviet Union.

1006 Dadamjan, G. "Paradoksy teatral'nogo myšlenija." (Paradoxes of Theatrical Thinking.) *TeatrM.* 1987; 2: 76-82. Lang.: Rus.

USSR. 1986-1988. Critical studies. ■Noted sociologist of theatre on socioeconomic, creative and ethical tasks of theatre and the essence of theatrical experiment.

1007 Danilova, G. "Prevratnosti ego sud'by." (The Vicissitudes of Its Fortune.) *TeatZ.* 1987; 14: 12-13. Lang.: Rus.

USSR: Kazan. 1917-1987. Historical studies. ■History and current situation of one of Russia's oldest theatres: Kazan Bol'šoj Drama Theatre.

1008 Demidova, A. "On žil tak—i pisal tak..." (He Lived Thus and Wrote Thus.) *LO.* 1987; 1: 93-96. Lang.: Rus.

USSR: Moscow. 1938-1980. Histories-sources. ■Actress's recollections of actor Vladimir Vysockij.

1009 Devine, Michael. "Vakhtangov Leaves Russia." *Theatrum.* 1987 Sum; 7: 25-30. 1. Lang.: Eng.

THEATRE IN GENERAL: —Performance/production

USSR. Canada. 1922-1987. Critical studies. ∎Discusses the explorations of acting styles of Jévgenij Vachtangov and their application to Canadian performers.

1010 Dmitriev, Ju. "Čto takoe iskusstvo Malogo teatra?" (What Is the Art of the Malyj Theatre?)*TeatrM.* 1987; 5: 123-128. Lang.: Rus.

USSR: Moscow. 1987. Historical studies. ∎The traditions and contemporary art of actors of the Malyj Theatre.

1011 Dybovskij, V. "Teatr dlja ljudej." (A Theatre for the People.) *TeatrM.* 1987; 6: 58-63. Lang.: Rus.

USSR. 1986-1988. Critical studies. ∎Problems of theatrical experimentation.

1012 Dzekun, A. "Čto ždut ot nas?" (What is Expected of Us?)*TeatZ.* 1987; 7: 5. Lang.: Rus.

USSR. 1987. Critical studies. ∎Current prospects for the development of Soviet theatrical art.

1013 Dzene, L. *Aktër protiv svoej voli: Dokument. rasskaz ob Je. Pavule.* (An Actor Against His Will: A Documentary Tale About Je. Pavule.) Riga: Liesma; 1987. 199 pp. Lang.: Lat.

USSR. 1929-1987. Biographical studies. ∎Latvian actor Je. Pavule.

1014 Fedorova, V. "Stajer." (The Stager.) *TeatZ.* 1987; 20: 16-19. Lang.: Rus.

USSR: Moscow. 1987. Biographical studies. ∎The work of Sergej Jašin, principal director of Gogol Theatre.

1015 Fokin, V. "Uroven' pravdy." (A Standard of Truth.) *TeatZ.* 1987; 7: 4. Lang.: Rus.

USSR. 1986-1988. Critical studies. ∎Creativity in the theatrical experiment.

1016 Gachramanov, A. *Nachičevanskij teatr. Puti i problemy razvitija: Avtoref. dis. kand. iskusstvovedenija.* (Nachičevan Theatre—Paths and Problems of Development: Abstract of a Dissertation by a Candidate in Art Criticism.) Taškent: Un-t iskusstvoznanija; 1987. 20 pp. Lang.: Rus.

USSR. 1900-1987. Historical studies.

1017 Gaevskij, V. "Obraz teatra." (The Image of the Theatre.) *TeatrM.* 1987; 10: 120-128. Lang.: Rus.

USSR: Moscow. 1960-1987. Critical studies. ∎Performances of Čechov plays directed by Oleg Jéfremov.

1018 Grueva, E.; Cimbler, A. "Razomknut' krug." (To Break the Circle.) *TeatZ.* 1987; 6: 28-29. Lang.: Rus.

USSR: Moscow. 1987. Critical studies. ∎Analysis of the successes and failures of the Moscow Lenin Comsomol's experimental group 'Debut'.

1019 Gul'čenko, V. "Pravdoljuby." (For the Sake of Truth.) *TeatrM.* 1987; 2: 52-75. Lang.: Rus.

USSR: Moscow. 1986-1987. Critical studies. ∎'Perestrojka' in the theatre: overview of the issues in the Moscow season.

1020 Gul'čenko, V. "Kak rasskazyvat' ob aktere?" (How Can One Talk About an Actor?)*TeatrM.* 1987; 6: 97-106. Lang.: Rus.

USSR. 1986. Critical studies. ∎Reflections of a theatre critic on the acting profession.

1021 Ivanov, V. "Mify i real'nost' tradicij." (Myths and the Reality of Traditions.) *TeatM.* 1987; 8: 147-154. Lang.: Rus.

USSR: Leningrad. 1909-1987. Biographical studies. ∎Portrait of actor Bruno Frejndlich of Leningrad Puškin Theatre.

1022 Ivanov, V. "Otkrytyj zvuk." (An Open Sound.) *TeatZ.* 1987; 20: 14-16. Lang.: Rus.

USSR: Moscow. 1986-1987. Histories-sources. ∎Playwrights, critics and directors discuss the Moscow season.

1023 Ivanov, V. "Pritjaženie talanta." (The Attraction of Talent.) *Druz.* 1987; 4: 129-134. Lang.: Rus.

USSR: Moscow. 1938-1980. Histories-sources. ∎Colleagues recall actor Vladimir Vysockij of Teat'r na Taganké.

1024 Jakobson, V.P. *Pavel Samojlov: Sceničeskaja biografija ego geroev.* (Pavel Samojlov: The Stage Biography of His Heroes.) Leningrad: Iskusstvo; 1987. 203 pp. Lang.: Rus.

USSR. 1836-1931. Biographical studies. ∎On the work of the well-known actor, Pavel Samojlov.

1025 Jakut, V.S. *Moj mir-teatr.* (My World-Theatre.) Moscow: Iskusstvo; 1987. 159 pp. Lang.: Rus.

USSR: Moscow. 1912-1980. Histories-sources. ∎Memoirs of actor V.S. Jakut at Jermolova Theatre.

1026 Janovskaja, G.; Ginkas, K. "Dialog ob učitele." (A Dialogue on Our Teacher.) *TeatZ.* 1987; 23: 8-11. Lang.: Rus.

USSR: Moscow. 1960-1987. Histories-sources. ∎Two Soviet directors on their teacher, director G.A. Tovstonogov.

1027 Kiselev, I. *Pojétessa ukrainskoj sceny.* (Poetess of the Ukrainian Stage.) Kiev: Mistectvo; 1987. 186 pp. Lang.: Rus.

USSR. 1898-1987. Biographical studies. ∎Life and work of Ukrainian folk artist N.N. Užvij.

1028 Klinov, V. "Vooružen i vzryvoopasen (Opyt momental'noj fotografii)." (Armed and Explosively Dangerous: The Experience of Instant Photography.) *TeatZ.* 1987; 11: 10-11. Lang.: Rus.

USSR: Omsk. 1980-1987. Biographical studies. ∎Portrait of director Gennadij Trostjaneckij.

1029 Knebel, M. "Aleksej Nikolaevič Gribov." *TeatrM.* 1987; 7: 34-45. Lang.: Rus.

USSR: Moscow. 1930-1979. Histories-sources. ∎Memoir on Aleksej Gribov, one of the most brilliant actors of Moscow Art Theatre's second generation.

1030 Korneva, O. "Prelest' putešestvija vverch po lestnice luny." (The Charm of a Journey up the Stairs of the Moon.) *TeatZ.* 1987; 13: 5-7. Lang.: Rus.

USSR: Leningrad. 1986-1987. Critical studies. ∎Review of the Leningrad theatre season.

1031 Kornienko, N. "Teatr 'preobraženija'." (A Theatre of 'Transformation'.) *TeatrM.* 1987; 9: 60-70. Lang.: Rus.

USSR. 1887-1942. Biographical studies. ∎Work of Ukrainian director L. Kurbas.

1032 Kostjukova, A. "Rol' prodolžaetsja..." (The Role Goes On.) *TeatZ.* 1987; 10: 6-7. Lang.: Rus.

USSR: Moscow. 1980-1987. Biographical studies. ∎Portrait of actor Oleg Jankovskij, Moscow Komsomol Theatre.

1033 Krymova, N. "O blagorodstve." (On Nobility.) *Ogonek.* 1987; 34: 22-24. Lang.: Rus.

USSR: Moscow. 1981-1982. Histories-sources. ∎From controversy between director/teacher Anatolij Efros and his directing students: his experiences, the art of directing, ethics of theatre work.

1034 Kuprin, O. "Demokratija i kompetentonost'." (Democracy and Competence.) *Kommunist.* 1987; 15: 45-52. Lang.: Rus.

USSR: Leningrad. 1980-1987. Histories-sources. ∎Interview with Georgij Tovstonogov, principal director of Leningrad Bolšoj Theatre, on continuity of theatrical art, role of artistic director's personality in the collective, life of the theatre under perestrojka.

1035 Kurbas, L. "Iz tvorčeskogo nasledija." (From the Creative Heritage.) *TeatrM.* 1987; 9: 55-60. Lang.: Rus.

USSR. 1887-1942. Histories-sources. ∎Collection of materials by Ukrainian director L. Kurdas on the centenary of his birth.

1036 Kušnir, S. "Intonacija." (Intonation.) *TeatZ.* 1987; 10: 30-31. Lang.: Rus.

USSR: Moscow. 1835-1987. Biographical studies. ∎Portrait of actor Sergej Jurskij.

1037 L'vov-Anochin, B. "Eduard Marcevič." *TeatZ.* 1987; 8: 29. Lang.: Rus.

USSR: Moscow. 1987. Biographical studies. ∎Portrait of Malyj Teat'r actor.

1038 Lamont, Rosette. "The Taganka of Anatoly Efros." *PerAJ.* 1987; 10(3): 96-101. Illus.: Photo. B&W. 3. Lang.: Eng.

USSR: Moscow. 1983-1987. Historical studies. ∎Life and work of Anatoly Efros, artistic director of the Taganka Theatre from 1983 to 1987.

1039 Law, Alma H. "Theatre in Moscow: The 1986-1987 Season." *SEEDTF.* 1987 Dec.; 7(2 & 3): 15-19. Lang.: Eng.

THEATRE IN GENERAL: —Performance/production

USSR: Moscow. 1986-1987. Historical studies. ■Overview of the 1986-1987 theatre season in Moscow finds a more open climate for producing previously controversial works.

1040 Levšina, E.; Orlov, Ju. "Predvaritel'nye itogi." (Preliminary Reviews.) *TeatZ*. 1987; 13: 22-23. Lang.: Rus.

USSR. 1986-1987. Historical studies. ■A composite experiment in children's theatre: conditions, problems, prospects.

1041 Levšina, I. "Žizn' artista." (Life of an Artist.) *TeatrM*. 1987; 8: 86-95. Lang.: Rus.

USSR. 1980-1987. Historical studies. ■Social problems of an actor's life and work from a sociological perspective.

1042 Macharadze, K. "Minuvšee prochodit predo mnoju." (The Past Passes Before Me.) *Avrora*. 1987; 7: 137-150. Lang.: Rus.

USSR. 1898-1987. Histories-sources. ■Recollections of actress Veriko Andžaparidze.

1043 Minkin, A. "Professija: režisser." (Profession: Director.) *Arrora*. 1987; 1: 135-142. Lang.: Rus.

USSR: Vilnius. 1980-1987. Critical studies. ■Work of E. Nekrošjus, director of Vil'njus Youth Theatre.

1044 Monastyrskij, P. "Razmyšlenija rukovoditelja teatra." (Reflections of a Theatre Director.) *TeatrM*. 1987; 8: 67-72. Lang.: Rus.

USSR. 1986-1988. Histories-sources. ■Principal director of Gorkij Theatre (Kubyšev) on results of theatrical experimentation.

1045 Morozov, B. "Razmyšlenija ob éksperimente." (Reflections on Experiment.) *SovD*. 1987; 1: 231-237. Lang.: Rus.

USSR: Moscow. 1986-1988. Histories-sources. ■A director's reflections on the creative and moral problems of a theatre collective.

1046 Petrova, A. "V uslovijach jéksperimenta." (In Experimental Conditions.) *TeatZ*. 1987; 5: 14-15. Lang.: Rus.

USSR: Moscow. 1986-1987. Histories-sources. ■Interview with A. Borodin, principal director of CDT, on the problems of theatrical experimentation.

1047 Pimenov, V. "Iz vospominanij." (From the Memoirs.) *TeatrM*. 1987; 2: 177-182. Lang.: Rus.

USSR: Moscow. 1940-1979. ■Memoirs of former director on actors of Vachtangov Theatre: N. Gricenko, N. Plotnikov, A. Abrikosov.

1048 Plavinskij, A. "Posle pervych šagov." (After the First Steps.) *MK*. 1987; 4: 81-88. Lang.: Rus.

USSR: Moscow. 1987. Critical studies. ■Plays performed for 27th Congress of Communist Party of Soviet Union.

1049 Pojurovskij, B. "Akterskaja 'Birža' Byloe i dumy." (Actor's 'Exchange': My Life and Thoughts.) *TeatZ*. 1987; 7: 26-27. Lang.: Rus.

USSR. 1980-1987. Critical studies. ■Problems of an actor's working conditions.

1050 Pojurovskij, B. "Uroki festivalja." (Lessons of the Festival.) *TeatZ*. 1987; 23: 6-7. Lang.: Rus.

USSR. 1987. Critical studies. ■Review of Baltic theatre festival.

1051 Potemkin, V.I. *Jévoljucija geroja v istoriko-revoljucionnych spektakljah G.A. Tovstonogova (1950-1980-e gody): Avtoref. dis. kand. iskusstvovedenija.* (The Evolution of the Hero in the Historical-Revolutionary Performances of G.A. Tovstonogov, 1950-1980: Abstract of a Dissertation by a Candidate in Art Criticism.) Leningrad: LGITMiK; 1987. 24 pp. Lang.: Rus.

USSR: Leningrad. 1950-1980. Critical studies.

1052 Rabinjanc, N. "Licedej." (The Actor.) *TeatZ*. 1987; 4: 15-17. Lang.: Rus.

USSR: Leningrad. 1980. Biographical studies. ■Portrait of Bolšoj Dramatic Theatre actor Valerij Ivčenko.

1053 Rachlina, A. "Spektakl' dlja vremeni peremen." (A Performance for a Time of Changes.) *TeatZ*. 1987; 10: 10-11. Lang.: Rus.

USSR: Moscow. 1980-1987. Biographical studies. ■Actor Oleg Borisov of Moscow Art Theatre.

1054 Roev, Ju. "Festivali, festivali..." (Festivals, Festivals.) *TeatrM*. 1987; 1: 39-49. Lang.: Rus.

USSR. 1986. Historical studies. ■Overview of the issues of 1986 Belorussian theatre festival.

1055 Romanov, A.V. *Ljubov' Orlova v iskusstve i žizni.* (Ljubov' Orlova in Art and Life.) Moscow: Iskusstvo; 1987. 241 pp. Lang.: Rus.

USSR: Moscow. 1902-1975. Biographical studies. ■Stage and screen actor Ljubov' Orlova. Related to Media: Film.

1056 Rubinštejn, A. "V polemike s ustarevšim myšleniem." (In Polemics with Old-Fashioned Thinking.) *TeatrM*. 1987 ; 5: 89-96. Lang.: Rus.

USSR. 1986-1988. Critical studies. ■Problems of theatre reform.

1057 Rudnickij, K. "Vdogonku za Terent'evym." (In Pursuit of Terent'ev.) *TeatrM*. 1987; 5: 58-80. Lang.: Rus.

USSR. 1920-1930. Biographical studies. ■Innovative director I.G. Terent'ev.

1058 Rudnickij, K. "Pervye p'esy russkich futuristov." (The First Plays of the Russian Futurists.) *SovD*. 1987; 2: 269-278. Lang.: Rus.

USSR. 1920-1929. Historical studies. ■Links between experimental theatre movement of the 1920s—Mejerchol'd, Radlov, Gripič—and early experiments of the Russian Futurists: Majakovskij, Chlebnikov, Blok. Grp/movt: Futurism.

1059 Rudnickij, K., ed. *Režisserskoe iskusstvo Tairova: (k 100-letiju so dnja roždenija).* (Tairov's Directorial Art: Toward the One Hundredth Anniversary of His Birth.) Moscow: VNII Iskusstrozianija; 1987. 148 pp. Lang.: Rus.

USSR: Moscow. 1885-1950. Critical studies.

1060 Rybakova, Ju. P. *Aleksandr Borisov.* Leningrad: Iskusstvo; 1987. 175 pp. Lang.: Rus.

USSR: Leningrad. 1905-1969. Biographical studies. ■Work of actor of Leningrad Puškin Theatre.

1061 Šangina, E.F. *Vyjavlenie tvorčeskoj odarennosti buduščich akterov i režisserov (Iz opyta raboty režisserskogo fakul'teta GITISa 1981-1986 gg.): Avtoref. dis. kand. iskusstvovedenija.* (Exposure of Creative Endowments of Future Actors and Directors—From the Experience of Work by the Directing Department of GITIS, 1981-1986: Abstract of a Dissertation by a Candidate in Art Criticism.) Moscow: GITIS; 1987. 24 pp. Lang.: Rus.

USSR: Moscow. 1981-1986. Historical studies.

1062 Savost'janov, A.I. *Problemy sceničeskoj zarazitel'nosti aktera: Avtoref. dis. kand. iskusstvovedenija.* (Problems of the Actor's Stage Infectiousness: Abstract of a Dissertation by a Candidate in Art Criticism.) Moscow: M-vo kul'tury RSFSR, GITIS; 1987. 23 pp. Lang.: Rus.

USSR. 1987. Instructional materials. ■The actor's art: teaching and directing the student actor.

1063 Sboeva, S.T. *Problema 'sintetičeskogo spektaklja' v kamernom teatre i evoljucija tvorčeskogo metoda A. Ja. Tairova, 1919-1933: Avtoref. dis. kand. iskusstvovedenija.* (The Problem of the 'Synthetic Performance' in the Chamber Theatre and the Evolution of A. Ja. Tairov's Creative Method, 1919-1933: Abstract of a Dissertation by a Candidate in Art Criticism.) Leningrad: M-vo kultury RSFSR/LGITMik; 1987. 25 pp. Lang.: Rus.

USSR: Moscow. 1919-1933. Critical studies.

1064 Sedych, M. "Deti Otvečajut za otcov." (The Children Answer for the Father.) *TeatrM*. 1987; 7: 60-66. Lang.: Rus.

USSR: Riga. 1985-1986. ■On Adol'f Šapiro's performances at Latvian Children's Theatre.

1065 Silina, I. "Infanty." (Infants.) *TeatrM*. 1987; 11: 82-99. Lang.: Rus.

USSR. 1980-1987. Critical studies. ■Theatre in the 1980s: absence of theatrical leadership.

1066 Smechov, V. "Fragmenty pamjati." (Fragments of Memory.) *TeatZ*. 1987; 7: 24-25. Lang.: Rus.

USSR: Moscow. 1938-1980. Histories-sources. ■An actor of the Taganka Theatre recalls actor Vladimir Vysockij.

CLASSED ENTRIES

THEATRE IN GENERAL: —Performance/production

1067 Smeljanskij, A.M. "Čem budem voskresat'?" (As What Shall We Rise Again?)*TeatrM*. 1987; 12: 42-52. Lang.: Rus.
USSR: Moscow. 1986-1987. Reviews of performances. ■Review of Moscow theatre season.

1068 Smeljanskij, A.M. "Čto že dal'še?" (And What Further?)*TeatZ*. 1987; 13: 3-6. Lang.: Rus.
USSR. 1986-1987. Critical studies. ■Problems of 1986-1987 Moscow theatre season, development of Soviet theatre.

1069 Smeljanskij, A.M., ed. *Klassika i sovremennost': problemy sovetskoj režissury 60-70 godov.* (The Classics and the Present: Problems of Soviet Directing of the Sixties and Seventies.) Moscow: Nauka; 1987. 368 pp. Lang.: Rus.
USSR. 1960-1979. Critical studies.

1070 Sologub, V. "Nakanune." (On the Eve.) *TeatZ*. 1987; 4: 11-12. Lang.: Rus.
USSR. 1986-1987. Histories-sources. ■Perestrojka in the theatre: interview with director Anatolij Vasiljëv.

1071 Suchanova, T.N. *Problemy aktërskogo iskusstva v sovetskom teatre 70-80-ch godov.* (Problems of the Actor's Art in the Soviet Union of the Seventies and Eighties.) Moscow: Gosudarstvennaja Biblioteka im. V.I. Lenina; 1987. 24 pp. (Zreliščnije iskusstva. Obzornaja informacija 1.) Lang.: Rus.
USSR. 1970-1987. Critical studies.

1072 Švedova, O.; Samarkina, O. "Čelovek novoj épochi." (A Man of the New Epoch.) *TeatZ*. 1987; 9: 20-21. Lang.: Rus.
USSR: Moscow. 1890-1942. Biographical studies. ■Life and work of N. Cereteli, leading actor of Tairov Chamber Theatre.

1073 Svobodin, A. "Gljadja na fotografii Kirill Lavrova." (Looking at the Photographs of Kirill Lavrov.) *TeatrM*. 1987; 6: 48-57. Lang.: Rus.
USSR: Leningrad. 1980. Histories-sources. ■Career of Kirill Lavrov, a leading actor of the Bolšoj Drama Theatre.

1074 Svobodin, A. "Neistovyj, Jéfremov." (Furious Jéfremov.) *KZ*. 1987; 10: 8-11. Lang.: Rus.
USSR: Moscow. 1927-1987. Biographical studies. ■Work of Oleg Jéfremov, artistic director of Moscow Art Theatre.

1075 Tabakov, O. "Teatry roždaet vremja." (Time Gives Rise to Theatres.) *Smena*. 1987; 3: 6-8. Lang.: Rus.
USSR: Moscow. 1980-1987. Histories-sources. ■Actor and director of Čaplygina Street Studio Theatre on creative and organizational principles of the theatre collective, recent changes in social life.

1076 Tenin, B.M. *Furgon komedianta: iz vospominanij.* (A Comedian's Van: Reminiscences.) Moscow: Iskusstvo; 1987. 383 pp. Lang.: Rus.
USSR: Moscow. 1920-1939. Histories-sources. ■Theatrical Moscow of the twenties and thirties: actor's recollections of personalities in theatre, vaudeville and film.

1077 Tovstonogov, G. "Monolog ob učenikah." (A Monologue on Students.) *TeatZ*. 1987; 23: 8. Lang.: Rus.
USSR: Leningrad. 1980-1987. Histories-sources. ■Principal director of Leningrad Bolšoj Theatre on educating young directors.

1078 Ul'janov, Michajl A. *Rabotaju akterom.* (I Work as an Actor.) Moscow: Iskusstvo; 1987. 394 pp. Lang.: Rus.
USSR. 1927-1987. Histories-sources. ■Soviet actor Michajl A. Ul'janov on his work.

1079 Velechova, N. "Sobirajuščij mgnovenija." (Gathering Moments.) *TeatrM*. 1987; 12: 125-140. Lang.: Eng.
USSR. 1980-1987. Biographical studies. ■Portrait of Mossovet actor Gennadij Bortnikov.

1080 Višnevskaja, I.L. *Artist Michajl Ul'janov.* Moscow: Sov. Rossija; 1987. 221 pp. Lang.: Rus.
USSR: Moscow. 1927-1987. Biographies.

1081 Vladi, M. "Ja živ toboj." (I Live Through You.) *Ogonek*. 1987; 18: 28-30. Lang.: Rus.
USSR. 1938-1980. Histories-sources. ■French actress discusses work and personality of actor Vladimir Vysockij.

1082 Vladimirov, I. "Utočnim predmet spora." (Let's Make the Subject of Dispute More Specific.) *TeatZ*. 1987; 14: 19-21. Lang.: Rus.

USSR. 1987. Critical studies. ■Considers the dilemma of successful theatre vs. a theatre of creative process.

1083 Žanturina, Z.N. *Process vzaimovlijanija sceničeskich kul'tur v teatral'nom iskusstve Kazachstana (1950-1980 gg.): Avtoref. dis. kand. iskusstvovedenija.* (The Process of Mutual Influence among Scenic Cultures in the Theatre Art of Kazakhstan, 1950-1980: Abstract of a Dissertation by a Candidate in Art Criticism.) Moscow: M-vo kul'tury RSFSR/GITIS; 1987. 22 pp. Lang.: Rus.
USSR. 1950-1980. Historical studies.

1084 Zelenaja, R.V. *Razroznennye stranicy.* (Random Pages.) Moscow: STD RSFSR; 1987. 250 pp. Lang.: Rus.
USSR: Moscow. Histories-sources. ■Memoirs of a Soviet actress of the variety stage, film. Related to Media: Film.

1085 Zingerman, B. "Zametki o Stanislavskom." (Notes on Stanislavskij.) *TeatrM*. 1987; 11: 31-37. Lang.: Rus.
USSR. 1863-1938. Historical studies.

1086 Zingerman, B. "Individual'nost' Tovstonogova." (The Individuality of Tovstonogov.) *TeatrM*. 1987; 1: 50-55. Lang.: Eng.
USSR: Leningrad. 1930-1987. Biographical studies. ■Principal director of Leningrad Bolšoj Theatre Georgij Aleksandrovič Tovstonogov.

1087 Zolotusskij, I. "Risk i Vybor." (Risk and Choice.) *TeatZ*. 1987; 22: 22-24. Lang.: Rus.
USSR. 1980-1987. Biographical studies. ■Work of Valerij Beljakovič, principal director of Teat'r-studija na Jugo-Zapade.

1088 Zverev, A. "Geroinja." (Heroine.) *TeatZ*. 1987; 10: 20-21. Lang.: Rus.
USSR: Moscow. 1980-1987. Biographical studies. ■Portrait of actress Ol'ga Jakovleva of Taganka Theatre.

1089 Zvezdočkin, V.A. *Plastika aktera v sovremennom dramaticeskom spektakle (interpretacija klassiki v rezissure G.A. Tovstonogova 1970-1980 o-dob). Avtoref.: dis. kand. iskusstvovedenija.* (The Plastic Art of the Actor in Contemporary Dramatic Performances—Interpretations of the Classics in the Directing of G.A. Tovstonogov in the 1970s and 1980s: Abstract of a Dissertation by a Candidate in Art Criticism.) Leningrad: LGITMiK; 1987. 25 pp. Lang.: Rus.
USSR. 1970-1987. Critical studies.

1090 Dzjubinskaja, O. "Pojdem za sinej pticej." (Let Us Go After the Bluebird.) *TeatrM*. 1987; 6: 170-179. Lang.: Rus.
Yugoslavia: Belgrade. 1986. Historical studies. ■Survey of the international theatre festival BITEF-88.

1091 Klaić, Dragan. "Yugoslavia: Even Summer Theatre Carries on the Business of Politics." *SEEDTF*. 1987 Dec.; 7(2 & 3): 20-23. Lang.: Eng.
Yugoslavia: Dubrovnik, Belgrade, Kotor, Budva, Subotica. 1987. Reviews of performances. ■Overview on the YU Fest organized by Ljubiša Ristić, director of the Subotica Theatre.

1092 Marin, Marko. "Miguel de Cervantes: Trois intermèdes." (Miguel de Cervantes: Three Interludes.) *MuK*. 1987; 33(1-2): 77-80. Lang.: Fre.
Yugoslavia. 1987. Critical studies.

1093 Ujes, Alojz. "Theaterfestivals in Jugoslawien als Teil des national-kulturellen Systems." (Theatre Festivals in Yugoslavia as a Part of the National Cultural System.) *MuK*. 1987; 33(1-2): 111-114. Lang.: Ger.
Yugoslavia. 1900-1987. Historical studies.

Performances spaces

1094 Moore, John D. "The New City Center." *PerfM*. 1983 May; 8(2): 3. Lang.: Eng.
USA: New York, NY. 1924-1983. Historical studies. ■Recent restoration and renovations, past events hosted and current season projected.

Plays/librettos/scripts

1095 Boucher, Denise. "Comment les femmes changent le théâtre." (How Women Change the Theatre.) 127-130 in Coca, Jordi, ed.; Conesa, Laura, comp. *Congrés Internacional de Teatre a Catalunya 1985. Actes. Volum III. Seccions 7, 8 i*

CLASSED ENTRIES

THEATRE IN GENERAL: —Plays/librettos/scripts

9. Barcelona: Institut del Teatre; 1987. 350 pp. [Section 8: Outlook for the Theatre.] Lang.: Fre.
1985. Critical studies. ■Social utility of women's theatre: a different point of view expressed in a different form.

1096 Dasgupta, Gautam. "From Science to Theatre: Dramas of Speculative Thought." *PerAJ.* 1987 Sum/Fall; 11(26/27): 237-246. Lang.: Eng.
1987. Critical studies. ■The commonality of science and theatre, how certain investigative disciplines have influenced drama.

1097 Richards, Alison. "We Can Work it Out: An Interview with Graham Pitts." *Meanjin.* 1987; 46(4): 487-495. Lang.: Eng.
Australia. 1987. Histories-sources. ■Left-wing playwright Graham Pitts discusses his life, comedy as a political weapon and source of his writing methods.

1098 Shine, Chris. "Interview: Jack Hibberd." *ADS.* 1987 Apr.; 10: 79-90. Lang.: Eng.
Australia. 1967-1986. Histories-sources. ■Discussion of Hibberd's work as a playwright and his views on current Australian theatre. His rejection of the mainstream and contributions to popular theatre.

1099 Bettis, Paul. "Michael Hollingsworth: Making History." *CTR.* 1987 Fall; 52: 36-44. Illus.: Photo. Print. B&W. 7. Lang.: Eng.
Canada. 1987. Historical studies. ■Synopsis of *The History of the Village of Small Huts.* History of Canada is revealed in 60 one-minute scenes using satiric devices.

1100 Cowan, Cindy. "*Doc* by Sharon Pollock." *CTR.* 1987 Fall; 52: 95-96. [Readings in Review.] Lang.: Eng.
Canada. 1987. Critical studies. ■Textual layering and collective sensibility propel action of Sharon Pollock's play *Doc.*

1101 Pavlovic, Diane. "Du décollage à l'envol." (From Taking it Off to Take-Off.) *JCT.* 1987; 42: 86-99. Illus.: Photo. Print. B&W. 13. Lang.: Fre.
Canada. 1987. Critical studies. ■Discussion of the art of Robert Lepage and the creative process as it applies to his work *Vinci.*

1102 Hulser, Kathleen. "Chileans Make Theatre in the Eye of the Storm." *AmTh.* 1987 Jan.; 3(10): 36-37. Illus.: Photo. B&W. 2. Lang.: Eng.
Chile: Santiago. 1967-1987. Histories-sources. ■Chilean theatre under the repressive Pinochet regime. Interview with Chilean playwright Antonio Skarmeto.

1103 Chiang, Jyh. "Shyu Fu Tzuoh Dih Sheng Pyng Her Juh Tzuoh." (The Biography and Literary Works of Shyu Fu Tzuoh.) *XYanj.* 1987; 8(19): 48-69. Lang.: Chi.
China: Beijing. 1526-1640. Bibliographical studies. ■The bibliography and works of the Chinese writer Shyu Fu Tzuoh.

1104 Jou, Goong Pyng. "Jang Dah Fu Shih Cheu Tzuoh Piin Kao Biann." (Criticism of the Dramatic Works of Jang Dah Fu.) *XYanj.* 1987; 8(19): 113-132. Lang.: Chi.
China: Beijing. 1620-1720. Critical studies. ■Criticism of the dramatic works of Jang Dah Fu.

1105 Lee, Fu Bo. "Yuann Yu Ling Sheng Pyng Kao Liueh." (Biography of Yuann Yu Ling.) *XYanj.* 1987; 8(19): 91-112. Lang.: Chi.
China: Beijing. 1592-1674. Bibliographical studies. ■Biography of Yuan Yu Ling.

1106 Luo, Di. "Wong jiang yu yuan zhen shu hui yi bian." (Discussion of Shu-Hui.) *XYishu.* 1987 Sum; 38: 23-33. Notes. Lang.: Chi.
China. 980-1600. Historical studies. ■Introduction to ancient Chinese Shu-Hui, which was a guild of playwrights.

1107 Shyong, Cheng Yu. "Jeang Shyh Chyuan Jiuh Tzuoh Dih Sy Sheang Ney Rong." (From Jean Shyh Chuan's Dramatic Works to See His Thoughts.) *XYanj.* 1987; 8(19): 133-259. Lang.: Chi.
China: Beijing. 1644-1875. Critical studies. ■Overview of Jeang Shyh Chyuan's thoughts from his dramatic works.

1108 Wey, Yih Jyy. "Yeh Shean Tzuu Jyi Chyi *Luan Yih Jih.*" (Yeh Shean Tzuu and His *Luan Yih Jih.*) *XYanj.* 1987; 8(19): 70-90. Lang.: Chi.
China: Beijing. 820-1641. Bibliographical studies. ■The bibliography of Yeh Shean Tzuu and his *Luan Yih Jih,* a literary work addressing the decline of the Tang Dynasty, contrasting it to the Ming Dynasty.

1109 Shen, Jian-Yi. "By lai xi te li lun pi pan." (Critique of Brecht.) *XYishu.* 1985 Spr; 29: 87-99. Notes. Lang.: Chi.
China, People's Republic of. 1949-1985. Critical studies. ■Brecht's theory of alienation in the Chinese theatre.

1110 Ciccotti, Eusebio. "Uno spettacolo praghese *Solitudine rumorosa* di Bohumil Hrabal." (A Prague Entertainment: *Too Loud a Solitude* by Bohumil Hrabal.) *TeatrC.* 1987; 7(15): 297-307. Lang.: Ita.
Czechoslovakia. 1914-1987. Critical studies. ■Analysis of *Příliš hlučna samota (Too Loud a Solitude).*

1111 Ciccotti, Eusebio, ed. "Numero speciale sul teatro cecoslovacco." (Special Issue on Czechoslovak Theatre.) *TeatrC.* 1987; 8(16/17). Lang.: Ita.
Czechoslovakia. 1980. Critical studies. ■Brief presentations of contemporary Czechoslovakian authors, with some short works translated into Italian.

1112 Fréchette, Carole. "L'ISTA et le Rôle Féminin." (ISTA and the Female Role.) *JCT.* 1987; 43: 43-47. Illus.: Photo. Print. B&W. 2. Lang.: Fre.
Denmark. Asia. 1986. Historical studies. ■The ISTA conference in September 1986 in Denmark examined the role of women in theatre.

1113 Jansen, Steen. "A proposito del *Pechinese azzurro* di Kield Abell." (With Regard to *The Blue Pekingese* by Kjeld Abell.) *QT.* 1987 Feb.; 9(35): 162-167. Lang.: Ita.
Denmark. 1901-1961. Critical studies. ■Analysis of *Den bla pekingeser (The Blue Pekingese).*

1114 Dauber, Antoinette B. "Allegory and Irony in *Othello.*" *ShS.* 1987; 40: 123-133. Lang.: Eng.
England. 1604. Critical studies. ■Exploration of themes developed allegorically and ironically in *Othello.*

1115 Hamel, Guy. "Time in *Richard III.*" *ShS.* 1987; 40: 41-49. Lang.: Eng.
England. 1592. Critical studies. ■A discussion of temporality in *Richard III.*

1116 Hawkes, Terence. "Take Me to Your Leda." *ShS.* 1987; 40: 21-32. Lang.: Eng.
England. 1604-1929. Historical studies. ■Comparative study of *Measure for Measure* by Shakespeare and the poem *Leda and the Swan* by William Butler Yeats.

1117 Jones, Ann Rosalind. "Italians and Others: Venice and the Irish in Coryat's *Crudities* and *The White Devil.*" *RenD.* 1987; 18: 101-119. Illus.: Dwg. B&W. 2. Lang.: Eng.
England. 1580-1612. Critical studies. ■Discussion of *Crudities* by Thomas Coryat and *The White Devil* by John Webster exploring Italian sensibilities.

1118 Jordan, Constance. "Gender and Justice in *Swetnam the Woman-Hater.*" *RenD.* 1987; 18: 149-169. Lang.: Eng.
England. 1600-1620. Critical studies. ■Discussion of feminist play: *Swetnam the Woman-Hater, Arraigned by Women,* written in 1620, in response to an anti-female pamphlet. Explores misogyny in a patriarchal society and androgyny.

1119 Kernan, Alvin. "Meaning and Emptiness in *King Lear* and *The Tempest.*" *RenD.* 1987: 225-236. Lang.: Eng.
England. 1605-1611. Critical studies. ■Discussion of theodicy and its connection to tragic drama in *King Lear* and *The Tempest.*

1120 Nevo, Ruth. "*Measure for Measure*: Mirror for Mirror." *ShS.* 1987; 40: 107-122. Lang.: Eng.
England. 1604. Critical studies. ■An analysis of the structure of *Measure for Measure.*

1121 Randall, Dale B.J. "The Rank and Earthy Background of Certain Physical Symbols in *The Duchess of Malfi.*" *RenD.* 1987; 18: 171-203. Illus.: Photo. Dwg. B&W. 4. Lang.: Eng.
England. 1613. Critical studies. ■Various symbols in Webster's *The Duchess of Malfi* and development of their possible meaning.

THEATRE IN GENERAL: —Plays/librettos/scripts

1122 Rozett, Martha Tuck. "Tragedies within Tragedies: Kent's Unmasking in *King Lear.*" *RenD.* 1987; 18: 237-258. Lang.: Eng.

England. 1605. Critical studies. ■Discussion of *King Lear*, with focus on the relationship of character of Kent to the overall tragedy of the play.

1123 Shapiro, James. "'Steale from the deade?': The Presence of Marlowe in Jonson's Early Plays." *RenD.* 1987; 18: 67-99. Lang.: Eng.

England. 1598-1602. Historical studies. ■Discussion of theory that Ben Jonson may be stylistically the 'heir to Christopher Marlowe'. Author refutes this notion in a comparison of their works.

1124 Walch, Gunter. "*Henry V* as Working House of Ideology." *ShS.* 1987; 40: 63-68. Lang.: Eng.

England. 1599. Critical studies. ■A study of *Henry V* in terms of its development of Prince Hal as an ideological monarch.

1125 Cordero, Anne D. "Marguerite Duras: *La Musica Deuxième*: Text Play Performance." 33-41 in Hartigan, Karelisa V., ed. *From the Bard to Broadway.* Lanham, MD: UP of America; 1987. 222 pp. (Univ. of Florida Dept. of Classics Comparative Drama Conference Papers 7.) Pref. Notes. Biblio. Lang.: Eng.

France: Paris. 1985-1987. Critical studies. ■Compares two versions of the play, including a 1985 performance. Also compares the production text to the written text to conclude how the dramatic dialogue is handled.

1126 Yeo, Seok-Gi. "Artaud wa Bali Yeon-Geuk." (Artaud and Bali Theatre.) 156-181 in *Study on the Comparison of Eastern Theatre and Western Theatre.* Seoul: Korea Univ.; 1987. 295 pp. Lang.: Kor.

France. Indonesia. 1931-1935. Historical studies. ■Contrasts theatre of Bali with its influence on playwright Antonin Artaud.

1127 Levesque, Solange. "Propositions autour d'un théâtre d'errances." (Thoughts on Dramatic Wanderings.) *JCT.* 1987; 43: 72-76. Illus.: Photo. Print. B&W. 3. Lang.: Fre.

Germany. 1970-1986. Critical studies. ■Examines the recurrent theme of traveling in German theatre and film from Siegfried to Handke's Gaspard Hauser. Related to Media: Film.

1128 Vinkó, József. "Egy drámaíró vallomásai. Lengyel Menyhértről naplói ürügyén." (Confessions of a Dramatist: On Menyhért Lengyel on the Basis of his Diary.) *Sz.* 1987 July; 20(7): 1-6. Illus.: Photo. B&W. 1. Lang.: Hun.

Hungary. 1907-1974. Biographical studies. ■Ideas on the life and career of Menyhért (Melchior) Lengyel in connection with the diary notes published in *Eletem könyve (The Book of My Life)*, Budapest, 1987.

1129 Alberti, Carmelo. "Carlo Gozzi e Antonio Sacchi: il drammaturgo e il suo doppio." (Carlo Gozzi and Antonio Sacchi: The Playwright and his Double.) *Ariel.* 1987; 2(8): 65-86. Notes. Illus.: Dwg. Lang.: Ita.

Italy: Venice. 1755. Critical studies. ■Analysis of the works of Carlo Gozzi and of his relationship with the Italian actor Antonio Sacchi as reported in his book: *Memorie inutili.*

1130 Bartalotta, Gianfranco. "Il *Lorenzaccio* di Carmelo Bene o L'illogicità del senso." (*Lorenzaccio* by Carmelo Bene or the Illogicality of Meaning.) *TeatrC.* 1987; 7(15): 269-279. Lang.: Ita.

Italy. 1986. Critical studies. ■Analysis of *Il Lorenzaccio* by Carmelo Bene.

1131 Bellezza, Ernesto, ed.; Franceschini, Maria, ed.; Piaggio, Rita, ed. *Umberto Fracchia direttore della Fiera Letteraria negli anni 1925-1926. Catalogo-regesto del carteggio tra Umberto Fracchia e i collaboratori della Fiera posseduto dalla Biblioteca Universitaria di Genova.* (Umberto Fracchia, Director of Fiera Letteraria, 1925-1926: Catalogue of the Card File on Fracchia and His Collaborators from University of Genoa Library.) Genoa: 1987. 383 pp. Tables. 15. Lang.: Ita.

Italy. 1925-1926. Histories-sources. ■Sources on Umberto Fracchia and the main exponents of literary and scientific culture of the time, in connection with their journal *La Fiera Letteraria.*

1132 Bosisio, Paolo. *La parola e la scena. Studi sul teatro italiano tra Settecento e Novecento.* (Word and Stage: Studies on Italian Theatre Between the Eighteenth and Twentieth Centuries.) Rome: Bulzoni; 1987. 470 pp. (Biblioteca di cultura 338.) Index. Pref. Lang.: Ita.

Italy. 1700-1900. Critical studies. ■Collection of essays on major Italian playwrights such as Gozzi, Gioia, Foscolo, Manzoni, Pirandello.

1133 Bragaglia, Leonardo. "Ruggero Ruggeri e Gabriele D'Annunzio." (Ruggero Ruggeri and Gabriele D'Annunzio.) *TeatrC.* 1987; 7(15): 238-248. Lang.: Ita.

Italy. 1901-1938. Biographical studies. ■The thirty years of friendship and collaboration between D'Annunzio and the actor Ruggero Ruggeri.

1134 Chiavarelli, Lucio. *100 idee per fare teatro.* (100 Ideas for Putting on Plays.) Bologna: A.C.E.R.; 1987. 118 pp. Pref. Illus.: Sketches. 10. Lang.: Ita.

Italy. 1987. Instructional materials. ■Summaries of one hundred plays, including number of characters, duration, type of company most appropriate.

1135 Guarino, Raimondo. "Gli umanisti e il teatro a Venezia nel Quattrocento. Scritture, ambienti, visioni." (The Humanists and Venetian Theatre in the Fifteenth Century.) *TeatroS.* 1987; 2(1): 135-166. Lang.: Ita.

Italy: Venice. 1400-1500. Historical studies. ■The Venetian *Commedia umanistica* and its links to the ideas and images of the ancient world in the context of the general intellectual climate.

1136 Isgrò, Giovanna. "Una commedia urbana nel teatro comico del Seicento. *Le notti di Palermu* di Tommaso Aversa." (A City Comedy in the Comic Theatre of the Seventeenth Century: *The Nights of Palermo* by Tommaso Aversa.) *QT.* 1987 May; 9(36): 134-147. Lang.: Ita.

Italy. 1600. Historical studies. ■Analysis of the Sicilian comic theatre through the work of Tommaso Aversa.

1137 Mancini, Andrea. "Rosso di San Secondo al Teatro del Convegno (lettere inedite)." (Rosso di San Secondo at the Theatre of the Convegno (Unpublished Letters).) *Ariel.* 1987; 2(2): 147-148. Lang.: Ita.

Italy: Milan. 1924-1925. Histories-sources. ■The unpublished letters of Rosso di San Secondo to Enzo Ferrieri, animators of the Teatro del Convegno.

1138 Mariani, Anna Laura. "Sibilla Aleramo. Significato di tre incontri col teatro: il personaggio di Nora, Giacinta Pezzana, Eleonora Duse." (Sibilla Aleramo: The Meaning of Three Encounters with the Theatre: The Character of Nora, Giacinta Pezzana, Eleonora Duse.) *TeatroS.* 1987; 2(1): 67-133. Lang.: Ita.

Italy. 1850-1930. Biographical studies. ■The connection between Sibilla Aleramo and other women of her time—Giacinta Pezzana, Eleonora Duse, Alessandrina Ravizza, Lina Poletti—reveal the central importance of the theatre as a means of expression for the history of women's liberation.

1139 Pagliai, Morena. "Caos e labirinto in *Amara* di Rosso di San Secondo." (Chaos and Labyrinth in *Bitter* by Rosso di San Secondo.) *QT.* 1987 Feb.; 9(35): 133-148. Lang.: Ita.

Italy. 1913-1917. Critical studies. ■Analysis of the work.

1140 Salsano, Roberto. "Drammaturgia gesuitica ed arcadica in un manifesto teatrale inedito di Simone Maria Poggi." (Arcadian and Jesuit Dramaturgy in an Unpublished Theatrical Manifesto by Simone Maria Poggi.) *Ariel.* 1987; 2(1): 62-72. Lang.: Ita.

Italy. 1700-1749. Critical studies. ■The theatrical production of a Jesuit and his idea of theatre.

1141 Savinio, Maria; Savinio, Angelica, ed. *Con Savinio: Ricordi e lettere.* (With Savinio: Recollections and Letters.) Palermo: Sellerio; 1987. 158 pp. (La diagonale 19.) Illus.: Pntg. Dwg. Photo. Print. B&W. Lang.: Ita.

Italy. 1923-1952. Biographies. ■Maria Savinio, her memories of her husband, writer Alberto Savinio and their correspondence.

1142 Scrivano, Riccardo. *La vocazione contesa. Note su Pirandello e il teatro.* (The Disputed Vocation: Notes and

THEATRE IN GENERAL: —Plays/librettos/scripts

Pirandello and the Theatre.) Rome: Bulzoni; 1987. 117 pp. (Strumenti di ricerca 48.) Pref. Index. Lang.: Ita.
Italy. 1910-1936. Critical studies. ■Collection of essays on Pirandello's theatrical activity.

1143 Verdone, Mario. *Teatro del Novecento.* (Theatre of the Twentieth-Century.) Brescia: La Scuola; 1987. 208 pp. (Sintesi dei documenti di letteratura italiana contemporanea 8.) Biblio. Index. [2d ed.] Lang.: Ita.
Italy. 1900-1987. Histories-specific. ■History of twentieth-century Italian theatre and its major playwrights.

1144 Yeo, Seok-Gi. "Brecht wa dong-yang yeon-geuk." (Brecht and Asian Theatre.) 131-155 in *Study on the Comparison of Eastern Theatre and Western Theatre.* Seoul, Korea: Korea Univ; 1987. 295 pp. Index. Lang.: Kor.
Japan. China. Germany. 1930-1940. Critical studies. ■The influence of Asian theatre on Brecht.

1145 Cho, Dong-Il. "Bongsantalchumui bunsuk." (The Analytical Investigation of Bongsan Mask Theatre.) 183-222 in *History & Theory of Mask Theatre.* Seoul: Hongik-SA; 1987. 406 pp. Lang.: Kor.
Korea. 57 B.C.-1987 A.D. Critical studies. ■The analysis of *Bongsantalchum*, a Korean mask play.

1146 Cho, Woo-Hyun. "Minsokkukui sikansungkwa gongkansung." (Time and Space in the Folk Drama.) *DongukDA.* 1983 Dec.; 14: 5-42. Lang.: Kor.
Korea. 57 B.C.-1987 A.D. Critical studies. ■Study of time and space in ancient Korean dramas.

1147 Lee, Yurina. "Keom-yol ŭi Yeoksa." (The Censorship of Plays.) *KTR.* 1987 Aug.; 8(1): 23-25. Illus.: Photo. B&W. 1. Lang.: Kor.
Korea. Japan. Germany. 1940-1987. Critical studies. ■An argument against the censorship of plays. Compares censorship in Korea with the situation in Japan and Germany.

1148 Park, Hang-Seo. "Hanguk yonkuk jungsinui saemgoomeong." (The Roots of Korean Theatrical Thought.) *DongukDA.* 1978 Apr.; 10-11: 37-43. Lang.: Kor.
Korea. 57 B.C. Historical studies. ■General study of ancient Korean plays.

1149 Yun, Cho-Pyeong; Kim, Kil-Su. "Hyong to kuk ui Yuk Seong kwa kaepal." (The Development and Improvement of the Folk Theatre.) *KTR.* 1987 June(5): 30-36. Lang.: Kor.
Korea. 1987-1987. Critical studies. ■Suggestions for the improvement of the plays and the production values of Korean folk theatre.

1150 Dowling, John. "Gorostiza's *Contigo Pan Y Cebolla*: From Romantic Farce to Nostalgic Musical Comedy." *ThS.* 1987 May; 28(1): 49-58. Notes. Biblio. Lang.: Eng.
Mexico: Mexico City. Spain: Madrid. 1833-1984. Critical studies. ■Examination of the qualities and appeal of original text of *Contigo pan y cebolla (With You, Bread and Onion)* produced in Mexico and Spain (1833) and popular musical adaptation in Mexico (1984). Related to Music-Drama: Musical theatre.

1151 Tello Díaz, Carlos. "Entrevista a Hugo Hiriart." (Interview with Hugo Hiriart.) *Universidad de Mexico.* 1987 Jun.; 17 (437): 41-44. Illus.: Dwg. B&W. 1. Lang.: Spa.
Mexico: Mexico City. 1987. Histories-sources. ■Interview with Mexican playwright Hugo Hiriart discussing his play *Vivir y Bebir (To Live and To Drink)* and the subject of alcoholism.

1152 Hunt, Nigel. "Controversy." *Theatrum.* 1987 Fall/Win; 8: 3-4, 40. Lang.: Eng.
North America. 1987. 1987. Critical studies. ■Discusses the lack of controversy in contemporary theatre.

1153 Hesse, G.H. "Die Toeval: P.G. du Plessis en Friedrich Dürrenmatt." (Chance: P.G. du Plessis and Friedrich Dürrenmatt.) *TvL.* 1987 Nov.; 25: 38-42. Lang.: Afr.
South Africa, Republic of. Switzerland. 1987. Critical studies. ■Use of chance in the plays of P.G. du Plessis and Friederich Dürrenmatt.

1154 Mouton, Marisa. "Tyd in die drameteks en in die opvoering." (Time in the Dramatic Text and Performance.) *JLS/ TLW.* 1987 Dec.; 3(4): 14-22. Lang.: Afr.

South Africa, Republic of. 1987. Critical studies. ■Study of dramatic time in the text versus actual physical time of the performance.

1155 Schutte, H.J. "Dramakroniek." (Drama Chronicle.) *TvL.* 1987 Feb.; 25: 87-97. Lang.: Afr.
South Africa, Republic of. 1985-1986. Critical studies. ■New Afrikaans drama and playwrights in South Africa, encouraged by 'Kamustoneel' of the ATKV. Related to Media: Video forms.

1156 Aszyk, Urszula. "Alfonso Vallejo: Pomimo wszystko życie jest możliwe." (Alfonso Vallejo: Life is Possible in Spite of Everything.) *DialogW.* 1987; 6: 108-111. Notes. Lang.: Pol.
Spain. 1976-1986. Biographical studies. ■Playwright Alfonso Vallejo's world view.

1157 Molas, Joaquim, ed.; Bou, Enric; Carbonell, Manuel; Gallén, Enric; Gustà, Marina; Murgades, Josep; Sullà, Enric. *Història de la literatura catalana. Volum 9.* (History of Catalan Literature, Volume 9.) Barcelona: Ariel; 1987. 512 pp. Index. Notes. Illus.: Design. Photo. Pntg. Print. Color. B&W. 105. Lang.: Cat.
Spain-Catalonia. 1902-1961. Histories-general. ■Chapters devoted to: Catalan theatrical life from the turn of the century to the Civil War, Josep Maria de Sagarra, Josep Carner and Josep Sebastià Pons.

1158 Gale, Steven H.; Gillen, Francis. "Editor's Column." *PintR.* 1987; 1: vii. Lang.: Eng.
UK-England. 1985-1987. Historical studies. ■Creation and editorial requirements of *The Pinter Review.*

1159 Gale, Steven H. "President's Column." *PintR.* 1987; 1: v-vi. Lang.: Eng.
UK-England. USA. 1985-1987. Historical studies. ■The founding of the Harold Pinter Society.

1160 Merritt, Susan Hollis. "Harold Pinter Bibliography, 1986-1987." *PintR.* 1987; 1: 77-82. Biblio. Lang.: Eng.
UK-England. USA. 1986-1987. Bibliographical studies. ■An annual bibliography of works by and about Harold Pinter, including all aspects of his writing (plays, films, television) and performances, as well as his acting and directing. Related to Media.

1161 "Behind the Scenes: Women in Theatre, OOB Updates." *DGQ.* 1987; 23(4): 44-49. Illus.: Sketches. 1. Lang.: Eng.
USA. 1987. Histories-sources. ■Seminar at Marymount College sponsored by the Women in Theatre Network of the Dramatists' Guild to exchange ideas with the public about women in theatre. The creation of new musicals at the Musical Theatre Workshop. Listings of playwriting contests and awards.

1162 "The Dramatists' Diary, Mid-October to Mid-January." *DGQ.* 1987; 23(4): 5064. Illus.: Sketches. 4. Lang.: Eng.
USA. 1987. Histories-sources. ■Notes on award to Wallace Shawn, upcoming Dramatists' Guild elections, plays being produced on Broadway, Off Broadway, regionally and abroad. Lists of new members. Plays optioned and published in acting and library versions.

1163 "1987-88 Directory of Institutional Theatres New York City and Cross Country." *DGQ.* 1987; 24(1): 20-56. Lang.: Eng.
USA. 1987. ■Directory of opportunities for playwrights to see their works produced in regional theatres. Logistics for submitting scripts. Listings for 150 theatres across the United States.

1164 "The Dramatists' Diary, May to August." *DGQ.* 1987; 24(2): 74-88. Illus.: Sketches. 3. Lang.: Eng.
USA. 1987. Histories-sources. ■Listing of members' plays produced from May to August on Broadway, Off Broadway, Off-off Broadway, regionally and abroad. Plays published in both library and acting editions, and new books by members.

1165 Bush, Max. "Serious Plays: A Playwright Responds." *YTJ.* 1987 Fall; 2(2): 12-13. Lang.: Eng.
USA. 1957-1987. Critical studies. ■Adaptations of fairy tales and fantasies for children's plays.

1166 Chinoy, Helen Krich; Jenkins, Linda Walsh. *Women in American Theatre.* New York, NY: Theatre Communications Group; 1987. 460 pp. Tables. Illus.: Photo. Print. B&W. [2nd ed.] Lang.: Eng.
USA. 1987. Historical studies. ■Interviews and essays on women in American theatre: their problems and successes. Includes lists of over 1000 plays, books, films and feminist theatres.

THEATRE IN GENERAL: —Plays/librettos/scripts

1167 Dietz, Steven. "Developed to Death?" *AmTh*. 1987 May; 4(2): 42-43. Notes. Lang.: Eng.
USA. 1987. Critical studies. ■How the developmental process and provisions made for playwrights by companies affect the outcome of the quality of plays and the playwright's knowledge of writing for the stage.

1168 Durang, Christopher. "Jules Feiffer Cartoonist-Playwright in Conversation with Christopher Durang." *DGQ*. 1987; 23(4): 8-17. Illus.: Sketches. 2. Lang.: Eng.
USA. 1950-1987. Histories-sources. ■Feiffer's childhood, work for the *New Yorker*, politics, decision to become a playwright, his film scripts. Related to Media: Film.

1169 Frome, Shelly. "Fault Finding Can Be Fun for All Except the Paranoid Playwright." *DGQ*. 1987; 24(3): 27-29. Illus.: Sketches. 1. Lang.: Eng.
USA. 1987. Critical studies. ■Humorous essay on the trials and tribulations of being a playwright in the current theatre scene. Describes a conversation with the board member of a local theatre and the difficulties of talking to non-theatre people about playwriting.

1170 Hale, Alice M. "Appalachian Spring." *AmTh*. 1987 June; 4(3): 4-5. Notes. Illus.: Photo. B&W. 1. Lang.: Eng.
USA: Whitesburg, KY. Critical studies. ■Roadside Theatre's production of *Leaving Egypt*, with brief history of its development and origins.

1171 Hansen, Holden. "Fairy Tales on Stage: A Need for New Adaptations." *YTJ*. 1987 Spr; 1(4): 12-14. Notes. Biblio. Lang.: Eng.
USA. 1972. Critical studies. ■Adaptations of fairy tales for stage fail to serve theatre or the development of the child because of playwrights' condescending point of view.

1172 Holmberg, Arthur. "Susan Sontag Interviewed by Arthur Holmberg." *PerAJ*. 1985 Spr; 9(25): 28-30. Lang.: Eng.
USA: Cambridge, MA. 1985. Histories-sources. ■Interview with Susan Sontag, who directed *Jacques and His Master*, Milan Kundera's adaptation of *Jacques le Fataliste* by Denis Diderot, at American Repertory Theatre.

1173 Holmberg, Arthur. "Milan Kundera Interviewed by Arthur Holmberg." *PerAJ*. 1985 Spr; 9(25): 25-27. Lang.: Eng.
USA: Cambridge, MA. 1985. Histories-sources. ■Interview with author Milan Kundera, whose play *Jacques and His Master* is adapted from *Jacques le Fataliste* by Denis Diderot.

1174 Hudson-Withers, Elenora. "Toni Morrison's World of Topsy-Turvydom: A Methodological Explication of New Black Literary Criticism." *WJBC*. 1986; 10(3): 132-136. Notes. Lang.: Eng.
USA. 1986. Critical studies. ■'Topsy-turvied' is a term used for survival technique for Blacks in Western society: positive affirmation contrasts traditional sterotyping of Blacks in plays and literature as evil.

1175 Londré, Felicia Hardison. "The Beast in Arrabal." *AmTh*. 1987 Feb; 3(11): 23-26. Illus.: Photo. B&W. 4. Lang.: Eng.
USA. France: Paris. 1959-1987. Historical studies. ■Playwright Fernando Arrabal and various productions of his work.

1176 Norman, Marsha. "FDG/CBC New Plays Conference: Why Do We Need New Plays? And Other Difficult Questions." *DGQ*. 1987; 23 (4): 18, 31-33. Lang.: Eng.
USA. 1987. Critical studies. ■Current situation in American playwriting. The relationship of theatre to movies and television. Economics of selecting, workshopping and producing a new play. Calls for a balance between new plays by established authors and new plays by new authors. Related to Media.

1177 Philips, Louis. "Without Reservations: Gleanings from a Playwright's Notebook." *DGQ*. 1987; 24(2): 57-59. Illus.: Sketches. 1. Lang.: Eng.
USA: New York, NY. 1987. Critical studies. ■Humorous suggestions by Arthur Wing Pinero: a time-sharing program for theatre seats, advice to aspiring dramatists, locking playwrights in their rooms to make them write.

1178 Rabkin, Gerald. "Milan and His Master." *PerAJ*. 1985 Spr; 9(25): 17-24. Illus.: Photo. B&W. 2. Lang.: Eng.

USA: Cambridge, MA. 1985. Critical studies. ■American Repertory Theatre production of Diderot's *Jacques le Fataliste (Jacques and His Master)*, adapted by Milan Kundera and directed by Susan Sontag.

1179 Ramsey, Dale. "Dramaturgs and Literary Managers: What's the Difference and How Do They Serve Playwrights?" *DGQ*. 1987; 24(1): 12, 14-17. Illus.: Sketches. 1. Lang.: Eng.
USA. 1987. Critical studies. ■Compares and contrasts the two jobs: process of choosing plays for a theatrical season, how specific theatres use literary managers and dramaturgs.

1180 Sweet, Jeffrey. "FDG/CBC New Plays Conference: Problems, Proposed Solutions, Warnings." *DGQ*. 1987; 23(4): 19-25. Illus.: Sketches. 1. Lang.: Eng.
USA: New York, NY. 1987. Histories-sources. ■Discussions among artistic directors, literary managers of more than twenty regional theatres and dramatists at FDG/CBC New Plays Program Conference. Unsolicited manuscripts, premieres versus previously produced works, the playwright-in-residence, developmental process.

1181 Trevens, Francine L. "TADA! An Exclamation Point of Opportunity in Children's Theatre." *DGQ*. 1987; 24(3): 30-31. Illus.: Sketches. 1. Lang.: Eng.
USA: New York, NY. 1987. Critical studies. ■Currently produced children's plays, their authors: kinds of plays sought by children's theatres.

1182 Whittlesey, Peregrine. "Dramaturgs and Literary Managers: After Literary Management." *DGQ*. 1987; 24(1): 18-19. Lang.: Eng.
USA: New York, NY. 1987. Critical studies. ■A literary manager becomes a playwright's agent because he wanted to become a more interested advocate for the writer. Reasons for becoming an agent over other careers in movies or television. Questions ability of anyone to stay in non-profit theatre.

1183 Winer, Laurie. "For Lucas and Rene, Teamwork Clicked." *AmTh*. 1987 Apr; 4(1): 36-37. Illus.: Photo. Print. B&W. 2. Lang.: Eng.
USA: New York, NY. 1985-1987. Critical studies. ■Collaboration between playwright Craig Lucas and director Norman Rene on *Blue Window*, *Three Postcards* and *Reckless*, focusing on structure of plays.

1184 Winer, Laurie. "People." *AmTh*. 1987 May; 4(2): 36-39. Illus.: Photo. B&W. 2. Lang.: Eng.
USA. 1987. Critical studies. ■Collaboration of Craig Lucas and Norman Rene on *Blue Window* and *Three Postcards*.

1185 "Teatr novogo zritelja." (The New Audience's Theatre.) *TeatZ*. 1987; 8: 6-7. Lang.: Rus.
USSR: Moscow. 1986-1987. Historical studies. ■Experiments of Moscow Children's Theatre, problems of children's theatre repertory.

1186 Giljarovskaja, Nadezna. "Contro l'archeologia nella scena teatrale." (Against Archaeology on the Stage.) *TeatrC*. 1987; 7(14): 157-162. Lang.: Ita.
USSR. 1987. Critical studies. ■Analysis of the works of Jakulov.

1187 Moskvičeva, G.V., ed. *Voprocy sjužeta i kompozicii: Mežvuzovskij sbornik.* (Questions of Plot and Composition: An Interinstitution Collection.) Gor'kij: Gor'k.un-t im. N.I. Lobačevskogo; 1987. 74 pp. Lang.: Rus.
USSR. 1987. Critical studies.

1188 Ninov, A.A. *Russkij teatr i dramaturgija épochi revoljucii 1905-1907 godov: sbornik naučnych trudov.* (Russian Theatre and Dramaturgy in the Revolutionary Period, 1905-1907: A Collection of Scientific Works.) Leningrad: LGIT-MiK; 1987. 187 pp. Lang.: Rus.
USSR. 1905-1907. Critical studies. ■Study of works by Maksim Gorkij, Leonid Andrejév, Jevgenij Čirikov, Innokentij Annenskij, Aleksand'r Blok, Valerij Brjusov and others. Also theatre events of the period of the first Russian revolution.

1189 Radsinskij, E. "Nužen dialog." (Dialogue Is Necssary.) *TeatZ*. 1987; 3: 22-23. Lang.: Rus.
USSR. 1987. Histories-sources. ■Interview with playwright Eduard Radsinskij on problems of contemporary theatre, foreign productions of his plays.

THEATRE IN GENERAL: —Plays/librettos/scripts

1190 Smeljanskij, A.M. "Porjadok slov." (The Order of Words.) *TeatrM.* 1987; 1: 4-21. Lang.: Rus.
USSR: Moscow. 1986-1987. Critical studies. ■Social and political themes in Moscow theatre performances of the 1986-87 season.

1191 Tuganova, O.V. *Vzaimodejstvie kul'tur SSSR i SSA 18-20 vv.: Sbornik statej.* (Interaction of the Cultures of the Soviet Union and the United States from the Eighteenth through the Twentieth Centuries: A Collection of Articles.) Moscow: Nauka; 1987. 228 pp. Lang.: Rus.
USSR. USA. 1700-1987. ■Interaction in science and culture, with emphasis on Čechov and Albee, O'Neill and Tairov.

Reference materials

1192 Brockett, Oscar G. *History of the Theatre.* Boston, MA: Allyn & Bacon; 1987. 779 pp. Index. Biblio. Illus.: Photo. Print. Color. B&W. 250. [5th ed.] Lang.: Eng.
500 B.C.-1987 A.D. Histories-general. ■Brockett's theatre history text updated to a 5th edition. Theatre history from the Greeks to the present.

1193 Carpenter, Charles A., comp. "Modern Drama Studies: An Annual Bibliography." *MD.* 1987 June; 30(2): 161-306. Lang.: Eng.
1986. ■Commentary on scholarship and criticism.

1194 Hay, Peter. *Theatrical Anecdotes.* New York, NY: Oxford UP; 1987. 392 pp. Notes. Biblio. Lang.: Eng.
500 B.C.-1987 A.D. Histories-sources. ■Collection of individual anecdotes create a portrait of the morals, manners and techniques of theatre artists and theatre itself through the ages.

1195 Hay, Peter. *Theatrical Anecdotes.* NY: Oxford UP; 1987. 392 pp. Pref. Index. Tables. Biblio. Lang.: Eng.
5 B.C.-1987 A.D. Historical studies. ■Compilation of stories about backstage rivalries, eccentricities of performers, indignities of touring and frugality of producers ranging from Aristophanes to Williams.

1196 Smiley, Sam. *Theatre: The Human Art.* New York, NY: Harper & Row; 1987. 433 pp. Index. Pref. Biblio. Append. Illus.: Photo. Print. B&W. 200. Lang.: Eng.
1987. Histories-general. ■Basic theatre history textbook for beginning students, from the perspective of human creativity. Explains how theatre is created and how audiences respond to it.

1197 *Annuaire du Spectacle de la Communauté Française de Belgique 1985-1986.* (Yearbook of Performing Arts in Belgium's French Community 1985-1986.) Bruxelles: Archives et Musée de la Littérature; 1987. 258 pp. Pref. Index. 174. Lang.: Fre.
Belgium. 1985-1986. Reviews of performances. ■Annals of theatre productions in Belgium's French community for the 1985-1986 season. Related to Dance-Drama.

1198 "Pao k'an wan tzai." (The Newspaper of the Select Article.) *XLunc.* 1984; 2: 125-126. Illus.: Photo. 3. Lang.: Chi.
China, People's Republic of. 1980-1984. ■Chinese drama yearbook. Selected problems within the sphere of Chinese drama are discussed and various opinions are offered.

1199 Lancashire, Ian. *Dramatic Texts and Records of Britain: A Chronological Topography to 1558.* Toronto, ON: Univ. of Toronto P; 1984. lxxi, 633. (Early English Drama 1.) Index. Biblio. Append. Illus.: Photo. Maps. Lang.: Eng.
England. 1558. ■Compiles the surviving records of British drama up to 1558. Includes records of play texts, dramatic performances, playing spaces, playwrights, visits by acting troupes, official acts of control over playing and other evidence relating to plays and their productions.

1200 Valentini, Valentina. *Teatro in immagine. Vol. 1: Eventi performativi e nuovi media. Vol. 2: Audiovisivi per il teatro.* (Theatre by Image: Vol. 1: Performative Events and New Media. Vol. 2: Audiovisuals for Theatre.) Rome: Bulzoni; 1987. 246 pp., 246 pp. (Videoteca teatrale 1/2.) Index. Notes. Illus.: Photo. Print. B&W. Lang.: Ita.
Europe. 1987. Instructional materials. ■Volume 1 discusses influence of new media, Volume 2 lists theatrical videos conserved in various European video libraries.

1201 Wickham, Glynne. *The Medieval Theatre.* New York, NY: Cambridge UP; 1987. 312 pp. Illus.: Photo. Dwg. Lang.: Eng.
Europe. 1000-1400. Histories-specific. ■Influence of religion, recreation and commerce upon the development of dramatic art in Christian Europe are described in this expanded history of medieval theatre.

1202 Blasting, Ralph. "Recent Publications—Notes from Germany." *REEDN.* 1987; 12(1): 19-21. Notes. Lang.: Eng.
Germany. 1986. Bibliographical studies. ■Description of the scope of Rolf Bergmann's *Katalog der deutschsprachigen geistlichen Spiele und Marienklagen des Mittelalters* and other related works in progress.

1203 Becker, Peter von, ed. "Dokumentation: Zahlen und Daten." (Documentation 1987: Figures and Dates.) *THeute.* 1987: 121-137. Lang.: Ger.
Germany, West. Austria. Switzerland. 1986-1987. ■Budgets and list of performances of 142 stages in German-speaking Europe (except G.D.R.). Figures also referring to subsidies, number of spectators, and average of seat-utilization.

1204 *Teatro italiano '86. Annuario I.D.I.-S.I.A.E. Stagione '85-'86.* (Italian Theatre '86. I.D.I.-S.I.A.E. Yearbook. Season '85-'86.) Rome: Società Italiana degli Autori ed Editori; 1987. 413 pp. Illus.: Photo. Print. B&W. 54. Lang.: Ita.
Italy. 1985-1986. Histories-sources. ■Productions by Italian companies, new Italian plays, festivals, exhibitions, summer theatre, prizes and competitions, television and radio broadcasts. Related to Media: Video forms.

1205 *Tutto teatro. Almanacco del teatro italiano 1987.* (All About Theatre: 1987 Italian Theatre Yearbook.) Rome: Gestione Editoriale AGIS; 1987. 334 pp. Index. Lang.: Ita.
Italy. 1987. Histories-sources. ■Names and addresses of institutions, companies, schools and theatres, geographically organized.

1206 *Il Patalogo dieci. Annuario 1987 dello spettacolo.* (The Patalogo Number Ten: 1987 Entertainment Yearbook.) Milan: Ubulibri; 1987. 286 pp. Illus.: Photo. Print. B&W. Lang.: Ita.
Italy. 1987. Histories-sources. ■Yearbook of theatre, cinema and television with brief critical annotations and statistical data. Related to Media: Film.

1207 Ente Teatrale Italiano. *Il teatro per ragazzi.* (Theatre for Youth.) Rome: ETI; 1987. 402 pp. (Documenti di teatro 6.) Pref. Index. Tables. Illus.: Sketches. Lang.: Ita.
Italy. 1986-1987. Histories-sources. ■Statistic and economic data of the Ente Teatrale Italiano system, catalogue of E.T.I. children's productions.

1208 Nowak, Maciej, ed.; Barcikowska, Małgorzata. "Bibliografia tytułów czasopism teatralnych 1758-1950. Suplement." (Bibliography of Theatre Magazines, 1758-1950: Supplement.) *PaT.* 1987; 3: 397-450. Pref. Notes. Index. Lang.: Pol.
Poland. 1758-1950. ■Listing of titles in Yiddish, German and Czech as well as Polish. Supplements bibliography by Straus.

1209 Comediants, Els. *La nit.* (The Night.) Graphic Design by Salvador Saura, Ramon Torrente and Els Comediants. Design. Pntg. Photo. Print. Color. B&W. 139. Lang.: Cat.
Spain-Catalonia. 1987. Histories-sources. ■Companion to Els Comediants' opening of *La Nit*, the book contains numerous illustrations related graphically and thematically to night.

1210 Molinas i Falgueras, Lluís. *El teatre a Palafrugell. Album-recull.* (The Theatre in Palafrugell: Album-Collection.) Palafrugell: Ajuntament de Palafrugell; 1987. 128 pp. Illus.: Design. Photo. Print. B&W. Lang.: Cat.
Spain-Catalonia: Palafrugell. 1900-1986. Histories-reconstruction. ■History of theatrical life in Palafrugell, divided into three periods: 1900-1939, 1940-1960, 1960-1986. Abundant visual documentation on the most significant individuals.

1211 Dreier, Martin. "Theater in Gegenwart und Geschichte: Dauerausstellung der Schweizer Theatersammlung." (Theatre Today and in History: Permanent Exhibition at Swiss Theatre Collection, Berne.) *ProScenium.* 1987 July; 15(3): 12-16. Illus.: Photo. B&W. 253. Lang.: Fre, Ger.

THEATRE IN GENERAL: —Reference materials

Switzerland: Berne. 1987. Historical studies. ■Since May 1987 the permanent exhibition entitled 'Theatre Today and in History' has been accessible to the public. Article informs as to contents (tracing theatre from antique Greek to present-day European) and didactic aim of the running exhibition.

1212 Rauch, Gaby, ed. *Bibliographie zur deutschsprachigen Schweizer-literatur (BSL).* (Bibliography of German-speaking Swiss Literature.) Bern: Schweizerische Landesbibliothek; 1987. (Vol 10 (1985).) Lang.: Ger.

Switzerland. 1987. ■Bibliography (begun in 1976) containing all authors living and working in German-speaking Switzerland: primary and secondary texts, reviews, critical analyses.

1213 Barbour, Sheena, ed. *British Performing Arts Yearbook 1988.* London: Rhinegold; 1987. 1081 pp. Pref. Index. Illus.: Maps. B&W. Chart. 5. [1st ed.] Lang.: Eng.

UK-England. 1987. Critical studies. ■Emphasizes venues and companies, producing managements, orchestras, music agencies, arts festivals, support organizations, suppliers and agents.

1214 Conway, Robert, ed.; McGillivray, David, ed. *British Alternative Theatre Directory 1987.* London: Conway McGillivray; 1987. Index. Illus.: Photo. Maps. B&W. 80. [8th ed.] Lang.: Eng.

UK-England. 1986-1987. Historical studies. ■Lists fringe, touring, dance and puppet companies, young people's theatre, venues, arts associations, festivals.

1215 Holland, Ann, ed. *British Theatre Directory 1987-88.* London: Richmond House; 1987. 572 pp. Illus.: Photo. Maps. B&W. 7. [16th ed.] Lang.: Eng.

UK-England. 1986-1987. Critical studies. ■Sections for venues, municipal entertainment, facilities, production (managements, companies, orchestras), agents, publishing, training and education, supplies and services.

1216 Hale, Alice M. "Living and Working in L.A." *ThCr.* 1985 Jan.; 19(1): 32-37, 96-97. Lang.: Eng.

USA: Los Angeles, CA. 1987. Instructional materials. ■Introductory survival guide for theatre professionals.

1217 Hill, Philip G. "Doctoral Projects in Progress in Theatre Arts, 1987." *TJ.* 1987 May; 39(2): 228-231. Lang.: Eng.

USA. 1987. Histories-sources. ■Listing of current doctoral projects in progress (1987).

Relation to other fields

1218 Gründ, Françoise. "La tradition vivante, élément dynamique de la créativité contemporaine?" (Living Tradition, Dynamic Element of Contemporary Creativity?)9-22 in Coca, Jordi, ed.; Conesa, Laura, comp. *Congrés Internacional de Teatre a Catalunya 1985. Actes. Volum III. Seccions 4, 5 i 6.* Barcelona: Institut del Teatre; 1987. 302 pp. Notes. [Section 4: Tradition and Modernity.] Lang.: Fre.

Asia. Africa. 1985. Critical studies. ■Analysis of the role of tradition informing dramaturgies of different cultures, especially Asian, African and Arab. Related to Dance.

1219 Helbo, André; Johansen, J. Dines; Pavis, Patrice; Carlson, Marvin; De Marinis, Marco; Larsen, Svend Erik; Østergaard, Ane Grethe; Ruffini, Franco; Seeberg, Lars; Ubersfeld, Anne, ed. *Théâtre Modes d'approche.* (Theatre Modes of Approach.) Brussels/Paris: Labor/Méridiens Klincksieck; 1987. 270 pp. Pref. Biblio. Illus.: Photo. B&W. 9. Lang.: Fre.

Belgium: Brussels. France: Paris. Denmark: Odense. 1983-1985. Histories-sources. ■Accounts of an experimental theatre training course conducted by the Association Internationale pour la Sémiologie du Spectacle and sponsored by the European Community. Includes discussion of *A Midsummer Night's Dream* staged by Peter Brook and *The Seagull* staged by Antoine Vitez.

1220 Davis, Irene. "Free Trade: The Cultural Issue." *PAC.* 1986 Jan.; 22(4): 8-10. Notes. Illus.: Photo. Print. 3. Lang.: Eng.

Canada. USA. 1986. Critical studies. ■Free trade between Canada and the United States and its effect on Canadian economy and performing arts.

1221 Hale, Amanda. "Ballrooms and Boardroom Tables." *CTR.* 1987 Win; 53: 29-34. Illus.: Photo. Print. B&W. 2. [Meanwhile in Toronto.../3.] Lang.: Eng.

Canada: Toronto, ON. 1987. Critical studies. ■Critical account of *The Working People's Picture Show,* created by the Ground Zero company to address women's experience in the workforce, as well as women's historical role, highlighting need for change: songs, dance, comedy are tools used to subvert and question authority. Excerpts are provided.

1222 Matsui, Judith. "Now More Than Ever." *CTR.* 1987 Win; 53: 7-10. Notes. Illus.: Photo. Print. B&W. 5. [Notes on Popular Theatre.../2.] Lang.: Eng.

Canada. 1987. Critical studies. ■Canadian popular theatre is examined as a necessary tool for critical analysis or social development. Beyond therapeutic benefits of communication between theatre and its audience, other positive aspects include self-expression and self-recognition over foreign content.

1223 Weiss, Peter Eliot. "Vancouver Give My Regards to Hell's Kitchen." *CTR.* 1987 Fall; 52: 89-91. Illus.: Photo. Print. B&W. 1. Lang.: Eng.

Canada: Vancouver, BC. USA: New York, NY. 1987. Critical studies. ■Plight of Canadian playwrights contrasted to their American counterparts. Colonialist attitudes of critics and reluctance of patrons to recognize special relationship of Canadian playwrights with their audience/country.

1224 Liao, Pen. "Song Yuan Beei Fang Tzar Cheu Fa Jean Shiuh Lieh Dih Lih Shyy Chern Ji." (The History and Development of Northern Chinese Drama during the Song and Yuan Dynasties.) *XYanj.* 1987; 8(19): 23-47. Lang.: Chi.

China. 960-1368. Historical studies. ■According to sculptures, statues and stone tablets discovered in the provinces of Honan and Shansi.

1225 Peng, Fei. "Yuan dai zhi shi fen zi min yun." (The Intellectuals under the Mongols in China.) *XYishu.* 1987 Spr; 37: 97-107. Notes. Lang.: Chi.

China. 1279-1368. Historical studies. ■Social phenomena, specifically the relationship of intellectuals and the religious, during the Yuan Dynasty (the Mongols).

1226 "A Few More Flowers Bloom." *Econ.* 1987 16 May; 303: 97. Illus.: Photo. B&W. 1. Lang.: Eng.

China, People's Republic of. 1987. Historical studies. ■Following recent conservative political restrictions, writers and artists wait to see how far party leaders will allow artistic expression to go.

1227 Ding, Luo-Nan. "Zai fan si han tan suo zhong qian jin." (The Progression Under Self-Examination and Search.) *XYishu.* 1987 Spr; 37: 37-46. Lang.: Chi.

China, People's Republic of. 1949-1987. Historical studies. ■Characterization in modern drama.

1228 Peng, Hao-Xian. "Xin xi she hui yu xi ju xue." (Information and Theatre.) *XYishu.* 1985 Spr; 29: 140-153. Lang.: Chi.

China, People's Republic of. 1948-1974. Historical studies. ■Theatre and its lively relationship to society.

1229 Dacal, Enrique. "Educación, Cultura y Teatro." (Education, Culture and Theatre.) *Cjo.* 1987 July/Sept; 73: 29-30. Lang.: Spa.

Cuba. 1987. Critical studies. ■Proposes an alternative to the perception of culture and education held by society and intelligensia.

1230 Muguercia, Magaly. "Nuevos Caminos en el Teatro Latinoamericano?" (New Roads in Latin American Theatre?)*Cjo.* 1987 July/Sept; 73: 15-28. Notes. Illus.: Design. Photo. B&W. 4. Lang.: Spa.

Cuba. 1973-1986. Critical studies. ■Characterizes general tendencies in Latin American theatre that may have influenced its evolution.

1231 Orkin, Martin. "Cruelty, *King Lear* and the South African Land Act in 1913." *ShS.* 1987; 40: 135-143. Lang.: Eng.

England. South Africa, Republic of. 1605-1913. Critical studies. ■Study of the connection between *King Lear* and the South African Land Act of 1913 in terms of land distribution.

1232 Riggs, David. "Ben Jonson's Family." *RORD.* 1987; 29: 1-5. Lang.: Eng.

England. 1602-1604. Biographical studies. ■Discusses the psychological effect of Ben Jonson's family life on his writings.

THEATRE IN GENERAL: —Relation to other fields

1233 Montesarchio, Gianni; Sardi, Paola. *Dal teatro della spontaneità allo psicodramma classico. Contributo per una revisione del pensiero di J.L. Moreno.* (From the Theatre of Spontaneity to Classic Psychodrama: Contribution to a Revision of the Ideas of J.L. Moreno.) Milan: Angeli; 1987. 117 pp. (Collana di psicologia sociale 2.) Pref. Biblio. Gloss. Lang.: Ita.
Europe. North America. 1900-1987. Critical studies. ■Development of psychodrama in clinical and classroom situations. Moreno's work as a bridge between classical theatre and the forms of non-conventional dramaturgy in contemporary theatre research.

1234 Sarmela, Matti; Poom, Ritva, transl. "Death of the Bear: An Old Finnish Hunting Drama." *TDR.* 1982 Fall; 26(3): 57-66. Lang.: Eng.
Finland. 1600-1982. Historical studies. ■Description of Finnish bear-hunting ritual drawn from several texts. Includes poetry presented at various stages of the ritual and hunters' incantations.

1235 "International Conference in Paris Studies Role of Today's Actor in Society." *EN.* 1982 Dec.; 67(12): 3. Illus.: Photo. B&W. 1. Lang.: Eng.
France: Paris. 1982. Historical studies. ■International Federation of Actors meets in Paris to discuss the economic, technical and social realities facing the actor.

1236 Wischenbart, Ruediger; Honegger, Gitta. "Jean Genet: The Intellectual as Guerrilla." *PerAJ.* 1985 Spr; 9(25): 36-45. Illus.: Photo. Print. B&W. 1. Lang.: Eng.
France. 1967-1985. Histories-sources. ■Interview with playwright Jean Genet regarding his political involvements around the world.

1237 Schumacher, Ernst. "Das 750järige Berlin und seine Theater: Zur Theatergeschichte einer Stadt." (750 Years of Berlin and Her Theatres: On the History of a City's Theatres.) *TZ.* 1987; 42(3): 8-13. Illus.: Photo. Dwg. 30. Lang.: Ger.
Germany: Berlin. 1700-1987. Historical studies. ■Cultural and social role of Berlin theatres, including role of theatre in East Berlin after 1945.

1238 Sperber, Heinz; Stampfer, Friedrich; Mehring, Franz; Märten, Lu; Bürgel, Tanja, ed. *Tendenzkunst-Debatte. 1910-1912. Dokumente zur Literaturtheorie und Literaturkritik der revolutionären deutschen Sozialdemokratie.* (Debate on Tendentious Art, 1910-1912: Documents of Literary Theory and Criticism by the Revolutionary German Social Democrats.) Berlin (East): Akademie-Verlag; 1987. 173 pp. Pref. Index. Lang.: Ger.
Germany: Berlin. 1910-1912. Critical studies. ■Debate on function of proletarian art, role of theatre and drama in workers' education, repertory for workers audience.

1239 Zwiauer, Herbert; Trumler, Gerhard, photo. *Papiertheater: Bühnenwelt en Miniature.* (Paper Theatre: Reproductions of Stage Settings.) Wien: Herold Verlag; 1987. 72 pp. Biblio. Illus.: Photo. Color. Lang.: Ger.
Germany. Switzerland. 1900-1930. Historical studies. ■What was considered educational toys for children are now authentic reproductions of 19th-century stage settings of great theatre and opera productions. The lost tradition of Paper Theatre gives insight into 19th century attitudes to theatre and education.

1240 van Erven, Eugène. "The Theatre of Liberation of India, Indonesia and The Philippines." *ADS.* 1987 Apr.; 10: 5-18. Lang.: Eng.
India. Indonesia. 1970-1986. Critical studies. ■Failure of political theatre in the West, success of third world theatre of liberation, which emphasizes process rather than performance, with the people as participants rather than observers, learning through improvisation and discussion.

1241 Furman, Lou. "Child Drama in Israel: Two Perspectives." *YTJ.* 1987 Spr; 1(4): 9-11. Notes. Lang.: Eng.
Israel. 1973. Critical studies. ■Developmental stages and needs of children's drama in Israel, incorporating it into education.

1242 De Marinis, Marco. "Attraverso lo specchio." (Through the Mirror.) *BiT.* 1987; 8: 19-44. Biblio. Lang.: Ita.
Italy. 1900-1987. Critical studies. ■The relationship between theatre and everyday life is no longer regarded as reproduction, reflection, imitation but increasingly as analysis, modeling and production. Any definition of the stage event that is not based on pragmatic criteria (i.e., 'intentio spectatoris') is impossible and unproductive.

1243 Francastel, Pierre. *Guardare il teatro.* (Looking at the Theatre.) Bologna: Mulino; 1987. 253 pp. (Intersezioni 34.) Illus.: Pntg. 16. Lang.: Ita.
Italy. 1987. Critical studies. ■Translation of several essays from French.

1244 Grotowski, Jerzy. "Tu es le fils de quelqu'un [You Are Someone's Son]." *TDR.* 1987 Fall; 31(3): 30-41. Lang.: Eng.
Italy: Florence. 1985. Critical studies. ■Excerpt from a speech by Jerzy Grotowski that examines the actor's technique both psychologically and philosophically.

1245 Lombardi, Giovanni, ed.; Alonge, Roberto; Valeri, Mario; Lapini, Lia; Gulotta, Baldassare; Pedrini, Giovanni. "Il teatro e la scuola." (Theatre and School.) *QT.* 1987 Aug.; 10(37): 3-77. Lang.: Ita.
Italy. 1970-1987. Critical studies. ■Collection of articles on theatre as a teaching tool: difficulties of including it in the national educational agenda.

1246 Han-Ki, Chang. "Hamil minsok-ui bigyo yeongu." (Comparative Study on Folklore of Japan and Korea.) *DongukDA.* 1987 Jun.; 17(1): 5-28. Pref. Tables. Illus.: Photo. B&W. 7. Lang.: Kor.
Korea. Japan: Kyushu. 1987. Historical studies. ■Mask plays and their relation to folklore. Related to Puppetry.

1247 Han, Jai-Soo. "Changjojeok yonkuksungkwa simlikuk." (Creative Dramatists and Psychodrama.) *DongukDA.* 1978 Apr.; 10-11: 57-65. Lang.: Kor.
Korea. 1978. Critical studies. ■Theoretical examination of psychodrama, creative drama.

1248 *Dejatel'nost' kompartii Litvy po razvitiju teatral'nogo iskusstva v respublike (1966-1980 gg.): Avtoref. dis. kand. istor. nauk.* (The Activity of the Lithuanian Communist Party in the Development of Theatrical Art in the Republic, 1966-1980: Abstract of a Dissertation by a Candidate in History.) Vil'njus: Vil'njus.un-t im. V. Kapsukasa; 1987. 23 pp. Lang.: Rus.
Lithuania. 1966-1980. Historical studies.

1249 Berg, Kent. "Private and Public Funding and Management on National, Regional, and Local Levels: Norwegian Cultural Policy for the 1980s." *JAML.* 1984 Fall; 14(3): 63-68. Lang.: Eng.
Norway. 1980-1984. Historical studies. ■Norwegian cultural policy for the 1980s: development, background and a look to the future.

1250 Langslet, Lars Roar. "Challenges and Perspectives for the 1980s: View from Norway." *JAML.* 1984 Fall; 14(3): 53-62. Lang.: Eng.
Norway. 1984. Historical studies. ■State of cultural similarities and differences between the United States and Norway.

1251 Eichbaum, Julius. "The U.N. Blacklist—A Counterproductive Farce and the Thin Edge of the Wedge." *Scenaria.* 1987 Aug.; 79: 3-4. Lang.: Eng.
South Africa, Republic of. 1987. Critical studies. ■United Nations cultural boycott on artists who have performed in South Africa: its effect on apartheid and on audiences of the country.

1252 Sole, Kelwyn. "Identities and Priorities in Recent Black Literature and Performance: A Preliminary Investigation." *SATJ.* 1987; 1(1): 45-113. Lang.: Eng.
South Africa, Republic of. 1970-1987. Historical studies. ■Influences of Black political and economic life on Black literature and performance in South Africa.

1253 Evers, Bernadette. "Wieviele Frauen verkraftet das Theater?" (How Many Women Can a Theatre Bear?) *Theater Morgen.* 1987 May; 1(2): 3-6. Tables. Illus.: Photo. B&W. Lang.: Ger.
Switzerland. 1987. Histories-sources. ■Report of a discussion among women concerning managers at Swiss theatres, organized by FiT

THEATRE IN GENERAL: —Relation to other fields

(Women in Theatre). Added to text is a catalogue stating demands as to social security for women working in the theatrical field.

1254 Evers, Bernadette; Gödrös, Margot. "FiT—Frauen im Theater." (WiT—Women in Theatre.) ix-xii in Apothéloz, Anne-Lise. *Szene Schweiz-Scène Suisse-Scena Svizzera.* Bonstetten: Theaterkultur-Verlag; 1987. 214 pp. (SSSS 14—1986/87.) Tables. Lang.: Ger, Fre.

Switzerland. 1985-1986. ■Although many women are engaged in theatre activities, most of them are in assisting positions. FiT (Women in Theatre) introduces its organization and proclaims its function and aims.

1255 Meier, Peter. *'Schlagt ihn tot, den Hund! Er ist ein Rezensent'.* ('Beat him dead, that dog! He's a critic'.) Bern: Zytglogge Verlag; 1987. 143 pp. Pref. Lang.: Ger.

Switzerland. 1960-1985. ■The critic is presented as being torn between social realities and party-political views as to the function of culture. The discrepancy between aesthetic and political criteria in theatrical and literary art is laid bare.

1256 Moser-Ehinger, Hansueli. "Freies Theater in einer freien Wirtschaft: Zensur durch den Geldhahn." (Free Theatre on the Free Market: Censored by Cash Flow Shortage.) *ASTEJ-Information.* 1987 Mar.(44): 9-14. Illus.: Diagram. Lang.: Ger.

Switzerland. 1987. Critical studies. ■Theatre in Switzerland is highly subsidized by the state. Financial support is, however, mostly restricted to the official playhouses and operas, whereas alternative theatre has to beg for every penny, and room to play in as well. Diagram illustrates the state finance situation concerning theatre.

1257 "Queen Margaret or Shakespeare Goes to the Falklands." *Econ.* 1982 25 Dec.: 13-20. Illus.: Sketches. 5. Lang.: Eng.

UK-England. 1982. Historical studies. ■Political satire emulating writing style of Shakespeare on Britain's conflict in the Falkland Islands using public figures and politicians as characters.

1258 Davis, Tracy C. "Victorian Charity and Self-Help for Women Performers." *TN.* 1987; 41(3): 114-128. Notes. Tables. Lang.: Eng.

UK-England. 1851-1920. Historical studies. ■Charitable and self-help welfare schemes for theatre personnel, focus on experiences of women.

1259 Donohue, Joseph, ed. "The Empire Theatre of Varieties Licensing Controversy of 1894: Testimony of Laura Ormiston Chant before the Theatres and Music Halls Committee of the London County Council, Sessions House, Clerkenwell, 10 October 1894." *NCT.* 1987; 15(1): 5-60. Notes. Lang.: Eng.

UK-England: London. 1890. Histories-sources. ■Contemporaneous evidence about prostitution activities in the Promenade section of the Empire Theatre of Varieties.

1260 Martin, Carol. "Charabanc Theatre Company." *TDR.* 1987 Sum; 31(2): 88-99. Illus.: Photo. B&W. 4. Lang.: Eng.

UK-Ireland. 1970-1987. Histories-sources. ■Interview with the founders of the Charabanc Theatre Company: Marie Jones, Carol Scanlan, Eleanor Methven, Maureen Macauley and Brenda Winter. Focus on women's theatrical rights in Ireland.

1261 "Equity Launches New Affirmative Action Program for Greater Employment of Minorities and Women." *EN.* 1982 Feb.; 67(2): 1. Illus.: Photo. B&W. 2. Lang.: Eng.

USA: New York, NY. 1982. Critical studies. ■Actors' Equity's affirmative action program for minorities and women.

1262 "Equity's Plan for a National Theatre of the United States." *EN.* 1982 Sep.; 67(9): 3. Lang.: Eng.

USA. 1982. Critical studies. ■Equity's National Theatre Plan as the only historical solution for providing steady, long-term employment to its average unemployed of 80.

1263 Bentley, Eric. "Writing for a Political Theatre." *PerAJ.* 1985 Sum/Fall; 9(26-27): 45-58. Lang.: Eng.

USA. 1985. Critical studies. ■Political viewpoints in drama and other art forms: what constitutes a political/propagandist theatre.

1264 Blair, Sarah Boyd; Diener, Mick; Lewis, Steven; St. John, Maria. "Mudpeople There and Here: Three Reports." *TDR.* 1987 Win; 31(4): 24-35. 6. Lang.: Eng.

USA: Providence, RI, New York, NY. New Guinea. 1986-1987. Historical studies. ■Three reports discussing appearance and symbolism of New Guinea Mudmen, a ritual tourist attraction.

1265 Blau, Herbert. "The Audition of Dream and Events." *TDR.* 1987 Fall; 31(3): 59-73. Notes. Biblio. Lang.: Eng.

USA. 1958-1985. Critical studies. ■Artaud's philosophy of theatre mediating between dream and history.

1266 Brooks, Colette. "The Marginal Body." *AmTh.* 1987 Oct.; 4(7): 30-31. Illus.: Dwg. 1. Lang.: Eng.

USA. 1950-1987. Technical studies. ■Analysis of past and current perceptions of the human body, how they affect the human experience and the arts.

1267 Burnham, Linda Frye. "Hands Across Skid Row." *TDR.* 1987 Sum; 31(2): 126-149. Notes. Biblio. Illus.: Photo. B&W. 13. Lang.: Eng.

USA: Los Angeles, CA. 1984-1987. Histories-sources. ■John Malpede's performance workshop for the homeless of Los Angeles: performance notes, sections of script, interview with Malpede.

1268 Colby, Robert W. "A Rationale for Drama as Education." *YTJ.* 1987 Spr; 1(4): 3-7. Notes. Lang.: Eng.

USA. 1987. Critical studies. ■Theoretical framework for the role of drama as education, exploring its history and development in relation to education.

1269 Courtney, Richard. "On Dramatic Instruction: Towards a Taxonomy of Methods." *YTJ.* 1987 Sum; 2(1): 3-7. Biblio. 1. Lang.: Eng.

USA. 1987. Critical studies. ■Potential methods for instructors working with dramatic action in educational drama, drama therapy, social drama and theatre.

1270 Dolan, Jill. "The Dynamics of Desire: Sexuality and Gender in Pornography and Performance." *TJ.* 1987 May; 39(2): 156-174. Illus.: Photo. B&W. 2. Lang.: Eng.

USA. 1987. Critical studies. ■Analysis of the role of sexuality and desire in performance.

1271 Flannery, James. "Southern Theatre and the Paradox of Progress." *PerAJ.* 1985 Sum/Fall; 9(26-27): 106-116. Lang.: Eng.

USA. 1985. Critical studies. ■Specific problems facing Southern theatre in America.

1272 Gates, Tom. "Al Hirschfeld: Drawing on Experience." *TheaterW.* 1987 Nov 9; 1(13): 6-9. Illus.: Photo. B&W. 4. Lang.: Eng.

USA: New York, NY. 1925-1981. Histories-sources. ■Interview with caricaturist Al Hirschfeld: his life and career in drawing theatrical sketches of Broadway theatre.

1273 Golodner, Jack. "Sweeping Changes in Policies Affect Future Arts Programs Nationwide." *EN.* 1982 May; 67(5): 3. Illus.: Dwg. 1. Lang.: Eng.

USA: Washington, DC. 1982. Critical studies. ■National Endowment for the Arts suffers severe cutbacks due to re-direction of wealth and government.

1274 Hulder, Kathleen; Bartow, Arthur. "Rehearsal for an Absence of Racism." *AmTh.* 1987 Feb.; 3(11): 20-22. Illus.: Photo. B&W. 4. Lang.: Eng.

USA. 1979-1987. Historical studies. ■Nontraditional casting and debate over casting minority actors in roles typically given to Anglo-Saxon actors.

1275 Kase-Polisini, Judith. "Getting Our Act Together." *YTJ.* 1987 Spr; 1(4): 15-17.

USA. 1987. Critical studies. ■Making all aspects of theatre and creative drama a full-time part of kindergarten through twelfth grade curriculum.

1276 Katz, Stanley. "History, Cultural Policy and International Exchange in the Performing Arts." *PerAJ.* 1985 Sum/Fall; 9(26-27): 76-88. Lang.: Eng.

USA. 1985. Critical studies. ■Need for a national policy regarding international artistic exchange.

THEATRE IN GENERAL: —Relation to other fields

1277 Klein, Jeanne. "Children's Processing of Theatre as a Function of Verbal and Visual Recall." *YTJ*. 1987 Sum; 2(1): 9-13. Notes. Biblio. Lang.: Eng.

USA. 1964. Empirical research. ■Comparing cognitive processing of theatre with television research: importance of visual imagery over aural and verbal modes. Related to Media: Video forms.

1278 Koste, Virgina Glasgow. *Dramatic Play in Childhood: Rehearsal for Life.* Lanham, MD: UP of America; 1987. 222 pp. Lang.: Eng.

USA. 1987. Historical studies. ■The nature and working of dramatic imagination in the natural play of childhood. Issues covered are: seriousness of play, importance of play and the process of dramatic play as a way for a child to order, clarify and understand human experience.

1279 Mangham, Iain H.; Overington, Michael A. *Organizations as Theatre: A Social Psychology of Dramatic Appearances.* New York, NY: Wiley; 1987. 218 pp. Index. Notes. Biblio. Lang.: Eng.

USA. 1987. Critical studies. ■Application of theatre analogy and metaphor to social action within organizations.

1280 Mankin, Lawrence D. "The National Endowment for the Arts: The Biddle Years and After." *JAML*. 1984 Sum; 14(2): 59-80. Notes. Lang.: Eng.

USA. 1977-1981. Historical studies. ■Historical look at the NEA during the term of office of Livingston Biddle (1977-1981). Background and financial information.

1281 Morris, Valerie. "The State of Arts Education: A Round Table." *JAML*. 1984 Sum; 14(2): 21-39. Lang.: Eng.

USA. 1984. Histories-sources. ■Participants included representatives from *JAML*, National Institute of Education, Music Educators National Conference and the National Endowment for the Arts.

1282 Munk, Erika. "INS Fights Foreign Invaders." *TDR*. 1987 Spr; 31(1): 117-119. Lang.: Eng.

USA. 1986. Critical studies. ■Problems American presenters confront with Immigration and Naturalization Service when bringing over foreign artists whose political ideologies do not conform with INS policy.

1283 Rokem, Freddie. "Acting and Psychoanalysis: Street Scenes, Private Scenes, and Transference." *TJ*. 1987 May; 39(2): 175-184. Lang.: Eng.

USA. 1987. Critical studies. ■Analysis of the cultural, social and psychological assumptions made by an audience while viewing a work of theatre and by the actor while performing.

1284 Savage, Jack. "Soviets Get Elbow Room." *AmTh*. 1987 Sep.; 4(6): 34-35. Lang.: Eng.

USA: New York, NY. USSR: Moscow. 1987. Historical studies. ■Recent exchange of ideas between Soviets and US theatre artists. Opinions on the effect of 'glasnost' on future theatre.

1285 Schechner, Richard; Renzi, Vince. "So You Wanna Be a Teacher." *TDR*. 1987 Sum; 31(2): 4-21. Notes. Biblio. Illus.: Graphs. B&W. 8. Lang.: Eng.

USA. 1986-1987. Critical studies. ■Evaluation of teaching opportunities in theatre and dance at the university level.

1286 Stover, Carl F. "A Public Interest in Art: Its Recognition and Stewardship." *JAML*. 1984 Fall; 14(3): 5-12. Lang.: Eng.

USA. 1987. Critical studies. ■Art as a 'public interest' exhibited through its partnerships with private philanthropy and state and local governments.

1287 Surface, Mary Hall. "The Professional Connection: Playwriting for Young Audiences and Multicultural Influences: Does Sleeping Beauty Have Anything to do With Them?" *YTJ*. 1987 Sum; 2(1): 22-25. Lang.: Eng.

USA. 1986. Critical studies. ■Cultural mix of public school classroom and ways for playwrights to reach children without writing a specifically 'ethnic' play.

1288 Townsend, Jane. "Wondering Questions in Creative Drama." *YTJ*. 1987 Sum; 2(1): 14-18. Notes. Biblio. Lang.: Eng.

USA. 1970-1977. Critical studies. ■Creative drama's potential to support 'wondering' and encourage learning.

1289 Versenyi, Adam. "Camera Theatron: Sherman/Steichen." *ThM*. 1987; 18(2): 14-21. Illus.: Photo. B&W. 6. Lang.: Eng.

USA. 1900-1987. Critical studies. ■Self-conscious theatricality of photographer Cindy Sherman's work. Compared to lack of theatricality in Edward Steichen's work. Sees the study of photography as a way to articulate a theatre of images.

1290 Zeisler, Peter. "The Mirror Cracked." *AmTh*. 1987 Sep.; 4(6): 3. Lang.: Eng.

USA. 1987. Historical studies. ■Diminishing ethics in society in areas of business, politics and education. Reflection of this breakdown in the theatre.

1291 Zesch, Lindy. "The Tangled Politics of Cultural Exchange." *AmTh*. 1987 Oct.; 4(7): 57-58. Lang.: Eng.

USA: Washington, DC. USSR: Moscow. China, People's Republic of: Peking. 1987. Historical studies. ■Recent cultural exchange pacts the USA has made with the Soviet Union and with China: how these pacts affect and are affected by the political climate in the countries.

1292 "Glasnost's Artifice." *Econ*. 1987 29 Aug.; 304: 84. Lang.: Eng.

USSR. 1987. Historical studies. ■Effects of glasnost's policy on exportation and expression of Russian arts.

1293 "Ponjat' i poljubit' ili poljubit' i ponjat'?" (To Understand and Come to Love or to Come to Love and Understand?) *TeatrM*. 1987; 2: 116-129. Lang.: Rus.

USSR. 1980-1987. Histories-sources. ■Theatre critics V. Siljunos, A. Bartoševič and M. Švydkoj on new political thinking, problems of the word and of theatrical culture.

1294 "Kul'turnye svjazi—doroga s dvustoronnim dviženiem." (Cultural Ties: A Two-Way Street.) *TeatZ*. 1987; 16: 18-21. Lang.: Rus.

USSR. 1980-1987. Histories-sources. ■Round-table discussion on international cultural ties by critics and playwrights: A. Bartoševič, Aleksand'r Galin, G. Gorin, V. Ivanov, Eduard Radsinskij, M. Švydkoj, V. Šechovcev.

1295 Fecht-Babuškin, Ju. "Napravit' goru k Magometu." (Send the Mountain to Mohammed.) *SovD*. 1987; 4: 194-200. Lang.: Rus.

USSR. 1980-1987. Histories-sources. ■Sociologist discusses the influence of art, ways of developing artistic culture.

1296 Titov, Ju. K. *Rol' sovremennogo teatra v idejno-nravstvennom vospitanii molodeži: Avtoref. dis. kand filosof. nauk.* (The Role of the Contemporary Theatre in the Ideational and Moral Education of Youth: Abstract of a Dissertation by a Candidate in Philosophy.) Moscow: Mosk. in-t kul'tury; 1987. 16 pp. Lang.: Rus.

USSR. 1987. Critical studies.

Research/historiography

1297 Draudt, Manfred. "The Rationale of Current Bibliographical Methods: Printing House Studies, Computer-Aided Compositor Studies, and the Use of Statistical Methods." *ShS*. 1987; 40: 145-153. Lang.: Eng.

1987. Critical studies. ■Shakespeare texts: discussion of the different types of bibliographic methodology, pro and con.

1298 Gibson, Colin. "Elizabethan and Stuart Dramatists in *Wit's Creation* (1640)." *RORD*. 1987; 29: 15-23. Lang.: Eng.

England: London. 1640. Textual studies. ■Discussion of the miscellany called *Wit's Creation, Selected from the Finest Fancies of Modern Muses, with Outlandish Proverbs*, published in London in 1640.

1299 Miola, Robert S. "Shakespeare and His Source: Observations on the Critical History of *Julius Caesar*." *ShS*. 1987; 40: 69-76. Lang.: Eng.

England. 1599-1987. Critical studies. ■Critical history of *Julius Caesar*.

1300 *Le forze in campo. Per una nuova cartografia del teatro.* (Forces in the Field: Toward a New Cartography of Theatre.) Modena: Mucchi; 1987. Lang.: Ita.

Italy. 1986. Critical studies. ■Reports and papers based on a conference in Modena, 1986 on theatre research in Italy.

1301 Mullaly, Edward. "Computers and Theatre Research." *ThS*. 1987 May; 28(1): 59-70. Notes. Lang.: Eng.

THEATRE IN GENERAL: —Research/historiography

North America. 1987. Critical studies. ▪Discussions and examples of database manipulation to yield patterns of information.

1302 Brockett, Oscar G. "The American Theatre, 1961-1986: An Address Delivered Before the National Educational Theatre Conference in August, 1986." *THSt.* 1987; 7: 99-116. Lang.: Eng.

USA. 1961-1986. Historical studies. ▪Expansion, diversification and artistic innovation in the American theatre.

1303 Moody, Richard. "The American Theatre, 1936-1961: An Address Delivered Before the National Educational Theatre Conference in August, 1986." *THSt.* 1987; 7: 84-98. Lang.: Eng.

USA. 1937-1961. Historical studies. ▪Trends, movements and notable productions and theatrical figures in the development of American theatre.

1304 Koroleva, O.I. *Formirovanie metodologii sovetskogo teatrovedenija (1920-1929): Avtoref. dis. kand. iskusstvovedenija.* (Formation of the Methodology of Soviet Theatre Science, 1920-1929: Abstract of a Dissertation by a Candidate in Art Criticism.) Moscow: GITIS; 1987. 24 pp. Lang.: Rus.

USSR. 1920-1929. Historical studies.

Theory/criticism

1305 *Heitere Poetik, Von der Kantine zum Theater.* (Hilarious Poetics: From the Canteen to the Theatre.) Halle, Lepizig: Mitteldeutscher Verlag; 1987. 288 pp. Lang.: Ger.

1987. Critical studies. ▪Reflections on the nature of theatre, of humor and the relation between art and reality.

1306 Blau, Herbert. *The Eye of Prey: Subversions of the Postmodern.* Bloomington, IN: Indiana UP; 1987. 213 pp. (Theories of the Contemporary Culture 9.) Pref. Index. Notes. Lang.: Eng.

1960-1987. Critical studies. ▪Series of essays by theorist Herbert Blau on the state of modern theatre from the 1960s to the present.

1307 Breslow, Maurice. "Theatre of the Theories." *Queen's Quarterly.* 1987 Fall; 94(4): 591-601. Lang.: Eng.

1987. Critical studies. ▪Citing somewhat polar positions in works by Marvin Carlson (*Theories of the Theatre*) and Terry Eagleton (*The Function of Criticism*), Breslow comments on relationships between theory and practice in theatre criticism.

1308 Davidson, Clifford. "Iconography and Some Problems of Terminology in the Study of the Drama and Theatre of the Renaissance." *RORD.* 1987; 29: 7-14. Lang.: Eng.

1987. Critical studies. ▪Critical discussion of iconography and terminology in researching Shakespeare and other Renaissance drama.

1309 Eagleton, Terry. *The Function of Criticism: From the Spectator to Post-Structuralism.* Toronto: Oxford UP; 1984. 128 pp. Index. Biblio. Lang.: Eng.

1984. Historical studies. ▪Examines the history of theatre criticism.

1310 Féral, Josette; Bermingham, Ron, transl. "Alienation Theory in Multi-Media Performance." *TJ.* 1987; 39(4): 461-472. Notes. Biblio. Lang.: Eng.

1960-1970. Historical studies. ▪Alienation effect in acting understood through the unification of the actor, spectator and social context by the director or author. Evidence of the alienation effect in contemporary multi-media performances and performance art. Related to Mixed Entertainment: Performance art.

1311 Hu, Miao-Sheng. "Xi ju de ben xing." (The Nature of Theatre.) *XYishu.* 1987 Spr; 37: 4-18. Notes. Lang.: Chi.

1949-1987. Historical studies. ▪Theatre communicates with people by language, tone, facial expression, action, spacing, color, shape, sound and music.

1312 Kim, Heung-Woo. "Yonkug mihakui-sajukkochal." (Historical Investigations of Theatre Aesthetics.) *DongukDA.* 1987; 18: 5-23. Lang.: Kor.

1987. Historical studies. ▪General introduction to aesthetics in theatre from the ancient Greeks to the present.

1313 Kirby, Michael. *A Formalist Theatre.* Philadelphia, PA: Univ of Pennsylvania P; 1987. 159 pp. Index. Lang.: Eng.

1987. Critical studies. ▪A formalist experience and analysis of theatre performance. Explains the formalist approach to theatre. Theatre performance should be viewed in a systematic, objective fashion, observing its form as meaning.

1314 Sanchis Sinisterra, José. "Teatro en un baño turco." (The Theatre in a Turkish Bath.) 131-145 in Coca, Jordi, ed.; Conesa, Laura, comp. *Congrés Internacional de Teatre a Catalunya 1985. Actes. Volum III. Seccions 7, 8 i 9.* Barcelona: Institut del Teatre; 1987. 350 pp. [Section 8: Outlook for the Theatre.] Lang.: Spa.

1985. Critical studies. ▪Based on concepts expressed by Gordon Craig, considers the return to 'conviviality' over 'spectacularity' in theatre. Theatre of the future must be centered in the implied receiver.

1315 Eccles, Jeremy. "Filling the Hole: Theatre Criticism in Australia." *ATR.* 1987; 1(13): 37-66. Lang.: Eng.

Australia. 1985-1986. Historical studies. ▪Report on two conferences on theatre reviewing in Australian newspapers and journals, with special reference to the power structures and economics of these publications and the ways in which these affect the craft and the livelihood of theatre critics.

1316 Holloway, Peter. *Contemporary Australian Drama.* Sydney: Currency; 1987. 628 pp. [Rev. ed.] Lang.: Eng.

Australia. 1955-1987. Critical studies. ▪Reprints of articles by various authors on Australian drama since 1955, most of them dealing with the work of specific playwrights. Revised edition of the work published in 1981, with several more recent articles added.

1317 Devine, Michael. "Change." *Theatrum.* 1987 Sum; 7: 3-4. Lang.: Eng.

Canada: Toronto, ON. 1987. Critical studies. ▪The editor reacts to a radio review of the 1987 Stratford Festival, and criticizes the current school of Canadian theatre criticism. Devine stresses the need for more artists to be involved in Canadian theatre criticism.

1318 Vais, Michel. "De qui se moque *Le Devoir*?" (Whom is *Le Devoir* Belittling?)*JCT.* 1987; 45: 5-7. Illus.: Photo. Print. B&W. 1. Lang.: Fre.

Canada: Montreal, PQ. 1987. Critical studies. ▪A critique of the misleading and incomplete reporting by the Montreal newspaper *Le Devoir* of the awards ceremony of the Quebec Association of Theatre Critics.

1319 Liu, Yeng Jiun. "Sung Jen Shih Jiuh Pi Ping Lun." (Dramatic Criticism by Literate Men of the Sung Dynasty.) *XYanj.* 1987; 8(19): 1-22. Lang.: Chi.

China: Beijing. 960-1279. Critical studies. ▪Criticism of the dramatic form, structure, language and skill of the performers.

1320 Zhou, Yu-De. "Tang, Xian zu xin tan." (Theory of Tang Theatre.) *XYishu.* 1987 Spr; 37: 82-96. Lang.: Chi.

China. 618-905. Historical studies. ▪General thoughts on theatre during the Tang dynasty: specifically, the relationship between human beings and nature.

1321 Chen, Shi-Xiong. "Bu lai xi te zhen shi guan." (Critique of the Realism of Brecht.) *XYishu.* 1985 Spr; 29: 79-85. Notes. Lang.: Chi.

China, People's Republic of. 1949-1985. Critical studies. ▪The purpose of a play is to reflect society.

1322 Chern, Shean Luu. "Lun Shih Cheu Yih Shuh Dih 'Shiee Yi Shing'." (The Impressionistic Character of Chinese Drama.) *XYanj.* 1987; 8(19): 191-211. Lang.: Chi.

China, People's Republic of: Beijing. 1271-1986. Critical studies. ▪The impressionistic character of Chinese drama. The art form is an impression, not an imitation and is outreaching, energetic and rhythmic.

1323 Gau, Shin Sheng. "Jiau Jyu Yiin Shian Sheng Dih Huah Jiuh Min Tzwu Huah Sy Sheang." (Nationalistic Thoughts on Chinese Drama of Mr. Jiau Jyu Yiin.) *XYanj.* 1987; 8(19): 259-280. Lang.: Chi.

China, People's Republic of: Beijing. 1929-1956. Critical studies. ▪Suggestions for nationalizing the modern Chinese play, which is a Western form.

1324 Murray, Timothy. *Theatrical Legitimation: Allegories of Genius in Seventeenth-Century England and France.* New

THEATRE IN GENERAL: —Theory/criticism

York, NY: Oxford UP; 1987. 292 pp. Pref. Index. Notes. Illus.: Photo. Print. B&W. 9. Lang.: Eng.

England. France. 1600-1700. Critical studies. ■Performance aspects of theatricality, relation between ideology and theatrical representation, rhetorical structures of performance, and the antitheatre prejudice from point of view of both theatre professionals and the audience.

1325 Ronk Lifson, Martha. "Learning by Talking: Conversation in *As You Like It*." *ShS*. 1987; 40: 91-105. Lang.: Eng.

England. 1599. Critical studies. ■Study of the conversations in Shakespeare's *As You Like It* in terms of their semiotic meaning.

1326 Rosenberg, Marvin. "Sign Theory and Shakespeare." *ShS*. 1987; 40: 33-40. Lang.: Eng.

England. USA. 1590-1987. Critical studies. ■A study of Shakespeare in terms of gesture and sign in performance.

1327 Scott, William O. "The Speculative Eye: Problematic Self-Knowledge in *Julius Caesar*." *ShS*. 1987; 40: 77-89. Lang.: Eng.

England. 1599. Critical studies. ■Study of the phenomenon of self-awareness or knowledge in Shakespeare's *Julius Caesar*.

1328 Berghaus, Günter. "A Theatre of Image, Sound and Motion: On Synaesthesia and the Idea of a Total Work of Art." *MuK*. 1986; 32(1-2): 7-29. Lang.: Eng.

Europe. 1804-1930. Historical studies.

1329 Lidova, N.R. *Teorija i praktika teatral'nogo postmodernizma (po materialam Venecianskoj biennale 1985 g.).* (The Theory and Practice of Theatrical Postmodernism—From Materials of the Venice Biennial, 1985.) Kul'tura i iskusstvo za rubežam. Moscow: Gosudarstvennaja Biblioteka im. V.I. Lenina; 1987. 20 pp. (Serija: reli n e iskusstva: Express-informacija 1.) Lang.: Rus.

Europe. 1985. Critical studies.

1330 "Canudo nelle avanguardie della musica e dello spettacolo degli anni Venti." (Canudo in the Vanguard of Music and Entertainment in the Twenties.) *TeatrC*. 1987; 7(14): 149-179. Lang.: Ita.

France. Italy. 1877-1923. Biographical studies. ■The eclectic critical and theoretical career of Ricciotto Canudo: dance, theatre, film. Related to Media: Film.

1331 Banu, Georges; Deprats, Jean-Michel; Durand, Regis; Millon, Martine; Sallenave, Danièle. "Les risques de la création. Les risques de l'institution." (Risks of Creation, Risks of Institution.) *AdT*. 1987 Sum; 1(7): 13-22. Illus.: Dwg. 1. Lang.: Fre.

France. 1987. Critical studies. ■How to make risk remain alive in theatre. Theatre seen as being easily deprived of risks because of its double nature of art and merchandise.

1332 Lafont, Robert. "Le sens véritable de la modernité." (The True Sense of Modernity.) 45-59 in Coca, Jordi, ed.; Conesa, Laura, comp. *Congrés Internacional de Teatre a Catalunya 1985. Actes. Volum III. Seccions 4, 5 i 6.* Barcelona: Institut del Teatre; 1987. 302 pp. [Section 4: Tradition and Modernity.] Lang.: Fre.

France. Spain-Catalonia: Barcelona. 1539-1985. Critical studies. ■Examines modernity as a dialectical concept defined by a place and dominant class. Compares the evolution of the concept in Occitania and Catalonia.

1333 Opl, Eberhard. "Versuch einer Annäherung an Artaud. Die Theaterkonzeption Antonin Artauds vor dem Hintergrund seines Weltbildes." (Trying an Approach to Artaud: Antonin Artaud's Conception of Theatre Against the Background of His Vision of the World.) *MuK*. 1986; 32(1-2): 61-114. Lang.: Ger.

France. 1896-1949. Historical studies.

1334 Pavis, Patrice. "Hacia una semiologia de la mise en scéne?" (Towards a Semiology of the Mise en Scène?)*Cjo*. 1987 Apr/July; 72: 104-114. Notes. Biblio. Lang.: Spa.

France. 1987. Critical studies. ■Specific relations between text and the representation of the mise en scène.

1335 Piemme, Jean-Marie. "Le risque du contemporain." (The Risk of the Contemporary.) *AdT*. 1987 Sum; 1(7): 23-27. Lang.: Fre.

France. 1887-1987. Critical studies. ■The risk for theatre today: how not to be any longer the business substance (as for opera) for the industries of reproduction. Director André Antoine's approach seen as a model for succeeding in building a repertory theatre with old plays addressing contemporary audiences.

1336 Sallenave, Danièle. "Les épreuves de l'art (V): A quoi bon des théâtres au temps du clip?" (The Tests of Art (V): What Good are Theatres in the Age of the Video Clip?)*AdT*. 1987 Spr; 1(6): 109-116. Notes. Illus.: Dwg. 1. Lang.: Fre.

France. 1987. Critical studies. ■Based on Heidegger's *The Question Concerning Technology*, considers how theatre faces the modern danger of infatuation with technology.

1337 Sarrazac, Jean-Pierre. "Le mot de naturalisme." (The Word of Naturalism.) *AdT*. 1987 Spr; 1(6): 119-123. Lang.: Fre.

France. 1887-1987. Critical studies. ■On the occasion of the one hundredth anniversary of André Antoine's Théâtre Libre, reflections on the opposition between symbolism and naturalism, proposal of a 'subjective realism' presenting both the world of dream and the world of reality on stage.

1338 Turim, Maureen. "French Melodrama: Theory of a Specific History." *TJ*. 1987 Oct.; 39(3): 307-327. Notes. Lang.: Eng.

France. 1770-1987. Critical studies. ■Melodrama as it makes a shift in the conception of theatrical performance in France beginning 1770.

1339 Vitez, Antoine. "Ici et maintenant, ailleurs et autrefois, ici et autrefois, ailleurs et maintenant." (Here and Now, Elsewhere and Before, Here and Before, Elsewhere and Now.) *AdT*. 1987 Spr; 1(6): 103-105. Lang.: Fre.

France. 1987. Critical studies. ■Movement of modern society toward audiovisual media forces theatre to restrict itself to representations of the past, destroying its function of representing the here and now.

1340 Heise, Wolfgang, ed. *Brecht 88. Anregungen zum Dialog über die Vernunft am Jahrtausendende.* (Brecht 88: Suggestions for Talks on Reason at the End of the Millennium.) Berlin: Henschelverlag; 1987. 351 pp. Notes. Lang.: Ger.

Germany, East. 1918-1987. Critical studies. ■Seventeen essays on different aspects of Brecht's theories, aesthetics and philosophy of theatre and their productivity in our time.

1341 Kröplin, Wolfgang. "Polnische Dramatik und DDR-Theater in Theaterhistorischer Sicht." (Polish Drama and GDR Theatre Seen from a Historical Point of View.) *ZS*. 1987; 32(2): 276-279. Lang.: Ger.

Germany, East. Poland. 1949-1987. Critical studies. ■Problems in staging and audience reception of Polish drama in the GDR, caused by differing national theatre developments and aesthetics.

1342 Wekwerth, Manfred. "Aus: Fragen, Brecht betreffend." (From: Questions Concerning Brecht.) 301-324 in Heise, Wolfgang, ed. *Brecht 88. Anregungen zum Dialog über die Vernunft am Jahrtausendende.* Berlin: Henschelverlag; 1987. 351 pp. Lang.: Ger.

Germany, East. Berlin, East. 1948-1956. Critical studies. ■On seven aspects of Brecht's theory and practice of theatre: changing of the world, gestus, pleasure, reason, naivety, distance/identification, realism.

1343 Hwu, Yaw Heng. "Poetic de bianben jiqizau yiao yin wun fan yi jian shu Aristotle zhuzue de di deuang." (The Versions and the English Translations of *Poetics*. Plus an Explanation of Aristotle's Conveying Method.) *ChWai*. 1987 Feb.; 15(9): 4-47. Notes. Biblio. Illus.: Diagram. Print. B&W. 1. Lang.: Chi.

Greece: Athens. Egypt: Alexandria. Europe. 70 B.C.-1981 A.D. Historical studies. ■Analysis of various versions and translations of Aristotle's *Poetics*.

1344 "Ariel: Special Issue Devoted to Silvio d'Amico." *Ariel*. 1987; 2(3): 5-205 (40). Lang.: Ita.

Italy. 1887-1987. Biographical studies. ■Collection of essays on the Italian theatre critic Silvio d'Amico published on the occasion of the centenary of his birth.

THEATRE IN GENERAL: —Theory/criticism

1345 Aufiero, Raffaele. *L'attor critico. Piero Gobetti e il teatro della crisi.* (Actor as Critic: Piero Gobetti and the Theatre of Crisis.) Rome: E & A; 1987. 40 pp. Lang.: Ita.
Italy. 1918-1926. Histories-sources. ■Gobetti's theatre criticism on plays, acting, directing, audience.

1346 Bobkova, Hana. "De Geschiedenis van de kritiek moet nog geschreven worden." (The History of Criticism Is Yet To Be Written.) *Toneel.* 1987 Jan.; 1: 22-24. Lang.: Dut.
Netherlands. 1987. Critical studies. ■Theatre criticism in the Netherlands: lack of good reviews, criticism years behind theatre research. Discussion of different types of reviews and the need for well supported criticism.

1347 Tomaselli, Keyan; Muller, Johan. "Class, Race and Oppression: Metaphor and Metonymy in 'Black' South African Theatre." *CrAr.* 1987; 4(3): 40-58. Illus.: Dwg. 2. Lang.: Eng.
South Africa, Republic of. 1980. Critical studies. ■Theory of semiotic production in popular performance that has not been created in isolation from current social movements.

1348 Eynat-Confino, Irène. *Beyond the Mask: Gordon Craig, Movement, and the Actor.* Carbondale, IL: Southern Illinois UP; 1987. 239 pp. Biblio. Pref. Index. Notes. Illus.: Diagram. Sketches. Photo. Print. B&W. 13. Lang.: Eng.
UK-England. 1872-1966. Historical studies. ■The nature and development of Edward Gordon Craig's concept of movement. Concentrates on a three year period—1904 to 1906. First part of book is chronology of his formative years.

1349 "Zen and the Heart of Physical Comedy: The Revenge of Murphy's Law." *ThM.* 1987; 18(3): 21-29. Illus.: Photo. Sketches. B&W. 8. Lang.: Eng.
USA. 1987. Critical studies. ■Re-emergence of physical comedy as a response to the complexities of modern life.

1350 Bentley, Eric. *Thinking About the Playwright: Eric Bentley Comments from Four Decades.* Evanston, IL: Northwestern UP; 1987. 364 pp. Index. Lang.: Eng.
USA. 1952-1986. Critical studies. ■Collection of critical essays on theatre artists, movements, political theatre, acting, and theatre criticism with a primary focus on the role of the playwright in each area.

1351 Brustein, Robert. *Who Needs Theatre.* New York, NY: Atlantic Monthly P; 320 pp. Lang.: Eng.
USA. 1980-1986. Critical studies. ■Collection of critical essays and reviews on theatre artists, plays, Broadway theatre, theatre from abroad and theatre criticism that reflect the author's personal views on the social significance of theatre.

1352 Chin, Daryl. "The Avant-Garde Industry." *PerAJ.* 1985 Sum/Fall; 9(26-27): 59-75. Lang.: Eng.
USA. 1985. Critical studies. ■Lack of an avant-garde in America: definition of the term and discussion of its use as a marketing tool.

1353 Copeland, Roger. "Shades of Brecht." *AmTh.* 1987 Feb.; 3(11): 12-19, 45. Illus.: Photo. B&W. 6. Lang.: Eng.
USA. Europe. 1950-1987. Historical studies. ■Brechtian influence on modern theatre, arts, architecture, dance and film.

1354 Kauffmann, Stanley. "Why We Need Broadway—Some Notes." *PerAJ.* 1985 May-Sep.; 9(2-3): 193-198. Lang.: Eng.
USA: New York, NY. 1985. Critical studies. ■Economic and social need for a Broadway theatre.

1355 Levin, Harry. "From Play to Play: The Folklore of Comedy." *CompD.* 1982 Sum; 16(2): 130-147. Notes. Lang.: Eng.
USA. 1982. Critical studies. ■Aesthetics of the pleasure principle, ga.nes and play in comedy, folklore and literature.

1356 Magruder, James. "How Much is That Royal Doulton Greyhound in the Vitrine?" *ThM.* 1987; 19(1): 24-30. Notes. Illus.: Photo. B&W. 2. Lang.: Eng.
USA: New York, NY. 1987. Critical studies. ■Ralph Lauren's flagship store as the epitome of theatre in America under Reagan. The vacancy of American mythology is performed by the merchandise and design of the store through its social, historic and economic amnesia.

1357 Malpede, Karen. "We Need an Aesthetic Fit for a Nuclear Age." *TT.* 1987 May; 6(4): 4-5. Illus.: Dwg. B&W. 7. Lang.: Eng.
USA: New York, NY. 1987. Critical studies. ■Theatres in distress as a direct reflection of our societal condition.

1358 Marowitz, Charles. "Reconstructing Shakespeare or Harlotry in Bardolatry." *ShS.* 1987; 40: 1-10. Lang.: Eng.
USA. 1987. Critical studies. ■Reconstruction of Shakespeare in performance.

1359 Marranca, Bonnie. "PAJ, A Personal History." *PerAJ.* 1985; 9(2-3): 23-42. Lang.: Eng.
USA: New York, NY. 1975-1985. Histories-sources. ■History and motivation behind the creation of *Performing Arts Journal* on the occasion of its 10th anniversary.

1360 Marranca, Bonnie. "Performance World, Performance Culture." *PerAJ.* 1987; 10(3): 21-29. Lang.: Eng.
USA. 1800-1987. Historical studies. ■How theatre fits into contemporary culture, including its development in the last century.

1361 Marranca, Bonnie; Dasgupta, Gautam. "The Theatre and Literary Culture." *PerAJ.* 1985 Spr; 9(25): 6-8.
USA. 1985. Critical studies. ■The absence of thoughtful essays on the theatre and its literature in major periodicals in America.

1362 Marranca, Bonnie. "Acts of Criticism." *PerAJ.* 1985 Spr; 9(25): 9-11. Lang.: Eng.
USA. Histories-sources. ■Author discusses writing for and about the theatre on receiving the 1983-84 George Jean Nathan Award.

1363 McNally, Terrence. "Frank Rich in Conversation with Terrence McNally." *DGQ.* 1987; 24(3): 11-26. Illus.: Sketches. 2. Lang.: Eng.
USA. 1960-1987. Histories-sources. ■Rich's beginnings in the theatre, his education, his work at the *New York Times* and his relationship with the theatre.

1364 Merritt, Susan Hollis. "Recent Developments in Pinter Criticism." *PintR.* 1987; 1: 68-76. Notes. Biblio. Lang.: Eng.
USA. UK-England. Germany, West. 1978-1987. Critical studies. ■Brief survey of critical reactions to Harold Pinter's work since 1978.

1365 Myers, Larry. "Desires Have Great Appetites: A Profile of Maria Piscator." *TheaterW.* 1987 Nov 16; 1(14): 14-16. Illus.: Photo. B&W. 2. Lang.: Eng.
USA. 1938-1987. Histories-sources. ■Symposium on Erwin Piscator conducted by his wife Maria: brief overview of her career, her collaboration with her husband and Bertolt Brecht.

1366 Rogoff, Gordon. *Theatre is Not Safe.* Evanston, IL: Northwestern UP; 1987. xiii, 296 pp. Index. Lang.: Eng.
USA. 1960-1986. Historical studies. ■Collection of essays and reviews on productions, theatre artists, plays, theatre companies and movements.

1367 Rogoff, Gordon. "Theatre Criticism: The Elusive Object, The Fading Craft." *PerAJ.* 1985 May-Sep.; 9(2-3): 133-141. Lang.: Eng.
USA: New York, NY. 1917-1985. Historical studies. ■The progression of theatre criticism in America.

1368 Rogoff, Gordon. "In Praise of Eric Bentley." *ThM.* 1987; 18(2): 73-74. Illus.: Photo. B&W. 1. Lang.: Eng.
USA. 1986. Histories-sources. ■Speech delivered, on the occasion of Eric Bentley's birthday, on Bentley's place in and impact on the theatre.

1369 Whitehead, Greg. "Bones Have Their Fates." *PerAJ.* 1987 Sum/Fall; 9(26/27): 234-236. Lang.: Eng.
USA. 1987. Critical studies. ■'The theatre of bones': a discussion of what is left of the theatre when the theatre as we know it is 'dead'.

1370 Yeo, Seok-Gi. "Mi-Guk-Geuk eui Su-Yong-Gwa-Jeong gwa Yeong-Hyang." (The Reception Process and the Influence of American Theatre in Korea.) 262-288 in *Study on the Comparison of Eastern Theatre and Western Theatre.* Seoul: Korea Univ.; 1987. 295 pp. Lang.: Kor.
USA. Korea. 1926-1970. Historical studies. ■Reception theory, performance and American influence in Korea.

1371 Zeisler, Peter. "The Critical Void." *AmTh.* 1987 June; 4(3): 3. Notes. Lang.: Eng.

THEATRE IN GENERAL: —Theory/criticism

USA. 1987. Critical studies. ■Discusses cultural reporting, uninformed critics, national standards for arts criticism.

1372 "Problema konflikta v sovremennom teatral'nom iskusstve." (The Problem of Conflict in Contemporary Theatre Art.) *TeatrM.* 1987; 11: 63-76. Lang.: Rus.

USSR. 1980-1987. Histories-sources. ■Round-table discussion by directors, playwrights, critics and philosophers. Continued in *TeatrM* 12 (1987), 112-124.

1373 Efremov, O.; Ščerbakov, K. "Zavlit." (Head of the Literary Section.) *TeatZ.* 1987; 7: 22-23. Lang.: Rus.

USSR. 1910-1959. Histories-sources. ■A conversation about the role of critic Pavel A. Markov in the Moscow Art Theatre.

1374 Gvozdev, A. *Teatral'naja kritika.* (Theatre Criticism.) Leningrad: Iskusstvo; 1987. 280 pp. Lang.: Rus.

USSR. 1920-1930. Critical studies. ■Collection of articles and reviews by theatre critic A. Gvozdev, reflecting theatrical and social life of the 1920s.

1375 Kjubomudrov, M. "...kak slovo naše otzovetsja: otvet opponentam." (How Our Word Will Echo: An Answer to Our Opponents.) *NasSovr.* 1987; 7: 167-175. Lang.: Rus.

USSR. 1980-1987. Critical studies. ■Theatre historian and critic of contemporary theatre appraises current Soviet theatre.

1376 Kokšeneva, K. "Nazyvat' vešči svoimi imenami." (To Call Things by Their Own Names.) *MolGvar.* 1987; 9: 245-249. Lang.: Rus.

USSR. 1980-1987. Critical studies. ■Problems of new theatre criticism current studio theatre movement.

Training

1377 Scher, Anna; Verrall, Charles. *Another 100 Ideas for Drama.* London: Heinemann; 1987. 108 pp. Illus.: Photo. Print. B&W. 1. Lang.: Eng.

1987. Instructional materials. ■Guidebook of improvisation exercises for teachers of theatre. Lessons applicable to adults and children. Treats improvisation as a means to production.

1378 Berghe, P.; Dardenne, A. *Avant les trois coups...: exercices pratiques d'art dramatique à l'usage de l'enseignement secondaire rénové.* (Before the Curtain Rises: Practical Drama Exercises for Reformed Secondary Education.) Brussels: De Boeck-Wesmael; 1987. 85 pp. Pref. Biblio. B&W. 4. [2d ed.] Lang.: Fre.

Belgium. 1987. Instructional materials. ■Basics of theatrical training—acting, voice, movement, etc.—for children twelve years and over. Includes exercises.

1379 Xiang, Qi. "Xie yi xi ju yu biao yan jiao xue." (Theatre and Teaching.) *XYishu.* 1985 Spr; 29: 126-128. Notes. Lang.: Chi.

China, People's Republic of. 1985. Instructional materials. ■Using masks to stimulate the imagination when teaching.

1380 Yu, Zi-Tao. "Dao yan jin xiu ban de jiao xu." (The Curriculum of Directing Classes.) *XYishu.* 1987 Sum; 38: 62-65. Lang.: Chi.

China, People's Republic of: Shanghai. 1949-1987. Historical studies. ■The classes of a master directing teacher, from experimentation to directing a performance.

1381 Drury, Martin. "Making Drama Work for Young People." *ThIr.* 1987; 12: 50-51. Illus.: Photo. B&W. 1. Lang.: Eng.

Ireland. 1979-1987. Historical studies. ■Overview of the state of theatre provision for the young in the republic of Ireland.

1382 Quarenghi, Paola, ed.; De Lellis, Aida, ed. *Orazio Costa pedagogia e didattica del teatro.* (Orazio Costa: Pedagogy and Didactics of the Theatre.) Rome: Univ di Roma 'La Sapienza'. Dept of Music and Theatre; 1987. (Storia del Teatro e dello Spettacolo.) Lang.: Ita.

Italy. 1935-1987. Critical studies. ■Collection of essays on the teaching of Orazio Costa, on the occasion of a seminar at the Centro Teatro Ateneo.

1383 Dalrymple, Lynn. "Some Thoughts on Identity, Culture and the Curriculum and the Future of South African Theatre." *SATJ.* 1987; 1(2): 20-51. Lang.: Eng.

South Africa, Republic of. 1960-1987. Historical studies. ■Drama teaching in South Africa since 1960: how syllabi could be adapted to facilitate indigenous drama in curriculum.

1384 Torras i Porti, Josep. *Juguem fent teatre.* (Let's Enjoy Making Theatre.) Alella: Edicions Pleniluni, S.A.; 1987. 206 pp. (Manuals Pleniluni 4.) Index. Tables. Append. Illus.: Design. Plan. 20. Lang.: Cat.

Spain-Catalonia. 1987. Instructional materials. ■Teachers' manual detailing various theatrical activities for recreational and educational use in the classroom.

1385 Campbell, Donna; Fait, Susan A. "The London Exchange." *PerfM.* 1985 Win; 11(1): 6-7. Illus.: Photo. B&W. 1. Lang.: Eng.

UK-England: London. USA: New York, NY. 1985. Historical studies. ■Exchange program for graduate students in arts administration at Brooklyn College and City University of London: significant differences, internships.

1386 "Feeding the Future." *ThIr.* 1987; 12: 59. Lang.: Eng.

UK-Ireland. 1987. Histories-sources. ■Interview with Michael Poyner, director of the Ulster Youth Theatre.

1387 Grant, David. "The Network Effect." *ThIr.* 1987; 12: 60-61. Illus.: Photo. B&W. 1. Lang.: Eng.

UK-Ireland. 1987. Historical studies. ■Assessment of the current state and importance of Northern Ireland's young theatre community.

1388 Vernon, Michael. "Management, Eicochets and Musicals: The Development of Youth Theatre in Ulster." *ThIr.* 1987; 12: 53-58. Illus.: Photo. B&W. 9. Lang.: Eng.

UK-Ireland. 1979-1987. Historical studies. ■Genesis and development of various youth theatre groups in Northern Ireland.

1389 Gordon, Cate. "Interns from the Employer's Viewpoint." *PerfM.* 1985 Win; 11(1): 5. Lang.: Eng.

USA: Brooklyn, NY. 1985. Critical studies. ■How an employer shapes an intern's position with a company based upon skills, time commitment and the company's needs. Survey of several managers of arts organizations on value of a management internship.

1390 Law, Alma H. "An Actor's Director Debuts in the West." *AmTh.* 1987 June; 4(3): 17-19, 45. Notes. Illus.: Photo. B&W. 2. Lang.: Eng.

USA. 1987. Critical studies. ■Interview with Georgij Tovstonogov, head of Leningrad Bolshoi Dramatic Theatre.

1391 Gončarov, A. "Kogo učit'? Kak učit'?" (Whom to Teach? How to Teach?) *TeatZ.* 1987; 13: 3-4. Lang.: Rus.

USSR: Moscow. 1987. Histories-sources. ■Problems of theatrical education.

1392 Kozljaninova, I. "A golos tak divno zvučal..." (And the Voice Resounded So Marvelously...) *TeatZ.* 1987; 3: 22. Lang.: Rus.

USSR. 1987. Critical studies. ■Problems of perfecting the teaching of stage speech in leading theatrical universities.

1393 Kuzjakina, N. "Vosspitat' učenika." (To Educate a Pupil.) *TeatrM.* 1987; 9: 71-79. Lang.: Rus.

USSR. 1887-1942. Historical studies. ■On the pedagogical activities of Ukrainian director L. Kurbas.

1394 Lifatova, N. "Proverki na dorogach." (Checkups Enroute.) *TeatZ.* 1987; 24: 28-30. Lang.: Rus.

USSR. 1980-1987. Critical studies. ■Problems of students graduating from theatre schools.

1395 Monastyrskij, P.; Novikova, L. "Vychod? V reforme obrazovanija." (Entrance? In Reform of Education.) *TeatZ.* 1987; 3: 12-13. Lang.: Rus.

USSR: Kujbyšev. 1987. Histories-sources. ■Principal director of Kujbyšev drama theatre on problems of theatrical education.

1396 Sidorov, A. "Aukcion." (The Action.) *TeatZ.* 1987; 6: 26-27. Lang.: Rus.

USSR. 1986-1987. Critical studies. ■Problems of young drama school graduates.

DANCE

General

Administration

1397   "Career Transition for Dancers Subject of Day-Long Conference." *EN*. 1982 Aug.; 67(8): 2. Illus.: Photo. B&W. 2. Lang.: Eng.
USA: New York, NY. 1982. Historical studies. ■Conference on career transitions for dancers investigating creation of programs to assist them.

Basic theatrical documents

1398   Mee, Charles L., Jr.; Smith, Amanda. "Martha Clarke's *Vienna: Lusthaus.*" *TDR*. 1987 Fall; 31(3): 42-58. Pref. Notes. Biblio. Illus.: Photo. B&W. 12. Lang.: Eng.
Austria: Vienna. 1986. Critical studies. ■Play text and photo essay of Martha Clarke's *Vienna: Lusthaus* describing Freud's influence in the work.

Design/technology

1399   Pavlovic, Diane. "La scene peuplée d'écrans." (The Stage Filled with Screens.) *JCT*. 1987; 44: 91-92. Print. B&W. 1. Lang.: Fre.
Canada. 1985. Critical studies. ■The increasing use of projected stage images and the new type of theatre they may be encouraging.

1400   Daly, Ann. "Shades of Blu." *LDim*. 1987 Sep/Oct.; 11(5): 46-51. Illus.: Photo. Color. 8. Lang.: Eng.
USA: New York, NY. 1987. Technical studies. ■Study of the work of dance lighting designer Blu.

1401   Sisk, Douglass F. "When the Dance Speaks..." *LDim*. 1987 Jan/Feb.; 11(1): 28-33, 48-49. Illus.: Photo. Lighting. 8. Lang.: Eng.
USA: New York, NY. 1987. Histories-sources. ■Designer Allen Lee Hughes discusses lighting of dance shows, allowing choreography to inspire environment of light.

Performance/production

1402   Rolando, Piero. *Il ballo da sala: teoria e tecnica delle figure più significative.* (Ballroom Dancing: Theory and Technique of the More Significant Figures.) Padua: MEB; 1987. 207 pp. (Manuali oratici hobby e lavoro 13.) Lang.: Ita.
1987. Instructional materials. ■Manual of ballroom dances, including waltz, tango, fox trot and charleston.

1403   Krishna, Swami Deva. "Carol Martin's *The Last Wave.*" *TDR*. 1983 Sum; 27(2): 94-96. Illus.: Photo. Sketches. B&W. 3. Lang.: Eng.
Belgium: Antwerp. 1982. Historical studies. ■Description of production, the choreography and themes of the piece. Includes diagram of dance steps.

1404   Citron, Paula. "Desrosiers: A Philosopher of Dance." *PAC*. 1986 Jan.; 22(4): 32-35. Notes. Illus.: Photo. Print. 4. Lang.: Eng.
Canada. 1985. Biographical studies. ■Top Canadian choreographer Robert Desrosiers and his company.

1405   Gelinas, Aline. "*Human sex* mystère de l'immense beauté." (*Human Sex* Mystery of the Great Beauty.) *JCT*. 1987 ; 43: 22-30. Illus.: Photo. B&W. 4. Lang.: Fre.
Canada: Vancouver, BC. 1985-1986. Critical studies. ■Discusses the structure, theme, background and performance of Edward Locke's *Human Sex.*

1406   Levesque, Solange. "Le corps politique/festival de chorégraphie et de performance engagées." (The Body Politic/Festival of Choreography and Performance Art.) *JCT*. 1987; 44: 67-74. Illus.: Photo. Print. B&W. 7. Lang.: Fre.
Canada: Montreal, PQ. 1986. Reviews of performances. ■Davida's 'Le festival annuel Moment'homme de chorégraphie et de danse masculin', which in 1986 allowed women to participate for the first time, and changed its name to 'Le corps politique: festival de chorégraphie et de performance engagées'.

1407   Rebling, Eberhard. "Vom Ausdruckstanz zum Tanztheater." (From Expressional Dance to the Dance Theatre.) *TZ*. 1987; 42(5) : 25-28. Illus.: Photo. Dwg. 4. Lang.: Ger.
Germany: Berlin. 1920-1986. Historical studies. ■Description of the stormy development of dance, its various schools, forms and methods.

1408   Graham, Desmond. "Dance Season Report." *ThIr*. 1987; 13: 28-29. Illus.: Photo. B&W. 1. Lang.: Eng.
Ireland: Dublin. 1987. Reviews of performances. ■The 1987 dance season in Dublin: focus on the Irish National Ballet and Dublin Contemporary Dance Theatre.

1409   "Dance Forum—Round Up." *Scenaria*. 1987 Jan.; 72: 7-12. Illus.: Photo. Print. B&W. 7. Lang.: Eng.
South Africa, Republic of: Durban. 1986. Reviews of performances. ■Review of six-week dance festival representing forms of dance in South Africa.

1410   Llorens, Pilar; Aviñoa, Xosé; Rubio, Isidre; Vida, Anna; Catany, Toni, photo. *Història de la Dansa a Catalunya.* (History of the Dance in Catalonia.) Barcelona: Caixa de Barcelona; 1987. 276 pp. Index. Tables. Gloss. Illus.: Design. Photo. Pntg. Dwg. Sketches. Print. Color. B&W. 263. Lang.: Cat.
Spain-Catalonia. 1300-1987. Histories-specific. ■History of dance in Catalonia including folk-dance and dance-drama. Emphasis on dancers and institutions of the nineteenth and twentieth centuries.

1411   Merz, Richard. "Dance in Switzerland: No Risk of Romanticizing." *Bal*. 1987 June; 10(6): 6-12. Illus.: Photo. B&W. Lang.: Ger, Eng.
Switzerland. 1950-1986. Histories-specific. ■Historical survey of professional (i.e. traditionally established) dancing and its opponent, free dance. Attention is drawn especially to the problematic financial situation free dance artists find themselves in, mostly due to the romantic notion of artists being granted exclusive freedom and institutions claiming objective criteria for assessing the artists' work.

1412   Allen, Bonnie. "Katherine Dunham: A Living Legend." *Essence*. 1987 Dec.; 18(8): 54, 112, 114, 116. Illus.: Photo. Color. 1. Lang.: Eng.
USA: New York, NY, Chicago, IL, Las Vegas, NV. 1909-1987. Historical studies. ■The dancing career of Katherine Dunham from the 1950s to present.

1413   Bromberg, Craig. "Art on the Beach." *ThCr*. 1985 Jan.; 19(1): 42-44, 76-79. Print. B&W. 6. Lang.: Eng.
USA: New York, NY. 1984-1985. Critical studies. ■Summer series of dance and performance art in a collaborative struggle for an outdoor production.

1414   Copeland, Roger. "Theatrical Dance: How Do We Know it When We See it If We Can't Define It." *PerAJ*. 1985 May-Sep.; 9 (2-3): 174-184. Illus.: Photo. B&W. 6. Lang.: Eng.
USA. 1985. Historical studies. ■How to recognize theatricality in the dance medium.

1415   Goldberg, Marianne. "Ballerinas and Ball Passing." *WPerf*. 1987-88; 3(2): 7-31. Notes. Biblio. Illus.: Photo. B&W. 32. Lang.: Eng.
USA. 1987. Critical studies. ■Published version of Goldberg's dance/lecture focusing on images of gender in dance.

1416   Goldberg, Marianne; Albright, Ann Cooper. "Roundtable Interview: Post-Modernism and Feminism in Dance." *WPerf*. 1987-88; 3(2): 41-56. Notes. Illus.: Photo. B&W. 7. Lang.: Eng.
USA. 1987. Histories-sources. ■Five women choreographers and critics discuss conceptions of the female body, body in performance context, relation of the dance to the audience and the impact of expected gender roles on dance.

1417   Kilkelly, Ann Gavere. "Brenda Bufalino's Too Small Blues." *WPerf*. 1987-88; 3(2): 67-77. Biblio. Illus.: Photo. B&W. 3. Lang.: Eng.
USA. 1987. Historical studies. ■Examines career of the largely unacknowledged yet premiere woman tap dancer in the US, Brenda Bufalino. Lack of recognition of women as solo dancers versus chorus members.

DANCE: General—Performance/production

1418 Mazur, Käthe; Sandford, Danny. "Anne Bogart's *Women and Men: A Big Dance.*" *TDR*. 1983 Sum; 27(2): 77-83. Illus.: Photo. B&W. 2. Lang.: Eng.
USA: New York, NY. 1983. Historical studies. ■Description of production at P.S. 122 and its blend of dance, music and text. Its development, themes, and the ensemble.

Plays/librettos/scripts

1419 Angove, Colleen. "The Inescapable Bond with a Predetermined Heritage: A Phenomenon Illustrated by Representative Characters from Three Athol Fugard Plays." *Literator*. 1987; 8(3): 1-11. Lang.: Eng.
South Africa, Republic of. 1970. Critical studies. ■Black and white characters in three Athol Fugard plays reflect their perceptions of bondage to their cultures.

1420 "'Ličnaja žizn'' na scene i v žizni." ('Private Life' on the Stage and in Life.) *SovD*. 1987; 3: 226-237. Lang.: Rus.
USSR. 1980-1987. Critical studies. ■Love, marriage and family relationships in contemporary drama.

1421 Lukin, Ju. "O teatral'noj perestrojke, repertuare i nekotoryh spornych postulatach." (On Theatrical Perestrojka, Its Repertoire and Some Controversial Postulates.) Lang.: Rus.
USSR. 1987. Critical studies. ■On the problem of the socially active hero in Soviet dramaturgy.

1422 Poličineckaja, I. "Ljubit li avtor svoego geroja?" (Does the Author Like His Hero?) *TeatZ*. 1987; 7: 14-15. Lang.: Rus.
USSR. 1975-1985. Critical studies. ■The social hero in recent Soviet dramaturgy.

1423 Šechter, N. "Sovremennyi geroj—naraschvat." (The Contemporary Hero: A Hot Item.) Lang.: Rus.
USSR. 1980-1987. Histories-sources. ■Interview with playwright S. Alešin on critical problems facing contemporary Soviet dramaturgy.

1424 Sverbilova, T. "Dviženie." (Motion.) *SovD*. 1987; 3: 238-246. Lang.: Rus.
USSR. 1980-1987. Critical studies. ■Genre and stylistic innovation in new Ukrainian dramaturgy.

Relation to other fields

1425 Hinz, Evelyn J., ed. *'For Better or Worse': Attitudes Towards Marriage in Literature.* Winnepeg, MB: Mosaic; 1985. xx, 282 pp. Lang.: Eng.
England. Norway. 1300-1985. Critical studies. ■Collection of essays examining the various representations of marriage and relationships in literature from Chaucer to contemporary work. Includes essays by Anne Parton on Shakespeare and Peter Buitenhaus on Ibsen. Introduction by Evelyn Hinz.

1426 Brooks, Colette. "'The Play's the Thing'—A Polemic." *PerAJ*. 1985 Sum/Fall; 9(26-27): 160-162. Lang.: Eng.
USA. 1985. Critical studies. ■Modern trend away from reading and studying individual plays as literature.

1427 Daly, Ann. "At Issue: Gender in Dance." *TDR*. 1987 Sum; 31(2): 22-26. Lang.: Eng.
USA. 1970-1987. Critical studies. ■Rebuttal to an article by Judith Lynne Hanna on gender hierarchy in dance: includes a response from Hanna.

Ballet

Administration

1428 Einhorn, Cathy. "The Ford Foundation as Patron and Innovator in the Dance Field." *PerfM*. 1985 Spr; 10(2): 3-4. Illus.: Photo. B&W. 2. Lang.: Eng.
USA. 1984. Historical studies. ■Ford Foundation's support for dance: funding, audience surveys, companies and training programs.

Design/technology

1429 Pritchard, Jane. "*The Seven Deadly Sins* at Brighton." *KWN*. 1987 Fall; 5(2): 10-11. Illus.: Photo. Poster. Print. B&W. 4. Lang.: Eng.
France: Paris. UK-England: London. 1933-1987. Histories-reconstruction. ■Description of the exhibit of costumes, set pieces and photographs from the original 1933 production of the ballet *The Seven Deadly Sins*, designed by Caspar Neher, now in the collection of the Brighton Art Gallery and Museum.

Institutions

1430 Pastori, Jean-Pierre. "The Emancipation of Dance in the Municipal Theatres." *Bal.* 1987 June; 10(6): 12-18. Illus.: Photo. B&W. Lang.: Eng, Ger.
Switzerland. 1955-1987. Histories-specific. ■Elaborating on the situation of the municipal theatres in the major cities of Basel, Zurich, and Geneva, Pastori traces the history of ballet companies from being mere attributes to opera productions to ensembles expressing an individual form of art. Related to Music-Drama: Opera.

Performance/production

1431 Šichlinskaja, L.F. *Osnovnye étapy vozniknovenija i stanovlenija azerbajdžanskogo baletnogo iskusstva (20-80-ch gg.): Avtoref. dis. kand. iskusstvovedenija.* (The Basic Stages of the Emergence and Formation of Azerbaijani Ballet Art from the Twenties to the Eighties: Abstract of a Dissertation by a Candidate in Art Criticism.) Tbilisi: Gruz. teatr. in-t; 1987. 21 pp. Lang.: Rus.
Azerbaijan. 1920-1980. Historical studies.

1432 Citron, Paula. "Gizella Witkowsky: The Duckling Becomes a Swan." *PAC*. 1984 Spr/Sum; 21(1): 18-21. Illus.: Photo. Print. 4. Lang.: Eng.
Canada: Toronto, ON. 1984. Biographical studies. ■Ballerina Gizella Witkowsky's debut, at the age of 25, in the lead role of *Swan Lake* with the National Ballet of Canada.

1433 Vašut, Vladimír. "Šedesátka no pochodu (Rozhovor s Pavlem Šmokem)." (Marching Sixty: Interview with Pavel Šmok.) *ScenaP*. 1987; 12(25-26): 10. Illus.: Photo. B&W. 2. Lang.: Cze.
Czechoslovakia: Prague. 1987. Histories-sources. ■Interview with Pavel Šmok about his production with Prague Chamber Ballet.

1434 Daly, Ann. "Classical Ballet: A Discourse of Difference." *WPerf.* 1987-88; 3(2): 57-66. Notes. Biblio. Lang.: Eng.
France. USA. 1720-1987. Historical studies. ■Issues of gender in ballet, especially the emergence of the ballerina and the patriarchal nature of ballet. Position of women in the ballet, passive and acted upon. Critical reaction to gender critique.

1435 Gaevskij, V. "Bežar prodolžaetsja." (Béjart Continues.) *TeatrM.* 1987; 12: 169-177. Lang.: Rus.
France. 1927-1987. Biographical studies. ■Choreographer Maurice Béjart's creative principles.

1436 Garafola, Lynn. "Bronislava Nijinska: A Legacy Uncovered." *WPerf.* 1987; 3(2): 78-89. Notes. Illus.: Photo. Sketches. B&W. 10. Lang.: Eng.
France. USA. 1891-1930. Historical studies. ■Career of choreographer/dancer Bronislava Nižinska, sister of Vaslav Nižinskij. Her talent was equal to Nižinskij's but because of her gender she has been erased from history. One of the first choreographers to use modernist abstractions.

1437 Baló, Júlia. "Találkozás Róna Viktorral. 'Az én szivem dobog tanítványaimban.'" (Interview with Viktor Róna: 'It Is My Heart that Beats in My Students.) *FSM.* 1987; 31(42): 15-17. Illus.: Photo. B&W. Color. 4. Lang.: Hun.
Hungary. Norway: Oslo. 1980-1987. Histories-sources. ■The oustanding ballet dancer speaks about his career and his present work as balletmaster and choreographer at famous foreign ballet ensembles. He has been working for some years now in Oslo.

1438 Molnár Gál, Péter. "'Minden eltáncolható...' Balett Szegeden." ('Everything Can Be Expressed in Dance': Ballet in Szeged.) *Mozgo.* 1987 Dec.; 13(12): 108-111. Lang.: Hun.
Hungary: Szeged. 1987. Reviews of performances. ■Notes on the introductory performance of the new dance company, Szeged Ballet, with a brief historical survey on Hungarian ballet companies.

1439 "Gregorio Lambrazzi: un 'maestro di ballo' da Venezia a Norimberga." (Gregorio Lambrazzi, a Ballet Teacher from

CLASSED ENTRIES

DANCE: Ballet—Performance/production

Venice to Nuremberg.) *BiT.* 1987; 8: 61-82. Illus.: Pntg. Lang.: Ita.

Italy: Venice. Germany: Nuremberg. 1700-1799. Historical studies. ■The *Nuova e curiosa scuola de' balli teatrali*, by dance master Gregorio Lambrazzi, documents Italian, German and French traditions of theatrical dance. 101 engravings.

1440 "Scenaria Interviews Ashley Killar." *Scenaria.* 1987 June(77): 11-13. 2. Lang.: Eng.

South Africa, Republic of. 1987. Histories-sources. ■Interview with choreographer Ashley Killar, his move to NAPAC and views on the arts in South Africa.

1441 "Scenaria Interviews Vincent Hantam." *Scenaria.* 1987 June(77): 33-36. Illus.: Photo. 6. Lang.: Eng.

South Africa, Republic of. 1987. Histories-sources. ■Interview with dancer Vincent Hantam on relationship of dance to music and areas in which dancers need to develop.

1442 Olsson-Dunér, Sonja. "Från Amorin till Eldfågel." (From Cupid to Firebird.) *MuD.* 1987; 9(3): 29. Illus.: Photo. Lang.: Swe.

Sweden. 1927-1987. Histories-sources. ■Interview with ballerina and teacher Ellen Rasch.

1443 Kappel, Mark. "A New Career Direction for Hilda Morales." *Nuestro.* 1983 Jan/Feb.: 25-27. Lang.: Eng.

USA: New York, NY. 1983. Biographical studies. ■Review and discussion of the work of Hilda Morales, principal dancer with the American Ballet Theatre, who is now free-lancing as a teacher in New York City.

1444 "Baletmejster Jurij Grigorovič." (Ballet-Master Jurij Grigorovič.) *TeatrM.* 1987; 1: 28-33. Lang.: Rus.

USSR: Moscow. 1927-1987. Biographical studies. ■Collection of articles on the work of ballet-master Jurij Grigorovič by cultural figures: T. Vasiljéva, L. Semenjaka, A. Ešpaj and Krzysztof Penderecki.

1445 Čepalov, A.I. *Poiski novych form vyrazitel'nosti v revoljucionnom teatre 20-h godov i tvorčestvo N.M. Foreggera: Avtoref. dis. kand. iskusstvovedenija.* (Searches for New Forms of Expressivity in the Revolutionary Theatre of the Twenties and the Work of N.M. Foregger: Abstract of a Dissertation by a Candidate in Art Criticism.) Leningrad: LGITMiK; 1987. Lang.: Rus.

USSR. 1920-1929. Historical studies.

1446 Davlekamova, S. "Andris Liepa." *TeatrM.* 1987; 11: 98-100. Lang.: Rus.

USSR: Moscow. 1980-1987. Biographical studies. ■Portrait of the Moscow Bolšoj soloist.

1447 Gabovič, M.M. *Principy biomehaniki v metodike prepodavanija klassiceskogo tanca: Avtoref. dis. kand. iskusstvovedenija.* (The Principles of Biomechanics in the Method of Teaching Classical Dance: Abstract of a Dissertation by a Candidate in Art Criticism.) Moscow: GITIS; 1987. 16 pp. Lang.: Rus.

USSR. 1987. Technical studies.

1448 Gaevskij, V. "Prima-balerina." (Prima Ballerina.) *TeatrM.* 1987; 8: 84-85. Lang.: Eng.

USSR: Leningrad. 1912-1987. Biographical studies. ■Portrait of ballerina Natal'ja Dudinskaja of the Kirov Ballet.

1449 Mušinskaja, T.M. *Garmonija duéta.* (The Harmony of the Duet.) Minsk: Belarus'; 1987. 414 pp. Lang.: Rus.

USSR. 1980. Biographical studies. ■Belorussian ballet soloists L. Bržozovskaja and Ju. Trojan.

1450 Smakov, Gennady; Trombetta, Sergio, ed. *I grandi danzatori russi.* (The Great Russian Dancers.) Rome: Gremese; 1987. 213 pp. (Biblioteca della Arti.) Index. Illus.: Photo. Print. B&W. Lang.: Ita.

USSR. 1890-1987. Biographical studies. ■The Russian style of dance described by a Russian critic through the sketches of thirty-three Russian dancers.

1451 Žjurajtis, A.A. *Litovskij ballet. Stanovlenie i razvitie žanra: Avtoref. dis. kand. iskusstvovedenija.* (Lithuanian Ballet—Its Establishment and Development: Abstract of a Dissertation

by a Candidate in Art Criticism.) Vil'njus: Gos.konservatorija LitSSR; 1987. 23 pp. Lang.: Rus.

USSR. 1920-1987. Historical studies. ■Regional theatre.

1452 Zozulina, N.N. *Alla Osipenko.* Leningrad: Iskusstvo; 1987. 220 pp. Lang.: Rus.

USSR: Leningrad. 1932-1980. Biographical studies. ■Ballet artist of the Kirov theatre.

1453 *Ballet narodnogo teatra v Belgrade (1923-1941): Avtoref. dis. kand. iskusstvovedenija.* (Ballet of the Belgrade Folk Theatre, 1923-1941: Abstract of a Dissertation by a Candidate in Art Criticism.) Moscow: GITIS; 1987. 26 pp. Lang.: Rus.

Yugoslavia: Belgrade. 1923-1941. Historical studies.

Plays/librettos/scripts

1454 Pečman, Rudolf. "Heroický balet Leopolda Koželuha." (The Heroic Ballet of Leopold Koželuh.) *Prog.* 1987; 58(6-9): 207-212, 243-246, 282-284, 330-331. Lang.: Cze.

Austria-Hungary: Vienna. 1794. Historical studies. ■The history of the inception of the work *Dcera Oty II. znovu nalezena (The Daughter of Ota II Was Found Again)* by Leopold Koželuh.

1455 Kant, Marion. "Ballett als eine Auskunft zur Frauenfrage." (Ballet as Information Source on the Women's Rights Question.) *WB.* 1987; 33(12): 2026-2043. Lang.: Ger.

France. Germany. Russia. 1830-1920. Historical studies. ■Treatise on the role of the 19th-century female dancer and changes in women's image in the romantic ballet.

Relation to other fields

1456 Strasser, Hannes. "Der Stellenwert des Balletts in den Schweizer Theatern." (Position and Function of Ballet in Swiss Theatres.) 71-76 in Reich, Dietbert; Waltisbühl, Christine. *Opernhaus Zürich—Jahrbuch 87/88.* Zürich: Orell Füssli Verlag; 1987. 184 pp. (Jahrbuch 87/88.) Lang.: Ger.

Switzerland. 1987. ■Insights into status of the Swiss ballet scene: reference to social security and education of dancers.

Theory/criticism

1457 Daly, Ann. "The Balanchine Woman of Humming Birds and Channel Swimmers." *TDR.* 1987 Spr; 31(1): 8-21. Notes. Biblio. Illus.: Photo. Print. B&W. 5. Lang.: Eng.

USA. 1946-1987. Histories-specific. ■Survey of Balanchine ballerinas: even during backlash against feminism, why men have never dominated the world of ballet.

1458 Hanna, Judith Lynne. "Patterns of Dominance—Men, Women, and Homosexuality in Dance." *TDR.* 1987 Spr; 31(1): 23-47. Notes. Biblio. Illus.: Photo. Print. B&W. 11. Lang.: Eng.

USA. 1700-1987. Histories-specific. ■Why women and gay men outnumber other groups in Western dance.

Ethnic dance

Institutions

1459 Davis, Chick. "African-American Dance Ensemble." *WJBS.* 1987 Sum; 11(2): 74, 75. Illus.: Photo. B&W. 3. Lang.: Eng.

USA: New York, NY. 1968-1987. Historical studies. ■History and development of the African-American Dance Ensemble and the Chuck Davis Dance Company.

Performance/production

1460 Pór, Anna. "*Boszorkányok, varázslatok*, Néptáncgála Szegeden." (*Witches and Witchcraft*: Folklore Dance Festival in Szeged.) *Sz.* 1987 Nov.; 20(11): 25-26. Illus.: Photo. B&W. 1. Lang.: Hun.

Hungary: Szeged. 1987. Reviews of performances. ■The traditional international folk-dance show was presented in the framework of a folk play called *Witches and Witchcraft* at the Szeged Open-Air Festival.

1461 Erdman, Joan L. "Performance as Translation—Uday Shankar in the West." *TDR.* 1987 Spr; 31(1): 64-87. Notes. Biblio. Illus.: Photo. Print. B&W. 14. Lang.: Eng.

DANCE: Ethnic dance—Performance/production

India. France: Paris. UK-England: London. 1924-1940. Historical studies. ■Uday Shankar's translation of classical Indian dance into authentic productions for Western audiences.

1462 Ju, Kang-hyoun. "Han Puly." (An Exorcism.) *KTR*. 1987 Aug.; 8(1): 60. Illus.: Photo. B&W. 1. Lang.: Kor.
Korea. 1500-1987. Historical studies. ■*Han Puly*, a form of exorcism, and its relationship with dance-drama. Related to Dance-Drama.

1463 Avila, Norma. "La Mixmedia: Una Necesidad de Expresión." (Mixed Media: A Necessity of Expression.) *Universidad de Mexico*. 1987 Jan.; 12(432): 42-44. Illus.: Photo. B&W. Grd.Plan. 3. Lang.: Spa.
Mexico: Mexico City. 1987. Historical studies. ■Describes the combination of dance theatre and music in productions given by the Department of Dance at University of Mexico.

1464 Abud, Ronald; Turner, Elaine; Clarke, Margaret. "Revolution as Self-Expression: The Folklore Ballet of Nicaragua." *NTQ*. 1987 Feb.; 3(9): 89-92. Illus.: Photo. Print. B&W. 2. Lang.: Eng.
Nicaragua. 1986. Histories-sources. ■The founder and director of the Ballet Folklórico Nacional de Nicaragua explains the work and aims of the company which has become closely identified with Nicaragua's revolution.

1465 Daigre, Edna. "Ewajo Dance Workshop." *WJBS*. 1985; 9(2): 103-105. Biblio. Illus.: Photo. B&W. 3. Lang.: Eng.
USA: Seattle, WA. 1975-1985. Historical studies. ■A new approach to dance as an art form: includes interfusion of break-dancing, ballet, modern, traditional and social jazz dances.

Relation to other fields

1466 Turner, Edith. "Zambia's KanKanga Dances: The Changing Life of Ritual." *PerAJ*. 1987; 10(3): 57-71. Illus.: Photo. B&W. 7. Lang.: Eng.
Zambia. 1951-1985. Historical studies. ■Evolution of ritual and ritual dances for the initiation of young girls in the Nolembu tribe.

Modern dance

Institutions

1467 Draeger, Volkmar. "Choreographien von glasklarer Konstruktion. Zum Gastpiel der Martha Graham Dance Company." (Choreographies of a Translucent Construction: On the Guest Performance of the Martha Graham Dance Company in Berlin.) *TZ*. 1987; 42(4): 25-26. Illus.: Photo. 2. Lang.: Ger.
USA. 1926-1986. Historical studies. ■Outline of Graham's biography and significance, history of the company, description of dancing style.

Performance/production

1468 Orlin, Merle. "The European Challenge." *Scenaria*. 1987 July; 78: 47-48. Lang.: Eng.
France: Paris. UK-England: London. South Africa, Republic of. 1987. Critical studies. ■Young choreographers in Europe, their development of new images and the need for South Africa to discover its own direction.

1469 *Palucca. Zum Fünfundachtzigsten. Glückwünsche, Selbstzeugnisse, Ausserungen.* (Palucca: A Present on Her 85th Birthday. Congratulations, Self-Testimonies, Statements.) Berlin: Akademie der Künste der DDR; 1987. 119 pp. Illus.: Photo. Dwg. Color. B&W. 38. Lang.: Ger.
Germany, East: Dresden. 1922-1987. Histories-sources. ■Letters to Gret Palucca by various artists. Six short contributions by herself, chronological list of her dances.

1470 Hammergren, Lena. "Arbete med text och rörelse." (Work with Text and Movement.) *NT*. 1987; 39: 12-15. Illus.: Photo. Lang.: Swe.
Sweden: Stockholm. 1970-1987. Biographical studies. ■A portrait of Efva Lilja, her way of creating through naked movements and even through the written word, and the difficult situation of a choreographer today.

1471 Wilhelmsson, Siv. "Unga Atalante, sjösand och mångtydiga bilder." (Young Atalanta, Sea Sand and Ambiguous Pictures.) *NT*. 1987; 37: 38-39. Illus.: Photo. Lang.: Swe.
Sweden: Gothenburg. 1987. Historical studies. ■In an old cinema filled with sand, Rubicon, the dance group which looks for the enigma of the ordinary, has staged *Allting rasar inför en naken skuldra* (*Everything Gives Way to a Naked Shoulder*).

1472 Daly, Ann. "Interview with Senta Driver." *WPerf*. 1987; 3(2): 90-96. Illus.: Photo. B&W. 3. Lang.: Eng.
USA. 1987. Histories-sources. ■Choreographer discusses her critique of traditional male/female partnering and dance styles, strength and power in dancers, disruption of traditional ideas of masculine and feminine, compares work to other choreographers.

1473 Falk, Bertril. "Koreograf Vaslav Nijinskij: 'Han var först, han var pionjären'." (Choreographer Vaslav Nižinskij: 'He Was the First, He Was the Pioneer'.) *MuD*. 1987; 9(1): 11-13. Illus.: Photo. Dwg. Lang.: Swe.
USA: Los Angeles, CA. 1913-1987. Histories-sources. ■Millicent Hodson speaks about how she managed to reconstruct Nižinskij's *Le sacre du printemps*.

1474 Layson, J. *Isadora Duncan: Her Life, Work and Contribution to Western Theatre Dance*. Ph.D. thesis, *Index to Theses*, 37-4375. Leeds: University of Leeds; 1987. Notes. Biblio. Lang.: Eng.
USA. Europe. 1877-1927. Biographical studies. ■Examines Duncan's life, work and role in the foundation and development of modern dance. Employs a specifically devised methodology to discuss her choreography and identifies several important innovations.

Relation to other fields

1475 Casini-Ropa, Eugenia. "Il corpo ritrovato. Danza e teatro tra pedagogia, ginnastica e arte." (The Rediscovered Body: Dance and Drama Between Pedagogy, Gymnastics and Art.) *TeatroS*. 1987; 2(2): 295-346. Lang.: Ita.
Germany. 1900-1930. Historical studies. ■Rediscovery of the body, psychophysical education through rhythm and expressive movement: educational gymnastics, eurythmics and free dance. The art of movement as a foundation for theatrical research.

1476 *Künstler um Palucca. Ausstellung zu Ehren des 85. Geburtstages.* (Artists Around Palucca: Exhibition in Honour of Her 85th Birthday.) Dresden: Staatliche Kunstsammlungen Dresden; 1987. 63 pp. Illus.: Photo. Color. B&W. 41. [May-August 1987, Dresden.] Lang.: Ger.
Germany, East: Dresden. 1922-1987. Histories-sources. ■Gret Palucca, dancer and teacher, as seen by other artists.

Theory/criticism

1477 Hughes, David. "Moving Forwards and Backwards in Time." *PM*. 1987(50/51): 25-29. Illus.: Photo. B&W. 5. Lang.: Eng.
USA. 1962-1987. Historical studies. ■Relationship of Merce Cunningham and John Cage's work to the urban environment. Discusses recent works produced by the Merce Cunningham Dance Company.

Other entries with significant content related to Dance: 376, 396, 1218, 1480, 1671, 3228, 3296.

DANCE-DRAMA

General

1478 Harris, David Alan. "Johanna Boyce's *With Longings to Realize*." *TDR*. 1983 Sum; 27(2): 86-91. Illus.: Photo. B&W. 2. Lang.: Eng.
USA: New York, NY. 1983. Historical studies. ■Boyce's dance piece presented by the Performance Group. Description of collage structure of piece, weave of dance, music and narration and themes of the play.

DANCE-DRAMA: General

Performance/production

1479 Ryan, Pete. "Les Ballets Jazz de Montréal: A Day in the Life of a Dancer." *PAC*. 1986 Jan.; 22(4): 12-13. Notes. Illus.: Photo. Print. 9. Lang.: Eng.
Canada: Montreal, PQ. 1985. Biographical studies. ∎Photo-story of dancer Bobby Thompson and daily routine of a dancer as member of Les Ballets Jazz de Montréal.

1480 Swiderski, Richard M. "Representing Representing: A *Cavittunatakam* Performance." *ATJ*. 1987 Fall; 4(2): 177-190. Biblio. Illus.: Photo. Color. 7. Lang.: Eng.
India: Kerala. 1984. Reviews of performances. ∎History and description of a performance of *Cavittunatakam*, a stamping drama performed by actors on a wooden stage recounting stories of the lives of the saints. Related to Dance: Ethnic dance.

1481 Kam, Garrett. "Wayang Wong in the Court of Yogyakarta: The Enduring Significance of Javanese Dance Drama." *ATJ*. 1987 Spr; 4(1): 29-51. Notes. Biblio. Illus.: Diagram. Photo. B&W. 4: var. sizes. Lang.: Eng.
Indonesia. 930-1986. Technical studies. ∎*Wayang wong*, dance drama of the central Javanese royal court: set designs, dramatic structure, training of dancers, style, and revival in 1981.

1482 Asahi shimbun, ed. *Sengo geinōshi monogatari*. (The Story of Theatrical Performance in the Postwar Period.) Tokyo: Asahi shimbunsha; 1987. 296 pp. Illus.: Photo. Print. B&W. Lang.: Jap.
Japan. 1945-1986. Historical studies. ∎A history of theatrical performance after World War II, focusing primarily on *shingeki*.

1483 Hoff, Frank. "What He Saw." *Theatrum*. 1987 Sum; 7(9-12). Illus.: Photo. B&W. 1. Lang.: Eng.
Japan. 1930-1986. Biographical studies. ∎Describes the work of Honda Yasuji on *kagura* (Japanese folk performance).

1484 Pack, Gin-Tae. *Hanguk kamyunguk-yonku*. (Korean Mask Theatre.) Seoul: Saemoom-SA; 1985. 220 pp. Lang.: Kor.
Korea. 57 B.C.-1907 A.D. Histories-specific. ∎The masked dance-drama of ancient Korea.

1485 Sung, Kyung-Lin. *Hangukui mooyong*. (Korean Traditional Dance.) Seoul: Kyoyang Guksa; 1976. 217 pp. Lang.: Kor.
Korea. 57 B.C.-1976 A.D. Historical studies. ∎The origin and theory of Korean traditional dance-theatre.

1486 Schechner, Richard. "The Struggle to Make Form: Leonardo Shapiro, Julie Lyonn Lieberman, and Philip Arnoult." *TDR*. 1987 Spr; 31(1): 131-136. Illus.: Photo. Print. B&W. 3. Lang.: Eng.
USA. 1960-1987. Histories-sources. ∎Interview discussing *The Yellow House* and Van Gogh's influence on the production, and people involved in original production.

1487 Shapiro, Leonardo. "Shaliko's *The Yellow House*: Swimming Upstream through the '80's." *TDR*. 1987 Spr; 31(1): 119-130. Illus.: Photo. Print. B&W. 10. Lang.: Eng.
USA: Baltimore, MD. 1982-1987. Technical studies. ∎Notes on script and staging of Shaliko's *The Yellow House*: background, theme, structure, set and character development.

Plays/librettos/scripts

1488 Dong-Il, Cho. "Yangjusandae-bunsuk." (The Analytical Investigation of Yangjusandae.) 223-278 in *History & Theory of Mask Theatre*. Seoul: Hongik-SA; 1987. 406 pp. Lang.: Kor.
Korea. 57 B.C.-1987 A.D. Critical studies. ∎Analysis of *Yangjusandae nolyee*, a Korean mask play.

1489 Kim, Sung Hee. "Theory of Lee Kang Bak." 71-97 pp in Han'guk Yŏn'guk p'yŏngnon'ga Hyŏphoe, ed. *Han'guk Hyŏnyŏk Kŭk Chakkaron*. Yent: Sin. Youngchul; 1987. 140 pp. Biblio. Illus.: Lighting. 5. Lang.: Kor.
Korea. 1970-1987. Critical studies. ∎Theory and plays of playwright Lee Kang Bak.

Kabuki

Audience

1490 Gerstle, C. Andrew. "Flowers of Edo: Eighteenth-Century *Kabuki* and Its Patrons." *ATJ*. 1987 Spr; 4(1): 52-75. Notes. Biblio. Illus.: Photo. Pntg. Dwg. Print. Color. B&W. 13. Lang.: Eng.
Japan: Tokyo. 1603-1868. Critical studies. ∎Patronage of *kabuki* in Tokyo: role of the samurai class, elements of *aragoto* acting and *onnagata* performers.

Basic theatrical documents

1491 Kabuki daichō kenkyūkai, ed. *Kabuki daichō shūsei*. (*Kabuki* Playtexts Series.) Tokyo: Benseisha; 1987. 503, 488, 670 pp.. Color. 1, 1, 1. [Vols 13, 14, 15.] Lang.: Jap.
Japan. 1600-1800. ∎Vol 13: *Kanazōshi Kousenya jitsuroku, Keisei Sajikogoku*, Vol 14: *Keisei Katsuodera, Kiritarō tengu sakamori*, Vol 15: *Akiba-gongen kaisengatari, Keisei Kamakurayama, Takebera Tarō kaidanki*.

Performance/production

1492 National Theatre of Japan, ed. *Kindai kabuki nenpyō Ōsaka-hen dai-ni-kan*. (The Chronological Record of *Kabuki* in Osaka.) Tokyo: Yagi-shoten; 1987. 710 pp. [Vol. 2.] Lang.: Jap.
Japan: Osaka. 1885-1893. Historical studies. ∎Contains the record of *kabuki* plays performed, with names of theatres and actors.

1493 Yakusha hyōbanki kenkyūkai, ed. *Kabuki hyōbanki shūsei—dainiki dai-ikkan*. (A Collection of Who is Who in *Kabuki*.) Tokyo: Iwanami-shoten; 1987. 573 pp.. (2nd series 1.) [Series 2, Volume 1.] Lang.: Jap.
Japan. 1600-1800. Critical studies. ∎First volume of the second series of a Who's Who in *kabuki* during the Edo period.

1494 Nishiyama, Matsunosuke. *Ichikawa Danjūrō*. Tokyo: Yoshikawa kōbunkan; 1987. 342 pp. Tables. Biblio. B&W. 4. Lang.: Jap.
Japan. 1791-1859. Biographies. ∎Articles on Edo Period actors who carried the name Ichikawa Danjūrō.

Plays/librettos/scripts

1495 Shigetoshi, Kawatake. *Kawatake Mokuami*. Tokyo: Yoshikawa kōbunkan; 1987. 271 pp. Tables. Biblio. B&W. 1. [2d ed.] Lang.: Jap.
Japan. 1816-1893. Biographies. ∎New edition of the classic study on Mokuami.

Kathakali

Performance/production

1496 Martin, Carol. "Feminist Analysis Across Cultures: Performing Gender in India." *WPerf*. 1987-88; 3(2): 32-40. Notes. Illus.: Photo. B&W. 1. Lang.: Eng.
India. USA. 1983-1987. Critical studies. ∎Western readings of other cultures: role of feminist in cultural critique.

Nō

Design/technology

1497 Nakamura, Yasuo. *Nakamura Naohiko nōmen isakushū*. (Collection of *Nō* Masks Carved by Nakamura Naohiko.) Kyoto: Tankōsha; 1987. 321 pp. Illus.: Photo. B&W. Color. Lang.: Jap.
Japan. 1900-1940. Histories-sources. ∎Illustrations of the life-work of *nō* mask sculptor Nakamura Naohiko.

Performance/production

1498 Gillespie, John K. "Interior Action: The Impact of Noh on Jean-Louis Barrault." *CompD*. 1982-83 Win; 16(4): 325-344. Notes. Lang.: Eng.
France. 1910-1982. Historical studies. ∎Influence of *nō* theatre on director Jean-Louis Barrault: his collaboration with Antonin Artaud,

DANCE-DRAMA: *Nō*—Performance/production

Paul Claudel, Etienne Marcel Decroux and Charles Dullin. Barrault's use of mime in his plays. Related to Mime.

1499 Emmert, Richard. "Training of the *Nō* Performer." *ThR.* 1987; 12(2): 123-133. Notes. Lang.: Eng.
Japan. 1987. Historical studies. ■Institutions and techniques involved in contemporary training of *nō* actors.

1500 Ishii, Tatsuro. "Zeami's Mature Thoughts on Acting." *ThR.* 1987; 12(2): 110-123. Notes. Illus.: Diagram. Print. B&W. 4. Lang.: Eng.
Japan. 1363-1443. Critical studies. ■Zeami's concept of the actor and the ideal performance.

1501 Johnson, Irmgard. "Priestly *Nō* at Chūsonji." *ATJ.* 1987 Fall; 4(2): 215-229. Notes. Illus.: Photo. B&W. 1. Lang.: Eng.
Japan: Hiraizumi. 1987. Reviews of performances. ■Present-day performances of *nō* plays by priests at Hiraizumi, including a new play *Hidehira*.

1502 Kawamura, Hatsue. *Nō no Japonism.* (Japonism of the *Nō*.) Tokyo: Shichigatsudō; 1987. 237 pp. Lang.: Jap.
Japan. 1300-1600. Critical studies. ■How *nō* acting expresses Japanese feelings.

1503 Nakamura, Hachirō. *Nō Chūgoku mono no butai to rekishi.* (Performance and History of *Nō* Plays with Chinese Subjects.) Tokyo: Nōgaku Shorin; 1987. 195 pp.. Illus.: Photo. Print. B&W. Lang.: Jap.
Japan. 1300-1500. Historical studies. ■Discussion of *nō* plays with subjects from Chinese history.

1504 Shigeyama, Sennojō. *Kyōgen yakusha.* (*Kyōgen* Actors.) Tokyo: Iwanami Shoten; 1987. 231 pp. Illus.: Photo. B&W. Lang.: Jap.
Japan. 1940-1987. Histories-sources. ■The author's ironic view of his own achievements as a *kyōgen* actor.

Plays/librettos/scripts

1505 Chūsei Minshū no Shinkō to Bunka. *Jishū bungei to Ippen Hōgo.* (The Literature of the Jishū Sect and Ippen Hōgo.) Tokyo: Tokyo Bijutsu; 1987. 548 pp. Notes. Biblio. Lang.: Jap.
Japan. 1200-1400. Critical studies. ■Work of the monk Ippen Hōgo, its reflection in the *nō*.

1506 Andō, Tsunejirō. *Yōkyoku Kyōgen* to kindai no bungei. (*Nō* and *Kyōgen* Plays and Contemporary Literature.) Tokyo: Wanya-shoten; 1986. 255 pp. Lang.: Jap.
Japan. 1300-1986. Critical studies. ■Relationships between traditional *nō* and *kyōgen* texts and modern literature.

1507 Matsuda, Tamotsu. *Waka to yōkyoku kō.* (Considerations on *Waka* and *Nō* Texts.) Tokyo: Āfūsha; 1987. 315 pp. Notes. Biblio. Lang.: Jap.
Japan. 700-1300. Critical studies. ■Study of *waka* poetry as it appears quoted in the 245 standard *nō* texts.

1508 Tashiro, Keiichirō. *Yōkyoku o yomu.* (Reading the *Nō* Texts.) Tokyo: Asahi Shimbunsha; 1987. 335 pp. Lang.: Jap.
Japan. 1300-1500. Critical studies. ■How to read the *nō* texts as poetry.

Reference materials

1509 Nishino, Haruo, ed.; Hata, Higashi, ed. *Nō kyōgen jiten.* (Dictionary of *Nō* and *Kyōgen*.) Tokyo: Heibonsha; 1987. 503 pp. Biblio. Illus.: Photo. Print. Color. B&W. Lang.: Jap.
Japan. 1100-1987.

Theory/criticism

1510 Rodowicz, Jadwiga. "Rola w teatrze *Nō*." (Actor's Role in the *Nō* Theatre.) *DialogW.* 1985 Apr.; 30(4): 119-126. Notes. Lang.: Pol.
Japan. 712-1980. Historical studies. ■Metaphysical and philosophical implications of the actor's role in the *nō* theatre.

Other entries with significant content related to Dance-Drama: 663, 664, 858, 1197, 1462, 1737.

DRAMA

Administration

1511 Souissi, Moncef. "L'état législatif du théâtre arabe." (Legislative Status of Arab Theatre.) 163-168 in Coca, Jordi, ed.; Conesa, Laura, comp. *Congrés Internacional de Teatre a Catalunya 1985. Actes. Volum III., Seccions 4, 5 i 6.* Barcelona: Institut del Teatre; 1987. 302 pp. [Section 5: Policy and Legislation.] Lang.: Fre.
Arabic countries. 1938-1985. Critical studies. ■The Arabic world lacks a theatrical tradition. Theatre boomed after the Egyptian revolution of 1952, declined after the military defeat of 1967 and grew in the 1980s, with the appearance of professional actors' syndicates. Emphasis on Tunisia.

1512 Atkinson, Roslyn; Fotheringham, Richard. "Dramatic Copyright in Australia to 1912." *ADS.* 1987 Oct.; 11: 47-63. Lang.: Eng.
Australia. UK-England. USA. 1870-1912. Critical studies. ■Describes the legal situation relating to the copyright of Australian plays prior to Australia's adoption of the British Copyright Act in 1912, and details several law cases concerned with breach of copyright.

1513 DuToit, Simon. "The Production Dramaturg." *Theatrum.* 1987 Spr; 6: 17-20. Lang.: Eng.
Canada. USA. Germany. 1980-1987. Critical studies. ■A discussion of the emerging role of dramaturgy in Canadian theatre. A comparison of American and European traditions is given as well as definitions of the task, function and role of dramaturgy in production and in theatre in general.

1514 Garebian, Keith. "Devaluation: The 1987 Shaw Festival." *JCNREC.* 1987/88 Win; 22(4): 128-141. Illus.: Photo. B&W. 3. Lang.: Eng.
Canada: Niagara-on-the-Lake, ON. 1987. Critical studies. ■Lower standards and loss of artistic purpose in season's Shaw Festival.

1515 Harrison, James. "Of Vision and Space (Dollars and Sense)." *Theatrum.* 1987 Spr; 6: 3-4. Lang.: Eng.
Canada: Toronto, ON. 1986-1987. Historical studies. ■Opinions concerning the recent merger of CentreStage and the Toronto Free Theatre: theatrical climate, financial conditions and artists involved.

1516 Tromly, F.B. "An Autumnal Season: Stratford's Thirty-Fifth Anniversary." *JCNREC.* 1987/88 Win; 22(4): 115-128. Lang.: Eng.
Canada: Stratford, ON. 1987. Historical studies. ■Good performances and poor attendance at the Stratford Festival.

1517 Goldstein, Robert Justin. "Political Censorship of the Theatre in Nineteenth-Century Europe." *ThR.* 1987; 12(3): 220-241 . Notes. Lang.: Eng.
England. Russia. France. Germany. 1800-1899. Historical studies. ■Debilitating effect of political censorship on theatre in nineteenth-century Europe.

1518 Reichel, Peter. "DDR-Dramatik Mitte der achtziger Jahre. Beobachtungen und Überlegungen." (GDR Drama in the Middle of the 80s: Observations and Reflections.) *WB.* 1987; 33(9): 1524-1551. Lang.: Ger.
Germany, East. 1985-1986. Historical studies. ■Situation of GDR drama and playwrights, promotional measures, author/theatre relationship.

1519 "Sodom and Begorrah Revisited." *Econ.* 1986 July 12; 300(7454): 88. Lang.: Eng.
Ireland. UK. 1986. Critical studies. ■Success of Irish theatre in Great Britain and abroad. Financial state of Dublin theatres, brief profile of Irish dramatists and their work.

1520 Thorell, Bernt. "Hamlet i Florens." (Hamlet in Florence.) *ProScen.* 1987; 10(1-2): 5-12. Illus.: Photo. 5. Lang.: Swe.
Italy: Florence. Sweden: Stockholm. 1986. Technical studies. ■How the guest performance of Ingmar Bergman's production of *Hamlet* was realized from a technical point of view.

1521 Lee, Sang-Il. "Sokūk'Jang Wŭndong." (Little Theatre Movement.) 121-126 in Seoul P'yongnon'ga Group, ed.

DRAMA: —Administration

Han'guk Yŏnguk kwa Chŏlmon Ŭislk. Mineum SA: Park. Mazngho; 1979. 262 pp. Notes. Lang.: Kor.
Korea: Seoul. 1960-1979. Historical studies. ■The little theatre movement in Korea: issues of control.

1522 Pierstorff, Erik. "Vesleøy Haslund vs. The National Theatre of Oslo." *TDR.* 1982 Fall; 26(3): 81-83. Lang.: Eng.
Norway: Oslo. 1979-1982. Historical studies. ■Actress fights her termination from the National Theatre in court with the backing of Norwegian Actors Equity. Regulations, legal arguments.

1523 "Scenaria Interviews Rodney Phillips." *Scenaria.* 1987 May(76): 35-39. Illus.: Photo. 6. Lang.: Eng.
South Africa, Republic of. 1987. Histories-sources. ■Achievements of NAPAC under Rodney Phillips, company's policy on political conditions in South Africa and state funding.

1524 "Ellen Burstyn Interviews Peter Sellars." *EN.* 1985 June; 70(6): 1, 2, 10. Illus.: Photo. B&W. 1.
USA: Washington, DC. 1985. Histories-sources. ■Director Peter Sellars discusses his new theatre operations at John F. Kennedy Center and opinions on theatre in general.

1525 Agapova, T. "'Netvorčeskie' grani tvorčeskogo processa." ('Non-Creative' Facets of the Creative Process.) *SovD.* 1987; 4: 201-207. Lang.: Rus.
USSR. 1980-1987. Critical studies. ■Ways of developing repertory.

1526 Melnjace, R. "V poiskach p'esy." (In Search of the Play.) *SovD.* 1987; 1: 249-252. Lang.: Rus.
USSR: Latvia. 1986-1988. Histories-sources. ■Literary director of Latvian Upit Theatre on one of the theatre's most critical problems: lack of information on contemporary dramaturgy.

1527 Roščin, Michajl. "'Sekret' éksperimenta." (The 'Secret' of Experiment.) *SovD.* 1987; 1: 238-241. Lang.: Rus.
USSR. 1986-1988. Histories-sources. ■A dramatist's opinion of repertorial policy under new conditions: democratization of theatre business.

1528 Sigaev, A. "Trudnosti teatra." (Difficulties of the Theatre.) *SovD.* 1987; 2: 255-259. Lang.: Rus.
USSR: Kazachstan. 1980-1987. Historical studies. ■Repertorial problems of Kazachstan's theatres, overview of recent Kazach dramaturgy.

1529 Tarasenko, A. "Teatr: tradicii i iskanija..." (The Theatre: Its Traditions and Strivings.) *Raduga.* 1987; 7: 116-120. Lang.: Rus.
USSR. 1986-1987. Historical studies. ■Theatrical experimentation on the Ukrainian stage: politics of repertory, new plays by Ukrainian dramatists.

Audience

1530 Blokdijk, Tom. "De Slag om de burg." (The Attack on the 'Burg'.) *Toneel.* 1987 June; 6(4): 23-26. Illus.: Dwg. Photo. 2. Lang.: Dut.
Austria: Vienna. 1986-1987. Historical studies. ■Claus Peymann, new artistic director of the Vienna Burgtheater: his theatrical 'attack' on Austrian society and his dealings with negative press, antisemitism and audience reactions.

1531 Féral, Josette; Gill, Rosalind, transl. "Face to Face with the Actor." *CTR.* 1987 Spr; 50: 78-81. Pref. Notes. Print. B&W. 1. Lang.: Eng.
Canada: Montreal, PQ. 1986. Critical studies. ■Analysis of Anne-Marie Provencher's *La Tour (The Tower),* which features one actor relating wordlessly with one audience member.

1532 Gurr, Andrew. *Playgoing in Shakespeare's London.* New York, NY: Cambridge UP; 1987. xv, 284 pp. Pref. Index. Notes. Biblio. Append. Illus.: Plan. Maps. Pntg. Dwg. Fr.Elev. R.Elev. Grd.Plan. 22. Lang.: Eng.
England: London. 1567-1642. Historical studies. ■Shakespeare's original audiences: their social and cultural backgrounds and what it was like to attend a play in London's playhouses.

1533 Haynes, Jonathan. "The Elizabethan Audience Onstage." *TID.* 1987; 9: 59-68. Notes. Lang.: Eng.
England. 1585-1625. Critical studies. ■The particular moment when the actor steps out of the dramatic moment and enters the present with the audience. Relation of theatre space in performance to the materiality of society and history. Theatre as an instrument of social thought.

1534 Muir, Lynette. "Audiences in the French Medieval Theatre." *MET.* 1987; 9(1): 8-22. Notes. Lang.: Eng.
France. 1450-1550. Historical studies. ■Assembly, composition, accommodation and response of spectators to civic and religious plays.

1535 Cairns, David; Richards, Shaun. "Reading a Riff: The 'Reading Formation' of Synge's Abbey Audience." *L&H.* 1987 Fall; 13 (2): 219-237. Notes. Lang.: Eng.
Ireland: Dublin. 1907. Historical studies. ■The political causes of the audience's hostile response to the first production of *The Playboy of the Western World.*

1536 Filipowicz, Halina. "Gardzienice—A Polish Expedition to Baltimore." *TDR.* 1987 Spr; 31(1): 137-163. Notes. Biblio. Illus.: Photo. Print. B&W. 10. Lang.: Eng.
Poland: Gardzienice. 1666-1987. Historical studies. ■Style of and American response to the Polish Gardzienice Theatre Association's production at the Theatre of Nations in Baltimore.

1537 Marsillach, Adolfo. "Se muere el teatro?" (Is the Theatre Dying?)109-125 in Coca, Jordi, ed.; Conesa, Laura, comp. *Congrés Internacional de Teatre a Catalunya 1985. Actes. Volum III. Seccions 7, 8 i 9.* Barcelona: Institut del Teatre; 1987. 350 pp. [Section 8: Outlook for the Theatre.] Lang.: Spa.
Spain. 1985. Critical studies. ■The current theatrical crisis is one of both authors and audience. Theatre has not surpassed the level of film and television. Boom in public theatre marginalizes private theatre.

1538 Pasto, David J. "The Origin of Public Attendance at the Spanish Court Theatre in the Seventeenth Century." *ThS.* 1987 Nov.; 28(2): 41-49. Notes. Lang.: Eng.
Spain: Madrid. 1630-1670. Historical studies. ■Unsatisfied with private performances, King Philip IV and Queen Isabella enjoyed seeing plays at the Coliseo in the company of a cross-section of Spanish society.

1539 Neuringer, Charles; Willis, Ronald A. "The Psychodynamics of Theatrical Spectatorship." *JDTC.* 1987; 2(1): 95-109. Notes. Lang.: Eng.
USA. 1987. Critical studies. ■Discussion of special qualities of live performance using psychoanalytic theory. Psychological transformation occuring in spectators during performance.

1540 Zarrilli, Phillip B. "Structure and Subjunctivity: Puta Wijaya's Theatre of Surprise." *TDR.* 1987 Fall; 31(3): 126-159. Pref. Notes. Biblio. Illus.: Photo. Plan. B&W. Grd.Plan. 15. Lang.: Eng.
USA: Madison, WI. 1986-1987. Critical studies. ■Audience reactions to *Geez,* a play by Indonesian playwright Putu Wijaya.

Basic theatrical documents

1541 Schnitzler, Arthur; Orduña, Javier, intro. *La ronda. (Round.)* Barcelona: Institut del Teatre; 1987. 111 pp. (Biblioteca Teatral 57.) Biblio. Lang.: Cat.
1862-1931. ■Catalan translation of Schnitzler's *Reigen.* Orduña's prologue discusses turn-of-the century Viennese culture, impressionism.

1542 Berreby, Elie Georges; Reich, John, transl.; Bobkoff, Ned, transl. "Jonah." *MID.* 1987; 20(2): 5-27. Lang.: Eng.
Belgium. 1987. ■A two-act comedy with four characters, all four to be played by the same actor. Inspired by the story of Jonah and the whale.

1543 Crommelynck, Fernand; Duvignaud, Jean, pref.; Emond, Paul, ed. *Le Cocu magnifique. (The Magnificent Cuckold.)* Brussels: Labor; 1987. 154 pp. (Espace Nord 44.) Pref. Biblio. Illus.: Photo. B&W. 8. Lang.: Fre.
Belgium. 1920. ■Edition of Crommelynck's play, followed by a study of the play and its author.

1544 Bessai, Diane, ed.; Kerv, Don, ed. *NeWest Plays by Women.* Saskatoon: NeWest P; 1987. Biblio. Illus.: Photo. Lang.: Eng.
Canada. 1987. Histories-sources. ■Collection of plays by four Canadian women dramatists: Sharon Pollock, Joanna Glass, Wendy Lill and Pamela Boyd. Introduction supplies brief biographies, production histories and text analyses.

1545 Dorge, Claude. "Le Roitelet." (The Kinglet.) *CDr.* 1985 Sum; 11(2): 340-375. Lang.: Fre.

DRAMA: —Basic theatrical documents

Canada: Montreal, PQ. 1976. ■Text of Claude Dorge's *Le Roitelet (The Kinglet)* first performed on April 30, 1976 at Cercle Molière.

1546 Dubois, René-Daniel; Gaboriau, Linda, transl. "Being at Home with Claude." *CTR*. 1987 Spr; 50: 37-58. Notes. Illus.: Photo. Print. B&W. 5. Lang.: Eng.

Canada: Montreal, PQ. 1986. ■English translation of René-Daniel Dubois' *Being at Home with Claude*, about the criminal investigation of a murder.

1547 Lambert, Betty. *Jennie's Story* and *Under the Skin*. Toronto, ON: Playwrights Canada P; 1987. 194 pp. Lang.: Eng.

Canada. 1987. ■Publication of two plays by Lambert, both of which derive their energy from anger at the injustices suffered by women.

1548 Petch, Steve. "Another Morning." *CTR*. 1987 Fall; 52: 58-81. Illus.: Photo. Print. B&W. 5. Lang.: Eng.

Canada: Vancouver, BC. 1987. Histories-sources. ■Illustration of social and political issues in *Another Morning*, in which a white Canadian boy meets a Japanese-Canadian girl in 1942.

1549 Tremblay, Michel; Plocher, Hanspeter, transl. *Schwesterherzchen*. (*Les Belles-Soeurs*.) Tübingen: Max Niemeyer V; 1987. 83 pp. Pref. Biblio. Lang.: Ger.

Canada: Quebec, PQ. Germany. 1987. ■Michel Tremblay's *Les Belles-Soeurs*, first performed in 1968, is now translated into German with an introduction on French Canadian theatre, 'joual', an interpretation of the play and a bio-bibliography of Tremblay.

1550 Milner, Arthur. "*Zero Hour*." *CTR*. 1987 Win; 53: 49-69. Illus.: Photo. 4. Lang.: Eng.

Costa Rica: San José. 1987. ■Three men, ranging from 22 to 38 years of age inhabit a Costa Rican jail cell. Discussion focuses on fighting Communism and the Contras. A context is provided for audience members to be educated in the politics of war in South America, from a U.S., rather than Canadian bias.

1551 Kundera, Milan. *Jacques i elseu amo: homenatge a Denis Diderot*. (*Jacques and His Master: Homage to Denis Diderot*.) Barcelona: Edicions del Mall; 1987. 117 pp. (Llibres del Mall. Sèrie oberta.) Lang.: Cat.

Czechoslovakia: Prague. 1968-1981. Critical studies. ■Catalan translation of Kundera's *Jacques at son maître*, with introductory remarks by the author.

1552 Emeljanow, Victor. "Komisarjevsky's *Three Sisters*, The Prompt Book." *TN*. 1987; 41(2): 56-66. Illus.: Diagram. B&W. 4. Lang.: Eng.

England: London. 1901. ■Constance Garnett's translation accommodating a converted theatre space and English taste of the period.

1553 Yliruusi, Tauno; Stone, Steve, transl. "*What, No Ashes?*." *MID*. 1987; 21(1): 27-52. Lang.: Eng.

Finland. 1987. ■Translation of a five-act comedy dealing with the relation of journalism to politics and religion.

1554 Rostand, Edmond; Smith, Kay Nolte, transl. *Chantecler*. A Play in Four Acts. Lanham, MD: UP of America; 1987. 242 pp. Lang.: Eng.

France. 1880-1987. ■First English translation of Rostand's *Chantecler* in over sixty years.

1555 Hammer, Klaus, ed. *Dramaturgische Schriften des 19. Jahrhunderts*. (19th Century Dramaturgic Writings, 2 vol.) Berlin: Henschelverlag; 1987. 1379 pp. Pref. Index. Notes. Lang.: Ger.

Germany. 1794-1906. ■About 150 texts by 19th-century writers, playwrights, scholars and critics, found in hidden sources, convey the outlines of dramatic theory of the period.

1556 Masen, Jacob; Halbig, Michael C., transl. *The Jesuit Theatre of Jacob Masen: Three Plays in Translation with an Introduction*. Amer. Univ. Studies. New York, NY: Peter Lang P; 1987. 300 pp. (Series xvii, Classical Languages & Literature 1.) Lang.: Eng.

Germany. 1606-1681. ■English translation of three of Jacob Masen's plays: *Androphilus*, *Rusticus imperans* and *Maurice*.

1557 Strauss, Botha; López, Yasmine F., intro. *Cares conegudes, sentiments barrejats*. (*Known Faces, Mixed Feelings*.) Barcelona: Institut del Teatre; 1987. 79 pp. (Biblioteca Teatral 56.) Biblio. Lang.: Cat.

Germany. 1944-1978. ■Catalan translation of *Bekannte Gesichter, Gemischte Gefühle (Known Faces, Mixed Feelings)* by Botho Strauss. López' prologue covers plot, characters.

1558 Beyaz'i, Bahram; Morad, Gowhar-e; Na'lbandian, Abbas; Kapuscinski, Gisele, transl. *Modern Persian Drama: An Anthology*. Lanham, MD: UP of America; 1987. 248 pp. Lang.: Eng.

Iran. 1987. ■Translations of five contemporary Persian plays, never before seen in the West.

1559 Mittelpunkt, Hillel; Taub, Michael, transl. "*Buba*." *MID*. 1987; 21(1): 5-26. Lang.: Eng.

Israel. 1987. ■A translation of a one-act, five character play dealing with male-female romantic and sexual relationships.

1560 Fo, Dario; Jenkins, Ron, transl. "Almost by Chance a Woman: Elizabeth." *ThM*. 1987; 18(3): 63-96. Illus.: Photo. B&W. 7. Lang.: Eng.

Italy. USA. 1987. ■Translation of *Elisabetta: Quasi per caso una donna*. Satiric look at Elizabethan empire.

1561 Fukuda, Tsuneari. *Fukuda Tsuneari zenshū*. (The Complete Works of Fukuda Tsuneari.) Tokyo: Bungei shunjū; 1987. Vol. 2, 675 pp., Vol. 4, 640 pp., Vol. 5, 638 pp. [5 vols.] Lang.: Jap.

Japan. 1912-1987.

1562 Terayama, Shūji. *Terayama Shūji no gikyoku*. (Plays of Terayama Shūji.) Tokyo: Shinchōsha; 1987. 369/369 pp. B&W. 8, 4. [Vols. 7 & 8.] Lang.: Jap.

Japan. 1950-1980. ■Vol 7: *Jinriki hikōki Soromon (Man-Powered Plane Solomon)*, *Kankyakuseki (Spectator's Seat)*, *Ahen-sensō (Opium War)*, Vol 8: *Kurumawari-ningyō (Nutcracker Suite)*, *Takarajima (Treasure Island)*.

1563 Lee, Song-Il. "*Sin'jang 70 ŭi Ŭimi*." 10-15 pp in Seoul P'yongnon'ga Group, ed. *Han'guk Yŏnguk kwa Chŏlmon Ŭislk*. Mineum SA: Park. Mazngho; 1979. 262 pp. Notes. Lang.: Kor.

Korea. 1908-1977. ■Text of adaptation of realistic play from early twentieth century Korean theatre.

1564 Lim, Je-Bok. "Yajunbyungwon." (Field Hospital.) *DongukDA*. 1976 Dec.; 9: 136-150. Lang.: Kor.

Korea. 1970. Critical studies. ■Text of *Yajunbyungwon (Field Hospital)* by Lim Je-Bok.

1565 Mrożek, Sławomir; Dwora, Gilula, transl. "*Vatslave*." *Bamah*. 1987; 21(107): 27-72. Illus.: Photo. Print. B&W. Lang.: Heb.

Poland: Cracow. Israel: Jerusalem. 1968-1984. ■Text of Sławomir Mrożek's *Vatslave* in a Hebrew translation.

1566 *Afrique: New Plays*. New York, NY: Theatre Communications Group; 1987. 340 pp. Lang.: Eng.

Senegal. Zaire. 1987. ■English translations of contemporary African plays *The Daughters of the Gods*, *Equatorium*, *Lost Voices*, *The Second Ark* and *The Eye*.

1567 Alcàntara Penya, Pere d'; Janer Manila, Gabriel, intro. *Teatre*. (Theatre.) Palma de Mallorca: Editorial Moll; 1987. 171 pp. Biblio. Lang.: Cat.

Spain. 1823-1906. Critical studies. ■Text of plays by Alcàntara Penya. Introduction focuses on *El cordó de la vila (The Village Cord)*, *Un criat nou (A New Manservant)* and *La peste groga (The Yellow Plague)*.

1568 López Mozo, Jerónimo; Hudson, Susanne, transl. "*Friday, July 29, 1983, Early in the Morning*." *MID*. 1987; 21(1): 53-66. Lang.: Eng.

Spain. 1987. ■Translation of *Viernes, 29 de julio de 1983, de madrugada*, a two-character one-act play on the subjects of death and friendship. Inspired by anecdotes about Pablo Picasso and Luis Buñuel.

1569 Moyà, Llorenç; Nadal, Antoni, intro. *Fàlaris/Orfeu*. Palma de Mallorca: Editorial Moll; 1987. 123 pp. (Biblioteca Bàsica de Mallorca 17.) Biblio. Lang.: Cat.

Spain. 1968-1981. Critical studies. ■Text of two plays. Introduction studies Moyà's theatrical works.

1570 Valle Inclán, Ramón del; Creel, Bryant, transl. "*The Horns of Don Friolera*." *MID*. 1987; 20(2): 29-68. Lang.: Eng.

DRAMA: —Basic theatrical documents

Spain. 1930. ■Translation of *Los cuernos de don Friolera*, a one-act play with twelve scenes, an epilogue and fifteen characters. Written before the Revolution, it deals with the military and the arts.

1571 Bartra, Agustí; Salvat, Ricard; Soldevila, Llorenç, ed. *Obres completes, IV.* (Complete Works, IV.) Barcelona: Edicions 62; 1987. 470 pp. (Clàssics catalans del segle XX.) Lang.: Cat.

Spain-Catalonia. Mexico. 1937-1982. Critical studies. ■Study of Bartra's poetry, fiction, theatre, importance in Catalonian culture. Texts include *La noia del gira-sol* (The Sunflower Girl), *Octubre* (October), *El tren de cristall* (The Crystal Train), *Cora i la Magrana* (Cora and the Pomegranate) and *L'hivern plora gebre damunt el gerani* (Winter Weeps Frost on the Geranium).

1572 Fontanella, Francesc; Rossich, Albert, intro. *El desengany.* (*The Disappointment.*) Barcelona: Quaderns Crema; 1987. 118 pp. (Minima de butxaca 28.) Lang.: Cat.

Spain-Catalonia: Barcelona. 1622-1680. ■Edition of the play. Introduction by the adapter of the play, includes biographical information on the author, with analyses of *Lo desengany* and *Amor, firmesa i porfia* (Love, Firmness and Stubborness).

1573 Oliver, Joan; Puimedon, Pilar, intro. *Allò que tal vegada s'esdevingué.* (*What Happened Then.*) Barcelona: Edicions 62; 1987. 94 pp. (El Garbell 22.) Biblio. Lang.: Cat.

Spain-Catalonia. 1899-1986. Histories-sources. ■Edition of Oliver's play. Introduction analyzes structure, theme, technique, language. Includes biography, a bibliography and overview of works by Joan Oliver.

1574 Vicenç Garcia, Francesc; Massip, Àngels, ed.; Massip, Josep Francesc, ed. *Comèdia famosa de la gloriosa Verge i Màrtir Santa Bàrbara.* (Famous Comedy of the Glorious Virgin and Martyr St. Barbara.) Barcelona: Publicacions i Edicions de la Universitat de Barcelona; 1987. 164 pp. Notes. Lang.: Cat.

Spain-Catalonia. 1581-1623. Critical studies. ■Edition of the play with critical analysis and biographical information on the author.

1575 Pinter, Harold. "*The Dwarfs.*" *PintR.* 1987; 1: 4-6. Lang.: Eng.

UK-England. 1958-1987. ■First printing of chapter from Harold Pinter's unpublished novel *The Dwarfs* which was subsequently rewritten for the stage.

1576 Acker, Kathy. "*Lulu.*" *PerAJ.* 1987; 10(3): 102-117. 1. Lang.: Eng.

USA. 1986. ■Complete text of play *Lulu* by Kathy Acker.

1577 Akalaitis, JoAnne. "*Green Card.*" *ThM.* 1987; 18(2): 37-64. Illus.: Photo. Maps. Sketches. B&W. 11. Lang.: Eng.

USA. 1986. ■A ten-person experimental play about the issues surrounding immigration in the US. Links international struggles and domestic events.

1578 Bert, Norman A. *One-Act Plays for Acting Students: An Anthology of Short One-Act Plays for One, Two or Three Actors.* Colorado Springs, CO: Meriwether; 1987. 284 pp. Pref. Biblio. Illus.: Photo. Print. B&W. 2. Lang.: Eng.

USA. 1987. ■One-act plays for acting students. Includes text and guides on how to secure rights for productions, how to schedule and conduct rehearsals and book lists of theatre how-tos and additional plays.

1579 Cleage, Pearl. "*Hospice.*" *Callaloo.* 1987 Win; 10(1): 120-159. Lang.: Eng.

USA. 1986-1987. ■Text of a one-act play about love between mother and daughter.

1580 Fugard, Athol. "*A Place with the Pigs.*" *ThM.* 1987; 19(1): 51-69. Illus.: Photo. B&W. 8. Lang.: Eng.

USA. South Africa, Republic of. 1987. ■Inspired by the true story of a deserter from the Soviet army who spent forty-one years of self-imposed exile in a pigsty.

1581 Osborn, M. Elizabeth, ed. "On New Ground: Contemporary Hispanic-American Plays." Lang.: Eng.

USA. Mexico. 1987. ■Plays by Milcha Sanchez-Scott, Lynne Alvarez, Maria Irene Fornes, José Rivera, John Jesurun and Eduardo Machado.

1582 Shengold, Nina, ed. *The Actor's Book of Contemporary Stage Monologues.* New York, NY: Penguin; 1987. xx, 355 pp. Pref. Biblio. Chart. 14. Lang.: Eng.

USA. 1960-1987. ■Monologues organized by gender, age range, comedic and dramatic. Includes interviews with Swoosie Kurtz, Lanford Wilson, Christopher Durang and Tina Howe on process of writing and performing monologues.

1583 Wright, Jay. "*Daughters of the Water.*" *Callaloo.* 1987 Spr; 10(2): 215-281. Lang.: Eng.

USA. 1987. ■Text of play about Spanish Americans in California.

1584 Green, Michael, ed. *The Russian Symbolist Theatre: An Anthology of Plays and Critical Tools.* Ann Arbor, MI: Ardis; 1986. 371 pp. Notes. Lang.: Eng.

USSR. 1880-1986. ■Plays of the Russian symbolist movement. Includes critical essays by playwrights. Grp/movt: Symbolism.

Design/technology

1585 Worth, Katharine. "Pinter's Scenic Imagery." *PintR.* 1987; 1: 31-39. Notes. Lang.: Eng.

1958-1987. Technical studies. ■Pinter's scenic designs extend visual language of stage realism as well as reflect themes.

1586 Lennon, Maureen. "Illusions in Theatre." *PAC.* 1985 Sep.; 22(3): 33-35, 38. Illus.: Photo. Print. B&W. 2. Lang.: Eng.

Canada: Toronto, ON. 1985. Histories-sources. ■Interview with several production managers and designers, including Jim Plaxton, about the special requirements for certain effects and costumes in various productions.

1587 Milliken, Paul. "Jim Plaxton." *PAC.* 1982 Fall; 19(3): 39-42. Illus.: Photo. Print. B&W. 4. Lang.: Eng.

Canada: Toronto, ON. 1982. Biographical studies. ■A profile of Canadian designer, Jim Plaxton, and the difficulties of designing for open or unconventional stages in Toronto and at the Shaw Festival.

1588 Vais, Michel. "Entre le jouet de pacotille et la voûte céleste." (From Shoddy Toys to the Vaults of Heaven.) *JCT.* 1987; 45: 98-110. Illus.: Photo. Print. B&W. 10. Lang.: Fre.

Canada. 1987. Critical studies. ■The symbolism of the objects used in *La Trilogie des dragons* enhances the action.

1589 MacIntyre, Jean. "'One that Hath Two Gowns': Costume Change in Some Elizabethan Plays." *English Studies in Canada.* 1987 Mar.; 13(1): 12-22. Notes. Lang.: Eng.

England. 1561-1633. Histories-reconstruction. ■Analysis of the written text for conventions of costuming in Shakespeare's and other Elizabethan plays.

1590 Wilson, Michael S. "*Ut pictura tragoedia*: An Extrinsic Approach to British Neoclassical and Romantic Theatre." *ThR.* 1987; 12(3): 201-220. Notes. Lang.: Eng.

England. 1700-1899. Critical studies. ■Influence of aesthetic philosophies and public taste on scenic painting in British theatre in the eighteenth and nineteenth centuries.

1591 Carlson, Marvin. "The Eighteenth Century Pioneers in French Costume Reform." *ThS.* 1987 May; 28(1): 37-47. Notes. Illus.: Dwg. 3. Lang.: Eng.

France: Paris. England: London. 1734-1765. Historical studies. ■Examination of the exact sequence of French costume experimentation during the 1750s.

1592 Ézsiás, Erzsébet. "Találkozás Csányi Árpáddal. 'Az alkotó energiája a kivitelezésre megy el'." (Interview with Árpád Csányi. 'Creative Energy is Spent on Execution'.) *FSM.* 1987 Feb.; 31(9): 18-19. Illus.: Photo. B&W. Color. 5. Lang.: Hun.

Hungary. 1987. Histories-sources. ■Árpád Csányi stage designer of the National Theatre in Budapest, speaks about the status of his profession—the complexity of the work, the relation with director and costume designer.

1593 Long, Joseph; Dowling, Joe; Flood, Frank Hallinan. "Shylock Versus the Rest." *ThIr.* 1985 Spr-Sum; 9/10: 132, 133, 134. B&W. 3. Lang.: Eng.

DRAMA: —Design/technology

Ireland: Dublin. 1985. Histories-sources. ■Scenic designer Frank Hallinan Flood represents architectural structure and other production elements in his set for *The Merchant of Venice* at the Abbey Theatre.

1594 Benedetti, Tere. "Il Teleobbiettivo per la *Finta Pazza*." (Close-up Look at *Fake Madwoman*.) *BiT*. 1987; 5/6: 307-314. Lang.: Ita.
Italy: Venice. 1641-1987. Critical studies. ■The *Finta Pazza* by Francesco Sacrati and Giulio Strozzi, performed in Venice in 1641, proposed again in July 1987. Are the 'wonders' of the baroque scene by Giacomo Torelli still up-to-date?.

1595 Jonson, Per A. "Pygmalion på Orionteatern, scenografiska anteckningar." (Pygmalion at the Orionteatern, Scenographic Notes.) *ProScen*. 1987; 10(1-2): 24-28. Illus.: Plan. Grd.Plan. Lang.: Swe.
Sweden: Stockholm. 1986. Histories-sources. ■The scenographer discusses his contribution to the production of *Pygmalion* in an old mechanical workshop.

1596 Garebian, Keith. "Desmond Heeley: Premier Designer." *PAC*. 1984 Win; 21(3): 49-52. Illus.: Photo. Print. B&W. 4. Lang.: Eng.
UK-England: London. USA: New York, NY. Canada: Stratford, ON. 1940-1984. Histories-sources. ■An interview with designer Desmond Heeley on the occasion of his 25th Stratford Festival production—he talks of his career, his start at the Old Vic in London, his training and the influences on his career.

1597 Howard, Pamela. "Designing the Shrew." *NTQ*. 1987 May; 3(10): 184-187. Illus.: Design. Sketches. B&W. 7. Lang.: Eng.
UK-England. 1985. Critical studies. ■Preliminary sketches for the Royal Shakespeare Company's regional tour of *The Taming of the Shrew*, showing the evolution of the design.

1598 Toogood, John. "Technical Review: *Bartholomew Fair/Midsummer Night's Dream*." *Sin*. 1987; 21(2): 38. Illus.: Photo. B&W. 1. Lang.: Eng.
UK-England: London. 1987. Reviews of performances. ■Review of *Bartholomew Fair* and *A Midsummer Night's Dream* in the Open Air Theatre, Regent's Park, London.

1599 Sultan, James L. "*A Streetcar Named Desire*." *L&DA*. 1987 Jan.; 17(1): 26. Illus.: Photo. 1. Lang.: Eng.
USA: San Diego, CA. 1986. Technical studies. ■Techniques of James Sultan, lighting designer, used in Lamplighter Community Theatre's production of *A Streetcar Named Desire*.

1600 Thomas, Veona. "Charles McClennahan: Designer's Advocate." *BlackM*. 1987 May-June; 3(9): 4, 10. Illus.: Photo. B&W. 2. Lang.: Eng.
USA: New York, NY. USA: Winston-Salem, NC. 1981-1987. Histories-sources. ■The career of Charles McClennahan, African-American designers and technicians in America. Also discusses the Black Design League.

1601 Thomas, Veona. "Judy Dearing: Costume Designer Supreme." *BlackM*. 1987 Nov-Dec.; 4(3): 4-5, 11. Illus.: Photo. B&W. 2. Lang.: Eng.
USA: New York, NY. Africa. 1970-1987. Historical studies. ■The theatrical career of Judy Dearing as costume designer, dancer and actress.

Institutions

1602 Brunner, Astrid. "Theatre New Brunswick: Promoting Greek in Fredericton's Mirror Lane." *ArtsAtl*. 1987 Sum/Fall; 8(1): 43-44. Illus.: Photo. B&W. 8. Lang.: Eng.
Canada: Fredericton, NB. 1964-1987. Historical studies. ■Theatre New Brunswick's history traced through three directors and plays produced.

1603 Day, Maria; Potts, Marilyn. "Elizabeth Sterling Haynes: Initiator of Alberta Theatre." *ET*. 1987 Spr; 8(1): 8-35. Notes. Illus.: Photo. Print. B&W. 3. Lang.: Eng.
Canada. 1916-1957. Biographical studies. ■Haynes' contributions to the Little Theatre Movement in Alberta and New Brunswick: her training at the University of Toronto and work in education.

1604 Grace-Warrick, Christa. "Vancouver Notes from the Fringe/1." *CTR*. 1987 Sum; 51: 78-80. Illus.: Photo. Print. B&W. 1. [Carte Blanche.] Lang.: Eng.
Canada: Vancouver, BC. 1987. Critical studies. ■Critical analysis of Vancouver's fringe festival. Details the non-juried, first-come-first-served format. Publicized as a whole event featuring alternative theatre and performance art. Purpose: to break down barriers between established and experimental theatre.

1605 Harrison, James. "In the Heart of the Heart of Stratford: An Interview with John Neville." *Theatrum*. 1985 Fall/Win; 3: 3-6. Pref. Illus.: Sketches. B&W. 2. Lang.: Eng.
Canada: Stratford, ON. 1985-1986. Histories-sources. ■The new Artistic Director discusses future plans for the future scope of the Stratford Festival. Outlines necessary ingredients for good performance, production and audience attendance.

1606 Harrison, James. "The Doras: One Hand Clapping." *Theatrum*. 1986 Sum; 2: 3-4. Lang.: Eng.
Canada: Toronto, ON. 1986. Critical studies. ■Discusses the importance of the Toronto theatre community's Dora Mavor Moore awards in the form of a fictionalized dialogue.

1607 Levesque, Solange. "Brecht au Milieu du Cercle de Craie: Conférences et Tables Rondes." (Brecht in the Middle of the Chalk Circle: Conferences and Round Tables.) *JCT*. 1987; 43: 136-137. Lang.: Fre.
Canada: Toronto, ON. 1985. Historical studies. ■The colloquium 'Brecht 30 Years After' brings together, in Toronto, a group of specialists to exchange ideas and share conclusions.

1608 Levine, Meredith. "Feminist Theatre—Toronto 1987." *Theatrum*. 1987 Spr; 6: 5-10. Illus.: Photo. B&W. 1. Lang.: Eng.
Canada: Toronto, ON. 1960-1987. Histories-specific. ■Historical overviews of the development of feminist theatre. An overview of three groups is given, detailing styles, content, and policy.

1609 Page, Malcolm. "Vancouver Notes from the Fringe/2." *CTR*. 1987 Sum; 51: 80-82. Illus.: Photo. Print. B&W. 2. [Carte Blanche.] Lang.: Eng.
Canada: Vancouver, BC. 1987. Reviews of performances. ■A report citing many of the acts and events present for the Fringe Festival, with critical comments. Brief descriptions of International participants' work quickly survey range of diversity.

1610 Vais, Michel. "Brecht 30 ans Après/Convergences à Toronto." (Brecht Thirty Years After: Meetings in Toronto.) *JCT*. 1987; 43: 130-135. Illus.: Photo. Print. B&W. 3. Lang.: Fre.
Canada: Toronto, ON. 1986. Historical studies. ■Discusses the films, lectures and performances organized in Toronto for the 30th anniversary of Brecht's death.

1611 Brown, Arvin. "Hands Across the Sea." *AmTh*. 1987 Mar.; 3(12): 24-25. Illus.: Photo. Print. B&W. 3. Lang.: Eng.
China, People's Republic of: Beijing. USA. 1986-1987. Critical studies. ■Arvin Brown, artistic director of the Long Wharf Theatre, travels to Beijing to direct *Farewell My Lovely* and *In a Grove* with National Theatre of the Deaf.

1612 Branald, Adolf. "Dvě stě let (k Roku českého divadla)." (Two Hundred Years: The Year of the Czech Theatre.) *Scena*. 1987; 8(7-8): 1-4. Illus.: Photo. B&W. 1. Lang.: Cze.
Czechoslovakia: Prague. 1783-1983. Historical studies. ■The present and the past of the Stavovské Theatre.

1613 Srba, Bořivoj. "Komorní hry v Brně 1942-1944 (Z historie zápasů o druhou brněnskou činohru)." (Chamber Plays in Brno 1942-1944: From the History of the Struggle for Brno Drama Company.) *Prog*. 1986-1987; 58(2-9): 62-65, 102-106, 142-146, 182-187, 222-227, 262-267, 302-307, 371-372. Illus.: Photo. B&W. 26. Lang.: Cze.
Czechoslovakia: Brno. 1942-1944. Historical studies. ■The history of the Komorní hry stage of Rudolf Walter.

1614 Bowers, Rick. "John Lowin: Actor-Manager of the King's Company." *ThS*. 1987 May; 28(1): 15-35. Notes. Lang.: Eng.

DRAMA: —Institutions

England: London. 1576-1653. Historical studies. ■Description of King's Company under Lowin's management: repertory, performance conditions and management practices.

1615 Hemmings, F.W.J. "The Training of Actors at the Paris Conservatoire During the Nineteenth Century." *ThR.* 1987; 12(3): 241-253. Notes. Lang.: Eng.
France: Paris. 1800-1899. Historical studies. ■The Paris Conservatoire provided an academic and conservative training which was well suited to acting in the classical repertory.

1616 Freydank, Ruth. "Die Volksbühnenbewegung." (The *Volksbühne* Movement.) *TZ.* 1987; 42(12): 25-28. Illus.: Photo. B&W. 6. Lang.: Ger.
Germany: Berlin. 1889-1914. Historical studies. ■Political background, aims, repertory and organizing forms of the workers' audience societies, *Freie Volksbühne* and *Neue Freie Volksbühne.*

1617 King, Marna. "Theatertreffen '86." *Gestus.* 1986 Win; 11(4): 282-292. Illus.: Photo. B&W. 4. Lang.: Eng.
Germany: Berlin. 1986. Historical studies. ■Profile of the seven theatre companies and their productions, chosen for Theatertreffen Festival: *Oidípous Týrannos* by Sophocles, (Thalia Theater, Hamburg). *Le triomphe de l'amour (The Triumph of Love)* by Marivaux, (Schaubühne am Lehniner Platz, West Berlin). *Amphitryon* by Kleist, (Bühnen der Stadt Bonn). *Der Theatermacher (The Theatre Maker)* by Thomas Bernhard, (Schauspielhaus Bochum). *Gust* by Achternbusch, (Bayerisches Staatsschauspielhaus, Munich). *Glengarry Glen Ross (Hanglage Meerblick)* by David Mamet, (Schauspiel Staatstheater, Stuttgart). *Föhn* by Hoffman, (Bremen Tanztheater).

1618 Donkes, Janny. "De Berlijnse Schaubühne onder Vuur." (The Berlin Schaubühne Under Fire.) *Toneel.* 1987 June; 6 (4): 12-15. Illus.: Photo. B&W. 3. Lang.: Dut.
Germany, West: Berlin, West. 1970-1987. Historical studies. ■The Berlin Schaubühne, formed in 1970 by Peter Stein and Claus Peymann as a politically left-wing theatre group is now Berlin's costliest theatre. Trouble with bad press and their current comeback with production of *Schuld und Sühne (Crime and Punishment).*

1619 St. Peter, Christine. "Denis Johnston, the Abbey and the Spirit of the Age." *IUR.* 1987 Fall; 17(2): 187-206. Notes. Lang.: Eng.
Ireland: Dublin. 1927-1935. Historical studies. ■Analysis of playwright Denis Johnston's struggle to make the Abbey Theatre more open to young, experimental playwrights in the late 1920s. Emphasis is given to the Dublin Drama League's introduction of world avant-garde trends and Abbey leaders' negative assessments of Johnston's plays and other plays the Abbey producers rejected.

1620 Bar-Shovit, Shlomo. "Veani Rayiti et Ahchalom." (I Saw the Dream.) *Bamah.* 1987; 22(109-110): 27-33. Illus.: Photo. Print. B&W. 2. [Interviews with HaBimah Theatre People.] Lang.: Heb.
Israel: Tel Aviv. USSR: Moscow. 1921-1987. Histories-sources. ■Interview with actress Fannia Lubitch: her involvement with the HaBimah Theatre from its inception in Moscow to the present in Tel Aviv.

1621 Bar-Shovit, Shlomo. "Beshvil Latete Yoter, Tatchili Meefess." (In Order To Give More, Start from Zero.) *Bamah.* 1987; 22(109-110): 42-48. Illus.: Photo. B&W. 4. [Interviews with HaBimah Theatre People.] Lang.: Heb.
Israel: Tel Aviv. USSR: Moscow. 1922-1987. Histories-sources. ■Interview with Dvora Bektonov, daughter of Joshua Bektonov, a HaBimah actor. She discusses her father's work in the theatre in Moscow and Tel Aviv, and her own work as a dancer.

1622 Hallman, Jukka. "Världens ända palestinska teater berättar om Ali, flykting och främling i sitt eget land." (The Only Palestine Theatre of the World: Narrative about Ali, Refugee and Stranger in the Country of His Own.) *NT.* 1985; 11(28): 46-47. Illus.: Photo. Print. Lang.: Swe.
Israel: Jerusalem. 1982-1985. Historical studies. ■Visit to the El-Hakawati theatre, an independent performance group, specializing in theatre for and about the Palestinians.

1623 Nilzan, Omri. "Eazo Mein Demama, Eazo Mein Hitrotzetzout." (Such Silence! Such Concentration!) *Bamah.*

1987; 22(109-110): 34-35. [Interviews with HaBimah Theatre People.] Lang.: Heb.
Israel: Tel Aviv. USSR: Moscow. 1922-1987. Histories-sources. ■Interview with Israel Mintz on the importance of the HaBimah Theatre for Jewish culture and the Jewish people.

1624 Nilzan, Omri. "Ani Rotze Lyirot Besora." (I Want To See the News.) *Bamah.* 1987; 22(109-110): 36-41. Illus.: Photo. B&W. 1. [Interviews with HaBimah Theatre People.] Lang.: Heb.
Israel: Tel Aviv. Germany: Berlin. 1923-1987. Histories-sources. ■Interview with Shimon Finkel on being an actor, director and producer of the HaBimah Theatre over the years.

1625 Galich, Franz. "Una Busqueda de un Lenguaje Propio." (The Search for a Personal Language.) *Cjo.* 1987 Apr/July; 72: 60-65. Illus.: Photo. Dwg. B&W. 5. Lang.: Spa.
Nicaragua. 1980-1986. Historical studies. ■Formation and development of the Justo Rufino Garay Group.

1626 Hoaas, Harald. "Norwegian Theatre: A Subsidized Complexity." *TDR.* 1982 Fall; 26(3): 67-74. Illus.: Photo. B&W. 7. Lang.: Eng.
Norway. 1971-1982. Historical studies. ■Expansion of regional theatres: state subsidies, productions, political theatre, trends.

1627 Kvamme, Elsa; Bromberg, Buffalo, transl.; Leovic, Pete, transl. "The Children Who Stayed at Home: Grenland Friteater from Porsgrunn." *TDR.* 1982 Fall; 26(3): 75-80. Illus.: Photo. B&W. 4. Lang.: Eng.
Norway: Porsgrunn. 1982. Historical studies. ■Profile of Grenland Friteater, an independent, self-trained, self-produced company comprised of community members. Their vision, productions, collective process and techniques.

1628 Osiński, Zbigniew. "Important Initiative of Young Artists." (Une importante entreprise de jeunes.) *TP.* 1987 Apr-June(4-6): 24. Illus.: Photo. Print. B&W. 5. Lang.: Eng, Fre.
Poland: Zakopane. 1982-1986. Historical studies. ■History of the Stanisław Ignacy Witkiewicz Theatre, in Zakopane, as well as their artistic purpose.

1629 Rudnicki, Adolf. *Teatr zawsze grany.* (Theatre Always Played.) Warsaw: Czytelnik; 1987. 127 pp. Lang.: Pol.
Poland: Warsaw. 1899-1987. Biographical studies. ■Essay on Zydowski Teatr w Warszawie (Jewish Theatre of Warsaw) and its director Ida Kamińska written by an eminent Polish novelist.

1630 "1986 Teatre Lliure: una alternativa de teatre públic." (1986 Teatre Lliure: An Alternative to Public Theatre.) 284-287 in *Teatre Lliure 1976-1987.* Barcelona: Institut del Teatre; 1987. 297 pp. Lang.: Cat.
Spain-Catalonia: Barcelona. 1976-1987. Histories-sources. ■Teatre Lliure as a public theatre. Plans for the future, including judicious restructuring, more productions and management, better outreach, new activities, a new theatre center.

1631 "1976 Manifest fundacional." (1976 Founding Manifest.) 274-280 in *Teatre Lliure 1976-1987.* Barcelona: Institut del Teatre; 1987. 297 pp. Lang.: Cat.
Spain-Catalonia: Barcelona. 1976. ■Founding manifesto of Teatre Lliure.

1632 Burguet i Ardiaca, Francesc. "Lliure per molts anys, Lliure!" (Free for Many Years, Lliure!) *Arrel.* 1987 Feb.; 17: 119-123. Illus.: Photo. Color. 2. Lang.: Cat.
Spain-Catalonia: Barcelona. 1976-1986. Critical studies. ■Present situation of Teatre Lliure and the necessity of growth. Argues that the theatre should relocate.

1633 Puigserver, Fabià. "Una experiència entre la utopia i la realitat." (An Experience Between Utopia and Reality.) *Arrel.* 1987 Feb.; 17: 114-118. Illus.: Photo. Color. 4. Lang.: Cat.
Spain-Catalonia: Barcelona. 1976-1986. Histories-sources. ■Teatro Lliure's present and future. Calls for its transformation into a true public theatre in the service of Catalan society.

1634 Racionero, Lluís; Bartomeus, Antoni; Boadella, Albert, intro. *Mester de Joglaria: Els Joglars. Vint-i-cinc anys.* (Profession of Minstrelsy: Els Joglars: Twenty-five Years.)

DRAMA: —Institutions

Barcelona: (Edicions 62) Department de Cultura de la Generalitat de Catalunya; 1987. xxix, 175 pp. Index. Biblio. Append. Illus.: Photo. Design. Print. Color. B&W. 140. [Résumé in English translated by James Eddy.] Lang.: Cat. Spain-Catalonia. 1962-1987. Histories-sources. ■History of Catalan theatre company Els Joglars, including details of each production.

1635 Teixidor, Jordi. "El teatre català, deu anys després." (The Catalan Theatre, Ten Years After.) *Arrel.* 1987 Feb. ; 17: 124-128. Illus.: Photo. Color. 3. Lang.: Cat.
Spain-Catalonia: Barcelona. 1976-1986. Histories-sources. ■Evaluation of Catalan theatrical policy since the founding of Teatre Lliure. Condemns failure to create a theatrical infrastructure.

1636 Vilà i Folch, Joaquim. "Deu anys de Teatre Lliure." (Ten Years of Teatre Lliure.) *SdO.* 1987 Jan.; 29(328): 61-65. Tables. Illus.: Photo. Print. B&W. 5. Lang.: Cat.
Spain-Catalonia: Barcelona. 1976-1986. Historical studies. ■Evaluates all productions staged at Teatre Lliure in its first ten years, with emphasis on direction.

1637 Flakes, Susan. "Theatre in Swedish Society." *TDR.* 1982 Fall; 26(3): 84-96. Lang.: Eng.
Sweden. 1982. Critical studies. ■Dramaten's attempt to reach more people with more theatre: construction of new theatres and more touring groups. Role of free theatres.

1638 Hoogland, Rikard. "En minatyr av nittonhundratalets svenska teaterhistoria." (A Miniature of the Twentieth Century History of the Swedish Theatre.) *Teaterf.* 1987; 20(1): 8-10. Illus.: Photo. Lang.: Swe.
Sweden: Stockholm. 1921-1987. Historical studies. ■The history of the student theatre in Stockholm, and their policy now to be open to any amateur who would like to do a production.

1639 Hoogland, Rikard. "Ormen i Hyresgästföreningens kvar-tersgård." (The Snake and the Union of Tenants.) *Teaterf.* 1987; 20(2-3): 14-16. Illus.: Photo. Lang.: Swe.
Sweden: Haninge. 1979-1987. Historical studies. ■A report on how the socialist group Ormen, in spite of more elaborate performances, manage to remain democratic in their inner work.

1640 Hoogland, Rikard. "Den svarta triangeln." (The Black Triangle.) *Teaterf.* 1987; 20(2-3): 21-23. Illus.: Photo. Lang.: Swe.
Sweden: Stockholm. 1917-1987. Historical studies. ■Under Folkkul-turcentrum (The People's Cultural Center) the Folketeatergruppen has developed from free improvisations to productions like *Antigone-nu (Antigone Now)* where the war has been replaced by the nuclear catastrophe at Chernobyl.

1641 Jönsson, Ulf. "På väg mot en ny teater." (On the Way to a New Theatre.) *NT.* 1987; 39: 28-34. Illus.: Photo. Lang.: Swe.
Sweden: Gävle. 1982-1987. Historical studies. ■A survey of Folketearn i Gävleborgs län, its many successes and some failures, its integration into the community.

1642 Niemi, Sibylla. "Amatörteaterns vårflod i Tornedalen." (The Spring Flood of the Amateur Theatre in Tornedalen.) *Teaterf.* 1987; 20(6): 10-11. Illus.: Photo. Lang.: Swe.
Sweden: Pajala. 1986-1987. Historical studies. ■A presentation of Tornedalsteatern and their cooperation with the director Ulla Lyttkens.

1643 Sandelin, Ann-Charlotte. "En handfull eldsjälar." (A Handful of Fiery Spirits.) *Teaterf.* 1987; 20(2-3): 6-8. Illus.: Photo. Lang.: Swe.
Sweden: Simrishamn. 1983-1987. Histories-sources. ■A discussion with members of the amateur group Teater Phoenix about management of the group, policy and the necessity of the difficulty of agreeing on meeting other groups.

1644 Sandelin, Ann-Charlotte. "Lustspel och bygdespel." (Comedies and Local Plays.) *Teaterf.* 1987; 20(4): 5-6. Illus.: Photo. Lang.: Swe.
Sweden: Gagnef. 1975-1987. Historical studies. ■Gagnef Teaterföreningen, which started as children's theatre, has produced a local play *Där älvarna samman flyta (Where the Rivers Meet)* about a criminal case from the 18th century in Dalecarlia.

1645 Sandelin, Ann-Charlotte. "Det är inte fint med sådana här lustspel." (It Is No Choice With Such Comedies.) *Teaterf.* 1987; 20(4): 7-8. Illus.: Photo. Lang.: Swe.
Sweden: Bollnäs. 1979-1987. Historical studies. ■A survey of Arbrå Teaterförening's different activities, like revues and comedies, among children and adults.

1646 Nixon, Jon. "The Dimensions of Drama: The Case for Cross-Curricular Planning." *NTQ.* 1987 Feb.; 3(9): 71-81. Notes. Lang.: Eng.
UK-England. 1980. Empirical studies. ■Drama teaching in schools takes a three-dimensional form: as social interaction, as discourse and as a mode of cognition. Drama should play a vital role in the development of communication and expressive skills across the curriculum.

1647 Raymond, Gerard. "National Theatre, International Influ-ence." *TheaterW.* 1987 Nov 2; 1(12): 17-18. Illus.: Photo. B&W. 1. Lang.: Eng.
UK-England: London. 1848-1987. Historical studies. ■History and current season of the National Theatre: past productions, performance spaces, directors and playwrights.

1648 Smith, R.J.B. *The Influence and Effect of German Expres-sionist Drama on Theatrical Practice in Britain and the United States between the Wars, 1910-1940.* London: Royal Holloway College; 1987. Notes. Biblio. [Ph.D. thesis, Index to Theses, 37-0090.] Lang.: Eng.
UK-England. USA. Germany. 1910-1940. Historical studies. ■Considers the impact of German expressionist theatre on the provincial British and the American literary theatre, especially its political influence. Primary sources from the period are analysed. Grp/movt: Expressionism.

1649 Bassnett, Susan. "Women Experiment with Theatre: Mag-dalena 1986." *NTQ.* 1987 Aug.; 3(11): 224-234. Illus.: Photo. B&W. 6. Lang.: Eng.
UK-Wales: Cardiff. 1986. Historical studies. ■First festival of women's work in experimental theatre.

1650 Anderson, Wayne. "Blind Ambition." *TheaterW.* 1987 28 Dec.-1988 3 Jan.; 1(20): 30-31. Illus.: Photo. B&W. 1. Lang.: Eng.
USA: New York, NY. 1981-1987. Critical studies. ■Brief history of Theatre by the Blind, a producing group integrating blind and sighted actors.

1651 French, William W. "A Double-Threaded Life: Maryat Lee's Ecotheatre." *TDR.* 1983 Sum; 27(2): 26-35. Illus.: Photo. B&W. 5. Lang.: Eng.
USA: Hinton, WV. 1951-1983. Historical studies. ■Profile of Ecotheatre and its artistic director: their creation of indigenous theatre for rural and isolated people. Productions, audience relationship. Excerpts from *A Double-Threaded Life: The Hinton Play.*

1652 Gray, Edward. "The Ridiculous Dilemma." *TheaterW.* 1987 Dec 21-27; 1(19): 24-26. 5. Lang.: Eng.
USA: New York, NY. 1965-1987. Critical studies. ■Review of the Ridiculous Theatre Company and its founder Charles Ludlam. Presents the questions facing the company since Ludlam's death.

1653 Howell, Ron. "The Negro Ensemble Company: 20 Years of Theatrical Excellence." *Ebony.* 1987 Mar.; 42(5): 92, 94, 96, 98. Illus.: Photo. B&W. 11. Lang.: Eng.
USA: New York, NY. 1969-1987. Historical studies. ■The history of the Negro Ensemble Company under the direction of Douglas Turner Ward.

1654 Kerns, Ruth B. "Color and Music and Movement: The Federal Theatre Project Lives on in the Pages of its Production Bulletins." *PAA.* 1987: 52-77. Illus.: Photo. Design. Sketches. Poster. Print. Color. B&W. 37. Lang.: Eng.
USA. 1936-1939. Histories-reconstruction. ■Production synopses: direc-tors', composers' and technical reports provide a vivid picture of the Federal Theatre Project.

1655 Kisselman, I.A. "Like a Fresh Air Fund for Actors and Playwrights: A Look at the O'Neill Theater Center." *TheaterW.* 1987 Aug 31; 3: 26-27. Illus.: Photo. 3. Lang.: Eng.

DRAMA: —Institutions

USA: Waterford, CT. 1985-1986. Histories-sources. ■Ned Eisenberg, author of *Soulful Scream at a Chosen Son*, describes working at the O'Neill Theatre Center from perspective of the actor and the director.

1656 Kruse, Kevin. "The New Dramatists: A Profile." *PerfM.* 1982 Dec.; 8(1): 4-5. Illus.: Photo. B&W. 2. Lang.: Eng.
USA: New York, NY. 1982. Historical studies. ■Profile of New Dramatists: its focus on the services it provides for member playwrights, reading series and development of new plays.

1657 Londré, Felicia Hardison. "Louisville's 'Classics in Context'." *TheaterW.* 1987 28 Dec.-1988 3 Jan.; 1(20): 18-21. Illus.: Photo. B&W. 6. Lang.: Eng.
USA: Louisville, KY. 1986-1988. Critical studies. ■Actors Theatre of Louisville's 'Classics in Context' festival examines classics of drama in the context they were written. Expansion of festival.

1658 Martin, Dan. "CSC Repertory: A Profile." *PerfM.* 1982 Dec.; 7(1): 3. Lang.: Eng.
USA: New York, NY. 1982. Historical studies. ■History and development of CSC Repertory: its focus on world classics and major modern plays as base texts. Artistic director Christopher Martin discusses company's goals, audience and season.

1659 McConachie, Bruce A. "William B. Wood and the 'Pathos of Paternalism'." *ThS.* 1987 May; 28(1): 1-14. Notes. Lang.: Eng.
USA: Philadelphia, PA. 1803-1855. Historical studies. ■Wood's paternalistic vision was characteristic of his times and led to his failures as a theatrical manager in the 1820s.

1660 McCosker, Susan. "La Compañia de Teatro de Alburquerque." *TDR.* 1983 Sum; 27(2): 50-60. Illus.: Photo. B&W. 7. Lang.: Eng.
USA: Albuquerque, NM. 1977-1983. Historical studies. ■Bilingual theatre company devoted to bringing theatre in Spanish and English to Hispanic population. Founder José Rodríguez discusses productions, philosophy of company, techniques.

1661 Nance, Bradley W. "The Circle Repertory Company: A Profile." *PerfM.* 1982 Dec.; 8(1): 6. Illus.: Photo. B&W. 1. Lang.: Eng.
USA: New York, NY. 1982. Historical studies. ■Origins of the Circle Repertory Company and its focus on plays of lyric realism.

1662 Paterson, Doug. "Theatre for a People: The Dakota Theatre Caravan." *TDR.* 1983 Sum; 27(2): 4-14. Illus.: Photo. B&W. 3. Lang.: Eng.
USA: Yankton, SD. 1977-1983. Historical atudies. ■Profile of Dakota Theatre Caravan: productions, audience relationship, collective process of development, use of historical material from region to create works. Excerpts from *Dakota Roads: The Story of a Prairie Family*.

1663 Pereira, John W. "The Manhattan Theatre Club Advancing Step by Step." *TheaterW.* 1987 Dec 14-20; 1(18): 19-23. FO. 3. Lang.: Eng.
USA: New York, NY. 1969-1987. Historical studies. ■History of the Manhattan Theatre Club: its expansion, results and setbacks.

1664 Salas, Jo. "Culture and Community: Playback Theatre." *TDR.* 1983 Sum; 27(2): 15-25. Illus.: Photo. B&W. 4. Lang.: Eng.
USA: Poughkeepsie, NY. 1975-1983. Historical studies. ■Profile of Playback Theatre. Teaching and performing improvisation, personal storytelling, audience relationship. Excerpts from a theatre performance.

1665 Thomas, Veona. "Alive at TUI." *BlackM.* 1986-1987 Dec/Jan.; 3(4): 4, 9. Illus.: Photo. B&W. 2. Lang.: Eng.
USA: Newark, NJ, New York, NY. 1981-1987. Historical studies. ■The Theatre of Universal Images, its general manager, Osoyande Baruti, and its upcoming season.

1666 Turner, Beth. "North Carolina Black Repertory Company: Look Out New York." *BlackM.* 1987 Apr-May; 3(7): 2, 3. Illus.: Photo. B&W. 1. Lang.: Eng.
USA: Winston-Salem, NC. 1979-1987. Historical studies. ■The founding of the North Carolina Black Repertory Company under the direction of Larry Leon Hamlin.

Performance spaces

1667 Souchotte, Sandra. "The Curtain Rises." *PAC.* 1985 Apr.; 22(1): 12-14. Illus.: Photo. Print. B&W. 3. Lang.: Eng.
Canada: Yellowknife, NT. 1980-1985. Historical studies. ■The planning, building and opening of the Northern Arts and Cultural Centre.

1668 King, Pamela. "Spacial Semantics and the Medieval Theatre." *TID.* 1987; 9: 45-58. Notes. Illus.: Dwg. 2. Lang.: Eng.
England. 1300-1576. Critical studies. ■Use of church interiors in liturgical tropes, nature of outdoor playing spaces in the middle ages, designation of locus and platea.

1669 Alexander, David. "Peraon chou Be-yom chage." (Paying a Debt on a Festive Occasion.) *Bamah.* 1987; 22(109-110): 7-8. Lang.: Heb.
Israel: Tel Aviv. 1917-1987. Histories-sources. ■The 70th birthday of the HaBimah theatre and its celebration with an exhibit on the Yiddish theatre in Moscow and Tel Aviv.

1670 Pasqual, Lluís. "La república del Lliure: deu anys d'utopia." (The Lliure's Republic: Ten Years of Utopia.) 22-25 in *Teatre Lliure 1976-1987.* Barcelona: Institut del Teatre; 1987. 297 pp. Lang.: Cat.
Spain-Catalonia: Barcelona. 1976-1987. Historical studies. ■Origin and growth of Teatr Lliure.

1671 Ros Ribas, Josep, photo.; Martí Pol, Miguel, intro. *Teatre Lliure 1976-1987.* Pref. Append. Photo. Design. Dwg. Color. B&W. 350. Lang.: Cat.
Spain-Catalonia: Barcelona. 1976-1987. Histories-sources. ■Collection of photographs relevant to the history of Teatre Lliure and its performances. Related to Dance: Modern dance.

1672 Suero Roca, Maria Teresa. *El teatre representat a Barcelona de 1800 a 1830.* (Theatre Performed in Barcelona, 1800-1830.) Barcelona: Institut del Teatre; 1987. 296 pp, 456 pp. (Estudis 2, I/II.) Pref. Index. Notes. Biblio. [2 vols.] Lang.: Cat.
Spain-Catalonia: Barcelona. 1800-1830. Histories-reconstruction. ■Theatrical activity at a time when only two theatres existed in Barcelona: Teatre de la Santa Creu and Teatre dels Gegants. Vol. I discusses theatre functioning, administration and performance. Vol. II transcribes the Santa Creu playlist, 1800-1815.

1673 Teixidor, Emili. "Petita història dels primers deu anys del Lliure." (Brief History of the Lliure's First Ten Years.) 11-21 in *Teatre Lliure 1976-1987.* Barcelona: Institut del Teatre; 1987. 297 pp. Lang.: Cat.
Spain-Catalonia: Barcelona. 1976-1987. Historical studies. ■The team of the theatre's founders, most significant productions and future prospects.

1674 Abramson, Kjell. "Kungliga Dramatiska Teaterns ombyggnad." (The Rebuilding of the Royal Dramatic Theatre, Part 1.) *ProScen.* 1987; 10(3): 5-9. Illus.: Photo. 11. Lang.: Swe.
Sweden: Stockholm. 1987. Technical studies. ■Some notes about the restoration to original appearance of the audience areas of the Royal Dramatic Theatre.

1675 Abramson, Kjell; Thorell, Bernt. "Kungliga Dramatiska Teaterns ombyggnad." (The Reconstruction of the Royal Dramatic Theatre, Part 2.) *ProScen.* 1987; 10(4): 23-32. Illus.: Photo. Dwg. 7. Lang.: Swe.
Sweden: Stockholm. 1987. Historical studies. ■How the front of house has been restored to the original design, and equipped with the best technical facilities.

1676 Frick, John. "Stock Companies on Union Square." *MarqJTHS.* 1987; 19(4): 10. Notes. Illus.: Photo. B&W. 11. Lang.: Eng.
USA: New York, NY. 1850-1889. Historical studies. ■Descriptions and histories of Wallack's Theatre and the Union Square Theatre.

Performance/production

1677 Hobson, Harold. "Political Slant." *Drama.* 1987; 3(165): 17-18. Illus.: Photo. B&W. 2. Lang.: Eng.
1956. Critical studies. ■Assessment of Kenneth Tynan's review of the first production of John Osborne's *Look Back in Anger*.

DRAMA: —Performance/production

1678 Quinn, Michael. "'Reading' and Directing the Play." *NTQ*. 1987 Aug.; 3(11): 218-223. Notes. Lang.: Eng.
Critical studies. ■A stage production carries the stamp of a director's initial reading of the text, and these influences should be properly recognized.

1679 Dominguez, Carlos Espinosa. "Facundia: teatro con todas las letras." (Facundia: Theatre with All the Letters.) *LATR*. 1987 Fall; 21(1): 99-106. Lang.: Spa.
Argentina: Buenos Aires. 1981. Critical studies. ■Analysis of the play *Facundia* which helps trace the development of a theatre form that emphasizes non-verbal expression.

1680 Labrenz, Ted. "Il Festival Latinoamericano de Teatro." (The Festival of Latin American Theatre.) *TDR*. 1987 Fall; 31(3). Biblio. Illus.: Photo. B&W. 10. Lang.: Eng.
Argentina: Córdoba. 1984-1987. Historical studies. ■Brief history of the Latin American Theatre Festival with notes on participants from Chile, Poland, Wales and Brazil.

1681 Blokdijk, Tom. "Studie in collaboratie." (Study in Collaboration.) *Toneel*. 1987 May; 5(4). Illus.: Photo. B&W. 10. Lang.: Dut.
Austria: Vienna. Netherlands: Amsterdam. 1987. Historical studies. ■Comparison of directing styles: Claus Peymann, new artistic director at Vienna's Burgtheater and Gerardjan Rijnders, new artistic director of Toneelgroep Amsterdam. Their productions of *Richard III* and *Hamlet*, their shared views of modern society.

1682 *50 ans de théâtre en wallon. Le grand prix du roi Albert.* (50 Years of Theatre in Walloon: The Grand Prix du Roi Albert.) Liège: Centre de recherche et d'information du wallon à l'école; 1987. 68 pp. (avec la collaboration du Conseil et de l'Exécutif de la Communauté française de Belgique.) Pref. Illus.: Photo. B&W. 70. Lang.: Fre.
Belgium. 1932-1987. Histories-sources. ■Retrospective of performances having won the King Albert competition among Walloon-language theatre companies.

1683 Bonté, Patrick. "*Solo*: Moins à mourir toujours moins." (*Solo*: Less To Die, Ever Less.) *AltT*. 1987 Dec.; 28: 48-51. Illus.: Photo. B&W. 3. Lang.: Fre.
Belgium: Brussels. 1987. Critical studies. ■Brief critique of *Solo* by Samuel Beckett, directed by Pascal Crochet.

1684 Cabes, Nicole. "*La théorie du mouchoir*: un grand carré de consolation." (*The Handkerchief Theory*: A Great Comfort.) *AltT*. 1987 Dec.; 28: 20-25. Illus.: Photo. B&W. 2. Lang.: Fre.
Belgium: Brussels. 1987. Critical studies. ■Review of the play followed by an interview with the playwright and director, Martine Wijckaert.

1685 Degan, Catherine. "*Mister Knight*: Sacrilège, forcément sacrilège." (*Mister Knight*: Sacrilege, Sheer Sacrilege.) *AltT*. 1987 Dec.; 28: 52-55. Illus.: Photo. B&W. 3. Lang.: Fre.
Belgium: Brussels. 1986. Critical studies. ■Brief review of *Mister Knight*, written and directed by Bruce Ellison at Théâtre de la Mandragore.

1686 Letessier, Dorothée. "'L'Histoire commence à 20 heures' Mirages à tous les étages." ('The Story Starts at 8 p.m.' A Mirage on Every Corner.) *AltT*. 1987 Dec.; 28: 26-30. Illus.: Photo. B&W. 1. Lang.: Fre.
Belgium: Liège. 1986. Histories-sources. ■The author of the novel *Voyage à Paimpol (Journey to Paimpol)* discusses its adaptation and staging by Richard Kalisz.

1687 Groupov. "*Koniec*." *AltT*. 1987 Dec.; 28: 12-19. Illus.: Photo. B&W. 3. Lang.: Fre.
Belgium: Liège. 1987. Histories-sources. ■Brief essay on the production of *Koniec* by the ensemble Groupov, directed by Jacques Delcuvellerie.

1688 George, David. "Os Comediantes and *Bridal Gown*." *LATR*. 1987 Fall; 21(1): 29-40. Lang.: Eng.
Brazil. 1943-1984. Critical studies. ■First of two articles examining forty-year cycle of modern Brazilian stage that begins and ends with stagings of plays by Nelson Rodrigues.

1689 Michalski, Yan. "El Teatro Brasileño en los Ochenta." (Brazilian Theatre in the Eighties.) *Cjo*. 1987 Apr/July; 72: 11-22. Pref. Illus.: Photo. Dwg. B&W. 10. Lang.: Spa.

Brazil. 1980-1984. Critical studies. ■The new direction and development of Brazilian theatre in the 1980s under the new political regime.

1690 Millaret, Margo. "Acting into Action: Teatro Arena's *Zumbi*." *LATR*. 1987 Fall; 21(1): 19-26. Lang.: Eng.
Brazil: São Paulo. 1965. Critical studies. ■Teatro Arena de São Paulo's production of *Arena Conta Zumbi*, a chronicle of resistance efforts of ex-slaves in Brazil in the late 17th Century.

1691 Peixoto, Fernando. "Teatro Brasileño e Identidad Nacional." (Brazilian Theatre and National Identity.) *Cjo*. 1987 July/Sept; 73: 3-14. Illus.: Photo. Dwg. B&W. 2. Lang.: Spa.
Brazil. 1987. Historical studies. ■Condensed historical account of the development of Brazilian theatre.

1692 Fol'kovič, Je. "Na bolgarskih spektakljah. Včera, segodnja, zavtra..." (At Bulgarian Performances: Yesterday, Today and Tomorrow.) *TeatrM*. 1987; 7: 178-185. Lang.: Rus.
Bulgaria: Sofia. USSR: Moscow. 1980. Reviews of performances. ■On performers of Vasov National Theatre and the 'Tears of Laughter' Theatre of Sofia, on tour in Moscow.

1693 Cansino, Barbara. "Ouzounian at MTC: Turning Things Around." *PAC*. 1982 Sum; 19(2): 19-21. B&W. 3. Lang.: Eng.
Canada: Winnipeg, MB. 1982. Biographical studies. ■A profile of Richard Ouzounian, the artistic director of the Manitoba Theatre Centre and the controversy around his modern dress *The Taming of the Shrew*, set in Winnipeg.

1694 Crowder, Eleanor. "Standin' the Gaff: Assessing Boal." *CTR*. 1987 Win; 53: 73-76. Illus.: Photo. B&W. 3. [Carte Blanche.] Lang.: Eng.
Canada: Sydney, NS. 1987. Historical studies. ■A critical analysis of the theatre of Augusto Boal, who conducted a workshop at the 1986 Standin' the Gaff festival. Approach to theatre combines systematic theory and practical vision. Expresses view that popular theatre is culturally specific, yet the fact that the oppressed must free themselves is universal.

1695 Downton, Dawn Rae. "Glen Cairns in the Theatre." *ArtsAtl*. 1987 Winter; 7(3): 30-31. Illus.: Photo. Print. B&W. 2. Lang.: Eng.
Canada: Halifax, NS. 1977-1987. Biographical studies. ■Writer-director Glen Cairns and surrealistic drama at the Neptune Theatre.

1696 Fréchette, Carole; Pavlovic, Diane. "Thèmes et formes." (Themes and Forms.) *JCT*. 1987; 42: 40-48. Illus.: Photo. Print. B&W. 6. Lang.: Fre.
Canada: Quebec, PQ. 1986. Reviews of performances. ■Reflections by the authors and Alexander Hausvater on La Quinzaine festival, which presented twenty-seven plays.

1697 Gaines, Robert A. *John Neville Takes Command: The Story of the Stratford Shakespearean Festival in Production.* Stratford, ON: William Street P; 1987. 338 pp. Index. Illus.: Photo. Print. B&W. 14. Lang.: Eng.
Canada: Stratford, ON. 1986. Historical studies. ■Rehearsals and performance process of the Stratford Shakespeare Festival's 1986 season, artistic director John Neville.

1698 Garebian, Keith. "The 1984 Stratford Festival." *JCNREC*. 1985 Mar.; 19(4): 136-143. Biblio. Lang.: Eng.
Canada: Stratford, ON. 1984. Reviews of performances. ■Negative review of the 1984 season. Radiant fantasy of Gilbert and Sullivan made the Shakespearean productions seem ponderous. Brilliant acting from John Neville and Patricia Conolly prevented *Separate Tables* and *A Streetcar Named Desire* from going awry.

1699 Garebian, Keith. "Ensemble Distinction." *JCNREC*. 1985 Mar.; 19(4): 143-148. Lang.: Eng.
Canada: Niagara-on-the-Lake, ON. 1984. Reviews of performances. ■Comedy came into its own at the Shaw Festival in 1984. The company is praised for its efficiency, wonderful variety and skillful acting in presenting plays by Shaw, Coward, Wilder and Ion Caragiale.

1700 Garebian, Keith. "The 1983 Stratford Festival: Commentary." *JCNREC*. 1984 Jan.; 18(3): 149-157. Lang.: Eng.
Canada: Stratford, ON. 1983. Reviews of performances. ■Critical overview of the productions during the 1983 season.

DRAMA: —Performance/production

1701 Garebian, Keith. "The 1982 Stratford Festival: Commentary." *JCNREC*. 1983 May; 17(4): 102-111. Lang.: Eng.
Canada: Stratford, ON. 1982. Reviews of performances. ■Critical overview of the productions during the 1982 season.

1702 Garebian, Keith. "Spinoza: From First Night to Opening." *PAC*. 1982 Spr; 19(1): 47-54. B&W. 6. Lang.: Eng.
Canada: Montreal, PQ. 1982. Histories-reconstruction. ■A diary of the production of the play, *Spinoza*, by Dmitri Frinkel Frank at the Saidye Bronfman Centre from the first rehearsal to the opening night, with reference to various aspects of production.

1703 Garebian, Keith. "The 1982 Shaw Festival: Commentary." *JCNREC*. 1983 May; 17(4): 112-118. Lang.: Eng.
Canada: Niagara-on-the-Lake, ON. 1982. Reviews of performances. ■Critical overview of the productions during the 1982 season.

1704 Hunt, Nigel. "The Moving Language of Robert Lepage." *Theatrum*. 1987 Spr; 6: 25-28, 32. Illus.: Photo. B&W. 1. Lang.: Eng.
Canada: Montreal, PQ. Canada: Toronto, ON. 1980-1987. Critical studies. ■Playwright Lepage's working methods and background, roots and influences of his theatre. Brief consideration is given to the common characteristics of his major plays.

1705 Lavoie, Pierre; Camerlain, Lorraine. "Points de repère/ entretien avec les créateurs." (Indicators/Interviews with the Artists.) *JCT*. 1987; 45: 177-208. Illus.: Photo. B&W. 23. Lang.: Fre.
Canada. 1987. Histories-sources. ■The actors in *La Trilogie des dragons (Dragons' Trilogy)* by Robert Lepage discuss their feelings about the production.

1706 Lavoie, Pierre. "Du hasard et de la nécéssité." (On Chance and Necessity.) *JCT*. 1987; 45: 169-170. Illus.: Photo. Print. B&W. 1. Lang.: Fre.
Canada. 1987. Histories-sources. ■The author interviewed the participants in Robert Lepage's *La Trilogie des dragons (Dragons' Trilogy)* in order to understand the way in which it was created.

1707 Lefebvre, Paul. "Lorne Brass: enfant de la télé." (Lorne Brass: Child of TV.) *JCT*. 1987; 44: 124-125. Illus.: Photo. Print. B&W. 1. Lang.: Fre.
Canada: Montreal, PQ. 1986. Histories-sources. ■Actor with the Carbone 14 troupe sees media and theatre as two sides of the same thing.

1708 McDonald, Larry. "Politics, Playwriting and *Zero Hour*." *CTR*. 1987 Win; 53: 43-48. Illus.: Photo. Print. B&W. 6. [Starting from Scratch.] Lang.: Eng.
Canada: Ottawa, ON. 1987. Histories-sources. ■Interview with playwright-in-residence Patrick McDonald, also artistic director at the Great Canadian. Focus is on how to write political theatre for politically uneducated audience while staying true to art. References to Milner's plays.

1709 McGawley, Laurie-Ann. "Super(Stack) Inspiration." *CTR*. 1987 Win; 53: 35-38. Illus.: Photo. Print. B&W. 3. Lang.: Eng.
Canada: Sudbury, ON. 1930-1987. Historical studies. ■Historical survey of popular theatre in Sudbury, ON, which has largely dealt with economic oppression by INCO Metals, Ltd., and feminist issues.

1710 Milliken, Paul. "Allan Stratton Gambles on Commercial Theatre." *PAC*. 1982 Spr; 19(1): 25-26. B&W. 2. Lang.: Eng.
Canada: Toronto, ON. 1982. Biographical studies. ■Profile of the Canadian playwright Allan Stratton, author of *Nurse Jane Goes to Hawaii* and *Rexy*.

1711 Milliken, Paul. "Erika Ritter's Search for Integrity on the Stage." *PAc*. 1982 Sum; 19(2): 33-37. Illus.: Photo. Print. B&W. 1. Lang.: Eng.
Canada: Toronto, ON. 1982. Biographical studies. ■A profile of Canadian playwright, Erika Ritter, and discussion of her plays, *The Splits* and *Automatic Pilot*.

1712 Pavlovic, Diane; Vais, Michel. "Splendeurs et Misères." (Magnificence and Wretchedness.) *JCT*. 1987; 42: 27-39. Illus.: Photo. Print. B&W. 9. Lang.: Fre.

Canada: Quebec, PQ. 1986-1986. Critical studies. ■The second international amateur theatre competition called La Quinzaine is discussed.

1713 Pavlovic, Diane. "Figures." (Faces.) *JCT*. 1987; 45: 141-158. Illus.: Photo. Print. B&W. 10. Lang.: Fre.
Canada. 1987. Biographical studies. ■Sketches of ten people (actors, the director and the person in charge of music) who were responsible for *La Trilogie des dragons* by Robert Lepage.

1714 Sawyer, Deborah C. "Ann Mortifee." *PAC*. 1982 Spr; 19(1): 43-46. B&W. 2. Lang.: Eng.
Canada: Vancouver, BC, Toronto, ON. 1982. Biographical studies. ■A profile of singer-songwriter-performer, Ann Mortifee, a discussion of her career, and her recent productions, *Journey to Kairos* and *Reflections on Crooked Walking*.

1715 Sher, Emil. "Canada: Apartheid on Tour." *CTR*. 1987 Spr(50): 59-62. Notes. Illus.: Photo. Print. B&W. 2. Lang.: Eng.
Canada. South Africa, Republic of. 1987. Critical studies. ■Content and North American reception of *Asinimali! (We Have No Money!)* by Mbongeni Ngema. American perception of apartheid.

1716 Soldevila, Philippe. "Magie et mysticisme: comment (ne pas) expliquer l'inexplicable." (Magic and Mysticism: How (Not) to Explain the Unexplainable.) *JCT*. 1987; 45: 171-176. Illus.: Photo. B&W. 3. Lang.: Fre.
Canada. 1987. Technical studies. ■The director Robert Lepage discusses the creation and development of *La Trilogie des dragons (Dragons' Trilogy)*.

1717 Stephenson, Craig. "Going Out for Chinese (Acting Styles)." *Theatrum*. 1987 Sum; 7: 5-8. Lang.: Eng.
Canada: Toronto, ON. China, People's Republic of: Shanghai. 1987. Histories-sources. ■A participant in a series of workshops relates the experience of studying traditional Chinese techniques as well as renewed western and Soviet-influenced methods currently in use in China.

1718 Stuart, Otis. "Confronting Complexities: A Conversation With Roberta Maxwell." *TheaterW*. 1987 Dec 14-20; 1(18): 24-30. Illus.: Photo. 3. Lang.: Eng.
Canada. 1987. Histories-sources. ■Interview with Roberta Maxwell in which she discusses her training, performance experience and acting philosophy emphasizing Shakespearean heroines and famous directors.

1719 Thompson, M.B. "Capital Losses." *BooksC*. 1983 Apr.; 12(4): 4-5. Lang.: Eng.
Canada: Ottawa, ON. 1960-1983. Historical studies. ■Overview of theatre in Ottawa: lack of attendance at alternative theatre despite high quality productions.

1720 Bravo-Elizondo, Pedro. "Un director chileño en el Berliner Ensemble (Entrevista con Alejandro Quintana Contreras)." (A Chilean Director in the Berliner Ensemble: An Interview with Alejandro Quintana Contreras.) *LATR*. 1987 Spr; 20(2): 113-117. Illus.: Photo. B&W. 1. Lang.: Spa.
Chile. Germany, East: Berlin, East. 1987. Histories-sources. ■Interview with Chilean director Alejandro Quintana Contreras. His work with the Berliner Ensemble and the difference between his 'Latin' approach and German theatre.

1721 Chen, Jia-Lin. "*Deng dai guo tuo* dao yan hou ji." (I Directed *Waiting for Godot*.) *XYishu*. 1987 Sum; 38: 66-71. Lang.: Chi.
China, People's Republic of: Shanghai. 1986-1987. Histories-sources. ■Record of a Chinese production of Samuel Beckett's *En attendant Godot (Waiting for Godot)*.

1722 Morley, Michael. "Brecht in Hong Kong." *KWN*. 1987 Spr; 5(1): 9-10. Illus.: Dwg. Print. B&W. Lang.: Eng.
China, People's Republic of: Beijing, Hong Kong. Japan: Tokyo. 1986. Reviews of performances. ■Review of the 9th International Brecht Symposium. Focus was 'how Eastern cultures and theatrical traditions approach staging of Brecht's work and the understanding of his theatrical methods.' Emphasis upon Chinese and Japanese productions.

1723 T'ung, Ch'ao. "Hua Chü Ch'a Kuan Tui Hsi Ch'ü Ch'uan Te Chieh Chien Han Yün Yung." (The Play *Tea House*: Its

DRAMA: —Performance/production

Practical Production Borrowed from the Theory of Conventional Theatre.) *XYanj.* 1987 June; 22: 1-13. Notes. Lang.: Chi.
China, People's Republic of. 1957-1959. Critical studies. ■Playwright Chiao Chü Yin borrowed from the style and techniques of Western theatre to create *Ch'a Kuan (Tea House)*, which demonstrates his theory.

1724 Mendia, Raquel Carrio. "La experimentación como principio metodológico en la formación de nuevos teatristas. Crónica de una experiencia." (Experimentation as the Principal Method in the Formation of New Dramatists: Chronicle of an Experiment.) *Cjo.* 1987 Apr/July; 72: 45-54. Illus.: Dwg. 5. Lang.: Spa.
Cuba. 1920-1986. Critical studies. ■Importance of experimental theatre to open new possibilities in Cuban drama.

1725 Muguercia, Magaly. "Veinte dias, noche a noche." (Twenty Days, Night After Night.) *Cjo.* 1987 Apr/July; 72: 23-40. Illus.: Photo. Dwg. B&W. 23. Lang.: Spa.
Cuba: Camagüey. 1986. Reviews of performances. ■Day by day account of the performances of the 1986 Festival of Camagüey.

1726 Lukavský, Radovan. "Herecké umĕné a vĕda." (Dramatic Art and Science.) *Scena.* 1987; 8(11): 3. Lang.: Cze.
Czechoslovakia: Prague. 1987. Histories-sources. ■Account of a seminar on dramatic art.

1727 Stuber, Andrea. "'A színházért kiabálok'. Beszélgetés Jozef Bednárikkal." ('I Shout for the Theatre': Interview with Jozef Bednárik.) *FSM.* 1987 Apr.; 31(16): 8. Illus.: Photo. B&W. 1. Lang.: Hun.
Czechoslovakia: Nitra. 1987. Histories-sources. ■Jozef Bednárik, stage manager of the Andrej Bagar Theatre, speaks about his career as actor and director, how he tries to affect his audience.

1728 Barba, Eugenio. "The Actor's Energy: Male/Female versus Animus/Anima." *NTQ.* 1987 Aug.; 3(11): 237-240. Lang.: Eng.
Denmark: Holstebro. 1986. Histories-sources. ■Speech delivered at 1986 Congress of the International School of Theatre Anthropology (ISTA): balance between the qualities of 'animus' and 'anima' necessary to the actor's energy.

1729 Bassnett, Susan. "Perceptions of the Female Role: the ISTA Congress." *NTQ.* 1987 Aug.; 3(11): 234-236. Lang.: Eng.
Denmark: Holstebro. 1986. Historical studies. ■Events and debates at the International School of Theatre Anthropology Congress.

1730 Fallenius-Braun, Ann-Marie, photo.; Voight, Torben, photo. "Billedstofteater: Theatre of Images." *TDR.* 1982 Fall; 26(3): 29-34. Illus.: Photo. B&W. 10. Lang.: Eng.
Denmark. 1977-1982. Historical studies. ■Photo essay on Billedstofteater, a site-specific theatre company that creates original works based on the surrounding architecture and atmosphere of the performance space.

1731 Bond, David. "Some Notes on Nell Gwyn's Stage Career 1663-1668." *TN.* 1987; 41(3): 107-114. Notes. Lang.: Eng.
England: London. 1663-1668. Biographical studies. ■Evidence suggests that Nell Gwyn did not play 'Lady Wealthy', but generally the 'madcap'.

1732 Cave, Richard Allen. "Romantic Drama in Performance." 79-104 in Cave, Richard Allen. *The Romantic Theatre: An International Symposium.* Totowa, NJ: Barnes & Noble; 1986. 130 pp. Index. Notes. Biblio. Lang.: Eng.
England. 1700-1987. Historical studies. ■By studying English Romantic drama in performance, we can better understand how the Romantics anticipated modern theatre.

1733 Copeland, Nancy E. "'Simple Art and Simple Nature': Sarah Siddons Versus Ann Crawford." *Restor.* 1987 Sum; 2(1): 54-61. Notes. Lang.: Eng.
England. 1783-1784. Historical studies. ■Interpretations of Lady Randolph in *Douglas* illustrate transition from Garrick to Kemble style of acting.

1734 Hazelton, Nancy J. Doran. *Historical Consciousness in Nineteenth-Century Shakespearean Staging.* Ann Arbor, MI: UMI Research P; 1987. 113 pp. (Theatre and Dramatic Studies 46.) Index. Notes. Biblio. Illus.: Pntg. Sketches. Print. B&W. 29. Lang.: Eng.
England: London. 1800-1900. Historical studies. ■New historical demands placed on theatre production, especially Shakespeare. Set design, acting, costuming and different theatre companies.

1735 Hughes, Alan. "Art and Eighteenth-Century Acting Style, Part III: Passions." *TN.* 1987; 41(3): 128-139. Notes. Illus.: Dwg. Pntg. B&W. 7. Lang.: Eng.
England. 1700. Historical studies. ■Actors studied Baroque style of visual arts to portray passions in style accesible to audience of era.

1736 Hughes, Alan. "Art and Eighteenth-Century Acting Style, Part One: Aesthetics." *TN.* 1987; 41(1): 24-31. Notes. Illus.: Photo. B&W. 1. Lang.: Eng.
England. 1672-1799. Historical studies. ■Historians lack evidence in evaluating acting styles, but suggest naturalistic aesthetic in 18th century.

1737 Hyland, Peter. "'A Kind of Woman': The Elizabethan Boy-Actor and the Kabuki *Onnagata.*" *ThR.* 1987; 12(1): 1-8. Notes. Lang.: Eng.
England. Japan. 1580-1987. Critical studies. ■Comparison of transvestite *onnagata* actors in *kabuki* with boy actors in Elizabethan theatre to explore interpretations of female roles. Related to Dance-Drama: *Kabuki.*

1738 Langhans, Edward A. *Eighteenth Century British and Irish Promptbooks: A Descriptive Bibliography.* New York, NY: Greenwood P; 1987. 268 pp. Index. Notes. Biblio. Append. Illus.: Dwg. Sketches. Architec. Grd.Plan. Fr.Elev. 17. Lang.: Eng.
England. Ireland. 1700-1799. Historical studies. ■Descriptions and details of over 380 promptbooks and related documents from the 18th century. Includes marked rehearsal and preparation copies, sides, role of the prompter, prompter's script notations and glossary of their abbreviations, speculation on how books were used. Brief description of wing and shutter staging system.

1739 Law, M.J. *Aspects of Theatre in Liverpool.* Liverpool: Univ. of Liverpool; 1987. Notes. Biblio. [M. Phil. dissertation, *Index to Theses,* 36: 6918.] Lang.: Eng.
England: Liverpool. 1850-1900. Histories-specific. ■Study of theatre in Liverpool in relation to the city's cultural history, focus on Liverpool careers of four actors.

1740 Lomax, Marion. *Stage Images and Traditions: Shakespeare to Ford.* Cambridge, UK: Cambridge UP; 1987. 202 pp. Pref. Index. Notes. Biblio. Illus.: Photo. Sketches. Print. B&W. 13. Lang.: Eng.
England. 1607-1987. Histories-specific. ■Interdependence of themes in performances of plays by Shakespeare and his contemporaries.

1741 McLuskie, Kathleen. "The Act, the Role and the Actor: Boy Actresses on the Elizabethan Stage." *NTQ.* 1987 May; 3(10): 120-130. Notes. Illus.: Photo. B&W. 2. Lang.: Eng.
England: London. 1580-1630. Historical studies. ■Conflicting approaches to the sensuality of performance in the Elizabethan and Jacobean theatre, and their reflection in theatrical conventions and in contemporary attitudes toward the plays and the 'boy actresses'.

1742 Pedicord, Harry William. "On-Stage with David Garrick: Garrick's Acting Companies in Performance." *ThS.* 1987 Nov.; 28(2): 51-74. Notes. Tables. Lang.: Eng.
England: London. 1737-1776. Historical studies. ■Assessment of quality of actors assembled by Garrick for season of 1771-1772, leading to conclusion that his company had declined, and that his continued success depended heavily upon innovations in scenic design and lighting.

1743 Sturgess, Keith. *Jacobean Private Theatre.* New York, NY: Routledge & Kegan Paul; 1987. 228 pp. (Theatre Production Studies.) Pref. Index. Notes. Biblio. Illus.: Design. Photo. Maps. Dwg. Sketches. Print. B&W. Grd.Plan. 24. Lang.: Eng.
England. 1596-1633. Histories-specific. ■Reassessment of a group of Jacobean plays from modern theatrical viewpoint.

1744 Twycross, Meg. "Two Maid Marians and a Jewess." *MET.* 1987; 9(1): 6-7. Notes. Lang.: Eng.

DRAMA: —Performance/production

England. 1510-1519. Histories-sources. ■Three more named transvestites are added to list published in *MET* 1983: 5(2): 123-180. Related to Mixed Entertainment: Pageants/parades.

1745 Davis, Nicholas. "Spectacula Christiana: A Roman Christian Template for Medieval Drama." *MET*. 1987; 9(2): 125-152. Notes. Illus.: Photo. B&W. 1. Lang.: Eng.

Europe. 160-1578. Historical studies. ■Relationship between two views of theatre: the condemnation of the Roman *ludi* by the early Church fathers and the creative impulse behind medieval drama.

1746 Esslin, Martin. "Actors Acting Actors." *MD*. 1987 Mar.; 30(1): 72-79. Notes. Lang.: Eng.

Europe. 1590-1987. Critical studies. ■'Showing' is an essential part of all acting.

1747 Hughes, Alan. "Art and Eighteenth-Century Acting Style, Part II: Attitudes." *TN*. 1987; 41(2): 79-89. Illus.: Pntg. Print. B&W. 4. Lang.: Eng.

Europe. 1700. Historical studies. ■Sources of attitudes for serious dramatic acting and acting for low comedy.

1748 Quinn, Michael. "The Semiosis of Brechtian Acting: a Prague School Analysis." *Gestus*. 1986 Win; 11(4): 265-275. Notes. Lang.: Eng.

Europe. 1986. Critical studies. ■Analysis of the communicative procedures and aesthetic functions of Brechtian acting employing the categories and principles found in the Prague School writings on acting.

1749 Louhija, Marja; Helminen, Jussi; Wigelius, Staffan, transl. "EPT:S manifest Vettlöshetens vettighet." (The Manifesto of EPT: The Sense of Senselessness.) *NT*. 1987; 37: 4-10. Lang.: Swe.

Finland. Oulu. 1986. Historical studies. ■Elemänpalvelusteatteri 981 (Life Service Theatre 981), is an experiment at the city theatre of Uleåborg to create a really topical theatre. In two months they produced nineteen different performances. Related to Mixed Entertainment.

1750 Centre de Documentació i d'Animació de Cultura Catalana. *De la literature popular a les tradicions de Pasqües*. (From Popular Literature to Easter Traditions.) Perpignan: Centre de Documentació i d'Animació de la Cultura Catalana; 1987. 30 pp. Notes. Biblio. Illus.: Design. 1. Lang.: Cat, Fre.

France. 1415-1987. Histories-sources. ■Catalogue of an exhibition on popular theatre, Perpignan, France. Includes a lecture by Pep Vila, reproductions of articles on popular celebrations and important individuals in Roussillon theatre. Related to Mixed Entertainment.

1751 Banu, Georges. "*Le mariage de Figaro*: Le spectacle de la plénitude." (*The Marriage of Figaro*: The Spectacle of Plenitude.) *AltT*. 1987 Dec.; 28: 38-43. Illus.: Photo. B&W. 2. Lang.: Fre.

France: Paris. 1987. Critical studies. ■Review of Beaumarchais' play as directed by Jean-Pierre Vincent, Théâtre National de Chaillot.

1752 Banu, Georges; Bassnett, Susan, transl. "Peter Brook's Six Days." *NTQ*. 1987 May; 3(10): 99-106. Illus.: Photo. Print. B&W. 3. Lang.: Eng.

France: Paris. 1986. Critical studies. ■Following the production of *The Mahabharata* by the Centre International de Recherche Théâtrale, a number of its earlier members met to share their approaches and experiences.

1753 Collin, Francise. "*L'hypothèse, Clytemnestre, Mystère bouffe* au Théâtre de la Bastille." (*The Hypothesis, Clytemnestra* and *Mystère-Bouffe* at Théâtre de la Bastille.) *AltT*. 1987 Dec.; 28: 56-61. Illus.: Photo. B&W. 3. Lang.: Fre.

France: Paris. 1987. Critical studies. ■Overview of three productions: *L'hypothèse (The Hypothesis)* by Robert Pinget, staged by Joël Jouanneau, *Clytemnestra* by Euripides, staged by Suzuki Tadashi, and *Mystère bouffe* by Théâtre du Rideau, staged by François Tanguy.

1754 Dort, Bernard. "Saint Strehler." *AdT*. 1987 Spr; 1(6): 52-56. Notes. Lang.: Fre.

France. Italy. 1921-1987. Biographical studies. ■Strehler as the incarnation of the 20th-century director, in its splendor and its misery.

1755 Heed, Sven Åke. "Kärleken som utslagsmekanism." (Love As Mechanism of Elimination.) *NT*. 1987; 38: 10-13. Illus.: Photo. Lang.: Swe.

France: Nanterre. 1982-1987. Historical studies. ■About Patrice Chéreau's influence on the École des Comédiens at the Théâtre des Amandiers, and the joint project of *Platonov* and a modern film version named *Hôtel de France*. Related to Media: Film.

1756 Hemmings, F.W.J. "Child Actors on the Paris Stage in the Eighteenth and Nineteenth Centuries." *ThR*. 1987; 12(1): 9-22. Notes. Lang.: Eng.

France: Paris. 1769-1850. Historical studies. ■Study of child actors in juvenile companies and at Comédie-Française.

1757 Jacques, Brigitte. "'Un dieu est toujours plus grand que son champ' (Hölderlin)." ('A God Is Always Taller Than His Field': Hölderlin.) *AdT*. 1987 Spr; 1(6): 31-34. Lang.: Fre.

France. 1987. Critical studies. ■The true author and maker of theatre is the director. The director historically is seen as the one who keeps theatre alive by challenging new spaces and by being the only validator of the actor's art.

1758 Knowlson, James. "Beckett as Director: The Manuscript Production Notebooks and Critical Interpretation." *MD*. 1987 Dec.; 30(4): 451-465. Notes. Lang.: Eng.

France. 1969-1984. Critical studies. ■How Beckett's notes can illuminate the plays, with sample notebook pages.

1759 Lassalle, Jacques. "Une crise salutaire?" (A Salutary Crisis?)*AdT*. 1987 Spr; 1(6): 35-40. Notes. Lang.: Fre.

France. 1987. Critical studies. ■Directing is not a title or a function. It is a challenge to one's own condition as an artist, starting with the desire to share and communicate a play.

1760 Lavoie, Pierre. "Des voix à decouvrir/3e festival de la francophonie Haute-Vienne, Limoges et Limousin." (Voices to Discover: Third Festival of the French Language of Haute-Vienne, Limoges and Limousin.) *JCT*. 1987; 44: 79-87. Illus.: Photo. Print. B&W. 6. Lang.: Fre.

France. Belgium. 1986. Reviews of performances. ■The multiple-venue festival of French-language theatre shows the need for a continuing exchange of culture.

1761 Norén, Kjerstin. "I skuggan av ljuset." (In the Shadow of the Light.) *NT*. 1987; 37: 11-14. Illus.: Photo. Lang.: Swe.

France: Paris. 1987. Critical studies. ■An analysis of Bernard-Marie Koltès' *Dans la solitude des champs de coton (In the Solitude of the Cotton Fields)* compared to Patrice Chéreau's staging.

1762 Pasquier, Marie-Claire. "Claude Régy: garder le secret du livre." (Claude Régy: Keeping the Secret of the Book.) *AdT*. 1987 Spr; 1(6): 62-69. Notes. Biblio. Lang.: Fre.

France. 1955-1987. Biographical studies. ■Claude Régy's directing work seen as an incessant work of reading and of a constant inner listening. His principle is to give birth, to open the way, to break down barriers, so the unconscious of the author and the actors can flow freely and reach the spectator's unconscious too.

1763 Regnault, François. "Juger sur les grands." (To Judge From the Great Ones.) *AdT*. 1987 Spr; 1(6): 51. Lang.: Fre.

France. 1987. Critical studies. ■Judging directors and directing by analyzing minor shows is a mistake. One should judge directing from the great directors' work and see how close they are to the actor.

1764 Regnault, François. "*Elvire Jouvet 40*: Paradoxes d'Elvire." (*Elvire Jouvet 40*: Elvira's Paradoxes.) *AltT*. 1987 Dec.; 28: 30-37. Illus.: Photo. B&W. 4. Lang.: Fre.

France: Strasbourg. 1940-1986. Critical studies. ■Analysis of Molière's *Dom Juan*, focusing on the performance of Brigitte Jacques in the role of Elvire. Her characterization based on preserved notes of Louis Jouvet.

1765 Ronconi, Luca. "Je ne suis pas un médiateur innocent." (I Am Not an Innocent Mediator.) *AdT*. 1987 Spr; 1(6): 91-100 . Lang.: Fre.

France. Italy. 1987. Critical studies. ■Ronconi's approach to directing: neither interpretation nor critical reevaluation, but a work of variation suggested by the place, the time and the actors.

DRAMA: —Performance/production

1766 Thibaudat, Jean-Pierre. "'Puis-je vous dire une toute petite chose?'." ('May I Tell You One Little Thing?'.) *AdT.* 1987 Spr; 1(6): 57-61. Lang.: Fre.
France. Germany. 1945-1987. Biographical studies. ■The characteristics of Klaus Michael Grüber's work as a director compared to that of an engineer: how to work on tension and density more than on direction.

1767 Ubersfeld, Anne. "*Le soulier de satin* ou la frontière de l'univers." (*The Satin Slipper* or the Frontiers of the Universe.) *AltT.* 1987 Dec.; 28: 4-11. Illus.: Photo. B&W. 3. Lang.: Fre.
France: Avignon. 1987. Critical studies. ■Critique of Antoine Vitez's production of Claudel's play at the Festival of Avignon.

1768 Vincent, Jean-Pierre. "The Go-Between." *AdT.* 1987 Spr; 1(6): 47-50. Illus.: Dwg. 1. Lang.: Fre.
France. 1987. Critical studies. ■The work of the director is to be the faithful interpreter of the text and to show the relation between the present and the pre-existent play.

1769 Zaslavskaja, A. "Uroki fonetiki." (Lessons in Phonetics.) *TeatrM.* 1987; 4: 132-135. Lang.: Rus.
France. USSR. 1980-1987. ■On a Soviet Union Tour of Molière's *Le Misanthrope* (The Misanthrope), directed by Jean-Pierre Vincent and performed by the Comédie-Française.

1770 Bojadžieva, L.V. *Rejnhardt.* (Reinhardt.) Leningrad: Iskusstvo; 1987. 220 pp. Lang.: Rus.
Germany. 1873-1943. Biographies. ■Life and work of actor, director, theatrical figure Max Reinhardt.

1771 Evenden, Michael. "Beyond *Verfremdung*: Notes Toward a Brecht 'Theaterturgy'." 129-147 in Cardullo, Bert, ed. *Before His Eyes: Essays in Honor of Stanley Kauffmann.* Lanham, MD: UP of America; 1986. 185 pp. Notes. Biblio. Lang.: Eng.
Germany. 1925-1987. Historical studies. ■By analyzing Brecht's directing style in his original productions, more can be learned about his dramaturgy and the principles of his 'theaterturgy.' The play as written becomes a guide to understanding Brecht's staging and the staging reveals the play.

1772 Fetting, Hugo, ed. *Von der Freien Bühne zum politischen Theater. Drama und Theater im Spiegel der Kritik 1889-1918, 1919-1933.* (From *Freie Bühne* to Political Theatre: Drama and Theatre in the Mirror of Criticism. Vol. 1: 1889-1918, vol. 2: 1919-1933.) Leipzig: Reclam; 1987. 677 pp. Pref. Index. Notes. Lang.: Ger.
Germany: Berlin. 1889-1933. Reviews of performances. ■Press reviews by very influential critics reflect the most important Berlin productions of that time: documentation.

1773 Freydank, Ruth. "'Es ist Ihr Triumph, nicht meiner...' Ifflands Berliner Schiller-Inszenierungen." ('It's Your Triumph, Not Mine': Iffland's Schiller Productions in Berlin.) *TZ.* 1987; 42(5): 22-25. Illus.: Dwg. B&W. 3. Lang.: Ger.
Germany: Berlin. 1796-1806. Historical studies. ■August Wilhelm Iffland's work as manager and director at the Königlisches National Theatre, especially on his productions of Friedrich von Schiller's *Die Piccolomini, Die Jungfrau von Orleans* (The Maid of Orleans), *Die Braut von Messina* (The Bride of Messina) and *Wilhelm Tell*.

1774 Fuegi, John. *Bertolt Brecht: Chaos, According to Plan.* New York, NY: Cambridge UP; 1987. 223 pp. (Directors in Perspective Series.) Pref. Notes. Index. Biblio. Illus.: Photo. Print. B&W. 52. Lang.: Eng.
Germany. 1922-1956. Historical studies. ■Practical exploration of how Brecht actually worked in rehearsal and performance.

1775 Grange, William. "Shakespeare in the Weimar Republic." *ThS.* 1987 Nov.; 28(2): 89-100. Notes. Lang.: Eng.
Germany. 1919-1930. Historical studies. ■In the face of political and social unrest, theatre artists brought new relevance to the plays of Shakespeare through reinterpretation and new theatrical forms.

1776 Günzel, Klaus. *Romantikerschicksale. Eine Portratgalerie.* (Fates of Romantics: A Portrait Gallery.) Berlin: Verlag der Nation; 1987. 383 pp. Pref. Index. Biblio. Illus.: Graphs. Photo. B&W. 67. Lang.: Ger.
Germany. 1795-1830. Biographical studies. ■Fourteen essays on romantic personalities, among them Ludwig Tieck, C.M. v. Weber, E.T.A. Hoffmann and the actor Ludwig Devrient. Grp/movt: Romanticism.

1777 Hörnigk, Therese. "Brecht-Aufführungen im Spiegel der Berliner Presse 1922 bis 1933." (Performances of Brecht's Plays 1922 to 1933 Reflected in the Berlin Press.) 79-121 in Wruck, Peter, ed. *Literarisches Leben in Berlin, vol. 2.* Berlin: Akademie-Verlag; 1987. 358 pp. Notes. Lang.: Ger.
Germany: Berlin. 1922-1933. Critical studies. ■Early Berlin productions of Brecht's *Trommeln in der Nacht* (Drums in the Night), *Baal, Die Dreigroschenoper* (The Three Penny Opera), *Mann ist Mann* (A Man's a Man), *Die Mutter* (The Mother), *Die Massnahme* (The Measures Taken).

1778 Albiro, Hartwig; Bleyhoeffer, Christian; Manrd, Günzel Lutz; Hofmann, Frank; Kayser, Karl Georg; Volkmer, Rüdiger. "Wie entsteht Ensemblekunst heute?" (What's Come of Ensemble Art Today?)*TZ.* 1984 Jan.; 39(1): 18-25. Lang.: Ger.
Germany, East: Berlin, East. 1983. Histories-sources. ■A round-table discussion with stage directors on the principles and methods of working with an ensemble company.

1779 Földes, Anna. "Berlini színházi levél." (Theatre Letter from Berlin.) *Sz.* 1987; 20(6): 40-45. Illus.: Photo. B&W. 3. Lang.: Hun.
Germany, East: Berlin, East. 1987. Reviews of performances. ■Review of four performances in Berlin.

1780 Funke, Christophe. *Marianne Wünscher—Ansichten und Absichten einer Schauspielerin.* (Marianne Wünscher: Views and Intentions of an Actress.) Berlin: Der Morgen; 1987. 97 pp. Illus.: Photo. Print. B&W. 30. Lang.: Ger.
Germany, East: Berlin, East. 1930-1986. Biographies. ■Training, engagements, roles and personality of the comic actress.

1781 Gleib, Jochen. "Feuer für fremde Abenteuer. Über den Schauspieler Arno Wyzniewski, Berliner Ensemble." (A Passion for Strange Adventures: On the Actor Arno Wyzniewski.) *TZ.* 1987; 42(6): 17-20. Illus.: Photo. B&W. 8. Lang.: Ger.
Germany, East: Berlin, East. 1956-1987. Biographical studies. ■Portrait of the Berliner Ensemble actor Arno Wyzniewski.

1782 Hamburger, Mark. "New Concepts of Staging *A Midsummer Night's Dream*." *ShS.* 1987; 40: 51-61. Notes. Illus.: Photo. Print. B&W. 5. Lang.: Eng.
Germany, East. 1960-1980. Historical studies. ■Change from sociopolitical emphasis to individual themes in productions of *A Midsummer Night's Dream* by Christoph Schroth and Alexander Lang.

1783 Kerber, Jan. "Shakespeare und der 'dritte Zweck'. *Troilus und Cressida* als Probe im Theaterwürfel." (Shakespeare and the 'Third Aim': *Troilus and Cressida* as a Test in the Group Theaterwürfel.) 165-170 in Klotz, Günther; Kuckhoff, Armin-Gerd. *Deutsche Shakespeare-Gesellschaft Jahrbuch.* Weimar: Böhlau; 1987. 305 pp. (SJW 123.) Lang.: Ger.
Germany, East: Berlin, East. 1985. Critical studies. ■Conception of a production of scenes from *Troilus and Cressida* on the theme of war/peace/love, shown by young Berlin actors of various theatres.

1784 Kuckhoff, Armin-Gerd. "Shakespeare auf den Bühnen der DDR im Jahre 1985." (Shakespeare on the Stages of the German Democratic Republic in 1985.) 153-164 in Klotz, Günther, ed.; Kuckhoff, Armin-Gerd, ed. *Deutsche Shakespeare-Gesellschaft Jahrbuch.* Weimar: Böhlau; 1987. 305 pp. (SJW 123.) Lang.: Ger.
Germany, East. 1985. Reviews of performances. ■List and short reviews of Shakespearean productions listed according to city.

1785 Martineau, Maureen. "Mettre en scène selon Brecht." (Play Production According to Brecht.) *JCT.* 1987; 43: 111-114. Illus.: Photo. Diagram. Print. B&W. 4. Lang.: Fre.
Germany, East. 1985. Critical studies. ■The author describes a two-week acting workshop in East Germany, during which director Konrad Zschiedrich studies texts of Brecht, using Brecht's theories of dramatic staging.

DRAMA: —Performance/production

1786 Molnár Gál, Péter. "Előadás után." (After Performance.) *Krit.* 1987 Dec.(12): 20. Illus.: Photo. B&W. 1. Lang.: Hun.
Germany, East: Berlin, East. Hungary. 1980-1987. Biographical studies. ■Remembering Mária Sulyok, Hungarian actress who died in October 1987, the article describes one of her last great successes as Mrs. Orbán in István Örkény's *Macskajáték (Catsplay)* at Volksbühne in Berlin, staged by Brigitte Soubeyran.

1787 Pietzsch, Ingeborg. "Eine Berliner Schauspielerin. Porträt-Versuch über Marianne Wünscher." (A Berlin Actress: Trying to Portray Marianne Wünscher.) *TZ.* 1987; 42(11): 19-22. Illus.: Photo. B&W. 10. Lang.: Ger.
Germany, East: Berlin, East. 1948-1987. Biographical studies.

1788 Volz, Ruprecht. "Strindberg-Premieren in Deutschland 1984-1986." (Strindberg Productions in Germany 1984-1986.) *Strind.* 1987; 2: 54-60. Lang.: Ger.
Germany, West. Germany, East. Sweden. 1984-1986. Critical studies. ■Recent productions of Strindberg plays in West and East Germany with citations from newspaper reviews.

1789 "Színikritikusok díja 1986/87." (Theatre Critics Prizes 1986/87.) *Sz.* 1987 Oct.; 20(10): 1-11. Illus.: Photo. B&W. 9. Lang.: Hun.
Hungary. 1987. Critical studies. ■The best Hungarian play, production, actor and actress, supporting actor and actress, stage design, costumes of the season as decided by twenty-three theatre critics.

1790 "Perújrafelvétel. Németh László *Galilei* jérő." (Retrial: On László Németh's *Galileo*.) *Sz.* 1987 Oct.; 20(10): 20-29. Illus.: Photo. B&W. 5. Lang.: Hun.
Hungary. 1952-1987. Historical studies. ■In connection with Ferenc Sík's production of Németh's *Galilei (Galileo)* at the Castle Theatre in 1987, the history of the birth and difficult fate of the drama in the light of the critics.

1791 Ablonczy, László. "'Elfáradtam'...Találkozás Ruszt József-fel." ('I Got Tired:' Interview with József Ruszt.) *FSM.* 1987 Feb.; 31(9): 6-7. Illus.: Photo. B&W. 2. Lang.: Hun.
Hungary. 1983-1987. Histories-sources. ■József Ruszt was the director, art director and stage manager of the Hevesi Sándor Theatre in Zalaegerszeg until 1987. He speaks about his resignation, his plans and his successes.

1792 Ablonczy, László. "'Orgon lettem'... Szegedi találkozás Mensáros Lászlóval." ('I Became Orgon': Interview with László Mensáros in Szeged.) *FSM.* 1987 Mar.; 31(10): 8-9. Illus.: Photo. B&W. 2. Lang.: Hun.
Hungary. 1952-1987. Histories-sources. ■László Mensáros speaks about his decision to become a 'commuting actor' after his years in the capital, his most outstanding colleagues, his stagings.

1793 Ablonczy, László. "Találkozás Gábor Miklóssal. A tört-énelmi Idő't igen, a csodákat ne értelmezzük!'" (Interview with Miklós Gábor: Historical Time Should be Interpreted, Miracles Should Not.) *FSM.* 1987 Apr.; 31(16): 12-15. Illus.: Photo. B&W. Color. 5. Lang.: Hun.
Hungary. 1962-1987. Histories-sources. ■Miklós Gábor speaks about his career as an actor, his plans as director, and his political activity.

1794 Ablonczy, László. *Latinovits Zoltán tekintete: Dokumentu-mok, tünődések, beszélgetések.* (The Look of Zoltan Latinovits: Documents, Recollections, Interviews.) Budapest: Minerva; 1987. xxxii, 214 pp. Illus.: Photo. Dwg. B&W. 74. Lang.: Hun.
Hungary. 1931-1986. Histories-sources. ■The career of Zoltán Latinovits: actor, director, writer, film actor of tragic fate, in the light of his writings, recollections of contemporaries, original documents. Related to Media: Film.

1795 Almási, Miklós. "Christopher Hampton: *Veszedelmes viszonyok.*" (Christopher Hampton: *Les Liaisons Dangere-uses.*) *Krit.* 1987 Jan.(1): 34-35. Lang.: Hun.
Hungary: Budapest. 1986. Reviews of performances. ■Stage adaptation of Choderlos de Laclos' novel at the Pest Theatre directed by János Szikora.

1796 Almási, Miklós. "Lope de Vega: *Sevilla csillaga.*" (Lope de Vega: *The Star of Seville.*) *Krit.* 1987 Apr.(4): 35-36. Illus.: Photo. B&W. 1. Lang.: Hun.

Hungary: Budapest. 1986. Reviews of performances. ■Modern pro-duction of *La estrella de Sevilla (The Star of Seville)*, last staged in Hungary in the nineteenth century, staged by László Márton at the Comedy Theatre.

1797 Almási, Miklós. "Arthur Miller: *Az ügynök halála.*" (Arthur Miller: *Death of A Salesman.*) *Krit.* 1987 May(5): 33-34. Lang.: Hun.
Hungary: Budapest. 1987. Reviews of performances. ■In the Comedy Theatre's new production, director János Szikora has given the role of Willy Loman to Géza Tordy, an actor who is and looks considerably younger than the usual image of the salesman.

1798 Almási, Miklós. "Sütő András: *Álomkommandó.*" (András Sütő: *Dream Commando.*) *Krit.* 1987 Nov.(11): 33-34. Lang.: Hun.
Hungary. 1987. Critical studies. ■After its summer run in Gyula, András Sütő's play was also produced at the Comedy Theatre in Budapest. The drama of the Hungarian writer living in Romania was staged by Ferenc Sík.

1799 Baló, Júlia. "Találkozás Andorai Péterrel. 'Mindent át-meneti állapotnak tekintek'." (Interview with Péter An-dorai: 'I consider everything as a transitory status'.) *FSM.* 1987 Jan.; 31(4): 10-11. Illus.: Photo. B&W. 1. Lang.: Hun.
Hungary. 1980-1987. Histories-sources. ■Péter Andorai speaks about his career, his theatre and film roles following the years of failure, his experiences in America. Related to Media: Film.

1800 Baló, Júlia. "Találkozás Ascher Tamással. 'Mestercsapat—Stuttgartban.'" (Interview with Tamás Ascher: 'Master Team' in Stuttgart.) *FSM.* 1987; 31(30): 6. Illus.: Photo. B&W. 2. Lang.: Hun.
Hungary. 1987. Histories-sources. ■On his staging of Čechov's *Tri sestry (Three Sisters)* at World Theatre Festival, performed by Katona József Theatre.

1801 Baló, Júlia. "Találkozás Udvaros Dorottyával. 'Bármi történhet'." (Interview with Dorottya Udvaros: 'Anything May Happen'.) *FSM.* 1987; 31(46): 8-9. Illus.: Photo. B&W. 1. Lang.: Hun.
Hungary. 1978-1987. Histories-sources. ■Interview with one of the leading young actresses of Budapest Katona József Theatre about her successful starting on her career.

1802 Bán, Magda. "'A kor nekem kedvezett'. Beszélgetés Tóth Judittal.'" ('The Age Favored Me': Interview with Judit Tóth.) *FSM.* 1987 Feb.; 31(7): 5. Illus.: Photo. B&W. 1. Lang.: Hun.
Hungary: Budapest. 1962-1987. Histories-sources. ■Judit Tóth, actress, speaks about her career, the nineteen years spent in the József Attila Theatre in Budapest and why she changed theatres.

1803 Bécsy, Tamás. "Ami megnyilatkozik, és ami rejtve marad. T.S. Eliot drámája a Várszínházban." (What Can Be Seen and What Remains Hidden: T.S. Eliot's Drama at the Castle Theatre.) *Sz.* 1987 July; 20(7): 27-32. Illus.: Photo. B&W. 2. Lang.: Hun.
Hungary: Budapest. 1987. Critical studies. ■Short analysis of Eliot's *The Cocktail Party* and evaluation of the performance at the Castle Theatre directed by János Mrsán.

1804 Bécsy, Tamás. "Camus: *Caligula.*" *Krit.* 1987 Apr.(4): 34-35. Illus.: Photo. B&W. 1. Lang.: Hun.
Hungary: Budapest. 1986. Reviews of performances. ■Director György Lengyel tries to probe into several layers of the drama. He brings out the psychological aspects that reflect the thoughts of the author about the world and himself, and also uncovers some universally valid ideas of the text.

1805 Bécsy, Tamás. "Csehov: *Cseresznyéskert.*" (Čechov: *The Cherry Orchard.*) *Krit.* 1987 July(7): 44-45. Lang.: Hun.
Hungary: Budapest. 1987. Reviews of performances. ■Višněvyj sad (The Cherry Orchard) drama of posing, conventions, lack of values at the Madách Theatre staged by Ottó Ádám.

1806 Bécsy, Tamás. "Az etikusság szépsége. A *Bölcs Náthán* Zalaegerszegen." (The Beauty of Ethics: *Nathan the Wise* in Zalaegerszeg.) *Sz.* 1987 Feb.; 20(2): 18-24. Illus.: Photo. B&W. 4. Lang.: Hun.

DRAMA: —Performance/production

Hungary: Zalaegerszeg. 1986. Critical studies. ■Lessing's drama directed by József Ruszt at the Hevesi Sándor Theatre of Zalaegerszeg.

1807 Bécsy, Tamás. "A becsület drámája. A *Sevilla csillaga* a Vígszínházban." (The Drama of Honesty: The *Star of Seville* at the Comedy Theatre.) *Sz.* 1987 Mar.; 20(3): 8-14. Illus.: Photo. B&W. 5. Lang.: Hun.
Hungary: Budapest. 1986. Reviews of performances. ■Lope de Vega's *La estrella de Sevilla* directed by László Márton at the Comedy Theatre.

1808 Bécsy, Tamás. "A kimúlt *Kék róka.* Herczeg Ferenc és utókora." (The Dead *Silver Fox*: Ferenc Herczeg and Posteriority.) *Sz.* 1987 Jan.; 20(1): 5-14. Illus.: Photo. B&W. 3. Lang.: Hun.
Hungary: Budapest. 1986. Critical studies. ■Short analysis of the play compared with earlier stagings in connection with the performance staged by Zsuzsa Bencze on Radnóti Miklós Stage.

1809 Bérczes, László. "Beszélgetés Nagy Zoltánnal. Egy amatőr profi." (Interview with Zoltán Nagy: An Amateur Professional.) *FSM.* 1987 Apr.; 31(14): 8-9. Illus.: Photo. B&W. 1. Lang.: Hun.
Hungary. 1962-1987. Histories-sources. ■Zoltán Nagy, having become an actor without having studied the profession, speaks about his career and plans.

1810 Bérczes, László. "Harrytól Henrikig. Shakespeare-királydrámák a Nemzeti Színházban." (From Harry to Henry: Shakespeare's King Plays at the National Theatre.) *Sz.* 1987; 20(3): 18-24. Illus.: Photo. B&W. 6. Lang.: Hun.
Hungary: Budapest. 1986. Critical studies. ■Both parts of *Henry IV* staged by László Vámos and *Henry V* staged by Imre Kerényi performed by the National Theatre Ensemble at the Castle Theatre.

1811 Bérczes, László. "Kép, kép, kép...A *Lear király* Pécsett." (Picture, Picture, Picture...*King Lear* in Pécs.) *Sz.* 1987 Jan.; 20(1): 18-21. Illus.: Photo. B&W. 2. Lang.: Hun.
Hungary: Pécs. 1986. Reviews of performances. ■Shakespeare's drama at the National Theatre in Pécs staged by Menyhért Szegvári.

1812 Blaha, Lujza; Csillag, Ilona, ed. *Blaha Lujza naplója.* (Lujza Blaha's Diary.) Budapest: Gondolat; 1987. 341 pp. Lang.: Hun.
Hungary. 1862-1905. Histories-sources. ■Diary of early life of the legendary actress and singer called 'the nation's nightingale': roles, friends, contemporaries, social life of Pest, Vienna and Paris.

1813 Brogyányi, Eugene. "An Absurdoid Evening in Binghamton." *SEEDTF.* 1987 Dec.; 7(2 & 3): 51-53. Lang.: Eng.
Hungary. USA: Binghamton, NY. 1987. Historical studies. ■Brief plot summations of five short plays by Géza Páskándi as presented by Threshold Theatre Company at the 20th anniversary celebration of *Modern International Drama* at SUNY Binghamton.

1814 Csáki, Judit; Keleti, Éva, photo.; Rédei, Ferenc, photo. *1 420828 0076: Közelkép Szilágyi Tiborról.* (1 420828 0076: Close-Up of Tibor Szilágyi.) Budapest: IPV; 1987. 221 pp. Illus.: Photo. B&W. 56. Lang.: Hun.
Hungary. 1950-1986. Biographical studies. ■Series of interviews on the actor's career, artistic beliefs, human relations.

1815 Csáki, Judit. "Munkácsi Miklós: *Lisszaboni eső.*" (Miklós Munkácsi: *Rain in Lisbon.*) *Krit.* 1987 July(7): 43. Lang.: Hun.
Hungary: Budapest. 1987. Reviews of performances. ■Notes on the performance directed by Menyhért Szegvári at The Stage.

1816 Csáki, Judit. "Tükör nélkül. A *Caligula* a Madách Kamaraszínházban." (Without a Mirror: *Caligula* at Madách Chamber Theatre.) *Sz.* 1987; 20(2): 24-27. Illus.: Photo. B&W. 2. Lang.: Hun.
Hungary: Budapest. 1986. Reviews of performances. ■Notes on the performance directed by György Lengyel at Madách Chamber Theatre.

1817 Csáki, Judit. "Gábor Andor: *Dollárpapa.*" (Andor Gábor: *Dollar Daddy.*) *Krit.* 1987 Dec.(12): 40. Lang.: Hun.
Hungary: Budapest. 1987. Reviews of performances. ■Notes on a 'clumsy and slow' performance staged by Gábor Berényi in the Chamber Theatre of the National Theatre, i.e. at the Castle Theatre.

1818 Csáki, Judit. "A divatos realizmus. Az *Örökösök* Szolnokon." (The Fashionable Realism: *Heirs* in Szolnok.) *Sz.* 1987 May; 20(5): 28-31. Illus.: Photo. B&W. 3. Lang.: Hun.
Hungary: Szolnok. 1987. Reviews of performances. ■Revival of Maksim Gorkij's 1910 version of *Vassa Železnova* directed by Tamás Fodor under the title *Örökösök (Heirs)*.

1819 Csáki, Judit. "Tamási Áron: *Énekes madár.*" (Áron Tamási: *The Song Bird.*) *Krit.* 1987 Sep.(9): 33. Lang.: Hun.
Hungary: Budapest. 1987. Reviews of performances. ■This work by Áron Tamási brought back to the stage the magic of fairy tales and poetry. The Transylvanian 'Székler' folk play at the National Theatre was staged by Imre Kerényi.

1820 Csizner, Ildikó. "A visszafeleselő századelő. *A rablólovag* és *A nagy fejedelem* Veszprémben." (The Early Century Talking Back: *The Gallant Kidnapper* and *The Great Prince* in Veszprém.) *Sz.* 1987 July ; 20(7): 11-16. Illus.: Photo. B&W. 3. Lang.: Hun.
Hungary: Veszprém. 1987. Reviews of performances. ■Short evaluation of the 1986/87 openings of the 25-year-old Petőfi Theatre, including Menyhért Lengyel's *A nagy fejedelem (The Great Prince)* directed by István Paál and Lajos Biró's *A rablólovag (The Gallant Kidnapper)* directed by József Szabó.

1821 Csizner, Ildikó. "A titokzatos utazók. Krúdy-bemutató Veszprémben, Remenyik-premier Nyíregyházán." (The Mysterious Travellers: Krúdy Opening in Veszprém, Remenyik Opening in Nyíregyháza.) *Sz.* 1987 Feb.; 20(2): 11-17. Illus.: Photo. B&W. 4. Lang.: Hun.
Hungary: Veszprém, Nyíregyháza. 1986. Reviews of performances. ■Notes on two theatre nights: Gyula Krúdy's drama *A vörös postakocsi (The Red Mail Coach)* at Petőfi Theatre in Veszprém staged by Dezső Kapás and Zsigmond Remenyik's play *Az atyai ház (The Paternal Roof)* staged by Péter Lener at Móricz Zsigmond Theatre in Nyíregyháza.

1822 Csizner, Ildikó. "Prózaian. Három előadás Győrben." (In a Prosaic Way: Three Performances in Győr.) *Sz.* 1987 Mar.; 20(3): 29-33. Illus.: Photo. B&W. 3. Lang.: Hun.
Hungary: Győr. 1986. Reviews of performances. ■Aladár Kovách's play about János Apáczai Csere titled *Teli zsoltár (Winter Psalm)* staged by István Illés, Shakespeare's *Much Ado About Nothing* staged by Ferenc Sík and Miklós Gerencsér's *Ferde ház (The Leaning House)* staged by Péter Gágyor, Kisfaludy Theatre.

1823 Csizner, Ildikó. "Az átöltöztetett Molière. A *Tudós nők* a Várszínházban." (Molière Redressed: *The Learned Ladies* at the Castle Theatre.) *Sz.* 1987 Sep.; 20(9): 22-25. Illus.: Photo. B&W. 4. Lang.: Hun.
Hungary: Budapest. 1987. Reviews of performances. ■Molière's *Les femmes savantes (The Learned Ladies)* in modern dress directed by László Vámos at Várszínház.

1824 Duró, Győző. "Az értelmezés: véleményalkotás." (Interpretation: Formation of Opinion.) *Krit.* 1987 Sep.(9): 13-14. Illus.: Photo. B&W. 2. Lang.: Hun.
Hungary. 1987. Critical studies. ■On the basis of the performances of the 6th National Theatre Meeting the author studies the ways a play can be interpreted from the selection of the play through dramaturgical intervention up to the use of costumes and props.

1825 Erdei, János. "A hatalom tükre. A *Hóhér és bolond* a Radnóti Miklós Színpadon." (The Mirror of Power: *The Hangman and the Madman* on Radnóti Miklós Stage.) *Sz.* 1987 July; 20(7): 23-26. Illus.: Photo. B&W. 3. Lang.: Hun.
Hungary: Budapest. 1986. Reviews of performances. ■Jan Werick's and Jiří Voskovec's play *Kat a blázen (The Hangman and the Madman)* with Jaroslav Jezek's songs on the Radnóti Miklós Stage, directed by Miklós Szurdi.

1826 Erdei, János. "Jobb az eredetinél! Brecht Galileije Csiszár Imre színpadán." (Better than the Original! Brecht's Galileo on Imre Csiszár's Stage.) *Sz.* 1987 June; 20(6): 24-27. Illus.: Photo. B&W. 2. Lang.: Hun.
Hungary: Miskolc. 1987. Reviews of performances. ■While the original Brechtian intention suggests unbroken faith in scientific development as the token of the advancement of man and the renewal of the world,

DRAMA: —Performance/production

director Imre Csiszár shifts the emphasis to the ambiguous role of science today.

1827 Erdei, János. "Élni és játszani—Anouilh-dráma Miskolcon és a Józsefvárosi Színházban." (To Live and to Play: Anouilh Drama in Miskolc and at the Theatre of Józsefváros.) *Sz.* 1987 Mar.; 20 (3): 33-39. Illus.: Photo. B&W. 3. Lang.: Hun.
Hungary: Miskolc, Budapest. 1987. Reviews of performances. ■Notes on two plays of Jean Anouilh: *Eurydice* directed by János Szűcs at the National Theatre of Miskolc and *Colombe* directed by Mátyás Giricz at the Theatre in the Józsefváros.

1828 Ferenci, Vera. "*Amit a szívedbe rejtesz*. Jordán Tamás József Attilája." (*Hidden in Your Heart*. Tamás Jordán's Attila József.) *Confes.* 1987; 11(3): 119-120. Lang.: Hun.
Hungary: Budapest. 1987. Reviews of performances. ■A compilation of the autobiographical confessions by the poet Attila József presented by Tamás Jordán at the Radnóti Miklós Theatre staged by János Gáspár.

1829 Földes, Anna. "A *Vendégség—tizenöt év után. Páskándi-dráma a Játékszínben.*" (*The Host and the Guest—After 15 Years: Páskándi Drama at The Stage.*) *Sz.* 1987 Feb.; 20(2): 1-4. Illus.: Photo. B&W. 2. Lang.: Hun.
Hungary: Budapest. 1986. Reviews of performances. ■Géza Páskándi's play directed by János Taub at Játékszín.

1830 Földes, Anna. "Oszlopos Simeonok." (The Men on the Pillar.) *Sz.* 1987 June; 20(6): 7-13. Illus.: Photo. B&W. 7. Lang.: Hun.
Hungary: Szeged, Budapest. 1967-1987. Critical studies. ■Two revivals of Imre Sarkadi's play, *Oszlopos Simeon (The Man on the Pillar)*: at the National Theatre in Szeged directed by Árpád Árkosi and at the Pesti Theatre directed by István Horvai. Comparison of the two plays and with the performances since the 1967 world premiere.

1831 Földes, Anna. *Színésznek született: Interjúk.* (Born to Be an Actor: Interviews.) Budapest: Kossuth: MNOT; 1987. 219 pp. Pref. Illus.: Photo. B&W. 27. Lang.: Hun.
Hungary. 1980-1986. Histories-sources. ■Interviews with successful Hungarian actors.

1832 Földes, Anna. "Paál István *Forgatókönyve*. Örkény István tragédiája Veszprémben." (István Paál's *Screenplay*: István Örkény's Tragedy in Veszprém.) *Sz.* 1987; 20(4): 4-7 . Illus.: Photo. B&W. 2. Lang.: Hun.
Hungary: Veszprém. 1987. Reviews of performances. ■Örkény's play directed by István Paál at the Petőfi Theatre.

1833 Forgách, András. "'Az új szomorúság korszaka'. Jeles Andrással Forgách András beszélget." ('The Age of New Sadness': András Forgách Interviews András Jeles.) *Sz.* 1987 Apr.; 20(4): 24-29. Lang.: Hun.
Hungary. 1985-1987. Histories-sources. ■András Jeles, leader of the Monteverdi Group, speaks of his career as stage manager, of his ideas.

1834 Futaky, Hajna. "Színészportrék pécsi háttérrel 9. Kézdy György." (Portraits of Actors with a Background in Pécs 9: György Kézdy.) *Jelenkor.* 1987 Oct.; 30(10): 915-921. Lang.: Hun.
Hungary: Pécs. 1953-1987. Histories-sources. ■Interview with György Kézdy about his career and prominent roles.

1835 Gách, Marianne. "Gách Marianne beszélgetése—Sinkovits Imrével. 'A vígjátékban mindig feloldódom'." (Marianne Gách Interview with Imre Sinkovits: 'I Am Dissolved in Comedy'.) *FSM.* 1987; 31(36): 6-7. Illus.: Photo. B&W. 1. Lang.: Hun.
Hungary: Budapest. 1951-1987. Histories-sources. ■A conversation with Imre Sinkovits on his career focusing on his recent performance in *Mózes (Moses)* at the National Theatre.

1836 Garai, László. "József Attila ötleteinek szabadsága. Jordán Tamás monodrámája a Radnóti Színpadon." (The Liberty of Attila József's Ideas: Monodrama of Tamás Jordán at the Radnóti Miklós Theatre.) *Krit.* 1987 Sep.(9): 31-32. Lang.: Hun.
Hungary: Budapest. 1987. Critical studies. ■Actor Tamás Jordán made a theatre play *Amit a szívedbe rejtesz (Hidden in Your Heart)* from the notes of the free associations of the poet Attila József known to

Hungarian literary history as 'The List of Free Ideas': reactions to the special performance.

1837 Gervai, András. "Látogatóban Tolnay Klárinál." (Visit to Klári Tolnay: Higher and Higher.) *FSM.* 1987 Apr.; 31(15): 12-13. Illus.: Photo. B&W. 7. Lang.: Hun.
Hungary. 1984-1987. Histories-sources. ■Klári Tolnay, actress, speaks about her last roles, hobbies, relationships.

1838 Julian, Ria. "'A pályán vagyok': Portrévázlat Vári Eváról." ('I Am on the Path of Vocation': Draft Portrait of Eva Vári.) *Sz.* 1987 Feb.; 20(2): 46-47. Illus.: Photo. B&W. 1. Lang.: Hun.
Hungary: Pécs. 1963-1986. Histories-sources. ■Interview and portrait of actress Éva Vári.

1839 Kállai, Katalin. "Bertolt Brecht: *Galilei élete*." (Bertolt Brecht: *The Life of Galileo*.) *Krit.* 1987 June(6) : 38-39. Lang.: Hun.
Hungary: Miskolc. 1987. Reviews of performances. ■Péter Blaskó, who plays the title role, bears the main burden of the production. This Galileo is fundamentally a man of intellect, whose flaming mind glows in calmer wisdom by the end of the performance. Brecht's play at Miskolc National Theatre directed by Imre Csiszár.

1840 Kállai, Katalin. "Móricz Zsigmond: *Fortunátus*." (Zsigmond Móricz: *Fortunátus*.) *Krit.* 1987 Oct. (10): 32. Lang.: Hun.
Hungary: Zalaegerszeg. 1987. Reviews of performances. ■Premiere of newly discovered Móricz drama (1916) about Imre Fortunátus, a Jew converted to Christianity, treasurer to King Louis II. The play was staged by Péter Tömöry at the Hevesi Sándor Theatre.

1841 Kárpáti, György. *Domján Edit.* (Edit Domján.) Budapest: Zeneműkiadó; 1987. 158 pp. Illus.: Photo. B&W. 67. Lang.: Hun.
Hungary. 1932-1972. Biographies. ■Life and career of late actress Edit Domján on the basis of interviews and the recollections of her contemporaries.

1842 Kerényi, Ferenc. "Romantikus színészdrámákról—a Kean ürügyén." (On Romantic Actor Dramas: In Connection with Kean.) *Sz.* 1987 Mar.; 20(3): 40-41. Lang.: Hun.
Hungary: Budapest. 1836-1847. Historical studies. ■A look back at actor-dramas produced at the National Theatre, on the occasion of the production of *Kean* by Dumas père, adapted by Sartre, directed by Tamás Szirtes.

1843 Kerényi, Imre. "Csiksomlyó és a világ." (Csiksomlyó and the World.) *FSM.* 1987; 31(37): 6-7. Illus.: Photo. B&W. 3. Lang.: Hun.
Hungary. 1982-1987. Histories-sources. ■Director Imre Kerényi's report on the successful guest performance series of *Passion Play of Csiksomlyó*. This 18th-century Transylvanian school play was already shown in Sofia, Le Havre, Warsaw, Rome, Cologne. Article continued in *FSM* 1987, 31(38): 4-5.

1844 Kocsis, L. Mihály. *Van itt valaki: Major Tamás.* (There Is Someone Present: Tamás Major.) Budapest: Minerva; 1987. xxxii, 434 pp. Illus.: Photo. B&W. 50. Lang.: Hun.
Hungary. 1910-1986. Biographies. ■Biography of Hungarian actor and director, based on interviews. Reviewed by Gábor Antal, *Sz* 20:12 (1987 Dec.), 46-48.

1845 Kőháti, Zsolt. "Egy népszínmű rétegei. Móricz *Sári bírója* Kisvárdán." (The Strata of a Folk Play: Móricz's *Judge Sári* in Kisvárda.) *Sz.* 1987 Nov.; 20(11): 28-29. Illus.: Photo. B&W. 1. Lang.: Hun.
Hungary: Kisvárda. 1987. Reviews of performances. ■Zsigmond Móricz's play with István Mikó's music at the Kisvárda Castle Theatre, directed by Imre Halasi on the summer program in Kisvárda.

1846 Koltai, Tamás. "Calderón: *Az élet álom*." (Calderón: *Life Is a Dream*.) *Krit.* 1987 Jan.(1): 33. Lang.: Hun.
Hungary: Budapest. 1986. Reviews of performances. ■Calderón's *La vida es sueño* at the Radnóti Miklós Theatre directed by Miklós Szinetár.

1847 Koltai, Tamás. "Páger Antal alakváltozásai." (Antal Páger's Metamorphoses.) *Krit.* 1987 Feb.(2): 17. Illus.: Photo. B&W. 2. Lang.: Hun.

DRAMA: —Performance/production

Hungary. 1919-1986. Critical studies. ■Analysis of acting style and interpretation of the actor Antal Páger with an overview of his career.

1848 Koltai, Tamás. "Gorkij: *Örökösök.*" (Gorkij: *Heirs.*) *Krit.* 1987 Apr.(4): 35. Illus.: Photo. B&W. 1. Lang.: Hun.

Hungary: Szolnok. 1987. Reviews of performances. ■Tamás Fodor's direction revealed that this first version of Gorkij's *Vassa Železnova*, though the writer himself considered it less successful, is a stirring drama that offers the insight of excellent psychological portrayal.

1849 Koltai, Tamás. "Sarkadi Imre: *Oszlopos Simeon.*" (Imre Sarkadi: *The Man on the Pillar.*) *Krit.* 1987 June(6): 39. Lang.: Hun.

Hungary: Budapest. 1987. Reviews of performances. ■István Horvai, one-time friend and associate of the dramatist Imre Sarkadi gave the play a mature and analytical interpretation at the Pest Theatre.

1850 Koltai, Tamás. "O'Neill: *Utazás az éjszakába.*" (O'Neill: *Long Day's Journey into Night.*) *Krit.* 1987 July(7): 42. Lang.: Hun.

Hungary: Eger. 1987. Reviews of performances. ■Ideas on the production of Katona József Theatre directed by Gábor Zsámbéki.

1851 Koltai, Tamás. "Németh László: *Galilei.*" (László Németh: *Galileo.*) *Krit.* 1987 Sep.(9): 32-33. Lang.: Hun.

Hungary: Budapest. 1987. Reviews of performances. ■Staging without inspiration among uncomfortable and artificial scenery: László Németh's play on the stage of Castle Theatre staged by Ferenc Sík.

1852 Koltai, Tamás. "A Katona József Színház rangot jelent. Beszélgetés Udvaros Dorottyával." (The Katona József Theatre Represents a Rank: Interview with Dorottya Udvaros.) *Krit.* 1987 Oct.(10): 8-9. Illus.: Photo. B&W. 1. [Close-Up of Katona József Theatre I.] Lang.: Hun.

Hungary. 1977-1987. Histories-sources. ■Actress Dorottya Udvaros, member of the Katona József Theatre at the time of the interview, speaks about her career.

1853 Koltai, Tamás. "Alapélményem maga az élet. Beszélgetés Ascher Tamással." (My Basic Experience Is Life Itself: Interview with Tamás Ascher.) *Krit.* 1987 Nov.(11): 6-8. Illus.: Photo. B&W. 2. [Close-Up of Katona József Theatre II.] Lang.: Hun.

Hungary. 1970-1987. Histories-sources. ■A director of the Csiky Gergely Theatre in Kaposvár speaks about the changes in Hungarian theatrical life, about his ideas as director.

1854 Koltai, Tamás. "Shakespeare: *A velencei kalmár.*" (Shakespeare: *The Merchant of Venice.*) *Krit.* 1987 Dec.(12): 40. Lang.: Hun.

Hungary: Pécs. 1987. Reviews of performances. ■Possibilities of interpreting the play, comparison of István Szőke's production with previous performances.

1855 Kovács, Dezső. "Folyamodvány életben maradásért. Sütő András új drámája a Gyulai Várszínházban." (Application for Survival: András Sütő's New Drama at the Castle Theatre of Gyula.) *Sz.* 1987 Nov.; 20(11): 2-5. Illus.: Photo. B&W. 2. Lang.: Hun.

Hungary: Gyula. 1987. Reviews of performances. ■András Sütő's *Álomkommandó (Dream Commando)* directed by Ferenc Sík at Gyulai Várszinház.

1856 Kovács, Dezső. "Schwajda György: *Mari.*" (György Schwajda: *Mari.*) *Krit.* 1987 Mar.(3): 41. Lang.: Hun.

Hungary: Pécs. 1986. Reviews of performances. ■At Pécsi National Theatre István Szőke directs *Mari*, a 'grotesque ballad' by György Schwajda, one of the foremost representatives of central East European absurdism.

1857 Kovács, Dezső. "Füst Milán: *Catullus.*" (Milán Füst: *Catullus.*) *Krit.* 1987 June(6): 37-38. Lang.: Hun.

Hungary: Budapest. 1987. Reviews of performances. ■The noted Hungarian writer and poet Milán Füst's play on the Roman poet was presented at the Katona József Theatre as a major production of the season.

1858 Kovács, Dezső. "Észrevétlen tragédiák. A *Lisszaboni eső* a Játékszínben." (Unnoticed Tragedies: *Rain in Lisbon* at The Stage.) *Sz.* 1987 June; 20(6): 18-20. Illus.: Photo. B&W. 4. Lang.: Hun.

Hungary: Budapest. 1987. Reviews of performances. ■Premiere of Miklós Munkácsi's play directed by Menyhért Szegvári at Játékszín.

1859 Kovács, Dezső. "Barokk mutatvány, plexiháttérrel. Corneille-bemutató a Katona József Színházban." (Baroque Show with Artificial Background: Opening of a Corneille Play at Katona József Theatre.) *Sz.* 1987 Mar.; 20(3): 6-8. Illus.: Photo. B&W. 2. Lang.: Hun.

Hungary: Budapest. 1986. Reviews of performances. ■*L'illusion comique (The Comic Illusion)* by Pierre Corneille directed by János Szikora at the Katona József Theatre.

1860 Léner, Péter. "'Élete drámákban telt'." ('His Life Was Spent in Dramas'.) *FSM.* 1987; 31(38): 8-9. Illus.: Photo. B&W. 2. Lang.: Hun.

Hungary. 1941-1978. Biographical studies. ■Memoir of stage director Endre Márton: survey of his career from the Comedy Theatre to the National Theatre.

1861 Mihályi, Gábor. "Ki tudja? Töprengések a kaposvári *Szent Johanna* alkalmából." (Who Knows? Meditation on *Saint Joan* Performed by Csiky Gergely Theatre, Kaposvár.) *Sz.* 1987 Aug.; 20(8): 22-28. Illus.: Photo. B&W. 4. Lang.: Hun.

Hungary: Kaposvár. 1983-1987. Critical studies. ■Analysis of the production of Shaw's play as the benefit performance of actress Eszter Csákányi directed by László Babarczy and evaluation of three seasons of the Csiky Gergely Theatre.

1862 Mihályi, Gábor. "Haumann Péter 'jutalomjátéka'. Dumas-Sartre: *Kean, a színész* című darabja a Madách Színházban." (Benefit Performance of Péter Haumann. Dumas-Sartre: *Edmund Kean or the Genius and the Libertine* at the Madách Theatre.) *Sz.* 1987 Mar.; 20(3): 15-17. Illus.: Photo. B&W. 3. Lang.: Hun.

Hungary: Budapest. 1986. Reviews of performances. ■Dumas's play as adapted by Sartre at the Madách Theatre directed by Tamás Szirtes.

1863 Molnár Gál, Péter. "Háy Mohácsa." (Háy's Mohács.) *Mozgo.* 1987 Nov.; 13(11): 125-127. Lang.: Hun.

Hungary. 1987. Critical studies. ■Madách Theatre production of *Mohács (The Mohács Disaster)* by Gyula Háy, staged by Tamás Szirtes.

1864 Müller, Péter P. "Önérvényesítés—önsorsrontás. A Pécsi Nyári Színház két bemutatójáról." (Self-Realization—Damaging One's Own Fate: On Two First Nights of the Summer Theatre in Pécs.) *Sz.* 1987 Nov.; 20(11): 5-9. Illus.: Photo. B&W. 4. Lang.: Hun.

Hungary: Pécs. 1987. Reviews of performances. ■Shakespeare's *Macbeth* directed by László Bagossy and Móricz's *Uri Muri (Gentlemen's Spree)* directed by the actor Tamás Jordán on the program of Pécs Summer Theatre.

1865 Müller, Péter P. "Zubbonyból zubbonyba. *Az apa* a Katona József Szinházban." (From Jacket to Jacket: *The Father* at the Katona József Theatre.) *Sz.* 1987 Dec.; 20(12): 9-12. Illus.: Photo. B&W. 3. Lang.: Hun.

Hungary: Budapest. 1987. Reviews of performances. ■Strindberg's *Fadren* at the Katona József Theatre staged by guest director Kalle Holmberg.

1866 Müller, Péter P. "Lessing: *Bölcs Náthán.*" (Lessing: *Nathan the Wise.*) *Krit.* 1987 Feb.(2): 34. Lang.: Hun.

Hungary: Zalaegerszeg. 1986. Reviews of performances. ■Lessing's drama in József Ruszt's production at the Hevesi Sándor Theatre speaks about the humanistic and timely message of tolerance, religious and otherwise.

1867 Müller, Péter P. "G.B. Shaw: *Szent Johanna.*" (G.B. Shaw: *Saint Joan.*) *Krit.* 1987 May(5): 35. Lang.: Hun.

Hungary: Kaposvár. 1987. Reviews of performances. ■The Csiky Gergely Theatre of Kaposvár put on G.B. Shaw's play in the production of László Babarczy, managing director of the company. Eszter Csákányi in the title role emphasized Joan's indestructible life force.

1868 Müller, Péter P. "Kaposvári terecske. Goldoni-bemutató Kaposvárott." (The Public Square in Kaposvár: Goldoni Opening in Kaposvár.) *Sz.* 1987 June; 20(6): 20-24. Illus.: Photo. B&W. 4. Lang.: Hun.

DRAMA: —Performance/production

Hungary: Kaposvár. 1987. Reviews of performances. ■Notes on Goldoni's *The Public Square (Il campiello)* performed by the Csiky Gergely Theatre of Kaposvár, staged by Tamás Ascher.

1869 Müller, Péter P. "Az öncsalás bűne és joga. *Az ügynök halála* a Vígszínházban." (The Right and Sin of Self-Deceit: *Death of a Salesman* at the Comedy Theatre.) *Sz.* 1987 May; 20(5): 31-36. Illus.: Photo. B&W. 3. Lang.: Hun.
Hungary: Budapest. 1987. Reviews of performances. ■Arthur Miller's play directed by János Szikora at the Comedy Theatre in Budapest.

1870 Müller, Péter P. "Világtünetek a világtengerparton. A *Világszezon* Szegeden." (World Phenomena on the World Shore: *World Tourist Season* in Szeged.) *Sz.* 1987 Mar.; 20(3): 4-6. Illus.: Photo. B&W. 2. Lang.: Hun.
Hungary: Szeged. 1986. Reviews of performances. ■Miklós Vámos' play directed by János Sándor at the National Theatre of Szeged.

1871 Müller, Péter P. "A tragikum iróniája. A *Csirkefej* a Katona József Színházban." (Irony of the Tragedy: *Chickenhead* at the Katona József Theatre.) *Sz.* 1987 Jan.; 20(1): 1-5. Illus.: Photo. B&W. 6. Lang.: Hun.
Hungary: Budapest. 1986. Reviews of performances. ■György Spiró's play directed by Gábor Zsámbéki.

1872 Müller, Péter P. "Népi játék—mai érvénnyel. Az *Énekes madár* a Nemzetiben." (Folkloric Play with a Validity for Today: *The Song Bird* at the National Theatre.) *Sz.* 1987 Aug.; 20(8): 5-8. Illus.: Photo. B&W. 4. Lang.: Hun.
Hungary: Budapest. 1987. Reviews of performances. ■Áron Tamási's play at the National Theatre revised by the author in 1956, directed by Imre Kerényi.

1873 Nádra, Valéria. "Békés Pál: *A női partőrség szeme láttára.*" (Pál Békés: *In Sight of the Spar.*) *Krit.* 1987 Jun.(6): 40-41. Lang.: Hun.
Hungary: Budapest. 1987. Reviews of performances. ■Satire of modern intellectual life presented at the Madách Chamber Theatre directed by the actor Péter Huszti.

1874 Nagy, Ibolya Cs. "Csendes László ecsetvonásai." (László Csendes' Brush Strokes.) *FSM.* 1987 Feb.; 31 (8): 15. Illus.: Photo. B&W. 1. Lang.: Hun.
Hungary. Czechoslovakia. 1970-1987. Histories-sources. ■László Csendes, Hungarian actor living in Czechoslovakia.

1875 Nagy, István Attila. "Edward Bond: *A bolond.*" (Edward Bond: *The Fool.*) *Krit.* 1987 Feb.(2): 36. Lang.: Hun.
Hungary: Nyíregyháza. 1986. Reviews of performances. ■Play about John Clare, a 19th-century English poet, was presented at the Móricz Zsigmond Theatre under László Salamon Suba's direction.

1876 Nagy, István Attila. "Páskándi Géza: *Lélekharang.*" (Géza Páskándi: *Death Knell.*) *Krit.* 1987 Oct.(10): 32. Lang.: Hun.
Hungary: Nyíregyháza. 1987. Reviews of performances. ■First night of Géza Páskándi's play directed by Péter Léner at the Móricz Zsigmond Theatre in Nyíregyháza.

1877 Nánay, István. "A reformer kudarca. Az *Uri muri* Békéscsabán." (The Failure of the Reformist: *Gentlemen's Spree* in Békéscsaba.) *Sz.* 1987; 20(2): 8-10. Illus.: Photo. B&W. 2. Lang.: Hun.
Hungary: Békéscsaba. 1986. Reviews of performances. ■The play of Zsigmond Móricz directed by Mátyás Giricz at Jókai Theatre.

1878 Nánay, István. "*Catullus.* Füst Milán drámája a Katona József Színházban." (*Catullus*: The Play of Milán Füst at the Katona József Theatre.) *Sz.* 1987 June; 20(6): 1-6. Illus.: Photo. B&W. 5. Lang.: Hun.
Hungary: Budapest. 1987. Reviews of performances. ■Notes on the performance directed by Gábor Székely.

1879 Nánay, István. "Az új dráma esélyei. Dramaturgiai tanácskozás Egervárott." (The Chances of New Drama: Conference on Dramaturgy in Egervár.) *Sz.* 1987 Mar.; 20(3): 42-45. Illus.: Photo. B&W. 2. Lang.: Hun.
Hungary: Egervár. 1987. Critical studies. ■Review of the 2nd Open Forum organized by Hevesi Sándor Theatre in Zalaegerszeg in order to analyze Hungarian drama of today.

1880 Nánay, István. "A groteszk torzulásai. Örkény-drámák utóélete." (The Distorsions of Grotesque: After-Life of the Örkény Dramas.) *Sz.* 1987 Apr.; 20(4): 8-11. Illus.: Photo. B&W. 2. Lang.: Hun.
Hungary: Veszprém, Budapest, Debrecen. 1986-1987. Critical studies. ■Revival of Örkény's *Forgatókönyv (Screenplay)* at the Petőfi Theatre in Veszprém staged by István Paál and *Tóték (The Tót Family)* in two new performances at Népszinház staged by János Meczner and at Csokonai Theatre in Debrecen staged by István Pinczés.

1881 Nánay, István. "Öncélú ötletek színháza. A *Szentivánéji álom* Egerben és Szolnokon." (Theatre of l'art pour l'art: *A Midsummer Night's Dream* in Eger and Szolnok.) *Sz.* 1987 Jan.; 20(1): 14-18. Illus.: Photo. B&W. 3. Lang.: Hun.
Hungary: Eger, Szolnok. 1986. Reviews of performances. ■*A Midsummer Night's Dream* staged by Tibor Csizmadia at the Agria Festival in Eger and Szolnok performed by Szigligeti Theatre ensemble of Szolnok.

1882 Novák, Mária. "*Amerikai bölény.* David Mamet darabja Pécsett." (*American Buffalo*: David Mamet's Play in Pécs.) *Sz.* 1987 Mar.; 20(3): 39-40. Illus.: Photo. B&W. 1. Lang.: Hun.
Hungary: Pécs. 1986. Reviews of performances. ■David Mamet's play directed by Péter Dezsényi at the National Theatre of Pécs.

1883 Pályi, András. "Ami nyers és ami igaz. Petrusevszkaja: *Három lány kékben.*" (What Is Rude and What Is True. Petruševskaja: *Three Girls in Blue.*) *Sz.* 1987 Aug.; 20(8): 1-4. Illus.: Photo. B&W. 4. Lang.: Hun.
Hungary: Budapest. USSR. 1987. Reviews of performances. ■*Tri devuški v golubom (Three Girls in Blue)*, a controversial play by 'new wave' Soviet playwright Ljudmila Petruševskaja, directed by Tamás Ascher at Katona József Theatre.

1884 Pályi, András. "A kamaszkor apoteózisa? Az *Übü király* Boglárlellén." (Apotheosis of Teen-Age? *King Ubu* in Boglárlelle.) *Sz.* 1987 Nov.; 20(11): 15-18. Illus.: Photo. B&W. 2. Lang.: Hun.
Hungary: Boglárelle. 1987. Reviews of performances. ■Alfred Jarry's *Ubu roi* performed by Csiky Gergely Theatre of Kaposvar directed by the actor Andor Lukács.

1885 Pályi, András. "Szinházi előadások Budapesten. (Spiró György: *Csirkefej*, Páskándi Géza: *Vendégség*.)" (Theatre Performances in Budapest—György Spiró: *Chickenhead*, Géza Páskándi: *The Host and the Guest*.) *Jelenkor.* 1987 Jan.; 30(1): 60-65. Lang.: Hun.
Hungary: Budapest. 1986. Reviews of performances. ■Outstanding premieres of two contemporary Hungarian plays: György Spiró's *Chickenhead* at the Katona József Theatre and Géza Páskándi's *The Host and the Guest* at the Stage.

1886 Pályi, András. "Szinházi előadások Budapesten. Füst Milán: *Catullus*, Sarkadi Imre: *Oszlopos Simeon*." (Theatre Performances in Budapest. Milán Füst: *Catullus*, Imre Sarkadi: *The Man on the Pillar*.) *Jelenkor.* 1987 May; 30(5): 442-447. Lang.: Hun.
Hungary: Budapest. 1987. Reviews of performances. ■Analysis of two productions in Budapest.

1887 Pályi, András. "Szinházi előadások Budapesten." (Theatre Performances in Budapest.) *Jelenkor.* 1987 July/Aug.; 30(7-8): 701-706. Lang.: Hun.
Hungary: Budapest. 1987. Reviews of performances. ■Analysis of three productions of the Radnóti Miklós Theatre: *Lepkék a kalapon (Butterflies on Your Hat)* by László Márton, *Amit a szivedbe rejtesz (Hidden in Your Heart)* by Tamás Jordán and *Kölcsey* by Ferenc Kulin.

1888 Papp, Lajos. "Szinház, nehéz időkben. A Miskolci Nemzeti Szinház két újabb bemutatójáról." (Theatre in Hard Times: On Two New First Nights of the Miskolc National Theatre.) *Napj.* 1987 Mar.; 26 (3): 38. Lang.: Hun.
Hungary: Miskolc. 1987. Reviews of performances. ■Jean Anouilh's *Eurydice* directed by János Szűcs. Hungarian premiere of Boris Vian's *Tête de Méduse (Medusa Head)* directed by István Szőke at the National Theatre of Miskolc.

1889 Papp, Lajos. "Az üres ládafia rendjéről. *Galilei élete.* Bertolt Brechttől és más újabb bemutatók a Miskolci Nemzeti

DRAMA: —Performance/production

Szinházban.'' (On the Order of the Empty Drawer: Bertolt Brecht's *The Life of Galileo* and Other New Premieres at the National Theatre of Mickolc.) *Napj.* 1987 June; 26(6): 37-38. Lang.: Hun.

Hungary: Miskolc. 1987. Reviews of performances. ■New productions of the National Theatre of Miskolc focusing on Brecht's *Galileo*, awarded three of the prizes at the National Theatre Meeting for best direction, best actor and best stage design.

1890 Pomogáts, Béla. "Sütő András szolgálata.'' (The Ministry of András Sütő.) *Confes.* 1987; 11(4): 79-83. Illus.: Photo. B&W. 1. Lang.: Hun.

Hungary. Romania: Tîrgu-Mures. 1949-1987. Biographical studies. ■Survey on the career of Transylvanian prose-writer, novelist and playwright András Sütő, on the occasion of the 60th anniversary of his birth.

1891 Reményi, József Tamás. "'Ha megölsz, se látok nyomot'. Az Ördögök a Vígszínházban.'' (Even If You Kill Me I Do Not See Any Trace: *The Devils* at the Comedy Theatre.) *Sz.* 1987 Jan.; 20(1): 21-23. Illus.: Photo. B&W. 3. Lang.: Hun.

Hungary: Budapest. 1986. Reviews of performances. ■Tamás Ascher directs *Ördögök (The Devils)*, a stage adaptation of Dostojévskij's *Besy (The Possessed)*, at Vígszínház.

1892 Róna, Katalin. "Találkozás Csiszár Imrével. Fokozottabb az egyén felelőssége.'' (Interview with Imre Csiszár: The Individual's Responsibility Is Much Greater.) *FSM.* 1987 Apr.; 31(15): 6-7. Illus.: Photo. B&W. 1. Lang.: Hun.

Hungary: Miskolc. 1986-1987. Histories-sources. ■Imre Csiszár speaks about directing Brecht in the National Theatre of Miskolc, about how the theatre reflects reality, his experience as artistic director.

1893 Róna, Katalin. "Hárman *Az ügynök halálában*.'' (Three Actors in *Death of a Salesman*.) *Sz.* 1987 May; 20(5): 36-39. Illus.: Photo. B&W. 3. Lang.: Hun.

Hungary: Budapest. 1987. Reviews of performances. ■Géza Tordy as Willy Loman, Géza Hegedűs D. and Attila Kaszás as Biff and Happy in Arthur Miller's play at the Comedy Theatre.

1894 Róna, Katalin. "Arcok és szerepek a *Csirkefej*ben.'' (Faces and Roles in *Chickenhead*.) *Sz.* 1987 Apr.; 20(4): 30-32. Illus.: Photo. B&W. 3. Lang.: Hun.

Hungary: Budapest. 1986. Reviews of performances. ■György Spiró's play *Csirkefej (Chickenhead)*: main roles and the actors. Notes on the play staged by Gábor Zsámbéki at Katona József Theatre.

1895 Schreiber, György. "Fel a Csirkefejjel?! Spiró György: *Csirkefej*-Katona József Szinház.'' (Up with the Chickenhead?! György Spiró: *Chickenhead* at the Katona József Theatre.) *Mozgo.* 1987 Jan.; 13(1): 125-127. Lang.: Hun.

Hungary: Budapest. 1986. Reviews of performances. ■Production of *Chickenhead* by György Spiró at the Katona József Theatre, directed by Gábor Zsámbéki: a play about wasted lives, squandered love and the pain of human relations that no longer have meaning.

1896 Sík, Ferenc. "Kegyelmi kérvény. Az *Álomkommandó*ról.'' (Application for Pardon: On *Dream Commando*.) *Alfold.* 1987 June; 38(6): 50-51. Lang.: Hun.

Hungary. 1987. Histories-sources. ■Using the form of theatre within the theatre András Sütő presents the hell of Auschwitz concentration camp as the theme of a theatre production in our days, raising parallel issues of reactions of individual and collective conscience.

1897 Stuber, Andrea. "Szomory Dezső: *Takáts Alice*.'' (Dezső Szomory: *Alice Takáts*.) *Krit.* 1987 Oct.(10): 31-32. Lang.: Hun.

Hungary: Budapest. 1987. Reviews of performances. ■Dezső Szomory's play treats the problem of euthanasia. The drama presented at the Madách Chamber Theatre was staged by Tamás Puskás, who was first graduated with a diploma in acting and is now finishing his studies at the Stage Directing Department.

1898 Stuber, Andrea. "Roger Vitrac: *Viktor, avagy a gyermekuralom*.'' (Roger Vitrac: *Victor, or the Children in Power*.) *Krit.* 1987 Oct.(10): 32. Lang.: Hun.

Hungary: Pécs. 1987. Reviews of performances. ■Notes on the performance directed by István Szőke at the Pécs National Theatre.

1899 Szakolczay, Lajos. "Szerelem és halál a pincén. Határ Győző nyíregyházi honfoglalása.'' (Love and Death in the Cellar: Győző Határ's Conquest in Nyíregyháza.) *Sz.* 1987 Apr.; 20(4): 11-15. Illus.: Photo. B&W. 2. Lang.: Hun.

Hungary: Nyíregyháza. 1987. Critical studies. ■Notes on the world premiere of Győző Határ's *A patkánykirály (The King of the Rats)*, staged by László Salamon Suba at the Móricz Zsigmond Theatre.

1900 Szántó, Judit. "A Vörös Malom mint Golgota. *A búsképű lovag* a Hilton-szálló udvarán.'' (The Red Mill as Golgotha: *The Sad-Faced Knight* in the Court of Hotel Hilton.) *Sz.* 1987 Nov.; 20(11): 18-20. Illus.: Photo. B&W. 2.

Hungary: Budapest. 1987. Reviews of performances. ■In the offer of 1987 summer productions László Gyurkó's play *A búsképű lovag (The Sad-Faced Knight)* in the Dominican Court of Hotel Hilton directed by István Malgot.

1901 Szántó, Judit. "Határ Győző: *Patkánykirály*.'' (Győző Határ: *The King of the Rats*.) *Krit.* 1987 Mar.(3): 42. Lang.: Hun.

Hungary: Nyíregyháza. 1987. Reviews of performances. ■Határ's play for two actors, about a man and a woman living in a cellar, directed by László Salamon Suba at Móricz Zsigmond Theatre.

1902 Szántó, Judit. "Ketten, angolszászok. *Mint két tojás—A bolond*.'' (Two Anglo-Saxons: *Talley's Folly—The Fool*.) *Sz.* 1987 Feb.; 20(2): 27-31. Illus.: Photo. B&W. 3. Lang.: Hun.

Hungary: Dunaujváros, Nyíregyháza. 1986. Reviews of performances. ■Lanford Wilson's *Talley's Folly* of Dunaujváros and Edward Bond's *The Fool* performed by Móricz Zsigmond Theatre in Nyíregyháza put on the stage by László Salamon Suba.

1903 Szántó, Judit. "Háy Gyula: *Mohács*.'' (Gyula Háy: *The Mohács Disaster*.) *Krit.* 1987 Nov.(11): 34-35. Lang.: Hun.

Hungary: Gyula. 1987. Critical studies. ■The world premiere of this important Hungarian drama on a national turning point of our history took place in 1970 in Luzerne. Its present homecoming is both a literary discovery and a source of pure theatrical enjoyment. Director: Tamás Szirtes.

1904 Szántó, Judit. "Egy nap Károlyéknál. *Viktor avagy A gyermekuralom* című Vitrac-színmű Pécsett.'' (One Day with the Charleses. Vitrac Play in Pécs: *Victor or the Children Take Over*.) *Sz.* 1987 June; 20(6): 28-30. Illus.: Photo. B&W. 2. Lang.: Hun.

Hungary: Pécs. 1987. Reviews of performances. ■Collision of the director's and writer's intentions, or ideas on the Hungarian premiere of Roger Vitrac's *Victor ou les enfants au pouvoir (Victor, or The Children in Power)* directed by István Szőke on the stage of the National Theatre in Pécs.

1905 Szántó, Judit. "Kalifornia, palatáblán. A *Szabóky Zsigmond Rafael* a Játékszínben.'' (California, on the Chalkboard: *Zsigmond Rafael Szabóky* at The Stage.) *Sz.* 1987 Mar.; 20(3): 1-4. Illus.: Photo. B&W. 2. Lang.: Hun.

Hungary: Budapest. 1986. Reviews of performances. ■Dezső Szomory's play at The Stage directed by István Verebes.

1906 Szántó, Judit. "Dr. Takáts Alice. Szomory Dezső drámája a Madách Kamarában.'' (Dr. Alice Takáts: Dezső Szomory's Play at the Madách Chamber Theatre.) *Sz.* 1987 Aug.; 20(8): 9-11. Illus.: Photo. B&W. 2. Lang.: Hun.

Hungary: Budapest. 1987. Reviews of performances. ■The misinterpretation of the 'play of second choice': Dezső Szomory's play *Dr. Alice Takáts* with a slightly abbreviated title—at the Madách Chamber Theatre, directed by Tamás Puskás.

1907 Szigethy, Gábor. "Dajka Margit utolsó mosolya.'' (The Last Smile of Margit Dajkma.) *Sz.* 1987 Nov.; 20(11): 31-35. Illus.: Photo. B&W. 4. Lang.: Hun.

Hungary. 1907-1986. Biographical studies. ■Commemoration of late actress Margit Dajka.

1908 Szűcs, Katalin. "Spiró György: *Csirkefej*.'' (György Spiró: *Chickenhead*.) *Krit.* 1987 Jan.(1): 32-33. Lang.: Hun.

Hungary: Budapest. 1986. Reviews of performances. ■Gábor Zsámbéki's direction has lifted this sociologically authentic drama from naturalism. With tableau-like scenes he rendered the dramaturgy symbolic.

DRAMA: —Performance/production

1909 Szűcs, Katalin. "Vámos Miklós: *Világszezon.*" (Miklós Vámos: *World Tourist Season.*) *Krit.* 1987 Apr.(4): 36-37. Lang.: Hun.
Hungary: Szeged. 1986. Reviews of performances. ■Miklós Vámos' play was presented at the Szeged National Theatre in János Sándor's production.

1910 Szűcs, Katalin. "Németh László: *Harc a jólét ellen.*" (László Németh: *The Fight Against Prosperity.*) *Krit.* 1987 June(6): 40. Lang.: Hun.
Hungary: Budapest. 1986. Reviews of performances. ■The Thália Theatre put on a forgotten work by László Németh, one of the great Hungarian dramatists of our times. The play is a social satire on the intellectual heroes set in the period immediately after the World War II. It was staged by Károly Kazimir.

1911 Szűcs, Katalin. "A konformizálódás drámája. Calderón drámája a Radnóti Miklós Színpadon." (The Drama of Conformation: Calderón's Play at the Radnóti Miklós Theatre.) *Sz.* 1987 Feb.; 20(2): 31-33. Illus.: Photo. B&W. 2. Lang.: Hun.
Hungary: Budapest. 1987. Reviews of performances. ■Pedro Calderón de la Barca's *Life Is a Dream (La vida es sueño)* at the Radnóti Miklós Theatre directed by Miklós Szinetár.

1912 Szűcs, Katalin. "Bohumil Hrabal: *Őfelsége pincére voltam.*" (Bohumil Hrabal: *I Served the King of Britain.*) *Krit.* 1987 Sep.(9): 34-35. Lang.: Hun.
Hungary: Nyíregyháza. 1987. Reviews of performances. ■A stage montage of writings by Bohumil Hrabal, the excellent Czech author, guest-directed by Ivo Krobot, of the Cinoherny Club of Prague at the Móricz Zsigmond Theatre in Nyíregyháza.

1913 Szűcs, Katalin. "Alfred Jarry: *Übü király.*" (Alfred Jarry: *King Ubu.*) *Krit.* 1987 Oct.(10): 31. Lang.: Hun.
Hungary: Kaposvár. 1987. Reviews of performances. ■The Csiky Gergely Theatre of Kaposvár staged Alfred Jarry's grotesque play, with Andor Lukáks, a leading actor of the company, directing the play.

1914 Szűcs, Katalin. "Szomory-szomor. Koós Olga és Bozóky István Szomory-szerepben." (Szomory-Sadness: Olga Koós and István Bozóky in Szomory Roles.) *Sz.* 1987 Apr.; 20(4): 33. Illus.: Photo. B&W. 1. Lang.: Hun.
Hungary: Budapest. 1987. Reviews of performances. ■Olga Koós and István Bozóky in the role of the grandparents in Dezső Szomory's play *Szabóky Zsigmond Rafael (Zsigmond Rafael Szabóky)* at The Stage.

1915 Szűcs, Katalin. "Történelmi színlelők. Páskándi Géza Lélekharangja Nyíregyházán." (Historical Pretenders: Géza Páskándi's *Death Knell* in Nyíregyháza.) *Sz.* 1987 Aug.; 20(8): 20-22. Illus.: Photo. B&W. 3. Lang.: Hun.
Hungary: Nyíregyháza. 1987. Reviews of performances. ■Notes on the world premiere performance directed by Péter Léner at the Móricz Zsigmond Theatre.

1916 Tarján, Tamás. "Próbababák Marivaux: *A szerelem és véletlen játéka—Miskolcon.*" (Mannequins. Marivaux: *The Game of Love and Chance* in Miskolc.) *Sz.* 1987 July; 20(7): 33-35. Illus.: Photo. B&W. 2. Lang.: Hun.
Hungary: Miskolc. 1987. Reviews of performances. ■Marivaux's *Le jeu de l'amour et du hasard* at the National Theatre of Miskolc directed by Péter Valló.

1917 Tarján, Tamás. "Jules Romains: *Knock.*" *Krit.* 1987 Jan.(1): 35. Lang.: Hun.
Hungary: Kaposvár. 1986. Reviews of performances. ■Romains' play presented by the Csiky Gergely Theatre in Kaposvár directed by the actor Gábor Máté.

1918 Tarján, Tamás. "Corneille: *L'Illusion comique.*" (Corneille: *The Comic Illusion.*) *Krit.* 1987 Apr.(4): 36. Illus.: Photo. B&W. 1. Lang.: Hun.
Hungary: Budapest. 1986. Reviews of performances. ■Pierre Corneille's play about the nature of acting and reality directed by János Szikora at Katona József Theatre.

1919 Tarján, Tamás. "Mrozek: *Egy nyári nap.*" (Mrozek: *A Summer's Day.*) *Krit.* 1987 July(7): 44. Lang.: Hun.

Hungary: Budapest. 1987. Reviews of performances. ■Sławomir Mrozek's *Letni dzień (A Summer's Day)* on the stage of Thália Stúdió directed by Zoltán Seregi.

1920 Tarján, Tamás. "Petrusevszkaja: *Három lány kékben.*" (Petruševskaja: *Three Girls in Blue.*) *Krit.* 1987 Sep.(9): 31. Lang.: Hun.
Hungary: Budapest. 1987. Reviews of performances. ■Ljudmila Petruševskaja's play about today's Soviet reality, reaffirmed the appeal of director Tamás Ascher.

1921 Tarján, Tamás. "Csatornátlan ország. *A tanítónő* Zalaegerszegen." (Country Without Canalization: The *Schoolmistress* in Zalaegerszeg.) *Sz.* 1987 Feb.; 20(2): 5-8. Illus.: Photo. B&W. 2. Lang.: Hun.
Hungary: Zalaegerszeg. 1986. Reviews of performances. ■Sándor Bródy's play at the Hevesi Sándor Theatre directed by Péter Tömöry.

1922 Tarján, Tamás. "*Velencei terecske.* Goldoni-bemutató Kaposváron." (*Il campiello*: First Night of a Goldoni Play in Kaposvár.) *Somo.* 1987 July-Aug.; 15(4): 96-98. Lang.: Hun.
Hungary: Kaposvár. 1987. Reviews of performances. ■Hungarian premiere of Carlo Goldoni's play at the Csiky Gergely Theatre directed by Tamás Ascher.

1923 Tarján, Tamás. "A mű működ. A *Lepkék a kalapon* bemutatójáról." (The Work is Operating: On the First Night of *Butterflies on Your Hat.*) *Sz.* 1987; 20(5): 19-23. Illus.: Photo. B&W. 3. Lang.: Hun.
Hungary: Budapest. 1987. Reviews of performances. ■László Márton's play *Lepkék a Kalapon (Butterflies on Your Hat)* based on Elek Gozdu's novel *Köd (The Fog)* at the Radnóti Miklós Theatre directed by István Verebes.

1924 Tarján, Tamás. "Cockpit. Békés Pál: *A női partőrség szeme láttára.*" (Cockpit: Pál Békés: *In Sight of the Spar.*) *Sz.* 1987 Apr.; 20(4): 1-3. Illus.: Photo. B&W. 2. Lang.: Hun.
Hungary: Budapest. 1987. Reviews of performances. ■The comedy of Pál Békés directed by Péter Huszti at the Madách Chamber Theatre.

1925 Tarján, Tamás. "Arany, ezüst, ólom. Két kecskeméti bemutatóról." (Gold, Silver, Lead: On Two Premieres in Kecskemét.) *Forras.* 1987 June; 19(6): 91-93. Lang.: Hun.
Hungary: Kecskemét. 1987. Reviews of performances. ■Shakespeare's *The Merchant of Venice* under Árpád Jutocsa Hegyi's direction and László Németh's *Villám fénynél (By the Stroke of Lightning)* directed by Attila Seprődi Kiss at the Katona József Theatre.

1926 Tarján, Tamás. "Éjfájdalmú szinjáték. A *Csongor és Tünde* Zalaegerszegen." (Stage Play of the Pain of Night: *Csongor and Tünde* in Zalaegerszeg.) *Sz.* 1987 Dec.; 20(12): 12-16. Illus.: Photo. B&W. 3. Lang.: Hun.
Hungary: Zalaegerszeg. 1987. Reviews of performances. ■Mihály Vörösmarty's 'fairy-play' *Csongor and Tünde* directed by Béla Merő at Hevesi Sándor Színház.

1927 Ungár, Júlia. "A *Koldusopera* Magyarországon. Az 1929-es bemutatótól napjainkig." (*The Three Penny Opera* in Hungary: From the First Night in 1929 Up to the Present.) *Sz.* 1987 June; 20(6): 35-39. Lang.: Hun.
Hungary. 1929-1987. Historical studies. ■Review of the stagings of *Die Dreigroschenoper (The Three Penny Opera)* in Hungary and short evaluation in the light of contemporary critics.

1928 Varga, György. "Hrabal-idézés Nyíregyházán." (Hrabal Citation in Nyíregyháza.) *Mozgo.* 1987 Sep.; 13(9): 81-84. Lang.: Hun.
Hungary: Nyíregyháza. 1987. Histories-sources. ■Ivo Krobot of Cinoherní Klub in Prague directed a stage adaptation of works by Czech writer Bohumil Hrabal (*Obsluhoval jsem anglického krale [I Served the King of Britain]*) at Móricz Zsigmond Theatre, under the title *Őfelsége pincére voltam.*

1929 Zsigmond, Gyula. "*Szent Bertalan nappala.* Szabó Magda történelmi drámája a Madách Szinházban." (*St. Bartholomew's Day*: Magda Szabó's Historical Play at the Madách Theatre.) *Confes.* 1987; 11(1): 96-98. Lang.: Hun.
Hungary: Budapest. 1987. Reviews of performances. ■The hero of Magda Szabó's new play is Mihály Csokonai Vitéz, 18th-century

DRAMA: —Performance/production

Hungarian poet, student of the Calvinist College of Debrecen, who presented a danger to the famed school with his rebel Jacobin ideas.

1930 Bharucha, Rustom. "Kroetz's *Request Concert* in India. Part One: Calcutta." *NTQ.* 1987 Aug.; 3(11): 241-257. Illus.: Photo. Print. B&W. 4. Lang.: Eng.
India: Calcutta. 1980. Critical studies. ■Kroetz's play transposed to Calcutta: theatrical and social problems posed by the transposition, and similarities and differences between East and West which were revealed.

1931 Bharucha, Rustom. "Kroetz's *Request Concert* in India, Part Two: Bombay." *NTQ.* 1987 Nov.; 3(12): 377-388. Illus.: Photo. B&W. 1. Lang.: Eng.
India: Bombay. 1986. Critical studies. ■Franz Xaver Kroetz's *Wunschkonzert (Request Concert)* transposed to Bombay, the perceptions of actress Sulabha Deshpande concerning her role and its technical requirements.

1932 Dasgupta, Gautam. "*The Mahabharata*: Peter Brook's 'Orientalism'." *PerAJ.* 1987; 10(3): 9-16. 4. Lang.: Eng.
India. USA: New York, NY. 400 B.C.-1987 A.D. Critical studies. ■Element of orientalism and other interpretive choices in Peter Brook's production of *The Mahabharata*.

1933 Gabnai, Katalin. "Mit ér az ember, ha ír? Színházi esték." (What is the Man Worth if he Writes? Theatre Evenings in Dublin.) *Sz.* 1987 Apr.; 20(4): 46-48. Illus.: Photo. B&W. 1. Lang.: Hun.
Ireland: Dublin. 1987. Reviews of performances. ■Notes on three theatre evenings in Dublin.

1934 Griffin, Christopher. "Visions and Revisions." *ThIr.* 1985 Spr-Sum; 9/10: 145-151. Lang.: Eng.
Ireland: Dublin. 1900-1985. Histories-sources. ■Eric Bentley discusses his production of *La Casa de Bernarda Alba (The House of Bernarda Alba)* at the Abbey Theatre, and evaluates the dramas of Shaw and O'Neill.

1935 Mason, Patrick. "Directing *The Gigli Concert*: An Interview." *IUR.* 1987 Spr; 17(1): 100-113. Notes. Lang.: Eng.
Ireland: Dublin. 1983. Histories-sources. ■A 1987 interview (by Christopher Murray) of Patrick Mason, director of *The Gigli Concert* at the Abbey Theatre, 1983. Emphasis is on relationship between script and director, other productions, evaluation of Murphy as a playwright.

1936 Blumert, Ruth. "Edna Fliedel, Sachkanit yim Nochechout." (Actress with Presence, an Interview with Edna Fliedel.) *Bamah.* 1987; 22(108): 86-96. Illus.: Photo. B&W. 7. [The Meir Margalith Prize 1987.] Lang.: Heb.
Israel: Tel Aviv. 1980-1987. Histories-sources. ■Actress Edna Fliedel's role in the development of original theatre in Israel.

1937 Blumert, Ruth. "AhaBamay Hanan Snir-Achdut AhaniGudim." (Unifying the Opposites, an Interview with Hanan Snir.) *Bamah.* 1987; 22(108): 97-109. Illus.: Photo. B&W. 6. Lang.: Heb.
Israel. 1976-1987. Histories-sources. ■Development of a director and his achievement in the theatre and opera, working with students and professional actors.

1938 Chu, Fa. "Eharot lebimhi *Vatslav*." (Some Comments on the Directing of *Vatslave*.) *Bamah.* 1987; 21(107): 73-75. Illus.: Photo. Print. B&W. 4. Lang.: Heb.
Israel: Jerusalem. Poland. 1984-1984. Histories-sources. ■Director's approach to the play *Vatslave* by Sławomir Mrożek: political and psychological interpretation.

1939 Scolnicov, Hanna. "*The Marriage of Wit and Wisdom.*" *MET.* 1987; 9(1): 64-69. Notes. Illus.: Photo. 5. Lang.: Eng.
Israel: Jerusalem. 1987. Reviews of performances. ■Production by David Parry of Merbury's interlude in the Botanical Garden of the Hebrew University, Jerusalem.

1940 Tal, Ada. "Lengoss Be-Chekhov." (Tasting Chechov.) *Bamah.* 1987; 21(107): 76-78. Illus.: Photo. Print. B&W. 1. Lang.: Heb.
Israel: Tel Aviv. USSR. 1987. Histories-sources. ■The actress Ada Tal's experience of performing in Chekhov's *Diadia Vania (Uncle Vanya)* as Sonia and then again twenty years later as Marina. Character approaches and analysis.

1941 Bassnett, Susan. "Pirandello's Debut as Director: The Opening of the Teatro d'Arte." *NTQ.* 1987 Nov.; 3(12): 349-351. Notes. Lang.: Eng.
Italy. 1925-1928. Historical studies. ■Events leading to the opening of Pirandello's company Teatro d'Arte, and its inaugural productions.

1942 Genet, Jean. *Conversation with Hubert Fichte.* Milan: Ubulibri; 1987. 87 pp. (La collanina.) Lang.: Ita.
Italy. 1975-1985. Biographical studies. ■Italian translation of *Hubert Fichte Jean Genet*.

1943 Giardi, Orietta. "Sulle principali compagnie che recitavano a Venezia alla fine del Settecento." (On the Principal Companies Performing in Venice at the End of the Eighteenth Century.) *BiT.* 1987; 5/6: 219-233. Lang.: Ita.
Italy: Venice. 1700-1800. Historical studies. ■Goldoni's reform and the ensuing change of repertoire contribute to causing great changes in the structure and organization of comic companies.

1944 Meldolesi, Claudio. *Fra Totò e Gadda. Sei invenzioni sprecate dal teatro italiano.* (Between Totò and Gadda: Six Inventions Wasted by Italian Theatre.) Rome: Bulzoni; 1987. 209 pp. (Memorie di teatro 4.) Pref. Index. Lang.: Ita.
Italy. 1930-1950. Critical studies. ■Examples of missed opportunities in modern Italian theatre.

1945 Róna, Katalin. "'Avagy a szinházi szenvedély'. Olaszországi jegyzet." ('Or the Theatre Passion': Notes from Italy.) *FSM.* 1987; 31(27): 8. Illus.: Photo. B&W. 1. Lang.: Hun.
Italy: Milan. 1947-1987. Historical studies. ■Brief survey of the history of Piccolo Teatro di Milano, Giorgio Strehler's theatre, on the occasion of its 40th anniversary.

1946 Scaccia, Mario. "Io e Molière." (Molière and I.) *Ariel.* 1987; 2(2): 96-103. Lang.: Ita.
Italy. 1949-1987. Histories-sources. ■The Italian actor Mario Scaccia narrates his interpretations of Molierian characters.

1947 Tinterri, Alessandro; Bassnett, Susan, transl. "*The Gods of the Mountain* at the Oceanside Theatre." *NTQ.* 1987 Nov.; 3 (12): 352-357. Illus.: Photo. Sketches. B&W. 10. Lang.: Eng.
Italy. 1923-1928. Historical studies. ■The encounter between Pirandello and Lord Dunsany during Pirandello's production of *I pazzi sulla montagna (The Gods of the Mountain)* by Alessandro De Stefani at his Teatro d'Arte.

1948 Trousdell, Richard. "Giorgio Strehler in Rehearsal." *TDR.* 1986 Win; 30(4): 65-83. Biblio. Illus.: Photo. B&W. 11. Lang.: Eng.
Italy. 1944-1986. Biographical studies. ■Biographical study of Giorgio Strehler's direction of *L'illusion comique (The Comic Illusion)*: a rehearsal journal of how leading directors present productions.

1949 Vasile, Turi. "Crisi della drammaturgia italiana e responsabilità della critica." (The Crisis of Italian Dramaturgy and the Responsibility of Criticism.) *Ariel.* 1987; 2(1): 84-90. Lang.: Ita.
Italy. 1987. Critical studies. ■A report on some aspects of Italian theatrical life discussed at a conference held at the Ente Teatrale Italiano.

1950 "Arashi no yō na *gekisei*, kaze no yōna *chūkan*." (Storm-like *Theatricality*, Wind-like *Central Feeling*.) *Sg.* 1987 Apr.; 409: 22-27. Illus.: Handbill. Photo. B&W. 5. Lang.: Jap.
Japan: Tokyo. 1987. Critical studies. ■Comments on four plays in the light of director Betsuyaku Minoru's statement that recent drama tends to deal only with *daijōkyō*, a large situation, and *shōjōkyō*, a small situation. *Hanare no aru ie (A House with an Annex)*, performed by Mingei, is seen as having *chūjōkyō*, a medium situation. *Black Comedy*, performed by Hakuhinkan Production, *Ashes*, performed by RINK and *Biloxi Blues*, performed by Parco and Shō-kikaku also discussed.

1951 Duró, Gyözö. "Távol-keleti színjátékok—másodkézből." (Plays from the Far-East—Secondhand.) *Sz.* 1987 Feb.; 20(2): 36-42. Illus.: Photo. B&W. 3. Lang.: Hun.
Japan. Indonesia. 1986. Reviews of performances. ■Three interesting but not original performances from the program of the Budapest Artistic Weeks of 1986 autumn: 'buyo' performances of the Fuji Dance

DRAMA: —Performance/production

and Music ensemble, professional show of Tom Cots *Puputan* on the dance theatre of Bali and performance of the Tōtōkai Nō Theatre.

1952   Földes, Anna. "*Tóték*, Tojamából." (*The Tót Family* from Toyama.) *Nvilag.* 1987 Sep.; 32(9): 1407-1409. Lang.: Hun.
Japan: Toyama. 1986. Reviews of performances. ■According to director István Pinczés, it was the express request of the Toyama theatre not to 'Japanize' the play, but to show typical Hungarian characters and situations.

1953   Ōtori, Hidenaga. "Sekai wa b-kyu kankaku." (Society's Low-Class Sensations.) *Sg.* 1987 Feb.; 407: 22-27. Illus.: Handbill. Photo. B&W. 9. Lang.: Jap.
Japan: Tokyo. 1986. Critical studies. ■New themes (e.g., crime, computer games) in Japanese theatre. Popularity of little theatres performing in non-theatrical venues. Discussion of *Keredo sukuriin ippai no hoshi (But the Screen Is Filled with Stars)*, performed by Shōma, *Nemuranai boku no yoru (My Sleepless Night)*, performed by Yūkikai Zenjidō shiatā and *Hassha-bai (Hushabye)*, performed by Daisan butai.

1954   Ōtori, Hidenaga. "Ofu shiatā dansō." (Some Comments on the Little Theatres.) *Sg.* 1987 June; 411: 18-23. Illus.: Photo. B&W. 6. Lang.: Jap.
Japan: Tokyo. 1987. Critical studies. ■Difficulty of interpreting the plays of Marguerite Duras on stage, problems of out-door theatre. Focus on *Agatha* and *The Passport*, performed by Bungakuza Atorie no kai, *Shin yozora no rū sanraizu sansetto in sunshine (New Lipstick of Night Sky, Sunrise Sunset in Sunshine)*, performed by Hihōreibankan, *Namida nashi ni tamanegi no kawa o muku hōhō (How to Peel an Onion without Tears)*, performed by Yūkikai Zenjidō shiatā and *Budori– Nemurenu natsu no tsuki (Budori, Sleepless Summer Moon)*, performed by 21 Seiki Fox.

1955   Ōtori, Hidenaga. "Ōi naru tanjun, karei naru kūkyo." (Great Simplicity, Gorgeous Emptiness.) *Sg.* 1987 May; 410: 22-27. Illus.: Photo. B&W. 7. Lang.: Jap.
Japan: Tokyo. 1960-1987. Critical studies. ■Comments on subjects formerly considered taboo on the Japanese stage, including freaks. Discusses *Uketsuke (The Reception)*, performed by Daisan erochika, *Heya (A Room)*, performed by Katatsumuri no kai and Hayūza gekijō, and *Yasashii inu (A Gentle Dog)*, performed by Ryūzanji jimushō. Focus on *Carmen*, with emphasis on Peter Brook's staging. Related to Music-Drama: Opera.

1956   Sasaki, Mikiro. "Kotoba wa shishimura no uchi ni hagukamareru." (Words Are Nurtured within One's Body.) *Sg.* 1987 Mar.; 408: 28-33. Illus.: Handbill. Photo. B&W. 8. Lang.: Jap.
Japan: Tokyo. 1986-1987. Critical studies. ■Discusses *Hanshin (Demigod)*, performed by Yume no yūminsha, *Hinmin kurabu (A Slum Club)* by Tōhō, *Kokoro enerugii–Hagoromo densetsu (Heart Energy: The Tale of the Feather Robe)* by Parco and Kansai Superstudio and *Nanbonomonjai! My Love (Who Cares?! My Love)* by Tsukumo Hajime. Focuses on Nakamura za's *Taketori monogatari–Honda shōgakkō hen (The Tale of the Bamboo Princess–Honda Elementary School Version)*, an experimental treatment of a poem.

1957   Sasaki, Mikiro. "Henbō no tāningu pointo." (A Turning Point.) *Sg.* 1987 Apr.; 409: 28-33. Illus.: Handbill. Photo. B&W. 6. Lang.: Jap.
Japan: Tokyo. 1987. Critical studies. ■Analysis of *Sindbad High Noon*, performed by Jitensha konkuriito, *Kago no tori (Birds in a Cage)*, performed by Hakuhinkan Productions. Focus on *Dai manzai (A Big Comic Dialogue)*, performed by Tokyo ichikumi: about changes in Japan after World War II. The play locates a turning point in 1964, the year of the Tokyo Olympics.

1958   Sasaki, Mikiro. "Gekisakka no hangeki." (Counterattacks from Playwrights.) *Sg.* 1987 Feb.; 407: 28-33. Illus.: Handbill. Photo. B&W. 9. Lang.: Jap.
Japan: Tokyo. 1986. Critical studies. ■Overview of the season highlights *Kaze no eki (The Station of Winds)* by Ohta Shogo, performed by Tenkei gekijō, *Good Night Oyasuminasai (Good Night)*, by Sugama Yu, performed by Manji and *Yume sarite, Orphe (The Dream Is Gone, Orpheus)* by Shimizu Kunio, performed by Mokutōsha.

1959   Sasaki, Mikiro. "Toshi no katachi." (Shape of a City.) *Sg.* 1987 June; 411: 24-29. Illus.: Photo. B&W. 9. Lang.: Jap.
Japan: Tokyo. 1987. Critical studies. ■Influence on theatre of the dependency on signs in everyday life. Sense of space replacing the idea of ground in people's minds. Comments on *Kaze no takishīdo (A Tuxedo of the Winds)*, performed by Tokyo vōdovirushō and Minami-kouchi banzai ichiza, *Za Sumidagawa (The Sumida River)*, performed by Hanagumi shibai, *The Passport* and *Agatha*, performed by Bungakuza- Atorie no kai.

1960   Sasaki, Mikiro. "Kankyaku to butai no deaikata." *Sg.* 1987 May; 410: 28-33. Illus.: Photo. B&W. 7. Lang.: Jap.
Japan: Tokyo. 1960-1987. Critical studies. ■Comments on *Carmen*, directed by Peter Brook, and recalls how the actors in Brook's *King Lear* tour were influenced by audience members in different countries. Also *Freaks* performed by Daisan erochika and *The Real Inspector Hound* performed by En.

1961   Watanabe, Tamotsu. "Kaze no eki no kandō." (Impressed by *The Station of Winds*.) *Sg.* 1987 Feb.; 407: 34-39. Illus.: Handbill. Photo. B&W. 8. Lang.: Jap.
Japan: Tokyo. 1986. Critical studies. ■Discusses *Kaze no eki (The Station of Winds)* by Ohta Shogo, performed by Tenkei gekijō, *Yumeyumeshii onnatachi (The Dreaming Women)*, performed by Bungakuza, *Kyubikku naitomeā (The Cubic Nightmare)*, performed by Tao and *Nemuranai boku no yoru (My Sleepless Night)*, performed by Yūkikai Zenjidō shiatā.

1962   Watanabe, Tamotsu. "Shōgekiteki na *Konna hanashi*." (A Shocking *Story Like This*.) *Sg.* 1987 Mar.; 408: 34-39. Illus.: Handbill. Photo. B&W. 6. Lang.: Jap.
Japan: Tokyo. 1987. Critical studies. ■Analysis of *Teiburu manā (Table Manners)* performed by Hayūza gekijō, *Jenii no shōzō (Portrait of Jenny)* performed by Katsuta jimosho and *Kokoro enerugii–Hagoromo densetsu (Heart Energy: The Tale of the Feather Robe)* performed by Parco and Kansai Superstudio. Focus on *Konna hanashi (A Story Like This)*, performed by Chijinkai, about apartheid. Discusses problems of performing translated plays.

1963   Watanabe, Tamotsu. "Guntai shibai no munashisa." (Vanity in Military Plays.) *Sg.* 1987 Apr.; 409: 34-39. Illus.: Photo. B&W. 6. Lang.: Jap.
Japan: Tokyo. 1944-1987. Critical studies. ■Criticism of overly optimistic Japanese versions of two plays about the military: Charles Fuller's *A Soldier's Play*, performed by Atorie Dankan and Yasuzawa jimūsho and Neil Simon's *Biloxi Blues*, performed by Parco and Shō-kikaku. Also discusses *Dai manzai (A Big Comic Dialogue)*, performed by Tokyo ichikumi and *Hanare no aru ie (A House with an Annex)*, performed by Mingei.

1964   Watanabe, Tamotsu. "Gekihyōka satsujin jiken." (Murder of a Theatre Critic.) *Sg.* 1987 May; 410: 34-39. Illus.: Photo. B&W. 9. Lang.: Jap.
Japan: Tokyo. 1987. Critical studies. ■Lack of plot in real life related to treatment of dramatic plot in *Carmen*, directed by Peter Brook, and *Puzzler*, performed by Shōma. Also discusses *Satsujin no sutōrī– Gekihyōka satsujin jiken (A Story of Murder–Murder of a Theatre Critic)*, performed by Theatre Daikanyama, *The Real Inspector Hound*, performed by En, *Freaks*, performed by Daisan erochika and *Zeami* by Yamazaki Masakazu.

1965   Watanabe, Tamotsu. "Shūkaku-nashi." (Nothing Special.) *Sg.* 1987 June; 411: 30-35. Illus.: Photo. B&W. 8. Lang.: Jap.
Japan: Tokyo. 1987. Critical studies. ■Criticizes choice of plays: *The Passport* and *Agatha*, performed by Bungakuza Atorie no kai, *Shārokku Hōmuzu Tantei monogatari–Chi no jūjika (Sherlock Holmes Mystery Tale–The Crucifer of Blood)*, performed by Parco and Office Nine.

1966   Watanabe, Tamotsu. "Karaashi." (A False Step.) *Sg.* 1987 Jan.; 406: 38-43. Illus.: Handbill. Photo. B&W. 8. Lang.: Jap.
Japan: Tokyo. 1986. Critical studies. ■Overview of six plays of the season: *Sarada satsujin jiken (A Murder Caused by a Salad Pack)*, by Yamazaki Tetsu, performed by Bungakuza Atorie no kai, *Harvey* performed by Hayūza gekijō, *Yūwaku megami (The Tempting Goddess)* performed by Waseda doramakan, *Tenraku no nochi ni (After the Fall)*

DRAMA: —Performance/production

by Arthur Miller, directed by Betsuyaku Minoru and performed by the Mingei, *Aimaya (The Obscure House)* performed by Main Stage MGS and *Karasawagi (Much Ado About Nothing)* by William Shakespeare performed by the Raimingu. Focuses on the direction of Betsuyaku Minoru.

1967 Go, Sul-Bong. "Yonkilon." (Theory of Acting.) 68-77 in *The Development of Korean Modern Theatre in the First Half of the Twentieth Century.* Seoul: Shin Hyup Theatre Company; 1986. 105 pp. Lang.: Kor.
Korea. 1986. Histories-sources. ■A personal view of acting.

1968 Go, Sul-Bong. "Hanguk yunguk-bansaeki." (The Development of Modern Korean Theatre in the First Half of the Twentieth Century.) 87-105 in *The Development of Korean Modern Theatre in the First Half of the Twentieth Century.* Seoul: Shin Hyup Theatre Company; 1986. 105 pp. Lang.: Kor.
Korea. 1900-1986. Histories-specific. ■The development of modern Korean theatre.

1969 Ha, Tae-jin. "Kongyoun Seonghyang." (The Performance Disposition.) *KTR.* 1987 Aug.; 8(1): 74-77. Illus.: Plan. B&W. 1. Lang.: Kor.
Korea: Seoul. 1987. Critical studies. ■Overview of the past theatre season, preview of the following.

1970 Kang, Gyu-Sik. "Hangukui yungukin." (Korean Actors and Theatre People of the Past.) 49-66 in *The Development of Korean Modern Theatre in the First Half of the Twentieth Century.* Seoul: Shin Hyup Theatre Company; 1986. 105 pp. Lang.: Kor.
Korea. 1900-1986. Biographical studies. ■Biographies of Korean actors and other theatre people of the twentieth century.

1971 Kim, Ki-Tae. "Yeonkŭk Balgeon Juhae Yoso." (What Makes a Play Good or Bad.) *KTR.* 1987 June; 6(1): 74-77. Illus.: Photo. Plan. 1. Lang.: Kor.
Korea: Seoul. 1986-1987. Empirical research. ■Essay, based on a survey, on factors contributing to the continued development of Korean theatre.

1972 Kim, Kyung-Ok. "Hankuk Sokŭkjang ŭi Hyosī." (The First Instance of Korean Little Theatre.) *KTR.* 1987 June ; 6(1): 42-45. Illus.: Photo. B&W. 1. Lang.: Kor.
Korea: Seoul. 1908-1965. Historical studies. ■History of Wonkaksa, the first Korean Little Theatre, and its influence.

1973 Kim, Mido. "Yonguk Yu 1930s." (Plays of the 1930s.) *KTR.* 1987 Mar.; 3(1): 21-26. Illus.: Photo. Pntg. Diagram. Lang.: Kor.
Korea: Seoul. 1930-1939. Historical studies. ■History of Korean theatre in the thirties. Includes photographs.

1974 Capetillo, Manuel. "*Miss fuegos artificiales*: yo he ganado: yo he perdido." (*Miss Firecracker*: I Have Won, I Have Lost.) *UMex.* 1987 Nov.; 42(442): 36-38. Illus.: Dwg. B&W. 1. Lang.: Spa.
Mexico: Mexico City. 1987. Reviews of performances. ■Review of a production of Beth Henley's *The Miss Firecracker Contest* and its use of language as socio-political commentary.

1975 Muro, María. "Teatro Experimental en nuestras días." (Experimental Theatre in Our Time.) *Universidad de Mexico.* 1987 May; 17(436): 36-39. Illus.: Photo. B&W. 3. Lang.: Spa.
Mexico: Mexico City. 1987. Critical studies. ■Various experimental theatre groups in Mexico City: absurdist theatrical techniques and performances.

1976 Muro, María. "*I Poli (El Pueblo)*: Obra Modelo del teatro." (*I Poli (The Town)*: A Model Work of the Contemporary Theatre.) *Universidad de Mexico.* 1987 Mar.; 17(434). Illus.: Photo. B&W. 2. Lang.: Spa.
Mexico: Mexico City. 1987. Reviews of performances. ■Review of *I Poli (The Town)* by Alejandra Gutierrez, based on Greek theatre tradition and performed in absurdist style. Grp/movt: Absurdism.

1977 Muro, María. "*La Alegría de Las Tandas*." (*The Happiness of the Groups.*) *Universidad de Mexico.* 1987 Apr.; 17(435): 42-43. Illus.: Photo. B&W. 2. Lang.: Spa.

Mexico: Mexico City. 1987. Reviews of performances. ■Review of *La Alegría de las Tandas (The Happiness of the Groups)* by Enrique Alonso, a satire of daily life in Mexico.

1978 Muro, María. "Más Alla Del Absurdo." (Beyond the Absurd.) *Universidad de Mexico.* 1987 Jan.; 12(432): 46-47. Illus.: Photo. B&W. 1. Lang.: Spa.
Mexico: Mexico City. 1987. Reviews of performances. ■Review of production of *El Balcón (The Balcony)* by Jean Genet. Development of language, symbolism and staging.

1979 Blokdijk, Tom. "'Ik wind me op over het onwaasachtige'." ('I Get Agitated by Untruthfulness'.) *Toneel.* 1987 Mar.; 3(6): 4-9. Illus.: Photo. B&W. 7. Lang.: Dut.
Netherlands. 1987. Histories-sources. ■Interview with Frans Strijards, enfant terrible of the Dutch theatre, director and playwright. Discussion of his production of *Višněvyj sad (The Cherry Orchard)* at Art & Pro, his new theatre group with fragment of his play *Hensbergen*.

1980 Houtman, Dirkje. "Acteur Jules Hamel: 'Ik laat liever niets zien dan onzin'." (Actor Jules Hamel: 'I'd Rather Show Nothing Than Show Nonsense'.) *Toneel.* 1987 Mar.; 3(5): 18-22. Illus.: Photo. B&W. 4. Lang.: Dut.
Netherlands. 1987. Histories-sources. ■Interview with actor Jules Hamel and his role as 'angry young man'. His association of 14 years with Centrum. His ideas of acting.

1981 Oranje, Hans. "Het heroïsch temperament." (The Heroic Temperament.) *Toneel.* 1987 June; 6(4): 6-9. Illus.: Photo. B&W. 3. Lang.: Dut.
Netherlands. USA. 1987. Historical studies. ■Production of *Ajax* directed by Peter Sellars, adapted from the original by Sophocles by Robert Auletta, performed by the American National Theatre at Holland Festival. Comparison with original text. Athena as the 'American dream'.

1982 Rutten, André. "Veertig Jaar Nederlands Toneel XV (slot)." (Forty Years of Dutch Theatre XV.) *Toneel.* 1987 Feb.; 2 (4): 35-37. Illus.: Photo. B&W. 3. Lang.: Dut.
Netherlands. 1975-1985. Historical studies. ■Final part of a history of Dutch theatre post-World War II. Growth of small experimental theatres and workshops. Financial room for new groups. Return to 'new' classics (Shaw, Ibsen). Actor becomes the focal point. Erik Vos's De Appel is formed in The Hague as the new adventure-seeking theatre group.

1983 Törnqvist, Egil. "Strindberg i Nederländerna." (Strindberg in the Netherlands.) *Strind.* 1987; 2: 43-47. Lang.: Swe.
Netherlands. Sweden. 1984-1986. Critical studies. ■Survey of recent productions of Strindberg plays in the Netherlands.

1984 Van der Jagt, Marijn. "De Aids en het Fatsoen." (AIDS and the 'Socially Acceptable'.) *Toneel.* 1987 Feb.; 2: 20-23. Lang.: Dut.
Netherlands. USA. 1987. Historical studies. ■Several AIDS plays: what's acceptable on stage, superficiality in some works, fear of offending.

1985 Féral, Josette; Mehdid, Malika, transl. "There Are at Least Three Americas." *NTQ.* 1987 Feb.; 3(9): 82-88. Illus.: Photo. Print. B&W. 3. Lang.: Eng.
North America. South America. Central America. 1985. Critical studies. ■The Theatre Festival of the Americas attempts to bring the continent to mutual self-awareness. The companies represented at the inaugural festival and their work.

1986 van Erven, Eugène. "Theatre of Liberation in Action: The People's Theatre Network of the Philippines." *NTQ.* 1987 May; 3(10): 131-149. Notes. Illus.: Photo. Print. B&W. 6. Lang.: Eng.
Philippines. 1970-1987. Historical studies. ■Theatre played a significant part in the Filipino revolution. Organization and work of the Philippine Educational Theatre Association (PETA).

1987 Baniewicz, Elżbieta. "Old and New Trends in the Contemporary Polish Theatre." (Anciennes at nouvelles tendances du théâtre polonais contemporain.) *TP.* 1987 Jan-Mar.(1-3): 3-18. Illus.: Photo. Print. B&W. 10. Lang.: Eng, Fre.

CLASSED ENTRIES

DRAMA: —Performance/production

Poland: Warsaw, Cracow, Wrocław. 1980-1987. Historical studies. ■Overview of theatre in Poland in the 1980s, especially political theatre. Includes theatre companies, playwrights, productions and actors.

1988 Baniewicz, Elżbieta; Wójcik, Lidia; Chynowski, Paweł. "New Productions." (Nouveaux spectacles.) *TP.* 1987 Sep-Oct.(9-10): 3-27. Illus.: Photo. Print. B&W. 23. Lang.: Eng, Fre.

Poland: Warsaw. 1986-1987. Reviews of performances. ■Three reviewers review four new productions in Poland—*The Master and Margarita, Passion Scenes, Fetters,* and *Nienasycenie (Insatiability).*

1989 Grodzicki, August, ed.; Baniewicz, Elżbieta; Ogrodzińska, Teresa; Sieradzki, Jacek. *El teatro polaco de hoy.* (Polish Theatre Today.) Warsaw: Agencja Autorska; 1987. 47 pp. Illus.: Photo. Print. B&W. 25. Lang.: Spa.

Poland. 1987. Critical studies. ■Survey of contemporary Polish theatre prepared for the XXII Congress of the International Theatre Institute in Havana.

1990 Howard, Tony; Kuhiwczak, Piotr; Plebanek, Barbara, transl. "Empty Stages: Teatr Provisorium and the Polish Alternative Theatre." *NTQ.* 1987 Aug.; 3(11): 258-272. Illus.: Photo. B&W. 9. Lang.: Eng.

Poland: Lublin. 1971-1987. Histories-sources. ■Teatr Prowizorium and an interview with its director Janusz Oprynski.

1991 Limanowski, Mieczysław; Osterwa, Juliusz; Osiński, Zbigniew, ed. *Listy.* (Letters.) Warsaw: Państwowy Instytut Wydawniczy; 1987. 225 pp. Pref. Index. Notes. Append. Illus.: Photo. Print. B&W. 5. Lang.: Pol.

Poland: Warsaw, Wilno. 1921-1947. Histories-sources. ■Correspondence between two creators of the Polish experimental theatre Reduta (1919-1939), working in Warsaw and Wilno.

1992 Miklaszewski, Krzysztof. "Konteksty Kantora." (Kantor's Contexts.) *DialogW.* 1987; 9: 91-94. Notes. Lang.: Pol.

Poland. 1933-1987. Biographical studies. ■Director Tadeusz Kantor's inspirations in early career in Cracow. Polish stage designers Pronaszko and Frycz, Polish writers Schulz, Gombrowicz, Witkacy, also Duchamp and Dada. Grp/movt: Dadaism.

1993 Robinson, Marc. "Zbigniew Cynkutis: 1938-1987." *SEEDTF.* 1987 Dec.; 7(2 & 3): 42-43. Lang.: Eng.

Poland: Wrocław. 1972-1987. Historical studies. ■Obituary of Zbigniew Cynkutis and his work with Second Studio Wrocław, his teaching and his influence on young actors.

1994 Schiller, Leon; Timoszewicz, Jerzy, ed. *Theatrum militans 1939-1945.* (Militant Theatre: 1939-1945.) Warsaw: Państwowy Instytut Wydawniczy; 1987. 351 pp. Index. Notes. Pref. Biblio. Illus.: Photo. Print. B&W. 37. Lang.: Pol.

Poland. Germany. Roman Empire. 275-1945. ■The third volume of writings by director Leon Schiller, written in captivity during World War II. Theatre of ancient Rome, twentieth-century Poland.

1995 Sieradzki, Jacek. "Polish Drama in the Early Eighties." (La dramaturgie polonaise au début des années quatre-vingt.) *TP.* 1987 Jan-Mar.(1-3): 19-32. Illus.: Photo. Print. B&W. 10. Lang.: Eng, Fre.

Poland: Warsaw. 1981-1987. Historical studies. ■An in-depth look at the shape and form of contemporary Polish theatre. Includes detailed synopses of specific plays and playwrights.

1996 Wierzyński, Kazimierz; Waszkiel, Halina, ed.; Waszkiel, Marek, ed. *Wrażenia teatralne.* (Theatre Impressions.) Warsaw: Państwowy Instytut Wydawnicza; 1987. 518 pp. Pref. Index. Illus.: Photo. Print. B&W. 33. Lang.: Pol.

Poland: Warsaw. 1932-1939. Reviews of performances. ■Selection of the reviews of the performances in Warsaw theatres written by an eminent Polish poet.

1997 Wysińska, Elżbieta. "Tadeusz Bradecki: Teatr podwojny." (Tadeusz Bradecki: Theatre Doubled.) *DialogW.* 1987; 2: 143-148. Notes. Lang.: Pol.

Poland: Cracow. 1977-1987. Critical studies. ■Tadeusz Bradecki's activity as a director, playwright and director of the Stary Theatre.

1998 Zeleński, Tadeusz; Hen, Józef, ed. *Romanse cieniów.* (Romances of Shadows.) Warsaw: Państwowy Instytut Wydawniczy; 1987. 618 pp. Pref. Lang.: Pol.

Poland: Cracow, Warsaw. 1919-1941. Reviews of performances. ■Selection of the reviews of the performances in Cracow and Warsaw theatres written by an eminent Polish critic and translator.

1999 Żurowski, Andrzej; Kuhiwczak, Piotr, transl. "Old and New in the Polish Theatre: A Season at the Stary." *NTQ.* 1987 May; 3(10): 178-183. Illus.: Photo. B&W. 4. Lang.: Eng.

Poland: Cracow. 1987. Critical studies. ■Three productions in recent season at the Stary show the theatre in the vanguard of experimental work: Wajda's *Crime and Punishment,* Pasolini's *Affabulazione* staged by Babicki and Bradecki's *Wrorzec dowodów metafizycznych (A Pattern of Metaphysical Proofs).*

2000 Abramson, Jan. "*Pelikanen* i Portugal." (*The Pelican* in Portugal.) *Teaterf.* 1987; 20(5): 14. Illus.: Photo. Lang.: Swe.

Portugal: Lisbon. 1987. Histories-sources. ■A report from the first amateur festival of Associação Portuguesa do Teatre de Amadores, APTA.

2001 Horváth Sz., István. "A szóhoz illesztett cselekvény. Sorok a kolozsvári *Hamletről.*" (Action Adjusted to Words: Lines on *Hamlet* in Kolozsvár.) *Mozgo.* 1987 Sep.; 13(9): 96-106. Illus.: Photo. B&W. 5. Lang.: Hun.

Romania: Cluj. 1987. Critical studies. ■Analysis of Shakespeare's play presented by the Hungarian Theatre of Kolozsvár (Cluj) directed by Gábor Tompa.

2002 Gordon, Mel. "Michael Chekhov's Life and Work: A Descriptive Chronology." *TDR.* 1983 Fall; 27(3): 3-21. Illus.: Photo. B&W. 16. Lang.: Eng.

Russia: Moscow. 1901-1980. Historical studies.

2003 Gordon, Mel. *The Stanislavsky Technique: Russia.* New York, NY: Applause; 1987. xv, 252 pp. (The Applause Acting Series.) Pref. Biblio. Gloss. Lang.: Eng.

Russia: Moscow. 1906-1938. Historical studies. ■Profile of the development of the Stanislavskij Acting System as taught by Konstantin Stanislavskij and disciples Jevgenij Vachtangov and Michajl Čechov.

2004 Ferm, Peter. "Romantikernas renässans." (The Renaissance of the Romantics.) *NT.* 1987; 37: 17-21. Illus.: Photo. Lang.: Swe.

Scandinavia. 1986-1987. Historical studies. ■The Romantic 'closet dramas' have lately become fruitful and Goethe, Schiller, Kleist and Stagnelius are suddenly means to individual stagings.

2005 Coplan, David. "Dialectics in Tradition in Southern African Black Popular Theatre." *CrAr.* 1987; 4(3): 5-27. Illus.: Dwg. 3. Lang.: Eng.

South Africa, Republic of. England: London. USA: New York, NY. 1586-1987. Historical studies. ■Black theatre in South Africa: its influences from traditional forms and how cultural dynamics have transformed traditions into political vehicles.

2006 Davis, Myra. "*Vuka*: Sharing the Image." *CrAr.* 1987; 4(3): 29-38. Lang.: Eng.

South Africa, Republic of: Soweto. 1976-1987. Reviews of performances. ■Review of *Vuka* by Matsemela Manaka from the Soyikwa African Theatre Group.

2007 James, Geoffrey. "*Othello* Revisited." *Scenaria.* 1987 Nov.(82): 9-10. Illus.: Photo. 2. Lang.: Eng.

South Africa, Republic of: Johannesburg. 1987. Reviews of performances. ■Critique of controversial production of *Othello* directed by Janet Suzman.

2008 Gornitz, Deborah. "Fiesta de Pobres. Crónica del II Festival de Teatro Latinoamericano de Córdoba." (Festival of the Poor: Chronicles of the Second Festival of Latin American Theatre of Córdoba.) *Conjunto.* 1987 Apr/July; 72: 2-9. Pref. Illus.: Design. Photo. B&W. 9. Lang.: Spa.

Spain: Córdoba. 1986. Reviews of performances. ■Review of the performances of the participating groups from Latin America and Europe.

2009 Burguet i Ardiaca, Francesc. "Els espectacles." (The Performances.) 40-271 in *Teatre Lliure 1976-1987.* Barcelona: Institut del Teatre; 1987. 297 pp. Lang.: Cat.

Spain-Catalonia: Barcelona. 1976-1987. Histories-reconstruction. ■Details and evolution of all Teatre Lliure productions.

DRAMA: —Performance/production

2010 Fàbregas, Xavier; Badiou, Maryse, ed., intro.; Melendres, Jaume, intro. *Teatre en viu (1969-1972)*. (Theatre Alive, 1969-1972.) Barcelona: Institut del Teatre; 1987. 284 pp. (Monografies de Teatre 23.) Pref. Index. Notes. Tables. Illus.: Photo. B&W. 35. Lang.: Cat.
Spain-Catalonia. 1969-1972. Critical studies. ■Collection of theatre reviews from *Serra d'Or* by Xavier Fàbregas. Emphasis on productions outside Barcelona, with attention to the director's role and commentary.

2011 García Giménez, Arturo, ed. *Resum de la temporada teatral a Barcelona 1986-1987*. (Summary of the Barcelona Theatrical Season, 1986-1987.) Barcelona: Institut del Teatre; 1987. 28 pp. Illus.: Design. Photo. B&W. 15. [Catalogue of the exhibition with the same title. Barcelona, July 13th to November 15th, 1987.] Lang.: Cat.
Spain-Catalonia: Barcelona. 1986-1987. Histories-sources. ■Catalogue of an exhibition on the 1986-87 season. Articles by six Barcelona theatre critics. Production details on 304 professional and semi-professional productions.

2012 Bergström, Johan. "En saknad." (A Loss.) *NT*. 1987; 36: 46-47. Illus.: Photo. Lang.: Swe.
Sweden. 1916-1979. Biographical studies. ■Evaluation of actor Anders Ek.

2013 Busk, Yvonne. "Klassrumsteater, närhet och starka reaktioner." (Classroom Theatre, Closeness and Violent Responses.) *NT*. 1987; 36: 14-15. Illus.: Photo. Lang.: Swe.
Sweden. 1986-1987. Histories-sources. ■Two actors Sören Hagdahl and Jonas Grafström, discuss *Brev på villovägar (A Letter Goes Astray)* about a quarrel that ends up in a murder, the youth of schools and problems of communication.

2014 Elenius, Lars. "Urpremiär i Pajala." (First Performance in Pajala.) *Teaterf*. 1987; 20(6): 8-9. Illus.: Photo. Lang.: Swe.
Sweden: Pajala. 1986. Historical studies. ■The second production of the Swedish Tornedalsteatern's *Kuutot* by Bengt Pohjanen was in Finnish because it's about the dilemma of languages in Tornedalen.

2015 Forser, Tomas; Harlén, Carl; Melldahl, Åsa; Janzon, Leif; Palo, Elisabet; Sjögren, Frederik; Lysell, Roland; Hägglund, Kent; Heed, Sven Åke; Claesson, Christer. "Då började jag fundera..." (Then I Began to Think...)*NT*. 1987; 37: 34-37. Lang.: Swe.
Sweden. 1986-1987. Histories-sources. ■Ten persons with connection to theatre speak about a performance which has changed their way of thinking.

2016 Marklund, Björn. "Ur paraplytäckta kartonger." (From Umbrella Covered Cartons.) *Teaterf*. 1987; 20(2-3): 17. Illus.: Photo. Lang.: Swe.
Sweden: Köping. 1987. Historical studies. ■A report from the amateur festival of children's and youth theatre.

2017 Ollén, Gunnar. "Strindbergspremiärer 1984-85-86." (Strindberg Productions 1984-85-86.) *Strind*. 1987; 2: 5-42. Illus.: Photo. Print. B&W. 8. Lang.: Swe.
Sweden. 1984-1986. Critical studies. ■Recent productions of Strindberg plays in Sweden and other countries with citations from newspaper reviews.

2018 Ring, Lars. "Plikten, lusten och lustan. Några skärvor eklekticism, Beckett, sex och politik." (Duty, Pleasure and Lust: Some Pieces of Eclecticism, Beckett, Sex and Politics.) *TArsb*. 1987; 6: 14-16. Illus.: Photo. Print. B&W. 10. Lang.: Swe.
Sweden. 1986-1987. Historical studies. ■Review of important theatre productions during the past season.

2019 Samuelsson, Björn. "När Kerim från Turkiet ringer till Hasse Tellemar." (When Kerim From Turkey Phones to Hasse Tellemar.) *Teaterf*. 1987; 20(1): 3-7. Illus.: Photo. 5. Lang.: Swe.
Sweden: Södertälje. 1986. Historical studies. ■How Musikteatergruppen Oktober, together with amateurs among the immigrants, produced *Hemma i Södertälje (At Home in Södertälje)* by Björn Runeborg.

2020 Samuelsson, Björn. "Till snällhetens lov." (In Praise of Goodness.) *Teaterf*. 1987; 20(1): 11-12. Illus.: Photo. Lang.: Swe.

Sweden: Stockholm. 1986-1987. Histories-sources. ■The director Marika Lagercrantz tells about the co-operation of Jordcirkus and amateur group Näktergalningarna in staging Dickens' *A Christmas Carol*.

2021 Sandelin, Ann-Charlotte. "Karikatyrens uppblåsta grepp." (The Inflated Grip of the Caricature.) *Teaterf*. 1987; 20 (2-3): 9-11. Illus.: Photo. Lang.: Swe.
Sweden: Nyköping. 1986-1987. Historical studies. ■The fringe theatre Nyköpings Teater has cooperated with amateurs in staging *Revizor (The Government Inspector)* under Orlanda Cook's direction, with great success.

2022 Sander, Anki. "*Landskronapågen*—ett sätt att förändra." (*The Boy From Landskrona*—A Way to Change.) *Teaterf*. 1987; 20(4): 3-4. Illus.: Photo. Lang.: Swe.
Sweden: Landskrona. 1982-1987. Histories-sources. ■Bruno Nilsson speaks about the big project of the amateur group Harlekin to involve youth in a local play which had 18 performances after two years' preparation.

2023 Sander, Anki. "Att bevista ATR-festivalen är en fascinerande upplevelse." (To Attend the Festival of ATR is a Fascinating Experience.) *Teaterf*. 1987; 20(4): 9-12. Illus.: Photo. Lang.: Swe.
Sweden: Västerås. 1987. Historical studies. ■A report from Västerås Amateur Theatre Festival, with groups from all Sweden and two guesting groups from Ireland and Soviet Georgia. Discussions about good and bad amateur ambitions.

2024 Sverenius, Torsten. "Finns det ett val?" (Is There Any Choice?)*NT*. 1987; 36: 10-13. Illus.: Photo. Lang.: Swe.
Sweden: Landskrona. 1982-1987. Historical studies. ■From the background of the project of *Landskronapågen (The Boy from Landskrona)* which involved youth of the town, and what a story of the eighteenth century could tell us today.

2025 Westling, Barbro. "Nu gäller det livet—men vad är livet?" (Now It Is For Life—But What Is Life?)*TArsb*. 1987; 6: 9-13. Illus.: Photo. Print. B&W. 5. Lang.: Swe.
Sweden. 1986-1987. Historical studies. ■Review of most important theatre productions during the past season.

2026 Arnold, Peter, comp; Cathonas, Vreni, comp. *Theater ohne Theater*. (Theatre Without a Theatre.) Kinder- und Jugendtheatre. Basel: Lenos Verlag; 1987. 189 pp. (Jahrbuch 1987/88.) Pref. Illus.: Photo. B&W. Lang.: Ger.
Switzerland. 1986-1988. ■Essays analyzing the situation and perspective of theatrical activities outside playhouses and the 'fuss about theatre', with regard especially to productions for children and young adults. Yearbook also contains two integral playtexts, plus addresses and descriptions of various youth theatres extant in Switzerland.

2027 Hennenberg, Fritz. "Simon Parmet, Paul Burkhard: Die Musik zur Uraufführung von *Mutter Courage und ihre Kinder*." (Simon Parmet, Paul Burkhard: Music to the Première of *Mother Courage*.) *NIMBZ*. 1987 July; 10(4): 10-12. Notes. Illus.: Photo. B&W. Lang.: Ger.
Switzerland: Zürich. Finland. 1939-1947. Historical studies. ■Detailed analysis of the origins of music written for Brecht's *Mutter Courage (Mother Courage)* concentrating on the versions by Simon Parmet from Finland and Paul Burkhard, composer and conductor at Zürich playhouse.

2028 Loeffler, Peter. *Ein Zürcher Faust*. (Faustus in Zürich.) Basel: Boston: Stuttgart: Birkhäuser; 1987. 120 pp. Illus.: Design. B&W. Lang.: Ger.
Switzerland: Zürich. 1949. Historical studies. ■Leonard Steckel's attempt at a modern staging of Goethe's *Faust II* was crucial as a turning point towards modern Swiss theatre. Includes illustrations of costume designs by Caspar Neher (to be seen in original form at the Swiss Theatre Collection, Berne), reviews and commentary.

2029 Mignonne, Patricia. "*Dom Juan* de Besson ou la désaffection des paysannes." (Besson's *Dom Juan*, or The Loveless Peasant Women.) *AltT*. 1987 Dec.; 28: 44-47. Illus.: Photo. B&W. 2. Lang.: Fre.
Switzerland: Geneva. 1987. Critical studies. ■Review of Molière's *Dom Juan*, directed by Benno Besson at the Comédie.

DRAMA: —Performance/production

2030   Tailby, John E. "The Role of the Director in the Lucerne Passion Play." *MET.* 1987; 9(2): 80-92. Notes. Lang.: Eng.
Switzerland: Lucerne. 1453-1616. Historical studies. ■Role of the director in text, casting, properties, costumes and rehearsals. Typical of methodology in other German-speaking countries of the time.

2031   "Reviews of Productions." *LTR.* 1987; 7(2): 67-95. Lang.: Eng.
UK. 1987. ■*The Amen Corner* by James Baldwin, dir by Anton Phillips at the Carib Theatre: rev by de Jongh, Gardner, Hirschhorn, King, Renton, Rose, Thorncroft. *The Cid* by Pierre Corneille, translated by David Bryer, dir by Declan Donnellan at Donmar Warehouse: rev by Billington, de Jongh, Edwardes, King, Nathan, Ratcliffe, Ray, Shorter, Sutcliffe, Woddis. *Road* by Jim Cartwright, dir by Simon Curtis at the Royal Court Theatre: rev by Armistead, Billington, Connor, Hiley, McFerran, Renton. *Fallen* by Polly Teale, dir by Julia Bardsley at Drill Hall Theatre (Edinburgh): rev by Armistead, Billington, Edwardes, Hayes, Smith. *The Merry Wives of Windsor* by William Shakespeare, dir by Bill Alexander at the Barbican Theatre: rev by Edwards, Hiley, Osborne. *Death of a Salesman* by Arthur Miller, dir by Giles Havergal at Citizens Theatre (Glasgow): rev by Hemming.

2032   Green, Michael. *The Art of Coarse Acting.* New York, NY: Limelight; 1987. 128 pp. Pref. Illus.: Photo. Dwg. B&W. 16. [New revised edition.] Lang.: Eng.
UK. 1987. Historical studies. ■Collection of humorous amateur theatre anecdotes on how to destroy a production. Focus on poor acting and directing in community theatre companies.

2033   "Reviews of Productions." *LTR.* 1987; 7(1): 5-17. Lang.: Eng.
UK-England. 1987. ■*Intensive Care* by Christoph Gahl, dir by Dominic Cassidy at the Tabard Theatre: rev by de Jongh, Dixon, Hopkinson. *Losing Venice* by John Clifford, dir by Jenny Killick at Traverse Theatre: rev by Armistead, de Jongh, Edwardes, Gardner, Ratcliffe. *Siegfried Sassoon: The Story of the Young Soldier-Poet* dir by Peter Barkworth, devised and performed by Hampstead Theatre: rev by Braybrooke, Connor, Ezard, Horner, Hoyle, Lawson, Pascal, Pearce, Ratcliffe, Ray, Rose, Say, Shulman, Tinker. *Coming In To Land* by Stephen Poliakoff, dir by Peter Hall at National Theatre: rev by Billington, Couling, Edwardes, Edwards, Hiley, Hirschhorn, Horner, Hoyle, Hurren, Jameson, King, Laffan, Nathan, Ratcliffe, Ray, Rissik, Shorter, Shulman, Smith.

2034   "Reviews of Productions." *LTR.* 1986; 6(25/26): 1332-1353. Lang.: Eng.
UK-England: London. 1986. ■*A Mouthful of Birds* by Caryl Churchill and David Lan, dir by Ian Spink and Les Waters at the Royal Court: rev by Coveney, de Jongh, Edwardes, Edwards, Hiley, King, Nathan, Radin, Ray, Renton, Shulman, Woddis. *Brighton Beach Memoirs* by Neil Simon, dir by Michael Rudman (a National Theatre production), at Aldwych Theatre: rev by de Jongh, Edwardes, Edwards, Hiley, Hirschhorn, Hoyle, Hurren, Jacobs, King, Shorter, Shulman, Smith, Tinker, Woddis.

2035   "Reviews of Productions." *LTR.* 1986; 6(25/26): 1353-1356. Lang.: Eng.
UK-England: London. 1986. ■*I Ought To Be In Pictures* by Neil Simon, dir by Robert Gillespie at Offstage Downstairs: rev by Billington, Hoyle, King, Nathan, Robinson, Sanderson, Shorter. *Spring Awakening* by Frank Wedekind, transl. by Tom Osborn, dir by Margaret Gordon at the Young Vic: rev by Bardsley, de Jongh, King, Murdin, Nathan, Nurse, Rose.

2036   "Reviews of Productions." *LTR.* 1986; 6(25/26): 1356-1357. Lang.: Eng.
UK-England: London. 1986. ■*Sandra Mellor* by Simon Cherry, dir by Richard Hansom at the Old Red Lion: rev by Gore-Langton, Woddis. *Hey! Luciani: The Times, Life and Codex of Albino Luciani* by Mark E. Smith and Craig Scanlon, dir by Smith at the Riverside Studios: rev by Gore-Langton, Lawson, Robinson.

2037   "Reviews of Productions." *LTR.* 1986; 6(25/26): 1358-1361. Lang.: Eng.
UK-England: London. 1986. ■*Candida* by George Bernard Shaw, dir by Frank Hauser at the King's Head Theatre: rev by Armistead, Atkins, de Jongh, King, McFerran, Murdin, Nathan, Wolf. *The Bijers Sunbird*

written and dir by Robert Kirby at the Lyric Studio: rev by Graham-Dixon, Kaye, Kenyon, Radin, Shorter, Vidal.

2038   "Reviews of Productions." *LTR.* 1986; 6(25/26): 1361-1362. Lang.: Eng.
UK-England: London. 1986. ■Two Indian *bhavai* plays: *Tejo Vanio (Tejo the Miser)* and *Zanda Zulan (Zulan, The Flag Bearer)* by Asaitha Thaker, dir by Jatinder Verma at the Tricycle Theatre: rev by Edwardes, Khan. *Dory Previn Singing Songs and Telling Tails* by Dory Previn, dir by Kate Young at Donmar Warehouse Theatre: rev by Clark, Cotton, Grove, Rosenbaum, Smith.

2039   "Reviews of Productions." *LTR.* 1986; 6(25/26): 1363-1369. Lang.: Eng.
UK-England: London. 1986. ■*When I Was a Girl, I Used To Scream and Shout* by Sharman MacDonald, dir by Simon Stokes at the Whitehall Theatre: rev by Armistead, Billington, Hiley, Hirschhorn, Hurren, King, Nathan, Ratcliffe, Ray, Rissik, Rose, Shannon, Shorter, Shulman, Smith, Tinker, Woddis. *The Hobbit* by Rony Robinson and Graham Watkins, dir by Watkins at the Fortune Theatre: rev by Hiley, Hoyle, Khan, McFerran, Steyn, Sutcliffe.

2040   "Reviews of Productions." *LTR.* 1986; 6(25-26): 1405-1409. Lang.: Eng.
UK-England: London. 1986. ■*An Italian Straw Hat (Un Chapeau de Paille d'Italie)* by Eugène Labiche, transl by Barnett Shaw, dir by Ray Cooney at the Shaftsbury Arts Centre: rev by Coveney, De Jongh, Hiley, Hirschhorn, Hurren, Kemp, King, Pearce, Ratcliffe, Shulman, Smith, Tinker. *The Lion, the Witch and the Wardrobe* by Glyn Robbins, dir by Richard Williams at the Westminster Theatre: rev by Chapman.

2041   "Reviews of Productions." *LTR.* 1986; 6(25-26): 1409-1410. Lang.: Eng.
UK-England: London. 1986. ■*Aladdin* by Terry Duggan and Ian Barnett, dir by Ben Benison at the Shaw Theatre: rev by Asquith, Clarke, Rose. *The Wind in the Willows* by David Conville and David Gooderson, music by Carl Davis, dir by Terry Wale at the Mermaid Theatre: rev by Armistead, Horner, Robinson.

2042   "Reviews of Productions." *LTR.* 1986; 6(25-26): 1410-1411. Lang.: Eng.
UK-England: London. 1986. ■*The Adventures of Mr. Toad* written and dir by Piers Chater Robinson at the Bloomsbury Theatre: rev by Armistead, Hayes. *Pinocchio* by Vince Foxall and Colin Sell, dir by Jonathan Martin at Theatre Royal: rev by Armistead, Gow, McKenley.

2043   "Reviews of Productions." *LTR.* 1986; 6(25-26): 1369-1372. Lang.: Eng.
UK-England: London. 1986. ■*Please Please Please* by Théâtre de Complicité, dir by Annabel Arden at Institute of Contemporary Arts: rev by Edwardes, Ratcliffe, Shack, St. George, Walker, Wolf. *The Mother (Die Mutter)* by Bertolt Brecht, transl. by Steve Gooch, dir by Di Trevis at the Cottesloe Theatre: rev by Atkins, Billington, Coveney, Radin, Ratcliffe, Rissik, Robinson, Rose.

2044   "Reviews of Productions." *LTR.* 1986; 6(25-26): 1373-1386. Lang.: Eng.
UK-England: London. 1986. ■*King Lear* by William Shakespeare, dir by David Hare (a National Theatre production) at the Olivier Theatre: rev by Anderson, Billington, Couling, Edwardes, Edwards, Hiley, Hirschhorn, Horner, Hoyle, Hurren, King, Lawson, Mars-Jones, Nathan, Radin, Ratcliffe, Ray, Shannon, Shorter, Shulman, Smith, Tinker. *What About Luv?* by Murray Schisgal, Jeffrey Sweet, Howard Marren and Susan Birkenhead, dir by Kim Grant at the Orange Tree Theatre: rev by Alexander, Billington, Hopkinson.

2045   "Reviews of Productions." *LTR.* 1986; 6(25/26): 1387-1393. Lang.: Eng.
UK-England: London. 1986. ■*Night Must Fall* by Emlyn Williams, dir by John Dove at the Greenwich Theatre: rev by de Jongh, Hoyle, King, Lyttle, McFerran, Rissik, Shorter, Tinker. *Heresies* by Deborah Levy, dir by Susan Todd at The Pit: rev by Billington, Coveney, Edwardes, Gardner, Hirschhorn, King, Nathan, Ratcliffe, Shorter, Shulman, Smith, Warner.

2046   "Reviews of Productions." *LTR.* 1986; 6(25/26): 1393-1398. Lang.: Eng.
UK-England: London. 1986. ■*The King and the Corpse* written and dir by Donald Sumpter at the Almeida Theatre: rev by de Jongh, Hoyle,

DRAMA: —Performance/production

Ratcliffe, Rose. *A Penny for a Song* by John Whiting, performed by the Royal Shakespeare Company, dir by Howard Davies at the Barbican Theatre: rev by Billington, Coveney, Gardner, Hirschhorn, Hurren, King, Nathan, Ratcliffe, Rissik, Rose, Shorter, Shulman, Tinker.

2047 "Reviews of Productions." *LTR.* 1986; 6(25/26): 1398-1402. Lang.: Eng.

UK-England: London. 1986. ∎*The American Clock* by Arthur Miller, dir by Peter Wood at the Olivier Theatre: rev by de Jongh, Edwardes, Hoyle, Nathan, Pearce. *Alice in Wonderland* by John Wells and Carl Davis, dir by Ian Forrest at the Lyric Hammersmith: rev by Asquith, Billington, Coveney, Grove, Harries, Hiley, Hirschhorn, Hurren, King, McFerran, Shorter.

2048 "Reviews of Productions." *LTR.* 1986; 6(25/26): 1403-1405. Lang.: Eng.

UK-England: London. 1986. ∎*Flash Trash* by Barbara Gloudon, dir by Yvonne Brewster at the Half Moon Theatre: rev by Connor, Hiley, Khan, Pearce, Renton, Rose. *Joseph and the Amazing Technicolor Dreamcoat* by Tim Rice and Andrew Lloyd Webber, dir by Bill Kenwright at the Royalty Theatre: rev by Coveney, Khan, Shorter, Sonin.

2049 "Reviews of Productions." *LTR.* 1986; 6(23): 1244-1249. Lang.: Eng.

UK-England: London. 1986. ∎*The Infernal Machine (La Machine Infernale)* by Jean Cocteau, transl. and dir by Simon Callow at the Lyric Hammersmith: rev by Asquith, Billington, Edwards, Hirschhorn, Hoyle, Hurren, Jones, Morley, Nathan, O'Shaughnessy, Radin, Ratcliffe, Rissik, Rose, Shulman. *The Old Man of Lochnagar* written and dir by David Wood at Sadler's Wells: rev by Barker, Hoyle, McHardy, Shannon.

2050 "Reviews of Productions." *LTR.* 1986; 6(23): 1250-1254. Lang.: Eng.

UK-England: London. 1986. ∎*The Pied Piper* by Adrian Mitchell, music by Dominic Muldowney, dir by Alan Cohen at the Olivier Theatre: rev by Atkins, Denselow, Hoyle, Klein, McFerran, Morrison, Rissik. *I Want* by Nell Dunn and Adrian Henri, dir by Michael Elwyn at the Old Red Lion: rev by Connor, de Jongh, Hoyle, Ratcliffe, Rose, Smith.

2051 "Reviews of Productions." *LTR.* 1986; 6(23): 1254-1255. Lang.: Eng.

UK-England: London. 1986. ∎*A Gothic Triple Bill* by Howard Brenton, Steven Berkoff, dir by Bright Red Theatre Co. at King's Head Theatre: rev by Conquest, Kaye. *Pinocchio Boys* by Jim Morris, dir by Pip Broughton at Young Vic Studio: rev by Coveney, de Jongh, Edwardes, Harron, Wahlberg, Woddis.

2052 "Reviews of Productions." *LTR.* 1986; 6(23): 1256-1260. Lang.: Eng.

UK-England: London. 1986. ∎*Treatment* written and dir by Jonathan Moore at the Donmar Warehouse: rev by Asquith, Grant, Harron, Lawson, Nurse, Shulman. *A Funny Thing Happened on the Way to the Forum* by Burt Shevelove and Larry Gelbart, music and lyrics by Stephen Sondheim, dir by Gelbart at the Piccadilly: rev by Atkins, Billington, Coveney, Grant, Harron, Nathan, Robinson, Shulman, Steyn, Usher.

2053 "Reviews of Productions." *LTR.* 1986; 6(23): 1265-1275. Lang.: Eng.

UK-England: London. 1986. ∎*Me and Mrs. Nobody* by Keith Water-house, dir by Ned Sherrin at the Garrick Theatre: rev by Billington, Coveney, Edwards, Gardner, Harron, Hurren, Jameson, King, Lawson, Morley, Nathan, Rose, Shannon, Shorter, Shulman, Smith, Twisk, Usher. *Wildfire* by N. Richard Nash, dir by Peter Wood at the Phoenix Theatre: rev by Asquith, Billington, Edwardes, Edwards, Hirschhorn, Hoyle, Hurren, Kemp, King, Morley, Nathan, Ratcliffe, Roper, Shannon, Shorter, Shulman, Smith, Twisk, Usher.

2054 "Reviews of Productions." *LTR.* 1986; 6(23): 1275-1301. Lang.: Eng.

UK-England: London. 1986. ∎*Bust* by Gregory Day, dir by Tony Craven at the Tabard Theatre: rev by Cotton, Robertson, Shack, Smith.

2055 "Reviews of Productions." *LTR.* 1986; 6(24): 1302-1305. Lang.: Eng.

UK-England: London. 1986. ∎*Killing Jessica* by David Rogers, dir by Bryan Forbes at the Savoy: rev by Edwardes, Grant, Harron, Hirschhorn, Hoyle, Hurren, Jameson, King, Nathan, Ray, Shorter, Shulman, Smith, Twisk, Usher, Wolf. *The Bernoulli Effect* by Burnt Bridges, dir by Birte Pedersen at the Oval House: rev by Hayes, Hoyle, Sanderson.

2056 "Reviews of Productions." *LTR.* 1986; 6(24): 1306-1309. Lang.: Eng.

UK-England: London. 1986. ∎*The Last Waltz* by Gillian Richmond, dir by Sue Dunderdale at the Soho Poly Theatre: rev by Carne, Coveney, Gardner, Rose, Smith. *Ashes* by David Rudkin, dir by Rob Walker at the Bush Theatre: rev by Billington, Grant, Hoyle, Nathan, Nurse, Shulman, Sutcliffe, Wolf.

2057 "Reviews of Productions." *LTR.* 1986; 6(24): 1309-1310. Lang.: Eng.

UK-England: London. 1986. ∎*Midnight in Moscow* by James Duke, dir by Terry Adams at the Bridge Lane Theatre: rev by McFerran, Quinn. *Ghosts* by Henrik Ibsen, transl. by Peter Watts, dir by David Thacker at Wyndham's: rev by Billington, Hirschhorn, Rose, Shorter.

2058 "Reviews of Productions." *LTR.* 1986; 6(24): 1311-1315. Lang.: Eng.

UK-England: London. 1986. ∎*Byrthrite* by Sarah Daniels, dir by Carole Hayman at Theatre Upstairs: rev by Armistead, Billington, Edwardes, Gardner, Harron, Lawson, Nathan, Shorter. *The Great Hunger* by Tom MacIntyre, dir by Patrick Mason at the Almeida Theatre: rev by de Jongh, Gardner, Hoyle, Kemp, Murdin, Rose, St. George.

2059 "Reviews of Productions." *LTR.* 1986; 6(24): 1315-1316. Lang.: Eng.

UK-England: London. 1986. ∎*Blood of Angels* written and dir by Jon Pope at the Gate Theatre: rev by Laffan, Rose. *Gold in the Streets* by Marie Jones, dir by Ian McElhinney at the Drill Hall Theatre: rev by Carne, Hayes, Rose, Smith.

2060 "Reviews of Productions." *LTR.* 1986; 6(24): 1317-1331. Lang.: Eng.

UK-England: London. 1986. ∎*The Women* by Clare Booth Luce, dir by Keith Hack at the Old Vic Theatre: rev by Asquith, Billington, Coveney, Edwards, Harron, Hirschhorn, Hurren, King, McFerran, Nathan, Ray, Shannon, Shorter, Shulman, Smith, Tinker. *Selling the Sizzle* by Peter Gibbs, dir by Robert Chetwys at the Hampstead Theatre: rev by Coveney, de Jongh, Edwards, Gardner, Grant, Harron, Hay, Hiley, Hirschhorn, Horner, Hurren, Kemp, King, Nathan, Shorter, Shulman, Tinker.

2061 "Reviews of Productions." *LTR.* 1986; 6(20): 1081-1083. Lang.: Eng.

UK-England: London. 1986. ∎*Mother Courage and Her Children (Mutter Courage und ihre Kinder)* by Bertolt Brecht, transl. by Eric Bentley, dir by Sam Walters at the Orange Tree Theatre: rev by Caplan, Sanderson. *Catherine of Siena* by Retta Taney, dir by Joan Kemp-Welch at King's Head Theatre: rev by Asquith, Carne, McFerran, Shulman, Smith.

2062 "Reviews of Productions." *LTR.* 1986; 6(20): 1083-1089. Lang.: Eng.

UK-England: London. 1986. ∎*Massage* written and dir by Michael Wilcox at the Lyric Studio: rev by Armistead, Billington, Edwardes, Morrison, Rissik, Shulman, Wolf. *Compromised Immunity* by Andy Kirby, dir by Philip Osment at the Drill Hall: rev by Connor, de Jongh.

2063 "Reviews of Productions." *LTR.* 1986; 6(20): 1090-1096. Lang.: Eng.

UK-England: London. 1986. ∎*Principia scriptoriae* by Richard Nelson, dir by David Jones at The Pit: rev by Armistead, Billington, Edwardes, King, Nathan, Ratcliffe, Rissik, Shulman, Smith, Woddis. *Ghosts (Gengangere)* by Henrik Ibsen, transl. by Peter Watts, dir by David Thacker at the Young Vic: rev by de Jongh, Gardner, Hiley, Hurren, Lawson, Murdin, O'Shaughnessy, Ratcliffe, Rose, Say, Tinker, Thorncroft.

2064 "Reviews of Productions." *LTR.* 1986; 6(20): 1109-1114. Lang.: Eng.

UK-England: London. 1986. ∎*Misalliance* by George Bernard Shaw, dir by John Caird at the Barbican: rev by Billington, Coveney, Couling, Edwards, Gardner, Grant, Hiley, Hurren, Jameson, King, Morley, Morrison, Nathan, Shorter, Shrimpton, Shulman, Smith, Tinker. *The*

DRAMA: —Performance/production

Asylum of Antonin Artaud by Mike Downey and Dennis Akers, dir by Sheena Wrigley and Downey at the Gate, Notting Hill: rev by Gore-Langton, Woddis.

2065 "Reviews of Productions." *LTR.* 1986; 6(20): 1114-1124. Lang.: Eng.

UK-England: London. 1986. ■*Line One* with book and lyrics by Volker Ludwig, music by Birger Heymann, transl. by Peter Gilbert, David Beer and Nick Fisher, dir by Wolfgang Kolneder at the Shaw: rev by Billington, Gardner, Khan, Matthews, Ratcliffe. *Phantom of the Opera*, music by Andrew Lloyd Webber, lyrics by Charles Hart, book by Richard Stilgoe and Webber, dir by Harold Prince at Her Majesty's Theatre: rev by Asquith, Barber, Barkley, Billington, Blake, Coveney, Couling, Edwardes, Edwards, Harron, Hiley, Hurren, Jameson, King, Morley, Nathan, Ratcliffe, Shannon, Shulman, Smith, Steyn, Tinker, Williamson.

2066 "Reviews of Productions." *LTR.* 1986; 6(20): 1124-1128. Lang.: Eng.

UK-England: London. 1986. ■*Anarkali* by British Asian Theatre Co., dir by Raj Patel at the Cockpit: rev by Remnant. *The Hostage* by Brendan Behan, dir by Nicholas Kent at the Tricycle: rev by de Jongh, Denselow, Hiley, Hoyle, Khan, King, Lubbock, Morley, Nathan, Nurse, Ratcliffe, Sanderson, Shulman.

2067 "Reviews of Productions." *LTR.* 1986; 6(21): 1129-1133. Lang.: Eng.

UK-England: London. 1986. ■*Les Liaisons Dangereuses* by Christopher Hampton, dir by Howard Davies, performed by the Royal Shakespeare Company at Ambassadors Theatre: rev by Asquith, de Jongh, Hiley, Hudson, Hurren, King, O'Shaughnessy, Ratcliffe, Smith, Tinker. *Rebel!* by Donna Franceschild and Richie Rich, dir by Colin Hicks at Albany Empire: rev by Billington, Hoyle, Sanderson, Woddis.

2068 "Reviews of Productions." *LTR.* 1986; 6(21): 1133-1135. Lang.: Eng.

UK-England: London. 1986. ■*Super Goodnight/Carthage* by Teatr Akademia Ruchu (Poland), dir by Wojciech Krukowski at the Almeida Theatre: rev by Allthorpe-Guyton, Rea, Rose. *Request Programme* by Franz Xaver Kroetz, dir by Nancy Diuguid at the Bush: rev by Grant, Shulman, Sutcliffe.

2069 "Reviews of Productions." *LTR.* 1986; 6(21): 1135-1144. Lang.: Eng.

UK-England: London. 1986. ■*The Spanish Play* by Seamus Finnegan, dir by Julia Pascal at The Place: rev by Lyttle, McFerran, Wolfe. *The Secret Life of Cartoons* by Clive Barker, dir by Tudor Davies at the Aldwych: rev by Barkley, Billington, Coveney, Edwardes, Hiley, Hurren, Kemp, King, Morley, Nathan, O'Shaughnessy, Shulman, Smith, St. George, Tinker, Wolf.

2070 "Reviews of Productions." *LTR.* 1986; 6(21): 1144-1146. Lang.: Eng.

UK-England: London. 1986. ■*Behind Heaven* by Jonathan Moore, dir by Gregory Hersov at Donmar Warehouse: rev by Billington, Grant, Hopkins, Lawson, Wolf. *Body Cell* by Melissa Murray, dir by Sue Dunderdale at Soho Poly: rev by Cotton, Hay, Smith.

2071 "Reviews of Productions." *LTR.* 1986; 6(21): 1147-1149. Lang.: Eng.

UK-England: London. 1986. ■*Revo* by Shango Baku, dir by A.J. Simon at the Battersea Arts Centre: rev by Alborough, Armistead, Lee. *Lillian* by William Luce, dir by Corin Redgrave at the Lyric Hammersmith: rev by Billington, Coveney, Hurren, Morley, Nathan, Nurse, Say, Woddis.

2072 "Reviews of Productions." *LTR.* 1986; 6(21): 1150-1158. Lang.: Eng.

UK-England: London. 1986. ■*Under Milkwood* by Dylan Thomas, dir by Anthony Cornish at the Greenwich Theatre: rev by Atkins, Coveney, de Jongh, Hurren, King, Lee, Rissik, Rose. *Breaking the Code* by Hugh Whitemore, dir by Clifford Williams at the Theatre Royal, Haymarket: rev by Barker, Billington, Christie, Couling, Coveney, Edwards, Gill, Hiley, Hirschhorn, Hurren, King, Khan, Lumsden, Mars-Jones, Morley, Nathan, Ratcliffe, Shannon, Shulman, Smith, Tinker.

2073 "Reviews of Productions." *LTR.* 1987; 7(11): 657-670. Lang.: Eng.

UK-England: London. 1987. ■*The Two Noble Kinsmen* attributed to John Fletcher and William Shakespeare, dir by Barry Kyle for the Royal Shakespeare Company at the Mermaid Theatre: rev by Billington, Billen, Coveney, Gordon, Hinton, Hirschhorn, Kemp, King, Nathan, Osborne, Ray, Remnant, Sanderson, Tinker. *Moses* by and with Rose English at the Drill Hall: rev by Osborne. *My Sister in This House* by Wendy Kesselman, dir by Nancy Meckler at the Hampstead Theatre: rev by Billington, Edwards, Edwardes, Gordon, Hirschhorn, Hiley, Hurren, King, Nathan, Osborne, Radin, Ratcliffe, Ray, Taylor. *Pain of Youth* by Ferdinand Bruckner dir by Patti Love at the Gate Theatre: rev by Coveney, de Jongh, Gordon, Hiley, Hudson, King, Looch, Radin, Rose, Rissik, Wolf.

2074 "How Bernard Shaw Produces Plays (As Told by Lillah McCarthy)." 163-168 in Leary, Daniel, ed. *Shaw's Plays in Performance*. University Park/London: Pennsylvania State UP; 1983. vi, 262 pp. (Shaw: The Annual of Bernard Shaw Studies 3 (ShawR).) Lang.: Eng.

UK-England. 1914-1927. Histories-sources. ■Reprint of manuscript of interview with Lillah McCarthy, revised by Shaw and published in New York's *American* (18 September 1927). Describes Shaw's techniques as a producer of his own plays.

2075 "Reviews of Productions." *LTR.* 1986; 6(11): 589-590. Lang.: Eng.

UK-England: London. 1986. ■*Philoctetes* by Sophocles, dir by Martyn Richards at the Offstage Downstairs: rev by Woddis. *On Humans* by Robin Driscoll and Tony Haase, dir by John Dale at the Lyric Studio: rev by Gardner, Rea, Rose, Shulman.

2076 "Reviews of Productions." *LTR.* 1986; 6(7): 314-315. Lang.: Eng.

UK-England: London. 1986. ■*The Bolt-Hole* by Jairo Anibal Niño, transl. and dir by Hal Brown at the Gate Theatre: rev by Connor, de Jongh, Rose. *QRs and AIs Clearly State* written and dir by Anthony Stanford-Tuck at King's Head Theatre: rev by Alexander, de Jongh, Nathan, Shorter. *Vintage Moving Pic* written and dir by Paul Filipiak, David Gaines and Toby Sedgwick at the Shaw Theatre: rev by Rea.

2077 "Reviews of Productions." *LTR.* 1986; 6(10): 527-531. Lang.: Eng.

UK-England: London. 1986. ■*Creditors* by August Strindberg, dir by the cast (Aryanne Bertish, Ian McDiarmida and Jonathan Kent) at the Almeida Theatre: rev by Barber, de Jongh, Edwardes, Edwards, Gardner, Harron, Hiley, Hoyle, Hurren, King, Shulman, Wheen. *The Normal Heart* by Larry Kramer, dir by David Hayman at the Albery: rev by Asquith, de Jongh, Edwardes, Hirschhorn, Hoyle, Hurren, Ratcliffe, Tinker.

2078 "Reviews of Productions." *LTR.* 1986; 6(7): 309-314. Lang.: Eng.

UK-England: London. 1986. ■*Judy* by Terry Wale, dir by Bill Kenwright at the Strand Theatre: rev by de Jongh, Edwardes, Gay, Hiley, Hoyle, Hirschhorn, Hurren, Jameson, Morley, Ratcliffe, Renton, Shannon, Shorter, St. George, Thorncroft, Usher, Wheen, Wolf. *Road* by Jim Cartwright, dir by Simon Curtis at Theatre Upstairs: rev by Hay, King, Rudin, Shorter. *The Company Forgives a Moment of Madness* by Rodolfo Santana, transl. and dir by Hal Brown at the Gate Theatre: rev by Connor, de Jongh, Rose.

2079 "Reviews of Productions." *LTR.* 1986; 6(7): 316-318. Lang.: Eng.

UK-England: London. 1986. ■*All the Fun of the Fair* by John McGrath, dir by Christopher Bond at the Half Moon Theatre and later at the Albany Empire Theatre: rev by Bardsley, Gardner, Hay, Hiley, Hoyle, Jay, Murdin. *Medea* by Euripides, dir by Toby Robertson at the Young Vic: rev by de Jongh, Hay, Hurren, King, McKenley, Morley, Shorter. *Bouncers* written and dir by John Godber at the Arts Theatre Club: rev by Shannon.

2080 "Reviews of Productions." *LTR.* 1986; 6(7): 321-326. Lang.: Eng.

UK-England: London. 1986. ■*Three Sisters* by Anton Pavlovič Čechov, dir by Mike Alfreds at the Bloomsbury: rev by Billington, Coveney, Fox, King, Nathan, Ratcliffe, Rose, Shorter. *Il Candelario (The Candlemaker)* by Giordano Bruno, dir by Clifford Williams at The Pit: rev by Billington, Gardner, Hiley, Hirschhorn, Hoyle, Morley, Nathan, Nightingale, Ratcliffe, Shannon, Shorter, Shulman. *People Show No. 91: A Romance* written and dir by Collette Walker, Jeremy Swift,

DRAMA: —Performance/production

George Khan and Mark Long at the Almeida: rev by Connor, Covenay, Rose.

2081 "Reviews of Productions." *LTR.* 1986; 7(7): 326-328. Lang.: Eng.

UK-England: London. 1986. ■*Relatively Speaking* by Alan Ayckbourn, dir by Alan Strachan at the Greenwich: rev by Curtis, de Jongh, Masters, McFerran, Say, Scafe, Shorter.

2082 "Reviews of Productions." *LTR.* 1986; 6(7): 369-380. Lang.: Eng.

UK-England: London. 1986. ■*Mephisto* by Ariane Mnouchkine, dir by Adrian Noble at the Barbican: rev by Bardsley, Billington, Coveney, Couling, Edwards, Hiley, Hirschhorn, Hurren, King, Jameson, Lawson, Nathan, Nightingale, Ratcliffe, Shannon, Shorter, Shulman, Usher, Wheen. *Cold Storage* by Ronald Ribman, dir by Peter Symond at the Offstage Downstairs: rev by Cotton, Radin, Sanderson. *The Beaux' Stratagem* by George Farquhar, dir by Peter James at the Lyric Hammersmith: rev by de Jongh, Edwards, Fox, King, McFerran, Nathan, Shannon, Shorter, Shulman, Smurthwaite, Thorncroft.

2083 "Reviews of Productions." *LTR.* 1986; 6(8): 407-408. Lang.: Eng.

UK-England: London. 1986. ■*The First Show* written and dir by Andy Walker at Oval House and Battersea Arts Centre: rev by Gardner. *The Suburbs of Hell* by Brian Lipson, dir by Andy Wilson at the Institute of Contemporary Arts: rev by Gardner, Gill, Ratcliffe. *Swim Visit* by Wesley Moore, dir by Christopher Payton at the Half Moon Theatre: rev by King, Murdin, Scafe, Shorter, Smurthwaite, Rose.

2084 "Reviews of Productions." *LTR.* 1986; 6(7): 381-403. Lang.: Eng.

UK-England: London. 1986. ■*The Carrier Frequency* by Impact Theatre Co-operative, dir by Russell Hoban at the Place Theatre: rev by Ashford, Parry, Rea. *Chiaroscuro* by Jackie Kay, dir by Joan Ann Maynard at Drill Hall: rev by Bardsley, Horsford, Rose. *Time* by Dave Clark, dir by Larry Fuller at the Dominion: rev by Barber, Billington, Couling, Gill, Hiley, Hirschhorn, Hoyle, Hurren, Jameson, King, Morley, Nightingale, Paton, Ratcliffe, Shulman, St. George, Usher, Wheen.

2085 "Reviews of Productions." *LTR.* 1986; 6(7): 404-407. Lang.: Eng.

UK-England: London. 1986. ■*Edmund Ironside*, attributed to William Shakespeare, dir by Tim Heath at the Bridge Lane: rev by Fox, Keatley, Neumark, Renton, Say. *Orphans* by Lyle Kessler, dir by Gary Sinise at the Apollo Theatre: rev by Murdin, Shannon. *The Lower Depths—An East End Story* by Maksim Gorkij, dir by Roland Rees at the Tricycle Theatre: rev by de Jongh, Edwardes, Grier, Hiley, Keatley, McKenley, Ratcliffe, Shorter.

2086 "Reviews of Productions." *LTR.* 1986; 6(8): 410-411. Lang.: Eng.

UK-England: London. 1986. ■*American Ballroom Theatre* at Sadler's Wells Theatre: rev by Clarke, Crisp, Parry, Thorpe. *Seh-Zan* by Hossein Karimbeik and *Someone Else's Child* by Jalal Al-E-Ahmad, dir by Karimbeik: rev by Edwardes. *Everyman* dir by Mark Strickson at Cottesloe Theatre: rev by Loosely, Nichols.

2087 "Reviews of Productions." *LTR.* 1986; 6(8): 412-421. Lang.: Eng.

UK-England: London. 1986. ■*The Gambler* by Peter Brewis, Bob Goody and Mel Smith at the Hampstead Theatre: rev by Barber, Billington, Connor, Coveney, Grant, Hiley, Hurren, King, Morley, Nathan, Nightingale, Ratcliffe, Shannon, Shulman, Tinker, Tressider. *The Merchant of Venice* by William Shakespeare, dir by Michael Joyce at the Almeida Theatre. *Force and Hypocrisy* by Doug Lucie, dir by Paul Tomlinson at the Young Vic Studio: rev by Edwards, Fox, Gardner, Shorter.

2088 "Reviews of Productions." *LTR.* 1986; 6(9): 457-462. Lang.: Eng.

UK-England: London. 1986. ■*Ballroom* by Robert Pugh, dir by Jonathan Martin at Theatre Royal, Stratford East: rev by Barber, Bryce, Connor, Fox, Hay, Hoyle, King, Morrison, Nathan, Nightingale, Shannon, Shulman. *Angry Housewives* by A.M. Collins and Chad Henry, dir by Art Wolff at the Lyric Studio: rev by Edwardes, Fox,

Hiley, Hurren, King, Morley, Shannon, Shulman, Thorncroft, Wheen, Wolf.

2089 "Reviews of Productions." *LTR.* 1986; 6(8): 422-454. Lang.: Eng.

UK-England: London. 1986. ■*The Wow Show* written and dir by Mark Arden, Lee Cornes, Mark Elliott and Stephen Frost at Wyndham's Theatre: rev by Barkley, Barber, Billington, Coveney, King, Herbert, Hiley, Hurren, Nathan, Nichols, Ratcliffe, Shulman, Tinker. *HMS Pinafore* by W.S. Gilbert and Arthur Sullivan, dir by Joe Dowling at the Old Vic: rev by Asquith, Barber, Billington, Grant, Hoyle, Hurren, Jameson, King, Morley, Nightingale, Norman, Ratcliffe, Shannon, Shulman, Tinker, Wheen.

2090 "Reviews of Productions." *LTR.* 1986; 6(9): 454-456. Lang.: Eng.

UK-England: London. 1986. ■*One of the Fair Sex* by Lin Dennis, dir by Peter Southcott at the Man in the Moon Theatre: rev by Alexander, Woddis. *Watching* by Jim Hitchmough, dir by Tony Mulholland at the Bush Theatre: rev by Billington, Connor, Coveney, Couling, Hurren, Nightingale, Ratcliffe, Rose, Shulman.

2091 "Reviews of Productions." *LTR.* 1986; 6(9): 462-466. Lang.: Eng.

UK-England: London. 1986. ■*Baal* by Bertolt Brecht, dir by Nancy Meckler at the Almeida Theatre: rev by Billington, Morrison, Murdin, Murray, Say. *Shirley* by Andrea Dunbar, dir by Carole Hayman at Theatre Upstairs: rev by Billington, Gardner, Grant, Herbert, Hirschhorn, Hoyle, Morley, Nightingale, Say, Shulman.

2092 "Reviews of Productions." *LTR.* 1986; 6(9): 466-471. Lang.: Eng.

UK-England: London. 1986. ■*The Voyage Home* by Sylvia Freedman, dir by Andrew Harmon at King's Head Theatre: rev by de Jongh, Murdin, Rose. *Possum in the Bughouse* by Caroline Behr, dir by Tim Luscombe at the Old Red Lion: rev by Asquith, Barber, de Jongh, Sanderson.

2093 "Reviews of Productions." *LTR.* 1986; 6(9): 472-473. Lang.: Eng.

UK-England: London. 1986. ■*A Midsummer Night's Dream* by William Shakespeare, dir by David Thacker and Jeremy Bell at Young Vic: rev by Coveney, de Jongh, Gardner, Wheen. *Fail/Safe* by Ayshe Raif, dir by Sue Dunderdale at the Soho Poly Theatre: rev by de Jongh, Edwardes.

2094 "Reviews of Productions." *LTR.* 1986; 6(9): 472-473. Lang.: Eng.

UK-England: London. 1986. ■*Can You Help?* written and dir by Jeremy Paul at the Latchmere Theatre: rev by Edwards.

2095 "Reviews of Productions." *LTR.* 1986; 6(9): 474-503. Lang.: Eng.

UK-England: London. 1986. ■*Troilus and Cressida* by William Shakespeare, dir by Howard Davies at the Barbican Theatre: rev by Billington, Coveney, du Bois, Edwards, Grant, Herbert, Nathan, Nightingale, Ratcliffe, Say, Shannon, Shorter, Shulman, Tinker. *La Cage aux Folles* by Jerry Herman, Harvey Fierstein and Jean Poiret, dir by Arthur Laurents at the London Palladium: rev by Barber, Billington, Connors, Coveney, Davis, Hiley, Hirschhorn, Hurren, Nightingale, Norley, Nathan, Ratcliffe, Robertson, Say, Shannon, Shulman, St. George, Tinker, Wheen.

2096 "Reviews of Productions." *LTR.* 1986; 6(10): 505-507. Lang.: Eng.

UK-England: London. 1986. ■*Double Cross* by Thomas Kilroy, dir by Jim Sheridan at the Royal Court Theatre: rev by Barber, Coveney, Cohen, Hurren, King, Lawson, Lawton, Morley, Murdin, Woddis. *Alas Poor Fred* by James Saunders, dir by Carmen Munroe at Drill Hall Theatre: rev by Edwardes, Woddis.

2097 "Reviews of Productions." *LTR.* 1986; 6(10): 508-515. Lang.: Eng.

UK-England: London. 1986. ■*Chess* by Tim Rice, Benny Anderssen and Bjorn Ulvaeus, dir by Trevor Nunn at the Prince Edward: rev by Asquith, Barber, Billington, Christie, Coveney, Denselow, Edwards, Grant, Hiley, Hirschhorn, Hurren, Jameson, King, Miller, Morley, Nathan, Nightingale, Ratcliffe, Shulman, Tinker, Wheen. *Incident*

DRAMA: —Performance/production

written and dir by Jan Lauwers at Riverside Studios: rev by Couling, Hiley, Hoyle, Rea, Rose.

2098 "Reviews of Productions." *LTR*. 1986; 6(10): 518-526. Lang.: Eng.

UK-England: London. 1986. ■*Real Dreams* by Trevor Griffiths, dir by Ron Daniels at The Pit: rev by Asquith, Barber, Billington, Coveney, Edwards, Grant, Hiley, Hurren, Morley, Nathan, Nightingale, Ratcliffe, Shannon, Shulman, Wheen. *Entertaining Strangers* written and dir by Hilary Westlake at the Lyric Studio: rev by de Jongh, Gardner, Salvadori.

2099 "Reviews of Productions." *LTR*. 1986; 6(10): 531-537. Lang.: Eng.

UK-England: London. 1986. ■*Son of Cain* by David Williamson, dir by John Noble at Wyndham's Theatre: rev by Barber, Billington, Coveney, Grant, Harron, Hiley, Hirschhorn, Hurren, Jacobs, Jameson, King, Nightingale, Shannon, Shulman, St. George, Tinker, Wheen. *Who Killed Hilda Murrell?* by Chris Martin, dir by Jane Collins at Tricycle Theatre: rev by Billington, Gardner, Harron, Nathan, Rose, Shannon, Shorter, Young.

2100 "Reviews of Productions." *LTR*. 1986; 6(11): 557-560. Lang.: Eng.

UK-England: London. 1986. ■*The Orphan* by Thomas Otway, dir by Philip Prowse at the Greenwich Theatre: rev by Barber, Billington, Coveney, Grant, Harron, Hurren, King, Wolf. *I've Been Running* by Clare McIntyre, dir by Terry Johnson at the Old Red Lion: rev by de Jongh, Hoyle, Rose, Woddis.

2101 "Reviews of Productions." *LTR*. 1986; 6(11): 559-566. Lang.: Eng.

UK-England: London. 1986. ■*Candy and Shelley Go to the Desert* by Paul Cizmar, dir by Terry Johnson at the Old Red Lion: rev by de Jongh, Hoyle, Rose, Woddis. *Antony and Cleopatra* by William Shakespeare, dir by Toby Robertson and Christopher Selbie at the Theatre Royal, Haymarket: rev by Barber, Billington, Coveney, Harron, Hiley, Hirschhorn, Hulme, Hurren, King, Morley, Nathan, Nightingale, O'Shaughnessy, Rose, Shulman, Tinker, Wheen, Woddis.

2102 "Reviews of Productions." *LTR*. 1986; 6(11): 567-573. Lang.: Eng.

UK-England: London. 1986. ■*Dalliance* by Tom Stoppard, dir by Peter Wood at the Lyttelton Theatre: rev by Barber, Billington, Bryce, Christie, Coveney, Edwardes, Harron, Hiley, Hirschhorn, Hurren, King, Morley, Nathan, Nightingale, O'Shaughnessy, Pascal, Shannon, Shulman, Tinker, Wheen. *Hamlet* by William Shakespeare, dir by Ian Thompson at the Young Vic Studio: rev by de Jongh, Gardner, Rose, Wheen.

2103 "Reviews of Productions." *LTR*. 1986; 6(11): 574-579. Lang.: Eng.

UK-England: London. 1986. ■*The Nest (Das Nest)* by Franz Xaver Kroetz, dir by Sarah Pia Anderson at the Bush Theatre: rev by Billington, Coveney, Gardner, Grant, Harron, Shulman. *Madonna in Slag City* written and dir by Jude Alderson at the Oval House: rev by Rose, Woddis.

2104 "Reviews of Productions." *LTR*. 1986; 6(11): 580-581. Lang.: Eng.

UK-England: London. 1986. ■*Heyday* by Herbert Appleman, dir by Nica Burns at King's Head Theatre: rev by Asquith, Barber, de Jongh, Griffiths, Hoyle, Hurren, King, Nathan, Shulman. *Woyzeck* by Georg Büchner, dir by Laurence Sach at the Latchmere: rev by Bardsley.

2105 "Reviews of Productions." *LTR*. 1986; 6(11): 582-585. Lang.: Eng.

UK-England: London. 1986. ■*Medea* by Euripides, dir by Mary McMurray at the Lyric Hammersmith: rev by Barber, de Jongh, Harren, Hiley, Hoyle, Hurren, King, Nathan, Nightingale, Rose, Shannon, Woddis. *The Flight to Venice* by Georg Kaiser, dir by David Graham-Young at the Gate, Notting Hill: rev by Billington, Hoyle, Robinson.

2106 "Reviews of Productions." *LTR*. 1986; 6(11): 586-589. Lang.: Eng.

UK-England: London. 1986. ■*Romeo and Juliet* by William Shakespeare, dir by Declan Donnellan at the Open Air Theatre, Regents' Park: rev by Coveney, King, McFerran, Shannon, Shorter,

Shulman, Tinker. *Jug* by Henry Livings (adapted from Heinrich von Kleist's *Der zerbrochene Krug*), dir by Philip Hedley at the Theatre Royal, Stratford East: rev by Coveney, de Jongh, Lee, Say.

2107 "Reviews of Productions." *LTR*. 1986; 6(14): 723-724. Lang.: Eng.

UK-England: London. 1986. ■*Travelling Light* written and dir by Meryl Tankard at the Institute of Contemporary Arts: rev by Connor, Coveney, Rea, Robertson. *I Do Like To Be* by Shane Connaughton, dir by Jeff Teare at the Tricycle Theatre: rev by Christy, Sanderson, Shulman, Woddis.

2108 "Reviews of Productions." *LTR*. 1986; 6(14): 725-729. Lang.: Eng.

UK-England: London. 1986. ■*Metamorphosis* written and dir by Steven Berkoff at the Mermaid: rev by Billington, Connor, Couling, Grier, Harron, Hay, King, Nurse, Pascal, Shannon, St. George, Tinker. *The Gambler* written and dir by Peter Brewis, Bob Goody and Mel Smith at the Comedy Theatre: rev by Asquith, Denselow, Hirschhorn, Jacobs, Keegan, Thorncroft, Wheen.

2109 "Reviews of Productions." *LTR*. 1986; 6(14): 729-732. Lang.: Eng.

UK-England: London. 1986. ■*Side by Side by Sondheim* by David Kernan, dir by Lindsay Dolan at Donmar Warehouse: rev by Barber, Couling, Coveney, Hay, Hiley, Hurren, Jacobs, Morley, Wolf. *Moll Flanders* by Claire Luckham, lyrics by Chris Bond and Luckham, dir by Bond at the Half Moon: rev by Billington, Connor, Grier, Jacobs, Loheen, Nurse, Rose, St. George.

2110 "Reviews of Productions." *LTR*. 1986; 6(14): 733-734. Lang.: Eng.

UK-England: London. 1986. ■*The Miss Firecracker Contest* by Beth Henley, dir by Simon Stokes at the Greenwich: rev by Barber, de Jongh, King, Lee, Pascal, Rose, Shulman. *The Parquet Floor* and *The Passport* by Desmond Adams, dir by Mark Freeland at the Young Vic: rev by Hay.

2111 "Reviews of Productions." *LTR*. 1986; 6(14): 739-771. Lang.: Eng.

UK-England: London. 1986. ■*The Danton Affair* by Pam Gems, dir by Ron Daniels featuring the Royal Shakespeare Company at the Barbican: rev by Barber, Billingon, Coveney, Grant, Harran, Hiley, Hirschhorn, Hurren, King, Morley, Nightingale, Pascal, Shulman, Smith, St. George, Tinker, Woddis. *The Dead Monkey* by Nick Darke, featuring the Royal Shakespeare Company, dir by Roger Michell at The Pit: rev by Billington, Coveney, Gardner, Harran, Hurren, King, Nightingale, Nurse, Shulman, Tinker.

2112 "Reviews of Productions." *LTR*. 1986; 6(14): 771-773. Lang.: Eng.

UK-England: London. 1986. ■*Dybbuk* written and dir by Bruce Myers at the Almeida: rev by Coveney, Edwards, Frazer, Gardner, Hay, Nurse.

2113 "Reviews of Productions." *LTR*. 1986; 6(18): 938-940. Lang.: Eng.

UK-England: London. 1986. ■*Flies By Night* by Peter Lloyd, dir by Nigel Halon at the Old Red Lion: rev by Rose, Wolf. *For King and Country* by John Wilson, dir by Alan Strachan at the Greenwich: rev by de Jongh, Hoyle, Matheou, McFerran, Nurse.

2114 "Reviews of Productions." *LTR*. 1986; 6(13): 678-680. Lang.: Eng.

UK-England: London. 1986. ■*An Evening With Barbara Cook* written and dir by Barbara Cook and Wally Harper at Donmar Warehouse: rev by Barber, Hirschhorn, Hurren, Murdin, Nathan, Ratcliffe, Robertson, Say, Sutcliffe, Tinker, Thorncroft, Wolf. *Sparkle Plenty* written and dir by Beatrice Reading at King's Head: rev by Edwardes, Hurren, Lee.

2115 "Reviews of Productions." *LTR*. 1986; 6(13): 681-687. Lang.: Eng.

UK-England: London. 1986. ■*Infidelities* written and dir by Sean Mathias at the Boulevard Theatre: rev by Asquith, Coveney, de Jongh, Denselow, Gordon, Gore-Langton, Hurren, Nathan, Say, Shannon, Shorter, Shulman, Woddis. *The Dragon* by Yevgeny Schwartz, dir by James MacDonald at Bridge Lane Battersea Theatre: rev by Gawthrop.

2116 "Reviews of Productions." *LTR*. 1986; 6(13): 688-690. Lang.: Eng.

DRAMA: —Performance/production

UK-England: London. 1986. ■*She Also Dances* by Kenneth Arnold, dir by Debbie Wolfe at Offstage Downstairs: rev by Barber, Carne, Nathan, Neumark, Wolf. *An Echo in the Bone* by Dennis Scott, dir by Yvonne Brewster at Drill Hall: rev by Asquith, Carne, Connor, Edwardes. *Let Us Go Then, You and I* written and dir by Josephine Hart at Lyric Studio: rev by Grove, Hoyle.

2117 "Reviews of Productions." *LTR*. 1986; 6(13): 691-696. Lang.: Eng.

UK-England: London. 1986. ■*Making Noise Quietly* by Robert Holman, dir by John Dove at the Bush: rev by Billington, Coveney, Edwardes, Gardner, Gordon, Nathan, Nightingale, Ratcliffe, Say, Shulman, Wheen. *A Lovely Sunday for Creve-Coeur* by Tennessee Williams, dir by Sydnee Blake at the Old Red Lion: rev by Billington, Coveney, King, Pascal, Rose.

2118 "Reviews of Productions." *LTR*. 1986; 6(13): 694-717. Lang.: Eng.

UK-England: London. 1986. ■*Fulfilling Koch's Postulate* and *Cabin Fever* by Joan Schenkar, dir by Paddi Taylor at the Gate, Notting Hill: rev by Gardner, Hoyle, Sanderson. *Neaptide* by Sarah Daniels, dir by John Burgess at Cottesloe Theatre: rev by Asquith, Barber, Billington, Coveney, Devlin, Hurren, King, Nightingale, Pascal, Ratcliffe, Shulman, Wheen, Woddis.

2119 "Reviews of Productions." *LTR*. 1986; 6(13): 717-722. Lang.: Eng.

UK-England: London. 1986. ■*I'm Not Rappaport* by Herb Gardner, dir by Daniel Sullivan at the Apollo: rev by Asquith, Christie, Coveney, Grant, Hirschhorn, Hurren, Jameson, King, Morley, Nightingale, Pascal, Ratcliffe, Shannon, Shorter, Shulman, Tinker, Wheen. *Narnia* by Jules Tasca, Thomas Tierney and Ted Drachman, dir by Christopher Biggins at All Hallows by the Tower: rev by Clements, Gardner.

2120 "Reviews of Productions." *LTR*. 1986; 6(13): 674-676. Lang.: Eng.

UK-England: London. 1986. ■*Deadly Nightcap* by Francis Durbridge, dir by Val May at Westminster Theatre: rev by Asquith, Barber, Hurren, Lee, Shannon. *Hedda Gabler* by Henrik Ibsen, dir by Clare Davidson at the Bloomsbury: rev by de Jongh, Hoyle, Ratcliffe.

2121 "Reviews of Productions." *LTR*. 1986; 6(12): 635-642. Lang.: Eng.

UK-England: London. 1986. ■*Krapp's Last Tape* dir by Ewan Hooper and *Endgame* dir by Charlie Hanson, both plays by Samuel Beckett at Riverside Studios: rev by Carne, Couling, Connor, Gore-Langton, Hoyle, Morrison, Shorter. *The Taming of the Shrew* by William Shakespeare, dir by Toby Robertson and Christopher Selbie at Theatre Royal, Haymarket: rev by Barber, Couling, Coveney, de Jongh, Edwardes, Edwards, Gardner, Hiley, Hirschhorn, Hurren, Jameson, King, Morley, Nathan, Ratcliffe, Shannon, Shulman, Tinker, Wheen.

2122 "Reviews of Productions." *LTR*. 1986; 6(12): 642-647. Lang.: Eng.

UK-England: London. 1986. ■*A Chorus of Disapproval* written and dir by Alan Ayckbourn at the Lyric: rev by Barber, Connor, Coveney, de Jongh, Edwardes, Hiley, Masters, Nathan, Say, Shannon, Tinker. *Double Double* by Eric Elice and Roger Rees, dir by Leon Rubin at the Fortune: rev by Hiley, Hurren, King, Nightingale, Rissik, Ratcliffe, Shannon, Shulman, Tinker, Wheen, Woddis.

2123 "Reviews of Productions." *LTR*. 1986; 6(12): 647-667. Lang.: Eng.

UK-England: London. 1986. ■*Road* by Jim Cartwright, dir by Simon Curtis at the Royal Court: rev by Asquith, Barber, Coveney, de Jongh, Edwardes, Hiley, Hirschhorn, King, Morley, Nathan, Nightingale, Ratcliffe, Shulman, St. George, Wheen. *A Midsummer Night's Dream* by William Shakespeare, dir by David Conville and Emma Freud at the Open Air Theatre in Regent's Park: rev by Bardsley, de Jongh, Edwards, Edwardes, Gordon, King, Nathan, Shannon, Williamson.

2124 "Reviews of Productions." *LTR*. 1986; 6(12): 667-673. Lang.: Eng.

UK-England: London. 1986. ■*My Life, by Josef Mengele* written and dir by Janek Alexander at Institute of Contemporary Arts: rev by Carne, Hoyle, Pascal. *Charlie Girl* by Hugh and Margaret Williams with Ray Cooney, music and lyrics by David Heneker and John Taylor,

dir by Stewart Trotter at Victoria Palace: rev by Barber, Christie, Connor, Coveney, de Jongh, Edwardes, Hiley, Hirschhorn, Hurren, King, Morley, Nathan, Ratcliffe, Shannon, Shulman, St. George, Tinker, Wheen.

2125 "Reviews of Productions." *LTR*. 1986; 6(13): 676-677. Lang.: Eng.

UK-England: London. 1986. ■*Some Kind of Hero* by Les Smith, dir by David Thacker at the Young Vic: rev by Coveney, de Jongh, Gardner, Hay, Nightingale, Wheen. *To All in Tents* by Rony Robinson, dir by Michael Hucks at the Young Vic: rev by Carne, Remnant, Rose.

2126 "Reviews of Productions." *LTR*. 1986; 6(12): 605-610. Lang.: Eng.

UK-England: London. 1986. ■*Ross* by Terrence Rattigan, dir by Roger Redfarn at the Old Vic: rev by Barber, Billington, Coveney, Couling, Edwards, Harron, Hiley, Hirschhorn, Hurren, Jameson, King, Lawson, Lubbock, Morley, Nathan, Pascal, Shannon, Shulman, Tinker. *The Art of Perspective* written and dir by Malcolm Sherman at Duke of Cambridge Theatre: rev by McFerran, Sanderson, Scaife, Woddis.

2127 "Reviews of Productions." *LTR*. 1986; 6(12): 610-611. Lang.: Eng.

UK-England: London. 1986. ■*The Sin Eaters* by Jacqueline Holborough, dir by Ann Mitchell at the Albany Empire: rev by McFerran, Woddis. *Waiting for Hannibal* written and dir by Burt Caesar at Drill Hall: rev by Carne, Hay, McKenley.

2128 "Reviews of Productions." *LTR*. 1986; 6(12): 611-624. Lang.: Eng.

UK-England: London. 1986. ■*Circe & Bravo* by Donald Freed, dir by Harold Pinter at the Hampstead Theatre: rev by Barber, Billington, Coveney, Denselow, Edwards, Harron, Hiley, Hirschhorn, Hurren, Jameson, King, Lubbock, Morley, Nathan, Nightingale, Rose, Shulman, Tinker, Woddis. *The Entertainer* by John Osborne, dir by Robin Lefevre at the Shaftsbury: rev by Barber, Billington, Connor, Couling, Coveney, Edwards, Grant, Hiley, Hirschhorn, Hurren, King, Lubbock, Morley, Nathan, Nightingale, Ratcliffe, Shannon, Shulman, St. George, Tinker.

2129 "Reviews of Productions." *LTR*. 1986; 6(12): 624-626. Lang.: Eng.

UK-England: London. 1986. ■*Film Film Film* by Farrukh Dhondy, dir by Laurens C. Postma at the Shaw: rev by Bhegani, de Jongh, Denselow, Hiley, Hoyle, Morrison. *Leaving Home* by Julia Kearsley, dir by Brian Stirner at Soho Poly: rev by de Jongh, Hoyle, Matheou, Nightingale.

2130 "Reviews of Productions." *LTR*. 1986; 6(12): 627. Lang.: Eng.

UK-England: London. 1986. ■*Dark Water Closing* written and dir by Steve Shull at Institute of Contemporary Arts: rev by Bardsley, Woddis. *Fanny Kemble At Home* written and dir by Laurier Lister at Watermans: rev by Fox.

2131 "Reviews of Productions." *LTR*. 1986; 6(12): 628-634. Lang.: Eng.

UK-England: London. 1986. ■*The Shawl* dir by Richard Eyre and *Prairie du Chien* dir by Max Stafford-Clark, both plays by David Mamet at Theatre Upstairs: rev by Barber, Coveney, de Jongh, Hay, Hirschhorn, Nathan, Nightingale, Ratcliffe, Shulman, Woddis. *Herman* by Stewart Conn, dir by Eric Standidge at the Old Red Lion: rev by Carne, Hoyle, Lee.

2132 "Reviews of Productions." *LTR*. 1986; 6(16): 831-840. Lang.: Eng.

UK-England: London. 1986. ■*The American Clock* by Arthur Miller, dir by Peter Wood at the Cottesloe: rev by Billington, Coveney, Edwards, Freedman, Hiley, Hirschhorn, Hurren, King, Morley, Morrison, Nathan, Pascal, Rissik, Shorter, Shulman. *Arms and the Man* by George Bernard Shaw, dir by David Conville at the Open Air Theatre in Regent's Park: rev by Alexander, Cotton, de Jongh, King, Nathan, Nurse, Shulman, Tinker, Young. *Suz O Suz* written and dir by La Fura Dels Baus Company at Isle of Dogs Theatre: rev by Hoyle, Jones, Thorpe.

2133 "Reviews of Productions." *LTR*. 1986; 6(16): 864-865. Lang.: Eng.

DRAMA: —Performance/production

UK-England: London. 1986. ■*Nightshriek* by Trisha Ward, dir by Edward Wilson at the Shaw: rev by Billington, Hoyle, Rose, Shorter, Woddis. *A Proper Place* by Edward Kemp, dir by Bill Buffery at Jeanetta Cochrane Theatre: rev by Thorncroft.

2134 "Reviews of Productions." *LTR*. 1986; 6(16): 844-850. Lang.: Eng.

UK-England: London. 1986. ■*Wonderful Town!* with book by Joseph A. Fields and Jerome Chodorov, music by Leonard Bernstein, and lyrics by Betty Comden and Adolph Green, dir by Martin Connor at Queen's Theatre: rev by Billington, Christie, Edwardes, Hirschhorn, Hoyle, Hurren, Jameson, King, Nathan, Nurse, Shannon, Shulman, St. George, Tinker, Woddis. *Garden Girls* by Jacqueline Holborough, dir by Simon Stokes at the Bush: rev by de Jongh, Hoyle, Nathan, Rose, Shorter, Shulman, Wheen, Woddis.

2135 "Reviews of Productions." *LTR*. 1986; 6(16): 850-864. Lang.: Eng.

UK-England: London. 1986. ■*Key Exchange* by Kevin Wade, dir by Anthony Allen at the Old Red Lion: rev by de Jongh, Rose, Villa. *Romeo and Juliet* by William Shakespeare, dir by Kenneth Branagh at the Lyric Studio: rev by de Jongh, Edwardes, Edwardes, Hoyle, Khan, Shannon, Shorter, Shulman, Wheen.

2136 "Reviews of Productions." *LTR*. 1986; 6(16): 866-868. Lang.: Eng.

UK-England: London. 1986. ■*The Riot Act* by Tom Paulin, dir by Gillian Reynolds at the Tabard Theatre: rev by King, Robinson, Sanderson. *Marlowe* by Leo Rost and Jimmy Horowitz, dir by Robert Gillespie at the King's Head Theatre: rev by Asquith, Atkins, de Jongh, Hay, King, Shulman, Smith, Thorncroft.

2137 "Reviews of Productions." *LTR*. 1986; 6(16): 933-938. Lang.: Eng.

UK-England: London. 1986. ■*Ourselves Alone* by Anne Devlin, dir by Simon Curtis at the Royal Court: rev by de Jongh, Edwardes, Hurren, King, Morley, Murdin, Nathan, Pascal, Shorter, Young. *Noël and Gertie* by Sheridan Morley and Noël Coward, dir by David Horlock at Donmar Warehouse: rev by Barkley, Edwardes, Edwardes, Gordon, Hiley, Hurren, Khan, King, Thorncroft, Tinker.

2138 "Reviews of Productions." *LTR*. 1986; 6(18): 975-976. Lang.: Eng.

UK-England: London. 1986. ■*Lorca* written and dir by Trater Faulkner at the Lyric Studio: rev by Carne, Hay, Robinson, Shulman. *Henry V* by William Shakespeare, dir by Michael Croft and Graham Chinn at the Open Air Theatre, Regent's Park: rev by Atkins, Young.

2139 "Reviews of Productions." *LTR*. 1986; 6(18): 964. Lang.: Eng.

UK-England: London. 1986. ■*Birth of the Beast* by Sam Dowling, dir by Tal Rubins at the Tabard: rev by Sanderson, Woddis. *The Tunnel* by Malcolm Sherman, dir by Anne Harris and Sherman at Duke of Cambridge Theatre: rev by Robinson, Rose.

2140 "Reviews of Productions." *LTR*. 1986; 6(18): 940-943. Lang.: Eng.

UK-England: London. 1986. ■*How the Vote Was Won* by Evelyn Glover, Inez Bensusan, Cicely Hamilton, and Christopher St. John, dir by Tamara Hincho at the Gate Theatre: rev by Alexander, Woddis. *Cramp* by John Godber and Tim Robinson, dir by Godber at the Bloomsbury: rev by Coveney, de Jongh, Gardner, Grant, Harron, Murdin, Shorter, Smith, St. George.

2141 "Reviews of Productions." *LTR*. 1986; 6(18): 943-951. Lang.: Eng.

UK-England: London. 1986. ■*The Maintenance Man* by Richard Harris, dir by Roger Clissold at the Comedy Theatre: rev by Billington, Edwardes, Edwardes, Gordon, Hiley, Hirschhorn, Hurren, Jameson, King, Nathan, Ratcliffe, Shorter, Shulman, Smith, St. George, Wolf, Young. *Rookery Nook* by Ben Travers, dir by Mark Kingston at the Shaftsbury: rev by Billington, Connor, Edwardes, Gordon, Grant, Hiley, Hirschhorn, Hurren, Jameson, King, Nathan, Ratcliffe, Shannon, Shorter, Shulman, Smith, Tinker, Young.

2142 "Reviews of Productions." *LTR*. 1986; 6(18): 952-962. Lang.: Eng.

UK-England: London. 1986. ■*Suna* and *Sand* by J.A. Seazer and Yutaka Nemota, dir by Seazer at Institute of Contemporary Arts: rev by

Connor, Grant, Hall, Hoyle. *Woman in Mind* written and dir by Alan Ayckbourn at the Vaudeville: rev by Asquith, Billington, Coveney, Gordon, Grant, Hiley, Hirschhorn, Hurren, Jameson, King, Nathan, Radin, Ratcliffe, Shorter, Shulman, Smith, Tinker.

2143 "Reviews of Productions." *LTR*. 1986; 6(18): 962-964. Lang.: Eng.

UK-England: London. 1986. ■*The Double* written and dir by Jonathan Holloway at the Bridge Lane Battersea Theatre: rev by Gardner, Hoyle, McFerran. *The Broken Thigh* by Bhasa, dir by Jatinder Verma at Drill Hall Theatre: rev by Billington, Edwardes, Scaife.

2144 "Reviews of Productions." *LTR*. 1986; 6(22): 1191-1199. Lang.: Eng.

UK-England. 1986. ■*Gaudete* written and dir by Julia Bardsley and Phelim McDermott at the Almeida Theatre: rev by Allnut, Armistead, Carne, Edwardes, Ford, Jones, Nathan, Ratcliffe, Shulman. *The Archbishop's Ceiling* by Arthur Miller, dir by Nick Hamm at The Pit: rev by Billington, Edwardes, Edwardes, Gardner, Hiley, Hirschhorn, Hoyle, Hurren, Jones, Licht, Morley, Ratcliffe, Rissik, Shorter, Shulman, Smith.

2145 "Reviews of Productions." *LTR*. 1986; 6(18): 977-978. Lang.: Eng.

UK-England: London. 1986. ■*Sink the Belgrano!* written and dir by Steven Berkoff at the Half Moon Theatre: rev by Connor, de Jongh, Gordon, Murdin, Rose, Shannon, Toberman. *Tele-Men* written and dir by Carlo Boso at Institute of Contemporary Arts: rev by Connor, Edwardes.

2146 "Reviews of Productions." *LTR*. 1986; 6(18): 979-996. Lang.: Eng.

UK-England: London. 1986. ■*Albertine in Five Times* by Michel Tremblay, transl. by John Van Burek and Bill Glassco, dir by Glassco at the Donmar Warehouse: rev by Billington, Conn, Edwardes, Gardner, Rose. *The Swap* by Mark McCrum, dir by Jenny Romya and McCrum at the Boulevard Theatre: rev by Atkins, Bardsley, Coveney, Gordon, King, Mavor.

2147 "Reviews of Productions." *LTR*. 1986; 6(18): 997-1000. Lang.: Eng.

UK-England: London. 1986. ■*Private Means* by Stephen Gilbert, dir by Brian Stirner at Soho Poly Theatre: rev by Armistead, de Jongh, Sanderson, Wolf. *Tuesday's Child* by Terry Johnson and Kate Lock, dir by Mike Bradwell at Theatre Royal, Stratford East: rev by Coveney, Edwardes, Gordon, Grant, Hiley, Ratcliffe, Shulman, Shorter, Woddis.

2148 "Reviews of Productions." *LTR*. 1986; 6(18): 1000-1005. Lang.: Eng.

UK-England: London. 1986. ■*Wait 'til You See Her* by Bob West, dir by Wally Harper at the Albery: rev by Billington, Conquest, Gardner, Hiley, Hopkins, Hudson, Hurren, King, Ratcliffe, St. George, Tinker. *Ask for the Moon* by Shirley Gee, dir by John Dove at the Hampstead: rev by Billington, Coveney, Edwardes, Gardner, Hirschhorn, Hurren, King, Nathan, Shorter, Shulman.

2149 "Reviews of Productions." *LTR*. 1986; 6(15): 774-779. Lang.: Eng.

UK-England: London. 1986. ■*Cabaret* with book by Joe Masteroff, music by John Kander and lyrics by Fred Ebb, dir by Gillian Lynne at the Strand: rev by Billington, Bonner, Christie, Coveney, Harron, Hiley, Hurren, Jacobs, Jameson, King, Morley, Robertson, Shannon, Shulman, Tinker, Shorter, Wheen, Woddis. *A Colder Climate* by Karim Alrawi, dir by Simon Curtis and Max Stafford-Clark at the Royal Court: rev by Billington, Coveney, Gardner, Hiley, Hudson, Hurren, King, McFerran, Ratcliffe, Shorter, Wheen.

2150 "Reviews of Productions." *LTR*. 1986; 6(15): 782-792. Lang.: Eng.

UK-England: London. 1986. ■*Jacobowsky and the Colonel* by Franz Werfel, dir by Jonathan Lynn at the National Theatre: rev by Billington, Coveney, Grant, Hiley, Hirschhorn, Hurren, Jameson, King, Morley, Nathan, Pascal, Ratcliffe, Shorter, Shulman, Tinker, Wheen. *I'll Go On* by Barry McGovern and Gerry Dukes, dir by Colm O'Brian at Riverside Studios: rev by Couling, Coveney, de Jongh, Ratcliffe, Rose, Wolf.

2151 "Reviews of Productions." *LTR*. 1986; 6(15): 793-796. Lang.: Eng.

DRAMA: —Performance/production

UK-England: London. 1986. ■*Observe the Sons of Ulster Marching Towards the Somme* by Frank McGuinness, dir by Michael Attenborough at the Hampstead: rev by Billington, Coveney, Edwards, Gardner, Grant, Hiley, Hurren, King, Morley, Nathan, Shorter, Shulman, Ratcliffe. *Cafe Tabou* by Vince Foxall, dir by John Turner at the Old Red Lion: rev by Hay.

2152 "Reviews of Productions." *LTR.* 1986; 6(15): 797-802. Lang.: Eng.

UK-England: London. 1986. ■*The Cocktail Party* by T. S. Eliot, dir by John Dexter at the Phoenix: rev by Barber, Billington, Coveney, Edwardes, Gardner, Hiley, Hirschhorn, Hurren, King, Morley, Ratcliffe, Shannon, Shulman, Tinker. *Einstein* by Ron Elisha, dir by Babs McMillan at the Gate Theatre: rev by de Jongh, Edwardes, Hayes.

2153 "Reviews of Productions." *LTR.* 1986; 6(15): 803-821. Lang.: Eng.

UK-England: London. 1986. ■*Annie Get Your Gun* with music and lyrics by Irving Berlin, book by Herbert and Dorothy Fields, dir by David Gilmore at the Aldwych: rev by Atyeo, Barber, Hirschhorn, Hoyle, Hurren, Jameson, Say, Shulman, Wolf. *The Petition* by Brian Clark, dir by Peter Hall at the Lyttelton: rev by Barber, Billington, Bryce, Couling, Coveney, Edwards, Hiley, Hirschhorn, Hurren, Grant, Jameson, King, Morley, Nathan, Ratcliffe, Shannon, Shulman, Tinker, Wheen, Woddis.

2154 "Reviews of Productions." *LTR.* 1986; 6(15): 822-831. Lang.: Eng.

UK-England: London. 1986. ■*Deadwood* by Hilary Westlake, Wendy Houstoun and Trevor Stuart, dir by Westlake at Kew Garden Theatre: rev by Billington, Hoyle, Rea, Rose. *Long Day's Journey into Night* by Eugene O'Neill, dir by Jonathan Miller at Theatre Royal, Haymarket: rev by Billington, Couling, Coveney, Edwardes, Edwards, Freedman, Hiley, Hirschhorn, Hurren, Jameson, King, Morley, Morrison, Nathan, Pascal, Shannon, Shorter, Shulman, Tinker.

2155 "Reviews of Productions." *LTR.* 1986; 6(22): 1200-1207. Lang.: Eng.

UK-England: London. 1986. ■*Dave Allen Live* written and dir by Dave Allen at the Albery Theatre: rev by Asquith, Billington, Hirschhorn, Hoyle, Hurren, Jones, Nathan, Sanderson, Smith, Tinker. *A Dream Play (Ett Drömspel)* by August Strindberg, adapt. by Ingmar Bergman, transl. by Michael Meyer, dir by Karina Micallef at King's Head: rev by de Jongh, Robinson, Rose, Shulman.

2156 "Reviews of Productions." *LTR.* 1986; 6(22): 1208-1213. Lang.: Eng.

UK-England: London. 1986. ■*'Allo 'Allo* by Jeremy Lloyd and David Croft, dir by Peter Farago at the Prince of Wales: rev by Armistead, Billington, Christie, Harron, Hirschhorn, Hurren, King, Morley, Nathan, Nurse, Preston, Shannon, Shulman, Steyn, Tinker. *Heads Held High* by Alan McDonald and Alan Hull, dir by Terry Conder at the Shaw: rev by Coveney, de Jongh, Edwardes. Khan, Woddis.

2157 "Reviews of Productions." *LTR.* 1986; 6(22): 1233-1236. Lang.: Eng.

UK-England: London. 1986. ■*The German Connection* by Seamus Finnegan, dir by Julia Pascal at Young Vic: rev by Connor, Gore-Langton, Rissik, Wolf. *Too True To Be Good* by George Bernard Shaw, dir by Mike Alfreds at Riverside Studios: rev by Billington, Couling, Coveney, Gardner, King, McFerran, Morley, Nathan, Ratcliffe, Shrimpton.

2158 "Reviews of Productions." *LTR.* 1986; 6(22): 1237-1239. Lang.: Eng.

UK-England: London. 1986. ■*Elizabeth (Elisabetta)* by Dario Fo, transl. by Gillian Hanna, dir by Michael Batz and Christopher Bond at the Half Moon Theatre: rev by Atkins, Bardsley, Carne, Hoyle, McFerran, Renton. *Hans Kohlhaas* by James Saunders, dir by Sam Walters at the Orange Tree: rev by Hays, Sanderson.

2159 "Reviews of Productions." *LTR.* 1986; 6(22): 1239-1243. Lang.: Eng.

UK-England: London. 1986. ■*Tons of Money* by Will Evans and Valentine, dir by Alan Ayckbourn at the Lyttelton Theatre: rev by Asquith, Billington, Carr, Couling, Coveney, Grant, Harron, Hirschhorn, Hurren, King, Morley, Nathan, Nurse, Shulman, Tinker. *The Girls in the Big Picture*

by Marie Jones, dir by Andy Hinds at the Drill Hall Theatre: rev by Gardner, McFerran.

2160 "Reviews of Productions." *LTR.* 1986; 6(21): 1159. Lang.: Eng.

UK-England: London. 1986. ■*Banjo Man* by Roderick Walcott, dir by Allan Weekes at the Commonwealth Institute: rev by Armistead, Hay, Woddis. *Ti Jean and His Brothers* by Derek Walcott, dir by George Alphonse at the Commonwealth Institute: rev by Armistead, Hay, Woddis.

2161 "Reviews of Productions." *LTR.* 1986; 6(21): 1160-1161. Lang.: Eng.

UK-England: London. 1986. ■*The Plague Year* by Theresa Heskins, dir by Hettie Macdonald at the Royal Court: rev by Asquith, Carne, Harron, Hoyle, Rissik, Rose. *William* by Shaun Duggan, dir by Hettie Macdonald at the Royal Court: rev by Asquith, Carne, Harron, Hoyle, Rissik, Rose.

2162 "Reviews of Productions." *LTR.* 1986; 6(21): 1161-1182. Lang.: Eng.

UK-England: London. 1986. ■*Ficky Stingers* by Eve Lewis, dir by Lindsay Posner at the Royal Court: rev by Asquith, Carne, Harron, Hoyle, Rissik. *Banged Up* by Tunde Ikoli, dir by Roland Rees at the Young Vic: rev by Coveney, de Jongh, Harron, Hay, Woddis.

2163 "Reviews of Productions." *LTR.* 1986; 6(21): 1182-1183. Lang.: Eng.

UK-England: London. 1986. ■*Dirty Dishes* by Nick Whitby, dir by Tim Whitby at the Boulevard Theatre: rev by Hay, Nathan, Shulman, Wolf. *The Day the Sheep Turned Pink* by Cordelia Ditton and Maggie Ford, dir by Ford at the Drill Hall Theatre: rev by Lee, Rose.

2164 "Reviews of Productions." *LTR.* 1986; 6(21): 1183-1187. Lang.: Eng.

UK-England: London. 1986. ■*Antigone* by Jean Anouilh, dir by Malcolm Sherman at the Duke of Cambridge: rev by Robinson, Rose. *Scenes From a Marriage* by Peter Barnes, dir by Terry Hands, performed by the Royal Shakespeare Company at the Barbican Theatre: rev by Barker, Billington, Edwards, Hiley, Hirschhorn, Hurren, King, Shulman, Wolf.

2165 "Reviews of Productions." *LTR.* 1986; 6(21): 1188-1191. Lang.: Eng.

UK-England: London. 1986. ■*Between the Devil and the Deep Blue Sea* by the Shadow Syndicate, dir by Peter Granger-Taylor at the Gate, Notting Hill: rev by Mavor, Nathan, Ratcliffe, Remnant, Renton. *School's Out* by Trevor Rhone, dir by Yvonne Brewster at Theatre Royal, Stratford East: rev by Armistead, Billington, Edwards, Morley, Rissik, Shorter, Woddis.

2166 "Reviews of Productions." *LTR.* 1986; 6(19): 1005-1009. Lang.: Eng.

UK-England: London. 1986. ■*Coriolanus* by William Shakespeare, dir by Deborah Warner at the Almeida Theatre: rev by Asquith, Billington, Coveney, Edwardes, Gordon, Nurse, Ratcliffe. *The News* by Paul Pulse, David Rotenberg and R. Vincent Park, dir by Kevin Williams at Paramount City: rev by Carne, Connor, Grant, Hiley, Hoyle, Hurren, Murdin, Nathan, Shorter.

2167 "Reviews of Productions." *LTR.* 1986; 6(19): 1010-1045. Lang.: Eng.

UK-England: London. 1986. ■*The Lemmings Are Coming* written and dir by John Baraldi at Riverside Studios: rev by Atkins, de Jongh, Gardner, Rose. *Kafka's Dick* by Alan Bennett, dir by Richard Eyre at the Royal Court: rev by Asquith, Billington, Coveney, Gordon, Grant, Hiley, Hirschhorn, Hopkins, Hurren, King, Nathan, Ratcliffe, Roper, Shannon, Shaugnessy, Shulman, Smith, St. George.

2168 "Reviews of Productions." *LTR.* 1986; 6(19): 1045-1047. Lang.: Eng.

UK-England: London. 1986. ■*Talk to Me* by William Humble, dir by Wyn Jones at the New End, Hampstead: rev by Armistead, Atkins, Gardner, Nathan, Rose, Sweeting. *Our Lady* by Deborah Levy, dir by Sallie Aprahamian at Drill Hall Theatre: rev by Carne, Hoyle, McKenley, Rose.

2169 "Reviews of Productions." *LTR.* 1986; 6(19): 1048-1076. Lang.: Eng.

DRAMA: —Performance/production

UK-England: London. 1986. ■*Intimate Memoirs of an Irish Taxidermist* written and dir by Marcia Kahan and *Hooligans Say* written and dir by Jon Gaunt at the Donmar Warehouse: rev by Billington, Brennan, Carne, Gardner, Hoyle, Hurren, Mavor, McHean, McMillan. *The Magistrate* by Arthur Wing Pinero, dir by Michael Rudman at the National Theatre: rev by Christy, Coveney, Gardner, Gordon, Grant, Hiley, Hirschhorn, Hurren, Jameson, King, Nathan, Ratcliffe, Shorter, Shulman, Smith.

2170 "Reviews of Productions." *LTR.* 1986; 6(19): 1077-1078. Lang.: Eng.

UK-England: London. 1986. ■*A Betrothal* by Lanford Wilson, dir by Alison Sutcliffe at the Man in the Moon: rev by Barker, Billington, Gardner, Hiley, Hudson, Hurren, King, Ratcliffe, Sanderson. *The Lucky Ones* by Tony Marchant, dir by Richard Hansom at the Old Red Lion: rev by Khan, Mavor.

2171 "Reviews of Productions." *LTR.* 1986; 6(19): 1079-1081. Lang.: Eng.

UK-England: London. 1986. ■*Nicholson Fights Croydon* by Simon Callow and Angus MacKay, dir by Callow at Offstage Downstairs: rev by Carne, Coveney, Edwardes, Hiley, King, Morley, Nathan, Ratcliffe, Remnant. *Heritage* by Teatr Provisorium (Lublin), dir by Janusz Oprynski at the Institute of Contemporary Arts: rev by Billington, Joseph, King, Rea.

2172 "Reviews of Productions." *LTR.* 1986; 6(18): 965-974. Lang.: Eng.

UK-England: London. 1986. ■*The House of Bernarda Alba (La Casa de Bernarda Alba)* by Federico García Lorca, dir by Nuria Espert at the Lyric Hammersmith: rev by Billington, Coveney, Edwards, Gordon, Grant, Hiley, Hirschhorn, Hurren, Jameson, King, Nathan, Pascal, Radin, Ratcliffe, Shorter, Shulman, Tinker. *The Bay at Nice* and *Wrecked Eggs* written and dir by David Hare at the Cottesloe: rev by Asquith, Billington, Edwardes, Gordon, Hiley, Hirschhorn, Hurren, Jacobs, Jameson, King, Ratcliffe, Shorter, Smith.

2173 "Reviews of Productions." *LTR.* 1987; 7(5): 277-281. Lang.: Eng.

UK-England: London. 1987. ■*Beached* by Kevin Hood, dir by Celia Bannerman at the Warehouse Theatre: rev by Gardner, Gordon, Hoyle, King, Ratcliffe, Warner, Vidal. *No Worries* by David Holman, dir by Jeremy Bell at the Young Vic Theatre: rev by Arnott, Asquith, McFerran. *Dantons Tod (Danton's Death)* by Georg Büchner, dir by Margarethe Forsyth at the Young Vic Studio Theatre: rev by Edwards, Gordon, King, Pearce, Rissik, Robinson, Vidal.

2174 "Reviews of Productions." *LTR.* 1987; 7(21): 1305-1315. Lang.: Eng.

UK-England: London. 1987. ■*Adult Child/Dead Child* written and dir by Claire Dowie at King's Head Theatre: rev by Hay, Hayes, Lewis. *The Hypochondriac (Le Malade imaginaire)* by Molière, dir by Nancy Meckler at the Lyric Hammersmith: rev by Billington, Couling, Coveney, Edwards, Gore-Langton, Grant, Hiley, Hurren, Jameson, King, Morley, Osborne, Paton, Ratcliffe, Rissik, Shulman, Wolf. *I'm Dreaming the Hardest* by Vince Foxall, dir by Ian Forrest at the Old Red Lion: rev by Clark, Church, de Jongh, Lavender, Renton. *Separation* by Tom Kempinski, dir by Michael Attenborough at the Hampstead: rev by Billington, Couling, Coveney, Hiley, Hirschhorn, Hurren, Kellaway, Khan, King, Morley, Nathan, Osborne, Sanderson, Shulman.

2175 "Reviews of Productions." *LTR.* 1987; 7(22): 1396- 1409. Lang.: Eng.

UK-England. 1987. ■*Sanctuary* by Ralph Brown, dir by Paulette Randall at Drill Hall: rev by Appio, de Jongh, Hardner, Kellaway, Steyn, Thorncroft. *Tewodros* by Tsegaye Gabre-Mednhin, dir by Jatinder Verma at the Arts (Cambridge): rev by Allan, Hiley, Rose, Taylor. *It's a Girl!* by John Burrows and Andy Whitfield, dir by Burrows at the Bush: rev by Allen, Gardner, Hoyle, Kellaway, Morton, Nathan, Rose, Spencer, Vidal. *The Importance of Being Earnest* by Oscar Wilde, dir by Lou Stein at the Whitehall: rev by Coveney, de Jongh, Edwards, Gordon, Hirschhorn, Hurren, Jameson, King, Morley, Nathan, Osborne, Paton, Rose, Steyn, Tinker, Wolf.

2176 "Reviews of Productions." *LTR.* 1987; 7(1): 18-26. Lang.: Eng.

UK-England: London. 1987. ■*Taken Out* by Gregg Cullen, dir by Sue Glanville, for Spark Theatre Company: rev by Bell, de Jongh, Woddis. *The Triumph of Love (Le triomphe de l'amour)* by Marivaux, dir by Guy Callan at the Gate Theatre: rev by Billington, Gardner, Hay, Hoyle, Ratcliffe, Shack. *Bopha! (Arrest!)* written and dir by Percy Mtwa, presented by the Market Theatre (Johannesburg): rev by Billington, Connor, Edwardes, Edwards, Hirschhorn, Hoyle, Hurren, Kemp, King, Pearce, Ratcliffe, Shulman, Smith, Tinker. *Woza Albert!* by Percy Mtwa, Mbongeni Ngema and Barney Simon, dir by Alby James at the Young Vic: rev by Armistead, de Jongh, Kamba, McFerran, Pearce, Renton.

2177 "Reviews of Productions." *LTR.* 1987; 7(1): 26-33. Lang.: Eng.

UK-England: London. 1987. ■*Monopoly* by Nicholas McIrney, dir by Jonathan Myerson at Touring Theatre: rev by Hay, Renton, Robinson. *An Imitation of Life* created by Peter Brook and Claire MacDonald, dir by Brook at Bush Theatre: rev by Billington, Gardner, Hiley, Hoyle, Rose, Shorter, Sutcliffe. *Twelfth Night* by William Shakespeare, dir by Declan Donnellan at Donmar Warehouse: rev by de Jongh, Edwards, Hiley, Hoyle, Kemp, King, Nathan, Pearce, Ratcliffe, Rose, Woddis. *Pour un oui ou pour un non* by Nathalie Sarraute, dir by Simone Benmussa at the Artaud Theatre, Institut Français de Londres: rev by Billington.

2178 "Reviews of Productions." *LTR.* 1987; 7(1): 33-65. Lang.: Eng.

UK-England: London. 1987. ■*Spotted Dick* by Ben Travers, dir by Lou Stein at the Palace Theatre: rev by Billington, Games, Hoyle, King, Shorter. *The Divided Soul* by Christine Rickey, dir by Christopher Davies at Canal Cafe Theatre: rev by Mayor, Robinson. *The House of Bernarda Alba (La casa de Bernarda Alba)* by Federico García Lorca, translated by Robert David MacDonald, dir by Nuria Espert at The Globe Theatre: rev by Asquith, Billington, Edwardes, Edwards, Hiley, Hoyle, Hurren, Rissik, Shorter, Smith, Tinker. *Faust, Part I* by Johann Wolfgang von Goethe, dir by Margarethe Forsyth at Young Vic Studio: rev by Armistead, Johnson, Ratcliffe, Renton, Sanderson, Woddis.

2179 "Reviews of Productions." *LTR.* 1987; 7(3): 112-122. Lang.: Eng.

UK-England: London. 1987. ■*Frozen Assets* by Barrie Keefe, dir by Paul Tomlinson for the Docklands Theatre Company at the Half Moon Theatre in London: rev by Armistead, de Jongh, Gardner, McFerran, Smith. *School for Wives (L'École des femmes)* by Molière, dir by Di Trevis at the Lyttelton Theatre: rev by Asquith, Billington, Couling, Edwards, Hiley, Hirschhorn, Hoyle, Hurren, Jameson, King, Mars-Jones, Nathan, Ratcliffe, Ray, Shorter, Shulman, Tinker. *The Viewing* by David Pownall, dir by Alan Strachan at the Greenwich Theatre: rev by Billington, Edwardes, Gardner, Hiley, Hoyle, King, Nathan, Osborne, Ratcliffe, Ray, Renton, Shulman.

2180 "Reviews of Productions." *LTR.* 1987; 7(3): 123-126. Lang.: Eng.

UK-England: London. 1987. ■*The Lady from the Sea (Fruen fra Havet)* by Henrik Ibsen, dir by Paddi Taylor for the Signs of Life Theatre Company at the Gate Theatre: rev by de Jongh, King, McFerran, Walsh, Wolf. *Cannibal* by Richard Crowe and Richard Zajdlic for the Ratskins Theatre Company at the Warehouse Theatre: rev by Armistead, Hayes, McFerran. *The Guest Room* by James Hogan, dir by Simon Usher at the Old Red Lion Theatre: rev by Armistead, de Jongh, Gore-Langton, Pearce.

2181 "Reviews of Productions." *LTR.* 1987; 7(3): 126-132. Lang.: Eng.

UK-England: London. 1987. ■*Alarms* by Susan Yankowitz, dir by Penny Cherns for the Monstrous Regiment Theatre Company at the Riverside Studios: rev by Billington, Edwards, Gardner, Hoyle, Nathan, Pearce, Ray, Shulman, Smith. *Largo Desolato* by Vaclav Havel, dir by Sam Walters at the Orange Tree Theatre: rev by Pearce, Sanderson, Woddis, de Jongh. *Lillian* by William Luce, dir by Corin Redgrave at the Fortune Theatre: rev by Armistead, Barkley, Barlow, Edwards, Gardner, Grant, Hiley, Horner, Hughes-Onslow, Mars-Jones, Pearce, Ratcliffe, Ray. *Popular Truth* written and dir by Niall Brooks at the Photographers Gallery: rev by Connor, Hay.

2182 "Reviews of Productions." *LTR.* 1987; 7(3): 133-143. Lang.: Eng.

DRAMA: —Performance/production

UK-England: London. 1987. ∎*Scout's Honor* by Christopher Douglas, dir by Mike Bradwell at the Lyric Hammersmith Theatre: rev by Billington, Gardner, Gill, Hoyle, Jameson, King, Nathan, Osborne, Ratcliffe, Ray, Shulman, Smith, Sutcliffe, Tinker. *Scrape Off the Black* by Tunde Ikoli, dir by Philip Hedley at the Theatre Royal: rev by de Jongh, Hiley, Robinson, Sanderson, Shorter, Shulman. *Siegfried Sassoon: The Story of the Young Soldier-Poet* written and dir by Peter Barkworth at the Apollo Theatre: rev by Edwards, Hiley.

2183   "Reviews of Productions." *LTR.* 1987; 7(3): 143-146, 169-176. Lang.: Eng.

UK-England: London. 1987. ∎*The Hamlet of Stepney Green* by Bernard Kops, dir by James Marcus at the New End Theatre: rev by Conway, Gore-Langton, Pascal, Shorter. *This Story of Yours* by John Hopkins, dir by Jack Gould at the Hampstead Theatre: rev by Billington, Edwards, Gardner, Horner, Hoyle, Hurren, King, Nathan, Radin, Ratcliffe, Ray, Renton, Rose, Shorter, Tinker. *A View from the Bridge* by Arthur Miller, dir by Alan Ayckbourn for the National Theatre Company at the Cottesloe Theatre: rev by Barnes, Barkley, Benedictus, Billington, Couling, Edwardes, Edwards, Hiley, Horner, Hoyle, Hurren, Kemp, King, Osborne, Radin, Ratcliffe, Ray, Shannon, Tinker, Wolf.

2184   "Reviews of Productions." *LTR.* 1987; 7(4): 176-190. Lang.: Eng.

UK-England: London. 1987. ∎*More Light* by Snoo Wilson, dir by Simon Stokes at the Bush Theatre: rev by Asquith, de Jongh, Gore-Langton, Hiley, Hoyle, Nathan, Rissik, Shorter, Shulman. *Deals* written and dir by Cindy Oswin for Burnt Bridges Theatre Company at the Drill Hall Theatre: rev by de Jongh, Gardner, McFerran. *Yardsale and Whatever Happened to Betty Lemon?* written and dir by Arnold Wesker at the Lyric Studio: rev by de Jongh, Edwardes, Gordon, Hiley, Hoyle, Hurren, King, Laffan, Nathan, Osborne, Ray, Rissik, Shulman. *Who's Afraid of Virginia Woolf?* by Edward Albee dir by David Thacker at the Young Vic Theatre: rev by Armistead, Asquith, Barkley, Couling, Edwards, Hoyle, Hurren, Kemp, King, Nathan, Osborne, Radin, Ray, Rose, Shulman, Smith, Tinker, Vidal.

2185   "Reviews of Productions." *LTR.* 1987; 7(4): 190-193. Lang.: Eng.

UK-England: London. 1987. ∎*The Bhangra Dancer* by H.O. Nazareth, dir by Sue Pomeroy for the Asian Co-Operative Theatre at the Young Vic Studio Theatre: rev by Lyttle, Neumark, Vidal. *Desire Caught by the Tail* by Pablo Picasso, dir by Gail Sagman at the Riverside Studios Theatre: rev by Asquith, Goldman, Osborne, Pascal. *Fascinating Aida*, a cabaret piece by Billie Keane, Adele Anderson and Denise Wharmley, dir by Nica Burns at the Piccadilly Theatre: rev by Connor, Hay, Khan, King, Nathan, Walsh.

2186   "Reviews of Productions." *LTR.* 1987; 7(5): 243-248. Lang.: Eng.

UK-England: London. 1987. ∎*Decadence* written and dir by Steven Berkoff at the Wyndham's Theatre: rev by Couling, Edwards, Edwardes, Goldman, Hiley, Hurren, Ratcliffe, Ray, Robinson, Shannon, Shorter, Spencer. *Missing Links* by John Antrobus, dir by Robert Huguenin and Jeremy Stockwell at the Latchmere Theatre: rev by Laffan, Rose. *Moses* by Rose English, dir by Luke Dixon at the Drill Hall Theatre: rev by Brown, Carne, Coveney, Edwardes, Hiley, Pascal, Rissik, Wolf.

2187   "Reviews of Productions." *LTR.* 1987; 7(4): 193-208. Lang.: Eng.

UK-England: London. 1987. ∎*Munich-Athens* by Lars Norén, dir by Brian Stirner at the Soho Poly Theatre: rev by Armistead, de Jongh, Edwardes, Hiley, Ratcliffe, Ray, Renton, Woddis. *The Dead* by Anne Caulfield, dir by Anna Furse for the Heaven and the Victorians Theatre Company at the Old Red Lion Theatre: rev by King, McFerran, Smith, Vidal. *High Society*, music and lyrics by Cole Porter, book by Richard Eyre, based on the book *Philadelphia Story* by Philip Barry, dir by Richard Eyre at the Victoria Palace Theatre: rev by Barkley, de Jongh, Edwards, Edwardes, Gardner, Gordon, Hiley, Horner, Hoyle, Hurren, King, Nathan, Osborne, Radin, Ratcliffe, Ray, Shulman, Smith, Steyn, St. George, Tinker.

2188   "Reviews of Productions." *LTR.* 1987; 7(4-5): 209-242. Lang.: Eng.

UK-England: London. 1987. ∎*Lady Day* written and dir by Stephen Stahl at the Donmar Warehouse Theatre: rev by Gelly, Gill, Hopkins,

King, Murdin, Nathan, Ray, Rissik, Thorncraft, Tinker, Vidal, Walsh, Woddis. *Kathie y el hipopótamo (Kathy and the Hippopotamus)* by Mario Vargas Llosa, dir by Stephen Unwin at the Almeida Theatre: rev by de Jongh, Gordon, Hoyle, Hurren, King, Nathan, Osborne, Ray, Rissik, Sanderson. *Anatol* by Arthur Schnitzler, dir by Michael Robertson at the Gate Theatre: rev by de Jongh, Gardner, Kemp, Osborne, Ratcliffe, Ray, Rose, Walsh. *The Arkley Barnet Show* by Patrick Fyffe and George Logan, dir by Michael White at the Comedy Theatre: rev by Connor, Coveney, Hirschhorn, Hurren, King, Murdin, Nathan, Sanderson, Stringer, Tinker.

2189   "Reviews of Productions." *LTR.* 1987; 7(6): 301-307. Lang.: Eng.

UK-England: London. 1987. ∎*Above All, Courage* by Max Arthur, dir by Wyn Jones at the New End Theatre: rev by de Jongh, Hay, Spencer, Wolf. *The Triumph of Love* written and dir by Guy Callan for Anchord Dolphin Theatre Company at the King's Head Theatre: rev by de Jongh, Grant, Ray. *Ghetto* by Seamus Finnegan, dir by Julia Pascal at the Riverside Theatre: rev by Couling, de Jongh, Gordon, Hiley, Hoyle, King, Lyttle, Nathan, Pearce, Radin, Ratcliffe, Rissik, Rose, Shulman. *The Lost Ring* written and dir by Jeff Teare at the Theatre Royal: rev by Armistead, Khan, Renton, Robinson, Sanderson.

2190   "Reviews of Productions." *LTR.* 1987; 7(6): 308-315. Lang.: Eng.

UK-England: London. 1987. ∎*A Smile on the End of the Line (Les Travaux et les jours)* by Michel Vinaver, dir by Sam Walters at the Orange Tree Theatre: rev by de Jongh, Mavor, Pearce, Woddis. *The Emperor* written and dir by Michael Hastings and Jonathan Miller at the Theatre Upstairs: rev by Billington, Coveney, Edwards, Edwardes, Hiley, Hurren, Kemp, King, Pearce, Radin, Ratcliffe, Shulman, Spencer, Winney, Woddis. *The Marriage of Panurge* by Julian Hilton, dir by Carl Heap at Regents College Theatre: rev by Armistead, Ratcliffe.

2191   "Reviews of Productions." *LTR.* 1987; 7(6): 315-321. Lang.: Eng.

UK-England: London. 1987. ∎*Thatcher's Women* by Kay Adshead, dir by Pip Broughton at the Tricycle Theatre: rev by Billington, Gordon, Harron, Hiley, Ray, Rose, Shorter, Thorncraft, Woddis. *1919—An Incident* by Sadat Hassan Manto, dir by Jatinder Verma at Tara Arts Centre: rev by Vidal. *The Amen Corner* by James Baldwin, dir by Anton Phillips at the Lyric Theatre: rev by Asquith, Billington, Couling, Coveney, Edwardes, Gordon, Pascal, Radin, Ratcliffe, Ray, Shannon, Shorter, Tinker, Wroe.

2192   "Reviews of Productions." *LTR.* 1987; 7(6): 321-336. Lang.: Eng.

UK-England: London. 1987. ∎*Mummy* by Bryony Lavey, dir by Ljiljana Ortolja at the Drill Hall Theatre: rev by Carne, Connor, Rose. *Six Characters in Search of an Author* by Luigi Pirandello, dir by Michael Rudman at the Olivier Theatre: rev by Asquith, Billington, Couling, Coveney, Edwards, Edwardes, Gordon, Hiley, Hirschhorn, Horner, Hurren, Jameson, King, Pascal, Radin, Ratcliffe, Ray, Rissik, Shorter, Shulman, St. George, Tinker. *Needles of Light* by James Pettifer, dir by Roland Rees at the Riverside Theatre: rev by Anderson, de Jongh, Edwards, Frazer, Gordon, Kemp, King, Pearce, Ratcliffe, Robinson, Shulman, Young. *Pier Paolo Pasolini* by Mickel Azama, dir by Tim Luscombe at the Offstage Downstairs Theatre: rev by Kamba, Sanderson.

2193   "Reviews of Productions." *LTR.* 1987; 7(6): 337-348. Lang.: Eng.

UK-England: London. 1987. ∎*The Henrys* by William Shakespeare, dir by Michael Bogdanov at the Old Vic Theatre: rev by Barkley, Billington, Coveney, Edwards, Gordon, Grant, Hurren, Jameson, King, Ratcliffe, Ray, Rissik, Shorter, Shulman, Tinker, Wolf. *Shades of the Jelly Woman* written and dir by Peter Sheridan at the Watermans Theatre: rev by Perera. *Nunsense* by Dan Goggin, dir by Richard Digby Day at the Fortune Theatre: rev by de Jongh, Gardner, Gordon, Harron, Hiley, Horner, Hurren, Jameson, McAfee, Ray, Sanderson, Shannon, Shorter, Shulman, Tinker.

2194   "Reviews of Productions." *LTR.* 1987; 7(26): 1659-1661. Lang.: Eng.

UK-England: London. 1987. ∎*Cinderella* by Ben Benison and Ken Bolam, dir by Ben Benison at the Shaw Theatre: rev by Coveney, Hiley,

DRAMA: —Performance/production

Khan, Lister, Paton. *Beauty and the Beast* by David Gregan and Brian Protheroe, dir by Philip Hedley at Stratford Theatre Royal: rev by Gow, McKane, McKenley, Sanderson, Thorncroft. *Jack and the Beanstalk* dir by Bob Mason at Half Moon Theatre: rev by Armistead, Brown, McFerran, McKenley.

2195   "Reviews of Productions." *LTR.* 1987; 7(6): 348-356.
      Lang.: Eng.
UK-England: London. 1987. ■*Twilight Freedom* by Bryan Oliver, dir by Hieronimo Selvi at the Tabard Theatre: rev by Conway. *Tri sestry (Three Sisters)* by Anton Pavlovič Čechov, dir by Elijah Moshinsky at the Greenwich Theatre: rev by Billington, Coveney, Hiley, Horner, King, Nathan, Pearce, Ratcliffe, Rissik, Rose, Spencer, Walsh. *March of the Falsettos* by William Finn, dir by Roger Haynes at the Albery Theatre: rev by Billington, Coveney, Gardner, Hiley, Hirschhorn, Hurren, Jameson, Nathan, Ratcliffe, Ray, Robertson, Shorter, Shulman, St. George, Tinker, Wroe.

2196   "Reviews of Productions." *LTR.* 1987; 7(7-8): 369-384.
      Lang.: Eng.
UK-England: London. 1987. ■*Serious Money* by Caryl Churchill, dir by Max Stafford-Clark at the Royal Court: rev by Asquith, Barker, Billington, Collins, Coveny, Edwards, Edwardes, Gilford, Gordon, Hiley, Hirschhorn, King, Nathan, Radin, Ratcliffe, Rissik, Shulman. *From Morning till Midnight* by Georg Kaiser, dir by Sue Dunderdale at the Soho Poly Theatre: rev by de Jongh, Gardner, Renton, Rose, Shorter, Spencer. *Yerma* by Federico García Lorca, dir by Di Trevis at the Cottesloe Theatre: rev by Armistead, Billington, Couling, Edwards, Gardner, Gordon, Hiley, Hirschhorn, Kemp, King, Nathan, Osborne, Radin, Ratcliffe, Rose, Shulman. *Country Dancing* by Nigel Williams, dir by Bill Alexander at The Pit: rev by de Jongh, Gordon, Hiley, Hurren, King, Laffan, Sanderson, Shorter, Shulman.

2197   "Reviews of Productions." *LTR.* 1987; 7(7-8): 425-431.
      Lang.: Eng.
UK-England: London. 1987. ■*Mainland* by Daniel Magee and and *Ronnie's Doing Well* by Michael McKnight, dir by Adrian Dunbar at the Watermans Theatre: rev by Brown, Gardner. *Spin of the Wheel* written and dir by Timothy Prager, music and lyrics by Geoff Morrow at the Comedy Theatre: rev by Hiley, Hoyle, Jameson, Lyttle, Middlehurst, Nathan, Osborne, Ray, Sanderson, Shulman. *The Tourist Guide (Die Fremdenführerin)* by Botho Strauss, dir by Pierre Audi at the Almeida Theatre: rev by Asquith, Couling, Coveney, de Jongh, Edwards, Harron, Mars-Jones, Radin, Rose.

2198   "Reviews of Productions." *LTR.* 1987; 7(7-8): 432-434.
      Lang.: Eng.
UK-England: London. 1987. ■*What About Luv?* by Jeffrey Sweet, music by Howard Marren, lyrics by Susan Birkenhead, dir by Kim Grant at the Lyric Hammersmith: rev by Harron, Hinton, Laffan, Nathan, Robertson, Shannon, Shorter, Spencer, Steyn, Stringer, Thorncroft. *Antony & Cleopatra* by William Shakespeare, dir by Peter Hall at the Olivier Theatre by the National Theatre Company: rev by Anderson, Asquith, Billington, Couling, Coveney, Grant, Hiley, Hirschhorn, Hurren, Jameson, Jones Evans, Kemp, King, Nathan, Osborne, Owen, Ratcliffe, Ray, Shannon, Shulman, St. George. *The Hole in the Top of the World* by Fay Weldon, dir by Stephanie Turner at the Orange Tree Theatre: rev by Armistead, de Jongh, Denford, Gardner, Renton, Shorter, Spencer. *Chicken* by Gregory Motton, dir by Kate Harwood at Riverside Studios: rev by Gardner, Gordon, Ratcliffe, Rose.

2199   "Reviews of Productions." *LTR.* 1987; 7(7-8): 414-425.
      Lang.: Eng.
UK-England. 1987. ■*Owners* by Caryl Churchill, dir by Annie Castledine at the Young Vic: rev by Gardner, Renton, Salvadori, Vidal. *The Resistible Rise of Arturo Ui (Der Aufhaltsame Aufstieg des Arturo Ui)* by Bertolt Brecht, dir by David Gilmore at the Queen's Theatre: rev by *Billington, Connor, Coveney, Couling, Dunn, Edwards, Edwardes, Gordon, Harron, Hiley, Horner, Hurren, Jameson, King, Middlehurst, Nathan, Osborne, Ray, Rissik, Shannon, Shulman.* Heaven Bent, Hell Bound* by John Clifford, dir by Mark Brickman at the Bridge Lane Battersea Theatre: rev by Edwardes, Gordon, Laffan, Martin, Ratcliffe, Rissik, Young.

2200   "Reviews of Productions." *LTR.* 1987; 7(7-8): 448-456.
      Lang.: Eng.

UK-England: London. 1987. ■*Every Man in His Humour* by Ben Jonson, dir by John Caird at the Mermaid Theatre by the Royal Shakespeare Company: rev by de Jongh, Gardner, Gordon, Grant, Hoyle, Hurren, Osborne, Ray, Shannon, Shulman, Sutcliffe. *The Greatest Story Ever Told* by Patrick Barlow, dir by Martin Duncan at the Tricycle Theatre: rev by Arnott, Billington, Harron, Hiley, Norman, Rissik, Rose, Spencer, St. George, Woddis. *Romeo and Juliet* by William Shakespeare, dir by Michael Bogdanov at the Barbican by the Royal Shakespeare Company: rev by Asquith, Couling, de Jongh, Gordon, Grant, Hirschhorn, Kemp, Shorter, Shulman.

2201   "Reviews of Productions." *LTR.* 1987; 7(7-8): 457-464.
      Lang.: Eng.
UK-England: London. 1987. ■*When Did You Last See Your...Trousers?* by Ray Galton and John Antrobus, dir by Roger Smith at the Garrick Theatre: rev by Armistead, Harron, Hay, Hiley, Hinton, Hirschhorn, Hurren, Kennedy, Middlehurst, Osborne, Ray, Shannon, Spencer, Steyn, Stringer, Wolf. *Diary of a Somebody* by John Lahr, based on diaries of Joe Orton. Dir by Jonathan Myerson at King's Head Theatre: rev by de Jongh, Edwards, Gordon, Hurren, Osborne, Sanderson, Walsh. *Volpone* by Ben Jonson, dir by Richard Ireson at Half Moon Theatre: rev by Carne, Connor, Hay, Rissik, Stringer.

2202   "Reviews of Productions." *LTR.* 1987; 7(7-8): 467-476.
      Lang.: Eng.
UK-England: London. 1987. ■*Sarcophagus* by Vladimir Gubaryev, dir by Jude Kelly for the Royal Shakespeare Company at The Pit: rev by Asquith, Billington, Gill, Hiley, Hoyle, Hurren, Kemp, King, Nathan, Osborne, Radin, Ratcliffe, Ray, Shulman, St. George, Tinker. *Dog Lady* and *The Cuban Swimmer* by Milcha Sanchez-Scott, dir by Christa van Raalte at the Gate Theatre: rev by de Jongh, Gardner, Gordon, Renton, Sanderson. *Yr. Obedient Servant* by Kay Eldredge, dir by Andrew Dallmeyer at the Lyric Studio: rev by Connor, Grant, Horner, Hoyle, Jones, Ratcliffe, Renton, Richler, Shannon, Spencer, Vidal. *Lessons in Love* by Bill Studdiford, dir by Judith Joseph at the Warehouse Theatre: rev by Hayes, Renton, Rose.

2203   "Reviews of Productions." *LTR.* 1987; 7(7-8): 477-492.
      Lang.: Eng.
UK-England: London. 1987. ■*Court in the Act!* by Maurice Hennequin and Pierre Veber, dir by Braham Murray at the Phoenix Theatre: rev by Billington, Coveney, Edwardes, Gordon, Hiley, Hirschhorn, Horner, Hurren, Jones, Jones-Evans, Mars-Jones, Nathan, Osborne, Ratcliffe, Robinson, Shannon, Shulman, Tinker. *Spookhouse* by Harvey Fierstein, dir by Robin Lefevre at the Hampstead Theatre: rev by Billington, Coveney, Edwardes, Gardner, Gordon, Grant, Hiley, Hirschhorn, Horner, Hurren, Jones, Kemp, Osborne, Ratcliffe, Rose, Shulman. *Home Work*, a collection of short theatre pieces by different authors and directors at the Mall by the Institute of Contemporary Arts: rev by Armistead, Connor, Coveney, de Jongh, Dunn, Edwardes, Gardner, Harron, Hiley, Kemp, LaFrenais, Nathan, Rea, Rose, Spencer, St. George.

2204   "Reviews of Productions." *LTR.* 1987; 7(9): 521-528.
      Lang.: Eng.
UK-England: London. 1987. ■*Emilia Galotti* by Gotthold Ephraim Lessing, dir by Malcolm Edwards at the Young Vic: rev by Billington, Brown, Goldman, Hoyle, Shorter, Spencer, Woddis. *Canaries Sometimes Sing* by Frederick Lonsdale, dir by Patrick Garland at the Albery Theatre: rev by Billington, Coveney, Gordon, Harron, Hiley, Hirschhorn, Horner, Hurren, Jameson, Jones-Evans, King, Nathan, Osborne, Ray, Renton, Rose, Shannon, Shulman, Tinker, Woddis. *Fathers Day* by Oliver Hailey, dir by Nigel P. Draycott at the Finborough Theatre Club: rev by Gore-Langton, Laffan.

2205   "Reviews of Productions." *LTR.* 1987; 7(9): 529-535.
      Lang.: Eng.
UK-England: London. 1987. ■*Hamlet* by William Shakespeare, dir by Chris Fisher at the Latchmere Theatre: rev by Brown, Denford, Gore-Langton, Shorter, Vidal. *Up on the Roof* written and dir by Simon Moore and Jane Prowse at the Donmar Warehouse: rev by Billington, Hoyle, Kemp, Osborne, Ray, Robinson, Saddler, Shulman, Spencer. *Black Flowers* by Robert Jakobsson, dir by Lars Mattsson and John Bergstrom for Teater Albatross of Sweden at the Soho Poly Theatre: rev by Alexander, Carne, Hoyle, Pascal, Renton, Rose, Spencer. *Star Turns*

DRAMA: —Performance/production

by Steve Gooch, dir by Ted Craig at the Warehouse Theatre: rev by Armistead, Carne, Hayes, Renton, Rose.

2206 "Reviews of Productions." *LTR.* 1987; 7(10): 593-599. Lang.: Eng.

UK-England: London. 1987. ■*A Toot Suit* written and dir by Pat van Hemelriejk at the Institute of Contemporary Arts: rev by Rea. *The Hairy Ape* by Eugene O'Neill, dir by Peter Stein for Schaubühne of West Berlin at the Lyttelton: rev by Billington, Couling, Coveney, Edwardes, Edwards, Gordon, Harron, Hiley, Hirschhorn, Hurren, Jones, Kemp, Kift, Osborne, Rickler, Tinker. *Mariana Pineda* by Federico García Lorca, dir by Tessa Schneideman at the Oval House Theatre: rev by de Jongh, Woddis.

2207 "Reviews of Productions." *LTR.* 1987; 7(10): 600-604. Lang.: Eng.

UK-England: London. 1987. ■*The Ticket-of-Leave Man* by Tom Taylor, dir by Philip Hedley at the Theatre Royal: rev by Connor, Hiley, Rose, Spencer, Taylor, Vidal. *Call Grandad* written and dir by Allen Frame at the Old Red Lion: rev by Bartlett, de Jongh. *Built on Sand* by Daniel Mornin, dir by Lindsay Posner at Theatre Upstairs: rev by Armistead, Billington, Gordon, Gore-Langton, Hudson, Kemp, Nathan, Osborne, Woddis.

2208 "Reviews of Productions." *LTR.* 1987; 7(10): 604-612. Lang.: Eng.

UK-England: London. 1987. ■*An Inspector Calls* by J.B. Priestley, dir by Peter Dews at the Westminster: rev by Ellis, Hiley, Horner, Hoyle, Hurren, Jones, Laffan, Nathan, Osborne, Ray, Rissik, Sanderson, Shulman, Spencer, Tinker. *Measure for Measure* by William Shakespeare, dir by David Thacker at the Young Vic: rev by Hay, Renton, Richler, Robinson, St. George, Young. *11 Josephine House* by Alfred Fagon, dir by Malcolm Frederick and Gloria Hamilton at Riverside Studios: rev by Bartholomew, McKenley, Ratcliffe, Renton. *Never the Sinner* by John Logan, dir by Debbie Wolfe at Offstage Downstairs: rev by Arnott, de Jongh, Grant, Griffith, Hoyle, Woddis.

2209 "Reviews of Productions." *LTR.* 1987; 7(7-8): 384-388. Lang.: Eng.

UK-England: London. 1987. ■*Love Field* by Stephen Davis, dir by Simon Stokes at the Bush Theatre: rev by Billington, Coveney, Gardner, Hudson, Hurren, Nathan, Pearce, Spencer, Sutcliffe. *Obscene Fables (Fabulazzo osceno)* by Dario Fo and *Comedy Without Title (Comedia sin título)* by Federico García Lorca, dir by Michael Batz at the Young Vic: rev by Billington, Connor, Langston, Osborne. *Hot Stuff* written and dir by Les Miller at the Old Red Lion Theatre: rev by Alexander.

2210L TR. 1987; 7(7-8): 389-403. Lang.: Eng.

UK-England: London. 1987. ■*Panic* written and dir by Hilary Westlake at The Place Theatre: rev by Adams, Armistead, Gardner, Hemmings, Hiley, Ratcliffe, Rea, Rose. *Macbeth* by William Shakespeare, dir by Adrian Noble at the Barbican Theatre: rev by Anderson, Asquith, Couling, de Jongh, Edwardes, Gordon, Hiley, Horner, Hoyle, Hurren, King, Pascal, Ray, Shannon, Shorter, Walsh. *A Piece of My Mind* by Peter Nichols, dir by Justin Greene at the Apollo Theatre: rev by Barkley, Billington, Coveney, Edwards, Harron, Hay, Hiley, Horner, Hurren, King, Nathan, Osborne, Ray, Rissik, Shannon, Shulman, Spencer, St. George, Wolf.

2211 "Reviews of Productions." *LTR.* 1987; 7(7-8): 404-413. Lang.: Eng.

UK-England: London. 1987. ■*This Is My Dream* by Henry Livings, dir by Philip Hedley at Theatre Royal: rev by Bartlett, Davis, de Jongh, Kemp, McAfee, Stringer, Woddis. *The Fair Maid of the West* by Thomas Middleton, dir by Trevor Nunn for the Royal Shakespeare Company at the Mermaid Theatre: rev by Billington, Couling, Gordon, Hiley, Hoyle, Hurren, Nathan, Osborne, Rissik, Rose, Shulman, Woddis. *Strokes of Genius* written and dir by Anna Furse and Suzy Gilmour at the Drill Hall Theatre: rev by Renton, Salvadori. *The Heat of the Day*, written and dir by Felicity Brown and Giles Havergal at the Donmar Warehouse Theatre: rev by Coveney, de Jongh, Kemp, Radin, Ratcliffe, Rose, Shorter, Spencer, Stringer, Woddis.

2212 "Reviews of Productions." *LTR.* 1987; 7(9): 536-543. Lang.: Eng.

UK-England: London. 1987. ■*Whistle Stop* written by the People Show No. 92 at the Bush Theatre: rev by Billington, Coveney, Gordon, Lyttle, Renton, Stringer, Taylor. *Mystère Bouffe* by Le Théâtre du Radeau of

Le Mans dir by François Tanguy at the Almeida: rev by Billington, Gardner, Harron, Kemp, Robertson, Sorley, Spencer. *Richard II* by William Shakespeare, dir by Barry Kyle at the Barbican by the Royal Shakespeare Company: rev by Couling, Gordon, Hay, Hirschhorn, Horner, Hoyle, Jones, Osborne, Ray, Rissik, Robinson, Shulman, Tinker.

2213 "Reviews of Productions." *LTR.* 1987; 7(9): 544-581. Lang.: Eng.

UK-England: London. 1987. ■*Jeeves Takes Charge* by Edward Duke, dir by Gillian Lynne at Wyndham's Theatre: rev by Asquith, Gore-Langton, Hurren, Jones-Evans, Nathan, Osborne, Rissik, Spencer, Vidal, Walsh. *Rosmersholm* by Henrik Ibsen, dir by Sarah Pia Anderson at the Cottesloe Theatre by the National Theatre Company: rev by Billington, Couling, Coveney, Gardner, Gordon, Harron, Hiley, Hirschhorn, Hurren, Jameson, Jones, Kemp, Nathan, Osborne, Ray, Rose, Shulman. *Minna von Barnhelm* by Gotthold Ephraim Lessing, dir by John Steer at the Young Vic Studio: rev by Brown, de Jongh, Hopkinson, Robinson.

2214 "Reviews of Productions." *LTR.* 1987; 7(10): 582-593. Lang.: Eng.

UK-England: London. 1987. ■*The Mystery of Edwin Drood* by Rupert Holmes, dir by Wilford Leach at the Savoy Theatre (London): rev by Barker, Billington, Coveney, Ellis, Gardner, Harron, Hiley, Hirschhorn, Horner, Hurren, Jameson, Jones, Nathan, Ray, Rose, Shulman, Steyn, St. George, Tinker. *Rosencrantz and Guildenstern Are Dead* by Tom Stoppard, dir by Chris Fisher and Mark Freeland at the Latchmere Theatre: rev by Brown, Langton, Robinson. *Worlds Apart* by José Triana, dir by Nick Hamm for the Royal Shakespeare Company at The Pit: rev by Armistead, de Jongh, Hiley, Radin, Rissik, Sanderson, Spencer, Thornber, Wolf. *Desire Under the Elms* by Eugene O'Neill, dir by Patrick Mason at the Greenwich Theatre: rev by Billington, Harron, Hoyle, Jones, Kemp, Richler, Rose, Shorter, Spencer, Wolf.

2215 "Reviews of Productions." *LTR.* 1987; 7(20): 1252-1256. Lang.: Eng.

UK-England: London. 1987. ■*Job Rocking* by Benjamin Zephaniah, dir by Charlie Hanson and Anna Furse at the Riverside Studios: rev by Armistead, Davis, Hay, McKenley. *Definitely the Bahamas* by Martin Crimp, dir by Alec McCowen at the Orange Tree: rev by Alexander, Billington, Clark, Coveney, Edwards, King, Morley, Rissik, Spencer. *Kafka* and *Stand Up* by Jack Klaff, dir by Anna Furse and Graham Callan at the Bloomsbury Theatre: rev by Connor, Hay. *Lear's Daughters* by Elaine Feinstein, dir by Women's Theatre Group at the Battersea Arts Center: rev by Butcher, Gardner.

2216 "Reviews of Productions." *LTR.* 1987; 7(20): 1256-1264. Lang.: Eng.

UK-England: London. 1987. ■*Victoria—A Most Unusual Woman* by George Pensotti, dir by Valerie Colgan at the Oval House by the Torn Curtain Theatre Company: rev by Gardner. *Blues in the Night* by Sheldon Epps, dir by Steve Whatley at the Piccadilly Theatre: rev by Henriques, Hiley, Hirschhorn, Tinker. *Tattoo Theatre* written and dir by Mladen Materic at the Almeida Theatre: rev by Alexander, Billen, Church, Coveney, Edwardes, Hiley, King, Nathan, Radin, Rissik, Vidal. *Moon Dance Night* by Edgar White, dir by Yvonne Brewster at the Arts Theatre (Cambridge): rev by Armistead, Buss, Connor, Gilbert, Grant, Kellaway, King, Rissik, Vidal.

2217 "Reviews of Productions." *LTR.* 1987; 7(20): 1264-1265. Lang.: Eng.

UK-England: London. 1987. ■*The Cocoa Party* by Ruth Dunlap Bartlett, dir by Malcolm Frederick at Drill Hall Theatre: rev by Hay, Kellaway, Kemp, St. George, Sweeting, Woddis. *The One Before the Last* by Kate Parker, dir by Valerie Doulton at the Offstage Downstairs Theatre: rev by Brown, Denford, King, Nathan, Sanderson, Sweeting. *Waterloo Road* by Robert Gordon and Vera Gottlieb, dir by Gottlieb at the Young Vic Studio: rev by Gilbert, Robinson, Rose, Shulman, Spencer. *The Fire Raisers (Biedermann und die Brandstifte)* by Max Frisch, dir by Peter Wilson at the Watermans Theatre: rev by Billington, Coleman, King, Laffan, Nathan, Osborne, Taylor.

2218 "Reviews of Productions." *LTR.* 1987; 7(20): 1270-1281. Lang.: Eng.

DRAMA: —Performance/production

UK-England: London. 1987. ■*Top Storey* by the Trestle Theatre Company, dir by John Wright and Sally Cook at the Shaw Theatre: rev by Baker, Connor, Coveney. *And Then There Were None* by Agatha Christie, dir by Kenneth Alan Taylor at the Duke of York's Theatre: rev by Asquith, Billington, Crookenden, Grant, Hiley, Hirschhorn, Hoyle, Hurren, Jameson, King, Morley, Nathan, Osborne, Paton, Shulman, Tinker. *Savage in Limbo* by John Patrick Shanley, dir by Robert Hickson at the Gate Theatre: rev by Billington, King, Radin, Renton, Sanderson, Spencer, Woddis. *Mary Queen of Scots Got Her Head Chopped Off* by Liz Lochhead, dir by Gerry Mulgrew at the Donmar Warehouse: rev by Clark.

2219 "Reviews of Productions." *LTR*. 1987; 7(20-21): 1283-1304. Lang.: Eng.

UK-England: London. 1987. ■*Innocent Erendira (La Cándida Eréndira)* by Gabriel García Márquez, dir by Michael Mulkerrin at Donmar Warehouse: rev by Farrell, Hurren, Rose, Sweeting. *Teechers* written and dir by John Godber at Donmar Warehouse: rev by Clark, Farrell, Gardner, Hornber. *Macbeth* by William Shakespeare dir by Chris Bond at the Half Moon: rev by Buss, McFerran, McKenley, Osborne, Rissik, St. George, Vidal. *Sarcophagus* by Vladimir Gubaryev, dir by Jude Kelly at the Mermaid Theatre: rev by Connor, Coveney, Hirschhorn, Hughes-Hallett, Morley, Paton, Renton.

2220 "Reviews of Productions." *LTR*. 1987; 7(21): 1315-1325. Lang.: Eng.

UK-England: London. 1987. ■*Upside Down at the Bottom of the World* by David Allen, dir by Ted Craig at the Croydon Warehouse: rev by Brown, Laffan, Warren. *The Winter's Tale* by William Shakespeare, dir by Terry Hands at the Barbican by the Royal Shakespeare Company: rev by Cotton, Grant, Hoyle, Lewis, Paton, Shorter, Taylor. *Entertaining Strangers* by David Edgar, dir by Peter Hall at the Cottesloe by the National Theatre Company: rev by Billington, Edwardes, Gore-Langton, Hiley, Hirschhorn, Hoyle, Hurren, Kemp, King, Morley, Osborne, Ratcliffe, Robinson, Shulman, St. George. *Conversations on a Homecoming* by Tom Murphy, dir by Garry Hines at Donmar Warehouse by the Druid Theatre Company of Galway: rev by de Jongh, Hughes-Hallett, Kellaway, Kemp, McFerran, Shorter, Wolf.

2221 "Reviews of Productions." *LTR*. 1987; 7(21): 1326-1339. Lang.: Eng.

UK-England: London. 1987. ■*Girlfriends* by Howard Goodall and John Retallack (dir) at the Playhouse Theatre: rev by Bandsley, Billington, Couling, Coveney, Grant, Hiley, Hirschhorn, Hurren, King, Morley, Osborne, Paton, Ratcliffe, Shulman, Taylor, Tinker. *A Man for All Seasons* by Robert Bolt, dir by Frank Hauser at the Savoy: rev by Billington, Coveney, Gore-Langton, Hiley, Hurren, King, Maxwell, Morley, Morrison, Osborne, Paton, Rissik, Shulman. *Falling Prey* by Max Hafler, dir by Stuart Wood at the Man in the Moon: rev by Clark, Coveney, de Jongh. *A Prayer for my Daughter* by Thomas Babe, dir by Bill Merrow at the New End: rev by Morton.

2222 "Reviews of Productions." *LTR*. 1987; 7(21): 1339-1347. Lang.: Eng.

UK-England: London. 1987. ■*Angelus* by Tony Craze, dir by Sue Dunderdale at Soho Poly: rev by de Jongh, Hay, Morton, Renton, Shorter, Woddis. *A Lie of the Mind* by Sam Shepard, dir by Simon Curtis at the Royal Court: rev by Billington, Couling, Coveney, Hiley, Hirschhorn, Hurren, Kemp, King, Morley, Morrison, Nathan, Osborne, Radin, Rose, Tinker, Wolf. *Atonement* by Barry Collins, dir by Clare Davidson at the Lyric Studio: rev by Gordon, Hoyle, Maxwell, McFerran, Shorter, Woddis. *A Vision of Love Revealed in Sleep* by Neil Bartlett, dir by Robin Whitmore at Butler's Wharf: rev by Griffiths, Hiley, Kellaway, Robinson, Taylor.

2223 "Reviews of Productions." *LTR*. 1987; 7(22): 1376-1390. Lang.: Eng.

UK-England: London. 1987. ■*Deathwatch (Haute surveillance)* and *The Maids (Les Bonnes)* by Jean Genet, dir by Gerard Murphy Ultz at The Pit: rev by Billington, Couling, Coveney, Dunn, Gordon, Hiley, Jones, Kellaway, Rissik, Sanderson, Spencer, Woddis. *Romeo and Juliet* by William Shakespeare, dir by David Thacker and Jeremy Bell at the Young Vic: rev by Armistead, Gardner, Hay, Marriott, Rissik, Spencer, Vidal. *No More A-Roving* by John Whiting, dir by Sam Walters at the Orange Tree: rev by Arnott, de Jongh, Hoyle, Khan, McFerran, Morley, Spencer. *Lettice and Lovage* by Peter Shaffer, dir by Michael

Blakemore at the Globe Theatre: rev by Asquith, Billington, Bonner, Couling, Grant, Hiley, Hirschhorn, Hoyle, Hurren, Jameson, Jones, Kemp, Morley, Nathan, Osborne, Paton, Ratcliffe, Tinker, Wapshott.

2224 "Reviews of Productions." *LTR*. 1987; 7(22): 1390-1396. Lang.: Eng.

UK-England: London. 1987. ■*The Small Poppies* by David Holman, dir by Matthew Marsh at the Young Vic: rev by Morton, Robinson, Rose. *The Life of Napoleon* by John Sessions, dir by Kenneth Branagh at the Albery: rev by Asquith, Gore-Langton, Hirschhorn, Vidal. *The Tuscan* by Alan Osborne, dir by Jamie Garren at the Watermans: rev by Pascal. *Tomorrow Was War* by Boris Vassiliev, dir by A.A. Goncharov at the Lyttelton: rev by Billington, Couling, Hiley, Jones, Hoyle, Kemp, Morley, Osborne, Radin, Ratcliffe, Shulman, Tinker.

2225 "Reviews of Productions." *LTR*. 1987; 7(24): 1519-1524. Lang.: Eng.

UK-England: London. 1987. ■*Twelfth Night* by William Shakespeare dir by Kenneth Branagh at the Young Vic: rev by Rissik, Wolf. *Doctor Faustus* by Christopher Marlowe, dir by Mark Brickman at the Lyric Studio: rev by de Jongh, Edwardes, Kellaway, King, Renton, Spencer, Taylor, Woddis, Young. *Crowned with Fame* by Michael Ellis, dir by Sue Pomeroy at the Battersea Arts Centre: rev by Cotton, Martin, Steyn, St. George, Urpeth. *Whistle Stop* by People Show No. 92 at the Boulevard Theatre: rev by Hay, Lavender.

2226 "Reviews of Productions." *LTR*. 1987; 7(24): 1525-1543. Lang.: Eng.

UK-England: London. 1987. ■*Waiting for Godot* by Samuel Beckett, dir by Michael Rudman at the Lyttelton by the National Theatre Company: rev by Billington, Connor, Edwardes, Hiley, Hirschhorn, Hurren, Jameson, Kellaway, Kemp, King, Morley, Nathan, Osborne, Paton, Radin, Shulman, Tinker, White. *Old Year's Eve* by Peter Speyer, dir by Sarah Pia Anderson at The Pit: rev by Billington, Coveney, Gardner, Hiley, Hirschhorn, Hurren, Kellaway, Kemp, King, Maxwell, Morley, Sanderson, Shulman, Spencer. *Dreams of San Francisco* by Jacqueline Holborough, dir by Simon Stokes at the Bush Theatre: rev by Billington, Coveney, Edwardes, Gardner, Hiley, Hurren, Kellaway, Kemp, Nathan, Radin, Shulman, Spencer, Tinker. *Naomi* by Paul Chand, dir by Giles Croft at the Gate Theatre: rev by Cotton, de Jongh, Edwardes, Taylor.

2227 "Reviews of Productions." *LTR*. 1987; 7(24): 1544-1548. Lang.: Eng.

UK-England: London. 1987. ■*Private Members* by Go-Go Boys at the Half Moon Theatre: rev by Davies, Hiley, Robinson, Sanderson. *Camille* by Nancy Sweet, dir by Catherine Carney at the Old Red Lion: rev by de Jongh, Gore-Langton, Taylor, Woddis. *King John* by William Shakespeare, dir by David Massarella at Bridge Lane: rev by Denford, Goldman, Hopkinson, Tanner. *Othello* by William Shakespeare, dir by Joseph Marcell at the Arts (Cambridge): rev by de Jongh, Lavender, Osborne, Rose, Taylor.

2228 "Reviews of Productions." *LTR*. 1987; 7(24): 1548-1580. Lang.: Eng.

UK-England: London. 1987. ■*The Way to Go Home* by Rona Munro, dir by Pip Broughton at Theatre Upstairs by the Parnes Plough Company: rev by Billington, Clark, Gardner, Hoyle, Hurren, Kellaway, Shorter, Shulman, Taylor. *Lyle* by Charles Strouse, dir by Peter James at the Lyric Hammersmith. *Twelfth Night* by William Shakespeare, dir by Kenneth Branagh at the Riverside Studios by the Renaissance Theatre Company: rev by Battersby, Billington, Edwards, Hiley, Hirschhorn, Hoyle, Hurren, Jameson, Jones, Kellaway, Kemp, Morley, Pascal, Paton, Rose, Shulman, Spencer, Tinker, Wolf. *Bells Are Ringing* by Jules Styne, Betty Comden and Adolph Green, dir by John Doyle at the Greenwich: rev by Billington, Coveney, Edwardes, Jameson, King, Nathan, Osborne, Tinker, Wolf.

2229 "Reviews of Productions." *LTR*. 1987; 7(25): 1581-1585. Lang.: Eng.

UK-England: London. 1987. ■*The Cape Orchard* by Michael Picardie, dir by Roland Rees at the Young Vic: rev by Billington, Dungate, Hurren, Kemp, Ratcliffe, Rose, Saddler, Shulman, Woddis. *Death of a Dragonfly* by Matthew Brady, dir by Seamus Newham at the Tabard: rev by Lavender, Rose. *Separation* by Tom Kempinski, dir by Michael Attenborough at the Comedy Theatre: rev by Bell, Grant, Hurren,

DRAMA: —Performance/production

Paton, Tinker. *Sturdy Beggars* by the Medieval Players, dir by Carl Heap at The Place Theatre: rev by Hoyle, Rea, Taylor.

2230   "Reviews of Productions." *LTR.* 1987; 7(25): 1586-1592. Lang.: Eng.

UK-England: London. 1987. ∎*Bicharo* by Bhadrakani Zaveri, dir by Jatinder Verma at Tara Arts Centre: rev by Butcher, Goldman, Lavender. *The Traveller* by Jean-Claude van Itallie, dir by Keith Boak at the Almeida: rev by Coveney, de Jongh, Edwardes, Nathan, St. George, Tinker. *Brel* by Bill Bryden, Sebastian Graham-Jones and Linda Thompson, dir by Bob Crowley at Donmar Warehouse: rev by Coldstream, de Jongh, Hurren, King, Lavender, Nathan, Rose, Steyn, Tinker, Thorncroft. *Outbreak of God in Area* by Kenny Murray and Neil Oram, dir by Ken Campbell at the Young Vic: rev by Billington, Coveney, Gardner, Marriott, Ratcliffe, Rose, Taylor.

2231   "Reviews of Productions." *LTR.* 1987; 7(26): 1649-1656. Lang.: Eng.

UK-England: London. 1987. ∎*James Bond—The Panto* by Tony Haase and Pete McCarthy, dir by McCarthy at the Institute of Contemporary Arts: rev by Connor, Hay, Hoyle, Renton, Spencer. *The See-Saw Tree* by David Wood by the Whirligig Theatre at Sadler's Wells: rev by Kaye, McHardy. *The Wind in the Willows* by David Gooderson and David Conville at the Vaudeville Theatre: rev by Coverley, Hiley, Warman. *Winnie-the-Pooh* by Glyn Robbins, dir by Richard Williams at the Royalty: rev by Cotton, Paton, Steyn.

2232   "Reviews of Productions." *LTR.* 1987; 7(26): 1656-1659. Lang.: Eng.

UK-England: London. 1987. ∎*The Lion, the Witch and the Wardrobe* by Glyn Robbins, dir by Richard Williams at the Westminster Theatre: rev by Kettle. *Sinbad* by Connie Stewart, dir by Andy Arnold at the Bloomsbury Theatre: rev by Armistead, Morrison. *Pinocchio* by Lou Stein at the Watford Palace: rev by Coveney, Sonin. *Cinderella—The Real True Story* by Cheryl Moch and Holly Gewandter, dir by Nona Sheppard at Drill Hall Theatre: rev by Armistead, Asquith, Middleton, Rose.

2233   "Reviews of Productions." *LTR.* 1987; 7(16): 937-948. Lang.: Eng.

UK-England: London. 1987. ∎*The Two Gentlemen of Verona* by William Shakespeare, dir by Ian Talbot for the New Shakespeare Company at the Open Air, Regent's Park Theatre: rev by Billington, Edwardes, Hurren, King, Lavender, Nathan, Paton, Rissik, Sanderson, Shulman, Spencer. *Maguire Speaking* by Nial Ward, dir by James Marcus at Etcetera Theatre: rev by Brown, Cotton, Rose. *Mr. Bennett and Miss Smith* by Marion Baraister, dir by Richard Hansom at the Old Red Lion Theatre: rev by Arnott, King, Looch, Rose, Woddis. *The Wandering Jew* adapted from Eugène Sue's novel by Michelene Wandor and Mike Alfreds, dir by Alfreds at the Lyttelton Theatre for the National Theatre Company: rev by Billington, Hirschhorn, Hoyle, Hurren, Kemp, Nathan, Osborne, Paton, Radin, Ratcliffe, Rose, Sheridan, Shulman, Wolf.

2234   "Reviews of Productions." *LTR.* 1987; 7(16): 949-990. Lang.: Eng.

UK-England: London. 1987. ∎*Diary of a Somebody*, adapted by John Lahr from the diaries of Joe Orton, dir by Jonathan Myerson at the King's Head Theatre Club: rev by Gill, Rissik, Robinson, Thorncroft. *Bless the Bride* by Vivian Ellis, book & lyrics by A.P. Herbert, dir by Christopher Renshaw at Sadler's Wells Theatre: rev by Cotton, Hirschhorn, Hoyle, Jacobus, Jones, Hurren, Paton, Osborne, Sanderson, Shannon, Shulman, Steyn. *Royal Borough* by Marty Cruickshank, dir by Simon Curtis at the Theatre Upstairs: rev by Asquith, Hoyle, Radin, Rose, Shorter, Shulman, Taylor, Vidal. *Henceforward* written and dir by Alan Ayckbourn at Stephen Joseph Theatre: rev by Brown, Lawson, Osborne, Ratcliffe.

2235   "Reviews of Productions." *LTR.* 1987; 7(16): 990-1007. Lang.: Eng.

UK-England: London. 1987. ∎*Bells Are Ringing*, a revival of the musical by Jules Styne, book and lyrics by Betty Comden and Adolph Green, dir by John Doyle at Everyman, Cheltenham: rev by Foot, Hurren, Young. *Kip's War* by Carl Davis, book and lyrics by Hiawyn Oram, dir by Robin Midgley at the Haymarket Theatre, Leicester: rev by Billington, Hiley, Osborne, Steyn, Young. *Groucho—A Life in Revue* by Arthur Marx and Robert Fisher, dir by Marx at the Yvonne Arnaud Theatre, Guildford: rev by Steyn. *Portraits* by William Douglas Home, dir by John Dexter at the Savoy: rev by Edwards, Goldman, Grant, Hiley, Hirschhorn, Hoyle, Hurren, Jones, Laffan, Magenis, Morley, Nathan, Paton, Shulman, Spencer.

2236   "Reviews of Productions." *LTR.* 1987; 7(17): 1007-1018. Lang.: Eng.

UK-England: London. 1987. ∎*Jehad* by Francis McNeil, dir by Jenny Lee at the Gate Theatre: rev by Brown, Reed, Woddis. *Mary Rose* by J.M. Barrie, dir by Matthew Francis at the Greenwich Theatre: rev by Curtis, de Jongh, Gill, King, Lavender, Nathan, Osborne, Shulman, Taylor. *A Midsummer Night's Dream* by William Shakespeare, dir by Bill Alexander at the Barbican Theatre for the Royal Shakespeare Company: rev by Couling, de Jongh, Edwardes, Edwards, Jameson, Morley, Nathan, Osborne, Shulman, Taylor, Wolf, Young. *The Art of Success* by Nick Dear, dir by Adrian Noble at The Pit for the Royal Shakespeare Company: rev by de Jongh, Edwardes, Januszczak, King, Morley, Nathan, Shulman, Spencer, Wolf, Young.

2237   "Reviews of Productions." *LTR.* 1987; 7(17): 1018-1068. Lang.: Eng.

UK-England: London. 1987. ∎*Brzeska* by Ros Green, dir by Alasdair Middleton at the Canal Cafe: rev by Lavender, Rose. *Judgment* by Barry Collins, dir by Paul Jepson at the Man in the Moon Theatre: rev by Lavender, Sanderson, Spencer, Taylor. *The Great White Hope* by Howard Sackler, dir by Nicholas Kent at the Mermaid Theatre for the Royal Shakespeare Company: rev by Armistead, Cotton, de Jongh, Grant, Hiley, Hirschhorn, Hurren, Kemp, Morley, Morrison, Nathan, Radin, Shulman. *The Life of Napoleon* by John Sessions, dir by Kenneth Branagh at the Riverside Studio 2: rev by Grant, Hoyle, Morley, Nathan, Paton, Radin, Richler, Robinson, Shannon, Shorter, Taylor, Tinker, Vidal.

2238   "Reviews of Productions." *LTR.* 1987; 7(17): 1068-1079. Lang.: Eng.

UK-England: London. 1987. ∎*As Is* by William M. Hoffman, dir by Chris Bond at the Half Moon Theatre: rev by Armistead, de Jongh, Gill, Hiley, Lyttle, Morley, Morrison, Radin, Shorter, Taylor. *Infidelities (La Double Inconstance)* by Marivaux, translation by William Gaskill, dir by Gaskill at the Lyric Hammersmith Theatre: rev by Morley, Billington, Hiley, Hirschhorn, Hoyle, Hurren, King, Morrison, Nathan, Paton, Rissik, Robertson, Shorter, Shulman, Tinker, Wolf. *Vinci* written and directed by Robert Lepage at the ICA Theatre: rev by Billington, Connor, Edwardes, Taylor. *Chakravyuha* adapted from the Drona Parva section of *The Mahabharata*, dir by Ratan Thiyan at the Riverside Studios: rev by de Jongh, Edwardes, Gardner, Mackrell, Walker.

2239   "Reviews of Productions." *LTR.* 1987; 7(10): 624-633. Lang.: Eng.

UK-England: London. 1987. ∎*Kiss Me Kate* by Cole Porter, book by Sam and Bella Spewack, dir by Adrian Noble for the Royal Shakespeare Company at the Old Vic: rev by Bonner, Coveney, Edwards, Ellis, Grant, Gordon, Hiley, Hirschhorn, Jameson, Jones, Jurren, Nathan, Osborne, Tinker, Walsh. *Chicken Soup with Barley* by Arnold Wesker, dir by Rebecca Wollman at the Half Moon Theatre: rev by de Jongh, Hay, Laffan, Spencer, Taylor. *Out of Sight* by Sheila Dewey, dir by David Kester at the Tabard Theatre: rev by Robinson, Salvadori. *The Pink Briefcase* by Michael Birch, dir by Jude Kelly at the Lyric Studio: rev by Billington, Connor, Coveney, Edwardes, Kenton, Looch, Richler. *The Westwoods* by Alan Ayckbourn, dir by Vivienne Cozens at the Etcetera Theatre: rev by Carne, Denford, Hoyle, Hurren, Rose, Steyn, Stringer.

2240   "Reviews of Productions." *LTR.* 1987; 7(12): 709-721. Lang.: Eng.

UK-England: London. 1987. ∎*A Small Family Business* written and dir by Alan Ayckbourn at the Olivier Theatre for the National Theatre Company: rev by Asquith, Couling, Coveney, de Jongh, Edwards, Edwardes, Gordon, Hiley, Hirschhorn, Horner, Hurren, Jones-Evans, Kemp, King, Morley, Nathan, Osborne, Ratcliffe, Tinker, Walsh. *The Tooth of Crime* by Sam Shepard, dir by Phil Setren at the Bridge Lane Theatre: rev by de Jongh, Gore-Langton, McKenley, Renton. *Starts in the Middle* by Sally Jane Heit, dir by Jonathan Cohen at the Offstage Theatre: rev by Gordon, Grant, Hopkinson, Laffan, Looch, Steyn. *Julie What Is Wrong?* by Jorg Friedrich and Thomas Ahrens, dir by Ian

DRAMA: —Performance/production

Bowater at the Shaw Theatre: rev by Klein, Rose. *Up on the Roof* written and dir by Simon Moore and Jane Prowse at the Apollo Theatre: rev by de Jongh, Hay, Hiley, Hirschhorn, Hurren, Jameson, Jones-Evans, Nathan, Ratcliffe, Tinker, Wolf.

2241 "Reviews of Productions." *LTR.* 1987; 7(12): 721-729. Lang.: Eng.

UK-England: London. 1987. ■*Fremsley* written and dir by Ivor Cutler at the Shaw Theatre: rev by Nichols. *All the Arts of Hurting* by Roger Stennett, dir by Mark Dornford-May at the Man in the Moon Theatre: rev by Edwardes, Robinson. *Demon Lovers* written and dir by Stephen Lowe at the Warehouse Theatre: rev by Connor, Gordon, Gore-Langton, Hoyle, King, Shorter. *Don't* by Jean Binnie, dir by Seamus Newham at the Tabard Theatre: rev by Bartlett, Cotton. *Hamlet* by William Shakespeare, dir by Ingmar Bergman at the Lyttelton Theatre by the Royal Dramatic Theatre Company (Stockholm): rev by Billington, Couling, Gordon, Hiley, Hoyle, King, Mars-Jones, Morley, Morrison, Osborne, Radin, Stringer, St. George, Tinker.

2242 "Reviews of Productions." *LTR.* 1987; 7(10): 612-623. Lang.: Eng.

UK-England: London. 1987. ■*S/He* written and dir by Andy Walker at The Place: rev by Rea. *Mumbo Jumbo* by Robin Glendinning, dir by Nicholas Hytner at the Lyric Hammersmith: rev by Billington, Coveney, Edwardes, Gordon, Jones, Harron, Hiley, Hurren, Nathan, Remnant, Shorter, Shulman, Sutcliffe, Tinker. *Burning Point* by John Cooper, dir by Joan-Ann Maynard at the Tricycle Theatre: rev by Coveney, de Jongh, Denford, Gordon, Kemp, Ratcliffe. *Fragments of Isabella* by Isabella Leitner, Michael Scott and Gabrielle Reidy, dir by Scott at Watermans Theatre: rev by Carne, Gardner, Hopkinson, Nathan, Taylor.

2243 "Reviews of Productions." *LTR.* 1987; 7(12): 730-742. Lang.: Eng.

UK-England: London. 1987. ■*A Night of Passion on Butterman Drive* by Bob Mason, dir by Wyn Jones at the New End Theatre: rev by Edwardes, Hayes, Hurren, Shorter. *Blues in the Night* written and dir by Sheldon Epps at the Donmar Warehouse Theatre: rev by Brown, Edwards, Hurren, King, Middlehurst, Morley, Nathan, Osborne, Richler, Scafe, Steyn. *Getting Through* by Nona Sheppard and Helen Glavin, dir by Sheppard at the Drill Hall Theatre: rev by Connor, Kemp, Rose. *Rosencrantz and Guildenstern Are Dead* by Tom Stoppard, dir by Peter Wilson at the Piccadilly Theatre: rev by Billington, Edwards, Hiley, Hirschhorn, Horner, Hoyle, Kenneth, King, Morley, Nathan, Rissik, Sanderson, Shannon, Shorter, Shulman, Spencer, Tinker, Wolf.

2244 "Reviews of Productions." *LTR.* 1987; 7(12): 743-769. Lang.: Eng.

UK-England: London. 1987. ■*Jenkin's Ear* by Dusty Hughes, dir by David Hayman at the Royal Court: rev by Billington, Couling, Coveney, Edwardes, Edwards, Gardner, Gordon, Hiley, Hirschhorn, Hurren, Jameson, Kemp, King, Morley, Nathan, Osborne, Ratcliffe, Shannon, Shulman. *Miss Julie* by August Strindberg, dir by Ingmar Bergman at the Cottesloe Theatre by the Royal Dramatic Theatre Company (Stockholm): rev by Billington, Couling, Coveney, Gordon, King, Radin, Rissik, Shulman, Tinker. *A Midsummer Night's Dream* by William Shakespeare, dir by Caroline Smith at the Open Air Theatre in Regent's Park: rev by Carne, Hopkinson, Horner, Hoyle, Jameson, Morley, Osborne, Richler, Robinson, Spencer, Wroe. *Hard Times* by Stephen Jeffreys, dir by Dilys Hamlett at the King's Head Theatre: rev by Asquith, de Jongh, Gordon, Hirshhorn, Horner, Hurren, Morley, Nathan, Renton, Rose, Shorter, Shulman.

2245 "Reviews of Productions." *LTR.* 1987; 7(13): 770-783. Lang.: Eng.

UK-England: London. 1987. ■*Let Us Go Then, You and I* by Peter Ackroyd, dir by Josephine Hart at the Lyric Hammersmith: rev by Billington, Hirschhorn, Horner, King, Morley, Osborne, Ratcliffe, Rissik, Robertson, Shulman, Spencer, St. George, Wolf. *The Air Fix* written and dir by James Castle at the Gate Theatre: rev by Asquith, Gardner, Renton, Rose. *Every Good Boy Deserves Favour* by Tom Stoppard and André Previn, dir by Jonathan Myerson at the Queen Elizabeth Hall Theatre: rev by Henderson, Hoyle, Morley, Sonin, Spencer, Stringer. *Melon* by Simon Gray, dir by Christopher Morahan at the Theatre Royal, Haymarket: rev by Asquith, Billington, Couling,

Coveney, Edwardes, Edwards, Gordon, Hiley, Hirschhorn, Horner, Hurren, Kemp, King, Morley, Nathan, Osborne, Radin, Ratcliffe, Shannon, Shulman.

2246 "Reviews of Productions." *LTR.* 1987; 7(13): 783-794. Lang.: Eng.

UK-England: London. 1987. ■*Close to the Bone* by Rupert Creed and Mary Cooper, music by Helen Porter, dir by Creed at the Warehouse Theatre: rev by Bartlett, Lavender, Spencer. *The Lover* and *A Slight Ache* by Harold Pinter, dir by Kevin Billington at the Young Vic: rev by Connor, Coveney, Edwards, Gordon, Hay, Hirschhorn, King, Morley, Osborne, Renton, Richler. *Love on the Plastic* by Julia Schofield, dir by Chris Bond at the Half Moon Theatre: rev by Billington, Gardner, Gordon, Hoyle, Kemp, Morley, Radin, Ratcliffe, Sanderson, Shorter, Stringer. *Teenage Trash* by Jon Jon, Phil Booth and the Bloolips Company, dir by Phyllis Stein at the Shaw Theatre: rev by Griffiths, Hiley, Lyttle, Rea, Renton.

2247 "Reviews of Productions." *LTR.* 1987; 7(15, 19): 921, 1177-1183. Lang.: Eng.

UK-England: London. 1987. ■*Made in Spain* by Tony Grounds, dir by Wyn Jones at the New End Theatre: rev by Alexander, Hopkinson, Rissik. *Pacific Overtures* by Stephen Sondheim and John Weidman, dir by Keith Warner at the Coliseum by the English National Opera: rev by Grier, Henderson, Hiley, Hirschhorn, Hurren, Jones, Kenyon, Loppert, Linker, Milnes, Ratcliffe, Robertson, Sonin, Sutcliffe, White, Wolf. *Somewhere Over the Balcony* by Marie Jones, dir by Peter Sheridan at the Drill Hall Theatre: rev by Brown, Rose, Woddis. *Cauldron* by Sam Dowling and Andrea Kealy, dir by Tal Rubins at the Tabard Theatre: rev by Butcher, Lavender.

2248 "Reviews of Productions." *LTR.* 1987; 7(19): 1184-1192. Lang.: Eng.

UK-England: London. 1987. ■*The Importance of Being Earnest* by Oscar Wilde, dir by Donald Sinder at the Royalty Theatre: rev by Billington, Edwards, Hiley, King, Laffan, Morley, Osborne, Paton, Ratcliffe, Richler, Robertson, Shannon, Steyn, Tinker, Young. *Judgment Day* by Michael K. Stark, dir by Evan Dunstan at the Pentameters Theatre: rev by Gilbert, Hay, Laffan. *Skullduggery* written and dir by Philip Davis at the Old Red Lion: rev by Brown, Coveney, Lavender, Ratcliffe, Sanderson. *Pork Pies* by Vince Foxall, dir by Jeff Teare at the Theatre Royal, Stratford: rev by Armistead, Billington, Gardner, Hay, Hiley, Paton, Spencer, Stringer, Taylor.

2249 "Reviews of Productions." *LTR.* 1987; 7(19): 1193-1203. Lang.: Eng.

UK-England: London. 1987. ■*Exile in the Forest* by G. Shankara Pillai, B. Bahi and Jatinder Verma, dir by Pillai and Verma at The Place: rev by Billington, Hiley, Kellaway, Khan, McFerran, Woddis. *Groucho—A Life in Revue* by Arthur Marx and Robert Fisher, dir by Marx at the Comedy Theatre: rev by Arnott, Connor, Coveney, Gill, Hiley, Hirshhorn, Hurren, Jameson, Kellaway, King, Morley, Osborne, Paton, Shannon, Shulman, St. George, Tinker. *Article Eleven* by Frank Tallis, dir by Patrick Duncan at the Etcetera Theatre: rev by Arnott, Sanderson. *Macbeth* by William Shakespeare, dir by Yukio Ninagawa at the Lyttelton Theatre by the Ninagawa Company (Tokyo): rev by Billington, Couling, Edwards, Hoyle, King, Osborne, Shulman, Taylor, Tinker.

2250 "Reviews of Productions." *LTR.* 1987; 7(19): 1203-1218. Lang.: Eng.

UK-England: London. 1987. ■*Medea* by Euripides, dir by Yukio Ninagawa at the Olivier Theatre by the Ninagawa Company (Tokyo): rev by Billington, Couling, Coveney, Edwards, Spencer, Tinker. *Ambulance* by Gregory Motton, dir by Lindsay Posner at Theatre Upstairs: rev by Brown, Connor, Hiley, Hoyle, Kellaway, Nathan, Rose, Spencer, Vidal. *The Big Knife* by Clifford Odets, dir by Robin Lefevre at the Albery Theatre: rev by Billington, Bonner, Coveney, Gardner, Hiley, Hirschhorn, Hurren, Jameson, Kellaway, King, Morley, Nathan, Paton, Rose, Shulman, Shorter, Steyn, St. George, Usher. *Comedians* by Trevor Griffiths, dir by David Thacker at the Young Vic: rev by Brown, Cotton, Hay, Hiley, Stringer, Sweeting.

2251 "Reviews of Productions." *LTR.* 1987; 7(19): 1219-1234. Lang.: Eng.

UK-England: London. 1987. ■*Beyond Reasonable Doubt* by Jeffrey Archer, dir by David Gilmore at the Queen's Theatre: rev by Asquith,

DRAMA: —Performance/production

Billington, Coghlan, Couling, Coveney, Edwards, Grant, Hiley, Hirschhorn, Hurren, Jameson, King, Lawson, Morley, Nathan, Osborne, Paton, Ratcliffe, Shulman, St. George, Tinker. *Ting Tang Mine* by Nick Darke, dir by Michael Rudman at the Cottesloe by the National Theatre Company: rev by Billington, Gardner, Grant, Hoyle, Kemp, King, Morley, Ratcliffe, Shulman, Spencer, St. George. National Youth Theatre of Great Britain, 1987 Season: rev by Armistead, Bartlett, Cotton, Dennford, Edwards, Hanks, Laffan, Looch, Magenis, Ratcliffe, Rissik, Rose, Sanderson.

2252 "Reviews of Productions." *LTR*. 1987; 7(11): 670-679. Lang.: Eng.

UK-England: London. 1987. ■*Bartholomew Fair* by Ben Jonson, dir by Peter Barnes for the New Shakespeare Company in an open air production at Regent's Park: rev by Coveney, Connor, de Jongh, Gordon, Hiley, Horner, Hurren, King, Nathan, Ratcliffe, Rose, Shorter, St. George, Tinker, Walsh. *No Worries* by David Holman, dir by Jeremy Bell at the Young Vic: rev by Khan, McAfee. *Releevo* by David Spencer, dir by Sue Dunderdale at the Soho Poly: rev by Atkins, Carne, Edwardes, Hoyle, Morrison, Renton, Spencer, Woddis. *Grimaldi* by Michael Bath, dir by Geoffrey Buckley for the Dual Control Theatre Company at the Old Red Lion Theatre: rev by Bartlett, Gordon, King, Renton. *Bet Noir* by James Mundy, dir by Robin Soans at the Young Vic: rev by Carne, Denford, Jones-Evans, Renton, Rose, Shorter.

2253 "Reviews of Productions." *LTR*. 1987; 7(11): 680-699. Lang.: Eng.

UK-England: London. 1987. ■*Three Sisters (Tri sestry)* by Anton Čechov in a translation by Michael Frayn, dir by Elijah Moshinksy at the Albery Theatre: rev by de Jongh, Edwards, Edwardes, Hiley, Hirschorn, Horner, Hoyle, Hurren, Jameson, King, Mars-Jones, Middlehurst, Osborne, Pascal, Richler, St. George, Tinker. *The Sleep*, text by Claire MacDonald, music by Jeremy Peyton Jones, dir by Peter Brook at the Riverside Studios: rev by Allen, Brown, Coveney, Gardner, Hemming, Hiley, Morrison, Rea, Spencer. Peter Stein's Schaubühne production of *The Hairy Ape* by Eugene O'Neill, presented by the National Theatre: rev by Radin. *Kiss Me Kate*, music and lyrics by Cole Porter, book by Sam and Bella Spewack, dir by Adrian Noble, presented by the Royal Shakespeare Company at the Old Vic: rev by Ray, St. George. *Chicken Soup with Barley* by Arnold Wesker, dir by Rebecca Wollman, presented by the East End Theatre Company at the the Half Moon Theatre: rev by Armistead, Grant. *Mumbo Jumbo* by Robin Glendinning, dir by Nicholas Hytner at the Lyric Hammersmith: rev by Ray.

2254 "Reviews of Productions." *LTR*. 1987; 7(18): 1108-1153. Lang.: Eng.

UK-England: London. 1987. ■*This Savage Parade* by Anthony Shaffer, dir by Jonathan Myerson at the King's Head Theatre: rev by Asquith, Corney, Coveney, de Jongh, Osborne, Radin, Sanderson, Shulman, Taylor, Tinker. *The Emperor* by Michael Hastings and Jonathan Miller, dir by Miller at the Royal Court: rev by Connor, Couling, de Jongh, Hurren, Osborne, Sanderson, Shannon. *Vespers* dir by Ritsaertten Cate at the ICA Theatre: rev by Arnott, Bartlett, Coveney, Rea, Robinson.

2255 "Reviews of Productions." *LTR*. 1987; 7(18): 1162-1168. Lang.: Eng.

UK-England: London. 1987. ■*The Taming of the Shrew* by William Shakespeare, dir by Jonathan Miller for the Royal Shakespeare Company: rev by Billington, Coveney, Edwardes, Gardner, King, Morley, Paton, Ratcliffe, Rissik, Shorter. *A Question of Geography* by John Berger and Nella Bielski, dir by John Caird at The Other Place: rev by Billington, Coveney, Edwardes, Gardner, Rissik.

2256 "Reviews of Productions." *LTR*. 1987; 7(18): 1154-1162. Lang.: Eng.

UK-England: London. 1987. ■*Thursday's Ladies* by Loleh Bellon, dir by Frank Hauser at the Apollo Theatre: rev by Alexander, Brown, Couling, Coveney, de Jongh, Edwards, Grant, Hiley, Hirschhorn, King, Paton, Radin, Ratcliffe, Rose, Shannon, Shulman, Spencer, Tinker. *Now You See Me* written and dir by Polly Teale and *Like Dolls or Ladies* by Stephen Jeffreys, dir by Mark Freeland at Young Vic: rev by Brown, Gardner, Lockerbie, Rose. *The Innocent Mistress* by Mary Pix, adapted by Elizabeth Rothschild, dir by Annie Castledine at the Derby Playhouse: rev by Hoyle, Shorter, Taylor, Thornber. *The School for*

Scandal by Richard Brinsley Sheridan, dir by Giles Havergal at the Citizens Theatre: rev by Hemming, McMillan, Shorter.

2257 "Reviews of Productions." *LTR*. 1987; 7(23): 1437-1440. Lang.: Eng.

UK-England: London. 1987. ■*Apart from George* written and dir by Nick Ward at Theatre Upstairs: rev by Billington, Christopher, Clark, Edwards, Hurren, Myer, Rissik, Shulman, Woddis. *Theme and Variations* by Samuel Alyoshin, translated by Michael Glenny, dir by Stuart Wood at Offstage Downstairs: rev by Brown, Cotton. *Naked (Vestire gli ignudi)* by Luigi Pirandello, translated by Diane Cilento, dir by Roland Jacuarello at Old Red Lion Theatre: rev by Brown, de Jongh, Robinson, Sanderson, Spencer. *The Bolt Hole* by Jairo Anibal Niño, translated and dir by Hal Brown, and *Trial by Fire (Prueba de fuego)* by Ugo Ulive, translated by Walter Acosta, dir by Brown at Bolivar Hall: rev by Denford.

2258 "Reviews of Productions." *LTR*. 1987; 7(22): 1410-1421. Lang.: Eng.

UK-England: London. 1987. ■*A View from the Bridge* by Arthur Miller, dir by Alan Ayckbourn at the Aldwych: rev by Asquith, Billington, Coveney, Edwards, Grant, Hiley, Hirschhorn, Hurren, Jameson, King, Morley, Nathan, Osborne, Paton, Purnell, Shulman, Tinker, White. *Hamlet Machine (Hamletmaschine)* by Heiner Müller, dir by Robert Wilson at the Almeida: rev by Billington, Couling, Coveney, Gill, Gordon, Jordan, Kemp, King, Nathan, Ratcliffe, Shorter, Wolf. *The Thousand Cherry Trees of Yoshitsune (Yoshitsune senbonzakura)* by the Ichakawa Ennosuke Kabuki Company at the Sadler's Wells Theatre: rev by de Jongh, Gordon, Mackrell, Radin, Walker. *The Kunju Macbeth*, *The Woman Warrior* and *The Peony Pavilion (Mu dan ting)* by the Shanghai Kunju Theatre at the London Palladium: rev by Hurren, Shulman.

2259 "Reviews of Productions." *LTR*. 1987; 7(22): 1422-1514. Lang.: Eng.

UK-England: London. 1987. ■*The Pied Piper* by Adrian Mitchell, dir by Alan Cohen at the Olivier Theatre: rev by Hiley, Hurren, Khan, McKenley, Sanderson. *Pushkin* by Richard Crane, dir by Faynia Williams and *Funeral Games* by Joe Orton, dir by Catharine Arakelian at the Bloomsbury. *American Buffalo* by David Mamet, dir by Timothy Veglio at the Young Vic: rev by Hay, McKenley, Renton. *Under the Web* by Julia Kearsley, dir by Brian Stirner at the Soho Poly: rev by Billington, Clark, Coveney, Hiley, Kemp, Shorter, Woddis.

2260 "Reviews of Productions." *LTR*. 1987; 7(24): 1515-1518. Lang.: Eng.

UK-England: London. 1987. ■*Praise Be to God* and *Reg* by Graeme Fife, *Houdini* by Barry Killerby, dir by Killerby at the Orange Tree: rev by Hopkinson, Hoyle, Kettle, Shorter. *A Month in the Country (Mesjats v derevne)* by Ivan Turgenev, dir by Bill Pryde at the Richmond Theatre: rev by Coveney, de Jongh, Kellaway, Lane, Osborne. *Effie's Burning* by Valerie Windsor, dir by Susan Mayo at the Offstage Downstairs: rev by de Jongh, Edwardes, Gardner, Hoyle. *Sell Out* by Jonathan Rich, dir by Patrick Wilde at the Latchmere: rev by McFerran.

2261 "Reviews of Productions." *LTR*. 1987; 7(25): 1593-1608. Lang.: Eng.

UK-England. 1987. ■*Love's a Luxury* by Guy Paxton and Edward V. Hoile, dir by Sam Walters at the Orange Tree: rev by Billington, Cotton, Gore-Langton, Spencer. *Countrymania* by Mike Alfreds after Carlo Goldoni, dir by Alfreds at the Olivier for the National Theatre Company: rev by Billington, Coveney, Edwardes, Gardner, Hurren, Kemp, King, Nathan, Osborne, Paton, Ratcliffe, Shulman. *The Servant of Two Masters (Il servitore di due padroni)* by Carlo Goldoni, dir by Ted Craig at the Warehouse, Croydon: rev by Gardner, Hay, Sutcliffe. *Acting Shakespeare* written and dir by Ian McKellan at the Playhouse: rev by Billington, Coveney, Hirschhorn, Hurren, Jameson, Kemp, King, Nathan, Osborne, Paton, Ratcliffe, Shulman, Tinker.

2262 "Reviews of Productions." *LTR*. 1987; 7(25): 1608-1616. Lang.: Eng.

UK-England. 1987. ■*Heart of Ice* by David Gale and Jeremy Peyton Jones, dir by Hilary Westlake at The Place: rev by Armistead, Rea, Robinson, Rose. *Stars* by Stephen Lowe, dir by Tom Knight at Waterman's Theatre: rev by Bartlett, de Jongh, Gardner, Nathan, Steyn. *The Foreigner* by Larry Shue, dir by Nick Broadhurst at the

DRAMA: —Performance/production

Albery Theatre: rev by Coveney, de Jongh, Hirschhorn, King, Lavender, Nathan, Osborne, Paton, Purnell, Rissik, Sanderson, Shulman, Tinker. *Speculators* by Tony Marchant, dir by Barry Kyle at The Pit: rev by Billington, Gardner, Gore-Langton, Hirschhorn, Hoyle, Hurren, Kemp, Stringer.

2263 "Reviews of Productions." *LTR*. 1987; 7(25): 1617-1649.
Lang.: Eng.
UK-England. 1987. ■*Between East and West* by Richard Nelson, dir by David Jones at the Hampstead Theatre: rev by Billington, Coveney, Edwardes, Kellaway, King, Nathan, Rissik, Sanderson, Woddis. *You Never Can Tell* by Bernard Shaw, dir by Toby Richardson at the Haymarket: rev by Billington, Coveney, Edwards, Jameson, Hiley, Hirschhorn, Kellaway, Kemp, McFerran, Morley, Nathan, Osborne, Paton, Shulman, Tinker, Williams, Wolf. *The Wizard of Oz* by John Kane, dir by Ian Judge at the Barbican for the Royal Shakespeare Company: rev by Asquith, Billington, Couling, Coveney, Edwardes, Hiley, Hirschhorn, Hurren, Jameson, King, Morley, Nathan, Paton, Radin, Ratcliffe, Shorter, Shulman, Steyn, Tinker. *Babes in the Woods* by Bryan Blackburn, dir by Michael Hurll at the London Palladium: rev by Billington, Bonner, Connor, Coveney, Hiley, Hurren, Jameson, Nathan, Ratcliffe, Shulman, Spencer, Tinker.

2264 "Reviews of Productions." *LTR*. 1987; 7(23): 1440-1445.
Lang.: Eng.
UK-England: London. 1987. ■*I Stand in a Land of Roses* devised and performed by The Raving Beauties, dir by Fanny Viner at Young Vic Studio: rev by McFerran. *The Rover* by Aphra Behn, adaptation and dir by John Barton, performed by Royal Shakespeare Company at the Mermaid: rev by Armistead, Billington, Edwardes, Hirschhorn, Hurren, Jameson, Marriott, Nathan, Osborne, Paton, Radin, Renton, Shaw, Shulman, Usher, Woddis. *Avenging Angel* adapted and dir by Joel Fisher from the novel *The Lodger* by Mrs. H. Belloc-Lowndes at Etcetera Theatre: rev by Caplan, Clark, Renton. *Height of Passion* by Maria Tsvetayeva presented by Labyrinth Productions, dir by Francesca Hamilton: rev by Hopkinson, Laffan.

2265 "Reviews of Productions." *LTR*. 1987; 7(23): 1444-1453.
Lang.: Eng.
UK-England: London. 1987. ■*Dangerous Obsession* by N.J. Crisp, dir by Roger Smith at the Apollo Theatre: rev by Billington, Bonner, Coveney, Grant, Hiley, Hirschhorn, Jameson, Kellaway, King, Lavender, Morley, Nathan, Paton, Shulman, Shorter, Spencer, Spencer, Taylor. *Fighting Kite* by Harwant Bains, dir by Jeff Teare at Theatre Royal: rev by Armistead, Goldman, Gordon, Hiley, Renton, Sanderson, Woddis. *The Lady Aoi* and *Hanjo*, two modern *nō* plays by Yukio Mishima, dir by Robert J. Carson at the Gate Theatre: rev by de Jongh, Gordon, Hay, Kemp, Lyttle, St. George. *Last Summer in Chulimsk (Prošlym letom v Čulimske)* by Aleksand'r Vampilov, adapted by Paul Thompson for Cambridge Theatre Company, dir by Bill Pryde at Riverside Studios: rev by de Jongh, Edwardes, Hoyle, Martin, Nathan, Short, Taylor, Woddis.

2266 "Reviews of Productions." *LTR*. 1987; 7(23): 1453-1459.
Lang.: Eng.
UK-England: London. 1987. ■*The Best Years of Your Life* by Clive Jermain presented by Shirk Productions, dir by Rod Bolt at Man in the Moon. *Canadian Gothic* by Joanna M. Glass, presented by Delirium Theatre Company, dir by Riel Karny-Jones at Man in the Moon Theatre: rev by McFerran. *Peter Pan* by J.M. Barrie, dir by John Newman at Cambridge Theatre: rev by Asquith, Bonner, Grant, Hirschhorn, Hoyle, Jameson, Hurren, King, Marriott, Maxwell, Morley, Oldfield, Osborne, Paton, Shulman, Steyn, Tinker.

2267 "Reviews of Productions." *LTR*. 1987; 7(13): 795-800.
Lang.: Eng.
UK-England: London. 1987. ■*The Mill on the Floss* by Robin Brown, dir by Jonathan Holloway at the Gate Theatre: rev by Carne, Gore-Langton, King, Robinson. *No Man's Land* by Bernard Wright and Jenny Frazer, dir by Philip Grout at the Latchmere Theatre: rev by Pascal, Rose. *Cuckoo* by Station House Opera at Riverside Studios: rev by Rea, Rogus, Rose. *The Perfect Party* by A.R. Gurney, Jr., dir by Alan Strachan at the Greenwich Theatre: rev by Billington, Coveney, Gordon, Hiley, Hirschhorn, Hurren, King, Osborne, Pascal, Ratcliffe, Rissik, Sanderson, Shannon, Shulman, Wolf.

2268 "Reviews of Productions." *LTR*. 1987; 7(13): 801-822.
Lang.: Eng.
UK-England. London. 1987. ■*Bodycount* by Les Smith, dir by Pip Broughton at the Old Red Lion Theatre: rev by Spencer, St. George, Vidal, Woddis. *Little Footsteps* by Ted Tally, dir by Robin Saphra at the Tabard Theatre: rev by Alexander, Billington, Edwardes, Looch. *Effie's Burning* by Valerie Windsor, dir by Susan Mayo at the Cottesloe Theatre: rev by Billington, Kemp, Ratcliffe. *Prometheus in Evin* written and dir by Iraj Jannatie Ataie at Theatre Upstairs: rev by Armistead, Brittain, Connor, Renton, Sanderson.

2269 "Reviews of Productions." *LTR*. 1987; 7(14): 822-831.
Lang.: Eng.
UK-England: London. 1987. ■*Pity of War* by Peter Florence, dir by Norman Florence at the Lyric Studio: rev by Laffon, Lavender, Sanderson. *Serious Money* by Caryl Churchill, dir by Max Stafford-Clark at Wyndham's Theatre: rev by Collins, Connor, Grant, Hiley, Horner, Hoyle, Hurren, Morley, Sonin, St. George, Sutcliffe. *Helen Lederer and Raw Sex* by Helen Lederer, dir by Robin Driscoll at the King's Head Theatre: rev by Carne, Connor, Pascal. *Fathers and Sons* by Brian Friel, dir by Michael Rudman at the Lyttelton Theatre for the National Theatre Company: rev by Asquith, Barkley, Billington, Coveney, Edwards, Gordon, Hiley, Horner, Hurren, Kemp, King, Morley, Osborne, Pascal, Ratcliffe, Rose, Shulman, Tinker.

2270 "Reviews of Productions." *LTR*. 1987; 7(14): 832-842.
Lang.: Eng.
UK-England: London. 1987. ■*That Summer* by David Edgar, dir by Michael Attenborough at the Hampstead Theatre: rev by Billington, Coveney, Edwards, French, Gordon, Hiley, Kemp, Lyttle, Pascal, Rose, Shorter, Shulman, Tinker. *The Attractions* by Tony Marchant, dir by Brian Stirner at the Soho Poly Theatre: rev by Gardner, Gordon, Hay, Khan, Renton, Shorter. *Hotel Vietnam* by Phil Melling, dir by Jay Vaughan at the Gate Theatre: rev by Alexander, de Jongh, Rose. *The Storm (Groza)* by Aleksand'r Ostrovskij, dir by Nick Hamm at The Pit: rev by Bartlett, de Jongh, French, Gordon, Hiley, Hoyle, Hurren, Kemp, King, Nathan, Osborne, Shulman.

2271 "Reviews of Productions." *LTR*. 1987; 7(14): 842-855.
Lang.: Eng.
UK-England: London. 1987. ■*Vanavasa (Exile)* by Calicut University Little Theatre Company at Drill Hall Theatre: rev by Connor, St. George. *The Balcony (Le Balcon)* by Jean Genet, dir by Terry Hands at the Barbican Theatre, for the Royal Shakespeare Company: rev by Billington, Coveney, Gordon, Grant, Hiley, Hirschhorn, Hurren, Kemp, King, Ratcliffe, Remnant, Shorter, Shulman. *Corpse!* written and dir by Gerald Moon at the Strand Theatre: rev by Horner, Osborne, Sanderson, Shannon, Shulman, Young. *Public Enemy* by Kenneth Branagh, dir by Malcolm McKay at the Lyric Hammersmith: rev by Coveney, Davis, de Jongh, Edwards, Gardner, Grant, Maxwell, Osborne, Ratcliffe, Richler, Rissik, Tinker.

2272 "Reviews of Productions." *LTR*. 1987; 7(14): 856-858.
Lang.: Eng.
UK-England: London. 1987. ■*Three Men on a Horse* by John Cecil Holm and George Abbott, dir by Jonathan Lynn at the Vaudeville Theatre: rev by Bartlett, de Jongh, Denford, Gordon, Horner, Shorter, Tinker, Young. *Lindsay Kemp Season* written and dir by Lindsay Kemp at Sadler's Wells Theatre: rev by Armistead, de Jongh, Hiley, Looch, Mackrell, Shorter, Spencer. *They Shoot Horses, Don't They?* by Ray Herman, dir by Ron Daniels at the Mermaid, performed by the Royal Shakespeare Company: rev by Billington, Edwardes, Gordon, Hiley, Hirschhorn, Hurren, Jameson, King, Morley, Nathan, Osborne, Ratcliffe, Shannon, Shulman, St. George, Taylor, Tinker, Young. *Canterbury Tales* by Geoffrey Chaucer, Michael Bogdanov and Phil Woods, dir by Bogdanov at the Prince of Wales Theatre: rev by Goldman, Hiley, Hopkinson, Laffan, Maxwell.

2273 "Reviews of Productions." *LTR*. 1987; 7(15): 886-908.
Lang.: Eng.
UK-England: London. 1987. ■*Rebel in Paradise* by Howard Zinn, dir by Paulette Randall at the Young Vic: rev by Carne, Gordon, Hopkinson, King, Looch, Robinson. *Sammy Cahn—Words & Music* by Sammy Cahn, dir by Peter Daniels at the Duke of York's Theatre: rev by Christie, Davis, Hurren, Morley, Nathan, Osborne, Sanderson, Steyn, Stringer, Sweeting, Thorncroft, Tinker, Wolf. *Follies* by Stephen

DRAMA: —Performance/production

Sondheim and James Goldman, dir by Mike Ockrent at the Shaftesbury Theatre: rev by Asquith, Billington, Coveney, Edwards, Gordon, Hiley, Hirschhorn, Horner, Hurren, Jameson, King, Middlehurst, Morley, Nathan, Osborne, Radin, Ratcliffe, Rose, Shulman, St. George, Steyn, Tinker. *Mean Tears* written and dir by Peter Gill at Cottesloe by the National Theatre Company: rev by Billington, Gordon, Grant, Hiley, Hirschhorn, Hurren, Kemp, King, Maxwell, Morley, Osborne, Ratcliffe, Shulman, Tinker, Woddis.

2274 "Reviews of Productions." *LTR*. 1987; 7(15): 909-921. Lang.: Eng.

UK-England: London. 1987. ■*The Fling* by Asher, translated by Mike Stott, dir by Brian Peck at King's Head Theatre: rev by Billington, Hoyle, Lavender, Looch, McAfee, Shulman, Steyn. *Mystery of the Rose Bouquet (Misterio del ramo de rosas)* by Manuel Puig, dir by Robert Allan Ackerman at the Donmar Warehouse Theatre: Atkins, Billington, Edwards, Gardner, Hiley, Hoyle, Hurren, Nathan, Ratcliffe, Rissik, Rose, Shulman. *Flight* by David Lan, dir by Howard Davies at The Pit: rev by de Jongh, Hiley, Looch, Nathan, Robinson, Sanderson, Shulman, Taylor. *Light Up the Sky* by Moss Hart, dir by Elijah Moshinsky at the Globe Theatre: rev by Asquith, Billington, Coveney, Grant, Hiley, Hinton, Hirschhorn, Hurren, King, Osborne, Ratcliffe, Shannon, Shulman, Steyn, Tinker.

2275 "Reviews of Productions." *LTR*. 1987; 7(17): 1079-1096. Lang.: Eng.

UK-England: London. 1987. ■*True Love Romances* by Graham Alborough, dir by Simon Usher at the Old Red Lion: rev by Herbert, Sanderson. *Beyond Reasonable Doubt* by Jeffrey Archer, dir by David Gilmore at the Theatre Royal: rev by Sexton. *The Light of Day* by Graham Swannell, dir by Peter James at the Lyric Studio: rev by Billington, Gardner, Hirschhorn, Hopkinson, Hurren, King, Morley, Osborne, Paton, Ratcliffe, Stringer, Taylor, Young. *Kiddush* written and dir by Shmuel Has'Fari at the Bloomsbury Theatre: rev by Rose.

2276 "Reviews of Productions." *LTR*. 1987; 7(18): 1097-1099. Lang.: Eng.

UK-England: London. 1987. ■*Nightmare Abbey* adapted from Thomas Love Peacock's novel by Eleanor Zeal, dir by Paul Dodwell at the Etcetera Theatre: rev by Connor, Sanderson. *Another Saturday Night* devised and presented by Buster Theatre, dir by Sarah Harper at the Latchmere Theatre: rev by Bartlett, Brown, Gardner. *The Image of the Beast* written and dir by Jonathan Holloway at the Croydon Warehouse: rev by Armistead, Gardner, King, Rose. *Tom Tom* by Nick Vivian and Tom Morris, dir by Vivian at the Corner Theatre: rev by Gardner, Mavor.

2277 "Reviews of Productions." *LTR*. 1987; 7(18): 1099-1107. Lang.: Eng.

UK-England: London. 1987. ■*When the Moon Has Set, The Shadow of the Glen* and *Riders to the Sea* by John Millington Synge, presented by the Four Corners Theatre Company, dir by Nigel P. Draycott at the Gate Theatre: rev by Gilber, Lavender, Hopkinson. *Curtains* by Stephen Bill, dir by Stuart Burge at the Hampstead Theatre: rev by Billington, Coveney, Edwards, Gardner, Grant, Hiley, Hirschhorn, Hurren, King, Morley, Osborne, Ratcliffe, Rissik, Rose, Shulman, Tinker. *Remembrance* by Derek Walcott, dir by Carmen Munroe at the Arts Theatre: rev by de Jongh, Foster, Edwardes, Radin, Taylor, Woddis. *Broken Promises* by David Henry, dir by Tony Craven at the Soho Poly: rev by Arnott, Cotton, Rose, Rubikowicz.

2278 Ashcroft, Peggy; Ewbank, Inga-Stina, ed. "Playing Shakespeare." *ShS*. 1987; 40: 11-19. Illus.: Photo. Print. B&W. 4. Lang.: Eng.

UK-England. 1930-1986. Histories-sources. ■Personal views of Dame Peggy Ashcroft on parts she has played and directors worked with.

2279 Bérczes, László. "Ködös Stratford." (Foggy Stratford.) *FSM*. 1987; 31(36): 8-9. Illus.: Photo. B&W. 3. Lang.: Hun.

UK-England: Stratford. 1987. Reviews of performances. ■Brief survey of four productions presented by the Royal Shakespeare Company and visiting the memorial places of Shakespeare.

2280 Booth, Michael R.; Heckenberg, Pamela. "Touring the Empire." *ET*. 1987 Nov.; 6(1): 49-60. Notes. Lang.: Eng.

UK-England. North America. Australia. 1870-1929. Historical studies. ■British touring companies: repertoire, hazards, travel, personal experiences.

2281 Brook, Peter. *The Shifting Point: 1946-1987*. New York, NY: Harper & Row; 1987. 254 pp. Pref. Index. Illus.: Photo. Print. B&W. 100. Lang.: Eng.

UK-England. 1946-1987. Biographies. ■Autobiography of stage and film director. Influences on his life and work and his productions through the years. Related to Media: Film.

2282 Brown, Peter; Butcher, Andrew. "Teaching 'Crisis, Text and Image'." *L&H*. 1987 Spr; 13(1): 3-13. Append. Lang.: Eng.

UK-England: Canterbury. 1983-1987. Historical studies. ■Undergraduate students stage the York Crucifixion play at the University of Kent as part of a course in medieval literature.

2283 Cohen, Dan Baron. "Staging *Struggle for Freedom*." *RLtrs*. 1987 July(21): 15-32. Illus.: Photo. Poster. B&W. 3. Lang.: Eng.

UK-England: Manchester. 1987. Historical studies. ■Production of *Struggle for Freedom: The Life and Work of Len Johnson* by the Youth of the Len Johnson Schools Project in collaboration with Frontline: Culture and Education.

2284 Cox, Brian. "Brian Cox Reflects on his Year at Stratford and Why He Returned from Films to Work in the Theatre." *Drama*. 1987; 3(165): 15-16. Illus.: Photo. B&W. 2. Lang.: Eng.

UK-England: Stratford, London. USA: New York, NY. 1968-1987. Histories-sources. ■Brian Cox's return to the Royal Shakespeare Company. Related to Media: Film.

2285 Dale, Tish. "The London Scene: There's More than Just Phantom to See." *TheaterW*. 1987 Aug 17; 1: 19-21. Illus.: Photo. 3. Lang.: Eng.

UK-England: London. 1987. Critical studies. ■Tish Dale discusses the West End season by comparing and contrasting 4 plays: Simon Gray's *Melon*, Hugh Whitmore's *Breaking the Code, Alan Turing: The Secret War*, and Wendy Kesselman's *My Sister in This House*.

2286 Elliot, Vivian. "Genius Loci: The Malvern Festival Tradition." 191-218 in Leary, Daniel, ed. *Shaw's Plays in Performance*. University Park/London: Pennsylvania State UP; 1983. vi, 262 pp. (Shaw: The Annual of Bernard Shaw Studies 3 (ShawR).) Notes. Illus.: Photo. Dwg. B&W. 5. Lang.: Eng.

UK-England: Malvern. 1904-1977. Historical studies. ■The founding of the Malvern Festival and its later history.

2287 Elliott, Bridget. "New & Not So 'New Women' on the London Stage: Aubrey Beardsley's Yellow Book Images of Mrs. Patrick Campbell and Réjane." *VS*. 1987 Fall; 31(1): 33-57. Notes. Illus.: Dwg. B&W. 7. Lang.: Eng.

UK-England: London. 1890. Historical studies. ■Beardsley's drawings outraged because they were of categories of women whose very existence challenged middle-class ideals of womanhood. Such deviant types, including actresses, were associated with 'New Women' or Victorian feminists.

2288 Evans, T.F. "*Man and Superman*: Notes for a Stage History." 79-101 in Leary, Daniel, ed. *Shaw's Plays in Performance*. University Park/London: Pennsylvania State UP; 1983. vi, 262 pp. (Shaw: The Annual of Bernard Shaw Studies (ShawR).) Notes. Lang.: Eng.

UK-England. North America. 1901-1982. Historical studies. ■Survey of productions (England and North America only) with commentary on various aspects (more about the automobile than the female leads) and critical reception.

2289 Földes, Anna. "Csoportkép—sztárokkal. Londoni levél." (Tableau with Stars: Letter from London.) *Sz*. 1987 Apr.; 20(4): 38-45. Illus.: Photo. B&W. 2. Lang.: Hun.

UK-England: London, Stratford. 1987. Reviews of performances. ■Review of a one-week stay in England: six interesting theatre evenings in London and Stratford.

2290 Hawkins-Dady, Mark. "Gogol's *The Government Inspector* at the National Theatre, 1985." *NTQ*. 1987 Nov.; 3(12): 358-376. Notes. Illus.: Photo. B&W. 10. Lang.: Eng.

UK-England: London. USSR. 1985. Critical studies. ■Revival of *Revizor (The Government Inspector)* at the National Theatre, directed

DRAMA: —Performance/production

by Richard Eyre, adhered to the metaphorical truth of the social ambience depicted by Gogol.

2291 Holland, Peter. "The Director and the Playwright: Control over the Means of Production." *NTQ.* 1987 Aug.; 3(11): 207-217. Notes. Lang.: Eng.

UK-England. 1800-1987. Critical studies. ■The relationship between the director and the playwright from contrasting historical perspectives.

2292 Hutson, William. "Elizabethan Stagings of *Hamlet*: George Pierce Baker and William Poel." *ThR.* 1987; 12(3): 253-260. Notes. Illus.: Photo. Print. B&W. 4. Lang.: Eng.

UK-England: London. USA. 1900-1904. Historical studies. ■Comparison of two early twentieth-century productions of *Hamlet* in an 'Elizabethan' style.

2293 Jackson, George. "Angus Neill." *Scenaria.* 1987 Oct.(81): 33-36. Illus.: Photo. 6. Lang.: Eng.

UK-England: London. South Africa, Republic of. 1952. Biographical studies. ■Career of Angus Neill from his work in art to his switch to drama as actor and director.

2294 Lawson, Mark. "Shaping up to Shakespeare: Antony Sher in Interview with Mark Lawson." *Drama.* 1987; 4(166): 27-30. Illus.: Photo. B&W. 2. Lang.: Eng.

UK-England: Stratford. 1987. Histories-sources. ■Actor discusses upcoming RSC season, especially his characterization of Shylock in *The Merchant of Venice*.

2295 Lawson, Mark. "The Gambon Effect." *Drama.* 1987; 3(165): 4-8. Illus.: Photo. B&W. 8: var. sizes. Lang.: Eng.

UK-England. 1987. Histories-sources. ■Interview with actor Michael Gambon, his technique and methodology.

2296 Mazer, Cary M. "Finders Keepers: Recent Scholarship on Granville-Barker." *NCT.* 1987; 15(1): 34-49. Lang.: Eng.

UK-England. Critical studies. ■A review essay examining six book-length studies of Harley Granville-Barker published between 1983 and 1986.

2297 Meewezen, Judy. "Espen Skjønberg." *Drama.* 1987; 4(166): 23-24. Illus.: Photo. B&W. 1. Lang.: Eng.

UK-England: London. Norway. 1986-1987. Histories-sources. ■Norwegian actor talks about theatre practice in Norway and compares it to his acting experience in England.

2298 Meyer, Michael. "Strindberg Productions in Great Britain, 1984-1986." *Strind.* 1987; 2: 48-53. Lang.: Eng.

UK-England. Sweden. 1984-1986. Critical studies. ■Recent productions of Strindberg plays in Great Britain with citations from newspaper reviews.

2299 Mills, David. "The *Chester Cycle* of Mystery Plays at Chester." *MET.* 1987; 9(1): 69-76. Lang.: Eng.

UK-England: Chester. 1987. Reviews of performances. ■Eighteen plays in a new text by Edward Burns, each performed by a different company on a versatile four-level acting area on the Cathedral Green and directed by Bob Cheeseman.

2300 Mullin, Donald, comp. *Victorian Plays: A Record of Significant Productions on the London Stage, 1837-1901.* New York, NY: Greenwood P; 1987. 444 pp. (Bibliographies and Indexes in the Performing Arts 4.) Pref. Index. Tables. Lang.: Eng.

UK-England: London. 1837-1901. Historical studies. ■Directory of London productions. Arranged alphabetically with a short history of each production and list of personnel involved.

2301 Robertson, Tony. "Survival of the Classics." *Drama.* 1987; 3(165): 21. Illus.: Photo. B&W. 1. Lang.: Eng.

UK-England: London, Liverpool. UK-Scotland: Edinburgh. 1987. Critical studies. ■Classical theatre is diminishing in the provinces due to financial cutbacks.

2302 Rosenberg, Marvin. "Sign Theory and Shakespeare." *ShS.* 1987; 40: 33-40. Notes. Lang.: Eng.

UK-England. 1870-1987. Technical studies. ■Gestures and movements implicit in Shakespeare's texts and their interpretation by different actors, with suggestions for a methodology of their study.

2303 Shaw, George Bernard. "Less Scenery Would Mean Better Drama." 25-27 in Leary, Daniel, ed. *Shaw's Plays in Performance.* University Park/London: Pennsylvania State UP; 1983. vi, 262 pp. (Shaw: The Annual of Bernard Shaw Studies 3 (ShawR).) Lang.: Eng.

UK-England. 1909. Historical studies. ■The advantages of what Shaw considered the Elizabethan stage to have been.

2304 Shortland, Michael. "Unnatural Acts: Art and Passion on the Mid-Eighteenth Century Stage." *ThR.* 1987; 12(2): 93-110. Notes. Lang.: Eng.

UK-England. 1740-1760. Historical studies. ■Acting styles on English stages.

2305 Small, Barbara J. "On Speaking Shaw: An Interview with Ann Casson." 169-179 in Leary, Daniel, ed. *Shaw's Plays in Performance.* University Park/London: Pennsylvania State UP; 1983. vi, 262 pp. (Shaw: The Annual of Bernard Shaw Studies 3 (ShawR).) Notes. Lang.: Eng.

UK-England. 1924-1981. Histories-sources. ■Actress Ann Casson talks about the significance of proper line speaking in Shaw productions.

2306 Sommers, Michael. "Russian Dressing." *ThCr.* 1987 Jan.; 21(1): 26-27, 45-51. Illus.: Maps. Color. 3. Lang.: Eng.

UK-England: London. 1986. Critical studies. ■Review of production and staging aspects of *Wild Honey* by Anton Čechov.

2307 Sternhagen, Frances. "Off Broadway in London." *EN.* 1985 June; 70(6): 7. Illus.: Photo. B&W. 2. Lang.: Eng.

UK-England: London. USA: New York, NY. 1985. Histories-sources. ■Author's experiences as an American actress working in the London theatre through British Equity's exchange program.

2308 Teitel, Carol. "Love Letters from Nottingham." *EN.* 1985 June; 70(6): 4-5. Lang.: Eng.

UK-England: London. USA: New York, NY. 1985. Histories-sources. ■The author describes her experiences as an American actress performing in the London theatre through British Equity's exchange program.

2309 Etherton, Michael. "The Field Day Theatre Company and the New Irish Drama." *NTQ.* 1987 Feb.; 3(9): 64-70. Notes. Illus.: Photo. Print. B&W. 2. Lang.: Eng.

UK-Ireland: Londonderry. 1986-1987. Critical studies. ■The company's aims, which extend beyond the theatrical, and three of their productions reflect the 'poetic and political' view the company has nurtured.

2310 Jesipenko, R. *V internacional'nom edinenii: Dramatur gija narodov SSSR v teatrach sovetskoj Ukrainy.* (In International Unity: Dramaturgy of the Peoples of the Soviet Union in the Theatres of the Ukraine.) Kiev: Mistectvo; 1987. 132 pp. Lang.: Rus.

Ukraine. 1917-1987. Histories-specific. ■Soviet dramaturgy on the Ukrainian stage.

2311 "Reviews of Productions." *NYTCR.* 1987; 48(8): 256-263. Lang.: Eng.

USA: New York, NY. 1987. ■*Les Liaisons Dangereuses* by Christopher Hampton, dir by Howard Davis, a Royal Shakespeare Company production imported to Broadway, at the Music Box Theater: rev by Barnes, Beaufort, Curry, Edwin, Henry, Kissel, Kroll, Lida, Rich, Wallach, Watt, Wilson. *Pygmalion* by George Bernard Shaw, dir by Val May at the Plymouth Theatre: rev by Barnes, Beaufort, Curry, Henry, Kissel, Lida, Rich, Wallach, Watt, Wilson. *The Comedy of Errors* by William Shakespeare, dir by Robert Woodruff at the Vivian Beaumont Theatre: rev by Barnes, Beaufort, Curry, Gussow, Henry, Kissel, Lida, Wallach, Watt. *Sleight of Hand* by John Pielmeier, dir by Walton Jones at the Cort Theatre: rev by Barnes, Cohen, Curry, Nelson, Rich, Wallach.

2312 "Reviews of Productions." *NYTCR.* 1987; 48(10): 224-242. Lang.: Eng.

USA: New York, NY. 1987. ■*Educating Rita* by Willy Russell, dir by Jeff Perry at the Westside Arts Theatre: rev by Barnes, Beaufort, Cohen, Gussow, Henry, Kissel, Wallach, Watt. *The Lucky Spot* by Beth Henley dir by Stephen Tobolowsky at Manhattan Theatre Club: rev by Barnes, Beaufort, Kissel, Lida, Rich, Wallach, Watt. *The Knife*, a musical by David Hare (book), Nick Bicat (music) and Tim Rose Price (lyrics) dir by Hare at the Public Theatre: rev by Barnes, Beaufort, Curry, Gold, Kissel, Lida, Rich, Wallach, Watt. *Hunting Cockroaches* by Janusz Glowacki, dir by Arthur Penn at Manhattan Theatre Club: rev by Barnes, Gold, Henry, Kissel, Rich, Watt.

DRAMA: —Performance/production

2313 "Reviews of Productions." *NYTCR.* 1987; 48: 86-98. Lang.: Eng.
USA: New York, NY. 1987. ■*Tamara* by John Krizanc, dir by Michael Rose at the Seventh Regiment Armory: rev by Barnes, Beaufort, Gussow, Kissel, Lida, Stearns, Wallach, Watt. *Real Estate* by Louise Page, dir by Brian Murray at Theatre at St. Peter's Church: rev by Barnes, Beaufort, Cohen, Gold, Kissel, Rich, Wallach. *The Milk Train Doesn't Stop Here Anymore* by Tennessee Williams, dir by Kevin Conway at WPA Theatre: rev by Barnes, Beaufort, Gold, Gussow, Kissel, Lida, Wallach.

2314 "No Accident: A Profile of Ethyl Eichelberger." *TheaterW.* 1987 7-13 Sep.(4): 16-19, 27. Illus.: Photo. B&W. 7. Lang.: Eng.
USA: New York, NY. 1987. Histories-sources. ■Interview with male performer Ethyl Eichelberger on his education and career as an actor.

2315 "Reviews of Productions." *NYTCR.* 1987; 48: 99-109. Lang.: Eng.
USA: New York, NY. 1987. ■*Laughing Wild* by Christopher Durang, dir by Ron Lagomarsino at Playwrights Horizons: rev by Barnes, Gold, Lida, Rich, Wallach, Watt. *The Mahabharata* adapted by Jean-Claude Carrière, dir by Peter Brook at the Majestic Theatre: rev by DeVries, Henry, Kissel, Kroll, Lida, Rich, Stasio, Wallach. *Bouncers* by John Godber, dir by Ron Link at the Minetta Lane Theatre: rev by Beaufort, Cohen, Gold, Kissel, Rich, Stasio, Wallach, Watt.

2316 "Reviews of Productions." *NYTCR.* 1987; 48: 116-143. Lang.: Eng.
USA: New York, NY. 1987. ■*Breaking the Code* by Hugh Whitemore, dir by Clifford Williams at the Neil Simon Theatre: rev by Barnes, Beaufort, Curry, Gussow, Kissel, Lida, Rich, Wallach, Watt, Whitemore, Wilson. *Teddy and Alice* by Jerome Alden, dir by John Driver at the Minskoff Theatre: rev by Barnes, Beaufort, Donlon, Kissel, Rich, Wallach, Watt, Wilson. *Into the Woods* by Stephen Sondheim, dir by James Lapine at the Martin Beck Theatre: rev by Barnes, Beaufort, Henry, Kissel, Kroll, Lida, Rich, Siegel, Stearns, Wallach, Watt, Wilson. *Don't Get God Started* written and dir by Ron Milner at the Longacre Theatre: rev by Barnes, Beaufort, Holden, Kissel, Wallach.

2317 "Reviews of Productions." *NYTCR.* 1987; 48: 146-166. Lang.: Eng.
USA: New York, NY. 1987. ■*Cabaret* by John Kander and Fred Ebb, dir by Harold Prince at Imperial Theatre: rev by Barnes, Beaufort, Kissel, Henry, Rich, Siegel, Wallach, Watt, Wilson. *Anything Goes* by Cole Porter, dir by Jerry Zaks at the Vivian Beaumont Theatre: rev by Barnes, Beaufort, Cohen, Henry, Kissel, Rich, Siegel, Stearns, Wallach, Watt. *Burn This* by Lanford Wilson, dir by Marshall W. Mason at the Plymouth Theatre: rev by Barnes, Beaufort, Curry, Henry, Kissel, Lida, Rich, Siegel, Wallach, Wilson.

2318 "Reviews of Productions." *NYTCR.* 1987; 48: 167-178. Lang.: Eng.
USA: New York, NY. 1987. ■*Late Nite Comic* by Allan Knee at the Ritz Theatre: rev by Barnes, Gussow, Kissel, Siegel, Wallach, Wilson. *Mort Sahl on Broadway!* by Mort Sahl at the Neil Simon Theatre: rev by Barnes, Gussow, Kissel, Siegel, Sterritt, Wallach, Wilson. *Roza* by Julian More, dir by Harold Prince at the Royale Theatre: rev by Barnes, Beaufort, Kissel, Rich, Roush, Siegel, Wallach.

2319 "Reviews of Productions." *NYTCR.* 1987; 48(12): 180-195. Lang.: Eng.
USA: New York, NY. 1987. ■*Holy Ghosts* by Romulus Linney, dir by Douglas Jacobs at the Theatre 890: rev by Beaufort, Nelson, Rich, Seligsohn, Stasio. *Self Defense* by Joe Cacaci, dir by Arvin Brown at the Joyce Theatre: rev by Barnes, Beaufort, Gold, Gussow, O'Haire, Wallach. *Talk Radio* by Eric Bogosian, dir by Frederick Zollo at the Public Theatre: rev by Barnes, Gussow, Kissel, Lida, Sterritt, Wallach, Watt. *Three Postcards* by Craig Lucas and Craig Carnelia, dir by Norman Rene at Playwrights Horizons: rev by Barnes, Cohen, Gussow, Henry, Kissel, Wallach, Watt.

2320 "Reviews of Productions." *NYTCR.* 1987; 48(7): 195-269. Lang.: Eng.
USA: New York, NY. 1987. ■*Driving Miss Daisy* by Alfred Uhry, dir by Ron Lagomarsino at Playwrights Horizons: rev by Barnes, Beaufort, Cohen, Gold, Gussow, Henry, Wallach, Watt. *Steel Magnolias* by Robert Harling, dir by Pamela Berlin at the Lucille Lortel Theatre:

rev by Barnes, Cohen, Curry, Gold, Gussow, Kissel, Richards, Wallach, Watt. *Pygmalion* by George Bernard Shaw, dir by Val May at the Plymouth Theatre: rev by Beaufort, Curry, Henry, Kissel, Lisa, Rich, Wallach, Watt, Wilson.

2321 "Reviews of Productions." *NYTCR.* 1987; 48(7): 272-288. Lang.: Eng.
USA: New York, NY. 1987. ■*All My Sons* by Arthur Miller, dir by Arvin Brown at the John Golden Theatre: rev by Barnes, Beaufort, Curry, Henry, Kissel, Lida, Rich, Siegel, Wallach, Watt, Wilson. *A Month of Sundays* by Bob Larbey, dir by Gene Saks at the Ritz Theatre: rev by Barnes, Beaufort, Curry, Rich, Wallach. *Barbara Cook: A Concert for the Theatre* by Barbara Cook, conducted by Wally Harper at the Ambassador Theatre: rev by Beaufort, Curry, Kissel, Lida, Rich, Wallach, Watt, Wilson.

2322 "Reviews of Productions." *NYTCR.* 1987; 48(6): 290-308. Lang.: Eng.
USA: New York, NY. 1987. ■*The Regard of Flight* by Bill Irwin, dir by Gregory Mosher at the Vivian Beaumont Theatre: rev by Barnes, Beaufort, Gussow, Lida, Nelson, Wallach, Wilson. *The Musical Comedy Murders of 1940* by John Bishop, dir by Bishop at the Circle Repertory: rev by Barnes, Beaufort, Curry, Gussow, Kissel, Siegel, Wallach, Watt. *Safe Sex* by Harvey Fierstein, dir by Eric Conklin at the Lyceum Theatre: rev by Barnes, Beaufort, Cohen, Curry, Kissel, Rich, Siegel, Wallach. *Blithe Spirit* by Noël Coward, dir by Brian Murray at the Neil Simon Theatre: rev by Barnes, Beaufort, Cohen, Curry, Henry, Kissel, Kroll, Rich, Wallach.

2323 "Reviews of Productions." *NYTCR.* 1987; 48(4): 352-389. Lang.: Eng.
USA: New York, NY. 1987. ■*The Rise of David Levinsky* by Isaiah Sheffer and Bobby Paul, dir by Sue Lawless at John Houseman Theatre: rev by Barnes, Beaufort, Gold, Holder, Kissel, Wallach, Watt. *North Shore Fish* by Israel Horovitz, dir by Stephen Zuckerman at the WPA Theatre: rev by Barnes, Beaufort, Cohen, Gold, Gussow, Kissel, Wallach, Watt. *Les Misérables* by Alain Boublil and Claude-Michel Schönberg, dir by Trevor Nunn and John Caird at the Broadway Theatre: rev by Barnes, Beaufort, Curry, Henry, Kissel, Kroll, Lida, Rich, Siegel, Wallach, Wilson. *South Pacific* by Richard Rodgers and Oscar Hammerstein, dir by Gerald Freedman at the New York City Opera: rev by Barnes, Eckert, Goodman, Hoelterhoff, Rockwell, Stearns, Watt, Zalariasen. *Sarafina!* by Mbongeni Ngema, dir by Ngema at Mitzi E. Newhouse Theatre: rev by Barnes, Beaufort, Kissel, Lida, Rich, Wallach, Watt.

2324 "Reviews of Productions." *NYTCR.* 1987; 48(1, 2): 310-400. Lang.: Eng.
USA: New York, NY. 1987. ■*Stepping Out* by Richard Harris, dir by Tommy Tune at John Golden Theatre: rev by Barnes, Beaufort, Kissel, Lida, Siegel, Story, Wallach, Watt. *Sweet Sue* by A.R. Gurney, Jr., dir by John Tillinger at the Music Box Theatre: rev by Barnes, Cohen, Gussow, Kissel, Siegel, Story, Wallach, Watt, Wilson. *The Mikado* by Gilbert and Sullivan, dir by Brian MacDonald at the City Center Theatre. *Stardust* written and dir by Albert Harris at St. Johns Episcopal Church: rev by Barnes, Beaufort, Cohen, Curry, Holden, Kissel, Wallach, Watt.

2325 "Reviews of Productions." *NYTCR.* 1987; 48(5): 323-343. Lang.: Eng.
USA: New York, NY. 1987. ■*The Nerd* by Larry Shue, dir by Charles Nelson Reilly at the Helen Hayes Theatre: rev by Barnes, Beaufort, Curry, Kissel, Lida, Rich, Siegel, Wallach, Wilson. *Starlight Express* by Andrew Lloyd Webber, dir by Trevor Nunn at the Gershwin Theatre: rev by Barnes, Beaufort, Cohen, Curry, Henry, Kissel, Kroll, Rich, Siegel, Wallach, Watt, Wilson. *The Hunger Artist* by Franz Kafka, dir by Martha Clarke at St. Clements Theatre: rev by Barnes, Gold, Henry, Kissel, Lida, Rich, Wallach. *Kvetch* written and dir by Steven Berkoff at the Westside Arts Theatre: rev by Beaufort, Cohen, Gussow, Kissel, Stasio, Wallach, Watt.

2326 "Reviews of Productions." *NYTCR.* 1987; 48(2): 314-382. Lang.: Eng.
USA: New York, NY. 1987. ■*Death and the King's Horsemen* written and dir by Wole Soyinka at the Vivian Beaumont Theatre: rev by Barnes, Beaufort, Cohen, Curry, Kissel, Rich, Wallach. *Fences* by August Wilson, dir by Lloyd Richards: rev by Barnes, Beaufort, Curry,

DRAMA: —Performance/production

Henry, Kissel, Kroll, Lida, Rich, Siegel, Wallach, Watt, Wilson. *Danger: Memory!* by Arthur Miller, dir by Gregory Mosher at the Mitzi E. Newhouse Theatre: rev by Beaufort, Curry, Kissel, Henry, Lida, Stasio, Rich, Wallach, Watt. *My Gene* by Barbara Gelb, dir by Andre Ernotte at the Public Theatre: rev by Barnes, Beaufort, Cohen, Kaplan, Kissel, Wallach, Watt.

2327   Barbour, David. "Driving Ron Lagomarsino." *TheaterW.* 1987 28 Dec.-1988 3 Jan.; 1(20): 32-35. Illus.: Photo. B&W. 2. Lang.: Eng.
USA. 1987. Biographical studies. ■Career of director Ron Lagomarsino, his style and technique.

2328   Barnes, Noreen C.; Wolf, Laurie J. "Actresses of All Work: Nineteenth-Century Sources on Women in Nineteenth-Century Theatre." *PAR.* 1987; 12: 98-134. Lang.: Eng.
USA. 1800-1900. Bibliographical studies. ■A survey/bibliography of nineteenth century women in theatre.

2329   Bartow, Arthur. "Both Halves of Richard Foreman: The Director." *AmTh.* 1987 July/Aug.; 4(4): 15-18, 49. Illus.: Photo. B&W. 2. Lang.: Eng.
USA: New York, NY. 1962-1987. Histories-sources. ■Interview with Richard Foreman, discussion of his development as a director, style and techniques.

2330   Bertin, Michael. "'Riding on a Smile and a Shoeshine': The Broadway *Salesman*." 103-107 in Cardullo, Bert, ed. *Before His Eyes: Essays in Honor of Stanley Kauffmann.* Lanham, MD: UP of America; 1986. 185 pp. Notes. Biblio. Lang.: Eng.
USA: New York, NY. 1984. Critical studies. ■Extended critical analysis of the 1984 Broadway production of *Death of a Salesman*.

2331   Coe, Robert. "What Makes Sellars Run?" *AmTh.* 1987 Dec.; 4(9): 12-49. Illus.: Photo. B&W. 11. Lang.: Eng.
USA: Washington, DC. 1981-1987. Biographical studies. ■The work and methodology of director Peter Sellars, and his association with the American National Theatre.

2332   Cronin, Mari. "The Growing Influence of Literary Managers and Dramaturgs in Theatre." *TheaterW.* 1987 7-13 Sep.(4): 33-34. Illus.: Photo. B&W. 2. Lang.: Eng.
USA. 1987. Critical studies. ■Functions and growing influence of dramaturgs and literary managers.

2333   Degen, John A. "Camp and Burlesque: A Study in Contrasts." *JDTC.* 1987; 1(2): 87-94. Biblio. Lang.: Eng.
USA. 1987. Critical studies. ■Defining camp and burlesque as comedic styles through examination of several Dracula films and theatre productions to delineate the terms.

2334   Dobrin, Darlene. "Matthew Locricchio, Working Actor." *TheaterW.* 1987 Nov 16; 1(14): 6-8. Illus.: Photo. B&W. 3. Lang.: Eng.
USA: New York, NY. 1987. Biographical studies. ■Profile of character actor Matthew Locricchio: training, methodology, career. Focus on his role as Candy in Steinbeck's *Of Mice and Men*.

2335   Flatow, Sheryl. "Philip Bosco: Essence of Shaw." *AmTh.* 1987 Apr.; 4(1): 36-37. Illus.: Photo. Print. B&W. 1. Lang.: Eng.
USA. 1987. Critical studies. ■Philip Bosco discusses his experience playing various characters in George Bernard Shaw's *Major Barbara*, *Saint Joan*, *Heartbreak House*, and *Misalliance*.

2336   Fried, Ronald K. "John Jesurun's *Chang in a Void Moon*." *TDR.* 1983 Sum; 27(3): 73-77. Illus.: Photo. B&W. 3. Lang.: Eng.
USA: New York, NY. 1982-1983. Critical studies. ■Description of production: staging, performance space, cinematic techniques employed. Development of play.

2337   Gray, John. "Simone Forti's *Spring*." *TDR.* 1983 Fall; 27(3): 101-102. Lang.: Eng.
USA: New York, NY. 1983. Historical studies. ■Production of *Spring* presented at the Danspace at St. Mark's Church: production elements, description of space, use of improvisations within performance, movement.

2338   Holmberg, Arthur. "Getting a Fix on Pirandello." *AmTh.* 1987 Mar.; 3(12): 10-16. Illus.: Photo. Print. B&W. 6. Lang.: Eng.
USA. Italy. 1917-1987. Critical studies. ■Influence of Luigi Pirandello on 20th-century theatre and renewed interest in his plays. Productions at American Repertory Theatre and Actors Theatre of Louisville.

2339   Houseman, John. *Entertainers and the Entertained: Essays on Theatre, Film and Television.* New York, NY: Simon & Schuster; 1986. 336 pp. Index. Lang.: Eng.
USA: New York, NY. 1935-1985. Biographies. ■Autobiography of John Houseman beginning with his involvement in the Federal Theatre Project in 1934, his Broadway experiences, Shakespeare productions in theatre and film. Related to Media.

2340   Jackson, Caroline. "James Earl Jones: Triumphant Again." *BlackM.* 1987 May-Jun.; 3(9): 2, 3, 11. Illus.: Photo. B&W. 2. Lang.: Eng.
USA: New York, NY. 1953-1987. Histories-sources. ■Actor James Earl Jones discusses his career, especially his relationship to the character of Troy in *Fences*.

2341   Jackson, Caroline. "Mary Alice: An Actor in Search of Perfection." *BlackM.* 1987 Sep.; 3(10): 2-3, 10. Illus.: Photo. B&W. 1. Lang.: Eng.
USA: New York, NY, Chicago, IL. 1966-1987. Histories-sources. ■Career of Mary Alice.

2342   James, Robert. "Southern Theatre Chronicle." 109-122 in Cardullo, Bert, ed. *Before His Eyes: Essays in Honor of Stanley Kauffmann.* Lanham, MD: UP of America; 1986. 185 pp. Lang.: Eng.
USA: Houston, TX, Louisville, KY, Gainesville, FL. 1980. Reviews of performances. ■A year of critical reviews at four different US regional theatres: Dallas Theater Center (*Land of Fire* by Glen Allen Smith), Actors' Theatre of Louisville (*Terra Nova* by Ted Tally), Hippodrome Theatre in Gainesville, FL (*As You Like It* by William Shakespeare) and the Alley Theatre in Houston (*The Three Penny Opera* by Bertolt Brecht).

2343   Kalb, Jonathan. "Acting Beckett." *AmTh.* 1987 Dec.; 4(9): 21-27. Illus.: Photo. B&W. 10. Lang.: Eng.
USA. 1987. Histories-sources. ■Actors Billie Whitelaw, Alvin Epstein and David Warrilow discuss their methods and techniques for working on Samuel Beckett characters.

2344   Kalb, Jonathan. "*Rockaby* and the Art of Inadvertent Interpretation." *MD.* 1987 Dec.; 30(4): 466-479. Notes. Lang.: Eng.
USA. 1981-1984. Critical studies. ■The interpretive effect of Billie Whitelaw's performances in Buffalo and New York.

2345   Kanellos, Nicolás. "Two Centuries of Hispanic Theatre in the Southwest." *Revista Chicano.* 1983 Spr; 9(1): 19-39. Illus.: Photo. B&W. 16. Lang.: Eng.
USA. 1598-1965. Historical studies. ■Retrospective of two centuries of theatre produced north of the Rio Grande River.

2346   Londré, Felicia Hardison. "Kim Champions Classic in Nature's Setting." *AmTh.* 1987 Nov.; 4(8): 45-46. Illus.: Photo. B&W. 1. Lang.: Eng.
USA. 1966-1987. Historical studies. ■Career of actor/director Randall Duk Kim from his early days in Honolulu to his current productions at the APT Outdoor Theatre in Wisconsin.

2347   Loney, Glenn. "'To Porky, from Brecht'." *Gestus.* 1986 Win; 11(4): 277-281. Lang.: Eng.
USA: Los Angeles, CA. 1944-1986. Histories-sources. ■Actor Don Pietromonaco recalls his experiences as a young child with Bertolt Brecht, actor Charles Laughton, director Joseph Losey during the rehearsal and premiere opening of *Galileo*.

2348   Maschio, Geraldine. "Female Impersonation on the American Stage, 1860-1927: A Selected Bibliography of Performed Materials, and a Review of Literature." *PAR.* 1987; 12: 156-170. Lang.: Eng.
USA. 1860-1927. Bibliographical studies. ■Bibliography of books written about female impersonators in American theatre.

DRAMA: —Performance/production

2349 Meisner, Sanford; Longwell, Dennis. *Sanford Meisner on Acting.* New York, NY: Vintage; 1987. xix, 252 pp. Pref. Notes. Lang.: Eng.
USA: New York, NY. 1987. Histories-sources. ■Personal account of the Meisner concept of teaching acting using exercises in the classroom.

2350 Mekler, Eva. *The New Generation of Acting Teachers.* New York, NY: Penguin; 1987. xi, 384 pp. Pref. Gloss. Illus.: Photo. B&W. 22. Lang.: Eng.
USA: New York, NY, Los Angeles, CA. 1987. Histories-sources. ■Collection of interviews with today's major teachers of acting in New York, Los Angeles, university theatre departments discussing philosophies of theatre, acting and acting processes.

2351 Middendorp, Jan. "Het Amerikaanse Wonderkind." (The American Whiz Kid.) *Toneel.* 1987 Feb.; 2(4): 4-7. Illus.: Photo. B&W. 1. Lang.: Dut.
USA. Netherlands. 1987. Historical studies. ■Peter Sellars, whiz kid of American theatre, and his work at Kennedy Center with American National Theatre production of *Ajax* coming to Holland. Influenced by Europe.

2352 Nelson, Steve. "Tükak Teatret's *Inuit—Human Beings.*" *TDR.* 1983 Sum; 27(2): 92-93. Lang.: Eng.
USA: New York, NY. Denmark: Holstebro. 1975-1983. Historical studies. ■Group of native Inuit (Eskimo) actors perform at Museum of Natural History. Description of company and its theatre school, production's elements of mask and dance-drama, its derivation from Inuit legends and mythology.

2353 Novick, Julius. "On Directing Shaw: An Interview with Stephen Porter." 181-189 in Leary, Daniel, ed. *Shaw's Plays in Performance.* University Park/London: Pennsylvania State UP; 1983. vi, 262 pp. (Shaw: The Annual of Bernard Shaw Studies 3 (ShawR).) Lang.: Eng.
USA. 1924-1981. Histories-sources. ■Stephen Porter's experience directing Shaw's plays in a variety of US productions.

2354 Salinas, Mike. "From Chelsea to Connecticut: Robert Perring is On the Move." *TheaterW.* 1987 7-13 Sep.(4): 13-15. Illus.: Photo. B&W. 3. Lang.: Eng.
USA. Histories-sources. ■Interview with playwright/actor Robert Perring on his career.

2355 Sands, Jeffrey. "*Electra's* First Hazel: An Interview with Mary Arbenz." *EON.* 1987 Spr; 11(1): 34-37. Lang.: Eng.
USA: New York, NY. 1927. Histories-sources. ■Interview with Mary Arbenz on the original production of *Mourning Becomes Electra.*

2356 Shannon, Sandra G. "Amiri Baraka on Directing." *BALF.* 1987 Win; 21(4): 425-433. Notes. Lang.: Eng.
USA: Newark, NJ, New York, NY. 1965-1969. Histories-sources. ■Interview covering the use of music, sound effects, props which have been most successful dramatic effects in his plays from the 1960s. Includes use of masks, costumes and taped sound that makes the plays' concept vivid.

2357 Smith, Starla. "New Life for 'That Scottish Play'." *TheaterW.* 1987 Oct.; 1(8): 8-12. Illus.: Photo. B&W. 4. Lang.: Eng.
USA: New York, NY. 1987. Histories-sources. ■Director and leading actor discuss their new production of *Macbeth* set in Chicago 1927.

2358 Solomon, Alisa. "Denaturalizing Ibsen/Denaturing Hedda: A Polemical Sketch in Three Parts." 85-91 in Cardullo, Bert, ed. *Before His Eyes: Essays in Honor of Stanley Kauffmann.* Lanham, MD: UP of America; 1986. 185 pp. Pref. Notes. Biblio. Lang.: Eng.
USA: Pittsburgh, PA. 1987. Historical studies. ■By concentrating on a production of *Hedda Gabler* by the American Ibsen Theatre in Pittsburgh, author focuses on problems of staging Ibsen in America.

2359 Strasberg, Lee; Morphos, Evangeline, ed. *A Dream of Passion: The Development of the Method.* Boston, MA: Little, Brown; 1987. xvii, 201 pp. Pref. Notes. Illus.: Handbill. Photo. Dwg. Sketches. Poster. B&W. 37. Lang.: Eng.
USA: New York, NY. USSR: Moscow. 1923-1987. Biographies. ■Discussion of the Method, its origins and development.

2360 Stuart, Otis. "Ensemble and Eccentricity: A Conversation with Austin Pendleton." *TheaterW.* 1987 Dec 21-27; 1(19): 16-19. 4. Lang.: Eng.
USA. 1987. Histories-sources. ■Interview with actor/director Austin Pendleton.

2361 Theissen, Bennett. "Creation's *The American Mysteries.*" *TDR.* 1983 Sum; 27(2): 83-86. Illus.: Photo. B&W. 1. Lang.: Eng.
USA: New York, NY. 1983. Historical studies. ■Description of production at La Mama directed by Matthew Maguire. Staging, plot summation, structure of play.

2362 Thorpe, John C. "From Sierra Leone to the Stages of Brooklyn." *BlackM.* 1987 Oct-Nov.; 4(2): 6, 11. Illus.: Photo. B&W. 1. Lang.: Eng.
USA: Brooklyn, NY. Sierra Leone: Freetown. Italy: Rome. 1987. Histories-sources. ■The struggle of the native African actor in Africa, Italy and America through the eyes of David Kamara.

2363 Thorpe, John C. "Behind the Wings of the *Colored Museum.*" *BlackM.* 1987 Jan-Feb.; 3(5): 2, 3. Lang.: Photo. B&W. 2. Lang.: Eng.
USA: New York, NY, New Brunswick, NJ. 1987. Histories-sources. ■Interview with L. Kenneth Richardson and George C. Wolfe about their production of *The Colored Museum.*

2364 Turner, Beth. "Joe Seneca: New Challenges, New Horizons." *BlackM.* 1987 Apr-May; 3(8): 2, 3. Illus.: Photo. B&W. 1. Lang.: Eng.
USA: New York, NY, Cleveland, OH. 1957-1987. Histories-sources. ■Actor Joe Seneca discusses his performing and writing careers.

2365 Turner, Beth. "The Multi-Talented Samm-Art Williams." *BlackM.* 1987 Feb/Mar.; 3(6): 2, 3, 9, 10. Illus.: Photo. B&W. 1. Lang.: Eng.
USA: Philadelphia, PA. 1973-1987. Biographical studies. ■The career of actor and playwright Samm-Art Williams.

2366 Wainscott, Ronald H. "Exploring the Religion of the Dead: Philip Moeller Directs O'Neill's *Mourning Becomes Electra.*" *THSt.* 1987; 7: 28-39. Notes. Lang.: Eng.
USA: New York, NY. 1931. Historical studies. ■Philip Moeller's directorial methods and achievements in staging the premiere of Eugene O'Neill's *Mourning Becomes Electra.*

2367 Williams, Kelly. "Bert Andrews: Black Theatre's Premier Photo Journalist." *BlackM.* 1987 Oct-Nov.; 4(2): 4-5, 11. Illus.: Photo. B&W. 2. Lang.: Eng.
USA: New York, NY. 1950-1987. Historical studies. ■Career of photojournalist Bert Andrews and his contribution to Black theatre.

2368 Yarbro-Bejarano, Yvonne. "Teatropoesia de Chicanas en the Bay Area: *Tongues of Fire.*" (Poetic Theatre by Latin American Women in the Bay Area: *Tongues of Fire.*) *Revista Chicano.* 1983 Spr; 9(1): 78-94. Lang.: Spa.
USA. 1974-1983. Histories-specific. ■Historical discussion of the dramatic form of teatropoesia—a combination of theatre and poetry as related to women's theatre in northern California.

2369 Ybarra-Frausto, Tomas. "La Chata Noloesca: Figura del Donaire." (The 'Chata Noloesca': Figure of Grace.) *Revista Chicano.* 1983 Spr; 9(1): 41-51. Lang.: Spa.
USA: San Antonio, TX. 1903-1979. Biographical studies. ■Biographical account of Beatriz Escalona, comedienne known as La Chata Noloesca.

2370 Zelenak, Michael. "Ubu Rides Again: The Irondale Project and the Politics of Clowning." *ThM.* 1987; 18(3): 43-45. Illus.: Photo. B&W. 2. Lang.: Eng.
USA: New York, NY. 1984-1987. Critical studies. ■The Irondale Ensemble's production of *Ubu roi* was a starting point for improvisation, cabaret, and burlesque on the themes of class and theatre. Eclectic style, audience central to the project.

2371 "Anti-Gofman ili Teatr vremeni." (The Theatre of Time.) *TeatZ.* 1987; 7: 6-8. Lang.: Rus.
USSR: Moscow. 1938-1987. Critical studies. ■Dramaturgy of Eduard Radsinskij, production of his new plays.

2372 *Dramatičeskij teatr Sovetskoj Moldavii (1917-1960): Bibliografičeskij ukazatel' AN MSSR.* (Drama Theatre of Soviet Moldavija, 1917-1960: Bibliographic Index/Academy of

DRAM: —Performance/production

Sciences of the Moldavian Republic.) Kisinev: Stiinca; 1987. 214 pp. Lang.: Rus.
USSR. 1917-1960. Bibliographical studies.

2373 Anikst, A. "Vratar' iz El'sinora." (The Goalkeeper of Elsinore.) *LO.* 1987; 4: 104-105. Lang.: Rus.
USSR: Moscow. 1980-1987. Critical studies. ■Director Gleb Panfilov's interpretation of *Hamlet* at Komsomol Theatre.

2374 Bakanidze, D. "Vypolnjaja vysokuju missiju iskusstva." (Fulfilling the Elevated Mission of Art.) *LitGruzia.* 1987; 7: 196-200. Lang.: Rus.
USSR. 1943-1949. Historical studies. ■Productions in Georgia of plays by Georgian author Konstantin Simonov.

2375 Chačaturova, N. "Novaja Katarina i drugie." (A New Catherine and Others.) *MuZizn.* 1987; 13: 7. Lang.: Rus.
USSR. 1980-1987. Critical studies. ■Shaw productions at Belorussian Theatre of Musical Comedy.

2376 Chekhov, Michael; Agarkov-Miklashevsky, Tamar, transl. "Chekhov's Academy of Arts Questionnaire." *TDR.* 1983 Fall; 27(3) : 22-33. Illus.: Photo. B&W. 6. Lang.: Eng.
USSR: Moscow. 1923. Histories-sources. ■Actor Michajl Čechov's answers to a questionnaire sent out by the Theatrical Branch of the Russian Academy of Arts to investigate the psychology of acting.

2377 Chekhov, Michael. "Chekhov on Acting: A Collection of Unpublished Materials (1919-1942)." *TDR.* 1983 Fall; 27(3): 47-83. Illus.: Photo. B&W. 8. Lang.: Eng.
USSR: Moscow. 1942-1919. Histories-sources. ■Transcriptions from lectures and lessons give by Čechov on his technique: imagination, atmosphere, psychological gesture, concentration and characterization.

2378 Cugaeva, N.G. *Klassičeskaja dramaturgija na scene osetinskogo teatra: Avtoref.dis. kand. iskusstvovedenija.* (Classical Dramaturgy on the Stage of the Osetinskij Theatre: Abstract of a Dissertation by a Candidate in Art Criticism.) Moscow: GITIS; 1988. 16 pp. Lang.: Rus.
USSR. 1960-1987. Historical studies.

2379 Fel'dman, O.M., ed. *Gore ot uma* na russkoj i sovetskoj scene: Svidetel'stva sovremennikov. (*Wit Works Woe* on the Russian and Soviet Stage: Testimonies of Contemporaries.) Moscow: Iskusstvo; 1987. 406 pp. (Klassika na Russkoj i Sovetskoj Scene.) Lang.: Rus.
USSR. 1845-1987. Histories-sources.

2380 Hoffmeier, Dieter. "Ein produktiv weiterwirkendes Lebenswerk. Zwischen 125. Geburtstag und 50. Todestag: Anmerkungen zu Stanislawski." (A Continuously Productive Life's Work: Remarks on Stanislavskij Between the 125th Anniversary of His Birth and the 50th Anniversary of his Death.) *TZ.* 1988; 43(5): 11-15. Notes. Lang.: Ger.
USSR: Moscow. 1933-1988. Critical studies. ■Stanislavskij's later artistic principles and two aspects of his work: method of physical actions applied in the field of comedy and satire, the productive relation of director and actor in the process of rehearsing.

2381 Iglamov, R.M. *Vydajuščijsja dramaturg.* (A Leading Dramatist.) Kazan: Tat. kn. izdatelstvo; 1987. 111 pp. Lang.: Rus.
USSR. 1887-1947. Biographical studies. ■Soviet playwright, actor and director K.G. Tinčurin.

2382 Kaljagin, A. "Moment istiny." (Moment of Truth.) *TeatZ.* 1987; 4: 2-3. Lang.: Rus.
USSR: Moscow. 1987. Histories-sources. ■Popular actor on his role as Lenin in *Tak pobedim (This is How We Will Triumph).*

2383 Koltai, Tamás. "Szabálygyűjtemények pedig nincsenek. A Rusztaveli Színház vendégjátéka." (And There Are No Sets of Rules: Guest Play of the Rustaveli Theatre.) *Sz.* 1987 Feb.; 20(2): 34-36. Illus.: Photo. B&W. 3. Lang.: Hun.
USSR: Tbilisi. Hungary. 1987. Reviews of performances. ■Shakespeare's *Richard III* and Brecht's *The Caucasian Chalk Circle*— guest performance of the Rustaveli Theatre of Georgia, Robert Sturua, director.

2384 Kuchta, Je. A. *Problemy teatra N.V. Gogolja i sovetskaja dramatičeskaja scena 1970-h godov: Avtoref. dis. kand. iskusstvoznanija.* (Problems of Gogol's Theatre and the Soviet Dramatic Stage of the Seventies: Abstract of a

Dissertation by a Candidate in Art Theory.) Leningrad: M-vo kul'tury RSFSR, LGITMiK; 1987. 18. Lang.: Rus.
USSR. 1970-1987. Critical studies.

2385 Lavrov, K. "Perečityvaja zanovo..." (Re-reading Anew.) *Kommunist.* 1987; 6: 49-54. Lang.: Rus.
USSR: Leningrad. 1987. Histories-sources. ■Actor of Leningrad Bolšoj Theatre on Lenin's personality, Lenin as a character and his portrayal of Lenin.

2386 Law, Alma H. "Chekhov's Russian *Hamlet* (1924)." *TDR.* 1983 Fall; 27(3): 34-45. Illus.: Photo. B&W. 10. Lang.: Eng.
USSR: Moscow. 1924. Historical studies. ■Moscow Art Theatre's production of *Hamlet* with Michajl Čechov in the title role. Rehearsal process, staging, expressionistic interpretation, references to rehearsal notes by Čechov and other company members.

2387 Lazarev, A.M. *Teatr Sovetskoj Moldavii. Stranicy istorii: Sbornik statej.* (Soviet Moldavian Theatre—Pages of a History: A Collection of Articles.) Kišinev: Štiinca; 1987. 162 pp. Lang.: Rus.
USSR. 1920-1970. Historical studies. ■Articles on less-known Moldavian theatre history.

2388 Michajlov, A. "'Moja revoljucija': žizn poeta." ('My Revolution': The Life of a Poet.) *Oktiabr.* 1987; 5: 12-16. Lang.: Rus.
USSR. 1918-1921. ■On two productions of *Misterija-Buff (Mystery-Bouffe)*, written by Vladimir Majakovskij: one directed by Mejerchol'd, Theatre of Musical Drama Petrograd 1918, the other by Mejerchol'd and Bebutov, First Theatre of the Russian Republic, Moscow 1921.

2389 Minkin, A. "Ne byt'?" (Not to Be?) *SovD.* 1987; 2: 243-254. Lang.: Rus.
USSR. 1987. Historical studies. ■Difficulties in contemporary readings of Shakespeare's plays.

2390 Molnár Gál, Péter. "Grúzok Pannóniában." (Georgians in Pannonia.) *Krit.* 1987 Jan.(1): 33-34. Lang.: Hun.
USSR: Tbilisi. Hungary: Budapest. 1986. Reviews of performances. ■Guest performances of Rustaveli Theatre at the Madách Theatre: the ensemble presented Shakespeare's *Richard III* and Brecht's *Der Kaukasische Kreidekreis (The Caucasian Chalk Circle).*

2391 Pearson, Tony. "Evreinov and Pirandello: Twin Apostles of Theatricality." *ThR.* 1987; 12(2): 147-167. Notes. Illus.: Photo. Print. B&W. 4. [First of two parts.] Lang.: Eng.
USSR. 1879-1953. Critical studies. ■Examines development of Jėvrejnov's theories of theatricality and suggests parallels with Pirandello's.

2392 Pilipčuk, R. Ja., ed. *Vospominanija o Ivane Karpenko-Karom.* (Memoirs about Ivan Karpenko-Karyj.) Kiev: Mistectvo; 1987. 184 pp. Lang.: Rus.
USSR. 1845-1907. Histories-sources. ■Memoirs of the Ukrainian playwright and actor.

2393 Romanenko, A. "Prostranstvo pamjati." (The Expanse of Memory.) *SovD.* 1987; 4: 234-241. Lang.: Rus.
USSR. 1980-1987. Histories-sources. ■Interview with director I. Ungurjano on problem of historical drama.

2394 Rzhevsky, Nicholas. "Magical Subversions: *The Master and Margarita* in Performance." *MD.* 1987 Sep.; 30(3): 327-339. Notes. Lang.: Eng.
USSR. 1938-1979. Critical studies. ■Jurij Liubimov's 1979 Taganka Theatre production of *The Master and Margarita (Master i Margarita).*

2395 Sakalauskas, T. *Monologi: Žizn Mil'tinisa.* (Monologue: The Life of Mil'tinis.) Vil'njus: MINTIS; 1987. 261 pp. Lang.: Rus.
USSR. 1907-1987. Biographies. ■Life and work of Lithuanian director Ju. Mil'tinis, creator of Panevežskij Theatre.

2396 Šaropov, M.M. *Na scene—tadžikskaja komedija.* (On Stage—Tadžik Comedy.) Dušanbe: Irfon; 1987. 110 pp. Lang.: Rus.
USSR. 1987. Critical studies.

2397 Shaland, Irene. *Tennessee Williams on the Soviet Stage.* Lanham, MD: UP of America; 1987. 100 pp. Lang.: Eng.

DRAMA: —Performance/production

USSR. 1910-1987. Historical studies. ■Soviet productions of Tennessee Williams' plays reveal differences in cross-cultural artistic interpretations. Designs, directors conceptions, actors of and public response to *A Streetcar Named Desire*, *The Glass Menagerie*, *Orpheus Descending*, *Sweet Bird of Youth* and *Kingdom of Earth*.

2398 Strel'cova, E.I. *Teatr Aleksandra Vampilova i nekotorye problemy sovremennogo sceničeskogo iskusstva. Avtoref. dis. kand. iskusstvovedenija.* (The Theatre of Aleksand'r Vampilov and Some Problems in Contemporary Stage Art: Abstract of a Dissertation by a Candidate in Art Criticism.) Moscow: VNII iskusstvoznanija; 1987. 21 pp. Lang.: Rus.

USSR. 1937-1972. Critical studies.

2399 Ungár, Júlia. "Tragédia—groteszkben elbeszélve. Vachtangov." (Tragedy—Told in Grotesque: Vachtangov and the HaBimah Studio.) *Sz.* 1987 Sep.; 20(9): 32-37. Illus.: Photo. B&W. 4. Lang.: Hun.

USSR: Moscow. 1922. Histories-reconstruction. ■Vachtangov's HaBimah production of *HaDybbuk (The Dybbuk)* by Slojme Anski reconstructed on the basis of photographs and other contemporary documentation.

2400 Volkov, Solomon. "At The Scene of Lyubimov's 'Crime'." *AmTh.* 1987 Apr.; 4(1): 12-18. Illus.: Photo. B&W. 8. Lang.: Eng.

USSR: Moscow. USA: Washington, DC. 1984-1987. Critical studies. ■Russian director Jurij Liubimov and his productions in the USSR and USA, emphasis on *Crime and Punishment*.

2401 Zverev, A. "Ogonek neizvestno otkuda." (A Fire from Who Knows Where.) *NovyjMir.* 1987; 9: 227-241. Lang.: Rus.

USSR: Moscow, Leningrad. 1950-1987. Historical studies. ■Dramaturgy of Aleksandr Volodin as interpreted in the theatre and in films. Related to Media: Film.

2402 Mackerras, Colin. "Theatre in Vietnam." *ATJ.* 1987 Spr; 4(1): 1-28. Notes. Biblio. Illus.: Photo. B&W. 5. Lang.: Eng.

Vietnam. 980-1986. Historical studies. ■Vietnamese theatre (cheo and tuong): development through the centuries, training, facilities, Chinese and French influences.

2403 Bőgel, József. "Az avoni hattyú Bácskában." (The Swan of Avon in Bácska.) *Sz.* 1987 Jan.; 20(1): 33-38. Illus.: Photo. B&W. 2. Lang.: Hun.

Yugoslavia: Subotica, Palić. 1986. Reviews of performances. ■The events of 'Shakespeare Fest '86' held in Palica near Subotica and the work of Ljubiša Ristić, leader of the National Theatre in Subotica.

2404 Eörsi, István. "Ristić és Madách." (Ristić and Madách.) *Sz.* 1987 Jan.; 20(1): 30-33. Illus.: Photo. B&W. 2. Lang.: Hun.

Yugoslavia: Subotica. 1986. Reviews of performances. ■Madách's *Az ember tragédiája (The Tragedy of a Man)* revised and staged by Ljubiša Ristić, performed by the National Theatre in Subotica.

2405 Forgách, András. "The kalap of Voltimand: A palicsi Shakespeare—fesztivál." (The Hat of Voltimand: Shakespeare Festival in Palić.) *Sz.* 1987 Jan.; 20(1): 43-48. Lang.: Hun.

Yugoslavia: Palić. 1986. Critical studies. ■'Shakespeare Fest '86': *Hamlet* staged by Vito Taufer, *Julius Caesar* by Janez Pipan, *Titus Andronicus* by Dušan Jovanović.

2406 Gerold, László. "Tóték. Örkény-bemutató Ujvidéken." (*The Tót Family*: First Night of the Örkény Play in Novi Sad.) *Sz.* 1987 Nov.; 20(11): 46-48. Illus.: Photo. B&W. 2. Lang.: Hun.

Yugoslavia: Novi Sad. 1987. Reviews of performances. ■Notes on the performance of István Örkény's play presented by the Hungarian Theatre of Novi Sad directed by Gábor Székely as a guest.

2407 Gerold, László. "Sékszpiriáde—Palicson." (Shakespeare Events in Palić.) *Sz.* 1987 Jan.; 20(1): 38-42 . Illus.: Photo. B&W. 3. Lang.: Hun.

Yugoslavia: Palić. 1986. Reviews of performances. ■The events of the festival 'Shakespeare Fest '86' held in Palić near Subotica.

2408 Radics, Melinda. "Maszk nélkül. Ljubiša Ristić pályájáról." (Without Mask: On Ljubisa Ristić's Career.) *Sz.* 1987 Jan.; 20(1): 28-30. Lang.: Hun.

Yugoslavia: Subotica. 1947-1986. Histories-sources. ■Interview with the leader of the National Theatre in Subotica.

Plays/librettos/scripts

2409 Black, Stephen A. "America's First Tragedy." *English Studies in Canada.* 1987 June; 13(2): 195-203. Notes. Biblio. Lang.: Eng.

1918-1946. Critical studies. ■Reassessment of Eugene O'Neill's *Beyond the Horizon* within the context of the tragic vision of Sophocles and Euripides.

2410 Broer, Lawrence. "Beckett's Heroic Vision: Sounds of Hope, Exclamations of Grief in *Waiting for Godot*." 11-20 in Hartigan, Karelisa V., ed. *From the Bard to Broadway.* Lanham, MD: UP America; 1987. 222 pp. (Univ. of Florida Dept. of Classics Comparative Drama Conference Papers 7.) Pref. Notes. Biblio. Lang.: Eng.

1987. Critical studies. ■*Waiting for Godot* interpreted from a more optimistic perspective. Uses Shaw's prefaces to support part of this position.

2411 Brooks, Colette. "Love at the Margin: F.X. Kroetz's *Through the Leaves*." 31-34 in Cardullo, Bert, ed. *Before His Eyes: Essays in Honor of Stanley Kauffmann.* Lanham, MD: UP of America; 1986. 185 pp. Pref. Notes. Biblio. Lang.: Eng.

1986. Critical studies. ■Theme of love in Franz Xaver Kroetz's *Wer durchs Laub geht (Through the Leaves)*.

2412 Champagne, Lenora. "West From India with Brook and Carrière." *AmTh.* 1987 Dec.; 4(9): 28-30. Illus.: Photo. B&W. 2. Lang.: Eng.

1975-1987. Technical studies. ■Development of *The Mahabharata* directed by Peter Brook in collaboration with Jean-Claude Carrière.

2413 Crum, Jane Ann. "'I must get out of this into the air': Transfiguration and Ascent in Three Plays by Bernard Shaw." 5-13 in Cardullo, Bert, ed. *Before His Eyes: Essays in Honor of Stanley Kauffmann.* Lanham, MD: UP of America; 1986. 185 pp. Pref. Notes. Biblio. Illus.: Photo. Print. B&W. 1. Lang.: Eng.

1986. Critical studies. ■Theme of transfiguration in three plays by G.B. Shaw: *Misalliance, Major Barbara* and *Saint Joan*.

2414 Falkner, Thomas. "Strengthless, Friendless, Loveless: The Chorus and the Cultural Construction of Old Age in Sophocles' *Oedipus at Colonus*." 51-59 in Hartigan, Karelisa V., ed. *From the Bard to Broadway.* Lanham, MD: UP of America; 1987. 222 pp. (Univ. of Florida Dept. of Classics Comparative Drama Conference Papers 7.) Pref. Notes. Biblio. Lang.: Eng.

405 B.C. Critical studies. ■Considers Sophocles' age as a source for the view of old age expressed by chorus in his *Oedipus at Colonus*.

2415 Haffter, Peter. "Bartho Smit se *Don Juan onder die Boere* binne die raamwer van die Don Juan-makroteks." (Bartho Smit's *Don Juan among the Boers* within the Framework of the Don Juan Macrotext.) *JLS/TLW.* 1987 Dec.; 3(4): 1-13. Lang.: Afr.

1600-1987. Critical studies. ■Bartho Smit's *Don Juan onder die Boere (Don Juan among the Boers)* as a hypertextually related version of a well-known legend, with the original versions of Don Juan as macrotext.

2416 Harrell, Wade. "When the Parody Parodies Itself: The Problem with Michael Frayn's *Noises Off*." 87-93 in Hartigan, Karelisa V., ed. *From the Bard to Broadway.* Lanham, MD: UP of America; 1987. 222 pp. (Univ. of Florida Dept. of Classics Comparative Drama Conference Papers 7.) Pref. Notes. Biblio. Lang.: Eng.

1987. Critical studies. ■Frayn's *Noises Off*: is it parody, travesty or an improvisation?.

2417 Harris Smith, Susan. "Ironic Distance and the Theatre of Feigned Madness." *TJ.* 1987 Mar.; 39(1): 51-64. Notes. Lang.: Eng.

1987. Critical studies. ■The use of irony by the dramatist as a tool to test, define and assert the distance, relationship and expectations that evolve between the actor and the audience.

DRAMA: —Plays/librettos/scripts

2418 Jones, Calvin N. "The Dialectics of Despair and Hope: The Modernist Volksstück of Jura Soyfer." *MuK.* 1986; 32(1-2): 33-40. Lang.: Eng.
1836. Biographical studies.

2419 Kalb, Jonathan. "Mayakovsky's Tragic Comedy." 15-30 in Cardullo, Bert, ed. *Before His Eyes: Essays in Honor of Stanley Kauffmann.* Lanham, MD: UP of America; 1986. 185 pp. Pref. Notes. Biblio. Lang.: Eng.
1986. Textual studies. ■Analysis of *Bathhouse.*

2420 Kott, Jan; Praz, Mario, intro. *Shakespeare nostro contemporaneo.* (Shakespeare, Our Contemporary.) Milan: Feltrinelli; 1987. 249 pp. Pref. Lang.: Ita.
1596-1614. Critical studies. ■Reprint of the Italian translation of Kott's 1964 essay and preface by Marco Praz.

2421 Kubiak, Anthony. "Disappearance as History: The Stages of Terror." *TJ.* 1987 Mar.; 39(1): 78-88. Notes. Lang.: Eng.
Critical studies. ■The advent of 'terror' in the theatre as an act that is accompanied by disappearance and displacement.

2422 Lappin, Lou. "The Artist in Society: Bond, Shakespeare, and *Bingo.*" 57-70 in Cardullo, Bert, ed. *Before His Eyes: Essays in Honor of Stanley Kauffmann.* Lanham, MD: UP of America; 1986. 185 pp. Pref. Notes. Biblio. Lang.: Eng.
1975. Critical studies. ■By using a character named Shakespeare, playwright Edward Bond explores the dependence of human beings upon their society. This pact with society implies that individuals 'sell out' for money.

2423 Levy, Jonathan; Mahard, Martha. "Preliminary Checklist of Early Printed Children's Plays in English, 1780-1855." *PAR.* 1987; 12: 1-97. Lang.: Eng.
1780-1855. Bibliographical studies. ■Annotated bibliography of children's plays published in English between 1780 and 1855.

2424 Martin, William F. *The Indissoluble Knot:* King Lear *as Ironic Drama.* Lanham, MD: UP of America; 1987. 93 pp. Biblio. Lang.: Eng.
1590. Critical studies. ■*King Lear* is placed within the context of ironic drama to redefine the plays generic premises. Posits the superiority of ironical drama to tragedy.

2425 Mercer, Peter. Hamlet *and the Acting of Revenge.* Ames, IA: Univ. of Iowa P; 1987. 269 pp. Pref. Index. Notes. Append. Lang.: Eng.
1600. Critical studies. ■Elements of revenge/tragedy. *Hamlet* compared to plays of Seneca, Kyd, Marston and Tourneur.

2426 Milward, Peter. *Biblical Influences in Shakespeare's Great Tragedies.* Bloomington, IN: Indiana UP; 1987. 208 pp. Pref. Lang.: Eng.
Critical studies. ■Biblical influences and meanings in four of Shakespeare's works: *King Lear, Hamlet, Othello* and *Macbeth.* Biblical metaphors, parables, images, references, etc..

2427 Paster, Gail Kern. "Leaky Vessels: The Incontinent Women of City Comedy." *RenD.* 1987; 18: 43-65. Illus.: Photo. B&W. 1. Lang.: Eng.
1599-1632. Critical studies. ■Discusses female characters in European plays who suffer from bladder incontinence. Social effects and psychological theory.

2428 Patraka, Vivian M. "Contemporary Drama, Fascism, and the Holocaust." *TJ.* 1987 Mar.; 39(1): 65-78. Notes. Lang.: Eng.
1980-1987. Critical studies. ■Fascism and the Holocaust as a theme in modern drama. At the same time many plays testify to historical atrocity and abuse of power, they also assert our unwillingness to deal with these same issues.

2429 Troxel, Patricia M. "In the Name of Passion: A Comparison of Medieval Passion Plays and Peter Nichols' *Passion Play.*" 213-222 in Hartigan, Karelisa V., ed. *From the Bard to Broadway.* Lanham, MD: UP of America; 1987. 222 pp. (Univ. of Florida Dept. of Classics Comparative Drama Conference Papers 7.) Pref. Notes. Biblio. Lang.: Eng.
1986. Critical studies. ■Similarity between medieval passion plays and Nichols' *Passion Play.* Applying modern critical approaches to theatre's nature and purpose.

2430 Van Laan, Thomas. "*The Modern Ibsen*: A Reconsideration." *INC.* 1987; 8: 20-27. Lang.: Eng.
1850-1987. Critical studies. ■Extended consideration of Hermann J. Weigand's *The Modern Ibsen* published originally in 1925.

2431 Werner, Hans-Georg. "Zur Bestimmung der Historizität von dramatischen Handlungen." (Determination of the Historicity of Dramatic Actions.) *ZG.* 1987; 8(3): 311-319. Lang.: Ger.
1987. Critical studies. ■Proposal of a method to analyze historical plays using examples of German 18th/19th century drama.

2432 Ordaz, Luis. "Carta a un joven autor dramático nuestro." (Letter to One of Our Young Dramatic Authors.) *Cjo.* 1987 Apr/July; 72: 66-69. Lang.: Spa.
Argentina. 1949-1986. Critical studies. ■Comparison of the subject material between the new generation of playwrights and their well-known predecessors in Argentina.

2433 Baker, Candida. "Ray Lawler." 144-171 in Baker, Candida. *Yacker 2: Australian Writers Talk About their Work.* Sydney: Pan; 1987. 301 pp. Lang.: Eng.
Australia. Ireland. 1921-1987. Histories-sources. ■Interview concentrating on Lawler's classic Australian play *The Summer of the Seventeenth Doll*—his views on some of the major characters, on the film adaptation, on three recent production of the play, on his reasons for developing two companion plays for it and on his writing methods. Related to Media: Film.

2434 Baker, Candida. "Jack Hibberd." 94-115 in Baker, Candida. *Yacker 2: Australian Writers Talk about Their Work.* Sydney: Pan; 1987. 301 pp. Lang.: Eng.
Australia: Melbourne. 1967-1987. Histories-sources. ■Interview with playwright Jack Hibberd touching on his move back to his original profession in medicine, on the new conservatism in Australian theatre, his writing methods, his plans for future directions in his writing and on major plays.

2435 Cousins, Jane. "Gender and Genre: *The Summer of the Seventeenth Doll.*" *Continuum.* 1987; 1(1): 121-139. Lang.: Eng.
Australia. 1955-1987. Critical studies. ■Analyses of critical objections to the play which claim it fails to reach a unified and coherent expression of the authentic Australian experience/identity. Stresses the male nature of this identity and explores the function of women in frustrating the possibility of closure for the play.

2436 Fitzpatrick, Peter. *Williamson.* Methuen Australian Drama Series. North Ryde (NSW): Methuen Australia; 1987. 189 pp. Lang.: Eng.
Australia. 1970-1987. Critical studies. ■Survey of the work of David Williamson, Australia's most popular playwright, defending him against common critical charges that his plays are poorly structured and superficial. Makes strong claims for him as a shaper of cultural images and as a craftsman.

2437 Hainsworth, John. *Hibberd.* Methuen Australian Drama Series. North Ryde (NSW): Methuen Australia; 1987. 148 pp. Lang.: Eng.
Australia. 1966-1986. Critical studies. ■A survey of Jack Hibberd's plays under the categories 'Polemical Plays', 'Popular Plays', 'Adaptations', 'Monodramas' and 'Short Plays'. Outlines plots and provides analysis largely in terms of themes and characterization, with some comment on productions.

2438 Hopkins, Lekkie. "Language, Culture and Landscape in *The Man from Mukinupin.*" *ADS.* 1987 Apr.; 10: 91-106. Lang.: Eng.
Australia. 1979. Critical studies. ■Critical analysis of Dorothy Hewett's *The Man from Mukinupin* as a study in the failed colonization of the Australian landscape by culturally and linguistically bankrupt Europeans. The play's celebratory ending is viewed ironically.

2439 Kelly, Veronica. "George Essex Evans the Playwright." *Margin.* 1987(19): 1-16. Lang.: Eng.
Australia. 1891-1902. Historical studies. ■Queensland poet and journalist Essex Evans, his adaptations of H.J. Byron's pantomime *Robinson Crusoe* and *Musical Whist.*

DRAMA: —Plays/librettos/scripts

2440 Kelly, Veronica. "Explorers and Bushrangers in Nineteenth Century Australian Theatre." 119-132 in Singh, Kirpal. *The Writer's Sense of the Past: Essays on Southeast Asian and Australasian Literature.* Singapore: Singapore UP; 1987. Lang.: Eng.
Australia. 1861-1900. Critical studies. ■Studies the failure of the explorers (much celebrated in other arts forms) to make any impact as subject matter for the nineteenth century popular stage in Australia. Contrasts this with the appeal of bushranger melodramas.

2441 Lloyd, Vic. "Dymphna Cusack's *Morning Sacrifice.*" *ADS.* 1987 Apr.; 10: 67-77. Lang.: Eng.
Australia. 1942. Critical studies. ■Thematic analysis of *Morning Sacrifice*, set in a girls' school, in which manipulative power and jealousy backed by the conservatism of a male-dominated profession defeats the idealistic, humane and progressive forces.

2442 McCallum, John. *Buzo.* Methuen Australia Drama Series. North Ryde (NSW): Methuen Australia; 1987. 155 pp. Lang.: Eng.
Australia. 1969-1983. Critical studies. ■Provides a survey of Alex Buzo's plays, arguing that the Australian theatre has been insensitive to the theatrical demands of the texts, failing to go beyond the superficial realism and come to terms with the high formalism of the writing.

2443 Mitchell, Tony. "Italo-Australian Theatre: Multiculturalism and Neo-Colonialism: Part One." *ADS.* 1987 Apr.; 10: 31-48. Lang.: Eng.
Australia. 1860-1986. Historical studies. ■Plays in Italian by Italo-Australians. Stereotyped stage Italian accents and depiction of Italian immigrants. Distortion of Italian plays in mainstream Australian theatre.

2444 Myers, Larry. "The Tyranny of Distance." *TheaterW.* 1987 Nov 2; 1(12): 27-28. Illus.: Photo. B&W. 2. Lang.: Eng.
Australia. USA: New York, NY. 1979-1987. Histories-sources. ■Interview with playwright Daniel Keene: his career in Australia and New York, comparison of producing plays in each country, writing techniques.

2445 O'Regan, Tom. "The Historical Relations Between Theatre and Film: *The Summer of the Seventeenth Doll.*" *Continuum.* 1987; 1(1): 116-120. Lang.: Eng.
Australia. USA. 1950-1955. Critical studies. ■Argues that Australian critics of theatre and film are insensitive to the interdependence of these art forms. Suggests that Ray Lawler's seminal play *The Summer of the Seventeenth Doll* was heavily influenced by American realism and method acting as mediated through the films of Kazan.

2446 Perkins, Elizabeth. "Form and Transformation in the Plays of Alma de Groen." *ADS.* 1987 Oct.; 11: 5-21. Lang.: Eng.
Australia. 1987. Critical studies. ■Explores the way De Groen brings together dramatic structure and stage design to evoke fluid forms embodying the meaning of her plays.

2447 Rees, Leslie. *Australian Drama 1970-1985: A Historical and Critical Survey.* Sydney: Angus Robertson; 1987. 400 pp. Lang.: Eng.
Australia. 1970-1985. Critical studies. ■An introductory survey of recent Australian playwrights, with a somewhat traditional literary bias, written by a pioneer in the field. A revised, expanded and updated edition of *Australian Drama in the 1970's*, first published in 1978.

2448 Ryan, J.S. "The Theatre of Justin Fleming: Neo-Edwardian or Universal?" *Margin.* 1987(18): 1-6. Lang.: Eng.
Australia. 1981-1986. Critical studies. ■Survey of the early plays of Justin Fleming, including his first major production *Cobra*, performed by the Sydney Theatre Company in 1983. Focus on the plays' use of fantasy and their literary allusiveness.

2449 Turcotte, Gerry. "'The Circle Is Burst': Eschatological Discourse in Louis Nowra's *Sunrise* and *The Golden Age.*" *ADS.* 1987 Oct.; 11: 65-77. Lang.: Eng.
Australia. 1983-1985. Critical studies. ■*Sunrise* and *The Golden Age* by Louis Nowra: confrontation of old and new worlds. Role of language in conflict. Nowra's pessimism.

2450 Crosby, C.D. *The Fairy Tale on the Old Viennese Stage.* St. Andrews: Univ. of St. Andrews; 1987. Notes. Biblio. [Ph.D. dissertation, *Index to Theses*, 36: 6915.] Lang.: Eng.

Austria: Vienna. 1700-1848. Histories-specific. ■Origins of fairy tales on the Viennese stage and differences between staged and literary versions.

2451 Cvetkov, Ju. L. *Iskusstvo i dejstvitel'nost'v rannich dramax Gugo fon Gofmanstalja (Mirovozzrenie i žanr): Avtoref. dis. kand. fil. nauk.* (Art and Reality in the Early Work of Hugo von Hofmannsthal—World View and Genre: Abstract of a Dissertation by a Candidate in Philology.) Leningrad: Leningr. un-t; 1987. 16 pp. Lang.: Rus.
Austria. 1874-1929. Critical studies.

2452 Sokót, Lech. "The Metaphysics of Sex: Strindberg, Weininger and S.I. Witkiewicz." *ThR.* 1987; 12(1): 39-51. Notes. Lang.: Eng.
Austria: Vienna. 1880-1987. Critical studies. ■Comparative study of misogynist themes in Strindberg, Weininger and Witkiewicz.

2453 Beyen, Roland. *Bibliographie de Michel de Ghelderode.* (Michel de Ghelderode: A Bibliography.) Brussels: Académie Royale de Langue et de Littérature Française; 1987. iv, 833 pp. Pref. Index. Lang.: Fre.
Belgium. 1915-1987. Bibliographical studies. ■Includes both published and unpublished works, interviews, critical studies, reviews of performances of adaptations of Ghelderode's works.

2454 Descamps, Maryse. *Maurice Maeterlinck. Un livre: Pelléas et Mélisande. Une oeuvre.* (Maurice Maeterlinck. A Book: Pelleas and Melisande. A Play.) Brussels: Labor; 1986. 115 pp. (Un livre, une oeuvre 8.) Pref. Biblio. Lang.: Fre.
Belgium. 1800. Critical studies. ■Historical context of Maeterlinck's play, analysis of technique, style, characterization. Intended as a textbook.

2455 Reisel, Wanda. "'De Taal creërt het personage'. Paul Pourveur, rekstschrijver." ('Language Creates the Character': Paul Pourveur, Playwright.) *Toneel.* 1987 July; 7(5): 6-10. Illus.: Photo. B&W. 3. Lang.: Dut.
Belgium. 1987. Histories-sources. ■Interview with Belgian playwright, Paul Pourveur. Discussion of his postmodern plays, use of allegorical characters, his plays *Le Diable au Corps* and *Ik, Ali.* Also, the differences of writing for film and theatre.

2456 Albuquerque, Severino João. "Representando o irrespresentáve encenações de tortura do teatro brasileiro da ditadura militar." (Scenes of Military Torture in Brazilian Theatre.) *LATR.* 1987 Fall; 21(1): 5-17. Lang.: Por.
Brazil. 1964-1985. Critical studies. ■Plays written during Brazil's military dictatorship focus on themes of torture.

2457 Brennan, Brian. "Award Winning Playwright Still Feels Uneasy about Arts Awards." *PAC.* 1986 Jan.; 22(4): 24. Notes. Illus.: Photo. 1. Lang.: Eng.
Canada. 1985. Histories-sources. ■Interview with playwright Sharon Pollock focusing on social issues.

2458 Camerlain, Lorraine. "O.K. on change." (O.K. Let's Change.) *JCT.* 1987; 45: 83-97. Illus.: Photo. Print. B&W. 9. Lang.: Fre.
Canada: Montreal, PQ. 1987. Critical studies. ■The child's game in *La Trilogie des dragons* by Robert Lepage awakened in the author questions about the history and identity of Quebec theatre.

2459 Camerlain, Lorraine. "Questions sur des questions." (Questions About Questions.) *JCT.* 1987; 45: 164-168. Illus.: Photo. Print. B&W. 2. Lang.: Fre.
Canada. 1987. Critical studies. ■A reply to Jean-Luc Denis' condemnation (*JCT* 45 (1987), 159-163) of *La Trilogie de dragons* by Robert Lepage which raises questions about Quebec theatre.

2460 Cowan, Doris. "Charter of Wrights." *BooksC.* 1982 Apr.; 11(4): 11. Lang.: Eng.
Canada: Toronto, ON. 1972-1982. Historical studies. ■Playwrights Canada publishes 'minimal editions' of new plays within six weeks of their closing. In ten years of publishing and promoting scripts it has published five hundred plays.

2461 David, Gilbert. "Brecht au Québec: Au-Delà des Malentendus." (Brecht in Quebec: Beyond Misunderstandings.) *JCT.* 1987; 43: 115-126. Illus.: Photo. Print. B&W. 9. Lang.: Fre.
Canada. 1950-1986. ■Traces productions of Brecht in Quebec and their relationship to political and social issues in the province.

DRAMA: —Plays/librettos/scripts

2462 Denis, Jean-Luc. "Questions sur une démarche." (Questions About an Event.) *JCT*. 1987; 45: 159-163. Illus.: Photo. Print. B&W. 2. Lang.: Fre.
Canada. 1987. Critical studies. ■*La Trilogie des dragons* by Robert Lepage is seen as a disappointing return to traditionalism.

2463 Fairley, Anne. "No Surprise to Playwright that Women Dominate Drama Writing." *PAC*. 1986 Jan.; 22(4): 22. Notes. Illus.: Photo. Print. 1. Lang.: Eng.
Canada. 1985. Histories-sources. ■Interview with playwright Anne Chrislett on women playwrights and her career.

2464 Fréchette, Carole. "'L'arte è un veicolo' entretien avec Robert Lepage." (Art is a Vehicle, Interview with Robert Lepage.) *JCT*. 1987; 42: 109-126. Illus.: Photo. Print. B&W. 8. Lang.: Fre.
Canada. 1987. Histories-sources. ■Playwright Robert Lepage discusses his career and his opinions of the theatrical scene in Quebec.

2465 Fréchette, Carole. "Grandeur et misère du père sur la scène québécoise." (Greatness and Despair/The Return of the Father to the Quebec Stage.) *JCT*. 1987; 45: 16-35. Illus.: Photo. Print. B&W. 13. Lang.: Fre.
Canada: Quebec. 1980-1987. Critical studies. ■The 'father figure' has returned to the Quebec stage in three plays: *Le printemps, Monsieur Deslauriers, Ce qui reste du désir* and *Le vrai monde*.

2466 Goldie, Terry. "Collective Concern." *CTR*. 1987 Spr; 50: 81-83. Illus.: Photo. Print. B&W. 2. Lang.: Eng.
Canada: St. John's, NF. 1987. Critical studies. ■Analysis of the collective process, specifically on *The Daily News* and *Fishwharf*.

2467 Harrison, James. "Refractions After Seeing a Play in the Age of Wallace Shawn." *Theatrum*. 1987 Spr; 6: 21-24, 37. Lang.: Eng.
Canada: Toronto, ON. USA: New York, NY. 1986-1987. Reviews of performances. ■The reviewer considers the production of *Aunt Dan and Lemon* in the context of its advance publicity and its philosophical implications.

2468 Highway, Tomson. "On Native Mythology." *Theatrum*. 1987 Spr; 6: 29-31. Illus.: Photo. B&W. 1. Lang.: Eng.
Canada. 1960-1987. Histories-sources. ■Translation of native mythology into English in Highway's work.

2469 Hofsess, John. "Ms. Blood." *BooksC*. 1983 Apr.; 12(4): 3-4. Lang.: Eng.
Canada. 1970-1983. Biographical studies. ■Profile of Canadian playwright Sharon Pollock, comparing her plays of the 70s which focused on humanitarian issues and her plays of the 80s which are more commercially successful.

2470 Homel, David. "Baron of Beef." *BooksC*. 1984 May; 13(5): 4-5. Lang.: Eng.
Canada: Montreal, PQ, Verdun, PQ. 1984. Critical studies. ■David Fennario, writer and director of the bilingual play *Joe Beef*, is also spokesman for the socially aware group Black Rock. Play expresses social conflict in Quebec.

2471 Hunt, Nigel. "Decoding René-Daniel Dubois." *Theatrum*. 1987 Sum; 7: 21-24, 36. Illus.: Photo. B&W. 1. Lang.: Eng.
Canada: Toronto, ON, Montreal, PQ. 1983-1987. Critical studies. ■Discusses levels of language and political metaphor in both text and performance of Dubois' work.

2472 Hunt, Nigel. "Searching for a Visual Syntax: An Interview with Ping Chong." *Theatrum*. 1987 Fall/Win; 8: 5-8, 40. Illus.: Photo. B&W. 1. Lang.: Eng.
Canada: Montreal, PQ. USA: New York, NY. 1987. Histories-sources. ■Ping Chong's work with specific reference to *The Angels of Swedenborg* which played at the Montreal Theatre Festival of the Americas.

2473 Leverett, James. "North of the Border." *AmTh*. 1987 Mar.; 3(12): 30-31. Illus.: Photo. Print. B&W. 1. Lang.: Eng.
Canada: Quebec, PQ. USA: New York, NY. 1984-1985. Critical studies. ■Thematic context of René-Daniel Dubois's *Being at Home with Claude* and its implications for Canadian-U.S. cultural relationship.

2474 Levesque, Solange. "Harmonie et contrepoint." (Harmony and Counterpoint.) *JCT*. 1987; 42: 100-108. Illus.: Photo. Print. B&W. 7. Lang.: Fre.

Canada. 1986-1987. Critical studies. ■An examination of what makes a good play and why Lepage's *Vinci* is so successful.

2475 Levesque, Solange. "Des fleurs, des tomates et quelques perles/l'accueil critique réservé au *Paravents*." (Flowers, Tomatoes and a Few Pearls: Critical Reaction to *The Screens*.) *JCT*. 1987; 44: 61-66. Lang.: Fre.
Canada: Montreal, PQ, Ottawa, ON. 1987. Reviews of performances. ■The critical reception of Brassard's *The Screens* in Ottawa and Montreal.

2476 Levesque, Solange. "Tenir l'univers dans sa main." (Holding the Universe in One's Hand.) *JCT*. 1987; 45: 111-120. Illus.: Photo. Print. B&W. 7. Lang.: Fre.
Canada. 1987. Critical studies. ■The ways in which history (social, theatrical and linguistic) is built into *La Trilogie des dragons (Dragons' Trilogy)* by Robert Lepage.

2477 McNamara, Tim. "Three Desks: A Turning Point in James Reaney's Drama." *Queen's Quarterly*. 1987 Spr; 94(1): 15-32. Notes. Lang.: Eng.
Canada. 1960-1977. Critical studies. ■Contends that Reaney's often overlooked and undervalued play *Three Desks* represents, through both theme and structure, a maturing of the playwright's style and solutions to many of the problems of Reaney's earlier plays.

2478 Pavlovic, Diane. "Cartographie: l'Allemagne Québécoise Recherche Iconographique." (Map Making: German Quebecers in Search of an Iconography.) *JCT*. 1987; 43: 77-110. Biblio. Illus.: Photo. B&W. 41. Lang.: Fre.
Canada. Germany. 1850-1949. Critical studies. ■Discusses the influence of German culture on Quebec playwrights.

2479 Pavlovic, Diane. "Reconstitution de la trilogie." (Reconstruction of the Trilogy.) *JCT*. 1987; 45: 40-82. Illus.: Photo. Print. B&W. 37. Lang.: Fre.
Canada: Montreal, PQ. 1987. Reviews of performances. ■A full description of Robert Lepage's *La Trilogie des dragons*, discussing its structure, themes, and settings. The plays fuses an exploration of Québécois culture, Chinese immigrant experience and war.

2480 Pavlovic, Diane. "Le sable et les étoiles." (Sand and Stars.) *JCT*. 1987; 45: 121-140. Illus.: Photo. Print. B&W. 13. Lang.: Fre.
Canada. 1987. Critical studies. ■*La Trilogie des dragons* by Robert Lepage achieved a memorable impact through a complex use of images.

2481 Plant, Richard. "Opening Lines." *BooksC*. 1985 Apr.; 14(3): 22-24. Lang.: Eng.
Canada. 1958-1985. Critical studies. ■Four recently staged Canadian plays by Marco Micone, Judith Thompson, Rachel Wyatt and Ann Saddlemyer reflect their author's attempts to master their craft.

2482 Plant, Richard. "Dramatic Readings." *BooksC*. 1984 Apr.; 13(4): 13-17. Lang.: Eng.
Canada. 1983-1984. Critical studies. ■Drama published in Canada in 1983-84 has gone beyond the realism of the 70s. Non-realistic, anti-naturalistic themes explored in plays by Panych and Reaney, and the less successful playwrights, Skelton and Beissel.

2483 Simon, Sherry. "Speaking with Authority: The Theatre of Marco Micone." *CanL*. 1985; 106: 57-64. Notes. Lang.: Eng.
Canada. 1982-1985. Critical studies. ■Marco Micone, Italo-québecois playwright and essayist, uses language to describe power and authority within family relationships in his plays, which are set in Montreal.

2484 Stone-Blackburne, Susan. *Robertson Davies, Playwright: A Search for the Self on the Canadian Stage*. Vancouver, BC: Univ. of Vancouver P.; 1985. 259 pp. Index. Biblio. Lang.: Eng.
Canada. 1913-1985. Critical studies. ■Chronological examination of the plays of Robertson Davies. Considers themes such as the ideal of wholeness in both individual and national character as well as the effects of the material conditions of production on the plays.

2485 Vais, Michel. "Derrière *Les Paravents*/entretien avec André Brassard." (Behind *The Screens*: Interview with André Brassard.) *JCT*. 1987; 44: 42-60. Illus.: Photo. Print. B&W. 10. Lang.: Fre.

DRAMA: —Plays/librettos/scripts

Canada: Montreal, PQ, Ottawa, ON. 1987. Histories-sources. ■André Brassard discusses his production of *The Screens*.

2486 Weins, Mary. "Playwright Judith Thompson." *PAC.* 1986 Jan.; 22(4): 23. Notes. Illus.: Photo. Print. 1. Lang.: Eng.
Canada. 1985. Histories-sources. ■Interview with playwright Judith Thompson focusing on her characters.

2487 Wilson, Paul. "Blythe Spirit." *BooksC.* 1983 Apr.; 12(4): 10-13. Illus.: Photo. Print. B&W. 1. Lang.: Eng.
Canada: Blythe, ON, Toronto, ON. 1963-1983. Biographical studies. ■Paul Thompson, founder of the Blythe Summer Festival, and his work with Toronto's Theatre Passe Muraille. His plays focus on Canadian people, events and spirit.

2488 Wynne-Jones, Tim. "Acts of Darkness." *BooksC.* 1985 Apr.; 14(3): 11-14. Illus.: Photo. Print. B&W. 1. Lang.: Eng.
Canada. 1972-1985. Biographical studies. ■Reading George F. Walker's plays reveals structure and symbolism that are invisible in the excitement of a good production. Winner of the 1984 Chalmers award, Walker has devoted himself exclusively to playwriting for the past 10 years.

2489 Zichy, Francis. "Justifying the Ways of Lizzie Borden to Men: The Play Within the Play in Sharon Pollock's *Blood Relations.*" *TA.* 1987(42): 61-81. Notes. Lang.: Eng.
Canada. 1987. Historical studies. ■Normally a distancing, self-conscious technique, the play-within-a-play device, as employed by Sharon Pollock in *Blood Relations*, illuminates the character of Lizzie Borden and her actions.

2490 Boyle, Catherine M. "Egon Wolff's *La balsa de la Medusa*: Is the Bourgeoisie Waving or Drowning?" *LATR.* 1987 Fall; 21 (1): 43-51. Lang.: Eng.
Chile. 1964-1984. Critical studies. ■Egon Wolff's *La balsa de la Medusa (The Raft of the Medusa)*, *Los invasores (The Invaders)* and *Flores de papel (Paper Flowers)* create a trilogy about the Chilean bourgeoisie.

2491 Xu, Fu-Ming. "Jin ping mei yu min dai xi qu." (The Novel of the Ming Dynasty and Jin Ping Mei.) *XYishu.* 1987 Sum; 38: 34-42. Notes. Lang.: Chi.
China. 1368-1644. Historical studies. ■We can discover a lot about the theatre of the Ming dynasty by examining the text of the novels of the period. Influence of *Jin Ping Mei (The Golden Lotus, or the Adventures of Hsi Men and His Six Wives)*.

2492 Abkowicz, Jerzy. "Gao Xinjian: Sygnał ostrzegawczy dzikiego człowieka." (Gao Xinjian: The Warning Signal of the Wild Man.) *DialogW.* 1987; 9: 83-90. Notes. Lang.: Pol.
China, People's Republic of. 1983-1987. Critical studies. ■Contemporary Chinese society as seen by playwright Gao Xinjian: problems of ecology, frustration after the cultural revolution.

2493 Pauo, Jueng. "Shou twu xigu kung tzuo chè tzwo t'an hsyue hsi." (Seminar of the Metropolitan Dramatists' Workshop.) *XLunc.* 1984; 2: 47. Notes. Lang.: Chi.
China, People's Republic of. 1984. Histories-sources. ■Several Chinese playwrights discuss humanitarianism and its impact on society in this time of peace and its impact on contemporary drama. Includes some criticism and research.

2494 Shafer, Yvonne. "Ibsen in China: An Interview with Haiping Liu." *INC.* 1987; 8: 6-10. Lang.: Eng.
China, People's Republic of. Norway. 1917-1985. Histories-sources. ■Overview by Chinese university professor of Ibsen translations, productions, reception and influence.

2495 Suwu, Hsin. "Huang tso lin tzai 'sheng mieng, ai ch'ieng, tz iou,' chweng ta t'an suo." (To Search for 'Life.Love.Freedom' by Hueng Tsolin.) *XLunc.* 1984; 2: 114-118. Notes. Illus.: Photo. B&W. 1. Lang.: Chi.
China, People's Republic of. 1983. Critical studies. ■Chinese playwright Hueng Tsolin and his themes of love, life and freedom in his plays, as well as the poetic form of his plays.

2496 Lyakhovskaya, Nina D. "French-Language Comedy in Tropical Africa as a Form of Mass Literature." *RAL.* 1987 Win; 18(4): 458-471. Biblio. Lang.: Eng.
Congo: Brazzaville. Cameroon. Benin. France. 1700-1975. Critical studies. ■A comparative study of the farces, sketches and tragic comedies written in post-colonial French-speaking Africa and French

Enlightenment comedy and melodrama. Emphasis is placed on the use of the comic to educate the audience about the social ills of these newly independent nations.

2497 Armitage, Daniel. "The Dismemberment of Orpheus: Mythic Elements in Shakespeare's Romances." *ShS.* 1986; 39: 123-133. Notes. Lang.: Eng.
England: London. 1607-1614. Critical studies. ■Influence of the poet Ovid on the later plays of William Shakespeare. Exploration of the romances using the myth of Orpheus as an image.

2498 Ayers, P.K. "Dreams of the City: The Urban and the Urbane in Jonson's *Epicoene.*" *PQ.* 1987 Win; 66(1): 73-86. Notes. Lang.: Eng.
England. 1609-1987. Critical studies. ■The paradoxical nature of urbanity gives the play both its subject and its form.

2499 Baird, Lorrayne Y. "'Cockes face' and the Problem of *poydrace* in the Chester Passion." *CompD.* 1982 Fall; 16(3): 227-236. Notes. Lang.: Eng.
England. 1400-1550. Historical studies. ■Analysis of terms and their meanings in the text of the *Chester Cycle*.

2500 Baker, Susan. "Hamlet's Bloody Thoughts and the Illusion of Inwardness." *CompD.* 1987/88 Win; 21(4): 303-317. Notes. Lang.: Eng.
England. 1600. Critical studies. ■Hamlet's psychological progress in Shakespeare's *Hamlet*. Analysis of the text, particularly soliloquies, to determine how interiority may be represented on stage.

2501 Barnes, Peter. "Still Standing Upright: Ben Jonson, 350 Years Alive." *NTQ.* 1987 Aug.; 3(11): 202-206. Lang.: Eng.
England. 1600-1987. Historical studies. ■Playwright Ben Jonson's theatricality and relevance today.

2502 Berger, Harry, Jr. "Textual Dramaturgy: Representing the Limits of Theatre in *Richard II.*" *TJ.* 1987 May; 39(2): 135-155. Lang.: Eng.
England. 1987. Critical studies. ■Study of textual dramaturgy and Shakespeare's *Richard II*.

2503 Bergeron, David M. "Images of Rule in *Cymbeline.*" *JDTC.* 1987; 1(2): 31-37. Notes. Lang.: Eng.
England. 1400-1550. Critical studies. ■Connecting the reign of James I with an understanding of the idea of rule in Shakespeare's *Cymbeline*. Relations between characters, problems of succession and the ongoing process of interpretation.

2504 Berry, Edward. *Shakespeare's Comic Rites.* Cambridge: Cambridge UP; 1984. x, 221 pp. Index. Biblio. Lang.: Eng.
England. 1564-1616. Critical studies. ■Analysis of rites of separation, transition and incorporation in Shakespeare's eight romantic comedies.

2505 Bertelsen, Lance. "The Significance of the 1731 Revisions to *The Fall of Mortimer.*" *Restor.* 1987 Win; 2(2): 8-25. Notes. Lang.: Eng.
England. 1691-1731. Historical studies. ■Attack on Sir Robert Walpole through character of Mortimer in 18th-century adaptation of *King Edward the Third*.

2506 Boone, Blair W. "The Skill of Cain in the English Mystery Cycles." *CompD.* 1982 Sum; 16(2): 112-129. Notes. Lang.: Eng.
England. 1200-1576. Critical studies. ■Topological analysis of the structure and unity in medieval Cain and Abel plays of the mystery cycles. Moral action, character study, language.

2507 Brockett, Clyde W. "Modal and Motivic Coherence in the Music of the *Fleury Playbook.*" *CompD.* 1982-83 Win; 16(4): 345-371. Notes. Lang.: Eng.
England. 1500-1980. Historical studies. ■Melodies from liturgical dramas: analysis provides basis for comparing musical effects of other manuscripts.

2508 Butler, Martin. *Theatre and Crisis 1632-1642.* Cambridge, UK: Cambridge UP; 1987. 340 pp. Pref. Index. Notes. Tables. Append. Illus.: Photo. Dwg. Sketches. Print. B&W. 14. Lang.: Eng.
England. 1632-1642. Historical studies. ■Study of English theatre between 1632 and 1642 focusing on its treatment of political subjects and themes and its use of issues of state, society and religion.

DRAMA: —Plays/librettos/scripts

2509 Champion, Larry S. "Westward-Northward: Structural Development in Dekker's *Ho* Plays." *CompD.* 1982 Fall; 16(3): 251-266. Notes. Lang.: Eng.
England. 1605. Critical studies. ■Evaluating work of playwright Thomas Dekker and his contribution to the development of comedy in late Elizabethan and Jacobean England.

2510 Ciocca, Rossella. *Il cerchio d'oro: i Re sacri nel teatro shakespeariano.* (The Golden Circlet: Sacred Kings in Shakespearian Theatre.) Rome: Officina; 1987. 213 pp. (Cultura & Società 10.) Pref. Index. Append. Lang.: Ita.
England. 1539-1613. Critical studies. ■Shakespeare's treatment of the sacred power of the king in the author's histories and tragedies.

2511 Cohen, Derek. "The Alternating Styles of *The Plain Dealer.*" *Restor.* 1987 Sum; 2(2): 19-37. Notes. Lang.: Eng.
England. 1676. Critical studies. ■Shifting styles of speech create problems in characterizations of Olivia and Manly.

2512 Craft, Catherine A. "Granville's *Jew of Venice* and the Eighteenth-Century Stage." *Restor.* 1987 Win; 2(2): 38-54. Notes. Lang.: Eng.
England. 1596-1701. Critical studies. ■Alterations that brought *The Merchant of Venice* into conformity with eighteenth-century dramaturgy.

2513 Curran, Stuart. "Shelleyan Drama." 61-77 in Cave, Richard Allen, ed. *The Romantic Theatre: An International Symposium.* Totowa, NJ: Barnes & Noble; 1986. 130 pp. Index. Notes. Biblio. Lang.: Eng.
England. 1792-1822. Historical studies. ■Shelley's concept of the drama in context of Romantic theatre movement of his time.

2514 Daniel, Clay. "The Fall of George Barnwell." *Restor.* 1987 Win; 2(2): 26-37. Notes. Lang.: Eng.
England. 1731-1987. Critical studies. ■George Lillo's *The London Merchant* is an allegory of the Fall.

2515 Dawson, Anthony B. "Madness and Meaning: *The Spanish Tragedy.*" *JDTC.* 1987; 2(1): 53-67. Notes. Lang.: Eng.
England. 1589. Critical studies. ■Connection between madness and revenge in *The Spanish Tragedy.* Historical comparison to instability of Jacobean period.

2516 de Sousa, Geraldo U. "Closure and the Antimasque of *The Tempest.*" *JDTC.* 1987; 2(1): 41-51. Notes. Biblio. Lang.: Eng.
England. 1611. Critical studies. ■Place of the masque in *The Tempest,* its relationship to theme of play, and comparison to contemporary masques.

2517 DeRitter, Jones. "A Cult of Dependence: The Social Context of *The London Merchant.*" *CompD.* 1987/88 Win; 21(4): 374-386. Notes. Lang.: Eng.
England. 1731-1740. Historical studies. ■Ideology of English popular literature reflected cultural anxiety about the decline of the family as an economic unit. The insecurities that arose as a result created audience for plays based on criminal biographies, such as *The London Merchant.*

2518 Durbach, Errol. "Playing the Fool to Sorrow: 'Life-Lies' and 'Life-Truths' in *King Lear* and *The Wild Duck.*" *ET.* 1987 Nov.; 6(1): 5-17. Notes. Lang.: Eng.
England. Norway. 1605-1884. Critical studies. ■Compares and contrasts the ideologies of 'the life lie' and 'the life truth' in *King Lear* and *Vildanden (The Wild Duck).*

2519 Freeman, Neil. "Shakespeare for the Stage or Page?" *Theatrum.* 1987 Spr; 6: 11-16, 38-40. Lang.: Eng.
England. 1623-1987. Textual studies. ■In a comparison of First Folio texts to modern editions, the author illustrates through guided readings the changes in meaning and impact of the written text caused by editorial and stylistic alterations made to editions after 1700.

2520 Grabbe, Christian Dietrich. *Sulla shakespearomania.* (On Shakespeare-Mania.) Rome: E & A; 1987. 43 pp. Lang.: Ita.
England. Germany. 1594-1836. Critical studies. ■Italian translation of the 1836 edition of *Über die Shakespearomanie.*

2521 Guilfoyle, Cherrell. "The Way to Dover: Arthurian Imagery in *King Lear.*" *CompD.* 1987 Fall; 21(3): 214-228. Notes. Lang.: Eng.

England. 1605. Historical studies. ■Shakespeare's references to Dover in *King Lear* may have its origins in Arthurian legend where returning troops from France may have landed in Dover.

2522 Heinemann, Margot. "Utopie und Geschichte im Drama der Zeitgenossen Shakespeares." (Utopian Ideas and Historiography in the Dramas of Shakespeare's Contemporaries.) 103-109 in Klotz, Günther, ed.; Kuckhoff, Armin-Gerd, ed. *Deutsche Shakespeare-Gesellschaft Jahrbuch.* Weimar: Böhlau; 1987. 305 pp. (SJW 123.) Lang.: Ger.
England. 1600-1650. Critical studies. ■Ideas of Utopia in plays by Thomas Dekker, Thomas Middleton, Philip Massinger, Richard Brome, Inigo Jones and others.

2523 Hogdon, Barbara. "The Making of Virgins and Mothers: Sexual Signs, Substitute Scenes and Doubled Presences in *All's Well That Ends Well.*" *PQ.* 1987 Win; 66(1): 47-71. Notes. Lang.: Eng.
England. 1602-1987. Critical studies. ■Suppression, doubling and substitutions convey the play's concern with sexuality.

2524 Holderness, Graham. "*Romeo and Juliet*: Empathy and Alienation." 118-129 in Klotz, Günther, ed.; Kuckhoff, Armin-Gerd, ed. *Deutsche Shakespeare-Gesellschaft Jahrbuch.* Weimar: Böhlau; 1987. 305 pp. (SJW 123.) Lang.: Eng.
England. 1595-1596. Critical studies. ■On the play's qualities of metadrama, alienation-effect and self-reflexive fantasy.

2525 Hughes, Derek. "Vanbrugh and Cibber: Language, Place, and Social Order in *The Relapse.*" *CompD.* 1987 Spr; 21(1): 62-83 . Notes. Lang.: Eng.
England. 1696. Critical studies. ■Imagery of home as a common and central theme of Cibber and Vanbrugh. Emphasis on moral and sexual homelessness and social disorientation.

2526 Hughes, Derek. "Naming and Entitlement in Wycherley, Etherege, and Dryden." *CompD.* 1987 Fall; 21(3): 259-289. Notes. Lang.: Eng.
England. 1500-1699. Critical studies. ■Recovery of social and moral identity is associated with a recovery of name or title. Recovery demonstrated the natural and inescapable interdependence of linguistic and moral order.

2527 Jason, Philip K. "The Distinction of Otway and Betterton." *Restor.* 1987 Sum; 2(1): 6-18. Notes. Tables. Lang.: Eng.
England. 1675-1683. Critical studies. ■Subtlety of *Venice Preserv'd* as evidence of impact of Thomas Betterton's acting style on Thomas Otway.

2528 Kagarlickij, Ju.I. *Teatr na veka: Teatr épochi Prosveščenia tendencii i tradicii.* (Theatre for an Age—Theatre of the Renaissance:Tendencies and Traditions.) Moscow: Iskusstvo; 1987. 348 pp. Lang.: Rus.
England. 1600-1699. Histories-specific. ■On theory of drama, evolution of comedy and tragedy, theory and practice of the actor's craft.

2529 Kaplan, Joel H. "Reopening King Cambises' Vein." *ET.* 1987 May; 5(2): 103-114. Notes. Illus.: Pntg. Photo. Print. B&W. 6. Lang.: Eng.
England. 1562-1987. Critical studies. ■Sources, historical importance and production history of Thomas Preston's *Cambyses, King of Persia.*

2530 Kiernan, Ryan. "Die Sprache der Tragödie: Geschichte und Utopie in *Romeo und Julia.*" (The Language of Tragedy: History and Utopia in *Romeo and Juliet.*) 54-60 in Klotz, Günther, ed.; Kuckhoff, Armin-Gerd, ed. *Deutsche Shakespeare-Gesellschaft Jahrbuch.* Weimar: Böhlau; 1987. 305 pp. (SJW 123.) Lang.: Ger.
England. 1595-1596. Critical studies. ■Contradiction between social reality and utopian claim as cause for the tragic end in *Romeo and Juliet.*

2531 Klotz, Günther. "Shakespeares Umgang mit künstlichen Paradiesen." (Shakespeare's Approach to Artificial Paradises.) 24-31 pp in Klotz, Günther, ed.; Kuckhoff, Armin-Gerd, ed. *Deutsche Shakespeare-Gesellschaft Jahrbuch.* Weimar: Böhlau; 1987. 305 pp. (SJW 123.) Lang.: Ger.
England. 1590-1612. Critical studies. ■Representation of real history and Utopia in Shakespeare's plays.

DRAMA: —Plays/librettos/scripts

2532 Klotz, Günther. "Die Inversion des Maskenspiels im *Sturm*: Zeitgeschichte, 'Authority' und Utopie." (The Inversion of the Masks Play in *The Tempest*: Contemporary History, 'Authority' and Utopia.) 32-41 in Klotz, Günther, ed.; Kuckhoff, Armin-Gerd, ed. *Deutsche Shakespeare-Gesellschaft Jahrbuch*. Weimar: Böhlau; 1987. 305 pp. (SJW 123.) Lang.: Ger.
England. 1611-1612. Critical studies. ■Social reality and utopian historical imagination: function of the mask play in *The Tempest*.

2533 Klotz, Sebastian. "Why 'Music with Her Silver Sound'?" 130-138 in Klotz, Günther, ed.; Kuckhoff, Armin-Gerd, ed. *Deutsche Shakespeare-Gesellschaft Jahrbuch*. Weimar: Böhlau; 1987. 305 pp. (SJW 123.) Lang.: Ger.
England. 1580-1616. Critical studies. ■On Shakespeare's conception and usage of music as rooted in his time.

2534 Longsworth, Robert. "Two Medieval Cornish Versions of the Creation of the World." *CompD*. 1987 Fall; 21(3): 249-258. Notes. Lang.: Eng.
England. 1350. Critical studies. ■Relationship between texts of two surviving Cornish Corpus Christi plays. Theorizes that *Creation of the World* is not an expanded version of *Origo Mundi* but a separate work.

2535 Mace, Nancy A. "Fielding, Theobald, and *The Tragedy of Tragedies*." *PQ*. 1987 Fall; 66(4): 457-472. Notes. Lang.: Eng.
England. 1730-1731. Critical studies. ■Fielding rewrote *Tom Thumb* to satirize Lewis Theobald not only as a scholar, but as a playwright.

2536 Magister, Karl-Heinz. "Shakespeares 'Green World': Doppeldeutigkeit und Utopie in *Wie es euch gefällt*." (Shakespeare's 'Green World': Ambiguity and Utopia in *As You Like It*.) 74-80 in Klotz, Günther, ed.; Kuckhoff, Armin-Gerd, ed. *Deutsche Shakespeare-Gesellschaft Jahrbuch*. Weimar: Böhlau; 1987. 305 pp. (SJW 123.) Lang.: Ger.
England. 1599-1600. Critical studies. ■Contradiction between society and nature in *As You Like It*.

2537 Magnusson, Lynne A. "The Collapse of Shakespeare's High Style in *The Two Noble Kinsman*." *English Studies in Canada*. 1987 Dec.; 13(4): 375-390. Notes. Lang.: Eng.
England. 1591-1616. Critical studies. ■Analysis of Shakespeare's use of language in *The Two Noble Kinsmen*.

2538 Manvell, Roger. *Elizabeth Inchbald: England's Principal Woman Dramatist and Independent Woman of Letters in 18th Century London*. Lanham, MD: UP of America; 1987. 232 pp. Notes. Lang.: Eng.
England: London. 1760-1821. Biographies. ■Study of little-known English dramatist, Elizabeth Inchbald. Biography and discussion of her plays.

2539 Margolies, David. "Vergangenheitsvision als Utopie in Shakespeares Stücken." (Vision of the Past as Utopian Ideal in Shakespeare's Plays.) 81-88 in Klotz, Günther, ed.; Kuckhoff, Armin-Gerd, ed. *Deutsche Shakespeare-Gesellschaft Jahrbuch*. Weimar: Böhlau; 1987. 305 pp. (SJW 123.) Lang.: Ger.
England. 1591-1599. Critical studies. ■Creation of ideal future worlds based on historical past in *Henry IV, Henry V, Henry VI* and *King Lear*.

2540 McFarland, Ronald E. "The Vampire on Stage: A Study in Adaptations." *CompD*. 1987 Spr; 21(1): 19-33. Notes. Lang.: Eng.
England. Italy. France. 1800-1825. Critical studies. ■Analysis of vampire characters in the works of Byron, Polidori and Planché. Study of melodrama on the stage.

2541 McMillin, Scott. *The Elizabethan Theatre and the Book of Sir Thomas More*. Ithaca, NY: Cornell UP; 1987. 170 pp. Pref. Index. Append. Lang.: Eng.
England. 1595-1650. Critical studies. ■New questions about the Elizabethan play *Sir Thomas More*. Previously, questions had centered on possible authorship by Shakespeare. New questions on the acting companies that performed the work.

2542 Melchiori, Giorgio. "The Dramas of Byron." 47-60 in Cave, Richard Allen, ed. *The Romantic Theatre: An International Symposium*. Totowa, NJ: Barnes & Noble; 1986. 130 pp. Index. Notes. Biblio. Lang.: Eng.
England. 1788-1824. Critical studies. ■The structure of Byron's plays with an eye towards performance.

2543 Palmer, Barbara D. "'Towneley Plays' or 'Wakefield Cycle' Revisited." *CompD*. 1987/88 Win; 21(4): 318-348. Notes. Lang.: Eng.
England. Historical studies. ■Evidence that cycle plays were actually a peculiar phenomenon in the medieval period when measured against other dramatic activity of the era.

2544 Parker, Douglas H. "Shakespeare's Female Twins in *Twelfth Night*: In Defense of Olivia." *English Studies in Canada*. 1987 Mar.; 13: 23-24. Notes. Lang.: Eng.
England. 1599. Critical studies. ■Interpretation of the character of Olivia in *Twelfth Night*. Analysis of various situations and scenes in which Olivia and Viola mirror each other, resulting in a non-genetic twinning of the two characters.

2545 Ronthaler, Jürgen. "Zwischen historischem Abbild und utopischem Entwurf: Die Publikumsbezogenheit des Hamlet." (Between Historical Representation and Utopian Ideas: Hamlet's Directedness to the Public.) 93-98 in Klotz, Günther, ed.; Kuckhoff, Armin-Gerd, ed. *Deutsche Shakespeare-Gesellschaft Jahrbuch*. Weimar: Böhlau; 1987. 305 pp. (SJW 123.) Lang.: Ger.
England. 1600-1601. Critical studies. ■Relation of the character of Hamlet to the audience.

2546 Rosenberg, D.M. "Milton, Dryden, and the Ideology of Genre." *CompD*. 1987 Spr; 21(1): 1-18. Notes. Lang.: Eng.
England. 1608-1700. Historical studies. ■Comparison of the work of Milton and Dryden with primary focus on their heroic plays. Study of Restoration theatre and culture.

2547 Sahel, Pierre. "The Strangeness of a Dramatic Style: Rumour in *Henry VIII*." *ShS*. 1985; 38: 145-151. Notes. Lang.: Eng.
England: London. 1612-1614. Critical studies. ■Function of rumour as a political and social tool in *Henry VIII*.

2548 Schechter, Joel. "The Theater of Satire, or Politicians and the Arts." 123-127 in Cardullo, Bert, ed. *Before His Eyes: Essays in Honor of Stanley Kauffmann*. Lanham, MD: UP of America; 1986. 185 pp. Lang.: Eng.
England: London. Italy. USA. 1728-1984. Historical studies. ■Describes four separate instances of satire on leading political figures in defferent periods.

2549 Schwartz, Robert B. "Puritans, Libertines and the Green World of Utopia in *As You Like It*." 66-73 in Klotz, Günther, ed.; Kuckhoff, Armin-Gerd, ed. *Deutsche Shakespeare-Gesellschaft Jahrbuch*. Weimar: Böhlau; 1987. 305 pp. (SJW 123.) Lang.: Ger.
England. 1599-1600. Critical studies. ■Social reality in contrast with nature as allegory of utopian social fiction.

2550 Shafer, Yvonne. "Restoration Heroines: Reflections of Social Change." *Restor*. 1987 Sum; 2(1): 38-53. Notes. Lang.: Eng.
England. 1668-1700. Critical studies. ■Independence of Restoration women is reflected in comic heroines.

2551 Shaw, Catherine M. "The Tragic Substructure of the *Henry IV* Plays." *ShS*. 1985; 38: 61-67. Notes. Lang.: Eng.
England: London. 1594-1599. Critical studies. ■Scenes from Shakespeare's *Richard II* only partially fulfill the play's dramatic obligations: promise of full tragic resolution is to be found in the *Henry IV* plays.

2552 Slights, William W.E. "'Swear by Thy Gracious Self': Self-Referenced Oaths in Shakespeare." *English Studies in Canada*. 1987 June; 13(2): 147-160. Notes. Lang.: Eng.
England. 1594-1616. Critical studies. ■Examines the formal oath as a calling to witness of a higher authority. Examines the dramatic role of the self-referential oath as employed by Shakespeare's characters.

2553 Soellner, Rolf. "Revolution und Utopie im Theater: Die Plebejer im *Coriolan*." (Revolution and Utopia in Drama: The Plebeians in *Coriolanus*.) 110-117 in Klotz, Günther,

DRAMA: —Plays/librettos/scripts

ed.; Kuckhoff, Armin-Gerd, ed. *Deutsche Shakespeare-Gesellschaft Jahrbuch.* Weimar: Böhlau; 1987. 305 pp. (SJW 123.) Lang.: Ger.

England. 1600-1980. Critical studies. ■General relation of *Coriolanus* to the conflict of the classes in Shakespeare's time and how it has been seen in 19th/20th century theatre.

2554 Suzuki, Mikoko. "Truth tired with iteration: Myth and Fiction in Shakespeare's *Troilus and Cressida*." *PQ.* 1987 Spr; 66(2): 153-174. Notes. Lang.: Eng.

England. 1601. Critical studies. ■Play's critique of codification and classification represented by myth, gender roles, social hierarchy and genre.

2555 Szabó, László. *Shakespeare: Esszék.* (Shakespeare: Essays.) Budapest: Gondolat; 1987. 307 pp. Lang.: Hun.

England. 1589-1610. Critical studies. ■Collected essays 1957-1984, by a historian of culture: Shakespeare's life, plays, literary background and milieu.

2556 Tyler, Sharon. "Minding True Things: The Chorus, the Audience and *Henry V*." *TID.* 1987; 9: 69-79. Notes. Lang.: Eng.

England. 1599. Critical studies. ■Possible interpretations of the role of Chorus in Shakespeare's *Henry V*: to make epic action visible, unify diverse non-naturalistic spatial requirements, remind audience of theatrical spectacle, foregrounding the notions of performance, representation, interpretation.

2557 Webb, Timothy. "The Romantic Poet and the Stage: A Short, Sad History." 9-46 in Cave, Richard Allen, ed. *The Romantic Theatre: An International Symposium.* Totowa, NJ: Barnes & Noble; 1986. 130 pp. Index. Notes. Biblio. Lang.: Eng.

England. 1700-1800. Critical studies. ■Conflicts within the Romantic tradition: the paradox of poetry.

2558 Weimann, Robert. "Utopie und Geschichte bei Shakespeare." (Utopia and History in Shakespeare's Plays.) 7-23 pp in Klotz, Günther, ed.; Kuckhoff, Armin-Gerd, ed. *Deutsche Shakespeare-Gesellschaft Jahrbuch.* Weimar: Böhlau; 1987. 305 pp. (SJW 123.) Lang.: Ger.

England. 1589-1606. Critical studies. ■Relation of historiography and utopian ideas in *Henry VI, Henry IV* and *King Lear.*

2559 Weiss, Adrian. "A Pill to Purge Parody: Marston's Manipulation of the Paul's Environment in the *Antonio* Plays." *TID.* 1987; 9: 81-97. Notes. Lang.: Eng.

England: London. 1553-1608. Critical studies. ■Self-referentiality in plays for St. Paul's schoolboys, school performance tradition. Relationships among spaces: theatrical, religious, textual, architectural.

2560 Wiles, David. *Shakespeare's Clown: Actor and Text in the Elizabethan Playhouse.* New York, NY: Cambridge UP; 1987. 260 pp. Lang.: Eng.

England. 1585-1625. Histories-specific. ■Role of the clown in the plays of Shakespeare and other Elizabethan dramatists. Focus on Will Kemp, Shakespeare's famed comic clown. How the dramatist and actor worked together via improvisation.

2561 Wiltenburg, Robert. "The *Aeneid* in *The Tempest*." *ShS.* 1986; 39: 159-168. Notes. Lang.: Eng.

England: London. 1611. Critical studies. ■Relationship of the *Aeneid* to Shakespeare's *The Tempest*. Similarity of patterns in situation, development and resolution.

2562 Bialik, Ilana. "Ekronot shel hafakat mekorot Lyiddish Beteatron ha 'Shund'." (Adaptation in the 'Shund' Theatre.) *Bamah.* 1987; 21(107): 15-22. Illus.: Print. B&W. Lang.: Heb.

Europe. USA. 1853-1960. Histories-general. ■The Yiddish theatre and its development from Europe to the United States. Adapting stories into Yiddish plays.

2563 Blau, Herbert. "The Bloody Show and the Eye of Prey: Beckett and Deconstruction." *TJ.* 1987 Mar.; 39(1): 5-19. Notes. Lang.: Eng.

Europe. 1953-1987. Critical studies. ■Discusses theme of deconstruction as a pervading force in Beckett's writing. Compares characters from his works.

2564 Campbell, Thomas P. "The Two Cities in the *Fleury Playbook*." *CompD.* 1982 Sum; 16(2): 148-165. Notes. Lang.: Eng.

Europe. 1300. Critical studies. ■Assessment of literary value and principles of coherence of group of medieval plays collected in the *Fleury Playbook.*

2565 Gentili, Bruno, ed. *Edipo: il teatro greco e la cultura europea.* (Oedipus: Greek Theatre and European Culture.) Roma: Edizioni dell'Ateneo; 1986. 587 pp. (Quaderni Urbinati di cultura Classica, Atti di convegni 3.) Index. Lang.: Ita.

Europe. Greece. 1000 B.C.-1987 A.D. Critical studies. ■Papers from a 1982 international conference, Urbino.

2566 Konrad, Linn B. "Ariadne and the Labyrinth of the Creative Mind." 147-156 in Hartigan, Karelisa V., ed. *From the Bard to Broadway.* Lanham, MD: UP of America; 1987. 222 pp. (Univ. of Florida Dept. of Classics Comparative Drama Conference Papers.) Pref. Notes. Biblio. Lang.: Eng.

Europe. 1892-1902. Critical studies. ■The myth character of Ariadne in three European plays: Strindberg's *Ett Drömspel (A Dream Play),* Maeterlinck's *Ariane et Barbe-Bleue (Ariadne and Bluebeard)* and Ibsen's *Bygmester Solness (The Master Builder).*

2567 "Sacha Guitry: The Modern Man's Molière?" *Econ.* 1986 Jan 4; 298(7427): 83. Illus.: Photo. B&W. 1. Lang.: Eng.

France. 1920-1986. Historical studies. ■Career of playwright Sacha Guitry: plays and productions, political content and themes, personal life.

2568 "Repertori de manuscrits de teatre rossellonès (2)." (Manuscripts of Roussillon Theatre Repertory, 2.) 329-342 in Massot i Muntaner, Josep. *Estudis de llengua i literatura catalana, XIV. Miscellània Antoni M. Badia i Margarit 6.* Barcelona: Publicacions de l'Abadia de Montserrat; 1987. 388 pp. Notes. Lang.: Cat.

France. 1696-1841. Bibliographical studies. ■Part Two of a bibliography of Roussillon theatre in Catalan based on the legacy of Josep-Sebastià Pons. Works in the Tolrà collection in Bordas, the municipal library of Montpellier and the Pons collection.

2569 Bartalotta, Gianfranco. "*Mouchoir de Nuages* di Tristan Tzara." (*Handkerchief of Clouds* by Tristan Tzara.) *TeatrC.* 1987; 7(14): 141-155. Lang.: Ita.

France. Critical studies. ■Analysis of the play.

2570 Belzil, Patricia. "L'emblème du pouvoir." (The Emblem of Power.) *JCT.* 1987; 44: 30-35. Illus.: Photo. Print. B&W. 2. Lang.: Fre.

France. Canada: Montreal, PQ, Ottawa, ON. 1961-1987. Critical studies. ■An analysis of the symbols of power in the Brassard production of *Les Paravents (The Screens).*

2571 Britton, David. "Theatre, Popular and Special: And the Perils of Cultural Piracy." *Westerly.* 1987 Dec.; 32(4): 66-73. Lang.: Eng.

France: Paris. India. Australia: Perth. 1987. Histories-sources. ■Peter Brook discusses his production of *The Mahabharata* in terms of the characteristic of myth: The use of a quarry as a theatre, and an international cast. The thematic preoccupations of the work, its use of popular elements, and its Shakespearean quality. Rejects charges of cultural imperialism.

2572 de Gaulmyn, Pierre. *Claudel, les campagnes épistolaires. L'époque du 'Partage de Midi', 1904-1909.* (Claudel's Epistolary Campaigns: The 'Break of Noon' Era, 1904-1909.) Brussels: De Boeck Univ.; 1987. 230 pp. (Prisme: Textes/Société 1.) Pref. Biblio. Index. Lang.: Fre.

France. 1904-1909. Critical studies. ■Study of Claudel as playwright and Catholic, based on his letters to various literary and artistic correspondents.

2573 Hanley, Katharine Rose. *Dramatic Approaches to Creative Fidelity: A Study in the Theatre and Philosophy of Gabriel Marcel (1889-1973).* Lanham, MD: UP of America; 1987. 226 pp. Pref. Index. Biblio. Append. Illus.: Photo. Dwg. Print. B&W. 6. Lang.: Eng.

DRAMA: —Plays/librettos/scripts

France. 1889-1973. Biographical studies. ■Examines life and work of Gabriel Marcel, dramatist and musician: his philosophical approach to writing and music.

2574 Howarth, William D. *Molière: uno scrittore di teatro e il suo pubblico.* (Molière: A Playwright and His Audience.) Bologna: Il Mulino; 1987. 367 pp. (Saggi 314.) Pref. Index. Biblio. Append. Illus.: Pntg. Dwg. Lang.: Ita.
France. 1622-1673. Critical studies. ■Italian translation of Howarth's 1982 study.

2575 Kim, Hyo-Kyung. "Pi (Chio-se)." (Adaptations of Sartre's *The Wall.*) *DongukDA.* 1976 Dec.; 9: 151-159. Lang.: Kor.
France. Korea. 1939-1976. ■Adaptation of *Le Mur (The Wall).*

2576 Kim, Tai-Kwan. "Carmuswa sartre heuikokui bunseokkochal." (Analytic Comparison of Plays by Camus and Sartre.) *DongukDA.* 1978 Apr.; 10-11: 16-28. Lang.: Kor.
France. 1905-1978. Critical studies. ■Comparison of plays by Camus and Sartre.

2577 Klein, Jeanne. "Jean Jullien's *La Sérénade*: A *Comédie Rosse* Study." *MD.* 1987 Dec.; 30(4): 528-534. Notes. Lang.: Eng.
France. 1887-1987. Critical studies. ■Jullien's violations of decorum and *honneur* in *La Sérénade (The Serenade).*

2578 Kolesnikova, A. "Antifašistskie p'esy Armana Gatti." (The Anti-Fascist Plays of Armand Gatti.) *VMGUf.* 1987; 5: 64-69. Lang.: Rus.
France. 1924-1987. Critical studies. ■Discusses *L'enfant-rat (The Rat Child)*, *La deuxième existence du camp de Tatenberg (The Second Life of Camp Tatenberg)* and *Chroniques d'une planète provisoire (Chronicle of a Temporary Planet).*

2579 Kolesnikova, V.V. *Dramaturgija Armana Gatti: Avtoref. dis. kand. filol. nauk.* (Dramaturgy of Armand Gatti: Abstract of a Dissertation by a Candidate in Philology.) Moscow: MGU im. M.V. Lomonosova; 1987. 24 pp. Lang.: Rus.
France. 1924-1987. Critical studies.

2580 Lamar, Celita. "Norodom Sihanouk, a Hero of Our Times: Character Development in Hélène Cixous' Cambodian Epic." 157-166 in Hartigan, Karelisa V., ed. *From the Bard to Broadway.* Lanham, MD: UP of America; 1987. 222 pp. (Univ. of Florida Dept. of Classics Comparative Drama Conference Papers 7.) Pref. Notes. Biblio. Lang.: Eng.
France: Paris. 1985-1987. Critical studies. ■Analysis of text of Cixous' long-running production *L'histoire terrible mais inachevé de Norodom Sihanouk, roi du Cambodia (The Terrible But Unfinished Story of Norodom Sihanouk, King of Cambodia)*: depiction of historical truth, symbolic truth and human reality.

2581 Laughlin, Karen. "'Looking for sense...': The Spectator's Response to Beckett's *Come and Go.*" *MD.* 1987 June; 30(2): 137-146. Notes. [Presented at the 1984 ATA Convention in San Francisco.] Lang.: Eng.
France. 1968-1987. Critical studies. ■The text's indeterminacy analyzed in terms of Wolfgang Iser's reader-response theory.

2582 Lemahieu, Daniel. "Pour Vinaver." (For Vinaver.) *AdT.* 1987 Spr; 1(6): 127-136. Notes. Illus.: Dwg. 2. Lang.: Fre.
France. 1927-1987. Critical studies. ■Study of the plays of Michel Vinaver: characters, writing, discontinuity. Comparison with film director Jean-Luc Godard. Related to Media: Film.

2583 Lepine, Stephanie. "*Les paravents*: le plaisir de jeu." (*The Screens*: The Pleasure of Acting.) *JCT.* 1987; 44: 17-28. Illus.: Photo. Print. B&W. 7. Lang.: Fre.
France. Canada: Montreal, PQ, Ottawa, ON. 1961-1987. Critical studies. ■In-depth study of Jean Genet's *The Screens* with reference to the 1987 Canadian production by André Brassard.

2584 Levitt, Annette Shandler. "The Domestic Tragedies of Roger Vitrac." *MD.* 1987 Dec.; 30(4): 514-527. Notes. Lang.: Eng.
France. 1922-1928. Critical studies. ■Vitrac's critiques of bourgeois family life. Grp/movt: Surrealism.

2585 Marchand, Alain Bernard. "D'un metteur en scène et d'un texte: André Brassard et *Les Paravents* de Jean Genet." (A Director and a Text: André Brassard and *The Screens.*) *JCT.* 1987; 44: 36-41. Illus.: Photo. Print. B&W. 2. Lang.: Fre.
France. Canada: Montreal, PQ, Ottawa, ON. 1961-1987. Critical studies. ■An investigation into the text with reference to Brassard's Canadian production.

2586 McMullan, Audrey. "The Space of Play in *L'Impromptu d'Ohio.*" *MD.* 1987 Mar.; 30(1): 23-34. Notes. Lang.: Eng.
France. 1981-1987. Critical studies. ■Interaction of scenic imagery and narrative in *Ohio Impromptu*, which liberates being from materiality and incarnates it in fiction.

2587 Piette, Alain. "Michel de Ghelderode's *La Balade du Grand Macabre*: The Triumph of Life." 51-56 in Cardullo, Bert, ed. *Before His Eyes: Essays in Honor of Stanley Kauffmann.* Lanham, MD: UP of America; 1986. 185 pp. Pref. Notes. Biblio. Lang.: Eng.
France. 1934. Critical studies. ■Theme of death in Ghelderode's *La Balade du Grand Macabre (The Grand Macabre's Stroll).*

2588 Shevtsova, Maria. "The Consumption of Empty Signs: Jean Genet's *The Balcony.*" *MD.* 1987 Mar.; 30(1): 35-45. Notes. Lang.: Eng.
France. 1958-1987. Critical studies. ■*Mise-en-abîme* produces, and simultaneously undermines, an allegory of capitalist society in *Le Balcon (The Balcony).*

2589 States, Bert O. "*Catastrophe*: Beckett's Laboratory/Theatre." *MD.* 1987 Mar.; 30(1): 14-22. Notes. Lang.: Eng.
France. 1982-1987. Critical studies. ■Beckett links the theme of political persecution to the voyeurism of the theatrical experience.

2590 Wellington, Marie. *The Art of Voltaire's Theatre: An Exploration of Possibility.* Amer. Univ. Studies. New York: Peter Lang P; 1987. 260 pp. (Series ii, Romance Languages & Literature 61.) Index. Notes. Biblio. Append. Lang.: Eng.
France. 1718-1778. Histories-sources. ■Examination of Voltaire's dramaturgy, emphasizing his approach to comedy. His technique, themes of character types and dramatic situations. Comedy and *drame* are examined.

2591 Böttcher, Kurt; Rosenberg, Rainer; Richter, Helmut; Krohn, Paul Günter; Wruck, Peter. *Geschichte der deutschen Literatur im 19. Jahrhundert. Vom Vormärz zum Naturalismus.* (History of German 19th-Century Literature. From *Vormärz* to Naturalism.) Berlin: Volk und Wissen; 1987. 747 pp. Pref. Index. Notes. Illus.: Photo. B&W. Lang.: Ger.
Germany. Austria. 1830-1900. Histories-general. ■History of 19th-century German literature, containing chapters on drama and theatre in each treated period. Grp/movt: Naturalism; *Vormärz.*

2592 Elwood, William R. "Ernst Toller's *Masse Mensch*: The Individual vs. The Collective." 43-50 in Hartigan, Karelisa V., ed. *From the Bard to Broadway.* Lanham, MD: UP of America; 1987. 222 pp. (Univ. of Florida Dept. of Classics Comparative Drama Conference Papers 7.) Pref. Notes. Biblio. Lang.: Eng.
Germany. 1921-1987. Critical studies. ■Reinterpretation of the theme of *Masse Mensch*: salvation of the indvidual vs. the salvation of the masses.

2593 Gadberry, Glen W. "Hauptmann's *Before Sunrise* (Berlin) and Wilbrandt's *Master of Palmyra* (Vienna): German Antipodes of 1889." 79-86 in Hartigan, Karelisa V., ed. *From the Bard to Broadway.* Lanham, MD: UP of America; 1987. 222 pp. (Univ. of Florida Dept. of Classics Comparative Drama Conference Papers 7.) Pref. Notes. Biblio. Lang.: Eng.
Germany: Berlin. Austria: Vienna. 1889-1987. Historical studies. ■Both Wilbrandt's *Der The Meister von Palmyra (Master of Palmyra)* and Hauptmann's *Vor Sonnenaufgang (Before Sunrise)* premiered in 1889. Hauptmann's drama was hailed as a triumph of German Naturalism, while Wilbrandt and his play have been forgotten. Author examines both plays as polar opposites of German drama of the period.

2594 Gallo, Pasquale. *Il teatro dialettico di Heiner Müller.* (The Dialectic Theatre of Heiner Müller.) Lecce: Milella; 1987. 147 pp. (Contemporanea 10.) Biblio. Lang.: Ita.

DRAMA: —Plays/librettos/scripts

Germany: Berlin. 1929-1987. Critical studies. ■Analysis of Müller's plays.

2595 Hammer, Klaus, ed. *Dramaturgische Schriften des 19. Jahrhunderts.* (Dramaturgical Studies of the 19th Century.) Berlin: Henschelverlag; 1987. 1379 pp. Pref. Notes. Biblio. Index. [2 vol.] Lang.: Ger.
Germany. 1800-1900. Critical studies. ■70 famous German 19th century authors: poets, dramaturgs, critics, historians on different aspects of theory and practice of drama, for mostly German but including Shakespeare and Greek tragedy.

2596 Hilliker, Rebecca. "Strindberg and Munch: The Powerlessness of the Individual Before the Great Forces of Love and Death." 107-124 in Hartigan, Karelisa V., ed. *From the Bard to Broadway.* Lanham, MD: UP of America; 1987. 222 pp. (Univ. of Florida Dept. of Classics Comparative Drama Conference Papers 7.) Pref. Notes. Biblio. Illus.: Photo. Print. B&W. 5. Lang.: Eng.
Germany: Berlin. 1892-1900. Critical studies. ■Strindberg and Munch's symbolic treatment of sexual confrontations depicting the individual as powerless before the great forces of love and death. Emphasizes Munch's influence on Strindberg.

2597 Lee, Yong-Hi. "Kandinsky *Der gelbe Klang* ui gujoya kineung." (The Structure and Function of Kandinsky's *The Yellow Sound.*) *DongukDA.* 1976 Dec.; 9: 64-79. Lang.: Kor.
Germany. 1896-1914. Critical studies. ■The theories of Wassily Kandinsky and analysis of his play *Der gelbe Klang (The Yellow Sound).*

2598 Müller, Péter P. "Aber die Geschichte schweigt nicht. Goethes *Geschichte Gottfriedens von Berlichingen mit der eisernen Hand,* dramatisiert als Beginn der deutschen Geschichtsdramatik." (But History Doesn't Keep Silence: Goethe's *Story of Gottfried von Berlichingen with the Iron Hand, Dramatized* as the Beginning of German Historical Drama.) *ZG.* 1987; 8(2): 141-159. Lang.: Ger.
Germany. 1749-1832. Critical studies. ■Analysis of plot and characters in *Geschichte Gottfriedens von Berlichingen mit der eisernen Hand, dramatisiert* (or *Götz von Berlichingen*) aims at showing the active individual in social revolutionary situations.

2599 Norton, Michael L. "Of 'Stages' and 'Types' in *Visitatione Sepulchri* (Part I)." *CompD.* 1987 Spr; 21(1): 34-61. Notes. MU. Lang.: Eng.
Germany. France. 900-1600. Historical studies. ■Examination of the stages of the *visitatio sepulchri.* Comparison of the staging theories of Carl Lange and Gustav Milchsack. Part II in CompD, 1987 Sum (21:2), 127-144.

2600 Nössig, Manfred. "Bertolt Brecht und die Berliner Arbeiter." (Bertolt Brecht and the Berlin Workers.) *TZ.* 1987; 42 (7): 14-19. Tables. Illus.: Photo. B&W. 3. Lang.: Ger.
Germany: Berlin. 1922-1932. Historical studies. ■Brecht's relation to events of the Berlin workers' movement and their reflection in his plays and stagings.

2601 Rohmer, Rolf. "Hauptmann und die anderen." (Hauptmann and the Others.) *TZ.* 1987; 42(11): 8-13. Illus.: Photo. B&W. 16. Lang.: Ger.
Germany. 1890-1987. Critical studies. ■On critical reception of naturalism and realism, influenced by present search for a European cultural identity: reception of Gerhart Hauptmann's later plays.

2602 Scamardi, Teodoro. *Teatro della quotidianità in Germania. Dagli psicogrammi sociali di M. Fleisser all'antitheater di R.W. Fassbinder.* (Theatre of the Ordinary in Germany: From the Social Psychograms of Fleisser to Fassbinder's Anti-Theatre.) Bari: Dedalo; 1987. 173 pp. Lang.: Ita.
Germany. 1900-1987. Critical studies. ■Analysis of the works of Marieluise Fleisser, Martin Sperr, Franz Xaver Kroetz and Rainer Werner Fassbinder.

2603 Schrader, Bärbel. "Brechts *Leben des Galilei.*" (Brecht's *The Life of Galilei.*) *WB.* 1988; 34(2): 199-212. Notes. Lang.: Ger.

Germany. USA. 1938-1956. Critical studies. ■Genesis and changes of Brecht's *The Life of Galileo* (several versions, depending on political development).

2604 Stellmacher, Wolfgang. "Schillers späte Dramen: Experimente im klassischen Stil." (Schiller's Late Dramas: Experiments in Classical Style.) *WB.* 1988; 34(5): 761-780. Lang.: Eng.
Germany. 1799-1805. Critical studies. ■Schiller's dramatic conception after his *Wallenstein* trilogy: growing neglect of historicity, growing aestheticization of historical processes and morality as centre of plot.

2605 Birringer, Johannes. "Brecht and Medea: Heiner Müller's Synthetic Fragments." *TA.* 1987; 42: 1-15. Notes. Lang.: Eng.
Germany, East. 1940-1984. Critical studies. ■Heiner Müller's earlier Brecht-inspired plays lead to post-modernist 'synthetic fragments' technique of his later plays. Comparison of Müller's and Brecht's style.

2606 Dieckmann, Friedrich. "*Galilei*-Komplikationen." (Complications in *Galilei.*) *WB.* 1988; 34(2): 213-229. Notes. Lang.: Ger.
Germany, East. 1938-1956. Critical studies. ■Analysis of the title character in Brecht's *The Life of Galileo,* emphasizing the contradiction of the treachery and the progressive scientific productivity.

2607 Fiebach, Joachim. "Nach Brecht—von Brecht aus—von ihm fort? Heiner Müllers Texte seit den siebziger Jahren." (After Brecht—Out of Brecht—Away from Him? Heiner Müller's Playtexts Since the Seventies.) 171-188 in Heise, Wolfgang. *Brecht 88. Anregungen zum Dialog über die Vernunft am Jahrtausendende.* Berlin: Henschelverlag; 1987. 351 pp. Notes. Lang.: Ger.
Germany, East: Berlin. 1972-1987. Critical studies. ■Significance of dream-structures in Müller's plays, compared with those in Brecht's.

2608 Ichikawa, Akira. "Heiner Müller's 'Vorgeschichte'-Dramen." (Heiner Müller's Prehistory Dramas.) *ZG.* 1988; 9(1): 59-64. Lang.: Ger.
Germany, East. 1976-1986. Critical studies. ■Heiner Müller's view on history as reflected in his plays.

2609 Klatt, Gudrun. "'Modebuch' und Diskussionen 'über das Leben selbst'. Ulrich Plenzdorfs *Die neuen Leiden des jungen W.*" (A 'Fashionable Book' and Discussions 'On Life as It Is': Ulrich Plenzdorf's *The New Sorrows of Young W.*) 361-397 in Münz-Koenen, Inge, ed. *Werke und Wirkungen. DDR-Literatur in der Diskussion.* Leipzig: Reclam; 1987. 397 pp. Notes. Lang.: Ger.
Germany, East. 1972-1987. Critical studies. ■On the play and its social context, its relations to Goethe's novel, *Werthers Leiden.*

2610 Lederer, Herbert. *Handbook of East German Drama 1945-1985.* New York: Peter Lang; 1987. 276 pp. (DDR-Studien/East German Studies.) Index. Lang.: Eng.
Germany, East. 1945-1985. ■Compilation of over 700 names of East German dramatists and their works. Brief biographical sketch, list of playwright's works in chronological order with dates, original German title and English translation.

2611 Lyon, James K. "Brecht and Money." *TJ.* 1987; 39(4): 487-497. Notes. Biblio. Lang.: Eng.
Germany, East. 1920-1930. Biographical studies. ■Brecht's conviction of the influential role of money in society—an insight he incorporated in his early dramas. Plays present conflicts in which people use money to repress others.

2612 Pietzsch, Ingeborg; Bereczky, Erzsébet, transl. "Uj drámák és rendezések az NDK-ban." (New Dramas and Stage Arrangements in the GDR.) *Sz.* 1987 June; 20(6): 45-48. Illus.: Photo. B&W. 1. Lang.: Hun.
Germany, East. 1985-1986. Critical studies. ■Overview of current theatrical tendencies, with discussion of few specific plays and outstanding directors.

2613 Reichel, Peter. *Resümee mit Trendmarkierungen. Autor—Werk—Wirkung. Die DDR-Dramatik in der Mitte der 80er Jahre.* (A Summary Showing Trends: Authors—Works—Effects. GDR Drama in the Mid-1980s.) Berlin: Verband

DRAMA: —Plays/librettos/scripts

der Theaterschaffenden der DDR; 1987. 124 pp. (MT 207.) Index. Lang.: Ger.

Germany, East. 1984-1986. Critical studies. ■Analysis of GDR drama and theatre: problems, conflicts, authors' positions, author/theatre relationship.

2614 Reichel, Peter. "En passant. Zitate und Notate zu Christoph Heins *Passage*." (In Passing: Quotations and Notes on Christoph Hein's *Passage*.) *TZ*. 1987; 42(5): 50-53. Illus.: Photo. B&W. 1. Lang.: Ger.

Germany, East. 1987. Critical studies. ■Subject, structure, language and historical background of *Passage*, relations to other works of Christoph Hein.

2615 Streisand, Marianne. "Heiner Müller's *Der Lohndrücker*. Zu verschiedenen Zeiten ein anderes Stück." (Heiner Müller's *Undercutting*: At Different Times Another Play.) 306-360 in Münz-Koenen, Inge, ed. *Werke und Wirkungen. DDR-Literatur in der Diskussion*. Leipzig: Reclam; 1987. 397 pp. Notes. Lang.: Ger.

Germany, East. 1956-1987. Critical studies. ■On the stage history of Heiner Müller's *Der Lohndrücker*: structure of the text as basis of various interpretations.

2616 Eisner, Nicholas. "*Theatertheater/Theaterspiele*: The Plays of Thomas Bernhard." *MD*. 1987 Mar.; 30(1): 104-114. Notes. [First presented before CAUTG section of Learned Societies Conference, Winnipeg, 1986.] Lang.: Eng.

Germany, West. 1974-1983. Critical studies. ■The metadramatic nature of Bernhard's plays.

2617 Jaspers, Karl. *Del tragico*. (On the Tragic.) Milan: Studio Editoriale; 1987. 82 pp. (Piccola Enciclopedia 35.) Lang.: Ita.

Germany, West. 1952. Critical studies. ■Italian translation *Über das Tragische*.

2618 Albini, Umberto. *Viaggio nel teatro classico*. (A Journey in the Classical Theatre.) Florence: Le Monnier; 1987. 185 pp. (Bibliotechina del Saggiatore 48.) Lang.: Ita.

Greece. 500 B.C.-1987 A.D. Critical studies. ■Collection of essays, some previously published, on Greek theatre and modern treatments and stagings.

2619 Baldry, H.C. *I greci a teatro. Spettacoli e forme della tragedia*. (The Greek Tragic Theatre.) Rome-Bari: Laterza; 1987. Lang.: Ita.

Greece. 500-400 B.C. Critical studies. ■Italian translation of *The Greek Tragic Theatre* by H.C. Baldry.

2620 Constantinidis, Stratos E. "The New Dionysus of Modern Greek Poetic Drama: Crucifix or Grapevine?" 21-31 in Hartigan, Karelisa V., ed. *From the Bard to Broadway*. Lanham, MD: UP of America; 1987. 222 pp. (Univ. of Florida Dept. of Classics Comparative Drama Conference Papers 7.) Pref. Notes. Biblio. Lang.: Eng.

Greece. 1987. Critical studies. ■New interpretation of modern Greek poetic drama using the Dionysian: a union between the conscious and the subconscious. Emphasizes Euripides' *The Bacchae*.

2621 Constantinidis, Stratos E. "The Rebirth of Tragedy: Protest and Evolution of Modern Greek Drama." *CompD*. 1987 Sum; 21 (2): 156-181. Notes. Lang.: Eng.

Greece. 1940-1987. Critical studies. ■Two styles of contemporary Greek theatre: realism/rationalism vs. imagination and poetry. Considers works of Sikelianos, Kazantzakis, Palamas and Politis.

2622 Kim, Jeang-Ho. "Heuilabbikukui hyungsikkwa keu euieui." (The Form and Meanings of Greek Tragedy.) *DongukDA*. 1978 Apr.; 10-11: 66-80. Lang.: Kor.

Greece. 500-400 B.C. Critical studies. ■Structure and plot of ancient Greek tragedies.

2623 Mihályi, Gábor. *A klasszikus görög dráma mult és jelen ütközésében*. (The Classical Greek Drama in the Conflict of Past and Present.) Budapest: Akadémiai K.; 1987. 187 pp. (Korunk tudományi.) Notes. Lang.: Hun.

Greece. 472-388 B.C. Critical studies. ■Analysis by type and dramaturgy of the Greek tragedy and comedy.

2624 Porter, David H. *'Only Connect': Three Studies in Greek Tragedy*. Lanham, MD: UP of America; 1987. 128 pp. Lang.: Eng.

Greece. 400 B.C.-500 A.D. Critical studies. ■New studies on three Greek tragedies: Aeschylus' *Seven Against Thebes*, Sophocles' *Antigone* and Euripides' *Heracles*.

2625 Slater, Niall W. "Transformations of Space in New Comedy." *TID*. 1987; 9: 1-10. Notes. Lang.: Eng.

Greece: Athens. Italy: Rome. 400 B.C.-180 A.D. Historical studies. ■Change in the use of physical theatre space when the New Comedy emerged in ancient Athens. Influence on Roman theatre through Terence.

2626 Stanton, Robert. "A Defense of the *Deus Ex Machina* in Euripides' *Orestes*." *TA*. 1987; 42: 53-59. Notes. Lang.: Eng.

Greece. 408 B.C. Critical studies. ■Argues that Euripides' use of *deus ex machina* is a fitting solution to a drama in which characters have invoked the god Apollo.

2627 "Róma pusztulásától a szanálásra itélt külvárosi házig (Spiró György drámáiról)." (From the Destruction of Rome to the Suburban House Condemned to 'Reorganization': On György Spiró's Dramas.) *Jelenkor*. 1987 Jan.; 30(1): 66-76. Lang.: Hun.

Hungary. 1982-1986. Critical studies. ■Study of the plays of György Spiró: he shares with other Eastern European writers a tendency to alternate between abstract philosophical plays and realism.

2628 Beck, András. "'Ki az a te vagy az?' Kornis Mihály: Ki vagy te?" ('Who Is the Is It You?' Mihály Kornis: Who Are You?)*Jelenkor*. 1987 Sep.; 30(9): 858-860. Lang.: Hun.

Hungary. 1980-1987. Critical studies. ■Study of three plays by Mihály Kornis: *Hallelluja*, *Büntetések (Punishments)* and a montage of Kafka's works, *Kozma*.

2629 Bécsy, Tamás. "Jó témák—álmonológokban." (Good Subjects—In Pseudo-Monologues.) *Sz*. 1987 Oct.; 20(10): 11-20. Illus.: Photo. B&W. 8. Lang.: Hun.

Hungary. 1986-1987. Critical studies. ■Ideas in connection with the Hungarian dramas performed in 1986/87—or, why do interesting subjects become uninteresting plays.

2630 Bécsy, Tamás. "Társasági normák és kettős jelentések. *Az ördög* a Madách Szinházban." (Social Norms and Double Meanings: *The Devil* at the Madách Theatre.) *Sz*. 1987 Aug.; 20(8): 11-20. Illus.: Photo. B&W. 4. Lang.: Hun.

Hungary: Budapest. 1987. Critical studies. ■In connection with *Az ördög* (*The Devil*) directed by György Lengyel considerations on Ferenc Molnár the playwright.

2631 Csizner, Ildikó. "Az újjászületo üdvtan. Négy Németh László-bemutatóról." (Salvation Science Reborn: On Four László Németh Openings.) *Sz*. 1987 May; 20(5): 23-28. Illus.: Photo. B&W. 4. Lang.: Hun.

Hungary. 1986-1987. Critical studies. ■Analysis of the plays of László Németh, one of the most important contemporary Hungarian playwrights, focusing on his permanent concern always present in his works: The conflicts of a person willing to make sacrifices for the sake of others, a group of people, a cause or a nation. The stage history of his plays.

2632 Katona, Anna B. "Ideological Implications of Absurd Drama." *TA*. 1987(42): 39-52. Notes. Lang.: Eng.

Hungary. 1970-1980. Historical studies. ■Absurdist plays by Hungarian playwrights including István Örkény, Istvan Csarka and Miklós Méjzöly as a response to failed Marxism. Definitions of absurdism by Esslin and Camus.

2633 Koltai, Tamás. "Számomra a dráma kísérletezo müfaj. Beszélgetés Spiró Györggyel." (Drama Is an Experimental Genre For Me: Interview with György Spiró.) *Krit*. 1987 Oct.(10): 11-13. Illus.: Photo. B&W. 2. [Close-Up of Katona József Theatre.] Lang.: Hun.

Hungary. 1962-1987. Histories-sources. ■György Spiró speaks about his career as dramaturg and playwright, his relation to Hungarian theatre in general and especially to Csiky Gergely Theatre in Kaposvár and

DRAMA: —Plays/librettos/scripts

Katona József Theatre in Budapest and about his outstanding play, *Chickenhead.*

2634 Lengyel, Menyhért; Vinkó, József, comp. *Életem könyve: Naplók, életrajzi töredékek.* (The Book of My Life: Diaries, Biographical Fragments.) Budapest: Gondolat; 1987. 517 pp. Pref. Notes. Index. Illus.: Photo. B&W. 1. Lang.: Hun.
Hungary. 1880-1974. Biographical studies. ∎Selections from diary of playwright and scenarist Ményhert (Melchior) Lengyel: Reviewed in *Sz* 20: 7 (1987 July), 7-11. Related to Media: Film.

2635 Márton, László. "Amíg a lepkéket kalapra tűzik." (Until the Butterflies are Fastened to the Hat.) *FSM.* 1987 Feb.; 31(8): 6. Illus.: Photo. B&W. 1. Lang.: Hun.
Hungary. 1982-1987. Histories-sources. ∎László Márton, young dramatist, speaks about the birth of his drama *Lepkék a Kalapon (Butterflies on Your Hat)*, a stage adaptation of Elek Gozsdu's novel *Köd (Fog)*.

2636 Brook, Peter. "A Storyteller with Many Heads." *AmTh.* 1987 Dec.; 4(9): 29-30. Lang.: Eng.
India. 1987. Histories-sources. ∎Director Peter Brook discusses his views on *The Mahabharata.*

2637 Bertha, Csilla. "Tragedies of National Fate: A Comparison Between Brian Friel's *Translations* and its Hungarian Counterpart, András Sütős *A szuzai menyegző.*" *IUR.* 1987 Fall; 17(2): 207-222. Notes. Lang.: Eng.
Ireland. Hungary. 1981. Critical studies. ∎Examination of Brian Friel's *Translations* in light of its themes of nationalism and imperialism concentrated in the issue of language.

2638 Blake, Ann. "Brian Friel and the Irish Theatre." *ADS.* 1987 Apr.; 10: 107-117. Lang.: Eng.
Ireland. 1929-1987. Critical studies. ∎Recurrent themes in Friel's plays: time and change, love and memory. Includes commentary on his attitudes towards politics and art.

2639 Evans, Thomas G. "The American Motif in the Irish Literary Renaissance: The Old Lady's Lost Children." *Eire.* 1987 Fall; 22(3): 4-14. Notes. Lang.: Eng.
Ireland. 1900-1930. Critical studies. ∎Irish Literary Renaissance writers' view of America, especially the link between Ireland and America. Themes of anti-Catholicism, the rebellion and optimism are discussed. Focus on novels and drama.

2640 Fitzgibbon, T. Gerald. "Thomas Murphy's Dramatic Vocabulary." *IUR.* 1987 Spr; 17(1): 41-50. Notes. Lang.: Eng.
Ireland. 1961-1984. Critical studies. ∎Analysis of playwright Thomas Murphy's use of theatrical language (as opposed to traditional literary language) in selected plays. Identification of and contrasting of each play's various 'languages' is paramount.

2641 Griffin, Christopher. "'The Audacity of Despair': *The Morning After Optimism.*" *IUR.* 1987 Spr; 17(1): 62-70. Notes. Lang.: Eng.
Ireland. 1971. Critical studies. ∎Brief analysis of Thomas Murphy's *The Morning After Optimism*: its fairytale qualities, theatrical conventions and manic, motley language styles. Some comparison to previous Irish playwrights, notably Samuel Beckett and Sean O'Casey.

2642 Hadfield, Paul. "Kazimierz Braun on Theatre." *ThIr.* 1983 Sep-Dec.; 4: 26-27. Illus.: Photo. B&W. 1. Lang.: Eng.
Ireland: Dublin. Poland. 1981-1983. Histories-sources. ∎Kazimierz Braun, noted Polish director, comments on transference of continental European drama to Irish stage, particularly the works of Różewicz, and speculates on how drama informs modern European political agendas.

2643 Harvey, Karen J.; Pry, Kevin B. "John O'Keeffe as an Irish Playwright Within the Theatrical, Social, and Economic Context of his Time." *Eire.* 1987 Spr; 22(1): 19-43. Notes. Lang.: Eng.
Ireland. England: London. 1767-1798. Critical studies. ∎A reassessment of 18th-century comic playwright John O'Keeffe, usually classified with British comedy of the period, as an Irish playwright. Concentrates on how O'Keeffe's plays comment on Ireland and the Irish from the viewpoint of a native Irishman.

2644 Holladay, William. "Song as Aesthetic Manipulation in Sean O'Casey's Dublin Trilogy." 125-137 in Hartigan, Karelisa V., ed. *From the Bard to Broadway.* Lanham, MD:

UP of America; 1987. 222 pp. (Univ. of Florida Dept. of Classics Comparative Drama Conference Papers 7.) Pref. Notes. Biblio. Lang.: Eng.
Ireland. 1923-1926. Critical studies. ∎Popular songs in the Dublin trilogy plays *The Shadow of a Gunman, Juno and the Paycock* and *The Plough and the Stars* by Sean O'Casey. Music manipulates an emotional response from the audience.

2645 Knapp, James F. "History Against Myth: Lady Gregory and Cultural Discourse." *Eire.* 1987 Fall; 22(3): 30-42. Notes. Lang.: Eng.
Ireland: Dublin. 1900-1930. Critical studies. ∎Mikhail Bakhtin's theory of cultural dialogue, an examination of how Irish Literary Revival writers used language to bridge Irish-Catholic and Protestant Ascendancy cultures.

2646 Laity, Cassandra. "Yeats' Changing Images of Maud Gonne." *Eire.* 1987 Sum; 22(2): 56-69. Lang.: Eng.
Ireland: Dublin. 1900-1930. Critical studies. ∎Analysis of Yeats's dramatic depictions of women in light of his use of the 'psychology' of Maud Gonne: his women characters as reflections of or warnings to his real-life love interest, actress and political revolutionary.

2647 McArdle, Kathy. "*The Blue Macushla*: Anatomy of a Failure." *IUR.* 1987 Spr; 17(1): 82-89. Notes. Lang.: Eng.
Ireland. 1980-1986. Critical studies. ∎Brief analysis of Thomas Murphy's *The Blue Macushla* in regard to its use of the gangster movie form and character role-playing. Also discussed is Americanism vs. Irishness. Related to Media: Film.

2648 Mercier, Vivian. "Noisy Desperation: Murphy and the Book of Job." *IUR.* 1987 Spr; 17(1): 18-23. Notes. Lang.: Eng.
Ireland. 1962-1983. Critical studies. ∎Analysis of Thomas Murphy's comic, protesting characters in light of the Book of Job.

2649 Mizejewski, Linda. "Patriarchy and the Female in Lady Gregory's *Grania.*" *Eire.* 1987 Spr; 22(1): 123-138. Notes. Lang.: Eng.
Ireland: Dublin. 1910-1930. Critical studies. ∎Analysis of Lady Gregory's tragedy *Grania* as a counterweight to the Deirdre tale often told in drama of the Irish Literary Revival. Also, an examination of the play's departures from the Gaelic folktale.

2650 Murray, Christopher. "Introduction: The Rough and Holy Theatre of Thomas Murphy." *IUR.* 1987 Spr; 17(1): 9-17. Notes. Illus.: Photo. B&W. 1. Lang.: Eng.
Ireland: Dublin. 1962-1986. Critical studies. ∎Analysis of the plays of Thomas Murphy in light of Peter Brook's idea of 'rough theatre' and 'holy theatre'.

2651 Niel, Ruth. "Digging into History: A Reading of Brian Friel's *Volunteers* and Seamus Heaney's *Viking Dublin: Trial Pieces.*" *IUR.* 1986 Spr; 16(1): 35-47. Notes. Lang.: Eng.
Ireland: Dublin. UK-Ireland. 1975. Critical studies. ∎Examination of the metaphor of archaeological digging in Brian Friel's play *Volunteers* and in Seamus Heaney's poetry. Emphasis is on the political and historical dimension of the past in the present.

2652 O'Dwyer, Riana. "Play-Acting and Myth-Making: The Western Plays of Thomas Murphy." *IUR.* 1987 Spr; 17(1): 31-40. Notes. Lang.: Eng.
Ireland. 1961-1986. Critical studies. ∎An exploration of the debunking of the myth of idyllic peasant life in western Ireland by playwright Thomas Murphy, especially in his plays set in Ireland's rural West.

2653 O'Toole, Fintan. "Homo Abscondius: The Apocalyptic Imagination in *The Gigli Concert.*" *IUR.* 1987 Spr; 17(1): 90-99. Notes. Lang.: Eng.
Ireland. 1983. Critical studies. ∎Brief analysis of Thomas Murphy's *The Gigli Concert* in light of the language and imagery of Christian thought, especially the legend of Faust and the ideas of damnation and salvation. Some reference to Jungian psychology.

2654 O'Valle, Violet M. "Deliberate Distortions of Grail Motifs, Solar Myth and Bird Metaphor in Sean O'Casey's *The Silver Tassie.*" *Eire.* 1987 Fall; 22(3): 58-74. Notes. Illus.: Sketches. 1. Lang.: Eng.

DRAMA: —Plays/librettos/scripts

Ireland. 1928. Critical studies. ▪Feminine life symbols in Sean O'Casey's *The Silver Tassie*. Symbols are related to the legend of the Holy Grail and Celtic sun worship.

2655 Roche, Anthony. "*Bailegangaire*: Storytelling into Drama." *IUR*. 1987 Spr; 17(1): 114-128. Notes. Lang.: Eng.

Ireland: Galway. 1985. Critical studies. ▪Brief analysis of Thomas Murphy's *Bailegangaire*, especially its Galway connections and significances. Emphasis is on Gaelic bases of its language and storytelling. Comparisons are drawn with Samuel Beckett.

2656 Stembridge, Gerard. "Murphy's Language of Theatrical Empathy." *IUR*. 1987 Spr; 17(1): 51-61. Notes. Lang.: Eng.

Ireland. 1962-1978. Critical studies. ▪Analysis of playwright Thomas Murphy's use of the alienating as well as liberating aspects of dramatic language in selected plays. Overall focus is on the plays' themes with regard to language.

2657 Toibin, Colm. "Thomas Murphy's Volcanic Ireland." *IUR*. 1987 Spr; 17(1): 24-30. Notes. Lang.: Eng.

Ireland. 1962-1986. Critical studies. ▪Examination of the historical accuracy of playwright Thomas Murphy's characters, especially those of the dispossessed class of Gaelic-Irish tenant farmers. Issues revolve around class, status and town vs. farm.

2658 White, Harry. "*The Sanctuary Lamp*: An Assessment." *IUR*. 1987 Spr; 17(1): 71-81. Lang.: Eng.

Ireland. 1976-1986. Critical studies. ▪Brief analysis of the text of Thomas Murphy's *The Sanctuary Lamp* in relation to the concept of spiritual mystery, that is, the irrational force of art. Comparison to Murphy's later (post-1976) plays.

2659 Wiley, Catherine. "Recreating Ballybeg: Two Translations by Brian Friel." *JDTC*. 1987; 1(2): 51-61. Notes. Lang.: Eng.

Ireland. 1987. Critical studies. ▪Playwright Brian Friel translates the imagined and material events of Ireland's history into the present time through his dramatic works. Focus on his plays *Aristocrats* and *Translations*.

2660 Ben-Shahar, Rina. "Bahayat Targuman shell Milot Pnyia, Kelalot, Keriyot Ve Kesharym Reykim Kefy shehy Mishtaakefet Be-machazot Sheturgemu Le-yiurit Me-anglyt Vetzarfatit." (Terms of Address in Plays Translated from English and French into Hebrew.) *Bamah*. 1987; 22(108): 51-57. Lang.: Heb.

Israel. 1987. Critical studies. ▪Difficulty that Hebrew translators experience in translating slang and everyday words.

2661 Andreoli, Annamaria. *Gabriele D'Annunzio*. Scandicci (Florence): La Nuova Italia; 1987. 280 pp. Index. Illus.: Dwg. Photo. Print. Color. B&W. Lang.: Ita.

Italy. 1863-1938. Biographies. ▪Biography of the playwright.

2662 Bazzoni, Jana O'Keefe. "The Carnival Motif in Pirandello's Drama." *MD*. 1987 Sep.; 30(3): 414-425. Notes. Lang.: Eng.

Italy. 1916-1929. Critical studies. ▪The carnival pattern in village, city and theatre plays from *Pensaci, Giacomino (Better Think Twice About It)* to *Questa sera si recita a soggetto (Tonight We Improvise)*.

2663 Biasin, Gian Paolo, ed.; Perella, Nicolas J., ed. *Pirandello 1986*. Rome: Bulzoni; 1987. 219 pp. (UC-Berkeley, Il Cerchio 3.) Lang.: Ita, Eng.

Italy. 1904-1936. Critical studies. ▪A collection of essays on Pirandello's literary works, from 1986 conference at the University of California, Berkeley.

2664 Bosisio, Paolo. "Un rendez-vous manqué: Marivaux e Goldoni." (A Missed Encounter: Marivaux and Goldoni.) *BiT*. 1987; 5/6: 189-217. Lang.: Ita.

Italy: Venice. France. 1707-1763. Critical studies. ▪The characters, the scenes, the skirmishes, the plots imply the two authors' affinities and differences, together with the cues, which they both offer and exploit, on the background of Italian actors in France.

2665 Cappello, Giovanni. *Quando Pirandello cambia titolo: occasionalità o strategia?* (When Pirandello Changed Titles: Chance or Strategy?)Milan: Mursia; 1986. 357 pp. (Civiltà letteraria del Novecento: saggi 38.) Lang.: Ita.

Italy. 1867-1936. Critical studies. ▪The problem of the change of titles in Pirandello's plays and narrative works.

2666 Ciarletta, Nicola. "*Lo spirito della morte* di Rosso di San Secondo confrontato con *La vita che ti diedi* di Pirandello." (*The Spirit of Death* by Rosso di San Secondo Compared with *The Life I Gave You* by Pirandello.) *TeatrC*. 1987; 7 (14): 133-140. Lang.: Ita.

Italy. 1923-1931. Critical studies. ▪A comparative analysis of the works.

2667 Čirva, A. Ju. *Dramaturgija Seneki i rimskij teatr ego vremeni: Avtoref. dis. kand. iskusstvovedenija.* (Seneca's Drama and Roman Theatre of His Time: Abstract of a Dissertation by a Candidate in Art Criticism.) Leningrad: LGITMiK; 1987. 20 pp. Lang.: Rus.

Italy: Rome. 4 B.C.-65 A.D. Historical studies.

2668 d'Amico, Alessandro. "Due 'Notizie' dal secondo volume di *Maschere nude*." (Two 'Notes' from the Second Volume of *Naked Masks*.) *TeatroS*. 1987; 2(2): 347-379. Lang.: Ita.

Italy. 1887-1986. Critical studies. ▪Pre-print of the introduction to Luigi Pirandello's plays *Ma non è una cosa seria (It's Nothing Serious)* and *Il giuoco delle parti (The Rules of the Game)*.

2669 Juralaro, Rosario. "Per una storia del teatro pugliese." (Toward a History of the Apulian Theatre.) *Ariel*. 1987; 2(1): 73-83. Lang.: Ita.

Italy. 1600-1900. Critical studies. ▪A study on three Apulian works: *Il martirio di s. Thèodoro (The Martyrdom of Saint Theodore)* by Antonio Monetta, *Li travianti fratelli (The Wayward Brothers)* by Pietro Suscio, *Nniccu Furcedda* by Girolamo Bax.

2670 Knapp, Bettina. "Machine and Magus in Pirandello's *Tonight We Improvise*." *MD*. 1987 Sep.; 30(3): 405-413. Notes. Lang.: Eng.

Italy. 1929-1987. Critical studies. ▪Machines—animate and inanimate—in *Tonight We Improvise (Questa sera si recita a soggetto)*.

2671 Mancini, Andrea. "*Amleto* di Bacchelli. Dall'Olimpico di Vicenza al Convegno di Milano." (*Amleto* by Bacchelli: From the Olimpico Theatre in Vicenza to the Convegno in Milan.) *Ariel*. 1987; 2(1): 93-145. Lang.: Ita.

Italy. 1919-1957. Critical studies. ▪Annotation about *Amleto (Hamlet)* by Riccardo Bacchelli and the eventual publication of the text.

2672 Mango, Achille. "Luigi Pirandello: il personaggio." (Luigi Pirandello: the Character.) *BiT*. 1987; 8: 1-18. Lang.: Ita.

Italy. 1867-1936. Critical studies. ▪The theme of the character is the central feature of Pirandello's theatre.

2673 Marinetti, Filippo Tommaso; Bertoni, Alberto, ed. *Taccuini 1915-1921*. (Note-books 1915-1921.) Bologna: Mulino; 1987. lxiii, 637 pp. (Storia/memoria.) Index. Notes. Append. Lang.: Ita.

Italy. 1915-1921. Histories-sources. ▪Playwright's unpublished journals reveal three major themes: war, women, politics.

2674 Patui, Paolo. *Luigi Candoni. Un sipario ancora aperto.* (Luigi Candoni: A Still Open Curtain.) Udine: Orazero; 1987. 199 pp. (Regione Autonoma del Friuli Venezia Giulia. Comune di Arta Terme.) Pref. Biblio. Append. Illus.: Photo. Print. B&W. Lang.: Ita.

Italy. 1921-1974. Critical studies. ▪Analysis of Luigi Candoni's theatrical works.

2675 Puppa, Paolo. "Benini tra Gallina e Bertolazzi." (Benini between Gallina and Bertolazzi.) *BiT*. 1987; 5/6: 249-264. Lang.: Ita.

Italy: Venice. 1870-1929. Critical studies. ▪The relationship between Giacinto Gallina and Carlo Bertolazzi is influenced by Ferruccio Benini's amazing career: Benini influenced both authors so that they abandoned their tendency towards a choral language and style in order to draw characters in full relief.

2676 Puppa, Paolo. *Dalle parti di Pirandello*. (On Pirandello's Side.) Rome: Bulzoni; 1987. 322 pp. (Biblioteca teatrale 49.) Index. Append. Lang.: Ita.

Italy. 1876-1936. Critical studies. ▪Collection of essays on the recurrent themes of Pirandellian theatre.

DRAMA: —Plays/librettos/scripts

2677 Rosada, Bruno. "Il successo del *Tieste* foscoliano." (The Success of Foscolo's *Thyestes*.) *BiT.* 1987; 5/6: 235-248. Lang.: Ita.

Italy: Venice. 1797-1827. Histories-sources. ■The Pellandi Company performs *Tieste (Thyestes)* by Ugo Foscolo, a tragedy that the author himself considered a failure but which was successful. His correspondence with Melchiorre Cesarotti concerning the tragedy.

2678 Vescovo, Piermario. "L'Accademia e la 'fantasia dei brighenti'." (The Academy and *Fantasy of the Brighenti*.) *BiT.* 1987; 5/6: 53-86. Lang.: Ita.

Italy. 1552-1553. Biographical studies. ■The peak of playwright Andrea Calmo's career. Also his interest in acting, the correspondence between actor and character.

2679 Witt, May Ann Frese. "*Six Characters in Search of an Author* and the Battle of the Lexis." *MD.* 1987 Sep.; 30(3): 396-404. Notes. Lang.: Eng.

Italy. 1921-1987. Critical studies. ■Conflict between the Father and Stepdaughter in Pirandello's *Sei personnaggi in cerca d'autore (Six Characters in Search of an Author)* is a gendered clash between the diegetic and mimetic modes.

2680 Zhao, Xiao-Li; Chu, Chang-Jiang. "Lun pi shi yu sha shi xi ju liang zhong." (*Henry IV* of Pirandello and *Hamlet* of Shakespeare.) *XYishu.* 1987 Spr; 37: 131-137. Notes. Lang.: Chi.

Italy. England. 1580-1936. Historical studies. ■Comparison between Pirandello's *Enrico Quarto (Henry IV)* and Shakespeare's *Hamlet*, including the influence of religion.

2681 Ōtori, Hidenaga. "Kietatezawari." (A Lost Feeling.) *Sg.* 1987 Jan.; 406: 26-31. Illus.: Handbill. Photo. B&W. 6. Lang.: Jap.

Japan: Tokyo. 1986. Critical studies. ■Changes in the way contemporary Japanese playwrights deal with the subject of crime. Discusses *Erian no shuki—Nakano Fujimi Chūgakkō jiken (A Note of Erian—Based on a Suicide at Nakano Fujimi Junior High School)* by Kiuchi Midori, *Sarada satsujin jiken (A Murder Caused by a Salad Pack)*, by Yamazaki Tetsu, *Tenraku no nochi ni (After the Fall)*, by Arthur Miller, directed by Betsuyaku Minoru and *Aoimi o tabeta (I Have Eaten a Blueberry)* by Watanabe Hiroko.

2682 Ōtori, Hidenaga. "Kotoba no rizumu wa dorama ni yorisō." (Drama Enhanced by the Rhythm of Language.) *Sg.* 1987 Mar.; 408: 22-27. Illus.: Photo. B&W. 6. Lang.: Jap.

Japan: Tokyo. 1986-1987. Critical studies. ■Focuses on *Nanbonomon-jai! My Love (Who Cares?! My Love)* by Tsukumo Hajime, in which the Osaka dialect enhances the dramatic atmosphere. Also discusses *Sayonara akuma no iru kurisumasu (Good-Bye to Christmas with a Devil)*, performed by Ryūzanji jimushō, *Jimusho (Office)* by Kaitasha, *Hans* by Shiki, *4H Club* by Masshu and *Hanshin (Demigod)* by Yume no yūminsha.

2683 Sasaki, Mikiro. "Shōnen no shitai wa aruku." (A Boy's Corpse is Walking.) *Sg.* 1987 Jan.; 406: 32-37. Illus.: Handbill. Photo. B&W. 7. Lang.: Jap.

Japan: Tokyo. 1986. Critical studies. ■Four plays about child suicides caused by bullying: *Erian no shuki—Nakano Fujimi Chūgakkō jiken (A Note of Erian—Based on a Suicide at Nakano Fujimi Junior High School)*, by Kiuchi Midori, *Sarada satsujin jiken (A Murder Caused by a Salad Pack)*, by Yamazaki Tetsu, *Jōen daihon (The Scenario)*, by Wada Shusaku and *Aoimi o tabeta (I Have Eaten a Blueberry)*, by Betsuyaku Minoru. Includes a personal opinion on the meaning of death in contemporary Japanese society.

2684 Kim, Jang-Ho. *Bulkyomunhakkwa heuilabbeekuk.* (Buddhist Literature and Greek Tragedy.) Seoul: Dongguk Univ; 1980. 156 pp. Lang.: Kor.

Korea. Greece. 57 B.C.-1392 A.D. Critical studies. ■Comparison of Greek tragedy and Korean Buddhist plays.

2685 Kim, Jeong-Ok. "Sae Yeonkŭk." (Traditional Plays and New Plays.) *KTR.* 1987 June; 6(1): 26-27. Illus.: Photo. B&W. 1. Lang.: Kor.

Korea: Seoul. 1910-1945. Historical studies. ■Differences between the traditional theatre of Korea and the new plays.

2686 Kim, Kyong Ok. "The Theory of Park Hyun Suk Ron." 31-52 in Han'guk Yŏn'guk p'yŏngnon'ga Hyŏphoe, ed. *Han'guk Hyŏnyŏk kŭk Chakkron.* Yeni: SIN. Youngchul; 1987. 140 pp. Biblio. Illus.: Diagram. Chart. Lang.: Kor.

Korea. Historical studies. ■Playwright Park Hyun Suk's dramatic theory.

2687 Kim, Mun Hwan. "Theory of Lee Kun Sam." 99-118 in Han'guk Yŏn'guk p'yŏngnon'ga Hyŏphoe, ed. *Han'guk Hyŏnyŏk kŭk Chakkron.* Yeni: SIN. Youngchul; 1987. 140 pp. Notes. Illus.: Lighting. 5. Lang.: Kor.

Korea. 1950-1987. Critical studies. ■Analysis of Lee Kun Sam's plays: relationship between theatre and political situations.

2688 Lee, Hai-Rang. "Yonkukui bonjil." (The Essence of the Drama.) *DongukDA.* 1978 Apr.; 10-11: 81-84. Lang.: Kor.

Korea. 1978. Critical studies. ■Subjective view of the essence of drama.

2689 Lee, Song-Il. "A Form of Drama." 87-95 pp in Seoul P'yongnon'ga Group, ed. *Han'guk Yŏnguk kwa Chŏlmon Ŭislk.* Mineum SA: Park. Mazngho; 1979. 262 pp. Notes. Lang.: Kor.

Korea. 1960-1979. Historical studies. ■Alteration of dramatic structure.

2690 Seo, Youn-Ho. "1910 nyundaeui heuikokinunhak." (Korean Drama in the 1910s.) *DongukDA.* 1976 Dec.; 9: 28-43. Lang.: Kor.

Korea. 1910-1919. Historical studies. ■The social and political background of the works of representative playwrights.

2691 Sheo, Yeon-Ho. "Hanguk Yonguk." (The Korean Play.) *KTR.* 1987 Aug.; 8(1): 32-36. Illus.: Photo. B&W. 1. Lang.: Kor.

Korea: Seoul. 1986. Critical studies. ■Calls on Korean playwrights to be more creative and to avoid facile formulas for commercial success.

2692 Sŏ, Yŏn-ho. "Sin'pa Gŭk." (Traditional Korean Theatre.) 28-33 pp in Seoul P'yongnon'ga Group, ed. *Han'guk Yŏnguk kwa Chŏlmon Ŭislk.* Mineum SA: Park. Mazngho; 1979. 262 pp. Notes. Lang.: Kor.

Korea. 1905-1979. Critical studies. ■Conventionality in the popular plays of Korea's early twentieth century.

2693 Sŏ, Yŏn-ho. "Theory of Yun Dae Sung." 53-71 in Han'guk Yŏn'guk p'yŏngnon'ga Hyŏphoe, ed. *Han'guk Hyŏnyŏk kŭk Chakkron.* Yeni: SIN. Youngchul; 1987. 140 pp. Notes. Lang.: Kor.

Korea. 1967-1987. Critical studies. ■Analysis of playwright Yun Dae Sung's theories of drama.

2694 Aponte, Barbara Bockus. "Estrategias dramáticas del feminismo en *El eterno femenino* de Rosario Castellanos." (Feminist Dramatic Strategies in *The Eternal Feminine* by Rosario Castellanos.) *LATR.* 1987 Spr; 20(2): 49-58. Lang.: Spa.

Mexico. Critical studies. ■Feminist themes in Rosario Castellanos' work: poetry, narrative, essays and play *El eterno femenino (The Eternal Feminine)*.

2695 Dial, Eleanore Maxwell. "A Pleasure and a Source: The Publications of the Teatro Clásico de México." *LATR.* 1987 Fall; 21(1): 53-64. Lang.: Eng.

Mexico. 1958-1973. Histories-sources. ■Notes and commentary of Alvario Custadio regarding his work with the Teatro Clásico de México.

2696 Galván, Delia V. "*Felipe Angeles* de Elena Garro: Sacrificio heroico." (*Felipe Angeles* by Elena Garro: Heroic Sacrifice.) *LATR.* 1987 Spr; 20(2): 29-35. Lang.: Spa.

Mexico. 1978. Critical studies. ■Analysis of Angeles' archetypal heroic figure, his redeemer image sacrificing himself to prevent more bloodshed with the hope of restoring the social fabric, the sacrificial ritual of his death sentence and trial.

2697 Muro, María. "*Los Que No Usan Smoking*: Melodrama Social." (*The Non-Smokers*, Social Melodrama.) *UMex.* 1987 July; 42(438): 41-42. Illus.: Photo. B&W. 2. Lang.: Spa.

Mexico: Mexico City. 1982-1987. Critical studies. ■Analysis of *The Non-Smokers*, by Gianfrancesco Guarnieri, a play with social compromise as its main theme.

DRAMA: —Plays/librettos/scripts

2698 Muro, María. "Un Nuevo Teatro Infantil." (A New Infantile Theatre.) *UMex.* 1987 Aug.; 42(439): 35-36. Illus.: Photo. B&W. 2. Lang.: Spa.
Mexico: Mexico City. 1987. Critical studies. ■A discussion of two plays: *Todo sucede en una noche (It All Happens in One Night)*, and *La rosa del tiempo (The Rose of Time)* in terms of the childlike use of imagination in theatre.

2699 Muro, María. "*De la calle*: Encuentro del origen." (*Of the Street*: A Meeting with Origins.) *UMex.* 1987 Sep.; 42 (440): 35-36. Illus.: Photo. B&W. 1. Lang.: Spa.
Mexico: Mexico City. 1987. Critical studies. ■*De la calle* by Jesús Gonzalez-Davila is an exploration of origin in terms of ethnic 'roots', the language of the play and its style.

2700 Muro, María. "Dos Dramas sobre La Realidad Mexicana." (Two Plays About The Mexican Reality.) *Universidad de Mexico.* 1987 Jun.; 17(437): 44-46. Illus.: Photo. B&W. 1. Lang.: Spa.
Mexico: Mexico City. 1987. Critical studies. ■Analysis and comparison of *El sueño de los peces (The Dream of the Fishes)* and *Casa llena (Full House)*.

2701 Nigro, Kirsten F. "Rhetoric and History in Three Mexican Plays." *LATR.* 1987 Fall; 21(1): 65-72. Lang.: Eng.
Mexico. 1958-1961. Critical studies. ■Use of rhetorical strategies by Celestino Gorostiza, Salvador Novo and Rodolfo Usigli in their plays *La Malinche, Cuauhtemac* and *Corona del Fuego (Heart of Fire)* which focus on the story of the Spanish Conquest.

2702 "Interview: Renée." *ADS.* 1987 Apr.; 10: 21-28. Lang.: Eng.
New Zealand. 1982-1987. Histories-sources. ■Playwright Renée discusses her plays and reviews in terms of their political and feminist concerns, their use of historical subject matter, naturalism and other styles.

2703 Unruh, Vicky. "*El Chinfonía burguesa*: A Linguistic Manifesto de Nicaragua's Avant-Garde." (*The Bourgeois Chinfonia*: A Linguistic Manifesto of Nicaragua's Avant-Garde.) *LATR.* 1987 Spr; 20(2): 37-48. Lang.: Spa.
Nicaragua. 1987. Critical studies. ■Linguistic absurdism of *El Chinfonía burguesa (The Bourgeois Chinfonia)* by Coronel Urtecho and Joaquin Pasos.

2704 Badejo, Diedre L. "Unmasking the Gods: Of Egungun and Demagogues in Three Works by Wole Soyinka." *TJ.* 1987 May; 39(2): 204-214. Lang.: Eng.
Nigeria. 1987. Critical studies. ■Study of three works by Soyinka: *A Dance of the Forests, Opera Wonyosi* and *A Play of Giants*.

2705 Crow, Brian. "Soyinka and His Radical Critics: A Review." *ThR.* 1987; 12(1): 61-73. Notes. Lang.: Eng.
Nigeria. 1973-1987. Critical studies. ■Polemic concerning Wole Soyinka's treatment of political themes.

2706 Degen, John A. "Cultural Identity and the Cross-Cultural Assimilation: The Case of Nigerian Drama in English." *SATJ.* 1987; 1(2): 52-62. Lang.: Eng.
Nigeria. 1940-1987. Textual studies. ■Use of English in Nigerian drama to reflect cultural values of a people whose native tongue is not English.

2707 Richards, Sandra L. "Nigerian Independence Onstage: Responses from 'Second Generation' Playwrights." *TJ.* 1987 May; 39 (2): 215-227. Lang.: Eng.
Nigeria. 1950-1987. Critical studies. ■Study of contemporary Nigerian playwrights: Soyinka, Clark, Sofola, Sowande, Osofisan.

2708 Richards, Sandra L. "Toward a Populist Nigerian Theatre: The Plays of Femi Osofisan." *NTQ.* 1987 Aug.; 3(11): 280-288. Notes. Illus.: Photo. B&W. 2. Lang.: Eng.
Nigeria. 1973-1987. Critical studies. ■Osofisan's work combines a radical perspective with a recognition of the importance of cultural traditions. Social analysis elicits an active response from audiences.

2709 Wright, Derek. "The Ritual Context of Two Plays by Soyinka." *ThR.* 1987; 12(1): 51-61. Notes. Lang.: Eng.
Nigeria. 1973-1987. Critical studies. ■*The Strong Breed* and *The Bacchae* (adaptation): how traditional New Year purification ceremony is transformed by Soyinka into a rite of passage and a symbol of political revolution.

2710 Hutchings, William. "*Equus* of Convent: *Agnes of God.*" 139-146 in Hartigan, Karelisa V., ed. *From the Bard to Broadway.* Lanham, MD: UP of America; 1987. 222 pp. (Univ. of Florida Dept. of Classics Comparative Drama Conference Papers 7.) Pref. Notes. Biblio. Lang.: Eng.
North America. 1973-1980. Critical studies. ■Similarities and differences in Peter Shaffer's *Equus* and John Pielmeier's *Agnes of God*. Author examines main difference of religion: traditional Christianity versus primitive worship.

2711 *Drámaértelmezések: Ibsen, Csehov, Beckett.* (Drama Interpretations: Ibsen, Čechov, Beckett.) Budapest: Tankönyvkiadó; 1987. 224 pp. (Müelemzések kiskönyvtára.) Lang.: Hun.
Norway. Ireland. Russia. 1987. Critical studies. ■Longing for freedom and the sense of tragicomedies on everyday life in Čechov's dramas, clowns on the stage of mystery in Beckett's work.

2712 Des Roches, Kay Unruh. "A Problem of Translation: Structural Patterns in the Language of Ibsen's *The Lady from the Sea.*" *MD.* 1987 Sep.; 30(3): 311-326. Notes. Lang.: Eng.
Norway. 1888-1987. Critical studies. ■The contribution of verbal repetition to the irony of *Fruen fra Havet (The Lady from the Sea)*.

2713 Dwora, Gilula. "*Vatslave*, shel Sławomir Marozek." (*Vatslave* by Sławomir Mrożek: A Wise, Funny and a Bit Tragic Play.) *Bamah.* 1987; 21(107): 23-26. Illus.: Photo. Print. B&W. Lang.: Heb.
Poland: Cracow. France: Paris. 1956-1987. Critical studies. ■History of Mrożek in Cracow and in Paris. History and analysis of his play *Vatslave*.

2714 Pietrasik, Zdzisław. "Dramaty najmłodsze: Azyl społeczny." (New Drama: Asylum in Society.) *DialogW.* 1987; 7 : 123-129. Lang.: Pol.
Poland. 1982-1987. Critical studies. ■Problems of Polish society as seen in new Polish dramas: frustrations, alienation, drugs, AIDS.

2715 Pysiak, Krzysztof. "Pawlikowska: Farsy i dwudziestolecie." (Pawlikowska: Farces and Twenties.) *DialogW.* 1987; 1: 113-120. Lang.: Pol.
Poland. 1918-1939. Critical studies. ■Problem of love and lovers in Maria Pawlikowska-Jasnorzewska's farces in comparison with her poems.

2716 Wilski, Zbigniew. "Bogusławski w Wilnie: Fikcja literacka i fakty." (Bogusławski in Vilnius: Fiction and Facts.) *DialogW.* 1987; 7: 119-122. Notes. Lang.: Pol.
Poland. Hungary. 1815-1987. Historical studies. ■Comparison of historical knowledge about Polish actor and theatre director Wojciech Bogusławski (1757-1829) and the artistic creation of Bogusławski's personality in György Spiró's play *Az imposztor (The Imposter)*.

2717 Szerdahelyi, István. "A feldobott pénz pillanatában. Sütő András hatvanéves." (At the Moment of the Money Cast Up: András Sütő Turns 60.) *Krit.* 1987 June(6): 18-20. Illus.: Photo. B&W. 4. Lang.: Hun.
Romania: Tirgu-Mures. Hungary. 1987. Histories-sources. ■Greeting András Sütő, the renowned Hungarian writer living in Romania, on the 60th anniversary of his birth.

2718 Lim, Un-Sup. "Heuikok *kalmaeki* ui bunsuk yon ku." (Analytical Study of *The Seagull*.) *DongukDA.* 1976 Dec.; 9: 7-20. Lang.: Kor.
Russia. 1896. Critical studies. ■Analysis of Čechov's *Čajka (The Seagull)*: symbols, characters, subject, concept.

2719 Lomidze, G.A. *Teorija dramy v gruzinskoj chudožestvennoj kritike i ésteticeskoj mysli XIX veka: Avtoref. dis. kand. filol. nauk.* (Drama Theory in Georgian Art Criticism and Esthetic Thought of the Nineteenth Century: Abstract of a Dissertation by a Candidate in Philology.) Tbilisi: Tbil.in-t; 1987. 35 pp. Lang.: Rus.
Russia. 1800-1900. Historical studies.

2720 Odesskij, M.P. *Russkaja drama épochi Petra 1 Avtoref. dis. kand. filol. nauk.* (Russian Drama of the Epoch of Peter the

DRAMA: —Plays/librettos/scripts

First: Abstract of a Dissertation by a Candidate in Philology.) Moscow: MGU im. M.V. Lomonosova; 1987. 24 pp. Lang.: Rus.
Russia. 1696-1725. Histories-specific.

2721 Rassadin, S. "Sekrety proizvodstva: O dramaturgii A.V. Suchovo-Kobylina." (Secrets of Production: On the Dramaturgy of A.V. Suchovo-Kobylin.) *Oktiabr.* 1987; 10: 193-204. Lang.: Rus.
Russia. 1861. Critical studies. ■*Delo (The Affair)* as a reflection of sociohistorical problems.

2722 Salamova, S.A. *Dramaturgija L.N. Tolstogo i zapadnoevropejskaja 'novaja drama' konca XIX-načala XX v.: Avtoref. dissertacii. kandidata filologičeskich nauk.* (The Plays of L.N. Tolstoj and Western European 'New Drama' in the Late Nineteenth and Early Twentieth Centuries: Abstract of a Dissertation by a Candidate in Philology.) Moscow: MGU im. M.V. Lomonosova; 1987. 30 pp. Lang.: Rus.
Russia. Europe. 1864-1910. Critical studies.

2723 Durbach, Errol. "*Master Harold...and the Boys*: Athol Fugard and the Psychopathology of Apartheid." *MD.* 1987 Dec.; 30 (4): 505-513. Notes. Lang.: Eng.
South Africa, Republic of. 1982-1987. Critical studies. ■A 'history' play that looks at apartheid in terms of human relationships.

2724 Green, Garth V. "Characterization in Pieter-Dirk Uys' *Appassionata.*" *UNISA English Studies.* 1987; 25(2): 18-22. Illus.: Photo. B&W. 2. Lang.: Eng.
South Africa, Republic of. 1987. Critical studies. ■Escape from rigid behavior demanded by societal structure in the play *Appassionata.*

2725 McKay, Kim. "*The Blood Knot* Reborn in the Eighties: A Reflection of the Artist and His Times." *MD.* 1987 Dec.; 30(4): 496-504. Notes. Lang.: Eng.
South Africa, Republic of. 1961-1985. Critical studies. ■How Fugard's revisions have changed the play.

2726 Prins, M.J. "Die Direktief as dramatiese taalhandeling ni *Krismis van Map Jacobs.*" (The Directive as Dramatic Speech Act in *Christmas of Map Jacobs.*) *Literator.* 1987; 8(3): 26-38. Lang.: Afr.
South Africa, Republic of. 1983. Technical studies. ■Nature of the directive as a speech act, strength of elocution to achieve objectives in Adam Small's play.

2727 Wertheim, Albert. "The Prison Theatre and the Theatre as Prison: Athol Fugard's *The Island.*" *TID.* 1987; 9: 229-237. Notes. Lang.: Eng.
South Africa, Republic of. 1987. Critical studies. ■The stage stands for Robben Island prison. It is not merely a representation of the idea of prison, but becomes a prison itself: society as prison.

2728 George, David. "*Poor Man's Bread*: A Spanish Version of Hauptmann's *The Weavers.*" *ThR.* 1987; 12(1): 23-38. Notes. Lang.: Eng.
Spain. 1894. Critical studies. ■Study of *El pan del pobre (Poor Man's Bread)*, adapted by Llana and Rodriguez from Hauptmann's *Die Weber (The Weavers).*

2729 Loftis, John. "Lope de Vega's and Webster's Amalfi Plays." *CompD.* 1982 Spr; 16(1): 64-77. Notes. Lang.: Eng.
Spain. 1612-1982. Critical studies. ■Comparative study of Lope de Vega's *El mayordomo de la Duquesa de Amalfi* and John Webster's *The Duchess of Malfi*: common source for both plays, elements of Spanish and English tragedy.

2730 Molas, Joaquim, ed.; Bou, Enric; Llanas, Manuel; Gallén, Enric; Gustà, Marina; Arnau, Carme; Manent, Albert; Medina, Jaume; Miralles, Carles; Pinyol i Torres, Ramon. *Història de la literatura catalana. Volum 10.* (History of Catalan Literature, Volume 10.) Barcelona: Ariel; 1987. 464 pp. Index. Notes. Illus.: Design. Photo. Pntg. Print. Color. B&W. 189. Lang.: Cat.
Spain-Catalonia. 1939-1975. Histories-general. ■Catalan literature after the Civil War. Theatre is not covered separately except in Chapter 8, on Salvador Espriu.

2731 Serrá i Campins, Antoni. *El teatre burlesc mallorquí, 1701-1850.* (Majorcan Burlesque Theatre, 1701-1850.) Barcelona: Curial Edicions Catalanes/Publicacions de l'Abadia de Montserrat; 1987. 248 pp. (Textos i Estudis de Cultura Catalana 15.) Index. Pref. Biblio. Append. Lang.: Cat.
Spain-Catalonia. 1701-1850. Critical studies. ■Analysis of the 51 extant interludes: the genre, its popularity and conventions.

2732 Sirera, Josep Lluís. "Literatura i pràctiques dramàtiques al país Valencià contemporani: dos segles d'indefinicions." (Literature and Dramatic Practices in the Contemporaneous Valencian Area Today: Two Centuries of Indefinitions.) 139-156 in Alemany Ferrer, Rafael. *Estudis de literatura catalana al País Valenciá.* Alacant: Ajuntament de Benidorm/Universitat d'Alacant; 1987. 182 pp. Notes. [Lecture to International Courses in Benidorm, organized by the University of Alicante in 1985 August.] Lang.: Cat.
Spain-Catalonia: Valencia. 1790-1985. Histories-general. ■Overview of two centuries of theatrical activity with emphasis on dramatic literature. Covers plays in both Catalan and Spanish.

2733 "Många kvinnor men få roller." (Many Women But Few Parts.) *Teaterf.* 1987; 20(2-3): 25-26. Lang.: Swe.
Sweden. 1987. Histories-sources. ■Four amateur theatre groups discuss the shortage of female parts, and how they manage.

2734 Bécsy, Tamás. "*A Dream Play*: It Is a Drama Indeed?" *Strind.* 1987; 2: 98-129. Notes. Lang.: Eng.
Sweden. 1901-1964. Critical studies. ■Attempt to analyze Strindberg's *A Dream Play (Ett Drömspel)* by means of drama theory, where conflict is stated as a key notion in contrast to earlier, literary interpretations.

2735 Hoogland, Rikard. "Besatt av Lasse-Maja." (Possessed By Lasse-Maja.) *NT.* 1987(39): 44. Illus.: Photo. Lang.: Swe.
Sweden: Järfälla. 1987. Histories-sources. ■Canni Möller speaks about her approach to children's theatre, her play *Stor tjuvens pojke (The Servant of the Master Thief)* and the difference in writing for a small ensemble or a big amateur group.

2736 Pettegrove, James P. "Karl Ragnar Gierow on O'Neill, October 6, 1970." *EON.* 1987 Spr; 11(1): 32-34. Lang.: Eng.
Sweden: Stockholm. 1920-1970. Histories-sources. ■Interview with Karl Ragnar Gierow on O'Neill's importance in Sweden.

2737 Ritzu, Merete Kjoller, ed. *La didascalia nella letteratura teatrale scandinava: testo drammatico e sintesi scenica.* (Stage Direction in Scandinavian Theatrical Literature: Dramatic Text and Stage Synthesis.) Rome: Bulzoni; 1987. 256 pp. Index. Pref. Illus.: Photo. Dwg. Print. B&W. Lang.: Ita.
Sweden. Norway. 1700-1987. Critical studies. ■Collection of papers on the theme of stage direction seen as a theatrical element of text. From a 1986 conference on Scandinavian studies, Florence.

2738 Thome, Eva. "Pistolteatern's Alice." *TDR.* 1982 Fall; 26(3): 105-110. Illus.: Photo. B&W. 2. Lang.: Eng.
Sweden: Stockholm. 1982. Critical studies. ■Description of adaptation of *Alice in Wonderland.* Techniques used in its development, emphasis on child's perceptions of difficulties in the adult world.

2739 Thorstensson, Guntha. "Vad spelar det för roll om pojkar spelar flickor eller tvärtom?" (What Difference Makes It if Boys Play Girls or Reverse?) *Teaterf.* 1987; 20(1): 13. Lang.: Swe.
Sweden. 1986. Critical studies. ■Why are all the plays mostly written for male parts, while the females of the amateur groups are in the majority?.

2740 Tjäder, Per Arne. "Mågen som försvann. En dramatisk detalj i Strindbergs *Pelikanen.*" (The Son-in-Law who Disappeared: A Dramatic Detail in Strindberg's *The Pelican.*) *Strind.* 1987; 2: 61-71. Notes. Lang.: Swe.
Sweden. 1907-1987. Critical studies. ■The ambiguous character of the son-in-law in August Strindberg's chamber play and its function in the dramatic structure.

2741 Wikander, Matthew H. "Strindberg's *Gustav III*: The Player King on the Stage of History." *MD.* 1987 Mar.; 30(1): 80-89. Notes. Lang.: Eng.

DRAMA: —Plays/librettos/scripts

Sweden. 1903-1987. Critical studies. ■Theatrical metaphor, particularly role-reversal and miscasting, used to make Gustav representative of man's entrapment in history.

2742 Agapova, L.A. *Maks Friš i problemy realizma v švejcarskom teatre vtoroj poloviny XX veka: Avtoref. dis. kand. iskusstvovedenija.* (Max Frisch and the Problems of Realism in the Swiss Theatre of the Second Half of the Twentieth Century: Abstract of a Dissertation by a Candidate in Art Criticism.) Leningrad: M-vo kul-tury RSFSR/LGITMiK; 1987. 21 pp. Lang.: Rus.

Switzerland. 1911-1987. Critical studies.

2743 Brater, Enoch. "*Play Strindberg* and the Theater of Adaptation." *CompD.* 1982 Spr; 16(1): 12-25. Notes. Lang.: Eng.

Switzerland. 1971-1982. Critical studies. ■Analysis and interpretation of Dürrenmatt's *Play Strindberg*, an adaptation of Strindberg's *Dödsdansen (The Dance of Death).* Production concepts for the play, language and character analysis.

2744 Jauslin, Christian, ed. *Mundart auf dem Berufstheater der deutschen Schweiz.* (Dialect on the Professional Stage in German-speaking Switzerland.) Schweizerische Gesellschaft für Theaterkul. Zürich: Theaterkultur-Verlag; 1987. 119 pp. (Schriften 17.) Pref. Notes. Biblio. Illus.: Photo. B&W. Lang.: Ger.

Switzerland. 1889-1984. Historical studies. ■Essays on political, social and artistic aspects of the relationship between standard German and Swiss German dialects on and off stage.

2745 Knopf, Jan. *Der Dramatiker Friedrich Dürrenmatt.* (The Playwright Friedrich Dürrenmatt.) Berlin: Henschelverlag; 1987. 232 pp. Notes. Biblio. Lang.: Ger.

Switzerland. Germany, West. 1945-1986. Critical studies. ■Analysis and interpretation of all plays by Dürrenmatt, evaluation of their social effect, comparison with Brecht's work.

2746 Muff, Heinz, ed. *Wedekind der Teufelskerl.* (Wedekind, Devil of a Fellow.) Lenzburg: Historisches Museum Aargau; 1987. 136 pp. Pref. Biblio. Illus.: Photo. B&W. Lang.: Ger.

Switzerland: Lenzburg. Germany: Berlin. France: Paris. 1864-1918. Biographies. ■Pictorial biography of Wedekind's life in Switzerland and Germany giving a slapstick portrait of the playwright.

2747 Pfefferkorn, Eli. "Faust Ve Hafisikaim." (Faust and the Physicists.) *Bamah.* 1987; 21(107): 5-14. Illus.: Photo. Print. B&W. Lang.: Heb.

Switzerland. 1987. Critical studies. ■Dürrenmatt's play *The Physicists (Die Physiker),* the theatre of protest and paradox, compared to *Doctor Faustus* and *Macbeth.*

2748 Ssansalo, Bede. "Unresolved Tension, Perpetual Conflict: The Works of E.N. Ziramu of Uganda." *Ufa.* 1986/87 Win; 15(3): 219-226. Biblio. Lang.: Eng.

Uganda: Buganda. 1962-1974. Critical studies. ■The plays of Ziramu which deal with characters who must negotiate the equally compelling demands of African traditional customs and of the progressive and technological inroads of modern society. Themes include middle-class acquisitiveness, religious satire, antiquated marriage rites and social ills.

2749 Mitchell, Jack. "Some Remarks on the Reflection of the Spanish Civil War in Irish, American and British Drama in the Thirties." *ZAA.* 1987; 35(2): 128-135. Lang.: Eng.

UK. Ireland. USA. 1930-1939. Critical studies. ■The theme of civil war in Hemingway's *The Fifth Column,* O'Casey's *The Silver Tassie, The Star Turns Red, Within the Gates* and other plays.

2750 Rabey, David Ian. *British and Irish Political Drama in the Twentieth Century: Implicating the Audience.* New York, NY: St. Martin's P; 1986. Pref. Index. Notes. Lang.: Eng.

UK. Ireland. 1890-1987. Critical studies. ■Trends and strategies expressing political dissatisfaction. Interaction of preconceptions, attitudes and dramatic tensions between audience and author in performance.

2751 Bakanova, E.R. *Mir i čelovek v tragedijah Marlo (k proleme chudožestvennogo metoda): Avtoref. dis. kand. filol. nauk.* (The World and Man in the Tragedies of Marlowe—Toward

the Problems of an Artistic Methods. Abstract of a Dissertation by a Candidate in Philology.) Moscow: MGU im. M.V. Lomonosova; 1987. 21 pp. Lang.: Rus.

UK-England. 1564-1593. Critical studies.

2752 Barton, Ann. "Livy, Machiavelli, and Shakespeare's *Coriolanus.*" *ShS.* 1985; 38: 115-129. Notes. Lang.: Eng.

UK-England: London. 1606-1610. Historical studies. ■Influence of Livy's *History* and Machiavelli's *Discorsi* on Shakespeare's *Coriolanus.*

2753 Berst, Charles A. "The Action of Shaw's Settings and Props." 41-65 in Leary, Daniel, ed. *Shaw's Plays in Performance.* University Park/London: Pennsylvania State UP; 1983. vi, 262 pp. (Shaw: The Annual of Bernard Shaw Studies (ShawR).) Notes. Lang.: Eng.

UK-England. 1883-1935. Critical studies. ■Demonstrates importance of settings and props to meaning in Shaw, emphasizing *Arms and the Man, Candida, Caesar and Cleopatra* and *Man and Superman.*

2754 Berst, Charles A. "*The Man of Destiny*: Shaw, Napoleon and the Theatre of Life." 85-118 in Turco, Alfred, Jr., ed. *Shaw: The Neglected Plays.* Shaw: The Annual of Bernard Shaw Studies 7. University Park and London: Pennsylvania State UP; 1987. vii, 368 pp. Illus.: Photo. B&W. 1. Lang.: Eng.

UK-England. 1894-1931. Critical studies. ■Literary, theatrical, historical sources as they are connected with predominant theme of the interrelationship of drama and life.

2755 Bertolini, John A. "Imagining *Saint Joan.*" 149-161 in Leary, Daniel, ed. *Shaw's Plays in Performance.* University Park/London: Pennsylvania State UP; 1983. vi, 262 pp. (Shaw: The Annual of Bernard Shaw Studies (ShawR).) Notes. Lang.: Eng.

UK-England. 1923. Critical studies. ■Explores theme of nature and function of imagination and its development through the play, culminating in the poetic ritual/tableau of the Epilogue.

2756 Bertolini, John A. "*The Doctor's Dilemma*: The Art of Undoing." 151-169 in Turco, Alfred, Jr., ed. *Shaw: The Neglected Plays.* Shaw: The Annual of Bernard Shaw Studies 7. University Park and London: Pennsylvania State UP; 1987. vii, 368 pp. Notes. Lang.: Eng.

UK-England. 1906. Critical studies. ■The *Doppelgänger* as archetype in characterization and theme of *The Doctor's Dilemma.*

2757 Bligh, John. "The Mind of Coriolanus." *English Studies in Canada.* 1987 Sept; 13(3): 256-270. Notes. Lang.: Eng.

UK-England. 1607. Critical studies. ■An interpretation of the character of Coriolanus based on an investigation of the character's inner vision of the ideal city of Rome.

2758 Bloom, Michael. "Intimacies and Enigmas." *AmTh.* 1987 Sep.; 4(6): 32-33. Illus.: Dwg. 1. Lang.: Eng.

UK-England: London. 1933-1987. Biographical studies. ■Recent release of playwright Joe Orton's diaries edited by John Lahr. Focus on his work and relationships.

2759 Braunmuller, A.R. "Pinter's *Silence*: Experience Without Character." 118-127 in Gale, Steven H., ed. *Harold Pinter: Critical Approaches.* London/Toronto: Associated University Presses; 1986. 232 pp. Notes. Lang.: Eng.

UK-England. 1964-1970. Critical studies. ■Deconstructionist analysis of Harold Pinter's *Silence.*

2760 Bryant, J.A., Jr. "*Julius Caesar* from a Euripidean Perspective." *CompD.* 1982 Sum; 16(2): 97-111. Notes. Lang.: Eng.

UK-England. 500 B.C.-1599 A.D. Critical studies. ■Comparison of Shakespeare's *Julius Caesar* with the drama and vision of Euripides. New perspective of text by departing from Aristotelian view of action and principal characters and adopting Euripidean principles.

2761 Burkman, Katherine H. "The Multiple Levels of Action in Harold Pinter's *Victoria Station.*" *PintR.* 1987; 1: 22-30. Notes. Biblio. Lang.: Eng.

UK-England. 1959-1982. Critical studies. ■*Victoria Station* as a continuation of Harold Pinter's probing of the struggle for power in terms of environment.

DRAMA: —Plays/librettos/scripts

2762 Carlson, Susan. "Comic Collisions: Convention, Rage and Order." *NTQ*. 1987 Nov.; 3(12): 303-316. Notes. Lang.: Eng.

UK-England. 1970-1987. Critical studies. ■Trevor Griffiths, Peter Barnes, Catherine Hayes and Caryl Churchill use the comic form to expose itself and the traditional comic ending which affirms the status quo.

2763 Cohen, Derek. "The Rite of Violence in *Henry IV, Part I*." *ShS*. 1985; 38: 77-84. Notes. Lang.: Eng.

UK-England: London. 1595-1598. Critical studies. ■Contrast of vivid depictions of dying moments of characters in drama with the stillness of the death of Hotspur.

2764 Cohn, Ruby. "Theatre in Recent English Theatre." *MD*. 1987 Mar.; 30(1): 1-13. Notes. Lang.: Eng.

UK-England. 1957-1985. Critical studies. ■Popular theatre in the legitimate theatre, how recent plays draw on theatre, self-reflexive plays and plays within plays, both historical and fictional.

2765 Crane, Gladys. "Directing Early Shaw: Acting and Meaning in *Mrs. Warren's Profession*." 29-39 in Leary, Daniel, ed. *Shaw's Plays in Performance*. University Park/London: Pennsylvania State UP; 1983. vi, 262 pp. (Shaw: The Annual of Bernard Shaw Studies (ShawR).) Lang.: Eng.

UK-England. 1902. Critical studies. ■Supports contention that in *Mrs. Warren's Profession* and other Shaw plays the ideas are embodied in the characters and revealed through their interactions.

2766 Degen, John A. "The Evolution of *The Shop Girl* and the Birth of 'Musical Comedy'." *THSt*. 1987; 7: 40-50. Notes. Lang.: Eng.

UK-England: London. 1830-1890. Historical studies. ■George Edwardes's productions of *In Town*, *A Gaiety Girl* and *The Shop Girl* contributed significantly to the development of the English musical comedy.

2767 Des Roches, Kay Unruh. "*The Sea*: Anarchy as Order." *MD*. 1987 Dec.; 30(4): 480-495. Notes. Lang.: Eng.

UK-England. 1973-1987. Critical studies. ■The structural incoherence of Edward Bond's play is the formal representation of the anarchy that is its subject.

2768 Dukore, Bernard F. "The Director as Interpreter: Shaw's *Pygmalion*." 129-147 in Leary, Daniel, ed. *Shaw's Plays in Performance*. University Park/London: Pennsylvania State UP; 1983. vi, 262 pp. (Shaw: The Annual of Bernard Shaw Studies (ShawR).) Notes. Lang.: Eng.

UK-England. 1894-1949. Critical studies. ■Shaw's ideas on directorial interpretation based on his own writing, his interpretation of *Pygmalion* and his revision of text to include interpretations arrived at in rehearsal.

2769 Dukore, Bernard F. "Lope Discovered: Barnes's *Actors*." *THSt*. 1987; 7: 12-27. Notes. Lang.: Eng.

UK-England: London. Spain: Madrid. 1983. Textual studies. ■A comparison of Peter Barnes's *Actors* to Lope de Vega's *Lo Fingido Verdadero (The Feigned Truth)* from which it is adapted.

2770 Dukore, Bernard F. "*Red Noses* and *Saint Joan*." *MD*. 1987 Sep.; 30(3): 340-351. Notes. Lang.: Eng.

UK-England. 1924-1985. Critical studies. ■*Red Noses* as Peter Barnes's response to Shaw's *Saint Joan*.

2771 Eccles, Christine. "The Unsolicited Playscript...and Its Almost Inevitable Return." *NTQ*. 1987 Feb.; 3(9): 24-28. Lang.: Eng.

UK-England. 1980. Critical studies. ■Various ways a script may reach the stage, and the sources of financial support for aspiring playwrights.

2772 Evans, T.F. "*In Good King Charles's Golden Days*: The Dramatist as Historian." 259-277 in Turco, Alfred, Jr., ed. *Shaw: The Neglected Plays*. Shaw: The Annual of Bernard Shaw Studies 7. University Park and London: Pennsylvania State UP; 1987. vii, 368 pp. Notes. Lang.: Eng.

UK-England. 1639. Critical studies. ■Shaw's method of transforming history into 'True History That Never Happened' (with a note on stage history).

2773 Everding, Robert. "*Village Wooing*: A Call for Individual Regeneration." 221-241 in Turco, Alfred, Jr., ed. *Shaw: The Neglected Plays*. Shaw: The Annual of Bernard Shaw Studies 7. University Park and London: Pennsylvania State UP; 1987. vii, 368 pp. Notes. Illus.: Photo. B&W. 1. Lang.: Eng.

UK-England. USA: Houston, TX. 1933-1984. Critical studies. ■Action of play as worked out during rehearsal for revival at Houston Shaw Festival (1984) with appendix on stage history.

2774 Everding, Robert. "Fusion of Character and Setting: Artistic Strategy in *Major Barbara*." 103-116 in Leary, Daniel, ed. *Shaw's Plays in Performance*. University Park/London: Pennsylvania State UP; 1983. vi, 262 pp. (Shaw: The Annual of Bernard Shaw Studies (ShawR).) Notes. Lang.: Eng.

UK-England. 1905. Critical studies. ■Character and setting function in Shaw's strategy: to establish an apparent point of view and then subvert it, challenging the audience's conventional assumptions.

2775 Fisher, Barbara N. "*Fanny's First Play*: A Critical Potboiler?" 187-205 in Turco, Alfred, Jr., ed. *Shaw: The Neglected Plays*. Shaw: The Annual of Bernard Shaw Studies 7. University Park and London: Pennsylvania State UP; 1987. vii, 368 pp. Notes. Illus.: Photo. B&W. 2. Lang.: Eng.

UK-England. 1911-1916. Critical studies. ■Play as demonstration of Bakhtinian *polyglossia* ('coexistence of multiple socially determined dialects...within a given culture').

2776 Fitzsimmons, Linda. "'I won't turn back for you or anyone': Caryl Churchill's Socialist-Feminist Theatre." *ET*. 1987 Nov.; 6(1): 19-29. Notes. Lang.: Eng.

UK-England. 1980-1987. Critical studies. ■Argues that Churchill's *Top Girls* and *Fen* are political socialist-feminist plays, and are optimistic in suggesting change and a way forward.

2777 Flores, Stephan P. "Mastering the Self: The Ideological Incorporation of Desire in Lillo's *The London Merchant*." *ET*. 1987 May; 5(2): 91-102. Notes. Lang.: Eng.

UK-England. 1731-1800. Critical studies. ■Text and characters of *The London Merchant* in terms of contemporary social, religious and economic ideologies.

2778 Gatton, John Spaulding. "'Put Into Scenery': Theatrical Space in Byron's Closet Historical Drama." *TID*. 1987; 9: 139-149. Notes. Illus.: Dwg. 1. Lang.: Eng.

UK-England: London. 1812-1822. Critical studies. ■Use of space in Byron's historical dramas: though meant to be closet dramas, they are specifically structured to the spatial and technical demands of contemporary London theatres.

2779 Gillen, Francis. "Introduction to Harold Pinter's Unpublished Novel: *The Dwarfs*." *PintR*. 1987; 1: 1-3. Lang.: Eng.

UK-England. 1958-1987. Histories-sources. ■Chapter 19 of Pinter's unpublished novel *The Dwarfs*, printed here for the first time, provides insights into playwright's later dramatic writing thematically and stylistically.

2780 Goodall, Jane. "Artaud's Revision of Shelley's *The Cenci*: The Text and Its Doubles." *CompD*. 1987 Sum; 21(2): 115-126. Notes. Lang.: Eng.

UK-England. France. 1819-1920. Critical studies. ■Artaud's concern with the theatre as a bridge from virtual to the actual, a convergence of physical and metaphysical operations and his quest for an 'alchemical theatre'. Comparison of his and Shelley's interpretation and production of *The Cenci*.

2781 Hark, Ina Rae. "Tomfooling with Melodrama in *Passion, Poison and Petrification*." 137-150 in Turco, Alfred, Jr., ed. *Shaw: The Neglected Plays*. Shaw: The Annual of Bernard Shaw Studies 7. University Park and London: Pennsylvania State UP; 1987. vii, 368 pp. Notes. Illus.: Photo. B&W. 1. Lang.: Eng.

UK-England. 1895-1926. Critical studies. ■Freudian reading of burlesque of romantic melodrama.

2782 Hornby, Richard. "Beyond the Verbal in *Pygmalion*." 121-127 in Leary, Daniel, ed. *Shaw's Plays in Performance*. University Park/London: Pennsylvania State UP; 1983. vi, 262 pp. (Shaw: The Annual of Bernard Shaw Studies (ShawR).) Notes. Lang.: Eng.

DRAMA: —Plays/librettos/scripts

UK-England. 1914. Critical studies. ∎Semiological approach showing connection of sets, props, costumes and all visual aspects to major themes of *Pygmalion*.

2783 Hu, Stephen. "Political Aesthetics of *Every Good Boy Deserves Favour*." *TA*. 1987; 42: 17-28. Notes. Lang.: Eng.
UK-England. USSR. 1974-1977. Critical studies. ∎André Previn invited Tom Stoppard to write a play that would include the use of a live symphony on stage. Originally apolitical in nature, the play became politicized after Stoppard visited Leningrad and learned of the government's use of psychiatry to imprison citizens.

2784 Innes, Christopher. "Somerset Maugham: A Test Case for Popular Comedy." *MD*. 1987 Dec.; 30(4): 549-559. Notes. Lang.: Eng.
UK-England. 1903-1933. Critical studies. ∎The potential for social influence in Maugham's comedies.

2785 Irvin, Eric. "Was John Lang Really a Four-Word Dramatist?" *ADS*. 1987 Oct.; 11: 23-36. Lang.: Eng.
UK-England. Australia. 1853. Historical studies. ∎John Lang's collaboration with Tom Taylor on *Plot and Passion* noting the inconsistency of Taylor's accounts. Details of Lang's career.

2786 Jackson, MacDonald P. "The Year's Work in Shakespearian Study: Editions and Textual Studies." *ShS*. 1986; 39: 236-252. Notes. Lang.: Eng.
UK-England. USA. 1981-1985. Textual studies. ∎Textual study of Stanley Wells' *Re-Editing Shakespeare for the Modern Reader* and the New Cambridge editions of *Richard II* (Andrew Gurr), *A Midsummer Night's Dream* (R. A. Foakes) and *Hamlet* (Philip Edwards).

2787 Jenckes, Norma. "The Political Function of Shaw's Destruction of Stage Irish Conventions in *John Bull's Other Island*." *ET*. 1987 May; 5(2): 115-126. Notes. Lang.: Eng.
UK-England. UK-Ireland. 1860-1925. Critical studies. ∎Shaw's use of Irish stereotypes and stage conventions in *John Bull's Other Island* makes political statement about Ireland's image and relationship with England.

2788 Jenkins, Anthony. *The Theatre of Tom Stoppard*. New York, NY: Cambridge UP; 1987. 208 pp. [2d ed.] Lang.: Eng.
UK-England. 1937-1987. Historical studies. ∎Playwright Tom Stoppard's career development: his radio and TV plays and his latest stage plays *The Real Thing*, *The Dog It Was That Died* and *Squaring the Circle*. Related to Media.

2789 Joyce, Steven. "The Ice Age Cometh: A Major Emendation of *Buoyant Billions* in Critical Perspective." 279-299 in Turco, Alfred, Jr., ed. *Shaw: The Neglected Plays*. Shaw: The Annual of Bernard Shaw Studies 7. University Park and London: Pennsylvania State UP; 1987. vii, 368 pp. Notes. Illus.: Photo. B&W. 4. Lang.: Eng.
UK-England. 1936-1946. Critical studies. ∎Contemporary approaches (structuralist criticism, speech-act theory, thematic analysis) applied to three versions of a segment of *Buoyant Billions* to understand effect of Shaw's revision process on dramatization of ideas, character and situation.

2790 Kaplan, Joel H. "Henry Arthur Jones and the Lime-Lit Imagination." *NCT*. 1987; 15(2): 115-141. Notes. Illus.: Dwg. Print. B&W. 2. Lang.: Eng.
UK-England: London. 1882-1900. Critical studies. ∎Movement of Henry Arthur Jones's dramaturgy from melodrama to modernity and its relationship to the stagecraft of his day.

2791 Keefer, Michael H. "History and the Canon: The Case of *Doctor Faustus*." *University of Toronto Quarterly*. 1987; 56(4): 498-522. Notes. Lang.: Eng.
UK-England. 1987. Textual studies. ∎A contextual analysis of both the A and B texts of Marlowe's *Doctor Faustus* in response to varying perspectives on canonicity.

2792 King, Rosalind. "'Then Murder's Out of Tune': The Music and Structure of *Othello*." *ShS*. 1986; 39: 149-158. Notes. Lang.: Eng.
UK-England: London. 1604. Critical studies. ∎Shakespeare's presentation of Iago's words and actions as part of an extensive pattern of

musical image which unites and expands the ideas of the play and provides terms of reference for both aesthetic and moral judgment.

2793 Klein, Jeanne. "Seeing Double: Theatrical Conceits in *Cloud 9*." *JDTC*. 1987; 1(2): 63-71. Notes. Lang.: Eng.
UK-England. 1978-1987. Critical studies. ∎Explores Caryl Churchill's conscious use of theatrical self-referentiality in *Cloud 9*. Churchill introduces enormous incongruities in order to foreground the artificiality of character, plot, and setting.

2794 Lamb, Mary Ellen. "The Nature of Topicality in *Love's Labour's Lost*." *ShS*. 1985; 38: 49-59. Notes. Lang.: Eng.
UK-England: London. 1590. Historical studies. ∎Explores the topicality of Shakespeare's *Love's Labour's Lost* and the play's availability to a wide audience. Valentine Pardieu as source for character of Moth.

2795 Lappin, Lou. "Gems Views History in a New Light." *AmTh*. 1987 Apr.; 4(1): 42-44. Illus.: Photo. B&W. 1. Lang.: Eng.
UK-England: London. 1984-1987. Critical studies. ∎Work of playwright Pam Gems, emphasis on themes of sex, power and politics.

2796 Leary, Daniel. "From Page to Stage to Audience in Shaw." 1-23 in Leary, Daniel, ed. *Shaw's Plays in Performance*. University Park/London: Pennsylvania State UP; 1983. vi, 262 pp. (Shaw: The Annual of Bernard Shaw Studies (ShawR).) Notes. Lang.: Eng.
UK-England. 1914. Critical studies. ∎Shaw's use of the audience to help create his play *Pygmalion* (Act I).

2797 Leggatt, Alexander. "*Henry VIII* and the Ideal England." *ShS*. 1985; 38: 131-143. Notes. Lang.: Eng.
UK-England: London. 1611-1614. Critical studies. ∎View of the ideal and mortal worlds explored through speeches of Cranmer in *Henry VIII*. Ideal vision versus our sense of the world as it really is.

2798 Longman, Stanley Vincent. "Fixed, Floating, and Fluid Stages." *TID*. 1987; 9: 151-160. Lang.: Eng.
UK-England. USA. 1947-1987. Critical studies. ∎Ways of characterizing stage space, a metaphor for larger world. Three categories for stage space: realism, epic and a generalized locale with specific sites.

2799 MacIntyre, Margaret; Buchbinder, David. "Having it Both Ways: Cross Dressing in Orton's *What the Butler Saw* and Churchill's *Cloud 9*." *JDTC*. 1987; 2(1): 23-39. Notes. Biblio. Lang.: Eng.
UK-England. 1987. Critical studies. ∎Use of transvestitism on stage, historical implications and roots of cross-dressing on stage.

2800 Marohl, Joseph. "De-realised Women: Performance and Identity in *Top Girls*." *MD*. 1987 Sep.; 30(3): 376-388. Notes. Lang.: Eng.
UK-England. 1982-1987. Critical studies. ∎Class conflict, rather than gender, emerges as the true subject of the play in the course of performance.

2801 Mayer, David. "*The Ticket-of-Leave Man* in Context." *ET*. 1987 Nov.; 6(1): 31-40. Notes.
UK-England. France. 1863. Historical studies. ∎Background of *The Ticket-of-Leave Man* by Tom Taylor, an appeal for justice and against a police state, based on Bisebarre's *Léonard*.

2802 Mazer, Cary M. "Bill Walker's Sovereign: A Note on Sources." 116-119 in Leary, Daniel, ed. *Shaw's Plays in Performance*. University Park/London: Pennsylvania State UP; 1983. vi, 262 pp. (Shaw: The Annual of Bernard Shaw Studies (ShawR).) Notes. Lang.: Eng.
UK-England. 1905. Critical studies. ∎Source of stage business by which Snobby Paice steals Bill Walker's sovereign (*Major Barbara*, Act II) is traced to Beerbohm Tree's production of *Much Ado About Nothing*.

2803 McDowell, Frederick P.W. "Shaw's 'Higher Comedy' Par Excellence: *You Never Can Tell*." 63-83 in Turco, Alfred, Jr., ed. *Shaw: The Neglected Plays*. Shaw: The Annual of Bernard Shaw Studies 7. University Park and London: Pennsylvania State UP; 1987. vii, 368 pp. Notes. Lang.: Eng.
UK-England. 1899. Critical studies. ∎Relation to contemporary comedy tradition, archetypal patterns in characters and themes.

2804 Meisel, Martin. "*John Bull's Other Island* and Other Working Partnerships." 119-136 in Turco, Alfred, Jr., ed. *Shaw:*

DRAMA: —Plays/librettos/scripts

The Neglected Plays. Shaw: The Annual of Bernard Shaw Studies 7. University Park and London: Pennsylvania State UP; 1987. vii, 368 pp. Notes. Lang.: Eng.
UK-England. 1904. Critical studies. ■Suggests autobiographical sources for 'private energies' underlying play's 'public actions and arguments', and shows how both interact to produce effect of the play. Character relationships and situations contrasted with other Shaw plays and contemporary drama.

2805 Mills, David. "Jean Genet." *Drama.* 1987; 4(166): 8-10. Illus.: Photo. B&W. 1. Lang.: Eng.
UK-England: London. 1987. Historical studies. ■An analysis of Genet's plays with particular reference to the RSC Genet Season at the Barbican in London.

2806 Mitchell, Tony. "The Red Theatre Under the Bed." *NTQ.* 1987 Aug.; 3(11): 195-201. Illus.: Photo. B&W. 2. Lang.: Eng.
UK-England. 1975-1987. Histories-sources. ■Interview with playwright Howard Brenton on his recent plays, including *The Romans in Britain* and *Pravda.*

2807 Paget, Derek. "'Verbatim Theatre': Oral History and Documentary Techniques." *NTQ.* 1987 Nov.; 3(12): 317-336. Notes. Illus.: Photo. B&W. 7. Lang.: Eng.
UK-England. 1970-1987. Critical studies. ■Leading practitioners and their methods used in that form of documentary dramas which employs (largely or exclusively) tape-recorded material from the 'real-life' originals of the characters and events depicted.

2808 Pálffy, István. *George Bernard Shaw Magyarországon (1904-1956).* (G.B. Shaw in Hungary, 1904-1956.) Budapest: Akadémiai K.; 1987. 216 pp. (Modern filológiai füzetek 40.) Lang.: Hun.
UK-England. 1904-1956. Historical studies. ■Reception of the plays of Shaw in Hungary.

2809 Parker, Douglas H. "Shakespeare's Use of Comic Inventions in *Titus Andronicus.*" *University of Toronto Quarterly.* 1987 ; 56(4): 487-497. Notes. Lang.: Eng.
UK-England. 1987. Critical studies. ■Shakespeare employed specific formal comic conventions to enhance tragedy in *Titus Andronicus.*

2810 Pechter, Edward. "Remembering *Hamlet:* Or, How it Feels to Go Like a Crab Backwards." *ShS.* 1986; 39: 135-147. Notes. Lang.: Eng.
UK-England: London. 1599-1603. Critical studies. ■Relationship between the well-made and unconventional elements of *Hamlet:* aesthetic, mythic and critical.

2811 Peters, Margot. "*The Millionairess:* Capitalism Bankrupt?" 243-258 in Turco, Alfred, Jr., ed. *Shaw: The Neglected Plays.* Shaw: The Annual of Bernard Shaw Studies 7. University Park and London: Pennsylvania State UP; 1987. vii, 368 pp. Notes. Illus.: Photo. B&W. 1. Lang.: Eng.
UK-England. 1936-1952. Critical studies. ■Traces shift in problem of capitalism from the source of the money to the use to which it is put as it appears in Shaw's plays and the problematics of Epifania as a capitalist heroine.

2812 Peters, Sally. "Shaw's Double Dethroned: *The Dark Lady of the Sonnets, Cymbeline Refinished,* and *Shakes Versus Shav.*" 301-316 in Turco, Alfred, Jr., ed. *Shaw: The Neglected Plays.* Shaw: The Annual of Bernard Shaw Studies 7. University Park and London: Pennsylvania State UP; 1987. vii, 368 pp. Notes. Lang.: Eng.
UK-England. 1882-1936. Critical studies. ■Traces ambivalent Shakespeare-Shaw double through the canon.

2813 Pierce, Robert B. "'Very Like a Whale': Scepticism and Seeing in *The Tempest.*" *ShS.* 1985; 38: 167-173. Notes. Lang.: Eng.
UK-England: London. 1611. Critical studies. ■Themes of perception in *The Tempest* where the ordinary is remote and dreams have clarity. Relationship between characters and audience and challenges of interpretation faced by both.

2814 Pullen, Charles. "Samuel Beckett and the Cultural Memory: How to Read Samuel Beckett." *Queen's Quarterly.* 1987 Sum; 94 (2): 288-299. Lang.: Eng.

UK-England. 1930-1987. Critical studies. ■Discusses strategies for reading Beckett's prose and drama within the context of cultural memory.

2815 Quigley, Austin E. "The Temporality of Structure in Pinter's Plays." *PintR.* 1987; 1: 7-21. Notes. Biblio. Lang.: Eng.
UK-England. 1958-1987. Critical studies. ■Interpreting Harold Pinter's dramas through focus on his play structures.

2816 Red'ko, N.A. *Tvorčeskaja évolucija D.Golsuorsi—dramaturga: Avtoref. dis. kand. filolog. nauk.* (The Creative Evolution of John Galsworthy, Dramatist: Abstract of a Dissertation by a Candidate in Philology.) Moscow: Mosk.obl.ped.in-t im. N.K. Krupskoj; 1987. 18 pp. Lang.: Rus.
UK-England. 1867-1933. Critical studies.

2817 Roche, S.W. *Travesties and Burlesques of Shakespeare's Plays on the British Stage during the Nineteenth Century.* London: Royal Holloway College; 1987. Notes. Biblio. [Ph.D. thesis, *Index to Theses,* 37-6474.] Lang.: Eng.
UK-England. 1800-1900. Historical studies. ■Places Shakespearean burlesque in the context of burlesque in general and shows how it reflects contemporary performances and criticism. Suggests that borrowings from other popular theatrical forms led to its demise.

2818 Shafer, Yvonne. "An Interview with Peter Barnes." *JDTC.* 1987; 2(1): 87-94. Lang.: Eng.
UK-England. USA. 1987. Histories-sources. ■Interview with Peter Barnes discussing state of playwriting in the US and England: naturalism versus non-naturalism.

2819 Šljahter, N.A. *Problema tragičeskogo v anglijskoj dramaturgii 1950-1960-ch godov: Avtoref. dis. kand. filol. nauk.* (The Problem of the Tragic in English Drama of the Fifties and Sixties: Abstract of a Dissertation by a Candidate in Philology.) Leningrad: Leningr. un-t; 1987. 14 pp. Lang.: Rus.
UK-England. 1950-1969. Critical studies.

2820 Stowell, Sheila. "'A Quaint and Comical Dismay': The Dramatic Strategies of Granville Barker's *The Voysey Inheritance.*" *ET.* 1987 May; 5(2): 127-138. Notes. Lang.: Eng.
UK-England. 1600-1938. Critical studies. ■Dramatic techniques, influences on the writing. Comparison with Shakespeare's *Henry IV* and plays of Shaw.

2821 Taylor, Gary. "The Fortunes of Oldcastle." *ShS.* 1985; 38: 85-100. Notes. Lang.: Eng.
UK-England: London. 1595-1598. Textual studies. ■Plea to restore Oldcastle to the text of *Henry IV, Part I* replacing Falstaff, arguing that the name of Falstaff trivializes the play's most memorable character.

2822 Thomson, Leslie. "The Subtext of *The Real Thing:* It's 'all right'." *MD.* 1987 Dec.; 30(4): 535-548. Notes. Lang.: Eng.
UK-England. 1986-1987. Critical studies. ■The subtextual meanings of the phrase 'all right' convey that Henry and Annie's relationship is 'the real thing' in Tom Stoppard's play.

2823 Turco, Alfred, Jr. "*The Philanderer:* Shaw's Poignant Romp." 47-62 in Turco, Alfred, Jr., ed. *Shaw: The Neglected Plays.* Shaw: The Annual of Bernard Shaw Studies 7. University Park and London: Pennsylvania State UP; 1987. vii, 368 pp. Illus.: Photo. B&W. 1. Lang.: Eng.
UK-England. 1905. Critical studies. ■The 'uncharacteristically bleak' ending comes from ideological shift from making society responsible to a recognition that characters are betrayed by their inner selves, leaving a sense that no redemptive process is likely.

2824 Vivis, V. Anthony. "Man to Man." *Drama.* 1987; 4(166): 18-19. Illus.: Photo. B&W. 2. Lang.: Eng.
UK-England. 1987. Histories-sources. ■Tilda Swinter talks about her role as a male and audience reaction to the difficulties of being the only character on stage for an hour and a half.

2825 Watson, Barbara B. "The Theatre of Love and the Theatre of Politics in *The Apple Cart.*" 207-220 in Turco, Alfred, Jr., ed. *Shaw: The Neglected Plays.* Shaw: The Annual of Bernard Shaw Studies 7. University Park and London:

DRAMA: —Plays/librettos/scripts

Pennsylvania State UP; 1987. vii, 368 pp. Notes. Lang.: Eng.

UK-England. 1918-1935. Critical studies. ▪Playacting and gamesmanship as the mode of conducting public and private affairs.

2826 Weintraub, Rosalie. "Johnny's Dream: *Misalliance*." 171-186 in Turco, Alfred, Jr., ed. *Shaw: The Neglected Plays.* Shaw: The Annual of Bernard Shaw Studies 7. University Park and London: Pennsylvania State UP; 1987. vii, 368 pp. Notes. Lang.: Eng.

UK-England. 1909-1911. Critical studies. ▪*Misalliance* as a Freudian dream play.

2827 Whitman, Robert F. "Shaw Listens to the Actors: The Completion of *The Devil's Disciple*." 67-78 in Leary, Daniel, ed. *Shaw's Plays in Performance.* University Park/London: Pennsylvania State UP; 1983. vi, 262 pp. (Shaw: The Annual of Bernard Shaw Studies (ShawR).) Notes. Lang.: Eng.

UK-England. 1896-1909. Critical studies. ▪Manuscript versions, letters and other documents reveal struggle to find a suitable ending for *The Devil's Disciple*.

2828 McIlroy, Brian. "An Interview with Playwright John Boyd." *IUR.* 1987 Fall; 17(2): 242-250. Notes. Lang.: Eng.

UK-Ireland: Belfast. 1930-1985. Histories-sources. ▪Interview by Brian McIlroy of Belfast playwright John Boyd: his life, plays, influences and involvement with Belfast's Lyric Theatre.

2829 Mengel, Hagal. "A Lost Heritage: Ulster Drama and the Work of Sam Thompson." *ThIr.* 1982 Sep-Dec.; 1: 18-19. Illus.: Photo. B&W. 2. Lang.: Eng.

UK-Ireland. 1900-1982. Historical studies. ▪Part I discusses the work of several obscure Irish playwrights writing before Sam Thompson. Part II (*ThIr* 1983 Jan-May, 2) considers Thompson's working-class dramas that deal with Protestant-Catholic conflict in the 1950s.

2830 Muinzer, Philomena. "Evacuating the Museum: The Crisis of Playwriting in Ulster." *NTQ.* 1987 Feb.; 3(9): 44-63. Illus.: Photo. Print. B&W. 8. Lang.: Eng.

UK-Ireland. 1979-1987. Critical studies. ▪Recent plays by Northern Irish writers do little to analyze the 'Troubles'. Plays fit too easily into old forms, and do not challenge politically nor aesthetically.

2831 Roll-Hansen, Diderik. "Dramatic Strategy in Christina Reid's *Tea in a China Cup*." *MD.* 1987 Sep.; 30(3): 389-395. Notes. Lang.: Eng.

UK-Ireland: Belfast. 1983-1987. Critical studies. ▪Reid shows Belfast from a female and social viewpoint, using non-naturalistic staging to dramatize her realistic subject-matter.

2832 Worthen, William B. "The Discipline of the Theatrical Sense: *At the Hawk's Well* and the Rhetoric of the Stage." *MD.* 1987 Mar.; 30(1): 90-103. Notes. Lang.: Eng.

UK-Ireland. 1916-1987. Critical studies. ▪Yeats's dance plays explore the effect of the elements of performance on text.

2833 *Ukrainskaja romantičeskaja drama 30-80-ch gov.: Avtoref. dis. kand. filo. nauk.* (Ukrainian Romantic Drama from the 1830s to the 1880s: Abstract of a Dissertation by a Candidate in Philology.) Kiev: In-t literatury; 1987. 17 pp. Lang.: Rus.

Ukraine. 1830-1889. Critical studies.

2834 Bojko, V. "Festival' ukrainskoj dramaturgii—na...Ukraine." (Festival of Ukrainian Dramaturgy—In the Ukraine.) *SovD.* 1987; 4: 228-233. Lang.: Rus.

Ukraine. 1980-1987. Critical studies. ▪Scarce attention paid to national dramaturgy by Ukrainian theatres.

2835 Kucenko, L.V. *Žanrovoe bogatstvo ukrainskoj sovetskoj dramaturgii 20-ch godov: Avtoref. dis. kand. filolog. nauk.* (The Wealth of Genres of Soviet Ukrainian Drama in the Twenties: Abstract of a Dissertation by a Candidate in Philology.) Kiev: Kiev. un-t.; 1987. 25 pp. Lang.: Rus.

Ukraine. 1920-1929. Historical studies.

2836 "John Oliver Killens: Through Him We Heard Thunder." *BlackM.* 1987 Nov-Dec.; 4(3): 12-13. Illus.: Photo. B&W. 1. Lang.: Eng.

USA: New York, NY. 1954-1987. Biographical studies. ▪Life of playwright John O. Killens, including an excerpt from his play *Youngblood.*

2837 "Mikuk Huikokae Natananun Mikuksahoi." (American Society Shown in the Playscripts of U.S.A.)*KTR.* 1987 Oct.(7): 62-76. Lang.: Kor.

USA. 1969-1982. Critical studies. ▪Views of American society and race relations in *The Great White Hope* by Howard Sackler, *That Championship Season* by Jason Miller and *A Soldier's Play* by Charles Fuller.

2838 Arnold, Stephanie K. "Multiple Spaces, Simultaneous Action and Illusion." *TID.* 1987; 9: 259-269. Notes. Lang.: Eng.

USA. 1950-1980. Critical studies. ▪Transformation of the audience/performer relationship in experimental theatre. Nature of theatre space in environmental theatre. Audience re-positioned in a non-confrontational but not passive manner.

2839 Austin, Gayle. "Women/Text/Theatre." *PerAJ.* 1985 Sum/Fall; 9(26-27): 185-190. Lang.: Eng.

USA: New York, NY. 1977-1985. Critical studies. ▪Need for integration of playwrights, directors and performers in creating women's theatre.

2840 Bermel, Albert. "A Crutch of the Poet." *EON.* 1987 Spr; 11(1): 10-14. Lang.: Eng.

USA. 1935. Historical studies. ▪Analysis of Eugene O'Neill's *A Touch of the Poet*: and his concept of 'pipe dreams'.

2841 Berry, David W. "Albee and the Iceman: O'Neill's Influence on *Who's Afraid of Virginia Woolf?*." *EON.* 1987 Win; 11(3): 18-21. Biblio. Lang.: Eng.

USA. 1949-1962. Critical studies. ▪Influence of O'Neill's *The Iceman Cometh* on Edward Albee's *Who's Afraid of Virginia Woolf?*.

2842 Black, Stephen A. "The War Among the Tyrones." *EON.* 1987 Sum/Fall; 11(2): 29-31. Lang.: Eng.

USA. 1940. Critical studies. ▪Psychological complexity of Eugene O'Neill's *Long Day's Journey into Night*.

2843 Borreca, Art. "*Old Times*: Pinter's Drama of the Invisible." 71-84 in Cardullo, Bert, ed. *Before His Eyes: Essays in Honor of Stanley Kauffmann.* Lanham, MD: UP of America; 1986. 185 pp. Pref. Notes. Biblio. Lang.: Eng.

USA: New York, NY. 1971-1984. Critical studies. ▪Structural analysis of Pinter's play *Old Times*. Author uses a 1984 New York production at the Roundabout Theatre to prove his thesis.

2844 Brown-Guillory, Elizabeth. "Alice Childress: A Pioneering Spirit." *Sage.* 1987 Spr; 4(1): 66-68. Lang.: Eng.

USA: New York, NY, Baltimore, MD. 1987. Histories-sources. ▪Interview with playwright: influential people and experiences, acting and directing with American Negro Theatre.

2845 Cadden, Michael. "Don Juan in the Age of AIDS." *AmTh.* 1987 Nov.; 4(8): 42-44. Illus.: Photo. B&W. 1. Lang.: Eng.

USA. 1987. Textual studies. ▪Transformation in symbolism of the Don Juan myth due to the AIDS health crisis. Recent production addressing this issue.

2846 Cameron, Lindsley. "The Forging of *Steel Magnolias*." *TheaterW.* 1987 Aug 24; 2: 29-32. Illus.: Photo. 4. Lang.: Eng.

USA: New York, NY. 1987. Histories-sources. ▪Playwright Robert Harling discusses his approach to *Steel Magnolias* and its cathartic impact on audience, playwright and cast. Cast members discuss experience of performing the play, and set designer Edward Gianfrancesco discusses his design.

2847 Capetillo, Manuel. "Festival de teatro latino." (Festival of Latin Theatre.) *UMex.* 1987 Dec.; 42(443): 33-35. Illus.: Photo. B&W. 2. Lang.: Spa.

USA: New York, NY. Latin America. Spain. 1987. Critical studies. ▪Description of Venezuelan, Argentinian and Spanish entries in the Festival of Latin Theatre. Includes discussion of the unifying themes in plays presented by these groups.

2848 Carpenter, John; Thomas, Craig; Omans, Stuart E. "A Suite from *King Lear*. A Collaborative Experiment in Critical Response." *JDTC.* 1987; 1(2): 113-143. MU. Lang.: Eng.

DRAMA: —Plays/librettos/scripts

USA. 1987. Critical studies. ■Experiment in musical composition conducted in critical response to *King Lear*. Musical responses for the emotional changes of three characters.

2849   Cattaneo, Anne. "'Stop Me Before I Write Another Act'." *AmTh.* 1987 Mar.; 3(12): 18-23. Illus.: Photo. Print. B&W. 8. Lang.: Eng.

USA. 1930-1987. Critical studies. ■One-act plays: history, structure and renewed interest in them. One-act festivals and specific productions.

2850   Clark, Larry D. "Female Characters on the New York Stage in the Year of Suffrage: Enter Advocacy, Quietly, Stage Left." *THSt.* 1987; 7: 51-60. Notes. Lang.: Eng.

USA: New York, NY. 1920. Historical studies. ■American women won the right to vote in 1920, but Broadway plays in this season with a few notable exceptions continued to reflect stereotyped characterizations of women.

2851   Cody, Gabrielle; Schechter, Joel. "An Interview with Athol Fugard." *ThM.* 1987; 19(1): 70-72. Lang.: Eng.

USA: New Haven, CT. 1987. Histories-sources. ■Interview on the production of his play *A Place with the Pigs* at the Yale Repertory Theatre. The play, the production and the sources.

2852   Cullen, Rosemary L. "A Checklist of American Civil War Drama: Beginning to 1900." *PAR.* 1987; 12: 135-155. Lang.: Eng.

USA. 1852-1900. Bibliographical studies. ■A bibliography of plays written between 1861 and 1900 specifically related to the Civil War period.

2853   Demastes, William W. "Understanding Sam Shepard's Realism." *CompD.* 1987 Fall; 21(3): 229-248. Notes. Lang.: Eng.

USA. 1960-1987. Critical studies. ■In-depth analysis and comparison of the characters and themes of playwright Sam Shepard's early and more recent plays. Progression toward the traditional reflects a maturation of technique rather than a loss of faith in the ideals of the 1960s.

2854   Demastes, William W. "Charles Fuller and *A Soldier's Play*: Attacking Prejudice, Challenging Form." *SAD.* 1987; 2: 43-56. Biblio. Illus.: Photo. B&W. 2. Lang.: Eng.

USA. 1976-1981. Critical studies. ■Connects the play's events to arguments over the most efficacious method of liberation for African-Americans. Debates between group militancy and personal liberation, weights the article in favor of the latter.

2855   Devries, Hilary. "A Song in Search of Itself." *AmTh.* 1987 Jan.; 3(10): 22-25. Illus.: Photo. B&W. 3. Lang.: Eng.

USA. 1970-1987. Histories-sources. ■Playwright August Wilson, his plays and their productions, and his contribution to Black American theatre.

2856   Digaetani, John. "An Interview with Albert Innaurato." *SAD.* 1987; 2: 87-95. Illus.: Photo. . B&W. 1. Lang.: Eng.

USA. 1986. Histories-sources. ■Discusses his work, his career, the state of contemporary theatre in America and the Italian-American experience.

2857   Dutton, Richard. "The Year's Contribution to Shakespearian Study: Shakespeare's Life, Times and Stage." *ShS.* 1986; 39: 223-236. Notes. Lang.: Eng.

USA. UK-England. 1564-1616. Biographical studies. ■Recent studies of the life of William Shakespeare with some attention to Shakespeare's contemporaries.

2858   Dyclos, Donald P. "A Plank in Faulkner's 'Lumber Room': *The Emperor Jones* and *Light in August*." *EON.* 1987 Sum/Fall; 11(2): 8-13. Biblio. Lang.: Eng.

USA: New York, NY. 1920-1962. Critical studies. ■Eugene O'Neill's influence on William Faulkner.

2859   Egan, Philip. "Ronald Ribman: A Classified Bibliography." *SAD.* 1987; 2: 97-117. Illus.: Photo. B&W. 1. Lang.: Eng.

USA. 1987. Bibliographical studies. ■Bibliography of Ribman's works, interviews with the playwright, criticism and reviews of his work, information on his life and works.

2860   Erben, Rudolf. "Women and Other Men in Sam Shepard Plays." *SAD.* 1987; 2: 29-41. Biblio. Illus.: Photo. B&W. 1. Lang.: Eng.

USA. 1960-1987. Critical studies. ■Gender roles in Shepard's plays. In early 1960s women represent the loss of individuality, in the 1970s women are responsible for the destruction of the family and in his most recent work he has begun to reassess his approach to a limited extent.

2861   Fielder, Mari Kathleen. "Green and Gold Reconsidered: The Identity and Assimilation Dilemma of the American Irish as Reflected in the Drama of Edward Everett Rose." *TheatreS.* 1983-84; 30: 29-42. Illus.: Photo. B&W. 3. Lang.: Eng.

USA. 1900-1920. Critical studies. ■Hibernian drama of early twentieth century.

2862   Frazier, Kermit; Leicht, John. "Journey to Justice." *AmTh.* 1987 Mar.; 3(12): 4-5. Illus.: Photo. Print. B&W. 1. Lang.: Eng.

USA: Milwaukee, WI. 1978-1987. Histories-sources. ■Research by playwrights of Milwaukee Repertory production, *An American Journey*. Includes interviews of people involved in murder case.

2863   Fu, Hong-Zhuo. "You jin ao ni er fen xi." (The Tragedy of Eugene O'Neill.) *XYishu.* 1985 Sum; 30: 54-62. Notes. Lang.: Chi.

USA. China, People's Republic of. 1930-1985. Critical studies. ■From a Chinese theatre standpoint, outlines the dramatic theory of Eugene O'Neill.

2864   Fuchs, Elinor. "Presence and the Revenge of Writing." *PerAJ.* 1985 Sum/Fall; 9(26-27): 163-173. Lang.: Eng.

USA. 1985. Critical studies. ■Dramatic writing as the focus in theatre ahead of performance itself.

2865   Garland, Phyl. "Wole Soyinka: Nobel Laureate Noted Nigerian Playwright is the First Black to Win Prize in Literature." *Ebony.* 1987 Apr.; 42(6): 141-142, 146. Illus.: Photo. Color. B&W. 3. Lang.: Eng.

USA: New York, NY. Nigeria. 1959-1986. Biographical studies. ■The career of playwright Wole Soyinka.

2866   Garner, Stanton B., Jr. "Visual Field in Beckett's Late Plays." *CompD.* 1987/88 Win; 21(4): 349-373. Notes. Lang.: Eng.

USA. 1970-1980. Critical studies. ■Study of Beckett's visual art. Exploration of his language with a parallel study of his vision as it is actualized in theatre.

2867   Garvey, Sheila Hickey. "Notes on a Work in Progress: An Interview with Barbara Gelb." *EON.* 1987 Spr; 11(1): 21-25. Lang.: Eng.

USA. 1962-1987. Critical studies. ■Barbara Gelb discusses the creation of *My Gene*.

2868   Guernsey, Otis L., Jr. "Conversation with Arthur Miller." *DGQ.* 1987; 24(2): 12-21. Illus.: Sketches. 2. Lang.: Eng.

USA. 1944-1987. Histories-sources. ■Discusses definition of plays, Miller's career, training, economics of being a playwright, reception of his plays.

2869   Harrop, John. "Ibsen Translated by Lewis Carroll: The Theatre of John Guare." *NTQ.* 1987 May; 3(10): 150-154. Illus.: Photo. B&W. 2. Lang.: Eng.

USA. 1960-1987. Critical studies. ■John Guare's work and his insights into American society.

2870   Harrop, John. "'Living in that Dark Room': The Playwright and his Audience." *NTQ.* 1987; 3(10): 155-159. Lang.: Eng.

USA. 1987. Histories-sources. ■Interview with playwright John Guare.

2871   Harrop, John. "NTQ Checklist No. 3: John Guare." *NTQ.* 1987 May; 3(10): 160-177. Biblio. Illus.: Photo. Poster. B&W. 8. Lang.: Eng.

USA. 1938-1987. Historical studies. ■Chronological listing of Guare's plays and first-performance details, together with bibliography and listing of reviews.

2872   Hinden, Michael. "When Playwrights Talk to God: Peter Shaffer and the Legacy of O'Neill." *CompD.* 1982 Spr; 16(1): 49-63 . Notes. Lang.: Eng.

USA. 1920-1982. Critical studies. ■Comparison of thematic concerns and dramaturgical techniques of Peter Shaffer and Eugene O'Neill. Shaffer considered heir to O'Neill's theatrical legacy.

DRAMA: —Plays/librettos/scripts

2873 Horovitz, Israel. "The Legacy of O'Neill." *EON.* 1987 Spr; 11(1): 3-10. Lang.: Eng.
USA: Boston, MA. France: Paris. 1939-1953. Biographical studies. ■Influences of Eugene O'Neill and Samuel Beckett on the life and career of playwright Israel Horovitz.

2874 Huerta, Jorge A. "The Influences of Latin American Theatre on Teatro Chicano." *Revista Chicano-Riquena.* 1983 Spr; 9(1): 68-75. Lang.: Eng.
USA. 1598-1983. Critical studies. ■Influences of Spanish-language theatre on Chicano theatre, historical development of dramatic form in performance.

2875 Hyman, Collette A. "Workers on Stage: An Annotated Bibliography of Labor Plays of the 1930's." *PAR.* 1987; 12: 171-195. Lang.: Eng.
USA. 1930-1940. Bibliographical studies. ■A short essay identifying the genre and a complete listing of all plays.

2876 Jackson, Caroline. "*Fences*: The Odyssey of a Play." *BlackM.* 1987 Feb-Mar.; 3(6): 4, 11. 1. Lang.: Eng.
USA: New York, NY. 1985-1987. Histories-sources. ■Playwright August Wilson discusses the development of his play *Fences*.

2877 Jefferson, Margo. "Portrait of the Artist as a Young Woman." *AmTh.* 1987 July/Aug.; 4(4): 36-37. Lang.: Eng.
USA: New York, NY. 1987. Biographical studies. ■Life and work of playwright Adrienne Kennedy. Discussion of her plays.

2878 Jones, Daniel R. "Peter Shaffer's Continued Quest for God in *Amadeus*." *CompD.* 1987 Sum; 21(2): 145-155. Notes. Lang.: Eng.
USA. UK-England. 1979-1984. Critical studies. ■Evolution of playwright Peter Shaffer's characters' search for God in his plays *Amadeus*, *Equus* and *The Royal Hunt of the Sun*.

2879 Kern, Edith. "*Not I*—Says Beckett." *JDTC.* 1987; 1(2): 73-85. Notes. Lang.: Eng.
USA. 1972-1987. Critical studies. ■Analysis of Samuel Beckett's *Not I* using psychoanalytical theory and Nietzsche.

2880 Koste, Virginia Glasgow. "Mere Giants: The Child Protagonist in Drama for Intergenerational Audiences." *YTJ.* 1987 Sum; 2(1): 19-21. Lang.: Eng.
USA. 1987. Critical studies. ■The child character in the role of protagonist, seeking meaning and learning to survive.

2881 Laerner, Richard. "Response to an Epidemic." *AmTh.* 1987 July/Aug.; 4(4): 31-32. Illus.: Photo. B&W. 1. Lang.: Eng.
USA: New York, NY, San Francisco, CA. 1987. Critical studies. ■Impact of AIDS crisis on the theatre. Recent plays and playwrights show commitment to explore social issues involved.

2882 Levy, Ellen. "Inspiration in its Roots: The Place of Poetry in the Theatre of Lee Breuer." *ThM.* 1987; 18(2): 66-68. Lang.: Eng.
USA. 1987. Critical studies. ■Breuer's animal analogies as a device to foreground human behavior and choices. The illusion of connections through language and art.

2883 Londré, Felicia Hardison. "Sam Shepard Works Out: The Masculinization of America." *SAD.* 1987; 2: 19-27. Biblio. Lang.: Eng.
USA. 1976-1987. Critical studies. ■Sam Shepard's evolving female characters influenced by changes in his personal life and his developing sense as a playwright. Focuses on the character of Beth in *A Lie of the Mind*.

2884 Lyons, Charles R. "Perceiving *Rockaby*—As a Text, As a Text by Samuel Beckett, As a Text for Performance." *CompD.* 1982-83 Win; 16(4): 297-311. Notes. Lang.: Eng.
USA. 1982. Critical studies. ■Analysis of text and characters in Beckett's *Rockaby*: textuality and intertextuality of his writing, processes audience employs when attending plays of Beckett.

2885 Manelle, Bette. "Family Ties: Landscape and Gender in *Desire Under the Elms*." *EON.* 1987 Sum/Fall; 11(2): 19-23. Biblio. Lang.: Eng.
USA. 1920. Critical studies. ■Family and male-female relationships in *Desire Under the Elms*.

2886 Manheim, Michael. "O'Neill's Transcendence of Melodrama in *A Touch of the Poet* and *A Moon for the Misbegotten*." *CompD.* 1982 Fall; 16(3): 238-250. Notes. Lang.: Eng.
USA. 1922-1947. Critical studies. ■Late O'Neill plays which transcend melodrama: their comparable plots, themes and characterizations.

2887 Mason, Jeffrey D. "Farcical Laughter in *True West*." *TA.* 1987; 42: 29-38. Notes. Lang.: Eng.
USA. 1981. Critical studies. ■Analysis of structure and character development to define the genre of farce. Focus on Sam Shepard's *True West* as an example of a farce in the guise of serious drama.

2888 Maufort, Marc. "The Legacy of Melville's *Pierre*: Family Relationships in *Mourning Becomes Electra*." *EON.* 1987 Sum/Fall; 11(2): 23-28. Notes. Lang.: Eng.
USA. 1927. Critical studies. ■The influence of Herman Melville on Eugene O'Neill.

2889 McConachie, Bruce A. "Herne's *Shore Acres* and the Family in the Tradition of the Irish-American Theatre." *TheatreS.* 1983-84; 30: 16-28. Lang.: Eng.
USA. 1839-1901. Critical studies. ■Irish influence on American theatre through Irish-American playwrights.

2890 McKelly, James C. "Ain't It the Truth: *Hughie* and the Power of Fiction." *EON.* 1987 Spr; 11(1): 15-19. Biblio. Lang.: Eng.
USA. 1941-1959. Critical studies. ■Importance of language in Eugene O'Neill's *Hughie*.

2891 Myers, Larry. "Alan Bowne: As Outspoken as His Plays." *TheaterW.* 1987 Oct.; 2(7): 34-35. Illus.: Photo. Poster. B&W. 3. Lang.: Eng.
USA: New York, NY. Biographical studies. ■Film and stage versions of *Forty Deuce* by Alan Bowne. Author's technique, actors who appeared in both versions.

2892 Myers, Larry. "Gordon Rogoff." *TheaterW.* 1987 Oct.; 1(8): 14-16. Illus.: Photo. B&W. 1. Lang.: Eng.
USA: New York, NY. 1931-1987. Biographical studies. ■Theatre critic Gordon Rogoff is awarded the George Jean Nathan Award. Discusses state of the art with author.

2893 Myers, Larry. "Leslie Lee: Sharing the Legacy." *BlackM.* 1987 Mar-Apr.; 3(7): 4, 10. Illus.: Photo. B&W. 1. Lang.: Eng.
USA: Bryn Mawr, PA, New York, NY. 1987. Histories-sources. ■Playwright Leslie Lee talks about his creative process and makes suggestions to new playwrights.

2894 Myers, Larry. "Knowing Where You're Going: A Conversation with John Ford Noonan." *TheaterW.* 1987 31 Aug.-6 Sep.; 1(3): 14-17. Illus.: Photo. B&W. 2. Lang.: Eng.
USA. 1970-1987. Histories-sources. ■Interview with playwright John Ford Noonan discussing his background and techniques for playwriting. Teaching playwriting, teachers actors and playwrights who have influenced him.

2895 Myers, Larry. "'Playwriting is Very Physical': A Conversation with Terrence McNally." *TheaterW.* 1987 Aug 17; 1: 32-34. Illus.: Photo. 3. Lang.: Eng.
USA: New York, NY. 1987. Histories-sources. ■Terrence McNally explains how he approaches the craft of playwriting: theme, character, scene development, comic lines and observation.

2896 Myers, Larry. "Making It Real: A Conversation with Christopher Hampton." *TheaterW.* 1987 Aug 24; 2: 24-26. Illus.: Photo. 3. Lang.: Eng.
USA: New York, NY. UK-England: London. 1987. Histories-sources. ■Christopher Hampton discusses techniques of playwriting: analysis of plot, structure and what makes a play successful.

2897 Orona-Cordova, Roberta. "*Zoot Suit* and the Pachuco Phenomenon: An Interview with Luis Valdez." *Revista Chicano-Riquena.* 1983 Spr; 9(1): 95-111. Lang.: Eng.
USA. 1940-1983. Histories-sources. ■Interview with playwright Luis Valdez, discussing thematic elements in *Zoot Suit*, including development of the pachuco character.

2898 Paller, Michael. "Driving the *Milk Train*: A Conversation with Elizabeth Ashley and Marian Seldes." *TheaterW.* 1987

DRAMA: —Plays/librettos/scripts

28 Dec.-1988 3 Jan.; 1(20): 8-11. Illus.: Photo. B&W. 5. Lang.: Eng.

USA: New York, NY. 1987. Histories-sources. ■Interview with actresses Elizabeth Ashley and Marian Seldes discussing *The Milk Train Doesn't Stop Here Anymore* and other Tennessee Williams plays.

2899 Paran, Janice. "Redressing Ibsen." *AmTh.* 1987 Nov.; 4(8): 14-20. Illus.: Photo. B&W. 7. Lang.: Eng.

USA. 1987. Historical studies. ■Directors Emily Mann, Maria Irene Fornes and Timothy Near direct 'feminist' productions of the plays of Henrik Ibsen. Discusses several plays and heroines.

2900 Patterson, Lindsay. "Alonzo D. Lamont, Jr., and *That Serious He-Man Ball*." *TheaterW.* 1987 Dec 7-13; 1(17): 20-22. Illus.: Photo. 3. Lang.: Eng.

USA: New York, NY. 1987. Critical studies. ■Alonzo Lamont's major themes in *That Serious He-Man Ball.*

2901 Paverman, V.M. *Amerikanskaja dramaturgija 60-ch godov XX veka.* (American Dramaturgy of the 1960s.) Sverdlovsk: Izd-vo Ural. un-ta; 1987. 169 pp. Lang.: Rus.

USA. 1960-1969. Historical studies. ■Chapter 1: Ideational-aesthetic Searching in the Theatre of Edward Albee. Ch. 2: The Struggle Against Racism. Ch. 3: The Politicization of American Drama.

2902 Putzel, Steven. "Expectation, Confutation, Revelation: Audience Complicity in the Plays of Sam Shepard." *MD.* 1987 June; 30(2): 147-160. Notes. Lang.: Eng.

USA. 1976-1986. Critical studies. ■How Shepard's plays have changed, or been altered in performance, to accommodate his changing audience.

2903 Rabillard, Sheila. "Sam Shepard: Theatrical Power and American Dreams." *MD.* 1987 Mar.; 30(1): 58-71. Notes. Lang.: Eng.

USA. 1965-1986. Critical studies. ■The exploration of theatricality links Shepard's early and later plays, revealing the theatricality of American culture.

2904 Rabkin, Gerald. "Is There a Text on This Stage?" *PerAJ.* 1985 Sum/Fall; 9(26-27): 160-162. Lang.: Eng.

USA. Critical studies. ■Privileges of dramatic authors concerning interpretation of their texts and emergence of the director as auteur.

2905 Radel, Nicholas F. "'What's the Meaning of This Corn, Tilden!': Mimesis in Sam Shepard's *Buried Child.*" 177-189 in Hartigan, Karelisa V., ed. *From the Bard to Broadway.* Lanham, MD: UP of America; 1987. 222 pp. (Univ. of Florida Dept. of Classics Comparative Drama Conference Papers 7.) Pref. Notes. Biblio. Lang.: Eng.

USA. 1978. Critical studies. ■The symbol of corn and its effect on the audience in Sam Shepard's *Buried Child.*

2906 Reed, Terry. "O'Neill's Nausikaa Episode." *EON.* 1987 Win; 11(2): 8-9. Biblio. Lang.: Eng.

USA. 1921. Critical studies. ■Parallels between O'Neill's *Anna Christie* and Homer's *Odyssey.*

2907 Salinas, Mike. "American Playwrights, American Politics: Why Are There No American Ibsens?" *TheaterW.* 1987 Aug 31; 3: 10-13. Illus.: Photo. 4. Lang.: Eng.

USA: New York, NY. 1987. Critical studies. ■Three of the few political dramas by American writers: David Shaber: *Bunker Reveries*, Larry Kramer: *The Normal Heart* and Emily Mann: *Execution of Justice.*

2908 Savran, David. "Both Halves of Richard Foreman: The Playwright." *AmTh.* 1987 July/Aug.; 4(4): 14, 19-21, 49-50. Illus.: Photo. Print. B&W. 5. Lang.: Eng.

USA: New York, NY. 1962-1987. Histories-sources. ■Interview with Richard Foreman and discussion of his work as playwright from his early career at Yale Drama School to the Ontological Hysteric Theatre.

2909 Savran, David. "Trading in the American Dream." *AmTh.* 1987 Sep.; 4(6): 12-18. Illus.: Photo. 5. Lang.: Eng.

USA: Chicago, IL, New York, NY. 1969-1987. Histories-sources. ■Interview with playwright David Mamet: background, early work, recurring themes in his plays.

2910 Schlueter, June. "*Keep Tightly Closed in a Cool Dry Place*: Megan Terry's Transformational Drama and the Possibilities of Self." *SAD.* 1987; 2: 59-69. Illus.: Photo. B&W. 1. Lang.: Eng.

USA. 1987. Critical studies. ■Examines author's 'transformational' plays written for the Open Theatre in the 1960s. Plays deal with shifting and multiple selves in unstable situations and contexts. Links plays to later feminist politics.

2911 Schvey, Henry I. "At the Deathbed: Edward Albee's *All Over.*" *MD.* 1987 Sep.; 30(3): 352-363. Notes. Lang.: Eng.

USA. 1971-1987. Critical studies. ■Edvard Munch's painting *Death in the Sickroom* used to demonstrate that Albee's subject is the spiritual death of the survivors.

2912 Sheaffer, Louis. "Taasinge or Tharsing?" *EON.* 1987 Spr; 11(1): 26. Lang.: Eng.

USA. 1890. Historical studies. ■Investigation of Eugene O'Neill's third wife's last name.

2913 Shirakawa, Sam. "Jewish Geography: From Second Avenue to Broadway." *TheaterW.* 1987 28 Dec.-1988 3 Jan.; 1(20): 22-26. Illus.: Poster. 9. Lang.: Eng.

USA: New York, NY. 1881-1987. Historical studies. ■Influence of Yiddish and Jewish theatre on mainstream American theatre. Plot/themes of four Off Broadway shows with strong Jewish focus.

2914 Shirakawa, Sam. "Play Money." *TheaterW.* 1987 Dec 21-27; 1(19): 20-23. 4. Lang.: Eng.

USA: New York, NY. 1987. Critical studies. ■Comparison of four plays: *Old Business* by Joe Cacaci, Bartlett Cormack's *The Racket*, Dario Fo's *About Face* and Caryl Churchill's *Serious Money*: themes of money, greed and power.

2915 Shirakawa, Sam. "Original Caste Dramas." *TheaterW.* 1987 Dec 14-20; 1(18): 32-35. Illus.: Photo. 5. Lang.: Eng.

USA: New York, NY. 1987. Critical studies. ■Depiction of the class struggle in contemporary theatre.

2916 Shirakawa, Sam. "Does Nerd Mean Monster?" *TheaterW.* 1987 Nov 2; 1(12): 14-16. Illus.: Photo. Sketches. B&W. 4. Lang.: Eng.

USA: New York, NY. 1987. Historical studies. ■Comparison of Larry Shue's *The Nerd*, Andrew Lloyd Webber's *Phantom of the Opera* and Peter Shaffer's *Amadeus*. Monstrous qualities of the main characters and their impact.

2917 Skloot, Robert. "The Drama of the Holocaust: Issues of Choice and Survival." *NTQ.* 1987 Nov.; 3(12): 337-348. Notes. Lang.: Eng.

USA. Germany, West. 1950-1987. Critical studies. ■Process of dramatically shaping material about the Holocaust forces an attitude to be taken by the dramatists towards the meaning of 'choice' and the 'acceptable' price of survival.

2918 Spencer, Jenny S. "Norman's *'Night, Mother*: Psychodrama of Female Identity." *MD.* 1987 Sep.; 30(3): 364-375. Notes. Lang.: Eng.

USA. 1983-1987. Critical studies. ■Examines the play as psychological drama in order to explain the different reactions of male and female audience members.

2919 Swortzell, Lowell. "O'Neill and the Marionette: Über and Otherwise." *EON.* 1987 Win; 11(3): 3-7. Biblio. Illus.: Sketches. 1. Lang.: Eng.

USA. 1937. Critical studies. ■Influence of puppetry on Eugene O'Neill. Related to Puppetry: Marionettes.

2920 Turi, Gábor. "Találkozás Barrie Stavisszel. 'A dráma csak nyersanyag'." (Interview with Barrie Stavis: 'Drama is But Raw Material'.) *FSM.* 1987; 31(44): 7. Illus.: Photo. B&W. 1. Lang.: Hun.

USA. 1987. Histories-sources. ■A conversation with Barrie Stavis, US dramatist, who spent a few days in Hungary in October. His play *Coat of Many Colors* was staged by István Pinczés at the Csokonai Theatre in Debrecen.

2921 Turner, Beth. "Charles Fuller: Black Pride, Integrity, Success." *BlackM.* 1987 Sep-Oct.; 4(1): 4-5, 11, 16. Illus.: Photo. B&W. 1. Lang.: Eng.

USA: Philadelphia, PA, New York, NY. Korea, South. 1959-1987. Histories-sources. ■The career of playwright Charles Fuller and discussion of other African-American playwrights.

2922 Valency, Maurice. "Maurice Valency Becomes Honorary Member of ISA." *INC.* 1986-87; 7(1): 2-5. Lang.: Eng.

CLASSED ENTRIES

DRAMA: —Plays/librettos/scripts

USA. 1985. Histories-sources. ■Text of author's acceptance speech to Ibsen Society of America. Discusses how tragedy and comedy are united in Ibsen's complex dramatic vision.

2923 Van Laan, Thomas. "*Rosmersholm* Program." *INC.* 1986-87; 7(1): 5-11. Lang.: Eng.

USA. Norway. 1886-1985. Histories-sources. ■Five different approaches to understanding and appreciating Ibsen's *Rosmersholm.* From panel discussion, meeting of Ibsen Society of America.

2924 Van Laan, Thomas. "Editorial." *INC.* 1987; 8: 1-4. Lang.: Eng.

USA. Norway. 1987. Critical studies. ■Much-needed annotations of English-language translations of Ibsen's plays should be facilitated by Ibsen database being developed in Norway.

2925 Viswanathan, R. "*The Jungle Books* and Eugene O'Neill." *EON.* 1987 Sum/Fall; 11(2): 3-7. Lang.: Eng.

USA. 1887-1950. Critical studies. ■Influence of Rudyard Kipling's *The Jungle Books* on Eugene O'Neill.

2926 Voelker, Paul D. "O'Neill's First Families: *Warnings* through *The Personal Equation.*" *EON.* 1987 Sum/Fall; 11(2): 13-17. Biblio. Lang.: Eng.

USA. 1913. Critical studies. ■Importance of family relationships in Eugene O'Neill's plays.

2927 Weales, Gerald. "Clifford's Children: Or, It's a Wise Playwright Who Knows His Own Children." *SAD.* 1987; 2: 3-18. Lang.: Eng.

USA. 1935-1987. Critical studies. ■Part of the 1985 Odets Symposium at the University of Wisconsin-Madison on the influence of Clifford Odets on mainstream American realism. Examines influences on Miller, Williams, Mamet, Shepard and on African-American theatre.

2928 Weber, Carl. "Problems of Trans-Atlantic Traffic." *PerAJ.* 1985 Sum/Fall; 9(26-27): 117-130. Lang.: Eng.

USA. Germany. 1985. Critical studies. ■Challenge of bringing German drama to the United States: how often done and how received.

2929 Whitlatch, Michael. "Eugene O'Neill and Class Consciousness in *The Hairy Ape.*" *ZAA.* 1987; 35(3): 223-227. Lang.: Eng.

USA. 1920-1922. Critical studies. ■Symbolism in the representation of the classes in O'Neill's *The Hairy Ape.*

2930 Wilcox, Leonard. "Modernism vs. Postmodernism: Shepard's *The Tooth of Crime* and the Discourses of Popular Culture." *MD.* 1987 Dec.; 30(4): 560-573. Notes. Lang.: Eng.

USA. 1972-1987. Critical studies. ■The battle between Hoss and Crow is a contest between modernism's futile longing for authenticity and postmodernism's ultimately destructive embrace of the surface.

2931 Wilmeth, Don B. "An Interview with Romulus Linney." *SAD.* 1987; 2: 71-84. Illus.: Photo. . B&W. 1. Lang.: Eng.

USA. 1986. Histories-sources. ■Interview with playwright conducted at Brown University. Discusses his beginnings in theatre, his influences, his directing and his choice of subject matter.

2932 Wilson, Ann. "Fool of Desire: The Spectator to the Plays of Sam Shepard." *MD.* 1987 Mar.; 30(1): 46-57. Notes. Lang.: Eng.

USA. 1967-1983. Critical studies. ■Shepard's exploitation of the tension between the audience's desire to believe what it sees and the deceptiveness of appearance.

2933 *Tvorčestvo Mikoly Zarudnogo i ego mesto v sovremennoj sovetskoj dramaturgii: Avtoref. diss. kand. fil. nauk.* (The Work of Mikola Zarudnyj and its Place in Contemporary Soviet Dramaturgy: Abstract of a Dissertation by a Candidate in Philology.) Odessa: Odes.in-t im. I.I. Mečnikova; 1987. 17 pp. Lang.: Rus.

USSR. 1921-1979. Critical studies.

2934 "Na idei my ne tak už bedny." (In Ideas We Are Not Impoverished.) *TeatZ.* 1987; 14: 24-25. Lang.: Rus.

USSR. 1986-1987. Histories-sources. ■Round-table discussion on Soviet multinational drama under perestrojka.

2935 "Sud'ba odnoaktnoj p'esy." (The Fate of the One-Act Play.) *SovD.* 1987; 4: 267-272. Lang.: Rus.

USSR. 1987. Histories-sources. ■Roundtable of playwrights on problems of the one-act play.

2936 Achmadullin, A.G. *Zaroždehie i formirovanie socialističeskogo realizma v tatarskoj dramaturgii: Avtoref. dis. kand. filol. nauk.* (Conception and Formation of Socialist Realism in Tatar Drama: Abstract of a Dissertation by a Candidate in Philology.) Alma-Ata: AN KazSSR, In-t literatury i iskusstva; 1987. 40. Lang.: Rus.

USSR. 1917-1987. Historical studies.

2937 Alekseev, A. "Diplomatija i ljubov'." (Diplomacy and Love.) *DalVostok.* 1987; 3: 145-149. Lang.: Rus.

USSR: Moscow. 1980-1987. Historical studies. ■Historical events underlying the plays of Andrej Vosnesenskij: *Junona (Juno)* and *Avos' (Perchance).*

2938 Allanzarov, T. *Nekotorye voprosy istorii karakalpakskoj sovetskoj dramaturgii.* (Some Issues in the History of Karakalpakskij Soviet Dramaturgy.) Nukus: Karakalpakstan; 1987. 265 pp. Lang.: Rus.

USSR. 1917-1987. Historical studies. ■History of dramaturgy in Karakalpak ASSR.

2939 Anikst, A., ed. *Šekspirovskie čtenija 1985.* (Shakespearean Readings 1985.) Moscow: Nauka; 1987. 275 pp. Lang.: Rus.

USSR. 1985. Critical studies.

2940 Babajan, I.K. *G. Sundukjan na gruzinskoj scene XIX veka (1874-1903): Avtoref. dis. kand. iskusstvovedenija.* (G. Sundukjan on the Georgian Stage of the Nineteenth Century, 1874-1903: Abstract of a Dissertation by a Candidate in Art Criticism.) Tbilisi: Gruz.gos.teatr.in-t; 1987. Lang.: Rus.

USSR. 1874-1903. Critical studies.

2941 Bobkovskij, V.N. *Problemy dokumental'nosti v sovetskoj dramaturgii 1960-1970 godov: Avtoref. dis. kand. iskusstvovedenija.* (Problems of Documentality in Soviet Drama of the Sixties and Seventies: Abstract of a Dissertation by a Candidate in Art Criticism.) Moscow: M-vo kul-tury RSFSR, LGITMiK; 1987. 24 pp. Lang.: Rus.

USSR. 1960-1979. Historical studies.

2942 Borodina, L.P. *Zanrovo-stilevye iskanija v sovetskoj dramaturgii 60-80-h godov: Avtoref. dis. kand. filolog. nauk.* (Genre and Stylistic Strivings in Soviet Dramaturgy from the 1960s through the 1980s: Abstract of a Dissertation by a Candidate in Philology.) Moscow: MGU im. M.V. Lomonosova; 1987. 17 pp. Lang.: Rus.

USSR. 1960-1987. Critical studies. ■Experiments in genre and style.

2943 Bugrov, B.S. *Geroj prinimaet rešenie: Dviženie dramy ot 50-ch godov.* (The Hero Decides: The Movement of Drama from the 1950s.) Moscow: Sov. pisatel'; 1987. 364 pp. Lang.: Rus.

USSR. 1950-1987. Critical studies.

2944 Daševskaja, O.A. *Structura dejstvija v sovremennoj sovetskoj dramaturgii (prostranstvenno-vremennaja organizacija): Avtoref. dis. kand. filol. nauk.* (The Structure of Action in Contemporary Soviet Drama (Time-Space Organization): Abstract of a Dissertation by a Candidate in Philology.) Tomsk: Tomskij un-t; 1987. 18 pp. Lang.: Rus.

USSR. 1980-1987. Critical studies.

2945 Golikova, N. "Anempodist, gde ty?" (Anempodist, Where Are You?)*SovD.* 1987; 4: 242-247. Lang.: Rus.

USSR. 1960-1979. Critical studies. ■The industrial theme in the plays of playwright I. Dvoreckij.

2946 Hekli, József. "Portrévázlat Leonyid Zorinról." (Draft Portrait of Leonid Zorin.) *Sz.* 1987 Oct.; 20(10) : 36-41. Lang.: Hun.

USSR. 1941-1980. Critical studies. ■Short review of Leonid Zorin, one of the most renowned and fertile Soviet dramatists.

2947 Ikramova, R.T. *Dramaturgija V. Šekspira v perevodach kazachskich sovetskich pisatelej (30-60 gg.): Avtoref. dis. kand. fil. nauk.* (The Drama of W. Shakespeare in the Translation of Soviet Kazakh Writers from the Thirties

DRAMA: —Plays/librettos/scripts

through the Sixties: Abstract of a Dissertation by a Candidate in Philology.) Alma-Ata: Kazah. un-t S.M. Kirova; 1987. 24 pp. Lang.: Rus.

USSR. 1930-1969. Critical studies.

2948 Kališ, V. "Dvoe v gorode." (A Duo in the City.) *TeatZ.* 1987; 11: 26-29. Lang.: Rus.

USSR. 1937-1972. Biographical studies. ■Work of playwright Aleksand'r Vampilov.

2949 Karaulov, A. "O slave dobroj i nedobroj." (On a Reputation Good and Bad.) *TeatZ.* 1987; 15: 28-29. Lang.: Rus.

USSR. 1980-1987. Critical studies. ■On the dramaturgy of Aleksand'r Galin.

2950 Katyšev, V. "Približenie: k 50-letiju so dnja roždenija Aleksandra Vampilova." (The Approach: Toward the Fiftieth Anniversary of the Birth of Aleksandr Vampilov.) *DalVostok.* 1987; 8: 145-153. Lang.: Rus.

USSR. 1937-1972. Critical studies. ■Poetics of Vampilov's dramaturgy.

2951 Kuznecov, S.N. *Chudožestvennaja priroda–'Višnevogo sada' A.P. Čechova: Avtoref. dis. kand. fil. nauk.* (The Artistic Nature of Čechov's *Cherry Orchard*: Abstract of a Dissertation by a Candidate in Philology.) Leningrad: Leningr.un-t; 1987. 22 pp. Lang.: Rus.

USSR. 1904. Critical studies.

2952 Lakšin, V. "Proval." (The Trap.) *TeatrM.* 1987; 4: 83-91. Lang.: Rus.

USSR. 1898-1987. Critical studies. ■On riddles in *Čajka (The Seagull)* by Anton Čechov.

2953 Law, Alma H. "On Radzinsky's *Jogging.*" *SEEDTF.* 1987 Dec.; 7(2 & 3): 62-63. Lang.: Eng.

USSR: Moscow. 1987. Critical studies. ■Based on a production of the play by Valerij Fokin at the Jermolova Theatre.

2954 Mal'gin, A. "Pochiščenie Svjatoslava." (The Abduction of Sviatoslav.) *TeatrM.* 1987; 9: 106-114. Lang.: Eng.

USSR. 1980-1987. Critical studies. ■Polemical reflections: people and events from the history of the fatherland in contemporary plays by M. Vartolomeev, P. Red'kin and P. Pavloskij.

2955 Mironov, V.L. *Idejno-chudožestvennye poiski v dramaturgii I.L. Sel'vinskogo: Avtoref. dis. kand. fil. nauk.* (Ideational-Artistic Quests in the Plays of I.L. Sel'vinskij: Abstract of a Dissertation by a Candidate in Philology.) Moscow: Ped.in-t im N.K. Krupskoj; 1987. 16 pp. Lang.: Rus.

USSR. 1899-1968. Critical studies.

2956 Mjagkov, B. "Zojkiny kvartiry." (Zojka's Apartments.) *Neva.* 1987; 7: 200-204. Lang.: Rus.

USSR: Moscow. 1926. Historical studies. ■Creation of *Zojkina kvartire (Zojka's Apartment)* by M.A. Bulgakov: prototypes of characters.

2957 Najdakov, V.C.; Impchelova, S.S. *Burjatskaja sovetskaja dramaturgija.* (Burjaskij Soviet Dramturgy.) Novosibirsk: Nauka; 1987. 269 pp. Lang.: Rus.

USSR: Burjatija. 1917-1987. Critical studies.

2958 Perchin, V.V. "Iz istorii izučenija poétiki V.V. Majakovskogo–dramaturga." (From the History of the Study of the Poetics of the Dramatist V.V. Majakovskij.) *RLit.* 1987; 2: 180-194. Lang.: Rus.

USSR. 1930-1939. Histories-sources. ■Majakovskij's dramatic works as seen by critics in the 1930s.

2959 Polley, J. Patrick. "When Cleanliness Was Next to Godlessness: The Proletarian Bathhouse." 167-176 in Hartigan, Karelisa V., ed. *From the Bard to Broadway.* Lanham, MD: UP of America; 1987. 222 pp. (Univ. of Florida Dept. of Classics Comparative Drama Conference Papers 7.) Pref. Notes. Biblio. Lang.: Eng.

USSR. 1925-1935. Critical studies. ■Analysis of three Russian works in terms of their use of the public bathhouse—not only as a public meeting place but as a metaphor for the Soviet State.

2960 Portes, Lisa. "The Poetry of Infidelity: An Interpretive Comparison of Eduard Radzinsky's *Jogging* to Edward Albee's *Who's Afraid of Virginia Woolf?.*" *SEEDTF.* 1987 Dec.; 7(2-3): 64-69. Notes. Lang.: Eng.

USSR. USA. 1987. Critical studies. ■Radsinskij's play seen as a subtle commentary on Soviet society.

2961 Rogačevskij, M. "Ékzamen na pravdu." (An Examination for Truth.) *TeatrM.* 1987; 11: 4-13. Lang.: Rus.

USSR. 1980-1987. Critical studies. ■Contemporary Soviet plays devoted to Leniniana.

2962 Rozov, V.S. *Putešestvie v raznye storony.* (A Journey in Different Directions.) Moscow: Sov. pisatel'; 1987. 493 pp. Lang.: Rus.

USSR. 1913-1987. Biographical studies. ■Autobiographical writings of playwright Viktor Rosov.

2963 Rudneva, L. "Komedija Nikolaja Érdmana, ee triumf i zabvenie." (The Comedy of Nikolaj Erdmann: Its Triumph and Oblivion.) *TeatrM.* 1987; 10: 28-33. Lang.: Rus.

USSR: Moscow. 1925. ■*Mandat (Mandate)* staged by Mejerchol'd, 1925. Mejerchol'd's rivalry with Stanislavskij to produce *Samoubijca (Suicide)*.

2964 Rybakov, N. "S čego načinaetsja teatr?" (What Does the Theatre Begin With?)*TeatZ.* 1987; 22: 20-21. Lang.: Rus.

USSR. 1980-1987. Critical studies. ■Overview of dramaturgy in Mari ASSR.

2965 Šach-Azizova, T. "Čechov vne jubileev." (Čechov Beyond Anniversary Celebrations.) *TeatrM.* 1987; 8: 131-141. Lang.: Rus.

USSR. 1980-1987. Critical studies. ■Analysis of socialist countries' interpretations of the plays of Čechov.

2966 Šatrov, M.F. "Voschoždenie k Leninu." (Going Back to Lenin.) *NiR.* 1987; 4: 2-5. Lang.: Rus.

USSR. 1980-1987. Histories-sources. ■Documentary dramatist explains his ideological and creative principles.

2967 Soroka, O. "Možno li v Šekspire najti novoe?" (Is It Possible to Find Something New in Shakespeare?)*InoLit.* 1987; 4: 215-221. Lang.: Rus.

USSR. 1980-1987. Critical studies. ■Contemporary interpretations of Shakespeare's work: criticism, translation, adaptation.

2968 Vampilov, A. "Emu bylo by nynče pjat'desjat...Perepiska A. Vampilova s E. Jakuškinoj." (Today He Would Be Fifty: The Correspondence of A. Vampilov and Je. Jakužkina.) Lang.: Rus.

USSR: Moscow. 1960-1975. Histories-sources. ■Playwright Aleksand'r Vampilov's personality, work, reception of his plays, through his letters to the head of the literary section of the Jermolova Theatre.

2969 Vinogradova, A. "Ežegodnaja šekspirovskaja konferencija." (Annual Shakespeare Conference.) *VLit.* 1987; 4: 262-268. Lang.: Rus.

USSR. 1987. Critical studies. ■Overview of papers on Shakespearean poetics, stage interpretation in the USSR.

2970 Zemnova, A. "Est' li v vašem gorode intelligentnyj čelovek?" (Is There a Cultured Person in Your Town?)*TeatrM.* 1987; 8: 155-162. Lang.: Rus.

USSR. Critical studies. ■Essay on the work of Azerbaijani playwright Anar.

2971 Zjukov, B.B. *Na scene i ékrane—Lesja Ukrainka.* (On Stage and Screen: Lesja Ukrainka.) Kiev: Mistectvo; 1987. 236 pp. Lang.: Rus.

USSR. 1987. Critical studies. ■Works by the Ukrainian poet on stage, in film and on television. Related to Media.

2972 Grehan, Stewart. "Fathers and Sons: Politics and Myth in Recent Zambian Drama." *NTQ.* 1987 Feb.; 3(9): 29-43. Notes. Illus.: Photo. Print. B&W. 5. Lang.: Eng.

Zambia. 1966-1987. Critical studies. ■Theme of aggression between fathers and sons in a number of plays staged in festivals of the Zambian National Theatre Arts Association (ZANTA), a theme with social and mythical dimensions.

Reference materials

2973 Magister, Karl-Heinz. "Shakespeare-Bibliographie für 1985." (Shakespearean Bibliography for 1985.) 224-299 in Klotz, Günther, ed.; Kuckhoff, Armin-Gerd, ed. *Deutsche Shakespeare-Gessellschaft Jahrbuch.* Weimar: Böhlau;

DRAMA: —Reference materials

1987. 305 pp. (SJW 123.) Lang.: Ger, Eng, Fre, Spa, Ita, Rus.
England. 1550-1985. ■International Shakespearean bibliography of 1593 items: research, reviews of performances, play editions, bibliographies and so on, deadline 2/28/86. Authors index.

2974 Cohn, Ruby. *From Desire to Godot: Pocket Theater of Postwar Paris.* Berkeley, CA: Univ of California P; 1987. 204 pp. Index. Pref. Notes. Illus.: Handbill. Photo. Maps. Dwg. Sketches. Print. B&W. 15. Lang.: Eng.
France: Paris. 1944-1953. Histories-specific. ■History of pocket theatres in Paris in the years after World War II: small, independent, avantgarde theatres doing new works, both European and American. Describes individual productions. Includes a chronology of the performances.

2975 Vàsquez Estévez, Anna; Blasco, Ricard, intro. *Fons de teatre valencià a les biblioteques de Barcelona.* (Holdings in Valencian Theatre at the Libraries of Barcelona.) Barcelona: Institut del Teatre; 1987. 288 pp. (Estudis 1.) Pref. Index. Lang.: Cat.
Spain: Valencia, Barcelona. Bibliographical studies. ■Lists 1,626 Valencian theatrical texts available in seven Barcelona libraries. Indexed by title, author, first line and opening performance. Related to Music-Drama: Musical theatre.

Relation to other fields

2976 Birringer, Johannes. "Texts, Plays and Instabilities." *SATJ.* 1987; 1(1): 4-16. Lang.: Eng.
1600-1987. Critical studies. ■Multiplicity and complexity of significations in dramatic performance results in a more 'literary' approach to dramatic texts.

2977 Esteva Fabregat, Claudi. "Ritual y dramaturgia: contexto antropológico del teatro." (Ritual and Drama: The Anthropological Context of Theatre.) 23-44 in Coca, Jordi, ed.; Conesa, Laura, comp. *Congrés Internacional de Teatre a Catalunya 1985. Actes. Volum III. Seccions 4, 5 i 6.* Barcelona: Institut del Teatre; 1987. 302 pp. Notes. [Section 4: Tradition and Modernity.] Lang.: Spa.
1985. Critical studies. ■Compares and contrasts the artistic role of theatre in contemporary urban society with the mystical role of ritual in traditional societies. Comedy as representation of normality, tragedy and drama as abnormality.

2978 Payne, Rhonda. "Via Newfoundland and Africa." *CTR.* 1987 Win; 53: 26-28. [Meanwhile in Toronto.../2.] Lang.: Eng.
Africa. Canada: St. John's, NF, Toronto, ON. 1978-1987. Critical studies. ■Discusses the 'African Theatre for Development' popular theatre movement, and applies its theories to Canadian theatre in Newfoundland and Toronto.

2979 Batchelder, Norma Woodward. "*El avión negro*: The Political and Structural Context." *LATR.* 1987 Spr; 20(2): 17-28. Lang.: Eng.
Argentina. 1969-1970. Critical studies. ■The collectively written drama *El avión negro (The Black Airplane)* effectively predicts Juan Perón's inability to reunify a fragmented Argentina and to restore political voice to the urban proletariat.

2980 Perry, Shauneille. "Ties that Bind (Impressions of Life/ Drama within the African Diaspora)." *BlackM.* 1987 Sep-Oct.; 4(1): 6, 14. Illus.: Dwg. B&W. 1. Lang.: Eng.
Barbados. Bermuda. Nigeria. 1987. Critical studies. ■Comparison of Caribbean, African and African-American theatre, spirituality and politics.

2981 Thomas, Gerald; Melo, Sergio Nunes; Hunt, Nigel. "An Exchange of Metaphors: The Theatre of Gerald Thomas." *Theatrum.* 1987 Spr; 6: 33-37. Pref. Lang.: Eng.
Brazil: Rio de Janeiro. North America. Europe. 1970-1987. Critical studies. ■Gerald Thomas discusses the philosophical foundations for his work in theatre, influences on his work.

2982 Filewod, Ian. "Underdeveloped Alliance." *CTR.* 1987 Win; 53: 39-42. Print. B&W. 4. Lang.: Eng.
Canada: Sydney, NS. Jamaica. Sudan. 1987. Critical studies. ■Discusses the 1986 Standin' the Gaff Festival. Critical analysis of theatre as an

educational bridge between theatre workers and non-governmental organizations. Popular theatre projects in the Sudan and Jamaica.

2983 Peterman, Michael. *Robertson Davies.* Boston, MA: Twayne; 1985. 178 pp. (TWAYNE World Author Series: Canadian Literature.) Index. Biblio. Lang.: Eng.
Canada. 1913-1985. Critical studies. ■Criticism and interpretation of Davies' work. Primarily focuses on the novels.

2984 Zabus, Chantal. "A Calibanic Tempest in Anglophone & Francophone New World Writings." *CanL.* 1985; 104: 35-50. Notes. Lang.: Eng.
Canada. Antilles. France. 1611-1977. Critical studies. ■*The Tempest* is described as a manifesto of decolonization and a myth of imperialism. Twentieth-century literary works from England and France, colonizing powers influenced by Prospero. Works from the Antilles and Canada show the Caliban influence.

2985 Boyle, C.M. *Thematic Development in Chilean Theatre since 1975: In Search of the Dramatic Conflict.* Liverpool: Univ. of Liverpool; 1987. Notes. Biblio. [Ph.D. dissertation, *Index to Theses,* 37-2144.] Lang.: Eng.
Chile. 1973-1986. Historical studies. ■Examines the role of theatre as an important medium of expression in a repressive environment, and studies the treatment on stage of social problems under authoritarian rule.

2986 Marker, Frederick J.; Marker, Lise-Lone. "Thalia in the Welfare State: Art and Politics in Contemporary Danish Theatre." *TDR.* 1982 Fall; 26(3): 3-14. Lang.: Eng.
Denmark. 1722-1982. Historical studies. ■Impact of politics upon funding of Danish theatre. Historical overview, commercial and experimental theatre, institutions.

2987 Amiard-Chevrel, Claudine, ed. *L'Ouvrier au théâtre. De 1871 à nos jours.* (The Worker at the Theatre from 1871 to the Present.) Travaux du Laboratoire de recherches sur les arts du spectacle du CNRS. Louvain-la-Neuve: Cahiers Théâtre Louvain; 1987. 354 pp. Pref. Biblio. Illus.: Photo. Dwg. B&W. 29. [Etude collective de l'Equipe 'Théâtre moderne'.] Lang.: Fre.
Europe. USA. 1871-1987. Historical studies. ■Collective study by the 'Théâtre moderne' team on the theatrical representation in Germany, France, Belgium, the U.S. and the U.S.S.R. of workers' lives and the labor movement. Includes interviews with authors and directors.

2988 Jones, Ernest; Caruso, Paolo, ed. *Amleto e Edipo.* (Hamlet and Oedipus.) Milan: Mondadori; 1987. 190 pp. (Saggi 116.) Pref. Lang.: Ita.
Europe. 1596-1949. Critical studies. ■Italian translation of Jones' 1949 *Hamlet and Oedipus.* The volume also contains an essay by Jean Starobinski: *Hamlet and Freud.*

2989 Carroll, Dennis; Carroll, Elsa. "Contemporary Finnish Theatre: National Myths and Beyond." *TDR.* 1982 Fall; 26(3): 35-56 . Illus.: Photo. B&W. 8. Lang.: Eng.
Finland. 1950-1982. Critical studies. ■Impact of myths of national character on the people of Finland, insight they provide into the great importance theatre has in their lives. Indigenous theatre, sociorealism, productions, Brecht's influence on development of their experimental theatre.

2990 Macchia, Giovanni. *La letteratura francese.* (French Literature.) Milan: Mondadori; 1987. 1518 pp. (I meridiani. Storia.) Pref. Index. Notes. Biblio. Lang.: Ita.
France. 800-1700. Histories-general. ■French theatre from the Middle Ages to the eighteenth century as a part of French literary history. Grp/movt: Neoclassicism.

2991 Grob, Michael. "Bertolt Brecht und die Philosophie." (Brecht and Philosophy.) *DZP.* 1988; 36(3): 213-221. Lang.: Ger.
Germany. 1918-1956. Critical studies. ■On Brecht's broad and intense interest in philosophical problems, which were vital to him for a vivid stage representation of social processes.

2992 Bathrick, David. "Patricide or Re-Generation: Brechts *Baal* and *Roundheads* in GDR." *TJ.* 1987 Dec.; 39(41): 439-447. Notes. Biblio. Illus.: Photo. Print. B&W. 2. Lang.: Eng.

DRAMA: —Relation to other fields

Germany, East: Berlin. 1987. Historical studies. ■The aesthetic dethronement of Brecht by his students through the plays *Baal* and *Die Rundköpfe und die Spitzköpfe (The Roundheads and the Pinheads)* which offered preferable behavioral alternatives to a stagnated status quo.

2993 Browne, Ivor W. "Thomas Murphy: The Madness of Genius." *IUR.* 1987 Spr; 17(1): 129-136. Notes. Lang.: Eng.

Ireland. 1961-1986. Critical studies. ■Brief commentary on the nature of the creative writer and the impetus to write. This is then applied to the playwright Thomas Murphy.

2994 Herr, Cheryl. "Subworlds, Props and Settings in Joyce's *Exiles.*" *TJ.* 1987 May; 39(2): 185-303. Lang.: Eng.

Ireland. 1900-1987. Critical studies. ■Irish playwrights, including James Joyce, and their approach to the issue of class in Ireland.

2995 O'Connor, Ulick. *All the Olympians: A Biographical Portrait of the Irish Literary Renaissance.* Holt; 1987. 292 pp. Pref. Index. Biblio. Illus.: Photo. Print. B&W. 65. Lang.: Eng.

Ireland. UK-Ireland. 1875-1938. Biographical studies. ■Literary figures of the Irish Literary Renaissance: W.B. Yeats, G.B. Shaw, James Joyce, Lady Gregory, George Moore, Oscar Wilde, Maud Gonne, John Millington Synge and Sean O'Casey.

2996 Rydström, Gunnar. "Gräv där du står i hela världen." (Dig Where You Are All Over the World.) *Teaterf.* 1987; 20(2-3): 18-20. Illus.: Photo. Lang.: Swe.

Jamaica. Zimbabwe. Bangladesh. 1987. Histories-sources. ■Three adult education teachers from Jamaica, Zimbabwe and Bangladesh discuss how creative drama is used for education and investigation of the peoples' living conditions.

2997 Pleśniarowicz, Krzysztof. "Labirynt Kantora." (Kantor's Labyrinth.) *DialogW.* 1987; 9: 95-99. Lang.: Pol.

Poland. 1915-1987. Critical studies. ■Director Tadeusz Kantor's ideas about art in the broad context of contemporary culture and philosophy.

2998 Luther, C.M. *South African Theatre: Aspects of the Collaborative.* Ph.D. dissertation, *Index to Theses,* 37-0088. Leeds: University of Leeds; 1987. Notes. Biblio. Lang.: Eng.

South Africa, Republic of. 1984. Historical studies. ■Studies interracial fringe productions in South Africa, focusing on projects staged at the Market Theatre and analyzing their function in terms of racial, class and sexual politics.

2999 Müller, Heiner. "The Wounded Woyzeck." *PerAJ.* 1987; 10(3): 73-75. Lang.: Eng.

South Africa, Republic of: Pretoria. 1985. Critical studies. ■Comparison of *Woyzeck* to Nelson Mandela and the politics of South Africa.

3000 Sander, Anki. "Lyckan." (Happiness.) *Teaterf.* 1987; 20(2-3): 3-5. Illus.: Photo. Dwg. Lang.: Swe.

Sweden: Gävle. 1978-1987. Historical studies. ■Some disabled persons in Sätrahöjden have joined a theatre group, under the leadership of Ulrike Hörberg, and show plays of their own for other mentally retarded.

3001 Arnold, Peter. *Auf den Spuren des 'anderen' Theaters: Claque Baden.* (On the Tracks of the 'Different' Theatre: Claque Baden.) Zürich: Limmat Verlag Genossenschaft; 1987. 326 pp. Pref. Index. Biblio. Append. Illus.: Photo. B&W. Lang.: Ger.

Switzerland: Baden. 1968-1987. Critical studies. ■Analysis of Claque Theatre, taken as a model for professional provincial ensembles in Switzerland.

3002 Jellonnek, Burkhard. "Totenfloss oder Traumschiff?" (Death Raft or Dream Boat?)*MuT.* 1987 Mar.; 8(3): 42-45. Illus.: Photo. B&W. Lang.: Ger.

Switzerland: Basel. Mönchengladbach. 1986-1987. Critical studies. ■Taking the production of a contemporary political play as the basis, the author tries to analyze and legitimate the importance of political drama on the European stage, not forgetting some problematic aspects (receptional, referential).

3003 Bate, Jonathan. "Hal and the Regent." *ShS.* 1985; 38: 69-75. Notes. Illus.: Photo. B&W. Lang.: Eng.

UK-England: London. 1790-1827. Historical studies. ■Public and parodic perceptions of the future George IV mediated through Shakespeare as a reference frame for their satire.

3004 Pope, Maurice. "Shakespeare's Medical Imagination." *ShS.* 1985; 38: 175-186. Notes. Lang.: Eng.

UK-England: London. 1589-1614. Historical studies. ■Shakespeare's pursuit of medical knowledge followed Reformation patterns to form his own opinion.

3005 Ryan, Paul. "Still Out There Pushing." *Drama.* 1987; 4(166): 5-7. Illus.: Photo. B&W. 3. Lang.: Eng.

UK-England. 1987. Histories-sources. ■Playwright/director Lindsay Anderson's analysis of attitudes to culture outlining its lack of radicalism. He cites the Royal Court Theatre as a sort of half-way house—a leftist branch of the establishment and the National Theatre as belonging to 'the other side'.

3006 Stovel, Nora Foster. "D.H. Lawrence, From Playwright to Novelist: 'Strife in Love' in *A Collier's Friday Night* and *Sons and Lovers.*" *English Studies in Canada.* 1987 Dec.; 13(4): 451-460. Notes. Lang.: Eng.

UK-England. 1906-1913. Critical studies. ■Discusses the impact of Lawrence's playwriting on his development as a novelist through analysis of *A Collier's Friday Night* and *Sons and Lovers.*

3007 Auslander, Philip. "Toward a Concept of the Political in Postmodern Theatre." *TJ.* 1987 Mar.; 39(1): 20-34. Notes. Illus.: Photo. 2. Lang.: Eng.

USA. 1987. Critical studies. ■Examination of crisis in theory and practice of today's political art. Focus on Wooster Group's production of *LSD* as example of contemporary political theatre.

3008 Melhem, D. H. "Black Nationalism and the Poet Activist: An Interview with Haki R. Madhubuti." *WJBS.* 1985; 9(2): 106-113 . Biblio. Notes. Lang.: Eng.

USA: Detroit, MI. Africa. Israel. 1942-1985. Histories-sources. ■Ex-military nationalist, Haki R. Madhubuti (Don L. Lee), talks of solutions to the problems of African-American communities.

3009 Gel'man, A. "Počemu my nazyvaem perestrojku revoljucionnoj?" (Why Do We Call Perestrojka Revolutionary-?)*TeatZ.* 1987 ; 7: 2. Lang.: Rus.

USSR. 1986-1987. Critical studies. ■Soviet dramatist on moral problems of perestrojka.

Research/historiography

3010 Drumbl, Johann. "Appunti sulla tradizione drammatica nell'alto medioevo." (Notes on the Dramatic Tradition of the Early Middle Ages.) *TeatroS.* 1987; 2(1): 205-249. Lang.: Ita.

Germany. 1000-1400. Historical studies. ■Methodological questions in the study of both 'origins' and 'tradition' of the liturgical drama in German countries. Analysis of the *Ordo Stellae* and the *Visitatio sepulchri.*

3011 Ayling, Ronald. "The Irish Dramatic Movement, 1891-1980: A Review Essay." *ET.* 1987 May; 5(2): 139-144. Lang.: Eng.

Ireland. UK-Ireland. Canada. 1891-1983. Critical studies. ■Short discussions of the Canadian dimension in Anglo-Irish literary scholarship. Examines positively D.E.S. Maxwell's *A Critical History of Modern Irish Drama 1891-1980.*

3012 Chang, Han-Gi. "Bikyoyonkukhakui yongubangbub." (The Research Method of Comparative Drama.) *DongukDA.* 1976 Dec.; 9: 130-135. Lang.: Kor.

Korea. 1970. Critical studies. ■The comparative method of drama study.

3013 Durbach, Errol. "Archer and Ibsen: A Review Essay." *ET.* 1987 May; 5(2): 145-148. Lang.: Eng.

UK-England. 1889-1919. Critical studies. ■Discusses William Archer's work and opinions on Ibsen, and Thomas Postlewait's two works on this subject. Grp/movt: Realism.

3014 Liao, Biing Huey. "Xin viskguan yu sha shi pi yia yian jiou." (A New Historical Theory and the Study of Shakespeare.) *ChWai.* 1987 Apr.; 15(11): 22-49. Notes. Biblio. Lang.: Chi.

DRAMA: —Research/historiography

UK-England. USA. 1900-1987. Critical studies. ∎Comparison of sociological and cultural perspectives on Shakespeare studies in the UK and the US.

Theory/criticism

3015   An, Chi. "Xi ju mei xue de xin tuo zhan." (The Development of Aesthetics in Drama.) *XYishu.* 1987 Spr; 37: 29-36. Notes. Lang.: Chi.
1949-1987. Critical studies. ∎Comparing impression with reality in drama.

3016   Hornby, Richard. *Script into Performance: A Structuralist View of Play Production.* Houston, TX: Univ. of Texas P; 1987. 215 pp. Notes. Index. Lang.: Eng.
500 B.C.-1987 A.D. Historical studies. ∎Structuralist approach to play interpretation to clarify relationship between text and performance. Current performance theories, critical methods and practical application of structuralist theory on productions directed by author.

3017   Liu, Yan-Jun. "Zhong guo xi ju jin nian fa zhan wo guan." (The Development of Contemporary Theatre in China.) *XYishu.* 1987 Spr; 37: 47-53. Lang.: Chi.
1949-1987. Historical studies. ∎Over time, the theatre has developed different forms of communication. Today, in contemporary drama, the form seems to be more psychological in nature.

3018   Reinert, Otto. "Articles on Ibsen, 1983-84." *INC.* 1987; 8: 15-20. Notes. Lang.: Eng.
1983-1984. Bibliographical studies. ∎Brief descriptions of 21 different scholarly articles.

3019   Styan, J.L. "The Discipline of Performance Criticism." *SATJ.* 1987; 1(2): 4-19. Lang.: Eng.
1987. Critical studies. ∎Suggests that dramatic theory gives little thought to relation between interpretation and actors and the audience and how this relationship influences criticism.

3020   Watson, Shawn. "The Ghost in *Hamlet*: Imminent Self in Tragedy." *JDTC.* 1987; 2(1): 3-21. Notes. Lang.: Eng.
500 B.C.-1987 A.D. Critical studies. ∎The nature of tragedy and dignity of the protagonists, exploration of theory that it denies the individual's need for self-definition.

3021   Yi, Guan-Hua. "Mo hu kong jian lun." (A Theory of Ambiguous Space.) *XYishu.* 1987 Spr; 37: 71-81. Notes. Illus.: Dwg. Print. B&W. 3. Lang.: Chi.
1949-1987. Historical studies. ∎The use of space can direct the time and place in the plot of a play.

3022   Pečman, Rudolf. "Tragédie a tragično v pojetí Otakara Hostinského (K 140. výročí narození)." (Tragedy and the Tragic in the Conception of Otakar Hostinský: On the 140th Anniversary of His Birth.) *Prog.* 1987; 58(4): 164-165. Lang.: Cze.
Austria-Hungary: Prague. 1906. Critical studies. ∎Hostinsky's analysis of the aesthetic categories of tragedy and the tragic.

3023   Beckers, Anne-Marie. *Michel de Ghelderode. Barabbas. Escurial. Une oeuvre.* (Michel de Ghelderode. Barabbas. Escurial. A Play.) Brussels: Labor; 1987. 109 pp. (Un livre, une oeuvre 13.) Biblio. Lang.: Fre.
Belgium. 1898. Instructional materials. ∎Brief biography of playwright Michel de Ghelderode, study of his plays *Escurial* and *Barabbas.* Intended as a textbook.

3024   Barnet, David. "Out of the Collectives." *CTR.* 1987 Win; 53: 5-6. Illus.: Photo. B&W. 3. [Notes on Popular Theatre.../1.] Lang.: Eng.
Canada. 1987. Critical studies. ∎Theory and methodology of popular theatre: beliefs common to performers and community. Two approaches.

3025   Hu, Zhi-Yi. "Wu-Si hua ju yu xi fang xing lang man zhu yi." (Neo-Romanticism and the Plays of the May Fourth Movement.) *XYishu.* 1987 Spr; 37: 118-130. Notes. Lang.: Chi.
China, People's Republic of. Norway. 1920-1950. Historical studies. ∎The influence and reflection of Henrik Ibsen's work on Chinese modern theatre.

3026   Molinaza, Luis. "Presencia del mito en el teatro Dominicano." (Presence of Myth in Dominican Theatre.) *Cjo.* 1987 July-Sep.(73): 82-87. Notes. Illus.: Dwg. Chart. 2. Lang.: Spa.
Dominican Republic. 1987. Critical studies. ∎Influence of myth (Greek, Hebrew, African, etc.) in the works of various Dominican playwrights.

3027   Canfield, J. Douglas. "Richard Flecknoe's Early Defense of the Stage: An Appeal to Cromwell." *Restor.* 1987 Win; 2(2): 1-7. Notes. Lang.: Eng.
England. 1654-1664. Historical studies. ∎Flecknoe's preface to *Love's Dominion*, relationship of theory to practice.

3028   Finkelstein, Richard. "Ben Jonson on Spectacle." *CompD.* 1987 Sum; 21(2): 103-114. Notes. Lang.: Eng.
England. 1572-1637. Historical studies. ∎Playwright Ben Jonson's view of similarities between spectacle plays and comic plays in performance. Power of images versus text.

3029   King, W.D. "An 'Exquisite' Memory: Henry Irving and Bernard Shaw at *Waterloo*." 35-49 in Cardullo, Bert, ed. *Before His Eyes: Essays in Honor of Stanley Kauffmann.* Lanham, MD: UP of America; 1986. 185 pp. Pref. Notes. Biblio. Lang.: Eng.
England: London. 1895-1905. Historical studies. ∎Account of early Shaw theatre criticism. Shaw critiques Henry Irving's production of Arthur Conan Doyle's *Waterloo.* Discusses Shaw's emerging genius as a critic as well as playwright.

3030   Kropf, Carl R. "Patriarchal Theory in Dryden's Early Drama." *ET.* 1987 Nov.; 6(1): 41-48. Notes.
England. 1679-1687. Critical studies. ∎Influence of philosophers, especially Plato and Aristotle, on Dryden's political ideas as expressed in his plays.

3031   Stallybrass, Peter. "Reading the Body: *The Revenger's Tragedy* and The Jacobean Theatre of Consumption." *RenD.* 1987; 18: 148. Lang.: Eng.
England. 1583. Critical studies. ∎The body as emblematic of a character's frame of mind. Focus on Shakespeare's *Othello* and Tourneur's *The Revenger's Tragedy.*

3032   Issacharoff, Michael. "Comic Space." *TID.* 1987; 9: 187-198. Notes. Lang.: Eng.
Europe. USA. Greece. 400 B.C.-1987 A.D. Critical studies. ∎Movement of comic space discursively through the transgressive treatment of implicit and explicit rules and conventions.

3033   Pavis, Patrice. "De la théorie considérée comme un des Beaux-Arts et de son influence limitée sur la dramaturgie contemporaine, majoritaire ou minoritaire." (Theory as a Fine Art and its Limited Influence on Present-Day Theatre of Greater or Lesser Diffusion.) 243-262 in Coca, Jordi, ed.; Conesa, Laura, comp. *Congrés Internacional de Teatre a Catalunya 1985. Actes. Volum IV. Seccions 7, 8 i 9.* Barcelona: Institut del Teatre; 1987. 350 pp. [Section 9: The Contribution of Theory to Performance.] Lang.: Fre.
Europe. 1985. Critical studies. ∎Contemporary theatrical theory has three major tendencies: pragmatic, anthropological and semiotic, causing standardization in both East and West. Theory has virtually no influence on commercial theatre.

3034   Schulte, Vera. *Das Gesicht einer gesichtslosen Welt: Zu Paradoxie und Groteske in F. Dürrenmatts dramatischem Werk.* (The Face of a Faceless World: Paradox and Grotesque in Dürrenmatt's Dramatic Work.) Bern/Frankfurt-am-Main: Peter Lang Verlag; 1987. 335 pp. (Europäische Hochschulschriften I/1002.) Pref. Notes. Biblio. Lang.: Ger.
Europe. 1986. Critical studies. ∎Doctoral thesis investigating the paradox and grotesque in Dürrenmatt's dramatic work. Society is criticized through analysis of its absurdities.

3035   Cooper, Barbara T. "The Space of Discourse and the Discourse of Space in Jacques Ancelot's *Louis IX*." *TID.* 1987; 9: 129-138. Notes. Illus.: Dwg. 1. Lang.: Eng.
France. 1800-1850. Critical studies. ∎Use of space in neo-classical tragedy. Debate between the adherence to Aristotelian notions of space

DRAMA: —Theory/criticism

and less deterministic notions of drama. The stage as space of discourse and tragedy as the place for the discourse of space.

3036   Gould, Evelyn. "Why Go to the Theatre?" *JDTC.* 1987; 2(1): 69-86. Notes. Lang.: Eng.
France. 1987. Critical studies. ▪Introduction to Mallarmé's *Crayonne au Théâtre* expresses ambivalence about theatre. Explores both actual events and metaphorical use of theatre.

3037   Martin, Mary Kay. "Space Invasions: Voice-Over in the Works by Samuel Beckett and Marguerite Duras." *TID.* 1987; 9: 239-246. Notes. Lang.: Eng.
France. 1977-1987. Critical studies. ▪Impact of cinematic techniques on non-realistic plays. Intrusions of conventions from one medium to the other. The disembodied voice in a physical space and laid over the live presence of the actors. Related to Media: Film.

3038   Milman, Yoseph. "Eyun Be-kama Yikarei Ieod shell Altpoetica Ahclasisistit Lefi Corni." (Principles of Corneille's Poetics.) *Bamah.* 1987; 22(108): 58-72. Lang.: Heb.
France. 1570-1660. Histories-specific. ▪Theories of Corneille in the 17th century. Transition from Baroque to classical in politics and thought.

3039   Poe, George. *The Rococo and Eighteenth Century French Literature: A Study through Marivaux's Theatre.* New York, NY: Peter Lang; 1987. 335 pp. (Series II: Romance Languages and Literature 30.) Pref. Index. Biblio. Illus.: Photo. Pntg. Dwg. Print. B&W. 27. Lang.: Eng.
France. 1715-1774. Critical studies. ▪Using Marivaux's plays as a medium, the rococo formula is examined. Elements of rococo society as well as the movement are examined.

3040   Reiss, Timothy J. "Corneille and Cornelia: Reason, Violence, and the Cultural Status of the Feminine. Or, How a Dominant Discourse Recuperated and Subverted the Advance of Women." *RenD.* 1987; 18: 3-41. Lang.: Eng.
France. 1540-1650. Critical studies. ▪Works of Pierre Corneille and the social role of women.

3041   Cascardi, Anthony J. "*Comedia* and *Trauerspiel:* On Benjamin and Calderón." *CompD.* 1982 Spr; 16(1): 1-11. Notes. Lang.: Eng.
Germany. 1916-1982. Critical studies. ▪Essays of critic Walter Benjamin: comparison of his views on Spanish baroque and *comedia* theatre and German plays. Stylistic qualities, representation of emotions and objects, particular focus on plays of Calderón.

3042   Harris, Brian L. "The Michelangelo Dramas of Friedrich Hebbel and Hugo Ball: From Historicism Toward Expressionism." 95-106 in Hartigan, Karelisa V., ed. *From the Bard to Broadway.* Lanham, MD: UP of America; 1987. 222 pp. (Univ. of Florida Dept. of Classics Comparative Drama Conference Papers 7.) Pref. Notes. Biblio. Lang.: Eng.
Germany. 1886-1927. Critical studies. ▪German playwright Hugo Ball's response to *Michel Angelo* (1855) by Friedrich Hebbel, and his own *Die Nase des Michelangelo (Michelangelo's Nose)* of 1908. Comparison of plays, development of Hebbel's ideas. Grp/movt: Expressionism.

3043   Lessing, Gothold Ephraim; Formosa, Feliu, transl.; Marí, Antoni, intro. *Dramatúrgia d'Hamburg.* (Hamburg Dramaturgy.) Barcelona: Institut del Teatre; 1987. 394 pp. (Monografies de Teatre 22.) Notes. Biblio. Lang.: Cat.
Germany: Hamburg. 1767-1769. Critical studies. ▪Catalan translation of *Hamburgische Dramaturgie*, Lessing's theory of drama that rejects the Aristotelian concept of catharsis and attempts to disengage German theatre from its dependency on French neoclassicism. Marí's prologue is on 'the critical spirit of the Aufklärung'.

3044   Yoon, Si-Hyang. "B. Brecht Jakpupsaekaeui yeejungsung." (An Inquiry into Brecht's Dualism.) *DonugukDA.* 1976 Dec.; 9: 44-63. Lang.: Kor.
Germany. 1878-1956. Critical studies. ▪Theories of Brecht as seen through an analysis of his *Die Dreigroschenoper (The Three Penny Opera).*

3045   Klaus, Völker. "Brecht Today: Classic or Challenge." *TJ.* 1987 Dec.; 39(4): 425-433. Lang.: Eng.
Germany, East: Berlin. 1960-1970. Historical studies. ▪Brecht's political and social criticism of government through his theories and drama

forced government to alienate him. Later examination proved truth in his writing and his plays were embraced as classics.

3046   Mittenzwei, Werner. "Das Brechtverständnis in den beiden deutschen Staaten." (Brecht Perception in the Two German States.) *SoF.* 1987; 39(6): 1265-1303.
Germany, East. Germany, West. 1948-1987. Historical studies. ▪The different and changing views on Brecht and his work in scholarly writing of the GDR and the FRG.

3047   Ahn, Min-Soo. "Samilcheebub sunglibui keunkeowa baekyung." (Historical Background of the Three Unities.) *DongukDA.* 1983 Dec.; 14: 79-104. Lang.: Kor.
Greece. France. Italy. 500 B.C.-1800 A.D. Critical studies. ▪Study of the development of the three unities.

3048   Gruber, William E. "'Non-Aristotelian' Theatre: Brecht's and Plato's Theories of Artistic Imitation." *CompD.* 1987 Fall; 21(3): 199-213. Notes. Lang.: Eng.
Greece. Germany. 300 B.C.-1956 A.D. Critical studies. ▪Elements essential to Brecht's theatre and how they can be appreciated with the overall logic of 'Platonic' poetics. Elements common to both authors including actor-audience relationship and the educative process of drama.

3049   Schmitt, Natalie Cronn. "Aristotle's Poetics and Aristotle's Nature." *JDTC.* 1987; 1(2): 3-15. Notes. Lang.: Eng.
Greece. 384-322 B.C. Critical studies. ▪Interpretation and reading of Aristotle's early works in natural science and biology: *Poetics* and Aristotle's thought seen as functional and biological and concerned with nature's processes.

3050   Connelly, Sean. "Dreaming History: Brian Friel's *Translations.*" *ThIr.* 1987; 13: 42-44. Illus.: Photo. B&W. 1. Lang.: Eng.
Ireland. 1987. Critical studies. ▪Brian Friel's play *Translations* about the mapping of new territories in Ireland by the British during the early 1830s.

3051   Geerts, W., ed.; Musarra, F., ed.; Vanvolsem, S., ed. *Luigi Pirandello: poetica e presenza.* (Luigi Pirandello: Poetics and Presence.) Rome: Bulzoni; 1987. 619 pp. Index. Pref. Illus.: Photo. Print. B&W. Lang.: Ita.
Italy. 1904-1936. Critical studies. ▪A collection of essays on Pirandello's poetics and its influence on other writers, from a 1986 conference, Universities of Louvain and Antwerp.

3052   Luk'jančuk, V.V. *Teatral'no-éstetičeskie vzgljady Luidži Pirandello: Avtoref.dis. kand. iskusstvovedenija.* (The Theatrical-Aesthetic Opinions of Luigi Pirandello: Abstract of a Dissertation by a Candidate in Art Criticism.) Leningrad: LGITMiK; 1987. 22 pp. Lang.: Rus.
Italy. 1867-1936. Historical studies.

3053   Chang, Han-Gi. "Zeamiwa keuui shikado lon." (Zeami and His Theory of *Shikadō.*) *DongukDA.* 1983 Dec.; 14: 119-128. Lang.: Kor.
Japan. 1363-1443. Critical studies. ▪Zeami's play *Shikadō.*

3054   Kim, Mun Hwan. "Yeok sa cheok sa sid chu ui ui kyokwaseo." (The Textbook of Realism.) *KTR.* 1987 Feb.; 2(3): 29-34. Lang.: Kor.
Korea: Seoul. 1986-1987. Reviews of performances. ▪Čechov's *Diadia Vania (Uncle Vanya)* performed by the National Theatre.

3055   Pavis, Patrice. "¿Hacia una semiologia de la mise en scéne? (II)." (Towards a Semiology of the Mise en Scène? (II).) *Cjo.* 1987 July-Sep.(73): 31-49. Notes. Biblio. Illus.: Dwg. 7. Lang.: Spa.
Latin America. Critical studies. ▪Relationship between the director and the text and its representation in the semiology of the mise en scène.

3056   de la Escalera, Ana-Maria. "El ojo y la escena." (The Eye and the Scene.) *UMex.* 1987 Dec.; 42(443): 31-33. Illus.: Photo. B&W. 2. Lang.: Spa.
Mexico: Mexico City. 1987. Critical studies. ▪Modern theatrical trends: possibilities for new ideas in contemporary theatre.

3057   Partida, Armando. "El Teatro en México antes y después del 68." (The Theatre in Mexico Before and After 1968.) *Universidad de Mexico.* 1987 Jan.; 17(432): 3-9. Lang.: Spa.

DRAMA: —Theory/criticism

Mexico: Mexico City. 1957-1987. Historical studies. ■Rise of contemporary theatre in Mexico. Style, content and artistic approach in institutional theatre in Mexico City.

3058 "Poética de la recepción: nueva teoría para un nuevo espectáculo (el primer teatro popular)." (Poetics of Reception: New Theory for a New Performance—The First Popular Theatre.) 203-231 in Coca, Jordi, ed.; Conesa, Laura, comp. *Congrés Internacional de Teatre a Catalunya 1985. Actes. Volum IV. Seccions 7, 8 i 9.* Barcelona: Institut del Teatre; 1987. 350 pp. Notes. [Section 9: The Contribution of Theory to Performance.] Lang.: Spa.
Spain. 1604-1690. Historical studies. ■Analysis of theatrical ideas of seventeenth-century Spain. Comedy as a product of the period's modernity with sociological, political and educational functions.

3059 Jones, Joseph R. "Isidore and the Theater." *CompD.* 1982 Spr; 16(1): 26-48. Notes. Lang.: Eng.
Spain. 560-636. Critical studies. ■Analysis of the writings of Saint Isidore of Seville on ancient Roman and Greek drama: observations on his sources, and medieval point of view on classical drama.

3060 "Retòrica i dramàtica: l'ambit de l'extraterritorialitat lingüística." (Rhetoric and Drama: Beyond Linguisitic Frontiers.) 233-241 in Coca, Jordi, ed.; Conesa, Laura, comp. *Congrés Internacional de Teatre a Catalunya 1985. Actes. Volum IV. Seccions 7, 8 i 9.* Barcelona: Institut del Teatre; 1987. 350 pp. [Section 9: The Contribution of Theory to Performance.] Lang.: Cat.
Spain-Catalonia. UK-England. 1600-1985. Critical studies. ■Translation of theatrical texts can effect communication between cultures and demonstrate the relations between art and life.

3061 Barr, Richard. "Perfect and Imperfect Illusion: Coercive and Collaborative Communities in Strindbergian Theatre." 1-10 in Hartigan, Karelisa V., ed. *From the Bard to Broadway.* Lanham, MD: UP of America; 1987. 222 pp. (Univ. of Florida Dept. of Classics Comparative Drama Conference Papers 7.) Pref. Notes. Biblio. Lang.: Eng.
Sweden. 1987. Critical studies. ■Strindberg's social and aesthetic theory changing from coercion to collaboration. Author postulates this moves Strindberg from naturalism to expressionism.

3062 Siebenhaar, Klaus. "'Bussort' und 'Korrektionsanstalt': Gottfried Kellers 'theatralische Sendung' im Berlin des Nachmärz." (Confession and Correction Institution: Keller's Theory of Drama. Berlin, 1850-1855.) *Tzs.* 1987 Spr(19): 41-53. Notes. Biblio. Illus.: Photo. B&W. Lang.: Ger.
Switzerland. Germany: Berlin. 1850-1855. Critical studies. ■Before the background of a societal change from the feudal to a more democratic state system, Gottfried Keller developed a bourgeois-capitalist theory of drama that was to be predominant up to Brecht.

3063 Epperly, Elizabeth. "Trollope Reading Old Drama." *English Studies in Canada.* 1987 Sep.; 13(3): 281-303. Notes. Lang.: Eng.
UK-England. 1866-1882. Histories-sources. ■Comments on the scope and nature of Trollope's critical response to Elizabethan and Jacobean drama using as a source Trollope's notes and marginalia written between 1866 and 1882 and contained within an 86-volume collection owned by the Folger Shakespeare Library in Washington, DC.

3064 Leiblein, Leanore. "Jan Kott, Peter Brook, and *King Lear.*" *JDTC.* 1987; 1(2): 39-49. Notes. Biblio. Lang.: Eng.
UK-England. 1962-1987. Historical studies. ■How Peter Brook took Jan Kott's interpretive model for reading Shakespeare centered on the reader's personal experience and translated it on to the stage, especially in *King Lear.* How Brook placed his production in the context of his historical moment.

3065 Brown, Terence. "History's Nightmare: Stewart Parker's *Northern Star.*" *ThIr.* 1987; 13: 40-41. Illus.: Photo. B&W. 1. Lang.: Eng.
UK-Ireland. 1984. Critical studies. ■Discussion of *Northern Star* by Irish playwright Stewart Parker which is about the Irish Rebellion of '98.

3066 Baker, Stuart E. "Tragedy Without Awe: A Rationalist View of an Irrational Form." *JDTC.* 1987; 1(2): 17-29. Biblio. Lang.: Eng.
USA. UK-England. Greece. 500 B.C.-1987 A.D. Critical studies. ■Re-examines the assumptions inherent in genre classifications, specifically that of tragedy, in order to offer a new understanding of tragedy linked with farce, rather than comedy, and shaped by historical circumstances.

3067 Boling, Becky. "From Pin-Ups to Striptease in Gambaro's *El despojamiento.*" *LATR.* 1987 Spr; 20(2): 59-65. Lang.: Eng.
USA. 1987. Critical studies. ■Semiotic approach to *El despojamiento (The Robbery)* by Griselda Gambaro, which concentrates on the idea of spectacle and semiotics of performance.

3068 Copeland, Roger. "Absorbing the Future." *AmTh.* 1987 July/Aug.; 4(4): 39-41. Illus.: Photo. B&W. 1. Lang.: Eng.
USA. 1987. Critical studies. ■Analysis of *On the Verge* by Eric Overmyer. Production history, plot synopsis and critical evaluation of play.

3069 Davis, Peter A. "Lawrence Barrett and *The Man O'Airlie*: The Genteel Tradition in Performance." *THSt.* 1987; 7: 61-72. Notes. Illus.: Photo. Print. B&W. 1. Lang.: Eng.
USA. 1870-1890. Historical studies. ■Lawrence Barrett's performances in 1871 as Harebell in W.G. Will's *The Man O'Airlie* is pivotal to understanding American aesthetic taste for 'genteelism' in late 19th century theatre.

3070 Findlay, Robert. "Practice/Theory/Practice/Theory: Excerpts from an Extended Interview/Dialogue with Zbigniew Cynkutis (1938-1987)." *JDTC.* 1987; 1(2): 145-150. Illus.: Photo. B&W. 1. Lang.: Eng.
USA. 1938-1987. Histories-sources. ■Combination interview, essay and dialogue, excerpts discussing connections between theory and practice.

3071 Hirsch, Foster. "The Critic as Subversive." *AmTh.* 1987 Nov.; 4(8): 36-37. Illus.: Photo. B&W. 2. Lang.: Eng.
USA. 1946-1987. Critical studies. ■The work and writings of theatre critics Eric Bentley and Gordon Rogoff.

3072 Novick, Julius. "The Critical Instinct." *AmTh.* 1987 July/Aug.; 4(4): 24-27. Illus.: Dwg. 1. Lang.: Eng.
USA. 1987. Histories-sources. ■Keynote address at Northern California Theatre Critics Conference. Duties and responsibilities of a critic.

3073 Raymond, Gerard. "An Intellectual of the Imagination." *TheaterW.* 1987 Dec 14-20; 1(18): 36-39. 3. Lang.: Eng.
USA: New York, NY. 1987. Histories-sources. ■Interview with Kathleen Tynan discussing her biography of her husband, critic Kenneth Tynan.

3074 Schechner, Richard. "A Call for 'Performaturgy'." *AmTh.* 1987 Oct.; 4(7): 84. Illus.: Photo. B&W. 1. Lang.: Eng.
USA: Tallahassee, FL. 1987. Technical studies. ■The author suggests a new offshoot of dramaturgical research called 'performaturgy', relating to concrete scenic actions from previous productions.

3075 Schneider, Michael. "Bottom's Dream, the Lion's Roar, and Hostility of Class Difference in *A Midsummer Night's Dream.*" 191-212 in Hartigan, Karelisa V., ed. *From the Bard to Broadway.* Lanham, MD: UP of America; 1987. 222 pp. (Univ. of Florida Dept. of Classics Comparative Drama Conference Papers 7.) Pref. Notes. Lang.: Eng.
USA. 1987. Critical studies. ■Refutation of Northrop Frye's critical analysis of *A Midsummer Night's Dream.* Encourages a more Marxist, cultural-materialist and Freudian approach.

3076 Schoolfield, George C. "Hermann J. Weigand (1892-1985)." *INC.* 1986-87; 7(1): 12-15. Notes. Illus.: Photo. 1. Lang.: Eng.
USA. 1892-1985. Biographical studies. ■Capsule summary of career and achievements of this noted Ibsen scholar.

3077 Wellman, Mac. "Poetry & Theatre." *TT.* 1987 June/July; 6(5): 4. Lang.: Eng.
USA. 1987. Critical studies. ■Role of language in plays and its relationship to characterization.

DRAMA: —Theory/criticism

3078 Harussi, Yael. "Drama VeFormalizem—Ahgisha Ahtechnologit shell S.D. Balukatyj." (Drama and Formalism According to S.D. Baluscatyj.) *Bamah*. 1987; 22(108): 73-83. Lang.: Heb.

USSR. Israel. 1921-1987. Critical studies. ■Relation of dramatic text to other written arts, and the formalist attempt to analyze Čechov's work.

Training

3079 Hametner, Michael. "Über die dritte Brecht-Werkstaat des DDR-Zentrums der AITA. Dokumentation." (Documentation of the 3rd Brecht Workshop of the GDR Centre of IATA.) *SzeneAT*. 1987; 22(1): 2-4. Illus.: Photo. B&W. 4. Lang.: Ger.

Germany, East: Berlin, East. 1986. Histories-sources. ■Structure, actions and working methods (amateur theatre) of an international Brecht course with 37 directors and actors from 16 countries.

3080 Sandelin, Ann-Charlotte. "Röst och psyke." (Voice and Psyche.) *Teaterf*. 1987; 20(2-3): 12-13. Illus.: Photo. Lang.: Swe.

Sweden. 1980-1987. Histories-sources. ■Orlanda Cook speaks about her activity as voice teacher among mostly amateur groups.

3081 Hurst, Deirdre du Prey. "Deirdre Hurst du Prey: Working with Chekhov." *TDR*. 1983 Fall; 27(3): 84-90. Illus.: Photo. B&W. 3. Lang.: Eng.

UK-England: Dartington. 1978. Histories-sources. ■Interview with one of the few remaining teachers of the Čechov Method who were personally taught by Michajl Čechov. Technique, methods, discussion of Čechov and some of his roles.

3082 Citron, Atay. "The Chekhov Technique Today." *TDR*. 1983 Fall; 27(3): 91-96. Illus.: Photo. B&W. 3. Lang.: Eng.

USA: New York, NY. 1930-1980. Historical studies. ■Focus on the remaining acting teachers who studied under Michajl Čechov. Beatrice Straight, Joanna Merlin, Blair Cutting. Work at the Michajl Čechov Studio, adapting the technique to new demands in the theatre.

MEDIA

General

Administration

3083 "International Actor Group Convenes in Israel, Meets 'Big Brother'." *EN*. 1987 Sep.; 72(9): 1. Lang.: Eng.

USA: New York, NY. Israel: Tel-Aviv. 1987. Historical studies. ■Conference on Secondary Use of Recorded Performances convened by the International Federation of Actors in Tel Aviv to discuss the use of digital sampling and holography to create a duplication of the human voice and human image.

3084 DuBoff, Leonard D. "Picking Up Blacked-Out Sports Events Via Satellite Dish Antenna: First Down and Goal to Go." *ColJL&A*. 1987 Spr; 11(3): 359-362. Notes. Lang.: Eng.

USA. 1976-1987. Technical studies. ■Introduction to a series of articles on pirating satellite signals of blacked-out sports events.

3085 Gentin, Adèle L. "A Picture is Worth a Thousand Words: The Basis for Copyrightability of Characters in Public Domain Works." *ColJL&A*. 1987 Fall; 12(1): 73-101. Notes. Lang.: Eng.

USA. 1986-1987. Technical studies. ■The *Silverman v. CBS* case and the issue of copyright protection for fictional characters.

3086 McManis, Charles R. "Satellite Dish Antenna Reception: Copyright Protection of Live Broadcasts and the Doctrine of Anticipatory Infringement." *ColJL&A*. 1987 Spr; 11(3): 387-402. Notes. Lang.: Eng.

USA. 1976-1987. Technical studies. ■Changes brought about in federal copyright law as a result of broadcasting's counter-offensive seeking FCC regulations restricting satellite reception.

3087 Murphy, Christopher A. "*Salinger v. Random House*: The Author's Interests in Unpublished Materials." *ColJL&A*. 1987 Fall; 12(1): 103-129. Notes. Lang.: Eng.

USA. 1986-1987. Critical studies. ■*Salinger v. Random House* and the nature of the author's interest in unpublished materials.

3088 Nevins, Frances M. "Antenna Dilemma: The Exemption from Copyright Liability for Public Performance Using Technology Common in the Home." *ColJL&A*. 1987 Spr; 11(3): 403-412. Notes. Lang.: Eng.

USA. 1976-1987. Critical studies. ■Exemption from copyright liability for public performance using common household technology.

3089 Osofsky, Howard R.; Schneiderman, Jan R. "The New California Gold Rush: SAG's 1980 Strike Revisited." *JAML*. 1982 Sum; 12(2): 5-32. Notes. Tables. Lang.: Eng.

USA. 1980. Historical studies. ■SAG/AFTRA strike of 1980. Nature and special demands of the television/motion picture industry, brief case study, explores the 1960, 1977 and 1980 'basic' and 'television' agreements between union and management.

3090 Roberts, Gary R. "Pirating Satellite Signals of Blacked-Out Sports Events: A Historical and Policy Perspective." *ColJL&A*. 1987 Spr; 11(3): 363-386. Notes. Illus.: Dwg. 1. Lang.: Eng.

USA. 1950-1987. Technical studies. ■History of blacked-out sports events and policy implications of enforcing their restrictions.

3091 Sparling, Tobin A. "The Resolution of Title to WPA Prints." *ColJL&A*. 1987 Fall; 12(1): 131-152. Notes. Illus.: Pntg. 1. Lang.: Eng.

USA. 1935-1987. Historical studies. ■History of ownerships of WPA prints and the current title disputes.

3092 Stim, Richard W. "The Reform of Notice Omission: *Crumb A.A. Sales, Inc.* as a Paradigm." *ColJL&A*. 1987 Sum; 11(4): 635-664. Notes. Lang.: Eng.

USA. 1968-1987. Historical studies. ■Effect of 1976 Copyright Act in reforming the loss of copyright through omission of notice as related to the illustration of Robert Crumb.

3093 Tigerman, Stephen M. "The Growing Problem of Involuntary Superstations." *JAML*. 1982 Fall; 12(3): 51-66. Notes. Lang.: Eng.

USA. 1970-1982. Historical studies. ■Voluntary and involuntary superstations: the interaction between copyright law and FCC regulation.

Audience

3094 Parfrey, Adam. "The Pre-Recorded Audience in Two Dimensions." *PerAJ*. 1985 Sum/Fall; 9(2-3): 213-218. Lang.: Eng.

USA. 1985. Critical studies. ■Public's perception of popular images as being real.

Performance/production

3095 Staples, Robert. "The Media as Opiate: Blacks in the Performing Arts." *WJBC*. 1987; 10(1): 6-11. Notes. Lang.: Eng.

USA. 1950-1987. Critical studies. ■Roles of Black Americans as entertainers in film industry: racist stereotypes subjected to exploitation and dehumanization.

Plays/librettos/scripts

3096 Frazer, Robbin. "All I Get is Static!" *PAC*. 1985 Apr.; 22(1): 3-7. Illus.: Photo. Print. B&W. 10. Lang.: Eng.

Canada: Ottawa, ON. 1984. Histories-reconstruction. ■A study of *All I Get is Static!*, a play commissioned by the National Museum of Science and Technology about Reginald Fessenden, the 'Father of Radio' in Canada.

3097 Davies, Anthony. "Shakespeare and the Media of Film, Radio and Television: A Retrospect." *ShS*. 1987; 39: 1-11. Notes. Lang.: Eng.

Europe. USA. 1899-1987. Critical studies. ■Two ways of adapting Shakespearean plays to other media, giving priority either to theatrical or to media concerns.

3098 MacKinnon, Kenneth. *Greek Tragedy into Film*. London: Crown Helm; 1987. 199 pp. Biblio. Index. Append. Illus.: Photo. Lang.: Eng.

Greece. 500 B.C.-1986 A.D. Histories-specific. ■Examination of how 16 films transferred Greek drama of 5th century into film medium.

MEDIA: General—Plays/librettos/scripts

3099 Rothwell, Kenneth S. "Representing *King Lear* on Screen: From Metatheatre to 'Meta-Cinema'." *ShS*. 1987; 39: 75-90. Notes. Illus.: Photo. B&W. 7. Lang.: Eng.
USA. UK-England. USSR. 1916-1983. Critical studies. ■Successful film versions of *King Lear*. Cinematic rather than literal interpretations of text as it appears for the stage.

Relation to other fields

3100 Magli, Adriano. *Mass-media e potere. discorso sul pubblico. La crisi della radio.* (Power and Mass-Media: A Speech on the Audience. The Crisis of Radio.) Rome: Bulzoni; 1987. 292 pp. (Biblioteca cinematografica e dei mass-media 22.) [Vol. 1, 2d ed.] Lang.: Ita.
Italy. 1900-1987. Critical studies. ■Diminishing political and economic power of radio with respect to audiovisual media. Role of radio compared to television, the press, media culture.

3101 Esslin, Martin. "The Arts in the Global Village." *JAML*. 1987 Win; 17(4): 51-56. Lang.: Eng.
USA. 1987. Critical studies. ■How aspects of media have affected arts around the world.

3102 Fuchs, Elinor. "The Theatricalization of American Politics." *AmTh*. 1987 Jan.; 3(10): 17-20, 44. Illus.: Photo. B&W. 3. Lang.: Eng.
USA. 1967-1987. Historical studies. ■Theatrical elements in U.S. politics and media. Aspects of social theatricalization in society, television, news and entertainment.

Theory/criticism

3103 Flesch, William. "Proximity and Power: Shakespearean and Cinematic Space." *TJ*. 1987 Oct.; 39(3): 277-293. Notes. Lang.: Eng.
USA. 1987. Critical studies. ■A theoretical account of the differences between cinematic and theatrical representations.

3104 Gates, Henry Louis, Jr. "The Black Person in Art: How Should S/he be Portrayed? (Part 1)." *BALF*. 1987 Spr-Sum; 21(2-1): 3-24. Lang.: Eng.
USA. 1926-1987. Critical studies. ■Portrayal of African-Americans in literature as compared to concerns of W.E.B. Dubois.

3105 Gates, Henry Louis, Jr. "The Black Person in Art: How Should S/he be Portrayed? (Part II)." *BALF*. 1987 Fall; 21(3): 317-332. Lang.: Eng.
USA. 1926-1987. Critical studies. ■Gates examines the portrayal of African-Americans in literature as compared to concerns of W.E.B. Dubois.

Audio forms

Administration

3106 Eichbaum, Julius. "The SABC—A Law Unto Itself." *Scenaria*. 1987 Jan.; 72: 3-6. Lang.: Eng.
South Africa, Republic of. 1987. Critical studies. ■Suggestion that SABC improve broadcasting standards to accommodate classical music lovers.

3107 Oman, Ralph. "Source Licensing: The Latest Skirmish in an Old Battle." *ColJL&A*. 1987 Win; 11(2): 251-281. Notes. Lang.: Eng.
USA. 1940-1987. Critical studies. ■Arguments for and against source licensing.

3108 Zieger, Joan. "How a Bequest Program Succeeded." *FundM*. 1987 Feb.; 17(12): 28-34. Illus.: Photo. Graphs. Diagram. Print. B&W. Color. 10. Lang.: Eng.
USA: Madison, WI. 1984-1987. Historical studies. ■New bequest program for Wisconsin Public Broadcasting results in over $1 million in bequests, indicating a significant future in planned giving.

Basic theatrical documents

3109 Fink, Howard, ed.; Jackson, John, ed. *All the Bright Company: Radio Drama Produced by Andrew Allan.* Kingston, ON: Quarry P and CBC Enterprises; 1987. xvi, 336. Biblio. Lang.: Eng.

Canada. 1942-1955. ■Collection of eleven radio plays, an introduction on Andrew Allan, early radio drama in Canada and an analysis of its legacy of theatre professionals.

Institutions

3110 Frick, Alice N. *Image in the Mind: CBC Radio Drama 1944 to 1954.* Toronto, ON: Canadian Stage Arts Publications; 1987. x, 176. Index. Biblio. Illus.: Photo. Lang.: Eng.
Canada. 1944-1954. Histories-sources. ■A personal chronicle of 'The Golden Age' of Canadian radio drama by Andrew Allan's script editor.

Performance/production

3111 Sibley, Brian. "Radio: Beyond *Milkwood*." *Drama*. 1987; 3(165): 46. Lang.: Eng.
UK-England. UK-Wales. 1987. Reviews of performances. ■Radio 4's Welsh Drama Week 1987 reviewed.

3112 Crutchfield, Will. "An Open Ear:...How to Listen to Historic Records." *OpN*. 1987 Aug.; 52(2): 18-20, 22-23. Illus.: Photo. B&W. 6. Lang.: Eng.
USA. Europe. 1877-1987. Histories-sources. ■Vocal style on antique phonograph records. Related to Music-Drama: Opera.

3113 Fisher, Martin; Poole, Jane L. "Nipper and His Friends." *OpN*. 1987 Aug.; 52(2): 7-12. Tables. Illus.: Photo. Color. 14. Lang.: Eng.
USA. Italy. Germany. 1904-1987. Histories-sources. ■Early phonograph records of opera singers. Related to Music-Drama: Opera.

3114 Livingstone, William. "Valhalla on Thirty-Fourth Street: Behind the Scenes at the First American Recording of Wagner's *Der Ring des Nibelungen*, a Joint Project of the Metropolitan Opera and Deutsche Grammophon." *OpN*. 1987 Aug.; 52(2): 34-36. Illus.: Photo. Color. 8. Lang.: Eng.
USA: New York, NY. 1987. Histories-sources. ■Backstage look at performance recording. Related to Music-Drama: Opera.

Plays/librettos/scripts

3115 Bull, Jill M. "John Hickling: Radio Drama Pioneer." *ADS*. 1987 Oct.; 11: 79-88. Lang.: Eng.
Australia. 1930-1960. Historical studies. ■Hickling's work as a producer and writer for programs for commercial radio, ranging from variety and dramatized documentary to dramatized novels and radio plays.

3116 Sherman, Jason. "Aural Dilemmas." *BooksC*. 1987 Mar.; 16(2): 5-6. Illus.: Design. B&W. 1. Lang.: Eng.
Canada. 1987. Critical studies. ■Six plays in CBC's Stereo Theatre *Sextet* examined in terms of relevance, structure and writing.

3117 Frost, Everett C. "Why Sound Art Works and the German Hörspiel." *TDR*. 1987 Win; 31(4): 109-124. Illus.: Photo. Dwg. Poster. B&W. 6. Lang.: Eng.
Germany, West: Cologne. USA. 1950-1985. Historical studies. ■The history of the German radio play *Hörspiel* from the 1950s to recent works. Includes detailed description of Faith Wilding's and Götz Naleppa's *Hildegarde & Ich*.

3118 Bolotova, Je. A. *Dokumental'naja drama v sovetskom radioteatre: Avtoref.dis. kand. iskusstvovedtnija.* (Documentary Drama in Soviet Radio Theatre: Abstract of a Dissertation by a Candidate in Art Criticism.) Moscow: GITIS; 1987. 24 pp. Lang.: Rus.
USSR. 1917-1987. Historical studies.

Film

Administration

3119 Vértessy, Péter. "A magyar filmesek nem gyerekek többé. Beszélgetés Jancsó Miklóssal." (Hungarian Film Makers Are Not Children Any More: Interview with Miklós Jancsó.) *Krit*. 1987 Sep.(9): 3-5. Illus.: Photo. B&W. 4. Lang.: Hun.
Hungary. 1987. Histories-sources. ■Director's view on the role of film production in a small country like Hungary, on the lack of patronage, sufficient intellectual and financial liberty, on the relation between film and television and on the need for competition.

MEDIA: Film—Administration

3120   Austin, Bruce A. "G-PG-R-X: The Purpose, Promise and Performance of the Movie Rating System." *JAML*. 1982 Sum; 12(2): 51-74. Notes. Lang.: Eng.
USA. 1968-1982. Historical studies. ■Reviews the scientific literature related to the Motion Picture Association of America's film rating system to ascertain the degree to which this self-regulatory policy has met its purpose and goal.

3121   Callagy, Robert; Karp, Irwin; Kovner, Victor A.; Rembor, Charles; Rossner, Judith. "Libel in Fiction: The Sylvia Plath Case and its Aftermath." *ColJL&A*. 1987 Sum; 11(4): 473-503. Notes. Lang.: Eng.
USA. 1986-1987. Historical studies. ■Discussion of the risk and element of libel in fiction following the Sylvia Plath case.

3122   King, Donald C. "The William Fox Story." *MarqJTHS*. 1987; 19(4): 25-27. Biblio. Illus.: Photo. B&W. 12. Lang.: Eng.
USA: New York, NY. 1879-1952. Historical studies. ■Fox's career, first as a cinema and variety theatre owner in New York and later as a Hollywood studio owner with a nation-wide chain of theatres.

3123   Lewis, Kevin. "Lee Shubert, Marcus Loew and the Founding of MGM." *PasShow*. 1986 Sum; 10(2): 6-8. Illus.: Photo. B&W. 2. Lang.: Eng.
USA: New York, NY. 1914-1924. Historical studies. ■Lee Shubert's role in the formation of the American film industry.

Audience

3124   Klimontovič, N. "Teatr i kino segodnja. Kino i zritel'." (Theatre and Film Today: The Cinema and Its Audience.) 21-32 in *Kino i zritel'*. Moscow: Sojuzinformkino; 1987. 275 pp. Lang.: Rus.
USSR. 1980-1987. Critical studies. ■Mutual relations of theatre and cinema.

Basic theatrical documents

3125   Rainer, Yvonne. "*The Man Who Envied Women*." *WPerf*. 1987; 3(2): 103-160. Illus.: Photo. B&W. 3. Lang.: Eng.
USA. 1985. ■Script of the film directed and written by Yvonne Rainer.

Design/technology

3126   Szabó, G. László. "'Fordult a kerék'. Prágai találkozás Theodor Pištěkkel, az Amadeus Oscar-dijas jelmeztervező-jével." ('The Wheel Turned': Interview in Prague with Theodor Pištěk, Oscar Winning Costume Designer of *Amadeus*.) *FSM*. 1987; 31(27): 18-19. Illus.: Design. Photo. Color. 4. Lang.: Hun.
Czechoslovakia. 1932-1987. Histories-sources. ■Interview with costume designer Theodor Pištěk.

3127   Baló, Júlia. "Találkozás Kende Jánossal. 'Az operatőr: beosztott társ'." (Interview with János Kende. 'The Cameraman Is a Subordinate Associate'.) *FSM*. 1987 Feb.; 31(7): 8-9. Illus.: Photo. B&W. 1. Lang.: Hun.
Hungary. 1965-1987. Histories-sources. ■Cameraman János Kende on his films, work with Miklós Jancsó, the qualities of good directors and cameramen, differences between television and film work.

3128   Nagy, Attila Miklós. "Mexikói beszélgetés Koltay Lajossal. 'A felelősség közös'." (Interview with Lajos Koltay in Mexico: The Responsibility Is Common.) *FSM*. 1987 Jan.; 31(3): 8-9. Illus.: Photo. B&W. 3. Lang.: Hun.
Hungary. 1986. Histories-sources. ■Lajos Koltay was the cameraman of the American film production *Gaby* directed by Louis Mandoki. He speaks about the scenario and working with the main actress Liv Ullmann.

3129   Allen, Woody; Forman, Milos; Pollack, Sydney; Rogers, Ginger; Silverstein, Elliott. "Colorization: The Arguments Against It." *JAML*. 1987 Fall; 17(3): 79-93. Lang.: Eng.
USA. 1987. Technical studies. ■Colorization of films and arguments against its use.

3130   Calhoun, John Leroy. "Design—Where Credit is Due." *ThCr*. 1987 Aug/Sep.; 21(7): 79-82. Illus.: Dwg. Diagram. Color. B&W. 12. Lang.: Eng.

USA: Los Angeles, CA. 1987. Technical studies. ■Current technology available and brief history of film credits.

3131   Gentry, Ric. "Defining Shades of Gray." *LDim*. 1987 Mar/Apr.; 11(2): 44-53. Illus.: Photo. B&W. 3. Lang.: Eng.
USA. 1986. Technical studies. ■The work of cinematographer Robby Muller.

3132   Gentry, Ric. "The Eastwood Aesthetic." *LDim*. 1987 Jan/Feb.; 11(1): 20-82. Illus.: Photo. B&W. 2. Lang.: Eng.
USA. 1982-1987. Technical studies. ■Analysis of the work of lighting designer Jack Green on the film *Heartbreak Ridge*.

3133   Maeder, Edward, comp. *Hollywood and History: Costume Design in Film*. Los Angeles, CA: Thomas & Hudson/L.A. County Museum of Art; 1987. 256 pp. Index. Notes. Tables. Illus.: Photo. Print. Color. B&W. 150. Lang.: Eng.
USA: Hollywood, CA. 1920-1986. Historical studies. ■Series of essays on historical costuming in films including a chronological filmography. Based on an exhibit *Hollywood History* at the Los Angeles County Museum of Art.

3134   Mayer, Roger L.; Word, Rob; Young, Buddy. "Colorization: The Arguments For." *JAML*. 1987 Fall; 17(3): 64-78. Lang.: Eng.
USA. 1987. Technical studies. ■Colorization of films and arguments for its use.

3135   Myers, Dennis; Ewing, Darrell. "Tar Heel Tinseltown: DeLaurentis Does it in North Carolina." *ThCr*. 1987 Apr.; 21(4): 53-54. Illus.: Photo. B&W. 2. Lang.: Eng.
USA: Wilmington, NC. 1987. Technical studies. ■DeLaurentis Entertainment Group's film studio venture.

3136   Pulleine, Tim. "Emotionally Correct Solutions." *LDim*. 1987 May/June; 11(3): 116-123. Illus.: Photo. B&W. 4. Lang.: Eng.
USA. 1987. Technical studies. ■Cinematographer Oliver Stapleton and his lighting work on the film *Prick Up Your Ears*.

3137   Pulleine, Tim. "Nature's Call." *LDim*. 1987 Sep/Oct.; 11(5): 55-74. Illus.: Photo. Color. 2. Lang.: Eng.
USA. 1987. Technical studies. ■Cinematography and lighting of the film *Castaway* by Harvey Harrison.

3138   Seidenberg, Robert. "Matewan: Nora Chavooshian Creates Major Miners." *ThCr*. 1987 Apr.; 21(4): 45-48. Illus.: Photo. Color. B&W. 5. Lang.: Eng.
USA. 1987. Technical studies. ■Production designer Nora Chavooshian and her collaborations with film director John Sayles.

3139   Williams, Mike. "*The Glass Menagerie*." *LDim*. 1987 Nov.; 11(5): 48-71. Illus.: Photo. Color. 2. Lang.: Eng.
USA. 1987. Technical studies. ■Cinematographer Michael Ballhaus' work on film version of Williams' *The Glass Menagerie* directed by Paul Newman.

Institutions

3140   Ballantine, Frank. "Non-Profit Entrepreneurship: The Astoria Motion Picture and Television Center." *JAML*. 1982 Spr; 12 (1): 5-25. Notes. Biblio. Lang.: Eng.
USA: Queens, NY. 1920-1982. Historical studies. ■A brief introduction to the history of the Astoria Studios and the process through which it has been restored to an operating film studio. Success depends on its nonprofit status and broad-based political and film industry coalition.

Performance spaces

3141   Bentham, Frederick. "The New Victoria in London: A Mermaid's Palace." *MarqJTHS*. 1987; 19(3): 5-9. Illus.: Photo. B&W. 5. Lang.: Eng.
UK-England: London. 1928-1987. Historical studies. ■The New Victoria as an example of the best of the British Super Cinemas. Description of the building and its history.

3142   House, John D.P. "Notes on the New Victoria." *MarqJTHS*. 1987; 19(3): 10-13. Illus.: Photo. Plan. B&W. 6. Lang.: Eng.
UK-England: London. 1930-1987. Historical studies. ■The New Victoria Theatre in the context of comparing British and American cinema theatre design.

MEDIA: Film—Performance spaces

3143 Bagley, Mary. "The Uptown Theatre." *MarqJTHS*. 1987; 19(4): 20-25. Notes. Illus.: Photo. B&W. 8. Lang.: Eng.
USA: Kansas City, MO. 1926-1987. Historical studies. ■This Eberson designed 'atmospheric' was a successful film house for 45 years. It was then used for dinner theatre, opera and the 1977 Republican Convention.

3144 Morrison, Andrew C.; Wheeler, Lucy Pope. "Garden Theatre, Pittsburgh, Pennsylvania." *MarqJTHS*. 1987; 19(3): 14-17. Illus.: Photo. Design. B&W. Fr.Elev. 6. Lang.: Eng.
USA: Pittsburgh, PA. 1915-1987. Historical studies. ■Description of the Garden Theatre designed by Thomas H. Scott.

3145 Potter, Elizabeth Walton; Wheeler, Lucy Pope; Meyers, Denys Peter. "Oriental Theatre, Portland Oregon." *MarqJTHS*. 1987; 19(1): 3-27. Notes. Illus.: Photo. Plan. Sketches. B&W. Architec. 49. Lang.: Eng.
USA: Portland, OR. 1927-1970. Historical studies. ■Interior of Oregon's second largest movie theatre, derived from Khmer sculpture in Angkor Wat, designed by Thomas & Mercier.

3146 Preston, Roy. "Pekin Theatre, Pekin, Ill." *MarqJTHS*. 1987; 19(1): 30-31. Illus.: Photo. B&W. 4. Lang.: Eng.
USA: Pekin, IL. 1927-1987. Historical studies. ■Structure and history of movie theatres, focusing on the Oriental-style Pekin Theatre designed by Elmer F. Behrns.

Performance/production

3147 Bharucha, Rustom. "The 'Boom' of David Lean's *A Passage to India*." 155-161 in Cardullo, Bert, ed. *Before His Eyes: Essays in Honor of Stanley Kauffmann*. Lanham, MD: UP of America; 1987. 185 pp. Lang.: Eng.
1983. Critical studies. ■Analysis of David Lean's film *A Passage to India*. Compares it to E.M. Forster's original novel with its disparaging views of India.

3148 Holderness, Graham; McCullough, Christopher. "Shakespeare on the Screen: A Selective Filmography." *ShS*. 1987; 39: 13-37. Notes. Lang.: Eng.
1899-1987. ■International coverage of straightforward film adaptations of Shakespeare, with distribution information given when available.

3149 Ju, Lih Min. "Laurence Olivier wei Hamlet zhen xin." (The Reconstruction of *Hamlet* by Laurence Olivier.) *ChWai*. 1987 Apr.; 15(11): 4-21. Notes. Lang.: Chi.
England. 1604-1948. Critical studies. ■Comparison of Olivier's film *Hamlet* with Shakespeare's theatrical text.

3150 Dévényi, Róbert. "Molière én vagyok! Szövegmagyarázat' Mnouchkine filmjéhez." (I am Molière! Text Explanation to Mnouchkine's Film.) *Sz*. 1987 May; 20(5): 45-48. Lang.: Hun.
France. 1987. Reviews of performances. ■Short review of Ariane Mnouchkine's Molière film.

3151 Baló, Júlia. "Találkozás Hanna Schygullával. 'Az ellentmondások izgatnak'." (Interview with Hanna Schygulla: 'Contradictions Excite Me.) *FSM*. 1987; 31(28): 6-7. Illus.: Photo. B&W. 1. Lang.: Hun.
Germany, West. 1987. Histories-sources. ■Interview with international film star Hanna Schygulla on the occasion of shooting 'Miss Arizona' in Hungary.

3152 Barna, Márta. "Hazát keresők. Beszélgetés Sára Sándorral." (Those Looking for a Fatherland: Interview with Sándor Sára.) *FSM*. 1987 Jan.; 31(5): 4-7. Illus.: Photo. B&W. 1. Lang.: Hun.
Hungary. 1980-1987. Histories-sources. ■Interview with film-maker Sándor Sára and his turn to documentary films.

3153 Cenner, Mihály; Geréb, Anna; Karcsai Kulcsár, István; Nemeskürty, István; Veress, József; Erdélyi Z., Agnes, ed. *Kabos Gyula, 1887-1941: Születésének századik évfordulójára*. (Gyula Kabos, 1887-1941: Centenary of His Birth.) Budapest: Magyar Filmintézet; 1987. 519 pp. Notes. Biblio. Filmography. Illus.: Photo. B&W. 108. Lang.: Hun.

Hungary. 1887-1941. Biographical studies. ■Studies and documents of film actor Gyula Kabos. Reviewed by Góbar Antal, *Sz* 20:9 (1987 Sep), 47-48.

3154 Harmat, György. "'Nem tudnék csak magamért élni'. Beszélgetés Nyakó Júliával." ('I Could Not Live for Myself Only': Interview with Júlia Nyakó.) *FSM*. 1987 Feb.; 31(8): 11. Illus.: Photo. B&W. 1. Lang.: Hun.
Hungary. 1978-1987. Histories-sources. ■Júlia Nyakó speaks about her roles, the acting profession and her relation to her colleagues.

3155 Kurcz, Béla. "'...Vonzódom a mesefilmhez...':Beszélgetés Sólyom Andrással." ('I am attracted by tale films': Interview with András Sólyom.) *FSM*. 1987 Jan.; 31(2): 7. Illus.: Photo. B&W. 1. Lang.: Hun.
Hungary. 1987. Histories-sources. ■Conversation about the relation between film and tale, specific features of making film.

3156 Baló, Júlia. "Találkozás Marcello Mastroiannival. 'Soha nem gondoltam: különleges az arcom'." (Interview with Marcello Mastroianni: 'I Have Never Thought: I Have a Special Face'.) *FSM*. 1987 Apr.; 31(17): 8-9. Illus.: Photo. B&W. 1. Lang.: Hun.
Italy. 1949-1987. Histories-sources. ■Mastroianni speaks about his roles, the stage and film directors to whom he is indebted, and his theatre work.

3157 Loren, Sophia; Hotchner, A.E.; Farkas, István, transl. *Élni és szeretni*. (Sophia: Living and Loving.) Budapest: Gondolat; 1987. xxxii, 254 pp. Filmography. Illus.: Photo. B&W. 52. Lang.: Hun.
Italy. 1934-1979. Biographies. ■Hungarian translation of Sophia Loren's autobiography (Victoria Pictures Ltd. and A.E. Hotchner, 1979).

3158 Schifano, Laurence. *I fuochi della passione. La vita di Luchino Visconti*. (The Fires of Passion: The Life of Luchino Visconti.) Milan: Longanesi; 1987. 429 pp. (Il cammeo 179.) Index. Biblio. Illus.: Photo. Print. B&W. 32. Lang.: Ita.
Italy. 1906-1976. Biographies. ■Italian translation of *Luchino Visconti*. *Les feux de la passion*.

3159 Villien, Bruno. *Visconti*. Milan: Garzanti; 1987. 254 pp. Notes. Index. Illus.: Photo. Print. Color. B&W. Lang.: Ita.
Italy. 1906-1976. Biographies. ■Film director Luchino Visconti.

3160 Zocaro, Ettore. "Ruggero Ruggeri attore nel cinema muto e sonoro." (The Actor Ruggero Ruggeri in the Sound and Silent Cinema.) *TeatrC*. 1987; 7(15): 249-258. Lang.: Ita.
Italy. 1914-1952. Biographical studies. ■The cinematographic activity of the theatre actor Ruggero Ruggeri.

3161 Lawson, Steve. "For Valor: The Career of Ingmar Bergman." 163-168 in Cardullo, Bert, ed. *Before His Eyes: Essays in Honor of Stanley Kauffmann*. Lanham, MD: UP of America; 1987. 185 pp. Lang.: Eng.
Sweden. 1944-1986. Biographical studies. ■Career of film director Ingmar Bergman.

3162 Enser, A.G.S. *Filmed Books and Plays*. Hampshire, England: Gower; 1987. 774 pp. Lang.: Eng.
UK-England. USA. 1926-1986. Historical studies. ■Listing of film titles, shoot locations and dates, authors, and producers of films made from books and plays: original authors and titles are included.

3163 Vardac, A. Nicholas. *Stage to Screen: Theatrical Method from Garrick to Griffith*. Da Capo P; 1987. 283 pp. Pref. Illus.: Photo. Print. B&W. 85. [First published in 1949.] Lang.: Eng.
UK-England: London. USA: Hollywood, CA, New York, NY. 1895-1915. Histories-specific. ■From the new theatrical realism of the late nineteenth century with its sense of a greater pictorial reality to the development of motion pictures. The connection between motion pictures and theatrical production.

3164 Cardullo, Bert. "The Real Fascination of *Citizen Kane*." 169-179 in Cardullo, Bert, ed. *Before His Eyes: Essays in Honor of Stanley Kauffmann*. Lanham, MD: UP of America; 1987. 185 pp. Lang.: Eng.

MEDIA: Film—Performance/production

USA. 1942. Critical studies. ■Critical questioning of filmmakers' approach in *Citizen Kane*. Why make Kane dead? Author posits that this choice was made to study the character's life after he was dead rather than allow audience to experience his life with him.

3165   Fried, Debra. "Hollywood Convention and Film Adaptation." *TJ.* 1987 Oct.; 39(3): 294-306. Notes. Lang.: Eng.
USA: Hollywood, CA. 1987. Technical studies. ■Speculation on ways in which stage classics are changed by conventions in classic Hollywood film: editing of dialogue, status of objects and the star system.

3166   Gentry, Ric. "Konchalovsky: The Force of Nature." *ThCr.* 1987 Mar.; 3(21): 63-66. Illus.: Photo. B&W. Color. 7. Lang.: Eng.
USA. USSR: Moscow. Critical studies. ■Film director Andrei Konchalovsky, his use of location and environment to create strong visual contexts.

3167   Henderson, Maurice. "Margaret Avery: A Place Among the Stars." *BlackM.* 1987 Sep.; 3(10): 4, 11. Illus.: Photo. B&W. 1. Lang.: Eng.
USA: San Diego, CA, Hollywood, CA. 1950-1987. Histories-sources. ■Actor Margaret Avery discusses her career, especially *The Color Purple*.

3168   Hepburn, Katherine. *The Making of the African Queen: Or How I Went to Africa with Bogart, Bacall and Huston and Almost Lost my Mind.* NY: Knopf; 1987. 129 pp. Illus.: Photo. Maps. Print. B&W. 45. Lang.: Eng.
USA: Hollywood, CA. 1950-1951. Histories-sources. ■Personal anecdotes and photographs from the making of *The African Queen*.

3169   Mailer, Norman; Bart, István, transl. *Marilyn.* Budapest: Corvina; 1987. 350 pp. Illus.: Photo. B&W. 16. [2d rev. ed.] Lang.: Hun.
USA. 1926-1962. Biographies. ■Hungarian translation of Norman Mailer's biography of Marilyn Monroe (Grosset and Dunlap, 1973).

3170   Paran, Janice. "My Keaton." 149-154 in Cardullo, Bert, ed. *Before His Eyes: Essays in Honor of Stanley Kauffmann.* Lanham, MD: UP of America; 1987. 185 pp. Lang.: Eng.
USA. 1895-1966. Historical studies. ■Analysis of Buster Keaton's screen persona. Traces his theatrical background and his film performances.

3171   Stensson, Ola. "Mario—syndaren." (Mario—The Sinner.) *MuD.* 1987; 9(2): 16-19. Illus.: Photo. 5. Lang.: Swe.
USA. 1921-1959. Biographical studies. ■Some short episodes from the life and career of Mario Lanza.

3172   Bán, Magda. "'Ha jó filmek készülnek...' Moszkvai beszelgetés Gleb Panfilovval." ('If Good Films are Made': Interview with Gleb Panfilov in Moscow.) *FSM.* 1987 Mar.; 31(12): 8. Illus.: Photo. B&W. 1. Lang.: Hun.
USSR. 1986-1987. Histories-sources. ■Gleb Panfilov, film director, speaks about his visit to Budapest, the impact of the changes in the Soviet Union on the possibilities of film art—the introduction of previously prohibited films, and his plans for two new films.

3173   Poplavskij, V. "V storonu teatra." (A Theatrical Aside.) *TeatZ.* 1987; 19: 11-14. Lang.: Rus.
USSR. 1987. Histories-sources. ■Theatre and film directors discuss interaction of the two forms: V. Uskov, V. Krasnopol'skij, V. Men'šov, K. Šachnazarov, M. Levitin, L. Chejfic.

3174   Sklovskij, Viktor Borisovič; Csala, Károly, transl. *Filmközelben.* (Close to Film.) Budapest: Gondolat-MOKÉP; 1987. 264 pp. Notes. Lang.: Hun.
USSR. 1923-1984. Critical studies. ■Writings of Viktor Sklovskij, Soviet aesthete, on the 'golden age' of Soviet film production.

Plays/librettos/scripts

3175   Fairley, Anne. "A Family Heritage Inspires Couple to Provide an Award Winning Film." *PAC.* 1986 Jan.; 22(4): 26-29. Notes. Filmography. Illus.: Photo. Print. 6. Lang.: Eng.
Canada: Winnipeg, MB. 1985. Critical studies. ■David and Toni Dueck produce docudrama as a result of their love for their Mennonite heritage.

3176   Gyertyán, Ervin. "Magyar film—magyar valóság." (Hungarian Film—Hungarian Reality.) *Krit.* 1987 Dec.(12): 11-14. Illus.: Photo. B&W. 8. Lang.: Hun.
Hungary. 1965-1987. Critical studies. ■To what extent does Hungarian film reflect reality, why are documentary films growing in number as compared to dramatic films and is there a need for these films expressed by the spectators.

3177   Mamone, Sara, ed. "Di scena in film." (From Stage to Film.) *QT.* 1987 Feb.; 9(35): 3-14. Lang.: Ita.
Italy. 1946-1983. Critical studies. ■Theatrical elements in Italian cinema after the Second World War.

3178   Verdone, Mario. "*Fumo* e *Lontano* cinescenari pirandelliani di Francesco Di Cocco." (*Smoke* and *Distant*: Pirandellian Filmscripts by Francesco di Cocco.) *TeatrC.* 1987; 7(15): 259-268. Lang.: Ita.
Italy. 1914-1934. Historical studies. ■Two cinematographic subjects taken from two of Pirandello's short stories proposed by Di Cocco but never realized.

3179   "Another World: The Shuberts and the Movies." *PasShow.* 1987 Sum; 11(7): 9-11. Illus.: Photo. B&W. 2. Lang.: Eng.
USA. 1914-1958. Historical studies. ■History of the World Film Corporation, a division of the Shubert Organization, and its adaptations of stage plays into films.

3180   Buchman, Lorne M. "Orson Welles's *Othello*: A Study of Time in Shakespeare's Tragedy." *ShS.* 1987; 39: 53-65. Notes. Lang.: Eng.
USA. 1952. Critical studies. ■Welles's use of cinematic technique exploits the concept of time in *Othello* leading to a fresh perception of the tragedy.

3181   Gill, Waliyy. "The Western Film Hollywood Myths and One Black Reality." *WJBC.* 1986; 10(1): 1-5. Notes. Biblio. Lang.: Eng.
USA. 1915-1986. Critical studies. ■Western film contributes to distortion of human relationships in the treatment of Black people as inferior, decadent and savage.

3182   Hapgood, Robert. "*Chimes at Midnight* from Stage to Screen: The Art of Adaptation." *ShS.* 1987; 39: 39-52. Notes. Illus.: Photo. Sketches. Print. B&W. 5. Lang.: Eng.
USA. Ireland. 1938-1965. Critical studies. ■Development of Welles's adaptation of *Henry IV* Parts I and II from stage to screen to clarify Shakespeare's vision.

3183   Pearlman, E. *Macbeth* on Film: Politics." *ShS.* 1987; 39: 67-74. Notes. Lang.: Eng.
USA. Japan. UK-England. 1948-1971. Critical studies. ■Directors Roman Polanski, Orson Welles and Akira Kurosawa's treatment of the theme of 'Divine Right' of monarchy in Shakespeare's *Macbeth*.

Relation to other fields

3184   Baldo, Jonathan. "Narrative Foiled in Bergman's *The Seventh Seal*." *TJ.* 1987; 39(3): 364-382. Notes. Lang.: Eng.
Critical studies. ■Examination of the film *The Seventh Seal* as a means of understanding why the narrative mode has become so predominant in our culture and how modern drama has been influenced by the ascendency of narrative fiction.

3185   Tomaselli, Keyan. "'Culture' as Theatre-Going, 'Arts' as Buildings: A Critique of 'Difference' in South African Propaganda Film." *SATJ.* 1987; 1(2): 63-75. Lang.: Eng.
South Africa, Republic of. 1970. Critical studies. ■South Africa Department of Information's film *South Africa's Performing Arts*, its political motivation and points of view on freedom.

3186   Mueller, Roswitha. "Montage in Brecht." *TJ.* 1987 Dec.; 39(4): 473-486. Notes. Biblio. Illus.: Photo. B&W. 23. Lang.: Eng.
USA. 1930. Historical studies. ■Brecht's art in montage technique in theatre and film and the usages of *gestus* brought a new and broad experience in many forms of art. Allows audience to make comparison with their personal experiences.

MEDIA: Film

Theory/criticism

3187 Conley, Tom. "Stages of Film Noir." *TJ.* 1987 Oct.; 39(3): 347-363. Notes. Illus.: Diagram. Photo. B&W. 5. Lang.: Eng.
1987. Critical studies. ■Emphasizes the closure offered by dramatic volume of film noir to study how the visual constriction articulates a space 'off' to convey the severity of the limits determining what is 'on'.

3188 Geldhill, Christine Ann, ed. *Home Is Where the Heart Is: Studies in Melodrama and Woman's Film.* London: British Film Institute; 1987. 364 pp. Pref. Index. Biblio. Notes. Illus.: Photo. Poster. B&W. 25. [Includes essays by Thomas Elsaesser, Geoffrey Nowell-Smith, Laura Mulvey.] Lang.: Eng.
USA: Los Angeles, CA. 1903-1987. Critical studies. ■Feminist anthology and analysis of essays examining gender and culture, class, race, historical and contemporary signposts within film theory as it relates to Hollywood's representation of women by film industry. Freudian and Marxist aspects.

3189 Gilman, Richard. "The Preemptive Image." *AmTh.* 1987 Oct.; 4(7): 28-29. Illus.: Photo. B&W. 1. Lang.: Eng.
USA. 1937-1987. Critical studies. ■Comparison of impact of film versus the theatrical experience. Discusses limitations of both art forms.

3190 Goldberg, Marianne. "The Body, Discourse, and *The Man Who Envied Women*." *WPerf.* 1987-88; 3(2): 97-102. Notes. Illus.: Photo. B&W. 5. Lang.: Eng.
USA. 1987. Critical studies. ■Analysis of Yvonne Rainer's film that attempts a feminist intervention in the male gaze. Breaking down voyeuristic codes of pleasure disrupts and negates Hollywood-generated fantasies of women. The body in representation.

Mixed media

Administration

3191 Kernochan, John M. "Imperatives for Enforcing Authors' Rights." *ColJL&A.* 1987 Sum; 11(4): 587-599. Notes. Lang.: Eng.
USA. 1987. Critical studies. ■Six recommendations of changes in US Copyright law to clarify author's rights regarding new technologies of video recording, cable and satellites.

Design/technology

3192 Accolas, Claude. "'Sesame, ouvre-toi' la pratique de l'ordinateur." ('Open Sesame': The Use of the Computer.) *JCT.* 1987 ; 44: 133-135. Illus.: Photo. Print. B&W. 1. Lang.: Fre.
Canada. 1987. Technical studies. ■Computers have become indispensable to theatre technicians.

Performance/production

3193 Lurie, John. "New Technology." 19-23, 81-96 in Coca, Jordi, ed.; Conesa, Laura, comp. *Congrés Internacional de Teatre a Catalunya 1985. Actes. Volum III. Seccions 7, 8 i 9.* Barcelona: Institut del Teatre; 1987. 350 pp. [Section 7: The New Technologies.] Lang.: Eng.
USA: New York, NY. 1985. Histories-sources. ■Argues the new technologies should not supplant theatrical aspects of a performance just as acting technique should not take precedence over the actor.

3194 Meyrowitz, Joshua. "TV's Covert Challenge." *AmTh.* 1987 Oct.; 4(7): 26-27, 97-103. Illus.: Dwg. 1. Lang.: Eng.
USA. 1950-1987. Historical studies. ■Analysis of TV: influence on the theatre, theatrical heritage and influence on society as compared to that of theatre.

3195 Shewey, Don. "Like a Movie: Readings in Contemporary Media Theatre." *TT.* 1987 Jan/Feb.; 6(2): 7-9. Illus.: Photo. B&W. 5. Lang.: Eng.
USA. 1986. Critical studies. ■Perspectives on modern media theatre.

3196 Shewey, Don. "Readings in Media Theatre." *AmTh.* 1987 Oct.; 4(7): 22-23, 90. Illus.: Photo. B&W. 1. Lang.: Eng.
USA: New York, NY. 1922-1987. Historical studies. ■History of incorporating film into a theatrical performance. Effect of the art of film and film industry on the art of the stage. Related to Media: Film.

Relations to other fields

3197 Silberman, Marc. "The Politics of Representation: Brecht and the Media." *TJ.* 1987; 39(4): 448-460. Notes. Biblio. Lang.: Eng.
Germany, East: Berlin, East. 1950. Historical studies. ■Brecht's perception of the media as a tool used by the bourgeois to isolate and pacify the masses. Television and radio displacing other realms of activity and experience and ultimately political intervention. Related to Media: Mixed media.

Video forms

3198 Köppl, Rainer Maria. "Basteln im Schatten des Rechts: Notiz zu Lessing und zum Status quo audiovisueller Theaterdokumentation." (Escaping Under the Protection of the Law: Note on Lessing and on the *status quo* of Audio-Visual Documentation.) *MuK.* 1986; 32(3-4): 13-28. Lang.: Ger.
Europe. 1986. Historical studies.

Audience

3199 Davis, Richard A. "TV Commercials and Management of Spoiled Identity." *WJBS.* 1987; 2(2): 59-63. Notes. Tables. Lang.: Eng.
USA. 1960-1987. Historical studies. ■Identity values are used by TV networks to see products through commercials.

3200 Johnson, Elizabeth. "Believability of Newscasters to Black Television Viewers." *WJBS.* 1987; 11(2): 64-68. Notes. Tables. Lang.: Eng.
USA. 1960-1987. Critical studies. ■Portrayal of Blacks in television newscasts and how Black audiences may be influenced.

Design/technology

3201 Heaton, Lorna. "L'holographie au théâtre." (Holography in the Theatre.) *JCT.* 1987; 44: 144-147. Illus.: Photo. Print. B&W. 2. Lang.: Fre.
Canada. 1987. Technical studies. ■How to use holography in theatre.

3202 Langlois, Christian; Pavlovic, Diane. "Les arts de la scène à l'heure de l'expérimentation vidéographique." (Stage Sets at a Time of Experiments in Video Special Effects.) *JCT.* 1987; 44: 126-132. Illus.: Photo. Print. B&W. 5. Lang.: Fre.
Canada. 1969-1987. Critical studies. ■New technologies in all areas of the arts are blurring the differences between genres.

3203 Lefebvre, Paul. "Dennis O'Sullivan: la disjonction entre la vie et l'écran." (Dennis O'Sullivan: The Disjunction Between Life and the Screen.) *JCT.* 1987; 44: 142-143. Illus.: Photo. Print. B&W. 1. Lang.: Fre.
Canada. 1986. Critical studies. ■The work of Dennis O'Sullivan, founder and director of Theatre Zoopsie, who uses film to enhance theatre productions.

3204 "*Sweeney Todd*—Live on Tape." *LDim.* 1982; 6(1): 18-23. Illus.: Photo. Lighting. 8. Lang.: Eng.
USA. 1982. Technical studies. ■Adapting lighting from a live theatre version of *Sweeney Todd* for videotape.

Performance/production

3205 Heaton, Lorna. "'Woyzeck': un exemple." ('Woyzeck': An Example.) *JCT.* 1987; 44: 148-150. Illus.: Photo. Print. B&W. 1. Lang.: Fre.
Canada: Banff, AB. 1987. Technical studies. ■Director Lorna Heaton describes how she integrated holography into the German drama *Woyzeck* in the InterArts program at the Banff Arts Centre.

3206 Knowles, Ronald. "*The Birthday Party*." *PintR.* 1987; 1: 46-49. Lang.: Eng.
UK-England. 1987. Reviews of performances. ■Production review of the 1987 BBC telecast of Pinter's *The Birthday Party*.

3207 Todd, Susan. "Jewel in the Crown." *ThCr.* 1985 Jan.; 19(1): 24-27, 98-99. Illus.: Photo. Color. 5. Lang.: Eng.
UK-England. India. 1986. Critical studies. ■Granada TV's production of the fourteen-part series *The Jewel in the Crown* based on Paul Scott's novel *The Raj Quartet*: political problems in England.

MEDIA: Video forms—Performance/production

3208 Walsh, John. "Television: Snobbery with Soap." *Drama*. 1987; 3(165): 45. Illus.: Photo. B&W. 1. Lang.: Eng.
UK-England. 1987. Reviews of performances. ■Dorothy L. Sayers' *Have His Carcase, Eastender* and *Intimate Contact* are reviewed.

3209 Collier, Arlen. "*The Dumb Waiter*." *PintR*. 1987; 1: 52-53. Lang.: Eng.
USA. 1987. Reviews of performances. ■Production review of ABC television's 1987 videocast of Pinter's *The Dumb Waiter*.

3210 Henderson, Heather. "The Well-Made Pray: Evangelism and the TV Stage." *ThM*. 1987; 19(1): 35-44. Illus.: Photo. B&W. 4. Lang.: Eng.
USA. 1987. Critical studies. ■Televised religion as a present-day communal, ritual performance. Theatre is the form and model at the heart of television evangelism. Difference in the varied programs currently available. Televangelism as melodrama.

3211 Hunter, Mead. "While You Were Out." *ThM*. 1987; 19(1): 45-48. Illus.: Photo. B&W. 2. Lang.: Eng.
USA. 1987. Critical studies. ■Televised wrestling from the World Wrestling Federation as sheer showmanship, the complete spectacle. Characters and clearly rehearsed scenarios in theatrical tradition. Private aspects of wrestlers manufactured to give commentary more dramatic emphasis.

3212 *Litovskij televizionnyj teatr (1957-1982): Avtoref.dis. kand. iskusstvovedenija*. (Lithuanian Television Theatre, 1957-1982: Abstract of a Dissertation by a Candidate in Art Criticism.) Leningrad: LGITMiK; 1987. 24 pp. Lang.: Rus.
USSR. 1957-1982. Historical studies.

3213 Belova, E. *Sintez baleta i TV*. (The Synthesis of Ballet and TV.) Moscow: 1987. Lang.: Rus.
USSR. 1980-1987. Critical studies. ■Traditional aspects of art in the age of SMK.

3214 Trusnova, E. "Teatral'nyj aktër: televizionnoe izmerenie." (A Theatre Actor: Television Survey.) 38-59 in *Televidenije v čera, sego nija, zavtra*. Moscow: Iskusstvo; 1987. 70 pp. Lang.: Rus.
USSR. 1980-1987. Histories-sources. ■Television actors' working conditions.

Plays/librettos/scripts

3215 Douglas, Robert L. "Black Males and Television: New Images versus Old Stereotypes." *WJBS*. 1987; 11(2): 69-73. Notes. Lang.: Eng.
USA. 1950-1987. Critical studies. ■Portrayal of Black male characters as being either subservient or supportive to dominant whites.

Relation to other fields

3216 Rodley, Chris. "Image After Image." *PM*. 1987(47): 17-19. Illus.: Photo. B&W. 4. Lang.: Eng.
UK-England: London. 1983-1987. Historical studies. ■Assesses the arts on television, with special reference to the series *Alter Image* show on Channel 4. Related to Mixed Entertainment: Performance art.

Theory/criticism

3217 Chien, Shi-Liang. "Dian shi ju shen mei gian shou de te shu xing." (The Characters of TV Plays in China.) *XYishu*. 1987 Sum; 38: 75-83. Notes. Lang.: Chi.
China, People's Republic of. 1970-1987. Historical studies. ■The influence of television on people and the difference between television and theatre performance.

3218 Harris, Claudia W. "A Living Mythology." *ThIr*. 1987; 13: 15-17. Illus.: Photo. B&W. 3. Lang.: Eng.
UK-Ireland. 1987. Histories-sources. ■Assessment of the television series *Lost Beginning* as well as the series' relation to Stewart Parker's latest play *Pentecost*.

———

Other entries with significant content related to Media: 6, 34, 63, 162, 165, 176, 201, 206, 224, 233, 281, 346, 450, 605, 624, 795, 839, 959, 1055, 1084, 1127, 1155, 1160, 1168, 1176, 1204, 1206, 1277, 1330, 1755, 1794, 1799, 2281, 2284, 2339, 2401, 2433, 2582, 2634, 2647, 2788, 2971, 3037, 3196, 3197, 3225, 3295, 3449, 3524, 3692, 3705,

3717, 3737, 3767, 3768, 3790, 3832, 3833, 3834, 3837, 3838, 3839, 3962, 4002.

MIME

General

Institutions

3219 Malo, Y., photo.; Bustros, J.C., photo. "Les Enfants du Paradis—Carbone 14, Montreal, Canada." *MimeJ*. 1982; 7: 58-69. Illus.: Photo. B&W. 15. Lang.: Eng.
Canada: Montreal, PQ. 1980-1982. Historical studies. ■Photographic essay of various works by Canadian mime troupe Les Enfants du Paradis—Carbone 14.

3220 Moynihan, Michael; Leigh, Barbara; Paul, Adolphe, photo. "Friends Mime Theatre, Milwaukee, Wisconsin." *MimeJ*. 1982; 7: 70-79. Illus.: Photo. B&W. 10. Lang.: Eng.
USA: Milwaukee, WI. 1980-1982. Historical studies. ■Profile of the Friends Mime Theatre: origins, performance methods and audience relationship.

Performance/production

3221 McKendrick, Kevin; Spino, Don; Birch, Randy; Gapihan, Jean-Pierre, photo. "Areté: Calgary, Alberta, Canada." *MimeJ*. 1982; 7: 22-27. Illus.: Photo. B&W. 4. Lang.: Eng.
Canada. 1980-1982. Historical studies. ■Evolution of the Areté Mime Troupe: its concepts, goals and performance methods.

3222 Ghumley, Daniel. "Going South: The San Francisco Mime Troupe in Nicaragua." *NTQ*. 1987 Nov.; 3(12): 291-302. Illus.: Photo. B&W. 6. Lang.: Eng.
Central America. 1986. Historical studies. ■San Francisco Mime Troupe's visit to Nicaragua's International Theatre Festival where they performed *Hotel Universe*.

3223 Lust, Annette. "From Pierrot to Bip and Beyond." *MimeJ*. 1982; 7: 9-15. Notes. Illus.: Sketches. B&W. 1. Lang.: Eng.
France: Paris. UK-England. USA: New York, NY. 1980-1982. Historical studies. ■The development of mime, pantomime and its related movements during the nineteenth and twentieth centuries: includes important individuals and training institutions.

3224 Rolfe, Bari. "And Now for Something Completely..." *MimeJ*. 1982; 7: 16-19. Illus.: Diagram. 1. Lang.: Eng.
France: Paris. Belgium. USA. 1980-1982. Historical studies. ■Contemporary mime forms with a discussion of their innovators.

3225 Ashwell, Ariel; Aguilar, Sigfrido; Clark, Edwardo, photo.; Gusky, Norman, photo. "Comediantes Pantomima-Teatro Guanajuato, Mexico." *MimeJ*. 1982; 7: 34-43. Illus.: Photo. B&W. 13. Lang.: Eng.
Mexico: Guanajuato. 1980-1982. Histories-sources. ■Authors discuss their use of movement, images, emotion and energy in their performance works as Comediantes Pantomima-Teatro. Related to Media: Performance art.

3226 Lindström, Kristina. "Vi är serietidningsmässiga." (We Are Like the Comics.) *NT*. 1987; 39: 16-19. Illus.: Photo. Lang.: Swe.
Sweden: Stockholm. 1985-1987. Historical studies. ■A presentation of Panopticon, which explores several movement oriented genres, like pantomime, dance or performance art, and the difficulties of life as a mime artist. Related to Mixed Entertainment: Performance art.

3227 Berky, Bob. "Bob Berky: New York, New York." *MimeJ*. 1982; 7: 28-33. Illus.: Photo. B&W. 4. Lang.: Eng.
USA: New York, NY. 1980. Histories-sources. ■Author's theories and philosophy as a clown and improvisational performer in relationship to the audience.

3228 Leabhart, Thomas; Fuchs, Alan, photo.; Vanderlende, Craig, photo.; Pieratt, Edward, photo. "Corporeal Theatre, Claremont, California." *MimeJ*. 1982; 6: 43-57. Illus.: Photo. B&W. 31. Lang.: Eng.

MIME: General—Performance/production

USA: Claremont, CA. 1980-1982. Histories-sources. ■Mime as a modern art form compared to paintings, dance, music, poetry and other forms of visual arts. Related to Dance: Ballet.

3229 Moore, Jim. "Jim Moore Photographs: 1972-1988." *MimeJ.* 1987/88: 21-232. Illus.: Photo. Print. B&W. 131. Lang.: Eng.
USA. Europe. 1972-1987. Histories-sources. ■Photographs of ninety-two different mimes, mime companies and performance artists from the United States and Europe with commentaries by the artists.

3230 Pedretti, Michael A. "A Stream of Consciousness Report: A Personal View from the Aqueducts." *MimeJ.* 1987/88: 8-14. Lang.: Eng.
USA. 1987. Critical studies. ■History that formed the mimes of the 1980s: how mime has affected and touched the author.

Pantomime

Audience

3231 Sweeney, Maxwell. "Pantomime: Preservation of a Tradition." *ThIr.* 1984 Fall; 7. Illus.: Photo. Poster. B&W. 2. Lang.: Eng.
Ireland: Dublin. 1900-1987. Historical studies. ■The enduring appeal of English pantomimes in Ireland, with notes on how audience-performer relationship has been manipulated over course of time.

Performance/production

3232 Markova, E.V. *Problemy razvitija sovremennoj zarubežnoj pantomimy: Avtoref.dis. kand. iskusstvovedenija.* (Problems in the Development of Contemporary Foreign Pantomime: Abstract of a Dissertation by a Candidate in Art Criticism.) Leningrad: LGITMiK; 1987. 18 pp. Lang.: Rus.
Europe. 1970-1987. Critical studies.

3233 Marceau, Marcel; Vicentini, Angela, ed. *Sull'arte del mimo. Riflessioni.* (On the Art of Mime: Reflections.) Montepulciano: Grifo; 1987. 221 pp. (Teatro 4.) Index. Pref. Biblio. Append. Illus.: Photo. Print. Color. B&W. Lang.: Ita.
France. Italy. 1982-1986. Critical studies.

3234 Jung, Jin Woo. "Pantomime." 81-86 in Seoul P'yongnon'ga Group, ed. *Han'guk Yŏnguk kwa Chŏlmon Úislk.* Mineum SA: Park. Mazngho; 1979. 262 pp. Notes. Lang.: Kor.
Korea. 1970-1979. Historical studies. ■Definition of a body language in mime.

3235 Schneider, Richard C. "Samy Molcho: Vom Mimen zum Manager." (Samy Molcho: From Mime to Management.) *MuT.* 1987 July/Aug. ; 8(7/8): 8-12. Illus.: Photo. B&W. Lang.: Ger.
Switzerland. 1987. Biographical studies. ■Pantomime artist Samy Molcho puts an early end to his artistic career in order to work as a lecturer for body-language in Vienna, as a director and as an author of books on body-language and creativity as a psychological phenomenon.

3236 Shewring, Margaret. "Reinhardt's 'Miracle' at Olympia: A Record and a Reconstruction." *NTQ.* 1987 Feb.; 3(9): 3-23. Notes. Illus.: Design. Photo. Sketches. B&W. 18. Lang.: Eng.
UK-England: London. 1911. Historical studies. ■The inaugural production of *The Miracle*, a Christmas pantomime, at the Olympia Exhibition Centre, directed by Max Reinhardt and produced by G.B. Cochran.

3237 Švedova, O.; Samarkina, O. "Poslednij P'ero Kamernogo Teatra." (The Last Pierrot of the Chamber Theatre.) *TeatZ.* 1987; 20: 26-27. Lang.: Rus.
USSR: Moscow. 1920-1939. Biographical studies. ■New light on A.A. Rušnev, actor of the Tairov Chamber Theatre.

Other entries with significant content related to Mime: 1498.

MIXED ENTERTAINMENT

General

Administration

3238 Edwards, Margaret. "Canada's Cultural Best at Expo '86." *PAC.* 1986 Jan.; 22(4): 54-55. Notes. Illus.: Photo. Print. 1. Lang.: Eng.
Canada: Vancouver, BC. 1986. Historical studies. ■$9.8 billion funded by Canadian government for Expo '86 cultural activities.

3239 Hewitt, Honorable James J. "British Columbia Inherits Expo '86 Legacy." *PAC.* 1986 Jan.; 22(4): 56-58. Notes. Illus.: Photo. Print. 4. Lang.: Eng.
Canada. 1986. Historical studies. ■Impact and legacy of World's Fair: time and expense versus its benefits to art, architecture and technology.

3240 Giancarelli, Roberto. "*Committenza* e spettacoli nella Roman Sistina: Il teatro tra liturgia e società civile." (Sponsorship and Performance in Sistine Rome: Theatre Between Liturgy and Secular Society.) *BiT.* 1987; 7: 1-37. Lang.: Ita.
Italy: Rome. 1585-1595. Historical studies. ■During the counter-Reformation, the Vatican court is forced to abandon the privileges of its traditional policy of being the high promoter of the festivals. Pope Sixtus V restructures the ancient theatrical 'Arena del Belvedere'.

3241 Erlich, Barbara Janowitz. "When to Tax a Writer." *AmTh.* 1987 Nov.; 4(8): 30-31. Lang.: Eng.
USA. 1987. Historical studies. ■Recent court decision over the IRS tax laws involving 'Uniform Organization Rules'. IRS seeks to pro-rate writer's deductions over a period of time.

Design/technology

3242 Ézsiás, Erzsébet. "'A könnyü müfajt nem lehet könnyen venni'." ('Light Genre Cannot Be Taken Easy'.) *FSM.* 1987; 31(41): 18-19. Illus.: Photo. B&W. 14. Lang.: Hun.
Hungary. 1927-1987. Histories-sources. ■An exhibition opened at the Pest Redoute Gallery of the set and costume designs of Eric Vogel who is now 80 and started out as a designer just 60 years ago. He is still working and is credited with designs for nearly 500 plays to date.

Performance spaces

3243 Barclay, Ian A. "Canada Place: A Legacy of Excellence and Grace to Live on After Expo '86." *PAC.* 1986 Jan.; 22(4): 59-61. Notes. Illus.: Photo. Print. 2. Lang.: Eng.
Canada: Vancouver, BC. 1986. Critical studies. ■Five buildings in Canada Place transform face of Vancouver.

3244 Frazer, Robin. "Extravangance of Entertainment and Culture Promised for Expo." *PAC.* 1986 Jan.; 22(4): 50-51. Notes. Illus.: Photo. Print. 2. Lang.: Eng.
Canada: Vancouver, BC. 1986. Historical studies. ■World's Fair to include over 14,000 performances from around the world.

3245 Iles, Chrissie. "Live Space for Tate North." *PM.* 1987(46): 24. Illus.: Photo. B&W. 3. Lang.: Eng.
UK-England: Liverpool. 1987. Historical studies. ■The Tate Gallery of the North in Liverpool has created a performance space within its premises.

3246 Hornsby, Kent L. "Garrett Coliseum Relighting." *L&DA.* 1987 June; 17(6): 10. Illus.: Photo. 1. Lang.: Eng.
USA: Montgomery, AL. 1987. Technical studies. ■Replacing lighting for the Garrett Coliseum's renovation required consideration of good color rendition, a brighter inner appearance, energy conservation, budget constraints and the wide range of activities that take place in the arena.

3247 Nibbelin, David A. "Cajundome Plays Many Roles." *L&DA.* 1987 Feb.; 17(2): 26. Illus.: Photo. 1. Lang.: Eng.

MIXED ENTERTAINMENT: General—Performance spaces

USA: Lafayette, LA. 1987. Technical studies. ■Various types of lighting are used to light the Cajundome, a multipurpose sports and entertainment arena. Indirect lighting gives uniform levels throughout the space.

Performance/production

3248 Abah, O.S. *Popular Theatre as a Strategy for Education and Development: The Example of Some African Countries.* Ph.D. thesis, *Index to Theses*, 37-4369. Leeds: University of Leeds; 1987. Notes. Biblio. Lang.: Eng.
Africa. 1987. Critical studies. ■Explores the role of radical popular theatre in non-formal education and in fighting for democracy. Discusses appropriate methodology and examines popular theatre practice in specific countries.

3249 Watson, Ian. "Third Theatre in Latin America." *TDR.* 1987 Win; 31(4): 18-24. Illus.: Photo. Print. B&W. 4. Lang.: Eng.
Argentina: Bahía Blanca. 1987. Historical studies. ■Description of 'Third Theatre' and a meeting of groups that performed together.

3250 "Il recinto dei sogni." (The Fence of Dreams.) *BiT.* 1987; 8: 115-120. Lang.: Ita.
Austria: Vienna. 1700-1799. Critical studies. ■The artistic personality of André Heller, the creator of *Luna Luna*, an unusual mixture of performances and fair-attractions, and the idea behind this original theatrical enterprise.

3251 Cripton, John; Bosse, Jean-Guy. "Technology and Arts at Canada Place Make for High Theatre." *PAC.* 1986 Jan.; 22(4): 52-53. Notes. Illus.: Photo. Print. 2. Lang.: Eng.
Canada: Vancouver, BC. 1986. Technical studies. ■Canada Place, including Amiga Studios Theatre, was built for Expo '86, features high-technology live theatre.

3252 Frazer, Robbin. "Vancouver's Expo '86 is Destined to be the Celebration of the Century." *PAC.* 1986 Jan.; 22(4): 46-49. Notes. Illus.: Photo. Print. 5. Lang.: Eng.
Canada: Vancouver, BC. 1986. Historical studies. ■World's Fair, Vancouver Expo '86 incorporating theme of transportation and communication through series of events and presentations.

3253 Porter, Helen. "Codco, A Unique Comic Theatre Troupe Reflects the Culture of Newfoundland." *PAC.* 1986 Jan.; 22(4): 36-38. Notes. Illus.: Photo. Print. 2. Lang.: Eng.
Canada: St. John's, NF. 1986. Critical studies. ■Codco, a comic theatrical troupe, creates characters using regional accents and idioms.

3254 White, Eileen. "Hewet, The Wait of York." *REEDN.* 1987; 12(2): 17-23. Notes. Lang.: Eng.
England: York. 1554-1597. Histories-sources. ■Examines conditions affecting itinerant musicians in Elizabethan England using entries from the Shuttleworth family and York records.

3255 Currell, David. *The Complete Book of Puppet Theatre.* Totowa, NJ: Barnes & Noble; 1985. 312 pp. Index. Tables. Biblio. Append. Illus.: Photo. Design. Plan. Dwg. Sketches. Explod.Sect. Detail. Schematic. 347. Lang.: Eng.
Europe. Asia. 400 B.C.-1985 A.D. Historical studies. ■Comprehensive guide to history, staging, techniques, designs and genres of puppet theatre. Instructions on puppet construction, use of puppets in education and their roles in cultures around the world. Focus on two premiere puppeteers and their companies.

3256 Staveacre, Tony. *Slapstick! The Illustrated Story of Knockabout Comedy.* North Ryde, NSW: Angus Robertson; 1987. 189 pp. Lang.: Eng.
Europe. North America. Australia. 480 B.C.-1986 A.D. Histories-specific. ■Popular account of comic entertainers, with reference to ritual performers, *commedia dell'arte*, vaudeville, pantomime, film and television.

3257 Strong, Roy C. *Arte e potere. Le feste del Rinascimento 1450-1650.* (Art and Power: Renaissance Festivals 1450-1650.) Saggiatore; 1987. (La Cultura 51.) Index. Pref. Notes. Append. Illus.: Dwg. Photo. Pntg. Design. Print. B&W. Lang.: Ita.
Europe. 1450-1650. Historical studies. ■Translation of Strong's 1984 *Art and Power.*

3258 McCormick, John. "Puppets in the Streets and Fairgrounds of Nineteenth-Century France." *MuK.* 1987; 33(1-2): 143-150. Lang.: Eng.
France. 1800-1899. Historical studies.

3259 Mollica, Vincenzo, ed. *Chez Josephine. Omaggio a Josephine Baker.* (Chez Josephine: Homage to Josephine Baker.) Montepulciano: Grifo; 1987. 165 pp. Illus.: Photo. Sketches. Poster. Lang.: Ita.
France: Paris. 1906-1975. Histories-sources. ■Catalogue of a 1987 exhibit, Taormina.

3260 Di Palma, Guido. "Prolegomeni allo studio della fabulazione. La voce del mito: oralità e racconto." (Prolegomena to the Study of Storytelling. The Voice of Myth: Orality and the Tale.) *BiT.* 1987; 7: 105-133. Lang.: Ita.
Italy. 1987. Critical studies. ■The action of telling a tale gives us the opportunity to investigate how an actor can establish a living contact with the public. The particular 'dramaturgy' of story-telling.

3261 Gori, Pietro. *La feste fiorentine attraverso i secoli. Le feste per San Giovanni.* (Florentine Feasts through the Centuries: The Feasts for San Giovanni.) Florence: Bemporad; 1987. 388 pp. Illus.: Photo. Pntg. Dwg. Lang.: Ita.
Italy: Florence. 1000-1926. Historical studies. ■Facsimile reprint of 1926 edition on Florentine feasts in honor of St. John.

3262 Pretini, Giancarlo. *Ambulante come spettacolo.* (Peddling as a Form of Entertainment.) Udine: Trapezio; 1987. 422 pp. (I grandi libri 4.) Index. Pref. Biblio. Gloss. Illus.: Photo. Dwg. Poster. Print. Color. B&W. Lang.: Ita.
Italy. Historical studies. ■Performance aspects of the cries of street vendors, story-tellers, etc..

3263 Trevisan, Albano. "Forme spettacolari minori a Venezia tra '800 e '900." (Minor Theatrical Forms in Nineteenth-Century Venice.) *BiT.* 1987; 5/6: 265-286. Lang.: Ita.
Italy: Venice. 1800-1900. Histories-sources. ■Sources and documents. Types and names of the itinerant performances: 'mechanical theatres,' 'landscapes,' 'scientific mechanical museums'.

3264 Martin, Randy; Ruf, Elizabeth. "Nicaragua—Performance After the 'Triumph': Two Views." *TDR.* 1987 Win; 31(4): 58-90. Notes. Biblio. Illus.: Photo. B&W. 15. Lang.: Eng.
Nicaragua. 1987. Historical studies. ■Nicaraguan theatre that emerged after the Sandinista war effort. Community theatre movement and rise and fall of Nicaraguan bougeoisie. Interview with Alan Bolt, creator of community Theatre Mut.

3265 Ivanova, N.A. *Teatral'no-zreliscnaja kul'tura Rusi XVII stoletija: Avtoref. dis. kand. iskusstvovedenija.* (The Theatre-Performance Culture of Seventeenth-Century Rus'—Aspects of Performance Intercourse: Abstract of a Dissertation by a Candidate in Art Criticism.) Moscow: In-t iskusstvovedenija, fol' klora i etnografii; 1987. 18 pp. Lang.: Rus.
Russia. 1600-1899. Historical studies.

3266 Thuynsma, Peter. "Xhosa Ntsomi: The Language of Gesture." *Ear.* 1987 Jan.; 4(77-89). Lang.: Eng.
South Africa, Republic of. 1987. Histories-specific. ■Xhosa story-telling uses verbal dramatization and language of gesture.

3267 Hilding, Malena. "Små saker." (Little Things.) *NT.* 1987; 36: 16-17. Illus.: Photo. Lang.: Swe.
Sweden: Järvsö. 1980-1987. Historical studies. ■Lasse Åkerlund is a clown, or one-man theatre, with his thumb, a cup of water and whispers: he tours the north of Sweden to visit children in the wilderness.

3268 Fletcher, Kathy. "Planché, Vestris, and the Transvestite Role: Sexuality and Gender in Victorian Popular Theatre." *NCT.* 1987; 15(1): 9-33. Notes. Illus.: Dwg. Print. B&W. 4. Lang.: Eng.
UK-England: London. 1830-1870. Historical studies. ■The psycho-social implications of women portraying male roles in the extravaganzas of James Robinson Planché in collaboration with Madame Vestris.

3269 George, J. Anne. "'Decent' Doggerel." *REEDN.* 1987; 12(2): 23-25. Notes. Lang.: Eng.

MIXED ENTERTAINMENT: General—Performance/production

UK-England: Stafford. 1616. Histories-sources. ■Comments on the linking of minstrelsy and its performers with ruffians and rascals through examination of public records detailing a charge of libel brought by a young woman against two men for the composition of a bawdy song.

3270 Van der Jagt, Marijn. "David Bowie: theater als veilig en controleerbaar medium." (David Bowie: Theatre as a Safe and Controllable Medium.) *Toneel.* 1987 July; 7(3): 33-35. Illus.: Photo. B&W. 2. Lang.: Dut.
UK-England. 1987. Reviews of performances. ■Critical evaluation of David Bowie's *Glass Spider Tour* and his use of scenes and characters, reaching away from pop towards theatre.

3271 Khan, Naseem. "Fringe: New Talents." *Drama.* 1987; 3(165): 33-34. Illus.: Photo. B&W. 2. Lang.: Eng.
UK-Scotland: Edinburgh. 1987. Reviews of performances. ■Review of the 1987 Edinburgh Fringe Festival.

3272 Bell, John. "Industrials: American Business Theatre in the 80's." *TDR.* 1987 Win; 31(4): 36-57. Illus.: Photo. B&W. 11. Lang.: Eng.
USA. 1985-1987. Historical studies. ■Survey of the industrial show, a theatrical performance commissioned by a business as a genre.

3273 Bilderback, Walter. "Juggling with No Balls." *ThM.* 1987; 18(3): 49-53. Illus.: Photo. B&W. 3. Lang.: Eng.
USA. 1977-1987. Critical studies. ■An assessment of the work of the New Vaudeville Group The Flying Karamazov Brothers as they moved from alternative underground venues into the legitimate theatre via the Goodman. Their adaptations of traditional theatre works. Grp/movt: New Vaudeville.

3274 Carlsson, Bengt. "Knee Plays." *NT.* 1987; 37: 15-16. Illus.: Photo. Dwg. Lang.: Swe.
USA. 1979-1987. Historical studies. ■Robert Wilson, his *CIVIL warS* and the small scenes *Knee Plays* that tie the parts together.

3275 Gerould, Daniel. "Imaginary Invalids: A Theatre of Simulated Patients." *ThM.* 1987; 19(1): 6-18. Notes. Illus.: Photo. B&W. 4. Lang.: Eng.
USA. 1987. Critical studies. ■The use of professional actors at medical conferences to enact specific illnesses for demonstration purposes. A theatre group specifically devoted to mastering the symptoms of specific illnesses in order to perform them. Representations of illness in theatre and literature.

3276 Pomanenko, A.I. *Razvitie tradicij agitacionno-revoljucionnogo teatra 20-ch godov v sovremennyh massovyh teatralizovannyh predstavlenijah: Avtoref. dis. kand. iskusstvovedenija.* (Development of Revolutionary-Propagandistic Theatre Traditions in the Twenties in Contemporary Mass Theatricalized Performances: Abstract of a Dissertation of a Candidate in Art Criticism.) Tbilisi: Gruz.gos.teatr, in-t; 1987. 22 pp. Lang.: Rus.
USSR. 1920-1929. Historical studies.

3277 "Soca Up de Party." *Econ.* 1987 29 Aug.; 304: 83-84. Lang.: Eng.
West Indies. Historical studies. ■Growth of West Indian carnival traditions: dance, masques, and their secular and pagan roots.

Plays/librettos/scripts

3278 Degen, John A. "Charles Mathews' *At Homes*: The Textual Morass." *ThS.* 1987 Nov.; 28(2): 75-88. Notes. Lang.: Eng.
UK-England. 1818-1834. Historical studies. ■Textual variations and ambiguities make a definitive reconstruction impossible, but suggest that *At Homes* were constantly changing, spontaneously adapted performances.

Reference materials

3279 Van Remoortere, Julien. *Le Guide des fêtes et du folklore en Belgique.* (Guide to Festivals and Folklore in Belgium.) Brussels: Didier Hatier; 1987. 432 pp. Pref. Illus.: Photo. Dwg. Color. B&W. 365. Lang.: Fre.
Belgium. 1987. Instructional materials. ■Description of some history and current status of fifty major folk festivals: folk elements described in detail. Includes practical information on museums, etc..

Relation to other fields

3280 Johnston, Alexandra F. "The Churchwarden Accounts of Great Marlow, Buckinghamshire." *REEDN.* 1987; 12(1): 9-12. Notes. Lang.: Eng.
England: Great Marlow. 1593-1674. Histories-sources. ■Seventeenth century references to Morris dancing gear and church ales in the account book of the churchwardens at Great Marlow, Buckinghamshire.

3281 van Erven, Eugène. "Philippine Political Theatre and the Fall of Ferdinand Marcos." *TDR.* 1987 Sum; 31(2): 57-78. Illus.: Photo. B&W. 13. Lang.: Eng.
Philippines. 1972-1986. Historical studies. ■Political use of theatre by Filipinos to voice opinions during political oppression.

3282 Hart, Steven. "Folktheatre in Poland." *SEEDTF.* 1987 Dec.; 7(2 & 3): 46-50. Lang.: Eng.
Poland: Tarnogród. 1985-1987. Histories-reconstruction. ■Factors in Polish farming that may contribute to folk theatre, and a festival of regional folk customs along with amateur productions of conventional drama.

Cabaret

Basic theatrical documents

3283 Valentin, Karl; Monterde, Pau, ed.; Melendres, Jaume, intro. *Teatre de Cabaret: Peces de Karl Valentin de l'espectacle Tafalitats.* (Cabaret Theatre: Karl Valentin's *Tafalitats* Skits.) Barcelona: Institut del Teatre; 1983. 90 pp. (Biblioteca Teatral 16.) Lang.: Cat.
Germany. 1882-1948. ■Comic texts of Karl Valentin.

Performance/production

3284 Shorto, Eric. "Paris: Cabaret Time." *Drama.* 1987; 3(165): 43. Illus.: Photo. B&W. 1. Lang.: Eng.
France: Paris. 1987. Reviews of performances. ■Parisian cabaret theatre performance reviews.

3285 Salamon, Béla; Furko, Zoltan. *Hej, szinmüvész! Visszaemlékezések.* (Oh, Actor! Recollections.) Budapest: Szépirod. Kvk.; 1987. 214 pp. (Kentaur könyvek.) Illus.: Photo. B&W. 11. Lang.: Hun.
Hungary: Budapest. 1885-1965. Biographies. ■Autobiography of Béla Salamon, Hungarian cabaret performer, includes recollections of old Budapest.

3286 Szuhay, Balázs. *Kiadom magam.* (I Deliver Myself.) Budapest: Szuhay B.; 1987. 396 pp. Index. Illus.: Photo. B&W. 52. Lang.: Hun.
Hungary. 1935-1986. Biographies. ■Recollections and biography of Balázs Szuhay, actor, cabaret author, director on his career, colleagues, several important actors of light entertainment.

3287 Zareba, Teodor. "Piwnica Pod Baranami—A Cabaret from Poland." *SEEDTF.* 1987 Dec.; 7(2 & 3): 44-45. Lang.: Eng.
Poland: Cracow. USA: New York, NY. 1987. Historical studies. ■A short sketch of Piwnica's beginnings and a performance at the CUNY Graduate School in New York on September 4, 1987.

3288 Lidington, Tony. "New Terms for Old Turns: The Rise of Alternative Cabaret." *NTQ.* 1987 May; 3(10): 107-119. Notes. Biblio. Illus.: Photo. Print. B&W. 3. Lang.: Eng.
UK-England. 1980. Critical studies. ■The development of alternative cabaret from the social and cultural beginnings and the current situation for performers.

3289 Barbour, David. "The Not-So-Hokey *Hokey-Pokey*: A Look at the *Oil City Symphony*." *TheaterW.* 1987 Dec 7-13; 1(17): 9-11. Illus.: Photo. 1. Lang.: Eng.
USA: New York, NY. 1987. Reviews of performances. ■The cabaret style musical revue *Oil City Symphony* mixes oddball musical novelties and pop culture.

3290 Bartlett, Neil. "Ethyl and Lily: Speaking Your Mind." *PM.* 1987(48): 20-27. Illus.: Photo. B&W. 6. Lang.: Eng.
USA. UK-England. 1987. Histories-sources. ■Parallel interviews with Ethyl Eichelberger and Lily Savage, two drag artists about their approaches to acting, audiences and women.

MIXED ENTERTAINMENT: Cabaret—Performance/production

3291 Gertsen, David. "Moonlighting: Broadway Stars Hit the Cabarets After Hours." *TheaterW*. 1987 Oct.; 2(7): 18-19. Illus.: Photo. Print. B&W. 8. Lang.: Eng.
USA: New York, NY. 1962-1987. Histories-sources. ■Discussions with actors who go from acting in Broadway shows to performing in cabaret acts after their Broadway show performances each night.

3292 Salinas, Mike. "Jack Gilford Comes to the Cabaret." *TheaterW*. 1987 Nov 9; 1(13): 20-21. Illus.: Photo. B&W. 1. Lang.: Eng.
USA: New York, NY. 1920-1987. Biographical studies. ■Actor Jack Gilford's long career in the theatre. Reprisal of some of his greatest hits from musicals for a cabaret audience.

Carnival

Performance spaces

3293 Mangini, Nicola. "Alle origini del teatro moderno: lo spettacolo pubblico nel Veneto tra Cinquecento e Seicento." (At the Origins of Modern Theatre: Public Performances in the Veneto in the Sixteenth and Seventeenth Centuries.) *BiT*. 1987; 5/6: 87-103. Lang.: Ita.
Italy: Venice. 1580-1700. Historical studies. ■The birth of the first public and permanent theatres in Venice, which started their activity during the Carnival in 1580-81.

Performance/production

3294 Revelard, Michel. *Le Carnaval traditionnel en Wallonie.* (Traditional Carnival in the Walloon Country.) Brussels/Liège: Pierre Mardaga; 1987. 15 pp. (Musées vivants de Wallonie et de Bruxelles 19.) Illus.: Photo. B&W. 16. Lang.: Fre.
Belgium. 1800-1987. Historical studies. ■Evolution and present status of Walloon masks and carnivals.

3295 Gruber, Klemens. "Piazza und Massenmedien." ('Piazza' and Mass Media.) *MuK*. 1987; 33(1-2): 51-60. Lang.: Ger.
Italy. 1980. Historical studies. ■Street theatre and mass media. Related to Media: Audio forms.

3296 Ju, Kang-hyoun. "Dan-o Je." (*Dan-o* Carnival.) *KTR*. 1987 Aug; 8(1): 58-59. Illus.: Photo. B&W. 1. Lang.: Kor.
Korea. 800-1987. Historical studies. ■Annual festival held on May 5, involving numerous folk songs, dances and performances. Related to Dance: Ethnic dance.

3297 Lee, Sang-Il. "'Daedong' Carnival." *KTR*. 1987 June; 6(1): 22-24. Illus.: Photo. B&W. 1. Lang.: Kor.
Korea: Seoul. 90-1987. Historical studies. ■The evolution and history of the carnival 'Daedong', how it brought people together and reflected the culture.

3298 Stadler, Edmund. "Die Fasnachtspiele im Alten Bern." (Carnival Activity in Berne, 1500-1800.) *Der Bund*. 1987 Feb 28-Mar 7. Illus.: Photo. B&W. Lang.: Ger.
Switzerland: Berne. 1416-1879. Histories-specific. ■Historical account of the carnival movement that was prohibited by the Protestant government in the 16th century but has never lost its subcultural function. Bernese carnival has been reactivated for several years now and is growing in popularity.

Relation to other fields

3299 Revelard, Michel, ed. *Fêtes et traditions masquées d'Autriche.* (Masked Festivals and Traditions of Austria.) Binche: Musée International du Carnaval et du Masque; 1987. 127 pp. Illus.: Photo. Color. B&W. 67. Lang.: Fre.
Austria. 1987. Histories-specific. ■Calendar of popular masked events with a description of the origins and development of each.

3300 *Confrérie folklorique des Blancs Moussis. Petite et grande histoire.* (The White Moussis' Folk Brotherhood: History and Stories.) Stavelot: J. Chauveheid; 1987. 128 pp. Pref. Illus.: Photo. Color. B&W. 155. Lang.: Fre.
Belgium: Stavelot. 1947-1987. Histories-specific. ■History, activity and role of a folk group that reformed after World War II.

3301 Lombardi Satriani, Luigi M. "La teatralizzazione della negazione." (The Theatricalization of Negation.) *Ariel*. 1987; 2 (2): 56-63. Lang.: Ita.
Europe. Critical studies. ■Carnival as theatricalized negation, in which a limited negativity is first assumed, then exorcised and conquered.

Circus

Performance/production

3302 White, John. "Le Charme du Cirque du Soleil." *CTR*. 1987 Sum; 51: 72-78. Illus.: Photo. Print. B&W. 7. [Carte Blanche.] Lang.: Eng.
Canada: Montreal, PQ. 1987. Technical studies. ■Practical account of performing with Cirque du Soleil—a one-ring circus which features no stars, no animal acts. Detailed history of formation and mandate. Innovative dramatic and comic contexts for featuring technical skills set Cirque du Soleil apart.

3303 Little, W. Kenneth. "Pitu's Doubt: Entree Clown Self-Fashioning in the Circus Tradition." *TDR*. 1986 Win; 30(4): 51-64. Notes. Biblio. Illus.: Photo. B&W. 8. Lang.: Eng.
France. 1956-1986. Critical studies. ■Critical study of Pitu, a whiteface clown, and the changing traditions of circuses and clowning.

3304 Jenkins, Ron; Schechter, Joel. "Entree (An Introduction)." *ThM*. 1987; 18(3): 4-5. Illus.: Photo. B&W. 2. Lang.: Eng.
USA. 1987. Critical studies. ■Introduction to a special issue surveying the growing number of performers who are moving the art of theatrical clowning forward. Connects clowning with theatre, current political scene.

3305 McNamara, Brooks. "Talking." *TDR*. 1987 Sum; 31(2): 39-56. Illus.: Photo. B&W. 9. Lang.: Eng.
USA: New York, NY. 1929-1987. Biographical studies. ■Doc Fred Foster Bloodgood, a pitchman who sold medicine to crowds between acts at circus and vaudeville shows in the 1930s.

3306 Slavskij, R.E. *Brat'ja Nikitiny.* (The Brothers Nikitin.) Moscow: Iskusstvo; 1987. 269 pp. (Žizn' v Iskusstve.) Lang.: Rus.
USSR. 1850-1950. Historical studies. ■Life and creative work of circus artists.

Training

3307 Fleury, Silvia; Urech, Christian. "Kinder spielen Circus." (Circus for Children by Children.) *Manege*. 1987 June; 26(3): 21-24. Illus.: Photo. B&W. Lang.: Ger.
Switzerland. 1987. Historical studies. ■Uncritical review of circus productions by the artists' children. Reference to the children's programs at Circus Knie and Circus Nock.

3308 Zollinger, Fritz; Urech, Christian. "Kinder spielen Circus." (Circus for Children by Children.) *Manege*. 1987 Aug.; 26 (4): 5-14. Illus.: Photo. B&W. Lang.: Ger.
Switzerland. 1987. Historical studies. ■Uncritical review of circus productions by the Children's Circuses 'Robinson' and 'Eva La Joie '87', and Youth Circus 'Basilisk'.

Commedia dell'arte

Design/technology

3309 Fulchignoni, Enrico. "La maschera dall'Oriente a Venezia." (Masks from the East to Venice.) *TeatrC*. 1987; 7(14): 195-205. Lang.: Ita.
Italy: Venice. 1500-1600. Historical studies. ■Use of masks in Venetian theatre.

Institutions

3310 Berson, Misha. "The Dell'Arte Players of Blue Lake, California." *TDR*. 1983 Sum; 27(2): 61-72. Illus.: Photo. Sketches. B&W. 11. Lang.: Eng.
USA: Blue Lake, CA. 1957-1983. Historical studies. ■Profile of Dell'Arte Players: theatrical style, influences, productions *The Loon's Rage, Intrigue at Ah-pah, Whiteman Meets Bigfoot* and *Performance Anxiety*. Attempts to blend old style *commedia* with contemporary themes.

MIXED ENTERTAINMENT: *Commedia dell'arte*—Institutions

Performance/production

3311 Coppola, Carmine. *Pulcinella. La maschera nella tradizione teatrale.* (The Mask in the Theatrical Tradition.) Naples: Edizioni Scientifiche Italiane; 1987. 79 pp. Illus.: Photo. Print. B&W. Lang.: Ita.
Italy: Naples. 1609-1975. Histories-specific. ■Interpreters of the character Pulcinella from Silvio Fiorillo to Carmine Coppola.

3312 Guccini, Gerardo. "Dall'Innamorato all'Autore. Strutture del teatro recitato a Venezia nel XVIII secolo." (From the *Innamorato* to the Writer: Patterns of the Acting Drama in Venice in the 18th Century.) *TeatroS.* 1987; 2(2): 251-293. Lang.: Ita.
Italy: Venice. 1700-1800. Historical studies. ■Weakness of the theatrical institutions. The S. Luca Theatre during the Vendramins' direct management. The organization of the companies. The character of *Innamorato* and four leading Lovers (Luigi Riccoboni, Bonaventura Navesi, Pompilio Miti, Antonio Franceschini).

3313 Suchanova, T.N. *Kul'turnaja tradicija komedii del' arte i ee sovremennoe bytovanie v zarubežnom teatre (na primere tvorčestva Dario Fo).* (The Cultural Tradition of the Commedia dell'Arte and Its Contemporary Existence in the Foreign Theatre in the Example of Dario Fo.) Kul'tura i iskusstvo za rubežom. Moscow: Gosudarstvennaja Biblioteka im. V.I. Lenina; 1987. 8 pp. (Zreliščnije iskusstva: Express-informacija 5.) Lang.: Rus.
Italy. 1550-1987. Historical studies.

3314 Fisher, James. "Edward Gordon Craig and the *Commedia Dell'Arte* in the Twentieth Century." 61-78 in Hartigan, Karelisa V., ed. *From the Bard to Broadway.* Lanham, MD: UP of America; 1987. 222 pp. (Univ. of Florida Dept. of Classics Comparative Drama Conference Papers 7.) Pref. Notes. Biblio. Lang.: Eng.
UK-England. Italy. 1872-1966. Historical studies. ■Craig's connection to tradition of *commedia dell'arte.* In his quest to escape naturalism and realism then prevalent, he explored other forms of theatre.

3315 Jent, Deanna. "Colombaioni Present *I Saltimbanchi.*" *ThM.* 1987; 18(3): 46-48. Illus.: Photo. B&W. 1. Lang.: Eng.
USA: Chicago, IL. 1986. Critical studies. ■Account of performance that combined circus clowning, *commedia* style work and modern improvisational techniques to bridge the language barrier.

Plays/librettos/scripts

3316 Alberti, Carmelo. *Pietro Chiari e il teatro europeo del Settecento.* (Pietro Chiari and the European Theatre of the Eighteenth Century.) Vicenza: Neri Pozza; 1986. 315 pp. (Nuova Biblioteca di Cultura 43.) Lang.: Ita.
Italy: Venice. 1747-1762. Critical studies. ■Collected studies of Venetian novelist and comic playwright Pietro Chiari, rival of Goldoni.

3317 Burattelli, Claudia. "L'eccezione e la regola nella *Commedia dell'arte*: *L'Inavvertito* di Niccolò Barbieri." (Rule and Exception in the *Commedia dell'arte*: *The Unperceived* by Niccolò Barbieri.) *Ariel.* 1987; 2(1): 42-61. Lang.: Ita.
Italy. 1629. Critical studies. ■An essay on one of the most successful scripts of the *commedia dell'arte.*

3318 Shin, Il-Soo. "*Commedia dell'arte* ui bunsukjuk yongu." (*Commedia dell'arte*: Its Characters and Costume.) *DongukDA.* 1983 Dec.; 14: 105-118. Lang.: Kor.
Italy. 1550-1700. Critical studies. ■Characters and costumes of the *commedia.*

Theory/criticism

3319 Sarabia, Rosa. "Darío y Lugones: dos visiones de Pierrot." (Darío and Lugones: Two Visions of Pierrot.) *LATR.* 1987 Fall; 21(1): 75-83. Lang.: Spa.
Spain. 1898-1909. Critical studies. ■Study of modernism through analysis of *Pierrot y Colombina (Pierrot and Columbine), La aventura eterna (The Eternal Adventure)* by Rubén Darío, and *El pierrot negro (The Black Pierrot)* by Leopoldo Lugones.

Court entertainment

Design/technology

3320 Oechslin, Werner; Buschow, Anja. *Architecture de fête: l'architecture comme metteur en scène.* (Festival Architecture: Architecture as Director.) Brussels/Liège: Pierre Mardaga; 1987. 164 pp. (Architecture: Architecture N documents.) Pref. Illus.: Photo. Dwg. B&W. Lang.: Fre.
Germany: Düsseldorf. France. Italy. 1700-1897. Historical studies. ■How the decors created for feasts and festivals by great artists prefigured architectural developments.

Performance/production

3321 Astington, John H. "The King and Queen Entertainment at Richmond." *REEDN.* 1987; 12(1): 12-18. Notes. Lang.: Eng.
England. 1636. Historical studies. ■Examines evidence concerning the location and staging of the 1636 Masque at Richmond Palace. Refutes the location proposed by H.M. Colvin and John Summerson.

3322 Allegri, Luigi, ed.; Di Benedetto, Renato, ed. *La Parma in festa. Spettacolarità e teatro nel ducato di Parma nel Settecento.* (Parma in Celebration: Performance and Theatre in the Duchy of Parma in the Eighteenth Century.) Modena: Mucchi; 1987. 217 pp. (Società e Cultura del Settecento in Emilia Romagna.) Lang.: Ita.
Italy: Parma. 1659-1807. Historical studies. ■Categories of festivals and performance.

3323 Pontremoli, Alessandro; La Rocca, Patrizia. *Il ballare lombardo: teoria e prassi coreutica nella festa di corte del XV secolo.* (Lombard Dancing: Theory and Practice in the Court Feasts of the Fifteenth-century.) Milano: Vita e Pensiero; 1987. 250 pp. (La città e lo spettacolo 1.) Index. Pref. Append. Lang.: Ita.
Italy: Milan. 1400-1500. Critical studies. ■History and theory of dances in spectacles of the Lombard court.

3324 Tamburini, Elena. "Patrimonio teatrale estense. Influenza e interventi nella Roma del Seicento." (The Theatrical Patrimony of the Ducal Family of Este: Influence and Interference in Seventeenth-Century Rome.) *BiT.* 1987; 7: 39-77. Lang.: Ita.
Italy: Rome. 1598-1645. Historical studies. ■The influence of the Este family on performance, which was so important during the sixteenth-century, becomes indirect after 1598. Three examples of these different interventions are given: the scenic landscape of Giovanni Guerra in *Amor pudico (Modest Love),* the cartels of Fulvio Testi in the *Giostra del Saracino (Joust of the Saracen),* the joust announced by Cardinal Este.

Plays/librettos/scripts

3325 Breight, Curtis C. "Entertainments of Elizabeth at Theobalds in the Early 1590s." *REEDN.* 1987; 12(2): 1-9. Notes. Append. Lang.: Eng.
England. 1591. Textual studies. ■Response to Marion Colthorpe's article on the Theobalds entertainment for Queen Elizabeth I in 1591 published in REEDN 12:1, 1987.

3326 Colthorpe, Marion. "The Theobalds Entertainment for Queen Elizabeth I in 1591, with a Transcript of the Gardener's Speech." *REEDN.* 1987; 12(1): 2-9. Notes. Lang.: Eng.
England. 1591-1885. Textual studies. ■Disputes questions of authorship and authenticity of three speeches purportedly given at the Theobalds in 1591. Response in REEDN 12:2 1987.

Relation to other fields

3327 Cruciani, Fabrizio. "Le feste per Isabella d'Este Gonzaga a Roma nel 1514-1515." (The Feasts for Isabella d'Este Gonzaga in Rome, 1514-1515.) *TeatroS.* 1987; 2(1): 167-185. Lang.: Ita.
Italy: Rome. 1514-1515. Historical studies. ■*Festa* may be understood as that which unifies languages and modalities, which have their own origins elsewhere, or as a combination of different expressive events and facts, which draw together cultural tensions.

MIXED ENTERTAINMENT: Court entertainment

Theory/criticism

3328   "'Those Beautiful Characters of Sense': Classical Deities and the Court Masque." *CompD*. 1982 Sum; 16(2): 166-179. Notes. Lang.: Eng.

Europe. 1982. Historical studies. ■Classical allusion and moral significance of court masques. Myths as source material, purpose of masques.

Pageants/parades

Performance spaces

3329   White, Eileen. "Places for Hearing the Corpus Christi Play in York." *MET*. 1987; 9(1): 23-63. Notes. Illus.: Photo. Plan. Maps. Diagram. B&W. 15. Lang.: Eng.

England: York. 1399-1569. Historical studies. ■Reconstructs processional route in which wagons stopped at set points for performance.

Performance/production

3330   Urban Padoan, Lina. "Ai primordi del teatro a Venezia: i ludi mariani ossia la festa delle Marie." (At the Origins of Venetian Theatre: The Marian Games, or, The Feast of the Marys.) *BiT*. 1987; 5/6: 5-27. Lang.: Ita.

Italy: Venice. 1000-1300. Historical studies. ■*La festa delle Marie*, a performance on the verge of sacred and profane. The story of the kidnapping of three young Venetian women by pirates.

3331   Ishii, Tatsuro. "The Festival of the Kasuga Wakamiya Shrine." *ThR*. 1987; 12(2): 134-147. Notes. Illus.: Dwg. Print. B&W. 7. Lang.: Eng.

Japan: Nara. 1136-1987. Historical studies. ■Description of annual *On-matsuri* festival at the Kasuga Wakamiya shrine.

3332   Gómez Lara, Manuel; Lester, Geoff; Portillo, Rafael. "Easter Processions in Puente Genil, Córdoba, Spain." *MET*. 1987; 9(2): 93-124. Notes. Illus.: Photo. B&W. 40. [Supplements survey of traditional religious festivals in Andalusia in *MET*, 1986: 8(2): 119-133.] Lang.: Eng.

Spain: Puente Genil. 1660-1987. Historical studies. ■Description of Easter processions, including a full list of characters with their symbols. Briefly discusses links with medieval drama.

3333   Muir, Lynette. "A Play of the Betrayal in Spain in 1579." *EDAM*. 1987 Spr; 9(2): 2-3. Lang.: Eng.

Spain: St. Ginar. 1579. Historical studies. ■*Corpus Christi* pageant in which a debtor playing the role of Christ was attacked by a creditor. Provides information about recruitment and staging as well as rehearsal practices.

3334   Slovenz, Madeline Anita. "'The Year is a Wild Animal': Lion Dancing in Chinatown." *TDR*. 1987 Fall; 31(3): 74-102. Biblio. Illus.: Photo. B&W. 17. Lang.: Eng.

USA: New York, NY. 1987. Historical studies. ■Celebration of the Chinese Lunar New Year: Lion dancing and its martial arts background.

3335   Solomon, Alisa. "Gay Rights and Revels: New York's Lesbian/Gay Pride Day." *ThM*. 1987; 19(1): 19-23. Illus.: Photo. B&W. 5. Lang.: Eng.

USA: New York, NY. 1987. Critical studies. ■The flamboyantly theatrical protest/celebration politics of the annual gay pride parade. Marching bands, floats and transvestites keep representation foregrounded. The parade as misrule/carnival.

Plays/librettos/scripts

3336   Bergeron, David M., ed. *Pageantry in the Shakespearean Theatre*. Athens: Univ. of Georgia P; 1985. 251 pp. Index. Notes. Illus.: Photo. Dwg. B&W. Lang.: Eng.

England. 1392-1642. Critical studies. ■Collection of essays examining various aspects and influence of English Renaissance Pageantry.

Relation to other fields

3337   Sanchis Guarner, Manuel; Llorens, Alfons, ed., intro. *Teatre i Festa (I). De Nadal a Falles.* (Theatre and Feast, I: From Christmas to St. Joseph's.) Prologued by Alfons Llorens. València: Eliseu Climent; 1987. 236 pp. (La Unitat 113/ Obra Completa de M. Sanchis Guarner 6.) Index. Notes. MU. Lang.: Cat.

Spain-Catalonia: Valencia. 1418-1981. Historical studies. ■Collection of articles on theatrical and paratheatrical activities from the Christmas cycle to St. Joseph's Day, March 19.

Performance art

Administration

3338   La Frenais, Rob. "Performance Support Slowly Spreading." *PM*. 1987(46): 34-35. Lang.: Eng.

UK-England. 1987. Historical studies. ■Sources of public funding for performance art. Arts Council's role is examined as well as other regional funding initiatives.

Audience

3339   Bartlett, Neil. "Who Are You Doing This For?" *PM*. 1987(48): 14-19. Illus.: Photo. B&W. 1. Lang.: Eng.

UK-England. 1987. Histories-sources. ■Sixteen performance art companies describe their current and potential audiences.

3340   Kröplin, Wolfgang. "Theater-Wunder. Die Oktoberrevolution und der erste Vorgriff auf ein neues Theaterkonzept." (The Theatre Miracle: The October Revolution and First Steps Towards New Theatrical Concepts.) *TZ*. 1987; 42(9): 37-40. Illus.: Photo. B&W. 5. Lang.: Ger.

USSR: Moscow. 1917-1924. Historical studies. ■Survey on mass (street) theatre in the Soviet Union after 1917, description of artistic means, forms of communication and the theatrical concept.

Basic theatrical documents

3341   Rosenthal, Rachel. "L.O.W. in Gaia: Chronicle of and Meditation on a 3-Week Vacation in the Mojave Desert, January 1986." *PerAJ*. 1987; 10(3): 76-94. 6. Lang.: Eng.

USA. 1986. ■Text of *L.O.W. in Gaia*, a performance art piece which parallels a woman's aging with the aging of the earth.

Design/technology

3342   Weisang, Myriam. "Masters of the Universe." *ThCr*. 1987 Jan.; 21(1): 28-29, 51-53. Illus.: Photo. B&W. 3. Lang.: Eng.

USA: San Francisco, CA. 1986. Technical studies. ■Three performance artists who build performing machines at their shop Survival Research Laboratories.

Performance spaces

3343   Herbert, Simon. "When Institutions Collide." *PM*. 1987(46): 32-33. Lang.: Eng.

UK-England. 1987. Historical studies. ■Trend for performance artists to work within municipal galleries and museums. Considers the status of performance art in today's culture and the potential conflicts created by the gradual integration of performance art into a traditional environment.

3344   Watson, Gray. "Beuys Line to Bond Street." *PM*. 1987(46): 10-14. Illus.: Photo. B&W. 4. Lang.: Eng.

UK-England. 1987. Histories-sources. ■Interview with Anthony D'Offay which discusses the relationship between the commercial gallery world and performance art with special reference to Joseph Beuys and Gilbert and George.

Performance/production

3345   Feldman, Peter. "Action to Image." *CTR*. 1987 Spr; 50: 4-9. Notes. Illus.: Photo. Print. B&W. 4. Lang.: Eng.

Canada. Europe. USA. 1987. Critical studies. ■Practical analysis of image theatre promoting its wider acceptance. Comparisons between text vs. image regarding implications each style has for actor and audience.

3346   Filip, Ray. "Dada Processing." *BooksC*. 1987 Nov.; 16(8): 4-5. Illus.: Design. B&W. 1. Lang.: Eng.

Canada: Montreal, PQ. 1987. Critical studies. ■Ultimatum II at Théâtre Le Milieu, a nine-day festival devoted to the avant garde, displays expensive technology, but cheap art.

3347   Lefebvre, Paul. "Robert Lepage: New Filters for Creation." *CTR*. 1987 Fall; 52: 30-35. Notes. Illus.: Photo. Print. B&W. 4. Lang.: Eng.

MIXED ENTERTAINMENT: Performance art—Performance/production

Canada: Montreal, PQ. 1987. Critical studies. ■Theatrical aesthetic of Robert Lepage, describing an imagistic over mimetic methodology.

3348   Wallace, Robert. "Image Theatre." *CTR*. 1987 Spr(50): 3. Illus.: Photo. Print. B&W. 2. Lang.: Eng.
Canada. 1987. Critical studies. ■Analysis of image theatre: methodology and creative practice.

3349   Babel, Tara. "Crossing the Desert." *PM*. 1987(49): 31-35. Illus.: Photo. B&W. 4. Lang.: Eng.
Europe. 1974-1987. Histories-sources. ■Interview with Egidio Alvaro about his involvement with performance art and his organization of many international festivals of performance art in Europe.

3350   Culshaw, Pete. "Going Abroad." *PM*. 1987(48): 28-30. Illus.: Photo. B&W. 3. Lang.: Eng.
Europe. 1987. Critical studies. ■International comparison of performance art, its status and style in its home context. Discusses work of the performance art reviewer.

3351   La Frenais, Rob. "When the Tunnel is Built." *PM*. 1987(49): 13-17. Illus.: Photo. B&W. 6. Lang.: Eng.
Europe. 1987. Critical studies. ■International review of contemporary work by performance artists throughout Europe.

3352   La Frenais, Rob; Rogers, Steve. "Perfo 4D, or The Artist Is in the Bar." *PM*. 1987(44/45): 28-31. Illus.: Photo. B&W. 8. Lang.: Eng.
Germany: Rotterdam. 1986. Historical studies. ■Description of Rotterdam's 1986 Perfo Festival.

3353   Gill, Ken. "Myths, Monsters and Mutations." *PM*. 1987(49): 25-28. Illus.: Photo. B&W. 3. Lang.: Eng.
Germany, West: Berlin, West. 1987. Historical studies. ■Description of the six-day performance art festival entitled *Myths, Monsters and Mutations* held in Berlin.

3354   Iles, Chrissie. "The Quintessential European Event." *PM*. 1987(49): 18-20. Illus.: Photo. B&W. 2. Lang.: Eng.
Germany, West: Kassel. 1987. Historical studies. ■Description of the 8th Documenta at Kassel: an international cultural event which combines visual and performance arts.

3355   Burzyński, Tadeusz. "The 4th International Festival of Street Theatres in Jelenia Góra." (4e Festival international du théâtre de rue à Jelenia Góra.) *TP*. 1987 Apr-June(4-6): 13-23. Illus.: Photo. Print. B&W. 11. Lang.: Eng, Fre.
Poland: Jelenia Góra. 1986. Historical studies. ■Qualities of the Festival, a brief history and a synopsis of theatre groups that attended.

3356   Gale, David; Westlake, Hilary. "Doff the Bonnet Before It Becomes a Tea Cosy." *PM*. 1987(44/45): 6-8. Illus.: Photo. B&W. 1. Lang.: Eng.
UK-England: London. 1986. Critical studies. ■Response to Steve Rogers' article 'Butterflies' (*PM*: 43) which attacked Lumière & Son's production *Deadwood* staged in Kew Gardens, London.

3357   Rogers, Steve. "The National Reviews of Live Art." *PM*. 1987(50/51): 44-45. Illus.: Photo. B&W. 2. Lang.: Eng.
UK-England: London. 1987. Histories-sources. ■Description of the 1987 National Review of Live Art, the first to be held in London rather than in Nottingham. Compares the two venues.

3358   Rogers, Steve; La Frenais, Rob. "The English Dream (Midlands Version)." *PM*. 1987(44/45): 36-39. Illus.: Photo. B&W. 5. Lang.: Eng.
UK-England: Nottingham. 1986. Historical studies. ■Description of Nottingham's National Review of Live Art festival.

3359   Warr, Tracey. "Look North." *PM*. 1987(47): 25-28. Illus.: Photo. B&W. 5. Lang.: Eng.
UK-England: Newcastle. 1986-1987. Historical studies. ■Previews performances, exhibitions, talks and workshops commissioned for *New Work Newcastle '87*.

3360   Kaylan, Mina. "Women Work Out." *PM*. 1987(44/45): 44-45. Illus.: Photo. B&W. 1. Lang.: Eng.
UK-Wales: Cardiff. 1986. Historical studies. ■Account of 'Magdalena 86': a three week festival of women's performances held at the Cardiff Laboratory Theatre.

3361   "*Hamlet Machine*: The Unique and Improbable Cooperation of Robert Wilson and Heiner Müller." *PM*. 1987(49): 10-12. Illus.: Photo. B&W. 2. Lang.: Eng.
USA: New York, NY. Germany, West: Hamburg. 1987. Histories-sources. ■Collaboration of Robert Wilson and Heiner Müller on *Hamlet Machine (Hamletmaschine)* staged in New York and Hamburg.

3362   Kisselman, I.A. "'A Very Old City With a Very Young Theatre': Show Biz in New Orleans." *TheaterW*. 1987 Aug 24; 2: 33-34. Illus.: Photo. 3. Lang.: Eng.
USA: New Orleans, LA, New York, NY. 1987. Histories-sources. ■Major native performance artists relate the frustrations of generating paid, unionized productions in New Orleans. Rita Sheffield describes her New York production of *Cleavage*, a New Orleans smash hit revue.

3363   La Frenais, Rob. "Technological Witch Doctors." *PM*. 1987(44/45): 9-13. Illus.: Photo. B&W. 4. Lang.: Eng.
USA. 1979-1987. Histories-sources. ■Interview with Mark Pauline and Steve Cripps of Survival Research Laboratories about their use of enormous robots to simulate futuristic battlefields.

3364   Milliken, Julia. "Escott and Zanarini's Associative Thinking: *The Way We Are At Home*." *TDR*. 1983 Fall; 27(3): 97-101. Illus.: Photo. B&W. 3. Lang.: Eng.
USA: Chicago, IL. 1981. Historical studies. ■Non-traditional theatre works presented by artists of the Clybourn Salon. Focus on production *The Way We Are At Home*, use of multi-media, themes.

3365   Munk, Erika. "Film is Ego: Radio is Food. Richard Foreman and the Art of Control." *TDR*. 1987 Win; 31(4): 143. Illus.: Photo. B&W. 2. Lang.: Eng.
USA: New York, NY. 1987. Histories-sources. ■Richard Foreman's production of *Film is Evil: Radio is Good*.

3366   Robinson, Marc. "Performance Strategies." *PerAJ*. 1987; 10(3): 31-55. Illus.: Photo. B&W. 8. Lang.: Eng.
USA. 1987. Histories-sources. ■Interviews with performance artists Ishmael Houston-Jones, John Kelly, Karen Finley and Richard Elovich.

3367   Sandford, Mariellen R. "Danny Mydlack, Suburban Culture Worker." *TDR*. 1987 Win; 31(4): 91-108. Illus.: Photo. B&W. 9. Lang.: Eng.
USA: Boston, MA. 1987. Histories-sources. ■Danny Mydlack's performance art *Living Room Project* in the individual's living room in suburbs of Boston. The artist creates his art projects in private homes, transforming them into his artistic environment.

3368   Schechner, Richard. "Richard Foreman on Richard Foreman." *TDR*. 1987 Win; 31(4): 125-142. Illus.: Photo. B&W. 7. Lang.: Eng.
USA: New York, NY. 1987. Histories-sources. ■Richard Foreman's works, rehearsal techniques and working process.

3369   Smith, Michael. "What's My Connection to Jim." *MimeJ*. 1987/88: 5-6. Lang.: Eng.
USA. 1987. ■Development of author from painter to performance artist: *Mike's Talent Show* at The Bottom Line.

Plays/librettos/scripts

3370   Zaloom, Paul. "The New Now." *MimeJ*. 1987/88: 7. Lang.: Eng.
USA. 1987. Critical studies. ■Satirical look at President and Vice President of the United States and potential for comedic performance material.

Relation to other fields

3371   La Frenais, Rob. "Behind the Aktion." *PM*. 1987(49): 21-24. Illus.: Photo. B&W. 2. Lang.: Eng.
Germany, West: Kassel. 1987. Histories-sources. ■Interview with Elizabeth Jappe about her organization of the performance art program for 'Documenta', the international arts event.

3372   Iles, Chrissie. "The Camera Is the Only Audience." *PM*. 1987(44/45): 14-17. Illus.: Photo. B&W. 4. Lang.: Eng.
UK. 1840-1987. Historical studies. ■Relationship of photographic records to the performance itself. Considers two recent exhibitions of photographic images.

3373   Warr, Tracey. "Extracurricular." *PM*. 1987(47): 29-30. Lang.: Eng.

MIXED ENTERTAINMENT: Performance art—Relation to other fields

UK-England. 1987. Historical studies. ■Introduces three performance art education projects: Alistair MacLennan's *Tree of Life* in Grizedale Forest, Stephen Taylor-Woodrow's 'living collage' in Newcastle, and Paul Burwell's performance at Hull Regatta.

Theory/criticism

3374   MacLennan, Alistair; McGonagle, Declan. "I See Danger." *PM*. 1987(47): 12-16. Illus.: Photo. B&W. 3. Lang.: Eng.
UK-Ireland: Belfast. 1975-1987. Histories-sources. ■Authors' development through social involvement and questioning into a major practitioner of live art.

3375   Demarco, Richard. "Ex-Cathedra." *PM*. 1987(50/51): 35-39. Illus.: Design. Photo. Dwg. B&W. 4. Lang.: Eng.
UK-Scotland: Edinburgh. 1987. Historical studies. ■Influence of author's native city and Catholicism on his development. Definition of performance art and work with the Edinburgh Festival.

3376   Iles, Chrissie. "Running at Great Speed Across a Great Distance." *PM*. 1987(46): 15-19. Illus.: Photo. B&W. 4. Lang.: Eng.
UK-Scotland: Edinburgh. 1970-1987. Histories-sources. ■Interview with Richard Demarco. Importance of performance art in the Edinburgh Festival. Demarco's plans for his new gallery.

3377   Breslauer, Jan. "Ollywood: Or, The Case of the Acting Lieutenant Colonel." *ThM*. 1987; 19(1): 31-34. Illus.: Photo. B&W. 2. Lang.: Eng.
USA: Hollywood, CA. 1987. Histories-sources. ■Account of a trip to California to see the performance art, political action piece protesting the Iran-Contra scandal. Two artists removed the H from the Hollywood sign to point up the false nature of the hearings. Written in 1940s detective fiction and film noir style.

3378   Kröplin, Wolfgang. "Kunst in der Revolution und Revolution in der Kunst. Oktoberrevolution, künstlerische Avantgarde und das neue Theaterkonzept." (Art in the Revolution and the Revolution in Art: October Revolution, Artistic Avant-Garde and the New Concept of Theatre.) *TZ*. 1987; 42(10): 14-19. Illus.: Photo. B&W. 5. Lang.: Ger.
USSR: Moscow. 1918-1930. Historical studies. ■Russian avant-garde theatre as source of a proletarian revolutionary and socialist theatre: technical revolution and art.

Shadow puppets

Plays/librettos/scripts

3379   Zurbechen, Mary Sabina. *The Language of Balinese Shadow Theatre*. Princeton, NJ: Princeton UP; 1987. 291 pp. Index. Biblio. Gloss. Append. Illus.: Photo. Sketches. 12. Lang.: Eng.
Indonesia. Historical studies. ■Interpreting and understanding linguistic forms and cultural, historical and social significance of Balinese shadow puppet theatre. Written texts and the verbal art itself are explored. History of the puppet theatre and its role in Balinese verbal communication.

Variety acts

Institutions

3380   Bomers, Bernard. "Tabootenay! Theatre to be Featured." *PAC*. 1986 Jan.; 22(4): 71. Notes. Illus.: Photo. Print. 2. Lang.: Eng.
Canada: Vancouver, BC. 1986. Critical studies. ■Tabootenay, a traveling troup offers street theatre of jugglers, musicians, poets, actors and clowns.

3381   Rátonyi, Robert; Vogel, Eric, illus. *Mulató a Nagymező utcában*. (Nightclub in Nagymező Street.) Budapest: IPV; 1987. 256 pp. Illus.: Dwg. Color. B&W. 37. Lang.: Hun.
Hungary: Budapest. 1932-1944. Histories-general. ■Adventurous and tragic story of the proprietors, artists and operation of the world famous nightclub and revue theatre.

3382   Knight, Athelia. "In Retrospect: Sherman H. Dudley—He Paved the Way for T.O.B.A." *BPM*. 1987 Fall; 15(2): 153-181. Notes. Append. Illus.: Handbill. Photo. Dwg. Print. B&W. 7. Lang.: Eng.
USA: Indianapolis, IN, Washington, DC. 1820-1922. Critical studies. ■After a brief history of Black musical theatre the article discusses Dudley's role as the primary force behind the creation of a Black circuit of theatres for booking vaudeville acts. Covers period from his establishment of the Dudley Circuit in 1912 to creation of Theatre Owner's Booking Agency in 1921.

Performance/production

3383   Busby, Cathy; Bean, Robert. "Mythmaking, History and the Nova Scotia Tattoo." *ArtsAtl*. 1987 Spr; 7(4): 52-53. Illus.: Photo. B&W. 2. Lang.: Eng.
Canada: Halifax, NS. 1978-1986. Critical studies. ■Nova Scotia Tattoo's family entertainment format provides a public relations function for the military.

3384   McKinley, Ann. "Debussy and American Minstrelsy." *BPM*. 1986 Fall; 14(3): 249-258. Lang.: Eng.
France: Paris. UK-England: London. 1893-1913. Critical studies. ■Various compositions by Debussy in their relationship to Afro-American music. Influences from songs from minstrel shows.

3385   Nelson, Steve. "Walt Disney's EPCOT and the World's Fair Performance Tradition." *TDR*. 1986 Win; 30(4): 106-146. Notes. Biblio. Illus.: Photo. B&W. 52. Lang.: Eng.
USA. 1893-1986. Historical studies. ■Comparison of three theatrical environmental entertainments: Chicago's 1893 Columbian Exposition, 1939 World's Fair and Walt Disney's Epcot Center.

Relation to other fields

3386   Jaffe, Harold. "Madonna." *PerAJ*. 1987; 10(3): 17-20. Lang.: Eng.
USA: New York, NY. UK-England: London. 1985-1987. Critical studies. ■Politics of what rock singer Madonna's image represents in the U.S. and what her popularity says about the culture.

———

Other entries with significant content related to Mixed Entertainment: 776, 977, 1310, 1744, 1749, 1750, 3216, 3226, 3621, 3622.

MUSIC-DRAMA

General

Administration

3387   Brainerd, Susan. "Creating an Organizational Climate to Motivate Volunteers." *JAML*. 1987 Sum; 17(2): 49-66. Notes. Illus.: Graphs. 3. Lang.: Eng.
USA: New York, NY. 1987. Critical studies. ■Volunteer-staff relationships in the New York Philharmonic. Effectiveness of policies and benefits.

Design/technology

3388   "Richard Pilbrow: A View of Lighting from Across the Water." *LDim*. 1982; 6(2): 16-17, 45. Illus.: Photo. 1. Lang.: Eng.
USA: Salt Lake City, UT. 1982. Technical studies. ■Innovative methods for theatrical and rock and roll lighting by designer Richard Pilbrow.

Institutions

3389   "Andrew Davis, the TS and Opera." *OC*. 1987 Sum; 28(2): 22-23. Illus.: Photo. B&W. 1. [Soundings.] Lang.: Eng.
Canada: Toronto, On. 1974-1987. Historical studies. ■Briefly discusses Andrew Davis' past contributions, upcoming and last season with the Toronto Symphony Orchestra.

3390   Mercer, Ruby. "The Royal Conservatory's 100th Birthday." *OC*. 1987 Spr; 28(1): 20-21. Illus.: Photo. B&W. 1. [Soundings.] Lang.: Eng.

MUSIC-DRAMA: General—Institutions

Canada: Toronto, ON. 1886-1986. Historical studies. ■Brief history of the Royal Conservatory of Music including details of its 100th Anniversary celebration, and its role in Canadian opera.

3391 Brauer, Regina. "Zur Geschichte des Leipziger Neuen Theaters von 1868 bis 1932." (On the History of Leipzig 'Neues Theater' from 1868 to 1932.) 20-40 in Seeger, Horst. *Oper heute.* Berlin: Henschelverlag; 1987. 301 pp. (Ein Almanach der Musikbühne 10.) Illus.: Photo. Print. B&W. 8. Lang.: Ger.
Germany: Leipzig. 1868-1932. Historical studies. ■Managements, repertory, finances, artistic questions of the Leipzig New Theatre.

3392 "The Edinburgh Festival: Glasgow's Miles Better." *Econ.* 1987 8 Aug.; 304: 82. Illus.: Photo. B&W. 1. Lang.: Eng.
UK-Scotland: Edinburgh. 1987. Critical studies. ■Flourishing European festival circuit has dented Edinburgh Festival's pre-eminence. Stressing theatre vs. music makes Edinburgh less competitive with other festivals.

Performance spaces

3393 Dell'Ira, Gino; Gualerzi, Giorgio. *I teatri di Pisa (1773-1986).* (The Theatres of Pisa, 1773-1986.) Pisa: Giardini; 1987. 403 pp. Pref. Index. Biblio. Illus.: Photo. Print. B&W. Lang.: Ita.
Italy: Pisa. 1773-1986. Historical studies. ■History of the various theatres and the musical works presented in them.

3394 "Bucklen Opera House, Elkhart, Indiana: 1884-1986." *MarqJTHS.* 1987; 19(3): 25-27. Illus.: Photo. Dwg. B&W. 5. Lang.: Eng.
USA: Elkhart, IN. 1884-1986. Historical studies. ■Illustrated chronology of the Bucklen Opera House built in 1884 and demolished in 1986.

3395 Rottenbach, Jane. "Light Plays Lead in Tampa: Tampa Bay Performing Arts Center." *L&DA.* 1987 Dec.; 17(12): 4-5, 36-37. Illus.: Photo. 4. Lang.: Eng.
USA: Tampa, FL. 1987. Technical studies. ■A new $55 milliion performing arts center in Tampa has special lighting and acoustical designs built into it. The designer of the lighting gives some background on design development.

Performance/production

3396 Sinclair, Lister. "Rossini: A Lion in the Path." *OC.* 1987 Fall; 28(3): 21, 43. Illus.: Photo. Dwg. 4. Lang.: Eng.
1792-1868. Biographical studies. ■Briefly discusses Rossini's impact, both during his lifetime and today.

3397 Ueng, Ou-Hueng. "Shiang ma juan iu ma shau liang." (The Story of the Robber and the Actor Ma Shau-Liang.) *XYanj.* 1987 Aug.: 46. Lang.: Chi.
China, People's Republic of. 1958-1986. Historical studies. ■The actor Ma Shau-Liang reproduced the play *Shiang ma juan (Story of the Robber).*

3398 Fallows, Colin. "Wash Your Brains." *PM.* 1987(47): 28. Illus.: Photo. B&W. 1. Lang.: Eng.
Europe. 1985. Historical studies. ■Previews a collection of neo-Dadaist dance soundtracks which simulate a Dada/Futurist variety club.

3399 Zucker, Stefan. "Changing Your Tune: Standards of Pitch Have Differed from Time to Time, Place to Place." *OpN.* 1987 Jan 3; 51(8): 32-34, 44. Lang.: Eng.
Europe. USA. 1500-1987. Historical studies. ■Standardization of musical pitch.

3400 Gábor, István. "Zenés előadások Szegeden." (Musical Performances in Szeged.) *Sz.* 1987 Nov.; 20(11): 20-25. Illus.: Photo. B&W. 4. Lang.: Hun.
Hungary: Szeged. 1987. Reviews of performances. ■Four musical productions of various genres in the program of the Open Air Stage in Szeged: Verdi's *Rigoletto* directed by András Békés, Lloyd Webber's *Requiem* directed by Gábor Koltay and László Tolcsvay and Béla Tolcsvay's *Hungarian Mass,* and *Les Misérables* by Alain Boublil and Claude-Michel Schönberg, directed by Miklós Szinetár.

3401 Molnár Gál, Péter. "A Szovjet Zenés Zsidó Kamaraszínház Budapesten." (The Soviet Musical Jewish Chamber Theatre in Budapest.) *Krit.* 1987 July(7): 44. Lang.: Hun.

Hungary: Budapest. USSR: Birobidjan. 1987. Reviews of performances. ■The Soviet Musical Jewish Chamber Theatre's guest play in Budapest in the frame of the series of events of the Budapest Spring Festival, at the Municipal Operetta Theatre. Notes on the performance.

3402 Rajk, András. "A *Koldusopera*—mint zenedráma." (*The Three Penny Opera*—As a Musical Drama.) *Sz.* 1987 June; 20 (6): 30-35. Illus.: Photo. B&W. 6. Lang.: Hun.
Hungary: Győr, Budapest. 1987. Critical studies. ■Comparison of three Hungarian productions of *Die Dreigroschenoper (The Three Penny Opera)* by Bertolt Brecht and Kurt Weill: as directed by Ferenc Sík, József Petrik and Miklós Szinetár.

3403 Fabbri, Paolo; Verti, Roberto. *Due secoli di teatro per musica a Reggio Emilia. Repertorio cronologico delle opere e dei balli 1645-1857.* (Two Centuries of Music Theatre in Reggio Emilia: A Chronological Repertoire of Operas and Ballets from 1645 to 1857.) Reggio Emilia: Teatro Municipale Valli; 1987. 481 pp. Pref. Index. Lang.: Ita.
Italy: Reggio Emilia. 1645-1857. Histories-sources. ■Chronological repertoire of operas and ballets performed in Reggio Emilia.

3404 *Koryeo saakjee.* (Theatre in Koryo Dynasty.) Seoul: Ulyumoonhwasa; 1982. 298 pp. Lang.: Kor.
Korea. China. 935-1392. Historical studies. ■Study of the origin, theory and instruments of music theatre in Koryo Dynasty.

3405 Jang, Sa-Hoon. *Gukakui yuksa.* (History of Musical Theatre.) Seoul: Kyoyang Guksa; 1977. 206 pp. Lang.: Kor.
Korea. 57 B.C.-1977 A.D. Historical studies. ■History of Korean music-drama.

3406 Kang, Han-Young. *Pansori.* Seoul: Kyoyang Guksa; 1977. 219 pp. Lang.: Kor.
Korea. 1392-1910. Historical studies. ■Origin of *pansori* music-drama, its influence on modern *changuk* drama.

3407 Lim, Young. "Chun Hyang Jeon." (*Chun Hyang* Music Drama.) *KTR.* 1987 Mar.; 3(1): 54-55. B&W. 1. Lang.: Kor.
Korea: Nam-won. 1400-1900. Historical studies. ■History of *Chun Hyang* musical drama.

3408 Park, Kwang. *Pansori sosa.* (Short History of Korean Musical Theatre—*Pansori.*) Seoul: Singumoonhwasa; 1983. 225 pp. [2d ed.] Lang.: Kor.
Korea. 1392-1910. Histories-specific. ■The origin and theory of Korean musical theatre, *pansori.*

3409 Fosdick, Scott. "Pablo Loves Gertrude." *AmTh.* 1987 Apr.; 4(1): 4-5. Illus.: Photo. B&W. 1. Lang.: Eng.
USA: Chicago, IL. 1986-1987. Critical studies. ■Goodman Theatre's series 'Celebration of Genius' with emphasis on *She Always Said, Pablo.*

3410 Kaufman, Rhoda Helfman. "The Yiddish Theatre in New York 1880-1920: A Secular Ritual." *TheatreS.* 1983-84; 30: 57-61. Lang.: Eng.
USA: New York, NY. 1930. Historical studies. ■Ritual elements and history of the Yiddish theatre.

3411 Linneman, Russell J. "Country Blues: Mirror of Southern Society." *WJBS.* 1985; 9(3): 183-187. Notes. Lang.: Eng.
USA. 1800-1985. Historical studies. ■Roots of blues music in the rural, agrarian culture of the South and how it mirrors the harsh oppressions and realities of that life.

3412 London, Todd. "Theatre Focus—Golden Fleece, Ltd." *TT.* 1987 Apr.; 6(3): 19. Illus.: Photo. B&W. 1. Lang.: Eng.
USA: New York, NY. 1987. Historical studies. ■Golden Fleece, Ltd. produces works by American composers, bridging classical music, opera and musical theatre.

3413 Shipow, Sandra. "Depression Era Trends in Popular Culture as Reflected in the Yiddish Theatre Career of Molly Picon." *TheatreS.* 1983-84; 30: 43-56. Illus.: Photo. B&W. 2. Lang.: Eng.
USA. 1930. Historical studies. ■Career of Depression-era Yiddish actress Molly Picon.

MUSIC-DRAMA: General—Performance/production

3414 Chamidova, M.A. *Akterskoe iskusstvo uzbekskoj muzykal'noj dramy.* (The Actor's Art in Uzbek Musical Drama.) Taškent: In-t iskusstvoznanija; 1987. 146 pp. Lang.: Rus.
USSR. 1920-1970. Historical studies.

3415 Chasanova, R.K. *Processy stanovlenija i razvitija ujgurskoj muzykal'noj dramy: Avtoref. dis. kand. iskusstvovedenija.* (The Processes of Establishment and Development of the Ujgur Musical Drama: Abstract of a Dissertation by a Candidate in Art Criticism.) Taškent: In-t iskusstvoznanija; 1987. 25 pp. Lang.: Rus.
USSR. 1920-1987. Historical studies.

3416 Kložin'š, A.E. *Ďoprosy muzykal'nogo i sceničeskogo tvorčestva v teatrach Latvii, Litvy, Estonii.* (Issues of Musical and Scenic Creativity in the Theatres of Latvia, Lithuania and Estonia.) Riga: 1987. 207 pp. (Pribaltijskij muzykovedčeskij.) Lang.: Rus.
USSR. 1980-1987. Critical studies.

3417 Mashiah, Selina. *"Petear Veltazeave."* (*Peter and the Wolf.*) *Bamah.* 1987; 21(107): 85-88. Illus.: Photo. Print. B&W. Lang.: Heb.
USSR: Moscow. 1930-1936. Historical studies. ▪Creation of a musical and writing a story for children in the USSR to educate them musically.

Plays/librettos/scripts

3418 Bianconi, Lorenzo, ed. *La drammaturgia musicale.* (Musical Dramaturgy.) Bologna: Mulino; 1986. ix, 450 pp. (Problemi e prospettive. Serie di musica e spettacolo.) Biblio. Pref. Illus.: Sketches. Lang.: Ita.
Europe. 1986. Critical studies. ▪Essays on the complex relationships between libretto, music and structure in musical drama.

3419 Uhry, Alfred. *"Driving Miss Daisy.* Making it at Long Last." *TheaterW.* 1987 Oct.; 1(8): 6-7. Illus.: Photo. B&W. 2. Lang.: Eng.
USA: New York, NY. 1976-1984. Histories-sources. ▪Playwright Alfred Uhry discusses the genesis of his hit play *Driving Miss Daisy.*

3420 Dmitrevskaja, M. "Prevraščenija melodramy." (The Transformation of Melodrama.) *SovD.* 1987; 2: 235-243. Lang.: Rus.
USSR. 1987. Historical studies. ▪The historical fate of melodrama, its place and significance in contemporary theatre.

Relation to other fields

3421 Komorowska, Małgorzata. "Nasza opera: Decydujące lata pięćdziesiąte." (Our Opera: The Crucial Fifties.) *DialogW.* 1987; 2: 134-142. Notes. Lang.: Pol.
Poland. 1950-1965. Historical studies. ▪Polish government's policy to promote opera, operetta and musical theatre in the 1950s: its positive and negative consequences.

Theory/criticism

3422 Fang, Hong-Lin. "Yin yue ju de xian dai shen mei jia zhi." (The Aesthetics of Musical Theatre in China.) *XYishu.* 1987 Sum; 38: 84-88. Notes. Lang.: Chi.
China, People's Republic of. 1975-1987. Historical studies. ▪The status of Chinese musical theatre includes elements of both Eastern and Western musical theatre.

3423 Chamidova, M.A. *Uzbekskaja muzykal'naja drama: Problemy zanra.* (Uzbek Musical Drama: Problems of Genre.) Taškent: Izd-vo lit. i is-va; 1987. 117 pp. Lang.: Rus.
USSR. 1917-1987. Critical studies.

Chinese opera

Administration

3424 Cheng, Mu; Jiang, Shi-U. "Uen ding iu duo bian d shing tai ho liu." (The Analysis of Aesthetical Intention of Audiences.) *XYanj.* 1987 Nov.: 25-35. Notes. Tables. 10. Lang.: Chi.
China, People's Republic of. 1987. Critical studies. ▪An investigation of the audience of Chinese classical drama.

3425 Chern, Der-Jen. "'Bao Day' wey hung lou jiuh twan." ('Bao Day' for Hung Lou Theatre.) *XYanj.* 1987 Spr: 71. Illus.: Photo. Print. B&W. Lang.: Chi.
China, People's Republic of. 1987. Historical studies. ▪Wang Wenn-Jiuann, who established the Hung Lou Theatre Company. It reformed Hsi Ch'u.

3426 Wu, Shi-Jian. "Jing ju yi shu nei bu guan li ti zhi grai lun." (The Management of the Beijing Opera.) *XYishu.* 1987 Sum; 38: 141-146. Lang.: Chi.
China, People's Republic of: Beijing. 1949-1987. Historical studies. ▪The difference between management styles of Beijing opera and other regional operas.

3427 Zhang, Geng. "Zhong guo xi qu yu zhong guo she bui." (Chinese Opera and the Chinese Society.) *XYanj.* 1987 Dec.; 24: 137-155. Lang.: Chi.
China, People's Republic of. 1279-1986. Historical studies. ▪Discussion of viability of Kun opera and the Beijing opera in modern China and the effects of nationalization and modernization on theatrical productions in China.

3428 Zhu, Ying-Hui. "Zhong guo xi qu de gai ge dao lu." (The Way of Reforming Chinese Opera.) *XYanj.* 1987 Dec.; 24: 156-177. Lang.: Chi.
China, People's Republic of: Beijing. 1942-1984. Critical studies. ▪The policy of reforming Chinese opera and theatre: encourage the variety of creative work, reform repertory, personnel and system of theatre. Plays should reflect modern life in China.

Audience

3429 Cheng, Mu; Jiang, Shi-U. "Uen ding iu duo bian d shing tai ho liu." (The Analysis of Aesthetical Intention of Audiences.) *XYanj.* 1987 Nov.: 25-35. Notes. Tables. 10. Lang.: Chi.
China, People's Republic of. 1987. Historical studies. ▪An investigation of the audience of Chinese classical drama.

3430 Chiu, Liew-Yii. "Man tarn hsi ch'ü yih shuh fu jaan de hong guan kuan shih." (The Art of Developing Audiences for Hsi Ch'ü.) *XYanj.* 1987 Spr: 4-6. Lang.: Chi.
China, People's Republic of. 1987. Historical studies. ▪How to develop more audiences for Hsi Ch'ü, a form of Chinese opera.

3431 Chiu, Shan-Lin. "Guu day chu luenn jung de guan jong shin lii shyue." (Audience Psychology in Chinese Opera.) *XYanj.* 1986 Win: 21-27. Lang.: Chi.
China, People's Republic of. 1987. Historical studies. ▪Audience psychology is very much a part of Hsi Ch'ü, an old form of Chinese opera.

3432 I, Kai. "Iong gan di jie shou pu lai shi te d tian jan." (Accepting the Challenge of Brecht.) *XYanj.* 1987 Dec.: 71-72. Lang.: Chi.
China, People's Republic of. 1987. Reviews of performances. ▪A comment on the Szechwan Opera adaptation of Brecht's *Der Gute Mensch von Sezuan (The Good Person of Szechwan).*

3433 Ju, Jian-Min. "Tang shen jeng luen j uo jian." (My Opinion About the Controversy Between Tang and Shen.) *XYanj.* 1987 Dec.: 52. Lang.: Chi.
China, People's Republic of. Critical studies. ▪The differences between two famous dramatists of the Chinese opera—Tang and Shen—and how ideally they should be combined.

3434 Li, Chun Xi. "Han guan zhong da jiao dao." (To Communicate with the Audience.) *XYanj.* 1987 Dec.; 24: 45-64. Lang.: Chi.
China, People's Republic of: Beijing. 1950-1986. Critical studies. ▪The communication between actor and audience in Chinese theatre is direct. Direct communication means the actor makes himself believe that he is a real person who lives on the stage, not a 'role' for the audience. Compares this to the Stanislavsky method. Also discusses the aesthetic, psychological and intellectual aspects of the communication.

3435 Liou, Fwu-Ho. "Jiann lih hsi ch'ü guan jong shyue." (Educating the Audience for Hsi Ch'ü.) *XYanj.* 1987 Spr: 56. Lang.: Chi.

MUSIC-DRAMA: Chinese opera—Audience

China, People's Republic of. 1987. Critical studies. ■Getting more audiences from schools involved in Chinese drama.

3436 Liou, Jing-Shian; Ho, J-Chian. "Guan jueng fan ing iu shi chiu shi kau." (The Reaction of Audience and Pondering of Chinese opera.) *XYanj.* 1987 May: 11-16. Tables. Lang.: Chi.

China, People's Republic of. 1986. Historical studies. ■The history of Chinese opera, including the reaction of audiences, to explain its decline.

3437 Liou, Yu-Cheng. "Hsi ch'ü shiaw tyau yuau in chu tann." (What Were the Reasons Why Hsi Ch'ü Was Abandoned.) *XYanj.* 1987 Spr: 7-10. Lang.: Chi.

China, People's Republic of. 1987. Historical studies. ■Ways to reform Hsi Ch'ü to bring it to life again.

3438 Shiun, Iu. "Shi chiu biao ian i shu iu shin shang." (The Performing Arts and Appreciation of Chinese Opera.) *XYanj.* 1987 June: 37-40. Lang.: Chi.

China, People's Republic of. 700-1986. Historical studies. ■Five steps to appreciate Chinese opera. The story, the personality of the character, the art of different schools, the beauty of free sketches and the beauty of describing things as they really are.

3439 Uen, Kai. "Guan Jueng Uei Shen Muo Shau Le?" (Why Did the Audience Become Smaller?)*XYanj.* 1987 Aug: 11-13. Lang.: Chi.

China, People's Republic of. 1987. Critical studies. ■Examination of methods of attracting audiences back to Chinese opera.

3440 Wang, Kuan-lung. "Fan rung jing chu ian chu san ti." (Three Topics on Beijing Opera's Performance.) *XYanj.* 1987 Nov.: 69-70. Lang.: Chi.

China, People's Republic of. 1987. Critical studies. ■From audience comments, there are three ways to keep improving the quality of the Beijing opera. One, to perform plays about the twelve kinds of animals. Two, to attract audiences by excellent acting skills. Three, to have famous actors and actresses play several roles in the same play.

3441 Wu, Guang-Yao. "Duo yang hua, jie jian, guan zhong xin shang." (Variety, Learning, Audience.) *XYishu.* 1985 Sum; 30: 24-37. Notes. Lang.: Chi.

China, People's Republic of. 1982-1985. Empirical research. ■How various audiences influence theatre.

Basic theatrical documents

3442 Guh, Shyi Tung. "Chang-le-gong (I)." (*The Palace of the Beatitudes* Part I: A Script of the Production by Zhejiang Xiau-bai-hua Yuejutuan.) *TaCh.* 1987 Jan.; 158: 66-73. Illus.: Photo. Print. B&W. 3. Lang.: Chi.

China: Binjiang. 1987. Historical studies. ■Text of the play by Guh Shyi Tung, as produced by Zhejiang Xiau-bai-hua Yuejutuan. (Continued in *Ta Cheng* 159 (1987 Feb 1), pp 67-73.

3443 Li, Hui-min. "Yu-wang-cheng-gue." (*The City of Desire.*) *ChWai.* 1987 Apr.; 15(11): 52-76. Notes. Lang.: Chi.

Taiwan. 1986. ■Text of play based on Shakespeare's *Macbeth*.

Design/technology

3444 I, Bor-kang. "Wuu tair chou lii dejii joong." (How to Handle Staging.) *XYanj.* 1986 Spr: 26-28. Lang.: Chi.

China, People's Republic of. 1986. Historical studies. ■Techniques to enhance visual variety and excitement in Chinese opera.

3445 Li, Yu. "Kuei chou nou shi mai chu." (The Masks of Kuei-chou-nou-shi.) *XYanj.* 1987 July: 4. Illus.: Photo. B&W. 1. Lang.: Chi.

China, People's Republic of. 700-1986. Technical studies. ■The production and style of the masks of Kuei-chou-nou-shi.

3446 Luan, Gan-Huah. "Gu dean shi chiu shyh jywe shyng chaing de pyng mam gou cheng." (The Visual Appearance of Chinese Classical Drama in the Structure of Flats.) *XYanj.* 1987 July: 47-55. Illus.: Sketches. 5. Lang.: Chi.

China, People's Republic of. 1856-1987. Technical studies. ■Scene design and its visual impact in Chinese opera.

3447 Wei, Suen. "Chi te de mian bu tzau shing i shu." (The Peculiar, Plastic Art of Facial Expression.) *XYanj.* 1987 May: 27. Illus.: Photo. Print. B&W. 2. Lang.: Chi.

China, People's Republic of. 1986. Historical studies. ■Explanation of the rules of the masks to understand Chinese drama—different colors mean different emotions.

3448 Yan, Shyh-Shii. "Choou jean lean puu." (Face Paintings Indicating Personality.) *XYanj.* 1986 Sum: 29-30. Illus.: Photo. Print. B&W. R.Elev. Lang.: Chi.

China, People's Republic of. 1986. Histories-sources. ■Face painting in Chinese opera reveals the comic dispositions of characters and their personalities.

3449 Mayfield, William F. "Music Computer Style." *BlackM.* 1987 Apr-May; 3(8): 4. Lang.: Eng.

USA. 1987. Historical studies. ■The composition and application of the musical instrument digital face as related to music and theatre. Related to Media: Audio forms.

Institutions

3450 Shang, Fang-Cheng; Cheng, Iuan-Lin. "Shau shing uen shi ho gau sheng u tai." (The Shau-Shing Opera and the Gau-Sheng Stage.) *XYanj.* 1987 Aug.: 49-51. Illus.: Sketches. B&W. 2. Lang.: Chi.

China. 1906-1934. Historical studies. ■The early history and development of the Shau-Shing opera.

Performance spaces

3451 Hwang, Wei-Ree. "Sung yuan ming san jong guo beei fang nong tsuen wuu tair de yan ger." (Improved Staging in Northern China During the Sung, Ming and Yuan Dynasties.) *XYanj.* 1986 Spr: 33. Tables. Illus.: Photo. Print. B&W. R.Elev. Lang.: Chi.

China. 960-1643. Historical studies. ■The relationship between theatre architecture and performance during the Sung, Ming and Yuan dynasties in Northern China. Talks about the changes these three different dynasties had on the theatre. Continued in *XYanj* (1987 Spr), 28-39, 45-51.

3452 Jeng, Kuangwei. "Ts'ung liao ning wen hua ch'uan t'ung t'an erh jen chuan te hsing ch'eng yü fa chan." (The Form and Development of Commune Theatre: From the Aspect of Liao Ning and Traditional Culture.) *XYanj.* 1987 June; 22: 82-94. Notes. Lang.: Chi.

China. 202 B.C.-1986 A.D. Historical studies. ■History of the development of the relationship between commune theatre and support areas.

3453 Liao, Pen. "Chin nan hsi pei ou lo." (A Collection from the Monument of Nan Hsi.) *XYanj.* 1987 June; 22: 269-281. Illus.: Photo. Print. B&W. 6. Lang.: Chi.

China. 960-1912. Histories-sources. ■Transcription of writings inscribed on a monument dedicated to Nan Hsi. A number of theatres are recorded.

3454 Shen, Ch'iunung. "Hsi te hsi shen t'ang chi." (Pleasures of the Discovery of a Monument.) *XYanj.* 1987 June; 22: 290-291 . Lang.: Chi.

China. 1742-1743. Histories-sources. ■Discusses a monument which describes the site of a playhouse in the Chiang Su province.

Performance/production

3455 Ch'ing, Chung. "Ching ying chin mei: kuan yü yün nan hua teng fa chan li ch'eng te fan szu." (The Beauty of Light: Studies of Yün Nan Hua Teng.) *XYanj.* 1987 June; 22: 31-43. Lang.: Chi.

China. 1456-1986. Historical studies. ■Studies of one local Chinese opera: Yün Nan Hua Teng.

3456 Chang, Kang. "Hsi ch'ü kuei lü yü hsi ch'ü chuang shih." (Hsi Ch'ü's Rules and Beginnings.) *XYanj.* 1986 Spr: 4-8. Lang.: Chi.

China. 1986. Historical studies. ■Conventions and origins of Chinese opera.

3457 Chi, Jin-Shen. "Maa lian liang shi shi le shi nian." (The 20th Anniversary of Maa Lian Liang's Death.) *TaCh.* 1987 Jan.; 158: 47-55. Illus.: Photo. Print. B&W. 7. Lang.: Chi.

MUSIC-DRAMA: Chinese opera—Performance/production

China: Beijing. 1929-1981. Biographical studies. ■As Maa Lian Liang's student, author reveals Maa's theatrical training, teaching principles and methods, and relationship with his students. Comments on Maa's major performances.

3458 Chuang, Yungp'ing. "Wo kuo ch'uan t'ung sheng ch'iang yin yüeh te yen chin han fa chan." (The Development of Chinese Theatrical Music.) *XYanj.* 1987 June; 22: 190-205. Lang.: Chi.
China. 1702-1986. Historical studies. ■Major development in Beijing opera vocal techniques and styles.

3459 Jen, Shi-Tsuen. "Shiu uei nan ts shiu lu ji duan ji shu d chan sh." (Several Fragmental Explanations of Shiu Uei's 'Nan-ts-shiu-lu'.) *XYanj.* 1987 Dec.: 41-44. Notes. Lang.: Chi.
China. 1521-1593. Critical studies. ■The basic characteristics of southern Chinese classical drama.

3460 Kong, Xiao-Ting. "Li Yuan Hao Jie 'Ji Ba Wang'." ('Ji Ba Wang'—The Hero of Beijing Opera.) *XYanj.* 1987; 8(22): 292-297. Lang.: Chi.
China: Beijing. 1937-1948. Histories-sources. ■Author's recollections of Beijing opera actor Ji Ba Wang (Ji Shao-Shan).

3461 Liao, Ben. "Song Yuan xi hua si kao." (Study of Four Theatrical Illustrations of Song Dynasty and Yuan Dynasty.) *XYanj.* 1987 Dec.; 24: 227-253. Illus.: Dwg. 4. Lang.: Chi.
China: Beijing. 960-1368. Histories-sources. ■Illustrations which depict theatrical performances in the Song Dynasty and Yuan Dynasty.

3462 Liu, Huich'un. "Hsi chü tsai wai shen te liu ch'uan yü ying hsiang." (The Development and Influence of Hsi Chü in China.) *XYanj.* 1987 June; 22: 129-146. Lang.: Chi.
China. 1600-1912. Historical studies. ■Development and influence of Hsi Chü.

3463 Liu, Shu-Kun. "Ji-Lin shi chiu iuan lio tan wei." (The Beginning of Ji-Lin Drama.) *XYanj.* 1987 Mar.: 61-69. Lang.: Chi.
China. 960 B.C.-1987 A.D. Historical studies. ■Chinese opera is drawn from all regions of China, incorporating many different styles of music, singing and dance. This long, traditional history is important to the development of Chinese opera. The opera of Ji-Lin helped to contribute to this development.

3464 Lu, Et'ing. "Su k'uen sheng yü kuen ch'iang." (Su Kuensheng and K'uen Ch'iang.) *XYanj.* 1987 June; 22: 95-116. Notes. Lang.: Chi.
China. 1600-1735. Biographical studies. ■Biography of Su Kuensheng.

3465 Mackerras, Colin. "Jueng guo chuan tueng shi chiu ho jueng guo feng jian tueng j jie ji." (The Traditional Chinese Opera and the Leading Class of Feudal China.) *XYanj.* 1987 Apr.: 8-14. Lang.: Chi.
China. 900. Historical studies. ■Traditional Chinese opera was strongly influenced by the leading feudal class, including the productions of Kun opera.

3466 Shen, Qiu-Yu. "Xi dao xi shen tang ji." (Propitious Find of The Chronicle of Happy Buddha Temple.) *XYanj.* 1987; 8(22): 290-291. Lang.: Chi.
China: Beijing. 1742-1911. Histories-sources. ■Discovery of writing—'the chronicle of happy Buddha temple'—on the monument of a Buddha temple.

3467 Shiu, Jin-biang. "Ming ching chuon chi iu ian iu in liu j liu bian." (The Development of the Language and Rhythm in the Classical Drama of the Ming and Ching Dynasties.) *XYanj.* 1987 Nov.: 54-59. Lang.: Chi.
China. 1386-1900. Histories-specific. ■The development of language and rhythm reflects certain rules and indicates the development of classical drama.

3468 Shu, Roun-Shan. "Leu jiuh chuang shy ren—sun jong shin." (The Creation of Liu Jiu—Sun Jong Shing.) *XYanj.* 1987 July: 61. Lang.: Chi.
China. 1852-1930. Biographical studies. ■Sun Jong-Shing created a dialect opera in Buo Shing county.

3469 Wang, Yen Yuann. "Lun tarn shin peir chang chiang yih shuh." (The Vocal Art Form of Tarn Shin Peir.) *XYanj.* 1987; 8(19) : 160-190. Lang.: Chi.
China: Beijing. 1847-1917. Textual studies. ■The vocal art form of Tarn Shin Peir of the Beijing Opera. He puts the dramatic movement into music and vocal parts and emphasizes unity and melody of the vocal elements.

3470 "Jing chu iu ba lei." (Chinese Opera and Ballet.) *XYanj.* 1987 June: 71-72. Lang.: Chi.
China, People's Republic of. 1986. Historical studies. ■Similarities and differences in Chinese opera and ballet. Chinese opera presents characters by singing, ballet by action.

3471 "Ren Min I Shu Jia De Tian J." (The Job of People's Artists.) *XYanj.* 1987 June: 81-82. Lang.: Chi.
China, People's Republic of. 1980-1986. Historical studies. ■The responsibility of artists to their audience.

3472 A, Jia. "U chiong u ha sh kueng kuo, bu duan ren liou shang shia chang." (The Endless Changes of Matters in Nature Passed the Time, the Characters Continually Go Up and Come Down the Stage.) *XYanj.* 1987 Aug.: 14-26. Lang.: Chi.
China, People's Republic of: Beijing. 1987. Critical studies. ■Representation of time and space in the highly conventionalized Chinese opera.

3473 A, Jia. "Hsing dang cheng sh d i i." (The Meaning of Character's Categorization.) *XYanj.* 1987 Dec.: 66-67. Lang.: Chi.
China, People's Republic of. 1987. Technical studies. ■The necessity of the character's categorization when the actor plays Chinese opera.

3474 A, Jia. "Xi qu wu tai yi shu xu ni yu cheng shi de zhi yue guan xi." (The Relationship Between the Imitation of Actions and the Technique of Acting.) *XYanj.* 1987 Dec.; 24: 1-15. Lang.: Chi.
China, People's Republic of: Beijing. 1027 B.C.-1986 A.D. Critical studies. ■The stylized, symbolic acting technique in Chinese theatre makes the imitation of real life practical on the limited space of the stage.

3475 Chang, Pyng. "Sheau ban yuh-shuang her ta de yean chang ii shuh." (Ban Yuh-Shuang's Singing Art.) *XYanj.* 1987 Spr: 69-72. Lang.: Chi.
China, People's Republic of. Biographical studies. ■The performances of Chinese opera star Ba Yuh-Shuang and her work in Hsi Ch'ü.

3476 Chen, Gu-Yu. "Tan shou yan shen fa bu." (The Acting Techniques of Chinese Opera.) *XYishu.* 1985 Sum; 30: 115-146. Lang.: Chi.
China, People's Republic of. 1985. Critical studies. ■Basic acting techniques found in Chinese theatre.

3477 Chen, Xiao Lu. "Xi qu xie yi xing." (The Impressionism of Chinese Drama.) *XYishu.* 1985 Spr; 29: 21-31. Notes. Lang.: Chi.
China, People's Republic of. 1924-1985. Critical studies. ■Impressionism in Chinese drama, specifically acting.

3478 Chen, You Han. "Xi qu xing shi mei." (The Aesthetics of Chinese Drama.) *XYishu.* 1985 Spr; 29: 4-16. Lang.: Chi.
China, People's Republic of. 1949-1985. Critical studies. ■The distinctive features of Chinese drama.

3479 Deng, Sheau-Chiou. "Bei shii jiau rong, yih ia yi shye." (Comedy and Tragedy, Pressing and Harmonious.) *XYanj.* 1986 Sum : 31-32. Lang.: Chi.
China, People's Republic of. 1986. Historical studies. ■Ways to blend comedy and tragedy in Hsi Ch'ü.

3480 Du, Qin Yuan. "Hua ju duo yuan hua." (The Pluralism of Chinese Drama.) *XYishu.* 1985 Spr; 29: 17-20. Lang.: Chi.
China, People's Republic of. 1949-1985. Critical studies. ■Creativity in the Chinese arts.

3481 Dueng, Ji-Chang. "Chin chiang iau tzai gai ge juang chian jin." (The Method of Singing of Chin School Can be Further Developed.) *XYanj.* 1987 July: 54. Lang.: Chi.
China, People's Republic of. 1987. Historical studies. ■The nourishment and development of the Chin school of Chinese drama is needed. The

MUSIC-DRAMA: Chinese opera—Performance/production

singing style of Chin and the actual plays also need to be promoted and developed. More research needs to be done.

3482 Fan, Lan. "Lun shi chiu in ian de cheng shi shing." (The Characteristics of Dramatic Language.) *XYanj.* 1987 Mar.: 58-59 . Lang.: Chi.

China, People's Republic of. 1986. Historical studies. ■The characteristics of dramatic language includes dancing, music and singing. They represent the appearance and beautiful style of Chinese opera.

3483 Fang, Xin. "Yan yu yi shu zao xing tan tao." (Outlines of Stage Language.) *XYishu.* 1985 Sum; 30: 82-88. Notes. Lang.: Chi.

China, People's Republic of. 1930-1985. Empirical research. ■A scientific method to outline stage language, especially the effect of speed on language.

3484 Feng, Li-Chiang. "Ta Tsueng Li Iuan Sh Jia Liai." (She Comes From a Dramatic Family.) *XYanj.* 1987 Feb.: 64. Lang.: Chi.

China, People's Republic of. 1947-1985. Histories-sources. ■Interview with Mei Bau-Iue, daughter of Mei Lanfang. She talks about her involvement with Chinese opera.

3485 Gueng, I-Jiang. "Nan Fang Jing Jiu Dan Jiau Giai Ge Be Shian Chu—Fueng Tz-He." (The Revolutionary Pioneer of Female Characters in Southern Chinese Opera—Fueng Tz-He.) *XYanj.* 1987 July: 69-72. Lang.: Chi.

China, People's Republic of: Shanghai. 1888-1941. Biographical studies. ■The famous actor, Fueng Tz-He, and his great contribution to Chinese opera.

3486 Han, Deng-Iong. "Jung guo shi chiu fa jan gai kuang." (An Outline on the Development of Chinese Opera.) *XYanj.* 1987 Dec.: 7. Lang.: Chi.

China, People's Republic of. 1644-1987. Histories-specific. ■Brief historical sketch of the development of Chinese opera from the Ching dynasty to the present.

3487 Ho, Wei. "Lun hsi ch'ü sheng in de teh shing." (The Characteristics of Hsi Ch'ü's Voice.) *XYanj.* 1987 Spr: 27-30. Lang.: Chi.

China, People's Republic of. 1987. Historical studies. ■The difference between Hsi Ch'ü's vocal music and Western vocal music. Also the development of Hsi Ch'ü's vocal music.

3488 Hong, Shin. "Shi chiu gai ge d tzuo biau shian." (The Starting Point of the Reform of Chinese Opera.) *XYanj.* 1987 Dec.: 3-4. Lang.: Chi.

China, People's Republic of. 1987. Critical studies. ■Three main thrusts of the reform of Chinese opera: modern conciousness, other art forms and the reform of music.

3489 Hu, Zhi Feng. "Cong shi jian zhong ren shi A Jia de xi qu biao yan li lun." (Understanding A Jia's Acting Theory from Practice.) *XYanj.* 1987 Dec.; 24: 65-76. Lang.: Chi.

China, People's Republic of: Beijing. 1935-1986. Critical studies. ■Discusses the unique features of acting in the Chinese theatre: how actors use their own experiences, how to recreate a character on stage and how to express emotion through a stylized, symbolic way of acting.

3490 Huang, Guo-Chiang. "Shi chiu in iue kai ke suei shiang." (To Improve the Music of Chinese Opera.) *XYanj.* 1987 Mar.: 56-57. Lang.: Chi.

China, People's Republic of. 1986. Historical studies. ■Improving the music of Chinese opera through innovation.

3491 Huang, Sh-Lin. "Tan fu-ing i shu tan ueu." (An Investigation of the Art of Tan Fu-Ing.) *XYanj.* 1987 Aug.: 41-42. Illus.: Photo. 1. Lang.: Chi.

China, People's Republic of. 1900-1950. Empirical research. ■The acting of Chinese opera star Tan Fu-Ing.

3492 Huang, Su. "Tsung xi qu jiao yu kan xi qu qian tu." (Institutes and Futures in Theatre.) *XYishu.* 1985 Sum; 30: 10-15. Lang.: Chi.

China, People's Republic of. 1985. Critical studies. ■Drama education in China.

3493 Huang, Zai-Min. "Xian dai xi wu tai jie zou xi qu hua." (The Rhythm of Modern Chinese Drama.) *XYishu.* 1985 Spr; 29: 44-51. Notes. Lang.: Chi.

China, People's Republic of. 1949-1985. Critical studies. ■The rhythm in the Chinese theatre consists of the rhythm of script, action, music and stage design.

3494 I, Iuen. "Shiue jiue shian uei iue chu shian shen shiu iu lan ian jiau se jiang ching." (Shiue Jiue-Shian Imerses Himself in the Drama and Shiu Iu-Lan Plays the Character to Her Heart's Content.) *XYanj.* 1987 Aug.: 51. Lang.: Chi.

China, People's Republic of. 1954-1979. Critical studies. ■The Chinese opera stars Shiue Jiue-Shian and Shiu Iu-Lan and their highly spiritual performances.

3495 Ian, Chang-Ke. "Man tan shi chiu chuan tueng ho shian dai hu." (The Tradition and Modernization of Chinese Drama.) *XYanj.* 1987 May: 6-8. Lang.: Chi.

China, People's Republic of. 1986. Historical studies. ■Modernization and broadening of the traditional drama.

3496 Ian, Jueng. "Chou En-Lai Iu *Horng Lou Meng.*" (Chou En-Lai and *Dream of the Red Chamber.*) *XYanj.* 1987 July: 74. Lang.: Chi.

China, People's Republic of: Shanghai. 1957. Histories-sources. ■Chou En-Lai gives comments on a dialect opera version of *Horng Lou Meng (Dream of the Red Chamber).*

3497 In, Ming. "Shi chiu in iue: Mian ling je sh dai d trau jan." (The Music of Chinese Opera Faces Today's Challenges.) *XYanj.* 1987 Dec.: 18-22. Lang.: Chi.

China, People's Republic of: Kiangsu. 1987. Critical studies. ■The results of the Conference of the Musical Theory of Chinese Opera demonstrate that more musical instruments should be added to Chinese opera.

3498 Iuan, Sh-Hai. "Tan gu-cheng-hei de sh gai." (The Adaptation of the Play *Gu Cheng-Hei.*) *XYanj.* 1987 Aug.: 43-46. Illus.: Photo. B&W. 1. Lang.: Chi.

China, People's Republic of. 1967. Empirical research. ■A discussion of the adaptation of the acting, characters, singing and plot of the play *Gu Cheng-Hei.*

3499 Jou, Chii-Fuh. "Jea ding shing shi chiu daw yean de faa bau." (A Supposition Is Good for a Hsi Ch'u Director.) *XYanj.* 1986 Spr: 24-25. Filmography. Lang.: Chi.

China, People's Republic of. 1986. Historical studies. ■The director's dilemma in Hsi Ch'ü—how to unite action and scenery.

3500 Lee, Mojan. "Wo Tiu hsi ch'ü te i te chih chieh." (My Theatre Idea.) *XYanj.* 1987 June; 22: 14-24. Lang.: Chi.

China, People's Republic of. 1900-1986. Histories-specific. ■Analysis of the acting theory of Chinese opera—argues its style, content and characteristics.

3501 Li, Ching-Chen. "Chuan tong shi chiu i shian shin." (A New Image of the Traditional Chinese Opera.) *XYanj.* 1987 Dec.: 12. Lang.: Chi.

China, People's Republic of: Beijing. 1987. Critical studies. ■Comments on the performances at the Chinese Art Festival which includes Beijing opera, Szechwan opera and Hunan opera.

3502 Li, Huoh-Tzeng. "'Gau liuh-guei' beau yean jing yann." (The 'Gau Liuh-Guei' of Performance Experience.) *XYanj.* 1986 Sum : 50-52. Illus.: Photo. Print. B&W. Lang.: Chi.

China, People's Republic of. 1986. Biographical studies. ■Discussion of the career of Chinese opera actor Gau Liuh-Guei.

3503 Li, Jing-Guang. "Jueng guo jin diai shi chiu shu liu." (Modern Chinese Opera.) *XYanj.* 1987 June: 58-62. Lang.: Chi.

China, People's Republic of. 1986. Historical studies. ■The development of modern Chinese opera, especially the influence of politics.

3504 Li, Rau Kuen. "Kai Tuo Shi Cheu De Shin Jiu Mian." (Open a New Situation for Chinese Opera.) *XYanj.* 1987 Aug.: 7-8. Lang.: Chi.

China, People's Republic of. 1987. Critical studies. ■Recent Chinese opera productions reveal a need for new ideas in acting.

3505 Li, Tsuen-Jie; U, Jiun-Da. "Shi shu change chiang bi shu jing shing shin de tan suo." (The Singing in Chinese Opera Has to Evolve Through New Research.) *XYanj.* 1987 Aug.: 37-40. MU. Lang.: Chi.

MUSIC-DRAMA: Chinese opera—Performance/production

China, People's Republic of. 1986. Critical studies. ■Introduction to the new way of producing singing, musical accompaniment and instrumentation for Chinese opera.

3506   Lio, Jeng-Wei. "Txai ia su de shuang gue tiang tan lu." (Looking for a Route Between High and Low.) *XYanj.* 1987 Feb.: 71-80. Lang.: Chi.

China, People's Republic of. 1987. Historical studies. ■Four steps to make *Da Peng Ge* more popular: mix, borrow and reproduce the music, melodize the singing style, personalize the characters and make the emotions exquisite.

3507   Liu, I-Jen. "Chueng shin ren sh guen jiu i shu de jia j." (Recognizing the Value of the Art of the Opera—*Kun-Jiu.*) *XYanj.* 1987 Aug.: 47-48. Lang.: Chi.

China, People's Republic of. 1956-1986. Critical studies. ■Improving the value and content of *Kun-Jiu* by improving the acting and cultivating the performers.

3508   Liu, Szuch'i. "Kuei chou ch'ien chü hua teng chü shen mei t'e cheng pi chiao." (Comparison of Kuei Chou *ch'ien chü* and *Hua Teng* chü.) *XYanj.* 1987 June; 24: 44-70. Notes. Lang.: Chi.

China, People's Republic of. 1908-1986. Historical studies. ■History and comparison of the different aesthetics between two local Chinese operas.

3509   Liu, Tziozi-Fu. "Jen shi shuo guo jin tsiun de li iuan shi." (Cherish the Only Li-Iuan Drama.) *XYanj.* 1987 Feb.: 76-77. Lang.: Chi.

China, People's Republic of. 1986. Historical studies. ■Ways actors should improve themselves in the Li-Iuan drama.

3510   Liu, Yi-Zhen. "A-jia xi qu biao yan li lun de ji ge zhu yao fang mian." (The Main Aspects of A Jia's Theory of Acting.) *XYanj.* 1987 Dec.; 24: 16-44. Lang.: Chi.

China, People's Republic of: Beijing. 1950-1986. Critical studies. ■The main aspects of Chinese acting, according to A Jia's theory. Also refers to Stanislavskij's and Brecht's theories of acting.

3511   Ma, Shau-Po. "Ching Guo Fei In Ching Guo Mau—Ma Shau Po Tan Ha Jiu *Iang Guei Fei.*" (Ruined the Country Not for the Sake of Beautiful Women: Man Shaa-Po Comments on *Iang Guei Fei.*) *XYanj.* 1987 July: 80. Illus.: Photo. B&W. 1. Lang.: Chi.

China, People's Republic of. 1987. Reviews of performances. ■The play *Iang Guei-Fei* and its success.

3512   Mackerras, Colin. "Theatre in China's Sichuan Province." *ATJ.* 1987 Fall; 4(2): 191-204. Notes. Biblio. Illus.: Photo. B&W. 3. Lang.: Eng.

China, People's Republic of: Chengdu. 1985-1986. Reviews of performances. ■Status of Sichuan Theatre focusing on Sichuan opera and spoken drama. Reviews six performances and documents development and changes in Experimental Sichuan Opera Company.

3513   Pimpaneau, J.; Cai, Ke Jian, transl. "Yi ge yang de zhong guo xi qu guan." (A Westerner's Concept of Chinese Theatre.) *XYanj.* 1987 Dec.; 24: 77-87. Lang.: Chi.

China, People's Republic of: 1947-1986. Critical studies. ■A comparison between Chinese theatre and Western theatre. Differences lie in history, language and style. Includes an introduction to Kun opera.

3514   Sheu, Sheau-Ming. "Tarn kuen jiuh *mu dan ting* de in yuen." (Music Design in *The Peony Pavilion.*) *XYanj.* 1987 Spr: 67-69. Lang.: Chi.

China, People's Republic of. 1987. Historical studies. ■A Hsi Ch'ü drama, *The Peony Pavilion* and its good music design.

3515   Shia, Fa. "Guan Shu-Shuan Iu Dai Chi-Shia." (The Famous Actresses Guan Shu-Shuan and Dai Chi-Shia.) *XYanj.* 1987 Aug.: 13. Lang.: Chi.

China, People's Republic of. 1987. Biographical studies. ■Analysis of the careers of two Chinese opera actresses—Guan Shu-Shuan and Dai Chi-Shia.

3516   Shiau, Chin-Iuan. "Jong guo gu dai shi chiu chai jiau j mei shiue jia j." (The Aesthetical Value of the Clown in Chinese Classical Drama.) *XYanj.* 1987 Dec.: 35-40. Notes. Lang.: Chi.

China, People's Republic of. 1987. Critical studies. ■The Chinese opera clown has a special acting style incorporating humor, exaggeration to attract audience's attention.

3517   Shin, Feng-Shya. "I duann jiaw shyh de hwei yih." (A Memoir.) *XYanj.* 1987 Spr: 65-66. Lang.: Chi.

China, People's Republic of. 1987. Histories-sources. ■The story of a Hsi Ch'u actress.

3518   Shiu, Cheng-Bei. "Lian shiu mau shian de ren." (One Who Has Continual Adventures.) *XYanj.* 1987 Feb.: 65-66. Lang.: Chi.

China, People's Republic of. 1986. Histories-sources. ■Interview with Li Sh-Ji, a performing student at the Cheng dramatic school. Her efforts and hard work make her successful.

3519   Shiu, Hong-Pei. "Man tan chi pai i shu." (A Casual Comment on the Art of 'Chi-Pai'.) *XYanj.* 1987 Dec.: 58-65. Notes. Lang.: Chi.

China, People's Republic of. 1987. Critical studies. ■Comments on several performances of Chinese opera actor Chi-Pai.

3520   Su, I. "Jieng jiu jian sh." (Short History of Chinese Opera.) *XYanj.* 1986 Apr.: 49-60. Lang.: Chi.

China, People's Republic of. 1922-1987. Histories-sources. ■Overview of Chinese opera divided into two parts: the magazines and periodicals that talk about Chinese opera and biographical information on playwrights and critics.

3521   Sui, Sii-Cheng. "Jing chu tzay jeylii jug'der le guan jong." (Peking Opera Audiences in England.) *XYanj.* 1986 Win: 20. Lang.: Chi.

China, People's Republic of. UK-England. 1987. Historical studies. ■Large English audience for Beijing Opera.

3522   Sven, Yuh-Min. "Shyun pay jih shuh de mey lih." (The Shyun Art of Charm.) *XYanj.* 1986 Spr: 63-64. Illus.: Photo. Print. B&W. Lang.: Chi.

China, People's Republic of. 1986. Critical studies. ■Discusses difference singing styles of Shyun schools and compares them.

3523   Tan, Tzu-Hua. "Shi chiu lian chang iu ian in fa sheng fa." (The Singing Practice and the Method of Making Sound from the Throat.) *XYanj.* 1987 June: 41-43. Lang.: Chi.

China, People's Republic of. 1986. Historical studies. ■Training the Chinese opera actor to produce high sounds and improve the quality of the sound by using Italian singing techniques.

3524   Tarng, Shiang-yun. "Hsi ch'ü meng t'ai ch'i shou fa chan hsueh." (The Hsi Ch'ü of Montage.) *XYanj.* 1986 Spr: 21-23. Filmography. B&W. Lang.: Chi.

China, People's Republic of. 1986. Historical studies. ■Film montage enhances Chinese opera performance. Related to Media: Film.

3525   Tau, Shueng. "I Ho Jim Ji—Tan Tan Shi Sheu J Bi Iu Tz Uo Geng Shin." (Art and Skill—The Shortcomings and Reform of Chinese Opera.) *XYanj.* 1987 Aug.: 9-10. Lang.: Chi.

China, People's Republic of. 1987. Technical studies. ■Chinese actors have to create a new situation for themselves.

3526   Wang, Iong-Jing. "Sh tan shi chiu u dan d te jeng." (The Features of the Dance in Chinese Opera.) *XYanj.* 1987 Dec.: 23-26. Lang.: Chi.

China, People's Republic of. 960-1987. Histories-specific. ■The features of dance in Chinese opera: costume and props, dancing and acrobatics, hand gestures and dramatic function.

3527   Wang, Li-Ha. "Tzian tan shi chiu cheng sh ji chi gai." (A Talk About the Formulas of Chinese Opera and its Reform.) *XYanj.* 1987 Dec.: 14-17. Lang.: Chi.

China, People's Republic of. 1987. Critical studies. ■The reformation of the four main formulas of the Beijing opera: singing, speaking, acting and acrobatics, all of which should be re-created by the actors to attract a more modern audience.

3528   Wang, Min-Ing. "Jing hu chieng in iue uen shi ji." (The Birth of 'Jing Hu'.) *XYanj.* 1987 June: 66. Lang.: Chi.

China, People's Republic of. 1985-1986. Historical studies. ■The light music of Jing-Hu was created by Ru-Jiun Li in 1985. It is an important breakthrough in Chinese traditional music.

MUSIC-DRAMA: Chinese opera—Performance/production

3529 Wang, Pei-kuei. "Hua ju yan yuan sheng yue jiao xue." (The Vocal Classes of Actors.) *XYishu.* 1987 Sum; 38: 72-74. Lang.: Chi.
China, People's Republic of: Shanghai. 1949-1987. Historical studies. ■Vocal classes in China—the relationship between vocal training and performance.

3530 Wang, Ren-Yuan. "Luenn hsi ch'ü in yueh de teh shing luo yi." (The Characteristics of Hsi Ch'ü Music.) *XYanj.* 1987 Spr: 57-64. Lang.: Chi.
China, People's Republic of. 1987. Historical studies. ■The theme of unity and harmony in the music of Chinese opera.

3531 Wang, Shian-Ching. "S du lai ji hua shon ching." (An In-Depth Interview with Famous Beijing Opera Actress—Du Jin-Fan.) *XYanj.* 1987 Nov.: 68. Lang.: Chi.
China, People's Republic of. 1987. Histories-sources. ■Chinese opera actress Du Jin-Fan discusses her performance in Shantung province.

3532 Wang, Syu-Chyi. "Tai wan juh ming jing chu neu yean yuan guo sheau juong." (Peking Opera Actress, Guo Sheau-Juang, Talks About her Career.) *XYanj.* 1987 Spr: 58-61. Lang.: Chi.
China, People's Republic of. 1987. Histories-sources. ■Interview with Beijing opera actress Guo Sheau-Juang.

3533 Werle-Burger, Helga; Jiang, Zhi, transl. "Zhong guo xi qu chuan tong yu yin du kerala di fang de fan ju de bi jiao." (The Comparison Between Traditional Chinese Opera and the Buddhist Drama in Kerala in Hindu.) *XYanj.* 1987 Dec.; 24: 113-136. Lang.: Chi.
China, People's Republic of: Beijing. India. 1050-1968. Critical studies. ■Comparison of Chinese opera and the Buddhist plays of Kerala: stages, props, music, languages, characters and acting.

3534 Xiang, Geng. "Xi qu li lun gai zao he geng xin." (The Renovation of Drama.) *XYishu.* 1985 Sum; 30: 4-7. Lang.: Chi.
China, People's Republic of. 1985. Critical studies. ■Characteristics of Chinese drama.

3535 Xu, Pei. "Xian dai ke ji yu xi qu bian ge." (Technique and Concept in Modern Drama.) *XYishu.* 1985 Spr; 29: 52-59. Lang.: Chi.
China, People's Republic of. 1949-1985. Critical studies. ■Modern techniques combine new ideas with modern drama.

3536 Yang, Min. "Dao yan tong yuau yuan de he zuo." (Cooperation Between Director and Actors.) *XYishu.* 1985 Sum; 30: 104-114 . Notes. Lang.: Chi.
China, People's Republic of. 1955-1985. Critical studies. ■Directing techniques found in Chinese theatre.

3537 Ye, Tao. "Hua ju biao yan yi shu te zheng." (Drama's Play in Theatre.) *XYishu.* 1985 Sum; 30: 63-74. Notes. Lang.: Chi.
China, People's Republic of. 1985. Critical studies. ■Chinese theatre acting theories on stage.

3538 Yei, Heh-Lao. "Jea bao yun syh yean *Hung lou meng.*" (*The Dream of the Red Chamber*—Yin Guey-Fang Played It Four Times.) *XYanj.* 1986 Spr: 72-73. Illus.: Photo. Print. B&W. Lang.: Chi.
China, People's Republic of. 1945-1983. Historical studies. ■Discusses Yin Guey-Fang, who acted in the *Hung lou meng (The Dream of the Red Chamber)* in 1945, 1951, 1962 and 1983. The play was taken from one of the great novels of the Ching Dynasty.

3539 Zhou, Xu-Geng. "Guan yu tang xian zu de gai bian yuan ju ji qi ta." (The Adaptation of Yuan Opera by Tang Xian-Zu and Others.) *XYanj.* 1987 Dec.; 24: 178-187. Lang.: Chi.
China, People's Republic of: Beijing. 1279-1986. Critical studies. ■Discusses how to keep spirit of traditional Chinese opera and yet instill it with a modern sense. Specifically talks of Kun opera and making its acting style acceptable to modern audiences.

3540 Ding, Ian-Jau. "Tai wan pi ing i ren shiu fu neng." (Taiwan's Puppeteer Shiu Fu-Neng.) *XYanj.* 1987 Dec.: 17. Lang.: Chi.
Taiwan. 1987. Biographical studies. ■The life and skills of Chinese puppeteer Shiu Fu-Neng.

3541 Hwu, Yaw Heng. "Xi fan shi ju gai bian wei pin ju de wunti yi 'Yu-Wang-Cheng-Gu' wei li." (The Problems of 'Chinese Opera' Based on Western Drama: The Example of *A City of Desire*.) *ChWai.* 1987 Apr.; 15(11): 77-84. Lang.: Chi.
Taiwan: Taipei. 1986. Reviews of performances. ■*Yu-wang-cheng-gue (A City of Desire)* by Li Hui-min based on *Macbeth* and performed in the style of Beijing opera.

3542 Peng, Ge. "Kan Guo Sheau-Juang *Yian de-yi yuan.*" (A Review of Guo Sheau-Juang's *A Marriage of Good Fortune.*) *TaCh.* 1987 Feb.; 159: 47-48. Illus.: Photo. Print. B&W. 1. Lang.: Chi.
Taiwan: Taipei. 1987. Reviews of performances. ■A review of *A Marriage of Good Fortune* by Guo Sheau-Juang and Ciao Fuh Yeong from the aspect of acting and singing in comparison with the traditional business line.

Plays/librettos/scripts

3543 Chao, Yinhsiang; Chen, Ch'angwen. "Cheng chih chen sheng p'ing shih liao te hsin fa hsien." (Discovery of Cheng Chihchen's Biography.) *XYanj.* 1987 June; 22: 250-251. Lang.: Chi.
China. 1518-1595. Biographical studies. ■New evidence that playwright Cheng Chihchen lived from 1518-1595.

3544 Chiu, Liou-I. "Jian li nuo shi shiu in ian." (The Production of Nuo Hsi.) *XYanj.* 1987 Feb.: 74-80. Lang.: Chi.
China. 900. Historical research. ■The Chinese opera form *Nuo Hsi* is still popular in many areas. There are many kinds and each has its own special characteristics. They are often intermixed with religious motifs. More research needs to be done on the development of this form.

3545 Fan, Jien-Hung. "Chong *Mu Dan Ting: Iu-iuan-jin-Mong* liu chiu kang Du-Li-Niang chi ren." (From the Play *The Chinese Pavilion*: Six Songs To Portray the Female Character Du-Li-Niang.) *XYanj.* 1987 Nov.: 60-63. Lang.: Chi.
China. 1600-1700. Histories-specific. ■Through the six songs in this play, the leading female character Du-Li-Niang expresses her love dream and psychological struggle of passion.

3546 Gong, Chong-Mo. "Tang xian-zu yi wen ji zhu." (The Collection of Lost Writings by Tang Xian-Zu.) *XYanj.* 1987 June; 22: 282-289. Lang.: Chi.
China: Beijing. 1610-1742. Histories-sources. ■Collection of notes on lost short writings of Beijing opera playwright Tang Xian-Zu.

3547 Jang, A-Li. "*Tao hua shan* ji gou shin luen." (New Commentary on the Structure of *The Peach Blossom Fan.*) *XYanj.* 1987 Nov.: 64-68. Notes. Lang.: Chi.
China. 1700-1800. Critical studies. ■The leading character's unfortunate fate is the structure of this play.

3548 Jou, Jian-Tz. "'Bei jiu' iu jong go gu dian shi chiu." (Tragedy and Chinese Classical Drama.) *XYanj.* 1987 Dec.: 27-34. Lang.: Chi.
China. 960-1644. Histories-specific. ■A correct definition of Chinese classical 'tragedy'. Characteristics include subjects, endings, structure.

3549 Pu, Chien. "Lee k'aihsien chia shih k'ao." (Biography of the Origin of Lee K'aihsien.) *XYanj.* 1987 June; 22: 234-249. Notes. Lang.: Chi.
China. 1566-1620. Biographical studies. ■Life, family and career of Chinese opera playwright Lee K'aihsien.

3550 Shiau, De-Min. "Li Shy Jiuh De Shiam Shyr Ju Yi Chin Cheng." (The Historical Progress of Drama in a Course of Realism.) *XYanj.* 1987 July: 34-42. Notes. Lang.: Chi.
China. 1111 B.C.-1856 A.D. Historical studies. ■The development of Chinese historical drama.

3551 Sun, Ch'ungt'ao. "Szu sheng yüan kuan k'uei." (A View on *Szu Sheng Yüan.*) *XYanj.* 1987 June; 22: 206-227. Notes. Lang.: Chi.
China. 1521-1593. Critical studies. ■Analysis of the play by Hsü Wei.

3552 Xie, Bo-Liang. "Lun gu dai qu xu de wen hua shi yi yi." (The Meaning of Preface and Postscript in Ancient Chinese Culture.) *XYishu.* 1987 Sum; 38: 12-22. Lang.: Chi.

MUSIC-DRAMA: Chinese opera—Plays/librettos/scripts

China. 1200-1987. Historical studies. ■Preface and postscript are unique in Chinese dramatic scripts. There are different schools of thought about what they should contain.

3553 Xu, Hong-Tu. "Shi 'Shao-Lai'." (Interpreting 'Shao-Lai'.) *XYanj.* 1987 Dec.; 24: 266-267. Lang.: Chi.
China: Beijing. 206 B.C.-1368 A.D. Critical studies. ■The explanation of the term 'Shao-Lai' in Yuan drama. It means unsophisticated, innocent, gullible young men.

3554 Xu, Shuo Fang. "Sha shi bi ya zhong guo xi qu." (Shakespeare and Chinese Theatre.) *XYanj.* 1987 Dec.; 24: 88-112. Lang.: Chi.
China. 1279-1616. Historical studies. ■A comparison between Shakespeare and Yuan Chinese opera playwrights, Tang Xian-Zu and Guan Hanqing. Compares their theatrical activity, their lives and their works.

3555 Ye, Chang-Hai. "Lun zhong guo xi qu de zong ti xing." (The System of Chinese Drama.) *XYishu.* 1987 Sum; 38: 4-11. Lang.: Chi.
China. 1200-1987. Historical studies. ■The development of traditional Chinese drama.

3556 You, Lyh Cherng. "Lun yuan zalu de yuyian de liang yuan duei bi." (A Discourse on the Duality of the Language of the Plays During the Yuan Dynasty.) *ChWai.* 1987 Jan.; 15(8): 110-129. Notes. Illus.: Diagram. Print. B&W. 4. Lang.: Chi.
China. 1260-1368. Critical studies. ■The use of noble and common speech in the plays of the Yuan dynasty.

3557 Chang, Suoo-Fen. "Jong guo hsi ch'ü yu shu chyng-ti shi jiuh." (Hsi Ch'ü and its Lyrical Style.) *XYanj.* 1987 Spr: 19-26. Lang.: Chi.
China, People's Republic of. 1987. Historical studies. ■The lyrical writing structure of Chinese opera form of Hsi Ch'ü.

3558 Chiu, Ian. "Jueng guo shi chu de ju ti i sh." (The Subjective Consciousness in Chinese Opera.) *XYanj.* 1987 Aug.: 27-28. Lang.: Chi.
China, People's Republic of. 1111 B.C.-1987 A.D. Histories-general. ■The playwright in Chinese opera expresses his subjective consciousness through the play.

3559 Chuan-Jia, Jo. "Guo jiun hueng jiu tzuo feng ge jie shi." (Explanation of the Dramatic Works of Guo Jiun.) *XYanj.* 1987 Aug.: 70. Lang.: Chi.
China, People's Republic of. 1987. Histories-sources. ■Chinese playwright Guo Jiun talks of style. He cites the influence of his traditional Chinese background in poetry and historic tales on his plays as well as his personal experiences.

3560 Guo, Han-Cheng; Tang, Chuh-hen. "Duei jong gwo chi chou hin hua hu tyah pou de tyai ren shyh." (The Re-Recognition of the Essence of Chinese Classical Drama.) *XYanj.* 1987 July: 29-33. Lang.: Chi.
China, People's Republic of. 1127-1987. Historical studies. ■The theme and essence of Chinese classical drama.

3561 Hiou, Ching-Po. "Dang day hsi ch'ü tzay sy cheang jea iya shahng de lieh shyh." (Hsi Ch'ü Plays Became Very Poor in Value.) *XYanj.* 1987 Spr: 17-18. Lang.: Chi.
China, People's Republic of. 1987. Historical studies. ■Changing the dramatic structure of Hsi Ch'ü plays to reflect new ideologies.

3562 Huang, Guang-Shien. "Ju min jiu tzuo uei ming lun pian lun." (A Fragment about the Famous Dramatist—Uei Ming-Lun.) *XYanj.* 1987 Dec.: 69-70. Notes. Lang.: Chi.
China, People's Republic of. 1987. Biographical studies. ■An introduction to the famous Chinese opera dramatist Uei Ming-Lun.

3563 Hwang, Chyang. "Uen guu dean hsi ch'ü de jin cherng shing." (Inheriting the Classics of Hsi Ch'ü.) *XYanj.* 1986 Spr: 41-46. Lang.: Chi.
China, People's Republic of. 1986. Historical studies. ■Studying the classics of Hsi Ch'ü by selecting materials from Chinese history.

3564 Iou-Su, Li. "Ts pan jin lian kan shi chiu tzueng ti i sh de bian ge." (The Change in Dramatic Ideology.) *XYanj.* 1987 Aug.: 71-73. Lang.: Chi.

China, People's Republic of. 1987. Critical studies. ■The tendency of modern drama in Chinese theatre is leaning toward philosophy. This tendency makes the artistic appeal of theatre stronger to the audience.

3565 Jang, I-Ho. "Jueng guo shi chiu luen—ren li pian." (Chinese Comedy—Characters.) *XYanj.* 1987 Feb.: 7-14. Lang.: Chi.
China, People's Republic of. 1986. Historical studies. ■Analysis of Chinese comedy: like tragedy, it has specialized characters whose stable characteristics are strongly emphasized and who have a childlike genius.

3566 Ji, Gin; Shan, Song-Lin; Cheng, Zhang. "Sui-chang fa xiang Tang Xian-Zu san pian lun wen." (Three Essays by Tang Xian-Zu are Discovered in Sui-Chang.) *XYanj.* 1987 Dec.; 24: 221-226. Lang.: Chi.
China, People's Republic of: Beijing. 1279-1983. Histories-sources. ■The discovery of essays by Tang Xian-Zu about his life and career.

3567 Juo, Guo-Chiong. "Jong guo go dian shi chiu ben r tzai tan." (The Discussion of Essential Qualities of Chinese Classical Comedy.) *XYanj.* 1987 Nov.: 17-24. Notes. Lang.: Chi.
China, People's Republic of. 1987. Critical studies. ■Falsehood as the essential quality of the Chinese classical comedy.

3568 Kuei, An. "Guan iu shi chiu ming iuen de tan suo." (Probe the Fate of Drama.) *XYanj.* 1987 June: 10-12. Lang.: Chi.
China, People's Republic of. 1986. Historical studies. ■How the needs of modern society and audiences are widening the emphasis on traditional ethics in Chinese opera.

3569 Liu, Bieng-Shian. "Sha jiu ian chu juong go hua shu ping." (A Comment on the Performance Which Adapts Shakespeare's Plays to Chinese Opera Style.) *XYanj.* 1987 Dec.: 75-80. Notes. Lang.: Chi.
China, People's Republic of. 1987. Critical studies. ■How to adapt Shakespeare to Chinese opera.

3570 Ma, Ie. "Shi chiu dan ha tzian i." (A Talk About 'Light' Conflict of Chinese Opera.) *XYanj.* 1987 Dec.: 13. Lang.: Chi.
China, People's Republic of. 1987. Critical studies. ■How to highlight the outer conflict and stress the inner struggle of the conflict and psychology of the characters.

3571 Mau, Shiau-iu. "Chong jian i uei je shin sheng." (Reconstruction Means Rebirth.) *XYanj.* 1987 Dec.: 9. Lang.: Chi.
China, People's Republic of. 1987. Critical studies. ■The modern playwright in the Chinese theatre should develop a 'modern sense' of dramaturgy to bridge the ancient, classical drama with the new forms of Chinese opera.

3572 Ming, Jou. "Jueng guo gu dian shi chiu de bei jiu jing shen." (The Tragic Spirit of Chinese Classical Opera.) *XYanj.* 1987 May: 45-47. Illus.: Photo. Print. B&W. 2. Lang.: Chi.
China, People's Republic of. 1986. Historical studies. ■Analysis of Chinese tragedy—characteristics, problems and spirit.

3573 Sheau, Shyong. "I gen syyjee duey shengjee de faang wenn." (The Dead Visit the Living.) *XYanj.* 1986 Sum: 53-54. Illus.: Photo. B&W. Lang.: Chi.
China, People's Republic of. 1987. Historical studies. ■The theme of 'all men are brothers' in Chinese opera.

3574 Tan, Jian-Jing. "Wei shi chiu wen shyue i biam." (An Augur for the Literature of Chinese Drama.) *XYanj.* 1987 July: 21. Lang.: Chi.
China, People's Republic of. 1987. Historical studies. ■Call for high quality of dramatic texts, especially for Beijing opera.

3575 Tzuoo, Shyan. "Dong hsi ch'ü guan tan daw kuen jiuh teh diem." (Characteristics of Hsi Ch'ü.) *XYanj.* 1987 Spr: 62-63. Lang.: Chi.
China, People's Republic of. 1987. Historical studies. ■Characteristics, value and development in Chinese drama.

3576 Wan, Yun Jun. "Li shi ju yu mei xue jia zhi." (Politicization and Aesthetics in Drama.) *XYishu.* 1985 Sum; 30: 49-53. Lang.: Chi.
China, People's Republic of. 1985. ■Historical people in the plays of Chinese theatre.

MUSIC-DRAMA: Chinese opera—Plays/librettos/scripts

3577   Xu, Qing-Shan. "Fou ding—Zhong guo xi qu de xi wang." (Negation—The Expectation of Chinese Theatre.) *XYishu*. 1985 Sum; 30: 8-9. Lang.: Chi.
China, People's Republic of. 1951-1985. ■The new Chinese drama.

3578   Yang, Yong. "Hsi ch'ü yan faan yinn shiann shyr sheng hiuo yaw shyh guan jong fuh meei chyng chiuh." (Hsi Ch'ü Needs to Reflect the Real Life of its Audience.) *XYanj*. 1987 Spr: 66. Lang.: Chi.
China, People's Republic of. 1987. Critical studies. ■The need for Hsi Ch'ü drama to reflect the life and needs of its current audience.

3579   Zhu, Ying-Hui. "Xi qu xing shi chuang xin." (The Alteration of Chinese Drama.) *XYishu*. 1985 Spr; 29: 34-43. Notes. Lang.: Chi.
China, People's Republic of. 1919-1985. Critical studies. ■The new situation of Chinese drama.

Reference materials

3580   Pong, Fei. "Jie shau bau tzuen iu Taiwan juong iang ian jiu iuan d jen guei shu ji." (Introduction to Precious Books Kept in the Academia Sinica in Taiwan.) *XYanj*. 1987 Dec.: 73-74. Lang.: Chi.
Taiwan. 1987. ■Source books containing many ancient references to Chinese folk songs, folklore, original scripts of the Beijing opera and the Kun opera.

Relation to other fields

3581   Kuo, Ying-de; Li, Zhen-yu. "Lun tang xian zhu wen hua yi shi de bei ju chong tu." (Tragic Conflicts within Tang Xian-Zhu's Cultural Sentiments.) *XYanj*. 1987 Dec.; 24: 203-220. Lang.: Chi.
China: Beijing. 1550-1616. Historical studies. ■Tragic conflicts in Tang Xian-Zu's cultural conscience from the view of aesthetics, philosophy of life and social conditions in the Yuan Dynasty.

3582   Shan, Dong Sheng. "Xi qu ren tsai cheng tsai gui lu." (Questionnaire on Training and Scholars' Inevitability.) *XYishu*. 1985 Sum; 30: 16-23. Lang.: Chi.
China, People's Republic of. 1983-1985. Empirical research. ■The results of a drama questionnaire reveal that parents influence children's drama education.

3583   Wang, Iuen-Mieng. "Dang dai i sh iu shi chiu ge shin." (The Reform of Drama and Contemporary Ideology.) *XYanj*. 1987 Sep.: 7-9. Lang.: Chi.
China, People's Republic of. 1987. Critical studies. ■The influence of current ideological movements on the development of modern Chinese plays. The characteristics of current plays are: open and broad, revolutionary and creative, competitive, democratic and political.

Research/historiography

3584   Wang, Ji-S. "Bian shi iuan min jian sh min jiu pien & clu bu she shiang." (A Rough Plan to Distinguish the Unknown Plays of the Iuan and Ming Dynasties.) *XYanj*. 1987 Nov.: 49-53. Lang.: Chi.
China. 1227-1644. Histories-specific. ■Understanding the original and developing conditions of Chinese northern classical drama, especially the unknown plays.

3585   Sun, Tsung-Tau. "Jong guo nan shi ian jiu r jian tiau." (An Examination of the Research of Chinese Southern Classical Drama.) *XYanj*. 1987 Nov.: 36-48. Lang.: Chi.
China, People's Republic of. 1960-1987. Historical studies. ■Three periods of research into Chinese classical southern drama.

Theory/criticism

3586   Gang, Chieng-Fu. "Li-iu de shi chiu iu ge w jiu." (The Opera of Li-Iu and Sing and Song Drama.) *XYanj*. 1987 Apr.: 45-48 . Lang.: Chi.
China. Japan. 1596-1876. Historical studies. ■The Chinese opera form, Li Li Ueng Sh Jueng Chiu, was very popular in Japan because it was close to Japanese song and dance drama.

3587   Jou, Gwo-Shong. "Jong Gwo Guo Dain Shi Tiuh Ben Jyr De Jer Shyue Tan Tao." (Philosophical Research into the

Essence of Chinese Classical Comedy.) *XYanj*. 1987 July: 15-21. Notes. Lang.: Chi.
China. 1127-1368. Histories-specific. ■The essence of Chinese classical comedy is 'untruth', which belongs to the subjective spirit of the main character.

3588   Nai, Li. "Jong guo shi chiu de shian juang ji chi wai la fa jan de yu tseh." (The Present Phenomenon and Prediction of Chinese Drama.) *XYanj*. 1987 July: 5-10. Illus.: Photo. B&W. 1. Lang.: Chi.
China. 1100 B.C.-1987 A.D. Historical studies. ■The development of Chinese traditional drama from ancient times to the present and a prediction for the future.

3589   Shian, Tzuo-Ming. "Gu dian mei shiue d shin gang shian." (The New Contribution of the Aesthetics of Classical Drama.) *XYanj*. 1987 Dec.: 45. Notes. Lang.: Chi.
China. 1386-1644. Critical studies. ■The famous dramatist and theoretician of Chinese opera Meng Cheng-Shuen and his theory of performance on stage.

3590   Suen, Sh-Ji. "Iue jiu ming ming de shin fa shian." (The New Discovery of the Denomination of Iue Drama.) *XYanj*. 1987 Jan.: 75. Lang.: Chi.
China. 1935-1938. Historical studies. ■Using new historical information, Iue drama actually began in 1935 in Ning-Po, three years earlier than in Shanghai.

3591   "Shi chiu huei shiao liang ma." (Is Chinese Opera Dying?)*XYanj*. 1987 Feb.: 4-5. Lang.: Chi.
China, People's Republic of. 1986. Historical studies. ■The defense of Chinese opera. It will not die because it has a deep historical background, the solid foundation of audiences and good Chinese opera troupes.

3592   Ch'ang, Chih-Ch'i. "Shi tai hy huan shi chiu de li hsing dain ha." (The Summons of Modern Time Lights the Nationality in Chinese Traditional Drama.) *XYanj*. 1987 July: 11-14. Lang.: Chi.
China, People's Republic of. 1787-1990. Critical studies. ■Recommends change in the conventional style of Chinese drama and the establishment of a new aesthetical idea.

3593   Chen, Jin-Iuan. "Li shi chiu chuang tzou de fan sze." (Historical Drama.) *XYanj*. 1987 Feb.: 15-20. Lang.: Chi.
China, People's Republic of. 1986. Historical studies. ■A discussion of the solutions and improvements to Chinese historical drama.

3594   Chiu, Iong-Chuen. "Mei guo ching shau nian iu jueng guo jing chu." (American Youth and Chinese Opera.) *XYanj*. 1987 May: 96. Lang.: Chi.
China, People's Republic of. 1985. Historical studies. ■The author's travels to the United States to teach Chinese opera to students. Their enthusiasm, interest and quick learning impressed the author.

3595   Chu, Da-Shu. "Shi Cheu Uei Ji Iu Shi Cheu Gai Ge." (The Crisis and Improvement in Chinese Opera.) *XYanj*. 1987 Aug.: 4-6 . Lang.: Chi.
China, People's Republic of. 1987. Histories-general. ■The crisis in Chinese opera and ways to improve it.

3596   Feng, Chi-Iueng. "Chu kan li iuan shi." (The First Sight of Chinese Opera.) *XYanj*. 1987 Feb.: 74-75. Lang.: Chi.
China, People's Republic of. 1986. Historical studies. ■A new way of looking at the history of Chinese opera—discovering new ideas from old traditions.

3597   Guo, Han-Cheng; Jang, I-Ho. "Luen jueng guo shi chiu de mei shiue s shiang." (The Idea of Aesthetics in Chinese Opera.) *XYanj*. 1987 Mar.: 10. Lang.: Chi.
China, People's Republic of. 960 B.C.-1987 A.D. Historical studies. ■The main characteristics of the Chinese aesthetic: directness in emotional portrayal and the happy ending.

3598   Jiang, Shing-I. "Shi chiu i shu tzuo shiang sh jie d bu sheng." (Chinese Opera Faces the World.) *XYanj*. 1987 Dec.: 5-7. Lang.: Chi.
China, People's Republic of. 1987. Histories-sources. ■Proceedings of the National Academic Conference of Chinese Classical Drama between Chinese opera academics and foreign professors.

MUSIC-DRAMA: Chinese opera—Theory/criticism

3599 Juo, Guo-Chiong. "Jong guo go dian shi chiu ben r tzai tan." (The Discussion of Essential Qualities of Chinese Classical Comedy.) *XYanj.* 1987 Nov.: 17-24. Notes. Lang.: Chi.

China, People's Republic of. 1987. Histories-specific. ■Falsehood as the essential quality of the Chinese classical comedy.

3600 Li, Jueng-Chiuan. "Ian an pieng jiu ian jiou iuan." (The Chinese Opera Research Center of Ian-An.) *XYanj.* 1987 June: 63-65. Lang.: Chi.

China, People's Republic of. 1942-1986. Historical studies. ■The formation of the Ian-An Chinese Opera Research Center, in 1942, to do research on Chinese opera and to improve it.

3601 Liang, Ding-Shan. "Shi chiu shu d shuong chiang tzu ho." (The Amphi-Construction on the Art of Chinese Opera.) *XYanj.* 1987 Dec.: 10-12. Lang.: Chi.

China, People's Republic of. 1987. Critical studies. ■A new aesthetic for the new forms of Chinese theatre.

3602 Liang, Sh-Sheng. "Iu jiu sheng shuai shiau jang luen." (The Growth and Decline of Iu Drama.) *XYanj.* 1987 June: 24-26. Lang.: Chi.

China, People's Republic of. 1986. Historical studies. ■History and some possible reasons for and solutions to the decline of Iu drama.

3603 Lin, Iu-Shi. "Bau chi shi chiu shian miang mei shiu ge shieng." (Maintaining the Aesthetic Characteristics of Chinese Opera.) *XYanj.* 1987 Oct.: 4. Lang.: Chi.

China, People's Republic of. 1987. Histories-sources. ■The author's personal response to productions presented during the Chinese Art Festival. The plays presented have tried to please the aesthetic desire of the public while introducing new aesthetic concepts to their audience.

3604 Lin, Ke Huan. "Hua ju gai ge bi tan." (Drama Reform in China.) *XYishu.* 1985 Spr; 29: 65-78. Lang.: Chi.

China, People's Republic of. 1949-1985. Historical studies. ■Seminar for the modern theatre in China.

3605 Liou, Ien-Pu. "Uang guo wei sueng iuan shi chiu shih pieng luen." (The Criticism of Wang Guo-Wei's Dramatic History of Sueng Iuan.) *XYanj.* 1987 Feb.: 38-44. Lang.: Chi.

China, People's Republic of. 1986. Historical studies. ■The problems and importance of Wang Guo-Wei's dramatic history of Iuen.

3606 Peng, Jau-Chi. "Tsueng shi chiu biao ian te jeng tan hua jiu jia chang." (From the Specialty of Performance to the Addition of Singing of Modern Drama.) *XYanj.* 1987 June: 29-30. Lang.: Chi.

China, People's Republic of. 1986. Technical studies. ■An important aspect of Chinese opera is its use of special body language to reveal character. It is not dependent upon spoken language.

3607 Sheng, Shou. "Ing dang iou fen shi de kan dai shi chiu shing shih." (We Should Treat Drama Style with Analytical Methods.) *XYanj.* 1987 June: 13-15. Lang.: Chi.

China, People's Republic of. 1986. Historical studies. ■Ways to improve Chinese opera.

3608 Shie, Bo-Liang. "Jueng kuo gu dai shi shu shiu ba de pi ping mu sh." (The Critical Form of the Preface and the Postscript in Chinese Classical Drama.) *XYanj.* 1987 Aug.: 29-36. Lang.: Chi.

China, People's Republic of. 1111 B.C.-1987 A.D. Critical studies. ■Using a certain critical form, we can categorize the preface and postscript of Chinese drama into four forms: historical, moral, stylistic and psychological criticism.

3609 Shiu, Shiang-Lin. "Tang xian zu iu ben se shuo." (Tang Xian-Zu and the Original Character.) *XYanj.* 1987 June: 55-57. Lang.: Chi.

China, People's Republic of. 700-1986. Historical studies. ■The theory of the 'original character' in Chinese opera developed by Tang Xian-Zu.

3610 Shung, Cheng-Iu. "Shuo chang dau duan." (Long or Short.) *XYanj.* 1987 June: 31-36. Lang.: Chi.

China, People's Republic of. 700-1986. Technical studies. ■The effect of aesthetics on the length of Chinese plays.

3611 Sun, Tsung-Tau. "Jong guo nan xi ian jiu r jian tiau." (An Examination of the Research of Chinese Southern Classical Drama.) *XYanj.* 1987 Nov.: 36-48. Lang.: Chi.

China, People's Republic of. 1960-1987. Historical studies. ■Three periods of research into Chinese classical southern drama.

3612 Wang, Chao. "Erh jen chuan te huo huo te erh jen chuan." (A Commune Theatre.) *XYanj.* 1987 June; 22: 71-81. Notes. Lang.: Chi.

China, People's Republic of. 1900-1986. Historical studies. ■Discussion of the commune and improvisation theory in the opera of Chi Lin.

3613 Wang, Kuei. "Hsi ch'ü ts'ung mei meng chung hsing lai." (Wake Up! Chinese Opera.) *XYanj.* 1987 June; 22: 25-30. Lang.: Chi.

China, People's Republic of. 1900-1986. Historical studies. ■Argues for modern ideas and revised concepts to reinvigorate Chinese drama.

3614 Wian, Wiou. "Shi dai shi shi chiu de iau lan." (Era is the Cradle of Chinese Opera.) *XYanj.* 1987 June: 17-20. Lang.: Chi.

China, People's Republic of. 1986. Technical studies. ■Improvements in the function and purpose of Chinese opera.

3615 Wu, Fang. "Xi qu gai ge yu guan nian gai ge." (Revolution of Drama and Its Concept in China.) *XYishu.* 1985 Spr; 29: 60-63. Lang.: Chi.

China, People's Republic of. 1949-1985. Historical studies. ■Different ideas leading to the modernization of Chinese drama.

3616 Hu, Jian. "Lai xin lun xi qu biao yan yi shu." (A Theory of Gotthold E. Lessing.) *XYishu.* 1985 Sum; 30: 75-78. Lang.: Chi.

Germany. China, People's Republic of. 1770-1985. Historical studies. ■Outlines the theories of G. E. Lessing and discusses how his theories can be practical in the Chinese theatre.

Musical theatre

Administration

3617 Shuster, Nan. "The Cat's Meow." *PAC.* 1985 Sum; 22(2): 15-20. Illus.: Photo. Print. B&W. 2. Lang.: Eng.

Canada: Toronto, ON. 1985. Biographical studies. ■A profile of Marlene Smith, the producer of the Canadian production of *Cats*, concerning its opening in Toronto.

3618 Kowalke, Kem H. "Is Anyone Minding the Score." *KWN.* 1987 Spr; 5(1): 4-5. Illus.: Photo. Print. B&W. 1. Lang.: Eng.

USA: New York, NY. Germany: Berlin. 1929-1987. Historical studies. ■Editorial response to attacks on the Weill Foundation on grounds of inconsistency in licensing of Weill scores. Justified position by reference to precedent established by Weill and Lenya.

Design/technology

3619 Jeary, Steve. "Fitting." *Sin.* 1987; 21(2): 13. Illus.: Photo. B&W. 1. Lang.: Eng.

UK-England: London. 1987. Technical studies. ■Machinery to be installed in Her Majesty's Theatre for *Phantom of the Opera*.

3620 Hale, Alice M. "Bringing a Smile to Broadway." *ThCr.* 1987 Jan.; 21(1): 18-22, 41-45. Illus.: Photo. Dwg. Lighting. B&W. 7. Lang.: Eng.

USA: New York, NY. 1986. Technical studies. ■Integration of the technical and staging aspects of the musical *Smile*.

3621 LaRue, Michèle. "Production Casebook: Barnum, Hokum and Humbug: Staging P.T.'s Life." *ThCr.* 1987 Jan.; 21(1): 30-31, 53-55. Illus.: Diagram. B&W. 4. Lang.: Eng.

USA: Memphis, TN. 1986. Technical studies. ■Design problems of simulating a circus for *Barnum*. Related to Mixed Entertainment: Circus.

3622 Libbon, Robert. "Don't Be a Sucker—Rig for Safety." *ThCr.* 1987 Jan.; 21(1): 32-33, 55-58. Illus.: Diagram. B&W. 6. Lang.: Eng.

USA. 1986. Technical studies. ■Directions for rigging all special circus effects for *Barnum*. Related to Mixed Entertainment: Circus.

MUSIC-DRAMA: Musical theatre—Design/technology

3623 Watson, Lee. "Watson on the Performing Arts." *L&DA.* 1987 Dec.; 17(12): 48. Lang.: Eng.
USA: New York, NY. 1987. Reviews of performances. ■Review of production and its lighting for *Anything Goes* at the Vivian Beaumont Theatre.

Institutions

3624 Marin, Ferenc. "Az Evitától a Szupersztárig. Beszélgetés Várkonyi Mátyással, a Rock Szinház igazgatójával." (From *Evita* to *Jesus Christ Superstar.* Interview with Mátyás Várkonyi, Director of the Rock Theatre.) *Krit.* 1987 June(6): 9-11. Illus.: Photo. B&W. 9. Lang.: Hun.
Hungary. 1980-1987. Histories-sources. ■This unusual theatrical venture, the Rock Theatre, has a real chance of rejuvenating the musical theatre traditions in Hungary. The director of the young theatrical company speaks about the best productions, guest performances and their difficulties.

3625 Rosenbaum, Helen. "Bruce Yeko: A Matter of Records." *TheaterW.* 1987 Oct.; 2(7): 30-32. Illus.: Photo. Poster. B&W. 5. Lang.: Eng.
USA: New York, NY. 1962-1981. Biographical studies. ■Profile of leading producer of the recorded theatre: career, and efforts to preserve music to the many versions of the *Forbidden Broadway* musicals.

Performance/production

3626 Jackson, Felix. "Your Place, or Mine?: An 'Un-German' Affair." *KWN.* 1987 Fall; 5(2): 5. Lang.: Eng.
Germany: Berlin. 1932. Historical studies. ■An excerpt from an unpublished biography *A Quiet Man: Kurt Weill, His Life and His Times* written by Felix Jackson circa 1970. Focuses on dinner at von Mendelssohn's at which Weill realizes the potential of the Nazi hatred of the Jews.

3627 Mercado, Mario R. "A Podium with a View: Recollections by Maurice Abravanel." *KWN.* 1987 Spr; 5(1): 6-8. Notes. 1. Lang.: Eng.
Germany: Berlin. 1922-1980. Histories-sources. ■The recollections of Kurt Weill's student who later became Weill's music director for his Broadway productions. Specific notes on *Knickerbocker Holiday, Lady in the Dark, One Touch of Venus* and *A Flag is Born.*

3628 Weill, Kurt; Hinton, Stephen. "Say No to Mediocrity! The Crisis of Musical Interpretation." *KWN.* 1987 Fall; 5(2): 6-7. Illus.: Photo. Print. B&W. 1. Lang.: Eng.
Germany: Berlin. 1925. Critical studies. ■Attack on the declining performance values accelerated by sociological and economic changes in the Weimar Republic.

3629 "A kaktusz virága." (The Cactus Flower.) *Krit.* 1987 Nov.(11): 35. Lang.: Hun.
Hungary: Budapest. 1987. Reviews of performances. ■The summer production of Barillet and Grédy's musical *Fleur de cactus* presented by the Gaiety Theatre at the Hild Court directed by István Kazán.

3630 Almási, Miklós. "A nyomorultak." (Les Misérables.) *Krit.* 1987 Dec.(12): 39-40. Lang.: Hun.
Hungary: Budapest. 1987. Reviews of performances. ■Miklós Szinetár's direction produced a fast-rolling, highly spectacular performance of Claude-Michel Schönberg and Alain Boublil's musical by the full company of the Budapest Rock Theatre, supported by some guest artists.

3631 Illisz, László. "Lionel Bart: Oliver." *Krit.* 1987 June(6): 41. Lang.: Hun.
Hungary: Budapest. 1986. Reviews of performances. ■Review of the successful production of Lionel Bart's musical at the Arany János Theatre staged by György Korcsmáros.

3632 Nánay, István. "Oliverek. Egy musical három előadása." (Olivers: Three Performances of a Musical.) *Sz.* 1987 Mar.; 20(3): 25-28. Illus.: Photo. B&W. 3. Lang.: Hun.
Hungary: Budapest, Békéscsaba, Zalaegerszeg. 1986. Reviews of performances. ■Notes on three performances of Lionel Bart's musical *Oliver* in Hungary.

3633 Stuber, Andrea. "A lovag és szíve hölgye. Szakácsi Sándor és Molnár Piroska a La Mancha lovagjá ban." (The Knight and His Heart's Lady: Sándor Szakácsi and Piroska Molnár

in *The Man of La Mancha.*) *Sz.* 1987 Nov.; 20(11): 29-31. Illus.: Photo. B&W. 1. Lang.: Hun.
Hungary: Pécs. 1987. Reviews of performances. ■Two outstanding actor performances at the Summer Theatre in Pécs: Sándor Szakácsi as Don Quijote and Piroska Molnár as Aldonza in *The Man of la Mancha* directed by László Bagossy.

3634 Burke, Michael. "Pact's *Pirates* and *Student Prince.*" *Scenaria.* 1987 Jan.; 72: 27-31. Illus.: Photo. B&W. 2. Lang.: Eng.
South Africa, Republic of: Johannesburg. 1986. Reviews of performances. ■Review of *Pirates* and *Student Prince* performed in Johannesburg and Durban and suggestions for improvement.

3635 Burke, Michael. "PACOF's *Hello Dolly.*" *Scenaria.* 1987 Apr.; 75: 39-41. Illus.: Photo. 3. Lang.: Eng.
South Africa, Republic of: Bloemfontein. 1987. Reviews of performances. ■Review of *Hello Dolly* in Bloemfontein, emphasis on audience interaction.

3636 Dahlberg, Christer. "Spelman på taket—en dagbok om teaterarbete." (Fiddler on the Roof—A Diary About the Work of Theatre.) *Teaterf.* 1987; 20(6): 12-13. Illus.: Dwg. Lang.: Swe.
Sweden: Bollnäs. 1987. Histories-sources. ■The director writes about the staging of the musical with amateurs.

3637 Skoglundh, Urban. "Drakar och demoner i Handen." (Dragons and Demons at Handen.) *Teaterf.* 1987; 20(5): 4-6. Illus.: Photo. Lang.: Swe.
Sweden: Handen. 1987. Historical studies. ■Collaboration of author Stefan Stenudd and amateur theatre group RoJ in rock-opera *Draker och Demoner (Dragons and Demons)* as part of work with pre-delinquent youth.

3638 Salinas, Mike. "The Follies of 1987: A Ghost Story with a Difference." *TheaterW.* 1987 Aug 17; 1: 8-16. Illus.: Photo. Chart. 10. Lang.: Eng.
UK-England: London. USA: New York, NY. 1987. Critical studies. ■Comparison between the failed 1971 production and critically and commercially successful 1987 London revival of Stephen Sondheim's *Follies* directed by Harold Prince.

3639 "Singing Broadway and Popular Music Without Hurting Your Voice." *EN.* 1985 Oct.; 70(10): 5-6. Lang.: Eng.
USA: New York, NY. 1985. Critical studies. ■Music Theatre Committee of the New York Singing Teachers Association (NYSTA) held symposium with many teachers, doctors and performers giving advice to singers.

3640 Barbour, David. "The Red Menace Returns." *TheaterW.* 1987 Dec 21-27; 1(19): 31-34. 3. Lang.: Eng.
USA: New York, NY. 1965-1987. Reviews of performances. ■Reviews and comparisons of two productions of *Flora, the Red Menace.* Brief history of each production and notes on how the latest version differs from the original.

3641 Dobrin, Darlene. "Lillias White: A New Kind of Dreamgirl." *TheaterW.* 1987 Oct.; 2(7): 28-29. Illus.: Photo. B&W. 2.
USA: New York, NY. 1960-1987. Biographical studies. ■Profile of actress who recreated the role of Effie in *Dreamgirls.* Her origins in musical theatre and current accomplishments.

3642 Driscoll, Terry. "*Henry, Sweet Henry.*" *TheaterW.* 1987 Dec 7-13; 1(17): 35-37. Illus.: Photo. 3. Lang.: Eng.
USA: New York, NY. 1967. Reviews of performances. ■Comprehensive history and review of the 1967 musical *Henry, Sweet Henry.* Includes excerpts from reviews of the day.

3643 Driscoll, Terry. "*King of Hearts.*" *TheaterW.* 1987 9 Nov.; 1(13): 27-29. Illus.: Photo. B&W. 4. Lang.: Eng.
USA: New York, NY. 1978-1987. Historical studies. ■Producer and authors discuss financial, technical and critical reasons for the failure of *King of Hearts,* a musical with music and lyrics by Peter Link and Jacob Brackman, and book by Steve Tesich.

3644 Driscoll, Terry. "*Breakfast at Tiffany's.*" *TheaterW.* 1987 Dec 21-27; 1(19): 36-39. 3. Lang.: Eng.

MUSIC-DRAMA: Musical theatre—Performance/production

USA: New York, NY, Philadelphia, PA, Boston, MA. 1958-1966. Reviews of performances. ■History and reviews of *Breakfast at Tiffany's*, the 1966 musical that closed before it opened.

3645 Drutman, Brian. "The Birth of the Passing Show." *PasShow.* 1987 Sum; 11(1): 1-3. Illus.: Photo. B&W. 3. Lang.: Eng.

USA: New York, NY. 1912-1913. Historical studies. ■History of the first Passing Show: a challenge to the Ziegfeld Follies.

3646 Feldman, Helaine. "U.S., Soviets Complete Children's Theatre Exchange." *EN.* 1986 July; 71(7): 2. Illus.: Photo. 1. Lang.: Eng.

USA: New York, NY. USSR: Moscow. 1986. Histories-sources. ■Interview with Patricia B. Snyder, producer of *Rag Dolly* performed by U.S. and Soviet performers. New era of cultural exchange inaugurated by this joint venture.

3647 Filichia, Peter. "The Backstage Story of a Backstage Story." *TheaterW.* 1987 Dec 21-27; 1(19): 8-11. Illus.: Photo. 2. Lang.: Eng.

USA: New York, NY. 1987. Historical studies. ■Plot synopsis of the musical *Mademoiselle Colombe* by Michael Valenti, Ed Dulchin and Albert Harris from Jean Anouilh's play *Colombe*. Includes background of performers Tammy Grimes, Victoria Brasser and Keith Buterbaugh.

3648 Hersh, Amy. "Nancy and Alice Grow Up." *TheaterW.* 1987 7-13 Dec.; 1(17): 12-14. Illus.: Photo. B&W. 3. Lang.: Eng.

USA. 1977-1987. Biographical studies. ■Overview of the life of Nancy Hume focusing on those events leading to her Broadway acting debut in *Teddy and Alice*.

3649 Hersh, Amy. "Musical Director Paul Gemignani On Sound, Sets, and Sondheim." *TheaterW.* 1987 28 Dec.-1988 3 Jan.; 1(20): 16-17. Illus.: Photo. B&W. 2. Lang.: Eng.

USA: New York, NY. 1987. Histories-sources. ■Musical director Paul Gemignani discusses role and importance of conductor of a musical. Relationship between conductor and actor and conductor and composer.

3650 Kenney, William Howland, III. "The Influence of Black Vaudeville on Early Jazz." *BPM.* 1986 Fall; 14(3): 233-248. Notes. Lang.: Eng.

USA: New Orleans, LA, New York, NY, Chicago, IL. Critical studies. ■The urban and theatrical origins of jazz with emphasis on its development as novelty music on the vaudeville circuit and as songs in Black musical theatre. Songwriters and performers and their style.

3651 Ledford, Larry. "On Saving Musical Theatre. Georgia: What's On Her Mind." *TheaterW.* 1987 Oct.; 2(7): 4-5. Illus.: Photo. Print. B&W. 1. Lang.: Eng.

USA: New York, NY. UK-England: London. 1957-1985. Histories-sources. ■Actress Georgia Brown discusses her accomplishments as an actress in London and New York. Focus on her lead role in *Roza*.

3652 Lewis, Kevin. "Barbara Barondess MacLean." *PasShow.* 1987 Sum; 11(1): 8-9. Illus.: Photo. B&W. 2. Lang.: Eng.

USA: New York, NY. 1920-1930. Histories-sources. ■Interview with actress Barbara Barondess MacLean on her career with the Shubert Organization.

3653 Miller, Terry. "*Love Life* Begins at Forty." *KWN.* 1987 Fall; 5(2): 8-9. Illus.: Photo. Print. B&W. 8. Lang.: Eng.

USA: New York, NY, Ann Arbor, MI. 1945-1986. Reviews of performances. ■Review of the University of Michigan all-student revival of Weill-Lerner musical *Love Life*. Attempts to contrast 1948 production with U of M production and thus arrive at an evaluation of the original script.

3654 Salinas, Mike. "Getting Giancarlo Esposito Started." *TheaterW.* 1987 Nov 16; 1(14): 22, 26. Illus.: Photo. B&W. 2. Lang.: Eng.

USA: New York, NY. 1987. Histories-sources. ■Interview with actor Giancarlo Esposito on his career, Blacks in the theatre, his performance in *Don't Get God Started*.

3655 Shirakawa, Sam. "Is Musical Theatre Becoming Operatic?" *TheaterW.* 1987 Oct.; 1(8): 17-21. Illus.: Photo. B&W. Architec. Detail. Grd.Plan. 8. Lang.: Eng.

USA: New York, NY. 1956-1984. Critical studies. ■Broadway musical songs becoming more 'classical'. Examples: *Phantom of the Opera*, *Les Misérables*.

3656 Shirakawa, Sam. "The Gospel Gossip." *TheaterW.* 1987 Nov 16; 1(14): 17-21. Illus.: Photo. B&W. 6. Lang.: Eng.

USA: New York, NY. 1987. Critical studies. ■Trend of gospel musicals on and off Broadway. Themes of plays, audience response and staging.

3657 Smith, Starla. "Connie Day: The Standby Star." *TheaterW.* 1987 Nov 9; 1(13): 22-23. Illus.: Photo. B&W. 2. Lang.: Eng.

USA: New York, NY. 1987. Biographical studies. ■Career of actress Connie Day: hazards and benefits of being an understudy for a famous lead in a Broadway musical.

3658 Smith, Starla. "Martin Charnin: Thrills, Spills, Chills, and *No Frills*." *TheaterW.* 1987 Dec 7-13; 1(17): 28-31. Illus.: Photo. 3. Lang.: Eng.

USA: New York, NY. 1957-1987. Biographical studies. ■The professional career of lyricist, actor, director Martin Charnin.

3659 Smith, Starla. "Enchanted DeForest." *TheaterW.* 1987 Sep.; 1: 18-20. Illus.: Photo. 1. Lang.: Eng.

USA: New York, NY. 1987. Biographical studies. ■Profile of composer Charles DeForest's work, including his development of a new musical that parodies awards ceremonies.

3660 Smith, Starla. "William McCauley: Actor, Chameleon." *TheaterW.* 1987 Nov 2; 1(12): 21-26. Illus.: Photo. Color. 3. Lang.: Eng.

USA. 1987. Biographical studies. ■Profile of William McCauley and his career in musical theatre: productions, relationship with directors, training.

3661 Smith, Starla. "Lee Roy Reams: Star Turn." *TheaterW.* 1987 16 Nov.; 1(14): 27-31. Illus.: Photo. B&W. 5. Lang.: Eng.

USA: New York, NY. 1987. Biographical studies. ■Career of actor Lee Roy Reams: his experience of being cast in the Broadway musical *La Cage Aux Folles* just as it closed.

3662 Smith, Starla. "Holding It Together: A Conversation with Paula Kalustian, 'The Only Straight Answer in Town'." *TheaterW.* 1987 31 Aug.-6 Sep.; 1(3): 22-24. Illus.: Photo. B&W. 4. Lang.: Eng.

USA: New York, NY. 1984-1987. Histories-sources. ■Paula Kalustian discusses her directing career, specifically the planning, production and demise of *Rags*.

3663 Smith, Starla. "He Is What He Says: A Profile of Jack Eric Williams." *TheaterW.* 1987 7-13 Sep.(4): 6-9. Illus.: Photo. B&W. 4. Lang.: Eng.

USA: New York, NY. 1987. Histories-sources. ■Jack Eric Williams discusses his background in composing and performing in musical theatre. Focus on his musical *Mrs. Farmer's Daughter*.

3664 St. George, Victoria. "Soldier Shows and the Shuberts: The Archive U.S.O. Collection." *PasShow.* 1987 Sun; 11(1): 3-5. Illus.: Photo. Poster. B&W. 3. Lang.: Eng.

USA: New York, NY. 1942-1945. Historical studies. ■History of 'The Soldier Show' and the Shubert Archives U.S.O. collection.

3665 Steyn, Mark. "A Funny Thing Happened to Sondheim." *Drama.* 1987; 3(165): 11-13. Illus.: Photo. B&W. 4. Lang.: Eng.

USA: New York, NY. UK-England: London. 1962-1985. Critical studies. ■Study of the work of Stephen Sondheim.

3666 Stulman, Andrea; St. George, Victoria. "Shubert Alley: The Life and Times of the Musical Theatre Project." *PasShow.* 1986 Win; 10(1): 3-5. Illus.: Photo. B&W. 4. Lang.: Eng.

USA: New York, NY. 1984-1985. Historical studies. ■Brooks McNamara, Archive Director, initiates the Musical Theatre Project to explore Broadway musical material available in Shubert Archive.

3667 *Naš gorod—naš dom: Birobidžanu—50 let.* (Our City, Our Home: For the Fiftieth Anniversary of Birobidžan.) Chabarovsk: Chabarovsk knižnoe izdatelstvo; 1987. 175 pp. Lang.: Rus.

USSR: Birobidžan. 1937-1987. Historical studies. ■Jewish musical chamber theatre, independent theatres.

MUSIC-DRAMA: Musical theatre—Performance/production

3668 Sličenko, N.A. *Rodilsja ja v tabore.* (I Was Born in a Gypsy Camp.) Moscow: Molodaja guardija; 1987. 110 pp. Lang.: Rus.
USSR: Moscow. 1950-1987. Histories-sources. ■Actor and chief director of gypsy theatre Romen on his creative work.

3669 Tarakanov, M. "Dorogoj poiska." (The Road of Innovation.) *SovMuzyka.* 1987; 11: 47-54. Lang.: Rus.
USSR: Tbilisi. 1980-1987. Critical studies. ■Problem of development of the Paliašvili Opera Theatre.

Plays/librettos/scripts

3670 Midwinter, Eric. "W.S. Gilbert: Victorian Entertainer." *NTQ.* 1987 Aug.; 3(11): 273-279. Illus.: Photo. B&W. 2. Lang.: Eng.
England. 1836-1911. Critical studies. ■Ingredients of Gilbert's comic operas which contributed to their popular success, the industry of spin-offs they created and their contribution to the development of the musical play.

3671 Fielder, Mari Kathleen. "Chauncey Olcott: Irish-American Mother-Love, Romance and Nationalism." *Eire.* 1987 Sum; 22(2): 4-26. Notes. Append. Lang.: Eng.
USA. 1893-1918. Critical studies. ■Analysis of the plays and songs of Irish-American musical theatre star Chauncey Olcott. Sociological in thrust, the article examines the plays' themes, especially regarding nationalism, women and male-female relationships, in light of their Irish-American audiences.

3672 Gates, Tom. "The Making of *Mademoiselle Colombe.*" *TheaterW.* 1987 Dec 12-15; 1(19): 12-15. Illus.: Photo. 2. Lang.: Eng.
USA. 1987. Historical studies. ■History of the adaptation of Jean Anouilh's *Colombe* into the musical *Mademoiselle Colombe.*

3673 Salinas, Mike. "Michael Short, 1924-1987." *TheaterW.* 1987 Oct.; 1(8): 4-5. Illus.: Photo. B&W. 1. Lang.: Eng.
USA: New York, NY. UK-England. 1924-1987. Biographical studies. ■Career of Michael Short, one of the most prolific authors of Broadway musicals. Discussion with artists who collaborated with him.

3674 Schaeffer, Martin. "Joe Masteroff: How *Cabaret* Was Made Into a Brand New Musical." *TheaterW.* 1987 Nov 2; 1(12): 6-9. Illus.: Photo. B&W. 6. Lang.: Eng.
USA: New York, NY. 1963-1987. Histories-sources. ■Interview with Joe Masteroff, author of the book for *Cabaret*: script changes for revival, collaboration with director Hal Prince, comparison between original production and revival.

3675 Winer, Laurie. "The Road to Roza." *AmTh.* 1987 July/Aug.; 4(4): 6. Illus.: Photo. Print. B&W. 1. Lang.: Eng.
USA: Baltimore, MD. 1965-1987. Reviews of performances. ■History of the musical *Roza,* adapted from the novel *La Vie Devant Soi* by Emile Ajar and the film *Madame Rosa.* Music by Gilbert Bécaud and directed by Harold Prince.

3676 Chudabašjan, K. "Stepen' vernosti originalu." (The Degree of Fidelity to the Original.) *SovMuzyka.* 1987; 3: 40-45. Lang.: Rus.
USSR. 1980-1987. Critical studies. ■Problem of author's conception and stage version of a work.

Opera

Administration

3677 Nordwall, Trygve. "Wien, mina gagers stad." (Vienna, City of My Fees.) *MuD.* 1987; 9(4): 12-13. Illus.: Photo. Lang.: Swe.
Austria: Vienna. 1986-1987. Historical studies. ■A report from the Staatsoper in Vienna under the management of Claus Helmut Drese and Claudio Abbado.

3678 Mercer, Ruby. "How Opera Plans to Meet the Budget." *OC.* 1987 Spr; 28(1): 2-3. Lang.: Eng.
Canada: Toronto, ON. 1980-1987. Historical studies. ■Discusses recent and past strategies for marketing opera and other arts in Toronto.

3679 Roberts, Joy. "How Opera's Irving Guttman Won the West." *PAC.* 1985 Sum; 22(2): 12-14. Illus.: Photo. Print. B&W. 1. Lang.: Eng.
Canada: Edmonton, AB, Winnipeg, MB. 1972-1985. Biographical studies. ■A profile of Irving Guttman, the artistic director of both the Edmonton and Manitoba opera companies with his opinions on opera, government funding, and surtitles.

3680 Ardoin, John. "A Ring Diary (Part 1 of 2)." *OQ.* 1983 Sum; 1(2): 4-10. Pref. Lang.: Eng.
Germany, West: Bayreuth. Germany, West: Munich. 1980. Histories-sources. ■A diary kept by the author (a member of the team) of the filming preparation and process of the first complete performance of the Bayreuth Festival's production of Wagner's *Der Ring des Nibelungen* for television. Continued in *OQ* 1:3 (1983 Fall), 25-35.

3681 Bergström, Gunnel. "Vad händer på Operan?" (What Is Happening at the Opera?)*MuD.* 1987; 9(1): 18-20. Illus.: Photo. Swe.
Sweden: Stockholm. 1986. Critical studies. ■On the basis of a new production of Mozart's *Die Zauberflöte* at Royal Swedish Opera (Kungliga Teatern), author presents critical overview of Opera management.

3682 Ardoin, John. "Bing Remembers." *OQ.* 1987/88 Win; 5(4): 1-11. Illus.: Photo. 4. Lang.: Eng.
USA: New York, NY. 1950-1972. Historical studies. ■Career of Sir Rudolph Bing, former general manager of the Metropolitan Opera.

3683 Balk, H. Wesley. "The Craft of Creating Opera: Restoring a Lost Legacy Through the Workshop Process." *OQ.* 1983 Sum; 1 (2): 91-108. Notes. Illus.: Photo. Lang.: Eng.
USA. 1987. Critical studies. ■The collaboration of composer and librettist—called CLP (Composer-Librettist Partnership) and the importance of opera workshop process to support the creation of new opera.

3684 Buchau, Stephanie von. "Funding Opera: An Endearing Attitude: Gordon Peter Getty—Patron, Baritone, Composer of *Plump Jack...*" *OpN.* 1987 June; 51(17): 14, 16. Illus.: Photo. Color. 1. Lang.: Eng.
USA: San Francisco, CA. 1987. Biographical studies. ■Gordon Peter Getty, composer of *Plump Jack,* patron of San Francisco Opera and Concert Opera Association.

3685 Commissiona, Sergiu. "Vitamins of Happiness: Sergiu Commissiona, Who This Month Becomes Music Director of New York City Opera, Talks about the Rejuvenating Challenges of His New Post." *OpN.* 1987 July; 52(1): 26-27. Illus.: Photo. Color. 1. Lang.: Eng.
USA: New York, NY. Romania. 1987. Histories-sources.

3686 Mayer, Marion. "Sound Ambitions, Unsteady Resources: Opera Companies in the 1980's." *JAML.* 1987 Spr; 17(1): 5-22. Lang.: Eng.
USA. 1980-1987. Technical studies. ■Financial crises of opera companies and new methods to regain financial resources.

3687 Schmidgall, Gary. "General Director David Gockley, Houston's Best Grand Opera Seller." *OpN.* 1987 Oct.; 52(4): 20, 70. Illus.: Photo. Color. 1. Lang.: Eng.
USA: Houston, TX. 1970-1987. Histories-sources. ■Interview with David Gockley, General Director, Houston Grand Opera.

3688 "Leningradskij kamernyj est'!" (Leningrad Chamber Exists.) *MuZizn.* 1987; 21: 8-9. Lang.: Rus.
USSR: Leningrad. 1987. Historical studies. ■Creation of Leningrad Chamber Opera Theatre.

Audience

3689 Crocker, Janet. "Opera Goes Atlantic." *OC.* 1987 Win; 28(4): 18-21, 41. Illus.: Photo. B&W. 4. Lang.: Eng.
Canada. 1987. Critical studies. ■Profile of opera in Canada's four Atlantic provinces in response to the Canadian Opera Company's Fall 1987 tour.

3690 Witsen, Leo van. "To Look or To Listen." *OQ.* 1983 Sum; 1(2): 48-53. Notes. Lang.: Eng.
Europe. 1781-1983. Critical studies. ■Debating the importance of both the vocal and visual aspects of opera.

MUSIC-DRAMA: Opera—Audience

3691 Pokrovskij, B. "Opera i zritel'." (Opera and Its Audience.) *SovMuzyka*. 1987; 1: 7-12. Lang.: Rus.

USSR: Moscow. 1980-1987. Histories-sources. ■Principal director of Moscow Musical Chamber Theatre on perceptions of the art of opera.

Basic theatrical documents

3692 Mercer, Ruby. "Videocassettes." *OC*. 1987 Win; 28(4): 52. Lang.: Eng.

Italy: Verona. Australia: Sydney. 1987. Reviews of performances. ■Brief reviews of two productions on videocassette: The Verona Arena production of Puccini's *Tosca* and Poulenc's *Dialogues des Carmélites* filmed at the Opera House in Sydney, Australia. Related to Media: Video forms.

Design/technology

3693 Ward, Mariellan. "The House of Malabar." *OC*. 1987 Win; 28(4): 13-17. Illus.: Photo. Sketches. B&W. 17. Lang.: Eng.

Canada: Toronto, ON. 1900-1987. Instructional materials. ■Malabar Costume's approach to the business of costume rental and provision to primarily opera. Includes discussions on cutting, fitting, etc..

3694 Beacham, Richard C. "Adolphe Appia and the Staging of Wagnerian Opera." *OQ*. 1983 Fall; 1(3): 114-139. Notes. Illus.: Photo. Lang.: Eng.

Germany. Switzerland. 1873-1928. Critical studies. ■Swiss theoretician and designer Adolphe Appia's ideas, concepts, staging and scenery of Wagner's opera.

3695 Mammitzsch, Dagmar. "...das hat auch mit Besessenheit zu tun. Sechs Fragen an Marion Schöne, Deutsche Staatsoper Berlin." (...That Has Also To Do with Obsession. Six Questions to Marion Schöne of the Deutsche Staatsoper, Berlin.) *TZ*. 1987 ; 42(5): 14-17. Illus.: Photo. B&W. 8. Lang.: Ger.

Germany, East: Berlin, East. 1987. Histories-sources. ■On the craftsmanship of a stage photographer and the specifics of photographing music-drama.

3696 Ézsiás, Erzsébet. "Ézsiás Erszébet beszélgetése Forray Gáborral. 'Jó színház nincsen saját műhely nélkül'." (Erzsébet Ézsiás' Interview with Gábor Forray. 'Good Theatre Cannot Do Without a Workshop of Its Own'.) *FSM*. 1987 Mar.; 31(13): 14-15. Illus.: Photo. Color. 3. Lang.: Hun.

Hungary: Budapest. 1950-1987. Histories-sources. ■Gábor Forray, stage designer of the Hungarian State Opera House for more than 30 years, speaks about his career, working conditions, style changes in stage designing.

3697 Pasi, Mario; Weaver, William, transl. *Versace teatro dalla Scala all'Hermitage*. (Versace: Theatre from the Scala to the Hermitage.) Milan: Ricci; 1987. 273 pp. Illus.: Photo. Dwg. Sketches. Print. Color. B&W. Lang.: Ita.

Italy. 1982-1987. Biographical studies. ■The work of Italian couturier Gianni Versace as costume designer.

3698 Bentham, Fred. "A Light at the Opera." *Sin*. 1987; 21(1): 27-33. Illus.: Photo. Diagram. B&W. 8. Lang.: Eng.

UK-England: London. 1928-1987. Technical studies. ■Lighting design and technology for opera and ballet.

3699 Crutchfield, Will. "Still More on the Mapleson Cylinder." *OQ*. 1987/88 Win; 5(4): 37-45. Notes. Lang.: Eng.

USA. 1901-1987. Critical studies. ■Ascertaining who recorded soprano role in 1901 Mapleson cylinder version of *Les Huguenots*.

3700 Hamilton, David. "The Mapleson *Huguenots* Cylinder Again." *OQ*. 1987 Spr; 5(1): 11-21. Notes. Illus.: Photo. Plan. 2. Lang.: Eng.

USA: New York, NY. 1947. Critical studies. ■Controversy over wax cylinder recordings of New York Met librarian Lionel Mapleson: inability to discern soprano part in Meyerbeer's *Les Huguenots*.

3701 Mobley, Cole. "Light Shows: Behind the Scenes with Gil Wechsler and His Staff, Who Illuminate the Metropolitan Opera Stage." *OpN*. 1987 Mar 14; 51(13): 14-17. Illus.: Photo. Color. 3. Lang.: Eng.

USA: New York, NY. 1967-1987. Histories-sources. ■Gil Wechsler, resident lighting designer, Metropolitan Opera.

Institutions

3702 "Roundup." *OC*. 1987 Sum; 28(2): 29-43. Illus.: Photo. B&W. 21. Lang.: Eng.

1987. Reviews of performances. ■Brief reviews of over 43 productions in Canada, the U.S. and internationally.

3703 "Roundup." *OC*. 1987 Fall; 28(3): 28-43. Illus.: Photo. B&W. 21. Lang.: Eng.

1987. Reviews of performances. ■Brief reviews of over 50 productions in Canada, the U.S. and around the world.

3704 "Roundup." *OC*. 1987 Win; 28(4): 26-30, 32-41. Illus.: Photo. B&W. 14. Lang.: Eng.

1987. Reviews of performances. ■Brief reviews of over 47 productions including Festivals, opera and musical theatre in Canada, U.S. and abroad.

3705 Crory, Neil. "Compact Discs." *OC*. 1987 Sum; 28(2): 50, 48. Illus.: Photo. B&W. 1. Lang.: Eng.

1987. Reviews of performances. ■Discusses the quality and availability of Maria Callas's work on compact disc. Notes the soon-to-be released Angel/EMI collection, and includes a table of available compact discs. Related to Media: Audio forms.

3706 Iacono, Julia. "Calendar." *OC*. 1987 Win; 28(4): 42-48. Lang.: Eng.

1988. Histories-sources. ■A 1988 calendar of productions listing the producing institution, stage director, conductor, designers, choreographer, opening date, number of performances and status as a world or Canadian premiere. Covers Canada, U.S. and abroad. Includes table of CBC radio and television opera broadcasts.

3707 LeBarge, Lawrence. "Calendar." *OC*. 1987 Spr; 28(1): 44-48. Lang.: Eng.

1987. Histories-sources. ■A 1987 calendar of productions listing the producing institution, stage director, conductor, designer, costume and lighting designers, choreographer, opening date, number of performances and status as a world or Canadian premiere. Covers USA, Canada and international information.

3708 LeBarge, Lawrence. "Calendar." *OC*. 1987 Sum; 28(2): 44-48. Lang.: Eng.

1987. Histories-sources. ■A 1987 calendar of summer productions listing the producing institution, stage director, conductor, designer, costume and lighting designers, choreographer, opening date, number of performances and status as a world or Canadian premiere. Covers U.S., Canada and international.

3709 LeBarge, Lawrence. "Calendar." *OC*. 1987 Fall; 28(3): 44-48. Lang.: Eng.

1987. Histories-sources. ■A 1987-88 calendar of fall productions listing the producing institution, stage director, conductor, designer, costume and lighting designers, choreographer, opening date, number of performances and status as a world or Canadian premiere. Covers Canada, U.S. and abroad.

3710 Höslinger, Clemens. "Eine Korrespondenz Richard Wagners mit dem Wiener Operndirektor Matteo Salvi." (A Correspondence of Richard Wagner with the Viennese Managing Opera Director Matteo Salvi.) 7-19 in Seeger, Horst. *Oper heute*. Berlin: Henschelverlag; 1987. 301 pp. (Ein Almanach der Musikbühne 10.) Lang.: Ger.

Austria: Vienna. 1861-1967. Histories-sources. ■Recently discovered letters in the Vienna Haus-, Hof- and Staatsarchiv: fruitless negotiations about first staging of *Tristan und Isolde* in the Wiener Hofoper.

3711 Piemme, Jean-Marie, ed.; Van Dam, José; Pols, Reinder; Oechslin, Henri; Mortier, Gérard. *Un théâtre d'opéra—l'équipe de Gérard Mortier*. (An Opera Theatre—Gérard Mortier's Team at La Monnaie.) Paris/Gembloux: Duculot; 1986. 245 pp. Pref. Index. Illus.: Photo. Dwg. Color. B&W. 354. Lang.: Fre.

Belgium: Brussels. 1981-1986. Histories-specific. ■Study of Mortier's work as director of Théâtre Royal de la Monnaie.

3712 "Roundup." *OC*. 1987 Spr; 28(1): 26-43. Illus.: Photo. B&W. 20. Lang.: Eng.

Canada. USA. 1986-1987. Reviews of performances. ■A collection of over 50 reviews of operas produced in Canada, the United States and internationally. By various critics.

MUSIC-DRAMA: Opera—Institutions

3713 Allen, Richard. "Saskatoon Opera Association Builds for the Future." *OC.* 1987 Win; 28(4): 22-23. Illus.: Photo. B&W. 1. [Soundings.] Lang.: Eng.
Canada: Saskatoon, SK. 1978-1987. Historical studies. ■History and contemporary plans of the Saskatoon Opera Association.

3714 Charles, John. "Critically Speaking." *OC.* 1987 Fall; 28(3): 51. Lang.: Eng.
Canada. 1987. Critical studies. ■Conditions surrounding the creation and production of operas by Canadian composers.

3715 Cooper, Dorith R. "Opera on CBC." *OC.* 1987 Spr; 28(1): 12-15, 22-23. Illus.: Photo. B&W. 10. Lang.: Eng.
Canada. 1936-1987. Historical studies. ■Discusses the changing role of the CBC in promoting Canadian Operatic activity over the past 50 years.

3716 Crocker, Janet. "On the Cover." *OC.* 1987 Fall; 28(3): 4. Lang.: Eng.
Canada: Toronto, ON. 1987. Historical studies. ■A look backstage at the Canadian Opera Company. Discusses in particular the rehearsals and preparations for the 1987 production of Donizetti's *Lucia di Lammermoor*.

3717 Crory, Neil. "Compact Discs." *OC.* 1987 Fall; 28(3): 50. Illus.: Photo. B&W. 3. Lang.: Eng.
Canada. 1987. Reviews of performances. ■Casting and performances on a compact disc release of *Ariadne auf Naxos* by Richard Strauss and librettist Hugo von Hofmannsthal on Deutsche Grammophon, and a recital by Edita Gruberova on Orfeo. Related to Media: Audio forms.

3718 Davidson, Hugh. "Critically Speaking." *OC.* 1987 Spr; 28(1): 49. Illus.: Photo. B&W. 5. Lang.: Eng.
Canada. 1987. Critical studies. ■Discusses the need for Canadian producers to produce more works by Canadian librettists and composers.

3719 DeLong, Kenneth. "On the Cover." *OC.* 1987 Spr; 28(1): 4, 22. Illus.: Photo. B&W. 1. Lang.: Eng.
Canada: Calgary, AB. 1971-1987. Historical studies. ■A brief history of opera in Calgary.

3720 Dyson, Peter. "Goldschmidt Leaves Guelph Spring Festival." *OC.* 1987 Spr; 28(1): 20-21. Illus.: Photo. B&W. 1. [Soundings.] Lang.: Eng.
Canada: Guelph, ON. 1967-1987. Biographical studies. ■Briefly discusses Nicholas Goldschmidt's contribution to Opera at the Guelph Spring Festival since 1967.

3721 Godfrey, Stephen. "On the Cover." *OC.* 1987 Win; 28(4): 4. Illus.: Photo. B&W. 1. Lang.: Eng.
Canada: Vancouver, BC. UK-Wales. 1983-1987. Historical studies. ■Discusses the impact of artistic director Brian McMaster on the Vancouver Opera, including his connection with the Welsh National Opera.

3722 Hammond, Anthony. "Opera Hamilton Looks to the Future." *OC.* 1987 Sum; 28(2): 22-23. Illus.: Photo. B&W. 1. [Soundings.] Lang.: Eng.
Canada: Hamilton, ON. 1986-1987. Historical studies. ■Briefly discusses the impact of recently appointed artistic director Daniel Lipton on Opera Hamilton.

3723 Kaplan, Jon. "Jeannette Aster: A New Future for Ottawa's Opera Lyra." *OC.* 1987 Fall; 28(3): 22-23. Illus.: Photo. B&W. 1. [Soundings.] Lang.: Eng.
Canada: Ottawa, ON. 1984-1987. Historical studies. ■Proposed changes to Ottawa's Opera Lyra on the occasion of its recent appointment of Jeannette Aster as artistic director.

3724 Maggiorotti, Aldo. "Food for Thought." *OC.* 1987 Win; 28(4): 52. Lang.: Eng.
Canada: Toronto, ON. 1987. Critical studies. ■The hesitancy of Toronto's Canadian Opera Company to follow the trend of producing institutions in other North American cities to stage greater numbers of operettas. Also discusses cuts to operatic performances.

3725 Mercer, Ruby. "Time for Celebration." *OC.* 1987 Fall; 28(3): 2-3. Illus.: Photo. B&W. 1. Lang.: Eng.
Canada. 1987. Critical studies. ■Discusses the coming of age of opera in Canada.

3726 Stompor, Stephan. "'Den Mächtigen passte unsere Richtung nicht': Die Kroll-Oper in Berlin." ('The Mighty Did Not Like Our Tack': The Kroll-Oper in Berlin.) *TZ.* 1987; 42(6): 12-16. Illus.: Photo. B&W. 6. Lang.: Ger.
Germany: Berlin. 1927-1931. Historical studies. ■History of the opera house, description of its accomplishments, ensemble, repertory and audience.

3727 Stompor, Stephan. "Die erste Komische Oper in Berlin. Das bedeutende Reformwerk Hans Gregors 1905-1911." (The First Komische Oper in Berlin. Hans Gregor's Significant Reform Work.) *TZ.* 1987; 42(12): 6-12. Illus.: Photo. B&W. 8. Lang.: Ger.
Germany: Berlin. 1905-1911. Historical studies. ■Conception, repertory, and reasons for the early demise of a progressive Berlin opera house (Komische Oper).

3728 Littler, William. "Dutch Treat in Amsterdam." *OC.* 1987 Spr; 28(1): 20-21. Illus.: Photo. B&W. 1. [Soundings.] Lang.: Eng.
Netherlands: Amsterdam. 1987. Histories-sources. ■Notes the circumstances surrounding the official opening of Amsterdam's Muziektheater.

3729 Husebye, Alexander. "Fair play—herrar kritiker!" (Fair Play—Gentlemen Critics.) *MuD.* 1987; 9(2): 3-5. Illus.: Dwg. Lang.: Swe.
Sweden: Stockholm. 1985-1987. Critical studies. ■An estimation of Lars af Malmborg's period as manager for the Royal Swedish Opera, and the negative critics of the press.

3730 Strömblom, Bengt. "Vart tog Lille Petter vägen?" (Whatever Became of Little Petter?) *MuD.* 1987; 9(4): 4-5. Illus.: Photo. Dwg. Lang.: Swe.
Sweden: Stockholm. 1960-1985. Critical studies. ■A discussion about Willmar Sauter's analysis of the attendance at the Royal Swedish Opera, compared with the 1960s and what to do to attract younger audiences.

3731 Gormley, R. James. "Requiem for an Opera Company." *OQ.* 1983 Win; 1(4): 12-21. Notes. Lang.: Eng.
USA: Chicago, IL. 1946-1947. Histories-sources. ■The beginnings and failure of the United States Opera Company in Chicago.

3732 Holden, Randall L. "The Opera Workshop From 'Rags' to 'Riches': The Story of the University of Louisville Opera Theatre." *OQ.* 1983 Win; 1(4): 22-43. Tables. Illus.: Photo. Lang.: Eng.
USA: Louisville, KY. 1952-1983. Instructional materials. ■Introduction of opera theatre program at the University of Louisville and its productions.

3733 Mobley, Cole. "What It's All About: Launching Careers and Building Audiences Are the Mission of Affiliate Artists." *OpN.* 1987 July; 52(1): 32-35. Illus.: Photo. B&W. 2. Lang.: Eng.
USA: New York, NY. 1967-1987. Historical studies. ■Affiliate Artists, performance training, audience development.

3734 Moriarty, John. "The Opera Workshop: Opera Training in Boston: Looking Toward the Future." *OQ.* 1983 Sum; 1(2): 54-68. Notes. Illus.: Photo. Lang.: Eng.
USA: Boston, MA. 1973-1983. Histories-sources. ■Program descriptions of the opera workshop in Boston Conservatory of Music.

3735 Rich, Maria F. "Opera USA—Perspective: The Popularization of Opera." *OQ.* 1983 Sum; 1(2): 19-27. Lang.: Eng.
USA. 1940-1983. Histories-specific. ■Study on the booming of opera companies, and the increasing popularization of opera in USA.

Performance spaces

3736 Kask, Jan. "'Här rivs för att få luft och ljus'." ('Here We Have Torn Down to Get Air and Light'.) *MuD.* 1987; 9(2): 5-6. Illus.: Photo. Lang.: Swe.
Sweden: Stockholm. 1985-1987. Critical studies. ■Recommends renovation or reconstruction of the Royal Swedish Opera building of Kungliga Teatern.

3737 Jentzen, Reinhold. "Operndirektübertragung vom Basler Stadttheater auf Grossleinwand/Münsterplatz (5/14/86)." (Opera Live: Telecast from Basel Opera House on to Screen

MUSIC-DRAMA: Opera—Performance spaces

on Munster Square (May 14, 1986).) *ProScenium*. 1987 Apr.; 15(2): 13-23. Illus.: Photo. Plan. B&W. Lang.: Fre, Ger.
Switzerland: Basel. 1986. Technical studies. ■On May 14, 1986, Donizetti's *Lucia di Lammermoor* was directly telecast from the stage of Basel playhouse onto the square in front of the Munster holding about 10,000 people. Report refers to all technical and organizational details, includes illustrations and press reactions. Related to Media: Video forms.

3738 Irwin, Alfreda L. "Second Century for Chautauqua: Second Half-Century for Opera." *OJ*. 1987; 20(2): 3-10. Notes. Illus.: Photo. 1. Lang.: Eng.
USA: Chautauqua, NY. 1928-1987. Historical studies. ■Renovations at Norton Hall at the Chautauqua Institution. Direction of the company and its unique position in the local community.

3739 Schmidgall, Gary; Caldwell, Jim, photo. "Can Do: Houston, A City That Thinks Big, This Month Officially Christens the Wortham Theatre Center, A Sterling New Home for Opera." *OpN*. 1987 Oct.; 52(4): 13-16. Illus.: Photo. Color. 11. Lang.: Eng.
USA: Houston, TX. 1977-1987. Histories-sources. ■Wortham Theatre Center, Eugene Aubry, architect.

3740 West, William D. "Summer Night's Dream: Glimmerglass Opera Opens Its New Home on June 27." *OpN*. 1987 June; 15(17): 34-35. Illus.: Dwg. Photo. Color. 3. Lang.: Eng.
USA: Cooperstown, NY. 1975-1987. Historical studies. ■Alice Busch Theatre, Glimmerglass Opera.

Performance/production

3741 Barber, David. *Bach, Beethoven, and the Boys: Music History As It Ought to be Taught*. Toronto, ON: Sound & Vision; 1987. 148 pp. Lang.: Eng.
Historical studies. ■A history of opera.

3742 Holliday, Thomas. "Amadeus: The Man in the Child, The Child in the Man." *OJ*. 1987; 20(3): 7-20. Notes. Lang.: Eng.
Austria: Vienna. 1756-1781. Biographical studies. ■Analysis of relationship between Wolfgang Amadeus Mozart and his father. Effects of his disciplined upbringing on his music and personal life.

3743 Lundberg, Carmilla. "Lulu—ett barn som aldrig fått växa." (Lulu—A Child Who Never Was Allowed to Grow Up.) *MuD*. 1987; 9(1): 4-8. Illus.: Photo. 6. Lang.: Swe.
Austria. France: Paris. 1937-1979. Historical studies. ■The story of how Alban Berg's *Lulu* had to wait for forty-two years for a first complete performance with Patrice Chéreau staging in Paris.

3744 Thamsen, Gisela. "Förändringens vindar." (The Winds of Innovation.) *MuD*. 1987; 9(3): 14-17. Illus.: Photo. Lang.: Swe.
Austria: Salzburg. 1987. Critical studies. ■A report from Salzburg Festspiele.

3745 Schrader, Steven W. "A Critic's Nightmare: To Judge and Be Judged Was the Fate of Writer Edouard Hanslick When He Reviewed the First Performance of *La Bohème*." *OpN*. 1987 Jan 3; 51(8): 20-21. Illus.: Photo. B&W. 1. Lang.: Eng.
Austro-Hungarian Empire: Vienna. 1896-1987. Histories-sources. ■Opera criticism of Edouard Hanslick and his opposition to *La Bohème* by Giacomo Puccini.

3746 *Opéra Royal de Wallonie 1967-1987*. (Royal Walloon Opera, 1967-1987.) Liège: Opéra Royal de Wallonie; 1987. 144 pp. Illus.: Photo. B&W. Color. 294. Lang.: Fre.
Belgium: Liège. 1967-1987. Histories-sources. ■Illustrated retrospective of the Royal Walloon Opera, including a list of performances for each season.

3747 "People Are Talking About..." *OC*. 1987 Spr; 28(1): 5-9. Illus.: Photo. B&W. 21. Lang.: Eng.
Canada. 1930-1987. 1987. Biographical studies. ■Brief biographical updates on over thirty selected individuals.

3748 Forrester, Maureen; McDonald, Marci. *Maureen Forrester, Out of Character*. Toronto, ON: McClelland Stewart; 1986. 326 pp. Lang.: Eng.
Canada. 1930-1986. Biographical studies. ■Memoir of opera singer.

3749 Kraglund, John. "John Kraglund Remembers." *OC*. 1987 Fall; 28(3): 17-19, 24. Illus.: Photo. B&W. 8. Lang.: Eng.
Canada: Toronto, ON. 1947-1987. Histories-sources. ■Recently retired music critic of the *Globe & Mail* recalls 40 years of Toronto opera: personalities, institutions, criticism.

3750 Mercer, Ruby. "All This and Opera Too!" *OC*. 1987 Win; 28(4): 2-3. Illus.: Photo. B&W. Lang.: Eng.
Canada. 1987. Critical studies. ■Comments on the changing face of opera as designers and stage directors impose novel interpretations of time and place.

3751 Mercer, Ruby. "*Carmen*: The Beloved Opera Is To Be Performed in Vancouver." *PAC*. 1986 Jan.; 22(4): 30. Notes. MU. Lang.: Eng.
Canada: Vancouver, BC. 1986. Reviews of performances. ■Presentation of *Carmen* at Expo '86 in Vancouver, imported from Wales to Queen Elizabeth Theatre.

3752 Mercer, Ruby. "Spotlight." *OC*. 1987 Spr; 28(1): 10-11. Illus.: Photo. B&W. 3. Lang.: Eng.
Canada. 1987. Histories-sources. ■Interview with Odette Beaupré in which she discusses her training in acting, staging and music as well as her experience with operettas.

3753 Mercer, Ruby. "It Looks So Easy..." *OC*. 1987 Sum; 28(2): 2-3. Illus.: Photo. B&W. 1. Lang.: Eng.
Canada. USA. 1987. Histories-sources. ■Comments on the rigours and availability of opera training in North America.

3754 Mercer, Ruby. "Spotlight." *OC*. 1987 Sum; 28(2): 11, 13. Illus.: Photo. B&W. 1. Lang.: Eng.
Canada. UK-England. 1987. Histories-sources. ■Interview with Canadian soprano Jane MacKenzie. Discusses her roles, awards and the division of her career between England and Canada.

3755 Mercer, Ruby. "Spotlight." *OC*. 1987 Fall; 28(3): 13-14. Illus.: Photo. B&W. 3. Lang.: Eng.
Canada. 1987. Histories-sources. ■Interview with Canadian soprano Tracy Dahl. Discusses training, approach to roles and repertoire.

3756 Mercer, Ruby. "Spotlight." *OC*. 1987 Win; 28(4): 11-12. Illus.: Photo. B&W. 3. Lang.: Eng.
Canada. 1987. Histories-sources. ■Gaétan Laperrière discusses his career, family, training, and approach to a role.

3757 Roberts, Joy. "Edmonton Festival Honoring Violet Archer Billed as a Canadian 'First'." *PAC*. 1986; 22(4): 11. Notes. MU. Illus.: Photo. Print. 1. Lang.: Eng.
Canada: Edmonton, AB. 1985. Critical studies. ■Festival of composer Violet Archer and premiere of her one-act opera *The Meal*.

3758 Scott, Iain. "Stuart Hamilton, the Genius Behind Opera in Concert." *OC*. 1987 Win; 28(4): 22-23. Illus.: Photo. B&W. 1. [Soundings.] Lang.: Eng.
Canada: Toronto, ON. 1929-1987. Historical studies. ■Stuart Hamilton's work as opera broadcaster, pianist, founder and co-ordinator of 'Opera in Concert'.

3759 Graff, Yveta Synek. "Water Nymph: Dvořák's *Rusalka* Surfaces This Month at Carnegie Hall, Thanks to Opera Orchestra of New York." *OpN*. 1987 Feb 28; 51(12): 32-33. Illus.: Photo. B&W. 3. Lang.: Eng.
Czechoslovakia: Prague. USA: New York, NY. 1900-1987. Historical studies. ■Anton Dvořák's *Rusalka* at Carnegie Hall.

3760 Sutcliffe, James Helme. "Touch of Venus: Czech Mezzo Eva Randová Adds the Metropolitan to her Conquests." *OpN*. 1987 Jan 17; 51(9): 34-35. Illus.: Photo. B&W. 2. Lang.: Eng.
Czechoslovakia. 1987. Biographical studies. ■Profile of mezzo-soprano Eva Randová.

3761 Burling, William J. "Four Casts for Early Eighteenth-Century London Operas." *Restor*. 1987 Sum; 2(1): 1-5. Notes. Lang.: Eng.

MUSIC-DRAMA: Opera—Performance/production

England: London. 1712-1717. Histories-sources. ■Cast lists and publication information.

3762 "People Are Talking About..." *OC*. 1987 Fall; 28(2): 5-9. Illus.: Photo. B&W. 20. Lang.: Eng.
Europe. North America. 1987. Biographical studies. ■Provides brief biographical updates on over fifty artists working in opera in Canada, the U.S. and abroad. Also provides information on producing institutions.

3763 "People Are Talking About..." *OC*. 1987 Fall; 28(3): 5-11. Illus.: Photo. B&W. 21. Lang.: Eng.
Europe. North America. 1987. Biographical studies. ■Provides brief biographical updates on over sixty artists working in opera and music theatre in Canada, the U.S. and abroad. Also provides information on producing institutions.

3764 "People are Talking About..." *OC*. 1987 Win; 28(4): 5-10. Illus.: Photo. B&W. 20. Lang.: Eng.
Europe. North America. 1987. Biographical studies. ■Brief biographical updates on over forty-three artists working in opera and music theatre in Canada, the U.S. and abroad. Also provides information on producing institutions.

3765 Heed, Sven Åke. "Katolsk kitsch." (Catholic Kitsch.) *MuD*. 1987; 9(3): 4-7. Illus.: Photo. Lang.: Swe.
Europe. 1986-1987. Critical studies. ■A comparison between Verdi's French *Don Carlos* (1867) and his Italian *Don Carlo*, and how the directors of today manage the Catholic ingredients.

3766 Maggiorotti, Aldo. "Food for Thought." *OC*. 1987 Sum; 28(2): 52. Lang.: Eng.
Europe. North America. 1887-1987. Critical studies. ■Comments on the shift in opera over the past century from a focus on the singer, to the contemporary focus on the conductor and stage director, resulting in interpretations which adapt music setting and character.

3767 Maggiorotti, Aldo. "Food for Thought." *OC*. 1987 Fall; 28(3): 51. Lang.: Eng.
Europe. North America. 1987. Critical studies. ■Film versions of Puccini's *La Bohème* in Paris and Offenbach's *Tales of Hoffmann* with Plácido Domingo. Also discusses conventional response to audience applause during a scene. Related to Media: Film.

3768 Stanbrook, Alan. "The Sight of Music." *SiSo*. 1987; 56(2): 132-135. Illus.: Photo. B&W. 7. Lang.: Eng.
Europe. 1951-1986. Empirical research. ■Attempts to film operas, notably Powell and Pressburger's *Tales of Hoffmann* and Menotti's *The Medium*. Related to Media: Film.

3769 Stern, Kenneth. "In Defense of Embellishment." *OpN*. 1987 Feb 14; 51(11): 18-21. Illus.: Dwg. Plan. Photo. Color. B&W. 5. Lang.: Eng.
Europe. 1767-1987. Historical studies. ■Vocal ornamentation in opera.

3770 Verdino-Süllwold, Carla Maria. "The Heldentenor in the 20th Century: Refining a Rare Breed." *OJ*. 1987; 20(3): 24-40 . Notes. Lang.: Eng.
Europe. North America. 1987. Critical studies. ■Definition of the Heldentenor in Wagnerian opera. Profile of Lauritz Melchior, Set Svanholm, Wolfgang Windgassen, Peter Hoffmann.

3771 Eaton, Quaintance. "Beau Idéal: Baritone Martial Singher, Featured in the Metropolitan Opera's New Historic Album of *Les Contes d'Hoffmann*, Has Set a Standard of Excellence as Both Singer and Teacher." *OpN*. 1987 Apr 11; 51(15): 10-14. Illus.: Photo. B&W. 12. Lang.: Eng.
France. USA: Santa Barbara, CA. 1904-1987. Histories-sources. ■Profile, interview with French tenor, Martial Singher.

3772 Eckert, Thor, Jr. "Singer for Life: French Stylist Michel Sénéchal." *OpN*. 1987 Feb 28; 51(12): 26. Illus.: Photo. B&W. 1. Lang.: Eng.
France: Paris. 1987. Histories-sources. ■Profile, interview with French comprimario baritone, Michel Sénéchal.

3773 Halévy, Ludovic; Meilhac, Henri; Russell, Clarence H., transl. "Breaking the Rules. In 1904, on the Occasion of the 1,000th Performance of *Carmen*, Co-Librettist Ludovic Halévy Recalled the Difficult Birth of Bizet's Masterpiece." *OpN*. 1987 Mar 14; 51(13): 36-37, 47. Illus.: Photo. B&W. 2. Lang.: Eng.

France: Paris. 1873-1875. Histories-sources. ■From an article in *Le Théâtre*, 1904.

3774 Harris, Dale. "Rien de Trop, 'Nothing in Excess' Is the Motto of Manuel Rosenthal, Who Conducts This Month's Metropolitan Telecast of *Dialogues des Carmélites*." *OpN*. 1987 May; 51(16): 10-11, 14. Illus.: Photo. Color. 1. Lang.: Eng.
France: Paris. 1904-1987. Histories-sources. ■Interview with conductor Manuel Rosenthal.

3775 Harris, Dale. "Full Cycle: How the *Ring* Has Been Staged Since Wagner's Day." *OpN*. 1987 Feb 28; 51(12): 12-14, 45. Illus.: Design. Diagram. Plan. Dwg. Photo. Print. Color. B&W. 10. Lang.: Eng.
Germany: Bayreuth. Italy: Milan. USA: New York, NY. 1876-1987. Historical studies. ■Production history of *Der Ring des Nibelungen*.

3776 Siegmund-Schultze, Walther; Rienäcker, Gerd. "Zum 200. Todestag von Christoph Willibald Gluck." (On the Bicentenary of C.W. Gluck's Death.) *MusGes*. 1987; 37(11): 561-579. Illus.: Photo. B&W. 9. Lang.: Ger.
Germany. Germany, East: Halle. 1762-1986. Critical studies. ■On Gluck as opera composer and productions of his works in the GDR, analysis of *Orfeo ed Euridice* in Halle 1986, staged by Peter Konwitschny.

3777 "Wie beschreibt man Opern?" (How to Describe Operas.) 41-73 in Seeger, Horst. *Oper heute*. Berlin: Henschelverlag; 1987. 301 pp. (Ein Almanach der Musikbühne 10.) Lang.: Ger.
Germany, East. Germany, West. 1988. Histories-sources.

3778 Hänsel, Dieter; Hykel, Edgard; Franke, Gotthard; Jäckel, Manfred. "Vom Beruf des Chorsängers." (On the Profession of the Chorus-Singer.) *TZ*. 1987; 42(1): 45-48. [Teil 1.] Lang.: Ger.
Germany, East. 1986. Instructional materials. ■Contributions of 4 opera chorus conductors.

3779 Heed, Sven Åke. "I dödens landskap." (In the Landscape of Death.) *MuD*. 1987; 9(4): 10-11. Illus.: Photo. Lang.: Swe.
Germany, East: Berlin, East. 1987. Critical studies. ■A presentation of Harry Kupfer's staging of *Don Giovanni*.

3780 Herz, Joachim. "Wir Heiben uns hoffen." (We Dare to Hope.) *TZ*. 1987; 42(4): 31-32. Lang.: Ger.
Germany, East. 1987. Historical studies. ■Opera singers' profession and craftsmanship, related to special necessities in their training.

3781 Lange, Wolfgang. "Bewegung und Bewegtheit. Betrachtungen zum DDR-Musiktheater(2): Zu Orchestern, Dirigenten und anderem." (Movement and Movability. Reflections on Musical Theatre in the GDR, Part II: Orchestras, Conductors and Other Things.) *TZ*. 1987; 42(4): 36-38. Illus.: Photo. 2. Lang.: Ger.
Germany, East. 1980-1986. Critical studies.

3782 Lange, Wolfgang. "Hans-Dieter Pflüger." *TZ*. 1987; 42(1): 42-44. Illus.: Photo. B&W. 2. Lang.: Ger.
Germany, East: Dresden. 1979-1986. Histories-sources. ■Talk with the chorus director of the Staatsoper Dresdner (Semperoper) on his professional practice and the profession of a chorus singer.

3783 Lange, Wolfgang. "Und das ist gut so. Betrachtungen zum DDR-Musiktheater(1): Regisseure-Präsenz, Nutzung, Kontinuität." (It's Good That Way: Reflections on Musical Theatre in the GDR, Part 1: Directors—Presence, Efficiency, Continuity.) *TZ*. 1987; 42(3): 35-37. Illus.: Photo. 2. Lang.: Ger.
Germany, East. 1980-1987. Critical studies. ■Overview of East German opera theatre: directors.

3784 Neef, Sigrid. "Ein Anfang und kein Ende, Bühnenwerke des 20. Jahrhunderts an der Deutschen Staatsoper Berlin." (A Beginning and No End: 20th-Century Stage Works at the Deutsche Staatsoper, Berlin.) *MusGes*. 1987; 37(5): 252-258. Illus.: Photo. B&W. 8. Lang.: Ger.
Germany, East: Berlin, East. 1945-1987. Historical studies.

3785 Neef, Sigrid, ed. *Ruth Berghaus inszeniert Die Verurteilung des Lukullus, Oper von Paul Dessau. Text von Bertolt*

MUSIC-DRAMA: Opera—Performance/production

Brecht. (Ruth Berghaus Stages *The Condemnation of Lucullus.* Music by Paul Dessau, Text by Bertolt Brecht.) Berlin: Verband der Theaterschaffenden der DDR; 1987. 156 pp. (TD.DR 14.) Biblio. Illus.: Photo. B&W. 72. Lang.: Ger.
Germany, East: Berlin, East. 1983. Histories-sources. ■Documentation of R. Berghaus' production of *Die Verurteilung des Lukullus* in the Deutsche Staatsoper Berlin, consisting of various materials: detailed description, theses, interviews, reviews, articles, list of Berghaus' productions.

3786 Schlegel, Dietrich; Däbritz, Anita; Liesk, Wolfgang. "Vom Beruf des Chorsängers." (On the Profession of the Chorus-Singer.) *TZ.* 1987; 42(2): 29-31. [Teil 2.] Lang.: Ger.
Germany, East. 1986. Instructional materials. ■Contributions of three opera chorus conductors.

3787 Tüngler, Irene. "Eine fast heilige Begeisterung. Über den Sänger Michael Rabsilber, Komische Oper Berlin." (An Almost Sacred Passion: On the Singer Michael Rabsilber, Komische Oper Berlin.) *TZ.* 1987; 42(2): 25-29. Illus.: Photo. 7. Lang.: Ger.
Germany, East. 1982-1986. Biographical studies. ■Career of young tenor, including remarks by and about director Harry Kupfer.

3788 Heed, Sven Åke. "Oedipus i Västberlin." (Oedipus in West Berlin.) *MuD.* 1987; 9(4): 8-9. Illus.: Photo. Lang.: Swe.
Germany, West: Berlin, West. 1987. Critical studies. ■A presentation of Wolfgang Rihm's *Oedipus* and the staging by Götz Friedrich.

3789 Sutcliffe, James Helme. "Birthdays in Berlin, II: Like the City Itself, Opera Houses Old and New Are Celebrating a String of Anniversaries." *OpN.* 1987 Mar 28; 51(14): 32-35, 45. Illus.: Plan. Color. 1. Lang.: Eng.
Germany, West: Berlin, West. Germany, East: Berlin, East. 1237-1987. Histories-sources. ■Anniversaries at Kleine Oper, Deutsche Oper, Städtische Oper and Deutsche Staatsoper.

3790 Scott, Michael. "A Connoisseur's Callas: Ten Years After Her Death...the Soprano's Achievement as Preserved in Memory and Through Recordings." *OpN.* 1987 Sep.; 52(3): 29-30, 32, 69. Illus.: Photo. B&W. 8. Lang.: Eng.
Greece. Italy. USA. 1923-1977. Histories-sources. ■Evaluation of soprano Maria Meneghini Callas. Related to Media: Audio forms.

3791 "Placido Domingo Budapesten. Radamesként tért vissza." (Plácido Domingo in Budapest: He Returned as Radames.) *FSM.* 1987 May; 31(18): 12-13. Illus.: Photo. B&W. 2. Lang.: Hun.
Hungary: Budapest. 1961-1987. Histories-sources. ■Opera singer Plácido Domingo speaks about his life, his roles, and his artistic faith.

3792 Gábor, István. "Szeged nincs messze Budapesttől." (Szeged Is Not Far Away From Budapest.) *Sz.* 1987 Aug.; 20 (8): 37-40. Illus.: Photo. B&W. 2. Lang.: Hun.
Hungary: Szeged. 1987. Reviews of performances. ■Some of the productions of the 4th opera ensemble meeting in Szeged: Sándor Szokolay's *Vérnász (Blood Wedding)* directed and conducted by Géza Oberfrank, Offenbach's *La vie parisienne (Parisian Life)*, Mozart's *Le nozze di Figaro (The Marriage of Figaro)*.

3793 Gách, Marianne. "Gách Marianne beszélgetése Gregor Józseffel. 'Hivatalos rangja: állandó vendég'." (Marianne Gách Interviews József Gregor: 'His Official Rank: Permanent Guest'.) *FSM.* 1987 Feb.; 31(9): 12-13. Illus.: Photo. B&W. 1. Lang.: Hun.
Hungary. 1963-1987. Histories-sources. ■Singer József Gregor speaks about his early career full of failure, his plans and artistic principles.

3794 Gách, Marianne. "Gách Marianne beszélgetése Gulyás Dénessel. 'Eszményképem, a polihisztor'." (Marianne Gách Interviews Dénes Gulyás: 'My Ideal, the Polihistor'.) *FSM.* 1987 Mar.; 31(13): 8-9. Illus.: Photo. B&W. 1. Lang.: Hun.
Hungary. 1983-1987. Histories-sources. ■The young Hungarian opera singer speaks about his performance abroad, his experiences gained in the Metropolitan, his ideals, working methods and plans.

3795 Hadai, Győző; Mag, László. *Sárdy János.* (János Sárdy.) Budapest: Zenemükiadó; 1987. 124 pp. Illus.: Photo. B&W. 93. Lang.: Hun.

Hungary. 1907-1969. Biographies. ■Career of tenor of opera and operetta: recollections of contemporaries and anecdotes.

3796 Kőháti, Zsolt. "Kettévált esernyő. Operaegyütteseink IV. találkozója." (Umbrella Divided into Two Parts: 4th Meeting of Opera Ensembles.) *Sz.* 1987 Aug.; 20(8): 34-37. Illus.: Photo. B&W. 2. Lang.: Hun.
Hungary: Szeged. 1987. Reviews of performances.

3797 Lanier, Thomas P. "Showing Emotions: Eva Marton Faces the Enigma of Turandot." *OpN.* 1987 Mar 28; 51(14): 18-19. Illus.: Photo. Color. 1. Lang.: Eng.
Hungary. 1943-1987. Histories-sources. ■Hungarian soprano Eva Marton analyzes the role of Turandot.

3798 Róna, Katalin. "Még a hold is feljő. A *Hamupipőke* Szentendrén." (Even the Moon Rises: *La Cenerentola* in Szentendre.) *Sz.* 1987 Nov.; 20(11): 27-28. Illus.: Photo. B&W. 1. Lang.: Hun.
Hungary: Szentendre. 1987. Reviews of performances. ■Rossini's comic opera *La Cenerentola* at the Szentendre Theatre directed by András Békés.

3799 "Bellini—den lycklige." (Bellini—The Happy One.) *MuD.* 1987; 9(4): 6-7. Illus.: Photo. Lang.: Swe.
Italy. 1837. Critical studies. ■Wagner's view on the Italian *bel canto* and the greatness of Vincenzo Bellini.

3800 Ardoin, John. "Verdi on Record: The Early Years." *OQ.* 1987 Sum; 5(2/3): 48-58. Notes. Lang.: Eng.
Italy. France. USA. 1900-1945. Historical studies. ■History of first recordings of Verdi's operas: singers who interpreted original roles.

3801 Battaglia, Carl. "In Quest of Rossini: Pesaro, Birthplace of the Composer, Has Become a Center for Research and Performance Style." *OpN.* 1987 Aug.; 52(2): 30-31, 45. Illus.: Photo. B&W. 2. Lang.: Eng.
Italy: Pesaro. 1984-1987. Histories-sources. ■Vocal style and authenticity of performances at the Rossini Festival.

3802 Battaglia, Carl. "Keepers of the Flame: Virginia Zeani and Nicola Rossi-Lemeni, After Rewarding Careers Onstage, Now Strive to Pass on Their Knowledge to a Younger Generation." *OpN.* 1987 Nov.; 52(5): 28-30, 32. Illus.: Photo. B&W. 3. Lang.: Eng.
Italy. 1920-1987. Histories-sources. ■Interview and profile of soprano Virginia Zeani and bass Nicola Rossi-Lemeni, new singing teachers.

3803 Duffie, Bruce. "Conversation Piece: Max Rudolf." *OJ.* 1987; 20(2): 36-40. Lang.: Eng.
Italy. USA: New York, NY. 1945-1987. Critical studies. ■Conductor Max Rudolf's career, his views on conducting and on educating aspiring conductors.

3804 Fallenius, Göran. "Det doftar..." (There Is a Scent.) *MuD.* 1987; 9(4): 15-17. Illus.: Photo. Lang.: Swe.
Italy: Sant' Agate. 1987. Histories-sources. ■Impressions from a tour to Sant'Agate and a *Nabucco* performance in the square of Rancole.

3805 Giannini, Vera. "Italo Tajo: A Great Basso Looks at his Repertoire." *OQ.* 1987/88 Win; 5(4): 58-66. Notes. Illus.: Photo. 2. Lang.: Eng.
Italy: Turin. 1935-1982. Historical studies. ■Analysis of basso singer Italo Tajo's style and adaptation of roles in the operatic repertoire.

3806 Keyser, Dorothy. "Cross-Sexual Casting in Baroque Opera Musical and Theatrical Conventions." *OQ.* 1987/88; 5(4): 46-57. Notes. Lang.: Eng.
Italy: Venice, Rome. 1550-1987. Historical studies. ■Cross-gender casting in Italian Baroque opera: use of boy *castrati* and relationship to women performers.

3807 Krauss, Malvyn. "Testa Dura: Mirella Freni...Claims the Secret of Her Success Is a Hard Head." *OpN.* 1987 Oct.; 52(4): 33-34. Illus.: Photo. Color. 1. Lang.: Eng.
Italy: Modena. USA. 1935-1987. Histories-sources. ■Interview with soprano Mirella Freni.

3808 Lebrecht, Norman. "Muti of Milan: La Scala's Artistic Director Talks About His New Job and Political Pressures in the Music World." *OpN.* 1987 Jan 17; 51(9): 18-19, 42. Illus.: Photo. Color. 1. Lang.: Eng.

MUSIC-DRAMA: Opera —Performance/production

Italy: Milan. 1970-1987. Histories-sources. ■Interview with Italian conductor Riccardo Muti, artistic director, Teatro alla Scala.

3809   Strehler, Giorgio; Heed, Sven Åke, transl. *"Tolvskillingsope-ran."* (*The Three Penny Opera*.) *NT.* 1987; 36: 4-9. Illus.: Photo. Lang.: Swe.

Italy: Milan. France: Paris. 1928-1986. Critical studies. ■An analysis of the difficulties of staging *Die Dreigroschenoper (The Three Penny Opera).*

3810   Briede, V. *Latyšskij opernyj teatr.* (Latvian Opera Theatre.) Riga: Zinatne; 1987. 246 pp. Lang.: Rus.

Latvia. 1913-1982. Historical studies.

3811   Muro, María. *"Puesta en escena de La Flauta Magica."* (Production of *The Magic Flute*.) *UMex.* 1987 Oct.; 42(441): 46-48. Illus.: Pntg. B&W. 2. Lang.: Spa.

Mexico: Mexico City. 1987. Reviews of performances. ■A children's production of Mozart's *The Magic Flute* performed in Spanish.

3812   Sachs, Harvey. "Domingo and Otello-Mania." *OC.* 1987 Sum; 28(2): 18-21. Illus.: Photo. B&W. 4. Lang.: Eng.

Mexico. 1941-1987. Biographical studies. ■Examines the career of Plácido Domingo at forty-six years of age, his commitments to the role of Otello in the centenary year of the opera's premiere, his growing career as a conductor and his family life.

3813   Scovell, Jane. "Domingo: Giving His Best: The Tenor Has Become a Multimedia Star, and This Fall He Opens Seasons in Los Angeles, New York and Houston." *OpN.* 1987 Sep.; 52(3): 14-17. Illus.: Photo. Color. 3. Lang.: Eng.

Mexico: Mexico City. USA: New York, NY, Los Angeles, CA, Houston, TX. 1941-1987. Histories-sources. ■Interview with tenor Plácido Domingo.

3814   Arian, Max; Brink, Nic. "'Ik was van natuur als episch'. Dario Fo over Rossini, Goldoni, Strehler en Politiek." ('I was already epic by nature': Dario Fo on Rossini, Goldoni, Strehler and Politics.) *Toneel.* 1987 June; 6(4): 30-33. Illus.: Photo. B&W. 1. Lang.: Dut.

Netherlands. Italy. 1987. Histories- sources. ■Interview with Dario Fo about his production of *Il barbiere di Siviglia* with the Nederlandse Opera and his ideas about Rossini, Goldoni, and his relationship with Strehler and his political ideas.

3815   Eichbaum, Julius. *"Der Fliegende Holländer*—A Stunning Achievement by NAPAC." *Scenaria.* 1987 Apr.; 75: 33-35. Illus.: Photo. 4. Lang.: Eng.

South Africa, Republic of: Durban. 1987. Reviews of performances. ■Review of *Der Fliegende Holländer* at the Natal Playhouse, directed by James Conrad. First Wagnerian opera to be performed in Natal.

3816   Eichbaum, Julius. *"Die Meistersinger von Nürnberg*—An Introduction." *Scenaria.* 1987 July; 78: 5-8. Illus.: Design. Handbill. Photo. Dwg. 8. Lang.: Eng.

South Africa, Republic of: Cape Town. Germany, West: Munich. 1868-1987. Histories-reconstruction. ■Development of *Die Meistersinger von Nürnberg* to its contemporary performance at the Nico Malan Operahouse, background on Wagner.

3817   Kinkaid, Frank. "Spell It M-A-D-R-I-D: Spain's Capital City Is Being Revitalized Operatically—But It's a Well-Kept Secret." *OpN.* 1987 May; 51(16): 50-51. Illus.: Photo. B&W. 2. Lang.: Eng.

Spain: Madrid. 1925-1987. Histories-specific. ■Focuses on Teatro Lirico Nacional La Zarzuela.

3818   Tassel, Janet. "Return to Barcelona: This Month the Gran Teatre del Liceu Features Catalan Opera Stars Montserrat Caballé and José Carreras in the World Premiere of Native Composer Leonardo Balada's *Cristobal Colón*." *OpN.* 1987 Sep.; 52(3): 41-42. Illus.: Photo. B&W. 4. Lang.: Eng.

Spain-Catalonia: Barcelona. 1987. Histories-sources.

3819   Bergström, Gunnel. "Musik som 'ångvält' och yta." (Music as 'Steamroller' and as Surface.) *MuD.* 1987; 9(1): 14-165. Illus.: Photo. Lang.: Swe.

Sweden. 1986. Histories-sources. ■Hans Gefors' view of the libretto versus his music to *Christina.*

3820   Davis, Peter G. "Saying It All." *OpN.* 1987 Feb 14; 51(11): 12. Lang.: Eng.

Sweden: Stockholm. 1927-1987. Biographical studies. ■Evaluation of soprano Elisabeth Söderström.

3821   Frankenstein, Alfred. "Kerstin Thorborg—altarnas Caruso." (Kerstin Thorborg: The Caruso of the Contraltos.) *MuD.* 1987; 9(2): 12-13. Illus.: Photo. Lang.: Swe.

Sweden. Germany. 1932-1970. Biographical studies. ■Memories of the great singer and her career in Europe.

3822   Friberg, Tomas; Sjöberg, Lars; Bergström, Gunnel. "Christina—ett mode. Sillös rappakalja." (Christina—a Fashion: Rubbish Without Style.) *MuD.* 1987; 9(1): 15-17. Notes. Illus.: Photo. Lang.: Swe.

Sweden: Stockholm. 1987. Critical studies. ■Discussion for and against Hans Gefors' *Christina* at the Royal Swedish Opera.

3823   Johansson, Stefan. "Grand Opera—eller drömspel? Om årets musikteaterhändelse: Christina." (Grand Opera—or a Dream Play? About the Event of the Year in Music Drama: *Christina*.) *TArsb.* 1987; 6: 20-25. Illus.: Photo. Print. B&W. 3. Lang.: Swe.

Sweden: Stockholm. 1986-1987. Historical studies. ■Review of the newly written opera *Christina* based on the play by August Strindberg: music by Hans Gefors, libretto by Lars Forssell.

3824   Loney, Glenn. "Pure and Simple: Göran Järvefelt, Soon to Stage *Die Schweigsame Frau* at Santa Fe Opera, May Have Outraged Traditionalists, But He Insists He's Following the Score." *OpN.* 1987 June; 51(17): 18-20, 22. Illus.: Photo. B&W. 1. Lang.: Eng.

Sweden. USA: Santa Fe, NM. 1948-1987. Biographical studies. ■Career of Swedish director Göran Järvefelt.

3825   Saarsen-Karlstedt, Karin. "Prins! Rövare! Förförare! Poet?" (Prince! Robber! Seducer! Poet?)*MuD.* 1987; 9(1): 44-45. Illus.: Photo. Lang.: Swe.

Sweden: Stockholm. Ethiopia. 1944-1987. Histories-sources. ■Esias Tewolde-Berhan speaks about his background in Eritrea and his career as tenor at the Royal Swedish Opera.

3826   Cahn, Roger. "Othmar Schoeck: Der schwierige Schweizer." (Othmar Schoeck: The Difficult Swiss Composer.) *MuT.* 1987 Jan. ; 8(1): 56-58. Illus.: Photo. B&W. Lang.: Ger.

Switzerland. 1886-1986. Biographies. ■Due to the celebrations to his 100th anniversary Schoeck has been talked about in wider circles. Being a composer of only a medium reputation he has left a work unfortunately not wide enough in range, often too complex for an unexperienced audience to grasp, to gain the credit he merits according to some musical critics.

3827   Kenyon, Nicholas. "Vintage Debut: Tenor Hugues Cuénod Is at the Met at Last." *OpN.* 1987 Mar 28; 51(14): 24, 44. Illus.: Photo. Color. B&W. 2. Lang.: Eng.

Switzerland: Vevey. 1902-1987. Histories-sources. ■Interview with Swiss tenor Hugues Cuénod.

3828   Roth, Jean-Jacques. *Opéras: Moments d'exception.* (Operas: Moments of Exception.) Fribourg: Office du Livre; 1987. 264 pp. Pref. Index. Append. Illus.: Photo. Color. B&W. Lang.: Fre.

Switzerland: Geneva. 1980-1987. ■Analyses of 20 opera productions at the Grand Théâtre de Genève under the managing direction of Hugues Gall.

3829   Bartlett, Neil. "Opera." *PM.* 1987(48): 9-13. Illus.: Photo. B&W. 2. Lang.: Eng.

UK-England. 1973-1987. Histories-sources. ■Interview with David Freeman, the director of the Opera Factory. Public perception of opera and David Freeman's approach to the art form are discussed.

3830   Kozinn, Alan. "No Mere Curiosity: Paul Esswood and the Resurging Art of the Countertenor." *OpN.* 1987 Aug.; 52(2): 26-29 . Illus.: Photo. B&W. 1. Lang.: Eng.

UK-England: London. 1942-1987. Histories-sources. ■Interview with countertenor Paul Esswood.

3831   Mortimer, John. "Open: Unabashed Emotion." *Drama.* 1987; 3(165): 44. Illus.: Photo. B&W. 1. Lang.: Eng.

UK-England: London. 1987. Reviews of performances. ■Review of *Otello* at the Royal Opera House, London.

MUSIC-DRAMA: Opera—Performance/production

3832 "Lyric Opera of Chicago: Radio Broadcast Performances." *OpN.* 1987; 51. Illus.: Photo. Color. B&W. [*Un Ballo in Maschera* (May): 26, *Die Zauberflöte* (May): 27, *Kát'a Kabanová* (May): 28, *La Bohéme* (May): 29, *Orlando* (June): 38, *La Gioconda* (June): 39, *Parsifal* (June): 40, *Lucia di Lammermoor* (June): 41, *The Merry Widow* (June): 42.] Lang.: Eng.
USA: Chicago, IL. 1987. Histories-sources. ■Photographs, lists of principals, conductors, production staff, synopses. Related to Media: Audio forms.

3833 "San Francisco on the Air: A Guide to the Company's 1987 Broadcast Season." *OpN.* 1987; 52. Illus.: Photo. B&W. [*Otello* (Sep): 46, *Khovanshchina* (Sep): 47, *Manon Lescaut* (Sep): 48, *Jen0ufa* (Oct): 28, *Don Carlos* (Oct): 29, *Le Nozze di Figaro* (Oct): 30, *Eugene Onegin* (Oct): 32, *Macbeth* (Nov): 44, *La Gioconda* (Nov): 45, *Falstaff* (Nov):46.] Lang.: Eng.
USA: San Francisco, CA. 1987. Histories-sources. ■Photographs, lists of principals, conductors, production staff, synopses. Related to Media: Audio forms.

3834 "Opera Company of Philadelphia: Telecast Performance." *OpN.* 1987; 52. Illus.: Design. Diagram. Dwg. Photo. Color. B&W. [*Un Ballo in Maschera* (Dec 20): 33.] Lang.: Eng.
USA: Philadelphia, PA. 1987. Histories-sources. ■Telecast stills, list of principals, conductors, production staff, synopsis. Related to Media: Video forms.

3835 Ardoin, John. "A Pride of Prima Donnas." *OQ.* 1987 Spr; 5(1): 58-70. Illus.: Photo. 3. Lang.: Eng.
USA. 1952-1981. Biographical studies. ■Careers of three female opera stars: Mary McCormic, Maria Jeritza, Bidú Sayão.

3836 Battaglia, Carl. "Staged by Scotto." *OpN.* 1987 Jan 17; 51(9): 10-13. Illus.: Photo. B&W. 9. Lang.: Eng.
USA: New York, NY. 1987. Histories-sources. ■Italian soprano Renata Scotto directs a Metropolitan Opera production of *Madama Butterfly* by Giacomo Puccini.

3837 Bergman, Beth; Flatow, Sheryl; Waleson, Heidi; Ostlere, Hilary; Schmidgall, Gary. "Metropolitan Opera: Radio Broadcast Performances." *OpN.* 1987; 51. Discography. Illus.: Design. Diagram. Dwg. Photo. Color. B&W. [*La Bohème* (Jan 3): 22-25, *Rigoletto* (Jan 3): 26-29, *Madama Butterfly* (Jan 17): 20-23, *Tannhäuser* (Jan 17): 26-29, *Manon Lescaut* (Jan 31): 18-20, 23, *Le Nozze di Figaro* (Jan 31): 24-27, *La Clemenza di Tito* (Feb 14): 22-24, 26, *Der Rosenkavalier* (Feb 14): 28-31, *Manon Lescaut* (Feb 14): 22-24, *Die Walküre* (Feb 14): 28-31, *Boris Godunov* (Mar 14): 20, 22-24, *Carmen* (Mar 14): 26, 28-30, *Turandot* (Mar 28):19-20, 22-23, *Dialogues des Carmélites* (Mar 28): 26-29, *Parsifal* (Apr 11): 20, 22-24, *Samson et Dalila* (Apr 11), 26-28, 30.] Lang.: Eng.
USA: New York, NY. 1987. Histories-sources. ■Photographs, lists of principals, conductors, production staff, biographies, synopses, discographies. Related to Media: Audio forms.

3838 Bergman, Beth; McGovern, Dennis; Flatow, Sheryl. "Metropolitan Opera: Radio Broadcast Performances ." *OpN.* 1987; 52. Illus.: Design. Diagram. Dwg. Photo. Color. B&W. [*Tosca* (Dec 5): 26-28, 30, *Die Entführung aus dem Serail* (Dec 5): 32-34, 36, *Il Trovatore* (Dec 19): 22-23, 26, *La Traviata* (Dec 19): 28-30, 32.] Lang.: Eng.
USA: New York, NY. 1987. Histories-sources. ■Photographs, lists of principals, conductors, production staff, biographies, synopses, discographies. Related to Media: Audio forms.

3839 Bergman, Beth. "Metropolitan Opera: Telecast Performances." *OpN.* 1987; 51. Discography. Illus.: Design. Diagram. Dwg. Photo. Color. B&W. [The Sutherland/Pavarotti Anniversary Gala (Feb 28): 40-41, *Carmen* (Mar 14): 26, 28-30, *Dialogues des Carmélites* (May): 12-13.] Lang.: Eng.
USA: New York, NY. 1987. Histories-sources. ■Photographs, telecast stills, lists of principals, conductors, production staff, biographies, discographies, synopses. Related to Media: Video forms.

3840 Blumenfeld, Harold. "A Breakthrough Season in St. Louis." *OJ.* 1987; 20(3): 3-6. Illus.: Photo. B&W. 1. Lang.: Eng.
USA: St. Louis, MO. 1987. Critical studies. ■1987 season of the Opera Theatre of St. Louis, its mingling of traditional classics with new commissioned works.

3841 Brisk, Barry. "Leopold Stokowski and *Wozzeck*: An American premiere in 1931." *OQ.* 1987 Spr; 5(1): 71-82. Notes. Lang.: Eng.
USA: New York, NY. 1931. Critical studies. ■Retrospective on American premiere of Alban Berg's *Wozzeck* under the leadership of conductor Leopold Stokowski.

3842 Buchau, Stephanie von. "Barbary Coast Bonanza: A Rich Lode Rewards Opera-Lovers in and Near San Francisco." *OpN.* 1987 Sep.; 52(3): 18, 20, 22, 68. Illus.: Photo. B&W. 4. Lang.: Eng.
USA: San Francisco, CA. 1900-1987. Histories-sources. ■Regional opera in the Bay Area.

3843 Buchau, Stephanie von. "Not Just Entertainment." *OpN.* 1987 Oct.; 52(4): 24, 26. Illus.: Photo. B&W. 2. Lang.: Eng.
USA: Houston, TX. 1987. Histories-sources. ■Premiere of the docu-opera, *Nixon in China*, John Adams (composer), Alice Goodman (librettist), Peter Sellars (director), Wortham Center, Houston Grand Opera.

3844 Duffie, Bruce. "Conversation Piece: Vasile Moldoveanu." *OJ.* 1987; 20(1): 36-40. Lang.: Eng.
USA. 1987. Histories-sources. ■Tenor Vasile Moldoveanu on assuming new roles at a fast pace and how to prepare for the production. Public and critics of the works.

3845 Duffie, Bruce. "Conversation Piece: Jane Klaviter." *OJ.* 1987; 20(4): 28-32. Lang.: Eng.
USA: Chicago, IL. 1987. Histories-sources. ■Jane Klaviter discusses her career as a prompter, use of techniques to communicate with singers onstage.

3846 Eckert, Thor, Jr. "No Nonsense: A Pragmatist, Barbara Daniels Has Built Her Career by Considering Every Step." *OpN.* 1987 Jan 3; 51(8): 16-19. Illus.: Photo. Color. B&W. 3. Lang.: Eng.
USA: New York, NY. 1987. Histories-sources. ■Interview and profile of American soprano Barbara Daniels.

3847 Flatow, Sheryl. "Double Play: John Mauceri and Paul Gemignani Like Both Sides of the Street, Conducting in the Opera House and on Broadway." *OpN.* 1987 June; 51(17): 10-13, 36. Tables. Illus.: Photo. Color. 1. Lang.: Eng.
USA: New York, NY. 1980-1987. Historical studies. ■Opera conductors who also conduct in Broadway musicals.

3848 Freeman, John. "Sharing the Music: John Wustman, Master Accompanist amd Mentor of Susan Dunn, Talks About His Specialities." *OpN.* 1987 July; 52(1): 16-18, 52. Illus.: Photo. B&W. 4. Lang.: Eng.
USA. 1960-1987. Histories-sources. ■American accompanist/voice teacher, John Wustman.

3849 Heymont, George. "A Painful Process: Opera in America Has Changed Drastically,...But There Are Still Difficult Issues to Face." *OpN.* 1987 Nov.; 52(5): 12-25. Illus.: Pntg. Plan. Color. 1. [Opera in America, an Overview.] Lang.: Eng.
USA. 1987. Histories-sources. ■Problems of opera funding and repertory.

3850 Heymont, George. "In It Together: Thirteen Companies Across the U.S. Share the Profits and Problems of Co-Producing *Porgy and Bess*, in a Program Sponsored by Opera America." *OpN.* 1987 Mar 28; 51(14): 10-13. Illus.: Photo. B&W. 6. Lang.: Eng.
USA. 1987. Historical studies. ■Cooperative finance in touring productions of Gershwin's *Porgy and Bess*.

3851 Heymont, George. "Music Director John DeMain: The Real Thing." *OpN.* 1987 Oct.; 52(4): 22. Illus.: Photo. B&W. 1. Lang.: Eng.
USA: Houston, TX. 1944-1987. Histories-sources. ■Interview with John DeMain, music director, Houston Grand Opera.

MUSIC-DRAMA: Opera—Performance/production

3852 Kandell, Leslie. "An Angel's Way: Lloyd E. Rigler, a Major Benefactor of the New York City Opera, Keeps Close Tabs on Where His Money Goes." *OpN.* 1987 Jan 31; 51(10): 8-10. Illus.: Photo. Color. 1. [Funding: the private donor.] Lang.: Eng.
USA: New York, NY. 1980-1987. Biographical studies. ■Profile of Lloyd Rigler, benefactor of the New York City Opera.

3853 Mayer, Martin. "The Altmeyer Story." *OpN.* 1987 Feb 28; 51(12): 8-10. Illus.: Photo. Color. 3. Lang.: Eng.
USA: New York, NY. 1950-1987. Histories-sources. ■Profile of soprano Jeannine Altmeyer.

3854 Mayer, Martin. "Make Me a Star: The Request Once Made by Soprano Susan Dunn Has Become a Reality." *OpN.* 1987 July; 52 (1): 10-14. Illus.: Photo. Color. B&W. 5. Lang.: Eng.
USA: New York, NY. 1955-1987. Biographical studies. ■Profile of soprano Susan Dunn.

3855 McGovern, Dennis. "Singing Day to Day: James McCracken...Ruminates on the Rewards and Frustrations of His Thirty-Five-Year Career." *OpN.* 1987 Oct.; 52(4): 38, 40-41. Illus.: Photo. Color. 2. Lang.: Eng.
USA: Gary, IN. Europe. 1926-1987. Histories-sources. ■Interview with tenor James McCracken.

3856 Price, Walter. "Irreplaceable: For Many, Risë Stevens Remains the Carmen of All Time—Though at First She Had to Fight for the Role." *OpN.* 1987 Mar 14; 51(13): 8-12. Illus.: Photo. Color. B&W. 10. Lang.: Eng.
USA: New York, NY. Biographical studies. ■Profile of mezzo soprano Risë Stevens.

3857 Rich, Maria F. "Opera in America. Playing It Safe." *OpN.* 1987 Nov.; 52(5): 20, 22, 24, 26-27, 78. Illus.: Pntg. Plan. Color. 1. Lang.: Eng.
USA. 1986-1987. Histories-sources. ■Survey of recent American opera reveals unadventurous repertory, few experimental works.

3858 Scherer, Barrymore Laurence. "Academic Questions: Twelve Major Figures from the World of Opera Confront Some Thorny Aspects of Educating the American Singer." *OpN.* 1987 Nov.; 52(5): 16-18, 71. Illus.: Pntg. Plan. Color. 1. [Opera in America, an Overview.] Lang.: Eng.
USA. 1987. Histories-sources. ■Experts discuss vocal training.

3859 Schmidgall, Gary. "Our Favorite Force of Nature: Birgit Nilsson's Master Classes Generously Combine Common Sense and Inspiration." *OpN.* 1987 July; 52(1): 20-22, 24. Illus.: Photo. B&W. 8. Lang.: Eng.
USA: New York, NY. 1983-1987. Histories-sources. ■Birgit Nilsson's master voice class at Manhattan School of Music.

3860 Schmidgall, Gary. "Dramatic Leanings: Leona Mitchell Enters a New Phase in Her Career." *OpN.* 1987 Jan 31; 51(10): 21-22 . Illus.: Photo. Color. 1. Lang.: Eng.
USA: New York, NY. 1940-1987. Biographical studies. ■Profile of American soprano Leona Mitchell.

3861 Seward, William. "Golden Days: Bidú Sayão Celebrates the Fiftieth Anniversary of Her Metropolitan Opera Debut." *OpN.* 1987 Feb 28; 51(12): 20. Illus.: Photo. B&W. 3. Lang.: Eng.
USA: New York, NY. Brazil. 1902-1987. Biographical studies. ■Brazilian soprano Bidú Sayão.

3862 Sills, Beverly; Linderman, Lawrence. *Beverly, an Autobiography.* Toronto, ON: Bantam; 1987. xii, 352 pp. Illus.: Photo. 30. Lang.: Eng.
USA: New York, NY. 1929-1987. Biographical studies. ■Autobiographical account of Beverly Sills' personal life and opera and concert career in the United States and Europe.

3863 Soria, Dorle. "Treasures and Trifles: The Metropolitan Opera Archives, Revitalized by Its Director, Robert Tuggle, Is a Storehouse for Priceless Memorabilia and Fascinating Marginalia." *OpN.* 1987 Sep.; 52(3): 24-26, 27. Illus.: Photo. Color. B&W. 3. Lang.: Eng.
USA: New York, NY. 1883-1987. Histories-sources. ■Metropolitan Opera archives.

3864 Winer, Deborah Grace; McGovern, Dennis. "Arias Alfresco: For Two Decades. the Metropolitan Opera Has Rounded Out Its Seasons with Concert Performances in New York City Parks, This Year Adding New Jersey to Its Itinerary." *OpN.* 1987 June; 15(17): 24, 26. Illus.: Photo. B&W. 2. Lang.: Eng.
USA: New York, NY. 1967-1987. Historical studies. ■Outdoor performances in city parks.

3865 Abukova, F.A. *Turkmenskaja opera (puti formirovanija, žanrovaja tipoligija).* (Turkmenian Opera: Its Paths of Formation, Genre Typology.) Ašchabad: Ylym; 1987. 162 pp. Lang.: Rus.
USSR. 1900-1987. Historical studies.

3866 Apakidze, Ju. *Nodar Andguladze.* Tbilisi: Helovneva; 1987. 107 pp. Lang.: Rus.
USSR: Georgia. 1927-1987. Biographical studies. ■Work of Georgian opera singer Nodar Andguladze.

3867 Čurova, M., ed. *Bol'šoj teatr Sojuza SSR.* (The Bolšoj Theatre of the Soviet Union.) Moscow: Sovetskij Kompozitor; 1987. 400 pp. Lang.: Rus.
USSR: Moscow. 1974-1980. Critical studies. ■Its creative, productive and sociopolitical life over six seasons.

3868 Faku, M. "Četyre večera v Per'mi." (Four Evenings in Perm'.) *SovMuzyka.* 1987; 5: 52-58. Lang.: Rus.
USSR: Perm. 1980-1987. Critical studies. ■Analysis of the work of Perm Opera Theatre.

3869 Kazenin, I. "Bravo Tamara Janko!" *MuZizn.* 1987; 17: 9. Lang.: Rus.
USSR. 1970-1987. Biographical studies. ■Portrait of folk artist.

3870 Korobkov, S. "Spektakli i sud'by." (Performances and Fates.) *SovMuzyka.* 1987; 5: 58-66. Lang.: Rus.
USSR: Perm. 1980-1987. Critical studies. ■Analysis of Perm Opera Theatre.

3871 Kucharskij, V. "Pravda i chudožestvennaja trebovatel'nost'." (Truth and Artistic Demands.) *TeatrM.* 1987; 8: 73-81. Lang.: Rus.
USSR. 1980-1987. Critical studies. ■Problems and perspectives on the recent development of opera.

3872 Kuusk, P. *Anu Kaal' narodnaja artistka SSSR.* (Anu Kaal': Folk Artist of the Soviet Union.) Tallinn: Periodika; 1987. 36 pp. Lang.: Rus.
USSR. 1960-1987. Biographical studies. ■Creative path of soloist of Estonija Theatre.

3873 Kuznecov, N. "Postavit' improvizaciju." (To Stage an Improvisation.) *MuZizn.* 1987; 1: 5-6. Lang.: Rus.
USSR: Moscow. 1912-1987. Biographical studies. ■Portrait of B.A. Pokrovskij, principal director of Moscow Musical Chamber Theatre, on his 75th birthday.

3874 Loney, Glenn. "Reviving the Dinosaur: Yuri Lyubimov, the Iconoclastic Soviet Director Who This Month Stages Berg's *Lulu* for Lyric Opera of Chicago, Seeks to Make Opera Live." *OpN.* 1987 Nov.; 52(5): 34-36. Illus.: Photo. B&W. 1. Lang.: Eng.
USSR: Moscow. USA: Chicago, IL. 1987. Histories-sources. ■Profile of Jurij Liubimov of Teat'r na Taganke, directing *Lulu* in Chicago.

3875 Magomaev, M.M. *O muzykal'nom iskusstve Azerbajdžana.* (On the Musical Art of Azerbaijan.) Baku: 1987. 156 pp. Lang.: Rus.
USSR. 1935-1987. Historical studies. ■Problems of musical art, opera theatre. Creation of opera *Nargiz*.

3876 Morozov, D. "Tbilisskij opernyj." (Tbilisi Opera.) *MuZizn.* 1987; 18: 2-14. Lang.: Rus.
USSR: Tbilisi. 1980-1987. Critical studies. ■Problems of the Tbilisi Opera Theatre.

3877 Morozov, D. "Sud'ba chudožnika—sud'ba teatra." (Fate of the Artist, Fate of the Theatre.) *SovMuzyka.* 1987; 8: 69-77 . Lang.: Rus.
USSR. 1980-1987. Biographical studies. ■Director A. Viljumanis of Latvian Opera Theatre.

MUSIC-DRAMA: Opera—Performance/production

3878 Pokrovskij, B. "Znanie i mnenie." (Knowledge and Opinion.) *TeatZ.* 1987; 7: 3. Lang.: Rus.
USSR. 1987. Critical studies. ■Issues of current Soviet opera.

3879 Rachmanova, M. "Tvorčestvo 'neslychannych peremen'." (Works of 'Unprecedented Changes'.) *SovMuzyka.* 1987; 12: 41-49. Lang.: Rus.
USSR. 1980-1987. Critical studies. ■New realizations of Mussorgskij operas on the contemporary Soviet stage.

3880 Saakjanc, S. "Lisician i dom Lisiciana." (Lisician and Lisician's Home.) *MuZizn.* 1987: 6-7. Lang.: Rus.
USSR. 1980-1987. Biographical studies. ■Singer and folk artist P. Lisician.

3881 Šaljapin, F.I. *Stranicy iz moej žizni.* (Pages from My Life.) Kiev: Muz. Ukrajna; 1987. 325 pp. Lang.: Rus.
USSR. 1873-1938. Histories-sources. ■Autobiographical memoirs of actor F.I. Šaljapin.

3882 Savenkov, A. "'Ya podarju vam celyj mir'." ('I Present You With the Entire World'.) *Zvezda.* 1987; 10: 176-185. Lang.: Rus.
USSR: Leningrad. 1980-1987. Critical studies. ■Director S. Taudasinskij of Leningrad Malyj Opera Theatre: overview of his productions.

3883 Stachorskij, S.V. *Problemy stilja sovremennoj opernoj režissury (na materiale tvorčestva B.A. Pokrovskogo): Avtoref. dis. kand. iskusstvovedenija.* (Problems of Style in Contemporary Opera Directing, Based on the Work of B.A. Pokrovskij: Abstract of a Dissertation by a Candidate in Art Criticism.) Moscow: GITIS; 1987. 20 pp. Lang.: Rus.
USSR. 1980-1987. Critical studies.

3884 Tartakov, G.I. *Kniga o I.V. Tartakove.* (A Book about I.V. Tartakov.) Leningrad: Muzyka; 1987. 86 pp. Lang.: Rus.
USSR. 1860-1923. Biographical studies. ■Life and work of the opera singer and director.

3885 Velikanova, O. "Ol'ga Basistjuk." *MuZizn.* 1987; 16: 8. Lang.: Rus.
USSR: Kiev. 1980-1987. Biographical studies. ■Portrait of opera soloist of Kiev Opera Theatre.

3886 Vjark, M. *Tijt Kuuzik, Narodnyj artist SSSR.* (Tijt Kuuzik, Folk Artist of the Soviet Union.) Tallinn: Periodika; 1987. 39 pp. Lang.: Rus.
USSR: Estonia. 1911-1987. Biographical studies. ■Tijt Kuuzik (Dmitri Janovič), Estonian opera singer and teacher.

Plays/librettos/scripts

3887 Bernick, Joan. "*The Marriage of Figaro*: Genesis of a Dramatic Masterpiece." *OQ.* 1983 Sum; 1(2): 79-90 aa no. Lang.: Eng.
1784-1786. Critical studies. ■Comparison of da Ponte's libretto for *Le Nozze di Figaro* by Mozart with its source, *Le mariage de Figaro (The Marriage of Figaro)* by Beaumarchais. Analysis of the major characters.

3888 Bowen, Meirion. "A Fusion of Words and Music." *OC.* 1987 Sum; 28(2): 14-17. Illus.: Photo. B&W. 5. Lang.: Eng.
1946-1987. Critical studies. ■Discusses the influence of Sir Michael Tippett on contemporary opera. Includes discussion of Tippett's eclecticism and the fusion created by Tippett's composition of both words and music.

3889 Davies, Robertson. "Critically Speaking." *OC.* 1987 Win; 28(4): 49. Lang.: Eng.
1835. Critical studies. ■Robertson Davies' fictionalized interview with the librettist of Donizetti's *Lucia di Lammermoor* about the treatment of Walter Scott's novel within the libretto.

3890 Ganz, Arthur. "Transformations of the Child Temptress: Mélisande, Salomé, Lulu." *OQ.* 1987/88 Win; 5(4): 12-20. Notes. Lang.: Eng.
1893-1987. Critical studies. ■Adaptation of literary works to opera: focus on *Salome, Lulu* and *Pelléas et Mélisande*.

3891 Gurewitsch, Matthew. "In the Mazes of Light and Shadow: A Thematic Comparison of *The Magic Flute* and *Die Frau ohne Schatten*." *OQ.* 1983 Sum; 1(2): 11-18. Notes. Lang.: Eng.
Austria: Vienna. 1980. Critical studies. ■Analogies between Mozart's *The Magic Flute* and Strauss and Hofmannsthal's *Die Frau ohne Schatten* in music, plot and characters.

3892 Peterson, Hans-Gunnar. "Den häftigaste av kvinnor." (The Hottest of Women.) *MuD.* 1987; 9(1): 9-10. Illus.: Photo. Lang.: Swe.
Austria. 1937-1985. Critical studies. ■George Perle's analysis of Alban Berg's opera *Lulu*.

3893 Dismore, Margaret. "A Lost People: Fierce and Fair, the Philistines Were Exotics on the Landscape of the Middle East, and Delilah Was One of Them." *OpN.* 1987 Apr 11; 51(15): 32-33, 49. Illus.: Maps. B&W. 1. Lang.: Eng.
Canaan. 3000-1000 B.C. Historical studies. ■Background on historical Philistines.

3894 Barber, David. "Winthrop: An Opera by István Anhalt." *Queen's Quarterly.* 1987 Sum; 94(2): 471-472. Lang.: Eng.
Canada: Kitchener, ON. USA. 1987. Critical studies. ■Creation, form, content and premiere of Anhalt's opera based on the life of John Winthrop, a 17th-century puritan and founder of Boston whose followers and descendants had great impact on Maritime Canada.

3895 Baldwin, Olive; Wilson, Thelma. "The Music for D'Urfey's *Cinthia and Endimion*." *TN.* 1987; 41(2): 70-74. Notes. Lang.: Eng.
England: London. 1697. Historical studies. ■Evidence that Daniel Purcell, Jeremiah Clarke and Richard Leveridge collaborated in setting songs for *Cinthia and Endimion*.

3896 Brown, Leslie Ellen. "Metaphor and Music: The Landscape Garden in Eighteenth-Century Operatic Sets." *OQ.* 1983 Win; 2(1): 37-55. Notes. Lang.: Eng.
Europe. 1700-1800. Critical studies. ■Study of the 'garden landscape scene' in the eighteenth-century opera libretto.

3897 Peterson, Hans-Gunnar. "1900-talets musikdramatik—epilog." (The Musical Drama of the 20th Century—Epilogue.) *MuD.* 1987; 9(1): 32-33. Illus.: Photo. Lang.: Swe.
Europe. 1900-1987. Critical studies. ■An overview of operas, mostly very solemn ones, and an inquiry for more relaxed means of expression.

3898 Berges, Ruth. "The Organ Professor As Opera Composer." *OJ.* 1987; 20(4): 23-27. Lang.: Eng.
France: Paris. 1822-1896. Biographical studies. ■César Franck as composer who thrived in an atmosphere of mediocrity where less talented composers were rewarded by the government.

3899 Kestner, Joseph. "Reign of Pleasure: In *Manon* Massenet Chronicled the Sensuality and Materialism of the Belle Époque." *OpN.* 1987 Feb 28; 51(12): 16-19, 39. Illus.: Plan. Dwg. Pntg. Photo. Color. B&W. 8. Lang.: Eng.
France: Paris. 1831-1910. Historical studies. ■Social/historical background and sources of *Manon* by Jules Massenet.

3900 Kestner, Joseph. "The Feared Woman: In *Samson et Dalila*, Saint-Saëns Seized Upon a Subject That Coursed Through Nineteenth-Century Literature and Art—the *Femme Fatale*." *OpN.* 1987 Apr 11; 51(15): 34-37, 49. Illus.: Pntg. Plan. Color. 4. Lang.: Eng.
France. 1800-1899. Critical studies. ■Background of the opera's theme.

3901 Merkling, Frank. "Escape from the Shadow: Poulenc's *Dialogues des Carmélites* and Its Fear-Haunted Heroine." *OpN.* 1987 Mar 28; 51(14): 30-31, 45. MU. Illus.: Photo. B&W. 7. Lang.: Eng.
France: Paris. 1957-1987. Critical studies. ■Role analysis of Blanche in *Dialogues des Carmélites* by Francis Poulenc.

3902 Ratner, Sabina. "Richard Wagner and Camille Saint-Saëns." *OQ.* 1983 Fall; 1(3): 101-113. Notes. Lang.: Eng.
France: Paris. 1859-1916. Histories-sources. ■Documentation on musical and personal relationship between Saint-Saëns and Wagner, how they viewed each other's music.

3903 Scherer, Barrymore Laurence. "Storyteller: Prosper Mérimée—Quiet Witty Author of *Carmen*-Captivated Readers Hungry for Sensation." *OpN.* 1987 Mar 14; 51(13): 32, 34-35. Illus.: Photo. Pntg. B&W. 2. Lang.: Eng.
France: Paris. 1803-1870. Biographical studies. ■Background of Mérimée's novella *Carmen*, on which Bizet's opera is based.

MUSIC-DRAMA: Opera—Plays/librettos/scripts

3904 Stampp, Kenneth M., Jr. "Reviving Daniel Auber." *OQ.* 1983 Win; 1(4): 82-89. Notes. Lang.: Eng.
France. 1782-1871. Critical studies. ■Study of French composer Daniel Auber and his works. Analysis of technique and style.

3905 Brody, Elaine. "The Jewish Wagnerites." *OQ.* 1983 Fall; 1(3): 66-83. Lang.: Eng.
Germany. 1813-1882. Historical studies. ■Study of the sources for Richard and Cosima Wagner's obsession with Jews and Judaism.

3906 Harden Borwick, Susan. "Perspective on Lenya: Through the Looking Glass." *OQ.* 1987/88 Win; 5(4): 21-36. Notes. Illus.: Photo. 3. Lang.: Eng.
Germany: Berlin. 1929-1970. Biographical studies. ■Career of singer/actress Lotte Lenya, her standards for interpretations of roles written by her husband Kurt Weill.

3907 Lee, M. Owen. "Who Is the Grail?" *OpN.* 1987 Apr 11; 51(15): 16-19. Illus.: Dwg. Photo. B&W. 8. Lang.: Eng.
Germany. 1882-1987. Critical studies. ■Interpretations of the Grail in Wagner's *Parsifal*: myth, Jungian collective unconscious, psychoanalytic theory.

3908 Nelson, Robert B. "Beyond the Tone Poems: The Eclectic Richard Strauss." *OJ.* 1987; 20(4): 3-16. Notes. Illus.: Dwg. 1. Lang.: Eng.
Germany: Dresden. 1864-1949. Critical studies. ■Composer Richard Strauss as an eclectic artist: his style, and neo-classical elements of his work.

3909 Potter, John; Potter, Suzanne. "An Artist's Salvation: In *Tannhäuser* Wagner Reworked a Myth That Obsessed Him Throughout His Life." *OpN.* 1987 Jan 17; 51(9): 30-33, 43. Illus.: Pntg. Color. 5. Lang.: Eng.
Germany. 1813-1883. Critical studies. ■Woman, salvation and love in *Tannhäuser*, *Der Fliegende Hollander* and *Parsifal*.

3910 Strasfogel, Ian. "The Other Side of the Churchyard Wall: Refined, Thoughtful, Beautifully Turned-Out, Composer Hans Werner Henze Claims To Be a Rebel." *OpN.* 1987 May; 51(16): 30-32, 35. Illus.: Photo. B&W. 3. Lang.: Eng.
Germany: Guterslöh. 1926-1987. Biographical studies. ■West German opera composer, Hans Werner Henze.

3911 White, Pamela C. "Two Vampires of 1828." *OQ.* 1987 Spr; 5(1): 22-57. Notes. Append. Lang.: Eng.
Germany: Leipzig, Stuttgart. 1828. Critical studies. ■Analysis of Heinrich Marschner's *Der Vampyr* and Peter Josef von Lindpaintner's opera of the same name.

3912 Münz-Koenen, Inge. "*Johann Faustus*—ein Werk, das Fragment blieb, und eine Debatte, die Legende wurde." (*Johann Faustus*: A Work that Remained a Fragment, and a Debate that Became a Legend.) 256-305 in Münz-Koenen, Inge, ed. *Werke und Wirkungen. DDR-Literatur in der Diskussion.* Leipzig: Reclam; 1987. 397 pp. Notes. Lang.: Ger.
Germany, East. 1953-1987. Critical studies. ■On the qualities of the libretto (or play) *Johann Faustus* by Hanns Eisler that met severe criticism, which stopped him composing the music for the planned opera.

3913 Ulrich, Roland. "'Die Kunst zu erben.' Probleme der *Faust*-Rezeption in der DDR bis 1955." ('The Art of Inheriting': Problems of GDR *Faust* Interpretation up to 1955.) *WB.* 1988; 34(2): 230-250. Notes. Lang.: Ger.
Germany, East: Berlin, East. 1949-1955. Historical studies. ■Hanns Eisler's adaptation of Goethe's *Faust* in his opera *Johann Faustus* and the political and aesthetic debate over his libretto.

3914 Del Bontà, Robert J. "Songs of India." *OQ.* 1983 Spr; 2(1): 5-14. Notes. Lang.: Eng.
India. Europe. 1730-1904. Critical studies. ■Operas that contain Indian related themes and music.

3915 Eliraz, Israel. "Mitoch Michtavim La Malchin." (A Letter to a Composer.) *Bamah.* 1987; 22(108): 17-18. Illus.: Photo. Print. B&W. Lang.: Heb.
Israel: Jerusalem. 1987. Critical studies. ■Analysis of the themes and ideas in the libretto for *The Garden of Adam and Eve*.

3916 Eliraz, Israel. "*Hagan*, Opera Be-sheva tmunot." (*The Garden*, a Libretto in Seven Pictures.) Print. B&W. Lang.: Heb.
Israel: Jerusalem. 1987. Critical studies. ■The opera *The Garden of Adam and Eve* by Israel Eliraz: contemporary look at the limitation of choices in the modern world.

3917 Busch, Hans. "Destined to Meet." *OQ.* 1987 Sum; 5(2/3): 4-23. Notes. Illus.: Photo. B&W. 6. Lang.: Eng.
Italy: Milan. 1862-1879. Biographical studies. ■Artistic collaboration of Giuseppe Verdi and Arrigo Boito on *Otello*.

3918 Chailly, Luciano. *Buzzati in musica. L'opera italiana nel dopoguerra.* (Buzzati in Music: Postwar Italian Opera.) Turin: Eda; 1987. 331 pp. Lang.: Ita.
Italy. 1933-1972. Biographical studies. ■Dino Buzzati's relations with the musical world: his narrative opera, his activity as librettist, scenographer and costumer.

3919 Davis, Peter G. "The Man *Turandot* Finished: Franco Alfano and His Operas are Neglected Unjustly." *OpN.* 1987 Mar 28; 51(14): 14-17. Illus.: Photo. B&W. 5. Lang.: Eng.
Italy. 1876-1954. Biographical studies. ■Franco Alfano the unpopularity of his work completing Puccini's *Turandot* ruined his career.

3920 Ducloux, Walter. "A Centennial Perspective *Cantiamo*." *OQ.* 1987 Sum; 5(2/3): 24-32. Notes. Illus.: Photo. 2. Lang.: Eng.
Italy: Milan. 1887. Critical studies. ■Analysis of characters in Verdi's *Otello* and its relation to other contemporary works.

3921 Lee, M. Owen. "Elemental, Furious, Wholly True." *OQ.* 1983 Win; 1(4): 3-11. Notes. Lang.: Eng.
Italy. 1983. Critical studies. ■Analysis of the plot of Verdi's opera *Il Trovatore*.

3922 Maehder, Jürgen. "Leoncavallos rutige byxor." (The Check Trousers of Leoncavallo.) *MuD.* 1987; 9(2 & 3): 8-11, 10-13. Illus.: Photo. Lang.: Swe.
Italy. 1893-1897. Historical studies. ■A presentation of Leoncavallo's work as librettist and composer of *La Bohème*, compared with that of Puccini and the original novel by Henri Murget.

3923 Marek, George R. "Falstaff—Boito's Alchemy." *OQ.* 1983 Sum; 1(2): 69-72. Lang.: Eng.
Italy. 1893. Critical studies. ■Analysis of the plot of *Falstaff* by Boito and how it is derived from Shakespeare's *Henry IV* and *The Merry Wives of Windsor*.

3924 Martin, George. "Posa in *Don Carlos*: The Flawed Hero." *OQ.* 1987 Sum; 5(2/3): 59-80. Notes. Illus.: Handbill. 1. Lang.: Eng.
Italy: Milan. 1867. Critical studies. ■Characters and political themes in Verdi's *Don Carlos*.

3925 Parker, Roger. "The Critical Edition of *Nabucco*." *OQ.* 1987 Sum; 5(2/3): 91-98. Lang.: Eng.
Italy: Milan. 1987. Textual studies. ■Analysis of score of Verdi's *Nabucco*: problems in adapting it to modern edition.

3926 Stern, Kenneth. "A Puccini Bouquet: In His Works the Composer Cultivated Floral Imagery." *OpN.* 1987 Jan 17; 51(9): 14-16. Illus.: Dwg. Photo. B&W. 7. Lang.: Eng.
Italy. 1858-1924. Critical studies. ■Floral imagery in the operas of Giacomo Puccini.

3927 Valente, Mario. "Giuseppina Strepponi Verdi." *OQ.* 1987 Sum; 5(2/3): 81-90. Notes. Illus.: Photo. 1. Lang.: Eng.
Italy: Milan. 1836-1901. Biographical studies. ■Relationship of Verdi and his wife Giuseppina, how she aided in his creative process.

3928 Shepherd, Gregory. "Non-Western Japanese Opera." *OJ.* 1987; 20(4): 17-21. Notes. Lang.: Eng.
Japan. 1975-1987. Critical studies. ■Modern Japanese opera as music that incorporates traditional Japanese and classical western elements to create new style.

3929 Schwinger, Wolfram. "Dämonen, Engel und Gespenster. Der Opernkomponist Krzysztof Penderecki." (Demons, Angels and Ghosts: The Opera-Composer K. Penderecki.)

MUSIC-DRAMA: Opera—Plays/librettos/scripts

175-204 in Seeger, Horst. *Oper heute*. Berlin: Henschelverlag; 1987. 301 pp. (Ein Almanach der Musikbühne 10.) Illus.: . Print. B&W. 13. Lang.: Ger.
Poland. 1969-1987. Critical studies. ■Short biography of Krzystof Penderecki and analysis of his works.

3930 Brunet, Manuel Chapa; García del Busto, José Luis; Reverter, Arturo; Mayo, Angel F.; Echevarria, Nestor. "Manuel de Falla (1876-1946)." 75-126 in Seeger, Horst. *Oper heute*. Berlin: Henschelverlag; 1987. 301 pp. (Ein Almanach der Musikbühne 10.) Illus.: Dwg. 1. Lang.: Ger.
Spain: Madrid. France: Paris. 1876-1946. Critical studies. ■Life, artistic profile and works of the composer, especially the opera *Atlántida*.

3931 Gozulova, N.G. *Epiceskoe v sovetskoj ukrainskoj opere (na materiale oper 20-60-h gg.): Avtoref. dis. kand. iskusstvovedenija*. (The Epic in Soviet Ukrainian Opera, 1920s-1960s: Abstract of a Dissertation by a Candidate in Art Criticism.) Kiev: Kiev. konservatorija; 1987. 18 pp. Lang.: Rus.
Ukraine. 1920-1969. Historical studies.

3932 Flatow, Sheryl. "Risky Business: Adapting the Classics for the Broadway Stage and Casting Them with Blacks Has Always Been a Gamble—Financial, Artistic and Social—But It Can Pay Off." *OpN*. 1987 May; 51(16): 18-20, 22, 57. Illus.: Photo. B&W. 7. Lang.: Eng.
USA: New York, NY. 1935-1987. Historical studies. ■Opera adaptations, Broadway, African-American performers.

3933 Hillard, Quincy C. "*The Tender Land* Revisited." *OJ*. 1987; 20(1): 27-35. Notes. Lang.: Eng.
USA. 1900. Critical studies. ■Analysis of plot and music of Aaron Copland's *The Tender Land*. Author's views on the work.

3934 Lassetter, Leslie. "The Position of *Satyagraha* in the Operatic Trilogy of Philip Glass." *OJ*. 1987; 20(1): 3-14. Notes. Illus.: Photo. B&W. 1. Lang.: Eng.
USA. 1980. Critical studies. ■Philip Glass's portrait of Gandhi in the opera *Satyagraha*. Analysis of his technique.

3935 Myrén, Carl. "Minimalism, vad ör det?" (Minimalism, What is That?)*MuD*. 1987; 9(1): 22-25. Illus.: Photo. 3. Lang.: Swe.
USA. 1937-1987. Histories-sources. ■Philip Glass speaks about his life and works.

Reference materials

3936 Milnes, Rodney, ed. *Opera Index 1987*. London: Opera; 1987. 83 pp. Lang.: Eng.
UK-England. USA. 1987. Historical studies. ■General subject index for vol. 38 of *Opera*, with separate listings of contributors, operas and artists.

3937 Chusid, Martin. "The American Institute for Verdi Studies and the Verdi Archive at New York University." *OQ*. 1987 Sum; 5(2/3): 33-47. Notes. Illus.: Handbill. 3. Lang.: Eng.
USA: New York, NY. Italy: Milan. 1976. Historical studies. ■Description of collections at Verdi Archive at New York University.

Relation to other fields

3938 Polkart, Ronald H. "The Bayreuth of South America: Wagnerian Opera in Buenos Aires." *OQ*. 1983 Fall; 1(3): 84-100. Notes. Illus.: Photo. Lang.: Eng.
Argentina: Buenos Aires. 1858-1983. Histories-general. ■The development, popularity, influence of Wagnerian opera in Argentina.

3939 Nattiez, Jean-Jacques. "How Can One Be Wagnerian?" *OQ*. 1983 Fall; 1(3): 3-10. Notes. Lang.: Eng.
Europe. 1860-1950. Critical studies. ■Background on Wagner: the philosophies expressed by Charles Baudelaire, Nietzsche and Thomas Mann.

3940 Reel, Jerome V., Jr. "The Image of the Child in Opera." *OQ*. 1983 Sum; 1(2): 73-78. Notes. Lang.: Eng.
Europe. 1800-1983. Historical studies. ■Children in opera reflect public perception of childhood and government policy on education.

3941 Littler, William. "Opéra—Bastille: A Political Football." *OC*. 1987 Spr; 28(1): 16-19, 22. Illus.: Photo. Dwg. B&W. 5. Lang.: Eng.
France: Paris. 1983-1987. Historical studies. ■Examines the politics of François Mitterand's commissioning of the Opéra-Bastille and subsequent changes under the new conservative government. Discusses Canadian architect Charles Ott's role.

3942 Marek, George R. "The Death of King Ludwig." *OQ*. 1983 Fall; 1(3): 140-147. Notes. Lang.: Eng.
Germany. 1864-1880. Historical studies. ■Life of King Ludwig II, and his relationship with composer Richard Wagner.

3943 Lowe, David A. "Opera in Pushkin's Life and Works." *OQ*. 1983 Win; 1(4): 44-49. Notes. Lang.: Eng.
Russia: St. Petersburg. 1799-1837. Critical studies. ■Study of Aleksand'r Puškin's life and works, and the influence of Rossini on Puškin.

3944 Rather, L.J. "Tolstoy and Wagner: The Shared Vision." *OQ*. 1983 Fall; 1(3): 11-24. Notes. Lang.: Eng.
Russia. Germany. 1860-1908. Critical studies. ■Wagner and Tolstoy's view of music, humanity, religion and politics.

3945 Magee, Bryan. "Schopenhauer and Wagner." *OQ*. 1983 Fall; 1(3): 148-171. Notes. Lang.: Eng.
Switzerland. 1834-1870. Critical studies. ■Influence of philosopher Schopenhauer on Richard Wagner's works and his theories about art. Continued *OQ* 1:4 (1983 Win), 50-73.

3946 Law, Joe K. "Daring to Eat a Peach: Literary Allusion in *Albert Herring*." *OQ*. 1987 Spr; 5(1): 1-10. Notes. Lang.: Eng.
UK-England. 1947. Critical studies. ■Adaptation of Guy de Maupassant's *Le Rosier de Madame Husson* to the opera *Albert Herring*, music by Benjamin Britten and libretto by Eric Crozier.

3947 Hansen, Robert. "Opera on Campus: An Interdisciplinary Approach." *OJ*. 1987; 20(2): 11-17. Notes. Lang.: Eng.
USA. 1987. Critical studies. ■Opera program in a university environment. Its viability as an academic discipline.

Research/historiography

3948 Lee, M. Owen. "Wagner's *Ring*: Turning the Sky Round." *OQ*. 1983 Sum; 1(2): 28-47. Notes. Lang.: Eng.
Germany: Dresden. 1813-1883. Critical studies. ■Influences on plot, structure and characterization in Wagner's *Ring* cycle: contemporary history and revolution, philosophy, etc..

Theory/criticism

3949 Neef, Sigrid. "Die kühnen Budetljany zum Begriff des 'Zukünftigen' in der russischen Oper des 20. Jahrhunderts." (The Bold Budetljany and Their Conception of 'Future People' in Russian 20th Century Opera.) *TZ*. 1987; 42(10): 26-29. Illus.: Photo. B&W. 6. Lang.: Ger.
USSR: Moscow. 1913-1987. Critical studies. ■History and aesthetics of the 'Budetljany' (term coined by the opera composer Velimir Chlebnikov: 'people on the way to manhood') and their significance for the development of Russian 20th-century opera.

Training

3950 Citron, Paula. "On the Cover." *OC*. 1987 Sum; 28(2): 4. 1. Lang.: Eng.
Canada: Banff, AB. 1933-1987. Historical studies. ■Discusses the changes which have taken place in the approach to teaching at the Banff Centre School of Fine Arts in the opera program, the Academy of Singing and the music theatre program.

3951 "Scenaria Interviews Hanno Blaschke." *Scenaria*. 1987 Nov.(82): 17-19. Illus.: Photo. 1. Lang.: Eng.
South Africa, Republic of. 1987. Histories-sources. ■Interview with singing master Hanno Blaschke on his experiences and views on opera training.

3952 Battaglia, Carl; Needham, Steven Mark. "A Joyful Noise: The Gospel of Singing Well, According to Five New York Voice Teachers." *OpN*. 1987 Jan 3; 51(8): 10-15. Illus.: Photo. B&W. 11. Lang.: Eng.

MUSIC-DRAMA: Opera—Training

USA: New York, NY. 1987. Histories-sources. ■Interviews with singing teachers Malena Malas, Rita Patanè, Robert Leonard, Margaret Hoswell and Franco Iglesias.

3953 "Spor vedut molodye." (The Young Conduct a Debate.) *SovMuzyka.* 1987; 2: 22-29. Lang.: Rus.
USSR: Kiev. 1980-1987. Histories-sources. ■Round-table of students of Kiev Conservatory on opera, education, creation.

Operetta

Institutions

3954 Allen, Richard. "Utopia '87: An International Toast to G&S." *OC.* 1987 Fall; 28(3): 22-23. Illus.: Sketches. 1. Lang.: Eng.
Canada: Toronto, ON. 1987. Histories-sources. ■Discusses the proceedings of the two-day Gilbert and Sullivan Symposium held at the University of Toronto in May 1987. Includes mention of the symposium production of *Utopia Limited* at the MacMillan Theatre.

3955 Scott, Iain. "Silva-Marin Meets the Challenge of TOT." *OC.* 1987 Fall; 28(3): 22-23. Illus.: Photo. B&W. 1. [Soundings.] Lang.: Eng.
Canada: Toronto, ON. 1985-1987. Historical studies. ■The Toronto Operetta Theatre under artistic director, impresario and performer Guillermo Silva-Marin.

3956 Lotz, Rainer E. "Will Garland and the Negro Operetta Company." *BPM.* 1986 Fall; 14(3): 290-302. Notes. Append. Illus.: Photo. Print. B&W. 1. Lang.: Eng.
UK-England. Finland: Helsinki. Russia. 1905-1917. Critical studies. ■Biographical sketch of Garland and discussion of the British Foreign Office's aid with the Negro Operetta Company tour of Finland and Russia.

Performance/production

3957 "Zerkovitz–Szilágyi: *Csókos asszony.*" (Zerkovitz–Szilágyi: *A Woman Made for Kissing.*) *Krit.* 1987 Sep. (9): 33. Lang.: Hun.
Hungary: Budapest. 1987. Reviews of performances. ■The original premiere of the ever-popular operetta by Béla Zerkovitz, was held at the Municipal Theatre of prewar years. Now the Comedy Theatre came out with the operetta, this time in István Iglódi's direction.

3958 Csáki, Judit. "Fo(ri)ntos siker. A *Csókos asszony* a Vígszínházban." (An Important Success: *A Woman Made for Kissing* at the Comedy Theatre.) *Sz.* 1987 Oct.; 20(10): 29-32. Illus.: Photo. B&W. 3. Lang.: Hun.
Hungary: Budapest. 1987. Reviews of performances. ■István Iglódi directs Zerkovits' *Csokos asszony (A Woman Made for Kissing)* at Comedy Theatre. With László Szilágyi.

3959 Gábor, István. "Cigányromantika? Bor József két rendezése a győri Kisfaludy Színházban." (Gypsy Romanticism? Two Stagings by József Bor at the Kisfaludy Theatre in Győr.) *Sz.* 1987 Apr.; 20 (4): 15-19. Illus.: Photo. B&W. 2. Lang.: Hun.
Hungary: Győr. 1912-1986. Reviews of performances. ■Imre Kálmán's *Cigányprimás (Sari)* and Bizet's *Carmen* at Kisfaludy Theatre staged by József Bor.

3960 Tauberg, L.Z. *Žak Offenbach i drugie.* (Jacques Offenbach and Others.) Moscow: Iskusstvo; 1987. 317 pp. Lang.: Rus.
Russia. 1860-1889. Biographical studies. ■Origin and development of operetta: sketches of the masters of the genre.

Other entries with significant content related to Music-Drama: 875, 892, 1150, 1430, 1955, 2975, 3112, 3113, 3114.

PUPPETRY

General

Design/technology

3961 Ni, Rong-Chuan. "Xuan li duo tsai de mu ou yi shu." (The Beauty Puppets.) *XYishu.* 1987 Sum; 38: 93-119. Lang.: Chi.
China, People's Republic of. Europe. 1986-1987. Historical studies. ■In a survey of world puppetry, the home of Chinese puppets—Fukien province—is mentioned.

3962 Bunin, Louis. "Computer Puppets." *PuJ.* 1987 Fall; 39(1): 14-15. Illus.: Photo. B&W. 3. Lang.: Eng.
USA. 1985-1987. Historical studies. ■Technological breakthroughs for puppetry. Electronic computer generated images on tape, film and stage. Related to Media.

3963 Frazier, Nancy; Renfro, Nancy. *Imagination: At Play With Puppets and Creative Drama.* Austin, TX: Nancy Renfro Studios; 1987. 96 pp. Biblio. Illus.: Design. Sketches. Print. B&W. 50. Lang.: Eng.
USA. 1987. Instructional materials. ■Puppet making projects for children. Includes designs and instructions for making different types of puppets. Incorporates creative drama techniques for children.

3964 Nash, Carolyn. "Therapy: Working with Blind Children." *PuJ.* 1987 Spr; 38(3): 27-28. Illus.: Photo. B&W. 3. Lang.: Eng.
USA. 1987. Instructional materials. ■An exercise in making and manipulating puppets for the visually handicapped.

Institutions

3965 Palmer, Honor. "Ramayana '87." *Anim.* 1987; 10(4): 72. Illus.: Photo. B&W. 2. Lang.: Eng.
UK-England: London. 1987. Critical studies. ■Puppet Centre's involvement in Ramayana '87, an Inner London Education Authority project based on the Hindu epic.

3966 Chessé, Ralph. "The Federal Theatre's Puppet Unit in California." *PuJ.* 1987 Fall; 39(1): 16-17. Illus.: Photo. B&W. 3. Lang.: Eng.
USA: San Francisco, CA. 1934-1987. Historical studies. ■The development of the Federal Theatre Project's California Puppetry Unit out of the Works Progress Administration.

3967 Lund, Leslie. "The Little Players Inc." *PuJ.* 1987 Sum; 38(4): 5. Illus.: Photo. B&W. 1. Lang.: Eng.
USA: New York, NY. 1960-1985. Historical studies. ■A brief history of the Little Players' five-hand puppet theatre that existed for twenty-five years in New York City.

3968 Sterling, Carol. "How to Be an Artist in the Schools, Part II." *PuJ.* 1987 Spr; 38(3): 24-25. Illus.: Photo. B&W. 2. Lang.: Eng.
USA. 1987. Historical studies. ■Exploring professional associations and organizations: contacts for puppeteer-educators.

Performance/production

3969 Navarro, Mayra. "Di Mauro avanza con sus titeres por Sudamerica." (Di Mauro and his Puppets Advance Throughout South America.) *Cjo.* 1987 July-Sep.(73): 100-106. Illus.: Photo. B&W. 5. Lang.: Spa.
Argentina. Venezuela. 1940-1987. Biographical studies. ■Eduardo Di Mauro and his puppets.

3970 Phillips, John. "Tradition in Europe: The Poesje of Antwerp." *Anim.* 1987; 10(6): 103-116. Illus.: Photo. B&W. 3. Lang.: Eng.
Belgium: Antwerp. 1812-1987. Historical studies. ■Survival of regional puppet theatre in Flemish in spite of Nazi suppression.

3971 Francis, Penny; Feng, Yang. "Hand Puppet Operating: Chinese Style." *Anim.* 1987; 10(5): 86-87. Illus.: Dwg. Photo. B&W. 2. Lang.: Eng.
China, People's Republic of. 1987. Histories-sources. ■Interview with Yang Feng, director of Zhangzhou company, on Chinese hand puppet operation.

CLASSED ENTRIES

PUPPETRY: General—Performance/production

3972 Hořínek, Zdeněk. "Drak v divadelním kontextu." (Drak Theatre in the Theatrical Context.) *CeskL.* 1987; 37 (6): 128-131. Illus.: Photo. B&W. 4. Lang.: Cze.
Czechoslovakia: Hradec Králové. 1987. Critical studies. ■Drak puppet theatre, criticism of their new play.

3973 Pilátová, Agáta. "O amatérském divadle ve Východočeském kraji." (On Amateur Theatre in East Bohemia.) *AmS.* 1985; 22(2): 12-13. Illus.: Photo. B&W. 1. Lang.: Cze.
Czechoslovakia: Hradec Králové. 1985. Histories-sources. ■Interview with Miroslava Císařovská on problems of amateur theatre in Eastern Bohemia.

3974 Gilula, Dwora. "Roni Nelken—Amanit Regisha, Keina Ume-anyenet." (Roni Nelken—A Sensitive and Sincere Artist.) *Bamah.* 1987; 22(108): 40-41. Lang.: Heb.
Israel: Jerusalem. 1987. Technical studies. ■Creation of a puppet character, its visual originality and impact on audience in the puppet theatre.

3975 Nelken, Roni. "Devarim Achadim Ahll Theatron Booboth Bechlal Ve-Ahlll 'Yosef Beferath'." (A Few Words about Puppet Theatre.) *Bamah.* 1987; 22(108): 42-50. Illus.: Photo. Print. B&W. 2. Lang.: Heb.
Israel: Jerusalem. 1987. Historical studies. ■Puppet theatre and the two ways of communicating with audiences: through identification with the action and alienation. Experimental work with children through puppet theatre, their reactions.

3976 Ostolani, Marisa; Byron, Michael, transl. "How Pulcinella Cetrula is Making a Comeback." *Anim.* 1987; 10(4): 64. Illus.: Photo. B&W. 2. [Originally published in *Burattini*, 4, Sep/Oct, 1985.] Lang.: Eng.
Italy: Naples. 1979-1987. Critical studies. ■Training, technique and performance of Bruno Leone, who is seeking to re-establish the Neapolitan culture of Guaratelle.

3977 Jones, Kenneth Lee. "Foot Puppetry in Korea." *PuJ.* 1987 Sum; 38(4): 14. Illus.: Photo. B&W. 1. Lang.: Eng.
Korea, South. 1977. Historical studies. ■An unusual form of folk puppetry: puppeteers manipulate puppets from a horizontal position using feet and hand rods.

3978 Chojnacki, Lech. "Wokół 'Błękitnego Pajaca'. Lalkarze poznańscy 1919-1939." (Around the 'Blue Puppet': Puppeteers in Poznań 1919-1939.) *PaT.* 1987; 1-2: 279-296. Notes. Illus.: Photo. Print. B&W. 19. Lang.: Pol.
Poland: Poznań. 1919-1939. Historical studies. ■Education, technical problems on tour, repertory, critics.

3979 Warzecha, Andrzej S. "Z tradycji teatru lalek w Łodzi." (Traditions of Puppet Theatre in Lodz.) *PaT.* 1987; 1-2: 297-310. Notes. Illus.: Photo. Print. B&W. 2. Lang.: Pol.
Poland: Łódź. 1900-1939. Historical studies. ■Activity of Polish puppeteers in Lodz.

3980 Waszkiel, Marek. "Dzieje teatru lalek w Polsce do 1945 roku. Kronika." (History of Puppet Theatre in Poland to 1945: A Chronicle.) *PaT.* 1987; 1-2: 3-135. Pref. Notes. Illus.: Photo. Print. B&W. 110. Lang.: Pol.
Poland. 1490-1945. Historical studies. ■Activity of puppeteers in Poland. Description of performances, discussion of documentation available in Polish archives, description of puppets and marionettes in poems and narrative fiction, visits of foreign performers to Poland.

3981 Meschke, Michael. "Förmåga till naivitet men med helgjuten övertygelse." (A Gift for Naiveté, But With Sterling Conviction.) *NT.* 1987; 39: 20-25. Illus.: Photo. 10. Lang.: Swe.
Sweden. 1987. Critical studies. ■About the difference between directing actors and puppeteers in the staging process, and the responsibilities of the director for children's theatre.

3982 Bridle, Martin. "Punch with a Personality." *Anim.* 1987; 10(4): 75. Illus.: Photo. B&W. 2. Lang.: Eng.
UK-England. 1987. Critical studies. ■Puppeteer's analysis of the range of characters in traditional Punch and Judy show.

3983 Hall, Mary. "The Puppeteers Company." *Anim.* 1987; 10(3): 59-60. Illus.: Photo. B&W. 4. Lang.: Eng.

UK-England: Norwich. 1971-1987. Historical studies. ■History of the Puppeteers Company charting its development.

3984 Fedas, I. *Ukrainskij narodnyj vertep: (v issledovanijach XIX-XX vv.).* (The Ukrainian Folk Den: Research on the Nineteenth and Twentieth Centuries.) Kiev: Naukova dumka; 1987. 184 pp. Lang.: Ukr.
Ukraine. 1800-1987. Histories-sources. ■Materials on traditional Ukrainian folk puppet theatre.

3985 Ballard, Frank. "Design—Part II." *PuJ.* 1987 Spr; 38(3): 9-14. Illus.: Photo. B&W. 7. Lang.: Eng.
USA. 1600-1987. Historical studies. ■Designing puppets and special considerations of manipulation for classical works.

3986 Bell, John. "The Nineteenth Annual Domestic Resurrection Circus." *ThM.* 1987; 18(3): 35-42. Notes. Illus.: Photo. B&W. 7. Lang.: Eng.
USA: Glover, VT. 1987. Critical studies. ■Annual two-day total-theatre event by the Bread and Puppet Theatre uses 150 volunteers and two acres of playing space. Theme was hunger.

3987 Sears, David. "Simply Zaloom." *PuJ.* 1987 Win; 39(2): 5-7. Illus.: Photo. B&W. 3. Lang.: Eng.
USA. 1970-1987. Histories-sources. ■Interview with puppeteer Paul Zaloom, who uses his puppets to express his political ideas, and trash to create scene designs.

3988 Sherzer, Dina, ed.; Sherzer, Joel, ed. *Humor and Comedy in Puppetry: Celebration in Popular Culture.* Bowling Green, OH: Bowling Green State Univ. Popular P; 1987. 151 pp. Notes. Append. Illus.: Photo. Pntg. Dwg. B&W. 24. Lang.: Eng.
USA. Italy. Belgium. Indonesia. 1987. Histories-specific. ■Essays on puppetry as an expression of popular and folk culture from the American southwest to Europe and Asia. Role of comedy and humor in puppetry performances.

3989 "Ljudi li Kukly?" (Are the Puppets People?) *TeatrM.* 1987; 7: 97-150. Lang.: Rus.
USSR. 1986. Critical studies. ■Collection of articles and speeches on the problems of Soviet puppet theatres.

3990 Wehle, Philippa; Khê, Trân Vân. "Vietnamese Water Puppets." *PerAJ.* 1985 Spr; 9(25): 73-82. Illus.: Photo. Dwg. B&W. 9. Lang.: Eng.
Vietnam. 900-1985. Historical studies. ■History, description, methods of manipulation, venues and operators of Vietnamese water puppets.

Plays/librettos/scripts

3991 Zucker, Mitchell. "Hermann—The Puppet Anti-Hero." *TDR.* 1987 Sum; 31(2): 79-87. Illus.: Photo. B&W. 10. Lang.: Eng.
Germany. Poland: Bielsko Biala. 1978-1987. Historical studies. ■The play *Hermann*, a puppet production for adult audiences about people coping with oppression.

3992 Goldovskij, B. "P'esa dlja prišel'cev." (A Play for Newcomers.) *SovD.* 1987; 4: 207-216. Lang.: Rus.
USSR. 1980-1987. Critical studies. ■Problems of dramaturgy for puppet theatres.

Relation to other fields

3993 Brooks, Zoe. "Some Thoughts on Mr. Punch." *Anim.* 1987; 10(4): 63. Illus.: Dwg. B&W. 1. Lang.: Eng.
England: London. 1662-1987. Historical studies. ■Examines character of Mr. Punch, how it reflects public attitudes and will change with audience responses.

3994 Szacsvay, Éva. *Bábtáncoltató bethlehemezés Magyarországon és Közép-Kelet-Európában.* (Puppet Dancing Bethlehem Plays in Hungary and in Middle East Europe.) Budapest: Akadémiai K.; 1987. xxvi, 195 pp. (Néprajzi tanulmányok.) Pref. Biblio. Illus.: Photo. Dwg. B&W. 46. Lang.: Hun.
Hungary. 1877-1967. Historical studies. ■The spread of one of the specific nativity plays: appearance in space and time, texts, scores.

PUPPETRY: General—Relation to other fields

3995 Waszkiel, Marek. "Teatr lalek w literaturze polskiej." (Puppet Theatre in Polish Fiction.) *PaT*. 1987; 1-2: 135-186. Lang.: Pol.
Poland. 1500-1945. Histories-sources. ■Anthology of texts of Polish poets and novelists speaking about puppets and marionettes.

3996 Cardich, Lily. "History Puppets in Catalonia." *Anim*. 1987; 10(3): 43-44. Illus.: Photo. B&W. 2. Lang.: Eng.
Spain-Catalonia. 500 B.C.-1987 A.D. Historical studies. ■History of puppetry in Catalonia, importance in preserving language and culture.

3997 Carroll, Fiona. "Puppets in Community Development Projects." *Anim*. 1987; 10(2): 32-33. Illus.: Photo. B&W. 1. Lang.: Eng.
UK-England: London. 1987. Critical studies. ■Workshop aimed at developing communication and community action.

3998 Leach, Robert. "Edwardian Punch and Judy, or, When the True Tradition was Nearly Traduced." *Anim*. 1987; 10(5): 83-84. Notes. Illus.: Photo. B&W. 4. Lang.: Eng.
UK-England. 1860-1910. Historical studies. ■Survival of Punch and Judy shows during the Edwardian period, cultural effects and practitioners.

Bunraku

Performance/production

3999 Drummond, Andrew; Coppola, Nicolas. "Sharing the Stage: Puppets and Actors." *PuJ*. 1987 Spr; 38(3): 15-17. Illus.: Photo. Dwg. B&W. 5. Lang.: Eng.
USA: Brooklyn, NY. 1985-1987. Historical studies. ■The working relationship between actors and puppets sharing the same stage, and the preparation involved.

Marionettes

Institutions

4000 Chessé, Ralph. *The Marionette Actor*. Fairfax, VA: George Mason UP; 1987. 69 pp. Notes. Biblio. Illus.: Photo. Sketches. Poster. Print. B&W. 30. Lang.: Eng.
USA. 1927-1987. Histories-specific. ■History of the Chessé Marionettes: its classic repertory, contribution to recognition of puppetry as a theatre art. The influence of Edward Gordon Craig.

Performance/production

4001 Amico, Nino. "Allied Against the Devil: A Study of a Sacred Play of the Opera dei Pupi." *Anim*. 1987; 10(2): 23-35. [Reproduced from *Burattini*, 5 Nov. 1985.] Lang.: Eng.
Italy. 1651-1987. Historical studies. ■Traditional performance of an adaptation of a 17th-century nativity, combining cultural and popular elements.

4002 Jones, Bob. "Getting It All Together." *PuJ*. 1987 Fall; 39(1): 7-8. Illus.: Photo. B&W. 1. Lang.: Eng.
USA. 1987. Historical studies. ■Comparing a puppeteer's problems with manipulation to those of a cartoon animator as described in *Disney Animation: An Illusion of Life*. Related to Media.

4003 Bez'jazyčnaja, Ju.; Simakovskaja, I. "Energija dobra." (The Energy of Good.) *LitGruzia*. 1987; 8: 212-217. Lang.: Rus.
USSR. 1980-1987. Historical studies. ■R. Gobriadze, director of marionette theatre.

Rod puppets

Basic theatrical documents

4004 "Kokdukagsi-nolum yonheuibon." (The Play of Korean Puppet Theatre: *Kokdugaksi*.) 23-36 in Kim, Jae-chel. *Puppet Theatre: Kokdugaksi*. Seoul: Korean Traditional Drama Inst; 1986. 165 pp. Lang.: Kor.

Korea. 600-1987. Historical studies. ■Playtext of *kokdugaksi* puppet theatre.

Design/technology

4005 Pack, Yong-Tae. "Kokdukagsi inhyung mandnun bup." (The Way of Making the Korean Puppet: *kokdugaksi*.) in Jae-chel, Kim. *Puppet Theatre: Kokdugaksi*. Seoul: Korean Traditional Drama Inst; 1986. 165 pp. Lang.: Kor.
Korea. 1987. Instructional materials. ■The way of making the Korean puppet, *kokdugaksi*.

Performance/production

4006 Ogrodzińska, Teresa. "Three Trends, Three Generations in the Polish Puppet Theatre." (Trois courants, trois générations au théâtre polonais de marionettes.) *TP*. 1987 Jan-Mar.(1-3): 33-46. Illus.: Photo. Print. B&W. 10. Lang.: Eng, Fre.
Poland: Wrocław, Białystock. Austria: Mistelbach. 1979-1987. Historical studies. ■Overview of Poland's puppet theatre from 1979 to 1987. Includes specific productions, especially by younger artists who are revitalizing the art form.

Theory/criticism

4007 Kim, Jae-chel, ed. *Kokdukagsi-nolum*. (Puppet Theatre: Kogdogaksi.) Seoul: Korean Traditional Drama Inst; 1986. 165 pp. Lang.: Kor.
Korea. 600-1987. Histories-specific. ■Theory of Korean puppet theatre and the way of making the puppets.

Shadow puppets

Basic theatrical documents

4008 Rajeg, I Nyoman; deBoer, Fredrik E., transl. "The *Dimba and Dimbi* of I Nyoman Rajeg: A Balinese Shadow Play." *ATJ*. 1987 Spr; 4(1): 76-107. Notes. Biblio. Illus.: Photo. B&W. 6. Lang.: Eng.
Indonesia. 1987. ■The complete text in English translation, accompanied by background material on shadow theatre, performance preparation and repertoire.

Performance spaces

4009 Belloli, Jo. "Not Just a Pretty Place." *Anim*. 1987; 11(1): 13. Illus.: Photo. B&W. 2. Lang.: Eng.
UK-England: London. 1987. Critical studies. ■Performances and workshops for children presented in converted church hall.

Performance/production

4010 Di Bernardi, Vito. "I Dalang, maestri di verità. Note su composizione e improvvisazione nel teatro delle ombre a Bali." (The Dalang, Teachers of Truth: Notes on Composition and Improvisation in the Shadow Theatre of Bali.) *BiT*. 1987; 7: 79-104. Lang.: Ita.
Indonesia. 1987. Historical studies. ■The shadow theatre as ritual and performance. *Dalang's* mythological background. The theatrical work: basic techniques (voice, puppet movement, music), scene sequences and improvisation.

Relation to other fields

4011 Down, Pauline. "A Drama and Shadow Puppet Project with Children who Have Profound Hearing Disabilities." *Anim*. 1987; 10 (3): 53. Lang.: Eng.
UK-England: London. 1987. Critical studies. ■Evaluation of workshop created to build confidence, communication skills and creativity in children.

———

Other entries with significant content related to Puppetry: 391, 1246, 2919. [QW]

SUBJECT INDEX

A, Jia
Performance/production
The stylized, symbolic acting technique in Chinese theatre. China, People's Republic of: Beijing. 1027 B.C.-1986 A.D. Lang.: Chi. 3474

Acting techniques in Chinese opera. China, People's Republic of: Beijing. 1935-1986. Lang.: Chi. 3489

Acting theories in Chinese opera. China, People's Republic of: Beijing. 1950-1986. Lang.: Chi. 3510

Abba, Marta
Performance/production
Pirandello as director: contemporary reviews and interviews. Italy. 1915-1936. Lang.: Ita. 838

Abbado, Claudio
Administration
Staatsoper under management of Claus Helmut Drese and Claudio Abbado. Austria: Vienna. 1986-1987. Lang.: Swe. 3677

Abbey Theatre (Dublin)
Design/technology
F.H. Flood's scene design for *The Merchant of Venice*. Ireland: Dublin. 1985. Lang.: Eng. 1593

Institutions
Playwright Denis Johnston and avant-garde theatre at the Abbey. Ireland: Dublin. 1927-1935. Lang.: Eng. 1619

Performance/production
Interview with Eric Bentley, director of *La Casa de Bernarda Alba* at the Abbey. Ireland: Dublin. 1900-1985. Lang.: Eng. 1934

Interview with Patrick Mason, director of Thomas Murphy's *The Gigli Concert*. Ireland: Dublin. 1983. Lang.: Eng. 1935

Plays/librettos/scripts
Lady Gregory's *Grania*. Ireland: Dublin. 1910-1930. Lang.: Eng. 2649

Relation to other fields
Literary figures of the Irish Literary Renaissance. Ireland. UK-Ireland. 1875-1938. Lang.: Eng. 2995

Research/historiography
Overview of Canadian research on twentieth-century Irish drama. Ireland. UK-Ireland. Canada. 1891-1983. Lang.: Eng. 3011

Abbott, George
Performance/production
Collection of newspaper reviews by London theatre critics. UK-England: London. 1987. Lang.: Eng. 2272

Two productions of *Flora, the Red Menace*. USA: New York, NY. 1965-1987. Lang.: Eng. 3640

Abduction from the Seraglio, The
SEE
Entführung aus dem Serail, Die.

Abell, Kjeld
Plays/librettos/scripts
Analysis of Kjeld Abell's *Der bla pekingeser (The Blue Pekingese)*. Denmark. 1901-1961. Lang.: Ita. 1113

Abhinayadarpanam
Performance/production
Discussion of text on classical Indian performance. India. 1987. Lang.: Eng. 814

Abortion
Plays/librettos/scripts
Family relationships in Eugene O'Neill's early plays. USA. 1913. Lang.: Eng. 2926

About Face
Plays/librettos/scripts
Money, greed and power in plays by Fo, Churchill, Cacaci and Cormack. USA: New York, NY. 1987. Lang.: Eng. 2914

Above All, Courage
Performance/production
Collection of newspaper reviews by London theatre critics. UK-England: London. 1987. Lang.: Eng. 2189

Abramow, Jarosław
Performance/production
The shape and form of contemporary Polish theatre. Poland: Warsaw. 1981-1987. Lang.: Eng, Fre. 1995

Abramson, Jan
Performance/production
Västerås Amateur Theatre Festival. Sweden: Västerås. 1987. Lang.: Swe. 2023

Abravanel, Maurice
Performance/production
Opera conductors who also conduct in Broadway musicals. USA: New York, NY. 1980-1987. Lang.: Eng. 3847

Abrikosov, A.
Performance/production
Director V. Pimenov's recollections of actors Gricenko, Plotnikov and Abrikosov. USSR: Moscow. 1940-1979. Lang.: Rus. 1047

Absurdism
Performance/production
Review of *I Poli (The Town)* based on Greek theatre tradition and performed in absurdist style. Mexico: Mexico City. 1987. Lang.: Spa. 1976

ABTT
SEE
Association of British Theatre Technicians.

Abujar Lila, O
Plays/librettos/scripts
Theme of torture in Brazilian drama. Brazil. 1964-1985. Lang.: Por. 2456

Academia Sinica (Taiwan)
Reference materials
Source materials on development of Chinese opera. Taiwan. 1987. Lang.: Chi. 3580

Accidental Death of an Anarchist
SEE
Morte accidentale di un anarchico.

Accounting
Administration
Objectives and strategies of pricing for the performing arts. USA: Bowling Green, OH. 1986. Lang.: Eng. 136

Fiduciary responsibilities of the museum trustee. USA. 1987. Lang.: Eng. 192

Financial problems of theatres. USSR. 1986-1987. Lang.: Rus. 273

Acevedo, Carlos
  Theory/criticism
    Myth in the plays of the Dominican Republic. Dominican Republic.
    1987. Lang.: Spa.   3026
Achmeteli, Aleksand'r
  Performance/production
    Articles on director Aleksand'r Achmeteli by leading theatre figures.
    USSR. 1886-1937. Lang.: Rus.   986
Achorn, John
  Performance/production
    New Vaudeville Festival. USA: San Francisco, CA. 1987. Lang.:
    Eng.   948
Achternbusch, Herbert
  Institutions
    Seven productions chosen for Theatertreffen '86. Germany: Berlin.
    1986. Lang.: Eng.   1617
Acid Rain Theatre Company (Sudbury, ON)
  Performance/production
    Popular theatre, mostly on economic, feminist themes. Canada:
    Sudbury, ON. 1930-1987. Lang.: Eng.   1709
Acker, Kathy
  Basic theatrical documents
    Complete text of *Lulu* by Kathy Acker. USA. 1986. Lang.: Eng.
                                                                         1576
Ackerman, Robert Allan
  Performance/production
    Collection of newspaper reviews by London theatre critics. UK-
    England: London. 1987. Lang.: Eng.   2274
Ackroyd, Peter
  Performance/production
    Collection of newspaper reviews by London theatre critics. UK-
    England: London. 1987. Lang.: Eng.   2245
Acosta, Walter
  Performance/production
    Collection of newspaper reviews by London theatre critics. UK-
    England: London. 1987. Lang.: Eng.   2257
Acrobatics
  Performance/production
    Production of Cirque du Soleil. Canada: Montreal, PQ. 1987. Lang.:
    Eng.   3302
    The four main elements of dance in Chinese opera. China, People's
    Republic of. 960-1987. Lang.: Chi.   3526
    Attempted reforms of the main aspects of Chinese opera. China,
    People's Republic of. 1987. Lang.: Chi.   3527
Acting
  SEE ALSO
    Training, actor.
    Behavior/psychology, actor.
  Administration
    The tenant rights of New York actors working elsewhere. USA:
    New York, NY. 1987. Lang.: Eng.   60
    The pros and cons of tax reform from the actor's point of view.
    USA. 1987. Lang.: Eng.   184
    Growth and decline of theatrical activity. Arabic countries. 1938-
    1985. Lang.: Fre.   1511
    Creating human voices and images with digital, holographic
    techniques: actors' conference. USA: New York, NY. Israel: Tel-
    Aviv. 1987. Lang.: Eng.   3083
  Audience
    Relationship between script, actors and audience. China, People's
    Republic of. 1985. Lang.: Chi.   279
    Actor and audience in Elizabethan theatre. England. 1585-1625.
    Lang.: Eng.   1533
    English pantomime in Irish productions. Ireland: Dublin. 1900-1987.
    Lang.: Eng.   3231
    Chinese acting: direct communication with audience. China, People's
    Republic of: Beijing. 1950-1986. Lang.: Chi.   3434
    Audiences suggest ways to improve the Beijing opera. China,
    People's Republic of. 1987. Lang.: Chi.   3440
  Basic theatrical documents
    Scenes and monologues for actors. USA. 1987. Lang.: Eng.   297
    Collection of stage monologues, interviews with playwrights. USA.
    1960-1987. Lang.: Eng.   1582
  Design/technology
    Career of costumer, dancer, actress Judy Dearing. USA: New York,
    NY. Africa. 1970-1987. Lang.: Eng.   1601

Institutions
    Archival documents of the Vendramin Theatre. Italy: Venice. 1700-
    1733. Lang.: Ita.   548
    History of Werkteater. Netherlands: Amsterdam. 1969-1985. Lang.:
    Eng.   554
    Texts and photos about the Teatre Grec. Spain-Catalonia: Barcelona.
    1929-1986. Lang.: Cat.   558
    Second City improvisational comedy troupe. USA: Chicago, IL.
    Canada: Toronto, ON. 1959-1987. Lang.: Eng.   605
    King's Company under actor-manager John Lowin. England:
    London. 1576-1653. Lang.: Eng.   1614
    Interview with actress Fannia Lubitch. Israel: Tel Aviv. USSR:
    Moscow. 1921-1987. Lang.: Heb.   1620
    The Stanisław Ignacy Witkiewicz Theatre. Poland: Zakopane. 1982-
    1986. Lang.: Eng, Fre.   1628
    Analysis of all the productions performed by Els Joglars in their
    twenty-five years of existence. Spain-Catalonia. 1962-1987. Lang.:
    Cat.   1634
    Experience of artists working at the O'Neill Theatre Center. USA:
    Waterford, CT. 1985-1986. Lang.: Eng.   1655
  Performance spaces
    History of Teatro San Carlo, its artists and performances. Italy:
    Naples. 1737-1987. Lang.: Ita.   648
    Reconstruction of theatrical activity in Barcelona. Spain-Catalonia:
    Barcelona. 1800-1830. Lang.: Cat.   1672
  Performance/production
    Performance as an 'enunciative event'. Lang.: Ita.   714
    Overview of acting styles since the ancient Greeks. 500 B.C.-1987
    A.D. Lang.: Chi.   716
    Transvestitism in the theatre. 1987. Lang.: Ita.   717
    Characteristics of Asian theatre. Asia. 1987. Lang.: Kor.   720
    Short eulogy for actress Janine Angers. Canada. 1987. Lang.: Fre.
                                                                         742
    Overview of the 1982 Stratford Festival. Canada: Stratford, ON.
    1982. Lang.: Eng.   749
    The influence of the audience on the actor's performance. China,
    People's Republic of. 1985. Lang.: Chi.   763
    Actors Jaromír Hanzlík and Viktor Preiss in Rostand's *Cyrano*,
    directed by Jaroslov Dudek at Vinohradské Theatre. Czechoslovakia:
    Prague. 1986. Lang.: Cze.   771
    Irony in *Gammer Gurton's Needle*: its interpretation and presentation
    to the audience. England. 1575-1982. Lang.: Eng.   777
    Actors and comics of the early eighteenth century. Europe. 1700-
    1750. Lang.: Ita.   778
    Directing as creation of a dimension that enhances the actor's desire.
    France. 1987. Lang.: Fre.   785
    Teamwork concept of directing. France. 1987. Lang.: Fre.   789
    Documentation on melodramatic acting style. France: Paris. 1800-
    1830. Lang.: Eng.   791
    Evolution of directing toward working closely with actors. France.
    1987. Lang.: Fre.   793
    Acting manual by Dario Fo. Italy. 1987. Lang.: Ita.   827
    Francesco de' Nobili, Renaissance actor. Italy: Venice. 1500-1600.
    Lang.: Ita.   829
    Relation between dramatic text, staging and the actor. Italy. France.
    1500-1700. Lang.: Ita.   830
    Life and career of actress Anna Maria Guarnieri. Italy. 1954-1987.
    Lang.: Ita.   833
    Photos and documentation: actor Angelo Musco. Italy: Catania.
    1904-1937. Lang.: Ita.   840
    Career of actor Angelo Musco. Italy. 1872-1937. Lang.: Ita.   841
    Actors Kawakami Otojirō and his wife, Sadayacco. Japan. 1899-
    1946. Lang.: Ita.   843
    Advice for novice actors. Korea. 1987. Lang.: Kor.   851
    Relation of actors and audiences. Korea: Seoul. 1987. Lang.: Kor.
                                                                         854
    Festival of Polish plays. Poland: Wrocław. 1987. Lang.: Eng, Fre.
                                                                         871
    Interview with Polish playwright Tadeusz Kantor. Poland: Cracow.
    Germany, West: Kassel. Italy: Milan. Italy: Sicily. 1987. Lang.: Eng,
    Fre.   876

Acting — cont'd

Acting — cont'd

Interview with male performer Ethyl Eichelberger. USA: New York, NY. 1987. Lang.: Eng. 2314

Profile of character actor Matthew Locricchio. USA: New York, NY. 1987. Lang.: Eng. 2334

Interview with actor James Earl Jones. USA: New York, NY. 1953-1987. Lang.: Eng. 2340

Interview with actress Mary Alice. USA: New York, NY, Chicago, IL. 1966-1987. Lang.: Eng. 2341

Recollections of actor Don Pietromonaco on his work with Bertolt Brecht, Charles Laughton and Joseph Losey. USA: Los Angeles, CA. 1944-1986. Lang.: Eng. 2347

Sanford Meisner's method of teaching acting. USA: New York, NY. 1987. Lang.: Eng. 2349

Interviews with teachers of acting. USA: New York, NY, Los Angeles, CA. 1987. Lang.: Eng. 2350

Interview with playwright/actor Robert Perring. USA. Lang.: Eng. 2354

Method acting: its origins and development. USA: New York, NY. USSR: Moscow. 1923-1987. Lang.: Eng. 2359

Interview with actor/director Austin Pendleton. USA. 1987. Lang.: Eng. 2360

The African actor in Africa, Italy and the United States. USA: Brooklyn, NY. Sierra Leone: Freetown. Italy: Rome. 1987. Lang.: Eng. 2362

Interview with actor and playwright Joe Seneca. USA: New York, NY, Cleveland, OH. 1957-1987. Lang.: Eng. 2364

The career of actor and playwright Samm-Art Williams. USA: Philadelphia, PA. 1973-1987. Lang.: Eng. 2365

Biographical account of Beatriz Escalona, La Chata Noloesca. USA: San Antonio, TX. 1903-1979. Lang.: Spa. 2369

Actor Michajl Čechov's answers to a questionnaire investigating the psychology of acting. USSR: Moscow. 1923. Lang.: Eng. 2376

Transcriptions from lectures and lessons given by actor Michajl Čechov on his technique. USSR: Moscow. 1942-1919. Lang.: Eng. 2377

Moscow Art Theatre's production of *Hamlet* with Michajl Čechov in the title role. USSR: Moscow. 1924. Lang.: Eng. 2386

Interpretation and critique of Olivier's film *Hamlet*. England. 1604-1948. Lang.: Chi. 3149

Centenary volume on actor Gyula Kabos. Hungary. 1887-1941. Lang.: Hun. 3153

Film career of stage actor Ruggero Ruggeri. Italy. 1914-1952. Lang.: Ita. 3160

Interview with actress Margaret Avery. USA: San Diego, CA, Hollywood, CA. 1950-1987. Lang.: Eng. 3167

Screen persona and performances of screen actor Buster Keaton. USA. 1895-1966. Lang.: Eng. 3170

Evolution of the Areté Mime Troupe: its concepts, goals and performance methods. Canada. 1980-1982. Lang.: Eng. 3221

Development of mime, pantomime and its related movements. France: Paris. UK-England. USA: New York, NY. 1980-1982. Lang.: Eng. 3223

Contemporary mime forms and their innovators. France: Paris. Belgium. USA. 1980-1982. Lang.: Eng. 3224

Performers Ariel Ashwell and Sigfrido Aguilar discuss their work with Comediantes Pantomima-Teatro. Mexico: Guanajuato. 1980-1982. Lang.: Eng. 3225

Philosophy of mime and improvisation performer Bob Berky. USA: New York, NY. 1980. Lang.: Eng. 3227

Mime compared with other forms of visual arts. USA: Claremont, CA. 1980-1982. Lang.: Eng. 3228

Marcel Marceau's reflections on his art. France. Italy. 1982-1986. Lang.: Ita. 3233

Body language in Korean mime. Korea. 1970-1979. Lang.: Kor. 3234

Story-teller as actor: establishing contact with audience. Italy. 1987. Lang.: Ita. 3260

Transvestite roles in extravaganzas of J.R. Planché and Mme. Vestris. UK-England: London. 1830-1870. Lang.: Eng. 3268

Review of the 1987 Edinburgh Fringe Festival. UK-Scotland: Edinburgh. 1987. Lang.: Eng. 3271

The cabaret-style musical revue *Oil City Symphony*. USA: New York, NY. 1987. Lang.: Eng. 3289

Ethyl Eichelberger and Lily Savage: their approaches to acting. USA. UK-England. 1987. Lang.: Eng. 3290

Broadway actors who moonlight in cabaret acts. USA: New York, NY. 1962-1987. Lang.: Eng. 3291

Career of actor Jack Gilford. USA: New York, NY. 1920-1987. Lang.: Eng. 3292

Interpreters of the *commedia dell'arte* character Pulcinella. Italy: Naples. 1609-1975. Lang.: Ita. 3311

Actors and institutions of eighteenth-century Venice. Italy: Venice. 1700-1800. Lang.: Ita. 3312

Pageant wagon presentation in Spain provides information on recruitment, staging and rehearsal practices. Spain: St. Ginar. 1579. Lang.: Eng. 3333

Chinese opera star Ma Shau-Liang reproduces the play *Shiang ma juan (Story of the Robber)*. China, People's Republic of. 1958-1986. Lang.: Chi. 3397

Studies of a local Chinese opera: Yün Nan Hua Teng. China. 1456-1986. Lang.: Chi. 3455

Career of Chinese opera actor and teacher Maa Lian Liang. China: Beijing. 1929-1981. Lang.: Chi. 3457

Beijing opera actor Ji Ba Wang. China: Beijing. 1937-1948. Lang.: Chi. 3460

Illustrations depicting theatrical performances, Song and Yuan dynasties. China: Beijing. 960-1368. Lang.: Chi. 3461

Biography of actor Su Kuensheng. China. 1600-1735. Lang.: Chi. 3464

Dialect opera—Liu Jiu—in China. China. 1852-1930. Lang.: Chi. 3468

Similarities and differences in Chinese opera and ballet. China, People's Republic of. 1986. Lang.: Chi. 3470

The responsibility of artists to their audience. China, People's Republic of. 1980-1986. Lang.: Chi. 3471

Conventions of time and space in Chinese opera. China, People's Republic of: Beijing. 1987. Lang.: Chi. 3472

Conventionalized characters in Chinese opera. China, People's Republic of. 1987. Lang.: Chi. 3473

The stylized, symbolic acting technique in Chinese theatre. China, People's Republic of: Beijing. 1027 B.C.-1986 A.D. Lang.: Chi. 3474

Chinese opera star Ba Yuh-Shuang. China, People's Republic of. Lang.: Chi. 3475

Basic acting technqiues of Chinese theatre. China, People's Republic of. 1985. Lang.: Chi. 3476

Impressionism in the acting of Chinese drama. China, People's Republic of. 1924-1985. Lang.: Chi. 3477

The distinctive features of Chinese drama. China, People's Republic of. 1949-1985. Lang.: Chi. 3478

Ways to blend comedy and tragedy in Hsi Ch'ü. China, People's Republic of. 1986. Lang.: Chi. 3479

Creativity in the Chinese arts. China, People's Republic of. 1949-1985. Lang.: Chi. 3480

Interview with Chinese opera actress Mei Bau-Iue. China, People's Republic of. 1947-1985. Lang.: Chi. 3484

Actor Fueng Tz-He: his contribution to Chinese opera. China, People's Republic of: Shanghai. 1888-1941. Lang.: Chi. 3485

Acting techniques in Chinese opera. China, People's Republic of: Beijing. 1935-1986. Lang.: Chi. 3489

The acting of Chinese opera star Tan Fu-Ing. China, People's Republic of. 1900-1950. Lang.: Chi. 3491

The rhythm of Chinese theatre—parts of the whole. China, People's Republic of. 1949-1985. Lang.: Chi. 3493

Chinese opera stars Shiue Jiue-Shian and Shiu Iu-Lan. China, People's Republic of. 1954-1979. Lang.: Chi. 3494

Chou En-Lai and *Horng Lou Meng (Dream of the Red Chamber)*. China, People's Republic of: Shanghai. 1957. Lang.: Chi. 3496

Overview of *Gu Cheng-Hei*. China, People's Republic of. 1967. Lang.: Chi. 3498

Acting theory of Chinese opera. China, People's Republic of. 1900-1986. Lang.: Chi. 3500

Chinese opera actor Gau Liuh-Guei. China, People's Republic of. 1986. Lang.: Chi. 3502

Acting — cont'd

New ideas in acting for Chinese opera. China, People's Republic of. 1987. Lang.: Chi.   3504

Ways to improve the Chinese opera style *Kun-Jiu*. China, People's Republic of. 1956-1986. Lang.: Chi.   3507

History of two local Chinese operas. China, People's Republic of. 1908-1986. Lang.: Chi.   3508

Ways actors should improve themselves in the Li-Iuan drama. China, People's Republic of. 1986. Lang.: Chi.   3509

Acting theories in Chinese opera. China, People's Republic of: Beijing. 1950-1986. Lang.: Chi.   3510

The play *Iang Guei-Fei* and its success. China, People's Republic of. 1987. Lang.: Chi.   3511

Differences between Chinese and Western theatre. China, People's Republic of: Beijing. 1947-1986. Lang.: Chi.   3513

The careers of two Chinese opera actresses—Guan Shu-Shuan and Dai Chi-Shia. China, People's Republic of. 1987. Lang.: Chi.   3515

Memoir of Chinese opera actress Shin Feng-Shya. China, People's Republic of. 1987. Lang.: Chi.   3517

Interview with a performing student at the Cheng Dramatic School. China, People's Republic of. 1986. Lang.: Chi.   3518

Chinese opera actor Chi-Pai. China, People's Republic of. 1987. Lang.: Chi.   3519

The Beijing Opera in England and its large audiences. China, People's Republic of. UK-England. 1987. Lang.: Chi.   3521

Training the Chinese opera actor in Italian singing techniques. China, People's Republic of. 1986. Lang.: Chi.   3523

Acting criticism of the Chinese opera. China, People's Republic of. 1987. Lang.: Chi.   3525

The four main elements of dance in Chinese opera. China, People's Republic of. 960-1987. Lang.: Chi.   3526

Attempted reforms of the main aspects of Chinese opera. China, People's Republic of. 1987. Lang.: Chi.   3527

Vocal training and performance in China. China, People's Republic of: Shanghai. 1949-1987. Lang.: Chi.   3529

Interview with Chinese opera actress Du Jin-Fan. China, People's Republic of. 1987. Lang.: Chi.   3531

Beijing opera actress Guo Sheau-Juang. China, People's Republic of. 1987. Lang.: Chi.   3532

Comparison between Chinese opera and Buddhist plays of Kerala. China, People's Republic of: Beijing. India. 1050-1968. Lang.: Chi.   3533

Directing techniques found in Chinese theatre. China, People's Republic of. 1955-1985. Lang.: Chi.   3536

The acting theories of the Chinese theatre. China, People's Republic of. 1985. Lang.: Chi.   3537

Actor Yin Guey-Fang's work in *The Dream of the Red Chamber*. China, People's Republic of. 1945-1983. Lang.: Chi.   3538

The modernization of Chinese opera—keeping the traditional spirit. China, People's Republic of: Beijing. 1279-1986. Lang.: Chi.   3539

A review of *Yian de-yi yuan* (*A Marriage of Good Fortune*). Taiwan: Taipei. 1987. Lang.: Chi.   3542

Two productions of *Flora, the Red Menace*. USA: New York, NY. 1965-1987. Lang.: Eng.   3640

Lillias White and her performance in the musical *Dreamgirls*. USA: New York, NY. 1960-1987.   3641

History of musical version, *Breakfast at Tiffany's*. USA: New York, NY, Philadelphia, PA, Boston, MA. 1958-1966. Lang.: Eng.   3644

Children's musical *Rag Dolly* jointly produced and performed by U.S. and Soviets. USA: New York, NY. USSR: Moscow. 1986. Lang.: Eng.   3646

Plot synopsis of musical *Mademoiselle Colombe* based on Anouilh's *Colombe*. USA: New York, NY. 1987. Lang.: Eng.   3647

Life and career of actress Nancy Hume. USA. 1977-1987. Lang.: Eng.   3648

Interview with actress Georgia Brown. USA: New York, NY. UK-England: London. 1957-1985. Lang.: Eng.   3651

Interview with actor Giancarlo Esposito. USA: New York, NY. 1987. Lang.: Eng.   3654

Career of Broadway actress Connie Day. USA: New York, NY. 1987. Lang.: Eng.   3657

Martin Charnin's work in musical theatre. USA: New York, NY. 1957-1987. Lang.: Eng.   3658

Career of actor William McCauley. USA. 1987. Lang.: Eng.   3660

Career of actor Lee Roy Reams. USA: New York, NY. 1987. Lang.: Eng.   3661

Plays/librettos/scripts

Works of Carlo Gozzi, his relationship with actor Antonio Sacchi. Italy: Venice. 1755. Lang.: Ita.   1129

Collaboration and friendship of writer Gabriele D'Annunzio and actor Ruggero Ruggeri. Italy. 1901-1938. Lang.: Ita.   1133

Influence of Sibilla Aleramo on women in Italian theatre. Italy. 1850-1930. Lang.: Ita.   1138

Improvement of Korean folk theatre. Korea. 1987-1987. Lang.: Kor.   1149

Self-referentiality and kinds of space in plays of John Marston. England: London. 1553-1608. Lang.: Eng.   2559

Improvisational clowning in Elizabethan theatre. England. 1585-1625. Lang.: Eng.   2560

Comparison of Marivaux and Goldoni. Italy: Venice. France. 1707-1763. Lang.: Ita.   2664

Playwright and actor Andrea Calmo. Italy. 1552-1553. Lang.: Ita.   2678

Analysis of 51 short farces written in Majorca. Spain-Catalonia. 1701-1850. Lang.: Cat.   2731

Pistolteatern's adaptation of *Alice in Wonderland*. Sweden: Stockholm. 1982. Lang.: Eng.   2738

Actress Tilda Swinter talks about her performance as a male. UK-England. 1987. Lang.: Eng.   2824

The inner and outer psychology of characters in Chinese opera. China, People's Republic of. 1987. Lang.: Chi.   3570

Reference materials

Theatrical anecdotes. 500 B.C.-1987 A.D. Lang.: Eng.   1194

History of theatrical activity in Palafrugell. Spain-Catalonia: Palafrugell. 1900-1986. Lang.: Cat.   1210

Relation to other fields

Theatre as an analogy and metaphor for studying social interaction. USA. 1987. Lang.: Eng.   1279

Assumptions by the actors and the audience in live theatre. USA. 1987. Lang.: Eng.   1283

Comparison of the role of theatre in urban society with that of traditional ritual. 1985. Lang.: Spa.   2977

Theory/criticism

Re-evaluation of Brecht's alienation effect in the context of contemporary performances. 1960-1970. Lang.: Eng.   1310

A formalist approach and interpretation of theatre performance. 1987. Lang.: Eng.   1313

Criticism by actor Piero Gobetti. Italy. 1918-1926. Lang.: Ita.   1345

Eric Bentley's critical essays on theatre. USA. 1952-1986. Lang.: Eng.   1350

Collection of critical essays and reviews by Robert Brustein. USA. 1980-1986. Lang.: Eng.   1351

Essays and reviews by Gordon Rogoff. USA. 1960-1986. Lang.: Eng.   1366

Rise of contemporary theatre in Mexico. Mexico: Mexico City. 1957-1987. Lang.: Spa.   3057

Actor Lawrence Barrett and the genteel tradition in acting. USA. 1870-1890. Lang.: Eng.   3069

Main characteristics of the Chinese theatre aesthetic. China, People's Republic of. 960 B.C.-1987 A.D. Lang.: Chi.   3597

Training

Teachers' handbook for theatre in education. Spain-Catalonia. 1987. Lang.: Cat.   1384

Acting teachers who studied under Michajl Čechov: making the Technique fit contemporary needs. USA: New York, NY. 1930-1980. Lang.: Eng.   3082

Acting

Administration

Interim report on the Renaissance Theatre Company. UK-England: London. 1987. Lang.: Eng.   54

Circle Repertory Theatre's plan to increase roles for minority actors. USA: New York, NY. 1983. Lang.: Eng.   116

Instructions for Actors' Equity members regarding new regulations in unemployment. USA: New York, NY. 1982. Lang.: Eng.   240

Long-term planning in artistic culture. USSR. 1987. Lang.: Rus.   263

Acting — cont'd

Audience

Role of samurai class in development and patronage of *kabuki*. Japan: Tokyo. 1603-1868. Lang.: Eng. 1490

Critical analysis of Anne-Marie Provencher's *La Tour*. Canada: Montreal, PQ. 1986. Lang.: Eng. 1531

Design/technology

Effects of mixed media on traditional dramatic components of theatre. Europe. 1900-1987. Lang.: Fre. 318

Influences on costume designs for Ellen Terry. UK-England: London. 1856-1902. Lang.: Eng. 372

Different casting and design approaches to *Brighton Beach Memoirs*. USA. 1983-1987. Lang.: Eng. 427

Stage space in performance. USSR. 1970-1987. Lang.: Rus. 498

Review of *Bartholomew Fair* and *A Midsummer Night's Dream*. UK-England: London. 1987. Lang.: Eng. 1598

Institutions

The Theatre Museum, Covent Garden, which opened on April 23, 1987. UK-England: London. 1924-1987. Lang.: Eng. 565

History of the Conservatoire, training for classical repertory. France: Paris. 1800-1899. Lang.: Eng. 1615

Review of a production of *Ariadne auf Naxos*. Canada. 1987. Lang.: Eng. 3717

Performance/production

Development of Azerbaijani theatre. Azerbaijan. 1875-1925. Lang.: Rus. 723

Interview with actress Tanja Jacobs. Canada: Toronto, ON. 1987. Lang.: Eng. 727

Lack of a theatre 'star' system. Canada. 1960-1987. Lang.: Fre. 729

Reviews of alternative theatre in Toronto. Canada: Toronto, ON, Montreal, PQ. 1987. Lang.: Eng. 731

Reviews of productions by Stratford Festival, Toronto companies. Canada: Toronto, ON, Stratford, ON. 1987. Lang.: Eng. 732

John Neville's first season as artistic director at the Stratford Festival. Canada: Stratford, ON. 1986. Lang.: Eng. 734

Review of Richard Epp's *Intimate Admiration*. Canada: Stratford, ON. 1987. Lang.: Eng. 735

Review of Joanna Glass's *Play Memory*. Canada: Toronto, ON. 1987. Lang.: Eng. 736

Review of August Wilson's play, *Ma Rainey's Black Bottom*. Canada: Toronto, ON. 1987. Lang.: Eng. 737

Hillar Liitoja's experimental theatre. Canada. 1987. Lang.: Eng. 739

Overview of the 1987 Theatre Festival of the Americas. Canada: Montreal, PQ. 1987. Lang.: Eng. 740

Analysis of directorial style of Gilles Maheu. Canada. 1987. Lang.: Eng. 745

Canadian actors and directors discuss their theatre experiences. Canada: Calgary, AB. 1987. Lang.: Eng. 748

Chinese acting technique. China, People's Republic of: Beijing. 1368-1986. Lang.: Chi. 758

History of Slovak school of acting. Czechoslovakia. 1830-1987. Lang.: Rus. 766

Extension of Adolphe Appia's ideas on the role of the actor. France. 1900-1987. Lang.: Fre. 786

Actor-director Friedrich Ludwig Schröder. Germany. 1744-1816. Lang.: Rus. 798

Biography of actor-singer Ernst Busch. Germany, East: Berlin, East. 1900-1980. Lang.: Ger. 799

Interview with actor-director Desző Garas. Hungary. 1983-1987. Lang.: Hun. 803

Reviews of drama students' final examination performances. Hungary: Budapest. 1986-1987. Lang.: Hun. 804

Interview with actress Ida Turay. Hungary: Pécs. 1924-1986. Lang.: Hun. 805

Letters illustrating development of professional theatre in Hungary. Hungary. 1790-1837. Lang.: Hun. 807

Origins of theatre and its relationship to the spectator. India. Japan. Sri Lanka. 1987. Lang.: Eng. 813

Actor Robert Eddison's diary of a Far Eastern tour. Japan. 1979. Lang.: Eng. 842

Progression of Malawian theatre. Malawi. 1987. Lang.: Eng. 859

Role of theatre in the face of political turmoil. Nicaragua: Managua. Uganda. 1987. Lang.: Eng. 864

Peter Feldman's techniques for training actors. North America. 1987. Lang.: Eng. 867

Work and influence of actors Robert and Rafail Adel'gejm. Russia. 1860-1938. Lang.: Rus. 880

Matsemela Manaka's play *Pula* and its anti-apartheid expressions. South Africa, Republic of: Soweto. 1969-1984. Lang.: Eng. 883

Career of actor Lord Laurence Olivier. UK-England. 1907-1987. Lang.: Rus. 898

Interview with actress Dame Peggy Ashcroft. UK-England. 1935-1964. Lang.: Eng. 899

Life and work of actress Ellen Terry. UK-England: London. 1847-1928. Lang.: Eng. 902

Theatre productions in Southwest England. UK-England: Bristol. 1987. Lang.: Eng. 903

Two productions of Pinter's *Old Times*. UK-England: London. USA: New York, NY, St. Louis, MO. 1971-1985. Lang.: Eng. 907

Emergence of feminist theatre groups within the alternative theatre movement. UK-England. 1970-1987. Lang.: Eng. 908

Review of theatre in the South of England. UK-England: Salisbury. 1987. Lang.: Eng. 911

Review of repertory theatre in Northern England. UK-England: Liverpool. 1987. Lang.: Eng. 912

Review of current theatre productions. UK-England: London. 1987. Lang.: Eng. 914

Review of productions in the Midlands region. UK-England. 1987. Lang.: Eng. 915

Carte-de-visite actors' photographs preserve acting styles. UK-England. France. USA. 1850-1920. Lang.: Eng. 916

Review of Scottish theatre for the first 6 months of 1987. UK-Scotland: Edinburgh. 1987. Lang.: Eng. 921

An experimental women's theatre workshop. UK-Wales: Cardiff. 1986-1987. Lang.: Eng. 922

Ukrainian theatrical process. Ukraine. 1970-1979. Lang.: Rus. 923

Organizational and production history of the American Shakespeare Festival. USA: Stratford, CT. 1955-1985. Lang.: Eng. 934

Eulogy of actor Charles Ludlam. USA. 1973-1987. Lang.: Eng. 947

Overview of the Theatre of Nations Festival. USA: Baltimore, MD. 1981-1986. Lang.: Eng. 949

Life and works of playwright, director, designer Charles Ludlam. USA: New York, NY. 1967-1987. Lang.: Eng. 952

Review of several productions in New York. USA: New York, NY. 1987. Lang.: Eng. 953

Career of actor, director, playwright Charles Ludlam. USA: New York, NY. 1964-1987. Lang.: Eng. 956

Influence and impact of the electronic media, live theatre experience. USA: Los Angeles, CA. 1987. Lang.: Eng. 959

Los Angeles theatre performances reviewed. USA: Los Angeles, CA. 1987. Lang.: Eng. 961

A Green Party that mixes politics, experimental theatre. USA: New Haven, CT. 1983-1987. Lang.: Eng. 973

Interview with director Robert Brustein. USA: Cambridge, MA. 1987. Lang.: Eng. 974

Théâtre de la Jeune Lune, its origins and influences. USA: Minneapolis, MN. France: Paris. 1980-1987. Lang.: Eng. 977

Critics' round-table on Leningrad theatre season. USSR: Leningrad. 1986-1987. Lang.: Rus. 983

Review of Moscow theatre season. USSR: Moscow. 1986-1987. Lang.: Rus. 984

Collection of materials on actor-poet Vladimir Vysockij. USSR. 1972-1987. Lang.: Rus. 985

Portrait of actor Eugenij Leonov, Moscow Komsomol Theatre. USSR: Moscow. 1926-1987. Lang.: Rus. 990

Actors discuss contemporary theatrical process. USSR: Moscow. 1987. Lang.: Rus. 993

Sergej Jurskij, director of Mossovet Theatre. USSR: Moscow. 1970-1980. Lang.: Rus. 995

Actors discuss their profession. USSR. 1987. Lang.: Eng. 996

Problems of raising standards in the professional actor's craft. USSR. 1987. Lang.: Rus. 997

Actor and playwright A.I. Sumbatov-Južin. USSR: Moscow. 1857-1927. Lang.: Rus. 998

Acting — cont'd

Actor Vladimir Vysockij remembered. USSR: Moscow. 1938-1980.
Lang.: Rus.   999

Actor Babken Nersisjan. USSR. 1917-1987. Lang.: Rus.   1000

Actor Jevgenij Gerčakov of the Theatre of Miniatures. USSR:
Moscow. 1980-1987. Lang.: Rus.   1002

History of Moscow State University student theatre. USSR: Moscow.
1960-1980. Lang.: Rus.   1004

Bibliography of Soviet Latvian actors. USSR. 1987. Lang.: Rus. 1005

Actress Alla Demidova recalls Vladimir Vysockij. USSR: Moscow.
1938-1980. Lang.: Rus.   1008

Acting style of Vachtangov. USSR. Canada. 1922-1987. Lang.: Eng.
                                                               1009

Tradition and art of acting at Malyj Theatre. USSR: Moscow. 1987.
Lang.: Rus.   1010

Current prospects for the development of Soviet theatrical art.
USSR. 1987. Lang.: Rus.   1012

Latvian actor Je. Pavule. USSR. 1929-1987. Lang.: Lat.   1013

Overview of issues in Moscow theatre season. USSR: Moscow. 1986-
1987. Lang.: Rus.   1019

Reflections of a theatre critic on the acting profession. USSR. 1986.
Lang.: Rus.   1020

Portrait of actor Bruno Frejndlich of Leningrad Puškin Theatre.
USSR: Leningrad. 1909-1987. Lang.: Rus.   1021

Actor Vladimir Vysockij of Taganka Theatre. USSR: Moscow. 1938-
1980. Lang.: Rus.   1023

Actor Pavel Samojlov. USSR. 1836-1931. Lang.: Rus.   1024

Memoirs of actor V.S. Jakut. USSR: Moscow. 1912-1980. Lang.:
Rus.   1025

Ukrainian actor N.N. Užvij. USSR. 1898-1987. Lang.: Rus.   1027

Actor Aleksej Nikolaevič Gribov of Moscow Art Theatre. USSR:
Moscow. 1930-1979. Lang.: Rus.   1029

Review of the Leningrad theatre season. USSR: Leningrad. 1986-
1987. Lang.: Rus.   1030

Portrait of actor Oleg Jankovskij, Moscow Komsomol Theatre.
USSR: Moscow. 1980-1987. Lang.: Rus.   1032

Portrait of actor Sergej Jurskij. USSR: Moscow. 1835-1987. Lang.:
Rus.   1036

Portrait of actor Eduard Marcevič. USSR: Moscow. 1987. Lang.:
Rus.   1037

Sociological study of actors. USSR. 1980-1987. Lang.: Rus.   1041

Recollections of actress Veriko Andžaparidze. USSR. 1898-1987.
Lang.: Rus.   1042

Creative and moral problems of a theatre collective. USSR: Moscow.
1986-1988. Lang.: Rus.   1045

Director V. Pimenov's recollections of actors Gricenko, Plotnikov and
Abrikosov. USSR: Moscow. 1940-1979. Lang.: Rus.   1047

Problems of an actor's working conditions. USSR. 1980-1987. Lang.:
Rus.   1049

Bolšoj actor Valerij Ivčenko. USSR: Leningrad. 1980. Lang.: Rus.
                                                               1052

Actor Oleg Borisov of Moscow Art Theatre. USSR: Moscow. 1980-
1987. Lang.: Rus.   1053

Overview of the issues of 1986 Belorussian theatre festival. USSR.
1986. Lang.: Rus.   1054

Stage and screen actor Ljubov' Orlova. USSR: Moscow. 1902-1975.
Lang.: Rus.   1055

Aleksandr Borisov, actor of the Leningrad Puškin Theatre. USSR:
Leningrad. 1905-1969. Lang.: Rus.   1060

Recognizing and developing talent: experiences of the Lunačarskij
School. USSR: Moscow. 1981-1986. Lang.: Rus.   1061

Teaching and directing the student actor. USSR. 1987. Lang.: Rus.
                                                               1062

Recollections of actor Vladimir Vysockij. USSR: Moscow. 1938-1980.
Lang.: Rus.   1066

Review of Moscow theatre season. USSR: Moscow. 1986-1987.
Lang.: Rus.   1067

The Moscow season and an overview of Soviet theatre. USSR. 1986-
1987. Lang.: Rus.   1068

Issues in acting. USSR. 1970-1987. Lang.: Rus.   1071

Life and work of N. Cereteli, leading actor of Tairov Chamber
Theatre. USSR: Moscow. 1890-1942. Lang.: Rus.   1072

Career of actor Kirill Lavrov. USSR: Leningrad. 1980. Lang.: Rus.
                                                               1073

Memoirs of actor Boris Tenin. USSR: Moscow. 1920-1939. Lang.:
Rus.   1076

Soviet actor Michajl A. Ul'janov on his work. USSR. 1927-1987.
Lang.: Rus.   1078

Portrait of actor Gennadij Bortnikov of Mossovet Theatre. USSR.
1980-1987. Lang.: Eng.   1079

Actor Michajl Ul'janov. USSR: Moscow. 1927-1987. Lang.: Rus.
                                                               1080

Actress Marina Vladi recalls Vladimir Vysockij. USSR. 1938-1980.
Lang.: Rus.   1081

Portrait of actress Ol'ga Jakovleva of Taganka Theatre. USSR:
Moscow. 1980-1987. Lang.: Rus.   1088

The actor's art as directed by G.A. Tovstonogov. USSR. 1970-1987.
Lang.: Rus.   1089

History and description of a performance of *Cavittunatakam*, a
drama recounting lives of the saints. India: Kerala. 1984. Lang.:
Eng.   1480

Institutions, techniques in training of *nō* actors. Japan. 1987. Lang.:
Eng.   1499

Zeami's concept of the actor and the ideal performance. Japan.
1363-1443. Lang.: Eng.   1500

Performances of *nō* plays by priests and description of a new play.
Japan: Hiraizumi. 1987. Lang.: Eng.   1501

Writer-director Glen Cairns and surrealistic drama at the Neptune
Theatre. Canada: Halifax, NS. 1977-1987. Lang.: Eng.   1695

Interview with actor Lorne Brass. Canada: Montreal, PQ. 1986.
Lang.: Fre.   1707

La Quinzaine acting competition. Canada: Quebec, PQ. 1986-1986.
Lang.: Fre.   1712

Content and North American reception of *Asinimali! (We Have No
Money!)* by Mbongeni Ngema. Canada. South Africa, Republic of.
1987. Lang.: Eng.   1715

Workshop in Chinese acting methods. Canada: Toronto, ON. China,
People's Republic of: Shanghai. 1987. Lang.: Eng.   1717

Interview with actor-director Jozef Bednárik. Czechoslovakia: Nitra.
1987. Lang.: Hun.   1727

Roles portrayed by stage actress Nell Gwyn. England: London.
1663-1668. Lang.: Eng.   1731

Examples of transition in acting style. England. 1783-1784. Lang.:
Eng.   1733

Use of visual arts conventions in acting techniques. England. 1700.
Lang.: Eng.   1735

Evaluation of acting styles in 18th century. England. 1672-1799.
Lang.: Eng.   1736

Comparison of *onnagata* actors with Elizabethan boy actors.
England. Japan. 1580-1987. Lang.: Eng.   1737

Study of theatre in Liverpool in relation to the city's cultural history.
England: Liverpool. 1850-1900. Lang.: Eng.   1739

'Boy actresses' and attitudes toward sensuality in performance.
England: London. 1580-1630. Lang.: Eng.   1741

Additions to list of transvestite actors. England. 1510-1519. Lang.:
Eng.   1744

'Showing' is an essential part of all acting. Europe. 1590-1987.
Lang.: Eng.   1746

Sources of attitudes for serious dramatic acting and acting for low
comedy. Europe. 1700. Lang.: Eng.   1747

Company members of Centre International de Recherche Théâtrale
discuss *The Mahabharata*. France: Paris. 1986. Lang.: Eng.   1752

Child actors in juvenile companies, Comédie-Française. France: Paris.
1769-1850. Lang.: Eng.   1756

Biography of Max Reinhardt. Germany. 1873-1943. Lang.: Rus. 1770

Reviews of major Berlin performances. Germany: Berlin. 1889-1933.
Lang.: Ger.   1772

Essays on major figures of the Romantic period. Germany. 1795-
1830. Lang.: Ger.   1776

Biography of comic actress Marianne Wünscher. Germany, East:
Berlin, East. 1930-1986. Lang.: Ger.   1780

Actor Arno Wyzniewski of Berliner Ensemble. Germany, East: Berlin,
East. 1956-1987. Lang.: Ger.   1781

Annual Brecht workshop. Germany, East. 1985. Lang.: Fre.   1785

Acting — cont'd

Acting — cont'd

Interview with actor Marcello Mastroianni. Italy. 1949-1987. Lang.: Hun. 3156

Sophia Loren's autobiography translated into Hungarian. Italy. 1934-1979. Lang.: Hun. 3157

Personal anecdotes and photographs from the making of *The African Queen*. USA: Hollywood, CA. 1950-1951. Lang.: Eng. 3168

Hungarian translation of Norman Mailer's biography of Marilyn Monroe. USA. 1926-1962. Lang.: Hun. 3169

Dorothy L. Sayers' *Have His Carcase, Eastender* and *Intimate Contact* are reviewed. UK-England. 1987. Lang.: Eng. 3208

Theatrical nature of televised wrestling. USA. 1987. Lang.: Eng. 3211

Television actors' working conditions. USSR. 1980-1987. Lang.: Rus. 3214

Photographs of mimes, mime companies and performance artists with commentary. USA. Europe. 1972-1987. Lang.: Eng. 3229

History that formed the mimes of the 1980s. USA. 1987. Lang.: Eng. 3230

Development of contemporary pantomime. Europe. 1970-1987. Lang.: Rus. 3232

Mime Samy Molcho: his new work as lecturer and author. Switzerland. 1987. Lang.: Ger. 3235

Actor A.A. Rušnev of Tairov Chamber Theatre. USSR: Moscow. 1920-1939. Lang.: Rus. 3237

Description of 'Third Theatre'. Argentina: Bahía Blanca. 1987. Lang.: Eng. 3249

Codco, a comic theatrical troupe, creates regional characters. Canada: St. John's, NF. 1986. Lang.: Eng. 3253

Community theatre movement after Sandinista war effort. Nicaragua. 1987. Lang.: Eng. 3264

Xhosa story-telling uses verbal dramatization and language of gesture. South Africa, Republic of. 1987. Lang.: Eng. 3266

Use of actors to simulate symptoms at medical conferences. USA. 1987. Lang.: Eng. 3275

Parisian cabaret theatre performance reviews. France: Paris. 1987. Lang.: Eng. 3284

Autobiography of cabaret actor Béla Salamon. Hungary: Budapest. 1885-1965. Lang.: Hun. 3285

Memoirs of cabaret artist Balázs Szuhay. Hungary. 1935-1986. Lang.: Hun. 3286

Doc Fred Foster Bloodgood, vaudevillian, who sold medicine to crowds between acts. USA: New York, NY. 1929-1987. Lang.: Eng. 3305

Life and work of the Nikitiny Circus artists. USSR. 1850-1950. Lang.: Rus. 3306

Dario Fo's use of *commedia dell'arte*. Italy. 1550-1987. Lang.: Rus. 3313

Techniques of the image theatre and effects on actor and audience. Canada. Europe. USA. 1987. Lang.: Eng. 3345

The work of director Robert Lepage. Canada: Montreal, PQ. 1987. Lang.: Eng. 3347

Image theatre methodology. Canada. 1987. Lang.: Eng. 3348

The performance art piece, *Living Room Project*, of Danny Mydlack. USA: Boston, MA. 1987. Lang.: Eng. 3367

Depression-era Yiddish actress Molly Picon. USA. 1930. Lang.: Eng. 3413

Acting in musical drama. USSR. 1920-1970. Lang.: Rus. 3414

Music-drama in the Baltics. USSR. 1980-1987. Lang.: Rus. 3416

Status of Sichuan theatre and opera. China, People's Republic of: Chengdu. 1985-1986. Lang.: Eng. 3512

Actors Sándor Szakácsi and Piroska Molnár in *Man of La Mancha* directed by László Bagossy. Hungary: Pécs. 1987. Lang.: Hun. 3633

Review of *Pirates* and *Student Prince*. South Africa, Republic of: Johannesburg. 1986. Lang.: Eng. 3634

Review of *Hello Dolly* in Bloemfontein. South Africa, Republic of: Bloemfontein. 1987. Lang.: Eng. 3635

Interview with actress Barbara Barondess MacLean. USA: New York, NY. 1920-1930. Lang.: Eng. 3652

N.A. Sličenko of Romen Gypsy Theatre. USSR: Moscow. 1950-1987. Lang.: Rus. 3668

Interview with opera star Gaétan Laperrière. Canada. 1987. Lang.: Eng. 3756

Shift in opera from the singer to the conductor. Europe. North America. 1887-1987. Lang.: Eng. 3766

Biography of tenor János Sárdy. Hungary. 1907-1969. Lang.: Hun. 3795

Review of *Otello* at the Royal Opera House. UK-England: London. 1987. Lang.: Eng. 3831

Study of the Moscow Bolšoj Theatre. USSR: Moscow. 1974-1980. Lang.: Rus. 3867

Folk artist Tamara F. Janko. USSR. 1970-1987. Lang.: Rus. 3869

Memoirs of actor Fëdor I. Šaljapin. USSR. 1873-1938. Lang.: Rus. 3881

Béla Zerkovitz's operetta *Csókos asszony (A Woman Made for Kissing)* directed by István Iglódi. Hungary: Budapest. 1987. Lang.: Hun. 3957

Plays/librettos/scripts

An annual bibliography of works by and about Harold Pinter. UK-England. USA. 1986-1987. Lang.: Eng. 1160

Elia Kazan's influence on playwright Ray Lawler. Australia. USA. 1950-1955. Lang.: Eng. 2445

Venice Preserv'd: impact of Betterton's acting style on Otway. England. 1675-1683. Lang.: Eng. 2527

Theoretical considerations of English Renaissance theatre. England. 1600-1699. Lang.: Rus. 2528

Directive as a speech act in *Krismis van Map Jacobs (Christmas of Map Jacobs)* by Adam Small. South Africa, Republic of. 1983. Lang.: Afr. 2726

Yeats's dance plays: effect of the elements of performance on text. UK-Ireland. 1916-1987. Lang.: Eng. 2832

Reference materials

Compilation of anecdotes on life in the theatre from Aristophanes to Williams. 5 B.C.-1987 A.D. Lang.: Eng. 1195

Relation to other fields

Excerpt from a speech by Jerzy Grotowski that examines the actor's technique. Italy: Florence. 1985. Lang.: Eng. 1244

Nontraditional casting of minority actors. USA. 1979-1987. Lang.: Eng. 1274

Survival of Punch and Judy shows during the Edwardian period. UK-England. 1860-1910. Lang.: Eng. 3998

Theory/criticism

Dramatic criticism in the Sung Dynasty. China: Beijing. 960-1279. Lang.: Chi. 1319

Gesture and sign in Shakespearean performance. England. USA. 1590-1987. Lang.: Eng. 1326

Metaphysical and philosophical implications of the actor's role in *nō* theatre. Japan. 712-1980. Lang.: Pol. 1510

Influence of actors' interpretation and audience on criticism. 1987. Lang.: Eng. 3019

Training

Interview with Georgij Tovstonogov. USA. 1987. Lang.: Eng. 1390

Vocal training in Soviet dramatic education. USSR. 1987. Lang.: Rus. 1392

Problems of students graduating from theatre schools. USSR. 1980-1987. Lang.: Rus. 1394

Problems of young drama school graduates. USSR. 1986-1987. Lang.: Rus. 1396

Acting Company (New York, NY)
Performance spaces

John Houseman on the New York home of the Acting Company. USA: New York, NY. 1972-1986. Lang.: Eng. 695

Acting Company (Toronto, ON)
Performance/production

Workshop in Chinese acting methods. Canada: Toronto, ON. China, People's Republic of: Shanghai. 1987. Lang.: Eng. 1717

Acting Shakespeare
Performance/production

Collection of newspaper reviews by London theatre critics. UK-England. 1987. Lang.: Eng. 2261

Action
Plays/librettos/scripts

Modernism and postmodernism as themes in Sam Shepard's plays. USA. 1972-1987. Lang.: Eng. 2930

Action Design
Design/technology

Action Design, a new theory of scenography emerging in Eastern Europe. Czechoslovakia: Prague. 1980-1987. Lang.: Eng. 315

Actors' Equity Association (USA) – cont'd

Institutions

Actors' Equity and Black History Month. USA: New York, NY.
1986. Lang.: Eng.   572

Actors' Equity strike against Producing Managers Association. USA:
New York, NY. 1921-1925. Lang.: Eng.   573

Nominees for Actors' Equity Association council state qualifications.
USA: New York, NY. 1986. Lang.: Eng.   574

Debate on 99-seat waiver. USA: Los Angeles, CA. 1986. Lang.: Eng.
                                                               577

New York Shakespeare Festival's Joseph Papp receives AEA's Paul
Robeson Award. USA: New York, NY. 1987. Lang.: Eng.   578

Actors' Equity outreach to encourage performers and new theatres.
USA. 1985-1986. Lang.: Eng.   596

A Season of Concern, an AIDS fundraising benefit in Chicago. USA:
Chicago, IL. 1987. Lang.: Eng.   609

The work of AEA's Equity Fights AIDS Committee. USA: New
York, NY. 1987. Lang.: Eng.   619

Performance spaces

Morosco Theatre torn down despite efforts by Actors' Equity. USA:
New York, NY. 1982. Lang.: Eng.   677

Performance/production

The AEA approved definition for nontraditional casting. USA: New
York, NY. 1987. Lang.: Eng.   925

Actor discusses Equity exchanges for *Les Misérables*. USA: New
York, NY. UK-England: London. 1987. Lang.: Eng.   926

Nontraditional casting in a production of *The Cherry Orchard*. USA:
San Francisco, CA. 1986. Lang.: Eng.   928

Issues in nontraditional casting. USA: New York, NY. 1986. Lang.:
Eng.   936

Actors' Equity symposium on nontraditional casting. USA. 1987.
Lang.: Eng.   981

Relation to other fields

Actors' Equity's affirmative action program. USA: New York, NY.
1982. Lang.: Eng.   1261

Equity's National Theatre Plan. USA. 1982. Lang.: Eng.   1262

Actors' Fund (New York, NY)

Institutions

The role of the Actors' Fund in New York's theatre industry. USA:
New York, NY. 1987. Lang.: Eng.   570

Actors' Theatre of Louisville (Louisville, KY)

Performance/production

Four productions in Southern regional theatres. USA: Houston, TX,
Louisville, KY, Gainesville, FL. 1980. Lang.: Eng.   2342

Adam le Bossu

SEE

Adam de la Halle.

Adám, Ottó

Performance/production

Ottó Adám directs Anton Pavlovič Čechov's *Višněvyj sad (The
Cherry Orchard)* at Madách Theatre under the title *Cseresznyéskert*.
Hungary: Budapest. 1987. Lang.: Hun.   1805

Adams, Desmond

Performance/production

Collection of newspaper reviews by London theatre critics. UK-
England: London. 1986. Lang.: Eng.   2110

Adams, John

Performance/production

Premiere of the docu-opera, *Nixon in China*, Houston Grand Opera.
USA: Houston, TX. 1987. Lang.: Eng.   3843

Adams, Suzanne

Design/technology

Controversy over 1901 cylinder recording of *Les Huguenots*. USA.
1901-1987. Lang.: Eng.   3699

Mapleson cylinders: controversy over *Les Huguenots*. USA: New
York, NY. 1947. Lang.: Eng.   3700

Adams, Terry

Performance/production

Collection of newspaper reviews by London theatre critics. UK-
England: London. 1986. Lang.: Eng.   2057

Adaptations

Basic theatrical documents

New English translation of Rostand's *Chantecler*. France. 1880-1987.
Lang.: Eng.   1554

Chapter 19 of Harold Pinter's unpublished novel *The Dwarfs*. UK-
England. 1958-1987. Lang.: Eng.   1575

Performance/production

Transformation of *La Cage aux Folles* from movie to a Broadway
musical. USA: New York, NY. 1983-1987. Lang.: Eng.   940

Dorothée Letessier's comments on the adaptation and staging of her
novel *Voyage à Paimpol (Journey to Paimpol)*. Belgium: Liège. 1986.
Lang.: Fre.   1686

Richard Ouzounian, director, Manitoba Theatre Centre. Canada:
Winnipeg, MB. 1982. Lang.: Eng.   1693

Peter Sellars and American National Theatre present *Ajax*, Holland
Festival. Netherlands. USA. 1987. Lang.: Dut.   1981

Jurij Liubimov's 1979 Taganka Theatre production of *The Master
and Margarita (Master i Margarita)*. USSR. 1938-1979. Lang.: Eng.
                                                             2394

International coverage of film adaptations of Shakespeare. 1899-
1987. Lang.: Eng.   3148

Listing of films made from books or plays and their production
information. UK-England. USA. 1926-1986. Lang.: Eng.   3162

Granada TV's production of *The Jewel in the Crown*. UK-England.
India. 1986. Lang.: Eng.   3207

Overview of *Gu Cheng-Hei*. China, People's Republic of. 1967.
Lang.: Chi.   3498

Beijing opera *Yu-wang-cheng-gue (A City of Desire)*, based on
Shakespeare's *Macbeth*. Taiwan: Taipei. 1986. Lang.: Chi.   3541

History of musical version, *Breakfast at Tiffany's*. USA: New York,
NY, Philadelphia, PA, Boston, MA. 1958-1966. Lang.: Eng.   3644

Increasingly novel adaptations of opera settings. Canada. 1987.
Lang.: Eng.   3750

Shift in opera from the singer to the conductor. Europe. North
America. 1887-1987. Lang.: Eng.   3766

Christina, opera based on Strindberg play by Hans Gefors and Lars
Forssell. Sweden: Stockholm. 1986-1987. Lang.: Swe.   3823

Adaptation of Nativity puppet play. Italy. 1651-1987. Lang.: Eng.
                                                             4001

Plays/librettos/scripts

Interview with playwright Antonio Skarmento. Chile: Santiago. 1967-
1987. Lang.: Eng.   1102

Musical adaptation of Gorostiza's *Contigo pan y cebolla (With You,
Bread and Onion)*. Mexico: Mexico City. Spain: Madrid. 1833-1984.
Lang.: Eng.   1150

Adaptations of fairy tales and fantasies for children's plays. USA.
1957-1987. Lang.: Eng.   1165

Playwrights' condescension to child audiences. USA. 1972. Lang.:
Eng.   1171

Interview with Susan Sontag, director of *Jacques and His Master*.
USA: Cambridge, MA. 1985. Lang.: Eng.   1172

Interview with Milan Kundera on *Jacques and His Master*. USA:
Cambridge, MA. 1985. Lang.: Eng.   1173

Playwright Fernando Arrabal and productions of his work. USA.
France: Paris. 1959-1987. Lang.: Eng.   1175

Kundera's adaptation of *Jacques le Fataliste (Jacques and His
Master)* by Diderot. USA: Cambridge, MA. 1985. Lang.: Eng.   1178

Experiments of Moscow Children's Theatre. USSR: Moscow. 1986-
1987. Lang.: Rus.   1185

Development of *The Mahabharata* directed by Peter Brook and
Jean-Claude Carrière. 1975-1987. Lang.: Eng.   2412

Essex Evans' adaptations of *Robinson Crusoe* and *Musical Whist*.
Australia. 1891-1902. Lang.: Eng.   2439

Productions of Brecht in Quebec. Canada. 1950-1986. Lang.: Fre.
                                                             2461

Brassard discusses his adaptation of Genet's *Les Paravents (The
Screens)*. Canada: Montreal, PQ, Ottawa, ON. 1987. Lang.: Fre.
                                                             2485

Attack on Sir Robert Walpole in 18th-century adaptation of *King
Edward the Third*. England. 1691-1731. Lang.: Eng.   2505

Eighteenth-century alterations to Shakespeare's *The Merchant of
Venice*. England. 1596-1701. Lang.: Eng.   2512

History of Yiddish theatre and development of its plays. Europe.
USA. 1853-1960. Lang.: Heb.   2562

Peter Brook discusses his production of *The Mahabharata*. France:
Paris. India. Australia: Perth. 1987. Lang.: Eng.   2571

Korean stage adaptation of *Le Mur (The Wall)* by Sartre. France.
Korea. 1939-1976. Lang.: Kor.   2575

Adaptations — cont'd

André Brassard's production of Jean Genet's *Les Paravents (The Screens)*. France. Canada: Montreal, PQ, Ottawa, ON. 1961-1987. Lang.: Fre.　　2583

Investigating the text of Genet's *Les Paravents (The Screens)*. France. Canada: Montreal, PQ, Ottawa, ON. 1961-1987. Lang.: Fre.　　2585

Interview with director Kazimierz Braun. Ireland: Dublin. Poland. 1981-1983. Lang.: Eng.　　2642

The Strong Breed and *The Bacchae*: Soyinka's symbolic use of ritual and ceremony. Nigeria. 1973-1987. Lang.: Eng.　　2709

Study of *El pan del pobre (Poor Man's Bread)*, adapted from Hauptmann's *Die Weber (The Weavers)*. Spain. 1894. Lang.: Eng.　　2728

Pistolteatern's adaptation of *Alice in Wonderland*. Sweden: Stockholm. 1982. Lang.: Eng.　　2738

Analysis of Dürrenmatt's *Play Strindberg*, adaptation of Strindberg's *Dödsdansen (The Dance of Death)*. Switzerland. 1971-1982. Lang.: Eng.　　2743

Comparison of Peter Barnes's *Actors* to Lope de Vega's *Lo Fingido Verdadero (The Feigned Truth)*. UK-England: London. Spain: Madrid. 1983. Lang.: Eng.　　2769

Introduction to Chapter 19 of Pinter's unpublished novel *The Dwarfs*. UK-England. 1958-1987. Lang.: Eng.　　2779

John Lang's collaboration with Tom Taylor on *Plot and Passion*. UK-England. Australia. 1853. Lang.: Eng.　　2785

Shakespearean burlesque in context. UK-England. 1800-1900. Lang.: Eng.　　2817

Productions exhibit changes in symbolism of the Don Juan myth due to AIDS crisis. USA. 1987. Lang.: Eng.　　2845

Adaptation of Alan Bowne's *Forty Deuce* as stage play and film. USA: New York, NY. Lang.: Eng.　　2891

Legal and ethical rights of playwrights regarding interpretations of their works. USA. Lang.: Eng.　　2904

Producing German drama in the United States. USA. Germany. 1985. Lang.: Eng.　　2928

Contemporary interpretations of Shakespeare's work. USSR. 1980-1987. Lang.: Rus.　　2967

Stage and screen adaptations of the poetry of Lesja Ukrainka. USSR. 1987. Lang.: Rus.　　2971

Two forms of adaptations of Shakespeare for other media. Europe. USA. 1899-1987. Lang.: Eng.　　3097

Translating ancient Greek theatre into film. Greece. 500 B.C.-1986 A.D. Lang.: Eng.　　3098

Successful film versions of Shakespeare's *King Lear*. USA. UK-England. USSR. 1916-1983. Lang.: Eng.　　3099

Orson Welles's adaptation of *Othello*: cinematic technique and time. USA. 1952. Lang.: Eng.　　3180

Development of Welles's adaptation of *Henry IV* Parts I and II from stage to screen. USA. Ireland. 1938-1965. Lang.: Eng.　　3182

Polanski, Welles and Kurosawa's versions of Shakespeare's *Macbeth*. USA. Japan. UK-England. 1948-1971. Lang.: Eng.　　3183

How to adapt Shakespeare to Chinese opera. China, People's Republic of. 1987. Lang.: Chi.　　3569

How Anouilh's *Colombe* was adapted as a musical. USA. 1987. Lang.: Eng.　　3672

History of the musical *Roza*. USA: Baltimore, MD. 1965-1987. Lang.: Eng.　　3675

Problems of adapting literary works to the stage. USSR. 1980-1987. Lang.: Rus.　　3676

Imagined interview with librettist of *Lucia di Lammermoor*. 1835. Lang.: Eng.　　3889

Adaptation of literary works to opera. 1893-1987. Lang.: Eng.　　3890

Background and sources of Massenet's *Manon Lescaut*. France: Paris. 1831-1910. Lang.: Eng.　　3899

Mérimée novella, source of Bizet's *Carmen*. France: Paris. 1803-1870. Lang.: Eng.　　3903

Making of Verdi's *Otello*. Italy: Milan. 1862-1879. Lang.: Eng.　　3917

Comparison of Puccini's and Leoncavallo's treatments of *La Bohème*. Italy. 1893-1897. Lang.: Swe.　　3922

Creating modern critical edition of score of Verdi's *Nabucco*. Italy: Milan. 1987. Lang.: Eng.　　3925

Opera adaptations for Broadway with African-American artists. USA: New York, NY. 1935-1987. Lang.: Eng.　　3932

Relation to other fields

Benjamin Britten's *Albert Herring* as an adaptation of a story by Maupassant. UK-England. 1947. Lang.: Eng.　　3946

Adel'gejm, Rafail

Performance/production

Work and influence of actors Robert and Rafail Adel'gejm. Russia. 1860-1938. Lang.: Rus.　　880

Adel'gejm, Robert

Performance/production

Work and influence of actors Robert and Rafail Adel'gejm. Russia. 1860-1938. Lang.: Rus.　　880

Adler, Stella

Performance/production

Development of the Stanislavskij Acting System. Russia: Moscow. 1906-1938. Lang.: Eng.　　2003

Administration

SEE ALSO

Classed Entries.

Design/technology

Managing director of theatre equipment manufacturer Donmar examines business aspects. UK-England: London. 1987. Lang.: Eng.　　371

Managing director of Raxcrest Electrical reviews the trade. UK-England. 1987. Lang.: Eng.　　378

Comprehensive look at touring theatre. USA. 1987. Lang.: Eng.　　464

Institutions

Aims and scope of the Olympic Arts Festival. Canada: Calgary, AB. 1987. Lang.: Eng.　　507

Atlantic Canada theatre companies' conferences. Canada. 1985-1986. Lang.: Eng.　　514

History of Theatre Plus theatre company. Canada: Toronto, ON. 1972-1982. Lang.: Eng.　　520

Previews 1982 International Children's Festival. Canada: Toronto, ON. 1982. Lang.: Eng.　　524

New York State Council on the Arts' Presenting Organizations Program. USA: New York. 1960-1983. Lang.: Eng.　　601

Profile and history of Symphony Space. USA: New York, NY. 1977-1984. Lang.: Eng.　　602

Profile of the theatre collective, Mabou Mines. USA: New York, NY. 1987. Lang.: Eng.　　617

Profile and history of Colden Center for the Performing Arts. USA: Flushing, NY. 1961-1984. Lang.: Eng.　　618

King's Company under actor-manager John Lowin. England: London. 1576-1653. Lang.: Eng.　　1614

Evaluation of theatrical policy in Catalonia. Spain-Catalonia: Barcelona. 1976-1986. Lang.: Cat.　　1635

Theatre manager William Wood's paternalism. USA: Philadelphia, PA. 1803-1855. Lang.: Eng.　　1659

Andrew Davis' role as Toronto Symphony Orchestra conductor. Canada: Toronto, On. 1974-1987. Lang.: Eng.　　3389

Daniel Lipton, new artistic director Opera Hamilton. Canada: Hamilton, ON. 1986-1987. Lang.: Eng.　　3722

Jeannette Aster, new artistic director of Opera Lyra. Canada: Ottawa, ON. 1984-1987. Lang.: Eng.　　3723

Lack of operetta productions by the Canadian Opera Company. Canada: Toronto, ON. 1987. Lang.: Eng.　　3724

Overview of Lars af Malmborg's management of Swedish Royal Opera. Sweden: Stockholm. 1985-1987. Lang.: Swe.　　3729

The popularization of opera companies since 1940. USA. 1940-1983. Lang.: Eng.　　3735

Operations of the Toronto Operetta Theatre. Canada: Toronto, ON. 1985-1987. Lang.: Eng.　　3955

Performance spaces

Interview with stage manager Michael Dembowicz about the new Swan Theatre. UK-England: Stratford. 1986. Lang.: Eng.　　673

Process of setting up a second performing space, includes guidelines. USA. 1980-1986. Lang.: Eng.　　684

History of the Alice Arts Center, new home of the Oakland Ensemble Theatre. USA: Oakland, CA. 1983-1987. Lang.: Eng.　　696

Reconstruction of theatrical activity in Barcelona. Spain-Catalonia: Barcelona. 1800-1830. Lang.: Cat.　　1672

Histories of Wallack's Theatre and the Union Square Theatre. USA: New York, NY. 1850-1889. Lang.: Eng.　　1676

Administration — cont'd

Performance/production

John Neville's first season as artistic director at the Stratford Festival. Canada: Stratford, ON. 1986. Lang.: Eng. 734

Grand Theatre: failed establishment of repertory theatre. Canada: London, ON. 1983-1984. Lang.: Eng. 738

Director discusses the needs of regional theatres. Hungary. 1986-1987. Lang.: Hun. 811

Theatre groups existing in small countries and communities. South America. UK-Wales. 1960-1987. Lang.: Eng. 884

Organizational and production history of the American Shakespeare Festival. USA: Stratford, CT. 1955-1985. Lang.: Eng. 934

Review of 1984 Shaw Festival season. Canada: Niagara-on-the-Lake, ON. 1984. Lang.: Eng. 1699

Overview of the 1983 Stratford Festival. Canada: Stratford, ON. 1983. Lang.: Eng. 1700

Overview of the 1982 Shaw Festival. Canada: Niagara-on-the-Lake, ON. 1982. Lang.: Eng. 1703

History of musical version, *Breakfast at Tiffany's*. USA: New York, NY, Philadelphia, PA, Boston, MA. 1958-1966. Lang.: Eng. 3644

Cooperative financing of Gershwin's *Porgy and Bess*. USA. 1987. Lang.: Eng. 3850

History of the Puppeteers Company. UK-England: Norwich. 1971-1987. Lang.: Eng. 3983

Relation to other fields

Actors' Equity's affirmative action program. USA: New York, NY. 1982. Lang.: Eng. 1261

Polish official promotion of music theatre. Poland. 1950-1965. Lang.: Pol. 3421

Training

Shaping of an arts management internship from an employer's point of view. USA: Brooklyn, NY. 1985. Lang.: Eng. 1389

Administration, top

Performance/production

Problems of theatre reform. USSR. 1986-1988. Lang.: Rus. 1056

Adolfo and Maria

Performance/production

Performance artists Ishmael Houston-Jones, John Kelly, Karen Finley, Richard Elovich. USA. 1987. Lang.: Eng. 3366

Adshead, Kay

Performance/production

Collection of newspaper reviews by London theatre critics. UK-England: London. 1987. Lang.: Eng. 2191

Adult Child/Dead Child

Performance/production

Collection of newspaper reviews by London theatre critics. UK-England: London. 1987. Lang.: Eng. 2174

Adventures of Mr. Toad, The

Performance/production

Collection of newspaper reviews by London theatre critics. UK-England: London. 1986. Lang.: Eng. 2042

Advertising

Administration

Form and content of Warsaw playbills. Poland: Warsaw. 1765-1915. Lang.: Pol. 38

Non-profit organizations benefit from use of computer modems. USA: New York, NY. 1987. Lang.: Eng. 151

Influence of TV ads on success of Broadway plays. USA: New York, NY. 1984-1987. Lang.: Eng. 179

History of the Russian theatre poster. USSR. 1870-1979. 261

Aeneid

Plays/librettos/scripts

Relationship of the *Aeneid* to Shakespeare's *The Tempest*. England: London. 1611. Lang.: Eng. 2561

Aerialists

Performance/production

Production of Cirque du Soleil. Canada: Montreal, PQ. 1987. Lang.: Eng. 3302

Aeschylus

Plays/librettos/scripts

Study of classical Greek dramaturgy. Greece. 472-388 B.C. Lang.: Hun. 2623

Study of works by Sophocles, Aeschylus and Euripides. Greece. 400 B.C.-500 A.D. Lang.: Eng. 2624

Aesthetics

Audience

Chinese acting: direct communication with audience. China, People's Republic of: Beijing. 1950-1986. Lang.: Chi. 3434

Five steps to appreciate Chinese opera. China, People's Republic of. 700-1986. Lang.: Chi. 3438

Basic theatrical documents

Texts on dramatic theory by nineteenth-century authors. Germany. 1794-1906. Lang.: Ger. 1555

Design/technology

Evolution of the principles of scene design. USSR. 1987. Lang.: Rus. 496

Aesthetic influences on scene design. England. 1700-1899. Lang.: Eng. 1590

Masks in Chinese drama. China, People's Republic of. 1986. Lang.: Chi. 3447

Performance/production

Directing in Western Europe: artistic concepts, sociocultural aspects. Europe. 1980-1987. Lang.: Rus. 782

Ukrainian theatrical process. Ukraine. 1970-1979. Lang.: Rus. 923

Influences within Kazakh theatre culture. USSR. 1950-1980. Lang.: Rus. 1083

Zeami's concept of the actor and the ideal performance. Japan. 1363-1443. Lang.: Eng. 1500

Use of visual arts conventions in acting techniques. England. 1700. Lang.: Eng. 1735

Evaluation of acting styles in 18th century. England. 1672-1799. Lang.: Eng. 1736

Sources of attitudes for serious dramatic acting and acting for low comedy. Europe. 1700. Lang.: Eng. 1747

Analysis of Brecht's original directing style and dramaturgy. Germany. 1925-1987. Lang.: Eng. 1771

Impressionism in the acting of Chinese drama. China, People's Republic of. 1924-1985. Lang.: Chi. 3477

The distinctive features of Chinese drama. China, People's Republic of. 1949-1985. Lang.: Chi. 3478

Creativity in the Chinese arts. China, People's Republic of. 1949-1985. Lang.: Chi. 3480

The promotion and development of the Chin school of Chinese drama. China, People's Republic of. 1987. Lang.: Chi. 3481

Dramatic language in Chinese opera: dancing, music and singing. China, People's Republic of. 1986. Lang.: Chi. 3482

Improving the music of Chinese opera through innovation. China, People's Republic of. 1986. Lang.: Chi. 3490

Four steps to make *Da Peng Ge* more popular. China, People's Republic of. 1987. Lang.: Chi. 3506

The importance of Jing-Hu music in Chinese opera. China, People's Republic of. 1985-1986. Lang.: Chi. 3528

Characteristics of Chinese drama. China, People's Republic of. 1985. Lang.: Chi. 3534

Plays/librettos/scripts

Temporality in Shakespeare's *Richard III*. England. 1592. Lang.: Eng. 1115

Swetnam the Woman-Hater, Arraigned by Women written in response to an anti-female pamphlet. England. 1600-1620. Lang.: Eng. 1118

Theodicy and tragic drama in *King Lear* and *The Tempest*. England. 1605-1611. Lang.: Eng. 1119

Traditional *nō* and *kyōgen* texts compared to modern literature. Japan. 1300-1986. Lang.: Jap. 1506

Waka poetry in *nō* plays. Japan. 700-1300. Lang.: Jap. 1507

Reading *nō* plays as poetry. Japan. 1300-1500. Lang.: Jap. 1508

Theoretical considerations of English Renaissance theatre. England. 1600-1699. Lang.: Rus. 2528

Collection of nineteenth-century theoretical writings on theatre and drama. Germany. 1800-1900. Lang.: Ger. 2595

Georgian criticism and theatrical art. Russia. 1800-1900. Lang.: Rus. 2719

Life and work of playwright Adrienne Kennedy. USA: New York, NY. 1987. Lang.: Eng. 2877

The Chinese opera form *Nou Hsi* and its characteristics. China. 900. Lang.: Chi. 3544

Theme and essence of Chinese classical drama. China, People's Republic of. 1127-1987. Lang.: Chi. 3560

Aesthetics — cont'd

Analysis of Chinese tragedy. China, People's Republic of. 1986. Lang.: Chi. 3572

Debate over Hanns Eisler's opera *Johann Faustus*. Germany, East: Berlin, East. 1949-1955. Lang.: Ger. 3913

Relation to other fields

Debate over proletarian art among Social Democrats. Germany: Berlin. 1910-1912. Lang.: Ger. 1238

Tragic conflicts in playwright's Tang Xian-Zu's cultural conscience. China: Beijing. 1550-1616. Lang.: Chi. 3581

Theory/criticism

Comedy, theatre, art and reality. 1987. Lang.: Ger. 1305

How theatre communicates with its audience. 1949-1987. Lang.: Chi. 1311

Overview of theoretical aesthetics throughout history. 1987. Lang.: Kor. 1312

Themes of the Chinese theatre during the Tang dynasty. China. 618-905. Lang.: Chi. 1320

Chinese critique of Brechtian realism. China, People's Republic of. 1949-1985. Lang.: Chi. 1321

The concept of theatre as a total work of art. Europe. 1804-1930. Lang.: Eng. 1328

Postmodernism in theatre. Europe. 1985. Lang.: Rus. 1329

How to maintain an element of risk in theatre. France. 1987. Lang.: Fre. 1331

Avoiding the risk of commercialism: the example of Antoine's Théâtre Libre. France. 1887-1987. Lang.: Fre. 1335

Theatre and the infatuation with technology. France. 1987. Lang.: Fre. 1336

Centenary of Théâtre Libre: proposes 'subjective realism'. France. 1887-1987. Lang.: Fre. 1337

Effect of audiovisual media on theatre. France. 1987. Lang.: Fre. 1339

Essays on Bertolt Brecht's theories, aesthetics and philosophy. Germany, East. 1918-1987. Lang.: Ger. 1340

Reception of Polish theatre in East Germany. Germany, East. Poland. 1949-1987. Lang.: Ger. 1341

Aspects of Bertolt Brecht's theory and practice of theatre. Germany, East: Berlin, East. 1948-1956. Lang.: Ger. 1342

Analysis of various versions and translations of Aristotle's *Poetics*. Greece: Athens. Egypt: Alexandria. Europe. 70 B.C.-1981 A.D. Lang.: Chi. 1343

Brechtian influence on contemporary art. USA. Europe. 1950-1987. Lang.: Eng. 1353

Aesthetics of the pleasure principle in comedy, folklore and literature. USA. 1982. Lang.: Eng. 1355

Correlation of a troubled society and its theatre. USA: New York, NY. 1987. Lang.: Eng. 1357

Reconstruction of Shakespeare in performance. USA. 1987. Lang.: Eng. 1358

Poetic discourse on the death of the theatre. USA. 1987. Lang.: Eng. 1369

Reception theory, performance and American influence in Korea. USA. Korea. 1926-1970. Lang.: Kor. 1370

National standards for arts criticism. USA. 1987. Lang.: Eng. 1371

Round-table discussion by philosophers and theatre professionals on conflict in contemporary drama. USSR. 1980-1987. Lang.: Rus. 1372

Collection of articles by theatre critic A. Gvozdev. USSR. 1920-1930. Lang.: Rus. 1374

Environment and the works of Merce Cunningham and John Cage. USA. 1962-1987. Lang.: Eng. 1477

Metaphysical and philosophical implications of the actor's role in the *nō* theatre. Japan. 712-1980. Lang.: Pol. 1510

Comparing impression with reality in drama. 1949-1987. Lang.: Chi. 3015

Structuralist approach to play interpretation. 500 B.C.-1987 A.D. Lang.: Eng. 3016

The use of space in plot to indicate time and place. 1949-1987. Lang.: Chi. 3021

Otakar Hostinský's conception of tragedy and the tragic. Austria-Hungary: Prague. 1906. Lang.: Cze. 3022

Analysis of *Escurial* and *Barabbas* by Michel de Ghelderode. Belgium. 1898. Lang.: Fre. 3023

Discussion of theory of popular theatre. Canada. 1987. Lang.: Eng. 3024

Flecknoe's preface to *Love's Dominion*, relationship of theory to practice. England. 1654-1664. Lang.: Eng. 3027

Ben Jonson's view of similarities between spectacle plays and comic plays. England. 1572-1637. Lang.: Eng. 3028

Evaluation of the present state of theatrical theory and its influence on theatrical practice. Europe. 1985. Lang.: Fre. 3033

Catalan translation of Lessing's *Hamburgische Dramaturgie*. Germany: Hamburg. 1767-1769. Lang.: Cat. 3043

Brecht's theories, *Die Dreigroschenoper (The Three Penny Opera)*. Germany. 1878-1956. Lang.: Kor. 3044

Challenge of Brecht's plays to communism. Germany, East: Berlin. 1960-1970. Lang.: Eng. 3045

East and West German views of Bertolt Brecht. Germany, East. Germany, West. 1948-1987. 3046

Development of the three unities. Greece. France. Italy. 500 B.C.-1800 A.D. Lang.: Kor. 3047

Pirandello's aesthetic views. Italy. 1867-1936. Lang.: Rus. 3052

Review of Korean National Theatre production of Čechov's *Diadia Vania (Uncle Vanya)*. Korea: Seoul. 1986-1987. Lang.: Kor. 3054

The issue of new ideas in contemporary theatre. Mexico: Mexico City. 1987. Lang.: Spa. 3056

Rise of contemporary theatre in Mexico. Mexico: Mexico City. 1957-1987. Lang.: Spa. 3057

Functions of comedy in the seventeenth century. Spain. 1604-1690. Lang.: Spa. 3058

Shift of August Strindberg from naturalism to expressionism. Sweden. 1987. Lang.: Eng. 3061

Gottfried Keller's theory of drama. Switzerland. Germany: Berlin. 1850-1855. Lang.: Ger. 3062

On the Verge by Eric Overmyer. Production history, plot synopsis, critical evaluation. USA. 1987. Lang.: Eng. 3068

Actor Lawrence Barrett and the genteel tradition in acting. USA. 1870-1890. Lang.: Eng. 3069

The work and writings of theatre critics Eric Bentley and Gordon Rogoff. USA. 1946-1987. Lang.: Eng. 3071

Suggestion for new form of dramaturgical research based on concrete scenic action from past productions. USA: Tallahassee, FL. 1987. Lang.: Eng. 3074

Career and achievements of Ibsen scholar Hermann J. Weigand. USA. 1892-1985. Lang.: Eng. 3076

Relation of dramatic text to other written arts. USSR. Israel. 1921-1987. Lang.: Heb. 3078

Fundamental differences between stage and cinema. USA. 1987. Lang.: Eng. 3103

Comparison of impact of film versus the theatrical experience. USA. 1937-1987. Lang.: Eng. 3189

Characterization in theatre and television. China, People's Republic of. 1970-1987. Lang.: Chi. 3217

Assessment of the series *Lost Beginning*, its relation to Stewart Parker's *Pentecost*. UK-Ireland. 1987. Lang.: Eng. 3218

Performance artists Declan McGonagle and Alistair MacLennan. UK-Ireland: Belfast. 1975-1987. Lang.: Eng. 3374

Influences on work of performance artist Richard Demarco. UK-Scotland: Edinburgh. 1987. Lang.: Eng. 3375

Richard Demarco on performance art. UK-Scotland: Edinburgh. 1970-1987. Lang.: Eng. 3376

Post-Revolutionary Soviet theatre. USSR: Moscow. 1918-1930. Lang.: Ger. 3378

Chinese and Western elements in Chinese musical theatre. China, People's Republic of. 1975-1987. Lang.: Chi. 3422

Genres of Uzbek musical drama. USSR. 1917-1987. Lang.: Rus. 3423

Influence of Chinese opera on Japanese drama. China. Japan. 1596-1876. Lang.: Chi. 3586

Theory of Chinese classical comedy. China. 1127-1368. Lang.: Chi. 3587

Chinese opera dramatist and theoretician Meng Cheng-Shuen. China. 1386-1644. Lang.: Chi. 3589

A defense of the Chinese opera. China, People's Republic of. 1986. Lang.: Chi. 3591

Aesthetics — cont'd

The new aesthetics of Chinese drama. China, People's Republic of. 1787-1990. Lang.: Chi. 3592

Solutions and improvements to Chinese historical drama. China, People's Republic of. 1986. Lang.: Chi. 3593

A new way of looking at the history of Chinese opera. China, People's Republic of. 1986. Lang.: Chi. 3596

Main characteristics of the Chinese theatre aesthetic. China, People's Republic of. 960 B.C.-1987 A.D. Lang.: Chi. 3597

Falsehood as the essential quality of the Chinese classical comedy. China, People's Republic of. 1987. Lang.: Chi. 3599

The history of the Ian-An Chinese Opera Research Center. China, People's Republic of. 1942-1986. Lang.: Chi. 3600

New aesthetics for the new Chinese theatre. China, People's Republic of. 1987. Lang.: Chi. 3601

The changing aesthetic characteristics of Chinese opera. China, People's Republic of. 1987. Lang.: Chi. 3603

Seminar for the modern theatre in China. China, People's Republic of. 1949-1985. Lang.: Chi. 3604

Wang Guo-Wei's dramatic history of Iuen. China, People's Republic of. 1986. Lang.: Chi. 3605

The importance of body language, as opposed to spoken language, to reveal character in Chinese opera. China, People's Republic of. 1986. Lang.: Chi. 3606

Ways to improve Chinese opera. China, People's Republic of. 1986. Lang.: Chi. 3607

Tang Xian-Zu's theory of 'original character' in Chinese opera. China, People's Republic of. 700-1986. Lang.: Chi. 3609

The effect of aesthetics on the length of Chinese plays. China, People's Republic of. 700-1986. Lang.: Chi. 3610

Commune and improvisation theatre in Chi Lin. China, People's Republic of. 1900-1986. Lang.: Chi. 3612

A new aesthetic theory of Chinese opera. China, People's Republic of. 1900-1986. Lang.: Chi. 3613

Improvements in the function and purpose of Chinese opera. China, People's Republic of. 1986. Lang.: Chi. 3614

Different ideas leading to the modernization of Chinese drama. China, People's Republic of. 1949-1985. Lang.: Chi. 3615

The theories of G. E. Lessing applied to Chinese theatre. Germany. China, People's Republic of. 1770-1985. Lang.: Chi. 3616

Chlebnikov and futurism in Russian opera. USSR: Moscow. 1913-1987. Lang.: Ger. 3949

Theory and construction of Korean rod puppetry *kokdugaksi-nolum*. Korea. 600-1987. Lang.: Kor. 4007

Affabulazione
Performance/production
Experimental theatre at the Stary in three recent productions. Poland: Cracow. 1987. Lang.: Eng. 1999

Affiliate Artists (New York, NY)
Institutions
Affiliate Artists, performance training, audience development. USA: New York, NY. 1967-1987. Lang.: Eng. 3733

African Queen, The
Performance/production
Personal anecdotes and photographs from the making of *The African Queen*. USA: Hollywood, CA. 1950-1951. Lang.: Eng. 3168

African-American Dance Ensemble (New York, NY)
Institutions
African-American Dance Ensemble, Chuck Davis Dance Company. USA: New York, NY. 1968-1987. Lang.: Eng. 1459

After the Fall
Performance/production
Six plays of the Tokyo season, focus on director Betsuyaku Minoru. Japan: Tokyo. 1986. Lang.: Jap. 1966

Plays/librettos/scripts
Contemporary Japanese plays about crime. Japan: Tokyo. 1986. Lang.: Jap. 2681

Agatha
Performance/production
New Tokyo productions. Japan: Tokyo. 1987. Lang.: Jap. 1954

Space and sign in various Tokyo productions. Japan: Tokyo. 1987. Lang.: Jap. 1959

Unsuitable choice of plays for Tokyo performances. Japan: Tokyo. 1987. Lang.: Jap. 1965

Agel i Barrière, Guillem
Performance/production
Exhibition catalogue: popular theatre in Catalan. France. 1415-1987. Lang.: Cat, Fre. 1750

Agents
Administration
Career of theatrical agent Milton Goldman. USA. 1930-1987. Lang.: Eng. 155

Exploitation of artists' work in the marketplace. USA. 1984-1986. Lang.: Eng. 169

Editorial response to attacks on the Weill Foundation. USA: New York, NY. Germany: Berlin. 1929-1987. Lang.: Eng. 3618

Plays/librettos/scripts
Motivation for literary manager becoming playwright's agent. USA: New York, NY. 1987. Lang.: Eng. 1182

Ages
Performance/production
Shakespeare and contemporaries: tradition, intertextuality in performance. England. 1607-1987. Lang.: Eng. 1740

Agnes of God
Plays/librettos/scripts
Religion in Pielmeier's *Agnes of God* and Shaffer's *Equus*. North America. 1973-1980. Lang.: Eng. 2710

Aguilar, Sigfrido
Performance/production
Performers Ariel Ashwell and Sigfrido Aguilar discuss their work with Comediantes Pantomima-Teatro. Mexico: Guanajuato. 1980-1982. Lang.: Eng. 3225

Aguiló i Cortès, Tomàs
Plays/librettos/scripts
Analysis of 51 short farces written in Majorca. Spain-Catalonia. 1701-1850. Lang.: Cat. 2731

Agyö, kedvesem
SEE
Adié, milacku!.

Ahen-senso (Opium War)
Basic theatrical documents
Plays of Terayama Shūji. Japan. 1950-1980. Lang.: Jap. 1562

Ahrens, Thomas
Performance/production
Collection of newspaper reviews by London theatre critics. UK-England: London. 1987. Lang.: Eng. 2240

Aibel, Doug
Institutions
Experience of artists working at the O'Neill Theatre Center. USA: Waterford, CT. 1985-1986. Lang.: Eng. 1655

Aida
Performance/production
Initial recordings of Verdi's operas. Italy. France. USA. 1900-1945. Lang.: Eng. 3800

AIDS Show, The
Plays/librettos/scripts
Impact of AIDS crisis on the theatre. USA: New York, NY, San Francisco, CA. 1987. Lang.: Eng. 2881

Ailey, Alvin
Performance/production
The career of dancer/choreographer Katherine Dunham. USA: New York, NY, Chicago, IL, Las Vegas, NV. 1909-1987. Lang.: Eng. 1412

Aimaya (Obscure House, The)
Performance/production
Six plays of the Tokyo season, focus on director Betsuyaku Minoru. Japan: Tokyo. 1986. Lang.: Jap. 1966

Air Fix, The
Performance/production
Collection of newspaper reviews by London theatre critics. UK-England: London. 1987. Lang.: Eng. 2245

Aja, Ron
Administration
Interview with Ron Aja of Actors' Equity Association. USA. 1987. Lang.: Eng. 238

Ajax
Performance/production
Peter Sellars and American National Theatre present *Ajax*, Holland Festival. Netherlands. USA. 1987. Lang.: Dut. 1981

Peter Sellars' American National Theatre on European tour. USA. Netherlands. 1987. Lang.: Dut. 2351

Ajtmatov, Čingiz
Performance/production
Jaroslav Dudek directs *A Day Lasts Longer than a Century* by
Čingiz Ajmatov, Vinohradské Theatre. Czechoslovakia: Prague. 1987.
Lang.: Cze. 774

Akademičeskij Teat'r Dramy im. A.S. Puškina (Leningrad)
Performance/production
Portrait of actor Bruno Frejndlich of Leningrad Puškin Theatre.
USSR: Leningrad. 1909-1987. Lang.: Rus. 1021

Aleksandr Borisov, actor of the Leningrad Puškin Theatre. USSR:
Leningrad. 1905-1969. Lang.: Rus. 1060

**Akademičeskij Teat'r Opery i Baleta im. S.M. Kirova
(Leningrad)**
Performance/production
Portrait of ballerina Natal'ja Dudinskaja of the Kirov Ballet. USSR:
Leningrad. 1912-1987. Lang.: Rus. 1448

Alla Osipenko, dancer of Kirov Theatre. USSR: Leningrad. 1932-
1980. Lang.: Rus. 1452

Akalaitis, JoAnne
Basic theatrical documents
Text of *Green Card* by JoAnne Akalaitis. USA. 1986. Lang.: Eng.
1577

Performance/production
Summarizes events of Directors' Colloquium. Canada: Calgary, AB.
1987. Lang.: Eng. 728

Directors' Colloquium: individual directorial techniques. Canada:
Calgary, AB. 1987. Lang.: Eng. 743

Plays/librettos/scripts
Conference on women in theatre, emphasis on playwriting. USA.
1987. Lang.: Eng. 1161

Åkerlund, Lasse
Performance/production
Lasse Åkerlund, a clown touring northern Sweden. Sweden: Järvsö.
1980-1987. Lang.: Swe. 3267

Akers, Dennis
Performance/production
Collection of newspaper reviews by London theatre critics. UK-
England: London. 1986. Lang.: Eng. 2064

Akers, Karen
Performance/production
Broadway actors who moonlight in cabaret acts. USA: New York,
NY. 1962-1987. Lang.: Eng. 3291

Akiba-gongen kaisengatari
Basic theatrical documents
Texts of seven *kabuki* plays. Japan. 1600-1800. Lang.: Jap. 1491

Akutagawa, Ryunosuke
Institutions
National Theatre of the Deaf productions of *Farewell My Lovely*
and *In a Grove* directed by Arvin Brown in Beijing. China, People's
Republic of: Beijing. USA. 1986-1987. Lang.: Eng. 1611

Performance/production
Actors and puppets sharing the same stage. USA: Brooklyn, NY.
1985-1987. Lang.: Eng. 3999

Al-E-Ahmad, Jalal
Performance/production
Collection of newspaper reviews by London theatre critics. UK-
England: London. 1986. Lang.: Eng. 2086

Alabama Shakespeare Festival (Montgomery, AL)
Institutions
Six books that discuss the origins and development of different
American regional theatres. USA: Cleveland, OH, Los Angeles, CA,
Houston, TX, Detroit, MI, Ashland, OR, Montgomery, AL. 1987.
Lang.: Eng. 612

Aladdin
Performance/production
Collection of newspaper reviews by London theatre critics. UK-
England: London. 1986. Lang.: Eng. 2041

Alan Turing: The Secret War
Performance/production
Comparison and review of *Melon, Breaking the Code, Alan Turing:
The Secret War* and *My Sister in This House*. UK-England: London.
1987. Lang.: Eng. 2285

Alarms
Performance/production
Collection of newspaper reviews by London theatre critics. UK-
England: London. 1987. Lang.: Eng. 2181

Alas Poor Fred
Performance/production
Collection of newspaper reviews by London theatre critics. UK-
England: London. 1986. Lang.: Eng. 2096

Albano, Michael
Institutions
Summary of proceedings from a Gilbert and Sullivan symposium.
Canada: Toronto, ON. 1987. Lang.: Eng. 3954

Albany Empire Theatre (London)
Performance/production
Collection of newspaper reviews by London theatre critics. UK-
England: London. 1986. Lang.: Eng. 2067

Collection of newspaper reviews by London theatre critics. UK-
England: London. 1986. Lang.: Eng. 2079

Collection of newspaper reviews by London theatre critics. UK-
England: London. 1986. Lang.: Eng. 2127

Albee, Edward
Performance/production
Collection of newspaper reviews by London theatre critics. UK-
England: London. 1987. Lang.: Eng. 2184

History of musical version, *Breakfast at Tiffany's*. USA: New York,
NY, Philadelphia, PA, Boston, MA. 1958-1966. Lang.: Eng. 3644

Plays/librettos/scripts
Russian and Soviet interaction with the U.S. USSR. USA. 1700-
1987. Lang.: Rus. 1191

Eugene O'Neill's influence on Edward Albee. USA. 1949-1962.
Lang.: Eng. 2841

One-act play: brief history and recent productions. USA. 1930-1987.
Lang.: Eng. 2849

Albee, racism, politics in American theatre of the sixties. USA. 1960-
1969. Lang.: Rus. 2901

Edvard Munch's painting *Death in the Sickroom* used to
demonstrate Albee's subject matter. USA. 1971-1987. Lang.: Eng.
2911

Radsinskij's *Jogging* directed by Fokin. USSR: Moscow. 1987. Lang.:
Eng. 2953

Comparison between Albee's *Who's Afraid of Virginia Woolf?* and
Radsinskij's *Jogging*. USSR. USA. 1987. Lang.: Eng. 2960

Albert Herring
Relation to other fields
Benjamin Britten's *Albert Herring* as an adaptation of a story by
Maupassant. UK-England. 1947. Lang.: Eng. 3946

Albertine in Five Times
Performance/production
Collection of newspaper reviews by London theatre critics. UK-
England: London. 1986. Lang.: Eng. 2146

Albery Theatre (London)
Performance/production
Collection of newspaper reviews by London theatre critics. UK-
England: London. 1986. Lang.: Eng. 2077

Collection of newspaper reviews by London theatre critics. UK-
England: London. 1986. Lang.: Eng. 2148

Collection of newspaper reviews by London theatre critics. UK-
England: London. 1986. Lang.: Eng. 2155

Collection of newspaper reviews by London theatre critics. UK-
England: London. 1987. Lang.: Eng. 2195

Collection of newspaper reviews by London theatre critics. UK-
England: London. 1987. Lang.: Eng. 2204

Collection of newspaper reviews by London theatre critics. UK-
England: London. 1987. Lang.: Eng. 2224

Collection of newspaper reviews by London theatre critics. UK-
England: London. 1987. Lang.: Eng. 2250

Collection of newspaper reviews by London theatre critics. UK-
England: London. 1987. Lang.: Eng. 2253

Collection of newspaper reviews by London theatre critics. UK-
England. 1987. Lang.: Eng. 2262

Albiro, Hartwig
Performance/production
A round-table discussion with stage directors on the principles and
methods of working with an ensemble company. Germany, East:
Berlin, East. 1983. Lang.: Ger. 1778

Alborough, Graham
Performance/production
Collection of newspaper reviews by London theatre critics. UK-
England: London. 1987. Lang.: Eng. 2275

Alcantara, Antonio
Performance/production
Examination of modern Brazilian theatre focusing on plays by
Nelson Rodrigues. Brazil. 1943-1984. Lang.: Eng.   1688

Aldea, Mercedes de la
Institutions
Texts and photos about the Teatre Grec. Spain-Catalonia: Barcelona.
1929-1986. Lang.: Cat.   558

Alden, Jerome
Performance/production
Collection of newspaper reviews by New York theatre critics. USA:
New York, NY. 1987. Lang.: Eng.   2316

Alderson, Jude
Performance/production
Collection of newspaper reviews by London theatre critics. UK-
England: London. 1986. Lang.: Eng.   2103

Aldwych Theatre (London)
Performance/production
Collection of newspaper reviews by London theatre critics. UK-
England: London. 1986. Lang.: Eng.   2034

Collection of newspaper reviews by London theatre critics. UK-
England: London. 1986. Lang.: Eng.   2069

Collection of newspaper reviews by London theatre critics. UK-
England: London. 1986. Lang.: Eng.   2153

Collection of newspaper reviews by London theatre critics. UK-
England: London. 1987. Lang.: Eng.   2258

Aleandro, Norma
Plays/librettos/scripts
Themes in the Festival of Latin Theatre. USA: New York, NY.
Latin America. Spain. 1987. Lang.: Spa.   2847

Alegría de las Tandas, La (Happiness of the Groups, The)
Performance/production
Review of *La Alegría de las Tandas (The Happiness of the Groups)*
by Enrique Alonso. Mexico: Mexico City. 1987. Lang.: Spa.   1977

Aleramo, Sibilla
Plays/librettos/scripts
Influence of Sibilla Aleramo on women in Italian theatre. Italy.
1850-1930. Lang.: Ita.   1138

Alexander, Bill
Performance/production
Collection of newspaper reviews by London theatre critics. UK.
1987. Lang.: Eng.   2031

Collection of newspaper reviews by London theatre critics. UK-
England: London. 1987. Lang.: Eng.   2196

Collection of newspaper reviews by London theatre critics. UK-
England: London. 1987. Lang.: Eng.   2236

Alexander, Jane
Performance/production
Two productions of Pinter's *Old Times*. UK-England: London. USA:
New York, NY, St. Louis, MO. 1971-1985. Lang.: Eng.   907

Alexander, Janek
Performance/production
Collection of newspaper reviews by London theatre critics. UK-
England: London. 1986. Lang.: Eng.   2124

Alfano, Franco
Plays/librettos/scripts
Franco Alfano, who completed Puccini's *Turandot*. Italy. 1876-1954.
Lang.: Eng.   3919

Alfaro, Emilio
Plays/librettos/scripts
Themes in the Festival of Latin Theatre. USA: New York, NY.
Latin America. Spain. 1987. Lang.: Spa.   2847

Alfreds, Mike
Performance/production
Collection of newspaper reviews by London theatre critics. UK-
England: London. 1986. Lang.: Eng.   2080

Collection of newspaper reviews by London theatre critics. UK-
England: London. 1986. Lang.: Eng.   2157

Collection of newspaper reviews by London theatre critics. UK-
England: London. 1987. Lang.: Eng.   2233

Collection of newspaper reviews by London theatre critics. UK-
England. 1987. Lang.: Eng.   2261

Alice Arts Center (Oakland, CA)
Performance spaces
History of the Alice Arts Center, new home of the Oakland
Ensemble Theatre. USA: Oakland, CA. 1983-1987. Lang.: Eng.   696

Alice Busch Theatre (Cooperstown, NY)
Performance spaces
Glimmerglass Opera inaugurates Alice Busch Theatre. USA:
Cooperstown, NY. 1975-1987. Lang.: Eng.   3740

Alice in Wonderland
Performance/production
Collection of newspaper reviews by London theatre critics. UK-
England: London. 1986. Lang.: Eng.   2047

Plays/librettos/scripts
Pistolteatern's adaptation of *Alice in Wonderland*. Sweden:
Stockholm. 1982. Lang.: Eng.   2738

The child character in the role of protagonist. USA. 1987. Lang.:
Eng.   2880

Alice, Mary
Performance/production
Interview with actress Mary Alice. USA: New York, NY, Chicago,
IL. 1966-1987. Lang.: Eng.   2341

All for Love
Plays/librettos/scripts
Name and entitlement in Dryden, Wycherley and Etherege. England.
1500-1699. Lang.: Eng.   2526

All Hallows by the Tower (London)
Performance/production
Collection of newspaper reviews by London theatre critics. UK-
England: London. 1986. Lang.: Eng.   2119

All I Get is Static!
Plays/librettos/scripts
The historical radio drama *All I Get is Static!*. Canada: Ottawa,
ON. 1984. Lang.: Eng.   3096

All My Sons
Performance/production
Collection of newspaper reviews by New York theatre critics. USA:
New York, NY. 1987. Lang.: Eng.   2321

All Over
Plays/librettos/scripts
Edvard Munch's painting *Death in the Sickroom* used to
demonstrate Albee's subject matter. USA. 1971-1987. Lang.: Eng.
                                                          2911

All the Arts of Hurting
Performance/production
Collection of newspaper reviews by London theatre critics. UK-
England: London. 1987. Lang.: Eng.   2241

All the Fun of the Fair
Performance/production
Collection of newspaper reviews by London theatre critics. UK-
England: London. 1986. Lang.: Eng.   2079

All's Well that Ends Well
Plays/librettos/scripts
Devices that convey concern with sexuality in Shakespeare's *All's
Well that Ends Well*. England. 1602-1987. Lang.: Eng.   2523

Állami Magyar Szinház (Cluj)
Performance/production
Gábor Tompa directs *Hamlet* at Hungarian Theatre of Kolozsvár.
Romania: Cluj. 1987. Lang.: Hun.   2001

Allan, Andrew
Basic theatrical documents
Collection of radio plays produced by Andrew Allan. Canada. 1942-
1955. Lang.: Eng.   3109

Institutions
Script editor's recollections of CBC radio dramas. Canada. 1944-
1954. Lang.: Eng.   3110

Allardyce, Nicoll
Plays/librettos/scripts
Analysis of vampire characters in the works of Byron, Polidori and
Planché. England. Italy. France. 1800-1825. Lang.: Eng.   2540

Allen, Anthony
Performance/production
Collection of newspaper reviews by London theatre critics. UK-
England: London. 1986. Lang.: Eng.   2135

Allen, David
Performance/production
Collection of newspaper reviews by London theatre critics. UK-
England: London. 1986. Lang.: Eng.   2155

Collection of newspaper reviews by London theatre critics. UK-
England: London. 1987. Lang.: Eng.   2220

Allers, Franz

Performance/production

Opera conductors who also conduct in Broadway musicals. USA: New York, NY. 1980-1987. Lang.: Eng.　　　3847

Alley Theatre (Houston, TX)

Institutions

Six books that discuss the origins and development of different American regional theatres. USA: Cleveland, OH, Los Angeles, CA, Houston, TX, Detroit, MI, Ashland, OR, Montgomery, AL. 1987. Lang.: Eng.　　　612

Performance/production

Four productions in Southern regional theatres. USA: Houston, TX, Louisville, KY, Gainesville, FL. 1980. Lang.: Eng.　　　2342

Alliance of Resident Theatres/New York (ART/NY)

Administration

Interview with Karen Brookes Hopkins (Brooklyn Academy of Music) and Kate Busch (ART/NY). USA: New York, NY. 1987. Lang.: Eng.　　　158

'Allo 'Allo

Performance/production

Collection of newspaper reviews by London theatre critics. UK-England: London. 1986. Lang.: Eng.　　　2156

Allò que tal vegada s'esdevingué (What Happened Then)

Basic theatrical documents

Edition and analysis, *Allò que tal vegada s'esdevingué (What Happened Then)* by Joan Oliver. Spain-Catalonia. 1899-1986. Lang.: Cat.　　　1573

Allting rasar inför en naken skuldra (Everything Gives Way to a Naked Shoulder)

Performance/production

Rubicon's choreography of *Allting rasar inför en naken skuldra (Everything Gives Way to a Naked Shoulder)*. Sweden: Gothenburg. 1987. Lang.: Swe.　　　1471

Almeida Theatre (London)

Performance/production

Collection of newspaper reviews by London theatre critics. UK-England: London. 1986. Lang.: Eng.　　　2046

Collection of newspaper reviews by London theatre critics. UK-England: London. 1986. Lang.: Eng.　　　2058

Collection of newspaper reviews by London theatre critics. UK-England: London. 1986. Lang.: Eng.　　　2068

Collection of newspaper reviews by London theatre critics. UK-England: London. 1986. Lang.: Eng.　　　2077

Collection of newspaper reviews by London theatre critics. UK-England: London. 1986. Lang.: Eng.　　　2080

Collection of newspaper reviews by London theatre critics. UK-England: London. 1986. Lang.: Eng.　　　2087

Collection of newspaper reviews by London theatre critics. UK-England: London. 1986. Lang.: Eng.　　　2091

Collection of newspaper reviews by London theatre critics. UK-England: London. 1986. Lang.: Eng.　　　2112

Collection of newspaper reviews by London theatre critics. UK-England. 1986. Lang.: Eng.　　　2144

Collection of newspaper reviews by London theatre critics. UK-England: London. 1986. Lang.: Eng.　　　2166

Collection of newspaper reviews by London theatre critics. UK-England: London. 1987. Lang.: Eng.　　　2188

Collection of newspaper reviews by London theatre critics. UK-England: London. 1987. Lang.: Eng.　　　2197

Collection of newspaper reviews by London theatre critics. UK-England: London. 1987. Lang.: Eng.　　　2212

Collection of newspaper reviews by London theatre critics. UK-England: London. 1987. Lang.: Eng.　　　2216

Collection of newspaper reviews by London theatre critics. UK-England: London. 1987. Lang.: Eng.　　　2230

Collection of newspaper reviews by London theatre critics. UK-England: London. 1987. Lang.: Eng.　　　2258

Álomkommandó (Dream Commando)

Performance/production

András Sütő's *Álomkommandó (Dream Commando)* directed by Ferenc Sík at Vigszinház. Hungary: Budapest. 1987. Lang.: Hun.　　　1798

Ferenc Sík directs András Sütő's *Álomkommandó (Dream Commando)*, Gyulai Várszinház. Hungary: Gyula. 1987. Lang.: Hun.　　　1855

Director Ferenc Sík discusses *Álomkommandó (Dream Commando)* by András Sütő. Hungary. 1987. Lang.: Hun.　　　1896

Alonso, Enrique

Performance/production

Review of *La Alegría de las Tandas (The Happiness of the Groups)* by Enrique Alonso. Mexico: Mexico City. 1987. Lang.: Spa.　　　1977

Alphonse, George

Performance/production

Collection of newspaper reviews by London theatre critics. UK-England: London. 1986. Lang.: Eng.　　　2160

Alrawi, Karim

Performance/production

Collection of newspaper reviews by London theatre critics. UK-England: London. 1986. Lang.: Eng.　　　2149

Alter Image

Relation to other fields

Assessment of arts on television. UK-England: London. 1983-1987. Lang.: Eng.　　　3216

Alternative theatre

SEE ALSO

Shōgekijō undō.

Experimental theatre.

Avant-garde theatre.

Administration

Ground Zero Theatre Company's project for the homeless. Canada: Toronto, ON. 1987. Lang.: Eng.　　　6

Financial profile of West End Theatre. UK-England: London. 1983-1986. Lang.: Eng.　　　45

Audience

Theatre education project for teaching about sexuality. Canada: Toronto, ON. 1987. Lang.: Eng.　　　278

Institutions

History of Alberta theatre companies. Canada: Edmonton, AB, Calgary, AB. 1987. Lang.: Eng.　　　506

Two community-based popular theatre projects. Canada. 1987. Lang.: Eng.　　　522

Overview of the Vancouver Fringe Festival. Canada: Vancouver, BC. 1987. Lang.: Eng.　　　1604

1987 Vancouver Fringe Festival: specific performances. Canada: Vancouver, BC. 1987. Lang.: Eng.　　　1609

Performance/production

Collective production of popular theatre. Canada: Edmonton, AB. 1987. Lang.: Eng.　　　726

Emergence of feminist theatre groups within the alternative theatre movement. UK-England. 1970-1987. Lang.: Eng.　　　908

Relationship of theatre, class and gender. UK-England. USA. 1969-1985. Lang.: Eng.　　　918

Work of actor/director Augusto Boal. Canada: Sydney, NS. 1987. Lang.: Eng.　　　1694

Interview with playwright Patrick McDonald. Canada: Ottawa, ON. 1987. Lang.: Eng.　　　1708

Popular theatre, mostly on economic, feminist themes. Canada: Sudbury, ON. 1930-1987. Lang.: Eng.　　　1709

Overview of theatre in Ottawa. Canada: Ottawa, ON. 1960-1983. Lang.: Eng.　　　1719

Amateur participation in Nyköpings Teater production of Gogol's *Revizor (The Government Inspector)*. Sweden: Nyköping. 1986-1987. Lang.: Swe.　　　2021

Reference materials

Directory of fringe, touring, dance and puppet companies, arts associations, festivals. UK-England. 1986-1987. Lang.: Eng.　　　1214

Relation to other fields

Description of *The Working People's Picture Show*. Canada: Toronto, ON. 1987. Lang.: Eng.　　　1221

Social implications of popular theatre. Canada. 1987. Lang.: Eng.　　　1222

Government funding of official theatre and opera companies. Switzerland. 1987. Lang.: Ger.　　　1256

Applications of African 'Theatre for Development' movement to Canadian popular theatre. Africa. Canada: St. John's, NF, Toronto, ON. 1978-1987. Lang.: Eng.　　　2978

Theory/criticism

Discussion of theory of popular theatre. Canada. 1987. Lang.: Eng.　　　3024

Altés, Emili
Performance/production
History of dance in Catalonia. Spain-Catalonia. 1300-1987. Lang.:
Cat.   1410
Altman, Robert
Performance/production
Review of ABC videocast of Pinter's *The Dumb Waiter*. USA. 1987.
Lang.: Eng.   3209
Altmeyer, Jeannine
Performance/production
Profile of soprano Jeannine Altmeyer. USA: New York, NY. 1950-
1987. Lang.: Eng.   3853
Altra Fedra, si us plau, Una (Another Phaedra, Please)
Plays/librettos/scripts
Catalan playwrights after the Spanish Civil War. Spain-Catalonia.
1939-1975. Lang.: Cat.   2730
Theory/criticism
Reflections on the value of theatrical translations. Spain-Catalonia.
UK-England. 1600-1985. Lang.: Cat.   3060
Alvarez, Lynne
Basic theatrical documents
Six plays detailing the Hispanic experience in the United States.
USA. Mexico. 1987. Lang.: Eng.   1581
Alvaro, Egidio
Performance/production
Egidio Alvaro and performance art festivals. Europe. 1974-1987.
Lang.: Eng.   3349
Alves de Souza, Naum
Performance/production
New regime ends theatrical censorship. Brazil. 1980-1984. Lang.:
Spa.   1689
Alvin Ailey Dance Theatre
Design/technology
Lighting reviews for several New York productions. USA: New
York, NY. 1987. Lang.: Eng.   474
Alyoshin, Samuel
Performance/production
Collection of newspaper reviews by London theatre critics. UK-
England: London. 1987. Lang.: Eng.   2257
Amadeus
Plays/librettos/scripts
Comparison of themes and dramaturgical techniques in plays of
Eugene O'Neill and Peter Shaffer. USA. 1920-1982. Lang.: Eng.
                                                                                    2872
Characters' search for God in plays of Peter Shaffer. USA. UK-
England. 1979-1984. Lang.: Eng.   2878
Comparison of main characters in three contemporary plays. USA:
New York, NY. 1987. Lang.: Eng.   2916
Amara (Bitter)
Plays/librettos/scripts
Analysis of Rosso di San Secondo's *Amara (Bitter)*. Italy. 1913-1917.
Lang.: Ita.   1139
AMAS Repertory (New York, NY)
Administration
Diversity of Letter of Agreement theatres that operate in New York
City. USA: New York, NY. 1987. Lang.: Eng.   204
Amateur Stage (England)
Administration
Editor of *Amateur Stage*, Charles Vance, talks about the amateur
world. UK-England. 1987. Lang.: Eng.   56
Amateur theatre
Administration
Cooperation between theatre association and county council to
promote theatrical activities. Sweden: Uddevalla. 1987. Lang.: Swe.
                                                                                     40
Institutions
A history of Brisbane's leading amateur theatre companies. Australia:
Brisbane. 1936-1986. Lang.: Eng.   502
Amateur theatre programs of rural Belgium. Belgium: Cerfontaine,
Soumoy. 1912-1961. Lang.: Fre.   504
Memoir of the papers and debates organized at the First Congress
of Amateur Theatre in Catalonia. Spain-Catalonia. 1850-1685. Lang.:
Cat.   560
Future of amateur theatre in Sweden. Sweden. 1987. Lang.: Swe.
                                                                                     561
Stockholms Studentteater now welcomes amateur participation.
Sweden: Stockholm. 1921-1987. Lang.: Swe.   1638

Socialist amateur theatre group Ormen. Sweden: Haninge. 1979-1987.
Lang.: Swe.   1639
Folkteatergruppen's productions, including *Antigone-nu (Antigone
Now)*. Sweden: Stockholm. 1917-1987. Lang.: Swe.   1640
Tornedalsteatern and director Ulla Lyttkens. Sweden: Pajala. 1986-
1987. Lang.: Swe.   1642
Interview with members of amateur group Teater Phoenix. Sweden:
Simrishamn. 1983-1987. Lang.: Swe.   1643
Gagnef Teaterförening's production of a play based on local history.
Sweden: Gagnef. 1975-1987. Lang.: Swe.   1644
Arbrå Teaterförening's theatrical activities for adults and children.
Sweden: Bollnäs. 1979-1987. Lang.: Swe.   1645
Performance/production
Impressions of Nordkalottfestivalen, conditions of Norwegian amateur
theatre. Norway: Hammerfest. 1987. Lang.: Swe.   868
A class for amateur directors. Sweden: Katrineberg. 1987. Lang.:
Swe.   887
Listing of Walloon theatre performances, winners of the Grand Prix
du Roi Albert. Belgium. 1932-1987. Lang.: Fre.   1682
Report from Portuguese amateur theatre festival. Portugal: Lisbon.
1987. Lang.: Swe.   2000
Swedish-Finnish language problems dramatized by Tornedalsteatern.
Sweden: Pajala. 1986. Lang.: Swe.   2014
Children's and youth theatre amateur festival. Sweden: Köping.
1987. Lang.: Swe.   2016
Musikteatergruppen Oktober collaborates with immigrant amateurs.
Sweden: Södertälje. 1986. Lang.: Swe.   2019
Jordcirkus and amateur group Näktergalningarna stage *A Christmas
Carol*. Sweden: Stockholm. 1986-1987. Lang.: Swe.   2020
Harlekin's efforts to involve youth in amateur theatre. Sweden:
Landskrona. 1982-1987. Lang.: Swe.   2022
Västerås Amateur Theatre Festival. Sweden: Västerås. 1987. Lang.:
Swe.   2023
Amateur theatre anecdotes: how to destroy a production. UK. 1987.
Lang.: Eng.   2032
Director on staging amateur *Fiddler on the Roof*. Sweden: Bollnäs.
1987. Lang.: Swe.   3636
Rock opera *Drakar och Demoner (Dragons and Demons)* about
youth at risk. Sweden: Handen. 1987. Lang.: Swe.   3637
Problems of amateur theatre, Eastern Bohemia. Czechoslovakia:
Hradec Králové. 1985. Lang.: Cze.   3973
Plays/librettos/scripts
Summary of plays, information for amateur companies. Italy. 1987.
Lang.: Ita.   1134
Dearth of female roles: how amateur theatres cope. Sweden. 1987.
Lang.: Swe.   2733
Interview with playwright Cannie Möller. Sweden: Järfälla. 1987.
Lang.: Swe.   2735
Contrasts mostly male parts in plays with mostly female membership
in amateur groups. Sweden. 1986. Lang.: Swe.   2739
Relation to other fields
Teachers discuss creative drama's role in adult education. Jamaica.
Zimbabwe. Bangladesh. 1987. Lang.: Swe.   2996
Sätrahöjdens teatergrupp, producing plays by and for the retarded.
Sweden: Gävle. 1978-1987. Lang.: Swe.   3000
Effect of farming practices on folk theatre. Poland: Tarnogród. 1985-
1987. Lang.: Eng.   3282
Training
Orlanda Cook on her work as voice teacher. Sweden. 1980-1987.
Lang.: Swe.   3080
Amatörteaterns Riksförbund (Västerås)
Institutions
Future of amateur theatre in Sweden. Sweden. 1987. Lang.: Swe.
                                                                                    561
Performance/production
Västerås Amateur Theatre Festival. Sweden: Västerås. 1987. Lang.:
Swe.   2023
Amaya, Carmen
Performance/production
History of dance in Catalonia. Spain-Catalonia. 1300-1987. Lang.:
Cat.   1410
Ambasador (Ambassador, The)
Performance/production
Polish theatre. Poland: Warsaw, Cracow, Wrocław. 1980-1987. Lang.:
Eng, Fre.   1987

Andrews, Bert
Performance/production
Theatre career of photo-journalist Bert Andrews. USA: New York,
NY. 1950-1987. Lang.: Eng. 2367
Androphilus
Basic theatrical documents
English translations of three plays by Jacob Masen. Germany. 1606-
1681. Lang.: Eng. 1556
Andžaparidze, Veriko
Performance/production
Recollections of actress Veriko Andžaparidze. USSR. 1898-1987.
Lang.: Rus. 1042
Angel City
Plays/librettos/scripts
Development of Sam Shepard's plays in response to audience. USA.
1976-1986. Lang.: Eng. 2902
Angel Knife
SEE
Ange couteau, L'.
Angeles, Felipe
Plays/librettos/scripts
Archetypal nature of title character in *Felipe Angeles* by Elena
Garro. Mexico. 1978. Lang.: Spa. 2696
Angels of Swedenbourg, The
Plays/librettos/scripts
Interview with playwright Ping Chong. Canada: Montreal, PQ. USA:
New York, NY. 1987. Lang.: Eng. 2472
Angelus
Performance/production
Collection of newspaper reviews by London theatre critics. UK-
England: London. 1987. Lang.: Eng. 2222
Angers, Janine
Performance/production
Short eulogy for actress Janine Angers. Canada. 1987. Lang.: Fre.
742
Angry Housewives
Performance/production
Collection of newspaper reviews by London theatre critics. UK-
England: London. 1986. Lang.: Eng. 2088
Angry Tenants and the Subterranean Sun
SEE
Inquilinos de la ira y el sol subterráneo, Los.
Anhalt, István
Institutions
Conditions affecting Canadian opera composers. Canada. 1987.
Lang.: Eng. 3714
Plays/librettos/scripts
Critical analysis of István Anhalt's opera, *Winthrop*. Canada:
Kitchener, ON. USA. 1987. Lang.: Eng. 3894
Anna Christie
Plays/librettos/scripts
Parallels between O'Neill's *Anna Christie* and Homer's *Odyssey*.
USA. 1921. Lang.: Eng. 2906
Anna Scher Children's Theatre (London)
Training
Guide to teaching through improvisation for children and adults.
1987. Lang.: Eng. 1377
Anne of Green Gables
Institutions
A history of the Charlottetown Festival. Canada: Charlottetown, PE.
1965-1987. Lang.: Eng. 505
Overview of the Charlottetown Festival, 1986 season. Canada:
Charlottetown, PE. 1965-1985. Lang.: Eng. 525
Annenkov, N.
Performance/production
Actors discuss their profession. USSR. 1987. Lang.: Eng. 996
Annenskij, Innokentij
Basic theatrical documents
Russian symbolist plays and essays. USSR. 1880-1986. Lang.: Eng.
1584
Plays/librettos/scripts
Theatre and dramaturgy of the first Russian revolution. USSR. 1905-
1907. Lang.: Rus. 1188
Annie
Performance/production
Martin Charnin's work in musical theatre. USA: New York, NY.
1957-1987. Lang.: Eng. 3658

Annie Get Your Gun
Performance/production
Collection of newspaper reviews by London theatre critics. UK-
England: London. 1986. Lang.: Eng. 2153
Another Morning
Basic theatrical documents
Text of *Another Morning* by Steve Petch. Canada: Vancouver, BC.
1987. Lang.: Eng. 1548
Another Saturday Night
Performance/production
Collection of newspaper reviews by London theatre critics. UK-
England: London. 1987. Lang.: Eng. 2276
Anouilh, Jean
Performance/production
Reviews of two Anouilh plays: *Eurydice* directed by János Szűcs,
Colombe directed by Mátyás Giricz. Hungary: Miskolc, Budapest.
1987. Lang.: Hun. 1827
Anouilh's *Eurydice*, Vian's *Tête de Méduse (Medusa Head)* at
National Theatre of Miskolc. Hungary: Miskolc. 1987. Lang.: Hun.
1888
Collection of newspaper reviews by London theatre critics. UK-
England: London. 1986. Lang.: Eng. 2164
Plot synopsis of musical *Mademoiselle Colombe* based on Anouilh's
Colombe. USA: New York, NY. 1987. Lang.: Eng. 3647
Plays/librettos/scripts
How Anouilh's *Colombe* was adapted as a musical. USA. 1987.
Lang.: Eng. 3672
Anski, Slojme (Rapoport, Slojme Zainvil)
Performance/production
Reconstruction of *The Dybbuk* as directed by Vachtangov with
HaBimah. USSR: Moscow. 1922. Lang.: Hun. 2399
ANTA
SEE
American National Theatre and Academy.
Anthony, Charles
Institutions
The formation of the North Carolina Black Repertory Company.
USA: Winston-Salem, NC. 1979-1987. Lang.: Eng. 1666
Anthropology
Basic theatrical documents
About aging: *L.O.W. in Gaia* by Rachel Rosenthal. USA. 1986.
Lang.: Eng. 3341
Design/technology
Use and evolution of masks. Lang.: Ita. 299
Effects of mixed media on traditional dramatic components of
theatre. Europe. 1900-1987. Lang.: Fre. 318
Performance/production
Origins of theatre and its relationship to the spectator. India. Japan.
Sri Lanka. 1987. Lang.: Eng. 813
Comparison of Samoan healing ritual and village theatre. Samoa.
1884-1980. Lang.: Eng. 881
History and description of a performance of *Cavittunatakam*, a
drama recounting lives of the saints. India: Kerala. 1984. Lang.:
Eng. 1480
Analysis of the play *Facundia*. Argentina: Buenos Aires. 1981. Lang.:
Spa. 1679
Events and debates at the ISTA Congress. Denmark: Holstebro.
1986. Lang.: Eng. 1729
Plays/librettos/scripts
Anthropological analysis of Shakespeare's romantic comedies.
England. 1564-1616. Lang.: Eng. 2504
Linguistic forms, historical-cultural significance of shadow puppet
theatre. Indonesia. Lang.: Eng. 3379
Relation to other fields
Analysis of the role of tradition in theatrical forms of different
cultures. Asia. Africa. 1985. Lang.: Fre. 1218
New light on Northern Chinese drama. China. 960-1368. Lang.: Chi.
1224
Tendencies in Latin American theatre that may have influenced its
evolution. Cuba. 1973-1986. Lang.: Spa. 1230
Korean mask plays, folklore and puppet theatre. Korea. Japan:
Kyushu. 1987. Lang.: Kor. 1246
Appearance and symbolism of New Guinea Mudmen. USA:
Providence, RI, New York, NY. New Guinea. 1986-1987. Lang.:
Eng. 1264

Anthropology — cont'd

Analysis of past and current perceptions of the human body, how they affect the human experience and the arts. USA. 1950-1987. Lang.: Eng. 1266

Evolution of ritual and ritual dances in the Nolembu tribe. Zambia. 1951-1985. Lang.: Eng. 1466

Comparison of the role of theatre in urban society with that of traditional ritual. 1985. Lang.: Spa. 2977

Effect of farming practices on folk theatre. Poland: Tarnogród. 1985-1987. Lang.: Eng. 3282

Descriptive calendar of masked festivals. Austria. 1987. Lang.: Fre. 3299

History of folk group Les Blancs Moussis. Belgium: Stavelot. 1947-1987. Lang.: Fre. 3300

Carnival as theatricalized negativity. Europe. Lang.: Ita. 3301

Popular entertainment in Valencian region from December to March. Spain-Catalonia: Valencia. 1418-1981. Lang.: Cat. 3337

Comparison between Wagner and Tolstoy. Russia. Germany. 1860-1908. Lang.: Eng. 3944

History of puppetry in Catalonia. Spain-Catalonia. 500 B.C.-1987 A.D. Lang.: Eng. 3996

Theory/criticism

The body as emblematic of a character's frame of mind. England. 1583. Lang.: Eng. 3031

Antígona

Plays/librettos/scripts

Catalan playwrights after the Spanish Civil War. Spain-Catalonia. 1939-1975. Lang.: Cat. 2730

Antigone

Performance/production

Collection of newspaper reviews by London theatre critics. UK-England: London. 1986. Lang.: Eng. 2164

Plays/librettos/scripts

Study of works by Sophocles, Aeschylus and Euripides. Greece. 400 B.C.-500 A.D. Lang.: Eng. 2624

Antigone-nu (Antigone-Now)

Institutions

Folkteatergruppen's productions, including *Antigone-nu (Antigone Now)*. Sweden: Stockholm. 1917-1987. Lang.: Swe. 1640

Antoine, André

Performance/production

Major directors of the early twentieth century. Europe. North America. 1900-1950. Lang.: Kor. 779

Reference materials

History of pocket theatre. France: Paris. 1944-1953. Lang.: Eng. 2974

Theory/criticism

Avoiding the risk of commercialism: the example of Antoine's Théâtre Libre. France. 1887-1987. Lang.: Fre. 1335

Centenary of Théâtre Libre: proposes 'subjective realism'. France. 1887-1987. Lang.: Fre. 1337

Antonio and Mellida

Plays/librettos/scripts

Self-referentiality and kinds of space in plays of John Marston. England: London. 1553-1608. Lang.: Eng. 2559

Antonio's Revenge

Plays/librettos/scripts

Structure of revenge tragedy in Shakespeare's *Hamlet*. 1600. Lang.: Eng. 2425

Self-referentiality and kinds of space in plays of John Marston. England: London. 1553-1608. Lang.: Eng. 2559

Antony & Cleopatra

Performance/production

Collection of newspaper reviews by London theatre critics. UK-England: London. 1987. Lang.: Eng. 2198

Antony and Cleopatra

Performance/production

Collection of newspaper reviews by London theatre critics. UK-England: London. 1986. Lang.: Eng. 2101

Antrobus, John

Performance/production

Collection of newspaper reviews by London theatre critics. UK-England: London. 1987. Lang.: Eng. 2186

Collection of newspaper reviews by London theatre critics. UK-England: London. 1987. Lang.: Eng. 2201

Anything Goes

Design/technology

Lighting review for *Anything Goes* at the Vivian Beaumont Theatre. USA: New York, NY. 1987. Lang.: Eng. 3623

Performance/production

Collection of newspaper reviews by New York theatre critics. USA: New York, NY. 1987. Lang.: Eng. 2317

Aoi, Yōji

Performance/production

Discussion of four Tokyo productions. Japan: Tokyo. 1944-1987. Lang.: Jap. 1963

Aoimi o tabeta (I Have Eaten a Blueberry)

Plays/librettos/scripts

Contemporary Japanese plays about crime. Japan: Tokyo. 1986. Lang.: Jap. 2681

Plays about child suicide in Japan. Japan: Tokyo. 1986. Lang.: Jap. 2683

Aoitori (Tokyo)

Plays/librettos/scripts

Contemporary Japanese plays about crime. Japan: Tokyo. 1986. Lang.: Jap. 2681

Plays about child suicide in Japan. Japan: Tokyo. 1986. Lang.: Jap. 2683

Apáczai Csere, János

Performance/production

Reviews of *Téli zsoltár (A Winter Psalm)* by Kovách, Shakespeare's *Much Ado About Nothing* and *Ferde ház (The Leaning House)* by Gerencsér performed at Kisfaludy Theatre. Hungary: Győr. 1986. Lang.: Hun. 1822

Apart from George

Performance/production

Collection of newspaper reviews by London theatre critics. UK-England: London. 1987. Lang.: Eng. 2257

Apollo Theatre (London)

Performance/production

Collection of newspaper reviews by London theatre critics. UK-England: London. 1986. Lang.: Eng. 2085

Collection of newspaper reviews by London theatre critics. UK-England: London. 1986. Lang.: Eng. 2119

Collection of newspaper reviews by London theatre critics. UK-England: London. 1987. Lang.: Eng. 2182

Collection of newspaper reviews by London theatre critics. UK-England: London. 1987. Lang.: Eng. 2210

Collection of newspaper reviews by London theatre critics. UK-England: London. 1987. Lang.: Eng. 2240

Collection of newspaper reviews by London theatre critics. UK-England: London. 1987. Lang.: Eng. 2256

Collection of newspaper reviews by London theatre critics. UK-England: London. 1987. Lang.: Eng. 2265

Apollonio, Mario

Performance/production

Examples of missed opportunities in modern Italian theatre. Italy. 1930-1950. Lang.: Ita. 1944

Appassionata

Plays/librettos/scripts

Characterization in Pieter-Dirk Uys' *Appassionata*. South Africa, Republic of. 1987. Lang.: Eng. 2724

Appel (Den Haag)

Performance/production

Postwar Dutch theatre: growth of small theatre groups. Netherlands. 1975-1985. Lang.: Dut. 1982

Appia, Adolphe

Design/technology

Designer Adolphe Appia's concepts and scenery for Wagner's operas. Germany. Switzerland. 1873-1928. Lang.: Eng. 3694

Performance/production

Major directors of the early twentieth century. Europe. North America. 1900-1950. Lang.: Kor. 779

Extension of Adolphe Appia's ideas on the role of the actor. France. 1900-1987. Lang.: Fre. 786

Production history of *Der Ring des Nibelungen*. Germany: Bayreuth. Italy: Milan. USA: New York, NY. 1876-1987. Lang.: Eng. 3775

Apple Butter

Plays/librettos/scripts

Critical analysis of James Reaney's *Three Desks*. Canada. 1960-1977. Lang.: Eng. 2477

Apple Cart, The
Plays/librettos/scripts
Playacting and gamesmanship: Shaw's *The Apple Cart*. UK-England. 1918-1935. Lang.: Eng.   2825

Appleman, Herbert
Performance/production
Collection of newspaper reviews by London theatre critics. UK-England: London. 1986. Lang.: Eng.   2104

Apprenticeship
Institutions
Burt Reynolds Institute apprenticeship program. USA: Miami, FL. 1987. Lang.: Eng.   587

Performance/production
Classical theatre is diminishing in the provinces due to financial cutbacks. UK-England: London, Liverpool. UK-Scotland: Edinburgh. 1987. Lang.: Eng.   2301

Training
Teachers' handbook for theatre in education. Spain-Catalonia. 1987. Lang.: Cat.   1384
Exchange program for graduate students in arts administration. UK-England: London. USA: New York, NY. 1985. Lang.: Eng.   1385
Genesis and development of various youth theatre groups. UK-Ireland. 1979-1987. Lang.: Eng.   1388
Shaping of an arts management internship from an employer's point of view. USA: Brooklyn, NY. 1985. Lang.: Eng.   1389
Problems of students graduating from theatre schools. USSR. 1980-1987. Lang.: Rus.   1394
Problems of young drama school graduates. USSR. 1986-1987. Lang.: Rus.   1396
Circus productions by performers' children. Switzerland. 1987. Lang.: Ger.   3307
Review of circus acts by children. Switzerland. 1987. Lang.: Ger.   3308
Round-table discussion of music students from Conservatory on art, education, creativity. USSR: Kiev. 1980-1987. Lang.: Rus. 3953

Aprahamian, Sallie
Performance/production
Collection of newspaper reviews by London theatre critics. UK-England: London. 1986. Lang.: Eng.   2168

Aragall, Giacomo
Basic theatrical documents
Review of video productions of *Tosca* and *Dialogues des Carmélites*. Italy: Verona. Australia: Sydney. 1987. Lang.: Eng. 3692

Arakelian, Catherine
Performance/production
Collection of newspaper reviews by London theatre critics. UK-England: London. 1987. Lang.: Eng.   2259

Arany János Szinház (Budapest)
Performance/production
György Korcsmáros directs Lionel Bart's *Oliver* at Arany János Theatre. Hungary: Budapest. 1986. Lang.: Hun.   3631
Performances of *Oliver* staged by György Korcsmáros, Antol Rencz and Imre Halasi. Hungary: Budapest, Békéscsaba, Zalaegerszeg. 1986. Lang.: Hun.   3632

Arbenz, Mary
Performance/production
Interview with Mary Arbenz on the original production of *Mourning Becomes Electra*. USA: New York, NY. 1927. Lang.: Eng.   2355

Arbrå Teaterförening (Bollnäs)
Institutions
Arbrå Teaterförening's theatrical activities for adults and children. Sweden: Bollnäs. 1979-1987. Lang.: Swe.   1645

Archbishop's Ceiling, The
Performance/production
Collection of newspaper reviews by London theatre critics. UK-England. 1986. Lang.: Eng.   2144

Archer, Jeffrey
Performance/production
Collection of newspaper reviews by London theatre critics. UK-England: London. 1987. Lang.: Eng.   2251
Collection of newspaper reviews by London theatre critics. UK-England: London. 1987. Lang.: Eng.   2275

Archer, Robyn
Performance/production
International Brecht symposium. China, People's Republic of: Beijing, Hong Kong. Japan: Tokyo. 1986. Lang.: Eng.   1722

Archer, Violet
Performance/production
Violet Archer festival, premiere of her one-act opera *The Meal*. Canada: Edmonton, AB. 1985. Lang.: Eng.   3757

Archer, William
Research/historiography
Views of the literary relationship between William Archer and Henrik Ibsen. UK-England. 1889-1919. Lang.: Eng.   3013

Architecture
Design/technology
Hungarian exhibition, Prague Quadrennial theatre design competition. Czechoslovakia: Prague. 1987. Lang.: Hun.   307
First American participation in Prague Quadrennial theatre design contest. Czechoslovakia: Prague. USA. 1967-1987. Lang.: Eng. 311
A report from the Prague Quadrennial theatre design contest. Czechoslovakia: Prague. 1987. Lang.: Swe.   312
Introductory textbook on scene and production design. USA. 1987. Lang.: Eng.   408
Influence of theatrical technology on restaurant design. USA. 1980-1985. Lang.: Eng.   451
Principles of theatre lighting applied to architectural lighting. USA: New York, NY. 1987. Lang.: Eng.   484
Decors of feasts and festivals prefigured architectural developments. Germany: Düsseldorf. France. Italy. 1700-1897. Lang.: Fre. 3320

Institutions
Texts and photos about the Teatre Grec. Spain-Catalonia: Barcelona. 1929-1986. Lang.: Cat.   558

Performance spaces
Italian translation, *Buildings for Music* by Michael Forsyth. 1600-1985. Lang.: Ita.   625
Modern theatre architecture. Canada: Montreal, PQ. 1900-1987. Lang.: Fre.   627
The lack of performance space for small theatre companies. Canada: Toronto, ON. 1987. Lang.: Eng.   629
Design for Richard Ryder's Exeter theatre. England: London. 1663. Lang.: Eng.   631
Analysis of theatre designs by Inigo Jones and John Webb. England. 1573-1672. Lang.: Eng.   632
Examining current needs of theatre artists vs. historical examination to determine theatre space design. France. Germany, West. UK-England. 1987. Lang.: Eng.   634
Theatrical equipment of the new Friedrichstadtpalast. Germany, East: Berlin, East. 1984. Lang.: Hun.   637
Designer of new Hungarian National Theatre on site and design considerations. Hungary: Budapest. 1987. Lang.: Hun.   639
Design and construction considerations: renovation of József Attila Theatre. Hungary: Budapest. 1985-1986. Lang.: Hun.   640
Comparison of two Nemzeti Szinház sites. Hungary: Budapest. 1983. Lang.: Hun.   641
Reprinted interview with Nemzeti Szinház architect Csaba Virág. Hungary: Budapest. 1966. Lang.: Hun.   646
Recent trends in Italian theatre. Italy. 1980. Lang.: Eng.   650
Plans for unrealized Roman auditorium and theatres. Italy: Rome. 1789-1953. Lang.: Ita.   655
History of San Carlo Theatre: structure, scenography, costumes. Italy: Naples. 1737-1987. Lang.: Ita.   656
Results of theatre design competition. Japan. 1986. Lang.: Hun.   658
Paul Shelving's contribution to stage design exhibited by Birmingham Museum. UK-England. 1888-1968. Lang.: Eng.   670
Mermaid Theatre, London home of Royal Shakespeare Company. UK-England: London. 1959-1987. Lang.: Eng.   671
Design of new Swan Theatre recreates Elizabethan atmosphere. UK-England: Stratford. 1987. Lang.: Eng.   672
Guidelines for preservation of theatres. USA: New York, NY. 1985-1986. Lang.: Eng.   675
Hearings for granting landmark status to forty-five Broadway theatres. USA: New York, NY. 1982. Lang.: Eng.   678
Theatre's relation to society, poor theatre design as reasons for state of theatre today. USA. 1987. Lang.: Eng.   680
Loeb Drama Center at Harvard. USA: Cambridge, MA. 1960-1987. Lang.: Eng.   682
Architect Roger Morgan discusses plans for restoring seven Broadway theatres. USA: New York, NY. 1984. Lang.: Eng.   683

SUBJECT INDEX

Architecture — cont'd

Directory of extant theatres built in the U.S. before 1915. USA. 1809-1915. Lang.: Eng. 689

Architectural and design information on the short-lived Earl Carroll Theatre. USA: New York, NY. 1931-1933. Lang.: Hun. 690

Architecture of La Jolla Playhouse and challenges it presents for designers. USA: La Jolla, CA. 1947-1987. Lang.: Eng. 694

The Tampa Bay Performing Arts Center. USA: Tampa, FL. 1987. Lang.: Eng. 698

Major expansion of the facilities at the Omaha Community Playhouse. USA: Omaha, NE. 1984-1987. Lang.: Eng. 699

Renovations at the Bayfront Center. USA: St. Petersburg, FL. 1960-1987. Lang.: Eng. 700

Recently completed Wortham Theatre Center. USA: Houston, TX. 1987. Lang.: Eng. 701

Rebuilding theatres constructed in the 1960s. USA. 1960-1986. Lang.: Eng. 702

Performimg arts centers covered in *ThCr* architecture issue. USA. 1987. Lang.: Eng. 703

Query about whether theatre architects learn from mistakes. USA. UK. 1960-1987. Lang.: Eng. 704

Renovation of the Seattle Center Playhouse into the new home of the Intiman Theatre. USA: Seattle, WA. 1983-1987. Lang.: Eng. 705

Construction and present condition of the Krannert Center for the Performing Arts. USA: Urbana, IL. 1969-1987. Lang.: Eng. 710

Design of the San Francisco Ballet Building. USA: San Francisco, CA. 1987. Lang.: Eng. 712

Northern Arts and Cultural Centre: planning and building. Canada: Yellowknife, NT. 1980-1985. Lang.: Eng. 1667

Restoration of audience areas of Kungliga Dramatiska Teatern. Sweden: Stockholm. 1987. Lang.: Swe. 1675

Architecture and history of the New Victoria Theatre. UK-England: London. 1928-1987. Lang.: Eng. 3141

Comparison of British and American cinema theatre design. UK-England: London. 1930-1987. Lang.: Eng. 3142

History of the Garden Theatre designed by Thomas H. Scott. USA: Pittsburgh, PA. 1915-1987. Lang.: Eng. 3144

Interior design of the Oriental Theatre. USA: Portland, OR. 1927-1970. Lang.: Eng. 3145

Theatre designed by Elmer F. Behrns. USA: Pekin, IL. 1927-1987. Lang.: Eng. 3146

Five buildings in Canada Place, built for Expo '86. Canada: Vancouver, BC. 1986. Lang.: Eng. 3243

Theatrical changes in Chinese opera during the Sung, Ming and Yuan dynasties. China. 960-1643. Lang.: Chi. 3451

Relation to other fields
Political context of the constructing of the Opéra-Bastille. France: Paris. 1983-1987. Lang.: Eng. 3941

Archives/libraries
The *status quo* of audio-visual documentation. Europe. 1986. Lang.: Ger. 3198

Administration
Interview with manager, historian and producer Anna Sosenko. USA: New York, NY. 1930-1987. Lang.: Eng. 154

Design/technology
Catalogue of exhibit on Viennese costume. Austria: Vienna. 1888-1972. Lang.: Fre, Dut. 301

Baroque stage machinery described in archives. Italy: Parma. 1675-1700. Lang.: Eng. 347

Institutions
Theatre department, National Museum, Prague. Czechoslovakia: Prague. 1987. Lang.: Cze. 527

Italian theatrical archives and libraries. Italy. 1987. Lang.: Ita. 547

Archival documents of the Vendramin Theatre. Italy: Venice. 1700-1733. Lang.: Ita. 548

Performance/production
Maintaining theatre archives and designating a coordinator. USA: New York, NY. 1987. Lang.: Eng. 938

Interview with Kathryn Lynch, manager of Shubert's Century Library. USA. 1945-1986. Lang.: Eng. 950

Resources of the Billy Rose Collection at Lincoln Center Performing Arts Library. USA: New York, NY. 1987. Lang.: Eng. 965

History of 'The Soldier Show', Shubert Archives U.S.O. collection. USA: New York, NY. 1942-1945. Lang.: Eng. 3664

Musical Theatre Project explores Broadway musical material available in Shubert Archive. USA: New York, NY. 1984-1985. Lang.: Eng. 3666

Metropolitan Opera archives. USA: New York, NY. 1883-1987. Lang.: Eng. 3863

Arden, Annabel
Performance/production
Collection of newspaper reviews by London theatre critics. UK-England: London. 1986. Lang.: Eng. 2043

Arden, Mark
Performance/production
Collection of newspaper reviews by London theatre critics. UK-England: London. 1986. Lang.: Eng. 2089

Are You Lonesome Tonight
Institutions
A history of the Charlottetown Festival. Canada: Charlottetown, PE. 1965-1987. Lang.: Eng. 505

Arena Conta Zumbi
Performance/production
Teatro Arena de São Paulo's production of *Arena Conta Zumbi*. Brazil: São Paulo. 1965. Lang.: Eng. 1690

Arena del Belvedere (Rome)
Administration
Vatican court's withdrawal from festival promotion under Sixtus V. Italy: Rome. 1585-1595. Lang.: Ita. 3240

Arena Stage (Washington, DC)
Institutions
Current trends in American theatre. USA. 1967-1987. Lang.: Eng. 621

Performance/production
Russian director Jurij Liubimov and his productions in the USSR and USA. USSR: Moscow. USA: Washington, DC. 1984-1987. Lang.: Eng. 2400

Areté Mime Troupe (Alberta)
Performance/production
Evolution of the Areté Mime Troupe: its concepts, goals and performance methods. Canada. 1980-1982. Lang.: Eng. 3221

Ariadne auf Naxos
Institutions
Review of a production of *Ariadne auf Naxos*. Canada. 1987. Lang.: Eng. 3717

Ariane et Barbe-Bleue (Ariadne and Bluebeard)
Plays/librettos/scripts
Ariadne in plays of Ibsen, Strindberg, Maeterlinck. Europe. 1892-1902. Lang.: Eng. 2566

Aristocrats
Plays/librettos/scripts
Themes of Brian Friel's plays. Ireland. 1929-1987. Lang.: Eng. 2638

Brian Friel's interpretation of Irish history through his plays *Aristocrats* and *Translations*. Ireland. 1987. Lang.: Eng. 2659

Aristophanes
Plays/librettos/scripts
Study of classical Greek dramaturgy. Greece. 472-388 B.C. Lang.: Hun. 2623

Changes in theatre space as a result of New Comedy. Greece: Athens. Italy: Rome. 400 B.C.-180 A.D. Lang.: Eng. 2625

Theory/criticism
Comic space from the ancient Greeks to the present. Europe. USA. Greece. 400 B.C.-1987 A.D. Lang.: Eng. 3032

Aristoteles
Theory/criticism
Analysis of various versions and translations of Aristotle's *Poetics*. Greece: Athens. Egypt: Alexandria. Europe. 70 B.C.-1981 A.D. Lang.: Chi. 1343

Politics, patriarchy in Dryden's plays. England. 1679-1687. 3030

Catalan translation of Lessing's *Hamburgische Dramaturgie*. Germany: Hamburg. 1767-1769. Lang.: Cat. 3043

Reading of Aristotle's early scientific works. Greece. 384-322 B.C. Lang.: Eng. 3049

Aristoti, Attilio
Performance/production
Cast lists for some early London operas. England: London. 1712-1717. Lang.: Eng. 3761

Aristotle
SEE
Aristoteles.

International Bibliography of Theatre: 1987

219

Arizona Mulató (Budapest)
Institutions
Proprietors, artists and operation of Jardin d'Hiver, nightclub and revue theatre. Hungary: Budapest. 1932-1944. Lang.: Hun.　　3381

Arkin, Alan
Plays/librettos/scripts
Interview with cartoonist-playwright Jules Feiffer. USA. 1950-1987. Lang.: Eng.　　1168

Arkley Barnet Show, The
Performance/production
Collection of newspaper reviews by London theatre critics. UK-England: London. 1987. Lang.: Eng.　　2188

Árkosi, Árpád
Performance/production
Comparison of the premiere of Imre Sarkadi's *Oszlopos Simeon (The Man on the Pillar)* and two revivals by Árpad Árkosi and István Horvai. Hungary: Szeged, Budapest. 1967-1987. Lang.: Hun.　　1830

Arm Yourself, or Harm Yourself
Performance/production
Interview with playwright Amiri Baraka. USA: Newark, NJ, New York, NY. 1965-1969. Lang.: Eng.　　2356

Arms and the Man
Performance/production
Collection of newspaper reviews by London theatre critics. UK-England: London. 1986. Lang.: Eng.　　2132

Plays/librettos/scripts
How settings and props convey meaning in plays by Shaw. UK-England. 1883-1935. Lang.: Eng.　　2753

Arnold, Andy
Performance/production
Collection of newspaper reviews by London theatre critics. UK-England: London. 1987. Lang.: Eng.　　2232

Arnold, Kenneth
Performance/production
Collection of newspaper reviews by London theatre critics. UK-England: London. 1986. Lang.: Eng.　　2116

Arnone, John
Design/technology
Philosophy of set designer John Arnone. USA: New York, NY. 1987. Lang.: Eng.　　430

Arnoult, Philip
Administration
Philip Arnoult, founding director of the Baltimore Theatre Project, and his search for new works. USA: Baltimore, MD. 1971-1987. Lang.: Eng.　　157

Audience
American response to Gardzienice Theatre Association. Poland: Gardzienice. 1666-1987. Lang.: Eng.　　1536

Performance/production
Interview with people who staged *The Yellow House*. USA. 1960-1987. Lang.: Eng.　　1486

Aronson, Boris
Design/technology
Career of Broadway set designer Boris Aronson. USA. 1925-1979. Lang.: Eng.　　449

Performance/production
Successful London revival of *Follies* by Stephen Sondheim. UK-England: London. USA: New York, NY. 1987. Lang.: Eng.　　3638

Aronstein, Martin
Performance/production
Review of production and staging aspects of *Wild Honey* by Anton Čechov. UK-England: London. 1986. Lang.: Eng.　　2306

Arrabal, Fernando
Performance/production
Directing and the desire to communicate. France. 1987. Lang.: Fre.　　1759

Plays/librettos/scripts
Playwright Fernando Arrabal and productions of his work. USA. France: Paris. 1959-1987. Lang.: Eng.　　1175

Theory/criticism
Comic space from the ancient Greeks to the present. Europe. USA. Greece. 400 B.C.-1987 A.D. Lang.: Eng.　　3032

Ars Veneta (Venice)
Performance/production
Letters documenting Ars Veneta, a dialect theatre company. Italy: Venice. 1921-1922. Lang.: Ita.　　820

Art & Pro (Netherlands)
Performance/production
Interview with Frans Strijards, playwright and director. Netherlands. 1987. Lang.: Dut.　　1979

Art of Perspective, The
Performance/production
Collection of newspaper reviews by London theatre critics. UK-England: London. 1986. Lang.: Eng.　　2126

Art of Success, The
Performance/production
Collection of newspaper reviews by London theatre critics. UK-England: London. 1987. Lang.: Eng.　　2236

Art Theatre (Budapest)
SEE
Müvész Szinház.

Artaud Theatre, Institut Français (London)
Performance/production
Collection of newspaper reviews by London theatre critics. UK-England: London. 1987. Lang.: Eng.　　2177

Artaud, Antonin
Design/technology
The impact of twentieth-century technology on theatre. Canada. 1900-1987. Lang.: Fre.　　302

Effects of mixed media on traditional dramatic components of theatre. Europe. 1900-1987. Lang.: Fre.　　318

Performance/production
Influence of *nō* theatre on director Jean-Louis Barrault and his colleagues. France. 1910-1982. Lang.: Eng.　　1498

New interpretation of Jacobean theatre. England: London. 1596-1633. Lang.: Eng.　　1743

Method acting: its origins and development. USA: New York, NY. USSR: Moscow. 1923-1987. Lang.: Eng.　　2359

Techniques of the image theatre and effects on actor and audience. Canada. Europe. USA. 1987. Lang.: Eng.　　3345

Plays/librettos/scripts
Influence of Balinese theatre on Antonin Artaud. France. Indonesia. 1931-1935. Lang.: Kor.　　1126

Antonin Artaud's interpretation of Shelley's *The Cenci*. UK-England. France. 1819-1920. Lang.: Eng.　　2780

Reference materials
History of pocket theatre. France: Paris. 1944-1953. Lang.: Eng.　　2974

Relation to other fields
Artaud's philosophy of theatre mediating between dream and history. USA. 1958-1985. Lang.: Eng.　　1265

Theory/criticism
Artaud's conception of theatre. France. 1896-1949. Lang.: Ger.　　1333

Theatre and contemporary culture. USA. 1800-1987. Lang.: Eng.　　1360

Comparison of impact of film versus the theatrical experience. USA. 1937-1987. Lang.: Eng.　　3189

Arthur, Max
Performance/production
Collection of newspaper reviews by London theatre critics. UK-England: London. 1987. Lang.: Eng.　　2189

Article Eleven
Performance/production
Collection of newspaper reviews by London theatre critics. UK-England: London. 1987. Lang.: Eng.　　2249

Arts Council (Canada)
SEE
Canada Council.

Arts Council of Great Britain (London)
Administration
Funding for performance art. UK-England. 1987. Lang.: Eng.　　3338

Arts Theatre (Cambridge, UK)
Performance/production
Collection of newspaper reviews by London theatre critics. UK-England. 1987. Lang.: Eng.　　2175

Collection of newspaper reviews by London theatre critics. UK-England: London. 1987. Lang.: Eng.　　2216

Collection of newspaper reviews by London theatre critics. UK-England: London. 1987. Lang.: Eng.　　2227

Collection of newspaper reviews by London theatre critics. UK-England: London. 1987. Lang.: Eng.　　2277

SUBJECT INDEX

Atorie Dankan (Tokyo)
Performance/production
Discussion of four Tokyo productions. Japan: Tokyo. 1944-1987.
Lang.: Jap. 1963

ATR
SEE
Amatörteaterns Riksförbund.

Attenborough, Michael
Performance/production
Collection of newspaper reviews by London theatre critics. UK-
England: London. 1986. Lang.: Eng. 2151

Collection of newspaper reviews by London theatre critics. UK-
England: London. 1987. Lang.: Eng. 2174

Collection of newspaper reviews by London theatre critics. UK-
England: London. 1987. Lang.: Eng. 2229

Collection of newspaper reviews by London theatre critics. UK-
England: London. 1987. Lang.: Eng. 2270

Attila Theatre
SEE
József Attila Szinház.

Attractions, The
Performance/production
Collection of newspaper reviews by London theatre critics. UK-
England: London. 1987. Lang.: Eng. 2270

Atyai ház, Az (Paternal Roof, The)
Performance/production
Reviews: *A vörös postakocsi (The Red Mail Coach)* by Gyula Krúdy,
staged by Dezső Kapás and *Az atyai ház (The Paternal Roof)* by
Zsigmond Remenyik, staged by Péter Lener. Hungary: Veszprém,
Nyíregyháza. 1986. Lang.: Hun. 1821

Auber, Daniel
Plays/librettos/scripts
Study of French composer Daniel Auber and his works. France.
1782-1871. Lang.: Eng. 3904

Aubrey, Diane
Performance/production
Theatre career of photo-journalist Bert Andrews. USA: New York,
NY. 1950-1987. Lang.: Eng. 2367

Aubry, Eugene
Performance spaces
Wortham Theatre Center, designed by Eugene Aubry. USA:
Houston, TX. 1977-1987. Lang.: Eng. 3739

Aucamp, Hennie
Plays/librettos/scripts
New Afrikaans drama and playwrights. South Africa, Republic of.
1985-1986. Lang.: Afr. 1155

Audi, Pierre
Performance/production
Collection of newspaper reviews by London theatre critics. UK-
England: London. 1987. Lang.: Eng. 2197

Audience
SEE ALSO
Behavior/psychology, audience.
Classed Entries.
Administration
Comprehensive guide to establishing and running a box office. USA:
New York, NY. 1980. Lang.: Eng. 126

Computer analysis of mailing lists and response enhancement. USA:
New York, NY. 1986. Lang.: Eng. 139

Results of market research survey for a small arts center. USA.
1984. Lang.: Eng. 171

Financial analysis of problems facing American theatre. USA. 1987.
Lang.: Eng. 219

An investigation of the audience of Chinese classical drama. China,
People's Republic of. 1987. Lang.: Chi. 3424
Design/technology
Advice on systems for hard of hearing in theatres. UK. 1987. Lang.:
Eng. 370

Creating access for hearing and visually impaired theatregoers. USA:
Washington, DC. 1987. Lang.: Eng. 413
Institutions
History of Theatre Plus theatre company. Canada: Toronto, ON.
1972-1982. Lang.: Eng. 520

Profile and history of Colden Center for the Performing Arts. USA:
Flushing, NY. 1961-1984. Lang.: Eng. 618

Interview with Stratford Festival's artistic director John Neville.
Canada: Stratford, ON. 1985-1986. Lang.: Eng. 1605

On audience societies Freie Volksbühne and Neue Freie Volksbühne.
Germany: Berlin. 1889-1914. Lang.: Ger. 1616

The popularization of opera companies since 1940. USA. 1940-1983.
Lang.: Eng. 3735
Performance spaces
Providing access to the handicapped in existing theatres. USA. 1987.
Lang.: Eng. 693

Reconstruction of theatrical activity in Barcelona. Spain-Catalonia:
Barcelona. 1800-1830. Lang.: Cat. 1672
Performance/production
Relationship of theatre, class and gender. UK-England. USA. 1969-
1985. Lang.: Eng. 918

Gays and lesbians on the American stage. USA. 1896-1987. Lang.:
Eng. 935

Decentralization of American theatre. USA. 1960-1980. Lang.: Eng.
958

New interpretation of Jacobean theatre. England: London. 1596-
1633. Lang.: Eng. 1743

Survey of critical reactions to contemporary Korean theatre. Korea:
Seoul. 1986-1987. Lang.: Kor. 1971

The responsibility of artists to their audience. China, People's
Republic of. 1980-1986. Lang.: Chi. 3471

The Beijing Opera in England and its large audiences. China,
People's Republic of. UK-England. 1987. Lang.: Chi. 3521

The use of film montage in Chinese theatre. China, People's
Republic of. 1986. Lang.: Chi. 3524
Plays/librettos/scripts
Playwrights' condescension to child audiences. USA. 1972. Lang.:
Eng. 1171

Old age in the plays of Sophocles, especially *Oedipus at Colonus*.
405 B.C. Lang.: Eng. 2414

Political, social and religious issues in Caroline drama. England.
1632-1642. Lang.: Eng. 2508

Political dissatisfaction in drama. UK. Ireland. 1890-1987. Lang.:
Eng. 2750

Shaw's artistic strategy in *Major Barbara*. UK-England. 1905. Lang.:
Eng. 2774

Historical context for Tom Taylor's *The Ticket-of-Leave Man*. UK-
England. France. 1863. 2801

Themes of perception in *The Tempest*. UK-England: London. 1611.
Lang.: Eng. 2813

Philosophical themes in modern Chinese drama: their audience
appeal. China, People's Republic of. 1987. Lang.: Chi. 3564

Chinese opera should reflect the concerns of its audience. China,
People's Republic of. 1987. Lang.: Chi. 3578
Relation to other fields
Debate over proletarian art among Social Democrats. Germany:
Berlin. 1910-1912. Lang.: Ger. 1238

Relationship between theatre and everyday life. Italy. 1900-1987.
Lang.: Ita. 1242

Theatre in the American South. USA. 1985. Lang.: Eng. 1271

Wagnerian opera in Argentina. Argentina: Buenos Aires. 1858-1983.
Lang.: Eng. 3938
Theory/criticism
How theatre communicates with its audience. 1949-1987. Lang.: Chi.
1311

Plays that attempt to legitimize theatre. England. France. 1600-1700.
Lang.: Eng. 1324

Criticism by actor Piero Gobetti. Italy. 1918-1926. Lang.: Ita. 1345

Advantage of having a Broadway theatre. USA: New York, NY.
1985. Lang.: Eng. 1354

The changing aesthetic characteristics of Chinese opera. China,
People's Republic of. 1987. Lang.: Chi. 3603

Audience areas
Performance spaces
Documentation of layout, operations: Teatro dei Comici. Italy:
Mantua. 1688-1800. Lang.: Eng. 654

Restoration of audience areas of Kungliga Dramatiska Teatern.
Sweden: Stockholm. 1987. Lang.: Swe. 1675

Audience composition
Administration
Ground Zero Theatre Company's project for the homeless. Canada:
Toronto, ON. 1987. Lang.: Eng. 6

Audio forms — cont'd

Compact disc recordings of Maria Callas's opera performances. 1987.
Lang.: Eng.   3705

Calendar of international opera productions and broadcasts for 1988
winter season. 1988. Lang.: Eng.   3706

Review of a production of *Ariadne auf Naxos*. Canada. 1987. Lang.:
Eng.   3717

Performance/production

West Coast artists explore audiovisual effects. USA. 1987. Lang.:
Eng.   969

Street theatre and mass media. Italy. 1980. Lang.: Ger.   3295

Stuart Hamilton's career in opera broadcasting. Canada: Toronto,
ON. 1929-1987. Lang.: Eng.   3758

Evaluation of soprano Maria Meneghini Callas. Greece. Italy. USA.
1923-1977. Lang.: Eng.   3790

Background on Lyric Opera radio broadcast performances. USA:
Chicago, IL. 1987. Lang.: Eng.   3832

Background on San Francisco opera radio broadcasts. USA: San
Francisco, CA. 1987. Lang.: Eng.   3833

Background on Metropolitan radio broadcast performances. USA:
New York, NY. 1987. Lang.: Eng.   3837

Background on Metropolitan radio broadcast performances. USA:
New York, NY. 1987. Lang.: Eng.   3838

Plays/librettos/scripts

Two forms of adaptations of Shakespeare for other media. Europe.
USA. 1899-1987. Lang.: Eng.   3097

Reference materials

New Italian productions in all areas. Italy. 1985-1986. Lang.: Ita.
                                                               1204

Audiovisual

SEE ALSO

Classed Entries under MEDIA.

Auditorium

Performance spaces

Questions spending $50 million on a new concert hall in Los
Angeles. USA: Los Angeles, CA. 1987. Lang.: Eng.   711

Lighting design in Tampa's new performing arts center. USA:
Tampa, FL. 1987. Lang.: Eng.   3395

Auditoriums

Performance spaces

Plans for unrealized Roman auditorium and theatres. Italy: Rome.
1789-1953. Lang.: Ita.   655

Providing access to the handicapped in existing theatres. USA. 1987.
Lang.: Eng.   693

Aufhaltsame Aufstieg des Arturo Ui, Der (Resistible Rise of Arturo Ui, The)

Performance/production

Collection of newspaper reviews by London theatre critics. UK-
England. 1987. Lang.: Eng.   2199

Auftrag, Der (Mission, The)

Plays/librettos/scripts

Brecht's influence on technique and style of playwright Heiner
Müller. Germany, East. 1940-1984. Lang.: Eng.   2605

Significance of dream-structures in Heiner Müller's plays, compared
with those in Brecht's. Germany, East: Berlin, East. 1972-1987.
Lang.: Ger.   2607

Augustine, Saint

Performance/production

Church condemnation of Roman *ludi*, creative impulse behind
medieval drama. Europe. 160-1578. Lang.: Eng.   1745

Auletta, Robert

Performance/production

Peter Sellars and American National Theatre present *Ajax*, Holland
Festival. Netherlands. USA. 1987. Lang.: Dut.   1981

Aunt Dan and Lemon

Plays/librettos/scripts

Review of Wallace Shawn's *Aunt Dan and Lemon*. Canada:
Toronto, ON. USA: New York, NY. 1986-1987. Lang.: Eng.   2467

Aunt Máli

SEE

Máli néni.

Austrian Federal Theatres

SEE

Österreichische Bundestheater.

Automatic Pilot

Performance/production

Playwright Erika Ritter. Canada: Toronto, ON. 1982. Lang.: Eng.
                                                               1711

Avant-garde theatre

SEE ALSO

Experimental theatre.

Shōgekijō undō.

Alternative theatre.

Design/technology

Oskar Schlemmer, head of Bauhaus stage workshop. Germany. 1888-
1943. Lang.: Dut.   323

Performance spaces

The streets of New York as experimental performance space. USA:
New York, NY. 1960-1975. Lang.: Eng.   688

Performance/production

Avant-garde theatre: focus on performance rather than dramaturgy.
1900-1987. Lang.: Ita.   718

Avant-garde theatres, authors and directors in Argentina. Argentina.
1950-1983. Lang.: Spa.   719

Bragaglia's Theatre of the Independent. Italy: Rome. 1911-1932.
Lang.: Ita.   836

Avant-garde performances presented at International Open Theatre
meeting. Poland: Wrocław. 1982-1987. Lang.: Pol, Eng, Fre.   877

History of experimental and alternative theatre. UK-England. 1800-
1987. Lang.: Eng.   904

Reference materials

History of pocket theatre. France: Paris. 1944-1953. Lang.: Eng.
                                                               2974

Relation to other fields

Interracial fringe productions: racial, class, sexual politics. South
Africa, Republic of. 1984. Lang.: Eng.   2998

Theory/criticism

Argument challenging existence of an avant-garde in America. USA.
1985. Lang.: Eng.   1352

Post-Revolutionary Soviet theatre. USSR: Moscow. 1918-1930. Lang.:
Ger.   3378

Avenging Angel

Performance/production

Collection of newspaper reviews by London theatre critics. UK-
England: London. 1987. Lang.: Eng.   2264

Aventura eterna, La (Eternal Adventure, The)

Theory/criticism

Study of modernism through analysis of three plays. Spain. 1898-
1909. Lang.: Spa.   3319

Aversa, Tommaso

Plays/librettos/scripts

Tommaso Aversa's Sicilian comedy *Le notti di Palermu (The Nights
of Palermo)*. Italy. 1600. Lang.: Ita.   1136

Avery, Margaret

Performance/production

Interview with actress Margaret Avery. USA: San Diego, CA,
Hollywood, CA. 1950-1987. Lang.: Eng.   3167

Aves (Conference of the Birds)

Performance/production

Autobiography of film and stage director Peter Brook. UK-England.
1946-1987. Lang.: Eng.   2281

Ávila, Maria de

Performance/production

History of dance in Catalonia. Spain-Catalonia. 1300-1987. Lang.:
Cat.   1410

Avión negro, El (Black Airplane, The)

Relation to other fields

Political predictions in *El avión negro (The Black Airplane)*.
Argentina. 1969-1970. Lang.: Eng.   2979

Avos' (Perchance)

Plays/librettos/scripts

Historical themes in plays of Andrej Vosnesenskij. USSR: Moscow.
1980-1987. Lang.: Rus.   2937

Awake and Sing

Plays/librettos/scripts

Influence of Clifford Odets on mainstream American realism. USA.
1935-1987. Lang.: Eng.   2927

Awards

Administration

Vancouver theatre scene, Jesse Richardson Theatre Awards. Canada:
Vancouver, BC. 1983-1984. Lang.: Eng.   18

Bacchae, The
SEE
    Bákchai.
Plays/librettos/scripts
    The Strong Breed and *The Bacchae*: Soyinka's symbolic use of ritual and ceremony. Nigeria. 1973-1987. Lang.: Eng.   2709

Bacchelli, Riccardo
Plays/librettos/scripts
    Riccardo Bacchelli's *Amleto (Hamlet)*. Italy. 1919-1957. Lang.: Ita.   2671

Bacci Barba, Roberto
Performance/production
    Theatre groups existing in small countries and communities. South America. UK-Wales. 1960-1987. Lang.: Eng.   884

Back Alley Theatre (Vancouver)
Institutions
    Survey of Vancouver theatre companies. Canada: Vancouver, BC. 1987. Lang.: Eng.   516

Backstage
SEE
    Support areas.

Bagaardeatre (Svendborg)
Relation to other fields
    Impact of politics upon funding of theatre. Denmark. 1722-1982. Lang.: Eng.   2986

Bagarozy, Edgar Richard
Institutions
    The beginnings and failure of the United States Opera Company. USA: Chicago, IL. 1946-1947. Lang.: Eng.   3731

Bagossy, László
Performance/production
    László Bagossy directs *Macbeth*, Tamás Jordán directs Zsigmond Móricz's *Uri muri (Gentlemen's Spree)* at Pécs Summer Theatre. Hungary: Pécs. 1987. Lang.: Hun.   1864

Bahi, B.
Performance/production
    Collection of newspaper reviews by London theatre critics. UK-England: London. 1987. Lang.: Eng.   2249

Bailegangaire
Plays/librettos/scripts
    Theatrical language in the plays of Thomas Murphy. Ireland. 1961-1984. Lang.: Eng.   2640
    Comic characters and the Book of Job in the plays of Thomas Murphy. Ireland. 1962-1983. Lang.: Eng.   2648
    The myth of the idyllic peasant life in the plays of Thomas Murphy. Ireland. 1961-1986. Lang.: Eng.   2652
    Analysis of Thomas Murphy's *Bailegangaire*, its connections with the Irish language, story-telling. Ireland: Galway. 1985. Lang.: Eng. 2655
    Historical accuracy of characters in the plays of Thomas Murphy. Ireland. 1962-1986. Lang.: Eng.   2657

Bains, Harwant
Performance/production
    Collection of newspaper reviews by London theatre critics. UK-England: London. 1987. Lang.: Eng.   2265

Bajo el Volcán (Below the Volcano)
Plays/librettos/scripts
    Interview with playwright Hugo Hiriart. Mexico: Mexico City. 1987. Lang.: Spa.   1151

Bákchai (Bacchae, The)
Plays/librettos/scripts
    Greek poetic drama through Nietzschean theory. Greece. 1987. Lang.: Eng.   2620

Baker, George Pierce
Performance/production
    Comparison of two 'Elizabethan' productions of *Hamlet*. UK-England: London. USA. 1900-1904. Lang.: Eng.   2292

Baker, Josephine
Performance/production
    Catalogue of an exhibit on singer-dancer Josephine Baker. France: Paris. 1906-1975. Lang.: Ita.   3259

Bakst, Léon
Design/technology
    Set and costume designs of major designers. UK-England. 1902-1980. Lang.: Eng.   376

Baku, Shango
Performance/production
    Collection of newspaper reviews by London theatre critics. UK-England: London. 1986. Lang.: Eng.   2071

Balade du Grand Macabre, La (Grand Macabre's Stroll, The)
Plays/librettos/scripts
    Death in Ghelderode's *La Balade du Grand Macabre (The Grand Macabre's Stroll)*. France. 1934. Lang.: Eng.   2587

Balanchine, George
Performance/production
    The career of dancer/choreographer Katherine Dunham. USA: New York, NY, Chicago, IL, Las Vegas, NV. 1909-1987. Lang.: Eng.   1412
    Theatricality of dance. USA. 1985. Lang.: Eng.   1414
    Roles of women in the field of ballet. France. USA. 1720-1987. Lang.: Eng.   1434
Theory/criticism
    Balanchine ballerinas: female domination in the ballet. USA. 1946-1987. Lang.: Eng.   1457
    Domination of women and gay men in Western dance. USA. 1700-1987. Lang.: Eng.   1458

Balanda i Sicart, Josep
Performance/production
    Exhibition catalogue: popular theatre in Catalan. France. 1415-1987. Lang.: Cat, Fre.   1750

Balarda, Leonardo
Performance/production
    Premiere of Leonardo Balarda's opera *Cristobal Colón*. Spain-Catalonia: Barcelona. 1987. Lang.: Eng.   3818

Balcon, Le (Balcony, The)
Performance/production
    Review of *El Balcón*: production of Genet's *Le Balcon (The Balcony)*. Mexico: Mexico City. 1987. Lang.: Spa.   1978
    Collection of newspaper reviews by London theatre critics. UK-England: London. 1987. Lang.: Eng.   2271
Plays/librettos/scripts
    The allegory of capitalist society in Genet's *Le Balcon (The Balcony)*. France. 1958-1987. Lang.: Eng.   2588

Bald Soprano, The
SEE
    Cantatrice chauve, La.

Baldwin, James
Performance/production
    Collection of newspaper reviews by London theatre critics. UK. 1987. Lang.: Eng.   2031
    Collection of newspaper reviews by London theatre critics. UK-England: London. 1987. Lang.: Eng.   2191
Plays/librettos/scripts
    Interview with playwright Charles Fuller. USA: Philadelphia, PA, New York, NY. Korea, South. 1959-1987. Lang.: Eng.   2921

Bálint, András
Performance/production
    Reviews of Wilson's *Talley's Folly* staged by András Bálint and Bond's *The Fool* staged by László Salamon Suba. Hungary: Dunaujváros, Nyíregyháza. 1986. Lang.: Hun.   1902

Balk, Wesley
Institutions
    Program of opera workshop, Boston Conservatory. USA: Boston, MA. 1973-1983. Lang.: Eng.   3734

Ball de titelles (Puppet Dance)
Plays/librettos/scripts
    General history of Catalan literature, including theatre. Spain-Catalonia. 1902-1961. Lang.: Cat.   1157

Ball, Hugo
Theory/criticism
    Comparison of Ball's *Michelangelo's Nose* and Hebbel's *Michel Angelo*. Germany. 1886-1927. Lang.: Eng.   3042

Ballester, Alexandre
Performance/production
    Collection of theatre reviews by Xavier Fàbregas. Spain-Catalonia. 1969-1972. Lang.: Cat.   2010

Ballet
SEE ALSO
    Training, ballet.
    Classed Entries under DANCE-Ballet.
Design/technology
    Picasso's theatrical work. France. Spain. 1917-1965. Lang.: Ita.   321
    Set and costume designs of major designers. UK-England. 1902-1980. Lang.: Eng.   376
    Lighting design and technology for opera and ballet. UK-England: London. 1928-1987. Lang.: Eng.   3698

Ballet — cont'd

Performance/production

Opera, ballet, theatre and music in South Africa. South Africa, Republic of. 1977-1987. Lang.: Eng.   882

Dancers' daily routine in Les Ballets Jazz de Montréal. Canada: Montreal, PQ. 1985. Lang.: Eng.   1479

Four new productions in Poland. Poland: Warsaw. 1986-1987. Lang.: Eng, Fre.   1988

Ballet on television. USSR. 1980-1987. Lang.: Rus.   3213

Mime compared with other forms of visual arts. USA: Claremont, CA. 1980-1982. Lang.: Eng.   3228

Similarities and differences in Chinese opera and ballet. China, People's Republic of. 1986. Lang.: Chi.   3470

Ballet Folklórico Nacional de Nicaragua

Performance/production

Founder and director of the Ballet Folklórico Nacional de Nicaragua discusses the company and its goals. Nicaragua. 1986. Lang.: Eng.   1464

Ballets Jazz de Montréal

Performance/production

Dancers' daily routine in Les Ballets Jazz de Montréal. Canada: Montreal, PQ. 1985. Lang.: Eng.   1479

Ballhaus, Michael

Design/technology

Cinematographer Michael Ballhaus' work on film version of Williams' *The Glass Menagerie* directed by Paul Newman. USA. 1987. Lang.: Eng.   3139

Ballo in Maschera, Un

Performance/production

Background on Lyric Opera radio broadcast performances. USA: Chicago, IL. 1987. Lang.: Eng.   3832

Background on Opera Company of Philadelphia telecast, *Un Ballo in Maschera*. USA: Philadelphia, PA. 1987. Lang.: Eng.   3834

Ballroom

Performance/production

Collection of newspaper reviews by London theatre critics. UK-England: London. 1986. Lang.: Eng.   2088

Balsa de la Medusa, La (Raft of the Medusa, The)

Plays/librettos/scripts

Egon Wolff's trilogy of plays focusing on Chilean bourgeoisie. Chile. 1964-1984. Lang.: Eng.   2490

Baltimore Theatre Project (Baltimore, MD)

Administration

Philip Arnoult, founding director of the Baltimore Theatre Project, and his search for new works. USA: Baltimore, MD. 1971-1987. Lang.: Eng.   157

BAM

SEE

Brooklyn Academy of Music.

Bán Bánk

SEE

Bánk Bán.

Banden (Odense)

Relation to other fields

Impact of politics upon funding of theatre. Denmark. 1722-1982. Lang.: Eng.   2986

Banff Arts Centre (AB)

Performance/production

Lorna Heaton's use of holograms in *Woyzeck*. Canada: Banff, AB. 1987. Lang.: Fre.   3205

Banff Centre School of Fine Arts (Banff, AB)

Institutions

Elizabeth Sterling Haynes and the Little Theatre movement. Canada. 1916-1957. Lang.: Eng.   1603

Training

Changes in music teaching methods at the Banff Centre. Canada: Banff, AB. 1933-1987. Lang.: Eng.   3950

Banged Up

Performance/production

Collection of newspaper reviews by London theatre critics. UK-England: London. 1986. Lang.: Eng.   2162

Bania (Bathhouse)

Plays/librettos/scripts

Textual analysis of Majakovskij's *Bathhouse*. 1986. Lang.: Eng.   2419

Use of public bathhouses as metaphors in Russian drama. USSR. 1925-1935. Lang.: Eng.   2959

Bania i Liudi (Bathhouse and People)

Plays/librettos/scripts

Use of public bathhouses as metaphors in Russian drama. USSR. 1925-1935. Lang.: Eng.   2959

Banjo Man

Performance/production

Collection of newspaper reviews by London theatre critics. UK-England: London. 1986. Lang.: Eng.   2160

Bannerman, Celia

Performance/production

Collection of newspaper reviews by London theatre critics. UK-England: London. 1987. Lang.: Eng.   2173

Bánus Bánk

SEE

Bánk Bán.

Barabbas

Theory/criticism

Analysis of *Escurial* and *Barabbas* by Michel de Ghelderode. Belgium. 1898. Lang.: Fre.   3023

Baraister, Marion

Performance/production

Collection of newspaper reviews by London theatre critics. UK-England: London. 1987. Lang.: Eng.   2233

Baraka, Imamu Amiri (Jones, LeRoi)

Performance/production

Interview with playwright Amiri Baraka. USA: Newark, NJ, New York, NY. 1965-1969. Lang.: Eng.   2356

Plays/librettos/scripts

Charles Fuller's *A Soldier's Play*: debate on means of liberation. USA. 1976-1981. Lang.: Eng.   2854

Baraldi, John

Performance/production

Collection of newspaper reviews by London theatre critics. UK-England: London. 1986. Lang.: Eng.   2167

Barba, Eugenio

Design/technology

Effects of mixed media on traditional dramatic components of theatre. Europe. 1900-1987. Lang.: Fre.   318

Performance/production

Analysis of the play *Facundia*. Argentina: Buenos Aires. 1981. Lang.: Spa.   1679

Barbeau, Anne

Theory/criticism

Politics, patriarchy in Dryden's plays. England. 1679-1687.   3030

Barber of Seville, The (opera)

SEE

Barbiere di Siviglia, Il.

Barbican Theatre (London)

SEE ALSO

Royal Shakespeare Company.

Performance/production

Collection of newspaper reviews by London theatre critics. UK. 1987. Lang.: Eng.   2031

Collection of newspaper reviews by London theatre critics. UK-England: London. 1986. Lang.: Eng.   2046

Collection of newspaper reviews by London theatre critics. UK-England: London. 1986. Lang.: Eng.   2064

Collection of newspaper reviews by London theatre critics. UK-England: London. 1986. Lang.: Eng.   2082

Collection of newspaper reviews by London theatre critics. UK-England: London. 1986. Lang.: Eng.   2095

Collection of newspaper reviews by London theatre critics. UK-England: London. 1986. Lang.: Eng.   2111

Collection of newspaper reviews by London theatre critics. UK-England: London. 1986. Lang.: Eng.   2164

Collection of newspaper reviews by London theatre critics. UK-England: London. 1987. Lang.: Eng.   2200

Collection of newspaper reviews by London theatre critics. UK-England: London. 1987. Lang.: Eng.   2210

Collection of newspaper reviews by London theatre critics. UK-England: London. 1987. Lang.: Eng.   2212

Collection of newspaper reviews by London theatre critics. UK-England: London. 1987. Lang.: Eng.   2220

Collection of newspaper reviews by London theatre critics. UK-England: London. 1987. Lang.: Eng.   2236

Barbican Theatre (London) — cont'd

Collection of newspaper reviews by London theatre critics. UK-England. 1987. Lang.: Eng.   2263

Collection of newspaper reviews by London theatre critics. UK-England: London. 1987. Lang.: Eng.   2271

Barbier, George
Design/technology
Set and costume designs of major designers. UK-England. 1902-1980. Lang.: Eng.   376

Barbiere di Siviglia, Il
Performance/production
Interview with Dario Fo. Netherlands. Italy. 1987. Lang.: Dut. 3814

Barbieri, Niccolò
Plays/librettos/scripts
Essay on *L'Inavvertito (The Unperceived)* by Niccolò Barbieri. Italy. 1629. Lang.: Ita.   3317

Bardsley, Julia
Performance/production
Collection of newspaper reviews by London theatre critics. UK. 1987. Lang.: Eng.   2031

Collection of newspaper reviews by London theatre critics. UK-England. 1986. Lang.: Eng.   2144

Barezzi, Margherita
Plays/librettos/scripts
Impact of Giuseppina Strepponi Verdi on her husband's creativity. Italy: Milan. 1836-1901. Lang.: Eng.   3927

Barillet, Pierre
Performance/production
István Kazán directs *Fleur de cactus (Cactus Flower)* at Vidám Színpad as *A kaktusz virága*. Hungary: Budapest. 1987. Lang.: Hun.   3629

Barker, Clive
Performance/production
Collection of newspaper reviews by London theatre critics. UK-England: London. 1986. Lang.: Eng.   2069

Barker, Howard
Performance/production
Interview with actress Tanja Jacobs. Canada: Toronto, ON. 1987. Lang.: Eng.   727

Barkworth, Peter
Performance/production
Collection of newspaper reviews by London theatre critics. UK-England. 1987. Lang.: Eng.   2033

Collection of newspaper reviews by London theatre critics. UK-England: London. 1987. Lang.: Eng.   2182

Barlow, Curtis
Relation to other fields
Pros and cons of free trade with respect to the performing arts. Canada. USA. 1986. Lang.: Eng.   1220

Barlow, Patrick
Performance/production
Collection of newspaper reviews by London theatre critics. UK-England: London. 1987. Lang.: Eng.   2200

Barnes, Ben
Performance/production
TEAM, an educational theatre company. Ireland: Dublin. 1984-1987. Lang.: Eng.   818

Barnes, Djuna
Performance/production
Directorial style of Claude Régy. France. 1955-1987. Lang.: Fre.   1762

Barnes, Peter
Performance/production
Collection of newspaper reviews by London theatre critics. UK-England: London. 1986. Lang.: Eng.   2164

Collection of newspaper reviews by London theatre critics. UK-England: London. 1987. Lang.: Eng.   2252

Plays/librettos/scripts
Political use of traditional comic structure by contemporary playwrights. UK-England. 1970-1987. Lang.: Eng.   2762

Comparison of Peter Barnes's *Actors* to Lope de Vega's *Lo Fingido Verdadero (The Feigned Truth)*. UK-England: London. Spain: Madrid. 1983. Lang.: Eng.   2769

Red Noses as Peter Barnes's response to Shaw's *Saint Joan*. UK-England. 1924-1985. Lang.: Eng.   2770

Interview with playwright Peter Barnes. UK-England. USA. 1987. Lang.: Eng.   2818

Barnett, Ian
Performance/production
Collection of newspaper reviews by London theatre critics. UK-England: London. 1986. Lang.: Eng.   2041

Barnum
Design/technology
Design problems of simulating a circus for *Barnum*. USA: Memphis, TN. 1986. Lang.: Eng.   3621

Rigging special circus effects for *Barnum*. USA. 1986. Lang.: Eng.   3622

Barnum and Bailey Circus (Sarasota, FL)
SEE ALSO
Ringling Brothers and Barnum & Bailey Circus.

Barnum, Phineas Taylor
Design/technology
Design problems of simulating a circus for *Barnum*. USA: Memphis, TN. 1986. Lang.: Eng.   3621

Baron, Carlos
Plays/librettos/scripts
Influences of Spanish-language theatre on Chicano theatre. USA. 1598-1983. Lang.: Eng.   2874

Baroque theatre
SEE ALSO
Geographical-Chronological Index under: Europe and other European countries, 1594-1702.

Theory/criticism
Functions of comedy in the seventeenth century. Spain. 1604-1690. Lang.: Spa.   3058

Barr, Larry
Institutions
Astoria Studios' restoration to operating film studio. USA: Queens, NY. 1920-1982. Lang.: Eng.   3140

Barrault, Jean-Louis
Performance/production
Influence of *nō* theatre on director Jean-Louis Barrault and his colleagues. France. 1910-1982. Lang.: Eng.   1498

Development of mime, pantomime and its related movements. France: Paris. UK-England. USA: New York, NY. 1980-1982. Lang.: Eng.   3223

Theory/criticism
Reconstruction of Shakespeare in performance. USA. 1987. Lang.: Eng.   1358

Barrett, Lawrence
Theory/criticism
Actor Lawrence Barrett and the genteel tradition in acting. USA. 1870-1890. Lang.: Eng.   3069

Barrett, Wilson
Performance/production
British theatrical touring companies. UK-England. North America. Australia. 1870-1929. Lang.: Eng.   2280

Barrie, J.M.
Performance/production
Collection of newspaper reviews by London theatre critics. UK-England: London. 1987. Lang.: Eng.   2266

Barrie, James M.
Performance/production
Collection of newspaper reviews by London theatre critics. UK-England: London. 1987. Lang.: Eng.   2236

Barriero, Juan José
Plays/librettos/scripts
Comparison of the plays *Todo sucede en una noche (It All Happens in One Night)* and *La rosa del tiempo (The Rose of Time)*. Mexico: Mexico City. 1987. Lang.: Spa.   2698

Barrington, Rutland
Plays/librettos/scripts
W.S. Gilbert's contribution to the development of the musical play. England. 1836-1911. Lang.: Eng.   3670

Barry of Ballymore
Plays/librettos/scripts
Analysis of the plays and songs of Irish-American musical theatre star Chauncey Olcott. USA. 1893-1918. Lang.: Eng.   3671

Barry, Philip
Performance/production
Collection of newspaper reviews by London theatre critics. UK-England: London. 1987. Lang.: Eng.   2187

Bart, Lionel
Performance/production
György Korcsmáros directs Lionel Bart's *Oliver* at Arany János Theatre. Hungary: Budapest. 1986. Lang.: Hun. 3631

Performances of *Oliver* staged by György Korcsmáros, Antol Rencz and Imre Halasi. Hungary: Budapest, Békéscsaba, Zalaegerszeg. 1986. Hun. 3632

Bartered Bride, The
SEE
Prodana Nevesla.

Barthes, Roland
Performance/production
Directing as guiding actors, not imposing a subjective interpretation. France. 1987. Lang.: Fre. 784

Evolution of directing toward working closely with actors. France. 1987. Lang.: Fre. 793

Directing and the desire to communicate. France. 1987. Lang.: Fre. 1759

Bartholomew Fair
Design/technology
Review of *Bartholomew Fair* and *A Midsummer Night's Dream.* UK-England: London. 1987. Lang.: Eng. 1598

Performance/production
Collection of newspaper reviews by London theatre critics. UK-England: London. 1987. Lang.: Eng. 2252

Bartlett, Neil
Performance/production
Collection of newspaper reviews by London theatre critics. UK-England: London. 1987. Lang.: Eng. 2222

Bartlett, Ruth Dunlap
Performance/production
Collection of newspaper reviews by London theatre critics. UK-England: London. 1987. Lang.: Eng. 2217

Barton, John
Performance/production
Collection of newspaper reviews by London theatre critics. UK-England: London. 1987. Lang.: Eng. 2264

Barton, Samuel P.
Institutions
Members of Negro Ensemble Company, New Federal Theatre and American Place Theatre on artistic agendas. USA: New York, NY. 1987. Lang.: Eng. 592

Bartoševič, A.
Relation to other fields
Theatre critics discuss political issues. USSR. 1980-1987. Lang.: Rus. 1293

Soviet critics and playwrights on international cultural tics. USSR. 1980-1987. Lang.: Rus. 1294

Bartra, Agustí
Basic theatrical documents
Study of the poetic, narrative and theatrical work of Agustí Bartra, edition of complete works, vol. 4. Spain-Catalonia. Mexico. 1937-1982. Lang.: Cat. 1571

Baruti, Osoyande
Institutions
The Theatre of Universal Images and its upcoming season. USA: Newark, NJ, New York, NY. 1981-1987. Lang.: Eng. 1665

Bascetta, Howard
Institutions
Operations of the Saskatoon Opera Association. Canada: Saskatoon, SK. 1978-1987. Lang.: Eng. 3713

Basic theatrical documents
SEE ALSO
Classed Entries.

Basistjuk, Ol'ga
Performance/production
Ol'ga Basistjuk, soloist of Kiev Opera Theatre. USSR: Kiev. 1980-1987. Lang.: Rus. 3885

Baskin, Irene
Performance/production
Life and work of Anatolij Efros. USSR: Moscow. 1983-1987. Lang.: Eng. 1038

Bateman, Kate
Performance/production
Carte-de-visite actors' photographs preserve acting styles. UK-England. France. USA. 1850-1920. Lang.: Eng. 916

Bates, Alan
Performance/production
Comparison and review of *Melon, Breaking the Code, Alan Turing: The Secret War* and *My Sister in This House.* UK-England: London. 1987. Lang.: Eng. 2285

Bath, Michael
Performance/production
Collection of newspaper reviews by London theatre critics. UK-England: London. 1987. Lang.: Eng. 2252

Batiste, Jaume
Performance/production
Collection of theatre reviews by Xavier Fàbregas. Spain-Catalonia. 1969-1972. Lang.: Cat. 2010

Battersea Arts Center (London)
Performance/production
Collection of newspaper reviews by London theatre critics. UK-England: London. 1987. Lang.: Eng. 2215

Battersea Arts Centre (London)
Performance/production
Collection of newspaper reviews by London theatre critics. UK-England: London. 1986. Lang.: Eng. 2071

Collection of newspaper reviews by London theatre critics. UK-England: London. 1986. Lang.: Eng. 2083

Collection of newspaper reviews by London theatre critics. UK-England: London. 1987. Lang.: Eng. 2225

Battersea Latchmere Theatre
SEE
Latchmere Theatre (London).

Batz, Michael
Performance/production
Collection of newspaper reviews by London theatre critics. UK-England: London. 1986. Lang.: Eng. 2158

Collection of newspaper reviews by London theatre critics. UK-England: London. 1987. Lang.: Eng. 2209

Bausch, Pina
Performance/production
Overview of performing artists that toured Japan. Japan: Tokyo. 1986. Lang.: Jap. 844

Development of dance. Germany: Berlin. 1920-1986. Lang.: Ger. 1407

New European choreographers and their development of new images. France: Paris. UK-England: London. South Africa, Republic of. 1987. Lang.: Eng. 1468

Bavarian State Opera
SEE
Bayerische Staatsoper im Nationaltheater.

Bawden, Nina
Institutions
Forms of teaching drama in schools and its role in communication skills. UK-England. 1980. Lang.: Eng. 1646

Bax, Girolamo
Plays/librettos/scripts
Plays of Antonio Monetta, Pietro Suscio and Girolamo Bax. Italy. 1600-1900. Lang.: Ita. 2669

Bay at Nice, The
Performance/production
Collection of newspaper reviews by London theatre critics. UK-England: London. 1986. Lang.: Eng. 2172

Bayen, Bruno
Performance/production
Directing as textual interpretation, relating performance to text. France. 1987. Lang.: Fre. 1768

Bayerisches Staatsschauspielhaus (Munich)
Institutions
Seven productions chosen for Theatertreffen '86. Germany: Berlin. 1986. Lang.: Eng. 1617

Bayfront Center (St. Petersburg, FL)
Performance spaces
Renovations at the Bayfront Center. USA: St. Petersburg, FL. 1960-1987. Lang.: Eng. 700

Bayreuth Festspiele (Bayreuth)
Administration
Filming Wagner's *Der Ring des Nibelungen* at Bayreuth. Germany, West: Bayreuth. Germany, West: Munich. 1980. Lang.: Eng. 3680

BDT
SEE
Bolšoj Dramatičeskij Teat'r.

Be Good Till Death
SEE
Légy jó mindhalálig.

Beached
Performance/production
Collection of newspaper reviews by London theatre critics. UK-England: London. 1987. Lang.: Eng. 2173

Beardsley, Aubrey
Performance/production
Aubrey Beardsley's drawings of actresses: impact on society. UK-England: London. 1890. Lang.: Eng. 2287

Beaumarchais, Pierre Augustin Caron de
Performance/production
Jean-Pierre Vincent directs *Le mariage de Figaro (The Marriage of Figaro)* by Beaumarchais. France: Paris. 1987. Lang.: Fre. 1751

Beaumarchais, Pierre-Augustin Caron de
Plays/librettos/scripts
Compares plays of Enlightenment France, Francophone Africa. Congo: Brazzaville. Cameroon. Benin. France. 1700-1975. Lang.: Eng. 2496

Mozart's *Nozze di Figaro* compared with Beaumarchais source. 1784-1786. Lang.: Eng. 3887

Beaumont, Francis
Theory/criticism
Trollope's writings on Elizabethan and Jacobean drama. UK-England. 1866-1882. Lang.: Eng. 3063

Beaupré, Odette
Performance/production
Interview with Odette Beaupré. Canada. 1987. Lang.: Eng. 3752

Beauty and the Beast
Performance/production
Collection of newspaper reviews by London theatre critics. UK-England: London. 1987. Lang.: Eng. 2194

Repertoire and artistic achievement of the Opera Theatre of St. Louis. USA: St. Louis, MO. 1987. Lang.: Eng. 3840

Beaux' Stratagem, The
Performance/production
Collection of newspaper reviews by London theatre critics. UK-England: London. 1986. Lang.: Eng. 2082

Bécaud, Gilbert
Plays/librettos/scripts
History of the musical *Roza*. USA: Baltimore, MD. 1965-1987. Lang.: Eng. 3675

Becher, Josef
Performance/production
Review of Wagner's *Der Fliegende Holländer* at the Natal Playhouse. South Africa, Republic of: Durban. 1987. Lang.: Eng. 3815

Beckett, Samuel
Performance/production
Pascal Crochet directs Samuel Beckett's *Solo*. Belgium: Brussels. 1987. Lang.: Fre. 1683

Chinese production of Beckett's *Waiting for Godot*. China, People's Republic of: Shanghai. 1986-1987. Lang.: Chi. 1721

Giorgio Strehler as the quintessential director of the century. France. Italy. 1921-1987. Lang.: Eng. 1754

Personal notes of Samuel Beckett, how they illuminate his plays. France. 1969-1984. Lang.: Eng. 1758

Collection of newspaper reviews by London theatre critics. UK-England: London. 1986. Lang.: Eng. 2121

Collection of newspaper reviews by London theatre critics. UK-England: London. 1987. Lang.: Eng. 2226

Three actors discuss their approaches to the characters of Samuel Beckett. USA. 1987. Lang.: Eng. 2343

Billie Whitelaw's performances in the plays of Samuel Beckett. USA. 1981-1984. Lang.: Eng. 2344

Plays/librettos/scripts
Optimistic interpretation of Beckett's *En attendant Godot (Waiting for Godot)*. 1987. Lang.: Eng. 2410

Theme of deconstruction in Samuel Beckett's writings. Europe. 1953-1987. Lang.: Eng. 2563

Iser's reader-response theory and Beckett's *Come and Go*. France. 1968-1987. Lang.: Eng. 2581

Interaction of scenic imagery and narrative in *Ohio Impromptu*. France. 1981-1987. Lang.: Eng. 2586

Beckett links theme of political persecution to voyeurism of the theatrical experience. France. 1982-1987. Lang.: Eng. 2589

Thomas Murphy's *The Morning After Optimism*: comparisons with Beckett, O'Casey. Ireland. 1971. Lang.: Eng. 2641

Analysis of Thomas Murphy's *Bailegangaire*, its connections with the Irish language, story-telling. Ireland: Galway. 1985. Lang.: Eng. 2655

Interpretations of the plays of Ibsen, Čechov and Beckett. Norway. Ireland. Russia. 1987. Lang.: Hun. 2711

Critical methodology for studying Beckett's works. UK-England. 1930-1987. Lang.: Eng. 2814

Study of playwright Samuel Beckett's visual art in his plays. USA. 1970-1980. Lang.: Eng. 2866

Influence of O'Neill and Beckett on Israel Horovitz. USA: Boston, MA. France. 1939-1953. Lang.: Eng. 2873

Nietzschean and psychoanalytical interpretation of Beckett's *Not I*. USA. 1972-1987. Lang.: Eng. 2879

Analysis of text of Samuel Beckett's *Rockaby* as literature and performance piece. USA. 1982. Lang.: Eng. 2884

Reference materials
History of pocket theatre. France: Paris. 1944-1953. Lang.: Eng. 2974

Research/historiography
Overview of Canadian research on twentieth-century Irish drama. Ireland. UK-Ireland. Canada. 1891-1983. Lang.: Eng. 3011

Theory/criticism
Theorist Herbert Blau on modern theatre. 1960-1987. Lang.: Eng. 1306

Comic space from the ancient Greeks to the present. Europe. USA. Greece. 400 B.C.-1987 A.D. Lang.: Eng. 3032

Impact of cinematic technique on plays by Beckett and Duras. France. 1977-1987. Lang.: Eng. 3037

Beckwith, John
Institutions
Need for more Canadian productions of Canadian-composed opera. Canada. 1987. Lang.: Eng. 3718

Bednárik, Jozef
Performance/production
Interview with actor-director Jozef Bednárik. Czechoslovakia: Nitra. 1987. Lang.: Hun. 1727

Beehive
Design/technology
Lighting reviews for some New York productions. USA: New York, NY. 1987. Lang.: Eng. 477

Beer, David
Performance/production
Collection of newspaper reviews by London theatre critics. UK-England: London. 1986. Lang.: Eng. 2065

Beerbohm, Max
Theory/criticism
Keynote address at Northern California Theatre Critics Conference. USA. 1987. Lang.: Eng. 3072

Beeston, Christopher
Performance spaces
Analysis of theatre designs by Inigo Jones and John Webb. England. 1573-1672. Lang.: Eng. 632

Begg, Heather
Basic theatrical documents
Review of video productions of *Tosca* and *Dialogues des Carmélites*. Italy: Verona. Australia: Sydney. 1987. Lang.: Eng. 3692

Beggar's Opera, The
Plays/librettos/scripts
Changing economic conditions created an audience for plays about criminals. England. 1731-1740. Lang.: Eng. 2517

Theme of political satire in plays of Fo and Gay. England: London. Italy. USA. 1728-1984. Lang.: Eng. 2548

Behan, Brendan
Performance/production
Collection of newspaper reviews by London theatre critics. UK-England: London. 1986. Lang.: Eng. 2066

Behavior/psychology, actor
Audience
Critical analysis of Anne-Marie Provencher's *La Tour*. Canada: Montreal, PQ. 1986. Lang.: Eng. 1531

Performance/production
Actor Michajl Čechov's answers to a questionnaire investigating the psychology of acting. USSR: Moscow. 1923. Lang.: Eng. 2376

Behavior/psychology, actor — cont'd

Techniques of the image theatre and effects on actor and audience. Canada. Europe. USA. 1987. Lang.: Eng.   3345

The work of director Robert Lepage. Canada: Montreal, PQ. 1987. Lang.: Eng.   3347

Behavior/psychology, audience
Audience

Repercussions of cinema and television on theatrical language and practice. Europe. 1885-1985. Lang.: Cat.   281

Critical analysis of Anne-Marie Provencher's *La Tour*. Canada: Montreal, PQ. 1986. Lang.: Eng.   1531

Causes and characteristics of the present theatrical crisis. Spain. 1985. Lang.: Spa.   1537

Performance/production

Hillar Liitoja's experimental theatre. Canada. 1987. Lang.: Eng.   739

Techniques of the image theatre and effects on actor and audience. Canada. Europe. USA. 1987. Lang.: Eng.   3345

The work of director Robert Lepage. Canada: Montreal, PQ. 1987. Lang.: Eng.   3347

Behind Heaven
Performance/production

Collection of newspaper reviews by London theatre critics. UK-England: London. 1986. Lang.: Eng.   2070

Behn, Aphra
Performance/production

Collection of newspaper reviews by London theatre critics. UK-England: London. 1987. Lang.: Eng.   2264

Behr, Caroline
Performance/production

Collection of newspaper reviews by London theatre critics. UK-England: London. 1986. Lang.: Eng.   2092

Behrns, Elmer F.
Performance spaces

Theatre designed by Elmer F. Behrns. USA: Pekin, IL. 1927-1987. Lang.: Eng.   3146

Beijing opera
SEE ALSO

Chinese opera.

Administration

Management of Beijing Opera. China, People's Republic of: Beijing. 1949-1987. Lang.: Chi.   3426

Basic theatrical documents

Text of *Yu-wang-cheng-gue (A City of Desire)* by Li Hui-min, based on Shakespeare's *Macbeth*. Taiwan. 1986. Lang.: Chi.   3443

Performance/production

Beijing opera actor Ji Ba Wang. China: Beijing. 1937-1948. Lang.: Chi.   3460

The vocal art form of Tarn Shin Peir of the Beijing Opera. China: Beijing. 1847-1917. Lang.: Chi.   3469

Comments on the performances at the Chinese Art Festival. China, People's Republic of: Beijing. 1987. Lang.: Chi.   3501

Attempted reforms of the main aspects of Chinese opera. China, People's Republic of. 1987. Lang.: Chi.   3527

Beijing opera *Yu-wang-cheng-gue (A City of Desire)*, based on Shakespeare's *Macbeth*. Taiwan: Taipei. 1986. Lang.: Chi.   3541

Plays/librettos/scripts

Lost short writings of Beijing opera playwright Tang Xian-Zu. China: Beijing. 1610-1742. Lang.: Chi.   3546

Call for high quality of dramatic texts, especially for Beijing opera. China, People's Republic of. 1987. Lang.: Chi.   3574

Reference materials

Source materials on development of Chinese opera. Taiwan. 1987. Lang.: Chi.   3580

Being at Home with Claude
Basic theatrical documents

Translation of *Being at Home with Claude*. Canada: Montreal, PQ. 1986. Lang.: Eng.   1546

Plays/librettos/scripts

Language and metaphor in plays of René-Daniel Dubois. Canada: Toronto, ON, Montreal, PQ. 1983-1987. Lang.: Eng.   2471

Theme of René-Daniel Dubois's *Being at Home with Claude*. Canada: Quebec, PQ. USA: New York, NY. 1984-1985. Lang.: Eng.   2473

Beirut
Plays/librettos/scripts

Impact of AIDS crisis on the theatre. USA: New York, NY, San Francisco, CA. 1987. Lang.: Eng.   2881

Beissel, Henry
Plays/librettos/scripts

New Canadian drama: non-realistic, anti-naturalistic. Canada. 1983-1984. Lang.: Eng.   2482

Béjart, Maurice
Performance/production

Development of dance. Germany: Berlin. 1920-1986. Lang.: Ger.   1407

Choreographer Maurice Béjart's creative principles. France. 1927-1987. Lang.: Rus.   1435

Bekannte Gesichter, Gemischte Gefühle (Known Faces, Mixed Feelings)
Basic theatrical documents

Catalan translation of *Bekannte Gesichter, Gemischte Gefühle (Known Faces, Mixed Feelings)* by Botho Strauss. Germany. 1944-1978. Lang.: Cat.   1557

Békés, András
Performance/production

Reviews of *Rigoletto*, Lloyd Webber's *Requiem*, *Les Misérables* and the Hungarian Mass of the Tolcsvays. Hungary: Szeged. 1987. Lang.: Hun.   3400

Review of performances at an assembly of opera ensembles. Hungary: Szeged. 1987. Lang.: Hun.   3796

András Békés directs Rossini's *La Cenerentola* at Szentendrei Teátrum under the title *Hamupipőke*. Hungary: Szentendre. 1987. Lang.: Hun.   3798

Békés, Pál
Performance/production

Péter Huszti directs *A női partőrség szeme láttára (In Sight of the Spar)* by Pál Békés at Madách Szinház Chamber Theatre. Hungary: Budapest. 1987. Lang.: Hun.   1873

Péter Huszti directs *A női partőrség szeme láttára (In Sight of the Spar)* by Pál Békés at Madách Chamber Theatre. Hungary: Budapest. 1987. Lang.: Hun.   1924

Bekker, Rien
Design/technology

Interview with costume designer Rien Bekkers. Netherlands. 1987. Lang.: Dut.   357

Bektonov, Dvora
Institutions

Interview with dancer Dvora Bektonov on her work and her father's acting. Israel: Tel Aviv. USSR: Moscow. 1922-1987. Lang.: Heb.   1621

Bektonov, Joshua
Institutions

Interview with dancer Dvora Bektonov on her work and her father's acting. Israel: Tel Aviv. USSR: Moscow. 1922-1987. Lang.: Heb.   1621

Belasco Theatre (New York, NY)
Performance spaces

Broadway theatres given landmark status. USA: New York, NY. 1982. Lang.: Eng.   692

Belasco, David
Performance/production

Influence of a director's initial impressions of a text on a production. Lang.: Eng.   1678

Relationship between motion pictures and realistic theatrical productions. UK-England: London. USA: Hollywood, CA, New York, NY. 1895-1915. Lang.: Eng.   3163

Beljaković, Valerij R.
Performance/production

Valerij Beljaković, director, Teat'r-studija na Jugo-Zapade. USSR: Moscow. 1980-1987. Lang.: Rus.   1087

Bell, Daniel
Plays/librettos/scripts

Research for *An American Journey* produced by Milwaukee Repertory. USA: Milwaukee, WI. 1978-1987. Lang.: Eng.   2862

Bell, Jeremy
Performance/production

Collection of newspaper reviews by London theatre critics. UK-England: London. 1986. Lang.: Eng.   2093

Collection of newspaper reviews by London theatre critics. UK-England: London. 1987. Lang.: Eng.   2173

Collection of newspaper reviews by London theatre critics. UK-England: London. 1987. Lang.: Eng.   2223

Collection of newspaper reviews by London theatre critics. UK-England: London. 1987. Lang.: Eng.   2252

Bell, Sylvia
Plays/librettos/scripts
Research for *An American Journey* produced by Milwaukee
Repertory. USA: Milwaukee, WI. 1978-1987. Lang.: Eng.   2862

Bella addormentata, La (Sleeping Beauty)
Performance/production
Collaboration of actor-director Virgilio Talli with playwright Pier
Maria Rosso di San Secondo. Italy. 1917-1920. Lang.: Ita.   835

Bellefeuille, Robert
Performance/production
Personnel associated with production of Lepage's *La Trilogie des
dragons*. Canada. 1987. Lang.: Fre.   1713

Belles-Soeurs, Les
Basic theatrical documents
German translation of Tremblay's *Les Belles-Soeurs*. Canada:
Quebec, PQ. Germany. 1987. Lang.: Ger.   1549

Bellgrave, Cynthia
Performance/production
Lillias White and her performance in the musical *Dreamgirls*. USA:
New York, NY. 1960-1987.   3641

Bellini, Vincenzo
Performance/production
Reprint of Richard Wagner's views on *bel canto*, Bellini. Italy. 1837.
Lang.: Swe.   3799

Bellon, Loleh
Performance/production
Collection of newspaper reviews by London theatre critics. UK-
England: London. 1987. Lang.: Eng.   2256

Bells Are Ringing
Performance/production
Collection of newspaper reviews by London theatre critics. UK-
England: London. 1987. Lang.: Eng.   2228
Collection of newspaper reviews by London theatre critics. UK-
England: London. 1987. Lang.: Eng.   2235

Belushi, John
Institutions
Second City improvisational comedy troupe. USA: Chicago, IL.
Canada: Toronto, ON. 1959-1987. Lang.: Eng.   605

Belyj, Andrej (Bugaev, Boris Nikolejevič)
Basic theatrical documents
Russian symbolist plays and essays. USSR. 1880-1986. Lang.: Eng.
    1584

Bemba, Sylvan
Plays/librettos/scripts
Compares plays of Enlightenment France, Francophone Africa.
Congo: Brazzaville. Cameroon. Benin. France. 1700-1975. Lang.: Eng.
    2496

Bemutató Színpad (Dunaújváros)
Performance/production
Reviews of Wilson's *Talley's Folly* staged by András Bálint and
Bond's *The Fool* staged by László Salamon Suba. Hungary:
Dunaújváros, Nyíregyháza. 1986. Lang.: Hun.   1902

Bencze, Zsuzsa
Performance/production
Analysis of *Kék róka (The Silver Fox)* by Ferenc Herczeg compares
Zsuzsa Bencze's staging with previous productions. Hungary:
Budapest. 1986. Lang.: Hun.   1808

Bene, Carmelo
Institutions
History of new and experimental theatre companies. Europe. North
America. 1947-1970. Lang.: Ita.   529

Performance/production
Carmelo Bene's production of *Otello/Secondo*. Italy: Florence. 1985.
Lang.: Eng.   823

Plays/librettos/scripts
Carmelo Bene's *Il Lorenzaccio*. Italy. 1986. Lang.: Ita.   1130

Benedetti, Robert
Performance/production
Directors' Colloquium: individual directorial techniques. Canada:
Calgary, AB. 1987. Lang.: Eng.   743
The Directors Colloquium: director/playwright relationship. Canada:
Calgary, AB. 1987. Lang.: Eng.   747

Benet i Jornet, Josep M.
Performance/production
Collection of theatre reviews by Xavier Fàbregas. Spain-Catalonia.
1969-1972. Lang.: Cat.   2010

Benini, Ferruccio
Plays/librettos/scripts
Influence of playwright Ferruccio Benini. Italy: Venice. 1870-1929.
Lang.: Ita.   2675

Benison, Ben
Performance/production
Collection of newspaper reviews by London theatre critics. UK-
England: London. 1986. Lang.: Eng.   2041
Collection of newspaper reviews by London theatre critics. UK-
England: London. 1987. Lang.: Eng.   2194

Benjamin, Walter
Theory/criticism
Critic Walter Benjamin's comparison of representation in Spanish
baroque theatre and German plays. Germany. 1916-1982. Lang.:
Eng.   3041

Benmussa, Simone
Performance/production
Collection of newspaper reviews by London theatre critics. UK-
England: London. 1987. Lang.: Eng.   2177

Bennett, Alan
Performance/production
Collection of newspaper reviews by London theatre critics. UK-
England: London. 1986. Lang.: Eng.   2167

Bennett, Colin
Plays/librettos/scripts
Avoidance of political themes in drama of Northern Ireland. UK-
Ireland. 1979-1987. Lang.: Eng.   2830

Bennett, Michael
Performance/production
Short history of *A Chorus Line*. USA: New York, NY. 1975-1987.
Lang.: Eng.   941
History and review of 1967 musical *Henry, Sweet Henry*. USA: New
York, NY. 1967. Lang.: Eng.   3642

Benois, Alexandre
Design/technology
Set and costume designs of major designers. UK-England. 1902-
1980. Lang.: Eng.   376

Benstock, Bernard
Relation to other fields
Theatrical themes and the class issue in the work of Irish
playwrights. Ireland. 1900-1987. Lang.: Eng.   2994

Bensusan, Inez
Performance/production
Collection of newspaper reviews by London theatre critics. UK-
England: London. 1986. Lang.: Eng.   2140

Bentley-Fisher, Tom
Institutions
Analysis of co-productions between Saskatoon theatre companies.
Canada: Saskatoon, SK. 1987. Lang.: Eng.   518

Bentley, Eric
Performance/production
Interview with Eric Bentley, director of *La Casa de Bernarda Alba*
at the Abbey. Ireland: Dublin. 1900-1985. Lang.: Eng.   1934
Collection of newspaper reviews by London theatre critics. UK-
England: London. 1986. Lang.: Eng   2061

Theory/criticism
The language of theatrical criticism. USA: New York, NY. 1917-
1985. Lang.: Eng.   1367
Speech praising work of critic Eric Bentley. USA. 1986. Lang.: Eng.
    1368
The work and writings of theatre critics Eric Bentley and Gordon
Rogoff. USA. 1946-1987. Lang.: Eng.   3071

Berényi, Gábor
Performance/production
Andor Gábor's *Dollárpapa (Dollar Daddy)* directed by Gábor
Berényi. Hungary: Budapest. 1987. Lang.: Hun.   1817

Berg, Alban
Performance/production
Stage history of Alban Berg's opera *Lulu*. Austria. France: Paris.
1937-1979. Lang.: Swe.   3743
American premiere of Alban Berg's *Wozzeck*. USA: New York, NY.
1931. Lang.: Eng.   3841
Jurij Liubimov of Taganka Theatre directs *Lulu* in Chicago. USSR:
Moscow. USA: Chicago, IL. 1987. Lang.: Eng.   3874

Plays/librettos/scripts
Adaptation of literary works to opera. 1893-1987. Lang.: Eng.   3890

Bessho, Bunsaku
  Performance/production
    Analysis of four Tokyo productions. Japan: Tokyo. 1987. Lang.: Jap.
    1957
Besson, Benno
  Performance/production
    Benno Besson directs Molière's *Dom Juan*. Switzerland: Geneva.
    1987. Lang.: Fre.   2029
Best Years of Your Life, The
  Performance/production
    Collection of newspaper reviews by London theatre critics. UK-
    England: London. 1987. Lang.: Eng.   2266
Besy (Possessed, The)
  Performance/production
    Ördögök (The Devils), based on Dostojévskij novel, directed by
    Tamás Ascher. Hungary: Budapest. 1986. Lang.: Hun.   1891
Bet Noir
  Performance/production
    Collection of newspaper reviews by London theatre critics. UK-
    England: London. 1987. Lang.: Eng.   2252
Betrayal
  Plays/librettos/scripts
    Interpreting Harold Pinter's dramas through focus on his play
    structures. UK-England. 1958-1987. Lang.: Eng.   2815
Betrayed
  SEE
    Vendidas.
Betrothal, A
  Performance/production
    Collection of newspaper reviews by London theatre critics. UK-
    England: London. 1986. Lang.: Eng.   2170
Betsuyaku, Minoru
  Performance/production
    Four Tokyo productions in light of ideas of Betsuyaku Minoru.
    Japan: Tokyo. 1987. Lang.: Jap.   1950
    Focus on several Tokyo productions. Japan: Tokyo. 1960-1987.
    Lang.: Jap.   1955
    Six plays of the Tokyo season, focus on director Betsuyaku Minoru.
    Japan: Tokyo. 1986. Lang.: Jap.   1966
  Plays/librettos/scripts
    Contemporary Japanese plays about crime. Japan: Tokyo. 1986.
    Lang.: Jap.   2681
    Plays about child suicide in Japan. Japan: Tokyo. 1986. Lang.: Jap.
    2683
Betterton, Thomas
  Performance/production
    Acting styles on English stages. UK-England. 1740-1760. Lang.: Eng.
    2304
  Plays/librettos/scripts
    Venice Preserv'd: impact of Betterton's acting style on Otway.
    England. 1675-1683. Lang.: Eng.   2527
Between East and West
  Performance/production
    Collection of newspaper reviews by London theatre critics. UK-
    England. 1987. Lang.: Eng.   2263
Between the Devil and the Deep Blue Sea
  Performance/production
    Collection of newspaper reviews by London theatre critics. UK-
    England: London. 1986. Lang.: Eng.   2165
Between Two Women
  SEE
    Fausse suivante, La.
Beutov, V.
  Performance/production
    Two productions of *Misterija-Buff (Mystery-Bouffe)* by Majakovskij.
    USSR. 1918-1921. Lang.: Rus.   2388
Beuys, Joseph
  Performance spaces
    Performance art and the commercial gallery world. UK-England.
    1987. Lang.: Eng.   3344
Beyaz'i, Bahram
  Basic theatrical documents
    Translation of five contemporary Persian plays. Iran. 1987. Lang.:
    Eng.   1558
Beyond Reasonable Doubt
  Performance/production
    Collection of newspaper reviews by London theatre critics. UK-
    England: London. 1987. Lang.: Eng.   2251

Collection of newspaper reviews by London theatre critics. UK-
England: London. 1987. Lang.: Eng.   2275
Beyond the Horizon
  Plays/librettos/scripts
    Compares tragedies of Sophocles and Euripides with those of
    Eugene O'Neill. 1918-1946. Lang.: Eng.   2409
Bhangra Dancer, The
  Performance/production
    Collection of newspaper reviews by London theatre critics. UK-
    England: London. 1987. Lang.: Eng.   2185
Bhasa
  Performance/production
    Collection of newspaper reviews by London theatre critics. UK-
    England: London. 1986. Lang.: Eng.   2143
Bhavai
  Performance/production
    Collection of newspaper reviews by London theatre critics. UK-
    England: London. 1986. Lang.: Eng.   2038
Białystock Puppet Theatre (Białystock)
  Performance/production
    Poland's puppet theatre. Poland: Wrocław, Białystock. Austria:
    Mistelbach. 1979-1987. Lang.: Eng, Fre.   4006
Bibliographies
  Basic theatrical documents
    German translation of Tremblay's *Les Belles-Soeurs*. Canada:
    Quebec, PQ. Germany. 1987. Lang.: Ger.   1549
  Institutions
    Tandem database system used by the Deutsches Theatermuseum.
    Germany, West: Munich. 1987. Lang.: Eng.   533
  Performance/production
    Yearbook of Swiss theatrical activity, with bibliography. Switzerland.
    1987-1988. Lang.: Fre, Ger, Ita.   892
    Bibliography of Soviet Latvian actors. USSR. 1987. Lang.: Rus. 1005
    Books written about female impersonators in American theatre. USA.
    1860-1927. Lang.: Eng.   2348
    Bibliographic index of Moldavian drama. USSR. 1917-1960. Lang.:
    Rus.   2372
  Plays/librettos/scripts
    An annual bibliography of works by and about Harold Pinter. UK-
    England. USA. 1986-1987. Lang.: Eng.   1160
    Annotated bibliography of children's plays published in English.
    1780-1855. Lang.: Eng.   2423
    Bibliography of playwright Ronald Ribman's works, interviews,
    criticisms, reviews. USA. 1987. Lang.: Eng.   2859
    Chronological listing of John Guare's plays, bibliography, list of
    reviews. USA. 1938-1987. Lang.: Eng.   2871
    Annotated bibliography of Labor plays. USA. 1930-1940. Lang.:
    Eng.   2875
  Reference materials
    Commentary on scholarship and criticism. 1986. Lang.: Eng.   1193
    Bibliography of Polish theatre magazines. Poland. 1758-1950. Lang.:
    Pol.   1208
    Bibliography of texts, reviews, and criticism of German-speaking
    Swiss theatrical activity. Switzerland. 1987. Lang.: Ger.   1212
    International Shakespeare bibliography. England. 1550-1985. Lang.:
    Ger, Eng, Fre, Spa, Ita, Rus.   2973
Bicat, Nick
  Performance/production
    Collection of newspaper reviews by New York theatre critics. USA:
    New York, NY. 1987. Lang.: Eng.   2312
Bicharo
  Performance/production
    Collection of newspaper reviews by London theatre critics. UK-
    England: London. 1987. Lang.: Eng.   2230
Biches, Les
  Performance/production
    Career of choreographer/dancer Bronislava Nižinska. France. USA.
    1891-1930. Lang.: Eng.   1436
Bichols, Dandy
  Performance/production
    Review of the BBC telecast of *The Birthday Party* by Harold Pinter.
    UK-England. 1987. Lang.: Eng.   3206
Biddle, Livingston
  Relation to other fields
    Historical look at the National Endowment for the Arts. USA. 1977-
    1981. Lang.: Eng.   1280

Bidermann und die Brandstifte (Fire Raisers, The)
Performance/production
Collection of newspaper reviews by London theatre critics. UK-England: London. 1987. Lang.: Eng.   2217
Bielski, Nella
Performance/production
Collection of newspaper reviews by London theatre critics. UK-England: London. 1987. Lang.: Eng.   2255
Bien, Peter
Plays/librettos/scripts
Imagistic versus realistic drama in contemporary Greek plays. Greece. 1940-1987. Lang.: Eng.   2621
Big Knife, The
Performance/production
Collection of newspaper reviews by London theatre critics. UK-England: London. 1987. Lang.: Eng.   2250
Big River
Administration
Influence of TV ads on success of Broadway plays. USA: New York, NY. 1984-1987. Lang.: Eng.   179
Biggins, Christopher
Performance/production
Collection of newspaper reviews by London theatre critics. UK-England: London. 1986. Lang.: Eng.   2119
Bijers Sunbird, The
Performance/production
Collection of newspaper reviews by London theatre critics. UK-England: London. 1986. Lang.: Eng.   2037
Bikel, Theodore
Administration
Ellen Burstyn succeeds Theodore Bikel as Actors' Equity president. USA: New York, NY. 1982. Lang.: Eng.   98
Contracts, actors and union negotiations. USA. 1986. Lang.: Eng.   235

Relation to other fields
International Federation of Actors discusses actors' conditions. France: Paris. 1982. Lang.: Eng.   1235
Biko, Stephen
Performance/production
Matsemela Manaka's play *Pula* and its anti-apartheid expressions. South Africa, Republic of: Soweto. 1969-1984. Lang.: Eng.   883
Bill, Stephen
Performance/production
Collection of newspaper reviews by London theatre critics. UK-England: London. 1987. Lang.: Eng.   2277
Billedstofteater (Copenhagen)
Performance/production
Photo essay on theatre company Billedstofteater. Denmark. 1977-1982. Lang.: Eng.   1730
Billington, Ken
Design/technology
Design aspects of *The Glory of Easter*: computerized lighting, lasers and pyrotechnics. USA. 1982. Lang.: Eng.   387
Influence of theatrical technology on restaurant design. USA. 1980-1985. Lang.: Eng.   451
Current Broadway shows and their lighting designers. USA: New York, NY. 1987. Lang.: Eng.   460
Billington, Kevin
Performance/production
Reviews of Pinter's *The Lover* and *A Slight Ache*. UK-England: London. 1987. Lang.: Eng.   901
Collection of newspaper reviews by London theatre critics. UK-England: London. 1987. Lang.: Eng.   2246
Billy Bishop Goes to War
Institutions
A history of the Charlottetown Festival. Canada: Charlottetown, PE. 1965-1987. Lang.: Eng.   505
Biloxi Blues
Performance/production
Four Tokyo productions in light of ideas of Betsuyaku Minoru. Japan: Tokyo. 1987. Lang.: Jap.   1950
Discussion of four Tokyo productions. Japan: Tokyo. 1944-1987. Lang.: Jap.   1963
Biltmore Theatre (New York, NY)
Performance spaces
Broadway theatres given landmark status. USA: New York, NY. 1982. Lang.: Eng.   692

Bing, Sir Rudolph
Administration
Career of Sir Rudolph Bing, challenges of managing the Metropolitan Opera. USA: New York, NY. 1950-1972. Lang.: Eng.   3682
Bingo
Plays/librettos/scripts
Societal dependence in Bond's *Bingo*. 1975. Lang.: Eng.   2422
Binnie, Jean
Performance/production
Collection of newspaper reviews by London theatre critics. UK-England: London. 1987. Lang.: Eng.   2241
Biographies
Performance/production
Resources on Chinese opera. China, People's Republic of. 1922-1987. Lang.: Chi.   3520
Birch, Michael
Performance/production
Collection of newspaper reviews by London theatre critics. UK-England: London. 1987. Lang.: Eng.   2239
Birkenhead, Susan
Performance/production
Collection of newspaper reviews by London theatre critics. UK-England: London. 1986. Lang.: Eng.   2044
Collection of newspaper reviews by London theatre critics. UK-England: London. 1987. Lang.: Eng.   2198
Bíró, Lajos
Performance/production
Season openings at Petőfi Theatre, including Lengyel's *A nagy fejedelem (The Great Prince)* and Bíró's *A rablólovag (The Gallant Kidnapper)*. Hungary: Veszprém. 1987. Lang.: Hun.   1820
Biros, Jim
Performance/production
The Directors Colloquium: director/playwright relationship. Canada: Calgary, AB. 1987. Lang.: Eng.   747
Birth of the Beast
Performance/production
Collection of newspaper reviews by London theatre critics. UK-England: London. 1986. Lang.: Eng.   2139
Birth of Tragedy, The
SEE
Geburt der Tragödie, Die.
Birthday Party, The
Performance/production
Review of the BBC telecast of *The Birthday Party* by Harold Pinter. UK-England. 1987. Lang.: Eng.   3206
Plays/librettos/scripts
Characterizations of stage spaces: examples from Brecht, Pinter, Douglas Turner Ward. UK-England. USA. 1947-1987. Lang.: Eng.   2798
Interpreting Harold Pinter's dramas through focus on his play structures. UK-England. 1958-1987. Lang.: Eng.   2815
Bisebarre, Edouard
Plays/librettos/scripts
Historical context for Tom Taylor's *The Ticket-of-Leave Man*. UK-England. France. 1863.   2801
Bishop, John
Performance/production
Collection of newspaper reviews by New York theatre critics. USA: New York, NY. 1987. Lang.: Eng.   2322
Bitterli, Dieter
Performance/production
Yearly productions of Calderón's *El gran teatro del mundo (The Great Stage of the World)*. Switzerland: Einsiedeln. 1987. Lang.: Ger.   893
Bitva na kopci (Battle on a Hill, A)
Performance/production
Plays of Ladislav Smoček at Činoherní klub. Czechoslovakia: Prague. 1965-1987. Lang.: Cze.   768
Bizet, Georges
Performance/production
Carmen presented at Expo '86. Canada: Vancouver, BC. 1986. Lang.: Eng.   3751
The original production of *Carmen*. France: Paris. 1873-1875. Lang.: Eng.   3773
Background on Metropolitan telecast performances. USA: New York, NY. 1987. Lang.: Eng.   3839

Bizet, Georges — cont'd

Mezzo soprano Risë Stevens. USA: New York, NY. Lang.: Eng.
3856

Imre Kálmán's *Cigányprimás (Sari)* and Bizet's *Carmen* at Kisfaludy Theatre staged by József Bor. Hungary: Győr. 1912-1986. Lang.: Hun.
3959

Plays/librettos/scripts
Mérimée novella, source of Bizet's *Carmen*. France: Paris. 1803-1870. Lang.: Eng.
3903

Operas that contain Indian-related themes and music. India. Europe. 1730-1904. Lang.: Eng.
3914

Opera adaptations for Broadway with African-American artists. USA: New York, NY. 1935-1987. Lang.: Eng.
3932

Bjornson, Bjornstjerne
Plays/librettos/scripts
Theme of stage direction in the work of Scandinavian authors. Sweden. Norway. 1700-1987. Lang.: Ita.
2737

Björnson, Maria
Performance/production
Successful London revival of *Follies* by Stephen Sondheim. UK-England: London. USA: New York, NY. 1987. Lang.: Eng.
3638

Bla pekingeser, Der (Blue Pekingese, The)
Plays/librettos/scripts
Analysis of Kjeld Abell's *Der bla pekingeser (The Blue Pekingese)*. Denmark. 1901-1961. Lang.: Ita.
1113

Black Comedy
Performance/production
Four Tokyo productions in light of ideas of Betsuyaku Minoru. Japan: Tokyo. 1987. Lang.: Jap.
1950

Analysis of four Tokyo productions. Japan: Tokyo. 1987. Lang.: Jap.
1957

Black Design League
Design/technology
Interview with designer Charles McClennahan: Black Design League. USA: New York, NY. USA: Winston-Salem, NC. 1981-1987. Lang.: Eng.
1600

Black Dog
Relation to other fields
Interracial fringe productions: racial, class, sexual politics. South Africa, Republic of. 1984. Lang.: Eng.
2998

Black Flowers
Performance/production
Collection of newspaper reviews by London theatre critics. UK-England: London. 1987. Lang.: Eng.
2205

Black Horizons Theatre (Pittsburgh)
Plays/librettos/scripts
Interview with playwright August Wilson. USA. 1970-1987. Lang.: Eng.
2855

Black Mass
Performance/production
Interview with playwright Amiri Baraka. USA: Newark, NJ, New York, NY. 1965-1969. Lang.: Eng.
2356

Black Rock (Verdun, PQ)
Plays/librettos/scripts
David Fennario's *Joe Beef*. Canada: Montreal, PQ, Verdun, PQ. 1984. Lang.: Eng.
2470

Black theatre
Design/technology
Interview with designer Charles McClennahan: Black Design League. USA: New York, NY. USA: Winston-Salem, NC. 1981-1987. Lang.: Eng.
1600

Career of costumer, dancer, actress Judy Dearing. USA: New York, NY. Africa. 1970-1987. Lang.: Eng.
1601

Institutions
Interview with Elizabeth Clark, director of Temba Theatre Company. UK-England: London. Caribbean. Lang.: Eng.
567

Actors' Equity and Black History Month. USA: New York, NY. 1986. Lang.: Eng.
572

Members of Negro Ensemble Company, New Federal Theatre and American Place Theatre on artistic agendas. USA: New York, NY. 1987. Lang.: Eng.
592

Black community theatre and its decline. USA. 1960-1987. Lang.: Eng.
593

Black theatre as an art and industry. USA: New York, NY. 1915-1987. Lang.: Eng.
600

Debate among Black theatre people whether Black theatre really exists. USA. 1987. Lang.: Eng.
610

The Theatre of Universal Images and its upcoming season. USA: Newark, NJ, New York, NY. 1981-1987. Lang.: Eng.
1665

The formation of the North Carolina Black Repertory Company. USA: Winston-Salem, NC. 1979-1987. Lang.: Eng.
1666

Sherman H. Dudley and the Black vaudeville circuit. USA: Indianapolis, IN, Washington, DC. 1820-1922. Lang.: Eng.
3382

Will Garland and European tour of Negro Operetta Company. UK-England. Finland: Helsinki. Russia. 1905-1917. Lang.: Eng.
3956

Performance/production
Review of August Wilson's play, *Ma Rainey's Black Bottom*. Canada: Toronto, ON. 1987. Lang.: Eng.
737

Matsemela Manaka's play *Pula* and its anti-apartheid expressions. South Africa, Republic of: Soweto. 1969-1984. Lang.: Eng.
883

Ethnic and minority casting opportunities. USA. 1986. Lang.: Eng.
939

The influence of African music on America. USA. 1600-1987. Lang.: Eng.
943

Interview with playwright Amiri Baraka. USA: Newark, NJ, New York, NY. 1965-1969. Lang.: Eng.
2356

The African actor in Africa, Italy and the United States. USA: Brooklyn, NY. Sierra Leone: Freetown. Italy: Rome. 1987. Lang.: Eng.
2362

George C. Wolfe and L. Kenneth Richardson discuss *The Colored Museum*. USA: New York, NY, New Brunswick, NJ. 1987. Lang.: Eng.
2363

Theatre career of photo-journalist Bert Andrews. USA: New York, NY. 1950-1987. Lang.: Eng.
2367

Compositions by Debussy in their relationship to Afro-American music. France: Paris. UK-England: London. 1893-1913. Lang.: Eng.
3384

Southern rural background of blues music. USA. 1800-1985. Lang.: Eng.
3411

Origins of jazz, its evolution in vaudeville. USA: New Orleans, LA, New York, NY, Chicago, IL. Lang.: Eng.
3650

Interview with actor Giancarlo Esposito. USA: New York, NY. 1987. Lang.: Eng.
3654

Plays/librettos/scripts
Life of playwright John O. Killens. USA: New York, NY. 1954-1987. Lang.: Eng.
2836

Korean views of American society based on plays of Howard Sackler, Charles Fuller and Jason Miller. USA. 1969-1982. Lang.: Kor.
2837

Interview with playwright Alice Childress. USA: New York, NY, Baltimore, MD. 1987. Lang.: Eng.
2844

Charles Fuller's *A Soldier's Play*: debate on means of liberation. USA. 1976-1981. Lang.: Eng.
2854

Interview with playwright August Wilson. USA. 1970-1987. Lang.: Eng.
2855

Interview with playwright Leslie Lee. USA: Bryn Mawr, PA, New York, NY. 1987. Lang.: Eng.
2893

Alonzo Lamont's major themes in *That Serious He-Man Ball*. USA: New York, NY. 1987. Lang.: Eng.
2900

Opera adaptations for Broadway with African-American artists. USA: New York, NY. 1935-1987. Lang.: Eng.
3932

Relation to other fields
Interview with poet and activist Haki R. Madhubuti (Don L. Lee). USA: Detroit, MI. Africa. Israel. 1942-1985. Lang.: Eng.
3008

Black, Malcolm
Performance/production
Review of Joanna Glass's *Play Memory*. Canada: Toronto, ON. 1987. Lang.: Eng.
736

Blackburn, Bryan
Performance/production
Collection of newspaper reviews by London theatre critics. UK-England. 1987. Lang.: Eng.
2263

Blackfriars Theatre (London)
Performance/production
Shakespeare and contemporaries: tradition, intertextuality in performance. England. 1607-1987. Lang.: Eng.
1740

New interpretation of Jacobean theatre. England: London. 1596-1633. Lang.: Eng.
1743

Blaha, Lujza
Performance/production
Diaries of singer-actress Lujza Blaha. Hungary. 1862-1905. Lang.: Hun.
1812

Blake, Sydnee
Performance/production
Collection of newspaper reviews by London theatre critics. UK-England: London. 1986. Lang.: Eng.   2117

Blakely, Colin
Performance/production
Review of the BBC telecast of *The Birthday Party* by Harold Pinter. UK-England. 1987. Lang.: Eng.   3206

Blakemore, Michael
Performance/production
Collection of newspaper reviews by London theatre critics. UK-England: London. 1987. Lang.: Eng.   2223

Blaschke, Hanno
Training
Interview with singing master Hanno Blaschke. South Africa, Republic of. 1987. Lang.: Eng.   3951

Blaskó, Péter
Performance/production
Péter Blaskó in the title role of Brecht's *Leben des Galilei (The Life of Galileo)* directed as *Galilei élete* by Imre Csiszár at Miskolc National Theatre. Hungary: Miskolc. 1987. Lang.: Hun.   1839

Blau, Herbert
Theory/criticism
Theorist Herbert Blau on modern theatre. 1960-1987. Lang.: Eng.   1306

Bless the Bride
Performance/production
Collection of newspaper reviews by London theatre critics. UK-England: London. 1987. Lang.: Eng.   2234

Bless Them All
Institutions
A history of the Charlottetown Festival. Canada: Charlottetown, PE. 1965-1987. Lang.: Eng.   505

Bletz, Zacharias
Performance/production
Role of the director in the Lucerne Passion play. Switzerland: Lucerne. 1453-1616. Lang.: Eng.   2030

Bleyhoeffer, Christian
Performance/production
A round-table discussion with stage directors on the principles and methods of working with an ensemble company. Germany, East: Berlin, East. 1983. Lang.: Ger.   1778

Blin, Roger
Theory/criticism
How to maintain an element of risk in theatre. France. 1987. Lang.: Fre.   1331

Blithe Spirit
Design/technology
Lighting reviews for some New York productions. USA: New York, NY. 1987. Lang.: Eng.   472

Performance/production
Collection of newspaper reviews by New York theatre critics. USA: New York, NY. 1987. Lang.: Eng.   2322

Block, Giles
Performance/production
Play scripts as literary texts and as performance texts. UK-England. 1977-1987. Lang.: Eng.   905

Blok, Aleksand'r Aleksandrovič
Basic theatrical documents
Russian symbolist plays and essays. USSR. 1880-1986. Lang.: Eng.   1584

Performance/production
Links between experimental theatre movement and the Russian Futurists. USSR. 1920-1929. Lang.: Rus.   1058

Plays/librettos/scripts
Theatre and dramaturgy of the first Russian revolution. USSR. 1905-1907. Lang.: Rus.   1188

Blokdijk, Tom
Administration
Funding of small theatre groups in the Netherlands. Netherlands. 1987. Lang.: Dut.   33

Blood Knot, The
Plays/librettos/scripts
Cultural predetermination in three Athol Fugard plays. South Africa, Republic of. 1970. Lang.: Eng.   1419

How Athol Fugard's revisions have changed *The Blood Knot*. South Africa, Republic of. 1961-1985. Lang.: Eng.   2725

Blood of Angels
Performance/production
Collection of newspaper reviews by London theatre critics. UK-England: London. 1986. Lang.: Eng.   2059

Blood of Colonel Lamb, The
Plays/librettos/scripts
Interview with playwright John Boyd: influences and plays. UK-Ireland: Belfast. 1930-1985. Lang.: Eng.   2828

Blood Relations
Plays/librettos/scripts
Play within a play in *Blood Relations* by Sharon Pollock. Canada. 1987. Lang.: Eng.   2489

Blood Sports
Plays/librettos/scripts
Depiction of the class struggle in contemporary theatre. USA: New York, NY. 1987. Lang.: Eng.   2915

Bloodgood, Fred Foster
Performance/production
Doc Fred Foster Bloodgood, vaudevillian, who sold medicine to crowds between acts. USA: New York, NY. 1929-1987. Lang.: Eng.   3305

Bloody Poetry
Design/technology
Interview with lighting designer Dennis Parichy. USA: New York, NY. 1986-1987. Lang.: Eng.   428

Bloolips Company (New York, NY)
Performance/production
Collection of newspaper reviews by London theatre critics. UK-England: London. 1987. Lang.: Eng.   2246

Bloomsbury Theatre (London)
Performance/production
Collection of newspaper reviews by London theatre critics. UK-England: London. 1986. Lang.: Eng.   2042

Collection of newspaper reviews by London theatre critics. UK-England: London. 1986. Lang.: Eng.   2080

Collection of newspaper reviews by London theatre critics. UK-England: London. 1986. Lang.: Eng.   2120

Collection of newspaper reviews by London theatre critics. UK-England: London. 1986. Lang.: Eng.   2140

Collection of newspaper reviews by London theatre critics. UK-England: London. 1987. Lang.: Eng.   2215

Collection of newspaper reviews by London theatre critics. UK-England: London. 1987. Lang.: Eng.   2232

Collection of newspaper reviews by London theatre critics. UK-England: London. 1987. Lang.: Eng.   2259

Collection of newspaper reviews by London theatre critics. UK-England: London. 1987. Lang.: Eng.   2275

Blu (Lambert, William Alfred, Jr.)
Design/technology
Study of the work of dance lighting designer Blu. USA: New York, NY. 1987. Lang.: Eng.   1400

Blue Macushla, The
Plays/librettos/scripts
Characters and the gangster movie form in Thomas Murphy's *The Blue Macushla*. Ireland. 1980-1986. Lang.: Eng.   2647

Comic characters and the Book of Job in the plays of Thomas Murphy. Ireland. 1962-1983. Lang.: Eng.   2648

The plays of Thomas Murphy. Ireland: Dublin. 1962-1986. Lang.: Eng.   2650

Blue Window
Plays/librettos/scripts
Collaboration between playwright Craig Lucas and director Norman Rene. USA: New York, NY. 1985-1987. Lang.: Eng.   1183

Collaboration of Craig Lucas and Norman Rene on *Blue Window* and *Three Postcards*. USA. 1987. Lang.: Eng.   1184

Blues
Performance/production
Southern rural background of blues music. USA. 1800-1985. Lang.: Eng.   3411

Blues in the Night
Performance/production
Collection of newspaper reviews by London theatre critics. UK-England: London. 1987. Lang.: Eng.   2216

Collection of newspaper reviews by London theatre critics. UK-England: London. 1987. Lang.: Eng.   2243

Blythe Summer Festival (Blythe, ON)
Plays/librettos/scripts
Playwright Paul Thompson. Canada: Blythe, ON, Toronto, ON. 1963-1983. Lang.: Eng. 2487

Boadella, Albert
Institutions
Analysis of all the productions performed by Els Joglars in their twenty-five years of existence. Spain-Catalonia. 1962-1987. Lang.: Cat. 1634

Boak, Keith
Performance/production
Collection of newspaper reviews by London theatre critics. UK-England: London. 1987. Lang.: Eng. 2230

Boal, Augusto
Performance/production
Teatro Arena de São Paulo's production of *Arena Conta Zumbi*. Brazil: São Paulo. 1965. Lang.: Eng. 1690
Work of actor/director Augusto Boal. Canada: Sydney, NS. 1987. Lang.: Eng. 1694

Theory/criticism
Semiotic production in popular performance. South Africa, Republic of. 1980. Lang.: Eng. 1347

Bobrov, E.
Plays/librettos/scripts
Playwrights discuss problems of one-act play. USSR. 1987. Lang.: Rus. 2935

Bodnár, Sándor
Performance/production
Interview with actor Imre Sinkovits. Hungary: Budapest. 1951-1987. Lang.: Hun. 1835

Body Cell
Performance/production
Collection of newspaper reviews by London theatre critics. UK-England: London. 1986. Lang.: Eng. 2070

Body, Jim
Relation to other fields
Survival of Punch and Judy shows during the Edwardian period. UK-England. 1860-1910. Lang.: Eng. 3998

Bodycount
Performance/production
Collection of newspaper reviews by London theatre critics. UK-England: London. 1987. Lang.: Eng. 2268

Bogart, Anne
Performance/production
Director Anne Bogart's production of *Women and Men: A Big Dance*. USA: New York, NY. 1983. Lang.: Eng. 1418

Bogart, Humphrey
Performance/production
Personal anecdotes and photographs from the making of *The African Queen*. USA: Hollywood, CA. 1950-1951. Lang.: Eng. 3168

Bogdanov, Michael
Performance/production
Collection of newspaper reviews by London theatre critics. UK-England: London. 1987. Lang.: Eng. 2193
Collection of newspaper reviews by London theatre critics. UK-England: London. 1987. Lang.: Eng. 2200
Collection of newspaper reviews by London theatre critics. UK-England: London. 1987. Lang.: Eng. 2272

Bogosian, Eric
Performance/production
Collection of newspaper reviews by New York theatre critics. USA: New York, NY. 1987. Lang.: Eng. 2319

Bogusławski, Wojciech
Performance/production
Poland's puppet theatre. Poland: Wrocław, Białystock. Austria: Mistelbach. 1979-1987. Lang.: Eng, Fre. 4006

Plays/librettos/scripts
Actor-manager Wojciech Bogusławski in life and in György Spiró's play *Az imposztor (The Imposter)*. Poland. Hungary. 1815-1987. Lang.: Pol. 2716

Bohème, La
Performance/production
Opera critic Edouard Hanslick and his opposition to *La Bohème* by Puccini. Austro-Hungarian Empire: Vienna. 1896-1987. Lang.: Eng. 3745
Film versions of Puccini's *La Bohème*, Offenbach's *Tales of Hoffmann*. Europe. North America. 1987. Lang.: Eng. 3767

Background on Lyric Opera radio broadcast performances. USA: Chicago, IL. 1987. Lang.: Eng. 3832
Background on Metropolitan radio broadcast performances. USA: New York, NY. 1987. Lang.: Eng. 3837

Plays/librettos/scripts
Comparison of Puccini's and Leoncavallo's treatments of *La Bohème*. Italy. 1893-1897. Lang.: Swe. 3922
Floral imagery in the operas of Giacomo Puccini. Italy. 1858-1924. Lang.: Eng. 3926

Boito, Arrigo
Plays/librettos/scripts
Making of Verdi's *Otello*. Italy: Milan. 1862-1879. Lang.: Eng. 3917
Analysis and success of Boito's libretto for Verdi's opera *Falstaff*. Italy. 1893. Lang.: Eng. 3923

Bokor, Roland
Performance/production
Premiere performance of new ballet company, Szegedi Balett. Hungary: Szeged. 1987. Lang.: Hun. 1438

Bola de neu (Snowball)
Plays/librettos/scripts
General history of Catalan literature, including theatre. Spain-Catalonia. 1902-1961. Lang.: Cat. 1157

Bolam, Ken
Performance/production
Collection of newspaper reviews by London theatre critics. UK-England: London. 1987. Lang.: Eng. 2194

Bolivar Hall (London)
Performance/production
Collection of newspaper reviews by London theatre critics. UK-England: London. 1987. Lang.: Eng. 2257

Bolshoi (Moscow)
SEE
Bolšoj Teat'r Opery i Baleta Sojuza SSR.

Bolshoi Ballet
SEE
Bolšoj Teat'r Opery i Baleta Sojuza SSR.

Bolshoi Opera
SEE
Bolšoj Teat'r Opery i Baleta Sojuza SSR.

Bolšoj Dramatičeskij Teat'r im. M. Gorkogo (BDT, Leningrad)
Performance/production
Interview with director Georgij Tovstonogov. USSR: Leningrad. 1980-1987. Lang.: Rus. 1034
Bolšoj actor Valerij Ivčenko. USSR: Leningrad. 1980. Lang.: Rus. 1052
Career of actor Kirill Lavrov. USSR: Leningrad. 1980. Lang.: Rus. 1073
Director on training directors. USSR: Leningrad. 1980-1987. Lang.: Rus. 1077
Portrait of director G.A. Tovstonogov. USSR: Leningrad. 1930-1987. Lang.: Eng. 1086
Lenin as a theatrical character. USSR: Leningrad. 1987. Lang.: Rus. 2385

Training
Interview with Georgij Tovstonogov. USA. 1987. Lang.: Eng. 1390

Bolšoj Teat'r Opery i Baleta Sojuza SSR (Moscow)
Performance/production
Moscow Bolšoj dancer Andris Liepa. USSR: Moscow. 1980-1987. Lang.: Rus. 1446
Study of the Moscow Bolšoj Theatre. USSR: Moscow. 1974-1980. Lang.: Rus. 3867

Relation to other fields
Cultural exchange pacts made between the USA and the Soviet Union and China. USA: Washington, DC. USSR: Moscow. China, People's Republic of: Peking. 1987. Lang.: Eng. 1291

Bolt Hole, The
Performance/production
Collection of newspaper reviews by London theatre critics. UK-England: London. 1987. Lang.: Eng. 2257

Bolt-Hole, The
Performance/production
Collection of newspaper reviews by London theatre critics. UK-England: London. 1986. Lang.: Eng. 2076

Bolt, Alan
Performance/production
Community theatre movement after Sandinista war effort. Nicaragua. 1987. Lang.: Eng. 3264

Boulez, Pierre
Performance/production
Stage history of Alban Berg's opera *Lulu*. Austria. France: Paris. 1937-1979. Lang.: Swe.   3743

Bouncers
Performance/production
Interview with director Ron Link. USA: New York, NY. 1987. Lang.: Eng.   963

Collection of newspaper reviews by London theatre critics. UK-England: London. 1986. Lang.: Eng.   2079

Collection of newspaper reviews by New York theatre critics. USA: New York, NY. 1987. Lang.: Eng.   2315

Bourne, Elizabeth
Performance/production
Libel suit against a minstrel. UK-England: Stafford. 1616. Lang.: Eng.   3269

Bouwer, Duncan
Performance/production
Review of *Hello Dolly* in Bloemfontein. South Africa, Republic of: Bloemfontein. 1987. Lang.: Eng.   3635

Bowater, Ian
Performance/production
Collection of newspaper reviews by London theatre critics. UK-England: London. 1987. Lang.: Eng.   2240

Bowie, David
Performance/production
David Bowie's *Glass Spider Tour*. UK-England. 1987. Lang.: Dut.   3270

Bowman, Ned
Design/technology
Third international scene painting seminar at the Mozarteum. Austria: Salzburg. 1986. Lang.: Eng.   300

Bowmer, Angus
Institutions
Six books that discuss the origins and development of different American regional theatres. USA: Cleveland, OH, Los Angeles, CA, Houston, TX, Detroit, MI, Ashland, OR, Montgomery, AL. 1987. Lang.: Eng.   612

Bowne, Alan
Plays/librettos/scripts
Adaptation of Alan Bowne's *Forty Deuce* as stage play and film. USA: New York, NY. Lang.: Eng.   2891

Boyce, Johanna
Performance/produciton
Johanna Boyce's *With Longings to Realize* presented by the Performance Group. USA: New York, NY. 1983. Lang.: Eng.   1478

Performance/production
Five women choreographers and critics discuss conceptions of the female body. USA. 1987. Lang.: Eng.   1416

Boyd, John
Plays/librettos/scripts
Interview with playwright John Boyd: influences and plays. UK-Ireland: Belfast. 1930-1985. Lang.: Eng.   2828

Boyd, Pamela
Basic theatrical documents
Collection of four plays by Canadian women dramatists. Canada. 1987. Lang.: Eng.   1544

Boyle, Wickham
Performance/production
Essays on the future of the theatre. USA: New York, NY. 1970-1987. Lang.: Eng.   955

Boyle, William
Plays/librettos/scripts
Irish Literary Renaissance writers' view of America. Ireland. 1900-1930. Lang.: Eng.   2639

Bozóky, István
Performance/production
Reviews of actors Olga Koós and István Bozóky in *Szabóky Zsigmond Rafael (Zsigmond Rafael Szabóky)* at Játékszín. Hungary: Budapest. 1987. Lang.: Hun.   1914

Brackman, Jacob
Performance/production
Brief Broadway run of *King of Hearts*. USA: New York, NY. 1978-1987. Lang.: Eng.   3643

Bradecki, Tadeusz
Performance/production
The 17th Warsaw theatre conference. Poland: Warsaw. 1987. Lang.: Eng, Fre.   872

Polish theatre. Poland: Warsaw, Cracow, Wrocław. 1980-1987. Lang.: Eng, Fre.   1987

The shape and form of contemporary Polish theatre. Poland: Warsaw. 1981-1987. Lang.: Eng, Fre.   1995

Tadeusz Bradecki, director and playwright. Poland: Cracow. 1977-1987. Lang.: Pol.   1997

Experimental theatre at the Stary in three recent productions. Poland: Cracow. 1987. Lang.: Eng.   1999

Bradwell, Mike
Performance/production
Collection of newspaper reviews by London theatre critics. UK-England: London. 1986. Lang.: Eng.   2147

Collection of newspaper reviews by London theatre critics. UK-England: London. 1987. Lang.: Eng.   2182

Brady, Alice
Performance/production
Philip Moeller's premiere of *Mourning Becomes Electra* by O'Neill. USA: New York, NY. 1931. Lang.: Eng.   2366

Brady, Matthew
Performance/production
Collection of newspaper reviews by London theatre critics. UK-England: London. 1987. Lang.: Eng.   2229

Bragaglia, Anton Giulio
Performance/production
Bragaglia's Theatre of the Independent. Italy: Rome. 1911-1932. Lang.: Ita.   836

Brahm, Otto
Institutions
On audience societies Freie Volksbühne and Neue Freie Volksbühne. Germany: Berlin. 1889-1914. Lang.: Ger.   1616

Performance/production
Reviews of major Berlin performances. Germany: Berlin. 1889-1933. Lang.: Ger.   1772

Brambilla, George
Institutions
Program of opera workshop, Boston Conservatory. USA: Boston, MA. 1973-1983. Lang.: Eng.   3734

Branagh, Kenneth
Administration
Interim report on the Renaissance Theatre Company. UK-England: London. 1987. Lang.: Eng.   54

Performance/production
Collection of newspaper reviews by London theatre critics. UK-England: London. 1986. Lang.: Eng.   2135

Collection of newspaper reviews by London theatre critics. UK-England: London. 1987. Lang.: Eng.   2224

Collection of newspaper reviews by London theatre critics. UK-England: London. 1987. Lang.: Eng.   2225

Collection of newspaper reviews by London theatre critics. UK-England: London. 1987. Lang.: Eng.   2228

Collection of newspaper reviews by London theatre critics. UK-England: London. 1987. Lang.: Eng.   2237

Collection of newspaper reviews by London theatre critics. UK-England: London. 1987. Lang.: Eng.   2271

Brännström, Lena
Institutions
Stockholms Studentteater now welcomes amateur participation. Sweden: Stockholm. 1921-1987. Lang.: Swe.   1638

Brask, Per
Administration
Dramaturgy in Canadian theatre. Canada. USA. Germany. 1980-1987. Lang.: Eng.   1513

Brass, Lorne
Performance/production
Interview with actor Lorne Brass. Canada: Montreal, PQ. 1986. Lang.: Fre.   1707

Brassard, André
Plays/librettos/scripts
Critical response to Brassard's *Les Paravents (The Screens)*. Canada: Montreal, PQ, Ottawa, ON. 1987. Lang.: Fre.   2475

Brassard discusses his adaptation of Genet's *Les Paravents (The Screens)*. Canada: Montreal, PQ, Ottawa, ON. 1987. Lang.: Fre.   2485

Symbols of power in Genet's *Les Paravents (The Screens)*. France. Canada: Montreal, PQ, Ottawa, ON. 1961-1987. Lang.: Fre.   2570

Brecht, Bertolt — cont'd

Kaukasische Kreidekreis (The Caucasian Chalk Circle). USSR: Tbilisi. Hungary: Budapest. 1986. Lang.: Hun.   2390

Comparison of *Die Dreigroschenoper (The Three Penny Opera)* as directed by Ferenc Sík, József Petrik and Miklós Szinetár under the title *Koldusopera*. Hungary: Győr, Budapest. 1987. Lang.: Hun.   3402

Acting theories in Chinese opera. China, People's Republic of: Beijing. 1950-1986. Lang.: Chi.   3510

Documentation of performance of *Die Verurteilung des Lukullus (The Condemnation of Lucullus)* by Bertolt Brecht and Paul Dessau, staged by Ruth Berghaus. Germany, East: Berlin, East. 1983. Lang.: Ger.   3785

Giorgio Strehler on staging *Die Dreigroschenoper (The Three Penny Opera)*. Italy: Milan. France: Paris. 1928-1986. Lang.: Swe.   3809

Plays/librettos/scripts

Brecht's theory of alienation in the Chinese theatre. China, People's Republic of. 1949-1985. Lang.: Chi.   1109

The influence of Asian theatre on Brecht. Japan. China. Germany. 1930-1940. Lang.: Kor.   1144

Productions of Brecht in Quebec. Canada. 1950-1986. Lang.: Fre.
                                                2461

Bertolt Brecht and the Berlin workers' movement. Germany: Berlin. 1922-1932. Lang.: Ger.   2600

Textual history of Brecht's *Leben des Galilei (The Life of Galileo)*. Germany. USA. 1938-1956. Lang.: Ger.   2603

Brecht's influence on technique and style of playwright Heiner Müller. Germany, East. 1940-1984. Lang.: Eng.   2605

Analysis of the title character of Brecht's *Leben des Galilei (The Life of Galileo)*. Germany, East. 1938-1956. Lang.: Ger.   2606

Significance of dream-structures in Heiner Müller's plays, compared with those in Brecht's. Germany, East: Berlin, East. 1972-1987. Lang.: Ger.   2607

Focus of money in Brecht's dramas. Germany, East. 1920-1930. Lang.: Eng.   2611

Analysis of plays of Friedrich Dürrenmatt, comparison with Bertolt Brecht. Switzerland. Germany, West. 1945-1986. Lang.: Ger.   2745

Characterizations of stage spaces: examples from Brecht, Pinter, Douglas Turner Ward. UK-England. USA. 1947-1987. Lang.: Eng.
                                                2798

Interview with playwright Howard Brenton. UK-England. 1975-1987. Lang.: Eng.   2806

Interview with playwright and director Richard Foreman. USA: New York, NY. 1962-1987. Lang.: Eng.   2908

Career of singer/actress Lotte Lenya. Germany: Berlin. 1929-1970. Lang.: Eng.   3906

Relation to other fields

Assumptions by the actors and the audience in live theatre. USA. 1987. Lang.: Eng.   1283

Approaching dramatic texts similarly to other literary texts. 1600-1987. Lang.: Eng.   2976

Development of theatre influenced by myths of national character. Finland. 1950-1982. Lang.: Eng.   2989

Bertolt Brecht's interest in philosophy. Germany. 1918-1956. Lang.: Ger.   2991

New generation of Brecht's students created avant-garde movement. Germany, East: Berlin. 1987. Lang.: Eng.   2992

Compares Brecht's montages and the film work of Sergei Eisenstein and the use and definition of *gestus*. USA. 1930. Lang.: Eng.   3186

Relations to other fields

Brecht's theories on the media's negative impact on the activity and politics of the public. Germany, East: Berlin, East. 1950. Lang.: Eng.
                                                3197

Theory/criticism

Re-evaluation of Brecht's alienation effect in the context of contemporary performances. 1960-1970. Lang.: Eng.   1310

Chinese critique of Brechtian realism. China, People's Republic of. 1949-1985. Lang.: Chi.   1321

Essays on Bertolt Brecht's theories, aesthetics and philosophy. Germany, East. 1918-1987. Lang.: Ger.   1340

Aspects of Bertolt Brecht's theory and practice of theatre. Germany, East: Berlin, East. 1948-1956. Lang.: Ger.   1342

Theatre and contemporary culture. USA. 1800-1987. Lang.: Eng.
                                                1360

Career and collaborations of Maria Piscator. USA. 1938-1987. Lang.: Eng.   1365

Evaluation of the present state of theatrical theory and its influence on theatrical practice. Europe. 1985. Lang.: Fre.   3033

Brecht's theories, *Die Dreigroschenoper (The Three Penny Opera)*. Germany. 1878-1956. Lang.: Kor.   3044

Challenge of Brecht's plays to communism. Germany, East: Berlin. 1960-1970. Lang.: Eng.   3045

East and West German views of Bertolt Brecht. Germany, East. Germany, West. 1948-1987. Lang.: Eng.   3046

Platonism in the plays of Brecht. Greece. Germany. 300 B.C.-1956 A.D. Lang.: Eng.   3048

The work and writings of theatre critics Eric Bentley and Gordon Rogoff. USA. 1946-1987. Lang.: Eng.   3071

Suggestion for new form of dramaturgical research based on concrete scenic action from past productions. USA: Tallahassee, FL. 1987. Lang.: Eng.   3074

Training

Brecht workshop of International Amateur Theatre Association. Germany, East: Berlin, East. 1986. Lang.: Ger.   3079

Brel

Performance/production

Collection of newspaper reviews by London theatre critics. UK-England: London. 1987. Lang.: Eng.   2230

Bremen Tanztheater (Bremen)

Institutions

Seven productions chosen for Theatertreffen '86. Germany: Berlin. 1986. Lang.: Eng.   1617

Brenner, David

Performance/production

Career of director/author Andre Ernotte. USA: New York, NY. 1987. Lang.: Eng.   954

Brenton, Howard

Design/technology

Interview with lighting designer Dennis Parichy. USA: New York, NY. 1986-1987. Lang.: Eng.   428

Performance/production

Collection of newspaper reviews by London theatre critics. UK-England: London. 1986. Lang.: Eng.   2051

Plays/librettos/scripts

Theme of theatre in recent plays. UK-England. 1957-1985. Lang.: Eng.   2764

Interview with playwright Howard Brenton. UK-England. 1975-1987. Lang.: Eng.   2806

Breuer, Lee

Plays/librettos/scripts

Animal imagery in plays of Lee Breuer. USA. 1987. Lang.: Eng.
                                                2882

Brev på villovägar (Letter Goes Astray, A)

Performance/production

Two actors discuss youth, communication. Sweden. 1986-1987. Lang.: Swe.   2013

Brewis, Peter

Performance/production

Collection of newspaper reviews by London theatre critics. UK-England: London. 1986. Lang.: Eng.   2087

Collection of newspaper reviews by London theatre critics. UK-England: London. 1986. Lang.: Eng.   2108

Brewster, Yvonne

Performance/production

Collection of newspaper reviews by London theatre critics. UK-England: London. 1986. Lang.: Eng.   2048

Collection of newspaper reviews by London theatre critics. UK-England: London. 1986. Lang.: Eng.   2116

Collection of newspaper reviews by London theatre critics. UK-England: London. 1986. Lang.: Eng.   2165

Collection of newspaper reviews by London theatre critics. UK-England: London. 1987. Lang.: Eng.   2216

Brickman, Mark

Performance/production

Collection of newspaper reviews by London theatre critics. UK-England. 1987. Lang.: Eng.   2199

Collection of newspaper reviews by London theatre critics. UK-England: London. 1987. Lang.: Eng.   2225

Bridal Gown

Performance/production

Examination of modern Brazilian theatre focusing on plays by Nelson Rodrigues. Brazil. 1943-1984. Lang.: Eng.   1688

Bridge Lane Battersea Theatre (London)
Performance/production

Collection of newspaper reviews by London theatre critics. UK-England: London. 1986. Lang.: Eng. 2057

Collection of newspaper reviews by London theatre critics. UK-England: London. 1986. Lang.: Eng. 2085

Collection of newspaper reviews by London theatre critics. UK-England: London. 1986. Lang.: Eng. 2115

Collection of newspaper reviews by London theatre critics. UK-England: London. 1986. Lang.: Eng. 2143

Collection of newspaper reviews by London theatre critics. UK-England. 1987. Lang.: Eng. 2199

Collection of newspaper reviews by London theatre critics. UK-England: London. 1987. Lang.: Eng. 2227

Collection of newspaper reviews by London theatre critics. UK-England: London. 1987. Lang.: Eng. 2240

Bright Red Theatre Company (London)
Performance/production

Collection of newspaper reviews by London theatre critics. UK-England: London. 1986. Lang.: Eng. 2051

Development of alternative cabaret. UK-England. 1980. Lang.: Eng. 3288

Bright, Charles
Performance/production

Career of actor/director Randall Duk Kim. USA. 1966-1987. Lang.: Eng. 2346

Brightman, Sarah
Administration

Phantom of the Opera exchange: British, U.S. Equity agreement. UK-England: London. USA: New York, NY. 1987. Lang.: Eng. 49

Equity's policy on U.S. performances by foreign artists. USA: New York, NY. 1987. Lang.: Eng. 131

Brighton Beach Memoirs
Design/technology

Different casting and design approaches to *Brighton Beach Memoirs.* USA. 1983-1987. Lang.: Eng. 427

Performance/production

Collection of newspaper reviews by London theatre critics. UK-England: London. 1986. Lang.: Eng. 2034

Brink, Jos
Performance/production

Dutch and American plays about AIDS. Netherlands. USA. 1987. Lang.: Dut. 1984

British Actors' Equity Association
Administration

Issues of conflict in the international exchange of artists. UK-England. Denmark: Copenhagen. 1982. Lang.: Eng. 55

British Actors' Equity Association (London)
Administration

Phantom of the Opera exchange: British, U.S. Equity agreement. UK-England: London. USA: New York, NY. 1987. Lang.: Eng. 49

U.S. and British Equity associations: actor exchange, union reciprocity. UK-England. USA. 1981-1987. Lang.: Eng. 50

The first Anglo-American commercial Broadway production, the musical *Carrie.* USA: New York, NY. UK-England: London. 1987. Lang.: Eng. 61

Actor exchange: discussions of Equity, Royal Shakespeare Company. USA. UK-England. 1985. Lang.: Eng. 74

Meeting between Actors' Equity and British Equity. USA: Washington, DC. UK-England. 1984. Lang.: Eng. 76

Performance/production

Actor discusses Equity exchanges for *Les Misérables.* USA: New York, NY. UK-England: London. 1987. Lang.: Eng. 926

Working in London through Equity actor exchange. UK-England: London. USA: New York, NY. 1985. Lang.: Eng. 2307

First-hand account of Equity actor exchange. UK-England: London. USA: New York, NY. 1985. Lang.: Eng. 2308

British Asian Theatre Company (London)
Performance/production

Collection of newspaper reviews by London theatre critics. UK-England: London. 1986. Lang.: Eng. 2066

British Broadcasting Corporation (BBC, London)
Performance/production

Review of the BBC telecast of *The Birthday Party* by Harold Pinter. UK-England. 1987. Lang.: Eng. 3206

Plays/librettos/scripts

Two forms of adaptations of Shakespeare for other media. Europe. USA. 1899-1987. Lang.: Eng. 3097

Britten, Benjamin
Relation to other fields

Benjamin Britten's *Albert Herring* as an adaptation of a story by Maupassant. UK-England. 1947. Lang.: Eng. 3946

Brjusov, Valerij
Basic theatrical documents

Russian symbolist plays and essays. USSR. 1880-1986. Lang.: Eng. 1584

Plays/librettos/scripts

Theatre and dramaturgy of the first Russian revolution. USSR. 1905-1907. Lang.: Rus. 1188

Broadhurst Theatre (New York, NY)
Performance spaces

Broadway theatres given landmark status. USA: New York, NY. 1982. Lang.: Eng. 692

Broadhurst, Nick
Performance/production

Collection of newspaper reviews by London theatre critics. UK-England. 1987. Lang.: Eng. 2262

Broadway Bound
Design/technology

Current Broadway shows and their lighting designers. USA: New York, NY. 1987. Lang.: Eng. 460

Lighting reviews for several New York productions. USA: New York, NY. 1987. Lang.: Eng. 474

Broadway theatre
Administration

The first Anglo-American commercial Broadway production, the musical *Carrie.* USA: New York, NY. UK-England: London. 1987. Lang.: Eng. 61

Endangered Theatres Production contract. USA: New York, NY. 1986-1987. Lang.: Eng. 77

Sophisticated Ladies taped for cable television amid controversy. USA: New York, NY. 1982. Lang.: Eng. 112

Sexual discrimination in American theatres. USA: New York, NY. 1976-1984. Lang.: Eng. 133

Comprehensive guide to play production. USA: New York, NY. 1987. Lang.: Eng. 150

Influence of TV ads on success of Broadway plays. USA: New York, NY. 1984-1987. Lang.: Eng. 179

Broadway producer Dorothy Olim on commercial theatre. USA: New York, NY. 1983. Lang.: Eng. 189

Design/technology

Index of Broadway costume designs and designers. USA: New York, NY. 1915-1985. Lang.: Eng. 444

Career of Broadway set designer Boris Aronson. USA. 1925-1979. Lang.: Eng. 449

Current Broadway shows and their lighting designers. USA: New York, NY. 1987. Lang.: Eng. 460

Bob Crowley's set designs for *Les Liaisons Dangereuses.* USA: New York, NY. UK-England: London. 1985-1987. Lang.: Eng. 463

Lighting reviews for some New York productions. USA: New York, NY. 1987. Lang.: Eng. 472

Lighting reviews of several Broadway shows. USA: New York, NY. 1987. Lang.: Eng. 473

Lighting reviews for several New York productions. USA: New York, NY. 1987. Lang.: Eng. 474

Lighting reviews for several New York productions. USA: New York, NY. 1987. Lang.: Eng. 475

Lighting reviews for several New York shows. USA: New York, NY. 1987. Lang.: Eng. 476

Lighting reviews for some New York productions. USA: New York, NY. 1987. Lang.: Eng. 477

Lighting review for *Anything Goes* at the Vivian Beaumont Theatre. USA: New York, NY. 1987. Lang.: Eng. 3623

Institutions

List of resources for playwrights. USA. 1987-1988. Lang.: Eng. 582

Meetings of various Dramatists' Guild committees, members' plays in production. USA: New York, NY. 1987. Lang.: Eng. 584

The work of AEA's Equity Fights AIDS Committee. USA: New York, NY. 1987. Lang.: Eng. 619

Broadway theatre — cont'd

Performance spaces

Guidelines for preservation of theatres. USA: New York, NY. 1985-1986. Lang.: Eng. 675

Debate over landmark status for Broadway theatres. USA: New York, NY. 1986. Lang.: Eng. 676

Morosco Theatre torn down despite efforts by Actors' Equity. USA: New York, NY. 1982. Lang.: Eng. 677

Hearings for granting landmark status to forty-five Broadway theatres. USA: New York, NY. 1982. Lang.: Eng. 678

History of theatres in the Times Square area. USA: New York, NY. 1883-1984. Lang.: Eng. 685

Commitment of Shubert Organization to cleaning up Broadway theatre district. USA: New York, NY. 1984. Lang.: Eng. 691

Broadway theatres given landmark status. USA: New York, NY. 1982. Lang.: Eng. 692

Renovation and subsequent failure of the New Apollo Theatre. USA: New York, NY. 1977-1984. Lang.: Eng. 697

Proposal for renovations of Broadway theatres. USA: New York, NY. 1984. Lang.: Eng. 713

Performance/production

Gays and lesbians on the American stage. USA. 1896-1987. Lang.: Eng. 935

The end of the out-of-town tryout system for Broadway openings. USA: New York, NY. 1965-1987. Lang.: Eng. 937

Index of Broadway productions which ran for one night only. USA: New York, NY. 1923-1983. Lang.: Eng. 951

Critique of the 1984 Broadway production of *Death of a Salesman*. USA: New York, NY. 1984. Lang.: Eng. 2330

Autobiography of director, producer and writer John Houseman. USA: New York, NY. 1935-1985. Lang.: Eng. 2339

Broadway actors who moonlight in cabaret acts. USA: New York, NY. 1962-1987. Lang.: Eng. 3291

Brief Broadway run of *King of Hearts*. USA: New York, NY. 1978-1987. Lang.: Eng. 3643

Life and career of actress Nancy Hume. USA. 1977-1987. Lang.: Eng. 3648

Broadway musical's shift from song and dance to aria and recitative. USA: New York, NY. 1956-1984. Lang.: Eng. 3655

Career of Broadway actress Connie Day. USA: New York, NY. 1987. Lang.: Eng. 3657

Musical Theatre Project explores Broadway musical material available in Shubert Archive. USA: New York, NY. 1984-1985. Lang.: Eng. 3666

Opera conductors who also conduct in Broadway musicals. USA: New York, NY. 1980-1987. Lang.: Eng. 3847

Plays/librettos/scripts

Notes on Dramatists' Guild activities and concerns. USA. 1987. Lang.: Eng. 1162

Career of Broadway musical author Michael Short. USA: New York, NY. UK-England. 1924-1987. Lang.: Eng. 3673

Opera adaptations for Broadway with African-American artists. USA: New York, NY. 1935-1987. Lang.: Eng. 3932

Relation to other fields

Interview with caricaturist Al Hirschfeld. USA: New York, NY. 1925-1981. Lang.: Eng. 1272

Research/historiography

Overview of two and a half decades of American theatre. USA. 1937-1961. Lang.: Eng. 1303

Theory/criticism

Collection of critical essays and reviews by Robert Brustein. USA. 1980-1986. Lang.: Eng. 1351

Advantage of having a Broadway theatre. USA: New York, NY. 1985. Lang.: Eng. 1354

Broadway Theatre (New York, NY)

Performance/production

Collection of newspaper reviews by New York theatre critics. USA: New York, NY. 1987. Lang.: Eng. 2323

Brocka, Lino

Performance/production

Role of theatre in the Filipino revolution. Philippines. 1970-1987. Lang.: Eng. 1986

Bródy, Sándor

Performance/production

A tanítóno (The Schoolmistress) by Sándor Bródy, directed by Péter Tömöry at Hevesi Sándor Theatre. Hungary: Zalaegerszeg. 1986. Lang.: Hun. 1921

Broken Heart, The

Performance/production

Shakespeare and contemporaries: tradition, intertextuality in performance. England. 1607-1987. Lang.: Eng. 1740

Broken Promises

Performance/production

Collection of newspaper reviews by London theatre critics. UK-England: London. 1987. Lang.: Eng. 2277

Broken Thigh, The

Performance/production

Collection of newspaper reviews by London theatre critics. UK-England: London. 1986. Lang.: Eng. 2143

Brome, Richard

Plays/librettos/scripts

Utopian ideas in Tudor and Stuart playwrights. England. 1600-1650. Lang.: Ger. 2522

Brook, Peter

Institutions

History of new and experimental theatre companies. Europe. North America. 1947-1970. Lang.: Ita. 529

Performance spaces

Performance spaces and audience-performer relationship. France. Germany, West. 1875-1987. Lang.: Eng. 633

Performance/production

Eastern theatre forms in Western artists' productions. Canada: Vancouver, BC. 1987. Lang.: Eng. 725

Productions by directors Patrice Chéreau, Claude Régy, Ariane Mnouchkine. France. 1980-1987. Lang.: Rus. 792

Company members of Centre International de Recherche Théâtrale discuss *The Mahabharata*. France: Paris. 1986. Lang.: Eng. 1752

Director as true author and maker of theatre. France. 1987. Lang.: Fre. 1757

Orientalism in Peter Brook's production of *The Mahabharata*. India. USA: New York, NY. 400 B.C.-1987 A.D. Lang.: Eng. 1932

Focus on several Tokyo productions. Japan: Tokyo. 1960-1987. Lang.: Jap. 1955

Reviews and discussion of Tokyo productions. Japan: Tokyo. 1960-1987. Lang.: Jap. 1960

Comments on Tokyo performances. Japan: Tokyo. 1987. Lang.: Jap. 1964

Collection of newspaper reviews by London theatre critics. UK-England: London. 1987. Lang.: Eng. 2177

Collection of newspaper reviews by London theatre critics. UK-England: London. 1987. Lang.: Eng. 2253

Autobiography of film and stage director Peter Brook. UK-England. 1946-1987. Lang.: Eng. 2281

Collection of newspaper reviews by New York theatre critics. USA: New York, NY. 1987. Lang.: Eng. 2315

Plays/librettos/scripts

Development of *The Mahabharata* directed by Peter Brook and Jean-Claude Carrière. 1975-1987. Lang.: Eng. 2412

Critical overview of the playwrights in Argentina. Argentina. 1949-1986. Lang.: Spa. 2432

Peter Brook discusses his production of *The Mahabharata*. France: Paris. India. Australia: Perth. 1987. Lang.: Eng. 2571

Director Peter Brook discusses his views on *The Mahabharata*. India. 1987. Lang.: Eng. 2636

The plays of Thomas Murphy. Ireland: Dublin. 1962-1986. Lang.: Eng. 2650

Successful film versions of Shakespeare's *King Lear*. USA. UK-England. USSR. 1916-1983. Lang.: Eng. 3099

Relation to other fields

Experimental theatre course, Assoc. Internationale pour la Sémiologie du Spectacle. Belgium: Brussels. France: Paris. Denmark: Odense. 1983-1985. Lang.: Fre. 1219

Theory/criticism

Reconstruction of Shakespeare in performance. USA. 1987. Lang.: Eng. 1358

Peter Brook's implementation of Jan Kott's theory in his approach to *King Lear*. UK-England. 1962-1987. Lang.: Eng. 3064

Brookes, Chris
Institutions
A history of documentary theatre in English Canada. Canada. 1970-1986. Lang.: Eng.   508
Brooklyn Academy of Music (BAM, New York, NY)
Administration
Interview with Karen Brookes Hopkins (Brooklyn Academy of Music) and Kate Busch (ART/NY). USA: New York, NY. 1987. Lang.: Eng.   158
Legal difficulties facing producers who present foreign artists and dance troupes. USA. 1987. Lang.: Eng.   244
Institutions
Profile of Brooklyn Academy of Music's Next Wave Festival. USA: New York, NY. 1984. Lang.: Eng.   590
Performance/production
The 1984 season of the Next Wave at BAM. USA: New York, NY. 1984. Lang.: Eng.   967
Evolution of the Flying Karamazov Brothers. USA. 1977-1987. Lang.: Eng.   3273
Brooks Atkinson Theatre (New York, NY)
Performance spaces
Broadway theatres given landmark status. USA: New York, NY. 1982. Lang.: Eng.   692
Brooks, Niall
Performance/production
Collection of newspaper reviews by London theatre critics. UK-England: London. 1987. Lang.: Eng.   2181
Brothers and Sisters
SEE
Bratja i sestry.
Brothers Karamazov, The
SEE
Bratja Karamazov.
Broughton, Pip
Performance/production
Collection of newspaper reviews by London theatre critics. UK-England: London. 1986. Lang.: Eng.   2051
Collection of newspaper reviews by London theatre critics. UK-England: London. 1987. Lang.: Eng.   2191
Collection of newspaper reviews by London theatre critics. UK-England: London. 1987. Lang.: Eng.   2228
Collection of newspaper reviews by London theatre critics. UK-England: London. 1987. Lang.: Eng.   2268
Brown Birds
Institutions
Will Garland and European tour of Negro Operetta Company. UK-England. Finland: Helsinki. Russia. 1905-1917. Lang.: Eng.   3956
Brown, Arvin
Institutions
National Theatre of the Deaf productions of *Farewell My Lovely* and *In a Grove* directed by Arvin Brown in Beijing. China, People's Republic of: Beijing. USA. 1986-1987. Lang.: Eng.   1611
Performance/production
Collection of newspaper reviews by New York theatre critics. USA: New York, NY. 1987. Lang.: Eng.   2319
Collection of newspaper reviews by New York theatre critics. USA: New York, NY. 1987. Lang.: Eng.   2321
Brown, Felicity
Performance/production
Collection of newspaper reviews by London theatre critics. UK-England: London. 1987. Lang.: Eng.   2211
Brown, Georgia
Performance/production
Interview with actress Georgia Brown. USA: New York, NY. UK-England: London. 1957-1985. Lang.: Eng.   3651
Brown, Hal
Performance/production
Collection of newspaper reviews by London theatre critics. UK-England: London. 1986. Lang.: Eng.   2076
Collection of newspaper reviews by London theatre critics. UK-England: London. 1986. Lang.: Eng.   2078
Collection of newspaper reviews by London theatre critics. UK-England: London. 1987. Lang.: Eng.   2257
Brown, Ralph
Performance/production
Collection of newspaper reviews by London theatre critics. UK-England. 1987. Lang.: Eng.   2175

Brown, Robin
Performance/production
Collection of newspaper reviews by London theatre critics. UK-England: London. 1987. Lang.: Eng.   2267
Brown, Trisha
Performance/production
Theatricality of dance. USA. 1985. Lang.: Eng.   1414
Browne, Roscoe Lee
Performance/production
Theatre career of photo-journalist Bert Andrews. USA: New York, NY. 1950-1987. Lang.: Eng.   2367
Bru et Descallar, Melchior de
Performance/production
Exhibition catalogue: popular theatre in Catalan. France. 1415-1987. Lang.: Cat, Fre.   1750
Bruckner, Ferdinand
Performance/production
Collection of newspaper reviews by London theatre critics. UK-England: London. 1987. Lang.: Eng.   2073
Bruno
Performance/production
Festival of Polish plays. Poland: Wrocław. 1987. Lang.: Eng, Fre.   871
Bruno, Giordano
Performance/production
Collection of newspaper reviews by London theatre critics. UK-England: London. 1986. Lang.: Eng.   2080
Bruscambille
SEE
Gracieux, Jean.
Brustein, Robert
Performance/production
Interview with director Robert Brustein. USA: Cambridge, MA. 1987. Lang.: Eng.   974
Influence of Pirandello on modern theatre. USA. Italy. 1917-1987. Lang.: Eng.   2338
Plays/librettos/scripts
Development of themes and characters in plays of Sam Shepard. USA. 1960-1987. Lang.: Eng.   2853
Theory/criticism
National standards for arts criticism. USA. 1987. Lang.: Eng.   1371
Bryceland, Yvonne
Administration
Equity's policy on U.S. performances by foreign artists. USA: New York, NY. 1987. Lang.: Eng.   131
Bryden, Bill
Performance/production
Collection of newspaper reviews by London theatre critics. UK-England: London. 1987. Lang.: Eng.   2230
Bryer, David
Performance/production
Collection of newspaper reviews by London theatre critics. UK. 1987. Lang.: Eng.   2031
Brzeska
Performance/production
Collection of newspaper reviews by London theatre critics. UK-England: London. 1987. Lang.: Eng.   2237
Brzezinski, Jacek
Performance/production
Teatr Prowizorium: interview with director Janusz Oprynski. Poland: Lublin. 1971-1987. Lang.: Eng.   1990
Bržozovskaja, L.
Performance/production
Belorussian ballet soloists L. Bržozovskaja and Ju. Trojan. USSR. 1980. Lang.: Rus.   1449
Buba
Basic theatrical documents
English translation of *Buba* by Hillel Mittelpunkt. Israel. 1987. Lang.: Eng.   1559
Buch mit sieben Siegeln, Das
Performance/production
Report from Salzburger Festspiele: Mozart's *Don Giovanni*, Schoenberg's *Moses und Aron*, Schmidt's *Das Buch mit sieben Siegeln*. Austria: Salzburg. 1987. Lang.: Swe.   3744
Buchanan, Isobel
Basic theatrical documents
Review of video productions of *Tosca* and *Dialogues des Carmélites*. Italy: Verona. Australia: Sydney. 1987. Lang.: Eng.   3692

Büchner, Georg
Performance/production
Collection of newspaper reviews by London theatre critics. UK-England: London. 1986. Lang.: Eng.   2104
Collection of newspaper reviews by London theatre critics. UK-England: London. 1987. Lang.: Eng.   2173
Lorna Heaton's use of holograms in *Woyzeck*. Canada: Banff, AB. 1987. Lang.: Fre.   3205

Buckley, Geoffrey
Performance/production
Collection of newspaper reviews by London theatre critics. UK-England: London. 1987. Lang.: Eng.   2252

Budapest Art Theatre
SEE
Müvész Szinház (Budapest).

Budapest Opera
SEE
Magyar Állami Operaház.

Buddies in Bad Times (Toronto, ON)
Performance spaces
The lack of performance space for small theatre companies. Canada: Toronto, ON. 1987. Lang.: Eng.   629

Budori—Nemurenu natsu no tsuki (Budori, Sleepless Summer Moon)
Performance/production
New Tokyo productions. Japan: Tokyo. 1987. Lang.: Jap.   1954

Bufalino, Brenda
Performance/production
Career of tap dancer Brenda Bufalino, and exploration of women's roles as lead dancers. USA. 1987. Lang.: Eng.   1417

Buffery, Bill
Performance/production
Collection of newspaper reviews by London theatre critics. UK-England: London. 1986. Lang.: Eng.   2133

Buffman, Zev
Design/technology
Four Broadway designers discuss redesigning shows for road tours. USA. 1987. Lang.: Eng.   414

Bühnen der Stadt Bonn (Bonn)
Institutions
Seven productions chosen for Theatertreffen '86. Germany: Berlin. 1986. Lang.: Eng.   1617

Built on Sand
Performance/production
Collection of newspaper reviews by London theatre critics. UK-England: London. 1987. Lang.: Eng.   2207

Buitenhaus, Peter
Relation to other fields
Essays on the theme of marriage in literature. England. Norway. 1300-1985. Lang.: Eng.   1425

Bulgakov, Michajl Afanasjevič
Basic theatrical documents
Michajl Bulgakov's letters about theatrical life in Moscow. USSR: Moscow. 1924-1931. Lang.: Rus.   298

Performance/production
The 4th International Theatre Conference: includes list of participants and their contributions. Poland: Warsaw. 1986. Lang.: Eng, Fre.   873
Polish theatre. Poland: Warsaw, Cracow, Wrocław. 1980-1987. Lang.: Eng, Fre.   1987
Four new productions in Poland. Poland: Warsaw. 1986-1987. Lang.: Eng, Fre.   1988
Jurij Liubimov's 1979 Taganka Theatre production of *The Master and Margarita (Master i Margarita)*. USSR. 1938-1979. Lang.: Eng.   2394

Plays/librettos/scripts
Prototypes of characters in Bulgakov's *Zojkina kvartira (Zojka's Apartment)*. USSR: Moscow. 1926. Lang.: Rus.   2956

Bullough, Geoffrey
Research/historiography
Critical history of *Julius Caesar*. England. 1599-1987. Lang.: Eng.   1299

Bungakuza (Tokyo)
Performance/production
Productions of Bungakuza, Yūkikai Zenjidō shiatā, Tao and Tenkei gekijō. Japan: Tokyo. 1986. Lang.: Jap.   1961

Bungakuza Atorie no kai (Tokyo)
Performance/production
New Tokyo productions. Japan: Tokyo. 1987. Lang.: Jap.   1954
Space and sign in various Tokyo productions. Japan: Tokyo. 1987. Lang.: Jap.   1959
Unsuitable choice of plays for Tokyo performances. Japan: Tokyo. 1987. Lang.: Jap.   1965
Six plays of the Tokyo season, focus on director Betsuyaku Minoru. Japan: Tokyo. 1986. Lang.: Jap.   1966
Plays/librettos/scripts
Contemporary Japanese plays about crime. Japan: Tokyo. 1986. Lang.: Jap.   2681
Plays about child suicide in Japan. Japan: Tokyo. 1986. Lang.: Jap.   2683

Bungeiza Gekidan
Performance/production
István Pinczés directs Örkény's *Tóték (The Tót Family)* in Japan. Japan: Toyama. 1986. Lang.: Hun.   1952

Bunker Reveries
Plays/librettos/scripts
David Shaber, Larry Kramer, Emily Mann: Three of the few American political dramatists. USA: New York, NY. 1987. Lang.: Eng.   2907

Bunraku
Design/technology
Puppetmaking projects for children. USA. 1987. Lang.: Eng.   3963
Performance/production
Eastern theatre forms in Western artists' productions. Canada: Vancouver, BC. 1987. Lang.: Eng.   725
Relation to other fields
Analysis of the role of tradition in theatrical forms of different cultures. Asia. Africa. 1985. Lang.: Fre.   1218

Büntetések (Punishments)
Plays/librettos/scripts
Study of three plays by Mihály Kornis: *Halleluja, Büntetések (Punishments)* and *Kozma*. Hungary. 1980-1987. Lang.: Hun.   2628

Buñuel, Luis
Plays/librettos/scripts
Egon Wolff's trilogy of plays focusing on Chilean bourgeoisie. Chile. 1964-1984. Lang.: Eng.   2490

Buoyant Billions
Plays/librettos/scripts
Approaches to Shaw's *Buoyant Billions*. UK-England. 1936-1946. Lang.: Eng.   2789

Burbage, James
Performance/production
New interpretation of Jacobean theatre. England: London. 1596-1633. Lang.: Eng.   1743

Burdonsky, A.
Performance/production
Soviet productions of five Tennessee Williams plays. USSR. 1910-1987. Lang.: Eng.   2397

Burge, Stuart
Performance/production
Collection of newspaper reviews by London theatre critics. UK-England: London. 1987. Lang.: Eng.   2277

Burger, Peter
Plays/librettos/scripts
Linguistic absurdism in *El Chinfónia burguesa (The Bourgeois Chinfonia)*. Nicaragua. 1987. Lang.: Spa.   2703

Burgess, John
Performance/production
Collection of newspaper reviews by London theatre critics. UK-England: London. 1986. Lang.: Eng.   2118

Burgos, Franklin Mieses
Theory/criticism
Myth in the plays of the Dominican Republic. Dominican Republic. 1987. Lang.: Spa.   3026

Burgtheater (Vienna)
Audience
Claus Peymann, new artistic director of the Vienna Burgtheater. Austria: Vienna. 1986-1987. Lang.: Dut.   1530
Performance/production
Productions by Claus Peymann, new artistic director of Vienna's Burgtheater. Austria: Vienna. 1986-1987. Lang.: Dut.   721
Directors Claus Peymann (Burgtheater) and Gerardjan Rijnders (Toneelgroep). Austria: Vienna. Netherlands: Amsterdam. 1987. Lang.: Dut.   1681

Burian, Jarka
Design/technology
Work of noted set designer and technological innovator Josef
Svoboda. Czechoslovakia: Prague. 1940-1987. Lang.: Eng. 305

Buried Child
Plays/librettos/scripts
Development of themes and characters in plays of Sam Shepard.
USA. 1960-1987. Lang.: Eng. 2853

Evolution of female characters in the plays of Sam Shepard. USA.
1976-1987. Lang.: Eng. 2883

Corn as a symbol in Sam Shepard's *Buried Child*. USA. 1978.
Lang.: Eng. 2905

Sam Shepard's manipulation of an audience's desire to believe what
it sees. USA. 1967-1983. Lang.: Eng. 2932

Burkhard, Paul
Performance/production
Music for Brecht's *Mutter Courage und ihre Kinder (Mother Courage
and Her Children)*. Switzerland: Zürich. Finland. 1939-1947. Lang.:
Ger. 2027

Burkov, G.
Performance/production
Actors discuss contemporary theatrical process. USSR: Moscow. 1987.
Lang.: Rus. 993

Burlesque
SEE ALSO
Classed Entries under MIXED ENTERTAINMENT–Variety acts.

Performance/production
Irondale Ensemble's production of *Ubu roi (King Ubu)* by Alfred
Jarry. USA: New York, NY. 1984-1987. Lang.: Eng. 2370

Plays/librettos/scripts
Shakespearean burlesque in context. UK-England. 1800-1900. Lang.:
Eng. 2817

Burn This
Performance/production
Collection of newspaper reviews by New York theatre critics. USA:
New York, NY. 1987. Lang.: Eng. 2317

Burning Point
Performance/production
Collection of newspaper reviews by London theatre critics. UK-
England: London. 1987. Lang.: Eng. 2242

Burns, Bree
Design/technology
Comprehensive look at touring theatre. USA. 1987. Lang.: Eng. 464

Burns, Edward
Performance/production
Modern production of the *Chester Cycle*. UK-England: Chester. 1987.
Lang.: Eng. 2299

Burns, Nica
Performance/production
Collection of newspaper reviews by London theatre critics. UK-
England: London. 1986. Lang.: Eng. 2104

Collection of newspaper reviews by London theatre critics. UK-
England: London. 1987. Lang.: Eng. 2185

Burnt Bridges (London)
Performance/production
Collection of newspaper reviews by London theatre critics. UK-
England: London. 1986. Lang.: Eng. 2055

Burnt Bridges Theatre Company (London)
Performance/production
Collection of newspaper reviews by London theatre critics. UK-
England: London. 1987. Lang.: Eng. 2184

Burrows, John
Performance/production
Collection of newspaper reviews by London theatre critics. UK-
England: London. 1987. Lang.: Eng. 2175

Burstyn, Ellen
Administration
Ellen Burstyn succeeds Theodore Bikel as Actors' Equity president.
USA: New York, NY. 1982. Lang.: Eng. 98

Actors' Equity president Ellen Burstyn on employment for minorities
and women. USA: New York, NY. 1982. Lang.: Eng. 109

Opposition to Equity National Theatre plan in favor of regional
theatre. USA. 1985. Lang.: Eng. 132

Interview with director Peter Sellars. USA: Washington, DC. 1985.
1524

Burt Reynolds Institute for Theatre Training (Miami, FL)
Institutions
Burt Reynolds Institute apprenticeship program. USA: Miami, FL.
1987. Lang.: Eng. 587

Burwell, Paul
Relation to other fields
Three performance art education projects. UK-England. 1987. Lang.:
Eng. 3373

Bury, John
Design/technology
Harold Pinter's scenic designs. 1958-1987. Lang.: Eng. 1585

Busch, Ernst
Performance/production
Biography of actor-singer Ernst Busch. Germany, East: Berlin, East.
1900-1980. Lang.: Ger. 799

Busch, Fritz
Performance/production
Career of basso Italo Tajo. Italy: Turin. 1935-1982. Lang.: Eng.
3805

Relation to other fields
Wagnerian opera in Argentina. Argentina: Buenos Aires. 1858-1983.
Lang.: Eng. 3938

Busch, Kate
Administration
Interview with Karen Brookes Hopkins (Brooklyn Academy of
Music) and Kate Busch (ART/NY). USA: New York, NY. 1987.
Lang.: Eng. 158

Bush Theatre (London)
Performance/production
Collection of newspaper reviews by London theatre critics. UK-
England: London. 1986. Lang.: Eng. 2056

Collection of newspaper reviews by London theatre critics. UK-
England: London. 1986. Lang.: Eng. 2068

Collection of newspaper reviews by London theatre critics. UK-
England: London. 1986. Lang.: Eng. 2090

Collection of newspaper reviews by London theatre critics. UK-
England: London. 1986. Lang.: Eng. 2103

Collection of newspaper reviews by London theatre critics. UK-
England: London. 1986. Lang.: Eng. 2117

Collection of newspaper reviews by London theatre critics. UK-
England: London. 1986. Lang.: Eng. 2134

Collection of newspaper reviews by London theatre critics. UK-
England. 1987. Lang.: Eng. 2175

Collection of newspaper reviews by London theatre critics. UK-
England: London. 1987. Lang.: Eng. 2177

Collection of newspaper reviews by London theatre critics. UK-
England: London. 1987. Lang.: Eng. 2184

Collection of newspaper reviews by London theatre critics. UK-
England: London. 1987. Lang.: Eng. 2209

Collection of newspaper reviews by London theatre critics. UK-
England: London. 1987. Lang.: Eng. 2212

Collection of newspaper reviews by London theatre critics. UK-
England: London. 1987. Lang.: Eng. 2226

Búsképü lovag, A (Sad-Faced Knight, The)
Performance/production
István Malgot directs *A búsképü lovag (The Sad-Faced Knight)* by
László Gyurko in the Dominican Court of the Budapest Hilton.
Hungary: Budapest. 1987. 1900

Bust
Performance/production
Collection of newspaper reviews by London theatre critics. UK-
England: London. 1986. Lang.: Eng. 2054

Buster Theatre Company (London)
Performance/production
Collection of newspaper reviews by London theatre critics. UK-
England: London. 1987. Lang.: Eng. 2276

Buterbaugh, Keith
Performance/production
Plot synopsis of musical *Mademoiselle Colombe* based on Anouilh's
Colombe. USA: New York, NY. 1987. Lang.: Eng. 3647

Butler, Brenda
Training
Proposed changes in teaching methodology to include indigenous
drama. South Africa, Republic of. 1960-1987. Lang.: Eng. 1383

Butler, Neil
Performance/production
Development of alternative cabaret. UK-England. 1980. Lang.: Eng.
3288

Butler's Wharf (London)
Performance/production
Collection of newspaper reviews by London theatre critics. UK-England: London. 1987. Lang.: Eng.
2222

Butō
Relation to other fields
Analysis of the role of tradition in theatrical forms of different cultures. Asia. Africa. 1985. Lang.: Fre.
1218

Buxton, Judy
Performance/production
Reviews of Pinter's *The Lover* and *A Slight Ache*. UK-England: London. 1987. Lang.: Eng.
901

Buzo, Alex
Plays/librettos/scripts
Survey of Alex Buzo's plays and analysis of the demands of the text. Australia. 1969-1983. Lang.: Eng.
2442

Buzzati, Dino
Plays/librettos/scripts
Operatic/theatrical activities of Dino Buzzati. Italy. 1933-1972. Lang.: Ita.
3918

Bygmester Solness (Master Builder, The)
Plays/librettos/scripts
Ariadne in plays of Ibsen, Strindberg, Maeterlinck. Europe. 1892-1902. Lang.: Eng.
2566

Byron, George Gordon, Lord
Performance/production
Stanislavskij's rehearsal notes for Byron's *Cain*. USSR. 1920. Lang.: Rus.
988
Romantic drama in performance: effect on modern theatre. England. 1700-1987. Lang.: Eng.
1732
Plays/librettos/scripts
Analysis of vampire characters in the works of Byron, Polidori and Planché. England. Italy. France. 1800-1825. Lang.: Eng.
2540
Structure of Byron's plays. England. 1788-1824. Lang.: Eng.
2542
Byron's 'closet' dramas structured for performance at London theatres. UK-England: London. 1812-1822. Lang.: Eng.
2778

Byrthrite
Performance/production
Collection of newspaper reviews by London theatre critics. UK-England: London. 1986. Lang.: Eng.
2058

Cabal of Saintly Hypocrites, The
SEE
Kabala sviatov.

Caballé, Montserrat
Performance/production
Premiere of Leonardo Balarda's opera *Cristobal Colón*. Spain-Catalonia: Barcelona. 1987. Lang.: Eng.
3818

Cabaret
Performance/production
Four approaches to the role of Sally Bowles in *Cabaret*. USA: New York, NY. Germany. 1966-1987. Lang.: Eng.
968
Collection of newspaper reviews by London theatre critics. UK-England: London. 1986. Lang.: Eng.
2149
Collection of newspaper reviews by New York theatre critics. USA: New York, NY. 1987. Lang.: Eng.
2317
Plays/librettos/scripts
Interview with Joe Masteroff, author of the book for *Cabaret*. USA: New York, NY. 1963-1987. Lang.: Eng.
3674

Cabaret
SEE ALSO
Classed Entries under MIXED ENTERTAINMENT–Cabaret.

Performance/production
Irondale Ensemble's production of *Ubu roi (King Ubu)* by Alfred Jarry. USA: New York, NY. 1984-1987. Lang.: Eng.
2370

Cabin Fever
Performance/production
Collection of newspaper reviews by London theatre critics. UK-England: London. 1986. Lang.: Eng.
2118

Cabral, Hector Inchaustegui
Theory/criticism
Myth in the plays of the Dominican Republic. Dominican Republic. 1987. Lang.: Spa.
3026

Cacaci, Joe
Performance/production
Collection of newspaper reviews by New York theatre critics. USA: New York, NY. 1987. Lang.: Eng.
2319
Plays/librettos/scripts
Money, greed and power in plays by Fo, Churchill, Cacaci and Cormack. USA: New York, NY. 1987. Lang.: Eng.
2914

Caesar and Cleopatra
Plays/librettos/scripts
How settings and props convey meaning in plays by Shaw. UK-England. 1883-1935. Lang.: Eng.
2753

Caesar, Burt
Performance/production
Collection of newspaper reviews by London theatre critics. UK-England: London. 1986. Lang.: Eng.
2127

Café de la Marina, El (Marina's Café)
Plays/librettos/scripts
General history of Catalan literature, including theatre. Spain-Catalonia. 1902-1961. Lang.: Cat.
1157

Café Muller
Performance/production
Overview of performing artists that toured Japan. Japan: Tokyo. 1986. Lang.: Jap.
844

Cafe Tabou
Performance/production
Collection of newspaper reviews by London theatre critics. UK-England: London. 1986. Lang.: Eng.
2151

Cage aux Folles, La
Performance/production
Transformation of *La Cage aux Folles* from movie to a Broadway musical. USA: New York, NY. 1983-1987. Lang.: Eng.
940

Cage Aux Folles, La
Performance/production
Collection of newspaper reviews by London theatre critics. UK-England: London. 1986. Lang.: Eng.
2095
Career of actor Lee Roy Reams. USA: New York, NY. 1987. Lang.: Eng.
3661

Cage, John
Institutions
History of new and experimental theatre companies. Europe. North America. 1947-1970. Lang.: Ita.
529

Performance/production
University of Mexico: music of dance theatre. Mexico: Mexico City. 1987. Lang.: Spa.
1463

Theory/criticism
Environment and the works of Merce Cunningham and John Cage. USA. 1962-1987. Lang.: Eng.
1477

Cahn, Sammy
Performance/production
Collection of newspaper reviews of London theatre critics. UK-England: London. 1987. Lang.: Eng.
2273

Cain
Performance/production
Stanislavskij's rehearsal notes for Byron's *Cain*. USSR. 1920. Lang.: Rus.
988

Caird, John
Performance/production
Collection of newspaper reviews by London theatre critics. UK-England: London. 1986. Lang.: Eng.
2064
Collection of newspaper reviews by London theatre critics. UK-England: London. 1987. Lang.: Eng.
2200
Collection of newspaper reviews by London theatre critics. UK-England: London. 1987. Lang.: Eng.
2255
Collection of newspaper reviews by New York theatre critics. USA: New York, NY. 1987. Lang.: Eng.
2323

Caird, Mona
Performance/production
Aubrey Beardsley's drawings of actresses: impact on society. UK-England: London. 1890. Lang.: Eng.
2287

Cairns, Glen
Performance/production
Writer-director Glen Cairns and surrealistic drama at the Neptune Theatre. Canada: Halifax, NS. 1977-1987. Lang.: Eng.
1695

Čajka (Seagull, The)
Plays/librettos/scripts
Analysis of *Čajka (The Seagull)* by Anton Čechov. Russia. 1896. Lang.: Kor.
2718

Carmen — cont'd

Reviews and discussion of Tokyo productions. Japan: Tokyo. 1960-1987. Lang.: Jap. 1960

Comments on Tokyo performances. Japan: Tokyo. 1987. Lang.: Jap. 1964

Autobiography of film and stage director Peter Brook. UK-England. 1946-1987. Lang.: Eng. 2281

Carmen presented at Expo '86. Canada: Vancouver, BC. 1986. Lang.: Eng. 3751

The original production of *Carmen*. France: Paris. 1873-1875. Lang.: Eng. 3773

Background on Metropolitan radio broadcast performances. USA: New York, NY. 1987. Lang.: Eng. 3837

Background on Metropolitan telecast performances. USA: New York, NY. 1987. Lang.: Eng. 3839

Mezzo soprano Risë Stevens. USA: New York, NY. Lang.: Eng. 3856

Imre Kálmán's *Cigányprimás (Sari)* and Bizet's *Carmen* at Kisfaludy Theatre staged by József Bor. Hungary: Györ. 1912-1986. Lang.: Hun. 3959

Plays/librettos/scripts

Mérimée novella, source of Bizet's *Carmen*. France: Paris. 1803-1870. Lang.: Eng. 3903

Opera adaptations for Broadway with African-American artists. USA: New York, NY. 1935-1987. Lang.: Eng. 3932

Carmen Jones

Plays/librettos/scripts

Opera adaptations for Broadway with African-American artists. USA: New York, NY. 1935-1987. Lang.: Eng. 3932

Carnegie Hall (New York, NY)

Performance spaces

The lighting restoration of Carnegie Hall. USA: New York, NY. 1986. Lang.: Eng. 708

Carnelia, Craig

Performance/production

Collection of newspaper reviews by New York theatre critics. USA: New York, NY. 1987. Lang.: Eng. 2319

Carner, Joseph

Plays/librettos/scripts

General history of Catalan literature, including theatre. Spain-Catalonia. 1902-1961. Lang.: Cat. 1157

Carney, Catherine

Performance/production

Collection of newspaper reviews by London theatre critics. UK-England: London. 1987. Lang.: Eng. 2227

Carnival

SEE ALSO

Classed Entries under MIXED ENTERTAINMENT—Carnival.

Performance/production

André Heller, creator of *Luna Luna*. Austria: Vienna. 1700-1799. Lang.: Ita. 3250

Growth of West Indian carnival traditions. West Indies. Lang.: Eng. 3277

Doc Fred Foster Bloodgood, vaudevillian, who sold medicine to crowds between acts. USA: New York, NY. 1929-1987. Lang.: Eng. 3305

Theatrical elements of gay rights parade. USA: New York, NY. 1987. Lang.: Eng. 3335

Caroline theatre

Plays/librettos/scripts

Political, social and religious issues in Caroline drama. England. 1632-1642. Lang.: Eng. 2508

Carolinian theatre

Plays/librettos/scripts

Political, social and religious issues in Caroline drama. England. 1632-1642. Lang.: Eng. 2508

Carr, Allan

Performance/production

Transformation of *La Cage aux Folles* from movie to a Broadway musical. USA: New York, NY. 1983-1987. Lang.: Eng. 940

Carreras, José

Performance/production

Film versions of Puccini's *La Bohème*, Offenbach's *Tales of Hoffmann*. Europe. North America. 1987. Lang.: Eng. 3767

Premiere of Leonardo Balarda's opera *Cristobal Colón*. Spain-Catalonia: Barcelona. 1987. Lang.: Eng. 3818

Carrie

Administration

The first Anglo-American commercial Broadway production, the musical *Carrie*. USA: New York, NY. UK-England: London. 1987. Lang.: Eng. 61

Carrier Frequency, The

Performance/production

Collection of newspaper reviews by London theatre critics. UK-England: London. 1986. Lang.: Eng. 2084

Carrière, Jean-Claude

Performance/production

Orientalism in Peter Brook's production of *The Mahabharata*. India. USA: New York, NY. 400 B.C.-1987 A.D. Lang.: Eng. 1932

Collection of newspaper reviews by New York theatre critics. USA: New York, NY. 1987. Lang.: Eng. 2315

Plays/librettos/scripts

Development of *The Mahabharata* directed by Peter Brook and Jean-Claude Carrière. 1975-1987. Lang.: Eng. 2412

Carrion, Ambrosi

Plays/librettos/scripts

General history of Catalan literature, including theatre. Spain-Catalonia. 1902-1961. Lang.: Cat. 1157

Carroll, Vinnette

Institutions

The formation of the North Carolina Black Repertory Company. USA: Winston-Salem, NC. 1979-1987. Lang.: Eng. 1666

Carson, Robert J.

Performance/production

Collection of newspaper reviews by London theatre critics. UK-England: London. 1987. Lang.: Eng. 2265

Cartwright, Fabian

Training

Current state of Northern Ireland's young theatre community. UK-Ireland. 1987. Lang.: Eng. 1387

Cartwright, Jim

Performance/production

Collection of newspaper reviews by London theatre critics. UK. 1987. Lang.: Eng. 2031

Collection of newspaper reviews by London theatre critics. UK-England: London. 1986. Lang.: Eng. 2078

Collection of newspaper reviews by London theatre critics. UK-England: London. 1986. Lang.: Eng. 2123

Caruso, Enrico

Performance/production

Initial recordings of Verdi's operas. Italy. France. USA. 1900-1945. Lang.: Eng. 3800

Casa de Bernarda Alba, La (House of Bernarda Alba, The)

Performance/production

Interview with Eric Bentley, director of *La Casa de Bernarda Alba* at the Abbey. Ireland: Dublin. 1900-1985. Lang.: Eng. 1934

Collection of newspaper reviews by London theatre critics. UK-England: London. 1986. Lang.: Eng. 2172

Collection of newspaper reviews by London theatre critics. UK-England: London. 1987. Lang.: Eng. 2178

Casa llena (Full House)

Plays/librettos/scripts

Comparison of plays by Leonor Azcarate and Estela Lenero. Mexico: Mexico City. 1987. Lang.: Spa. 2700

Casault, Jean

Performance/production

Personnel associated with production of Lepage's *La Trilogie des dragons*. Canada. 1987. Lang.: Fre. 1713

Cash, Rosalind

Plays/librettos/scripts

Interview with playwright Charles Fuller. USA: Philadelphia, PA, New York, NY. Korea, South. 1959-1987. Lang.: Eng. 2921

Cassidy, Dominic

Performance/production

Collection of newspaper reviews by London theatre critics. UK-England. 1987. Lang.: Eng. 2033

Casson, Ann

Performance/production

Actress Ann Casson on proper line speaking in Shaw. UK-England. 1924-1981. Lang.: Eng. 2305

CAST (Cartoon Archetypal Slogan Theatre)

Performance/production

Development of alternative cabaret. UK-England. 1980. Lang.: Eng. 3288

Castellanos, Rosario
  Plays/librettos/scripts
  Feminist themes in Rosario Castellanos' *El eterno femenino (The Eternal Feminine)*. Mexico. Lang.: Spa.   2694
Castillo, Julio
  Plays/librettos/scripts
  Ethnic roots in *De la calle (Of the Street)* by Jesús Gonzalez-Davila. Mexico: Mexico City. 1987. Lang.: Spa.   2699
Casting
  Administration
  Interview with Hans Kemna, casting director. Netherlands. 1987. Lang.: Dut.   34
  Strike by Hispanic Organization of Latin Americans (HOLA) due to inadequate casting of Hispanic actors. USA: New York, NY. 1982. Lang.: Eng.   110
  Circle Repertory Theatre's plan to increase roles for minority actors. USA: New York, NY. 1983. Lang.: Eng.   116
  Advisory Committee on Chorus Affairs and Equity devise procedures for chorus calls. USA: New York, NY. 1983. Lang.: Eng.   117
  Reactions to first national symposium on nontraditional casting. USA: New York, NY. 1986-1987. Lang.: Eng.   144
  Career of theatrical agent Milton Goldman. USA. 1930-1987. Lang.: Eng.   155
  Nontraditional casting: types, rationale and examples. USA: New York, NY. 1987. Lang.: Eng.   203
  First nontraditional casting symposium. USA: New York, NY. 1975-1987. Lang.: Eng.   208
  Producer's comments on first national symposium on nontraditional casting. USA: New York, NY. 1986-1987. Lang.: Eng.   215

  Institutions
  Review of a production of *Ariadne auf Naxos*. Canada. 1987. Lang.: Eng.   3717

  Performance/production
  The AEA approved definition for nontraditional casting. USA: New York, NY. 1987. Lang.: Eng.   925
  Nontraditional casting in a production of *The Cherry Orchard*. USA: San Francisco, CA. 1986. Lang.: Eng.   928
  Issues in nontraditional casting. USA: New York, NY. 1986. Lang.: Eng.   936
  Ethnic and minority casting opportunities. USA. 1986. Lang.: Eng.   939
  Actors' Equity symposium on nontraditional casting. USA. 1987. Lang.: Eng.   981

  Relation to other fields
  Actors' Equity's affirmative action program. USA: New York, NY. 1982. Lang.: Eng.   1261
  Nontraditional casting of minority actors. USA. 1979-1987. Lang.: Eng.   1274
Castle of Perseverance, The
  Performance spaces
  Use of space in medieval theatre: outdoor areas, churches. England. 1300-1576. Lang.: Eng.   1668

  Performance/production
  The medieval tournament tradition in the original staging of *The Castle of Perseverance*. England. 1425. Lang.: Eng.   776
Castle Theatre (Budapest)
  SEE
  Várszínház.
Castle Theatre (Gyula)
  SEE
  Gyulai Várszínház.
Castle Theatre (Kisvárda)
  SEE
  Kisvárdai Várszínház.
Castle Theatre (Kőszeg)
  SEE
  Kőszegi Várszínház.
Castle, James
  Performance/production
  Collection of newspaper reviews by London theatre critics. UK-England: London. 1987. Lang.: Eng.   2245
Castle, The
  Performance/production
  Interview with actress Tanja Jacobs. Canada: Toronto, ON. 1987. Lang.: Eng.   727

Castledine, Annie
  Performance/production
  Collection of newspaper reviews by London theatre critics. UK-England. 1987. Lang.: Eng.   2199
  Collection of newspaper reviews by London theatre critics. UK-England: London. 1987. Lang.: Eng.   2256
Castrati
  Performance/production
  Cross-gender casting in Italian Baroque opera. Italy: Venice, Rome. 1550-1987. Lang.: Eng.   3806
Català, Víctor
  SEE
  Albert, Caterina.
Catalogues
  Design/technology
  Catalogue of exhibit on Viennese costume. Austria: Vienna. 1888-1972. Lang.: Fre, Dut.   301
  Catalogue of costume exhibit: Fortuny, Caramba. Italy. 1906-1936. Lang.: Ita.   345

  Performance/production
  Catalogue of an exhibit on singer-dancer Josephine Baker. France: Paris. 1906-1975. Lang.: Ita.   3259

  Reference materials
  Rolf Bergmann's catalogue of medieval German drama. Germany. 1986. Lang.: Eng.   1202
  Children's productions by Ente Teatrale Italiano. Italy. 1986-1987. Lang.: Ita.   1207

  Relation to other fields
  Exhibition devoted to modern dancer Gret Palucca. Germany, East: Dresden. 1922-1987. Lang.: Ger.   1476
Catalyst Theatre (Edmonton, AB)
  Institutions
  A history of documentary theatre in English Canada. Canada. 1970-1986. Lang.: Eng.   508
  Two community-based popular theatre projects. Canada. 1987. Lang.: Eng.   522

  Performance/production
  Collective production of popular theatre. Canada: Edmonton, AB. 1987. Lang.: Eng.   726
Catastrophe
  Plays/librettos/scripts
  Beckett links theme of political persecution to voyeurism of the theatrical experience. France. 1982-1987. Lang.: Eng.   2589
Catch Chang Hui-tsan Alive
  SEE
  Chu yen ch'u tong ho hsi.
Cate, Ritsaertten
  Performance/production
  Collection of newspaper reviews by London theatre critics. UK-England: London. 1987. Lang.: Eng.   2254
Catherine of Siena
  Performance/production
  Collection of newspaper reviews by London theatre critics. UK-England: London. 1986. Lang.: Eng.   2061
Cats
  Administration
  Producer Marlene Smith. Canada: Toronto, ON. 1985. Lang.: Eng.   3617
Catullus
  Performance/production
  Gábor Székely directs Milán Füst's *Catullus* at Katona József Theatre. Hungary: Budapest. 1987. Lang.: Hun.   1857
  Gábor Székely directs Milán Füst's *Catullus* at Katona József Theatre. Hungary: Budapest. 1987. Lang.: Hun.   1878
  Milán Füst's *Catullus* and Imre Sarkadi's *Oszlopos Simeon (The Man on the Pillar)* reviewed. Hungary: Budapest. 1987. Lang.: Hun.   1886
Caucasian Chalk Circle, The
  SEE
  Kaukasische Kreidekreis, Der.
Cauldron
  Performance/production
  Collection of newspaper reviews by London theatre critics. UK-England: London. 1987. Lang.: Eng.   2247
Caulfield, Anne
  Performance/production
  Collection of newspaper reviews by London theatre critics. UK-England: London. 1987. Lang.: Eng.   2187

Caux, Robert
Performance/production
Personnel associated with production of Lepage's *La Trilogie des dragons*. Canada. 1987. Lang.: Fre.   1713
Cave of Salamanca, The
SEE
Cueva de Salamanca, La.
Cavittunatakam
Performance/production
History and description of a performance of *Cavittunatakam*, a drama recounting lives of the saints. India: Kerala. 1984. Lang.: Eng.   1480
CCT Theatre Lighting Limited (UK)
Design/technology
Interview with Don Hindle and Phil Rose of CCT Theatre Lighting Ltd. UK-England. 1864-1987. Lang.: Hun.   374
Ce qui reste du désir (What's Left of Desire)
Plays/librettos/scripts
The role of the father-figure in recent plays from Quebec. Canada: Quebec. 1980-1987. Lang.: Fre.   2465
Čechov, Anton Pavlovič
Basic theatrical documents
Constance Garnett's translation of *Tri sestry (Three Sisters)* by Čechov. England: London. 1901. Lang.: Eng.   1552
Russian symbolist plays and essays. USSR. 1880-1986. Lang.: Eng.   1584
Design/technology
V. Levental's scenery for Čechov's *Diadia Vania (Uncle Vanya)* at Moscow Art Theatre. USSR: Moscow. 1985. Lang.: Rus.   493
Performance/production
Revolutionary approach to directing. France. 1987. Lang.: Fre.   794
Plays of Čechov interpreted by director Oleg Jefremov. USSR: Moscow. 1960-1987. Lang.: Rus.   1017
Life and work of Anatolij Efros. USSR: Moscow. 1983-1987. Lang.: Eng.   1038
Patrice Chéreau and Théâtre des Amandiers create stage and film versions of Čechov's *Platonov*. France: Nanterre. 1982-1987. Lang.: Swe.   1755
Interview with director Tamás Ascher. Hungary. 1987. Lang.: Hun.   1800
Ottó Ádám directs Anton Pavlovič Čechov's *Višnëvyj sad (The Cherry Orchard)* at Madách Theatre under the title *Cseresznyéskert*. Hungary: Budapest. 1987. Lang.: Hun.   1805
Actress Ada Tal on playing different Čechov roles. Israel: Tel Aviv. USSR. 1987. Lang.: Heb.   1940
Collection of newspaper reviews by London theatre critics. UK-England: London. 1986. Lang.: Eng.   2080
Collection of newspaper reviews by London theatre critics. UK-England: London. 1987. Lang.: Eng.   2195
Collection of newspaper reviews by London theatre critics. UK-England: London. 1987. Lang.: Eng.   2253
Review of production and staging aspects of *Wild Honey* by Anton Čechov. UK-England: London. 1986. Lang.: Eng.   2306
Plays/librettos/scripts
Russian and Soviet interaction with the U.S. USSR. USA. 1700-1987. Lang.: Rus.   1191
Critical reception of realism and naturalism. Germany. 1890-1987. Lang.: Ger.   2601
Interpretations of the plays of Ibsen, Čechov and Beckett. Norway. Ireland. Russia. 1987. Lang.: Hun.   2711
Analysis of *Čajka (The Seagull)* by Anton Čechov. Russia. 1896. Lang.: Kor.   2718
Višnëvyj sad (The Cherry Orchard): Čechov's artistry. USSR. 1904. Lang.: Rus.   2951
Riddles in Čechov's *Čajka (The Seagull)*. USSR. 1898-1987. Lang.: Rus.   2952
Čechov interpretations in socialist countries. USSR. 1980-1987. Lang.: Rus.   2965
Relation to other fields
Experimental theatre course, Assoc. Internationale pour la Sémiologie du Spectacle. Belgium: Brussels. France: Paris. Denmark: Odense. 1983-1985. Lang.: Fre.   1219
Theory/criticism
Exploration of the nature of tragedy. 500 B.C.-1987 A.D. Lang.: Eng.   3020

Review of Korean National Theatre production of Čechov's *Diadia Vania (Uncle Vanya)*. Korea: Seoul. 1986-1987. Lang.: Kor.   3054
Relation of dramatic text to other written arts. USSR. Israel. 1921-1987. Lang.: Heb.   3078
Čechov, Michajl A.
Performance/production
History of teaching method of Michajl Čechov. USA. USSR. 1891-1955. Lang.: Eng.   931
Michajl Čechov's life and work: a descriptive chronology. Russia: Moscow. 1901-1980. Lang.: Eng.   2002
Development of the Stanislavskij Acting System. Russia: Moscow. 1906-1938. Lang.: Eng.   2003
Actor Michajl Čechov's answers to a questionnaire investigating the psychology of acting. USSR: Moscow. 1923. Lang.: Eng.   2376
Transcriptions from lectures and lessons given by actor Michajl Čechov on his technique. USSR: Moscow. 1942-1919. Lang.: Eng.   2377
Moscow Art Theatre's production of *Hamlet* with Michajl Čechov in the title role. USSR: Moscow. 1924. Lang.: Eng.   2386
Training
Interview with acting teacher Deirdre Hurst du Prey, specialist in the Chekhov Method. UK-England: Dartington. 1978. Lang.: Eng.   3081
Acting teachers who studied under Michajl Čechov: making the Technique fit contemporary needs. USA: New York, NY. 1930-1980. Lang.: Eng.   3082
Cecil, Robert
Plays/librettos/scripts
Argument against authenticity of three Elizabethan documents. England. 1591-1885. Lang.: Eng.   3326
Cële-Cële, un mauvais cadre agricole (Cële-Cële, or Bad Farm Manager)
Plays/librettos/scripts
Compares plays of Enlightenment France, Francophone Africa. Congo: Brazzaville. Cameroon. Benin. France. 1700-1975. Lang.: Eng.   2496
Cele, Thami
Performance/production
Content and North American reception of *Asinimali! (We Have No Money!)* by Mbongeni Ngema. Canada. South Africa, Republic of. 1987. Lang.: Eng.   1715
Cenci, The
Plays/librettos/scripts
Antonin Artaud's interpretation of Shelley's *The Cenci*. UK-England. France. 1819-1920. Lang.: Eng.   2780
Theory/criticism
Structuralist approach to play interpretation. 500 B.C.-1987 A.D. Lang.: Eng.   3016
Cenerentola, La
Performance/production
András Békés directs Rossini's *La Cenerentola* at Szentendrei Teátrum under the title *Hamupipöke*. Hungary: Szentendre. 1987. Lang.: Hun.   3798
Censorship
Administration
Impact of the proposed anti-pornography legislation. Canada: Quebec, PQ. 1985-1988. Lang.: Fre.   10
Role of the Master of the Revels as censor. England: London. 1662-1737. Lang.: Eng.   22
Censorship, sociology and constitutional law. Korea. 1987. Lang.: Kor.   31
Questions about the role of private sponsorship in publicly funded theatre. Switzerland. 1987. Lang.: Ger.   43
Fight against censorship in theatre. USA: New York, NY. 1986. Lang.: Eng.   68
Copyright laws governing Soviet publications. USA. USSR. 1973-1987. Lang.: Eng.   253
Political censorship of theatre. England. Russia. France. Germany. 1800-1899. Lang.: Eng.   1517
Little theatre and control. Korea: Seoul. 1960-1979. Lang.: Kor.   1521
The film rating system of the Motion Picture Association of America (MPAA). USA. 1968-1982. Lang.: Eng.   3120
Performance/production
New regime ends theatrical censorship. Brazil. 1980-1984. Lang.: Spa.   1689

Censorship — cont'd

The influence of the feudal class on traditional Chinese opera. China. 900. Lang.: Chi. 3465

Plays/librettos/scripts

Comparative view of play censorship. Korea. Japan. Germany. 1940-1987. Lang.: Kor. 1147

Political protest in Tom Stoppard's *Every Good Boy Deserves Favour*. UK-England. USSR. 1974-1977. Lang.: Eng. 2783

Relation to other fields

Artists and writers affected by political decisions. China, People's Republic of. 1987. Lang.: Eng. 1226

Protest of US Immigration and Naturalization Service policies by American presenting organizations. USA. 1986. Lang.: Eng. 1282

Effects of glasnost's policy on Russian arts. USSR. 1987. Lang.: Eng. 1292

South Africa Department of Information's film *South Africa's Performing Arts*. South Africa, Republic of. 1970. Lang.: Eng. 3185

Political theatre and the fall of Ferdinand Marcos. Philippines. 1972-1986. Lang.: Eng. 3281

Census, The
SEE
Censo, El.

Central Puppet Theatre (Moscow)
SEE
Gosudarstvénnyj Centralnyj Teat'r Kukol.

Centre Dramàtic de la Generalitat de Catalunya (Barcelona)
Institutions

Evaluation of theatrical policy in Catalonia. Spain-Catalonia: Barcelona. 1976-1986. Lang.: Cat. 1635

Centre International de Recherche Théâtrale (Paris)
Performance/production

Eastern theatre forms in Western artists' productions. Canada: Vancouver, BC. 1987. Lang.: Eng. 725

Company members of Centre International de Recherche Théâtrale discuss *The Mahabharata*. France: Paris. 1986. Lang.: Eng. 1752

CentreStage (Toronto, ON)
Administration

The merger of two Toronto theatre companies. Canada: Toronto, ON. 1987. Lang.: Eng. 7

Merger of CentreStage and Toronto Free Theatre. Canada: Toronto, ON. 1986-1987. Lang.: Eng. 1515

Centro de Experimentación Teatral (CET, Mexico City)
Performance/production

Review of *El Balcón*: production of Genet's *Le Balcon (The Balcony)*. Mexico: Mexico City. 1987. Lang.: Spa. 1978

Centro Richerche Teatrali (Milan)
Performance/production

Interview with Polish playwright Tadeusz Kantor. Poland: Cracow. Germany, West: Kassel. Italy: Milan. Italy: Sicily. 1987. Lang.: Eng, Fre. 876

Centrum (Netherlands)
Performance/production

Interview with Jules Hamel, actor. Netherlands. 1987. Lang.: Dut. 1980

Cercle Molière (Montreal, PQ)
Basic theatrical documents

Text of *Le Roitelet (The Kinglet)* by Claude Dorge. Canada: Montreal, PQ. 1976. Lang.: Fre. 1545

Cereteli, N.
Performance/production

Life and work of N. Cereteli, leading actor of Tairov Chamber Theatre. USSR: Moscow. 1890-1942. Lang.: Rus. 1072

Cerha, Friedrich
Performance/production

Stage history of Alban Berg's opera *Lulu*. Austria. France: Paris. 1937-1979. Lang.: Swe. 3743

Černyševskij Opera Theatre
SEE
Teat'r Opery i Baleta im. N. Černyševskovo (Saratov).

Cervantes Saavedra, Miguel de
Performance/production

Review of three interludes by Cervantes. Yugoslavia. 1987. Lang.: Fre. 1092

Theory/criticism

Functions of comedy in the seventeenth century. Spain. 1604-1690. Lang.: Spa. 3058

Cesarotti, Melchiorre
Plays/librettos/scripts

Correspondence of playwright Ugo Foscolo regarding *Tieste (Thyestes)*. Italy: Venice. 1797-1827. Lang.: Ita. 2677

Ch'a Kuan (Tea House)
Performance/production

Chiao Chü Yin's *Ch'a Kuan (Tea House)* uses Western style. China, People's Republic of. 1957-1959. Lang.: Chi. 1723

Ch'iu, Shengjung
Performance/production

Acting theory of Chinese opera. China, People's Republic of. 1900-1986. Lang.: Chi. 3500

Chaikin, Joseph
Audience

Letters written by Joseph Chaikin regarding actor-audience relationship. USA: Washington, DC, New York, NY. 1974-1984. Lang.: Eng. 291

Performance/production

Rehearsals and performance of Joseph Chaikin's *A War Within*. USA: San Francisco, CA. 1987. Lang.: Eng. 930

Plays/librettos/scripts

Megan Terry's transformational plays for the Open Theatre. USA. 1987. Lang.: Eng. 2910

Chaises, Les (Chairs, The)
Reference materials

History of pocket theatre. France: Paris. 1944-1953. Lang.: Eng. 2974

Chakravyuha
Performance/production

Collection of newspaper reviews by London theatre critics. UK-England: London. 1987. Lang.: Eng. 2238

Chalmers, Floyd S.
Institutions

Critical discussion of the Chalmers Awards. Canada: Toronto, ON. 1987. Lang.: Eng. 513

Chamber Theatre (Moscow)
SEE
Kamernyj Teat'r.

Chamber Theatre (Munich)
SEE
Kammerspiele.

Chamber Theatre (Pest)
SEE
Kamaraszinház.

Chamber Theatre (Sopot)
SEE
Teatr Wybrzeżne.

Chamber Theatre (Tel Aviv)
SEE
Kameri.

Chamberlain, Richard
Performance/production

History of musical version, *Breakfast at Tiffany's*. USA: New York, NY, Philadelphia, PA, Boston, MA. 1958-1966. Lang.: Eng. 3644

Chand, Paul
Performance/production

Collection of newspaper reviews by London theatre critics. UK-England: London. 1987. Lang.: Eng. 2226

Chandler, Raymond
Performance/production

Autobiography of director, producer and writer John Houseman. USA: New York, NY. 1935-1985. Lang.: Eng. 2339

Chang in a Void Moon
Performance/production

Production of John Jesurun's *Chang in a Void Moon*. USA: New York, NY. 1982-1983. Lang.: Eng. 2336

Chang-le-gong (Palace of the Beatitudes, The)
Basic theatrical documents

Text of the play *Chang-le-gong (The Palace of the Beatitudes)* by Guh Shyi Tung. China: Binjiang. 1987. Lang.: Chi. 3442

Chang, Ren-Xia
Performance/production

Comparison between Chinese opera and Buddhist plays of Kerala. China, People's Republic of: Beijing. India. 1050-1968. Lang.: Chi. 3533

Chang, Tisa
Administration

Nontraditional casting: types, rationale and examples. USA: New York, NY. 1987. Lang.: Eng. 203

Chang, Tisa — cont'd

Relation to other fields
Nontraditional casting of minority actors. USA. 1979-1987. Lang.:
Eng.   1274

Changeling, The
Performance/production
Shakespeare and contemporaries: tradition, intertextuality in
performance. England. 1607-1987. Lang.: Eng.   1740

Changuk
Performance spaces
Performance space and staging of traditional Korean genres. Korea.
Japan. 57 B.C.-1986 A.D. Lang.: Kor.   663
Stages of traditional theatre in Asia, and development of *Changuk*
dance drama. Korea. China. India. 57 B.C.-1987 A.D. Lang.: Kor.
                                                                         664

Performance/production
Origin and influence of *pansori* music-drama. Korea. 1392-1910.
Lang.: Kor.   3406

Chantecler
Basic theatrical documents
New English translation of Rostand's *Chantecler*. France. 1880-1987.
Lang.: Eng.   1554

Chapeau de Paille d'Italie, Un (Italian Straw Hat, An)
Performance/production
Collection of newspaper reviews by London theatre critics. UK-
England: London. 1986. Lang.: Eng.   2040

Chapin, Ted
Administration
Current computer vendor developments in information systems. USA.
1983-1984. Lang.: Eng.   249

Chaplin, Charlie
Performance/production
Autobiography of director, producer and writer John Houseman.
USA: New York, NY. 1935-1985. Lang.: Eng.   2339

Chapman, John
Theory/criticism
Balanchine ballerinas: female domination in the ballet. USA. 1946-
1987. Lang.: Eng.   1457
Trollope's writings on Elizabethan and Jacobean drama. UK-
England. 1866-1882. Lang.: Eng.   3063

Charabanc Theatre Company
Relation to other fields
Interview with founders of the Charabanc Theatre Company. UK-
Ireland. 1970-1987. Lang.: Eng.   1260

Characters/roles
Administration
Phantom of the Opera exchange: British, U.S. Equity agreement. UK-
England: London. USA: New York, NY. 1987. Lang.: Eng.   49
Copyrightability of fictional characters. USA. 1986-1987. Lang.: Eng.
                                                                       3085

Basic theatrical documents
Catalan translation of Milan Kundera's *Jacques et son maître
(Jacques and His Master)*, with introduction. Czechoslovakia: Prague.
1968-1981. Lang.: Cat.   1551
Catalan translation of *Bekannte Gesichter, Gemischte Gefühle (Known
Faces, Mixed Feelings)* by Botho Strauss. Germany. 1944-1978.
Lang.: Cat.   1557
Study of the poetic, narrative and theatrical work of Agustí Bartra,
edition of complete works, vol. 4. Spain-Catalonia. Mexico. 1937-
1982. Lang.: Cat.   1571
Edition and analysis, *Allò que tal vegada s'esdevingué (What
Happened Then)* by Joan Oliver. Spain-Catalonia. 1899-1986. Lang.:
Cat.   1573

Design/technology
Face painting and character in Chinese opera. China, People's
Republic of. 1986. Lang.: Chi.   3448
Controversy over 1901 cylinder recording of *Les Huguenots*. USA.
1901-1987. Lang.: Eng.   3699

Performance/production
Chinese acting technique. China, People's Republic of: Beijing. 1368-
1986. Lang.: Chi.   758
Two productions of Pinter's *Old Times*. UK-England: London. USA:
New York, NY, St. Louis, MO. 1971-1985. Lang.: Eng.   907
Actresses discuss role of Joan in Shaw's *Saint Joan*. USA. Canada.
UK-England. 1987. Lang.: Eng.   944
Four approaches to the role of Sally Bowles in *Cabaret*. USA: New
York, NY. Germany. 1966-1987. Lang.: Eng.   968

Evolution of the heroes in plays directed by G.A. Tovstonogov.
USSR: Leningrad. 1950-1980. Lang.: Rus.   1051
Kenneth Tynan's review of the first production of Osborne's *Look
Back in Anger*. 1956. Lang.: Eng.   1677
Theatre of playwright Robert Lepage. Canada: Montreal, PQ.
Canada: Toronto, ON. 1980-1987. Lang.: Eng.   1704
Creations' of *La Trilogie des dragons (Dragon Trilogy)* by Robert
Lepage. Canada. 1987. Lang.: Fre.   1706
Interview with actress Roberta Maxwell. Canada. 1987. Lang.: Eng.
                                                                       1718
Roles portrayed by stage actress Nell Gwyn. England: London.
1663-1668. Lang.: Eng.   1731
Examples of transition in acting style. England. 1783-1784. Lang.:
Eng.   1733
Comparison of *onnagata* actors with Elizabethan boy actors.
England. Japan. 1580-1987. Lang.: Eng.   1737
Semiotics of Brechtian acting. Europe. 1986. Lang.: Eng.   1748
Franz Xaver Kroetz's *Wunschkonzert (Request Concert)* in Bombay:
observations of actress Sulabha Deshpande. India: Bombay. 1986.
Lang.: Eng.   1931
Actress Ada Tal on playing different Čechov roles. Israel: Tel Aviv.
USSR. 1987. Lang.: Heb.   1940
Actor Mario Scaccia and his Molière interpretations. Italy. 1949-1987.
Lang.: Ita.   1946
Roles of Dame Peggy Ashcroft and directors she has worked with.
UK-England. 1930-1986. Lang.: Eng.   2278
Actor Antony Sher talks about his upcoming season at Stratford.
UK-England: Stratford. 1987. Lang.: Eng.   2294
Philip Bosco's portrayals of characters in the plays of George
Bernard Shaw. USA. 1987. Lang.: Eng.   2335
Interview with actor James Earl Jones. USA: New York, NY. 1953-
1987. Lang.: Eng.   2340
Three actors discuss their approaches to the characters of Samuel
Beckett. USA. 1987. Lang.: Eng.   2343
Codco, a comic theatrical troupe, creates regional characters. Canada:
St. John's, NF. 1986. Lang.: Eng.   3253
Transvestite roles in extravaganzas of J.R. Planché and Mme.
Vestris. UK-England: London. 1830-1870. Lang.: Eng.   3268
David Bowie's *Glass Spider Tour*. UK-England. 1987. Lang.: Dut.
                                                                       3270
Interpreters of the *commedia dell'arte* character Pulcinella. Italy:
Naples. 1609-1975. Lang.: Ita.   3311
Actors and institutions of eighteenth-century Venice. Italy: Venice.
1700-1800. Lang.: Ita.   3312
Conventionalized characters in Chinese opera. China, People's
Republic of. 1987. Lang.: Chi.   3473
Overview of *Gu Cheng-Hei*. China, People's Republic of. 1967.
Lang.: Chi.   3498
Four steps to make *Da Peng Ge* more popular. China, People's
Republic of. 1987. Lang.: Chi.   3506
Comparison between Chinese opera and Buddhist plays of Kerala.
China, People's Republic of: Beijing. India. 1050-1968. Lang.: Chi.
                                                                       3533
History of musical version, *Breakfast at Tiffany's*. USA: New York,
NY, Philadelphia, PA, Boston, MA. 1958-1966. Lang.: Eng.   3644
Plot synopsis of musical *Mademoiselle Colombe* based on Anouilh's
Colombe. USA: New York, NY. 1987. Lang.: Eng.   3647
Interview with soprano Jane MacKenzie. Canada. UK-England. 1987.
Lang.: Eng.   3754
Shift in opera from the singer to the conductor. Europe. North
America. 1887-1987. Lang.: Eng.   3766
Soprano Eva Marton discusses Turandot. Hungary. 1943-1987. Lang.:
Eng.   3797
Career of basso Italo Tajo. Italy: Turin. 1935-1982. Lang.: Eng.
                                                                       3805
Cross-gender casting in Italian Baroque opera. Italy: Venice, Rome.
1550-1987. Lang.: Eng.   3806
Vasile Moldoveanu's views on the current state of opera. USA.
1987. Lang.: Eng.   3844
Puppeteer's analysis of characters in Punch and Judy show. UK-
England. 1987. Lang.: Eng.   3982

Characters/roles — cont'd

Plays/librettos/scripts

Summary and critical analysis of *Doc* by Sharon Pollock. Canada. 1987. Lang.: Eng. 1100

Discusses the 1986 ISTA conference. Denmark. Asia. 1986. Lang.: Fre. 1112

King Lear focusing on the character of Kent. England. 1605. Lang.: Eng. 1122

Shakespeare's *Henry V*: development of Prince Hal as an ideological monarch. England. 1599. Lang.: Eng. 1124

Theme of journeys in German theatre and film. Germany. 1970-1986. Lang.: Fre. 1127

The new Black literary criticism. USA. 1986. Lang.: Eng. 1174

Cultural predetermination in three Athol Fugard plays. South Africa, Republic of. 1970. Lang.: Eng. 1419

Perestrojka and the theatre: the socially active hero. USSR. 1987. Lang.: Rus. 1421

The social hero in recent Soviet dramaturgy. USSR. 1975-1985. Lang.: Rus. 1422

Female roles and images in the romantic ballet. France. Germany. Russia. 1830-1920. Lang.: Ger. 1455

Optimistic interpretation of Beckett's *En attendant Godot (Waiting for Godot)*. 1987. Lang.: Eng. 2410

Bartho Smit's *Don Juan onder die Boere (Don Juan among the Boers)*. 1600-1987. Lang.: Afr. 2415

Female characters in city comedy who suffer from bladder incontinence. 1599-1632. Lang.: Eng. 2427

Reconsideration of Weigand's *The Modern Ibsen* (1925). 1850-1987. Lang.: Eng. 2430

Interview with playwright Ray Lawler. Australia. Ireland. 1921-1987. Lang.: Eng. 2433

Ray Lawler's *The Summer of the Seventeenth Doll* and the Australian experience. Australia. 1955-1987. Lang.: Eng. 2435

Focus on the plays of David Williamson and their cultural impact. Australia. 1970-1987. Lang.: Eng. 2436

Survey of the plays of Jack Hibberd: themes and characterization. Australia. 1966-1986. Lang.: Eng. 2437

Paucity of explorers in nineteenth-century Australian drama. Australia. 1861-1900. Lang.: Eng. 2440

Introductory survey of recent Australian playwrights. Australia. 1970-1985. Lang.: Eng. 2447

Misogynist themes in Strindberg, Weininger and Witkiewicz. Austria: Vienna. 1880-1987. Lang.: Eng. 2452

Analysis of *Pelléas et Mélisande* by Maeterlinck. Belgium. 1800. Lang.: Fre. 2454

Interview with playwright Paul Pourveur. Belgium. 1987. Lang.: Dut. 2455

The theme of a child's game in Lepage's *La Trilogie des dragons*. Canada: Montreal, PQ. 1987. Lang.: Fre. 2458

The role of the father-figure in recent plays from Quebec. Canada: Quebec. 1980-1987. Lang.: Fre. 2465

Collective theatre projects in Newfoundland. Canada: St. John's, NF. 1987. Lang.: Eng. 2466

Playwright Tomson Highway's use of native mythology. Canada. 1960-1987. Lang.: Eng. 2468

Playwright Sharon Pollock. Canada. 1970-1983. Lang.: Eng. 2469

Robert Lepage's play *Vinci*. Canada. 1986-1987. Lang.: Fre. 2474

Critical analysis of James Reaney's *Three Desks*. Canada. 1960-1977. Lang.: Eng. 2477

La Trilogie des dragons by Robert Lepage. Canada: Montreal, PQ. 1987. Lang.: Fre. 2479

Plays by Micone, Saddlemyer, Thompson, Wyatt. Canada. 1958-1985. Lang.: Eng. 2481

Survey of Robertson Davies' plays. Canada. 1913-1985. Lang.: Eng. 2484

Interview with playwright Judith Thompson. Canada. 1985. Lang.: Eng. 2486

Play within a play in *Blood Relations* by Sharon Pollock. Canada. 1987. Lang.: Eng. 2489

Shakespeare's *Hamlet*: representation of interiority onstage. England. 1600. Lang.: Eng. 2500

Attack on Sir Robert Walpole in 18th-century adaptation of *King Edward the Third*. England. 1691-1731. Lang.: Eng. 2505

Analysis of medieval Cain and Abel mystery plays. England. 1200-1576. Lang.: Eng. 2506

Styles of speech in Wycherley's *The Plain Dealer*. England. 1676. Lang.: Eng. 2511

The London Merchant by Lillo is an allegory of the Fall. England. 1731-1987. Lang.: Eng. 2514

Changing economic conditions created an audience for plays about criminals. England. 1731-1740. Lang.: Eng. 2517

Comparison of *King Lear* and *Vildanden (The Wild Duck)*. England. Norway. 1605-1884. Lang.: Eng. 2518

Devices that convey concern with sexuality in Shakespeare's *All's Well that Ends Well*. England. 1602-1987. Lang.: Eng. 2523

Venice Preserv'd: impact of Betterton's acting style on Otway. England. 1675-1683. Lang.: Eng. 2527

Analysis of vampire characters in the works of Byron, Polidori and Planché. England. Italy. France. 1800-1825. Lang.: Eng. 2540

Productions of *Sir Thomas More* by Elizabethan theatre companies. England. 1595-1650. Lang.: Eng. 2541

Character analysis of Olivia in *Twelfth Night*. England. 1599. Lang.: Eng. 2544

Title character's relation to the audience in Shakespeare's *Hamlet*. England. 1600-1601. Lang.: Ger. 2545

Independence of Restoration women is reflected in comic heroines. England. 1668-1700. Lang.: Eng. 2550

Classification and social hierarchy in Shakespeare's *Troilus and Cressida*. England. 1601. Lang.: Eng. 2554

Role of Chorus in Shakespeare's *Henry V*. England. 1599. Lang.: Eng. 2556

Improvisational clowning in Elizabethan theatre. England. 1585-1625. Lang.: Eng. 2560

Theme of deconstruction in Samuel Beckett's writings. Europe. 1953-1987. Lang.: Eng. 2563

Ariadne in plays of Ibsen, Strindberg, Maeterlinck. Europe. 1892-1902. Lang.: Eng. 2566

Playwright Michel Vinaver and his works. France. 1927-1987. Lang.: Fre. 2582

Techniques, themes, characters and dramaturgy of Voltaire. France. 1718-1778. Lang.: Eng. 2590

Analysis of the title character of Brecht's *Leben des Galilei (The Life of Galileo)*. Germany, East. 1938-1956. Lang.: Ger. 2606

Maud Gonne and Yeats's portrayal of women in his plays. Ireland: Dublin. 1900-1930. Lang.: Eng. 2646

Characters and the gangster movie form in Thomas Murphy's *The Blue Macushla*. Ireland. 1980-1986. Lang.: Eng. 2647

Comic characters and the Book of Job in the plays of Thomas Murphy. Ireland. 1962-1983. Lang.: Eng. 2648

Historical accuracy of characters in the plays of Thomas Murphy. Ireland. 1962-1986. Lang.: Eng. 2657

Comparison of Marivaux and Goldoni. Italy: Venice. France. 1707-1763. Lang.: Ita. 2664

Machines—animate and inanimate—in *Tonight We Improvise (Questa sera si recita a soggetto)* by Pirandello. Italy. 1929-1987. Lang.: Eng. 2670

Centrality of characters in the plays of Luigi Pirandello. Italy. 1867-1936. Lang.: Ita. 2672

Gender conflict in Pirandello's *Sei personaggi in cerca d'autore (Six Characters in Search of an Author)*. Italy. 1921-1987. Lang.: Eng. 2679

Archetypal nature of title character in *Felipe Angeles* by Elena Garro. Mexico. 1978. Lang.: Spa. 2696

Actor-manager Wojciech Bogusławski in life and in György Spiró's play *Az imposztor (The Imposter)*. Poland. Hungary. 1815-1987. Lang.: Pol. 2716

Analysis of *Čajka (The Seagull)* by Anton Čechov. Russia. 1896. Lang.: Kor. 2718

Athol Fugard's *Master Harold...and the Boys* examines apartheid in terms of human relationships. South Africa, Republic of. 1982-1987. Lang.: Eng. 2723

Characterization in Pieter-Dirk Uys' *Appassionata*. South Africa, Republic of. 1987. Lang.: Eng. 2724

How Athol Fugard's revisions have changed *The Blood Knot*. South Africa, Republic of. 1961-1985. Lang.: Eng. 2725

Characters/roles — cont'd

Directive as a speech act in *Krismis van Map Jacobs (Christmas of Map Jacobs)* by Adam Small. South Africa, Republic of. 1983. Lang.: Afr. 2726

Analysis of 51 short farces written in Majorca. Spain-Catalonia. 1701-1850. Lang.: Cat. 2731

Dearth of female roles: how amateur theatres cope. Sweden. 1987. Lang.: Swe. 2733

Dramatic vs. literary interpretation of *Ett Drömspel (A Dream Play)* by August Strindberg. Sweden. 1901-1964. Lang.: Eng. 2734

Contrasts mostly male parts in plays with mostly female membership in amateur groups. Sweden. 1986. Lang.: Swe. 2739

The son-in-law in *Pelikanen (The Pelican)* by August Strindberg. Sweden. 1907-1987. Lang.: Swe. 2740

Theatrical metaphor in Strindberg's *Gustav III*. Sweden. 1903-1987. Lang.: Eng. 2741

Analysis of Dürrenmatt's *Play Strindberg*, adaptation of Strindberg's *Dödsdansen (The Dance of Death)*. Switzerland. 1971-1982. Lang.: Eng. 2743

Analysis of the plays of E.N. Ziramu. Uganda: Buganda. 1962-1974. Lang.: Eng. 2748

The *Doppelgänger* in *The Doctor's Dilemma* by G.B. Shaw. UK-England. 1906. Lang.: Eng. 2756

Interpretation of the title character of Shakespeare's *Coriolanus*. UK-England. 1607. Lang.: Eng. 2757

Depictions of dying moments of characters in drama, specifically that of Hotspur in *Henry IV, Part I*. UK-England: London. 1595-1598. Lang.: Eng. 2763

Mrs. Warren's Profession: Shaw's ideas embodied in characters. UK-England. 1902. Lang.: Eng. 2765

Shaw's artistic strategy in *Major Barbara*. UK-England. 1905. Lang.: Eng. 2774

Ideological content of Lillo's *The London Merchant*. UK-England. 1731-1800. Lang.: Eng. 2777

Antonin Artaud's interpretation of Shelley's *The Cenci*. UK-England. France. 1819-1920. Lang.: Eng. 2780

Shaw's use of Irish stereotypes in *John Bull's Other Ireland*. UK-England. UK-Ireland. 1860-1925. Lang.: Eng. 2787

Focus on patterns of musical images in character of Iago which unite ideas of *Othello*. UK-England: London. 1604. Lang.: Eng. 2792

The topicality of Shakespeare's *Love's Labour's Lost*. UK-England: London. 1590. Lang.: Eng. 2794

Transvestitism in plays of Caryl Churchill. UK-England. 1987. Lang.: Eng. 2799

Class conflict as theme of *Top Girls*. UK-England. 1982-1987. Lang.: Eng. 2800

Stage business in *Major Barbara* traced to Beerbohm Tree. UK-England. 1905. Lang.: Eng. 2802

Analysis of Shaw's *You Never Can Tell*. UK-England. 1899. Lang.: Eng. 2803

Use of oral history material to develop characters and events in plays. UK-England. 1970-1987. Lang.: Eng. 2807

Comic conventions in Shakespeare's *Titus Andronicus*. UK-England. 1987. Lang.: Eng. 2809

The problem of capitalism in Shaw's *The Millionairess*. UK-England. 1936-1952. Lang.: Eng. 2811

Themes of perception in *The Tempest*. UK-England: London. 1611. Lang.: Eng. 2813

Restoring character originally intended for role of Falstaff in *Henry IV, Part I*. UK-England: London. 1595-1598. Lang.: Eng. 2821

Relationships in Tom Stoppard's *The Real Thing*. UK-England. 1986-1987. Lang.: Eng. 2822

Actress Tilda Swinter talks about her performance as a male. UK-England. 1987. Lang.: Eng. 2824

Christina Reid's *Tea in a China Cup*: a woman's view of Belfast. UK-Ireland: Belfast. 1983-1987. Lang.: Eng. 2831

Psychological complexity of Eugene O'Neill's *Long Day's Journey into Night*. USA. 1940. Lang.: Eng. 2842

Interview with playwright Robert Harling, designer Edward Gianfrancesco. USA: New York, NY. 1987. Lang.: Eng. 2846

Experiment in musical composition based on *King Lear*. USA. 1987. Lang.: Eng. 2848

Women's roles in Broadway plays at the time of women's suffrage. USA: New York, NY. 1920. Lang.: Eng. 2850

Development of themes and characters in plays of Sam Shepard. USA. 1960-1987. Lang.: Eng. 2853

Gender roles in Sam Shepard's plays. USA. 1960-1987. Lang.: Eng. 2860

Barbara Gelb discusses the creation of *My Gene*. USA. 1962-1987. Lang.: Eng. 2867

Interview with playwright August Wilson. USA: New York, NY. 1985-1987. Lang.: Eng. 2876

Characters' search for God in plays of Peter Shaffer. USA. UK-England. 1979-1984. Lang.: Eng. 2878

The child character in the role of protagonist. USA. 1987. Lang.: Eng. 2880

Evolution of female characters in the plays of Sam Shepard. USA. 1976-1987. Lang.: Eng. 2883

Family and male-female relationships in O'Neill's *Desire Under the Elms*. USA. 1920. Lang.: Eng. 2885

Interview with playwright Luis Valdez. USA. 1940-1983. Lang.: Eng. 2897

Three feminist productions of plays by Henrik Ibsen. USA. 1987. Lang.: Eng. 2899

Interview with playwright and director Richard Foreman. USA: New York, NY. 1962-1987. Lang.: Eng. 2908

Comparison of main characters in three contemporary plays. USA: New York, NY. 1987. Lang.: Eng. 2916

Male and female responses to Marsha Norman's *'Night, Mother*. USA. 1983-1987. Lang.: Eng. 2918

Family relationships in Eugene O'Neill's early plays. USA. 1913. Lang.: Eng. 2926

Modernism and postmodernism as themes in Sam Shepard's plays. USA. 1972-1987. Lang.: Eng. 2930

Sam Shepard's manipulation of an audience's desire to believe what it sees. USA. 1967-1983. Lang.: Eng. 2932

Evolution of the hero. USSR. 1950-1987. Lang.: Rus. 2943

Historical themes in recent plays by M. Vartolomeev, P. Red'kin and P. Pavlovskij. USSR. 1980-1987. Lang.: Rus. 2954

Prototypes of characters in Bulgakov's *Zojkina kvartira (Zojka's Apartment)*. USSR: Moscow. 1926. Lang.: Rus. 2956

V.I. Lenin in contemporary Soviet dramaturgy. USSR. 1980-1987. Lang.: Rus. 2961

Distorted race relations in Western films. USA. 1915-1986. Lang.: Eng. 3181

Roles of Black males in American TV. USA. 1950-1987. Lang.: Eng. 3215

Commedia dell'arte: its characters and their costumes. Italy. 1550-1700. Lang.: Kor. 3318

Satirical look at President and Vice President of the United States. USA. 1987. Lang.: Eng. 3370

How music reveals character in Chinese opera. China. 1600-1700. Lang.: Chi. 3545

The explanation of the term 'Shao-Lai' in Yuan drama. China: Beijing. 206 B.C.-1368 A.D. Lang.: Chi. 3553

Stock characters in Chinese comedy. China, People's Republic of. 1986. Lang.: Chi. 3565

The inner and outer psychology of characters in Chinese opera. China, People's Republic of. 1987. Lang.: Chi. 3570

Historical people in the plays of Chinese theatre. China, People's Republic of. 1985. Lang.: Chi. 3576

Mozart's *Nozze di Figaro* compared with Beaumarchais source. 1784-1786. Lang.: Eng. 3887

Adaptation of literary works to opera. 1893-1987. Lang.: Eng. 3890

Comparison of Mozart's *The Magic Flute* and Strauss's *Die Frau ohne Schatten*. Austria: Vienna. 1980. Lang.: Eng. 3891

Background on Philistines of Saint-Saëns' *Samson et Dalila*. Canaan. 3000-1000 B.C. Lang.: Eng. 3893

Role analysis of Blanche in Poulenc's *Dialogues des Carmélites*. France: Paris. 1957-1987. Lang.: Eng. 3901

Career of singer/actress Lotte Lenya. Germany: Berlin. 1929-1970. Lang.: Eng. 3906

Musical sources in the operas of Richard Strauss. Germany: Dresden. 1864-1949. Lang.: Eng. 3908

Characters/roles — cont'd

Analysis of Heinrich Marschner's and Peter Josef von Lindpaintner's operas *Der Vampyr*. Germany: Leipzig, Stuttgart. 1828. Lang.: Eng.
3911

Characters in Verdi's *Otello*. Italy: Milan. 1887. Lang.: Eng. 3920

Characters and political themes in Verdi's *Don Carlos*. Italy: Milan. 1867. Lang.: Eng.
3924

Philip Glass's non-traditional approach to opera. USA. 1980. Lang.: Eng.
3934

Relation to other fields
Characterization in modern drama. China, People's Republic of. 1949-1987. Lang.: Chi.
1227

Nontraditional casting of minority actors. USA. 1979-1987. Lang.: Eng.
1274

Comparison of *Woyzeck* to Nelson Mandela. South Africa, Republic of: Pretoria. 1985. Lang.: Eng.
2999

Audience responses determine character of Mr. Punch. England: London. 1662-1987. Lang.: Eng.
3993

Survival of Punch and Judy shows during the Edwardian period. UK-England. 1860-1910. Lang.: Eng.
3998

Research/historiography
Influences on Wagner's *Ring* cycle. Germany: Dresden. 1813-1883. Lang.: Eng.
3948

Theory/criticism
Self-awareness in Shakespeare's *Julius Caesar*. England. 1599. Lang.: Eng.
1327

Role of poetry in contemporary plays. USA. 1987. Lang.: Eng. 3077

Characterization in theatre and television. China, People's Republic of. 1970-1987. Lang.: Chi.
3217

Tang Xian-Zu's theory of 'original character' in Chinese opera. China, People's Republic of. 700-1986. Lang.: Chi.
3609

Charcot, Jean-Martin
Performance/production
Use of actors to simulate symptoms at medical conferences. USA. 1987. Lang.: Eng.
3275

Charlie Girl
Performance/production
Collection of newspaper reviews by London theatre critics. UK-England: London. 1986. Lang.: Eng.
2124

Charlottetown Festival (Charlottetown, PE)
Institutions
A history of the Charlottetown Festival. Canada: Charlottetown, PE. 1965-1987. Lang.: Eng.
505

Overview of the Charlottetown Festival, 1986 season. Canada: Charlottetown, PE. 1965-1985. Lang.: Eng.
525

Charnin, Martin
Performance/production
Martin Charnin's work in musical theatre. USA: New York, NY. 1957-1987. Lang.: Eng.
3658

Charpentier, Gabriel
Institutions
Need for more Canadian productions of Canadian-composed opera. Canada. 1987. Lang.: Eng.
3718

Chartrand, Linda
Administration
Ground Zero Theatre Company's project for the homeless. Canada: Toronto, ON. 1987. Lang.: Eng.
6

Chater Robinson, Piers
Performance/production
Collection of newspaper reviews by London theatre critics. UK-England: London. 1986. Lang.: Eng.
2042

Chaucer, Geoffrey
Performance/production
Collection of newspaper reviews by London theatre critics. UK-England: London. 1987. Lang.: Eng.
2272

Chautauqua Opera Company (Chautauqua, NY)
Performance spaces
Renovations and new directions for the Chautauqua Opera Company. USA: Chautauqua, NY. 1928-1987. Lang.: Eng.
3738

Chavooshian, Nora
Design/technology
Design work of Nora Chavooshian. USA. 1987. Lang.: Eng. 3138

Checheno-Ingush Drama Theatre
SEE
Čečeno-Ingusskij Dramaticeskij Teat'r im. Ch. Nuradilova.

Cheeseman, Bob
Performance/production
Modern production of the *Chester Cycle*. UK-England: Chester. 1987. Lang.: Eng.
2299

Cheeseman, Peter
Plays/librettos/scripts
Use of oral history material to develop characters and events in plays. UK-England. 1970-1987. Lang.: Eng.
2807

Chejfic, Leonid
Performance/production
Theatre and film directors on interaction of two forms. USSR. 1987. Lang.: Rus.
3173

Chekhov, Anton
SEE
Čechov, Anton Pavlovič.

Chekhov, Michael
SEE
Čechov, Michajl A..

Chelsea Theatre Center (New York, NY)
Administration
Financial challenges of four former artistic directors. USA. 1981-1987. Lang.: Eng.
239

Chen, Chaozheng
Performance/production
Status of Sichuan theatre and opera. China, People's Republic of: Chengdu. 1985-1986. Lang.: Eng.
3512

Chen, Shufang
Performance/production
Status of Sichuan theatre and opera. China, People's Republic of: Chengdu. 1985-1986. Lang.: Eng.
3512

Cheng, Chihchen
Plays/librettos/scripts
Biographical information on playwright Cheng Chihchen. China. 1518-1595. Lang.: Chi.
3543

Chéreau, Patrice
Administration
Filming Wagner's *Der Ring des Nibelungen* at Bayreuth. Germany, West: Bayreuth. Germany, West: Munich. 1980. Lang.: Eng. 3680

Performance/production
Directing as creation of a dimension that enhances the actor's desire. France. 1987. Lang.: Fre.
785

Productions by directors Patrice Chéreau, Claude Régy, Ariane Mnouchkine. France. 1980-1987. Lang.: Rus.
792

Patrice Chéreau and Théâtre des Amandiers create stage and film versions of Čechov's *Platonov*. France: Nanterre. 1982-1987. Lang.: Swe.
1755

Analysis of *Dans la solitude des champs de coton (In the Solitude of the Cotton Fields)* by Bernard-Marie Koltès. France: Paris. 1987. Lang.: Swe.
1761

Directing should be judged by the work of great directors. France. 1987. Lang.: Fre.
1763

Luca Ronconi's view of directing. France. Italy. 1987. Lang.: Fre.
1765

Stage history of Alban Berg's opera *Lulu*. Austria. France: Paris. 1937-1979. Lang.: Swe.
3743

Production history of *Der Ring des Nibelungen*. Germany: Bayreuth. Italy: Milan. USA: New York, NY. 1876-1987. Lang.: Eng. 3775

Cherns, Penny
Performance/production
Collection of newspaper reviews by London theatre critics. UK-England: London. 1987. Lang.: Eng.
2181

Cherry Creek Theatre (St. Peter, MN)
Institutions
History and goals of Cherry Creek Theatre. USA: St. Peter, MN. 1979-1983. Lang.: Eng.
598

Cherry Orchard, The
SEE
Višnëvyj sad.

Cherry, Simon
Performance/production
Collection of newspaper reviews by London theatre critics. UK-England: London. 1986. Lang.: Eng.
2036

Chesley, Robert
Plays/librettos/scripts
Impact of AIDS crisis on the theatre. USA: New York, NY, San Francisco, CA. 1987. Lang.: Eng.
2881

SUBJECT INDEX

Chess
Performance/production
Collection of newspaper reviews by London theatre critics. UK-England: London. 1986. Lang.: Eng.   2097

Chessé, Ralph
Institutions
History of Chessé Marionettes. USA. 1927-1987. Lang.: Eng.   4000

Chester Cycle
Performance/production
Modern production of the *Chester Cycle*. UK-England: Chester. 1987. Lang.: Eng.   2299

Plays/librettos/scripts
Analysis of terms and their meanings in the text of the *Chester Cycle*. England. 1400-1550. Lang.: Eng.   2499

Comparison of Shakespeare's *Cymbeline* with the reign of James I. England. 1400-1550. Lang.: Eng.   2503

Chestnut Street Theatre (Philadelphia, PA)
Institutions
Theatre manager William Wood's paternalism. USA: Philadelphia, PA. 1803-1855. Lang.: Eng.   1659

Chetwys, Robert
Performance/production
Collection of newspaper reviews by London theatre critics. UK-England: London. 1986. Lang.: Eng.   2060

Chevauchée sur le lac de Constance, La (Ride on Lake Constance, A)
Plays/librettos/scripts
Theme of journeys in German theatre and film. Germany. 1970-1986. Lang.: Fre.   1127

Chi-Pai
Performance/production
Chinese opera actor Chi-Pai. China, People's Republic of. 1987. Lang.: Chi.   3519

Chiao, Chü Yin
Performance/production
Chiao Chü Yin's *Ch'a Kuan (Tea House)* uses Western style. China, People's Republic of. 1957-1959. Lang.: Chi.   1723

Chiari, Pietro
Plays/librettos/scripts
Playwright Pietro Chiari. Italy: Venice. 1747-1762. Lang.: Ita.   3316

Chiaroscuro
Performance/production
Collection of newspaper reviews by London theatre critics. UK-England: London. 1986. Lang.: Eng.   2084

Chicago
Plays/librettos/scripts
Gender roles in Sam Shepard's plays. USA. 1960-1987. Lang.: Eng.   2860

Chicago Gypsies, The
Plays/librettos/scripts
The child character in the role of protagonist. USA. 1987. Lang.: Eng.   2880

Chicano theatre
SEE
Ethnic theatre.

Chicken
Performance/production
Collection of newspaper reviews by London theatre critics. UK-England: London. 1987. Lang.: Eng.   2198

Chicken Soup with Barley
Performance/production
Collection of newspaper reviews by London theatre critics. UK-England: London. 1987. Lang.: Eng.   2239

Collection of newspaper reviews by London theatre critics. UK-England: London. 1987. Lang.: Eng.   2253

Childe Byron
Plays/librettos/scripts
Interview with playwright Romulus Linney. USA. 1986. Lang.: Eng.   2931

Childe Harold
Plays/librettos/scripts
Structure of Byron's plays. England. 1788-1824. Lang.: Eng.   2542

Children's theatre
SEE ALSO
Creative drama.

Administration
Interview with Madeleine Rivest. Canada: Montreal, PQ. 1987. Lang.: Fre.   14

Collection of articles on children's theatre. USSR. 1986-1987. Lang.: Rus.   258

Work and problems of a children's theatre. USSR. 1987. Lang.: Rus.   274

Audience
Theatre education project for teaching about sexuality. Canada: Toronto, ON. 1987. Lang.: Eng.   278

Importance of children's theatre and community theatre to the community. Israel. 1987. Lang.: Heb.   283

Early development of children's theatre. USA. 1900-1910. Lang.: Eng.   293

Design/technology
Puppetmaking projects for children. USA. 1987. Lang.: Eng.   3963

Institutions
Previews 1982 International Children's Festival. Canada: Toronto, ON. 1982. Lang.: Eng.   524

History of Theaterworks/USA, a national theatre for young people. USA: New York, NY. 1961-1987. Lang.: Eng.   613

Arbrå Teaterförening's theatrical activities for adults and children. Sweden: Bollnäs. 1979-1987. Lang.: Swe.   1645

Performance spaces
Performances, workshops for children in converted church hall. UK-England: London. 1987. Lang.: Eng.   4009

Performance/production
Improvisation and other forms in children's theatre. China, People's Republic of. 1975-1987. Lang.: Chi.   764

Theatrical activity at the concentration camp Theresienstadt. Czechoslovakia: Terezín. 1938-1968. Lang.: Heb.   772

Wet Paint, a young people's theatre group. Ireland: Dublin. 1985. Lang.: Eng.   815

DYT (Dublin Youth Theatre). Ireland: Dublin. 1980-1987. Lang.: Eng.   816

TEAM, an educational theatre company. Ireland: Dublin. 1984-1987. Lang.: Eng.   818

Listing and bibliography of children's theatre productions. Italy: Cesena. 1987. Lang.: Ita.   825

Children's theatre in Holland: financial, artistic growth. Netherlands. 1987. Lang.: Dut.   863

Festival of Polish plays. Poland: Wrocław. 1987. Lang.: Eng, Fre.   871

Overview of Polish theatre scene. Poland: Warsaw, Cracow. 1987. Lang.: Eng.   874

Report from a children's theatre festival. Sweden: Gothenburg. 1987. Lang.: Swe.   888

A report from the first European Youth theatre encounter. UK-England: Stratford. 1987. Lang.: Swe.   910

Soviet directors discuss children's theatre. USSR. 1987. Lang.: Rus.   991

Work of Moscow Children's Theatre. USSR: Moscow. 1980-1987. Lang.: Rus.   992

Problems and prospects in children's theatre. USSR. 1986-1987. Lang.: Rus.   1040

Work of E. Nekrošjus, director of Vil'njus Youth Theatre. USSR: Vilnius. 1980-1987. Lang.: Rus.   1043

Children's and youth theatre amateur festival. Sweden: Köping. 1987. Lang.: Swe.   2016

Harlekin's efforts to involve youth in amateur theatre. Sweden: Landskrona. 1982-1987. Lang.: Swe.   2022

Background on *Landskronapågen (The Boy from Landskrona)*. Sweden: Landskrona. 1982-1987. Lang.: Swe.   2024

Children's theatrical productions outside of theatres. Includes playtexts. Switzerland. 1986-1988. Lang.: Ger.   2026

Collection of newspaper reviews by London theatre critics. UK-England: London. 1987. Lang.: Eng.   2231

Collection of newspaper reviews by London theatre critics. UK-England: London. 1987. Lang.: Eng.   2232

Production of *Struggle for Freedom: The Life and Work of Len Johnson*. UK-England: Manchester. 1987. Lang.: Eng.   2283

Lasse Åkerlund, a clown touring northern Sweden. Sweden: Järvsö. 1980-1987. Lang.: Swe.   3267

Creation and production of *Peter and the Wolf* by Prokofjèv. USSR: Moscow. 1930-1936. Lang.: Heb.   3417

Children's theatre — cont'd

Rock opera *Drakar och Demoner (Dragons and Demons)* about youth at risk. Sweden: Handen. 1987. Lang.: Swe.   3637

Children's musical *Rag Dolly* jointly produced and performed by U.S. and Soviets. USA: New York, NY. USSR: Moscow. 1986. Lang.: Eng.   3646

A children's production of Mozart's *The Magic Flute* performed in Spanish. Mexico: Mexico City. 1987. Lang.: Spa.   3811

Communicating with young audiences with puppet theatre. Israel: Jerusalem. 1987. Lang.: Heb.   3975

Difference between directing actors and puppeteers, responsibility of children's theatre. Sweden. 1987. Lang.: Swe.   3981

Collection of articles on puppet theatre. USSR. 1986. Lang.: Rus.   3989

Plays/librettos/scripts
Adaptations of fairy tales and fantasies for children's plays. USA. 1957-1987. Lang.: Eng.   1165

Playwrights' condescension to child audiences. USA. 1972. Lang.: Eng.   1171

Plays and playwrights of children's theatre. USA: New York, NY. 1987. Lang.: Eng.   1181

Experiments of Moscow Children's Theatre. USSR: Moscow. 1986-1987. Lang.: Rus.   1185

Annotated bibliography of children's plays published in English. 1780-1855. Lang.: Eng.   2423

Interview with playwright Cannie Möller. Sweden: Järfälla. 1987. Lang.: Swe.   2735

Problems of dramaturgy for puppet theatres. USSR. 1980-1987. Lang.: Rus.   3992

Reference materials
Children's productions by Ente Teatrale Italiano. Italy. 1986-1987. Lang.: Ita.   1207

Relation to other fields
Psychodrama in the clinic, the classroom and contemporary research. Europe. North America. 1900-1987. Lang.: Ita.   1233

Role of theatre in moral education. USSR. 1987. Lang.: Rus.   1296

Puppetry in education of hearing-impaired. UK-England: London. 1987. Lang.: Eng.   4011

Training
Guide to teaching through improvisation for children and adults. 1987. Lang.: Eng.   1377

Basic theatrical techniques for secondary school. Belgium. 1987. Lang.: Fre.   1378

Interview with Michael Poyner, director of Ulster Youth Theatre. UK-Ireland. 1987. Lang.: Eng.   1386

Current state of Northern Ireland's young theatre community. UK-Ireland. 1987. Lang.: Eng.   1387

Genesis and development of various youth theatre groups. UK-Ireland. 1979-1987. Lang.: Eng.   1388

Circus productions by performers' children. Switzerland. 1987. Lang.: Ger.   3307

Children's Theatre (Moscow)
SEE
Oblastnoj Teat'r Junovo Zritelia.

Childress, Alice
Plays/librettos/scripts
Interview with playwright Alice Childress. USA: New York, NY, Baltimore, MD. 1987. Lang.: Eng.   2844

Childs, Lucinda
Design/technology
Modern dance production *Portraits in Reflection*. USA. 1986. Lang.: Eng.   396

Chimes at Midnight
Plays/librettos/scripts
Development of Welles's adaptation of *Henry IV* Parts I and II from stage to screen. USA. Ireland. 1938-1965. Lang.: Eng.   3182

Chimombo, Steve
Performance/production
Progression of Malawian theatre. Malawi. 1987. Lang.: Eng.   859

China Youth Art Theatre (Hong Kong)
Performance/production
Review of International Brecht Festival. China, People's Republic of: Hong Kong. 1986. Lang.: Dut.   759

Chinese opera
SEE ALSO
Classed Entries under MUSIC-DRAMA—Chinese opera.

Administration
Wang Wenn-Jiuann and the establishment of Hung Lou Theatre Company. China, People's Republic of. 1987. Lang.: Chi.   3425

Performance/production
Overview of performing artists that toured Japan. Japan: Tokyo. 1986. Lang.: Jap.   844

Chinfónia Burguesa, El (Bourgeois Chinfonia, The)
Plays/librettos/scripts
Linguistic absurdism in *El Chinfónia burguesa (The Bourgeois Chinfonia)*. Nicaragua. 1987. Lang.: Spa.   2703

Chinn, Graham
Performance/production
Collection of newspaper reviews by London theatre critics. UK-England: London. 1986. Lang.: Eng.   2138

Chislett, Anne
Plays/librettos/scripts
New Canadian drama: non-realistic, anti-naturalistic. Canada. 1983-1984. Lang.: Eng.   2482

Chklovski, V.V.
Theory/criticism
Re-evaluation of Brecht's alienation effect in the context of contemporary performances. 1960-1970. Lang.: Eng.   1310

Chlebnikov, Velimir
Performance/production
Links between experimental theatre movement and the Russian Futurists. USSR. 1920-1929. Lang.: Rus.   1058

Theory/criticism
Chlebnikov and futurism in Russian opera. USSR: Moscow. 1913-1987. Lang.: Ger.   3949

Chmielnik, Jacek
Performance/production
The 17th Warsaw theatre conference. Poland: Warsaw. 1987. Lang.: Eng, Fre.   872

Chodorov, Jerome
Performance/production
Collection of newspaper reviews by London theatre critics. UK-England: London. 1986. Lang.: Eng.   2134

Choice, The
SEE
Vybor.

Chong, Ping
Performance/production
The 1984 season of the Next Wave at BAM. USA: New York, NY. 1984. Lang.: Eng.   967

Plays/librettos/scripts
Interview with playwright Ping Chong. Canada: Montreal, PQ. USA: New York, NY. 1987. Lang.: Eng.   2472

Choondal, Chummar
Performance/production
History and description of a performance of *Cavittunatakam*, a drama recounting lives of the saints. India: Kerala. 1984. Lang.: Eng.   1480

Choreographers
SEE
Choreography.

Choreography
Design/technology
Modern dance production *Portraits in Reflection*. USA. 1986. Lang.: Eng.   396

Interview with dance lighting designer Allen Lee Hughes. USA: New York, NY. 1987. Lang.: Eng.   1401

Institutions
Calendar of international opera productions and broadcasts for 1988 winter season. 1988. Lang.: Eng.   3706

International survey of early 1987 opera productions. 1987. Lang.: Eng.   3707

International calendar of summer 1987 opera productions. 1987. Lang.: Eng.   3708

International calendar of fall 1987 opera productions. 1987. Lang.: Eng.   3709

Performance/production
Choreographer Carol Martin's production of *The Last Wave*. Belgium: Antwerp. 1982. Lang.: Eng.   1403

Canadian choreographer Robert Desrosiers. Canada. 1985. Lang.: Eng.   1404

Review of touring production of Edward Lock's *Human Sex*. Canada: Vancouver, BC. 1985-1986. Lang.: Fre.   1405

Choreography — cont'd

Review, 'Le corps politique' festival. Canada: Montreal, PQ. 1986.
Lang.: Fre. 1406

Review of six-week dance festival representing forms of dance in
South Africa. South Africa, Republic of: Durban. 1986. Lang.: Eng.
1409

The career of dancer/choreographer Katherine Dunham. USA: New
York, NY, Chicago, IL, Las Vegas, NV. 1909-1987. Lang.: Eng.
1412

Theatricality of dance. USA. 1985. Lang.: Eng. 1414

Development of ballet in Azerbaijan. Azerbaijan. 1920-1980. Lang.:
Rus. 1431

Interview with choreographer Pavel Šmok. Czechoslovakia: Prague.
1987. Lang.: Cze. 1433

Choreographer Maurice Béjart's creative principles. France. 1927-
1987. Lang.: Rus. 1435

Interview with dancer-choreographer Viktor Róna. Hungary. Norway:
Oslo. 1980-1987. Lang.: Hun. 1437

Interview with choreographer Ashley Killar. South Africa, Republic
of.. 1987. Lang.: Eng. 1440

History of Lithuanian ballet. USSR. 1920-1987. Lang.: Rus. 1451

Belgrade folk ballet. Yugoslavia: Belgrade. 1923-1941. Lang.: Rus.
1453

New European choreographers and their development of new
images. France: Paris. UK-England: London. South Africa, Republic
of. 1987. Lang.: Eng. 1468

Portrait of choreographer Efva Lilja. Sweden: Stockholm. 1970-1987.
Lang.: Swe. 1470

Rubicon's choreography of *Allting rasar inför en naken skuldra*
(*Everything Gives Way to a Naked Shoulder*). Sweden: Gothenburg.
1987. Lang.: Swe. 1471

Millicent Hodson speaks about how she managed to reconstruct
Nižinskij's *Le sacre du printemps*. USA: Los Angeles, CA. 1913-
1987. Lang.: Swe. 1473

Ballet on television. USSR. 1980-1987. Lang.: Rus. 3213

Collaboration of Robert Wilson and Heiner Müller on *Hamlet
Machine* (*Hamletmaschine*). USA: New York, NY. Germany, West:
Hamburg. 1987. Lang.: Eng. 3361

Theory/criticism

Balanchine ballerinas: female domination in the ballet. USA. 1946-
1987. Lang.: Eng. 1457

Chorus Line, A

Performance/production

Overview of performing artists that toured Japan. Japan: Tokyo.
1986. Lang.: Jap. 844

Short history of *A Chorus Line*. USA: New York, NY. 1975-1987.
Lang.: Eng. 941

Chorus of Disapproval

Plays/librettos/scripts

Theme of theatre in recent plays. UK-England. 1957-1985. Lang.:
Eng. 2764

Chorus of Disapproval, A

Performance/production

Collection of newspaper reviews by London theatre critics. UK-
England: London. 1986. Lang.: Eng. 2122

Chorus singing

Performance/production

Three opera chorus conductors. Germany, East. 1986. Lang.: Ger.
3786

Chōryō (Chang-Liang)

Performance/production

Nō plays with Chinese historical subjects. Japan. 1300-1500. Lang.:
Jap. 1503

Chosen, The

Plays/librettos/scripts

Influence of Yiddish and Jewish theatre on mainstream American
theatre. USA: New York, NY. 1881-1987. Lang.: Eng. 2913

Chou, En-Lai

Performance/production

Chou En-Lai and *Horng Lou Meng* (*Dream of the Red Chamber*).
China, People's Republic of: Shanghai. 1957. Lang.: Chi. 3496

Chovanščina

Performance/production

Background on San Francisco opera radio broadcasts. USA: San
Francisco, CA. 1987. Lang.: Eng. 3833

Chrislett, Anne

Plays/librettos/scripts

Interview with playwright Anne Chrislett. Canada. 1985. Lang.: Eng.
2463

Christiani Wallace Brothers Combined

SEE

Wallace Brothers Circus.

Christie, Agatha

Performance/production

Collection of newspaper reviews by London theatre critics. UK-
England: London. 1987. Lang.: Eng. 2218

Christie, Bunny

Design/technology

Preliminary sketches for the Royal Shakespeare Company's *The
Taming of the Shrew*. UK-England. 1985. Lang.: Eng. 1597

Christie, John

Relation to other fields

Benjamin Britten's *Albert Herring* as an adaptation of a story by
Maupassant. UK-England. 1947. Lang.: Eng. 3946

Christina

Performance/production

Christina, opera based on Strindberg play by Hans Gefors and Lars
Forssell. Sweden: Stockholm. 1986-1987. Lang.: Swe. 3823

Christmas Carol, A

Performance/production

Jordcirkus and amateur group Näktergalningarna stage *A Christmas
Carol*. Sweden: Stockholm. 1986-1987. Lang.: Swe. 2020

Chroniques d'une planète provisoire (Chronicle of a Temporary Planet)

Plays/librettos/scripts

Anti-fascist plays of Armand Gatti. France. 1924-1987. Lang.: Rus.
2578

Chuck Davis Dance Company (New York, NY)

Institutions

African-American Dance Ensemble, Chuck Davis Dance Company.
USA: New York, NY. 1968-1987. Lang.: Eng. 1459

Chudožestvènnyj Teat'r (Moscow)

SEE

Moskovskij Chudožestvènnyj Akademičèskij Teat'r.

Chumacero, Oliva

Performance/production

Teatropoesia, a combination of theatre and poetry. USA. 1974-1983.
Lang.: Spa. 2368

Chun Hyang

Performance/production

History of *Chun Hyang* musical drama. Korea: Nam-won. 1400-
1900. Lang.: Kor. 3407

Churchill Play, The

Plays/librettos/scripts

Theme of theatre in recent plays. UK-England. 1957-1985. Lang.:
Eng. 2764

Churchill, Caryl

Performance/production

Relationship of theatre, class and gender. UK-England. USA. 1969-
1985. Lang.: Eng. 918

Collection of newspaper reviews by London theatre critics. UK-
England: London. 1986. Lang.: Eng. 2034

Collection of newspaper reviews by London theatre critics. UK-
England: London. 1987. Lang.: Eng. 2196

Collection of newspaper reviews by London theatre critics. UK-
England. 1987. Lang.: Eng. 2199

Collection of newspaper reviews by London theatre critics. UK-
England: London. 1987. Lang.: Eng. 2269

Plays/librettos/scripts

Political use of traditional comic structure by contemporary
playwrights. UK-England. 1970-1987. Lang.: Eng. 2762

Socialist-feminist nature of Caryl Churchill's plays. UK-England.
1980-1987. Lang.: Eng. 2776

Transvestitism in plays of Caryl Churchill. UK-England. 1987. Lang.:
Eng. 2799

Class conflict as theme of *Top Girls*. UK-England. 1982-1987. Lang.:
Eng. 2800

Money, greed and power in plays by Fo, Churchill, Cacaci and
Cormack. USA: New York, NY. 1987. Lang.: Eng. 2914

Ciao, Fuh Yeong
Performance/production
A review of *Yian de-yi yuan (A Marriage of Good Fortune)*. Taiwan: Taipei. 1987. Lang.: Chi. 3542

Ciascuno a suo modo (Each in His Own Way)
Performance/production
'Showing' is an essential part of all acting. Europe. 1590-1987. Lang.: Eng. 1746

Cibber, Colley
Plays/librettos/scripts
Changing economic conditions created an audience for plays about criminals. England. 1731-1740. Lang.: Eng. 2517
Themes of home and homelessness in plays of Cibber and Vanbrugh. England. 1696. Lang.: Eng. 2525

Cibber, Theophilus
Administration
Theatrical season of 1723 at the Drury Lane Theatre. England: London. 1723. Lang.: Eng. 21

Cicle de Teatre per a nois i noies 'Cavall Fort' (Barcelona)
Performance/production
Collection of theatre reviews by Xavier Fàbregas. Spain-Catalonia. 1969-1972. Lang.: Cat. 2010

Cid, Le (Cid, The)
Performance/production
Collection of newspaper reviews by London theatre critics. UK. 1987. Lang.: Eng. 2031

Cigányprimás (Sari)
Performance/production
Imre Kálmán's *Cigányprimás (Sari)* and Bizet's *Carmen* at Kisfaludy Theatre staged by József Bor. Hungary: Győr. 1912-1986. Lang.: Hun. 3959

Cilento, Diane
Performance/production
Collection of newspaper reviews by London theatre critics. UK-England: London. 1987. Lang.: Eng. 2257

Cinderella
Performance/production
Collection of newspaper reviews by London theatre critics. UK-England: London. 1987. Lang.: Eng. 2194

Cinderella by Kalmár
SEE
Hamupipőke.

Cinderella—The Real True Story
Performance/production
Collection of newspaper reviews by London theatre critics. UK-England: London. 1987. Lang.: Eng. 2232

Cine Mexico (Chicago, IL)
SEE
Congress Theatre.

Cinematography
Design/technology
Interview with cameraman János Kende. Hungary. 1965-1987. Lang.: Hun. 3127
Interview with cameraman Lajos Koltay. Hungary. 1986. Lang.: Hun. 3128

Performance/production
Interview with film-maker Sándor Sára. Hungary. 1980-1987. Lang.: Hun. 3152

Cinnabar Opera Theater (Petaluma, CA)
Performance/production
Bay Area opera companies. USA: San Francisco, CA. 1900-1987. Lang.: Eng. 3842

Činoherní klub (Prague)
Performance/production
Noises Off by Michael Frayn, directed by Jiří Menzel, Činoherní klub. Czechoslovakia: Prague. 1987. Lang.: Cze. 765
Plays of Ladislav Smoček at Činoherní klub. Czechoslovakia: Prague. 1965-1987. Lang.: Cze. 768

Cinthia and Endimion
Plays/librettos/scripts
Collaboration on songs for *Cinthia and Endimion*. England: London. 1697. Lang.: Eng. 3895

Cinthio
SEE
Giraldi Cinthio, Giovanbattista.

Cinzio
SEE
Giraldi Cinthio, Giovanbattista.

Circé
Institutions
Production of *Circé* by the Comédiens du Roy, Hôtel Guénégaud. France: Paris. 1673-1679. Lang.: Eng. 530

Circe & Bravo
Performance/production
Collection of newspaper reviews by London theatre critics. UK-England: London. 1986. Lang.: Eng. 2128

Circle Repertory (New York, NY)
Administration
Circle Repertory Theatre's plan to increase roles for minority actors. USA: New York, NY. 1983. Lang.: Eng. 116
Production sharing among non-profit theatres in effort to develop new works. USA. 1987. Lang.: Eng. 255

Design/technology
Interview with lighting designer Dennis Parichy. USA: New York, NY. 1986-1987. Lang.: Eng. 428

Institutions
Profile of Circle Repertory Company. USA: New York, NY. 1982. Lang.: Eng. 1661

Performance/production
Maintaining theatre archives and designating a coordinator. USA: New York, NY. 1987. Lang.: Eng. 938
Collection of newspaper reviews by New York theatre critics. USA: New York, NY. 1987. Lang.: Eng. 2322

Circle Theatre (Budapest)
SEE
Körszinház.

Circle, The
Plays/librettos/scripts
The potential for social influence in W. Somerset Maugham's comedies. UK-England. 1903-1933. Lang.: Eng. 2784

Circulations
Performance/production
Theatre of playwright Robert Lepage. Canada: Montreal, PQ. Canada: Toronto, ON. 1980-1987. Lang.: Eng. 1704

Circus
SEE ALSO
Classed Entries under MIXED ENTERTAINMENT—Circus.

Administration
Long-term planning in artistic culture. USSR. 1987. Lang.: Rus. 263

Design/technology
Design problems of simulating a circus for *Barnum*. USA: Memphis, TN. 1986. Lang.: Eng. 3621
Rigging special circus effects for *Barnum*. USA. 1986. Lang.: Eng. 3622

Performance/production
The 4th International Festival of Street Theatres. Poland: Jelenia Góra. 1986. Lang.: Eng, Fre. 3355

Čirikov, Jevgenij
Plays/librettos/scripts
Theatre and dramaturgy of the first Russian revolution. USSR. 1905-1907. Lang.: Rus. 1188

Cirka Teater (Norway)
Performance/production
The 4th International Festival of Street Theatres. Poland: Jelenia Góra. 1986. Lang.: Eng, Fre. 3355

Cirque du Soleil (Montreal, PQ)
Performance/production
Production of Cirque du Soleil. Canada: Montreal, PQ. 1987. Lang.: Eng. 3302

Císařovská, Miroslava
Performance/production
Problems of amateur theatre, Eastern Bohemia. Czechoslovakia: Hradec Králové. 1985. Lang.: Cze. 3973

Citadel Theatre (Edmonton, AB)
Institutions
History of Alberta theatre companies. Canada: Edmonton, AB, Calgary, AB. 1987. Lang.: Eng. 506

Citizen Kane
Performance/production
New questions about Welles' *Citizen Kane*. USA. 1942. Lang.: Eng. 3164

Citizens Theatre (Glasgow)
Performance/production
Collection of newspaper reviews by London theatre critics. UK. 1987. Lang.: Eng. 2031

Clowning — cont'd

The Polish cabaret performance group Piwnica. Poland: Cracow. USA: New York, NY. 1987. Lang.: Eng.   3287

Production of Cirque du Soleil. Canada: Montreal, PQ. 1987. Lang.: Eng.   3302

Profile of Pitu, a whiteface clown, and changing traditions of circuses and clowning. France. 1956-1986. Lang.: Eng.   3303

Introduction to articles on art of theatrical clowning. USA. 1987. Lang.: Eng.   3304

Performance by the Colombaioni combining *commedia*, improvisation and clowning. USA: Chicago, IL. 1986. Lang.: Eng.   3315

The 4th International Festival of Street Theatres. Poland: Jelenia Góra. 1986. Lang.: Eng, Fre.   3355

The special acting style of the clown in Chinese opera. China, People's Republic of. 1987. Lang.: Chi.   3516

Plays/librettos/scripts
Improvisational clowning in Elizabethan theatre. England. 1585-1625. Lang.: Eng.   2560

Theory/criticism
Physical comedy in high-tech society. USA. 1987. Lang.: Eng.   1349

Clurman, Harold
Plays/librettos/scripts
Humorous article on playwriting. USA: New York, NY. 1987. Lang.: Eng.   1177

Influence of Clifford Odets on mainstream American realism. USA. 1935-1987. Lang.: Eng.   2927

Cluró, Honorat
Performance/production
Exhibition catalogue: popular theatre in Catalan. France. 1415-1987. Lang.: Cat, Fre.   1750

Clybourn Salon (Chicago, IL)
Performance/production
Artists Beth Escott and Tom Zanarini present *The Way We Are At Home* at the Clybourn Salon. USA: Chicago, IL. 1981. Lang.: Eng.   3364

Clytemnestra
Performance/production
Plays of Pinget, Euripides and Théâtre du Rideau staged by Jouanneau, Suzuki and Tanguy, Théâtre de la Bastille. France: Paris. 1987. Lang.: Fre.   1753

Coastal Disturbances
Design/technology
Interview with lighting designer Dennis Parichy. USA: New York, NY. 1986-1987. Lang.: Eng.   428

Lighting designer Dennis Parichy's work on *Coastal Disturbances*. USA: New York, NY. 1987. Lang.: Eng.   461

Lighting reviews for some New York productions. USA: New York, NY. 1987. Lang.: Eng.   477

Coat of Many Colors
Plays/librettos/scripts
Interview with playwright Barrie Stavis. USA. 1987. Lang.: Hun.   2920

Cobra
Plays/librettos/scripts
The early plays of Justin Fleming, especially *Cobra*. Australia. 1981-1986. Lang.: Eng.   2448

Coche, Michael
Performance/production
Musikteatergruppen Oktober collaborates with immigrant amateurs. Sweden: Södertälje. 1986. Lang.: Swe.   2019

Cochran, G.B.
Performance/production
Christmas pantomime *The Miracle* directed by Max Reinhardt. UK-England: London. 1911. Lang.: Eng.   3236

Cockpit Theatre (London)
Performance/production
Collection of newspaper reviews by London theatre critics. UK-England: London. 1986. Lang.: Eng.   2066

Cocktail Party, The
Performance/production
János Mrsán directs *The Cocktail Party* by T.S. Eliot at Várszinház under the title *Koktél hatkor*. Hungary: Budapest. 1987. Lang.: Hun.   1803

Collection of newspaper reviews by London theatre critics. UK-England: London. 1986. Lang.: Eng.   2152

Coco, William
Institutions
Symposium: 'The Significance and Legacy of the Living Theatre'. USA: New York, NY. 1986. Lang.: Eng.   614

Cocoa Party, The
Performance/production
Collection of newspaper reviews by London theatre critics. UK-England: London. 1987. Lang.: Eng.   2217

Cocteau, Jean
Design/technology
Exhibition of theatrical design by Léger, Cocteau, Kokoschka and Kandinsky. France. Lang.: Eng.   322

Performance/production
Collection of newspaper reviews by London theatre critics. UK-England: London. 1986. Lang.: Eng.   2049

Theory/criticism
Comic space from the ancient Greeks to the present. Europe. USA. Greece. 400 B.C.-1987 A.D. Lang.: Eng.   3032

Cocu imaginaire, Le
SEE
Sganarelle.

Cocu magnifique, Le (Magnificent Cuckold, The)
Basic theatrical documents
Text of Fernand Crommelynck's *Le Cocu magnifique (The Magnificent Cuckold)*. Belgium. 1920. Lang.: Fre.   1543

Codco (St. John's, NF)
Performance/production
Codco, a comic theatrical troupe, creates regional characters. Canada: St. John's, NF. 1986. Lang.: Eng.   3253

Codina, Josep Anton
Performance/production
Collection of theatre reviews by Xavier Fàbregas. Spain-Catalonia. 1969-1972. Lang.: Cat.   2010

Coeur des autres, Le (Rebellious Heart, The)
Plays/librettos/scripts
Life and works of French dramatist Gabriel Marcel. France. 1889-1973. Lang.: Eng.   2573

Coffee House, The
SEE
Bottega del caffè, La.

Coffey, Denise
Performance/production
Summarizes events of Directors' Colloquium. Canada: Calgary, AB. 1987. Lang.: Eng.   728

Directors' Colloquium: individual directorial techniques. Canada: Calgary, AB. 1987. Lang.: Eng.   743

Cohen, Alan
Performance/production
Collection of newspaper reviews by London theatre critics. UK-England: London. 1986. Lang.: Eng.   2050

Collection of newspaper reviews by London theatre critics. UK-England: London. 1987. Lang.: Eng.   2259

Cohen, Jonathan
Performance/production
Collection of newspaper reviews by London theatre critics. UK-England: London. 1987. Lang.: Eng.   2240

Cold Storage
Performance/production
Collection of newspaper reviews by London theatre critics. UK-England: London. 1986. Lang.: Eng.   2082

Colden Center for the Performing Arts (Queens College, Flushing, NY)
Institutions
Profile and history of Colden Center for the Performing Arts. USA: Flushing, NY. 1961-1984. Lang.: Eng.   618

Colder Climate, A
Performance/production
Collection of newspaper reviews by London theatre critics. UK-England: London. 1986. Lang.: Eng.   2149

Cole, Richard
Performance/production
Libel suit against a minstrel. UK-England: Stafford. 1616. Lang.: Eng.   3269

Coles, Honi
Performance/production
Career of tap dancer Brenda Bufalino, and exploration of women's roles as lead dancers. USA. 1987. Lang.: Eng.   1417

Coles, Tom
Institutions
The formation of the North Carolina Black Repertory Company.
USA: Winston-Salem, NC. 1979-1987. Lang.: Eng.   1666

Colgan, Valerie
Performance/production
Collection of newspaper reviews by London theatre critics. UK-
England: London. 1987. Lang.: Eng.   2216

Coliseo (Madrid)
Audience
Public attendance at Spanish court theatre. Spain: Madrid. 1630-
1670. Lang.: Eng.   1538

Coliseum Theatre (London)
Performance/production
Collection of newspaper reviews by London theatre critics. UK-
England: London. 1987. Lang.: Eng.   2247

Collected materials
Administration
Six articles on theatrical business published in the *St. James Gazette*.
UK-England: London. 1885. Lang.: Eng.   53
Institutions
Family letters and business papers of the Shuberts. USA: New York,
NY. 1900-1953. Lang.: Eng.   620
Performance/production
Staging Shakespeare in the twentieth century. Europe. 1596-1987.
Lang.: Ita.   781
Collection of reviews by Arnaldo Mariotti. Italy. 1958-1982. Lang.:
Ita.   834
History of British Theatre Museum, its collections and exhibition
spaces. UK-England: London. 1987. Lang.: Eng.   919
Description of scope and content of new museum in Covent Garden.
UK-England: London. 1987. Lang.: Eng.   920
Maintaining theatre archives and designating a coordinator. USA:
New York, NY. 1987. Lang.: Eng.   938
History of 'The Soldier Show', Shubert Archives U.S.O. collection.
USA: New York, NY. 1942-1945. Lang.: Eng.   3664
Plays/librettos/scripts
Notes and commentary of Alvario Custadio on Teatro Clásico de
México. Mexico. 1958-1973. Lang.: Eng.   2695
Theme of stage direction in the work of Scandinavian authors.
Sweden. Norway. 1700-1987. Lang.: Ita.   2737
Playwright Pietro Chiari. Italy: Venice. 1747-1762. Lang.: Ita.   3316
Reference materials
Compilation of anecdotes on life in the theatre from Aristophanes to
Williams. 5 B.C.-1987 A.D. Lang.: Eng.   1195
Surviving records of British drama before 1558. England. 1558.
Lang.: Eng.   1199
Picture book to accompany production of *La Nit (The Night)* by Els
Comediants. Spain-Catalonia. 1987. Lang.: Cat.   1209
History of theatrical activity in Palafrugell. Spain-Catalonia:
Palafrugell. 1900-1986. Lang.: Cat.   1210
Theory/criticism
Trollope's writings on Elizabethan and Jacobean drama. UK-
England. 1866-1882. Lang.: Eng.   3063

Collection, The
Plays/librettos/scripts
Interpreting Harold Pinter's dramas through focus on his play
structures. UK-England. 1958-1987. Lang.: Eng.   2815

Collective creations
Institutions
Profile of street theatre company Earthcirkus. Sweden: Stockholm.
1977-1982. Lang.: Eng.   562
History and goals of Cherry Creek Theatre. USA: St. Peter, MN.
1979-1983. Lang.: Eng.   598
Profile of community theatre Grenland Friteater. Norway: Porsgrunn.
1982. Lang.: Eng.   1627
History of Dakota Theatre Caravan. USA: Yankton, SD. 1977-1983.
Lang.: Eng.   1662
Performance/production
Popular theatre, mostly on economic, feminist themes. Canada:
Sudbury, ON. 1930-1987. Lang.: Eng.   1709

College of Theatre Arts (Warsaw)
SEE
Panstova Akademia Sztuk Teatralnych.

College theatre
SEE
University theatre.

Collier, John Payne
Plays/librettos/scripts
Argument against authenticity of three Elizabethan documents.
England. 1591-1885. Lang.: Eng.   3326

Collier's Friday Night, A
Relation to other fields
Comparison of D.H. Lawrence's dramatic and novel writings. UK-
England. 1906-1913. Lang.: Eng.   3006

Collins, A.M.
Performance/production
Collection of newspaper reviews by London theatre critics. UK-
England: London. 1986. Lang.: Eng.   2088

Collins, Barry
Performance/production
Collection of newspaper reviews by London theatre critics. UK-
England: London. 1987. Lang.: Eng.   2222
Collection of newspaper reviews by London theatre critics. UK-
England: London. 1987. Lang.: Eng.   2237

Collins, Jane
Performance/production
Collection of newspaper reviews by London theatre critics. UK-
England: London. 1986. Lang.: Eng.   2099

Collins, Maury
Institutions
A Season of Concern, an AIDS fundraising benefit in Chicago. USA:
Chicago, IL. 1987. Lang.: Eng.   609

Colman, George
Audience
Influence of audience on George Colman's artistic choices. England:
London. 1767-1774. Lang.: Eng.   280

Colombaioni, Alberto
Performance/production
Performance by the Colombaioni combining *commedia*, improvisation
and clowning. USA: Chicago, IL. 1986. Lang.: Eng.   3315

Colombaioni, Carlo
Performance/production
Performance by the Colombaioni combining *commedia*, improvisation
and clowning. USA: Chicago, IL. 1986. Lang.: Eng.   3315

Colombe
Performance/production
Reviews of two Anouilh plays: *Eurydice* directed by János Szűcs,
Colombe directed by Mátyás Giricz. Hungary: Miskolc, Budapest.
1987. Lang.: Hun.   1827
Plot synopsis of musical *Mademoiselle Colombe* based on Anouilh's
Colombe. USA: New York, NY. 1987. Lang.: Eng.   3647
Plays/librettos/scripts
How Anouilh's *Colombe* was adapted as a musical. USA. 1987.
Lang.: Eng.   3672

Color of Chambalén, The
SEE
Color de Chambalén, El.

Color Purple, The
Performance/production
Interview with actress Margaret Avery. USA: San Diego, CA,
Hollywood, CA. 1950-1987. Lang.: Eng.   3167

Colored Balls
SEE
Bolles de colors.

Colored Museum, The
Design/technology
Lighting reviews for several New York productions. USA: New
York, NY. 1987. Lang.: Eng.   475
Performance/production
George C. Wolfe and L. Kenneth Richardson discuss *The Colored
Museum*. USA: New York, NY, New Brunswick, NJ. 1987. Lang.:
Eng.   2363

Colosseum Theatre (Johannesburg)
Performance spaces
Theatres built, influences on design. South Africa, Republic of:
Johannesburg. 1887-1940. Lang.: Afr.   667

Colours in the Dark
Plays/librettos/scripts
Critical analysis of James Reaney's *Three Desks*. Canada. 1960-1977.
Lang.: Eng.   2477

Colthorpe, Marion
Plays/librettos/scripts
Argument for authenticity of three Elizabethan documents. England.
1591. Lang.: Eng.   3325

Comedy — cont'd

Comic space from the ancient Greeks to the present. Europe. USA. Greece. 400 B.C.-1987 A.D. Lang.: Eng.   3032

Rococo elements in the comedies of Marivaux. France. 1715-1774. Lang.: Eng.   3039

Catalan translation of Lessing's *Hamburgische Dramaturgie*. Germany: Hamburg. 1767-1769. Lang.: Cat.   3043

Functions of comedy in the seventeenth century. Spain. 1604-1690. Lang.: Spa.   3058

Analysis of the writings of Isidore of Seville on ancient Roman and Greek drama. Spain. 560-636. Lang.: Eng.   3059

Refutes Frye's analysis of Shakespeare's *A Midsummer Night's Dream*. USA. 1987. Lang.: Eng.   3075

Theory of Chinese classical comedy. China. 1127-1368. Lang.: Chi.   3587

Comedy of Errors, The
Performance/production
Collection of newspaper reviews by New York theatre critics. USA: New York, NY. 1987. Lang.: Eng.   2311

Comedy Theatre (Budapest)
SEE
Vigszinház.

Comedy Theatre (London)
Performance/production
Collection of newspaper reviews by London theatre critics. UK-England: London. 1986. Lang.: Eng.   2108

Collection of newspaper reviews by London theatre critics. UK-England: London. 1986. Lang.: Eng.   2141

Collection of newspaper reviews by London theatre critics. UK-England: London. 1987. Lang.: Eng.   2188

Collection of newspaper reviews by London theatre critics. UK-England: London. 1987. Lang.: Eng.   2197

Collection of newspaper reviews by London theatre critics. UK-England: London. 1987. Lang.: Eng.   2229

Collection of newspaper reviews by London theatre critics. UK-England: London. 1987. Lang.: Eng.   2249

Comic Illusion, The
SEE
Illusion comique, L'.

Coming In To Land
Performance/production
Collection of newspaper reviews by London theatre critics. UK-England. 1987. Lang.: Eng.   2033

Coming of Age in Soho
Plays/librettos/scripts
Interview with playwright Albert Innaurato. USA. 1986. Lang.: Eng.   2856

Comings and Goings
Plays/librettos/scripts
Megan Terry's transformational plays for the Open Theatre. USA. 1987. Lang.: Eng.   2910

Comissiona, Sergiu
Administration
Sergiu Comissiona, new music director, New York City Opera. USA: New York, NY. Romania. 1987. Lang.: Eng.   3685

Commedia dell'arte
SEE ALSO
Classed Entries under MIXED ENTERTAINMENT—*Commedia dell'arte*.

Performance/production
Théâtre de la Jeune Lune, its origins and influences. USA: Minneapolis, MN. France: Paris. 1980-1987. Lang.: Eng.   977

Popular account of comic entertainers. Europe. North America. Australia. 480 B.C.-1986 A.D. Lang.: Eng.   3256

Commody of the Moste Vertuous and Godlye Susanna
SEE
Comedy of Virtuous and Godly Susanna.

Commonwealth Institute (London)
Performance/production
Collection of newspaper reviews by London theatre critics. UK-England: London. 1986. Lang.: Eng.   2160

Community relations
Administration
Interview with Madeleine Rivest. Canada: Montreal, PQ. 1987. Lang.: Fre.   14

Panel discussion on the importance of volunteers in the arts. USA. 1987. Lang.: Eng.   82

Interview with Actor's Work Program director, Ronda Ormont. USA: New York, NY. 1987. Lang.: Eng.   93

Evaluation of volunteers in an arts organization. USA. 1987. Lang.: Eng.   148

Integration of creative process in society. USA: New York, NY. 1986. Lang.: Eng.   168

Volunteer organizations and their role in the community. USA. 1700-1987. Lang.: Eng.   195

Function of a board member. USA. 1987. Lang.: Eng.   250

Volunteer-staff relationships in the New York Philharmonic. USA: New York, NY. 1987. Lang.: Eng.   3387

Institutions
Contribution of non-commercial theatre to the New York community. USA: New York, NY. 1987. Lang.: Eng.   608

Folkteatern i Gävleborgs län: integration into the community. Sweden: Gävle. 1982-1987. Lang.: Swe.   1641

Performance spaces
Renovations and new directions for the Chautauqua Opera Company. USA: Chautauqua, NY. 1928-1987. Lang.: Eng.   3738

Performance/production
Public relations function of the Nova Scotia Tattoo. Canada: Halifax, NS. 1978-1986. Lang.: Eng.   3383

Relation to other fields
Puppets used in community development workshops. UK-England: London. 1987. Lang.: Eng.   3997

Community theatre
Audience
Death Defying Theatre's development of the play *Coal Town*. Australia: Collinsville. 1984-1985. Lang.: Eng.   276

Importance of children's theatre and community theatre to the community. Israel. 1987. Lang.: Heb.   283

Institutions
Two community-based popular theatre projects. Canada. 1987. Lang.: Eng.   522

Profile of community theatre Grenland Friteater. Norway: Porsgrunn. 1982. Lang.: Eng.   1627

Performance/production
Staging community theatre. UK-England. 1987. Lang.: Eng.   909

Casting community theatre. UK-England: Dorchester. 1987. Lang.: Eng.   913

Amateur theatre anecdotes: how to destroy a production. UK. 1987. Lang.: Eng.   2032

Production of *Struggle for Freedom: The Life and Work of Len Johnson*. UK-England: Manchester. 1987. Lang.: Eng.   2283

Plays/librettos/scripts
Interview with playwright Graham Pitts. Australia. 1987. Lang.: Eng.   1097

Relation to other fields
Social implications of popular theatre. Canada. 1987. Lang.: Eng.   1222

Theory/criticism
Discussion of theory of popular theatre. Canada. 1987. Lang.: Eng.   3024

Compagnie Jo Bithume (France)
Performance/production
The 4th International Festival of Street Theatres. Poland: Jelenia Góra. 1986. Lang.: Eng, Fre.   3355

Compagnie Renaud-Barrault
SEE
Compagnie Madeleine Renaud—Jean-Louis Barrault.

Compañia Ciudad Condal (Barcelona)
Institutions
Texts and photos about the Teatre Grec. Spain-Catalonia: Barcelona. 1929-1986. Lang.: Cat.   558

Companies
SEE
Institutions, producing.

Company Forgives a Moment of Madness, The
Performance/production
Collection of newspaper reviews by London theatre critics. UK-England: London. 1986. Lang.: Eng.   2078

Company of Sirens (Toronto, ON)
Institutions
Development of feminist theatre in Toronto. Canada: Toronto, ON. 1960-1987. Lang.: Eng.   1608

Company of Sirens (Toronto, ON) — cont'd

Relation to other fields

Description of *The Working People's Picture Show*. Canada: Toronto, ON. 1987. Lang.: Eng.   1221

Applications of African 'Theatre for Development' movement to Canadian popular theatre. Africa. Canada: St. John's, NF, Toronto, ON. 1978-1987. Lang.: Eng.   2978

Competitions

Design/technology

Report on the Prague Quadrennial computer symposium. Czechoslovakia: Prague. 1987. Lang.: Eng.   306

Hungarian exhibition, Prague Quadrennial theatre design competition. Czechoslovakia: Prague. 1987. Lang.: Hun.   307

The contribution of Josef Svoboda to the 1987 Prague Quadrennial exhibition. Czechoslovakia: Prague. 1987. Lang.: Eng.   308

Judge of Prague Quadrennial design competition describes jury's work. Czechoslovakia: Prague. 1987. Lang.: Eng.   310

First American participation in Prague Quadrennial theatre design contest. Czechoslovakia: Prague. USA. 1967-1987. Lang.: Eng.   311

A report from the Prague Quadrennial theatre design contest. Czechoslovakia: Prague. 1987. Lang.: Swe.   312

Stage designer reviews 1987 Prague Quadrennial exhibits. Europe. 1987. Lang.: Eng.   319

Institutions

List of resources for playwrights. USA. 1987-1988. Lang.: Eng.   582

Performance spaces

East German exhibition at Prague Quadrennial '87: Gold medal for theatre reconstruction exhibit. Germany, East: Berlin, East. 1742-1986. Lang.: Hun.   636

Results of theatre design competition. Japan. 1986. Lang.: Hun.   658

Performance/production

Theory, problems of folk-arts competitions. Korea. 1986-1987. Lang.: Kor.   857

Composers

SEE

Music.

Performance/production

Study of the work of Stephen Sondheim. USA: New York, NY. UK-England: London. 1962-1985. Lang.: Eng.   3665

Wolfgang Amadeus Mozart: a psychological profile. Austria: Vienna. 1756-1781. Lang.: Eng.   3742

Work of composer Othmar Schoeck. Switzerland. 1886-1986. Lang.: Ger.   3826

Plays/librettos/scripts

Musical sources in the operas of Richard Strauss. Germany: Dresden. 1864-1949. Lang.: Eng.   3908

Composition

SEE

Plays/librettos/scripts.

Compromise of 1867

SEE

Kiegyezés.

Compromised Immunity

Performance/production

Collection of newspaper reviews by London theatre critics. UK-England: London. 1986. Lang.: Eng.   2062

Computers

Administration

Guide to establishing data bases for subscription, marketing. USA. 1981-1983. Lang.: Eng.   134

National Information Systems Project. USA. 1977-1984. Lang.: Eng.   138

Computer analysis of mailing lists and response enhancement. USA: New York, NY. 1986. Lang.: Eng.   139

Economic analyses of arts organizations. USA. 1984. Lang.: Eng.   140

Art Museum Association of America's Computer Software Project. USA. 1981-1983. Lang.: Eng.   145

Non-profit organizations benefit from use of computer modems. USA: New York, NY. 1987. Lang.: Eng.   151

How to computerize your non-profit organization. USA: New York, NY. 1986. Lang.: Eng.   152

Computer glossary for new users. USA. 1981-1984. Lang.: Eng.   161

TCG's National Computer Project for the Performing Arts. USA. 1980-1983. Lang.: Eng.   172

Impact of computers on not-for-profit organizations. USA. 1980-1984. Lang.: Eng.   196

Information systems for local arts agencies. USA. 1982-1983. Lang.: Eng.   223

Technical information for the new computer user. USA. 1983. Lang.: Eng.   228

Impact of computer-based information system on an arts organization: case study. USA. 1979-1983. Lang.: Eng.   236

Evaluation of computer support systems in arts organizations. USA. 1983-1984. Lang.: Eng.   241

Information systems used in arts organizations. USA. 1977-1984. Lang.: Eng.   242

Use of computers in planned giving. USA. 1987. Lang.: Eng.   247

Current computer vendor developments in information systems. USA. 1983-1984. Lang.: Eng.   249

Design/technology

Report on the Prague Quadrennial computer symposium. Czechoslovakia: Prague. 1987. Lang.: Eng.   306

Contribution of Modelbox Computer Aided Design. UK. 1984-1987. Lang.: Eng.   369

AutoCAD software applied to lighting design. USA. 1987. Lang.: Eng.   419

The effect of computer synthesizers on theatrical composition. USA. 1986. Lang.: Eng.   424

Purchasing a computer system for a theatre. USA. 1987. Lang.: Eng.   438

Technology of computerized dimming systems. USA. 1987. Lang.: Eng.   457

Current computer-assisted lighting controllers. USA. 1987. Lang.: Eng.   459

Interview with lighting designer Marilyn Lowey. USA. 1987. Lang.: Eng.   462

The use of computers to enhance theatre technology. Canada. 1987. Lang.: Fre.   3192

The use of holography in theatre. Canada. 1987. Lang.: Fre.   3201

Application of the musical instrument digital face. USA. 1987. Lang.: Eng.   3449

Computer and technological breakthroughs for puppetry. USA. 1985-1987. Lang.: Eng.   3962

Institutions

Tandem database system used by the Deutsches Theatermuseum. Germany, West: Munich. 1987. Lang.: Eng.   533

Performance/production

Lorna Heaton's use of holograms in *Woyzeck*. Canada: Banff, AB. 1987. Lang.: Fre.   3205

Plays/librettos/scripts

Ibsen database now being developed. USA. Norway. 1987. Lang.: Eng.   2924

Research/historiography

Database manipulation in theatre research. North America. 1987. Lang.: Eng.   1301

Comsomol Theatre

SEE

Teat'r im. Leninskovo Komsomola.

Concert Opera Association (San Francisco, CA)

Administration

Gordon Peter Getty, philanthropist, composer. USA: San Francisco, CA. 1987. Lang.: Eng.   3684

Condemned of Altona, The

SEE

Séquestrés d'Altona, Les.

Condemned Village

SEE

Pueblo rechazado.

Conder, Terry

Performance/production

Collection of newspaper reviews by London theatre critics. UK-England: London. 1986. Lang.: Eng.   2156

Conducting

Performance/production

Interview with musical conductor Paul Gemignani. USA: New York, NY. 1987. Lang.: Eng.   3649

Interview with conductor Manuel Rosenthal. France: Paris. 1904-1987. Lang.: Eng.   3774

Career of conductor/educator Max Rudolf. Italy. USA: New York, NY. 1945-1987. Lang.: Eng.   3803

Conducting — cont'd

Interview, Italian conductor Riccardo Muti, artistic director, Teatro alla Scala. Italy: Milan. 1970-1987. Lang.: Eng.   3808

Opera conductors who also conduct in Broadway musicals. USA: New York, NY. 1980-1987. Lang.: Eng.   3847

Interview with John DeMain, music director, Houston Grand Opera. USA: Houston, TX. 1944-1987. Lang.: Eng.   3851

Conductors
  SEE
    Music.

Conference of the Birds
  SEE
    Aves (Conference of the Birds).

Conferences
  Administration
    National Actors' Equity conference. USA: New York, NY. 1985. Lang.: Eng.   63

    Panel discussion on the importance of volunteers in the arts. USA. 1987. Lang.: Eng.   82

    Conference on Equity's plan to create a National Theatre in America. USA: New York, NY. 1982. Lang.: Eng.   111

    Actors' Equity urges communication between chapters and main office. USA: New York, NY. 1982. Lang.: Eng.   113

    Labor-sponsored conference for Chicago Equity members. USA: Chicago, IL. 1986. Lang.: Eng.   221

    Contracts, actors and union negotiations. USA. 1986. Lang.: Eng.   235

    Conference on career transitions for dancers. USA: New York, NY. 1982. Lang.: Eng.   1397

    Creating human voices and images with digital, holographic techniques: actors' conference. USA: New York, NY. Israel: Tel-Aviv. 1987. Lang.: Eng.   3083

  Design/technology
    Report on the Prague Quadrennial computer symposium. Czechoslovakia: Prague. 1987. Lang.: Eng.   306

    A report from the Prague Quadrennial theatre design contest. Czechoslovakia: Prague. 1987. Lang.: Swe.   312

    Possible uses of electronics in theatre technology. Hungary: Szeged. 1987. Lang.: Hun.   333

    Current status of theatre technology. Hungary: Szeged. 1987. Lang.: Hun.   334

    Director, Szegedi Nemzeti Szinház, on theatre technology. Hungary: Szeged. 1987. Lang.: Hun.   337

    Product exhibit, theatre technology convention. Hungary: Szeged. 1987. Lang.: Hun.   338

    Summary of theatre technology conference. Hungary: Szeged. 1987. Lang.: Hun.   339

    Scene design training at Academy of Performing Arts, Bratislava. Hungary: Szeged. Czechoslovakia: Bratislava. 1980-1987. Lang.: Hun.   344

    Report on OISTAT conference. Netherlands: Amsterdam. 1987. Lang.: Swe.   356

    OISTAT theatre technology meeting. Netherlands: Amsterdam. 1987. Lang.: Hun.   358

    1987 USITT convention. USA: Minneapolis/St. Paul, MN. 1987. Lang.: Eng.   446

  Institutions
    Atlantic Canada theatre companies' conferences. Canada. 1985-1986. Lang.: Eng.   514

    International Association of Theatre Critics conference on theatre as language of the people. Hungary: Budapest. 1987. Lang.: Hun.   536

    Director of Hungarian Theatre Institute addresses conference on national theatres in Europe. Hungary. 1987. Lang.: Hun.   538

    International conference on national theatres in Europe. Hungary: Budapest. 1987. Lang.: Hun.   541

    Director of National Theatre of Budapest addresses conference on national theatres in Europe. Hungary. 1987. Lang.: Hun.   544

    Memoir of the papers and debates organized at the First Congress of Amateur Theatre in Catalonia. Spain-Catalonia. 1850-1685. Lang.: Cat.   560

    Conference of Dramatists' Guild Women's Committee. USA. 1987. Lang.: Eng.   583

    Closing remarks, FDG/CBS conference on new plays. USA. 1987. Lang.: Eng.   586

1987 USITT conference. USA: Minneapolis, MN. 1987. Lang.: Eng.   603

XV Congress, All-Russian Theatre Society. USSR. 1986. Lang.: Rus.   622

Colloquium on 'Brecht 30 Years After'. Canada: Toronto, ON. 1985. Lang.: Fre.   1607

Brecht was the theme of the 1986 International Theatre Festival and Conference. Canada: Toronto, ON. 1986. Lang.: Fre.   1610

Summary of proceedings from a Gilbert and Sullivan symposium. Canada: Toronto, ON. 1987. Lang.: Eng.   3954

  Performance spaces
    Theatre renovation plans and survey. Hungary. 1980-1986. Lang.: Hun.   645

  Performance/production
    Summarizes events of Directors' Colloquium. Canada: Calgary, AB. 1987. Lang.: Eng.   728

    Directors' Colloquium: individual directorial techniques. Canada: Calgary, AB. 1987. Lang.: Eng.   743

    The Directors Colloquium: director/playwright relationship. Canada: Calgary, AB. 1987. Lang.: Eng.   747

    Canadian actors and directors discuss their theatre experiences. Canada: Calgary, AB. 1987. Lang.: Eng.   748

    Analysis of the playwright/director relationship in Canada. Canada. 1987. Lang.: Eng.   750

    Essays on theatre of the twenties. Europe. 1920-1930. Lang.: Ita. 783

    Consideration of plays performed at national theatre meeting. Hungary. 1986-1987. Lang.: Hun.   812

    Avant-garde performances presented at International Open Theatre meeting. Poland: Wrocław. 1982-1987. Lang.: Pol, Eng, Fre.   877

    Events and debates at the ISTA Congress. Denmark: Holstebro. 1986. Lang.: Eng.   1729

    Essay on interpretive methods in performance and production. Hungary. 1987. Lang.: Hun.   1824

    Review of conference on contemporary Hungarian drama. Hungary: Egervár. 1987. Lang.: Hun.   1879

    Aspects of contemporary Italian theatrical life. Italy. 1987. Lang.: Ita.   1949

  Plays/librettos/scripts
    Conference on women in theatre, emphasis on playwriting. USA. 1987. Lang.: Eng.   1161

    FDG/CBS New Plays Program Conferences. USA: New York, NY. 1987. Lang.: Eng.   1180

    Ancient Greek theatre and European culture. Europe. Greece. 1000 B.C.-1987 A.D. Lang.: Ita.   2565

    Acts of Pirandello conference. Italy. 1904-1936. Lang.: Ita, Eng.   2663

    Theme of stage direction in the work of Scandinavian authors. Sweden. Norway. 1700-1987. Lang.: Ita.   2737

  Relation to other fields
    International Federation of Actors discusses actors' conditions. France: Paris. 1982. Lang.: Eng.   1235

  Theory/criticism
    Pirandello's poetics and influence on other writers. Italy. 1904-1936. Lang.: Ita.   3051

    Keynote address at Northern California Theatre Critics Conference. USA. 1987. Lang.: Eng.   3072

    Proceedings of a conference on Chinese opera. China, People's Republic of. 1987. Lang.: Chi.   3598

Confession of a Wood
  SEE
    Spowiedź w driewnie.

Congreve, William
  Plays/librettos/scripts
    Independence of Restoration women is reflected in comic heroines. England. 1668-1700. Lang.: Eng.   2550

Conklin, Eric
  Performance/production
    Collection of newspaper reviews by New York theatre critics. USA: New York, NY. 1987. Lang.: Eng.   2322

Conn, Stewart
  Performance/production
    Collection of newspaper reviews by London theatre critics. UK-England: London. 1986. Lang.: Eng.   2131

Copyright — cont'd

Court ruling protecting the copyright of audio-visual works. USA: New York, NY. 1976-1982. Lang.: Eng. 165

Legal issues of record rental and copyright infringement. USA. 1964-1987. Lang.: Eng. 176

The 'Proof of Harm' doctrine in copyright law. USA. 1985. Lang.: Eng. 182

Historical look at the Copyright Act. USA. 1984. Lang.: Eng. 206

Trademark protection as related to merchandising. USA. 1987. Lang.: Eng. 209

Aspects of paying for works in the public domain. USA: New York, NY. 1983. Lang.: Eng. 213

Copyright law regarding ownership of works for hire. USA. 1987. 217

Legislative remedies for home video recordings of copyrighted works. USA: Los Angeles, CA. 1980-1982. Lang.: Eng. 224

Fair use standards of the Copyright Act of 1976. USA. 1976-1984. Lang.: Eng. 229

Copyright laws governing Soviet publications. USA. USSR. 1973-1987. Lang.: Eng. 253

The copyright of Australian plays prior to adoption of British Copyright Act. Australia. UK-England. USA. 1870-1912. Lang.: Eng. 1512

Introduction to articles on satellite transmission pirating. USA. 1976-1987. Lang.: Eng. 3084

Copyrightability of fictional characters. USA. 1986-1987. Lang.: Eng. 3085

Copyright protection of live broadcasts. USA. 1976-1987. Lang.: Eng. 3086

The *Salinger v. Random House* copyright case. USA. 1986-1987. Lang.: Eng. 3087

Public performance exemptions from copyright liability. USA. 1976-1987. Lang.: Eng. 3088

Enforcing restrictions on blacked-out sports events. USA. 1950-1987. Lang.: Eng. 3090

Title disputes over WPA prints. USA. 1935-1987. Lang.: Eng. 3091

Reform of copyright notice omission. USA. 1968-1987. Lang.: Eng. 3092

Copyright law, FCC regulations and involuntary superstations. USA. 1970-1982. Lang.: Eng. 3093

Arguments for and against source licensing. USA. 1940-1987. Lang.: Eng. 3107

Recommended changes to copyright law. USA. 1987. Lang.: Eng. 3191

Plays/librettos/scripts
Legal and ethical rights of playwrights regarding interpretations of their works. USA. Lang.: Eng. 2904

Cora i la Magrana (Cora and the Pomegranate)
Basic theatrical documents
Study of the poetic, narrative and theatrical work of Agustí Bartra, edition of complete works, vol. 4. Spain-Catalonia. Mexico. 1937-1982. Lang.: Cat. 1571

Cordó de la vila, El (Village Cord, The)
Basic theatrical documents
Theatrical works of Pere d'Alcàntara Penya: texts and analysis. Spain. 1823-1906. Lang.: Cat. 1567

Coriolanus
Performance/production
Collection of newspaper reviews by London theatre critics. UK-England: London. 1986. Lang.: Eng. 2166

Plays/librettos/scripts
Class conflict in Shakespeare's *Coriolanus* as viewed in 17th and 20th century. England. 1600-1980. Lang.: Ger. 2553

Influence of Livy's *History* and Machiavelli's *Discorsi* on Shakespeare's *Coriolanus*. UK-England: London. 1606-1610. Lang.: Eng. 2752

Interpretation of the title character of Shakespeare's *Coriolanus*. UK-England. 1607. Lang.: Eng. 2757

Cork Opera House (Cork)
Institutions
Difficulty in obtaining funding for theatre building repair. Ireland: Dublin, Cork. UK-Ireland: Belfast. 1965-1984. Lang.: Eng. 545

Cormack, Bartlett
Plays/librettos/scripts
Money, greed and power in plays by Fo, Churchill, Cacaci and Cormack. USA: New York, NY. 1987. Lang.: Eng. 2914

Corneille, Pierre
Performance/production
'Showing' is an essential part of all acting. Europe. 1590-1987. Lang.: Eng. 1746

L'illusion comique (The Comic Illusion) by Pierre Corneille directed by János Szikora at the Katona József Theatre. Hungary: Budapest. 1986. Lang.: Hun. 1859

János Szikora directs Corneille's *L'illusion comique (The Comic Illusion)* at Katona József Theatre. Hungary: Budapest. 1986. Lang.: Hun. 1918

Giorgio Strehler's staging of *L'illusion comique (The Comic Illusion)* by Corneille. Italy. 1944-1986. Lang.: Eng. 1948

Collection of newspaper reviews by London theatre critics. UK. 1987. Lang.: Eng. 2031

Theory/criticism
Principles and theories of playwright Pierre Corneille. France. 1570-1660. Lang.: Heb. 3038

Works of Pierre Corneille and the social role of women. France. 1540-1650. Lang.: Eng. 3040

Catalan translation of Lessing's *Hamburgische Dramaturgie*. Germany: Hamburg. 1767-1769. Lang.: Cat. 3043

Corner Theatre (London)
Performance/production
Collection of newspaper reviews by London theatre critics. UK-England: London. 1987. Lang.: Eng. 2276

Cornes, Lee
Performance/production
Collection of newspaper reviews by London theatre critics. UK-England: London. 1986. Lang.: Eng. 2089

Cornish, Anthony
Performance/production
Collection of newspaper reviews by London theatre critics. UK-England: London. 1986. Lang.: Eng. 2072

Corona del Fuego (Heart of Fire)
Plays/librettos/scripts
Plays by Gorostiza, Usigli and Novo on Spanish conquest of Mexico. Mexico. 1958-1961. Lang.: Eng. 2701

Corona of Light
SEE
Corona de luz.

Coronation of Poppea, The
SEE
Incoronazione di Poppea, L'.

Corpse!
Performance/production
Collection of newspaper reviews by London theatre critics. UK-England: London. 1987. Lang.: Eng. 2271

Corpus Christi
Performance spaces
Reconstructs processional route of *Corpus Christi* performances. England: York. 1399-1569. Lang.: Eng. 3329

Performance/production
Pageant wagon presentation in Spain provides information on recruitment, staging and rehearsal practices. Spain: St. Ginar. 1579. Lang.: Eng. 3333

Plays/librettos/scripts
Two Cornish *Corpus Christi* plays. England. 1350. Lang.: Eng. 2534

Medieval cycle plays as the exception rather than the norm. England. Lang.: Eng. 2543

Corsaro, Frank
Audience
The vocal versus the visual aspects of opera. Europe. 1781-1983. Lang.: Eng. 3690

Cort Theatre (New York, NY)
Performance/production
Collection of newspaper reviews by New York theatre critics. USA: New York, NY. 1987. Lang.: Eng. 2311

Cosmos Kolej (France)
Performance/production
The 4th International Festival of Street Theatres. Poland: Jelenia Góra. 1986. Lang.: Eng, Fre. 3355

Cottesloe Theatre (London) — cont'd

Collection of newspaper reviews by London theatre critics. UK-England: London. 1986. Lang.: Eng.   2172

Collection of newspaper reviews by London theatre critics. UK-England: London. 1987. Lang.: Eng.   2183

Collection of newspaper reviews by London theatre critics. UK-England: London. 1987. Lang.: Eng.   2196

Collection of newspaper reviews by London theatre critics. UK-England: London. 1987. Lang.: Eng.   2213

Collection of newspaper reviews by London theatre critics. UK-England: London. 1987. Lang.: Eng.   2220

Collection of newspaper reviews by London theatre critics. UK-England: London. 1987. Lang.: Eng.   2244

Collection of newspaper reviews by London theatre critics. UK-England: London. 1987. Lang.: Eng.   2251

Collection of newspaper reviews by London theatre critics. UK-England: London. 1987. Lang.: Eng.   2268

Collection of newspaper reviews of London theatre critics. UK-England: London. 1987. Lang.: Eng.   2273

Council of Stock Theatres (COST)
   Administration

New Council of Stock Theatres contract and its impact. USA: New York, NY. 1986. Lang.: Eng.   122

Countess Cathleen, The
   Plays/librettos/scripts

Maud Gonne and Yeats's portrayal of women in his plays. Ireland: Dublin. 1900-1930. Lang.: Eng.   2646

Country Dancing
   Performance/production

Collection of newspaper reviews by London theatre critics. UK-England: London. 1987. Lang.: Eng.   2196

Country Wife, The
   Plays/librettos/scripts

Name and entitlement in Dryden, Wycherley and Etherege. England. 1500-1699. Lang.: Eng.   2526

Countrymania
   Performance/production

Collection of newspaper reviews by London theatre critics. UK-England. 1987. Lang.: Eng.   2261

Court entertainment
   SEE ALSO

Classed Entries under MIXED ENTERTAINMENTS—Court entertainment.

   Performance/production

The medieval tournament tradition in the original staging of *The Castle of Perseverance*. England. 1425. Lang.: Eng.   776

Court in the Act!
   Performance/production

Collection of newspaper reviews by London theatre critics. UK-England: London. 1987. Lang.: Eng.   2203

Court Theatre (London)
   SEE

Royal Court Theatre.

Courtney, Richard
   Relation to other fields

Creative drama's potential to stimulate wonder. USA. 1970-1977. Lang.: Eng.   1288

Covent Garden
   SEE

Royal Opera House, Covent Garden.

Coward, Noël
   Performance/production

Review of 1984 Shaw Festival season. Canada: Niagara-on-the-Lake, ON. 1984. Lang.: Eng.   1699

Collection of newspaper reviews by London theatre critics. UK-England: London. 1986. Lang.: Eng.   2137

Collection of newspaper reviews by New York theatre critics. USA: New York, NY. 1987. Lang.: Eng.   2322

Cowboys #2
   Plays/librettos/scripts

Sam Shepard's manipulation of an audience's desire to believe what it sees. USA. 1967-1983. Lang.: Eng.   2932

Cox, Brian
   Performance/production

Brian Cox's work with the Royal Shakespeare Company. UK-England: Stratford, London. USA: New York, NY. 1968-1987. Lang.: Eng.   2284

Cox, Ida
   Performance/production

Origins of jazz, its evolution in vaudeville. USA: New Orleans, LA, New York, NY, Chicago, IL. Lang.: Eng.   3650

Cox, Veanne
   Performance/production

Two productions of *Flora, the Red Menace*. USA: New York, NY. 1965-1987. Lang.: Eng.   3640

Cozens, Vivienne
   Performance/production

Collection of newspaper reviews by London theatre critics. UK-England: London. 1987. Lang.: Eng.   2239

Cracow KTO (Cracow)
   Performance/production

The 4th International Festival of Street Theatres. Poland: Jelenia Góra. 1986. Lang.: Eng, Fre.   3355

Craig, Edward Gordon
   Institutions

History of Chessé Marionettes. USA. 1927-1987. Lang.: Eng.   4000

   Performance spaces

Performance spaces and audience-performer relationship. France. Germany, West. 1875-1987. Lang.: Eng.   633

   Performance/production

Major directors of the early twentieth century. Europe. North America. 1900-1950. Lang.: Kor.   779

Directing as guiding actors, not imposing a subjective interpretation. France. 1987. Lang.: Fre.   784

Florentine theatrical culture. Italy: Florence. 1800-1900. Lang.: Ita.   832

Edward Gordon Craig's use of *commedia dell'arte* in his work. UK-England. Italy. 1872-1966. Lang.: Eng.   3314

   Theory/criticism

Conviviality vs. spectacularity in theatre. 1985. Lang.: Spa.   1314

Edward Gordon Craig's concept of movement and his theory of theatre. UK-England. 1872-1966. Lang.: Eng.   1348

Craig, Ted
   Performance/production

Collection of newspaper reviews by London theatre critics. UK-England: London. 1987. Lang.: Eng.   2205

Collection of newspaper reviews by London theatre critics. UK-England: London. 1987. Lang.: Eng.   2220

Collection of newspaper reviews by London theatre critics. UK-England: London. 1987. Lang.: Eng.   2261

Cramp
   Performance/production

Collection of newspaper reviews by London theatre critics. UK-England: London. 1986. Lang.: Eng.   2140

Crane, Richard
   Performance/production

Collection of newspaper reviews by London theatre critics. UK-England: London. 1987. Lang.: Eng.   2259

Cranes Are Flying, The
   SEE

Večno živyjė.

Cranham, Kenneth
   Performance/production

Review of the BBC telecast of *The Birthday Party* by Harold Pinter. UK-England. 1987. Lang.: Eng.   3206

Cranko, John
   Performance/production

New European choreographers and their development of new images. France: Paris. UK-England: London. South Africa, Republic of. 1987. Lang.: Eng.   1468

Craon, Guy
   Performance/production

Production of Cirque du Soleil. Canada: Montreal, PQ. 1987. Lang.: Eng.   3302

Craufurd, Russell
   Performance/production

British theatrical touring companies. UK-England. North America. Australia. 1870-1929. Lang.: Eng.   2280

Craven, Tony
   Performance/production

Collection of newspaper reviews by London theatre critics. UK-England: London. 1986. Lang.: Eng.   2054

Collection of newspaper reviews by London theatre critics. UK-England: London. 1987. Lang.: Eng.   2277

Craver, Mike
Performance/production
The cabaret-style musical revue *Oil City Symphony*. USA: New
York, NY. 1987. Lang.: Eng. 3289
Crawford, Ann
Performance/production
Examples of transition in acting style. England. 1783-1784. Lang.:
Eng. 1733
Crawford, Cheryl
Performance/production
Development of the Stanislavskij Acting System. Russia: Moscow.
1906-1938. Lang.: Eng. 2003
Crayonne au Théâtre
Theory/criticism
Introduction to Mallarmé's *Crayonne au Théâtre*. France. 1987.
Lang.: Eng. 3036
Craze, Tony
Performance/production
Collection of newspaper reviews by London theatre critics. UK-
England: London. 1987. Lang.: Eng. 2222
Creation (New York, NY)
Performance/production
Director Matthew Maguire's production of *The American Mysteries*
presented by Creation at La Mama. USA: New York, NY. 1983.
Lang.: Eng. 2361
Creation of the World
Plays/librettos/scripts
Two Cornish *Corpus Christi* plays. England. 1350. Lang.: Eng. 2534
Creative drama
SEE ALSO
Children's theatre.

Relation to other fields
Theoretical examination of psychodrama, creative drama. Korea.
1978. Lang.: Kor. 1247
Teachers discuss creative drama's role in adult education. Jamaica.
Zimbabwe. Bangladesh. 1987. Lang.: Swe. 2996
Creditors
Performance/production
Collection of newspaper reviews by London theatre critics. UK-
England: London. 1986. Lang.: Eng. 2077
Theory/criticism
Shift of August Strindberg from naturalism to expressionism. Sweden.
1987. Lang.: Eng. 3061
Creed, Rupert
Performance/production
Collection of newspaper reviews by London theatre critics. UK-
England: London. 1987. Lang.: Eng. 2246
Crehuet, Pompeu
Plays/librettos/scripts
General history of Catalan literature, including theatre. Spain-
Catalonia. 1902-1961. Lang.: Cat. 1157
Criat nou, Un (New Manservant, A)
Basic theatrical documents
Theatrical works of Pere d'Alcàntara Penya: texts and analysis.
Spain. 1823-1906. Lang.: Cat. 1567
Cricoteka (Cracow)
Performance/production
Interview with Polish playwright Tadeusz Kantor. Poland: Cracow.
Germany, West: Kassel. Italy: Milan. Italy: Sicily. 1987. Lang.: Eng,
Fre. 876
Crime and Punishment
SEE
Prestuplenijė i nakazanijė.
Crimp, Martin
Performance/production
Collection of newspaper reviews by London theatre critics. UK-
England: London. 1987. Lang.: Eng. 2215
Crippa, Maddalena
Performance/production
Luca Ronconi's view of directing. France. Italy. 1987. Lang.: Fre.
1765
Cripps, Steve
Performance/production
Futuristic performance art. USA. 1979-1987. Lang.: Eng. 3363
Crisp, N.J.
Performance/production
Collection of newspaper reviews by London theatre critics. UK-
England: London. 1987. Lang.: Eng. 2265

Cristobal Colón
Performance/production
Premiere of Leonardo Balarda's opera *Cristobal Colón*. Spain-
Catalonia: Barcelona. 1987. Lang.: Eng. 3818
Criticism
SEE
Theory/criticism.
Croatian National Theatre (Drama and Opera)
SEE
Hravatsko Narodno Kazalište.
Crochet, Pascal
Performance/production
Pascal Crochet directs Samuel Beckett's *Solo*. Belgium: Brussels.
1987. Lang.: Fre. 1683
Croft, David
Performance/production
Collection of newspaper reviews by London theatre critics. UK-
England: London. 1986. Lang.: Eng. 2156
Croft, Giles
Performance/production
Collection of newspaper reviews by London theatre critics. UK-
England: London. 1987. Lang.: Eng. 2226
Croft, Michael
Performance/production
Collection of newspaper reviews by London theatre critics. UK-
England: London. 1986. Lang.: Eng. 2138
Crommelynck, Fernand
Basic theatrical documents
Text of Fernand Crommelynck's *Le Cocu magnifique (The
Magnificent Cuckold)*. Belgium. 1920. Lang.: Fre. 1543
Crossmith, George
Plays/librettos/scripts
W.S. Gilbert's contribution to the development of the musical play.
England. 1836-1911. Lang.: Eng. 3670
Crothers, Rachel
Plays/librettos/scripts
Women's roles in Broadway plays at the time of women's suffrage.
USA: New York, NY. 1920. Lang.: Eng. 2850
Crow's Theatre (Toronto, ON)
Performance spaces
The lack of performance space for small theatre companies. Canada:
Toronto, ON. 1987. Lang.: Eng. 629
Crowe, Richard
Performance/production
Collection of newspaper reviews by London theatre critics. UK-
England: London. 1987. Lang.: Eng. 2180
Crowley, Bob
Design/technology
Bob Crowley's set designs for *Les Liaisons Dangereuses*. USA: New
York, NY. UK-England: London. 1985-1987. Lang.: Eng. 463

Performance/production
Collection of newspaper reviews by London theatre critics. UK-
England: London. 1987. Lang.: Eng. 2230
Crown of Light
SEE
Corona de luz.
Crowned with Fame
Performance/production
Collection of newspaper reviews by London theatre critics. UK-
England: London. 1987. Lang.: Eng. 2225
Croydon Warehouse (London)
Performance/production
Collection of newspaper reviews by London theatre critics. UK-
England: London. 1987. Lang.: Eng. 2276
Crozier, Eric
Relation to other fields
Benjamin Britten's *Albert Herring* as an adaptation of a story by
Maupassant. UK-England. 1947. Lang.: Eng. 3946
Crucial Week in the Life of a Grocer's Assistant, A
Plays/librettos/scripts
Comic characters and the Book of Job in the plays of Thomas
Murphy. Ireland. 1962-1983. Lang.: Eng. 2648
The plays of Thomas Murphy. Ireland: Dublin. 1962-1986. Lang.:
Eng. 2650
The myth of the idyllic peasant life in the plays of Thomas
Murphy. Ireland. 1961-1986. Lang.: Eng. 2652
Theme and language in the plays of Thomas Murphy. Ireland. 1962-
1978. Lang.: Eng. 2656

Da Peng Ge
Performance/production
Four steps to make *Da Peng Ge* more popular. China, People's Republic of. 1987. Lang.: Chi. 3506

da Ponte, Lorenzo
Plays/librettos/scripts
Mozart's *Nozze di Figaro* compared with Beaumarchais source. 1784-1786. Lang.: Eng. 3887

Dadaism
Design/technology
Oskar Schlemmer, head of Bauhaus stage workshop. Germany. 1888-1943. Lang.: Dut. 323

Performance/production
Director Tadeusz Kantor's inspirations in early career. Poland. 1933-1987. Lang.: Pol. 1992
Dance soundtracks simulate a Dada/Futurist variety club. Europe. 1985. Lang.: Eng. 3398

Dahl, Tracy
Performance/production
Interview with soprano Tracy Dahl. Canada. 1987. Lang.: Eng. 3755

Dahlberg, Christer
Performance/production
Director on staging amateur *Fiddler on the Roof*. Sweden: Bollnäs. 1987. Lang.: Swe. 3636

Dai manzai (Big Comic Dialogue, A)
Performance/production
Analysis of four Tokyo productions. Japan: Tokyo. 1987. Lang.: Jap. 1957
Discussion of four Tokyo productions. Japan: Tokyo. 1944-1987. Lang.: Jap. 1963

Dai, Chi-Shia
Performance/production
The careers of two Chinese opera actresses—Guan Shu-Shuan and Dai Chi-Shia. China, People's Republic of. 1987. Lang.: Chi. 3515

Daigre, Edna
Performance/production
Ewajo Dance Workshop's new approach to dance as an art form. USA: Seattle, WA. 1975-1985. Lang.: Eng. 1465

Dainty Shapes and Hairy Apes
SEE
Nabodnisie i koczkodany.

Daisan butai (Tokyo)
Performance/production
New themes and styles in Japanese theatre. Japan: Tokyo. 1986. Lang.: Jap. 1953

Daisan erochika (Tokyo)
Performance/production
Focus on several Tokyo productions. Japan: Tokyo. 1960-1987. Lang.: Jap. 1955
Reviews and discussion of Tokyo productions. Japan: Tokyo. 1960-1987. Lang.: Jap. 1960
Comments on Tokyo performances. Japan: Tokyo. 1987. Lang.: Jap. 1964

Dajka, Margit
Performance/production
Commemoration of actress Margit Dajka. Hungary. 1907-1986. Lang.: Hun. 1907

Dakota Roads: The Story of a Prairie Family
Institutions
History of Dakota Theatre Caravan. USA: Yankton, SD. 1977-1983. Lang.: Eng. 1662

Dakota Theatre Caravan (Yankton, SD)
Institutions
History of Dakota Theatre Caravan. USA: Yankton, SD. 1977-1983. Lang.: Eng. 1662

Dalang
Performance/production
Mythological background and performance aspects of *dalang*. Indonesia. 1987. Lang.: Ita. 4010

Dale, John
Performance/production
Collection of newspaper reviews by London theatre critics. UK-England: London. 1986. Lang.: Eng. 2075

Dallas Theater Center (Dallas, TX)
Performance/production
Four productions in Southern regional theatres. USA: Houston, TX, Louisville, KY, Gainesville, FL. 1980. Lang.: Eng. 2342

Dallas Theatre Center (Dallas, TX)
Administration
Production sharing among non-profit theatres in effort to develop new works. USA. 1987. Lang.: Eng. 255

Dalliance
Performance/production
Collection of newspaper reviews by London theatre critics. UK-England: London. 1986. Lang.: Eng. 2102

Dallmeyer, Andrew
Performance/production
Collection of newspaper reviews by London theatre critics. UK-England: London. 1987. Lang.: Eng. 2202

Dalton, Timothy
Performance/production
English Shakespearean productions. UK-England: London, Manchester, Stratford. 1985-1986. Lang.: Eng. 917

Dana, F. Mitchell
Design/technology
Interview with designer F. Mitchell Dana. USA: New York, NY. 1987. Lang.: Eng. 433

Dance
SEE ALSO
Classed Entries under DANCE.
Choreography.
Design/technology
Set and costume designs of major designers. UK-England. 1902-1980. Lang.: Eng. 376
Modern dance production *Portraits in Reflection*. USA. 1986. Lang.: Eng. 396
Performance spaces
Collection of photographs on the history of the Teatre Lliure. Spain-Catalonia: Barcelona. 1976-1987. Lang.: Cat. 1671
Performance/production
History and description of a performance of *Cavittunatakam*, a drama recounting lives of the saints. India: Kerala. 1984. Lang.: Eng. 1480
Mime compared with other forms of visual arts. USA: Claremont, CA. 1980-1982. Lang.: Eng. 3228
Dan-o festival of folk performances. Korea. 800-1987. Lang.: Kor. 3296
Relation to other fields
Analysis of the role of tradition in theatrical forms of different cultures. Asia. Africa. 1985. Lang.: Fre. 1218

Dance Forum Design Exhibition
Performance/production
Review of six-week dance festival representing forms of dance in South Africa. South Africa, Republic of: Durban. 1986. Lang.: Eng. 1409

Dance of Death, The
SEE
Dödsdansen.

Dance of the Forests, A
Plays/librettos/scripts
Study of three plays by Wole Soyinka. Nigeria. 1987. Lang.: Eng. 2704

Dance-Drama
SEE ALSO
Classed Entries under DANCE-DRAMA.
Performance spaces
Performance space and staging of traditional Korean genres. Korea. Japan. 57 B.C.-1986 A.D. Lang.: Kor. 663
Stages of traditional theatre in Asia, and development of *Changuk* dance drama. Korea. China. India. 57 B.C.-1987 A.D. Lang.: Kor. 664
Performance/production
Origins, theory of traditional Korean mask theatre. Korea. 57 B.C.-1985 A.D. Lang.: Kor. 858
Han Puly, Korean exorcism dance. Korea. 1500-1987. Lang.: Kor. 1462
Comparison of *onnagata* actors with Elizabethan boy actors. England. Japan. 1580-1987. Lang.: Eng. 1737
Reference materials
French-language Belgian theatre. Belgium. 1985-1986. Lang.: Fre. 1197

Dancing
SEE ALSO
Training, dance.

Dancing — cont'd

Design/technology

Picasso's theatrical work. France. Spain. 1917-1965. Lang.: Ita. 321

Study of the work of dance lighting designer Blu. USA: New York, NY. 1987. Lang.: Eng. 1400

Career of costumer, dancer, actress Judy Dearing. USA: New York, NY. Africa. 1970-1987. Lang.: Eng. 1601

Lighting design and technology for opera and ballet. UK-England: London. 1928-1987. Lang.: Eng. 3698

Institutions

History of ballet companies: their origins in opera companies, later autonomy. Switzerland. 1955-1987. Lang.: Eng, Ger. 1430

Overview of Martha Graham Dance Company. USA. 1926-1986. Lang.: Ger. 1467

Performance/production

Theory, problems of folk-arts competitions. Korea. 1986-1987. Lang.: Kor. 857

Overview of the Theatre of Nations Festival. USA: Baltimore, MD. 1981-1986. Lang.: Eng. 949

History of dance marathons. USA. 1920-1987. Lang.: Eng. 957

Manual of ballroom dances. 1987. Lang.: Ita. 1402

Canadian choreographer Robert Desrosiers. Canada. 1985. Lang.: Eng. 1404

Review of touring production of Edward Lock's *Human Sex.* Canada: Vancouver, BC. 1985-1986. Lang.: Fre. 1405

Review, 'Le corps politique' festival. Canada: Montreal, PQ. 1986. Lang.: Fre. 1406

Development of dance. Germany: Berlin. 1920-1986. Lang.: Ger. 1407

Overview of Dublin dance season. Ireland: Dublin. 1987. Lang.: Eng. 1408

Review of six-week dance festival representing forms of dance in South Africa. South Africa, Republic of: Durban. 1986. Lang.: Eng. 1409

History of dance in Catalonia. Spain-Catalonia. 1300-1987. Lang.: Cat. 1410

Problems of dancers outside established companies. Switzerland. 1950-1986. Lang.: Ger, Eng. 1411

The career of dancer/choreographer Katherine Dunham. USA: New York, NY, Chicago, IL, Las Vegas, NV. 1909-1987. Lang.: Eng. 1412

Dance/lecture focusing on images of gender in dance. USA. 1987. Lang.: Eng. 1415

Five women choreographers and critics discuss conceptions of the female body. USA. 1987. Lang.: Eng. 1416

Career of tap dancer Brenda Bufalino, and exploration of women's roles as lead dancers. USA. 1987. Lang.: Eng. 1417

Development of ballet in Azerbaijan. Azerbaijan. 1920-1980. Lang.: Rus. 1431

Ballerina Gizella Witkowsky: debut, National Ballet of Canada. Canada: Toronto, ON. 1984. Lang.: Eng. 1432

Roles of women in the field of ballet. France. USA. 1720-1987. Lang.: Eng. 1434

Career of choreographer/dancer Bronislava Nižinska. France. USA. 1891-1930. Lang.: Eng. 1436

Interview with dancer-choreographer Viktor Róna. Hungary. Norway: Oslo. 1980-1987. Lang.: Hun. 1437

Premiere performance of new ballet company, Szegedi Balett. Hungary: Szeged. 1987. Lang.: Hun. 1438

Theatrical dance tradition as presented by dance teacher Gregorio Lambranzi. Italy: Venice. Germany: Nuremberg. 1700-1799. Lang.: Ita. 1439

Interview with dancer Vincent Hantam. South Africa, Republic of. 1987. Lang.: Eng. 1441

Interview with ballerina and teacher Ellen Rasch. Sweden. 1927-1987. Lang.: Swe. 1442

Career of American Ballet Theatre dancer Hilda Morales. USA: New York, NY. 1983. Lang.: Eng. 1443

N.M. Foregger's experimental dance performances. USSR. 1920-1929. Lang.: Rus. 1445

Moscow Bolšoj dancer Andris Liepa. USSR: Moscow. 1980-1987. Lang.: Rus. 1446

Principles of biomechanics in teaching ballet. USSR. 1987. Lang.: Rus. 1447

Portrait of ballerina Natal'ja Dudinskaja of the Kirov Ballet. USSR: Leningrad. 1912-1987. Lang.: Eng. 1448

Belorussian ballet soloists L. Bržozovskaja and Ju. Trojan. USSR. 1980. Lang.: Rus. 1449

Russian ballet style seen through sketches of dancers. USSR. 1890-1987. Lang.: Ita. 1450

Alla Osipenko, dancer of Kirov Theatre. USSR: Leningrad. 1932-1980. Lang.: Rus. 1452

Belgrade folk ballet. Yugoslavia: Belgrade. 1923-1941. Lang.: Rus. 1453

International folk dance presentation: the folk play *Witches and Witchcraft.* Hungary: Szeged. 1987. Lang.: Hun. 1460

Uday Shankar's translation of Indian dance for Western audiences. India. France: Paris. UK-England: London. 1924-1940. Lang.: Eng. 1461

Han Puly, Korean exorcism dance. Korea. 1500-1987. Lang.: Kor. 1462

University of Mexico: music of dance theatre. Mexico: Mexico City. 1987. Lang.: Spa. 1463

Founder and director of the Ballet Folklórico Nacional de Nicaragua discusses the company and its goals. Nicaragua. 1986. Lang.: Eng. 1464

Ewajo Dance Workshop's new approach to dance as an art form. USA: Seattle, WA. 1975-1985. Lang.: Eng. 1465

Memorial album by and about dancer Gret Palucca. Germany, East: Dresden. 1922-1987. Lang.: Ger. 1469

Interview with choreographer Senta Driver. USA. 1987. Lang.: Eng. 1472

Life and work of of dancer/choreographer Isadora Duncan. USA. Europe. 1877-1927. Lang.: Eng. 1474

Dancers' daily routine in Les Ballets Jazz de Montréal. Canada: Montreal, PQ. 1985. Lang.: Eng. 1479

History and description of a performance of *Cavittunatakam,* a drama recounting lives of the saints. India: Kerala. 1984. Lang.: Eng. 1480

Complete description of all aspects of *Wayang wong.* Indonesia. 930-1986. Lang.: Eng. 1481

Honda Yasuji's work on Japanese folk theatre. Japan. 1930-1986. Lang.: Eng. 1483

Role of feminist in cultural critique. India. USA. 1983-1987. Lang.: Eng. 1496

Ballet on television. USSR. 1980-1987. Lang.: Rus. 3213

Description of 'Third Theatre'. Argentina: Bahía Blanca. 1987. Lang.: Eng. 3249

Genre of business theatre. USA. 1985-1987. Lang.: Eng. 3272

Growth of West Indian carnival traditions. West Indies. Lang.: Eng. 3277

History and theory of dances in spectacles of the Lombard court. Italy: Milan. 1400-1500. Lang.: Ita. 3323

Celebration of Chinese Lunar New Year: Lion dancing and its martial arts background. USA: New York, NY. 1987. Lang.: Eng. 3334

Dance soundtracks simulate a Dada/Futurist variety club. Europe. 1985. Lang.: Eng. 3398

Chronological repertoire of operas and ballets performed in Reggio Emilia. Italy: Reggio Emilia. 1645-1857. Lang.: Ita. 3403

Career of Chinese opera actor and teacher Maa Lian Liang. China: Beijing. 1929-1981. Lang.: Chi. 3457

Similarities and differences in Chinese opera and ballet. China, People's Republic of. 1986. Lang.: Chi. 3470

Dramatic language in Chinese opera: dancing, music and singing. China, People's Republic of. 1986. Lang.: Chi. 3482

The four main elements of dance in Chinese opera. China, People's Republic of. 960-1987. Lang.: Chi. 3526

Plays/librettos/scripts

Yeats's dance plays: effect of the elements of performance on text. UK-Ireland. 1916-1987. Lang.: Eng. 2832

Reference materials

French-language Belgian theatre. Belgium. 1985-1986. Lang.: Fre. 1197

Relation to other fields

Rediscovery of the body in modern dance. Germany. 1900-1930. Lang.: Ita. 1475

Dancing — cont'd

Church records related to Morris dancing. England: Great Marlow. 1593-1674. Lang.: Eng.   3280

Theory/criticism

Balanchine ballerinas: female domination in the ballet. USA. 1946-1987. Lang.: Eng.   1457

Domination of women and gay men in Western dance. USA. 1700-1987. Lang.: Eng.   1458

Influence of Chinese opera on Japanese drama. China. Japan. 1596-1876. Lang.: Chi.   3586

Danger: Memory!

Performance/production

Collection of newspaper reviews by New York theatre critics. USA: New York, NY. 1987. Lang.: Eng.   2326

Dangerous Obsession

Performance/production

Collection of newspaper reviews by London theatre critics. UK-England: London. 1987. Lang.: Eng.   2265

Daniels, Barbara

Performance/production

Film versions of Puccini's *La Bohème*, Offenbach's *Tales of Hoffmann*. Europe. North America. 1987. Lang.: Eng.   3767

Interview with soprano Barbara Daniels. USA: New York, NY. 1987. Lang.: Eng.   3846

Daniels, Peter

Performance/production

Collection of newspaper reviews of London theatre critics. UK-England: London. 1987. Lang.: Eng.   2273

Daniels, Ron

Performance spaces

Mermaid Theatre, London home of Royal Shakespeare Company. UK-England: London. 1959-1987. Lang.: Eng.   671

Performance/production

Play scripts as literary texts and as performance texts. UK-England. 1977-1987. Lang.: Eng.   905

Collection of newspaper reviews by London theatre critics. UK-England: London. 1986. Lang.: Eng.   2098

Collection of newspaper reviews by London theatre critics. UK-England: London. 1986. Lang.: Eng.   2111

Collection of newspaper reviews by London theatre critics. UK-England: London. 1987. Lang.: Eng.   2272

Daniels, Sarah

Performance/production

Collection of newspaper reviews by London theatre critics. UK-England: London. 1986. Lang.: Eng.   2058

Collection of newspaper reviews by London theatre critics. UK-England: London. 1986. Lang.: Eng.   2118

Plays/librettos/scripts

Interview with playwright Howard Brenton. UK-England. 1975-1987. Lang.: Eng.   2806

Dans la solitude des champs de coton (In the Solitude of the Cotton Fields)

Performance/production

Analysis of *Dans la solitude des champs de coton (In the Solitude of the Cotton Fields)* by Bernard-Marie Koltès. France: Paris. 1987. Lang.: Swe.   1761

Danspace at St. Mark's Church (New York, NY)

Performance/production

Production of *Spring* by Simone Forti presented at the Danspace at St. Mark's Church. USA: New York, NY. 1983. Lang.: Eng.   2337

Danton Affair, The

Performance/production

Collection of newspaper reviews by London theatre critics. UK-England: London. 1986. Lang.: Eng.   2111

Dantons Tod (Danton's Death)

Performance/production

Collection of newspaper reviews by London theatre critics. UK-England: London. 1987. Lang.: Eng.   2173

Daphne

Plays/librettos/scripts

Musical sources in the operas of Richard Strauss. Germany: Dresden. 1864-1949. Lang.: Eng.   3908

Där älvarna samman flyta (Where the Rivers Meet)

Institutions

Gagnef Teaterförening's production of a play based on local history. Sweden: Gagnef. 1975-1987. Lang.: Swe.   1644

Darío, Rubén

Theory/criticism

Study of modernism through analysis of three plays. Spain. 1898-1909. Lang.: Spa.   3319

Dark Lady of the Sonnets, The

Plays/librettos/scripts

Shakespeare's influence on George Bernard Shaw. UK-England. 1882-1936. Lang.: Eng.   2812

Dark Water Closing

Performance/production

Collection of newspaper reviews by London theatre critics. UK-England: London. 1986. Lang.: Eng.   2130

Darke, Nick

Performance/production

Collection of newspaper reviews by London theatre critics. UK-England: London. 1986. Lang.: Eng.   2111

Collection of newspaper reviews by London theatre critics. UK-England: London. 1987. Lang.: Eng.   2251

Darkhorse Theatre (Vancouver, BC)

Institutions

Survey of Vancouver theatre companies. Canada: Vancouver, BC. 1987. Lang.: Eng.   516

Dasgupta, Gautam

Performance/production

Essays on the future of the theatre. USA: New York, NY. 1970-1987. Lang.: Eng.   955

Theory/criticism

Editor of *Performing Arts Journal* discusses its history. USA: New York, NY. 1975-1985. Lang.: Eng.   1359

DaSilva, Howard

Administration

Conference on Equity's plan to create a National Theatre in America. USA: New York, NY. 1982. Lang.: Eng.   111

DaSilva, Ray

Performance/production

History and aspects of puppet theatre: designs, genres and puppeteers. Europe. Asia. 400 B.C.-1985 A.D. Lang.: Eng.   3255

Daughter of Monsieur Occitania, The

SEE

Fille de Monsieur Occitania, La.

Daughters of the Gods, The

Basic theatrical documents

English translations of contemporary African plays. Senegal. Zaire. 1987. Lang.: Eng.   1566

Daughters of the Water

Basic theatrical documents

Text of *Daughters of the Water* by Jay Wright. USA. 1987. Lang.: Eng.   1583

Dave Allen Live

Performance/production

Collection of newspaper reviews by London theatre critics. UK-England: London. 1986. Lang.: Eng.   2155

David, Gerard

Plays/librettos/scripts

History and sources of Thomas Preston's *Cambyses, King of Persia*. England. 1562-1987. Lang.: Eng.   2529

Davida, Dena

Performance/production

Review, 'Le corps politique' festival. Canada: Montreal, PQ. 1986. Lang.: Fre.   1406

Davidson, Clare

Performance/production

Collection of newspaper reviews by London theatre critics. UK-England: London. 1986. Lang.: Eng.   2120

Collection of newspaper reviews by London theatre critics. UK-England: London. 1987. Lang.: Eng.   2222

Davies, Christopher

Performance/production

Collection of newspaper reviews by London theatre critics. UK-England: London. 1987. Lang.: Eng.   2178

Davies, Howard

Performance/production

Collection of newspaper reviews by London theatre critics. UK-England: London. 1986. Lang.: Eng.   2046

Collection of newspaper reviews by London theatre critics. UK-England: London. 1986. Lang.: Eng.   2067

Collection of newspaper reviews by London theatre critics. UK-England: London. 1986. Lang.: Eng.   2095

Davies, Howard — cont'd

Collection of newspaper reviews by London theatre critics. UK-England: London. 1987. Lang.: Eng. 2274

Collection of newspaper reviews by New York theatre critics. USA: New York, NY. 1987. Lang.: Eng. 2311

Davies, John
Plays/librettos/scripts
Argument against authenticity of three Elizabethan documents. England. 1591-1885. Lang.: Eng. 3326

Davies, Robertson
Plays/librettos/scripts
Survey of Robertson Davies' plays. Canada. 1913-1985. Lang.: Eng. 2484

Relation to other fields
Critical study of Robertson Davies' literature and drama. Canada. 1913-1985. Lang.: Eng. 2983

Davies, Tudor
Performance/production
Collection of newspaper reviews by London theatre critics. UK-England: London. 1986. Lang.: Eng. 2069

Davis, Andrew
Institutions
Andrew Davis' role as Toronto Symphony Orchestra conductor. Canada: Toronto, On. 1974-1987. Lang.: Eng. 3389

Performance spaces
The modern acoustics of Toronto's Thomson Hall. Canada: Toronto, ON. 1982. Lang.: Eng. 628

Davis, Barbara
Institutions
The role of the Actors' Fund in New York's theatre industry. USA: New York, NY. 1987. Lang.: Eng. 570

Davis, Carl
Performance/production
Collection of newspaper reviews by London theatre critics. UK-England: London. 1986. Lang.: Eng. 2041

Collection of newspaper reviews by London theatre critics. UK-England: London. 1986. Lang.: Eng. 2047

Collection of newspaper reviews by London theatre critics. UK-England: London. 1987. Lang.: Eng. 2235

Davis, Philip
Performance/production
Collection of newspaper reviews by London theatre critics. UK-England: London. 1987. Lang.: Eng. 2248

Davis, Stephen
Performance/production
Collection of newspaper reviews by London theatre critics. UK-England: London. 1987. Lang.: Eng. 2209

Davis, Thomas
Theory/criticism
Brian Friel's play *Translations*. Ireland. 1987. Lang.: Eng. 3050

Day of Absence
Plays/librettos/scripts
Characterizations of stage spaces: examples from Brecht, Pinter, Douglas Turner Ward. UK-England. USA. 1947-1987. Lang.: Eng. 2798

Day the Sheep Turned Pink, The
Performance/production
Collection of newspaper reviews by London theatre critics. UK-England: London. 1986. Lang.: Eng. 2163

Day, Connie
Performance/production
Career of Broadway actress Connie Day. USA: New York, NY. 1987. Lang.: Eng. 3657

Day, Gregory
Performance/production
Collection of newspaper reviews by London theatre critics. UK-England: London. 1986. Lang.: Eng. 2054

Dcera Oty II. znovu nalezena (Daughter of Ota II Was Found Again, The)
Plays/librettos/scripts
Inception of Leopold Koželuh's ballet *Dcera Oty II. znovu nalezena (The Daughter of Ota II Was Found Again)*. Austria-Hungary: Vienna. 1794. Lang.: Cze. 1454

De Beauvoir, Simone
SEE
Beauvoir, Simone de.

De Filippo, Luigi
Performance/production
Examples of missed opportunities in modern Italian theatre. Italy. 1930-1950. Lang.: Ita. 1944

De Groen, Alma
Plays/librettos/scripts
Dramatic and scenic structure, feminism, in plays of Alma De Groen. Australia. 1987. Lang.: Eng. 2446

De la calle (Of the Street)
Plays/librettos/scripts
Ethnic roots in *De la calle (Of the Street)* by Jesús Gonzalez-Davila. Mexico: Mexico City. 1987. Lang.: Spa. 2699

de la Tour, Andy
Performance/production
Development of alternative cabaret. UK-England. 1980. Lang.: Eng. 3288

De Lavallade, Carmen
Performance/production
The career of dancer/choreographer Katherine Dunham. USA: New York, NY, Chicago, IL, Las Vegas, NV. 1909-1987. Lang.: Eng. 1412

De Loutherbourg, Philippe James
Design/technology
Influence of scene designer Philippe James de Loutherbourg. England. 1700-1800. Lang.: Eng. 317

de Maligny, Bernier
Performance/production
Documentation on melodramatic acting style. France: Paris. 1800-1830. Lang.: Eng. 791

de Matta, Roberto
Performance/production
Teatro Arena de São Paulo's production of *Arena Conta Zumbi*. Brazil: São Paulo. 1965. Lang.: Eng. 1690

De Molina, Tirso
SEE
Molina, Tirso de.

de Rojas, Fernando
Plays/librettos/scripts
Themes in the Festival of Latin Theatre. USA: New York, NY. Latin America. Spain. 1987. Lang.: Spa. 2847

De Stefani, Alessandro
Performance/production
Encounter between Pirandello and Lord Dunsany during Pirandello's production of *I pazzi sulla montagna (The Gods of the Mountain)* by Alessandro De Stefani. Italy. 1923-1928. Lang.: Eng. 1947

de' Nobili, Francesco
Performance/production
Francesco de' Nobili, Renaissance actor. Italy: Venice. 1500-1600. Lang.: Ita. 829

Dead Class, The
SEE
Umerla Klasa.

Dead Monkey, The
Performance/production
Collection of newspaper reviews by London theatre critics. UK-England: London. 1986. Lang.: Eng. 2111

Dead, The
Performance/production
Collection of newspaper reviews by London theatre critics. UK-England: London. 1987. Lang.: Eng. 2187

Deadly Nightcap
Performance/production
Collection of newspaper reviews by London theatre critics. UK-England: London. 1986. Lang.: Eng. 2120

Deadwood
Performance/production
Collection of newspaper reviews by London theatre critics. UK-England: London. 1986. Lang.: Eng. 2154

View of Lumière & Son's production *Deadwood*. UK-England: London. 1986. Lang.: Eng. 3356

Deals
Performance/production
Collection of newspaper reviews by London theatre critics. UK-England: London. 1987. Lang.: Eng. 2184

Dean, Laura
Administration
Contracts, actors and union negotiations. USA. 1986. Lang.: Eng. 235

Dean, Phillip-Hayes
Institutions
The formation of the North Carolina Black Repertory Company. USA: Winston-Salem, NC. 1979-1987. Lang.: Eng. 1666

Dear, Nick
Performance/production
Collection of newspaper reviews by London theatre critics. UK-England: London. 1987. Lang.: Eng. 2236

Dearing, Judy
Design/technology
Career of costumer, dancer, actress Judy Dearing. USA: New York, NY. Africa. 1970-1987. Lang.: Eng. 1601

Death and Resurection of Monsieur Occitania
SEE
Mort et résurrection de Monsieur Occitania.

Death and the Fool
SEE
Tor und der Tod, Der.

Death and the King's Horsemen
Design/technology
Lighting reviews for several New York productions. USA: New York, NY. 1987. Lang.: Eng. 475

Performance/production
Collection of newspaper reviews by New York theatre critics. USA: New York, NY. 1987. Lang.: Eng. 2326

Death Defying Theatre (Sydney)
Audience
Death Defying Theatre's development of the play *Coal Town*. Australia: Collinsville. 1984-1985. Lang.: Eng. 276

Death of a Dragonfly
Performance/production
Collection of newspaper reviews by London theatre critics. UK-England: London. 1987. Lang.: Eng. 2229

Death of a Salesman
Performance/production
Géza Tordy as Willy Loman in Arthur Miller's *Death of a Salesman* directed, as *Az ügynök halála*, by János Szikora at Vigszinház. Hungary: Budapest. 1987. Lang.: Hun. 1797

Arthur Miller's *Death of a Salesman* directed by János Szikora at Vígszínház. Hungary: Budapest. 1987. Lang.: Hun. 1869

Review of actors Géza Tordy, Géza Hegedűs D. and Attila Kaszás in Arthur Miller's *Death of a Salesman*. Hungary: Budapest. 1987. Lang.: Hun. 1893

Collection of newspaper reviews by London theatre critics. UK. 1987. Lang.: Eng. 2031

Critique of the 1984 Broadway production of *Death of a Salesman*. USA: New York, NY. 1984. Lang.: Eng. 2330

Plays/librettos/scripts
Interview with playwright Arthur Miller. USA. 1944-1987. Lang.: Eng. 2868

Theory/criticism
Perceptions of tragedy and new perspective on its analysis. USA. UK-England. Greece. 500 B.C.-1987 A.D. Lang.: Eng. 3066

Death Round at Sinera
SEE
Ronda de mort a Sinera.

Deburau, Jean Gaspard
Performance/production
Development of mime, pantomime and its related movements. France: Paris. UK-England. USA: New York, NY. 1980-1982. Lang.: Eng. 3223

Debussy, Claude
Plays/librettos/scripts
Adaptation of literary works to opera. 1893-1987. Lang.: Eng. 3890

Decadence
Performance/production
Collection of newspaper reviews by London theatre critics. UK-England: London. 1987. Lang.: Eng. 2186

Deconstruction
Plays/librettos/scripts
Temporality in Shakespeare's *Richard III*. England. 1592. Lang.: Eng. 1115

Comparative study of *Measure for Measure* by Shakespeare and the poem *Leda and the Swan* by Yeats. England. 1604-1929. Lang.: Eng. 1116

Swetnam the Woman-Hater, Arraigned by Women written in response to an anti-female pamphlet. England. 1600-1620. Lang.: Eng. 1118

Theodicy and tragic drama in *King Lear* and *The Tempest*. England. 1605-1611. Lang.: Eng. 1119

An analysis of the structure of *Measure for Measure*. England. 1604. Lang.: Eng. 1120

Use of symbols in Webster's *The Duchess of Malfi*. England. 1613. Lang.: Eng. 1121

King Lear focusing on the character of Kent. England. 1605. Lang.: Eng. 1122

Theme of deconstruction in Samuel Beckett's writings. Europe. 1953-1987. Lang.: Eng. 2563

Deconstructionist analysis of Harold Pinter's *Silence*. UK-England. 1964-1970. Lang.: Eng. 2759

Examination of different editions of Marlowe's *Doctor Faustus*. UK-England. 1987. Lang.: Eng. 2791

Theory/criticism
Gesture and sign in Shakespearean performance. England. USA. 1590-1987. Lang.: Eng. 1326

Self-awareness in Shakespeare's *Julius Caesar*. England. 1599. Lang.: Eng. 1327

The body as emblematic of a character's frame of mind. England. 1583. Lang.: Eng. 3031

Works of Pierre Corneille and the social role of women. France. 1540-1650. Lang.: Eng. 3040

Decroux, Etienne Marcel
Performance/production
Influence of *nō* theatre on director Jean-Louis Barrault and his colleagues. France. 1910-1982. Lang.: Eng. 1498

Dederko, Henryk
Performance/production
Festival of Polish plays. Poland: Wrocław. 1987. Lang.: Eng, Fre. 871

Dee, Ruby
Plays/librettos/scripts
Life of playwright John O. Killens. USA: New York, NY. 1954-1987. Lang.: Eng. 2836

Definitely the Bahamas
Performance/production
Collection of newspaper reviews by London theatre critics. UK-England: London. 1987. Lang.: Eng. 2215

DeForest, Charles
Performance/production
Career of composer Charles DeForest. USA: New York, NY. 1987. Lang.: Eng. 3659

Deguchi, Norio
Performance/production
Four Tokyo productions in light of ideas of Betsuyaku Minoru. Japan: Tokyo. 1987. Lang.: Jap. 1950

Analysis of four Tokyo productions. Japan: Tokyo. 1987. Lang.: Jap. 1957

Déjazet, Virginie
Performance/production
Child actors in juvenile companies, Comédie-Française. France: Paris. 1769-1850. Lang.: Eng. 1756

Dekker, Thomas
Plays/librettos/scripts
Evaluation of *Westward Ho!* and *Northward Ho!* by Thomas Dekker and John Webster. England. 1605. Lang.: Eng. 2509

Utopian ideas in Tudor and Stuart playwrights. England. 1600-1650. Lang.: Ger. 2522

Del Valle-Inclán, Ramón
SEE
Valle-Inclán, Ramón del.

DeLaurentis, Dino
Design/technology
DeLaurentis Entertainment Group's film studio in North Carolina. USA: Wilmington, NC. 1987. Lang.: Eng. 3135

Delbo, Charlotte
Plays/librettos/scripts
Dramatic treatment of material about the Holocaust. USA. Germany, West. 1950-1987. Lang.: Eng. 2917

Delcuvellerie, Jacques
Performance/production
Groupov ensemble describes the creation of *Koniec*. Belgium: Liège. 1987. Lang.: Fre. 1687

Delirium Theatre Company (London)
　Performance/production
　　Collection of newspaper reviews by London theatre critics. UK-England: London. 1987. Lang.: Eng.　　2266
Dell'Arte Players (Blue Lake, CA)
　Institutions
　　Profile of Dell'Arte Players and their productions. USA: Blue Lake, CA. 1957-1983. Lang.: Eng.　　3310
　Performance/production
　　New Vaudeville Festival. USA: San Francisco, CA. 1987. Lang.: Eng.　　948
Delo (Affair, The)
　Plays/librettos/scripts
　　Analysis of *Delo (The Affair)* by A.V. Suchovo-Kobylin. Russia. 1861. Lang.: Rus.　　2721
DeMain, John
　Performance/production
　　Opera conductors who also conduct in Broadway musicals. USA: New York, NY. 1980-1987. Lang.: Eng.　　3847
　　Interview with John DeMain, music director, Houston Grand Opera. USA: Houston, TX. 1944-1987. Lang.: Eng.　　3851
Demarco, Richard
　Theory/criticism
　　Influences on work of performance artist Richard Demarco. UK-Scotland: Edinburgh. 1987. Lang.: Eng.　　3375
　　Richard Demarco on performance art. UK-Scotland: Edinburgh. 1970-1987. Lang.: Eng.　　3376
Demarczyk, Ewa
　Performance/production
　　The Polish cabaret performance group Piwnica. Poland: Cracow. USA: New York, NY. 1987. Lang.: Eng.　　3287
Dembowicz, Michael
　Performance spaces
　　Interview with stage manager Michael Dembowicz about the new Swan Theatre. UK-England: Stratford. 1986. Lang.: Eng.　　673
Demidova, Alla
　Performance/production
　　Actress Alla Demidova recalls Vladimir Vysockij. USSR: Moscow. 1938-1980. Lang.: Rus.　　1008
　　Life and work of Anatolij Efros. USSR: Moscow. 1983-1987. Lang.: Eng.　　1038
Demon Lovers
　Performance/production
　　Collection of newspaper reviews by London theatre critics. UK-England: London. 1987. Lang.: Eng.　　2241
Dempster, Curt
　Administration
　　Profile of Ensemble Studio Theatre. USA: New York, NY. 1987. Lang.: Eng.　　232
Dempsy, The
　Plays/librettos/scripts
　　Irish Literary Renaissance writers' view of America. Ireland. 1900-1930. Lang.: Eng.　　2639
Denis, Jean-Luc
　Plays/librettos/scripts
　　Rebuttal of review of Lepage's *La Trilogie des dragons*. Canada. 1987. Lang.: Fre.　　2459
Denmark, Leon
　Administration
　　Nontraditional casting: types, rationale and examples. USA: New York, NY. 1987. Lang.: Eng.　　203
　Performance/production
　　Theatre career of photo-journalist Bert Andrews. USA: New York, NY. 1950-1987. Lang.: Eng.　　2367
Dennis, Lin
　Performance/production
　　Collection of newspaper reviews by London theatre critics. UK-England: London. 1986. Lang.: Eng.　　2090
Derby Playhouse (London)
　Performance/production
　　Collection of newspaper reviews by London theatre critics. UK-England: London. 1987. Lang.: Eng.　　2256
Dernière bande, La
　SEE
　　Krapp's Last Tape.
Des Lauriers
　SEE
　　Gracieux, Jean.

Des Pres, Terrence
　Plays/librettos/scripts
　　Dramatic treatment of material about the Holocaust. USA. Germany, West. 1950-1987. Lang.: Eng.　　2917
Deschamps, Jérôme
　Performance/production
　　Directing as textual interpretation, relating performance to text. France. 1987. Lang.: Fre.　　1768
Descriptions of resources
　Performance/production
　　Description of scope and content of new museum in Covent Garden. UK-England: London. 1987. Lang.: Eng.　　920
　Reference materials
　　Source materials on development of Chinese opera. Taiwan. 1987. Lang.: Chi.　　3580
　　Description of the Verdi Archive at New York University. USA: New York, NY. Italy: Milan. 1976. Lang.: Eng.　　3937
Desengany, Lo (Disappointment, The)
　Basic theatrical documents
　　Text of *Lo desengany (The Disappointment)* by Francesc Fontanella, with analysis. Spain-Catalonia: Barcelona. 1622-1680. Lang.: Cat.　　1572
Deshpande, Sulabha
　Performance/production
　　Franz Xaver Kroetz's *Wunschkonzert (Request Concert)* in Bombay: observations of actress Sulabha Deshpande. India: Bombay. 1986. Lang.: Eng.　　1931
Design/technology
　SEE ALSO
　　Classed Entries.
　Administration
　　Creating human voices and images with digital, holographic techniques: actors' conference. USA: New York, NY. Israel: Tel-Aviv. 1987. Lang.: Eng.　　3083
　　Public performance exemptions from copyright liability. USA. 1976-1987. Lang.: Eng.　　3088
　　Recommended changes to copyright law. USA. 1987. Lang.: Eng.　　3191
　　Effect of hosting a World's Fair on region. Canada. 1986. Lang.: Eng.　　3239
　　Irving Guttman, artistic director, Edmonton Opera, Manitoba Opera. Canada: Edmonton, AB, Winnipeg, MB. 1972-1985. Lang.: Eng.　　3679
　Institutions
　　1987 USITT conference. USA: Minneapolis, MN. 1987. Lang.: Eng.　　603
　　Calendar of international opera productions and broadcasts for 1988 winter season. 1988. Lang.: Eng.　　3706
　　International survey of early 1987 opera productions. 1987. Lang.: Eng.　　3707
　　International calendar of summer 1987 opera productions. 1987. Lang.: Eng.　　3708
　　International calendar of fall 1987 opera productions. 1987. Lang.: Eng.　　3709
　Performance spaces
　　Plans for New Theatre of Bologna's machinery and stage. Italy: Bologna. 1763. Lang.: Eng.　　651
　　Theatres built, influences on design. South Africa, Republic of: Johannesburg. 1887-1940. Lang.: Afr.　　667
　　Technical team of Teatre Lliure. Spain-Catalonia: Barcelona. 1976-1987. Lang.: Cat.　　668
　　Paul Shelving's contribution to stage design exhibited by Birmingham Museum. UK-England. 1888-1968. Lang.: Eng.　　670
　　Design of new Swan Theatre recreates Elizabethan atmosphere. UK-England: Stratford. 1987. Lang.: Eng.　　672
　　Restoration of Ohio, State and Palace Theatres in Playhouse Square. USA: Cleveland, OH. 1964-1986. Lang.: Eng.　　681
　　Use of lighting in Hult Center's lobby and two performance halls. USA: Eugene, OR. 1987. Lang.: Eng.　　687
　　Directory of extant theatres built in the U.S. before 1915. USA. 1809-1915. Lang.: Eng.　　689
　　The Tampa Bay Performing Arts Center. USA: Tampa, FL. 1987. Lang.: Eng.　　698
　　Comparison of British and American cinema theatre design. UK-England: London. 1930-1987. Lang.: Eng.　　3142

Design/technology — cont'd

Lighting renovation in an amphitheatre and arena. USA: Montgomery, AL. 1987. Lang.: Eng.   3246

Performance/production

Conference proceedings on staging of Elizabethan plays. England. 1546-1616. Lang.: Eng.   775

Interview with people who staged *The Yellow House*. USA. 1960-1987. Lang.: Eng.   1486

Review of production and staging aspects of *Wild Honey* by Anton Čechov. UK-England: London. 1986. Lang.: Eng.   2306

Latest technology at Amiga Studio Theatre, Canada Place. Canada: Vancouver, BC. 1986. Lang.: Eng.   3251

Minor theatrical forms involving tableaux, mechanics. Italy: Venice. 1800-1900. Lang.: Ita.   3263

Critical discussion of the Ultimatum II festival. Canada: Montreal, PQ. 1987. Lang.: Eng.   3346

Comparison of three theatrical environmental entertainments. USA. 1893-1986. Lang.: Eng.   3385

Creativity in the Chinese arts. China, People's Republic of. 1949-1985. Lang.: Chi.   3480

Designing and using puppets in classical works. USA. 1600-1987. Lang.: Eng.   3985

Puppeteer Paul Zaloom discusses political ideas, scene design. USA. 1970-1987. Lang.: Eng.   3987

Desire Caught by the Tail

Performance/production

Collection of newspaper reviews by London theatre critics. UK-England: London. 1987. Lang.: Eng.   2185

Desire Under the Elms

Performance/production

Collection of newspaper reviews by London theatre critics. UK-England: London. 1987. Lang.: Eng.   2214

Plays/librettos/scripts

Family and male-female relationships in O'Neill's *Desire Under the Elms*. USA. 1920. Lang.: Eng.   2885

Desmarias, Lorraine

Performance/production

Production of Cirque du Soleil. Canada: Montreal, PQ. 1987. Lang.: Eng.   3302

Desperrier, Hélène

Relation to other fields

Representation of workers on stage. Europe. USA. 1871-1987. Lang.: Fre.   2987

Despojamiento, El (Robbery, The)

Theory/criticism

Semiotic study of Gambaro's *El despojamiento (The Robbery)*. USA. 1987. Lang.: Eng.   3067

Desrosiers, Robert

Performance/production

Canadian choreographer Robert Desrosiers. Canada. 1985. Lang.: Eng.   1404

Dessau, Paul

Performance/production

Documentation of performance of *Die Verurteilung des Lukullus (The Condemnation of Lucullus)* by Bertolt Brecht and Paul Dessau, staged by Ruth Berghaus. Germany, East: Berlin, East. 1983. Lang.: Ger.   3785

Dessen, Alan

Performance/production

Conference proceedings on staging of Elizabethan plays. England. 1546-1616. Lang.: Eng.   775

Deutsche Grammophon

Performance/production

Metropolitan/Deutsche Grammophon recording, Wagner's *Ring*, conducted by James Levine. USA: New York, NY. 1987. Lang.: Eng.   3114

Deutsche Oper Berlin (West Berlin)

Performance/production

Anniversaries of opera houses and theatres. Germany, West: Berlin, West. Germany, East: Berlin, East. 1237-1987. Lang.: Eng.   3789

Deutsche Staatsoper (East Berlin)

Design/technology

On opera photography. Germany, East: Berlin, East. 1987. Lang.: Ger.   3695

Performance/production

Contemporary opera at Deutsche Staatsoper. Germany, East: Berlin, East. 1945-1987. Lang.: Ger.   3784

Documentation of performance of *Die Verurteilung des Lukullus (The Condemnation of Lucullus)* by Bertolt Brecht and Paul Dessau, staged by Ruth Berghaus. Germany, East: Berlin, East. 1983. Lang.: Ger.   3785

Anniversaries of opera houses and theatres. Germany, West: Berlin, West. Germany, East: Berlin, East. 1237-1987. Lang.: Eng.   3789

Deutsches Theater (Berlin)

Institutions

Founding of Deutsches Theater. Germany: Berlin. 1854-1883. Lang.: Ger.   531

Deutsches Theater (East Berlin)

Performance/production

Change from sociopolitical emphasis to individual themes in productions of *A Midsummer Night's Dream*. Germany, East. 1960-1980. Lang.: Eng.   1782

Annual Brecht workshop. Germany, East. 1985. Lang.: Fre.   1785

Deutsches Theatermuseum (Munich)

Institutions

Tandem database system used by the Deutsches Theatermuseum. Germany, West: Munich. 1987. Lang.: Eng.   533

Deuxième existence du camp de Tatenberg, La (Second Life of Camp Tatenberg, The)

Plays/librettos/scripts

Anti-fascist plays of Armand Gatti. France. 1924-1987. Lang.: Rus.   2578

Development

Audience

Devices used to draw audiences to the theatre. USA. 1985. Lang.: Eng.   292

Devil Is an Ass, The

Audience

Actor and audience in Elizabethan theatre. England. 1585-1625. Lang.: Eng.   1533

Devil's Disciple, The

Plays/librettos/scripts

Shaw's struggle to find an apt ending for *The Devil's Disciple*. UK-England. 1896-1909. Lang.: Eng.   2827

Devlin, Ann

Plays/librettos/scripts

Avoidance of political themes in drama of Northern Ireland. UK-Ireland. 1979-1987. Lang.: Eng.   2830

Devlin, Anne

Performance/production

Collection of newspaper reviews by London theatre critics. UK-England: London. 1986. Lang.: Eng.   2137

Devoir, Le (Montreal, PQ)

Theory/criticism

Criticizes newspaper coverage of Montreal theatre awards. Canada: Montreal, PQ. 1987. Lang.: Fre.   1318

Devrient, Ludwig

Performance/production

Essays on major figures of the Romantic period. Germany. 1795-1830. Lang.: Ger.   1776

Dewey, Sheila

Performance/production

Collection of newspaper reviews by London theatre critics. UK-England: London. 1987. Lang.: Eng.   2239

Dewhurst, Colleen

Administration

Fight against censorship in theatre. USA: New York, NY. 1986. Lang.: Eng.   68

Plays/librettos/scripts

Barbara Gelb discusses the creation of *My Gene*. USA. 1962-1987. Lang.: Eng.   2867

Dews, Peter

Performance/production

Collection of newspaper reviews by London theatre critics. UK-England: London. 1987. Lang.: Eng.   2208

Dexter, John

Performance/production

Collection of newspaper reviews by London theatre critics. UK-England: London. 1986. Lang.: Eng.   2152

Collection of newspaper reviews by London theatre critics. UK-England: London. 1987. Lang.: Eng.   2235

Dezman, Peter

Institutions

Historical survey of opera in Calgary. Canada: Calgary, AB. 1971-1987. Lang.: Eng.   3719

Dezsényi, Péter
Performance/production
David Mamet's *American Buffalo* directed by Péter Dezsényi at National Theatre as *Amérikai bölény*. Hungary: Pécs. 1986. Lang.: Hun.   1882

Dhondy, Farrukh
Performance/production
Collection of newspaper reviews by London theatre critics. UK-England: London. 1986. Lang.: Eng.   2129

Di Cocco, Francesco
Plays/librettos/scripts
Two filmscripts by Francesco Di Cocco based on short stories of Pirandello. Italy. 1914-1934. Lang.: Ita.   3178

Di Mauro, Eduardo
Performance/production
Eduardo Di Mauro and his puppets. Argentina. Venezuela. 1940-1987. Lang.: Spa.   3969

Di Mauro, Hector
Performance/production
Eduardo Di Mauro and his puppets. Argentina. Venezuela. 1940-1987. Lang.: Spa.   3969

Diable au Corps, Le (Devil Inside, The)
Plays/librettos/scripts
Interview with playwright Paul Pourveur. Belgium. 1987. Lang.: Dut.   2455

Diableries
Design/technology
Scenic representations of Hell. Italy. France. 1300-1399. Lang.: Ita.   349

Diadia Vania (Uncle Vanya)
Design/technology
V. Levental's scenery for Čechov's *Diadia Vania (Uncle Vanya)* at Moscow Art Theatre. USSR: Moscow. 1985. Lang.: Rus.   493

Performance/production
Actress Ada Tal on playing different Čechov roles. Israel: Tel Aviv. USSR. 1987. Lang.: Heb.   1940

Theory/criticism
Review of Korean National Theatre production of Čechov's *Diadia Vania (Uncle Vanya)*. Korea: Seoul. 1986-1987. Lang.: Kor.   3054

Diaghilev, Serge
Performance/production
Career of choreographer/dancer Bronislava Nižinska. France. USA. 1891-1930. Lang.: Eng.   1436

Dialectics
Plays/librettos/scripts
Comparison of the works of Ben Jonson and Christopher Marlowe. England. 1598-1602. Lang.: Eng.   1123

Theory/criticism
Gesture and sign in Shakespearean performance. England. USA. 1590-1987. Lang.: Eng.   1326

Essays on Bertolt Brecht's theories, aesthetics and philosophy. Germany, East. 1918-1987. Lang.: Ger.   1340

Paradoxical and grotesque elements in plays of Dürrenmatt. Europe. 1986. Lang.: Ger.   3034

Works of Pierre Corneille and the social role of women. France. 1540-1650. Lang.: Eng.   3040

Dialogues des Carmélites
Performance/production
Interview with conductor Manuel Rosenthal. France: Paris. 1904-1987. Lang.: Eng.   3774

Background on Metropolitan radio broadcast performances. USA: New York, NY. 1987. Lang.: Eng.   3837

Background on Metropolitan telecast performances. USA: New York, NY. 1987. Lang.: Eng.   3839

Plays/librettos/scripts
Role analysis of Blanche in Poulenc's *Dialogues des Carmélites*. France: Paris. 1957-1987. Lang.: Eng.   3901

Diary of a Somebody
Performance/production
Collection of newspaper reviews by London theatre critics. UK-England: London. 1987. Lang.: Eng.   2201

Collection of newspaper reviews by London theatre critics. UK-England: London. 1987. Lang.: Eng.   2234

Diaz-Puilja, Catalina
Plays/librettos/scripts
Feminist themes in Rosario Castellanos' *El eterno femenino (The Eternal Feminine)*. Mexico. Lang.: Spa.   2694

Diaz, Jorge
Theory/criticism
Semiotic study of Gambaro's *El despojamiento (The Robbery)*. USA. 1987. Lang.: Eng.   3067

Dickens, Charles
Performance/production
Jordcirkus and amateur group Näktergalningarna stage *A Christmas Carol*. Sweden: Stockholm. 1986-1987. Lang.: Swe.   2020

Performances of *Oliver* staged by György Korcsmáros, Antol Rencz and Imre Halasi. Hungary: Budapest, Békéscsaba, Zalaegerszeg. 1986. Lang.: Hun.   3632

Dickson, Mwansa
Plays/librettos/scripts
Theme of aggression between fathers and sons: Zambian National Theatre Arts Association festival. Zambia. 1966-1987. Lang.: Eng.   2972

Diderot, Denis
Basic theatrical documents
Catalan translation of Milan Kundera's *Jacques et son maître (Jacques and His Master)*, with introduction. Czechoslovakia: Prague. 1968-1981. Lang.: Cat.   1551

Plays/librettos/scripts
Interview with Susan Sontag, director of *Jacques and His Master*. USA: Cambridge, MA. 1985. Lang.: Eng.   1172

Interview with Milan Kundera on *Jacques and His Master*. USA: Cambridge, MA. 1985. Lang.: Eng.   1173

Kundera's adaptation of *Jacques le Fataliste (Jacques and His Master)* by Diderot. USA: Cambridge, MA. 1985. Lang.: Eng.   1178

Theory/criticism
Catalan translation of Lessing's *Hamburgische Dramaturgie*. Germany: Hamburg. 1767-1769. Lang.: Cat.   3043

Diekmann, Nancy Kassak
Administration
Diversity of Letter of Agreement theatres that operate in New York City. USA: New York, NY. 1987. Lang.: Eng.   204

Digby Day, Richard
Performance/production
Collection of newspaper reviews by London theatre critics. UK-England: London. 1987. Lang.: Eng.   2193

Dimba and Dimbi
Basic theatrical documents
Complete text of *Dimba and Dimbi* with background materials and preparations. Indonesia. 1987. Lang.: Eng.   4008

Dimboola
Plays/librettos/scripts
Interview with playwright Jack Hibberd. Australia: Melbourne. 1967-1987. Lang.: Eng.   2434

Dingelstedt, Franz
Institutions
Founding of Deutsches Theater. Germany: Berlin. 1854-1883. Lang.: Ger.   531

Dining Table with Romeo and Freesia, The
SEE
Romeo to Freesia no aru shokutaku.

Dinner theatre
Administration
Contract between Actors' Equity and the American Dinner Theatre Institute. USA: New York, NY. 1985. Lang.: Eng.   83

Directing
SEE
Staging.

Directories
Institutions
List of resources for playwrights. USA. 1987-1988. Lang.: Eng.   582

Plays/librettos/scripts
Directory of institutional theatres: aimed at playwrights. USA. 1987. Lang.: Eng.   1163

Reference materials
Guide to theatrical resources and support organizations for the arts. UK-England. 1987. Lang.: Eng.   1213

Directory of fringe, touring, dance and puppet companies, arts associations, festivals. UK-England. 1986-1987. Lang.: Eng.   1214

Multi-purpose directory for theatrical resources, including training, supplies and services. UK-England. 1986-1987. Lang.: Eng.   1215

Directors
SEE
Staging.

Domján, Edit
Performance/production
Life and career of actress Edit Domján. Hungary. 1932-1972. Lang.:
Hun. 1841

Don Carlo
Performance/production
Catholic elements in two treatments of *Don Carlos* by Verdi.
Europe. 1986-1987. Lang.: Swe. 3765

Don Carlos
SEE ALSO
Don Carlo.
Performance/production
Catholic elements in two treatments of *Don Carlos* by Verdi.
Europe. 1986-1987. Lang.: Swe. 3765
Background on San Francisco opera radio broadcasts. USA: San
Francisco, CA. 1987. Lang.: Eng. 3833
Plays/librettos/scripts
Characters and political themes in Verdi's *Don Carlos*. Italy: Milan.
1867. Lang.: Eng. 3924

Don Giovanni
Performance/production
Report from Salzburger Festspiele: Mozart's *Don Giovanni*,
Schoenberg's *Moses und Aron*, Schmidt's *Das Buch mit sieben
Siegeln*. Austria: Salzburg. 1987. Lang.: Swe. 3744
Mozart's *Don Giovanni* staged by Harry Kupfer. Germany, East:
Berlin, East. 1987. Lang.: Swe. 3779

Don Juan Among the Peasants
SEE
Don Juan onder die Boere.

Don Juan by Molière
SEE
Dom Juan.

Don Juan by Tirso de Molina
SEE
Burlador de Sevilla, El.

Don Juan Continued
SEE
Don Chuan Prodolženijė.

Don Juan onder die Boere (Don Juan among the Boers)
Plays/librettos/scripts
Bartho Smit's *Don Juan onder die Boere (Don Juan among the
Boers)*. 1600-1987. Lang.: Afr. 2415

Don't
Performance/production
Collection of newspaper reviews by London theatre critics. UK-
England: London. 1987. Lang.: Eng. 2241

Don't Get God Started
Performance/production
Collection of newspaper reviews by New York theatre critics. USA:
New York, NY. 1987. Lang.: Eng. 2316
Interview with actor Giancarlo Esposito. USA: New York, NY. 1987.
Lang.: Eng. 3654
Trend of gospel musicals on and off Broadway. USA: New York,
NY. 1987. Lang.: Eng. 3656

Donizetti, Gaetano
Institutions
Operations of the Canadian Opera Company. Canada: Toronto, ON.
1987. Lang.: Eng. 3716
Performance spaces
Telecast of Donizetti's *Lucia di Lammermoor* into a large performing
area. Switzerland: Basel. 1986. Lang.: Fre, Ger. 3737
Performance/production
Background on Lyric Opera radio broadcast performances. USA:
Chicago, IL. 1987. Lang.: Eng. 3832
Plays/librettos/scripts
Imagined interview with librettist of *Lucia di Lammermoor*. 1835.
Lang.: Eng. 3889

Donmar Warehouse (London)
Performance/production
Collection of newspaper reviews by London theatre critics. UK.
1987. Lang.: Eng. 2031
Collection of newspaper reviews by London theatre critics. UK-
England: London. 1986. Lang.: Eng. 2038
Collection of newspaper reviews by London theatre critics. UK-
England: London. 1986. Lang.: Eng. 2052
Collection of newspaper reviews by London theatre critics. UK-
England: London. 1986. Lang.: Eng. 2070

Collection of newspaper reviews by London theatre critics. UK-
England: London. 1986. Lang.: Eng. 2109
Collection of newspaper reviews by London theatre critics. UK-
England: London. 1986. Lang.: Eng. 2114
Collection of newspaper reviews by London theatre critics. UK-
England: London. 1986. Lang.: Eng. 2137
Collection of newspaper reviews by London theatre critics. UK-
England: London. 1986. Lang.: Eng. 2146
Collection of newspaper reviews by London theatre critics. UK-
England: London. 1986. Lang.: Eng. 2169
Collection of newspaper reviews by London theatre critics. UK-
England: London. 1987. Lang.: Eng. 2177
Collection of newspaper reviews by London theatre critics. UK-
England: London. 1987. Lang.: Eng. 2188
Collection of newspaper reviews by London theatre critics. UK-
England: London. 1987. Lang.: Eng. 2205
Collection of newspaper reviews by London theatre critics. UK-
England: London. 1987. Lang.: Eng. 2211
Collection of newspaper reviews by London theatre critics. UK-
England: London. 1987. Lang.: Eng. 2218
Collection of newspaper reviews by London theatre critics. UK-
England: London. 1987. Lang.: Eng. 2219
Collection of newspaper reviews by London theatre critics. UK-
England: London. 1987. Lang.: Eng. 2220
Collection of newspaper reviews by London theatre critics. UK-
England: London. 1987. Lang.: Eng. 2230
Collection of newspaper reviews by London theatre critics. UK-
England: London. 1987. Lang.: Eng. 2243
Collection of newspaper reviews by London theatre critics. UK-
England: London. 1987. Lang.: Eng. 2274

Donnellan, Declan
Performance/production
Collection of newspaper reviews by London theatre critics. UK.
1987. Lang.: Eng. 2031
Collection of newspaper reviews by London theatre critics. UK-
England: London. 1986. Lang.: Eng. 2106
Collection of newspaper reviews by London theatre critics. UK-
England: London. 1987. Lang.: Eng. 2177

Donnelly, Neil
Performance/production
TEAM, an educational theatre company. Ireland: Dublin. 1984-1987.
Lang.: Eng. 818

Donnellys, The
Plays/librettos/scripts
Critical analysis of James Reaney's *Three Desks*. Canada. 1960-1977.
Lang.: Eng. 2477

Dorge, Claude
Basic theatrical documents
Text of *Le Roitelet (The Kinglet)* by Claude Dorge. Canada:
Montreal, PQ. 1976. Lang.: Fre. 1545

Dorinda
Performance/production
Cast lists for some early London operas. England: London. 1712-
1717. Lang.: Eng. 3761

Dornford-May, Mark
Performance/production
Collection of newspaper reviews by London theatre critics. UK-
England: London. 1987. Lang.: Eng. 2241

Dort, Bernard
Performance/production
Staging as a form of translation. France. 1987. Lang.: Fre. 788

Dorval, Marie
Performance/production
Child actors in juvenile companies, Comédie-Française. France: Paris.
1769-1850. Lang.: Eng. 1756

Dory Previn Singing Songs and Telling Tails
Performance/production
Collection of newspaper reviews by London theatre critics. UK-
England: London. 1986. Lang.: Eng. 2038

Dostojèvskij, Fëdor Michajlovič
Design/technology
Action Design, a new theory of scenography emerging in Eastern
Europe. Czechoslovakia: Prague. 1980-1987. Lang.: Eng. 315
Performance/production
The 17th Warsaw theatre conference. Poland: Warsaw. 1987. Lang.:
Eng, Fre. 872

Dostojèvskij, Fëdor Michajlovič — cont'd

Ördögök (The Devils), based on Dostojèvskij novel, directed by Tamás Ascher. Hungary: Budapest. 1986. Lang.: Hun. 1891

Russian director Jurij Liubimov and his productions in the USSR and USA. USSR: Moscow. USA: Washington, DC. 1984-1987. Lang.: Eng. 2400

Dostoyevsky, Fyodor
SEE
Dostojèvskij, Fëdor Michajlovič.

Double Cross
Performance/production
Collection of newspaper reviews by London theatre critics. UK-England: London. 1986. Lang.: Eng. 2096

Double Double
Performance/production
Collection of newspaper reviews by London theatre critics. UK-England: London. 1986. Lang.: Eng. 2122

Double Expertise, La (Double Expertise, The)
Plays/librettos/scripts
Life and works of French dramatist Gabriel Marcel. France. 1889-1973. Lang.: Eng. 2573

Double Inconstance, La (Infidelities)
Performance/production
Collection of newspaper reviews by London theatre critics. UK-England: London. 1987. Lang.: Eng. 2238

Double-Threaded Life: The Hinton Play, A
Institutions
Profile of Ecotheatre and its artistic director Maryat Lee. USA: Hinton, WV. 1951-1983. Lang.: Eng. 1651

Double, The
Performance/production
Collection of newspaper reviews by London theatre critics. UK-England: London. 1986. Lang.: Eng. 2143

Douglas
Performance/production
Examples of transition in acting style. England. 1783-1784. Lang.: Eng. 1733

Douglas, Christopher
Performance/production
Collection of newspaper reviews by London theatre critics. UK-England: London. 1987. Lang.: Eng. 2182

Doulton, Valerie
Performance/production
Collection of newspaper reviews by London theatre critics. UK-England: London. 1987. Lang.: Eng. 2217

Dove, John
Performance/production
Collection of newspaper reviews by London theatre critics. UK-England: London. 1986. Lang.: Eng. 2045

Collection of newspaper reviews by London theatre critics. UK-England: London. 1986. Lang.: Eng. 2117

Collection of newspaper reviews by London theatre critics. UK-England: London. 1986. Lang.: Eng. 2148

Dowie, Claire
Performance/production
Collection of newspaper reviews by London theatre critics. UK-England: London. 1987. Lang.: Eng. 2174

Dowling, Joe
Design/technology
F.H. Flood's scene design for *The Merchant of Venice*. Ireland: Dublin. 1985. Lang.: Eng. 1593

Institutions
The touring company Irish Theatre Company. UK-Ireland. 1974-1987. Lang.: Eng. 569

Performance/production
TEAM, an educational theatre company. Ireland: Dublin. 1984-1987. Lang.: Eng. 818

Collection of newspaper reviews by London theatre critics. UK-England: London. 1986. Lang.: Eng. 2089

Dowling, Sam
Performance/production
Collection of newspaper reviews by London theatre critics. UK-England: London. 1986. Lang.: Eng. 2139

Collection of newspaper reviews by London theatre critics. UK-England: London. 1987. Lang.: Eng. 2247

Downey, Mike
Performance/production
Collection of newspaper reviews by London theatre critics. UK-England: London. 1986. Lang.: Eng. 2064

Doyle, Arthur Conan
Theory/criticism
Early theatre criticism of George Bernard Shaw. England: London. 1895-1905. Lang.: Eng. 3029

Doyle, John
Performance/production
Collection of newspaper reviews by London theatre critics. UK-England: London. 1987. Lang.: Eng. 2228

Collection of newspaper reviews by London theatre critics. UK-England: London. 1987. Lang.: Eng. 2235

Dr. Faustus
Institutions
The Stanisław Ignacy Witkiewicz Theatre. Poland: Zakopane. 1982-1986. Lang.: Eng, Fre. 1628

Dragon, The
Performance/production
Collection of newspaper reviews by London theatre critics. UK-England: London. 1986. Lang.: Eng. 2115

Dragone, Franco
Performance/production
Production of Cirque du Soleil. Canada: Montreal, PQ. 1987. Lang.: Eng. 3302

Drain, Millie
Institutions
The Dora Mavor Moore theatre awards. Canada: Toronto, ON. 1987. Lang.: Eng. 523

Drak (Hradec Králové)
Performance/production
On Drak puppet theatre. Czechoslovakia: Hradec Králové. 1987. Lang.: Cze. 3972

Drakar och Demoner (Dragons and Demons)
Performance/production
Rock opera *Drakar och Demoner (Dragons and Demons)* about youth at risk. Sweden: Handen. 1987. Lang.: Swe. 3637

Drama Theatre Sofia (Bulgaria)
Performance/production
The 4th International Theatre Conference: includes list of participants and their contributions. Poland: Warsaw. 1986. Lang.: Eng, Fre. 873

Dramaten (Stockholm)
SEE
Kungliga Dramatiska Teatern.

Dramatic structure
Audience
Audience reactions to *Geez*, by Putu Wijaya. USA: Madison, WI. 1986-1987. Lang.: Eng. 1540

Differences between two dramatists of Chinese opera—Tang and Shen. China, People's Republic of. Lang.: Chi. 3433

Basic theatrical documents
Text and analysis of *Fàlaris* and *Orfeu* by Llorenç Moyà. Spain. 1968-1981. Lang.: Cat. 1569

Study of the poetic, narrative and theatrical work of Agustí Bartra, edition of complete works, vol. 4. Spain-Catalonia. Mexico. 1937-1982. Lang.: Cat. 1571

Edition and analysis, *Allò que tal vegada s'esdevingué (What Happened Then)* by Joan Oliver. Spain-Catalonia. 1899-1986. Lang.: Cat. 1573

Chapter 19 of Harold Pinter's unpublished novel *The Dwarfs*. UK-England. 1958-1987. Lang.: Eng. 1575

Russian symbolist plays and essays. USSR. 1880-1986. Lang.: Eng. 1584

Design/technology
Effects of mixed media on traditional dramatic components of theatre. Europe. 1900-1987. Lang.: Fre. 318

Performance/production
Realism in Korean theatre. Korea. 1980-1987. Lang.: Kor. 855

Script and staging of Shaliko's *The Yellow House*. USA: Baltimore, MD. 1982-1987. Lang.: Eng. 1487

Theatre of playwright Robert Lepage. Canada: Montreal, PQ. Canada: Toronto, ON. 1980-1987. Lang.: Eng. 1704

Creations' of *La Trilogie des dragons (Dragon Trilogy)* by Robert Lepage. Canada. 1987. Lang.: Fre. 1706

Robert Lepage: creation, direction of *La Trilogie des dragons (Dragons' Trilogy)*. Canada. 1987. Lang.: Fre. 1716

Romantic drama in performance: effect on modern theatre. England. 1700-1987. Lang.: Eng. 1732

Dramatic structure — cont'd

'Showing' is an essential part of all acting. Europe. 1590-1987. Lang.: Eng. 1746

Xhosa story-telling uses verbal dramatization and language of gesture. South Africa, Republic of. 1987. Lang.: Eng. 3266

Plays/librettos/scripts

Summary and critical analysis of *Doc* by Sharon Pollock. Canada. 1987. Lang.: Eng. 1100

Works of playwright Jang Dah Fu. China: Beijing. 1620-1720. Lang.: Chi. 1104

Analysis of Kjeld Abell's *Der bla pekingeser (The Blue Pekingese)*. Denmark. 1901-1961. Lang.: Ita. 1113

Allegory and irony in *Othello*. England. 1604. Lang.: Eng. 1114

An analysis of the structure of *Measure for Measure*. England. 1604. Lang.: Eng. 1120

Comparison of the works of Ben Jonson and Christopher Marlowe. England. 1598-1602. Lang.: Eng. 1123

Theme of journeys in German theatre and film. Germany. 1970-1986. Lang.: Fre. 1127

Analysis of Rosso di San Secondo's *Amara (Bitter)*. Italy. 1913-1917. Lang.: Ita. 1139

Time and space in traditional Korean theatre. Korea. 57 B.C.-1987 A.D. Lang.: Kor. 1146

Study of dramatic time versus physical time of performance. South Africa, Republic of. 1987. Lang.: Afr. 1154

Collaboration between playwright Craig Lucas and director Norman Rene. USA: New York, NY. 1985-1987. Lang.: Eng. 1183

Analysis of the plays of G.B. Jakulov. USSR. 1987. Lang.: Ita. 1186

Essays on plot and composition. USSR. 1987. Lang.: Rus. 1187

Theatre and dramaturgy of the first Russian revolution. USSR. 1905-1907. Lang.: Rus. 1188

Love, marriage and family relationships in contemporary drama. USSR. 1980-1987. Lang.: Rus. 1420

Genre and stylistic innovation in new Ukrainian dramaturgy. USSR. 1980-1987. Lang.: Rus. 1424

Dramatic structure in Frayn's *Noises Off*. 1987. Lang.: Eng. 2416

Dramatic irony as an actor's tool. 1987. Lang.: Eng. 2417

Textual analysis of Majakovskij's *Bathhouse*. 1986. Lang.: Eng. 2419

Terror and terrorism in the theatre. Lang.: Eng. 2421

Structure of revenge tragedy in Shakespeare's *Hamlet*. 1600. Lang.: Eng. 2425

Modern theatrical treatment of Fascism and the Holocaust. 1980-1987. Lang.: Eng. 2428

Focus on the plays of David Williamson and their cultural impact. Australia. 1970-1987. Lang.: Eng. 2436

Dramatic and scenic structure, feminism, in plays of Alma De Groen. Australia. 1987. Lang.: Eng. 2446

Art and realism in works of Hugo von Hofmannsthal. Austria. 1874-1929. Lang.: Rus. 2451

Analysis of *Pelléas et Mélisande* by Maeterlinck. Belgium. 1800. Lang.: Fre. 2454

Traditionalism in Lepage's *La Trilogie des dragons*. Canada. 1987. Lang.: Fre. 2462

Collective theatre projects in Newfoundland. Canada: St. John's, NF. 1987. Lang.: Eng. 2466

Playwright Sharon Pollock. Canada. 1970-1983. Lang.: Eng. 2469

Language and metaphor in plays of René-Daniel Dubois. Canada: Toronto, ON, Montreal, PQ. 1983-1987. Lang.: Eng. 2471

Robert Lepage's play *Vinci*. Canada. 1986-1987. Lang.: Fre. 2474

Critical analysis of James Reaney's *Three Desks*. Canada. 1960-1977. Lang.: Eng. 2477

La Trilogie des dragons by Robert Lepage. Canada: Montreal, PQ. 1987. Lang.: Fre. 2479

Plays by Micone, Saddlemyer, Thompson, Wyatt. Canada. 1958-1985. Lang.: Eng. 2481

Work of playwright Marco Micone. Canada. 1982-1985. Lang.: Eng. 2483

Survey of Robertson Davies' plays. Canada. 1913-1985. Lang.: Eng. 2484

Brassard discusses his adaptation of Genet's *Les Paravents (The Screens)*. Canada: Montreal, PQ, Ottawa, ON. 1987. Lang.: Fre. 2485

Playwright George F. Walker. Canada. 1972-1985. Lang.: Eng. 2488

Ming dynasty novels as source of theatrical inspiration. China. 1368-1644. Lang.: Chi. 2491

The structures and themes of Chinese playwright Hueng Tsolin. China, People's Republic of. 1983. Lang.: Chi. 2495

Urbanity as subject and form of Jonson's *Epicoene*. England. 1609-1987. Lang.: Eng. 2498

Shakespeare's *Hamlet*: representation of interiority onstage. England. 1600. Lang.: Eng. 2500

Textual dramaturgy and *Richard II*. England. 1987. Lang.: Eng. 2502

Anthropological analysis of Shakespeare's romantic comedies. England. 1564-1616. Lang.: Eng. 2504

Analysis of medieval Cain and Abel mystery plays. England. 1200-1576. Lang.: Eng. 2506

Evaluation of *Westward Ho!* and *Northward Ho!* by Thomas Dekker and John Webster. England. 1605. Lang.: Eng. 2509

The London Merchant by Lillo is an allegory of the Fall. England. 1731-1987. Lang.: Eng. 2514

Italian translation of *Über die Shakespearomanie (On Shakespeare-Mania)* by Christian Dietrich Grabbe. England. Germany. 1594-1836. Lang.: Ita. 2520

Devices that convey concern with sexuality in Shakespeare's *All's Well that Ends Well*. England. 1602-1987. Lang.: Eng. 2523

Metadrama, alienation and fantasy in Shakespeare's *Romeo and Juliet*. England. 1595-1596. Lang.: Eng. 2524

Theoretical considerations of English Renaissance theatre. England. 1600-1699. Lang.: Rus. 2528

Utopianism in Shakespeare's *The Tempest*. England. 1611-1612. Lang.: Ger. 2532

Music in Shakespeare. England. 1580-1616. Lang.: Ger. 2533

Two Cornish *Corpus Christi* plays. England. 1350. Lang.: Eng. 2534

Henry Fielding rewrote *Tom Thumb* to satirize Lewis Theobald. England. 1730-1731. Lang.: Eng. 2535

Structure of Byron's plays. England. 1788-1824. Lang.: Eng. 2542

Comparison of works of Milton and Dryden. England. 1608-1700. Lang.: Eng. 2546

Shakespeare's use of formal self-referential oaths. England. 1594-1616. Lang.: Eng. 2552

Classification and social hierarchy in Shakespeare's *Troilus and Cressida*. England. 1601. Lang.: Eng. 2554

Analysis of medieval plays found in the *Fleury Playbook*. Europe. 1300. Lang.: Eng. 2564

Ariadne in plays of Ibsen, Strindberg, Maeterlinck. Europe. 1892-1902. Lang.: Eng. 2566

Jullien's violations of decorum and *honneur* in *La Sérénade (The Serenade)*. France. 1887-1987. Lang.: Eng. 2577

Anti-fascist plays of Armand Gatti. France. 1924-1987. Lang.: Rus. 2578

Dramaturgy of Armand Gatti. France. 1924-1987. Lang.: Rus. 2579

Analysis of Cixous' *Norodom Sihanouk*. France: Paris. 1985-1987. Lang.: Eng. 2580

Iser's reader-response theory and Beckett's *Come and Go*. France. 1968-1987. Lang.: Eng. 2581

Playwright Roger Vitrac's critiques of bourgeois family life. France. 1922-1928. Lang.: Eng. 2584

Interaction of scenic imagery and narrative in *Ohio Impromptu*. France. 1981-1987. Lang.: Eng. 2586

The allegory of capitalist society in Genet's *Le Balcon (The Balcony)*. France. 1958-1987. Lang.: Eng. 2588

Beckett links theme of political persecution to voyeurism of the theatrical experience. France. 1982-1987. Lang.: Eng. 2589

Techniques, themes, characters and dramaturgy of Voltaire. France. 1718-1778. Lang.: Eng. 2590

New interpretation of Toller's *Masse Mensch*. Germany. 1921-1987. Lang.: Eng. 2592

Comparison of works by Hauptmann and Wilbrandt. Germany: Berlin. Austria: Vienna. 1889-1987. Lang.: Eng. 2593

Theatrical works of Heiner Müller. Germany: Berlin. 1929-1987. Lang.: Ita. 2594

Dramatic structure — cont'd

Collection of nineteenth-century theoretical writings on theatre and drama. Germany. 1800-1900. Lang.: Ger. 2595

Munch's influence on Strindberg. Germany: Berlin. 1892-1900. Lang.: Eng. 2596

Der gelbe Klang (The Yellow Sound) by Wassily Kandinsky. Germany. 1896-1914. Lang.: Eng. 2597

Theories of staging the *visitatio sepulchri*. Germany. France. 900-1600. Lang.: Eng. 2599

Bertolt Brecht and the Berlin workers' movement. Germany: Berlin. 1922-1932. Lang.: Ger. 2600

Brecht's influence on technique and style of playwright Heiner Müller. Germany, East. 1940-1984. Lang.: Eng. 2605

Stage history and interpretations of Heiner Müller's *Der Lohndrücker (Undercutting)*. Germany, East. 1956-1987. Lang.: Ger. 2615

The metadramatic nature of Thomas Bernhard's plays. Germany, West. 1974-1983. Lang.: Eng. 2616

Italian translation of *Über das Tragische (On the Tragic)* by Karl Jaspers. Germany, West. 1952. Lang.: Ita. 2617

Italian translation, *The Greek Tragic Theatre* by H.C. Baldry. Greece. 500-400 B.C. Lang.: Ita. 2619

Imagistic versus realistic drama in contemporary Greek plays. Greece. 1940-1987. Lang.: Eng. 2621

Structure and plot of ancient Greek tragedies. Greece. 500-400 B.C. Lang.: Kor. 2622

Euripides' use of *deus ex machina* in *Orestes*. Greece. 408 B.C. Lang.: Eng. 2626

A critic's reflections on dramatic themes reflected in recent Hungarian plays. Hungary. 1986-1987. Lang.: Hun. 2629

Carnival patterns in the plays of Luigi Pirandello. Italy. 1916-1929. Lang.: Eng. 2662

Plays of Seneca and theatre of his time. Italy: Rome. 4 B.C.-65 A.D. Lang.: Rus. 2667

Plays of Antonio Monetta, Pietro Suscio and Girolamo Bax. Italy. 1600-1900. Lang.: Ita. 2669

Machines—animate and inanimate—in *Tonight We Improvise (Questa sera si recita a soggetto)* by Pirandello. Italy. 1929-1987. Lang.: Eng. 2670

Analysis of the plays of Luigi Candoni. Italy. 1921-1974. Lang.: Ita. 2674

Correspondence of playwright Ugo Foscolo regarding *Tieste (Thyestes)*. Italy: Venice. 1797-1827. Lang.: Ita. 2677

Gender conflict in Pirandello's *Sei personnaggi in cerca d'autore (Six Characters in Search of an Author)*. Italy. 1921-1987. Lang.: Eng. 2679

Comparison of Pirandello's *Enrico Quarto (Henry IV)* and Shakespeare's *Hamlet*. Italy. England. 1580-1936. Lang.: Chi. 2680

Comparison of Greek tragedy and Korean Buddhist plays. Korea. Greece. 57 B.C.-1392 A.D. Lang.: Kor. 2684

Korean drama: changes in structure. Korea. 1960-1979. Lang.: Kor. 2689

Korean drama: social and political background. Korea. 1910-1919. Lang.: Kor. 2690

Religion in Pielmeier's *Agnes of God* and Shaffer's *Equus*. North America. 1973-1980. Lang.: Eng. 2710

Irony in Ibsen's *Fruen fra Havet (Lady from the Sea, The)*. Norway. 1888-1987. Lang.: Eng. 2712

Analysis of *Čajka (The Seagull)* by Anton Čechov. Russia. 1896. Lang.: Kor. 2718

Georgian criticism and theatrical art. Russia. 1800-1900. Lang.: Rus. 2719

Russian drama under Peter I. Russia. 1696-1725. Lang.: Rus. 2720

Analysis of *Delo (The Affair)* by A.V. Suchovo-Kobylin. Russia. 1861. Lang.: Rus. 2721

Plays of Tolstoj and the 'New Drama' of Western Europe. Russia. Europe. 1864-1910. Lang.: Rus. 2722

Comparative study of Lope de Vega's *El mayordomo de la Duquesa de Amalfi* and Webster's *The Duchess of Malfi*. Spain. 1612-1982. Lang.: Eng. 2729

Catalan playwrights after the Spanish Civil War. Spain-Catalonia. 1939-1975. Lang.: Cat. 2730

Valencian playwrights writing in both Catalan and Castilian. Spain-Catalonia: Valencia. 1790-1985. Lang.: Cat. 2732

Dramatic vs. literary interpretation of *Ett Drömspel (A Dream Play)* by August Strindberg. Sweden. 1901-1964. Lang.: Eng. 2734

The son-in-law in *Pelikanen (The Pelican)* by August Strindberg. Sweden. 1907-1987. Lang.: Swe. 2740

Theatrical metaphor in Strindberg's *Gustav III*. Sweden. 1903-1987. Lang.: Eng. 2741

Realism in the plays of Max Frisch. Switzerland. 1911-1987. Lang.: Rus. 2742

Comparison of Dürrenmatt's *The Physicists (Die Physiker)*, *Macbeth* and *Doctor Faustus*. Switzerland. 1987. Lang.: Heb. 2747

The world and man in Marlowe's tragedies. UK-England. 1564-1593. Lang.: Rus. 2751

Political use of traditional comic structure by contemporary playwrights. UK-England. 1970-1987. Lang.: Eng. 2762

Theme of theatre in recent plays. UK-England. 1957-1985. Lang.: Eng. 2764

Role of playwright George Edwardes in development of musical comedy. UK-England: London. 1830-1890. Lang.: Eng. 2766

Structure of *The Sea* by Edward Bond. UK-England. 1973-1987. Lang.: Eng. 2767

Red Noses as Peter Barnes's response to Shaw's *Saint Joan*. UK-England. 1924-1985. Lang.: Eng. 2770

Shaw's artistic strategy in *Major Barbara*. UK-England. 1905. Lang.: Eng. 2774

Byron's 'closet' dramas structured for performance at London theatres. UK-England: London. 1812-1822. Lang.: Eng. 2778

Introduction to Chapter 19 of Pinter's unpublished novel *The Dwarfs*. UK-England. 1958-1987. Lang.: Eng. 2779

Antonin Artaud's interpretation of Shelley's *The Cenci*. UK-England. France. 1819-1920. Lang.: Eng. 2780

Stage, radio and television plays of Tom Stoppard. UK-England. 1937-1987. Lang.: Eng. 2788

Study of plays by Henry Arthur Jones. UK-England: London. 1882-1900. Lang.: Eng. 2790

Comic conventions in Shakespeare's *Titus Andronicus*. UK-England. 1987. Lang.: Eng. 2809

Interpreting Harold Pinter's dramas through focus on his play structures. UK-England. 1958-1987. Lang.: Eng. 2815

Creative evolution of playwright John Galsworthy. UK-England. 1867-1933. Lang.: Rus. 2816

Influences on *The Voysey Inheritance* by Granville Barker. UK-England. 1600-1938. Lang.: Eng. 2820

Ulster drama before Sam Thompson. UK-Ireland. 1900-1982. Lang.: Eng. 2829

Christina Reid's *Tea in a China Cup*: a woman's view of Belfast. UK-Ireland: Belfast. 1983-1987. Lang.: Eng. 2831

Yeats's dance plays: effect of the elements of performance on text. UK-Ireland. 1916-1987. Lang.: Eng. 2832

Ukrainian Romantic drama. Ukraine. 1830-1889. Lang.: Rus. 2833

Scarce attention paid to national dramaturgy by Ukrainian theatres. Ukraine. 1980-1987. Lang.: Rus. 2834

The many genres of Ukrainian theatre. Ukraine. 1920-1929. Lang.: Rus. 2835

Structural analysis of Pinter's *Old Times*. USA: New York, NY. 1971-1984. Lang.: Eng. 2843

One-act play: brief history and recent productions. USA. 1930-1987. Lang.: Eng. 2849

Development of themes and characters in plays of Sam Shepard. USA. 1960-1987. Lang.: Eng. 2853

Barbara Gelb discusses the creation of *My Gene*. USA. 1962-1987. Lang.: Eng. 2867

Influences of Spanish-language theatre on Chicano theatre. USA. 1598-1983. Lang.: Eng. 2874

Interview with playwright August Wilson. USA: New York, NY. 1985-1987. Lang.: Eng. 2876

The child character in the role of protagonist. USA. 1987. Lang.: Eng. 2880

Analysis of text of Samuel Beckett's *Rockaby* as literature and performance piece. USA. 1982. Lang.: Eng. 2884

Sam Shepard's *True West* as a farce in the guise of serious drama. USA. 1981. Lang.: Eng. 2887

Dramatic structure — cont'd

Interview with playwright Leslie Lee. USA: Bryn Mawr, PA, New York, NY. 1987. Lang.: Eng.   2893

Interview with playwright John Ford Noonan. USA. 1970-1987. Lang.: Eng.   2894

Terrence McNally discusses playwriting. USA: New York, NY. 1987. Lang.: Eng.   2895

Author Christopher Hampton discusses techniques of playwriting. USA: New York, NY. UK-England: London. 1987. Lang.: Eng.
2896

Albee, racism, politics in American theatre of the sixties. USA. 1960-1969. Lang.: Rus.   2901

Development of Sam Shepard's plays in response to audience. USA. 1976-1986. Lang.: Eng.   2902

Theatricality of Sam Shepard's early and late works. USA. 1965-1986. Lang.: Eng.   2903

Edvard Munch's painting *Death in the Sickroom* used to demonstrate Albee's subject matter. USA. 1971-1987. Lang.: Eng.
2911

Dramatic treatment of material about the Holocaust. USA. Germany, West. 1950-1987. Lang.: Eng.   2917

Interview with playwright Charles Fuller. USA: Philadelphia, PA, New York, NY. Korea, South. 1959-1987. Lang.: Eng.   2921

Symbolism in *The Hairy Ape* by Eugene O'Neill. USA. 1920-1922. Lang.: Eng.   2929

Sam Shepard's manipulation of an audience's desire to believe what it sees. USA. 1967-1983. Lang.: Eng.   2932

Plays of Mikola Zarudnyj. USSR. 1921-1979. Lang.: Rus.   2933

Socialist realism in Tatar drama. USSR. 1917-1987. Lang.: Rus.
2936

History of dramaturgy in Karakalpak ASSR. USSR. 1917-1987. Lang.: Rus.   2938

Current analysis of Shakespearean plays. USSR. 1985. Lang.: Rus.
2939

Career of actor G. Sundukjan. USSR. 1874-1903. Lang.: Rus.   2940

Documentality in Soviet drama. USSR. 1960-1979. Lang.: Rus. 2941

Genre and style in Soviet dramaturgy. USSR. 1960-1987. Lang.: Rus.   2942

Evolution of the hero. USSR. 1950-1987. Lang.: Rus.   2943

Structure of action in Soviet drama. USSR. 1980-1987. Lang.: Rus.
2944

Work of playwright Aleksand'r Vampilov. USSR. 1937-1972. Lang.: Rus.   2948

Playwright Aleksand'r Galin. USSR. 1980-1987. Lang.: Rus.   2949

Dramaturgy of Aleksandr Vampilov. USSR. 1937-1972. Lang.: Rus.
2950

Višněvyj sad (The Cherry Orchard): Čechov's artistry. USSR. 1904. Lang.: Rus.   2951

Riddles in Čechov's *Čajka (The Seagull)*. USSR. 1898-1987. Lang.: Rus.   2952

The quest in plays of I.L. Sel'vinskij. USSR. 1899-1968. Lang.: Rus.
2955

Soviet dramaturgy in the region of Burjatija. USSR: Burjatija. 1917-1987. Lang.: Rus.   2957

Majakovskij's dramatic works as seen by critics in the 1930s. USSR. 1930-1939. Lang.: Rus.   2958

Nikolaj Erdmann's plays, relations with major directors. USSR: Moscow. 1925. Lang.: Rus.   2963

Overview of dramaturgy in Mari ASSR. USSR. 1980-1987. Lang.: Rus.   2964

Čechov interpretations in socialist countries. USSR. 1980-1987. Lang.: Rus.   2965

Contemporary interpretations of Shakespeare's work. USSR. 1980-1987. Lang.: Rus.   2967

Conference on staging Shakespeare in USSR. USSR. 1987. Lang.: Rus.   2969

Essay on Azerbaijani playwright Anar. USSR. Lang.: Rus.   2970

Critical discussion of six plays in CBC's *Sextet* broadcast series. Canada. 1987. Lang.: Eng.   3116

Theatrical elements in Italian cinema after the Second World War. Italy. 1946-1983. Lang.: Ita.   3177

Playwright Pietro Chiari. Italy: Venice. 1747-1762. Lang.: Ita. 3316

Pageantry in Elizabethan theatre. England. 1392-1642. Lang.: Eng.
3336

Relationship between libretto and music in structure of musical drama. Europe. 1986. Lang.: Ita.   3418

Historical fate of melodrama. USSR. 1987. Lang.: Rus.   3420

Dramatic structure in Chinese opera play *Tao hua shan (The Peach Blossom Fan)*. China. 1700-1800. Lang.: Chi.   3547

A correct definition of Chinese classical 'tragedy'. China. 960-1644. Lang.: Chi.   3548

Preface and postscript in Chinese dramatic scripts. China. 1200-1987. Lang.: Chi.   3552

The development of traditional Chinese drama. China. 1200-1987. Lang.: Chi.   3555

The lyrical style of Chinese opera form. China, People's Republic of. 1987. Lang.: Chi.   3557

Interview with playwright Guo Jiun. China, People's Republic of. 1987. Lang.: Chi.   3559

New ideologies and dramatic structure in Chinese opera. China, People's Republic of. 1987. Lang.: Chi.   3561

Chinese opera dramatist Uei Ming-Lun. China, People's Republic of. 1987. Lang.: Chi.   3562

Classic works of Chinese opera. China, People's Republic of. 1986. Lang.: Chi.   3563

Philosophical themes in modern Chinese drama: their audience appeal. China, People's Republic of. 1987. Lang.: Chi.   3564

Bridging the gap between classical and modern forms of Chinese opera. China, People's Republic of. 1987. Lang.: Chi.   3571

Characteristics, value and development in Chinese drama. China, People's Republic of. 1987. Lang.: Chi.   3575

W.S. Gilbert's contribution to the development of the musical play. England. 1836-1911. Lang.: Eng.   3670

Tippett's influence on contemporary opera. 1946-1987. Lang.: Eng.
3888

Imagined interview with librettist of *Lucia di Lammermoor*. 1835. Lang.: Eng.   3889

Adaptation of literary works to opera. 1893-1987. Lang.: Eng. 3890

Critical analysis of István Anhalt's opera, *Winthrop*. Canada: Kitchener, ON. USA. 1987. Lang.: Eng.   3894

The garden landscape scene in opera. Europe. 1700-1800. Lang.: Eng.   3896

Study of French composer Daniel Auber and his works. France. 1782-1871. Lang.: Eng.   3904

Unique style of modern Japanese Opera. Japan. 1975-1987. Lang.: Eng.   3928

Relation to other fields

Current ideology: influence on Chinese theatre. China, People's Republic of. 1987. Lang.: Chi.   3583

Research/historiography

Influences on Wagner's *Ring* cycle. Germany: Dresden. 1813-1883. Lang.: Eng.   3948

Theory/criticism

Dramatic criticism in the Sung Dynasty. China: Beijing. 960-1279. Lang.: Chi.   1319

Themes of the Chinese theatre during the Tang dynasty. China. 618-905. Lang.: Chi.   1320

The impressionistic character of Chinese drama. China, People's Republic of: Beijing. 1271-1986. Lang.: Chi.   1322

Plays that attempt to legitimize theatre. England. France. 1600-1700. Lang.: Eng.   1324

Semiotic study of dialogue in *As You Like It*. England. 1599. Lang.: Eng.   1325

Psychological communication in contemporary drama. 1949-1987. Lang.: Chi.   3017

The use of space in plot to indicate time and place. 1949-1987. Lang.: Chi.   3021

Critic Walter Benjamin's comparison of representation in Spanish baroque theatre and German plays. Germany. 1916-1982. Lang.: Eng.   3041

Pirandello's poetics and influence on other writers. Italy. 1904-1936. Lang.: Ita.   3051

The issue of new ideas in contemporary theatre. Mexico: Mexico City. 1987. Lang.: Spa.   3056

Dramatic structure — cont'd

Main characteristics of the Chinese theatre aesthetic. China, People's Republic of. 960 B.C.-1987 A.D. Lang.: Chi.   3597

Dramatičeskij Teat'r im. M. Gorkogo (Kujbyšev)

Performance/production
Director of Gorkij Theatre on theatrical experimentation. USSR. 1986-1988. Lang.: Rus.   1044

Training
Director discusses problems of theatrical education. USSR: Kujbyšev. 1987. Lang.: Rus.   1395

Dramatičeskij Teat'r im. N. Gogolia (Moscow)

Performance/production
The work of Sergej Jašin, principal director of Gogol Theatre. USSR: Moscow. 1987. Lang.: Rus.   1014

Dramatiska Institutet (Stockholm)

Design/technology
First twelve theatre-technician graduates of Dramatiska Institutet. Sweden: Stockholm. 1987. Lang.: Swe.   361

Touring companies' set construction techniques. Sweden. 1986. Lang.: Swe.   362

Dramatists' Guild (New York, NY)

Institutions
News for playwrights about regional theatre activities. USA. 1987. Lang.: Eng.   580

Photos and list of those present at Dramatists' Guild award ceremony. USA: New York, NY. 1987. Lang.: Eng.   581

Conference of Dramatists' Guild Women's Committee. USA. 1987. Lang.: Eng.   583

Meetings of various Dramatists' Guild committees, members' plays in production. USA: New York, NY. 1987. Lang.: Eng.   584

Activities of Dramatists' Guild include writer's-block workshop. USA: New York, NY. 1987. Lang.: Eng.   585

Plays/librettos/scripts
Conference on women in theatre, emphasis on playwriting. USA. 1987. Lang.: Eng.   1161

Notes on Dramatists' Guild activities and concerns. USA. 1987. Lang.: Eng.   1162

Plays and books produced and published by Dramatists' Guild members. USA. 1987. Lang.: Eng.   1164

Dramaturgy

Administration
Dramaturgy in Canadian theatre. Canada. USA. Germany. 1980-1987. Lang.: Eng.   1513

Audience
Scientific and psychological study of the role of audience as dramaturgs. Italy. 1987. Lang.: Eng.   284

Institutions
Literary Managers and Dramaturgs of America (LMDA). USA: New York, NY. 1987. Lang.: Eng.   594

Performance/production
Analysis of the playwright/director relationship in Canada. Canada. 1987. Lang.: Eng.   750

Play scripts as literary texts and as performance texts. UK-England. 1977-1987. Lang.: Eng.   905

Analysis of Brecht's original directing style and dramaturgy. Germany. 1925-1987. Lang.: Eng.   1771

Essay on interpretive methods in performance and production. Hungary. 1987. Lang.: Hun.   1824

Review of conference on contemporary Hungarian drama. Hungary: Egervár. 1987. Lang.: Hun.   1879

Review of I Poli (The Town) based on Greek theatre tradition and performed in absurdist style. Mexico: Mexico City. 1987. Lang.: Spa.   1976

Functions, influence of dramaturgs and literary managers. USA. 1987. Lang.: Eng.   2332

Plays/librettos/scripts
Role of dramaturgs, literary managers. USA. 1987. Lang.: Eng.   1179

Textual dramaturgy and Richard II. England. 1987. Lang.: Eng.   2502

Eighteenth-century alterations to Shakespeare's The Merchant of Venice. England. 1596-1701. Lang.: Eng.   2512

Study of plays by Henry Arthur Jones. UK-England: London. 1882-1900. Lang.: Eng.   2790

Research for An American Journey produced by Milwaukee Repertory. USA: Milwaukee, WI. 1978-1987. Lang.: Eng.   2862

Theory/criticism
Rise of contemporary theatre in Mexico. Mexico: Mexico City. 1957-1987. Lang.: Spa.   3057

Reflections on the value of theatrical translations. Spain-Catalonia. UK-England. 1600-1985. Lang.: Cat.   3060

Suggestion for new form of dramaturgical research based on concrete scenic action from past productions. USA: Tallahassee, FL. 1987. Lang.: Eng.   3074

Draycott, Nigel P.

Performance/production
Collection of newspaper reviews by London theatre critics. UK-England: London. 1987. Lang.: Eng.   2204

Collection of newspaper reviews by London theatre critics. UK-England: London. 1987. Lang.: Eng.   2277

Dreamgirls

Design/technology
Lighting reviews for some New York productions. USA: New York, NY. 1987. Lang.: Eng.   477

Performance/production
Overview of performing artists that toured Japan. Japan: Tokyo. 1986. Lang.: Jap.   844

Lillias White and her performance in the musical Dreamgirls. USA: New York, NY. 1960-1987.   3641

Dreams of San Francisco

Performance/production
Collection of newspaper reviews by London theatre critics. UK-England: London. 1987. Lang.: Eng.   2226

Dreigroschenoper, Die (Three Penny Opera, The)

Administration
Editorial response to attacks on the Weill Foundation. USA: New York, NY. Germany: Berlin. 1929-1987. Lang.: Eng.   3618

Performance/production
Early productions of Brecht's plays reflected in the press. Germany: Berlin. 1922-1933. Lang.: Ger.   1777

History of Hungarian productions of Die Dreigroschenoper (The Three Penny Opera) by Brecht and Weill. Hungary. 1929-1987. Lang.: Hun.   1927

Four productions in Southern regional theatres. USA: Houston, TX, Louisville, KY, Gainesville, FL. 1980. Lang.: Eng.   2342

Comparison of Die Dreigroschenoper (The Three Penny Opera) as directed by Ferenc Sík, József Petrik and Miklós Szinetár under the title Koldusopera. Hungary: Győr, Budapest. 1987. Lang.: Hun. 3402

Giorgio Strehler on staging Die Dreigroschenoper (The Three Penny Opera). Italy: Milan. France: Paris. 1928-1986. Lang.: Swe.   3809

Theory/criticism
Brecht's theories, Die Dreigroschenoper (The Three Penny Opera). Germany. 1878-1956. Lang.: Kor.   3044

Challenge of Brecht's plays to communism. Germany, East: Berlin. 1960-1970. Lang.: Eng.   3045

Dresdner Hoftheater (Dresden)

Performance/production
Interview with choral director Hans-Dieter Pflüger of Dresdner Hoftheater. Germany, East: Dresden. 1979-1986. Lang.: Ger.   3782

Drese, Claus Helmut

Administration
Staatsoper under management of Claus Helmut Drese and Claudio Abbado. Austria: Vienna. 1986-1987. Lang.: Swe.   3677

Drews, Karen

Design/technology
Survey of 1960s stage machinery. USA. 1960-1987. Lang.: Eng.   456

Drill Hall Theatre (Edinburgh)

Performance/production
Collection of newspaper reviews by London theatre critics. UK. 1987. Lang.: Eng.   2031

Drill Hall Theatre (London)

Performance/production
Collection of newspaper reviews by London theatre critics. UK-England: London. 1986. Lang.: Eng.   2059

Collection of newspaper reviews by London theatre critics. UK-England: London. 1986. Lang.: Eng.   2062

Collection of newspaper reviews by London theatre critics. UK-England: London. 1987. Lang.: Eng.   2073

Collection of newspaper reviews by London theatre critics. UK-England: London. 1986. Lang.: Eng.   2084

Collection of newspaper reviews by London theatre critics. UK-England: London. 1986. Lang.: Eng.   2096

Drill Hall Theatre (London) — cont'd

Collection of newspaper reviews by London theatre critics. UK-England: London. 1986. Lang.: Eng.   2116

Collection of newspaper reviews by London theatre critics. UK-England: London. 1986. Lang.: Eng.   2127

Collection of newspaper reviews by London theatre critics. UK-England: London. 1986. Lang.: Eng.   2143

Collection of newspaper reviews by London theatre critics. UK-England. 1986. Lang.: Eng.   2159

Collection of newspaper reviews by London theatre critics. UK-England: London. 1986. Lang.: Eng.   2163

Collection of newspaper reviews by London theatre critics. UK-England: London. 1986. Lang.: Eng.   2168

Collection of newspaper reviews by London theatre critics. UK-England. 1987. Lang.: Eng.   2175

Collection of newspaper reviews by London theatre critics. UK-England: London. 1987. Lang.: Eng.   2184

Collection of newspaper reviews by London theatre critics. UK-England: London. 1987. Lang.: Eng.   2186

Collection of newspaper reviews by London theatre critics. UK-England: London. 1987. Lang.: Eng.   2192

Collection of newspaper reviews by London theatre critics. UK-England: London. 1987. Lang.: Eng.   2211

Collection of newspaper reviews by London theatre critics. UK-England: London. 1987. Lang.: Eng.   2217

Collection of newspaper reviews by London theatre critics. UK-England: London. 1987. Lang.: Eng.   2232

Collection of newspaper reviews by London theatre critics. UK-England: London. 1987. Lang.: Eng.   2243

Collection of newspaper reviews by London theatre critics. UK-England: London. 1987. Lang.: Eng.   2247

Collection of newspaper reviews by London theatre critics. UK-England: London. 1987. Lang.: Eng.   2271

Driscoll, Robin
Performance/production
Collection of newspaper reviews by London theatre critics. UK-England: London. 1986. Lang.: Eng.   2075

Collection of newspaper reviews by London theatre critics. UK-England: London. 1987. Lang.: Eng.   2269

Driver, John
Performance/production
Collection of newspaper reviews by New York theatre critics. USA: New York, NY. 1987. Lang.: Eng.   2316

Driver, Senta
Performance/production
Interview with choreographer Senta Driver. USA. 1987. Lang.: Eng.   1472

Driving Miss Daisy
Performance/production
Collection of newspaper reviews by New York theatre critics. USA: New York, NY. 1987. Lang.: Eng.   2320

Career of director Ron Lagomarsino, his style and technique. USA. 1987. Lang.: Eng.   2327

Plays/librettos/scripts
Alfred Uhry on *Driving Miss Daisy*. USA: New York, NY. 1976-1984. Lang.: Eng.   3419

Drömspel, Ett (Dream Play, A)
Performance/production
Collection of newspaper reviews by London theatre critics. UK-England: London. 1986. Lang.: Eng.   2155

Plays/librettos/scripts
Ariadne in plays of Ibsen, Strindberg, Maeterlinck. Europe. 1892-1902. Lang.: Eng.   2566

Dramatic vs. literary interpretation of *Ett Drömspel (A Dream Play)* by August Strindberg. Sweden. 1901-1964. Lang.: Eng.   2734

Theory/criticism
Shift of August Strindberg from naturalism to expressionism. Sweden. 1987. Lang.: Eng.   3061

Drottningholm
SEE
Kungliga Operahus (Stockholm).

Druid Theatre Company (Galway)
Performance/production
Collection of newspaper reviews by London theatre critics. UK-England: London. 1987. Lang.: Eng.   2220

Plays/librettos/scripts
Analysis of Thomas Murphy's *Bailegangaire*, its connections with the Irish language, story-telling. Ireland: Galway. 1985. Lang.: Eng.   2655

Drury Lane Theatre (London)
Administration
Theatrical season of 1723 at the Drury Lane Theatre. England: London. 1723. Lang.: Eng.   21

Role of the Master of the Revels as censor. England: London. 1662-1737. Lang.: Eng.   22

Design/technology
Influence of scene designer Philippe James de Loutherbourg. England. 1700-1800. Lang.: Eng.   317

Performance/production
Quality of ensembles declined in latter part of Garrick's career. England: London. 1737-1776. Lang.: Eng.   1742

Plays/librettos/scripts
Byron's 'closet' dramas structured for performance at London theatres. UK-England: London. 1812-1822. Lang.: Eng.   2778

Dry Cleaner's Integrity, The
Performance/production
Five short plays by Géza Páskándi at SUNY Binghamton. Hungary. USA: Binghamton, NY. 1987. Lang.: Eng.   1813

Dryden, John
Plays/librettos/scripts
Name and entitlement in Dryden, Wycherley and Etherege. England. 1500-1699. Lang.: Eng.   2526

Comparison of works of Milton and Dryden. England. 1608-1700. Lang.: Eng.   2546

Theory/criticism
Politics, patriarchy in Dryden's plays. England. 1679-1687.   3030

du Plessis, P.G.
Plays/librettos/scripts
Chance in the plays of P.G. du Plessis and Friedrich Dürrenmatt. South Africa, Republic of. Switzerland. 1987. Lang.: Afr.   1153

New Afrikaans drama and playwrights. South Africa, Republic of. 1985-1986. Lang.: Afr.   1155

du Prey, Deirdre Hurst
Training
Interview with acting teacher Deirdre Hurst du Prey, specialist in the Chekhov Method. UK-England: Dartington. 1978. Lang.: Eng.   3081

Du, Jin-Fan
Performance/production
Interview with Chinese opera actress Du Jin-Fan. China, People's Republic of. 1987. Lang.: Chi.   3531

Dual Control Theatre Company (London)
Performance/production
Collection of newspaper reviews by London theatre critics. UK-England: London. 1987. Lang.: Eng.   2252

Duan, Le
Performance/production
Development of Vietnamese theatre through the centuries. Vietnam. 980-1986. Lang.: Eng.   2402

Dube, Msiki
Performance/production
Content and North American reception of *Asinimali! (We Have No Money!)* by Mbongeni Ngema. Canada. South Africa, Republic of. 1987. Lang.: Eng.   1715

Dublin Contemporary Dance Theatre (Dublin)
Performance/production
Overview of Dublin dance season. Ireland: Dublin. 1987. Lang.: Eng.   1408

Dublin Drama League (Dublin)
Institutions
Playwright Denis Johnston and avant-garde theatre at the Abbey. Ireland: Dublin. 1927-1935. Lang.: Eng.   1619

Dublin Youth Theatre (DYT, Dublin)
Performance/production
DYT (Dublin Youth Theatre). Ireland: Dublin. 1980-1987. Lang.: Eng.   816

Dubois, René-Daniel
Basic theatrical documents
Translation of *Being at Home with Claude*. Canada: Montreal, PQ. 1986. Lang.: Eng.   1546

Plays/librettos/scripts
The role of the father-figure in recent plays from Quebec. Canada: Quebec. 1980-1987. Lang.: Fre.   2465

Language and metaphor in plays of René-Daniel Dubois. Canada: Toronto, ON, Montreal, PQ. 1983-1987. Lang.: Eng.   2471

Dubois, René-Daniel — cont'd

Theme of René-Daniel Dubois's *Being at Home with Claude.* Canada: Quebec, PQ. USA: New York, NY. 1984-1985. Lang.: Eng. 2473

Dubois, W.E.B.
Theory/criticism
Portrayals of African-Americans in media and literature. USA. 1926-1987. Lang.: Eng. 3104

Portrayal of African-American artists in literature. USA. 1926-1987. Lang.: Eng. 3105

Dubrowsky, Franz
Performance/production
Controversial production of *Othello* directed by Janet Suzman. South Africa, Republic of: Johannesburg. 1987. Lang.: Eng. 2007

Ducal Nuptials
SEE
Nopces ducales, Les.

Duchess of Malfi, The
Performance/production
Shakespeare and contemporaries: tradition, intertextuality in performance. England. 1607-1987. Lang.: Eng. 1740

Plays/librettos/scripts
Use of symbols in Webster's *The Duchess of Malfi.* England. 1613. Lang.: Eng. 1121

Comparative study of Lope de Vega's *El mayordomo de la Duquesa de Amalfi* and Webster's *The Duchess of Malfi.* Spain. 1612-1982. Lang.: Eng. 2729

Dudek, Jaroslav
Performance/production
Actors Jaromír Hanzlík and Viktor Preiss in Rostand's *Cyrano,* directed by Jaroslov Dudek at Vinohradské Theatre. Czechoslovakia: Prague. 1986. Lang.: Cze. 771

Jaroslav Dudek directs *A Day Lasts Longer than a Century* by Čingiz Ajmatov, Vinohradské Theatre. Czechoslovakia: Prague. 1987. Lang.: Cze. 774

Dudinskaja, Natal'ja
Performance/production
Portrait of ballerina Natal'ja Dudinskaja of the Kirov Ballet. USSR: Leningrad. 1912-1987. Lang.: Eng. 1448

Dueck, David
Plays/librettos/scripts
David and Toni Dueck's docudrama about their Mennonite heritage. Canada: Winnipeg, MB. 1985. Lang.: Eng. 3175

Dueck, Toni
Plays/librettos/scripts
David and Toni Dueck's docudrama about their Mennonite heritage. Canada: Winnipeg, MB. 1985. Lang.: Eng. 3175

Duet for One
Performance/production
Work of film director Andrei Konchalovsky. USA. USSR: Moscow. Lang.: Eng. 3166

Duffy, Craig
Institutions
1987 Vancouver Fringe Festival: specific performances. Canada: Vancouver, BC. 1987. Lang.: Eng. 1609

Duggan, Shaun
Performance/production
Collection of newspaper reviews by London theatre critics. UK-England: London. 1986. Lang.: Eng. 2161

Duggan, Terry
Performance/production
Collection of newspaper reviews by London theatre critics. UK-England: London. 1986. Lang.: Eng. 2041

Duke of Cambridge Theatre (London)
Performance/production
Collection of newspaper reviews by London theatre critics. UK-England: London. 1986. Lang.: Eng. 2126

Collection of newspaper reviews by London theatre critics. UK-England: London. 1986. Lang.: Eng. 2139

Collection of newspaper reviews by London theatre critics. UK-England: London. 1986. Lang.: Eng. 2164

Duke of York's Theatre (London)
Performance/production
Collection of newspaper reviews by London theatre critics. UK-England: London. 1987. Lang.: Eng. 2218

Collection of newspaper reviews of London theatre critics. UK-England: London. 1987. Lang.: Eng. 2273

Duke, Edward
Performance/production
Collection of newspaper reviews by London theatre critics. UK-England: London. 1987. Lang.: Eng. 2213

Duke, James
Performance/production
Collection of newspaper reviews by London theatre critics. UK-England: London. 1986. Lang.: Eng. 2057

Dukes, Gerry
Performance/production
Collection of newspaper reviews by London theatre critics. UK-England: London. 1986. Lang.: Eng. 2150

Dukkehjem, Et (Doll's House, A)
Plays/librettos/scripts
Three feminist productions of plays by Henrik Ibsen. USA. 1987. Lang.: Eng. 2899

Theory/criticism
Structuralist approach to play interpretation. 500 B.C.-1987 A.D. Lang.: Eng. 3016

Dulchin, Ed
Performance/production
Plot synopsis of musical *Mademoiselle Colombe* based on Anouilh's *Colombe.* USA: New York, NY. 1987. Lang.: Eng. 3647

Plays/librettos/scripts
How Anouilh's *Colombe* was adapted as a musical. USA. 1987. Lang.: Eng. 3672

Dullin, Charles
Performance/production
Influence of *nō* theatre on director Jean-Louis Barrault and his colleagues. France. 1910-1982. Lang.: Eng. 1498

Dumas, Alexandre (père)
Performance/production
Actor-dramas produced by National Theatre. Hungary: Budapest. 1836-1847. Lang.: Hun. 1842

Kean by Dumas and Sartre, directed by Tamás Szirtes, Madách Theatre. Hungary: Budapest. 1986. Lang.: Hun. 1862

Dumb Waiter, The
Performance/production
Review of ABC videocast of Pinter's *The Dumb Waiter.* USA. 1987. Lang.: Eng. 3209

Plays/librettos/scripts
Interpreting Harold Pinter's dramas through focus on his play structures. UK-England. 1958-1987. Lang.: Eng. 2815

Dunbar, Adrian
Performance/production
Collection of newspaper reviews by London theatre critics. UK-England: London. 1987. Lang.: Eng. 2197

Dunbar, Andrea
Performance/production
Collection of newspaper reviews by London theatre critics. UK-England: London. 1986. Lang.: Eng. 2091

Dunbar, Paul Laurence
Performance/production
Compositions by Debussy in their relationship to Afro-American music. France: Paris. UK-England: London. 1893-1913. Lang.: Eng. 3384

Duncan, Isadora
Performance/production
Life and work of of dancer/choreographer Isadora Duncan. USA. Europe. 1877-1927. Lang.: Eng. 1474

Edward Gordon Craig's use of *commedia dell'arte* in his work. UK-England. Italy. 1872-1966. Lang.: Eng. 3314

Duncan, Martin
Performance/production
Collection of newspaper reviews by London theatre critics. UK-England: London. 1987. Lang.: Eng. 2200

Duncan, Patrick
Performance/production
Collection of newspaper reviews by London theatre critics. UK-England: London. 1987. Lang.: Eng. 2249

Dunderdale, Sue
Performance/production
Collection of newspaper reviews by London theatre critics. UK-England: London. 1986. Lang.: Eng. 2056

Collection of newspaper reviews by London theatre critics. UK-England: London. 1986. Lang.: Eng. 2070

Collection of newspaper reviews by London theatre critics. UK-England: London. 1986. Lang.: Eng. 2093

Dunderdale, Sue — cont'd

Collection of newspaper reviews by London theatre critics. UK-England: London. 1987. Lang.: Eng.   2196

Collection of newspaper reviews by London theatre critics. UK-England: London. 1987. Lang.: Eng.   2222

Collection of newspaper reviews by London theatre critics. UK-England: London. 1987. Lang.: Eng.   2252

Dunham, Katherine
  Performance/production

The career of dancer/choreographer Katherine Dunham. USA: New York, NY, Chicago, IL, Las Vegas, NV. 1909-1987. Lang.: Eng.   1412

Dunn, Nell
  Performance/production

Relationship of theatre, class and gender. UK-England. USA. 1969-1985. Lang.: Eng.   918

Collection of newspaper reviews by London theatre critics. UK-England: London. 1986. Lang.: Eng.   2050

Dunn, Susan
  Performance/production

Soprano Susan Dunn. USA: New York, NY. 1955-1987. Lang.: Eng.   3854

Dunne, John
  Performance/production

DYT (Dublin Youth Theatre). Ireland: Dublin. 1980-1987. Lang.: Eng.   816

Dunsany, Edward John Morton Drax Plunkett, Baron
  Performance/production

Encounter between Pirandello and Lord Dunsany during Pirandello's production of *I pazzi sulla montagna (The Gods of the Mountain)* by Alessandro De Stefani. Italy. 1923-1928. Lang.: Eng.   1947

Dunstan, Evan
  Performance/production

Collection of newspaper reviews by London theatre critics. UK-England: London. 1987. Lang.: Eng.   2248

Dupak, Nikolaj
  Performance/production

Life and work of Anatolij Efros. USSR: Moscow. 1983-1987. Lang.: Eng.   1038

Durang, Christopher
  Performance/production

Collection of newspaper reviews by New York theatre critics. USA: New York, NY. 1987. Lang.: Eng.   2315

Duras, Marguerite
  Performance/production

Directorial style of Claude Régy. France. 1955-1987. Lang.: Fre.   1762

New Tokyo productions. Japan: Tokyo. 1987. Lang.: Jap.   1954

Unsuitable choice of plays for Tokyo performances. Japan: Tokyo. 1987. Lang.: Jap.   1965

  Plays/librettos/scripts

Comparison of two versions of Duras' *La Musica Deuxième*. France: Paris. 1985-1987. Lang.: Eng.   1125

  Theory/criticism

Impact of cinematic technique on plays by Beckett and Duras. France. 1977-1987. Lang.: Eng.   3037

Durbridge, Francis
  Performance/production

Collection of newspaper reviews by London theatre critics. UK-England: London. 1986. Lang.: Eng.   2120

Dürrenmatt, Friedrich
  Plays/librettos/scripts

Chance in the plays of P.G. du Plessis and Friedrich Dürrenmatt. South Africa, Republic of. Switzerland. 1987. Lang.: Afr.   1153

Analysis of Dürrenmatt's *Play Strindberg*, adaptation of Strindberg's *Dödsdansen (The Dance of Death)*. Switzerland. 1971-1982. Lang.: Eng.   2743

Analysis of plays of Friedrich Dürrenmatt, comparison with Bertolt Brecht. Switzerland. Germany, West. 1945-1986. Lang.: Ger.   2745

Comparison of Dürrenmatt's *The Physicists (Die Physiker)*, *Macbeth* and *Doctor Faustus*. Switzerland. 1987. Lang.: Heb.   2747

  Theory/criticism

Paradoxical and grotesque elements in plays of Dürrenmatt. Europe. 1986. Lang.: Ger.   3034

Duse, Eleonora
  Plays/librettos/scripts

Influence of Sibilla Aleramo on women in Italian theatre. Italy. 1850-1930. Lang.: Ita.   1138

Dutchman
  Performance/production

Interview with playwright Amiri Baraka. USA: Newark, NJ, New York, NY. 1965-1969. Lang.: Eng.   2356

Dutton, Charles S.
  Plays/librettos/scripts

Interview with playwright August Wilson. USA. 1970-1987. Lang.: Eng.   2855

Duvall, Robert
  Performance/production

Analysis of art of television and comparison to live theatre. USA. 1950-1987. Lang.: Eng.   3194

Dvořak, Anton
  Performance/production

Anton Dvořak's *Rusalka*. Czechoslovakia: Prague. USA: New York, NY. 1900-1987. Lang.: Eng.   3759

Dvoreckij, I.
  Plays/librettos/scripts

The industrial theme in the plays of playwright I. Dvoreckij. USSR. 1960-1979. Lang.: Rus.   2945

Dwarfs, The
  Basic theatrical documents

Chapter 19 of Harold Pinter's unpublished novel *The Dwarfs*. UK-England. 1958-1987. Lang.: Eng.   1575

  Plays/librettos/scripts

Introduction to Chapter 19 of Pinter's unpublished novel *The Dwarfs*. UK-England. 1958-1987. Lang.: Eng.   2779

Interpreting Harold Pinter's dramas through focus on his play structures. UK-England. 1958-1987. Lang.: Eng.   2815

Dybbuk, The
  SEE
    HaDybbuk.

Earl Carroll Theatre (New York, NY)
  Performance spaces

Architectural and design information on the short-lived Earl Carroll Theatre. USA: New York, NY. 1931-1933. Lang.: Hun.   690

Earthcirkus (Stockholm)
  Institutions

Profile of street theatre company Earthcirkus. Sweden: Stockholm. 1977-1982. Lang.: Eng.   562

East End Theatre Company (London)
  Performance/production

Collection of newspaper reviews by London theatre critics. UK-England: London. 1987. Lang.: Eng.   2253

Easter
  SEE
    Påsk.

Easter Egg, The
  Plays/librettos/scripts

Critical analysis of James Reaney's *Three Desks*. Canada. 1960-1977. Lang.: Eng.   2477

Eau Dormante, Une (Stagnant Water)
  Plays/librettos/scripts

Compares plays of Enlightenment France, Francophone Africa. Congo: Brazzaville. Cameroon. Benin. France. 1700-1975. Lang.: Eng.   2496

Ebb, Fred
  Performance/production

Collection of newspaper reviews by London theatre critics. UK-England: London. 1986. Lang.: Eng.   2149

Collection of newspaper reviews by New York theatre critics. USA: New York, NY. 1987. Lang.: Eng.   2317

Two productions of *Flora, the Red Menace*. USA: New York, NY. 1965-1987. Lang.: Eng.   3640

Eberson, John
  Performance spaces

Many uses of the Uptown Theatre. USA: Kansas City, MO. 1926-1987. Lang.: Eng.   3143

Echo (USSR)
  Performance/production

Oleg Tabakov's experimental group 'Echo'. USSR. 1980-1987. Lang.: Rus.   1001

Echo in the Bone, An
  Performance/production

Collection of newspaper reviews by London theatre critics. UK-England: London. 1986. Lang.: Eng.   2116

Education — cont'd

Getting more audiences from schools involved in Chinese drama. China, People's Republic of. 1987. Lang.: Chi. 3435

Design/technology

Puppetmaking projects for children. USA. 1987. Lang.: Eng. 3963

Institutions

Director Leon Schiller's plan for a drama department, Theatre Institute. Poland: Warsaw. 1943. Lang.: Pol. 555

Elizabeth Sterling Haynes and the Little Theatre movement. Canada. 1916-1957. Lang.: Eng. 1603

Forms of teaching drama in schools and its role in communication skills. UK-England. 1980. Lang.: Eng. 1646

Ramayana '87, an Inner London Education Authority project. UK-England: London. 1987. Lang.: Eng. 3965

Professional associations and organizations for puppeteers. USA. 1987. Lang.: Eng. 3968

Performance/production

TEAM, an educational theatre company. Ireland: Dublin. 1984-1987. Lang.: Eng. 818

Interview with playwright Patrick McDonald. Canada: Ottawa, ON. 1987. Lang.: Eng. 1708

Role of theatre in the Filipino revolution. Philippines. 1970-1987. Lang.: Eng. 1986

Life and career of Polish theatre professional Zbigniew Cynkutis. Poland: Wrocław. 1972-1987. Lang.: Eng. 1993

Undergraduate students stage the York Crucifixion play. UK-England: Canterbury. 1983-1987. Lang.: Eng. 2282

History and aspects of puppet theatre: designs, genres and puppeteers. Europe. Asia. 400 B.C.-1985 A.D. Lang.: Eng. 3255

Puppet companies from Poznań. Poland: Poznań. 1919-1939. Lang.: Pol. 3978

Plays/librettos/scripts

Playwrights' condescension to child audiences. USA. 1972. Lang.: Eng. 1171

Relation to other fields

Experimental theatre course, Assoc. Internationale pour la Sémiologie du Spectacle. Belgium: Brussels. France: Paris. Denmark: Odense. 1983-1985. Lang.: Fre. 1219

Alternative view of culture and education in theatre. Cuba. 1987. Lang.: Spa. 1229

Psychodrama in the clinic, the classroom and contemporary research. Europe. North America. 1900-1987. Lang.: Ita. 1233

Paper reproductions of 19th-century stage sets. Germany. Switzerland. 1900-1930. Lang.: Ger. 1239

Importance of theatre for youth and arts in education in Israel. Israel. 1973. Lang.: Eng. 1241

Theatre in education—uses and problems. Italy. 1970-1987. Lang.: Ita. 1245

Drama as education: current theory and practice. USA. 1987. Lang.: Eng. 1268

Criteria for instructors' use of dramatic action. USA. 1987. Lang.: Eng. 1269

Integrating theatre into primary and secondary education. USA. 1987. 1275

Children's interaction with theatre as compared to television. USA. 1964. Lang.: Eng. 1277

Dramatic imagination in childhood play. USA. 1987. Lang.: Eng. 1278

Roundtable discussion on the state of arts education. USA. 1984. Lang.: Eng. 1281

Statistics relating to teaching positions in the arts. USA. 1986-1987. Lang.: Eng. 1285

Multicultural plays for children. USA. 1986. Lang.: Eng. 1287

Creative drama's potential to stimulate wonder. USA. 1970-1977. Lang.: Eng. 1288

Role of theatre in moral education. USSR. 1987. Lang.: Rus. 1296

The role of ballet and ballet dancers in Swiss theatres. Switzerland. 1987. Lang.: Ger. 1456

Rediscovery of the body in modern dance. Germany. 1900-1930. Lang.: Ita. 1475

Applications of African 'Theatre for Development' movement to Canadian popular theatre. Africa. Canada: St. John's, NF, Toronto, ON. 1978-1987. Lang.: Eng. 2978

Teachers discuss creative drama's role in adult education. Jamaica. Zimbabwe. Bangladesh. 1987. Lang.: Swe. 2996

Sätrahöjdens teatergrupp, producing plays by and for the retarded. Sweden: Gävle. 1978-1987. Lang.: Swe. 3000

Three performance art education projects. UK-England. 1987. Lang.: Eng. 3373

Results of questionnaire on drama education. China, People's Republic of. 1983-1985. Lang.: Chi. 3582

Perceptions of childhood reflected in opera. Europe. 1800-1983. Lang.: Eng. 3940

College opera programs an an integral part of mainstream liberal arts education. USA. 1987. Lang.: Eng. 3947

Puppets used in community development workshops. UK-England: London. 1987. Lang.: Eng. 3997

Puppetry in education of hearing-impaired. UK-England: London. 1987. Lang.: Eng. 4011

Training

Basic theatrical techniques for secondary school. Belgium. 1987. Lang.: Fre. 1378

Exchange program for graduate students in arts administration. UK-England: London. USA: New York, NY. 1985. Lang.: Eng. 1385

Educational theatre

Performance/production

History of modern Dutch theatre. Netherlands. 1970-1985. Lang.: Dut. 862

Training

Teachers' handbook for theatre in education. Spain-Catalonia. 1987. Lang.: Cat. 1384

Edwardes, George

Plays/librettos/scripts

Role of playwright George Edwardes in development of musical comedy. UK-England: London. 1830-1890. Lang.: Eng. 2766

Edwards, Malcolm

Performance/production

Collection of newspaper reviews by London theatre critics. UK-England: London. 1987. Lang.: Eng. 2204

Eells, George

Performance/production

History of dance marathons. USA. 1920-1987. Lang.: Eng. 957

Effie's Burning

Performance/production

Collection of newspaper reviews by London theatre critics. UK-England: London. 1987. Lang.: Eng. 2260

Collection of newspaper reviews by London theatre critics. UK-England: London. 1987. Lang.: Eng. 2268

Efremov, Oleg

SEE

Jefremov, Oleg.

Efros, Anatolij

Performance/production

Director Anatolij Efros on directing, ethics. USSR: Moscow. 1981-1982. Lang.: Rus. 1033

Life and work of Anatolij Efros. USSR: Moscow. 1983-1987. Lang.: Eng. 1038

Egerton, George

Performance/production

Aubrey Beardsley's drawings of actresses: impact on society. UK-England: London. 1890. Lang.: Eng. 2287

Eich, Günther

Plays/librettos/scripts

The German radio play *Hörspiel* and its history. Germany, West: Cologne. USA. 1950-1985. Lang.: Eng. 3117

Eichelberger, Ethyl

Performance/production

Interview with male performer Ethyl Eichelberger. USA: New York, NY. 1987. Lang.: Eng. 2314

Ethyl Eichelberger and Lily Savage: their approaches to acting. USA. UK-England. 1987. Lang.: Eng. 3290

Eight Shining Palaces

SEE

Pa Chin Kung.

Eileen Asthore

Plays/librettos/scripts

Analysis of the plays and songs of Irish-American musical theatre star Chauncey Olcott. USA. 1893-1918. Lang.: Eng. 3671

Einen Jux will er sich machen
SEE
    Jux will er sich machen, Einen.

Einstein
Performance/production
    Collection of newspaper reviews by London theatre critics. UK-England: London. 1986. Lang.: Eng.   2152

Eisenberg, Alan
Administration
    U.S. and British Equity associations: actor exchange, union reciprocity. UK-England. USA. 1981-1987. Lang.: Eng.   50
    The first Anglo-American commercial Broadway production, the musical *Carrie*. USA: New York, NY. UK-England: London. 1987. Lang.: Eng.   61
    Equity's policy on U.S. performances by foreign artists. USA: New York, NY. 1987. Lang.: Eng.   131
    Effects of new immigration rules on performing arts organizations. USA: New York, NY. 1987. Lang.: Eng.   174
    Legal difficulties facing producers who present foreign artists and dance troupes. USA. 1987. Lang.: Eng.   244

Relation to other fields
    Actors' Equity's affirmative action program. USA: New York, NY. 1982. Lang.: Eng.   1261

Eisenberg, Eric
Performance/production
    Nontraditional casting in a production of *The Cherry Orchard*. USA: San Francisco, CA. 1986. Lang.: Eng.   928

Eisenberg, Ned
Institutions
    Experience of artists working at the O'Neill Theatre Center. USA: Waterford, CT. 1985-1986. Lang.: Eng.   1655

Eisenstein, Sergei Michajlovič
Relation to other fields
    Compares Brecht's montages and the film work of Sergei Eisenstein and the use and definition of *gestus*. USA. 1930. Lang.: Eng.   3186

Eisenstein, Sergej Michajlovič
Performance/production
    Links between experimental theatre movement and the Russian Futurists. USSR. 1920-1929. Lang.: Rus.   1058

Eisler, Hanns
Plays/librettos/scripts
    Why Hanns Eisler's opera *Johann Faustus* remained incomplete. Germany, East. 1953-1987. Lang.: Ger.   3912
    Debate over Hanns Eisler's opera *Johann Faustus*. Germany, East: Berlin, East. 1949-1955. Lang.: Ger.   3913

Ek, Anders
Performance/production
    Evaluation of actor Anders Ek. Sweden. 1916-1979. Lang.: Swe.   2012

El-Hakawati (Jerusalem)
Institutions
    Visit to the El-Hakawati theatre, an independent performance group, specializing in theatre for and about the Palestinians. Israel: Jerusalem. 1982-1985. Lang.: Swe.   1622

Elam, Keir
Theory/criticism
    Semiotic study of Gambaro's *El despojamiento (The Robbery)*. USA. 1987. Lang.: Eng.   3067

Elckerlijc
SEE
    Everyman.

Eldredge, Kay
Performance/production
    Collection of newspaper reviews by London theatre critics. UK-England: London. 1987. Lang.: Eng.   2202

Electra by Hofmannsthal
SEE
    Elektra.

Elemänpalvelusteatteri 981 (EPT, Oulu)
Performance/production
    Life Service Theatre experiment in topical theatre. Finland: Oulu. 1986. Lang.: Swe.   1749

Elias Gonzales, Adalberto
Performance/production
    Retrospective of two centuries of Hispanic theatre. USA. 1598-1965. Lang.: Eng.   2345

Elice, Eric
Performance/production
    Collection of newspaper reviews by London theatre critics. UK-England: London. 1986. Lang.: Eng.   2122

Eliot, Thomas Stearns
Administration
    Producer Marlene Smith. Canada: Toronto, ON. 1985. Lang.: Eng.   3617

Performance/production
    János Mrsán directs *The Cocktail Party* by T.S. Eliot at Várszinház under the title *Koktél hatkor*. Hungary: Budapest. 1987. Lang.: Hun.   1803
    Collection of newspaper reviews by London theatre critics. UK-England: London. 1986. Lang.: Eng.   2152

Eliraz, Israel
Plays/librettos/scripts
    Themes of Eliraz's *The Garden of Adam and Eve*. Israel: Jerusalem. 1987. Lang.: Heb.   3915
    Librettist on *The Garden of Adam and Eve*. Israel: Jerusalem. 1987. Lang.: Heb.   3916

Elisabetta: Quasi per caso una donna (Elizabeth: Almost By Chance a Woman)
Basic theatrical documents
    English text of *Elisabetta: Quasi per caso una donna (Elizabeth: Almost By Chance a Woman)* by Dario Fo. Italy. USA. 1987. Lang.: Eng.   1560
Performance/production
    Collection of newspaper reviews by London theatre critics. UK-England: London. 1986. Lang.: Eng.   2158

Elisha, Ron
Performance/production
    Collection of newspaper reviews by London theatre critics. UK-England: London. 1986. Lang.: Eng.   2152

Elizabethan theatre
    Popular history of theatre. Europe. 500 B.C.-1983 A.D. Lang.: Eng.   1

SEE ALSO
    Geographical-Chronological Index under England 1558-1603.
Audience
    Study of Shakespeare's original audiences. England: London. 1567-1642. Lang.: Eng.   1532
    Actor and audience in Elizabethan theatre. England. 1585-1625. Lang.: Eng.   1533
Design/technology
    Early use of the counterweight system. England. 1433-1579. Lang.: Eng.   316
    Discusses costuming in Elizabethan theatre. England. 1561-1633. Lang.: Eng.   1589
Performance spaces
    Analysis of theatre designs by Inigo Jones and John Webb. England. 1573-1672. Lang.: Eng.   632
    Design of new Swan Theatre recreates Elizabethan atmosphere. UK-England: Stratford. 1987. Lang.: Eng.   672
Performance/production
    Conference proceedings on staging of Elizabethan plays. England. 1546-1616. Lang.: Eng.   775
    Comparison of *onnagata* actors with Elizabethan boy actors. England. Japan. 1580-1987. Lang.: Eng.   1737
    'Boy actresses' and attitudes toward sensuality in performance. England: London. 1580-1630. Lang.: Eng.   1741
    Shaw's conception of the Elizabethan theatre. UK-England. 1909. Lang.: Eng.   2303
Plays/librettos/scripts
    Discussion of *Crudities* by Thomas Coryat and *The White Devil* by John Webster. England. 1580-1612. Lang.: Eng.   1117
    King Lear focusing on the character of Kent. England. 1605. Lang.: Eng.   1122
    Comparison of the works of Ben Jonson and Christopher Marlowe. England. 1598-1602. Lang.: Eng.   1123
    Female characters in city comedy who suffer from bladder incontinence. 1599-1632. Lang.: Eng.   2427
    Productions of *Sir Thomas More* by Elizabethan theatre companies. England. 1595-1650. Lang.: Eng.   2541
    Improvisational clowning in Elizabethan theatre. England. 1585-1625. Lang.: Eng.   2560
    Argument for authenticity of three Elizabethan documents. England. 1591. Lang.: Eng.   3325

Elizabethan theatre — cont'd

Argument against authenticity of three Elizabethan documents. England. 1591-1885. Lang.: Eng. 3326

Pageantry in Elizabethan theatre. England. 1392-1642. Lang.: Eng. 3336

Theory/criticism
The body as emblematic of a character's frame of mind. England. 1583. Lang.: Eng. 3031

Trollope's writings on Elizabethan and Jacobean drama. UK-England. 1866-1882. Lang.: Eng. 3063

Ellington, Duke
Performance/production
Origins of jazz, its evolution in vaudeville. USA: New Orleans, LA, New York, NY, Chicago, IL. Lang.: Eng. 3650

Elliot, Michael
Plays/librettos/scripts
Successful film versions of Shakespeare's *King Lear*. USA. UK-England. USSR. 1916-1983. Lang.: Eng. 3099

Elliot, Richard
Performance/production
History of dance marathons. USA. 1920-1987. Lang.: Eng. 957

Elliott, Mark
Performance/production
Collection of newspaper reviews by London theatre critics. UK-England: London. 1986. Lang.: Eng. 2089

Ellis, Michael
Performance/production
Collection of newspaper reviews by London theatre critics. UK-England: London. 1987. Lang.: Eng. 2225

Ellis, Vivian
Performance/production
Collection of newspaper reviews by London theatre critics. UK-England: London. 1987. Lang.: Eng. 2234

Ellison, Bruce
Performance/production
Bruce Ellison directs his *Mister Knight* at Théâtre de la Mandragore. Belgium: Brussels. 1986. Lang.: Fre. 1685

Elovich, Richard
Performance/production
Performance artists Ishmael Houston-Jones, John Kelly, Karen Finley, Richard Elovich. USA. 1987. Lang.: Eng. 3366

Elson, Elizabeth
Institutions
The Federal Theatre Project's California Puppetry Unit. USA: San Francisco, CA. 1934-1987. Lang.: Eng. 3966

Elton, Ben
Performance/production
Development of alternative cabaret. UK-England. 1980. Lang.: Eng. 3288

Elverhoj (Elfmound, The)
Institutions
Profile of political theatre company Solvognen. Denmark. 1969-1982. Lang.: Eng. 528

Elwyn, Michael
Performance/production
Collection of newspaper reviews by London theatre critics. UK-England: London. 1986. Lang.: Eng. 2050

Ember tragédiája, Az (Tragedy of a Man, The)
Performance/production
Ljubiša Ristić adapts and directs Imre Madách's *Az ember tragédiája (The Tragedy of a Man)*. Yugoslavia: Subotica. 1986. Lang.: Hun. 2404

Emilia Galotti
Performance/production
Collection of newspaper reviews by London theatre critics. UK-England: London. 1987. Lang.: Eng. 2204

Emmons, Beverly
Design/technology
Lighting design and instruments for production of *Nicholas Nickleby*. USA: New York, NY. 1982. Lang.: Eng. 478

Emperor Jones, The
Plays/librettos/scripts
Eugene O'Neill's influence on William Faulkner. USA: New York, NY. 1920-1962. Lang.: Eng. 2858

Influence of puppetry on Eugene O'Neill. USA. 1937. Lang.: Eng. 2919

Influence of Rudyard Kipling on Eugene O'Neill. USA. 1887-1950. Lang.: Eng. 2925

Emperor, The
Performance/production
Collection of newspaper reviews by London theatre critics. UK-England: London. 1987. Lang.: Eng. 2190

Collection of newspaper reviews by London theatre critics. UK-England: London. 1987. Lang.: Eng. 2254

Empire Theatre (London)
Relation to other fields
Documentation on prostitution at the Empire theatre. UK-England: London. 1890. Lang.: Eng. 1259

Employment
Administration
Protests against proposed labor policies for non-immigrant aliens. USA. 1987. Lang.: Eng. 72

Overview of activities of Actors' Equity Association. USA: New York, NY, Chicago, IL. 1961-1984. Lang.: Eng. 75

Actors' Equity president Ellen Burstyn on employment for minorities and women. USA: New York, NY. 1982. Lang.: Eng. 109

Strike by Hispanic Organization of Latin Americans (HOLA) due to inadequate casting of Hispanic actors. USA: New York, NY. 1982. Lang.: Eng. 110

Value of degree in arts management. USA: New York, NY. 1985. Lang.: Eng. 123

Relation to other fields
Equity's National Theatre Plan. USA. 1982. Lang.: Eng. 1262

Training
Shaping of an arts management internship from an employer's point of view. USA: Brooklyn, NY. 1985. Lang.: Eng. 1389

En (Tokyo)
Performance/production
Reviews and discussion of Tokyo productions. Japan: Tokyo. 1960-1987. Lang.: Jap. 1960

Comments on Tokyo performances. Japan: Tokyo. 1987. Lang.: Jap. 1964

En attendant Godot (Waiting for Godot)
Performance/production
Chinese production of Beckett's *Waiting for Godot*. China, People's Republic of: Shanghai. 1986-1987. Lang.: Chi. 1721

Personal notes of Samuel Beckett, how they illuminate his plays. France. 1969-1984. Lang.: Eng. 1758

Collection of newspaper reviews by London theatre critics. UK-England: London. 1987. Lang.: Eng. 2226

Plays/librettos/scripts
Optimistic interpretation of Beckett's *En attendant Godot (Waiting for Godot)*. 1987. Lang.: Eng. 2410

Nietzschean and psychoanalytical interpretation of Beckett's *Not I*. USA. 1972-1987. Lang.: Eng. 2879

Reference materials
History of pocket theatre. France: Paris. 1944-1953. Lang.: Eng. 2974

Endgame
SEE
Fin de partie.
Plays/librettos/scripts
Critical methodology for studying Beckett's works. UK-England. 1930-1987. Lang.: Eng. 2814

Énekes madár (Song Bird, The)
Performance/production
Imre Kerényi directs *Énekes madár (The Song Bird)* by Áron Tamási at the National Theatre. Hungary: Budapest. 1987. Lang.: Hun. 1819

Áron Tamási's *Énekes madár (The Song Bird)* directed by Imre Kerényi at National Theatre. Hungary: Budapest. 1987. Lang.: Hun. 1872

Enfant-rat, L' (Rat Child, The)
Plays/librettos/scripts
Anti-fascist plays of Armand Gatti. France. 1924-1987. Lang.: Rus. 2578

Enfants du Paradis—Carbone 14, Les (Montreal, PQ)
Institutions
Photographic essay of various works by Canadian mime troupe Les Enfants du Paradis—Carbone 14. Canada: Montreal, PQ. 1980-1982. Lang.: Eng. 3219

Engel, Erich
Performance/production
Politics and Shakespeare in Weimar Republic. Germany. 1919-1930. Lang.: Eng. 1775

Equipment — cont'd

Advice on systems for hard of hearing in theatres. UK. 1987. Lang.: Eng. 370

Managing director of theatre equipment manufacturer Donmar examines business aspects. UK-England: London. 1987. Lang.: Eng. 371

Survey on the performance of induction hoop systems. UK-England: London. 1987. Lang.: Eng. 375

Victorian under-stage machinery, Her Majesty's Theatre, London. UK-England: London. 1890-1987. Lang.: Eng. 377

Managing director of Raxcrest Electrical reviews the trade. UK-England. 1987. Lang.: Eng. 378

Restoration of the stage machinery at the Grand Theatre. UK-Wales: Llandudno. 1901-1987. Lang.: Eng. 381

How to make flexible negative molds. USA. 1987. Lang.: Eng. 382

Dimmer standards developed by the United States Institute for Theatre Technology. USA. 1987. Lang.: Eng. 384

Description of the Tracer, Inductive Amplifier and Tic Tracer cable tracers. USA. 1987. Lang.: Eng. 386

Design aspects of *The Glory of Easter*: computerized lighting, lasers and pyrotechnics. USA. 1982. Lang.: Eng. 387

Technology in post-modern theatre. USA. 1985. Lang.: Eng. 388

Procedures to photograph a production. USA. 1982. Lang.: Eng. 389

Construction of thinner furniture and prop pallets. USA. 1986. Lang.: Eng. 390

Sound designer Guy Sherman's innovations. USA: New York, NY. 1984-1987. Lang.: Eng. 392

Making a curved handrail out of Wep. USA. 1985. Lang.: Eng. 393

Mass producing styrofoam balusters economically. USA. 1985. Lang.: Eng. 394

Survey of theatrical fog machines. USA. 1987. Lang.: Eng. 395

Descriptions of three easily concealed lighting fixtures. USA. 1987. Lang.: Eng. 398

Stabilizing doors that bounce open when slammed. USA. 1987. Lang.: Eng. 399

Quantifying the response of theatrical structures. USA. 1987. Lang.: Eng. 401

Description of dimmers and how they work. USA. 1987. Lang.: Eng. 402

Economic construction of large laminated curves. USA. 1985. Lang.: Eng. 405

Comparison of four plastics as scenery glides. USA. 1986. Lang.: Eng. 406

Introductory textbook on scene and production design. USA. 1987. Lang.: Eng. 408

How to use wireless microphones. USA. 1987. Lang.: Eng. 409

Care and safe use of stage rigging equipment. USA. 1987. Lang.: Eng. 411

Retrospective of 1960s rigging installation. USA. 1960-1987. Lang.: Eng. 412

Creating access for hearing and visually impaired theatregoers. USA: Washington, DC. 1987. Lang.: Eng. 413

Techniques for achieving believable relief textures on stage. USA. 1987. Lang.: Eng. 416

A simultaneous vertical and horizontal travel-fly rigging system. USA. 1985. Lang.: Eng. 421

Using electret microphone element as a pick-up mike. USA. 1987. Lang.: Eng. 423

Construction of concealed hinges. USA. 1986. Lang.: Eng. 425

How to construct inner tube sandbag. USA. 1985. Lang.: Eng. 426

Update on the state of the wireless microphone. USA. 1985. Lang.: Eng. 432

Advances in theatre intercom systems. USA. 1960-1987. Lang.: Eng. 435

Use of side drill and conversion to simple drill press. USA. 1985. Lang.: Eng. 436

Purchasing a computer system for a theatre. USA. 1987. Lang.: Eng. 438

Construction of a versatile audio power meter. USA. 1986. Lang.: Eng. 442

LED circuits and possible theatrical applications. USA. 1985. Lang.: Eng. 443

1987 USITT convention. USA: Minneapolis/St. Paul, MN. 1987. Lang.: Eng. 446

Analog and digital sound equipment. USA. 1987. Lang.: Eng. 447

Rock 'n roll lighting control boards. USA. 1987. Lang.: Eng. 448

Instructions on how to make a fog machine silencer. USA. 1987. Lang.: Eng. 453

Survey of 1960s stage machinery. USA. 1960-1987. Lang.: Eng. 456

Technology of computerized dimming systems. USA. 1987. Lang.: Eng. 457

Current computer-assisted lighting controllers. USA. 1987. Lang.: Eng. 459

Devising a traveller track for light scenery pieces. USA. 1987. Lang.: Eng. 467

USITT standards for dimmers and controllers. USA. 1987. Lang.: Eng. 468

Idea and uses of white light. USA. 1982. Lang.: Eng. 471

Lighting design and instruments for production of *Nicholas Nickleby*. USA: New York, NY. 1982. Lang.: Eng. 478

Challenges of repertory lighting. USA. 1982. Lang.: Eng. 479

Clamps used when duplicating steel tube frames. USA. 1987. Lang.: Eng. 480

Use of neon lights from film making to theatrical productions. USA. 1982. Lang.: Eng. 481

Brief history of development of lighting equipment. USA. 1700-1987. Lang.: Eng. 486

The use of computers to enhance theatre technology. Canada. 1987. Lang.: Fre. 3192

Mark Pauline, Matthew Heckert and Eric Werner: performance artists who construct performing machines. USA: San Francisco, CA. 1986. Lang.: Eng. 3342

Application of the musical instrument digital face. USA. 1987. Lang.: Eng. 3449

Machinery to be installed in Her Majesty's Theatre for *Phantom of the Opera*. UK-England: London. 1987. Lang.: Eng. 3619

Performance spaces

Theatrical equipment of the new Friedrichstadtpalast. Germany, East: Berlin, East. 1984. Lang.: Hun. 637

Equity Library Theatre (New York, NY)

Performance spaces

George Wojtasik, managing director of Equity Library Theatre (ELT). USA: New York, NY. 1943-1987. Lang.: Eng. 674

Equus

Plays/librettos/scripts

Religion in Pielmeier's *Agnes of God* and Shaffer's *Equus*. North America. 1973-1980. Lang.: Eng. 2710

Comparison of themes and dramaturgical techniques in plays of Eugene O'Neill and Peter Shaffer. USA. 1920-1982. Lang.: Eng. 2872

Characters' search for God in plays of Peter Shaffer. USA. UK-England. 1979-1984. Lang.: Eng. 2878

Erdmann, Nikolaj

Performance/production

Overview of 1986-1987 Moscow theatre season. USSR: Moscow. 1986-1987. Lang.: Eng. 1039

Plays/librettos/scripts

Nikolaj Erdmann's plays, relations with major directors. USSR: Moscow. 1925. Lang.: Rus. 2963

Erian no shuki—Nakano Fujimi Chūgakkō jiken (Note of Erian—Based on a Suicide at Nakano Fujimi Junior High School, A)

Plays/librettos/scripts

Contemporary Japanese plays about crime. Japan: Tokyo. 1986. Lang.: Jap. 2681

Plays about child suicide in Japan. Japan: Tokyo. 1986. Lang.: Jap. 2683

ERIC

SEE

Educational Resources Information Center.

Ernotte, Andre

Performance/production

Career of director/author Andre Ernotte. USA: New York, NY. 1987. Lang.: Eng. 954

Collection of newspaper reviews by New York theatre critics. USA: New York, NY. 1987. Lang.: Eng. 2326

Erskine, Julian
Institutions
The touring company Irish Theatre Company. UK-Ireland. 1974-
1987. Lang.: Eng.   569
Erté (de Tirtoff, Romain)
Design/technology
Set and costume designs of major designers. UK-England. 1902-
1980. Lang.: Eng.   376
Ervine, St. John
Plays/librettos/scripts
Women's roles in Broadway plays at the time of women's suffrage.
USA: New York, NY. 1920. Lang.: Eng.   2850
Éry-Kovacs, András
Performance/production
Review of productions at opera ensembles meeting. Hungary: Szeged.
1987. Lang.: Hun.   3792
Escalante i Mateu, Eduard
Plays/librettos/scripts
Valencian playwrights writing in both Catalan and Castilian. Spain-
Catalonia: Valencia. 1790-1985. Lang.: Cat.   2732
Escalante Mateu, Eduard
Reference materials
Catalogue of Valencian playtexts available at libraries of Barcelona.
Spain: Valencia, Barcelona. Lang.: Cat.   2975
Escalona, Beatriz
Performance/production
Biographical account of Beatriz Escalona, La Chata Noloesca. USA:
San Antonio, TX. 1903-1979. Lang.: Spa.   2369
Escape, The
SEE
Bég.
Escola Bolera (Barcelona)
Performance/production
History of dance in Catalonia. Spain-Catalonia. 1300-1987. Lang.:
Cat.   1410
Escola Catalana d'Art Dramàtic (Barcelona)
Plays/librettos/scripts
General history of Catalan literature, including theatre. Spain-
Catalonia. 1902-1961. Lang.: Cat.   1157
Escott, Beth
Performance/production
Artists Beth Escott and Tom Zanarini present *The Way We Are At
Home* at the Clybourn Salon. USA: Chicago, IL. 1981. Lang.: Eng.
                                                                           3364
Escudero, Vicente
Performance/production
History of dance in Catalonia. Spain-Catalonia. 1300-1987. Lang.:
Cat.   1410
Escurial
Theory/criticism
Analysis of *Escurial* and *Barabbas* by Michel de Ghelderode.
Belgium. 1898. Lang.: Fre.   3023
Espace Libre (Montreal, PQ)
Audience
Critical analysis of Anne-Marie Provencher's *La Tour*. Canada:
Montreal, PQ. 1986. Lang.: Eng.   1531
Ešpaj, A.
Performance/production
Articles on ballet-master Jurij Grigorovič by other artists. USSR:
Moscow. 1927-1987. Lang.: Rus.   1444
Espert, Nuria
Institutions
Texts and photos about the Teatre Grec. Spain-Catalonia: Barcelona.
1929-1986. Lang.: Cat.   558

Performance/production
Collection of newspaper reviews by London theatre critics. UK-
England: London. 1986. Lang.: Eng.   2172
Collection of newspaper reviews by London theatre critics. UK-
England: London. 1987. Lang.: Eng.   2178
Esposito, Giancarlo
Performance/production
Interview with actor Giancarlo Esposito. USA: New York, NY. 1987.
Lang.: Eng.   3654
Espriu, Salvador
Plays/librettos/scripts
Catalan playwrights after the Spanish Civil War. Spain-Catalonia.
1939-1975. Lang.: Cat.   2730

Theory/criticism
Reflections on the value of theatrical translations. Spain-Catalonia.
UK-England. 1600-1985. Lang.: Cat.   3060
Esswood, Paul
Performance/production
Interview with countertenor Paul Esswood. UK-England: London.
1942-1987. Lang.: Eng.   3830
Este family
Performance/production
Influence of the Este family on theatrical performance. Italy: Rome.
1598-1645. Lang.: Ita.   3324
Estrella de Sevilla, La (Star of Seville, The)
Performance/production
László Márton directs *La estrella de Sevilla (The Star of Seville)* by
Lope de Vega at Vigszinház under the title *Sevilla csillaga*.
Hungary: Budapest. 1986. Lang.: Hun.   1796
La estrella de Sevilla (The Star of Seville) by Lope de Vega, staged
by László Márton at Vigszinház. Hungary: Budapest. 1986. Lang.:
Hun.   1807
Etcetera Theatre (London)
Performance/production
Collection of newspaper reviews by London theatre critics. UK-
England: London. 1987. Lang.: Eng.   2233
Collection of newspaper reviews by London theatre critics. UK-
England: London. 1987. Lang.: Eng.   2239
Collection of newspaper reviews by London theatre critics. UK-
England: London. 1987. Lang.: Eng.   2249
Collection of newspaper reviews by London theatre critics. UK-
England: London. 1987. Lang.: Eng.   2264
Collection of newspaper reviews by London theatre critics. UK-
England: London. 1987. Lang.: Eng.   2276
Eterno femenino, El (Eternal Feminine, The)
Plays/librettos/scripts
Feminist themes in Rosario Castellanos' *El eterno femenino (The
Eternal Feminine)*. Mexico. Lang.: Spa.   2694
Ethel Barrymore Theatre (New York, NY)
Performance spaces
Broadway theatres given landmark status. USA: New York, NY.
1982. Lang.: Eng.   692
Etherege, George
Plays/librettos/scripts
Name and entitlement in Dryden, Wycherley and Etherege. England.
1500-1699. Lang.: Eng.   2526
Independence of Restoration women is reflected in comic heroines.
England. 1668-1700. Lang.: Eng.   2550
Ethics
Administration
Literal and imaginative perceptions of work. USA. 1986. Lang.: Eng.
                                                                           199
Performance/production
Director Anatolij Efros on directing, ethics. USSR: Moscow. 1981-
1982. Lang.: Rus.   1033
Creative and moral problems of a theatre collective. USSR: Moscow.
1986-1988. Lang.: Rus.   1045
Difference between directing actors and puppeteers, responsibility of
children's theatre. Sweden. 1987. Lang.: Swe.   3981
Plays/librettos/scripts
Structure of revenge tragedy in Shakespeare's *Hamlet*. 1600. Lang.:
Eng.   2425
The quest in plays of I.L. Sel'vinskij. USSR. 1899-1968. Lang.: Rus.
                                                                           2955
Wagner's obsession with Jews and Judaism. Germany. 1813-1882.
Lang.: Eng.   3905
Relation to other fields
Role of theatre in moral education. USSR. 1987. Lang.: Rus.   1296
Playwright A. Gelman on perestrojka. USSR. 1986-1987. Lang.: Rus.
                                                                           3009
Ethnic dance
SEE ALSO
Classed Entries under DANCE.
Performance/production
History and description of a performance of *Cavittunatakam*, a
drama recounting lives of the saints. India: Kerala. 1984. Lang.:
Eng.   1480
Complete description of all aspects of *Wayang wong*. Indonesia. 930-
1986. Lang.: Eng.   1481

Ethnic dance — cont'd

Dan-o festival of folk performances. Korea. 800-1987. Lang.: Kor.
3296

Relation to other fields
Analysis of the role of tradition in theatrical forms of different cultures. Asia. Africa. 1985. Lang.: Fre. 1218

Ethnic Folk Arts Center (New York, NY)
Institutions
Profile of Ethnic Folk Arts Center. USA: New York, NY. 1966-1984. Lang.: Eng. 611

Ethnic theatre
Basic theatrical documents
Six plays detailing the Hispanic experience in the United States. USA. Mexico. 1987. Lang.: Eng. 1581

Institutions
Two community-based popular theatre projects. Canada. 1987. Lang.: Eng. 522

Brief history of HaBimah. Russia: Moscow. Israel. 1912-1980. Lang.: Hun. 557

Interview with Rodrigo Duarte of Teatro de la Esperanza. USA: Santa Barbara, CA. 1971-1983. Lang.: Eng. 597

History and goals of Cherry Creek Theatre. USA: St. Peter, MN. 1979-1983. Lang.: Eng. 598

Debate among Black theatre people whether Black theatre really exists. USA. 1987. Lang.: Eng. 610

Profile of Ethnic Folk Arts Center. USA: New York, NY. 1966-1984. Lang.: Eng. 611

Visit to the El-Hakawati theatre, an independent performance group, specializing in theatre for and about the Palestinians. Israel: Jerusalem. 1982-1985. Lang.: Swe. 1622

Profile of community theatre Grenland Friteater. Norway: Porsgrunn. 1982. Lang.: Eng. 1627

Profile of Ecotheatre and its artistic director Maryat Lee. USA: Hinton, WV. 1951-1983. Lang.: Eng. 1651

Performance spaces
History of the Alice Arts Center, new home of the Oakland Ensemble Theatre. USA: Oakland, CA. 1983-1987. Lang.: Eng. 696

Celebration of the birthday of the HaBimah Theatre. Israel: Tel Aviv. 1917-1987. Lang.: Heb. 1669

Performance/production
Hungarian-language theatre in an ethnic Hungarian region of Czechoslovakia. Czechoslovakia: Kosice, Komarno. 1953-1987. Lang.: Hun. 769

History of Hausa theatre. Niger, Republic of. 1876-1982. Lang.: Eng. 865

Comprehensive survey of Romansh theatre. Switzerland. 1984-1987. Lang.: Ger. 894

Overview of Mexican-American theatre. USA. Mexico. 1850-1987. Lang.: Eng. 946

Honda Yasuji's work on Japanese folk theatre. Japan. 1930-1986. Lang.: Eng. 1483

Listing of Walloon theatre performances, winners of the Grand Prix du Roi Albert. Belgium. 1932-1987. Lang.: Fre. 1682

Black theatre in South Africa: influence of traditional forms. South Africa, Republic of. England: London. USA: New York, NY. 1586-1987. Lang.: Eng. 2005

Xhosa story-telling uses verbal dramatization and language of gesture. South Africa, Republic of. 1987. Lang.: Eng. 3266

Celebration of Chinese Lunar New Year: Lion dancing and its martial arts background. USA: New York, NY. 1987. Lang.: Eng. 3334

Performance of Soviet Musical Jewish Chamber Theatre. Hungary: Budapest. USSR: Birobidjan. 1987. Lang.: Hun. 3401

Survival of Flemish puppet theatre. Belgium: Antwerp. 1812-1987. Lang.: Eng. 3970

Work of Bruno Leone and his attempts to re-establish the Neapolitan culture of Guaratelle. Italy: Naples. 1979-1987. Lang.: Eng. 3976

Plays/librettos/scripts
Italo-Australian drama, in English and Italian. Australia. 1860-1986. Lang.: Eng. 2443

History of Yiddish theatre and development of its plays. Europe. USA. 1853-1960. Lang.: Heb. 2562

Ethnic roots in *De la calle (Of the Street)* by Jesús Gonzalez-Davila. Mexico: Mexico City. 1987. Lang.: Spa. 2699

Wole Soyinka's treatment of political themes. Nigeria. 1973-1987. Lang.: Eng. 2705

Use of English in Nigerian drama. Nigeria. 1940-1987. Lang.: Eng. 2706

Themes in the Festival of Latin Theatre. USA: New York, NY. Latin America. Spain. 1987. Lang.: Spa. 2847

Irish assimilation in plays of Edward Everett Rose. USA. 1900-1920. Lang.: Eng. 2861

Influences of Spanish-language theatre on Chicano theatre. USA. 1598-1983. Lang.: Eng. 2874

Irish influence on American theatre through Irish-American playwrights. USA. 1839-1901. Lang.: Eng. 2889

Influence of Yiddish and Jewish theatre on mainstream American theatre. USA: New York, NY. 1881-1987. Lang.: Eng. 2913

Relation to other fields
Influences of Black political and economic life on literature, performance. South Africa, Republic of. 1970-1987. Lang.: Eng. 1252

Development of theatre influenced by myths of national character. Finland. 1950-1982. Lang.: Eng. 2989

History of puppetry in Catalonia. Spain-Catalonia. 500 B.C.-1987 A.D. Lang.: Eng. 3996

Theory/criticism
Semiotic production in popular performance. South Africa, Republic of. 1980. Lang.: Eng. 1347

Training
Proposed changes in teaching methodology to include indigenous drama. South Africa, Republic of. 1960-1987. Lang.: Eng. 1383

Euripides
Performance/production
Plays of Pinget, Euripides and Théâtre du Rideau staged by Jouanneau, Suzuki and Tanguy, Théâtre de la Bastille. France: Paris. 1987. Lang.: Fre. 1753

Collection of newspaper reviews by London theatre critics. UK-England: London. 1986. Lang.: Eng. 2079

Collection of newspaper reviews by London theatre critics. UK-England: London. 1986. Lang.: Eng. 2105

Collection of newspaper reviews by London theatre critics. UK-England: London. 1987. Lang.: Eng. 2250

Plays/librettos/scripts
Compares tragedies of Sophocles and Euripides with those of Eugene O'Neill. 1918-1946. Lang.: Eng. 2409

Greek poetic drama through Nietzschean theory. Greece. 1987. Lang.: Eng. 2620

Study of classical Greek dramaturgy. Greece. 472-388 B.C. Lang.: Hun. 2623

Study of works by Sophocles, Aeschylus and Euripides. Greece. 400 B.C.-500 A.D. Lang.: Eng. 2624

Euripides' use of *deus ex machina* in *Orestes*. Greece. 408 B.C. Lang.: Eng. 2626

Comparison of Shakespeare's *Julius Caesar* to the drama and vision of Euripides. UK-England. 500 B.C.-1599 A.D. Lang.: Eng. 2760

Theory/criticism
Catalan translation of Lessing's *Hamburgische Dramaturgie*. Germany: Hamburg. 1767-1769. Lang.: Cat. 3043

Europe, James Resse
Performance/production
Origins of jazz, its evolution in vaudeville. USA: New Orleans, LA, New York, NY, Chicago, IL. Lang.: Eng. 3650

European Youth Theatre Encounter (Stratford, UK)
Performance/production
A report from the first European Youth theatre encounter. UK-England: Stratford. 1987. Lang.: Swe. 910

Eurydice
Performance/production
Reviews of two Anouilh plays: *Eurydice* directed by János Szűcs, *Colombe* directed by Mátyás Giricz. Hungary: Miskolc, Budapest. 1987. Lang.: Hun. 1827

Anouilh's *Eurydice*, Vian's *Tête de Méduse (Medusa Head)* at National Theatre of Miskolc. Hungary: Miskolc. 1987. Lang.: Hun. 1888

Evans, George Essex
Plays/librettos/scripts
Essex Evans' adaptations of *Robinson Crusoe* and *Musical Whist*. Australia. 1891-1902. Lang.: Eng. 2439

Experimental theatre — cont'd

Introduction to article on paratheatre. USA. 1987. Lang.: Eng. 971

A Green Party that mixes politics, experimental theatre. USA: New Haven, CT. 1983-1987. Lang.: Eng. 973

Oleg Tabakov's experimental group 'Echo'. USSR. 1980-1987. Lang.: Rus. 1001

Theatre sociologist's view of theatrical work and experimentation. USSR. 1986-1988. Lang.: Rus. 1006

Problems of theatrical experimentation. USSR. 1986-1988. Lang.: Rus. 1011

Creativity in experimental theatre. USSR. 1986-1988. Lang.: Rus. 1015

Moscow Lenin Comsomol's 'Debut', an experimental group. USSR: Moscow. 1987. Lang.: Rus. 1018

Director of Gorkij Theatre on theatrical experimentation. USSR. 1986-1988. Lang.: Rus. 1044

Creative and moral problems of a theatre collective. USSR: Moscow. 1986-1988. Lang.: Rus. 1045

Links between experimental theatre movement and the Russian Futurists. USSR. 1920-1929. Lang.: Rus. 1058

Director Anne Bogart's production of *Women and Men: A Big Dance.* USA: New York, NY. 1983. Lang.: Eng. 1418

N.M. Foregger's experimental dance performances. USSR. 1920-1929. Lang.: Rus. 1445

Teatro Arena de São Paulo's production of *Arena Conta Zumbi*. Brazil: São Paulo. 1965. Lang.: Eng. 1690

Overview of theatre in Ottawa. Canada: Ottawa, ON. 1960-1983. Lang.: Eng. 1719

Experimental theatre opening new possibilities in Cuban drama. Cuba. 1920-1986. Lang.: Spa. 1724

Events and debates at the ISTA Congress. Denmark: Holstebro. 1986. Lang.: Eng. 1729

Photo essay on theatre company Billedstofteater. Denmark. 1977-1982. Lang.: Eng. 1730

Life Service Theatre experiment in topical theatre. Finland: Oulu. 1986. Lang.: Swe. 1749

Company members of Centre International de Recherche Théâtrale discuss *The Mahabharata*. France: Paris. 1986. Lang.: Eng. 1752

Franz Xaver Kroetz's *Wunschkonzert (Request Concert)* transposed to Calcutta. India: Calcutta. 1980. Lang.: Eng. 1930

Experimental theatre groups in Mexico City. Mexico: Mexico City. 1987. Lang.: Spa. 1975

Review of *El Balcón*: production of Genet's *Le Balcon (The Balcony)*. Mexico: Mexico City. 1987. Lang.: Spa. 1978

Postwar Dutch theatre: growth of small theatre groups. Netherlands. 1975-1985. Lang.: Dut. 1982

Teatr Prowizorium: interview with director Janusz Oprynski. Poland: Lublin. 1971-1987. Lang.: Eng. 1990

Experimental theatre at the Stary in three recent productions. Poland: Cracow. 1987. Lang.: Eng. 1999

Director Robert Wilson, his *CIVIL warS* and connecting *Knee Plays*. USA. 1979-1987. Lang.: Swe. 3274

Critical discussion of the Ultimatum II festival. Canada: Montreal, PQ. 1987. Lang.: Eng. 3346

Artists Beth Escott and Tom Zanarini present *The Way We Are At Home* at the Clybourn Salon. USA: Chicago, IL. 1981. Lang.: Eng. 3364

Plays/librettos/scripts

Playwright Alfonso Vallejo's world view. Spain. 1976-1986. Lang.: Pol. 1156

Experiments of Moscow Children's Theatre. USSR: Moscow. 1986-1987. Lang.: Rus. 1185

Genre and stylistic innovation in new Ukrainian dramaturgy. USSR. 1980-1987. Lang.: Rus. 1424

New interpretation of Toller's *Masse Mensch*. Germany. 1921-1987. Lang.: Eng. 2592

Munch's influence on Strindberg. Germany: Berlin. 1892-1900. Lang.: Eng. 2596

Linguistic absurdism in *El Chinfónia burguesa (The Bourgeois Chinfonia)*. Nicaragua. 1987. Lang.: Spa. 2703

Space and audience-performer relationship–examples from Ellen Sebastian and Maria Irene Fornes. USA. 1950-1980. Lang.: Eng. 2838

Development of themes and characters in plays of Sam Shepard. USA. 1960-1987. Lang.: Eng. 2853

Analysis of text of Samuel Beckett's *Rockaby* as literature and performance piece. USA. 1982. Lang.: Eng. 2884

Relation to other fields

Impact of politics upon funding of theatre. Denmark. 1722-1982. Lang.: Eng. 2986

Development of theatre influenced by myths of national character. Finland. 1950-1982. Lang.: Eng. 2989

Research/historiography

Expansion, diversification and artistic innovation in the American theatre. USA. 1961-1986. Lang.: Eng. 1302

Theory/criticism

Theorist Herbert Blau on modern theatre. 1960-1987. Lang.: Eng. 1306

Re-evaluation of Brecht's alienation effect in the context of contemporary performances. 1960-1970. Lang.: Eng. 1310

Artaud's conception of theatre. France. 1896-1949. Lang.: Ger. 1333

Essays and reviews by Gordon Rogoff. USA. 1960-1986. Lang.: Eng. 1366

Expo '86 (Vancouver, BC)
Administration

Effect of hosting a World's Fair on region. Canada. 1986. Lang.: Eng. 3239

Institutions

Tabootenay, a collaborative street theatre troupe. Canada: Vancouver, BC. 1986. Lang.: Eng. 3380

Performance spaces

Five buildings in Canada Place, built for Expo '86. Canada: Vancouver, BC. 1986. Lang.: Eng. 3243

Vancouver's Expo '86: 14,000 performances. Canada: Vancouver, BC. 1986. Lang.: Eng. 3244

Performance/production

World's Fair, Vancouver Expo '86. Canada: Vancouver, BC. 1986. Lang.: Eng. 3252

Carmen presented at Expo '86. Canada: Vancouver, BC. 1986. Lang.: Eng. 3751

Expressionism
Institutions

Impact of German expressionist theatre. UK-England. USA. Germany. 1910-1940. Lang.: Eng. 1648

Plays/librettos/scripts

New interpretation of Toller's *Masse Mensch*. Germany. 1921-1987. Lang.: Eng. 2592

Munch's influence on Strindberg. Germany: Berlin. 1892-1900. Lang.: Eng. 2596

Theory/criticism

Comparison of Ball's *Michelangelo's Nose* and Hebbel's *Michel Angelo*. Germany. 1886-1927. Lang.: Eng. 3042

Shift of August Strindberg from naturalism to expressionism. Sweden. 1987. Lang.: Eng. 3061

Exter, Alexandra
Design/technology

Set and costume designs of major designers. UK-England. 1902-1980. Lang.: Eng. 376

Performance/production

Career of choreographer/dancer Bronislava Nižinska. France. USA. 1891-1930. Lang.: Eng. 1436

Eye, The
Basic theatrical documents

English translations of contemporary African plays. Senegal. Zaire. 1987. Lang.: Eng. 1566

Eyre, Richard
Performance/production

Collection of newspaper reviews by London theatre critics. UK-England: London. 1986. Lang.: Eng. 2131

Collection of newspaper reviews by London theatre critics. UK-England: London. 1986. Lang.: Eng. 2167

Collection of newspaper reviews by London theatre critics. UK-England: London. 1987. Lang.: Eng. 2187

Revival of *Revizor (The Government Inspector)* at the National Theatre directed by Richard Eyre. UK-England: London. USSR. 1985. Lang.: Eng. 2290

Eyre, Ronald
Institutions

Recent work by the National Theatre of Great Britain. UK-England: London. 1985-1987. Lang.: Eng. 568

Fabregas, Virginia
Performance/production
Retrospective of two centuries of Hispanic theatre. USA. 1598-1965.
Lang.: Eng. 2345

Fabulazzo osceno (Obscene Fables)
Performance/production
Collection of newspaper reviews by London theatre critics. UK-
England: London. 1987. Lang.: Eng. 2209

Facing North
Plays/librettos/scripts
Interview with playwright John Boyd: influences and plays. UK-
Ireland: Belfast. 1930-1985. Lang.: Eng. 2828

Facundia
Performance/production
Analysis of the play *Facundia*. Argentina: Buenos Aires. 1981. Lang.:
Spa. 1679

Facundia, Miranda
Performance/production
Analysis of the play *Facundia*. Argentina: Buenos Aires. 1981. Lang.:
Spa. 1679

Fadren (Father, The)
Performance/production
Fadren (The Father) by August Strindberg presented under the title
Az apa at Katona József Theatre, guest director Kalle Holmberg.
Hungary: Budapest. 1987. Lang.: Hun. 1865
Plays/librettos/scripts
Munch's influence on Strindberg. Germany: Berlin. 1892-1900. Lang.:
Eng. 2596
Theory/criticism
Shift of August Strindberg from naturalism to expressionism. Sweden.
1987. Lang.: Eng. 3061

Fagon, Alfred
Performance/production
Collection of newspaper reviews by London theatre critics. UK-
England: London. 1987. Lang.: Eng. 2208

Fail/Safe
Performance/production
Collection of newspaper reviews by London theatre critics. UK-
England: London. 1986. Lang.: Eng. 2093

Fair Maid of the West, The
Performance/production
Collection of newspaper reviews by London theatre critics. UK-
England: London. 1987. Lang.: Eng. 2211

Fairgrounds
Performance spaces
Performance space of traditional Korean theatre. Korea. 57 B.C.
Lang.: Kor. 659
Original performing area of Korean mask theatre. Korea. 57 B.C.-
1987 A.D. Lang.: Kor. 660
Vancouver's Expo '86: 14,000 performances. Canada: Vancouver,
BC. 1986. Lang.: Eng. 3244
Performance/production
Puppetry on the streets and fairgrounds. France. 1800-1899. Lang.:
Eng. 3258

Faison, George
Performance/production
The career of dancer/choreographer Katherine Dunham. USA: New
York, NY, Chicago, IL, Las Vegas, NV. 1909-1987. Lang.: Eng.
1412

Faith Healer
Plays/librettos/scripts
Themes of Brian Friel's plays. Ireland. 1929-1987. Lang.: Eng. 2638

Fàlaris
Basic theatrical documents
Text and analysis of *Fàlaris* and *Orfeu* by Llorenç Moyà. Spain.
1968-1981. Lang.: Cat. 1569

Falco, Raul
Plays/librettos/scripts
Comparison of the plays *Todo sucede en una noche (It All Happens
in One Night)* and *La rosa del tiempo (The Rose of Time)*. Mexico:
Mexico City. 1987. Lang.: Spa. 2698

Fall of Mortimer, The
Plays/librettos/scripts
Attack on Sir Robert Walpole in 18th-century adaptation of *King
Edward the Third*. England. 1691-1731. Lang.: Eng. 2505

Falla, Manuel de
Plays/librettos/scripts
Life and career of Manuel de Falla: his opera *Atlántida*. Spain:
Madrid. France: Paris. 1876-1946. Lang.: Ger. 3930

Fallen
Performance/production
Collection of newspaper reviews by London theatre critics. UK.
1987. Lang.: Eng. 2031

Falling Prey
Performance/production
Collection of newspaper reviews by London theatre critics. UK-
England: London. 1987. Lang.: Eng. 2221

Falls, Robert
Performance/production
Influence and impact of the electronic media, live theatre experience.
USA: Los Angeles, CA. 1987. Lang.: Eng. 959

False Confidences
SEE
Fausses confidences, Les.

Falstaff
Performance/production
Initial recordings of Verdi's operas. Italy. France. USA. 1900-1945.
Lang.: Eng. 3800
Background on San Francisco opera radio broadcasts. USA: San
Francisco, CA. 1987. Lang.: Eng. 3833
Plays/librettos/scripts
Analysis and success of Boito's libretto for Verdi's opera *Falstaff*.
Italy. 1893. Lang.: Eng. 3923

Family Spear
Plays/librettos/scripts
Analysis of the plays of E.N. Ziramu. Uganda: Buganda. 1962-1974.
Lang.: Eng. 2748

Family Voices
Plays/librettos/scripts
Interpreting Harold Pinter's dramas through focus on his play
structures. UK-England. 1958-1987. Lang.: Eng. 2815

Famine
Plays/librettos/scripts
Theatrical language in the plays of Thomas Murphy. Ireland. 1961-
1984. Lang.: Eng. 2640
Comic characters and the Book of Job in the plays of Thomas
Murphy. Ireland. 1962-1983. Lang.: Eng. 2648
The plays of Thomas Murphy. Ireland: Dublin. 1962-1986. Lang.:
Eng. 2650
The myth of the idyllic peasant life in the plays of Thomas
Murphy. Ireland. 1961-1986. Lang.: Eng. 2652
Historical accuracy of characters in the plays of Thomas Murphy.
Ireland. 1962-1986. Lang.: Eng. 2657

Fanal, Le (Lantern, The)
Plays/librettos/scripts
Life and works of French dramatist Gabriel Marcel. France. 1889-
1973. Lang.: Eng. 2573

Fanciulla del West, La
Plays/librettos/scripts
Floral imagery in the operas of Giacomo Puccini. Italy. 1858-1924.
Lang.: Eng. 3926

Fanny Kemble At Home
Performance/production
Collection of newspaper reviews by London theatre critics. UK-
England: London. 1986. Lang.: Eng. 2130

Fanny's First Play
Plays/librettos/scripts
Bakhtinian analysis of *Fanny's First Play* by Shaw. UK-England.
1911-1916. Lang.: Eng. 2775

Fantasia dei brighenti (Fantasy of the Brighenti)
Plays/librettos/scripts
Playwright and actor Andrea Calmo. Italy. 1552-1553. Lang.: Ita.
2678

Farago, Peter
Performance/production
Collection of newspaper reviews by London theatre critics. UK-
England: London. 1986. Lang.: Eng. 2156
Theory/criticism
Stewart Parker's *Northern Star*. UK-Ireland. 1984. Lang.: Eng. 3065

Farce
Plays/librettos/scripts
Sam Shepard's *True West* as a farce in the guise of serious drama.
USA. 1981. Lang.: Eng. 2887
Theory/criticism
Comic space from the ancient Greeks to the present. Europe. USA.
Greece. 400 B.C.-1987 A.D. Lang.: Eng. 3032

Farce — cont'd

Perceptions of tragedy and new perspective on its analysis. USA.
UK-England. Greece. 500 B.C.-1987 A.D. Lang.: Eng.   3066

Farce of Master Pierre Pathelin, The
SEE
Farce de Maître Pierre Pathelin, La.

Farewell My Lovely
Institutions
National Theatre of the Deaf productions of *Farewell My Lovely*
and *In a Grove* directed by Arvin Brown in Beijing. China, People's
Republic of: Beijing. USA. 1986-1987. Lang.: Eng.   1611

Farewell Performance
Performance/production
The 4th International Festival of Street Theatres. Poland: Jelenia
Góra. 1986. Lang.: Eng, Fre.   3355

Fargas, Antonio
Institutions
The formation of the North Carolina Black Repertory Company.
USA: Winston-Salem, NC. 1979-1987. Lang.: Eng.   1666

Farm, The
Plays/librettos/scripts
Interview with playwright John Boyd: influences and plays. UK-
Ireland: Belfast. 1930-1985. Lang.: Eng.   2828

Farmer, Frances
Performance/production
Interview with composer Jack Eric Williams, focus on his musical
Mrs. Farmer's Daughter. USA: New York, NY. 1987. Lang.: Eng.
3663

Farquhar, George
Performance/production
Collection of newspaper reviews by London theatre critics. UK-
England: London. 1986. Lang.: Eng.   2082

Farr, Florence
Performance/production
Aubrey Beardsley's drawings of actresses: impact on society. UK-
England: London. 1890. Lang.: Eng.   2287

Farrell, Bernard
Performance/production
TEAM, an educational theatre company. Ireland: Dublin. 1984-1987.
Lang.: Eng.   818

Fascinating Aida
Performance/production
Collection of newspaper reviews by London theatre critics. UK-
England: London. 1987. Lang.: Eng.   2185

Fascism
Plays/librettos/scripts
Modern theatrical treatment of Fascism and the Holocaust. 1980-
1987. Lang.: Eng.   2428

Fassbinder, Rainer Werner
Plays/librettos/scripts
Four German playwrights: Fleisser, Sperr, Kroetz, Fassbinder.
Germany. 1900-1987. Lang.: Ita.   2602

Fathers and Sons
Performance/production
Collection of newspaper reviews by London theatre critics. UK-
England: London. 1987. Lang.: Eng.   2269

Fathers Day
Performance/production
Collection of newspaper reviews by London theatre critics. UK-
England: London. 1987. Lang.: Eng.   2204

Faulkner, Trater
Performance/production
Collection of newspaper reviews by London theatre critics. UK-
England: London. 1986. Lang.: Eng.   2138

Faulkner, William
Plays/librettos/scripts
Eugene O'Neill's influence on William Faulkner. USA: New York,
NY. 1920-1962. Lang.: Eng.   2858

Faust
Performance/production
The 4th International Theatre Conference: includes list of
participants and their contributions. Poland: Warsaw. 1986. Lang.:
Eng, Fre.   873

Collection of newspaper reviews by London theatre critics. UK-
England: London. 1987. Lang.: Eng.   2178

Plays/librettos/scripts
Debate over Hanns Eisler's opera *Johann Faustus*. Germany, East:
Berlin, East. 1949-1955. Lang.: Ger.   3913

Faust II
Performance/production
Leonard Steckel's production of *Faust II* as a turning point of Swiss
theatre. Switzerland: Zürich. 1949. Lang.: Ger.   2028

Fay, Léontine
Performance/production
Child actors in juvenile companies, Comédie-Française. France: Paris.
1769-1850. Lang.: Eng.   1756

Federació Catalana de Societats de Teatre Amateur (Catalonia)
Institutions
Memoir of the papers and debates organized at the First Congress
of Amateur Theatre in Catalonia. Spain-Catalonia. 1850-1685. Lang.:
Cat.   560

Federació de Teatre Amateur de Catalunya (Catalonia)
Institutions
Memoir of the papers and debates organized at the First Congress
of Amateur Theatre in Catalonia. Spain-Catalonia. 1850-1685. Lang.:
Cat.   560

Federal Theatre Project
Institutions
The Federal Theatre Project's California Puppetry Unit. USA: San
Francisco, CA. 1934-1987. Lang.: Eng.   3966

History of Chessé Marionettes. USA. 1927-1987. Lang.: Eng.   4000

Performance/production
Autobiography of director, producer and writer John Houseman.
USA: New York, NY. 1935-1985. Lang.: Eng.   2339

Federal Theatre Project (Washington, DC)
Institutions
Production bulletins of the Federal Theatre Project. USA. 1936-1939.
Lang.: Eng.   1654

Fefu and Her Friends
Plays/librettos/scripts
Space and audience-performer relationship—examples from Ellen
Sebastian and Maria Irene Fornes. USA. 1950-1980. Lang.: Eng.
2838

Fehling, Jurgen
Performance/production
Politics and Shakespeare in Weimar Republic. Germany. 1919-1930.
Lang.: Eng.   1775

Feiffer, Jules
Plays/librettos/scripts
Interview with cartoonist-playwright Jules Feiffer. USA. 1950-1987.
Lang.: Eng.   1168

Feinstein, Elaine
Performance/production
Collection of newspaper reviews by London theatre critics. UK-
England: London. 1987. Lang.: Eng.   2215

Feldman, Peter
Performance/production
Peter Feldman's techniques for training actors. North America. 1987.
Lang.: Eng.   867

Feminism
Administration
Sexual discrimination in American theatres. USA: New York, NY.
1976-1984. Lang.: Eng.   133

Performance/production
History of experimental and alternative theatre. UK-England. 1800-
1987. Lang.: Eng.   904

Relationship of theatre, class and gender. UK-England. USA. 1969-
1985. Lang.: Eng.   918

Dance/lecture focusing on images of gender in dance. USA. 1987.
Lang.: Eng.   1415

Roles of women in the field of ballet. France. USA. 1720-1987.
Lang.: Eng.   1434

Role of feminist in cultural critique. India. USA. 1983-1987. Lang.:
Eng.   1496

Popular theatre, mostly on economic, feminist themes. Canada:
Sudbury, ON. 1930-1987. Lang.: Eng.   1709

Events and debates at the ISTA Congress. Denmark: Holstebro.
1986. Lang.: Eng.   1729

Aubrey Beardsley's drawings of actresses: impact on society. UK-
England: London. 1890. Lang.: Eng.   2287

A survey/bibliography of nineteenth century women in theatre. USA.
1800-1900. Lang.: Eng.   2328

Transvestite roles in extravaganzas of J.R. Planché and Mme.
Vestris. UK-England: London. 1830-1870. Lang.: Eng.   3268

Feminism — cont'd

Festivals — cont'd

John Hirsch, artistic director of the Stratford Festival. Canada: Stratford, ON. 1982. Lang.: Eng.   16

Methods of funding the Edinburgh Festival. UK-Scotland: Edinburgh. 1982. Lang.: Eng.   57

Negative review of the Shaw Festival season. Canada: Niagara-on-the-Lake, ON. 1987. Lang.: Eng.   1514

Good performances and poor attendance at the Stratford Festival. Canada: Stratford, ON. 1987. Lang.: Eng.   1516

Government funding for Expo '86. Canada: Vancouver, BC. 1986. Lang.: Eng.   3238

Effect of hosting a World's Fair on region. Canada. 1986. Lang.: Eng.   3239

Vatican court's withdrawal from festival promotion under Sixtus V. Italy: Rome. 1585-1595. Lang.: Ita.   3240

Filming Wagner's *Der Ring des Nibelungen* at Bayreuth. Germany, West: Bayreuth. Germany, West: Munich. 1980. Lang.: Eng.   3680

Audience
Low demand for summer theatre. Canada. 1964-1984. Lang.: Fre.   277

American response to Gardzienice Theatre Association. Poland: Gardzienice. 1666-1987. Lang.: Eng.   1536

Design/technology
Profile of designer Jim Plaxton. Canada: Toronto, ON. 1982. Lang.: Eng.   1587

Interview with designer Desmond Heeley. UK-England: London. USA: New York, NY. Canada: Stratford, ON. 1940-1984. Lang.: Eng.   1596

Institutions
A history of the Charlottetown Festival. Canada: Charlottetown, PE. 1965-1987. Lang.: Eng.   505

Aims and scope of the Olympic Arts Festival. Canada: Calgary, AB. 1987. Lang.: Eng.   507

The 1987 Edmonton Fringe Festival. Canada: Edmonton, AB. 1987. Lang.: Eng.   512

Critical discussion of the Chalmers Awards. Canada: Toronto, ON. 1987. Lang.: Eng.   513

The advantages and disadvantages of the Jesse Awards. Canada: Vancouver, BC. 1983. Lang.: Eng.   517

Analysis of co-productions between Saskatoon theatre companies. Canada: Saskatoon, SK. 1987. Lang.: Eng.   518

History of the Stratford Festival. Canada: Stratford, ON. 1953-1982. Lang.: Eng.   521

The Dora Mavor Moore theatre awards. Canada: Toronto, ON. 1987. Lang.: Eng.   523

Previews 1982 International Children's Festival. Canada: Toronto, ON. 1982. Lang.: Eng.   524

Texts and photos about the Teatre Grec. Spain-Catalonia: Barcelona. 1929-1986. Lang.: Cat.   558

Overview of the Vancouver Fringe Festival. Canada: Vancouver, BC. 1987. Lang.: Eng.   1604

Interview with Stratford Festival's artistic director John Neville. Canada: Stratford, ON. 1985-1986. Lang.: Eng.   1605

Colloquium on 'Brecht 30 Years After'. Canada: Toronto, ON. 1985. Lang.: Fre.   1607

1987 Vancouver Fringe Festival: specific performances. Canada: Vancouver, BC. 1987. Lang.: Eng.   1609

Brecht was the theme of the 1986 International Theatre Festival and Conference. Canada: Toronto, ON. 1986. Lang.: Fre.   1610

First festival of women's work in experimental theatre. UK-Wales: Cardiff. 1986. Lang.: Eng.   1649

Actors Theatre of Louisville's 'Classics in Context' festival. USA: Louisville, KY. 1986-1988. Lang.: Eng.   1657

Edinburgh Festival's productions less competitive. UK-Scotland: Edinburgh. 1987. Lang.: Eng.   3392

Summary review of spring 1987 international opera productions. 1987. Lang.: Eng.   3702

International survey and review of summer 1987 opera productions. 1987. Lang.: Eng.   3704

Calendar of international opera productions and broadcasts for 1988 winter season. 1988. Lang.: Eng.   3706

International survey of early 1987 opera productions. 1987. Lang.: Eng.   3707

International calendar of summer 1987 opera productions. 1987. Lang.: Eng.   3708

International calendar of fall 1987 opera productions. 1987. Lang.: Eng.   3709

Nicholas Goldschmidt's tenure as artistic director, Guelph Spring Festival. Canada: Guelph, ON. 1967-1987. Lang.: Eng.   3720

Performance spaces
Vancouver's Expo '86: 14,000 performances. Canada: Vancouver, BC. 1986. Lang.: Eng.   3244

Performance/production
Reviews of productions by Stratford Festival, Toronto companies. Canada: Toronto, ON, Stratford, ON. 1987. Lang.: Eng.   732

John Neville's first season as artistic director at the Stratford Festival. Canada: Stratford, ON. 1986. Lang.: Eng.   734

Overview of the 1987 Theatre Festival of the Americas. Canada: Montreal, PQ. 1987. Lang.: Eng.   740

Role of festivals in Canadian theatre. Canada. 1987. Lang.: Eng.   746

Review of International Brecht Festival. China, People's Republic of: Hong Kong. 1986. Lang.: Dut.   759

Criticism of Bayreuth festival. Germany: Bayreuth. 1876-1987. Lang.: Ger.   797

Plays presented at eleventh Seoul theatre festival. Korea: Seoul. 1987. Lang.: Kor.   852

Interviews with some Korean directors. Korea: Seoul. 1987. Lang.: Kor.   856

Children's theatre in Holland: financial, artistic growth. Netherlands. 1987. Lang.: Eng.   863

Role of theatre in the face of political turmoil. Nicaragua: Managua. Uganda. 1987. Lang.: Eng.   864

Impressions of Nordkalottfestivalen, conditions of Norwegian amateur theatre. Norway: Hammerfest. 1987. Lang.: Swe.   868

Festival of Polish plays. Poland: Wrocław. 1987. Lang.: Eng, Fre.   871

Interview with Polish playwright Tadeusz Kantor. Poland: Cracow. Germany, West: Kassel. Italy: Milan. Italy: Sicily. 1987. Lang.: Eng, Fre.   876

Report from a children's theatre festival. Sweden: Gothenburg. 1987. Lang.: Swe.   888

Theatre activities in Baden. Switzerland: Baden. 1967-1987. Lang.: Ger.   895

Open-air theatre and festivals. Switzerland. 1987. Lang.: Ger.   896

Role of festivals in Turkish theatre. Turkey. 1900-1987. Lang.: Ger.   897

History of the London International Festival of Theatre. UK-England: London. 1967-1987. Lang.: Eng.   906

New Vaudeville Festival. USA: San Francisco, CA. 1987. Lang.: Eng.   948

Overview of the Theatre of Nations Festival. USA: Baltimore, MD. 1981-1986. Lang.: Eng.   949

Los Angeles Theatre Center Festival of 1987. USA: Los Angeles, CA. 1987. Lang.: Eng.   966

Review of Baltic theatre festival. USSR. 1987. Lang.: Rus.   1050

Overview of the issues of 1986 Belorussian theatre festival. USSR. 1986. Lang.: Rus.   1054

Survey of the international theatre festival BITEF-88. Yugoslavia: Belgrade. 1986. Lang.: Rus.   1090

Yugoslav theatre festivals. Yugoslavia. 1900-1987. Lang.: Ger.   1093

Review, 'Le corps politique' festival. Canada: Montreal, PQ. 1986. Lang.: Fre.   1406

Outdoor summer series of dance and performance art. USA: New York, NY. 1984-1985. Lang.: Eng.   1413

International folk dance presentation: the folk play *Witches and Witchcraft*. Hungary: Szeged. 1987. Lang.: Hun.   1460

Brief history of the Latin American Theatre Festival. Argentina: Córdoba. 1984-1987. Lang.: Eng.   1680

Work of actor/director Augusto Boal. Canada: Sydney, NS. 1987. Lang.: Eng.   1694

Description of La Quinzaine theatre festival. Canada: Quebec, PQ. 1986. Lang.: Fre.   1696

Review of the 1984 Stratford Festival. Canada: Stratford, ON. 1984. Lang.: Eng.   1698

Festivals — cont'd

Review of 1984 Shaw Festival season. Canada: Niagara-on-the-Lake, ON. 1984. Lang.: Eng. 1699

Overview of the 1983 Stratford Festival. Canada: Stratford, ON. 1983. Lang.: Eng. 1700

Overview of the 1982 Stratford Festival. Canada: Stratford, ON. 1982. Lang.: Eng. 1701

Overview of the 1982 Shaw Festival. Canada: Niagara-on-the-Lake, ON. 1982. Lang.: Eng. 1703

La Quinzaine acting competition. Canada: Quebec, PQ. 1986-1986. Lang.: Fre. 1712

Day by day account of the 1986 Festival of Camagüey. Cuba: Camagüey. 1986. Lang.: Spa. 1725

Review of the 1986 Festival de la Francophonie. France. Belgium. 1986. Lang.: Fre. 1760

Antoine Vitez directs *Le soulier de satin* (*The Satin Slipper*) by Paul Claudel, Festival of Avignon. France: Avignon. 1987. Lang.: Fre. 1767

Shakespeare's *A Midsummer Night's Dream* staged by Tibor Csizmadia. Hungary: Eger, Szolnok. 1986. Lang.: Hun. 1881

Peter Sellars and American National Theatre present *Ajax*, Holland Festival. Netherlands. USA. 1987. Lang.: Dut. 1981

Companies and productions at Theatre Festival of the Americas. North America. South America. Central America. 1985. Lang.: Eng. 1985

Report from Portuguese amateur theatre festival. Portugal: Lisbon. 1987. Lang.: Swe. 2000

Review of Second Festival of Latin American Theatre. Spain: Córdoba. 1986. Lang.: Spa. 2008

Collection of theatre reviews by Xavier Fàbregas. Spain-Catalonia. 1969-1972. Lang.: Cat. 2010

Overview of theatre season. Spain-Catalonia: Barcelona. 1986-1987. Lang.: Cat. 2011

Västerås Amateur Theatre Festival. Sweden: Västerås. 1987. Lang.: Swe. 2023

The founding and history of the Malvern Festival. UK-England: Malvern. 1904-1977. Lang.: Eng. 2286

Teatropoesia, a combination of theatre and poetry. USA. 1974-1983. Lang.: Spa. 2368

Director Ljubiša Ristić and 'Shakespeare Fest '86'. Yugoslavia: Subotica, Palić. 1986. Lang.: Hun. 2403

Review of *Hamlet*, *Julius Caesar* and *Titus Andronicus* at 'Shakespeare Fest '86'. Yugoslavia: Palić. 1986. Lang.: Hun. 2405

'Shakespeare Fest '86' reviews. Yugoslavia: Palić. 1986. Lang.: Hun. 2407

San Francisco Mime Troupe's visit to Nicaragua's International Theatre Festival. Central America. 1986. Lang.: Eng. 3222

Latest technology at Amiga Studio Theatre, Canada Place. Canada: Vancouver, BC. 1986. Lang.: Eng. 3251

World's Fair, Vancouver Expo '86. Canada: Vancouver, BC. 1986. Lang.: Eng. 3252

Florentine festivals honoring St. John. Italy: Florence. 1000-1926. Lang.: Ita. 3261

Review of the 1987 Edinburgh Fringe Festival. UK-Scotland: Edinburgh. 1987. Lang.: Eng. 3271

Dan-o festival of folk performances. Korea. 800-1987. Lang.: Kor. 3296

Performance aspects of festivals in the Duchy of Parma. Italy: Parma. 1659-1807. Lang.: Ita. 3322

Description of annual *On-matsuri* festival at the Kasuga Wakamiya shrine. Japan: Nara. 1136-1987. Lang.: Eng. 3331

Description of Easter processions. Spain: Puente Genil. 1660-1987. Lang.: Eng. 3332

Critical discussion of the Ultimatum II festival. Canada: Montreal, PQ. 1987. Lang.: Eng. 3346

Egidio Alvaro and performance art festivals. Europe. 1974-1987. Lang.: Eng. 3349

Description of Rotterdam's 1986 Perfo Festival. Germany: Rotterdam. 1986. Lang.: Eng. 3352

Description of the *Myths, Monsters and Mutations* festival. Germany, West: Berlin, West. 1987. Lang.: Eng. 3353

Overview of the 8th Documenta festival. Germany, West: Kassel. 1987. Lang.: Eng. 3354

The 4th International Festival of Street Theatres. Poland: Jelenia Góra. 1986. Lang.: Eng, Fre. 3355

Description of London's National Review of Live Art festival. UK-England: London. 1987. Lang.: Eng. 3357

Description of Nottingham's National Review of Live Art festival. UK-England: Nottingham. 1986. Lang.: Eng. 3358

Overview of *New Work Newcastle '87* festival. UK-England: Newcastle. 1986-1987. Lang.: Eng. 3359

Overview of the 'Magdalena 86' festival. UK-Wales: Cardiff. 1986. Lang.: Eng. 3360

Goodman Theatre's series 'Celebration of Genius'. USA: Chicago, IL. 1986-1987. Lang.: Eng. 3409

Comments on the performances at the Chinese Art Festival. China, People's Republic of: Beijing. 1987. Lang.: Chi. 3501

Report from Salzburger Festspiele: Mozart's *Don Giovanni*, Schoenberg's *Moses und Aron*, Schmidt's *Das Buch mit sieben Siegeln*. Austria: Salzburg. 1987. Lang.: Swe. 3744

Violet Archer festival, premiere of her one-act opera *The Meal*. Canada: Edmonton, AB. 1985. Lang.: Eng. 3757

Bread and Puppet Theatre's annual festival. USA: Glover, VT. 1987. Lang.: Eng. 3986

Poland's puppet theatre. Poland: Wrocław, Białystock. Austria: Mistelbach. 1979-1987. Lang.: Eng, Fre. 4006

Plays/librettos/scripts

Interview with playwright Ping Chong. Canada: Montreal, PQ. USA: New York, NY. 1987. Lang.: Eng. 2472

Themes in the Festival of Latin Theatre. USA: New York, NY. Latin America. Spain. 1987. Lang.: Spa. 2847

One-act play: brief history and recent productions. USA. 1930-1987. Lang.: Eng. 2849

Influences of Spanish-language theatre on Chicano theatre. USA. 1598-1983. Lang.: Eng. 2874

Theme of aggression between fathers and sons: Zambian National Theatre Arts Association festival. Zambia. 1966-1987. Lang.: Eng. 2972

Reference materials

New Italian productions in all areas. Italy. 1985-1986. Lang.: Ita. 1204

Major festivals of Belgium: folklore, history, description. Belgium. 1987. Lang.: Fre. 3279

Relation to other fields

Popular theatre and non-governmental funding agencies. Canada: Sydney, NS. Jamaica. Sudan. 1987. Lang.: Eng. 2982

Effect of farming practices on folk theatre. Poland: Tarnogród. 1985-1987. Lang.: Eng. 3282

Elizabeth Jappe and the performance art program for the Documenta festival. Germany, West: Kassel. 1987. Lang.: Eng. 3371

Fetters

Performance/production

Four new productions in Poland. Poland: Warsaw. 1986-1987. Lang.: Eng, Fre. 1988

Fialka, Ladislav

Performance/production

Contemporary mime forms and their innovators. France: Paris. Belgium. USA. 1980-1982. Lang.: Eng. 3224

Fichandler, Zelda

Administration

Contracts, actors and union negotiations. USA. 1986. Lang.: Eng. 235

Fichte, Hubert

Performance/production

Italian translation of *Hubert Fichte Jean Genet*. Italy. 1975-1985. Lang.: Ita. 1942

Ficky Stingers

Performance/production

Collection of newspaper reviews by London theatre critics. UK-England: London. 1986. Lang.: Eng. 2162

Fiddler on the Roof

Performance/production

Director on staging amateur *Fiddler on the Roof*. Sweden: Bollnäs. 1987. Lang.: Swe. 3636

Field Day Theatre Company (Londonderry)

Performance/production

Productions and political philosophy of Field Day Theatre Company. UK-Ireland: Londonderry. 1986-1987. Lang.: Eng. 2309

Field, Crystal
Performance/production
Essays on the future of the theatre. USA: New York, NY. 1970-1987. Lang.: Eng. 955
Fielding, Henry
Plays/librettos/scripts
Henry Fielding rewrote *Tom Thumb* to satirize Lewis Theobald. England. 1730-1731. Lang.: Eng. 2535
Fields, Dorothy
Performance/production
Collection of newspaper reviews by London theatre critics. UK-England: London. 1986. Lang.: Eng. 2153
Fields, Herbert
Performance/production
Collection of newspaper reviews by London theatre critics. UK-England: London. 1986. Lang.: Eng. 2153
Fields, Joseph A.
Performance/production
Collection of newspaper reviews by London theatre critics. UK-England: London. 1986. Lang.: Eng. 2134
Fierstein, Harvey
Performance/production
Transformation of *La Cage aux Folles* from movie to a Broadway musical. USA: New York, NY. 1983-1987. Lang.: Eng. 940
Collection of newspaper reviews by London theatre critics. UK-England: London. 1986. Lang.: Eng. 2095
Collection of newspaper reviews by London theatre critics. UK-England: London. 1987. Lang.: Eng. 2203
Collection of newspaper reviews by New York theatre critics. USA: New York, NY. 1987. Lang.: Eng. 2322
Career of actor Lee Roy Reams. USA: New York, NY. 1987. Lang.: Eng. 3661
Fife, Graeme
Performance/production
Collection of newspaper reviews by London theatre critics. UK-England: London. 1987. Lang.: Eng. 2260
Fifth Column, The
Plays/librettos/scripts
The Spanish Civil War in works by Ernest Hemingway and Sean O'Casey. UK. Ireland. USA. 1930-1939. Lang.: Eng. 2749
Fifth Season
SEE
Quinta Temporada.
Fighting Kite
Performance/production
Collection of newspaper reviews by London theatre critics. UK-England: London. 1987. Lang.: Eng. 2265
Fighting Parson, The
Plays/librettos/scripts
New Canadian drama: non-realistic, anti-naturalistic. Canada. 1983-1984. Lang.: Eng. 2482
Figurative arts
Design/technology
Aesthetic influences on scene design. England. 1700-1899. Lang.: Eng. 1590

Performance/production
Introduction to articles on theatre and photography. USA. 1987. Lang.: Eng. 972
Script and staging of Shaliko's *The Yellow House.* USA: Baltimore, MD. 1982-1987. Lang.: Eng. 1487
Use of visual arts conventions in acting techniques. England. 1700. Lang.: Eng. 1735
Italian translation, Roy Strong, *Art and Power.* Europe. 1450-1650. Lang.: Ita. 3257

Plays/librettos/scripts
Edvard Munch's painting *Death in the Sickroom* used to demonstrate Albee's subject matter. USA. 1971-1987. Lang.: Eng. 2911

Relation to other fields
Translation of several essays from French. Italy. 1987. Lang.: Ita. 1243
Appearance and symbolism of New Guinea Mudmen. USA: Providence, RI, New York, NY. New Guinea. 1986-1987. Lang.: Eng. 1264
Interview with caricaturist Al Hirschfeld. USA: New York, NY. 1925-1981. Lang.: Eng. 1272

Theatricality in works of photographers Cindy Sherman and Edward Steichen. USA. 1900-1987. Lang.: Eng. 1289
Exhibition devoted to modern dancer Gret Palucca. Germany, East: Dresden. 1922-1987. Lang.: Ger. 1476
Satirical perceptions of George IV using Shakespeare as a frame of reference. UK-England: London. 1790-1827. Lang.: Eng. 3003
Assessment of arts on television. UK-England: London. 1983-1987. Lang.: Eng. 3216
Elizabeth Jappe and the performance art program for the Documenta festival. Germany, West: Kassel. 1987. Lang.: Eng. 3371
Relation of photographic records to the performance. UK. 1840-1987. Lang.: Eng. 3372
Theory/criticism
Rococo elements in the comedies of Marivaux. France. 1715-1774. Lang.: Eng. 3039
Fiji Company (New York)
Plays/librettos/scripts
Interview with playwright Ping Chong. Canada: Montreal, PQ. USA: New York, NY. 1987. Lang.: Eng. 2472
Filho, Antunes
Performance/production
Examination of modern Brazilian theatre focusing on plays by Nelson Rodrigues. Brazil. 1943-1984. Lang.: Eng. 1688
New regime ends theatrical censorship. Brazil. 1980-1984. Lang.: Spa. 1689
Filipiak, Paul
Performance/production
Collection of newspaper reviews by London theatre critics. UK-England: London. 1986. Lang.: Eng. 2076
Filla del Carmesí, La (Carmesí's Daughter)
Plays/librettos/scripts
General history of Catalan literature, including theatre. Spain-Catalonia. 1902-1961. Lang.: Cat. 1157
Fillis' Circus (Johannesburg)
Performance spaces
Theatres built, influences on design. South Africa, Republic of: Johannesburg. 1887-1940. Lang.: Afr. 667
Film
SEE ALSO
Classed Entries under MEDIA—Film.
Audience
Repercussions of cinema and television on theatrical language and practice. Europe. 1885-1985. Lang.: Cat. 281
Design/technology
Complete guide to make-up. Italy. 1987. Lang.: Ita. 346
Set and costume designs of major designers. UK-England. 1902-1980. Lang.: Eng. 376
Comparison of roles of sound designer in film and theatrical productions. USA. 1987. Lang.: Eng. 450
Institutions
Actor, union leader Michajl A. Ul'janov on social changes, their effect on theatre and film. USSR. 1970-1987. Lang.: Rus. 624
Performance/production
Influence of filmmaker Jean Renoir's techniques in the theatre. France. 1987. Lang.: Eng. 795
History of performance in Italy. Italy. Lang.: Ita. 839
Stage and screen actor Ljubov' Orlova. USSR: Moscow. 1902-1975. Lang.: Rus. 1055
Memoirs of actress Rina Zelenaja. USSR: Moscow. Lang.: Rus. 1084
Patrice Chéreau and Théâtre des Amandiers create stage and film versions of Čechov's *Platonov.* France: Nanterre. 1982-1987. Lang.: Swe. 1755
Career of actor, director, writer Zoltán Latinovits. Hungary. 1931-1986. Lang.: Hun. 1794
Interview with Péter Andorai. Hungary. 1980-1987. Lang.: Hun. 1799
Autobiography of film and stage director Peter Brook. UK-England. 1946-1987. Lang.: Eng. 2281
Brian Cox's work with the Royal Shakespeare Company. UK-England: Stratford, London. USA: New York, NY. 1968-1987. Lang.: Eng. 2284
Plays of A.M. Volodin on stage and screen. USSR: Moscow, Leningrad. 1950-1987. Lang.: Rus. 2401
History of incorporating film into a theatrical performance. USA: New York, NY. 1922-1987. Lang.: Eng. 3196

Film — cont'd

SUBJECT INDEX

Financial operations — cont'd

Influence of mergers and corporate takeovers on corporate giving. USA. 1985-1987. Lang.: Eng. 130

Marketing the concept of planned giving. USA. 1987. Lang.: Eng. 135

Crisis of financial survival in arts organizations. USA. 1976-1987. Lang.: Eng. 137

Economic analyses of arts organizations. USA. 1984. Lang.: Eng. 140

Marketing research methods as applied to specific areas of arts management. USA: Iowa City, IA. 1982. Lang.: Eng. 143

Art Museum Association of America's Computer Software Project. USA. 1981-1983. Lang.: Eng. 145

How to computerize your non-profit organization. USA: New York, NY. 1986. Lang.: Eng. 152

Effects of the 1986 Tax Reform Act on non-profit organizations. USA. 1986. Lang.: Eng. 153

Training volunteer fundraisers through role playing. USA. 1987. Lang.: Eng. 159

Competition between marketing and non-profit fundraising. USA: New York, NY. 1980-1987. Lang.: Eng. 164

Tax Reform Act of 1986 and how it affects theatre professionals. USA. 1987. Lang.: Eng. 166

Changes in tax laws affect Actors' Equity members. USA: New York, NY. 1982. Lang.: Eng. 170

Survey of financial results for nonprofit theatres. USA. 1986. Lang.: Eng. 173

Government funding of art. USA. 1980-1987. Lang.: Eng. 175

Self-hypnosis techniques for fundraising. USA: Los Angeles, CA. 1986-1987. Lang.: Eng. 178

Real estate alternatives for arts organizations. USA. 1982. Lang.: Eng. 180

Questions and answers regarding tax returns. USA: New York, NY. 1986-1987. Lang.: Eng. 183

The pros and cons of tax reform from the actor's point of view. USA. 1987. Lang.: Eng. 184

Information on artists' taxes. USA: New York, NY. 1986. Lang.: Eng. 185

Surviving an IRS tax audit. USA: New York, NY. 1987. Lang.: Eng. 186

Employees Witholding Allowance Certificate (W-4 Form): effect on actors. USA: New York, NY. 1987. Lang.: Eng. 187

1987 tax law and its impact on actors. USA: New York, NY. 1987. Lang.: Eng. 188

Broadway producer Dorothy Olim on commercial theatre. USA: New York, NY. 1983. Lang.: Eng. 189

Fiduciary responsibilities of the museum trustee. USA. 1987. Lang.: Eng. 192

Attempts to cut funding to the National Endowment for the Arts. USA. 1965-1985. Lang.: Eng. 194

Survey on what attracts volunteers. USA. 1987. Lang.: Eng. 202

Training volunteer fundraisers. USA. 1987. Lang.: Eng. 205

Techniques for attracting qualified volunteers. USA: New York, NY. 1987. Lang.: Eng. 207

Attracting volunteers to non-profit organizations. USA. 1987. Lang.: Eng. 212

Impact of the arts on the economy, politics and society. USA: Baton Rouge, LA. 1986. Lang.: Eng. 214

Financial analysis of problems facing American theatre. USA. 1987. Lang.: Eng. 219

Fundraising for Orange County Performing Arts Center. USA: Los Angeles, CA. 1980-1986. Lang.: Eng. 222

Advantages of planned giving to the donor's heirs. USA. 1985-1987. Lang.: Eng. 225

Techniques for securing planned gifts. USA. 1987. Lang.: Eng. 230

Supporting the arts through government-instituted tax programs. USA. 1987. Lang.: Eng. 231

Impact of new laws on nonprofit theatre funding. USA. 1984-1987. Lang.: Eng. 234

Donation of funds for arts buildings versus funding for artists themselves. USA. 1987. Lang.: Eng. 237

Instructions for Actors' Equity members regarding new regulations in unemployment. USA: New York, NY. 1982. Lang.: Eng. 240

Successful volunteers and their methods of fundraising. USA: Chicago, IL. 1987. Lang.: Eng. 243

Use of computers in planned giving. USA. 1987. Lang.: Eng. 247

Influence of Baumol/Bowen report on arts funding. USA. 1966-1985. Lang.: Eng. 248

Relationship of philanthropy to the arts and public policy. USA. 1987. Lang.: Eng. 251

Production sharing among non-profit theatres in effort to develop new works. USA. 1987. Lang.: Eng. 255

Debate over the National Endowment for the Arts' new guidelines. USA. 1977-1987. Lang.: Eng. 256

Economic questions of the theatrical experiment. USSR. 1986-1987. Lang.: Rus. 259

Problems of arts patronage, cooperation between theatres and businesses. USSR. 1987. Lang.: Rus. 260

Financial problems of theatres. USSR. 1986-1987. Lang.: Rus. 273

Ford Foundation's support for the field of dance. USA. 1984. Lang.: Eng. 1428

State of Irish theatre in Dublin and abroad. Ireland. UK. 1986. Lang.: Eng. 1519

Interview with NAPAC director Rodney Phillips. South Africa, Republic of. 1987. Lang.: Eng. 1523

Bequest program for Wisconsin Public Broadcasting. USA: Madison, WI. 1984-1987. Lang.: Eng. 3108

Interview with film director Miklós Jancsó. Hungary. 1987. Lang.: Hun. 3119

Government funding for Expo '86. Canada: Vancouver, BC. 1986. Lang.: Eng. 3238

Effect of hosting a World's Fair on region. Canada. 1986. Lang.: Eng. 3239

Recent court decision over the IRS tax laws affecting writers' deductions. USA. 1987. Lang.: Eng. 3241

Funding for performance art. UK-England. 1987. Lang.: Eng. 3338

Volunteer-staff relationships in the New York Philharmonic. USA: New York, NY. 1987. Lang.: Eng. 3387

Gordon Peter Getty, philanthropist, composer. USA: San Francisco, CA. 1987. Lang.: Eng. 3684

Financial crises of opera companies. USA. 1980-1987. Lang.: Eng. 3686

Basic theatrical documents

Percy family records in relation to Elizabethan theatre. England. 1582-1639. Lang.: Eng. 296

Institutions

Analysis of co-productions between Saskatoon theatre companies. Canada: Saskatoon, SK. 1987. Lang.: Eng. 518

Production of *Circé* by the Comédiens du Roy, Hôtel Guénégaud. France: Paris. 1673-1679. Lang.: Eng. 530

Difficulty in obtaining funding for theatre building repair. Ireland: Dublin, Cork. UK-Ireland: Belfast. 1965-1984. Lang.: Eng. 545

Meetings of various Dramatists' Guild committees, members' plays in production. USA: New York, NY. 1987. Lang.: Eng. 584

Conditions affecting Canadian opera composers. Canada. 1987. Lang.: Eng. 3714

Performance spaces

The lack of performance space for small theatre companies. Canada: Toronto, ON. 1987. Lang.: Eng. 629

Performance/production

The end of the out-of-town tryout system for Broadway openings. USA: New York, NY. 1965-1987. Lang.: Eng. 937

Overview of the 1983 Stratford Festival. Canada: Stratford, ON. 1983. Lang.: Eng. 1700

Overview of the 1982 Stratford Festival. Canada: Stratford, ON. 1982. Lang.: Eng. 1701

Overview of the 1982 Shaw Festival. Canada: Niagara-on-the-Lake, ON. 1982. Lang.: Eng. 1703

Postwar Dutch theatre: growth of small theatre groups. Netherlands. 1975-1985. Lang.: Dut. 1982

Classical theatre is diminishing in the provinces due to financial cutbacks. UK-England: London, Liverpool. UK-Scotland: Edinburgh. 1987. Lang.: Eng. 2301

Relation to other fields

Government funding of official theatre and opera companies. Switzerland. 1987. Lang.: Ger. 1256

Fliegende Holländer, Der — cont'd

Plays/librettos/scripts
Woman, salvation and love in operas of Richard Wagner. Germany. 1813-1883. Lang.: Eng. 3909

Flies By Night
Performance/production
Collection of newspaper reviews by London theatre critics. UK-England: London. 1986. Lang.: Eng. 2113

Flight
Performance/production
Collection of newspaper reviews by London theatre critics. UK-England: London. 1987. Lang.: Eng. 2274

Flight to Venice, The
Performance/production
Collection of newspaper reviews by London theatre critics. UK-England: London. 1986. Lang.: Eng. 2105

Flimm, Jürgen
Performance/production
The 4th International Theatre Conference: includes list of participants and their contributions. Poland: Warsaw. 1986. Lang.: Eng, Fre. 873

Fling, The
Performance/production
Collection of newspaper reviews by London theatre critics. UK-England: London. 1987. Lang.: Eng. 2274

Flood, Frank Hallinan
Design/technology
F.H. Flood's scene design for *The Merchant of Venice*. Ireland: Dublin. 1985. Lang.: Eng. 1593

Flora, the Red Menace
Performance/production
Two productions of *Flora, the Red Menace*. USA: New York, NY. 1965-1987. Lang.: Eng. 3640

Florence
Plays/librettos/scripts
Interview with playwright Alice Childress. USA: New York, NY, Baltimore, MD. 1987. Lang.: Eng. 2844

Florence, Norman
Performance/production
Collection of newspaper reviews by London theatre critics. UK-England: London. 1987. Lang.: Eng. 2269

Florence, Peter
Performance/production
Collection of newspaper reviews by London theatre critics. UK-England: London. 1987. Lang.: Eng. 2269

Flores de papel (Paper Flowers)
Plays/librettos/scripts
Egon Wolff's trilogy of plays focusing on Chilean bourgeoisie. Chile. 1964-1984. Lang.: Eng. 2490

Flying Karamazov Brothers
Performance/production
Evolution of the Flying Karamazov Brothers. USA. 1977-1987. Lang.: Eng. 3273

Fo, Dario
Performance/production
Acting manual by Dario Fo. Italy. 1987. Lang.: Ita. 827

Collection of newspaper reviews by London theatre critics. UK-England: London. 1986. Lang.: Eng. 2158

Collection of newspaper reviews by London theatre critics. UK-England: London. 1987. Lang.: Eng. 2209

Introduction to articles on art of theatrical clowning. USA. 1987. Lang.: Eng. 3304

Dario Fo's use of *commedia dell'arte*. Italy. 1550-1987. Lang.: Rus. 3313

Interview with Dario Fo. Netherlands. Italy. 1987. Lang.: Dut. 3814

Plays/librettos/scripts
Theme of political satire in plays of Fo and Gay. England: London. Italy. USA. 1728-1984. Lang.: Eng. 2548

Money, greed and power in plays by Fo, Churchill, Cacaci and Cormack. USA: New York, NY. 1987. Lang.: Eng. 2914

Fodor, Tamás
Performance/production
Örökösök (Heirs) by Gorkij directed by Tamás Fodor. Hungary: Szolnok. 1987. Lang.: Hun. 1818

Tamás Fodor directs *Örökösök (Heirs)* based on Gorkij's *Vassa Železnova*. Hungary: Szolnok. 1987. Lang.: Hun. 1848

Fohn
Institutions
Seven productions chosen for Theatertreffen '86. Germany: Berlin. 1986. Lang.: Eng. 1617

Fokin, Michajl
Performance/production
Development of dance. Germany: Berlin. 1920-1986. Lang.: Ger. 1407

Fokin, Valerij
Performance/production
Round-table of Soviet directors. USSR: Moscow. 1980-1987. Lang.: Rus. 989

Creativity in experimental theatre. USSR. 1986-1988. Lang.: Rus. 1015

Plays/librettos/scripts
Radsinskij's *Jogging* directed by Fokin. USSR: Moscow. 1987. Lang.: Eng. 2953

Folk puppetry
Performance/production
Korean folk puppetry using hands and feet. Korea, South. 1977. Lang.: Eng. 3977

Folklore
Institutions
Profile of Roadside Theatre: story-telling, use of folklore. USA. 1971-1983. Lang.: Eng. 599
Performance/production
Puppetry as an expression of popular and folk culture. USA. Italy. Belgium. Indonesia. 1987. Lang.: Eng. 3988
Reference materials
Major festivals of Belgium: folklore, history, description. Belgium. 1987. Lang.: Fre. 3279
Relation to other fields
Effect of farming practices on folk theatre. Poland: Tarnogród. 1985-1987. Lang.: Eng. 3282

History of puppet Nativity plays. Hungary. 1877-1967. Lang.: Hun. 3994
Theory/criticism
Aesthetics of the pleasure principle in comedy, folklore and literature. USA. 1982. Lang.: Eng. 1355

Folkteatergruppen (Stockholm)
Institutions
Folkteatergruppen's productions, including *Antigone-nu (Antigone Now)*. Sweden: Stockholm. 1917-1987. Lang.: Swe. 1640

Folkteatern i Gävleborgs län (Gävleborg)
Institutions
Folkteatern i Gävleborgs län: integration into the community. Sweden: Gävle. 1982-1987. Lang.: Swe. 1641

Follies
Performance/production
Collection of newspaper reviews of London theatre critics. UK-England: London. 1987. Lang.: Eng. 2273

Fontainebleau
Plays/librettos/scripts
New findings on 18th-century Irish comic playwright John O'Keeffe. Ireland. England: London. 1767-1798. Lang.: Eng. 2643

Fontanella, Francesc
Basic theatrical documents
Text of *Lo desengany (The Disappointment)* by Francesc Fontanella, with analysis. Spain-Catalonia: Barcelona. 1622-1680. Lang.: Cat. 1572

Fool for Love
Plays/librettos/scripts
Development of themes and characters in plays of Sam Shepard. USA. 1960-1987. Lang.: Eng. 2853

Evolution of female characters in the plays of Sam Shepard. USA. 1976-1987. Lang.: Eng. 2883

Development of Sam Shepard's plays in response to audience. USA. 1976-1986. Lang.: Eng. 2902

Sam Shepard's manipulation of an audience's desire to believe what it sees. USA. 1967-1983. Lang.: Eng. 2932

Fool, The
Performance/production
Edward Bond's *The Fool* under the title *A bolond* directed by László Salamon Suba at Móricz Zsigmond Theatre. Hungary: Nyíregyháza. 1986. Lang.: Hun. 1875

Reviews of Wilson's *Talley's Folly* staged by András Bálint and Bond's *The Fool* staged by László Salamon Suba. Hungary: Dunaujváros, Nyíregyháza. 1986. Lang.: Hun. 1902

For King and Country
Performance/production
Collection of newspaper reviews by London theatre critics. UK-England: London. 1986. Lang.: Eng. 2113

Forbes, Bryan
Performance/production
Collection of newspaper reviews by London theatre critics. UK-England: London. 1986. Lang.: Eng. 2055

Forbidden Broadway
Institutions
Record producer Bruce Yeko's accomplishments. USA: New York, NY. 1962-1981. Lang.: Eng. 3625

Force and Hypocrisy
Performance/production
Collection of newspaper reviews by London theatre critics. UK-England: London. 1986. Lang.: Eng. 2087

Ford, John
Performance/production
Play scripts as literary texts and as performance texts. UK-England. 1977-1987. Lang.: Eng. 905

Shakespeare and contemporaries: tradition, intertextuality in performance. England. 1607-1987. Lang.: Eng. 1740

New interpretation of Jacobean theatre. England: London. 1596-1633. Lang.: Eng. 1743

Theory/criticism
Trollope's writings on Elizabethan and Jacobean drama. UK-England. 1866-1882. Lang.: Eng. 3063

Ford, Maggie
Performance/production
Collection of newspaper reviews by London theatre critics. UK-England: London. 1986. Lang.: Eng. 2163

Foregger, N.M.
Performance/production
N.M. Foregger's experimental dance performances. USSR. 1920-1929. Lang.: Rus. 1445

Foreigner, The
Performance/production
Collection of newspaper reviews by London theatre critics. UK-England. 1987. Lang.: Eng. 2262

Foreman, Richard
Performance/production
Interview with director Richard Foreman. USA: New York, NY. 1962-1987. Lang.: Eng. 2329

Richard Foreman's production of *Film is Evil: Radio is Good*. USA: New York, NY. 1987. Lang.: Eng. 3365

The theatre techniques of performance artist Richard Foreman. USA: New York, NY. 1987. Lang.: Eng. 3368

Plays/librettos/scripts
Interview with playwright and director Richard Foreman. USA: New York, NY. 1962-1987. Lang.: Eng. 2908

Forgatókönyv (Screenplay)
Performance/production
István Paál directs István Örkény's *Forgatókönyv (Screenplay)* at Petőfi Theatre. Hungary: Veszprém. 1987. Lang.: Hun. 1832

Reviews of two plays by István Örkény: *Forgatókönyv (Screenplay)* directed by István Paál and two productions of *Tóték (The Tót Family)* staged by János Meczner and István Pinczés. Hungary: Veszprém, Budapest, Debrecen. 1986-1987. Lang.: Hun. 1880

Formosa, Feliu
Performance/production
Collection of theatre reviews by Xavier Fàbregas. Spain-Catalonia. 1969-1972. Lang.: Cat. 2010

Fornes, Maria Irene
Basic theatrical documents
Six plays detailing the Hispanic experience in the United States. USA. Mexico. 1987. Lang.: Eng. 1581

Plays/librettos/scripts
Space and audience-performer relationship—examples from Ellen Sebastian and Maria Irene Fornes. USA. 1950-1980. Lang.: Eng. 2838

Three feminist productions of plays by Henrik Ibsen. USA. 1987. Lang.: Eng. 2899

Forray, Gábor
Design/technology
Interview with set designer Gábor Forray. Hungary: Budapest. 1950-1987. Lang.: Hun. 3696

Forrest, Ian
Performance/production
Collection of newspaper reviews by London theatre critics. UK-England: London. 1986. Lang.: Eng. 2047

Collection of newspaper reviews by London theatre critics. UK-England: London. 1987. Lang.: Eng. 2174

Forrester, Alice
Relation to other fields
Sexuality and desire in performance. USA. 1987. Lang.: Eng. 1270

Forrester, Maureen
Performance/production
Autobiography of opera star Maureen Forrester. Canada. 1930-1986. Lang.: Eng. 3748

Forssell, Lars
Performance/production
Composer Hans Gefors on his opera *Christina*. Sweden. 1986. Lang.: Swe. 3819

Reviews of *Christina* by Hans Gefors and Lars Forssell. Sweden: Stockholm. 1987. Lang.: Swe. 3822

Christina, opera based on Strindberg play by Hans Gefors and Lars Forssell. Sweden: Stockholm. 1986-1987. Lang.: Swe. 3823

Forsyth, Margarethe
Performance/production
Collection of newspaper reviews by London theatre critics. UK-England: London. 1987. Lang.: Eng. 2173

Collection of newspaper reviews by London theatre critics. UK-England: London. 1987. Lang.: Eng. 2178

Forti, Simone
Performance/production
Production of *Spring* by Simone Forti presented at the Danspace at St. Mark's Church. USA: New York, NY. 1983. Lang.: Eng. 2337

Fortunátus
Performance/production
Péter Tömöry directs premiere of Zsigmond Móricz's 1916 *Fortunátus*. Hungary: Zalaegerszeg. 1987. Lang.: Hun. 1840

Fortune My Foe
Plays/librettos/scripts
Survey of Robertson Davies' plays. Canada. 1913-1985. Lang.: Eng. 2484

Fortune Theatre (London)
Performance/production
Collection of newspaper reviews by London theatre critics. UK-England: London. 1986. Lang.: Eng. 2039

Collection of newspaper reviews by London theatre critics. UK-England: London. 1986. Lang.: Eng. 2122

Collection of newspaper reviews by London theatre critics. UK-England: London. 1987. Lang.: Eng. 2181

Collection of newspaper reviews by London theatre critics. UK-England: London. 1987. Lang.: Eng. 2193

Fortuny y Madrazo, Mariano
Design/technology
Catalogue of costume exhibit: Fortuny, Caramba. Italy. 1906-1936. Lang.: Ita. 345

Forty Deuce
Plays/librettos/scripts
Adaptation of Alan Bowne's *Forty Deuce* as stage play and film. USA: New York, NY. Lang.: Eng. 2891

Foscolo, Ugo
Plays/librettos/scripts
Essays on various Italian playwrights. Italy. 1700-1900. Lang.: Ita. 1132

Correspondence of playwright Ugo Foscolo regarding *Tieste (Thyestes)*. Italy: Venice. 1797-1827. Lang.: Ita. 2677

Foster, Barry
Performance/production
Reviews of Pinter's *The Lover* and *A Slight Ache*. UK-England: London. 1987. Lang.: Eng. 901

Foster, Hal
Relation to other fields
Examination of crisis in theory and practice of political art. USA. 1987. Lang.: Eng. 3007

Found spaces
Administration
Real estate alternatives for arts organizations. USA. 1982. Lang.: Eng. 180

Found spaces — cont'd

Design/technology
Scene designer discusses production of *Pygmalion* in former mechanical workshop. Sweden: Stockholm. 1986. Lang.: Swe. 1595

Performance spaces
The lack of performance space for small theatre companies. Canada: Toronto, ON. 1987. Lang.: Eng. 629

Conversion of ferryboat *Innvik* into theatre and its production of *Splint*. Norway. 1982. Lang.: Eng. 666

Reconstructs processional route of *Corpus Christi* performances. England: York. 1399-1569. Lang.: Eng. 3329

Performance art in traditional environs. UK-England. 1987. Lang.: Eng. 3343

Telecast of Donizetti's *Lucia di Lammermoor* into a large performing area. Switzerland: Basel. 1986. Lang.: Fre, Ger. 3737

Foundation for the Extension and Development of the American Professional Theatre (FEDAPT, New York, NY)
Performance/production
Production of open-air historical drama. USA. 1985. Lang.: Eng. 978

Four Corners Theatre Company (London)
Performance/production
Collection of newspaper reviews by London theatre critics. UK-England: London. 1987. Lang.: Eng. 2277

Fourie, C.
Plays/librettos/scripts
New Afrikaans drama and playwrights. South Africa, Republic of. 1985-1986. Lang.: Afr. 1155

Fővárosi Operettszinház (Budapest)
Performance/production
Biography of tenor János Sárdy. Hungary. 1907-1969. Lang.: Hun. 3795

Fox, William
Administration
Career of theatre owner William Fox. USA: New York, NY. 1879-1952. Lang.: Eng. 3122

Foxall, Vince
Performance/production
Collection of newspaper reviews by London theatre critics. UK-England: London. 1986. Lang.: Eng. 2042

Collection of newspaper reviews by London theatre critics. UK-England: London. 1986. Lang.: Eng. 2151

Collection of newspaper reviews by London theatre critics. UK-England: London. 1987. Lang.: Eng. 2174

Collection of newspaper reviews by London theatre critics. UK-England: London. 1987. Lang.: Eng. 2248

Fracchia, Umberto
Plays/librettos/scripts
Sources on Umberto Fracchia and his literary magazine *La Fiera Letteraria*. Italy. 1925-1926. Lang.: Ita. 1131

Fragments of Isabella
Performance/production
Collection of newspaper reviews by London theatre critics. UK-England: London. 1987. Lang.: Eng. 2242

Frame, Allen
Performance/production
Collection of newspaper reviews by London theatre critics. UK-England: London. 1987. Lang.: Eng. 2207

Franceschild, Donna
Performance/production
Collection of newspaper reviews by London theatre critics. UK-England: London. 1986. Lang.: Eng. 2067

Franceschini, Antonio
Performance/production
Actors and institutions of eighteenth-century Venice. Italy: Venice. 1700-1800. Lang.: Ita. 3312

Francis, Matthew
Performance/production
Collection of newspaper reviews by London theatre critics. UK-England: London. 1987. Lang.: Eng. 2236

Franck, César
Plays/librettos/scripts
Operas of César Franck. France: Paris. 1822-1896. Lang.: Eng. 3898

Francos Rodriguez, José
Plays/librettos/scripts
Study of *El pan del pobre* (*Poor Man's Bread*), adapted from Hauptmann's *Die Weber* (*The Weavers*). Spain. 1894. Lang.: Eng. 2728

Frank, Dmitri Frinkel
Performance/production
Production account, Frank's *Spinoza*, Saidye Bronfman Centre. Canada: Montreal, PQ. 1982. Lang.: Eng. 1702

Frankel, Kenneth
Performance/production
Two productions of Pinter's *Old Times*. UK-England: London. USA: New York, NY, St. Louis, MO. 1971-1985. Lang.: Eng. 907

Fraser, Helen
Performance/production
Review of the BBC telecast of *The Birthday Party* by Harold Pinter. UK-England. 1987. Lang.: Eng. 3206

Frau ohne Schatten, Die
Plays/librettos/scripts
Comparison of Mozart's *The Magic Flute* and Strauss's *Die Frau ohne Schatten*. Austria: Vienna. 1980. Lang.: Eng. 3891

Frayn, Michael
Performance/production
Noises Off by Michael Frayn, directed by Jiří Menzel, Činoherní klub. Czechoslovakia: Prague. 1987. Lang.: Cze. 765

Collection of newspaper reviews by London theatre critics. UK-England: London. 1987. Lang.: Eng. 2253

Review of production and staging aspects of *Wild Honey* by Anton Čechov. UK-England: London. 1986. Lang.: Eng. 2306

Plays/librettos/scripts
Dramatic structure in Frayn's *Noises Off*. 1987. Lang.: Eng. 2416

Theme of theatre in recent plays. UK-England. 1957-1985. Lang.: Eng. 2764

Frazer, Jenny
Performance/production
Collection of newspaper reviews by London theatre critics. UK-England: London. 1987. Lang.: Eng. 2267

Frazier, Kermit
Plays/librettos/scripts
Research for *An American Journey* produced by Milwaukee Repertory. USA: Milwaukee, WI. 1978-1987. Lang.: Eng. 2862

Freaks
Performance/production
Reviews and discussion of Tokyo productions. Japan: Tokyo. 1960-1987. Lang.: Jap. 1960

Comments on Tokyo performances. Japan: Tokyo. 1987. Lang.: Jap. 1964

Fréchette, Richard
Performance/production
Personnel associated with production of Lepage's *La Trilogie des dragons*. Canada. 1987. Lang.: Fre. 1713

Frederick, Malcolm
Performance/production
Collection of newspaper reviews by London theatre critics. UK-England: London. 1987. Lang.: Eng. 2208

Collection of newspaper reviews by London theatre critics. UK-England: London. 1987. Lang.: Eng. 2217

Fredro, Aleksander
Performance/production
The 17th Warsaw theatre conference. Poland: Warsaw. 1987. Lang.: Eng, Fre. 872

Free Southern Theatre (New Orleans, LA)
Institutions
Black community theatre and its decline. USA. 1960-1987. Lang.: Eng. 593

Freed, Donald
Performance/production
Collection of newspaper reviews by London theatre critics. UK-England: London. 1986. Lang.: Eng. 2128

Freedman, Gerald
Performance/production
Collection of newspaper reviews by New York theatre critics. USA: New York, NY. 1987. Lang.: Eng. 2323

Freedman, Sylvia
Performance/production
Collection of newspaper reviews by London theatre critics. UK-England: London. 1986. Lang.: Eng. 2092

Freedom of the City, The
Plays/librettos/scripts
Themes of Brian Friel's plays. Ireland. 1929-1987. Lang.: Eng. 2638

Brian Friel's interpretation of Irish history through his plays *Aristocrats* and *Translations*. Ireland. 1987. Lang.: Eng. 2659

Funding — cont'd

Fundraising — cont'd

Marketing the concept of planned giving. USA. 1987. Lang.: Eng.
135

Marketing research methods as applied to specific areas of arts
management. USA: Iowa City, IA. 1982. Lang.: Eng.
143

Comprehensive guide to play production. USA: New York, NY.
1987. Lang.: Eng.
150

Training volunteer fundraisers through role playing. USA. 1987.
Lang.: Eng.
159

Competition between marketing and non-profit fundraising. USA:
New York, NY. 1980-1987. Lang.: Eng.
164

Self-hypnosis techniques for fundraising. USA: Los Angeles, CA.
1986-1987. Lang.: Eng.
178

Survey on what attracts volunteers. USA. 1987. Lang.: Eng.   202

Training volunteer fundraisers. USA. 1987. Lang.: Eng.   205

Techniques for attracting qualified volunteers. USA: New York, NY.
1987. Lang.: Eng.
207

Fundraising for Orange County Performing Arts Center. USA: Los
Angeles, CA. 1980-1986. Lang.: Eng.
222

Techniques for securing planned gifts. USA. 1987. Lang.: Eng.   230

Successful volunteers and their methods of fundraising. USA:
Chicago, IL. 1987. Lang.: Eng.
243

Use of computers in planned giving. USA. 1987. Lang.: Eng.   247

Bequest program for Wisconsin Public Broadcasting. USA: Madison,
WI. 1984-1987. Lang.: Eng.
3108

Institutions
Profile and history of Symphony Space. USA: New York, NY.
1977-1984. Lang.: Eng.
602

Funeral Games
Performance/production
Collection of newspaper reviews by London theatre critics. UK-
England: London. 1987. Lang.: Eng.
2259

Funny Feet
Design/technology
Lighting reviews for several New York shows. USA: New York,
NY. 1987. Lang.: Eng.
476

Funny Thing Happened on the Way to the Forum, A
Performance/production
Collection of newspaper reviews by London theatre critics. UK-
England: London. 1986. Lang.: Eng.
2052

Funnyhouse of a Negro
Plays/librettos/scripts
Life and work of playwright Adrienne Kennedy. USA: New York,
NY. 1987. Lang.: Eng.
2877

Fura dels Baus, La (Barcelona & Moià)
Performance/production
Collection of newspaper reviews by London theatre critics. UK-
England: London. 1986. Lang.: Eng.
2132

*Furcht und Elend des III Reiches (Fear and Misery of the Third
Reich)*
Performance/production
Interview with Chilean director Alejandro Quintana Contreras. Chile.
Germany, East: Berlin, East. 1987. Lang.: Spa.
1720

Furse, Anna
Performance/production
Collection of newspaper reviews by London theatre critics. UK-
England: London. 1987. Lang.: Eng.
2187

Collection of newspaper reviews by London theatre critics. UK-
England: London. 1987. Lang.: Eng.
2211

Collection of newspaper reviews by London theatre critics. UK-
England: London. 1987. Lang.: Eng.
2215

Füst, Milán
Performance/production
Gábor Székely directs Milán Füst's *Catullus* at Katona József
Theatre. Hungary: Budapest. 1987. Lang.: Hun.
1857

Gábor Székely directs Milán Füst's *Catullus* at Katona József
Theatre. Hungary: Budapest. 1987. Lang.: Hun.
1878

Milán Füst's *Catullus* and Imre Sarkadi's *Oszlopos Simeon (The Man
on the Pillar)* reviewed. Hungary: Budapest. 1987. Lang.: Hun.   1886

Futurism
Design/technology
Futurism in the scenographic work of Jiři Kroha. Czechoslovakia.
1918-1923. Lang.: Ita.
314

Performance/production
Theory and practice of Italian Futurist theatre. Italy. 1909. Lang.:
Ita.
831

Links between experimental theatre movement and the Russian
Futurists. USSR. 1920-1929. Lang.: Rus.
1058

Dance soundtracks simulate a Dada/Futurist variety club. Europe.
1985. Lang.: Eng.
3398

Plays/librettos/scripts
Notebooks of playwright Filippo Tommaso Marinetti. Italy. 1915-
1921. Lang.: Ita.
2673

Theory/criticism
Chlebnikov and futurism in Russian opera. USSR: Moscow. 1913-
1987. Lang.: Ger.
3949

Fyffe, Patrick
Performance/production
Collection of newspaper reviews by London theatre critics. UK-
England: London. 1987. Lang.: Eng.
2188

Gábor, Andor
Performance/production
Andor Gábor's *Dollárpapa (Dollar Daddy)* directed by Gábor
Berényi. Hungary: Budapest. 1987. Lang.: Hun.
1817

Gábor, Miklós
Performance/production
Interview with actor-director Miklós Gábor. Hungary. 1962-1987.
Lang.: Hun.
1793

Gabre-Medhnin, Tsegaye
Performance/production
Collection of newspaper reviews by London theatre critics. UK-
England. 1987. Lang.: Eng.
2175

Gaby
Design/technology
Interview with cameraman Lajos Koltay. Hungary. 1986. Lang.: Hun.
3128

Gadda, Carlo Emilio
Performance/production
Examples of missed opportunities in modern Italian theatre. Italy.
1930-1950. Lang.: Ita.
1944

Gado K'Arhin Alla
Performance/production
History of Hausa theatre. Niger, Republic of. 1876-1982. Lang.: Eng.
865

Gaevskij, V.
Performance/production
Choreographer Maurice Béjart's creative principles. France. 1927-
1987. Lang.: Rus.
1435

Gagnef Teaterförening (Gagnef)
Institutions
Gagnef Teaterförening's production of a play based on local history.
Sweden: Gagnef. 1975-1987. Lang.: Swe.
1644

Gágyor, Péter
Performance/production
Reviews of *Téli zsoltár (A Winter Psalm)* by Kovách, Shakespeare's
Much Ado About Nothing and *Ferde ház (The Leaning House)* by
Gerencsér performed at Kisfaludy Theatre. Hungary: Győr. 1986.
Lang.: Hun.
1822

Gahl, Christoph
Performance/production
Collection of newspaper reviews by London theatre critics. UK-
England. 1987. Lang.: Eng.
2033

Gaiety Theatre (Budapest)
SEE
Vigszinház.

Gaiety Theatre (Dublin)
Institutions
Difficulty in obtaining funding for theatre building repair. Ireland:
Dublin, Cork. UK-Ireland: Belfast. 1965-1984. Lang.: Eng.   545

Gaiety Theatre (London)
Plays/librettos/scripts
Role of playwright George Edwardes in development of musical
comedy. UK-England: London. 1830-1890. Lang.: Eng.
2766

Gaines, David
Performance/production
Collection of newspaper reviews by London theatre critics. UK-
England: London. 1986. Lang.: Eng.
2076

Galati, Frank
Institutions
Analysis of the changing scene in Chicago's theatres. USA: Chicago,
IL. 1987. Lang.: Eng.
589

Performance/production
Goodman Theatre's series 'Celebration of Genius'. USA: Chicago,
IL. 1986-1987. Lang.: Eng.
3409

Gardzienice, Grotowski
Performance/production
Teatr Prowizorium: interview with director Janusz Oprynski. Poland: Lublin. 1971-1987. Lang.: Eng. 1990
Garland, Patrick
Performance/production
Collection of newspaper reviews by London theatre critics. UK-England: London. 1987. Lang.: Eng. 2204
Garland, Will
Institutions
Will Garland and European tour of Negro Operetta Company. UK-England. Finland: Helsinki. Russia. 1905-1917. Lang.: Eng. 3956
Garnett, Constance
Basic theatrical documents
Constance Garnett's translation of *Tri sestry (Three Sisters)* by Čechov. England: London. 1901. Lang.: Eng. 1552
Garren, Jamie
Performance/production
Collection of newspaper reviews by London theatre critics. UK-England: London. 1987. Lang.: Eng. 2224
Garrette, Collette
Institutions
Stockholms Studentteater now welcomes amateur participation. Sweden: Stockholm. 1921-1987. Lang.: Swe. 1638
Garrick Theatre (London)
Performance/production
Collection of newspaper reviews by London theatre critics. UK-England: London. 1986. Lang.: Eng. 2053
Collection of newspaper reviews by London theatre critics. UK-England: London. 1987. Lang.: Eng. 2201
Garrick, David
Design/technology
Influence of scene designer Philippe James de Loutherbourg. England. 1700-1800. Lang.: Eng. 317

Performance/production
Examples of transition in acting style. England. 1783-1784. Lang.: Eng. 1733
Quality of ensembles declined in latter part of Garrick's career. England: London. 1737-1776. Lang.: Eng. 1742
Acting styles on English stages. UK-England. 1740-1760. Lang.: Eng. 2304
Relationship between motion pictures and realistic theatrical productions. UK-England: London. USA: Hollywood, CA, New York, NY. 1895-1915. Lang.: Eng. 3163
Garrucho, Cecilia
Performance/production
Role of theatre in the Filipino revolution. Philippines. 1970-1987. Lang.: Eng. 1986
Gaskill, William
Performance/production
Collection of newspaper reviews by London theatre critics. UK-England: London. 1987. Lang.: Eng. 2238
Gáspár, János
Performance/production
Tamás Jordán's *Amit a szívedbe rejtesz (Hidden in Your Heart)* directed by János Gáspár. Hungary: Budapest. 1987. Lang.: Hun. 1828
János Gáspar directs *Amit a szívedbe rejtesz (Hidden in Your Heart)* by Tamás Jordán, based on notes by poet Attila József, at Radnóti Miklós Theatre. Hungary: Budapest. 1987. Lang.: Hun. 1836
Productions of plays by László Márton, Tamás Jordán and Ferenc Kulin at Radnóti Miklós Theatre. Hungary: Budapest. 1987. Lang.: Hun. 1887
Gassol, Ventura
Plays/librettos/scripts
General history of Catalan literature, including theatre. Spain-Catalonia. 1902-1961. Lang.: Cat. 1157
Gate Theatre (Notting Hill, London)
Performance/production
Collection of newspaper reviews by London theatre critics. UK-England: London. 1986. Lang.: Eng. 2059
Collection of newspaper reviews by London theatre critics. UK-England: London. 1986. Lang.: Eng. 2064
Collection of newspaper reviews by London theatre critics. UK-England: London. 1987. Lang.: Eng. 2073
Collection of newspaper reviews by London theatre critics. UK-England: London. 1986. Lang.: Eng. 2078

Collection of newspaper reviews by London theatre critics. UK-England: London. 1986. Lang.: Eng. 2105
Collection of newspaper reviews by London theatre critics. UK-England: London. 1986. Lang.: Eng. 2118
Collection of newspaper reviews by London theatre critics. UK-England: London. 1986. Lang.: Eng. 2140
Collection of newspaper reviews by London theatre critics. UK-England: London. 1986. Lang.: Eng. 2152
Collection of newspaper reviews by London theatre critics. UK-England: London. 1986. Lang.: Eng. 2165
Collection of newspaper reviews by London theatre critics. UK-England: London. 1987. Lang.: Eng. 2176
Collection of newspaper reviews by London theatre critics. UK-England: London. 1987. Lang.: Eng. 2180
Collection of newspaper reviews by London theatre critics. UK-England: London. 1987. Lang.: Eng. 2188
Collection of newspaper reviews by London theatre critics. UK-England: London. 1987. Lang.: Eng. 2202
Collection of newspaper reviews by London theatre critics. UK-England: London. 1987. Lang.: Eng. 2218
Collection of newspaper reviews by London theatre critics. UK-England: London. 1987. Lang.: Eng. 2226
Collection of newspaper reviews by London theatre critics. UK-England: London. 1987. Lang.: Eng. 2236
Collection of newspaper reviews by London theatre critics. UK-England: London. 1987. Lang.: Eng. 2245
Collection of newspaper reviews by London theatre critics. UK-England: London. 1987. Lang.: Eng. 2265
Collection of newspaper reviews by London theatre critics. UK-England: London. 1987. Lang.: Eng. 2267
Collection of newspaper reviews by London theatre critics. UK-England: London. 1987. Lang.: Eng. 2270
Collection of newspaper reviews by London theatre critics. UK-England: London. 1987. Lang.: Eng. 2277
Gates, Henry Louis, Jr.
Theory/criticism
Portrayals of African-Americans in media and literature. USA. 1926-1987. Lang.: Eng. 3104
Portrayal of African-American artists in literature. USA. 1926-1987. Lang.: Eng. 3105
Gatti, Armand
Plays/librettos/scripts
Anti-fascist plays of Armand Gatti. France. 1924-1987. Lang.: Rus. 2578
Dramaturgy of Armand Gatti. France. 1924-1987. Lang.: Rus. 2579
Relation to other fields
Representation of workers on stage. Europe. USA. 1871-1987. Lang.: Fre. 2987
Gatti, Carlo
Plays/librettos/scripts
Impact of Giuseppina Strepponi Verdi on her husband's creativity. Italy: Milan. 1836-1901. Lang.: Eng. 3927
Gau, Liuh-Guei
Performance/production
Chinese opera actor Gau Liuh-Guei. China, People's Republic of. 1986. Lang.: Chi. 3502
Gaudete
Performance/production
Collection of newspaper reviews by London theatre critics. UK-England. 1986. Lang.: Eng. 2144
Gaunt, Jon
Performance/production
Collection of newspaper reviews by London theatre critics. UK-England: London. 1986. Lang.: Eng. 2169
Gay Sweatshop (London)
Performance/production
Relationship of theatre, class and gender. UK-England. USA. 1969-1985. Lang.: Eng. 918
Gay theatre
Performance/production
Relationship of theatre, class and gender. UK-England. USA. 1969-1985. Lang.: Eng. 918
Gays and lesbians on the American stage. USA. 1896-1987. Lang.: Eng. 935

Genres — cont'd

Effects of new technologies on theatre. Canada. 1969-1987. Lang.:
Fre.   3202

Institutions

Two community-based popular theatre projects. Canada. 1987. Lang.:
Eng.   522

Development of feminist theatre in Toronto. Canada: Toronto, ON.
1960-1987. Lang.: Eng.   1608

Performance/production

Characteristics of Asian theatre. Asia. 1987. Lang.: Kor.   720

Canadian popular theatre. Canada. Africa. Asia. 1987. Lang.: Eng.
                                                                       733

Analysis of directorial style of Gilles Maheu. Canada. 1987. Lang.:
Eng.   745

Complete description of all aspects of *Wayang wong*. Indonesia. 930-
1986. Lang.: Eng.   1481

Honda Yasuji's work on Japanese folk theatre. Japan. 1930-1986.
Lang.: Eng.   1483

Staging of Romantic 'closet dramas'. Scandinavia. 1986-1987. Lang.:
Swe.   2004

Differentiation between camp and burlesque styles. USA. 1987.
Lang.: Eng.   2333

Teatropoesia, a combination of theatre and poetry. USA. 1974-1983.
Lang.: Spa.   2368

Popular account of comic entertainers. Europe. North America.
Australia. 480 B.C.-1986 A.D. Lang.: Eng.   3256

Genre of business theatre. USA. 1985-1987. Lang.: Eng.   3272

Edward Gordon Craig's use of *commedia dell'arte* in his work. UK-
England. Italy. 1872-1966. Lang.: Eng.   3314

Techniques of the image theatre and effects on actor and audience.
Canada. Europe. USA. 1987. Lang.: Eng.   3345

Image theatre methodology. Canada. 1987. Lang.: Eng.   3348

Ways to blend comedy and tragedy in Hsi Ch'ü. China, People's
Republic of. 1986. Lang.: Chi.   3479

Offenbach and the origin and development of operetta. Russia.
1860-1889. Lang.: Rus.   3960

Plays/librettos/scripts

Comparison of two versions of Duras' *La Musica Deuxième*. France:
Paris. 1985-1987. Lang.: Eng.   1125

Theme of journeys in German theatre and film. Germany. 1970-
1986. Lang.: Fre.   1127

Genre and stylistic innovation in new Ukrainian dramaturgy. USSR.
1980-1987. Lang.: Rus.   1424

Shakespeare's *King Lear* in the context of ironic drama. 1590.
Lang.: Eng.   2424

Art and realism in works of Hugo von Hofmannsthal. Austria. 1874-
1929. Lang.: Rus.   2451

Anthropological analysis of Shakespeare's romantic comedies.
England. 1564-1616. Lang.: Eng.   2504

Theoretical considerations of English Renaissance theatre. England.
1600-1699. Lang.: Rus.   2528

Dramatic vs. literary interpretation of *Ett Drömspel (A Dream Play)*
by August Strindberg. Sweden. 1901-1964. Lang.: Eng.   2734

Comic conventions in Shakespeare's *Titus Andronicus*. UK-England.
1987. Lang.: Eng.   2809

Critical methodology for studying Beckett's works. UK-England.
1930-1987. Lang.: Eng.   2814

Problem of the tragic in English drama. UK-England. 1950-1969.
Lang.: Rus.   2819

Influences on *The Voysey Inheritance* by Granville Barker. UK-
England. 1600-1938. Lang.: Eng.   2820

The many genres of Ukrainian theatre. Ukraine. 1920-1929. Lang.:
Rus.   2835

Sam Shepard's *True West* as a farce in the guise of serious drama.
USA. 1981. Lang.: Eng.   2887

Genre and style in Soviet dramaturgy. USSR. 1960-1987. Lang.:
Rus.   2942

Historical fate of melodrama. USSR. 1987. Lang.: Rus.   3420

A correct definition of Chinese classical 'tragedy'. China. 960-1644.
Lang.: Chi.   3548

Stock characters in Chinese comedy. China, People's Republic of.
1986. Lang.: Chi.   3565

Theme of falsehood in Chinese classical comedy. China, People's
Republic of. 1987. Lang.: Chi.   3567

Analysis of Chinese tragedy. China, People's Republic of. 1986.
Lang.: Chi.   3572

Unique style of modern Japanese Opera. Japan. 1975-1987. Lang.:
Eng.   3928

Relation to other fields

Social implications of popular theatre. Canada. 1987. Lang.: Eng.
                                                                      1222

Comparison of the role of theatre in urban society with that of
traditional ritual. 1985. Lang.: Spa.   2977

Church records related to Morris dancing. England: Great Marlow.
1593-1674. Lang.: Eng.   3280

Theory/criticism

Exploration of the nature of tragedy. 500 B.C.-1987 A.D. Lang.:
Eng.   3020

Discussion of theory of popular theatre. Canada. 1987. Lang.: Eng.
                                                                      3024

Rise of contemporary theatre in Mexico. Mexico: Mexico City. 1957-
1987. Lang.: Spa.   3057

Perceptions of tragedy and new perspective on its analysis. USA.
UK-England. Greece. 500 B.C.-1987 A.D. Lang.: Eng.   3066

Genres of Uzbek musical drama. USSR. 1917-1987. Lang.: Rus.
                                                                      3423

Theory of Chinese classical comedy. China. 1127-1368. Lang.: Chi.
                                                                      3587

Gentleman Dancing Master, The

Plays/librettos/scripts

Independence of Restoration women is reflected in comic heroines.
England. 1668-1700. Lang.: Eng.   2550

Geography Match

Plays/librettos/scripts

Critical analysis of James Reaney's *Three Desks*. Canada. 1960-1977.
Lang.: Eng.   2477

Georgia Minstrels

Institutions

Sherman H. Dudley and the Black vaudeville circuit. USA:
Indianapolis, IN, Washington, DC. 1820-1922. Lang.: Eng.   3382

Georgian Academic Theatre (Tbilisi)

SEE

Gruzinskij Akademičeskij Teat'r im. Kote Mordžanišvili.

Gerald, Frank

Performance/production

British theatrical touring companies. UK-England. North America.
Australia. 1870-1929. Lang.: Eng.   2280

Gerčakov, Jevgenij

Performance/production

Actor Jevgenij Gerčakov of the Theatre of Miniatures. USSR:
Moscow. 1980-1987. Lang.: Rus.   1002

Gerencsér, Miklós

Performance/production

Reviews of *Téli zsoltár (A Winter Psalm)* by Kovách, Shakespeare's
Much Ado About Nothing and *Ferde ház (The Leaning House)* by
Gerencsér performed at Kisfaludy Theatre. Hungary: Győr. 1986.
Lang.: Hun.   1822

Gergely, Géza

Institutions

Memoirs of director and teacher Géza Gergely on Hungarian
theatrical training in Romania. Romania: Tîrgu-Mures. Hungary.
1946-1986. Lang.: Hun.   556

German Connection, The

Performance/production

Collection of newspaper reviews by London theatre critics. UK-
England: London. 1986. Lang.: Eng.   2157

Gershwin Theatre (New York, NY)

Design/technology

Gershwin Theatre's accommodation of RSC touring productions.
USA: New York, NY. 1984. Lang.: Eng.   420

Performance/production

Collection of newspaper reviews by New York theatre critics. USA:
New York, NY. 1987. Lang.: Eng.   2325

Gershwin, George

Performance/production

Cooperative financing of Gershwin's *Porgy and Bess*. USA. 1987.
Lang.: Eng.   3850

Gersten, Bernard
Performance/production
Essays on the future of the theatre. USA: New York, NY. 1970-1987. Lang.: Eng.   955

Gert, Valesca
Performance/production
Development of dance. Germany: Berlin. 1920-1986. Lang.: Ger.   1407

Gervais, C.H.
Plays/librettos/scripts
New Canadian drama: non-realistic, anti-naturalistic. Canada. 1983-1984. Lang.: Eng.   2482

Gestiefelte Kater, Der (Puss in Boots)
Performance/production
'Showing' is an essential part of all acting. Europe. 1590-1987. Lang.: Eng.   1746

Gesture
Performance/production
Actors' interpretations of gestures and movements implicit in Shakespeare's texts. UK-England. 1870-1987. Lang.: Eng.   2302

Gestus
Relation to other fields
Compares Brecht's montages and the film work of Sergei Eisenstein and the use and definition of *gestus*. USA. 1930. Lang.: Eng.   3186

Getting Through
Performance/production
Collection of newspaper reviews by London theatre critics. UK-England: London. 1987. Lang.: Eng.   2243

Getty, Gordon Peter
Administration
Gordon Peter Getty, philanthropist, composer. USA: San Francisco, CA. 1987. Lang.: Eng.   3684

Gewandter, Holly
Performance/production
Collection of newspaper reviews by London theatre critics. UK-England: London. 1987. Lang.: Eng.   2232

Ghelderode, Michel de
Plays/librettos/scripts
Bibliography of Michel de Ghelderode. Belgium. 1915-1987. Lang.: Fre.   2453

Death in Ghelderode's *La Balade du Grand Macabre (The Grand Macabre's Stroll)*. France. 1934. Lang.: Eng.   2587

Theory/criticism
Analysis of *Escurial* and *Barabbas* by Michel de Ghelderode. Belgium. 1898. Lang.: Fre.   3023

Ghetto
Performance/production
Collection of newspaper reviews by London theatre critics. UK-England: London. 1987. Lang.: Eng.   2189

Ghosts
SEE
Gengangere.

Gi, Yan-Ming
Administration
History of Chinese theatre reform. China, People's Republic of: Beijing. 1942-1984. Lang.: Chi.   3428

Gianfrancesco, Edward
Design/technology
Interview with set designer Edward Gianfrancesco. USA: New York, NY. 1987. Lang.: Eng.   429

Plays/librettos/scripts
Interview with playwright Robert Harling, designer Edward Gianfrancesco. USA: New York, NY. 1987. Lang.: Eng.   2846

Gibbs, Peter
Performance/production
Collection of newspaper reviews by London theatre critics. UK-England: London. 1986. Lang.: Eng.   2060

Gibson, Mel
Performance/production
Analysis of art of television and comparison to live theatre. USA. 1950-1987. Lang.: Eng.   3194

Gide, André
Plays/librettos/scripts
Study of playwright Paul Claudel based on his letters. France. 1904-1909. Lang.: Fre.   2572

Gielgud, John
Performance/production
Interview with actress Dame Peggy Ashcroft. UK-England. 1935-1964. Lang.: Eng.   899

Gierow, Karl Ragnar
Plays/librettos/scripts
Karl Ragnar Gierow on O'Neill and his importance in Sweden. Sweden: Stockholm. 1920-1970. Lang.: Eng.   2736

Giganti della montagna, I (Giants of the Mountain, The)
Performance/production
Renato Simoni's staging of *I giganti della montagna (The Giants of the Mountain)* by Luigi Pirandello. Italy: Florence. 1937. Lang.: Ita.   821

Gigli Concert, The
Performance/production
Interview with Patrick Mason, director of Thomas Murphy's *The Gigli Concert*. Ireland: Dublin. 1983. Lang.: Eng.   1935

Plays/librettos/scripts
Theatrical language in the plays of Thomas Murphy. Ireland. 1961-1984. Lang.: Eng.   2640

Comic characters and the Book of Job in the plays of Thomas Murphy. Ireland. 1962-1983. Lang.: Eng.   2648

The plays of Thomas Murphy. Ireland: Dublin. 1962-1986. Lang.: Eng.   2650

The myth of the idyllic peasant life in the plays of Thomas Murphy. Ireland. 1961-1986. Lang.: Eng.   2652

Christian thought in Thomas Murphy's *The Gigli Concert*. Ireland. 1983. Lang.: Eng.   2653

Historical accuracy of characters in the plays of Thomas Murphy. Ireland. 1962-1986. Lang.: Eng.   2657

Gignac, Marie
Performance/production
Personnel associated with production of Lepage's *La Trilogie des dragons*. Canada. 1987. Lang.: Fre.   1713

Gilbert, Peter
Performance/production
Collection of newspaper reviews by London theatre critics. UK-England: London. 1986. Lang.: Eng.   2065

Gilbert, Sky
Institutions
The Dora Mavor Moore theatre awards. Canada: Toronto, ON. 1987. Lang.: Eng.   523

Performance/production
Toronto directors discuss their training and craft. Canada: Toronto, ON. 1987. Lang.: Eng.   730

Hillar Liitoja's experimental theatre. Canada. 1987. Lang.: Eng.   739

Gilbert, Stephen
Performance/production
Collection of newspaper reviews by London theatre critics. UK-England: London. 1986. Lang.: Eng.   2147

Gilbert, William Schwenck
Institutions
Summary of proceedings from a Gilbert and Sullivan symposium. Canada: Toronto, ON. 1987. Lang.: Eng.   3954

Performance/production
Collection of newspaper reviews by London theatre critics. UK-England: London. 1986. Lang.: Eng.   2089

Collection of newspaper reviews by New York critics. USA: New York, NY. 1987. Lang.: Eng.   2324

Review of *Pirates* and *Student Prince*. South Africa, Republic of: Johannesburg. 1986. Lang.: Eng.   3634

Plays/librettos/scripts
W.S. Gilbert's contribution to the development of the musical play. England. 1836-1911. Lang.: Eng.   3670

Opera adaptations for Broadway with African-American artists. USA: New York, NY. 1935-1987. Lang.: Eng.   3932

Gilford, Jack
Performance/production
Career of actor Jack Gilford. USA: New York, NY. 1920-1987. Lang.: Eng.   3292

Gill, Peter
Performance/production
Collection of newspaper reviews of London theatre critics. UK-England: London. 1987. Lang.: Eng.   2273

Gillespie, Robert
Performance/production
Collection of newspaper reviews by London theatre critics. UK-England: London. 1986. Lang.: Eng.   2035

Collection of newspaper reviews by London theatre critics. UK-England: London. 1986. Lang.: Eng.   2136

Grant, Cynthia
Institutions
Development of feminist theatre in Toronto. Canada: Toronto, ON.
1960-1987. Lang.: Eng. 1608

Grant, Kim
Performance/production
Collection of newspaper reviews by London theatre critics. UK-
England: London. 1986. Lang.: Eng. 2044
Collection of newspaper reviews by London theatre critics. UK-
England: London. 1987. Lang.: Eng. 2198

Grant, Micki
Institutions
Debate among Black theatre people whether Black theatre really
exists. USA. 1987. Lang.: Eng. 610

Granville-Barker, Harley
Performance/production
Interview with actress Dame Peggy Ashcroft. UK-England. 1935-
1964. Lang.: Eng. 899
Recent scholarly books on Harley Granville-Barker. UK-England.
Lang.: Eng. 2296

Plays/librettos/scripts
Influences on *The Voysey Inheritance* by Granville Barker. UK-
England. 1600-1938. Lang.: Eng. 2820

Theory/criticism
Reconstruction of Shakespeare in performance. USA. 1987. Lang.:
Eng. 1358

Granville, George
Plays/librettos/scripts
Eighteenth-century alterations to Shakespeare's *The Merchant of
Venice*. England. 1596-1701. Lang.: Eng. 2512

Grassman, Sven
Administration
Criticism of reduced government funding for the arts. Sweden. 1976-
1987. Lang.: Swe. 41

Gray, Alexander
Institutions
Historical survey of opera in Calgary. Canada: Calgary, AB. 1971-
1987. Lang.: Eng. 3719

Gray, Simon
Performance/production
Collection of newspaper reviews by London theatre critics. UK-
England: London. 1987. Lang.: Eng. 2245
Comparison and review of *Melon, Breaking the Code, Alan Turing:
The Secret War* and *My Sister in This House*. UK-England: London.
1987. Lang.: Eng. 2285

Gray, Spalding
Performance/production
Performance artists Ishmael Houston-Jones, John Kelly, Karen
Finley, Richard Elovich. USA. 1987. Lang.: Eng. 3366

Theory/criticism
Theatre and contemporary culture. USA. 1800-1987. Lang.: Eng.
1360

Greager, Richard
Basic theatrical documents
Review of video productions of *Tosca* and *Dialogues des Carmélites*.
Italy: Verona. Australia: Sydney. 1987. Lang.: Eng. 3692

Great Canadian Theatre Company (Ottawa, ON)
Performance/production
Interview with playwright Patrick McDonald. Canada: Ottawa, ON.
1987. Lang.: Eng. 1708

Relation to other fields
Popular theatre and non-governmental funding agencies. Canada:
Sydney, NS. Jamaica. Sudan. 1987. Lang.: Eng. 2982

Great God Brown, The
Plays/librettos/scripts
Comparison of themes and dramaturgical techniques in plays of
Eugene O'Neill and Peter Shaffer. USA. 1920-1982. Lang.: Eng.
2872

Great Goodness of Life
Performance/production
Interview with playwright Amiri Baraka. USA: Newark, NJ, New
York, NY. 1965-1969. Lang.: Eng. 2356

Great Hunger, The
Performance/production
Collection of newspaper reviews by London theatre critics. UK-
England: London. 1986. Lang.: Eng. 2058

Great Theatre of the World, The
SEE
Gran Teatro del Mundo, El.

Great Wallace Circus
SEE
Wallace Brothers Circus.

Great White Hope, The
Performance/production
Collection of newspaper reviews by London theatre critics. UK-
England: London. 1987. Lang.: Eng. 2237

Plays/librettos/scripts
Korean views of American society based on plays of Howard
Sackler, Charles Fuller and Jason Miller. USA. 1969-1982. Lang.:
Kor. 2837

Greatest Story Ever Told, The
Performance/production
Collection of newspaper reviews by London theatre critics. UK-
England: London. 1987. Lang.: Eng. 2200

Grédy, Jean-Pierre
Performance/production
István Kazán directs *Fleur de cactus (Cactus Flower)* at Vidám
Színpad as *A kaktusz virága*. Hungary: Budapest. 1987. Lang.: Hun.
3629

Greek Amphitheatre (Syracuse)
SEE
Teatro Greco.

Green Bird, The
SEE
Augellino belverde, L'.

Green Card
Basic theatrical documents
Text of *Green Card* by JoAnne Akalaitis. USA. 1986. Lang.: Eng.
1577

Green Cockatoo, The
SEE
Grüne Kakadu, Der.

Green, Adolph
Performance/production
Collection of newspaper reviews by London theatre critics. UK-
England: London. 1986. Lang.: Eng. 2134
Collection of newspaper reviews by London theatre critics. UK-
England: London. 1987. Lang.: Eng. 2228
Collection of newspaper reviews by London theatre critics. UK-
England: London. 1987. Lang.: Eng. 2235

Green, Jack
Design/technology
Analysis of the work of lighting designer Jack Green on the film
Heartbreak Ridge. USA. 1982-1987. Lang.: Eng. 3132

Green, John
Institutions
Summary of proceedings from a Gilbert and Sullivan symposium.
Canada: Toronto, ON. 1987. Lang.: Eng. 3954

Green, Ros
Performance/production
Collection of newspaper reviews by London theatre critics. UK-
England: London. 1987. Lang.: Eng. 2237

Greene, Justin
Performance/production
Collection of newspaper reviews by London theatre critics. UK-
England: London. 1987. Lang.: Eng. 2210

Greene, Robert
Theory/criticism
Trollope's writings on Elizabethan and Jacobean drama. UK-
England. 1866-1882. Lang.: Eng. 3063

Greenhalgh, Jill
Institutions
First festival of women's work in experimental theatre. UK-Wales:
Cardiff. 1986. Lang.: Eng. 1649

Performance/production
An experimental women's theatre workshop. UK-Wales: Cardiff.
1986-1987. Lang.: Eng. 922

Greenwich Street Theatre (New York, NY)
Performance spaces
Subverting alienating effect of some performance spaces. USA. 1800-
1910. Lang.: Eng. 706

Gross, Allen Robert
Institutions
Opera theatre program at the University of Louisville. USA:
Louisville, KY. 1952-1983. Lang.: Eng.   3732

Gross, Sally
Design/technology
Study of the work of dance lighting designer Blu. USA: New York,
NY. 1987. Lang.: Eng.   1400

Grotowski, Jerzy
Institutions
History of new and experimental theatre companies. Europe. North
America. 1947-1970. Lang.: Ita.   529

Development of El Teatro Carmen. USA: Tucson, AZ. 1915-1923.
Lang.: Spa.   606

Performance/production
Director as true author and maker of theatre. France. 1987. Lang.:
Fre.   1757

Experimental theatre groups in Mexico City. Mexico: Mexico City.
1987. Lang.: Spa.   1975

Method acting: its origins and development. USA: New York, NY.
USSR: Moscow. 1923-1987. Lang.: Eng.   2359

Techniques of the image theatre and effects on actor and audience.
Canada. Europe. USA. 1987. Lang.: Eng.   3345

Theory/criticism
Interview with Zbigniew Cynkutis on theatrical theory and practice.
USA. 1938-1987. Lang.: Eng.   3070

Comparison of impact of film versus the theatrical experience. USA.
1937-1987. Lang.: Eng.   3189

Groucho—A Life in Revue
Performance/production
Collection of newspaper reviews by London theatre critics. UK-
England: London. 1987. Lang.: Eng.   2235

Collection of newspaper reviews by London theatre critics. UK-
England: London. 1987. Lang.: Eng.   2249

Ground Zero Theatre Company (Toronto, ON)
Administration
Ground Zero Theatre Company's project for the homeless. Canada:
Toronto, ON. 1987. Lang.: Eng.   6

Relation to other fields
Description of *The Working People's Picture Show*. Canada: Toronto,
ON. 1987. Lang.: Eng.   1221

Applications of African 'Theatre for Development' movement to
Canadian popular theatre. Africa. Canada: St. John's, NF, Toronto,
ON. 1978-1987. Lang.: Eng.   2978

Grounds, Tony
Performance/production
Collection of newspaper reviews by London theatre critics. UK-
England: London. 1987. Lang.: Eng.   2247

Group Theatre (New York, NY)
Plays/librettos/scripts
Influence of Clifford Odets on mainstream American realism. USA.
1935-1987. Lang.: Eng.   2927

Groupov (Liège)
Performance/production
Groupov ensemble describes the creation of *Koniec*. Belgium: Liège.
1987. Lang.: Fre.   1687

Grout, Philip
Performance/production
Collection of newspaper reviews by London theatre critics. UK-
England: London. 1987. Lang.: Eng.   2267

Grove, Barry
Institutions
History of Manhattan Theatre Club. USA: New York, NY. 1969-
1987. Lang.: Eng.   1663

Grown Ups
Plays/librettos/scripts
Interview with cartoonist-playwright Jules Feiffer. USA. 1950-1987.
Lang.: Eng.   1168

Groza (Storm, The)
Performance/production
Collection of newspaper reviews by London theatre critics. UK-
England: London. 1987. Lang.: Eng.   2270

Grüber, Klaus Michael
Performance/production
Directing methods of Klaus Michael Grüber. France. Germany.
1945-1987. Lang.: Fre.   1766

Gruberova, Edita
Institutions
Review of a production of *Ariadne auf Naxos*. Canada. 1987. Lang.:
Eng.   3717

Grüne Kakadu, Der (Green Cockatoo, The)
Performance/production
'Showing' is an essential part of all acting. Europe. 1590-1987.
Lang.: Eng.   1746

Grupa Ghwilowa (Lublin)
Performance/production
Teatr Prowizorium: interview with director Janusz Oprynski. Poland:
Lublin. 1971-1987. Lang.: Eng.   1990

Grupo Justo Rufino Garay (Nicaragua)
Institutions
Formation and development of the Justo Rufino Garay Group.
Nicaragua. 1980-1986. Lang.: Spa.   1625

Grupo Rajatabla (Caracas)
Plays/librettos/scripts
Themes in the Festival of Latin Theatre. USA: New York, NY.
Latin America. Spain. 1987. Lang.: Spa.   2847

Gruza, Jerzy
Performance/production
Overview of Polish theatre scene. Poland: Warsaw, Cracow. 1987.
Lang.: Eng.   874

Gu Cheng-Hei
Performance/production
Overview of *Gu Cheng-Hei*. China, People's Republic of. 1967.
Lang.: Chi.   3498

Guan, Hanqing
Performance/production
The modernization of Chinese opera—keeping the traditional spirit.
China, People's Republic of: Beijing. 1279-1986. Lang.: Chi.   3539

Plays/librettos/scripts
Shakespeare compared to writers of Chinese opera. China. 1279-
1616. Lang.: Chi.   3554

Guan, Shu-Shuan
Performance/production
The careers of two Chinese opera actresses—Guan Shu-Shuan and
Dai Chi-Shia. China, People's Republic of. 1987. Lang.: Chi.   3515

Guare, John
Design/technology
Tony Walton's set designs at the Vivian Beaumont Theatre. USA:
New York, NY. 1986-1987. Lang.: Eng.   465

Plays/librettos/scripts
John Guare's work and his insights into American society. USA.
1960-1987. Lang.: Eng.   2869

Interview with playwright John Guare. USA. 1987. Lang.: Eng.   2870

Chronological listing of John Guare's plays, bibliography, list of
reviews. USA. 1938-1987. Lang.: Eng.   2871

Guarnieri, Anna Maria
Performance/production
Life and career of actress Anna Maria Guarnieri. Italy. 1954-1987.
Lang.: Ita.   833

Guarnieri, Gianfrancesco
Plays/librettos/scripts
The Non-Smokers by Gianfrancesco Guarnieri. Mexico: Mexico City.
1982-1987. Lang.: Spa.   2697

Gubaryev, Vladimir
Performance/production
Collection of newspaper reviews by London theatre critics. UK-
England: London. 1987. Lang.: Eng.   2202

Collection of newspaper reviews by London theatre critics. UK-
England: London. 1987. Lang.: Eng.   2219

Gudden, Bernhard
Relation to other fields
Life of King Ludwig II, and his relationship with composer Richard
Wagner. Germany. 1864-1880. Lang.: Eng.   3942

Guerrola, Juan José
Plays/librettos/scripts
Comparison of the plays *Todo sucede en una noche (It All Happens
in One Night)* and *La rosa del tiempo (The Rose of Time)*. Mexico:
Mexico City. 1987. Lang.: Spa.   2698

Guest Room, The
Performance/production
Collection of newspaper reviews by London theatre critics. UK-
England: London. 1987. Lang.: Eng.   2180

Guests
Plays/librettos/scripts
Interview with playwright John Boyd: influences and plays. UK-Ireland: Belfast. 1930-1985. Lang.: Eng. 2828

Guh, Shyi Tung
Basic theatrical documents
Text of the play *Chang-le-gong (The Palace of the Beatitudes)* by Guh Shyi Tung. China: Binjiang. 1987. Lang.: Chi. 3442

Guides
Administration
New Actors' Equity handbook published for membership. USA: New York, NY. 1982. Lang.: Eng. 107

Survey of financial results for nonprofit theatres. USA. 1986. Lang.: Eng. 173

Design/technology
Purchasing a computer system for a theatre. USA. 1987. Lang.: Eng. 438

Technology of computerized dimming systems. USA. 1987. Lang.: Eng. 457

Reference materials
Guide to theatrical resources and support organizations for the arts. UK-England. 1987. Lang.: Eng. 1213

Multi-purpose directory for theatrical resources, including training, supplies and services. UK-England. 1986-1987. Lang.: Eng. 1215

Introductory survival guide for theatre professionals. USA: Los Angeles, CA. 1987. Lang.: Eng. 1216

Major festivals of Belgium: folklore, history, description. Belgium. 1987. Lang.: Fre. 3279

Guidote, Cecilia Reyes
Performance/production
Role of theatre in the Filipino revolution. Philippines. 1970-1987. Lang.: Eng. 1986

Guilla, Louis
Performance/production
Exhibition catalogue: popular theatre in Catalan. France. 1415-1987. Lang.: Cat, Fre. 1750

Guilty, The
SEE
Vinotavye.

Guitry, Sacha
Plays/librettos/scripts
Career of playwright Sacha Guitry. France. 1920-1986. Lang.: Eng. 2567

Gulyás, Dénes
Performance/production
Interview with singer Dénes Gulyás. Hungary. 1983-1987. Lang.: Hun. 3794

Gundersen, Arne
Administration
U.S. and British Equity associations: actor exchange, union reciprocity. UK-England. USA. 1981-1987. Lang.: Eng. 50

Gunter, John
Performance/production
Revival of *Revizor (The Government Inspector)* at the National Theatre directed by Richard Eyre. UK-England: London. USSR. 1985. Lang.: Eng. 2290

Review of production and staging aspects of *Wild Honey* by Anton Čechov. UK-England: London. 1986. Lang.: Eng. 2306

Guo, Jiun
Plays/librettos/scripts
Interview with playwright Guo Jiun. China, People's Republic of. 1987. Lang.: Chi. 3559

Guo, Moruo
Performance/production
Status of Sichuan theatre and opera. China, People's Republic of: Chengdu. 1985-1986. Lang.: Eng. 3512

Guo, Sheau-Juang
Performance/production
Beijing opera actress Guo Sheau-Juang. China, People's Republic of. 1987. Lang.: Chi. 3532

A review of *Yian de-yi yuan (A Marriage of Good Fortune)*. Taiwan: Taipei. 1987. Lang.: Chi. 3542

Gurney, A.R., Jr.
Performance/production
Collection of newspaper reviews by London theatre critics. UK-England: London. 1987. Lang.: Eng. 2267

Collection of newspaper reviews by New York critics. USA: New York, NY. 1987. Lang.: Eng. 2324

Gussow, Mel
Theory/criticism
The language of theatrical criticism. USA: New York, NY. 1917-1985. Lang.: Eng. 1367

Gust
Institutions
Seven productions chosen for Theatertreffen '86. Germany: Berlin. 1986. Lang.: Eng. 1617

Gustabe, Shorsh
Performance/production
Theatrical activity at the concentration camp Theresienstadt. Czechoslovakia: Terezín. 1938-1968. Lang.: Heb. 772

Gustav III
Plays/librettos/scripts
Theatrical metaphor in Strindberg's *Gustav III*. Sweden. 1903-1987. Lang.: Eng. 2741

Gute Mensch von Sezuan, Der (Good Person of Szechwan, The)
Audience
Szechwan Opera adaptation of Brecht's *Der Gute Mensch von Sezuan (The Good Person of Szechwan)*. China, People's Republic of. 1987. Lang.: Chi. 3432

Performance/production
International Brecht symposium. China, People's Republic of: Beijing, Hong Kong. Japan: Tokyo. 1986. Lang.: Eng. 1722

Analysis of Brecht's original directing style and dramaturgy. Germany. 1925-1987. Lang.: Eng. 1771

Guthrie Theatre (Minneapolis, MN)
Performance/production
Career of director Garland Wright. USA. 1972-1987. Lang.: Eng. 975

Guthrie, Tyrone
Administration
Founder Tom Patterson's description of the opening of the Stratford Festival. Canada: Stratford, ON. 1952-1953. Lang.: Eng. 13

Performance/production
Interview with actress Roberta Maxwell. Canada. 1987. Lang.: Eng. 1718

Gutierrez, Alejandra
Performance/production
Review of *I Poli (The Town)* based on Greek theatre tradition and performed in absurdist style. Mexico: Mexico City. 1987. Lang.: Spa. 1976

Guttman, Irving
Administration
Irving Guttman, artistic director, Edmonton Opera, Manitoba Opera. Canada: Edmonton, AB, Winnipeg, MB. 1972-1985. Lang.: Eng. 3679

Institutions
Current strength of opera in Canada. Canada. 1987. Lang.: Eng. 3725

Gvozdev, A.
Theory/criticism
Collection of articles by theatre critic A. Gvozdev. USSR. 1920-1930. Lang.: Rus. 1374

Gwala, Pascal
Relation to other fields
Influences of Black political and economic life on literature, performance. South Africa, Republic of. 1970-1987. Lang.: Eng. 1252

Gwyn, Nell
Performance/production
Roles portrayed by stage actress Nell Gwyn. England: London. 1663-1668. Lang.: Eng. 1731

Gyroscope
Plays/librettos/scripts
New Canadian drama: non-realistic, anti-naturalistic. Canada. 1983-1984. Lang.: Eng. 2482

Gyulai Várszinház (Gyula)
Performance/production
Ferenc Sík directs András Sütő's *Álomkommandó (Dream Commando)*, Gyulai Várszinház. Hungary: Gyula. 1987. Lang.: Hun. 1855

Gyula Háy's *Mohács (The Mohács Disaster)* staged by Tamás Szirtes, Gyulai Várszinház. Hungary: Gyula. 1987. Lang.: Hun. 1903

Gyurkó, László
Performance/production
István Malgot directs *A búsképű lovag (The Sad-Faced Knight)* by László Gyurko in the Dominican Court of the Budapest Hilton. Hungary: Budapest. 1987. 1900

Haase, Tony
Performance/production
Collection of newspaper reviews by London theatre critics. UK-England: London. 1986. Lang.: Eng. 2075

Collection of newspaper reviews by London theatre critics. UK-England: London. 1987. Lang.: Eng. 2231

HaBimah (Moscow)
Performance/production
Reconstruction of *The Dybbuk* as directed by Vachtangov with HaBimah. USSR: Moscow. 1922. Lang.: Hun. 2399

HaBimah (Tel Aviv)
Institutions
Brief history of HaBimah. Russia: Moscow. Israel. 1912-1980. Lang.: Hun. 557

Creation and history of the HaBimah Theatre. USSR: Moscow. Israel: Tel Aviv. 1913-1955. Lang.: Heb. 623

Interview with actress Fannia Lubitch. Israel: Tel Aviv. USSR: Moscow. 1921-1987. Lang.: Heb. 1620

Interview with dancer Dvora Bektonov on her work and her father's acting. Israel: Tel Aviv. USSR: Moscow. 1922-1987. Lang.: Heb. 1621

Interview with Israel Mintz on the HaBimah Theatre. Israel: Tel Aviv. USSR: Moscow. 1922-1987. Lang.: Heb. 1623

Interview with actor, director and producer Shimon Finkel. Israel: Tel Aviv. Germany: Berlin. 1923-1987. Lang.: Heb. 1624

Performance spaces
Celebration of the birthday of the HaBimah Theatre. Israel: Tel Aviv. 1917-1987. Lang.: Heb. 1669

Hack, Keith
Performance/production
Collection of newspaper reviews by London theatre critics. UK-England: London. 1986. Lang.: Eng. 2060

Hadfield, Paul
Training
Genesis and development of various youth theatre groups. UK-Ireland. 1979-1987. Lang.: Eng. 1388

HaDybbuk (Dybbuk, The)
Audience
Letters written by Joseph Chaikin regarding actor-audience relationship. USA: Washington, DC, New York, NY. 1974-1984. Lang.: Eng. 291

Performance/production
Collection of newspaper reviews by London theatre critics. UK-England: London. 1986. Lang.: Eng. 2112

Reconstruction of *The Dybbuk* as directed by Vachtangov with HaBimah. USSR: Moscow. 1922. Lang.: Hun. 2399

Haffenden, Audley
Institutions
The formation of the North Carolina Black Repertory Company. USA: Winston-Salem, NC. 1979-1987. Lang.: Eng. 1666

Hafler, Max
Performance/production
Collection of newspaper reviews by London theatre critics. UK-England: London. 1987. Lang.: Eng. 2221

Hagan (Garden of Adam and Eve, The)
Plays/librettos/scripts
Themes of Eliraz's *The Garden of Adam and Eve*. Israel: Jerusalem. 1987. Lang.: Heb. 3915

Librettist on *The Garden of Adam and Eve*. Israel: Jerusalem. 1987. Lang.: Heb. 3916

Hagdahl, Sören
Performance/production
Two actors discuss youth, communication. Sweden. 1986-1987. Lang.: Swe. 2013

Hagio, Moto
Plays/librettos/scripts
Productions by several Tokyo companies. Japan: Tokyo. 1986-1987. Lang.: Jap. 2682

Haifa Municipal Theatre
SEE
Teatron HaIroni (Haifa).

Hailey, Oliver
Performance/production
Collection of newspaper reviews by London theatre critics. UK-England: London. 1987. Lang.: Eng. 2204

Haimes, Todd
Institutions
League of Resident Theatres' role in labor and contract negotiations. USA. 1987. Lang.: Eng. 607

Haines, Richard
Performance/production
Controversial production of *Othello* directed by Janet Suzman. South Africa, Republic of: Johannesburg. 1987. Lang.: Eng. 2007

Haire, Wilson John
Plays/librettos/scripts
Avoidance of political themes in drama of Northern Ireland. UK-Ireland. 1979-1987. Lang.: Eng. 2830

Hairy Ape, The
Performance/production
Collection of newspaper reviews by London theatre critics. UK-England: London. 1987. Lang.: Eng. 2206

Collection of newspaper reviews by London theatre critics. UK-England: London. 1987. Lang.: Eng. 2253

Plays/librettos/scripts
Influence of Rudyard Kipling on Eugene O'Neill. USA. 1887-1950. Lang.: Eng. 2925

Symbolism in *The Hairy Ape* by Eugene O'Neill. USA. 1920-1922. Lang.: Eng. 2929

Hakuhinkan Production (Tokyo)
Performance/production
Four Tokyo productions in light of ideas of Betsuyaku Minoru. Japan: Tokyo. 1987. Lang.: Jap. 1950

Analysis of four Tokyo productions. Japan: Tokyo. 1987. Lang.: Jap. 1957

Halasi, Imre
Performance/production
Imre Halasi directs *Sári bíró (Judge Sári)* by Zsigmond Móricz, music by István Mikó, at Kisvarda Castle Theatre. Hungary: Kisvárda. 1987. Lang.: Hun. 1845

Performances of *Oliver* staged by György Korcsmáros, Antol Rencz and Imre Halasi. Hungary: Budapest, Békéscsaba, Zalaegerszeg. 1986. Lang.: Hun. 3632

Halévy, Ludovic
Performance/production
The original production of *Carmen*. France: Paris. 1873-1875. Lang.: Eng. 3773

Half Moon Theatre (London)
Performance/production
Collection of newspaper reviews by London theatre critics. UK-England: London. 1986. Lang.: Eng. 2048

Collection of newspaper reviews by London theatre critics. UK-England: London. 1986. Lang.: Eng. 2079

Collection of newspaper reviews by London theatre critics. UK-England: London. 1986. Lang.: Eng. 2083

Collection of newspaper reviews by London theatre critics. UK-England: London. 1986. Lang.: Eng. 2109

Collection of newspaper reviews by London theatre critics. UK-England: London. 1986. Lang.: Eng. 2145

Collection of newspaper reviews by London theatre critics. UK-England: London. 1986. Lang.: Eng. 2158

Collection of newspaper reviews by London theatre critics. UK-England: London. 1987. Lang.: Eng. 2179

Collection of newspaper reviews by London theatre critics. UK-England: London. 1987. Lang.: Eng. 2194

Collection of newspaper reviews by London theatre critics. UK-England: London. 1987. Lang.: Eng. 2201

Collection of newspaper reviews by London theatre critics. UK-England: London. 1987. Lang.: Eng. 2219

Collection of newspaper reviews by London theatre critics. UK-England: London. 1987. Lang.: Eng. 2227

Collection of newspaper reviews by London theatre critics. UK-England: London. 1987. Lang.: Eng. 2238

Collection of newspaper reviews by London theatre critics. UK-England: London. 1987. Lang.: Eng. 2239

Collection of newspaper reviews by London theatre critics. UK-England: London. 1987. Lang.: Eng. 2246

SUBJECT INDEX

Hanslick, Edouard
Performance/production
Opera critic Edouard Hanslick and his opposition to *La Bohème* by Puccini. Austro-Hungarian Empire: Vienna. 1896-1987. Lang.: Eng.
3745

Hansom, Richard
Performance/production
Collection of newspaper reviews by London theatre critics. UK-England: London. 1986. Lang.: Eng.
2036
Collection of newspaper reviews by London theatre critics. UK-England: London. 1986. Lang.: Eng.
2170
Collection of newspaper reviews by London theatre critics. UK-England: London. 1987. Lang.: Eng.
2233

Hanson, Brian
Institutions
Historical survey of opera in Calgary. Canada: Calgary, AB. 1971-1987. Lang.: Eng.
3719

Hanson, Charlie
Performance/production
Collection of newspaper reviews by London theatre critics. UK-England: London. 1986. Lang.: Eng.
2121
Collection of newspaper reviews by London theatre critics. UK-England: London. 1987. Lang.: Eng.
2215

Hantam, Vincent
Performance/production
Interview with dancer Vincent Hantam. South Africa, Republic of. 1987. Lang.: Eng.
1441

Hanzlík, Jaromír
Performance/production
Actors Jaromír Hanzlík and Viktor Preiss in Rostand's *Cyrano*, directed by Jaroslov Dudek at Vinohradské Theatre. Czechoslovakia: Prague. 1986. Lang.: Cze.
771

Harc a jólét ellen (Fight Against Prosperity, The)
Performance/production
Károly Kazimir directs László Németh's *Harc a jólét ellen (The Fight Against Prosperity)*. Hungary: Budapest. 1986. Lang.: Hun.
1910

Hard Times
Performance/production
Collection of newspaper reviews by London theatre critics. UK-England: London. 1987. Lang.: Eng.
2244

Hardwick, Mark
Performance/production
The cabaret-style musical revue *Oil City Symphony*. USA: New York, NY. 1987. Lang.: Eng.
3289

Hare, David
Performance/production
Relationship of theatre, class and gender. UK-England. USA. 1969-1985. Lang.: Eng.
918
Collection of newspaper reviews by London theatre critics. UK-England: London. 1986. Lang.: Eng.
2044
Collection of newspaper reviews by London theatre critics. UK-England: London. 1986. Lang.: Eng.
2172
Collection of newspaper reviews by New York theatre critics. USA: New York, NY. 1987. Lang.: Eng.
2312
Plays/librettos/scripts
Theme of theatre in recent plays. UK-England. 1957-1985. Lang.: Eng.
2764
Interview with playwright Howard Brenton. UK-England. 1975-1987. Lang.: Eng.
2806
Interview with playwright John Guare. USA. 1987. Lang.: Eng. 2870

Harlekin (Landskrona)
Performance/production
Harlekin's efforts to involve youth in amateur theatre. Sweden: Landskrona. 1982-1987. Lang.: Swe.
2022
Background on *Landskronapågen (The Boy from Landskrona)*. Sweden: Landskrona. 1982-1987. Lang.: Swe.
2024

Harley, Margot
Performance spaces
John Houseman on the New York home of the Acting Company. USA: New York, NY. 1972-1986. Lang.: Eng.
695

Harling, Robert
Administration
Financial considerations in transferring *Steel Magnolias* to an Off Broadway theatre. USA: New York, NY. 1987. Lang.: Eng.
226

Performance/production
Collection of newspaper reviews by New York theatre critics. USA: New York, NY. 1987. Lang.: Eng.
2320
Plays/librettos/scripts
Interview with playwright Robert Harling, designer Edward Gianfrancesco. USA: New York, NY. 1987. Lang.: Eng.
2846

Harmon, Andrew
Performance/production
Collection of newspaper reviews by London theatre critics. UK-England: London. 1986. Lang.: Eng.
2092

Harnick, Jay
Institutions
History of Theaterworks/USA, a national theatre for young people. USA: New York, NY. 1961-1987. Lang.: Eng.
613

Harper, Kyra
Performance/production
Canadian actors and directors discuss their theatre experiences. Canada: Calgary, AB. 1987. Lang.: Eng.
748

Harper, Sarah
Performance/production
Collection of newspaper reviews by London theatre critics. UK-England: London. 1987. Lang.: Eng.
2276

Harper, Wally
Performance/production
Collection of newspaper reviews by London theatre critics. UK-England: London. 1986. Lang.: Eng.
2114
Collection of newspaper reviews by London theatre critics. UK-England: London. 1986. Lang.: Eng.
2148
Collection of newspaper reviews by New York theatre critics. USA: New York, NY. 1987. Lang.: Eng.
2321

Harris, Albert
Performance/production
Collection of newspaper reviews by New York critics. USA: New York, NY. 1987. Lang.: Eng.
2324
Plot synopsis of musical *Mademoiselle Colombe* based on Anouilh's *Colombe*. USA: New York, NY. 1987. Lang.: Eng.
3647
Plays/librettos/scripts
How Anouilh's *Colombe* was adapted as a musical. USA. 1987. Lang.: Eng.
3672

Harris, Anne
Performance/production
Collection of newspaper reviews by London theatre critics. UK-England: London. 1986. Lang.: Eng.
2139

Harris, Barbara
Institutions
Second City improvisational comedy troupe. USA: Chicago, IL. Canada: Toronto, ON. 1959-1987. Lang.: Eng.
605

Harris, Jed
Performance/production
Autobiography of director, producer and writer John Houseman. USA: New York, NY. 1935-1985. Lang.: Eng.
2339

Harris, Richard
Administration
Illness of star rule arbitrated *re*: Richard Harris in *Camelot*. USA: New York, NY. 1983. Lang.: Eng.
115
Performance/production
Collection of newspaper reviews by London theatre critics. UK-England: London. 1986. Lang.: Eng.
2141
Collection of newspaper reviews by New York critics. USA: New York, NY. 1987. Lang.: Eng.
2324

Harrison, Harvey
Design/technology
Cinematography and lighting of the film *Castaway* by Harvey Harrison. USA. 1987. Lang.: Eng.
3137

Harrison, Jane
Performance/production
Origins of theatre and its relationship to the spectator. India. Japan. Sri Lanka. 1987. Lang.: Eng.
813

Hart House Theatre (Toronto, ON)
Institutions
Elizabeth Sterling Haynes and the Little Theatre movement. Canada. 1916-1957. Lang.: Eng.
1603

Hart, Charles
Performance/production
Collection of newspaper reviews by London theatre critics. UK-England: London. 1986. Lang.: Eng.
2065

International Bibliography of Theatre: 1987

339

Hart, Josephine
Performance/production
Collection of newspaper reviews by London theatre critics. UK-England: London. 1986. Lang.: Eng.　　2116
Collection of newspaper reviews by London theatre critics. UK-England: London. 1987. Lang.: Eng.　　2245
Hart, Moss
Performance/production
Collection of newspaper reviews by London theatre critics. UK-England: London. 1987. Lang.: Eng.　　2274
Hartman Theatre (New York, NY)
Administration
Financial challenges of four former artistic directors. USA. 1981-1987. Lang.: Eng.　　239
Harvest
Plays/librettos/scripts
Irish Literary Renaissance writers' view of America. Ireland. 1900-1930. Lang.: Eng.　　2639
Harvey
Performance/production
Six plays of the Tokyo season, focus on director Betsuyaku Minoru. Japan: Tokyo. 1986. Lang.: Jap.　　1966
Harwood, Kate
Performance/production
Collection of newspaper reviews by London theatre critics. UK-England: London. 1987. Lang.: Eng.　　2198
Has'Fari, Shmuel
Performance/production
Collection of newspaper reviews by London theatre critics. UK-England: London. 1987. Lang.: Eng.　　2275
Hashhia
SEE
Zakat.
Haslund, Vesleøy
Administration
Actress Vesleøy Haslund fights termination from the National Theatre. Norway: Oslo. 1979-1982. Lang.: Eng.　　1522
Hassha-bai (Hushabye)
Performance/production
New themes and styles in Japanese theatre. Japan: Tokyo. 1986. Lang.: Jap.　　1953
Hastings, Michael
Performance/production
Collection of newspaper reviews by London theatre critics. UK-England: London. 1987. Lang.: Eng.　　2190
Collection of newspaper reviews by London theatre critics. UK-England: London. 1987. Lang.: Eng.　　2254
Határ, Győző
Performance/production
A patkánykirály (The King of the Rats) by Győző Határ staged by László Salamon Suba at Móricz Zsigmond Theatre. Hungary: Nyíregyháza. 1987. Lang.: Hun.　　1899
László Salamon Suba directs *A patkánykirály (The King of the Rats)* by Győző Határ at Móricz Zsigmond Theatre. Hungary: Nyíregyháza. 1987. Lang.: Hun.　　1901
Hato poppa shōkai (Tokyo)
Performance/production
Analysis of four Tokyo productions. Japan: Tokyo. 1987. Lang.: Jap.　　1957
Hauptfleisch, Temple
Plays/librettos/scripts
New Afrikaans drama and playwrights. South Africa, Republic of. 1985-1986. Lang.: Afr.　　1155
Hauptman, William
Administration
Influence of TV ads on success of Broadway plays. USA: New York, NY. 1984-1987. Lang.: Eng.　　179
Hauptmann, Gerhart
Plays/librettos/scripts
Comparison of works by Hauptmann and Wilbrandt. Germany: Berlin. Austria: Vienna. 1889-1987. Lang.: Eng.　　2593
Critical reception of realism and naturalism. Germany. 1890-1987. Lang.: Ger.　　2601
Study of *El pan del pobre (Poor Man's Bread)*, adapted from Hauptmann's *Die Weber (The Weavers)*. Spain. 1894. Lang.: Eng.　　2728

Hausa theatre
Performance/production
History of Hausa theatre. Niger, Republic of. 1876-1982. Lang.: Eng.　　865
Hauser, Frank
Performance/production
Collection of newspaper reviews by London theatre critics. UK-England: London. 1986. Lang.: Eng.　　2037
Collection of newspaper reviews by London theatre critics. UK-England: London. 1987. Lang.: Eng.　　2221
Collection of newspaper reviews by London theatre critics. UK-England: London. 1987. Lang.: Eng.　　2256
Hausvater, Alexander
Performance/production
Description of La Quinzaine theatre festival. Canada: Quebec, PQ. 1986. Lang.: Fre.　　1696
Haute surveillance (Deathwatch)
Performance/production
Collection of newspaper reviews by London theatre critics. UK-England: London. 1987. Lang.: Eng.　　2223
Have His Carcase, Eastender
Performance/production
Dorothy L. Sayers' *Have His Carcase, Eastender* and *Intimate Contact* are reviewed. UK-England. 1987. Lang.: Eng.　　3208
Havel, Vaclav
Performance/production
Collection of newspaper reviews by London theatre critics. UK-England: London. 1987. Lang.: Eng.　　2181
Havergal, Giles
Performance/production
Collection of newspaper reviews by London theatre critics. UK. 1987. Lang.: Eng.　　2031
Collection of newspaper reviews by London theatre critics. UK-England: London. 1987. Lang.: Eng.　　2211
Collection of newspaper reviews by London theatre critics. UK-England: London. 1987. Lang.: Eng.　　2256
Hawling, Francis
Administration
Theatrical season of 1723 at the Drury Lane Theatre. England: London. 1723. Lang.: Eng.　　21
Hawthorn, Pamela
Institutions
The advantages and disadvantages of the Jesse Awards. Canada: Vancouver, BC. 1983. Lang.: Eng.　　517
Performance/production
The Directors Colloquium: director/playwright relationship. Canada: Calgary, AB. 1987. Lang.: Eng.　　747
Háy, Gyula
Performance/production
Tamás Szirtes directs Gyula Háy's *Mohács (The Mohács Disaster)* at Madách Színház. Hungary. 1987. Lang.: Hun.　　1863
Gyula Háy's *Mohács (The Mohács Disaster)* staged by Tamás Szirtes, Gyulai Várszinház. Hungary: Gyula. 1987. Lang.: Hun.　　1903
Hayes, Catherine
Plays/librettos/scripts
Political use of traditional comic structure by contemporary playwrights. UK-England. 1970-1987. Lang.: Eng.　　2762
Haym, Nicola
Performance/production
Cast lists for some early London operas. England: London. 1712-1717. Lang.: Eng.　　3761
Hayman, Carole
Performance/production
Collection of newspaper reviews by London theatre critics. UK-England: London. 1986. Lang.: Eng.　　2058
Collection of newspaper reviews by London theatre critics. UK-England: London. 1986. Lang.: Eng.　　2091
Hayman, David
Performance/production
Collection of newspaper reviews by London theatre critics. UK-England: London. 1986. Lang.: Eng.　　2077
Collection of newspaper reviews by London theatre critics. UK-England: London. 1987. Lang.: Eng.　　2244
Haymarket Theatre (Leicester)
Performance/production
Collection of newspaper reviews by London theatre critics. UK-England: London. 1987. Lang.: Eng.　　2235

Haymarket Theatre (London)
Performance/production

Two productions of Pinter's *Old Times*. UK-England: London. USA: New York, NY, St. Louis, MO. 1971-1985. Lang.: Eng.   907

Collection of newspaper reviews by London theatre critics. UK-England. 1987. Lang.: Eng.   2263

Haynes, Ed
Performance/production

Review of Wagner's *Der Fliegende Holländer* at the Natal Playhouse. South Africa, Republic of: Durban. 1987. Lang.: Eng.   3815

Haynes, Elizabeth Sterling
Institutions

Elizabeth Sterling Haynes and the Little Theatre movement. Canada. 1916-1957. Lang.: Eng.   1603

Haynes, Roger
Performance/production

Collection of newspaper reviews by London theatre critics. UK-England: London. 1987. Lang.: Eng.   2195

Hays, David
Institutions

National Theatre of the Deaf productions of *Farewell My Lovely* and *In a Grove* directed by Arvin Brown in Beijing. China, People's Republic of: Beijing. USA. 1986-1987. Lang.: Eng.   1611

Hayūza gekijō (Tokyo)
Performance/production

Focus on several Tokyo productions. Japan: Tokyo. 1960-1987. Lang.: Jap.   1955

Productions of several Tokyo companies. Japan: Tokyo. 1987. Lang.: Jap.   1962

Six plays of the Tokyo season, focus on director Betsuyaku Minoru. Japan: Tokyo. 1986. Lang.: Jap.   1966

Hayworth, Jill
Performance/production

Four approaches to the role of Sally Bowles in *Cabaret*. USA: New York, NY. Germany. 1966-1987. Lang.: Eng.   968

Heads Held High
Performance/production

Collection of newspaper reviews by London theatre critics. UK-England: London. 1986. Lang.: Eng.   2156

Health/safety
Administration

Revisions in eligibility, insurance coverage rules, Equity League Welfare Fund. USA. 1985. Lang.: Eng.   65

Changes in Equity welfare benefits. USA: New York, NY. 1985. Lang.: Eng.   67

Information pension and health claim forms on Equity. USA: New York, NY. 1986. Lang.: Eng.   69

Changes to Equity League Health Plan's second opinion program. USA: New York, NY. 1987. Lang.: Eng.   80

Fundraising for Equity Fights AIDS. USA: New York, NY. 1987. Lang.: Eng.   87

Equity-League Pension and Health Fund annual report, FY86. USA: New York, NY. 1987. Lang.: Eng.   97

New Council of Stock Theatres contract and its impact. USA: New York, NY. 1986. Lang.: Eng.   122

Report on Equity League Welfare Fund program. USA. 1985. Lang.: Eng.   147

Labor-sponsored conference for Chicago Equity members. USA: Chicago, IL. 1986. Lang.: Eng.   221

Audience

Theatre education project for teaching about sexuality. Canada: Toronto, ON. 1987. Lang.: Eng.   278

Design/technology

Survey of theatrical fog machines. USA. 1987. Lang.: Eng.   395

Institutions

The role of the Actors' Fund in New York's theatre industry. USA: New York, NY. 1987. Lang.: Eng.   570

First health care institution specifically for performers. USA: New York, NY. 1985. Lang.: Eng.   576

A Season of Concern, an AIDS fundraising benefit in Chicago. USA: Chicago, IL. 1987. Lang.: Eng.   609

The work of AEA's Equity Fights AIDS Committee. USA: New York, NY. 1987. Lang.: Eng.   619

Performance spaces

Safety problems of new, cooperative Jurta theatre. Hungary: Budapest. 1987. Lang.: Hun.   638

Relation to other fields

Charitable and self-help welfare schemes for theatre personnel, focus on experiences of women. UK-England. 1851-1920. Lang.: Eng. 1258

Healy, Derek
Institutions

Need for more Canadian productions of Canadian-composed opera. Canada. 1987. Lang.: Eng.   3718

Heaney, Seamus
Plays/librettos/scripts

Metaphor of archaeology in Friel's *Volunteers*, poems of Heaney. Ireland: Dublin. UK-Ireland. 1975. Lang.: Eng.   2651

Heap, Carl
Performance/production

Collection of newspaper reviews by London theatre critics. UK-England: London. 1987. Lang.: Eng.   2190

Collection of newspaper reviews by London theatre critics. UK-England: London. 1987. Lang.: Eng.   2229

Heart of Ice
Performance/production

Collection of newspaper reviews by London theatre critics. UK-England. 1987. Lang.: Eng.   2262

Heart of Paddy Whack, The
Plays/librettos/scripts

Analysis of the plays and songs of Irish-American musical theatre star Chauncey Olcott. USA. 1893-1918. Lang.: Eng.   3671

Heartbreak House
Performance/production

Philip Bosco's portrayals of characters in the plays of George Bernard Shaw. USA. 1987. Lang.: Eng.   2335

Heartbroken Boat, The
SEE

Barca dels afligits, La.

Heat of the Day, The
Performance/production

Collection of newspaper reviews by London theatre critics. UK-England: London. 1987. Lang.: Eng.   2211

Heath, Tim
Performance/production

Collection of newspaper reviews by London theatre critics. UK-England: London. 1986. Lang.: Eng.   2085

Heatly, Stephen
Institutions

Analysis of co-productions between Saskatoon theatre companies. Canada: Saskatoon, SK. 1987. Lang.: Eng.   518

Heaton, Lorna
Performance/production

Lorna Heaton's use of holograms in *Woyzeck*. Canada: Banff, AB. 1987. Lang.: Fre.   3205

Heaven and Earth
Plays/librettos/scripts

Structure of Byron's plays. England. 1788-1824. Lang.: Eng.   2542

Heaven and the Victorians Theatre Company (London)
Performance/production

Collection of newspaper reviews by London theatre critics. UK-England: London. 1987. Lang.: Eng.   2187

Heaven Bent, Hell Bound
Performance/production

Collection of newspaper reviews by London theatre critics. UK-England. 1987. Lang.: Eng.   2199

Hebbel, Friedrich
Theory/criticism

Comparison of Ball's *Michelangelo's Nose* and Hebbel's *Michel Angelo*. Germany. 1886-1927. Lang.: Eng.   3042

Hebrew University (Jerusalem)
Performance/production

Production of Merbury's *The Marriage of Wit and Wisdom* by David Parry. Israel: Jerusalem. 1987. Lang.: Eng.   1939

Hecht, Ben
Design/technology

Tony Walton's set designs at the Vivian Beaumont Theatre. USA: New York, NY. 1986-1987. Lang.: Eng.   465

Heckert, Matthew
Design/technology
Mark Pauline, Matthew Heckert and Eric Werner: performance artists who construct performing machines. USA: San Francisco, CA. 1986. Lang.: Eng.   3342

Hedda Gabler
Performance spaces
Theatre space and theatrical space in theatre from the ancient Greeks to the present. Germany. England. Greece. 400 B.C.-1987 A.D. Lang.: Eng.   635

Performance/production
Collection of newspaper reviews by London theatre critics. UK-England: London. 1986. Lang.: Eng.   2120

Hedda Gabler at American Ibsen Theatre. USA: Pittsburgh, PA. 1987. Lang.: Eng.   2358

Plays/librettos/scripts
Three feminist productions of plays by Henrik Ibsen. USA. 1987. Lang.: Eng.   2899

Theory/criticism
Exploration of the nature of tragedy. 500 B.C.-1987 A.D. Lang.: Eng.   3020

Hedley, Philip
Performance/production
Collection of newspaper reviews by London theatre critics. UK-England: London. 1986. Lang.: Eng.   2106

Collection of newspaper reviews by London theatre critics. UK-England: London. 1987. Lang.: Eng.   2182

Collection of newspaper reviews by London theatre critics. UK-England: London. 1987. Lang.: Eng.   2194

Collection of newspaper reviews by London theatre critics. UK-England: London. 1987. Lang.: Eng.   2207

Collection of newspaper reviews by London theatre critics. UK-England: London. 1987. Lang.: Eng.   2211

Heeley, Desmond
Design/technology
Interview with designer Desmond Heeley. UK-England: London. USA: New York, NY. Canada: Stratford, ON. 1940-1984. Lang.: Eng.   1596

Hegedűs D., Géza
Performance/production
Review of actors Géza Tordy, Géza Hegedűs D. and Attila Kaszás in Arthur Miller's *Death of a Salesman*. Hungary: Budapest. 1987. Lang.: Hun.   1893

Hegyi, Árpad Jutocsa
Performance/production
Two premieres: Shakespeare, *The Merchant of Venice*, directed by Árpád Jutacsa Hegyi. Németh's *Villámfénynél (By the Stroke of Lightning)*, directed by Attila Seprődi Kiss. Hungary: Kecskemét. 1987. Lang.: Hun.   1925

Height of Passion
Performance/production
Collection of newspaper reviews by London theatre critics. UK-England: London. 1987. Lang.: Eng.   2264

Heijermans, Herman
Relation to other fields
Debate over proletarian art among Social Democrats. Germany: Berlin. 1910-1912. Lang.: Ger.   1238

Hein, Christoph
Plays/librettos/scripts
Study of *Passage* by Christoph Hein. Germany, East. 1987. Lang.: Ger.   2614

Heit, Sally Jane
Performance/production
Collection of newspaper reviews by London theatre critics. UK-England: London. 1987. Lang.: Eng.   2240

Helen Hayes Theatre (New York, NY)
Performance/production
Collection of newspaper reviews by New York theatre critics. USA: New York, NY. 1987. Lang.: Eng.   2325

Helen Lederer and Raw Sex
Performance/production
Collection of newspaper reviews by London theatre critics. UK-England: London. 1987. Lang.: Eng.   2269

Heller, André
Performance/production
André Heller, creator of *Luna Luna*. Austria: Vienna. 1700-1799. Lang.: Ita.   3250

Hellman, Lillian
Plays/librettos/scripts
Interview with playwright Alice Childress. USA: New York, NY, Baltimore, MD. 1987. Lang.: Eng.   2844

Hello Dolly
Performance/production
Review of *Hello Dolly* in Bloemfontein. South Africa, Republic of: Bloemfontein. 1987. Lang.: Eng.   3635

Help
Institutions
Two community-based popular theatre projects. Canada. 1987. Lang.: Eng.   522

Help the King!
SEE
Segitsd a királyst!.

Help Wanted
SEE
Furcht und Hoffnung der BRD.

Helsingin Kaupunginteatteri (Helsinki)
Performance/production
The 4th International Theatre Conference: includes list of participants and their contributions. Poland: Warsaw. 1986. Lang.: Eng, Fre.   873

Helsinki City Theatre
SEE
Helsingin Kaupunginteatteri.

Hemingway, Ernest
Plays/librettos/scripts
The Spanish Civil War in works by Ernest Hemingway and Sean O'Casey. UK. Ireland. USA. 1930-1939. Lang.: Eng.   2749

Hemma i Södertälje (At Home in Södertälje)
Performance/production
Musikteatergruppen Oktober collaborates with immigrant amateurs. Sweden: Södertälje. 1986. Lang.: Swe.   2019

Henceforward
Performance/production
Collection of newspaper reviews by London theatre critics. UK-England: London. 1987. Lang.: Eng.   2234

Heneker, David
Performance/production
Collection of newspaper reviews by London theatre critics. UK-England: London. 1986. Lang.: Eng.   2124

Henley, Beth
Performance/production
Examination of language in Beth Henley's *The Miss Firecracker Contest*. Mexico: Mexico City. 1987. Lang.: Spa.   1974

Collection of newspaper reviews by London theatre critics. UK-England: London. 1986. Lang.: Eng.   2110

Collection of newspaper reviews by New York theatre critics. USA: New York, NY. 1987. Lang.: Eng.   2312

Hennequin, Maurice
Performance/production
Collection of newspaper reviews by London theatre critics. UK-England: London. 1987. Lang.: Eng.   2203

Henri, Adrian
Performance/production
Collection of newspaper reviews by London theatre critics. UK-England: London. 1986. Lang.: Eng.   2050

Henry IV
Performance/production
Shakespeare at Várszinház: László Vámos directs *Henry IV* Parts I and II, Imre Kerényi directs *Henry V*. Hungary: Budapest. 1986. Lang.: Hun.   1810

Collection of newspaper reviews by London theatre critics. UK-England: London. 1987. Lang.: Eng.   2193

Plays/librettos/scripts
The creation of ideal future worlds based on the historical past in some plays of Shakespeare. England. 1591-1599. Lang.: Ger.   2539

Structure of tragic elements in plays of William Shakespeare. England: London. 1594-1599. Lang.: Eng.   2551

History and utopianism in some plays of Shakespeare. England. 1589-1606. Lang.: Ger.   2558

Depictions of dying moments of characters in drama, specifically that of Hotspur in *Henry IV, Part I*. UK-England: London. 1595-1598. Lang.: Eng.   2763

Influences on *The Voysey Inheritance* by Granville Barker. UK-England. 1600-1938. Lang.: Eng.   2820

Henry IV – cont'd

Restoring character originally intended for role of Falstaff in *Henry IV, Part I*. UK-England: London. 1595-1598. Lang.: Eng. 2821

Development of Welles's adaptation of *Henry IV* Parts I and II from stage to screen. USA. Ireland. 1938-1965. Lang.: Eng. 3182

Analysis and success of Boito's libretto for Verdi's opera *Falstaff*. Italy. 1893. Lang.: Eng. 3923

Henry IV by Pirandello
SEE
Enrico Quarto.

Henry V
Performance/production
Shakespeare at Várszinház: László Vámos directs *Henry IV* Parts I and II, Imre Kerényi directs *Henry V*. Hungary: Budapest. 1986. Lang.: Hun. 1810

Collection of newspaper reviews by London theatre critics. UK-England: London. 1986. Lang.: Eng. 2138

Plays/librettos/scripts
Shakespeare's *Henry V*: development of Prince Hal as an ideological monarch. England. 1599. Lang.: Eng. 1124

The creation of ideal future worlds based on the historical past in some plays of Shakespeare. England. 1591-1599. Lang.: Ger. 2539

Role of Chorus in Shakespeare's *Henry V*. England. 1599. Lang.: Eng. 2556

Henry VI
Plays/librettos/scripts
The creation of ideal future worlds based on the historical past in some plays of Shakespeare. England. 1591-1599. Lang.: Ger. 2539

History and utopianism in some plays of Shakespeare. England. 1589-1606. Lang.: Ger. 2558

Henry VIII
Plays/librettos/scripts
Rumour as a political and social tool in *Henry VIII*. England: London. 1612-1614. Lang.: Eng. 2547

View of the ideal and mortal worlds explored in *Henry VIII*. UK-England: London. 1611-1614. Lang.: Eng. 2797

Henry, Chad
Performance/production
Collection of newspaper reviews by London theatre critics. UK-England: London. 1986. Lang.: Eng. 2088

Henry, David
Performance/production
Collection of newspaper reviews by London theatre critics. UK-England: London. 1987. Lang.: Eng. 2277

Henry, Martha
Performance/production
Grand Theatre: failed establishment of repertory theatre. Canada: London, ON. 1983-1984. Lang.: Eng. 738

Henry, Sweet Henry
Performance/production
History and review of 1967 musical *Henry, Sweet Henry*. USA: New York, NY. 1967. Lang.: Eng. 3642

Hensbergen
Performance/production
Interview with Frans Strijards, playwright and director. Netherlands. 1987. Lang.: Dut. 1979

Henschke, Alfred
SEE
Klabund.

Henshaw, James
Plays/librettos/scripts
Use of English in Nigerian drama. Nigeria. 1940-1987. Lang.: Eng. 2706

Henslowe, Philip
Relation to other fields
Psychological effect of Ben Jonson's family life on his writings. England. 1602-1604. Lang.: Eng. 1232

Henze, Hans Werner
Plays/librettos/scripts
Opera composer, Hans Werner Henze. Germany: Gutersloh. 1926-1987. Lang.: Eng. 3910

Hepburn, Katherine
Performance/production
Personal anecdotes and photographs from the making of *The African Queen*. USA: Hollywood, CA. 1950-1951. Lang.: Eng. 3168

Her Majesty's Theatre (London)
Design/technology
Victorian under-stage machinery, Her Majesty's Theatre, London. UK-England: London. 1890-1987. Lang.: Eng. 377

Machinery to be installed in Her Majesty's Theatre for *Phantom of the Opera*. UK-England: London. 1987. Lang.: Eng. 3619

Performance/production
Collection of newspaper reviews by London theatre critics. UK-England: London. 1986. Lang.: Eng. 2065

Heracles
Plays/librettos/scripts
Study of works by Sophocles, Aeschylus and Euripides. Greece. 400 B.C.-500 A.D. Lang.: Eng. 2624

Herbert, A.P.
Performance/production
Collection of newspaper reviews by London theatre critics. UK-England: London. 1987. Lang.: Eng. 2234

Herbert, Victor
Performance/production
Review of *Pirates* and *Student Prince*. South Africa, Republic of: Johannesburg. 1986. Lang.: Eng. 3634

Herbert, Zbigniew
Performance/production
Festival of Polish plays. Poland: Wrocław. 1987. Lang.: Eng, Fre. 871

Herczeg, Ferenc
Performance/production
Analysis of *Kék róka (The Silver Fox)* by Ferenc Herczeg compares Zsusza Bencze's staging with previous productions. Hungary: Budapest. 1986. Lang.: Hun. 1808

Heresies
Performance/production
Collection of newspaper reviews by London theatre critics. UK-England: London. 1986. Lang.: Eng. 2045

Heritage
Performance/production
Collection of newspaper reviews by London theatre critics. UK-England: London. 1986. Lang.: Eng. 2171

Herman
Performance/production
Collection of newspaper reviews by London theatre critics. UK-England: London. 1986. Lang.: Eng. 2131

Herman, Jerry
Performance/production
Transformation of *La Cage aux Folles* from movie to a Broadway musical. USA: New York, NY. 1983-1987. Lang.: Eng. 940

Collection of newspaper reviews by London theatre critics. UK-England: London. 1986. Lang.: Eng. 2095

Career of actor Lee Roy Reams. USA: New York, NY. 1987. Lang.: Eng. 3661

Study of the work of Stephen Sondheim. USA: New York, NY. UK-England: London. 1962-1985. Lang.: Eng. 3665

Herman, Ray
Performance/production
Collection of newspaper reviews by London theatre critics. UK-England: London. 1987. Lang.: Eng. 2272

Hermann
Plays/librettos/scripts
Hermann, a puppet production for adults about coping with oppression. Germany. Poland: Bielsko Biala. 1978-1987. Lang.: Eng. 3991

Herne, James A.
Plays/librettos/scripts
Irish influence on American theatre through Irish-American playwrights. USA. 1839-1901. Lang.: Eng. 2889

Herr Puntila und sein Knecht Matti (Mr. Puntila and His Hired Man, Matti)
Performance/production
International Brecht symposium. China, People's Republic of: Beijing, Hong Kong. Japan: Tokyo. 1986. Lang.: Eng. 1722

Hersey, David
Design/technology
Current Broadway shows and their lighting designers. USA: New York, NY. 1987. Lang.: Eng. 460

Lighting design and instruments for production of *Nicholas Nickleby*. USA: New York, NY. 1982. Lang.: Eng. 478

Hersov, Gregory
Performance/production
Collection of newspaper reviews by London theatre critics. UK-England: London. 1986. Lang.: Eng. 2070

Heskins, Theresa
Performance/production
Collection of newspaper reviews by London theatre critics. UK-England: London. 1986. Lang.: Eng. 2161

Heston, Charlton
Performance/production
Creative self-knowledge and the mystical path of actors. UK-England: London. USA. 1977-1987. Lang.: Eng. 900

Hevesi Sándor Szinház (Zalaegerszeg)
Design/technology
Technical innovation in scene design at Hevesi Sándor Theatre. Hungary: Zalaegerszeg. 1982-1986. Lang.: Hun. 336

Performance/production
Interview with director József Ruszt. Hungary. 1983-1987. Lang.: Hun. 1791

G.E. Lessing's *Nathan der Weise (Nathan the Wise)* staged by József Ruszt, Hevesi Sándor Theatre. Hungary: Zalaegerszeg. 1986. Lang.: Hun. 1806

Péter Tömöry directs premiere of Zsigmond Móricz's 1916 *Fortunátus*. Hungary: Zalaegerszeg. 1987. Lang.: Hun. 1840

József Ruszt directs G.E. Lessing's *Nathan der Weise (Nathan the Wise)* at Hevesi Sándor Theatre under the title *Bölcs Náthán*. Hungary: Zalaegerszeg. 1986. Lang.: Hun. 1866

Review of conference on contemporary Hungarian drama. Hungary: Egervár. 1987. Lang.: Hun. 1879

A tanítónő (The Schoolmistress) by Sándor Bródy, directed by Péter Tömöry at Hevesi Sándor Theatre. Hungary: Zalaegerszeg. 1986. Lang.: Hun. 1921

Mihály Vörösmarty's 'fairy-play' *Csongor and Tünde* directed by Béla Merő at Hevesi Sándor Színház. Hungary: Zalaegerszeg. 1987. Lang.: Hun. 1926

Performances of *Oliver* staged by György Korcsmáros, Antol Rencz and Imre Halasi. Hungary: Budapest, Békéscsaba, Zalaegerszeg. 1986. Lang.: Hun. 3632

Hewett, Dorothy
Plays/librettos/scripts
Critical analysis of Dorothy Hewett's *The Man from Mukinupin*. Australia. 1979. Lang.: Eng. 2438

Hey! Luciani: The Times, Life and Codex of Albino Luciani
Performance/production
Collection of newspaper reviews by London theatre critics. UK-England: London. 1986. Lang.: Eng. 2036

Heya (Room, A)
Performance/production
Focus on several Tokyo productions. Japan: Tokyo. 1960-1987. Lang.: Jap. 1955

Heyday
Performance/production
Collection of newspaper reviews by London theatre critics. UK-England: London. 1986. Lang.: Eng. 2104

Heymann, Birger
Performance/production
Collection of newspaper reviews by London theatre critics. UK-England: London. 1986. Lang.: Eng. 2065

Heywood, Thomas
Performance/production
Shakespeare and contemporaries: tradition, intertextuality in performance. England. 1607-1987. Lang.: Eng. 1740

'Boy actresses' and attitudes toward sensuality in performance. England: London. 1580-1630. Lang.: Eng. 1741

Theory/criticism
Trollope's writings on Elizabethan and Jacobean drama. UK-England. 1866-1882. Lang.: Eng. 3063

Hibberd, Jack
Plays/librettos/scripts
Interview with playwright Jack Hibberd. Australia. 1967-1986. Lang.: Eng. 1098

Survey of the plays of Jack Hibberd: themes and characterization. Australia. 1966-1986. Lang.: Eng. 2437

Hickling, John
Plays/librettos/scripts
Producer and writer John Hickling's work for commercial radio. Australia. 1930-1960. Lang.: Eng. 3115

Hicks, Colin
Performance/production
Collection of newspaper reviews by London theatre critics. UK-England: London. 1986. Lang.: Eng. 2067

Hicks, Laura
Theory/criticism
On the Verge by Eric Overmyer. Production history, plot synopsis, critical evaluation. USA. 1987. Lang.: Eng. 3068

Hicks, Seymour
Performance/production
British theatrical touring companies. UK-England. North America. Australia. 1870-1929. Lang.: Eng. 2280

Hickson, Robert
Performance/production
Collection of newspaper reviews by London theatre critics. UK-England: London. 1987. Lang.: Eng. 2218

Higby, ShaSha
Design/technology
Costume sculpture performance of ShaSha Higby. USA. 1987. Lang.: Eng. 482

High Society
Performance/production
Collection of newspaper reviews by London theatre critics. UK-England: London. 1987. Lang.: Eng. 2187

Highway, Tomson
Plays/librettos/scripts
Playwright Tomson Highway's use of native mythology. Canada. 1960-1987. Lang.: Eng. 2468

Hihōreibankan (Tokyo)
Performance/production
New Tokyo productions. Japan: Tokyo. 1987. Lang.: Jap. 1954

Hildegarde & Ich (Hildegard & I)
Plays/librettos/scripts
The German radio play *Hörspiel* and its history. Germany, West: Cologne. USA. 1950-1985. Lang.: Eng. 3117

Hill, Aaron
Performance/production
Acting styles on English stages. UK-England. 1740-1760. Lang.: Eng. 2304

Hiller, Wendy
Performance/production
The founding and history of the Malvern Festival. UK-England: Malvern. 1904-1977. Lang.: Eng. 2286

Hilpert, Heinz
Performance/production
Reviews of major Berlin performances. Germany: Berlin. 1889-1933. Lang.: Ger. 1772

Hilton, Julian
Performance/production
Collection of newspaper reviews by London theatre critics. UK-England: London. 1987. Lang.: Eng. 2190

Hincho, Tamara
Performance/production
Collection of newspaper reviews by London theatre critics. UK-England: London. 1986. Lang.: Eng. 2140

Hinds, Andy
Performance/production
Collection of newspaper reviews by London theatre critics. UK-England. 1986. Lang.: Eng. 2159

Hines, Garry
Performance/production
Collection of newspaper reviews by London theatre critics. UK-England: London. 1987. Lang.: Eng. 2220

Hinmin kurabu (Slum Club, A)
Performance/production
Productions from Yume no yūminsha, Tōhō, Parco, Tsukumo and Nakamura za. Japan: Tokyo. 1986-1987. Lang.: Jap. 1956

Hippodrome Theatre (Gainesville, FL)
Performance/production
Four productions in Southern regional theatres. USA: Houston, TX, Louisville, KY, Gainesville, FL. 1980. Lang.: Eng. 2342

Hiriart, Hugo
Plays/librettos/scripts
Interview with playwright Hugo Hiriart. Mexico: Mexico City. 1987. Lang.: Spa. 1151

Hirsch, John
Administration
Excerpts, John Hirsch's farewell lecture, Stratford Festival. Canada: Stratford, ON. 1947-1985. Lang.: Eng. 9

Holborough, Jacqueline — cont'd

Collection of newspaper reviews by London theatre critics. UK-England: London. 1987. Lang.: Eng. 2226

Holcroft, Thomas
Plays/librettos/scripts
Analysis of vampire characters in the works of Byron, Polidori and Planché. England. Italy. France. 1800-1825. Lang.: Eng. 2540

Hole in the Top of the World, The
Performance/production
Collection of newspaper reviews by London theatre critics. UK-England: London. 1987. Lang.: Eng. 2198

Hollaender, Felix
Performance/production
Reviews of major Berlin performances. Germany: Berlin. 1889-1933. Lang.: Ger. 1772

Holland Festival (Netherlands)
Performance/production
Peter Sellars and American National Theatre present *Ajax*, Holland Festival. Netherlands. USA. 1987. Lang.: Dut. 1981

Hollingsworth, Michael
Plays/librettos/scripts
Michael Hollingsworth's *The History of the Village of Small Huts*. Canada. 1987. Lang.: Eng. 1099

Holloway, Jonathan
Performance/production
Collection of newspaper reviews by London theatre critics. UK-England: London. 1986. Lang.: Eng. 2143

Collection of newspaper reviews by London theatre critics. UK-England: London. 1987. Lang.: Eng. 2267

Collection of newspaper reviews by London theatre critics. UK-England: London. 1987. Lang.: Eng. 2276

Holloway, W.H.
Performance/production
British theatrical touring companies. UK-England. North America. Australia. 1870-1929. Lang.: Eng. 2280

Holm, John Cecil
Performance/production
Collection of newspaper reviews by London theatre critics. UK-England: London. 1987. Lang.: Eng. 2272

Holman, David
Performance/production
Collection of newspaper reviews by London theatre critics. UK-England: London. 1987. Lang.: Eng. 2173

Collection of newspaper reviews by London theatre critics. UK-England: London. 1987. Lang.: Eng. 2224

Collection of newspaper reviews by London theatre critics. UK-England: London. 1987. Lang.: Eng. 2252

Holman, Robert
Performance/production
Collection of newspaper reviews by London theatre critics. UK-England: London. 1986. Lang.: Eng. 2117

Holmberg, Kalle
Performance/production
Fadren (The Father) by August Strindberg presented under the title *Az apa* at Katona József Theatre, guest director Kalle Holmberg. Hungary: Budapest. 1987. Lang.: Hun. 1865

Holmes, Rupert
Performance/production
Collection of newspaper reviews by London theatre critics. UK-England: London. 1987. Lang.: Eng. 2214

Holograms
Design/technology
The use of holography in theatre. Canada. 1987. Lang.: Fre. 3201

Performance/production
Lorna Heaton's use of holograms in *Woyzeck*. Canada: Banff, AB. 1987. Lang.: Fre. 3205

Holst, Gustav
Plays/librettos/scripts
Operas that contain Indian-related themes and music. India. Europe. 1730-1904. Lang.: Eng. 3914

Holy Ghosts
Design/technology
Lighting reviews for some New York productions. USA: New York, NY. 1987. Lang.: Eng. 477

Performance/production
Collection of newspaper reviews by New York theatre critics. USA: New York, NY. 1987. Lang.: Eng. 2319

Plays/librettos/scripts
Interview with playwright Romulus Linney. USA. 1986. Lang.: Eng. 2931

Home on the Range
Performance/production
Interview with playwright Amiri Baraka. USA: Newark, NJ, New York, NY. 1965-1969. Lang.: Eng. 2356

Home Work
Performance/production
Collection of newspaper reviews by London theatre critics. UK-England: London. 1987. Lang.: Eng. 2203

Home, John
Performance/production
Examples of transition in acting style. England. 1783-1784. Lang.: Eng. 1733

Home, William Douglas
Performance/production
Collection of newspaper reviews by London theatre critics. UK-England: London. 1987. Lang.: Eng. 2235

Homecoming, The
Plays/librettos/scripts
Interpreting Harold Pinter's dramas through focus on his play structures. UK-England. 1958-1987. Lang.: Eng. 2815

Theory/criticism
Structuralist approach to play interpretation. 500 B.C.-1987 A.D. Lang.: Eng. 3016

Homer
Plays/librettos/scripts
Parallels between O'Neill's *Anna Christie* and Homer's *Odyssey*. USA. 1921. Lang.: Eng. 2906

Homme qui tua le crocodile, L' (Man Who Killed the Crocodile, The)
Plays/librettos/scripts
Compares plays of Enlightenment France, Francophone Africa. Congo: Brazzaville. Cameroon. Benin. France. 1700-1975. Lang.: Eng. 2496

Honda, Jifu
Performance/production
Four Tokyo productions in light of ideas of Betsuyaku Minoru. Japan: Tokyo. 1987. Lang.: Jap. 1950

Honda, Yasuji
Performance/production
Honda Yasuji's work on Japanese folk theatre. Japan. 1930-1986. Lang.: Eng. 1483

Honer, Chris
Plays/librettos/scripts
Use of oral history material to develop characters and events in plays. UK-England. 1970-1987. Lang.: Eng. 2807

Hong Kong Repertory Theatre (Hong Kong)
Performance/production
Review of International Brecht Festival. China, People's Republic of: Hong Kong. 1986. Lang.: Dut. 759

Hood, Kevin
Performance/production
Collection of newspaper reviews by London theatre critics. UK-England: London. 1987. Lang.: Eng. 2173

Hooker, John Lee
Performance/production
Southern rural background of blues music. USA. 1800-1985. Lang.: Eng. 3411

Hooligans Say
Performance/production
Collection of newspaper reviews by London theatre critics. UK-England: London. 1986. Lang.: Eng. 2169

Hooper, Ewan
Performance/production
Collection of newspaper reviews by London theatre critics. UK-England: London. 1986. Lang.: Eng. 2121

Hopkins, Anthony
Performance/production
Two productions of Pinter's *Old Times*. UK-England: London. USA: New York, NY, St. Louis, MO. 1971-1985. Lang.: Eng. 907

Hopkins, John
Performance/production
Collection of newspaper reviews by London theatre critics. UK-England: London. 1987. Lang.: Eng. 2183

Hopkins, Karen Brookes
Administration
Interview with Karen Brookes Hopkins (Brooklyn Academy of Music) and Kate Busch (ART/NY). USA: New York, NY. 1987. Lang.: Eng.   158

Hoplands, Bernard
Performance/production
Canadian actors and directors discuss their theatre experiences. Canada: Calgary, AB. 1987. Lang.: Eng.   748

Hörberg, Ulrike
Relation to other fields
Sätrahöjdens teatergrupp, producing plays by and for the retarded. Sweden: Gävle. 1978-1987. Lang.: Swe.   3000

Horlock, David
Performance/production
Collection of newspaper reviews by London theatre critics. UK-England: London. 1986. Lang.: Eng.   2137

Hornbrook, David
Institutions
Forms of teaching drama in schools and its role in communication skills. UK-England. 1980. Lang.: Eng.   1646

Horne, Lena
Institutions
Lena Horne, 1984 recipient of Paul Robeson Award. USA. 1985. Lang.: Eng.   575

Horng Lou Meng (Dream of the Red Chamber)
Performance/production
Chou En-Lai and *Horng Lou Meng (Dream of the Red Chamber)*. China, People's Republic of: Shanghai. 1957. Lang.: Chi.   3496

Horniman, Annie
Audience
Political roots of rioting on opening of Synge's *The Playboy of the Western World*. Ireland: Dublin. 1907. Lang.: Eng.   1535

Horns of Don Friolera, The
Basic theatrical documents
The Horns of Don Friolera, translation of *Los cuernos de don Friolera* by Ramón del Valle-Inclán. Spain. 1930. Lang.: Eng.   1570

Hornsby, Kent L.
Performance spaces
Lighting renovation in an amphitheatre and arena. USA: Montgomery, AL. 1987. Lang.: Eng.   3246

Horovitz, Israel
Performance/production
Collection of newspaper reviews by New York theatre critics. USA: New York, NY. 1987. Lang.: Eng.   2323

Plays/librettos/scripts
Influence of O'Neill and Beckett on Israel Horovitz. USA: Boston, MA. France: Paris. 1939-1953. Lang.: Eng.   2873

Horowitz, Jimmy
Performance/production
Collection of newspaper reviews by London theatre critics. UK-England: London. 1986. Lang.: Eng.   2136

Hortense Couldn't Care Less
SEE
Hortense a dit: 'Je m'en fous!'.

Horton, Priscilla
Performance/production
Transvestite roles in extravaganzas of J.R. Planché and Mme. Vestris. UK-England: London. 1830-1870. Lang.: Eng.   3268

Horvai, István
Performance/production
Comparison of the premiere of Imre Sarkadi's *Oszlopos Simeon (The Man on the Pillar)* and two revivals by Árpad Árkosi and István Horvai. Hungary: Szeged, Budapest. 1967-1987. Lang.: Hun.   1830

István Horvai directs Imre Sarkadi's *Oszlopos Simeon (The Man on the Pillar)* at the Pesti Theatre. Hungary: Budapest. 1987. Lang.: Hun.   1849

Milán Füst's *Catullus* and Imre Sarkadi's *Oszlopos Simeon (The Man on the Pillar)* reviewed. Hungary: Budapest. 1987. Lang.: Hun.   1886

Hospice
Basic theatrical documents
Text of *Hospice*, a one-act play by Pearl Cleage. USA. 1986-1987. Lang.: Eng.   1579

Hostage, The
Performance/production
Collection of newspaper reviews by London theatre critics. UK-England: London. 1986. Lang.: Eng.   2066

Hostal de la Glòria, L' (Gloria's Hostel)
Plays/librettos/scripts
General history of Catalan literature, including theatre. Spain-Catalonia. 1902-1961. Lang.: Cat.   1157

Hostinský, Otakar
Theory/criticism
Otakar Hostinský's conception of tragedy and the tragic. Austria-Hungary: Prague. 1906. Lang.: Cze.   3022

Hoswell, Margaret
Training
Interviews with singing teachers in New York City. USA: New York, NY. 1987. Lang.: Eng.   3952

Hot Mikado, The
Plays/librettos/scripts
Opera adaptations for Broadway with African-American artists. USA: New York, NY. 1935-1987. Lang.: Eng.   3932

Hot Stuff
Performance/production
Collection of newspaper reviews by London theatre critics. UK-England: London. 1987. Lang.: Eng.   2209

Hotel Universe
Performance/production
San Francisco Mime Troupe's visit to Nicaragua's International Theatre Festival. Central America. 1986. Lang.: Eng.   3222

Hotel Vietnam
Performance/production
Collection of newspaper reviews by London theatre critics. UK-England: London. 1987. Lang.: Eng.   2270

Houdini
Performance/production
Collection of newspaper reviews by London theatre critics. UK-England: London. 1987. Lang.: Eng.   2260

Houlihan, Curtis
Design/technology
Comprehensive look at touring theatre. USA. 1987. Lang.: Eng.   464

House management
SEE
Management, house.

House of Blue Leaves, The
Design/technology
Tony Walton's set designs at the Vivian Beaumont Theatre. USA: New York, NY. 1986-1987. Lang.: Eng.   465

Houseman, John
Performance spaces
John Houseman on the New York home of the Acting Company. USA: New York, NY. 1972-1986. Lang.: Eng.   695

Performance/production
Autobiography of director, producer and writer John Houseman. USA: New York, NY. 1935-1985. Lang.: Eng.   2339

Houston Grand Opera (Houston, TX)
Administration
Interview with David Gockley, General Director, Houston Grand Opera. USA: Houston, TX. 1970-1987. Lang.: Eng.   3687

Performance/production
Premiere of the docu-opera, *Nixon in China*, Houston Grand Opera. USA: Houston, TX. 1987. Lang.: Eng.   3843

Interview with John DeMain, music director, Houston Grand Opera. USA: Houston, TX. 1944-1987. Lang.: Eng.   3851

Houston-Jones, Ishmael
Performance/production
Performance artists Ishmael Houston-Jones, John Kelly, Karen Finley, Richard Elovich. USA. 1987. Lang.: Eng.   3366

Houstoun, Wendy
Performance/production
Collection of newspaper reviews by London theatre critics. UK-England: London. 1986. Lang.: Eng.   2154

How the Vote Was Won
Performance/production
Collection of newspaper reviews by London theatre critics. UK-England: London. 1986. Lang.: Eng.   2140

Howard-Brooks, Dorothy
Institutions
Operations of the Saskatoon Opera Association. Canada: Saskatoon, SK. 1978-1987. Lang.: Eng.   3713

Howard, Bronson
Plays/librettos/scripts
Humorous article on playwriting. USA: New York, NY. 1987. Lang.: Eng.   1177

Howe, Tina
Design/technology
Interview with lighting designer Dennis Parichy. USA: New York, NY. 1986-1987. Lang.: Eng. 428

Hrabal, Bohumil
Performance/production
Bohumil Hrabal's *Obsluhoval jsem anglického krale (I Served the King of Britain)* directed by Ivo Krobot as *Öfelsége pincére voltam.* Hungary: Nyíregyháza. 1987. Lang.: Hun. 1912

Ivo Krobot directs *Öfelsége pincére voltam (I Served the King of Britain)*, based on writings of Bohumil Hrabal. Hungary: Nyíregyháza. 1987. Lang.: Hun. 1928

Plays/librettos/scripts
Příliš hlučna samota (Too Loud a Solitude) by Bohumil Hrabal. Czechoslovakia. 1914-1987. Lang.: Ita. 1110

Hruby, Mária
Design/technology
Interview with costume designer Mária Hruby. Hungary. 1970-1987. Lang.: Hun. 332

Hsi ch'ü
SEE
Classed Entries under MUSIC-DRAMA—Chinese opera.

Hsü, Wei
Plays/librettos/scripts
Ming dynasty novels as source of theatrical inspiration. China. 1368-1644. Lang.: Chi. 2491

Hsü Wei's *Szu Sheng Yüan (Four Famous Apes)*. China. 1521-1593. Lang.: Chi. 3551

Huaju
Performance/production
Creativity in the Chinese arts. China, People's Republic of. 1949-1985. Lang.: Chi. 3480

The acting theories of the Chinese theatre. China, People's Republic of. 1985. Lang.: Chi. 3537

Theory/criticism
Seminar for the modern theatre in China. China, People's Republic of. 1949-1985. Lang.: Chi. 3604

Hübner, Zygmunt
Performance/production
Festival of Polish plays. Poland: Wrocław. 1987. Lang.: Eng, Fre. 871

Polish theatre. Poland: Warsaw, Cracow, Wrocław. 1980-1987. Lang.: Eng, Fre. 1987

Hucks, Michael
Performance/production
Collection of newspaper reviews by London theatre critics. UK-England: London. 1986. Lang.: Eng. 2125

Hudson Guild Theatre (New York, NY)
Institutions
Duma Ndlovu, the Woza Afrika Foundation and the Hudson Guild Theatre. USA: New York, NY. South Africa, Republic of. 1976-1986. Lang.: Eng. 604

Huebert, Ronald
Performance/production
Conference proceedings on staging of Elizabethan plays. England. 1546-1616. Lang.: Eng. 775

Hueng, Tsolin
Plays/librettos/scripts
The structures and themes of Chinese playwright Hueng Tsolin. China, People's Republic of. 1983. Lang.: Chi. 2495

Huff, Mike
Performance/production
Review of *Hello Dolly* in Bloemfontein. South Africa, Republic of: Bloemfontein. 1987. Lang.: Eng. 3635

Hughes Jones, Lis
Institutions
First festival of women's work in experimental theatre. UK-Wales: Cardiff. 1986. Lang.: Eng. 1649

Hughes, Allen Lee
Design/technology
Interview with dance lighting designer Allen Lee Hughes. USA: New York, NY. 1987. Lang.: Eng. 1401

Hughes, Dusty
Performance/production
Collection of newspaper reviews by London theatre critics. UK-England: London. 1987. Lang.: Eng. 2244

Hughie
Plays/librettos/scripts
Importance of language in Eugene O'Neill's *Hughie.* USA. 1941-1959. Lang.: Eng. 2890

Hugo, Victor
Performance/production
Miklós Szinetár directs *Les Misérables* at Rock Szinház. Hungary: Budapest. 1987. Lang.: Hun. 3630

Theory/criticism
Tragedy, space and discourse in neoclassical dramatic theory. France. 1800-1850. Lang.: Eng. 3035

Huguenin, Robert
Performance/production
Collection of newspaper reviews by London theatre critics. UK-England: London. 1987. Lang.: Eng. 2186

Huguenots, Les
Design/technology
Controversy over 1901 cylinder recording of *Les Huguenots.* USA. 1901-1987. Lang.: Eng. 3699

Mapleson cylinders: controversy over *Les Huguenots.* USA: New York, NY. 1947. Lang.: Eng. 3700

Huis clos (No Exit)
Reference materials
History of pocket theatre. France: Paris. 1944-1953. Lang.: Eng. 2974

Hull, Alan
Performance/production
Collection of newspaper reviews by London theatre critics. UK-England: London. 1986. Lang.: Eng. 2156

Hult Center (Eugene, OR)
Performance spaces
Use of lighting in Hult Center's lobby and two performance halls. USA: Eugene, OR. 1987. Lang.: Eng. 687

Human Sex
Performance/production
Review of touring production of Edward Lock's *Human Sex.* Canada: Vancouver, BC. 1985-1986. Lang.: Fre. 1405

Humanism
Plays/librettos/scripts
Role of the *commedia umanistica* in the intellectual life of Renaissance Venice. Italy: Venice. 1400-1500. Lang.: Ita. 1135

Humble, William
Performance/production
Collection of newspaper reviews by London theatre critics. UK-England: London. 1986. Lang.: Eng. 2168

Hume, Nancy
Performance/production
Life and career of actress Nancy Hume. USA. 1977-1987. Lang.: Eng. 3648

Humphrey, Doris
Performance/production
Interview with choreographer Senta Driver. USA. 1987. Lang.: Eng. 1472

Hunan opera
Performance/production
Comments on the performances at the Chinese Art Festival. China, People's Republic of: Beijing. 1987. Lang.: Chi. 3501

Hung lou meng (Dream of the Red Chamber, The)
Performance/production
Actor Yin Guey-Fang's work in *The Dream of the Red Chamber.* China, People's Republic of. 1945-1983. Lang.: Chi. 3538

Hung Lou Theatre Company (People's Republic of China)
Administration
Wang Wenn-Jiuann and the establishment of Hung Lou Theatre Company. China, People's Republic of. 1987. Lang.: Chi. 3425

Hungarian National Theatre
SEE
Nemzeti Szinház.

Hungarian State Opera
SEE
Magyar Állami Operaház.

Hungarian State Puppet Theatre
SEE
Állami Bábszinház.

Hungarian State Theatre (Kolozsvár)
SEE
Állami Magyar Szinház (Cluj).

Ibsen, Henrik — cont'd

Ibsen translation, production, reception and influence in China. China, People's Republic of. Norway. 1917-1985. Lang.: Eng.   2494

Comparison of *King Lear* and *Vildanden (The Wild Duck)*. England. Norway. 1605-1884. Lang.: Eng.   2518

Ariadne in plays of Ibsen, Strindberg, Maeterlinck. Europe. 1892-1902. Lang.: Eng.   2566

Critical reception of realism and naturalism. Germany. 1890-1987. Lang.: Ger.   2601

Interpretations of the plays of Ibsen, Čechov and Beckett. Norway. Ireland. Russia. 1987. Lang.: Hun.   2711

Irony in Ibsen's *Fruen fra Havet (Lady from the Sea, The)*. Norway. 1888-1987. Lang.: Eng.   2712

Theme of stage direction in the work of Scandinavian authors. Sweden. Norway. 1700-1987. Lang.: Ita.   2737

The son-in-law in *Pelikanen (The Pelican)* by August Strindberg. Sweden. 1907-1987. Lang.: Swe.   2740

Three feminist productions of plays by Henrik Ibsen. USA. 1987. Lang.: Eng.   2899

Tragedy and comedy in Ibsen's dramatic vision. USA. 1985. Lang.: Eng.   2922

Varied approaches to Ibsen's *Rosmersholm*. USA. Norway. 1886-1985. Lang.: Eng.   2923

Ibsen database now being developed. USA. Norway. 1987. Lang.: Eng.   2924

Research/historiography

Views of the literary relationship between William Archer and Henrik Ibsen. UK-England. 1889-1919. Lang.: Eng.   3013

Theory/criticism

Centenary of Théâtre Libre: proposes 'subjective realism'. France. 1887-1987. Lang.: Fre.   1337

Structuralist approach to play interpretation. 500 B.C.-1987 A.D. Lang.: Eng.   3016

Brief descriptions of 21 articles on Ibsen. 1983-1984. Lang.: Eng.   3018

Exploration of the nature of tragedy. 500 B.C.-1987 A.D. Lang.: Eng.   3020

Ibsen's influence on modern Chinese theatre. China, People's Republic of. Norway. 1920-1950. Lang.: Chi.   3025

Career and achievements of Ibsen scholar Hermann J. Weigand. USA. 1892-1985. Lang.: Eng.   3076

Icarus's Mother

Plays/librettos/scripts

Theatricality of Sam Shepard's early and late works. USA. 1965-1986. Lang.: Eng.   2903

Ice Break

Plays/librettos/scripts

Tippett's influence on contemporary opera. 1946-1987. Lang.: Eng.   3888

Iceman Cometh, The

Plays/librettos/scripts

Eugene O'Neill's influence on Edward Albee. USA. 1949-1962. Lang.: Eng.   2841

Comparison of themes and dramaturgical techniques in plays of Eugene O'Neill and Peter Shaffer. USA. 1920-1982. Lang.: Eng.   2872

Ichakawa Ennosuke Kabuki Company

Performance/production

Collection of newspaper reviews by London theatre critics. UK-England: London. 1987. Lang.: Eng.   2258

Ichikawa, Danjūrō

Performance/production

Articles on Edo period *kabuki* actors. Japan. 1600-1800. Lang.: Jap.   1493

Kabuki actors who carried the name Ichikawa Danjūrō. Japan. 1791-1859. Lang.: Jap.   1494

Iconography

Institutions

Tandem database system used by the Deutsches Theatermuseum. Germany, West: Munich. 1987. Lang.: Eng.   533

Performance/production

Documentation on melodramatic acting style. France: Paris. 1800-1830. Lang.: Eng.   791

Iffland, August Wilhelm

Performance/production

August Wilhelm Iffland's productions of plays by Friedrich von Schiller. Germany: Berlin. 1796-1806. Lang.: Ger.   1773

Ifigenia (Iphigeneia)

Performance/production

Actors and comics of the early eighteenth century. Europe. 1700-1750. Lang.: Ita.   778

Iglesias, Franco

Training

Interviews with singing teachers in New York City. USA: New York, NY. 1987. Lang.: Eng.   3952

Iglódi, István

Performance/production

Béla Zerkovitz's operetta *Csókos asszony (A Woman Made for Kissing)* directed by István Iglódi. Hungary: Budapest. 1987. Lang.: Hun.   3957

István Iglódi directs *Csókos asszony (A Woman Made for Kissing)* by Béla Zerkovitz at Vigszinház. Hungary: Budapest. 1987. Lang.: Hun.   3958

Ignoramus

Plays/librettos/scripts

Critical analysis of James Reaney's *Three Desks*. Canada. 1960-1977. Lang.: Eng.   2477

Ihering, Herbert

Performance/production

Early productions of Brecht's plays reflected in the press. Germany: Berlin. 1922-1933. Lang.: Ger.   1777

Iijima, Sanae

Performance/production

Analysis of four Tokyo productions. Japan: Tokyo. 1987. Lang.: Jap.   1957

Ik, Ali

Plays/librettos/scripts

Interview with playwright Paul Pourveur. Belgium. 1987. Lang.: Dut.   2455

Ikoli, Tunde

Performance/production

Collection of newspaper reviews by London theatre critics. UK-England: London. 1986. Lang.: Eng.   2162

Collection of newspaper reviews by London theatre critics. UK-England: London. 1987. Lang.: Eng.   2182

Ikuta, Man

Performance/production

Focus on several Tokyo productions. Japan: Tokyo. 1960-1987. Lang.: Jap.   1955

Illés, István

Performance/production

Reviews of *Téli zsoltár (A Winter Psalm)* by Kovách, Shakespeare's *Much Ado About Nothing* and *Ferde ház (The Leaning House)* by Gerencsér performed at Kisfaludy Theatre. Hungary: Győr. 1986. Lang.: Hun.   1822

Illusion comique, L' (Comic Illusion, The)

Performance/production

'Showing' is an essential part of all acting. Europe. 1590-1987. Lang.: Eng.   1746

L'illusion comique (The Comic Illusion) by Pierre Corneille directed by János Szikora at the Katona József Theatre. Hungary: Budapest. 1986. Lang.: Hun.   1859

János Szikora directs Corneille's *L'illusion comique (The Comic Illusion)* at Katona József Theatre. Hungary: Budapest. 1986. Lang.: Hun.   1918

Giorgio Strehler's staging of *L'illusion comique (The Comic Illusion)* by Corneille. Italy. 1944-1986. Lang.: Eng.   1948

Image of the Beast, The

Performance/production

Collection of newspaper reviews by London theatre critics. UK-England: London. 1987. Lang.: Eng.   2276

Image theatre

Performance/production

Techniques of the image theatre and effects on actor and audience. Canada. Europe. USA. 1987. Lang.: Eng.   3345

Image theatre methodology. Canada. 1987. Lang.: Eng.   3348

Iman, Yusef

Performance/production

Interview with playwright Amiri Baraka. USA: Newark, NJ, New York, NY. 1965-1969. Lang.: Eng.   2356

Imitation of Life, An
Performance/production
Collection of newspaper reviews by London theatre critics. UK-England: London. 1987. Lang.: Eng. 2177

Immanuel Kant
Plays/librettos/scripts
The metadramatic nature of Thomas Bernhard's plays. Germany, West. 1974-1983. Lang.: Eng. 2616

Impact Theatre Co-operative (London)
Performance/production
Collection of newspaper reviews by London theatre critics. UK-England: London. 1986. Lang.: Eng. 2084

Imperial Theatre (New York, NY)
Performance/production
Collection of newspaper reviews by New York theatre critics. USA: New York, NY. 1987. Lang.: Eng. 2317

Importance of Being Earnest, The
Performance/production
Collection of newspaper reviews by London theatre critics. UK-England. 1987. Lang.: Eng. 2175

Collection of newspaper reviews by London theatre critics. UK-England: London. 1987. Lang.: Eng. 2248

Impossible Theatre (Baltimore, MD)
Design/technology
Multimedia experts discuss the creation of special effects. USA. 1987. Lang.: Eng. 422

Imposztor, Az (Imposter, The)
Plays/librettos/scripts
Actor-manager Wojciech Bogusławski in life and in György Spiró's play Az imposztor (The Imposter). Poland. Hungary. 1815-1987. Lang.: Pol. 2716

Impressionism
Basic theatrical documents
Catalan translation of Arthur Schnitzler's Reigen (Round). 1862-1931. Lang.: Cat. 1541

Improvisation
Institutions
A history of documentary theatre in English Canada. Canada. 1970-1986. Lang.: Eng. 508

History of Werkteater. Netherlands: Amsterdam. 1969-1985. Lang.: Eng. 554

Performance spaces
Form and development of the commune theatre. China. 202 B.C.-1986 A.D. Lang.: Chi. 3452

Performance/production
Improvisation and other forms in children's theatre. China, People's Republic of. 1975-1987. Lang.: Chi. 764

Memorial album by and about dancer Gret Palucca. Germany, East: Dresden. 1922-1987. Lang.: Ger. 1469

Irondale Ensemble's production of Ubu roi (King Ubu) by Alfred Jarry. USA: New York, NY. 1984-1987. Lang.: Eng. 2370

Codco, a comic theatrical troupe, creates regional characters. Canada: St. John's, NF. 1986. Lang.: Eng. 3253

Performance by the Colombaioni combining commedia, improvisation and clowning. USA: Chicago, IL. 1986. Lang.: Eng. 3315

Mythological background and performance aspects of dalang. Indonesia. 1987. Lang.: Ita. 4010

Plays/librettos/scripts
Dramatic structure in Frayn's Noises Off. 1987. Lang.: Eng. 2416

Improvisational clowning in Elizabethan theatre. England. 1585-1625. Lang.: Eng. 2560

Theory/criticism
Commune and improvisation theatre in Chi Lin. China, People's Republic of. 1900-1986. Lang.: Chi. 3612

Training
Guide to teaching through improvisation for children and adults. 1987. Lang.: Eng. 1377

In a Grove
Institutions
National Theatre of the Deaf productions of Farewell My Lovely and In a Grove directed by Arvin Brown in Beijing. China, People's Republic of: Beijing. USA. 1986-1987. Lang.: Eng. 1611

In Dahomey
Performance/production
Compositions by Debussy in their relationship to Afro-American music. France: Paris. UK-England: London. 1893-1913. Lang.: Eng. 3384

In Good King Charles's Golden Days
Plays/librettos/scripts
Imaginary history: Shaw's In Good King Charles's Golden Days. UK-England. 1639. Lang.: Eng. 2772

In the Jungle of the Cities
SEE
Im Dickicht der Städte.

Inavvertito L' (Unperceived, The)
Plays/librettos/scripts
Essay on L'Inavvertito (The Unperceived) by Niccolò Barbieri. Italy. 1629. Lang.: Ita. 3317

Inchbald, Elizabeth
Plays/librettos/scripts
Biography of playwright Elizabeth Inchbald. England: London. 1760-1821. Lang.: Eng. 2538

Incident
Performance/production
Collection of newspaper reviews by London theatre critics. UK-England: London. 1986. Lang.: Eng. 2097

Independent Booking Office (New York, NY)
Administration
Services and operations of Independent Booking Office. USA: New York, NY. 1983. Lang.: Eng. 211

Indexes
Design/technology
Index of Broadway costume designs and designers. USA: New York, NY. 1915-1985. Lang.: Eng. 444

Performance/production
Directory of London productions. UK-England: London. 1837-1901. Lang.: Eng. 2300

Plays/librettos/scripts
Index of East German dramatists and their works. Germany, East. 1945-1985. Lang.: Eng. 2610

Reference materials
General subject index for vol. 38 of Opera. UK-England. USA. 1987. Lang.: Eng. 3936

India Song
Theory/criticism
Impact of cinematic technique on plays by Beckett and Duras. France. 1977-1987. Lang.: Eng. 3037

Indoor Games
SEE
Jeu d'intérieur.

Industrials
Performance/production
Genre of business theatre. USA. 1985-1987. Lang.: Eng. 3272

Infernal Machine, The
SEE
Machine Infernale, La.

Infidelities
Performance/production
Collection of newspaper reviews by London theatre critics. UK-England: London. 1986. Lang.: Eng. 2115

Ingram, Michael R.
Design/technology
Design problems of simulating a circus for Barnum. USA: Memphis, TN. 1986. Lang.: Eng. 3621

Innaurato, Albert
Plays/librettos/scripts
Interview with playwright Albert Innaurato. USA. 1986. Lang.: Eng. 2856

Innocent Mistress, The
Performance/production
Collection of newspaper reviews by London theatre critics. UK-England: London. 1987. Lang.: Eng. 2256

Innvik Theatre (Norway)
Performance spaces
Conversion of ferryboat Innvik into theatre and its production of Splint. Norway. 1982. Lang.: Eng. 666

Inoue, Tomoaki
Performance/production
Space and sign in various Tokyo productions. Japan: Tokyo. 1987. Lang.: Jap. 1959

Inside Images of Motion
SEE
Innere Bewegungsbilder.

Institutions, producing — cont'd

Institutions, producing — cont'd

Brecht was the theme of the 1986 International Theatre Festival and Conference. Canada: Toronto, ON. 1986. Lang.: Fre.   1610

National Theatre of the Deaf productions of *Farewell My Lovely* and *In a Grove* directed by Arvin Brown in Beijing. China, People's Republic of: Beijing. USA. 1986-1987. Lang.: Eng.   1611

History of Stavovské Theatre. Czechoslovakia: Prague. 1783-1983. Lang.: Cze.   1612

Rudolf Walter's theatre, Komorní hry. Czechoslovakia: Brno. 1942-1944. Lang.: Cze.   1613

King's Company under actor-manager John Lowin. England: London. 1576-1653. Lang.: Eng.   1614

Seven productions chosen for Theatertreffen '86. Germany: Berlin. 1986. Lang.: Eng.   1617

Schaubühne's comeback with production of *Schuld und Sühne (Crime and Punishment)*. Germany, West: Berlin, West. 1970-1987. Lang.: Dut.   1618

Playwright Denis Johnston and avant-garde theatre at the Abbey. Ireland: Dublin. 1927-1935. Lang.: Eng.   1619

Interview with actress Fannia Lubitch. Israel: Tel Aviv. USSR: Moscow. 1921-1987. Lang.: Heb.   1620

Interview with dancer Dvora Bektonov on her work and her father's acting. Israel: Tel Aviv. USSR: Moscow. 1922-1987. Lang.: Heb.   1621

Visit to the El-Hakawati theatre, an independent performance group, specializing in theatre for and about the Palestinians. Israel: Jerusalem. 1982-1985. Lang.: Swe.   1622

Interview with Israel Mintz on the HaBimah Theatre. Israel: Tel Aviv. USSR: Moscow. 1922-1987. Lang.: Heb.   1623

Interview with actor, director and producer Shimon Finkel. Israel: Tel Aviv. Germany: Berlin. 1923-1987. Lang.: Heb.   1624

Formation and development of the Justo Rufino Garay Group. Nicaragua. 1980-1986. Lang.: Spa.   1625

Trends in regional theatre. Norway. 1971-1982. Lang.: Eng.   1626

Profile of community theatre Grenland Friteater. Norway: Porsgrunn. 1982. Lang.: Eng.   1627

The Stanisław Ignacy Witkiewicz Theatre. Poland: Zakopane. 1982-1986. Lang.: Eng, Fre.   1628

Ida Kamińska, director of Jewish Theatre of Warsaw. Poland: Warsaw. 1899-1987. Lang.: Pol.   1629

The Teatre Lliure as a public theatre: future prospects. Spain-Catalonia: Barcelona. 1976-1987. Lang.: Cat.   1630

Founding manifesto of the Teatre Lliure. Spain-Catalonia: Barcelona. 1976. Lang.: Cat.   1631

Evaluation of the first ten years of Teatre Lliure. Spain-Catalonia: Barcelona. 1976-1986. Lang.: Cat.   1632

Present and future of Teatre Lliure. Spain-Catalonia: Barcelona. 1976-1986. Lang.: Cat.   1633

Analysis of all the productions performed by Els Joglars in their twenty-five years of existence. Spain-Catalonia. 1962-1987. Lang.: Cat.   1634

Evaluation of theatrical policy in Catalonia. Spain-Catalonia: Barcelona. 1976-1986. Lang.: Cat.   1635

Evaluation of the plays performed during the first ten years of Teatre Lliure. Spain-Catalonia: Barcelona. 1976-1986. Lang.: Cat.   1636

Dramaten's attempts at greater community outreach. Sweden. 1982. Lang.: Eng.   1637

Folkteatern i Gävleborgs län: integration into the community. Sweden: Gävle. 1982-1987. Lang.: Swe.   1641

Tornedalsteatern and director Ulla Lyttkens. Sweden: Pajala. 1986-1987. Lang.: Swe.   1642

Interview with members of amateur group Teater Phoenix. Sweden: Simrishamn. 1983-1987. Lang.: Swe.   1643

Gagnef Teaterförening's production of a play based on local history. Sweden: Gagnef. 1975-1987. Lang.: Swe.   1644

Arbrå Teaterförening's theatrical activities for adults and children. Sweden: Bollnäs. 1979-1987. Lang.: Swe.   1645

Forms of teaching drama in schools and its role in communication skills. UK-England. 1980. Lang.: Eng.   1646

History and current season of the National Theatre. UK-England: London. 1848-1987. Lang.: Eng.   1647

Impact of German expressionist theatre. UK-England. USA. Germany. 1910-1940. Lang.: Eng.   1648

First festival of women's work in experimental theatre. UK-Wales: Cardiff. 1986. Lang.: Eng.   1649

Theatre by the Blind, integrating blind and sighted actors. USA: New York, NY. 1981-1987. Lang.: Eng.   1650

Profile of Ecotheatre and its artistic director Maryat Lee. USA: Hinton, WV. 1951-1983. Lang.: Eng.   1651

The Ridiculous Theatre Company and its founder Charles Ludlam. USA: New York, NY. 1965-1987. Lang.: Eng.   1652

History of the Negro Ensemble Company. USA: New York, NY. 1969-1987. Lang.: Eng.   1653

Production bulletins of the Federal Theatre Project. USA. 1936-1939. Lang.: Eng.   1654

Experience of artists working at the O'Neill Theatre Center. USA: Waterford, CT. 1985-1986. Lang.: Eng.   1655

Profile of New Dramatists. USA: New York, NY. 1982. Lang.: Eng.   1656

Actors Theatre of Louisville's 'Classics in Context' festival. USA: Louisville, KY. 1986-1988. Lang.: Eng.   1657

Profile of CSC Repertory, artistic director Christopher Martin. USA: New York, NY. 1982. Lang.: Eng.   1658

Theatre manager William Wood's paternalism. USA: Philadelphia, PA. 1803-1855. Lang.: Eng.   1659

Profile of bilingual theatre company La Compañia de Teatro de Alburquerque. USA: Albuquerque, NM. 1977-1983. Lang.: Eng.   1660

Profile of Circle Repertory Company. USA: New York, NY. 1982. Lang.: Eng.   1661

History of Dakota Theatre Caravan. USA: Yankton, SD. 1977-1983. Lang.: Eng.   1662

History of Manhattan Theatre Club. USA: New York, NY. 1969-1987. Lang.: Eng.   1663

History and interactive techniques of Playback Theatre. USA: Poughkeepsie, NY. 1975-1983. Lang.: Eng.   1664

The Theatre of Universal Images and its upcoming season. USA: Newark, NJ, New York, NY. 1981-1987. Lang.: Eng.   1665

The formation of the North Carolina Black Repertory Company. USA: Winston-Salem, NC. 1979-1987. Lang.: Eng.   1666

Script editor's recollections of CBC radio dramas. Canada. 1944-1954. Lang.: Eng.   3110

Astoria Studios' restoration to operating film studio. USA: Queens, NY. 1920-1982. Lang.: Eng.   3140

Photographic essay of various works by Canadian mime troupe Les Enfants du Paradis—Carbone 14. Canada: Montreal, PQ. 1980-1982. Lang.: Eng.   3219

Profile of Friends Mime Theatre. USA: Milwaukee, WI. 1980-1982. Lang.: Eng.   3220

Profile of Dell'Arte Players and their productions. USA: Blue Lake, CA. 1957-1983. Lang.: Eng.   3310

Tabootenay, a collaborative street theatre troupe. Canada: Vancouver, BC. 1986. Lang.: Eng.   3380

Proprietors, artists and operation of Jardin d'Hiver, nightclub and revue theatre. Hungary: Budapest. 1932-1944. Lang.: Hun.   3381

Andrew Davis' role as Toronto Symphony Orchestra conductor. Canada: Toronto, On. 1974-1987. Lang.: Eng.   3389

History of the Royal Conservatory of Music. Canada: Toronto, ON. 1886-1986. Lang.: Eng.   3390

History of Leipzig Neues Theater. Germany: Leipzig. 1868-1932. Lang.: Ger.   3391

Edinburgh Festival's productions less competitive. UK-Scotland: Edinburgh. 1987. Lang.: Eng.   3392

The early history and development of the Shau-Shing opera. China. 1906-1934. Lang.: Chi.   3450

Interview with Mátyás Várkanyi, director of Rock Theatre. Hungary. 1980-1987. Lang.: Hun.   3624

Record producer Bruce Yeko's accomplishments. USA: New York, NY. 1962-1981. Lang.: Eng.   3625

Summary review of spring 1987 international opera productions. 1987. Lang.: Eng.   3702

International survey and review of summer 1987 opera productions. 1987. Lang.: Eng.   3703

Institutions, producing — cont'd

Performance spaces

Performance/production

Institutions, producing — cont'd

Listings for the 1987-1988 theatre season. USA: New York, NY. 1987. Lang.: Eng. 929

Organizational and production history of the American Shakespeare Festival. USA: Stratford, CT. 1955-1985. Lang.: Eng. 934

Decentralization of American theatre. USA. 1960-1980. Lang.: Eng. 958

Review, 'Le corps politique' festival. Canada: Montreal, PQ. 1986. Lang.: Fre. 1406

Problems of dancers outside established companies. Switzerland. 1950-1986. Lang.: Ger, Eng. 1411

Founder and director of the Ballet Folklórico Nacional de Nicaragua discusses the company and its goals. Nicaragua. 1986. Lang.: Eng. 1464

Richard Ouzounian, director, Manitoba Theatre Centre. Canada: Winnipeg, MB. 1982. Lang.: Eng. 1693

Writer-director Glen Cairns and surrealistic drama at the Neptune Theatre. Canada: Halifax, NS. 1977-1987. Lang.: Eng. 1695

Rehearsal and performance process, Stratford Shakespeare Festival. Canada: Stratford, ON. 1986. Lang.: Eng. 1697

Production account, Frank's *Spinoza*, Saidye Bronfman Centre. Canada: Montreal, PQ. 1982. Lang.: Eng. 1702

Creations' of *La Trilogie des dragons (Dragon Trilogy)* by Robert Lepage. Canada. 1987. Lang.: Fre. 1706

Personnel associated with production of Lepage's *La Trilogie des dragons*. Canada. 1987. Lang.: Fre. 1713

Content and North American reception of *Asinimali! (We Have No Money!)* by Mbongeni Ngema. Canada. South Africa, Republic of. 1987. Lang.: Eng. 1715

Robert Lepage: creation, direction of *La Trilogie des dragons (Dragons' Trilogy)*. Canada. 1987. Lang.: Fre. 1716

Photo essay on theatre company Billedstofteater. Denmark. 1977-1982. Lang.: Eng. 1730

Child actors in juvenile companies, Comédie-Française. France: Paris. 1769-1850. Lang.: Eng. 1756

A round-table discussion with stage directors on the principles and methods of working with an ensemble company. Germany, East: Berlin, East. 1983. Lang.: Ger. 1778

Interview with director József Ruszt. Hungary. 1983-1987. Lang.: Hun. 1791

Interview with director Imre Csiszár. Hungary: Miskolc. 1986-1987. Lang.: Hun. 1892

Luigi Pirandello's company Teatro d'Arte and its inaugural productions. Italy. 1925-1928. Lang.: Eng. 1941

Structure and organization of comic acting companies. Italy: Venice. 1700-1800. Lang.: Ita. 1943

Encounter between Pirandello and Lord Dunsany during Pirandello's production of *I pazzi sulla montagna (The Gods of the Mountain)* by Alessandro De Stefani. Italy. 1923-1928. Lang.: Eng. 1947

Experimental theatre groups in Mexico City. Mexico: Mexico City. 1987. Lang.: Spa. 1975

Postwar Dutch theatre: growth of small theatre groups. Netherlands. 1975-1985. Lang.: Dut. 1982

Polish theatre. Poland: Warsaw, Cracow, Wrocław. 1980-1987. Lang.: Eng, Fre. 1987

Four new productions in Poland. Poland: Warsaw. 1986-1987. Lang.: Eng, Fre. 1988

The shape and form of contemporary Polish theatre. Poland: Warsaw. 1981-1987. Lang.: Eng, Fre. 1995

Description of the performances played in the Teatre Lliure. Spain-Catalonia: Barcelona. 1976-1987. Lang.: Cat. 2009

Collection of theatre reviews by Xavier Fàbregas. Spain-Catalonia. 1969-1972. Lang.: Cat. 2010

Overview of theatre season. Spain-Catalonia: Barcelona. 1986-1987. Lang.: Cat. 2011

British theatrical touring companies. UK-England. North America. Australia. 1870-1929. Lang.: Eng. 2280

Brian Cox's work with the Royal Shakespeare Company. UK-England: Stratford, London. USA: New York, NY. 1968-1987. Lang.: Eng. 2284

The founding and history of the Malvern Festival. UK-England: Malvern. 1904-1977. Lang.: Eng. 2286

Productions and political philosophy of Field Day Theatre Company. UK-Ireland: Londonderry. 1986-1987. Lang.: Eng. 2309

Four productions in Southern regional theatres. USA: Houston, TX, Louisville, KY, Gainesville, FL. 1980. Lang.: Eng. 2342

Evolution of the Areté Mime Troupe: its concepts, goals and performance methods. Canada. 1980-1982. Lang.: Eng. 3221

Development of mime, pantomime and its related movements. France: Paris. UK-England. USA: New York, NY. 1980-1982. Lang.: Eng. 3223

Photographs of mimes, mime companies and performance artists with commentary. USA. Europe. 1972-1987. Lang.: Eng. 3229

Actors and institutions of eighteenth-century Venice. Italy: Venice. 1700-1800. Lang.: Ita. 3312

Critical discussion of the Ultimatum II festival. Canada: Montreal, PQ. 1987. Lang.: Eng. 3346

The 4th International Festival of Street Theatres. Poland: Jelenia Góra. 1986. Lang.: Eng, Fre. 3355

Status of Sichuan theatre and opera. China, People's Republic of: Chengdu. 1985-1986. Lang.: Eng. 3512

History of the first Passing Show. USA: New York, NY. 1912-1913. Lang.: Eng. 3645

History of 'The Soldier Show', Shubert Archives U.S.O. collection. USA: New York, NY. 1942-1945. Lang.: Eng. 3664

Musical Theatre Project explores Broadway musical material available in Shubert Archive. USA: New York, NY. 1984-1985. Lang.: Eng. 3666

Retired critic recalls Toronto opera. Canada: Toronto, ON. 1947-1987. Lang.: Eng. 3749

Stuart Hamilton's career in opera broadcasting. Canada: Toronto, ON. 1929-1987. Lang.: Eng. 3758

International biographical survey of opera performers and productions. Europe. North America. 1987. Lang.: Eng. 3762

Biographical survey of Canadian opera performers. Europe. North America. 1987. Lang.: Eng. 3763

Biographical survey of international opera stars. Europe. North America. 1987. Lang.: Eng. 3764

Twenty opera productions at Grand Théâtre. Switzerland: Geneva. 1980-1987. Lang.: Fre. 3828

Repertoire and artistic achievement of the Opera Theatre of St. Louis. USA: St. Louis, MO. 1987. Lang.: Eng. 3840

History of the Puppeteers Company. UK-England: Norwich. 1971-1987. Lang.: Eng. 3983

Poland's puppet theatre. Poland: Wrocław, Białystock. Austria: Mistelbach. 1979-1987. Lang.: Eng, Fre. 4006

Plays/librettos/scripts

Effects of developmental playwriting process. USA. 1987. Lang.: Eng. 1167

Roadside Theatre's production of *Leaving Egypt*. USA: Whitesburg, KY. Lang.: Eng. 1170

Collective theatre projects in Newfoundland. Canada: St. John's, NF. 1987. Lang.: Eng. 2466

La Trilogie des dragons by Robert Lepage. Canada: Montreal, PQ. 1987. Lang.: Fre. 2479

Productions of *Sir Thomas More* by Elizabethan theatre companies. England. 1595-1650. Lang.: Eng. 2541

André Brassard's production of Jean Genet's *Les Paravents (The Screens)*. France. Canada: Montreal, PQ, Ottawa, ON. 1961-1987. Lang.: Fre. 2583

Pistolteatern's adaptation of *Alice in Wonderland*. Sweden: Stockholm. 1982. Lang.: Eng. 2738

Research for *An American Journey* produced by Milwaukee Repertory. USA: Milwaukee, WI. 1978-1987. Lang.: Eng. 2862

Reference materials

Theatre demographics in German-speaking Europe. Germany, West. Austria. Switzerland. 1986-1987. Lang.: Ger. 1203

Names and addresses of Italian theatrical institutions. Italy. 1987. Lang.: Ita. 1205

Picture book to accompany production of *La Nit (The Night)* by Els Comediants. Spain-Catalonia. 1987. Lang.: Cat. 1209

History of theatrical activity in Palafrugell. Spain-Catalonia: Palafrugell. 1900-1986. Lang.: Cat. 1210

Directory of fringe, touring, dance and puppet companies, arts associations, festivals. UK-England. 1986-1987. Lang.: Eng. 1214

Relation to other fields

Cultural and social role of Berlin theatres. Germany: Berlin. 1700-1987. Lang.: Ger.   1237

Government funding of official theatre and opera companies. Switzerland. 1987. Lang.: Ger.   1256

Sätrahöjdens teatergrupp, producing plays by and for the retarded. Sweden: Gävle. 1978-1987. Lang.: Swe.   3000

Political context of the constructing of the Opéra-Bastille. France: Paris. 1983-1987. Lang.: Eng.   3941

Theory/criticism

Essays and reviews by Gordon Rogoff. USA. 1960-1986. Lang.: Eng.   1366

Rise of contemporary theatre in Mexico. Mexico: Mexico City. 1957-1987. Lang.: Spa.   3057

Institutions, research

Institutions

Tandem database system used by the Deutsches Theatermuseum. Germany, West: Munich. 1987. Lang.: Eng.   533

Theatre collection of the Museum of the City of New York. USA: New York, NY. 1987. Lang.: Eng.   616

Plays/librettos/scripts

Discusses the 1986 ISTA conference. Denmark. Asia. 1986. Lang.: Fre.   1112

Institutions, service

Administration

Volunteer organizations and their role in the community. USA. 1700-1987. Lang.: Eng.   195

Institutions

The role of the Actors' Fund in New York's theatre industry. USA: New York, NY. 1987. Lang.: Eng.   570

First health care institution specifically for performers. USA: New York, NY. 1985. Lang.: Eng.   576

Profile of New Dramatists. USA: New York, NY. 1982. Lang.: Eng.   1656

Institutions, special

Administration

Effects of new immigration rules on performing arts organizations. USA: New York, NY. 1987. Lang.: Eng.   174

Institutions

Critical discussion of the Chalmers Awards. Canada: Toronto, ON. 1987. Lang.: Eng.   513

Theatre department, National Museum, Prague. Czechoslovakia: Prague. 1987. Lang.: Cze.   527

Italian theatrical archives and libraries. Italy. 1987. Lang.: Ita.   547

Failure of a Swiss project to promote playwrights. Switzerland. 1982-1986. Lang.: Ger.   563

Opening of Britain's first permanent theatre museum. UK-England: London. Lang.: Eng.   564

Actors' Equity and Black History Month. USA: New York, NY. 1986. Lang.: Eng.   572

Lena Horne, 1984 recipient of Paul Robeson Award. USA. 1985. Lang.: Eng.   575

New York State Council on the Arts' Presenting Organizations Program. USA: New York. 1960-1983. Lang.: Eng.   601

League of Resident Theatres' role in labor and contract negotiations. USA. 1987. Lang.: Eng.   607

Dora Mavor Moore Awards: their importance. Canada: Toronto, ON. 1986. Lang.: Eng.   1606

On audience societies Freie Volksbühne and Neue Freie Volksbühne. Germany: Berlin. 1889-1914. Lang.: Ger.   1616

Sherman H. Dudley and the Black vaudeville circuit. USA: Indianapolis, IN, Washington, DC. 1820-1922. Lang.: Eng.   3382

Ramayana '87, an Inner London Education Authority project. UK-England: London. 1987. Lang.: Eng.   3965

Relation to other fields

Protest of US Immigration and Naturalization Service policies by American presenting organizations. USA. 1986. Lang.: Eng.   1282

Institutions, training

Design/technology

Third international scene painting seminar at the Mozarteum. Austria: Salzburg. 1986. Lang.: Eng.   300

Interview with designer Desmond Heeley. UK-England: London. USA: New York, NY. Canada: Stratford, ON. 1940-1984. Lang.: Eng.   1596

Institutions

Survey of liberal arts and professional training courses. Australia. 1987. Lang.: Eng.   503

Historical background of National Theatre School. Canada: Montreal, PQ. 1960-1985. Lang.: Eng.   519

Creative teaching of theatre. Israel: Tel Aviv. 1987. Lang.: Heb.   546

Director Leon Schiller's plan for a drama department, Theatre Institute. Poland: Warsaw. 1943. Lang.: Pol.   555

Memoirs of director and teacher Géza Gergely on Hungarian theatrical training in Romania. Romania: Tîrgu-Mures. Hungary. 1946-1986. Lang.: Hun.   556

Burt Reynolds Institute apprenticeship program. USA: Miami, FL. 1987. Lang.: Eng.   587

History of the Conservatoire, training for classical repertory. France: Paris. 1800-1899. Lang.: Eng.   1615

Opera theatre program at the University of Louisville. USA: Louisville, KY. 1952-1983. Lang.: Eng.   3732

Affiliate Artists, performance training, audience development. USA: New York, NY. 1967-1987. Lang.: Eng.   3733

Program of opera workshop, Boston Conservatory. USA: Boston, MA. 1973-1983. Lang.: Eng.   3734

Performance spaces

Design of the San Francisco Ballet Building. USA: San Francisco, CA. 1987. Lang.: Eng.   712

Performance/production

Institutions, techniques in training of nō actors. Japan. 1987. Lang.: Eng.   1499

Workshop in Chinese acting methods. Canada: Toronto, ON. China, People's Republic of: Shanghai. 1987. Lang.: Eng.   1717

Development of mime, pantomime and its related movements. France: Paris. UK-England. USA: New York, NY. 1980-1982. Lang.: Eng.   3223

Quality of and access to opera training in North America. Canada. USA. 1987. Lang.: Eng.   3753

Interview with opera star Gaétan Laperrière. Canada. 1987. Lang.: Eng.   3756

Training

Changes in music teaching methods at the Banff Centre. Canada: Banff, AB. 1933-1987. Lang.: Eng.   3950

Instituto Torcuato Di Tella (Argentina)

Performance/production

Avant-garde theatres, authors and directors in Argentina. Argentina. 1950-1983. Lang.: Spa.   719

Instituut voor Theateronderzoek (Netherlands)

Administration

Funding of small theatre groups in the Netherlands. Netherlands. 1987. Lang.: Dut.   33

INTAR (New York, NY)

Plays/librettos/scripts

Playwright Fernando Arrabal and productions of his work. USA. France: Paris. 1959-1987. Lang.: Eng.   1175

Intensive Care

Performance/production

Collection of newspaper reviews by London theatre critics. UK-England. 1987. Lang.: Eng.   2033

Inter-American Music Festival

Performance/production

Violet Archer festival, premiere of her one-act opera *The Meal.* Canada: Edmonton, AB. 1985. Lang.: Eng.   3757

Interludes

Performance/production

Production of Merbury's *The Marriage of Wit and Wisdom* by David Parry. Israel: Jerusalem. 1987. Lang.: Eng.   1939

International Alliance of Theatrical Stage Employees (IATSE)

Design/technology

Effort to find union representation for theatrical sound designers. USA. 1985-1987. Lang.: Eng.   469

International Amateur Theatre Association

Training

Brecht workshop of International Amateur Theatre Association. Germany, East: Berlin, East. 1986. Lang.: Ger.   3079

International Brecht Festival (Hong Kong)

Performance/production

Review of International Brecht Festival. China, People's Republic of: Hong Kong. 1986. Lang.: Dut.   759

Isle of Dogs Theatre (London)
　　Performance/production
　　　Collection of newspaper reviews by London theatre critics. UK-
　　　England: London. 1986. Lang.: Eng.　　　　　　　　2132
ISTA
　　SEE
　　　International School of Theatre Anthropology.
It's a Girl!
　　Performance/production
　　　Collection of newspaper reviews by London theatre critics. UK-
　　　England. 1987. Lang.: Eng.　　　　　　　　　　　2175
It's Raining in My House
　　SEE
　　　Il pleut dans ma maison.
Italian Straw Hat, An
　　SEE
　　　Chapeau de paille d'Italie, Un.
Iue drama
　　Theory/criticism
　　　The beginning of *Iue* drama in 1935. China. 1935-1938. Lang.: Chi.
　　　　　　　　　　　　　　　　　　　　　　　　3590
Iván, a rettentő
　　SEE
　　　Ivan Vasiljěvič.
Ivanov, Viačeslav
　　Basic theatrical documents
　　　Russian symbolist plays and essays. USSR. 1880-1986. Lang.: Eng.
　　　　　　　　　　　　　　　　　　　　　　　　1584
　　Relation to other fields
　　　Soviet critics and playwrights on international cultural ties. USSR.
　　　1980-1987. Lang.: Rus.　　　　　　　　　　　　1294
Ivčenko, Valerij
　　Performance/production
　　　Bolšoj actor Valerij Ivčenko. USSR: Leningrad. 1980. Lang.: Rus.
　　　　　　　　　　　　　　　　　　　　　　　　1052
Ives, Kenneth
　　Performance/production
　　　Review of the BBC telecast of *The Birthday Party* by Harold Pinter.
　　　UK-England. 1987. Lang.: Eng.　　　　　　　　　3206
Ivey, Dana
　　Plays/librettos/scripts
　　　Alfred Uhry on *Driving Miss Daisy.* USA: New York, NY. 1976-
　　　1984. Lang.: Eng.　　　　　　　　　　　　　　3419
Izenour, George
　　Design/technology
　　　Survey of 1960s stage machinery. USA. 1960-1987. Lang.: Eng.　456
Jack and the Beanstalk
　　Performance/production
　　　Collection of newspaper reviews by London theatre critics. UK-
　　　England: London. 1987. Lang.: Eng.　　　　　　　2194
Jack Straw
　　Plays/librettos/scripts
　　　The potential for social influence in W. Somerset Maugham's
　　　comedies. UK-England. 1903-1933. Lang.: Eng.　　　2784
Jackson, Barry
　　Performance/production
　　　The founding and history of the Malvern Festival. UK-England:
　　　Malvern. 1904-1977. Lang.: Eng.　　　　　　　　2286
Jackson, Glenda
　　Performance/production
　　　Creative self-knowledge and the mystical path of actors. UK-
　　　England: London. USA. 1977-1987. Lang.: Eng.　　　900
Jackson, Nagle
　　Administration
　　　American theatre's view of the commissioning process. USA: New
　　　York, NY. 1987. Lang.: Eng.　　　　　　　　　　118
Jacobean theatre
　　SEE ALSO
　　　Geographical-Chronological Index under: England, 1603-1625.
　　Performance/production
　　　'Boy actresses' and attitudes toward sensuality in performance.
　　　England: London. 1580-1630. Lang.: Eng.　　　　　1741
　　　New interpretation of Jacobean theatre. England: London. 1596-
　　　1633. Lang.: Eng.　　　　　　　　　　　　　　1743
　　Plays/librettos/scripts
　　　Female characters in city comedy who suffer from bladder
　　　incontinence. 1599-1632. Lang.: Eng.　　　　　　　2427

　　　Madness and revenge in Kyd's *The Spanish Tragedy.* England. 1589.
　　　Lang.: Eng.　　　　　　　　　　　　　　　　　2515
　　Theory/criticism
　　　The body as emblematic of a character's frame of mind. England.
　　　1583. Lang.: Eng.　　　　　　　　　　　　　　3031
　　　Trollope's writings on Elizabethan and Jacobean drama. UK-
　　　England. 1866-1882. Lang.: Eng.　　　　　　　　3063
Jacobi, Derek
　　Performance/production
　　　Comparison and review of *Melon, Breaking the Code, Alan Turing:
　　　The Secret War* and *My Sister in This House.* UK-England: London.
　　　1987. Lang.: Eng.　　　　　　　　　　　　　　2285
Jacobowsky and the Colonel
　　Performance/production
　　　Collection of newspaper reviews by London theatre critics. UK-
　　　England: London. 1986. Lang.: Eng.　　　　　　　2150
Jacobs, Douglas
　　Performance/production
　　　Collection of newspaper reviews by New York theatre critics. USA:
　　　New York, NY. 1987. Lang.: Eng.　　　　　　　　2319
Jacques and His Master
　　Plays/librettos/scripts
　　　Interview with Susan Sontag, director of *Jacques and His Master.*
　　　USA: Cambridge, MA. 1985. Lang.: Eng.　　　　　　1172
　　　Interview with Milan Kundera on *Jacques and His Master.* USA:
　　　Cambridge, MA. 1985. Lang.: Eng.　　　　　　　　1173
　　　Kundera's adaptation of *Jacques le Fataliste (Jacques and His
　　　Master)* by Diderot. USA: Cambridge, MA. 1985. Lang.: Eng.　1178
Jacques et son maître (Jacques and His Master)
　　Basic theatrical documents
　　　Catalan translation of Milan Kundera's *Jacques et son maître
　　　(Jacques and His Master),* with introduction. Czechoslovakia: Prague.
　　　1968-1981. Lang.: Cat.　　　　　　　　　　　　1551
Jacques, Brigitte
　　Performance/production
　　　Directing as creation of a dimension that enhances the actor's desire.
　　　France. 1987. Lang.: Fre.　　　　　　　　　　　785
　　　Brigitte Jacques as Elvire in Molière's *Dom Juan.* France:
　　　Strasbourg. 1940-1986. Lang.: Fre.　　　　　　　　1764
Jacuarello, Roland
　　Performance/production
　　　Collection of newspaper reviews by London theatre critics. UK-
　　　England: London. 1987. Lang.: Eng.　　　　　　　2257
Jagdgesellschaft, Die (Hunting Party, The)
　　Plays/librettos/scripts
　　　The metadramatic nature of Thomas Bernhard's plays. Germany,
　　　West. 1974-1983. Lang.: Eng.　　　　　　　　　　2616
Jakobsson, Robert
　　Performance/production
　　　Collection of newspaper reviews by London theatre critics. UK-
　　　England: London. 1987. Lang.: Eng.　　　　　　　2205
Jakovlev, A.
　　Design/technology
　　　Mejerchol'd's collaboration with artists A. Jakovlev, V. Suchaev.
　　　USSR. 1935-1939. Lang.: Rus.　　　　　　　　　491
Jakovleva, Ol'ga
　　Performance/production
　　　Life and work of Anatolij Efros. USSR: Moscow. 1983-1987. Lang.:
　　　Eng.　　　　　　　　　　　　　　　　　　　1038
　　　Portrait of actress Ol'ga Jakovleva of Taganka Theatre. USSR:
　　　Moscow. 1980-1987. Lang.: Rus.　　　　　　　　1088
Jakreškina, Je.
　　Plays/librettos/scripts
　　　Correspondence of playwright Aleksand'r Vampilov. USSR: Moscow.
　　　1960-1975. Lang.: Rus.　　　　　　　　　　　　2968
Jakulov, G.B.
　　Plays/librettos/scripts
　　　Analysis of the plays of G.B. Jakulov. USSR. 1987. Lang.: Ita.　1186
Jakut, V.S.
　　Performance/production
　　　Memoirs of actor V.S. Jakut. USSR: Moscow. 1912-1980. Lang.:
　　　Rus.　　　　　　　　　　　　　　　　　　　1025
Jakutskij Dramatičeskij Teat'r im. P.A. Ojunskij (Jakutsk)
　　Performance/production
　　　Work of Andrej Borisov, principal director of Jakutskij Drama
　　　Theatre. USSR: Yakutsk. 1980-1987. Lang.: Rus.　　1003

Jehad
Performance/production
Collection of newspaper reviews by London theatre critics. UK-England: London. 1987. Lang.: Eng.   2236

Jeles, András
Performance/production
Interview with director András Jeles of Monteverdi Birkózókör (Budapest). Hungary. 1985-1987. Lang.: Hun.   1833

Jenkin, Len
Design/technology
Philosophy of set designer John Arnone. USA: New York, NY. 1987. Lang.: Eng.   430

Performance/production
Career of director Garland Wright. USA. 1972-1987. Lang.: Eng.
                                    975

Jenkin's Ear
Performance/production
Collection of newspaper reviews by London theatre critics. UK-England: London. 1987. Lang.: Eng.   2244

Jenkins, Paulie
Design/technology
Work of lighting designer Paulie Jenkins. USA. 1987. Lang.: Eng.
                                    404

Jennie's Story
Basic theatrical documents
Publication of two playtexts by Betty Lambert. Canada. 1987. Lang.: Eng.   1547

Jenůfa
Performance/production
Background on San Francisco opera radio broadcasts. USA: San Francisco, CA. 1987. Lang.: Eng.   3833

Jepson, Paul
Performance/production
Collection of newspaper reviews by London theatre critics. UK-England: London. 1987. Lang.: Eng.   2237

Jeritza, Maria
Performance/production
Careers of three female opera stars: Mary McCormic, Maria Jeritza, Bidú Sayão. USA. 1952-1981. Lang.: Eng.   3835

Jermain, Clive
Performance/production
Collection of newspaper reviews by London theatre critics. UK-England: London. 1987. Lang.: Eng.   2266

Jessner, Leopold
Performance/production
Reviews of major Berlin performances. Germany: Berlin. 1889-1933. Lang.: Ger.   1772
Politics and Shakespeare in Weimar Republic. Germany. 1919-1930. Lang.: Eng.   1775

Jesuit theatre
Basic theatrical documents
English translations of three plays by Jacob Masen. Germany. 1606-1681. Lang.: Eng.   1556

Jesurun, John
Basic theatrical documents
Six plays detailing the Hispanic experience in the United States. USA. Mexico. 1987. Lang.: Eng.   1581

Performance/production
Production of John Jesurun's *Chang in a Void Moon*. USA: New York, NY. 1982-1983. Lang.: Eng.   2336
History of incorporating film into a theatrical performance. USA: New York, NY. 1922-1987. Lang.: Eng.   3196

Jeu de l'amour et du hasard, Le (Game of Love and Chance, The)
Performance/production
Le jeu de l'amour et du hasard (*The Game of Love and Chance*) by Marivaux directed at National Theatre by Péter Valló as *A szerelem és véletlen játéka*. Hungary: Miskolc. 1987. Lang.: Hun.   1916

Jevrejnov, Nikolaj Nikolajevič
Performance/production
'Showing' is an essential part of all acting. Europe. 1590-1987. Lang.: Eng.   1746
Jevrejnov's theories of theatricality, parallels with Pirandello's. USSR. 1879-1953. Lang.: Eng.   2391

Jew of Venice, The
Plays/librettos/scripts
Eighteenth-century alterations to Shakespeare's *The Merchant of Venice*. England. 1596-1701. Lang.: Eng.   2512

Jewel in the Crown, The
Performance/production
Granada TV's production of *The Jewel in the Crown*. UK-England. India. 1986. Lang.: Eng.   3207

Jewish theatre
SEE
Yiddish theatre.

Jezek, Jaroslav
Performance/production
Miklós Szurdi directs *Kat a blázen* (*The Hangman and the Madman*) by Jan Werick and Jiři Voskovec, songs by Jaroslav Jezek, at Radnóti Miklós Szinpad as *Hóhér és Bolond*. Hungary: Budapest. 1986. Lang.: Hun.   1825

Ji-Lin opera
Performance/production
Role of Ji-Lin opera in development of Chinese opera. China. 960 B.C.-1987 A.D. Lang.: Chi.   3463

Ji, Shao-Shan (Ji Ba Wang)
Performance/production
Beijing opera actor Ji Ba Wang. China: Beijing. 1937-1948. Lang.: Chi.   3460

Jia-Li, Tuo-Suo
Performance/production
Comparison between Chinese opera and Buddhist plays of Kerala. China, People's Republic of: Beijing. India. 1050-1968. Lang.: Chi.
                                    3533

Jiang, Xing-Yi
Performance/production
Comparison between Chinese opera and Buddhist plays of Kerala. China, People's Republic of: Beijing. India. 1050-1968. Lang.: Chi.
                                    3533

Jig for the Gypsy, A
Plays/librettos/scripts
Survey of Robertson Davies' plays. Canada. 1913-1985. Lang.: Eng.
                                    2484

Jimenez, Carlos
Performance/production
Brief history of the Latin American Theatre Festival. Argentina: Córdoba. 1984-1987. Lang.: Eng.   1680

Jimusho (Office)
Plays/librettos/scripts
Productions by several Tokyo companies. Japan: Tokyo. 1986-1987. Lang.: Jap.   2682

Jin Ping Mei (Golden Lotus, The)
Plays/librettos/scripts
Ming dynasty novels as source of theatrical inspiration. China. 1368-1644. Lang.: Chi.   2491

Jinriki hikōki Soromon (Man-Powered Plane Solomon)
Basic theatrical documents
Plays of Terayama Shūji. Japan. 1950-1980. Lang.: Jap.   1562

Jitensha konkuriito (Tokyo)
Performance/production
Analysis of four Tokyo productions. Japan: Tokyo. 1987. Lang.: Jap.
                                    1957

Job Rocking
Performance/production
Collection of newspaper reviews by London theatre critics. UK-England: London. 1987. Lang.: Eng.   2215

Joe Beef
Plays/librettos/scripts
David Fennario's *Joe Beef*. Canada: Montreal, PQ, Verdun, PQ. 1984. Lang.: Eng.   2470

Jōen daihon (Scenario, The)
Plays/librettos/scripts
Plays about child suicide in Japan. Japan: Tokyo. 1986. Lang.: Jap.
                                    2683

Jogging
Plays/librettos/scripts
Comparison between Albee's *Who's Afraid of Virginia Woolf?* and Radsinskij's *Jogging*. USSR. USA. 1987. Lang.: Eng.   2960

Joglars, Els (Catalonia)
Institutions
Analysis of all the productions performed by Els Joglars in their twenty-five years of existence. Spain-Catalonia. 1962-1987. Lang.: Cat.   1634

Johann Faustus
Plays/librettos/scripts
Why Hanns Eisler's opera *Johann Faustus* remained incomplete. Germany, East. 1953-1987. Lang.: Ger.   3912

Johann Faustus — cont'd

Debate over Hanns Eisler's opera *Johann Faustus*. Germany, East: Berlin, East. 1949-1955. Lang.: Ger. 3913

John Bull's Other Island
Plays/librettos/scripts
Shaw's use of Irish stereotypes in *John Bull's Other Ireland*. UK-England. UK-Ireland. 1860-1925. Lang.: Eng. 2787
Background of *John Bull's Other Island* by G.B. Shaw. UK-England. 1904. Lang.: Eng. 2804

John F. Kennedy Center (Washington, DC)
Administration
Interview with director Peter Sellars. USA: Washington, DC. 1985. 1524

John Golden Theatre (New York, NY)
Performance/production
Collection of newspaper reviews by New York theatre critics. USA: New York, NY. 1987. Lang.: Eng. 2321
Collection of newspaper reviews by New York critics. USA: New York, NY. 1987. Lang.: Eng. 2324

John Houseman Theatre (New York, NY)
Performance/production
Collection of newspaper reviews by New York theatre critics. USA: New York, NY. 1987. Lang.: Eng. 2323

Johnson, J. Rosamund
Performance/production
Origins of jazz, its evolution in vaudeville. USA: New Orleans, LA, New York, NY, Chicago, IL. Lang.: Eng. 3650

Johnson, Jill
Performance/production
Reviews of Pinter's *The Lover* and *A Slight Ache*. UK-England: London. 1987. Lang.: Eng. 901

Johnson, Nunnally
Performance/production
History and review of 1967 musical *Henry, Sweet Henry*. USA: New York, NY. 1967. Lang.: Eng. 3642
History of musical version, *Breakfast at Tiffany's*. USA: New York, NY, Philadelphia, PA, Boston, MA. 1958-1966. Lang.: Eng. 3644

Johnson, Samuel
Research/historiography
Critical history of *Julius Caesar*. England. 1599-1987. Lang.: Eng. 1299

Johnson, Terry
Performance/production
Collection of newspaper reviews by London theatre critics. UK-England: London. 1986. Lang.: Eng. 2100
Collection of newspaper reviews by London theatre critics. UK-England: London. 1986. Lang.: Eng. 2101
Collection of newspaper reviews by London theatre critics. UK-England: London. 1986. Lang.: Eng. 2147

Johnston, Denis
Institutions
Playwright Denis Johnston and avant-garde theatre at the Abbey. Ireland: Dublin. 1927-1935. Lang.: Eng. 1619

Johnstone, Jennifer
Plays/librettos/scripts
Avoidance of political themes in drama of Northern Ireland. UK-Ireland. 1979-1987. Lang.: Eng. 2830

Johnstone, Keith
Performance/production
Summarizes events of Directors' Colloquium. Canada: Calgary, AB. 1987. Lang.: Eng. 728

Joint Stock Theater Group (England)
Plays/librettos/scripts
Self-referential techniques in Caryl Churchill's *Cloud 9*. UK-England. 1978-1987. Lang.: Eng. 2793

Jókai Szinház (Békéscsaba)
Performance/production
Performances of *Oliver* staged by György Korcsmáros, Antol Rencz and Imre Halasi. Hungary: Budapest, Békéscsaba, Zalaegerszeg. 1986. Lang.: Hun. 3632

Jókai Szinház (Budapest)
Performance/production
Uri muri (Gentlemen's Spree) by Zsigmond Móricz staged by Mátyás Giricz at Jókai Theatre. Hungary: Békéscsaba. 1986. Lang.: Hun. 1877

Jókai, Mór
Performance spaces
Mór Jókai's recollections of the old, gas-lit National Theatre building. Hungary: Budapest. 1900. Lang.: Hun. 642

Jomfru Ane Theatre (Denmark)
Relation to other fields
Impact of politics upon funding of theatre. Denmark. 1722-1982. Lang.: Eng. 2986

Jon, Jon
Performance/production
Collection of newspaper reviews by London theatre critics. UK-England: London. 1987. Lang.: Eng. 2246

Jonah
Basic theatrical documents
English translation of *Jonah* by Elie Georges Berreby. Belgium. 1987. Lang.: Eng. 1542

Jones-Meadows, Karen
Institutions
Members of Negro Ensemble Company, New Federal Theatre and American Place Theatre on artistic agendas. USA: New York, NY. 1987. Lang.: Eng. 592

Jones, David
Performance/production
Two productions of Pinter's *Old Times*. UK-England: London. USA: New York, NY, St. Louis, MO. 1971-1985. Lang.: Eng. 907
Collection of newspaper reviews by London theatre critics. UK-England: London. 1986. Lang.: Eng. 2063

Jones, Emrys
Research/historiography
Critical history of *Julius Caesar*. England. 1599-1987. Lang.: Eng. 1299

Jones, Henry Arthur
Plays/librettos/scripts
Study of plays by Henry Arthur Jones. UK-England: London. 1882-1900. Lang.: Eng. 2790

Jones, Inigo
Performance spaces
Analysis of theatre designs by Inigo Jones and John Webb. England. 1573-1672. Lang.: Eng. 632
Performance/production
Location and staging of a 1636 royal masque. England. 1636. Lang.: Eng. 3321
Plays/librettos/scripts
Utopian ideas in Tudor and Stuart playwrights. England. 1600-1650. Lang.: Ger. 2522
Theory/criticism
Ben Jonson's view of similarities between spectacle plays and comic plays. England. 1572-1637. Lang.: Eng. 3028

Jones, James Earl
Performance/production
Interview with actor James Earl Jones. USA: New York, NY. 1953-1987. Lang.: Eng. 2340
Theatre career of photo-journalist Bert Andrews. USA: New York, NY. 1950-1987. Lang.: Eng. 2367
Plays/librettos/scripts
Interview with playwright August Wilson. USA. 1970-1987. Lang.: Eng. 2855

Jones, LeRoi
SEE
Baraka, Imamu Amiri.

Jones, Marie
Performance/production
Collection of newspaper reviews by London theatre critics. UK-England: London. 1986. Lang.: Eng. 2059
Collection of newspaper reviews by London theatre critics. UK-England. 1986. Lang.: Eng. 2159
Collection of newspaper reviews by London theatre critics. UK-England: London. 1987. Lang.: Eng. 2247
Relation to other fields
Interview with founders of the Charabanc Theatre Company. UK-Ireland. 1970-1987. Lang.: Eng. 1260

Jones, Robert Edmond
Performance/production
Philip Moeller's premiere of *Mourning Becomes Electra* by O'Neill. USA: New York, NY. 1931. Lang.: Eng. 2366
History of incorporating film into a theatrical performance. USA: New York, NY. 1922-1987. Lang.: Eng. 3196
American premiere of Alban Berg's *Wozzeck*. USA: New York, NY. 1931. Lang.: Eng. 3841

Jones, Walton
Performance/production
Collection of newspaper reviews by New York theatre critics. USA:
New York, NY. 1987. Lang.: Eng.   2311

Jones, Wyn
Performance/production
Collection of newspaper reviews by London theatre critics. UK-
England: London. 1986. Lang.: Eng.   2168

Collection of newspaper reviews by London theatre critics. UK-
England: London. 1987. Lang.: Eng.   2189

Collection of newspaper reviews by London theatre critics. UK-
England: London. 1987. Lang.: Eng.   2243

Collection of newspaper reviews by London theatre critics. UK-
England: London. 1987. Lang.: Eng.   2247

Jonson, Ben
Audience
Actor and audience in Elizabethan theatre. England. 1585-1625.
Lang.: Eng.   1533

Design/technology
Review of *Bartholomew Fair* and *A Midsummer Night's Dream.* UK-
England: London. 1987. Lang.: Eng.   1598

Performance/production
'Boy actresses' and attitudes toward sensuality in performance.
England: London. 1580-1630. Lang.: Eng.   1741

New interpretation of Jacobean theatre. England: London. 1596-
1633. Lang.: Eng.   1743

Collection of newspaper reviews by London theatre critics. UK-
England: London. 1987. Lang.: Eng.   2200

Collection of newspaper reviews by London theatre critics. UK-
England: London. 1987. Lang.: Eng.   2201

Collection of newspaper reviews by London theatre critics. UK-
England: London. 1987. Lang.: Eng.   2252

Plays/librettos/scripts
Comparison of the works of Ben Jonson and Christopher Marlowe.
England. 1598-1602. Lang.: Eng.   1123

Female characters in city comedy who suffer from bladder
incontinence. 1599-1632. Lang.: Eng.   2427

Urbanity as subject and form of Jonson's *Epicoene.* England. 1609-
1987. Lang.: Eng.   2498

Playwright Ben Jonson's theatricality and relevance today. England.
1600-1987. Lang.: Eng.   2501

Characters in Verdi's *Otello.* Italy: Milan. 1887. Lang.: Eng.   3920

Relation to other fields
Psychological effect of Ben Jonson's family life on his writings.
England. 1602-1604. Lang.: Eng.   1232

Research/historiography
Discussion of the miscellany called *Wit's Creation.* England: London.
1640. Lang.: Eng.   1298

Theory/criticism
Ben Jonson's view of similarities between spectacle plays and comic
plays. England. 1572-1637. Lang.: Eng.   3028

Trollope's writings on Elizabethan and Jacobean drama. UK-
England. 1866-1882. Lang.: Eng.   3063

Jonson, Per A.
Design/technology
Scene designer discusses production of *Pygmalion* in former
mechanical workshop. Sweden: Stockholm. 1986. Lang.: Swe.   1595

Jooss, Kurt
Performance/production
Development of dance. Germany: Berlin. 1920-1986. Lang.: Ger.
                                                                   1407

Jordán, Tamás
Performance/production
Tamás Jordán's *Amit a szívedbe rejtesz (Hidden in Your Heart)*
directed by János Gáspár. Hungary: Budapest. 1987. Lang.: Hun.
                                                                   1828

János Gáspar directs *Amit a szívedbe rejtesz (Hidden in Your Heart)*
by Tamás Jordán, based on notes by poet Attila József, at Radnóti
Miklós Theatre. Hungary: Budapest. 1987. Lang.: Hun.   1836

László Bagossy directs *Macbeth,* Tamás Jordán directs Zsigmond
Móricz's *Úri muri (Gentlemen's Spree)* at Pécs Summer Theatre.
Hungary: Pécs. 1987. Lang.: Hun.   1864

Productions of plays by László Márton, Tamás Jordán and Ferenc
Kulin at Radnóti Miklós Theatre. Hungary: Budapest. 1987. Lang.:
Hun.   1887

Jordcirkus (Stockholm)
Performance/production
Jordcirkus and amateur group Näktergalningarna stage *A Christmas
Carol.* Sweden: Stockholm. 1986-1987. Lang.: Swe.   2020

Jory, Jon
Institutions
Actors Theatre of Louisville's 'Classics in Context' festival. USA:
Louisville, KY. 1986-1988. Lang.: Eng.   1657

Performance/production
Influence of Pirandello on modern theatre. USA. Italy. 1917-1987.
Lang.: Eng.   2338

Joseph and the Amazing Technicolor Dreamcoat
Performance/production
Collection of newspaper reviews by London theatre critics. UK-
England: London. 1986. Lang.: Eng.   2048

Joseph, Judith
Performance/production
Collection of newspaper reviews by London theatre critics. UK-
England: London. 1987. Lang.: Eng.   2202

Jouanneau, Joël
Performance/production
Plays of Pinget, Euripides and Théâtre du Rideau staged by
Jouanneau, Suzuki and Tanguy, Théâtre de la Bastille. France: Paris.
1987. Lang.: Fre.   1753

Joudry, Patricia
Basic theatrical documents
Collection of radio plays produced by Andrew Allan. Canada. 1942-
1955. Lang.: Eng.   3109

Journey to Kairos
Performance/production
Ann Mortifee, singer, songwriter, performer. Canada: Vancouver, BC,
Toronto, ON. 1982. Lang.: Eng.   1714

Jours heureux, Les (Happy Days)
Performance/production
Personal notes of Samuel Beckett, how they illuminate his plays.
France. 1969-1984. Lang.: Eng.   1758

Jouvet, Louis
Performance/production
Directing as creation of a dimension that enhances the actor's desire.
France. 1987. Lang.: Fre.   785

Brigitte Jacques as Elvire in Molière's *Dom Juan.* France:
Strasbourg. 1940-1986. Lang.: Fre.   1764

Jovanović, Dušan
Performance/production
Review of *Hamlet, Julius Caesar* and *Titus Andronicus* at
'Shakespeare Fest '86'. Yugoslavia: Palić. 1986. Lang.: Hun.   2405

Joyce Theatre (New York, NY)
Performance/production
Collection of newspaper reviews by New York theatre critics. USA:
New York, NY. 1987. Lang.: Eng.   2319

Joyce, James
Relation to other fields
Theatrical themes and the class issue in the work of Irish
playwrights. Ireland. 1900-1987. Lang.: Eng.   2994

Literary figures of the Irish Literary Renaissance. Ireland. UK-
Ireland. 1875-1938. Lang.: Eng.   2995

Joyce, Michael
Performance/production
Collection of newspaper reviews by London theatre critics. UK-
England: London. 1986. Lang.: Eng.   2087

József Attila Színház (Budapest)
Performance spaces
Design and construction considerations: renovation of József Attila
Theatre. Hungary: Budapest. 1985-1986. Lang.: Hun.   640

Details of the renovation of József Attila Theatre. Hungary:
Budapest. 1985-1986. Lang.: Hun.   644

Performance/production
Interview with actress Judit Tóth. Hungary: Budapest. 1962-1987.
Lang.: Hun.   1802

Comparison of *Die Dreigroschenoper (The Three Penny Opera)* as
directed by Ferenc Sík, József Petrik and Miklós Szinetár under the
title *Koldusopera.* Hungary: Győr, Budapest. 1987. Lang.: Hun.   3402

József Katona Theatre
SEE
Katona József Színház.

József, Attila
Performance/production

Tamás Jordán's *Amit a szívedbe rejtesz (Hidden in Your Heart)* directed by János Gáspár. Hungary: Budapest. 1987. Lang.: Hun.
1828

János Gáspar directs *Amit a szívedbe rejtesz (Hidden in Your Heart)* by Tamás Jordán, based on notes by poet Attila József, at Radnóti Miklós Theatre. Hungary: Budapest. 1987. Lang.: Hun.
1836

Productions of plays by László Márton, Tamás Jordán and Ferenc Kulin at Radnóti Miklós Theatre. Hungary: Budapest. 1987. Lang.: Hun.
1887

Józsefvárosi Szinház (Budapest)
Performance/production

Reviews of two Anouilh plays: *Eurydice* directed by János Szűcs, *Colombe* directed by Mátyás Giricz. Hungary: Miskolc, Budapest. 1987. Lang.: Hun.
1827

Comparison of *Die Dreigroschenoper (The Three Penny Opera)* as directed by Ferenc Sík, József Petrik and Miklós Szinetár under the title *Koldusopera*. Hungary: Győr, Budapest. 1987. Lang.: Hun. 3402

Judge, Ian
Performance/production

Collection of newspaper reviews by London theatre critics. UK-England. 1987. Lang.: Eng.
2263

Judgment
Performance/production

Collection of newspaper reviews by London theatre critics. UK-England: London. 1987. Lang.: Eng.
2237

Judgment Day
Performance/production

Collection of newspaper reviews by London theatre critics. UK-England: London. 1987. Lang.: Eng.
2248

Judson Dance Theatre (New York, NY)
Performance/production

Five women choreographers and critics discuss conceptions of the female body. USA. 1987. Lang.: Eng.
1416

Judy
Performance/production

Collection of newspaper reviews by London theatre critics. UK-England: London. 1986. Lang.: Eng.
2078

Jug
Performance/production

Collection of newspaper reviews by London theatre critics. UK-England: London. 1986. Lang.: Eng.
2106

Juggling
Performance/production

Description of 'Third Theatre'. Argentina: Bahía Blanca. 1987. Lang.: Eng.
3249

Evolution of the Flying Karamazov Brothers. USA. 1977-1987. Lang.: Eng.
3273

Production of Cirque du Soleil. Canada: Montreal, PQ. 1987. Lang.: Eng.
3302

Juilliard School (New York, NY)
Performance spaces

John Houseman on the New York home of the Acting Company. USA: New York, NY. 1972-1986. Lang.: Eng.
695

Julie What Is Wrong?
Performance/production

Collection of newspaper reviews by London theatre critics. UK-England: London. 1987. Lang.: Eng.
2240

Julius Caesar
Performance/production

Review of *Hamlet*, *Julius Caesar* and *Titus Andronicus* at 'Shakespeare Fest '86'. Yugoslavia: Palić. 1986. Lang.: Hun. 2405

Plays/librettos/scripts

Comparison of Shakespeare's *Julius Caesar* to the drama and vision of Euripides. UK-England. 500 B.C.-1599 A.D. Lang.: Eng. 2760

Research/historiography

Critical history of *Julius Caesar*. England. 1599-1987. Lang.: Eng.
1299

Theory/criticism

Self-awareness in Shakespeare's *Julius Caesar*. England. 1599. Lang.: Eng.
1327

Jullien, Jean
Plays/librettos/scripts

Jullien's violations of decorum and *honneur* in *La Sérénade (The Serenade)*. France. 1887-1987. Lang.: Eng.
2577

Theory/criticism

Centenary of Théâtre Libre: proposes 'subjective realism'. France. 1887-1987. Lang.: Fre.
1337

Jungfrau von Orleans, Die (Maid of Orleans, The)
Performance/production

August Wilhelm Iffland's productions of plays by Friedrich von Schiller. Germany: Berlin. 1796-1806. Lang.: Ger.
1773

Plays/librettos/scripts

Friedrich von Schiller's late works: new conception of drama. Germany. 1799-1805. Lang.: Eng.
2604

Junkies Are Full of Shhh
Performance/production

Interview with playwright Amiri Baraka. USA: Newark, NJ, New York, NY. 1965-1969. Lang.: Eng.
2356

Juno and the Paycock
Plays/librettos/scripts

Popular music in the Dublin trilogy plays of Sean O'Casey. Ireland. 1923-1926. Lang.: Eng.
2644

Junona (Juno)
Plays/librettos/scripts

Historical themes in plays of Andrej Vosnesenskij. USSR: Moscow. 1980-1987. Lang.: Rus.
2937

Jurskij, Sergej
Performance/production

Sergej Jurskij, director of Mossovet Theatre. USSR: Moscow. 1970-1980. Lang.: Rus.
995

Actors discuss their profession. USSR. 1987. Lang.: Eng.
996

Portrait of actor Sergej Jurskij. USSR: Moscow. 1835-1987. Lang.: Rus.
1036

Jurta Szinház (Budapest)
Performance spaces

Safety problems of new, cooperative Jurta theatre. Hungary: Budapest. 1987. Lang.: Hun.
638

Jusqu'à nouvel avis (Until Further Notice)
Plays/librettos/scripts

Compares plays of Enlightenment France, Francophone Africa. Congo: Brazzaville. Cameroon. Benin. France. 1700-1975. Lang.: Eng.
2496

Justification for the Bloodshed
SEE

Opravdanijė krovi.

Kâ, Abdov Anta
Basic theatrical documents

English translations of contemporary African plays. Senegal. Zaire. 1987. Lang.: Eng.
1566

Kaaitheater (Belgium)
Performance/production

History of Kaaitheater. Belgium. 1980-1987. Lang.: Eng.
724

Kaal', Anu
Performance/production

Anu Kaal', Estonian opera singer. USSR. 1960-1987. Lang.: Rus.
3872

Kabos, Gyula
Performance/production

Centenary volume on actor Gyula Kabos. Hungary. 1887-1941. Lang.: Hun.
3153

Kabuki
SEE ALSO

Classed Entries under DANCE-DRAMA—*Kabuki.*

Performance/production

Comparison of *onnagata* actors with Elizabethan boy actors. England. Japan. 1580-1987. Lang.: Eng.
1737

Kadashima, Yūshi
Performance/production

Six plays of the Tokyo season, focus on director Betsuyaku Minoru. Japan: Tokyo. 1986. Lang.: Jap.
1966

Kafka
Performance/production

Collection of newspaper reviews by London theatre critics. UK-England: London. 1987. Lang.: Eng.
2215

Kafka, Franz
Performance/production

Collection of newspaper reviews by New York theatre critics. USA: New York, NY. 1987. Lang.: Eng.
2325

Plays/librettos/scripts

Study of three plays by Mihály Kornis: *Halleluja*, *Büntetések (Punishments)* and *Kozma*. Hungary. 1980-1987. Lang.: Hun. 2628

Kafka, Franz — cont'd

Theory/criticism
Evaluation of the present state of theatrical theory and its influence
on theatrical practice. Europe. 1985. Lang.: Fre.   3033

Kafka's Dick
Performance/production
Collection of newspaper reviews by London theatre critics. UK-
England: London. 1986. Lang.: Eng.   2167

Kaggai, Ghisulo
Plays/librettos/scripts
Theme of aggression between fathers and sons: Zambian National
Theatre Arts Association festival. Zambia. 1966-1987. Lang.: Eng.
2972

Kago no tori (Birds in a Cage)
Performance/production
Analysis of four Tokyo productions. Japan: Tokyo. 1987. Lang.: Jap.
1957

Kagura
Performance/production
Honda Yasuji's work on Japanese folk theatre. Japan. 1930-1986.
Lang.: Eng.   1483

Kahan, Marcia
Performance/production
Collection of newspaper reviews by London theatre critics. UK-
England: London. 1986. Lang.: Eng.   2169

Kahn, Michael
Relation to other fields
Nontraditional casting of minority actors. USA. 1979-1987. Lang.:
Eng.   1274

Kahn, Rick
Performance/production
George C. Wolfe and L. Kenneth Richardson discuss *The Colored
Museum*. USA: New York, NY, New Brunswick, NJ. 1987. Lang.:
Eng.   2363

Kaiser, Georg
Performance/production
Collection of newspaper reviews by London theatre critics. UK-
England: London. 1986. Lang.: Eng.   2105
Collection of newspaper reviews by London theatre critics. UK-
England: London. 1987. Lang.: Eng.   2196

Kaitasha (Tokyo)
Plays/librettos/scripts
Productions by several Tokyo companies. Japan: Tokyo. 1986-1987.
Lang.: Jap.   2682

Kalevala
Performance/production
The 4th International Theatre Conference: includes list of
participants and their contributions. Poland: Warsaw. 1986. Lang.:
Eng, Fre.   873

Kalfin, Bob
Administration
Financial challenges of four former artistic directors. USA. 1981-
1987. Lang.: Eng.   239

Kalinska, Zofia
Performance/production
An experimental women's theatre workshop. UK-Wales: Cardiff.
1986-1987. Lang.: Eng.   922

Kalisz, Richard
Performance/production
Dorothée Letessier's comments on the adaptation and staging of her
novel *Voyage à Paimpol (Journey to Paimpol)*. Belgium: Liège. 1986.
Lang.: Fre.   1686

Kaljagin, A.
Performance/production
Actor A. Kaljagin on his role as Lenin. USSR: Moscow. 1987.
Lang.: Rus.   2382

Kálmán, Imre
Performance/production
Imre Kálmán's *Cigányprimás (Sari)* and Bizet's *Carmen* at Kisfaludy
Theatre staged by József Bor. Hungary: Győr. 1912-1986. Lang.:
Hun.   3959

Kamal Theatre
SEE
Tatarskij Gosudarstvěnnyj Akademičeskij Teat'r im. Kamala.

Kamara, David
Performance/production
The African actor in Africa, Italy and the United States. USA:
Brooklyn, NY. Sierra Leone: Freetown. Italy: Rome. 1987. Lang.:
Eng.   2362

Kamatsuda, Rinnosuke
Performance/production
Honda Yasuji's work on Japanese folk theatre. Japan. 1930-1986.
Lang.: Eng.   1483

Kamernyj Muzykal'nyj Teat'r (Moscow)
Performance/production
Life and work of N. Cereteli, leading actor of Tairov Chamber
Theatre. USSR: Moscow. 1890-1942. Lang.: Rus.   1072
Actor A.A. Rušnev of Tairov Chamber Theatre. USSR: Moscow.
1920-1939. Lang.: Rus.   3237
B.A. Pokrovskij, principal director, Moscow Musical Chamber
Theatre. USSR: Moscow. 1912-1987. Lang.: Rus.   3873

Kamernyj Opernyj Teat'r (Leningrad)
Administration
Creation of Leningrad Chamber Opera Theatre. USSR: Leningrad.
1987. Lang.: Rus.   3688

Kamernyj Teat'r (Moscow)
Performance/production
Work of director Aleksandr Tairov with Kamernyj Teat'r. USSR:
Moscow. 1919-1933. Lang.: Rus.   1063

Kamińska, Ida
Institutions
Ida Kamińska, director of Jewish Theatre of Warsaw. Poland:
Warsaw. 1899-1987. Lang.: Pol.   1629

Kamiyama, Shigeru
Performance/production
Reviews and discussion of Tokyo productions. Japan: Tokyo. 1960-
1987. Lang.: Jap.   1960
Comments on Tokyo performances. Japan: Tokyo. 1987. Lang.: Jap.
1964

Kanazōshi Kokusenya jitsuroku
Basic theatrical documents
Texts of seven *kabuki* plays. Japan. 1600-1800. Lang.: Jap.   1491

Kander, John
Performance/production
Collection of newspaper reviews by London theatre critics. UK-
England: London. 1986. Lang.: Eng.   2149
Collection of newspaper reviews by New York theatre critics. USA:
New York, NY. 1987. Lang.: Eng.   2317
Two productions of *Flora, the Red Menace*. USA: New York, NY.
1965-1987. Lang.: Eng.   3640

Kandinsky, Wassily
Design/technology
Exhibition of theatrical design by Léger, Cocteau, Kokoschka and
Kandinsky. France. Lang.: Eng.   322
Plays/librettos/scripts
Der gelbe Klang (The Yellow Sound) by Wassily Kandinsky.
Germany. 1896-1914. Lang.: Kor.   2597
Theory/criticism
The concept of theatre as a total work of art. Europe. 1804-1930.
Lang.: Eng.   1328

Kane, John
Performance/production
Collection of newspaper reviews by London theatre critics. UK-
England. 1987. Lang.: Eng.   2263

Kanellos, Nicolas
Institutions
Development of El Teatro Carmen. USA: Tucson, AZ. 1915-1923.
Lang.: Spa.   606

Kani, John
Performance/production
Black theatre in South Africa: influence of traditional forms. South
Africa, Republic of. England: London. USA: New York, NY. 1586-
1987. Lang.: Eng.   2005
Controversial production of *Othello* directed by Janet Suzman. South
Africa, Republic of: Johannesburg. 1987. Lang.: Eng.   2007
Plays/librettos/scripts
Stage space as prison in *The Island* by Athol Fugard with John
Kani and Winston Ntshona. South Africa, Republic of. 1987. Lang.:
Eng.   2727

KanKanga
Relation to other fields
Evolution of ritual and ritual dances in the Nolembu tribe. Zambia.
1951-1985. Lang.: Eng.   1466

Kankyakuseki (Spectator Seat)
Basic theatrical documents
Plays of Terayama Shūji. Japan. 1950-1980. Lang.: Jap.   1562

Katona József Szinház (Budapest) — cont'd

Gábor Zsámbéki directs *Csirkefej (Chickenhead)* by György Spiró, Katona József Theatre. Hungary: Budapest. 1986. Lang.: Hun.   1895

György Spiró's *Csirkefej (Chickenhead)* directed by Gábor Zsámbéki, Katona József Theatre. Hungary: Budapest. 1986. Lang.: Hun.   1908

János Szikora directs Corneille's *L'illusion comique (The Comic Illusion)* at Katona József Theatre. Hungary: Budapest. 1986. Lang.: Hun.   1918

Ljudmila Petruševskaja's controversial play, *Tri devuški v golubom (Three Girls in Blue)*, directed by Tamás Ascher at Katona József Theatre. Hungary: Budapest. 1987. Lang.: Hun.   1920

Plays/librettos/scripts
Interview with playwright György Spiró. Hungary. 1962-1987. Lang.: Hun.   2633

Katona József Szinház (Kecskemét)
Performance/production
Two premieres: Shakespeare, *The Merchant of Venice*, directed by Árpád Jutacsa Hegyi. Németh's *Villámfénynél (By the Stroke of Lightning)*, directed by Attila Seprődi Kiss. Hungary: Kecskemét. 1987. Lang.: Hun.   1925

Katsuta, Yasuhiko
Performance/production
Productions of several Tokyo companies. Japan: Tokyo. 1987. Lang.: Jap.   1962

Kauffmann, Stanley
Plays/librettos/scripts
Structural analysis of Pinter's *Old Times*. USA: New York, NY. 1971-1984. Lang.: Eng.   2843

Kaukasische Kreidekreis, Der (Caucasian Chalk Circle, The)
Performance/production
International Brecht symposium. China, People's Republic of: Beijing, Hong Kong. Japan: Tokyo. 1986. Lang.: Eng.   1722

Analysis of Brecht's original directing style and dramaturgy. Germany. 1925-1987. Lang.: Eng.   1771

Rustaveli Theatre of Georgia, directed by Robert Sturua, presents Shakespeare's *Richard III* and Brecht's *Der Kaukasische Kreidekreis (The Caucasian Chalk Circle)* in Hungary. USSR: Tbilisi. Hungary. 1987. Lang.: Hun.   2383

Guest performances by Teat'r im. Šato Rustaveli of Tbilisi at Madách Theatre: Shakespeare's *Richard III*, Brecht's *Der Kaukasische Kreidekreis (The Caucasian Chalk Circle)*. USSR: Tbilisi. Hungary: Budapest. 1986. Lang.: Hun.   2390

Kaupunginteatteri (Helsinki)
SEE
Helsingin Kaupunginteatteri.

Kavanaugh, Robert
Performance/production
Review of *Vuka* by Matsemela Manaka. South Africa, Republic of: Soweto. 1976-1987. Lang.: Eng.   2006

Kawakami, Otojirō
Performance/production
Actors Kawakami Otojirō and his wife, Sadayacco. Japan. 1899-1946. Lang.: Ita.   843

Kawakami, Sadayacco
Performance/production
Actors Kawakami Otojirō and his wife, Sadayacco. Japan. 1899-1946. Lang.: Ita.   843

Kawamura, Takeshi
Audience
Contemporary influences on Japanese theatre and its audience. Japan: Tokyo. 1960-1986. Lang.: Jap.   285

Performance/production
New themes and styles in Japanese theatre. Japan: Tokyo. 1986. Lang.: Jap.   1953

Kawamura, Tsuyoshi
Performance/production
Focus on several Tokyo productions. Japan: Tokyo. 1960-1987. Lang.: Jap.   1955

Reviews and discussion of Tokyo productions. Japan: Tokyo. 1960-1987. Lang.: Jap.   1960

Comments on Tokyo performances. Japan: Tokyo. 1987. Lang.: Jap.   1964

Kawatake, Mokuami
Plays/librettos/scripts
Biography of *kabuki* author Kawatake Mokuami. Japan. 1816-1893. Lang.: Jap.   1495

Kay, Jackie
Performance/production
Collection of newspaper reviews by London theatre critics. UK-England: London. 1986. Lang.: Eng.   2084

Kaye, Pooh
Performance/production
Five women choreographers and critics discuss conceptions of the female body. USA. 1987. Lang.: Eng.   1416

Kayser, Karl Georg
Performance/production
A round-table discussion with stage directors on the principles and methods of working with an ensemble company. Germany, East: Berlin, East. 1983. Lang.: Ger.   1778

Kazan, Elia
Plays/librettos/scripts
Elia Kazan's influence on playwright Ray Lawler. Australia. USA. 1950-1955. Lang.: Eng.   2445

Kazán, István
Performance/production
István Kazán directs *Fleur de cactus (Cactus Flower)* at Vidám Színpad as *A kaktusz virága*. Hungary: Budapest. 1987. Lang.: Hun.   3629

Kazanskij Bolšoj Dramatičeskij Teat'r im. V.I. Kačalov (Kazan)
Performance/production
History of Kazan Bolšoj Drama Theatre. USSR: Kazan. 1917-1987. Lang.: Rus.   1007

Kazantsev, Aleksei
Performance/production
Overview of 1986-1987 Moscow theatre season. USSR: Moscow. 1986-1987. Lang.: Eng.   1039

Kazantzakis, Nikos
Plays/librettos/scripts
Greek poetic drama through Nietzschean theory. Greece. 1987. Lang.: Eng.   2620

Imagistic versus realistic drama in contemporary Greek plays. Greece. 1940-1987. Lang.: Eng.   2621

Kaze no eki (Station of Winds, The)
Performance/production
Productions by Tenkei gekijō, Manji and Mokutōsha. Japan: Tokyo. 1986. Lang.: Jap.   1958

Productions of Bungakuza, Yūkikai Zenjidō shiatā, Tao and Tenkei gekijō. Japan: Tokyo. 1986. Lang.: Jap.   1961

Kaze no takishīdo (Tuxedo of the Winds, A)
Performance/production
Space and sign in various Tokyo productions. Japan: Tokyo. 1987. Lang.: Jap.   1959

Kazimir, Károly
Performance/production
Károly Kazimir directs László Németh's *Harc a jólét ellen (The Fight Against Prosperity)*. Hungary: Budapest. 1986. Lang.: Hun.   1910

Kealy, Andrea
Performance/production
Collection of newspaper reviews by London theatre critics. UK-England: London. 1987. Lang.: Eng.   2247

Kean ou désordre et génie (Edmund Kean, or the Genius and the Libertine)
Performance/production
Actor-dramas produced by National Theatre. Hungary: Budapest. 1836-1847. Lang.: Hun.   1842

Kean by Dumas and Sartre, directed by Tamás Szirtes, Madách Theatre. Hungary: Budapest. 1986. Lang.: Hun.   1862

Kean, Charles
Performance/production
Historical accuracy in 19th-century London theatre productions. England: London. 1800-1900. Lang.: Eng.   1734

Kean, Edmund
Performance/production
Actor-dramas produced by National Theatre. Hungary: Budapest. 1836-1847. Lang.: Hun.   1842

Kean by Dumas and Sartre, directed by Tamás Szirtes, Madách Theatre. Hungary: Budapest. 1986. Lang.: Hun.   1862

Keane, Billie
Performance/production
Collection of newspaper reviews by London theatre critics. UK-England: London. 1987. Lang.: Eng.   2185

Kerényi, Imre
Performance/production
Shakespeare at Várszinház: László Vámos directs *Henry IV* Parts I and II, Imre Kerényi directs *Henry V*. Hungary: Budapest. 1986. Lang.: Hun. 1810

Imre Kerényi directs *Énekes madár (The Song Bird)* by Áron Tamási at the National Theatre. Hungary: Budapest. 1987. Lang.: Hun. 1819

Director Imre Kerényi discusses *Csiksomlyó passió (Passion Play of Csiksomlyó)*. Hungary. 1982-1987. Lang.: Hun. 1843

Áron Tamási's *Énekes madár (The Song Bird)* directed by Imre Kerényi at National Theatre. Hungary: Budapest. 1987. Lang.: Hun. 1872

Productions of plays by László Márton, Tamás Jordán and Ferenc Kulin at Radnóti Miklós Theatre. Hungary: Budapest. 1987. Lang.: Hun. 1887

Kerényi, Miklós Gábor
Performance/production
Review of performances at an assembly of opera ensembles. Hungary: Szeged. 1987. Lang.: Hun. 3796

Kernan, David
Performance/production
Collection of newspaper reviews by London theatre critics. UK-England: London. 1986. Lang.: Eng. 2109

Kerr, Alfred
Performance/production
Early productions of Brecht's plays reflected in the press. Germany: Berlin. 1922-1933. Lang.: Ger. 1777

Kerr, Walter
Theory/criticism
The language of theatrical criticism. USA: New York, NY. 1917-1985. Lang.: Eng. 1367

Kertész, Ákos
Performance/production
The 4th International Theatre Conference: includes list of participants and their contributions. Poland: Warsaw. 1986. Lang.: Eng, Fre. 873

Kertész, Gyula
Institutions
Interview with Gyula Kertész and István Pinczés of the Csokonai Theatre. Hungary: Debrecen. 1987. Lang.: Hun. 543

Performance/production
Review of performances at an assembly of opera ensembles. Hungary: Szeged. 1987. Lang.: Hun. 3796

Kertész, László
Performance/production
Review of productions at opera ensembles meeting. Hungary: Szeged. 1987. Lang.: Hun. 3792

Kesselman, Wendy
Performance/production
Collection of newspaper reviews by London theatre critics. UK-England: London. 1987. Lang.: Eng. 2073

Comparison and review of *Melon, Breaking the Code, Alan Turing: The Secret War* and *My Sister in This House*. UK-England: London. 1987. Lang.: Eng. 2285

Kessler, Lyle
Performance/production
Collection of newspaper reviews by London theatre critics. UK-England: London. 1986. Lang.: Eng. 2085

Kester, David
Performance/production
Collection of newspaper reviews by London theatre critics. UK-England: London. 1987. Lang.: Eng. 2239

Kew Garden Theatre (London)
Performance/production
Collection of newspaper reviews by London theatre critics. UK-England: London. 1986. Lang.: Eng. 2154

Key Exchange
Performance/production
Collection of newspaper reviews by London theatre critics. UK-England: London. 1986. Lang.: Eng. 2135

Kézdy, György
Performance/production
Interview with actor György Kézdy. Hungary: Pécs. 1953-1987. Lang.: Hun. 1834

Khan, George
Performance/production
Collection of newspaper reviews by London theatre critics. UK-England: London. 1986. Lang.: Eng. 2080

Khovanshchina
SEE
Chovanščina.

Kidd, Ross
Performance/production
Canadian popular theatre. Canada. Africa. Asia. 1987. Lang.: Eng. 733

Relation to other fields
Applications of African 'Theatre for Development' movement to Canadian popular theatre. Africa. Canada: St. John's, NF, Toronto, ON. 1978-1987. Lang.: Eng. 2978

Theory/criticism
Semiotic production in popular performance. South Africa, Republic of. 1980. Lang.: Eng. 1347

Kiddush
Performance/production
Collection of newspaper reviews by London theatre critics. UK-England: London. 1987. Lang.: Eng. 2275

Killander, Birgitta
Performance/production
Background on *Landskronapågen (The Boy from Landskrona)*. Sweden: Landskrona. 1982-1987. Lang.: Swe. 2024

Killar, Ashley
Performance/production
Interview with choreographer Ashley Killar. South Africa, Republic of.. 1987. Lang.: Eng. 1440

Killdeer, The
Plays/librettos/scripts
Critical analysis of James Reaney's *Three Desks*. Canada. 1960-1977. Lang.: Eng. 2477

Killens, John O.
Plays/librettos/scripts
Life of playwright John O. Killens. USA: New York, NY. 1954-1987. Lang.: Eng. 2836

Killerby, Barry
Performance/production
Collection of newspaper reviews by London theatre critics. UK-England: London. 1987. Lang.: Eng. 2260

Killick, Jenny
Performance/production
Collection of newspaper reviews by London theatre critics. UK-England: London. 1987. Lang.: Eng. 2033

Killigrew, Charles
Administration
Role of the Master of the Revels as censor. England: London. 1662-1737. Lang.: Eng. 22

Killigrew, Thomas
Administration
Role of the Master of the Revels as censor. England: London. 1662-1737. Lang.: Eng. 22

Killing Jessica
Performance/production
Collection of newspaper reviews by London theatre critics. UK-England: London. 1986. Lang.: Eng. 2055

Kilroy, Thomas
Performance/production
Collection of newspaper reviews by London theatre critics. UK-England: London. 1986. Lang.: Eng. 2096

Productions and political philosophy of Field Day Theatre Company. UK-Ireland: Londonderry. 1986-1987. Lang.: Eng. 2309

Kim, Ho-kyung
Plays/librettos/scripts
Korean stage adaptation of *Le Mur (The Wall)* by Sartre. France. Korea. 1939-1976. Lang.: Kor. 2575

Kim, Jung-Whan
Design/technology
Scene designer Kim Jung-Whan. Korea. 1978. Lang.: Kor. 354

Kim, Randall Duk
Performance/production
Career of actor/director Randall Duk Kim. USA. 1966-1987. Lang.: Eng. 2346

Kimotsuki, Kenta
Performance/production
New Tokyo productions. Japan: Tokyo. 1987. Lang.: Jap. 1954

Kimura, Kōichi
Performance/production
Productions of several Tokyo companies. Japan: Tokyo. 1987. Lang.:
Jap.   1962
King and the Corpse, The
Performance/production
Collection of newspaper reviews by London theatre critics. UK-
England: London. 1986. Lang.: Eng.   2046
King Edward the Third, with the Fall of Mortimer
Plays/librettos/scripts
Attack on Sir Robert Walpole in 18th-century adaptation of *King
Edward the Third*. England. 1691-1731. Lang.: Eng.   2505
King Goes Forth to France, The
SEE
Kuningas lähtee Ranskaan.
King John
Performance/production
Collection of newspaper reviews by London theatre critics. UK-
England: London. 1987. Lang.: Eng.   2227
King Lear
Plays/librettos/scripts
Influences of Arthurian legend on Shakespeare's *King Lear*. England.
1605. Lang.: Eng.   2521
King Lear
Performance/production
Shakespeare's *King Lear* staged by Menyhért Szegvári at the
National Theatre. Hungary: Pécs. 1986. Lang.: Hun.   1811
Collection of newspaper reviews by London theatre critics. UK-
England: London. 1986. Lang.: Eng.   2044
Plays/librettos/scripts
Theodicy and tragic drama in *King Lear* and *The Tempest*. England.
1605-1611. Lang.: Eng.   1119
King Lear focusing on the character of Kent. England. 1605. Lang.:
Eng.   1122
Shakespeare's *King Lear* in the context of ironic drama. 1590.
Lang.: Eng.   2424
Comparison of *King Lear* and *Vildanden (The Wild Duck)*. England.
Norway. 1605-1884. Lang.: Eng.   2518
The creation of ideal future worlds based on the historical past in
some plays of Shakespeare. England. 1591-1599. Lang.: Ger.   2539
History and utopianism in some plays of Shakespeare. England.
1589-1606. Lang.: Ger.   2558
Experiment in musical composition based on *King Lear*. USA. 1987.
Lang.: Eng.   2848
Relation to other fields
Comparison of *King Lear* and South African Land Act regarding
land distribution. England. South Africa, Republic of. 1605-1913.
Lang.: Eng.   1231
Theory/criticism
Peter Brook's implementation of Jan Kott's theory in his approach
to *King Lear*. UK-England. 1962-1987. Lang.: Eng.   3064
King of Hearts
Performance/production
Brief Broadway run of *King of Hearts*. USA: New York, NY. 1978-
1987. Lang.: Eng.   3643
King Phoenix
Plays/librettos/scripts
Survey of Robertson Davies' plays. Canada. 1913-1985. Lang.: Eng.
                                                                        2484
King Priam
Plays/librettos/scripts
Tippett's influence on contemporary opera. 1946-1987. Lang.: Eng.
                                                                        3888
King Stephen
SEE
István, a király.
King, T.J.
Performance/production
Conference proceedings on staging of Elizabethan plays. England.
1546-1616. Lang.: Eng.   775
King, Woodie
Design/technology
Career of costumer, dancer, actress Judy Dearing. USA: New York,
NY. Africa. 1970-1987. Lang.: Eng.   1601
King, Woodie, Jr.
Performance/production
Essays on the future of the theatre. USA: New York, NY. 1970-
1987. Lang.: Eng.   955

King's Company (London)
Institutions
King's Company under actor-manager John Lowin. England:
London. 1576-1653. Lang.: Eng.   1614
King's Head Theatre (London)
Performance/production
Collection of newspaper reviews by London theatre critics. UK-
England: London. 1986. Lang.: Eng.   2037
Collection of newspaper reviews by London theatre critics. UK-
England: London. 1986. Lang.: Eng.   2051
Collection of newspaper reviews by London theatre critics. UK-
England: London. 1986. Lang.: Eng.   2061
Collection of newspaper reviews by London theatre critics. UK-
England: London. 1986. Lang.: Eng.   2076
Collection of newspaper reviews by London theatre critics. UK-
England: London. 1986. Lang.: Eng.   2092
Collection of newspaper reviews by London theatre critics. UK-
England: London. 1986. Lang.: Eng.   2104
Collection of newspaper reviews by London theatre critics. UK-
England: London. 1986. Lang.: Eng.   2114
Collection of newspaper reviews by London theatre critics. UK-
England: London. 1986. Lang.: Eng.   2136
Collection of newspaper reviews by London theatre critics. UK-
England: London. 1986. Lang.: Eng.   2155
Collection of newspaper reviews by London theatre critics. UK-
England: London. 1987. Lang.: Eng.   2174
Collection of newspaper reviews by London theatre critics. UK-
England: London. 1987. Lang.: Eng.   2189
Collection of newspaper reviews by London theatre critics. UK-
England: London. 1987. Lang.: Eng.   2201
Collection of newspaper reviews by London theatre critics. UK-
England: London. 1987. Lang.: Eng.   2234
Collection of newspaper reviews by London theatre critics. UK-
England: London. 1987. Lang.: Eng.   2244
Collection of newspaper reviews by London theatre critics. UK-
England: London. 1987. Lang.: Eng.   2254
Collection of newspaper reviews by London theatre critics. UK-
England: London. 1987. Lang.: Eng.   2269
Collection of newspaper reviews by London theatre critics. UK-
England: London. 1987. Lang.: Eng.   2274
King's Men, The (London)
Performance/production
Shakespeare and contemporaries: tradition, intertextuality in
performance. England. 1607-1987. Lang.: Eng.   1740
New interpretation of Jacobean theatre. England: London. 1596-
1633. Lang.: Eng.   1743
Plays/librettos/scripts
Productions of *Sir Thomas More* by Elizabethan theatre companies.
England. 1595-1650. Lang.: Eng.   2541
Kingdom of Earth
Performance/production
Soviet productions of five Tennessee Williams plays. USSR. 1910-
1987. Lang.: Eng.   2397
Kingston, Mark
Performance/production
Collection of newspaper reviews by London theatre critics. UK-
England: London. 1986. Lang.: Eng.   2141
Kip's War
Performance/production
Collection of newspaper reviews by London theatre critics. UK-
England: London. 1987. Lang.: Eng.   2235
Kipling, Rudyard
Plays/librettos/scripts
Influence of Rudyard Kipling on Eugene O'Neill. USA. 1887-1950.
Lang.: Eng.   2925
Kirby, Andy
Performance/production
Collection of newspaper reviews by London theatre critics. UK-
England: London. 1986. Lang.: Eng.   2062
Kirby, Robert
Performance/production
Collection of newspaper reviews by London theatre critics. UK-
England: London. 1986. Lang.: Eng.   2037

Kirchner, Alfred
Theory/criticism
Challenge of Brecht's plays to communism. Germany, East: Berlin.
1960-1970. Lang.: Eng.   3045

Kiritarō tengu sakamori
Basic theatrical documents
Texts of seven *kabuki* plays. Japan. 1600-1800. Lang.: Jap.   1491

Kirkwood, James
Performance/production
Short history of *A Chorus Line*. USA: New York, NY. 1975-1987.
Lang.: Eng.   941

Kirley, E.T.
Performance/production
Origins of theatre and its relationship to the spectator. India. Japan.
Sri Lanka. 1987. Lang.: Eng.   813

Kirov Ballet
SEE
Akademičeskij Teat'r Opery i Baleta im. S.M. Kirova.

Kirov Opera
SEE
Akademičeskij Teat'r Opery i Baleta im. S.M. Kirova.

Kirov Theatre (Leningrad)
SEE
Akademičeskij Teat'r Opery i Baleta im. S.M. Kirova.

Kirstein, Lincoln
Performance/production
Theatricality of dance. USA. 1985. Lang.: Eng.   1414

Kis Színház (Budapest)
Performance/production
Evaluation of the season's productions of Kis Színház and its
chamber theatre, the Vidám Szinpad. Hungary: Budapest. 1987.
Lang.: Hun.   806

Kisfaludy Színház (Győr)
Performance/production
Reviews of *Téli zsoltár (A Winter Psalm)* by Kovách, Shakespeare's
Much Ado About Nothing and *Ferde ház (The Leaning House)* by
Gerencsér performed at Kisfaludy Theatre. Hungary: Győr. 1986.
Lang.: Hun.   1822

Comparison of *Die Dreigroschenoper (The Three Penny Opera)* as
directed by Ferenc Sík, József Petrik and Miklós Szinetár under the
title *Koldusopera*. Hungary: Győr, Budapest. 1987. Lang.: Hun. 3402

Imre Kálmán's *Cigányprímás (Sari)* and Bizet's *Carmen* at Kisfaludy
Theatre staged by József Bor. Hungary: Győr. 1912-1986. Lang.:
Hun.   3959

Kiss Me Kate
Performance/production
Collection of newspaper reviews by London theatre critics. UK-
England: London. 1987. Lang.: Eng.   2239

Collection of newspaper reviews by London theatre critics. UK-
England: London. 1987. Lang.: Eng.   2253

Kisvárdai Várszínház (Kisvárda)
Performance/production
Imre Halasi directs *Sári bíró (Judge Sári)* by Zsigmond Móricz,
music by István Mikó, at Kisvarda Castle Theatre. Hungary:
Kisvárda. 1987. Lang.: Hun.   1845

Kitaev, M.
Design/technology
Theatre artists M. Kitaev and E. Kočergin. USSR. 1970-1987. Lang.:
Rus.   499

Kitamura, Soh
Performance/production
New Tokyo productions. Japan: Tokyo. 1987. Lang.: Jap.   1954

Plays/librettos/scripts
Productions by several Tokyo companies. Japan: Tokyo. 1986-1987.
Lang.: Jap.   2682

Kitchen, The (New York, NY)
Performance/production
Performance artists Ishmael Houston-Jones, John Kelly, Karen
Finley, Richard Elovich. USA. 1987. Lang.: Eng.   3366

Kiuchi, Midori
Plays/librettos/scripts
Contemporary Japanese plays about crime. Japan: Tokyo. 1986.
Lang.: Jap.   2681

Plays about child suicide in Japan. Japan: Tokyo. 1986. Lang.: Jap.
                                                           2683

Klaff, Jack
Performance/production
Collection of newspaper reviews by London theatre critics. UK-
England: London. 1987. Lang.: Eng.   2215

Klages, Bill
Design/technology
Adapting lighting from a live theatre version of *Sweeney Todd* for
videotape. USA. 1982. Lang.: Eng.   3204

Klaviter, Jane
Performance/production
Interview with professional opera prompter. USA: Chicago, IL. 1987.
Lang.: Eng.   3845

Kleber, Pia
Institutions
Brecht was the theme of the 1986 International Theatre Festival and
Conference. Canada: Toronto, ON. 1986. Lang.: Fre.   1610

Kleinberg, Seymour
Theory/criticism
Domination of women and gay men in Western dance. USA. 1700-
1987. Lang.: Eng.   1458

Kleine Oper (West Berlin)
Performance/production
Anniversaries of opera houses and theatres. Germany, West: Berlin,
West. Germany, East: Berlin, East. 1237-1987. Lang.: Eng. 3789

Kleist, Heinrich von
Institutions
Seven productions chosen for Theatertreffen '86. Germany: Berlin.
1986. Lang.: Eng.   1617

Performance/production
Staging of Romantic 'closet dramas'. Scandinavia. 1986-1987. Lang.:
Swe.   2004

Collection of newspaper reviews by London theatre critics. UK-
England: London. 1986. Lang.: Eng.   2106

Klemperer, Otto
Institutions
History of Kroll-Oper. Germany: Berlin. 1927-1931. Lang.: Ger. 3726

Klockare, Roland
Performance/production
A class for amateur directors. Sweden: Katrineberg. 1987. Lang.:
Swe.   887

Knapp, Alain
Performance/production
The work of director Robert Lepage. Canada: Montreal, PQ. 1987.
Lang.: Eng.   3347

Knee Plays
Performance/production
Director Robert Wilson, his *CIVIL warS* and connecting *Knee Plays*.
USA. 1979-1987. Lang.: Swe.   3274

Knee, Allan
Performance/production
Collection of newspaper reviews by New York theatre critics. USA:
New York, NY. 1987. Lang.: Eng.   2318

Knickerbocker Holiday
Performance/production
Former Weill student talks about his work on Weill's Broadway
productions. Germany: Berlin. 1922-1980. Lang.: Eng.   3627

Knife, The
Design/technology
Lighting reviews for several New York productions. USA: New
York, NY. 1987. Lang.: Eng.   475

Performance/production
Collection of newspaper reviews by New York theatre critics. USA:
New York, NY. 1987. Lang.: Eng.   2312

Knight of the Burning Pestle, The
Audience
Actor and audience in Elizabethan theatre. England. 1585-1625.
Lang.: Eng.   1533

Knight, Tom
Performance/production
Collection of newspaper reviews by London theatre critics. UK-
England. 1987. Lang.: Eng.   2262

*Knock ou triomphe de la médicine (Doctor Knock, or the
Triumph of Medicine)*
Performance/production
Jules Romains' *Knock* directed by Gábor Máté at Csiky Gergely
Theatre. Hungary: Kaposvár. 1986. Lang.: Hun.   1917

Knot Garden, The
Plays/librettos/scripts
Tippett's influence on contemporary opera. 1946-1987. Lang.: Eng.
3888

Kočergin, E.
Design/technology
Theatre artists M. Kitaev and E. Kočergin. USSR. 1970-1987. Lang.: Rus.
499

Koch, Howard
Performance/production
Autobiography of director, producer and writer John Houseman. USA: New York, NY. 1935-1985. Lang.: Eng.
2339

Kogami, Shōji
Audience
Contemporary influences on Japanese theatre and its audience. Japan: Tokyo. 1960-1986. Lang.: Jap.
285

Performance/production
New themes and styles in Japanese theatre. Japan: Tokyo. 1986. Lang.: Jap.
1953

Kokdugaksi
Basic theatrical documents
Text of a *kokdugaksi* puppet play. Korea. 600-1987. Lang.: Kor.
4004

Design/technology
How to construct *kokdugaksi* rod puppets. Korea. 1987. Lang.: Kor.
4005

Theory/criticism
Theory and construction of Korean rod puppetry *kokdugaksi-nolum.* Korea. 600-1987. Lang.: Kor.
4007

Kokoro enerugii—Hagoromo densetsu (Heart Energy: The Tale of the Feather Robe)
Performance/production
Productions from Yume no yūminsha, Tōhō, Parco, Tsukumo and Nakamura za. Japan: Tokyo. 1986-1987. Lang.: Jap.
1956
Productions of several Tokyo companies. Japan: Tokyo. 1987. Lang.: Jap.
1962

Kokoschka, Oskar
Design/technology
Exhibition of theatrical design by Léger, Cocteau, Kokoschka and Kandinsky. France. Lang.: Eng.
322

Kölcsey
Performance/production
Productions of plays by László Márton, Tamás Jordán and Ferenc Kulin at Radnóti Miklós Theatre. Hungary: Budapest. 1987. Lang.: Hun.
1887

Kolneder, Wolfgang
Performance/production
Collection of newspaper reviews by London theatre critics. UK-England: London. 1986. Lang.: Eng.
2065

Kolozsvár State Theatre
SEE
Állami Magyar Szinház (Cluj).

Koltai, Ralph
Design/technology
Gershwin Theatre's accommodation of RSC touring productions. USA: New York, NY. 1984. Lang.: Eng.
420

Koltay, Gábor
Performance/production
Reviews of *Rigoletto*, Lloyd Webber's *Requiem*, *Les Misérables* and the Hungarian Mass of the Tolcsvays. Hungary: Szeged. 1987. Lang.: Hun.
3400

Koltay, Lajos
Design/technology
Interview with cameraman Lajos Koltay. Hungary. 1986. Lang.: Hun.
3128

Koltès, Bernard-Marie
Performance/production
Director as true author and maker of theatre. France. 1987. Lang.: Fre.
1757
Analysis of *Dans la solitude des champs de coton (In the Solitude of the Cotton Fields)* by Bernard-Marie Koltès. France: Paris. 1987. Lang.: Swe.
1761

Komische Oper (Berlin)
Institutions
The first Komische Oper. Germany: Berlin. 1905-1911. Lang.: Ger.
3727

Komische Oper (East Berlin)
Performance/production
Life and career of tenor Michael Rabsilber. Germany, East. 1982-1986. Lang.: Ger.
3787
Anniversaries of opera houses and theatres. Germany, West: Berlin, West. Germany, East: Berlin, East. 1237-1987. Lang.: Eng.
3789

Kommisarževskij, Modest
Basic theatrical documents
Constance Garnett's translation of *Tri sestry (Three Sisters)* by Čechov. England: London. 1901. Lang.: Eng.
1552

Komorní hry (Brno)
Institutions
Rudolf Walter's theatre, Komorní hry. Czechoslovakia: Brno. 1942-1944. Lang.: Cze.
1613

Komsomol Theatre (USSR)
SEE
Teat'r im. Leninskovo Komsomola.

Konchalovsky, Andrei
Performance/production
Work of film director Andrei Konchalovsky. USA. USSR: Moscow. Lang.: Eng.
3166

Konflikt (Conflict)
Performance/production
Three plays performed by the Dutch Orkater ensemble company. Netherlands. 1986. Lang.: Hun.
861

Kong, Xiao-Ting
Performance/production
Beijing opera actor Ji Ba Wang. China: Beijing. 1937-1948. Lang.: Chi.
3460

Koniec
Performance/production
Groupov ensemble describes the creation of *Koniec*. Belgium: Liège. 1987. Lang.: Fre.
1687

Konieczny, Zygmunt
Performance/production
The Polish cabaret performance group Piwnica. Poland: Cracow. USA: New York, NY. 1987. Lang.: Eng.
3287

Königlisches Nationaltheater (Berlin)
Performance/production
August Wilhelm Iffland's productions of plays by Friedrich von Schiller. Germany: Berlin. 1796-1806. Lang.: Ger.
1773

Königsmark, Václav
Performance/production
Miroslav Krobot directs Steigerwald's *Dobové tance (Period Dances)*, Nejedlý Realistic Theatre. Czechoslovakia: Prague. 1987. Lang.: Cze.
770

Konna hanashi (Story Like This, A)
Performance/production
Productions of several Tokyo companies. Japan: Tokyo. 1987. Lang.: Jap.
1962

Konstanty, Ildefons
Performance/production
Poland's puppet theatre. Poland: Wrocław, Białystock. Austria: Mistelbach. 1979-1987. Lang.: Eng, Fre.
4006

Kontrakt (Contract)
Performance/production
Festival of Polish plays. Poland: Wrocław. 1987. Lang.: Eng, Fre.
871
Polish theatre. Poland: Warsaw, Cracow, Wrocław. 1980-1987. Lang.: Eng, Fre.
1987

Konwitschny, Peter
Performance/production
Gluck as opera composer: his *Orfeo ed Euridice* staged by Peter Konwitschny. Germany. Germany, East: Halle. 1762-1986. Lang.: Ger.
3776

Koós, Olga
Performance/production
Reviews of actors Olga Koós and István Bozóky in *Szabóky Zsigmond Rafael (Zsigmond Rafael Szabóky)* at Játékszín. Hungary: Budapest. 1987. Lang.: Hun.
1914

Kops, Bernard
Performance/production
Collection of newspaper reviews by London theatre critics. UK-England: London. 1987. Lang.: Eng.
2183

Korcsmáros, György
Performance/production
György Korcsmáros directs Lionel Bart's *Oliver* at Arany János Theatre. Hungary: Budapest. 1986. Lang.: Hun.
3631

Korcsmáros, György — cont'd

Performances of *Oliver* staged by György Korcsmáros, Antol Rencz and Imre Halasi. Hungary: Budapest, Békéscsaba, Zalaegerszeg. 1986. Lang.: Hun.   3632

Korean puppet theatre
Relation to other fields
Korean mask plays, folklore and puppet theatre. Korea. Japan: Kyushu. 1987. Lang.: Kor.   1246

Koreya, Senda
Performance/production
International Brecht symposium. China, People's Republic of: Beijing, Hong Kong. Japan: Tokyo. 1986. Lang.: Eng.   1722

Kornis, Mihály
Plays/librettos/scripts
Study of three plays by Mihály Kornis: *Halleluja, Büntetések (Punishments)* and *Kozma*. Hungary. 1980-1987. Lang.: Hun.   2628

Kortner, Fritz
Performance/production
Politics and Shakespeare in Weimar Republic. Germany. 1919-1930. Lang.: Eng.   1775

Koste, Virginia
Relation to other fields
Creative drama's potential to stimulate wonder. USA. 1970-1977. Lang.: Eng.   1288

Kostolevskij, I.
Performance/production
Actors discuss their profession. USSR. 1987. Lang.: Eng.   996

Kott, Jan
Theory/criticism
Peter Brook's implementation of Jan Kott's theory in his approach to *King Lear*. UK-England. 1962-1987. Lang.: Eng.   3064

Kōu (Hsiang Yu)
Performance/production
Nō plays with Chinese historical subjects. Japan. 1300-1500. Lang.: Jap.   1503

Kovách, Aladár
Performance/production
Reviews of *Téli zsoltár (A Winter Psalm)* by Kovách, Shakespeare's *Much Ado About Nothing* and *Ferde ház (The Leaning House)* by Gerencsér performed at Kisfaludy Theatre. Hungary: Győr. 1986. Lang.: Hun.   1822

Koželuh, Leopold
Plays/librettos/scripts
Inception of Leopold Koželuh's ballet *Dcera Oty II. znovu nalezena (The Daughter of Ota II Was Found Again)*. Austria-Hungary: Vienna. 1794. Lang.: Cze.   1454

Kozintsev, Grigori
Plays/librettos/scripts
Successful film versions of Shakespeare's *King Lear*. USA. UK-England. USSR. 1916-1983. Lang.: Eng.   3099

Kozma
Plays/librettos/scripts
Study of three plays by Mihály Kornis: *Halleluja, Büntetések (Punishments)* and *Kozma*. Hungary. 1980-1987. Lang.: Hun.   2628

Kraft, Johann
Performance/production
Role of the director in the Lucerne Passion play. Switzerland: Lucerne. 1453-1616. Lang.: Eng.   2030

Kraglund, John
Performance/production
Retired critic recalls Toronto opera. Canada: Toronto, ON. 1947-1987. Lang.: Eng.   3749

Krakowiacy i górale (Cracovians and Mountaineers)
Performance/production
Poland's puppet theatre. Poland: Wrocław, Białystock. Austria: Mistelbach. 1979-1987. Lang.: Eng, Fre.   4006

Kramer, Ken
Institutions
A history of documentary theatre in English Canada. Canada. 1970-1986. Lang.: Eng.   508

Kramer, Larry
Performance/production
Collection of newspaper reviews by London theatre critics. UK-England: London. 1986. Lang.: Eng.   2077
Plays/librettos/scripts
Impact of AIDS crisis on the theatre. USA: New York, NY, San Francisco, CA. 1987. Lang.: Eng.   2881

David Shaber, Larry Kramer, Emily Mann: Three of the few American political dramatists. USA: New York, NY. 1987. Lang.: Eng.   2907

Krannert Center for the Performing Arts (Urbana, IL)
Performance spaces
Construction and present condition of the Krannert Center for the Performing Arts. USA: Urbana, IL. 1969-1987. Lang.: Eng.   710

Krapp's Last Tape
Performance/production
Personal notes of Samuel Beckett, how they illuminate his plays. France. 1969-1984. Lang.: Eng.   1758

Collection of newspaper reviews by London theatre critics. UK-England: London. 1986. Lang.: Eng.   2121
Plays/librettos/scripts
Critical methodology for studying Beckett's works. UK-England. 1930-1987. Lang.: Eng.   2814

Study of playwright Samuel Beckett's visual art in his plays. USA. 1970-1980. Lang.: Eng.   2866

Krasiński, Janusz
Performance/production
Overview of 1986-1987 Moscow theatre season. USSR: Moscow. 1986-1987. Lang.: Eng.   1039

Kreacja (Creation)
Performance/production
The shape and form of contemporary Polish theatre. Poland: Warsaw. 1981-1987. Lang.: Eng, Fre.   1995

Krejca, Octomar
Design/technology
Work of noted set designer and technological innovator Josef Svoboda. Czechoslovakia: Prague. 1940-1987. Lang.: Eng.   305

Krismis van Map Jacobs (Christmas of Map Jacobs)
Plays/librettos/scripts
Directive as a speech act in *Krismis van Map Jacobs (Christmas of Map Jacobs)* by Adam Small. South Africa, Republic of. 1983. Lang.: Afr.   2726

Krizanc, John
Performance/production
Collection of newspaper reviews by New York theatre critics. USA: New York, NY. 1987. Lang.: Eng.   2313

Krobot, Ivo
Performance/production
Bohumil Hrabal's *Obsluhoval jsem anglického krale (I Served the King of Britain)* directed by Ivo Krobot as *Ôfelsége pincére voltam*. Hungary: Nyíregyháza. 1987. Lang.: Hun.   1912

Ivo Krobot directs *Ôfelsége pincére voltam (I Served the King of Britain)*, based on writings of Bohumil Hrabal. Hungary: Nyíregyháza. 1987. Lang.: Hun.   1928

Krobot, Miroslav
Performance/production
Miroslav Krobot directs Steigerwald's *Dobové tance (Period Dances)*, Nejedlý Realistic Theatre. Czechoslovakia: Prague. 1987. Lang.: Cze.   770

Kroetz, Franz Xaver
Performance/production
Franz Xaver Kroetz's *Wunschkonzert (Request Concert)* transposed to Calcutta. India: Calcutta. 1980. Lang.: Eng.   1930

Franz Xaver Kroetz's *Wunschkonzert (Request Concert)* in Bombay: observations of actress Sulabha Deshpande. India: Bombay. 1986. Lang.: Eng.   1931

Collection of newspaper reviews by London theatre critics. UK-England: London. 1986. Lang.: Eng.   2068

Collection of newspaper reviews by London theatre critics. UK-England: London. 1986. Lang.: Eng.   2103
Plays/librettos/scripts
Love in Kroetz's *Wer durchs Laub geht (Through the Leaves)*. 1986. Lang.: Eng.   2411

Four German playwrights: Fleisser, Sperr, Kroetz, Fassbinder. Germany. 1900-1987. Lang.: Ita.   2602

Kroha, Jiří
Design/technology
Futurism in the scenographic work of Jiří Kroha. Czechoslovakia. 1918-1923. Lang.: Ita.   314

Kroll-Oper (Berlin)
Institutions
History of Kroll-Oper. Germany: Berlin. 1927-1931. Lang.: Ger.   3726

Krúdy, Gyula
Performance/production
Reviews: *A vörös postakocsi (The Red Mail Coach)* by Gyula Krúdy, staged by Dezső Kapás and *Az atyai ház (The Paternal Roof)* by Zsigmond Remenyik, staged by Péter Lener. Hungary: Veszprém, Nyíregyháza. 1986. Lang.: Hun.   1821

Krukowaska, Jolanta
Institutions
First festival of women's work in experimental theatre. UK-Wales:
Cardiff. 1986. Lang.: Eng.   1649
Krukowski, Wojciech
Performance/production
Collection of newspaper reviews by London theatre critics. UK-
England: London. 1986. Lang.: Eng.   2068
Kulin, Ferenc
Performance/production
Productions of plays by László Márton, Tamás Jordán and Ferenc
Kulin at Radnóti Miklós Theatre. Hungary: Budapest. 1987. Lang.:
Hun.   1887
Kulturföreningen RoJ (Handen)
Performance/production
Rock opera *Drakar och Demoner (Dragons and Demons)* about
youth at risk. Sweden: Handen. 1987. Lang.: Swe.   3637
Kumquat Seed, The
SEE
Kinkan Shonen.
Kun opera
Administration
Effects of nationalization and modernization on Chinese theatre.
China, People's Republic of: Beijing. 1279-1986. Lang.: Chi. 3427
Performance/production
The influence of the feudal class on traditional Chinese opera.
China. 900. Lang.: Chi.   3465
Ways to improve the Chinese opera style *Kun-Jiu*. China, People's
Republic of. 1956-1986. Lang.: Chi.   3507
Differences between Chinese and Western theatre. China, People's
Republic of: Beijing. 1947-1986. Lang.: Chi.   3513
Reference materials
Source materials on development of Chinese opera. Taiwan. 1987.
Lang.: Chi.   3580
Kundera, Milan
Basic theatrical documents
Catalan translation of Milan Kundera's *Jacques et son maître
(Jacques and His Master)*, with introduction. Czechoslovakia: Prague.
1968-1981. Lang.: Cat.   1551
Plays/librettos/scripts
Interview with Susan Sontag, director of *Jacques and His Master.*
USA: Cambridge, MA. 1985. Lang.: Eng.   1172
Interview with Milan Kundera on *Jacques and His Master.* USA:
Cambridge, MA. 1985. Lang.: Eng.   1173
Kundera's adaptation of *Jacques le Fataliste (Jacques and His
Master)* by Diderot. USA: Cambridge, MA. 1985. Lang.: Eng.   1178
Kungliga Dramatiska Teatern (Stockholm)
Administration
Technical details of guest performance of *Hamlet* by Kungliga
Dramatiska Teatern, directed by Ingmar Bergman. Italy: Florence.
Sweden: Stockholm. 1986. Lang.: Swe.   1520
Institutions
Dramaten's attempts at greater community outreach. Sweden. 1982.
Lang.: Eng.   1637
Performance spaces
Restoration of the house, Kungliga Dramatiska Teatern. Sweden:
Stockholm. 1987. Lang.: Swe.   1674
Restoration of audience areas of Kungliga Dramatiska Teatern.
Sweden: Stockholm. 1987. Lang.: Swe.   1675
Performance/production
Collection of newspaper reviews by London theatre critics. UK-
England: London. 1987. Lang.: Eng.   2241
Collection of newspaper reviews by London theatre critics. UK-
England: London. 1987. Lang.: Eng.   2244
Plays/librettos/scripts
Karl Ragnar Gierow on O'Neill and his importance in Sweden.
Sweden: Stockholm. 1920-1970. Lang.: Eng.   2736
Productions exhibit changes in symbolism of the Don Juan myth
due to AIDS crisis. USA. 1987. Lang.: Eng.   2845
Kungliga Teatern (Stockholm)
Administration
Royal Swedish Opera: new production of *Die Zauberflöte*, overview
of management. Sweden: Stockholm. 1986. Lang.: Swe.   3681
Institutions
Overview of Lars af Malmborg's management of Swedish Royal
Opera. Sweden: Stockholm. 1985-1987. Lang.: Swe.   3729
Attendance at Royal Swedish Opera: analysis, how to improve it.
Sweden: Stockholm. 1960-1985. Lang.: Swe.   3730

Performance spaces
Recommendation that Royal Swedish Opera house be rebuilt.
Sweden: Stockholm. 1985-1987. Lang.: Swe.   3736
Performance/production
Composer Hans Gefors on his opera *Christina*. Sweden. 1986. Lang.:
Swe.   3819
Reviews of *Christina* by Hans Gefors and Lars Forssell. Sweden:
Stockholm. 1987. Lang.: Swe.   3822
Interview with tenor Esias Tewolde-Berhan of Kungliga Teatern.
Sweden: Stockholm. Ethiopia. 1944-1987. Lang.: Swe.   3825
Kunju Macbeth, The
Performance/production
Collection of newspaper reviews by London theatre critics. UK-
England: London. 1987. Lang.: Eng.   2258
Kupfer, Harry
Performance/production
Mozart's *Don Giovanni* staged by Harry Kupfer. Germany, East:
Berlin, East. 1987. Lang.: Swe.   3779
Life and career of tenor Michael Rabsilber. Germany, East. 1982-
1986. Lang.: Ger.   3787
Kurahashi, Takeshi
Performance/production
Four Tokyo productions in light of ideas of Betsuyaku Minoru.
Japan: Tokyo. 1987. Lang.: Jap.   1950
Analysis of four Tokyo productions. Japan: Tokyo. 1987. Lang.: Jap.
                                                             1957
Unsuitable choice of plays for Tokyo performances. Japan: Tokyo.
1987. Lang.: Jap.   1965
Six plays of the Tokyo season, focus on director Betsuyaku Minoru.
Japan: Tokyo. 1986. Lang.: Jap.   1966
Kurbas, L.
Performance/production
Work of Ukrainian director L. Kurbas. USSR. 1887-1942. Lang.:
Rus.   1031
Centenary collection of materials by director L. Kurbas. USSR.
1887-1942. Lang.: Rus.   1035
Training
Pedagogy of director L. Kurbas. USSR. 1887-1942. Lang.: Rus. 1393
Kurnitz, Julie
Performance/production
Broadway actors who moonlight in cabaret acts. USA: New York,
NY. 1962-1987. Lang.: Eng.   3291
Kuroi, Senji
Performance/production
Four Tokyo productions in light of ideas of Betsuyaku Minoru.
Japan: Tokyo. 1987. Lang.: Jap.   1950
Discussion of four Tokyo productions. Japan: Tokyo. 1944-1987.
Lang.: Jap.   1963
Kurosawa, Akira
Plays/librettos/scripts
Polanski, Welles and Kurosawa's versions of Shakespeare's *Macbeth*.
USA. Japan. UK-England. 1948-1971. Lang.: Eng.   3183
Theory/criticism
Reconstruction of Shakespeare in performance. USA. 1987. Lang.:
Eng.   1358
Kurtz, Leo
Design/technology
Exhibition of the design renderings of designer Leo Kurtz who
worked closely with Bertolt Brecht and Erwin Piscator. USA:
Cambridge, MA. 1986. Lang.: Eng.   455
Kurumawari-ningyō (Nutcracker Suite)
Basic theatrical documents
Plays of Terayama Shūji. Japan. 1950-1980. Lang.: Jap.   1562
Kuuto
Performance/production
Swedish-Finnish language problems dramatized by Tornedalsteatern.
Sweden: Pajala. 1986. Lang.: Swe.   2014
Kuuzik, Tijt (Janovič, Dmitrij)
Performance/production
Tijt Kuuzik, operatic artist and teacher. USSR: Estonia. 1911-1987.
Lang.: Rus.   3886
Kuzmin, Michajl
Basic theatrical documents
Russian symbolist plays and essays. USSR. 1880-1986. Lang.: Eng.
                                                             1584

Kvapil, Jaroslav
Performance/production
Jaroslav Kvapil's role in establishing the profession of director. Czechoslovakia. 1900-1918. Lang.: Rus.   773

Kvetch
Performance/production
Collection of newspaper reviews by New York theatre critics. USA: New York, NY. 1987. Lang.: Eng.   2325

Kyd, Thomas
Plays/librettos/scripts
Comparison of the works of Ben Jonson and Christopher Marlowe. England. 1598-1602. Lang.: Eng.   1123

Structure of revenge tragedy in Shakespeare's *Hamlet*. 1600. Lang.: Eng.   2425

Madness and revenge in Kyd's *The Spanish Tragedy*. England. 1589. Lang.: Eng.   2515

Theory/criticism
Trollope's writings on Elizabethan and Jacobean drama. UK-England. 1866-1882. Lang.: Eng.   3063

Kyle, Barry
Performance/production
Play scripts as literary texts and as performance texts. UK-England. 1977-1987. Lang.: Eng.   905

English Shakespearean productions. UK-England: London, Manchester, Stratford. 1985-1986. Lang.: Eng.   917

Collection of newspaper reviews by London theatre critics. UK-England: London. 1987. Lang.: Eng.   2073

Collection of newspaper reviews by London theatre critics. UK-England: London. 1987. Lang.: Eng.   2212

Collection of newspaper reviews by London theatre critics. UK-England. 1987. Lang.: Eng.   2262

Kyōgen
Plays/librettos/scripts
Traditional *nō* and *kyōgen* texts compared to modern literature. Japan. 1300-1986. Lang.: Jap.   1506

Reference materials
Dictionary of *nō* and *kyōgen*. Japan. 1100-1987. Lang.: Jap.   1509

Kyubikku naitomea (Cubic Nightmare, The)
Performance/production
Productions of Bungakuza, Yūkikai Zenjidō shiatā, Tao and Tenkei gekijō. Japan: Tokyo. 1986. Lang.: Jap.   1961

L.A. Law
Performance/production
Analysis of art of television and comparison to live theatre. USA. 1950-1987. Lang.: Eng.   3194

L.O.W. in Gaia
Basic theatrical documents
About aging: *L.O.W. in Gaia* by Rachel Rosenthal. USA. 1986. Lang.: Eng.   3341

L'Arronge, Adolphe
Institutions
Founding of Deutsches Theater. Germany: Berlin. 1854-1883. Lang.: Ger.   531

La Compañia de Teatro de Alburquerque (Albuquerque, NM)
Institutions
Profile of bilingual theatre company La Compañia de Teatro de Alburquerque. USA: Albuquerque, NM. 1977-1983. Lang.: Eng.   1660

La Fenice (Venice)
SEE
Teatro La Fenice.

la Garde, Philippe Bridart, Abbé de
Design/technology
French costume experimentation. France: Paris. England: London. 1734-1765. Lang.: Eng.   1591

La Grange, Charles de
Institutions
Production of *Circé* by the Comédiens du Roy, Hôtel Guénégaud. France: Paris. 1673-1679. Lang.: Eng.   530

La Jolla Playhouse (La Jolla, CA)
Performance spaces
Architecture of La Jolla Playhouse and challenges it presents for designers. USA: La Jolla, CA. 1947-1987. Lang.: Eng.   694

Performance/production
Influence and impact of the electronic media, live theatre experience. USA: Los Angeles, CA. 1987. Lang.: Eng.   959

Plays/librettos/scripts
Three feminist productions of plays by Henrik Ibsen. USA. 1987. Lang.: Eng.   2899

La Mama (New York, NY)
Performance/production
Director Matthew Maguire's production of *The American Mysteries* presented by Creation at La Mama. USA: New York, NY. 1983. Lang.: Eng.   2361

Plays/librettos/scripts
Playwright Fernando Arrabal and productions of his work. USA. France: Paris. 1959-1987. Lang.: Eng.   1175

La Scala
SEE
Teatro alla Scala.

Labad, Lutgardo
Performance/production
Role of theatre in the Filipino revolution. Philippines. 1970-1987. Lang.: Eng.   1986

Labiche, Eugène
Performance/production
Collection of newspaper reviews by London theatre critics. UK-England: London. 1986. Lang.: Eng.   2040

Labor relations
Administration
Situation of performing artists in capitalist countries. Europe. 1987. Lang.: Rus.   24

Phantom of the Opera exchange: British, U.S. Equity agreement. UK-England: London. USA: New York, NY. 1987. Lang.: Eng.   49

Issues of conflict in the international exchange of artists. UK-England: Copenhagen. 1982. Lang.: Eng.   55

AEA Actors' Work Program, a re-training program for actors. USA: New York, NY. 1986-1987. Lang.: Eng.   59

The first Anglo-American commercial Broadway production, the musical *Carrie*. USA: New York, NY. UK-England: London. 1987. Lang.: Eng.   61

Potential for League of Resident Theatres strike. USA: New York, NY. 1985. Lang.: Eng.   62

Equity ratifies League of Resident Theatres pact: gains for members. USA: New York, NY. 1985. Lang.: Eng.   66

Actor exchange: discussions of Equity, Royal Shakespeare Company. USA. UK-England. 1985. Lang.: Eng.   74

Meeting between Actors' Equity and British Equity. USA: Washington, DC. UK-England. 1984. Lang.: Eng.   76

Panel discussion on the importance of volunteers in the arts. USA. 1987. Lang.: Eng.   82

Exchange of British and American artists. USA: New York, NY. UK-England. 1982. Lang.: Eng.   84

Equity wins court battle against producer David Merrick. USA: New York, NY. 1982. Lang.: Eng.   92

Outdoor Musical Stock agreement. USA: New York, NY. 1982. Lang.: Eng.   96

Chicago Equity celebrates anniversary of labor's fight for eight-hour day. USA: Chicago, IL. 1986. Lang.: Eng.   99

Actors' Equity status report. USA: New York, NY. 1982. Lang.: Eng.   100

Admission and employment of non-immigrant aliens. USA: Washington, DC. 1982. Lang.: Eng.   101

Dispute over compensation for cast of *The First*. USA: New York, NY. 1982. Lang.: Eng.   102

Lawsuits against artists' groups may have impact on all labor unions. USA: New York, NY. 1982. Lang.: Eng.   105

Actors' Equity president Ellen Burstyn on employment for minorities and women. USA: New York, NY. 1982. Lang.: Eng.   109

Actors' Equity urges communication between chapters and main office. USA: New York, NY. 1982. Lang.: Eng.   113

Circle Repertory Theatre's plan to increase roles for minority actors. USA: New York, NY. 1983. Lang.: Eng.   116

Working relationship of League of Resident Theatres and Actors' Equity Association. USA. 1987. Lang.: Eng.   128

Sexual discrimination in American theatres. USA: New York, NY. 1976-1984. Lang.: Eng.   133

Evaluation of volunteers in an arts organization. USA. 1987. Lang.: Eng.   148

Ziegfeld Follies strike. USA: New York, NY. 1919. Lang.: Eng.   167

Integration of creative process in society. USA: New York, NY. 1986. Lang.: Eng.   168

Labor relations — cont'd

Labor and the arts as advocates of social and cultural democracy. USA. 1982. Lang.: Eng.   193

San Francisco Bay Area Advisory Committee and its goals. USA: San Francisco, CA. 1987. Lang.: Eng.   197

Literal and imaginative perceptions of work. USA. 1986. Lang.: Eng.   199

Labor-sponsored conference for Chicago Equity members. USA: Chicago, IL. 1986. Lang.: Eng.   221

Contracts, actors and union negotiations. USA. 1986. Lang.: Eng.   235

Interview with Ron Aja of Actors' Equity Association. USA. 1987. Lang.: Eng.   238

Legal difficulties facing producers who present foreign artists and dance troupes. USA. 1987. Lang.: Eng.   244

New legal terms to describe old ideas. USA. 1986. Lang.: Eng.   245

Creation and tasks of Union of Theatre Workers of the Russian SFSR. USSR. 1986-1988. Lang.: Rus.   271

Actress Vesleøy Haslund fights termination from the National Theatre. Norway: Oslo. 1979-1982. Lang.: Eng.   1522

SAG/AFTRA strikes in the television/motion picture industry. USA. 1980. Lang.: Eng.   3089

Volunteer-staff relationships in the New York Philharmonic. USA: New York, NY. 1987. Lang.: Eng.   3387

Design/technology
Merger of United Scenic Artists locals into a national union. USA. 1987. Lang.: Eng.   403

Effort to find union representation for theatrical sound designers. USA. 1985-1987. Lang.: Eng.   469

Institutions
Actors' Equity strike against Producing Managers Association. USA: New York, NY. 1921-1925. Lang.: Eng.   573

League of Resident Theatres' role in labor and contract negotiations. USA. 1987. Lang.: Eng.   607

Performance/production
Actor discusses Equity exchanges for *Les Misérables*. USA: New York, NY. UK-England: London. 1987. Lang.: Eng.   926

Problems of an actor's working conditions. USSR. 1980-1987. Lang.: Rus.   1049

Working in London through Equity actor exchange. UK-England: London. USA: New York, NY. 1985. Lang.: Eng.   2307

First-hand account of Equity actor exchange. UK-England: London. USA: New York, NY. 1985. Lang.: Eng.   2308

Plays/librettos/scripts
Annotated bibliography of Labor plays. USA. 1930-1940. Lang.: Eng.   2875

Relation to other fields
Actors' Equity's affirmative action program. USA: New York, NY. 1982. Lang.: Eng.   1261

Equity's National Theatre Plan. USA. 1982. Lang.: Eng.   1262

Laboratory Theatre (Poland)
SEE
Teatr Laboratorium.

Labowitz, Leslie
Relation to other fields
Sexuality and desire in performance. USA. 1987. Lang.: Eng.   1270

Labyrinth Productions (London)
Performance/production
Collection of newspaper reviews by London theatre critics. UK-England: London. 1987. Lang.: Eng.   2264

Lady Aoi, The
Performance/production
Collection of newspaper reviews by London theatre critics. UK-England: London. 1987. Lang.: Eng.   2265

Lady Day
Design/technology
Lighting reviews for several New York productions. USA: New York, NY. 1987. Lang.: Eng.   474

Performance/production
Collection of newspaper reviews by London theatre critics. UK-England: London. 1987. Lang.: Eng.   2188

Lady Frederick
Plays/librettos/scripts
The potential for social influence in W. Somerset Maugham's comedies. UK-England. 1903-1933. Lang.: Eng.   2784

Lady from Tacna, The
SEE
Señorita de Tacna, La.

Lady in the Dark
Performance/production
Former Weill student talks about his work on Weill's Broadway productions. Germany: Berlin. 1922-1980. Lang.: Eng.   3627

Lagercrantz, Marika
Performance/production
Jordcirkus and amateur group Näktergalningarna stage *A Christmas Carol*. Sweden: Stockholm. 1986-1987. Lang.: Swe.   2020

Lagomarsino, Ron
Performance/production
Collection of newspaper reviews by New York theatre critics. USA: New York, NY. 1987. Lang.: Eng.   2315

Collection of newspaper reviews by New York theatre critics. USA: New York, NY. 1987. Lang.: Eng.   2320

Career of director Ron Lagomarsino, his style and technique. USA. 1987. Lang.: Eng.   2327

Lahr, John
Performance/production
Collection of newspaper reviews by London theatre critics. UK-England: London. 1987. Lang.: Eng.   2201

Collection of newspaper reviews by London theatre critics. UK-England: London. 1987. Lang.: Eng.   2234

Plays/librettos/scripts
Recent release of playwright Joe Orton's diaries. UK-England: London. 1933-1987. Lang.: Eng.   2758

Laliberté, Guy
Performance/production
Production of Cirque du Soleil. Canada: Montreal, PQ. 1987. Lang.: Eng.   3302

Lambert, Betty
Basic theatrical documents
Publication of two playtexts by Betty Lambert. Canada. 1987. Lang.: Eng.   1547

Lamberts, Heath
Performance/production
Overview of the 1982 Shaw Festival. Canada: Niagara-on-the-Lake, ON. 1982. Lang.: Eng.   1703

Lambranzi, Gregorio
Performance/production
Theatrical dance tradition as presented by dance teacher Gregorio Lambranzi. Italy: Venice. Germany: Nuremberg. 1700-1799. Lang.: Ita.   1439

Lamont, Alonzo D., Jr.
Plays/librettos/scripts
Alonzo Lamont's major themes in *That Serious He-Man Ball*. USA: New York, NY. 1987. Lang.: Eng.   2900

Depiction of the class struggle in contemporary theatre. USA: New York, NY. 1987. Lang.: Eng.   2915

Lampe, Jutte
Performance/production
Ten theatre people on a performance that changed their thinking. Sweden. 1986-1987. Lang.: Swe.   2015

Lamplighter Community Theatre (San Diego, CA)
Design/technology
Lighting designer James Sultan's design for *A Streetcar Named Desire*. USA: San Diego, CA. 1986. Lang.: Eng.   1599

Lan, David
Performance/production
Collection of newspaper reviews by London theatre critics. UK-England: London. 1986. Lang.: Eng.   2034

Collection of newspaper reviews by London theatre critics. UK-England: London. 1987. Lang.: Eng.   2274

Lanavoj, V.
Performance/production
Actors discuss contemporary theatrical process. USSR: Moscow. 1987. Lang.: Rus.   993

Land of Fire
Performance/production
Four productions in Southern regional theatres. USA: Houston, TX, Louisville, KY, Gainesville, FL. 1980. Lang.: Eng.   2342

Land, The
Plays/librettos/scripts
Irish Literary Renaissance writers' view of America. Ireland. 1900-1930. Lang.: Eng.   2639

Landesman, Heidi
Design/technology
Four Broadway designers discuss redesigning shows for road tours. USA. 1987. Lang.: Eng. 414

Landesman, Rocco
Performance/production
Functions, influence of dramaturgs and literary managers. USA. 1987. Lang.: Eng. 2332

Landestheater (Halle)
Performance/production
Change from sociopolitical emphasis to individual themes in productions of *A Midsummer Night's Dream*. Germany, East. 1960-1980. Lang.: Eng. 1782

Landestheater (Salzburg)
Performance/production
Two German productions of *A Midsummer Night's Dream*. Germany, West. 1970-1975. Lang.: Eng. 801

Landscape
Plays/librettos/scripts
Interpreting Harold Pinter's dramas through focus on his play structures. UK-England. 1958-1987. Lang.: Eng. 2815

Landskronapågen (Boy from Landskrona, The)
Performance/production
Harlekin's efforts to involve youth in amateur theatre. Sweden: Landskrona. 1982-1987. Lang.: Swe. 2022

Background on *Landskronapågen (The Boy from Landskrona)*. Sweden: Landskrona. 1982-1987. Lang.: Swe. 2024

Lane, John
Performance/production
Aubrey Beardsley's drawings of actresses: impact on society. UK-England: London. 1890. Lang.: Eng. 2287

Lang, Alexander
Performance/production
Two German productions of *A Midsummer Night's Dream*. Germany, West. 1970-1975. Lang.: Eng. 801

Change from sociopolitical emphasis to individual themes in productions of *A Midsummer Night's Dream*. Germany, East. 1960-1980. Lang.: Eng. 1782

Lang, John
Plays/librettos/scripts
John Lang's collaboration with Tom Taylor on *Plot and Passion*. UK-England. Australia. 1853. Lang.: Eng. 2785

Lang, Robert
Performance/production
Review of the BBC telecast of *The Birthday Party* by Harold Pinter. UK-England. 1987. Lang.: Eng. 3206

Langella, Frank
Performance/production
Director A.J. Antoon discusses *Sherlock's Last Case*. USA: New York, NY. 1987. Lang.: Eng. 970

Langer, Lawrence
Plays/librettos/scripts
Modern theatrical treatment of Fascism and the Holocaust. 1980-1987. Lang.: Eng. 2428

Language
Basic theatrical documents
German translation of Tremblay's *Les Belles-Soeurs*. Canada: Quebec, PQ. Germany. 1987. Lang.: Ger. 1549

Edition and analysis, *Allò que tal vegada s'esdevingué (What Happened Then)* by Joan Oliver. Spain-Catalonia. 1899-1986. Lang.: Cat. 1573

Design/technology
The impact of twentieth-century technology on theatre. Canada. 1900-1987. Lang.: Fre. 302

Effects of mixed media on traditional dramatic components of theatre. Europe. 1900-1987. Lang.: Fre. 318

Performance/production
Review of the 1986 Festival de la Francophonie. France. Belgium. 1986. Lang.: Fre. 1760

Examination of language in Beth Henley's *The Miss Firecracker Contest*. Mexico: Mexico City. 1987. Lang.: Spa. 1974

Codco, a comic theatrical troupe, creates regional characters. Canada: St. John's, NF. 1986. Lang.: Eng. 3253

Xhosa story-telling uses verbal dramatization and language of gesture. South Africa, Republic of. 1987. Lang.: Eng. 3266

The development of Chinese classical drama. China. 1386-1900. Lang.: Chi. 3467

Effect of speed on language in Chinese theatre. China, People's Republic of. 1930-1985. Lang.: Chi. 3483

Comparison between Chinese opera and Buddhist plays of Kerala. China, People's Republic of: Beijing. India. 1050-1968. Lang.: Chi. 3533

Professionals explain their methods of verbal description of opera. Germany, East. Germany, West. 1988. Lang.: Ger. 3777

Plays/librettos/scripts
Comparison of the works of Ben Jonson and Christopher Marlowe. England. 1598-1602. Lang.: Eng. 1123

Reading *nō* plays as poetry. Japan. 1300-1500. Lang.: Jap. 1508

Conflict of worlds in plays by Louis Nowra. Australia. 1983-1985. Lang.: Eng. 2449

Uses of history in Lepage's *La Trilogie des dragons*. Canada. 1987. Lang.: Fre. 2476

Work of playwright Marco Micone. Canada. 1982-1985. Lang.: Eng. 2483

Brassard discusses his adaptation of Genet's *Les Paravents (The Screens)*. Canada: Montreal, PQ, Ottawa, ON. 1987. Lang.: Fre. 2485

Playwright George F. Walker. Canada. 1972-1985. Lang.: Eng. 2488

Analysis of terms and their meanings in the text of the *Chester Cycle*. England. 1400-1550. Lang.: Eng. 2499

Styles of speech in Wycherley's *The Plain Dealer*. England. 1676. Lang.: Eng. 2511

Venice Preserv'd: impact of Betterton's acting style on Otway. England. 1675-1683. Lang.: Eng. 2527

Shakespeare's use of language in *The Two Noble Kinsmen*. England. 1591-1616. Lang.: Eng. 2537

The paradox and problems of poetry in Romantic theatre. England. 1700-1800. Lang.: Eng. 2557

History of Yiddish theatre and development of its plays. Europe. USA. 1853-1960. Lang.: Heb. 2562

André Brassard's production of Jean Genet's *Les Paravents (The Screens)*. France. Canada: Montreal, PQ, Ottawa, ON. 1961-1987. Lang.: Fre. 2583

Investigating the text of Genet's *Les Paravents (The Screens)*. France. Canada: Montreal, PQ, Ottawa, ON. 1961-1987. Lang.: Fre. 2585

Comparison of Brian Friel's *Translations* and András Sütő's *A szuzai menyegző*. Ireland. Hungary. 1981. Lang.: Eng. 2637

Theatrical language in the plays of Thomas Murphy. Ireland. 1961-1984. Lang.: Eng. 2640

Thomas Murphy's *The Morning After Optimism*: comparisons with Beckett, O'Casey. Ireland. 1971. Lang.: Eng. 2641

Interview with director Kazimierz Braun. Ireland: Dublin. Poland. 1981-1983. Lang.: Eng. 2642

Bakhtinian analysis of Irish Literary Renaissance. Ireland: Dublin. 1900-1930. Lang.: Eng. 2645

Analysis of Thomas Murphy's *Bailegangaire*, its connections with the Irish language, story-telling. Ireland: Galway. 1985. Lang.: Eng. 2655

Theme and language in the plays of Thomas Murphy. Ireland. 1962-1978. Lang.: Eng. 2656

Problems of translating from English and French into Hebrew. Israel. 1987. Lang.: Heb. 2660

Influence of playwright Ferruccio Benini. Italy: Venice. 1870-1929. Lang.: Ita. 2675

Productions by several Tokyo companies. Japan: Tokyo. 1986-1987. Lang.: Jap. 2682

Ethnic roots in *De la calle (Of the Street)* by Jesús Gonzalez-Davila. Mexico: Mexico City. 1987. Lang.: Spa. 2699

Plays by Gorostiza, Usigli and Novo on Spanish conquest of Mexico. Mexico. 1958-1961. Lang.: Eng. 2701

Linguistic absurdism in *El Chinfónia burguesa (The Bourgeois Chinfonia)*. Nicaragua. 1987. Lang.: Spa. 2703

Use of English in Nigerian drama. Nigeria. 1940-1987. Lang.: Eng. 2706

Irony in Ibsen's *Fruen fra Havet (Lady from the Sea, The)*. Norway. 1888-1987. Lang.: Eng. 2712

How Athol Fugard's revisions have changed *The Blood Knot*. South Africa, Republic of. 1961-1985. Lang.: Eng. 2725

Language — cont'd

Directive as a speech act in *Krismis van Map Jacobs (Christmas of Map Jacobs)* by Adam Small. South Africa, Republic of. 1983. Lang.: Afr.   2726

Analysis of 51 short farces written in Majorca. Spain-Catalonia. 1701-1850. Lang.: Cat.   2731

Analysis of Dürrenmatt's *Play Strindberg*, adaptation of Strindberg's *Dödsdansen (The Dance of Death)*. Switzerland. 1971-1982. Lang.: Eng.   2743

Standard German and the German Swiss dialects on and off stage. Switzerland. 1889-1984. Lang.: Ger.   2744

Relationships in Tom Stoppard's *The Real Thing*. UK-England. 1986-1987. Lang.: Eng.   2822

Influences of Spanish-language theatre on Chicano theatre. USA. 1598-1983. Lang.: Eng.   2874

Importance of language in Eugene O'Neill's *Hughie*. USA. 1941-1959. Lang.: Eng.   2890

Theatricality of Sam Shepard's early and late works. USA. 1965-1986. Lang.: Eng.   2903

Ibsen database now being developed. USA. Norway. 1987. Lang.: Eng.   2924

Modernism and postmodernism as themes in Sam Shepard's plays. USA. 1972-1987. Lang.: Eng.   2930

Genre and style in Soviet dramaturgy. USSR. 1960-1987. Lang.: Rus.   2942

Conference on staging Shakespeare in USSR. USSR. 1987. Lang.: Rus.   2969

Linguistic forms, historical-cultural significance of shadow puppet theatre. Indonesia. Lang.: Eng.   3379

The explanation of the term 'Shao-Lai' in Yuan drama. China: Beijing. 206 B.C.-1368 A.D. Lang.: Chi.   3553

Language of Chinese classical plays. China. 1260-1368. Lang.: Chi.   3556

Call for high quality of dramatic texts, especially for Beijing opera. China, People's Republic of. 1987. Lang.: Chi.   3574

Floral imagery in the operas of Giacomo Puccini. Italy. 1858-1924. Lang.: Eng.   3926

Relation to other fields
Idea of *festa* in relation to celebrations honoring Isabella d'Este Gonzaga. Italy: Rome. 1514-1515. Lang.: Ita.   3327

History of puppetry in Catalonia. Spain-Catalonia. 500 B.C.-1987 A.D. Lang.: Eng.   3996

Theory/criticism
Theorist Herbert Blau on modern theatre. 1960-1987. Lang.: Eng.   1306

Dramatic criticism in the Sung Dynasty. China: Beijing. 960-1279. Lang.: Chi.   1319

Plays that attempt to legitimize theatre. England. France. 1600-1700. Lang.: Eng.   1324

Semiotic study of dialogue in *As You Like It*. England. 1599. Lang.: Eng.   1325

Rococo elements in the comedies of Marivaux. France. 1715-1774. Lang.: Eng.   3039

Role of poetry in contemporary plays. USA. 1987. Lang.: Eng.   3077

The importance of body language, as opposed to spoken language, to reveal character in Chinese opera. China, People's Republic of. 1986. Lang.: Chi.   3606

Lanza, Mario
Performance/production
Life and career of singer Mario Lanza. USA. 1921-1959. Lang.: Swe.   3171

Laperrière, Gaétan
Performance/production
Interview with opera star Gaétan Laperrière. Canada. 1987. Lang.: Eng.   3756

Lapine, James
Performance/production
Collection of newspaper reviews by New York theatre critics. USA: New York, NY. 1987. Lang.: Eng.   2316

Larbey, Bob
Performance/production
Collection of newspaper reviews by New York theatre critics. USA: New York, NY. 1987. Lang.: Eng.   2321

Largo Desolato
Performance/production
Collection of newspaper reviews by London theatre critics. UK-England: London. 1987. Lang.: Eng.   2181

Lassale, Jacques
Performance/production
Luca Ronconi's view of directing. France. Italy. 1987. Lang.: Fre.   1765

Lasser, Louise
Performance/production
History and review of 1967 musical *Henry, Sweet Henry*. USA: New York, NY. 1967. Lang.: Eng.   3642

Lassgård, Rolf
Institutions
Folkteatern i Gävleborgs län: integration into the community. Sweden: Gävle. 1982-1987. Lang.: Swe.   1641

Last Bus, The
Institutions
Analysis of co-productions between Saskatoon theatre companies. Canada: Saskatoon, SK. 1987. Lang.: Eng.   518

Last Call
Plays/librettos/scripts
New Canadian drama: non-realistic, anti-naturalistic. Canada. 1983-1984. Lang.: Eng.   2482

Last Waltz, The
Performance/production
Collection of newspaper reviews by London theatre critics. UK-England: London. 1986. Lang.: Eng.   2056

Last Wave, The
Performance/production
Choreographer Carol Martin's production of *The Last Wave*. Belgium: Antwerp. 1982. Lang.: Eng.   1403

Latchmere Theatre (London)

Performance/production
Collection of newspaper reviews by London theatre critics. UK-England: London. 1986. Lang.: Eng.   2094

Collection of newspaper reviews by London theatre critics. UK-England: London. 1986. Lang.: Eng.   2104

Collection of newspaper reviews by London theatre critics. UK-England: London. 1987. Lang.: Eng.   2186

Collection of newspaper reviews by London theatre critics. UK-England: London. 1987. Lang.: Eng.   2205

Collection of newspaper reviews by London theatre critics. UK-England: London. 1987. Lang.: Eng.   2214

Collection of newspaper reviews by London theatre critics. UK-England: London. 1987. Lang.: Eng.   2260

Collection of newspaper reviews by London theatre critics. UK-England: London. 1987. Lang.: Eng.   2267

Collection of newspaper reviews by London theatre critics. UK-England: London. 1987. Lang.: Eng.   2276

Late Nite Comic
Performance/production
Collection of newspaper reviews by New York theatre critics. USA: New York, NY. 1987. Lang.: Eng.   2318

Laterna magika (Prague)
Performance/production
Antonín Máša directs his play *Vivisekce (Vivisection)* at Laterna magika. Czechoslovakia: Prague. 1987. Lang.: Cze.   767

Latinovits, Zoltán
Performance/production
Career of actor, director, writer Zoltán Latinovits. Hungary. 1931-1986. Lang.: Hun.   1794

Latvijskij Akademičeskij Teat'r Dramy im. A. Upit
Administration
Problem of lack of information about contemporary dramaturgy. USSR: Latvia. 1986-1988. Lang.: Rus.   1526

Latvijskij Opernyj Teat'r
Performance/production
Director A. Viljumanis of Latvian Opera Theatre. USSR. 1980-1987. Lang.: Rus.   3877

Latz, Dolly
Institutions
Texts and photos about the Teatre Grec. Spain-Catalonia: Barcelona. 1929-1986. Lang.: Cat.   558

Legal aspects — cont'd

Actors' Equity plans National Theatre project. USA. 1985. Lang.: Eng. 125

Comprehensive guide to establishing and running a box office. USA: New York, NY. 1980. Lang.: Eng. 126

Overview of the highlights of Trademark Law. USA: New York, NY. 1970-1982. Lang.: Eng. 129

Opposition to Equity National Theatre plan in favor of regional theatre. USA. 1985. Lang.: Eng. 132

Sexual discrimination in American theatres. USA: New York, NY. 1976-1984. Lang.: Eng. 133

Marketing the concept of planned giving. USA. 1987. Lang.: Eng. 135

1986-87 US legislation pending and approved by congress. USA. 1985-1987. Lang.: Eng. 142

History of Volunteer Lawyers for the Arts. USA: New York, NY. 1969-1982. Lang.: Eng. 146

Report on Equity League Welfare Fund program. USA. 1985. Lang.: Eng. 147

National laws for employed authors. USA. 1986-1987. Lang.: Eng. 149

Effects of the 1986 Tax Reform Act on non-profit organizations. USA. 1986. Lang.: Eng. 153

Laws governing music and performance piracy. USA: New York, NY. 1954-1982. Lang.: Eng. 162

Court ruling protecting the copyright of audio-visual works. USA: New York, NY. 1976-1982. Lang.: Eng. 165

Exploitation of artists' work in the marketplace. USA. 1984-1986. Lang.: Eng. 169

Changes in tax laws affect Actors' Equity members. USA: New York, NY. 1982. Lang.: Eng. 170

Effects of new immigration rules on performing arts organizations. USA: New York, NY. 1987. Lang.: Eng. 174

Legal issues of record rental and copyright infringement. USA. 1964-1987. Lang.: Eng. 176

The 'Proof of Harm' doctrine in copyright law. USA. 1985. Lang.: Eng. 182

Surviving an IRS tax audit. USA: New York, NY. 1987. Lang.: Eng. 186

1987 tax law and its impact on actors. USA: New York, NY. 1987. Lang.: Eng. 188

Broadway producer Dorothy Olim on commercial theatre. USA: New York, NY. 1983. Lang.: Eng. 189

Legal ramifications and remedies for artists whose work is fake or forged. USA. 1986. Lang.: Eng. 190

Customs regulations over imports. USA. 1986-1987. Lang.: Eng. 198

Literal and imaginative perceptions of work. USA. 1986. Lang.: Eng. 199

Negative effects of injunctions. USA. 1958-1982. Lang.: Eng. 201

Diversity of Letter of Agreement theatres that operate in New York City. USA: New York, NY. 1987. Lang.: Eng. 204

Historical look at the Copyright Act. USA. 1984. Lang.: Eng. 206

Trademark protection as related to merchandising. USA. 1987. Lang.: Eng. 209

Aspects of paying for works in the public domain. USA: New York, NY. 1983. Lang.: Eng. 213

Impact of the arts on the economy, politics and society. USA: Baton Rouge, LA. 1986. Lang.: Eng. 214

Copyright law regarding ownership of works for hire. USA. 1987. 217

Actress wins suit against theatre termination without just cause. USA: Chicago, IL. 1985-1986. Lang.: Eng. 220

Legislative remedies for home video recordings of copyrighted works. USA: Los Angeles, CA. 1980-1982. Lang.: Eng. 224

Advantages of planned giving to the donor's heirs. USA. 1985-1987. Lang.: Eng. 225

Education for artists on legal problems. USA: San Francisco, CA. 1980-1987. Lang.: Eng. 227

Fair use standards of the Copyright Act of 1976. USA. 1976-1984. Lang.: Eng. 229

Techniques for securing planned gifts. USA. 1987. Lang.: Eng. 230

Problems associated with the deregulation of cable television. USA: New York, NY. 1934-1982. Lang.: Eng. 233

Contracts, actors and union negotiations. USA. 1986. Lang.: Eng. 235

Interview with Ron Aja of Actors' Equity Association. USA. 1987. Lang.: Eng. 238

New legal terms to describe old ideas. USA. 1986. Lang.: Eng. 245

Obtaining tax-exempt status as a not-for-profit arts organization. USA. 1982. Lang.: Eng. 246

Copyright laws governing Soviet publications. USA. USSR. 1973-1987. Lang.: Eng. 253

Relationships between artists and producers. USA. 1986. Lang.: Eng. 257

Growth and decline of theatrical activity. Arabic countries. 1938-1985. Lang.: Fre. 1511

The copyright of Australian plays prior to adoption of British Copyright Act. Australia. UK-England. USA. 1870-1912. Lang.: Eng. 1512

Political censorship of theatre. England. Russia. France. Germany. 1800-1899. Lang.: Eng. 1517

Situation of East German theatres and playwrights. Germany, East. 1985-1986. Lang.: Ger. 1518

Little theatre and control. Korea: Seoul. 1960-1979. Lang.: Kor. 1521

Actress Vesleøy Haslund fights termination from the National Theatre. Norway: Oslo. 1979-1982. Lang.: Eng. 1522

Creating human voices and images with digital, holographic techniques: actors' conference. USA: New York, NY. Israel: Tel-Aviv. 1987. Lang.: Eng. 3083

Introduction to articles on satellite transmission pirating. USA. 1976-1987. Lang.: Eng. 3084

Copyrightability of fictional characters. USA. 1986-1987. Lang.: Eng. 3085

Copyright protection of live broadcasts. USA. 1976-1987. Lang.: Eng. 3086

The *Salinger v. Random House* copyright case. USA. 1986-1987. Lang.: Eng. 3087

Public performance exemptions from copyright liability. USA. 1976-1987. Lang.: Eng. 3088

Enforcing restrictions on blacked-out sports events. USA. 1950-1987. Lang.: Eng. 3090

Title disputes over WPA prints. USA. 1935-1987. Lang.: Eng. 3091

Reform of copyright notice omission. USA. 1968-1987. Lang.: Eng. 3092

Copyright law, FCC regulations and involuntary superstations. USA. 1970-1982. Lang.: Eng. 3093

Arguments for and against source licensing. USA. 1940-1987. Lang.: Eng. 3107

The film rating system of the Motion Picture Association of America (MPAA). USA. 1968-1982. Lang.: Eng. 3120

The risk of libel in fiction: Sylvia Plath's case. USA. 1986-1987. Lang.: Eng. 3121

Recommended changes to copyright law. USA. 1987. Lang.: Eng. 3191

Institutions

Archival documents of the Vendramin Theatre. Italy: Venice. 1700-1733. Lang.: Ita. 548

Astoria Studios' restoration to operating film studio. USA: Queens, NY. 1920-1982. Lang.: Eng. 3140

Performance spaces

Reconstruction of theatrical activity in Barcelona. Spain-Catalonia: Barcelona. 1800-1830. Lang.: Cat. 1672

Performance/production

Libel suit against a minstrel. UK-England: Stafford. 1616. Lang.: Eng. 3269

Legal, Ernst

Institutions

History of Kroll-Oper. Germany: Berlin. 1927-1931. Lang.: Ger. 3726

Léger, Fernand

Design/technology

Exhibition of theatrical design by Léger, Cocteau, Kokoschka and Kandinsky. France. Lang.: Eng. 322

Lighting — cont'd

USITT standards for dimmers and controllers. USA. 1987. Lang.:
Eng.   468

How to devise a circuit to simulate TV light on stage. USA. 1987.
Lang.: Eng.   470

Idea and uses of white light. USA. 1982. Lang.: Eng.   471

Lighting reviews for some New York productions. USA: New York,
NY. 1987. Lang.: Eng.   472

Lighting reviews of several Broadway shows. USA: New York, NY.
1987. Lang.: Eng.   473

Lighting reviews for several New York productions. USA: New
York, NY. 1987. Lang.: Eng.   474

Lighting reviews for several New York productions. USA: New
York, NY. 1987. Lang.: Eng.   475

Lighting reviews for several New York shows. USA: New York,
NY. 1987. Lang.: Eng.   476

Lighting reviews for some New York productions. USA: New York,
NY. 1987. Lang.: Eng.   477

Lighting design and instruments for production of *Nicholas Nickleby*.
USA: New York, NY. 1982. Lang.: Eng.   478

Challenges of repertory lighting. USA. 1982. Lang.: Eng.   479

Use of neon lights from film making to theatrical productions. USA.
1982. Lang.: Eng.   481

Principles of theatre lighting applied to architectural lighting. USA:
New York, NY. 1987. Lang.: Eng.   484

Interview with lighting designer Ishii Motoko. USA: Boston, MA.
1987. Lang.: Eng.   485

Brief history of development of lighting equipment. USA. 1700-1987.
Lang.: Eng.   486

Study of the work of dance lighting designer Blu. USA: New York,
NY. 1987. Lang.: Eng.   1400

Interview with dance lighting designer Allen Lee Hughes. USA: New
York, NY. 1987. Lang.: Eng.   1401

Lighting designer James Sultan's design for *A Streetcar Named
Desire*. USA: San Diego, CA. 1986. Lang.: Eng.   1599

The work of cinematographer Robby Muller. USA. 1986. Lang.:
Eng.   3131

Analysis of the work of lighting designer Jack Green on the film
Heartbreak Ridge. USA. 1982-1987. Lang.: Eng.   3132

Cinematographer Oliver Stapleton and his lighting work on the film
Prick Up Your Ears. USA. 1987. Lang.: Eng.   3136

Cinematography and lighting of the film *Castaway* by Harvey
Harrison. USA. 1987. Lang.: Eng.   3137

Cinematographer Michael Ballhaus' work on film version of
Williams' *The Glass Menagerie* directed by Paul Newman. USA.
1987. Lang.: Eng.   3139

The use of computers to enhance theatre technology. Canada. 1987.
Lang.: Fre.   3192

Adapting lighting from a live theatre version of *Sweeney Todd* for
videotape. USA. 1982. Lang.: Eng.   3204

Lighting designer Richard Pilbrow's methods. USA: Salt Lake City,
UT. 1982. Lang.: Eng.   3388

Scene design and its visual impact in Chinese opera. China, People's
Republic of. 1856-1987. Lang.: Chi.   3446

Integration of the technical and staging aspects of the musical *Smile*.
USA: New York, NY. 1986. Lang.: Eng.   3620

Lighting review for *Anything Goes* at the Vivian Beaumont Theatre.
USA: New York, NY. 1987. Lang.: Eng.   3623

Lighting design and technology for opera and ballet. UK-England:
London. 1928-1987. Lang.: Eng.   3698

Gil Wechsler, lighting designer, Metropolitan Opera. USA: New
York, NY. 1967-1987. Lang.: Eng.   3701

Performance spaces

Use of lighting in Hult Center's lobby and two performance halls.
USA: Eugene, OR. 1987. Lang.: Eng.   687

The lighting restoration of Carnegie Hall. USA: New York, NY.
1986. Lang.: Eng.   708

Restoration of audience areas of Kungliga Dramatiska Teatern.
Sweden: Stockholm. 1987. Lang.: Swe.   1675

Lighting renovation in an amphitheatre and arena. USA:
Montgomery, AL. 1987. Lang.: Eng.   3246

Lighting design in a multipurpose sports and entertainment arena.
USA: Lafayette, LA. 1987. Lang.: Eng.   3247

Lighting design in Tampa's new performing arts center. USA:
Tampa, FL. 1987. Lang.: Eng.   3395

Liitoja, Hillar
Performance/production

Hillar Liitoja's experimental theatre. Canada. 1987. Lang.: Eng. 739

Reproduction and discussion of an annotated 'score' by director
Hillar Liitoja. Canada: Toronto, ON. 1987. Lang.: Eng.   744

Like Dolls or Ladies
Performance/production

Collection of newspaper reviews by London theatre critics. UK-
England: London. 1987. Lang.: Eng.   2256

Lilja, Efva
Performance/production

Portrait of choreographer Efva Lilja. Sweden: Stockholm. 1970-1987.
Lang.: Swe.   1470

Lill, Wendy
Basic theatrical documents

Collection of four plays by Canadian women dramatists. Canada.
1987. Lang.: Eng.   1544

Lilley, Clarence C.
Institutions

The Theatre of Universal Images and its upcoming season. USA:
Newark, NJ, New York, NY. 1981-1987. Lang.: Eng.   1665

Lillian
Performance/production

Collection of newspaper reviews by London theatre critics. UK-
England: London. 1986. Lang.: Eng.   2071

Collection of newspaper reviews by London theatre critics. UK-
England: London. 1987. Lang.: Eng.   2181

Lillo, George
Plays/librettos/scripts

The London Merchant by Lillo is an allegory of the Fall. England.
1731-1987. Lang.: Eng.   2514

Changing economic conditions created an audience for plays about
criminals. England. 1731-1740. Lang.: Eng.   2517

Ideological content of Lillo's *The London Merchant*. UK-England.
1731-1800. Lang.: Eng.   2777

Liltved, Oystein
Performance/production

Review of Wagner's *Der Fliegende Holländer* at the Natal
Playhouse. South Africa, Republic of: Durban. 1987. Lang.: Eng.
                                                                     3815

Lim, Je-Bok
Basic theatrical documents

Text of *Yajunbyungwon (Field Hospital)* by Lim Je-Bok. Korea.
1970. Lang.: Kor.   1564

Limacher, John
Institutions

Historical survey of opera in Calgary. Canada: Calgary, AB. 1971-
1987. Lang.: Eng.   3719

Limanowski, Mieczysław
Performance/production

Correspondence of Reduta directors Mieczysław Limanowski and
Juliusz Osterwa. Poland: Warsaw, Wilno. 1921-1947. Lang.: Pol.
                                                                     1991

Limon, Jerzy
Performance/production

Conference proceedings on staging of Elizabethan plays. England.
1546-1616. Lang.: Eng.   775

Lincoln Center for the Performing Arts (New York, NY)
Performance/production

Resources of the Billy Rose Collection at Lincoln Center Performing
Arts Library. USA: New York, NY. 1987. Lang.: Eng.   965

Lindpaintner, Peter Josef von
Plays/librettos/scripts

Analysis of Heinrich Marschner's and Peter Josef von Lindpaintner's
operas *Der Vampyr*. Germany: Leipzig, Stuttgart. 1828. Lang.: Eng.
                                                                     3911

Lindsay Kemp Season
Performance/production

Collection of newspaper reviews by London theatre critics. UK-
England: London. 1987. Lang.: Eng.   2272

Lindsay, David
Performance/production

The 4th International Theatre Conference: includes list of
participants and their contributions. Poland: Warsaw. 1986. Lang.:
Eng, Fre.   873

Line One
Performance/production
Collection of newspaper reviews by London theatre critics. UK-England: London. 1986. Lang.: Eng. 2065
Link, Peter
Performance/production
Brief Broadway run of *King of Hearts*. USA: New York, NY. 1978-1987. Lang.: Eng. 3643
Link, Ron
Performance/production
Collection of newspaper reviews by New York theatre critics. USA: New York, NY. 1987. Lang.: Eng. 2315
Linke, Hansjürgen
Reference materials
Rolf Bergmann's catalogue of medieval German drama. Germany. 1986. Lang.: Eng. 1202
Linney, Romulus
Performance/production
Collection of newspaper reviews by New York theatre critics. USA: New York, NY. 1987. Lang.: Eng. 2319
Plays/librettos/scripts
Interview with playwright Romulus Linney. USA. 1986. Lang.: Eng. 2931
Linton, E. Lynn
Performance/production
Aubrey Beardsley's drawings of actresses: impact on society. UK-England: London. 1890. Lang.: Eng. 2287
Lion, the Witch and the Wardrobe, The
Performance/production
Collection of newspaper reviews by London theatre critics. UK-England: London. 1986. Lang.: Eng. 2040
Collection of newspaper reviews by London theatre critics. UK-England: London. 1987. Lang.: Eng. 2232
Lipson, Brian
Performance/production
Collection of newspaper reviews by London theatre critics. UK-England: London. 1986. Lang.: Eng. 2083
Lipton, Daniel
Institutions
Daniel Lipton, new artistic director Opera Hamilton. Canada: Hamilton, ON. 1986-1987. Lang.: Eng. 3722
Current strength of opera in Canada. Canada. 1987. Lang.: Eng. 3725
Lisician, P.
Performance/production
Singer and folk artist P. Lisician. USSR. 1980-1987. Lang.: Rus. 3880
Lisszaboni eső (Rain in Lisbon)
Performance/production
Menyhért Szegvári directs Miklós Munkácsi's *Lisszaboni eső (Rain in Lisbon)* at Játékszín. Hungary: Budapest. 1987. Lang.: Hun. 1815
Menyhért Szegvári directs premiere of *Lisszaboni eső (Rain in Lisbon)* by Miklós Munkácsi at Játékszín. Hungary: Budapest. 1987. Lang.: Hun. 1858
Listen to the Wind
Plays/librettos/scripts
Critical analysis of James Reaney's *Three Desks*. Canada. 1960-1977. Lang.: Eng. 2477
Lister, Laurier
Performance/production
Collection of newspaper reviews by London theatre critics. UK-England: London. 1986. Lang.: Eng. 2130
Lists
Performance/production
Cast lists for some early London operas. England: London. 1712-1717. Lang.: Eng. 3761
Plays/librettos/scripts
Plays and books produced and published by Dramatists' Guild members. USA. 1987. Lang.: Eng. 1164
Bibliography of plays related to the Civil War. USA. 1852-1900. Lang.: Eng. 2852
Reference materials
Theatre demographics in German-speaking Europe. Germany, West. Austria. Switzerland. 1986-1987. Lang.: Ger. 1203
Children's productions by Ente Teatrale Italiano. Italy. 1986-1987. Lang.: Ita. 1207
Directory of fringe, touring, dance and puppet companies, arts associations, festivals. UK-England. 1986-1987. Lang.: Eng. 1214

General subject index for vol. 38 of *Opera*. UK-England. USA. 1987. Lang.: Eng. 3936
Liszt, Franz
Plays/librettos/scripts
Musical, personal relationship of Saint-Saëns and Wagner. France: Paris. 1859-1916. Lang.: Eng. 3902
Literary management
Institutions
Literary Managers and Dramaturgs of America (LMDA). USA: New York, NY. 1987. Lang.: Eng. 594
Plays/librettos/scripts
Role of dramaturgs, literary managers. USA. 1987. Lang.: Eng. 1179
FDG/CBS New Plays Program Conferences. USA: New York, NY. 1987. Lang.: Eng. 1180
Literary Managers and Dramaturgs of America (LMDA, New York, NY)
Institutions
Literary Managers and Dramaturgs of America (LMDA). USA: New York, NY. 1987. Lang.: Eng. 594
Literature
Administration
Copyrightability of fictional characters. USA. 1986-1987. Lang.: Eng. 3085
The *Salinger v. Random House* copyright case. USA. 1986-1987. Lang.: Eng. 3087
The risk of libel in fiction: Sylvia Plath's case. USA. 1986-1987. Lang.: Eng. 3121
Performance/production
Undergraduate students stage the York Crucifixion play. UK-England: Canterbury. 1983-1987. Lang.: Eng. 2282
Teatropoesia, a combination of theatre and poetry. USA. 1974-1983. Lang.: Spa. 2368
Plays/librettos/scripts
The new Black literary criticism. USA. 1986. Lang.: Eng. 1174
Traditional *nō* and *kyōgen* texts compared to modern literature. Japan. 1300-1986. Lang.: Jap. 1506
Waka poetry in *nō* plays. Japan. 700-1300. Lang.: Jap. 1507
Reading *nō* plays as poetry. Japan. 1300-1500. Lang.: Jap. 1508
Origins of fairy tales on the Viennese stage. Austria: Vienna. 1700-1848. Lang.: Eng. 2450
The paradox and problems of poetry in Romantic theatre. England. 1700-1800. Lang.: Eng. 2557
Investigating the text of Genet's *Les Paravents (The Screens)*. France. Canada: Montreal, PQ, Ottawa, ON. 1961-1987. Lang.: Fre. 2585
Maud Gonne and Yeats's portrayal of women in his plays. Ireland: Dublin. 1900-1930. Lang.: Eng. 2646
Introduction to Chapter 19 of Pinter's unpublished novel *The Dwarfs*. UK-England. 1958-1987. Lang.: Eng. 2779
Stage and screen adaptations of the poetry of Lesja Ukrainka. USSR. 1987. Lang.: Rus. 2971
Problems of adapting literary works to the stage. USSR. 1980-1987. Lang.: Rus. 3676
Adaptation of literary works to opera. 1893-1987. Lang.: Eng. 3890
Theme of *femme fatale* in *Samson et Dalila*. France. 1800-1899. Lang.: Eng. 3900
Relation to other fields
Plays as literature. USA. 1985. Lang.: Eng. 1426
Approaching dramatic texts similarly to other literary texts. 1600-1987. Lang.: Eng. 2976
Critical study of Robertson Davies' literature and drama. Canada. 1913-1985. Lang.: Eng. 2983
Theme of imperialism in *The Tempest*. Canada. Antilles. France. 1611-1977. Lang.: Eng. 2984
Overview of French literature including theatre. France. 800-1700. Lang.: Ita. 2990
New generation of Brecht's students created avant-garde movement. Germany, East: Berlin. 1987. Lang.: Eng. 2992
Literary figures of the Irish Literary Renaissance. Ireland. UK-Ireland. 1875-1938. Lang.: Eng. 2995
Comparison of D.H. Lawrence's dramatic and novel writings. UK-England. 1906-1913. Lang.: Eng. 3006
Interview with poet and activist Haki R. Madhubuti (Don L. Lee). USA: Detroit, MI. Africa. Israel. 1942-1985. Lang.: Eng. 3008

Literature — cont'd

Influence of narrative fiction on film and drama: Bergman's *Sjunde inseglet* (The Seventh Seal). Lang.: Eng.   3184

Study of Aleksand'r Puškin's life and works, and the influence of Rossini on Puškin. Russia: St. Petersburg. 1799-1837. Lang.: Eng.   3943

Benjamin Britten's *Albert Herring* as an adaptation of a story by Maupassant. UK-England. 1947. Lang.: Eng.   3946

Theme of puppets and marionettes in Polish literature. Poland. 1500-1945. Lang.: Pol.   3995

Theory/criticism

Lack of interest in dramatic literature. USA. 1985.   1361

Myth in the plays of the Dominican Republic. Dominican Republic. 1987. Lang.: Spa.   3026

Portrayals of African-Americans in media and literature. USA. 1926-1987. Lang.: Eng.   3104

Portrayal of African-American artists in literature. USA. 1926-1987. Lang.: Eng.   3105

Lithgow, Arthur
Plays/librettos/scripts

Interview with playwright Charles Fuller. USA: Philadelphia, PA, New York, NY. Korea, South. 1959-1987. Lang.: Eng.   2921

Little Eyolf
SEE

Lille Eyolf.

Little Footsteps
Performance/production

Collection of newspaper reviews by London theatre critics. UK-England: London. 1987. Lang.: Eng.   2268

Little Murders
Plays/librettos/scripts

Interview with cartoonist-playwright Jules Feiffer. USA. 1950-1987. Lang.: Eng.   1168

Little Players (New York, NY)
Institutions

History of New York's Little Players puppet theatre. USA: New York, NY. 1960-1985. Lang.: Eng.   3967

Little Tale of Horror
SEE

Pequeña historia de horror.

Little Theatre (Leningrad)
SEE

Malyj Dramatičeskij Teat'r.

Little Theatre (Moscow)
SEE

Malyj Teat'r.

Little Theatre movement
Institutions

Elizabeth Sterling Haynes and the Little Theatre movement. Canada. 1916-1957. Lang.: Eng.   1603

Performance/production

Wonkaksa, Korea's first Little Theatre. Korea: Seoul. 1908-1965. Lang.: Kor.   1972

Littlewood, Joan
Plays/librettos/scripts

Use of oral history material to develop characters and events in plays. UK-England. 1970-1987. Lang.: Eng.   2807

Liturgical drama
Performance spaces

Use of space in medieval theatre: outdoor areas, churches. England. 1300-1576. Lang.: Eng.   1668

Performance/production

History and description of a performance of *Cavittunatakam*, a drama recounting lives of the saints. India: Kerala. 1984. Lang.: Eng.   1480

Role of the director in the Lucerne Passion play. Switzerland: Lucerne. 1453-1616. Lang.: Eng.   2030

Description of Easter processions. Spain: Puente Genil. 1660-1987. Lang.: Eng.   3332

Pageant wagon presentation in Spain provides information on recruitment, staging and rehearsal practices. Spain: St. Ginar. 1579. Lang.: Eng.   3333

Adaptation of Nativity puppet play. Italy. 1651-1987. Lang.: Eng.   4001

Plays/librettos/scripts

Comparison between medieval passion plays and Peter Nichols' *Passion Play*. 1986. Lang.: Eng.   2429

Analysis of music contained in medieval plays of the *Fleury Playbook*. England. 1500-1980. Lang.: Eng.   2507

Two Cornish *Corpus Christi* plays. England. 1350. Lang.: Eng.   2534

Medieval cycle plays as the exception rather than the norm. England. Lang.: Eng.   2543

Theories of staging the *visitatio sepulchri*. Germany. France. 900-1600. Lang.: Eng.   2599

Relation to other fields

Popular entertainment in Valencian region from December to March. Spain-Catalonia: Valencia. 1418-1981. Lang.: Cat.   3337

Research/historiography

Research methods on origins and tradition of liturgical drama. Germany. 1000-1400. Lang.: Ita.   3010

Liubimov, Jurij Petrovič
Performance/production

Life and work of Anatolij Efros. USSR: Moscow. 1983-1987. Lang.: Eng.   1038

Jurij Liubimov's 1979 Taganka Theatre production of *The Master and Margarita* (Master i Margarita). USSR. 1938-1979. Lang.: Eng.   2394

Russian director Jurij Liubimov and his productions in the USSR and USA. USSR: Moscow. USA: Washington, DC. 1984-1987. Lang.: Eng.   2400

Jurij Liubimov of Taganka Theatre directs *Lulu* in Chicago. USSR: Moscow. USA: Chicago, IL. 1987. Lang.: Eng.   3874

Plays/librettos/scripts

Productions exhibit changes in symbolism of the Don Juan myth due to AIDS crisis. USA. 1987. Lang.: Eng.   2845

Living Newspaper
Institutions

Production bulletins of the Federal Theatre Project. USA. 1936-1939. Lang.: Eng.   1654

Living Room Project
Performance/production

The performance art piece, *Living Room Project*, of Danny Mydlack. USA: Boston, MA. 1987. Lang.: Eng.   3367

Living Theatre (New York, NY)
Institutions

History of new and experimental theatre companies. Europe. North America. 1947-1970. Lang.: Ita.   529

Symposium: 'The Significance and Legacy of the Living Theatre'. USA: New York, NY. 1986. Lang.: Eng.   614

Performance/production

Audience participation in Living Theatre's *Paradise Now*. USA: New York, NY. 1968. Lang.: Kor.   945

Livings, Henry
Performance/production

Collection of newspaper reviews by London theatre critics. UK-England: London. 1986. Lang.: Eng.   2106

Collection of newspaper reviews by London theatre critics. UK-England: London. 1987. Lang.: Eng.   2211

Ljungh, Esse W.
Institutions

Script editor's recollections of CBC radio dramas. Canada. 1944-1954. Lang.: Eng.   3110

Llerena, Cristobal de
Theory/criticism

Myth in the plays of the Dominican Republic. Dominican Republic. 1987. Lang.: Spa.   3026

Llorente, Teodor
Reference materials

Catalogue of Valencian playtexts available at libraries of Barcelona. Spain: Valencia, Barcelona. Lang.: Cat.   2975

Llot de Ribera, Miquel
Performance/production

Exhibition catalogue: popular theatre in Catalan. France. 1415-1987. Lang.: Cat, Fre.   1750

Lloyd Webber, Andrew
Administration

Phantom of the Opera exchange: British, U.S. Equity agreement. UK-England: London. USA: New York, NY. 1987. Lang.: Eng.   49

Producer Marlene Smith. Canada: Toronto, ON. 1985. Lang.: Eng.   3617

Design/technology

Machinery to be installed in Her Majesty's Theatre for *Phantom of the Opera*. UK-England: London. 1987. Lang.: Eng.   3619

Lloyd Webber, Andrew — cont'd

Performance/production

Collection of newspaper reviews by London theatre critics. UK-England: London. 1986. Lang.: Eng.   2048

Collection of newspaper reviews by London theatre critics. UK-England: London. 1986. Lang.: Eng.   2065

Collection of newspaper reviews by New York theatre critics. USA: New York, NY. 1987. Lang.: Eng.   2325

Reviews of *Rigoletto*, Lloyd Webber's *Requiem*, *Les Misérables* and the Hungarian Mass of the Tolcsvays. Hungary: Szeged. 1987. Lang.: Hun.   3400

Plays/librettos/scripts

Comparison of main characters in three contemporary plays. USA: New York, NY. 1987. Lang.: Eng.   2916

Lloyd, Jeremy

Performance/production

Collection of newspaper reviews by London theatre critics. UK-England: London. 1986. Lang.: Eng.   2156

Lloyd, Peter

Performance/production

Collection of newspaper reviews by London theatre critics. UK-England: London. 1986. Lang.: Eng.   2113

Lochhead, Liz

Performance/production

Collection of newspaper reviews by London theatre critics. UK-England: London. 1987. Lang.: Eng.   2218

Lock, Edward

Performance/production

Review of touring production of Edward Lock's *Human Sex*. Canada: Vancouver, BC. 1985-1986. Lang.: Fre.   1405

Lock, Kate

Performance/production

Collection of newspaper reviews by London theatre critics. UK-England: London. 1986. Lang.: Eng.   2147

Locricchio, Matthew

Performance/production

Profile of character actor Matthew Locricchio. USA: New York, NY. 1987. Lang.: Eng.   2334

Loeb Drama Center (Cambridge, MA)

Performance spaces

Loeb Drama Center at Harvard. USA: Cambridge, MA. 1960-1987. Lang.: Eng.   682

Loeffler, Mark

Design/technology

Comprehensive look at touring theatre. USA. 1987. Lang.: Eng.   464

Loene, Leonore

Administration

Analysis of how American Theatre Association ceased to exist. USA. 1983-1986. Lang.: Eng.   163

Loew, Marcus

Administration

Lee Shubert's role in the formation of the American film industry. USA: New York, NY. 1914-1924. Lang.: Eng.   3123

Logan, George

Performance/production

Collection of newspaper reviews by London theatre critics. UK-England: London. 1987. Lang.: Eng.   2188

Logan, John

Performance/production

Collection of newspaper reviews by London theatre critics. UK-England: London. 1987. Lang.: Eng.   2208

Logan, Joshua

Performance/production

Autobiography of director, producer and writer John Houseman. USA: New York, NY. 1935-1985. Lang.: Eng.   2339

Lohndrücker, Der (Undercutting)

Plays/librettos/scripts

Stage history and interpretations of Heiner Müller's *Der Lohndrücker (Undercutting)*. Germany, East. 1956-1987. Lang.: Ger.   2615

Lokalteatern i Kalmar

Performance/production

A performance for the deaf and the blind. Sweden: Kalmar. 1987. Lang.: Swe.   889

London Cuckolds, The

Plays/librettos/scripts

Independence of Restoration women is reflected in comic heroines. England. 1668-1700. Lang.: Eng.   2550

London Merchant, The

Plays/librettos/scripts

The London Merchant by Lillo is an allegory of the Fall. England. 1731-1987. Lang.: Eng.   2514

Changing economic conditions created an audience for plays about criminals. England. 1731-1740. Lang.: Eng.   2517

Ideological content of Lillo's *The London Merchant*. UK-England. 1731-1800. Lang.: Eng.   2777

London Palladium

Performance/production

Collection of newspaper reviews by London theatre critics. UK-England: London. 1987. Lang.: Eng.   2258

Collection of newspaper reviews by London theatre critics. UK-England. 1987. Lang.: Eng.   2263

London Palladium (London)

Performance/production

Collection of newspaper reviews by London theatre critics. UK-England: London. 1986. Lang.: Eng.   2095

Long Day's Journey into Night

Performance/production

Gábor Zsámbéki directs Eugene O'Neill's *Long Day's Journey into Night* under the title *Utazás az éjszakába*. Hungary: Eger. 1987. Lang.: Hun.   1850

Collection of newspaper reviews by London theatre critics. UK-England: London. 1986. Lang.: Eng.   2154

Plays/librettos/scripts

Psychological complexity of Eugene O'Neill's *Long Day's Journey into Night*. USA. 1940. Lang.: Eng.   2842

Long Wharf Theatre (New Haven, CT)

Institutions

National Theatre of the Deaf productions of *Farewell My Lovely* and *In a Grove* directed by Arvin Brown in Beijing. China, People's Republic of: Beijing. USA. 1986-1987. Lang.: Eng.   1611

Performance/production

Relations between acting, theatre photography. USA. Lang.: Eng.   942

Plays/librettos/scripts

Interview with playwright Arthur Miller. USA. 1944-1987. Lang.: Eng.   2868

Long, Mark

Performance/production

Collection of newspaper reviews by London theatre critics. UK-England: London. 1986. Lang.: Eng.   2080

Long, William Ivey

Design/technology

Integration of the technical and staging aspects of the musical *Smile*. USA: New York, NY. 1986. Lang.: Eng.   3620

Longacre Theatre (New York, NY)

Performance/production

Collection of newspaper reviews by New York theatre critics. USA: New York, NY. 1987. Lang.: Eng.   2316

Lonsdale, Frederick

Performance/production

Collection of newspaper reviews by London theatre critics. UK-England: London. 1987. Lang.: Eng.   2204

Look Back in Anger

Performance/production

Kenneth Tynan's review of the first production of Osborne's *Look Back in Anger*. 1956. Lang.: Eng.   1677

Looking for a Bride

SEE

Ženitba.

Loon's Rage, The

Institutions

Profile of Dell'Arte Players and their productions. USA: Blue Lake, CA. 1957-1983. Lang.: Eng.   3310

Loose Moose (Calgary, AB)

Institutions

History of Alberta theatre companies. Canada: Edmonton, AB, Calgary, AB. 1987. Lang.: Eng.   506

Loot

Plays/librettos/scripts

Recent release of playwright Joe Orton's diaries. UK-England: London. 1933-1987. Lang.: Eng.   2758

Lope de Vega

SEE

Vega Carpio, Lope Félix de.

López Mozo, Jeronimo
Basic theatrical documents
Translation of *Viernes, 29 de julio de 1983, de madrugada (Friday, July 29, 1983, Early in the Morning)* by Jerónimo López Moto. Spain. 1987. Lang.: Eng. 1568
Lorca
Performance/production
Collection of newspaper reviews by London theatre critics. UK-England: London. 1986. Lang.: Eng. 2138
Lorca, Federico García
SEE
García Lorca, Federico.
Lord, Alan
Performance/production
Critical discussion of the Ultimatum II festival. Canada: Montreal, PQ. 1987. Lang.: Eng. 3346
Loren, Sophia
Performance/production
Sophia Loren's autobiography translated into Hungarian. Italy. 1934-1979. Lang.: Hun. 3157
Lorenzaccio, Il
Plays/librettos/scripts
Carmelo Bene's *Il Lorenzaccio.* Italy. 1986. Lang.: Ita. 1130
Lorieau, Maurice
Institutions
Historical survey of opera in Calgary. Canada: Calgary, AB. 1971-1987. Lang.: Eng. 3719
Lortel, Lucille
Performance/production
Interview with producer Lucille Lortel. USA: Waterford, CT. 1987. Lang.: Eng. 964
Los Angeles Music Center (Los Angeles, CA)
Performance spaces
Questions spending $50 million on a new concert hall in Los Angeles. USA: Los Angeles, CA. 1987. Lang.: Eng. 711
Los Angeles Theatre Center
Performance/production
Los Angeles Theatre Center Festival of 1987. USA: Los Angeles, CA. 1987. Lang.: Eng. 966
Losey, Joseph
Performance/production
Recollections of actor Don Pietromonaco on his work with Bertolt Brecht, Charles Laughton and Joseph Losey. USA: Los Angeles, CA. 1944-1986. Lang.: Eng. 2347
Losing Venice
Performance/production
Collection of newspaper reviews by London theatre critics. UK-England. 1987. Lang.: Eng. 2033
Lost in the Stars
Administration
Editorial response to attacks on the Weill Foundation. USA: New York, NY. Germany: Berlin. 1929-1987. Lang.: Eng. 3618
Lost Ring, The
Performance/production
Collection of newspaper reviews by London theatre critics. UK-England: London. 1987. Lang.: Eng. 2189
Lost Voices
Basic theatrical documents
English translations of contemporary African plays. Senegal. Zaire. 1987. Lang.: Eng. 1566
Louis Riel
Institutions
Conditions affecting Canadian opera composers. Canada. 1987. Lang.: Eng. 3714
Louise, Merle
Performance/production
Broadway actors who moonlight in cabaret acts. USA: New York, NY. 1962-1987. Lang.: Eng. 3291
Louvet, Jean
Relation to other fields
Representation of workers on stage. Europe. USA. 1871-1987. Lang.: Fre. 2987
Love Field
Performance/production
Collection of newspaper reviews by London theatre critics. UK-England: London. 1987. Lang.: Eng. 2209

Love for Love
Plays/librettos/scripts
Independence of Restoration women is reflected in comic heroines. England. 1668-1700. Lang.: Eng. 2550
Love in a Camp or Patrick in Prussia
Plays/librettos/scripts
New findings on 18th-century Irish comic playwright John O'Keeffe. Ireland. England: London. 1767-1798. Lang.: Eng. 2643
Love Life
Performance/production
Revival of *Love Life* by Kurt Weill and Alan Jay Lerner. USA: New York, NY, Ann Arbor, MI. 1945-1986. Lang.: Eng. 3653
Love on the Plastic
Performance/production
Collection of newspaper reviews by London theatre critics. UK-England: London. 1987. Lang.: Eng. 2246
Love, Patti
Performance/production
Collection of newspaper reviews by London theatre critics. UK-England: London. 1987. Lang.: Eng. 2073
Love's a Luxury
Performance/production
Collection of newspaper reviews by London theatre critics. UK-England. 1987. Lang.: Eng. 2261
Love's Dominion
Theory/criticism
Flecknoe's preface to *Love's Dominion,* relationship of theory to practice. England. 1654-1664. Lang.: Eng. 3027
Love's Labour's Lost
Plays/librettos/scripts
The topicality of Shakespeare's *Love's Labour's Lost.* UK-England: London. 1590. Lang.: Eng. 2794
Love's Last Shift
Plays/librettos/scripts
Themes of home and homelessness in plays of Cibber and Vanbrugh. England. 1696. Lang.: Eng. 2525
Lovely Sunday for Creve-Coeur, A
Performance/production
Collection of newspaper reviews by London theatre critics. UK-England: London. 1986. Lang.: Eng. 2117
Lover, The
Performance/production
Reviews of Pinter's *The Lover* and *A Slight Ache.* UK-England: London. 1987. Lang.: Eng. 901
Collection of newspaper reviews by London theatre critics. UK-England: London. 1987. Lang.: Eng. 2246
Plays/librettos/scripts
Interpreting Harold Pinter's dramas through focus on his play structures. UK-England. 1958-1987. Lang.: Eng. 2815
Lowe, K. Elmo
Institutions
Six books that discuss the origins and development of different American regional theatres. USA: Cleveland, OH, Los Angeles, CA, Houston, TX, Detroit, MI, Ashland, OR, Montgomery, AL. 1987. Lang.: Eng. 612
Lowe, Stephen
Performance/production
Collection of newspaper reviews by London theatre critics. UK-England: London. 1987. Lang.: Eng. 2241
Collection of newspaper reviews by London theatre critics. UK-England: London. 1987. Lang.: Eng. 2262
Lowey, Marilyn
Design/technology
Interview with lighting designer Marilyn Lowey. USA. 1987. Lang.: Eng. 462
Lowin, John
Institutions
King's Company under actor-manager John Lowin. England: London. 1576-1653. Lang.: Eng. 1614
LSD
Relation to other fields
Examination of crisis in theory and practice of political art. USA. 1987. Lang.: Eng. 3007
Luan Yih Jih
Plays/librettos/scripts
Bibliography of Yeh Shean Tzuu and his *Luan Yih Jih.* China: Beijing. 820-1641. Lang.: Chi. 1108

Macklin, Charles
Performance/production
Acting styles on English stages. UK-England. 1740-1760. Lang.: Eng.
2304

MacLean, Barbara Barondess
Performance/production
Interview with actress Barbara Barondess MacLean. USA: New York, NY. 1920-1930. Lang.: Eng.
3652

Maclennan, Alistair
Relation to other fields
Three performance art education projects. UK-England. 1987. Lang.: Eng.
3373

MacLennan, Alistair
Theory/criticism
Performance artists Declan McGonagle and Alistair MacLennan. UK-Ireland: Belfast. 1975-1987. Lang.: Eng.
3374

MacMillan Theatre (Toronto, ON)
Institutions
Summary of proceedings from a Gilbert and Sullivan symposium. Canada: Toronto, ON. 1987. Lang.: Eng.
3954

Macready, William Charles
Performance/production
Historical accuracy in 19th-century London theatre productions. England: London. 1800-1900. Lang.: Eng.
1734

Macskajáték (Catsplay)
Performance/production
Mária Sulyok as Mrs. Orbán in Örkény's *Macskajáték (Catsplay)*. Germany, East: Berlin, East. Hungary. 1980-1987. Lang.: Hun. 1786

Macushla
Plays/librettos/scripts
Analysis of the plays and songs of Irish-American musical theatre star Chauncey Olcott. USA. 1893-1918. Lang.: Eng.
3671

Madách Kamaraszinház (Budapest)
Performance/production
György Lengyel directs Camus's *Caligula* at Madách Szinház Chamber Theatre. Hungary: Budapest. 1986. Lang.: Hun. 1804

Camus's *Caligula* staged by György Lengyel, Madách Chamber Theatre. Hungary: Budapest. 1986. Lang.: Hun.
1816

Péter Huszti directs *A női partőrség szeme láttára (In Sight of the Spar)* by Pál Békés at Madách Szinház Chamber Theatre. Hungary: Budapest. 1987. Lang.: Hun.
1873

Tamás Puskás directs *Takáts Alice (Alice Takáts)* by Dezső Szomory, Madách Chamber Theatre. Hungary: Budapest. 1987. Lang.: Hun.
1897

Tamás Puskás directs *Takáts Alice (Alice Takáts)* by Dezső Szomory at Madách Kamaraszinház. Hungary: Budapest. 1987. Lang.: Hun.
1906

Péter Huszti directs *A női partőrség szeme láttára (In Sight of the Spar)* by Pál Békés at Madách Chamber Theatre. Hungary: Budapest. 1987. Lang.: Hun.
1924

Madách Szinház (Budapest)
Performance/production
Ottó Adám directs Anton Pavlovič Čechov's *Višnëvyj sad (The Cherry Orchard)* at Madách Theatre under the title *Cseresznyéskert*. Hungary: Budapest. 1987. Lang.: Hun.
1805

Actor-dramas produced by National Theatre. Hungary: Budapest. 1836-1847. Lang.: Hun.
1842

Kean by Dumas and Sartre, directed by Tamás Szirtes, Madách Theatre. Hungary: Budapest. 1986. Lang.: Hun.
1862

György Lengyel directs *Szent Bertalan nappala (St. Bartholomew's Day)* by Magda Szabó at Madách Theatre. Hungary: Budapest. 1987. Lang.: Hun.
1929

Plays/librettos/scripts
Review of Ferenc Molnár's *Az ördög (The Devil)* directed by György Lengyel at Madách Theatre with discussion of the playwright and the play. Hungary: Budapest. 1987. Lang.: Hun.
2630

Madách, Imre
Performance/production
Interview with actor Imre Sinkovits. Hungary: Budapest. 1951-1987. Lang.: Hun.
1835

Ljubiša Ristić adapts and directs Imre Madách's *Az ember tragédiája (The Tragedy of a Man)*. Yugoslavia: Subotica. 1986. Lang.: Hun.
2404

Madama Butterfly
Performance/production
Soprano Renata Scotto directs Metropolitan Opera production of *Madama Butterfly*. USA: New York, NY. 1987. Lang.: Eng. 3836

Background on Metropolitan radio broadcast performances. USA: New York, NY. 1987. Lang.: Eng.
3837

Plays/librettos/scripts
Floral imagery in the operas of Giacomo Puccini. Italy. 1858-1924. Lang.: Eng.
3926

Madame Rosa
Plays/librettos/scripts
History of the musical *Roza*. USA: Baltimore, MD. 1965-1987. Lang.: Eng.
3675

Madden, John
Plays/librettos/scripts
Interview with cartoonist-playwright Jules Feiffer. USA. 1950-1987. Lang.: Eng.
1168

Made in Spain
Performance/production
Collection of newspaper reviews by London theatre critics. UK-England: London. 1987. Lang.: Eng.
2247

Mademoiselle Colombe
Performance/production
Plot synopsis of musical *Mademoiselle Colombe* based on Anouilh's *Colombe*. USA: New York, NY. 1987. Lang.: Eng. 3647

Plays/librettos/scripts
How Anouilh's *Colombe* was adapted as a musical. USA. 1987. Lang.: Eng.
3672

Madhubuti, Haki R. (Lee, Don L.)
Relation to other fields
Interview with poet and activist Haki R. Madhubuti (Don L. Lee). USA: Detroit, MI. Africa. Israel. 1942-1985. Lang.: Eng. 3008

Madingoane, Ingoapele
Relation to other fields
Influences of Black political and economic life on literature, performance. South Africa, Republic of. 1970-1987. Lang.: Eng. 1252

Madison Square Garden (New York, NY)
Performance spaces
Subverting alienating effect of some performance spaces. USA. 1800-1910. Lang.: Eng.
706

Madman and the Nun, The
SEE
Wariat i zakonnica.

Madonna
Relation to other fields
Image of rock singer Madonna in American culture. USA: New York, NY. UK-England: London. 1985-1987. Lang.: Eng. 3386

Madonna in Slag City
Performance/production
Collection of newspaper reviews by London theatre critics. UK-England: London. 1986. Lang.: Eng.
2103

Mądzik, Leszek
Performance/production
Four new productions in Poland. Poland: Warsaw. 1986-1987. Lang.: Eng, Fre.
1988

Maestro
Performance/production
The shape and form of contemporary Polish theatre. Poland: Warsaw. 1981-1987. Lang.: Eng, Fre.
1995

Maeterlinck, Maurice
Basic theatrical documents
Russian symbolist plays and essays. USSR. 1880-1986. Lang.: Eng.
1584

Plays/librettos/scripts
Analysis of *Pelléas et Mélisande* by Maeterlinck. Belgium. 1800. Lang.: Fre.
2454

Ariadne in plays of Ibsen, Strindberg, Maeterlinck. Europe. 1892-1902. Lang.: Eng.
2566

Maffei, Francesco Scipione
Theory/criticism
Catalan translation of Lessing's *Hamburgische Dramaturgie*. Germany: Hamburg. 1767-1769. Lang.: Cat.
3043

Magdalena Experiment (Cardiff, Wales)
Performance/production
An experimental women's theatre workshop. UK-Wales: Cardiff. 1986-1987. Lang.: Eng.
922

Magee, Daniel
Performance/production
Collection of newspaper reviews by London theatre critics. UK-England: London. 1987. Lang.: Eng.   2197

Magee, Patrick
Performance/production
Review of the BBC telecast of *The Birthday Party* by Harold Pinter. UK-England. 1987. Lang.: Eng.   3206

Maggio Musicale Fiorentino (Florence)
Performance/production
Renato Simoni's staging of *I giganti della montagna (The Giants of the Mountain)* by Luigi Pirandello. Italy: Florence. 1937. Lang.: Ita.
821

Maggiolo, Marcio Velez
Theory/criticism
Myth in the plays of the Dominican Republic. Dominican Republic. 1987. Lang.: Spa.   3026

Magic Flute, The
SEE
Zauberflöte, Die.

Magistrate, The
Performance/production
Collection of newspaper reviews by London theatre critics. UK-England: London. 1986. Lang.: Eng.   2169

Magomaev, M.M.
Performance/production
Musical art in opera: the creation of *Nargiz*. USSR. 1935-1987. Lang.: Rus.   3875

Magriñà, Joan
Performance/production
History of dance in Catalonia. Spain-Catalonia. 1300-1987. Lang.: Cat.   1410

Maguire Speaking
Performance/production
Collection of newspaper reviews by London theatre critics. UK-England: London. 1987. Lang.: Eng.   2233

Maguire, Matthew
Performance/production
Essays on the future of the theatre. USA: New York, NY. 1970-1987. Lang.: Eng.   955

Magwaza, Phakade
Performance/production
Content and North American reception of *Asinimali! (We Have No Money!)* by Mbongeni Ngema. Canada. South Africa, Republic of. 1987. Lang.: Eng.   1715

Magyar Állami Népi Együttes
Design/technology
Early working conditions of the Magyar Állami Népi Együttes (Hungarian State Folk Ensemble). Hungary. 1951-1987. Lang.: Hun.
343

Magyar Állami Operaház (Budapest)
Design/technology
Interview with set designer Gábor Forray. Hungary: Budapest. 1950-1987. Lang.: Hun.   3696

Performance/production
Biography of tenor János Sárdy. Hungary. 1907-1969. Lang.: Hun.
3795

Magyar Játékszin (Budapest)
Performance/production
Premiere of Spiró's *Csirkefej (Chickenhead)* and Páskándi's *Vendégség (The Host and the Guest)*. Hungary: Budapest. 1986. Lang.: Hun.   1885

Mahabharata, The
Performance/production
Company members of Centre International de Recherche Théâtrale discuss *The Mahabharata*. France: Paris. 1986. Lang.: Eng.   1752
Orientalism in Peter Brook's production of *The Mahabharata*. India. USA: New York, NY. 400 B.C.-1987 A.D. Lang.: Eng.   1932
Collection of newspaper reviews by London theatre critics. UK-England: London. 1987. Lang.: Eng.   2238
Autobiography of film and stage director Peter Brook. UK-England. 1946-1987. Lang.: Eng.   2281
Collection of newspaper reviews by New York theatre critics. USA: New York, NY. 1987. Lang.: Eng.   2315

Plays/librettos/scripts
Development of *The Mahabharata* directed by Peter Brook and Jean-Claude Carrière. 1975-1987. Lang.: Eng.   2412

Peter Brook discusses his production of *The Mahabharata*. France: Paris. India. Australia: Perth. 1987. Lang.: Eng.   2571
Director Peter Brook discusses his views on *The Mahabharata*. India. 1987. Lang.: Eng.   2636

Mahagonny
SEE
Aufstieg und Fall der Stadt Mahagonny.

Administration
Editorial response to attacks on the Weill Foundation. USA: New York, NY. Germany: Berlin. 1929-1987. Lang.: Eng.   3618

Maheu, Gilles
Performance/production
Analysis of directorial style of Gilles Maheu. Canada. 1987. Lang.: Eng.   745

Mahlmann, John
Relation to other fields
Roundtable discussion on the state of arts education. USA. 1984. Lang.: Eng.   1281

Mahomet
Plays/librettos/scripts
Techniques, themes, characters and dramaturgy of Voltaire. France. 1718-1778. Lang.: Eng.   2590

Main Stage MGS (Tokyo)
Performance/production
Six plays of the Tokyo season, focus on director Betsuyaku Minoru. Japan: Tokyo. 1986. Lang.: Jap.   1966

Mainland
Performance/production
Collection of newspaper reviews by London theatre critics. UK-England: London. 1987. Lang.: Eng.   2197

Maintenance Man, The
Performance/production
Collection of newspaper reviews by London theatre critics. UK-England: London. 1986. Lang.: Eng.   2141

Maison Québécoise du théâtre pour l'enfance et la jeunesse (Montreal, PQ)
Administration
Interview with Madeleine Rivest. Canada: Montreal, PQ. 1987. Lang.: Fre.   14

Majakovskij, Vladimir Vladimirovič
Performance/production
Links between experimental theatre movement and the Russian Futurists. USSR. 1920-1929. Lang.: Rus.   1058
Two productions of *Misterija-Buff (Mystery-Bouffe)* by Majakovskij. USSR. 1918-1921. Lang.: Rus.   2388

Plays/librettos/scripts
Textual analysis of Majakovskij's *Bathhouse*. 1986. Lang.: Eng.   2419
Majakovskij's dramatic works as seen by critics in the 1930s. USSR. 1930-1939. Lang.: Rus.   2958
Use of public bathhouses as metaphors in Russian drama. USSR. 1925-1935. Lang.: Eng.   2959

Majestic Theatre (Brooklyn, NY)
Performance/production
Collection of newspaper reviews by New York theatre critics. USA: New York, NY. 1987. Lang.: Eng.   2315

Major Barbara
Performance/production
Philip Bosco's portrayals of characters in the plays of George Bernard Shaw. USA. 1987. Lang.: Eng.   2335

Plays/librettos/scripts
Transfiguration in Shaw's *Misalliance, Saint Joan* and *Major Barbara*. 1986. Lang.: Eng.   2413
Shaw's artistic strategy in *Major Barbara*. UK-England. 1905. Lang.: Eng.   2774
Stage business in *Major Barbara* traced to Beerbohm Tree. UK-England. 1905. Lang.: Eng.   2802

Major, Tamás
Performance/production
Biography of actor-director Tamás Major. Hungary. 1910-1986. Lang.: Hun.   1844

Make-up
Design/technology
Complete guide to make-up. Italy. 1987. Lang.: Ita.   346
Theory of theatrical make-up in Korean theatre. Korea. 1987. Lang.: Kor.   353
Theory and application of make-up. Korea. 1976. Lang.: Kor.   355

Make-up — cont'd

Scene design and its visual impact in Chinese opera. China, People's Republic of. 1856-1987. Lang.: Chi. 3446

Face painting and character in Chinese opera. China, People's Republic of. 1986. Lang.: Chi. 3448

Make, Sello
Performance/production
Content and North American reception of *Asinimali! (We Have No Money!)* by Mbongeni Ngema. Canada. South Africa, Republic of. 1987. Lang.: Eng. 1715

Making Noise Quietly
Performance/production
Collection of newspaper reviews by London theatre critics. UK-England: London. 1986. Lang.: Eng. 2117

Makishi Theatre 2000
Plays/librettos/scripts
Theme of aggression between fathers and sons: Zambian National Theatre Arts Association festival. Zambia. 1966-1987. Lang.: Eng. 2972

Malabar Costume Company (Toronto, ON)
Design/technology
Malabar Costume Company's work for opera. Canada: Toronto, ON. 1900-1987. Lang.: Eng. 3693

Malade imaginaire, Le (Hypochondriac, The)
Performance/production
Collection of newspaper reviews by London theatre critics. UK-England: London. 1987. Lang.: Eng. 2174

Malas, Malena
Training
Interviews with singing teachers in New York City. USA: New York, NY. 1987. Lang.: Eng. 3952

Maleczech, Ruth
Institutions
Profile of the theatre collective, Mabou Mines. USA: New York, NY. 1987. Lang.: Eng. 617

Maleras, Emma
Performance/production
History of dance in Catalonia. Spain-Catalonia. 1300-1987. Lang.: Cat. 1410

Maleszko, Andrzej
Performance/production
Festival of Polish plays. Poland: Wrocław. 1987. Lang.: Eng, Fre. 871

Malgot, István
Performance/production
István Malgot directs *A búskepű lovag (The Sad-Faced Knight)* by László Gyurko in the Dominican Court of the Budapest Hilton. Hungary: Budapest. 1987. 1900

Malina, Jaroslav
Design/technology
Action Design, a new theory of scenography emerging in Eastern Europe. Czechoslovakia: Prague. 1980-1987. Lang.: Eng. 315

Malinche, La
Plays/librettos/scripts
Plays by Gorostiza, Usigli and Novo on Spanish conquest of Mexico. Mexico. 1958-1961. Lang.: Eng. 2701

Mallarmé, Stéphane
Theory/criticism
Centenary of Théâtre Libre: proposes 'subjective realism'. France. 1887-1987. Lang.: Fre. 1337

Introduction to Mallarmé's *Crayonne au Théâtre*. France. 1987. Lang.: Eng. 3036

Malmborg, Lars af
Institutions
Overview of Lars af Malmborg's management of Swedish Royal Opera. Sweden: Stockholm. 1985-1987. Lang.: Swe. 3729

Malory, Thomas, Sir
Plays/librettos/scripts
Influences of Arthurian legend on Shakespeare's *King Lear*. England. 1605. Lang.: Eng. 2521

Malpede, John
Relation to other fields
John Malpede's performance workshop for the homeless. USA: Los Angeles, CA. 1984-1987. Lang.: Eng. 1267

Malpede, Karen
Institutions
Symposium: 'The Significance and Legacy of the Living Theatre'. USA: New York, NY. 1986. Lang.: Eng. 614

Malvern Festival (Malvern, UK)
Performance/production
The founding and history of the Malvern Festival. UK-England: Malvern. 1904-1977. Lang.: Eng. 2286

Malvius, Georg
Performance/production
Catholic elements in two treatments of *Don Carlos* by Verdi. Europe. 1986-1987. Lang.: Swe. 3765

Malyj Teat'r (Moscow)
Performance/production
Tradition and art of acting at Malyj Theatre. USSR: Moscow. 1987. Lang.: Rus. 1010

Portrait of actor Eduard Marcevič. USSR: Moscow. 1987. Lang.: Rus. 1037

Malyj Teat'r Opery i Baleta (Leningrad)
Performance/production
Productions of S. Taudasinskij, Leningrad Malyj Opera Theatre. USSR: Leningrad. 1980-1987. Lang.: Rus. 3882

Mama, I Want to Sing
Performance/production
Trend of gospel musicals on and off Broadway. USA: New York, NY. 1987. Lang.: Eng. 3656

Mamet, David
Administration
Profile of Ensemble Studio Theatre. USA: New York, NY. 1987. Lang.: Eng. 232

Institutions
Analysis of the changing scene in Chicago's theatres. USA: Chicago, IL. 1987. Lang.: Eng. 589

Current trends in American theatre. USA. 1967-1987. Lang.: Eng. 621

Seven productions chosen for Theatertreffen '86. Germany: Berlin. 1986. Lang.: Eng. 1617

Performance/production
David Mamet's *American Buffalo* directed by Péter Dezsényi at National Theatre as *Amérikai bölény*. Hungary: Pécs. 1986. Lang.: Hun. 1882

Collection of newspaper reviews by London theatre critics. UK-England: London. 1986. Lang.: Eng. 2131

Collection of newspaper reviews by London theatre critics. UK-England: London. 1987. Lang.: Eng. 2259

Plays/librettos/scripts
Interview with playwright John Guare. USA. 1987. Lang.: Eng. 2870

Interview with playwright David Mamet. USA: Chicago, IL, New York, NY. 1969-1987. Lang.: Eng. 2909

Man and Superman
Performance/production
Various North American and English productions of *Man and Superman*. UK-England. North America. 1901-1982. Lang.: Eng. 2288

Plays/librettos/scripts
How settings and props convey meaning in plays by Shaw. UK-England. 1883-1935. Lang.: Eng. 2753

Man for All Seasons, A
Performance/production
Collection of newspaper reviews by London theatre critics. UK-England: London. 1987. Lang.: Eng. 2221

Man from Mukinupin, The
Plays/librettos/scripts
Critical analysis of Dorothy Hewett's *The Man from Mukinupin*. Australia. 1979. Lang.: Eng. 2438

Man in the Moon Theatre (London)
Performance/production
Collection of newspaper reviews by London theatre critics. UK-England: London. 1986. Lang.: Eng. 2090

Collection of newspaper reviews by London theatre critics. UK-England: London. 1986. Lang.: Eng. 2170

Collection of newspaper reviews by London theatre critics. UK-England: London. 1987. Lang.: Eng. 2221

Collection of newspaper reviews by London theatre critics. UK-England: London. 1987. Lang.: Eng. 2237

Collection of newspaper reviews by London theatre critics. UK-England: London. 1987. Lang.: Eng. 2241

Collection of newspaper reviews by London theatre critics. UK-England: London. 1987. Lang.: Eng. 2266

Man of Destiny, The
Plays/librettos/scripts
Themes and sources of Shaw's *The Man of Destiny*. UK-England.
1894-1931. Lang.: Eng.   2754
Man of La Mancha
Performance/production
Actors Sándor Szakácsi and Piroska Molnár in *Man of La Mancha*
directed by Lászlo Bagossy. Hungary: Pécs. 1987. Lang.: Hun. 3633
Man of Mode, The
Plays/librettos/scripts
Independence of Restoration women is reflected in comic heroines.
England. 1668-1700. Lang.: Eng.   2550
Man Who Envied Women, The
Basic theatrical documents
Script of *The Man Who Envied Women* by Yvonne Rainer. USA.
1985. Lang.: Eng.   3125
Theory/criticism
Yvonne Rainer's film *The Man Who Envied Women*. USA. 1987.
Lang.: Eng.   3190
Man, Animal and Virtue
SEE
Uomo, la bestia e la virtù, L'.
Management
SEE ALSO
Administration.
Administration
John Hirsch, artistic director of the Stratford Festival. Canada:
Stratford, ON. 1982. Lang.: Eng.   16
Value of degree in arts management. USA: New York, NY. 1985.
Lang.: Eng.   123
How to computerize your non-profit organization. USA: New York,
NY. 1986. Lang.: Eng.   152
Interview with manager, historian and producer Anna Sosenko. USA:
New York, NY. 1930-1987. Lang.: Eng.   154
Board presidents on their roles in nonprofit organizations. USA.
1987. Lang.: Eng.   177
Impact of computers on not-for-profit organizations. USA. 1980-1984.
Lang.: Eng.   196
Relationship of board of directors to artistic and managing directors.
USA. 1987. Lang.: Eng.   252
Merger of CentreStage and Toronto Free Theatre. Canada: Toronto,
ON. 1986-1987. Lang.: Eng.   1515
SAG/AFTRA strikes in the television/motion picture industry. USA.
1980. Lang.: Eng.   3089
Management of Beijing Opera. China, People's Republic of: Beijing.
1949-1987. Lang.: Chi.   3426
History of Chinese theatre reform. China, People's Republic of:
Beijing. 1942-1984. Lang.: Chi.   3428
Audience
Influence of audience on George Colman's artistic choices. England:
London. 1767-1774. Lang.: Eng.   280
Institutions
Archival documents of the Vendramin Theatre. Italy: Venice. 1700-
1733. Lang.: Ita.   548
Profile and history of Symphony Space. USA: New York, NY.
1977-1984. Lang.: Eng.   602
Profile of the theatre collective, Mabou Mines. USA: New York,
NY. 1987. Lang.: Eng.   617
History and current season of the National Theatre. UK-England:
London. 1848-1987. Lang.: Eng.   1647
Nicholas Goldschmidt's tenure as artistic director, Guelph Spring
Festival. Canada: Guelph, ON. 1967-1987. Lang.: Eng.   3720
Performance spaces
History of Teatro San Carlo, its artists and performances. Italy:
Naples. 1737-1987. Lang.: Ita.   648
Histories of Wallack's Theatre and the Union Square Theatre. USA:
New York, NY. 1850-1889. Lang.: Eng.   1676
Performance/production
Letters illustrating development of professional theatre in Hungary.
Hungary. 1790-1837. Lang.: Hun.   807
Maurizio Scaparro: critic, director, administrator. Italy. 1964-1987.
Lang.: Ita.   837
Plays/librettos/scripts
Motivation for literary manager becoming playwright's agent. USA:
New York, NY. 1987. Lang.: Eng.   1182

Training
Shaping of an arts management internship from an employer's point
of view. USA: Brooklyn, NY. 1985. Lang.: Eng.   1389
Management, literary
Performance/production
Functions, influence of dramaturgs and literary managers. USA.
1987. Lang.: Eng.   2332
Management, stage
Administration
Stage managers represented on Actors' Equity Council. USA: New
York, NY. 1982. Lang.: Eng.   104
Ratification of amendment allowing stage managers on Actors'
Equity Council. USA: New York, NY. 1982. Lang.: Eng.   108
Design/technology
Guide to stage management. USA. 1987. Lang.: Eng.   466
Performance/production
Detailed descriptions of numerous promptbooks: glossary, examples,
role of prompter. England. Ireland. 1700-1799. Lang.: Eng. 1738
Management, top
Administration
Royal Swedish Opera: new production of *Die Zauberflöte*, overview
of management. Sweden: Stockholm. 1986. Lang.: Swe.   3681
Career of Sir Rudolph Bing, challenges of managing the
Metropolitan Opera. USA: New York, NY. 1950-1972. Lang.: Eng.
                                                           3682
Institutions
King's Company under actor-manager John Lowin. England:
London. 1576-1653. Lang.: Eng.   1614
Theatre manager William Wood's paternalism. USA: Philadelphia,
PA. 1803-1855. Lang.: Eng.   1659
Manaka, Matsemela
Performance/production
Matsemela Manaka's play *Pula* and its anti-apartheid expressions.
South Africa, Republic of: Soweto. 1969-1984. Lang.: Eng. 883
Black theatre in South Africa: influence of traditional forms. South
Africa, Republic of. England: London. USA: New York, NY. 1586-
1987. Lang.: Eng.   2005
Review of *Vuka* by Matsemela Manaka. South Africa, Republic of:
Soweto. 1976-1987. Lang.: Eng.   2006
Mandat (Mandate)
Plays/librettos/scripts
Nikolaj Erdmann's plays, relations with major directors. USSR:
Moscow. 1925. Lang.: Rus.   2963
Mandela, Nelson
Relation to other fields
Comparison of *Woyzeck* to Nelson Mandela. South Africa, Republic
of: Pretoria. 1985. Lang.: Eng.   2999
Mandoki, Louis
Design/technology
Interview with cameraman Lajos Koltay. Hungary. 1986. Lang.: Hun.
                                                           3128
Manfred
Plays/librettos/scripts
Structure of Byron's plays. England. 1788-1824. Lang.: Eng. 2542
Mangan, James Clarence
Theory/criticism
Brian Friel's play *Translations*. Ireland. 1987. Lang.: Eng. 3050
Manganyi, N.C.
Training
Proposed changes in teaching methodology to include indigenous
drama. South Africa, Republic of. 1960-1987. Lang.: Eng.   1383
Manhattan Class Company (New York, NY)
Institutions
News of various theatres. USA: New York, NY. 1987. Lang.: Eng.
                                                           579
Manhattan School of Music (New York, NY)
Performance/production
Birgit Nilsson's master voice class at Manhattan School of Music.
USA: New York, NY. 1983-1987. Lang.: Eng.   3859
Manhattan Theatre Club (New York, NY)
Design/technology
Interview with lighting designer Dennis Parichy. USA: New York,
NY. 1986-1987. Lang.: Eng.   428
Institutions
History of Manhattan Theatre Club. USA: New York, NY. 1969-
1987. Lang.: Eng.   1663

Manhattan Theatre Club (New York, NY) — cont'd

Performance/production
Relations between acting, theatre photography. USA. Lang.: Eng.
942

Collection of newspaper reviews by New York theatre critics. USA:
New York, NY. 1987. Lang.: Eng.
2312

Manheim, Kate
Performance/production
Interview with director Richard Foreman. USA: New York, NY.
1962-1987. Lang.: Eng.
2329

Manitoba Opera Company (Winnipeg, MB)
Administration
Irving Guttman, artistic director, Edmonton Opera, Manitoba Opera.
Canada: Edmonton, AB, Winnipeg, MB. 1972-1985. Lang.: Eng.
3679

Manitoba Theatre Centre (Winnipeg, MB)
Performance/production
Richard Ouzounian, director, Manitoba Theatre Centre. Canada:
Winnipeg, MB. 1982. Lang.: Eng.
1693

Manji (Tokyo)
Performance/production
Productions by Tenkei gekijō, Manji and Mokutōsha. Japan: Tokyo.
1986. Lang.: Jap.
1958

Mankiewicz, Herman J.
Performance/production
New questions about Welles' *Citizen Kane*. USA. 1942. Lang.: Eng.
3164

Mann ist Mann (Man's a Man, A)
Performance/production
Early productions of Brecht's plays reflected in the press. Germany:
Berlin. 1922-1933. Lang.: Ger.
1777

Plays/librettos/scripts
Focus of money in Brecht's dramas. Germany, East. 1920-1930.
Lang.: Eng.
2611

Theory/criticism
Challenge of Brecht's plays to communism. Germany, East: Berlin.
1960-1970. Lang.: Eng.
3045

Mann, Emily
Plays/librettos/scripts
Conference on women in theatre, emphasis on playwriting. USA.
1987. Lang.: Eng.
1161

Three feminist productions of plays by Henrik Ibsen. USA. 1987.
Lang.: Eng.
2899

David Shaber, Larry Kramer, Emily Mann: Three of the few
American political dramatists. USA: New York, NY. 1987. Lang.:
Eng.
2907

Manon Lescaut
Performance/production
Background on San Francisco opera radio broadcasts. USA: San
Francisco, CA. 1987. Lang.: Eng.
3833

Background on Metropolitan radio broadcast performances. USA:
New York, NY. 1987. Lang.: Eng.
3837

Plays/librettos/scripts
Background and sources of Massenet's *Manon Lescaut*. France: Paris.
1831-1910. Lang.: Eng.
3899

Floral imagery in the operas of Giacomo Puccini. Italy. 1858-1924.
Lang.: Eng.
3926

Manrd, Günzel, Lutz
Performance/production
A round-table discussion with stage directors on the principles and
methods of working with an ensemble company. Germany, East:
Berlin, East. 1983. Lang.: Ger.
1778

Mantegna, Joe
Plays/librettos/scripts
Interview with playwright David Mamet. USA: Chicago, IL, New
York, NY. 1969-1987. Lang.: Eng.
2909

Manto, Sadat Hassan
Performance/production
Collection of newspaper reviews by London theatre critics. UK-
England: London. 1987. Lang.: Eng.
2191

Manzoni, Alessandro
Plays/librettos/scripts
Essays on various Italian playwrights. Italy. 1700-1900. Lang.: Ita.
1132

Mao, Tse-Tung
Administration
History of Chinese theatre reform. China, People's Republic of:
Beijing. 1942-1984. Lang.: Chi.
3428

Map of the World, A
Plays/librettos/scripts
Theme of theatre in recent plays. UK-England. 1957-1985. Lang.:
Eng.
2764

Mapleson, Lionel
Design/technology
Controversy over 1901 cylinder recording of *Les Huguenots*. USA.
1901-1987. Lang.: Eng.
3699

Mapleson cylinders: controversy over *Les Huguenots*. USA: New
York, NY. 1947. Lang.: Eng.
3700

Maponya, Maishe
Performance/production
Black theatre in South Africa: influence of traditional forms. South
Africa, Republic of. England: London. USA: New York, NY. 1586-
1987. Lang.: Eng.
2005

Review of *Vuka* by Matsemela Manaka. South Africa, Republic of:
Soweto. 1976-1987. Lang.: Eng.
2006

Relation to other fields
Interracial fringe productions: racial, class, sexual politics. South
Africa, Republic of. 1984. Lang.: Eng.
2998

Theory/criticism
Semiotic production in popular performance. South Africa, Republic
of. 1980. Lang.: Eng.
1347

Mapplethorpe, Robert
Design/technology
Modern dance production *Portraits in Reflection*. USA. 1986. Lang.:
Eng.
396

Marat/Sade
Performance/production
The 4th International Theatre Conference: includes list of
participants and their contributions. Poland: Warsaw. 1986. Lang.:
Eng, Fre.
873

Maratta, Joanna
Institutions
1987 Vancouver Fringe Festival: specific performances. Canada:
Vancouver, BC. 1987. Lang.: Eng.
1609

Marceau, Marcel
Performance/production
Development of mime, pantomime and its related movements.
France: Paris. UK-England. USA: New York, NY. 1980-1982. Lang.:
Eng.
3223

Contemporary mime forms and their innovators. France: Paris.
Belgium. USA. 1980-1982. Lang.: Eng.
3224

Marcel Marceau's reflections on his art. France. Italy. 1982-1986.
Lang.: Ita.
3233

Marcel, Gabriel
Plays/librettos/scripts
Life and works of French dramatist Gabriel Marcel. France. 1889-
1973. Lang.: Eng.
2573

Marcell, Joseph
Performance/production
Collection of newspaper reviews by London theatre critics. UK-
England: London. 1987. Lang.: Eng.
2227

March of the Falsettos
Performance/production
Collection of newspaper reviews by London theatre critics. UK-
England: London. 1987. Lang.: Eng.
2195

Marchant, Tony
Performance/production
Collection of newspaper reviews by London theatre critics. UK-
England: London. 1986. Lang.: Eng.
2170

Collection of newspaper reviews by London theatre critics. UK-
England: London. 1987. Lang.: Eng.
2262

Collection of newspaper reviews by London theatre critics. UK-
England: London. 1987. Lang.: Eng.
2270

Marchessault, Jovette
Plays/librettos/scripts
New Canadian drama: non-realistic, anti-naturalistic. Canada. 1983-
1984. Lang.: Eng.
2482

Marcus, Dr. Eliezer
Relation to other fields
Importance of theatre for youth and arts in education in Israel.
Israel. 1973. Lang.: Eng.
1241

Marcus, James
Performance/production
Collection of newspaper reviews by London theatre critics. UK-
England: London. 1987. Lang.: Eng.
2183

Marketing — cont'd

An investigation of the audience of Chinese classical drama. China, People's Republic of. 1987. Lang.: Chi. 3424

Marketing of opera and the arts in Toronto. Canada: Toronto, ON. 1980-1987. Lang.: Eng. 3678

Audience
Devices used to draw audiences to the theatre. USA. 1985. Lang.: Eng. 292

Audience reactions to the Canadian Opera Company's Atlantic tour. Canada. 1987. Lang.: Eng. 3689

Institutions
History of Alberta theatre companies. Canada: Edmonton, AB, Calgary, AB. 1987. Lang.: Eng. 506

Survey of Vancouver theatre companies. Canada: Vancouver, BC. 1987. Lang.: Eng. 516

Analysis of co-productions between Saskatoon theatre companies. Canada: Saskatoon, SK. 1987. Lang.: Eng. 518

Profile and history of Colden Center for the Performing Arts. USA: Flushing, NY. 1961-1984. Lang.: Eng. 618

Operations of the Saskatoon Opera Association. Canada: Saskatoon, SK. 1978-1987. Lang.: Eng. 3713

Role of the CBC in promoting Canadian opera. Canada. 1936-1987. Lang.: Eng. 3715

Plays/librettos/scripts
History of Playwrights Canada Press. Canada: Toronto, ON. 1972-1982. Lang.: Eng. 2460

Relation to other fields
Popular theatre and non-governmental funding agencies. Canada: Sydney, NS. Jamaica. Sudan. 1987. Lang.: Eng. 2982

Theory/criticism
Argument challenging existence of an avant-garde in America. USA. 1985. Lang.: Eng. 1352

Markov, Pavel A.
Theory/criticism
Critic Pavel A. Markov and the Moscow Art Theatre. USSR. 1910-1959. Lang.: Rus. 1373

Marlowe
Performance/production
Collection of newspaper reviews by London theatre critics. UK-England: London. 1986. Lang.: Eng. 2136

Marlowe, Christopher
Institutions
The Stanisław Ignacy Witkiewicz Theatre. Poland: Zakopane. 1982-1986. Lang.: Eng, Fre. 1628

Performance/production
Collection of newspaper reviews by London theatre critics. UK-England: London. 1987. Lang.: Eng. 2225

Plays/librettos/scripts
Comparison of the works of Ben Jonson and Christopher Marlowe. England. 1598-1602. Lang.: Eng. 1123

Comparison of Dürrenmatt's The Physicists (Die Physiker), Macbeth and Doctor Faustus. Switzerland. 1987. Lang.: Heb. 2747

The world and man in Marlowe's tragedies. UK-England. 1564-1593. Lang.: Rus. 2751

Examination of different editions of Marlowe's Doctor Faustus. UK-England. 1987. Lang.: Eng. 2791

Theory/criticism
Trollope's writings on Elizabethan and Jacobean drama. UK-England. 1866-1882. Lang.: Eng. 3063

Marowitz, Charles
Theory/criticism
Peter Brook's implementation of Jan Kott's theory in his approach to King Lear. UK-England. 1962-1987. Lang.: Eng. 3064

Marranca, Bonnie
Theory/criticism
Editor of Performing Arts Journal discusses its history. USA: New York, NY. 1975-1985. Lang.: Eng. 1359

Marren, Howard
Performance/production
Collection of newspaper reviews by London theatre critics. UK-England: London. 1986. Lang.: Eng. 2044

Collection of newspaper reviews by London theatre critics. UK-England: London. 1987. Lang.: Eng. 2198

Marriage A-La-Mode
Theory/criticism
Politics, patriarchy in Dryden's plays. England. 1679-1687. 3030

Marriage of Figaro, The (Opera)
SEE
Nozze di Figaro, Le.
Marriage of Panurge, The
Performance/production
Collection of newspaper reviews by London theatre critics. UK-England: London. 1987. Lang.: Eng. 2190

Marriage of Wit and Wisdom, The
Performance/production
Production of Merbury's The Marriage of Wit and Wisdom by David Parry. Israel: Jerusalem. 1987. Lang.: Eng. 1939

Marriage, The
SEE
Ženitba.
Mars, Mlle
Performance/production
Child actors in juvenile companies, Comédie-Française. France: Paris. 1769-1850. Lang.: Eng. 1756

Marschner, Heinrich
Plays/librettos/scripts
Analysis of Heinrich Marschner's and Peter Josef von Lindpaintner's operas Der Vampyr. Germany: Leipzig, Stuttgart. 1828. Lang.: Eng. 3911

Marsh, Matthew
Performance/production
Collection of newspaper reviews by London theatre critics. UK-England: London. 1987. Lang.: Eng. 2224

Marshall, Susan
Performance/production
New European choreographers and their development of new images. France: Paris. UK-England: London. South Africa, Republic of. 1987. Lang.: Eng. 1468

Marston, John
Performance/production
Play scripts as literary texts and as performance texts. UK-England. 1977-1987. Lang.: Eng. 905

'Boy actresses' and attitudes toward sensuality in performance. England: London. 1580-1630. Lang.: Eng. 1741

Plays/librettos/scripts
Structure of revenge tragedy in Shakespeare's Hamlet. 1600. Lang.: Eng. 2425

Theory/criticism
Trollope's writings on Elizabethan and Jacobean drama. UK-England. 1866-1882. Lang.: Eng. 3063

Martersteig, Max
Institutions
History of Leipzig Neues Theater. Germany: Leipzig. 1868-1932. Lang.: Ger. 3391

Martial arts
Performance/production
Celebration of Chinese Lunar New Year: Lion dancing and its martial arts background. USA: New York, NY. 1987. Lang.: Eng. 3334

Martin Beck Theatre (New York, NY)
Performance spaces
Broadway theatres given landmark status. USA: New York, NY. 1982. Lang.: Eng. 692
Performance/production
Collection of newspaper reviews by New York theatre critics. USA: New York, NY. 1987. Lang.: Eng. 2316

Martin-Harvey, John
Performance/production
British theatrical touring companies. UK-England. North America. Australia. 1870-1929. Lang.: Eng. 2280

Martin, Carol
Performance/production
Choreographer Carol Martin's production of The Last Wave. Belgium: Antwerp. 1982. Lang.: Eng. 1403

Martin, Chris
Performance/production
Collection of newspaper reviews by London theatre critics. UK-England: London. 1986. Lang.: Eng. 2099

Martin, Christopher
Administration
Relationship of board of directors to artistic and managing directors. USA. 1987. Lang.: Eng. 252
Institutions
Profile of CSC Repertory, artistic director Christopher Martin. USA: New York, NY. 1982. Lang.: Eng. 1658

Martin, Christopher — cont'd

Performance/production
Relations between acting, theatre photography. USA. Lang.: Eng.
942

Martin, Jonathan
Performance/production
Collection of newspaper reviews by London theatre critics. UK-England: London. 1986. Lang.: Eng.
2042

Collection of newspaper reviews by London theatre critics. UK-England: London. 1986. Lang.: Eng.
2088

Martínez Sierra, Gregorio
Performance/production
Collection of theatre reviews by J.M. de Sagarra. Spain-Catalonia: Barcelona. 1922-1927. Lang.: Cat.
885

Martinez, Humberto
Plays/librettos/scripts
Influences of Spanish-language theatre on Chicano theatre. USA. 1598-1983. Lang.: Eng.
2874

Martirio di s. Thëodoro, Il (Martyrdom of Saint Theodore, The)
Plays/librettos/scripts
Plays of Antonio Monetta, Pietro Suscio and Girolamo Bax. Italy. 1600-1900. Lang.: Ita.
2669

Martoglio, Nino
Performance/production
Career of actor Angelo Musco. Italy. 1872-1937. Lang.: Ita.
841

Márton, Endre
Performance/production
Director Endre Márton. Hungary. 1941-1978. Lang.: Hun.
1860

Marton, Eva
Basic theatrical documents
Review of video productions of *Tosca* and *Dialogues des Carmélites*. Italy: Verona. Australia: Sydney. 1987. Lang.: Eng.
3692

Performance/production
Soprano Eva Marton discusses Turandot. Hungary. 1943-1987. Lang.: Eng.
3797

Márton, László
Performance/production
László Márton directs *La estrella de Sevilla (The Star of Seville)* by Lope de Vega at Vigszinház under the title *Sevilla csillaga*. Hungary: Budapest. 1986. Lang.: Hun.
1796

La estrella de Sevilla (The Star of Seville) by Lope de Vega, staged by László Márton at Vigszinház. Hungary: Budapest. 1986. Lang.: Hun.
1807

Productions of plays by László Márton, Tamás Jordán and Ferenc Kulin at Radnóti Miklós Theatre. Hungary: Budapest. 1987. Lang.: Hun.
1887

László Márton's *Lepkék a kalapon (Butterflies on Your Hat)* directed by István Verebes at Radnóti Miklós Theatre. Hungary: Budapest. 1987. Lang.: Hun.
1923

Plays/librettos/scripts
Interview with László Márton, author of *Lepkék a kalapon (Butterflies on Your Hat)*. Hungary. 1982-1987. Lang.: Hun.
2635

Marx, Arthur
Performance/production
Collection of newspaper reviews by London theatre critics. UK-England: London. 1987. Lang.: Eng.
2235

Collection of newspaper reviews by London theatre critics. UK-England: London. 1987. Lang.: Eng.
2249

Marx, Karl
Administration
History of Chinese theatre reform. China, People's Republic of: Beijing. 1942-1984. Lang.: Chi.
3428

Mary Queen of Scots Got Her Head Chopped Off
Performance/production
Collection of newspaper reviews by London theatre critics. UK-England: London. 1987. Lang.: Eng.
2218

Mary Rose
Performance/production
Collection of newspaper reviews by London theatre critics. UK-England: London. 1987. Lang.: Eng.
2236

Máša, Antonín
Performance/production
Antonín Máša directs his play *Vivisekce (Vivisection)* at Laterna magika. Czechoslovakia: Prague. 1987. Lang.: Cze.
767

Masautso, Phiri
Plays/librettos/scripts
Theme of aggression between fathers and sons: Zambian National Theatre Arts Association festival. Zambia. 1966-1987. Lang.: Eng.
2972

Mascherin, Ginzia
Institutions
First festival of women's work in experimental theatre. UK-Wales: Cardiff. 1986. Lang.: Eng.
1649

Masen, Jacob
Basic theatrical documents
English translations of three plays by Jacob Masen. Germany. 1606-1681. Lang.: Eng.
1556

Mask of Aesop, A
Plays/librettos/scripts
Survey of Robertson Davies' plays. Canada. 1913-1985. Lang.: Eng.
2484

Mask plays
Performance/production
Tükak Teatret and its artistic director Reidar Nilsson present *Inuit—Human Beings*. USA: New York, NY. Denmark: Holstebro. 1975-1983. Lang.: Eng.
2352

Masks
Design/technology
Use and evolution of masks. Lang.: Ita.
299

Masks in popular entertainment. Japan. 110-1500. Lang.: Jap.
350

Exhibit of theatre crafts. Sweden: Gävle. 1987. Lang.: Swe.
365

Artistry of mask-maker Ralph Lee. USA: New York, NY. 1960-1987. Lang.: Eng.
391

Nō masks by Nakamura Naohiko. Japan. 1900-1940. Lang.: Jap.
1497

Use of masks in Venetian theatre. Italy: Venice. 1500-1600. Lang.: Ita.
3309

Masks of Kuei-chou-nou-shi. China, People's Republic of. 700-1986. Lang.: Chi.
3445

Masks in Chinese drama. China, People's Republic of. 1986. Lang.: Chi.
3447

Performance spaces
Original performing area of Korean mask theatre. Korea. 57 B.C.-1987 A.D. Lang.: Kor.
660

Performance space and staging of traditional Korean genres. Korea. Japan. 57 B.C.-1986 A.D. Lang.: Kor.
663

Performance/production
The development of Korean mask theatre. Korea. 57 B.C.-1987 A.D. Lang.: Kor.
847

Audience participation in the development of Korean mask theatre. Korea. 57 B.C.-1987 A.D. Lang.: Kor.
848

Origins, theory of traditional Korean mask theatre. Korea. 57 B.C.-1985 A.D. Lang.: Kor.
858

The masked dance-drama of ancient Korea. Korea. 57 B.C.-1907 A.D. Lang.: Kor.
1484

Walloon carnivals and masks. Belgium. 1800-1987. Lang.: Fre. 3294

Plays/librettos/scripts
The analysis of *Bongsantalchum*, a Korean mask play. Korea. 57 B.C.-1987 A.D. Lang.: Kor.
1145

Analysis of *Yangjusandae nolyee*. Korea. 57 B.C.-1987 A.D. Lang.: Kor.
1488

Reference materials
Major festivals of Belgium: folklore, history, description. Belgium. 1987. Lang.: Fre.
3279

Relation to other fields
Korean mask plays, folklore and puppet theatre. Korea. Japan: Kyushu. 1987. Lang.: Kor.
1246

Descriptive calendar of masked festivals. Austria. 1987. Lang.: Fre.
3299

Training
Using masks to stimulate the imagination when teaching. China, People's Republic of. 1985. Lang.: Chi.
1379

Mason, Bob
Performance/production
Collection of newspaper reviews by London theatre critics. UK-England: London. 1987. Lang.: Eng.
2194

Collection of newspaper reviews by London theatre critics. UK-England: London. 1987. Lang.: Eng.
2243

Mason, Marsha
Performance/production
Two productions of Pinter's *Old Times*. UK-England: London. USA: New York, NY, St. Louis, MO. 1971-1985. Lang.: Eng.
907

McCullers, Carson
Performance/production
Directorial style of Claude Régy. France. 1955-1987. Lang.: Fre.
1762

McDermott, Phelim
Performance/production
Collection of newspaper reviews by London theatre critics. UK-England. 1986. Lang.: Eng.
2144

McDiarmida, Ian
Performance/production
Collection of newspaper reviews by London theatre critics. UK-England: London. 1986. Lang.: Eng.
2077

McDonald, Alan
Performance/production
Collection of newspaper reviews by London theatre critics. UK-England: London. 1986. Lang.: Eng.
2156

McDonald, Anne-Marie
Basic theatrical documents
Review of video productions of *Tosca* and *Dialogues des Carmélites*. Italy: Verona. Australia: Sydney. 1987. Lang.: Eng.
3692

McDonald, Patrick
Performance/production
Interview with playwright Patrick McDonald. Canada: Ottawa, ON. 1987. Lang.: Eng.
1708

McElhinney, Ian
Performance/production
Collection of newspaper reviews by London theatre critics. UK-England: London. 1986. Lang.: Eng.
2059

McGaw, Charles
Performance/production
Beginning text on acting. USA. 1987. Lang.: Eng.
960

McGonagle, Declan
Theory/criticism
Performance artists Declan McGonagle and Alistair MacLennan. UK-Ireland: Belfast. 1975-1987. Lang.: Eng.
3374

McGovern, Barry
Performance/production
Collection of newspaper reviews by London theatre critics. UK-England: London. 1986. Lang.: Eng.
2150

McGrath, John
Performance/production
Relationship of theatre, class and gender. UK-England. USA. 1969-1985. Lang.: Eng.
918
Collection of newspaper reviews by London theatre critics. UK-England: London. 1986. Lang.: Eng.
2079

McGuinness, Frank
Performance/production
TEAM, an educational theatre company. Ireland: Dublin. 1984-1987. Lang.: Eng.
818
Collection of newspaper reviews by London theatre critics. UK-England: London. 1986. Lang.: Eng.
2151
Productions and political philosophy of Field Day Theatre Company. UK-Ireland: Londonderry. 1986-1987. Lang.: Eng.
2309

Training
Funding for youth theatre in Ireland. Ireland. 1979-1987. Lang.: Eng.
1381

McInnes, Allen
Performance/production
The Directors Colloquium: director/playwright relationship. Canada: Calgary, AB. 1987. Lang.: Eng.
747

McIntyre, Clare
Performance/production
Collection of newspaper reviews by London theatre critics. UK-England: London. 1986. Lang.: Eng.
2100

McIrney, Nicholas
Performance/production
Collection of newspaper reviews by London theatre critics. UK-England: London. 1987. Lang.: Eng.
2177

McKay, Malcolm
Performance/production
Collection of newspaper reviews by London theatre critics. UK-England: London. 1987. Lang.: Eng.
2271

McKechnie, Donna
Performance/production
Short history of *A Chorus Line*. USA: New York, NY. 1975-1987. Lang.: Eng.
941

McKellan, Ian
Performance/production
Collection of newspaper reviews by London theatre critics. UK-England. 1987. Lang.: Eng.
2261

McKnight, Michael
Performance/production
Collection of newspaper reviews by London theatre critics. UK-England: London. 1987. Lang.: Eng.
2197

McMaster, Brian
Institutions
Brian McMaster's direction of the Vancouver Opera. Canada: Vancouver, BC. UK-Wales. 1983-1987. Lang.: Eng.
3721
Current strength of opera in Canada. Canada. 1987. Lang.: Eng.
3725

McMillan, Babs
Performance/production
Collection of newspaper reviews by London theatre critics. UK-England: London. 1986. Lang.: Eng.
2152

McMullan, Frank
Performance/production
Influence of a director's initial impressions of a text on a production. Lang.: Eng.
1678

McMurray, Mary
Performance/production
Collection of newspaper reviews by London theatre critics. UK-England: London. 1986. Lang.: Eng.
2105

McNally, Terrence
Plays/librettos/scripts
Terrence McNally discusses playwriting. USA: New York, NY. 1987. Lang.: Eng.
2895

McNamara, Brooks
Performance/production
Musical Theatre Project explores Broadway musical material available in Shubert Archive. USA: New York, NY. 1984-1985. Lang.: Eng.
3666

McNeil, Francis
Performance/production
Collection of newspaper reviews by London theatre critics. UK-England: London. 1987. Lang.: Eng.
2236

McSorley, Gerald
Theory/criticism
Stewart Parker's *Northern Star*. UK-Ireland. 1984. Lang.: Eng. 3065

Me and Mrs. Nobody
Performance/production
Collection of newspaper reviews by London theatre critics. UK-England: London. 1986. Lang.: Eng.
2053

Me and My Girl
Design/technology
Current Broadway shows and their lighting designers. USA: New York, NY. 1987. Lang.: Eng.
460
Lighting reviews for several New York productions. USA: New York, NY. 1987. Lang.: Eng.
474

Meadow, Lynne
Institutions
History of Manhattan Theatre Club. USA: New York, NY. 1969-1987. Lang.: Eng.
1663

Meal, The
Performance/production
Violet Archer festival, premiere of her one-act opera *The Meal*. Canada: Edmonton, AB. 1985. Lang.: Eng.
3757

Mean Tears
Performance/production
Collection of newspaper reviews of London theatre critics. UK-England: London. 1987. Lang.: Eng.
2273

Measure for Measure
Performance/production
Collection of newspaper reviews by London theatre critics. UK-England: London. 1987. Lang.: Eng.
2208

Plays/librettos/scripts
Comparative study of *Measure for Measure* by Shakespeare and the poem *Leda and the Swan* by Yeats. England. 1604-1929. Lang.: Eng.
1116
An analysis of the structure of *Measure for Measure*. England. 1604. Lang.: Eng.
1120

Meckler, Nancy
Performance/production
Collection of newspaper reviews by London theatre critics. UK-England: London. 1987. Lang.: Eng.
2073

Meckler, Nancy — cont'd

Collection of newspaper reviews by London theatre critics. UK-England: London. 1986. Lang.: Eng. 2091

Collection of newspaper reviews by London theatre critics. UK-England: London. 1987. Lang.: Eng. 2174

Meczner, János

Performance/production

Reviews of two plays by István Örkény: *Forgatókönyv (Screenplay)* directed by István Paál and two productions of *Tóték (The Tót Family)* staged by János Meczner and István Pinczés. Hungary: Veszprém, Budapest, Debrecen. 1986-1987. Lang.: Hun. 1880

Medea

Performance/production

Collection of newspaper reviews by London theatre critics. UK-England: London. 1986. Lang.: Eng. 2079

Collection of newspaper reviews by London theatre critics. UK-England: London. 1986. Lang.: Eng. 2105

Collection of newspaper reviews by London theatre critics. UK-England: London. 1987. Lang.: Eng. 2250

Media

SEE ALSO

Classed Entries under MEDIA.

Administration

Ground Zero Theatre Company's project for the homeless. Canada: Toronto, ON. 1987. Lang.: Eng. 6

Interview with Hans Kemna, casting director. Netherlands. 1987. Lang.: Dut. 34

National Actors' Equity conference. USA: New York, NY. 1985. Lang.: Eng. 63

Laws governing music and performance piracy. USA: New York, NY. 1954-1982. Lang.: Eng. 162

Court ruling protecting the copyright of audio-visual works. USA: New York, NY. 1976-1982. Lang.: Eng. 165

Legal issues of record rental and copyright infringement. USA. 1964-1987. Lang.: Eng. 176

Negative effects of injunctions. USA. 1958-1982. Lang.: Eng. 201

Historical look at the Copyright Act. USA. 1984. Lang.: Eng. 206

Legislative remedies for home video recordings of copyrighted works. USA: Los Angeles, CA. 1980-1982. Lang.: Eng. 224

Problems associated with the deregulation of cable television. USA: New York, NY. 1934-1982. Lang.: Eng. 233

Creating human voices and images with digital, holographic techniques: actors' conference. USA: New York, NY. Israel: Tel-Aviv. 1987. Lang.: Eng. 3083

Audience

Repercussions of cinema and television on theatrical language and practice. Europe. 1885-1985. Lang.: Cat. 281

Basic theatrical documents

Review of video productions of *Tosca* and *Dialogues des Carmélites*. Italy: Verona. Australia: Sydney. 1987. Lang.: Eng. 3692

Design/technology

Complete guide to make-up. Italy. 1987. Lang.: Ita. 346

Comparison of roles of sound designer in film and theatrical productions. USA. 1987. Lang.: Eng. 450

Application of the musical instrument digital face. USA. 1987. Lang.: Eng. 3449

Computer and technological breakthroughs for puppetry. USA. 1985-1987. Lang.: Eng. 3962

Institutions

Second City improvisational comedy troupe. USA: Chicago, IL. Canada: Toronto, ON. 1959-1987. Lang.: Eng. 605

Actor, union leader Michajl A. Ul'janov on social changes, their effect on theatre and film. USSR. 1970-1987. Lang.: Rus. 624

Compact disc recordings of Maria Callas's opera performances. 1987. Lang.: Eng. 3705

Review of a production of *Ariadne auf Naxos*. Canada. 1987. Lang.: Eng. 3717

Performance spaces

Telecast of Donizetti's *Lucia di Lammermoor* into a large performing area. Switzerland: Basel. 1986. Lang.: Fre, Ger. 3737

Performance/production

Influence of filmmaker Jean Renoir's techniques in the theatre. France. 1987. Lang.: Eng. 795

History of performance in Italy. Italy. Lang.: Ita. 839

Influence and impact of the electronic media, live theatre experience. USA: Los Angeles, CA. 1987. Lang.: Eng. 959

Stage and screen actor Ljubov' Orlova. USSR: Moscow. 1902-1975. Lang.: Rus. 1055

Memoirs of actress Rina Zelenaja. USSR: Moscow. Lang.: Rus. 1084

Patrice Chéreau and Théâtre des Amandiers create stage and film versions of Čechov's *Platonov*. France: Nanterre. 1982-1987. Lang.: Swe. 1755

Career of actor, director, writer Zoltán Latinovits. Hungary. 1931-1986. Lang.: Hun. 1794

Interview with Péter Andorai. Hungary. 1980-1987. Lang.: Hun. 1799

Autobiography of film and stage director Peter Brook. UK-England. 1946-1987. Lang.: Eng. 2281

Brian Cox's work with the Royal Shakespeare Company. UK-England: Stratford, London. USA: New York, NY. 1968-1987. Lang.: Eng. 2284

Autobiography of director, producer and writer John Houseman. USA: New York, NY. 1935-1985. Lang.: Eng. 2339

Plays of A.M. Volodin on stage and screen. USSR: Moscow, Leningrad. 1950-1987. Lang.: Rus. 2401

History of incorporating film into a theatrical performance. USA: New York, NY. 1922-1987. Lang.: Eng. 3196

Performers Ariel Ashwell and Sigfrido Aguilar discuss their work with Comediantes Pantomima-Teatro. Mexico: Guanajuato. 1980-1982. Lang.: Eng. 3225

Street theatre and mass media. Italy. 1980. Lang.: Ger. 3295

The use of film montage in Chinese theatre. China, People's Republic of. 1986. Lang.: Chi. 3524

Film versions of Puccini's *La Bohème*, Offenbach's *Tales of Hoffmann*. Europe. North America. 1987. Lang.: Eng. 3767

Filming of operas *Tales of Hoffmann* and Menotti's *The Medium*. Europe. 1951-1986. Lang.: Eng. 3768

Evaluation of soprano Maria Meneghini Callas. Greece. Italy. USA. 1923-1977. Lang.: Eng. 3790

Background on Lyric Opera radio broadcast performances. USA: Chicago, IL. 1987. Lang.: Eng. 3832

Background on San Francisco opera radio broadcasts. USA: San Francisco, CA. 1987. Lang.: Eng. 3833

Background on Opera Company of Philadelphia telecast, *Un Ballo in Maschera*. USA: Philadelphia, PA. 1987. Lang.: Eng. 3834

Background on Metropolitan radio broadcast performances. USA: New York, NY. 1987. Lang.: Eng. 3837

Background on Metropolitan radio broadcast performances. USA: New York, NY. 1987. Lang.: Eng. 3838

Background on Metropolitan telecast performances. USA: New York, NY. 1987. Lang.: Eng. 3839

Comparison between the problems of puppeteers and cartoon animators. USA. 1987. Lang.: Eng. 4002

Plays/librettos/scripts

Theme of journeys in German theatre and film. Germany. 1970-1986. Lang.: Fre. 1127

New Afrikaans drama and playwrights. South Africa, Republic of. 1985-1986. Lang.: Afr. 1155

An annual bibliography of works by and about Harold Pinter. UK-England. USA. 1986-1987. Lang.: Eng. 1160

Interview with cartoonist-playwright Jules Feiffer. USA. 1950-1987. Lang.: Eng. 1168

Current American playwriting—link with film and TV, production, economics. USA. 1987. Lang.: Eng. 1176

Interview with playwright Ray Lawler. Australia. Ireland. 1921-1987. Lang.: Eng. 2433

Playwright Michel Vinaver and his works. France. 1927-1987. Lang.: Fre. 2582

Selections from diary of author Ményhert (Melchior) Lengyel. Hungary. 1880-1974. Lang.: Hun. 2634

Characters and the gangster movie form in Thomas Murphy's *The Blue Macushla*. Ireland. 1980-1986. Lang.: Eng. 2647

Stage, radio and television plays of Tom Stoppard. UK-England. 1937-1987. Lang.: Eng. 2788

Stage and screen adaptations of the poetry of Lesja Ukrainka. USSR. 1987. Lang.: Rus. 2971

Successful film versions of Shakespeare's *King Lear*. USA. UK-England. USSR. 1916-1983. Lang.: Eng. 3099

Media — cont'd

Reference materials

New Italian productions in all areas. Italy. 1985-1986. Lang.: Ita.
1204

Yearbook of Italian theatre, television and film. Italy. 1987. Lang.:
Ita.
1206

Relation to other fields

Children's interaction with theatre as compared to television. USA.
1964. Lang.: Eng.
1277

Image of rock singer Madonna in American culture. USA: New
York, NY. UK-England: London. 1985-1987. Lang.: Eng.
3386

Relations to other fields

Brecht's theories on the media's negative impact on the activity and
politics of the public. Germany, East: Berlin, East. 1950. Lang.: Eng.
3197

Theory/criticism

Criticizes newspaper coverage of Montreal theatre awards. Canada:
Montreal, PQ. 1987. Lang.: Fre.
1318

The career of critic Ricciotto Canudo. France. Italy. 1877-1923.
Lang.: Ita.
1330

Impact of cinematic technique on plays by Beckett and Duras.
France. 1977-1987. Lang.: Eng.
3037

Medicine

Performance/production

Use of actors to simulate symptoms at medical conferences. USA.
1987. Lang.: Eng.
3275

Relation to other fields

Shakespeare's use of medical knowledge in his plays. UK-England:
London. 1589-1614. Lang.: Eng.
3004

Medieval Players (London)

Performance/production

Collection of newspaper reviews by London theatre critics. UK-
England: London. 1987. Lang.: Eng.
2229

Medieval theatre

Popular history of theatre. Europe. 500 B.C.-1983 A.D. Lang.: Eng.
1

Audience

Assembly, composition, accommodation and response of spectators to
civic and religious plays. France. 1450-1550. Lang.: Eng.
1534

Basic theatrical documents

English translations of three plays by Jacob Masen. Germany. 1606-
1681. Lang.: Eng.
1556

Design/technology

Scenic representations of Hell. Italy. France. 1300-1399. Lang.: Ita.
349

Performance spaces

Use of space in medieval theatre: outdoor areas, churches. England.
1300-1576. Lang.: Eng.
1668

Reconstructs processional route of *Corpus Christi* performances.
England: York. 1399-1569. Lang.: Eng.
3329

Performance/production

The medieval tournament tradition in the original staging of *The
Castle of Perseverance*. England. 1425. Lang.: Eng.
776

Additions to list of transvestite actors. England. 1510-1519. Lang.:
Eng.
1744

Church condemnation of Roman *ludi*, creative impulse behind
medieval drama. Europe. 160-1578. Lang.: Eng.
1745

Role of the director in the Lucerne Passion play. Switzerland:
Lucerne. 1453-1616. Lang.: Eng.
2030

Modern production of the *Chester Cycle*. UK-England: Chester. 1987.
Lang.: Eng.
2299

Description of Easter processions. Spain: Puente Genil. 1660-1987.
Lang.: Eng.
3332

Plays/librettos/scripts

Comparison between medieval passion plays and Peter Nichols'
Passion Play. 1986. Lang.: Eng.
2429

Analysis of terms and their meanings in the text of the *Chester
Cycle*. England. 1400-1550. Lang.: Eng.
2499

Analysis of medieval Cain and Abel mystery plays. England. 1200-
1576. Lang.: Eng.
2506

Analysis of music contained in medieval plays of the *Fleury
Playbook*. England. 1500-1980. Lang.: Eng.
2507

Two Cornish *Corpus Christi* plays. England. 1350. Lang.: Eng. 2534

Medieval cycle plays as the exception rather than the norm.
England. Lang.: Eng.
2543

Analysis of medieval plays found in the *Fleury Playbook*. Europe.
1300. Lang.: Eng.
2564

Theories of staging the *visitatio sepulchri*. Germany. France. 900-
1600. Lang.: Eng.
2599

Reference materials

Influences on development of medieval theatre. Europe. 1000-1400.
Lang.: Eng.
1201

Rolf Bergmann's catalogue of medieval German drama. Germany.
1986. Lang.: Eng.
1202

Relation to other fields

Overview of French literature including theatre. France. 800-1700.
Lang.: Ita.
2990

Medium, The

Performance/production

Filming of operas *Tales of Hoffmann* and Menotti's *The Medium*.
Europe. 1951-1986. Lang.: Eng.
3768

Meeh, Gregory

Design/technology

Modern dance production *Portraits in Reflection*. USA. 1986. Lang.:
Eng.
396

Mehring, Franz

Institutions

On audience societies Freie Volksbühne and Neue Freie Volksbühne.
Germany: Berlin. 1889-1914. Lang.: Ger.
1616

Mei, Bau-Iue

Performance/production

Interview with Chinese opera actress Mei Bau-Iue. China, People's
Republic of. 1947-1985. Lang.: Chi.
3484

Mei, Lanfang

Performance/production

Interview with Chinese opera actress Mei Bau-Iue. China, People's
Republic of. 1947-1985. Lang.: Chi.
3484

Acting theory of Chinese opera. China, People's Republic of. 1900-
1986. Lang.: Chi.
3500

Meilhac, Henri

Performance/production

The original production of *Carmen*. France: Paris. 1873-1875. Lang.:
Eng.
3773

Meisner, Sanford

Performance/production

Sanford Meisner's method of teaching acting. USA: New York, NY.
1987. Lang.: Eng.
2349

Meister von Palmyra, Der (Master of Palmyra, The)

Plays/librettos/scripts

Comparison of works by Hauptmann and Wilbrandt. Germany:
Berlin. Austria: Vienna. 1889-1987. Lang.: Eng.
2593

Meistersinger von Nürnberg, Die

Performance/production

Development of Wagner's *Die Meistersinger von Nürnberg*. South
Africa, Republic of: Cape Town. Germany, West: Munich. 1868-
1987. Lang.: Eng.
3816

Mejerchol'd, Vsevolod Emiljevič

Basic theatrical documents

Russian symbolist plays and essays. USSR. 1880-1986. Lang.: Eng.
1584

Design/technology

Mejerchol'd's collaboration with artists A. Jakovlev, V. Suchaev.
USSR. 1935-1939. Lang.: Rus.
491

Performance/production

Acting style of Vachtangov. USSR. Canada. 1922-1987. Lang.: Eng.
1009

Links between experimental theatre movement and the Russian
Futurists. USSR. 1920-1929. Lang.: Rus.
1058

Two productions of *Misterija-Buff (Mystery-Bouffe)* by Majakovskij.
USSR. 1918-1921. Lang.: Rus.
2388

Plays/librettos/scripts

Nikolaj Erdmann's plays, relations with major directors. USSR:
Moscow. 1925. Lang.: Rus.
2963

Theory/criticism

Theatre and the infatuation with technology. France. 1987. Lang.:
Fre.
1336

Effect of audiovisual media on theatre. France. 1987. Lang.: Fre.
1339

Reconstruction of Shakespeare in performance. USA. 1987. Lang.:
Eng.
1358

Post-Revolutionary Soviet theatre. USSR: Moscow. 1918-1930. Lang.:
Ger.
3378

Méjzöly, Miklós
Plays/librettos/scripts
Political aspects of Hungarian absurdist drama. Hungary. 1970-1980.
Lang.: Eng.   2632
Melba, Nellie
Design/technology
Controversy over 1901 cylinder recording of *Les Huguenots*. USA.
1901-1987. Lang.: Eng.   3699
Melchior, Lauritz
Performance/production
The Heldentenor in Wagnerian opera. Europe. North America. 1987.
Lang.: Eng.   3770
Melillo, Joe
Administration
Legal difficulties facing producers who present foreign artists and
dance troupes. USA. 1987. Lang.: Eng.   244
Relation to other fields
Protest of US Immigration and Naturalization Service policies by
American presenting organizations. USA. 1986. Lang.: Eng.   1282
Melling, Phil
Performance/production
Collection of newspaper reviews by London theatre critics. UK-
England: London. 1987. Lang.: Eng.   2270
Melodrama
Performance/production
Documentation on melodramatic acting style. France: Paris. 1800-
1830. Lang.: Eng.   791
Ritual and theatrical nature of TV evangelism. USA. 1987. Lang.:
Eng.   3210
Plays/librettos/scripts
Paucity of explorers in nineteenth-century Australian drama.
Australia. 1861-1900. Lang.: Eng.   2440
Analysis of vampire characters in the works of Byron, Polidori and
Planché. England. Italy. France. 1800-1825. Lang.: Eng.   2540
The Non-Smokers by Gianfrancesco Guarnieri. Mexico: Mexico City.
1982-1987. Lang.: Spa.   2697
Freudian reading of Shaw's *Passion, Poison and Petrification*. UK-
England. 1895-1926. Lang.: Eng.   2781
John Lang's collaboration with Tom Taylor on *Plot and Passion*.
UK-England. Australia. 1853. Lang.: Eng.   2785
Study of plays by Henry Arthur Jones. UK-England: London. 1882-
1900. Lang.: Eng.   2790
Historical context for Tom Taylor's *The Ticket-of-Leave Man*. UK-
England. France. 1863.   2801
Influences on *The Voysey Inheritance* by Granville Barker. UK-
England. 1600-1938. Lang.: Eng.   2820
O'Neill's transcendence of melodrama in *A Touch of the Poet* and
A Moon for the Misbegotten. USA. 1922-1947. Lang.: Eng.   2886
Historical fate of melodrama. USSR. 1987. Lang.: Rus.   3420
Theory/criticism
Shift from classical traditions to melodrama. France. 1770-1987.
Lang.: Eng.   1338
Representation of women by Hollywood film industry. USA: Los
Angeles, CA. 1903-1987. Lang.: Eng.   3188
Melody Farm
Institutions
Analysis of co-productions between Saskatoon theatre companies.
Canada: Saskatoon, SK. 1987. Lang.: Eng.   518
Melon
Performance/production
Collection of newspaper reviews by London theatre critics. UK-
England: London. 1987. Lang.: Eng.   2245
Comparison and review of *Melon, Breaking the Code, Alan Turing:
The Secret War* and *My Sister in This House*. UK-England: London.
1987. Lang.: Eng.   2285
Melville, Herman
Plays/librettos/scripts
Influence of Herman Melville on Eugene O'Neill. USA. 1927. Lang.:
Eng.   2888
Menander
Plays/librettos/scripts
Changes in theatre space as a result of New Comedy. Greece:
Athens. Italy: Rome. 400 B.C.-180 A.D. Lang.: Eng.   2625
Theory/criticism
Catalan translation of Lessing's *Hamburgische Dramaturgie*.
Germany: Hamburg. 1767-1769. Lang.: Cat.   3043

Mendelssohn, Francesco von
Performance/production
Weill's realization of the Nazi threat. Germany: Berlin. 1932. Lang.:
Eng.   3626
Meng, Cheng-Shuen
Theory/criticism
Chinese opera dramatist and theoretician Meng Cheng-Shuen. China.
1386-1644. Lang.: Chi.   3589
Menotti, Gian Carlo
Performance/production
Filming of operas *Tales of Hoffmann* and Menotti's *The Medium*.
Europe. 1951-1986. Lang.: Eng.   3768
Mensáros, László
Performance/production
Interview with actor-director László Mensáros. Hungary. 1952-1987.
Lang.: Hun.   1792
Menzel, Jiří
Performance/production
Noises Off by Michael Frayn, directed by Jiří Menzel, Činoherní
klub. Czechoslovakia: Prague. 1987. Lang.: Cze.   765
Mephisto
Performance/production
Collection of newspaper reviews by London theatre critics. UK-
England: London. 1986. Lang.: Eng.   2082
Merbury, Francis
Performance/production
Production of Merbury's *The Marriage of Wit and Wisdom* by
David Parry. Israel: Jerusalem. 1987. Lang.: Eng.   1939
Merce Cunningham Dance Company (New York, NY)
Theory/criticism
Environment and the works of Merce Cunningham and John Cage.
USA. 1962-1987. Lang.: Eng.   1477
Merchant of Venice, The
Design/technology
F.H. Flood's scene design for *The Merchant of Venice*. Ireland:
Dublin. 1985. Lang.: Eng.   1593
Performance/production
Interview with actress Dame Peggy Ashcroft. UK-England. 1935-
1964. Lang.: Eng.   899
István Szőke directs Shakespeare's *Merchant of Venice*, Pécs
National Theatre. Hungary: Pécs. 1987. Lang.: Hun.   1854
Two premieres: Shakespeare, *The Merchant of Venice*, directed by
Árpád Jutacsa Hegyi. Németh's *Villámfénynél (By the Stroke of
Lightning)*, directed by Attila Seprődi Kiss. Hungary: Kecskemét.
1987. Lang.: Hun.   1925
Collection of newspaper reviews by London theatre critics. UK-
England: London. 1986. Lang.: Eng.   2087
Actor Antony Sher talks about his upcoming season at Stratford.
UK-England: Stratford. 1987. Lang.: Eng.   2294
Plays/librettos/scripts
Eighteenth-century alterations to Shakespeare's *The Merchant of
Venice*. England. 1596-1701. Lang.: Eng.   2512
Shakespeare's use of formal self-referential oaths. England. 1594-
1616. Lang.: Eng.   2552
Mercier, Paul
Training
Funding for youth theatre in Ireland. Ireland. 1979-1987. Lang.:
Eng.   1381
Merlin, Joanna
Training
Acting teachers who studied under Michajl Čechov: making the
Technique fit contemporary needs. USA: New York, NY. 1930-1980.
Lang.: Eng.   3082
Mermaid Theatre (London)
Performance spaces
Mermaid Theatre, London home of Royal Shakespeare Company.
UK-England: London. 1959-1987. Lang.: Eng.   671
Performance/production
Collection of newspaper reviews by London theatre critics. UK-
England: London. 1986. Lang.: Eng.   2041
Collection of newspaper reviews by London theatre critics. UK-
England: London. 1987. Lang.: Eng.   2073
Collection of newspaper reviews by London theatre critics. UK-
England: London. 1986. Lang.: Eng.   2108
Collection of newspaper reviews by London theatre critics. UK-
England: London. 1987. Lang.: Eng.   2200

Mermaid Theatre (London) — cont'd

Collection of newspaper reviews by London theatre critics. UK-England: London. 1987. Lang.: Eng.   2211

Collection of newspaper reviews by London theatre critics. UK-England: London. 1987. Lang.: Eng.   2219

Collection of newspaper reviews by London theatre critics. UK-England: London. 1987. Lang.: Eng.   2237

Collection of newspaper reviews by London theatre critics. UK-England: London. 1987. Lang.: Eng.   2264

Collection of newspaper reviews by London theatre critics. UK-England: London. 1987. Lang.: Eng.   2272

Merő, Béla
Performance/production
Mihály Vörösmarty's 'fairy-play' *Csongor and Tünde* directed by Béla Merő at Hevesi Sándor Színház. Hungary: Zalaegerszeg. 1987. Lang.: Hun.   1926

Merola, Gaetano
Performance/production
Opera conductors who also conduct in Broadway musicals. USA: New York, NY. 1980-1987. Lang.: Eng.   3847

Mérope
Plays/librettos/scripts
Techniques, themes, characters and dramaturgy of Voltaire. France. 1718-1778. Lang.: Eng.   2590

Merrick, David
Administration
Equity wins court battle against producer David Merrick. USA: New York, NY. 1982. Lang.: Eng.   92

Institutions
Record producer Bruce Yeko's accomplishments. USA: New York, NY. 1962-1981. Lang.: Eng.   3625

Performance/production
History of musical version, *Breakfast at Tiffany's*. USA: New York, NY, Philadelphia, PA, Boston, MA. 1958-1966. Lang.: Eng.   3644

Merrill, Bob
Performance/production
History and review of 1967 musical *Henry, Sweet Henry*. USA: New York, NY. 1967. Lang.: Eng.   3642

History of musical version, *Breakfast at Tiffany's*. USA: New York, NY, Philadelphia, PA, Boston, MA. 1958-1966. Lang.: Eng.   3644

Merrow, Bill
Performance/production
Collection of newspaper reviews by London theatre critics. UK-England: London. 1987. Lang.: Eng.   2221

Merry Wives of Windsor, The
Performance/production
Collection of newspaper reviews by London theatre critics. UK. 1987. Lang.: Eng.   2031

Plays/librettos/scripts
Analysis and success of Boito's libretto for Verdi's opera *Falstaff*. Italy. 1893. Lang.: Eng.   3923

Mesjats v derevne (Month in the Country, A)
Performance/production
Collection of newspaper reviews by London theatre critics. UK-England: London. 1987. Lang.: Eng.   2260

Message of the One-Eyed Magician, The
Performance/production
Three plays performed by the Dutch Orkater ensemble company. Netherlands. 1986. Lang.: Hun.   861

Mestre i Barceló, Bartomeu
Plays/librettos/scripts
Analysis of 51 short farces written in Majorca. Spain-Catalonia. 1701-1850. Lang.: Cat.   2731

Metadrama
Plays/librettos/scripts
The metadramatic nature of Thomas Bernhard's plays. Germany, West. 1974-1983. Lang.: Eng.   2616

Metamorphosis
Performance/production
Collection of newspaper reviews by London theatre critics. UK-England: London. 1986. Lang.: Eng.   2108

Metatheatre
Plays/librettos/scripts
Play within a play in *Blood Relations* by Sharon Pollock. Canada. 1987. Lang.: Eng.   2489

Metcalf, John
Training
Changes in music teaching methods at the Banff Centre. Canada: Banff, AB. 1933-1987. Lang.: Eng.   3950

Methodology
Audience
Sociological issues in theatre research. USSR. 1980-1987. Lang.: Rus.   294

Performance/production
Reproduction and discussion of an annotated 'score' by director Hillar Liitoja. Canada: Toronto, ON. 1987. Lang.: Eng.   744

Plays/librettos/scripts
Editorial discussion of contemporary theatre. North America. 1987. 1987. Lang.: Eng.   1152

Critical methodology for studying Beckett's works. UK-England. 1930-1987. Lang.: Eng.   2814

Research/historiography
Shakespeare texts: discussion of bibliographic methodology. 1987. Lang.: Eng.   1297

Critical history of *Julius Caesar*. England. 1599-1987. Lang.: Eng.   1299

Essays on theatre research in Italy. Italy. 1986. Lang.: Ita.   1300

Methodology of Soviet theatre science. USSR. 1920-1929. Lang.: Rus.   1304

Research methods on origins and tradition of liturgical drama. Germany. 1000-1400. Lang.: Ita.   3010

Overview of Canadian research on twentieth-century Irish drama. Ireland. UK-Ireland. Canada. 1891-1983. Lang.: Eng.   3011

Methodology of comparative drama. Korea. 1970. Lang.: Kor.   3012

Views of the literary relationship between William Archer and Henrik Ibsen. UK-England. 1889-1919. Lang.: Eng.   3013

Sociological view of American and English Shakespeare studies. UK-England. USA. 1900-1987. Lang.: Chi.   3014

Conditions of northern Chinese classical drama. China. 1227-1644. Lang.: Chi.   3584

Influences on Wagner's *Ring* cycle. Germany: Dresden. 1813-1883. Lang.: Eng.   3948

Theory/criticism
Theory and practice in theatre criticism. 1987. Lang.: Eng.   1307

Methven, Eleanor
Relation to other fields
Interview with founders of the Charabanc Theatre Company. UK-Ireland. 1970-1987. Lang.: Eng.   1260

Metro Theatre (Johannesburg)
Performance spaces
Theatres built, influences on design. South Africa, Republic of: Johannesburg. 1887-1940. Lang.: Afr.   667

Metro-Goldwyn-Mayer Film Studio
Administration
Lee Shubert's role in the formation of the American film industry. USA: New York, NY. 1914-1924. Lang.: Eng.   3123

Metropolitan Opera (New York, NY)
Administration
Career of Sir Rudolph Bing, challenges of managing the Metropolitan Opera. USA: New York, NY. 1950-1972. Lang.: Eng.   3682

Design/technology
Work of noted set designer and technological innovator Josef Svoboda. Czechoslovakia: Prague. 1940-1987. Lang.: Eng.   305

Lighting reviews for several New York productions. USA: New York, NY. 1987. Lang.: Eng.   474

Gil Wechsler, lighting designer, Metropolitan Opera. USA: New York, NY. 1967-1987. Lang.: Eng.   3701

Performance/production
Metropolitan/Deutsche Grammophon recording, Wagner's *Ring*, conducted by James Levine. USA: New York, NY. 1987. Lang.: Eng.   3114

Interview with conductor Manuel Rosenthal. France: Paris. 1904-1987. Lang.: Eng.   3774

Soprano Renata Scotto directs Metropolitan Opera production of *Madama Butterfly*. USA: New York, NY. 1987. Lang.: Eng.   3836

Background on Metropolitan telecast performances. USA: New York, NY. 1987. Lang.: Eng.   3839

Mezzo soprano Risë Stevens. USA: New York, NY. Lang.: Eng.   3856

Metropolitan Opera archives. USA: New York, NY. 1883-1987. Lang.: Eng.   3863

Expanded schedule of outdoor opera performances by Metropolitan Opera. USA: New York, NY. 1967-1987. Lang.: Eng.   3864

Metropolitan Opera (New York, NY) — cont'd

Relation to other fields
Cultural exchange pacts made between the USA and the Soviet Union and China. USA: Washington, DC. USSR: Moscow. China, People's Republic of: Peking. 1987. Lang.: Eng. 1291

Mettawee River Company (Salem, NY)
Design/technology
Artistry of mask-maker Ralph Lee. USA: New York, NY. 1960-1987. Lang.: Eng. 391

Meyer, Michael
Performance/production
Collection of newspaper reviews by London theatre critics. UK-England: London. 1986. Lang.: Eng. 2155

Meyerbeer, Giacomo
Design/technology
Controversy over 1901 cylinder recording of *Les Huguenots*. USA. 1901-1987. Lang.: Eng. 3699

Mapleson cylinders: controversy over *Les Huguenots*. USA: New York, NY. 1947. Lang.: Eng. 3700

Performance/production
Florentine theatrical culture. Italy: Florence. 1800-1900. Lang.: Ita. 832

Plays/librettos/scripts
Operas that contain Indian-related themes and music. India. Europe. 1730-1904. Lang.: Eng. 3914

Meyerhold, V.E.
SEE
Mejerchol'd, Vsevolod Emiljèvič.

Mgadi, Bheki
Performance/production
Content and North American reception of *Asinimali! (We Have No Money!)* by Mbongeni Ngema. Canada. South Africa, Republic of. 1987. Lang.: Eng. 1715

Mhangwane, Sam
Relation to other fields
Influences of Black political and economic life on literature, performance. South Africa, Republic of. 1970-1987. Lang.: Eng. 1252

Miami Vice
Performance/production
Analysis of art of television and comparison to live theatre. USA. 1950-1987. Lang.: Eng. 3194

Micallef, Karina
Performance/production
Collection of newspaper reviews by London theatre critics. UK-England: London. 1986. Lang.: Eng. 2155

Michaels, Stuart
Performance/production
Golden Fleece, Ltd. bridges classical music, opera and musical theatre. USA: New York, NY. 1987. Lang.: Eng. 3412

Michaelson, Jon
Performance/production
Review of August Wilson's play, *Ma Rainey's Black Bottom*. Canada: Toronto, ON. 1987. Lang.: Eng. 737

Michaud, Marie
Performance/production
Personnel associated with production of Lepage's *La Trilogie des dragons*. Canada. 1987. Lang.: Fre. 1713

Michel Angelo
Theory/criticism
Comparison of Ball's *Michelangelo's Nose* and Hebbel's *Michel Angelo*. Germany. 1886-1927. Lang.: Eng. 3042

Michell, Roger
Performance/production
Collection of newspaper reviews by London theatre critics. UK-England: London. 1986. Lang.: Eng. 2111

Micone, Marco
Plays/librettos/scripts
Plays by Micone, Saddlemyer, Thompson, Wyatt. Canada. 1958-1985. Lang.: Eng. 2481

Work of playwright Marco Micone. Canada. 1982-1985. Lang.: Eng. 2483

Microscope Stage
SEE
Mikroszkóp Szinpad.

Middleton, Alasdair
Performance/production
Collection of newspaper reviews by London theatre critics. UK-England: London. 1987. Lang.: Eng. 2237

Middleton, Thomas
Performance/production
Shakespeare and contemporaries: tradition, intertextuality in performance. England. 1607-1987. Lang.: Eng. 1740

New interpretation of Jacobean theatre. England: London. 1596-1633. Lang.: Eng. 1743

Collection of newspaper reviews by London theatre critics. UK-England: London. 1987. Lang.: Eng. 2211

Plays/librettos/scripts
Female characters in city comedy who suffer from bladder incontinence. 1599-1632. Lang.: Eng. 2427

Utopian ideas in Tudor and Stuart playwrights. England. 1600-1650. Lang.: Ger. 2522

Theory/criticism
Trollope's writings on Elizabethan and Jacobean drama. UK-England. 1866-1882. Lang.: Eng. 3063

Midgley, Robin
Performance/production
Collection of newspaper reviews by London theatre critics. UK-England: London. 1987. Lang.: Eng. 2235

Midnight in Moscow
Performance/production
Collection of newspaper reviews by London theatre critics. UK-England: London. 1986. Lang.: Eng. 2057

Midsummer Marriage, The
Plays/librettos/scripts
Tippett's influence on contemporary opera. 1946-1987. Lang.: Eng. 3888

Midsummer Night's Dream, A
Design/technology
Action Design, a new theory of scenography emerging in Eastern Europe. Czechoslovakia: Prague. 1980-1987. Lang.: Eng. 315

Review of *Bartholomew Fair* and *A Midsummer Night's Dream*. UK-England: London. 1987. Lang.: Eng. 1598

Performance/production
Two German productions of *A Midsummer Night's Dream*. Germany, West. 1970-1975. Lang.: Eng. 801

English Shakespearean productions. UK-England: London, Manchester, Stratford. 1985-1986. Lang.: Eng. 917

'Showing' is an essential part of all acting. Europe. 1590-1987. Lang.: Eng. 1746

Change from sociopolitical emphasis to individual themes in productions of *A Midsummer Night's Dream*. Germany, East. 1960-1980. Lang.: Eng. 1782

Shakespeare's *A Midsummer Night's Dream* staged by Tibor Csizmadia. Hungary: Eger, Szolnok. 1986. Lang.: Hun. 1881

Collection of newspaper reviews by London theatre critics. UK-England: London. 1986. Lang.: Eng. 2093

Collection of newspaper reviews by London theatre critics. UK-England: London. 1987. Lang.: Eng. 2236

Collection of newspaper reviews by London theatre critics. UK-England: London. 1987. Lang.: Eng. 2244

Relation to other fields
Experimental theatre course, Assoc. Internationale pour la Sémiologie du Spectacle. Belgium: Brussels. France: Paris. Denmark: Odense. 1983-1985. Lang.: Fre. 1219

Theory/criticism
Refutes Frye's analysis of Shakespeare's *A Midsummer Night's Dream*. USA. 1987. Lang.: Eng. 3075

Midummer Night's Dream, A
Performance/production
Collection of newspaper reviews by London theatre critics. UK-England: London. 1986. Lang.: Eng. 2123

Mikado, The
Performance/production
Collection of newspaper reviews by New York critics. USA: New York, NY. 1987. Lang.: Eng. 2324

Plays/librettos/scripts
Opera adaptations for Broadway with African-American artists. USA: New York, NY. 1935-1987. Lang.: Eng. 3932

Mike's Talent Show
Performance/production
Development of Michael Smith from painter to performance artist. USA. 1987. Lang.: Eng. 3369

Miki, Minoru
Plays/librettos/scripts
Unique style of modern Japanese Opera. Japan. 1975-1987. Lang.:
Eng.   3928

Mikó, István
Performance/production
Imre Halasi directs *Sári bíró (Judge Sári)* by Zsigmond Móricz,
music by István Mikó, at Kisvarda Castle Theatre. Hungary:
Kisvárda. 1987. Lang.: Hun.   1845

Mil'tinis, Ju.
Performance/production
Biography of director Ju. Mil'tinis. USSR. 1907-1987. Lang.: Rus.
                                                                                       2395

Milagre na Cela (Miracle in the Cell)
Plays/librettos/scripts
Theme of torture in Brazilian drama. Brazil. 1964-1985. Lang.: Por.
                                                                                       2456

Miles, Julia
Plays/librettos/scripts
Conference on women in theatre, emphasis on playwriting. USA.
1987. Lang.: Eng.   1161

Milk Train Doesn't Stop Here Anymore, The
Performance/production
Collection of newspaper reviews by New York theatre critics. USA:
New York, NY. 1987. Lang.: Eng.   2313

Plays/librettos/scripts
Interview with actresses Elizabeth Ashley and Marian Seldes. USA:
New York, NY. 1987. Lang.: Eng.   2898

Mill on the Floss, The
Performance/production
Collection of newspaper reviews by London theatre critics. UK-
England: London. 1987. Lang.: Eng.   2267

Millan, Jim
Performance/production
Toronto directors discuss their training and craft. Canada: Toronto,
ON. 1987. Lang.: Eng.   730

Millàs-Raurell, Josep
Plays/librettos/scripts
General history of Catalan literature, including theatre. Spain-
Catalonia. 1902-1961. Lang.: Cat.   1157

Miller, Arthur
Administration
Recent court decision over the IRS tax laws affecting writers'
deductions. USA. 1987. Lang.: Eng.   3241

Performance/production
Géza Tordy as Willy Loman in Arthur Miller's *Death of a
Salesman* directed, as *Az ügynök halála*, by János Szikora at
Vigszinház. Hungary: Budapest. 1987. Lang.: Hun.   1797

Arthur Miller's *Death of a Salesman* directed by János Szikora at
Vígszinház. Hungary: Budapest. 1987. Lang.: Hun.   1869

Review of actors Géza Tordy, Géza Hegedüs D. and Attila Kaszás
in Arthur Miller's *Death of a Salesman*. Hungary: Budapest. 1987.
Lang.: Hun.   1893

Six plays of the Tokyo season, focus on director Betsuyaku Minoru.
Japan: Tokyo. 1986. Lang.: Jap.   1966

Collection of newspaper reviews by London theatre critics. UK.
1987. Lang.: Eng.   2031

Collection of newspaper reviews by London theatre critics. UK-
England: London. 1986. Lang.: Eng.   2047

Collection of newspaper reviews by London theatre critics. UK-
England: London. 1986. Lang.: Eng.   2132

Collection of newspaper reviews by London theatre critics. UK-
England. 1986. Lang.: Eng.   2144

Collection of newspaper reviews by London theatre critics. UK-
England: London. 1987. Lang.: Eng.   2183

Collection of newspaper reviews by London theatre critics. UK-
England: London. 1987. Lang.: Eng.   2258

Collection of newspaper reviews by New York theatre critics. USA:
New York, NY. 1987. Lang.: Eng.   2321

Collection of newspaper reviews by New York theatre critics. USA:
New York, NY. 1987. Lang.: Eng.   2326

Critique of the 1984 Broadway production of *Death of a Salesman*.
USA: New York, NY. 1984. Lang.: Eng.   2330

Plays/librettos/scripts
Contemporary Japanese plays about crime. Japan: Tokyo. 1986.
Lang.: Jap.   2681

One-act play: brief history and recent productions. USA. 1930-1987.
Lang.: Eng.   2849

Development of themes and characters in plays of Sam Shepard.
USA. 1960-1987. Lang.: Eng.   2853

Interview with playwright Arthur Miller. USA. 1944-1987. Lang.:
Eng.   2868

Theory/criticism
Perceptions of tragedy and new perspective on its analysis. USA.
UK-England. Greece. 500 B.C.-1987 A.D. Lang.: Eng.   3066

Miller, Jason
Plays/librettos/scripts
Korean views of American society based on plays of Howard
Sackler, Charles Fuller and Jason Miller. USA. 1969-1982. Lang.:
Kor.   2837

Miller, Jonathan
Performance/production
Collection of newspaper reviews by London theatre critics. UK-
England: London. 1986. Lang.: Eng.   2154

Collection of newspaper reviews by London theatre critics. UK-
England: London. 1987. Lang.: Eng.   2190

Collection of newspaper reviews by London theatre critics. UK-
England: London. 1987. Lang.: Eng.   2254

Collection of newspaper reviews by London theatre critics. UK-
England: London. 1987. Lang.: Eng.   2255

Plays/librettos/scripts
Successful film versions of Shakespeare's *King Lear*. USA. UK-
England. USSR. 1916-1983. Lang.: Eng.   3099

Miller, Les
Performance/production
Collection of newspaper reviews by London theatre critics. UK-
England: London. 1987. Lang.: Eng.   2209

Miller, Roger
Administration
Influence of TV ads on success of Broadway plays. USA: New
York, NY. 1984-1987. Lang.: Eng.   179

Millionairess, The
Plays/librettos/scripts
The problem of capitalism in Shaw's *The Millionairess*. UK-England.
1936-1952. Lang.: Eng.   2811

Mills, John
Administration
Theatrical season of 1723 at the Drury Lane Theatre. England:
London. 1723. Lang.: Eng.   21

Milner, Arthur
Basic theatrical documents
Playtext of *Zero Hour* by Arthur Milner. Costa Rica: San José.
1987. Lang.: Eng.   1550

Performance/production
Interview with playwright Patrick McDonald. Canada: Ottawa, ON.
1987. Lang.: Eng.   1708

Plays/librettos/scripts
The historical radio drama *All I Get is Static!*. Canada: Ottawa,
ON. 1984. Lang.: Eng.   3096

Milner, Ron
Institutions
The formation of the North Carolina Black Repertory Company.
USA: Winston-Salem, NC. 1979-1987. Lang.: Eng.   1666

Performance/production
Collection of newspaper reviews by New York theatre critics. USA:
New York, NY. 1987. Lang.: Eng.   2316

Milton, John
Plays/librettos/scripts
Comparison of works of Milton and Dryden. England. 1608-1700.
Lang.: Eng.   2546

Milwaukee Repertory Theatre (Milwaukee, WI)
Institutions
Current trends in American theatre. USA. 1967-1987. Lang.: Eng.
                                                                                       621

Plays/librettos/scripts
Research for *An American Journey* produced by Milwaukee
Repertory. USA: Milwaukee, WI. 1978-1987. Lang.: Eng.   2862

Three feminist productions of plays by Henrik Ibsen. USA. 1987.
Lang.: Eng.   2899

Mime
SEE ALSO
Pantomime.

Classed Entries under MIME.

Mime — cont'd

Performance/production

Career of actor Angelo Musco. Italy. 1872-1937. Lang.: Ita. 841

Role of theatre in the face of political turmoil. Nicaragua: Managua. Uganda. 1987. Lang.: Eng. 864

Review of six-week dance festival representing forms of dance in South Africa. South Africa, Republic of: Durban. 1986. Lang.: Eng. 1409

Influence of *nō* theatre on director Jean-Louis Barrault and his colleagues. France. 1910-1982. Lang.: Eng. 1498

Popular account of comic entertainers. Europe. North America. Australia. 480 B.C.-1986 A.D. Lang.: Eng. 3256

The 4th International Festival of Street Theatres. Poland: Jelenia Góra. 1986. Lang.: Eng, Fre. 3355

Minamikouchi banzai ichiza (Tokyo)

Performance/production

Space and sign in various Tokyo productions. Japan: Tokyo. 1987. Lang.: Jap. 1959

Minelli, Liza

Performance/production

Two productions of *Flora, the Red Menace*. USA: New York, NY. 1965-1987. Lang.: Eng. 3640

Minelli, Vincent

Theory/criticism

Representation of women by Hollywood film industry. USA: Los Angeles, CA. 1903-1987. Lang.: Eng. 3188

Minetta Lane Theatre (New York, NY)

Performance/production

Collection of newspaper reviews by New York theatre critics. USA: New York, NY. 1987. Lang.: Eng. 2315

Minetti

Performance/production

'Showing' is an essential part of all acting. Europe. 1590-1987. Lang.: Eng. 1746

Plays/librettos/scripts

The metadramatic nature of Thomas Bernhard's plays. Germany, West. 1974-1983. Lang.: Eng. 2616

Mingei (Tokyo)

Performance/production

Four Tokyo productions in light of ideas of Betsuyaku Minoru. Japan: Tokyo. 1987. Lang.: Jap. 1950

Discussion of four Tokyo productions. Japan: Tokyo. 1944-1987. Lang.: Jap. 1963

Plays/librettos/scripts

Contemporary Japanese plays about crime. Japan: Tokyo. 1986. Lang.: Jap. 2681

Miniature Theatre (Moscow)

SEE

Teat'r Minjatjur.

Minna von Barnhelm

Performance/production

Collection of newspaper reviews by London theatre critics. UK-England: London. 1987. Lang.: Eng. 2213

Minnelli, Liza

Performance/production

Four approaches to the role of Sally Bowles in *Cabaret*. USA: New York, NY. Germany. 1966-1987. Lang.: Eng. 968

Minninger, Joan

Institutions

Activities of Dramatists' Guild include writer's-block workshop. USA: New York, NY. 1987. Lang.: Eng. 585

Minskoff Theatre (New York, NY)

Performance/production

Collection of newspaper reviews by New York theatre critics. USA: New York, NY. 1987. Lang.: Eng. 2316

Minstrel of Clare, The

Plays/librettos/scripts

Analysis of the plays and songs of Irish-American musical theatre star Chauncey Olcott. USA. 1893-1918. Lang.: Eng. 3671

Mintz, Israel

Institutions

Interview with Israel Mintz on the HaBimah Theatre. Israel: Tel Aviv. USSR: Moscow. 1922-1987. Lang.: Heb. 1623

Miracle, The

Performance/production

Christmas pantomime *The Miracle* directed by Max Reinhardt. UK-England: London. 1911. Lang.: Eng. 3236

Miraculous Mandarin, The

SEE

Csodálatos mandarin, A.

Mirošničenko, N.

Plays/librettos/scripts

Playwrights discuss problems of one-act play. USSR. 1987. Lang.: Rus. 2935

Misalliance

Performance/production

Collection of newspaper reviews by London theatre critics. UK-England: London. 1986. Lang.: Eng. 2064

Philip Bosco's portrayals of characters in the plays of George Bernard Shaw. USA. 1987. Lang.: Eng. 2335

Plays/librettos/scripts

Transfiguration in Shaw's *Misalliance*, *Saint Joan* and *Major Barbara*. 1986. Lang.: Eng. 2413

Shaw's *Misalliance* as a Freudian dream play. UK-England. 1909-1911. Lang.: Eng. 2826

Misanthrope, Le (Misanthrope, The)

Performance/production

Soviet tour of Comédie-Française: Jean-Pierre Vincent directs Molière's *Le Misanthrope*. France. USSR. 1980-1987. Lang.: Rus. 1769

Mišarin, Aleksand'r

Performance/production

Overview of 1986-1987 Moscow theatre season. USSR: Moscow. 1986-1987. Lang.: Eng. 1039

Miscellaneous texts

Basic theatrical documents

Percy family records in relation to Elizabethan theatre. England. 1582-1639. Lang.: Eng. 296

Michajl Bulgakov's letters about theatrical life in Moscow. USSR: Moscow. 1924-1931. Lang.: Rus. 298

Texts on dramatic theory by nineteenth-century authors. Germany. 1794-1906. Lang.: Ger. 1555

Performance/production

Brief historical sketch of Chinese opera. China, People's Republic of. 1644-1987. Lang.: Chi. 3486

Plays/librettos/scripts

Letters of Pier Maria Rosso di San Secondo to Enzo Ferrieri. Italy: Milan. 1924-1925. Lang.: Ita. 1137

Misérables, Les

Design/technology

Current Broadway shows and their lighting designers. USA: New York, NY. 1987. Lang.: Eng. 460

Lighting reviews for some New York productions. USA: New York, NY. 1987. Lang.: Eng. 472

Performance/production

Actor discusses Equity exchanges for *Les Misérables*. USA: New York, NY. UK-England: London. 1987. Lang.: Eng. 926

Collection of newspaper reviews by New York theatre critics. USA: New York, NY. 1987. Lang.: Eng. 2323

Reviews of *Rigoletto*, Lloyd Webber's *Requiem*, *Les Misérables* and the Hungarian Mass of the Tolcsvays. Hungary: Szeged. 1987. Lang.: Hun. 3400

Miklós Szinetár directs *Les Misérables* at Rock Szinház. Hungary: Budapest. 1987. Lang.: Hun. 3630

Broadway musical's shift from song and dance to aria and recitative. USA: New York, NY. 1956-1984. Lang.: Eng. 3655

Mishima, Yukio

Performance/production

Collection of newspaper reviews by London theatre critics. UK-England: London. 1987. Lang.: Eng. 2265

Miskolci Nemzeti Szinház (Miskolc)

Institutions

Evaluation of the theatrical season by a city official. Hungary: Miskolc. 1986-1987. Lang.: Hun. 537

Performance/production

Imre Csiszár directs Bertolt Brecht's *Leben des Galilei (The Life of Galileo)* at the National Theatre. Hungary: Miskolc. 1987. Lang.: Hun. 1826

Reviews of two Anouilh plays: *Eurydice* directed by János Szűcs, *Colombe* directed by Mátyás Giricz. Hungary: Miskolc, Budapest. 1987. Lang.: Hun. 1827

Péter Blaskó in the title role of Brecht's *Leben des Galilei (The Life of Galileo)* directed as *Galilei élete* by Imre Csiszár at Miskolc National Theatre. Hungary: Miskolc. 1987. Lang.: Hun. 1839

Miskolci Nemzeti Szinház (Miskolc) — cont'd

Anouilh's *Eurydice*, Vian's *Tête de Méduse (Medusa Head)* at National Theatre of Miskolc. Hungary: Miskolc. 1987. Lang.: Hun.
1888

Imre Csiszár's award-winning production of *Galileo élete*: Brecht's *Life of Galileo*. Hungary: Miskolc. 1987. Lang.: Hun.
1889

Interview with director Imre Csiszár. Hungary: Miskolc. 1986-1987. Lang.: Hun.
1892

Le jeu de l'amour et du hasard (The Game of Love and Chance) by Marivaux directed at National Theatre by Péter Valló as *A szerelem és véletten játéka*. Hungary: Miskolc. 1987. Lang.: Hun.
1916

Miss Firecracker Contest, The
Performance/production
Examination of language in Beth Henley's *The Miss Firecracker Contest*. Mexico: Mexico City. 1987. Lang.: Spa.
1974

Collection of newspaper reviews by London theatre critics. UK-England: London. 1986. Lang.: Eng.
2110

Miss Julie
SEE
Fröken Julie.

Missing Links
Performance/production
Collection of newspaper reviews by London theatre critics. UK-England: London. 1987. Lang.: Eng.
2186

Mission, The
SEE
Auftrag, Der.

Mister Knight
Performance/production
Bruce Ellison directs his *Mister Knight* at Théâtre de la Mandragore. Belgium: Brussels. 1986. Lang.: Fre.
1685

Misterija-Buff (Mystery-Bouffe)
Performance/production
Two productions of *Misterija-Buff (Mystery-Bouffe)* by Majakovskij. USSR. 1918-1921. Lang.: Rus.
2388

Misterio del ramo de rosas (Mystery of the Rose Bouquet)
Performance/production
Collection of newspaper reviews by London theatre critics. UK-England: London. 1987. Lang.: Eng.
2274

Mistress of the Inn
SEE
Locandiera, La.

Mitchell, Adrian
Performance/production
Collection of newspaper reviews by London theatre critics. UK-England: London. 1986. Lang.: Eng.
2050

Collection of newspaper reviews by London theatre critics. UK-England: London. 1987. Lang.: Eng.
2259

Mitchell, Ann
Performance/production
Collection of newspaper reviews by London theatre critics. UK-England: London. 1986. Lang.: Eng.
2127

Mitchell, David
Design/technology
Design problems of simulating a circus for *Barnum*. USA: Memphis, TN. 1986. Lang.: Eng.
3621

Mitchell, Leona
Performance/production
Profile, soprano Leona Mitchell. USA: New York, NY. 1940-1987. Lang.: Eng.
3860

Mitchell, Maggie
Performance/production
Carte-de-visite actors' photographs preserve acting styles. UK-England. France. USA. 1850-1920. Lang.: Eng.
916

Mitchell, Roy
Institutions
Elizabeth Sterling Haynes and the Little Theatre movement. Canada. 1916-1957. Lang.: Eng.
1603

Mitchell, W.O.
Basic theatrical documents
Collection of radio plays produced by Andrew Allan. Canada. 1942-1955. Lang.: Eng.
3109

Miti, Pompilio
Performance/production
Actors and institutions of eighteenth-century Venice. Italy: Venice. 1700-1800. Lang.: Ita.
3312

Mitmacher, Der (Mythmaker, The)
Plays/librettos/scripts
Chance in the plays of P.G. du Plessis and Friedrich Dürrenmatt. South Africa, Republic of. Switzerland. 1987. Lang.: Afr.
1153

Mittelpunkt, Hillel
Basic theatrical documents
English translation of *Buba* by Hillel Mittelpunkt. Israel. 1987. Lang.: Eng.
1559

Mitzi E. Newhouse Theatre (New York, NY)
Performance/production
Collection of newspaper reviews by New York theatre critics. USA: New York, NY. 1987. Lang.: Eng.
2323

Collection of newspaper reviews by New York theatre critics. USA: New York, NY. 1987. Lang.: Eng.
2326

Mixed entertainment
Administration
Long-term planning in artistic culture. USSR. 1987. Lang.: Rus. 263

Mixed Entertainment
SEE ALSO
Classed Entries under MIXED ENTERTAINMENT.
Design/technology
Restoration of the stage machinery at the Grand Theatre. UK-Wales: Llandudno. 1901-1987. Lang.: Eng.
381

Design problems of simulating a circus for *Barnum*. USA: Memphis, TN. 1986. Lang.: Eng.
3621

Rigging special circus effects for *Barnum*. USA. 1986. Lang.: Eng.
3622
Performance/production
The medieval tournament tradition in the original staging of *The Castle of Perseverance*. England. 1425. Lang.: Eng.
776

Théâtre de la Jeune Lune, its origins and influences. USA: Minneapolis, MN. France: Paris. 1980-1987. Lang.: Eng.
977

Additions to list of transvestite actors. England. 1510-1519. Lang.: Eng.
1744

Life Service Theatre experiment in topical theatre. Finland: Oulu. 1986. Lang.: Swe.
1749

Exhibition catalogue: popular theatre in Catalan. France. 1415-1987. Lang.: Cat, Fre.
1750

Mime troupe Panopticon. Sweden: Stockholm. 1985-1987. Lang.: Swe.
3226
Relation to other fields
Assessment of arts on television. UK-England: London. 1983-1987. Lang.: Eng.
3216
Theory/criticism
Re-evaluation of Brecht's alienation effect in the context of contemporary performances. 1960-1970. Lang.: Eng.
1310

Mixed media
SEE ALSO
Classed Entries under MEDIA.
Administration
Ground Zero Theatre Company's project for the homeless. Canada: Toronto, ON. 1987. Lang.: Eng.
6
Design/technology
The impact of twentieth-century technology on theatre. Canada. 1900-1987. Lang.: Fre.
302

The use and development of special effects in the theatre. Canada. 1977-1987. Lang.: Fre.
303

Effects of mixed media on traditional dramatic components of theatre. Europe. 1900-1987. Lang.: Fre.
318

Effects of new technologies on theatre. Canada. 1969-1987. Lang.: Fre.
3202

Dennis O'Sullivan's work with mixed media. Canada. 1986. Lang.: Fre.
3203
Relations to other fields
Brecht's theories on the media's negative impact on the activity and politics of the public. Germany, East: Berlin, East. 1950. Lang.: Eng.
3197

Mnouchkine, Ariane
Performance/production
Eastern theatre forms in Western artists' productions. Canada: Vancouver, BC. 1987. Lang.: Eng.
725

Productions by directors Patrice Chéreau, Claude Régy, Ariane Mnouchkine. France. 1980-1987. Lang.: Rus.
792

Collection of newspaper reviews by London theatre critics. UK-England: London. 1986. Lang.: Eng.
2082

Mnouchkine, Ariane — cont'd

Review of Ariane Mnouchkine's film *Molière*. France. 1987. Lang.:
Hun.   3150

Plays/librettos/scripts
Analysis of Cixous' *Norodom Sihanouk*. France: Paris. 1985-1987.
Lang.: Eng.   2580

Moch, Cheryl
Performance/production
Collection of newspaper reviews by London theatre critics. UK-
England: London. 1987. Lang.: Eng.   2232

Modern dance
SEE ALSO
Classed Entries under DANCE.
Design/technology
Modern dance production *Portraits in Reflection*. USA. 1986. Lang.:
Eng.   396
Performance spaces
Collection of photographs on the history of the Teatre Lliure. Spain-
Catalonia: Barcelona. 1976-1987. Lang.: Cat.   1671
Theory/criticism
Domination of women and gay men in Western dance. USA. 1700-
1987. Lang.: Eng.   1458

Modin, Jan
Performance/production
Background on *Landskronapågen (The Boy from Landskrona)*.
Sweden: Landskrona. 1982-1987. Lang.: Swe.   2024

***Modlitwa chorego przed noca (Sick Man's Prayer at Nightfall,
A)***
Performance/production
The 17th Warsaw theatre conference. Poland: Warsaw. 1987. Lang.:
Eng, Fre.   872

Moeller, Philip
Performance/production
Interview with Mary Arbenz on the original production of *Mourning
Becomes Electra*. USA: New York, NY. 1927. Lang.: Eng.   2355
Philip Moeller's premiere of *Mourning Becomes Electra* by O'Neill.
USA: New York, NY. 1931. Lang.: Eng.   2366

Mogilat, Serge
Performance/production
Maintaining theatre archives and designating a coordinator. USA:
New York, NY. 1987. Lang.: Eng.   938

Mohács (Mohács Disaster, The)
Performance/production
Tamás Szirtes directs Gyula Háy's *Mohács (The Mohács Disaster)* at
Madách Szinház. Hungary. 1987. Lang.: Hun.   1863
Gyula Háy's *Mohács (The Mohács Disaster)* staged by Tamás
Szirtes, Gyulai Várszinház. Hungary: Gyula. 1987. Lang.: Hun.   1903

Mokae, Zakes
Performance/production
Black theatre in South Africa: influence of traditional forms. South
Africa, Republic of. England: London. USA: New York, NY. 1586-
1987. Lang.: Eng.   2005

Mokutōsha (Tokyo)
Performance/production
Productions by Tenkei gekijō, Manji and Mokutōsha. Japan: Tokyo.
1986. Lang.: Jap.   1958

Molas, Antoni
Performance/production
Exhibition catalogue: popular theatre in Catalan. France. 1415-1987.
Lang.: Cat, Fre.   1750

Molchanov, V.V.
Performance/production
New themes and styles in Japanese theatre. Japan: Tokyo. 1986.
Lang.: Jap.   1953

Molcho, Samy
Performance/production
Mime Samy Molcho: his new work as lecturer and author.
Switzerland. 1987. Lang.: Ger.   3235

Moldoveanu, Vasile
Performance/production
Vasile Moldoveanu's views on the current state of opera. USA.
1987. Lang.: Eng.   3844

Molière
Performance/production
Review of Ariane Mnouchkine's film *Molière*. France. 1987. Lang.:
Hun.   3150

Molière (Poquelin, Jean-Baptiste)
Performance/production
Théâtre de la Jeune Lune, its origins and influences. USA:
Minneapolis, MN. France: Paris. 1980-1987. Lang.: Eng.   977

Brigitte Jacques as Elvire in Molière's *Dom Juan*. France:
Strasbourg. 1940-1986. Lang.: Fre.   1764
Soviet tour of Comédie-Française: Jean-Pierre Vincent directs
Molière's *Le Misanthrope*. France. USSR. 1980-1987. Lang.: Rus.
                                                                                             1769
László Vámos directs *Les femmes savantes (The Learned Ladies)* by
Molière at Várszinház under the title *Tudós nök*. Hungary: Budapest.
1987. Lang.: Hun.   1823
Actor Mario Scaccia and his Molière interpretations. Italy. 1949-1987.
Lang.: Ita.   1946
Benno Besson directs Molière's *Dom Juan*. Switzerland: Geneva.
1987. Lang.: Fre.   2029
Collection of newspaper reviews by London theatre critics. UK-
England: London. 1987. Lang.: Eng.   2174
Collection of newspaper reviews by London theatre critics. UK-
England: London. 1987. Lang.: Eng.   2179
Plays/librettos/scripts
Bartho Smit's *Don Juan onder die Boere (Don Juan among the
Boers)*. 1600-1987. Lang.: Afr.   2415
Italian translation of W. D. Howarth's *Molière: A Playwright and
His Audience*. France. 1622-1673. Lang.: Ita.   2574
Theory/criticism
Catalan translation of Lessing's *Hamburgische Dramaturgie*.
Germany: Hamburg. 1767-1769. Lang.: Cat.   3043
Suggestion for new form of dramaturgical research based on
concrete scenic action from past productions. USA: Tallahassee, FL.
1987. Lang.: Eng.   3074

Molina, Alfred
Performance/production
English Shakespearean productions. UK-England: London,
Manchester, Stratford. 1985-1986. Lang.: Eng.   917

Molina, Tirso de
Plays/librettos/scripts
Bartho Smit's *Don Juan onder die Boere (Don Juan among the
Boers)*. 1600-1987. Lang.: Afr.   2415

Moll Flanders
Performance/production
Collection of newspaper reviews by London theatre critics. UK-
England: London. 1986. Lang.: Eng.   2109

Möller, Cannie
Plays/librettos/scripts
Interview with playwright Cannie Möller. Sweden: Järfälla. 1987.
Lang.: Swe.   2735

Molnár, Ference
Plays/librettos/scripts
Review of Ferenc Molnár's *Az ördög (The Devil)* directed by
György Lengyel at Madách Theatre with discussion of the
playwright and the play. Hungary: Budapest. 1987. Lang.: Hun.
                                                                                             2630

Molnár, Piroska
Performance/production
Actors Sándor Szakácsi and Piroska Molnár in *Man of La Mancha*
directed by Lászlo Bagossy. Hungary: Pécs. 1987. Lang.: Hun.   3633

Molodëžnyj Teat'r (Vilnius)
Performance/production
Work of E. Nekrošjus, director of Vil'njus Youth Theatre. USSR:
Vilnius. 1980-1987. Lang.: Rus.   1043

Moment of Sincerity, A
Performance/production
Five short plays by Géza Páskándi at SUNY Binghamton. Hungary.
USA: Binghamton, NY. 1987. Lang.: Eng.   1813

Momojiri, Sumio
Performance/production
Six plays of the Tokyo season, focus on director Betsuyaku Minoru.
Japan: Tokyo. 1986. Lang.: Jap.   1966

Mompou, Frederic
Performance/production
History of dance in Catalonia. Spain-Catalonia. 1300-1987. Lang.:
Cat.   1410

Moms
Design/technology
Lighting reviews for some New York productions. USA: New York,
NY. 1987. Lang.: Eng.   477
Plays/librettos/scripts
Interview with playwright Alice Childress. USA: New York, NY,
Baltimore, MD. 1987. Lang.: Eng.   2844

Monastyrskij, P.
Performance/production
Director of Gorkij Theatre on theatrical experimentation. USSR. 1986-1988. Lang.: Rus.   1044

Training
Director discusses problems of theatrical education. USSR: Kujbyšev. 1987. Lang.: Rus.   1395

Monetta, Antonio
Plays/librettos/scripts
Plays of Antonio Monetta, Pietro Suscio and Girolamo Bax. Italy. 1600-1900. Lang.: Ita.   2669

Monette, Richard
Performance/production
Rehearsal process of 1987 Stratford Festival productions directed by Robin Phillips. Canada: Stratford, ON. 1987. Lang.: Eng.   741

Monk, Debra
Performance/production
The cabaret-style musical revue *Oil City Symphony*. USA: New York, NY. 1987. Lang.: Eng.   3289

Monk, Meredith
Performance/production
The 1984 season of the Next Wave at BAM. USA: New York, NY. 1984. Lang.: Eng.   967

Monodrama
Plays/librettos/scripts
Interview with playwright Jack Hibberd. Australia. 1967-1986. Lang.: Eng.   1098

Survey of the plays of Jack Hibberd: themes and characterization. Australia. 1966-1986. Lang.: Eng.   2437

Monopoly
Performance/production
Collection of newspaper reviews by London theatre critics. UK-England: London. 1987. Lang.: Eng.   2177

Monroe, Marilyn
Performance/production
Hungarian translation of Norman Mailer's biography of Marilyn Monroe. USA. 1926-1962. Lang.: Hun.   3169

Monstrous Regiment (London)
Performance/production
Relationship of theatre, class and gender. UK-England. USA. 1969-1985. Lang.: Eng.   918

Monstrous Regiment Theatre Company (London)
Performance/production
Collection of newspaper reviews by London theatre critics. UK-England: London. 1987. Lang.: Eng.   2181

Montaland, Cécile
Performance/production
Child actors in juvenile companies, Comédie-Française. France: Paris. 1769-1850. Lang.: Eng.   1756

Montanaro, Tony
Performance/production
Contemporary mime forms and their innovators. France: Paris. Belgium. USA. 1980-1982. Lang.: Eng.   3224

Montanyès, Josep
Performance/production
Collection of theatre reviews by Xavier Fàbregas. Spain-Catalonia. 1969-1972. Lang.: Cat.   2010

Monterey, Carlotta
SEE
O'Neill, Carlotta Monterey.

Montero, Joaquim
Performance/production
Collection of theatre reviews by J.M. de Sagarra. Spain-Catalonia: Barcelona. 1922-1927. Lang.: Cat.   885

Monteverdi Birkózókör (Budapest)
Performance/production
Interview with director András Jeles of Monteverdi Birkózókör (Budapest). Hungary. 1985-1987. Lang.: Hun.   1833

Montgomery, Lucy Maud
Institutions
Overview of the Charlottetown Festival, 1986 season. Canada: Charlottetown, PE. 1965-1985. Lang.: Eng.   525

Month of Sundays, A
Performance/production
Collection of newspaper reviews by New York theatre critics. USA: New York, NY. 1987. Lang.: Eng.   2321

Montreal, série noire
Design/technology
Dennis O'Sullivan's work with mixed media. Canada. 1986. Lang.: Fre.   3203

Montsalvatge, Xavier
Performance/production
History of dance in Catalonia. Spain-Catalonia. 1300-1987. Lang.: Cat.   1410

Monturiol, Carme
Plays/librettos/scripts
General history of Catalan literature, including theatre. Spain-Catalonia. 1902-1961. Lang.: Cat.   1157

Moon Dance Night
Performance/production
Collection of newspaper reviews by London theatre critics. UK-England: London. 1987. Lang.: Eng.   2216

Moon for the Misbegotten, A
Plays/librettos/scripts
O'Neill's transcendence of melodrama in *A Touch of the Poet* and *A Moon for the Misbegotten*. USA. 1922-1947. Lang.: Eng.   2886

Moon, Gerald
Performance/production
Collection of newspaper reviews by London theatre critics. UK-England: London. 1987. Lang.: Eng.   2271

Moore, George
Relation to other fields
Literary figures of the Irish Literary Renaissance. Ireland. UK-Ireland. 1875-1938. Lang.: Eng.   2995

Moore, Jim
Performance/production
Development of Michael Smith from painter to performance artist. USA. 1987. Lang.: Eng.   3369

Moore, Jonathan
Performance/production
Collection of newspaper reviews by London theatre critics. UK-England: London. 1986. Lang.: Eng.   2052

Collection of newspaper reviews by London theatre critics. UK-England: London. 1986. Lang.: Eng.   2070

Moore, Mary Tyler
Performance/production
History of musical version, *Breakfast at Tiffany's*. USA: New York, NY, Philadelphia, PA, Boston, MA. 1958-1966. Lang.: Eng.   3644

Moore, Simon
Performance/production
Collection of newspaper reviews by London theatre critics. UK-England: London. 1987. Lang.: Eng.   2205

Collection of newspaper reviews by London theatre critics. UK-England: London. 1987. Lang.: Eng.   2240

Moore, Wesley
Performance/production
Collection of newspaper reviews by London theatre critics. UK-England: London. 1986. Lang.: Eng.   2083

Morad, Gowhar-e
Basic theatrical documents
Translation of five contemporary Persian plays. Iran. 1987. Lang.: Eng.   1558

Moragas, Ricard
Performance/production
History of dance in Catalonia. Spain-Catalonia. 1300-1987. Lang.: Cat.   1410

Morahan, Christopher
Performance/production
Collection of newspaper reviews by London theatre critics. UK-England: London. 1987. Lang.: Eng.   2245

Review of production and staging aspects of *Wild Honey* by Anton Čechov. UK-England: London. 1986. Lang.: Eng.   2306

Morales de Molla, Laura
Performance/production
Retrospective of two centuries of Hispanic theatre. USA. 1598-1965. Lang.: Eng.   2345

Morales, Hilda
Performance/production
Career of American Ballet Theatre dancer Hilda Morales. USA: New York, NY. 1983. Lang.: Eng.   1443

Morality plays
Performance/production
The medieval tournament tradition in the original staging of *The Castle of Perseverance*. England. 1425. Lang.: Eng.   776

Mordžanišvili Theatre (Tbilisi)
SEE
Gruzinskij Akademičéskij Teat'r im. Kote Mordžanišvili.

More Light
Performance/production
Collection of newspaper reviews by London theatre critics. UK-
England: London. 1987. Lang.: Eng.   2184

More, Julian
Performance/production
Collection of newspaper reviews by New York theatre critics. USA:
New York, NY. 1987. Lang.: Eng.   2318

Moreau, Jeanne
Performance/production
Directing methods of Klaus Michael Grüber. France. Germany.
1945-1987. Lang.: Fre.   1766
Ten theatre people on a performance that changed their thinking.
Sweden. 1986-1987. Lang.: Swe.   2015

Moreno, Dorina
Performance/production
Teatropoesia, a combination of theatre and poetry. USA. 1974-1983.
Lang.: Spa.   2368

Moreno, J.L.
Relation to other fields
Psychodrama in the clinic, the classroom and contemporary research.
Europe. North America. 1900-1987. Lang.: Ita.   1233

Morera, Maria
Performance/production
Collection of theatre reviews by J.M. de Sagarra. Spain-Catalonia:
Barcelona. 1922-1927. Lang.: Cat.   885

Morgan, James
Design/technology
Four Broadway designers discuss redesigning shows for road tours.
USA. 1987. Lang.: Eng.   414

Morgan, Roger
Performance spaces
Architect Roger Morgan discusses plans for restoring seven
Broadway theatres. USA: New York, NY. 1984. Lang.: Eng.   683

Móricz Zsigmond Szinház (Nyíregyháza)
Performance/production
Reviews: *A vörös postakocsi (The Red Mail Coach)* by Gyula Krúdy,
staged by Dezső Kapás and *Az atyai ház (The Paternal Roof)* by
Zsigmond Remenyik, staged by Péter Lener. Hungary: Veszprém,
Nyíregyháza. 1986. Lang.: Hun.   1821
Edward Bond's *The Fool* under the title *A bolond* directed by László
Salamon Suba at Móricz Zsigmond Theatre. Hungary: Nyíregyháza.
1986. Lang.: Hun.   1875
Péter Léner directs Géza Páskandi's *Lélekharang (Death Knell)*,
Móricz Zsigmond Theatre. Hungary: Nyíregyháza. 1987. Lang.: Hun.
                                                                     1876
A patkánykirály (The King of the Rats) by Győző Határ staged by
László Salamon Suba at Móricz Zsigmond Theatre. Hungary:
Nyíregyháza. 1987. Lang.: Hun.   1899
László Salamon Suba directs *A patkánykirály (The King of the Rats)*
by Győző Határ at Móricz Zsigmond Theatre. Hungary:
Nyíregyháza. 1987. Lang.: Hun.   1901
Reviews of Wilson's *Talley's Folly* staged by András Bálint and
Bond's *The Fool* staged by László Salamon Suba. Hungary:
Dunaujváros, Nyíregyháza. 1986. Lang.: Hun.   1902
Péter Léner directs premiere of *Lélekharang (Death Knell)* by Géza
Páskandi at Móricz Zsigmond Theatre. Hungary: Nyíregyháza. 1987.
Lang.: Hun.   1915
Ivo Krobot directs *Ófelsége pincére voltam (I Served the King of
Britain)*, based on writings of Bohumil Hrabal. Hungary:
Nyíregyháza. 1987. Lang.: Hun.   1928

Bohumil Hrabal's *Obsluhoval jsem anglického krale (I Served the
King of Britain)* directed by Ivo Krobot as *Ófelsége pincére voltam.*
Hungary: Nyíregyháza. 1987. Lang.: Hun.   1912

Móricz, Zsigmond
Performance/production
Péter Tömöry directs premiere of Zsigmond Móricz's 1916
Fortunátus. Hungary: Zalaegerszeg. 1987. Lang.: Hun.   1840
Imre Halasi directs *Sári bíró (Judge Sári)* by Zsigmond Móricz,
music by István Mikó, at Kisvarda Castle Theatre. Hungary:
Kisvárda. 1987. Lang.: Hun.   1845

László Bagossy directs *Macbeth*, Tamás Jordán directs Zsigmond
Móricz's *Uri muri (Gentlemen's Spree)* at Pécs Summer Theatre.
Hungary: Pécs. 1987. Lang.: Hun.   1864
Uri muri (Gentlemen's Spree) by Zsigmond Móricz staged by Mátyás
Giricz at Jókai Theatre. Hungary: Békéscsaba. 1986. Lang.: Hun.
                                                                     1877

Morley, Sheridan
Performance/production
Collection of newspaper reviews by London theatre critics. UK-
England: London. 1986. Lang.: Eng.   2137

Mornin, Daniel
Performance/production
Collection of newspaper reviews by London theatre critics. UK-
England: London. 1987. Lang.: Eng.   2207
Plays/librettos/scripts
Avoidance of political themes in drama of Northern Ireland. UK-
Ireland. 1979-1987. Lang.: Eng.   2830

Morning After Optimism, The
Plays/librettos/scripts
Theatrical language in the plays of Thomas Murphy. Ireland. 1961-
1984. Lang.: Eng.   2640
Thomas Murphy's *The Morning After Optimism*: comparisons with
Beckett, O'Casey. Ireland. 1971. Lang.: Eng.   2641
Characters and the gangster movie form in Thomas Murphy's *The
Blue Macushla.* Ireland. 1980-1986. Lang.: Eng.   2647
Comic characters and the Book of Job in the plays of Thomas
Murphy. Ireland. 1962-1983. Lang.: Eng.   2648
The plays of Thomas Murphy. Ireland: Dublin. 1962-1986. Lang.:
Eng.   2650
Theme and language in the plays of Thomas Murphy. Ireland. 1962-
1978. Lang.: Eng.   2656

Morning Sacrifice
Plays/librettos/scripts
Thematic analysis of Dymphna Cusack's *Morning Sacrifice.*
Australia. 1942. Lang.: Eng.   2441

Morosco Theatre (New York, NY)
Performance spaces
Morosco Theatre torn down despite efforts by Actors' Equity. USA:
New York, NY. 1982. Lang.: Eng.   677

Morozov, B.
Performance/production
Round-table of Soviet directors. USSR: Moscow. 1980-1987. Lang.:
Rus.   989
Creative and moral problems of a theatre collective. USSR: Moscow.
1986-1988. Lang.: Rus.   1045

Morphos, Evangeline
Performance/production
Method acting: its origins and development. USA: New York, NY.
USSR: Moscow. 1923-1987. Lang.: Eng.   2359

Morris, Jim
Performance/production
Collection of newspaper reviews by London theatre critics. UK-
England: London. 1986. Lang.: Eng.   2051

Morris, Mark
Performance/production
The 1984 season of the Next Wave at BAM. USA: New York, NY.
1984. Lang.: Eng.   967

Morris, Tom
Performance/production
Collection of newspaper reviews by London theatre critics. UK-
England: London. 1987. Lang.: Eng.   2276

Morrison, Toni
Plays/librettos/scripts
The new Black literary criticism. USA. 1986. Lang.: Eng.   1174

Morrow, Geoff
Performance/production
Collection of newspaper reviews by London theatre critics. UK-
England: London. 1987. Lang.: Eng.   2197

Mort de César, La (Death of Caesar, The)
Plays/librettos/scripts
Techniques, themes, characters and dramaturgy of Voltaire. France.
1718-1778. Lang.: Eng.   2590

Mortier, Gérard
Institutions
Gérard Mortier, director of Théâtre Royal de la Monnaie. Belgium:
Brussels. 1981-1986. Lang.: Fre.   3711

Mortifee, Ann
Performance/production
Ann Mortifee, singer, songwriter, performer. Canada: Vancouver, BC,
Toronto, ON. 1982. Lang.: Eng.   1714
Moscow Art Theatre
SEE
Moskovskij Chudožestvénnyj Akademičeskij Teat'r.
Moscow Puppet Theatre
SEE
Gosudarstvénnyj Centralnyj Teat'r Kukol.
Moscow Theatre Institute, GITIS
SEE
Gosudarstvénnyj Institut Teatralnovo Iskusstva.
Moses
Performance/production
Collection of newspaper reviews by London theatre critics. UK-
England: London. 1987. Lang.: Eng.   2073
Collection of newspaper reviews by London theatre critics. UK-
England: London. 1987. Lang.: Eng.   2186
Moses und Aron
Performance/production
Report from Salzburger Festspiele: Mozart's *Don Giovanni*,
Schoenberg's *Moses und Aron*, Schmidt's *Das Buch mit sieben
Siegeln*. Austria: Salzburg. 1987. Lang.: Swe.   3744
Moses, Gil
Performance/production
Interview with playwright Amiri Baraka. USA: Newark, NJ, New
York, NY. 1965-1969. Lang.: Eng.   2356
Mosher, Gregory
Administration
Production sharing among non-profit theatres in effort to develop
new works. USA. 1987. Lang.: Eng.   255
Institutions
Analysis of the changing scene in Chicago's theatres. USA: Chicago,
IL. 1987. Lang.: Eng.   589
Current trends in American theatre. USA. 1967-1987. Lang.: Eng.
                                                                 621
Performance/production
Collection of newspaper reviews by New York theatre critics. USA:
New York, NY. 1987. Lang.: Eng.   2322
Collection of newspaper reviews by New York theatre critics. USA:
New York, NY. 1987. Lang.: Eng.   2326
Plays/librettos/scripts
Interview with playwright David Mamet. USA: Chicago, IL, New
York, NY. 1969-1987. Lang.: Eng.   2909
Moshinsky, Elijah
Performance/production
Collection of newspaper reviews by London theatre critics. UK-
England: London. 1987. Lang.: Eng.   2195
Collection of newspaper reviews by London theatre critics. UK-
England: London. 1987. Lang.: Eng.   2253
Collection of newspaper reviews by London theatre critics. UK-
England: London. 1987. Lang.: Eng.   2274
**Moskovskij Chudožestvénnyj Akademičeskij Teat'r (Moscow Art
Theatre)**
Basic theatrical documents
Russian symbolist plays and essays. USSR. 1880-1986. Lang.: Eng.
                                                                 1584
Design/technology
V. Levental's scenery for Čechov's *Diadia Vania (Uncle Vanya)* at
Moscow Art Theatre. USSR: Moscow. 1985. Lang.: Rus.   493
Performance/production
History of teaching method of Michajl Čechov. USA. USSR. 1891-
1955. Lang.: Eng.   931
Actor Aleksej Nikolaevič Gribov of Moscow Art Theatre. USSR:
Moscow. 1930-1979. Lang.: Rus.   1029
Actor Oleg Borisov of Moscow Art Theatre. USSR: Moscow. 1980-
1987. Lang.: Rus.   1053
Work of Oleg Jéfremov, artistic director of Moscow Art Theatre.
USSR: Moscow. 1927-1987. Lang.: Rus.   1074
Michajl Čechov's life and work: a descriptive chronology. Russia:
Moscow. 1901-1980. Lang.: Eng.   2002
The relationship between the director and the playwright from
contrasting historical perspectives. UK-England. 1800-1987. Lang.:
Eng.   2291
Moscow Art Theatre's production of *Hamlet* with Michajl Čechov in
the title role. USSR: Moscow. 1924. Lang.: Eng.   2386

Relation to other fields
Exchange of ideas between Soviets and US theatre artists. USA:
New York, NY. USSR: Moscow. 1987. Lang.: Eng.   1284
Theory/criticism
Critic Pavel A. Markov and the Moscow Art Theatre. USSR. 1910-
1959. Lang.: Rus.   1373
Mossovét Theatre
SEE
Teat'r im. Mossovéta.
Mother Courage and Her Children
SEE
Mutter Courage und ihre Kinder.
Motion Picture Association of America (Los Angeles, CA)
Administration
The film rating system of the Motion Picture Association of America
(MPAA). USA. 1968-1982. Lang.: Eng.   3120
Motton, Gregory
Performance/production
Collection of newspaper reviews by London theatre critics. UK-
England: London. 1987. Lang.: Eng.   2198
Collection of newspaper reviews by London theatre critics. UK-
England: London. 1987. Lang.: Eng.   2250
Mouchoir de Nuages (Handkerchief of Clouds)
Plays/librettos/scripts
Mouchoir de Nuages (Handkerchief of Clouds) by Tristan Tzara.
France. Lang.: Ita.   2569
Mourning Becomes Electra
Performance/production
Interview with Mary Arbenz on the original production of *Mourning
Becomes Electra*. USA: New York, NY. 1927. Lang.: Eng.   2355
Philip Moeller's premiere of *Mourning Becomes Electra* by O'Neill.
USA: New York, NY. 1931. Lang.: Eng.   2366
Plays/librettos/scripts
Influence of Herman Melville on Eugene O'Neill. USA. 1927. Lang.:
Eng.   2888
Moussorgsky, Modeste
SEE
Mussorgskij, Modest Pavlovič.
Mouthful of Birds, A
Performance/production
Collection of newspaper reviews by London theatre critics. UK-
England: London. 1986. Lang.: Eng.   2034
Movement
Performance/production
Career of actor Angelo Musco. Italy. 1872-1937. Lang.: Ita.   841
Actors' interpretations of gestures and movements implicit in
Shakespeare's texts. UK-England. 1870-1987. Lang.: Eng.   2302
Two aspects of Stanislavskij's work: physical comedy, rehearsal
process. USSR: Moscow. 1933-1988. Lang.: Ger.   2380
Mime troupe Panopticon. Sweden: Stockholm. 1985-1987. Lang.:
Swe.   3226
Body language in Korean mime. Korea. 1970-1979. Lang.: Kor.
                                                                 3234
Mime Samy Molcho: his new work as lecturer and author.
Switzerland. 1987. Lang.: Ger.   3235
The four main elements of dance in Chinese opera. China, People's
Republic of. 960-1987. Lang.: Chi.   3526
Training
Basic theatrical techniques for secondary school. Belgium. 1987.
Lang.: Fre.   1378
Movement Theatre International
Performance/production
History that formed the mimes of the 1980s. USA. 1987. Lang.:
Eng.   3230
Mowat, Barbara
Performance/production
Conference proceedings on staging of Elizabethan plays. England.
1546-1616. Lang.: Eng.   775
Moyà, Llorenç
Basic theatrical documents
Text and analysis of *Fàlaris* and *Orfeu* by Llorenç Moyà. Spain.
1968-1981. Lang.: Cat.   1569
Mozart, Wolfgang Amadeus
Administration
Royal Swedish Opera: new production of *Die Zauberflöte*, overview
of management. Sweden: Stockholm. 1986. Lang.: Swe.   3681

Mozart, Wolfgang Amadeus — cont'd

Audience
The vocal versus the visual aspects of opera. Europe. 1781-1983.
Lang.: Eng. 3690

Performance/production
Wolfgang Amadeus Mozart: a psychological profile. Austria: Vienna.
1756-1781. Lang.: Eng. 3742

Report from Salzburger Festspiele: Mozart's *Don Giovanni*,
Schoenberg's *Moses und Aron*, Schmidt's *Das Buch mit sieben
Siegeln*. Austria: Salzburg. 1987. Lang.: Swe. 3744

In defense of vocal ornamentation. Europe. 1767-1987. Lang.: Eng.
3769

Mozart's *Don Giovanni* staged by Harry Kupfer. Germany, East:
Berlin, East. 1987. Lang.: Swe. 3779

Review of productions at opera ensembles meeting. Hungary: Szeged.
1987. Lang.: Hun. 3792

A children's production of Mozart's *The Magic Flute* performed in
Spanish. Mexico: Mexico City. 1987. Lang.: Spa. 3811

Background on Lyric Opera radio broadcast performances. USA:
Chicago, IL. 1987. Lang.: Eng. 3832

Background on Metropolitan radio broadcast performances. USA:
New York, NY. 1987. Lang.: Eng. 3837

Background on Metropolitan radio broadcast performances. USA:
New York, NY. 1987. Lang.: Eng. 3838

Plays/librettos/scripts
Comparison of Mozart's *The Magic Flute* and Strauss's *Die Frau
ohne Schatten*. Austria: Vienna. 1980. Lang.: Eng. 3891

Mozarteum (Salzburg)

Design/technology
Third international scene painting seminar at the Mozarteum.
Austria: Salzburg. 1986. Lang.: Eng. 300

Mózes (Moses)

Performance/production
Interview with actor Imre Sinkovits. Hungary: Budapest. 1951-1987.
Lang.: Hun. 1835

Mr. Bennett and Miss Smith

Performance/production
Collection of newspaper reviews by London theatre critics. UK-
England: London. 1987. Lang.: Eng. 2233

Mrożek, Sławomir

Basic theatrical documents
Hebrew translation of Sławomir Mrożek's *Vatslave*. Poland: Cracow.
Israel: Jerusalem. 1968-1984. Lang.: Heb. 1565

Performance/production
Festival of Polish plays. Poland: Wrocław. 1987. Lang.: Eng, Fre.
871

Overview of 1986-1987 Moscow theatre season. USSR: Moscow.
1986-1987. Lang.: Eng. 1039

Zoltán Seregi directs Sławomir Mrożek's *Letni dzień (A Summer's
Day)* at Thália Stúdió under the title *Egy nyári nap*. Hungary:
Budapest. 1987. Lang.: Hun. 1919

Directing Mrożek's *Vatslave*. Israel: Jerusalem. Poland. 1984-1984.
Lang.: Heb. 1938

Polish theatre. Poland: Warsaw, Cracow, Wrocław. 1980-1987. Lang.:
Eng, Fre. 1987

Plays/librettos/scripts
History and analysis of Mrożek's play *Vatslave*. Poland: Cracow.
France: Paris. 1956-1987. Lang.: Heb. 2713

Mrs. Farmer's Daughter

Performance/production
Interview with composer Jack Eric Williams, focus on his musical
Mrs. Farmer's Daughter. USA: New York, NY. 1987. Lang.: Eng.
3663

Mrs. Warren's Profession

Plays/librettos/scripts
Mrs. Warren's Profession: Shaw's ideas embodied in characters. UK-
England. 1902. Lang.: Eng. 2765

Mrsán, János

Performance/production
János Mrsán directs *The Cocktail Party* by T.S. Eliot at Várszinház
under the title *Koktél hatkor*. Hungary: Budapest. 1987. Lang.: Hun.
1803

Mtshali, Oswald

Relation to other fields
Influences of Black political and economic life on literature,
performance. South Africa, Republic of. 1970-1987. Lang.: Eng. 1252

Mtwa, Percy

Performance/production
Collection of newspaper reviews by London theatre critics. UK-
England: London. 1987. Lang.: Eng. 2176

Mu dan ting (Peony Pavilion, The)

Performance/production
Collection of newspaper reviews by London theatre critics. UK-
England: London. 1987. Lang.: Eng. 2258

Music design of *Mu dan ting (The Peony Pavilion)*. China, People's
Republic of. 1987. Lang.: Chi. 3514

Plays/librettos/scripts
How music reveals character in Chinese opera. China. 1600-1700.
Lang.: Chi. 3545

Much Ado About Nothing

Design/technology
Gershwin Theatre's accommodation of RSC touring productions.
USA: New York, NY. 1984. Lang.: Eng. 420

Performance/production
Reviews of *Téli zsoltár (A Winter Psalm)* by Kovách, Shakespeare's
Much Ado About Nothing and *Ferde ház (The Leaning House)* by
Gerencsér performed at Kisfaludy Theatre. Hungary: Győr. 1986.
Lang.: Hun. 1822

Six plays of the Tokyo season, focus on director Betsuyaku Minoru.
Japan: Tokyo. 1986. Lang.: Jap. 1966

Plays/librettos/scripts
Stage business in *Major Barbara* traced to Beerbohm Tree. UK-
England. 1905. Lang.: Eng. 2802

Mueller, Harald

Relation to other fields
Analysis of the role of political drama in Europe. Switzerland: Basel.
Mönchengladbach. 1986-1987. Lang.: Ger. 3002

Muldoon, Roland

Performance/production
Development of alternative cabaret. UK-England. 1980. Lang.: Eng.
3288

Muldowney, Dominic

Performance/production
Collection of newspaper reviews by London theatre critics. UK-
England: London. 1986. Lang.: Eng. 2050

Mulet, Francesc

Reference materials
Catalogue of Valencian playtexts available at libraries of Barcelona.
Spain: Valencia, Barcelona. Lang.: Cat. 2975

Mulgrew, Gerry

Performance/production
Collection of newspaper reviews by London theatre critics. UK-
England: London. 1987. Lang.: Eng. 2218

Mulholland, Tony

Performance/production
Collection of newspaper reviews by London theatre critics. UK-
England: London. 1986. Lang.: Eng. 2090

Mulkerrin, Michael

Performance/production
Collection of newspaper reviews by London theatre critics. UK-
England: London. 1987. Lang.: Eng. 2219

Müller, Heiner

Performance/production
Collection of newspaper reviews by London theatre critics. UK-
England: London. 1987. Lang.: Eng. 2258

Collaboration of Robert Wilson and Heiner Müller on *Hamlet
Machine (Hamletmaschine)*. USA: New York, NY. Germany, West:
Hamburg. 1987. Lang.: Eng. 3361

Plays/librettos/scripts
Theatrical works of Heiner Müller. Germany: Berlin. 1929-1987.
Lang.: Ita. 2594

Brecht's influence on technique and style of playwright Heiner
Müller. Germany, East. 1940-1984. Lang.: Eng. 2605

Significance of dream-structures in Heiner Müller's plays, compared
with those in Brecht's. Germany, East: Berlin, East. 1972-1987.
Lang.: Ger. 2607

Study of playwright Heiner Müller's view of history. Germany, East.
1976-1986. Lang.: Ger. 2608

Stage history and interpretations of Heiner Müller's *Der Lohndrücker
(Undercutting)*. Germany, East. 1956-1987. Lang.: Ger. 2615

Theory/criticism
Theatre and contemporary culture. USA. 1800-1987. Lang.: Eng.
1360

Müller, Peter
Performance/production
The 4th International Festival of Street Theatres. Poland: Jelenia
Góra. 1986. Lang.: Eng, Fre. 3355
Muller, Robby
Design/technology
The work of cinematographer Robby Muller. USA. 1986. Lang.:
Eng. 3131
Multiculturalism
Administration
Reactions to first national symposium on nontraditional casting.
USA: New York, NY. 1986-1987. Lang.: Eng. 144
First nontraditional casting symposium. USA: New York, NY. 1975-
1987. Lang.: Eng. 208
Producer's comments on first national symposium on nontraditional
casting. USA: New York, NY. 1986-1987. Lang.: Eng. 215
Performance/production
Ethnic and minority casting opportunities. USA. 1986. Lang.: Eng.
939
Plays/librettos/scripts
Italo-Australian drama, in English and Italian. Australia. 1860-1986.
Lang.: Eng. 2443
Relation to other fields
Nontraditional casting of minority actors. USA. 1979-1987. Lang.:
Eng. 1274
Mumbo Jumbo
Performance/production
Collection of newspaper reviews by London theatre critics. UK-
England: London. 1987. Lang.: Eng. 2242
Collection of newspaper reviews by London theatre critics. UK-
England: London. 1987. Lang.: Eng. 2253
Mummer's Troupe (St. John's, NF)
Institutions
A history of documentary theatre in English Canada. Canada. 1970-
1986. Lang.: Eng. 508
Mummers Troupe (St. John's, NF)
Relation to other fields
Applications of African 'Theatre for Development' movement to
Canadian popular theatre. Africa. Canada: St. John's, NF, Toronto,
ON. 1978-1987. Lang.: Eng. 2978
Mummy
Performance/production
Collection of newspaper reviews by London theatre critics. UK-
England: London. 1987. Lang.: Eng. 2192
Münchener Festspiele
SEE
Bayerische Staatsoper im Nationaltheater.
Munday, Anthony
Plays/librettos/scripts
Productions of *Sir Thomas More* by Elizabethan theatre companies.
England. 1595-1650. Lang.: Eng. 2541
Mundy, James
Performance/production
Collection of newspaper reviews by London theatre critics. UK-
England: London. 1987. Lang.: Eng. 2252
Munich Opera
SEE
Bayerische Staatsoper im Nationaltheater.
Munich-Athens
Performance/production
Collection of newspaper reviews by London theatre critics. UK-
England: London. 1987. Lang.: Eng. 2187
Municipal Theatre (Haifa)
SEE
Teatron HaIroni (Haifa).
Municipal Theatre (Helsinki)
SEE
Helsingin Kaupunginteatteri.
Munkácsi, Miklós
Performance/production
Menyhért Szegvári directs Miklós Munkácsi's *Lisszaboni eső (Rain in
Lisbon)* at Játékszín. Hungary: Budapest. 1987. Lang.: Hun. 1815
Menyhért Szegvári directs premiere of *Lisszaboni eső (Rain in
Lisbon)* by Miklós Munkácsi at Játékszín. Hungary: Budapest. 1987.
Lang.: Hun. 1858

Munro, Rona
Performance/production
Collection of newspaper reviews by London theatre critics. UK-
England: London. 1987. Lang.: Eng. 2228
Munroe, Carmen
Performance/production
Collection of newspaper reviews by London theatre critics. UK-
England: London. 1986. Lang.: Eng. 2096
Collection of newspaper reviews by London theatre critics. UK-
England: London. 1987. Lang.: Eng. 2277
Mur, Le (Wall, The)
Plays/librettos/scripts
Korean stage adaptation of *Le Mur (The Wall)* by Sartre. France.
Korea. 1939-1976. Lang.: Kor. 2575
Murai, Shimako
Performance/production
Focus on several Tokyo productions. Japan: Tokyo. 1960-1987.
Lang.: Jap. 1955
Murdock, W. Gordon
Institutions
History of New York's Little Players puppet theatre. USA: New
York, NY. 1960-1985. Lang.: Eng. 3967
Murfitt, Mary
Performance/production
The cabaret-style musical revue *Oil City Symphony*. USA: New
York, NY. 1987. Lang.: Eng. 3289
Murphy, Eddie
Performance/production
How film industry has shaped racist attitudes toward Blacks. USA.
1950-1987. Lang.: Eng. 3095
Murphy, Gerard
Performance/production
Collection of newspaper reviews by London theatre critics. UK-
England: London. 1987. Lang.: Eng. 2223
Murphy, Thomas
Performance/production
Interview with Patrick Mason, director of Thomas Murphy's *The
Gigli Concert*. Ireland: Dublin. 1983. Lang.: Eng. 1935
Collection of newspaper reviews by London theatre critics. UK-
England: London. 1987. Lang.: Eng. 2220
Plays/librettos/scripts
Theatrical language in the plays of Thomas Murphy. Ireland. 1961-
1984. Lang.: Eng. 2640
Thomas Murphy's *The Morning After Optimism*: comparisons with
Beckett, O'Casey. Ireland. 1971. Lang.: Eng. 2641
Characters and the gangster movie form in Thomas Murphy's *The
Blue Macushla*. Ireland. 1980-1986. Lang.: Eng. 2647
Comic characters and the Book of Job in the plays of Thomas
Murphy. Ireland. 1962-1983. Lang.: Eng. 2648
The plays of Thomas Murphy. Ireland: Dublin. 1962-1986. Lang.:
Eng. 2650
The myth of the idyllic peasant life in the plays of Thomas
Murphy. Ireland. 1961-1986. Lang.: Eng. 2652
Christian thought in Thomas Murphy's *The Gigli Concert*. Ireland.
1983. Lang.: Eng. 2653
Analysis of Thomas Murphy's *Bailegangaire*, its connections with the
Irish language, story-telling. Ireland: Galway. 1985. Lang.: Eng. 2655
Theme and language in the plays of Thomas Murphy. Ireland. 1962-
1978. Lang.: Eng. 2656
Historical accuracy of characters in the plays of Thomas Murphy.
Ireland. 1962-1986. Lang.: Eng. 2657
Analysis of the text of Thomas Murphy's *The Sanctuary Lamp*.
Ireland. 1976-1986. Lang.: Eng. 2658
Relation to other fields
Playwright Thomas Murphy and the nature of creativity. Ireland.
1961-1986. Lang.: Eng. 2993
Murphy, Tom
Institutions
The touring company Irish Theatre Company. UK-Ireland. 1974-
1987. Lang.: Eng. 569
Performance/production
Productions and political philosophy of Field Day Theatre Company.
UK-Ireland: Londonderry. 1986-1987. Lang.: Eng. 2309
Murray, Bill
Institutions
Second City improvisational comedy troupe. USA: Chicago, IL.
Canada: Toronto, ON. 1959-1987. Lang.: Eng. 605

Music — cont'd

Violet Archer festival, premiere of her one-act opera *The Meal*. Canada: Edmonton, AB. 1985. Lang.: Eng. 3757

Professionals explain their methods of verbal description of opera. Germany, East. Germany, West. 1988. Lang.: Ger. 3777

Overview of East German opera theatre: conductors and orchestras. Germany, East. 1980-1986. Lang.: Ger. 3781

Wolfgang Rihm's new opera *Oedipus* staged by Götz Friedrich. Germany, West: Berlin, West. 1987. Lang.: Swe. 3788

Career of conductor/educator Max Rudolf. Italy. USA: New York, NY. 1945-1987. Lang.: Eng. 3803

Composer Hans Gefors on his opera *Christina*. Sweden. 1986. Lang.: Swe. 3819

Work of composer Othmar Schoeck. Switzerland. 1886-1986. Lang.: Ger. 3826

Interview with John DeMain, music director, Houston Grand Opera. USA: Houston, TX. 1944-1987. Lang.: Eng. 3851

Musical art in opera: the creation of *Nargiz*. USSR. 1935-1987. Lang.: Rus. 3875

Offenbach and the origin and development of operetta. Russia. 1860-1889. Lang.: Rus. 3960

Mythological background and performance aspects of *dalang*. Indonesia. 1987. Lang.: Ita. 4010

Plays/librettos/scripts

Comparison between medieval passion plays and Peter Nichols' *Passion Play*. 1986. Lang.: Eng. 2429

Music in Shakespeare. England. 1580-1616. Lang.: Ger. 2533

Life and works of French dramatist Gabriel Marcel. France. 1889-1973. Lang.: Eng. 2573

Popular music in the Dublin trilogy plays of Sean O'Casey. Ireland. 1923-1926. Lang.: Eng. 2644

Analysis of 51 short farces written in Majorca. Spain-Catalonia. 1701-1850. Lang.: Cat. 2731

Experiment in musical composition based on *King Lear*. USA. 1987. Lang.: Eng. 2848

Relationship between libretto and music in structure of musical drama. Europe. 1986. Lang.: Ita. 3418

Comparison of Mozart's *The Magic Flute* and Strauss's *Die Frau ohne Schatten*. Austria: Vienna. 1980. Lang.: Eng. 3891

Collaboration on songs for *Cinthia and Endimion*. England: London. 1697. Lang.: Eng. 3895

Operas of César Franck. France: Paris. 1822-1896. Lang.: Eng. 3898

Study of French composer Daniel Auber and his works. France. 1782-1871. Lang.: Eng. 3904

Opera composer, Hans Werner Henze. Germany: Gutersloh. 1926-1987. Lang.: Eng. 3910

Unique style of modern Japanese Opera. Japan. 1975-1987. Lang.: Eng. 3928

Aaron Copland's opera *The Tender Land*. USA. 1900. Lang.: Eng. 3933

Research/historiography

Influences on Wagner's *Ring* cycle. Germany: Dresden. 1813-1883. Lang.: Eng. 3948

Theory/criticism

Chinese and Western elements in Chinese musical theatre. China, People's Republic of. 1975-1987. Lang.: Chi. 3422

Music Box Theater (New York, NY)
Performance/production

Collection of newspaper reviews by New York theatre critics. USA: New York, NY. 1987. Lang.: Eng. 2311

Music Box Theatre (New York, NY)
Design/technology

Bob Crowley's set designs for *Les Liaisons Dangereuses*. USA: New York, NY. UK-England: London. 1985-1987. Lang.: Eng. 463

Performance/production

Collection of newspaper reviews by New York critics. USA: New York, NY. 1987. Lang.: Eng. 2324

Music for the Living
SEE

Muzyka dlja živych.

Music hall
SEE ALSO

Classed Entries under MIXED ENTERTAINMENT—Variety acts.

Music-Drama
SEE ALSO

Classed Entries under MUSIC-DRAMA.

Institutions

History of ballet companies: their origins in opera companies, later autonomy. Switzerland. 1955-1987. Lang.: Eng, Ger. 1430

Performance/production

Polish theatre in areas annexed by Austria-Hungary and Prussia. Poland. Austria-Hungary. Prussia. 1890-1918. Lang.: Pol. 875

Yearbook of Swiss theatrical activity, with bibliography. Switzerland. 1987-1988. Lang.: Fre, Ger, Ita. 892

Focus on several Tokyo productions. Japan: Tokyo. 1960-1987. Lang.: Jap. 1955

Vocal style on antique phonograph records. USA. Europe. 1877-1987. Lang.: Eng. 3112

Early phonograph records of opera singers. USA. Italy. Germany. 1904-1987. Lang.: Eng. 3113

Metropolitan/Deutsche Grammophon recording, Wagner's *Ring*, conducted by James Levine. USA: New York, NY. 1987. Lang.: Eng. 3114

Plays/librettos/scripts

Musical adaptation of Gorostiza's *Contigo pan y cebolla (With You, Bread and Onion)*. Mexico: Mexico City. Spain: Madrid. 1833-1984. Lang.: Eng. 1150

Reference materials

Catalogue of Valencian playtexts available at libraries of Barcelona. Spain: Valencia, Barcelona. Lang.: Cat. 2975

Musica Deuxième, La
Plays/librettos/scripts

Comparison of two versions of Duras' *La Musica Deuxième*. France: Paris. 1985-1987. Lang.: Eng. 1125

Musical Comedy Murders of 1940, The
Design/technology

Lighting reviews for several New York shows. USA: New York, NY. 1987. Lang.: Eng. 476

Performance/production

Collection of newspaper reviews by New York theatre critics. USA: New York, NY. 1987. Lang.: Eng. 2322

Musical theatre
SEE ALSO

Classed Entries under MUSIC-DRAMA—Musical theatre.

Administration

Advisory Committee on Chorus Affairs and Equity devise procedures for chorus calls. USA: New York, NY. 1983. Lang.: Eng. 117

Institutions

A history of the Charlottetown Festival. Canada: Charlottetown, PE. 1965-1987. Lang.: Eng. 505

International survey and review of summer 1987 opera productions. 1987. Lang.: Eng. 3704

Performance/production

Yearbook of Swiss theatrical activity, with bibliography. Switzerland. 1987-1988. Lang.: Fre, Ger, Ita. 892

Overview of Soviet Ukrainian theatre. Ukraine. 1917-1987. Lang.: Ukr. 924

University of Mexico: music of dance theatre. Mexico: Mexico City. 1987. Lang.: Spa. 1463

Ann Mortifee, singer, songwriter, performer. Canada: Vancouver, BC, Toronto, ON. 1982. Lang.: Eng. 1714

Golden Fleece, Ltd. bridges classical music, opera and musical theatre. USA: New York, NY. 1987. Lang.: Eng. 3412

International biographical survey of opera performers and productions. Europe. North America. 1987. Lang.: Eng. 3762

Biographical survey of international opera stars. Europe. North America. 1987. Lang.: Eng. 3764

Plays/librettos/scripts

Musical adaptation of Gorostiza's *Contigo pan y cebolla (With You, Bread and Onion)*. Mexico: Mexico City. Spain: Madrid. 1833-1984. Lang.: Eng. 1150

Role of playwright George Edwardes in development of musical comedy. UK-England: London. 1830-1890. Lang.: Eng. 2766

Reference materials

Catalogue of Valencian playtexts available at libraries of Barcelona. Spain: Valencia, Barcelona. Lang.: Cat. 2975

Theory/criticism

Current theatre compared to Ralph Lauren store. USA: New York, NY. 1987. Lang.: Eng. 1356

Musical Theatre Project (New York, NY)
Performance/production
Musical Theatre Project explores Broadway musical material
available in Shubert Archive. USA: New York, NY. 1984-1985.
Lang.: Eng. 3666

Musical Theatre Workshop (New York, NY)
Plays/librettos/scripts
Conference on women in theatre, emphasis on playwriting. USA.
1987. Lang.: Eng. 1161

Musical Whist
Plays/librettos/scripts
Essex Evans' adaptations of *Robinson Crusoe* and *Musical Whist*.
Australia. 1891-1902. Lang.: Eng. 2439

Musikteatergruppen Oktober (Södertälje)
Performance/production
Musikteatergruppen Oktober collaborates with immigrant amateurs.
Sweden: Södertälje. 1986. Lang.: Swe. 2019

Mussorgskij, Modest Pavlovič
Performance/production
Background on San Francisco opera radio broadcasts. USA: San
Francisco, CA. 1987. Lang.: Eng. 3833

Background on Metropolitan radio broadcast performances. USA:
New York, NY. 1987. Lang.: Eng. 3837

New realizations of Mussorgskij operas on the contemporary Soviet
stage. USSR. 1980-1987. Lang.: Rus. 3879

Muti, Riccardo
Performance/production
Interview, Italian conductor Riccardo Muti, artistic director, Teatro
alla Scala. Italy: Milan. 1970-1987. Lang.: Eng. 3808

*Mutter Courage und ihre Kinder (Mother Courage and Her
Children)*
Performance/production
Analysis of Brecht's original directing style and dramaturgy.
Germany. 1925-1987. Lang.: Eng. 1771

Music for Brecht's *Mutter Courage und ihre Kinder (Mother Courage
and Her Children)*. Switzerland: Zürich. Finland. 1939-1947. Lang.:
Ger. 2027

Collection of newspaper reviews by London theatre critics. UK-
England: London. 1986. Lang.: Eng. 2061

Theory/criticism
Suggestion for new form of dramaturgical research based on
concrete scenic action from past productions. USA: Tallahassee, FL.
1987. Lang.: Eng. 3074

Mutter, Die (Mother, The)
Performance/production
Analysis of Brecht's original directing style and dramaturgy.
Germany. 1925-1987. Lang.: Eng. 1771

Early productions of Brecht's plays reflected in the press. Germany:
Berlin. 1922-1933. Lang.: Ger. 1777

Collection of newspaper reviews by London theatre critics. UK-
England: London. 1986. Lang.: Eng. 2043

Plays/librettos/scripts
Bertolt Brecht and the Berlin workers' movement. Germany: Berlin.
1922-1932. Lang.: Ger. 2600

Muziektheater (Amsterdam)
Institutions
Opening of a new opera house in Amsterdam. Netherlands:
Amsterdam. 1987. Lang.: Eng. 3728

Mwale, John
Plays/librettos/scripts
Theme of aggression between fathers and sons: Zambian National
Theatre Arts Association festival. Zambia. 1966-1987. Lang.: Eng.
2972

My Gene
Performance/production
Collection of newspaper reviews by New York theatre critics. USA:
New York, NY. 1987. Lang.: Eng. 2326

Plays/librettos/scripts
Barbara Gelb discusses the creation of *My Gene*. USA. 1962-1987.
Lang.: Eng. 2867

My Life, by Josef Mengele
Performance/production
Collection of newspaper reviews by London theatre critics. UK-
England: London. 1986. Lang.: Eng. 2124

My Sister in This House
Performance/production
Collection of newspaper reviews by London theatre critics. UK-
England: London. 1987. Lang.: Eng. 2073

Comparison and review of *Melon, Breaking the Code, Alan Turing:
The Secret War* and *My Sister in This House*. UK-England: London.
1987. Lang.: Eng. 2285

Mydlack, Danny
Performance/production
The performance art piece, *Living Room Project*, of Danny Mydlack.
USA: Boston, MA. 1987. Lang.: Eng. 3367

Myers, Bruce
Performance/production
Collection of newspaper reviews by London theatre critics. UK-
England: London. 1986. Lang.: Eng. 2112

Myerson, Jonathan
Performance/production
Collection of newspaper reviews by London theatre critics. UK-
England: London. 1987. Lang.: Eng. 2177

Collection of newspaper reviews by London theatre critics. UK-
England: London. 1987. Lang.: Eng. 2201

Collection of newspaper reviews by London theatre critics. UK-
England: London. 1987. Lang.: Eng. 2234

Collection of newspaper reviews by London theatre critics. UK-
England: London. 1987. Lang.: Eng. 2245

Collection of newspaper reviews by London theatre critics. UK-
England: London. 1987. Lang.: Eng. 2254

Mystère bouffe
Performance/production
Plays of Pinget, Euripides and Théâtre du Rideau staged by
Jouanneau, Suzuki and Tanguy, Théâtre de la Bastille. France: Paris.
1987. Lang.: Fre. 1753

Mystère Bouffe
Performance/production
Collection of newspaper reviews by London theatre critics. UK-
England: London. 1987. Lang.: Eng. 2212

Mystères
Design/technology
Scenic representations of Hell. Italy. France. 1300-1399. Lang.: Ita.
349

Mystères de l'amour, Les (Mysteries of Love, The)
Plays/librettos/scripts
Playwright Roger Vitrac's critiques of bourgeois family life. France.
1922-1928. Lang.: Eng. 2584

Mystery of Edwin Drood, The
Performance/production
Collection of newspaper reviews by London theatre critics. UK-
England: London. 1987. Lang.: Eng. 2214

Mystery of Irma Vep, The
Performance/production
Life and works of playwright, director, designer Charles Ludlam.
USA: New York, NY. 1967-1987. Lang.: Eng. 952

Mystery plays
SEE ALSO
Passion plays.

Performance spaces
Reconstructs processional route of *Corpus Christi* performances.
England: York. 1399-1569. Lang.: Eng. 3329

Performance/production
Church condemnation of Roman *ludi*, creative impulse behind
medieval drama. Europe. 160-1578. Lang.: Eng. 1745

Modern production of the *Chester Cycle*. UK-England: Chester. 1987.
Lang.: Eng. 2299

Plays/librettos/scripts
Analysis of medieval Cain and Abel mystery plays. England. 1200-
1576. Lang.: Eng. 2506

Mythology
Institutions
Ramayana '87, an Inner London Education Authority project. UK-
England: London. 1987. Lang.: Eng. 3965

Performance/production
Orientalism in Peter Brook's production of *The Mahabharata*. India.
USA: New York, NY. 400 B.C.-1987 A.D. Lang.: Eng. 1932

Tükak Teatret and its artistic director Reidar Nilsson present *Inuit—
Human Beings*. USA: New York, NY. Denmark: Holstebro. 1975-
1983. Lang.: Eng. 2352

Mythology — cont'd

Plays/librettos/scripts

Origins of fairy tales on the Viennese stage. Austria: Vienna. 1700-1848. Lang.: Eng.   2450

Playwright Tomson Highway's use of native mythology. Canada. 1960-1987. Lang.: Eng.   2468

Exploration of mythic elements in the later plays of William Shakespeare. England: London. 1607-1614. Lang.: Eng.   2497

Classification and social hierarchy in Shakespeare's *Troilus and Cressida*. England. 1601. Lang.: Eng.   2554

Ariadne in plays of Ibsen, Strindberg, Maeterlinck. Europe. 1892-1902. Lang.: Eng.   2566

Peter Brook discusses his production of *The Mahabharata*. France: Paris. India. Australia: Perth. 1987. Lang.: Eng.   2571

Feminine life symbols in Sean O'Casey's *The Silver Tassie*. Ireland. 1928. Lang.: Eng.   2654

Archetypal nature of title character in *Felipe Angeles* by Elena Garro. Mexico. 1978. Lang.: Spa.   2696

Psychological interpretations of Wagner's *Parsifal*. Germany. 1882-1987. Lang.: Eng.   3907

Relation to other fields

Bear hunting ritual-drama: text, poetry, description of rites. Finland. 1600-1982. Lang.: Eng.   1234

Development of theatre influenced by myths of national character. Finland. 1950-1982. Lang.: Eng.   2989

Theory/criticism

Myth in the plays of the Dominican Republic. Dominican Republic. 1987. Lang.: Spa.   3026

Assessment of the series *Lost Beginning*, its relation to Stewart Parker's *Pentecost*. UK-Ireland. 1987. Lang.: Eng.   3218

Classical allusion and moral significance of court masques. Europe. 1982. Lang.: Eng.   3328

N-town Plays

Plays/librettos/scripts

Analysis of medieval Cain and Abel mystery plays. England. 1200-1576. Lang.: Eng.   2506

N'Debeka, Maxime

Basic theatrical documents

English translations of contemporary African plays. Senegal. Zaire. 1987. Lang.: Eng.   1566

N'Tumb, Diur

Basic theatrical documents

English translations of contemporary African plays. Senegal. Zaire. 1987. Lang.: Eng.   1566

Na dnè (Lower Depths, The)

Performance/production

The 4th International Theatre Conference: includes list of participants and their contributions. Poland: Warsaw. 1986. Lang.: Eng, Fre.   873

Life and work of Anatolij Efros. USSR: Moscow. 1983-1987. Lang.: Eng.   1038

Na dnè (Lower Depths, The)

Performance/production

Collection of newspaper reviews by London theatre critics. UK-England: London. 1986. Lang.: Eng.   2085

Na'lbandian, Abbas

Basic theatrical documents

Translation of five contemporary Persian plays. Iran. 1987. Lang.: Eng.   1558

Nabucco

Performance/production

On a performance of Verdi's *Nabucco*. Italy: Sant' Agate. 1987. Lang.: Swe.   3804

Plays/librettos/scripts

Creating modern critical edition of score of Verdi's *Nabucco*. Italy: Milan. 1987. Lang.: Eng.   3925

Nagy fejedelem, A (Great Prince, The)

Performance/production

Season openings at Petőfi Theatre, including Lengyel's *A nagy fejedelem (The Great Prince)* and Bíró's *A rablólovag (The Gallant Kidnapper)*. Hungary: Veszprém. 1987. Lang.: Hun.   1820

Nagy, László

Design/technology

Director, Szegedi Nemzeti Szinház, on theatre technology. Hungary: Szeged. 1987. Lang.: Hun.   337

Nagy, Zoltán

Performance/production

Interview with actor Zoltán Nagy. Hungary. 1962-1987. Lang.: Hun.   1809

Naitō, Yūkei

Performance/production

Space and sign in various Tokyo productions. Japan: Tokyo. 1987. Lang.: Jap.   1959

Nakamura za (Tokyo)

Performance/production

Productions from Yume no yūminsha, Tōhō, Parco, Tsukumo and Nakamura za. Japan: Tokyo. 1986-1987. Lang.: Jap.   1956

Nakamura, Naohiko

Design/technology

Nō masks by Nakamura Naohiko. Japan. 1900-1940. Lang.: Jap.   1497

Näktergalningarna (Skarpnäck)

Performance/production

Jordcirkus and amateur group Näktergalningarna stage *A Christmas Carol*. Sweden: Stockholm. 1986-1987. Lang.: Swe. 2020

Naleppa, Götz

Plays/librettos/scripts

The German radio play *Hörspiel* and its history. Germany, West: Cologne. USA. 1950-1985. Lang.: Eng.   3117

Nameday

Performance/production

The 4th International Theatre Conference: includes list of participants and their contributions. Poland: Warsaw. 1986. Lang.: Eng, Fre.   873

Names and Nicknames

Plays/librettos/scripts

Critical analysis of James Reaney's *Three Desks*. Canada. 1960-1977. Lang.: Eng.   2477

Namida nashi ni tamanegi no kawa o muku hōhō (How to Peel an Onion without Tears)

Performance/production

New Tokyo productions. Japan: Tokyo. 1987. Lang.: Jap.   1954

Nanbonomonjai! My Love (Who Cares?! My Love)

Performance/production

Productions from Yume no yūminsha, Tōhō, Parco, Tsukumo and Nakamura za. Japan: Tokyo. 1986-1987. Lang.: Jap.   1956

Plays/librettos/scripts

Productions by several Tokyo companies. Japan: Tokyo. 1986-1987. Lang.: Jap.   2682

Nanxi

Theory/criticism

Research on Chinese classical southern drama. China, People's Republic of. 1960-1987. Lang.: Chi.   3611

Naomi

Performance/production

Collection of newspaper reviews by London theatre critics. UK-England: London. 1987. Lang.: Eng.   2226

Nargiz

Performance/production

Musical art in opera: the creation of *Nargiz*. USSR. 1935-1987. Lang.: Rus.   3875

Narnia

Performance/production

Collection of newspaper reviews by London theatre critics. UK-England: London. 1986. Lang.: Eng.   2119

Narodno pozorište (Subotica)

Performance/production

Director Ljubiša Ristić and 'Shakespeare Fest '86'. Yugoslavia: Subotica, Palić. 1986. Lang.: Hun.   2403

Ljubiša Ristić adapts and directs Imre Madách's *Az ember tragédiája (The Tragedy of a Man)*. Yugoslavia: Subotica. 1986. Lang.: Hun.   2404

Interview with National Theatre director Ljubiša Ristić. Yugoslavia: Subotica. 1947-1986. Lang.: Hun.   2408

Nase des Michelangelo, Die (Michelangelo's Nose)

Theory/criticism

Comparison of Ball's *Michelangelo's Nose* and Hebbel's *Michel Angelo*. Germany. 1886-1927. Lang.: Eng.   3042

Nash, N. Richard

Performance/production

Collection of newspaper reviews by London theatre critics. UK-England: London. 1986. Lang.: Eng.   2053

Nat Horne Theatre (New York, NY)
Institutions
News of various theatres. USA: New York, NY. 1987. Lang.: Eng.
579

Natal Playhouse (Durban)
Performance/production
Review of Wagner's *Der Fliegende Holländer* at the Natal
Playhouse. South Africa, Republic of: Durban. 1987. Lang.: Eng.
3815

Nathan der Weise (Nathan the Wise)
Performance/production
G.E. Lessing's *Nathan der Weise (Nathan the Wise)* staged by József
Ruszt, Hevesi Sándor Theatre. Hungary: Zalaegerszeg. 1986. Lang.:
Hun.
1806

József Ruszt directs G.E. Lessing's *Nathan der Weise (Nathan the
Wise)* at Hevesi Sándor Theatre under the title *Bölcs Náthán.*
Hungary: Zalaegerszeg. 1986. Lang.: Hun.
1866

National Ballet of Canada (Toronto, ON)
Performance/production
Ballerina Gizella Witkowsky: debut, National Ballet of Canada.
Canada: Toronto, ON. 1984. Lang.: Eng.
1432

National Endowment for the Arts (NEA, Washington, DC)
Administration
Survey of financial results for nonprofit theatres. USA. 1986. Lang.:
Eng.
173

Government funding of art. USA. 1980-1987. Lang.: Eng.
175

Attempts to cut funding to the National Endowment for the Arts.
USA. 1965-1985. Lang.: Eng.
194

Report on a hearing to evaluate proposed cuts to NEA, NEH. USA:
Washington, DC. 1987. Lang.: Eng.
216

Debate over the National Endowment for the Arts' new guidelines.
USA. 1977-1987. Lang.: Eng.
256

Relation to other fields
National Endowment for the Arts suffers severe cutbacks. USA:
Washington, DC. 1982. Lang.: Eng.
1273

Historical look at the National Endowment for the Arts. USA. 1977-
1981. Lang.: Eng.
1280

**National Endowment for the Humanities (NEH, Washington,
DC)**
Administration
Report on a hearing to evaluate proposed cuts to NEA, NEH. USA:
Washington, DC. 1987. Lang.: Eng.
216

National Institute of Dramatic Art (Australia)
Institutions
Survey of liberal arts and professional training courses. Australia.
1987. Lang.: Eng.
503

National Theatre (Bratislava)
SEE
Slovenske Narodni Divadlo.

National Theatre (Budapest)
SEE
Nemzeti Szinház.

National Theatre (Dublin)
SEE
Abbey Theatre.

National Theatre (Helsinki)
SEE
Suomen Kansallisteatteri.

National Theatre (London)
Institutions
Recent work by the National Theatre of Great Britain. UK-England:
London. 1985-1987. Lang.: Eng.
568

History and current season of the National Theatre. UK-England:
London. 1848-1987. Lang.: Eng.
1647

Performance/production
Collection of newspaper reviews by London theatre critics. UK-
England: London. 1986. Lang.: Eng.
2034

Collection of newspaper reviews by London theatre critics. UK-
England: London. 1986. Lang.: Eng.
2044

Collection of newspaper reviews by London theatre critics. UK-
England: London. 1986. Lang.: Eng.
2150

Collection of newspaper reviews by London theatre critics. UK-
England: London. 1986. Lang.: Eng.
2169

Revival of *Revizor (The Government Inspector)* at the National
Theatre directed by Richard Eyre. UK-England: London. USSR.
1985. Lang.: Eng.
2290

Review of production and staging aspects of *Wild Honey* by Anton
Čechov. UK-England: London. 1986. Lang.: Eng.
2306

Plays/librettos/scripts
Interview with playwright Howard Brenton. UK-England. 1975-1987.
Lang.: Eng.
2806

National Theatre (Miskolc)
SEE
Miskolci Nemzeti Szinház.

National Theatre (Munich)
SEE
Bayerische Staatsoper im Nationaltheater.

National Theatre (New York, NY)
SEE
American National Theatre and Academy.

National Theatre (Pécs)
SEE
Pécsi Nemzeti Szinház.

National Theatre (Prague)
SEE
Národní Divadlo.

National Theatre (Szeged)
SEE
Szegedi Nemzeti Szinház.

National Theatre (Tel Aviv)
SEE
HaBimah (Tel Aviv).

National Theatre (Uganda)
Performance/production
Role of theatre in the face of political turmoil. Nicaragua: Managua.
Uganda. 1987. Lang.: Eng.
864

National Theatre Company (London)
Performance/production
Collection of newspaper reviews by London theatre critics. UK-
England. 1987. Lang.: Eng.
2033

Collection of newspaper reviews by London theatre critics. UK-
England: London. 1987. Lang.: Eng.
2183

Collection of newspaper reviews by London theatre critics. UK-
England: London. 1987. Lang.: Eng.
2198

Collection of newspaper reviews by London theatre critics. UK-
England: London. 1987. Lang.: Eng.
2213

Collection of newspaper reviews by London theatre critics. UK-
England: London. 1987. Lang.: Eng.
2220

Collection of newspaper reviews by London theatre critics. UK-
England: London. 1987. Lang.: Eng.
2226

Collection of newspaper reviews by London theatre critics. UK-
England: London. 1987. Lang.: Eng.
2233

Collection of newspaper reviews by London theatre critics. UK-
England: London. 1987. Lang.: Eng.
2240

Collection of newspaper reviews by London theatre critics. UK-
England: London. 1987. Lang.: Eng.
2251

Collection of newspaper reviews by London theatre critics. UK-
England: London. 1987. Lang.: Eng.
2253

Collection of newspaper reviews by London theatre critics. UK-
England. 1987. Lang.: Eng.
2261

Collection of newspaper reviews by London theatre critics. UK-
England: London. 1987. Lang.: Eng.
2269

Collection of newspaper reviews of London theatre critics. UK-
England: London. 1987. Lang.: Eng.
2273

Plays/librettos/scripts
Analysis of Jean Genet's plays. UK-England: London. 1987. Lang.:
Eng.
2805

Relation to other fields
Lindsay Anderson's analysis of the political role of theatre. UK-
England. 1987. Lang.: Eng.
3005

National Theatre of the Deaf (Waterford, CT)
Institutions
National Theatre of the Deaf productions of *Farewell My Lovely*
and *In a Grove* directed by Arvin Brown in Beijing. China, People's
Republic of: Beijing. USA. 1986-1987. Lang.: Eng.
1611

National Theatre School (Montreal, PQ)
Institutions
Historical background of National Theatre School. Canada: Montreal,
PQ. 1960-1985. Lang.: Eng.
519

National Youth Theatre of Great Britain (London)
Performance/production
Collection of newspaper reviews by London theatre critics. UK-England: London. 1987. Lang.: Eng. 2251

Nationaltheatret (Oslo)
Administration
Actress Vesleøy Haslund fights termination from the National Theatre. Norway: Oslo. 1979-1982. Lang.: Eng. 1522

Naturalism
Basic theatrical documents
Catalan translation of Arthur Schnitzler's *Reigen (Round)*. 1862-1931. Lang.: Cat. 1541

Plays/librettos/scripts
History of 19th-century German literature, including drama and theatre. Germany. Austria. 1830-1900. Lang.: Ger. 2591

Comparison of works by Hauptmann and Wilbrandt. Germany: Berlin. Austria: Vienna. 1889-1987. Lang.: Eng. 2593

Critical reception of realism and naturalism. Germany. 1890-1987. Lang.: Ger. 2601

Theory/criticism
Centenary of Théâtre Libre: proposes 'subjective realism'. France. 1887-1987. Lang.: Fre. 1337

Shift of August Strindberg from naturalism to expressionism. Sweden. 1987. Lang.: Eng. 3061

Navarro Gonzalvo, Eduard
Reference materials
Catalogue of Valencian playtexts available at libraries of Barcelona. Spain: Valencia, Barcelona. Lang.: Cat. 2975

Navarro Llombart, Carmelo
Reference materials
Catalogue of Valencian playtexts available at libraries of Barcelona. Spain: Valencia, Barcelona. Lang.: Cat. 2975

Navesi, Bonaventura
Performance/production
Actors and institutions of eighteenth-century Venice. Italy: Venice. 1700-1800. Lang.: Ita. 3312

Nazareth, H.O.
Performance/production
Collection of newspaper reviews by London theatre critics. UK-England: London. 1987. Lang.: Eng. 2185

Nazimova, Alla
Performance/production
Philip Moeller's premiere of *Mourning Becomes Electra* by O'Neill. USA: New York, NY. 1931. Lang.: Eng. 2366

Ndebele, Nimrod N.T.
Relation to other fields
Influences of Black political and economic life on literature, performance. South Africa, Republic of. 1970-1987. Lang.: Eng. 1252

Ndedi-Penda, Patrice
Plays/librettos/scripts
Compares plays of Enlightenment France, Francophone Africa. Congo: Brazzaville. Cameroon. Benin. France. 1700-1975. Lang.: Eng. 2496

Ndlovu, Duma
Institutions
Duma Ndlovu, the Woza Afrika Foundation and the Hudson Guild Theatre. USA: New York, NY. South Africa, Republic of. 1976-1986. Lang.: Eng. 604

Ne blâmez jamais les bedouins (Don't Blame the Bedouins)
Plays/librettos/scripts
Language and metaphor in plays of René-Daniel Dubois. Canada: Toronto, ON, Montreal, PQ. 1983-1987. Lang.: Eng. 2471

Neak, Larry
Plays/librettos/scripts
Interview with playwright Charles Fuller. USA: Philadelphia, PA, New York, NY. Korea, South. 1959-1987. Lang.: Eng. 2921

Neaptide
Performance/production
Collection of newspaper reviews by London theatre critics. UK-England: London. 1986. Lang.: Eng. 2118

Near, Timothy
Plays/librettos/scripts
Three feminist productions of plays by Henrik Ibsen. USA. 1987. Lang.: Eng. 2899

Necessary Angel Theatre Company (Toronto, ON)
Performance/production
Interview with actress Tanja Jacobs. Canada: Toronto, ON. 1987. Lang.: Eng. 727

Nederlandse Opera (Netherlands)
Performance/production
Interview with Dario Fo. Netherlands. Italy. 1987. Lang.: Dut. 3814

Needles of Light
Performance/production
Collection of newspaper reviews by London theatre critics. UK-England: London. 1987. Lang.: Eng. 2192

Negro Ensemble Company (NEC, New York, NY)
Administration
Nontraditional casting: types, rationale and examples. USA: New York, NY. 1987. Lang.: Eng. 203

Institutions
Members of Negro Ensemble Company, New Federal Theatre and American Place Theatre on artistic agendas. USA: New York, NY. 1987. Lang.: Eng. 592

Plays/librettos/scripts
Charles Fuller's *A Soldier's Play*: debate on means of liberation. USA. 1976-1981. Lang.: Eng. 2854

Negro Ensemble Company (New York, NY)
Institutions
History of the Negro Ensemble Company. USA: New York, NY. 1969-1987. Lang.: Eng. 1653

Negro Operetta Company
Institutions
Will Garland and European tour of Negro Operetta Company. UK-England. Finland: Helsinki. Russia. 1905-1917. Lang.: Eng. 3956

Neher, Caspar
Design/technology
Exhibition on ballet *The Seven Deadly Sins* by Kurt Weill and Edward James. France: Paris. UK-England: London. 1933-1987. Lang.: Eng. 1429

Performance/production
Leonard Steckel's production of *Faust II* as a turning point of Swiss theatre. Switzerland: Zürich. 1949. Lang.: Ger. 2028

Neighborhood Action (Sudbury, ON)
Performance/production
Popular theatre, mostly on economic, feminist themes. Canada: Sudbury, ON. 1930-1987. Lang.: Eng. 1709

Neighborhood Playhouse (New York, NY)
Performance/production
Sanford Meisner's method of teaching acting. USA: New York, NY. 1987. Lang.: Eng. 2349

Neil Simon Theatre (New York, NY)
Performance/production
Collection of newspaper reviews by New York theatre critics. USA: New York, NY. 1987. Lang.: Eng. 2316

Collection of newspaper reviews by New York theatre critics. USA: New York, NY. 1987. Lang.: Eng. 2318

Collection of newspaper reviews by New York theatre critics. USA: New York, NY. 1987. Lang.: Eng. 2322

Neill, Angus
Performance/production
Career of actor/director Angus Neill. UK-England: London. South Africa, Republic of. 1952. Lang.: Eng. 2293

Nekrošjus, Éjmuntas
Performance/production
Work of E. Nekrošjus, director of Vil'njus Youth Theatre. USSR: Vilnius. 1980-1987. Lang.: Rus. 1043

Nel.lo, Francesc
Performance/production
Collection of theatre reviews by Xavier Fàbregas. Spain-Catalonia. 1969-1972. Lang.: Cat. 2010

Nelken, Roni
Performance/production
Creation of an original puppet character in puppet theatre. Israel: Jerusalem. 1987. Lang.: Heb. 3974

Communicating with young audiences with puppet theatre. Israel: Jerusalem. 1987. Lang.: Heb. 3975

Nelson, Richard
Performance/production
Collection of newspaper reviews by London theatre critics. UK-England: London. 1986. Lang.: Eng. 2063

Collection of newspaper reviews by London theatre critics. UK-England. 1987. Lang.: Eng. 2263

Németh, László
Performance/production
Interview with director Ferenc Sík. Hungary. 1987. Lang.: Hun. 802

Németh, László — cont'd

Production history of *Galilei (Galileo)* by László Németh. Hungary. 1952-1987. Lang.: Hun.   1790

Ferenc Sík directs *Galilei (Galileo)* by László Németh at Várszinház. Hungary: Budapest. 1987. Lang.: Hun.   1851

Károly Kazimir directs László Németh's *Harc a jólét ellen (The Fight Against Prosperity)*. Hungary: Budapest. 1986. Lang.: Hun.   1910

Two premieres: Shakespeare, *The Merchant of Venice*, directed by Árpád Jutacsa Hegyi. Németh's *Villámfénynél (By the Stroke of Lightning)*, directed by Attila Seprődi Kiss. Hungary: Kecskemét. 1987. Lang.: Hun.   1925

Plays/librettos/scripts
Analysis of plays by László Németh. Hungary. 1986-1987. Lang.: Hun.   2631

Nemota, Yutaka
Performance/production
Collection of newspaper reviews by London theatre critics. UK-England: London. 1986. Lang.: Eng.   2142

Nemuranai boku no yoru (My Sleepless Night)
Performance/production
New themes and styles in Japanese theatre. Japan: Tokyo. 1986. Lang.: Jap.   1953

Productions of Bungakuza, Yūkikai Zenjidō shiatā, Tao and Tenkei gekijō. Japan: Tokyo. 1986. Lang.: Jap.   1961

Nemzeti Szinház (Budapest)
Design/technology
Pál Tolnay's original proposal for modernization of the lighting system at National Theatre. Hungary: Budapest. 1957. Lang.: Hun.   340

Detailed description of a light-weight revolving stage platform. Hungary: Budapest. 1930. Lang.: Hun.   341

Renovation plans for the Hungarian National Theatre. Hungary: Budapest. 1957. Lang.: Hun.   342

Interview with set designer Árpád Csányi. Hungary. 1987. Lang.: Hun.   1592

Institutions
International conference on national theatres in Europe. Hungary: Budapest. 1987. Lang.: Hun.   541

History of the Nemzeti Szinház. Hungary: Budapest. 1837-1987. Lang.: Hun.   542

Director of National Theatre of Budapest addresses conference on national theatres in Europe. Hungary. 1987. Lang.: Hun.   544

Performance spaces
Designer of new Hungarian National Theatre on site and design considerations. Hungary: Budapest. 1987. Lang.: Hun.   639

Comparison of two Nemzeti Szinház sites. Hungary: Budapest. 1983. Lang.: Hun.   641

Mór Jókai's recollections of the old, gas-lit National Theatre building. Hungary: Budapest. 1900. Lang.: Hun.   642

Reprinted interview with Nemzeti Szinház architect Csaba Virág. Hungary: Budapest. 1966. Lang.: Hun.   646

Performance/production
Imre Kerényi directs *Énekes madár (The Song Bird)* by Áron Tamási at the National Theatre. Hungary: Budapest. 1987. Lang.: Hun.   1819

Director Imre Kerényi discusses *Csiksomlyó passió (Passion Play of Csiksomlyó)*. Hungary. 1982-1987. Lang.: Hun.   1843

Director Endre Márton. Hungary. 1941-1978. Lang.: Hun.   1860

Áron Tamási's *Énekes madár (The Song Bird)* directed by Imre Kerényi at National Theatre. Hungary: Budapest. 1987. Lang.: Hun.   1872

Nemzeti Szinház (Miskolc)
SEE
Miskolci Nemzeti Szinház.

Nemzeti Szinház (Pécs)
SEE
Pécsi Nemzeti Szinház.

Nemzeti Szinház (Pest)
SEE
Pesti Nemzeti Szinház.

Nemzeti Szinház (Szeged)
SEE
Szegedi Nemzeti Szinház.

Neo-Dadaism
Performance/production
Dance soundtracks simulate a Dada/Futurist variety club. Europe. 1985. Lang.: Eng.   3398

Neoclassicism
SEE ALSO
Geographical-Chronological Index under Europe 1540-1660, France 1629-1660, Italy 1540-1576.

Design/technology
Aesthetic influences on scene design. England. 1700-1899. Lang.: Eng.   1590

Relation to other fields
Overview of French literature including theatre. France. 800-1700. Lang.: Ita.   2990

Theory/criticism
Tragedy, space and discourse in neoclassical dramatic theory. France. 1800-1850. Lang.: Eng.   3035

Catalan translation of Lessing's *Hamburgische Dramaturgie*. Germany: Hamburg. 1767-1769. Lang.: Cat.   3043

Nepszinház (Budapest)
Performance/production
Reviews of two plays by István Örkény: *Forgatókönyv (Screenplay)* directed by István Paál and two productions of *Tóték (The Tót Family)* staged by János Meczner and István Pinczés. Hungary: Veszprém, Budapest, Debrecen. 1986-1987. Lang.: Hun.   1880

Neptune Theatre (Halifax, NS)
Administration
The role of a board of directors for successful theatre companies. Canada: Toronto, ON, Halifax, NS. 1982. Lang.: Eng.   17

Performance/production
Writer-director Glen Cairns and surrealistic drama at the Neptune Theatre. Canada: Halifax, NS. 1977-1987. Lang.: Eng.   1695

Nerd, The
Design/technology
Lighting reviews for several New York productions. USA: New York, NY. 1987. Lang.: Eng.   475

Performance/production
Collection of newspaper reviews by New York theatre critics. USA: New York, NY. 1987. Lang.: Eng.   2325

Plays/librettos/scripts
Comparison of main characters in three contemporary plays. USA: New York, NY. 1987. Lang.: Eng.   2916

Nersisjan, Babken
Performance/production
Actor Babken Nersisjan. USSR. 1917-1987. Lang.: Rus.   1000

Nest of the Woodgrouse
SEE
Teterëvo gnezdo.

Nest, Das (Nest, The)
Performance/production
Collection of newspaper reviews by London theatre critics. UK-England: London. 1986. Lang.: Eng.   2103

Network
SEE
Netzwerk.

Neuen Leiden des jungen W., Die (New Sorrows of Young W., The)
Plays/librettos/scripts
On *Die Neuen Leiden des jungen W. (The New Sorrows of Young W.)* by Ulrich Plenzdorf. Germany, East. 1972-1987. Lang.: Ger.   2609

Neuer Künstlerischer Tanz
Performance/production
Memorial album by and about dancer Gret Palucca. Germany, East: Dresden. 1922-1987. Lang.: Ger.   1469

Relation to other fields
Exhibition devoted to modern dancer Gret Palucca. Germany, East: Dresden. 1922-1987. Lang.: Ger.   1476

Neues Theater (Leipzig)
Institutions
History of Leipzig Neues Theater. Germany: Leipzig. 1868-1932. Lang.: Ger.   3391

Neumann, Bernd
Reference materials
Rolf Bergmann's catalogue of medieval German drama. Germany. 1986. Lang.: Eng.   1202

Niccodemi, Dario
Performance/production
Collection of theatre reviews by J.M. de Sagarra. Spain-Catalonia:
Barcelona. 1922-1927. Lang.: Cat.   885

Nicholas Nickleby
Design/technology
Lighting design and instruments for production of *Nicholas Nickleby*.
USA: New York, NY. 1982. Lang.: Eng.   478

Nichols, Mike
Institutions
Second City improvisational comedy troupe. USA: Chicago, IL.
Canada: Toronto, ON. 1959-1987. Lang.: Eng.   605

Current trends in American theatre. USA. 1967-1987. Lang.: Eng.
                                                                              621

Nichols, Peter
Performance/production
Collection of newspaper reviews by London theatre critics. UK-
England: London. 1987. Lang.: Eng.   2210

Plays/librettos/scripts
Comparison between medieval passion plays and Peter Nichols'
Passion Play. 1986. Lang.: Eng.   2429

Theme of theatre in recent plays. UK-England. 1957-1985. Lang.:
Eng.   2764

Nicholson Fights Croydon
Performance/production
Collection of newspaper reviews by London theatre critics. UK-
England: London. 1986. Lang.: Eng.   2171

Nico Malan Operahouse (Cape Town, SA)
Performance/production
Development of Wagner's *Die Meistersinger von Nürnberg*. South
Africa, Republic of: Cape Town. Germany, West: Munich. 1868-
1987. Lang.: Eng.   3816

Niech sczezną artyści (Let the Artists Die)
Performance/production
Polish theatre. Poland: Warsaw, Cracow, Wrocław. 1980-1987. Lang.:
Eng, Fre.   1987

Nienasycenie (Insatiability)
Performance/production
Four new productions in Poland. Poland: Warsaw. 1986-1987. Lang.:
Eng, Fre.   1988

Nietzsche, Friedrich
Plays/librettos/scripts
Greek poetic drama through Nietzschean theory. Greece. 1987.
Lang.: Eng.   2620

Theory/criticism
Comparison of Ball's *Michelangelo's Nose* and Hebbel's *Michel
Angelo*. Germany. 1886-1927. Lang.: Eng.   3042

Nieuwe Dood, Een (New Death, A)
Performance/production
Dutch and American plays about AIDS. Netherlands. USA. 1987.
Lang.: Dut.   1984

Night Must Fall
Performance/production
Collection of newspaper reviews by London theatre critics. UK-
England: London. 1986. Lang.: Eng.   2045

Night of Legio, The
SEE
Nag van Legio, Die.

Night of Passion on Butterman Drive, A
Performance/production
Collection of newspaper reviews by London theatre critics. UK-
England: London. 1987. Lang.: Eng.   2243

Night of the Assassins, The
SEE
Noche de los asesinos, La.

'Night, Mother
Administration
Influence of TV ads on success of Broadway plays. USA: New
York, NY. 1984-1987. Lang.: Eng.   179

Plays/librettos/scripts
Male and female responses to Marsha Norman's *'Night, Mother*.
USA. 1983-1987. Lang.: Eng.   2918

Nightmare Abbey
Performance/production
Collection of newspaper reviews by London theatre critics. UK-
England: London. 1987. Lang.: Eng.   2276

Nightshriek
Performance/production
Collection of newspaper reviews by London theatre critics. UK-
England: London. 1986. Lang.: Eng.   2133

Nightwood Theatre (Toronto, ON)
Institutions
Development of feminist theatre in Toronto. Canada: Toronto, ON.
1960-1987. Lang.: Eng.   1608

Performance spaces
The lack of performance space for small theatre companies. Canada:
Toronto, ON. 1987. Lang.: Eng.   629

Nikitiny
Performance/production
Life and work of the Nikitiny Circus artists. USSR. 1850-1950.
Lang.: Rus.   3306

Nilsson, Birgit
Performance/production
Birgit Nilsson's master voice class at Manhattan School of Music.
USA: New York, NY. 1983-1987. Lang.: Eng.   3859

Nilsson, Bruno
Performance/production
Harlekin's efforts to involve youth in amateur theatre. Sweden:
Landskrona. 1982-1987. Lang.: Swe.   2022

Nilsson, Reidar
Performance/production
Tükak Teatret and its artistic director Reidar Nilsson present *Inuit–
Human Beings*. USA: New York, NY. Denmark: Holstebro. 1975-
1983. Lang.: Eng.   2352

Ninagawa Company (Tokyo)
Performance/production
Collection of newspaper reviews by London theatre critics. UK-
England: London. 1987. Lang.: Eng.   2249

Collection of newspaper reviews by London theatre critics. UK-
England: London. 1987. Lang.: Eng.   2250

Ninagawa, Yukio
Performance/production
Collection of newspaper reviews by London theatre critics. UK-
England: London. 1987. Lang.: Eng.   2249

Collection of newspaper reviews by London theatre critics. UK-
England: London. 1987. Lang.: Eng.   2250

Niño, Jairo Anibal
Performance/production
Collection of newspaper reviews by London theatre critics. UK-
England: London. 1986. Lang.: Eng.   2076

Collection of newspaper reviews by London theatre critics. UK-
England: London. 1987. Lang.: Eng.   2257

Nishiki, Kazuo
Performance/production
Productions of several Tokyo companies. Japan: Tokyo. 1987. Lang.:
Jap.   1962

Nit, La (Night, The)
Reference materials
Picture book to accompany production of *La Nit (The Night)* by Els
Comedians. Spain-Catalonia. 1987. Lang.: Cat.   1209

Nixon in China
Performance/production
Peter Sellars' American National Theatre on European tour. USA.
Netherlands. 1987. Lang.: Dut.   2351

Premiere of the docu-opera, *Nixon in China*, Houston Grand Opera.
USA: Houston, TX. 1987. Lang.: Eng.   3843

Nižinska, Bronislava
Performance/production
Career of choreographer/dancer Bronislava Nižinska. France. USA.
1891-1930. Lang.: Eng.   1436

Nižinskij, Vaslav
Performance/production
Career of choreographer/dancer Bronislava Nižinska. France. USA.
1891-1930. Lang.: Eng.   1436

Millicent Hodson speaks about how she managed to reconstruct
Nižinskij's *Le sacre du printemps*. USA: Los Angeles, CA. 1913-
1987. Lang.: Swe.   1473

Nkangia, Samuel
Plays/librettos/scripts
Compares plays of Enlightenment France, Francophone Africa.
Congo: Brazzaville. Cameroon. Benin. France. 1700-1975. Lang.: Eng.
                                                                            2496

Nniccu Furcedda
Plays/librettos/scripts
Plays of Antonio Monetta, Pietro Suscio and Girolamo Bax. Italy.
1600-1900. Lang.: Ita. 2669

Nō
SEE ALSO
Classed Entries under DANCE-DRAMA—Nō.

Performance/production
Eastern theatre forms in Western artists' productions. Canada:
Vancouver, BC. 1987. Lang.: Eng. 725

Origins of theatre and its relationship to the spectator. India. Japan.
Sri Lanka. 1987. Lang.: Eng. 813

Reviews of Oriental dance-drama performances. Japan. Indonesia.
1986. Lang.: Hun. 1951

Relation to other fields
Analysis of the role of tradition in theatrical forms of different
cultures. Asia. Africa. 1985. Lang.: Fre. 1218

Theory/criticism
Metaphysical and philosophical implications of the actor's role in the
nō theatre. Japan. 712-1980. Lang.: Pol. 1510

Analysis of Shikadō by Zeami. Japan. 1363-1443. Lang.: Kor. 3053

No Frills
Performance/production
Martin Charnin's work in musical theatre. USA: New York, NY.
1957-1987. Lang.: Eng. 3658

No Man's Land
Performance/production
Collection of newspaper reviews by London theatre critics. UK-
England: London. 1987. Lang.: Eng. 2267

Plays/librettos/scripts
Interpreting Harold Pinter's dramas through focus on his play
structures. UK-England. 1958-1987. Lang.: Eng. 2815

No More A-Roving
Performance/production
Collection of newspaper reviews by London theatre critics. UK-
England: London. 1987. Lang.: Eng. 2223

No Worries
Performance/production
Collection of newspaper reviews by London theatre critics. UK-
England: London. 1987. Lang.: Eng. 2173

Collection of newspaper reviews by London theatre critics. UK-
England: London. 1987. Lang.: Eng. 2252

Noble, Adrian
Performance/production
Collection of newspaper reviews by London theatre critics. UK-
England: London. 1986. Lang.: Eng. 2082

Collection of newspaper reviews by London theatre critics. UK-
England: London. 1987. Lang.: Eng. 2210

Collection of newspaper reviews by London theatre critics. UK-
England: London. 1987. Lang.: Eng. 2236

Collection of newspaper reviews by London theatre critics. UK-
England: London. 1987. Lang.: Eng. 2239

Collection of newspaper reviews by London theatre critics. UK-
England: London. 1987. Lang.: Eng. 2253

Noble, John
Performance/production
Collection of newspaper reviews by London theatre critics. UK-
England: London. 1986. Lang.: Eng. 2099

Noces, Les
Performance/production
Career of choreographer/dancer Bronislava Nižinska. France. USA.
1891-1930. Lang.: Eng. 1436

Noda, Hideki
Plays/librettos/scripts
Productions by several Tokyo companies. Japan: Tokyo. 1986-1987.
Lang.: Jap. 2682

Noël and Gertie
Performance/production
Collection of newspaper reviews by London theatre critics. UK-
England: London. 1986. Lang.: Eng. 2137

Női partőrség szeme láttára, A (In Sight of the Spar)
Performance/production
Péter Huszti directs A női partőrség szeme láttára (In Sight of the
Spar) by Pál Békés at Madách Szinház Chamber Theatre. Hungary:
Budapest. 1987. Lang.: Hun. 1873

Péter Huszti directs A női partőrség szeme láttára (In Sight of the
Spar) by Pál Békés at Madách Chamber Theatre. Hungary:
Budapest. 1987. Lang.: Hun. 1924

Noia del gira-sol, La (Sunflower Girl, The)
Basic theatrical documents
Study of the poetic, narrative and theatrical work of Agustí Bartra,
edition of complete works, vol. 4. Spain-Catalonia. Mexico. 1937-
1982. Lang.: Cat. 1571

Noises Off
Performance/production
Noises Off by Michael Frayn, directed by Jiří Menzel, Činoherní
klub. Czechoslovakia: Prague. 1987. Lang.: Cze. 765

Plays/librettos/scripts
Dramatic structure in Frayn's Noises Off. 1987. Lang.: Eng. 2416

Theme of theatre in recent plays. UK-England. 1957-1985. Lang.:
Eng. 2764

Nolan, Jim
Performance/production
TEAM, an educational theatre company. Ireland: Dublin. 1984-1987.
Lang.: Eng. 818

Nontraditional Casting Project (New York, NY)
Administration
Nontraditional casting: types, rationale and examples. USA: New
York, NY. 1987. Lang.: Eng. 203

Noonan, John Ford
Plays/librettos/scripts
Interview with playwright John Ford Noonan. USA. 1970-1987.
Lang.: Eng. 2894

Nordkalottfestivalen (Hammerfest)
Performance/production
Impressions of Nordkalottfestivalen, conditions of Norwegian amateur
theatre. Norway: Hammerfest. 1987. Lang.: Swe. 868

Norén, Lars
Performance/production
Collection of newspaper reviews by London theatre critics. UK-
England: London. 1987. Lang.: Eng. 2187

Norgård, Dag
Performance/production
Harlekin's efforts to involve youth in amateur theatre. Sweden:
Landskrona. 1982-1987. Lang.: Swe. 2022

Normal Heart, The
Performance/production
Collection of newspaper reviews by London theatre critics. UK-
England: London. 1986. Lang.: Eng. 2077

Plays/librettos/scripts
Impact of AIDS crisis on the theatre. USA: New York, NY, San
Francisco, CA. 1987. Lang.: Eng. 2881

David Shaber, Larry Kramer, Emily Mann: Three of the few
American political dramatists. USA: New York, NY. 1987. Lang.:
Eng. 2907

Norman, Marsha
Administration
Influence of TV ads on success of Broadway plays. USA: New
York, NY. 1984-1987. Lang.: Eng. 179

Profile of Ensemble Studio Theatre. USA: New York, NY. 1987.
Lang.: Eng. 232

Plays/librettos/scripts
Male and female responses to Marsha Norman's 'Night, Mother.
USA. 1983-1987. Lang.: Eng. 2918

Norodom Sihanouk
SEE
Histoire terrible mais inachevée de Norodom Sihanouk, roi du
Cambodge, L'.

North Carolina Black Repertory Company (Winston-Salem, NC)
Institutions
The formation of the North Carolina Black Repertory Company.
USA: Winston-Salem, NC. 1979-1987. Lang.: Eng. 1666

North Shore Fish
Performance/production
Collection of newspaper reviews by New York theatre critics. USA:
New York, NY. 1987. Lang.: Eng. 2323

North, Robert
Performance/production
New European choreographers and their development of new
images. France: Paris. UK-England: London. South Africa, Republic
of. 1987. Lang.: Eng. 1468

Northbay Lyric Opera (San Rafael, CA)
Performance/production
Bay Area opera companies. USA: San Francisco, CA. 1900-1987.
Lang.: Eng. 3842
Northern Arts and Cultural Centre (Yellowknife, NT)
Performance spaces
Northern Arts and Cultural Centre: planning and building. Canada:
Yellowknife, NT. 1980-1985. Lang.: Eng. 1667
Northern Star
Theory/criticism
Stewart Parker's *Northern Star*. UK-Ireland. 1984. Lang.: Eng. 3065
Northlight Theatre (Chicago, IL)
Institutions
Analysis of the changing scene in Chicago's theatres. USA: Chicago,
IL. 1987. Lang.: Eng. 589
Northward Ho!
Plays/librettos/scripts
Evaluation of *Westward Ho!* and *Northward Ho!* by Thomas Dekker
and John Webster. England. 1605. Lang.: Eng. 2509
Norup, Bent
Performance/production
Review of Wagner's *Der Fliegende Holländer* at the Natal
Playhouse. South Africa, Republic of: Durban. 1987. Lang.: Eng. 3815
Not I
Plays/librettos/scripts
Nietzschean and psychoanalytical interpretation of Beckett's *Not I*.
USA. 1972-1987. Lang.: Eng. 2879
Notebooks of a Cameraman, Serafino Gubbio
SEE
Quaderni di Serafino Gubbio operatore.
Notre fille ne se mariera pas (Our Daughter Will Not Marry)
Plays/librettos/scripts
Compares plays of Enlightenment France, Francophone Africa.
Congo: Brazzaville. Cameroon. Benin. France. 1700-1975. Lang.: Eng. 2496
Notti di Palermu, Le (Nights of Palermo, The)
Plays/librettos/scripts
Tommaso Aversa's Sicilian comedy *Le notti di Palermu (The Nights of Palermo)*. Italy. 1600. Lang.: Ita. 1136
Nou Hsi
Plays/librettos/scripts
The Chinese opera form *Nou Hsi* and its characteristics. China. 900.
Lang.: Chi. 3544
Novarina, Valère
Performance/production
Directing as creation of a dimension that enhances the actor's desire.
France. 1987. Lang.: Fre. 785
Noverre, Jean-Georges
Performance/production
Theatricality of dance. USA. 1985. Lang.: Eng. 1414
Novo, Salvador
Plays/librettos/scripts
Plays by Gorostiza, Usigli and Novo on Spanish conquest of
Mexico. Mexico. 1958-1961. Lang.: Eng. 2701
Novosadsko pozorište (Novi Sad)
Performance/production
Tóték (The Tót Family) by István Örkény at Hungarian Theatre,
guest director Gábor Székely. Yugoslavia: Novi Sad. 1987. Lang.:
Hun. 2406
Now They Sing Again
SEE
Nun singen sie wieder.
Now You See Me
Performance/production
Collection of newspaper reviews by London theatre critics. UK-
England: London. 1987. Lang.: Eng. 2256
Nowra, Louis
Plays/librettos/scripts
Conflict of worlds in plays by Louis Nowra. Australia. 1983-1985.
Lang.: Eng. 2449
Nozze di Figaro, Le
Performance/production
Review of productions at opera ensembles meeting. Hungary: Szeged.
1987. Lang.: Hun. 3792
Background on San Francisco opera radio broadcasts. USA: San
Francisco, CA. 1987. Lang.: Eng. 3833

Background on Metropolitan radio broadcast performances. USA:
New York, NY. 1987. Lang.: Eng. 3837
Plays/librettos/scripts
Mozart's *Nozze di Figaro* compared with Beaumarchais source. 1784-
1786. Lang.: Eng. 3887
Ntshona, Winston
Performance/production
Black theatre in South Africa: influence of traditional forms. South
Africa, Republic of. England: London. USA: New York, NY. 1586-
1987. Lang.: Eng. 2005
Plays/librettos/scripts
Stage space as prison in *The Island* by Athol Fugard with John
Kani and Winston Ntshona. South Africa, Republic of. 1987. Lang.:
Eng. 2727
Nunn, Trevor
Performance/production
Interview with actress Dame Peggy Ashcroft. UK-England. 1935-
1964. Lang.: Eng. 899
Collection of newspaper reviews by London theatre critics. UK-
England: London. 1986. Lang.: Eng. 2097
Collection of newspaper reviews by London theatre critics. UK-
England: London. 1987. Lang.: Eng. 2211
Collection of newspaper reviews by New York theatre critics. USA:
New York, NY. 1987. Lang.: Eng. 2323
Collection of newspaper reviews by New York theatre critics. USA:
New York, NY. 1987. Lang.: Eng. 2325
Nunsense
Performance/production
Collection of newspaper reviews by London theatre critics. UK-
England: London. 1987. Lang.: Eng. 2193
Nurse Jane Goes to Hawaii
Performance/production
Canadian playwright Allan Stratton. Canada: Toronto, ON. 1982.
Lang.: Eng. 1710
Nus, Eugène
Plays/librettos/scripts
Historical context for Tom Taylor's *The Ticket-of-Leave Man*. UK-
England. France. 1863. 2801
Nyakó, Júlia
Performance/production
Interview with actress Júlia Nyakó. Hungary. 1978-1987. Lang.: Hun. 3154
Nyköpings Teater
Performance/production
Amateur participation in Nyköpings Teater production of Gogol's
Revizor (The Government Inspector). Sweden: Nyköping. 1986-1987.
Lang.: Swe. 2021
O'Brian, Colm
Performance/production
Collection of newspaper reviews by London theatre critics. UK-
England: London. 1986. Lang.: Eng. 2150
O'Casey, Sean
Institutions
Playwright Denis Johnston and avant-garde theatre at the Abbey.
Ireland: Dublin. 1927-1935. Lang.: Eng. 1619
Plays/librettos/scripts
Thomas Murphy's *The Morning After Optimism*: comparisons with
Beckett, O'Casey. Ireland. 1971. Lang.: Eng. 2641
Popular music in the Dublin trilogy plays of Sean O'Casey. Ireland.
1923-1926. Lang.: Eng. 2644
Feminine life symbols in Sean O'Casey's *The Silver Tassie*. Ireland.
1928. Lang.: Eng. 2654
The Spanish Civil War in works by Ernest Hemingway and Sean
O'Casey. UK. Ireland. USA. 1930-1939. Lang.: Eng. 2749
Relation to other fields
Literary figures of the Irish Literary Renaissance. Ireland. UK-
Ireland. 1875-1938. Lang.: Eng. 2995
Research/historiography
Overview of Canadian research on twentieth-century Irish drama.
Ireland. UK-Ireland. Canada. 1891-1983. Lang.: Eng. 3011
O'Connor, Sara
Administration
American theatre's view of the commissioning process. USA: New
York, NY. 1987. Lang.: Eng. 118
O'Curry, Eugene
Theory/criticism
Brian Friel's play *Translations*. Ireland. 1987. Lang.: Eng. 3050

O'Dalaigh, Tony
Institutions
The touring company Irish Theatre Company. UK-Ireland. 1974-1987. Lang.: Eng.   569

O'Dwyer, Paddy
Performance/production
DYT (Dublin Youth Theatre). Ireland: Dublin. 1980-1987. Lang.: Eng.   816

O'Grady, Hubert
Relation to other fields
Theatrical themes and the class issue in the work of Irish playwrights. Ireland. 1900-1987. Lang.: Eng.   2994

O'Keeffe, John
Plays/librettos/scripts
New findings on 18th-century Irish comic playwright John O'Keeffe. Ireland. England: London. 1767-1798. Lang.: Eng.   2643

O'Malley, Mary
Performance/production
Relationship of theatre, class and gender. UK-England. USA. 1969-1985. Lang.: Eng.   918

O'Neill of Derry
Plays/librettos/scripts
Analysis of the plays and songs of Irish-American musical theatre star Chauncey Olcott. USA. 1893-1918. Lang.: Eng.   3671

O'Neill Theatre Center (Waterford, CT)
Institutions
Experience of artists working at the O'Neill Theatre Center. USA: Waterford, CT. 1985-1986. Lang.: Eng.   1655

O'Neill, Carlotta Monterey
Plays/librettos/scripts
Barbara Gelb discusses the creation of *My Gene*. USA. 1962-1987. Lang.: Eng.   2867

Investigation of Eugene O'Neill's third wife's last name. USA. 1890. Lang.: Eng.   2912

O'Neill, Eugene
Performance/production
Gábor Zsámbéki directs Eugene O'Neill's *Long Day's Journey into Night* under the title *Utazás az éjszakába*. Hungary: Eger. 1987. Lang.: Hun.   1850

Interview with Eric Bentley, director of *La Casa de Bernarda Alba* at the Abbey. Ireland: Dublin. 1900-1985. Lang.: Eng.   1934

Collection of newspaper reviews by London theatre critics. UK-England: London. 1986. Lang.: Eng.   2154

Collection of newspaper reviews by London theatre critics. UK-England: London. 1987. Lang.: Eng.   2206

Collection of newspaper reviews by London theatre critics. UK-England: London. 1987. Lang.: Eng.   2214

Collection of newspaper reviews by London theatre critics. UK-England: London. 1987. Lang.: Eng.   2253

Interview with Mary Arbenz on the original production of *Mourning Becomes Electra*. USA: New York, NY. 1927. Lang.: Eng.   2355

Philip Moeller's premiere of *Mourning Becomes Electra* by O'Neill. USA: New York, NY. 1931. Lang.: Eng.   2366

Plays/librettos/scripts
Russian and Soviet interaction with the U.S. USSR. USA. 1700-1987. Lang.: Rus.   1191

Compares tragedies of Sophocles and Euripides with those of Eugene O'Neill. 1918-1946. Lang.: Eng.   2409

Karl Ragnar Gierow on O'Neill and his importance in Sweden. Sweden: Stockholm. 1920-1970. Lang.: Eng.   2736

Pipe dreams in Eugene O'Neill's *A Touch of the Poet*. USA. 1935. Lang.: Eng.   2840

Eugene O'Neill's influence on Edward Albee. USA. 1949-1962. Lang.: Eng.   2841

Psychological complexity of Eugene O'Neill's *Long Day's Journey into Night*. USA. 1940. Lang.: Eng.   2842

Women's roles in Broadway plays at the time of women's suffrage. USA: New York, NY. 1920. Lang.: Eng.   2850

Development of themes and characters in plays of Sam Shepard. USA. 1960-1987. Lang.: Eng.   2853

Eugene O'Neill's influence on William Faulkner. USA: New York, NY. 1920-1962. Lang.: Eng.   2858

Chinese view of playwright Eugene O'Neill. USA. China, People's Republic of. 1930-1985. Lang.: Chi.   2863

Barbara Gelb discusses the creation of *My Gene*. USA. 1962-1987. Lang.: Eng.   2867

Comparison of themes and dramaturgical techniques in plays of Eugene O'Neill and Peter Shaffer. USA. 1920-1982. Lang.: Eng.   2872

Influence of O'Neill and Beckett on Israel Horovitz. USA: Boston, MA. France: Paris. 1939-1953. Lang.: Eng.   2873

Family and male-female relationships in O'Neill's *Desire Under the Elms*. USA. 1920. Lang.: Eng.   2885

O'Neill's transcendence of melodrama in *A Touch of the Poet* and *A Moon for the Misbegotten*. USA. 1922-1947. Lang.: Eng.   2886

Influence of Herman Melville on Eugene O'Neill. USA. 1927. Lang.: Eng.   2888

Importance of language in Eugene O'Neill's *Hughie*. USA. 1941-1959. Lang.: Eng.   2890

Parallels between O'Neill's *Anna Christie* and Homer's *Odyssey*. USA. 1921. Lang.: Eng.   2906

Investigation of Eugene O'Neill's third wife's last name. USA. 1890. Lang.: Eng.   2912

Influence of puppetry on Eugene O'Neill. USA. 1937. Lang.: Eng.   2919

Influence of Rudyard Kipling on Eugene O'Neill. USA. 1887-1950. Lang.: Eng.   2925

Family relationships in Eugene O'Neill's early plays. USA. 1913. Lang.: Eng.   2926

Symbolism in *The Hairy Ape* by Eugene O'Neill. USA. 1920-1922. Lang.: Eng.   2929

O'Shaunessy, Brian
Performance/production
Review of *Hello Dolly* in Bloemfontein. South Africa, Republic of: Bloemfontein. 1987. Lang.: Eng.   3635

O'Sullivan, Dennis
Design/technology
Dennis O'Sullivan's work with mixed media. Canada. 1986. Lang.: Fre.   3203

Oakland Ensemble Theatre (Oakland, CA)
Performance spaces
History of the Alice Arts Center, new home of the Oakland Ensemble Theatre. USA: Oakland, CA. 1983-1987. Lang.: Eng.   696

Oba l'instituteur (Oba the Teacher)
Plays/librettos/scripts
Compares plays of Enlightenment France, Francophone Africa. Congo: Brazzaville. Cameroon. Benin. France. 1700-1975. Lang.: Eng.   2496

Oberfrank, Géza
Performance/production
Review of productions at opera ensembles meeting. Hungary: Szeged. 1987. Lang.: Hun.   3792

Obraztsov Puppet Theatre
SEE
Gosudarstvénnyj Centralnyj Teat'r Kukol.

Observe the Sons of Ulster Marching Towards the Somme
Performance/production
Collection of newspaper reviews by London theatre critics. UK-England: London. 1986. Lang.: Eng.   2151

Obsluhoval jsem anglického krale (I Served the King of Britain)
Performance/production
Bohumil Hrabal's *Obsluhoval jsem anglického krale (I Served the King of Britain)* directed by Ivo Krobot as *Ófelsége pincére voltam*. Hungary: Nyíregyháza. 1987. Lang.: Hun.   1912

Ivo Krobot directs *Ófelsége pincére voltam (I Served the King of Britain)*, based on writings of Bohumil Hrabal. Hungary: Nyíregyháza. 1987. Lang.: Hun.   1928

Occhiogrosso, Anne
Performance/production
Career of actor/director Randall Duk Kim. USA. 1966-1987. Lang.: Eng.   2346

Occupation of Heather Rose, The
Basic theatrical documents
Collection of four plays by Canadian women dramatists. Canada. 1987. Lang.: Eng.   1544

Ochs, Adolph
Theory/criticism
The language of theatrical criticism. USA: New York, NY. 1917-1985. Lang.: Eng.   1367

Offstage Downstairs Theatre (London) — cont'd

Collection of newspaper reviews by London theatre critics. UK-England: London. 1987. Lang.: Eng. 2260

Offstage Theatre (London)
Performance/production
Collection of newspaper reviews by London theatre critics. UK-England: London. 1987. Lang.: Eng. 2240

Ogunba, Oyin
Plays/librettos/scripts
Use of English in Nigerian drama. Nigeria. 1940-1987. Lang.: Eng. 2706

Oh, Coward!
Design/technology
Lighting reviews for several New York productions. USA: New York, NY. 1987. Lang.: Eng. 474

Ohio Impromptu
Plays/librettos/scripts
Interaction of scenic imagery and narrative in *Ohio Impromptu*. France. 1981-1987. Lang.: Eng. 2586
Study of playwright Samuel Beckett's visual art in his plays. USA. 1970-1980. Lang.: Eng. 2866

Ohio Theatre (Cleveland, OH)
Performance spaces
Restoration of Ohio, State and Palace Theatres in Playhouse Square. USA: Cleveland, OH. 1964-1986. Lang.: Eng. 681

Ohta, Shogo
Performance/production
Productions by Tenkei gekijō, Manji and Mokutōsha. Japan: Tokyo. 1986. Lang.: Jap. 1958
Productions of Bungakuza, Yūkikai Zenjidō shiatā, Tao and Tenkei gekijō. Japan: Tokyo. 1986. Lang.: Jap. 1961

Ohtani, Ryōsuke
Performance/production
Analysis of four Tokyo productions. Japan: Tokyo. 1987. Lang.: Jap. 1957
Discussion of four Tokyo productions. Japan: Tokyo. 1944-1987. Lang.: Jap. 1963

Oide, Yoshi
Performance/production
Company members of Centre International de Recherche Théâtrale discuss *The Mahabharata*. France: Paris. 1986. Lang.: Eng. 1752

Oidípous Týrannos
Institutions
Seven productions chosen for Theatertreffen '86. Germany: Berlin. 1986. Lang.: Eng. 1617
Performance spaces
Theatre space and theatrical space in theatre from the ancient Greeks to the present. Germany. England. Greece. 400 B.C.-1987 A.D. Lang.: Eng. 635
Theory/criticism
Exploration of the nature of tragedy. 500 B.C.-1987 A.D. Lang.: Eng. 3020
Perceptions of tragedy and new perspective on its analysis. USA. UK-England. Greece. 500 B.C.-1987 A.D. Lang.: Eng. 3066

Oil City Symphony
Performance/production
The cabaret-style musical revue *Oil City Symphony*. USA: New York, NY. 1987. Lang.: Eng. 3289

OISTAT
SEE
Organisation Internationale de Scénographes, Techniciens et Architectes de Théâtre.

Old B Hanging on the Wall
Performance/production
Influences of Western culture on Chinese theatre reflected in performance of *Old B Hanging on the Wall*. China, People's Republic of. 1984-1986. Lang.: Eng. 761

Old Business
Plays/librettos/scripts
Money, greed and power in plays by Fo, Churchill, Cacaci and Cormack. USA: New York, NY. 1987. Lang.: Eng. 2914

Old Globe Theatre (San Diego, CA)
Performance spaces
New Old Globe Theatre replaces previous structure. USA: San Diego, CA. 1982. Lang.: Eng. 709

Old Lady Says 'No', The
Institutions
Playwright Denis Johnston and avant-garde theatre at the Abbey. Ireland: Dublin. 1927-1935. Lang.: Eng. 1619

Old Limerick Town
Plays/librettos/scripts
Analysis of the plays and songs of Irish-American musical theatre star Chauncey Olcott. USA. 1893-1918. Lang.: Eng. 3671

Old Man Go-It-Alone
SEE
Père va-tout-seul.

Old Man of Lochnagar, The
Performance/production
Collection of newspaper reviews by London theatre critics. UK-England: London. 1986. Lang.: Eng. 2049

Old Red Lion Theatre (London)
Performance/production
Collection of newspaper reviews by London theatre critics. UK-England: London. 1986. Lang.: Eng. 2036
Collection of newspaper reviews by London theatre critics. UK-England: London. 1986. Lang.: Eng. 2050
Collection of newspaper reviews by London theatre critics. UK-England: London. 1986. Lang.: Eng. 2092
Collection of newspaper reviews by London theatre critics. UK-England: London. 1986. Lang.: Eng. 2100
Collection of newspaper reviews by London theatre critics. UK-England: London. 1986. Lang.: Eng. 2101
Collection of newspaper reviews by London theatre critics. UK-England: London. 1986. Lang.: Eng. 2113
Collection of newspaper reviews by London theatre critics. UK-England: London. 1986. Lang.: Eng. 2117
Collection of newspaper reviews by London theatre critics. UK-England: London. 1986. Lang.: Eng. 2131
Collection of newspaper reviews by London theatre critics. UK-England: London. 1986. Lang.: Eng. 2135
Collection of newspaper reviews by London theatre critics. UK-England: London. 1986. Lang.: Eng. 2151
Collection of newspaper reviews by London theatre critics. UK-England: London. 1986. Lang.: Eng. 2170
Collection of newspaper reviews by London theatre critics. UK-England: London. 1987. Lang.: Eng. 2174
Collection of newspaper reviews by London theatre critics. UK-England: London. 1987. Lang.: Eng. 2180
Collection of newspaper reviews by London theatre critics. UK-England: London. 1987. Lang.: Eng. 2187
Collection of newspaper reviews by London theatre critics. UK-England: London. 1987. Lang.: Eng. 2207
Collection of newspaper reviews by London theatre critics. UK-England: London. 1987. Lang.: Eng. 2209
Collection of newspaper reviews by London theatre critics. UK-England: London. 1987. Lang.: Eng. 2227
Collection of newspaper reviews by London theatre critics. UK-England: London. 1987. Lang.: Eng. 2233
Collection of newspaper reviews by London theatre critics. UK-England: London. 1987. Lang.: Eng. 2248
Collection of newspaper reviews by London theatre critics. UK-England: London. 1987. Lang.: Eng. 2252
Collection of newspaper reviews by London theatre critics. UK-England: London. 1987. Lang.: Eng. 2257
Collection of newspaper reviews by London theatre critics. UK-England: London. 1987. Lang.: Eng. 2268
Collection of newspaper reviews by London theatre critics. UK-England: London. 1987. Lang.: Eng. 2275

Old Times
Plays/librettos/scripts
Interpreting Harold Pinter's dramas through focus on his play structures. UK-England. 1958-1987. Lang.: Eng. 2815
Structural analysis of Pinter's *Old Times*. USA: New York, NY. 1971-1984. Lang.: Eng. 2843

Old Vic Theatre (Bristol)
SEE
Bristol Old Vic Theatre.

Old Vic Theatre (London)
Design/technology
Interview with designer Desmond Heeley. UK-England: London. USA: New York, NY. Canada: Stratford, ON. 1940-1984. Lang.: Eng. 1596

Old Vic Theatre (London) — cont'd

Performance/production

Collection of newspaper reviews by London theatre critics. UK-England: London. 1986. Lang.: Eng. 2060

Collection of newspaper reviews by London theatre critics. UK-England: London. 1986. Lang.: Eng. 2089

Collection of newspaper reviews by London theatre critics. UK-England: London. 1986. Lang.: Eng. 2126

Collection of newspaper reviews by London theatre critics. UK-England: London. 1987. Lang.: Eng. 2193

Collection of newspaper reviews by London theatre critics. UK-England: London. 1987. Lang.: Eng. 2239

Collection of newspaper reviews by London theatre critics. UK-England: London. 1987. Lang.: Eng. 2253

Old Year's Eve

Performance/production

Collection of newspaper reviews by London theatre critics. UK-England: London. 1987. Lang.: Eng. 2226

Olim, Dorothy

Administration

Broadway producer Dorothy Olim on commercial theatre. USA: New York, NY. 1983. Lang.: Eng. 189

Oliver

Performance/production

György Korcsmáros directs Lionel Bart's *Oliver* at Arany János Theatre. Hungary: Budapest. 1986. Lang.: Hun. 3631

Performances of *Oliver* staged by György Korcsmáros, Antol Rencz and Imre Halasi. Hungary: Budapest, Békéscsaba, Zalaegerszeg. 1986. Lang.: Hun. 3632

Oliver, Bryan

Performance/production

Collection of newspaper reviews by London theatre critics. UK-England: London. 1987. Lang.: Eng. 2195

Oliver, Joan

Basic theatrical documents

Edition and analysis, *Allò que tal vegada s'esdevingué (What Happened Then)* by Joan Oliver. Spain-Catalonia. 1899-1986. Lang.: Cat. 1573

Plays/librettos/scripts

General history of Catalan literature, including theatre. Spain-Catalonia. 1902-1961. Lang.: Cat. 1157

Oliver, Stephen

Performance/production

Repertoire and artistic achievement of the Opera Theatre of St. Louis. USA: St. Louis, MO. 1987. Lang.: Eng. 3840

Olivier Theatre (London)

SEE ALSO

National Theatre (London).

Performance/production

Collection of newspaper reviews by London theatre critics. UK-England: London. 1986. Lang.: Eng. 2044

Collection of newspaper reviews by London theatre critics. UK-England: London. 1986. Lang.: Eng. 2047

Collection of newspaper reviews by London theatre critics. UK-England: London. 1986. Lang.: Eng. 2050

Collection of newspaper reviews by London theatre critics. UK-England: London. 1987. Lang.: Eng. 2192

Collection of newspaper reviews by London theatre critics. UK-England: London. 1987. Lang.: Eng. 2198

Collection of newspaper reviews by London theatre critics. UK-England: London. 1987. Lang.: Eng. 2240

Collection of newspaper reviews by London theatre critics. UK-England: London. 1987. Lang.: Eng. 2250

Collection of newspaper reviews by London theatre critics. UK-England: London. 1987. Lang.: Eng. 2259

Collection of newspaper reviews by London theatre critics. UK-England: London. 1987. Lang.: Eng. 2261

Olivier, Laurence

Institutions

History and current season of the National Theatre. UK-England: London. 1848-1987. Lang.: Eng. 1647

Performance/production

Career of actor Lord Laurence Olivier. UK-England. 1907-1987. Lang.: Rus. 898

Interview with actress Dame Peggy Ashcroft. UK-England. 1935-1964. Lang.: Eng. 899

'Showing' is an essential part of all acting. Europe. 1590-1987. Lang.: Eng. 1746

Interpretation and critique of Olivier's film *Hamlet*. England. 1604-1948. Lang.: Chi. 3149

Theory/criticism

Reconstruction of Shakespeare in performance. USA. 1987. Lang.: Eng. 1358

Olson, David Matthew

Institutions

History and goals of Cherry Creek Theatre. USA: St. Peter, MN. 1979-1983. Lang.: Eng. 598

Ołtarz wzniesiony sobie (Altar for Himself, An)

Performance/production

Festival of Polish plays. Poland: Wrocław. 1987. Lang.: Eng, Fre. 871

Olympia Theatre (Dublin)

Institutions

Difficulty in obtaining funding for theatre building repair. Ireland: Dublin, Cork. UK-Ireland: Belfast. 1965-1984. Lang.: Eng. 545

Olympic Arts Festival (Calgary, AB)

Institutions

Aims and scope of the Olympic Arts Festival. Canada: Calgary, AB. 1987. Lang.: Eng. 507

Olympie

Plays/librettos/scripts

Techniques, themes, characters and dramaturgy of Voltaire. France. 1718-1778. Lang.: Eng. 2590

Olympus on My Mind

Design/technology

Lighting reviews of several Broadway shows. USA: New York, NY. 1987. Lang.: Eng. 473

Omaha Community Playhouse (Omaha, NE)

Performance spaces

Major expansion of the facilities at the Omaha Community Playhouse. USA: Omaha, NE. 1984-1987. Lang.: Eng. 699

On Humans

Performance/production

Collection of newspaper reviews by London theatre critics. UK-England: London. 1986. Lang.: Eng. 2075

On Second Avenue

Plays/librettos/scripts

Influence of Yiddish and Jewish theatre on mainstream American theatre. USA: New York, NY. 1881-1987. Lang.: Eng. 2913

On the Outside

Plays/librettos/scripts

Comic characters and the Book of Job in the plays of Thomas Murphy. Ireland. 1962-1983. Lang.: Eng. 2648

The plays of Thomas Murphy. Ireland: Dublin. 1962-1986. Lang.: Eng. 2650

Historical accuracy of characters in the plays of Thomas Murphy. Ireland. 1962-1986. Lang.: Eng. 2657

On the Razzle

SEE ALSO

Jux will er sich machen, Einen.

On the Ruins of Carthage

SEE

Sur les ruines de Carthage.

On the Verge

Theory/criticism

On the Verge by Eric Overmyer. Production history, plot synopsis, critical evaluation. USA. 1987. Lang.: Eng. 3068

On the Wire, or The Ballad of the Phantom Train

SEE

Sur le fil ou La Ballade du train fantôme.

Once Upon a Time

Plays/librettos/scripts

Analysis of the plays and songs of Irish-American musical theatre star Chauncey Olcott. USA. 1893-1918. Lang.: Eng. 3671

One Before the Last, The

Performance/production

Collection of newspaper reviews by London theatre critics. UK-England: London. 1987. Lang.: Eng. 2217

One of the Fair Sex

Performance/production

Collection of newspaper reviews by London theatre critics. UK-England: London. 1986. Lang.: Eng. 2090

Ouaknine, Serge
Design/technology
The increasing use of projected images in theatre. Canada. 1985.
Lang.: Fre. 1399
Our Lady
Performance/production
Collection of newspaper reviews by London theatre critics. UK-England: London. 1986. Lang.: Eng. 2168
Ourselves Alone
Performance/production
Collection of newspaper reviews by London theatre critics. UK-England: London. 1986. Lang.: Eng. 2137
Out of Sight
Performance/production
Collection of newspaper reviews by London theatre critics. UK-England: London. 1987. Lang.: Eng. 2239
Outaouais Popular Theatre (Ottawa, ON)
Performance/production
Work of actor/director Augusto Boal. Canada: Sydney, NS. 1987.
Lang.: Eng. 1694
Outbreak of God in Area
Performance/production
Collection of newspaper reviews by London theatre critics. UK-England: London. 1987. Lang.: Eng. 2230
Outside Noises or: Don't Be Afraid of Mr. Kopa
Performance/production
Five short plays by Géza Páskándi at SUNY Binghamton. Hungary.
USA: Binghamton, NY. 1987. Lang.: Eng. 1813
Ouzounian, Richard
Performance/production
Summarizes events of Directors' Colloquium. Canada: Calgary, AB.
1987. Lang.: Eng. 728
Richard Ouzounian, director, Manitoba Theatre Centre. Canada:
Winnipeg, MB. 1982. Lang.: Eng. 1693
Oval House Theatre (London)
Performance/production
Collection of newspaper reviews by London theatre critics. UK-England: London. 1986. Lang.: Eng. 2055
Collection of newspaper reviews by London theatre critics. UK-England: London. 1986. Lang.: Eng. 2083
Collection of newspaper reviews by London theatre critics. UK-England: London. 1986. Lang.: Eng. 2103
Collection of newspaper reviews by London theatre critics. UK-England: London. 1987. Lang.: Eng. 2206
Collection of newspaper reviews by London theatre critics. UK-England: London. 1987. Lang.: Eng. 2216
Overlaid
Plays/librettos/scripts
Survey of Robertson Davies' plays. Canada. 1913-1985. Lang.: Eng.
2484
Overmyer, Eric
Design/technology
Philosophy of set designer John Arnone. USA: New York, NY.
1987. Lang.: Eng. 430
Theory/criticism
On the Verge by Eric Overmyer. Production history, plot synopsis,
critical evaluation. USA. 1987. Lang.: Eng. 3068
Ovid
Plays/librettos/scripts
Exploration of mythic elements in the later plays of William
Shakespeare. England: London. 1607-1614. Lang.: Eng. 2497
Owi-Okanza, Jacob
Plays/librettos/scripts
Compares plays of Enlightenment France, Francophone Africa.
Congo: Brazzaville. Cameroon. Benin. France. 1700-1975. Lang.: Eng.
2496
Owners
Performance/production
Collection of newspaper reviews by London theatre critics. UK-England. 1987. Lang.: Eng. 2199
Oyono-Mbia, Guillaume
Plays/librettos/scripts
Compares plays of Enlightenment France, Francophone Africa.
Congo: Brazzaville. Cameroon. Benin. France. 1700-1975. Lang.: Eng.
2496

Paál, István
Performance/production
Season openings at Petőfi Theatre, including Lengyel's *A nagy
fejedelem (The Great Prince)* and Bíró's *A rablólovag (The Gallant
Kidnapper)*. Hungary: Veszprém. 1987. Lang.: Hun. 1820
István Paál directs István Örkény's *Forgatókönyv (Screenplay)* at
Petőfi Theatre. Hungary: Veszprém. 1987. Lang.: Hun. 1832
Reviews of two plays by István Örkény: *Forgatókönyv (Screenplay)*
directed by István Paál and two productions of *Tóték (The Tót
Family)* staged by János Meczner and István Pinczés. Hungary:
Veszprém, Budapest, Debrecen. 1986-1987. Lang.: Hun. 1880
Pacific Overtures
Performance/production
Collection of newspaper reviews by London theatre critics. UK-England: London. 1987. Lang.: Eng. 2247
Page, Judy
Performance/production
Review of *Hello Dolly* in Bloemfontein. South Africa, Republic of:
Bloemfontein. 1987. Lang.: Eng. 3635
Page, Louise
Performance/production
Collection of newspaper reviews by New York theatre critics. USA:
New York, NY. 1987. Lang.: Eng. 2313
Pageants/parades
SEE ALSO
Classed Entries under MIXED ENTERTAINMENT—Pageants/
parades.
Processional theatre.
Performance/production
Additions to list of transvestite actors. England. 1510-1519. Lang.:
Eng. 1744
Páger, Antal
Performance/production
Style and career of actor Antal Páger. Hungary. 1919-1986. Lang.:
Hun. 1847
Pagett, Nicola
Performance/production
Two productions of Pinter's *Old Times*. UK-England: London. USA:
New York, NY, St. Louis, MO. 1971-1985. Lang.: Eng. 907
Pain blanc (White Bread)
Performance/production
Analysis of directorial style of Gilles Maheu. Canada. 1987. Lang.:
Eng. 745
Pain of Youth
Performance/production
Collection of newspaper reviews by London theatre critics. UK-England: London. 1987. Lang.: Eng. 2073
Palace Theatre (Cleveland, OH)
Performance spaces
Restoration of Ohio, State and Palace Theatres in Playhouse Square.
USA: Cleveland, OH. 1964-1986. Lang.: Eng. 681
Palace Theatre (London)
Performance/production
Collection of newspaper reviews by London theatre critics. UK-England: London. 1987. Lang.: Eng. 2178
Palamas, Kostis
Plays/librettos/scripts
Greek poetic drama through Nietzschean theory. Greece. 1987.
Lang.: Eng. 2620
Imagistic versus realistic drama in contemporary Greek plays.
Greece. 1940-1987. Lang.: Eng. 2621
Paliashvili Opera Theatre (Tbilisi)
SEE
Teat'r Opery i Baleta im. Z. Paliašvili.
Palladium Theatre (Johannesburg)
Performance spaces
Theatres built, influences on design. South Africa, Republic of:
Johannesburg. 1887-1940. Lang.: Afr. 667
Palmer, Alisa
Institutions
Development of feminist theatre in Toronto. Canada: Toronto, ON.
1960-1987. Lang.: Eng. 1608
Palmer, D.J.
Research/historiography
Critical history of *Julius Caesar*. England. 1599-1987. Lang.: Eng.
1299

Palucca, Gret
Performance/production
Development of dance. Germany: Berlin. 1920-1986. Lang.: Ger.
1407

Memorial album by and about dancer Gret Palucca. Germany, East: Dresden. 1922-1987. Lang.: Ger. 1469
Relation to other fields
Exhibition devoted to modern dancer Gret Palucca. Germany, East: Dresden. 1922-1987. Lang.: Ger. 1476

Pan Asian Repertory Theatre (New York, NY)
Administration
Nontraditional casting: types, rationale and examples. USA: New York, NY. 1987. Lang.: Eng. 203

Diversity of Letter of Agreement theatres that operate in New York City. USA: New York, NY. 1987. Lang.: Eng. 204

Pan Cogito (Mr. Cogito)
Performance/production
Festival of Polish plays. Poland: Wrocław. 1987. Lang.: Eng, Fre.
871

Pan del pobre, El (Poor Man's Bread)
Plays/librettos/scripts
Study of *El pan del pobre (Poor Man's Bread)*, adapted from Hauptmann's *Die Weber (The Weavers)*. Spain. 1894. Lang.: Eng.
2728

Pan Jowialski (Mr. Jowialski)
Performance/production
The 17th Warsaw theatre conference. Poland: Warsaw. 1987. Lang.: Eng, Fre. 872

Pan, Jinlian
Performance/production
Status of Sichuan theatre and opera. China, People's Republic of: Chengdu. 1985-1986. Lang.: Eng. 3512

Panfilov, Gleb
Performance/production
Director Gleb Panfilov's interpretation of *Hamlet* at Komsomol Theatre. USSR: Moscow. 1980-1987. Lang.: Rus. 2373

Interview with film director Gleb Panfilov. USSR. 1986-1987. Lang.: Hun. 3172

Panic
Performance/production
Collection of newspaper reviews by London theatre critics. UK-England: London. 1987. Lang.: Eng. 2210

Panic in Berlin
Performance/production
Three plays performed by the Dutch Orkater ensemble company. Netherlands. 1986. Lang.: Hun. 861

Panigrahi, Sanjukta
Performance/production
Role of feminist in cultural critique. India. USA. 1983-1987. Lang.: Eng. 1496

Panopticon (Stockholm)
Performance/production
Mime troupe Panopticon. Sweden: Stockholm. 1985-1987. Lang.: Swe. 3226

Pansori
Performance spaces
Performance space and staging of traditional Korean genres. Korea. Japan. 57 B.C.-1986 A.D. Lang.: Kor. 663
Performance/production
Origin and influence of *pansori* music-drama. Korea. 1392-1910. Lang.: Kor. 3406

History of *pansori*, Korean music-drama. Korea. 1392-1910. Lang.: Kor. 3408

Pantomime
SEE ALSO
Mime.
Classed Entries under MIME—Pantomime.
Design/technology
Restoration of the stage machinery at the Grand Theatre. UK-Wales: Llandudno. 1901-1987. Lang.: Eng. 381
Plays/librettos/scripts
Essex Evans' adaptations of *Robinson Crusoe* and *Musical Whist*. Australia. 1891-1902. Lang.: Eng. 2439

Panych, Morris
Plays/librettos/scripts
New Canadian drama: non-realistic, anti-naturalistic. Canada. 1983-1984. Lang.: Eng. 2482

Papa Highirte
Plays/librettos/scripts
Theme of torture in Brazilian drama. Brazil. 1964-1985. Lang.: Por.
2456

Paper Cage, The
Plays/librettos/scripts
New Canadian drama: non-realistic, anti-naturalistic. Canada. 1983-1984. Lang.: Eng. 2482

Papp, Joseph
Institutions
New York Shakespeare Festival's Joseph Papp receives AEA's Paul Robeson Award. USA: New York, NY. 1987. Lang.: Eng. 578

Contribution of non-commercial theatre to the New York community. USA: New York, NY. 1987. Lang.: Eng. 608
Performance spaces
The streets of New York as experimental performance space. USA: New York, NY. 1960-1975. Lang.: Eng. 688
Performance/production
Short history of *A Chorus Line*. USA: New York, NY. 1975-1987. Lang.: Eng. 941

Career of director/author Andre Ernotte. USA: New York, NY. 1987. Lang.: Eng. 954

Director A.J. Antoon discusses *Sherlock's Last Case*. USA: New York, NY. 1987. Lang.: Eng. 970
Plays/librettos/scripts
Barbara Gelb discusses the creation of *My Gene*. USA. 1962-1987. Lang.: Eng. 2867

Impact of AIDS crisis on the theatre. USA: New York, NY, San Francisco, CA. 1987. Lang.: Eng. 2881

Parades
SEE
Pageants/parades.

Paradise Lost by Sarkadi
SEE
Elveszett paradicsom.

Paradise Now
Performance/production
Audience participation in Living Theatre's *Paradise Now*. USA: New York, NY. 1968. Lang.: Kor. 945

Paramount City Theatre (London)
Performance/production
Collection of newspaper reviews by London theatre critics. UK-England: London. 1986. Lang.: Eng. 2166

Paravents, Les (Screens, The)
Plays/librettos/scripts
Critical response to Brassard's *Les Paravents (The Screens)*. Canada: Montreal, PQ, Ottawa, ON. 1987. Lang.: Fre. 2475

Brassard discusses his adaptation of Genet's *Les Paravents (The Screens)*. Canada: Montreal, PQ, Ottawa, ON. 1987. Lang.: Fre.
2485

Symbols of power in Genet's *Les Paravents (The Screens)*. France. Canada: Montreal, PQ, Ottawa, ON. 1961-1987. Lang.: Fre. 2570

André Brassard's production of Jean Genet's *Les Paravents (The Screens)*. France. Canada: Montreal, PQ, Ottawa, ON. 1961-1987. Lang.: Fre. 2583

Investigating the text of Genet's *Les Paravents (The Screens)*. France. Canada: Montreal, PQ, Ottawa, ON. 1961-1987. Lang.: Fre.
2585

Parco (Tokyo)
Performance/production
Four Tokyo productions in light of ideas of Betsuyaku Minoru. Japan: Tokyo. 1987. Lang.: Jap. 1950

Productions from Yume no yūminsha, Tōhō, Parco, Tsukumo and Nakamura za. Japan: Tokyo. 1986-1987. Lang.: Jap. 1956

Productions of several Tokyo companies. Japan: Tokyo. 1987. Lang.: Jap. 1962

Discussion of four Tokyo productions. Japan: Tokyo. 1944-1987. Lang.: Jap. 1963

Unsuitable choice of plays for Tokyo performances. Japan: Tokyo. 1987. Lang.: Jap. 1965

Parichy, Dennis
Design/technology
Interview with lighting designer Dennis Parichy. USA: New York, NY. 1986-1987. Lang.: Eng. 428

Current Broadway shows and their lighting designers. USA: New York, NY. 1987. Lang.: Eng. 460

Parichy, Dennis — cont'd

Lighting designer Dennis Parichy's work on *Coastal Disturbances*. USA: New York, NY. 1987. Lang.: Eng. 461

Paris Opera
SEE
Opéra de Paris.

Park Theatre (London)
SEE
Battersea Park Theatre.

Park, Hyun Suk
Plays/librettos/scripts
Playwright Park Hyun Suk's dramatic theory. Korea. Lang.: Kor. 2686

Park, R. Vincent
Performance/production
Collection of newspaper reviews by London theatre critics. UK-England: London. 1986. Lang.: Eng. 2166

Parker, Kate
Performance/production
Collection of newspaper reviews by London theatre critics. UK-England: London. 1987. Lang.: Eng. 2217

Parker, Stewart
Theory/criticism
Stewart Parker's *Northern Star*. UK-Ireland. 1984. Lang.: Eng. 3065
Assessment of the series *Lost Beginning*, its relation to Stewart Parker's *Pentecost*. UK-Ireland. 1987. Lang.: Eng. 3218

Parmet, Simon
Performance/production
Music for Brecht's *Mutter Courage und ihre Kinder (Mother Courage and Her Children)*. Switzerland: Zürich. Finland. 1939-1947. Lang.: Ger. 2027

Parnes Plough Company (London)
Performance/production
Collection of newspaper reviews by London theatre critics. UK-England: London. 1987. Lang.: Eng. 2228

Parquet Floor, The
Performance/production
Collection of newspaper reviews by London theatre critics. UK-England: London. 1986. Lang.: Eng. 2110

Parry, David
Performance/production
Production of Merbury's *The Marriage of Wit and Wisdom* by David Parry. Israel: Jerusalem. 1987. Lang.: Eng. 1939

Parsifal
Design/technology
Lighting reviews for several New York productions. USA: New York, NY. 1987. Lang.: Eng. 474
Performance/production
Background on Lyric Opera radio broadcast performances. USA: Chicago, IL. 1987. Lang.: Eng. 3832
Background on Metropolitan radio broadcast performances. USA: New York, NY. 1987. Lang.: Eng. 3837
Plays/librettos/scripts
Psychological interpretations of Wagner's *Parsifal*. Germany. 1882-1987. Lang.: Eng. 3907
Woman, salvation and love in operas of Richard Wagner. Germany. 1813-1883. Lang.: Eng. 3909

Parsons School of Design (New York, NY)
Design/technology
MFA program in lighting design at Parsons School of Design. USA: New York, NY. 1987. Lang.: Eng. 454

Partage de Midi (Break of Noon)
Plays/librettos/scripts
Study of playwright Paul Claudel based on his letters. France. 1904-1909. Lang.: Fre. 2572

Partner
SEE
Compañero.

Parton, Anne
Relation to other fields
Essays on the theme of marriage in literature. England. Norway. 1300-1985. Lang.: Eng. 1425

Pascal, Julia
Performance/production
Collection of newspaper reviews by London theatre critics. UK-England: London. 1986. Lang.: Eng. 2069
Collection of newspaper reviews by London theatre critics. UK-England: London. 1986. Lang.: Eng. 2157

Collection of newspaper reviews by London theatre critics. UK-England: London. 1987. Lang.: Eng. 2189

Páskándi, Géza
Performance/production
Five short plays by Géza Páskándi at SUNY Binghamton. Hungary. USA: Binghamton, NY. 1987. Lang.: Eng. 1813
Vendégség (The Host and the Guest) staged by János Taub at Játékszín. Hungary: Budapest. 1986. Lang.: Hun. 1829
Péter Léner directs Géza Páskándi's *Lélekharang (Death Knell)*, Móricz Zsigmond Theatre. Hungary: Nyíregyháza. 1987. Lang.: Hun. 1876
Premiere of Spiró's *Csirkefej (Chickenhead)* and Páskándi's *Vendégség (The Host and the Guest)*. Hungary: Budapest. 1986. Lang.: Hun. 1885
Péter Léner directs premiere of *Lélekharang (Death Knell)* by Géza Páskándi at Móricz Zsigmond Theatre. Hungary: Nyíregyháza. 1987. Lang.: Hun. 1915

Pasolini, Pier Paolo
Performance/production
Experimental theatre at the Stary in three recent productions. Poland: Cracow. 1987. Lang.: Eng. 1999

Pasos, Joaquin
Plays/librettos/scripts
Linguistic absurdism in *El Chinfónia burguesa (The Bourgeois Chinfonia)*. Nicaragua. 1987. Lang.: Spa. 2703

Pasqual, Lluís
Institutions
Evaluation of the plays performed during the first ten years of Teatre Lliure. Spain-Catalonia: Barcelona. 1976-1986. Lang.: Cat. 1636
Performance spaces
Collection of photographs on the history of the Teatre Lliure. Spain-Catalonia: Barcelona. 1976-1987. Lang.: Cat. 1671

Passage
Plays/librettos/scripts
Study of *Passage* by Christoph Hein. Germany, East. 1987. Lang.: Ger. 2614

Passage to India, A
Performance/production
Analysis of David Lean's film *A Passage to India*. 1983. Lang.: Eng. 3147

Passion According to Antígona Pérez, The
SEE
Pasión según Antígona Pérez, La.

Passion Machine (Dublin)
Training
Funding for youth theatre in Ireland. Ireland. 1979-1987. Lang.: Eng. 1381

Passion Play
Plays/librettos/scripts
Comparison between medieval passion plays and Peter Nichols' *Passion Play*. 1986. Lang.: Eng. 2429

Passion plays
SEE ALSO
Mystery plays.
Performance/production
Role of the director in the Lucerne Passion play. Switzerland: Lucerne. 1453-1616. Lang.: Eng. 2030
Pageant wagon presentation in Spain provides information on recruitment, staging and rehearsal practices. Spain: St. Ginar. 1579. Lang.: Eng. 3333
Reference materials
Rolf Bergmann's catalogue of medieval German drama. Germany. 1986. Lang.: Eng. 1202

Passion Scenes
Performance/production
Four new productions in Poland. Poland: Warsaw. 1986-1987. Lang.: Eng, Fre. 1988

Passion, Poison and Petrification
Plays/librettos/scripts
Freudian reading of Shaw's *Passion, Poison and Petrification*. UK-England. 1895-1926. Lang.: Eng. 2781

Passport, The
Performance/production
New Tokyo productions. Japan: Tokyo. 1987. Lang.: Jap. 1954
Space and sign in various Tokyo productions. Japan: Tokyo. 1987. Lang.: Jap. 1959

SUBJECT INDEX

Performance/production — cont'd

Productions of *Sir Thomas More* by Elizabethan theatre companies. England. 1595-1650. Lang.: Eng.   2541

Structure of Byron's plays. England. 1788-1824. Lang.: Eng.   2542

Improvisational clowning in Elizabethan theatre. England. 1585-1625. Lang.: Eng.   2560

Actress Tilda Swinter talks about her performance as a male. UK-England. 1987. Lang.: Eng.   2824

Interview with playwright Robert Harling, designer Edward Gianfrancesco. USA: New York, NY. 1987. Lang.: Eng.   2846

Chronological listing of John Guare's plays, bibliography, list of reviews. USA. 1938-1987. Lang.: Eng.   2871

Two forms of adaptations of Shakespeare for other media. Europe. USA. 1899-1987. Lang.: Eng.   3097

Interview with Joe Masteroff, author of the book for *Cabaret*. USA: New York, NY. 1963-1987. Lang.: Eng.   3674

Career of singer/actress Lotte Lenya. Germany: Berlin. 1929-1970. Lang.: Eng.   3906

Opera adaptations for Broadway with African-American artists. USA: New York, NY. 1935-1987. Lang.: Eng.   3932

Reference materials

French-language Belgian theatre. Belgium. 1985-1986. Lang.: Fre.   1197

New Italian productions in all areas. Italy. 1985-1986. Lang.: Ita.   1204

Relation to other fields

John Malpede's performance workshop for the homeless. USA: Los Angeles, CA. 1984-1987. Lang.: Eng.   1267

Sexuality and desire in performance. USA. 1987. Lang.: Eng.   1270

Approaching dramatic texts similarly to other literary texts. 1600-1987. Lang.: Eng.   2976

Theory/criticism

A formalist approach and interpretation of theatre performance. 1987. Lang.: Eng.   1313

Eric Bentley's critical essays on theatre. USA. 1952-1986. Lang.: Eng.   1350

Collection of critical essays and reviews by Robert Brustein. USA. 1980-1986. Lang.: Eng.   1351

Career and collaborations of Maria Piscator. USA. 1938-1987. Lang.: Eng.   1365

Essays and reviews by Gordon Rogoff. USA. 1960-1986. Lang.: Eng.   1366

Reception theory, performance and American influence in Korea. USA. Korea. 1926-1970. Lang.: Kor.   1370

Metaphysical and philosophical implications of the actor's role in the *nō* theatre. Japan. 712-1980. Lang.: Pol.   1510

Tragedy, space and discourse in neoclassical dramatic theory. France. 1800-1850. Lang.: Eng.   3035

Impact of cinematic technique on plays by Beckett and Duras. France. 1977-1987. Lang.: Eng.   3037

Chinese opera dramatist and theoretician Meng Cheng-Shuen. China. 1386-1644. Lang.: Chi.   3589

Performing institutions

SEE

Institutions, producing.

Pericles

Performance/production

Shakespeare's later plays at Stratford Festival. Canada: Stratford, ON. 1986. Lang.: Eng.   751

Plays/librettos/scripts

Comparison of Shakespeare's *Cymbeline* with the reign of James I. England. 1400-1550. Lang.: Eng.   2503

Perle, George

Plays/librettos/scripts

George Perle's analysis of Alban Berg's opera *Lulu*. Austria. 1937-1985. Lang.: Swe.   3892

Permskij Opernyj Teat'r (Perm)

Performance/production

Analysis of the work of Perm Opera Theatre. USSR: Perm. 1980-1987. Lang.: Rus.   3868

Analysis of Perm Opera Theatre. USSR: Perm. 1980-1987. Lang.: Rus.   3870

Perring, Robert

Performance/production

Interview with playwright/actor Robert Perring. USA. Lang.: Eng.   2354

Perron, Wendy

Performance/production

Five women choreographers and critics discuss conceptions of the female body. USA. 1987. Lang.: Eng.   1416

Perry, Jeff

Performance/production

Collection of newspaper reviews by New York theatre critics. USA: New York, NY. 1987. Lang.: Eng.   2312

Person, Ellis

Performance/production

Review of six-week dance festival representing forms of dance in South Africa. South Africa, Republic of: Durban. 1986. Lang.: Eng.   1409

Personal Equation, The

Plays/librettos/scripts

Family relationships in Eugene O'Neill's early plays. USA. 1913. Lang.: Eng.   2926

Personnel

Administration

Interview with Madeleine Rivest. Canada: Montreal, PQ. 1987. Lang.: Fre.   14

Interview with Hans Kemna, casting director. Netherlands. 1987. Lang.: Dut.   34

Phantom of the Opera exchange: British, U.S. Equity agreement. UK-England: London. USA: New York, NY. 1987. Lang.: Eng.   49

U.S. and British Equity associations: actor exchange, union reciprocity. UK-England. USA. 1981-1987. Lang.: Eng.   50

Issues of conflict in the international exchange of artists. UK-England. Denmark: Copenhagen. 1982. Lang.: Eng.   55

AEA Actors' Work Program, a re-training program for actors. USA: New York, NY. 1986-1987. Lang.: Eng.   59

The first Anglo-American commercial Broadway production, the musical *Carrie*. USA: New York, NY. UK-England: London. 1987. Lang.: Eng.   61

National Actors' Equity conference. USA: New York, NY. 1985. Lang.: Eng.   63

Actor exchange: discussions of Equity, Royal Shakespeare Company. USA. UK-England. 1985. Lang.: Eng.   74

Overview of activities of Actors' Equity Association. USA: New York, NY, Chicago, IL. 1961-1984. Lang.: Eng.   75

Meeting between Actors' Equity and British Equity. USA: Washington, DC. UK-England. 1984. Lang.: Eng.   76

Panel discussion on the importance of volunteers in the arts. USA. 1987. Lang.: Eng.   82

Exchange of British and American artists. USA: New York, NY. UK-England. 1982. Lang.: Eng.   84

Equity wins court battle against producer David Merrick. USA: New York, NY. 1982. Lang.: Eng.   92

Arbitration of Equity's Billie Whitelaw case. USA: New York, NY. 1982. Lang.: Eng.   94

Ellen Burstyn succeeds Theodore Bikel as Actors' Equity president. USA: New York, NY. 1982. Lang.: Eng.   98

Chicago Equity celebrates anniversary of labor's fight for eight-hour day. USA: Chicago, IL. 1986. Lang.: Eng.   99

Admission and employment of non-immigrant aliens. USA: Washington, DC. 1982. Lang.: Eng.   101

Actors' Equity president Ellen Burstyn on employment for minorities and women. USA: New York, NY. 1982. Lang.: Eng.   109

Strike by Hispanic Organization of Latin Americans (HOLA) due to inadequate casting of Hispanic actors. USA: New York, NY. 1982. Lang.: Eng.   110

Circle Repertory Theatre's plan to increase roles for minority actors. USA: New York, NY. 1983. Lang.: Eng.   116

Current trends and future of summer stock companies. USA. 1985. Lang.: Eng.   121

Value of degree in arts management. USA: New York, NY. 1985. Lang.: Eng.   123

Actors' Equity plans National Theatre project. USA. 1985. Lang.: Eng.   125

Comprehensive guide to establishing and running a box office. USA: New York, NY. 1980. Lang.: Eng.   126

Equity's policy on U.S. performances by foreign artists. USA: New York, NY. 1987. Lang.: Eng.   131

Personnel — cont'd

Opposition to Equity National Theatre plan in favor of regional theatre. USA. 1985. Lang.: Eng.   132

Reactions to first national symposium on nontraditional casting. USA: New York, NY. 1986-1987. Lang.: Eng.   144

Evaluation of volunteers in an arts organization. USA. 1987. Lang.: Eng.   148

Protecting rights of Actors' Equity members who appear in Off-off Broadway shows. USA: New York, NY. 1966-1982. Lang.: Eng.   156

Integration of creative process in society. USA: New York, NY. 1986. Lang.: Eng.   168

Board presidents on their roles in nonprofit organizations. USA. 1987. Lang.: Eng.   177

Results of a survey conducted by the New York Foundation for the Arts. USA: New York, NY. 1987. Lang.: Eng.   181

The Showcase Code and playwrights who supported it. USA: New York, NY. 1985. Lang.: Eng.   191

Fiduciary responsibilities of the museum trustee. USA. 1987. Lang.: Eng.   192

Volunteer organizations and their role in the community. USA. 1700-1987. Lang.: Eng.   195

San Francisco Bay Area Advisory Committee and its goals. USA: San Francisco, CA. 1987. Lang.: Eng.   197

Literal and imaginative perceptions of work. USA. 1986. Lang.: Eng.   199

Nontraditional casting: types, rationale and examples. USA: New York, NY. 1987. Lang.: Eng.   203

Training volunteer fundraisers. USA. 1987. Lang.: Eng.   205

First nontraditional casting symposium. USA: New York, NY. 1975-1987. Lang.: Eng.   208

Producer's comments on first national symposium on nontraditional casting. USA: New York, NY. 1986-1987. Lang.: Eng.   215

Survey of employment through Actors' Equity Association. USA. 1975-1985. Lang.: Eng.   218

Labor-sponsored conference for Chicago Equity members. USA: Chicago, IL. 1986. Lang.: Eng.   221

Contracts, actors and union negotiations. USA. 1986. Lang.: Eng.   235

Legal difficulties facing producers who present foreign artists and dance troupes. USA. 1987. Lang.: Eng.   244

New legal terms to describe old ideas. USA. 1986. Lang.: Eng.   245

Function of a board member. USA. 1987. Lang.: Eng.   250

Theatrical experiment and the director of literary affairs. USSR. 1986-1988. Lang.: Rus.   266

Problems of the enhancement of literary director's prestige. USSR. 1980-1987. Lang.: Rus.   270

Conference on career transitions for dancers. USA: New York, NY. 1982. Lang.: Eng.   1397

Growth and decline of theatrical activity. Arabic countries. 1938-1985. Lang.: Fre.   1511

Dramaturgy in Canadian theatre. Canada. USA. Germany. 1980-1987. Lang.: Eng.   1513

SAG/AFTRA strikes in the television/motion picture industry. USA. 1980. Lang.: Eng.   3089

Volunteer-staff relationships in the New York Philharmonic. USA: New York, NY. 1987. Lang.: Eng.   3387

Wang Wenn-Jiuann and the establishment of Hung Lou Theatre Company. China, People's Republic of. 1987. Lang.: Chi.   3425

Design/technology

Merger of United Scenic Artists locals into a national union. USA. 1987. Lang.: Eng.   403

Effort to find union representation for theatrical sound designers. USA. 1985-1987. Lang.: Eng.   469

Institutions

Need for more Canadian productions of Canadian-composed opera. Canada. 1987. Lang.: Eng.   3718

Performance/production

Toronto directors discuss their training and craft. Canada: Toronto, ON. 1987. Lang.: Eng.   730

Problems of an actor's working conditions. USSR. 1980-1987. Lang.: Rus.   1049

Oleg Tabakov on organization of a theatre collective under perestrojka. USSR: Moscow. 1980-1987. Lang.: Rus.   1075

Personnel associated with production of Lepage's *La Trilogie des dragons*. Canada. 1987. Lang.: Fre.   1713

Biographical survey of Canadian opera personnel. Canada. 1930-1987. 1987. Lang.: Eng.   3747

Autobiography of opera star Maureen Forrester. Canada. 1930-1986. Lang.: Eng.   3748

Quality of and access to opera training in North America. Canada. USA. 1987. Lang.: Eng.   3753

International biographical survey of opera performers and productions. Europe. North America. 1987. Lang.: Eng.   3762

Relation to other fields

Discussion by theatre women on management, social security. Switzerland. 1987. Lang.: Ger.   1253

Charitable and self-help welfare schemes for theatre personnel, focus on experiences of women. UK-England. 1851-1920. Lang.: Eng.   1258

Actors' Equity's affirmative action program. USA: New York, NY. 1982. Lang.: Eng.   1261

Perucci, Andrea
   Performance/production
   Adaptation of Nativity puppet play. Italy. 1651-1987. Lang.: Eng.   4001

Pervyj Teat'r RSFSR (Moscow)
   Performance/production
   Two productions of *Misterija-Buff (Mystery-Bouffe)* by Majakovskij. USSR. 1918-1921. Lang.: Rus.   2388

Peschka, Francis
   Institutions
   History of New York's Little Players puppet theatre. USA: New York, NY. 1960-1985. Lang.: Eng.   3967

Peste groga, La (Yellow Plague, The)
   Basic theatrical documents
   Theatrical works of Pere d'Alcàntara Penya: texts and analysis. Spain. 1823-1906. Lang.: Cat.   1567

Pesti Nemzeti Szinház (Budapest)
   Performance/production
   Comparison of the premiere of Imre Sarkadi's *Oszlopos Simeon (The Man on the Pillar)* and two revivals by Árpad Árkosi and István Horvai. Hungary: Szeged, Budapest. 1967-1987. Lang.: Hun.   1830

Pesti Szinház (Budapest)
   Performance/production
   Christopher Hampton's *Les Liaisons Dangereuses* directed by János Szikora at Pesti Szinház under the title *Veszedelmes viszonyok*. Hungary: Budapest. 1986. Lang.: Hun.   1795

   István Horvai directs Imre Sarkadi's *Oszlopos Simeon (The Man on the Pillar)* at the Pesti Theatre. Hungary: Budapest. 1987. Lang.: Hun.   1849

   Milán Füst's *Catullus* and Imre Sarkadi's *Oszlopos Simeon (The Man on the Pillar)* reviewed. Hungary: Budapest. 1987. Lang.: Hun.   1886

PETA (Philippines)
   Performance/production
   Review of International Brecht Festival. China, People's Republic of: Hong Kong. 1986. Lang.: Dut.   759

Petch, Steve
   Basic theatrical documents
   Text of *Another Morning* by Steve Petch. Canada: Vancouver, BC. 1987. Lang.: Eng.   1548

Peter Pan
   Performance/production
   Collection of newspaper reviews by London theatre critics. UK-England: London. 1987. Lang.: Eng.   2266

Peterson, Len
   Basic theatrical documents
   Collection of radio plays produced by Andrew Allan. Canada. 1942-1955. Lang.: Eng.   3109

Petherbridge, Edward
   Performance/production
   Dorothy L. Sayers' *Have His Carcase*, *Eastender* and *Intimate Contact* are reviewed. UK-England. 1987. Lang.: Eng.   3208

Petition, The
   Performance/production
   Collection of newspaper reviews by London theatre critics. UK-England: London. 1986. Lang.: Eng.   2153

Petőfi Szinház (Veszprém)
   Performance/production
   Season openings at Petőfi Theatre, including Lengyel's *A nagy fejedelem (The Great Prince)* and Bíró's *A rablólovag (The Gallant Kidnapper)*. Hungary: Veszprém. 1987. Lang.: Hun.   1820

Petőfi Szinház (Veszprém) — cont'd

István Paál directs István Örkény's *Forgatókönyv (Screenplay)* at Petőfi Theatre. Hungary: Veszprém. 1987. Lang.: Hun. 1832

Reviews of two plays by István Örkény: *Forgatókönyv (Screenplay)* directed by István Paál and two productions of *Tóték (The Tót Family)* staged by János Meczner and István Pinczés. Hungary: Veszprém, Budapest, Debrecen. 1986-1987. Lang.: Hun. 1880

Reviews: *A vörös postakocsi (The Red Mail Coach)* by Gyula Krúdy, staged by Dezső Kapás and *Az atyai ház (The Paternal Roof)* by Zsigmond Remenyik, staged by Péter Lener. Hungary: Veszprém, Nyíregyháza. 1986. Lang.: Hun. 1821

Petrie, George
Theory/criticism
Brian Friel's play *Translations*. Ireland. 1987. Lang.: Eng. 3050

Petrik, József
Performance/production
Comparison of *Die Dreigroschenoper (The Three Penny Opera)* as directed by Ferenc Sík, József Petrik and Miklós Szinetár under the title *Koldusopera*. Hungary: Győr, Budapest. 1987. Lang.: Hun. 3402

Petruševskaja, Ljudmila
Performance/production
Overview of 1986-1987 Moscow theatre season. USSR: Moscow. 1986-1987. Lang.: Eng. 1039

Tamás Ascher directs Ljudmila Petruševskaja's *Tri devuški v golubom (Three Girls in Blue)* at Katona József Theatre under the title *Három lány kékben*. Hungary: Budapest. USSR. 1987. Lang.: Hun. 1883

Ljudmila Petruševskaja's controversial play, *Tri devuški v golubom (Three Girls in Blue)*, directed by Tamás Ascher at Katona József Theatre. Hungary: Budapest. 1987. Lang.: Hun. 1920

Pettifer, James
Performance/production
Collection of newspaper reviews by London theatre critics. UK-England: London. 1987. Lang.: Eng. 2192

Pettijohn, Doris
Performance/production
Maintaining theatre archives and designating a coordinator. USA: New York, NY. 1987. Lang.: Eng. 938

Peydró Díez, Vicent
Reference materials
Catalogue of Valencian playtexts available at libraries of Barcelona. Spain: Valencia, Barcelona. Lang.: Cat. 2975

Peymann, Claus
Audience
Claus Peymann, new artistic director of the Vienna Burgtheater. Austria: Vienna. 1986-1987. Lang.: Dut. 1530

Institutions
Schaubühne's comeback with production of *Schuld und Sühne (Crime and Punishment)*. Germany, West: Berlin, West. 1970-1987. Lang.: Dut. 1618

Performance/production
Productions by Claus Peymann, new artistic director of Vienna's Burgtheater. Austria: Vienna. 1986-1987. Lang.: Dut. 721

Directors Claus Peymann (Burgtheater) and Gerardjan Rijnders (Toneelgroep). Austria: Vienna. Netherlands: Amsterdam. 1987. Lang.: Dut. 1681

Peyton Jones, Jeremy
Performance/production
Collection of newspaper reviews by London theatre critics. UK-England: London. 1987. Lang.: Eng. 2253

Collection of newspaper reviews by London theatre critics. UK-England. 1987. Lang.: Eng. 2262

Pezzana, Giacinta
Plays/librettos/scripts
Influence of Sibilla Aleramo on women in Italian theatre. Italy. 1850-1930. Lang.: Ita. 1138

Pflüger, Hans-Dieter
Performance/production
Interview with choral director Hans-Dieter Pflüger of Dresdner Hoftheater. Germany, East: Dresden. 1979-1986. Lang.: Ger. 3782

Phantom of the Opera
Administration
Phantom of the Opera exchange: British, U.S. Equity agreement. UK-England: London. USA: New York, NY. 1987. Lang.: Eng. 49

Equity's policy on U.S. performances by foreign artists. USA: New York, NY. 1987. Lang.: Eng. 131

Design/technology
Machinery to be installed in Her Majesty's Theatre for *Phantom of the Opera*. UK-England: London. 1987. Lang.: Eng. 3619

Performance/production
Collection of newspaper reviews by London theatre critics. UK-England: London. 1986. Lang.: Eng. 2065

Broadway musical's shift from song and dance to aria and recitative. USA: New York, NY. 1956-1984. Lang.: Eng. 3655

Plays/librettos/scripts
Comparison of main characters in three contemporary plays. USA: New York, NY. 1987. Lang.: Eng. 2916

Phelps, Samuel
Performance/production
Historical accuracy in 19th-century London theatre productions. England: London. 1800-1900. Lang.: Eng. 1734

Phenomenology
Theory/criticism
Self-awareness in Shakespeare's *Julius Caesar*. England. 1599. Lang.: Eng. 1327

The beginning of *Iue* drama in 1935. China. 1935-1938. Lang.: Chi. 3590

American students are exposed to Chinese opera. China, People's Republic of. 1985. Lang.: Chi. 3594

The history of the decline of Iu drama. China, People's Republic of. 1986. Lang.: Chi. 3602

Philadelphia Story
Performance/production
Collection of newspaper reviews by London theatre critics. UK-England: London. 1987. Lang.: Eng. 2187

Philadelphia, Here I Come
Plays/librettos/scripts
Themes of Brian Friel's plays. Ireland. 1929-1987. Lang.: Eng. 2638

Philanderer, The
Plays/librettos/scripts
Significance of the ending of Shaw's *The Philanderer*. UK-England. 1905. Lang.: Eng. 2823

Philistines
SEE
Varvary.

Phillippou, Nick
Training
Genesis and development of various youth theatre groups. UK-Ireland. 1979-1987. Lang.: Eng. 1388

Phillips, Anton
Performance/production
Collection of newspaper reviews by London theatre critics. UK. 1987. Lang.: Eng. 2031

Collection of newspaper reviews by London theatre critics. UK-England: London. 1987. Lang.: Eng. 2191

Phillips, Robin
Institutions
History of the Stratford Festival. Canada: Stratford, ON. 1953-1982. Lang.: Eng. 521

Performance/production
Grand Theatre: failed establishment of repertory theatre. Canada: London, ON. 1983-1984. Lang.: Eng. 738

Rehearsal process of 1987 Stratford Festival productions directed by Robin Phillips. Canada: Stratford, ON. 1987. Lang.: Eng. 741

Shakespeare's later plays at Stratford Festival. Canada: Stratford, ON. 1986. Lang.: Eng. 751

Play scripts as literary texts and as performance texts. UK-England. 1977-1987. Lang.: Eng. 905

Phillips, Rodney
Administration
Interview with NAPAC director Rodney Phillips. South Africa, Republic of. 1987. Lang.: Eng. 1523

Philoctetes
Performance/production
Collection of newspaper reviews by London theatre critics. UK-England: London. 1986. Lang.: Eng. 2075

Philosophy
Performance/production
Theatre sociologist's view of theatrical work and experimentation. USSR. 1986-1988. Lang.: Rus. 1006

Plays/librettos/scripts
Humanitarianism in contemporary Chinese drama. China, People's Republic of. 1984. Lang.: Chi. 2493

Philosophy — cont'd

Theme of deconstruction in Samuel Beckett's writings. Europe. 1953-1987. Lang.: Eng. 2563

Collection of nineteenth-century theoretical writings on theatre and drama. Germany. 1800-1900. Lang.: Ger. 2595

Analysis of Jean Genet's plays. UK-England: London. 1987. Lang.: Eng. 2805

Philosophical themes in modern Chinese drama: their audience appeal. China, People's Republic of. 1987. Lang.: Chi. 3564

Relation to other fields

Excerpt from a speech by Jerzy Grotowski that examines the actor's technique. Italy: Florence. 1985. Lang.: Eng. 1244

Nature and effectiveness of political theatre. USA. 1985. Lang.: Eng. 1263

Artaud's philosophy of theatre mediating between dream and history. USA. 1958-1985. Lang.: Eng. 1265

International exchange in the performing arts. USA. 1985. Lang.: Eng. 1276

Playwright Gerald Thomas discusses influences on his work. Brazil: Rio de Janeiro. North America. Europe. 1970-1987. Lang.: Eng. 2981

Bertolt Brecht's interest in philosophy. Germany. 1918-1956. Lang.: Ger. 2991

Playwright Thomas Murphy and the nature of creativity. Ireland. 1961-1986. Lang.: Eng. 2993

Director Tadeusz Kantor's views on art, culture, philosophy. Poland. 1915-1987. Lang.: Pol. 2997

Lindsay Anderson's analysis of the political role of theatre. UK-England. 1987. Lang.: Eng. 3005

Tragic conflicts in playwright's Tang Xian-Zu's cultural conscience. China: Beijing. 1550-1616. Lang.: Chi. 3581

Mann, Baudelaire and Nietzche on Wagnerian philosophy. Europe. 1860-1950. Lang.: Eng. 3939

Perceptions of childhood reflected in opera. Europe. 1800-1983. Lang.: Eng. 3940

Influence of Arthur Schopenhauer on Wagner's works. Switzerland. 1834-1870. Lang.: Eng. 3945

Research/historiography

Influences on Wagner's *Ring* cycle. Germany: Dresden. 1813-1883. Lang.: Eng. 3948

Theory/criticism

Theatre and the infatuation with technology. France. 1987. Lang.: Fre. 1336

Essays on Bertolt Brecht's theories, aesthetics and philosophy. Germany, East. 1918-1987. Lang.: Ger. 1340

Aspects of Bertolt Brecht's theory and practice of theatre. Germany, East: Berlin, East. 1948-1956. Lang.: Ger. 1342

Editor of *Performing Arts Journal* discusses its history. USA: New York, NY. 1975-1985. Lang: Eng. 1359

Round-table discussion by philosophers and theatre professionals on conflict in contemporary drama. USSR. 1980-1987. Lang.: Rus. 1372

Domination of women and gay men in Western dance. USA. 1700-1987. Lang.: Eng. 1458

Politics, patriarchy in Dryden's plays. England. 1679-1687. 3030

Phoenix Theatre (London)

Performance/production

Collection of newspaper reviews by London theatre critics. UK-England: London. 1986. Lang.: Eng. 2053

Collection of newspaper reviews by London theatre critics. UK-England: London. 1986. Lang.: Eng. 2152

Collection of newspaper reviews by London theatre critics. UK-England: London. 1987. Lang.: Eng. 2203

Phoenix Theatre (New York, NY)

Administration

Financial challenges of four former artistic directors. USA. 1981-1987. Lang.: Eng. 239

Photographers Gallery (London)

Performance/production

Collection of newspaper reviews by London theatre critics. UK-England: London. 1987. Lang.: Eng. 2181

Photography

Basic theatrical documents

Play text and photo essay of Martha Clarke's *Vienna: Lusthaus*. Austria: Vienna. 1986. Lang.: Eng. 1398

Design/technology

Procedures to photograph a production. USA. 1982. Lang.: Eng. 389

Modern dance production *Portraits in Reflection*. USA. 1986. Lang.: Eng. 396

Exhibition on ballet *The Seven Deadly Sins* by Kurt Weill and Edward James. France: Paris. UK-England: London. 1933-1987. Lang.: Eng. 1429

On opera photography. Germany, East: Berlin, East. 1987. Lang.: Ger. 3695

Institutions

Photos and list of those present at Dramatists' Guild award ceremony. USA: New York, NY. 1987. Lang.: Eng. 581

Performance spaces

Collection of photographs on the history of the Teatre Lliure. Spain-Catalonia: Barcelona. 1976-1987. Lang.: Cat. 1671

Performance/production

Photos and documentation: actor Angelo Musco. Italy: Catania. 1904-1937. Lang.: Ita. 840

Carte-de-visite actors' photographs preserve acting styles. UK-England. France. USA. 1850-1920. Lang.: Eng. 916

Criticizes failure to integrate photography into theatre productions. USA. 1987. Lang.: Eng. 932

Relations between acting, theatre photography. USA. Lang.: Eng. 942

Introduction to articles on theatre and photography. USA. 1987. Lang.: Eng. 972

Career of actor Kirill Lavrov. USSR: Leningrad. 1980. Lang.: Rus. 1073

Dancers' daily routine in Les Ballets Jazz de Montréal. Canada: Montreal, PQ. 1985. Lang.: Eng. 1479

Development of Korean theatre. Korea: Seoul. 1930-1939. Lang.: Kor. 1973

Theatre career of photo-journalist Bert Andrews. USA: New York, NY. 1950-1987. Lang.: Eng. 2367

Photographs of mimes, mime companies and performance artists with commentary. USA. Europe. 1972-1987. Lang.: Eng. 3229

Relation to other fields

Theatricality in works of photographers Cindy Sherman and Edward Steichen. USA. 1900-1987. Lang.: Eng. 1289

Relation of photographic records to the performance. UK. 1840-1987. Lang.: Eng. 3372

Physicists, The

SEE

Physiker, Die.

Physiker, Die (Physicists, The)

Plays/librettos/scripts

Chance in the plays of P.G. du Plessis and Friedrich Dürrenmatt. South Africa, Republic of. Switzerland. 1987. Lang.: Afr. 1153

Comparison of Dürrenmatt's The Physicists (Die Physiker), Macbeth and *Doctor Faustus*. Switzerland. 1987. Lang.: Heb. 2747

Piaf

Plays/librettos/scripts

Work of playwright Pam Gems. UK-England: London. 1984-1987. Lang.: Eng. 2795

Picardie, Michael

Performance/production

Collection of newspaper reviews by London theatre critics. UK-England: London. 1987. Lang.: Eng. 2229

Picasso, Lamberto

Performance/production

Encounter between Pirandello and Lord Dunsany during Pirandello's production of *I pazzi sulla montagna (The Gods of the Mountain)* by Alessandro De Stefani. Italy. 1923-1928. Lang.: Eng. 1947

Picasso, Pablo

Design/technology

Picasso's theatrical work. France. Spain. 1917-1965. Lang.: Ita. 321

Performance/production

Collection of newspaper reviews by London theatre critics. UK-England: London. 1987. Lang.: Eng. 2185

Piccadilly Theatre (London)

Performance/production

Collection of newspaper reviews by London theatre critics. UK-England: London. 1986. Lang.: Eng. 2052

Collection of newspaper reviews by London theatre critics. UK-England: London. 1987. Lang.: Eng. 2185

Collection of newspaper reviews by London theatre critics. UK-England: London. 1987. Lang.: Eng. 2216

Pinter, Harold — cont'd

The founding of the Harold Pinter Society. UK-England. USA.
1985-1987. Lang.: Eng.   1159

An annual bibliography of works by and about Harold Pinter. UK-
England. USA. 1986-1987. Lang.: Eng.   1160

Deconstructionist analysis of Harold Pinter's *Silence*. UK-England.
1964-1970. Lang.: Eng.   2759

Analysis of Harold Pinter's *Victoria Station*. UK-England. 1959-1982.
Lang.: Eng.   2761

Characterizations of stage spaces: examples from Brecht, Pinter,
Douglas Turner Ward. UK-England. USA. 1947-1987. Lang.: Eng.
    2798

Interpreting Harold Pinter's dramas through focus on his play
structures. UK-England. 1958-1987. Lang.: Eng.   2815

Structural analysis of Pinter's *Old Times*. USA: New York, NY.
1971-1984. Lang.: Eng.   2843

Interview with playwright John Ford Noonan. USA. 1970-1987.
Lang.: Eng.   2894

Author Christopher Hampton discusses techniques of playwriting.
USA: New York, NY. UK-England: London. 1987. Lang.: Eng.
    2896

Theory/criticism

Survey of critical reactions to Harold Pinter's work. USA. UK-
England. Germany, West. 1978-1987. Lang.: Eng.   1364

Structuralist approach to play interpretation. 500 B.C.-1987 A.D.
Lang.: Eng.   3016

Comic space from the ancient Greeks to the present. Europe. USA.
Greece. 400 B.C.-1987 A.D. Lang.: Eng.   3032

Pipan, Janez

Performance/production

Review of *Hamlet, Julius Caesar* and *Titus Andronicus* at
'Shakespeare Fest '86'. Yugoslavia: Palić. 1986. Lang.: Hun.   2405

Pirandello, Luigi

Institutions

Pirandello's experiences as director of the Teatro d'Arte. Italy. 1924-
1928. Lang.: Ita.   549

Performance/production

Renato Simoni's staging of *I giganti della montagna (The Giants of
the Mountain)* by Luigi Pirandello. Italy: Florence. 1937. Lang.: Ita.
    821

Pirandello as director: contemporary reviews and interviews. Italy.
1915-1936. Lang.: Ita.   838

Career of actor Angelo Musco. Italy. 1872-1937. Lang.: Ita.   841

'Showing' is an essential part of all acting. Europe. 1590-1987.
Lang.: Eng.   1746

Luigi Pirandello's company Teatro d'Arte and its inaugural
productions. Italy. 1925-1928. Lang.: Eng.   1941

Encounter between Pirandello and Lord Dunsany during Pirandello's
production of *I pazzi sulla montagna (The Gods of the Mountain)*
by Alessandro De Stefani. Italy. 1923-1928. Lang.: Eng.   1947

Collection of newspaper reviews by London theatre critics. UK-
England: London. 1987. Lang.: Eng.   2192

Collection of newspaper reviews by London theatre critics. UK-
England: London. 1987. Lang.: Eng.   2257

Influence of Pirandello on modern theatre. USA. Italy. 1917-1987.
Lang.: Eng.   2338

Jevrejnov's theories of theatricality, parallels with Pirandello's. USSR.
1879-1953. Lang.: Eng.   2391

Plays/librettos/scripts

Essays on various Italian playwrights. Italy. 1700-1900. Lang.: Ita.
    1132

Collection of essays on Pirandello's theatrical activity. Italy. 1910-
1936. Lang.: Ita.   1142

Carnival patterns in the plays of Luigi Pirandello. Italy. 1916-1929.
Lang.: Eng.   2662

Acts of Pirandello conference. Italy. 1904-1936. Lang.: Ita, Eng.
    2663

Change of titles of the works of Luigi Pirandello. Italy. 1867-1936.
Lang.: Ita.   2665

Comparison between *La vita che ti diedi (The Life I Gave You)* by
Pirandello and *Lo spirito della morte (The Spirit of Death)* by Rosso
di San Secondo. Italy. 1923-1931. Lang.: Ita.   2666

Advance publication of introduction to Volume II, *Maschere nude
(Naked Masks)*, by Pirandello. Italy. 1887-1986. Lang.: Ita.   2668

Machines—animate and inanimate—in *Tonight We Improvise (Questa
sera si recita a soggetto)* by Pirandello. Italy. 1929-1987. Lang.: Eng.
    2670

Centrality of characters in the plays of Luigi Pirandello. Italy. 1867-
1936. Lang.: Ita.   2672

Characteristic themes in the work of Pirandello. Italy. 1876-1936.
Lang.: Ita.   2676

Gender conflict in Pirandello's *Sei personnaggi in cerca d'autore (Six
Characters in Search of an Author)*. Italy. 1921-1987. Lang.: Eng.
    2679

Comparison of Pirandello's *Enrico Quarto (Henry IV)* and
Shakespeare's *Hamlet*. Italy. England. 1580-1936. Lang.: Chi.   2680

Two filmscripts by Francesco Di Cocco based on short stories of
Pirandello. Italy. 1914-1934. Lang.: Ita.   3178

Theory/criticism

Theatre and contemporary culture. USA. 1800-1987. Lang.: Eng.
    1360

Pirandello's poetics and influence on other writers. Italy. 1904-1936.
Lang.: Ita.   3051

Pirandello's aesthetic views. Italy. 1867-1936. Lang.: Rus.   3052

Pirates of Penzance, The

Performance/production

Review of *Pirates* and *Student Prince*. South Africa, Republic of:
Johannesburg. 1986. Lang.: Eng.   3634

Pirchan, Emil

Performance/production

Politics and Shakespeare in Weimar Republic. Germany. 1919-1930.
Lang.: Eng.   1775

Pirosmanašvili, Niko

Design/technology

Artist Niko Pirosmanašvili's theatrical work. USSR. Lang.: Rus.   494

Piscator, Erwin

Design/technology

Exhibition of the design renderings of designer Leo Kurtz who
worked closely with Bertolt Brecht and Erwin Piscator. USA:
Cambridge, MA. 1986. Lang.: Eng.   455

Performance/production

Reviews of major Berlin performances. Germany: Berlin. 1889-1933.
Lang.: Ger.   1772

Theory/criticism

Effect of audiovisual media on theatre. France. 1987. Lang.: Fre.
    1339

Career and collaborations of Maria Piscator. USA. 1938-1987. Lang.:
Eng.   1365

Piscator, Maria

Theory/criticism

Career and collaborations of Maria Piscator. USA. 1938-1987. Lang.:
Eng.   1365

Pištěk, Theodor

Design/technology

Interview with costume designer Theodor Pištěk. Czechoslovakia.
1932-1987. Lang.: Hun.   3126

Pistolteatern (Stockholm)

Plays/librettos/scripts

Pistolteatern's adaptation of *Alice in Wonderland*. Sweden:
Stockholm. 1982. Lang.: Eng.   2738

Pit, The (London)

SEE ALSO

Royal Shakespeare Company.

Performance/production

Collection of newspaper reviews by London theatre critics. UK-
England: London. 1986. Lang.: Eng.   2045

Collection of newspaper reviews by London theatre critics. UK-
England: London. 1986. Lang.: Eng.   2063

Collection of newspaper reviews by London theatre critics. UK-
England: London. 1986. Lang.: Eng.   2080

Collection of newspaper reviews by London theatre critics. UK-
England: London. 1986. Lang.: Eng.   2098

Collection of newspaper reviews by London theatre critics. UK-
England: London. 1986. Lang.: Eng.   2111

Collection of newspaper reviews by London theatre critics. UK-
England. 1986. Lang.: Eng.   2144

Collection of newspaper reviews by London theatre critics. UK-
England: London. 1987. Lang.: Eng.   2196

Collection of newspaper reviews by London theatre critics. UK-
England: London. 1987. Lang.: Eng.   2202

Planning/operation — cont'd

Plaston: DNS-kind (Plaston: DNA Child)

Plays/librettos/scripts

Platforms

Design/technology

Plath, Sylvia

Administration

Plato

Theory/criticism

Platonov

Performance/production

Playtexts — cont'd

Play text and photo essay of Martha Clarke's *Vienna: Lusthaus*. Austria: Vienna. 1986. Lang.: Eng.   1398

Texts of seven *kabuki* plays. Japan. 1600-1800. Lang.: Jap.   1491

Catalan translation of Arthur Schnitzler's *Reigen (Round)*. 1862-1931. Lang.: Cat.   1541

English translation of *Jonah* by Elie Georges Berreby. Belgium. 1987. Lang.: Eng.   1542

Text of Fernand Crommelynck's *Le Cocu magnifique (The Magnificent Cuckold)*. Belgium. 1920. Lang.: Fre.   1543

Collection of four plays by Canadian women dramatists. Canada. 1987. Lang.: Eng.   1544

Text of *Le Roitelet (The Kinglet)* by Claude Dorge. Canada: Montreal, PQ. 1976. Lang.: Fre.   1545

Translation of *Being at Home with Claude*. Canada: Montreal, PQ. 1986. Lang.: Eng.   1546

Publication of two playtexts by Betty Lambert. Canada. 1987. Lang.: Eng.   1547

Text of *Another Morning* by Steve Petch. Canada: Vancouver, BC. 1987. Lang.: Eng.   1548

German translation of Tremblay's *Les Belles-Soeurs*. Canada: Quebec, PQ. Germany. 1987. Lang.: Ger.   1549

Playtext of *Zero Hour* by Arthur Milner. Costa Rica: San José. 1987. Lang.: Eng.   1550

Catalan translation of Milan Kundera's *Jacques et son maître (Jacques and His Master)*, with introduction. Czechoslovakia: Prague. 1968-1981. Lang.: Cat.   1551

English translation of *What, No Ashes?* by Tauno Yliruusi. Finland. 1987. Lang.: Eng.   1553

New English translation of Rostand's *Chantecler*. France. 1880-1987. Lang.: Eng.   1554

English translations of three plays by Jacob Masen. Germany. 1606-1681. Lang.: Eng.   1556

Catalan translation of *Bekannte Gesichter, Gemischte Gefühle (Known Faces, Mixed Feelings)* by Botho Strauss. Germany. 1944-1978. Lang.: Cat.   1557

Translation of five contemporary Persian plays. Iran. 1987. Lang.: Eng.   1558

English translation of *Buba* by Hillel Mittelpunkt. Israel. 1987. Lang.: Eng.   1559

English text of *Elisabetta: Quasi per caso una donna (Elizabeth: Almost By Chance a Woman)* by Dario Fo. Italy. USA. 1987. Lang.: Eng.   1560

Complete works of Fukuda Tsuneari. Japan. 1912-1987. Lang.: Jap.   1561

Plays of Terayama Shūji. Japan. 1950-1980. Lang.: Jap.   1562

Realism in Korean theatre. Korea. 1908-1977. Lang.: Kor.   1563

Text of *Yajunbyungwon (Field Hospital)* by Lim Je-Bok. Korea. 1970. Lang.: Kor.   1564

Hebrew translation of Sławomir Mrożek's *Vatslave*. Poland: Cracow. Israel: Jerusalem. 1968-1984. Lang.: Heb.   1565

English translations of contemporary African plays. Senegal. Zaire. 1987. Lang.: Eng.   1566

Theatrical works of Pere d'Alcàntara Penya: texts and analysis. Spain. 1823-1906. Lang.: Cat.   1567

Translation of *Viernes, 29 de julio de 1983, de madrugada (Friday, July 29, 1983, Early in the Morning)* by Jerónimo López Moto. Spain. 1987. Lang.: Eng.   1568

Text and analysis of *Fàlaris* and *Orfeu* by Llorenç Moyà. Spain. 1968-1981. Lang.: Cat.   1569

The Horns of Don Friolera, translation of *Los cuernos de don Friolera* by Ramón del Valle-Inclán. Spain. 1930. Lang.: Eng.   1570

Study of the poetic, narrative and theatrical work of Agustí Bartra, edition of complete works, vol. 4. Spain-Catalonia. Mexico. 1937-1982. Lang.: Cat.   1571

Text of *Lo desengany (The Disappointment)* by Francesc Fontanella, with analysis. Spain-Catalonia: Barcelona. 1622-1680. Lang.: Cat.   1572

Edition and analysis, *Allò que tal vegada s'esdevingué (What Happened Then)* by Joan Oliver. Spain-Catalonia. 1899-1986. Lang.: Cat.   1573

Analysis and edition of *Comèdia famosa de la gloriosa Verge i Màrtir Santa Bàrbara*, by F. Vicenç Garcia. Spain-Catalonia. 1581-1623. Lang.: Cat.   1574

Complete text of *Lulu* by Kathy Acker. USA. 1986. Lang.: Eng.   1576

Text of *Green Card* by JoAnne Akalaitis. USA. 1986. Lang.: Eng.   1577

One-act plays for acting students. USA. 1987. Lang.: Eng.   1578

Text of *Hospice*, a one-act play by Pearl Cleage. USA. 1986-1987. Lang.: Eng.   1579

Text of *A Place with the Pigs* by Athol Fugard. USA. South Africa, Republic of. 1987. Lang.: Eng.   1580

Six plays detailing the Hispanic experience in the United States. USA. Mexico. 1987. Lang.: Eng.   1581

Text of *Daughters of the Water* by Jay Wright. USA. 1987. Lang.: Eng.   1583

Russian symbolist plays and essays. USSR. 1880-1986. Lang.: Eng.   1584

Collection of radio plays produced by Andrew Allan. Canada. 1942-1955. Lang.: Eng.   3109

Texts of cabaret artist and clown Karl Valentin. Germany. 1882-1948. Lang.: Cat.   3283

About aging: *L.O.W. in Gaia* by Rachel Rosenthal. USA. 1986. Lang.: Eng.   3341

Text of the play *Chang-le-gong (The Palace of the Beatitudes)* by Guh Shyi Tung. China: Binjiang. 1987. Lang.: Chi.   3442

Text of *Yu-wang-cheng-gue (A City of Desire)* by Li Hui-min, based on Shakespeare's *Macbeth*. Taiwan. 1986. Lang.: Chi.   3443

Text of a *kokdugaksi* puppet play. Korea. 600-1987. Lang.: Kor.   4004

Complete text of *Dimba and Dimbi* with background materials and preparations. Indonesia. 1987. Lang.: Eng.   4008

Performance/production
Children's theatrical productions outside of theatres. Includes playtexts. Switzerland. 1986-1988. Lang.: Ger.   2026

Reference materials
Catalogue of Valencian playtexts available at libraries of Barcelona. Spain: Valencia, Barcelona. Lang.: Cat.   2975

Playwrights
SEE
Plays/librettos/scripts.

Playwriting.

Playwrights Canada Press (Toronto, ON)
Plays/librettos/scripts
History of Playwrights Canada Press. Canada: Toronto, ON. 1972-1982. Lang.: Eng.   2460

Playwrights Horizons (New York, NY)
Performance/production
Collection of newspaper reviews by New York theatre critics. USA: New York, NY. 1987. Lang.: Eng.   2315

Collection of newspaper reviews by New York theatre critics. USA: New York, NY. 1987. Lang.: Eng.   2319

Collection of newspaper reviews by New York theatre critics. USA: New York, NY. 1987. Lang.: Eng.   2320

Playwriting
SEE ALSO
Plays/librettos/scripts.

Administration
American theatre's view of the commissioning process. USA: New York, NY. 1987. Lang.: Eng.   118

Recent court decision over the IRS tax laws affecting writers' deductions. USA. 1987. Lang.: Eng.   3241

Institutions
The Canadian Governor General's Awards. Canada. 1987. Lang.: Eng.   509

List of resources for playwrights. USA. 1987-1988. Lang.: Eng.   582

Closing remarks, FDG/CBS conference on new plays. USA. 1987. Lang.: Eng.   586

Literary Managers and Dramaturgs of America (LMDA). USA: New York, NY. 1987. Lang.: Eng.   594

Playwright Denis Johnston and avant-garde theatre at the Abbey. Ireland: Dublin. 1927-1935. Lang.: Eng.   1619

Profile of New Dramatists. USA: New York, NY. 1982. Lang.: Eng.   1656

Playwriting — cont'd

Script editor's recollections of CBC radio dramas. Canada. 1944-1954. Lang.: Eng. 3110

Performance/production

Collective production of popular theatre. Canada: Edmonton, AB. 1987. Lang.: Eng. 726

The Directors Colloquium: director/playwright relationship. Canada: Calgary, AB. 1987. Lang.: Eng. 747

Analysis of the playwright/director relationship in Canada. Canada. 1987. Lang.: Eng. 750

Description of La Quinzaine theatre festival. Canada: Quebec, PQ. 1986. Lang.: Fre. 1696

Theatre of playwright Robert Lepage. Canada: Montreal, PQ. Canada: Toronto, ON. 1980-1987. Lang.: Eng. 1704

Interview with playwright Patrick McDonald. Canada: Ottawa, ON. 1987. Lang.: Eng. 1708

Robert Lepage: creation, direction of *La Trilogie des dragons (Dragons' Trilogy)*. Canada. 1987. Lang.: Fre. 1716

Review of the 1986 Festival de la Francophonie. France. Belgium. 1986. Lang.: Fre. 1760

The relationship between the director and the playwright from contrasting historical perspectives. UK-England. 1800-1987. Lang.: Eng. 2291

Interview with playwright/actor Robert Perring. USA. Lang.: Eng. 2354

Interview with actor and playwright Joe Seneca. USA: New York, NY, Cleveland, OH. 1957-1987. Lang.: Eng. 2364

Resources on Chinese opera. China, People's Republic of. 1922-1987. Lang.: Chi. 3520

Plays/librettos/scripts

Work of playwright Robert Lepage. Canada. 1987. Lang.: Fre. 1101

Interview with playwright Hugo Hiriart. Mexico: Mexico City. 1987. Lang.: Spa. 1151

Notes on Dramatists' Guild activities and concerns. USA. 1987. Lang.: Eng. 1162

Directory of institutional theatres: aimed at playwrights. USA. 1987. Lang.: Eng. 1163

Plays and books produced and published by Dramatists' Guild members. USA. 1987. Lang.: Eng. 1164

Adaptations of fairy tales and fantasies for children's plays. USA. 1957-1987. Lang.: Eng. 1165

Prominent women in American theatre. USA. 1987. Lang.: Eng. 1166

Effects of developmental playwriting process. USA. 1987. Lang.: Eng. 1167

Current American playwriting—link with film and TV, production, economics. USA. 1987. Lang.: Eng. 1176

FDG/CBS New Plays Program Conferences. USA: New York, NY. 1987. Lang.: Eng. 1180

Plays and playwrights of children's theatre. USA: New York, NY. 1987. Lang.: Eng. 1181

Collaboration between playwright Craig Lucas and director Norman Rene. USA: New York, NY. 1985-1987. Lang.: Eng. 1183

Essays on plot and composition. USSR. 1987. Lang.: Rus. 1187

Interview with playwright S. Alešin. USSR. 1980-1987. Lang.: Rus. 1423

Critical overview of the playwrights in Argentina. Argentina. 1949-1986. Lang.: Spa. 2432

Interview with playwright Ray Lawler. Australia. Ireland. 1921-1987. Lang.: Eng. 2433

Survey of Alex Buzo's plays and analysis of the demands of the text. Australia. 1969-1983. Lang.: Eng. 2442

Interview with playwright Daniel Keene. Australia. USA: New York, NY. 1979-1987. Lang.: Eng. 2444

Introductory survey of recent Australian playwrights. Australia. 1970-1985. Lang.: Eng. 2447

Interview with playwright Paul Pourveur. Belgium. 1987. Lang.: Dut. 2455

Interview with playwright Robert Lepage. Canada. 1987. Lang.: Fre. 2464

Playwright Sharon Pollock. Canada. 1970-1983. Lang.: Eng. 2469

Language and metaphor in plays of René-Daniel Dubois. Canada: Toronto, ON, Montreal, PQ. 1983-1987. Lang.: Eng. 2471

Interview with playwright Ping Chong. Canada: Montreal, PQ. USA: New York, NY. 1987. Lang.: Eng. 2472

Robert Lepage's play *Vinci*. Canada. 1986-1987. Lang.: Fre. 2474

Critical response to Brassard's *Les Paravents (The Screens)*. Canada: Montreal, PQ, Ottawa, ON. 1987. Lang.: Fre. 2475

Plays by Micone, Saddlemyer, Thompson, Wyatt. Canada. 1958-1985. Lang.: Eng. 2481

Brecht's influence on technique and style of playwright Heiner Müller. Germany, East. 1940-1984. Lang.: Eng. 2605

Use of English in Nigerian drama. Nigeria. 1940-1987. Lang.: Eng. 2706

Karl Ragnar Gierow on O'Neill and his importance in Sweden. Sweden: Stockholm. 1920-1970. Lang.: Eng. 2736

Biography of Swiss playwright Frank Wedekind. Switzerland: Lenzburg. Germany: Berlin. France: Paris. 1864-1918. Lang.: Ger. 2746

Financial support for aspiring playwrights. UK-England. 1980. Lang.: Eng. 2771

Political protest in Tom Stoppard's *Every Good Boy Deserves Favour*. UK-England. USSR. 1974-1977. Lang.: Eng. 2783

Work of playwright Pam Gems. UK-England: London. 1984-1987. Lang.: Eng. 2795

Avoidance of political themes in drama of Northern Ireland. UK-Ireland. 1979-1987. Lang.: Eng. 2830

Life of playwright John O. Killens. USA: New York, NY. 1954-1987. Lang.: Eng. 2836

Eugene O'Neill's influence on Edward Albee. USA. 1949-1962. Lang.: Eng. 2841

Development of themes and characters in plays of Sam Shepard. USA. 1960-1987. Lang.: Eng. 2853

Interview with playwright August Wilson. USA. 1970-1987. Lang.: Eng. 2855

Eugene O'Neill's influence on William Faulkner. USA: New York, NY. 1920-1962. Lang.: Eng. 2858

Dramatic writing in the forefront of theatre. USA. 1985. Lang.: Eng. 2864

Barbara Gelb discusses the creation of *My Gene*. USA. 1962-1987. Lang.: Eng. 2867

Interview with playwright Arthur Miller. USA. 1944-1987. Lang.: Eng. 2868

Interview with playwright John Guare. USA. 1987. Lang.: Eng. 2870

Chronological listing of John Guare's plays, bibliography, list of reviews. USA. 1938-1987. Lang.: Eng. 2871

Influence of O'Neill and Beckett on Israel Horovitz. USA: Boston, MA. France: Paris. 1939-1953. Lang.: Eng. 2873

Interview with playwright August Wilson. USA: New York, NY. 1985-1987. Lang.: Eng. 2876

Impact of AIDS crisis on the theatre. USA: New York, NY, San Francisco, CA. 1987. Lang.: Eng. 2881

Interview with playwright Leslie Lee. USA: Bryn Mawr, PA, New York, NY. 1987. Lang.: Eng. 2893

Interview with playwright John Ford Noonan. USA. 1970-1987. Lang.: Eng. 2894

Terrence McNally discusses playwriting. USA: New York, NY. 1987. Lang.: Eng. 2895

Author Christopher Hampton discusses techniques of playwriting. USA: New York, NY. UK-England: London. 1987. Lang.: Eng. 2896

Legal and ethical rights of playwrights regarding interpretations of their works. USA. Lang.: Eng. 2904

Interview with playwright Charles Fuller. USA: Philadelphia, PA, New York, NY. Korea, South. 1959-1987. Lang.: Eng. 2921

Influence of Rudyard Kipling on Eugene O'Neill. USA. 1887-1950. Lang.: Eng. 2925

Playwrights discuss problems of one-act play. USSR. 1987. Lang.: Rus. 2935

Autobiographical writings of playwright Viktor Rosov. USSR. 1913-1987. Lang.: Rus. 2962

Dramatist M.F. Šatrov on his creative and ideological principles. USSR. 1980-1987. Lang.: Rus. 2966

Alfred Uhry on *Driving Miss Daisy*. USA: New York, NY. 1976-1984. Lang.: Eng. 3419

Playwriting — cont'd

Shakespeare compared to writers of Chinese opera. China. 1279-1616. Lang.: Chi. 3554

Interview with playwright Guo Jiun. China, People's Republic of. 1987. Lang.: Chi. 3559

Tippett's influence on contemporary opera. 1946-1987. Lang.: Eng. 3888

Relation to other fields
Psychological effect of Ben Jonson's family life on his writings. England. 1602-1604. Lang.: Eng. 1232

Multicultural plays for children. USA. 1986. Lang.: Eng. 1287

Essays on the theme of marriage in literature. England. Norway. 1300-1985. Lang.: Eng. 1425

Playwright Gerald Thomas discusses influences on his work. Brazil: Rio de Janeiro. North America. Europe. 1970-1987. Lang.: Eng. 2981

Playwright Thomas Murphy and the nature of creativity. Ireland. 1961-1986. Lang.: Eng. 2993

Theatrical themes and the class issue in the work of Irish playwrights. Ireland. 1900-1987. Lang.: Eng. 2994

Theory/criticism
Reprints of articles by various authors on Australian drama since 1955. Australia. 1955-1987. Lang.: Eng. 1316

Eric Bentley's critical essays on theatre. USA. 1952-1986. Lang.: Eng. 1350

Round-table discussion by philosophers and theatre professionals on conflict in contemporary drama. USSR. 1980-1987. Lang.: Rus. 1372

Plaza Theatre (Johannesburg)
Performance spaces
Theatres built, influences on design. South Africa, Republic of: Johannesburg. 1887-1940. Lang.: Afr. 667

Please Please Please
Performance/production
Collection of newspaper reviews by London theatre critics. UK-England: London. 1986. Lang.: Eng. 2043

Pleciuga Puppet Theatre (Szczecin)
Performance/production
Poland's puppet theatre. Poland: Wrocław, Białystock. Austria: Mistelbach. 1979-1987. Lang.: Eng, Fre. 4006

Pljatt, R.
Performance/production
Actors discuss their profession. USSR. 1987. Lang.: Eng. 996

Plot and Passion
Plays/librettos/scripts
John Lang's collaboration with Tom Taylor on *Plot and Passion*. UK-England. Australia. 1853. Lang.: Eng. 2785

Plot/subject/theme
Basic theatrical documents
Collection of four plays by Canadian women dramatists. Canada. 1987. Lang.: Eng. 1544

Catalan translation of Milan Kundera's *Jacques et son maître (Jacques and His Master)*, with introduction. Czechoslovakia: Prague. 1968-1981. Lang.: Cat. 1551

Text of *Lo desengany (The Disappointment)* by Francesc Fontanella, with analysis. Spain-Catalonia: Barcelona. 1622-1680. Lang.: Cat. 1572

Chapter 19 of Harold Pinter's unpublished novel *The Dwarfs*. UK-England. 1958-1987. Lang.: Eng. 1575

Design/technology
Effects of mixed media on traditional dramatic components of theatre. Europe. 1900-1987. Lang.: Fre. 318

Harold Pinter's scenic designs. 1958-1987. Lang.: Eng. 1585

Institutions
Previews 1982 International Children's Festival. Canada: Toronto, ON. 1982. Lang.: Eng. 524

Colloquium on 'Brecht 30 Years After'. Canada: Toronto, ON. 1985. Lang.: Fre. 1607

Development of feminist theatre in Toronto. Canada: Toronto, ON. 1960-1987. Lang.: Eng. 1608

Brecht was the theme of the 1986 International Theatre Festival and Conference. Canada: Toronto, ON. 1986. Lang.: Fre. 1610

Performance/produciton
Johanna Boyce's *With Longings to Realize* presented by the Performance Group. USA: New York, NY. 1983. Lang.: Eng. 1478

Performance/production
Reviews of alternative theatre in Toronto. Canada: Toronto, ON, Montreal, PQ. 1987. Lang.: Eng. 731

Canadian popular theatre. Canada. Africa. Asia. 1987. Lang.: Eng. 733

Overview of the 1987 Theatre Festival of the Americas. Canada: Montreal, PQ. 1987. Lang.: Eng. 740

Realism in Korean theatre. Korea. 1980-1987. Lang.: Kor. 855

Two productions of Pinter's *Old Times*. UK-England: London. USA: New York, NY, St. Louis, MO. 1971-1985. Lang.: Eng. 907

Career of actor, director, playwright Charles Ludlam. USA: New York, NY. 1964-1987. Lang.: Eng. 956

Review of touring production of Edward Lock's *Human Sex*. Canada: Vancouver, BC. 1985-1986. Lang.: Fre. 1405

Director Anne Bogart's production of *Women and Men: A Big Dance*. USA: New York, NY. 1983. Lang.: Eng. 1418

Script and staging of Shaliko's *The Yellow House*. USA: Baltimore, MD. 1982-1987. Lang.: Eng. 1487

Theatre of playwright Robert Lepage. Canada: Montreal, PQ. Canada: Toronto, ON. 1980-1987. Lang.: Eng. 1704

Creations' *La Trilogie des dragons (Dragon Trilogy)* by Robert Lepage. Canada. 1987. Lang.: Fre. 1706

Canadian playwright Allan Stratton. Canada: Toronto, ON. 1982. Lang.: Eng. 1710

Content and North American reception of *Asinimali! (We Have No Money!)* by Mbongeni Ngema. Canada. South Africa, Republic of. 1987. Lang.: Eng. 1715

Change from sociopolitical emphasis to individual themes in productions of *A Midsummer Night's Dream*. Germany, East. 1960-1980. Lang.: Eng. 1782

Production of scenes from Shakespeare's *Troilus and Cressida* on the themes of war, peace and love. Germany, East: Berlin, East. 1985. Lang.: Ger. 1783

Five short plays by Géza Páskándi at SUNY Binghamton. Hungary. USA: Binghamton, NY. 1987. Lang.: Eng. 1813

New themes and styles in Japanese theatre. Japan: Tokyo. 1986. Lang.: Jap. 1953

The shape and form of contemporary Polish theatre. Poland: Warsaw. 1981-1987. Lang.: Eng, Fre. 1995

Productions and political philosophy of Field Day Theatre Company. UK-Ireland: Londonderry. 1986-1987. Lang.: Eng. 2309

Libel suit against a minstrel. UK-England: Stafford. 1616. Lang.: Eng. 3269

Overview of *Gu Cheng-Hei*. China, People's Republic of. 1967. Lang.: Chi. 3498

The development of modern Chinese opera. China, People's Republic of. 1986. Lang.: Chi. 3503

Unity and harmony in the music of Chinese opera. China, People's Republic of. 1987. Lang.: Chi. 3530

Plot synopsis of musical *Mademoiselle Colombe* based on Anouilh's *Colombe*. USA: New York, NY. 1987. Lang.: Eng. 3647

Plays/librettos/scripts
Social value of women's dramatic literature. 1985. Lang.: Fre. 1095

Connection between artistic practice and scientific inquiry. 1987. Lang.: Eng. 1096

Michael Hollingsworth's *The History of the Village of Small Huts*. Canada. 1987. Lang.: Eng. 1099

Summary and critical analysis of *Doc* by Sharon Pollock. Canada. 1987. Lang.: Eng. 1100

Work of playwright Robert Lepage. Canada. 1987. Lang.: Fre. 1101

Ideas of playwright Jeang Shyh Chyuan. China: Beijing. 1644-1875. Lang.: Chi. 1107

Přílis hlučna samota (Too Loud a Solitude) by Bohumil Hrabal. Czechoslovakia. 1914-1987. Lang.: Ita. 1110

Contemporary Czechoslovakian authors, some works in Italian translation. Czechoslovakia. 1980. Lang.: Ita. 1111

Analysis of Kjeld Abell's *Der bla pekingeser (The Blue Pekingese)*. Denmark. 1901-1961. Lang.: Ita. 1113

Allegory and irony in *Othello*. England. 1604. Lang.: Eng. 1114

Temporality in Shakespeare's *Richard III*. England. 1592. Lang.: Eng. 1115

Comparative study of *Measure for Measure* by Shakespeare and the poem *Leda and the Swan* by Yeats. England. 1604-1929. Lang.: Eng. 1116

Plot/subject/theme — cont'd

Discussion of *Crudities* by Thomas Coryat and *The White Devil* by John Webster. England. 1580-1612. Lang.: Eng. 1117

Swetnam the Woman-Hater, Arraigned by Women written in response to an anti-female pamphlet. England. 1600-1620. Lang.: Eng. 1118

Theodicy and tragic drama in *King Lear* and *The Tempest*. England. 1605-1611. Lang.: Eng. 1119

Use of symbols in Webster's *The Duchess of Malfi*. England. 1613. Lang.: Eng. 1121

Comparison of two versions of Duras' *La Musica Deuxième*. France: Paris. 1985-1987. Lang.: Eng. 1125

Theme of journeys in German theatre and film. Germany. 1970-1986. Lang.: Fre. 1127

Works of Carlo Gozzi, his relationship with actor Antonio Sacchi. Italy: Venice. 1755. Lang.: Ita. 1129

Carmelo Bene's *Il Lorenzaccio*. Italy. 1986. Lang.: Ita. 1130

Role of the *commedia umanistica* in the intellectual life of Renaissance Venice. Italy: Venice. 1400-1500. Lang.: Ita. 1135

Tommaso Aversa's Sicilian comedy *Le notti di Palermu (The Nights of Palermo)*. Italy. 1600. Lang.: Ita. 1136

Influence of Sibilla Aleramo on women in Italian theatre. Italy. 1850-1930. Lang.: Ita. 1138

Analysis of Rosso di San Secondo's *Amara (Bitter)*. Italy. 1913-1917. Lang.: Ita. 1139

Comparative view of play censorship. Korea. Japan. Germany. 1940-1987. Lang.: Kor. 1147

Overview of ancient Korean plays. Korea. 57 B.C. Lang.: Kor. 1148

Interview with playwright Hugo Hiriart. Mexico: Mexico City. 1987. Lang.: Spa. 1151

Editorial discussion of contemporary theatre. North America. 1987. Lang.: Eng. 1152

Chance in the plays of P.G. du Plessis and Friedrich Dürrenmatt. South Africa, Republic of. Switzerland. 1987. Lang.: Afr. 1153

Playwright Alfonso Vallejo's world view. Spain. 1976-1986. Lang.: Pol. 1156

General history of Catalan literature, including theatre. Spain-Catalonia. 1902-1961. Lang.: Cat. 1157

Prominent women in American theatre. USA. 1987. Lang.: Eng. 1166

Effects of developmental playwriting process. USA. 1987. Lang.: Eng. 1167

Roadside Theatre's production of *Leaving Egypt*. USA: Whitesburg, KY. Lang.: Eng. 1170

Collaboration of Craig Lucas and Norman Rene on *Blue Window* and *Three Postcards*. USA. 1987. Lang.: Eng. 1184

Essays on plot and composition. USSR. 1987. Lang.: Rus. 1187

Interview with playwright Eduard Radsinskij. USSR. 1987. Lang.: Rus. 1189

Social and political themes in the Moscow theatre season. USSR: Moscow. 1986-1987. Lang.: Rus. 1190

Cultural predetermination in three Athol Fugard plays. South Africa, Republic of. 1970. Lang.: Eng. 1419

Interview with playwright S. Alešin. USSR. 1980-1987. Lang.: Rus. 1423

Nō playwright, monk Ippen Hōgo. Japan. 1200-1400. Lang.: Jap. 1505

Waka poetry in *nō* plays. Japan. 700-1300. Lang.: Jap. 1507

Compares tragedies of Sophocles and Euripides with those of Eugene O'Neill. 1918-1946. Lang.: Eng. 2409

Optimistic interpretation of Beckett's *En attendant Godot (Waiting for Godot)*. 1987. Lang.: Eng. 2410

Love in Kroetz's *Wer durchs Laub geht (Through the Leaves)*. 1986. Lang.: Eng. 2411

Transfiguration in Shaw's *Misalliance*, *Saint Joan* and *Major Barbara*. 1986. Lang.: Eng. 2413

Old age in the plays of Sophocles, especially *Oedipus at Colonus*. 405 B.C. Lang.: Eng. 2414

Bartho Smit's *Don Juan onder die Boere (Don Juan among the Boers)*. 1600-1987. Lang.: Afr. 2415

Dramatic structure in Frayn's *Noises Off*. 1987. Lang.: Eng. 2416

The comedies of Jura Soyfer. 1836. Lang.: Eng. 2418

Textual analysis of Majakovskij's *Bathhouse*. 1986. Lang.: Eng. 2419

Societal dependence in Bond's *Bingo*. 1975. Lang.: Eng. 2422

Shakespeare's *King Lear* in the context of ironic drama. 1590. Lang.: Eng. 2424

Structure of revenge tragedy in Shakespeare's *Hamlet*. 1600. Lang.: Eng. 2425

Biblical influences in *King Lear, Hamlet, Othello* and *Macbeth*. Lang.: Eng. 2426

Female characters in city comedy who suffer from bladder incontinence. 1599-1632. Lang.: Eng. 2427

Modern theatrical treatment of Fascism and the Holocaust. 1980-1987. Lang.: Eng. 2428

Comparison between medieval passion plays and Peter Nichols' *Passion Play*. 1986. Lang.: Eng. 2429

Reconsideration of Weigand's *The Modern Ibsen* (1925). 1850-1987. Lang.: Eng. 2430

Proposed method of analyzing historical plays. 1987. Lang.: Ger. 2431

Critical overview of the playwrights in Argentina. Argentina. 1949-1986. Lang.: Spa. 2432

Interview with playwright Jack Hibberd. Australia: Melbourne. 1967-1987. Lang.: Eng. 2434

Focus on the plays of David Williamson and their cultural impact. Australia. 1970-1987. Lang.: Eng. 2436

Survey of the plays of Jack Hibberd: themes and characterization. Australia. 1966-1986. Lang.: Eng. 2437

Critical analysis of Dorothy Hewett's *The Man from Mukinupin*. Australia. 1979. Lang.: Eng. 2438

Thematic analysis of Dymphna Cusack's *Morning Sacrifice*. Australia. 1942. Lang.: Eng. 2441

Survey of Alex Buzo's plays and analysis of the demands of the text. Australia. 1969-1983. Lang.: Eng. 2442

Italo-Australian drama, in English and Italian. Australia. 1860-1986. Lang.: Eng. 2443

The early plays of Justin Fleming, especially *Cobra*. Australia. 1981-1986. Lang.: Eng. 2448

Conflict of worlds in plays by Louis Nowra. Australia. 1983-1985. Lang.: Eng. 2449

Origins of fairy tales on the Viennese stage. Austria: Vienna. 1700-1848. Lang.: Eng. 2450

Misogynist themes in Strindberg, Weininger and Witkiewicz. Austria: Vienna. 1880-1987. Lang.: Eng. 2452

Theme of torture in Brazilian drama. Brazil. 1964-1985. Lang.: Por. 2456

Interview with playwright Sharon Pollock. Canada. 1985. Lang.: Eng. 2457

The theme of a child's game in Lepage's *La Trilogie des dragons*. Canada: Montreal, PQ. 1987. Lang.: Fre. 2458

Rebuttal of review of Lepage's *La Trilogie des dragons*. Canada. 1987. Lang.: Fre. 2459

Productions of Brecht in Quebec. Canada. 1950-1986. Lang.: Fre. 2461

Traditionalism in Lepage's *La Trilogie des dragons*. Canada. 1987. Lang.: Fre. 2462

The role of the father-figure in recent plays from Quebec. Canada: Quebec. 1980-1987. Lang.: Fre. 2465

Collective theatre projects in Newfoundland. Canada: St. John's, NF. 1987. Lang.: Eng. 2466

Review of Wallace Shawn's *Aunt Dan and Lemon*. Canada: Toronto, ON. USA: New York, NY. 1986-1987. Lang.: Eng. 2467

Playwright Tomson Highway's use of native mythology. Canada. 1960-1987. Lang.: Eng. 2468

Playwright Sharon Pollock. Canada. 1970-1983. Lang.: Eng. 2469

David Fennario's *Joe Beef*. Canada: Montreal, PQ, Verdun, PQ. 1984. Lang.: Eng. 2470

Language and metaphor in plays of René-Daniel Dubois. Canada: Toronto, ON, Montreal, PQ. 1983-1987. Lang.: Eng. 2471

Interview with playwright Ping Chong. Canada: Montreal, PQ. USA: New York, NY. 1987. Lang.: Eng. 2472

Theme of René-Daniel Dubois's *Being at Home with Claude*. Canada: Quebec, PQ. USA: New York, NY. 1984-1985. Lang.: Eng. 2473

Robert Lepage's play *Vinci*. Canada. 1986-1987. Lang.: Fre. 2474

Plot/subject/theme — cont'd

Critical response to Brassard's *Les Paravents (The Screens)*. Canada: Montreal, PQ, Ottawa, ON. 1987. Lang.: Fre. 2475

Uses of history in Lepage's *La Trilogie des dragons*. Canada. 1987. Lang.: Fre. 2476

Critical analysis of James Reaney's *Three Desks*. Canada. 1960-1977. Lang.: Eng. 2477

German influences on contemporary Quebecois theatre. Canada. Germany. 1850-1949. Lang.: Fre. 2478

La Trilogie des dragons by Robert Lepage. Canada: Montreal, PQ. 1987. Lang.: Fre. 2479

Imagery in Lepage's *La Trilogie des dragons*. Canada. 1987. Lang.: Fre. 2480

Plays by Micone, Saddlemyer, Thompson, Wyatt. Canada. 1958-1985. Lang.: Eng. 2481

New Canadian drama: non-realistic, anti-naturalistic. Canada. 1983-1984. Lang.: Eng. 2482

Work of playwright Marco Micone. Canada. 1982-1985. Lang.: Eng. 2483

Survey of Robertson Davies' plays. Canada. 1913-1985. Lang.: Eng. 2484

Brassard discusses his adaptation of Genet's *Les Paravents (The Screens)*. Canada: Montreal, PQ, Ottawa, ON. 1987. Lang.: Fre. 2485

Playwright Paul Thompson. Canada: Blythe, ON, Toronto, ON. 1963-1983. Lang.: Eng. 2487

Playwright George F. Walker. Canada. 1972-1985. Lang.: Eng. 2488

Play within a play in *Blood Relations* by Sharon Pollock. Canada. 1987. Lang.: Eng. 2489

Egon Wolff's trilogy of plays focusing on Chilean bourgeoisie. Chile. 1964-1984. Lang.: Eng. 2490

Playwright Gao Xinjian—view of Chinese society. China, People's Republic of. 1983-1987. Lang.: Pol. 2492

Humanitarianism in contemporary Chinese drama. China, People's Republic of. 1984. Lang.: Chi. 2493

The structures and themes of Chinese playwright Hueng Tsolin. China, People's Republic of. 1983. Lang.: Chi. 2495

Exploration of mythic elements in the later plays of William Shakespeare. England: London. 1607-1614. Lang.: Eng. 2497

Urbanity as subject and form of Jonson's *Epicoene*. England. 1609-1987. Lang.: Eng. 2498

Playwright Ben Jonson's theatricality and relevance today. England. 1600-1987. Lang.: Eng. 2501

Comparison of Shakespeare's *Cymbeline* with the reign of James I. England. 1400-1550. Lang.: Eng. 2503

Political, social and religious issues in Caroline drama. England. 1632-1642. Lang.: Eng. 2508

Sacred power of the king in Shakespeare's histories and tragedies. England. 1539-1613. Lang.: Ita. 2510

The London Merchant by Lillo is an allegory of the Fall. England. 1731-1987. Lang.: Eng. 2514

Madness and revenge in Kyd's *The Spanish Tragedy*. England. 1589. Lang.: Eng. 2515

Place of the masque in *The Tempest*. England. 1611. Lang.: Eng. 2516

Changing economic conditions created an audience for plays about criminals. England. 1731-1740. Lang.: Eng. 2517

Comparison of *King Lear* and *Vildanden (The Wild Duck)*. England. Norway. 1605-1884. Lang.: Eng. 2518

Influences of Arthurian legend on Shakespeare's *King Lear*. England. 1605. Lang.: Eng. 2521

Utopian ideas in Tudor and Stuart playwrights. England. 1600-1650. Lang.: Ger. 2522

Themes of home and homelessness in plays of Cibber and Vanbrugh. England. 1696. Lang.: Eng. 2525

Name and entitlement in Dryden, Wycherley and Etherege. England. 1500-1699. Lang.: Eng. 2526

History and sources of Thomas Preston's *Cambyses, King of Persia*. England. 1562-1987. Lang.: Eng. 2529

Tragic result of utopian ideas in Shakespeare's *Romeo and Juliet*. England. 1595-1596. Lang.: Ger. 2530

Representation of real history and Utopia in Shakespeare's plays. England. 1590-1612. Lang.: Ger. 2531

Two Cornish *Corpus Christi* plays. England. 1350. Lang.: Eng. 2534

Henry Fielding rewrote *Tom Thumb* to satirize Lewis Theobald. England. 1730-1731. Lang.: Eng. 2535

Society vs. nature in Shakespeare's *As You Like It*. England. 1599-1600. Lang.: Ger. 2536

Shakespeare's use of language in *The Two Noble Kinsmen*. England. 1591-1616. Lang.: Eng. 2537

The creation of ideal future worlds based on the historical past in some plays of Shakespeare. England. 1591-1599. Lang.: Ger. 2539

Medieval cycle plays as the exception rather than the norm. England. Lang.: Eng. 2543

Character analysis of Olivia in *Twelfth Night*. England. 1599. Lang.: Eng. 2544

Rumour as a political and social tool in *Henry VIII*. England: London. 1612-1614. Lang.: Eng. 2547

Theme of political satire in plays of Fo and Gay. England: London. Italy. USA. 1728-1984. Lang.: Eng. 2548

Social reality in contrast with nature as allegory of utopian social fiction. England. 1599-1600. Lang.: Eng. 2549

Structure of tragic elements in plays of William Shakespeare. England: London. 1594-1599. Lang.: Eng. 2551

Shakespeare's use of formal self-referential oaths. England. 1594-1616. Lang.: Eng. 2552

Class conflict in Shakespeare's *Coriolanus* as viewed in 17th and 20th century. England. 1600-1987. Lang.: Ger. 2553

Classification and social hierarchy in Shakespeare's *Troilus and Cressida*. England. 1601. Lang.: Eng. 2554

History and utopianism in some plays of Shakespeare. England. 1589-1606. Lang.: Ger. 2558

Self-referentiality and kinds of space in plays of John Marston. England: London. 1553-1608. Lang.: Eng. 2559

Relationship of the *Aeneid* to Shakespeare's *The Tempest*. England: London. 1611. Lang.: Eng. 2561

Theme of deconstruction in Samuel Beckett's writings. Europe. 1953-1987. Lang.: Eng. 2563

Ancient Greek theatre and European culture. Europe. Greece. 1000 B.C.-1987 A.D. Lang.: Ita. 2565

Ariadne in plays of Ibsen, Strindberg, Maeterlinck. Europe. 1892-1902. Lang.: Eng. 2566

Career of playwright Sacha Guitry. France. 1920-1986. Lang.: Eng. 2567

Mouchoir de Nuages (Handkerchief of Clouds) by Tristan Tzara. France. Lang.: Ita. 2569

Symbols of power in Genet's *Les Paravents (The Screens)*. France. Canada: Montreal, PQ, Ottawa, ON. 1961-1987. Lang.: Fre. 2570

Comparison of plays by Camus and Sartre. France. 1905-1978. Lang.: Kor. 2576

Jullien's violations of decorum and *honneur* in *La Sérénade (The Serenade)*. France. 1887-1987. Lang.: Eng. 2577

Iser's reader-response theory and Beckett's *Come and Go*. France. 1968-1987. Lang.: Eng. 2581

André Brassard's production of Jean Genet's *Les Paravents (The Screens)*. France. Canada: Montreal, PQ, Ottawa, ON. 1961-1987. Lang.: Fre. 2583

Playwright Roger Vitrac's critiques of bourgeois family life. France. 1922-1928. Lang.: Eng. 2584

Investigating the text of Genet's *Les Paravents (The Screens)*. France. Canada: Montreal, PQ, Ottawa, ON. 1961-1987. Lang.: Fre. 2585

Interaction of scenic imagery and narrative in *Ohio Impromptu*. France. 1981-1987. Lang.: Eng. 2586

Death in Ghelderode's *La Balade du Grand Macabre (The Grand Macabre's Stroll)*. France. 1934. Lang.: Eng. 2587

The allegory of capitalist society in Genet's *Le Balcon (The Balcony)*. France. 1958-1987. Lang.: Eng. 2588

Beckett links theme of political persecution to voyeurism of the theatrical experience. France. 1982-1987. Lang.: Eng. 2589

Techniques, themes, characters and dramaturgy of Voltaire. France. 1718-1778. Lang.: Eng. 2590

History of 19th-century German literature, including drama and theatre. Germany. Austria. 1830-1900. Lang.: Ger. 2591

Plot/subject/theme — cont'd

Comparison of works by Hauptmann and Wilbrandt. Germany: Berlin. Austria: Vienna. 1889-1987. Lang.: Eng.   2593

Munch's influence on Strindberg. Germany: Berlin. 1892-1900. Lang.: Eng.   2596

Analysis of Goethe's *Götz von Berlichingen*. Germany. 1749-1832. Lang.: Ger.   2598

Critical reception of realism and naturalism. Germany. 1890-1987. Lang.: Ger.   2601

Four German playwrights: Fleisser, Sperr, Kroetz, Fassbinder. Germany. 1900-1987. Lang.: Ita.   2602

Textual history of Brecht's *Leben des Galilei (The Life of Galileo)*. Germany. USA. 1938-1956. Lang.: Ger.   2603

Friedrich von Schiller's late works: new conception of drama. Germany. 1799-1805. Lang.: Eng.   2604

Significance of dream-structures in Heiner Müller's plays, compared with those in Brecht's. Germany, East: Berlin, East. 1972-1987. Lang.: Ger.   2607

Study of playwright Heiner Müller's view of history. Germany, East. 1976-1986. Lang.: Ger.   2608

On *Die Neuen Leiden des jungen W. (The New Sorrows of Young W.)* by Ulrich Plenzdorf. Germany, East. 1972-1987. Lang.: Ger.   2609

Focus of money in Brecht's dramas. Germany, East. 1920-1930. Lang.: Eng.   2611

Overview of contemporary East German drama and directors. Germany, East. 1985-1986. Lang.: Hun.   2612

Analysis of contemporary East German drama and theatre. Germany, East. 1984-1986. Lang.: Ger.   2613

Study of *Passage* by Christoph Hein. Germany, East. 1987. Lang.: Ger.   2614

Greek poetic drama through Nietzschean theory. Greece. 1987. Lang.: Eng.   2620

Structure and plot of ancient Greek tragedies. Greece. 500-400 B.C. Lang.: Kor.   2622

Study of works by Sophocles, Aeschylus and Euripides. Greece. 400 B.C.-500 A.D. Lang.: Eng.   2624

Changes in theatre space as a result of New Comedy. Greece: Athens. Italy: Rome. 400 B.C.-180 A.D. Lang.: Eng.   2625

Study of the plays of György Spiró. Hungary. 1982-1986. Lang.: Hun.   2627

A critic's reflections on dramatic themes reflected in recent Hungarian plays. Hungary. 1986-1987. Lang.: Hun.   2629

Review of Ferenc Molnár's *Az ördög (The Devil)* directed by György Lengyel at Madách Theatre with discussion of the playwright and the play. Hungary: Budapest. 1987. Lang.: Hun.   2630

Analysis of plays by László Németh. Hungary. 1986-1987. Lang.: Hun.   2631

Political aspects of Hungarian absurdist drama. Hungary. 1970-1980. Lang.: Eng.   2632

Interview with playwright György Spiró. Hungary. 1962-1987. Lang.: Hun.   2633

Interview with László Márton, author of *Lepkék a kalapon (Butterflies on Your Hat)*. Hungary. 1982-1987. Lang.: Hun.   2635

Director Peter Brook discusses his views on *The Mahabharata*. India. 1987. Lang.: Eng.   2636

Comparison of Brian Friel's *Translations* and András Sütő's *A szuzai menyegző*. Ireland. Hungary. 1981. Lang.: Eng.   2637

Themes of Brian Friel's plays. Ireland. 1929-1987. Lang.: Eng.   2638

Irish Literary Renaissance writers' view of America. Ireland. 1900-1930. Lang.: Eng.   2639

Thomas Murphy's *The Morning After Optimism*: comparisons with Beckett, O'Casey. Ireland. 1971. Lang.: Eng.   2641

New findings on 18th-century Irish comic playwright John O'Keeffe. Ireland. England: London. 1767-1798. Lang.: Eng.   2643

Characters and the gangster movie form in Thomas Murphy's *The Blue Macushla*. Ireland. 1980-1986. Lang.: Eng.   2647

Comic characters and the Book of Job in the plays of Thomas Murphy. Ireland. 1962-1983. Lang.: Eng.   2648

Lady Gregory's *Grania*. Ireland: Dublin. 1910-1930. Lang.: Eng.   2649

The plays of Thomas Murphy. Ireland: Dublin. 1962-1986. Lang.: Eng.   2650

Metaphor of archaeology in Friel's *Volunteers*, poems of Heaney. Ireland: Dublin. UK-Ireland. 1975. Lang.: Eng.   2651

The myth of the idyllic peasant life in the plays of Thomas Murphy. Ireland. 1961-1986. Lang.: Eng.   2652

Christian thought in Thomas Murphy's *The Gigli Concert*. Ireland. 1983. Lang.: Eng.   2653

Feminine life symbols in Sean O'Casey's *The Silver Tassie*. Ireland. 1928. Lang.: Eng.   2654

Analysis of Thomas Murphy's *Bailegangaire*, its connections with the Irish language, story-telling. Ireland: Galway. 1985. Lang.: Eng.   2655

Historical accuracy of characters in the plays of Thomas Murphy. Ireland. 1962-1986. Lang.: Eng.   2657

Analysis of the text of Thomas Murphy's *The Sanctuary Lamp*. Ireland. 1976-1986. Lang.: Eng.   2658

Brian Friel's interpretation of Irish history through his plays *Aristocrats* and *Translations*. Ireland. 1987. Lang.: Eng.   2659

Acts of Pirandello conference. Italy. 1904-1936. Lang.: Ita, Eng.   2663

Comparison of Marivaux and Goldoni. Italy: Venice. France. 1707-1763. Lang.: Ita.   2664

Comparison between *La vita che ti diedi (The Life I Gave You)* by Pirandello and *Lo spirito della morte (The Spirit of Death)* by Rosso di San Secondo. Italy. 1923-1931. Lang.: Ita.   2666

Machines—animate and inanimate—in *Tonight We Improvise (Questa sera si recita a soggetto)* by Pirandello. Italy. 1929-1987. Lang.: Eng.   2670

Riccardo Bacchelli's *Amleto (Hamlet)*. Italy. 1919-1957. Lang.: Ita.   2671

Centrality of characters in the plays of Luigi Pirandello. Italy. 1867-1936. Lang.: Ita.   2672

Notebooks of playwright Filippo Tommaso Marinetti. Italy. 1915-1921. Lang.: Ita.   2673

Analysis of the plays of Luigi Candoni. Italy. 1921-1974. Lang.: Ita.   2674

Characteristic themes in the work of Pirandello. Italy. 1876-1936. Lang.: Ita.   2676

Gender conflict in Pirandello's *Sei personnaggi in cerca d'autore (Six Characters in Search of an Author)*. Italy. 1921-1987. Lang.: Eng.   2679

Comparison of Pirandello's *Enrico Quarto (Henry IV)* and Shakespeare's *Hamlet*. Italy. England. 1580-1936. Lang.: Chi.   2680

Contemporary Japanese plays about crime. Japan: Tokyo. 1986. Lang.: Jap.   2681

Plays about child suicide in Japan. Japan: Tokyo. 1986. Lang.: Jap.   2683

Call for greater creativity in Korean theatre. Korea: Seoul. 1986. Lang.: Kor.   2691

Conventionality in the popular plays of Korea's early twentieth century. Korea. 1905-1979. Lang.: Kor.   2692

Feminist themes in Rosario Castellanos' *El eterno femenino (The Eternal Feminine)*. Mexico. Lang.: Spa.   2694

The Non-Smokers by Gianfrancesco Guarnieri. Mexico: Mexico City. 1982-1987. Lang.: Spa.   2697

Comparison of the plays *Todo sucede en una noche (It All Happens in One Night)* and *La rosa del tiempo (The Rose of Time)*. Mexico: Mexico City. 1987. Lang.: Spa.   2698

Ethnic roots in *De la calle (Of the Street)* by Jesús Gonzalez-Davila. Mexico: Mexico City. 1987. Lang.: Spa.   2699

Comparison of plays by Leonor Azcarate and Estela Lenero. Mexico: Mexico City. 1987. Lang.: Spa.   2700

Playwright Renée discusses her plays. New Zealand. 1982-1987. Lang.: Eng.   2702

Wole Soyinka's treatment of political themes. Nigeria. 1973-1987. Lang.: Eng.   2705

Plays by contemporary Nigerian authors. Nigeria. 1950-1987. Lang.: Eng.   2707

Analysis of plays of Femi Osofisan and audience response. Nigeria. 1973-1987. Lang.: Eng.   2708

The Strong Breed and *The Bacchae*: Soyinka's symbolic use of ritual and ceremony. Nigeria. 1973-1987. Lang.: Eng.   2709

Plot/subject/theme — cont'd

Religion in Pielmeier's *Agnes of God* and Shaffer's *Equus*. North America. 1973-1980. Lang.: Eng. 2710

History and analysis of Mrożek's play *Vatslave*. Poland: Cracow. France: Paris. 1956-1987. Lang.: Heb. 2713

Problems of Polish society reflected in contemporary theatre. Poland. 1982-1987. Lang.: Pol. 2714

Theme of love and lovers in plays and poems by Maria Pawlikowska-Jasnorzewska. Poland. 1918-1939. Lang.: Pol. 2715

Analysis of *Čajka (The Seagull)* by Anton Čechov. Russia. 1896. Lang.: Kor. 2718

Athol Fugard's *Master Harold...and the Boys* examines apartheid in terms of human relationships. South Africa, Republic of. 1982-1987. Lang.: Eng. 2723

Characterization in Pieter-Dirk Uys' *Appassionata*. South Africa, Republic of. 1987. Lang.: Eng. 2724

How Athol Fugard's revisions have changed *The Blood Knot*. South Africa, Republic of. 1961-1985. Lang.: Eng. 2725

Stage space as prison in *The Island* by Athol Fugard with John Kani and Winston Ntshona. South Africa, Republic of. 1987. Lang.: Eng. 2727

Study of *El pan del pobre (Poor Man's Bread)*, adapted from Hauptmann's *Die Weber (The Weavers)*. Spain. 1894. Lang.: Eng. 2728

Comparative study of Lope de Vega's *El mayordomo de la Duquesa de Amalfi* and Webster's *The Duchess of Malfi*. Spain. 1612-1982. Lang.: Eng. 2729

Catalan playwrights after the Spanish Civil War. Spain-Catalonia. 1939-1975. Lang.: Cat. 2730

Analysis of 51 short farces written in Majorca. Spain-Catalonia. 1701-1850. Lang.: Cat. 2731

Dramatic vs. literary interpretation of *Ett Drömspel (A Dream Play)* by August Strindberg. Sweden. 1901-1964. Lang.: Eng. 2734

Theme of stage direction in the work of Scandinavian authors. Sweden. Norway. 1700-1987. Lang.: Ita. 2737

Theatrical metaphor in Strindberg's *Gustav III*. Sweden. 1903-1987. Lang.: Eng. 2741

Analysis of plays of Friedrich Dürrenmatt, comparison with Bertolt Brecht. Switzerland. Germany, West. 1945-1986. Lang.: Ger. 2745

The Spanish Civil War in works by Ernest Hemingway and Sean O'Casey. UK. Ireland. USA. 1930-1939. Lang.: Eng. 2749

Political dissatisfaction in drama. UK. Ireland. 1890-1987. Lang.: Eng. 2750

Influence of Livy's *History* and Machiavelli's *Discorsi* on Shakespeare's *Coriolanus*. UK-England: London. 1606-1610. Lang.: Eng. 2752

How settings and props convey meaning in plays by Shaw. UK-England. 1883-1935. Lang.: Eng. 2753

Themes and sources of Shaw's *The Man of Destiny*. UK-England. 1894-1931. Lang.: Eng. 2754

Imagination in Shaw's *Saint Joan*. UK-England. 1923. Lang.: Eng. 2755

The *Doppelgänger* in *The Doctor's Dilemma* by G.B. Shaw. UK-England. 1906. Lang.: Eng. 2756

Interpretation of the title character of Shakespeare's *Coriolanus*. UK-England. 1607. Lang.: Eng. 2757

Recent release of playwright Joe Orton's diaries. UK-England: London. 1933-1987. Lang.: Eng. 2758

Deconstructionist analysis of Harold Pinter's *Silence*. UK-England. 1964-1970. Lang.: Eng. 2759

Comparison of Shakespeare's *Julius Caesar* to the drama and vision of Euripides. UK-England. 500 B.C.-1599 A.D. Lang.: Eng. 2760

Analysis of Harold Pinter's *Victoria Station*. UK-England. 1959-1982. Lang.: Eng. 2761

Structure of *The Sea* by Edward Bond. UK-England. 1973-1987. Lang.: Eng. 2767

Shaw's ideas on directorial interpretation in *Pygmalion*. UK-England. 1894-1949. Lang.: Eng. 2768

Red Noses as Peter Barnes's response to Shaw's *Saint Joan*. UK-England. 1924-1985. Lang.: Eng. 2770

Imaginary history: Shaw's *In Good King Charles's Golden Days*. UK-England. 1639. Lang.: Eng. 2772

Revival of Shaw's *Village Wooing*: staging and stage history. UK-England. USA: Houston, TX. 1933-1984. Lang.: Eng. 2773

Bakhtinian analysis of *Fanny's First Play* by Shaw. UK-England. 1911-1916. Lang.: Eng. 2775

Socialist-feminist nature of Caryl Churchill's plays. UK-England. 1980-1987. Lang.: Eng. 2776

Ideological content of Lillo's *The London Merchant*. UK-England. 1731-1800. Lang.: Eng. 2777

Introduction to Chapter 19 of Pinter's unpublished novel *The Dwarfs*. UK-England. 1958-1987. Lang.: Eng. 2779

Freudian reading of Shaw's *Passion, Poison and Petrification*. UK-England. 1895-1926. Lang.: Eng. 2781

Visual aspects of *Pygmalion* related to its theme. UK-England. 1914. Lang.: Eng. 2782

Political protest in Tom Stoppard's *Every Good Boy Deserves Favour*. UK-England. USSR. 1974-1977. Lang.: Eng. 2783

The potential for social influence in W. Somerset Maugham's comedies. UK-England. 1903-1933. Lang.: Eng. 2784

Shaw's use of Irish stereotypes in *John Bull's Other Ireland*. UK-England. UK-Ireland. 1860-1925. Lang.: Eng. 2787

Approaches to Shaw's *Buoyant Billions*. UK-England. 1936-1946. Lang.: Eng. 2789

Focus on patterns of musical images in character of Iago which unite ideas of *Othello*. UK-England: London. 1604. Lang.: Eng. 2792

Self-referential techniques in Caryl Churchill's *Cloud 9*. UK-England. 1978-1987. Lang.: Eng. 2793

The topicality of Shakespeare's *Love's Labour's Lost*. UK-England: London. 1590. Lang.: Eng. 2794

Work of playwright Pam Gems. UK-England: London. 1984-1987. Lang.: Eng. 2795

Shaw's use of the audience to help create his play *Pygmalion*. UK-England. 1914. Lang.: Eng. 2796

View of the ideal and mortal worlds explored in *Henry VIII*. UK-England: London. 1611-1614. Lang.: Eng. 2797

Characterizations of stage spaces: examples from Brecht, Pinter, Douglas Turner Ward. UK-England. USA. 1947-1987. Lang.: Eng. 2798

Transvestitism in plays of Caryl Churchill. UK-England. 1987. Lang.: Eng. 2799

Class conflict as theme of *Top Girls*. UK-England. 1982-1987. Lang.: Eng. 2800

Historical context for Tom Taylor's *The Ticket-of-Leave Man*. UK-England. France. 1863. 2801

Stage business in *Major Barbara* traced to Beerbohm Tree. UK-England. 1905. Lang.: Eng. 2802

Analysis of Shaw's *You Never Can Tell*. UK-England. 1899. Lang.: Eng. 2803

Background of *John Bull's Other Island* by G.B. Shaw. UK-England. 1904. Lang.: Eng. 2804

Analysis of Jean Genet's plays. UK-England: London. 1987. Lang.: Eng. 2805

Use of oral history material to develop characters and events in plays. UK-England. 1970-1987. Lang.: Eng. 2807

Comic conventions in Shakespeare's *Titus Andronicus*. UK-England. 1987. Lang.: Eng. 2809

Relationship between the well-made and unconventional elements of *Hamlet*. UK-England: London. 1599-1603. Lang.: Eng. 2810

The problem of capitalism in Shaw's *The Millionairess*. UK-England. 1936-1952. Lang.: Eng. 2811

Shakespeare's influence on George Bernard Shaw. UK-England. 1882-1936. Lang.: Eng. 2812

Themes of perception in *The Tempest*. UK-England: London. 1611. Lang.: Eng. 2813

Critical methodology for studying Beckett's works. UK-England. 1930-1987. Lang.: Eng. 2814

Problem of the tragic in English drama. UK-England. 1950-1969. Lang.: Rus. 2819

Influences on *The Voysey Inheritance* by Granville Barker. UK-England. 1600-1938. Lang.: Eng. 2820

Relationships in Tom Stoppard's *The Real Thing*. UK-England. 1986-1987. Lang.: Eng. 2822

Plot/subject/theme — cont'd

Plot/subject/theme — cont'd

Radsinskij's *Jogging* directed by Fokin. USSR: Moscow. 1987. Lang.: Eng.   2953

Historical themes in recent plays by M. Vartolomeev, P. Red'kin and P. Pavlovskij. USSR. 1980-1987. Lang.: Eng.   2954

The quest in plays of I.L. Sel'vinskij. USSR. 1899-1968. Lang.: Rus.   2955

Use of public bathhouses as metaphors in Russian drama. USSR. 1925-1935. Lang.: Eng.   2959

Comparison between Albee's *Who's Afraid of Virginia Woolf?* and Radsinskij's *Jogging*. USSR. USA. 1987. Lang.: Eng.   2960

V.I. Lenin in contemporary Soviet dramaturgy. USSR. 1980-1987. Lang.: Rus.   2961

Dramatist M.F. Šatrov on his creative and ideological principles. USSR. 1980-1987. Lang.: Rus.   2966

Correspondence of playwright Aleksand'r Vampilov. USSR: Moscow. 1960-1975. Lang.: Rus.   2968

Theme of aggression between fathers and sons: Zambian National Theatre Arts Association festival. Zambia. 1966-1987. Lang.: Eng.   2972

The historical radio drama *All I Get is Static!*. Canada: Ottawa, ON. 1984. Lang.: Eng.   3096

Critical discussion of six plays in CBC's *Sextet* broadcast series. Canada. 1987. Lang.: Eng.   3116

Documentary Soviet radio drama. USSR. 1917-1987. Lang.: Rus.   3118

David and Toni Dueck's docudrama about their Mennonite heritage. Canada: Winnipeg, MB. 1985. Lang.: Eng.   3175

Trends in contemporary Hungarian film-making. Hungary. 1965-1987. Lang.: Hun.   3176

Polanski, Welles and Kurosawa's versions of Shakespeare's *Macbeth*. USA. Japan. UK-England. 1948-1971. Lang.: Eng.   3183

Satirical look at President and Vice President of the United States. USA. 1987. Lang.: Eng.   3370

Dramatic structure in Chinese opera play *Tao hua shan (The Peach Blossom Fan)*. China. 1700-1800. Lang.: Chi.   3547

A correct definition of Chinese classical 'tragedy'. China. 960-1644. Lang.: Chi.   3548

The development of Chinese historical drama. China. 1111 B.C.-1856 A.D. Lang.: Chi.   3550

Hsü Wei's *Szu Sheng Yüan (Four Famous Apes)*. China. 1521-1593. Lang.: Chi.   3551

Subjectivity of Chinese opera playwrights. China, People's Republic of. 1111 B.C.-1987 A.D. Lang.: Chi.   3558

Theme and essence of Chinese classical drama. China, People's Republic of. 1127-1987. Lang.: Chi.   3560

Philosophical themes in modern Chinese drama: their audience appeal. China, People's Republic of. 1987. Lang.: Chi.   3564

Theme of falsehood in Chinese classical comedy. China, People's Republic of. 1987. Lang.: Chi.   3567

Modern audience needs and traditional values in Chinese opera. China, People's Republic of. 1986. Lang.: Chi.   3568

The inner and outer psychology of characters in Chinese opera. China, People's Republic of. 1987. Lang.: Chi.   3570

Bridging the gap between classical and modern forms of Chinese opera. China, People's Republic of. 1987. Lang.: Chi.   3571

The theme of 'all men are brothers' in Chinese opera. China, People's Republic of. 1987. Lang.: Chi.   3573

Characteristics, value and development in Chinese drama. China, People's Republic of. 1987. Lang.: Chi.   3575

Historical people in the plays of Chinese theatre. China, People's Republic of. 1985. Lang.: Chi.   3576

Chinese opera should reflect the concerns of its audience. China, People's Republic of. 1987. Lang.: Chi.   3578

Analysis of the plays and songs of Irish-American musical theatre star Chauncey Olcott. USA. 1893-1918. Lang.: Eng.   3671

Mozart's *Nozze di Figaro* compared with Beaumarchais source. 1784-1786. Lang.: Eng.   3887

Tippett's influence on contemporary opera. 1946-1987. Lang.: Eng.   3888

Imagined interview with librettist of *Lucia di Lammermoor*. 1835. Lang.: Eng.   3889

Comparison of Mozart's *The Magic Flute* and Strauss's *Die Frau ohne Schatten*. Austria: Vienna. 1980. Lang.: Eng.   3891

George Perle's analysis of Alban Berg's opera *Lulu*. Austria. 1937-1985. Lang.: Swe.   3892

Background on Philistines of Saint-Saëns' *Samson et Dalila*. Canaan. 3000-1000 B.C. Lang.: Eng.   3893

Operas of César Franck. France: Paris. 1822-1896. Lang.: Eng.   3898

Theme of *femme fatale* in *Samson et Dalila*. France. 1800-1899. Lang.: Eng.   3900

Psychological interpretations of Wagner's *Parsifal*. Germany. 1882-1987. Lang.: Eng.   3907

Woman, salvation and love in operas of Richard Wagner. Germany. 1813-1883. Lang.: Eng.   3909

Analysis of Heinrich Marschner's and Peter Josef von Lindpaintner's operas *Der Vampyr*. Germany: Leipzig, Stuttgart. 1828. Lang.: Eng.   3911

Why Hanns Eisler's opera *Johann Faustus* remained incomplete. Germany, East. 1953-1987. Lang.: Ger.   3912

Debate over Hanns Eisler's opera *Johann Faustus*. Germany, East: Berlin, East. 1949-1955. Lang.: Ger.   3913

Operas that contain Indian-related themes and music. India. Europe. 1730-1904. Lang.: Eng.   3914

Themes of Eliraz's *The Garden of Adam and Eve*. Israel: Jerusalem. 1987. Lang.: Heb.   3915

Librettist on *The Garden of Adam and Eve*. Israel: Jerusalem. 1987. Lang.: Heb.   3916

Analysis of the plot of Verdi's opera *Il Trovatore*. Italy. 1983. Lang.: Eng.   3921

Analysis and success of Boito's libretto for Verdi's opera *Falstaff*. Italy. 1893. Lang.: Eng.   3923

Characters and political themes in Verdi's *Don Carlos*. Italy: Milan. 1867. Lang.: Eng.   3924

Life and operatic works of composer Krzysztof Penderecki. Poland. 1969-1987. Lang.: Ger.   3929

Life and career of Manuel de Falla: his opera *Atlántida*. Spain: Madrid. France: Paris. 1876-1946. Lang.: Ger.   3930

Epic themes in Ukrainian opera. Ukraine. 1920-1969. Lang.: Rus.   3931

Aaron Copland's opera *The Tender Land*. USA. 1900. Lang.: Eng.   3933

Philip Glass's non-traditional approach to opera. USA. 1980. Lang.: Eng.   3934

Hermann, a puppet production for adults about coping with oppression. Germany. Poland: Bielsko Biala. 1978-1987. Lang.: Eng.   3991

Problems of dramaturgy for puppet theatres. USSR. 1980-1987. Lang.: Rus.   3992

Relation to other fields
Description of *The Working People's Picture Show*. Canada: Toronto, ON. 1987. Lang.: Eng.   1221

Comparison of *King Lear* and South African Land Act regarding land distribution. England. South Africa, Republic of. 1605-1913. Lang.: Eng.   1231

Research/historiography
Influences on Wagner's *Ring* cycle. Germany: Dresden. 1813-1883. Lang.: Eng.   3948

Theory/criticism
Themes of the Chinese theatre during the Tang dynasty. China. 618-905. Lang.: Chi.   1320

Semiotic study of dialogue in *As You Like It*. England. 1599. Lang.: Eng.   1325

Aesthetics of the pleasure principle in comedy, folklore and literature. USA. 1982. Lang.: Eng.   1355

The use of space in plot to indicate time and place. 1949-1987. Lang.: Chi.   3021

Ibsen's influence on modern Chinese theatre. China, People's Republic of. Norway. 1920-1950. Lang.: Chi.   3025

Politics, patriarchy in Dryden's plays. England. 1679-1687.   3030

On the Verge by Eric Overmyer. Production history, plot synopsis, critical evaluation. USA. 1987. Lang.: Eng.   3068

Chinese and Western elements in Chinese musical theatre. China, People's Republic of. 1975-1987. Lang.: Chi.   3422

Plot/subject/theme — cont'd

Main characteristics of the Chinese theatre aesthetic. China, People's Republic of. 960 B.C.-1987 A.D. Lang.: Chi. 3597

Falsehood as the essential quality of the Chinese classical comedy. China, People's Republic of. 1987. Lang.: Chi. 3599

Plotnikov, N.
Performance/production

Director V. Pimenov's recollections of actors Gricenko, Plotnikov and Abrikosov. USSR: Moscow. 1940-1979. Lang.: Rus. 1047

Plough and the Stars, The
Plays/librettos/scripts

Popular music in the Dublin trilogy plays of Sean O'Casey. Ireland. 1923-1926. Lang.: Eng. 2644

Plouviez, Peter
Administration

The first Anglo-American commercial Broadway production, the musical *Carrie*. USA: New York, NY. UK-England: London. 1987. Lang.: Eng. 61

Plowright, Joan
Performance/production

Review of the BBC telecast of *The Birthday Party* by Harold Pinter. UK-England. 1987. Lang.: Eng. 3206

Plump Jack
Administration

Gordon Peter Getty, philanthropist, composer. USA: San Francisco, CA. 1987. Lang.: Eng. 3684

Plymouth Theatre (New York, NY)
Performance/production

Collection of newspaper reviews by New York theatre critics. USA: New York, NY. 1987. Lang.: Eng. 2311

Collection of newspaper reviews by New York theatre critics. USA: New York, NY. 1987. Lang.: Eng. 2317

Collection of newspaper reviews by New York theatre critics. USA: New York, NY. 1987. Lang.: Eng. 2320

Poculi Ludique Societas (Toronto, ON)
Plays/librettos/scripts

History and sources of Thomas Preston's *Cambyses, King of Persia*. England. 1562-1987. Lang.: Eng. 2529

Podehl, Enno
Plays/librettos/scripts

Hermann, a puppet production for adults about coping with oppression. Germany. Poland: Bielsko Biala. 1978-1987. Lang.: Eng. 3991

Podivné odpoledne doktora Zvonka Burkeho (Strange Afternoon of Doctor Zvonek Burke, The)
Performance/production

Plays of Ladislav Smoček at Činoherní klub. Czechoslovakia: Prague. 1965-1987. Lang.: Cze. 768

Poel, William
Performance/production

Comparison of two 'Elizabethan' productions of *Hamlet*. UK-England: London. USA. 1900-1904. Lang.: Eng. 2292

Poetry
Administration

The risk of libel in fiction: Sylvia Plath's case. USA. 1986-1987. Lang.: Eng. 3121

Performance/production

Hillar Liitoja's experimental theatre. Canada. 1987. Lang.: Eng. 739

Collection of materials on actor-poet Vladimir Vysockij. USSR. 1972-1987. Lang.: Rus. 985

Actor Vladimir Vysockij remembered. USSR: Moscow. 1938-1980. Lang.: Rus. 999

Actress Alla Demidova recalls Vladimir Vysockij. USSR: Moscow. 1938-1980. Lang.: Rus. 1008

Actor Vladimir Vysockij of Taganka Theatre. USSR: Moscow. 1938-1980. Lang.: Rus. 1023

Recollections of actor Vladimir Vysockij. USSR: Moscow. 1938-1980. Lang.: Rus. 1066

Actress Marina Vladi recalls Vladimir Vysockij. USSR: Moscow. 1938-1980. Lang.: Rus. 1081

Tamás Jordán's *Amit a szívedbe rejtesz (Hidden in Your Heart)* directed by János Gáspár. Hungary: Budapest. 1987. Lang.: Hun. 1828

János Gáspar directs *Amit a szívedbe rejtesz (Hidden in Your Heart)* by Tamás Jordán, based on notes by poet Attila József, at Radnóti Miklós Theatre. Hungary: Budapest. 1987. Lang.: Hun. 1836

Productions of plays by László Márton, Tamás Jordán and Ferenc Kulin at Radnóti Miklós Theatre. Hungary: Budapest. 1987. Lang.: Hun. 1887

Teatropoesia, a combination of theatre and poetry. USA. 1974-1983. Lang.: Spa. 2368

Plays/librettos/scripts

The paradox and problems of poetry in Romantic theatre. England. 1700-1800. Lang.: Eng. 2557

Stage and screen adaptations of the poetry of Lesja Ukrainka. USSR. 1987. Lang.: Rus. 2971

Relation to other fields

Interview with poet and activist Haki R. Madhubuti (Don L. Lee). USA: Detroit, MI. Africa. Israel. 1942-1985. Lang.: Eng. 3008

Theory/criticism

Role of poetry in contemporary plays. USA. 1987. Lang.: Eng. 3077

Poggi, Simone Maria
Plays/librettos/scripts

On a theatrical manifesto of Simone Maria Poggi. Italy. 1700-1749. Lang.: Ita. 1140

Pohjanen, Bengt
Institutions

Tornedalsteatern and director Ulla Lyttkens. Sweden: Pajala. 1986-1987. Lang.: Swe. 1642

Performance/production

Swedish-Finnish language problems dramatized by Tornedalsteatern. Sweden: Pajala. 1986. Lang.: Swe. 2014

Pohl, Carla
Performance/production

Review of Wagner's *Der Fliegende Holländer* at the Natal Playhouse. South Africa, Republic of: Durban. 1987. Lang.: Eng. 3815

Points sur les i (Dot the I)
Plays/librettos/scripts

Life and works of French dramatist Gabriel Marcel. France. 1889-1973. Lang.: Eng. 2573

Poiret, Jean
Performance/production

Collection of newspaper reviews by London theatre critics. UK-England: London. 1986. Lang.: Eng. 2095

Career of actor Lee Roy Reams. USA: New York, NY. 1987. Lang.: Eng. 3661

Poissant, Claude
Plays/librettos/scripts

The role of the father-figure in recent plays from Quebec. Canada: Quebec. 1980-1987. Lang.: Fre. 2465

Pokrovskij, Boris A.
Audience

Boris Pokrovskij, Moscow Musical Chamber Theatre, on perceptions of opera. USSR: Moscow. 1980-1987. Lang.: Rus. 3691

Performance/production

B.A. Pokrovskij, principal director, Moscow Musical Chamber Theatre. USSR: Moscow. 1912-1987. Lang.: Rus. 3873

Style in opera directing, with reference to Boris A. Pokrovskij. USSR. 1980-1987. Lang.: Rus. 3883

Polanski, Roman
Plays/librettos/scripts

Polanski, Welles and Kurosawa's versions of Shakespeare's *Macbeth*. USA. Japan. UK-England. 1948-1971. Lang.: Eng. 3183

Poletti, Lina
Plays/librettos/scripts

Influence of Sibilla Aleramo on women in Italian theatre. Italy. 1850-1930. Lang.: Ita. 1138

Poli, I (Town, The)
Performance/production

Review of *I Poli (The Town)* based on Greek theatre tradition and performed in absurdist style. Mexico: Mexico City. 1987. Lang.: Spa. 1976

Poliakoff, Stephen
Performance/production

Collection of newspaper reviews by London theatre critics. UK-England. 1987. Lang.: Eng. 2033

Police
Performance/production

Interview with playwright Amiri Baraka. USA: Newark, NJ, New York, NY. 1965-1969. Lang.: Eng. 2356

Politics — cont'd

Audience

Basic theatrical documents

Institutions

Performance/production

Politics — cont'd

Puppeteer Paul Zaloom discusses political ideas, scene design. USA. 1970-1987. Lang.: Eng.   3987

Plays/librettos/scripts

Interview with playwright Antonio Skarmento. Chile: Santiago. 1967-1987. Lang.: Eng.   1102

Editorial discussion of contemporary theatre. North America. 1987. 1987. Lang.: Eng.   1152

Theatre and dramaturgy of the first Russian revolution. USSR. 1905-1907. Lang.: Rus.   1188

Social and political themes in the Moscow theatre season. USSR: Moscow. 1986-1987. Lang.: Rus.   1190

Russian and Soviet interaction with the U.S. USSR. USA. 1700-1987. Lang.: Rus.   1191

Cultural predetermination in three Athol Fugard plays. South Africa, Republic of. 1970. Lang.: Eng.   1419

Perestrojka and the theatre: the socially active hero. USSR. 1987. Lang.: Rus.   1421

Interview with playwright S. Alešin. USSR. 1980-1987. Lang.: Rus.   1423

Modern theatrical treatment of Fascism and the Holocaust. 1980-1987. Lang.: Eng.   2428

Critical analysis of Dorothy Hewett's *The Man from Mukinupin*. Australia. 1979. Lang.: Eng.   2438

Theme of torture in Brazilian drama. Brazil. 1964-1985. Lang.: Por.   2456

The theme of a child's game in Lepage's *La Trilogie des dragons*. Canada: Montreal, PQ. 1987. Lang.: Fre.   2458

Productions of Brecht in Quebec. Canada. 1950-1986. Lang.: Fre.   2461

Playwright Sharon Pollock. Canada. 1970-1983. Lang.: Eng.   2469

Language and metaphor in plays of René-Daniel Dubois. Canada: Toronto, ON, Montreal, PQ. 1983-1987. Lang.: Eng.   2471

German influences on contemporary Quebecois theatre. Canada. Germany. 1850-1949. Lang.: Fre.   2478

Playwright Gao Xinjian—view of Chinese society. China, People's Republic of. 1983-1987. Lang.: Pol.   2492

Comparison of Shakespeare's *Cymbeline* with the reign of James I. England. 1400-1550. Lang.: Eng.   2503

Attack on Sir Robert Walpole in 18th-century adaptation of *King Edward the Third*. England. 1691-1731. Lang.: Eng.   2505

Anti-fascist plays of Armand Gatti. France. 1924-1987. Lang.: Rus.   2578

Beckett links theme of political persecution to voyeurism of the theatrical experience. France. 1982-1987. Lang.: Eng.   2589

Analysis of Goethe's *Götz von Berlichingen*. Germany. 1749-1832. Lang.: Ger.   2598

Bertolt Brecht and the Berlin workers' movement. Germany: Berlin. 1922-1932. Lang.: Ger.   2600

Political aspects of Hungarian absurdist drama. Hungary. 1970-1980. Lang.: Eng.   2632

Themes of Brian Friel's plays. Ireland. 1929-1987. Lang.: Eng.   2638

Interview with director Kazimierz Braun. Ireland: Dublin. Poland. 1981-1983. Lang.: Eng.   2642

Metaphor of archaeology in Friel's *Volunteers*, poems of Heaney. Ireland: Dublin. UK-Ireland. 1975. Lang.: Eng.   2651

Theory and practice of playwright Lee Kun Sam. Korea. 1950-1987. Lang.: Kor.   2687

Korean drama: social and political background. Korea. 1910-1919. Lang.: Kor.   2690

Wole Soyinka's treatment of political themes. Nigeria. 1973-1987. Lang.: Eng.   2705

Use of English in Nigerian drama. Nigeria. 1940-1987. Lang.: Eng.   2706

The Strong Breed and *The Bacchae*: Soyinka's symbolic use of ritual and ceremony. Nigeria. 1973-1987. Lang.: Eng.   2709

Problems of Polish society reflected in contemporary theatre. Poland. 1982-1987. Lang.: Pol.   2714

Athol Fugard's *Master Harold...and the Boys* examines apartheid in terms of human relationships. South Africa, Republic of. 1982-1987. Lang.: Eng.   2723

Stage space as prison in *The Island* by Athol Fugard with John Kani and Winston Ntshona. South Africa, Republic of. 1987. Lang.: Eng.   2727

Standard German and the German Swiss dialects on and off stage. Switzerland. 1889-1984. Lang.: Ger.   2744

The Spanish Civil War in works by Ernest Hemingway and Sean O'Casey. UK. Ireland. USA. 1930-1939. Lang.: Eng.   2749

Socialist-feminist nature of Caryl Churchill's plays. UK-England. 1980-1987. Lang.: Eng.   2776

Political protest in Tom Stoppard's *Every Good Boy Deserves Favour*. UK-England. USSR. 1974-1977. Lang.: Eng.   2783

Shaw's use of Irish stereotypes in *John Bull's Other Ireland*. UK-England. UK-Ireland. 1860-1925. Lang.: Eng.   2787

The problem of capitalism in Shaw's *The Millionairess*. UK-England. 1936-1952. Lang.: Eng.   2811

Avoidance of political themes in drama of Northern Ireland. UK-Ireland. 1979-1987. Lang.: Eng.   2830

Christina Reid's *Tea in a China Cup*: a woman's view of Belfast. UK-Ireland: Belfast. 1983-1987. Lang.: Eng.   2831

Charles Fuller's *A Soldier's Play*: debate on means of liberation. USA. 1976-1981. Lang.: Eng.   2854

Albee, racism, politics in American theatre of the sixties. USA. 1960-1969. Lang.: Rus.   2901

Round-table on drama under perestrojka. USSR. 1986-1987. Lang.: Rus.   2934

Socialist realism in Tatar drama. USSR. 1917-1987. Lang.: Rus.   2936

Historical themes in recent plays by M. Vartolomeev, P. Red'kin and P. Pavlovskij. USSR. 1980-1987. Lang.: Eng.   2954

Dramatist M.F. Šatrov on his creative and ideological principles. USSR. 1980-1987. Lang.: Rus.   2966

Polanski, Welles and Kurosawa's versions of Shakespeare's *Macbeth*. USA. Japan. UK-England. 1948-1971. Lang.: Eng.   3183

New ideologies and dramatic structure in Chinese opera. China, People's Republic of. 1987. Lang.: Chi.   3561

Historical people in the plays of Chinese theatre. China, People's Republic of. 1985. Lang.: Chi.   3576

Operas of César Franck. France: Paris. 1822-1896. Lang.: Eng.   3898

Debate over Hanns Eisler's opera *Johann Faustus*. Germany, East: Berlin, East. 1949-1955. Lang.: Ger.   3913

Characters and political themes in Verdi's *Don Carlos*. Italy: Milan. 1867. Lang.: Eng.   3924

Relation to other fields

Description of *The Working People's Picture Show*. Canada: Toronto, ON. 1987. Lang.: Eng.   1221

Social implications of popular theatre. Canada. 1987. Lang.: Eng.   1222

Difficulties encountered by playwrights in Canada. Canada: Vancouver, BC. USA: New York, NY. 1987. Lang.: Eng.   1223

Situation of Chinese intellectuals during the Yuan Dynasty. China. 1279-1368. Lang.: Chi.   1225

Artists and writers affected by political decisions. China, People's Republic of. 1987. Lang.: Eng.   1226

Comparison of *King Lear* and South African Land Act regarding land distribution. England. South Africa, Republic of. 1605-1913. Lang.: Eng.   1231

Interview with playwright Jean Genet regarding his political commitments. France. 1967-1985. Lang.: Eng.   1236

Cultural and social role of Berlin theatres. Germany: Berlin. 1700-1987. Lang.: Ger.   1237

Debate over proletarian art among Social Democrats. Germany: Berlin. 1910-1912. Lang.: Ger.   1238

Political theatre East and West. India. Indonesia. 1970-1986. Lang.: Eng.   1240

Role of Communist Party in Lithuanian theatre. Lithuania. 1966-1980. Lang.: Rus.   1248

Cultural policy of Norway. Norway. 1980-1984. Lang.: Eng.   1249

UN cultural boycott on artists who have performed in South Africa. South Africa, Republic of. 1987. Lang.: Eng.   1251

Influences of Black political and economic life on literature, performance. South Africa, Republic of. 1970-1987. Lang.: Eng. 1252

Politics — cont'd

The sociopolitical role of the critic in theatrical criticism. Switzerland. 1960-1985. Lang.: Ger.   1255

Government funding of official theatre and opera companies. Switzerland. 1987. Lang.: Ger.   1256

Political satire on Britain's conflict in the Falkland Islands. UK-England. 1982. Lang.: Eng.   1257

Interview with founders of the Charabanc Theatre Company. UK-Ireland. 1970-1987. Lang.: Eng.   1260

Actors' Equity's affirmative action program. USA: New York, NY. 1982. Lang.: Eng.   1261

Equity's National Theatre Plan. USA. 1982. Lang.: Eng.   1262

Nature and effectiveness of political theatre. USA. 1985. Lang.: Eng.   1263

National Endowment for the Arts suffers severe cutbacks. USA: Washington, DC. 1982. Lang.: Eng.   1273

International exchange in the performing arts. USA. 1985. Lang.: Eng.   1276

Historical look at the National Endowment for the Arts. USA. 1977-1981. Lang.: Eng.   1280

Protest of US Immigration and Naturalization Service policies by American presenting organizations. USA. 1986. Lang.: Eng.   1282

Exchange of ideas between Soviets and US theatre artists. USA: New York, NY. USSR: Moscow. 1987. Lang.: Eng.   1284

Public interest politics and the arts. USA. 1987. Lang.: Eng.   1286

Diminishing ethics in society and its relation to the theatre. USA. 1987. Lang.: Eng.   1290

Cultural exchange pacts made between the USA and the Soviet Union and China. USA: Washington, DC. USSR: Moscow. China, People's Republic of: Peking. 1987. Lang.: Eng.   1291

Effects of glasnost's policy on Russian arts. USSR. 1987. Lang.: Eng.   1292

Theatre critics discuss political issues. USSR. 1980-1987. Lang.: Rus.   1293

Soviet critics and playwrights on international cultural ties. USSR. 1980-1987. Lang.: Rus.   1294

Role of theatre in moral education. USSR. 1987. Lang.: Rus.   1296

Political predictions in *El avión negro (The Black Airplane)*. Argentina. 1969-1970. Lang.: Eng.   2979

African-American theatre compared to Caribbean and African theatre. Barbados. Bermuda. Nigeria. 1987. Lang.: Eng.   2980

Popular theatre and non-governmental funding agencies. Canada: Sydney, NS. Jamaica. Sudan. 1987. Lang.: Eng.   2982

Theme of imperialism in *The Tempest*. Canada. Antilles. France. 1611-1977. Lang.: Eng.   2984

Theatre as medium of expression under repressive government. Chile. 1973-1986. Lang.: Eng.   2985

Impact of politics upon funding of theatre. Denmark. 1722-1982. Lang.: Eng.   2986

Representation of workers on stage. Europe. USA. 1871-1987. Lang.: Fre.   2987

Teachers discuss creative drama's role in adult education. Jamaica. Zimbabwe. Bangladesh. 1987. Lang.: Swe.   2996

Interracial fringe productions: racial, class, sexual politics. South Africa, Republic of. 1984. Lang.: Eng.   2998

Comparison of *Woyzeck* to Nelson Mandela. South Africa, Republic of: Pretoria. 1985. Lang.: Eng.   2999

Claque Theatre, a professional provincial ensemble. Switzerland: Baden. 1968-1987. Lang.: Ger.   3001

Analysis of the role of political drama in Europe. Switzerland: Basel. Mönchengladbach. 1986-1987. Lang.: Ger.   3002

Lindsay Anderson's analysis of the political role of theatre. UK-England. 1987. Lang.: Eng.   3005

Examination of crisis in theory and practice of political art. USA. 1987. Lang.: Eng.   3007

Interview with poet and activist Haki R. Madhubuti (Don L. Lee). USA: Detroit, MI. Africa. Israel. 1942-1985. Lang.: Eng.   3008

Playwright A. Gelman on perestrojka. USSR. 1986-1987. Lang.: Rus.   3009

Diminishing political and economic role of radio. Italy. 1900-1987. Lang.: Ita.   3100

Theatrical elements in American politics. USA. 1967-1987. Lang.: Eng.   3102

South Africa Department of Information's film *South Africa's Performing Arts*. South Africa, Republic of. 1970. Lang.: Eng.   3185

Political theatre and the fall of Ferdinand Marcos. Philippines. 1972-1986. Lang.: Eng.   3281

Image of rock singer Madonna in American culture. USA: New York, NY. UK-England: London. 1985-1987. Lang.: Eng.   3386

Polish official promotion of music theatre. Poland. 1950-1965. Lang.: Pol.   3421

Current ideology: influence on Chinese theatre. China, People's Republic of. 1987. Lang.: Chi.   3583

Perceptions of childhood reflected in opera. Europe. 1800-1983. Lang.: Eng.   3940

Political context of the constructing of the Opéra-Bastille. France: Paris. 1983-1987. Lang.: Eng.   3941

Life of King Ludwig II, and his relationship with composer Richard Wagner. Germany. 1864-1880. Lang.: Eng.   3942

Comparison between Wagner and Tolstoy. Russia. Germany. 1860-1908. Lang.: Eng.   3944

Relations to other fields

Brecht's theories on the media's negative impact on the activity and politics of the public. Germany, East: Berlin, East. 1950. Lang.: Eng.   3197

Theory/criticism

Historical survey of drama and theatre criticism. 1984. Lang.: Eng.   1309

Two conferences on theatre reviewing. Australia. 1985-1986. Lang.: Eng.   1315

Chinese critique of Brechtian realism. China, People's Republic of. 1949-1985. Lang.: Chi.   1321

Modernity as historical concept applied to Catalonia and Occitana. France. Spain-Catalonia: Barcelona. 1539-1985. Lang.: Fre.   1332

Semiotic production in popular performance. South Africa, Republic of. 1980. Lang.: Eng.   1347

Current theatre compared to Ralph Lauren store. USA: New York, NY. 1987. Lang.: Eng.   1356

Correlation of a troubled society and its theatre. USA: New York, NY. 1987. Lang.: Eng.   1357

Works of Pierre Corneille and the social role of women. France. 1540-1650. Lang.: Eng.   3040

Challenge of Brecht's plays to communism. Germany, East: Berlin. 1960-1970. Lang.: Eng.   3045

Functions of comedy in the seventeenth century. Spain. 1604-1690. Lang.: Spa.   3058

Performance art piece protesting Iran-Contra scandal. USA: Hollywood, CA. 1987. Lang.: Eng.   3377

Post-Revolutionary Soviet theatre. USSR: Moscow. 1918-1930. Lang.: Ger.   3378

Politis, Linos

Plays/librettos/scripts

Imagistic versus realistic drama in contemporary Greek plays. Greece. 1940-1987. Lang.: Eng.   2621

Polka Children's Theatre (London)

Performance spaces

Performances, workshops for children in converted church hall. UK-England: London. 1987. Lang.: Eng.   4009

Pollock, Sharon

Basic theatrical documents

Collection of four plays by Canadian women dramatists. Canada. 1987. Lang.: Eng.   1544

Plays/librettos/scripts

Summary and critical analysis of *Doc* by Sharon Pollock. Canada. 1987. Lang.: Eng.   1100

Interview with playwright Sharon Pollock. Canada. 1985. Lang.: Eng.   2457

Playwright Sharon Pollock. Canada. 1970-1983. Lang.: Eng.   2469

Play within a play in *Blood Relations* by Sharon Pollock. Canada. 1987. Lang.: Eng.   2489

Pomeroy, Sue

Performance/production

Collection of newspaper reviews by London theatre critics. UK-England: London. 1987. Lang.: Eng.   2185

Collection of newspaper reviews by London theatre critics. UK-England: London. 1987. Lang.: Eng.   2225

Ponchielli, Amilcare
Performance/production
Background on Lyric Opera radio broadcast performances. USA: Chicago, IL. 1987. Lang.: Eng. 3832

Background on San Francisco opera radio broadcasts. USA: San Francisco, CA. 1987. Lang.: Eng. 3833

Pons, Josep-Sebastià
Plays/librettos/scripts
General history of Catalan literature, including theatre. Spain-Catalonia. 1902-1961. Lang.: Cat. 1157

Index of theatrical manuscripts from Roussillon written in Catalan. France. 1696-1841. Lang.: Cat. 2568

Pons, Ventura
Performance/production
Collection of theatre reviews by Xavier Fàbregas. Spain-Catalonia. 1969-1972. Lang.: Cat. 2010

Pontiac and the Green Man
Plays/librettos/scripts
Survey of Robertson Davies' plays. Canada. 1913-1985. Lang.: Eng. 2484

Pop Music Festival '66
SEE
Táncdalfesztivál '66.

Pope, Deborah
Performance/production
Essays on the future of the theatre. USA: New York, NY. 1970-1987. Lang.: Eng. 955

Pope, Jon
Performance/production
Collection of newspaper reviews by London theatre critics. UK-England: London. 1986. Lang.: Eng. 2059

Poppy
Plays/librettos/scripts
Theme of theatre in recent plays. UK-England. 1957-1985. Lang.: Eng. 2764

Popular entertainment
SEE ALSO
Classed Entries under MIXED ENTERTAINMENT.

Institutions
Two community-based popular theatre projects. Canada. 1987. Lang.: Eng. 522

Performance/production
Canadian popular theatre. Canada. Africa. Asia. 1987. Lang.: Eng. 733

Relation to other fields
Social implications of popular theatre. Canada. 1987. Lang.: Eng. 1222

Applications of African 'Theatre for Development' movement to Canadian popular theatre. Africa. Canada: St. John's, NF, Toronto, ON. 1978-1987. Lang.: Eng. 2978

Theory/criticism
Discussion of theory of popular theatre. Canada. 1987. Lang.: Eng. 3024

Popular Truth
Performance/production
Collection of newspaper reviews by London theatre critics. UK-England: London. 1987. Lang.: Eng. 2181

Porgy and Bess
Performance/production
Cooperative financing of Gershwin's *Porgy and Bess*. USA. 1987. Lang.: Eng. 3850

Pork Pies
Performance/production
Collection of newspaper reviews by London theatre critics. UK-England: London. 1987. Lang.: Eng. 2248

Porter, Cole
Performance/production
Collection of newspaper reviews by London theatre critics. UK-England: London. 1987. Lang.: Eng. 2187

Collection of newspaper reviews by London theatre critics. UK-England: London. 1987. Lang.: Eng. 2239

Collection of newspaper reviews by London theatre critics. UK-England: London. 1987. Lang.: Eng. 2253

Collection of newspaper reviews by New York theatre critics. USA: New York, NY. 1987. Lang.: Eng. 2317

Porter, Helen
Performance/production
Collection of newspaper reviews by London theatre critics. UK-England: London. 1987. Lang.: Eng. 2246

Porter, Stephen
Performance/production
Stephen Porter on directing Shaw. USA. 1924-1981. Lang.: Eng. 2353

Portrait of Jenny
Performance/production
Productions of several Tokyo companies. Japan: Tokyo. 1987. Lang.: Jap. 1962

Portraits
Performance/production
Collection of newspaper reviews by London theatre critics. UK-England: London. 1987. Lang.: Eng. 2235

Portraits in Reflection
Design/technology
Modern dance production *Portraits in Reflection*. USA. 1986. Lang.: Eng. 396

Positive Man, The
Plays/librettos/scripts
New findings on 18th-century Irish comic playwright John O'Keeffe. Ireland. England: London. 1767-1798. Lang.: Eng. 2643

Posner, Lindsay
Performance/production
Collection of newspaper reviews by London theatre critics. UK-England: London. 1986. Lang.: Eng. 2162

Collection of newspaper reviews by London theatre critics. UK-England: London. 1987. Lang.: Eng. 2207

Collection of newspaper reviews by London theatre critics. UK-England: London. 1987. Lang.: Eng. 2250

Possum in the Bughouse
Performance/production
Collection of newspaper reviews by London theatre critics. UK-England: London. 1986. Lang.: Eng. 2092

Postma, Laurens C.
Performance/production
Collection of newspaper reviews by London theatre critics. UK-England: London. 1986. Lang.: Eng. 2129

Potter, Dennis
Plays/librettos/scripts
Interview with playwright Howard Brenton. UK-England. 1975-1987. Lang.: Eng. 2806

Poulenc, Francis
Basic theatrical documents
Review of video productions of *Tosca* and *Dialogues des Carmélites*. Italy: Verona. Australia: Sydney. 1987. Lang.: Eng. 3692

Performance/production
Background on Metropolitan radio broadcast performances. USA: New York, NY. 1987. Lang.: Eng. 3837

Background on Metropolitan telecast performances. USA: New York, NY. 1987. Lang.: Eng. 3839

Plays/librettos/scripts
Role analysis of Blanche in Poulenc's *Dialogues des Carmélites*. France: Paris. 1957-1987. Lang.: Eng. 3901

Poulter, Chrissie
Training
Genesis and development of various youth theatre groups. UK-Ireland. 1979-1987. Lang.: Eng. 1388

Pound, Ezra
Performance/production
Hillar Liitoja's experimental theatre. Canada. 1987. Lang.: Eng. 739

Theory/criticism
The language of theatrical criticism. USA: New York, NY. 1917-1985. Lang.: Eng. 1367

Pour un oui ou pour un non
Performance/production
Collection of newspaper reviews by London theatre critics. UK-England: London. 1987. Lang.: Eng. 2177

Powell, Arnold
Design/technology
Survey of 1960s stage machinery. USA. 1960-1987. Lang.: Eng. 456

Powell, Michael
Performance/production
Filming of operas *Tales of Hoffmann* and Menotti's *The Medium*. Europe. 1951-1986. Lang.: Eng. 3768

Pownall, David
 Performance/production
 Collection of newspaper reviews by London theatre critics. UK-England: London. 1987. Lang.: Eng. 2179

Poyner, Michael
 Training
 Interview with Michael Poyner, director of Ulster Youth Theatre. UK-Ireland. 1987. Lang.: Eng. 1386

Prager, Timothy
 Performance/production
 Collection of newspaper reviews by London theatre critics. UK-England: London. 1987. Lang.: Eng. 2197

Pragmatyści (Pragmatists, The)
 Institutions
 The Stanisław Ignacy Witkiewicz Theatre. Poland: Zakopane. 1982-1986. Lang.: Eng, Fre. 1628

Prague Quadrennial
 Design/technology
 Report on the Prague Quadrennial computer symposium. Czechoslovakia: Prague. 1987. Lang.: Eng. 306
 Hungarian exhibition, Prague Quadrennial theatre design competition. Czechoslovakia: Prague. 1987. Lang.: Hun. 307
 The contribution of Josef Svoboda to the 1987 Prague Quadrennial exhibition. Czechoslovakia: Prague. 1987. Lang.: Eng. 308
 Judge of Prague Quadrennial design competition describes jury's work. Czechoslovakia: Prague. 1987. Lang.: Eng. 310
 First American participation in Prague Quadrennial theatre design contest. Czechoslovakia: Prague. USA. 1967-1987. Lang.: Eng. 311
 A report from the Prague Quadrennial theatre design contest. Czechoslovakia: Prague. 1987. Lang.: Swe. 312
 Stage designer reviews 1987 Prague Quadrennial exhibits. Europe. 1987. Lang.: Eng. 319
 Performance spaces
 East German exhibition at Prague Quadrennial '87: Gold medal for theatre reconstruction exhibit. Germany, East: Berlin, East. 1742-1986. Lang.: Hun. 636

Prairie du Chien
 Performance/production
 Collection of newspaper reviews by London theatre critics. UK-England: London. 1986. Lang.: Eng. 2131

Praise Be to God
 Performance/production
 Collection of newspaper reviews by London theatre critics. UK-England: London. 1987. Lang.: Eng. 2260

Prampolini, Enrico
 Theory/criticism
 The concept of theatre as a total work of art. Europe. 1804-1930. Lang.: Eng. 1328

Präsident, Der (President, The)
 Plays/librettos/scripts
 The metadramatic nature of Thomas Bernhard's plays. Germany, West. 1974-1983. Lang.: Eng. 2616

Pratt, John
 Performance/production
 The career of dancer/choreographer Katherine Dunham. USA: New York, NY, Chicago, IL, Las Vegas, NV. 1909-1987. Lang.: Eng. 1412

Pravda
 Plays/librettos/scripts
 Interview with playwright Howard Brenton. UK-England. 1975-1987. Lang.: Eng. 2806

Prayer for my Daughter, A
 Performance/production
 Collection of newspaper reviews by London theatre critics. UK-England: London. 1987. Lang.: Eng. 2221

Pražsky Komorní Balet (Prague)
 Performance/production
 Interview with choreographer Pavel Šmok. Czechoslovakia: Prague. 1987. Lang.: Cze. 1433

Preetorius, Emil
 Performance/production
 Production history of *Der Ring des Nibelungen*. Germany: Bayreuth. Italy: Milan. USA: New York, NY. 1876-1987. Lang.: Eng. 3775

Preiss, Viktor
 Performance/production
 Actors Jaromír Hanzlík and Viktor Preiss in Rostand's *Cyrano*, directed by Jaroslov Dudek at Vinohradské Theatre. Czechoslovakia: Prague. 1986. Lang.: Cze. 771

Press
 Institutions
 Overview of Lars af Malmborg's management of Swedish Royal Opera. Sweden: Stockholm. 1985-1987. Lang.: Swe. 3729
 Plays/librettos/scripts
 History of Playwrights Canada Press. Canada: Toronto, ON. 1972-1982. Lang.: Eng. 2460
 Theory/criticism
 Two conferences on theatre reviewing. Australia. 1985-1986. Lang.: Eng. 1315
 Criticizes newspaper coverage of Montreal theatre awards. Canada: Montreal, PQ. 1987. Lang.: Fre. 1318

Pressburger, Giorgio
 Performance/production
 Filming of operas *Tales of Hoffmann* and Menotti's *The Medium*. Europe. 1951-1986. Lang.: Eng. 3768

Preston, Thomas
 Plays/librettos/scripts
 History and sources of Thomas Preston's *Cambyses, King of Persia*. England. 1562-1987. Lang.: Eng. 2529

Prestuplenič i nakazanič (Crime and Punishment)
 Performance/production
 The 17th Warsaw theatre conference. Poland: Warsaw. 1987. Lang.: Eng, Fre. 872

 Experimental theatre at the Stary in three recent productions. Poland: Cracow. 1987. Lang.: Eng. 1999
 Russian director Jurij Liubimov and his productions in the USSR and USA. USSR: Moscow. USA: Washington, DC. 1984-1987. Lang.: Eng. 2400

Previn, André
 Performance/production
 Collection of newspaper reviews by London theatre critics. UK-England: London. 1987. Lang.: Eng. 2245
 Plays/librettos/scripts
 Political protest in Tom Stoppard's *Every Good Boy Deserves Favour*. UK-England. USSR. 1974-1977. Lang.: Eng. 2783

Previn, Dory
 Performance/production
 Collection of newspaper reviews by London theatre critics. UK-England: London. 1986. Lang.: Eng. 2038

Price, Tim Rose
 Performance/production
 Collection of newspaper reviews by New York theatre critics. USA: New York, NY. 1987. Lang.: Eng. 2312

Prick Up Your Ears
 Design/technology
 Cinematographer Oliver Stapleton and his lighting work on the film *Prick Up Your Ears*. USA. 1987. Lang.: Eng. 3136

Priestley, J.B.
 Performance/production
 Collection of newspaper reviews by London theatre critics. UK-England: London. 1987. Lang.: Eng. 2208

Příliš hlučna samota (Too Loud a Solitude)
 Plays/librettos/scripts
 Příliš hlučna samota (Too Loud a Solitude) by Bohumil Hrabal. Czechoslovakia. 1914-1987. Lang.: Ita. 1110

Primera història d'Esther (First Story of Esther)
 Plays/librettos/scripts
 Catalan playwrights after the Spanish Civil War. Spain-Catalonia. 1939-1975. Lang.: Cat. 2730

Prince Edward Theatre (London)
 Performance/production
 Collection of newspaper reviews by London theatre critics. UK-England: London. 1986. Lang.: Eng. 2097

Prince of Wales Theatre (London)
 Performance/production
 Collection of newspaper reviews by London theatre critics. UK-England: London. 1986. Lang.: Eng. 2156
 Collection of newspaper reviews by London theatre critics. UK-England: London. 1987. Lang.: Eng. 2272

Prince, Harold
 Performance/production
 Four approaches to the role of Sally Bowles in *Cabaret*. USA: New York, NY. Germany. 1966-1987. Lang.: Eng. 968
 Collection of newspaper reviews by London theatre critics. UK-England: London. 1986. Lang.: Eng. 2065

Prince, Harold — cont'd

Collection of newspaper reviews by New York theatre critics. USA: New York, NY. 1987. Lang.: Eng.   2317

Collection of newspaper reviews by New York theatre critics. USA: New York, NY. 1987. Lang.: Eng.   2318

Successful London revival of *Follies* by Stephen Sondheim. UK-England: London. USA: New York, NY. 1987. Lang.: Eng.   3638

Two productions of *Flora, the Red Menace.* USA: New York, NY. 1965-1987. Lang.: Eng.   3640

Interview with actress Georgia Brown. USA: New York, NY. UK-England: London. 1957-1985. Lang.: Eng.   3651

Plays/librettos/scripts

Interview with Joe Masteroff, author of the book for *Cabaret.* USA: New York, NY. 1963-1987. Lang.: Eng.   3674

History of the musical *Roza.* USA: Baltimore, MD. 1965-1987. Lang.: Eng.   3675

Prince, Joe

Relation to other fields

Roundtable discussion on the state of arts education. USA. 1984. Lang.: Eng.   1281

Principia scriptoriae

Performance/production

Collection of newspaper reviews by London theatre critics. UK-England: London. 1986. Lang.: Eng.   2063

Printemps, Monsieur Deslauriers, Le (Spring, Mr. Deslauriers)

Plays/librettos/scripts

The role of the father-figure in recent plays from Quebec. Canada: Quebec. 1980-1987. Lang.: Fre.   2465

Prinz, Rosemary

Plays/librettos/scripts

Interview with playwright Robert Harling, designer Edward Gianfrancesco. USA: New York, NY. 1987. Lang.: Eng.   2846

Prisoner at Large, The

Plays/librettos/scripts

New findings on 18th-century Irish comic playwright John O'Keeffe. Ireland. England: London. 1767-1798. Lang.: Eng.   2643

Private Means

Performance/production

Collection of newspaper reviews by London theatre critics. UK-England: London. 1986. Lang.: Eng.   2147

Private Members

Performance/production

Collection of newspaper reviews by London theatre critics. UK-England: London. 1987. Lang.: Eng.   2227

Private Performances

Performance/production

Reproduction and discussion of an annotated 'score' by director Hillar Liitoja. Canada: Toronto, ON. 1987. Lang.: Eng.   744

Privates on Parade

Plays/librettos/scripts

Theme of theatre in recent plays. UK-England. 1957-1985. Lang.: Eng.   2764

Processional theatre

SEE ALSO

Pageants/parades.

Classed Entries under MIXED ENTERTAINMENT–Pageants/parades: 3421-3432.

Proctor's Pleasure Palace & Garden of Palms (New York, NY)

Performance spaces

Subverting alienating effect of some performance spaces. USA: 1800-1910. Lang.: Eng.   706

Producing

Administration

Biography of theatre manager Christopher Rich. England: London. 1647-1715. Lang.: Eng.   23

Cooperation between theatre association and county council to promote theatrical activities. Sweden: Uddevalla. 1987. Lang.: Swe.   40

Comparison of commercial and subsidized theatre. UK-England: London. 1986. Lang.: Eng.   46

Interim report on the Renaissance Theatre Company. UK-England: London. 1987. Lang.: Eng.   54

Editor of *Amateur Stage*, Charles Vance, talks about the amateur world. UK-England. 1987. Lang.: Eng.   56

American theatre's view of the commissioning process. USA: New York, NY. 1987. Lang.: Eng.   118

Objectives and strategies of pricing for the performing arts. USA: Bowling Green, OH. 1986. Lang.: Eng.   136

Comprehensive guide to play production. USA: New York, NY. 1987. Lang.: Eng.   150

Philip Arnoult, founding director of the Baltimore Theatre Project, and his search for new works. USA: Baltimore, MD. 1971-1987. Lang.: Eng.   157

Broadway producer Dorothy Olim on commercial theatre. USA: New York, NY. 1983. Lang.: Eng.   189

Alternative curtain times as a way to increase attendance. USA: New York, NY. 1986. Lang.: Eng.   200

Financial considerations in transferring *Steel Magnolias* to an Off Broadway theatre. USA: New York, NY. 1987. Lang.: Eng.   226

Profile of Ensemble Studio Theatre. USA: New York, NY. 1987. Lang.: Eng.   232

Career of theatre owner William Fox. USA: New York, NY. 1879-1952. Lang.: Eng.   3122

Lee Shubert's role in the formation of the American film industry. USA: New York, NY. 1914-1924. Lang.: Eng.   3123

Effects of nationalization and modernization on Chinese theatre. China, People's Republic of: Beijing. 1279-1986. Lang.: Chi.   3427

History of Chinese theatre reform. China, People's Republic of: Beijing. 1942-1984. Lang.: Chi.   3428

Producer Marlene Smith. Canada: Toronto, ON. 1985. Lang.: Eng.   3617

Irving Guttman, artistic director, Edmonton Opera, Manitoba Opera. Canada: Edmonton, AB, Winnipeg, MB. 1972-1985. Lang.: Eng.   3679

The collaboration of composer and librettist in workshops of new operas. USA. 1987. Lang.: Eng.   3683

Audience

Causes and characteristics of the present theatrical crisis. Spain. 1985. Lang.: Spa.   1537

Basic theatrical documents

Collection of radio plays produced by Andrew Allan. Canada. 1942-1955. Lang.: Eng.   3109

Institutions

Aims and scope of the Olympic Arts Festival. Canada: Calgary, AB. 1987. Lang.: Eng.   507

Closing remarks, FDG/CBS conference on new plays. USA. 1987. Lang.: Eng.   586

Family letters and business papers of the Shuberts. USA: New York, NY. 1900-1953. Lang.: Eng.   620

Script editor's recollections of CBC radio dramas. Canada. 1944-1954. Lang.: Eng.   3110

Operations of the Canadian Opera Company. Canada: Toronto, ON. 1987. Lang.: Eng.   3716

Attendance at Royal Swedish Opera: analysis, how to improve it. Sweden: Stockholm. 1960-1985. Lang.: Swe.   3730

Performance/production

Overview of Hungarian producers. Hungary. 1986-1987. Lang.: Hun.   810

Interview with Kathryn Lynch, manager of Shubert's Century Library. USA. 1945-1986. Lang.: Eng.   950

Interview with producer Lucille Lortel. USA: Waterford, CT. 1987. Lang.: Eng.   964

Richard Ouzounian, director, Manitoba Theatre Centre. Canada: Winnipeg, MB. 1982. Lang.: Eng.   1693

Production account, Frank's *Spinoza*, Saidye Bronfman Centre. Canada: Montreal, PQ. 1982. Lang.: Eng.   1702

Actress Lillah McCarthy, in an old interview, talks about Shaw. UK-England. 1914-1927. Lang.: Eng.   2074

British theatrical touring companies. UK-England. North America. Australia. 1870-1929. Lang.: Eng.   2280

Production of Cirque du Soleil. Canada: Montreal, PQ. 1987. Lang.: Eng.   3302

Golden Fleece, Ltd. bridges classical music, opera and musical theatre. USA: New York, NY. 1987. Lang.: Eng.   3412

History of musical version, *Breakfast at Tiffany's.* USA: New York, NY, Philadelphia, PA, Boston, MA. 1958-1966. Lang.: Eng.   3644

Interview with director Paula Kalustian. USA: New York, NY. 1984-1987. Lang.: Eng.   3662

Producing — cont'd

Autobiography of opera star Maureen Forrester. Canada. 1930-1986. Lang.: Eng.   3748

Professionals explain their methods of verbal description of opera. Germany, East. Germany, West. 1988. Lang.: Ger.   3777

Plays/librettos/scripts
Current American playwriting—link with film and TV, production, economics. USA. 1987. Lang.: Eng.   1176

FDG/CBS New Plays Program Conferences. USA: New York, NY. 1987. Lang.: Eng.   1180

Role of playwright George Edwardes in development of musical comedy. UK-England: London. 1830-1890. Lang.: Eng.   2766

Reference materials
Compilation of anecdotes on life in the theatre from Aristophanes to Williams. 5 B.C.-1987 A.D. Lang.: Eng.   1195

Producing Managers Association (New York, NY)
Institutions
Actors' Equity strike against Producing Managers Association. USA: New York, NY. 1921-1925. Lang.: Eng.   573

Production Company (New York, NY)
Administration
Financial challenges of four former artistic directors. USA. 1981-1987. Lang.: Eng.   239

Production histories
SEE
Staging.
Performance/production.

Programs
SEE ALSO
Collected materials.

Projections
Design/technology
The use and development of special effects in the theatre. Canada. 1977-1987. Lang.: Fre.   303

Work of noted set designer and technological innovator Josef Svoboda. Czechoslovakia: Prague. 1940-1987. Lang.: Eng.   305

The increasing use of projected images in theatre. Canada. 1985. Lang.: Fre.   1399

Colorization of films and arguments against its use. USA. 1987. Lang.: Eng.   3129

Technology and history of film credits. USA: Los Angeles, CA. 1987. Lang.: Eng.   3130

Colorization of films and arguments for its use. USA. 1987. Lang.: Eng.   3134

The use of holography in theatre. Canada. 1987. Lang.: Fre.   3201

Prokofjev, Sergej Sergejevič
Performance/production
Creation and production of *Peter and the Wolf* by Prokofjev. USSR: Moscow. 1930-1936. Lang.: Heb.   3417

Proloog (Netherlands)
Performance/production
History of modern Dutch theatre. Netherlands. 1970-1985. Lang.: Dut.   862

Prometheus in Evin
Performance/production
Collection of newspaper reviews by London theatre critics. UK-England: London. 1987. Lang.: Eng.   2268

Promptbooks
Basic theatrical documents
Constance Garnett's translation of *Tri sestry (Three Sisters)* by Čechov. England: London. 1901. Lang.: Eng.   1552

Pronaszko, Andrzej
Performance/production
Director Tadeusz Kantor's inspirations in early career. Poland. 1933-1987. Lang.: Pol.   1992

Proper Place, A
Performance/production
Collection of newspaper reviews by London theatre critics. UK-England: London. 1986. Lang.: Eng.   2133

Properties
Design/technology
Exhibit of theatre crafts. Sweden: Gävle. 1987. Lang.: Swe.   365

How to make flexible negative molds. USA. 1987. Lang.: Eng.   382

Introductory textbook on scene and production design. USA. 1987. Lang.: Eng.   408

Symbolism of stage props in Lepage's *La Trilogie des dragons*. Canada. 1987. Lang.: Fre.   1588

Scene design and its visual impact in Chinese opera. China, People's Republic of. 1856-1987. Lang.: Chi.   3446

Prošlym letom v Čulimske (Last Summer in Chulimsk)
Performance/production
Collection of newspaper reviews by London theatre critics. UK-England: London. 1987. Lang.: Eng.   2265

Protheroe, Brian
Performance/production
Collection of newspaper reviews by London theatre critics. UK-England: London. 1987. Lang.: Eng.   2194

Provencher, Anne-Marie
Audience
Critical analysis of Anne-Marie Provencher's *La Tour*. Canada: Montreal, PQ. 1986. Lang.: Eng.   1531

Provincial theatre
SEE
Regional theatre.

Prowse, Jane
Performance/production
Collection of newspaper reviews by London theatre critics. UK-England: London. 1987. Lang.: Eng.   2205

Collection of newspaper reviews by London theatre critics. UK-England: London. 1987. Lang.: Eng.   2240

Prowse, Philip
Performance/production
Play scripts as literary texts and as performance texts. UK-England. 1977-1987. Lang.: Eng.   905

Collection of newspaper reviews by London theatre critics. UK-England: London. 1986. Lang.: Eng.   2100

Prueba de fuego (Trial by Fire)
Performance/production
Collection of newspaper reviews by London theatre critics. UK-England: London. 1987. Lang.: Eng.   2257

Pryde, Bill
Performance/production
Collection of newspaper reviews by London theatre critics. UK-England: London. 1987. Lang.: Eng.   2260

Collection of newspaper reviews by London theatre critics. UK-England: London. 1987. Lang.: Eng.   2265

Pseudolus
Plays/librettos/scripts
Changes in theatre space as a result of New Comedy. Greece: Athens. Italy: Rome. 400 B.C.-180 A.D. Lang.: Eng.   2625

Psychodrama
Relation to other fields
Psychodrama in the clinic, the classroom and contemporary research. Europe. North America. 1900-1987. Lang.: Ita.   1233

Theoretical examination of psychodrama, creative drama. Korea. 1978. Lang.: Kor.   1247

Psychology
Administration
Results of a survey conducted by the New York Foundation for the Arts. USA: New York, NY. 1987. Lang.: Eng.   181

Long-term planning in artistic culture. USSR. 1987. Lang.: Rus.   263

Audience
Scientific and psychological study of the role of audience as dramaturgs. Italy. 1987. Lang.: Eng.   284

Analysis of live performance using psychoanalytic theory. USA. 1987. Lang.: Eng.   1539

Audience psychology in Chinese opera. China, People's Republic of. 1987. Lang.: Chi.   3431

Chinese acting: direct communication with audience. China, People's Republic of: Beijing. 1950-1986. Lang.: Chi.   3434

Basic theatrical documents
Play text and photo essay of Martha Clarke's *Vienna: Lusthaus*. Austria: Vienna. 1986. Lang.: Eng.   1398

Institutions
Activities of Dramatists' Guild include writer's-block workshop. USA: New York, NY. 1987. Lang.: Eng.   585

Performance/production
Creative self-knowledge and the mystical path of actors. UK-England: London. USA. 1977-1987. Lang.: Eng.   900

Sociological study of actors. USSR. 1980-1987. Lang.: Rus.   1041

Expression of Japanese feelings in *nō*. Japan. 1300-1600. Lang.: Jap.   1502

Mime Samy Molcho: his new work as lecturer and author. Switzerland. 1987. Lang.: Ger.   3235

Psychology — cont'd

Transvestite roles in extravaganzas of J.R. Planché and Mme. Vestris. UK-England: London. 1830-1870. Lang.: Eng.   3268

Wolfgang Amadeus Mozart: a psychological profile. Austria: Vienna. 1756-1781. Lang.: Eng.   3742

Plays/librettos/scripts

Love, marriage and family relationships in contemporary drama. USSR. 1980-1987. Lang.: Rus.   1420

Dramatic irony as an actor's tool. 1987. Lang.: Eng.   2417

Terror and terrorism in the theatre. Lang.: Eng.   2421

Female characters in city comedy who suffer from bladder incontinence. 1599-1632. Lang.: Eng.   2427

The role of the father-figure in recent plays from Quebec. Canada: Quebec. 1980-1987. Lang.: Fre.   2465

Shakespeare's *Hamlet*: representation of interiority onstage. England. 1600. Lang.: Eng.   2500

Madness and revenge in Kyd's *The Spanish Tragedy*. England. 1589. Lang.: Eng.   2515

Changing economic conditions created an audience for plays about criminals. England. 1731-1740. Lang.: Eng.   2517

Comparison of *King Lear* and *Vildanden (The Wild Duck)*. England. Norway. 1605-1884. Lang.: Eng.   2518

Christian thought in Thomas Murphy's *The Gigli Concert*. Ireland. 1983. Lang.: Eng.   2653

Athol Fugard's *Master Harold...and the Boys* examines apartheid in terms of human relationships. South Africa, Republic of. 1982-1987. Lang.: Eng.   2723

Freudian reading of Shaw's *Passion, Poison and Petrification*. UK-England. 1895-1926. Lang.: Eng.   2781

Shaw's *Misalliance* as a Freudian dream play. UK-England. 1909-1911. Lang.: Eng.   2826

Psychological complexity of Eugene O'Neill's *Long Day's Journey into Night*. USA. 1940. Lang.: Eng.   2842

Impact of AIDS crisis on the theatre. USA: New York, NY, San Francisco, CA. 1987. Lang.: Eng.   2881

Corn as a symbol in Sam Shepard's *Buried Child*. USA. 1978. Lang.: Eng.   2905

The inner and outer psychology of characters in Chinese opera. China, People's Republic of. 1987. Lang.: Chi.   3570

Chinese opera should reflect the concerns of its audience. China, People's Republic of. 1987. Lang.: Chi.   3578

Theme of *femme fatale* in *Samson et Dalila*. France. 1800-1899. Lang.: Eng.   3900

Wagner's obsession with Jews and Judaism. Germany. 1813-1882. Lang.: Eng.   3905

Psychological interpretations of Wagner's *Parsifal*. Germany. 1882-1987. Lang.: Eng.   3907

Relation to other fields

Psychological effect of Ben Jonson's family life on his writings. England. 1602-1604. Lang.: Eng.   1232

Psychodrama in the clinic, the classroom and contemporary research. Europe. North America. 1900-1987. Lang.: Eng.   1233

Excerpt from a speech by Jerzy Grotowski that examines the actor's technique. Italy: Florence. 1985. Lang.: Eng.   1244

Theoretical examination of psychodrama, creative drama. Korea. 1978. Lang.: Kor.   1247

Children's interaction with theatre as compared to television. USA. 1964. Lang.: Eng.   1277

Assumptions by the actors and the audience in live theatre. USA. 1987. Lang.: Eng.   1283

Italian translations of Ernest Jones' *Hamlet and Oedipus*, and Jean Starobinski's *Hamlet and Freud*. Europe. 1596-1949. Lang.: Ita.   2988

Playwright Thomas Murphy and the nature of creativity. Ireland. 1961-1986. Lang.: Eng.   2993

Perceptions of childhood reflected in opera. Europe. 1800-1983. Lang.: Eng.   3940

Theory/criticism

The concept of theatre as a total work of art. Europe. 1804-1930. Lang.: Eng.   1328

Public Enemy

Performance/production

Collection of newspaper reviews by London theatre critics. UK-England: London. 1987. Lang.: Eng.   2271

Public relations

Administration

The merger of two Toronto theatre companies. Canada: Toronto, ON. 1987. Lang.: Eng.   7

Interview with Madeleine Rivest. Canada: Montreal, PQ. 1987. Lang.: Fre.   14

Vancouver theatre scene, Jesse Richardson Theatre Awards. Canada: Vancouver, BC. 1983-1984. Lang.: Eng.   18

The purpose and impact of Canadian theatre awards. Canada. 1987. Lang.: Eng.   19

Form and content of Warsaw playbills. Poland: Warsaw. 1765-1915. Lang.: Pol.   38

Cooperation between theatre association and county council to promote theatrical activities. Sweden: Uddevalla. 1987. Lang.: Swe.   40

Questions about the role of private sponsorship in publicly funded theatre. Switzerland. 1987. Lang.: Ger.   43

Attempts by private sponsors to influence artistic decisions. Switzerland. 1987. Lang.: Ger.   44

Interview with Actor's Work Program director, Ronda Ormont. USA: New York, NY. 1987. Lang.: Eng.   93

New Actors' Equity handbook published for membership. USA: New York, NY. 1982. Lang.: Eng.   107

Sophisticated Ladies taped for cable television amid controversy. USA: New York, NY. 1982. Lang.: Eng.   112

Actors' Equity urges communication between chapters and main office. USA: New York, NY. 1982. Lang.: Eng.   113

Computer analysis of mailing lists and response enhancement. USA: New York, NY. 1986. Lang.: Eng.   139

Integration of creative process in society. USA: New York, NY. 1986. Lang.: Eng.   168

Results of market research survey for a small arts center. USA. 1984. Lang.: Eng.   171

Influence of TV ads on success of Broadway plays. USA: New York, NY. 1984-1987. Lang.: Eng.   179

Labor and the arts as advocates of social and cultural democracy. USA. 1982. Lang.: Eng.   193

History of the Russian theatre poster. USSR. 1870-1979.   261

Situation of East German theatres and playwrights. Germany, East. 1985-1986. Lang.: Ger.   1518

Suggestion that South African Broadcasting Company improve broadcasting standards. South Africa, Republic of. 1987. Lang.: Eng.   3106

Vatican court's withdrawal from festival promotion under Sixtus V. Italy: Rome. 1585-1595. Lang.: Ita.   3240

An investigation of the audience of Chinese classical drama. China, People's Republic of. 1987. Lang.: Chi.   3424

Marketing of opera and the arts in Toronto. Canada: Toronto, ON. 1980-1987. Lang.: Eng.   3678

Audience

The audience of Chinese classical drama. China, People's Republic of. 1987. Lang.: Chi.   3429

Audience reactions to the Canadian Opera Company's Atlantic tour. Canada. 1987. Lang.: Eng.   3689

Institutions

History of Alberta theatre companies. Canada: Edmonton, AB, Calgary, AB. 1987. Lang.: Eng.   506

Critical discussion of the Chalmers Awards. Canada: Toronto, ON. 1987. Lang.: Eng.   513

The advantages and disadvantages of the Jesse Awards. Canada: Vancouver, BC. 1983. Lang.: Eng.   517

Analysis of co-productions between Saskatoon theatre companies. Canada: Saskatoon, SK. 1987. Lang.: Eng.   518

History of Theatre Plus theatre company. Canada: Toronto, ON. 1972-1982. Lang.: Eng.   520

The Dora Mavor Moore theatre awards. Canada: Toronto, ON. 1987. Lang.: Eng.   523

Interview with Stratford Festival's artistic director John Neville. Canada: Stratford, ON. 1985-1986. Lang.: Eng.   1605

Operations of the Saskatoon Opera Association. Canada: Saskatoon, SK. 1978-1987. Lang.: Eng.   3713

Public relations — cont'd

Relation to other fields
UN cultural boycott on artists who have performed in South Africa. South Africa, Republic of. 1987. Lang.: Eng. 1251

Theory/criticism
Criticizes newspaper coverage of Montreal theatre awards. Canada: Montreal, PQ. 1987. Lang.: Fre. 1318

Public Theatre (New York, NY)

Administration
Arbitration of Equity's Billie Whitelaw case. USA: New York, NY. 1982. Lang.: Eng. 94

Institutions
New York Shakespeare Festival's Joseph Papp receives AEA's Paul Robeson Award. USA: New York, NY. 1987. Lang.: Eng. 578

Performance/production
Maintaining theatre archives and designating a coordinator. USA: New York, NY. 1987. Lang.: Eng. 938

Career of director/author Andre Ernotte. USA: New York, NY. 1987. Lang.: Eng. 954

Career of director Garland Wright. USA. 1972-1987. Lang.: Eng. 975

Collection of newspaper reviews by New York theatre critics. USA: New York, NY. 1987. Lang.: Eng. 2312

Collection of newspaper reviews by New York theatre critics. USA: New York, NY. 1987. Lang.: Eng. 2319

Collection of newspaper reviews by New York theatre critics. USA: New York, NY. 1987. Lang.: Eng. 2326

Plays/librettos/scripts
Animal imagery in plays of Lee Breuer. USA. 1987. Lang.: Eng. 2882

Relation to other fields
Nontraditional casting of minority actors. USA. 1979-1987. Lang.: Eng. 1274

Puccini, Giacomo

Audience
The vocal versus the visual aspects of opera. Europe. 1781-1983. Lang.: Eng. 3690

Basic theatrical documents
Review of video productions of *Tosca* and *Dialogues des Carmélites*. Italy: Verona. Australia: Sydney. 1987. Lang.: Eng. 3692

Performance/production
Opera critic Edouard Hanslick and his opposition to *La Bohème* by Puccini. Austro-Hungarian Empire: Vienna. 1896-1987. Lang.: Eng. 3745

Film versions of Puccini's *La Bohème*, Offenbach's *Tales of Hoffmann*. Europe. North America. 1987. Lang.: Eng. 3767

Review of performances at an assembly of opera ensembles. Hungary: Szeged. 1987. Lang.: Hun. 3796

Soprano Eva Marton discusses Turandot. Hungary. 1943-1987. Lang.: Eng. 3797

Background on Lyric Opera radio broadcast performances. USA: Chicago, IL. 1987. Lang.: Eng. 3832

Soprano Renata Scotto directs Metropolitan Opera production of *Madama Butterfly*. USA: New York, NY. 1987. Lang.: Eng. 3836

Background on Metropolitan radio broadcast performances. USA: New York, NY. 1987. Lang.: Eng. 3837

Background on Metropolitan radio broadcast performances. USA: New York, NY. 1987. Lang.: Eng. 3838

Plays/librettos/scripts
Franco Alfano, who completed Puccini's *Turandot*. Italy. 1876-1954. Lang.: Eng. 3919

Comparison of Puccini's and Leoncavallo's treatments of *La Bohème*. Italy. 1893-1897. Lang.: Swe. 3922

Floral imagery in the operas of Giacomo Puccini. Italy. 1858-1924. Lang.: Eng. 3926

Pugh, Robert

Performance/production
Collection of newspaper reviews by London theatre critics. UK-England: London. 1986. Lang.: Eng. 2088

Pugin, Augustus Welby Northmore

Performance/production
Historical accuracy in 19th-century London theatre productions. England: London. 1800-1900. Lang.: Eng. 1734

Puig, Manuel

Performance/production
Collection of newspaper reviews by London theatre critics. UK-England: London. 1987. Lang.: Eng. 2274

Puigserver, Fabià

Institutions
Evaluation of the plays performed during the first ten years of Teatre Lliure. Spain-Catalonia: Barcelona. 1976-1986. Lang.: Cat. 1636

Performance spaces
Collection of photographs on the history of the Teatre Lliure. Spain-Catalonia: Barcelona. 1976-1987. Lang.: Cat. 1671

History of the Teatre Lliure. Spain-Catalonia: Barcelona. 1976-1987. Lang.: Cat. 1673

Pula

Performance/production
Matsemela Manaka's play *Pula* and its anti-apartheid expressions. South Africa, Republic of: Soweto. 1969-1984. Lang.: Eng. 883

Pulapka (Trap, The)

Performance/production
Polish theatre. Poland: Warsaw, Cracow, Wrocław. 1980-1987. Lang.: Eng, Fre. 1987

The shape and form of contemporary Polish theatre. Poland: Warsaw. 1981-1987. Lang.: Eng, Fre. 1995

Pulse, Paul

Performance/production
Collection of newspaper reviews by London theatre critics. UK-England: London. 1986. Lang.: Eng. 2166

Puppet Centre (London)

Institutions
Ramayana '87, an Inner London Education Authority project. UK-England: London. 1987. Lang.: Eng. 3965

Puppet Theatre (Budapest)

SEE
Állami Bábszinház.

Puppeteers

Performance/production
Theatrical activity at the concentration camp Theresienstadt. Czechoslovakia: Terezín. 1938-1968. Lang.: Heb. 772

Writings of director Leon Schiller. Poland. Germany. Roman Empire. 275-1945. Lang.: Pol. 1994

History and aspects of puppet theatre: designs, genres and puppeteers. Europe. Asia. 400 B.C.-1985 A.D. Lang.: Eng. 3255

Puppetry on the streets and fairgrounds. France. 1800-1899. Lang.: Eng. 3258

The life of Chinese puppeteer Shiu Fu-Neng. Taiwan. 1987. Lang.: Chi. 3540

Eduardo Di Mauro and his puppets. Argentina. Venezuela. 1940-1987. Lang.: Spa. 3969

Survival of Flemish puppet theatre. Belgium: Antwerp. 1812-1987. Lang.: Eng. 3970

Interview with Yang Feng on technique of hand puppet operation. China, People's Republic of. 1987. Lang.: Eng. 3971

On Drak puppet theatre. Czechoslovakia: Hradec Králové. 1987. Lang.: Cze. 3972

Creation of an original puppet character in puppet theatre. Israel: Jerusalem. 1987. Lang.: Eng. 3974

Communicating with young audiences with puppet theatre. Israel: Jerusalem. 1987. Lang.: Heb. 3975

Work of Bruno Leone and his attempts to re-establish the Neapolitan culture of Guaratelle. Italy: Naples. 1979-1987. Lang.: Eng. 3976

Korean folk puppetry using hands and feet. Korea, South. 1977. Lang.: Eng. 3977

Puppet companies from Poznań. Poland: Poznań. 1919-1939. Lang.: Pol. 3978

Activity of Polish puppeteers in Lodz. Poland: Łodź. 1900-1939. Lang.: Pol. 3979

History of Polish puppet theatre. Poland. 1490-1945. Lang.: Pol. 3980

Puppeteer's analysis of characters in Punch and Judy show. UK-England. 1987. Lang.: Eng. 3982

History of the Puppeteers Company. UK-England: Norwich. 1971-1987. Lang.: Eng. 3983

Materials on traditional Ukrainian folk puppet theatre. Ukraine. 1800-1987. Lang.: Ukr. 3984

Designing and using puppets in classical works. USA. 1600-1987. Lang.: Eng. 3985

Puppeteers — cont'd

Bread and Puppet Theatre's annual festival. USA: Glover, VT. 1987. Lang.: Eng.   3986

Puppeteer Paul Zaloom discusses political ideas, scene design. USA. 1970-1987. Lang.: Eng.   3987

Puppetry as an expression of popular and folk culture. USA. Italy. Belgium. Indonesia. 1987. Lang.: Eng.   3988

Collection of articles on puppet theatre. USSR. 1986. Lang.: Rus.
3989

Vietnamese water puppets. Vietnam. 900-1985. Lang.: Eng.   3990

Actors and puppets sharing the same stage. USA: Brooklyn, NY. 1985-1987. Lang.: Eng.   3999

Adaptation of Nativity puppet play. Italy. 1651-1987. Lang.: Eng.
4001

Comparison between the problems of puppeteers and cartoon animators. USA. 1987. Lang.: Eng.   4002

Mythological background and performance aspects of *dalang*. Indonesia. 1987. Lang.: Ita.   4010

Puppeteers Company (Norwich, UK)
Performance/production
History of the Puppeteers Company. UK-England: Norwich. 1971-1987. Lang.: Eng.   3983

Puppetry
SEE ALSO
Classed Entries under PUPPETRY.

Design/technology
Exhibit of theatre crafts. Sweden: Gävle. 1987. Lang.: Swe.   365

Artistry of mask-maker Ralph Lee. USA: New York, NY. 1960-1987. Lang.: Eng.   391

Performance/production
Overview of the Theatre of Nations Festival. USA: Baltimore, MD. 1981-1986. Lang.: Eng.   949

Plays/librettos/scripts
Influence of puppetry on Eugene O'Neill. USA. 1937. Lang.: Eng.
2919

Relation to other fields
Analysis of the role of tradition in theatrical forms of different cultures. Asia. Africa. 1985. Lang.: Fre.   1218

Korean mask plays, folklore and puppet theatre. Korea. Japan: Kyushu. 1987. Lang.: Kor.   1246

Puppets
Design/technology
The home of Chinese puppetry. China, People's Republic of. Europe. 1986-1987. Lang.: Chi.   3961

Computer and technological breakthroughs for puppetry. USA. 1985-1987. Lang.: Eng.   3962

Puppetmaking projects for children. USA. 1987. Lang.: Eng.   3963

Making and using puppets for the visually handicapped. USA. 1987. Lang.: Eng.   3964

How to construct *kokdugaksi* rod puppets. Korea. 1987. Lang.: Kor.
4005

Institutions
History of New York's Little Players puppet theatre. USA: New York, NY. 1960-1985. Lang.: Eng.   3967

Performance/production
Overview of Polish theatre scene. Poland: Warsaw, Cracow. 1987. Lang.: Eng.   874

Interview with Polish playwright Tadeusz Kantor. Poland: Cracow. Germany, West: Kassel. Italy: Milan. Italy: Sicily. 1987. Lang.: Eng, Fre.   876

Designing and using puppets in classical works. USA. 1600-1987. Lang.: Eng.   3985

Comparison between the problems of puppeteers and cartoon animators. USA. 1987. Lang.: Eng.   4002

Purcell, Daniel
Plays/librettos/scripts
Collaboration on songs for *Cinthia and Endimion*. England: London. 1697. Lang.: Eng.   3895

Pushkin
Performance/production
Collection of newspaper reviews by London theatre critics. UK-England: London. 1987. Lang.: Eng.   2259

Pushkin Theatre (Leningrad)
SEE
Akademičeskij Teat'r Dramy im. A.S. Puškina.

Puskás, Tamás
Performance/production
Tamás Puskás directs *Takáts Alice (Alice Takáts)* by Dezső Szomory, Madách Chamber Theatre. Hungary: Budapest. 1987. Lang.: Hun.   1897

Tamás Puskás directs *Takáts Alice (Alice Takáts)* by Dezső Szomory at Madách Kamaraszinház. Hungary: Budapest. 1987. Lang.: Hun.
1906

Puškin, Aleksand'r Sergejevič
Relation to other fields
Study of Aleksand'r Puškin's life and works, and the influence of Rossini on Puškin. Russia: St. Petersburg. 1799-1837. Lang.: Eng.
3943

Puzzler
Performance/production
Comments on Tokyo performances. Japan: Tokyo. 1987. Lang.: Jap.
1964

Pygmalion
Design/technology
Scene designer discusses production of *Pygmalion* in former mechanical workshop. Sweden: Stockholm. 1986. Lang.: Swe.   1595

Performance/production
Collection of newspaper reviews by New York theatre critics. USA: New York, NY. 1987. Lang.: Eng.   2311

Collection of newspaper reviews by New York theatre critics. USA: New York, NY. 1987. Lang.: Eng.   2320

Plays/librettos/scripts
Shaw's ideas on directorial interpretation in *Pygmalion*. UK-England. 1894-1949. Lang.: Eng.   2768

Visual aspects of *Pygmalion* related to its theme. UK-England. 1914. Lang.: Eng.   2782

Shaw's use of the audience to help create his play *Pygmalion*. UK-England. 1914. Lang.: Eng.   2796

QRs and AIs Clearly State
Performance/production
Collection of newspaper reviews by London theatre critics. UK-England: London. 1986. Lang.: Eng.   2076

Qu'ils crèvent les artists
SEE
Niech sczezną artyści.

Quaigh Theatre (New York, NY)
Institutions
News of various theatres. USA: New York, NY. 1987. Lang.: Eng.
579

Que No Usan Smoking, Los (Non-Smokers, The)
Plays/librettos/scripts
The Non-Smokers by Gianfrancesco Guarnieri. Mexico: Mexico City. 1982-1987. Lang.: Spa.   2697

Queen Elizabeth Hall Theatre (London)
Performance/production
Collection of newspaper reviews by London theatre critics. UK-England: London. 1987. Lang.: Eng.   2245

Queen Elizabeth Theatre (Vancouver, BC)
Performance/production
Carmen presented at Expo '86. Canada: Vancouver, BC. 1986. Lang.: Eng.   3751

Queen of Spades
SEE
Pique Dame.

Queen's Theatre (London)
Performance/production
Collection of newspaper reviews by London theatre critics. UK-England: London. 1986. Lang.: Eng.   2134

Collection of newspaper reviews by London theatre critics. UK-England: London. 1987. Lang.: Eng.   2199

Collection of newspaper reviews by London theatre critics. UK-England: London. 1987. Lang.: Eng.   2251

Ques, Bonaventura
Performance/production
Exhibition catalogue: popular theatre in Catalan. France. 1415-1987. Lang.: Cat, Fre.   1750

Questa sera si recita a soggetto (Tonight We Improvise)
Performance/production
'Showing' is an essential part of all acting. Europe. 1590-1987. Lang.: Eng.   1746

Realism — cont'd

Research/historiography
Views of the literary relationship between William Archer and Henrik Ibsen. UK-England. 1889-1919. Lang.: Eng.   3013

Theory/criticism
The issue of new ideas in contemporary theatre. Mexico: Mexico City. 1987. Lang.: Spa.   3056

Realistické divadlo Z. Nejedlého (Prague)

Performance/production
Miroslav Krobot directs Steigerwald's *Dobové tance (Period Dances)*, Nejedlý Realistic Theatre. Czechoslovakia: Prague. 1987. Lang.: Cze.   770

Reams, Lee Roy

Performance/production
Career of actor Lee Roy Reams. USA: New York, NY. 1987. Lang.: Eng.   3661

Reaney, James

Plays/librettos/scripts
Critical analysis of James Reaney's *Three Desks*. Canada. 1960-1977. Lang.: Eng.   2477

New Canadian drama: non-realistic, anti-naturalistic. Canada. 1983-1984. Lang.: Eng.   2482

Rebel in Paradise

Performance/production
Collection of newspaper reviews of London theatre critics. UK-England: London. 1987. Lang.: Eng.   2273

Rebel!

Performance/production
Collection of newspaper reviews by London theatre critics. UK-England: London. 1986. Lang.: Eng.   2067

Rebels, The by Ignác Nagy

SEE
Pártütők, A.

Reckless

Plays/librettos/scripts
Collaboration between playwright Craig Lucas and director Norman Rene. USA: New York, NY. 1985-1987. Lang.: Eng.   1183

Reconstruction, performance

Institutions
Pirandello's experiences as director of the Teatro d'Arte. Italy. 1924-1928. Lang.: Ita.   549

Performance spaces
Reconstructs processional route of *Corpus Christi* performances. England: York. 1399-1569. Lang.: Eng.   3329

Performance/production
Uday Shankar's translation of Indian dance for Western audiences. India. France: Paris. UK-England: London. 1924-1940. Lang.: Eng.   1461

Millicent Hodson speaks about how she managed to reconstruct Nižinskij's *Le sacre du printemps*. USA: Los Angeles, CA. 1913-1987. Lang.: Swe.   1473

Interview with Mary Arbenz on the original production of *Mourning Becomes Electra*. USA: New York, NY. 1927. Lang.: Eng.   2355

Christmas pantomime *The Miracle* directed by Max Reinhardt. UK-England: London. 1911. Lang.: Eng.   3236

Development of Wagner's *Die Meistersinger von Nürnberg*. South Africa, Republic of: Cape Town. Germany, West: Munich. 1868-1987. Lang.: Eng.   3816

Theory/criticism
Reconstruction of Shakespeare in performance. USA. 1987. Lang.: Eng.   1358

Reconstruction, theatre

Institutions
Difficulty in obtaining funding for theatre building repair. Ireland: Dublin, Cork. UK-Ireland: Belfast. 1965-1984. Lang.: Eng.   545

Performance spaces
Preservation and maintenance of cultural sites in Prague. Czechoslovakia: Prague. 1987. Lang.: Eng.   630

East German exhibition at Prague Quadrennial '87: Gold medal for theatre reconstruction exhibit. Germany, East: Berlin, East. 1742-1986. Lang.: Hun.   636

History of Teatro La Fenice's construction and reconstruction. Italy: Venice. 1787-1976. Lang.: Ita.   652

Rebuilding theatres constructed in the 1960s. USA. 1960-1986. Lang.: Eng.   702

Red Kettle (Dublin)

Training
Funding for youth theatre in Ireland. Ireland. 1979-1987. Lang.: Eng.   1381

Red Noses

Plays/librettos/scripts
Red Noses as Peter Barnes's response to Shaw's *Saint Joan*. UK-England. 1924-1985. Lang.: Eng.   2770

Interview with playwright Peter Barnes. UK-England. USA. 1987. Lang.: Eng.   2818

Red'kin, P.

Plays/librettos/scripts
Historical themes in recent plays by M. Vartolomeev, P. Red'kin and P. Pavlovskij. USSR. 1980-1987. Lang.: Eng.   2954

Redfarn, Roger

Performance/production
Collection of newspaper reviews by London theatre critics. UK-England: London. 1986. Lang.: Eng.   2126

Redgrave, Corin

Performance/production
Collection of newspaper reviews by London theatre critics. UK-England: London. 1986. Lang.: Eng.   2071

Collection of newspaper reviews by London theatre critics. UK-England: London. 1987. Lang.: Eng.   2181

Reed, Allison

Performance/production
Four approaches to the role of Sally Bowles in *Cabaret*. USA: New York, NY. Germany. 1966-1987. Lang.: Eng.   968

Rees, Roger

Performance/production
Collection of newspaper reviews by London theatre critics. UK-England: London. 1986. Lang.: Eng.   2122

Rees, Roland

Performance/production
Collection of newspaper reviews by London theatre critics. UK-England: London. 1986. Lang.: Eng.   2085

Collection of newspaper reviews by London theatre critics. UK-England: London. 1986. Lang.: Eng.   2162

Collection of newspaper reviews by London theatre critics. UK-England: London. 1987. Lang.: Eng.   2192

Collection of newspaper reviews by London theatre critics. UK-England: London. 1987. Lang.: Eng.   2229

Reference materials

SEE ALSO
Classed Entries.

Administration
Comprehensive guide to establishing and running a box office. USA: New York, NY. 1980. Lang.: Eng.   126

Performance/production
Directory of London productions. UK-England: London. 1837-1901. Lang.: Eng.   2300

Reflections on Crooked Walking

Performance/production
Ann Mortifee, singer, songwriter, performer. Canada: Vancouver, BC, Toronto, ON. 1982. Lang.: Eng.   1714

Reformer, The

SEE
Reformátor, A.

Reg

Performance/production
Collection of newspaper reviews by London theatre critics. UK-England: London. 1987. Lang.: Eng.   2260

Regard of Flight, The

Performance/production
Collection of newspaper reviews by New York theatre critics. USA: New York, NY. 1987. Lang.: Eng.   2322

Theory/criticism
Physical comedy in high-tech society. USA. 1987. Lang.: Eng.   1349

Regents College Theatre (London)

Performance/production
Collection of newspaper reviews by London theatre critics. UK-England: London. 1987. Lang.: Eng.   2190

Regional theatre

Administration
Italian government subsidy of theatre. Italy. 1970-1985. Lang.: Fre.   28

Development of Korean regional theatre. Korea. 1970-1979. Lang.: Kor.   32

Findings of bankruptcy expert Kenneth Cork on the state of Britain's theatre. UK-England. 1985-1986. Lang.: Eng.   47

Regional theatre — cont'd

Rule books and employment contracts for summer stock. USA. 1987. Lang.: Eng. 73

Current trends and future of summer stock companies. USA. 1985. Lang.: Eng. 121

Opposition to Equity National Theatre plan in favor of regional theatre. USA. 1985. Lang.: Eng. 132

Philip Arnoult, founding director of the Baltimore Theatre Project, and his search for new works. USA: Baltimore, MD. 1971-1987. Lang.: Eng. 157

Production sharing among non-profit theatres in effort to develop new works. USA. 1987. Lang.: Eng. 255

Design/technology
Georgian scenography—Brecht's influences. USSR. 1960-1987. Lang.: Rus. 492

Institutions
Regional theatre directors encourage new relationships between Latin American and U.S. artists. Colombia: Bogotá. 1948-1987. Lang.: Eng. 526

News for playwrights about regional theatre activities. USA. 1987. Lang.: Eng. 580

Meetings of various Dramatists' Guild committees, members' plays in production. USA: New York, NY. 1987. Lang.: Eng. 584

Six books that discuss the origins and development of different American regional theatres. USA: Cleveland, OH, Los Angeles, CA, Houston, TX, Detroit, MI, Ashland, OR, Montgomery, AL. 1987. Lang.: Eng. 612

Survey of southeastern theatre organizations. USA. 1987. Lang.: Eng. 615

Trends in regional theatre. Norway. 1971-1982. Lang.: Eng. 1626

Present and future of Teatre Lliure. Spain-Catalonia: Barcelona. 1976-1986. Lang.: Cat. 1633

Gagnef Teaterförening's production of a play based on local history. Sweden: Gagnef. 1975-1987. Lang.: Swe. 1644

Performance spaces
History and technical data on Pittsburgh's Public Theatre. USA: Pittsburgh, PA. 1975-1987. Lang.: Eng. 686

Performance/production
Development of Azerbaijani theatre. Azerbaijan. 1875-1925. Lang.: Rus. 723

Director discusses the needs of regional theatres. Hungary. 1986-1987. Lang.: Hun. 811

Theatre productions in Southwest England. UK-England: Bristol. 1987. Lang.: Eng. 903

Review of theatre in the South of England. UK-England: Salisbury. 1987. Lang.: Eng. 911

Review of repertory theatre in Northern England. UK-England: Liverpool. 1987. Lang.: Eng. 912

Review of productions in the Midlands region. UK-England. 1987. Lang.: Eng. 915

Ukrainian theatrical process. Ukraine. 1970-1979. Lang.: Rus. 923

Overview of Soviet Ukrainian theatre. Ukraine. 1917-1987. Lang.: Ukr. 924

Review of several productions in New York. USA: New York, NY. 1987. Lang.: Eng. 953

Decentralization of American theatre. USA. 1960-1980. Lang.: Eng. 958

Los Angeles theatre performances reviewed. USA: Los Angeles, CA. 1987. Lang.: Eng. 961

Director Mary Robinson's career in regional theatre. USA. 1976-1987. Lang.: Eng. 976

History of Nachičevan theatre. USSR. 1900-1987. Lang.: Rus. 1016

Development of ballet in Azerbaijan. Azerbaijan. 1920-1980. Lang.: Rus. 1431

Harlekin's efforts to involve youth in amateur theatre. Sweden: Landskrona. 1982-1987. Lang.: Swe. 2022

Background on Landskronapågen (The Boy from Landskrona). Sweden: Landskrona. 1982-1987. Lang.: Swe. 2024

Classical theatre is diminishing in the provinces due to financial cutbacks. UK-England: London, Liverpool. UK-Scotland: Edinburgh. 1987. Lang.: Eng. 2301

Soviet dramaturgy on the Ukrainian stage. Ukraine. 1917-1987. Lang.: Rus. 2310

Bibliographic index of Moldavian drama. USSR. 1917-1960. Lang.: Rus. 2372

Events of Moldavian theatre history. USSR. 1920-1970. Lang.: Rus. 2387

Theatre-performance culture of Rus'. Russia. 1600-1899. Lang.: Rus. 3265

Goodman Theatre's series 'Celebration of Genius'. USA: Chicago, IL. 1986-1987. Lang.: Eng. 3409

Acting in musical drama. USSR. 1920-1970. Lang.: Rus. 3414

History of Ujgur musical drama. USSR. 1920-1987. Lang.: Rus. 3415

Overview of Latvian opera. Latvia. 1913-1982. Lang.: Rus. 3810

Bay Area opera companies. USA: San Francisco, CA. 1900-1987. Lang.: Eng. 3842

History of Turkmenian opera. USSR. 1900-1987. Lang.: Rus. 3865

Materials on traditional Ukrainian folk puppet theatre. Ukraine. 1800-1987. Lang.: Ukr. 3984

Plays/librettos/scripts
Directory of institutional theatres: aimed at playwrights. USA. 1987. Lang.: Eng. 1163

Roadside Theatre's production of Leaving Egypt. USA: Whitesburg, KY. Lang.: Eng. 1170

Index of theatrical manuscripts from Roussillon written in Catalan. France. 1696-1841. Lang.: Cat. 2568

Ukrainian Romantic drama. Ukraine. 1830-1889. Lang.: Rus. 2833

Scarce attention paid to national dramaturgy by Ukrainian theatres. Ukraine. 1980-1987. Lang.: Rus. 2834

The many genres of Ukrainian theatre. Ukraine. 1920-1929. Lang.: Rus. 2835

Research for An American Journey produced by Milwaukee Repertory. USA: Milwaukee, WI. 1978-1987. Lang.: Eng. 2862

History of dramaturgy in Karakalpak ASSR. USSR. 1917-1987. Lang.: Rus. 2938

Epic themes in Ukrainian opera. Ukraine. 1920-1969. Lang.: Rus. 3931

Reference materials
Catalogue of Valencian playtexts available at libraries of Barcelona. Spain: Valencia, Barcelona. Lang.: Cat. 2975

Relation to other fields
Role of Communist Party in Lithuanian theatre. Lithuania. 1966-1980. Lang.: Rus. 1248

Claque Theatre, a professional provincial ensemble. Switzerland: Baden. 1968-1987. Lang.: Ger. 3001

Research/historiography
Expansion, diversification and artistic innovation in the American theatre. USA. 1961-1986. Lang.: Eng. 1302

Overview of two and a half decades of American theatre. USA. 1937-1961. Lang.: Eng. 1303

Theory/criticism
Genres of Uzbek musical drama. USSR. 1917-1987. Lang.: Rus. 3423

Regulations
The status quo of audio-visual documentation. Europe. 1986. Lang.: Ger. 3198

Administration
Role of the Master of the Revels as censor. England: London. 1662-1737. Lang.: Eng. 22

New immigration ruling affects theatre workers. USA. 1987. Lang.: Eng. 58

National Actors' Equity conference. USA: New York, NY. 1985. Lang.: Eng. 63

Playwrights' opinion on showcase 'Letter of Agreement and Tiered Code'. USA: New York, NY. 1985. Lang.: Eng. 64

New immigration law and its effect on employment. USA: New York, NY. 1987. Lang.: Eng. 79

Exchange of British and American artists. USA: New York, NY. UK-England. 1982. Lang.: Eng. 84

Meeting of LORT member organizations to create stronger liaisons. USA: New York, NY, Chicago, IL. 1984. Lang.: Eng. 85

Arbitration of conversion rights dispute. USA: New York, NY. 1982. Lang.: Eng. 86

Granting permission for filming and recording productions under Equity contracts. USA: New York, NY. 1982. Lang.: Eng. 88

Regulations — cont'd

Tax regulations for performers working out of town. USA: New York, NY. 1982. Lang.: Eng. 103

Stage managers represented on Actors' Equity Council. USA: New York, NY. 1982. Lang.: Eng. 104

Actors' Equity case against Lyric Dinner Theatre. USA: La Mesa, CA. 1987. Lang.: Eng. 106

Ratification of amendment allowing stage managers on Actors' Equity Council. USA: New York, NY. 1982. Lang.: Eng. 108

Illness of star rule arbitrated *re*: Richard Harris in *Camelot*. USA: New York, NY. 1983. Lang.: Eng. 115

Advisory Committee on Chorus Affairs and Equity devise procedures for chorus calls. USA: New York, NY. 1983. Lang.: Eng. 117

Actors' Equity plans National Theatre project. USA. 1985. Lang.: Eng. 125

New York City's political structure, support of the arts. USA: New York, NY. 1987. Lang.: Eng. 141

1986-87 US legislation pending and approved by congress. USA. 1985-1987. Lang.: Eng. 142

Report on Equity League Welfare Fund program. USA. 1985. Lang.: Eng. 147

Evaluation of volunteers in an arts organization. USA. 1987. Lang.: Eng. 148

Comprehensive guide to play production. USA: New York, NY. 1987. Lang.: Eng. 150

Protecting rights of Actors' Equity members who appear in Off-off Broadway shows. USA: New York, NY. 1966-1982. Lang.: Eng. 156

Laws governing music and performance piracy. USA: New York, NY. 1954-1982. Lang.: Eng. 162

Tax Reform Act of 1986 and how it affects theatre professionals. USA. 1987. Lang.: Eng. 166

Changes in tax laws affect Actors' Equity members. USA: New York, NY. 1982. Lang.: Eng. 170

Legal issues of record rental and copyright infringement. USA. 1964-1987. Lang.: Eng. 176

Legal ramifications and remedies for artists whose work is fake or forged. USA. 1986. Lang.: Eng. 190

Customs regulations over imports. USA. 1986-1987. Lang.: Eng. 198

Diversity of Letter of Agreement theatres that operate in New York City. USA: New York, NY. 1987. Lang.: Eng. 204

Historical look at the Copyright Act. USA. 1984. Lang.: Eng. 206

Trademark protection as related to merchandising. USA. 1987. Lang.: Eng. 209

Aspects of paying for works in the public domain. USA: New York, NY. 1983. Lang.: Eng. 213

Legislative remedies for home video recordings of copyrighted works. USA: Los Angeles, CA. 1980-1982. Lang.: Eng. 224

Fair use standards of the Copyright Act of 1976. USA. 1976-1984. Lang.: Eng. 229

Problems associated with the deregulation of cable television. USA: New York, NY. 1934-1982. Lang.: Eng. 233

Instructions for Actors' Equity members regarding new regulations in unemployment. USA: New York, NY. 1982. Lang.: Eng. 240

Legal difficulties facing producers who present foreign artists and dance troupes. USA. 1987. Lang.: Eng. 244

Obtaining tax-exempt status as a not-for-profit arts organization. USA. 1982. Lang.: Eng. 246

Growth and decline of theatrical activity. Arabic countries. 1938-1985. Lang.: Fre. 1511

Actress Vesleøy Haslund fights termination from the National Theatre. Norway: Oslo. 1979-1982. Lang.: Eng. 1522

Copyright protection of live broadcasts. USA. 1976-1987. Lang.: Eng. 3086

Public performance exemptions from copyright liability. USA. 1976-1987. Lang.: Eng. 3088

Enforcing restrictions on blacked-out sports events. USA. 1950-1987. Lang.: Eng. 3090

Title disputes over WPA prints. USA. 1935-1987. Lang.: Eng. 3091

Suggestion that South African Broadcasting Company improve broadcasting standards. South Africa, Republic of. 1987. Lang.: Eng. 3106

Arguments for and against source licensing. USA. 1940-1987. Lang.: Eng. 3107

Recent court decision over the IRS tax laws affecting writers' deductions. USA. 1987. Lang.: Eng. 3241

Design/technology

Designer examines regulations and restrictions imposed on German theatre. Germany, West: Munich. 1982. Lang.: Eng. 328

Survey of theatrical fog machines. USA. 1987. Lang.: Eng. 395

Dimmer standards developed by the United States Institute for Theatre Technology. USA. 1986. Lang.: Eng. 458

Performance spaces

Providing access to the handicapped in existing theatres. USA. 1987. Lang.: Eng. 693

Relation to other fields

Artists and writers affected by political decisions. China, People's Republic of. 1987. Lang.: Eng. 1226

Discussion by theatre women on management, social security. Switzerland. 1987. Lang.: Ger. 1253

Actors' Equity's affirmative action program. USA: New York, NY. 1982. Lang.: Eng. 1261

International exchange in the performing arts. USA. 1985. Lang.: Eng. 1276

Protest of US Immigration and Naturalization Service policies by American presenting organizations. USA. 1986. Lang.: Eng. 1282

Régy, Claude

Performance/production

Productions by directors Patrice Chéreau, Claude Régy, Ariane Mnouchkine. France. 1980-1987. Lang.: Rus. 792

Directorial style of Claude Régy. France. 1955-1987. Lang.: Fre. 1762

Rehearsal

Performance/production

Two aspects of Stanislavskij's work: physical comedy, rehearsal process. USSR: Moscow. 1933-1988. Lang.: Ger. 2380

Reich, Carina

Performance/production

Mime troupe Panopticon. Sweden: Stockholm. 1985-1987. Lang.: Swe. 3226

Reid, Christina

Plays/librettos/scripts

Christina Reid's *Tea in a China Cup*: a woman's view of Belfast. UK-Ireland: Belfast. 1983-1987. Lang.: Eng. 2831

Training

Current state of Northern Ireland's young theatre community. UK-Ireland. 1987. Lang.: Eng. 1387

Reid, Graham

Plays/librettos/scripts

Avoidance of political themes in drama of Northern Ireland. UK-Ireland. 1979-1987. Lang.: Eng. 2830

Reid, Kate

Performance/production

Critique of the 1984 Broadway production of *Death of a Salesman*. USA: New York, NY. 1984. Lang.: Eng. 2330

Reidy, Gabrielle

Performance/production

Collection of newspaper reviews by London theatre critics. UK-England: London. 1987. Lang.: Eng. 2242

Reigen (Round)

Basic theatrical documents

Catalan translation of Arthur Schnitzler's *Reigen (Round)*. 1862-1931. Lang.: Cat. 1541

Reilly, Charles Nelson

Performance/production

Collection of newspaper reviews by New York theatre critics. USA: New York, NY. 1987. Lang.: Eng. 2325

Reinhardt, Max

Performance/production

Biography of Max Reinhardt. Germany. 1873-1943. Lang.: Rus. 1770

Reviews of major Berlin performances. Germany: Berlin. 1889-1933. Lang.: Ger. 1772

Christmas pantomime *The Miracle* directed by Max Reinhardt. UK-England: London. 1911. Lang.: Eng. 3236

Theory/criticism

Reconstruction of Shakespeare in performance. USA. 1987. Lang.: Eng. 1358

Reiter-Soffer, Domy

Performance/production

Overview of Dublin dance season. Ireland: Dublin. 1987. Lang.: Eng. 1408

Relapse, The
Plays/librettos/scripts
Themes of home and homelessness in plays of Cibber and Vanbrugh. England. 1696. Lang.: Eng.   2525

Relatively Speaking
Performance/production
Collection of newspaper reviews by London theatre critics. UK-England: London. 1986. Lang.: Eng.   2081

Releevo
Performance/production
Collection of newspaper reviews by London theatre critics. UK-England: London. 1987. Lang.: Eng.   2252

Religion
Administration
Growth and decline of theatrical activity. Arabic countries. 1938-1985. Lang.: Fre.   1511
Vatican court's withdrawal from festival promotion under Sixtus V. Italy: Rome. 1585-1595. Lang.: Ita.   3240

Design/technology
Use and evolution of masks. Lang.: Ita.   299

Performance/production
Ritual origins of Korean theatre. Korea. 57 B.C.-935 A.D. Lang.: Kor.   849
Comparison of Samoan healing ritual and village theatre. Samoa. 1884-1980. Lang.: Eng.   881
Creative self-knowledge and the mystical path of actors. UK-England: London. USA. 1977-1987. Lang.: Eng.   900
Han Puly, Korean exorcism dance. Korea. 1500-1987. Lang.: Kor.   1462
Performances of *nō* plays by priests and description of a new play. Japan: Hiraizumi. 1987. Lang.: Eng.   1501
Ritual and theatrical nature of TV evangelism. USA. 1987. Lang.: Eng.   3210
Florentine festivals honoring St. John. Italy: Florence. 1000-1926. Lang.: Ita.   3261
History of Bernese carnival. Switzerland: Berne. 1416-1879. Lang.: Ger.   3298
Description of annual *On-matsuri* festival at the Kasuga Wakamiya shrine. Japan: Nara. 1136-1987. Lang.: Eng.   3331
Description of Easter processions. Spain: Puente Genil. 1660-1987. Lang.: Eng.   3332

Plays/librettos/scripts
On a theatrical manifesto of Simone Maria Poggi. Italy. 1700-1749. Lang.: Ita.   1140
Biblical influences in *King Lear, Hamlet, Othello* and *Macbeth*. Lang.: Eng.   2426
Shakespeare's use of formal self-referential oaths. England. 1594-1616. Lang.: Eng.   2552
Self-referentiality and kinds of space in plays of John Marston. England: London. 1553-1608. Lang.: Eng.   2559
Christian thought in Thomas Murphy's *The Gigli Concert*. Ireland. 1983. Lang.: Eng.   2653
Comparison of Pirandello's *Enrico Quarto (Henry IV)* and Shakespeare's *Hamlet*. Italy. England. 1580-1936. Lang.: Chi.   2680
Religion in Pielmeier's *Agnes of God* and Shaffer's *Equus*. North America. 1973-1980. Lang.: Eng.   2710
David and Toni Dueck's docudrama about their Mennonite heritage. Canada: Winnipeg, MB. 1985. Lang.: Eng.   3175
Polanski, Welles and Kurosawa's versions of Shakespeare's *Macbeth*. USA. Japan. UK-England. 1948-1971. Lang.: Eng.   3183
The Chinese opera form *Nou Hsi* and its characteristics. China. 900. Lang.: Chi.   3544
Wagner's obsession with Jews and Judaism. Germany. 1813-1882. Lang.: Eng.   3905

Reference materials
Influences on development of medieval theatre. Europe. 1000-1400. Lang.: Eng.   1201

Relation to other fields
Analysis of the role of tradition in theatrical forms of different cultures. Asia. Africa. 1985. Lang.: Fre.   1218
Situation of Chinese intellectuals during the Yuan Dynasty. China. 1279-1368. Lang.: Chi.   1225
Interview with founders of the Charabanc Theatre Company. UK-Ireland. 1970-1987. Lang.: Eng.   1260

Essays on the theme of marriage in literature. England. Norway. 1300-1985. Lang.: Eng.   1425
African-American theatre compared to Caribbean and African theatre. Barbados. Bermuda. Nigeria. 1987. Lang.: Eng.   2980
Interview with poet and activist Haki R. Madhubuti (Don L. Lee). USA: Detroit, MI. Africa. Israel. 1942-1985. Lang.: Eng.   3008
Church records related to Morris dancing. England: Great Marlow. 1593-1674. Lang.: Eng.   3280
Popular entertainment in Valencian region from December to March. Spain-Catalonia: Valencia. 1418-1981. Lang.: Cat.   3337
Comparison between Wagner and Tolstoy. Russia. Germany. 1860-1908. Lang.: Eng.   3944

Religious theatre
Audience
Assembly, composition, accommodation and response of spectators to civic and religious plays. France. 1450-1550. Lang.: Eng.   1534

Design/technology
Scenic representations of Hell. Italy. France. 1300-1399. Lang.: Ita.   349
Design aspects of *The Glory of Easter*: computerized lighting, lasers and pyrotechnics. USA. 1982. Lang.: Eng.   387

Performance/production
History and description of a performance of *Cavittunatakam*, a drama recounting lives of the saints. India: Kerala. 1984. Lang.: Eng.   1480
Church condemnation of Roman *ludi*, creative impulse behind medieval drama. Europe. 160-1578. Lang.: Eng.   1745
Role of the director in the Lucerne Passion play. Switzerland: Lucerne. 1453-1616. Lang.: Eng.   2030
Adaptation of Nativity puppet play. Italy. 1651-1987. Lang.: Eng.   4001

Reference materials
Influences on development of medieval theatre. Europe. 1000-1400. Lang.: Eng.   1201

Relation to other fields
History of puppet Nativity plays. Hungary. 1877-1967. Lang.: Hun.   3994

Research/historiography
Research methods on origins and tradition of liturgical drama. Germany. 1000-1400. Lang.: Ita.   3010

Remembrance
Performance/production
Collection of newspaper reviews by London theatre critics. UK-England: London. 1987. Lang.: Eng.   2277

Remenyik, Zsigmond
Performance/production
Reviews: *A vörös postakocsi (The Red Mail Coach)* by Gyula Krúdy, staged by Dezső Kapás and *Az atyai ház (The Paternal Roof)* by Zsigmond Remenyik, staged by Péter Lener. Hungary: Veszprém, Nyíregyháza. 1986. Lang.: Hun.   1821

Remizov, Aleksei
Basic theatrical documents
Russian symbolist plays and essays. USSR. 1880-1986. Lang.: Eng.   1584

Renaissance theatre
SEE ALSO
Geographical-Chronological Index under Europe 1400-1600, France 1500-1700, Italy 1400-1600, Spain 1400-1600.

Performance/production
Essays on Italian Renaissance theatre. Italy. 1400-1500. Lang.: Ita.   822

Plays/librettos/scripts
Role of the *commedia umanistica* in the intellectual life of Renaissance Venice. Italy: Venice. 1400-1500. Lang.: Ita.   1135
Evaluation of *Westward Ho!* and *Northward Ho!* by Thomas Dekker and John Webster. England. 1605. Lang.: Eng.   2509

Relation to other fields
Psychological effect of Ben Jonson's family life on his writings. England. 1602-1604. Lang.: Eng.   1232
Overview of French literature including theatre. France. 800-1700. Lang.: Ita.   2990

Theory/criticism
Iconography and terminology in Renaissance drama. 1987. Lang.: Eng.   1308
Classical allusion and moral significance of court masques. Europe. 1982. Lang.: Eng.   3328

Renaissance Theatre Company (London)

Administration

Interim report on the Renaissance Theatre Company. UK-England: London. 1987. Lang.: Eng.   54

Performance/production

Collection of newspaper reviews by London theatre critics. UK-England: London. 1987. Lang.: Eng.   2228

Rencz, Antal

Performance/production

Performances of *Oliver* staged by György Korcsmáros, Antol Rencz and Imre Halasi. Hungary: Budapest, Békéscsaba, Zalaegerszeg. 1986. Lang.: Hun.   3632

Rene, Norman

Administration

Financial challenges of four former artistic directors. USA. 1981-1987. Lang.: Eng.   239

Performance/production

Collection of newspaper reviews by New York theatre critics. USA: New York, NY. 1987. Lang.: Eng.   2319

Plays/librettos/scripts

Collaboration between playwright Craig Lucas and director Norman Rene. USA: New York, NY. 1985-1987. Lang.: Eng.   1183

Collaboration of Craig Lucas and Norman Rene on *Blue Window* and *Three Postcards*. USA. 1987. Lang.: Eng.   1184

Renée

Plays/librettos/scripts

Playwright Renée discusses her plays. New Zealand. 1982-1987. Lang.: Eng.   2702

Renfro, Nancy

Design/technology

Puppetmaking projects for children. USA. 1987. Lang.: Eng.   3963

Renick, Kyle

Administration

Financial considerations in transferring *Steel Magnolias* to an Off Broadway theatre. USA: New York, NY. 1987. Lang.: Eng.   226

Renoir, Jean

Performance/production

Influence of filmmaker Jean Renoir's techniques in the theatre. France. 1987. Lang.: Eng.   795

Renovation

Performance spaces

Lighting renovation in an amphitheatre and arena. USA: Montgomery, AL. 1987. Lang.: Eng.   3246

Renovation, theatre

Design/technology

Pál Tolnay's original proposal for modernization of the lighting system at National Theatre. Hungary: Budapest. 1957. Lang.: Hun.   340

Performance spaces

The modern acoustics of Toronto's Thomson Hall. Canada: Toronto, ON. 1982. Lang.: Eng.   628

Design and construction considerations: renovation of József Attila Theatre. Hungary: Budapest. 1985-1986. Lang.: Hun.   640

Details of the renovation of József Attila Theatre. Hungary: Budapest. 1985-1986. Lang.: Hun.   644

Theatre renovation plans and survey. Hungary. 1980-1986. Lang.: Hun.   645

History of Teatro La Fenice's construction and reconstruction. Italy: Venice. 1787-1976. Lang.: Ita.   652

Details of several theatre renovation projects. USA. 1987. Lang.: Eng.   679

Restoration of Ohio, State and Palace Theatres in Playhouse Square. USA: Cleveland, OH. 1964-1986. Lang.: Eng.   681

Architect Roger Morgan discusses plans for restoring seven Broadway theatres. USA: New York, NY. 1984. Lang.: Eng.   683

Major expansion of the facilities at the Omaha Community Playhouse. USA: Omaha, NE. 1984-1987. Lang.: Eng.   699

Renovations at the Bayfront Center. USA: St. Petersburg, FL. 1960-1987. Lang.: Eng.   700

Renovation of the Seattle Center Playhouse into the new home of the Intiman Theatre. USA: Seattle, WA. 1983-1987. Lang.: Eng.   705

Proposal for renovations of Broadway theatres. USA: New York, NY. 1984. Lang.: Eng.   713

Renovations and new directions for the Chautauqua Opera Company. USA: Chautauqua, NY. 1928-1987. Lang.: Eng.   3738

Performances, workshops for children in converted church hall. UK-England: London. 1987. Lang.: Eng.   4009

Performances spaces

History and renovations of City Center. USA: New York, NY. 1924-1983. Lang.: Eng.   1094

Renshaw, Christopher

Performance/production

Collection of newspaper reviews by London theatre critics. UK-England: London. 1987. Lang.: Eng.   2234

Repertory

Administration

Theatrical experiment and the director of literary affairs. USSR. 1986-1988. Lang.: Rus.   266

Problems of the enhancement of literary director's prestige. USSR. 1980-1987. Lang.: Rus.   270

Ways of developing repertory. USSR. 1980-1987. Lang.: Rus.   1525

Problem of lack of information about contemporary dramaturgy. USSR: Latvia. 1986-1988. Lang.: Rus.   1526

Playwright Michajl Roščin on repertory under perestrojka. USSR. 1986-1988. Lang.: Rus.   1527

Kazach repertory and dramaturgy. USSR: Kazachstan. 1980-1987. Lang.: Rus.   1528

Institutions

King's Company under actor-manager John Lowin. England: London. 1576-1653. Lang.: Eng.   1614

Lack of operetta productions by the Canadian Opera Company. Canada: Toronto, ON. 1987. Lang.: Eng.   3724

Performance/production

Classical theatre is diminishing in the provinces due to financial cutbacks. UK-England: London, Liverpool. UK-Scotland: Edinburgh. 1987. Lang.: Eng.   2301

Repertoire and artistic achievement of the Opera Theatre of St. Louis. USA: St. Louis, MO. 1987. Lang.: Eng.   3840

Plays/librettos/scripts

Scarce attention paid to national dramaturgy by Ukrainian theatres. Ukraine. 1980-1987. Lang.: Rus.   2834

Problems of dramaturgy for puppet theatres. USSR. 1980-1987. Lang.: Rus.   3992

Repertory theatre

Design/technology

Gershwin Theatre's accommodation of RSC touring productions. USA: New York, NY. 1984. Lang.: Eng.   420

Challenges of repertory lighting. USA. 1982. Lang.: Eng.   479

Performance/production

Grand Theatre: failed establishment of repertory theatre. Canada: London, ON. 1983-1984. Lang.: Eng.   738

Contemporary opera at Deutsche Staatsoper. Germany, East: Berlin, East. 1945-1987. Lang.: Ger.   3784

Plays/librettos/scripts

Experiments of Moscow Children's Theatre. USSR: Moscow. 1986-1987. Lang.: Rus.   1185

Requiem

Performance/production

Reviews of *Rigoletto*, Lloyd Webber's *Requiem*, *Les Misérables* and the Hungarian Mass of the Tolcsvays. Hungary: Szeged. 1987. Lang.: Hun.   3400

Research tools

Research/historiography

Database manipulation in theatre research. North America. 1987. Lang.: Eng.   1301

Research/historiography

SEE ALSO

Classed Entries.

Performance/production

Documentation on melodramatic acting style. France: Paris. 1800-1830. Lang.: Eng.   791

Millicent Hodson speaks about how she managed to reconstruct Nižinskij's *Le sacre du printemps*. USA: Los Angeles, CA. 1913-1987. Lang.: Swe.   1473

Reference materials

Dissertations in progress in theatre arts. USA. 1987. Lang.: Eng.   1217

Theory/criticism

Evaluation of the present state of theatrical theory and its influence on theatrical practice. Europe. 1985. Lang.: Fre.   3033

Richard III — cont'd

Role of Chorus in Shakespeare's *Henry V*. England. 1599. Lang.:
Eng.   2556

Richards, Lloyd
Administration
Production sharing among non-profit theatres in effort to develop
new works. USA. 1987. Lang.: Eng.   255

Institutions
Current trends in American theatre. USA. 1967-1987. Lang.: Eng.
                                                                              621

Experience of artists working at the O'Neill Theatre Center. USA:
Waterford, CT. 1985-1986. Lang.: Eng.   1655

Performance/production
Collection of newspaper reviews by New York theatre critics. USA:
New York, NY. 1987. Lang.: Eng.   2326

Richards, Martyn
Performance/production
Collection of newspaper reviews by London theatre critics. UK-
England: London. 1986. Lang.: Eng.   2075

Richardson, Kenneth
Institutions
Members of Negro Ensemble Company, New Federal Theatre and
American Place Theatre on artistic agendas. USA: New York, NY.
1987. Lang.: Eng.   592

Richardson, L. Kenneth
Performance/production
George C. Wolfe and L. Kenneth Richardson discuss *The Colored
Museum*. USA: New York, NY, New Brunswick, NJ. 1987. Lang.:
Eng.   2363

Richardson, Toby
Performance/production
Collection of newspaper reviews by London theatre critics. UK-
England. 1987. Lang.: Eng.   2263

Richmond Theatre (London)
Performance/production
Collection of newspaper reviews by London theatre critics. UK-
England: London. 1987. Lang.: Eng.   2260

Richmond, Gillian
Performance/production
Collection of newspaper reviews by London theatre critics. UK-
England: London. 1986. Lang.: Eng.   2056

Rickey, Christine
Performance/production
Collection of newspaper reviews by London theatre critics. UK-
England: London. 1987. Lang.: Eng.   2178

Ricordo, Giulio
Plays/librettos/scripts
Making of Verdi's *Otello*. Italy: Milan. 1862-1879. Lang.: Eng.   3917

Riders to the Sea
Performance/production
Collection of newspaper reviews by London theatre critics. UK-
England: London. 1987. Lang.: Eng.   2277

Ridiculous Theatre Company, The (TRTC, New York, NY)
Institutions
The Ridiculous Theatre Company and its founder Charles Ludlam.
USA: New York, NY. 1965-1987. Lang.: Eng.   1652

Performance/production
Eulogy of actor Charles Ludlam. USA. 1973-1987. Lang.: Eng.   947

Life and works of playwright, director, designer Charles Ludlam.
USA: New York, NY. 1967-1987. Lang.: Eng.   952

Career of actor, director, playwright Charles Ludlam. USA: New
York, NY. 1964-1987. Lang.: Eng.   956

Riel, Louis
Basic theatrical documents
Text of *Le Roitelet (The Kinglet)* by Claude Dorge. Canada:
Montreal, PQ. 1976. Lang.: Fre.   1545

Riga Russian Drama Theatre
SEE
Teat'r Russkoj Dramy.

Rigdon, Kevin
Design/technology
Work of set/lighting designer Kevin Rigdon. USA. 1986. Lang.:
Eng.   400

Rigging
Design/technology
Care and safe use of stage rigging equipment. USA. 1987. Lang.:
Eng.   411

Retrospective of 1960s rigging installation. USA. 1960-1987. Lang.:
Eng.   412

A simultaneous vertical and horizontal travel-fly rigging system.
USA. 1985. Lang.: Eng.   421

Rigging special circus effects for *Barnum*. USA. 1986. Lang.: Eng.
                                                                            3622

Rigler, Lloyd
Performance/production
Profile of Lloyd Rigler, benefactor of the New York City Opera.
USA: New York, NY. 1980-1987. Lang.: Eng.   3852

Rigoletto
Performance/production
Reviews of *Rigoletto*, Lloyd Webber's *Requiem*, *Les Misérables* and
the Hungarian Mass of the Tolcsvays. Hungary: Szeged. 1987. Lang.:
Hun.   3400

Initial recordings of Verdi's operas. Italy. France. USA. 1900-1945.
Lang.: Eng.   3800

Background on Metropolitan radio broadcast performances. USA:
New York, NY. 1987. Lang.: Eng.   3837

Rihm, Wolfgang
Performance/production
Wolfgang Rihm's new opera *Oedipus* staged by Götz Friedrich.
Germany, West: Berlin, West. 1987. Lang.: Swe.   3788

Rijnders, Gerardjan
Institutions
Toneelgroep Amsterdam's theatrical mission in the eighties.
Netherlands: Amsterdam. 1987. Lang.: Dut.   553

Performance/production
Directors Claus Peymann (Burgtheater) and Gerardjan Rijnders
(Toneelgroep). Austria: Vienna. Netherlands: Amsterdam. 1987.
Lang.: Dut.   1681

Riley, Clayton
Plays/librettos/scripts
Interview with playwright Charles Fuller. USA: Philadelphia, PA,
New York, NY. Korea, South. 1959-1987. Lang.: Eng.   2921

Rimini, Giacomo
Performance/production
Initial recordings of Verdi's operas. Italy. France. USA. 1900-1945.
Lang.: Eng.   3800

Ring des Nibelungen, Der
Administration
Filming Wagner's *Der Ring des Nibelungen* at Bayreuth. Germany,
West: Bayreuth. Germany, West: Munich. 1980. Lang.: Eng.   3680

Performance/production
Metropolitan/Deutsche Grammophon recording, Wagner's *Ring*,
conducted by James Levine. USA: New York, NY. 1987. Lang.:
Eng.   3114

Production history of *Der Ring des Nibelungen*. Germany: Bayreuth.
Italy: Milan. USA: New York, NY. 1876-1987. Lang.: Eng.   3775

Plays/librettos/scripts
Theme of journeys in German theatre and film. Germany. 1970-
1986. Lang.: Fre.   1127

Research/historiography
Influences on Wagner's *Ring* cycle. Germany: Dresden. 1813-1883.
Lang.: Eng.   3948

Ringling Brothers and Barnum & Bailey Circus (Sarasota, FL)
SEE ALSO
Barnum and Bailey Circus.

Ringwood, Gwen Pharis
Institutions
Elizabeth Sterling Haynes and the Little Theatre movement. Canada.
1916-1957. Lang.: Eng.   1603

RINK (Tokyo)
Performance/production
Four Tokyo productions in light of ideas of Betsuyaku Minoru.
Japan: Tokyo. 1987. Lang.: Jap.   1950

Riot Act, The
Performance/production
Collection of newspaper reviews by London theatre critics. UK-
England: London. 1986. Lang.: Eng.   2136

Rise and Fall of the City of Mahagonny
SEE
Aufstieg und Fall der Stadt Mahagonny.

Rise of David Levinsky, The
Performance/production
Collection of newspaper reviews by New York theatre critics. USA:
New York, NY. 1987. Lang.: Eng.   2323

Riverside Studios (London) — cont'd

Collection of newspaper reviews by London theatre critics. UK-England: London. 1987. Lang.: Eng.   2189

Collection of newspaper reviews by London theatre critics. UK-England: London. 1987. Lang.: Eng.   2192

Collection of newspaper reviews by London theatre critics. UK-England: London. 1987. Lang.: Eng.   2198

Collection of newspaper reviews by London theatre critics. UK-England: London. 1987. Lang.: Eng.   2208

Collection of newspaper reviews by London theatre critics. UK-England: London. 1987. Lang.: Eng.   2215

Collection of newspaper reviews by London theatre critics. UK-England: London. 1987. Lang.: Eng.   2228

Collection of newspaper reviews by London theatre critics. UK-England: London. 1987. Lang.: Eng.   2237

Collection of newspaper reviews by London theatre critics. UK-England: London. 1987. Lang.: Eng.   2238

Collection of newspaper reviews by London theatre critics. UK-England: London. 1987. Lang.: Eng.   2253

Collection of newspaper reviews by London theatre critics. UK-England: London. 1987. Lang.: Eng.   2265

Collection of newspaper reviews by London theatre critics. UK-England: London. 1987. Lang.: Eng.   2267

Rivière, Jacques
Plays/librettos/scripts
Study of playwright Paul Claudel based on his letters. France. 1904-1909. Lang.: Fre.   2572

Road
Performance/production
Collection of newspaper reviews by London theatre critics. UK. 1987. Lang.: Eng.   2031

Collection of newspaper reviews by London theatre critics. UK-England: London. 1986. Lang.: Eng.   2078

Collection of newspaper reviews by London theatre critics. UK-England: London. 1986. Lang.: Eng.   2123

Road to Mecca
Administration
Equity's policy on U.S. performances by foreign artists. USA: New York, NY. 1987. Lang.: Eng.   131

Roadside Theatre (Whitesburg, KY)
Institutions
Profile of Roadside Theatre: story-telling, use of folklore. USA. 1971-1983. Lang.: Eng.   599

Survey of southeastern theatre organizations. USA. 1987. Lang.: Eng.   615

Plays/librettos/scripts
Roadside Theatre's production of *Leaving Egypt*. USA: Whitesburg, KY. Lang.: Eng.   1170

Robbins, Carrie
Design/technology
Work and career of costume designer Carrie Robbins. USA. 1966-1986. Lang.: Eng.   385

Robbins, Glyn
Performance/production
Collection of newspaper reviews by London theatre critics. UK-England: London. 1986. Lang.: Eng.   2040

Collection of newspaper reviews by London theatre critics. UK-England: London. 1987. Lang.: Eng.   2231

Collection of newspaper reviews by London theatre critics. UK-England: London. 1987. Lang.: Eng.   2232

Roberts, Denise
Performance/production
Overview of Dublin dance season. Ireland: Dublin. 1987. Lang.: Eng.   1408

Robertson, Alan
Performance/production
Canadian actors and directors discuss their theatre experiences. Canada: Calgary, AB. 1987. Lang.: Eng.   748

Robertson, Michael
Performance/production
Collection of newspaper reviews by London theatre critics. UK-England: London. 1987. Lang.: Eng.   2188

Robertson, Toby
Performance/production
Collection of newspaper reviews by London theatre critics. UK-England: London. 1986. Lang.: Eng.   2079

Collection of newspaper reviews by London theatre critics. UK-England: London. 1986. Lang.: Eng.   2101

Collection of newspaper reviews by London theatre critics. UK-England: London. 1986. Lang.: Eng.   2121

Robinson Crusoe
Plays/librettos/scripts
Essex Evans' adaptations of *Robinson Crusoe* and *Musical Whist*. Australia. 1891-1902. Lang.: Eng.   2439

Robinson, Lennox
Institutions
Playwright Denis Johnston and avant-garde theatre at the Abbey. Ireland: Dublin. 1927-1935. Lang.: Eng.   1619

Plays/librettos/scripts
Irish Literary Renaissance writers' view of America. Ireland. 1900-1930. Lang.: Eng.   2639

Robinson, Mary
Performance/production
Director Mary Robinson's career in regional theatre. USA. 1976-1987. Lang.: Eng.   976

Robinson, Rony
Performance/production
Collection of newspaper reviews by London theatre critics. UK-England: London. 1986. Lang.: Eng.   2039

Collection of newspaper reviews by London theatre critics. UK-England: London. 1986. Lang.: Eng.   2125

Plays/librettos/scripts
Use of oral history material to develop characters and events in plays. UK-England. 1970-1987. Lang.: Eng.   2807

Robinson, Tim
Performance/production
Collection of newspaper reviews by London theatre critics. UK-England: London. 1986. Lang.: Eng.   2140

Robman, Steve
Administration
Financial challenges of four former artistic directors. USA. 1981-1987. Lang.: Eng.   239

Roca i Seguí, Guillem
Plays/librettos/scripts
Analysis of 51 short farces written in Majorca. Spain-Catalonia. 1701-1850. Lang.: Cat.   2731

Rock opera
Design/technology
Rock 'n roll lighting control boards. USA. 1987. Lang.: Eng.   448

Lighting designer Richard Pilbrow's methods. USA: Salt Lake City, UT. 1982. Lang.: Eng.   3388

Institutions
Interview with Mátyás Várkanyi, director of Rock Theatre. Hungary. 1980-1987. Lang.: Hun.   3624

Performance/production
David Bowie's *Glass Spider Tour*. UK-England. 1987. Lang.: Dut.   3270

Rock opera *Drakar och Demoner (Dragons and Demons)* about youth at risk. Sweden: Handen. 1987. Lang.: Swe.   3637

Rock Szinház (Budapest)
Institutions
Interview with Mátyás Várkanyi, director of Rock Theatre. Hungary. 1980-1987. Lang.: Hun.   3624

Performance/production
Miklós Szinetár directs *Les Misérables* at Rock Szinház. Hungary: Budapest. 1987. Lang.: Hun.   3630

Rockaby
Performance/production
Billie Whitelaw's performances in the plays of Samuel Beckett. USA. 1981-1984. Lang.: Eng.   2344

Plays/librettos/scripts
Analysis of text of Samuel Beckett's *Rockaby* as literature and performance piece. USA. 1982. Lang.: Eng.   2884

Theory/criticism
Impact of cinematic technique on plays by Beckett and Duras. France. 1977-1987. Lang.: Eng.   3037

Rockefeller Foundation (New York, NY)
Administration
Relation of government spending to non-profit organizations. USA. 1987. Lang.: Eng.   254

Rocky Horror Show, The
Performance/production
Actor Tim Curry's career. USA. UK-England. 1987. Lang.: Eng.   980

Rod puppets
Design/technology
Puppetmaking projects for children. USA. 1987. Lang.: Eng.   3963
Roda i Fàbregas, Frederic
Performance/production
Collection of theatre reviews by Xavier Fàbregas. Spain-Catalonia. 1969-1972. Lang.: Cat.   2010
Rodgers, Richard
Performance/production
Collection of newspaper reviews by New York theatre critics. USA: New York, NY. 1987. Lang.: Eng.   2323
Rodrigues, Nelson
Performance/production
Examination of modern Brazilian theatre focusing on plays by Nelson Rodrigues. Brazil. 1943-1984. Lang.: Eng.   1688
Rodriguez, Jesusa
Plays/librettos/scripts
Productions exhibit changes in symbolism of the Don Juan myth due to AIDS crisis. USA. 1987. Lang.: Eng.   2845
Rodríguez, José
Institutions
Profile of bilingual theatre company La Compañia de Teatro de Alburquerque. USA: Albuquerque, NM. 1977-1983. Lang.: Eng. 1660
Rogers, David
Performance/production
Collection of newspaper reviews by London theatre critics. UK-England: London. 1986. Lang.: Eng.   2055
Rogers, Steve
Performance/production
View of Lumière & Son's production *Deadwood*. UK-England: London. 1986. Lang.: Eng.   3356
Rogoff, Gordon
Plays/librettos/scripts
Gordon Rogoff is recipient of George Jean Nathan Award. USA: New York, NY. 1931-1987. Lang.: Eng.   2892
Theory/criticism
The work and writings of theatre critics Eric Bentley and Gordon Rogoff. USA. 1946-1987. Lang.: Eng.   3071
Roitelet, Le (Kinglet, The)
Basic theatrical documents
Text of *Le Roitelet (The Kinglet)* by Claude Dorge. Canada: Montreal, PQ. 1976. Lang.: Fre.   1545
Roker, Roxie
Plays/librettos/scripts
Interview with playwright Charles Fuller. USA: Philadelphia, PA, New York, NY. Korea, South. 1959-1987. Lang.: Eng.   2921
Roles
SEE
Characters/roles.
Romains, Jules
Performance/production
Jules Romains' *Knock* directed by Gábor Máté at Csiky Gergely Theatre. Hungary: Kaposvár. 1986. Lang.: Hun.   1917
Roman theatre
SEE ALSO
Geographical-Chronological Index under Roman Republic 509-27 BC, Roman Empire 27 BC-476 AD.
Theory/criticism
Analysis of the writings of Isidore of Seville on ancient Roman and Greek drama. Spain. 560-636. Lang.: Eng.   3059
Romanca (Romance)
Performance/production
The 17th Warsaw theatre conference. Poland: Warsaw. 1987. Lang.: Eng, Fre.   872
Romance of Athlone, The
Plays/librettos/scripts
Analysis of the plays and songs of Irish-American musical theatre star Chauncey Olcott. USA. 1893-1918. Lang.: Eng.   3671
Romans in Britain, The
Plays/librettos/scripts
Interview with playwright Howard Brenton. UK-England. 1975-1987. Lang.: Eng.   2806
Romanticism
SEE ALSO
Geographical-Chronological Index under Europe 1800-1850, France 1810-1857, Germany 1798-1830, Italy 1815-1876, UK 1801-1850.
Design/technology
Aesthetic influences on scene design. England. 1700-1899. Lang.: Eng.   1590

Performance/production
Romantic drama in performance: effect on modern theatre. England. 1700-1987. Lang.: Eng.   1732
Essays on major figures of the Romantic period. Germany. 1795-1830. Lang.: Ger.   1776
Staging of Romantic 'closet dramas'. Scandinavia. 1986-1987. Lang.: Swe.   2004
Plays/librettos/scripts
Female roles and images in the romantic ballet. France. Germany. Russia. 1830-1920. Lang.: Ger.   1455
Structure of Byron's plays. England. 1788-1824. Lang.: Eng.   2542
The paradox and problems of poetry in Romantic theatre. England. 1700-1800. Lang.: Eng.   2557
Ukrainian Romantic drama. Ukraine. 1830-1889. Lang.: Rus.   2833
Romeo and Juliet
Performance/production
Interview with actress Dame Peggy Ashcroft. UK-England. 1935-1964. Lang.: Eng.   899
English Shakespearean productions. UK-England: London, Manchester, Stratford. 1985-1986. Lang.: Eng.   917
Théâtre de la Jeune Lune, its origins and influences. USA: Minneapolis, MN. France: Paris. 1980-1987. Lang.: Eng.   977
Collection of newspaper reviews by London theatre critics. UK-England: London. 1986. Lang.: Eng.   2106
Collection of newspaper reviews by London theatre critics. UK-England: London. 1986. Lang.: Eng.   2135
Collection of newspaper reviews by London theatre critics. UK-England: London. 1987. Lang.: Eng.   2200
Collection of newspaper reviews by London theatre critics. UK-England: London. 1987. Lang.: Eng.   2223
Plays/librettos/scripts
Metadrama, alienation and fantasy in Shakespeare's *Romeo and Juliet*. England. 1595-1596. Lang.: Eng.   2524
Tragic result of utopian ideas in Shakespeare's *Romeo and Juliet*. England. 1595-1596. Lang.: Ger.   2530
Shakespeare's use of formal self-referential oaths. England. 1594-1616. Lang.: Eng.   2552
Romya, Jenny
Performance/production
Collection of newspaper reviews by London theatre critics. UK-England: London. 1986. Lang.: Eng.   2146
Ron, Link
Performance/production
Interview with director Ron Link. USA: New York, NY. 1987. Lang.: Eng.   963
Róna, Viktor
Performance/production
Interview with dancer-choreographer Viktor Róna. Hungary. Norway: Oslo. 1980-1987. Lang.: Hun.   1437
Rondine, La
Plays/librettos/scripts
Floral imagery in the operas of Giacomo Puccini. Italy. 1858-1924. Lang.: Eng.   3926
Ronnie's Doing Well
Performance/production
Collection of newspaper reviews by London theatre critics. UK-England: London. 1987. Lang.: Eng.   2197
Rookery Nook
Performance/production
Collection of newspaper reviews by London theatre critics. UK-England: London. 1986. Lang.: Eng.   2141
Room, The
Performance spaces
Theatre space and theatrical space in theatre from the ancient Greeks to the present. Germany. England. Greece. 400 B.C.-1987 A.D. Lang.: Eng.   635
Plays/librettos/scripts
Characterizations of stage spaces: examples from Brecht, Pinter, Douglas Turner Ward. UK-England. USA. 1947-1987. Lang.: Eng.   2798
Roppeita, Kita
Performance/production
Performances of *nō* plays by priests and description of a new play. Japan: Hiraizumi. 1987. Lang.: Eng.   1501

Rorem, Ned
Performance/production
Golden Fleece, Ltd. bridges classical music, opera and musical theatre. USA: New York, NY. 1987. Lang.: Eng.   3412

Rosa del tiempo, La (Rose of Time, The)
Plays/librettos/scripts
Comparison of the plays *Todo sucede en una noche (It All Happens in One Night)* and *La rosa del tiempo (The Rose of Time)*. Mexico: Mexico City. 1987. Lang.: Spa.   2698

Roščin, Michajl
Administration
Playwright Michajl Roščin on repertory under perestrojka. USSR. 1986-1988. Lang.: Rus.   1527
Performance/production
Overview of 1986-1987 Moscow theatre season. USSR: Moscow. 1986-1987. Lang.: Eng.   1039

Rose, Edward Everett
Plays/librettos/scripts
Irish assimilation in plays of Edward Everett Rose. USA. 1900-1920. Lang.: Eng.   2861

Rose, Michael
Performance/production
Collection of newspaper reviews by New York theatre critics. USA: New York, NY. 1987. Lang.: Eng.   2313

Rose, Richard
Performance/production
Interview with actress Tanja Jacobs. Canada: Toronto, ON. 1987. Lang.: Eng.   727
Summarizes events of Directors' Colloquium. Canada: Calgary, AB. 1987. Lang.: Eng.   728
Toronto directors discuss their training and craft. Canada: Toronto, ON. 1987. Lang.: Eng.   730
Directors' Colloquium: individual directorial techniques. Canada: Calgary, AB. 1987. Lang.: Eng.   743
Canadian actors and directors discuss their theatre experiences. Canada: Calgary, AB. 1987. Lang.: Eng.   748

Rose, Ron
Plays/librettos/scripts
Use of oral history material to develop characters and events in plays. UK-England. 1970-1987. Lang.: Eng.   2807

Rosencrantz and Guildenstern Are Dead
Performance/production
Collection of newspaper reviews by London theatre critics. UK-England: London. 1987. Lang.: Eng.   2214
Collection of newspaper reviews by London theatre critics. UK-England: London. 1987. Lang.: Eng.   2243

Rosenkavalier, Der
Performance/production
Background on Metropolitan radio broadcast performances. USA: New York, NY. 1987. Lang.: Eng.   3837
Plays/librettos/scripts
Musical sources in the operas of Richard Strauss. Germany: Dresden. 1864-1949. Lang.: Eng.   3908

Rosenthal, Manuel
Performance/production
Interview with conductor Manuel Rosenthal. France: Paris. 1904-1987. Lang.: Eng.   3774

Rosenthal, Rachel
Basic theatrical documents
About aging: *L.O.W. in Gaia* by Rachel Rosenthal. USA. 1986. Lang.: Eng.   3341
Relation to other fields
Sexuality and desire in performance. USA. 1987. Lang.: Eng.   1270

Rosmersholm
Performance/production
Collection of newspaper reviews by London theatre critics. UK-England: London. 1987. Lang.: Eng.   2213
Plays/librettos/scripts
Varied approaches to Ibsen's *Rosmersholm*. USA. Norway. 1886-1985. Lang.: Eng.   2923

Rosov, Viktor S.
Plays/librettos/scripts
Autobiographical writings of playwright Viktor Rosov. USSR. 1913-1987. Lang.: Rus.   2962

Ross
Performance/production
Collection of newspaper reviews by London theatre critics. UK-England: London. 1986. Lang.: Eng.   2126

Ross, Bill
Institutions
Actors' Equity Council member Bill Ross receives award. USA: New York, NY. 1985. Lang.: Eng.   571

Ross, Justin
Performance/production
Broadway actors who moonlight in cabaret acts. USA: New York, NY. 1962-1987. Lang.: Eng.   3291

Rossi-Lemeni, Nicola
Performance/production
Singers/teachers Virginia Zeani and Nicola Rossi-Lemeni. Italy. 1920-1987. Lang.: Eng.   3802

Rossini Festival (Pesaro)
Performance/production
Style and authenticity at the Rossini festival. Italy: Pesaro. 1984-1987. Lang.: Eng.   3801

Rossini, Gioacchino
Performance/production
Musical influence of Gioacchino Rossini. 1792-1868. Lang.: Eng.   3396
Review of performances at an assembly of opera ensembles. Hungary: Szeged. 1987. Lang.: Hun.   3796
András Békés directs Rossini's *La Cenerentola* at Szentendrei Teátrum under the title *Hamupipőke*. Hungary: Szentendre. 1987. Lang.: Hun.   3798
Style and authenticity at the Rossini festival. Italy: Pesaro. 1984-1987. Lang.: Eng.   3801
Interview with Dario Fo. Netherlands. Italy. 1987. Lang.: Dut.   3814
Relation to other fields
Study of Aleksand'r Puškin's life and works, and the influence of Rossini on Puškin. Russia: St. Petersburg. 1799-1837. Lang.: Eng.   3943

Rosso di San Secondo, Pier Maria
Performance/production
Collaboration of actor-director Virgilio Talli with playwright Pier Maria Rosso di San Secondo. Italy. 1917-1920. Lang.: Ita.   835
Plays/librettos/scripts
Letters of Pier Maria Rosso di San Secondo to Enzo Ferrieri. Italy: Milan. 1924-1925. Lang.: Ita.   1137
Analysis of Rosso di San Secondo's *Amara (Bitter)*. Italy. 1913-1917. Lang.: Ita.   1139
Comparison between *La vita che ti diedi (The Life I Gave You)* by Pirandello and *Lo spirito della morte (The Spirit of Death)* by Rosso di San Secondo. Italy. 1923-1931. Lang.: Ita.   2666

Rost, Leo
Performance/production
Collection of newspaper reviews by London theatre critics. UK-England: London. 1986. Lang.: Eng.   2136

Rostand, Edmond
Basic theatrical documents
New English translation of Rostand's *Chantecler*. France. 1880-1987. Lang.: Eng.   1554
Design/technology
Gershwin Theatre's accommodation of RSC touring productions. USA: New York, NY. 1984. Lang.: Eng.   420
Performance/production
Actors Jaromír Hanzlík and Viktor Preiss in Rostand's *Cyrano*, directed by Jaroslav Dudek at Vinohradské Theatre. Czechoslovakia: Prague. 1986. Lang.: Cze.   771

Rotenberg, David
Performance/production
Collection of newspaper reviews by London theatre critics. UK-England: London. 1986. Lang.: Eng.   2166

Rothschild, Elizabeth
Performance/production
Collection of newspaper reviews by London theatre critics. UK-England: London. 1987. Lang.: Eng.   2256

Roundabout Theatre (New York, NY)
Performance/production
Two productions of Pinter's *Old Times*. UK-England: London. USA: New York, NY, St. Louis, MO. 1971-1985. Lang.: Eng.   907
Plays/librettos/scripts
Structural analysis of Pinter's *Old Times*. USA: New York, NY. 1971-1984. Lang.: Eng.   2843

Rousset, David
Plays/librettos/scripts
Modern theatrical treatment of Fascism and the Holocaust. 1980-1987. Lang.: Eng.   2428

Royal Shakespeare Company (RSC, Stratford & London) — cont'd

Hungarian reviewer's impressions of four Shakespeare productions. UK-England: Stratford. 1987. Lang.: Hun. 2279

Brian Cox's work with the Royal Shakespeare Company. UK-England: Stratford, London. USA: New York, NY. 1968-1987. Lang.: Eng. 2284

Actor Antony Sher talks about his upcoming season at Stratford. UK-England: Stratford. 1987. Lang.: Eng. 2294

Collection of newspaper reviews by New York theatre critics. USA: New York, NY. 1987. Lang.: Eng. 2311

Plays/librettos/scripts

Playwright Ben Jonson's theatricality and relevance today. England. 1600-1987. Lang.: Eng. 2501

Interview with playwright Peter Barnes. UK-England. USA. 1987. Lang.: Eng. 2818

Royale Theatre (New York, NY)
Performance/production

Collection of newspaper reviews by New York theatre critics. USA: New York, NY. 1987. Lang.: Eng. 2318

Royalty Theatre (London)
Performance/production

Collection of newspaper reviews by London theatre critics. UK-England: London. 1986. Lang.: Eng. 2048

Collection of newspaper reviews by London theatre critics. UK-England: London. 1987. Lang.: Eng. 2231

Collection of newspaper reviews by London theatre critics. UK-England: London. 1987. Lang.: Eng. 2248

Roza
Performance/production

Collection of newspaper reviews by New York theatre critics. USA: New York, NY. 1987. Lang.: Eng. 2318

Interview with actress Georgia Brown. USA: New York, NY. UK-England: London. 1957-1985. Lang.: Eng. 3651

Plays/librettos/scripts

History of the musical *Roza*. USA: Baltimore, MD. 1965-1987. Lang.: Eng. 3675

Różewicz, Tadeusz
Performance/production

Polish theatre. Poland: Warsaw, Cracow, Wrocław. 1980-1987. Lang.: Eng, Fre. 1987

The shape and form of contemporary Polish theatre. Poland: Warsaw. 1981-1987. Lang.: Eng, Fre. 1995

Plays/librettos/scripts

Interview with director Kazimierz Braun. Ireland: Dublin. Poland. 1981-1983. Lang.: Eng. 2642

Rozov, Viktor
Performance/production

Overview of 1986-1987 Moscow theatre season. USSR: Moscow. 1986-1987. Lang.: Eng. 1039

Rozovskij, M.
Performance/production

Round-table of Soviet directors. USSR: Moscow. 1980-1987. Lang.: Rus. 989

Rozsnyai, Sándor
Institutions

Proprietors, artists and operation of Jardin d'Hiver, nightclub and revue theatre. Hungary: Budapest. 1932-1944. Lang.: Hun. 3381

Rubess, Banuta
Performance/production

Toronto directors discuss their training and craft. Canada: Toronto, ON. 1987. Lang.: Eng. 730

Rubicon (Gothenburg)
Performance/production

Rubicon's choreography of *Allting rasar inför en naken skuldra (Everything Gives Way to a Naked Shoulder)*. Sweden: Gothenburg. 1987. Lang.: Swe. 1471

Rubin, Leon
Performance/production

Collection of newspaper reviews by London theatre critics. UK-England: London. 1986. Lang.: Eng. 2122

Rubins, Tal
Performance/production

Collection of newspaper reviews by London theatre critics. UK-England: London. 1986. Lang.: Eng. 2139

Collection of newspaper reviews by London theatre critics. UK-England: London. 1987. Lang.: Eng. 2247

Rudkin, David
Performance/production

Collection of newspaper reviews by London theatre critics. UK-England: London. 1986. Lang.: Eng. 2056

Rudman, Michael
Performance/production

Collection of newspaper reviews by London theatre critics. UK-England: London. 1986. Lang.: Eng. 2034

Collection of newspaper reviews by London theatre critics. UK-England: London. 1986. Lang.: Eng. 2169

Collection of newspaper reviews by London theatre critics. UK-England: London. 1987. Lang.: Eng. 2192

Collection of newspaper reviews by London theatre critics. UK-England: London. 1987. Lang.: Eng. 2226

Collection of newspaper reviews by London theatre critics. UK-England: London. 1987. Lang.: Eng. 2251

Collection of newspaper reviews by London theatre critics. UK-England: London. 1987. Lang.: Eng. 2269

Critique of the 1984 Broadway production of *Death of a Salesman*. USA: New York, NY. 1984. Lang.: Eng. 2330

Rudnicka, Zofia
Performance/production

Four new productions in Poland. Poland: Warsaw. 1986-1987. Lang.: Eng, Fre. 1988

Rudolf, Max
Performance/production

Career of conductor/educator Max Rudolf. Italy. USA: New York, NY. 1945-1987. Lang.: Eng. 3803

Rufino, Justo
Performance/production

San Francisco Mime Troupe's visit to Nicaragua's International Theatre Festival. Central America. 1986. Lang.: Eng. 3222

Ruggeri, Ruggero
Performance/production

Film career of stage actor Ruggero Ruggeri. Italy. 1914-1952. Lang.: Ita. 3160

Plays/librettos/scripts

Collaboration and friendship of writer Gabriele D'Annunzio and actor Ruggero Ruggeri. Italy. 1901-1938. Lang.: Ita. 1133

Rules of the Game, The
SEE
Giuoco delle parti, Il.

Ruling Class, The
Plays/librettos/scripts

Interview with playwright Peter Barnes. UK-England. USA. 1987. Lang.: Eng. 2818

Runaway Train
Performance/production

Work of film director Andrei Konchalovsky. USA. USSR: Moscow. Lang.: Eng. 3166

Rundköpfe und die Spitzköpfe, Die (Roundheads and the Pinheads, The)
Relation to other fields

New generation of Brecht's students created avant-garde movement. Germany, East: Berlin. 1987. Lang.: Eng. 2992

Runeborg, Björn
Performance/production

Musikteatergruppen Oktober collaborates with immigrant amateurs. Sweden: Södertälje. 1986. Lang.: Swe. 2019

Rusalka
Performance/production

Anton Dvořák's *Rusalka*. Czechoslovakia: Prague. USA: New York, NY. 1900-1987. Lang.: Eng. 3759

Rušnev, A.A.
Performance/production

Actor A.A. Rušnev of Tairov Chamber Theatre. USSR: Moscow. 1920-1939. Lang.: Rus. 3237

Russell, George W.
Plays/librettos/scripts

Lady Gregory's *Grania*. Ireland: Dublin. 1910-1930. Lang.: Eng. 2649

Russell, Willy
Performance/production

Collection of newspaper reviews by New York theatre critics. USA: New York, NY. 1987. Lang.: Eng. 2312

Training

Funding for youth theatre in Ireland. Ireland. 1979-1987. Lang.: Eng. 1381

Rusticus imperans, sive Mopsus
Basic theatrical documents
English translations of three plays by Jacob Masen. Germany. 1606-
1681. Lang.: Eng.   1556

Ruszt, József
Performance/production
G.E. Lessing's *Nathan der Weise (Nathan the Wise)* staged by József
Ruszt, Hevesi Sándor Theatre. Hungary: Zalaegerszeg. 1986. Lang.:
Hun.   1806

József Ruszt directs G.E. Lessing's *Nathan der Weise (Nathan the
Wise)* at Hevesi Sándor Theatre under the title *Bölcs Náthán.*
Hungary: Zalaegerszeg. 1986. Lang.: Hun.   1866

Ruzzante
SEE
Beolco, Angelo.

Ryan, Phyllis
Institutions
The touring company Irish Theatre Company. UK-Ireland. 1974-
1987. Lang.: Eng.   569

Ryūzanji jimushō (Tokyo)
Performance/production
Focus on several Tokyo productions. Japan: Tokyo. 1960-1987.
Lang.: Jap.   1955

Plays/librettos/scripts
Productions by several Tokyo companies. Japan: Tokyo. 1986-1987.
Lang.: Jap.   2682

S.C.O.T. Suzuki Company of Toga
Performance/production
Plays of Pinget, Euripides and Théâtre du Rideau staged by
Jouanneau, Suzuki and Tanguy, Théâtre de la Bastille. France: Paris.
1987. Lang.: Fre.   1753

S/He
Performance/production
Collection of newspaper reviews by London theatre critics. UK-
England: London. 1987. Lang.: Eng.   2242

Sacchi, Antonio
Plays/librettos/scripts
Works of Carlo Gozzi, his relationship with actor Antonio Sacchi.
Italy: Venice. 1755. Lang.: Ita.   1129

Sach, Laurence
Performance/production
Collection of newspaper reviews by London theatre critics. UK-
England: London. 1986. Lang.: Eng.   2104

Sackler, Howard
Performance/production
Collection of newspaper reviews by London theatre critics. UK-
England: London. 1987. Lang.: Eng.   2237

Plays/librettos/scripts
Korean views of American society based on plays of Howard
Sackler, Charles Fuller and Jason Miller. USA. 1969-1982. Lang.:
Kor.   2837

Sacramento Opera (Sacramento, CA)
Performance/production
Bay Area opera companies. USA: San Francisco, CA. 1900-1987.
Lang.: Eng.   3842

Sacrati, Francesco Paolo
Design/technology
Proposed new production of *La Finta Pazza (The Fake Madwoman)*
by Sacrati and Strozzi, with scene design by Torelli. Italy: Venice.
1641-1987. Lang.: Ita.   1594

Sacre du printemps, Le
Performance/production
Millicent Hodson speaks about how she managed to reconstruct
Nižinskij's *Le sacre du printemps.* USA: Los Angeles, CA. 1913-
1987. Lang.: Swe.   1473

Sada, Yacco
SEE
Kawakami, Sadayacco.

Saddlemyer, Ann
Plays/librettos/scripts
Plays by Micone, Saddlemyer, Thompson, Wyatt. Canada. 1958-
1985. Lang.: Eng.   2481

Sadler's Wells Theatre (London)
Performance/production
Collection of newspaper reviews by London theatre critics. UK-
England: London. 1986. Lang.: Eng.   2049

Collection of newspaper reviews by London theatre critics. UK-
England: London. 1986. Lang.: Eng.   2086

Collection of newspaper reviews by London theatre critics. UK-
England: London. 1987. Lang.: Eng.   2231

Collection of newspaper reviews by London theatre critics. UK-
England: London. 1987. Lang.: Eng.   2234

Collection of newspaper reviews by London theatre critics. UK-
England: London. 1987. Lang.: Eng.   2258

Collection of newspaper reviews by London theatre critics. UK-
England: London. 1987. Lang.: Eng.   2272

Safe Sex
Performance/production
Collection of newspaper reviews by New York theatre critics. USA:
New York, NY. 1987. Lang.: Eng.   2322

Plays/librettos/scripts
Impact of AIDS crisis on the theatre. USA: New York, NY, San
Francisco, CA. 1987. Lang.: Eng.   2881

Safety
SEE
Health/safety.

Saga des poules mouillées, La (Saga of the Wet Hens)
Plays/librettos/scripts
New Canadian drama: non-realistic, anti-naturalistic. Canada. 1983-
1984. Lang.: Eng.   2482

Sagarra, Josep Maria de
Performance/production
Collection of theatre reviews by J.M. de Sagarra. Spain-Catalonia:
Barcelona. 1922-1927. Lang.: Cat.   885
Plays/librettos/scripts
General history of Catalan literature, including theatre. Spain-
Catalonia. 1902-1961. Lang.: Cat.   1157

Sagman, Gail
Performance/production
Collection of newspaper reviews by London theatre critics. UK-
England: London. 1987. Lang.: Eng.   2185

Sahl, Mort
Performance/production
Collection of newspaper reviews by New York theatre critics. USA:
New York, NY. 1987. Lang.: Eng.   2318

Saidye Bronfman Centre (Montreal, PQ)
Institutions
The future of English-language theatre in Quebec. Canada: Montreal,
PQ. 1982. Lang.: Eng.   511
Performance/production
Production account, Frank's *Spinoza*, Saidye Bronfman Centre.
Canada: Montreal, PQ. 1982. Lang.: Eng.   1702

Saiki, Junya
Performance/production
Six plays of the Tokyo season, focus on director Betsuyaku Minoru.
Japan: Tokyo. 1986. Lang.: Jap.   1966

Saint Joan
Performance/production
Actresses discuss role of Joan in Shaw's *Saint Joan.* USA. Canada.
UK-England. 1987. Lang.: Eng.   944

Eszter Csákányi as *Saint Joan* by George Bernard Shaw, directed by
László Babarczy at Csiky Gergely Theatre as *Szent Johanna.*
Hungary: Kaposvár. 1983-1987. Lang.: Hun.   1861

Eszter Csákányi in the title role of Shaw's *Saint Joan*, directed
under the title *Szent Johanna* by László Babarczy at Csiky Gergely
Theatre. Hungary: Kaposvár. 1987. Lang.: Hun.   1867

Philip Bosco's portrayals of characters in the plays of George
Bernard Shaw. USA. 1987. Lang.: Eng.   2335

Plays/librettos/scripts
Transfiguration in Shaw's *Misalliance, Saint Joan* and *Major
Barbara.* 1986. Lang.: Eng.   2413

Imagination in Shaw's *Saint Joan.* UK-England. 1923. Lang.: Eng.
                                                                         2755

Red Noses as Peter Barnes's response to Shaw's *Saint Joan.* UK-
England. 1924-1985. Lang.: Eng.   2770
Theory/criticism
Perceptions of tragedy and new perspective on its analysis. USA.
UK-England. Greece. 500 B.C.-1987 A.D. Lang.: Eng.   3066

Saint-Croix, Gilles
Performance/production
Production of Cirque du Soleil. Canada: Montreal, PQ. 1987. Lang.:
Eng.   3302

Saint-Saëns, Camille
Performance/production
Background on Metropolitan radio broadcast performances. USA:
New York, NY. 1987. Lang.: Eng.   3837

Saint-Saëns, Camille — cont'd

Plays/librettos/scripts
Background on Philistines of Saint-Saëns' *Samson et Dalila*. Canaan. 3000-1000 B.C. Lang.: Eng. 3893

Theme of *femme fatale* in *Samson et Dalila*. France. 1800-1899. Lang.: Eng. 3900

Saito, Junya
Performance/production
Unsuitable choice of plays for Tokyo performances. Japan: Tokyo. 1987. Lang.: Jap. 1965

Sakata, Tōjūrō
Performance/production
Articles on Edo period *kabuki* actors. Japan. 1600-1800. Lang.: Jap. 1493

Saks, Gene
Performance/production
Collection of newspaper reviews by New York theatre critics. USA: New York, NY. 1987. Lang.: Eng. 2321

Salamon Suba, László
Performance/production
Edward Bond's *The Fool* under the title *A bolond* directed by László Salamon Suba at Móricz Zsigmond Theatre. Hungary: Nyíregyháza. 1986. Lang.: Hun. 1875

A patkánykirály (The King of the Rats) by Győző Határ staged by László Salamon Suba at Móricz Zsigmond Theatre. Hungary: Nyíregyháza. 1987. Lang.: Hun. 1899

László Salamon Suba directs *A patkánykirály (The King of the Rats)* by Győző Határ at Móricz Zsigmond Theatre. Hungary: Nyíregyháza. 1987. Lang.: Hun. 1901

Reviews of Wilson's *Talley's Folly* staged by András Bálint and Bond's *The Fool* staged by László Salamon Suba. Hungary: Dunaujváros, Nyíregyháza. 1986. Lang.: Hun. 1902

Salamon, Béla
Performance/production
Autobiography of cabaret actor Béla Salamon. Hungary: Budapest. 1885-1965. Lang.: Hun. 3285

Salamoso, Sandra
Institutions
First festival of women's work in experimental theatre. UK-Wales: Cardiff. 1986. Lang.: Eng. 1649

Salat, Hans
Performance/production
Role of the director in the Lucerne Passion play. Switzerland: Lucerne. 1453-1616. Lang.: Eng. 2030

Salinger, J.D.
Administration
The *Salinger v. Random House* copyright case. USA. 1986-1987. Lang.: Eng. 3087

Salinger, Leo
Research/historiography
Critical history of *Julius Caesar*. England. 1599-1987. Lang.: Eng. 1299

Šaljapin, Fëdor I.
Performance/production
Memoirs of actor Fëdor I. Šaljapin. USSR. 1873-1938. Lang.: Rus. 3881

Sallé, Marie
Design/technology
French costume experimentation. France: Paris. England: London. 1734-1765. Lang.: Eng. 1591

Salome
Plays/librettos/scripts
Adaptation of literary works to opera. 1893-1987. Lang.: Eng. 3890

Musical sources in the operas of Richard Strauss. Germany: Dresden. 1864-1949. Lang.: Eng. 3908

Salvat, Ricard
Performance/production
Collection of theatre reviews by Xavier Fàbregas. Spain-Catalonia. 1969-1972. Lang.: Cat. 2010

Salvi, Matteo
Institutions
Correspondence of Richard Wagner and Matteo Salvi on the staging of *Tristan und Isolde*. Austria: Vienna. 1861-1967. Lang.: Ger. 3710

Salzburger Festspiele (Salzburg)
Performance/production
Report from Salzburger Festspiele: Mozart's *Don Giovanni*, Schoenberg's *Moses und Aron*, Schmidt's *Das Buch mit sieben Siegeln*. Austria: Salzburg. 1987. Lang.: Swe. 3744

Sammy Cahn—Words & Music
Performance/production
Collection of newspaper reviews of London theatre critics. UK-England: London. 1987. Lang.: Eng. 2273

Samoe Glavnoe (Main Thing, The)
Performance/production
'Showing' is an essential part of all acting. Europe. 1590-1987. Lang.: Eng. 1746

Samojlov, Pavel V.
Performance/production
Actor Pavel Samojlov. USSR. 1836-1931. Lang.: Rus. 1024

Samoubijca (Suicide)
Plays/librettos/scripts
Nikolaj Erdmann's plays, relations with major directors. USSR: Moscow. 1925. Lang.: Rus. 2963

Samson Agonistes
Plays/librettos/scripts
Comparison of works of Milton and Dryden. England. 1608-1700. Lang.: Eng. 2546

Samson et Dalila
Performance/production
Background on Metropolitan radio broadcast performances. USA: New York, NY. 1987. Lang.: Eng. 3837

Plays/librettos/scripts
Background on Philistines of Saint-Saëns' *Samson et Dalila*. Canaan. 3000-1000 B.C. Lang.: Eng. 3893

Theme of *femme fatale* in *Samson et Dalila*. France. 1800-1899. Lang.: Eng. 3900

San Francisco Ballet (San Francisco, CA)
Performance spaces
Design of the San Francisco Ballet Building. USA: San Francisco, CA. 1987. Lang.: Eng. 712

San Francisco Mime Troupe (San Francisco, CA)
Performance/production
San Francisco Mime Troupe's visit to Nicaragua's International Theatre Festival. Central America. 1986. Lang.: Eng. 3222

San Francisco Opera (San Francisco, CA)
Administration
Gordon Peter Getty, philanthropist, composer. USA: San Francisco, CA. 1987. Lang.: Eng. 3684

Performance/production
Background on San Francisco opera radio broadcasts. USA: San Francisco, CA. 1987. Lang.: Eng. 3833

Bay Area opera companies. USA: San Francisco, CA. 1900-1987. Lang.: Eng. 3842

San Jose Civic Light Opera (San Jose, CA)
Design/technology
Design problems of simulating a circus for *Barnum*. USA: Memphis, TN. 1986. Lang.: Eng. 3621

Sanchez-Scott, Milcha
Basic theatrical documents
Six plays detailing the Hispanic experience in the United States. USA. Mexico. 1987. Lang.: Eng. 1581

Performance/production
Collection of newspaper reviews by London theatre critics. UK-England: London. 1987. Lang.: Eng. 2202

Sanctuary
Performance/production
Collection of newspaper reviews by London theatre critics. UK-England. 1987. Lang.: Eng. 2175

Sanctuary Lamp, The
Plays/librettos/scripts
Theatrical language in the plays of Thomas Murphy. Ireland. 1961-1984. Lang.: Eng. 2640

Comic characters and the Book of Job in the plays of Thomas Murphy. Ireland. 1962-1983. Lang.: Eng. 2648

The plays of Thomas Murphy. Ireland: Dublin. 1962-1986. Lang.: Eng. 2650

Analysis of the text of Thomas Murphy's *The Sanctuary Lamp*. Ireland. 1976-1986. Lang.: Eng. 2658

Sand
Performance/production
Collection of newspaper reviews by London theatre critics. UK-England: London. 1986. Lang.: Eng. 2142

Sandford, Kenneth
Institutions
Summary of proceedings from a Gilbert and Sullivan symposium. Canada: Toronto, ON. 1987. Lang.: Eng. 3954

SUBJECT INDEX

Scenery — cont'd

Oskar Schlemmer, head of Bauhaus stage workshop. Germany. 1888-1943. Lang.: Dut. 323

Interior and exterior in scene design. Germany, West. Germany, East. 1840-1986. Lang.: Ger. 327

Meeting of scenographers' committee of OISTAT. Germany, West: Friedrichshafen. 1986. Lang.: Hun. 329

Scene designer Jenő Kéméndy. Hungary. 1860-1925. Lang.: Hun. 331

Account of exhibition of Eric Vogel's scene and costume designs. Hungary: Budapest. 1927-1987. Lang.: Hun. 335

Technical innovation in scene design at Hevesi Sándor Theatre. Hungary: Zalaegerszeg. 1982-1986. Lang.: Hun. 336

Detailed description of a light-weight revolving stage platform. Hungary: Budapest. 1930. Lang.: Hun. 341

Baroque stage machinery described in archives. Italy: Parma. 1675-1700. Lang.: Eng. 347

Perspective and the piazzetta on the Venetian stage. Italy: Venice. 1500-1600. Lang.: Ita. 348

Scenic representations of Hell. Italy. France. 1300-1399. Lang.: Ita. 349

Theory of scenography. Korea. 1876. Lang.: Kor. 352

Scene designer Kim Jung-Whan. Korea. 1978. Lang.: Kor. 354

A portable, flexible podium system. Norway: Trondheim. 1986. Lang.: Swe. 359

Touring companies' set construction techniques. Sweden. 1986. Lang.: Swe. 362

An aluminum-wood girder for stage use. Sweden. 1980-1986. Lang.: Swe. 364

Chinese view of British stage design. UK. USA: New York, NY. 1982-1985. Lang.: Chi. 368

Contribution of Modelbox Computer Aided Design. UK. 1984-1987. Lang.: Eng. 369

Review of the British Theatre Design 83-87 exhibition. UK-England. 1983-1987. Lang.: Eng. 373

Set and costume designs of major designers. UK-England. 1902-1980. Lang.: Eng. 376

Technology in post-modern theatre. USA. 1985. Lang.: Eng. 388

Procedures to photograph a production. USA. 1982. Lang.: Eng. 389

Construction of thinner furniture and prop pallets. USA. 1986. Lang.: Eng. 390

Building contoured hill set with small budget. USA. 1985. Lang.: Eng. 397

Stabilizing doors that bounce open when slammed. USA. 1987. Lang.: Eng. 399

Work of set/lighting designer Kevin Rigdon. USA. 1986. Lang.: Eng. 400

Quantifying the response of theatrical structures. USA. 1987. Lang.: Eng. 401

Economic construction of large laminated curves. USA. 1985. Lang.: Eng. 405

Comparison of four plastics as scenery glides. USA. 1986. Lang.: Eng. 406

Introductory textbook on scene and production design. USA. 1987. Lang.: Eng. 408

Retrospective of 1960s rigging installation. USA. 1960-1987. Lang.: Eng. 412

Four Broadway designers discuss redesigning shows for road tours. USA. 1987. Lang.: Eng. 414

Techniques for achieving believable relief textures on stage. USA. 1987. Lang.: Eng. 416

Construction of concealed hinges. USA. 1986. Lang.: Eng. 425

Different casting and design approaches to *Brighton Beach Memoirs*. USA. 1983-1987. Lang.: Eng. 427

Interview with set designer Edward Gianfrancesco. USA: New York, NY. 1987. Lang.: Eng. 429

Philosophy of set designer John Arnone. USA: New York, NY. 1987. Lang.: Eng. 430

Instruction in scene painting. USA. 1600-1987. Lang.: Eng. 434

Laying out odd-shaped raked decks. USA. 1986. Lang.: Eng. 439

Set construction for portable stage sets and freestanding scenery. USA. 1987. Lang.: Eng. 440

Using plasticene to plug holes in styrofoam decks. USA. 1987. Lang.: Eng. 445

Career of Broadway set designer Boris Aronson. USA. 1925-1979. Lang.: Eng. 449

Interview with designer Pericles McCohen. USA. 1982. Lang.: Eng. 452

Exhibition of the design renderings of designer Leo Kurtz who worked closely with Bertolt Brecht and Erwin Piscator. USA: Cambridge, MA. 1986. Lang.: Eng. 455

Bob Crowley's set designs for *Les Liaisons Dangereuses*. USA: New York, NY. UK-England: London. 1985-1987. Lang.: Eng. 463

Tony Walton's set designs at the Vivian Beaumont Theatre. USA: New York, NY. 1986-1987. Lang.: Eng. 465

Devising a traveller track for light scenery pieces. USA. 1987. Lang.: Eng. 467

Clamps used when duplicating steel tube frames. USA. 1987. Lang.: Eng. 480

Stagecraft handbook. USA. 1987. Lang.: Eng. 483

Portrait of designer Vladimir Serebrovskij. USSR. Lang.: Rus. 487

Memoirs of set and costume designer M.V. Dobužinskij. USSR. 1875-1958. Lang.: Rus. 488

Theatrical art, a comparative analysis. USSR: Moscow, Leningrad. 1920-1939. Lang.: Rus. 489

Theory and practice of set design. USSR. 1987. Lang.: Rus. 490

Mejerchol'd's collaboration with artists A. Jakovlev, V. Suchaev. USSR. 1935-1939. Lang.: Rus. 491

Georgian scenography—Brecht's influences. USSR. 1960-1987. Lang.: Rus. 492

V. Levental's scenery for Čechov's *Diadia Vania (Uncle Vanya)* at Moscow Art Theatre. USSR: Moscow. 1985. Lang.: Rus. 493

Artist Niko Pirosmanašvili's theatrical work. USSR. Lang.: Rus. 494

Portrait of theatre artist Nina Gaponova. USSR. 1986. Lang.: Rus. 495

Evolution of the principles of scene design. USSR. 1987. Lang.: Rus. 496

Work of theatre artist Oleg Šejncis. USSR. 1987. Lang.: Rus. 497

Stage space in performance. USSR. 1970-1987. Lang.: Rus. 498

Theatre artists M. Kitaev and E. Kočergin. USSR. 1970-1987. Lang.: Rus. 499

Interview with theatrical artist A.P. Vasiljev. USSR. 1987. Lang.: Rus. 500

Exhibition on ballet *The Seven Deadly Sins* by Kurt Weill and Edward James. France: Paris. UK-England: London. 1933-1987. Lang.: Eng. 1429

Harold Pinter's scenic designs. 1958-1987. Lang.: Eng. 1585

Profile of designer Jim Plaxton. Canada: Toronto, ON. 1982. Lang.: Eng. 1587

Aesthetic influences on scene design. England. 1700-1899. Lang.: Eng. 1590

Interview with set designer Árpád Csányi. Hungary. 1987. Lang.: Hun. 1592

F.H. Flood's scene design for *The Merchant of Venice*. Ireland: Dublin. 1985. Lang.: Eng. 1593

Proposed new production of *La Finta Pazza (The Fake Madwoman)* by Sacrati and Strozzi, with scene design by Torelli. Italy: Venice. 1641-1987. Lang.: Ita. 1594

Scene designer discusses production of *Pygmalion* in former mechanical workshop. Sweden: Stockholm. 1986. Lang.: Swe. 1595

Preliminary sketches for the Royal Shakespeare Company's *The Taming of the Shrew*. UK-England. 1985. Lang.: Eng. 1597

Interview with designer Charles McClennahan: Black Design League. USA: New York, NY. USA: Winston-Salem, NC. 1981-1987. Lang.: Eng. 1600

Design work of Nora Chavooshian. USA. 1987. Lang.: Eng. 3138

An exhibition at the Pest Redoute Gallery of the set and costume designs of Eric Vogel. Hungary. 1927-1987. Lang.: Hun. 3242

Decors of feasts and festivals prefigured architectural developments. Germany: Düsseldorf. France. Italy. 1700-1897. Lang.: Fre. 3320

Scene design and its visual impact in Chinese opera. China, People's Republic of. 1856-1987. Lang.: Chi. 3446

Scenery — cont'd

Integration of the technical and staging aspects of the musical *Smile*. USA: New York, NY. 1986. Lang.: Eng.   3620

Design problems of simulating a circus for *Barnum*. USA: Memphis, TN. 1986. Lang.: Eng.   3621

Rigging special circus effects for *Barnum*. USA. 1986. Lang.: Eng.   3622

Designer Adolphe Appia's concepts and scenery for Wagner's operas. Germany. Switzerland. 1873-1928. Lang.: Eng.   3694

Interview with set designer Gábor Forray. Hungary: Budapest. 1950-1987. Lang.: Hun.   3696

Performance spaces

Recent trends in Italian theatre. Italy. 1980. Lang.: Eng.   650

Documentation of layout, operations: Teatro dei Comici. Italy: Mantua. 1688-1800. Lang.: Eng.   654

History of San Carlo Theatre: structure, scenography, costumes. Italy: Naples. 1737-1987. Lang.: Ita.   656

Architecture of La Jolla Playhouse and challenges it presents for designers. USA: La Jolla, CA. 1947-1987. Lang.: Eng.   694

Performance/production

Overview of the director's art. China, People's Republic of. 1985. Lang.: Chi.   757

Conference proceedings on staging of Elizabethan plays. England. 1546-1616. Lang.: Eng.   775

Historical accuracy in 19th-century London theatre productions. England: London. 1800-1900. Lang.: Eng.   1734

Theatre critics' awards of the season. Hungary. 1987. Lang.: Hun.   1789

Music-drama in the Baltics. USSR. 1980-1987. Lang.: Rus.   3416

The rhythm of Chinese theatre—parts of the whole. China, People's Republic of. 1949-1985. Lang.: Chi.   3493

How to unite action and scenery in Chinese opera. China, People's Republic of. 1986. Lang.: Chi.   3499

Increasingly novel adaptations of opera settings. Canada. 1987. Lang.: Eng.   3750

Shift in opera from the singer to the conductor. Europe. North America. 1887-1987. Lang.: Eng.   3766

Plays/librettos/scripts

La Trilogie des dragons by Robert Lepage. Canada: Montreal, PQ. 1987. Lang.: Fre.   2479

How settings and props convey meaning in plays by Shaw. UK-England. 1883-1935. Lang.: Eng.   2753

Visual aspects of *Pygmalion* related to its theme. UK-England. 1914. Lang.: Eng.   2782

Operatic/theatrical activities of Dino Buzzati. Italy. 1933-1972. Lang.: Ita.   3918

Relation to other fields

Paper reproductions of 19th-century stage sets. Germany. Switzerland. 1900-1930. Lang.: Ger.   1239

Scenes From a Marriage

Performance/production

Collection of newspaper reviews by London theatre critics. UK-England: London. 1986. Lang.: Eng.   2164

Scenes of Passion

Performance/production

Overview of Polish theatre scene. Poland: Warsaw, Cracow. 1987. Lang.: Eng.   874

Schaeffer, Bogusław

Performance/production

Festival of Polish plays. Poland: Wrocław. 1987. Lang.: Eng, Fre.   871

Schafer, R. Murray

Institutions

Need for more Canadian productions of Canadian-composed opera. Canada. 1987. Lang.: Eng.   3718

Schall, Ekkehard

Performance/production

Contemporary performances of Brecht plays. Canada: Toronto, ON. USA. 1987. Lang.: Eng.   752

Schaubühne (West Berlin)

Institutions

Schaubühne's comeback with production of *Schuld und Sühne (Crime and Punishment)*. Germany, West: Berlin, West. 1970-1987. Lang.: Dut.   1618

Schaubühne am Helleschen Ufer (West Berlin)

Performance/production

Collection of newspaper reviews by London theatre critics. UK-England: London. 1987. Lang.: Eng.   2206

Collection of newspaper reviews by London theatre critics. UK-England: London. 1987. Lang.: Eng.   2253

Schaubühne am Lehniner Platz (West Berlin)

Institutions

Seven productions chosen for Theatertreffen '86. Germany: Berlin. 1986. Lang.: Eng.   1617

Schauspiel Staatstheater (Stuttgart)

Institutions

Seven productions chosen for Theatertreffen '86. Germany: Berlin. 1986. Lang.: Eng.   1617

Schauspielhaus (Bochum)

Institutions

Seven productions chosen for Theatertreffen '86. Germany: Berlin. 1986. Lang.: Eng.   1617

Schechner, Richard

Institutions

Symposium: 'The Significance and Legacy of the Living Theatre'. USA: New York, NY. 1986. Lang.: Eng.   614

Performance/production

Interview with people who staged *The Yellow House*. USA. 1960-1987. Lang.: Eng.   1486

Role of feminist in cultural critique. India. USA. 1983-1987. Lang.: Eng.   1496

Schenkar, Joan

Performance/production

Collection of newspaper reviews by London theatre critics. UK-England: London. 1986. Lang.: Eng.   2118

Schepers, Rina-Maria

Performance/production

Review of *Hello Dolly* in Bloemfontein. South Africa, Republic of: Bloemfontein. 1987. Lang.: Eng.   3635

Scher, Anna

Training

Guide to teaching through improvisation for children and adults. 1987. Lang.: Eng.   1377

Schikaneder, Emmanuel

Performance/production

A children's production of Mozart's *The Magic Flute* performed in Spanish. Mexico: Mexico City. 1987. Lang.: Spa.   3811

Schiller, Friedrich von

Basic theatrical documents

Texts on dramatic theory by nineteenth-century authors. Germany. 1794-1906. Lang.: Ger.   1555

Performance/production

August Wilhelm Iffland's productions of plays by Friedrich von Schiller. Germany: Berlin. 1796-1806. Lang.: Ger.   1773

Staging of Romantic 'closet dramas'. Scandinavia. 1986-1987. Lang.: Swe.   2004

Plays/librettos/scripts

Friedrich von Schiller's late works: new conception of drama. Germany. 1799-1805. Lang.: Eng.   2604

Characters and political themes in Verdi's *Don Carlos*. Italy: Milan. 1867. Lang.: Eng.   3924

Schiller, Leon

Institutions

Director Leon Schiller's plan for a drama department, Theatre Institute. Poland: Warsaw. 1943. Lang.: Pol.   555

Performance/production

Innovative director Leon Schiller. Poland. 1920-1939. Lang.: Rus.   870

Writings of director Leon Schiller. Poland. Germany. Roman Empire. 275-1945. Lang.: Pol.   1994

Schilling, Tom

Performance/production

Development of dance. Germany: Berlin. 1920-1986. Lang.: Ger.   1407

Schisgal, Murray

Performance/production

Collection of newspaper reviews by London theatre critics. UK-England: London. 1986. Lang.: Eng.   2044

Schlegel, August Wilhem von

Performance/production

Two German productions of *A Midsummer Night's Dream*. Germany, West. 1970-1975. Lang.: Eng.   801

Scores — cont'd

Plays/librettos/scripts
Collaboration on songs for *Cinthia and Endimion*. England: London.
1697. Lang.: Eng. 3895

Creating modern critical edition of score of Verdi's *Nabucco*. Italy:
Milan. 1987. Lang.: Eng. 3925

Scott, Dennis
Performance/production
Collection of newspaper reviews by London theatre critics. UK-
England: London. 1986. Lang.: Eng. 2116

Scott, Fred
Institutions
Historical survey of opera in Calgary. Canada: Calgary, AB. 1971-
1987. Lang.: Eng. 3719

Scott, Michael
Performance/production
Collection of newspaper reviews by London theatre critics. UK-
England: London. 1987. Lang.: Eng. 2242

Scott, Thomas H.
Performance spaces
History of the Garden Theatre designed by Thomas H. Scott. USA:
Pittsburgh, PA. 1915-1987. Lang.: Eng. 3144

Scottish Theatre Company (Glasgow)
Performance/production
The 4th International Theatre Conference: includes list of
participants and their contributions. Poland: Warsaw. 1986. Lang.:
Eng, Fre. 873

Scotto, Ottavio
Institutions
The beginnings and failure of the United States Opera Company.
USA: Chicago, IL. 1946-1947. Lang.: Eng. 3731

Scotto, Renata
Audience
The vocal versus the visual aspects of opera. Europe. 1781-1983.
Lang.: Eng. 3690

Performance/production
Soprano Renata Scotto directs Metropolitan Opera production of
Madama Butterfly. USA: New York, NY. 1987. Lang.: Eng. 3836

Scout's Honor
Performance/production
Collection of newspaper reviews by London theatre critics. UK-
England: London. 1987. Lang.: Eng. 2182

Scrape off the Black
Performance/production
Collection of newspaper reviews by London theatre critics. UK-
England: London. 1987. Lang.: Eng. 2182

Screen Actors Guild (SAG, USA)
Administration
Granting permission for filming and recording productions under
Equity contracts. USA: New York, NY. 1982. Lang.: Eng. 88

Lawsuits against artists' groups may have impact on all labor
unions. USA: New York, NY. 1982. Lang.: Eng. 105

Screen Actors' Guild (SAG, USA)
Administration
SAG/AFTRA strikes in the television/motion picture industry. USA.
1980. Lang.: Eng. 3089

Screens, The
SEE
Paravents, Les.

Sea Theatre (Vancouver, BC)
Institutions
Survey of Vancouver theatre companies. Canada: Vancouver, BC.
1987. Lang.: Eng. 516

Sea, The
Plays/librettos/scripts
Theme of theatre in recent plays. UK-England. 1957-1985. Lang.:
Eng. 2764

Structure of *The Sea* by Edward Bond. UK-England. 1973-1987.
Lang.: Eng. 2767

Seagull, The
SEE
Čajka.

Seazer, J.A.
Performance/production
Collection of newspaper reviews by London theatre critics. UK-
England: London. 1986. Lang.: Eng. 2142

Sebastian, Ellen
Plays/librettos/scripts
Space and audience-performer relationship—examples from Ellen
Sebastian and Maria Irene Fornes. USA. 1950-1980. Lang.: Eng.
2838

Seboko, Louis
Performance/production
Content and North American reception of *Asinimali! (We Have No
Money!)* by Mbongeni Ngema. Canada. South Africa, Republic of.
1987. Lang.: Eng. 1715

Šechovcev, V.
Relation to other fields
Soviet critics and playwrights on international cultural ties. USSR.
1980-1987. Lang.: Rus. 1294

Second Ark, The
Basic theatrical documents
English translations of contemporary African plays. Senegal. Zaire.
1987. Lang.: Eng. 1566

Second City (Chicago, IL & Toronto, ON)
Institutions
Second City improvisational comedy troupe. USA: Chicago, IL.
Canada: Toronto, ON. 1959-1987. Lang.: Eng. 605

Second Look Arts Resource (Toronto, ON)
Relation to other fields
Applications of African 'Theatre for Development' movement to
Canadian popular theatre. Africa. Canada: St. John's, NF, Toronto,
ON. 1978-1987. Lang.: Eng. 2978

Second Mrs. Tanqueray, The
Theory/criticism
Perceptions of tragedy and new perspective on its analysis. USA.
UK-England. Greece. 500 B.C.-1987 A.D. Lang.: Eng. 3066

Second Shepherds Play
SEE
Secundum Pastorum.

Second Studio Wrocław
Performance/production
Life and career of Polish theatre professional Zbigniew Cynkutis.
Poland: Wrocław. 1972-1987. Lang.: Eng. 1993

Secret Dialogue
SEE
Diálogo secreto.

Secret Life of Cartoons, The
Performance/production
Collection of newspaper reviews by London theatre critics. UK-
England: London. 1986. Lang.: Eng. 2069

Secrétaire particulière, La (Private Secretary, The)
Plays/librettos/scripts
Compares plays of Enlightenment France, Francophone Africa.
Congo: Brazzaville. Cameroon. Benin. France. 1700-1975. Lang.: Eng.
2496

Sedgwick, Toby
Performance/production
Collection of newspaper reviews by London theatre critics. UK-
England: London. 1986. Lang.: Eng. 2076

See-Saw Tree, The
Performance/production
Collection of newspaper reviews by London theatre critics. UK-
England: London. 1987. Lang.: Eng. 2231

Seh-Zan
Performance/production
Collection of newspaper reviews by London theatre critics. UK-
England: London. 1986. Lang.: Eng. 2086

**Sei personaggi in cerca d'autore (Six Characters in Search of an
Author)**
Performance/production
'Showing' is an essential part of all acting. Europe. 1590-1987.
Lang.: Eng. 1746

Collection of newspaper reviews by London theatre critics. UK-
England: London. 1987. Lang.: Eng. 2192

Plays/librettos/scripts
Gender conflict in Pirandello's *Sei personnaggi in cerca d'autore (Six
Characters in Search of an Author)*. Italy. 1921-1987. Lang.: Eng.
2679

Seide, Stuart
Performance/production
Staging as a form of translation. France. 1987. Lang.: Fre. 788

Šejncis, Oleg
  Design/technology
    Work of theatre artist Oleg Šejncis. USSR. 1987. Lang.: Rus.   497
Sel'vinskij, I.L.
  Plays/librettos/scripts
    The quest in plays of I.L. Sel'vinskij. USSR. 1899-1968. Lang.: Rus.
                                                                    2955
Selbie, Christopher
  Performance/production
    Collection of newspaper reviews by London theatre critics. UK-
    England: London. 1986. Lang.: Eng.   2101
    Collection of newspaper reviews by London theatre critics. UK-
    England: London. 1986. Lang.: Eng.   2121
Seldes, Marian
  Plays/librettos/scripts
    Interview with actresses Elizabeth Ashley and Marian Seldes. USA:
    New York, NY. 1987. Lang.: Eng.   2898
Self Defense
  Performance/production
    Collection of newspaper reviews by New York theatre critics. USA:
    New York, NY. 1987. Lang.: Eng.   2319
Sell Out
  Performance/production
    Collection of newspaper reviews by London theatre critics. UK-
    England: London. 1987. Lang.: Eng.   2260
Sell, Colin
  Performance/production
    Collection of newspaper reviews by London theatre critics. UK-
    England: London. 1986. Lang.: Eng.   2042
Sellars, Peter
  Administration
    Interview with director Peter Sellars. USA: Washington, DC. 1985.
                                                                    1524
  Performance/production
    Interview with director Peter Sellars. Europe. USA. 1968-1987.
    Lang.: Swe.   780
    Influence and impact of the electronic media, live theatre experience.
    USA: Los Angeles, CA. 1987. Lang.: Eng.   959
    Peter Sellars and American National Theatre present *Ajax*, Holland
    Festival. Netherlands. USA. 1987. Lang.: Dut.   1981
    Work and methodology of director Peter Sellars. USA: Washington,
    DC. 1981-1987. Lang.: Eng.   2331
    Peter Sellars' American National Theatre on European tour. USA.
    Netherlands. 1987. Lang.: Dut.   2351
    Premiere of the docu-opera, *Nixon in China*, Houston Grand Opera.
    USA: Houston, TX. 1987. Lang.: Eng.   3843
  Plays/librettos/scripts
    Productions exhibit changes in symbolism of the Don Juan myth
    due to AIDS crisis. USA. 1987. Lang.: Eng.   2845
Selling the Sizzle
  Performance/production
    Collection of newspaper reviews by London theatre critics. UK-
    England: London. 1986. Lang.: Eng.   2060
Selman, Jan
  Institutions
    A history of documentary theatre in English Canada. Canada. 1970-
    1986. Lang.: Eng.   508
  Performance/production
    Canadian popular theatre. Canada. Africa. Asia. 1987. Lang.: Eng.
                                                                    733
Selvi, Hieronimo
  Performance/production
    Collection of newspaper reviews by London theatre critics. UK-
    England: London. 1987. Lang.: Eng.   2195
Semenjaka, L.
  Performance/production
    Articles on ballet-master Jurij Grigorovič by other artists. USSR:
    Moscow. 1927-1987. Lang.: Rus.   1444
Semiotics
  Performance/production
    Semiotics of Brechtian acting. Europe. 1986. Lang.: Eng.   1748
    Actors' interpretations of gestures and movements implicit in
    Shakespeare's texts. UK-England. 1870-1987. Lang.: Eng.   2302
  Plays/librettos/scripts
    Swetnam the Woman-Hater, Arraigned by Women written in response
    to an anti-female pamphlet. England. 1600-1620. Lang.: Eng.   1118

Theodicy and tragic drama in *King Lear* and *The Tempest*. England.
1605-1611. Lang.: Eng.   1119
Comparison of the works of Ben Jonson and Christopher Marlowe.
England. 1598-1602. Lang.: Eng.   1123
Uses of history in Lepage's *La Trilogie des dragons*. Canada. 1987.
Lang.: Fre.   2476
  Theory/criticism
    Iconography and terminology in Renaissance drama. 1987. Lang.:
    Eng.   1308
    Semiotic study of dialogue in *As You Like It*. England. 1599. Lang.:
    Eng.   1325
    Gesture and sign in Shakespearean performance. England. USA.
    1590-1987. Lang.: Eng.   1326
    Modernity as historical concept applied to Catalonia and Occitania.
    France. Spain-Catalonia: Barcelona. 1539-1985. Lang.: Fre.   1332
    Relations between text and representation of *mise en scène*. France.
    1987. Lang.: Spa.   1334
    Semiotic production in popular performance. South Africa, Republic
    of. 1980. Lang.: Eng.   1347
    Reconstruction of Shakespeare in performance. USA. 1987. Lang.:
    Eng.   1358
    Works of Pierre Corneille and the social role of women. France.
    1540-1650. Lang.: Eng.   3040
    Semiotic study of Gambaro's *El despojamiento (The Robbery)*. USA.
    1987. Lang.: Eng.   3067
    Role of poetry in contemporary plays. USA. 1987. Lang.: Eng. 3077
    Representation of women by Hollywood film industry. USA: Los
    Angeles, CA. 1903-1987. Lang.: Eng.   3188
    Yvonne Rainer's film *The Man Who Envied Women*. USA. 1987.
    Lang.: Eng.   3190
Sémiramis
  Plays/librettos/scripts
    Techniques, themes, characters and dramaturgy of Voltaire. France.
    1718-1778. Lang.: Eng.   2590
Semon, Larry
  Performance/production
    Comedian Larry Semon. USA. 1889-1928. Lang.: Ita.   962
Semper Court Theatre
  SEE
    Dresdner Hoftheater.
Semper Opera
  SEE
    Dresdner Hoftheater.
Sempronio
  SEE
    Artis, Avelli.
Sendin, Ashleigh
  Performance/production
    Review of *Hello Dolly* in Bloemfontein. South Africa, Republic of:
    Bloemfontein. 1987. Lang.: Eng.   3635
Seneca, Joe
  Performance/production
    Interview with actor and playwright Joe Seneca. USA: New York,
    NY, Cleveland, OH. 1957-1987. Lang.: Eng.   2364
Seneca, Lucius Annaeus
  Plays/librettos/scripts
    Structure of revenge tragedy in Shakespeare's *Hamlet*. 1600. Lang.:
    Eng.   2425
    Plays of Seneca and theatre of his time. Italy: Rome. 4 B.C.-65
    A.D. Lang.: Rus.   2667
Sénéchal, Michel
  Performance/production
    Interview with baritone Michel Sénéchal. France: Paris. 1987. Lang.:
    Eng.   3772
Senger Mária, Miss Arizona
  Institutions
    Proprietors, artists and operation of Jardin d'Hiver, nightclub and
    revue theatre. Hungary: Budapest. 1932-1944. Lang.: Hun.   3381
Señora Carrar's Rifles
  SEE
    Gewehre der Frau Carrar, Die.
Sense of Detachment, A
  Plays/librettos/scripts
    Theme of theatre in recent plays. UK-England. 1957-1985. Lang.:
    Eng.   2764

Shakespeare, William

Administration

Technical details of guest performance of *Hamlet* by Kungliga
Dramatiska Teatern, directed by Ingmar Bergman. Italy: Florence.
Sweden: Stockholm. 1986. Lang.: Swe.   1520

Audience

Study of Shakespeare's original audiences. England: London. 1567-
1642. Lang.: Eng.   1532

Basic theatrical documents

Texts on dramatic theory by nineteenth-century authors. Germany.
1794-1906. Lang.: Ger.   1555

Text of *Yu-wang-cheng-gue (A City of Desire)* by Li Hui-min, based
on Shakespeare's *Macbeth*. Taiwan. 1986. Lang.: Chi.   3443

Design/technology

Action Design, a new theory of scenography emerging in Eastern
Europe. Czechoslovakia: Prague. 1980-1987. Lang.: Eng. 315

Gershwin Theatre's accommodation of RSC touring productions.
USA: New York, NY. 1984. Lang.: Eng.   420

Discusses costuming in Elizabethan theatre. England. 1561-1633.
Lang.: Eng.   1589

F.H. Flood's scene design for *The Merchant of Venice*. Ireland:
Dublin. 1985. Lang.: Eng.   1593

Preliminary sketches for the Royal Shakespeare Company's *The
Taming of the Shrew*. UK-England. 1985. Lang.: Eng.   1597

Review of *Bartholomew Fair* and *A Midsummer Night's Dream*. UK-
England: London. 1987. Lang.: Eng.   1598

Dennis O'Sullivan's work with mixed media. Canada. 1986. Lang.:
Fre.   3203

Institutions

Interview with Elizabeth Clark, director of Temba Theatre Company.
UK-England: London. Caribbean. Lang.: Eng.   567

Performance/production

Evolution of directing toward working closely with actors. France.
1987. Lang.: Fre.   793

Interview with actress Dame Peggy Ashcroft. UK-England. 1935-
1964. Lang.: Eng.   899

Play scripts as literary texts and as performance texts. UK-England.
1977-1987. Lang.: Eng.   905

English Shakespearean productions. UK-England: London,
Manchester, Stratford. 1985-1986. Lang.: Eng.   917

Théâtre de la Jeune Lune, its origins and influences. USA:
Minneapolis, MN. France: Paris. 1980-1987. Lang.: Eng. 977

Directors Claus Peymann (Burgtheater) and Gerardjan Rijnders
(Toneelgroep). Austria: Vienna. Netherlands: Amsterdam. 1987.
Lang.: Dut.   1681

Richard Ouzounian, director, Manitoba Theatre Centre. Canada:
Winnipeg, MB. 1982. Lang.: Eng.   1693

Historical accuracy in 19th-century London theatre productions.
England: London. 1800-1900. Lang.: Eng.   1734

Shakespeare and contemporaries: tradition, intertextuality in
performance. England. 1607-1987. Lang.: Eng.   1740

'Boy actresses' and attitudes toward sensuality in performance.
England: London. 1580-1630. Lang.: Eng.   1741

'Showing' is an essential part of all acting. Europe. 1590-1987.
Lang.: Eng.   1746

Giorgio Strehler as the quintessential director of the century. France.
Italy. 1921-1987. Lang.: Fre.   1754

Politics and Shakespeare in Weimar Republic. Germany. 1919-1930.
Lang.: Eng.   1775

Change from sociopolitical emphasis to individual themes in
productions of *A Midsummer Night's Dream*. Germany, East. 1960-
1980. Lang.: Eng.   1782

Production of scenes from Shakespeare's *Troilus and Cressida* on the
themes of war, peace and love. Germany, East: Berlin, East. 1985.
Lang.: Ger.   1783

Listing of Shakespearean productions by city. Germany, East. 1985.
Lang.: Ger.   1784

Shakespeare at Várszinház: László Vámos directs *Henry IV* Parts I
and II, Imre Kerényi directs *Henry V*. Hungary: Budapest. 1986.
Lang.: Hun.   1810

Shakespeare's *King Lear* staged by Menyhért Szegvári at the
National Theatre. Hungary: Pécs. 1986. Lang.: Hun.   1811

Reviews of *Téli zsoltár (A Winter Psalm)* by Kovách, Shakespeare's
Much Ado About Nothing and *Ferde ház (The Leaning House)* by

Gerencsér performed at Kisfaludy Theatre. Hungary: Győr. 1986.
Lang.: Hun.   1822

István Szőke directs Shakespeare's *Merchant of Venice*, Pécs
National Theatre. Hungary: Pécs. 1987. Lang.: Hun.   1854

László Bagossy directs *Macbeth*, Tamás Jordán directs Zsigmond
Móricz's *Uri muri (Gentlemen's Spree)* at Pécs Summer Theatre.
Hungary: Pécs. 1987. Lang.: Hun.   1864

Shakespeare's *A Midsummer Night's Dream* staged by Tibor
Csizmadia. Hungary: Eger, Szolnok. 1986. Lang.: Hun.   1881

Two premieres: Shakespeare, *The Merchant of Venice*, directed by
Árpád Jutacsa Hegyi. Németh's *Villámfénynél (By the Stroke of
Lightning)*, directed by Attila Seprődi Kiss. Hungary: Kecskemét.
1987. Lang.: Hun.   1925

Six plays of the Tokyo season, focus on director Betsuyaku Minoru.
Japan: Tokyo. 1986. Lang.: Jap.   1966

Gábor Tompa directs *Hamlet* at Hungarian Theatre of Kolozsvár.
Romania: Cluj. 1987. Lang.: Hun.   2001

Controversial production of *Othello* directed by Janet Suzman. South
Africa, Republic of: Johannesburg. 1987. Lang.: Eng.   2007

Collection of newspaper reviews by London theatre critics. UK.
1987. Lang.: Eng.   2031

Collection of newspaper reviews by London theatre critics. UK-
England: London. 1986. Lang.: Eng.   2044

Collection of newspaper reviews by London theatre critics. UK-
England: London. 1987. Lang.: Eng.   2073

Collection of newspaper reviews by London theatre critics. UK-
England: London. 1986. Lang.: Eng.   2085

Collection of newspaper reviews by London theatre critics. UK-
England: London. 1986. Lang.: Eng.   2087

Collection of newspaper reviews by London theatre critics. UK-
England: London. 1986. Lang.: Eng.   2093

Collection of newspaper reviews by London theatre critics. UK-
England: London. 1986. Lang.: Eng.   2095

Collection of newspaper reviews by London theatre critics. UK-
England: London. 1986. Lang.: Eng.   2101

Collection of newspaper reviews by London theatre critics. UK-
England: London. 1986. Lang.: Eng.   2102

Collection of newspaper reviews by London theatre critics. UK-
England: London. 1986. Lang.: Eng.   2106

Collection of newspaper reviews by London theatre critics. UK-
England: London. 1986. Lang.: Eng.   2121

Collection of newspaper reviews by London theatre critics. UK-
England: London. 1986. Lang.: Eng.   2123

Collection of newspaper reviews by London theatre critics. UK-
England: London. 1986. Lang.: Eng.   2135

Collection of newspaper reviews by London theatre critics. UK-
England: London. 1986. Lang.: Eng.   2138

Collection of newspaper reviews by London theatre critics. UK-
England: London. 1986. Lang.: Eng.   2166

Collection of newspaper reviews by London theatre critics. UK-
England: London. 1987. Lang.: Eng.   2177

Collection of newspaper reviews by London theatre critics. UK-
England: London. 1987. Lang.: Eng.   2193

Collection of newspaper reviews by London theatre critics. UK-
England: London. 1987. Lang.: Eng.   2198

Collection of newspaper reviews by London theatre critics. UK-
England: London. 1987. Lang.: Eng.   2200

Collection of newspaper reviews by London theatre critics. UK-
England: London. 1987. Lang.: Eng.   2205

Collection of newspaper reviews by London theatre critics. UK-
England: London. 1987. Lang.: Eng.   2208

Collection of newspaper reviews by London theatre critics. UK-
England: London. 1987. Lang.: Eng.   2210

Collection of newspaper reviews by London theatre critics. UK-
England: London. 1987. Lang.: Eng.   2212

Collection of newspaper reviews by London theatre critics. UK-
England: London. 1987. Lang.: Eng.   2219

Collection of newspaper reviews by London theatre critics. UK-
England: London. 1987. Lang.: Eng.   2220

Collection of newspaper reviews by London theatre critics. UK-
England: London. 1987. Lang.: Eng.   2223

Shakespeare, William — cont'd

Collection of newspaper reviews by London theatre critics. UK-England: London. 1987. Lang.: Eng. 2225

Collection of newspaper reviews by London theatre critics. UK-England: London. 1987. Lang.: Eng. 2227

Collection of newspaper reviews by London theatre critics. UK-England: London. 1987. Lang.: Eng. 2228

Collection of newspaper reviews by London theatre critics. UK-England: London. 1987. Lang.: Eng. 2233

Collection of newspaper reviews by London theatre critics. UK-England: London. 1987. Lang.: Eng. 2236

Collection of newspaper reviews by London theatre critics. UK-England: London. 1987. Lang.: Eng. 2241

Collection of newspaper reviews by London theatre critics. UK-England: London. 1987. Lang.: Eng. 2244

Collection of newspaper reviews by London theatre critics. UK-England: London. 1987. Lang.: Eng. 2249

Collection of newspaper reviews by London theatre critics. UK-England: London. 1987. Lang.: Eng. 2255

Roles of Dame Peggy Ashcroft and directors she has worked with. UK-England. 1930-1986. Lang.: Eng. 2278

Comparison of two 'Elizabethan' productions of *Hamlet*. UK-England: London. USA. 1900-1904. Lang.: Eng. 2292

Actors' interpretations of gestures and movements implicit in Shakespeare's texts. UK-England. 1870-1987. Lang.: Eng. 2302

Collection of newspaper reviews by New York theatre critics. USA: New York, NY. 1987. Lang.: Eng. 2311

Autobiography of director, producer and writer John Houseman. USA: New York, NY. 1935-1985. Lang.: Eng. 2339

Four productions in Southern regional theatres. USA: Houston, TX, Louisville, KY, Gainesville, FL. 1980. Lang.: Eng. 2342

New production of *Macbeth* set in 1927 Chicago. USA: New York, NY. 1987. Lang.: Eng. 2357

Director Gleb Panfilov's interpretation of *Hamlet* at Komsomol Theatre. USSR: Moscow. 1980-1987. Lang.: Rus. 2373

Rustaveli Theatre of Georgia, directed by Robert Sturua, presents Shakespeare's *Richard III* and Brecht's *Der Kaukasische Kreidekreis (The Caucasian Chalk Circle)* in Hungary. USSR: Tbilisi. Hungary. 1987. Lang.: Hun. 2383

Difficulties in contemporary readings of Shakespeare's plays. USSR. 1987. Lang.: Rus. 2389

Guest performances by Teat'r im. Šato Rustaveli of Tbilisi at Madách Theatre: Shakespeare's *Richard III*, Brecht's *Der Kaukasische Kreidekreis (The Caucasian Chalk Circle)*. USSR: Tbilisi. Hungary: Budapest. 1986. Lang.: Hun. 2390

Director Ljubiša Ristić and 'Shakespeare Fest '86'. Yugoslavia: Subotica, Palić. 1986. Lang.: Hun. 2403

Review of *Hamlet*, *Julius Caesar* and *Titus Andronicus* at 'Shakespeare Fest '86'. Yugoslavia: Palić. 1986. Lang.: Hun. 2405

'Shakespeare Fest '86' reviews. Yugoslavia: Palić. 1986. Lang.: Hun. 2407

International coverage of film adaptations of Shakespeare. 1899-1987. Lang.: Eng. 3148

Interpretation and critique of Olivier's film *Hamlet*. England. 1604-1948. Lang.: Chi. 3149

Beijing opera *Yu-wang-cheng-gue (A City of Desire)*, based on Shakespeare's *Macbeth*. Taiwan: Taipei. 1986. Lang.: Chi. 3541

Plays/librettos/scripts

Allegory and irony in *Othello*. England. 1604. Lang.: Eng. 1114

Temporality in Shakespeare's *Richard III*. England. 1592. Lang.: Eng. 1115

Comparative study of *Measure for Measure* by Shakespeare and the poem *Leda and the Swan* by Yeats. England. 1604-1929. Lang.: Eng. 1116

Theodicy and tragic drama in *King Lear* and *The Tempest*. England. 1605-1611. Lang.: Eng. 1119

An analysis of the structure of *Measure for Measure*. England. 1604. Lang.: Eng. 1120

King Lear focusing on the character of Kent. England. 1605. Lang.: Eng. 1122

Shakespeare's *Henry V*: development of Prince Hal as an ideological monarch. England. 1599. Lang.: Eng. 1124

Italian translation, *Shakespeare, Our Contemporary* by Jan Kott. 1596-1614. Lang.: Ita. 2420

Shakespeare's *King Lear* in the context of ironic drama. 1590. Lang.: Eng. 2424

Structure of revenge tragedy in Shakespeare's *Hamlet*. 1600. Lang.: Eng. 2425

Biblical influences in *King Lear*, *Hamlet*, *Othello* and *Macbeth*. Lang.: Eng. 2426

Language and metaphor in plays of René-Daniel Dubois. Canada: Toronto, ON, Montreal, PQ. 1983-1987. Lang.: Eng. 2471

Exploration of mythic elements in the later plays of William Shakespeare. England: London. 1607-1614. Lang.: Eng. 2497

Shakespeare's *Hamlet*: representation of interiority onstage. England. 1600. Lang.: Eng. 2500

Playwright Ben Jonson's theatricality and relevance today. England. 1600-1987. Lang.: Eng. 2501

Textual dramaturgy and *Richard II*. England. 1987. Lang.: Eng. 2502

Comparison of Shakespeare's *Cymbeline* with the reign of James I. England. 1400-1550. Lang.: Eng. 2503

Anthropological analysis of Shakespeare's romantic comedies. England. 1564-1616. Lang.: Eng. 2504

Political, social and religious issues in Caroline drama. England. 1632-1642. Lang.: Eng. 2508

Sacred power of the king in Shakespeare's histories and tragedies. England. 1539-1613. Lang.: Ita. 2510

Eighteenth-century alterations to Shakespeare's *The Merchant of Venice*. England. 1596-1701. Lang.: Eng. 2512

Place of the masque in *The Tempest*. England. 1611. Lang.: Eng. 2516

Comparison of *King Lear* and *Vildanden (The Wild Duck)*. England. Norway. 1605-1884. Lang.: Eng. 2518

Italian translation of *Über die Shakespearomanie (On Shakespeare-Mania)* by Christian Dietrich Grabbe. England. Germany. 1594-1836. Lang.: Ita. 2520

Influences of Arthurian legend on Shakespeare's *King Lear*. England. 1605. Lang.: Eng. 2521

Devices that convey concern with sexuality in Shakespeare's *All's Well that Ends Well*. England. 1602-1987. Lang.: Eng. 2523

Metadrama, alienation and fantasy in Shakespeare's *Romeo and Juliet*. England. 1595-1596. Lang.: Eng. 2524

Themes of home and homelessness in plays of Cibber and Vanbrugh. England. 1696. Lang.: Eng. 2525

Tragic result of utopian ideas in Shakespeare's *Romeo and Juliet*. England. 1595-1596. Lang.: Ger. 2530

Representation of real history and Utopia in Shakespeare's plays. England. 1590-1612. Lang.: Ger. 2531

Utopianism in Shakespeare's *The Tempest*. England. 1611-1612. Lang.: Ger. 2532

Music in Shakespeare. England. 1580-1616. Lang.: Ger. 2533

Society vs. nature in Shakespeare's *As You Like It*. England. 1599-1600. Lang.: Ger. 2536

Shakespeare's use of language in *The Two Noble Kinsmen*. England. 1591-1616. Lang.: Eng. 2537

The creation of ideal future worlds based on the historical past in some plays of Shakespeare. England. 1591-1599. Lang.: Ger. 2539

Productions of *Sir Thomas More* by Elizabethan theatre companies. England. 1595-1650. Lang.: Eng. 2541

Character analysis of Olivia in *Twelfth Night*. England. 1599. Lang.: Eng. 2544

Title character's relation to the audience in Shakespeare's *Hamlet*. England. 1600-1601. Lang.: Ger. 2545

Rumour as a political and social tool in *Henry VIII*. England: London. 1612-1614. Lang.: Eng. 2547

Social reality in contrast with nature as allegory of utopian social fiction. England. 1599-1600. Lang.: Eng. 2549

Structure of tragic elements in plays of William Shakespeare. England: London. 1594-1599. Lang.: Eng. 2551

Shakespeare's use of formal self-referential oaths. England. 1594-1616. Lang.: Eng. 2552

Class conflict in Shakespeare's *Coriolanus* as viewed in 17th and 20th century. England. 1600-1980. Lang.: Ger. 2553

Classification and social hierarchy in Shakespeare's *Troilus and Cressida*. England. 1601. Lang.: Eng. 2554

Shakespeare, William — cont'd

Essays on Shakespeare by a historian of culture. England. 1589-1610. Lang.: Hun. 2555

Role of Chorus in Shakespeare's *Henry V*. England. 1599. Lang.: Eng. 2556

History and utopianism in some plays of Shakespeare. England. 1589-1606. Lang.: Ger. 2558

Improvisational clowning in Elizabethan theatre. England. 1585-1625. Lang.: Eng. 2560

Relationship of the *Aeneid* to Shakespeare's *The Tempest*. England: London. 1611. Lang.: Eng. 2561

Collection of nineteenth-century theoretical writings on theatre and drama. Germany. 1800-1900. Lang.: Ger. 2595

Comparison of Pirandello's *Enrico Quarto (Henry IV)* and Shakespeare's *Hamlet*. Italy. England. 1580-1936. Lang.: Chi. 2680

Comparison of Dürrenmatt's *The Physicists (Die Physiker)*, *Macbeth* and *Doctor Faustus*. Switzerland. 1987. Lang.: Heb. 2747

Influence of Livy's *History* and Machiavelli's *Discorsi* on Shakespeare's *Coriolanus*. UK-England: London. 1606-1610. Lang.: Eng. 2752

Interpretation of the title character of Shakespeare's *Coriolanus*. UK-England. 1607. Lang.: Eng. 2757

Comparison of Shakespeare's *Julius Caesar* to the drama and vision of Euripides. UK-England. 500 B.C.-1599 A.D. Lang.: Eng. 2760

Depictions of dying moments of characters in drama, specifically that of Hotspur in *Henry IV, Part I*. UK-England: London. 1595-1598. Lang.: Eng. 2763

Textual studies of several books on the plays of William Shakespeare and new editions of his plays. UK-England. USA. 1981-1985. Lang.: Eng. 2786

Focus on patterns of musical images in character of Iago which unite ideas of *Othello*. UK-England: London. 1604. Lang.: Eng. 2792

The topicality of Shakespeare's *Love's Labour's Lost*. UK-England: London. 1590. Lang.: Eng. 2794

View of the ideal and mortal worlds explored in *Henry VIII*. UK-England: London. 1611-1614. Lang.: Eng. 2797

Stage business in *Major Barbara* traced to Beerbohm Tree. UK-England. 1905. Lang.: Eng. 2802

Comic conventions in Shakespeare's *Titus Andronicus*. UK-England. 1987. Lang.: Eng. 2809

Relationship between the well-made and unconventional elements of *Hamlet*. UK-England: London. 1599-1603. Lang.: Eng. 2810

Shakespeare's influence on George Bernard Shaw. UK-England. 1882-1936. Lang.: Eng. 2812

Themes of perception in *The Tempest*. UK-England: London. 1611. Lang.: Eng. 2813

Shakespearean burlesque in context. UK-England. 1800-1900. Lang.: Eng. 2817

Influences on *The Voysey Inheritance* by Granville Barker. UK-England. 1600-1938. Lang.: Eng. 2820

Restoring character originally intended for role of Falstaff in *Henry IV, Part I*. UK-England: London. 1595-1598. Lang.: Eng. 2821

Experiment in musical composition based on *King Lear*. USA. 1987. Lang.: Eng. 2848

Recent studies of the life of William Shakespeare. USA. UK-England. 1564-1616. Lang.: Eng. 2857

Current analysis of Shakespearean plays. USSR. 1985. Lang.: Rus. 2939

Kazakh translations of Shakespeare. USSR. 1930-1969. Lang.: Rus. 2947

Contemporary interpretations of Shakespeare's work. USSR. 1980-1987. Lang.: Rus. 2967

Conference on staging Shakespeare in USSR. USSR. 1987. Lang.: Rus. 2969

Two forms of adaptations of Shakespeare for other media. Europe. USA. 1899-1987. Lang.: Eng. 3097

Orson Welles's adaptation of *Othello*: cinematic technique and time. USA. 1952. Lang.: Eng. 3180

Development of Welles's adaptation of *Henry IV* Parts I and II from stage to screen. USA. Ireland. 1938-1965. Lang.: Eng. 3182

Shakespeare compared to writers of Chinese opera. China. 1279-1616. Lang.: Chi. 3554

How to adapt Shakespeare to Chinese opera. China, People's Republic of. 1987. Lang.: Chi. 3569

Analysis and success of Boito's libretto for Verdi's opera *Falstaff*. Italy. 1893. Lang.: Eng. 3923

Reference materials

International Shakespeare bibliography. England. 1550-1985. Lang.: Ger, Eng, Fre, Spa, Ita, Rus. 2973

Relation to other fields

Experimental theatre course, Assoc. Internationale pour la Sémiologie du Spectacle. Belgium: Brussels. France: Paris. Denmark: Odense. 1983-1985. Lang.: Fre. 1219

Comparison of *King Lear* and South African Land Act regarding land distribution. England. South Africa, Republic of. 1605-1913. Lang.: Eng. 1231

Approaching dramatic texts similarly to other literary texts. 1600-1987. Lang.: Eng. 2976

Theme of imperialism in *The Tempest*. Canada. Antilles. France. 1611-1977. Lang.: Eng. 2984

Italian translations of Ernest Jones' *Hamlet and Oedipus*, and Jean Starobinski's *Hamlet and Freud*. Europe. 1596-1949. Lang.: Ita. 2988

Satirical perceptions of George IV using Shakespeare as a frame of reference. UK-England: London. 1790-1827. Lang.: Eng. 3003

Shakespeare's use of medical knowledge in his plays. UK-England: London. 1589-1614. Lang.: Eng. 3004

Research/historiography

Shakespeare texts: discussion of bibliographic methodology. 1987. Lang.: Eng. 1297

Critical history of *Julius Caesar*. England. 1599-1987. Lang.: Eng. 1299

Sociological view of American and English Shakespeare studies. UK-England. USA. 1900-1987. Lang.: Chi. 3014

Theory/criticism

Iconography and terminology in Renaissance drama. 1987. Lang.: Eng. 1308

Semiotic study of dialogue in *As You Like It*. England. 1599. Lang.: Eng. 1325

Gesture and sign in Shakespearean performance. England. USA. 1590-1987. Lang.: Eng. 1326

Self-awareness in Shakespeare's *Julius Caesar*. England. 1599. Lang.: Eng. 1327

Avoiding the risk of commercialism: the example of Antoine's Théâtre Libre. France. 1887-1987. Lang.: Fre. 1335

Effect of audiovisual media on theatre. France. 1987. Lang.: Fre. 1339

Reconstruction of Shakespeare in performance. USA. 1987. Lang.: Eng. 1358

The body as emblematic of a character's frame of mind. England. 1583. Lang.: Eng. 3031

Catalan translation of Lessing's *Hamburgische Dramaturgie*. Germany: Hamburg. 1767-1769. Lang.: Cat. 3043

Reflections on the value of theatrical translations. Spain-Catalonia. UK-England. 1600-1985. Lang.: Cat. 3060

Peter Brook's implementation of Jan Kott's theory in his approach to *King Lear*. UK-England. 1962-1987. Lang.: Eng. 3064

Perceptions of tragedy and new perspective on its analysis. USA. UK-England. Greece. 500 B.C.-1987 A.D. Lang.: Eng. 3066

Refutes Frye's analysis of Shakespeare's *A Midsummer Night's Dream*. USA. 1987. Lang.: Eng. 3075

Shaliko

Performance/production

Interview with people who staged *The Yellow House*. USA. 1960-1987. Lang.: Eng. 1486

Script and staging of Shaliko's *The Yellow House*. USA: Baltimore, MD. 1982-1987. Lang.: Eng. 1487

Shameen Dhu

Plays/librettos/scripts

Analysis of the plays and songs of Irish-American musical theatre star Chauncey Olcott. USA. 1893-1918. Lang.: Eng. 3671

Shang, Hsio Yu

Performance/production

Performance commemorating 85th birthday of playwright Shang Hsio Yu. China, People's Republic of. 1984. Lang.: Chi. 756

Shaw, George Bernard — cont'd

Political dissatisfaction in drama. UK. Ireland. 1890-1987. Lang.: Eng. 2750

How settings and props convey meaning in plays by Shaw. UK-England. 1883-1935. Lang.: Eng. 2753

Themes and sources of Shaw's *The Man of Destiny*. UK-England. 1894-1931. Lang.: Eng. 2754

Imagination in Shaw's *Saint Joan*. UK-England. 1923. Lang.: Eng. 2755

The *Doppelgänger* in *The Doctor's Dilemma* by G.B. Shaw. UK-England. 1906. Lang.: Eng. 2756

Mrs. Warren's Profession: Shaw's ideas embodied in characters. UK-England. 1902. Lang.: Eng. 2765

Shaw's ideas on directorial interpretation in *Pygmalion*. UK-England. 1894-1949. Lang.: Eng. 2768

Red Noses as Peter Barnes's response to Shaw's *Saint Joan*. UK-England. 1924-1985. Lang.: Eng. 2770

Imaginary history: Shaw's *In Good King Charles's Golden Days*. UK-England. 1639. Lang.: Eng. 2772

Revival of Shaw's *Village Wooing*: staging and stage history. UK-England. USA: Houston, TX. 1933-1984. Lang.: Eng. 2773

Shaw's artistic strategy in *Major Barbara*. UK-England. 1905. Lang.: Eng. 2774

Bakhtinian analysis of *Fanny's First Play* by Shaw. UK-England. 1911-1916. Lang.: Eng. 2775

Freudian reading of Shaw's *Passion, Poison and Petrification*. UK-England. 1895-1926. Lang.: Eng. 2781

Visual aspects of *Pygmalion* related to its theme. UK-England. 1914. Lang.: Eng. 2782

Shaw's use of Irish stereotypes in *John Bull's Other Ireland*. UK-England. UK-Ireland. 1860-1925. Lang.: Eng. 2787

Approaches to Shaw's *Buoyant Billions*. UK-England. 1936-1946. Lang.: Eng. 2789

Shaw's use of the audience to help create his play *Pygmalion*. UK-England. 1914. Lang.: Eng. 2796

Stage business in *Major Barbara* traced to Beerbohm Tree. UK-England. 1905. Lang.: Eng. 2802

Analysis of Shaw's *You Never Can Tell*. UK-England. 1899. Lang.: Eng. 2803

Background of *John Bull's Other Island* by G.B. Shaw. UK-England. 1904. Lang.: Eng. 2804

Reception of G.B. Shaw's plays in Hungary. UK-England. 1904-1956. Lang.: Hun. 2808

The problem of capitalism in Shaw's *The Millionairess*. UK-England. 1936-1952. Lang.: Eng. 2811

Shakespeare's influence on George Bernard Shaw. UK-England. 1882-1936. Lang.: Eng. 2812

Influences on *The Voysey Inheritance* by Granville Barker. UK-England. 1600-1938. Lang.: Eng. 2820

Significance of the ending of Shaw's *The Philanderer*. UK-England. 1905. Lang.: Eng. 2823

Playacting and gamesmanship: Shaw's *The Apple Cart*. UK-England. 1918-1935. Lang.: Eng. 2825

Shaw's *Misalliance* as a Freudian dream play. UK-England. 1909-1911. Lang.: Eng. 2826

Shaw's struggle to find an apt ending for *The Devil's Disciple*. UK-England. 1896-1909. Lang.: Eng. 2827

Relation to other fields

Literary figures of the Irish Literary Renaissance. Ireland. UK-Ireland. 1875-1938. Lang.: Eng. 2995

Research/historiography

Overview of Canadian research on twentieth-century Irish drama. Ireland. UK-Ireland. Canada. 1891-1983. Lang.: Eng. 3011

Theory/criticism

Early theatre criticism of George Bernard Shaw. England: London. 1895-1905. Lang.: Eng. 3029

Perceptions of tragedy and new perspective on its analysis. USA. UK-England. Greece. 500 B.C.-1987 A.D. Lang.: Eng. 3066

Shawl, The

Performance/production

Collection of newspaper reviews by London theatre critics. UK-England: London. 1986. Lang.: Eng. 2131

Shawn, Wallace

Plays/librettos/scripts

Notes on Dramatists' Guild activities and concerns. USA. 1987. Lang.: Eng. 1162

Review of Wallace Shawn's *Aunt Dan and Lemon*. Canada: Toronto, ON. USA: New York, NY. 1986-1987. Lang.: Eng. 2467

Shayna Maidel, A

Plays/librettos/scripts

Influence of Yiddish and Jewish theatre on mainstream American theatre. USA: New York, NY. 1881-1987. Lang.: Eng. 2913

She Also Dances

Performance/production

Collection of newspaper reviews by London theatre critics. UK-England: London. 1986. Lang.: Eng. 2116

She Always Said, Pablo

Performance/production

Goodman Theatre's series 'Celebration of Genius'. USA: Chicago, IL. 1986-1987. Lang.: Eng. 3409

She Would If She Could

Plays/librettos/scripts

Independence of Restoration women is reflected in comic heroines. England. 1668-1700. Lang.: Eng. 2550

She-Gallant, The

Plays/librettos/scripts

New findings on 18th-century Irish comic playwright John O'Keeffe. Ireland. England: London. 1767-1798. Lang.: Eng. 2643

Sheed, Wilfrid

Theory/criticism

Keynote address at Northern California Theatre Critics Conference. USA. 1987. Lang.: Eng. 3072

Sheffer, Isaiah

Performance/production

Collection of newspaper reviews by New York theatre critics. USA: New York, NY. 1987. Lang.: Eng. 2323

Sheffield, Rita

Performance/production

Performance artists and their work in New Orleans. USA: New Orleans, LA, New York, NY. 1987. Lang.: Eng. 3362

Shelley, Percy Bysshe

Performance/production

Romantic drama in performance: effect on modern theatre. England. 1700-1987. Lang.: Eng. 1732

Plays/librettos/scripts

The Romantic drama of Shelley. England. 1792-1822. Lang.: Eng. 2513

The paradox and problems of poetry in Romantic theatre. England. 1700-1800. Lang.: Eng. 2557

Antonin Artaud's interpretation of Shelley's *The Cenci*. UK-England. France. 1819-1920. Lang.: Eng. 2780

Theory/criticism

Structuralist approach to play interpretation. 500 B.C.-1987 A.D. Lang.: Eng. 3016

Shepard, Sam

Audience

Letters written by Joseph Chaikin regarding actor-audience relationship. USA: Washington, DC, New York, NY. 1974-1984. Lang.: Eng. 291

Performance/production

Collection of newspaper reviews by London theatre critics. UK-England: London. 1987. Lang.: Eng. 2222

Collection of newspaper reviews by London theatre critics. UK-England: London. 1987. Lang.: Eng. 2240

Plays/librettos/scripts

Development of themes and characters in plays of Sam Shepard. USA. 1960-1987. Lang.: Eng. 2853

John Guare's work and his insights into American society. USA. 1960-1987. Lang.: Eng. 2869

Interview with playwright John Guare. USA. 1987. Lang.: Eng. 2870

Evolution of female characters in the plays of Sam Shepard. USA. 1976-1987. Lang.: Eng. 2883

Sam Shepard's *True West* as a farce in the guise of serious drama. USA. 1981. Lang.: Eng. 2887

Interview with playwright John Ford Noonan. USA. 1970-1987. Lang.: Eng. 2894

Theatricality of Sam Shepard's early and late works. USA. 1965-1986. Lang.: Eng. 2903

Shepard, Sam — cont'd

Corn as a symbol in Sam Shepard's *Buried Child*. USA. 1978.
Lang.: Eng. 2905

Modernism and postmodernism as themes in Sam Shepard's plays.
USA. 1972-1987. Lang.: Eng. 2930

Sam Shepard's manipulation of an audience's desire to believe what
it sees. USA. 1967-1983. Lang.: Eng. 2932

Theory/criticism

Theorist Herbert Blau on modern theatre. 1960-1987. Lang.: Eng.
1306

Shepherd-Wilson, Clare
Performance/production

Review of six-week dance festival representing forms of dance in
South Africa. South Africa, Republic of: Durban. 1986. Lang.: Eng.
1409

Shepherds, The
SEE
Pastorets, Els.

Sheppard, Jack
Plays/librettos/scripts

Changing economic conditions created an audience for plays about
criminals. England. 1731-1740. Lang.: Eng. 2517

Sheppard, Nona
Performance/production

Collection of newspaper reviews by London theatre critics. UK-
England: London. 1987. Lang.: Eng. 2232

Collection of newspaper reviews by London theatre critics. UK-
England: London. 1987. Lang.: Eng. 2243

Sheppey
Plays/librettos/scripts

The potential for social influence in W. Somerset Maugham's
comedies. UK-England. 1903-1933. Lang.: Eng. 2784

Sher, Antony
Performance/production

Creative self-knowledge and the mystical path of actors. UK-
England. USA. 1977-1987. Lang.: Eng. 900

Actor Antony Sher talks about his upcoming season at Stratford.
UK-England: Stratford. 1987. Lang.: Eng. 2294

Sheridan, Jim
Performance/production

Collection of newspaper reviews by London theatre critics. UK-
England: London. 1986. Lang.: Eng. 2096

Sheridan, Peter
Performance/production

DYT (Dublin Youth Theatre). Ireland: Dublin. 1980-1987. Lang.:
Eng. 816

Collection of newspaper reviews by London theatre critics. UK-
England: London. 1987. Lang.: Eng. 2193

Collection of newspaper reviews by London theatre critics. UK-
England: London. 1987. Lang.: Eng. 2247

Sheridan, Richard Brinsley
Performance/production

Collection of newspaper reviews by London theatre critics. UK-
England: London. 1987. Lang.: Eng. 2256

Sherman, Cindy
Relation to other fields

Theatricality in works of photographers Cindy Sherman and Edward
Steichen. USA. 1900-1987. Lang.: Eng. 1289

Sherman, Guy
Design/technology

Sound designer Guy Sherman's innovations. USA: New York, NY.
1984-1987. Lang.: Eng. 392

Sherman, Malcolm
Performance/production

Collection of newspaper reviews by London theatre critics. UK-
England: London. 1986. Lang.: Eng. 2126

Collection of newspaper reviews by London theatre critics. UK-
England: London. 1986. Lang.: Eng. 2139

Collection of newspaper reviews by London theatre critics. UK-
England: London. 1986. Lang.: Eng. 2164

Sherrin, Ned
Performance/production

Collection of newspaper reviews by London theatre critics. UK-
England: London. 1986. Lang.: Eng. 2053

Shevelove, Burt
Performance/production

Collection of newspaper reviews by London theatre critics. UK-
England: London. 1986. Lang.: Eng. 2052

Shewey, Don
Theory/criticism

National standards for arts criticism. USA. 1987. Lang.: Eng. 1371

Shezi, Mutwa
Relation to other fields

Influences of Black political and economic life on literature,
performance. South Africa, Republic of. 1970-1987. Lang.: Eng. 1252

Shiang ma juan (Story of the Robber)
Performance/production

Chinese opera star Ma Shau-Liang reproduces the play *Shiang ma
juan (Story of the Robber)*. China, People's Republic of. 1958-1986.
Lang.: Chi. 3397

Shigeyama, Sennojō
Performance/production

Kyōgen actor Shigeyama Sennojō on his profession. Japan. 1940-
1987. Lang.: Jap. 1504

Shikadō
Theory/criticism

Analysis of *Shikadō* by Zeami. Japan. 1363-1443. Lang.: Kor. 3053

Shiki (Tokyo)
Plays/librettos/scripts

Productions by several Tokyo companies. Japan: Tokyo. 1986-1987.
Lang.: Jap. 2682

Shikitei, Sanba
Audience

Role of samurai class in development and patronage of *kabuki*.
Japan: Tokyo. 1603-1868. Lang.: Eng. 1490

Shimizu, Kunio
Performance/production

Productions by Tenkei gekijō, Manji and Mokutōsha. Japan: Tokyo.
1986. Lang.: Jap. 1958

Shimizu, Shinji
Plays/librettos/scripts

Productions by several Tokyo companies. Japan: Tokyo. 1986-1987.
Lang.: Jap. 2682

***Shin yozora no rū sanraizu sansetto in sunshine (New Lipstick of
Night Sky, Sunrise Sunset in Sunshine)***
Performance/production

New Tokyo productions. Japan: Tokyo. 1987. Lang.: Jap. 1954

Shin, Feng-Shya
Performance/production

Memoir of Chinese opera actress Shin Feng-Shya. China, People's
Republic of. 1987. Lang.: Chi. 3517

Shingeki
Performance/production

History of postwar *shingeki* performance. Japan. 1945-1986. Lang.:
Jap. 1482

Shirk Productions (London)
Performance/production

Collection of newspaper reviews by London theatre critics. UK-
England: London. 1987. Lang.: Eng. 2266

Shirley
Performance/production

Collection of newspaper reviews by London theatre critics. UK-
England: London. 1986. Lang.: Eng. 2091

Shirley, James
Theory/criticism

Trollope's writings on Elizabethan and Jacobean drama. UK-
England. 1866-1882. Lang.: Eng. 3063

Shiu, Fu-Neng
Performance/production

The life of Chinese puppeteer Shiu Fu-Neng. Taiwan. 1987. Lang.:
Chi. 3540

Shiu, Iu-Lan
Performance/production

Chinese opera stars Shiue Jiue-Shian and Shiu Iu-Lan. China,
People's Republic of. 1954-1979. Lang.: Chi. 3494

Shiue, Jiue-Shian
Performance/production

Chinese opera stars Shiue Jiue-Shian and Shiu Iu-Lan. China,
People's Republic of. 1954-1979. Lang.: Chi. 3494

Shō kikaku (Tokyo)
Performance/production

Four Tokyo productions in light of ideas of Betsuyaku Minoru.
Japan: Tokyo. 1987. Lang.: Jap. 1950

Discussion of four Tokyo productions. Japan: Tokyo. 1944-1987.
Lang.: Jap. 1963

Singing — cont'd

Life and career of singer Mario Lanza. USA. 1921-1959. Lang.: Swe. 3171

Conditions affecting Elizabethan minstrels. England: York. 1554-1597. Lang.: Eng. 3254

Libel suit against a minstrel. UK-England: Stafford. 1616. Lang.: Eng. 3269

David Bowie's *Glass Spider Tour*. UK-England. 1987. Lang.: Dut. 3270

Genre of business theatre. USA. 1985-1987. Lang.: Eng. 3272

The Polish cabaret performance group Piwnica. Poland: Cracow. USA: New York, NY. 1987. Lang.: Eng. 3287

Dan-o festival of folk performances. Korea. 800-1987. Lang.: Kor. 3296

Standardization of musical pitch. Europe. USA. 1500-1987. Lang.: Eng. 3399

Chronological repertoire of operas and ballets performed in Reggio Emilia. Italy: Reggio Emilia. 1645-1857. Lang.: Ita. 3403

Southern rural background of blues music. USA. 1800-1985. Lang.: Eng. 3411

Acting in musical drama. USSR. 1920-1970. Lang.: Rus. 3414

Career of Chinese opera actor and teacher Maa Lian Liang. China: Beijing. 1929-1981. Lang.: Chi. 3457

The developmental history of Chinese theatrical music. China. 1702-1986. Lang.: Chi. 3458

Basic characteristics of southern Chinese classical drama. China. 1521-1593. Lang.: Chi. 3459

The development of Chinese classical drama. China. 1386-1900. Lang.: Chi. 3467

The vocal art form of Tarn Shin Peir of the Beijing Opera. China: Beijing. 1847-1917. Lang.: Chi. 3469

Chinese opera star Ba Yuh-Shuang. China, People's Republic of. Lang.: Chi. 3475

Dramatic language in Chinese opera: dancing, music and singing. China, People's Republic of. 1986. Lang.: Chi. 3482

Singing style of Chinese opera. China, People's Republic of. 1987. Lang.: Chi. 3487

The addition of more musical instruments into Chinese opera. China, People's Republic of: Kiangsu. 1987. Lang.: Chi. 3497

Overview of *Gu Cheng-Hei*. China, People's Republic of. 1967. Lang.: Chi. 3498

A new way to produce the music in Chinese opera. China, People's Republic of. 1986. Lang.: Chi. 3505

Four steps to make *Da Peng Ge* more popular. China, People's Republic of. 1987. Lang.: Chi. 3506

Different singing styles of Shyun Chinese opera schools. China, People's Republic of. 1986. Lang.: Chi. 3522

Attempted reforms of the main aspects of Chinese opera. China, People's Republic of. 1987. Lang.: Chi. 3527

Review of *Pirates* and *Student Prince*. South Africa, Republic of: Johannesburg. 1986. Lang.: Eng. 3634

Music Theatre Committee of the New York Singing Teachers Association (NYSTA) symposium on singing popular music. USA: New York, NY. 1985. Lang.: Eng. 3639

Lillias White and her performance in the musical *Dreamgirls*. USA: New York, NY. 1960-1987. 3641

Interview with actress Georgia Brown. USA: New York, NY. UK-England: London. 1957-1985. Lang.: Eng. 3651

Broadway musical's shift from song and dance to aria and recitative. USA: New York, NY. 1956-1984. Lang.: Eng. 3655

Biographical survey of Canadian opera personnel. Canada. 1930-1987. 1987. Lang.: Eng. 3747

Autobiography of opera star Maureen Forrester. Canada. 1930-1986. Lang.: Eng. 3748

Retired critic recalls Toronto opera. Canada: Toronto, ON. 1947-1987. Lang.: Eng. 3749

Interview with Odette Beaupré. Canada. 1987. Lang.: Eng. 3752

Quality of and access to opera training in North America. Canada. USA. 1987. Lang.: Eng. 3753

Interview with soprano Jane MacKenzie. Canada. UK-England. 1987. Lang.: Eng. 3754

Interview with soprano Tracy Dahl. Canada. 1987. Lang.: Eng. 3755

Interview with opera star Gaétan Laperrière. Canada. 1987. Lang.: Eng. 3756

Stuart Hamilton's career in opera broadcasting. Canada: Toronto, ON. 1929-1987. Lang.: Eng. 3758

Profile of mezzo-soprano Eva Randová. Czechoslovakia. 1987. Lang.: Eng. 3760

Cast lists for some early London operas. England: London. 1712-1717. Lang.: Eng. 3761

International biographical survey of opera performers and productions. Europe. North America. 1987. Lang.: Eng. 3762

Biographical survey of Canadian opera performers. Europe. North America. 1987. Lang.: Eng. 3763

Biographical survey of international opera stars. Europe. North America. 1987. Lang.: Eng. 3764

Film versions of Puccini's *La Bohème*, Offenbach's *Tales of Hoffmann*. Europe. North America. 1987. Lang.: Eng. 3767

In defense of vocal ornamentation. Europe. 1767-1987. Lang.: Eng. 3769

The Heldentenor in Wagnerian opera. Europe. North America. 1987. Lang.: Eng. 3770

Interview with tenor Martial Singher. France. USA: Santa Barbara, CA. 1904-1987. Lang.: Eng. 3771

Interview with baritone Michel Sénéchal. France: Paris. 1987. Lang.: Eng. 3772

Directors' notes on the profession of choral singing in opera. Germany, East. 1986. Lang.: Ger. 3778

Special needs in operatic training. Germany, East. 1987. Lang.: Ger. 3780

Interview with choral director Hans-Dieter Pflüger of Dresdner Hoftheater. Germany, East: Dresden. 1979-1986. Lang.: Ger. 3782

Three opera chorus conductors. Germany, East. 1986. Lang.: Ger. 3786

Life and career of tenor Michael Rabsilber. Germany, East. 1982-1986. Lang.: Ger. 3787

Evaluation of soprano Maria Meneghini Callas. Greece. Italy. USA. 1923-1977. Lang.: Eng. 3790

Interview with tenor Plácido Domingo. Hungary: Budapest. 1961-1987. Lang.: Hun. 3791

Interview with singer József Gregor. Hungary. 1963-1987. Lang.: Hun. 3793

Interview with singer Dénes Gulyás. Hungary. 1983-1987. Lang.: Hun. 3794

Biography of tenor János Sárdy. Hungary. 1907-1969. Lang.: Hun. 3795

Review of performances at an assembly of opera ensembles. Hungary: Szeged. 1987. Lang.: Hun. 3796

Soprano Eva Marton discusses Turandot. Hungary. 1943-1987. Lang.: Eng. 3797

Reprint of Richard Wagner's views on *bel canto*, Bellini. Italy. 1837. Lang.: Swe. 3799

Initial recordings of Verdi's operas. Italy. France. USA. 1900-1945. Lang.: Eng. 3800

Style and authenticity at the Rossini festival. Italy: Pesaro. 1984-1987. Lang.: Eng. 3801

Singers/teachers Virginia Zeani and Nicola Rossi-Lemeni. Italy. 1920-1987. Lang.: Eng. 3802

Career of basso Italo Tajo. Italy: Turin. 1935-1982. Lang.: Eng. 3805

Cross-gender casting in Italian Baroque opera. Italy: Venice, Rome. 1550-1987. Lang.: Eng. 3806

Interview with soprano Mirella Freni. Italy: Modena. USA. 1935-1987. Lang.: Eng. 3807

Overview of Latvian opera. Latvia. 1913-1982. Lang.: Rus. 3810

Career of singer Plácido Domingo. Mexico. 1941-1987. Lang.: Eng. 3812

Interview with tenor Plácido Domingo. Mexico: Mexico City. USA: New York, NY, Los Angeles, CA, Houston, TX. 1941-1987. Lang.: Eng. 3813

Teatro Lirico Nacional La Zarzuela. Spain: Madrid. 1925-1987. Lang.: Eng. 3817

Evaluation of soprano, Elisabeth Söderström. Sweden: Stockholm. 1927-1987. Lang.: Eng. 3820

Singing — cont'd

Memories of contralto Kerstin Thorborg. Sweden. Germany. 1932-1970. Lang.: Swe. 3821

Interview with tenor Esias Tewolde-Berhan of Kungliga Teatern. Sweden: Stockholm. Ethiopia. 1944-1987. Lang.: Swe. 3825

Interview with Swiss tenor Hugues Cuénod. Switzerland: Vevey. 1902-1987. Lang.: Eng. 3827

Interview with countertenor Paul Esswood. UK-England: London. 1942-1987. Lang.: Eng. 3830

Careers of three female opera stars: Mary McCormic, Maria Jeritza, Bidú Sayão. USA. 1952-1981. Lang.: Eng. 3835

Repertoire and artistic achievement of the Opera Theatre of St. Louis. USA: St. Louis, MO. 1987. Lang.: Eng. 3840

American premiere of Alban Berg's *Wozzeck*. USA: New York, NY. 1931. Lang.: Eng. 3841

Vasile Moldoveanu's views on the current state of opera. USA. 1987. Lang.: Eng. 3844

Interview with professional opera prompter. USA: Chicago, IL. 1987. Lang.: Eng. 3845

Interview with soprano Barbara Daniels. USA: New York, NY. 1987. Lang.: Eng. 3846

Accompanist/voice teacher, John Wustman. USA. 1960-1987. Lang.: Eng. 3848

Profile of soprano Jeannine Altmeyer. USA: New York, NY. 1950-1987. Lang.: Eng. 3853

Soprano Susan Dunn. USA: New York, NY. 1955-1987. Lang.: Eng. 3854

Interview with tenor James McCracken. USA: Gary, IN. Europe. 1926-1987. Lang.: Eng. 3855

Mezzo soprano Risë Stevens. USA: New York, NY. Lang.: Eng. 3856

Experts discuss vocal training. USA. 1987. Lang.: Eng. 3858

Birgit Nilsson's master voice class at Manhattan School of Music. USA: New York, NY. 1983-1987. Lang.: Eng. 3859

Profile, soprano Leona Mitchell. USA: New York, NY. 1940-1987. Lang.: Eng. 3860

Soprano Bidú Sayão. USA: New York, NY. Brazil. 1902-1987. Lang.: Eng. 3861

Autobiography of opera star Beverly Sills. USA: New York, NY. 1929-1987. Lang.: Eng. 3862

Expanded schedule of outdoor opera performances by Metropolitan Opera. USA: New York, NY. 1967-1987. Lang.: Eng. 3864

History of Turkmenian opera. USSR. 1900-1987. Lang.: Rus. 3865

Georgian opera singer Nodar Andguladze. USSR: Georgia. 1927-1987. Lang.: Rus. 3866

Analysis of Perm Opera Theatre. USSR: Perm. 1980-1987. Lang.: Rus. 3870

Anu Kaal', Estonian opera singer. USSR. 1960-1987. Lang.: Rus. 3872

Problems of the Tbilisi Opera Theatre. USSR: Tbilisi. 1980-1987. Lang.: Rus. 3876

Singer and folk artist P. Lisician. USSR. 1980-1987. Lang.: Rus. 3880

Opera singer, director I.V. Tartakov. USSR. 1860-1923. Lang.: Rus. 3884

Ol'ga Basistjuk, soloist of Kiev Opera Theatre. USSR: Kiev. 1980-1987. Lang.: Rus. 3885

Tijt Kuuzik, operatic artist and teacher. USSR: Estonia. 1911-1987. Lang.: Rus. 3886

Plays/librettos/scripts

Career of singer/actress Lotte Lenya. Germany: Berlin. 1929-1970. Lang.: Eng. 3906

Unique style of modern Japanese Opera. Japan. 1975-1987. Lang.: Eng. 3928

Theory/criticism

Influence of Chinese opera on Japanese drama. China. Japan. 1596-1876. Lang.: Chi. 3586

Training

Interview with singing master Hanno Blaschke. South Africa, Republic of. 1987. Lang.: Eng. 3951

Interviews with singing teachers in New York City. USA: New York, NY. 1987. Lang.: Eng. 3952

Sinise, Gary
Performance/production
Collection of newspaper reviews by London theatre critics. UK-England: London. 1986. Lang.: Eng. 2085

Sink the Belgrano!
Performance/production
Collection of newspaper reviews by London theatre critics. UK-England: London. 1986. Lang.: Eng. 2145

Sir Thomas More
Plays/librettos/scripts
Productions of *Sir Thomas More* by Elizabethan theatre companies. England. 1595-1650. Lang.: Eng. 2541

Siren, Paul
Relation to other fields
Pros and cons of free trade with respect to the performing arts. Canada. USA. 1986. Lang.: Eng. 1220

Sirera, Rodolf
Plays/librettos/scripts
Valencian playwrights writing in both Catalan and Castilian. Spain-Catalonia: Valencia. 1790-1985. Lang.: Cat. 2732

Sirk, David
Theory/criticism
Representation of women by Hollywood film industry. USA: Los Angeles, CA. 1903-1987. Lang.: Eng. 3188

Sister Suzie Cinema
Plays/librettos/scripts
Animal imagery in plays of Lee Breuer. USA. 1987. Lang.: Eng. 2882

Sistren Jamaica Theatre Collective
Relation to other fields
Popular theatre and non-governmental funding agencies. Canada: Sydney, NS. Jamaica. Sudan. 1987. Lang.: Eng. 2982

Sita, Ari
Theory/criticism
Semiotic production in popular performance. South Africa, Republic of. 1980. Lang.: Eng. 1347

Six Characters in Search of an Author
SEE
Sei personaggi in cerca d'autore.

Sjunde inseglet (Seventh Seal, The)
Relation to other fields
Influence of narrative fiction on film and drama: Bergman's *Sjunde inseglet (The Seventh Seal).* Lang.: Eng. 3184

Skarmento, Antonio
Institutions
Regional theatre directors encourage new relationships between Latin American and U.S. artists. Colombia: Bogotá. 1948-1987. Lang.: Eng. 526

Plays/librettos/scripts
Interview with playwright Antonio Skarmento. Chile: Santiago. 1967-1987. Lang.: Eng. 1102

Skelton, Robin
Plays/librettos/scripts
New Canadian drama: non-realistic, anti-naturalistic. Canada. 1983-1984. Lang.: Eng. 2482

Skjelstad, Björn
Performance/production
Director training course at Dalsland Folkhögskola. Sweden. 1987. Lang.: Swe. 886

Rock opera *Drakar och Demoner (Dragons and Demons)* about youth at risk. Sweden: Handen. 1987. Lang.: Swe. 3637

Skjønberg, Espen
Performance/production
Actor Espen Skjønberg talks about acting in Norway and England. UK-England: London. Norway. 1986-1987. Lang.: Eng. 2297

Skloot, Robert
Plays/librettos/scripts
Modern theatrical treatment of Fascism and the Holocaust. 1980-1987. Lang.: Eng. 2428

Sklovskij, Viktor Borisovič
Performance/production
Golden age of Soviet film production. USSR. 1923-1984. Lang.: Hun. 3174

Skop, Sloawomir
Performance/production
Teatr Prowizorium: interview with director Janusz Oprynski. Poland: Lublin. 1971-1987. Lang.: Eng. 1990

Sociology — cont'd

The Non-Smokers by Gianfrancesco Guarnieri. Mexico: Mexico City. 1982-1987. Lang.: Spa. 2697

Use of English in Nigerian drama. Nigeria. 1940-1987. Lang.: Eng. 2706

Problems of Polish society reflected in contemporary theatre. Poland. 1982-1987. Lang.: Pol. 2714

Analysis of *Delo (The Affair)* by A.V. Suchovo-Kobylin. Russia. 1861. Lang.: Rus. 2721

Athol Fugard's *Master Harold...and the Boys* examines apartheid in terms of human relationships. South Africa, Republic of. 1982-1987. Lang.: Eng. 2723

Characterization in Pieter-Dirk Uys' *Appassionata*. South Africa, Republic of. 1987. Lang.: Eng. 2724

Standard German and the German Swiss dialects on and off stage. Switzerland. 1889-1984. Lang.: Ger. 2744

Class conflict as theme of *Top Girls*. UK-England. 1982-1987. Lang.: Eng. 2800

Christina Reid's *Tea in a China Cup*: a woman's view of Belfast. UK-Ireland: Belfast. 1983-1987. Lang.: Eng. 2831

Irish assimilation in plays of Edward Everett Rose. USA. 1900-1920. Lang.: Eng. 2861

Impact of AIDS crisis on the theatre. USA: New York, NY, San Francisco, CA. 1987. Lang.: Eng. 2881

Theatricality of Sam Shepard's early and late works. USA. 1965-1986. Lang.: Eng. 2903

Comparison between Albee's *Who's Afraid of Virginia Woolf?* and Radsinskij's *Jogging*. USSR. USA. 1987. Lang.: Eng. 2960

Roles of Black males in American TV. USA. 1950-1987. Lang.: Eng. 3215

Linguistic forms, historical-cultural significance of shadow puppet theatre. Indonesia. Lang.: Eng. 3379

Chinese opera should reflect the concerns of its audience. China, People's Republic of. 1987. Lang.: Chi. 3578

Analysis of the plays and songs of Irish-American musical theatre star Chauncey Olcott. USA. 1893-1918. Lang.: Eng. 3671

Relation to other fields

Analysis of the role of tradition in theatrical forms of different cultures. Asia. Africa. 1985. Lang.: Fre. 1218

Description of *The Working People's Picture Show*. Canada: Toronto, ON. 1987. Lang.: Eng. 1221

Social implications of popular theatre. Canada. 1987. Lang.: Eng. 1222

Difficulties encountered by playwrights in Canada. Canada: Vancouver, BC. USA: New York, NY. 1987. Lang.: Eng. 1223

Situation of Chinese intellectuals during the Yuan Dynasty. China. 1279-1368. Lang.: Chi. 1225

Characterization in modern drama. China, People's Republic of. 1949-1987. Lang.: Chi. 1227

Theatre and its relationship to society. China, People's Republic of. 1948-1974. Lang.: Chi. 1228

Relationship between theatre and everyday life. Italy. 1900-1987. Lang.: Ita. 1242

Cultural similarities and differences between the United States and Norway. Norway. 1984. Lang.: Eng. 1250

Influences of Black political and economic life on literature, performance. South Africa, Republic of. 1970-1987. Lang.: Eng. 1252

Discussion by theatre women on management, social security. Switzerland. 1987. Lang.: Ger. 1253

The functions and aims of FiT (Women in Theatre). Switzerland. 1985-1986. Lang.: Ger, Fre. 1254

The sociopolitical role of the critic in theatrical criticism. Switzerland. 1960-1985. Lang.: Ger. 1255

Charitable and self-help welfare schemes for theatre personnel, focus on experiences of women. UK-England. 1851-1920. Lang.: Eng. 1258

Documentation on prostitution at the Empire theatre. UK-England: London. 1890. Lang.: Eng. 1259

Nature and effectiveness of political theatre. USA. 1985. Lang.: Eng. 1263

John Malpede's performance workshop for the homeless. USA: Los Angeles, CA. 1984-1987. Lang.: Eng. 1267

Sexuality and desire in performance. USA. 1987. Lang.: Eng. 1270

Theatre in the American South. USA. 1985. Lang.: Eng. 1271

Nontraditional casting of minority actors. USA. 1979-1987. Lang.: Eng. 1274

Theatre as an analogy and metaphor for studying social interaction. USA. 1987. Lang.: Eng. 1279

Assumptions by the actors and the audience in live theatre. USA. 1987. Lang.: Eng. 1283

Diminishing ethics in society and its relation to the theatre. USA. 1987. Lang.: Eng. 1290

Sociologist on art and society. USSR. 1980-1987. Lang.: Rus. 1295

Essays on the theme of marriage in literature. England. Norway. 1300-1985. Lang.: Eng. 1425

Rebuttal to article on gender hierarchy in dance. USA. 1970-1987. Lang.: Eng. 1427

Applications of African 'Theatre for Development' movement to Canadian popular theatre. Africa. Canada: St. John's, NF, Toronto, ON. 1978-1987. Lang.: Eng. 2978

African-American theatre compared to Caribbean and African theatre. Barbados. Bermuda. Nigeria. 1987. Lang.: Eng. 2980

Representation of workers on stage. Europe. USA. 1871-1987. Lang.: Fre. 2987

Theatrical themes and the class issue in the work of Irish playwrights. Ireland. 1900-1987. Lang.: Eng. 2994

Analysis of the role of political drama in Europe. Switzerland: Basel. Mönchengladbach. 1986-1987. Lang.: Ger. 3002

Interview with poet and activist Haki R. Madhubuti (Don L. Lee). USA: Detroit, MI. Africa. Israel. 1942-1985. Lang.: Eng. 3008

Theatrical elements in American politics. USA. 1967-1987. Lang.: Eng. 3102

Idea of *festa* in relation to celebrations honoring Isabella d'Este Gonzaga. Italy: Rome. 1514-1515. Lang.: Ita. 3327

Image of rock singer Madonna in American culture. USA: New York, NY. UK-England: London. 1985-1987. Lang.: Eng. 3386

Polish official promotion of music theatre. Poland. 1950-1965. Lang.: Pol. 3421

Tragic conflicts in playwright's Tang Xian-Zu's cultural conscience. China: Beijing. 1550-1616. Lang.: Chi. 3581

Results of questionnaire on drama education. China, People's Republic of. 1983-1985. Lang.: Chi. 3582

Current ideology: influence on Chinese theatre. China, People's Republic of. 1987. Lang.: Chi. 3583

Wagnerian opera in Argentina. Argentina: Buenos Aires. 1858-1983. Lang.: Eng. 3938

Perceptions of childhood reflected in opera. Europe. 1800-1983. Lang.: Eng. 3940

Audience responses determine character of Mr. Punch. England: London. 1662-1987. Lang.: Eng. 3993

History of puppetry in Catalonia. Spain-Catalonia. 500 B.C.-1987 A.D. Lang.: Eng. 3996

Puppets used in community development workshops. UK-England: London. 1987. Lang.: Eng. 3997

Survival of Punch and Judy shows during the Edwardian period. UK-England. 1860-1910. Lang.: Eng. 3998

Research/historiography

Sociological view of American and English Shakespeare studies. UK-England. USA. 1900-1987. Lang.: Chi. 3014

Theory/criticism

Semiotic production in popular performance. South Africa, Republic of. 1980. Lang.: Eng. 1347

Advantage of having a Broadway theatre. USA: New York, NY. 1985. Lang.: Eng. 1354

Current theatre compared to Ralph Lauren store. USA: New York, NY. 1987. Lang.: Eng. 1356

Correlation of a troubled society and its theatre. USA: New York, NY. 1987. Lang.: Eng. 1357

Balanchine ballerinas: female domination in the ballet. USA. 1946-1987. Lang.: Eng. 1457

The body as emblematic of a character's frame of mind. England. 1583. Lang.: Eng. 3031

Paradoxical and grotesque elements in plays of Dürrenmatt. Europe. 1986. Lang.: Ger. 3034

Rococo elements in the comedies of Marivaux. France. 1715-1774. Lang.: Eng. 3039

Sociology — cont'd

Works of Pierre Corneille and the social role of women. France. 1540-1650. Lang.: Eng.   3040

Functions of comedy in the seventeenth century. Spain. 1604-1690. Lang.: Spa.   3058

Shift of August Strindberg from naturalism to expressionism. Sweden. 1987. Lang.: Eng.   3061

Portrayal of African-American artists in literature. USA. 1926-1987. Lang.: Eng.   3105

Söderberg, Margareta
Institutions
Folkteatergruppen's productions, including *Antigone-nu (Antigone Now)*. Sweden: Stockholm. 1917-1987. Lang.: Swe.   1640

Söderström, Elisabeth
Performance/production
Evaluation of soprano, Elisabeth Söderström. Sweden: Stockholm. 1927-1987. Lang.: Eng.   3820

Södra Teatern (Stockholm)
Design/technology
Newly computerized fly equipment of old Södra Theatre. Sweden: Stockholm. 1985-1987. Lang.: Swe.   363

Sofola, Zulu
Plays/librettos/scripts
Plays by contemporary Nigerian authors. Nigeria. 1950-1987. Lang.: Eng.   2707

Soho Poly Theatre (London)
Performance/production
Collection of newspaper reviews by London theatre critics. UK-England: London. 1986. Lang.: Eng.   2056

Collection of newspaper reviews by London theatre critics. UK-England: London. 1986. Lang.: Eng.   2070

Collection of newspaper reviews by London theatre critics. UK-England: London. 1986. Lang.: Eng.   2093

Collection of newspaper reviews by London theatre critics. UK-England: London. 1986. Lang.: Eng.   2129

Collection of newspaper reviews by London theatre critics. UK-England: London. 1986. Lang.: Eng.   2147

Collection of newspaper reviews by London theatre critics. UK-England: London. 1987. Lang.: Eng.   2187

Collection of newspaper reviews by London theatre critics. UK-England: London. 1987. Lang.: Eng.   2196

Collection of newspaper reviews by London theatre critics. UK-England: London. 1987. Lang.: Eng.   2205

Collection of newspaper reviews by London theatre critics. UK-England: London. 1987. Lang.: Eng.   2222

Collection of newspaper reviews by London theatre critics. UK-England: London. 1987. Lang.: Eng.   2252

Collection of newspaper reviews by London theatre critics. UK-England: London. 1987. Lang.: Eng.   2259

Collection of newspaper reviews by London theatre critics. UK-England: London. 1987. Lang.: Eng.   2270

Collection of newspaper reviews by London theatre critics. UK-England: London. 1987. Lang.: Eng.   2277

Sojuz Teatral'nych Dejatelej RSFSR
Administration
Creation and tasks of Union of Theatre Workers of the Russian SFSR. USSR. 1986-1988. Lang.: Rus.   271

Soldaten, Die
Plays/librettos/scripts
Overview of modern opera criticizing its solemnity. Europe. 1900-1987. Lang.: Swe.   3897

Soldene, Emily
Performance/production
British theatrical touring companies. UK-England. North America. Australia. 1870-1929. Lang.: Eng.   2280

Soldevila, Carles
Plays/librettos/scripts
General history of Catalan literature, including theatre. Spain-Catalonia. 1902-1961. Lang.: Cat.   1157

Soldevila, Carlota
Performance spaces
History of the Teatre Lliure. Spain-Catalonia: Barcelona. 1976-1987. Lang.: Cat.   1673

Soldevila, Ferran
Plays/librettos/scripts
General history of Catalan literature, including theatre. Spain-Catalonia. 1902-1961. Lang.: Cat.   1157

Soldier's Play, A
Performance/production
Discussion of four Tokyo productions. Japan: Tokyo. 1944-1987. Lang.: Jap.   1963

Plays/librettos/scripts
Korean views of American society based on plays of Howard Sackler, Charles Fuller and Jason Miller. USA. 1969-1982. Lang.: Kor.   2837

Charles Fuller's *A Soldier's Play*: debate on means of liberation. USA. 1976-1981. Lang.: Eng.   2854

Solo
Performance/production
Pascal Crochet directs Samuel Beckett's *Solo*. Belgium: Brussels. 1987. Lang.: Fre.   1683

Solodovnikov, A.
Administration
Director A. Solodovnikov discusses foundation of Sovremennik Theatre. USSR: Moscow. 1956-1957. Lang.: Rus.   268

Sologub, Fyodor
Basic theatrical documents
Russian symbolist plays and essays. USSR. 1880-1986. Lang.: Eng.   1584

Solomin, V.
Performance/production
Actors discuss contemporary theatrical process. USSR: Moscow. 1987. Lang.: Rus.   993

Solvognen (Denmark)
Institutions
Profile of political theatre company Solvognen. Denmark. 1969-1982. Lang.: Eng.   528

Sólyom, András
Performance/production
Interview with film director András Sólyom. Hungary. 1987. Lang.: Hun.   3155

Som om jag inte fanns (As if I Didn't Exist)
Institutions
Socialist amateur theatre group Ormen. Sweden: Haninge. 1979-1987. Lang.: Swe.   1639

Some Kind of Hero
Performance/production
Collection of newspaper reviews by London theatre critics. UK-England: London. 1986. Lang.: Eng.   2125

Someone Else's Child
Performance/production
Collection of newspaper reviews by London theatre critics. UK-England: London. 1986. Lang.: Eng.   2086

Somers, Harry
Institutions
Conditions affecting Canadian opera composers. Canada. 1987. Lang.: Eng.   3714

Need for more Canadian productions of Canadian-composed opera. Canada. 1987. Lang.: Eng.   3718

Somewhere Over the Balcony
Performance/production
Collection of newspaper reviews by London theatre critics. UK-England: London. 1987. Lang.: Eng.   2247

Son of Cain
Performance/production
Collection of newspaper reviews by London theatre critics. UK-England: London. 1986. Lang.: Eng.   2099

Sondheim, Stephen
Performance/production
Collection of newspaper reviews by London theatre critics. UK-England: London. 1986. Lang.: Eng.   2052

Collection of newspaper reviews by London theatre critics. UK-England: London. 1986. Lang.: Eng.   2109

Collection of newspaper reviews by London theatre critics. UK-England: London. 1987. Lang.: Eng.   2247

Collection of newspaper reviews of London theatre critics. UK-England: London. 1987. Lang.: Eng.   2273

Collection of newspaper reviews by New York theatre critics. USA: New York, NY. 1987. Lang.: Eng.   2316

Successful London revival of *Follies* by Stephen Sondheim. UK-England: London. USA: New York, NY. 1987. Lang.: Eng.   3638

Interview with musical conductor Paul Gemignani. USA: New York, NY. 1987. Lang.: Eng.   3649

Soyfer, Jura
Plays/librettos/scripts
The comedies of Jura Soyfer. 1836. Lang.: Eng.   2418
Soyikwa African Theatre Group (Soweto)
Performance/production
Review of *Vuka* by Matsemela Manaka. South Africa, Republic of: Soweto. 1976-1987. Lang.: Eng.   2006
Soyinka, Wole
Performance/production
Collection of newspaper reviews by New York theatre critics. USA: New York, NY. 1987. Lang.: Eng.   2326

Plays/librettos/scripts
Study of three plays by Wole Soyinka. Nigeria. 1987. Lang.: Eng.   2704
Wole Soyinka's treatment of political themes. Nigeria. 1973-1987. Lang.: Eng.   2705
Use of English in Nigerian drama. Nigeria. 1940-1987. Lang.: Eng.   2706
Plays by contemporary Nigerian authors. Nigeria. 1950-1987. Lang.: Eng.   2707
Analysis of plays of Femi Osofisan and audience response. Nigeria. 1973-1987. Lang.: Eng.   2708
The Strong Breed and *The Bacchae*: Soyinka's symbolic use of ritual and ceremony. Nigeria. 1973-1987. Lang.: Eng.   2709
The career of playwright Wole Soyinka. USA: New York, NY. Nigeria. 1959-1986. Lang.: Eng.   2865
Spalding, George
Administration
Current computer vendor developments in information systems. USA. 1983-1984. Lang.: Eng.   249
Spanish Play, The
Performance/production
Collection of newspaper reviews by London theatre critics. UK-England: London. 1986. Lang.: Eng.   2069
Spanish Tragedy, The
Plays/librettos/scripts
Structure of revenge tragedy in Shakespeare's *Hamlet*. 1600. Lang.: Eng.   2425
Madness and revenge in Kyd's *The Spanish Tragedy*. England. 1589. Lang.: Eng.   2515
Spark Theatre Company (London)
Performance/production
Collection of newspaper reviews by London theatre critics. UK-England: London. 1987. Lang.: Eng.   2176
Sparkle Plenty
Performance/production
Collection of newspaper reviews by London theatre critics. UK-England: London. 1986. Lang.: Eng.   2114
Speca, Luigi
Design/technology
Malabar Costume Company's work for opera. Canada: Toronto, ON. 1900-1987. Lang.: Eng.   3693
Special effects
Design/technology
The impact of twentieth-century technology on theatre. Canada. 1900-1987. Lang.: Fre.   302
The use and development of special effects in the theatre. Canada. 1977-1987. Lang.: Fre.   303
Early use of the counterweight system. England. 1433-1579. Lang.: Eng.   316
Effects of mixed media on traditional dramatic components of theatre. Europe. 1900-1987. Lang.: Fre.   318
Baroque stage machinery described in archives. Italy: Parma. 1675-1700. Lang.: Eng.   347
Restoration of the stage machinery at the Grand Theatre. UK-Wales: Llandudno. 1901-1987. Lang.: Eng.   381
Experiments with light. USA. 1987. Lang.: Eng.   383
Design aspects of *The Glory of Easter*: computerized lighting, lasers and pyrotechnics. USA. 1982. Lang.: Eng.   387
Creating lighting effects to work in rhythm with music. USA. 1987. Lang.: Eng.   415
Multimedia experts discuss the creation of special effects. USA. 1987. Lang.: Eng.   422
Instructions on how to make a fog machine silencer. USA. 1987. Lang.: Eng.   453

Comprehensive look at touring theatre. USA. 1987. Lang.: Eng.   464
How to devise a circuit to simulate TV light on stage. USA. 1987. Lang.: Eng.   470
Special effects technology in theatre. Canada: Toronto, ON. 1985. Lang.: Eng.   1586
Colorization of films and arguments against its use. USA. 1987. Lang.: Eng.   3129
Colorization of films and arguments for its use. USA. 1987. Lang.: Eng.   3134
The use of computers to enhance theatre technology. Canada. 1987. Lang.: Fre.   3192
The use of holography in theatre. Canada. 1987. Lang.: Fre.   3201
Effects of new technologies on theatre. Canada. 1969-1987. Lang.: Fre.   3202
Dennis O'Sullivan's work with mixed media. Canada. 1986. Lang.: Fre.   3203
Mark Pauline, Matthew Heckert and Eric Werner: performance artists who construct performing machines. USA: San Francisco, CA. 1986. Lang.: Eng.   3342
Three ways to avoid being boring in Hsi Ch'u while on stage. China, People's Republic of. 1986. Lang.: Chi.   3444
Machinery to be installed in Her Majesty's Theatre for *Phantom of the Opera*. UK-England: London. 1987. Lang.: Eng.   3619
Rigging special circus effects for *Barnum*. USA. 1986. Lang.: Eng.   3622

Performance/production
West Coast artists explore audiovisual effects. USA. 1987. Lang.: Eng.   969
Lorna Heaton's use of holograms in *Woyzeck*. Canada: Banff, AB. 1987. Lang.: Fre.   3205
Minor theatrical forms involving tableaux, mechanics. Italy: Venice. 1800-1900. Lang.: Ita.   3263
Speculators
Performance/production
Collection of newspaper reviews by London theatre critics. UK-England. 1987. Lang.: Eng.   2262
Speers, David
Institutions
Historical survey of opera in Calgary. Canada: Calgary, AB. 1971-1987. Lang.: Eng.   3719
Spencer, David
Performance/production
Collection of newspaper reviews by London theatre critics. UK-England: London. 1987. Lang.: Eng.   2252
Speranza's Boy
Plays/librettos/scripts
Interview with playwright John Boyd: influences and plays. UK-Ireland: Belfast. 1930-1985. Lang.: Eng.   2828
Sperr, Martin
Plays/librettos/scripts
Four German playwrights: Fleisser, Sperr, Kroetz, Fassbinder. Germany. 1900-1987. Lang.: Ita.   2602
Spesivcev, Vjačeslav
Performance/production
Jaroslav Dudek directs *A Day Lasts Longer than a Century* by Čingiz Ajmatov, Vinohradské Theatre. Czechoslovakia: Prague. 1987. Lang.: Cze.   774
Spewack, Bella
Performance/production
Collection of newspaper reviews by London theatre critics. UK-England: London. 1987. Lang.: Eng.   2239
Collection of newspaper reviews by London theatre critics. UK-England: London. 1987. Lang.: Eng.   2253
Spewack, Sam
Performance/production
Collection of newspaper reviews by London theatre critics. UK-England: London. 1987. Lang.: Eng.   2253
Speyer, Peter
Performance/production
Collection of newspaper reviews by London theatre critics. UK-England: London. 1987. Lang.: Eng.   2226
Spielberg, Stephen
Theory/criticism
Portrayals of African-Americans in media and literature. USA. 1926-1987. Lang.: Eng.   3104

Staging — cont'd

SUBJECT INDEX

Staging — cont'd

Innovative director Leon Schiller. Poland. 1920-1939. Lang.: Rus.
870

Festival of Polish plays. Poland: Wrocław. 1987. Lang.: Eng, Fre.
871

The 17th Warsaw theatre conference. Poland: Warsaw. 1987. Lang.: Eng, Fre.
872

The 4th International Theatre Conference: includes list of participants and their contributions. Poland: Warsaw. 1986. Lang.: Eng, Fre.
873

Overview of Polish theatre scene. Poland: Warsaw, Cracow. 1987. Lang.: Eng.
874

Interview with Polish playwright Tadeusz Kantor. Poland: Cracow. Germany, West: Kassel. Italy: Milan. Italy: Sicily. 1987. Lang.: Eng, Fre.
876

Avant-garde performances presented at International Open Theatre meeting. Poland: Wrocław. 1982-1987. Lang.: Pol, Eng, Fre.   877

Early life of director Konrad Swinarski. Poland. 1929-1955. Lang.: Pol.
878

Soviet tours of Teatrul C.I. Nottara. Romania: Bucharest. 1980-1987. Lang.: Rus.
879

Collection of theatre reviews by J.M. de Sagarra. Spain-Catalonia: Barcelona. 1922-1927. Lang.: Cat.
885

Director training course at Dalsland Folkhögskola. Sweden. 1987. Lang.: Swe.
886

A class for amateur directors. Sweden: Katrineberg. 1987. Lang.: Swe.
887

Yearly productions of Calderón's *El gran teatro del mundo (The Great Stage of the World)*. Switzerland: Einsiedeln. 1987. Lang.: Ger.
893

Reviews of Pinter's *The Lover* and *A Slight Ache*. UK-England: London. 1987. Lang.: Eng.
901

History of experimental and alternative theatre. UK-England. 1800-1987. Lang.: Eng.
904

Two productions of Pinter's *Old Times*. UK-England: London. USA: New York, NY, St. Louis, MO. 1971-1985. Lang.: Eng.
907

Staging community theatre. UK-England. 1987. Lang.: Eng.   909

Casting community theatre. UK-England: Dorchester. 1987. Lang.: Eng.
913

English Shakespearean productions. UK-England: London, Manchester, Stratford. 1985-1986. Lang.: Eng.
917

Relationship of theatre, class and gender. UK-England. USA. 1969-1985. Lang.: Eng.
918

Ukrainian theatrical process. Ukraine. 1970-1979. Lang.: Rus.   923

Overview of Soviet Ukrainian theatre. Ukraine. 1917-1987. Lang.: Ukr.
924

Rehearsals and performance of Joseph Chaikin's *A War Within*. USA: San Francisco, CA. 1987. Lang.: Eng.
930

Protest theatre, its social and artistic aspects. USA. 1960-1979. Lang.: Rus.
933

Gays and lesbians on the American stage. USA. 1896-1987. Lang.: Eng.
935

Transformation of *La Cage aux Folles* from movie to a Broadway musical. USA: New York, NY. 1983-1987. Lang.: Eng.   940

Audience participation in Living Theatre's *Paradise Now*. USA: New York, NY. 1968. Lang.: Kor.
945

Overview of Mexican-American theatre. USA. Mexico. 1850-1987. Lang.: Eng.
946

Career of director/author Andre Ernotte. USA: New York, NY. 1987. Lang.: Eng.
954

Career of actor, director, playwright Charles Ludlam. USA: New York, NY. 1964-1987. Lang.: Eng.
956

Interview with director Ron Link. USA: New York, NY. 1987. Lang.: Eng.
963

West Coast artists explore audiovisual effects. USA. 1987. Lang.: Eng.
969

Director A.J. Antoon discusses *Sherlock's Last Case*. USA: New York, NY. 1987. Lang.: Eng.
970

Interview with director Robert Brustein. USA: Cambridge, MA. 1987. Lang.: Eng.
974

Career of director Garland Wright. USA. 1972-1987. Lang.: Eng.
975

Director Mary Robinson's career in regional theatre. USA. 1976-1987. Lang.: Eng.
976

Threat of extinction of live performance. USA. 1987. Lang.: Eng.
979

Critics' round-table on Leningrad theatre season. USSR: Leningrad. 1986-1987. Lang.: Rus.
983

Review of Moscow theatre season. USSR: Moscow. 1986-1987. Lang.: Rus.
984

Articles on director Aleksand'r Achmeteli by leading theatre figures. USSR. 1886-1937. Lang.: Rus.
986

Young studio theatre artists of Moscow. USSR: Moscow. 1980-1987.
987

Stanislavskij's rehearsal notes for Byron's *Cain*. USSR. 1920. Lang.: Rus.
988

Round-table of Soviet directors. USSR: Moscow. 1980-1987. Lang.: Rus.
989

Soviet directors discuss children's theatre. USSR. 1987. Lang.: Rus.
991

Actors discuss contemporary theatrical process. USSR: Moscow. 1987. Lang.: Rus.
993

Overview of Michajl Levitin's direction of Theatre of Miniatures. USSR: Moscow. 1980-1987. Lang.: Rus.
994

Sergej Jurskij, director of Mossovet Theatre. USSR: Moscow. 1970-1980. Lang.: Rus.
995

Actor and playwright A.I. Sumbatov-Južin. USSR: Moscow. 1857-1927. Lang.: Rus.
998

Oleg Tabakov's experimental group 'Echo'. USSR. 1980-1987. Lang.: Rus.
1001

Work of Andrej Borisov, principal director of Jakutskij Drama Theatre. USSR: Yakutsk. 1980-1987. Lang.: Rus.   1003

History of Moscow State University student theatre. USSR: Moscow. 1960-1980. Lang.: Rus.
1004

Theatre sociologist's view of theatrical work and experimentation. USSR. 1986-1988. Lang.: Rus.   1006

History of Kazan Bolšoj Drama Theatre. USSR: Kazan. 1917-1987. Lang.: Rus.
1007

Problems of theatrical experimentation. USSR. 1986-1988. Lang.: Rus.
1011

Current prospects for the development of Soviet theatrical art. USSR. 1987. Lang.: Rus.
1012

The work of Sergej Jašin, principal director of Gogol Theatre. USSR: Moscow. 1987. Lang.: Rus.   1014

Creativity in experimental theatre. USSR. 1986-1988. Lang.: Rus.
1015

History of Nachičevan theatre. USSR. 1900-1987. Lang.: Rus.   1016

Plays of Čechov interpreted by director Oleg Jefremov. USSR: Moscow. 1960-1987. Lang.: Rus.
1017

Moscow Lenin Comsomol's 'Debut', an experimental group. USSR: Moscow. 1987. Lang.: Rus.
1018

Overview of issues in Moscow theatre season. USSR: Moscow. 1986-1987. Lang.: Rus.
1019

Playwrights, critics and directors discuss the Moscow season. USSR: Moscow. 1986-1987. Lang.: Rus.
1022

Directors discuss their training under G.A. Tovstonogov. USSR: Moscow. 1960-1987. Lang.: Rus.
1026

Portrait of director Gennadij Trostjaneckij. USSR: Omsk. 1980-1987. Lang.: Rus.
1028

Review of the Leningrad theatre season. USSR: Leningrad. 1986-1987. Lang.: Rus.
1030

Work of Ukrainian director L. Kurbas. USSR. 1887-1942. Lang.: Rus.
1031

Director Anatolij Efros on directing, ethics. USSR: Moscow. 1981-1982. Lang.: Rus.
1033

Interview with director Georgij Tovstonogov. USSR: Leningrad. 1980-1987. Lang.: Rus.
1034

Centenary collection of materials by director L. Kurbas. USSR. 1887-1942. Lang.: Rus.
1035

Life and work of Anatolij Efros. USSR: Moscow. 1983-1987. Lang.: Eng.
1038

Overview of 1986-1987 Moscow theatre season. USSR: Moscow. 1986-1987. Lang.: Eng.
1039

Staging — cont'd

Staging — cont'd

Popular theatre, mostly on economic, feminist themes. Canada: Sudbury, ON. 1930-1987. Lang.: Eng. 1709

Canadian playwright Allan Stratton. Canada: Toronto, ON. 1982. Lang.: Eng. 1710

Playwright Erika Ritter. Canada: Toronto, ON. 1982. Lang.: Eng. 1711

Personnel associated with production of Lepage's *La Trilogie des dragons.* Canada. 1987. Lang.: Fre. 1713

Robert Lepage: creation, direction of *La Trilogie des dragons (Dragons' Trilogy).* Canada. 1987. Lang.: Fre. 1716

Workshop in Chinese acting methods. Canada: Toronto, ON. China, People's Republic of: Shanghai. 1987. Lang.: Eng. 1717

Overview of theatre in Ottawa. Canada: Ottawa, ON. 1960-1983. Lang.: Eng. 1719

Interview with Chilean director Alejandro Quintana Contreras. Chile. Germany, East: Berlin, East. 1987. Lang.: Spa. 1720

Chinese production of Beckett's *Waiting for Godot.* China, People's Republic of: Shanghai. 1986-1987. Lang.: Chi. 1721

International Brecht symposium. China, People's Republic of: Beijing, Hong Kong. Japan: Tokyo. 1986. Lang.: Eng. 1722

Interview with actor-director Jozef Bednárik. Czechoslovakia: Nitra. 1987. Lang.: Hun. 1727

Photo essay on theatre company Billedstofteater. Denmark. 1977-1982. Lang.: Eng. 1730

Romantic drama in performance: effect on modern theatre. England. 1700-1987. Lang.: Eng. 1732

Historical accuracy in 19th-century London theatre productions. England: London. 1800-1900. Lang.: Eng. 1734

Shakespeare and contemporaries: tradition, intertextuality in performance. England. 1607-1987. Lang.: Eng. 1740

'Boy actresses' and attitudes toward sensuality in performance. England: London. 1580-1630. Lang.: Eng. 1741

New interpretation of Jacobean theatre. England: London. 1596-1633. Lang.: Eng. 1743

Church condemnation of Roman *ludi*, creative impulse behind medieval drama. Europe. 160-1578. Lang.: Eng. 1745

Jean-Pierre Vincent directs *Le mariage de Figaro (The Marriage of Figaro)* by Beaumarchais. France: Paris. 1987. Lang.: Fre. 1751

Plays of Pinget, Euripides and Théâtre du Rideau staged by Jouanneau, Suzuki and Tanguy, Théâtre de la Bastille. France: Paris. 1987. Lang.: Fre. 1753

Giorgio Strehler as the quintessential director of the century. France. Italy. 1921-1987. Lang.: Fre. 1754

Patrice Chéreau and Théâtre des Amandiers create stage and film versions of Čechov's *Platonov.* France: Nanterre. 1982-1987. Lang.: Swe. 1755

Director as true author and maker of theatre. France. 1987. Lang.: Fre. 1757

Personal notes of Samuel Beckett, how they illuminate his plays. France. 1969-1984. Lang.: Eng. 1758

Directing and the desire to communicate. France. 1987. Lang.: Fre. 1759

Review of the 1986 Festival de la Francophonie. France. Belgium. 1986. Lang.: Fre. 1760

Analysis of *Dans la solitude des champs de coton (In the Solitude of the Cotton Fields)* by Bernard-Marie Koltès. France: Paris. 1987. Lang.: Swe. 1761

Directorial style of Claude Régy. France. 1955-1987. Lang.: Fre. 1762

Directing should be judged by the work of great directors. France. 1987. Lang.: Fre. 1763

Brigitte Jacques as Elvire in Molière's *Dom Juan.* France: Strasbourg. 1940-1986. Lang.: Fre. 1764

Luca Ronconi's view of directing. France. Italy. 1987. Lang.: Fre. 1765

Directing methods of Klaus Michael Grüber. France. Germany. 1945-1987. Lang.: Fre. 1766

Antoine Vitez directs *Le soulier de satin (The Satin Slipper)* by Paul Claudel, Festival of Avignon. France: Avignon. 1987. Lang.: Fre. 1767

Directing as textual interpretation, relating performance to text. France. 1987. Lang.: Fre. 1768

Soviet tour of Comédie-Française: Jean-Pierre Vincent directs Molière's *Le Misanthrope.* France. USSR. 1980-1987. Lang.: Rus. 1769

Biography of Max Reinhardt. Germany. 1873-1943. Lang.: Rus. 1770

Analysis of Brecht's original directing style and dramaturgy. Germany. 1925-1987. Lang.: Eng. 1771

Reviews of major Berlin performances. Germany: Berlin. 1889-1933. Lang.: Ger. 1772

August Wilhelm Iffland's productions of plays by Friedrich von Schiller. Germany: Berlin. 1796-1806. Lang.: Ger. 1773

Brecht as director. Germany. 1922-1956. Lang.: Eng. 1774

Politics and Shakespeare in Weimar Republic. Germany. 1919-1930. Lang.: Eng. 1775

Early productions of Brecht's plays reflected in the press. Germany: Berlin. 1922-1933. Lang.: Ger. 1777

A Hungarian reviewer's impressions of several theatre productions in East Berlin. Germany, East: Berlin, East. 1987. Lang.: Hun. 1779

Change from sociopolitical emphasis to individual themes in productions of *A Midsummer Night's Dream.* Germany, East. 1960-1980. Lang.: Eng. 1782

Annual Brecht workshop. Germany, East. 1985. Lang.: Fre. 1785

German productions of Strindberg plays. Germany, West. Germany, East. Sweden. 1984-1986. Lang.: Ger. 1788

Theatre critics' awards of the season. Hungary. 1987. Lang.: Hun. 1789

Production history of *Galilei (Galileo)* by László Németh. Hungary. 1952-1987. Lang.: Hun. 1790

Interview with director József Ruszt. Hungary. 1983-1987. Lang.: Hun. 1791

Interview with actor-director László Mensáros. Hungary. 1952-1987. Lang.: Hun. 1792

Interview with actor-director Miklós Gábor. Hungary. 1962-1987. Lang.: Hun. 1793

Christopher Hampton's *Les Liaisons Dangereuses* directed by János Szikora at Pesti Szinház under the title *Veszedelmes viszonyok.* Hungary: Budapest. 1986. Lang.: Hun. 1795

László Márton directs *La estrella de Sevilla (The Star of Seville)* by Lope de Vega at Vigszinház under the title *Sevilla csillaga.* Hungary: Budapest. 1986. Lang.: Hun. 1796

Géza Tordy as Willy Loman in Arthur Miller's *Death of a Salesman* directed, as *Az ügynök halála*, by János Szikora at Vigszinház. Hungary: Budapest. 1987. Lang.: Hun. 1797

András Sütő's *Álomkommandó (Dream Commando)* directed by Ferenc Sík at Vigszinház. Hungary: Budapest. 1987. Lang.: Hun. 1798

Interview with director Tamás Ascher. Hungary. 1987. Lang.: Hun. 1800

János Mrsán directs *The Cocktail Party* by T.S. Eliot at Várszinház under the title *Koktél hatkor.* Hungary: Budapest. 1987. Lang.: Hun. 1803

György Lengyel directs Camus's *Caligula* at Madách Szinház Chamber Theatre. Hungary: Budapest. 1986. Lang.: Hun. 1804

Ottó Ádám directs Anton Pavlovič Čechov's *Višněvyj sad (The Cherry Orchard)* at Madách Theatre under the title *Cseresznyéskert.* Hungary: Budapest. 1987. Lang.: Hun. 1805

G.E. Lessing's *Nathan der Weise (Nathan the Wise)* staged by József Ruszt, Hevesi Sándor Theatre. Hungary: Zalaegerszeg. 1986. Lang.: Hun. 1806

La estrella de Sevilla (The Star of Seville) by Lope de Vega, staged by László Márton at Vigszinház. Hungary: Budapest. 1986. Lang.: Hun. 1807

Analysis of *Kék róka (The Silver Fox)* by Ferenc Herczeg compares Zsuzsa Bencze's staging with previous productions. Hungary: Budapest. 1986. Lang.: Hun. 1808

Shakespeare at Várszinház: László Vámos directs *Henry IV* Parts I and II, Imre Kerényi directs *Henry V.* Hungary: Budapest. 1986. Lang.: Hun. 1810

Shakespeare's *King Lear* staged by Menyhért Szegvári at the National Theatre. Hungary: Pécs. 1986. Lang.: Hun. 1811

Five short plays by Géza Páskándi at SUNY Binghamton. Hungary. USA: Binghamton, NY. 1987. Lang.: Eng. 1813

Menyhért Szegvári directs Miklós Munkácsi's *Lisszaboni eső (Rain in Lisbon)* at Játékszín. Hungary: Budapest. 1987. Lang.: Hun. 1815

Staging — cont'd

Camus's *Caligula* staged by György Lengyel, Madách Chamber Theatre. Hungary: Budapest. 1986. Lang.: Hun. 1816

Andor Gábor's *Dollárpapa (Dollar Daddy)* directed by Gábor Berényi. Hungary: Budapest. 1987. Lang.: Hun. 1817

Örökösök (Heirs) by Gorkij directed by Tamás Fodor. Hungary: Szolnok. 1987. Lang.: Hun. 1818

Imre Kerényi directs *Énekes madár (The Song Bird)* by Áron Tamási at the National Theatre. Hungary: Budapest. 1987. Lang.: Hun. 1819

Season openings at Petőfi Theatre, including Lengyel's *A nagy fejedelem (The Great Prince)* and Bíró's *A rablólovag (The Gallant Kidnapper)*. Hungary: Veszprém. 1987. Lang.: Hun. 1820

Reviews: *A vörös postakocsi (The Red Mail Coach)* by Gyula Krúdy, staged by Dezső Kapás and *Az atyai ház (The Paternal Roof)* by Zsigmond Remenyik, staged by Péter Lener. Hungary: Veszprém, Nyíregyháza. 1986. Lang.: Hun. 1821

Reviews of *Téli zsoltár (A Winter Psalm)* by Kovách, Shakespeare's *Much Ado About Nothing* and *Ferde ház (The Leaning House)* by Gerencsér performed at Kisfaludy Theatre. Hungary: Győr. 1986. Lang.: Hun. 1822

László Vámos directs *Les femmes savantes (The Learned Ladies)* by Molière at Várszinház under the title *Tudós nők.* Hungary: Budapest. 1987. Lang.: Hun. 1823

Essay on interpretive methods in performance and production. Hungary. 1987. Lang.: Hun. 1824

Miklós Szurdi directs *Kat a blázen (The Hangman and the Madman)* by Jan Werick and Jiří Voskoveč, songs by Jaroslav Jezek, at Radnóti Miklós Szinpad as *Hóhér és Bolond.* Hungary: Budapest. 1986. Lang.: Hun. 1825

Imre Csiszár directs Bertolt Brecht's *Leben des Galilei (The Life of Galileo)* at the National Theatre. Hungary: Miskolc. 1987. Lang.: Hun. 1826

Reviews of two Anouilh plays: *Eurydice* directed by János Szűcs, *Colombe* directed by Mátyás Giricz. Hungary: Miskolc, Budapest. 1987. Lang.: Hun. 1827

Tamás Jordán's *Amit a szívedbe rejtesz (Hidden in Your Heart)* directed by János Gáspár. Hungary: Budapest. 1987. Lang.: Hun. 1828

Vendégség (The Host and the Guest) staged by János Taub at Játékszín. Hungary: Budapest. 1986. Lang.: Hun. 1829

Comparison of the premiere of Imre Sarkadi's *Oszlopos Simeon (The Man on the Pillar)* and two revivals by Árpad Árkosi and István Horvai. Hungary: Szeged, Budapest. 1967-1987. Lang.: Hun. 1830

István Paál directs István Örkény's *Forgatókönyv (Screenplay)* at Petőfi Theatre. Hungary: Veszprém. 1987. Lang.: Hun. 1832

Interview with director András Jeles of Monteverdi Birkózókör (Budapest). Hungary. 1985-1987. Lang.: Hun. 1833

János Gáspar directs *Amit a szívedbe rejtesz (Hidden in Your Heart)* by Tamás Jordán, based on notes by poet Attila József, at Radnóti Miklós Theatre. Hungary: Budapest. 1987. Lang.: Hun. 1836

Péter Blaskó in the title role of Brecht's *Leben des Galilei (The Life of Galileo)* directed as *Galilei élete* by Imre Csiszár at Miskolc National Theatre. Hungary: Miskolc. 1987. Lang.: Hun. 1839

Péter Tömöry directs premiere of Zsigmond Móricz's 1916 *Fortunátus.* Hungary: Zalaegerszeg. 1987. Lang.: Hun. 1840

Director Imre Kerényi discusses *Csiksomlyó passió (Passion Play of Csiksomlyó)*. Hungary. 1982-1987. Lang.: Hun. 1843

Imre Halasi directs *Sári bíró (Judge Sári)* by Zsigmond Móricz, music by István Mikó, at Kisvarda Castle Theatre. Hungary: Kisvárda. 1987. Lang.: Hun. 1845

La vida es sueño (Life Is a Dream) directed by Miklós Szinetár at Radnóti Miklós Theatre under the title *Az élet álom.* Hungary: Budapest. 1986. Lang.: Hun. 1846

Tamás Fodor directs *Örökösök (Heirs)* based on Gorkij's *Vassa Železnova.* Hungary: Szolnok. 1987. Lang.: Hun. 1848

István Horvai directs Imre Sarkadi's *Oszlopos Simeon (The Man on the Pillar)* at the Pesti Theatre. Hungary: Budapest. 1987. Lang.: Hun. 1849

Gábor Zsámbéki directs Eugene O'Neill's *Long Day's Journey into Night* under the title *Utazás az éjszakába.* Hungary: Eger. 1987. Lang.: Hun. 1850

Ferenc Sík directs *Galilei (Galileo)* by László Németh at Várszinház. Hungary: Budapest. 1987. Lang.: Hun. 1851

Interview with director Tamás Ascher. Hungary. 1970-1987. Lang.: Hun. 1853

István Szőke directs Shakespeare's *Merchant of Venice*, Pécs National Theatre. Hungary: Pécs. 1987. Lang.: Hun. 1854

Ferenc Sík directs András Sütő's *Álomkommandó (Dream Commando)*, Gyulai Várszinház. Hungary: Gyula. 1987. Lang.: Hun. 1855

István Szőke directs *Mari* by György Schwajda at Pécsi Nemzeti Szinház. Hungary: Pécs. 1986. Lang.: Hun. 1856

Gábor Székely directs Milán Füst's *Catullus* at Katona József Theatre. Hungary: Budapest. 1987. Lang.: Hun. 1857

Menyhért Szegvári directs premiere of *Lisszaboni eső (Rain in Lisbon)* by Miklós Munkácsi at Játékszín. Hungary: Budapest. 1987. Lang.: Hun. 1858

L'illusion comique (The Comic Illusion) by Pierre Corneille directed by János Szikora at the Katona József Theatre. Hungary: Budapest. 1986. Lang.: Hun. 1859

Director Endre Márton. Hungary. 1941-1978. Lang.: Hun. 1860

Eszter Csákányi as *Saint Joan* by George Bernard Shaw, directed by László Babarczy at Csiky Gergely Theatre as *Szent Johanna.* Hungary: Kaposvár. 1983-1987. Lang.: Hun. 1861

Kean by Dumas and Sartre, directed by Tamás Szirtes, Madách Theatre. Hungary: Budapest. 1986. Lang.: Hun. 1862

Tamás Szirtes directs Gyula Háy's *Mohács (The Mohács Disaster)* at Madách Szinház. Hungary. 1987. Lang.: Hun. 1863

László Bagossy directs *Macbeth*, Tamás Jordán directs Zsigmond Móricz's *Úri muri (Gentlemen's Spree)* at Pécs Summer Theatre. Hungary: Pécs. 1987. Lang.: Hun. 1864

Fadren (The Father) by August Strindberg presented under the title *Az apa* at Katona József Theatre, guest director Kalle Holmberg. Hungary: Budapest. 1987. Lang.: Hun. 1865

József Ruszt directs G.E. Lessing's *Nathan der Weise (Nathan the Wise)* at Hevesi Sándor Theatre under the title *Bölcs Náthán.* Hungary: Zalaegerszeg. 1986. Lang.: Hun. 1866

Eszter Csákányi in the title role of Shaw's *Saint Joan*, directed under the title *Szent Johanna* by László Babarczy at Csiky Gergely Theatre. Hungary: Kaposvár. 1987. Lang.: Hun. 1867

Tamás Ascher directs *Il campiello (The Public Square)* by Goldoni at Csiky Gergely Theatre. Hungary: Kaposvár. 1987. Lang.: Hun. 1868

Arthur Miller's *Death of a Salesman* directed by János Szikora at Vígszínház. Hungary: Budapest. 1987. Lang.: Hun. 1869

Miklós Vámos' *Világszezon (World Tourist Season)* staged by János Sándor at National Theatre. Hungary: Szeged. 1986. Lang.: Hun. 1870

Review of *Csirkefej (Chickenhead)* by György Spiró, directed by Gábor Zsámbécki at Katona József Theatre. Hungary: Budapest. 1986. Lang.: Hun. 1871

Áron Tamási's *Énekes madár (The Song Bird)* directed by Imre Kerényi at National Theatre. Hungary: Budapest. 1987. Lang.: Hun. 1872

Péter Huszti directs *A női partőrség szeme láttára (In Sight of the Spar)* by Pál Békés at Madách Szinház Chamber Theatre. Hungary: Budapest. 1987. Lang.: Hun. 1873

Edward Bond's *The Fool* under the title *A bolond* directed by László Salamon Suba at Móricz Zsigmond Theatre. Hungary: Nyíregyháza. 1986. Lang.: Hun. 1875

Péter Léner directs Géza Páskandi's *Lélekharang (Death Knell)*, Móricz Zsigmond Theatre. Hungary: Nyíregyháza. 1987. Lang.: Hun. 1876

Úri muri (Gentlemen's Spree) by Zsigmond Móricz staged by Mátyás Giricz at Jókai Theatre. Hungary: Békéscsaba. 1986. Lang.: Hun. 1877

Gábor Székely directs Milán Füst's *Catullus* at Katona József Theatre. Hungary: Budapest. 1987. Lang.: Hun. 1878

Reviews of two plays by István Örkény: *Forgatókönyv (Screenplay)* directed by István Paál and two productions of *Tóték (The Tót Family)* staged by János Meczner and István Pinczés. Hungary: Veszprém, Budapest, Debrecen. 1986-1987. Lang.: Hun. 1880

Shakespeare's *A Midsummer Night's Dream* staged by Tibor Csizmadia. Hungary: Eger, Szolnok. 1986. Lang.: Hun. 1881

David Mamet's *American Buffalo* directed by Péter Dezsényi at National Theatre as *Amerikai bölény.* Hungary: Pécs. 1986. Lang.: Hun. 1882

SUBJECT INDEX

Staging — cont'd

Encounter between Pirandello and Lord Dunsany during Pirandello's production of *I pazzi sulla montagna (The Gods of the Mountain)* by Alessandro De Stefani. Italy. 1923-1928. Lang.: Eng.   1947

Giorgio Strehler's staging of *L'illusion comique (The Comic Illusion)* by Corneille. Italy. 1944-1986. Lang.: Eng.   1948

Four Tokyo productions in light of ideas of Betsuyaku Minoru. Japan: Tokyo. 1987. Lang.: Jap.   1950

Reviews of Oriental dance-drama performances. Japan. Indonesia. 1986. Lang.: Hun.   1951

István Pinczés directs Örkény's *Tóték (The Tót Family)* in Japan. Japan: Toyama. 1986. Lang.: Hun.   1952

Six plays of the Tokyo season, focus on director Betsuyaku Minoru. Japan: Tokyo. 1986. Lang.: Jap.   1966

Korean theatre personalities. Korea. 1900-1986. Lang.: Kor.   1970

Survey of critical reactions to contemporary Korean theatre. Korea: Seoul. 1986-1987. Lang.: Kor.   1971

Development of Korean theatre. Korea: Seoul. 1930-1939. Lang.: Kor.   1973

Examination of language in Beth Henley's *The Miss Firecracker Contest*. Mexico: Mexico City. 1987. Lang.: Spa.   1974

Experimental theatre groups in Mexico City. Mexico: Mexico City. 1987. Lang.: Spa.   1975

Review of *I Poli (The Town)* based on Greek theatre tradition and performed in absurdist style. Mexico: Mexico City. 1987. Lang.: Spa.   1976

Review of *La Alegría de las Tandas (The Happiness of the Groups)* by Enrique Alonso. Mexico: Mexico City. 1987. Lang.: Spa.   1977

Review of *El Balcón*: production of Genet's *Le Balcon (The Balcony)*. Mexico: Mexico City. 1987. Lang.: Spa.   1978

Interview with Frans Strijards, playwright and director. Netherlands. 1987. Lang.: Dut.   1979

Peter Sellars and American National Theatre present *Ajax*, Holland Festival. Netherlands. USA. 1987. Lang.: Dut.   1981

Postwar Dutch theatre: growth of small theatre groups. Netherlands. 1975-1985. Lang.: Dut.   1982

Recent productions of Strindberg plays in the Netherlands. Netherlands. Sweden. 1984-1986. Lang.: Swe.   1983

Companies and productions at Theatre Festival of the Americas. North America. South America. Central America. 1985. Lang.: Eng.   1985

Role of theatre in the Filipino revolution. Philippines. 1970-1987. Lang.: Eng.   1986

Polish theatre. Poland: Warsaw, Cracow, Wrocław. 1980-1987. Lang.: Eng, Fre.   1987

Four new productions in Poland. Poland: Warsaw. 1986-1987. Lang.: Eng, Fre.   1988

Teatr Prowizorium: interview with director Janusz Oprynski. Poland: Lublin. 1971-1987. Lang.: Eng.   1990

Correspondence of Reduta directors Mieczysław Limanowski and Juliusz Osterwa. Poland: Warsaw, Wilno. 1921-1947. Lang.: Pol.   1991

Director Tadeusz Kantor's inspirations in early career. Poland. 1933-1987. Lang.: Pol.   1992

The shape and form of contemporary Polish theatre. Poland: Warsaw. 1981-1987. Lang.: Eng, Fre.   1995

Selection of theatre reviews by poet Kazimierz Wierzyński. Poland: Warsaw. 1932-1939. Lang.: Pol.   1996

Tadeusz Bradecki, director and playwright. Poland: Cracow. 1977-1987. Lang.: Pol.   1997

Selection of reviews by Tadeusz Zeleński. Poland: Cracow, Warsaw. 1919-1941. Lang.: Pol.   1998

Experimental theatre at the Stary in three recent productions. Poland: Cracow. 1987. Lang.: Eng.   1999

Gábor Tompa directs *Hamlet* at Hungarian Theatre of Kolozsvár. Romania: Cluj. 1987. Lang.: Hun.   2001

Staging of Romantic 'closet dramas'. Scandinavia. 1986-1987. Lang.: Swe.   2004

Controversial production of *Othello* directed by Janet Suzman. South Africa, Republic of: Johannesburg. 1987. Lang.: Eng.   2007

Description of the performances played in the Teatre Lliure. Spain-Catalonia: Barcelona. 1976-1987. Lang.: Cat.   2009

Collection of theatre reviews by Xavier Fàbregas. Spain-Catalonia. 1969-1972. Lang.: Cat.   2010

Overview of theatre season. Spain-Catalonia: Barcelona. 1986-1987. Lang.: Cat.   2011

Swedish-Finnish language problems dramatized by Tornedalsteatern. Sweden: Pajala. 1986. Lang.: Swe.   2014

Ten theatre people on a performance that changed their thinking. Sweden. 1986-1987. Lang.: Swe.   2015

Recent productions of Strindberg plays in Sweden and elsewhere. Sweden. 1984-1986. Lang.: Swe.   2017

Overview of the season's performances. Sweden. 1986-1987. Lang.: Swe.   2018

Jordcirkus and amateur group Näktergalningarna stage *A Christmas Carol*. Sweden: Stockholm. 1986-1987. Lang.: Swe.   2020

Amateur participation in Nyköpings Teater production of Gogol's *Revizor (The Government Inspector)*. Sweden: Nyköping. 1986-1987. Lang.: Swe.   2021

Harlekin's efforts to involve youth in amateur theatre. Sweden: Landskrona. 1982-1987. Lang.: Swe.   2022

Background on *Landskronapågen (The Boy from Landskrona)*. Sweden: Landskrona. 1982-1987. Lang.: Swe.   2024

Review of the season's productions. Sweden. 1986-1987. Lang.: Swe.   2025

Leonard Steckel's production of *Faust II* as a turning point of Swiss theatre. Switzerland: Zürich. 1949. Lang.: Ger.   2028

Benno Besson directs Molière's *Dom Juan*. Switzerland: Geneva. 1987. Lang.: Fre.   2029

Role of the director in the Lucerne Passion play. Switzerland: Lucerne. 1453-1616. Lang.: Eng.   2030

Collection of newspaper reviews by London theatre critics. UK. 1987. Lang.: Eng.   2031

Collection of newspaper reviews by London theatre critics. UK-England. 1987. Lang.: Eng.   2033

Collection of newspaper reviews by London theatre critics. UK-England: London. 1987. Lang.: Eng.   2073

Actress Lillah McCarthy, in an old interview, talks about Shaw. UK-England. 1914-1927. Lang.: Eng.   2074

Collection of newspaper reviews by London theatre critics. UK-England: London. 1987. Lang.: Eng.   2173

Collection of newspaper reviews by London theatre critics. UK-England: London. 1987. Lang.: Eng.   2174

Collection of newspaper reviews by London theatre critics. UK-England. 1987. Lang.: Eng.   2175

Collection of newspaper reviews by London theatre critics. UK-England: London. 1987. Lang.: Eng.   2176

Collection of newspaper reviews by London theatre critics. UK-England: London. 1987. Lang.: Eng.   2177

Collection of newspaper reviews by London theatre critics. UK-England: London. 1987. Lang.: Eng.   2178

Collection of newspaper reviews by London theatre critics. UK-England: London. 1987. Lang.: Eng.   2179

Collection of newspaper reviews by London theatre critics. UK-England: London. 1987. Lang.: Eng.   2180

Collection of newspaper reviews by London theatre critics. UK-England: London. 1987. Lang.: Eng.   2181

Collection of newspaper reviews by London theatre critics. UK-England: London. 1987. Lang.: Eng.   2182

Collection of newspaper reviews by London theatre critics. UK-England: London. 1987. Lang.: Eng.   2183

Collection of newspaper reviews by London theatre critics. UK-England: London. 1987. Lang.: Eng.   2184

Collection of newspaper reviews by London theatre critics. UK-England: London. 1987. Lang.: Eng.   2185

Collection of newspaper reviews by London theatre critics. UK-England: London. 1987. Lang.: Eng.   2186

Collection of newspaper reviews by London theatre critics. UK-England: London. 1987. Lang.: Eng.   2187

Collection of newspaper reviews by London theatre critics. UK-England: London. 1987. Lang.: Eng.   2188

Collection of newspaper reviews by London theatre critics. UK-England: London. 1987. Lang.: Eng.   2189

Staging — cont'd

Collection of newspaper reviews by London theatre critics. UK-England: London. 1987. Lang.: Eng.   2190

Collection of newspaper reviews by London theatre critics. UK-England: London. 1987. Lang.: Eng.   2191

Collection of newspaper reviews by London theatre critics. UK-England: London. 1987. Lang.: Eng.   2192

Collection of newspaper reviews by London theatre critics. UK-England: London. 1987. Lang.: Eng.   2193

Collection of newspaper reviews by London theatre critics. UK-England: London. 1987. Lang.: Eng.   2194

Collection of newspaper reviews by London theatre critics. UK-England: London. 1987. Lang.: Eng.   2195

Collection of newspaper reviews by London theatre critics. UK-England: London. 1987. Lang.: Eng.   2196

Collection of newspaper reviews by London theatre critics. UK-England: London. 1987. Lang.: Eng.   2197

Collection of newspaper reviews by London theatre critics. UK-England: London. 1987. Lang.: Eng.   2198

Collection of newspaper reviews by London theatre critics. UK-England. 1987. Lang.: Eng.   2199

Collection of newspaper reviews by London theatre critics. UK-England: London. 1987. Lang.: Eng.   2200

Collection of newspaper reviews by London theatre critics. UK-England: London. 1987. Lang.: Eng.   2201

Collection of newspaper reviews by London theatre critics. UK-England: London. 1987. Lang.: Eng.   2202

Collection of newspaper reviews by London theatre critics. UK-England: London. 1987. Lang.: Eng.   2203

Collection of newspaper reviews by London theatre critics. UK-England: London. 1987. Lang.: Eng.   2204

Collection of newspaper reviews by London theatre critics. UK-England: London. 1987. Lang.: Eng.   2205

Collection of newspaper reviews by London theatre critics. UK-England: London. 1987. Lang.: Eng.   2207

Collection of newspaper reviews by London theatre critics. UK-England: London. 1987. Lang.: Eng.   2208

Collection of newspaper reviews by London theatre critics. UK-England: London. 1987. Lang.: Eng.   2209

Collection of newspaper reviews by London theatre critics. UK-England: London. 1987. Lang.: Eng.   2210

Collection of newspaper reviews by London theatre critics. UK-England: London. 1987. Lang.: Eng.   2211

Collection of newspaper reviews by London theatre critics. UK-England: London. 1987. Lang.: Eng.   2212

Collection of newspaper reviews by London theatre critics. UK-England: London. 1987. Lang.: Eng.   2213

Collection of newspaper reviews by London theatre critics. UK-England: London. 1987. Lang.: Eng.   2214

Collection of newspaper reviews by London theatre critics. UK-England: London. 1987. Lang.: Eng.   2215

Collection of newspaper reviews by London theatre critics. UK-England: London. 1987. Lang.: Eng.   2216

Collection of newspaper reviews by London theatre critics. UK-England: London. 1987. Lang.: Eng.   2217

Collection of newspaper reviews by London theatre critics. UK-England: London. 1987. Lang.: Eng.   2218

Collection of newspaper reviews by London theatre critics. UK-England: London. 1987. Lang.: Eng.   2219

Collection of newspaper reviews by London theatre critics. UK-England: London. 1987. Lang.: Eng.   2220

Collection of newspaper reviews by London theatre critics. UK-England: London. 1987. Lang.: Eng.   2221

Collection of newspaper reviews by London theatre critics. UK-England: London. 1987. Lang.: Eng.   2222

Collection of newspaper reviews by London theatre critics. UK-England: London. 1987. Lang.: Eng.   2223

Collection of newspaper reviews by London theatre critics. UK-England: London. 1987. Lang.: Eng.   2224

Collection of newspaper reviews by London theatre critics. UK-England: London. 1987. Lang.: Eng.   2225

Collection of newspaper reviews by London theatre critics. UK-England: London. 1987. Lang.: Eng.   2226

Collection of newspaper reviews by London theatre critics. UK-England: London. 1987. Lang.: Eng.   2227

Collection of newspaper reviews by London theatre critics. UK-England: London. 1987. Lang.: Eng.   2228

Collection of newspaper reviews by London theatre critics. UK-England: London. 1987. Lang.: Eng.   2229

Collection of newspaper reviews by London theatre critics. UK-England: London. 1987. Lang.: Eng.   2230

Collection of newspaper reviews by London theatre critics. UK-England: London. 1987. Lang.: Eng.   2231

Collection of newspaper reviews by London theatre critics. UK-England: London. 1987. Lang.: Eng.   2232

Collection of newspaper reviews by London theatre critics. UK-England: London. 1987. Lang.: Eng.   2233

Collection of newspaper reviews by London theatre critics. UK-England: London. 1987. Lang.: Eng.   2234

Collection of newspaper reviews by London theatre critics. UK-England: London. 1987. Lang.: Eng.   2235

Collection of newspaper reviews by London theatre critics. UK-England: London. 1987. Lang.: Eng.   2236

Collection of newspaper reviews by London theatre critics. UK-England: London. 1987. Lang.: Eng.   2237

Collection of newspaper reviews by London theatre critics. UK-England: London. 1987. Lang.: Eng.   2238

Collection of newspaper reviews by London theatre critics. UK-England: London. 1987. Lang.: Eng.   2239

Collection of newspaper reviews by London theatre critics. UK-England: London. 1987. Lang.: Eng.   2240

Collection of newspaper reviews by London theatre critics. UK-England: London. 1987. Lang.: Eng.   2241

Collection of newspaper reviews by London theatre critics. UK-England: London. 1987. Lang.: Eng.   2242

Collection of newspaper reviews by London theatre critics. UK-England: London. 1987. Lang.: Eng.   2243

Collection of newspaper reviews by London theatre critics. UK-England: London. 1987. Lang.: Eng.   2244

Collection of newspaper reviews by London theatre critics. UK-England: London. 1987. Lang.: Eng.   2245

Collection of newspaper reviews by London theatre critics. UK-England: London. 1987. Lang.: Eng.   2246

Collection of newspaper reviews by London theatre critics. UK-England: London. 1987. Lang.: Eng.   2247

Collection of newspaper reviews by London theatre critics. UK-England: London. 1987. Lang.: Eng.   2248

Collection of newspaper reviews by London theatre critics. UK-England: London. 1987. Lang.: Eng.   2249

Collection of newspaper reviews by London theatre critics. UK-England: London. 1987. Lang.: Eng.   2250

Collection of newspaper reviews by London theatre critics. UK-England: London. 1987. Lang.: Eng.   2251

Collection of newspaper reviews by London theatre critics. UK-England: London. 1987. Lang.: Eng.   2252

Collection of newspaper reviews by London theatre critics. UK-England: London. 1987. Lang.: Eng.   2254

Collection of newspaper reviews by London theatre critics. UK-England: London. 1987. Lang.: Eng.   2255

Collection of newspaper reviews by London theatre critics. UK-England: London. 1987. Lang.: Eng.   2256

Collection of newspaper reviews by London theatre critics. UK-England: London. 1987. Lang.: Eng.   2257

Collection of newspaper reviews by London theatre critics. UK-England: London. 1987. Lang.: Eng.   2258

Collection of newspaper reviews by London theatre critics. UK-England: London. 1987. Lang.: Eng.   2259

Collection of newspaper reviews by London theatre critics. UK-England: London. 1987. Lang.: Eng.   2260

Collection of newspaper reviews by London theatre critics. UK-England. 1987. Lang.: Eng.   2261

Collection of newspaper reviews by London theatre critics. UK-England. 1987. Lang.: Eng.   2262

Collection of newspaper reviews by London theatre critics. UK-England. 1987. Lang.: Eng.   2263

Staging — cont'd

Collection of newspaper reviews by London theatre critics. UK-England: London. 1987. Lang.: Eng. 2264

Collection of newspaper reviews by London theatre critics. UK-England: London. 1987. Lang.: Eng. 2265

Collection of newspaper reviews by London theatre critics. UK-England: London. 1987. Lang.: Eng. 2266

Collection of newspaper reviews by London theatre critics. UK-England: London. 1987. Lang.: Eng. 2267

Collection of newspaper reviews by London theatre critics. UK-England: London. 1987. Lang.: Eng. 2268

Collection of newspaper reviews by London theatre critics. UK-England: London. 1987. Lang.: Eng. 2269

Collection of newspaper reviews by London theatre critics. UK-England: London. 1987. Lang.: Eng. 2270

Collection of newspaper reviews by London theatre critics. UK-England: London. 1987. Lang.: Eng. 2271

Collection of newspaper reviews by London theatre critics. UK-England: London. 1987. Lang.: Eng. 2272

Collection of newspaper reviews by London theatre critics. UK-England: London. 1987. Lang.: Eng. 2274

Collection of newspaper reviews by London theatre critics. UK-England: London. 1987. Lang.: Eng. 2275

Collection of newspaper reviews by London theatre critics. UK-England: London. 1987. Lang.: Eng. 2276

Collection of newspaper reviews by London theatre critics. UK-England: London. 1987. Lang.: Eng. 2277

Roles of Dame Peggy Ashcroft and directors she has worked with. UK-England. 1930-1986. Lang.: Eng. 2278

Hungarian reviewer's impressions of four Shakespeare productions. UK-England: Stratford. 1987. Lang.: Hun. 2279

Autobiography of film and stage director Peter Brook. UK-England. 1946-1987. Lang.: Eng. 2281

Undergraduate students stage the York Crucifixion play. UK-England: Canterbury. 1983-1987. Lang.: Eng. 2282

Production of *Struggle for Freedom: The Life and Work of Len Johnson.* UK-England: Manchester. 1987. Lang.: Eng. 2283

The founding and history of the Malvern Festival. UK-England: Malvern. 1904-1977. Lang.: Eng. 2286

Various North American and English productions of *Man and Superman.* UK-England. North America. 1901-1982. Lang.: Eng. 2288

Hungarian reviewer's impressions of several English productions. UK-England: London, Stratford. 1987. Lang.: Hun. 2289

Revival of *Revizor (The Government Inspector)* at the National Theatre directed by Richard Eyre. UK-England: London. USSR. 1985. Lang.: Eng. 2290

The relationship between the director and the playwright from contrasting historical perspectives. UK-England. 1800-1987. Lang.: Eng. 2291

Comparison of two 'Elizabethan' productions of *Hamlet.* UK-England: London. USA. 1900-1904. Lang.: Eng. 2292

Recent Strindberg productions in Great Britain. UK-England. Sweden. 1984-1986. Lang.: Eng. 2298

Modern production of the *Chester Cycle.* UK-England: Chester. 1987. Lang.: Eng. 2299

Shaw's conception of the Elizabethan theatre. UK-England. 1909. Lang.: Eng. 2303

Review of production and staging aspects of *Wild Honey* by Anton Čechov. UK-England: London. 1986. Lang.: Eng. 2306

Productions and political philosophy of Field Day Theatre Company. UK-Ireland: Londonderry. 1986-1987. Lang.: Eng. 2309

Soviet dramaturgy on the Ukrainian stage. Ukraine. 1917-1987. Lang.: Rus. 2310

Collection of newspaper reviews by New York theatre critics. USA: New York, NY. 1987. Lang.: Eng. 2311

Collection of newspaper reviews by New York theatre critics. USA: New York, NY. 1987. Lang.: Eng. 2312

Collection of newspaper reviews by New York theatre critics. USA: New York, NY. 1987. Lang.: Eng. 2313

Collection of newspaper reviews by New York theatre critics. USA: New York, NY. 1987. Lang.: Eng. 2315

Collection of newspaper reviews by New York theatre critics. USA: New York, NY. 1987. Lang.: Eng. 2316

Collection of newspaper reviews by New York theatre critics. USA: New York, NY. 1987. Lang.: Eng. 2317

Collection of newspaper reviews by New York theatre critics. USA: New York, NY. 1987. Lang.: Eng. 2318

Collection of newspaper reviews by New York theatre critics. USA: New York, NY. 1987. Lang.: Eng. 2319

Collection of newspaper reviews by New York theatre critics. USA: New York, NY. 1987. Lang.: Eng. 2320

Collection of newspaper reviews by New York theatre critics. USA: New York, NY. 1987. Lang.: Eng. 2321

Collection of newspaper reviews by New York theatre critics. USA: New York, NY. 1987. Lang.: Eng. 2322

Collection of newspaper reviews by New York theatre critics. USA: New York, NY. 1987. Lang.: Eng. 2323

Collection of newspaper reviews by New York critics. USA: New York, NY. 1987. Lang.: Eng. 2324

Collection of newspaper reviews by New York theatre critics. USA: New York, NY. 1987. Lang.: Eng. 2326

Career of director Ron Lagomarsino, his style and technique. USA. 1987. Lang.: Eng. 2327

Interview with director Richard Foreman. USA: New York, NY. 1962-1987. Lang.: Eng. 2329

Critique of the 1984 Broadway production of *Death of a Salesman.* USA: New York, NY. 1984. Lang.: Eng. 2330

Work and methodology of director Peter Sellars. USA: Washington, DC. 1981-1987. Lang.: Eng. 2331

Functions, influence of dramaturgs and literary managers. USA. 1987. Lang.: Eng. 2332

Production of John Jesurun's *Chang in a Void Moon.* USA: New York, NY. 1982-1983. Lang.: Eng. 2336

Production of *Spring* by Simone Forti presented at the Danspace at St. Mark's Church. USA: New York, NY. 1983. Lang.: Eng. 2337

Influence of Pirandello on modern theatre. USA. Italy. 1917-1987. Lang.: Eng. 2338

Autobiography of director, producer and writer John Houseman. USA: New York, NY. 1935-1985. Lang.: Eng. 2339

Four productions in Southern regional theatres. USA: Houston, TX, Louisville, KY, Gainesville, FL. 1980. Lang.: Eng. 2342

Career of actor/director Randall Duk Kim. USA. 1966-1987. Lang.: Eng. 2346

Peter Sellars' American National Theatre on European tour. USA. Netherlands. 1987. Lang.: Dut. 2351

Tükak Teatret and its artistic director Reidar Nilsson present *Inuit—Human Beings.* USA: New York, NY. Denmark: Holstebro. 1975-1983. Lang.: Eng. 2352

Stephen Porter on directing Shaw. USA. 1924-1981. Lang.: Eng. 2353

Interview with playwright Amiri Baraka. USA: Newark, NJ, New York, NY. 1965-1969. Lang.: Eng. 2356

New production of *Macbeth* set in 1927 Chicago. USA: New York, NY. 1987. Lang.: Eng. 2357

Hedda Gabler at American Ibsen Theatre. USA: Pittsburgh, PA. 1987. Lang.: Eng. 2358

Interview with actor/director Austin Pendleton. USA. 1987. Lang.: Eng. 2360

Director Matthew Maguire's production of *The American Mysteries* presented by Creation at La Mama. USA: New York, NY. 1983. Lang.: Eng. 2361

George C. Wolfe and L. Kenneth Richardson discuss *The Colored Museum.* USA: New York, NY, New Brunswick, NJ. 1987. Lang.: Eng. 2363

Philip Moeller's premiere of *Mourning Becomes Electra* by O'Neill. USA: New York, NY. 1931. Lang.: Eng. 2366

Theatre career of photo-journalist Bert Andrews. USA: New York, NY. 1950-1987. Lang.: Eng. 2367

Dramaturgy of Eduard Radsinskij, production of his new plays. USSR: Moscow. 1938-1987. Lang.: Rus. 2371

Director Gleb Panfilov's interpretation of *Hamlet* at Komsomol Theatre. USSR: Moscow. 1980-1987. Lang.: Rus. 2373

Staging — cont'd

Productions in Georgia of plays by Georgian author Konstantin Simonov. USSR. 1943-1949. Lang.: Rus. 2374

Shaw productions at Belorussian Theatre of Musical Comedy. USSR. 1980-1987. Lang.: Rus. 2375

Classical dramaturgy on the Osetinskij stage. USSR. 1960-1987. Lang.: Rus. 2378

Personal recollections of productions of Griboedov's *Gore ot uma (Wit Works Woe)*. USSR. 1845-1987. Lang.: Rus. 2379

Two aspects of Stanislavskij's work: physical comedy, rehearsal process. USSR: Moscow. 1933-1988. Lang.: Ger. 2380

Soviet playwright, actor and director K.G. Tinčurin. USSR. 1887-1947. Lang.: Rus. 2381

Rustaveli Theatre of Georgia, directed by Robert Sturua, presents Shakespeare's *Richard III* and Brecht's *Der Kaukasische Kreidekreis (The Caucasian Chalk Circle)* in Hungary. USSR: Tbilisi. Hungary. 1987. Lang.: Hun. 2383

Problems of Gogol's theatre. USSR. 1970-1987. Lang.: Rus. 2384

Moscow Art Theatre's production of *Hamlet* with Michajl Čechov in the title role. USSR: Moscow. 1924. Lang.: Eng. 2386

Events of Moldavian theatre history. USSR. 1920-1970. Lang.: Rus. 2387

Two productions of *Misterija-Buff (Mystery-Bouffe)* by Majakovskij. USSR. 1918-1921. Lang.: Rus. 2388

Difficulties in contemporary readings of Shakespeare's plays. USSR. 1987. Lang.: Rus. 2389

Guest performances by Teat'r im. Šato Rustaveli of Tbilisi at Madách Theatre: Shakespeare's *Richard III*, Brecht's *Der Kaukasische Kreidekreis (The Caucasian Chalk Circle)*. USSR: Tbilisi. Hungary: Budapest. 1986. Lang.: Hun. 2390

Jèvrejnov's theories of theatricality, parallels with Pirandello's. USSR. 1879-1953. Lang.: Eng. 2391

Interview with director I. Ungurjanu. USSR. 1980-1987. Lang.: Rus. 2393

Jurij Liubimov's 1979 Taganka Theatre production of *The Master and Margarita (Master i Margarita)*. USSR. 1938-1979. Lang.: Eng. 2394

Biography of director Ju. Mil'tinis. USSR. 1907-1987. Lang.: Rus. 2395

Soviet productions of five Tennessee Williams plays. USSR. 1910-1987. Lang.: Eng. 2397

Plays of Aleksand'r Vampilov in connection with problems of directing. USSR. 1937-1972. Lang.: Rus. 2398

Reconstruction of *The Dybbuk* as directed by Vachtangov with HaBimah. USSR: Moscow. 1922. Lang.: Hun. 2399

Russian director Jurij Liubimov and his productions in the USSR and USA. USSR: Moscow. USA: Washington, DC. 1984-1987. Lang.: Eng. 2400

Plays of A.M. Volodin on stage and screen. USSR: Moscow, Leningrad. 1950-1987. Lang.: Rus. 2401

Director Ljubiša Ristić and 'Shakespeare Fest '86'. Yugoslavia: Subotica, Palić. 1986. Lang.: Hun. 2403

Ljubiša Ristić adapts and directs Imre Madách's *Az ember tragédiája (The Tragedy of a Man)*. Yugoslavia: Subotica. 1986. Lang.: Hun. 2404

Review of *Hamlet*, *Julius Caesar* and *Titus Andronicus* at 'Shakespeare Fest '86'. Yugoslavia: Palić. 1986. Lang.: Hun. 2405

Tóték (The Tót Family) by István Örkény at Hungarian Theatre, guest director Gábor Székely. Yugoslavia: Novi Sad. 1987. Lang.: Hun. 2406

'Shakespeare Fest '86' reviews. Yugoslavia: Palić. 1986. Lang.: Hun. 2407

Interview with National Theatre director Ljubiša Ristić. Yugoslavia: Subotica. 1947-1986. Lang.: Hun. 2408

Analysis of David Lean's film *A Passage to India*. 1983. Lang.: Eng. 3147

Review of Ariane Mnouchkine's film *Molière*. France. 1987. Lang.: Hun. 3150

Interview with film-maker Sándor Sára. Hungary. 1980-1987. Lang.: Hun. 3152

Interview with film director András Sólyom. Hungary. 1987. Lang.: Hun. 3155

Biography of director Luchino Visconti. Italy. 1906-1976. Lang.: Ita. 3158

Biography of film director Luchino Visconti. Italy. 1906-1976. Lang.: Ita. 3159

Career of film director Ingmar Bergman. Sweden. 1944-1986. Lang.: Eng. 3161

Relationship between motion pictures and realistic theatrical productions. UK-England: London. USA: Hollywood, CA, New York, NY. 1895-1915. Lang.: Eng. 3163

New questions about Welles' *Citizen Kane*. USA. 1942. Lang.: Eng. 3164

Work of film director Andrei Konchalovsky. USA. USSR: Moscow. Lang.: Eng. 3166

Interview with film director Gleb Panfilov. USSR. 1986-1987. Lang.: Hun. 3172

Theatre and film directors on interaction of two forms. USSR. 1987. Lang.: Rus. 3173

Arguments against misuse of new technology in theatre. USA: New York, NY. 1985. Lang.: Eng. 3193

History of incorporating film into a theatrical performance. USA: New York, NY. 1922-1987. Lang.: Eng. 3196

Lorna Heaton's use of holograms in *Woyzeck*. Canada: Banff, AB. 1987. Lang.: Fre. 3205

Review of the BBC telecast of *The Birthday Party* by Harold Pinter. UK-England. 1987. Lang.: Eng. 3206

Review of ABC videocast of Pinter's *The Dumb Waiter*. USA. 1987. Lang.: Eng. 3209

Lithuanian television drama. USSR. 1957-1982. Lang.: Rus. 3212

San Francisco Mime Troupe's visit to Nicaragua's International Theatre Festival. Central America. 1986. Lang.: Eng. 3222

Christmas pantomime *The Miracle* directed by Max Reinhardt. UK-England: London. 1911. Lang.: Eng. 3236

History and aspects of puppet theatre: designs, genres and puppeteers. Europe. Asia. 400 B.C.-1985 A.D. Lang.: Eng. 3255

Minor theatrical forms involving tableaux, mechanics. Italy: Venice. 1800-1900. Lang.: Ita. 3263

Theatre-performance culture of Rus'. Russia. 1600-1899. Lang.: Rus. 3265

Director Robert Wilson, his *CIVIL warS* and connecting *Knee Plays*. USA. 1979-1987. Lang.: Swe. 3274

Agit-prop theatre traditions. USSR. 1920-1929. Lang.: Rus. 3276

Growth of West Indian carnival traditions. West Indies. Lang.: Eng. 3277

Production of Cirque du Soleil. Canada: Montreal, PQ. 1987. Lang.: Eng. 3302

Dario Fo's use of *commedia dell'arte*. Italy. 1550-1987. Lang.: Rus. 3313

Edward Gordon Craig's use of *commedia dell'arte* in his work. UK-England. Italy. 1872-1966. Lang.: Eng. 3314

Location and staging of a 1636 royal masque. England. 1636. Lang.: Eng. 3321

Analysis of *La Festa delle Marie*. Italy: Venice. 1000-1300. Lang.: Ita. 3330

Description of Easter processions. Spain: Puente Genil. 1660-1987. Lang.: Eng. 3332

Pageant wagon presentation in Spain provides information on recruitment, staging and rehearsal practices. Spain: St. Ginar. 1579. Lang.: Eng. 3333

Critical discussion of the Ultimatum II festival. Canada: Montreal, PQ. 1987. Lang.: Eng. 3346

The work of director Robert Lepage. Canada: Montreal, PQ. 1987. Lang.: Eng. 3347

Egidio Alvaro and performance art festivals. Europe. 1974-1987. Lang.: Eng. 3349

Comparative review of current performance art. Europe. 1987. Lang.: Eng. 3351

Description of Rotterdam's 1986 Perfo Festival. Germany: Rotterdam. 1986. Lang.: Eng. 3352

Description of the *Myths, Monsters and Mutations* festival. Germany, West: Berlin, West. 1987. Lang.: Eng. 3353

Overview of the 8th Documenta festival. Germany, West: Kassel. 1987. Lang.: Eng. 3354

The 4th International Festival of Street Theatres. Poland: Jelenia Góra. 1986. Lang.: Eng, Fre. 3355

Staging — cont'd

Staging — cont'd

András Békés directs Rossini's *La Cenerentola* at Szentendrei
Teátrum under the title *Hamupipőke*. Hungary: Szentendre. 1987.
Lang.: Hun.   3798

Giorgio Strehler on staging *Die Dreigroschenoper (The Three Penny
Opera)*. Italy: Milan. France: Paris. 1928-1986. Lang.: Swe.   3809

Overview of Latvian opera. Latvia. 1913-1982. Lang.: Rus.   3810

A children's production of Mozart's *The Magic Flute* performed in
Spanish. Mexico: Mexico City. 1987. Lang.: Spa.   3811

Interview with Dario Fo. Netherlands. Italy. 1987. Lang.: Dut. 3814

Review of Wagner's *Der Fliegende Holländer* at the Natal
Playhouse. South Africa, Republic of: Durban. 1987. Lang.: Eng.
                                                              3815

Development of Wagner's *Die Meistersinger von Nürnberg*. South
Africa, Republic of: Cape Town. Germany, West: Munich. 1868-
1987. Lang.: Eng.   3816

Premiere of Leonardo Balarda's opera *Cristobal Colón*. Spain-
Catalonia: Barcelona. 1987. Lang.: Eng.   3818

Reviews of *Christina* by Hans Gefors and Lars Forssell. Sweden:
Stockholm. 1987. Lang.: Swe.   3822

Christina, opera based on Strindberg play by Hans Gefors and Lars
Forssell. Sweden: Stockholm. 1986-1987. Lang.: Swe.   3823

Swedish opera director, Göran Järvefelt. Sweden: Stockholm. USA:
Santa Fe, NM. 1948-1987. Lang.: Eng.   3824

Twenty opera productions at Grand Théâtre. Switzerland: Geneva.
1980-1987. Lang.: Fre.   3828

Interview with David Freeman, the director of the Opera Factory.
UK-England. 1973-1987. Lang.: Eng.   3829

Background on Lyric Opera radio broadcast performances. USA:
Chicago, IL. 1987. Lang.: Eng.   3832

Background on San Francisco opera radio broadcasts. USA: San
Francisco, CA. 1987. Lang.: Eng.   3833

Background on Opera Company of Philadelphia telecast, *Un Ballo in
Maschera*. USA: Philadelphia, PA. 1987. Lang.: Eng.   3834

Soprano Renata Scotto directs Metropolitan Opera production of
Madama Butterfly. USA: New York, NY. 1987. Lang.: Eng.   3836

Background on Metropolitan radio broadcast performances. USA:
New York, NY. 1987. Lang.: Eng.   3837

Background on Metropolitan radio broadcast performances. USA:
New York, NY. 1987. Lang.: Eng.   3838

Background on Metropolitan telecast performances. USA: New York,
NY. 1987. Lang.: Eng.   3839

Repertoire and artistic achievement of the Opera Theatre of St.
Louis. USA: St. Louis, MO. 1987. Lang.: Eng.   3840

Bay Area opera companies. USA: San Francisco, CA. 1900-1987.
Lang.: Eng.   3842

Premiere of the docu-opera, *Nixon in China*, Houston Grand Opera.
USA: Houston, TX. 1987. Lang.: Eng.   3843

Problems of opera funding and repertory. USA. 1987. Lang.: Eng.
                                                              3849

Cooperative financing of Gershwin's *Porgy and Bess*. USA. 1987.
Lang.: Eng.   3850

Survey of opera repertory. USA. 1986-1987. Lang.: Eng.   3857

Metropolitan Opera archives. USA: New York, NY. 1883-1987.
Lang.: Eng.   3863

History of Turkmenian opera. USSR. 1900-1987. Lang.: Rus.   3865

Study of the Moscow Bolšoj Theatre. USSR: Moscow. 1974-1980.
Lang.: Rus.   3867

Analysis of the work of Perm Opera Theatre. USSR: Perm. 1980-
1987. Lang.: Rus.   3868

Analysis of Perm Opera Theatre. USSR: Perm. 1980-1987. Lang.:
Rus.   3870

Perspectives on modern opera. USSR. 1980-1987. Lang.: Rus.   3871

B.A. Pokrovskij, principal director, Moscow Musical Chamber
Theatre. USSR: Moscow. 1912-1987. Lang.: Rus.   3873

Jurij Liubimov of Taganka Theatre directs *Lulu* in Chicago. USSR:
Moscow. USA: Chicago, IL. 1987. Lang.: Eng.   3874

Problems of the Tbilisi Opera Theatre. USSR: Tbilisi. 1980-1987.
Lang.: Rus.   3876

Director A. Viljumanis of Latvian Opera Theatre. USSR. 1980-1987.
Lang.: Rus.   3877

Issues of current Soviet opera. USSR. 1987. Lang.: Rus.   3878

New realizations of Mussorgskij operas on the contemporary Soviet
stage. USSR. 1980-1987. Lang.: Rus.   3879

Productions of S. Taudasinskij, Leningrad Malyj Opera Theatre.
USSR: Leningrad. 1980-1987. Lang.: Rus.   3882

Style in opera directing, with reference to Boris A. Pokrovskij.
USSR. 1980-1987. Lang.: Rus.   3883

Opera singer, director I.V. Tartakov. USSR. 1860-1923. Lang.: Rus.
                                                              3884

Béla Zerkovitz's operetta *Csókos asszony (A Woman Made for
Kissing)* directed by István Iglódi. Hungary: Budapest. 1987. Lang.:
Hun.   3957

István Iglódi directs *Csókos asszony (A Woman Made for Kissing)*
by Béla Zerkovitz at Vigszinház. Hungary: Budapest. 1987. Lang.:
Hun.   3958

Imre Kálmán's *Cigányprimás (Sari)* and Bizet's *Carmen* at Kisfaludy
Theatre staged by József Bor. Hungary: Győr. 1912-1986. Lang.:
Hun.   3959

Problems of amateur theatre, Eastern Bohemia. Czechoslovakia:
Hradec Králové. 1985. Lang.: Cze.   3973

Korean folk puppetry using hands and feet. Korea, South. 1977.
Lang.: Eng.   3977

Difference between directing actors and puppeteers, responsibility of
children's theatre. Sweden. 1987. Lang.: Swe.   3981

R. Gobriadze, director of marionette theatre. USSR. 1980-1987.
Lang.: Rus.   4003

Poland's puppet theatre. Poland: Wrocław, Białystock. Austria:
Mistelbach. 1979-1987. Lang.: Eng, Fre.   4006

Plays/librettos/scripts

Michael Hollingsworth's *The History of the Village of Small Huts*.
Canada. 1987. Lang.: Eng.   1099

Work of playwright Robert Lepage. Canada. 1987. Lang.: Fre. 1101

Brecht's theory of alienation in the Chinese theatre. China, People's
Republic of. 1949-1985. Lang.: Chi.   1109

On a theatrical manifesto of Simone Maria Poggi. Italy. 1700-1749.
Lang.: Ita.   1140

Improvement of Korean folk theatre. Korea. 1987-1987. Lang.: Kor.
                                                              1149

Musical adaptation of Gorostiza's *Contigo pan y cebolla (With You,
Bread and Onion)*. Mexico: Mexico City. Spain: Madrid. 1833-1984.
Lang.: Eng.   1150

An annual bibliography of works by and about Harold Pinter. UK-
England. USA. 1986-1987. Lang.: Eng.   1160

Interview with Susan Sontag, director of *Jacques and His Master*.
USA: Cambridge, MA. 1985. Lang.: Eng.   1172

FDG/CBS New Plays Program Conferences. USA: New York, NY.
1987. Lang.: Eng.   1180

Collaboration between playwright Craig Lucas and director Norman
Rene. USA: New York, NY. 1985-1987. Lang.: Eng.   1183

Collaboration of Craig Lucas and Norman Rene on *Blue Window*
and *Three Postcards*. USA. 1987. Lang.: Eng.   1184

Development of *The Mahabharata* directed by Peter Brook and
Jean-Claude Carrière. 1975-1987. Lang.: Eng.   2412

Robert Lepage's play *Vinci*. Canada. 1986-1987. Lang.: Fre. 2474

Critical response to Brassard's *Les Paravents (The Screens)*. Canada:
Montreal, PQ, Ottawa, ON. 1987. Lang.: Fre.   2475

La Trilogie des dragons by Robert Lepage. Canada: Montreal, PQ.
1987. Lang.: Fre.   2479

Imagery in Lepage's *La Trilogie des dragons*. Canada. 1987. Lang.:
Fre.   2480

Plays by Micone, Saddlemyer, Thompson, Wyatt. Canada. 1958-
1985. Lang.: Eng.   2481

Work of playwright Marco Micone. Canada. 1982-1985. Lang.: Eng.
                                                              2483

Brassard discusses his adaptation of Genet's *Les Paravents (The
Screens)*. Canada: Montreal, PQ, Ottawa, ON. 1987. Lang.: Fre.
                                                              2485

Political, social and religious issues in Caroline drama. England.
1632-1642. Lang.: Eng.   2508

Productions of *Sir Thomas More* by Elizabethan theatre companies.
England. 1595-1650. Lang.: Eng.   2541

Peter Brook discusses his production of *The Mahabharata*. France:
Paris. India. Australia: Perth. 1987. Lang.: Eng.   2571

Staging — cont'd

André Brassard's production of Jean Genet's *Les Paravents (The Screens)*. France. Canada: Montreal, PQ, Ottawa, ON. 1961-1987. Lang.: Fre. 2583

Overview of contemporary East German drama and directors. Germany, East. 1985-1986. Lang.: Hun. 2612

Ancient Greek theatre, modern stagings. Greece. 500 B.C.-1987 A.D. Lang.: Ita. 2618

Analysis of 51 short farces written in Majorca. Spain-Catalonia. 1701-1850. Lang.: Cat. 2731

Theme of stage direction in the work of Scandinavian authors. Sweden. Norway. 1700-1987. Lang.: Ita. 2737

Pistolteatern's adaptation of *Alice in Wonderland*. Sweden: Stockholm. 1982. Lang.: Eng. 2738

Shaw's ideas on directorial interpretation in *Pygmalion*. UK-England. 1894-1949. Lang.: Eng. 2768

Visual aspects of *Pygmalion* related to its theme. UK-England. 1914. Lang.: Eng. 2782

Stage business in *Major Barbara* traced to Beerbohm Tree. UK-England. 1905. Lang.: Eng. 2802

Yeats's dance plays: effect of the elements of performance on text. UK-Ireland. 1916-1987. Lang.: Eng. 2832

Three feminist productions of plays by Henrik Ibsen. USA. 1987. Lang.: Eng. 2899

Development of Sam Shepard's plays in response to audience. USA. 1976-1986. Lang.: Eng. 2902

Legal and ethical rights of playwrights regarding interpretations of their works. USA. Lang.: Eng. 2904

Interview with playwright Romulus Linney. USA. 1986. Lang.: Eng. 2931

Nikolaj Erdmann's plays, relations with major directors. USSR: Moscow. 1925. Lang.: Rus. 2963

Conference on staging Shakespeare in USSR. USSR. 1987. Lang.: Rus. 2969

Successful film versions of Shakespeare's *King Lear*. USA. UK-England. USSR. 1916-1983. Lang.: Eng. 3099

Orson Welles's adaptation of *Othello*: cinematic technique and time. USA. 1952. Lang.: Eng. 3180

Distorted race relations in Western films. USA. 1915-1986. Lang.: Eng. 3181

Polanski, Welles and Kurosawa's versions of Shakespeare's *Macbeth*. USA. Japan. UK-England. 1948-1971. Lang.: Eng. 3183

Tippett's influence on contemporary opera. 1946-1987. Lang.: Eng. 3888

Critical analysis of István Anhalt's opera, *Winthrop*. Canada: Kitchener, ON. USA. 1987. Lang.: Eng. 3894

Reference materials

Theatrical anecdotes. 500 B.C.-1987 A.D. Lang.: Eng. 1194

History of theatrical activity in Palafrugell. Spain-Catalonia: Palafrugell. 1900-1986. Lang.: Cat. 1210

Relation to other fields

Playwright Gerald Thomas discusses influences on his work. Brazil: Rio de Janeiro. North America. Europe. 1970-1987. Lang.: Eng. 2981

Director Tadeusz Kantor's views on art, culture, philosophy. Poland. 1915-1987. Lang.: Pol. 2997

Research/historiography

Expansion, diversification and artistic innovation in the American theatre. USA. 1961-1986. Lang.: Eng. 1302

Theory/criticism

A formalist approach and interpretation of theatre performance. 1987. Lang.: Eng. 1313

Conviviality vs. spectacularity in theatre. 1985. Lang.: Spa. 1314

How to maintain an element of risk in theatre. France. 1987. Lang.: Fre. 1331

Relations between text and representation of *mise en scène*. France. 1987. Lang.: Spa. 1334

Effect of audiovisual media on theatre. France. 1987. Lang.: Fre. 1339

Criticism by actor Piero Gobetti. Italy. 1918-1926. Lang.: Ita. 1345

Eric Bentley's critical essays on theatre. USA. 1952-1986. Lang.: Eng. 1350

Collection of critical essays and reviews by Robert Brustein. USA. 1980-1986. Lang.: Eng. 1351

Reconstruction of Shakespeare in performance. USA. 1987. Lang.: Eng. 1358

Essays and reviews by Gordon Rogoff. USA. 1960-1986. Lang.: Eng. 1366

Round-table discussion by philosophers and theatre professionals on conflict in contemporary drama. USSR. 1980-1987. Lang.: Rus. 1372

New theatre criticism, Soviet studio theatre movement. USSR. 1980-1987. Lang.: Rus. 1376

Structuralist approach to play interpretation. 500 B.C.-1987 A.D. Lang.: Eng. 3016

The use of space in plot to indicate time and place. 1949-1987. Lang.: Chi. 3021

Evaluation of the present state of theatrical theory and its influence on theatrical practice. Europe. 1985. Lang.: Fre. 3033

Semiotics in the relationship between director and text. Latin America. Lang.: Spa. 3055

Training

Teachers' handbook for theatre in education. Spain-Catalonia. 1987. Lang.: Cat. 1384

Interview with Michael Poyner, director of Ulster Youth Theatre. UK-Ireland. 1987. Lang.: Eng. 1386

Interview with Georgij Tovstonogov. USA. 1987. Lang.: Eng. 1390

Pedagogy of director L. Kurbas. USSR. 1887-1942. Lang.: Rus. 1393

Problems of students graduating from theatre schools. USSR. 1980-1987. Lang.: Rus. 1394

Stagnelius, Erik Johan

Performance/production

Staging of Romantic 'closet dramas'. Scandinavia. 1986-1987. Lang.: Swe. 2004

Stahl, Stephen

Performance/production

Collection of newspaper reviews by London theatre critics. UK-England: London. 1987. Lang.: Eng. 2188

Stand Up

Performance/production

Collection of newspaper reviews by London theatre critics. UK-England: London. 1987. Lang.: Eng. 2215

Standidge, Eric

Performance/production

Collection of newspaper reviews by London theatre critics. UK-England: London. 1986. Lang.: Eng. 2131

Standin' the Gaff Festival (Sydney, NS)

Performance/production

Work of actor/director Augusto Boal. Canada: Sydney, NS. 1987. Lang.: Eng. 1694

Relation to other fields

Popular theatre and non-governmental funding agencies. Canada: Sydney, NS. Jamaica. Sudan. 1987. Lang.: Eng. 2982

Stanford-Tuck, Anthony

Performance/production

Collection of newspaper reviews by London theatre critics. UK-England: London. 1986. Lang.: Eng. 2076

Staniewski, Włodzimierz

Audience

American response to Gardzienice Theatre Association. Poland: Gardzienice. 1666-1987. Lang.: Eng. 1536

Performance/production

Polish theatre. Poland: Warsaw, Cracow, Wrocław. 1980-1987. Lang.: Eng, Fre. 1987

Teatr Prowizorium: interview with director Janusz Oprynski. Poland: Lublin. 1971-1987. Lang.: Eng. 1990

Stanislavskij, Konstantin Sergejěvič

Audience

Chinese acting: direct communication with audience. China, People's Republic of: Beijing. 1950-1986. Lang.: Chi. 3434

Institutions

Creation and history of the HaBimah Theatre. USSR: Moscow. Israel: Tel Aviv. 1913-1955. Lang.: Heb. 623

Performance/production

Major directors of the early twentieth century. Europe. North America. 1900-1950. Lang.: Kor. 779

Stanislavskij's rehearsal notes for Byron's *Cain*. USSR. 1920. Lang.: Rus. 988

Acting style of Vachtangov. USSR. Canada. 1922-1987. Lang.: Eng. 1009

Stanislavskij, Konstantin Sergejèvič — cont'd

Notes on Stanislavskij. USSR. 1863-1938. Lang.: Rus. 1085

Chiao Chü Yin's *Ch'a Kuan (Tea House)* uses Western style. China, People's Republic of. 1957-1959. Lang.: Chi. 1723

Michajl Čechov's life and work: a descriptive chronology. Russia: Moscow. 1901-1980. Lang.: Eng. 2002

Development of the Stanislavskij Acting System. Russia: Moscow. 1906-1938. Lang.: Eng. 2003

Method acting: its origins and development. USA: New York, NY. USSR: Moscow. 1923-1987. Lang.: Eng. 2359

Two aspects of Stanislavskij's work: physical comedy, rehearsal process. USSR: Moscow. 1933-1988. Lang.: Ger. 2380

Techniques of the image theatre and effects on actor and audience. Canada. Europe. USA. 1987. Lang.: Eng. 3345

Acting theories in Chinese opera. China, People's Republic of: Beijing. 1950-1986. Lang.: Chi. 3510

Plays/librettos/scripts
Nikolaj Erdmann's plays, relations with major directors. USSR: Moscow. 1925. Lang.: Rus. 2963

Relation to other fields
Assumptions by the actors and the audience in live theatre. USA. 1987. Lang.: Eng. 1283

Theory/criticism
Reconstruction of Shakespeare in performance. USA. 1987. Lang.: Eng. 1358

Stanley, Mark
Design/technology
Principles of theatre lighting applied to architectural lighting. USA: New York, NY. 1987. Lang.: Eng. 484

Stapleton, Oliver
Design/technology
Cinematographer Oliver Stapleton and his lighting work on the film *Prick Up Your Ears*. USA. 1987. Lang.: Eng. 3136

Star Turns
Performance/production
Collection of newspaper reviews by London theatre critics. UK-England: London. 1987. Lang.: Eng. 2205

Star Turns Red, The
Plays/librettos/scripts
The Spanish Civil War in works by Ernest Hemingway and Sean O'Casey. UK. Ireland. USA. 1930-1939. Lang.: Eng. 2749

Stardust
Design/technology
Lighting reviews for several New York productions. USA: New York, NY. 1987. Lang.: Eng. 475

Performance/production
Collection of newspaper reviews by New York critics. USA: New York, NY. 1987. Lang.: Eng. 2324

Stark, Michael K.
Performance/production
Collection of newspaper reviews by London theatre critics. UK-England: London. 1987. Lang.: Eng. 2248

Starlight Express
Design/technology
Current Broadway shows and their lighting designers. USA: New York, NY. 1987. Lang.: Eng. 460

Lighting reviews for some New York productions. USA: New York, NY. 1987. Lang.: Eng. 472

Performance/production
Collection of newspaper reviews by New York theatre critics. USA: New York, NY. 1987. Lang.: Eng. 2325

Stars
Performance/production
Collection of newspaper reviews by London theatre critics. UK-England. 1987. Lang.: Eng. 2262

Starts in the Middle
Performance/production
Collection of newspaper reviews by London theatre critics. UK-England: London. 1987. Lang.: Eng. 2240

Staruska
SEE
Latino, Staruska.

Stary Teatr (Cracow)
Performance/production
The 17th Warsaw theatre conference. Poland: Warsaw. 1987. Lang.: Eng, Fre. 872

Polish theatre. Poland: Warsaw, Cracow, Wrocław. 1980-1987. Lang.: Eng, Fre. 1987

The shape and form of contemporary Polish theatre. Poland: Warsaw. 1981-1987. Lang.: Eng, Fre. 1995

Tadeusz Bradecki, director and playwright. Poland: Cracow. 1977-1987. Lang.: Pol. 1997

Experimental theatre at the Stary in three recent productions. Poland: Cracow. 1987. Lang.: Eng. 1999

State Puppet Theatre (Budapest)
SEE
Állami Bábszinház.

State Puppet Theatre (Moscow)
SEE
Gosudarstvènnyj Centralnyj Teat'r Kukol.

State Theatre (Cleveland, OH)
Performance spaces
Restoration of Ohio, State and Palace Theatres in Playhouse Square. USA: Cleveland, OH. 1964-1986. Lang.: Eng. 681

State Theatre Institute (Moscow)
SEE
Gosudarstvènnyj Institut Teatralnogo Iskusstva.

Statements after an Arrest under the Immorality Act
Plays/librettos/scripts
Cultural predetermination in three Athol Fugard plays. South Africa, Republic of. 1970. Lang.: Eng. 1419

States, Bert O.
Plays/librettos/scripts
Dramatic irony as an actor's tool. 1987. Lang.: Eng. 2417

Station House Opera (London)
Performance/production
Collection of newspaper reviews by London theatre critics. UK-England: London. 1987. Lang.: Eng. 2267

Stavis, Barrie
Plays/librettos/scripts
Interview with playwright Barrie Stavis. USA. 1987. Lang.: Hun. 2920

Stavovské divadlo (Prague)
Institutions
History of Stavovské Theatre. Czechoslovakia: Prague. 1783-1983. Lang.: Cze. 1612

Steadman, Ian
Performance/production
Black theatre in South Africa: influence of traditional forms. South Africa, Republic of. England: London. USA: New York, NY. 1586-1987. Lang.: Eng. 2005

Theory/criticism
Semiotic production in popular performance. South Africa, Republic of. 1980. Lang.: Eng. 1347

Steel Magnolias
Administration
Financial considerations in transferring *Steel Magnolias* to an Off Broadway theatre. USA: New York, NY. 1987. Lang.: Eng. 226

Performance/production
Collection of newspaper reviews by New York theatre critics. USA: New York, NY. 1987. Lang.: Eng. 2320

Plays/librettos/scripts
Interview with playwright Robert Harling, designer Edward Gianfrancesco. USA: New York, NY. 1987. Lang.: Eng. 2846

Steele, Richard
Administration
Role of the Master of the Revels as censor. England: London. 1662-1737. Lang.: Eng. 22

Steer, John
Performance/production
Collection of newspaper reviews by London theatre critics. UK-England: London. 1987. Lang.: Eng. 2213

Steichen, Edward
Relation to other fields
Theatricality in works of photographers Cindy Sherman and Edward Steichen. USA. 1900-1987. Lang.: Eng. 1289

Steigerwald, Karel
Performance/production
Miroslav Krobot directs Steigerwald's *Dobové tance (Period Dances)*, Nejedlý Realistic Theatre. Czechoslovakia: Prague. 1987. Lang.: Cze. 770

Stein, Gertrude
Performance/production
Goodman Theatre's series 'Celebration of Genius'. USA: Chicago, IL. 1986-1987. Lang.: Eng. 3409

Stein, Lou
Performance/production
Collection of newspaper reviews by London theatre critics. UK-England. 1987. Lang.: Eng.   2175

Collection of newspaper reviews by London theatre critics. UK-England: London. 1987. Lang.: Eng.   2178

Collection of newspaper reviews by London theatre critics. UK-England: London. 1987. Lang.: Eng.   2232

Stein, Peter
Institutions
Schaubühne's comeback with production of *Schuld und Sühne (Crime and Punishment)*. Germany, West: Berlin, West. 1970-1987. Lang.: Dut.   1618

Performance/production
Collection of newspaper reviews by London theatre critics. UK-England: London. 1987. Lang.: Eng.   2206

Collection of newspaper reviews by London theatre critics. UK-England: London. 1987. Lang.: Eng.   2253

Stein, Phyllis
Performance/production
Collection of newspaper reviews by London theatre critics. UK-England: London. 1987. Lang.: Eng.   2246

Steinbeck, John
Performance/production
Profile of character actor Matthew Locricchio. USA: New York, NY. 1987. Lang.: Eng.   2334

Stembridge, Gerry
Performance/production
DYT (Dublin Youth Theatre). Ireland: Dublin. 1980-1987. Lang.: Eng.   816

Stennett, Roger
Performance/production
Collection of newspaper reviews by London theatre critics. UK-England: London. 1987. Lang.: Eng.   2241

Stenudd, Stefan
Performance/production
Rock opera *Drakar och Demoner (Dragons and Demons)* about youth at risk. Sweden: Handen. 1987. Lang.: Swe.   3637

Stephen Joseph Theatre (London)
Performance/production
Collection of newspaper reviews by London theatre critics. UK-England: London. 1987. Lang.: Eng.   2234

Steppenwolf Theatre (Chicago, IL)
Design/technology
Work of set/lighting designer Kevin Rigdon. USA. 1986. Lang.: Eng.   400

Institutions
Analysis of the changing scene in Chicago's theatres. USA: Chicago, IL. 1987. Lang.: Eng.   589

Stepping Out
Design/technology
Lighting reviews for several New York productions. USA: New York, NY. 1987. Lang.: Eng.   474

Performance/production
Collection of newspaper reviews by New York critics. USA: New York, NY. 1987. Lang.: Eng.   2324

Sternhagen, Frances
Performance/production
Working in London through Equity actor exchange. UK-England: London. USA: New York, NY. 1985. Lang.: Eng.   2307

Stevens, Risë
Performance/production
Mezzo soprano Risë Stevens. USA: New York, NY. Lang.: Eng.   3856

Stewart, Chuck
Performance/production
Theatre career of photo-journalist Bert Andrews. USA: New York, NY. 1950-1987. Lang.: Eng.   2367

Stewart, Connie
Performance/production
Collection of newspaper reviews by London theatre critics. UK-England: London. 1987. Lang.: Eng.   2232

Stewart, Ellen
Administration
Diversity of Letter of Agreement theatres that operate in New York City. USA: New York, NY. 1987. Lang.: Eng.   204

Stewart, Nellie
Performance/production
British theatrical touring companies. UK-England. North America. Australia. 1870-1929. Lang.: Eng.   2280

Sticks and Stones
Plays/librettos/scripts
Critical analysis of James Reaney's *Three Desks*. Canada. 1960-1977. Lang.: Eng.   2477

Sticks and Stones (Sudbury, ON)
Performance/production
Popular theatre, mostly on economic, feminist themes. Canada: Sudbury, ON. 1930-1987. Lang.: Eng.   1709

Stilgoe, Richard
Performance/production
Collection of newspaper reviews by London theatre critics. UK-England: London. 1986. Lang.: Eng.   2065

Stinchi, Nilde
Performance/production
Career of basso Italo Tajo. Italy: Turin. 1935-1982. Lang.: Eng.   3805

Stirner, Brian
Performance/production
Collection of newspaper reviews by London theatre critics. UK-England: London. 1986. Lang.: Eng.   2129

Collection of newspaper reviews by London theatre critics. UK-England: London. 1986. Lang.: Eng.   2147

Collection of newspaper reviews by London theatre critics. UK-England: London. 1987. Lang.: Eng.   2187

Collection of newspaper reviews by London theatre critics. UK-England: London. 1987. Lang.: Eng.   2259

Collection of newspaper reviews by London theatre critics. UK-England: London. 1987. Lang.: Eng.   2270

Stockholm Opera
SEE
Kungliga Operahus.

Stockholms Studentteater
Institutions
Stockholms Studentteater now welcomes amateur participation. Sweden: Stockholm. 1921-1987. Lang.: Swe.   1638

Stockwell, Jeremy
Performance/production
Collection of newspaper reviews by London theatre critics. UK-England: London. 1987. Lang.: Eng.   2186

Stokes, Simon
Performance/production
Collection of newspaper reviews by London theatre critics. UK-England: London. 1986. Lang.: Eng.   2039

Collection of newspaper reviews by London theatre critics. UK-England: London. 1986. Lang.: Eng.   2110

Collection of newspaper reviews by London theatre critics. UK-England: London. 1986. Lang.: Eng.   2134

Collection of newspaper reviews by London theatre critics. UK-England: London. 1987. Lang.: Eng.   2184

Collection of newspaper reviews by London theatre critics. UK-England: London. 1987. Lang.: Eng.   2209

Collection of newspaper reviews by London theatre critics. UK-England: London. 1987. Lang.: Eng.   2226

Stokowski, Leopold
Performance/production
American premiere of Alban Berg's *Wozzeck*. USA: New York, NY. 1931. Lang.: Eng.   3841

Stone, Peter
Institutions
Photos and list of those present at Dramatists' Guild award ceremony. USA: New York, NY. 1987. Lang.: Eng.   581

Stoppard, Tom
Performance/production
Reviews and discussion of Tokyo productions. Japan: Tokyo. 1960-1987. Lang.: Jap.   1960

Comments on Tokyo performances. Japan: Tokyo. 1987. Lang.: Jap.   1964

Collection of newspaper reviews by London theatre critics. UK-England: London. 1986. Lang.: Eng.   2102

Collection of newspaper reviews by London theatre critics. UK-England: London. 1987. Lang.: Eng.   2214

Strauss, Richard — cont'd

Performance/production

Background on Metropolitan radio broadcast performances. USA: New York, NY. 1987. Lang.: Eng.   3837

Plays/librettos/scripts

Adaptation of literary works to opera. 1893-1987. Lang.: Eng.   3890

Comparison of Mozart's *The Magic Flute* and Strauss's *Die Frau ohne Schatten*. Austria: Vienna. 1980. Lang.: Eng.   3891

Musical sources in the operas of Richard Strauss. Germany: Dresden. 1864-1949. Lang.: Eng.   3908

Street theatre

Audience

Street theatre after the Russian Revolution: new theatrical concepts. USSR: Moscow. 1917-1924. Lang.: Ger.   3340

Institutions

Tabootenay, a collaborative street theatre troupe. Canada: Vancouver, BC. 1986. Lang.: Eng.   3380

Performance spaces

The streets of New York as experimental performance space. USA: New York, NY. 1960-1975. Lang.: Eng.   688

Performance/production

Examples of Nigerian street theatre. Nigeria. 1900-1987. Lang.: Eng.   866

Puppetry on the streets and fairgrounds. France. 1800-1899. Lang.: Eng.   3258

Street theatre and mass media. Italy. 1980. Lang.: Ger.   3295

The 4th International Festival of Street Theatres. Poland: Jelenia Góra. 1986. Lang.: Eng, Fre.   3355

Plays/librettos/scripts

Interview with playwright Luis Valdez. USA. 1940-1983. Lang.: Eng.   2897

Relation to other fields

Tendencies in Latin American theatre that may have influenced its evolution. Cuba. 1973-1986. Lang.: Spa.   1230

Street, The

Plays/librettos/scripts

Interview with playwright John Boyd: influences and plays. UK-Ireland: Belfast. 1930-1985. Lang.: Eng.   2828

Streetcar Named Desire, A

Design/technology

Lighting designer James Sultan's design for *A Streetcar Named Desire*. USA: San Diego, CA. 1986. Lang.: Eng.   1599

Performance/production

Soviet productions of five Tennessee Williams plays. USSR. 1910-1987. Lang.: Eng.   2397

Reference materials

History of pocket theatre. France: Paris. 1944-1953. Lang.: Eng.   2974

Strehler, Giorgio

Performance/production

Giorgio Strehler as the quintessential director of the century. France. Italy. 1921-1987. Lang.: Fre.   1754

Examples of missed opportunities in modern Italian theatre. Italy. 1930-1950. Lang.: Ita.   1944

Brief history of Piccolo Teatro. Italy: Milan. 1947-1987. Lang.: Hun.   1945

Giorgio Strehler's staging of *L'illusion comique (The Comic Illusion)* by Corneille. Italy. 1944-1986. Lang.: Eng.   1948

Giorgio Strehler on staging *Die Dreigroschenoper (The Three Penny Opera)*. Italy: Milan. France: Paris. 1928-1986. Lang.: Swe.   3809

Interview with Dario Fo. Netherlands. Italy. 1987. Lang.: Dut.   3814

Strepponi, Giuseppina

Plays/librettos/scripts

Impact of Giuseppina Strepponi Verdi on her husband's creativity. Italy: Milan. 1836-1901. Lang.: Eng.   3927

Reference materials

Description of the Verdi Archive at New York University. USA: New York, NY. Italy: Milan. 1976. Lang.: Eng.   3937

Stretch of the Imagination, A

Plays/librettos/scripts

Interview with playwright Jack Hibberd. Australia: Melbourne. 1967-1987. Lang.: Eng.   2434

Strickson, Mark

Performance/production

Collection of newspaper reviews by London theatre critics. UK-England: London. 1986. Lang.: Eng.   2086

Strijards, Frans

Performance/production

Interview with Frans Strijards, playwright and director. Netherlands. 1987. Lang.: Dut.   1979

Strindberg, August

Performance/production

German productions of Strindberg plays. Germany, West. Germany, East. Sweden. 1984-1986. Lang.: Ger.   1788

Fadren (The Father) by August Strindberg presented under the title *Az apa* at Katona József Theatre, guest director Kalle Holmberg. Hungary: Budapest. 1987. Lang.: Hun.   1865

Recent productions of Strindberg plays in the Netherlands. Netherlands. Sweden. 1984-1986. Lang.: Swe.   1983

Recent productions of Strindberg plays in Sweden and elsewhere. Sweden. 1984-1986. Lang.: Swe.   2017

Västerås Amateur Theatre Festival. Sweden: Västerås. 1987. Lang.: Swe.   2023

Collection of newspaper reviews by London theatre critics. UK-England: London. 1986. Lang.: Eng.   2077

Collection of newspaper reviews by London theatre critics. UK-England: London. 1986. Lang.: Eng.   2155

Collection of newspaper reviews by London theatre critics. UK-England: London. 1987. Lang.: Eng.   2244

Recent Strindberg productions in Great Britain. UK-England. Sweden. 1984-1986. Lang.: Eng.   2298

Composer Hans Gefors on his opera *Christina*. Sweden. 1986. Lang.: Swe.   3819

Christina, opera based on Strindberg play by Hans Gefors and Lars Forssell. Sweden: Stockholm. 1986-1987. Lang.: Swe.   3823

Plays/librettos/scripts

Misogynist themes in Strindberg, Weininger and Witkiewicz. Austria: Vienna. 1880-1987. Lang.: Eng.   2452

Ariadne in plays of Ibsen, Strindberg, Maeterlinck. Europe. 1892-1902. Lang.: Eng.   2566

Munch's influence on Strindberg. Germany: Berlin. 1892-1900. Lang.: Eng.   2596

Critical reception of realism and naturalism. Germany. 1890-1987. Lang.: Ger.   2601

Theme of stage direction in the work of Scandinavian authors. Sweden. Norway. 1700-1987. Lang.: Ita.   2737

The son-in-law in *Pelikanen (The Pelican)* by August Strindberg. Sweden. 1907-1987. Lang.: Swe.   2740

Theatrical metaphor in Strindberg's *Gustav III*. Sweden. 1903-1987. Lang.: Eng.   2741

Analysis of Dürrenmatt's *Play Strindberg*, adaptation of Strindberg's *Dödsdansen (The Dance of Death)*. Switzerland. 1971-1982. Lang.: Eng.   2743

Theory/criticism

Centenary of Théâtre Libre: proposes 'subjective realism'. France. 1887-1987. Lang.: Fre.   1337

Exploration of the nature of tragedy. 500 B.C.-1987 A.D. Lang.: Eng.   3020

Shift of August Strindberg from naturalism to expressionism. Sweden. 1987. Lang.: Eng.   3061

Strokes of Genius

Performance/production

Collection of newspaper reviews by London theatre critics. UK-England: London. 1987. Lang.: Eng.   2211

Strong Breed, The

Plays/librettos/scripts

The Strong Breed and *The Bacchae*: Soyinka's symbolic use of ritual and ceremony. Nigeria. 1973-1987. Lang.: Eng.   2709

Strong, Roy

Performance/production

History of British Theatre Museum, its collections and exhibition spaces. UK-England: London. 1987. Lang.: Eng.   919

Strouse, Charles

Performance/production

Collection of newspaper reviews by London theatre critics. UK-England: London. 1987. Lang.: Eng.   2228

Golden Fleece, Ltd. bridges classical music, opera and musical theatre. USA: New York, NY. 1987. Lang.: Eng.   3412

Interview with director Paula Kalustian. USA: New York, NY. 1984-1987. Lang.: Eng.   3662

Swartz, Marlene
 Administration
 American theatre's view of the commissioning process. USA: New
 York, NY. 1987. Lang.: Eng. 118
Swedish Society for Theatre Technicians
 SEE
 Svensk Teaterteknisk Förening.
Sweeney Todd
 Design/technology
 Adapting lighting from a live theatre version of *Sweeney Todd* for
 videotape. USA. 1982. Lang.: Eng. 3204
Sweet Bird of Youth
 Performance/production
 Soviet productions of five Tennessee Williams plays. USSR. 1910-
 1987. Lang.: Eng. 2397
Sweet Charity
 Design/technology
 Lighting reviews for several New York productions. USA: New
 York, NY. 1987. Lang.: Eng. 475
Sweet Inniscarra
 Plays/librettos/scripts
 Analysis of the plays and songs of Irish-American musical theatre
 star Chauncey Olcott. USA. 1893-1918. Lang.: Eng. 3671
Sweet Sue
 Design/technology
 Lighting reviews of several Broadway shows. USA: New York, NY.
 1987. Lang.: Eng. 473

 Performance/production
 Collection of newspaper reviews by New York critics. USA: New
 York, NY. 1987. Lang.: Eng. 2324
Sweet, Jeffrey
 Performance/production
 Collection of newspaper reviews by London theatre critics. UK-
 England: London. 1986. Lang.: Eng. 2044
 Collection of newspaper reviews by London theatre critics. UK-
 England: London. 1987. Lang.: Eng. 2198
Sweet, Nancy
 Performance/production
 Collection of newspaper reviews by London theatre critics. UK-
 England: London. 1987. Lang.: Eng. 2227
Swetnam the Woman-Hater, Arraigned by Women
 Plays/librettos/scripts
 Swetnam the Woman-Hater, Arraigned by Women written in response
 to an anti-female pamphlet. England. 1600-1620. Lang.: Eng. 1118
Swift, Jeremy
 Performance/production
 Collection of newspaper reviews by London theatre critics. UK-
 England: London. 1986. Lang.: Eng. 2080
Swim Visit
 Performance/production
 Collection of newspaper reviews by London theatre critics. UK-
 England: London. 1986. Lang.: Eng. 2083
Swinarski, Konrad
 Performance/production
 Early life of director Konrad Swinarski. Poland. 1929-1955. Lang.:
 Pol. 878
Swinter, Tilda
 Plays/librettos/scripts
 Actress Tilda Swinter talks about her performance as a male. UK-
 England. 1987. Lang.: Eng. 2824
Swire, Willard
 Administration
 U.S. and British Equity associations: actor exchange, union
 reciprocity. UK-England. USA. 1981-1987. Lang.: Eng. 50
Swiss Union of Theatre Makers
 SEE
 Vereinigten Theaterschaffenden der Schweiz.
Symbolism
 Basic theatrical documents
 Russian symbolist plays and essays. USSR. 1880-1986. Lang.: Eng.
 1584

 Theory/criticism
 Centenary of Théâtre Libre: proposes 'subjective realism'. France.
 1887-1987. Lang.: Fre. 1337
Symond, Peter
 Performance/production
 Collection of newspaper reviews by London theatre critics. UK-
 England: London. 1986. Lang.: Eng. 2082

Symonds, Vic
 Performance/production
 Granada TV's production of *The Jewel in the Crown*. UK-England.
 India. 1986. Lang.: Eng. 3207
Symphony Space (New York, NY)
 Institutions
 Profile and history of Symphony Space. USA: New York, NY.
 1977-1984. Lang.: Eng. 602
Synge, John Millington
 Audience
 Political roots of rioting on opening of Synge's *The Playboy of the
 Western World*. Ireland: Dublin. 1907. Lang.: Eng. 1535
 Performance/production
 Collection of newspaper reviews by London theatre critics. UK-
 England: London. 1987. Lang.: Eng. 2277
 Plays/librettos/scripts
 Irish Literary Renaissance writers' view of America. Ireland. 1900-
 1930. Lang.: Eng. 2639
 Lady Gregory's *Grania*. Ireland: Dublin. 1910-1930. Lang.: Eng.
 2649

 Relation to other fields
 Literary figures of the Irish Literary Renaissance. Ireland. UK-
 Ireland. 1875-1938. Lang.: Eng. 2995

 Research/historiography
 Overview of Canadian research on twentieth-century Irish drama.
 Ireland. UK-Ireland. Canada. 1891-1983. Lang.: Eng. 3011

 Theory/criticism
 Assessment of the series *Lost Beginning*, its relation to Stewart
 Parker's *Pentecost*. UK-Ireland. 1987. Lang.: Eng. 3218
Szabó, József
 Performance/production
 Season openings at Petőfi Theatre, including Lengyel's *A nagy
 fejedelem (The Great Prince)* and Bíró's *A rablólovag (The Gallant
 Kidnapper)*. Hungary: Veszprém. 1987. Lang.: Hun. 1820
Szabó, Magda
 Performance/production
 György Lengyel directs *Szent Bertalan nappala (St. Bartholomew's
 Day)* by Magda Szabó at Madách Theatre. Hungary: Budapest.
 1987. Lang.: Hun. 1929
Szabóky Zsigmond Rafael (Zsigmond Rafael Szabóky)
 Performance/production
 Dezső Szomary's *Szabóky Zsigmond Rafael (Zsigmond Rafael
 Szabóky)* staged by István Verebes at Játékszín (Budapest).
 Hungary: Budapest. 1986. Lang.: Hun. 1905
 Reviews of actors Olga Koós and István Bozóky in *Szabóky
 Zsigmond Rafael (Zsigmond Rafael Szabóky)* at Játékszín. Hungary:
 Budapest. 1987. Lang.: Hun. 1914
Szakácsi, Sándor
 Performance/production
 Actors Sándor Szakácsi and Piroska Molnár in *Man of La Mancha*
 directed by Lászlo Bagossy. Hungary: Pécs. 1987. Lang.: Hun. 3633
Szechwan opera
 Performance/production
 Comments on the performances at the Chinese Art Festival. China,
 People's Republic of: Beijing. 1987. Lang.: Chi. 3501
Szechwan Opera (People's Republic of China)
 Audience
 Szechwan Opera adaptation of Brecht's *Der Gute Mensch von
 Sezuan (The Good Person of Szechwan)*. China, People's Republic
 of. 1987. Lang.: Chi. 3432
Szegedi Balett (Szeged)
 Performance/production
 Premiere performance of new ballet company, Szegedi Balett.
 Hungary: Szeged. 1987. Lang.: Hun. 1438
Szegedi Nemzeti Színház (Szeged)
 Design/technology
 Technical details of Szegedi Nemzeti Színház. Hungary: Szeged.
 1987. Lang.: Hun. 330
 Director, Szegedi Nemzeti Színház, on theatre technology. Hungary:
 Szeged. 1987. Lang.: Hun. 337

 Performance/production
 Comparison of the premiere of Imre Sarkadi's *Oszlopos Simeon (The
 Man on the Pillar)* and two revivals by Árpad Árkosi and István
 Horvai. Hungary: Szeged, Budapest. 1967-1987. Lang.: Hun. 1830
 Miklós Vámos' *Világszezon (World Tourist Season)* staged by János
 Sándor at National Theatre. Hungary: Szeged. 1986. Lang.: Hun.
 1870

Szegedi Nemzeti Szinház (Szeged) — cont'd

János Sándor directs *Világszezon (World Tourist Season)* by Miklós Vámos at Szegedi Nemzeti Szinház. Hungary: Szeged. 1986. Lang.: Hun.   1909

Szegedi Szabadtéri Játékok (Szeged)
Performance/production
Reviews of *Rigoletto*, Lloyd Webber's *Requiem*, *Les Misérables* and the Hungarian Mass of the Tolcsvays. Hungary: Szeged. 1987. Lang.: Hun.   3400

Szegvári, Menyhért
Performance/production
Shakespeare's *King Lear* staged by Menyhért Szegvári at the National Theatre. Hungary: Pécs. 1986. Lang.: Hun.   1811

Menyhért Szegvári directs Miklós Munkácsi's *Lisszaboni eső (Rain in Lisbon)* at Játékszín. Hungary: Budapest. 1987. Lang.: Hun.   1815

Menyhért Szegvári directs premiere of *Lisszaboni eső (Rain in Lisbon)* by Miklós Munkácsi at Játékszín. Hungary: Budapest. 1987. Lang.: Hun.   1858

Székely, Gábor
Performance/production
Interview with director Gábor Székely. Hungary: Budapest. 1982-1987. Lang.: Hun.   809

Gábor Székely directs Milán Füst's *Catullus* at Katona József Theatre. Hungary: Budapest. 1987. Lang.: Hun.   1857

Gábor Székely directs Milán Füst's *Catullus* at Katona József Theatre. Hungary: Budapest. 1987. Lang.: Hun.   1878

Milán Füst's *Catullus* and Imre Sarkadi's *Oszlopos Simeon (The Man on the Pillar)* reviewed. Hungary: Budapest. 1987. Lang.: Hun.   1886

Tóték (The Tót Family) by István Örkény at Hungarian Theatre, guest director Gábor Székely. Yugoslavia: Novi Sad. 1987. Lang.: Hun.   2406

Szenariusz dla trzech aktorów (Script for Three Actors, A)
Performance/production
Festival of Polish plays. Poland: Wrocław. 1987. Lang.: Eng, Fre.   871

Szent Bertalan nappala (St. Bartholomew's Day)
Performance/production
György Lengyel directs *Szent Bertalan nappala (St. Bartholomew's Day)* by Magda Szabó at Madách Theatre. Hungary: Budapest. 1987. Lang.: Hun.   1929

Szentendrei Teátrum (Szentendre)
Performance/production
András Békés directs Rossini's *La Cenerentola* at Szentendrei Teátrum under the title *Hamupipőke*. Hungary: Szentendre. 1987. Lang.: Hun.   3798

Szentgyörgyi István Szinmüvészeti Főiskola (Marosvásárhely)
Institutions
Memoirs of director and teacher Géza Gergely on Hungarian theatrical training in Romania. Romania: Tirgu-Mures. Hungary. 1946-1986. Lang.: Hun.   556

Szigligeti Szinház (Szolnok)
Performance/production
Örökösök (Heirs) by Gorkij directed by Tamás Fodor. Hungary: Szolnok. 1987. Lang.: Hun.   1818

Tamás Fodor directs *Örökösök (Heirs)* based on Gorkij's *Vassa Železnova*. Hungary: Szolnok. 1987. Lang.: Hun.   1848

Shakespeare's *A Midsummer Night's Dream* staged by Tibor Csizmadia. Hungary: Eger, Szolnok. 1986. Lang.: Hun.   1881

Szikora, János
Performance/production
Christopher Hampton's *Les Liaisons Dangereuses* directed by János Szikora at Pesti Szinház under the title *Veszedelmes viszonyok*. Hungary: Budapest. 1986. Lang.: Hun.   1795

Géza Tordy as Willy Loman in Arthur Miller's *Death of a Salesman* directed, as *Az ügynök halála*, by János Szikora at Vigszinház. Hungary: Budapest. 1987. Lang.: Hun.   1797

L'illusion comique (The Comic Illusion) by Pierre Corneille directed by János Szikora at the Katona József Theatre. Hungary: Budapest. 1986. Lang.: Hun.   1859

Arthur Miller's *Death of a Salesman* directed by János Szikora at Vígszínház. Hungary: Budapest. 1987. Lang.: Hun.   1869

János Szikora directs Corneille's *L'illusion comique (The Comic Illusion)* at Katona József Theatre. Hungary: Budapest. 1986. Lang.: Hun.   1918

Szilágyi, László
Performance/production
Béla Zerkovitz's operetta *Csókos asszony (A Woman Made for Kissing)* directed by István Iglódi. Hungary: Budapest. 1987. Lang.: Hun.   3957

István Iglódi directs *Csókos asszony (A Woman Made for Kissing)* by Béla Zerkovitz at Vigszinház. Hungary: Budapest. 1987. Lang.: Hun.   3958

Szilágyi, Tibor
Performance/production
Series of interviews with actor Tibor Szilágyi. Hungary. 1950-1986. Lang.: Hun.   1814

Szinetár, Miklós
Performance/production
La vida es sueño (Life Is a Dream) directed by Miklós Szinetár at Radnóti Miklós Theatre under the title *Az élet álom*. Hungary: Budapest. 1986. Lang.: Hun.   1846

Calderón's *La vida es sueño (Life Is a Dream)* staged by Miklós Szinetár under the title *Az élet álom*. Hungary: Budapest. 1987. Lang.: Hun.   1911

Comparison of *Die Dreigroschenoper (The Three Penny Opera)* as directed by Ferenc Sík, József Petrik and Miklós Szinetár under the title *Koldusopera*. Hungary: Győr, Budapest. 1987. Lang.: Hun.   3402

Miklós Szinetár directs *Les Misérables* at Rock Szinház. Hungary: Budapest. 1987. Lang.: Hun.   3630

Szinmüvészeti Főiskola (Budapest)
Performance/production
Reviews of drama students' final examination performances. Hungary: Budapest. 1986-1987. Lang.: Hun.   804

Szirtes, Tamás
Performance/production
Actor-dramas produced by National Theatre. Hungary: Budapest. 1836-1847. Lang.: Hun.   1842

Kean by Dumas and Sartre, directed by Tamás Szirtes, Madách Theatre. Hungary: Budapest. 1986. Lang.: Hun.   1862

Tamás Szirtes directs Gyula Háy's *Mohács (The Mohács Disaster)* at Madách Szinház. Hungary: Budapest. 1987. Lang.: Hun.   1863

Gyula Háy's *Mohács (The Mohács Disaster)* staged by Tamás Szirtes, Gyulai Várszinház. Hungary: Gyula. 1987. Lang.: Hun.   1903

Szőke, István
Performance/production
István Szőke directs Shakespeare's *Merchant of Venice*, Pécs National Theatre. Hungary: Pécs. 1987. Lang.: Hun.   1854

István Szőke directs *Mari* by György Schwajda at Pécsi Nemzeti Szinház. Hungary: Pécs. 1986. Lang.: Hun.   1856

Anouilh's *Eurydice*, Vian's *Tête de Méduse (Medusa Head)* at National Theatre of Miskolc. Hungary: Miskolc. 1987. Lang.: Hun.   1888

Vitrac's *Victor, ou les enfants au pouvoir (Victor, or the Children in Power)* directed by István Szőke as *Viktor, avagy a gyermekuralom*. Hungary: Pécs. 1987. Lang.: Hun.   1898

István Szőke directs *Victor ou les enfants au pouvoir (Victor, or The Children in Power)* by Roger Vitrac at National Theatre. Hungary: Pécs. 1987. Lang.: Hun.   1904

Szokolay, Sándor
Performance/production
Review of productions at opera ensembles meeting. Hungary: Szeged. 1987. Lang.: Hun.   3792

Szomory, Dezső
Performance/production
Tamás Puskás directs *Takáts Alice (Alice Takáts)* by Dezső Szomory, Madách Chamber Theatre. Hungary: Budapest. 1987. Lang.: Hun.   1897

Dezső Szomary's *Szabóky Zsigmond Rafael (Zsigmond Rafael Szabóky)* staged by István Verebes at Játékszín (Budapest). Hungary: Budapest. 1986. Lang.: Hun.   1905

Tamás Puskás directs *Takáts Alice (Alice Takáts)* by Dezső Szomory at Madách Kamaraszinház. Hungary: Budapest. 1987. Lang.: Hun.   1906

Reviews of actors Olga Koós and István Bozóky in *Szabóky Zsigmond Rafael (Zsigmond Rafael Szabóky)* at Játékszín. Hungary: Budapest. 1987. Lang.: Hun.   1914

Szu Sheng Yüan (Four Famous Apes)
Plays/librettos/scripts
Hsü Wei's *Szu Sheng Yüan (Four Famous Apes)*. China. 1521-1593. Lang.: Chi.   3551

Tales of Hoffmann, The
SEE
Contes d'Hoffmann, Les.

Talk Radio
Performance/production
Collection of newspaper reviews by New York theatre critics. USA: New York, NY. 1987. Lang.: Eng. 2319

Talk to Me
Performance/production
Collection of newspaper reviews by London theatre critics. UK-England: London. 1986. Lang.: Eng. 2168

Talking Dirty
Plays/librettos/scripts
New Canadian drama: non-realistic, anti-naturalistic. Canada. 1983-1984. Lang.: Eng. 2482

Talley's Folly
Performance/production
Reviews of Wilson's *Talley's Folly* staged by András Bálint and Bond's *The Fool* staged by László Salamon Suba. Hungary: Dunaujváros, Nyíregyháza. 1986. Lang.: Hun. 1902

Talli, Virgilio
Performance/production
Collaboration of actor-director Virgilio Talli with playwright Pier Maria Rosso di San Secondo. Italy. 1917-1920. Lang.: Ita. 835

Tallis, Frank
Performance/production
Collection of newspaper reviews by London theatre critics. UK-England: London. 1987. Lang.: Eng. 2249

Tally, Ted
Performance/production
Collection of newspaper reviews by London theatre critics. UK-England: London. 1987. Lang.: Eng. 2268

Four productions in Southern regional theatres. USA: Houston, TX, Louisville, KY, Gainesville, FL. 1980. Lang.: Eng. 2342

Taluta Theatre
Plays/librettos/scripts
Theme of aggression between fathers and sons: Zambian National Theatre Arts Association festival. Zambia. 1966-1987. Lang.: Eng. 2972

Tamara
Performance/production
Collection of newspaper reviews by New York theatre critics. USA: New York, NY. 1987. Lang.: Eng. 2313

Tamási, Áron
Performance/production
Imre Kerényi directs *Énekes madár (The Song Bird)* by Áron Tamási at the National Theatre. Hungary: Budapest. 1987. Lang.: Hun. 1819

Áron Tamási's *Énekes madár (The Song Bird)* directed by Imre Kerényi at National Theatre. Hungary: Budapest. 1987. Lang.: Hun. 1872

Taming of the Shrew, The
Design/technology
Preliminary sketches for the Royal Shakespeare Company's *The Taming of the Shrew*. UK-England. 1985. Lang.: Eng. 1597

Performance/production
English Shakespearean productions. UK-England: London, Manchester, Stratford. 1985-1986. Lang.: Eng. 917

Richard Ouzounian, director, Manitoba Theatre Centre. Canada: Winnipeg, MB. 1982. Lang.: Eng. 1693

Collection of newspaper reviews by London theatre critics. UK-England: London. 1986. Lang.: Eng. 2121

Collection of newspaper reviews by London theatre critics. UK-England: London. 1987. Lang.: Eng. 2255

Plays/librettos/scripts
Shakespeare's use of formal self-referential oaths. England. 1594-1616. Lang.: Eng. 2552

Tampa Bay Performing Arts Center (Tampa, FL)
Performance spaces
The Tampa Bay Performing Arts Center. USA: Tampa, FL. 1987. Lang.: Eng. 698

Lighting design in Tampa's new performing arts center. USA: Tampa, FL. 1987. Lang.: Eng. 3395

Tan, Fu-Ing
Performance/production
The acting of Chinese opera star Tan Fu-Ing. China, People's Republic of. 1900-1950. Lang.: Chi. 3491

Taney, Retta
Performance/production
Collection of newspaper reviews by London theatre critics. UK-England: London. 1986. Lang.: Eng. 2061

Tang, Xian-Zu
Audience
Differences between two dramatists of Chinese opera—Tang and Shen. China, People's Republic of. Lang.: Chi. 3433

Performance/production
The modernization of Chinese opera—keeping the traditional spirit. China, People's Republic of: Beijing. 1279-1986. Lang.: Chi. 3539

Plays/librettos/scripts
How music reveals character in Chinese opera. China. 1600-1700. Lang.: Chi. 3545

Lost short writings of Beijing opera playwright Tang Xian-Zu. China: Beijing. 1610-1742. Lang.: Chi. 3546

Shakespeare compared to writers of Chinese opera. China. 1279-1616. Lang.: Chi. 3554

New light on playwright Tang Xian-Zu. China, People's Republic of: Beijing. 1279-1983. Lang.: Chi. 3566

Relation to other fields
Tragic conflicts in playwright's Tang Xian-Zu's cultural conscience. China: Beijing. 1550-1616. Lang.: Chi. 3581

Theory/criticism
Tang Xian-Zu's theory of 'original character' in Chinese opera. China, People's Republic of. 700-1986. Lang.: Chi. 3609

Tangente (Montreal, PQ)
Performance/production
Review, 'Le corps politique' festival. Canada: Montreal, PQ. 1986. Lang.: Fre. 1406

Tanguy, François
Performance/production
Plays of Pinget, Euripides and Théâtre du Rideau staged by Jouanneau, Suzuki and Tanguy, Théâtre de la Bastille. France: Paris. 1987. Lang.: Fre. 1753

Collection of newspaper reviews by London theatre critics. UK-England: London. 1987. Lang.: Eng. 2212

Taniguchi, Shūichi
Plays/librettos/scripts
Productions by several Tokyo companies. Japan: Tokyo. 1986-1987. Lang.: Jap. 2682

Tanítónő, A (Schoolmistress, The)
Performance/production
A tanítónő (The Schoolmistress) by Sándor Bródy, directed by Péter Tömöry at Hevesi Sándor Theatre. Hungary: Zalaegerszeg. 1986. Lang.: Hun. 1921

Tanizaki, Junichirō
Performance/production
Six plays of the Tokyo season, focus on director Betsuyaku Minoru. Japan: Tokyo. 1986. Lang.: Jap. 1966

Tankard, Meryl
Performance/production
Collection of newspaper reviews by London theatre critics. UK-England: London. 1986. Lang.: Eng. 2107

Tannhäuser
Performance/production
Background on Metropolitan radio broadcast performances. USA: New York, NY. 1987. Lang.: Eng. 3837

Plays/librettos/scripts
Woman, salvation and love in operas of Richard Wagner. Germany. 1813-1883. Lang.: Eng. 3909

Tansi, Sony Lab'ou
Basic theatrical documents
English translations of contemporary African plays. Senegal. Zaire. 1987. Lang.: Eng. 1566

Tantara-rara, Rogues All
Plays/librettos/scripts
New findings on 18th-century Irish comic playwright John O'Keeffe. Ireland. England: London. 1767-1798. Lang.: Eng. 2643

Tao (Tokyo)
Performance/production
Productions of Bungakuza, Yūkikai Zenjidō shiatā, Tao and Tenkei gekijō. Japan: Tokyo. 1986. Lang.: Jap. 1961

Tao hua shan (Peach Blossom Fan, The)
Plays/librettos/scripts
Dramatic structure in Chinese opera play *Tao hua shan (The Peach Blossom Fan)*. China. 1700-1800. Lang.: Chi. 3547

Teaching methods — cont'd

Development of the Stanislavskij Acting System. Russia: Moscow. 1906-1938. Lang.: Eng. 2003

Quality of and access to opera training in North America. Canada. USA. 1987. Lang.: Eng. 3753

Comparison between the problems of puppeteers and cartoon animators. USA. 1987. Lang.: Eng. 4002

Relation to other fields

Drama as education: current theory and practice. USA. 1987. Lang.: Eng. 1268

Criteria for instructors' use of dramatic action. USA. 1987. Lang.: Eng. 1269

Integrating theatre into primary and secondary education. USA. 1987. 1275

Creative drama's potential to stimulate wonder. USA. 1970-1977. Lang.: Eng. 1288

Puppetry in education of hearing-impaired. UK-England: London. 1987. Lang.: Eng. 4011

Training

Guide to teaching through improvisation for children and adults. 1987. Lang.: Eng. 1377

Basic theatrical techniques for secondary school. Belgium. 1987. Lang.: Fre. 1378

Using masks to stimulate the imagination when teaching. China, People's Republic of. 1985. Lang.: Chi. 1379

The classes of a master directing teacher. China, People's Republic of: Shanghai. 1949-1987. Lang.: Chi. 1380

Funding for youth theatre in Ireland. Ireland. 1979-1987. Lang.: Eng. 1381

Essays on theatre teacher Orazio Costa. Italy. 1935-1987. Lang.: Ita. 1382

Proposed changes in teaching methodology to include indigenous drama. South Africa, Republic of. 1960-1987. Lang.: Eng. 1383

Interview with Michael Poyner, director of Ulster Youth Theatre. UK-Ireland. 1987. Lang.: Eng. 1386

Interview with Georgij Tovstonogov. USA. 1987. Lang.: Eng. 1390

Problems of theatrical education. USSR: Moscow. 1987. Lang.: Rus. 1391

Vocal training in Soviet dramatic education. USSR. 1987. Lang.: Rus. 1392

Pedagogy of director L. Kurbas. USSR. 1887-1942. Lang.: Rus. 1393

Problems of students graduating from theatre schools. USSR. 1980-1987. Lang.: Rus. 1394

Director discusses problems of theatrical education. USSR: Kujbyšev. 1987. Lang.: Rus. 1395

Brecht workshop of International Amateur Theatre Association. Germany, East: Berlin, East. 1986. Lang.: Ger. 3079

Interview with acting teacher Deirdre Hurst du Prey, specialist in the Chekhov Method. UK-England: Dartington. 1978. Lang.: Eng. 3081

Acting teachers who studied under Michajl Čechov: making the Technique fit contemporary needs. USA: New York, NY. 1930-1980. Lang.: Eng. 3082

Changes in music teaching methods at the Banff Centre. Canada: Banff, AB. 1933-1987. Lang.: Eng. 3950

Interview with singing master Hanno Blaschke. South Africa, Republic of. 1987. Lang.: Eng. 3951

Interviews with singing teachers in New York City. USA: New York, NY. 1987. Lang.: Eng. 3952

Teale, Polly

Performance/production

Collection of newspaper reviews by London theatre critics. UK. 1987. Lang.: Eng. 2031

Collection of newspaper reviews by London theatre critics. UK-England: London. 1987. Lang.: Eng. 2256

Team Theatre (Denmark)

Relation to other fields

Impact of politics upon funding of theatre. Denmark. 1722-1982. Lang.: Eng. 2986

Teare, Jeff

Performance/production

Collection of newspaper reviews by London theatre critics. UK-England: London. 1986. Lang.: Eng. 2107

Collection of newspaper reviews by London theatre critics. UK-England: London. 1987. Lang.: Eng. 2189

Collection of newspaper reviews by London theatre critics. UK-England: London. 1987. Lang.: Eng. 2248

Collection of newspaper reviews by London theatre critics. UK-England: London. 1987. Lang.: Eng. 2265

Teat'r Dramy i Komedii (Moscow)

SEE

Teat'r na Tagankė.

Teat'r Estonija (Tallinn)

Performance/production

Anu Kaal', Estonian opera singer. USSR. 1960-1987. Lang.: Rus. 3872

Teat'r im. Je. Vachtangova (Moscow)

Performance/production

Director V. Pimenov's recollections of actors Gricenko, Plotnikov and Abrikosov. USSR: Moscow. 1940-1979. Lang.: Rus. 1047

Relation to other fields

Exchange of ideas between Soviets and US theatre artists. USA: New York, NY. USSR: Moscow. 1987. Lang.: Eng. 1284

Teat'r im. Kamala

SEE

Tatarskij Gosudarstvėnnyj Akademičėskij Teat'r im. Kamala.

Teat'r im. Leninskogo Komsomola (Moscow)

Performance/production

Portrait of actor Eugenij Leonov, Moscow Komsomol Theatre. USSR: Moscow. 1926-1987. Lang.: Rus. 990

Moscow Lenin Comsomol's 'Debut', an experimental group. USSR: Moscow. 1987. Lang.: Rus. 1018

Portrait of actor Oleg Jankovskij, Moscow Komsomol Theatre. USSR: Moscow. 1980-1987. Lang.: Rus. 1032

Director Gleb Panfilov's interpretation of *Hamlet* at Komsomol Theatre. USSR: Moscow. 1980-1987. Lang.: Rus. 2373

Plays/librettos/scripts

Historical themes in plays of Andrej Vosnesenskij. USSR: Moscow. 1980-1987. Lang.: Rus. 2937

Teat'r im. M. Jėrmolovoj (Moscow)

Performance/production

Young studio theatre artists of Moscow. USSR: Moscow. 1980-1987. 987

Memoirs of actor V.S. Jakut. USSR: Moscow. 1912-1980. Lang.: Rus. 1025

Plays/librettos/scripts

Radsinskij's *Jogging* directed by Fokin. USSR: Moscow. 1987. Lang.: Eng. 2953

Correspondence of playwright Aleksand'r Vampilov. USSR: Moscow. 1960-1975. Lang.: Rus. 2968

Teat'r im. Mossovėta (Moscow)

Performance/production

Sergej Jurskij, director of Mossovet Theatre. USSR: Moscow. 1970-1980. Lang.: Rus. 995

Portrait of actor Gennadij Bortnikov of Mossovet Theatre. USSR. 1980-1987. Lang.: Eng. 1079

Teat'r im. Šato Rustaveli (Tbilisi)

Performance/production

Rustaveli Theatre of Georgia, directed by Robert Sturua, presents Shakespeare's *Richard III* and Brecht's *Der Kaukasische Kreidekreis (The Caucasian Chalk Circle)* in Hungary. USSR: Tbilisi. Hungary. 1987. Lang.: Hun. 2383

Guest performances by Teat'r im. Šato Rustaveli of Tbilisi at Madách Theatre: Shakespeare's *Richard III*, Brecht's *Der Kaukasische Kreidekreis (The Caucasian Chalk Circle)*. USSR: Tbilisi. Hungary: Budapest. 1986. Lang.: Hun. 2390

Teat'r Junogo Zritelja (Moscow)

Performance/production

Work of Moscow Children's Theatre. USSR: Moscow. 1980-1987. Lang.: Rus. 992

Plays/librettos/scripts

Experiments of Moscow Children's Theatre. USSR: Moscow. 1986-1987. Lang.: Rus. 1185

Teat'r Junogo Zritelja im. Leninskogo Komsomola (Riga)

Performance/production

Performances by Adol'f Šapiro Latvian Children's Theatre. USSR: Riga. 1985-1986. Lang.: Rus. 1064

Teat'r Malyj (Moscow)

Performance/production

Actor and playwright A.I. Sumbatov-Južin. USSR: Moscow. 1857-1927. Lang.: Rus. 998

Tembe, Bongane
Performance/production
Review of Wagner's *Der Fliegende Holländer* at the Natal
Playhouse. South Africa, Republic of: Durban. 1987. Lang.: Eng.
3815

Tempest, The
Institutions
Interview with Elizabeth Clark, director of Temba Theatre Company.
UK-England: London. Caribbean. Lang.: Eng.   567

Plays/librettos/scripts
Theodicy and tragic drama in *King Lear* and *The Tempest*. England.
1605-1611. Lang.: Eng.   1119

Place of the masque in *The Tempest*. England. 1611. Lang.: Eng.
2516

Utopianism in Shakespeare's *The Tempest*. England. 1611-1612.
Lang.: Ger.   2532

Relationship of the *Aeneid* to Shakespeare's *The Tempest*. England:
London. 1611. Lang.: Eng.   2561

Themes of perception in *The Tempest*. UK-England: London. 1611.
Lang.: Eng.   2813

Relation to other fields
Theme of imperialism in *The Tempest*. Canada. Antilles. France.
1611-1977. Lang.: Eng.   2984

Ten-i 21 (Tokyo)
Plays/librettos/scripts
Contemporary Japanese plays about crime. Japan: Tokyo. 1986.
Lang.: Jap.   2681

Plays about child suicide in Japan. Japan: Tokyo. 1986. Lang.: Jap.
2683

Tender Land, The
Plays/librettos/scripts
Aaron Copland's opera *The Tender Land*. USA. 1900. Lang.: Eng.
3933

Tenin, Boris
Performance/production
Memoirs of actor Boris Tenin. USSR: Moscow. 1920-1939. Lang.:
Rus.   1076

Tenkei gekijō (Tokyo)
Performance/production
Productions by Tenkei gekijō, Manji and Mokutōsha. Japan: Tokyo.
1986. Lang.: Jap.   1958

Productions of Bungakuza, Yūkikai Zenjidō shiatā, Tao and Tenkei
gekijō. Japan: Tokyo. 1986. Lang.: Jap.   1961

Tennyson, Henrietta
Performance/production
Overview of Dublin dance season. Ireland: Dublin. 1987. Lang.:
Eng.   1408

Terayama, Shūji
Basic theatrical documents
Plays of Terayama Shūji. Japan. 1950-1980. Lang.: Jap.   1562

Terent'ev, I.G.
Performance/production
Innovative director I.G. Terent'ev. USSR. 1920-1930. Lang.: Rus.
1057

Terentius Afer, Publius
Plays/librettos/scripts
Changes in theatre space as a result of New Comedy. Greece:
Athens. Italy: Rome. 400 B.C.-180 A.D. Lang.: Eng.   2625

Theory/criticism
Catalan translation of Lessing's *Hamburgische Dramaturgie*.
Germany: Hamburg. 1767-1769. Lang.: Cat.   3043

Terra Nova
Performance/production
Four productions in Southern regional theatres. USA: Houston, TX,
Louisville, KY, Gainesville, FL. 1980. Lang.: Eng.   2342

Terroryści (Terrorists, The)
Performance/production
The shape and form of contemporary Polish theatre. Poland:
Warsaw. 1981-1987. Lang.: Eng, Fre.   1995

Terry, Ellen
Design/technology
Influences on costume designs for Ellen Terry. UK-England: London.
1856-1902. Lang.: Eng.   372

Performance/production
Life and work of actress Ellen Terry. UK-England: London. 1847-
1928. Lang.: Eng.   902

Plays/librettos/scripts
Themes and sources of Shaw's *The Man of Destiny*. UK-England.
1894-1931. Lang.: Eng.   2754

Terry, Marion
Plays/librettos/scripts
W.S. Gilbert's contribution to the development of the musical play.
England. 1836-1911. Lang.: Eng.   3670

Terry, Megan
Plays/librettos/scripts
Megan Terry's transformational plays for the Open Theatre. USA.
1987. Lang.: Eng.   2910

Tertullian
Performance/production
Church condemnation of Roman *ludi*, creative impulse behind
medieval drama. Europe. 160-1578. Lang.: Eng.   1745

Teseo
Performance/production
Cast lists for some early London operas. England: London. 1712-
1717. Lang.: Eng.   3761

Tesich, Steve
Performance/production
Brief Broadway run of *King of Hearts*. USA: New York, NY. 1978-
1987. Lang.: Eng.   3643

Tête de Méduse (Medusa Head)
Performance/production
Anouilh's *Eurydice*, Vian's *Tête de Méduse (Medusa Head)* at
National Theatre of Miskolc. Hungary: Miskolc. 1987. Lang.: Hun.
1888

Teufel von Loudun, Die (Devils of Loudun, The)
Plays/librettos/scripts
Life and operatic works of composer Krzysztof Penderecki. Poland.
1969-1987. Lang.: Ger.   3929

Tewodros
Performance/production
Collection of newspaper reviews by London theatre critics. UK-
England. 1987. Lang.: Eng.   2175

Tewolde-Berhan, Esias
Performance/production
Interview with tenor Esias Tewolde-Berhan of Kungliga Teatern.
Sweden: Stockholm. Ethiopia. 1944-1987. Lang.: Swe.   3825

Thacker, David
Performance/production
Collection of newspaper reviews by London theatre critics. UK-
England: London. 1986. Lang.: Eng.   2057

Collection of newspaper reviews by London theatre critics. UK-
England: London. 1986. Lang.: Eng.   2063

Collection of newspaper reviews by London theatre critics. UK-
England: London. 1986. Lang.: Eng.   2093

Collection of newspaper reviews by London theatre critics. UK-
England: London. 1986. Lang.: Eng.   2125

Collection of newspaper reviews by London theatre critics. UK-
England: London. 1987. Lang.: Eng.   2184

Collection of newspaper reviews by London theatre critics. UK-
England: London. 1987. Lang.: Eng.   2208

Collection of newspaper reviews by London theatre critics. UK-
England: London. 1987. Lang.: Eng.   2223

Collection of newspaper reviews by London theatre critics. UK-
England: London. 1987. Lang.: Eng.   2250

Plays/librettos/scripts
Use of oral history material to develop characters and events in
plays. UK-England. 1970-1987. Lang.: Eng.   2807

Thaker, Asaitha
Performance/production
Collection of newspaper reviews by London theatre critics. UK-
England: London. 1986. Lang.: Eng.   2038

Thalaba, the Destroyer
Plays/librettos/scripts
Analysis of vampire characters in the works of Byron, Polidori and
Planché. England. Italy. France. 1800-1825. Lang.: Eng.   2540

Thália Stúdió (Budapest)
Performance/production
Zoltán Seregi directs Sławomir Mrożek's *Letni dzień (A Summer's
Day)* at Thália Stúdió under the title *Egy nyári nap*. Hungary:
Budapest. 1987. Lang.: Hun.   1919

Thália Színház (Budapest)
Performance/production
Károly Kazimir directs László Németh's *Harc a jólét ellen (The Fight Against Prosperity)*. Hungary: Budapest. 1986. Lang.: Hun.
1910

Thalia Theater (Hamburg)
Institutions
Seven productions chosen for Theatertreffen '86. Germany: Berlin. 1986. Lang.: Eng.
1617

Performance/production
The 4th International Theatre Conference: includes list of participants and their contributions. Poland: Warsaw. 1986. Lang.: Eng, Fre.
873

Thanhouser, Edwin
Plays/librettos/scripts
Successful film versions of Shakespeare's *King Lear*. USA. UK-England. USSR. 1916-1983. Lang.: Eng.
3099

That Championship Season
Plays/librettos/scripts
Korean views of American society based on plays of Howard Sackler, Charles Fuller and Jason Miller. USA. 1969-1982. Lang.: Kor.
2837

That Serious He-Man Ball
Plays/librettos/scripts
Alonzo Lamont's major themes in *That Serious He-Man Ball*. USA: New York, NY. 1987. Lang.: Eng.
2900
Depiction of the class struggle in contemporary theatre. USA: New York, NY. 1987. Lang.: Eng.
2915

That Summer
Performance/production
Collection of newspaper reviews by London theatre critics. UK-England: London. 1987. Lang.: Eng.
2270

Thatcher's Women
Performance/production
Collection of newspaper reviews by London theatre critics. UK-England: London. 1987. Lang.: Eng.
2191

Theatermacher, Der (Theatermaker, The)
Institutions
Seven productions chosen for Theatertreffen '86. Germany: Berlin. 1986. Lang.: Eng.
1617

Performance/production
Productions by Claus Peymann, new artistic director of Vienna's Burgtheater. Austria: Vienna. 1986-1987. Lang.: Dut.
721

Theaterworks/USA (New York, NY)
Institutions
History of Theaterworks/USA, a national theatre for young people. USA: New York, NY. 1961-1987. Lang.: Eng.
613

Theatre at St. Peter's Church (New York, NY)
Performance/production
Collection of newspaper reviews by New York theatre critics. USA: New York, NY. 1987. Lang.: Eng.
2313

Théâtre aux Bouffes du Nord
SEE
Bouffes du Nord.

Theatre by the Blind (New York, NY)
Institutions
Theatre by the Blind, integrating blind and sighted actors. USA: New York, NY. 1981-1987. Lang.: Eng.
1650

Theatre Calgary (Calgary, AB)
Institutions
History of Alberta theatre companies. Canada: Edmonton, AB, Calgary, AB. 1987. Lang.: Eng.
506

Theatre Columbus (Toronto, ON)
Performance spaces
The lack of performance space for small theatre companies. Canada: Toronto, ON. 1987. Lang.: Eng.
629

Theatre Communications Group (TCG, New York, NY)
Administration
TCG's National Computer Project for the Performing Arts. USA. 1980-1983. Lang.: Eng.
172
Survey of financial results for nonprofit theatres. USA. 1986. Lang.: Eng.
173

Plays/librettos/scripts
Interview with playwright John Guare. USA. 1987. Lang.: Eng. 2870

Theatre Daikanyama (Tokyo)
Performance/production
Comments on Tokyo performances. Japan: Tokyo. 1987. Lang.: Jap.
1964

Théâtre de Complicité (London)
Performance/production
Collection of newspaper reviews by London theatre critics. UK-England: London. 1986. Lang.: Eng.
2043

Théâtre de la Balsamine (Brussels)
Performance/production
La théorie du mouchoir (The Handkerchief Theory) written and directed by Martine Wijckaert. Belgium: Brussels. 1987. Lang.: Fre.
1684

Théâtre de la Bastille (Paris)
Performance/production
Plays of Pinget, Euripides and Théâtre du Rideau staged by Jouanneau, Suzuki and Tanguy, Théâtre de la Bastille. France: Paris. 1987. Lang.: Fre.
1753

Théâtre de la Communauté (Seraing)
Performance/production
Dorothée Letessier's comments on the adaptation and staging of her novel *Voyage à Paimpol (Journey to Paimpol)*. Belgium: Liège. 1986. Lang.: Fre.
1686

Théâtre de la Fondation Jacques Gueux (Brussels)
Performance/production
Dorothée Letessier's comments on the adaptation and staging of her novel *Voyage à Paimpol (Journey to Paimpol)*. Belgium: Liège. 1986. Lang.: Fre.
1686

Théâtre de la Jeune Lune (Minneapolis, MN)
Performance/production
Théâtre de la Jeune Lune, its origins and influences. USA: Minneapolis, MN. France: Paris. 1980-1987. Lang.: Eng. 977

Théâtre de la Mandragore (Brussels)
Performance/production
Bruce Ellison directs his *Mister Knight* at Théâtre de la Mandragore. Belgium: Brussels. 1986. Lang.: Fre.
1685

Théâtre des Amandiers (Nanterre)
Performance/production
Patrice Chéreau and Théâtre des Amandiers create stage and film versions of Čechov's *Platonov*. France: Nanterre. 1982-1987. Lang.: Swe.
1755

Théâtre du Nouveau Monde (Montreal, PQ)
Plays/librettos/scripts
Critical response to Brassard's *Les Paravents (The Screens)*. Canada: Montreal, PQ, Ottawa, ON. 1987. Lang.: Fre. 2475
Brassard discusses his adaptation of Genet's *Les Paravents (The Screens)*. Canada: Montreal, PQ, Ottawa, ON. 1987. Lang.: Fre.
2485
Symbols of power in Genet's *Les Paravents (The Screens)*. France. Canada: Montreal, PQ, Ottawa, ON. 1961-1987. Lang.: Fre. 2570
André Brassard's production of Jean Genet's *Les Paravents (The Screens)*. France. Canada: Montreal, PQ, Ottawa, ON. 1961-1987. Lang.: Fre.
2583
Investigating the text of Genet's *Les Paravents (The Screens)*. France. Canada: Montreal, PQ, Ottawa, ON. 1961-1987. Lang.: Fre.
2585

Théâtre du Nouvel Ontario (Sudbury, ON)
Performance/production
Popular theatre, mostly on economic, feminist themes. Canada: Sudbury, ON. 1930-1987. Lang.: Eng.
1709

Théâtre du Radeau (Le Mans)
Performance/production
Collection of newspaper reviews by London theatre critics. UK-England: London. 1987. Lang.: Eng.
2212

Théâtre du Rideau (Brussels)
Performance/production
Plays of Pinget, Euripides and Théâtre du Rideau staged by Jouanneau, Suzuki and Tanguy, Théâtre de la Bastille. France: Paris. 1987. Lang.: Fre.
1753

Théâtre du Rond-Point (Paris)
Plays/librettos/scripts
Comparison of two versions of Duras' *La Musica Deuxième*. France: Paris. 1985-1987. Lang.: Eng.
1125

Théâtre du Soleil (Paris)
Performance/production
Eastern theatre forms in Western artists' productions. Canada: Vancouver, BC. 1987. Lang.: Eng.
725

Theatre Royal, Haymarket (London)
Performance/production
Collection of newspaper reviews by London theatre critics. UK-England: London. 1986. Lang.: Eng.   2072

Collection of newspaper reviews by London theatre critics. UK-England: London. 1986. Lang.: Eng.   2101

Collection of newspaper reviews by London theatre critics. UK-England: London. 1986. Lang.: Eng.   2121

Collection of newspaper reviews by London theatre critics. UK-England: London. 1986. Lang.: Eng.   2154

Collection of newspaper reviews by London theatre critics. UK-England: London. 1987. Lang.: Eng.   2245

Theatre Royal, Stratford East (London)
Performance/production
Collection of newspaper reviews by London theatre critics. UK-England: London. 1986. Lang.: Eng.   2042

Collection of newspaper reviews by London theatre critics. UK-England: London. 1986. Lang.: Eng.   2088

Collection of newspaper reviews by London theatre critics. UK-England: London. 1986. Lang.: Eng.   2106

Collection of newspaper reviews by London theatre critics. UK-England: London. 1986. Lang.: Eng.   2147

Collection of newspaper reviews by London theatre critics. UK-England: London. 1986. Lang.: Eng.   2165

Collection of newspaper reviews by London theatre critics. UK-England: London. 1987. Lang.: Eng.   2182

Collection of newspaper reviews by London theatre critics. UK-England: London. 1987. Lang.: Eng.   2189

Collection of newspaper reviews by London theatre critics. UK-England: London. 1987. Lang.: Eng.   2194

Collection of newspaper reviews by London theatre critics. UK-England: London. 1987. Lang.: Eng.   2207

Collection of newspaper reviews by London theatre critics. UK-England: London. 1987. Lang.: Eng.   2211

Collection of newspaper reviews by London theatre critics. UK-England: London. 1987. Lang.: Eng.   2248

Collection of newspaper reviews by London theatre critics. UK-England: London. 1987. Lang.: Eng.   2265

Plays/librettos/scripts
Byron's 'closet' dramas structured for performance at London theatres. UK-England: London. 1812-1822. Lang.: Eng.   2778

Theatre Upstairs (London)
SEE ALSO
English Stage Company.
Performance/production
Collection of newspaper reviews by London theatre critics. UK-England: London. 1986. Lang.: Eng.   2058

Collection of newspaper reviews by London theatre critics. UK-England: London. 1986. Lang.: Eng.   2078

Collection of newspaper reviews by London theatre critics. UK-England: London. 1986. Lang.: Eng.   2091

Collection of newspaper reviews by London theatre critics. UK-England: London. 1986. Lang.: Eng.   2131

Collection of newspaper reviews by London theatre critics. UK-England: London. 1987. Lang.: Eng.   2190

Collection of newspaper reviews by London theatre critics. UK-England: London. 1987. Lang.: Eng.   2207

Collection of newspaper reviews by London theatre critics. UK-England: London. 1987. Lang.: Eng.   2228

Collection of newspaper reviews by London theatre critics. UK-England: London. 1987. Lang.: Eng.   2234

Collection of newspaper reviews by London theatre critics. UK-England: London. 1987. Lang.: Eng.   2250

Collection of newspaper reviews by London theatre critics. UK-England: London. 1987. Lang.: Eng.   2257

Collection of newspaper reviews by London theatre critics. UK-England: London. 1987. Lang.: Eng.   2268

Theatre X (Milwaukee, WI)
Performance/production
Criticizes failure to integrate photography into theatre productions. USA. 1987. Lang.: Eng.   932

Theatre Zoopsie (Montreal, PQ)
Design/technology
Dennis O'Sullivan's work with mixed media. Canada. 1986. Lang.: Fre.   3203

Theatre 890 (New York, NY)
Performance/production
Collection of newspaper reviews by New York theatre critics. USA: New York, NY. 1987. Lang.: Eng.   2319

Theatres
Administration
Tong-Yang theatre, first commercial theatre in Korea. Korea: Seoul. 1935-1945. Lang.: Kor.   30
Audience
Audience reactions to the Canadian Opera Company's Atlantic tour. Canada. 1987. Lang.: Eng.   3689
Design/technology
Renovation plans for the Hungarian National Theatre. Hungary: Budapest. 1957. Lang.: Hun.   342

Tony Walton's set designs at the Vivian Beaumont Theatre. USA: New York, NY. 1986-1987. Lang.: Eng.   465

Machinery to be installed in Her Majesty's Theatre for *Phantom of the Opera*. UK-England: London. 1987. Lang.: Eng.   3619
Institutions
Profile and history of Colden Center for the Performing Arts. USA: Flushing, NY. 1961-1984. Lang.: Eng.   618
Performance spaces
Multi-purpose halls and the Canberra Theatre Centre. Australia: Canberra. 1925-1965. Lang.: Eng.   626

Modern theatre architecture. Canada: Montreal, PQ. 1900-1987. Lang.: Fre.   627

The lack of performance space for small theatre companies. Canada: Toronto, ON. 1987. Lang.: Eng.   629

Preservation and maintenance of cultural sites in Prague. Czechoslovakia: Prague. 1987. Lang.: Eng.   630

Design for Richard Ryder's Exeter theatre. England: London. 1663. Lang.: Eng.   631

Analysis of theatre designs by Inigo Jones and John Webb. England. 1573-1672. Lang.: Eng.   632

Performance spaces and audience-performer relationship. France. Germany, West. 1875-1987. Lang.: Eng.   633

Examining current needs of theatre artists vs. historical examination to determine theatre space design. France. Germany, West. UK-England. 1987. Lang.: Eng.   634

East German exhibition at Prague Quadrennial '87: Gold medal for theatre reconstruction exhibit. Germany, East: Berlin, East. 1742-1986. Lang.: Hun.   636

Theatrical equipment of the new Friedrichstadtpalast. Germany, East: Berlin, East. 1984. Lang.: Hun.   637

Safety problems of new, cooperative Jurta theatre. Hungary: Budapest. 1987. Lang.: Hun.   638

Designer of new Hungarian National Theatre on site and design considerations. Hungary: Budapest. 1987. Lang.: Hun.   639

Design and construction considerations: renovation of József Attila Theatre. Hungary: Budapest. 1985-1986. Lang.: Hun.   640

Comparison of two Nemzeti Szinház sites. Hungary: Budapest. 1983. Lang.: Hun.   641

Mór Jókai's recollections of the old, gas-lit National Theatre building. Hungary: Budapest. 1900. Lang.: Hun.   642

Report on OISTAT's future plans. Hungary: Budapest. 1987. Lang.: Swe.   643

Details of the renovation of József Attila Theatre. Hungary: Budapest. 1985-1986. Lang.: Hun.   644

Theatre renovation plans and survey. Hungary. 1980-1986. Lang.: Hun.   645

Reprinted interview with Nemzeti Szinház architect Csaba Virág. Hungary: Budapest. 1966. Lang.: Hun.   646

History of Teatro San Carlo, its artists and performances. Italy: Naples. 1737-1987. Lang.: Ita.   648

Index of Roman theatres. Italy: Rome. 1531-1981. Lang.: Ita.   649

Recent trends in Italian theatre. Italy. 1980. Lang.: Eng.   650

Plans for New Theatre of Bologna's machinery and stage. Italy: Bologna. 1763. Lang.: Eng.   651

History of Teatro La Fenice's construction and reconstruction. Italy: Venice. 1787-1976. Lang.: Ita.   652

Theatres — cont'd

Study of Teatro San Carlo. Italy: Naples. 1737-1987. Lang.: Ita. 653

Documentation of layout, operations: Teatro dei Comici. Italy: Mantua. 1688-1800. Lang.: Eng. 654

Plans for unrealized Roman auditorium and theatres. Italy: Rome. 1789-1953. Lang.: Ita. 655

History of San Carlo Theatre: structure, scenography, costumes. Italy: Naples. 1737-1987. Lang.: Ita. 656

Documentation on the San Giovanni Grisostomo Theatre. Italy: Venice. 1675-1750. Lang.: Ita. 657

Results of theatre design competition. Japan. 1986. Lang.: Hun. 658

History of Tong-Yang Theatre, Korea's first dramatic theatre. Korea: Seoul. 1930-1935. Lang.: Kor. 661

Criticism of Kwang-ju's theatres. Korea: Kwang-ju. 1986-1987. Lang.: Kor. 662

Performance space and staging of traditional Korean genres. Korea. Japan. 57 B.C.-1986 A.D. Lang.: Kor. 663

Restoration of Maputo's only theatre, Teatro Avenida. Mozambique: Maputo. 1986-1987. Lang.: Swe. 665

Theatres built, influences on design. South Africa, Republic of: Johannesburg. 1887-1940. Lang.: Afr. 667

Technical team of Teatre Lliure. Spain-Catalonia: Barcelona. 1976-1987. Lang.: Cat. 668

Paul Shelving's contribution to stage design exhibited by Birmingham Museum. UK-England. 1888-1968. Lang.: Eng. 670

Mermaid Theatre, London home of Royal Shakespeare Company. UK-England: London. 1959-1987. Lang.: Eng. 671

Interview with stage manager Michael Dembowicz about the new Swan Theatre. UK-England: Stratford. 1986. Lang.: Eng. 673

George Wojtasik, managing director of Equity Library Theatre (ELT). USA: New York, NY. 1943-1987. Lang.: Eng. 674

Guidelines for preservation of theatres. USA: New York, NY. 1985-1986. Lang.: Eng. 675

Debate over landmark status for Broadway theatres. USA: New York, NY. 1986. Lang.: Eng. 676

Morosco Theatre torn down despite efforts by Actors' Equity. USA: New York, NY. 1982. Lang.: Eng. 677

Hearings for granting landmark status to forty-five Broadway theatres. USA: New York, NY. 1982. Lang.: Eng. 678

Details of several theatre renovation projects. USA. 1987. Lang.: Eng. 679

Theatre's relation to society, poor theatre design as reasons for state of theatre today. USA. 1987. Lang.: Eng. 680

Restoration of Ohio, State and Palace Theatres in Playhouse Square. USA: Cleveland, OH. 1964-1986. Lang.: Eng. 681

Loeb Drama Center at Harvard. USA: Cambridge, MA. 1960-1987. Lang.: Eng. 682

Architect Roger Morgan discusses plans for restoring seven Broadway theatres. USA: New York, NY. 1984. Lang.: Eng. 683

History of theatres in the Times Square area. USA: New York, NY. 1883-1984. Lang.: Eng. 685

History and technical data on Pittsburgh's Public Theatre. USA: Pittsburgh, PA. 1975-1987. Lang.: Eng. 686

Directory of extant theatres built in the U.S. before 1915. USA. 1809-1915. Lang.: Eng. 689

Architectural and design information on the short-lived Earl Carroll Theatre. USA: New York, NY. 1931-1933. Lang.: Hun. 690

Commitment of Shubert Organization to cleaning up Broadway theatre district. USA: New York, NY. 1984. Lang.: Eng. 691

Broadway theatres given landmark status. USA: New York, NY. 1982. Lang.: Eng. 692

Providing access to the handicapped in existing theatres. USA. 1987. Lang.: Eng. 693

Architecture of La Jolla Playhouse and challenges it presents for designers. USA: La Jolla, CA. 1947-1987. Lang.: Eng. 694

John Houseman on the New York home of the Acting Company. USA: New York, NY. 1972-1986. Lang.: Eng. 695

History of the Alice Arts Center, new home of the Oakland Ensemble Theatre. USA: Oakland, CA. 1983-1987. Lang.: Eng. 696

Renovation and subsequent failure of the New Apollo Theatre. USA: New York, NY. 1977-1984. Lang.: Eng. 697

The Tampa Bay Performing Arts Center. USA: Tampa, FL. 1987. Lang.: Eng. 698

Major expansion of the facilities at the Omaha Community Playhouse. USA: Omaha, NE. 1984-1987. Lang.: Eng. 699

Renovations at the Bayfront Center. USA: St. Petersburg, FL. 1960-1987. Lang.: Eng. 700

Recently completed Wortham Theatre Center. USA: Houston, TX. 1987. Lang.: Eng. 701

Rebuilding theatres constructed in the 1960s. USA. 1960-1986. Lang.: Eng. 702

Performimg arts centers covered in *ThCr* architecture issue. USA. 1987. Lang.: Eng. 703

Query about whether theatre architects learn from mistakes. USA. UK. 1960-1987. Lang.: Eng. 704

Renovation of the Seattle Center Playhouse into the new home of the Intiman Theatre. USA: Seattle, WA. 1983-1987. Lang.: Eng. 705

Larger theatre buildings threaten subtleties in acting. USA: New York, NY. 1986. Lang.: Eng. 707

New Old Globe Theatre replaces previous structure. USA: San Diego, CA. 1982. Lang.: Eng. 709

Construction and present condition of the Krannert Center for the Performing Arts. USA: Urbana, IL. 1969-1987. Lang.: Eng. 710

Questions spending $50 million on a new concert hall in Los Angeles. USA: Los Angeles, CA. 1987. Lang.: Eng. 711

Design of the San Francisco Ballet Building. USA: San Francisco, CA. 1987. Lang.: Eng. 712

Proposal for renovations of Broadway theatres. USA: New York, NY. 1984. Lang.: Eng. 713

Northern Arts and Cultural Centre: planning and building. Canada: Yellowknife, NT. 1980-1985. Lang.: Eng. 1667

Celebration of the birthday of the HaBimah Theatre. Israel: Tel Aviv. 1917-1987. Lang.: Heb. 1669

Birth and growth of the Teatre Lliure. Spain-Catalonia: Barcelona. 1976-1987. Lang.: Cat. 1670

Collection of photographs on the history of the Teatre Lliure. Spain-Catalonia: Barcelona. 1976-1987. Lang.: Cat. 1671

Reconstruction of theatrical activity in Barcelona. Spain-Catalonia: Barcelona. 1800-1830. Lang.: Cat. 1672

History of the Teatre Lliure. Spain-Catalonia: Barcelona. 1976-1987. Lang.: Cat. 1673

Restoration of the house, Kungliga Dramatiska Teatern. Sweden: Stockholm. 1987. Lang.: Swe. 1674

Restoration of audience areas of Kungliga Dramatiska Teatern. Sweden: Stockholm. 1987. Lang.: Swe. 1675

Histories of Wallack's Theatre and the Union Square Theatre. USA: New York, NY. 1850-1889. Lang.: Eng. 1676

Architecture and history of the New Victoria Theatre. UK-England: London. 1928-1987. Lang.: Eng. 3141

Comparison of British and American cinema theatre design. UK-England: London. 1930-1987. Lang.: Eng. 3142

Many uses of the Uptown Theatre. USA: Kansas City, MO. 1926-1987. Lang.: Eng. 3143

History of the Garden Theatre designed by Thomas H. Scott. USA: Pittsburgh, PA. 1915-1987. Lang.: Eng. 3144

Interior design of the Oriental Theatre. USA: Portland, OR. 1927-1970. Lang.: Eng. 3145

Theatre designed by Elmer F. Behrns. USA: Pekin, IL. 1927-1987. Lang.: Eng. 3146

Five buildings in Canada Place, built for Expo '86. Canada: Vancouver, BC. 1986. Lang.: Eng. 3243

Performance space at Tate Gallery of the North. UK-England: Liverpool. 1987. Lang.: Eng. 3245

First public theatres in Venice. Italy: Venice. 1580-1700. Lang.: Ita. 3293

Theatres of Pisa, musical performances. Italy: Pisa. 1773-1986. Lang.: Ita. 3393

Illustrated chronology of the Bucklen Opera House. USA: Elkhart, IN. 1884-1986. Lang.: Eng. 3394

Lighting design in Tampa's new performing arts center. USA: Tampa, FL. 1987. Lang.: Eng. 3395

Theatrical changes in Chinese opera during the Sung, Ming and Yuan dynasties. China. 960-1643. Lang.: Chi. 3451

Form and development of the commune theatre. China. 202 B.C.-1986 A.D. Lang.: Chi. 3452

Theatres — cont'd

Inscription on Nan Hsi opera monument. China. 960-1912. Lang.: Chi. 3453

Documentation on a playhouse in Chiang Su province. China. 1742-1743. Lang.: Chi. 3454

Recommendation that Royal Swedish Opera house be rebuilt. Sweden: Stockholm. 1985-1987. Lang.: Swe. 3736

Wortham Theatre Center, designed by Eugene Aubry. USA: Houston, TX. 1977-1987. Lang.: Eng. 3739

Glimmerglass Opera inaugurates Alice Busch Theatre. USA: Cooperstown, NY. 1975-1987. Lang.: Eng. 3740

Performances, workshops for children in converted church hall. UK-England: London. 1987. Lang.: Eng. 4009

Performance/production

Overview of the director's art. China, People's Republic of. 1985. Lang.: Chi. 757

Record of *kabuki* performances, names of theatres, actors. Japan: Osaka. 1885-1893. Lang.: Jap. 1492

Collection of theatre reviews by Xavier Fàbregas. Spain-Catalonia. 1969-1972. Lang.: Cat. 2010

Performances spaces

History and renovations of City Center. USA: New York, NY. 1924-1983. Lang.: Eng. 1094

Reference materials

History of theatrical activity in Palafrugell. Spain-Catalonia: Palafrugell. 1900-1986. Lang.: Cat. 1210

Theme parks

SEE

Amusement parks.

Theobald, Lewis

Plays/librettos/scripts

Henry Fielding rewrote *Tom Thumb* to satirize Lewis Theobald. England. 1730-1731. Lang.: Eng. 2535

Théorie du mouchoir, La (Handkerchief Theory, The)

Performance/production

La théorie du mouchoir (The Handkerchief Theory) written and directed by Martine Wijckaert. Belgium: Brussels. 1987. Lang.: Fre. 1684

Theory/criticism

SEE ALSO

Classed Entries.

Audience

Actor and audience in Elizabethan theatre. England. 1585-1625. Lang.: Eng. 1533

Street theatre after the Russian Revolution: new theatrical concepts. USSR: Moscow. 1917-1924. Lang.: Ger. 3340

Basic theatrical documents

Russian symbolist plays and essays. USSR. 1880-1986. Lang.: Eng. 1584

Institutions

The Canadian Governor General's Awards. Canada. 1987. Lang.: Eng. 509

Functions of theatre in post-war Germany. Germany, West. 1945-1948. Lang.: Eng. 535

International Association of Theatre Critics conference on theatre as language of the people. Hungary: Budapest. 1987. Lang.: Hun. 536

Performance spaces

The streets of New York as experimental performance space. USA: New York, NY. 1960-1975. Lang.: Eng. 688

Subverting alienating effect of some performance spaces. USA. 1800-1910. Lang.: Eng. 706

Performance/production

Performance as an 'enunciative event'. Lang.: Ita. 714

Avant-garde theatre: focus on performance rather than dramaturgy. 1900-1987. Lang.: Ita. 718

Shakespeare's later plays at Stratford Festival. Canada: Stratford, ON. 1986. Lang.: Eng. 751

Influences of Western culture on Chinese theatre reflected in performance of *Old B Hanging on the Wall*. China, People's Republic of. 1984-1986. Lang.: Eng. 761

Irony in *Gammer Gurton's Needle*: its interpretation and presentation to the audience. England. 1575-1982. Lang.: Eng. 777

Discussion of text on classical Indian performance. India. 1987. Lang.: Eng. 814

Dario Fo on comic actor Totò. Italy. 1898-1978. Lang.: Eng. 826

Collection of reviews by Arnaldo Mariotti. Italy. 1958-1982. Lang.: Ita. 834

Maurizio Scaparro: critic, director, administrator. Italy. 1964-1987. Lang.: Ita. 837

Origins, theory of traditional Korean mask theatre. Korea. 57 B.C.-1985 A.D. Lang.: Kor. 858

Interview with Polish playwright Tadeusz Kantor. Poland: Cracow. Germany, West: Kassel. Italy: Milan. Italy: Sicily. 1987. Lang.: Eng, Fre. 876

Collection of theatre reviews by J.M. de Sagarra. Spain-Catalonia: Barcelona. 1922-1927. Lang.: Cat. 885

Play scripts as literary texts and as performance texts. UK-England. 1977-1987. Lang.: Eng. 905

The 1984 season of the Next Wave at BAM. USA: New York, NY. 1984. Lang.: Eng. 967

Reflections of a theatre critic on the acting profession. USSR. 1986. Lang.: Rus. 1020

Dance/lecture focusing on images of gender in dance. USA. 1987. Lang.: Eng. 1415

Five women choreographers and critics discuss conceptions of the female body. USA. 1987. Lang.: Eng. 1416

Roles of women in the field of ballet. France. USA. 1720-1987. Lang.: Eng. 1434

Work of actor/director Augusto Boal. Canada: Sydney, NS. 1987. Lang.: Eng. 1694

Evaluation of acting styles in 18th century. England. 1672-1799. Lang.: Eng. 1736

Semiotics of Brechtian acting. Europe. 1986. Lang.: Eng. 1748

Analysis of Brecht's original directing style and dramaturgy. Germany. 1925-1987. Lang.: Eng. 1771

Franz Xaver Kroetz's *Wunschkonzert (Request Concert)* transposed to Calcutta. India: Calcutta. 1980. Lang.: Eng. 1930

Interview with Eric Bentley, director of *La Casa de Bernarda Alba* at the Abbey. Ireland: Dublin. 1900-1985. Lang.: Eng. 1934

Aspects of contemporary Italian theatrical life. Italy. 1987. Lang.: Ita. 1949

Collection of theatre reviews by Xavier Fàbregas. Spain-Catalonia. 1969-1972. Lang.: Cat. 2010

Overview of theatre season. Spain-Catalonia: Barcelona. 1986-1987. Lang.: Cat. 2011

Various North American and English productions of *Man and Superman*. UK-England. North America. 1901-1982. Lang.: Eng. 2288

Critique of the 1984 Broadway production of *Death of a Salesman*. USA: New York, NY. 1984. Lang.: Eng. 2330

Influence of Pirandello on modern theatre. USA. Italy. 1917-1987. Lang.: Eng. 2338

Four productions in Southern regional theatres. USA: Houston, TX, Louisville, KY, Gainesville, FL. 1980. Lang.: Eng. 2342

Jevrejnov's theories of theatricality, parallels with Pirandello's. USSR. 1879-1953. Lang.: Eng. 2391

Ritual and theatrical nature of TV evangelism. USA. 1987. Lang.: Eng. 3210

History and theory of dances in spectacles of the Lombard court. Italy: Milan. 1400-1500. Lang.: Ita. 3323

Theatrical elements of gay rights parade. USA: New York, NY. 1987. Lang.: Eng. 3335

Acting techniques in Chinese opera. China, People's Republic of: Beijing. 1935-1986. Lang.: Chi. 3489

Acting theories in Chinese opera. China, People's Republic of: Beijing. 1950-1986. Lang.: Chi. 3510

Perspectives on modern opera. USSR. 1980-1987. Lang.: Rus. 3871

Puppeteer's analysis of characters in Punch and Judy show. UK-England. 1987. Lang.: Eng. 3982

Plays/librettos/scripts

Connection between artistic practice and scientific inquiry. 1987. Lang.: Eng. 1096

Shakespeare's *Henry V*: development of Prince Hal as an ideological monarch. England. 1599. Lang.: Eng. 1124

An annual bibliography of works by and about Harold Pinter. UK-England. USA. 1986-1987. Lang.: Eng. 1160

Effects of developmental playwriting process. USA. 1987. Lang.: Eng. 1167

Theory/criticism — cont'd

Kundera's adaptation of *Jacques le Fataliste (Jacques and His Master)* by Diderot. USA: Cambridge, MA. 1985. Lang.: Eng. 1178

Traditional *nō* and *kyōgen* texts compared to modern literature. Japan. 1300-1986. Lang.: Jap. 1506

Transfiguration in Shaw's *Misalliance*, *Saint Joan* and *Major Barbara*. 1986. Lang.: Eng. 2413

Proposed method of analyzing historical plays. 1987. Lang.: Ger. 2431

Ray Lawler's *The Summer of the Seventeenth Doll* and the Australian experience. Australia. 1955-1987. Lang.: Eng. 2435

Rebuttal of review of Lepage's *La Trilogie des dragons*. Canada. 1987. Lang.: Fre. 2459

Critical response to Brassard's *Les Paravents (The Screens)*. Canada: Montreal, PQ, Ottawa, ON. 1987. Lang.: Fre. 2475

Play within a play in *Blood Relations* by Sharon Pollock. Canada. 1987. Lang.: Eng. 2489

Egon Wolff's trilogy of plays focusing on Chilean bourgeoisie. Chile. 1964-1984. Lang.: Eng. 2490

Analysis of medieval Cain and Abel mystery plays. England. 1200-1576. Lang.: Eng. 2506

Role of Chorus in Shakespeare's *Henry V*. England. 1599. Lang.: Eng. 2556

Analysis of medieval plays found in the *Fleury Playbook*. Europe. 1300. Lang.: Eng. 2564

New interpretation of Toller's *Masse Mensch*. Germany. 1921-1987. Lang.: Eng. 2592

Der gelbe Klang (The Yellow Sound) by Wassily Kandinsky. Germany. 1896-1914. Lang.: Kor. 2597

Greek poetic drama through Nietzschean theory. Greece. 1987. Lang.: Eng. 2620

Political aspects of Hungarian absurdist drama. Hungary. 1970-1980. Lang.: Eng. 2632

Comparison of plays by Leonor Azcarate and Estela Lenero. Mexico: Mexico City. 1987. Lang.: Spa. 2700

Plays by Gorostiza, Usigli and Novo on Spanish conquest of Mexico. Mexico. 1958-1961. Lang.: Eng. 2701

Comparative study of Lope de Vega's *El mayordomo de la Duquesa de Amalfi* and Webster's *The Duchess of Malfi*. Spain. 1612-1982. Lang.: Eng. 2729

Dramatic vs. literary interpretation of *Ett Drömspel (A Dream Play)* by August Strindberg. Sweden. 1901-1964. Lang.: Eng. 2734

Comparison of Shakespeare's *Julius Caesar* to the drama and vision of Euripides. UK-England. 500 B.C.-1599 A.D. Lang.: Eng. 2760

Characterizations of stage spaces: examples from Brecht, Pinter, Douglas Turner Ward. UK-England. USA. 1947-1987. Lang.: Eng. 2798

Interpreting Harold Pinter's dramas through focus on his play structures. UK-England. 1958-1987. Lang.: Eng. 2815

Pipe dreams in Eugene O'Neill's *A Touch of the Poet*. USA. 1935. Lang.: Eng. 2840

Eugene O'Neill's influence on Edward Albee. USA. 1949-1962. Lang.: Eng. 2841

Influence of O'Neill and Beckett on Israel Horovitz. USA: Boston, MA. France: Paris. 1939-1953. Lang.: Eng. 2873

Nietzschean and psychoanalytical interpretation of Beckett's *Not I*. USA. 1972-1987. Lang.: Eng. 2879

Analysis of text of Samuel Beckett's *Rockaby* as literature and performance piece. USA. 1982. Lang.: Eng. 2884

O'Neill's transcendence of melodrama in *A Touch of the Poet* and *A Moon for the Misbegotten*. USA. 1922-1947. Lang.: Eng. 2886

Influence of Herman Melville on Eugene O'Neill. USA. 1927. Lang.: Eng. 2888

Parallels between O'Neill's *Anna Christie* and Homer's *Odyssey*. USA. 1921. Lang.: Eng. 2906

Influence of Rudyard Kipling on Eugene O'Neill. USA. 1887-1950. Lang.: Eng. 2925

Family relationships in Eugene O'Neill's early plays. USA. 1913. Lang.: Eng. 2926

Majakovskij's dramatic works as seen by critics in the 1930s. USSR. 1930-1939. Lang.: Rus. 2958

Contemporary interpretations of Shakespeare's work. USSR. 1980-1987. Lang.: Rus. 2967

Translating ancient Greek theatre into film. Greece. 500 B.C.-1986 A.D. Lang.: Eng. 3098

Call for high quality of dramatic texts, especially for Beijing opera. China, People's Republic of. 1987. Lang.: Chi. 3574

Reference materials

Bibliography of texts, reviews, and criticism of German-speaking Swiss theatrical activity. Switzerland. 1987. Lang.: Ger. 1212

Relation to other fields

Relationship between theatre and everyday life. Italy. 1900-1987. Lang.: Ita. 1242

The sociopolitical role of the critic in theatrical criticism. Switzerland. 1960-1985. Lang.: Ger. 1255

Theatre as an analogy and metaphor for studying social interaction. USA. 1987. Lang.: Eng. 1279

Approaching dramatic texts similarly to other literary texts. 1600-1987. Lang.: Eng. 2976

Applications of African 'Theatre for Development' movement to Canadian popular theatre. Africa. Canada: St. John's, NF, Toronto, ON. 1978-1987. Lang.: Eng. 2978

Examination of crisis in theory and practice of political art. USA. 1987. Lang.: Eng. 3007

Research/historiography

Discussion of the miscellany called *Wit's Creation*. England: London. 1640. Lang.: Eng. 1298

Theory/criticism

Trollope's writings on Elizabethan and Jacobean drama. UK-England. 1866-1882. Lang.: Eng. 3063

Interview with Kathleen Tynan about Kenneth Tynan. USA: New York, NY. 1987. Lang.: Eng. 3073

They Shoot Horses, Don't They?
Performance/production

Collection of newspaper reviews by London theatre critics. UK-England: London. 1987. Lang.: Eng. 2272

Thief of a Christmas, A
Plays/librettos/scripts

Theatrical language in the plays of Thomas Murphy. Ireland. 1961-1984. Lang.: Eng. 2640

The myth of the idyllic peasant life in the plays of Thomas Murphy. Ireland. 1961-1986. Lang.: Eng. 2652

Thief of Souls
SEE
Ladro di anime, Il.

This Is My Dream
Performance/production

Collection of newspaper reviews by London theatre critics. UK-England: London. 1987. Lang.: Eng. 2211

This Savage Parade
Performance/production

Collection of newspaper reviews by London theatre critics. UK-England: London. 1987. Lang.: Eng. 2254

This Story of Yours
Performance/production

Collection of newspaper reviews by London theatre critics. UK-England: London. 1987. Lang.: Eng. 2183

Thiyan, Ratan
Performance/production

Collection of newspaper reviews by London theatre critics. UK-England: London. 1987. Lang.: Eng. 2238

Thomas, Betty
Institutions

Second City improvisational comedy troupe. USA: Chicago, IL. Canada: Toronto, ON. 1959-1987. Lang.: Eng. 605

Thomas, Dylan
Performance/production

Collection of newspaper reviews by London theatre critics. UK-England: London. 1986. Lang.: Eng. 2072

Thomas, Gerald
Relation to other fields

Playwright Gerald Thomas discusses influences on his work. Brazil: Rio de Janeiro. North America. Europe. 1970-1987. Lang.: Eng. 2981

Thomas, Sian
Performance/production

English Shakespearean productions. UK-England: London, Manchester, Stratford. 1985-1986. Lang.: Eng. 917

Thompson, Bobby
Performance/production
Dancers' daily routine in Les Ballets Jazz de Montréal. Canada: Montreal, PQ. 1985. Lang.: Eng. 1479

Thompson, Ian
Performance/production
Collection of newspaper reviews by London theatre critics. UK-England: London. 1986. Lang.: Eng. 2102

Thompson, Judith
Plays/librettos/scripts
Plays by Micone, Saddlemyer, Thompson, Wyatt. Canada. 1958-1985. Lang.: Eng. 2481
Interview with playwright Judith Thompson. Canada. 1985. Lang.: Eng. 2486

Thompson, Linda
Performance/production
Collection of newspaper reviews by London theatre critics. UK-England: London. 1987. Lang.: Eng. 2230

Thompson, Paul
Institutions
A history of documentary theatre in English Canada. Canada. 1970-1986. Lang.: Eng. 508

Performance/production
Collection of newspaper reviews by London theatre critics. UK-England: London. 1987. Lang.: Eng. 2265

Plays/librettos/scripts
Playwright Paul Thompson. Canada: Blythe, ON, Toronto, ON. 1963-1983. Lang.: Eng. 2487

Thompson, Sam
Plays/librettos/scripts
Ulster drama before Sam Thompson. UK-Ireland. 1900-1982. Lang.: Eng. 2829

Thomson Hall (Toronto, ON)
Performance spaces
The modern acoustics of Toronto's Thomson Hall. Canada: Toronto, ON. 1982. Lang.: Eng. 628

Thorborg, Kerstin
Performance/production
Memories of contralto Kerstin Thorborg. Sweden. Germany. 1932-1970. Lang.: Swe. 3821

Three Desks
Plays/librettos/scripts
Critical analysis of James Reaney's *Three Desks*. Canada. 1960-1977. Lang.: Eng. 2477

Three Girls in Blue
SEE
Tri devuški v golubom.

Three Men on a Horse
Performance/production
Collection of newspaper reviews by London theatre critics. UK-England: London. 1987. Lang.: Eng. 2272

Three Penny Opera, The
SEE
Dreigroschenoper, Die.

Three Postcards
Performance/production
Collection of newspaper reviews by New York theatre critics. USA: New York, NY. 1987. Lang.: Eng. 2319

Plays/librettos/scripts
Collaboration between playwright Craig Lucas and director Norman Rene. USA: New York, NY. 1985-1987. Lang.: Eng. 1183
Collaboration of Craig Lucas and Norman Rene on *Blue Window* and *Three Postcards*. USA. 1987. Lang.: Eng. 1184

Three Sisters
SEE
Tri sestry.

Threshold Theatre Company (Binghamton, NY)
Performance/production
Five short plays by Géza Páskándi at SUNY Binghamton. Hungary. USA: Binghamton, NY. 1987. Lang.: Eng. 1813

Thursday's Ladies
Performance/production
Collection of newspaper reviews by London theatre critics. UK-England: London. 1987. Lang.: Eng. 2256

Thyestes
Plays/librettos/scripts
Structure of revenge tragedy in Shakespeare's *Hamlet*. 1600. Lang.: Eng. 2425

Ti Jean and His Brothers
Performance/production
Collection of newspaper reviews by London theatre critics. UK-England: London. 1986. Lang.: Eng. 2160

Tian, Shi-Lin
Performance/production
Comparison between Chinese opera and Buddhist plays of Kerala. China, People's Republic of: Beijing. India. 1050-1968. Lang.: Chi. 3533

Ticket-of-Leave Man, The
Performance/production
Collection of newspaper reviews by London theatre critics. UK-England: London. 1987. Lang.: Eng. 2207

Plays/librettos/scripts
Historical context for Tom Taylor's *The Ticket-of-Leave Man*. UK-England. France. 1863. 2801

TIE (Theatre in Education, Ireland)
Performance/production
Graffiti Theatre Company which tours schools in southern Ireland. Ireland: Cork. 1987. Lang.: Eng. 817

Tieck, Ludwig
Performance/production
'Showing' is an essential part of all acting. Europe. 1590-1987. Lang.: Eng. 1746
Essays on major figures of the Romantic period. Germany. 1795-1830. Lang.: Ger. 1776

Tierney, Thomas
Performance/production
Collection of newspaper reviews by London theatre critics. UK-England: London. 1986. Lang.: Eng. 2119

Tieste (Thyestes)
Plays/librettos/scripts
Correspondence of playwright Ugo Foscolo regarding *Tieste (Thyestes)*. Italy: Venice. 1797-1827. Lang.: Ita. 2677

Till Damaskus (To Damaskus)
Plays/librettos/scripts
Munch's influence on Strindberg. Germany: Berlin. 1892-1900. Lang.: Eng. 2596

Tillinger, John
Performance/production
Collection of newspaper reviews by New York critics. USA: New York, NY. 1987. Lang.: Eng. 2324

Time
Performance/production
Collection of newspaper reviews by London theatre critics. UK-England: London. 1986. Lang.: Eng. 2084

Timoneda, Joan
Reference materials
Catalogue of Valencian playtexts available at libraries of Barcelona. Spain: Valencia, Barcelona. Lang.: Cat. 2975

Tinčurin, K.G.
Performance/production
Soviet playwright, actor and director K.G. Tinčurin. USSR. 1887-1947. Lang.: Rus. 2381

Ting Tang Mine
Performance/production
Collection of newspaper reviews by London theatre critics. UK-England: London. 1987. Lang.: Eng. 2251

Tippett, Sir Michael
Plays/librettos/scripts
Tippett's influence on contemporary opera. 1946-1987. Lang.: Eng. 3888

Tipton, Jennifer
Design/technology
Interview with lighting designer Jennifer Tipton. USA: New York, NY. 1986. Lang.: Eng. 431

'Tis Pity She's a Whore
Performance/production
Shakespeare and contemporaries: tradition, intertextuality in performance. England. 1607-1987. Lang.: Eng. 1740

Titanic, Le (Titanic, The)
Performance/production
Analysis of directorial style of Gilles Maheu. Canada. 1987. Lang.: Eng. 745

Tito Manlio
Performance/production
Cast lists for some early London operas. England: London. 1712-1717. Lang.: Eng. 3761

Titus Andronicus
Performance/production
Review of *Hamlet*, *Julius Caesar* and *Titus Andronicus* at 'Shakespeare Fest '86'. Yugoslavia: Palić. 1986. Lang.: Hun. 2405

Plays/librettos/scripts
Comic conventions in Shakespeare's *Titus Andronicus*. UK-England. 1987. Lang.: Eng. 2809

To All in Tents
Performance/production
Collection of newspaper reviews by London theatre critics. UK-England: London. 1986. Lang.: Eng. 2125

Tobolowsky, Stephen
Performance/production
Collection of newspaper reviews by New York theatre critics. USA: New York, NY. 1987. Lang.: Eng. 2312

Todd, Susan
Performance/production
Collection of newspaper reviews by London theatre critics. UK-England. 1986. Lang.: Eng. 2045

Todo sucede en una noche (It All Happens in One Night)
Plays/librettos/scripts
Comparison of the plays *Todo sucede en una noche (It All Happens in One Night)* and *La rosa del tiempo (The Rose of Time)*. Mexico: Mexico City. 1987. Lang.: Spa. 2698

Tofano, Sergio
Performance/production
Pirandello as director: contemporary reviews and interviews. Italy. 1915-1936. Lang.: Ita. 838

Tōhō (Tokyo)
Performance/production
Productions from Yume no yūminsha, Tōhō, Parco, Tsukumo and Nakamura za. Japan: Tokyo. 1986-1987. Lang.: Jap. 1956

Tokolonga ou le socialisme vaincu (Tokolonga or Socialism Vanquished)
Plays/librettos/scripts
Compares plays of Enlightenment France, Francophone Africa. Congo: Brazzaville. Cameroon. Benin. France. 1700-1975. Lang.: Eng. 2496

Tokyo ichikumi (Tokyo)
Performance/production
Analysis of four Tokyo productions. Japan: Tokyo. 1987. Lang.: Jap. 1957

Discussion of four Tokyo productions. Japan: Tokyo. 1944-1987. Lang.: Jap. 1963

Tokyo vōdoviru shō (Tokyo)
Performance/production
Space and sign in various Tokyo productions. Japan: Tokyo. 1987. Lang.: Jap. 1959

Tolcsvay, Béla
Performance/production
Reviews of *Rigoletto*, Lloyd Webber's *Requiem*, *Les Misérables* and the Hungarian Mass of the Tolcsvays. Hungary: Szeged. 1987. Lang.: Hun. 3400

Tolcsvay, László
Performance/production
Reviews of *Rigoletto*, Lloyd Webber's *Requiem*, *Les Misérables* and the Hungarian Mass of the Tolcsvays. Hungary: Szeged. 1987. Lang.: Hun. 3400

Toller, Ernst
Plays/librettos/scripts
New interpretation of Toller's *Masse Mensch*. Germany. 1921-1987. Lang.: Eng. 2592

Tolney, Klári
Performance/production
Interview with actress Klári Tolnay. Hungary. 1984-1987. Lang.: Hun. 1837

Tolstoj, Lev Nikolajèvič
Plays/librettos/scripts
Plays of Tolstoj and the 'New Drama' of Western Europe. Russia. Europe. 1864-1910. Lang.: Rus. 2722

Relation to other fields
Comparison between Wagner and Tolstoy. Russia. Germany. 1860-1908. Lang.: Eng. 3944

Tom Tom
Performance/production
Collection of newspaper reviews by London theatre critics. UK-England: London. 1987. Lang.: Eng. 2276

Tomaselli, Keyan G.
Performance/production
Black theatre in South Africa: influence of traditional forms. South Africa, Republic of. England: London. USA: New York, NY. 1586-1987. Lang.: Eng. 2005

Tomlinson, Paul
Performance/production
Collection of newspaper reviews by London theatre critics. UK-England: London. 1986. Lang.: Eng. 2087

Collection of newspaper reviews by London theatre critics. UK-England: London. 1987. Lang.: Eng. 2179

Tomorrow Was War
Performance/production
Collection of newspaper reviews by London theatre critics. UK-England: London. 1987. Lang.: Eng. 2224

Tömöry, Péter
Performance/production
Péter Tömöry directs premiere of Zsigmond Móricz's 1916 *Fortunátus*. Hungary: Zalaegerszeg. 1987. Lang.: Hun. 1840

A tanítónő (The Schoolmistress) by Sándor Bródy, directed by Péter Tömöry at Hevesi Sándor Theatre. Hungary: Zalaegerszeg. 1986. Lang.: Hun. 1921

Tompa, Gábor
Performance/production
Gábor Tompa directs *Hamlet* at Hungarian Theatre of Kolozsvár. Romania: Cluj. 1987. Lang.: Hun. 2001

Toneelgroep (Amsterdam)
Institutions
Toneelgroep Amsterdam's theatrical mission in the eighties. Netherlands: Amsterdam. 1987. Lang.: Dut. 553

Performance/production
Directors Claus Peymann (Burgtheater) and Gerardjan Rijnders (Toneelgroep). Austria: Vienna. Netherlands: Amsterdam. 1987. Lang.: Dut. 1681

Tong-Yang Kuk Chang (Seoul)
Administration
Tong-Yang theatre, first commercial theatre in Korea. Korea: Seoul. 1935-1945. Lang.: Kor. 30

Institutions
Closing of Tong-Yang theatre. Korea: Seoul. 1940-1947. Lang.: Kor. 552

Performance spaces
History of Tong-Yang Theatre, Korea's first dramatic theatre. Korea: Seoul. 1930-1935. Lang.: Kor. 661

Tongues of Fire
Performance/production
Teatropoesia, a combination of theatre and poetry. USA. 1974-1983. Lang.: Spa. 2368

Tonight Show, The
Performance/production
Analysis of art of television and comparison to live theatre. USA. 1950-1987. Lang.: Eng. 3194

Tons of Money
Performance/production
Collection of newspaper reviews by London theatre critics. UK-England. 1986. Lang.: Eng. 2159

Too True To Be Good
Performance/production
Collection of newspaper reviews by London theatre critics. UK-England: London. 1986. Lang.: Eng. 2157

Toot Suit, A
Performance/production
Collection of newspaper reviews by London theatre critics. UK-England: London. 1987. Lang.: Eng. 2206

Tooth of Crime, The
Performance/production
Collection of newspaper reviews by London theatre critics. UK-England: London. 1987. Lang.: Eng. 2240

Plays/librettos/scripts
Gender roles in Sam Shepard's plays. USA. 1960-1987. Lang.: Eng. 2860

Modernism and postmodernism as themes in Sam Shepard's plays. USA. 1972-1987. Lang.: Eng. 2930

Top Girls
Plays/librettos/scripts
Socialist-feminist nature of Caryl Churchill's plays. UK-England. 1980-1987. Lang.: Eng. 2776

Touring companies — cont'd

Overview of performing artists that toured Japan. Japan: Tokyo. 1986. Lang.: Jap.   844

Overview of Mexican-American theatre. USA. Mexico. 1850-1987. Lang.: Eng.   946

British theatrical touring companies. UK-England. North America. Australia. 1870-1929. Lang.: Eng.   2280

Puppet companies from Poznań. Poland: Poznań. 1919-1939. Lang.: Pol.   3978

Reference materials
Compilation of anecdotes on life in the theatre from Aristophanes to Williams. 5 B.C.-1987 A.D. Lang.: Eng.   1195

Touring Theatre (London)
Performance/production
Collection of newspaper reviews by London theatre critics. UK-England: London. 1987. Lang.: Eng.   2177

Tourneur, Cyril
Plays/librettos/scripts
Structure of revenge tragedy in Shakespeare's *Hamlet*. 1600. Lang.: Eng.   2425

Theory/criticism
The body as emblematic of a character's frame of mind. England. 1583. Lang.: Eng.   3031

Tovstonogov, Georgij Aleksandrovič
Performance/production
Round-table of Soviet directors. USSR: Moscow. 1980-1987. Lang.: Rus.   989

Directors discuss their training under G.A. Tovstonogov. USSR: Moscow. 1960-1987. Lang.: Rus.   1026

Interview with director Georgij Tovstonogov. USSR: Leningrad. 1980-1987. Lang.: Rus.   1034

Evolution of the heroes in plays directed by G.A. Tovstonogov. USSR: Leningrad. 1950-1980. Lang.: Rus.   1051

Director on training directors. USSR: Leningrad. 1980-1987. Lang.: Rus.   1077

Portrait of director G.A. Tovstonogov. USSR: Leningrad. 1930-1987. Lang.: Eng.   1086

The actor's art as directed by G.A. Tovstonogov. USSR. 1970-1987. Lang.: Rus.   1089

Training
Interview with Georgij Tovstonogov. USA. 1987. Lang.: Eng.   1390

Tower of Babel, The
SEE
Tour de Babel, La.

Towneley Cycle
Plays/librettos/scripts
Analysis of medieval Cain and Abel mystery plays. England. 1200-1576. Lang.: Eng.   2506

Medieval cycle plays as the exception rather than the norm. England. Lang.: Eng.   2543

Toy, The
Plays/librettos/scripts
New findings on 18th-century Irish comic playwright John O'Keeffe. Ireland. England: London. 1767-1798. Lang.: Eng. 2643

Toyama, Shizu
Performance spaces
Theatre's relation to society, poor theatre design as reasons for state of theatre today. USA. 1987. Lang.: Eng.   680

Tragedy
Design/technology
Scenic representations of Hell. Italy. France. 1300-1399. Lang.: Ita.   349

Performance/production
Ways to blend comedy and tragedy in Hsi Ch'ü. China, People's Republic of. 1986. Lang.: Chi.   3479

Plays/librettos/scripts
Compares tragedies of Sophocles and Euripides with those of Eugene O'Neill. 1918-1946. Lang.: Eng.   2409

Old age in the plays of Sophocles, especially *Oedipus at Colonus*. 405 B.C. Lang.: Eng.   2414

Structure of revenge tragedy in Shakespeare's *Hamlet*. 1600. Lang.: Eng.   2425

Biblical influences in *King Lear, Hamlet, Othello* and *Macbeth*. Lang.: Eng.   2426

Tragic result of utopian ideas in Shakespeare's *Romeo and Juliet*. England. 1595-1596. Lang.: Ger.   2530

Techniques, themes, characters and dramaturgy of Voltaire. France. 1718-1778. Lang.: Eng.   2590

Italian translation of *Über das Tragische (On the Tragic)* by Karl Jaspers. Germany, West. 1952. Lang.: Ita.   2617

Italian translation, *The Greek Tragic Theatre* by H.C. Baldry. Greece. 500-400 B.C. Lang.: Ita.   2619

Structure and plot of ancient Greek tragedies. Greece. 500-400 B.C. Lang.: Kor.   2622

Study of classical Greek dramaturgy. Greece. 472-388 B.C. Lang.: Hun.   2623

Comparison of Greek tragedy and Korean Buddhist plays. Korea. Greece. 57 B.C.-1392 A.D. Lang.: Kor.   2684

The world and man in Marlowe's tragedies. UK-England. 1564-1593. Lang.: Rus.   2751

Problem of the tragic in English drama. UK-England. 1950-1969. Lang.: Rus.   2819

Chinese view of playwright Eugene O'Neill. USA. China, People's Republic of. 1930-1985. Lang.: Chi.   2863

Orson Welles's adaptation of *Othello*: cinematic technique and time. USA. 1952. Lang.: Eng.   3180

A correct definition of Chinese classical 'tragedy'. China. 960-1644. Lang.: Chi.   3548

Analysis of Chinese tragedy. China, People's Republic of. 1986. Lang.: Chi.   3572

Relation to other fields
Comparison of the role of theatre in urban society with that of traditional ritual. 1985. Lang.: Spa.   2977

Theory/criticism
Exploration of the nature of tragedy. 500 B.C.-1987 A.D. Lang.: Eng.   3020

Otakar Hostinský's conception of tragedy and the tragic. Austria-Hungary: Prague. 1906. Lang.: Cze.   3022

Tragedy, space and discourse in neoclassical dramatic theory. France. 1800-1850. Lang.: Eng.   3035

Catalan translation of Lessing's *Hamburgische Dramaturgie*. Germany: Hamburg. 1767-1769. Lang.: Cat.   3043

Tragedy of a Man, The
SEE
Ember tragédiája, Az.

Tragedy of Tragedies, The
Plays/librettos/scripts
Henry Fielding rewrote *Tom Thumb* to satirize Lewis Theobald. England. 1730-1731. Lang.: Eng.   2535

Training
SEE ALSO
Classed Entries.

Administration
AEA Actors' Work Program, a re-training program for actors. USA: New York, NY. 1986-1987. Lang.: Eng.   59

Sexual discrimination in American theatres. USA: New York, NY. 1976-1984. Lang.: Eng.   133

Articles on changing realities: effect on theatre. USSR. 1985-1987. Lang.: Rus.   267

Institutions
Historical background of National Theatre School. Canada: Montreal, PQ. 1960-1985. Lang.: Eng.   519

Creative teaching of theatre. Israel: Tel Aviv. 1987. Lang.: Heb.   546

Performance/production
A report from the first European Youth theatre encounter. UK-England: Stratford. 1987. Lang.: Swe.   910

Complete description of all aspects of *Wayang wong*. Indonesia. 930-1986. Lang.: Eng.   1481

Mime Samy Molcho: his new work as lecturer and author. Switzerland. 1987. Lang.: Ger.   3235

Drama education in China. China, People's Republic of. 1985. Lang.: Chi.   3492

Status of Sichuan theatre and opera. China, People's Republic of: Chengdu. 1985-1986. Lang.: Eng.   3512

Career of conductor/educator Max Rudolf. Italy. USA: New York, NY. 1945-1987. Lang.: Eng.   3803

Work of Bruno Leone and his attempts to re-establish the Neapolitan culture of Guaratelle. Italy: Naples. 1979-1987. Lang.: Eng.   3976

Training — cont'd

Relation to other fields

Importance of theatre for youth and arts in education in Israel. Israel. 1973. Lang.: Eng. 1241

Drama as education: current theory and practice. USA. 1987. Lang.: Eng. 1268

Training aids

Design/technology

Use of stereographs in costume design. USA. 1987. Lang.: Eng. 437

Beginner's guide to stage lighting. USA. 1987. Lang.: Eng. 441

Training, actor

Institutions

Survey of liberal arts and professional training courses. Australia. 1987. Lang.: Eng. 503

Director Leon Schiller's plan for a drama department, Theatre Institute. Poland: Warsaw. 1943. Lang.: Pol. 555

Performance/production

Canadian actors and directors discuss their theatre experiences. Canada: Calgary, AB. 1987. Lang.: Eng. 748

History of Slovak school of acting. Czechoslovakia. 1830-1987. Lang.: Rus. 766

Reviews of drama students' final examination performances. Hungary: Budapest. 1986-1987. Lang.: Hun. 804

Advice for novice actors. Korea. 1987. Lang.: Kor. 851

Peter Feldman's techniques for training actors. North America. 1987. Lang.: Eng. 867

History of teaching method of Michajl Čechov. USA. USSR. 1891-1955. Lang.: Eng. 931

Organizational and production history of the American Shakespeare Festival. USA: Stratford, CT. 1955-1985. Lang.: Eng. 934

Beginning text on acting. USA. 1987. Lang.: Eng. 960

Acting style of Vachtangov. USSR. Canada. 1922-1987. Lang.: Eng. 1009

Recognizing and developing talent: experiences of the Lunačarskij School. USSR: Moscow. 1981-1986. Lang.: Rus. 1061

Teaching and directing the student actor. USSR. 1987. Lang.: Rus. 1062

Notes on Stanislavskij. USSR. 1863-1938. Lang.: Rus. 1085

Institutions, techniques in training of nō actors. Japan. 1987. Lang.: Eng. 1499

Zeami's concept of the actor and the ideal performance. Japan. 1363-1443. Lang.: Eng. 1500

Work of actor/director Augusto Boal. Canada: Sydney, NS. 1987. Lang.: Eng. 1694

Workshop in Chinese acting methods. Canada: Toronto, ON. China, People's Republic of: Shanghai. 1987. Lang.: Eng. 1717

Interview with actress Roberta Maxwell. Canada. 1987. Lang.: Eng. 1718

Use of visual arts conventions in acting techniques. England. 1700. Lang.: Eng. 1735

Sources of attitudes for serious dramatic acting and acting for low comedy. Europe. 1700. Lang.: Eng. 1747

Patrice Chéreau and Théâtre des Amandiers create stage and film versions of Čechov's *Platonov*. France: Nanterre. 1982-1987. Lang.: Swe. 1755

Interview with actor Zoltán Nagy. Hungary. 1962-1987. Lang.: Hun. 1809

Discussion of acting techniques. Korea. 1986. Lang.: Kor. 1967

Life and career of Polish theatre professional Zbigniew Cynkutis. Poland: Wrocław. 1972-1987. Lang.: Eng. 1993

Development of the Stanislavskij Acting System. Russia: Moscow. 1906-1938. Lang.: Eng. 2003

Interview with actor Michael Gambon. UK-England. 1987. Lang.: Eng. 2295

Acting styles on English stages. UK-England. 1740-1760. Lang.: Eng. 2304

Actress Ann Casson on proper line speaking in Shaw. UK-England. 1924-1981. Lang.: Eng. 2305

Profile of character actor Matthew Locricchio. USA: New York, NY. 1987. Lang.: Eng. 2334

Sanford Meisner's method of teaching acting. USA: New York, NY. 1987. Lang.: Eng. 2349

Interviews with teachers of acting. USA: New York, NY, Los Angeles, CA. 1987. Lang.: Eng. 2350

Method acting: its origins and development. USA: New York, NY. USSR: Moscow. 1923-1987. Lang.: Eng. 2359

Transcriptions from lectures and lessons given by actor Michajl Čechov on his technique. USSR: Moscow. 1942-1919. Lang.: Eng. 2377

Techniques of the image theatre and effects on actor and audience. Canada. Europe. USA. 1987. Lang.: Eng. 3345

Career of Chinese opera actor and teacher Maa Lian Liang. China: Beijing. 1929-1981. Lang.: Chi. 3457

Training the Chinese opera actor in Italian singing techniques. China, People's Republic of. 1986. Lang.: Chi. 3523

Vocal training and performance in China. China, People's Republic of: Shanghai. 1949-1987. Lang.: Chi. 3529

Career of actor William McCauley. USA. 1987. Lang.: Eng. 3660

Relation to other fields

Popular theatre and non-governmental funding agencies. Canada: Sydney, NS. Jamaica. Sudan. 1987. Lang.: Eng. 2982

Research/historiography

Expansion, diversification and artistic innovation in the American theatre. USA. 1961-1986. Lang.: Eng. 1302

Training

Guide to teaching through improvisation for children and adults. 1987. Lang.: Eng. 1377

Proposed changes in teaching methodology to include indigenous drama. South Africa, Republic of. 1960-1987. Lang.: Eng. 1383

Problems of theatrical education. USSR: Moscow. 1987. Lang.: Rus. 1391

Vocal training in Soviet dramatic education. USSR. 1987. Lang.: Rus. 1392

Problems of students graduating from theatre schools. USSR. 1980-1987. Lang.: Rus. 1394

Problems of young drama school graduates. USSR. 1986-1987. Lang.: Rus. 1396

Brecht workshop of International Amateur Theatre Association. Germany, East: Berlin, East. 1986. Lang.: Ger. 3079

Interview with acting teacher Deirdre Hurst du Prey, specialist in the Chekhov Method. UK-England: Dartington. 1978. Lang.: Eng. 3081

Acting teachers who studied under Michajl Čechov: making the Technique fit contemporary needs. USA: New York, NY. 1930-1980. Lang.: Eng. 3082

Training, dance

Performance/production

Interview with dancer-choreographer Viktor Róna. Hungary. Norway: Oslo. 1980-1987. Lang.: Hun. 1437

Interview with ballerina and teacher Ellen Rasch. Sweden. 1927-1987. Lang.: Swe. 1442

Principles of biomechanics in teaching ballet. USSR. 1987. Lang.: Rus. 1447

Relation to other fields

Rediscovery of the body in modern dance. Germany. 1900-1930. Lang.: Ita. 1475

Exhibition devoted to modern dancer Gret Palucca. Germany, East: Dresden. 1922-1987. Lang.: Ger. 1476

Training, design

Design/technology

Scene design training at Academy of Performing Arts, Bratislava. Hungary: Szeged. Czechoslovakia: Bratislava. 1980-1987. Lang.: Hun. 344

Interview with costume designer Rien Bekkers. Netherlands. 1987. Lang.: Dut. 357

Problems associated with setting up a training course in design. UK-Scotland: Glasgow. 1987. Lang.: Eng. 380

MFA program in lighting design at Parsons School of Design. USA: New York, NY. 1987. Lang.: Eng. 454

Institutions

Director Leon Schiller's plan for a drama department, Theatre Institute. Poland: Warsaw. 1943. Lang.: Pol. 555

Training, director

Institutions

Director Leon Schiller's plan for a drama department, Theatre Institute. Poland: Warsaw. 1943. Lang.: Pol. 555

Training, director — cont'd

Memoirs of director and teacher Géza Gergely on Hungarian theatrical training in Romania. Romania: Tîrgu-Mureş. Hungary. 1946-1986. Lang.: Hun.   556

Performance/production

Summarizes events of Directors' Colloquium. Canada: Calgary, AB. 1987. Lang.: Eng.   728

Toronto directors discuss their training and craft. Canada: Toronto, ON. 1987. Lang.: Eng.   730

Directors' Colloquium: individual directorial techniques. Canada: Calgary, AB. 1987. Lang.: Eng.   743

The Directors Colloquium: director/playwright relationship. Canada: Calgary, AB. 1987. Lang.: Eng.   747

Canadian actors and directors discuss their theatre experiences. Canada: Calgary, AB. 1987. Lang.: Eng.   748

Analysis of the playwright/director relationship in Canada. Canada. 1987. Lang.: Eng.   750

Overview of the director's art. China, People's Republic of. 1985. Lang.: Chi.   757

Reviews of drama students' final examination performances. Hungary: Budapest. 1986-1987. Lang.: Hun.   804

Director training course at Dalsland Folkhögskola. Sweden. 1987. Lang.: Swe.   886

A class for amateur directors. Sweden: Katrineberg. 1987. Lang.: Swe.   887

Directors discuss their training under G.A. Tovstonogov. USSR: Moscow. 1960-1987. Lang.: Rus.   1026

Director Anatolij Efros on directing, ethics. USSR: Moscow. 1981-1982. Lang.: Rus.   1033

Recognizing and developing talent: experiences of the Lunačarskij School. USSR: Moscow. 1981-1986. Lang.: Rus.   1061

Director on training directors. USSR: Leningrad. 1980-1987. Lang.: Rus.   1077

Interview with director Richard Foreman. USA: New York, NY. 1962-1987. Lang.: Eng.   2329

Training

The classes of a master directing teacher. China, People's Republic of: Shanghai. 1949-1987. Lang.: Chi.   1380

Problems of theatrical education. USSR: Moscow. 1987. Lang.: Rus.   1391

Problems of students graduating from theatre schools. USSR. 1980-1987. Lang.: Rus.   1394

Brecht workshop of International Amateur Theatre Association. Germany, East: Berlin, East. 1986. Lang.: Ger.   3079

Training, singer

Institutions

Jeannette Aster, new artistic director of Opera Lyra. Canada: Ottawa, ON. 1984-1987. Lang.: Eng.   3723

Program of opera workshop, Boston Conservatory. USA: Boston, MA. 1973-1983. Lang.: Eng.   3734

Performance/production

Training the Chinese opera actor in Italian singing techniques. China, People's Republic of. 1986. Lang.: Chi.   3523

Vocal training and performance in China. China, People's Republic of: Shanghai. 1949-1987. Lang.: Chi.   3529

Music Theatre Committee of the New York Singing Teachers Association (NYSTA) symposium on singing popular music. USA: New York, NY. 1985. Lang.: Eng.   3639

Autobiography of opera star Maureen Forrester. Canada. 1930-1986. Lang.: Eng.   3748

Interview with Odette Beaupré. Canada. 1987. Lang.: Eng.   3752

Quality of and access to opera training in North America. Canada. USA. 1987. Lang.: Eng.   3753

Interview with soprano Jane MacKenzie. Canada. UK-England. 1987. Lang.: Eng.   3754

Interview with soprano Tracy Dahl. Canada. 1987. Lang.: Eng.   3755

Interview with opera star Gaétan Laperrière. Canada. 1987. Lang.: Eng.   3756

Stuart Hamilton's career in opera broadcasting. Canada: Toronto, ON. 1929-1987. Lang.: Eng.   3758

Directors' notes on the profession of choral singing in opera. Germany, East. 1986. Lang.: Ger.   3778

Special needs in operatic training. Germany, East. 1987. Lang.: Ger.   3780

Three opera chorus conductors. Germany, East. 1986. Lang.: Ger.   3786

Singers/teachers Virginia Zeani and Nicola Rossi-Lemeni. Italy. 1920-1987. Lang.: Eng.   3802

Vasile Moldoveanu's views on the current state of opera. USA. 1987. Lang.: Eng.   3844

Accompanist/voice teacher, John Wustman. USA. 1960-1987. Lang.: Eng.   3848

Experts discuss vocal training. USA. 1987. Lang.: Eng.   3858

Tijt Kuuzik, operatic artist and teacher. USSR: Estonia. 1911-1987. Lang.: Rus.   3886

Training

Interview with singing master Hanno Blaschke. South Africa, Republic of. 1987. Lang.: Eng.   3951

Interviews with singing teachers in New York City. USA: New York, NY. 1987. Lang.: Eng.   3952

Round-table discussion of music students from Conservatory on art, education, creativity. USSR: Kiev. 1980-1987. Lang.: Rus.   3953

Training, technician

Design/technology

Third international scene painting seminar at the Mozarteum. Austria: Salzburg. 1986. Lang.: Eng.   300

First twelve theatre-technician graduates of Dramatiska Institutet. Sweden: Stockholm. 1987. Lang.: Swe.   361

Report on two-week theatre technician course. Sweden: Gothenburg. 1987. Lang.: Swe.   367

Instruction in scene painting. USA. 1600-1987. Lang.: Eng.   434

Transfiguration of Benno Blimpie, The

Plays/librettos/scripts

Interview with playwright Albert Innaurato. USA. 1986. Lang.: Eng.   2856

Translations

Plays/librettos/scripts

Comparison of Brian Friel's *Translations* and András Sütő's *A szuzai menyegző*. Ireland. Hungary. 1981. Lang.: Eng.   2637

Themes of Brian Friel's plays. Ireland. 1929-1987. Lang.: Eng.   2638

Brian Friel's interpretation of Irish history through his plays *Aristocrats* and *Translations*. Ireland. 1987. Lang.: Eng.   2659

Theory/criticism

Brian Friel's play *Translations*. Ireland. 1987. Lang.: Eng.   3050

Translations

Basic theatrical documents

English translation of *Jonah* by Elie Georges Berreby. Belgium. 1987. Lang.: Eng.   1542

Translation of *Being at Home with Claude*. Canada: Montreal, PQ. 1986. Lang.: Eng.   1546

German translation of Tremblay's *Les Belles-Soeurs*. Canada: Quebec, PQ. Germany. 1987. Lang.: Ger.   1549

Constance Garnett's translation of *Tri sestry (Three Sisters)* by Čechov. England: London. 1901. Lang.: Eng.   1552

English translation of *What, No Ashes?* by Tauno Yliruusi. Finland. 1987. Lang.: Eng.   1553

English translations of three plays by Jacob Masen. Germany. 1606-1681. Lang.: Eng.   1556

Translation of five contemporary Persian plays. Iran. 1987. Lang.: Eng.   1558

English translation of *Buba* by Hillel Mittelpunkt. Israel. 1987. Lang.: Eng.   1559

Hebrew translation of Sławomir Mrożek's *Vatslave*. Poland: Cracow. Israel: Jerusalem. 1968-1984. Lang.: Heb.   1565

English translations of contemporary African plays. Senegal. Zaire. 1987. Lang.: Eng.   1566

Translation of *Viernes, 29 de julio de 1983, de madrugada (Friday, July 29, 1983, Early in the Morning)* by Jerónimo López Moto. Spain. 1987. Lang.: Eng.   1568

The Horns of Don Friolera, translation of *Los cuernos de don Friolera* by Ramón del Valle-Inclán. Spain. 1930. Lang.: Eng.   1570

Complete text of *Dimba and Dimbi* with background materials and preparations. Indonesia. 1987. Lang.: Eng.   4008

Performance spaces

Italian translation, *Buildings for Music* by Michael Forsyth. 1600-1985. Lang.: Ita.   625

Translations — cont'd

Performance/production

Italian translation of *Hubert Fichte Jean Genet*. Italy. 1975-1985. Lang.: Ita.   1942

Biography of director Luchino Visconti. Italy. 1906-1976. Lang.: Ita.   3158

Hungarian translation of Norman Mailer's biography of Marilyn Monroe. USA. 1926-1962. Lang.: Hun.   3169

Italian translation, Roy Strong, *Art and Power*. Europe. 1450-1650. Lang.: Ita.   3257

Plays/librettos/scripts

Italian translation, *Shakespeare, Our Contemporary* by Jan Kott. 1596-1614. Lang.: Ita.   2420

Ibsen translation, production, reception and influence in China. China, People's Republic of. Norway. 1917-1985. Lang.: Eng.   2494

Italian translation of *Über die Shakespearomanie (On Shakespeare-Mania)* by Christian Dietrich Grabbe. England. Germany. 1594-1836. Lang.: Ita.   2520

Italian translation of *Über das Tragische (On the Tragic)* by Karl Jaspers. Germany, West. 1952. Lang.: Ita.   2617

Problems of translating from English and French into Hebrew. Israel. 1987. Lang.: Heb.   2660

Ibsen database now being developed. USA. Norway. 1987. Lang.: Eng.   2924

Kazakh translations of Shakespeare. USSR. 1930-1969. Lang.: Rus.   2947

Contemporary interpretations of Shakespeare's work. USSR. 1980-1987. Lang.: Rus.   2967

Relation to other fields

Italian translations of Ernest Jones' *Hamlet and Oedipus*, and Jean Starobinski's *Hamlet and Freud*. Europe. 1596-1949. Lang.: Ita. 2988

Theory/criticism

Analysis of various versions and translations of Aristotle's *Poetics*. Greece: Athens. Egypt: Alexandria. Europe. 70 B.C.-1981 A.D. Lang.: Chi.   1343

Catalan translation of Lessing's *Hamburgische Dramaturgie*. Germany: Hamburg. 1767-1769. Lang.: Cat.   3043

Reflections on the value of theatrical translations. Spain-Catalonia. UK-England. 1600-1985. Lang.: Cat.   3060

Transposed Heads, The
SEE
> *Vertauschten Köpfe, Die*.

Transvestism
Performance/production

Transvestite roles in extravaganzas of J.R. Planché and Mme. Vestris. UK-England: London. 1830-1870. Lang.: Eng.   3268

Trap, The
SEE
> *Pulapka*.

Travaux et les jours, Les (Smile on the End of the Line, A)
Performance/production

Collection of newspaper reviews by London theatre critics. UK-England: London. 1987. Lang.: Eng.   2190

Traveler without Baggage
SEE
> *Voyageur sans bagages, Le*.

Traveller, The
Performance/production

Collection of newspaper reviews by London theatre critics. UK-England: London. 1987. Lang.: Eng.   2230

Travelling Jewish Theatre (San Francisco, CA)
Performance/production

Rehearsals and performance of Joseph Chaikin's *A War Within*. USA: San Francisco, CA. 1987. Lang.: Eng.   930

Travelling Light
Performance/production

Collection of newspaper reviews by London theatre critics. UK-England: London. 1986. Lang.: Eng.   2107

Travers, Ben
Performance/production

Collection of newspaper reviews by London theatre critics. UK-England: London. 1986. Lang.: Eng.   2141

Collection of newspaper reviews by London theatre critics. UK-England: London. 1987. Lang.: Eng.   2178

Traverse Theatre Company (Edinburgh)
Performance/production

Collection of newspaper reviews by London theatre critics. UK-England. 1987. Lang.: Eng.   2033

Travesties
Plays/librettos/scripts

Theme of theatre in recent plays. UK-England. 1957-1985. Lang.: Eng.   2764

Travianti fratelli, Li (Wayward Brothers, The)
Plays/librettos/scripts

Plays of Antonio Monetta, Pietro Suscio and Girolamo Bax. Italy. 1600-1900. Lang.: Ita.   2669

Traviata, La
Performance/production

Initial recordings of Verdi's operas. Italy. France. USA. 1900-1945. Lang.: Eng.   3800

Background on Metropolitan radio broadcast performances. USA: New York, NY. 1987. Lang.: Eng.   3838

Travolta, John
Performance/production

Review of ABC videocast of Pinter's *The Dumb Waiter*. USA. 1987. Lang.: Eng.   3209

Treatment
Performance/production

Collection of newspaper reviews by London theatre critics. UK-England: London. 1986. Lang.: Eng.   2052

Tree of Life
Relation to other fields

Three performance art education projects. UK-England. 1987. Lang.: Eng.   3373

Tree, Herbert Beerbohm
Plays/librettos/scripts

Stage business in *Major Barbara* traced to Beerbohm Tree. UK-England. 1905. Lang.: Eng.   2802

Theory/criticism

Reconstruction of Shakespeare in performance. USA. 1987. Lang.: Eng.   1358

Tremblay, Michel
Basic theatrical documents

German translation of Tremblay's *Les Belles-Soeurs*. Canada: Quebec, PQ. Germany. 1987. Lang.: Ger.   1549

Performance/production

Collection of newspaper reviews by London theatre critics. UK-England: London. 1986. Lang.: Eng.   2146

Plays/librettos/scripts

The role of the father-figure in recent plays from Quebec. Canada: Quebec. 1980-1987. Lang.: Fre.   2465

Tren de cristall, El (Crystal Train, The)
Basic theatrical documents

Study of the poetic, narrative and theatrical work of Agustí Bartra, edition of complete works, vol. 4. Spain-Catalonia. Mexico. 1937-1982. Lang.: Cat.   1571

Trestle Theatre Company (London)
Performance/production

Collection of newspaper reviews by London theatre critics. UK-England: London. 1987. Lang.: Eng.   2218

Trevis, Di
Design/technology

Preliminary sketches for the Royal Shakespeare Company's *The Taming of the Shrew*. UK-England. 1985. Lang.: Eng.   1597

Performance/production

English Shakespearean productions. UK-England: London, Manchester, Stratford. 1985-1986. Lang.: Eng.   917

Collection of newspaper reviews by London theatre critics. UK-England: London. 1986. Lang.: Eng.   2043

Collection of newspaper reviews by London theatre critics. UK-England: London. 1987. Lang.: Eng.   2179

Collection of newspaper reviews by London theatre critics. UK-England: London. 1987. Lang.: Eng.   2196

Tri devuški v golubom (Three Girls in Blue)
Performance/production

Tamás Ascher directs Ljudmila Petruševskaja's *Tri devuški v golubom (Three Girls in Blue)* at Katona József Theatre under the title *Három lány kékben*. Hungary: Budapest. USSR. 1987. Lang.: Hun.   1883

Ljudmila Petruševskaja's controversial play, *Tri devuški v golubom (Three Girls in Blue)*, directed by Tamás Ascher at Katona József Theatre. Hungary: Budapest. 1987. Lang.: Hun.   1920

Tynan, Kenneth — cont'd

Performance/production

Kenneth Tynan's review of the first production of Osborne's *Look Back in Anger*. 1956. Lang.: Eng.   1677

Plays/librettos/scripts

Financial support for aspiring playwrights. UK-England. 1980. Lang.: Eng.   2771

Theory/criticism

Interview with theatre critic Frank Rich. USA. 1960-1987. Lang.: Eng.   1363

Interview with Kathleen Tynan about Kenneth Tynan. USA: New York, NY. 1987. Lang.: Eng.   3073

Tyson, Cicely

Performance/production

Theatre career of photo-journalist Bert Andrews. USA: New York, NY. 1950-1987. Lang.: Eng.   2367

Tzara, Tristan

Plays/librettos/scripts

Mouchoir de Nuages (Handkerchief of Clouds) by Tristan Tzara. France. Lang.: Ita.   2569

Ubersfeld, Anne

Performance/production

Directing as guiding actors, not imposing a subjective interpretation. France. 1987. Lang.: Fre.   784

Ubu roi (King Ubu)

Performance/production

Andor Lukács directs Alfred Jarry's *Ubu roi (King Ubu)* at Csiky Gergely Theatre as *Übü király*. Hungary: Boglárelle. 1987. Lang.: Hun.   1884

Jarry's *Ubu roi (King Ubu)* directed by Andor Lukáks at Csiky Gergely Theatre under the title *Übü király*. Hungary: Kaposvár. 1987. Lang.: Hun.   1913

Irondale Ensemble's production of *Ubu roi (King Ubu)* by Alfred Jarry. USA: New York, NY. 1984-1987. Lang.: Eng.   2370

Uciechy Staropolskie (Old Polish Revels, The)

Performance/production

Polish theatre. Poland: Warsaw, Cracow, Wrocław. 1980-1987. Lang.: Eng, Fre.   1987

Udall, Nicholas

Performance/production

Irony in *Gammer Gurton's Needle*: its interpretation and presentation to the audience. England. 1575-1982. Lang.: Eng.   777

Udvaros, Dorottya

Performance/production

Interview with actress Dorottya Udvaros. Hungary. 1978-1987. Lang.: Hun.   1801

Interview with actress Dorottya Udvaros. Hungary. 1977-1987. Lang.: Hun.   1852

Uei, Ming-Lun

Plays/librettos/scripts

Chinese opera dramatist Uei Ming-Lun. China, People's Republic of. 1987. Lang.: Chi.   3562

Ugone, Casimiro Ruggeri

Performance/production

Adaptation of Nativity puppet play. Italy. 1651-1987. Lang.: Eng.   4001

Uhry, Alfred

Performance/production

Collection of newspaper reviews by New York theatre critics. USA: New York, NY. 1987. Lang.: Eng.   2320

Plays/librettos/scripts

Alfred Uhry on *Driving Miss Daisy*. USA: New York, NY. 1976-1984. Lang.: Eng.   3419

Uketsuke (Reception, The)

Performance/production

Focus on several Tokyo productions. Japan: Tokyo. 1960-1987. Lang.: Jap.   1955

Ukrainka, Lesja

Plays/librettos/scripts

Stage and screen adaptations of the poetry of Lesja Ukrainka. USSR. 1987. Lang.: Rus.   2971

Ul'janov, Michajl A.

Administration

Problem of theatre as business. USSR. 1986-1988. Lang.: Rus.   272

Institutions

Actor, union leader Michajl A. Ul'janov on social changes, their effect on theatre and film. USSR. 1970-1987. Lang.: Rus.   624

Performance/production

Soviet actor Michajl A. Ul'janov on his work. USSR. 1927-1987. Lang.: Rus.   1078

Actor Michajl Ul'janov. USSR: Moscow. 1927-1987. Lang.: Rus.   1080

Relation to other fields

Exchange of ideas between Soviets and US theatre artists. USA: New York, NY. USSR: Moscow. 1987. Lang.: Eng.   1284

Ulive, Ugo

Performance/production

Collection of newspaper reviews by London theatre critics. UK-England: London. 1987. Lang.: Eng.   2257

Ullmann, Liv

Design/technology

Interview with cameraman Lajos Koltay. Hungary. 1986. Lang.: Hun.   3128

Performance/production

Creative self-knowledge and the mystical path of actors. UK-England: London. USA. 1977-1987. Lang.: Eng.   900

Two productions of Pinter's *Old Times*. UK-England: London. USA: New York, NY, St. Louis, MO. 1971-1985. Lang.: Eng.   907

Ulster Youth Theatre

Training

Interview with Michael Poyner, director of Ulster Youth Theatre. UK-Ireland. 1987. Lang.: Eng.   1386

Ultimatum II

Performance/production

Critical discussion of the Ultimatum II festival. Canada: Montreal, PQ. 1987. Lang.: Eng.   3346

Ulvaeus, Bjorn

Performance/production

Collection of newspaper reviews by London theatre critics. UK-England: London. 1986. Lang.: Eng.   2097

Ulysses in Traction

Plays/librettos/scripts

Interview with playwright Albert Innaurato. USA. 1986. Lang.: Eng.   2856

Ulysses von Ithaca (Ulysses of Ithaca)

Performance/production

'Showing' is an essential part of all acting. Europe. 1590-1987. Lang.: Eng.   1746

Umerla Klasa (Dead Class, The)

Performance/production

Polish theatre. Poland: Warsaw, Cracow, Wrocław. 1980-1987. Lang.: Eng, Fre.   1987

Umino, Hiroshi

Audience

Contemporary influences on Japanese theatre and its audience. Japan: Tokyo. 1960-1986. Lang.: Jap.   285

Uncle Vanya

SEE

Diadia Vania.

Under Coyote's Eye?

Plays/librettos/scripts

New Canadian drama: non-realistic, anti-naturalistic. Canada. 1983-1984. Lang.: Eng.   2482

Under Milkwood

Performance/production

Collection of newspaper reviews by London theatre critics. UK-England: London. 1986. Lang.: Eng.   2072

Under the Skin

Basic theatrical documents

Publication of two playtexts by Betty Lambert. Canada. 1987. Lang.: Eng.   1547

Under the Web

Performance/production

Collection of newspaper reviews by London theatre critics. UK-England: London. 1987. Lang.: Eng.   2259

Undivine Comedy, The

SEE

Ne-boska komedia.

Unga Atalante (Gothenburg)

Performance/production

Rubicon's choreography of *Allting rasar inför en naken skuldra (Everything Gives Way to a Naked Shoulder)*. Sweden: Gothenburg. 1987. Lang.: Swe.   1471

Ungurjano, I.
Performance/production
Interview with director I. Ungurjanu. USSR. 1980-1987. Lang.: Rus.
2393

Union Square Theatre (New York, NY)
Performance spaces
Histories of Wallack's Theatre and the Union Square Theatre. USA: New York, NY. 1850-1889. Lang.: Eng.
1676

United Scenic Artists (USA)
Design/technology
Merger of United Scenic Artists locals into a national union. USA. 1987. Lang.: Eng.
403

Effort to find union representation for theatrical sound designers. USA. 1985-1987. Lang.: Eng.
469

United States Institute for Theatre Technology (USITT)
Design/technology
Dimmer standards developed by the United States Institute for Theatre Technology. USA. 1987. Lang.: Eng.
384

1987 USITT convention. USA: Minneapolis/St. Paul, MN. 1987. Lang.: Eng.
446

Dimmer standards developed by the United States Institute for Theatre Technology. USA. 1986. Lang.: Eng.
458

USITT standards for dimmers and controllers. USA. 1987. Lang.: Eng.
468

Institutions
United States Institute for Theatre Technology and its future. USA. 1986. Lang.: Eng.
588

1987 USITT conference. USA: Minneapolis, MN. 1987. Lang.: Eng.
603

Performance spaces
Performance spaces and audience-performer relationship. France. Germany, West. 1875-1987. Lang.: Eng.
633

United States Opera Company (Chicago, IL)
Institutions
The beginnings and failure of the United States Opera Company. USA: Chicago, IL. 1946-1947. Lang.: Eng.
3731

United Vaudeville Circuit
Institutions
Sherman H. Dudley and the Black vaudeville circuit. USA: Indianapolis, IN, Washington, DC. 1820-1922. Lang.: Eng.
3382

Unity Theatre (Bengal)
Performance/production
Review of International Brecht Festival. China, People's Republic of: Hong Kong. 1986. Lang.: Dut.
759

Universal Theatre Society
Institutions
Evolution of the International Theatre Institute and its relations with UNESCO. 1927-1985. Lang.: Fre.
501

Unwin, Stephen
Performance/production
Collection of newspaper reviews by London theatre critics. UK-England: London. 1987. Lang.: Eng.
2188

Plays/librettos/scripts
Actress Tilda Swinter talks about her performance as a male. UK-England. 1987. Lang.: Eng.
2824

Uotinen, Jorma
Performance/production
The 4th International Theatre Conference: includes list of participants and their contributions. Poland: Warsaw. 1986. Lang.: Eng, Fre.
873

Up on the Roof
Performance/production
Collection of newspaper reviews by London theatre critics. UK-England: London. 1987. Lang.: Eng.
2205

Collection of newspaper reviews by London theatre critics. UK-England: London. 1987. Lang.: Eng.
2240

Upside Down at the Bottom of the World
Performance/production
Collection of newspaper reviews by London theatre critics. UK-England: London. 1987. Lang.: Eng.
2220

Upsy-Daisy, We Are Alive
SEE
Hoppla, wir leben!.

Uptown Theatre (Kansas City, MO)
Performance spaces
Many uses of the Uptown Theatre. USA: Kansas City, MO. 1926-1987. Lang.: Eng.
3143

Ureña, Pedro Henrique
Theory/criticism
Myth in the plays of the Dominican Republic. Dominican Republic. 1987. Lang.: Spa.
3026

Uri muri (Gentlemen's Spree)
Performance/production
László Bagossy directs Macbeth, Tamás Jordán directs Zsigmond Móricz's Uri muri (Gentlemen's Spree) at Pécs Summer Theatre. Hungary: Pécs. 1987. Lang.: Hun.
1864

Uri muri (Gentlemen's Spree) by Zsigmond Móricz staged by Mátyás Giricz at Jókai Theatre. Hungary: Békéscsaba. 1986. Lang.: Hun.
1877

Urrutia, Elena
Plays/librettos/scripts
Archetypal nature of title character in Felipe Angeles by Elena Garro. Mexico. 1978. Lang.: Spa.
2696

Urtecho, Coronel
Plays/librettos/scripts
Linguistic absurdism in El Chinfónia burguesa (The Bourgeois Chinfonia). Nicaragua. 1987. Lang.: Spa.
2703

Usher, Simon
Performance/production
Collection of newspaper reviews by London theatre critics. UK-England: London. 1987. Lang.: Eng.
2180

Collection of newspaper reviews by London theatre critics. UK-England: London. 1987. Lang.: Eng.
2275

Usigli, Rodolfo
Plays/librettos/scripts
Plays by Gorostiza, Usigli and Novo on Spanish conquest of Mexico. Mexico. 1958-1961. Lang.: Eng.
2701

Utopia Limited
Institutions
Summary of proceedings from a Gilbert and Sullivan symposium. Canada: Toronto, ON. 1987. Lang.: Eng.
3954

Uyama, Hitoshi
Performance/production
New Tokyo productions. Japan: Tokyo. 1987. Lang.: Jap.
1954

Space and sign in various Tokyo productions. Japan: Tokyo. 1987. Lang.: Jap.
1959

Unsuitable choice of plays for Tokyo performances. Japan: Tokyo. 1987. Lang.: Jap.
1965

Uys, Pieter-Dirk
Plays/librettos/scripts
Characterization in Pieter-Dirk Uys' Appassionata. South Africa, Republic of. 1987. Lang.: Eng.
2724

Užvij, N.N.
Performance/production
Ukrainian actor N.N. Užvij. USSR. 1898-1987. Lang.: Rus.
1027

Vacationists, The
SEE
Dačniki.

Vaccaro, John
Performance/production
Life and works of playwright, director, designer Charles Ludlam. USA: New York, NY. 1967-1987. Lang.: Eng.
952

Vachtangov, Jevgenij Bogrationovič
Institutions
Creation and history of the HaBimah Theatre. USSR: Moscow. Israel: Tel Aviv. 1913-1955. Lang.: Heb.
623

Performance/production
Acting style of Vachtangov. USSR. Canada. 1922-1987. Lang.: Eng.
1009

Michajl Čechov's life and work: a descriptive chronology. Russia: Moscow. 1901-1980. Lang.: Eng.
2002

Development of the Stanislavskij Acting System. Russia: Moscow. 1906-1938. Lang.: Eng.
2003

Reconstruction of The Dybbuk as directed by Vachtangov with HaBimah. USSR: Moscow. 1922. Lang.: Hun.
2399

Vakhtangov Theatre
SEE
Teat'r im. Je. Vachtangova.

Valadié, Dominique
Performance/production
Teamwork concept of directing. France. 1987. Lang.: Fre.
789

Velz, John W.
    Research/historiography
        Critical history of *Julius Caesar*. England. 1599-1987. Lang.: Eng.
        1299

Venceslas
    Performance/production
        Cast lists for some early London operas. England: London. 1712-1717. Lang.: Eng.
        3761

Vendégség (Host and the Guest, The)
    Performance/production
        Vendégség (The Host and the Guest) staged by János Taub at Játékszín. Hungary: Budapest. 1986. Lang.: Hun.
        1829
        Premiere of Spiró's *Csirkefej (Chickenhead)* and Páskándi's *Vendégség (The Host and the Guest)*. Hungary: Budapest. 1986. Lang.: Hun.
        1885

Venice Preserv'd
    Plays/librettos/scripts
        Venice Preserv'd: impact of Betterton's acting style on Otway. England. 1675-1683. Lang.: Eng.
        2527

Verdi Archive, New York University
    Reference materials
        Description of the Verdi Archive at New York University. USA: New York, NY. Italy: Milan. 1976. Lang.: Eng.
        3937

Verdi, Giuseppe
    Performance/production
        Reviews of *Rigoletto*, Lloyd Webber's *Requiem*, *Les Misérables* and the Hungarian Mass of the Tolcsvays. Hungary: Szeged. 1987. Lang.: Hun.
        3400
        Catholic elements in two treatments of *Don Carlos* by Verdi. Europe. 1986-1987. Lang.: Swe.
        3765
        Review of performances at an assembly of opera ensembles. Hungary: Szeged. 1987. Lang.: Hun.
        3796
        On a performance of Verdi's *Nabucco*. Italy: Sant' Agate. 1987. Lang.: Swe.
        3804
        Career of singer Plácido Domingo. Mexico. 1941-1987. Lang.: Eng.
        3812
        Review of *Otello* at the Royal Opera House. UK-England: London. 1987. Lang.: Eng.
        3831
        Background on Lyric Opera radio broadcast performances. USA: Chicago, IL. 1987. Lang.: Eng.
        3832
        Background on San Francisco opera radio broadcasts. USA: San Francisco, CA. 1987. Lang.: Eng.
        3833
        Background on Opera Company of Philadelphia telecast, *Un Ballo in Maschera*. USA: Philadelphia, PA. 1987. Lang.: Eng.
        3834
        Background on Metropolitan radio broadcast performances. USA: New York, NY. 1987. Lang.: Eng.
        3837
        Background on Metropolitan radio broadcast performances. USA: New York, NY. 1987. Lang.: Eng.
        3838
    Plays/librettos/scripts
        Making of Verdi's *Otello*. Italy: Milan. 1862-1879. Lang.: Eng. 3917
        Analysis of the plot of Verdi's opera *Il Trovatore*. Italy. 1983. Lang.: Eng.
        3921
        Analysis and success of Boito's libretto for Verdi's opera *Falstaff*. Italy. 1893. Lang.: Eng.
        3923
        Characters and political themes in Verdi's *Don Carlos*. Italy: Milan. 1867. Lang.: Eng.
        3924
        Creating modern critical edition of score of Verdi's *Nabucco*. Italy: Milan. 1987. Lang.: Eng.
        3925
        Impact of Giuseppina Strepponi Verdi on her husband's creativity. Italy: Milan. 1836-1901. Lang.: Eng.
        3927
    Reference materials
        Description of the Verdi Archive at New York University. USA: New York, NY. Italy: Milan. 1976. Lang.: Eng.
        3937

Verdict, The
    SEE
        Veredicto, El.

Verebes, István
    Performance/production
        Productions of plays by László Márton, Tamás Jordán and Ferenc Kulin at Radnóti Miklós Theatre. Hungary: Budapest. 1987. Lang.: Hun.
        1887
        Dezső Szomary's *Szabóky Zsigmond Rafael (Zsigmond Rafael Szabóky)* staged by István Verebes at Játékszín (Budapest). Hungary: Budapest. 1986. Lang.: Hun.
        1905

László Márton's *Lepkék a kalapon (Butterflies on Your Hat)* directed by István Verebes at Radnóti Miklós Theatre. Hungary: Budapest. 1987. Lang.: Hun.
        1923

Vergani, Vera
    Performance/production
        Collection of theatre reviews by J.M. de Sagarra. Spain-Catalonia: Barcelona. 1922-1927. Lang.: Cat.
        885

Verkommenes Ufer Medeamaterial Landschaft mit Argonauten (Deserted Shore Material for Medea Landscape with Argonauts)
    Plays/librettos/scripts
        Brecht's influence on technique and style of playwright Heiner Müller. Germany, East. 1940-1984. Lang.: Eng.
        2605

Verlorene Paradies, Das (Paradise Lost)
    Plays/librettos/scripts
        Life and operatic works of composer Krzysztof Penderecki. Poland. 1969-1987. Lang.: Ger.
        3929

Verma, Jatinder
    Performance/production
        Collection of newspaper reviews by London theatre critics. UK-England: London. 1986. Lang.: Eng.
        2038
        Collection of newspaper reviews by London theatre critics. UK-England: London. 1986. Lang.: Eng.
        2143
        Collection of newspaper reviews by London theatre critics. UK-England: London. 1987. Lang.: Eng.
        2175
        Collection of newspaper reviews by London theatre critics. UK-England: London. 1987. Lang.: Eng.
        2191
        Collection of newspaper reviews by London theatre critics. UK-England: London. 1987. Lang.: Eng.
        2230
        Collection of newspaper reviews by London theatre critics. UK-England: London. 1987. Lang.: Eng.
        2249

Vérnász
    Performance/production
        Review of productions at opera ensembles meeting. Hungary: Szeged. 1987. Lang.: Hun.
        3792

Vernon, Timothy
    Institutions
        Current strength of opera in Canada. Canada. 1987. Lang.: Eng.
        3725

Versace, Gianni
    Design/technology
        Costume designs of couturier Gianni Versace. Italy. 1982-1987. Lang.: Ita.
        3697

Verurteilung des Lukullus, Die (Condemnation of Lucullus, The)
    Performance/production
        Documentation of performance of *Die Verurteilung des Lukullus (The Condemnation of Lucullus)* by Bertolt Brecht and Paul Dessau, staged by Ruth Berghaus. Germany, East: Berlin, East. 1983. Lang.: Ger.
        3785

Vespers
    Performance/production
        Collection of newspaper reviews by London theatre critics. UK-England: London. 1987. Lang.: Eng.
        2254

Vestire gli ignudi (Naked)
    Performance/production
        Collection of newspaper reviews by London theatre critics. UK-England: London. 1987. Lang.: Eng.
        2257

Vestris, Madame
    Performance/production
        Transvestite roles in extravaganzas of J.R. Planché and Mme. Vestris. UK-England: London. 1830-1870. Lang.: Eng.
        3268

Vian, Boris
    Performance/production
        Anouilh's *Eurydice*, Vian's *Tête de Méduse (Medusa Head)* at National Theatre of Miskolc. Hungary: Miskolc. 1987. Lang.: Hun.
        1888

Vicenç Garcia, Francesc
    Basic theatrical documents
        Analysis and edition of *Comèdia famosa de la gloriosa Verge i Màrtir Santa Bàrbara*, by F. Vicenç Garcia. Spain-Catalonia. 1581-1623. Lang.: Cat.
        1574

Victims of Duty
    SEE
        Victimes du devoir.

Victor, ou les enfants au pouvoir (Victor, or the Children in Power)

Performance/production

Vitrac's *Victor, ou les enfants au pouvoir (Victor, or the Children in Power)* directed by István Szőke as *Viktor, avagy a gyermekuralom.* Hungary: Pécs. 1987. Lang.: Hun. 1898

Plays/librettos/scripts

Playwright Roger Vitrac's critiques of bourgeois family life. France. 1922-1928. Lang.: Eng. 2584

Victoria Palace Theatre (London)

Performance/production

Collection of newspaper reviews by London theatre critics. UK-England: London. 1986. Lang.: Eng. 2124

Collection of newspaper reviews by London theatre critics. UK-England: London. 1987. Lang.: Eng. 2187

Victoria Station

Plays/librettos/scripts

Analysis of Harold Pinter's *Victoria Station.* UK-England. 1959-1982. Lang.: Eng. 2761

Victoria—A Most Unusual Woman

Performance/production

Collection of newspaper reviews by London theatre critics. UK-England: London. 1987. Lang.: Eng. 2216

Victorian theatre

SEE ALSO

Geographical-Chronological Index under England 1837-1901.

Performance/production

Transvestite roles in extravaganzas of J.R. Planché and Mme. Vestris. UK-England: London. 1830-1870. Lang.: Eng. 3268

Plays/librettos/scripts

Study of plays by Henry Arthur Jones. UK-England: London. 1882-1900. Lang.: Eng. 2790

Relation to other fields

Documentation on prostitution at the Empire theatre. UK-England: London. 1890. Lang.: Eng. 1259

Vida es sueño, La (Life Is a Dream)

Institutions

The Stanisław Ignacy Witkiewicz Theatre. Poland: Zakopane. 1982-1986. Lang.: Eng, Fre. 1628

Performance/production

The 17th Warsaw theatre conference. Poland: Warsaw. 1987. Lang.: Eng, Fre. 872

La vida es sueño (Life Is a Dream) directed by Miklós Szinetár at Radnóti Miklós Theatre under the title *Az élet álom.* Hungary: Budapest. 1986. Lang.: Hun. 1846

Calderón's *La vida es sueño (Life Is a Dream)* staged by Miklós Szinetár under the title *Az élet álom.* Hungary: Budapest. 1987. Lang.: Hun. 1911

Theory/criticism

Critic Walter Benjamin's comparison of representation in Spanish baroque theatre and German plays. Germany. 1916-1982. Lang.: Eng. 3041

Vidal Alcover, Jaume

Performance/production

Collection of theatre reviews by Xavier Fàbregas. Spain-Catalonia. 1969-1972. Lang.: Cat. 2010

Vidám Szinpad (Budapest)

Performance/production

István Kazán directs *Fleur de cactus (Cactus Flower)* at Vidám Színpad as *A kaktusz virága.* Hungary: Budapest. 1987. Lang.: Hun. 3629

Vidám Szinpad (Budapest)

Performance/production

Evaluation of the season's productions of Kis Szinház and its chamber theatre, the Vidám Szinpad. Hungary: Budapest. 1987. Lang.: Hun. 806

Video forms

SEE ALSO

Classed Entries under MEDIA—Video forms.

Administration

Interview with Hans Kemna, casting director. Netherlands. 1987. Lang.: Dut. 34

Copyright disputes over simultaneous distribution of cable broadcasts. Netherlands. 1981-1987. Lang.: Eng. 35

Sophisticated Ladies taped for cable television amid controversy. USA: New York, NY. 1982. Lang.: Eng. 112

Contract for videotaping of theatre production for cable TV distribution. USA: New York, NY. 1982. Lang.: Eng. 114

Laws governing music and performance piracy. USA: New York, NY. 1954-1982. Lang.: Eng. 162

Court ruling protecting the copyright of audio-visual works. USA: New York, NY. 1976-1982. Lang.: Eng. 165

Influence of TV ads on success of Broadway plays. USA: New York, NY. 1984-1987. Lang.: Eng. 179

Historical look at the Copyright Act. USA. 1984. Lang.: Eng. 206

Legislative remedies for home video recordings of copyrighted works. USA: Los Angeles, CA. 1980-1982. Lang.: Eng. 224

Problems associated with the deregulation of cable television. USA: New York, NY. 1934-1982. Lang.: Eng. 233

Creating human voices and images with digital, holographic techniques; actors' conference. USA: New York, NY. Israel: Tel-Aviv. 1987. Lang.: Eng. 3083

Introduction to articles on satellite transmission pirating. USA. 1976-1987. Lang.: Eng. 3084

Enforcing restrictions on blacked-out sports events. USA. 1950-1987. Lang.: Eng. 3090

Recommended changes to copyright law. USA. 1987. Lang.: Eng. 3191

Filming Wagner's *Der Ring des Nibelungen* at Bayreuth. Germany, West: Bayreuth. Germany, West: Munich. 1980. Lang.: Eng. 3680

Audience

The vocal versus the visual aspects of opera. Europe. 1781-1983. Lang.: Eng. 3690

Basic theatrical documents

Review of video productions of *Tosca* and *Dialogues des Carmélites.* Italy: Verona. Australia: Sydney. 1987. Lang.: Eng. 3692

Design/technology

Multimedia experts discuss the creation of special effects. USA. 1987. Lang.: Eng. 422

Institutions

Second City improvisational comedy troupe. USA: Chicago, IL. Canada: Toronto, ON. 1959-1987. Lang.: Eng. 605

History of Chessé Marionettes. USA. 1927-1987. Lang.: Eng. 4000

Performance spaces

Telecast of Donizetti's *Lucia di Lammermoor* into a large performing area. Switzerland: Basel. 1986. Lang.: Fre, Ger. 3737

Performance/production

West Coast artists explore audiovisual effects. USA. 1987. Lang.: Eng. 969

Recent productions of Strindberg plays in Sweden and elsewhere. Sweden. 1984-1986. Lang.: Swe. 2017

Analysis of art of television and comparison to live theatre. USA. 1950-1987. Lang.: Eng. 3194

Popular account of comic entertainers. Europe. North America. Australia. 480 B.C.-1986 A.D. Lang.: Eng. 3256

Background on Opera Company of Philadelphia telecast, *Un Ballo in Maschera.* USA: Philadelphia, PA. 1987. Lang.: Eng. 3834

Background on Metropolitan telecast performances. USA: New York, NY. 1987. Lang.: Eng. 3839

Plays/librettos/scripts

New Afrikaans drama and playwrights. South Africa, Republic of. 1985-1986. Lang.: Afr. 1155

Two forms of adaptations of Shakespeare for other media. Europe. USA. 1899-1987. Lang.: Eng. 3097

Successful film versions of Shakespeare's *King Lear.* USA. UK-England. USSR. 1916-1983. Lang.: Eng. 3099

Reference materials

New Italian productions in all areas. Italy. 1985-1986. Lang.: Ita. 1204

Relation to other fields

Children's interaction with theatre as compared to television. USA. 1964. Lang.: Eng. 1277

Theatrical elements in American politics. USA. 1967-1987. Lang.: Eng. 3102

Relations to other fields

Brecht's theories on the media's negative impact on the activity and politics of the public. Germany, East: Berlin, East. 1950. Lang.: Eng. 3197

Videographies

Performance/production

International coverage of film adaptations of Shakespeare. 1899-1987. Lang.: Eng. 3148

Reference materials

Theatre on video. Europe. 1987. Lang.: Ita. 1200

Virág, Csaba

Performance spaces

Reprinted interview with Nemzeti Szinház architect Csaba Virág.
Hungary: Budapest. 1966. Lang.: Hun.   646

Virgil, Publius Maro

Plays/librettos/scripts

Relationship of the *Aeneid* to Shakespeare's *The Tempest*. England:
London. 1611. Lang.: Eng.   2561

Visconti, Luchino

Performance/production

Biography of director Luchino Visconti. Italy. 1906-1976. Lang.: Ita.
                                                        3158

Biography of film director Luchino Visconti. Italy. 1906-1976. Lang.:
Ita.   3159

Vision of Love Revealed in Sleep, A

Performance/production

Collection of newspaper reviews by London theatre critics. UK-
England: London. 1987. Lang.: Eng.   2222

Visions

SEE

Látomások.

Visit, The

SEE

Besuch der alten Dame, Der.

Visitatio sepulchri

Plays/librettos/scripts

Theories of staging the *visitatio sepulchri*. Germany. France. 900-
1600. Lang.: Eng.   2599

Research/historiography

Research methods on origins and tradition of liturgical drama.
Germany. 1000-1400. Lang.: Ita.   3010

Višněvyj sad (Cherry Orchard, The)

Performance/production

Nontraditional casting in a production of *The Cherry Orchard*. USA:
San Francisco, CA. 1986. Lang.: Eng.   928

Life and work of Anatolij Efros. USSR: Moscow. 1983-1987. Lang.:
Eng.   1038

Ottó Adám directs Anton Pavlovič Čechov's *Višněvyj sad (The
Cherry Orchard)* at Madách Theatre under the title *Cseresznyéskert*.
Hungary: Budapest. 1987. Lang.: Hun.   1805

Interview with Frans Strijards, playwright and director. Netherlands.
1987. Lang.: Dut.   1979

Autobiography of film and stage director Peter Brook. UK-England.
1946-1987. Lang.: Eng.   2281

Plays/librettos/scripts

Višněvyj sad (The Cherry Orchard): Čechov's artistry. USSR. 1904.
Lang.: Rus.   2951

Visser, Colin

Institutions

Brecht was the theme of the 1986 International Theatre Festival and
Conference. Canada: Toronto, ON. 1986. Lang.: Fre.   1610

Vita che ti diedi, La (Life I Gave You, The)

Plays/librettos/scripts

Comparison between *La vita che ti diedi (The Life I Gave You)* by
Pirandello and *Lo spirito della morte (The Spirit of Death)* by Rosso
di San Secondo. Italy. 1923-1931. Lang.: Ita.   2666

Vitez, Antoine

Performance/production

Directing as guiding actors, not imposing a subjective interpretation.
France. 1987. Lang.: Fre.   784

Directing as creation of a dimension that enhances the actor's desire.
France. 1987. Lang.: Fre.   785

Direction as unveiling: Antoine Vitez. France. 1987. Lang.: Fre.   787

Staging as a form of translation. France. 1987. Lang.: Fre.   788

Teamwork concept of directing. France. 1987. Lang.: Fre.   789

Directing should be judged by the work of great directors. France.
1987. Lang.: Fre.   1763

Luca Ronconi's view of directing. France. Italy. 1987. Lang.: Fre.
                                                        1765

Antoine Vitez directs *Le soulier de satin (The Satin Slipper)* by Paul
Claudel, Festival of Avignon. France: Avignon. 1987. Lang.: Fre.
                                                        1767

Relation to other fields

Experimental theatre course, Assoc. Internationale pour la Sémiologie
du Spectacle. Belgium: Brussels. France: Paris. Denmark: Odense.
1983-1985. Lang.: Fre.   1219

Vitrac, Roger

Performance/production

Vitrac's *Victor, ou les enfants au pouvoir (Victor, or the Children in
Power)* directed by István Szőke as *Viktor, avagy a gyermekuralom*.
Hungary: Pécs. 1987. Lang.: Hun.   1898

István Szőke directs *Victor ou les enfants au pouvoir (Victor, or The
Children in Power)* by Roger Vitrac at National Theatre. Hungary:
Pécs. 1987. Lang.: Hun.   1904

Plays/librettos/scripts

Playwright Roger Vitrac's critiques of bourgeois family life. France.
1922-1928. Lang.: Eng.   2584

Vivian Beaumont Theatre (New York, NY)

Design/technology

Tony Walton's set designs at the Vivian Beaumont Theatre. USA:
New York, NY. 1986-1987. Lang.: Eng.   465

Lighting review for *Anything Goes* at the Vivian Beaumont Theatre.
USA: New York, NY. 1987. Lang.: Eng.   3623

Performance/production

Collection of newspaper reviews by New York theatre critics. USA:
New York, NY. 1987. Lang.: Eng.   2311

Collection of newspaper reviews by New York theatre critics. USA:
New York, NY. 1987. Lang.: Eng.   2317

Collection of newspaper reviews by New York theatre critics. USA:
New York, NY. 1987. Lang.: Eng.   2322

Collection of newspaper reviews by New York theatre critics. USA:
New York, NY. 1987. Lang.: Eng.   2326

Vivian, Nick

Performance/production

Collection of newspaper reviews by London theatre critics. UK-
England: London. 1987. Lang.: Eng.   2276

Vivir y Bebir (To Live and To Drink)

Plays/librettos/scripts

Interview with playwright Hugo Hiriart. Mexico: Mexico City. 1987.
Lang.: Spa.   1151

Vivisekce (Vivisection)

Performance/production

Antonín Máša directs his play *Vivisekce (Vivisection)* at Laterna
magika. Czechoslovakia: Prague. 1987. Lang.: Cze.   767

Vladi, Marina

Performance/production

Actress Marina Vladi recalls Vladimir Vysockij. USSR. 1938-1980.
Lang.: Rus.   1081

Vogel, Eric

Design/technology

Account of exhibition of Eric Vogel's scene and costume designs.
Hungary: Budapest. 1927-1987. Lang.: Hun.   335

An exhibition at the Pest Redoute Gallery of the set and costume
designs of Eric Vogel. Hungary. 1927-1987. Lang.: Hun. 3242

Voice

Performance/production

Evaluation of actor Anders Ek. Sweden. 1916-1979. Lang.: Swe.
                                                        2012

Actress Ann Casson on proper line speaking in Shaw. UK-England.
1924-1981. Lang.: Eng.   2305

Vocal training and performance in China. China, People's Republic
of: Shanghai. 1949-1987. Lang.: Chi.   3529

Training

Basic theatrical techniques for secondary school. Belgium. 1987.
Lang.: Fre.   1378

Vocal training in Soviet dramatic education. USSR. 1987. Lang.:
Rus.   1392

Orlanda Cook on her work as voice teacher. Sweden. 1980-1987.
Lang.: Swe.   3080

Interviews with singing teachers in New York City. USA: New
York, NY. 1987. Lang.: Eng.   3952

Voice of McConnell, The

Plays/librettos/scripts

Analysis of the plays and songs of Irish-American musical theatre
star Chauncey Olcott. USA. 1893-1918. Lang.: Eng.   3671

Volksbühne (East Berlin)

Performance/production

Biography of comic actress Marianne Wünscher. Germany, East:
Berlin, East. 1930-1986. Lang.: Ger.   1780

Mária Sulyok as Mrs. Orbán in Örkény's *Macskajáték (Catsplay)*.
Germany, East: Berlin, East. Hungary. 1980-1987. Lang.: Hun. 1786

Volksbühne (East Berlin) — cont'd

Portrait of actress Marianne Wünscher. Germany, East: Berlin, East.
1948-1987. Lang.: Ger.   1787

Relation to other fields
Debate over proletarian art among Social Democrats. Germany:
Berlin. 1910-1912. Lang.: Ger.   1238

Volodin, Aleksandr Mojsejěvič
Performance/production
Plays of A.M. Volodin on stage and screen. USSR: Moscow,
Leningrad. 1950-1987. Lang.: Rus.   2401

Volpone
Performance/production
Collection of newspaper reviews by London theatre critics. UK-
England: London. 1987. Lang.: Eng.   2201

Voltaire (Arouet, François-Marie)
Plays/librettos/scripts
Techniques, themes, characters and dramaturgy of Voltaire. France.
1718-1778. Lang.: Eng.   2590

Theory/criticism
Catalan translation of Lessing's *Hamburgische Dramaturgie*.
Germany: Hamburg. 1767-1769. Lang.: Cat.   3043

Volunteer Firemen
Performance/production
Five short plays by Géza Páskándi at SUNY Binghamton. Hungary.
USA: Binghamton, NY. 1987. Lang.: Eng.   1813

Volunteer Lawyers for the Arts (New York, NY)
Administration
History of Volunteer Lawyers for the Arts. USA: New York, NY.
1969-1982. Lang.: Eng.   146

Volunteers
Plays/librettos/scripts
Metaphor of archaeology in Friel's *Volunteers*, poems of Heaney.
Ireland: Dublin. UK-Ireland. 1975. Lang.: Eng.   2651

Vor Sonnenaufgang (Before Sunrise)
Plays/librettos/scripts
Comparison of works by Hauptmann and Wilbrandt. Germany:
Berlin. Austria: Vienna. 1889-1987. Lang.: Eng.   2593

Vormärz
Plays/librettos/scripts
History of 19th-century German literature, including drama and
theatre. Germany. Austria. 1830-1900. Lang.: Ger.   2591

Vörös postakocsi, A (Red Mail Coach, The)
Performance/production
Reviews: *A vörös postakocsi (The Red Mail Coach)* by Gyula Krúdy,
staged by Dezső Kapás and *Az atyai ház (The Paternal Roof)* by
Zsigmond Remenyik, staged by Péter Lener. Hungary: Veszprém,
Nyíregyháza. 1986. Lang.: Hun.   1821

Vörösmarty, Mihály
Performance/production
Mihály Vörösmarty's 'fairy-play' *Csongor and Tünde* directed by
Béla Merő at Hevesi Sándor Színház. Hungary: Zalaegerszeg. 1987.
Lang.: Hun.   1926

Vos, Erik
Performance/production
Postwar Dutch theatre: growth of small theatre groups. Netherlands.
1975-1985. Lang.: Dut.   1982

Voskovec, Jiří
Performance/production
Miklós Szurdi directs *Kat a blázen (The Hangman and the Madman)*
by Jan Werick and Jiří Voskovec, songs by Jaroslav Jezek, at
Radnóti Miklós Szinpad as *Hóhér és Bolond*. Hungary: Budapest.
1986. Lang.: Hun.   1825

Voyage à Paimpol (Journey to Paimpol)
Performance/production
Dorothée Letessier's comments on the adaptation and staging of her
novel *Voyage à Paimpol (Journey to Paimpol)*. Belgium: Liège. 1986.
Lang.: Fre.   1686

Voyage Home, The
Performance/production
Collection of newspaper reviews by London theatre critics. UK-
England: London. 1986. Lang.: Eng.   2092

Voysey Inheritance, The
Plays/librettos/scripts
Influences on *The Voysey Inheritance* by Granville Barker. UK-
England. 1600-1938. Lang.: Eng.   2820

Vrai monde, Le (Real World, The)
Plays/librettos/scripts
The role of the father-figure in recent plays from Quebec. Canada:
Quebec. 1980-1987. Lang.: Fre.   2465

Vuka
Performance/production
Review of *Vuka* by Matsemela Manaka. South Africa, Republic of:
Soweto. 1976-1987. Lang.: Eng.   2006

Vychodil, Ladislav
Design/technology
Czech scenographers Josef Svoboda and Ladislav Vychodil.
Czechoslovakia: Prague. USA. 1950-1987. Lang.: Eng.   309

Vysockij, Vladimir
Performance/production
Collection of materials on actor-poet Vladimir Vysockij. USSR. 1972-
1987. Lang.: Rus.   985

Actor Vladimir Vysockij remembered. USSR: Moscow. 1938-1980.
Lang.: Rus.   999

Actress Alla Demidova recalls Vladimir Vysockij. USSR: Moscow.
1938-1980. Lang.: Rus.   1008

Actor Vladimir Vysockij of Taganka Theatre. USSR: Moscow. 1938-
1980. Lang.: Rus.   1023

Recollections of actor Vladimir Vysockij. USSR: Moscow. 1938-1980.
Lang.: Rus.   1066

Actress Marina Vladi recalls Vladimir Vysockij. USSR. 1938-1980.
Lang.: Rus.   1081

Wada, Shusaku
Plays/librettos/scripts
Plays about child suicide in Japan. Japan: Tokyo. 1986. Lang.: Jap.
     2683

Wade, Kevin
Performance/production
Collection of newspaper reviews by London theatre critics. UK-
England: London. 1986. Lang.: Eng.   2135

Wagner, Cosima
Performance/production
Production history of *Der Ring des Nibelungen*. Germany: Bayreuth.
Italy: Milan. USA: New York, NY. 1876-1987. Lang.: Eng.   3775

Plays/librettos/scripts
Wagner's obsession with Jews and Judaism. Germany. 1813-1882.
Lang.: Eng.   3905

Wagner, Richard
Administration
Filming Wagner's *Der Ring des Nibelungen* at Bayreuth. Germany,
West: Bayreuth. Germany, West: Munich. 1980. Lang.: Eng.   3680

Design/technology
Designer Adolphe Appia's concepts and scenery for Wagner's
operas. Germany. Switzerland. 1873-1928. Lang.: Eng.   3694

Institutions
Correspondence of Richard Wagner and Matteo Salvi on the staging
of *Tristan und Isolde*. Austria: Vienna. 1861-1967. Lang.: Ger.   3710

Performance/production
Metropolitan/Deutsche Grammophon recording, Wagner's *Ring*,
conducted by James Levine. USA: New York, NY. 1987. Lang.:
Eng.   3114

The Heldentenor in Wagnerian opera. Europe. North America. 1987.
Lang.: Eng.   3770

Production history of *Der Ring des Nibelungen*. Germany: Bayreuth.
Italy: Milan. USA: New York, NY. 1876-1987. Lang.: Eng.   3775

Reprint of Richard Wagner's views on *bel canto*, Bellini. Italy. 1837.
Lang.: Swe.   3799

Review of Wagner's *Der Fliegende Holländer* at the Natal
Playhouse. South Africa, Republic of: Durban. 1987. Lang.: Eng.
     3815

Development of Wagner's *Die Meistersinger von Nürnberg*. South
Africa, Republic of: Cape Town. Germany, West: Munich. 1868-
1987. Lang.: Eng.   3816

Background on Lyric Opera radio broadcast performances. USA:
Chicago, IL. 1987. Lang.: Eng.   3832

Background on Metropolitan radio broadcast performances. USA:
New York, NY. 1987. Lang.: Eng.   3837

Profile of soprano Jeannine Altmeyer. USA: New York, NY. 1950-
1987. Lang.: Eng.   3853

Plays/librettos/scripts
Musical, personal relationship of Saint-Saëns and Wagner. France:
Paris. 1859-1916. Lang.: Eng.   3902

Wagner's obsession with Jews and Judaism. Germany. 1813-1882.
Lang.: Eng.   3905

Psychological interpretations of Wagner's *Parsifal*. Germany. 1882-
1987. Lang.: Eng.   3907

Wagner, Richard — cont'd

Woman, salvation and love in operas of Richard Wagner. Germany.
1813-1883. Lang.: Eng. 3909

Analysis of Heinrich Marschner's and Peter Josef von Lindpaintner's
operas *Der Vampyr*. Germany: Leipzig, Stuttgart. 1828. Lang.: Eng.
3911

Characters in Verdi's *Otello*. Italy: Milan. 1887. Lang.: Eng. 3920

Relation to other fields
Wagnerian opera in Argentina. Argentina: Buenos Aires. 1858-1983.
Lang.: Eng. 3938

Mann, Baudelaire and Nietzsche on Wagnerian philosophy. Europe.
1860-1950. Lang.: Eng. 3939

Life of King Ludwig II, and his relationship with composer Richard
Wagner. Germany. 1864-1880. Lang.: Eng. 3942

Comparison between Wagner and Tolstoy. Russia. Germany. 1860-
1908. Lang.: Eng. 3944

Influence of Arthur Schopenhauer on Wagner's works. Switzerland.
1834-1870. Lang.: Eng. 3945

Research/historiography
Influences on Wagner's *Ring* cycle. Germany: Dresden. 1813-1883.
Lang.: Eng. 3948

Wague, George
Performance/production
Development of mime, pantomime and its related movements.
France: Paris. UK-England. USA: New York, NY. 1980-1982. Lang.:
Eng. 3223

Wailing for the Janitress
Plays/librettos/scripts
Political aspects of Hungarian absurdist drama. Hungary. 1970-1980.
Lang.: Eng. 2632

Wait 'til You See Her
Performance/production
Collection of newspaper reviews by London theatre critics. UK-
England: London. 1986. Lang.: Eng. 2148

Waiting for Godot
SEE
En attendant Godot.

Plays/librettos/scripts
Critical methodology for studying Beckett's works. UK-England.
1930-1987. Lang.: Eng. 2814

Waiting for Hannibal
Performance/production
Collection of newspaper reviews by London theatre critics. UK-
England: London. 1986. Lang.: Eng. 2127

Wajda, Andrzej
Audience
American response to Gardzienice Theatre Association. Poland:
Gardzienice. 1666-1987. Lang.: Eng. 1536

Performance/production
Experimental theatre at the Stary in three recent productions.
Poland: Cracow. 1987. Lang.: Eng. 1999

Wakefield Cycle
Plays/librettos/scripts
Medieval cycle plays as the exception rather than the norm.
England. Lang.: Eng. 2543

Walcott, Derek
Performance/production
Collection of newspaper reviews by London theatre critics. UK-
England: London. 1986. Lang.: Eng. 2160

Collection of newspaper reviews by London theatre critics. UK-
England: London. 1987. Lang.: Eng. 2277

Walcott, Roderick
Performance/production
Collection of newspaper reviews by London theatre critics. UK-
England: London. 1986. Lang.: Eng. 2160

Wale, Terry
Performance/production
Collection of newspaper reviews by London theatre critics. UK-
England: London. 1986. Lang.: Eng. 2041

Collection of newspaper reviews by London theatre critics. UK-
England: London. 1986. Lang.: Eng. 2078

Walker, Alice
Theory/criticism
Portrayals of African-Americans in media and literature. USA. 1926-
1987. Lang.: Eng. 3104

Walker, Andy
Performance/production
Collection of newspaper reviews by London theatre critics. UK-
England: London. 1986. Lang.: Eng. 2083

Collection of newspaper reviews by London theatre critics. UK-
England: London. 1987. Lang.: Eng. 2242

Walker, Collette
Performance/production
Collection of newspaper reviews by London theatre critics. UK-
England: London. 1986. Lang.: Eng. 2080

Walker, George
Institutions
Sherman H. Dudley and the Black vaudeville circuit. USA:
Indianapolis, IN, Washington, DC. 1820-1922. Lang.: Eng. 3382

Performance/production
Compositions by Debussy in their relationship to Afro-American
music. France: Paris. UK-England: London. 1893-1913. Lang.: Eng.
3384

Walker, Rob
Performance/production
Collection of newspaper reviews by London theatre critics. UK-
England: London. 1986. Lang.: Eng. 2056

Walküre, Die
Design/technology
Lighting reviews for several New York productions. USA: New
York, NY. 1987. Lang.: Eng. 474

Performance/production
Background on Metropolitan radio broadcast performances. USA:
New York, NY. 1987. Lang.: Eng. 3837

Wallace, Michelle
Theory/criticism
Portrayals of African-Americans in media and literature. USA. 1926-
1987. Lang.: Eng. 3104

Wallack's Theatre (New York, NY)
Performance spaces
Histories of Wallack's Theatre and the Union Square Theatre. USA:
New York, NY. 1850-1889. Lang.: Eng. 1676

Wallenstein
Plays/librettos/scripts
Friedrich von Schiller's late works: new conception of drama.
Germany. 1799-1805. Lang.: Eng. 2604

Waller, Fats
Performance/production
Origins of jazz, its evolution in vaudeville. USA: New Orleans, LA,
New York, NY, Chicago, IL. Lang.: Eng. 3650

Walpole, Sir Robert
Plays/librettos/scripts
Attack on Sir Robert Walpole in 18th-century adaptation of *King
Edward the Third*. England. 1691-1731. Lang.: Eng. 2505

Walsh, Des
Plays/librettos/scripts
Collective theatre projects in Newfoundland. Canada: St. John's, NF.
1987. Lang.: Eng. 2466

Walter, Froied
Performance/production
Theatrical activity at the concentration camp Theresienstadt.
Czechoslovakia: Terezín. 1938-1968. Lang.: Heb. 772

Walter, Harriet
Performance/production
Dorothy L. Sayers' *Have His Carcase, Eastender* and *Intimate
Contact* are reviewed. UK-England. 1987. Lang.: Eng. 3208

Walter, Rudolf
Institutions
Rudolf Walter's theatre, Komorní hry. Czechoslovakia: Brno. 1942-
1944. Lang.: Cze. 1613

Walters, Julie
Performance/production
Review of the BBC telecast of *The Birthday Party* by Harold Pinter.
UK-England. 1987. Lang.: Eng. 3206

Walters, Sam
Performance/production
Collection of newspaper reviews by London theatre critics. UK-
England: London. 1986. Lang.: Eng. 2061

Collection of newspaper reviews by London theatre critics. UK-
England: London. 1986. Lang.: Eng. 2158

Collection of newspaper reviews by London theatre critics. UK-
England: London. 1987. Lang.: Eng. 2181

Walters, Sam — cont'd

Collection of newspaper reviews by London theatre critics. UK-England: London. 1987. Lang.: Eng. 2190

Collection of newspaper reviews by London theatre critics. UK-England: London. 1987. Lang.: Eng. 2223

Collection of newspaper reviews by London theatre critics. UK-England. 1987. Lang.: Eng. 2261

Walton, Tony
Design/technology
Four Broadway designers discuss redesigning shows for road tours. USA. 1987. Lang.: Eng. 414

Tony Walton's set designs at the Vivian Beaumont Theatre. USA: New York, NY. 1986-1987. Lang.: Eng. 465

Performance/production
Essays on the future of the theatre. USA: New York, NY. 1970-1987. Lang.: Eng. 955

Wandering Jew, The
Performance/production
Collection of newspaper reviews by London theatre critics. UK-England: London. 1987. Lang.: Eng. 2233

Wandor, Michelene
Performance/production
Collection of newspaper reviews by London theatre critics. UK-England: London. 1987. Lang.: Eng. 2233

Wang, Guo-Wa
Plays/librettos/scripts
Shakespeare compared to writers of Chinese opera. China. 1279-1616. Lang.: Chi. 3554

Wang, Shi-Fu
Performance/production
The modernization of Chinese opera—keeping the traditional spirit. China, People's Republic of: Beijing. 1279-1986. Lang.: Chi. 3539

Wang, Wenn-Jiuann
Administration
Wang Wenn-Jiuann and the establishment of Hung Lou Theatre Company. China, People's Republic of. 1987. Lang.: Chi. 3425

War Within, A
Performance/production
Rehearsals and performance of Joseph Chaikin's *A War Within*. USA: San Francisco, CA. 1987. Lang.: Eng. 930

Ward, Charles
Performance/production
Director A.J. Antoon discusses *Sherlock's Last Case*. USA: New York, NY. 1987. Lang.: Eng. 970

Ward, Douglas Turner
Design/technology
Career of costumer, dancer, actress Judy Dearing. USA: New York, NY. Africa. 1970-1987. Lang.: Eng. 1601

Institutions
Debate among Black theatre people whether Black theatre really exists. USA. 1987. Lang.: Eng. 610

History of the Negro Ensemble Company. USA: New York, NY. 1969-1987. Lang.: Eng. 1653

Performance/production
Theatre career of photo-journalist Bert Andrews. USA: New York, NY. 1950-1987. Lang.: Eng. 2367

Plays/librettos/scripts
Characterizations of stage spaces: examples from Brecht, Pinter, Douglas Turner Ward. UK-England. USA. 1947-1987. Lang.: Eng. 2798

Interview with playwright Charles Fuller. USA: Philadelphia, PA, New York, NY. Korea, South. 1959-1987. Lang.: Eng. 2921

Ward, Genevieve
Performance/production
Carte-de-visite actors' photographs preserve acting styles. UK-England. France. USA. 1850-1920. Lang.: Eng. 916

British theatrical touring companies. UK-England. North America. Australia. 1870-1929. Lang.: Eng. 2280

Ward, Malcolm
Performance/production
Reviews of Pinter's *The Lover* and *A Slight Ache*. UK-England: London. 1987. Lang.: Eng. 901

Ward, Nial
Performance/production
Collection of newspaper reviews by London theatre critics. UK-England: London. 1987. Lang.: Eng. 2233

Ward, Nick
Performance/production
Collection of newspaper reviews by London theatre critics. UK-England: London. 1987. Lang.: Eng. 2257

Ward, Trisha
Performance/production
Collection of newspaper reviews by London theatre critics. UK-England: London. 1986. Lang.: Eng. 2133

Warehouse Theatre (London)
Performance/production
Collection of newspaper reviews by London theatre critics. UK-England: London. 1987. Lang.: Eng. 2173

Collection of newspaper reviews by London theatre critics. UK-England: London. 1987. Lang.: Eng. 2180

Collection of newspaper reviews by London theatre critics. UK-England: London. 1987. Lang.: Eng. 2202

Collection of newspaper reviews by London theatre critics. UK-England: London. 1987. Lang.: Eng. 2205

Collection of newspaper reviews by London theatre critics. UK-England: London. 1987. Lang.: Eng. 2220

Collection of newspaper reviews by London theatre critics. UK-England: London. 1987. Lang.: Eng. 2241

Collection of newspaper reviews by London theatre critics. UK-England: London. 1987. Lang.: Eng. 2246

Collection of newspaper reviews by London theatre critics. UK-England. 1987. Lang.: Eng. 2261

Warmiński, Janusz
Performance/production
Polish theatre. Poland: Warsaw, Cracow, Wrocław. 1980-1987. Lang.: Eng, Fre. 1987

Warner, Deborah
Performance/production
Collection of newspaper reviews by London theatre critics. UK-England: London. 1986. Lang.: Eng. 2166

Warner, Keith
Performance/production
Collection of newspaper reviews by London theatre critics. UK-England: London. 1987. Lang.: Eng. 2247

Warnings
Plays/librettos/scripts
Family relationships in Eugene O'Neill's early plays. USA. 1913. Lang.: Eng. 2926

Warren, Robert Penn
Theory/criticism
Keynote address at Northern California Theatre Critics Conference. USA. 1987. Lang.: Eng. 3072

Warrilow, David
Performance/production
Three actors discuss their approaches to the characters of Samuel Beckett. USA. 1987. Lang.: Eng. 2343

Waseda Doramakan (Tokyo)
Performance/production
Six plays of the Tokyo season, focus on director Betsuyaku Minoru. Japan: Tokyo. 1986. Lang.: Jap. 1966

Wassermann, Dale
Performance/production
Actors Sándor Szakácsi and Piroska Molnár in *Man of La Mancha* directed by Lászlo Bagossy. Hungary: Pécs. 1987. Lang.: Hun. 3633

Wasserstein, Wendy
Administration
Profile of Ensemble Studio Theatre. USA: New York, NY. 1987. Lang.: Eng. 232

Watanabe, Hiroko
Performance/production
Four Tokyo productions in light of ideas of Betsuyaku Minoru. Japan: Tokyo. 1987. Lang.: Jap. 1950

Discussion of four Tokyo productions. Japan: Tokyo. 1944-1987. Lang.: Jap. 1963

Six plays of the Tokyo season, focus on director Betsuyaku Minoru. Japan: Tokyo. 1986. Lang.: Jap. 1966

Plays/librettos/scripts
Contemporary Japanese plays about crime. Japan: Tokyo. 1986. Lang.: Jap. 2681

Watching
Performance/production
Collection of newspaper reviews by London theatre critics. UK-England: London. 1986. Lang.: Eng. 2090

Wilcox, Michael
Performance/production
Collection of newspaper reviews by London theatre critics. UK-England: London. 1986. Lang.: Eng. 2062

Wild Duck, The
SEE
Vildanden.

Wild Honey
SEE ALSO
Platonov.
Design/technology
Lighting reviews of several Broadway shows. USA: New York, NY. 1987. Lang.: Eng. 473
Performance/production
Patrice Chéreau and Théâtre des Amandiers create stage and film versions of Čechov's *Platonov*. France: Nanterre. 1982-1987. Lang.: Swe. 1755
Review of production and staging aspects of *Wild Honey* by Anton Čechov. UK-England: London. 1986. Lang.: Eng. 2306

Wild Oats
Plays/librettos/scripts
New findings on 18th-century Irish comic playwright John O'Keeffe. Ireland. England: London. 1767-1798. Lang.: Eng. 2643

Wilde, Oscar
Performance/production
Collection of newspaper reviews by London theatre critics. UK-England. 1987. Lang.: Eng. 2175
Collection of newspaper reviews by London theatre critics. UK-England: London. 1987. Lang.: Eng. 2248
Aubrey Beardsley's drawings of actresses: impact on society. UK-England. 1890. Lang.: Eng. 2287
Plays/librettos/scripts
Adaptation of literary works to opera. 1893-1987. Lang.: Eng. 3890
Relation to other fields
Literary figures of the Irish Literary Renaissance. Ireland. UK-Ireland. 1875-1938. Lang.: Eng. 2995

Wilde, Patrick
Performance/production
Collection of newspaper reviews by London theatre critics. UK-England: London. 1987. Lang.: Eng. 2260

Wilder, Thornton
Performance/production
Review of 1984 Shaw Festival season. Canada: Niagara-on-the-Lake, ON. 1984. Lang.: Eng. 1699

Wildfire
Performance/production
Collection of newspaper reviews by London theatre critics. UK-England: London. 1986. Lang.: Eng. 2053

Wilding, Faith
Plays/librettos/scripts
The German radio play *Hörspiel* and its history. Germany, West: Cologne. USA. 1950-1985. Lang.: Eng. 3117

Wilhelm Tell
Performance/production
August Wilhelm Iffland's productions of plays by Friedrich von Schiller. Germany: Berlin. 1796-1806. Lang.: Ger. 1773
Plays/librettos/scripts
Friedrich von Schiller's late works: new conception of drama. Germany. 1799-1805. Lang.: Eng. 2604

Wilke, Hannah
Relation to other fields
Sexuality and desire in performance. USA. 1987. Lang.: Eng. 1270

Wilkowski, Jan
Performance/production
Poland's puppet theatre. Poland: Wrocław, Białystock. Austria: Mistelbach. 1979-1987. Lang.: Eng, Fre. 4006

Wilks, William, Jr.
Administration
Theatrical season of 1723 at the Drury Lane Theatre. England: London. 1723. Lang.: Eng. 21

Wille, Bruno
Institutions
On audience societies Freie Volksbühne and Neue Freie Volksbühne. Germany: Berlin. 1889-1914. Lang.: Ger. 1616

William
Performance/production
Collection of newspaper reviews by London theatre critics. UK-England: London. 1986. Lang.: Eng. 2161

Williams, Bert
Institutions
Sherman H. Dudley and the Black vaudeville circuit. USA: Indianapolis, IN, Washington, DC. 1820-1922. Lang.: Eng. 3382
Performance/production
Compositions by Debussy in their relationship to Afro-American music. France: Paris. UK-England: London. 1893-1913. Lang.: Eng. 3384

Williams, Clifford
Performance/production
Collection of newspaper reviews by London theatre critics. UK-England: London. 1986. Lang.: Eng. 2072
Collection of newspaper reviews by London theatre critics. UK-England: London. 1986. Lang.: Eng. 2080
Collection of newspaper reviews by New York theatre critics. USA: New York, NY. 1987. Lang.: Eng. 2316

Williams, David
Performance/production
John Neville's first season as artistic director at the Stratford Festival. Canada: Stratford, ON. 1986. Lang.: Eng. 734
Shakespeare's later plays at Stratford Festival. Canada: Stratford, ON. 1986. Lang.: Eng. 751

Williams, Emlyn
Performance/production
Collection of newspaper reviews by London theatre critics. UK-England: London. 1986. Lang.: Eng. 2045

Williams, Faynia
Performance/production
Collection of newspaper reviews by London theatre critics. UK-England: London. 1987. Lang.: Eng. 2259

Williams, Hugh
Performance/production
Collection of newspaper reviews by London theatre critics. UK-England: London. 1986. Lang.: Eng. 2124

Williams, Jack Eric
Performance/production
Interview with composer Jack Eric Williams, focus on his musical *Mrs. Farmer's Daughter*. USA: New York, NY. 1987. Lang.: Eng. 3663

Williams, Kevin
Performance/production
Collection of newspaper reviews by London theatre critics. UK-England: London. 1986. Lang.: Eng. 2166

Williams, Margaret
Performance/production
Collection of newspaper reviews by London theatre critics. UK-England: London. 1986. Lang.: Eng. 2124

Williams, Nigel
Performance/production
Collection of newspaper reviews by London theatre critics. UK-England: London. 1987. Lang.: Eng. 2196

Williams, Raymond
Plays/librettos/scripts
Dramatic vs. literary interpretation of *Ett Drömspel (A Dream Play)* by August Strindberg. Sweden. 1901-1964. Lang.: Eng. 2734
Training
Proposed changes in teaching methodology to include indigenous drama. South Africa, Republic of. 1960-1987. Lang.: Eng. 1383

Williams, Richard
Performance/production
Collection of newspaper reviews by London theatre critics. UK-England: London. 1986. Lang.: Eng. 2040
Collection of newspaper reviews by London theatre critics. UK-England: London. 1987. Lang.: Eng. 2231
Collection of newspaper reviews by London theatre critics. UK-England: London. 1987. Lang.: Eng. 2232

Williams, Ron
Training
Genesis and development of various youth theatre groups. UK-Ireland. 1979-1987. Lang.: Eng. 1388

Williams, Samm-Art
Institutions
The formation of the North Carolina Black Repertory Company. USA: Winston-Salem, NC. 1979-1987. Lang.: Eng. 1666
Performance/production
The career of actor and playwright Samm-Art Williams. USA: Philadelphia, PA. 1973-1987. Lang.: Eng. 2365

Williams, Simon
Performance/production
Reviews of Pinter's *The Lover* and *A Slight Ache*. UK-England: London. 1987. Lang.: Eng. 901
Williams, Tennessee
Design/technology
Cinematographer Michael Ballhaus' work on film version of Williams' *The Glass Menagerie* directed by Paul Newman. USA. 1987. Lang.: Eng. 3139

Performance/production
Collection of newspaper reviews by London theatre critics. UK-England: London. 1986. Lang.: Eng. 2117
Collection of newspaper reviews by New York theatre critics. USA: New York, NY. 1987. Lang.: Eng. 2313
Soviet productions of five Tennessee Williams plays. USSR. 1910-1987. Lang.: Eng. 2397

Plays/librettos/scripts
One-act play: brief history and recent productions. USA. 1930-1987. Lang.: Eng. 2849
Author Christopher Hampton discusses techniques of playwriting. USA: New York, NY. UK-England: London. 1987. Lang.: Eng. 2896
Interview with actresses Elizabeth Ashley and Marian Seldes. USA: New York, NY. 1987. Lang.: Eng. 2898

Reference materials
History of pocket theatre. France: Paris. 1944-1953. Lang.: Eng. 2974

Williams, Terri
Performance/production
Theatre career of photo-journalist Bert Andrews. USA: New York, NY. 1950-1987. Lang.: Eng. 2367
Williamson, David
Performance/production
Collection of newspaper reviews by London theatre critics. UK-England: London. 1986. Lang.: Eng. 2099

Plays/librettos/scripts
Focus on the plays of David Williamson and their cultural impact. Australia. 1970-1987. Lang.: Eng. 2436
Willis, Frank
Institutions
Script editor's recollections of CBC radio dramas. Canada. 1944-1954. Lang.: Eng. 3110
Wilson, Andy
Performance/production
Collection of newspaper reviews by London theatre critics. UK-England: London. 1986. Lang.: Eng. 2083
Wilson, August
Administration
Production sharing among non-profit theatres in effort to develop new works. USA. 1987. Lang.: Eng. 255

Institutions
Current trends in American theatre. USA. 1967-1987. Lang.: Eng. 621

Performance/production
Review of August Wilson's play, *Ma Rainey's Black Bottom*. Canada: Toronto, ON. 1987. Lang.: Eng. 737
Collection of newspaper reviews by New York theatre critics. USA: New York, NY. 1987. Lang.: Eng. 2326
Interview with actor James Earl Jones. USA: New York, NY. 1953-1987. Lang.: Eng. 2340
Interview with actor and playwright Joe Seneca. USA: New York, NY, Cleveland, OH. 1957-1987. Lang.: Eng. 2364

Plays/librettos/scripts
Interview with playwright August Wilson. USA: New York, NY. 1985-1987. Lang.: Eng. 2876
Depiction of the class struggle in contemporary theatre. USA: New York, NY. 1987. Lang.: Eng. 2915
Wilson, Edward
Performance/production
Collection of newspaper reviews by London theatre critics. UK-England: London. 1986. Lang.: Eng. 2133
Wilson, John
Performance/production
Collection of newspaper reviews by London theatre critics. UK-England: London. 1986. Lang.: Eng. 2113

Wilson, Julie
Performance/production
Broadway actors who moonlight in cabaret acts. USA: New York, NY. 1962-1987. Lang.: Eng. 3291
Wilson, Lanford
Design/technology
Interview with lighting designer Dennis Parichy. USA: New York, NY. 1986-1987. Lang.: Eng. 428

Performance/production
Reviews of Wilson's *Talley's Folly* staged by András Bálint and Bond's *The Fool* staged by László Salamon Suba. Hungary: Dunaujváros, Nyíregyháza. 1986. Lang.: Hun. 1902
Collection of newspaper reviews by London theatre critics. UK-England: London. 1986. Lang.: Eng. 2170
Collection of newspaper reviews by New York theatre critics. USA: New York, NY. 1987. Lang.: Eng. 2317

Plays/librettos/scripts
John Guare's work and his insights into American society. USA. 1960-1987. Lang.: Eng. 2869
Interview with playwright John Guare. USA. 1987. Lang.: Eng. 2870
Wilson, Peter
Performance/production
Collection of newspaper reviews by London theatre critics. UK-England: London. 1987. Lang.: Eng. 2217
Collection of newspaper reviews by London theatre critics. UK-England: London. 1987. Lang.: Eng. 2243
Wilson, Robert
Institutions
Schaubühne's comeback with production of *Schuld und Sühne (Crime and Punishment)*. Germany, West: Berlin, West. 1970-1987. Lang.: Dut. 1618

Performance/production
The 1984 season of the Next Wave at BAM. USA: New York, NY. 1984. Lang.: Eng. 967
Director as true author and maker of theatre. France. 1987. Lang.: Fre. 1757
Collection of newspaper reviews by London theatre critics. UK-England: London. 1987. Lang.: Eng. 2258
Director Robert Wilson, his *CIVIL warS* and connecting *Knee Plays*. USA. 1979-1987. Lang.: Swe. 3274
Collaboration of Robert Wilson and Heiner Müller on *Hamlet Machine (Hamletmaschine)*. USA: New York, NY. Germany, West: Hamburg. 1987. Lang.: Eng. 3361

Plays/librettos/scripts
Brecht's influence on technique and style of playwright Heiner Müller. Germany, East. 1940-1984. Lang.: Eng. 2605
Interview with playwright John Guare. USA. 1987. Lang.: Eng. 2870

Theory/criticism
Theatre and contemporary culture. USA. 1800-1987. Lang.: Eng. 1360

Wilson, Snoo
Performance/production
Collection of newspaper reviews by London theatre critics. UK-England: London. 1987. Lang.: Eng. 2184
Wincelberg, Shimon
Plays/librettos/scripts
Dramatic treatment of material about the Holocaust. USA. Germany, West. 1950-1987. Lang.: Eng. 2917
Wind in the Willows, The
Performance/production
Collection of newspaper reviews by London theatre critics. UK-England: London. 1986. Lang.: Eng. 2041
Collection of newspaper reviews by London theatre critics. UK-England: London. 1987. Lang.: Eng. 2231
Windgassen, Wolfgang
Performance/production
The Heldentenor in Wagnerian opera. Europe. North America. 1987. Lang.: Eng. 3770
Window-Cleaner, The
Plays/librettos/scripts
Political aspects of Hungarian absurdist drama. Hungary. 1970-1980. Lang.: Eng. 2632
Windsor, Valerie
Performance/production
Collection of newspaper reviews by London theatre critics. UK-England: London. 1987. Lang.: Eng. 2260

Windsor, Valerie — cont'd

Collection of newspaper reviews by London theatre critics. UK-England: London. 1987. Lang.: Eng. 2268

Winler, Claus-Martin
Performance/production
A round-table discussion with stage directors on the principles and methods of working with an ensemble company. Germany, East: Berlin, East. 1983. Lang.: Ger. 1778

Winnie-the-Pooh
Performance/production
Collection of newspaper reviews by London theatre critics. UK-England: London. 1987. Lang.: Eng. 2231

Winter, Brenda
Relation to other fields
Interview with founders of the Charabanc Theatre Company. UK-Ireland. 1970-1987. Lang.: Eng. 1260

Winter, William
Theory/criticism
Actor Lawrence Barrett and the genteel tradition in acting. USA. 1870-1890. Lang.: Eng. 3069

Winter's Tale, The
Performance/production
Shakespeare's later plays at Stratford Festival. Canada: Stratford, ON. 1986. Lang.: Eng. 751

English Shakespearean productions. UK-England: London, Manchester, Stratford. 1985-1986. Lang.: Eng. 917

Collection of newspaper reviews by London theatre critics. UK-England: London. 1987. Lang.: Eng. 2220

Winthrop
Institutions
Conditions affecting Canadian opera composers. Canada. 1987. Lang.: Eng. 3714

Plays/librettos/scripts
Critical analysis of István Anhalt's opera, *Winthrop*. Canada: Kitchener, ON. USA. 1987. Lang.: Eng. 3894

Wisdom Bridge Theatre (Chicago, IL)
Institutions
Analysis of the changing scene in Chicago's theatres. USA: Chicago, IL. 1987. Lang.: Eng. 589

Wiśniewski, Janusz
Performance/production
The 17th Warsaw theatre conference. Poland: Warsaw. 1987. Lang.: Eng, Fre. 872

Polish theatre. Poland: Warsaw, Cracow, Wrocław. 1980-1987. Lang.: Eng, Fre. 1987

Wit Works Woe
SEE
Gore ot uma.

Wit's Creation, Selected from the Finest Fancies of Modern Muses, with Outlandish Proverbs
Research/historiography
Discussion of the miscellany called *Wit's Creation*. England: London. 1640. Lang.: Eng. 1298

With Longings to Realize
Performance/produciton
Johanna Boyce's *With Longings to Realize* presented by the Performance Group. USA: New York, NY. 1983. Lang.: Eng. 1478

Within the Gates
Plays/librettos/scripts
The Spanish Civil War in works by Ernest Hemingway and Sean O'Casey. UK. Ireland. USA. 1930-1939. Lang.: Eng. 2749

Witkacy
SEE
Witkiewicz, Stanisław Ignacy.

Witkacy-Autoparodia (Witkacy-Self-Parody)
Institutions
The Stanisław Ignacy Witkiewicz Theatre. Poland: Zakopane. 1982-1986. Lang.: Eng, Fre. 1628

Witkiewicz, Stanisław Ignacy
Institutions
The Stanisław Ignacy Witkiewicz Theatre. Poland: Zakopane. 1982-1986. Lang.: Eng, Fre. 1628

Performance/production
Director Tadeusz Kantor's inspirations in early career. Poland. 1933-1987. Lang.: Pol. 1992

The shape and form of contemporary Polish theatre. Poland: Warsaw. 1981-1987. Lang.: Eng, Fre. 1995

Plays/librettos/scripts
Misogynist themes in Strindberg, Weininger and Witkiewicz. Austria: Vienna. 1880-1987. Lang.: Eng. 2452

Witkowsky, Gizella
Performance/production
Ballerina Gizella Witkowsky: debut, National Ballet of Canada. Canada: Toronto, ON. 1984. Lang.: Eng. 1432

Wixell, Ingmar
Basic theatrical documents
Review of video productions of *Tosca* and *Dialogues des Carmélites*. Italy: Verona. Australia: Sydney. 1987. Lang.: Eng. 3692

Wizard of Oz, The
Performance/production
Collection of newspaper reviews by London theatre critics. UK-England. 1987. Lang.: Eng. 2263

Woe from Wit
SEE
Gore ot uma.

Wojewodski, Stan, Jr.
Performance/production
Overview of the Theatre of Nations Festival. USA: Baltimore, MD. 1981-1986. Lang.: Eng. 949

Wojtasik, George
Performance spaces
George Wojtasik, managing director of Equity Library Theatre (ELT). USA: New York, NY. 1943-1987. Lang.: Eng. 674

Wolfe, Debbie
Performance/production
Collection of newspaper reviews by London theatre critics. UK-England: London. 1986. Lang.: Eng. 2116

Collection of newspaper reviews by London theatre critics. UK-England: London. 1987. Lang.: Eng. 2208

Wolfe, George C.
Institutions
Photos and list of those present at Dramatists' Guild award ceremony. USA: New York, NY. 1987. Lang.: Eng. 581

Performance/production
George C. Wolfe and L. Kenneth Richardson discuss *The Colored Museum*. USA: New York, NY, New Brunswick, NJ. 1987. Lang.: Eng. 2363

Wolff, Art
Performance/production
Collection of newspaper reviews by London theatre critics. UK-England: London. 1986. Lang.: Eng. 2088

Wolff, Egon
Plays/librettos/scripts
Egon Wolff's trilogy of plays focusing on Chilean bourgeoisie. Chile. 1964-1984. Lang.: Eng. 2490

Wolfson, John
Institutions
Summary of proceedings from a Gilbert and Sullivan symposium. Canada: Toronto, ON. 1987. Lang.: Eng. 3954

Wollman, Rebecca
Performance/production
Collection of newspaper reviews by London theatre critics. UK-England: London. 1987. Lang.: Eng. 2239

Collection of newspaper reviews by London theatre critics. UK-England: London. 1987. Lang.: Eng. 2253

Woman in Mind
Performance/production
Collection of newspaper reviews by London theatre critics. UK-England: London. 1986. Lang.: Eng. 2142

Woman of Paradise
SEE
Donna del Paradiso.

Woman of Paris, The
SEE
Parisienne, La.

Woman Warrior, The
Performance/production
Collection of newspaper reviews by London theatre critics. UK-England: London. 1987. Lang.: Eng. 2258

Women and Men: A Big Dance
Performance/production
Director Anne Bogart's production of *Women and Men: A Big Dance*. USA: New York, NY. 1983. Lang.: Eng. 1418

Workers' theatre
Plays/librettos/scripts
Annotated bibliography of Labor plays. USA. 1930-1940. Lang.:
Eng.   2875
Relation to other fields
Debate over proletarian art among Social Democrats. Germany:
Berlin. 1910-1912. Lang.: Ger.   1238
Working People's Picture Show, The
Relation to other fields
Description of *The Working People's Picture Show*. Canada: Toronto,
ON. 1987. Lang.: Eng.   1221
Workshops
Administration
The collaboration of composer and librettist in workshops of new
operas. USA. 1987. Lang.: Eng.   3683
Performance/production
Casting community theatre. UK-England: Dorchester. 1987. Lang.:
Eng.   913
World in a Village
Plays/librettos/scripts
New findings on 18th-century Irish comic playwright John O'Keeffe.
Ireland. England: London. 1767-1798. Lang.: Eng.   2643
World of Statistics or: We Know Why, The
Performance/production
Five short plays by Géza Páskándi at SUNY Binghamton. Hungary.
USA: Binghamton, NY. 1987. Lang.: Eng.   1813
Worlds Apart
Performance/production
Collection of newspaper reviews by London theatre critics. UK-
England: London. 1987. Lang.: Eng.   2214
Wortham Theatre Center (Houston, TX)
Performance spaces
Recently completed Wortham Theatre Center. USA: Houston, TX.
1987. Lang.: Eng.   701
Wortham Theatre Center, designed by Eugene Aubry. USA:
Houston, TX. 1977-1987. Lang.: Eng.   3739
Wow Show, The
Performance/production
Collection of newspaper reviews by London theatre critics. UK-
England: London. 1986. Lang.: Eng.   2089
Wowro, Jędrzej
Performance/production
Poland's puppet theatre. Poland: Wrocław, Białystock. Austria:
Mistelbach. 1979-1987. Lang.: Eng, Fre.   4006
Woyzeck
Performance/production
Collection of newspaper reviews by London theatre critics. UK-
England: London. 1986. Lang.: Eng.   2104
Lorna Heaton's use of holograms in *Woyzeck*. Canada: Banff, AB.
1987. Lang.: Fre.   3205
Relation to other fields
Comparison of *Woyzeck* to Nelson Mandela. South Africa, Republic
of: Pretoria. 1985. Lang.: Eng.   2999
Woza Albert!
Performance/production
Collection of newspaper reviews by London theatre critics. UK-
England: London. 1987. Lang.: Eng.   2176
Woźniak, Roman
Performance/production
Four new productions in Poland. Poland: Warsaw. 1986-1987. Lang.:
Eng, Fre.   1988
Wozzeck
Performance/production
American premiere of Alban Berg's *Wozzeck*. USA: New York, NY.
1931. Lang.: Eng.   3841
WPA Theatre (New York, NY)
Administration
Financial considerations in transferring *Steel Magnolias* to an Off
Broadway theatre. USA: New York, NY. 1987. Lang.: Eng.   226
Design/technology
Interview with set designer Edward Gianfrancesco. USA: New York,
NY. 1987. Lang.: Eng.   429
Performance/production
Collection of newspaper reviews by New York theatre critics. USA:
New York, NY. 1987. Lang.: Eng.   2313
Collection of newspaper reviews by New York theatre critics. USA:
New York, NY. 1987. Lang.: Eng.   2323

Wrecked Eggs
Performance/production
Collection of newspaper reviews by London theatre critics. UK-
England: London. 1986. Lang.: Eng.   2172
Wright, Bernard
Performance/production
Collection of newspaper reviews by London theatre critics. UK-
England: London. 1987. Lang.: Eng.   2267
Wright, Garland
Design/technology
Philosophy of set designer John Arnone. USA: New York, NY.
1987. Lang.: Eng.   430
Performance/production
Career of director Garland Wright. USA. 1972-1987. Lang.: Eng.
                                                                                         975
Théâtre de la Jeune Lune, its origins and influences. USA:
Minneapolis, MN. France: Paris. 1980-1987. Lang.: Eng.   977
Theory/criticism
On the Verge by Eric Overmyer. Production history, plot synopsis,
critical evaluation. USA. 1987. Lang.: Eng.   3068
Wright, Jay
Basic theatrical documents
Text of *Daughters of the Water* by Jay Wright. USA. 1987. Lang.:
Eng.   1583
Wright, John
Performance/production
Collection of newspaper reviews by London theatre critics. UK-
England: London. 1987. Lang.: Eng.   2218
Wright, Thomas
Performance/production
Libel suit against a minstrel. UK-England: Stafford. 1616. Lang.:
Eng.   3269
Wrigley, Sheena
Performance/production
Collection of newspaper reviews by London theatre critics. UK-
England: London. 1986. Lang.: Eng.   2064
*Wrorzec dowodów metafizycznych (Pattern of Metaphysical
Proofs, A)*
Performance/production
The shape and form of contemporary Polish theatre. Poland:
Warsaw. 1981-1987. Lang.: Eng, Fre.   1995
Experimental theatre at the Stary in three recent productions.
Poland: Cracow. 1987. Lang.: Eng.   1999
Wu, Shu-fu
Performance/production
The biography of Wu Shu-fu. China. 1657-1720. Lang.: Chi.   754
Wu, Zetian
Performance/production
Status of Sichuan theatre and opera. China, People's Republic of:
Chengdu. 1985-1986. Lang.: Eng.   3512
Wünscher, Marianne
Performance/production
Biography of comic actress Marianne Wünscher. Germany, East:
Berlin, East. 1930-1986. Lang.: Ger.   1780
Portrait of actress Marianne Wünscher. Germany, East: Berlin, East.
1948-1987. Lang.: Ger.   1787
Wunschkonzert (Request Concert)
Performance/production
Franz Xaver Kroetz's *Wunschkonzert (Request Concert)* transposed to
Calcutta. India: Calcutta. 1980. Lang.: Eng.   1930
Franz Xaver Kroetz's *Wunschkonzert (Request Concert)* in Bombay:
observations of actress Sulabha Deshpande. India: Bombay. 1986.
Lang.: Eng.   1931
Collection of newspaper reviews by London theatre critics. UK-
England: London. 1986. Lang.: Eng.   2068
Wustman, John
Performance/production
Accompanist/voice teacher, John Wustman. USA. 1960-1987. Lang.:
Eng.   3848
Wyatt, Rachel
Plays/librettos/scripts
Plays by Micone, Saddlemyer, Thompson, Wyatt. Canada. 1958-
1985. Lang.: Eng.   2481
Wycherley, William
Plays/librettos/scripts
Styles of speech in Wycherley's *The Plain Dealer*. England. 1676.
Lang.: Eng.   2511

Wycherley, William — cont'd

Name and entitlement in Dryden, Wycherley and Etherege. England. 1500-1699. Lang.: Eng. 2526

Independence of Restoration women is reflected in comic heroines. England. 1668-1700. Lang.: Eng. 2550

Wyndham, Charles
Plays/librettos/scripts
Study of plays by Henry Arthur Jones. UK-England: London. 1882-1900. Lang.: Eng. 2790

Wyndham's Theatre (London)
Performance/production
Collection of newspaper reviews by London theatre critics. UK-England: London. 1986. Lang.: Eng. 2057

Collection of newspaper reviews by London theatre critics. UK-England: London. 1986. Lang.: Eng. 2089

Collection of newspaper reviews by London theatre critics. UK-England: London. 1986. Lang.: Eng. 2099

Collection of newspaper reviews by London theatre critics. UK-England: London. 1987. Lang.: Eng. 2186

Collection of newspaper reviews by London theatre critics. UK-England: London. 1987. Lang.: Eng. 2213

Collection of newspaper reviews by London theatre critics. UK-England: London. 1987. Lang.: Eng. 2269

Wysocki
Performance/production
The shape and form of contemporary Polish theatre. Poland: Warsaw. 1981-1987. Lang.: Eng, Fre. 1995

Wyspiański, Stanisław
Performance/production
Polish theatre. Poland: Warsaw, Cracow, Wrocław. 1980-1987. Lang.: Eng, Fre. 1987

Wyzniewski, Arno
Performance/production
Actor Arno Wyzniewski of Berliner Ensemble. Germany, East: Berlin, East. 1956-1987. Lang.: Ger. 1781

Wyzwolenie (Liberation)
Performance/production
Polish theatre. Poland: Warsaw, Cracow, Wrocław. 1980-1987. Lang.: Eng, Fre. 1987

Xirgu, Margarita
Performance/production
Collection of theatre reviews by J.M. de Sagarra. Spain-Catalonia: Barcelona. 1922-1927. Lang.: Cat. 885

Xu, Di-Shan
Performance/production
Comparison between Chinese opera and Buddhist plays of Kerala. China, People's Republic of: Beijing. India. 1050-1968. Lang.: Chi. 3533

Xu, Rong-lian
Performance/production
Workshop in Chinese acting methods. Canada: Toronto, ON. China, People's Republic of: Shanghai. 1987. Lang.: Eng. 1717

Yajunbyungwon (Field Hospital)
Basic theatrical documents
Text of Yajunbyungwon (Field Hospital) by Lim Je-Bok. Korea. 1970. Lang.: Kor. 1564

Yale Repertory Theatre (New Haven, CT)
Basic theatrical documents
English text of Elisabetta: Quasi per caso una donna (Elizabeth: Almost By Chance a Woman) by Dario Fo. Italy. USA. 1987. Lang.: Eng. 1560

Text of A Place with the Pigs by Athol Fugard. USA. South Africa, Republic of. 1987. Lang.: Eng. 1580

Performance/production
Relations between acting, theatre photography. USA. Lang.: Eng. 942

Plays/librettos/scripts
Interview with playwright Athol Fugard on A Place with the Pigs. USA: New Haven, CT. 1987. Lang.: Eng. 2851

Interview with playwright August Wilson. USA. 1970-1987. Lang.: Eng. 2855

Yamamoto, Kansai
Performance/production
Productions of several Tokyo companies. Japan: Tokyo. 1987. Lang.: Jap. 1962

Yamazaki, Masakazu
Performance/production
Comments on Tokyo performances. Japan: Tokyo. 1987. Lang.: Jap. 1964

Yamazaki, Tetsu
Plays/librettos/scripts
Contemporary Japanese plays about crime. Japan: Tokyo. 1986. Lang.: Jap. 2681

Plays about child suicide in Japan. Japan: Tokyo. 1986. Lang.: Jap. 2683

Yang, Hsiaolio
Performance/production
Acting theory of Chinese opera. China, People's Republic of. 1900-1986. Lang.: Chi. 3500

Yangjusandae nolyee
Plays/librettos/scripts
Analysis of Yangjusandae nolyee. Korea. 57 B.C.-1987 A.D. Lang.: Kor. 1488

Yankowitz, Susan
Performance/production
Collection of newspaper reviews by London theatre critics. UK-England: London. 1987. Lang.: Eng. 2181

Yardsale
Performance/production
Collection of newspaper reviews by London theatre critics. UK-England: London. 1987. Lang.: Eng. 2184

Yasashii inu (Gentle Dog, A)
Performance/production
Focus on several Tokyo productions. Japan: Tokyo. 1960-1987. Lang.: Jap. 1955

Yashiro, Seiichi
Performance/production
Productions of Bungakuza, Yūkikai Zenjidō shiatā, Tao and Tenkei gekijō. Japan: Tokyo. 1986. Lang.: Jap. 1961

Yasuzawa jimūsho (Tokyo)
Performance/production
Discussion of four Tokyo productions. Japan: Tokyo. 1944-1987. Lang.: Jap. 1963

Yearbooks
Performance/production
Yearbook of Swiss theatrical activity, with bibliography. Switzerland. 1987-1988. Lang.: Fre, Ger, Ita. 892

Soviet theatrical calendar. USSR. 1988. Lang.: Rus. 982

Children's theatrical productions outside of theatres. Includes playtexts. Switzerland. 1986-1988. Lang.: Ger. 2026

Reference materials
French-language Belgian theatre. Belgium. 1985-1986. Lang.: Fre. 1197

Chinese drama yearbook including selected problems, various opinions. China, People's Republic of. 1980-1984. Lang.: Chi. 1198

New Italian productions in all areas. Italy. 1985-1986. Lang.: Ita. 1204

Names and addresses of Italian theatrical institutions. Italy. 1987. Lang.: Ita. 1205

Yearbook of Italian theatre, television and film. Italy. 1987. Lang.: Ita. 1206

Yeats, William Butler
Institutions
Playwright Denis Johnston and avant-garde theatre at the Abbey. Ireland: Dublin. 1927-1935. Lang.: Eng. 1619

Plays/librettos/scripts
Comparative study of Measure for Measure by Shakespeare and the poem Leda and the Swan by Yeats. England. 1604-1929. Lang.: Eng. 1116

Maud Gonne and Yeats's portrayal of women in his plays. Ireland: Dublin. 1900-1930. Lang.: Eng. 2646

Lady Gregory's Grania. Ireland: Dublin. 1910-1930. Lang.: Eng. 2649

Yeats's dance plays: effect of the elements of performance on text. UK-Ireland. 1916-1987. Lang.: Eng. 2832

Relation to other fields
Literary figures of the Irish Literary Renaissance. Ireland. UK-Ireland. 1875-1938. Lang.: Eng. 2995

Research/historiography
Overview of Canadian research on twentieth-century Irish drama. Ireland. UK-Ireland. Canada. 1891-1983. Lang.: Eng. 3011

Yeats, William Butler — cont'd

Theory/criticism

Assessment of the series *Lost Beginning*, its relation to Stewart Parker's *Pentecost*. UK-Ireland. 1987. Lang.: Eng. 3218

Yeh, Shean Tzuu

Plays/librettos/scripts

Bibliography of Yeh Shean Tzuu and his *Luan Yih Jih*. China: Beijing. 820-1641. Lang.: Chi. 1108

Yeko, Bruce

Institutions

Record producer Bruce Yeko's accomplishments. USA: New York, NY. 1962-1981. Lang.: Eng. 3625

Yellow House, The

Performance/production

Interview with people who staged *The Yellow House*. USA. 1960-1987. Lang.: Eng. 1486

Script and staging of Shaliko's *The Yellow House*. USA: Baltimore, MD. 1982-1987. Lang.: Eng. 1487

Yerma

Performance/production

Collection of newspaper reviews by London theatre critics. UK-England: London. 1987. Lang.: Eng. 2196

Yévgeni Onegin

Performance/production

Background on San Francisco opera radio broadcasts. USA: San Francisco, CA. 1987. Lang.: Eng. 3833

Yian de-yi yuan (Marriage of Good Fortune, A)

Performance/production

A review of *Yian de-yi yuan (A Marriage of Good Fortune)*. Taiwan: Taipei. 1987. Lang.: Chi. 3542

Yiddish theatre

SEE ALSO

Ethnic theatre.

Performance spaces

Celebration of the birthday of the HaBimah Theatre. Israel: Tel Aviv. 1917-1987. Lang.: Heb. 1669

Performance/production

Ritual elements and history of the Yiddish theatre. USA: New York, NY. 1930. Lang.: Eng. 3410

Depression-era Yiddish actress Molly Picon. USA. 1930. Lang.: Eng. 3413

Plays/librettos/scripts

History of Yiddish theatre and development of its plays. Europe. USA. 1853-1960. Lang.: Heb. 2562

Influence of Yiddish and Jewish theatre on mainstream American theatre. USA: New York, NY. 1881-1987. Lang.: Eng. 2913

Yin, Guey-Fang

Performance/production

Actor Yin Guey-Fang's work in *The Dream of the Red Chamber*. China, People's Republic of. 1945-1983. Lang.: Chi. 3538

Ying hsi

SEE

Shadow puppets.

Yliruusi, Tauno

Basic theatrical documents

English translation of *What, No Ashes?* by Tauno Yliruusi. Finland. 1987. Lang.: Eng. 1553

Yōkihi (Yang Kuei-fei)

Performance/production

Nō plays with Chinese historical subjects. Japan. 1300-1500. Lang.: Jap. 1503

York Cycle

Performance/production

Undergraduate students stage the York Crucifixion play. UK-England: Canterbury. 1983-1987. Lang.: Eng. 2282

Yorunoki (Tokyo)

Plays/librettos/scripts

Plays about child suicide in Japan. Japan: Tokyo. 1986. Lang.: Jap. 2683

Yoshida, Hideo

Performance/production

Analysis of four Tokyo productions. Japan: Tokyo. 1987. Lang.: Jap. 1957

Discussion of four Tokyo productions. Japan: Tokyo. 1944-1987. Lang.: Jap. 1963

Yoshitsune senbonzakura (Thousand Cherry Trees of Yoshitsune, The)

Performance/production

Collection of newspaper reviews by London theatre critics. UK-England: London. 1987. Lang.: Eng. 2258

Yoshitsune, Minamoto

Performance/production

Performances of *nō* plays by priests and description of a new play. Japan: Hiraizumi. 1987. Lang.: Eng. 1501

Yoshizawa, Kōichi

Performance/production

New themes and styles in Japanese theatre. Japan: Tokyo. 1986. Lang.: Jap. 1953

Productions of Bungakuza, Yūkikai Zenjidō shiatā, Tao and Tenkei gekijō. Japan: Tokyo. 1986. Lang.: Jap. 1961

You Never Can Tell

Design/technology

Lighting reviews for several New York productions. USA: New York, NY. 1987. Lang.: Eng. 474

Performance/production

Collection of newspaper reviews by London theatre critics. UK-England. 1987. Lang.: Eng. 2263

Plays/librettos/scripts

Analysis of Shaw's *You Never Can Tell*. UK-England. 1899. Lang.: Eng. 2803

Young Vic (London)

Performance/production

Reviews of Pinter's *The Lover* and *A Slight Ache*. UK-England: London. 1987. Lang.: Eng. 901

Collection of newspaper reviews by London theatre critics. UK-England: London. 1986. Lang.: Eng. 2035

Collection of newspaper reviews by London theatre critics. UK-England: London. 1986. Lang.: Eng. 2051

Collection of newspaper reviews by London theatre critics. UK-England: London. 1986. Lang.: Eng. 2063

Collection of newspaper reviews by London theatre critics. UK-England: London. 1986. Lang.: Eng. 2079

Collection of newspaper reviews by London theatre critics. UK-England: London. 1986. Lang.: Eng. 2087

Collection of newspaper reviews by London theatre critics. UK-England: London. 1986. Lang.: Eng. 2093

Collection of newspaper reviews by London theatre critics. UK-England: London. 1986. Lang.: Eng. 2102

Collection of newspaper reviews by London theatre critics. UK-England: London. 1986. Lang.: Eng. 2110

Collection of newspaper reviews by London theatre critics. UK-England: London. 1986. Lang.: Eng. 2125

Collection of newspaper reviews by London theatre critics. UK-England: London. 1986. Lang.: Eng. 2157

Collection of newspaper reviews by London theatre critics. UK-England: London. 1986. Lang.: Eng. 2162

Collection of newspaper reviews by London theatre critics. UK-England: London. 1987. Lang.: Eng. 2173

Collection of newspaper reviews by London theatre critics. UK-England: London. 1987. Lang.: Eng. 2176

Collection of newspaper reviews by London theatre critics. UK-England: London. 1987. Lang.: Eng. 2178

Collection of newspaper reviews by London theatre critics. UK-England: London. 1987. Lang.: Eng. 2184

Collection of newspaper reviews by London theatre critics. UK-England: London. 1987. Lang.: Eng. 2185

Collection of newspaper reviews by London theatre critics. UK-England. 1987. Lang.: Eng. 2199

Collection of newspaper reviews by London theatre critics. UK-England: London. 1987. Lang.: Eng. 2204

Collection of newspaper reviews by London theatre critics. UK-England: London. 1987. Lang.: Eng. 2208

Collection of newspaper reviews by London theatre critics. UK-England: London. 1987. Lang.: Eng. 2209

Collection of newspaper reviews by London theatre critics. UK-England: London. 1987. Lang.: Eng. 2213

Collection of newspaper reviews by London theatre critics. UK-England: London. 1987. Lang.: Eng. 2217

Young Vic (London) — cont'd

Collection of newspaper reviews by London theatre critics. UK-England: London. 1987. Lang.: Eng. 2223

Collection of newspaper reviews by London theatre critics. UK-England: London. 1987. Lang.: Eng. 2224

Collection of newspaper reviews by London theatre critics. UK-England: London. 1987. Lang.: Eng. 2225

Collection of newspaper reviews by London theatre critics. UK-England: London. 1987. Lang.: Eng. 2229

Collection of newspaper reviews by London theatre critics. UK-England: London. 1987. Lang.: Eng. 2230

Collection of newspaper reviews by London theatre critics. UK-England: London. 1987. Lang.: Eng. 2246

Collection of newspaper reviews by London theatre critics. UK-England: London. 1987. Lang.: Eng. 2250

Collection of newspaper reviews by London theatre critics. UK-England: London. 1987. Lang.: Eng. 2252

Collection of newspaper reviews by London theatre critics. UK-England: London. 1987. Lang.: Eng. 2256

Collection of newspaper reviews by London theatre critics. UK-England: London. 1987. Lang.: Eng. 2259

Collection of newspaper reviews by London theatre critics. UK-England: London. 1987. Lang.: Eng. 2264

Collection of newspaper reviews of London theatre critics. UK-England: London. 1987. Lang.: Eng. 2273

Young, Kate
Performance/production
Collection of newspaper reviews by London theatre critics. UK-England: London. 1986. Lang.: Eng. 2038

Young, Stark
Theory/criticism
The language of theatrical criticism. USA: New York, NY. 1917-1985. Lang.: Eng. 1367

Youngblood
Plays/librettos/scripts
Life of playwright John O. Killens. USA: New York, NY. 1954-1987. Lang.: Eng. 2836

Your Place is No Longer With Us
Plays/librettos/scripts
Space and audience-performer relationship—examples from Ellen Sebastian and Maria Irene Fornes. USA. 1950-1980. Lang.: Eng. 2838

Youth theatre
SEE
Children's theatre.

Yr. Obedient Servant
Performance/production
Collection of newspaper reviews by London theatre critics. UK-England: London. 1987. Lang.: Eng. 2202

YU Fest (Budva, Yugoslavia)
Performance/production
Overview of the YU Fest. Yugoslavia: Dubrovnik, Belgrade, Kotor, Budva, Subotica. 1987. Lang.: Eng. 1091

Yu-wang-cheng-gue (City of Desire, A)
Basic theatrical documents
Text of *Yu-wang-cheng-gue (A City of Desire)* by Li Hui-min, based on Shakespeare's *Macbeth*. Taiwan. 1986. Lang.: Chi. 3443

Performance/production
Beijing opera *Yu-wang-cheng-gue (A City of Desire)*, based on Shakespeare's *Macbeth*. Taiwan: Taipei. 1986. Lang.: Chi. 3541

Yu, Da-Gang
Performance/production
Comparison between Chinese opera and Buddhist plays of Kerala. China, People's Republic of: Beijing. India. 1050-1968. Lang.: Chi. 3533

Yuan, Yu Ling
Plays/librettos/scripts
Biography of Yuan Yu Ling. China: Beijing. 1592-1674. Lang.: Chi. 1105

Yūkikai Zenjidō shiatā (Tokyo)
Performance/production
New themes and styles in Japanese theatre. Japan: Tokyo. 1986. Lang.: Jap. 1953

New Tokyo productions. Japan: Tokyo. 1987. Lang.: Jap. 1954

Productions of Bungakuza, Yūkikai Zenjidō shiatā, Tao and Tenkei gekijō. Japan: Tokyo. 1986. Lang.: Jap. 1961

Yume no yūminsha (Tokyo)
Performance/production
Productions from Yume no yūminsha, Tōhō, Parco, Tsukumo and Nakamura za. Japan: Tokyo. 1986-1987. Lang.: Jap. 1956

Plays/librettos/scripts
Productions by several Tokyo companies. Japan: Tokyo. 1986-1987. Lang.: Jap. 2682

Yume sarite, Orphe (Dream Is Gone, Orpheus, The)
Performance/production
Productions by Tenkei gekijō, Manji and Mokutōsha. Japan: Tokyo. 1986. Lang.: Jap. 1958

Yumeyumeshii onnatachi (Dreaming Women, The)
Performance/production
Productions of Bungakuza, Yūkikai Zenjidō shiatā, Tao and Tenkei gekijō. Japan: Tokyo. 1986. Lang.: Jap. 1961

Yun, Dae Sung
Plays/librettos/scripts
Dramatist Yun Dae Sung's theories. Korea. 1967-1987. Lang.: Kor. 2693

Yūwaku megami (Tempting Goddess, The)
Performance/production
Six plays of the Tokyo season, focus on director Betsuyaku Minoru. Japan: Tokyo. 1986. Lang.: Jap. 1966

Yvonne Arnaud Theatre (Guildford)
Performance/production
Collection of newspaper reviews by London theatre critics. UK-England: London. 1987. Lang.: Eng. 2235

Za Sumidagawa (Sumida River, The)
Performance/production
Space and sign in various Tokyo productions. Japan: Tokyo. 1987. Lang.: Jap. 1959

Zacconi, Ermete
Performance/production
Collection of theatre reviews by J.M. de Sagarra. Spain-Catalonia: Barcelona. 1922-1927. Lang.: Cat. 885

Zaire
Plays/librettos/scripts
Techniques, themes, characters and dramaturgy of Voltaire. France. 1718-1778. Lang.: Eng. 2590

Zajdlic, Richard
Performance/production
Collection of newspaper reviews by London theatre critics. UK-England: London. 1987. Lang.: Eng. 2180

Zaks, Jerry
Design/technology
Tony Walton's set designs at the Vivian Beaumont Theatre. USA: New York, NY. 1986-1987. Lang.: Eng. 465

Performance/production
Collection of newspaper reviews by New York theatre critics. USA: New York, NY. 1987. Lang.: Eng. 2317

Plays/librettos/scripts
Interview with playwright August Wilson. USA. 1970-1987. Lang.: Eng. 2855

Zaloom, Paul
Performance/production
Puppeteer Paul Zaloom discusses political ideas, scene design. USA. 1970-1987. Lang.: Eng. 3987

Zambian National Theatre Arts Association (ZANTA)
Plays/librettos/scripts
Theme of aggression between fathers and sons: Zambian National Theatre Arts Association festival. Zambia. 1966-1987. Lang.: Eng. 2972

Zamora, José de
Design/technology
Set and costume designs of major designers. UK-England. 1902-1980. Lang.: Eng. 376

Zampella, Nunzio
Performance/production
Work of Bruno Leone and his attempts to re-establish the Neapolitan culture of Guaratelle. Italy: Naples. 1979-1987. Lang.: Eng. 3976

Zanarini, Tom
Performance/production
Artists Beth Escott and Tom Zanarini present *The Way We Are At Home* at the Clybourn Salon. USA: Chicago, IL. 1981. Lang.: Eng. 3364

Zanda Zulan (Zulan, The Flag Bearer)
Performance/production
Collection of newspaper reviews by London theatre critics. UK-England: London. 1986. Lang.: Eng.   2038

Zaourov, Bernard Zadi
Basic theatrical documents
English translations of contemporary African plays. Senegal. Zaire. 1987. Lang.: Eng.   1566

Zap Club
Performance/production
Development of alternative cabaret. UK-England. 1980. Lang.: Eng.   3288

Zapata, Carmen
Performance/production
Retrospective of two centuries of Hispanic theatre. USA. 1598-1965. Lang.: Eng.   2345

Zarudnyj, Mikola
Plays/librettos/scripts
Plays of Mikola Zarudnyj. USSR. 1921-1979. Lang.: Rus.   2933

Zauberflöte, Die
Administration
Royal Swedish Opera: new production of *Die Zauberflöte*, overview of management. Sweden: Stockholm. 1986. Lang.: Swe.   3681
Design/technology
Lighting reviews for some New York productions. USA: New York, NY. 1987. Lang.: Eng.   477
Performance/production
A children's production of Mozart's *The Magic Flute* performed in Spanish. Mexico: Mexico City. 1987. Lang.: Spa.   3811
Background on Lyric Opera radio broadcast performances. USA: Chicago, IL. 1987. Lang.: Eng.   3832
Plays/librettos/scripts
Comparison of Mozart's *The Magic Flute* and Strauss's *Die Frau ohne Schatten*. Austria: Vienna. 1980. Lang.: Eng.   3891

Zavala-Rocha family
Plays/librettos/scripts
Musical adaptation of Gorostiza's *Contigo pan y cebolla (With You, Bread and Onion)*. Mexico: Mexico City. Spain: Madrid. 1833-1984. Lang.: Eng.   1150

Zaveri, Bhadrakani
Performance/production
Collection of newspaper reviews by London theatre critics. UK-England: London. 1987. Lang.: Eng.   2230

Zawistowski, Władysław
Performance/production
The shape and form of contemporary Polish theatre. Poland: Warsaw. 1981-1987. Lang.: Eng, Fre.   1995

Zeal, Eleanor
Performance/production
Collection of newspaper reviews by London theatre critics. UK-England: London. 1987. Lang.: Eng.   2276

Zeami, Motokiyo
Performance/production
Zeami's concept of the actor and the ideal performance. Japan. 1363-1443. Lang.: Eng.   1500
Nō plays with Chinese historical subjects. Japan. 1300-1500. Lang.: Jap.   1503
Plays/librettos/scripts
Nō playwright, monk Ippen Hōgo. Japan. 1200-1400. Lang.: Jap.   1505
Theory/criticism
Analysis of *Shikadō* by Zeami. Japan. 1363-1443. Lang.: Kor.   3053

Zeani, Virginia
Performance/production
Singers/teachers Virginia Zeani and Nicola Rossi-Lemeni. Italy. 1920-1987. Lang.: Eng.   3802

Zeder, Susan
Plays/librettos/scripts
Playwrights' condescension to child audiences. USA. 1972. Lang.: Eng.   1171

Żegnaj Judaszu (Farewell Judas)
Performance/production
The shape and form of contemporary Polish theatre. Poland: Warsaw. 1981-1987. Lang.: Eng, Fre.   1995

Zeisler, Peter
Relation to other fields
Exchange of ideas between Soviets and US theatre artists. USA: New York, NY. USSR: Moscow. 1987. Lang.: Eng.   1284

Zelenaja, Rina
Performance/production
Memoirs of actress Rina Zelenaja. USSR: Moscow. Lang.: Rus. 1084

Zeleński, Tadeusz
Performance/production
Selection of reviews by Tadeusz Zeleński. Poland: Cracow, Warsaw. 1919-1941. Lang.: Pol.   1998

Zemach, Nachoom
Institutions
Creation and history of the HaBimah Theatre. USSR: Moscow. Israel: Tel Aviv. 1913-1955. Lang.: Heb.   623

Zemlinskij, Aleksand'r
Institutions
History of Kroll-Oper. Germany: Berlin. 1927-1931. Lang.: Ger. 3726

Zemsta (Vengeance)
Performance/production
Polish theatre. Poland: Warsaw, Cracow, Wrocław. 1980-1987. Lang.: Eng, Fre.   1987

Zenchiku
Performance/production
Nō plays with Chinese historical subjects. Japan. 1300-1500. Lang.: Jap.   1503

Zephaniah, Benjamin
Performance/production
Collection of newspaper reviews by London theatre critics. UK-England: London. 1987. Lang.: Eng.   2215

Zerbrochene Krug, Der (Broken Jug, The)
Performance/production
Collection of newspaper reviews by London theatre critics. UK-England: London. 1986. Lang.: Eng.   2106

Zerkovitz, Béla
Performance/production
Béla Zerkovitz's operetta *Csókos asszony (A Woman Made for Kissing)* directed by István Iglódi. Hungary: Budapest. 1987. Lang.: Hun.   3957
István Iglódi directs *Csókos asszony (A Woman Made for Kissing)* by Béla Zerkovitz at Vigszinház. Hungary: Budapest. 1987. Lang.: Hun.   3958

Zero Hour
Basic theatrical documents
Playtext of *Zero Hour* by Arthur Milner. Costa Rica: San José. 1987. Lang.: Eng.   1550

Zhan, Ji-Ye
Performance/production
Comparison between Chinese opera and Buddhist plays of Kerala. China, People's Republic of: Beijing. India. 1050-1968. Lang.: Chi.   3533

Zhang, Geng
Performance/production
Comparison between Chinese opera and Buddhist plays of Kerala. China, People's Republic of: Beijing. India. 1050-1968. Lang.: Chi.   3533
The modernization of Chinese opera—keeping the traditional spirit. China, People's Republic of: Beijing. 1279-1986. Lang.: Chi.   3539

Zheng, Zhen-Duo
Performance/production
Comparison between Chinese opera and Buddhist plays of Kerala. China, People's Republic of: Beijing. India. 1050-1968. Lang.: Chi.   3533

Zhou, En-Lai
Administration
History of Chinese theatre reform. China, People's Republic of: Beijing. 1942-1984. Lang.: Chi.   3428

Zhou, Yi-Bai
Performance/production
Comparison between Chinese opera and Buddhist plays of Kerala. China, People's Republic of: Beijing. India. 1050-1968. Lang.: Chi.   3533

Zhu, Sheng-Hao
Plays/librettos/scripts
Shakespeare compared to writers of Chinese opera. China. 1279-1616. Lang.: Chi.   3554

Ziębiński, Andrzej
Performance/production
Overview of Polish theatre scene. Poland: Warsaw, Cracow. 1987. Lang.: Eng.   874

GEOGRAPHICAL - CHRONOLOGICAL INDEX

Australia — cont'd

1970-1985. **Plays/librettos/scripts.**
Introductory survey of recent Australian playwrights. Lang.:
Eng.   2447
1970-1987. **Plays/librettos/scripts.**
Focus on the plays of David Williamson and their cultural
impact. Lang.: Eng.   2436
1979. **Plays/librettos/scripts.**
Critical analysis of Dorothy Hewett's *The Man from
Mukinupin*. Lang.: Eng.   2438
1979-1987. **Plays/librettos/scripts.**
Interview with playwright Daniel Keene. New York, NY.
Lang.: Eng.   2444
1981-1986. **Plays/librettos/scripts.**
The early plays of Justin Fleming, especially *Cobra*. Lang.:
Eng.   2448
1983-1985. **Plays/librettos/scripts.**
Conflict of worlds in plays by Louis Nowra. Lang.: Eng.
                                                                 2449
1984-1985. **Audience.**
Death Defying Theatre's development of the play *Coal
Town*. Collinsville. Lang.: Eng.   276
1985-1986. **Theory/criticism.**
Two conferences on theatre reviewing. Lang.: Eng.   1315
1986. **Administration.**
Seminar in response to the McLeay Report, a government
paper on arts policy. Lang.: Eng.   2
1987. **Basic theatrical documents.**
Review of video productions of *Tosca* and *Dialogues des
Carmélites*. Verona. Sydney. Lang.: Eng.   3692
1987. **Institutions.**
Survey of liberal arts and professional training courses.
Lang.: Eng.   503
1987. **Plays/librettos/scripts.**
Interview with playwright Graham Pitts. Lang.: Eng.   1097
Dramatic and scenic structure, feminism, in plays of Alma
De Groen. Lang.: Eng.   2446
Peter Brook discusses his production of *The Mahabharata*.
Paris. India. Perth. Lang.: Eng.   2571

Austria
1700-1799. **Performance/production.**
André Heller, creator of *Luna Luna*. Vienna. Lang.: Ita.
                                                                 3250
1700-1848. **Plays/librettos/scripts.**
Origins of fairy tales on the Viennese stage. Vienna. Lang.:
Eng.   2450
1756-1781. **Performance/production.**
Wolfgang Amadeus Mozart: a psychological profile. Vienna.
Lang.: Eng.   3742
1830-1900. **Plays/librettos/scripts.**
History of 19th-century German literature, including drama
and theatre. Germany. Lang.: Ger.   2591
1861-1967. **Institutions.**
Correspondence of Richard Wagner and Matteo Salvi on the
staging of *Tristan und Isolde*. Vienna. Lang.: Ger.   3710
1874-1929. **Plays/librettos/scripts.**
Art and realism in works of Hugo von Hofmannsthal. Lang.:
Rus.   2451
1880-1987. **Plays/librettos/scripts.**
Misogynist themes in Strindberg, Weininger and Witkiewicz.
Vienna. Lang.: Eng.   2452
1888-1972. **Design/technology.**
Catalogue of exhibit on Viennese costume. Vienna. Lang.:
Fre, Dut.   301
1889-1987. **Plays/librettos/scripts.**
Comparison of works by Hauptmann and Wilbrandt. Berlin.
Vienna. Lang.: Eng.   2593
1937-1979. **Performance/production.**
Stage history of Alban Berg's opera *Lulu*. Paris. Lang.: Swe.
                                                                 3743
1937-1985. **Plays/librettos/scripts.**
George Perle's analysis of Alban Berg's opera *Lulu*. Lang.:
Swe.   3892
1979-1987. **Performance/production.**
Poland's puppet theatre. Wrocław. Białystock. Mistelbach.
Lang.: Eng, Fre.   4006
1980. **Plays/librettos/scripts.**
Comparison of Mozart's *The Magic Flute* and Strauss's *Die
Frau ohne Schatten*. Vienna. Lang.: Eng.   3891
1986. **Basic theatrical documents.**
Play text and photo essay of Martha Clarke's *Vienna:
Lusthaus*. Vienna. Lang.: Eng.   1398

1986. **Design/technology.**
Third international scene painting seminar at the Mozarteum.
Salzburg. Lang.: Eng.   300
1986-1987. **Administration.**
Staatsoper under management of Claus Helmut Drese and
Claudio Abbado. Vienna. Lang.: Swe.   3677
1986-1987. **Audience.**
Claus Peymann, new artistic director of the Vienna
Burgtheater. Vienna. Lang.: Dut.   1530
1986-1987. **Performance/production.**
Productions by Claus Peymann, new artistic director of
Vienna's Burgtheater. Vienna. Lang.: Dut.   721
1986-1987. **Reference materials.**
Theatre demographics in German-speaking Europe. Germany,
West. Switzerland. Lang.: Ger.   1203
1987. **Performance/production.**
Interview with Hungarian-born Viennese director George
Tabori. Vienna. Lang.: Hun.   722
Directors Claus Peymann (Burgtheater) and Gerardjan
Rijnders (Toneelgroep). Vienna. Amsterdam. Lang.: Dut.
                                                                 1681
Report from Salzburger Festspiele: Mozart's *Don Giovanni*,
Schoenberg's *Moses und Aron*, Schmidt's *Das Buch mit
sieben Siegeln*. Salzburg. Lang.: Swe.   3744
1987. **Relation to other fields.**
Descriptive calendar of masked festivals. Lang.: Fre.   3299

Austria-Hungary
1794. **Plays/librettos/scripts.**
Inception of Leopold Koželuh's ballet *Dcera Oty II. znovu
nalezena (The Daughter of Ota II Was Found Again)*.
Vienna. Lang.: Cze.   1454
1890-1918. **Performance/production.**
Polish theatre in areas annexed by Austria-Hungary and
Prussia. Poland. Prussia. Lang.: Pol.   875
1906. **Theory/criticism.**
Otakar Hostinský's conception of tragedy and the tragic.
Prague. Lang.: Cze.   3022

Austro-Hungarian Empire
1896-1987. **Performance/production.**
Opera critic Edouard Hanslick and his opposition to *La
Bohème* by Puccini. Vienna. Lang.: Eng.   3745

Azerbaijan
1875-1925. **Performance/production.**
Development of Azerbaijani theatre. Lang.: Rus.   723
1920-1980. **Performance/production.**
Development of ballet in Azerbaijan. Lang.: Rus.   1431

Bangladesh
1987. **Relation to other fields.**
Teachers discuss creative drama's role in adult education.
Jamaica. Zimbabwe. Lang.: Swe.   2996

Barbados
1987. **Relation to other fields.**
African-American theatre compared to Caribbean and African
theatre. Bermuda. Nigeria. Lang.: Eng.   2980

Belgium
1800. **Plays/librettos/scripts.**
Analysis of *Pelléas et Mélisande* by Maeterlinck. Lang.: Fre.
                                                                 2454
1800-1987. **Performance/production.**
Walloon carnivals and masks. Lang.: Fre.   3294
1812-1987. **Performance/production.**
Survival of Flemish puppet theatre. Antwerp. Lang.: Eng.
                                                                 3970
1898. **Theory/criticism.**
Analysis of *Escurial* and *Barabbas* by Michel de Ghelderode.
Lang.: Fre.   3023
1900-1987. **Administration.**
Legal status and rights of artists. Lang.: Fre.   4
1912-1961. **Institutions.**
Amateur theatre programs of rural Belgium. Cerfontaine.
Soumoy. Lang.: Fre.   504
1915-1987. **Plays/librettos/scripts.**
Bibliography of Michel de Ghelderode. Lang.: Fre.   2453
1920. **Basic theatrical documents.**
Text of Fernand Crommelynck's *Le Cocu magnifique (The
Magnificent Cuckold)*. Lang.: Fre.   1543
1932-1987. **Performance/production.**
Listing of Walloon theatre performances, winners of the
Grand Prix du Roi Albert. Lang.: Fre.   1682

Belgium — cont'd

1947-1987. **Relation to other fields.**
History of folk group Les Blancs Moussis. Stavelot. Lang.:
Fre. 3300

1967-1987. **Performance/production.**
Illustrated retrospective of Opéra Royal de Wallonie. Liège.
Lang.: Fre. 3746

1980-1982. **Performance/production.**
Contemporary mime forms and their innovators. Paris. USA.
Lang.: Eng. 3224

1980-1987. **Performance/production.**
History of Kaaitheater. Lang.: Eng. 724

1981-1986. **Institutions.**
Gérard Mortier, director of Théâtre Royal de la Monnaie.
Brussels. Lang.: Fre. 3711

1982. **Performance/production.**
Choreographer Carol Martin's production of *The Last Wave.*
Antwerp. Lang.: Eng. 1403

1983-1985. **Relation to other fields.**
Experimental theatre course, Assoc. Internationale pour la
Sémiologie du Spectacle. Brussels. Paris. Odense. Lang.: Fre.
1219

1985-1986. **Administration.**
Theatre as part of the consumer economy. Lang.: Fre. 3

1985-1986. **Reference materials.**
French-language Belgian theatre. Lang.: Fre. 1197

1986. **Performance/production.**
Bruce Ellison directs his *Mister Knight* at Théâtre de la
Mandragore. Brussels. Lang.: Fre. 1685

Dorothée Letessier's comments on the adaptation and staging
of her novel *Voyage à Paimpol (Journey to Paimpol).* Liège.
Lang.: Fre. 1686

Review of the 1986 Festival de la Francophonie. France.
Lang.: Fre. 1760

1987. **Basic theatrical documents.**
English translation of *Jonah* by Elie Georges Berreby. Lang.:
Eng. 1542

1987. **Performance/production.**
Pascal Crochet directs Samuel Beckett's *Solo.* Brussels. Lang.:
Fre. 1683

La théorie du mouchoir (The Handkerchief Theory) written
and directed by Martine Wijckaert. Brussels. Lang.: Fre.
1684

Groupov ensemble describes the creation of *Koniec.* Liège.
Lang.: Fre. 1687

Puppetry as an expression of popular and folk culture. USA.
Italy. Indonesia. Lang.: Eng. 3988

1987. **Plays/librettos/scripts.**
Interview with playwright Paul Pourveur. Lang.: Dut. 2455

1987. **Reference materials.**
Major festivals of Belgium: folklore, history, description.
Lang.: Fre. 3279

1987. **Training.**
Basic theatrical techniques for secondary school. Lang.: Fre.
1378

Benin

1700-1975. **Plays/librettos/scripts.**
Compares plays of Enlightenment France, Francophone
Africa. Brazzaville. Cameroon. France. Lang.: Eng. 2496

Bermuda

1987. **Relation to other fields.**
African-American theatre compared to Caribbean and African
theatre. Barbados. Nigeria. Lang.: Eng. 2980

Brazil

1902-1987. **Performance/production.**
Soprano Bidú Sayão. New York, NY. Lang.: Eng. 3861

1943-1984. **Performance/production.**
Examination of modern Brazilian theatre focusing on plays
by Nelson Rodrigues. Lang.: Eng. 1688

1964-1985. **Plays/librettos/scripts.**
Theme of torture in Brazilian drama. Lang.: Por. 2456

1965. **Performance/production.**
Teatro Arena de São Paulo's production of *Arena Conta
Zumbi.* São Paulo. Lang.: Eng. 1690

1970-1987. **Relation to other fields.**
Playwright Gerald Thomas discusses influences on his work.
Rio de Janeiro. North America. Europe. Lang.: Eng. 2981

1980-1984. **Performance/production.**
New regime ends theatrical censorship. Lang.: Spa. 1689

1987. **Performance/production.**
Search for a national identity through theatre. Lang.: Spa.
1691

Bulgaria

1980. **Performance/production.**
On performers of Vasov National Theatre and the 'Tears of
Laughter' Theatre of Sofia, on tour in Moscow. Sofia.
Moscow. Lang.: Rus. 1692

Cameroon

1700-1975. **Plays/librettos/scripts.**
Compares plays of Enlightenment France, Francophone
Africa. Brazzaville. Benin. France. Lang.: Eng. 2496

Canaan

3000-1000 B.C. **Plays/librettos/scripts.**
Background on Philistines of Saint-Saëns' *Samson et Dalila.*
Lang.: Eng. 3893

Canada

Administration.
Guide for trustees of cultural organizations. Lang.: Eng. 12

1611-1977. **Relation to other fields.**
Theme of imperialism in *The Tempest.* Antilles. France.
Lang.: Eng. 2984

1850-1949. **Plays/librettos/scripts.**
German influences on contemporary Quebecois theatre.
Germany. Lang.: Fre. 2478

1886-1986. **Institutions.**
History of the Royal Conservatory of Music. Toronto, ON.
Lang.: Eng. 3390

1891-1983. **Research/historiography.**
Overview of Canadian research on twentieth-century Irish
drama. Ireland. UK-Ireland. Lang.: Eng. 3011

1900-1987. **Design/technology.**
The impact of twentieth-century technology on theatre. Lang.:
Fre. 302

Malabar Costume Company's work for opera. Toronto, ON.
Lang.: Eng. 3693

1900-1987. **Performance spaces.**
Modern theatre architecture. Montreal, PQ. Lang.: Fre. 627

1913-1985. **Plays/librettos/scripts.**
Survey of Robertson Davies' plays. Lang.: Eng. 2484

1913-1985. **Relation to other fields.**
Critical study of Robertson Davies' literature and drama.
Lang.: Eng. 2983

1916-1957. **Institutions.**
Elizabeth Sterling Haynes and the Little Theatre movement.
Lang.: Eng. 1603

1922-1987. **Performance/production.**
Acting style of Vachtangov. USSR. Lang.: Eng. 1009

1929-1987. **Performance/production.**
Stuart Hamilton's career in opera broadcasting. Toronto, ON.
Lang.: Eng. 3758

1930-1986. **Performance/production.**
Autobiography of opera star Maureen Forrester. Lang.: Eng.
3748

1930-1987. **Performance/production.**
Popular theatre, mostly on economic, feminist themes.
Sudbury, ON. Lang.: Eng. 1709

Biographical survey of Canadian opera personnel. Lang.:
Eng. 3747

1933-1987. **Training.**
Changes in music teaching methods at the Banff Centre.
Banff, AB. Lang.: Eng. 3950

1936-1987. **Institutions.**
Role of the CBC in promoting Canadian opera. Lang.: Eng.
3715

1940-1984. **Design/technology.**
Interview with designer Desmond Heeley. London. New
York, NY. Stratford, ON. Lang.: Eng. 1596

1942-1955. **Basic theatrical documents.**
Collection of radio plays produced by Andrew Allan. Lang.:
Eng. 3109

1944-1954. **Institutions.**
Script editor's recollections of CBC radio dramas. Lang.:
Eng. 3110

1947-1985. **Administration.**
Excerpts, John Hirsch's farewell lecture, Stratford Festival.
Stratford, ON. Lang.: Eng. 9

1947-1987. **Performance/production.**
Retired critic recalls Toronto opera. Toronto, ON. Lang.:
Eng. 3749

Canada — cont'd

1950-1986. Plays/librettos/scripts.
Productions of Brecht in Quebec. Lang.: Fre. 2461

1952-1953. Administration.
Founder Tom Patterson's description of the opening of the Stratford Festival. Stratford, ON. Lang.: Eng. 13

1953-1982. Institutions.
History of the Stratford Festival. Stratford, ON. Lang.: Eng. 521

1953-1987. Performance/production.
Changes at the Stratford Festival since appointment of John Neville as artistic director. Stratford, ON. Lang.: Eng. 753

1958-1985. Plays/librettos/scripts.
Plays by Micone, Saddlemyer, Thompson, Wyatt. Lang.: Eng. 2481

1959-1987. Institutions.
Second City improvisational comedy troupe. Chicago, IL. Toronto, ON. Lang.: Eng. 605

1960-1977. Plays/librettos/scripts.
Critical analysis of James Reaney's *Three Desks*. Lang.: Eng. 2477

1960-1983. Performance/production.
Overview of theatre in Ottawa. Ottawa, ON. Lang.: Eng. 1719

1960-1985. Institutions.
Historical background of National Theatre School. Montreal, PQ. Lang.: Eng. 519

1960-1987. Institutions.
Development of feminist theatre in Toronto. Toronto, ON. Lang.: Eng. 1608

1960-1987. Performance/production.
Lack of a theatre 'star' system. Lang.: Fre. 729

1960-1987. Plays/librettos/scripts.
Playwright Tomson Highway's use of native mythology. Lang.: Eng. 2468

1961-1987. Plays/librettos/scripts.
Symbols of power in Genet's *Les Paravents (The Screens)*. France. Montreal, PQ. Ottawa, ON. Lang.: Fre. 2570

André Brassard's production of Jean Genet's *Les Paravents (The Screens)*. France. Montreal, PQ. Ottawa, ON. Lang.: Fre. 2583

Investigating the text of Genet's *Les Paravents (The Screens)*. France. Montreal, PQ. Ottawa, ON. Lang.: Fre. 2585

1963-1983. Plays/librettos/scripts.
Playwright Paul Thompson. Blythe, ON. Toronto, ON. Lang.: Eng. 2487

1964-1984. Audience.
Low demand for summer theatre. Lang.: Fre. 277

1964-1987. Institutions.
Historical overview of Theatre New Brunswick. Fredericton, NB. Lang.: Eng. 1602

1965-1985. Institutions.
Overview of the Charlottetown Festival, 1986 season. Charlottetown, PE. Lang.: Eng. 525

1965-1987. Institutions.
A history of the Charlottetown Festival. Charlottetown, PE. Lang.: Eng. 505

1967-1987. Institutions.
Nicholas Goldschmidt's tenure as artistic director, Guelph Spring Festival. Guelph, ON. Lang.: Eng. 3720

1969-1987. Design/technology.
Effects of new technologies on theatre. Lang.: Fre. 3202

1970-1983. Plays/librettos/scripts.
Playwright Sharon Pollock. Lang.: Eng. 2469

1970-1986. Institutions.
A history of documentary theatre in English Canada. Lang.: Eng. 508

1971-1987. Institutions.
Historical survey of opera in Calgary. Calgary, AB. Lang.: Eng. 3719

1972-1982. Institutions.
History of Theatre Plus theatre company. Toronto, ON. Lang.: Eng. 520

1972-1982. Plays/librettos/scripts.
History of Playwrights Canada Press. Toronto, ON. Lang.: Eng. 2460

1972-1985. Administration.
Irving Guttman, artistic director, Edmonton Opera, Manitoba Opera. Edmonton, AB. Winnipeg, MB. Lang.: Eng. 3679

1972-1985. Plays/librettos/scripts.
Playwright George F. Walker. Lang.: Eng. 2488

1974-1987. Institutions.
Andrew Davis' role as Toronto Symphony Orchestra conductor. Toronto, On. Lang.: Eng. 3389

1976. Basic theatrical documents.
Text of *Le Roitelet (The Kinglet)* by Claude Dorge. Montreal, PQ. Lang.: Fre. 1545

1977-1987. Design/technology.
The use and development of special effects in the theatre. Lang.: Fre. 303

1977-1987. Performance/production.
Writer-director Glen Cairns and surrealistic drama at the Neptune Theatre. Halifax, NS. Lang.: Eng. 1695

1978-1986. Performance/production.
Public relations function of the Nova Scotia Tattoo. Halifax, NS. Lang.: Eng. 3383

1978-1987. Institutions.
Operations of the Saskatoon Opera Association. Saskatoon, SK. Lang.: Eng. 3713

1978-1987. Relation to other fields.
Applications of African 'Theatre for Development' movement to Canadian popular theatre. Africa. St. John's, NF. Toronto, ON. Lang.: Eng. 2978

1980-1982. Institutions.
Photographic essay of various works by Canadian mime troupe Les Enfants du Paradis—Carbone 14. Montreal, PQ. Lang.: Eng. 3219

1980-1982. Performance/production.
Evolution of the Areté Mime Troupe: its concepts, goals and performance methods. Lang.: Eng. 3221

1980-1985. Performance spaces.
Northern Arts and Cultural Centre: planning and building. Yellowknife, NT. Lang.: Eng. 1667

1980-1987. Administration.
Dramaturgy in Canadian theatre. USA. Germany. Lang.: Eng. 1513

Marketing of opera and the arts in Toronto. Toronto, ON. Lang.: Eng. 3678

1980-1987. Performance/production.
Theatre of playwright Robert Lepage. Montreal, PQ. Toronto, ON. Lang.: Eng. 1704

1980-1987. Plays/librettos/scripts.
The role of the father-figure in recent plays from Quebec. Quebec. Lang.: Fre. 2465

1982. Administration.
The closing of the Festival Lennoxville. Lennoxville, PQ. Lang.: Eng. 8

John Hirsch, artistic director of the Stratford Festival. Stratford, ON. Lang.: Eng. 16

The role of a board of directors for successful theatre companies. Toronto, ON. Halifax, NS. Lang.: Eng. 17

1982. Design/technology.
Profile of designer Jim Plaxton. Toronto, ON. Lang.: Eng. 1587

1982. Institutions.
The future of English-language theatre in Quebec. Montreal, PQ. Lang.: Eng. 511

Previews 1982 International Children's Festival. Toronto, ON. Lang.: Eng. 524

1982. Performance spaces.
The modern acoustics of Toronto's Thomson Hall. Toronto, ON. Lang.: Eng. 628

1982. Performance/production.
Overview of the 1982 Stratford Festival. Stratford, ON. Lang.: Eng. 749

Richard Ouzounian, director, Manitoba Theatre Centre. Winnipeg, MB. Lang.: Eng. 1693

Overview of the 1982 Stratford Festival. Stratford, ON. Lang.: Eng. 1701

Production account, Frank's *Spinoza*, Saidye Bronfman Centre. Montreal, PQ. Lang.: Eng. 1702

Overview of the 1982 Shaw Festival. Niagara-on-the-Lake, ON. Lang.: Eng. 1703

Canadian playwright Allan Stratton. Toronto, ON. Lang.: Eng. 1710

Playwright Erika Ritter. Toronto, ON. Lang.: Eng. 1711

Ann Mortifee, singer, songwriter, performer. Vancouver, BC. Toronto, ON. Lang.: Eng. 1714

GEOGRAPHICAL - CHRONOLOGICAL INDEX

Canada — cont'd

Critical discussion of the Ultimatum II festival. Montreal, PQ. Lang.: Eng. 3346

The work of director Robert Lepage. Montreal, PQ. Lang.: Eng. 3347

Image theatre methodology. Lang.: Eng. 3348

Increasingly novel adaptations of opera settings. Lang.: Eng. 3750

Interview with Odette Beaupré. Lang.: Eng. 3752

Quality of and access to opera training in North America. USA. Lang.: Eng. 3753

Interview with soprano Jane MacKenzie. UK-England. Lang.: Eng. 3754

Interview with soprano Tracy Dahl. Lang.: Eng. 3755

Interview with opera star Gaétan Laperrière. Lang.: Eng. 3756

1987.   Plays/librettos/scripts.
Michael Hollingsworth's *The History of the Village of Small Huts*. Lang.: Eng. 1099

Summary and critical analysis of *Doc* by Sharon Pollock. Lang.: Eng. 1100

Work of playwright Robert Lepage. Lang.: Fre. 1101

The theme of a child's game in Lepage's *La Trilogie des dragons*. Montreal, PQ. Lang.: Fre. 2458

Rebuttal of review of Lepage's *La Trilogie des dragons*. Lang.: Fre. 2459

Traditionalism in Lepage's *La Trilogie des dragons*. Lang.: Fre. 2462

Interview with playwright Robert Lepage. Lang.: Fre. 2464

Collective theatre projects in Newfoundland. St. John's, NF. Lang.: Eng. 2466

Interview with playwright Ping Chong. Montreal, PQ. New York, NY. Lang.: Eng. 2472

Critical response to Brassard's *Les Paravents (The Screens)*. Montreal, PQ. Ottawa, ON. Lang.: Fre. 2475

Uses of history in Lepage's *La Trilogie des dragons*. Lang.: Fre. 2476

La Trilogie des dragons by Robert Lepage. Montreal, PQ. Lang.: Fre. 2479

Imagery in Lepage's *La Trilogie des dragons*. Lang.: Fre. 2480

Brassard discusses his adaptation of Genet's *Les Paravents (The Screens)*. Montreal, PQ. Ottawa, ON. Lang.: Fre. 2485

Play within a play in *Blood Relations* by Sharon Pollock. Lang.: Eng. 2489

Critical discussion of six plays in CBC's *Sextet* broadcast series. Lang.: Eng. 3116

Critical analysis of István Anhalt's opera, *Winthrop*. Kitchener, ON. USA. Lang.: Eng. 3894

1987.   Relation to other fields.
Description of *The Working People's Picture Show*. Toronto, ON. Lang.: Eng. 1221

Social implications of popular theatre. Lang.: Eng. 1222

Difficulties encountered by playwrights in Canada. Vancouver, BC. New York, NY. Lang.: Eng. 1223

Popular theatre and non-governmental funding agencies. Sydney, NS. Jamaica. Sudan. Lang.: Eng. 2982

1987.   Theory/criticism.
Editorial response to Canadian theatre criticism. Toronto, ON. Lang.: Eng. 1317

Criticizes newspaper coverage of Montreal theatre awards. Montreal, PQ. Lang.: Fre. 1318

Discussion of theory of popular theatre. Lang.: Eng. 3024

Caribbean

Institutions.
Interview with Elizabeth Clark, director of Temba Theatre Company. London. Lang.: Eng. 567

Catalonia
SEE
Spain-Catalonia.

Central America
1985.   Performance/production.
Companies and productions at Theatre Festival of the Americas. North America. South America. Lang.: Eng. 1985

1986.   Performance/production.
San Francisco Mime Troupe's visit to Nicaragua's International Theatre Festival. Lang.: Eng. 3222

Chile
1964-1984.   Plays/librettos/scripts.
Egon Wolff's trilogy of plays focusing on Chilean bourgeoisie. Lang.: Eng. 2490

1967-1987.   Plays/librettos/scripts.
Interview with playwright Antonio Skarmento. Santiago. Lang.: Eng. 1102

1973-1986.   Relation to other fields.
Theatre as medium of expression under repressive government. Lang.: Eng. 2985

1987.   Performance/production.
Interview with Chilean director Alejandro Quintana Contreras. Berlin, East. Lang.: Spa. 1720

China
1111 B.C.-1856 A.D.   Plays/librettos/scripts.
The development of Chinese historical drama. Lang.: Chi. 3550

1100 B.C.-1987 A.D.   Theory/criticism.
The development and future of Chinese traditional drama. Lang.: Chi. 3588

960 B.C.-1987 A.D.   Performance/production.
Role of Ji-Lin opera in development of Chinese opera. Lang.: Chi. 3463

206 B.C.-1368 A.D.   Plays/librettos/scripts.
The explanation of the term 'Shao-Lai' in Yuan drama. Beijing. Lang.: Chi. 3553

202 B.C.-1986 A.D.   Performance spaces.
Form and development of the commune theatre. Lang.: Chi. 3452

57 B.C.-1987 A.D.   Performance spaces.
Stages of traditional theatre in Asia, and development of *Changuk* dance drama. Korea. India. Lang.: Kor. 664

618-905.   Theory/criticism.
Themes of the Chinese theatre during the Tang dynasty. Lang.: Chi. 1320

820-1641.   Plays/librettos/scripts.
Bibliography of Yeh Shean Tzuu and his *Luan Yih Jih*. Beijing. Lang.: Chi. 1108

900.   Performance/production.
The influence of the feudal class on traditional Chinese opera. Lang.: Chi. 3465

900.   Plays/librettos/scripts.
The Chinese opera form *Nou Hsi* and its characteristics. Lang.: Chi. 3544

935-1392.   Performance/production.
Music theatre under Koryo dynasty. Korea. Lang.: Kor. 3404

960-1279.   Theory/criticism.
Dramatic criticism in the Sung Dynasty. Beijing. Lang.: Chi. 1319

960-1368.   Performance/production.
Illustrations depicting theatrical performances, Song and Yuan dynasties. Beijing. Lang.: Chi. 3461

960-1368.   Relation to other fields.
New light on Northern Chinese drama. Lang.: Chi. 1224

960-1643.   Performance spaces.
Theatrical changes in Chinese opera during the Sung, Ming and Yuan dynasties. Lang.: Chi. 3451

960-1644.   Plays/librettos/scripts.
A correct definition of Chinese classical 'tragedy'. Lang.: Chi. 3548

960-1912.   Performance spaces.
Inscription on Nan Hsi opera monument. Lang.: Chi. 3453

980-1600.   Plays/librettos/scripts.
Introduction to Shu-Hui, a guild of playwrights in ancient China. Lang.: Chi. 1106

1127-1368.   Theory/criticism.
Theory of Chinese classical comedy. Lang.: Chi. 3587

1200-1987.   Plays/librettos/scripts.
Preface and postscript in Chinese dramatic scripts. Lang.: Chi. 3552

The development of traditional Chinese drama. Lang.: Chi. 3555

1227-1644.   Research/historiography.
Conditions of northern Chinese classical drama. Lang.: Chi. 3584

1260-1368.   Plays/librettos/scripts.
Language of Chinese classical plays. Lang.: Chi. 3556

China — cont'd

China, People's Republic of — cont'd

1900-1986. **Theory/criticism.**
Commune and improvisation theatre in Chi Lin. Lang.: Chi.
3612

A new aesthetic theory of Chinese opera. Lang.: Chi. 3613

1908-1986. **Performance/production.**
History of two local Chinese operas. Lang.: Chi. 3508

1917-1985. **Plays/librettos/scripts.**
Ibsen translation, production, reception and influence in
China. Norway. Lang.: Eng. 2494

1919-1985. **Plays/librettos/scripts.**
The new situation of Chinese drama. Lang.: Chi. 3579

1920-1950. **Theory/criticism.**
Ibsen's influence on modern Chinese theatre. Norway. Lang.:
Chi. 3025

1922-1987. **Performance/production.**
Resources on Chinese opera. Lang.: Chi. 3520

1924-1985. **Performance/production.**
Impressionism in the acting of Chinese drama. Lang.: Chi.
3477

1929-1956. **Theory/criticism.**
Bringing modern Chinese drama into line with tradition.
Beijing. Lang.: Chi. 1323

1930-1985. **Performance/production.**
Effect of speed on language in Chinese theatre. Lang.: Chi.
3483

1930-1985. **Plays/librettos/scripts.**
Chinese view of playwright Eugene O'Neill. USA. Lang.:
Chi. 2863

1935-1986. **Performance/production.**
Acting techniques in Chinese opera. Beijing. Lang.: Chi. 3489

1942-1984. **Administration.**
History of Chinese theatre reform. Beijing. Lang.: Chi. 3428

1942-1986. **Theory/criticism.**
The history of the Ian-An Chinese Opera Research Center.
Lang.: Chi. 3600

1945-1983. **Performance/production.**
Actor Yin Guey-Fang's work in *The Dream of the Red
Chamber*. Lang.: Chi. 3538

1947-1985. **Performance/production.**
Interview with Chinese opera actress Mei Bau-Iue. Lang.:
Chi. 3484

1947-1986. **Performance/production.**
Differences between Chinese and Western theatre. Beijing.
Lang.: Chi. 3513

1948-1974. **Relation to other fields.**
Theatre and its relationship to society. Lang.: Chi. 1228

1949-1985. **Performance/production.**
The distinctive features of Chinese drama. Lang.: Chi. 3478

Creativity in the Chinese arts. Lang.: Chi. 3480

The rhythm of Chinese theatre—parts of the whole. Lang.:
Chi. 3493

Modern techniques combine new ideas with modern drama.
Lang.: Chi. 3535

1949-1985. **Plays/librettos/scripts.**
Brecht's theory of alienation in the Chinese theatre. Lang.:
Chi. 1109

1949-1985. **Theory/criticism.**
Chinese critique of Brechtian realism. Lang.: Chi. 1321

Seminar for the modern theatre in China. Lang.: Chi. 3604

Different ideas leading to the modernization of Chinese
drama. Lang.: Chi. 3615

1949-1987. **Administration.**
Management of Beijing Opera. Beijing. Lang.: Chi. 3426

1949-1987. **Performance/production.**
Using space in the theatre to communicate abstract concepts.
Lang.: Chi. 762

Vocal training and performance in China. Shanghai. Lang.:
Chi. 3529

1949-1987. **Relation to other fields.**
Characterization in modern drama. Lang.: Chi. 1227

1949-1987. **Training.**
The classes of a master directing teacher. Shanghai. Lang.:
Chi. 1380

1950-1986. **Audience.**
Chinese acting: direct communication with audience. Beijing.
Lang.: Chi. 3434

1950-1986. **Performance/production.**
Acting theories in Chinese opera. Beijing. Lang.: Chi. 3510

1951-1985. **Plays/librettos/scripts.**
The new Chinese drama. Lang.: Chi. 3577

1954-1979. **Performance/production.**
Chinese opera stars Shiue Jiue-Shian and Shiu Iu-Lan. Lang.:
Chi. 3494

1955-1985. **Performance/production.**
Directing techniques found in Chinese theatre. Lang.: Chi.
3536

1956-1986. **Performance/production.**
Ways to improve the Chinese opera style *Kun-Jiu*. Lang.:
Chi. 3507

1957. **Performance/production.**
Chou En-Lai and *Horng Lou Meng (Dream of the Red
Chamber)*. Shanghai. Lang.: Chi. 3496

1957-1959. **Performance/production.**
Chiao Chü Yin's *Ch'a Kuan (Tea House)* uses Western style.
Lang.: Chi. 1723

1958-1986. **Performance/production.**
Chinese opera star Ma Shau-Liang reproduces the play
Shiang ma juan (Story of the Robber). Lang.: Chi. 3397

1960-1987. **Research/historiography.**
Three periods of research into Chinese classical southern
drama. Lang.: Chi. 3585

1960-1987. **Theory/criticism.**
Research on Chinese classical southern drama. Lang.: Chi.
3611

1967. **Performance/production.**
Overview of *Gu Cheng-Hei*. Lang.: Chi. 3498

1970-1985. **Theory/criticism.**
Characterization in theatre and television. Lang.: Chi. 3217

1975-1987. **Performance/production.**
Improvisation and other forms in children's theatre. Lang.:
Chi. 764

1975-1987. **Theory/criticism.**
Chinese and Western elements in Chinese musical theatre.
Lang.: Chi. 3422

1980-1984. **Reference materials.**
Chinese drama yearbook including selected problems, various
opinions. Lang.: Chi. 1198

1980-1986. **Performance/production.**
The responsibility of artists to their audience. Lang.: Chi.
3471

1982-1985. **Audience.**
How various audiences influence theatre. Lang.: Chi. 3441

1983. **Plays/librettos/scripts.**
The structures and themes of Chinese playwright Hueng
Tsolin. Lang.: Chi. 2495

1983-1985. **Relation to other fields.**
Results of questionnaire on drama education. Lang.: Chi.
3582

1983-1987. **Plays/librettos/scripts.**
Playwright Gao Xinjian—view of Chinese society. Lang.: Pol.
2492

1984. **Performance/production.**
Performance commemorating 85th birthday of playwright
Shang Hsio Yu. Lang.: Chi. 756

1984. **Plays/librettos/scripts.**
Humanitarianism in contemporary Chinese drama. Lang.: Chi.
2493

1984-1985. **Design/technology.**
Basics of stage design. Lang.: Chi. 304

1984-1986. **Performance/production.**
Influences of Western culture on Chinese theatre reflected in
performance of *Old B Hanging on the Wall*. Lang.: Eng. 761

1985. **Audience.**
Relationship between script, actors and audience. Lang.: Chi.
279

1985. **Performance/production.**
Overview of the director's art. Lang.: Chi. 757

The influence of the audience on the actor's performance.
Lang.: Chi. 763

Basic acting technqiues of Chinese theatre. Lang.: Chi. 3476

Drama education in China. Lang.: Chi. 3492

Characteristics of Chinese drama. Lang.: Chi. 3534

The acting theories of the Chinese theatre. Lang.: Chi. 3537

1985. **Plays/librettos/scripts.**
Historical people in the plays of Chinese theatre. Lang.: Chi.
3576

China, People's Republic of — cont'd

Chinese opera dramatist Uei Ming-Lun. Lang.: Chi. 3562

Philosophical themes in modern Chinese drama: their audience appeal. Lang.: Chi. 3564

Theme of falsehood in Chinese classical comedy. Lang.: Chi. 3567

How to adapt Shakespeare to Chinese opera. Lang.: Chi. 3569

The inner and outer psychology of characters in Chinese opera. Lang.: Chi. 3570

Bridging the gap between classical and modern forms of Chinese opera. Lang.: Chi. 3571

The theme of 'all men are brothers' in Chinese opera. Lang.: Chi. 3573

Call for high quality of dramatic texts, especially for Beijing opera. Lang.: Chi. 3574

Characteristics, value and development in Chinese drama. Lang.: Chi. 3575

Chinese opera should reflect the concerns of its audience. Lang.: Chi. 3578

1987.   Relation to other fields.
Artists and writers affected by political decisions. Lang.: Eng. 1226

Cultural exchange pacts made between the USA and the Soviet Union and China. Washington, DC. Moscow. Peking. Lang.: Eng. 1291

Current ideology: influence on Chinese theatre. Lang.: Chi. 3583

1987.   Theory/criticism.
Crisis and reform in Chinese opera. Lang.: Chi. 3595

Proceedings of a conference on Chinese opera. Lang.: Chi. 3598

Falsehood as the essential quality of the Chinese classical comedy. Lang.: Chi. 3599

New aesthetics for the new Chinese theatre. Lang.: Chi. 3601

The changing aesthetic characteristics of Chinese opera. Lang.: Chi. 3603

Colombia
1948-1987.   Institutions.
Regional theatre directors encourage new relationships between Latin American and U.S. artists. Bogotá. Lang.: Eng. 526

Congo
1700-1975.   Plays/librettos/scripts.
Compares plays of Enlightenment France, Francophone Africa. Brazzaville. Cameroon. Benin. France. Lang.: Eng. 2496

Costa Rica
1987.   Basic theatrical documents.
Playtext of *Zero Hour* by Arthur Milner. San José. Lang.: Eng. 1550

Cuba
1920-1986.   Performance/production.
Experimental theatre opening new possibilities in Cuban drama. Lang.: Spa. 1724

1973-1986.   Relation to other fields.
Tendencies in Latin American theatre that may have influenced its evolution. Lang.: Spa. 1230

1986.   Performance/production.
Day by day account of the 1986 Festival of Camagüey. Camagüey. Lang.: Spa. 1725

1987.   Relation to other fields.
Alternative view of culture and education in theatre. Lang.: Spa. 1229

Czechoslovakia
1783-1983.   Institutions.
History of Stavovské Theatre. Prague. Lang.: Cze. 1612

1830-1987.   Performance/production.
History of Slovak school of acting. Lang.: Rus. 766

1900-1918.   Performance/production.
Jaroslav Kvapil's role in establishing the profession of director. Lang.: Rus. 773

1900-1987.   Performance/production.
Anton Dvořak's *Rusalka*. Prague. New York, NY. Lang.: Eng. 3759

1911-1939.   Design/technology.
Josef Čapek's work as set designer. Prague. Lang.: Cze. 313

1914-1987.   Plays/librettos/scripts.
Příliš hlučna samota (Too Loud a Solitude) by Bohumil Hrabal. Lang.: Ita. 1110

1918-1923.   Design/technology.
Futurism in the scenographic work of Jiří Kroha. Lang.: Ita. 314

1932-1987.   Design/technology.
Interview with costume designer Theodor Pištěk. Lang.: Hun. 3126

1938-1968.   Performance/production.
Theatrical activity at the concentration camp Theresienstadt. Terezín. Lang.: Heb. 772

1940-1987.   Design/technology.
Work of noted set designer and technological innovator Josef Svoboda. Prague. Lang.: Eng. 305

1942-1944.   Institutions.
Rudolf Walter's theatre, Komorní hry. Brno. Lang.: Cze. 1613

1950-1987.   Design/technology.
Czech scenographers Josef Svoboda and Ladislav Vychodil. Prague. USA. Lang.: Eng. 309

1953-1987.   Performance/production.
Hungarian-language theatre in an ethnic Hungarian region of Czechoslovakia. Kosice. Komarno. Lang.: Hun. 769

1965-1987.   Performance/production.
Plays of Ladislav Smoček at Činoherní klub. Prague. Lang.: Cze. 768

1967-1987.   Design/technology.
First American participation in Prague Quadrennial theatre design contest. Prague. USA. Lang.: Eng. 311

1968-1981.   Basic theatrical documents.
Catalan translation of Milan Kundera's *Jacques et son maître (Jacques and His Master)*, with introduction. Prague. Lang.: Cat. 1551

1970-1987.   Performance/production.
Interview with actor László Csendes. Hungary. Lang.: Hun. 1874

1980.   Plays/librettos/scripts.
Contemporary Czechoslovakian authors, some works in Italian translation. Lang.: Ita. 1111

1980-1987.   Design/technology.
Action Design, a new theory of scenography emerging in Eastern Europe. Prague. Lang.: Eng. 315

Scene design training at Academy of Performing Arts, Bratislava. Szeged. Bratislava. Lang.: Hun. 344

1985.   Performance/production.
Problems of amateur theatre, Eastern Bohemia. Hradec Králové. Lang.: Cze. 3973

1986.   Performance/production.
Actors Jaromír Hanzlík and Viktor Preiss in Rostand's *Cyrano*, directed by Jaroslov Dudek at Vinohradské Theatre. Prague. Lang.: Cze. 771

1987.   Design/technology.
Report on the Prague Quadrennial computer symposium. Prague. Lang.: Eng. 306

Hungarian exhibition, Prague Quadrennial theatre design competition. Prague. Lang.: Hun. 307

The contribution of Josef Svoboda to the 1987 Prague Quadrennial exhibition. Prague. Lang.: Eng. 308

Judge of Prague Quadrennial design competition describes jury's work. Prague. Lang.: Eng. 310

A report from the Prague Quadrennial theatre design contest. Prague. Lang.: Swe. 312

1987.   Institutions.
Theatre department, National Museum, Prague. Prague. Lang.: Cze. 527

1987.   Performance spaces.
Preservation and maintenance of cultural sites in Prague. Prague. Lang.: Eng. 630

1987.   Performance/production.
Noises Off by Michael Frayn, directed by Jiří Menzel, Činoherní klub. Prague. Lang.: Cze. 765

Antonín Máša directs his play *Vivisekce (Vivisection)* at Laterna magika. Prague. Lang.: Cze. 767

Miroslav Krobot directs Steigerwald's *Dobové tance (Period Dances)*, Nejedlý Realistic Theatre. Prague. Lang.: Cze. 770

Jaroslav Dudek directs *A Day Lasts Longer than a Century* by Čingiz Ajmatov, Vinohradské Theatre. Prague. Lang.: Cze. 774

England — cont'd

1589-1606.   **Plays/librettos/scripts.**
History and utopianism in some plays of Shakespeare. Lang.:
Ger.   2558
1589-1610.   **Plays/librettos/scripts.**
Essays on Shakespeare by a historian of culture. Lang.: Hun.
    2555
1590-1612.   **Plays/librettos/scripts.**
Representation of real history and Utopia in Shakespeare's
plays. Lang.: Ger.   2531
1590-1987.   **Theory/criticism.**
Gesture and sign in Shakespearean performance. USA. Lang.:
Eng.   1326
1591.   **Plays/librettos/scripts.**
Argument for authenticity of three Elizabethan documents.
Lang.: Eng.   3325
1591-1599.   **Plays/librettos/scripts.**
The creation of ideal future worlds based on the historical
past in some plays of Shakespeare. Lang.: Ger.   2539
1591-1616.   **Plays/librettos/scripts.**
Shakespeare's use of language in *The Two Noble Kinsmen.*
Lang.: Eng.   2537
1591-1885.   **Plays/librettos/scripts.**
Argument against authenticity of three Elizabethan
documents. Lang.: Eng.   3326
1592.   **Plays/librettos/scripts.**
Temporality in Shakespeare's *Richard III.* Lang.: Eng.   1115
1593-1674.   **Relation to other fields.**
Church records related to Morris dancing. Great Marlow.
Lang.: Eng.   3280
1594-1599.   **Plays/librettos/scripts.**
Structure of tragic elements in plays of William Shakespeare.
London. Lang.: Eng.   2551
1594-1616.   **Plays/librettos/scripts.**
Shakespeare's use of formal self-referential oaths. Lang.: Eng.
    2552
1594-1836.   **Plays/librettos/scripts.**
Italian translation of *Über die Shakespearomanie (On
Shakespeare-Mania)* by Christian Dietrich Grabbe. Germany.
Lang.: Ita.   2520
1595-1596.   **Plays/librettos/scripts.**
Metadrama, alienation and fantasy in Shakespeare's *Romeo
and Juliet.* Lang.: Eng.   2524
Tragic result of utopian ideas in Shakespeare's *Romeo and
Juliet.* Lang.: Ger.   2530
1595-1650.   **Plays/librettos/scripts.**
Productions of *Sir Thomas More* by Elizabethan theatre
companies. Lang.: Eng.   2541
1596-1633.   **Performance/production.**
New interpretation of Jacobean theatre. London. Lang.: Eng.
    1743
1596-1701.   **Plays/librettos/scripts.**
Eighteenth-century alterations to Shakespeare's *The Merchant
of Venice.* Lang.: Eng.   2512
1598-1602.   **Plays/librettos/scripts.**
Comparison of the works of Ben Jonson and Christopher
Marlowe. Lang.: Eng.   1123
1599.   **Plays/librettos/scripts.**
Shakespeare's *Henry V*: development of Prince Hal as an
ideological monarch. Lang.: Eng.   1124
Character analysis of Olivia in *Twelfth Night.* Lang.: Eng.
    2544
Role of Chorus in Shakespeare's *Henry V.* Lang.: Eng.   2556
1599.   **Theory/criticism.**
Semiotic study of dialogue in *As You Like It.* Lang.: Eng.
    1325
Self-awareness in Shakespeare's *Julius Caesar.* Lang.: Eng.
    1327
1599-1600.   **Plays/librettos/scripts.**
Society vs. nature in Shakespeare's *As You Like It.* Lang.:
Ger.   2536
Social reality in contrast with nature as allegory of utopian
social fiction. Lang.: Eng.   2549
1599-1987.   **Research/historiography.**
Critical history of *Julius Caesar.* Lang.: Eng.   1299
1600.   **Plays/librettos/scripts.**
Shakespeare's *Hamlet*: representation of interiority onstage.
Lang.: Eng.   2500
1600-1601.   **Plays/librettos/scripts.**
Title character's relation to the audience in Shakespeare's
Hamlet. Lang.: Ger.   2545

1600-1620.   **Plays/librettos/scripts.**
Swetnam the Woman-Hater, Arraigned by Women written in
response to an anti-female pamphlet. Lang.: Eng.   1118
1600-1650.   **Plays/librettos/scripts.**
Utopian ideas in Tudor and Stuart playwrights. Lang.: Ger.
    2522
1600-1699.   **Plays/librettos/scripts.**
Theoretical considerations of English Renaissance theatre.
Lang.: Rus.   2528
1600-1700.   **Theory/criticism.**
Plays that attempt to legitimize theatre. France. Lang.: Eng.
    1324
1600-1980.   **Plays/librettos/scripts.**
Class conflict in Shakespeare's *Coriolanus* as viewed in 17th
and 20th century. Lang.: Ger.   2553
1600-1987.   **Plays/librettos/scripts.**
Playwright Ben Jonson's theatricality and relevance today.
Lang.: Eng.   2501
1601.   **Plays/librettos/scripts.**
Classification and social hierarchy in Shakespeare's *Troilus
and Cressida.* Lang.: Eng.   2554
1602-1604.   **Relation to other fields.**
Psychological effect of Ben Jonson's family life on his
writings. Lang.: Eng.   1232
1602-1987.   **Plays/librettos/scripts.**
Devices that convey concern with sexuality in Shakespeare's
All's Well that Ends Well. Lang.: Eng.   2523
1604.   **Plays/librettos/scripts.**
Allegory and irony in *Othello.* Lang.: Eng.   1114
An analysis of the structure of *Measure for Measure.* Lang.:
Eng.   1120
1604-1929.   **Plays/librettos/scripts.**
Comparative study of *Measure for Measure* by Shakespeare
and the poem *Leda and the Swan* by Yeats. Lang.: Eng.
    1116
1604-1948.   **Performance/production.**
Interpretation and critique of Olivier's film *Hamlet.* Lang.:
Chi.   3149
1605.   **Plays/librettos/scripts.**
King Lear focusing on the character of Kent. Lang.: Eng.
    1122
Evaluation of *Westward Ho!* and *Northward Ho!* by Thomas
Dekker and John Webster. Lang.: Eng.   2509
Influences of Arthurian legend on Shakespeare's *King Lear.*
Lang.: Eng.   2521
1605-1611.   **Plays/librettos/scripts.**
Theodicy and tragic drama in *King Lear* and *The Tempest.*
Lang.: Eng.   1119
1605-1884.   **Plays/librettos/scripts.**
Comparison of *King Lear* and *Vildanden (The Wild Duck).*
Norway. Lang.: Eng.   2518
1605-1913.   **Relation to other fields.**
Comparison of *King Lear* and South African Land Act
regarding land distribution. South Africa, Republic of. Lang.:
Eng.   1231
1607-1614.   **Plays/librettos/scripts.**
Exploration of mythic elements in the later plays of William
Shakespeare. London. Lang.: Eng.   2497
1607-1987.   **Performance/production.**
Shakespeare and contemporaries: tradition, intertextuality in
performance. Lang.: Eng.   1740
1608-1700.   **Plays/librettos/scripts.**
Comparison of works of Milton and Dryden. Lang.: Eng.
    2546
1609-1987.   **Plays/librettos/scripts.**
Urbanity as subject and form of Jonson's *Epicoene.* Lang.:
Eng.   2498
1611.   **Plays/librettos/scripts.**
Place of the masque in *The Tempest.* Lang.: Eng.   2516
Relationship of the *Aeneid* to Shakespeare's *The Tempest.*
London. Lang.: Eng.   2561
1611-1612.   **Plays/librettos/scripts.**
Utopianism in Shakespeare's *The Tempest.* Lang.: Ger.   2532
1612-1614.   **Plays/librettos/scripts.**
Rumour as a political and social tool in *Henry VIII.*
London. Lang.: Eng.   2547
1613.   **Plays/librettos/scripts.**
Use of symbols in Webster's *The Duchess of Malfi.* Lang.:
Eng.   1121

Europe — cont'd

International biographical survey of opera performers and productions. North America. Lang.: Eng. 3762

Biographical survey of Canadian opera performers. North America. Lang.: Eng. 3763

Biographical survey of international opera stars. North America. Lang.: Eng. 3764

Film versions of Puccini's *La Bohème*, Offenbach's *Tales of Hoffmann*. North America. Lang.: Eng. 3767

The Heldentenor in Wagnerian opera. North America. Lang.: Eng. 3770

1987. **Reference materials.**
Theatre on video. Lang.: Ita. 1200

Federal Republic of Germany
SEE
Germany, West.

Finland
1600-1982. **Relation to other fields.**
Bear hunting ritual-drama: text, poetry, description of rites. Lang.: Eng. 1234

1905-1917. **Institutions.**
Will Garland and European tour of Negro Operetta Company. UK-England. Helsinki. Russia. Lang.: Eng. 3956

1939-1947. **Performance/production.**
Music for Brecht's *Mutter Courage und ihre Kinder (Mother Courage and Her Children)*. Zürich. Lang.: Ger. 2027

1950-1982. **Relation to other fields.**
Development of theatre influenced by myths of national character. Lang.: Eng. 2989

1986. **Performance/production.**
Life Service Theatre experiment in topical theatre. Oulu. Lang.: Swe. 1749

1987. **Basic theatrical documents.**
English translation of *What, No Ashes?* by Tauno Yliruusi. Lang.: Eng. 1553

France
Design/technology.
Exhibition of theatrical design by Léger, Cocteau, Kokoschka and Kandinsky. Lang.: Eng. 322
Plays/librettos/scripts.
Mouchoir de Nuages (Handkerchief of Clouds) by Tristan Tzara. Lang.: Ita. 2569

500 B.C.-1800 A.D. **Theory/criticism.**
Development of the three unities. Greece. Italy. Lang.: Kor. 3047

800-1700. **Relation to other fields.**
Overview of French literature including theatre. Lang.: Ita. 2990

900-1600. **Plays/librettos/scripts.**
Theories of staging the *visitatio sepulchri*. Germany. Lang.: Eng. 2599

1300-1399. **Design/technology.**
Scenic representations of Hell. Italy. Lang.: Ita. 349

1415-1987. **Performance/production.**
Exhibition catalogue: popular theatre in Catalan. Lang.: Cat, Fre. 1750

1450-1550. **Audience.**
Assembly, composition, accommodation and response of spectators to civic and religious plays. Lang.: Eng. 1534

1500-1700. **Performance/production.**
Relation between dramatic text, staging and the actor. Italy. Lang.: Ita. 830

1539-1985. **Theory/criticism.**
Modernity as historical concept applied to Catalonia and Occitania. Barcelona. Lang.: Fre. 1332

1540-1650. **Theory/criticism.**
Works of Pierre Corneille and the social role of women. Lang.: Eng. 3040

1570-1660. **Theory/criticism.**
Principles and theories of playwright Pierre Corneille. Lang.: Heb. 3038

1600-1700. **Theory/criticism.**
Plays that attempt to legitimize theatre. England. Lang.: Eng. 1324

1611-1977. **Relation to other fields.**
Theme of imperialism in *The Tempest*. Canada. Antilles. Lang.: Eng. 2984

1622-1673. **Plays/librettos/scripts.**
Italian translation of W. D. Howarth's *Molière: A Playwright and His Audience*. Lang.: Ita. 2574

1673-1679. **Institutions.**
Production of *Circé* by the Comédiens du Roy, Hôtel Guénégaud. Paris. Lang.: Eng. 530

1696-1841. **Plays/librettos/scripts.**
Index of theatrical manuscripts from Roussillon written in Catalan. Lang.: Cat. 2568

1700-1897. **Design/technology.**
Decors of feasts and festivals prefigured architectural developments. Düsseldorf. Italy. Lang.: Fre. 3320

1700-1975. **Plays/librettos/scripts.**
Compares plays of Enlightenment France, Francophone Africa. Brazzaville. Cameroon. Benin. Lang.: Eng. 2496

1707-1763. **Plays/librettos/scripts.**
Comparison of Marivaux and Goldoni. Venice. Lang.: Ita. 2664

1715-1774. **Theory/criticism.**
Rococo elements in the comedies of Marivaux. Lang.: Eng. 3039

1718-1778. **Plays/librettos/scripts.**
Techniques, themes, characters and dramaturgy of Voltaire. Lang.: Eng. 2590

1720-1987. **Performance/production.**
Roles of women in the field of ballet. USA. Lang.: Eng. 1434

1734-1765. **Design/technology.**
French costume experimentation. Paris. London. Lang.: Eng. 1591

1769-1850. **Performance/production.**
Child actors in juvenile companies, Comédie-Française. Paris. Lang.: Eng. 1756

1770-1987. **Theory/criticism.**
Shift from classical traditions to melodrama. Lang.: Eng. 1338

1782-1871. **Plays/librettos/scripts.**
Study of French composer Daniel Auber and his works. Lang.: Eng. 3904

1800-1825. **Plays/librettos/scripts.**
Analysis of vampire characters in the works of Byron, Polidori and Planché. England. Italy. Lang.: Eng. 2540

1800-1830. **Performance/production.**
Documentation on melodramatic acting style. Paris. Lang.: Eng. 791

1800-1850. **Theory/criticism.**
Tragedy, space and discourse in neoclassical dramatic theory. Lang.: Eng. 3035

1800-1899. **Administration.**
Political censorship of theatre. England. Russia. Germany. Lang.: Eng. 1517

1800-1899. **Institutions.**
History of the Conservatoire, training for classical repertory. Paris. Lang.: Eng. 1615

1800-1899. **Performance/production.**
Puppetry on the streets and fairgrounds. Lang.: Eng. 3258

1800-1899. **Plays/librettos/scripts.**
Theme of *femme fatale* in *Samson et Dalila*. Lang.: Eng. 3900

1803-1870. **Plays/librettos/scripts.**
Mérimée novella, source of Bizet's *Carmen*. Paris. Lang.: Eng. 3903

1819-1920. **Plays/librettos/scripts.**
Antonin Artaud's interpretation of Shelley's *The Cenci*. UK-England. Lang.: Eng. 2780

1822-1896. **Plays/librettos/scripts.**
Operas of César Franck. Paris. Lang.: Eng. 3898

1830-1920. **Plays/librettos/scripts.**
Female roles and images in the romantic ballet. Germany. Russia. Lang.: Ger. 1455

1831-1910. **Plays/librettos/scripts.**
Background and sources of Massenet's *Manon Lescaut*. Paris. Lang.: Eng. 3899

1850-1920. **Performance/production.**
Carte-de-visite actors' photographs preserve acting styles. UK-England. USA. Lang.: Eng. 916

1859-1916. **Plays/librettos/scripts.**
Musical, personal relationship of Saint-Saëns and Wagner. Paris. Lang.: Eng. 3902

1863. **Plays/librettos/scripts.**
Historical context for Tom Taylor's *The Ticket-of-Leave Man*. UK-England. 2801

GEOGRAPHICAL - CHRONOLOGICAL INDEX

France — cont'd

1864-1918. **Plays/librettos/scripts.**
Biography of Swiss playwright Frank Wedekind. Lenzburg. Berlin. Paris. Lang.: Ger. 2746

1873-1875. **Performance/production.**
The original production of *Carmen*. Paris. Lang.: Eng. 3773

1875-1987. **Performance spaces.**
Performance spaces and audience-performer relationship. Germany, West. Lang.: Eng. 633

1876-1946. **Plays/librettos/scripts.**
Life and career of Manuel de Falla: his opera *Atlántida*. Madrid. Paris. Lang.: Ger. 3930

1877-1923. **Theory/criticism.**
The career of critic Ricciotto Canudo. Italy. Lang.: Ita. 1330

1880-1987. **Basic theatrical documents.**
New English translation of Rostand's *Chantecler*. Lang.: Eng. 1554

1887-1987. **Plays/librettos/scripts.**
Jullien's violations of decorum and *honneur* in *La Sérénade (The Serenade)*. Lang.: Eng. 2577

1887-1987. **Theory/criticism.**
Avoiding the risk of commercialism: the example of Antoine's Théâtre Libre. Lang.: Fre. 1335

Centenary of Théâtre Libre: proposes 'subjective realism'. Lang.: Fre. 1337

1889-1973. **Plays/librettos/scripts.**
Life and works of French dramatist Gabriel Marcel. Lang.: Eng. 2573

1891-1930. **Performance/production.**
Career of choreographer/dancer Bronislava Nižinska. USA. Lang.: Eng. 1436

1893-1913. **Performance/production.**
Compositions by Debussy in their relationship to Afro-American music. Paris. London. Lang.: Eng. 3384

1896-1949. **Theory/criticism.**
Artaud's conception of theatre. Lang.: Ger. 1333

1900-1945. **Performance/production.**
Initial recordings of Verdi's operas. Italy. USA. Lang.: Eng. 3800

1900-1987. **Performance/production.**
Extension of Adolphe Appia's ideas on the role of the actor. Lang.: Fre. 786

1904-1909. **Plays/librettos/scripts.**
Study of playwright Paul Claudel based on his letters. Lang.: Fre. 2572

1904-1987. **Performance/production.**
Interview with tenor Martial Singher. Santa Barbara, CA. Lang.: Eng. 3771

Interview with conductor Manuel Rosenthal. Paris. Lang.: Eng. 3774

1905-1978. **Plays/librettos/scripts.**
Comparison of plays by Camus and Sartre. Lang.: Kor. 2576

1906-1975. **Performance/production.**
Catalogue of an exhibit on singer-dancer Josephine Baker. Paris. Lang.: Ita. 3259

1910-1982. **Performance/production.**
Influence of *nō* theatre on director Jean-Louis Barrault and his colleagues. Lang.: Eng. 1498

1917-1965. **Design/technology.**
Picasso's theatrical work. Spain. Lang.: Ita. 321

1920-1986. **Plays/librettos/scripts.**
Career of playwright Sacha Guitry. Lang.: Eng. 2567

1921-1987. **Performance/production.**
Giorgio Strehler as the quintessential director of the century. Italy. Lang.: Fre. 1754

1922-1928. **Plays/librettos/scripts.**
Playwright Roger Vitrac's critiques of bourgeois family life. Lang.: Eng. 2584

1924-1940. **Performance/production.**
Uday Shankar's translation of Indian dance for Western audiences. India. Paris. London. Lang.: Eng. 1461

1924-1987. **Plays/librettos/scripts.**
Anti-fascist plays of Armand Gatti. Lang.: Rus. 2578

Dramaturgy of Armand Gatti. Lang.: Rus. 2579

1927-1987. **Performance/production.**
Choreographer Maurice Béjart's creative principles. Lang.: Rus. 1435

1927-1987. **Plays/librettos/scripts.**
Playwright Michel Vinaver and his works. Lang.: Fre. 2582

1928-1986. **Performance/production.**
Giorgio Strehler on staging *Die Dreigroschenoper (The Three Penny Opera)*. Milan. Paris. Lang.: Swe. 3809

1931-1935. **Plays/librettos/scripts.**
Influence of Balinese theatre on Antonin Artaud. Indonesia. Lang.: Kor. 1126

1933-1987. **Design/technology.**
Exhibition on ballet *The Seven Deadly Sins* by Kurt Weill and Edward James. Paris. London. Lang.: Eng. 1429

1934. **Plays/librettos/scripts.**
Death in Ghelderode's *La Balade du Grand Macabre (The Grand Macabre's Stroll)*. Lang.: Eng. 2587

1937-1979. **Performance/production.**
Stage history of Alban Berg's opera *Lulu*. Austria. Paris. Lang.: Swe. 3743

1939-1953. **Plays/librettos/scripts.**
Influence of O'Neill and Beckett on Israel Horovitz. Boston, MA. Paris. Lang.: Eng. 2873

1939-1976. **Plays/librettos/scripts.**
Korean stage adaptation of *Le Mur (The Wall)* by Sartre. Korea. Lang.: Kor. 2575

1940-1986. **Performance/production.**
Brigitte Jacques as Elvire in Molière's *Dom Juan*. Strasbourg. Lang.: Fre. 1764

1944-1953. **Reference materials.**
History of pocket theatre. Paris. Lang.: Eng. 2974

1945-1987. **Performance/production.**
Directing methods of Klaus Michael Grüber. Germany. Lang.: Fre. 1766

1955-1987. **Performance/production.**
Directorial style of Claude Régy. Lang.: Fre. 1762

1956-1986. **Performance/production.**
Profile of Pitu, a whiteface clown, and changing traditions of circuses and clowning. Lang.: Eng. 3303

1956-1987. **Plays/librettos/scripts.**
History and analysis of Mrożek's play *Vatslave*. Cracow. Paris. Lang.: Heb. 2713

1957-1985. **Administration.**
New reforms and changes in the 1957 French copyright law. Paris. Lang.: Eng. 25

1957-1987. **Plays/librettos/scripts.**
Role analysis of Blanche in Poulenc's *Dialogues des Carmélites*. Paris. Lang.: Eng. 3901

1958-1987. **Plays/librettos/scripts.**
The allegory of capitalist society in Genet's *Le Balcon (The Balcony)*. Lang.: Eng. 2588

1959-1987. **Plays/librettos/scripts.**
Playwright Fernando Arrabal and productions of his work. USA. Paris. Lang.: Eng. 1175

1961-1987. **Plays/librettos/scripts.**
Symbols of power in Genet's *Les Paravents (The Screens)*. Montreal, PQ. Ottawa, ON. Lang.: Fre. 2570

André Brassard's production of Jean Genet's *Les Paravents (The Screens)*. Montreal, PQ. Ottawa, ON. Lang.: Fre. 2583

Investigating the text of Genet's *Les Paravents (The Screens)*. Montreal, PQ. Ottawa, ON. Lang.: Fre. 2585

1967-1985. **Relation to other fields.**
Interview with playwright Jean Genet regarding his political commitments. Lang.: Eng. 1236

1968-1987. **Plays/librettos/scripts.**
Iser's reader-response theory and Beckett's *Come and Go*. Lang.: Eng. 2581

1969-1984. **Performance/production.**
Personal notes of Samuel Beckett, how they illuminate his plays. Lang.: Eng. 1758

1977-1987. **Theory/criticism.**
Impact of cinematic technique on plays by Beckett and Duras. Lang.: Eng. 3037

1980-1982. **Performance/production.**
Development of mime, pantomime and its related movements. Paris. UK-England. New York, NY. Lang.: Eng. 3223

Contemporary mime forms and their innovators. Paris. Belgium. USA. Lang.: Eng. 3224

1980-1987. **Performance/production.**
Productions by directors Patrice Chéreau, Claude Régy, Ariane Mnouchkine. Lang.: Rus. 792

Théâtre de la Jeune Lune, its origins and influences. Minneapolis, MN. Paris. Lang.: Eng. 977

France — cont'd

Soviet tour of Comédie-Française: Jean-Pierre Vincent directs Molière's *Le Misanthrope*. USSR. Lang.: Rus.   1769

1981-1987.   Plays/librettos/scripts.
Interaction of scenic imagery and narrative in *Ohio Impromptu*. Lang.: Eng.   2586

1982.   Relation to other fields.
International Federation of Actors discusses actors' conditions. Paris. Lang.: Eng.   1235

1982-1986.   Performance/production.
Marcel Marceau's reflections on his art. Italy. Lang.: Ita.   3233

1982-1987.   Performance/production.
Patrice Chéreau and Théâtre des Amandiers create stage and film versions of Čechov's *Platonov*. Nanterre. Lang.: Swe.   1755

1982-1987.   Plays/librettos/scripts.
Beckett links theme of political persecution to voyeurism of the theatrical experience. Lang.: Eng.   2589

1983-1985.   Relation to other fields.
Experimental theatre course, Assoc. Internationale pour la Sémiologie du Spectacle. Brussels. Paris. Odense. Lang.: Fre.   1219

1983-1987.   Relation to other fields.
Political context of the constructing of the Opéra-Bastille. Paris. Lang.: Eng.   3941

1985-1987.   Plays/librettos/scripts.
Comparison of two versions of Duras' *La Musica Deuxième*. Paris. Lang.: Eng.   1125

Analysis of Cixous' *Norodom Sihanouk*. Paris. Lang.: Eng.   2580

1986.   Performance/production.
Company members of Centre International de Recherche Théâtrale discuss *The Mahabharata*. Paris. Lang.: Eng.   1752

Review of the 1986 Festival de la Francophonie. Belgium. Lang.: Fre.   1760

1987.   Administration.
In-depth look at funding systems for the arts. UK-England. USA. Lang.: Eng.   52

1987.   Performance spaces.
Examining current needs of theatre artists vs. historical examination to determine theatre space design. Germany, West. UK-England. Lang.: Eng.   634

1987.   Performance/production.
Directing as guiding actors, not imposing a subjective interpretation. Lang.: Fre.   784

Directing as creation of a dimension that enhances the actor's desire. Lang.: Fre.   785

Direction as unveiling: Antoine Vitez. Lang.: Fre.   787

Staging as a form of translation. Lang.: Fre.   788

Teamwork concept of directing. Lang.: Fre.   789

Concrete, specific style of young French directors. Lang.: Fre.   790

Evolution of directing toward working closely with actors. Lang.: Fre.   793

Revolutionary approach to directing. Lang.: Fre.   794

Influence of filmmaker Jean Renoir's techniques in the theatre. Lang.: Eng.   795

Directing today must counter perceived habits of perception. Lang.: Fre.   796

New European choreographers and their development of new images. Paris. London. South Africa, Republic of. Lang.: Eng.   1468

Jean-Pierre Vincent directs *Le mariage de Figaro (The Marriage of Figaro)* by Beaumarchais. Paris. Lang.: Fre.   1751

Plays of Pinget, Euripides and Théâtre du Rideau staged by Jouanneau, Suzuki and Tanguy, Théâtre de la Bastille. Paris. Lang.: Fre.   1753

Director as true author and maker of theatre. Lang.: Fre.   1757

Directing and the desire to communicate. Lang.: Fre.   1759

Analysis of *Dans la solitude des champs de coton (In the Solitude of the Cotton Fields)* by Bernard-Marie Koltès. Paris. Lang.: Swe.   1761

Directing should be judged by the work of great directors. Lang.: Fre.   1763

Luca Ronconi's view of directing. Italy. Lang.: Fre.   1765

Antoine Vitez directs *Le soulier de satin (The Satin Slipper)* by Paul Claudel, Festival of Avignon. Avignon. Lang.: Fre.   1767

Directing as textual interpretation, relating performance to text. Lang.: Fre.   1768

Review of Ariane Mnouchkine's film *Molière*. Lang.: Hun.   3150

Parisian cabaret theatre performance reviews. Paris. Lang.: Eng.   3284

Interview with baritone Michel Sénéchal. Paris. Lang.: Eng.   3772

1987.   Plays/librettos/scripts.
Peter Brook discusses his production of *The Mahabharata*. Paris. India. Perth. Lang.: Eng.   2571

1987.   Theory/criticism.
How to maintain an element of risk in theatre. Lang.: Fre.   1331

Relations between text and representation of *mise en scène*. Lang.: Spa.   1334

Theatre and the infatuation with technology. Lang.: Fre.   1336

Effect of audiovisual media on theatre. Lang.: Fre.   1339

Introduction to Mallarmé's *Crayonne au Théâtre*. Lang.: Eng.   3036

German Democratic Republic
SEE
Germany, East.

Germany
400 B.C.-1987 A.D.   Performance spaces.
Theatre space and theatrical space in theatre from the ancient Greeks to the present. England. Greece. Lang.: Eng.   635

300 B.C.-1956 A.D.   Theory/criticism.
Platonism in the plays of Brecht. Greece. Lang.: Eng.   3048
275-1945.   Performance/production.
Writings of director Leon Schiller. Poland. Roman Empire. Lang.: Pol.   1994
900-1600.   Plays/librettos/scripts.
Theories of staging the *visitatio sepulchri*. France. Lang.: Eng.   2599
1000-1400.   Research/historiography.
Research methods on origins and tradition of liturgical drama. Lang.: Ita.   3010
1594-1836.   Plays/librettos/scripts.
Italian translation of *Über die Shakespearomanie (On Shakespeare-Mania)* by Christian Dietrich Grabbe. England. Lang.: Ita.   2520
1606-1681.   Basic theatrical documents.
English translations of three plays by Jacob Masen. Lang.: Eng.   1556
1700-1799.   Performance/production.
Theatrical dance tradition as presented by dance teacher Gregorio Lambranzi. Venice. Nuremberg. Lang.: Ita.   1439
1700-1897.   Design/technology.
Decors of feasts and festivals prefigured architectural developments. Düsseldorf. France. Italy. Lang.: Fre.   3320
1700-1987.   Relation to other fields.
Cultural and social role of Berlin theatres. Berlin. Lang.: Ger.   1237
1744-1816.   Performance/production.
Actor-director Friedrich Ludwig Schröder. Lang.: Rus.   798
1749-1832.   Plays/librettos/scripts.
Analysis of Goethe's *Götz von Berlichingen*. Lang.: Ger.   2598
1762-1986.   Performance/production.
Gluck as opera composer: his *Orfeo ed Euridice* staged by Peter Konwitschny. Halle. Lang.: Ger.   3776
1767-1769.   Theory/criticism.
Catalan translation of Lessing's *Hamburgische Dramaturgie*. Hamburg. Lang.: Cat.   3043
1770-1985.   Theory/criticism.
The theories of G. E. Lessing applied to Chinese theatre. China, People's Republic of. Lang.: Chi.   3616
1794-1906.   Basic theatrical documents.
Texts on dramatic theory by nineteenth-century authors. Lang.: Ger.   1555
1795-1830.   Performance/production.
Essays on major figures of the Romantic period. Lang.: Ger.   1776

Greece — cont'd

500 B.C.-1800 A.D.   Theory/criticism.
Development of the three unities. France. Italy. Lang.: Kor.
3047

500 B.C.-1986 A.D.   Plays/librettos/scripts.
Translating ancient Greek theatre into film. Lang.: Eng. 3098

500 B.C.-1987 A.D.   Plays/librettos/scripts.
Ancient Greek theatre, modern stagings. Lang.: Ita.   2618

500 B.C.-1987 A.D.   Theory/criticism.
Perceptions of tragedy and new perspective on its analysis.
USA. UK-England. Lang.: Eng.   3066

472-388 B.C.   Plays/librettos/scripts.
Study of classical Greek dramaturgy. Lang.: Hun.   2623

408 B.C.   Plays/librettos/scripts.
Euripides' use of *deus ex machina* in *Orestes*. Lang.: Eng.
2626

400 B.C.-180 A.D.   Plays/librettos/scripts.
Changes in theatre space as a result of New Comedy.
Athens. Rome. Lang.: Eng.   2625

400 B.C.-500 A.D.   Plays/librettos/scripts.
Study of works by Sophocles, Aeschylus and Euripides.
Lang.: Eng.   2624

400 B.C.-1987 A.D.   Performance spaces.
Theatre space and theatrical space in theatre from the
ancient Greeks to the present. Germany. England. Lang.:
Eng.   635

400 B.C.-1987 A.D.   Theory/criticism.
Comic space from the ancient Greeks to the present. Europe.
USA. Lang.: Eng.   3032

384-322 B.C.   Theory/criticism.
Reading of Aristotle's early scientific works. Lang.: Eng.
3049

300 B.C.-1956 A.D.   Theory/criticism.
Platonism in the plays of Brecht. Germany. Lang.: Eng. 3048

70 B.C.-1981 A.D.   Theory/criticism.
Analysis of various versions and translations of Aristotle's
Poetics. Athens. Alexandria. Europe. Lang.: Chi.   1343

57 B.C.-1392 A.D.   Plays/librettos/scripts.
Comparison of Greek tragedy and Korean Buddhist plays.
Korea. Lang.: Kor.   2684

1923-1977.   Performance/production.
Evaluation of soprano Maria Meneghini Callas. Italy. USA.
Lang.: Eng.   3790

1940-1987.   Plays/librettos/scripts.
Imagistic versus realistic drama in contemporary Greek plays.
Lang.: Eng.   2621

1987.   Plays/librettos/scripts.
Greek poetic drama through Nietzschean theory. Lang.: Eng.
2620

Holland
SEE
Netherlands.

Hungary
1790-1837.   Performance/production.
Letters illustrating development of professional theatre in
Hungary. Lang.: Hun.   807

1815-1987.   Plays/librettos/scripts.
Actor-manager Wojciech Bogusławski in life and in György
Spiró's play *Az imposztor (The Imposter)*. Poland. Lang.: Pol.
2716

1836-1847.   Performance/production.
Actor-dramas produced by National Theatre. Budapest.
Lang.: Hun.   1842

1837-1987.   Institutions.
History of the Nemzeti Szinház. Budapest. Lang.: Hun.   542

1860-1925.   Design/technology.
Scene designer Jenő Kéméndy. Lang.: Hun.   331

1862-1905.   Performance/production.
Diaries of singer-actress Lujza Blaha. Lang.: Hun.   1812

1877-1967.   Relation to other fields.
History of puppet Nativity plays. Lang.: Hun.   3994

1880-1974.   Plays/librettos/scripts.
Selections from diary of author Ményhert (Melchior) Lengyel.
Lang.: Hun.   2634

1885-1965.   Performance/production.
Autobiography of cabaret actor Béla Salamon. Budapest.
Lang.: Hun.   3285

1887-1941.   Performance/production.
Centenary volume on actor Gyula Kabos. Lang.: Hun.   3153

1900.   Performance spaces.
Mór Jókai's recollections of the old, gas-lit National Theatre
building. Budapest. Lang.: Hun.   642

1907-1969.   Performance/production.
Biography of tenor János Sárdy. Lang.: Hun.   3795

1907-1974.   Plays/librettos/scripts.
Life and career of dramatist and director Menyhért
(Melchior) Lengyel. Lang.: Hun.   1128

1907-1986.   Performance/production.
Commemoration of actress Margit Dajka. Lang.: Hun.   1907

1910-1986.   Performance/production.
Biography of actor-director Tamás Major. Lang.: Hun.   1844

1912-1986.   Performance/production.
Imre Kálmán's *Cigányprimás (Sari)* and Bizet's *Carmen* at
Kisfaludy Theatre staged by József Bor. Győr. Lang.: Hun.
3959

1919-1986.   Performance/production.
Style and career of actor Antal Páger. Lang.: Hun.   1847

1924-1986.   Performance/production.
Interview with actress Ida Turay. Pécs. Lang.: Hun.   805

1927-1987.   Design/technology.
Account of exhibition of Eric Vogel's scene and costume
designs. Budapest. Lang.: Hun.   335
An exhibition at the Pest Redoute Gallery of the set and
costume designs of Eric Vogel. Lang.: Hun.   3242

1929-1987.   Performance/production.
History of Hungarian productions of *Die Dreigroschenoper
(The Three Penny Opera)* by Brecht and Weill. Lang.: Hun.
1927

1930.   Design/technology.
Detailed description of a light-weight revolving stage
platform. Budapest. Lang.: Hun.   341

1931-1986.   Performance/production.
Career of actor, director, writer Zoltán Latinovits. Lang.:
Hun.   1794

1932-1944.   Institutions.
Proprietors, artists and operation of Jardin d'Hiver, nightclub
and revue theatre. Budapest. Lang.: Hun.   3381

1932-1972.   Performance/production.
Life and career of actress Edit Domján. Lang.: Hun.   1841

1935-1986.   Performance/production.
Memoirs of cabaret artist Balázs Szuhay. Lang.: Hun.   3286

1941-1978.   Performance/production.
Director Endre Márton. Lang.: Hun.   1860

1943-1987.   Performance/production.
Soprano Eva Marton discusses Turandot. Lang.: Eng.   3797

1946-1986.   Institutions.
Memoirs of director and teacher Géza Gergely on Hungarian
theatrical training in Romania. Tîrgu-Mures. Lang.: Hun. 556

1949-1987.   Performance/production.
Career of playwright András Sütő. Tîrgu-Mures. Lang.: Hun.
1890

1950-1986.   Performance/production.
Series of interviews with actor Tibor Szilágyi. Lang.: Hun.
1814

1950-1987.   Design/technology.
Interview with set designer Gábor Forray. Budapest. Lang.:
Hun.   3696

1951-1987.   Design/technology.
Early working conditions of the Magyar Állami Népi
Együttes (Hungarian State Folk Ensemble). Lang.: Hun. 343

1951-1987.   Performance/production.
Interview with actor Imre Sinkovits. Budapest. Lang.: Hun.
1835

1952-1987.   Performance/production.
Production history of *Galilei (Galileo)* by László Németh.
Lang.: Hun.   1790
Interview with actor-director László Mensáros. Lang.: Hun.
1792

1953-1987.   Performance/production.
Interview with actor György Kézdy. Pécs. Lang.: Hun.   1834

1957.   Design/technology.
Pál Tolnay's original proposal for modernization of the
lighting system at National Theatre. Budapest. Lang.: Hun.
340
Renovation plans for the Hungarian National Theatre.
Budapest. Lang.: Hun.   342

1961-1987.   Performance/production.
Interview with tenor Plácido Domingo. Budapest. Lang.: Hun.
3791

1962-1987.   Performance/production.
Interview with actor-director Miklós Gábor. Lang.: Hun. 1793

Hungary — cont'd

Imre Kerényi directs *Énekes madár (The Song Bird)* by Áron Tamási at the National Theatre. Budapest. Lang.: Hun.
1819

Season openings at Petőfi Theatre, including Lengyel's *A nagy fejedelem (The Great Prince)* and Bíró's *A rablólovag (The Gallant Kidnapper).* Veszprém. Lang.: Hun.
1820

László Vámos directs *Les femmes savantes (The Learned Ladies)* by Molière at Várszinház under the title *Tudós nők.* Budapest. Lang.: Hun.
1823

Essay on interpretive methods in performance and production. Lang.: Hun.
1824

Imre Csiszár directs Bertolt Brecht's *Leben des Galilei (The Life of Galileo)* at the National Theatre. Miskolc. Lang.: Hun.
1826

Reviews of two Anouilh plays: *Eurydice* directed by János Szűcs, *Colombe* directed by Mátyás Giricz. Miskolc. Budapest. Lang.: Hun.
1827

Tamás Jordán's *Amit a szívedbe rejtesz (Hidden in Your Heart)* directed by János Gáspár. Budapest. Lang.: Hun.
1828

István Paál directs István Örkény's *Forgatókönyv (Screenplay)* at Petőfi Theatre. Veszprém. Lang.: Hun.
1832

János Gáspar directs *Amit a szívedbe rejtesz (Hidden in Your Heart)* by Tamás Jordán, based on notes by poet Attila József, at Radnóti Miklós Theatre. Budapest. Lang.: Hun.
1836

Péter Blaskó in the title role of Brecht's *Leben des Galilei (The Life of Galileo)* directed as *Galilei élete* by Imre Csiszár at Miskolc National Theatre. Miskolc. Lang.: Hun.
1839

Péter Tömöry directs premiere of Zsigmond Móricz's 1916 *Fortunátus.* Zalaegerszeg. Lang.: Hun.
1840

Imre Halasi directs *Sári bíró (Judge Sári)* by Zsigmond Móricz, music by István Mikó, at Kisvarda Castle Theatre. Kisvárda. Lang.: Hun.
1845

Tamás Fodor directs *Örökösök (Heirs)* based on Gorkij's *Vassa Železnova.* Szolnok. Lang.: Hun.
1848

István Horvai directs Imre Sarkadi's *Oszlopos Simeon (The Man on the Pillar)* at the Pesti Theatre. Budapest. Lang.: Hun.
1849

Gábor Zsámbéki directs Eugene O'Neill's *Long Day's Journey into Night* under the title *Utazás az éjszakába.* Eger. Lang.: Hun.
1850

Ferenc Sík directs *Galilei (Galileo)* by László Németh at Várszinház. Budapest. Lang.: Hun.
1851

István Szőke directs Shakespeare's *Merchant of Venice,* Pécs National Theatre. Pécs. Lang.: Hun.
1854

Ferenc Sík directs András Sütő's *Álomkommandó (Dream Commando),* Gyulai Várszinház. Gyula. Lang.: Hun.
1855

Gábor Székely directs Milán Füst's *Catullus* at Katona József Theatre. Budapest. Lang.: Hun.
1857

Menyhért Szegvári directs premiere of *Lisszaboni eső (Rain in Lisbon)* by Miklós Munkácsi at Játékszín. Budapest. Lang.: Hun.
1858

Tamás Szirtes directs Gyula Háy's *Mohács (The Mohács Disaster)* at Madách Szinház. Lang.: Hun.
1863

László Bagossy directs *Macbeth,* Tamás Jordán directs Zsigmond Móricz's *Uri muri (Gentlemen's Spree)* at Pécs Summer Theatre. Pécs. Lang.: Hun.
1864

Fadren (The Father) by August Strindberg presented under the title *Az apa* at Katona József Theatre, guest director Kalle Holmberg. Budapest. Lang.: Hun.
1865

Eszter Csákányi in the title role of Shaw's *Saint Joan,* directed under the title *Szent Johanna* by László Babarczy at Csiky Gergely Theatre. Kaposvár. Lang.: Hun.
1867

Tamás Ascher directs *Il campiello (The Public Square)* by Goldoni at Csiky Gergely Theatre. Kaposvár. Lang.: Hun.
1868

Arthur Miller's *Death of a Salesman* directed by János Szikora at Vígszínház. Budapest. Lang.: Hun.
1869

Áron Tamási's *Énekes madár (The Song Bird)* directed by Imre Kerényi at National Theatre. Budapest. Lang.: Hun.
1872

Péter Huszti directs *A női partőrség szeme láttára (In Sight of the Spar)* by Pál Békés at Madách Szinház Chamber Theatre. Budapest. Lang.: Hun.
1873

Péter Léner directs Géza Páskandi's *Lélekharang (Death Knell),* Móricz Zsigmond Theatre. Nyíregyháza. Lang.: Hun.
1876

Gábor Székely directs Milán Füst's *Catullus* at Katona József Theatre. Budapest. Lang.: Hun.
1878

Review of conference on contemporary Hungarian drama. Egervár. Lang.: Hun.
1879

Tamás Ascher directs Ljudmila Petruševskaja's *Tri devuški v golubom (Three Girls in Blue)* at Katona József Theatre under the title *Három lány kékben.* Budapest. USSR. Lang.: Hun.
1883

Andor Lukács directs Alfred Jarry's *Ubu roi (King Ubu)* at Csiky Gergely Theatre as *Übü király.* Boglárelle. Lang.: Hun.
1884

Milán Füst's *Catullus* and Imre Sarkadi's *Oszlopos Simeon (The Man on the Pillar)* reviewed. Budapest. Lang.: Hun.
1886

Productions of plays by László Márton, Tamás Jordán and Ferenc Kulin at Radnóti Miklós Theatre. Budapest. Lang.: Hun.
1887

Anouilh's *Eurydice,* Vian's *Tête de Méduse (Medusa Head)* at National Theatre of Miskolc. Miskolc. Lang.: Hun.
1888

Imre Csiszár's award-winning production of *Galileo élete:* Brecht's *Life of Galileo.* Miskolc. Lang.: Hun.
1889

Review of actors Géza Tordy, Géza Hegedűs D. and Attila Kaszás in Arthur Miller's *Death of a Salesman.* Budapest. Lang.: Hun.
1893

Director Ferenc Sík discusses *Álomkommandó (Dream Commando)* by András Sütő. Lang.: Hun.
1896

Tamás Puskás directs *Takáts Alice (Alice Takáts)* by Dezső Szomory, Madách Chamber Theatre. Budapest. Lang.: Hun.
1897

Vitrac's *Victor, ou les enfants au pouvoir (Victor, or the Children in Power)* directed by István Szőke as *Viktor, avagy a gyermekuralom.* Pécs. Lang.: Hun.
1898

A patkánykirály (The King of the Rats) by Győző Határ staged by László Salamon Suba at Móricz Zsigmond Theatre. Nyíregyháza. Lang.: Hun.
1899

István Malgot directs *A búsképű lovag (The Sad-Faced Knight)* by László Gyurko in the Dominican Court of the Budapest Hilton. Budapest.
1900

László Salamon Suba directs *A patkánykirály (The King of the Rats)* by Győző Határ at Móricz Zsigmond Theatre. Nyíregyháza. Lang.: Hun.
1901

Gyula Háy's *Mohács (The Mohács Disaster)* staged by Tamás Szirtes, Gyulai Várszinház. Gyula. Lang.: Hun.
1903

István Szőke directs *Victor ou les enfants au pouvoir (Victor, or The Children in Power)* by Roger Vitrac at National Theatre. Pécs. Lang.: Hun.
1904

Tamás Puskás directs *Takáts Alice (Alice Takáts)* by Dezső Szomory at Madách Kamaraszinház. Budapest. Lang.: Hun.
1906

Calderón's *La vida es sueño (Life Is a Dream)* staged by Miklós Szinetár under the title *Az élet álom.* Budapest. Lang.: Hun.
1911

Bohumil Hrabal's *Obsluhoval jsem anglického krale (I Served the King of Britain)* directed by Ivo Krobot as *Őfelsége pincére voltam.* Nyíregyháza. Lang.: Hun.
1912

Jarry's *Ubu roi (King Ubu)* directed by Andor Lukáks at Csiky Gergely Theatre under the title *Übü király.* Kaposvár. Lang.: Hun.
1913

Reviews of actors Olga Koós and István Bozóky in *Szabóky Zsigmond Rafael (Zsigmond Rafael Szabóky)* at Játékszín. Budapest. Lang.: Hun.
1914

Péter Léner directs premiere of *Lélekharang (Death Knell)* by Géza Páskandi at Móricz Zsigmond Theatre. Nyíregyháza. Lang.: Hun.
1915

Le jeu de l'amour et du hasard (The Game of Love and Chance) by Marivaux directed at National Theatre by Péter Valló as *A szerelem és véletten játéka.* Miskolc. Lang.: Hun.
1916

Hungary — cont'd

Zoltán Seregi directs Sławomir Mrożek's *Letni dzień (A Summer's Day)* at Thália Stúdió under the title *Egy nyári nap.* Budapest. Lang.: Hun. 1919

Ljudmila Petruševskaja's controversial play, *Tri devuški v golubom (Three Girls in Blue)*, directed by Tamás Ascher at Katona József Theatre. Budapest. Lang.: Hun. 1920

Goldoni's *Il campiello (The Public Square)* directed at Csiky Gergely Theatre as *Velencei terecske.* Kaposvár. Lang.: Hun. 1922

László Márton's *Lepkék a kalapon (Butterflies on Your Hat)* directed by István Verebes at Radnóti Miklós Theatre. Budapest. Lang.: Hun. 1923

Péter Huszti directs *A női partőrség szeme láttára (In Sight of the Spar)* by Pál Békés at Madách Chamber Theatre. Budapest. Lang.: Hun. 1924

Two premieres: Shakespeare, *The Merchant of Venice*, directed by Árpád Jutacsa Hegyi. Németh's *Villámfénynél (By the Stroke of Lightning)*, directed by Attila Seprődi Kiss. Kecskemét. Lang.: Hun. 1925

Mihály Vörösmarty's 'fairy-play' *Csongor and Tünde* directed by Béla Merő at Hevesi Sándor Színház. Zalaegerszeg. Lang.: Hun. 1926

Ivo Krobot directs *Öfelsége pincére voltam (I Served the King of Britain)*, based on writings of Bohumil Hrabal. Nyíregyháza. Lang.: Hun. 1928

György Lengyel directs *Szent Bertalan nappala (St. Bartholomew's Day)* by Magda Szabó at Madách Theatre. Budapest. Lang.: Hun. 1929

Rustaveli Theatre of Georgia, directed by Robert Sturua, presents Shakespeare's *Richard III* and Brecht's *Der Kaukasische Kreidekreis (The Caucasian Chalk Circle)* in Hungary. Tbilisi. Lang.: Hun. 2383

Interview with film director András Sólyom. Lang.: Hun. 3155

Reviews of *Rigoletto*, Lloyd Webber's *Requiem*, *Les Misérables* and the Hungarian Mass of the Tolcsvays. Szeged. Lang.: Hun. 3400

Performance of Soviet Musical Jewish Chamber Theatre. Budapest. Birobidjan. Lang.: Hun. 3401

Comparison of *Die Dreigroschenoper (The Three Penny Opera)* as directed by Ferenc Sík, József Petrik and Miklós Szinetár under the title *Koldusopera.* Győr. Budapest. Lang.: Hun. 3402

István Kazán directs *Fleur de cactus (Cactus Flower)* at Vidám Színpad as *A kaktusz virága.* Budapest. Lang.: Hun. 3629

Miklós Szinetár directs *Les Misérables* at Rock Szinház. Budapest. Lang.: Hun. 3630

Actors Sándor Szakácsi and Piroska Molnár in *Man of La Mancha* directed by Lászlo Bagossy. Pécs. Lang.: Hun. 3633

Review of productions at opera ensembles meeting. Szeged. Lang.: Hun. 3792

Review of performances at an assembly of opera ensembles. Szeged. Lang.: Hun. 3796

András Békés directs Rossini's *La Cenerentola* at Szentendrei Teátrum under the title *Hamupipőke.* Szentendre. Lang.: Hun. 3798

Béla Zerkovitz's operetta *Csókos asszony (A Woman Made for Kissing)* directed by István Iglódi. Budapest. Lang.: Hun. 3957

István Iglódi directs *Csókos asszony (A Woman Made for Kissing)* by Béla Zerkovitz at Vigszinház. Budapest. Lang.: Hun. 3958

1987. **Plays/librettos/scripts.**
Review of Ferenc Molnár's *Az ördög (The Devil)* directed by György Lengyel at Madách Theatre with discussion of the playwright and the play. Budapest. Lang.: Hun. 2630

Commemoration of 60th birthday of playwright András Sütő. Tîrgu-Mures. Lang.: Hun. 2717

India

400 B.C.-1987 A.D. **Performance/production.**
Orientalism in Peter Brook's production of *The Mahabharata.* New York, NY. Lang.: Eng. 1932

57 B.C.-1987 A.D. **Performance spaces.**
Stages of traditional theatre in Asia, and development of *Changuk* dance drama. Korea. China. Lang.: Kor. 664

1050-1968. **Performance/production.**
Comparison between Chinese opera and Buddhist plays of Kerala. Beijing. Lang.: Chi. 3533

1730-1904. **Plays/librettos/scripts.**
Operas that contain Indian-related themes and music. Europe. Lang.: Eng. 3914

1924-1940. **Performance/production.**
Uday Shankar's translation of Indian dance for Western audiences. Paris. London. Lang.: Eng. 1461

1970-1986. **Relation to other fields.**
Political theatre East and West. Indonesia. Lang.: Eng. 1240

1980. **Performance/production.**
Franz Xaver Kroetz's *Wunschkonzert (Request Concert)* transposed to Calcutta. Calcutta. Lang.: Eng. 1930

1983-1987. **Performance/production.**
Role of feminist in cultural critique. USA. Lang.: Eng. 1496

1984. **Performance/production.**
History and description of a performance of *Cavittunatakam*, a drama recounting lives of the saints. Kerala. Lang.: Eng. 1480

1986. **Performance/production.**
Franz Xaver Kroetz's *Wunschkonzert (Request Concert)* in Bombay: observations of actress Sulabha Deshpande. Bombay. Lang.: Eng. 1931

Granada TV's production of *The Jewel in the Crown.* UK-England. Lang.: Eng. 3207

1987. **Performance/production.**
Origins of theatre and its relationship to the spectator. Japan. Sri Lanka. Lang.: Eng. 813

Discussion of text on classical Indian performance. Lang.: Eng. 814

1987. **Plays/librettos/scripts.**
Peter Brook discusses his production of *The Mahabharata.* Paris. Perth. Lang.: Eng. 2571

Director Peter Brook discusses his views on *The Mahabharata.* Lang.: Eng. 2636

Indonesia

Plays/librettos/scripts.
Linguistic forms, historical-cultural significance of shadow puppet theatre. Lang.: Eng. 3379

930-1986. **Performance/production.**
Complete description of all aspects of *Wayang wong.* Lang.: Eng. 1481

1931-1935. **Plays/librettos/scripts.**
Influence of Balinese theatre on Antonin Artaud. France. Lang.: Kor. 1126

1970-1986. **Relation to other fields.**
Political theatre East and West. India. Lang.: Eng. 1240

1986. **Performance/production.**
Reviews of Oriental dance-drama performances. Japan. Lang.: Hun. 1951

1987. **Basic theatrical documents.**
Complete text of *Dimba and Dimbi* with background materials and preparations. Lang.: Eng. 4008

1987. **Performance/production.**
Puppetry as an expression of popular and folk culture. USA. Italy. Belgium. Lang.: Eng. 3988

Mythological background and performance aspects of *dalang.* Lang.: Ita. 4010

Iran

1987. **Basic theatrical documents.**
Translation of five contemporary Persian plays. Lang.: Eng. 1558

Ireland

1700-1799. **Performance/production.**
Detailed descriptions of numerous promptbooks: glossary, examples, role of prompter. England. Lang.: Eng. 1738

1767-1798. **Plays/librettos/scripts.**
New findings on 18th-century Irish comic playwright John O'Keeffe. London. Lang.: Eng. 2643

1875-1938. **Relation to other fields.**
Literary figures of the Irish Literary Renaissance. UK-Ireland. Lang.: Eng. 2995

1890-1987. **Plays/librettos/scripts.**
Political dissatisfaction in drama. UK. Lang.: Eng. 2750

Ireland — cont'd

1891-1983. **Research/historiography.**
Overview of Canadian research on twentieth-century Irish drama. UK-Ireland. Canada. Lang.: Eng.   3011

1900-1930. **Plays/librettos/scripts.**
Irish Literary Renaissance writers' view of America. Lang.: Eng.   2639

Bakhtinian analysis of Irish Literary Renaissance. Dublin. Lang.: Eng.   2645

Maud Gonne and Yeats's portrayal of women in his plays. Dublin. Lang.: Eng.   2646

1900-1985. **Performance/production.**
Interview with Eric Bentley, director of *La Casa de Bernarda Alba* at the Abbey. Dublin. Lang.: Eng.   1934

1900-1987. **Audience.**
English pantomime in Irish productions. Dublin. Lang.: Eng.   3231

1900-1987. **Relation to other fields.**
Theatrical themes and the class issue in the work of Irish playwrights. Lang.: Eng.   2994

1907. **Audience.**
Political roots of rioting on opening of Synge's *The Playboy of the Western World*. Dublin. Lang.: Eng.   1535

1910-1930. **Plays/librettos/scripts.**
Lady Gregory's *Grania*. Dublin. Lang.: Eng.   2649

1921-1987. **Plays/librettos/scripts.**
Interview with playwright Ray Lawler. Australia. Lang.: Eng.   2433

1923-1926. **Plays/librettos/scripts.**
Popular music in the Dublin trilogy plays of Sean O'Casey. Lang.: Eng.   2644

1927-1935. **Institutions.**
Playwright Denis Johnston and avant-garde theatre at the Abbey. Dublin. Lang.: Eng.   1619

1928. **Plays/librettos/scripts.**
Feminine life symbols in Sean O'Casey's *The Silver Tassie*. Lang.: Eng.   2654

1929-1987. **Plays/librettos/scripts.**
Themes of Brian Friel's plays. Lang.: Eng.   2638

1930-1939. **Plays/librettos/scripts.**
The Spanish Civil War in works by Ernest Hemingway and Sean O'Casey. UK. USA. Lang.: Eng.   2749

1938-1965. **Plays/librettos/scripts.**
Development of Welles's adaptation of *Henry IV* Parts I and II from stage to screen. USA. Lang.: Eng.   3182

1961-1984. **Plays/librettos/scripts.**
Theatrical language in the plays of Thomas Murphy. Lang.: Eng.   2640

1961-1986. **Plays/librettos/scripts.**
The myth of the idyllic peasant life in the plays of Thomas Murphy. Lang.: Eng.   2652

1961-1986. **Relation to other fields.**
Playwright Thomas Murphy and the nature of creativity. Lang.: Eng.   2993

1962-1978. **Plays/librettos/scripts.**
Theme and language in the plays of Thomas Murphy. Lang.: Eng.   2656

1962-1983. **Plays/librettos/scripts.**
Comic characters and the Book of Job in the plays of Thomas Murphy. Lang.: Eng.   2648

1962-1986. **Plays/librettos/scripts.**
The plays of Thomas Murphy. Dublin. Lang.: Eng.   2650

Historical accuracy of characters in the plays of Thomas Murphy. Lang.: Eng.   2657

1965-1984. **Institutions.**
Difficulty in obtaining funding for theatre building repair. Dublin. Cork. Belfast. Lang.: Eng.   545

1971. **Plays/librettos/scripts.**
Thomas Murphy's *The Morning After Optimism*: comparisons with Beckett, O'Casey. Lang.: Eng.   2641

1975. **Plays/librettos/scripts.**
Metaphor of archaeology in Friel's *Volunteers*, poems of Heaney. Dublin. UK-Ireland. Lang.: Eng.   2651

1976-1986. **Plays/librettos/scripts.**
Analysis of the text of Thomas Murphy's *The Sanctuary Lamp*. Lang.: Eng.   2658

1979-1987. **Training.**
Funding for youth theatre in Ireland. Lang.: Eng.   1381

1980-1986. **Plays/librettos/scripts.**
Characters and the gangster movie form in Thomas Murphy's *The Blue Macushla*. Lang.: Eng.   2647

1980-1987. **Performance/production.**
DYT (Dublin Youth Theatre). Dublin. Lang.: Eng.   816

1981. **Plays/librettos/scripts.**
Comparison of Brian Friel's *Translations* and András Sütő's *A szuzai menyegző*. Hungary. Lang.: Eng.   2637

1981-1983. **Plays/librettos/scripts.**
Interview with director Kazimierz Braun. Dublin. Poland. Lang.: Eng.   2642

1983. **Performance/production.**
Interview with Patrick Mason, director of Thomas Murphy's *The Gigli Concert*. Dublin. Lang.: Eng.   1935

1983. **Plays/librettos/scripts.**
Christian thought in Thomas Murphy's *The Gigli Concert*. Lang.: Eng.   2653

1984-1987. **Performance/production.**
TEAM, an educational theatre company. Dublin. Lang.: Eng.   818

1985. **Design/technology.**
F.H. Flood's scene design for *The Merchant of Venice*. Dublin. Lang.: Eng.   1593

1985. **Performance/production.**
Wet Paint, a young people's theatre group. Dublin. Lang.: Eng.   815

1985. **Plays/librettos/scripts.**
Analysis of Thomas Murphy's *Bailegangaire*, its connections with the Irish language, story-telling. Galway. Lang.: Eng.   2655

1986. **Administration.**
State of Irish theatre in Dublin and abroad. UK. Lang.: Eng.   1519

1987. **Performance/production.**
Graffiti Theatre Company which tours schools in southern Ireland. Cork. Lang.: Eng.   817

Overview of Dublin dance season. Dublin. Lang.: Eng.   1408

Hungarian reviewer's impressions of three Irish productions. Dublin. Lang.: Hun.   1933

1987. **Plays/librettos/scripts.**
Brian Friel's interpretation of Irish history through his plays *Aristocrats* and *Translations*. Lang.: Eng.   2659

Interpretations of the plays of Ibsen, Čechov and Beckett. Norway. Russia. Lang.: Hun.   2711

1987. **Theory/criticism.**
Brian Friel's play *Translations*. Lang.: Eng.   3050

Israel

1912-1980. **Institutions.**
Brief history of HaBimah. Moscow. Lang.: Hun.   557

1913-1955. **Institutions.**
Creation and history of the HaBimah Theatre. Moscow. Tel Aviv. Lang.: Heb.   623

1917-1987. **Performance spaces.**
Celebration of the birthday of the HaBimah Theatre. Tel Aviv. Lang.: Heb.   1669

1921-1987. **Institutions.**
Interview with actress Fannia Lubitch. Tel Aviv. Moscow. Lang.: Heb.   1620

1921-1987. **Theory/criticism.**
Relation of dramatic text to other written arts. USSR. Lang.: Heb.   3078

1922-1987. **Institutions.**
Interview with dancer Dvora Bektonov on her work and her father's acting. Tel Aviv. Moscow. Lang.: Heb.   1621

Interview with Israel Mintz on the HaBimah Theatre. Tel Aviv. Moscow. Lang.: Heb.   1623

1923-1987. **Institutions.**
Interview with actor, director and producer Shimon Finkel. Tel Aviv. Berlin. Lang.: Heb.   1624

1942-1985. **Relation to other fields.**
Interview with poet and activist Haki R. Madhubuti (Don L. Lee). Detroit, MI. Africa. Lang.: Eng.   3008

1968-1984. **Basic theatrical documents.**
Hebrew translation of Sławomir Mrożek's *Vatslave*. Cracow. Jerusalem. Lang.: Heb.   1565

1973. **Relation to other fields.**
Importance of theatre for youth and arts in education in Israel. Lang.: Eng.   1241

1976-1987. **Performance/production.**
Interview with director Hanan Snir. Lang.: Heb.   1937

1980-1987. **Performance/production.**
Interview with actress Edna Fliedel. Tel Aviv. Lang.: Heb.   1936

Italy — cont'd

1737-1987.　　**Performance spaces.**
History of Teatro San Carlo, its artists and performances.
Naples. Lang.: Ita.　　648

Study of Teatro San Carlo. Naples. Lang.: Ita.　　653

History of San Carlo Theatre: structure, scenography,
costumes. Naples. Lang.: Ita.　　656

1747-1762.　　**Plays/librettos/scripts.**
Playwright Pietro Chiari. Venice. Lang.: Ita.　　3316

1755.　　**Plays/librettos/scripts.**
Works of Carlo Gozzi, his relationship with actor Antonio
Sacchi. Venice. Lang.: Ita.　　1129

1763.　　**Performance spaces.**
Plans for New Theatre of Bologna's machinery and stage.
Bologna. Lang.: Eng.　　651

1773-1986.　　**Performance spaces.**
Theatres of Pisa, musical performances. Pisa. Lang.: Ita. 3393

1787-1976.　　**Performance spaces.**
History of Teatro La Fenice's construction and reconstruction.
Venice. Lang.: Ita.　　652

1789-1953.　　**Performance spaces.**
Plans for unrealized Roman auditorium and theatres. Rome.
Lang.: Ita.　　655

1797-1827.　　**Plays/librettos/scripts.**
Correspondence of playwright Ugo Foscolo regarding *Tieste
(Thyestes)*. Venice. Lang.: Ita.　　2677

1800-1825.　　**Plays/librettos/scripts.**
Analysis of vampire characters in the works of Byron,
Polidori and Planché. England. France. Lang.: Eng.　　2540

1800-1900.　　**Institutions.**
Performance in the context of theatrical organization. Reggio
Emilia. Lang.: Ita.　　550

1800-1900.　　**Performance/production.**
Florentine theatrical culture. Florence. Lang.: Ita.　　832

Minor theatrical forms involving tableaux, mechanics. Venice.
Lang.: Ita.　　3263

1836-1901.　　**Plays/librettos/scripts.**
Impact of Giuseppina Strepponi Verdi on her husband's
creativity. Milan. Lang.: Eng.　　3927

1837.　　**Performance/production.**
Reprint of Richard Wagner's views on *bel canto*, Bellini.
Lang.: Swe.　　3799

1850-1930.　　**Plays/librettos/scripts.**
Influence of Sibilla Aleramo on women in Italian theatre.
Lang.: Ita.　　1138

1858-1924.　　**Plays/librettos/scripts.**
Floral imagery in the operas of Giacomo Puccini. Lang.:
Eng.　　3926

1862-1879.　　**Plays/librettos/scripts.**
Making of Verdi's *Otello*. Milan. Lang.: Eng.　　3917

1863-1938.　　**Plays/librettos/scripts.**
Life and career of playwright Gabriele D'Annunzio. Lang.:
Ita.　　2661

1867.　　**Plays/librettos/scripts.**
Characters and political themes in Verdi's *Don Carlos*. Milan.
Lang.: Eng.　　3924

1867-1936.　　**Plays/librettos/scripts.**
Change of titles of the works of Luigi Pirandello. Lang.: Ita.
2665

Centrality of characters in the plays of Luigi Pirandello.
Lang.: Ita.　　2672

1867-1936.　　**Theory/criticism.**
Pirandello's aesthetic views. Lang.: Rus.　　3052

1870-1929.　　**Plays/librettos/scripts.**
Influence of playwright Ferruccio Benini. Venice. Lang.: Ita.
2675

1872-1937.　　**Performance/production.**
Career of actor Angelo Musco. Lang.: Ita.　　841

1872-1966.　　**Performance/production.**
Edward Gordon Craig's use of *commedia dell'arte* in his
work. UK-England. Lang.: Eng.　　3314

1876-1936.　　**Plays/librettos/scripts.**
Characteristic themes in the work of Pirandello. Lang.: Ita.
2676

1876-1954.　　**Plays/librettos/scripts.**
Franco Alfano, who completed Puccini's *Turandot*. Lang.:
Eng.　　3919

1876-1987.　　**Performance/production.**
Production history of *Der Ring des Nibelungen*. Bayreuth.
Milan. New York, NY. Lang.: Eng.　　3775

1877-1923.　　**Theory/criticism.**
The career of critic Ricciotto Canudo. France. Lang.: Ita.
1330

1887.　　**Plays/librettos/scripts.**
Characters in Verdi's *Otello*. Milan. Lang.: Eng.　　3920

1887-1986.　　**Plays/librettos/scripts.**
Advance publication of introduction to Volume II, *Maschere
nude (Naked Masks)*, by Pirandello. Lang.: Ita.　　2668

1887-1987.　　**Theory/criticism.**
Essays on critic Silvio d'Amico. Lang.: Ita.　　1344

1893.　　**Plays/librettos/scripts.**
Analysis and success of Boito's libretto for Verdi's opera
Falstaff. Lang.: Eng.　　3923

1893-1897.　　**Plays/librettos/scripts.**
Comparison of Puccini's and Leoncavallo's treatments of *La
Bohème*. Lang.: Swe.　　3922

1898-1978.　　**Performance/production.**
Dario Fo on comic actor Totò. Lang.: Eng.　　826

1900-1945.　　**Performance/production.**
Initial recordings of Verdi's operas. France. USA. Lang.:
Eng.　　3800

1900-1987.　　**Plays/librettos/scripts.**
Twentieth-century Italian theatre. Lang.: Ita.　　1143

1900-1987.　　**Relation to other fields.**
Relationship between theatre and everyday life. Lang.: Ita.
1242

Diminishing political and economic role of radio. Lang.: Ita.
3100

1901-1938.　　**Plays/librettos/scripts.**
Collaboration and friendship of writer Gabriele D'Annunzio
and actor Ruggero Ruggeri. Lang.: Ita.　　1133

1904-1936.　　**Plays/librettos/scripts.**
Acts of Pirandello conference. Lang.: Ita, Eng.　　2663

1904-1936.　　**Theory/criticism.**
Pirandello's poetics and influence on other writers. Lang.: Ita.
3051

1904-1937.　　**Performance/production.**
Photos and documentation: actor Angelo Musco. Catania.
Lang.: Ita.　　840

1904-1987.　　**Performance/production.**
Early phonograph records of opera singers. USA. Germany.
Lang.: Eng.　　3113

1906-1936.　　**Design/technology.**
Catalogue of costume exhibit: Fortuny, Caramba. Lang.: Ita.
345

1906-1976.　　**Performance/production.**
Biography of director Luchino Visconti. Lang.: Ita.　　3158

Biography of film director Luchino Visconti. Lang.: Ita. 3159

1909.　　**Performance/production.**
Theory and practice of Italian Futurist theatre. Lang.: Ita.
831

1910-1936.　　**Plays/librettos/scripts.**
Collection of essays on Pirandello's theatrical activity. Lang.:
Ita.　　1142

1911-1932.　　**Performance/production.**
Bragaglia's Theatre of the Independent. Rome. Lang.: Ita.
836

1913-1917.　　**Plays/librettos/scripts.**
Analysis of Rosso di San Secondo's *Amara (Bitter)*. Lang.:
Ita.　　1139

1914-1934.　　**Plays/librettos/scripts.**
Two filmscripts by Francesco Di Cocco based on short
stories of Pirandello. Lang.: Ita.　　3178

1914-1952.　　**Performance/production.**
Film career of stage actor Ruggero Ruggeri. Lang.: Ita. 3160

1915-1921.　　**Plays/librettos/scripts.**
Notebooks of playwright Filippo Tommaso Marinetti. Lang.:
Ita.　　2673

1915-1936.　　**Performance/production.**
Pirandello as director: contemporary reviews and interviews.
Lang.: Ita.　　838

1916-1929.　　**Plays/librettos/scripts.**
Carnival patterns in the plays of Luigi Pirandello. Lang.:
Eng.　　2662

1917-1920.　　**Performance/production.**
Collaboration of actor-director Virgilio Talli with playwright
Pier Maria Rosso di San Secondo. Lang.: Ita.　　835

1917-1987.　　**Performance/production.**
Influence of Pirandello on modern theatre. USA. Lang.: Eng.
2338

Italy — cont'd

1918-1926. **Theory/criticism.**
Criticism by actor Piero Gobetti. Lang.: Ita. 1345
1919-1957. **Plays/librettos/scripts.**
Riccardo Bacchelli's *Amleto (Hamlet)*. Lang.: Ita. 2671
1920-1987. **Performance/production.**
Singers/teachers Virginia Zeani and Nicola Rossi-Lemeni.
Lang.: Eng. 3802
1921-1922. **Performance/production.**
Letters documenting Ars Veneta, a dialect theatre company.
Venice. Lang.: Ita. 820
1921-1974. **Plays/librettos/scripts.**
Analysis of the plays of Luigi Candoni. Lang.: Ita. 2674
1921-1987. **Performance/production.**
Giorgio Strehler as the quintessential director of the century.
France. Lang.: Fre. 1754
1921-1987. **Plays/librettos/scripts.**
Gender conflict in Pirandello's *Sei personnaggi in cerca d'autore (Six Characters in Search of an Author)*. Lang.: Eng. 2679
1923-1928. **Performance/production.**
Encounter between Pirandello and Lord Dunsany during Pirandello's production of *I pazzi sulla montagna (The Gods of the Mountain)* by Alessandro De Stefani. Lang.: Eng. 1947
1923-1931. **Plays/librettos/scripts.**
Comparison between *La vita che ti diedi (The Life I Gave You)* by Pirandello and *Lo spirito della morte (The Spirit of Death)* by Rosso di San Secondo. Lang.: Ita. 2666
1923-1952. **Plays/librettos/scripts.**
Biography of writer Alberto Savinio by his wife. Lang.: Ita. 1141
1923-1977. **Performance/production.**
Evaluation of soprano Maria Meneghini Callas. Greece. USA.
Lang.: Eng. 3790
1924-1925. **Plays/librettos/scripts.**
Letters of Pier Maria Rosso di San Secondo to Enzo Ferrieri. Milan. Lang.: Ita. 1137
1924-1928. **Institutions.**
Pirandello's experiences as director of the Teatro d'Arte.
Lang.: Ita. 549
1925-1926. **Plays/librettos/scripts.**
Sources on Umberto Fracchia and his literary magazine *La Fiera Letteraria*. Lang.: Ita. 1131
1925-1928. **Performance/production.**
Luigi Pirandello's company Teatro d'Arte and its inaugural productions. Lang.: Eng. 1941
1928-1986. **Performance/production.**
Giorgio Strehler on staging *Die Dreigroschenoper (The Three Penny Opera)*. Milan. Paris. Lang.: Swe. 3809
1929-1987. **Plays/librettos/scripts.**
Machines—animate and inanimate—in *Tonight We Improvise (Questa sera si recita a soggetto)* by Pirandello. Lang.: Eng. 2670
1930-1950. **Performance/production.**
Examples of missed opportunities in modern Italian theatre.
Lang.: Ita. 1944
1933-1972. **Plays/librettos/scripts.**
Operatic/theatrical activities of Dino Buzzati. Lang.: Ita. 3918
1934-1979. **Performance/production.**
Sophia Loren's autobiography translated into Hungarian.
Lang.: Hun. 3157
1935-1982. **Performance/production.**
Career of basso Italo Tajo. Turin. Lang.: Eng. 3805
1935-1987. **Performance/production.**
Interview with soprano Mirella Freni. Modena. USA. Lang.: Eng. 3807
1935-1987. **Training.**
Essays on theatre teacher Orazio Costa. Lang.: Ita. 1382
1937. **Performance/production.**
Renato Simoni's staging of *I giganti della montagna (The Giants of the Mountain)* by Luigi Pirandello. Florence. Lang.: Ita. 821
1944-1986. **Performance/production.**
Giorgio Strehler's staging of *L'illusion comique (The Comic Illusion)* by Corneille. Lang.: Eng. 1948
1945-1987. **Performance/production.**
Career of conductor/educator Max Rudolf. New York, NY.
Lang.: Eng. 3803
1946-1983. **Plays/librettos/scripts.**
Theatrical elements in Italian cinema after the Second World War. Lang.: Ita. 3177

1947-1987. **Performance/production.**
Brief history of Piccolo Teatro. Milan. Lang.: Hun. 1945
1949-1987. **Performance/production.**
Actor Mario Scaccia and his Molière interpretations. Lang.: Ita. 1946
Interview with actor Marcello Mastroianni. Lang.: Hun. 3156
1954-1987. **Performance/production.**
Life and career of actress Anna Maria Guarnieri. Lang.: Ita. 833
1958-1982. **Performance/production.**
Collection of reviews by Arnaldo Mariotti. Lang.: Ita. 834
1964-1987. **Performance/production.**
Maurizio Scaparro: critic, director, administrator. Lang.: Ita. 837
1970-1985. **Administration.**
Italian government subsidy of theatre. Lang.: Fre. 28
1970-1987. **Performance/production.**
Interview, Italian conductor Riccardo Muti, artistic director, Teatro alla Scala. Milan. Lang.: Eng. 3808
1970-1987. **Relation to other fields.**
Theatre in education—uses and problems. Lang.: Ita. 1245
1975-1985. **Performance/production.**
Italian translation of *Hubert Fichte Jean Genet*. Lang.: Ita. 1942
1976. **Reference materials.**
Description of the Verdi Archive at New York University.
New York, NY. Milan. Lang.: Eng. 3937
1979-1987. **Performance/production.**
Work of Bruno Leone and his attempts to re-establish the Neapolitan culture of Guaratelle. Naples. Lang.: Eng. 3976
1980. **Performance spaces.**
Recent trends in Italian theatre. Lang.: Eng. 650
1980. **Performance/production.**
Street theatre and mass media. Lang.: Ger. 3295
1982. **Performance/production.**
Feminist theatre Teatro Viola's production of *Shoe-Show*.
Lang.: Eng. 824
1982-1986. **Performance/production.**
Marcel Marceau's reflections on his art. France. Lang.: Ita. 3233
1982-1987. **Design/technology.**
Costume designs of couturier Gianni Versace. Lang.: Ita. 3697
1983. **Plays/librettos/scripts.**
Analysis of the plot of Verdi's opera *Il Trovatore*. Lang.: Eng. 3921
1984-1987. **Performance/production.**
Style and authenticity at the Rossini festival. Pesaro. Lang.: Eng. 3801
1985. **Performance/production.**
Carmelo Bene's production of *Otello/Secondo*. Florence.
Lang.: Eng. 823
1985. **Relation to other fields.**
Excerpt from a speech by Jerzy Grotowski that examines the actor's technique. Florence. Lang.: Eng. 1244
1985-1986. **Reference materials.**
New Italian productions in all areas. Lang.: Ita. 1204
1986. **Administration.**
Technical details of guest performance of *Hamlet* by Kungliga Dramatiska Teatern, directed by Ingmar Bergman. Florence. Stockholm. Lang.: Swe. 1520
1986. **Plays/librettos/scripts.**
Carmelo Bene's *Il Lorenzaccio*. Lang.: Ita. 1130
1986. **Research/historiography.**
Essays on theatre research in Italy. Lang.: Ita. 1300
1986-1987. **Reference materials.**
Children's productions by Ente Teatrale Italiano. Lang.: Ita. 1207
1987. **Audience.**
Scientific and psychological study of the role of audience as dramaturgs. Lang.: Eng. 284
1987. **Basic theatrical documents.**
English text of *Elisabetta: Quasi per caso una donna (Elizabeth: Almost By Chance a Woman)* by Dario Fo. USA.
Lang.: Eng. 1560
Review of video productions of *Tosca* and *Dialogues des Carmélites*. Verona. Sydney. Lang.: Eng. 3692
1987. **Design/technology.**
Complete guide to make-up. Lang.: Ita. 346
1987. **Institutions.**
Italian theatrical archives and libraries. Lang.: Ita. 547

Japan — cont'd

1986-1987.   Performance/production.
Productions from Yume no yūminsha, Tōhō, Parco, Tsukumo and Nakamura za. Tokyo. Lang.: Jap.   1956
1986-1987.   Plays/librettos/scripts.
Productions by several Tokyo companies. Tokyo. Lang.: Jap.   2682
1987.   Performance/production.
Origins of theatre and its relationship to the spectator. India. Sri Lanka. Lang.: Eng.   813
Institutions, techniques in training of nō actors. Lang.: Eng.   1499
Performances of nō plays by priests and description of a new play. Hiraizumi. Lang.: Eng.   1501
Four Tokyo productions in light of ideas of Betsuyaku Minoru. Tokyo. Lang.: Jap.   1950
New Tokyo productions. Tokyo. Lang.: Jap.   1954
Analysis of four Tokyo productions. Tokyo. Lang.: Jap.   1957
Space and sign in various Tokyo productions. Tokyo. Lang.: Jap.   1959
Productions of several Tokyo companies. Tokyo. Lang.: Jap.   1962
Comments on Tokyo performances. Tokyo. Lang.: Jap.   1964
Unsuitable choice of plays for Tokyo performances. Tokyo. Lang.: Jap.   1965
1987.   Relation to other fields.
Korean mask plays, folklore and puppet theatre. Korea. Kyushu. Lang.: Kor.   1246

Korea

Plays/librettos/scripts.
Playwright Park Hyun Suk's dramatic theory. Lang.: Kor.   2686
57 B.C.   Performance spaces.
Performance space of traditional Korean theatre. Lang.: Kor.   659
57 B.C.   Plays/librettos/scripts.
Overview of ancient Korean plays. Lang.: Kor.   1148
57 B.C.-935 A.D.   Performance/production.
Ritual origins of Korean theatre. Lang.: Kor.   849
57 B.C.-1392 A.D.   Plays/librettos/scripts.
Comparison of Greek tragedy and Korean Buddhist plays. Greece. Lang.: Kor.   2684
57 B.C.-1907 A.D.   Performance/production.
The masked dance-drama of ancient Korea. Lang.: Kor.   1484
57 B.C.-1976 A.D.   Performance/production.
Origin and development of Korean dance-drama. Lang.: Kor.   1485
57 B.C.-1977 A.D.   Performance/production.
History of Korean music-drama. Lang.: Kor.   3405
57 B.C.-1985 A.D.   Performance/production.
Origins, theory of traditional Korean mask theatre. Lang.: Kor.   858
57 B.C.-1986 A.D.   Performance spaces.
Performance space and staging of traditional Korean genres. Japan. Lang.: Kor.   663
57 B.C.-1986 A.D.   Performance/production.
History of Korean theatre. Lang.: Kor.   846
57 B.C.-1987 A.D.   Performance spaces.
Original performing area of Korean mask theatre. Lang.: Kor.   660
Stages of traditional theatre in Asia, and development of Changuk dance drama. China. India. Lang.: Kor.   664
57 B.C.-1987 A.D.   Performance/production.
The development of Korean mask theatre. Lang.: Kor.   847
Audience participation in the development of Korean mask theatre. Lang.: Kor.   848
General history of Korean theatre. Lang.: Kor.   853
57 B.C.-1987 A.D.   Plays/librettos/scripts.
The analysis of Bongsantalchum, a Korean mask play. Lang.: Kor.   1145
Time and space in traditional Korean theatre. Lang.: Kor.   1146
Analysis of Yangjusandae nolyee. Lang.: Kor.   1488
90-1987.   Performance/production.
Evolution and history of the 'Daedong' carnival. Seoul. Lang.: Kor.   3297

600-1987.   Basic theatrical documents.
Text of a kokdugaksi puppet play. Lang.: Kor.   4004
600-1987.   Theory/criticism.
Theory and construction of Korean rod puppetry kokdugaksinolum. Lang.: Kor.   4007
800-1987.   Performance/production.
Dan-o festival of folk performances. Lang.: Kor.   3296
935-1392.   Performance/production.
Music theatre under Koryo dynasty. China. Lang.: Kor.   3404
1392-1910.   Performance/production.
History of theatre under Chosun dynasty. Lang.: Kor.   850
Origin and influence of pansori music-drama. Lang.: Kor.   3406
History of pansori, Korean music-drama. Lang.: Kor.   3408
1400-1900.   Performance/production.
History of Chun Hyang musical drama. Nam-won. Lang.: Kor.   3407
1500-1987.   Performance/production.
Han Puly, Korean exorcism dance. Lang.: Kor.   1462
1876.   Design/technology.
Theory of scenography. Lang.: Kor.   352
1900-1950.   Institutions.
Development of Korean theatre in the twentieth century. Lang.: Kor.   551
1900-1970.   Audience.
Role of theatre in Korean society. Lang.: Kor.   288
1900-1986.   Performance/production.
Development of modern Korean theatre. Lang.: Kor.   1968
Korean theatre personalities. Lang.: Kor.   1970
1905-1979.   Plays/librettos/scripts.
Conventionality in the popular plays of Korea's early twentieth century. Lang.: Kor.   2692
1908-1965.   Performance/production.
Wonkaksa, Korea's first Little Theatre. Seoul. Lang.: Kor.   1972
1908-1977.   Basic theatrical documents.
Realism in Korean theatre. Lang.: Kor.   1563
1910-1919.   Plays/librettos/scripts.
Korean drama: social and political background. Lang.: Kor.   2690
1910-1945.   Performance/production.
Korean theatre in Tokyo. Tokyo. Lang.: Kor.   845
1910-1945.   Plays/librettos/scripts.
Traditional and modern theatre in Korea. Seoul. Lang.: Kor.   2685
1926-1970.   Theory/criticism.
Reception theory, performance and American influence in Korea. USA. Lang.: Kor.   1370
1930-1935.   Performance spaces.
History of Tong-Yang Theatre, Korea's first dramatic theatre. Seoul. Lang.: Kor.   661
1930-1939.   Performance/production.
Development of Korean theatre. Seoul. Lang.: Kor.   1973
1935-1945.   Administration.
Tong-Yang theatre, first commercial theatre in Korea. Seoul. Lang.: Kor.   30
1939-1976.   Plays/librettos/scripts.
Korean stage adaptation of Le Mur (The Wall) by Sartre. France. Lang.: Kor.   2575
1940-1947.   Institutions.
Closing of Tong-Yang theatre. Seoul. Lang.: Kor.   552
1940-1987.   Plays/librettos/scripts.
Comparative view of play censorship. Japan. Germany. Lang.: Kor.   1147
1950-1987.   Plays/librettos/scripts.
Theory and practice of playwright Lee Kun Sam. Lang.: Kor.   2687
1960-1979.   Administration.
Little theatre and control. Seoul. Lang.: Kor.   1521
1960-1979.   Plays/librettos/scripts.
Korean drama: changes in structure. Lang.: Kor.   2689
1967-1987.   Plays/librettos/scripts.
Dramatist Yun Dae Sung's theories. Lang.: Kor.   2693
1970.   Basic theatrical documents.
Text of Yajunbyungwon (Field Hospital) by Lim Je-Bok. Lang.: Kor.   1564
1970.   Research/historiography.
Methodology of comparative drama. Lang.: Kor.   3012
1970-1979.   Administration.
Development of Korean regional theatre. Lang.: Kor.   32

Korea — cont'd

1970-1979.   **Audience.**
Lack of theatre consciousness in Korean audiences. Lang.:
Kor.   286
1970-1979.   **Performance/production.**
Body language in Korean mime. Lang.: Kor.   3234
1970-1987.   **Plays/librettos/scripts.**
Theory and plays of playwright Lee Kang Bak. Lang.: Kor.
  1489
1976.   **Audience.**
Essay on audience-performer relationship. Lang.: Kor.   287
1976.   **Design/technology.**
Theory and application of make-up. Lang.: Kor.   355
1978.   **Design/technology.**
Theory and history of lighting design. Lang.: Kor.   351
Scene designer Kim Jung-Whan. Lang.: Kor.   354
1978.   **Plays/librettos/scripts.**
Subjective view of the essence of drama. Lang.: Kor.   2688
1978.   **Relation to other fields.**
Theoretical examination of psychodrama, creative drama.
Lang.: Kor.   1247
1980-1987.   **Administration.**
Effect of copyright law on performing arts. Seoul. Lang.:
Kor.   29
1980-1987.   **Performance/production.**
Realism in Korean theatre. Lang.: Kor.   855
1986.   **Performance/production.**
Discussion of acting techniques. Lang.: Kor.   1967
1986.   **Plays/librettos/scripts.**
Call for greater creativity in Korean theatre. Seoul. Lang.:
Kor.   2691
1986-1987.   **Performance spaces.**
Criticism of Kwang-ju's theatres. Kwang-ju. Lang.: Kor.   662
1986-1987.   **Performance/production.**
Theory, problems of folk-arts competitions. Lang.: Kor.   857
Survey of critical reactions to contemporary Korean theatre.
Seoul. Lang.: Kor.   1971
1986-1987.   **Theory/criticism.**
Review of Korean National Theatre production of Čechov's
Diadia Vania (Uncle Vanya). Seoul. Lang.: Kor.   3054
1987.   **Administration.**
Censorship, sociology and constitutional law. Lang.: Kor.   31
1987.   **Design/technology.**
Theory of theatrical make-up in Korean theatre. Lang.: Kor.
  353
How to construct *kokdugaksi* rod puppets. Lang.: Kor.   4005
1987.   **Performance/production.**
Advice for novice actors. Lang.: Kor.   851
Plays presented at eleventh Seoul theatre festival. Seoul.
Lang.: Kor.   852
Relation of actors and audiences. Seoul. Lang.: Kor.   854
Interviews with some Korean directors. Seoul. Lang.: Kor.
  856
Seoul's theatre season. Seoul. Lang.: Kor.   1969
1987.   **Relation to other fields.**
Korean mask plays, folklore and puppet theatre. Kyushu.
Lang.: Kor.   1246
1987-1987.   **Plays/librettos/scripts.**
Improvement of Korean folk theatre. Lang.: Kor.   1149

Korea, South
1959-1987.   **Plays/librettos/scripts.**
Interview with playwright Charles Fuller. Philadelphia, PA.
New York, NY. Lang.: Eng.   2921
1977.   **Performance/production.**
Korean folk puppetry using hands and feet. Lang.: Eng.
  3977

Latin America
    Theory/criticism.
Semiotics in the relationship between director and text.
Lang.: Spa.   3055
1987.   **Plays/librettos/scripts.**
Themes in the Festival of Latin Theatre. New York, NY.
Spain. Lang.: Spa.   2847

Latvia
1913-1982.   **Performance/production.**
Overview of Latvian opera. Lang.: Rus.   3810

Lithuania
1966-1980.   **Relation to other fields.**
Role of Communist Party in Lithuanian theatre. Lang.: Rus.
  1248

Malawi
1987.   **Performance/production.**
Progression of Malawian theatre. Lang.: Eng.   859

Mexico
    Plays/librettos/scripts.
Feminist themes in Rosario Castellanos' *El eterno femenino
(The Eternal Feminine).* Lang.: Spa.   2694
1833-1984.   **Plays/librettos/scripts.**
Musical adaptation of Gorostiza's *Contigo pan y cebolla
(With You, Bread and Onion).* Mexico City. Madrid. Lang.:
Eng.   1150
1850-1987.   **Performance/production.**
Overview of Mexican-American theatre. USA. Lang.: Eng.
  946
1937-1982.   **Basic theatrical documents.**
Study of the poetic, narrative and theatrical work of Agustí
Bartra, edition of complete works, vol. 4. Spain-Catalonia.
Lang.: Cat.   1571
1941-1987.   **Performance/production.**
Career of singer Plácido Domingo. Lang.: Eng.   3812
Interview with tenor Plácido Domingo. Mexico City. New
York, NY. Los Angeles, CA. Houston, TX. Lang.: Eng.   3813
1957-1987.   **Theory/criticism.**
Rise of contemporary theatre in Mexico. Mexico City. Lang.:
Spa.   3057
1958-1961.   **Plays/librettos/scripts.**
Plays by Gorostiza, Usigli and Novo on Spanish conquest of
Mexico. Lang.: Eng.   2701
1958-1973.   **Plays/librettos/scripts.**
Notes and commentary of Alvario Custadio on Teatro
Clásico de México. Lang.: Spa.   2695
1978.   **Plays/librettos/scripts.**
Archetypal nature of title character in *Felipe Angeles* by
Elena Garro. Lang.: Spa.   2696
1980-1982.   **Performance/production.**
Performers Ariel Ashwell and Sigfrido Aguilar discuss their
work with Comediantes Pantomima-Teatro. Guanajuato.
Lang.: Eng.   3225
1982-1987.   **Plays/librettos/scripts.**
The Non-Smokers by Gianfrancesco Guarnieri. Mexico City.
Lang.: Spa.   2697
1987.   **Basic theatrical documents.**
Six plays detailing the Hispanic experience in the United
States. USA. Lang.: Eng.   1581
1987.   **Performance/production.**
University of Mexico: music of dance theatre. Mexico City.
Lang.: Spa.   1463
Examination of language in Beth Henley's *The Miss
Firecracker Contest.* Mexico City. Lang.: Spa.   1974
Experimental theatre groups in Mexico City. Mexico City.
Lang.: Spa.   1975
Review of *I Poli (The Town)* based on Greek theatre
tradition and performed in absurdist style. Mexico City.
Lang.: Spa.   1976
Review of *La Alegría de las Tandas (The Happiness of the
Groups)* by Enrique Alonso. Mexico City. Lang.: Spa.   1977
Review of *El Balcón:* production of Genet's *Le Balcon (The
Balcony).* Mexico City. Lang.: Spa.   1978
A children's production of Mozart's *The Magic Flute*
performed in Spanish. Mexico City. Lang.: Spa.   3811
1987.   **Plays/librettos/scripts.**
Interview with playwright Hugo Hiriart. Mexico City. Lang.:
Spa.   1151
Comparison of the plays *Todo sucede en una noche (It All
Happens in One Night)* and *La rosa del tiempo (The Rose of
Time).* Mexico City. Lang.: Spa.   2698
Ethnic roots in *De la calle (Of the Street)* by Jesús
Gonzalez-Davila. Mexico City. Lang.: Spa.   2699
Comparison of plays by Leonor Azcarate and Estela Lenero.
Mexico City. Lang.: Spa.   2700
1987.   **Theory/criticism.**
The issue of new ideas in contemporary theatre. Mexico City.
Lang.: Spa.   3056

Mongolia
1921-1986.   **Performance/production.**
Art and theatre in Mongolian People's Republic. Ulan-Bator.
Lang.: Ger.   860

North America — cont'd

Norway

1300-1985.   **Relation to other fields.**
Essays on the theme of marriage in literature. England.
Lang.: Eng.   1425

1605-1884.   **Plays/librettos/scripts.**
Comparison of *King Lear* and *Vildanden (The Wild Duck).*
England. Lang.: Eng.   2518

1700-1987.   **Plays/librettos/scripts.**
Theme of stage direction in the work of Scandinavian
authors. Sweden. Lang.: Ita.   2737

1886-1985.   **Plays/librettos/scripts.**
Varied approaches to Ibsen's *Rosmersholm.* USA. Lang.: Eng.
    2923

1888-1987.   **Plays/librettos/scripts.**
Irony in Ibsen's *Fruen fra Havet (Lady from the Sea, The).*
Lang.: Eng.   2712

1917-1985.   **Plays/librettos/scripts.**
Ibsen translation, production, reception and influence in
China. China, People's Republic of. Lang.: Eng.   2494

1920-1950.   **Theory/criticism.**
Ibsen's influence on modern Chinese theatre. China, People's
Republic of. Lang.: Chi.   3025

1971-1982.   **Institutions.**
Trends in regional theatre. Lang.: Eng.   1626

1979-1982.   **Administration.**
Actress Vesleøy Haslund fights termination from the National
Theatre. Oslo. Lang.: Eng.   1522

1980-1984.   **Relation to other fields.**
Cultural policy of Norway. Lang.: Eng.   1249

1980-1987.   **Performance/production.**
Interview with dancer-choreographer Viktor Róna. Hungary.
Oslo. Lang.: Hun.   1437

1982.   **Institutions.**
Profile of community theatre Grenland Friteater. Porsgrunn.
Lang.: Eng.   1627

1982.   **Performance spaces.**
Conversion of ferryboat *Innvik* into theatre and its
production of *Splint.* Lang.: Eng.   666

1984.   **Relation to other fields.**
Cultural similarities and differences between the United
States and Norway. Lang.: Eng.   1250

1986.   **Design/technology.**
A portable, flexible podium system. Trondheim. Lang.: Swe.
    359

1986-1987.   **Performance/production.**
Actor Espen Skjønberg talks about acting in Norway and
England. London. Lang.: Eng.   2297

1987.   **Performance/production.**
Impressions of Nordkalottfestivalen, conditions of Norwegian
amateur theatre. Hammerfest. Lang.: Swe.   868

1987.   **Plays/librettos/scripts.**
Interpretations of the plays of Ibsen, Čechov and Beckett.
Ireland. Russia. Lang.: Hun.   2711

Ibsen database now being developed. USA. Lang.: Eng. 2924

Ottoman Empire
SEE
    Turkey.

Philippines

1970-1987.   **Performance/production.**
Role of theatre in the Filipino revolution. Lang.: Eng.   1986

1972-1986.   **Performance/production.**
Survival of Philippine theatre during and after martial law.
Lang.: Eng.   869

1972-1986.   **Relation to other fields.**
Political theatre and the fall of Ferdinand Marcos. Lang.:
Eng.   3281

Poland

275-1945.   **Performance/production.**
Writings of director Leon Schiller. Germany. Roman Empire.
Lang.: Pol.   1994

1258-1980.   **Design/technology.**
History of stage lighting in Europe, especially Warsaw.
Warsaw. Europe. Lang.: Pol.   360

1490-1945.   **Performance/production.**
History of Polish puppet theatre. Lang.: Pol.   3980

1500-1945.   **Relation to other fields.**
Theme of puppets and marionettes in Polish literature. Lang.:
Pol.   3995

1666-1987.   **Audience.**
American response to Gardzienice Theatre Association.
Gardzienice. Lang.: Eng.   1536

1758-1950.   **Reference materials.**
Bibliography of Polish theatre magazines. Lang.: Pol.   1208

1765-1915.   **Administration.**
Form and content of Warsaw playbills. Warsaw. Lang.: Pol.
    38

1815-1987.   **Plays/librettos/scripts.**
Actor-manager Wojciech Bogusławski in life and in György
Spiró's play *Az imposztor (The Imposter).* Hungary. Lang.:
Pol.   2716

1890-1918.   **Performance/production.**
Polish theatre in areas annexed by Austria-Hungary and
Prussia. Austria-Hungary. Prussia. Lang.: Pol.   875

1899-1987.   **Institutions.**
Ida Kamińska, director of Jewish Theatre of Warsaw.
Warsaw. Lang.: Pol.   1629

1900-1939.   **Performance/production.**
Activity of Polish puppeteers in Lodz. Łodź. Lang.: Pol. 3979

1915-1987.   **Relation to other fields.**
Director Tadeusz Kantor's views on art, culture, philosophy.
Lang.: Pol.   2997

1918-1939.   **Plays/librettos/scripts.**
Theme of love and lovers in plays and poems by Maria
Pawlikowska-Jasnorzewska. Lang.: Pol.   2715

1919-1939.   **Performance/production.**
Puppet companies from Poznań. Poznań. Lang.: Pol.   3978

1919-1941.   **Performance/production.**
Selection of reviews by Tadeusz Zeleński. Cracow. Warsaw.
Lang.: Pol.   1998

1920-1939.   **Performance/production.**
Innovative director Leon Schiller. Lang.: Rus.   870

1921-1947.   **Performance/production.**
Correspondence of Reduta directors Mieczysław Limanowski
and Juliusz Osterwa. Warsaw. Wilno. Lang.: Pol.   1991

1929-1955.   **Performance/production.**
Early life of director Konrad Swinarski. Lang.: Pol.   878

1932-1939.   **Performance/production.**
Selection of theatre reviews by poet Kazimierz Wierzyński.
Warsaw. Lang.: Pol.   1996

1933-1987.   **Performance/production.**
Director Tadeusz Kantor's inspirations in early career. Lang.:
Pol.   1992

1943.   **Institutions.**
Director Leon Schiller's plan for a drama department,
Theatre Institute. Warsaw. Lang.: Pol.   555

1949-1987.   **Theory/criticism.**
Reception of Polish theatre in East Germany. Germany, East.
Lang.: Ger.   1341

1950-1965.   **Relation to other fields.**
Polish official promotion of music theatre. Lang.: Pol.   3421

1956-1987.   **Plays/librettos/scripts.**
History and analysis of Mrożek's play *Vatslave.* Cracow.
Paris. Lang.: Heb.   2713

1968-1984.   **Basic theatrical documents.**
Hebrew translation of Sławomir Mrożek's *Vatslave.* Cracow.
Jerusalem. Lang.: Heb.   1565

1969-1987.   **Plays/librettos/scripts.**
Life and operatic works of composer Krzysztof Penderecki.
Lang.: Ger.   3929

1971-1987.   **Performance/production.**
Teatr Prowizorium: interview with director Janusz Oprynski.
Lublin. Lang.: Eng.   1990

1972-1987.   **Performance/production.**
Life and career of Polish theatre professional Zbigniew
Cynkutis. Wrocław. Lang.: Eng.   1993

1977-1987.   **Performance/production.**
Tadeusz Bradecki, director and playwright. Cracow. Lang.:
Pol.   1997

1978-1987.   **Plays/librettos/scripts.**
Hermann, a puppet production for adults about coping with
oppression. Germany. Bielsko Biala. Lang.: Eng.   3991

1979-1987.   **Performance/production.**
Poland's puppet theatre. Wrocław. Białystock. Mistelbach.
Lang.: Eng, Fre.   4006

1980-1987.   **Performance/production.**
Polish theatre. Warsaw. Cracow. Wrocław. Lang.: Eng, Fre.
    1987

1981-1983.   **Plays/librettos/scripts.**
Interview with director Kazimierz Braun. Dublin. Lang.: Eng.
    2642

Poland — cont'd

1981-1987. **Performance/production.**
The shape and form of contemporary Polish theatre.
Warsaw. Lang.: Eng, Fre. 1995

1982-1986. **Institutions.**
The Stanisław Ignacy Witkiewicz Theatre. Zakopane. Lang.:
Eng, Fre. 1628

1982-1987. **Performance/production.**
Avant-garde performances presented at International Open
Theatre meeting. Wrocław. Lang.: Pol, Eng, Fre. 877

1982-1987. **Plays/librettos/scripts.**
Problems of Polish society reflected in contemporary theatre.
Lang.: Pol. 2714

1984-1984. **Performance/production.**
Directing Mrożek's *Vatslave*. Jerusalem. Lang.: Heb. 1938

1985-1987. **Relation to other fields.**
Effect of farming practices on folk theatre. Tarnogród. Lang.:
Eng. 3282

1986. **Performance/production.**
The 4th International Theatre Conference: includes list of
participants and their contributions. Warsaw. Lang.: Eng, Fre. 873

The 4th International Festival of Street Theatres. Jelenia
Góra. Lang.: Eng, Fre. 3355

1986-1987. **Performance/production.**
Four new productions in Poland. Warsaw. Lang.: Eng, Fre. 1988

1987. **Performance/production.**
Festival of Polish plays. Wrocław. Lang.: Eng, Fre. 871

The 17th Warsaw theatre conference. Warsaw. Lang.: Eng,
Fre. 872

Overview of Polish theatre scene. Warsaw. Cracow. Lang.:
Eng. 874

Interview with Polish playwright Tadeusz Kantor. Cracow.
Kassel. Milan. Sicily. Lang.: Eng, Fre. 876

ITI survey of Polish theatre. Lang.: Spa. 1989

Experimental theatre at the Stary in three recent productions.
Cracow. Lang.: Eng. 1999

The Polish cabaret performance group Piwnica. Cracow. New
York, NY. Lang.: Eng. 3287

Portugal
1987. **Performance/production.**
Report from Portuguese amateur theatre festival. Lisbon.
Lang.: Swe. 2000

Prussia
SEE
Germany.

1890-1918. **Performance/production.**
Polish theatre in areas annexed by Austria-Hungary and
Prussia. Poland. Austria-Hungary. Lang.: Pol. 875

Roman Empire
275-1945. **Performance/production.**
Writings of director Leon Schiller. Poland. Germany. Lang.:
Pol. 1994

Romania
1946-1986. **Institutions.**
Memoirs of director and teacher Géza Gergely on Hungarian
theatrical training in Romania. Tîrgu-Mureş. Hungary. Lang.:
Hun. 556

1949-1987. **Performance/production.**
Career of playwright András Sütő. Hungary. Tîrgu-Mureş.
Lang.: Hun. 1890

1980-1987. **Performance/production.**
Soviet tours of Teatrul C.I. Nottara. Bucharest. Lang.: Rus. 879

1987. **Administration.**
Sergiu Comissiona, new music director, New York City
Opera. New York, NY. Lang.: Eng. 3685

1987. **Performance/production.**
Gábor Tompa directs *Hamlet* at Hungarian Theatre of
Kolozsvár. Cluj. Lang.: Hun. 2001

1987. **Plays/librettos/scripts.**
Commemoration of 60th birthday of playwright András Sütő.
Tîrgu-Mureş. Hungary. Lang.: Hun. 2717

Russia
1600-1899. **Performance/production.**
Theatre-performance culture of Rus'. Lang.: Rus. 3265

1696-1725. **Plays/librettos/scripts.**
Russian drama under Peter I. Lang.: Rus. 2720

1799-1837. **Relation to other fields.**
Study of Aleksand'r Puškin's life and works, and the
influence of Rossini on Puškin. St. Petersburg. Lang.: Eng. 3943

1800-1899. **Administration.**
Political censorship of theatre. England. France. Germany.
Lang.: Eng. 1517

1800-1900. **Plays/librettos/scripts.**
Georgian criticism and theatrical art. Lang.: Rus. 2719

1830-1920. **Plays/librettos/scripts.**
Female roles and images in the romantic ballet. France.
Germany. Lang.: Ger. 1455

1860-1889. **Performance/production.**
Offenbach and the origin and development of operetta.
Lang.: Rus. 3960

1860-1908. **Relation to other fields.**
Comparison between Wagner and Tolstoy. Germany. Lang.:
Eng. 3944

1860-1938. **Performance/production.**
Work and influence of actors Robert and Rafail Adel'gejm.
Lang.: Rus. 880

1861. **Plays/librettos/scripts.**
Analysis of *Delo (The Affair)* by A.V. Suchovo-Kobylin.
Lang.: Rus. 2721

1864-1910. **Plays/librettos/scripts.**
Plays of Tolstoj and the 'New Drama' of Western Europe.
Europe. Lang.: Rus. 2722

1896. **Plays/librettos/scripts.**
Analysis of *Čajka (The Seagull)* by Anton Čechov. Lang.:
Kor. 2718

1901-1980. **Performance/production.**
Michajl Čechov's life and work: a descriptive chronology.
Moscow. Lang.: Eng. 2002

1905-1917. **Institutions.**
Will Garland and European tour of Negro Operetta
Company. UK-England. Helsinki. Lang.: Eng. 3956

1906-1938. **Performance/production.**
Development of the Stanislavskij Acting System. Moscow.
Lang.: Eng. 2003

1912-1980. **Institutions.**
Brief history of HaBimah. Moscow. Israel. Lang.: Hun. 557

1987. **Plays/librettos/scripts.**
Interpretations of the plays of Ibsen, Čechov and Beckett.
Norway. Ireland. Lang.: Hun. 2711

Samoa
1884-1980. **Performance/production.**
Comparison of Samoan healing ritual and village theatre.
Lang.: Eng. 881

Scandinavia
1986-1987. **Performance/production.**
Staging of Romantic 'closet dramas'. Lang.: Swe. 2004

Senegal
1987. **Basic theatrical documents.**
English translations of contemporary African plays. Zaire.
Lang.: Eng. 1566

Sierra Leone
1987. **Performance/production.**
The African actor in Africa, Italy and the United States.
Brooklyn, NY. Freetown. Rome. Lang.: Eng. 2362

South Africa, Republic of
1586-1987. **Performance/production.**
Black theatre in South Africa: influence of traditional forms.
London. New York, NY. Lang.: Eng. 2005

1605-1913. **Relation to other fields.**
Comparison of *King Lear* and South African Land Act
regarding land distribution. England. Lang.: Eng. 1231

1868-1987. **Performance/production.**
Development of Wagner's *Die Meistersinger von Nürnberg*.
Cape Town. Munich. Lang.: Eng. 3816

1887-1940. **Performance spaces.**
Theatres built, influences on design. Johannesburg. Lang.:
Afr. 667

1952. **Performance/production.**
Career of actor/director Angus Neill. London. Lang.: Eng. 2293

1960-1987. **Training.**
Proposed changes in teaching methodology to include
indigenous drama. Lang.: Eng. 1383

1961-1985. **Plays/librettos/scripts.**
How Athol Fugard's revisions have changed *The Blood Knot*.
Lang.: Eng. 2725

Spain — cont'd

1987.   **Basic theatrical documents.**
Translation of *Viernes, 29 de julio de 1983, de madrugada (Friday, July 29, 1983, Early in the Morning)* by Jerónimo López Moto. Lang.: Eng.   1568

1987.   **Plays/librettos/scripts.**
Themes in the Festival of Latin Theatre. New York, NY. Latin America. Lang.: Spa.   2847

Spain-Catalonia

500 B.C.-1987 A.D.   Relation to other fields.
History of puppetry in Catalonia. Lang.: Eng.   3996

1300-1987.   Performance/production.
History of dance in Catalonia. Lang.: Cat.   1410

1418-1981.   Relation to other fields.
Popular entertainment in Valencian region from December to March. Valencia. Lang.: Cat.   3337

1539-1985.   Theory/criticism.
Modernity as historical concept applied to Catalonia and Occitania. France. Barcelona. Lang.: Fre.   1332

1581-1623.   Basic theatrical documents.
Analysis and edition of *Comèdia famosa de la gloriosa Verge i Màrtir Santa Bàrbara*, by F. Vicenç Garcia. Lang.: Cat.   1574

1600-1985.   Theory/criticism.
Reflections on the value of theatrical translations. UK-England. Lang.: Cat.   3060

1622-1680.   Basic theatrical documents.
Text of *Lo desengany (The Disappointment)* by Francesc Fontanella, with analysis. Barcelona. Lang.: Cat.   1572

1701-1850.   Plays/librettos/scripts.
Analysis of 51 short farces written in Majorca. Lang.: Cat.   2731

1790-1985.   Plays/librettos/scripts.
Valencian playwrights writing in both Catalan and Castilian. Valencia. Lang.: Cat.   2732

1800-1830.   Performance spaces.
Reconstruction of theatrical activity in Barcelona. Barcelona. Lang.: Cat.   1672

1850-1685.   Institutions.
Memoir of the papers and debates organized at the First Congress of Amateur Theatre in Catalonia. Lang.: Cat.   560

1899-1986.   Basic theatrical documents.
Edition and analysis, *Allò que tal vegada s'esdevingué (What Happened Then)* by Joan Oliver. Lang.: Cat.   1573

1900-1986.   Reference materials.
History of theatrical activity in Palafrugell. Palafrugell. Lang.: Cat.   1210

1902-1961.   Plays/librettos/scripts.
General history of Catalan literature, including theatre. Lang.: Cat.   1157

1922-1927.   Performance/production.
Collection of theatre reviews by J.M. de Sagarra. Barcelona. Lang.: Cat.   885

1929-1986.   Institutions.
Texts and photos about the Teatre Grec. Barcelona. Lang.: Cat.   558

1937-1982.   Basic theatrical documents.
Study of the poetic, narrative and theatrical work of Agustí Bartra, edition of complete works, vol. 4. Mexico. Lang.: Cat.   1571

1939-1975.   Plays/librettos/scripts.
Catalan playwrights after the Spanish Civil War. Lang.: Cat.   2730

1962-1987.   Institutions.
Analysis of all the productions performed by Els Joglars in their twenty-five years of existence. Lang.: Cat.   1634

1969-1972.   Performance/production.
Collection of theatre reviews by Xavier Fàbregas. Lang.: Cat.   2010

1975-1985.   Institutions.
Proposes database for Catalan theatre. Lang.: Spa.   559

1976.   Institutions.
Founding manifesto of the Teatre Lliure. Barcelona. Lang.: Cat.   1631

1976-1986.   Institutions.
Evaluation of the first ten years of Teatre Lliure. Barcelona. Lang.: Cat.   1632
Present and future of Teatre Lliure. Barcelona. Lang.: Cat.   1633
Evaluation of theatrical policy in Catalonia. Barcelona. Lang.: Cat.   1635

Evaluation of the plays performed during the first ten years of Teatre Lliure. Barcelona. Lang.: Cat.   1636

1976-1987.   Institutions.
The Teatre Lliure as a public theatre: future prospects. Barcelona. Lang.: Cat.   1630

1976-1987.   Performance spaces.
Technical team of Teatre Lliure. Barcelona. Lang.: Cat.   668
Birth and growth of the Teatre Lliure. Barcelona. Lang.: Cat.   1670
Collection of photographs on the history of the Teatre Lliure. Barcelona. Lang.: Cat.   1671
History of the Teatre Lliure. Barcelona. Lang.: Cat.   1673

1976-1987.   Performance/production.
Description of the performances played in the Teatre Lliure. Barcelona. Lang.: Cat.   2009

1986-1987.   Performance/production.
Overview of theatre season. Barcelona. Lang.: Cat.   2011

1987.   Performance/production.
Premiere of Leonardo Balarda's opera *Cristobal Colón*. Barcelona. Lang.: Eng.   3818

1987.   Reference materials.
Picture book to accompany production of *La Nit (The Night)* by Els Comediants. Lang.: Cat.   1209

1987.   Training.
Teachers' handbook for theatre in education. Lang.: Cat.   1384

Sri Lanka

1987.   Performance/production.
Origins of theatre and its relationship to the spectator. India. Japan. Lang.: Eng.   813

Sudan

1987.   Relation to other fields.
Popular theatre and non-governmental funding agencies. Sydney, NS. Jamaica. Lang.: Eng.   2982

Sweden

1700-1987.   Plays/librettos/scripts.
Theme of stage direction in the work of Scandinavian authors. Norway. Lang.: Ita.   2737

1901-1964.   Plays/librettos/scripts.
Dramatic vs. literary interpretation of *Ett Drömspel (A Dream Play)* by August Strindberg. Lang.: Eng.   2734

1903-1987.   Plays/librettos/scripts.
Theatrical metaphor in Strindberg's *Gustav III*. Lang.: Eng.   2741

1907-1987.   Plays/librettos/scripts.
The son-in-law in *Pelikanen (The Pelican)* by August Strindberg. Lang.: Swe.   2740

1916-1979.   Performance/production.
Evaluation of actor Anders Ek. Lang.: Swe.   2012

1917-1987.   Institutions.
Folkteatergruppen's productions, including *Antigone-nu (Antigone Now)*. Stockholm. Lang.: Swe.   1640

1920-1970.   Plays/librettos/scripts.
Karl Ragnar Gierow on O'Neill and his importance in Sweden. Stockholm. Lang.: Eng.   2736

1921-1987.   Institutions.
Stockholms Studentteater now welcomes amateur participation. Stockholm. Lang.: Swe.   1638

1927-1987.   Performance/production.
Interview with ballerina and teacher Ellen Rasch. Lang.: Swe.   1442
Evaluation of soprano, Elisabeth Söderström. Stockholm. Lang.: Eng.   3820

1932-1970.   Performance/production.
Memories of contralto Kerstin Thorborg. Germany. Lang.: Swe.   3821

1944-1986.   Performance/production.
Career of film director Ingmar Bergman. Lang.: Eng.   3161

1944-1987.   Performance/production.
Interview with tenor Esias Tewolde-Berhan of Kungliga Teatern. Stockholm. Ethiopia. Lang.: Swe.   3825

1948-1987.   Performance/production.
Swedish opera director, Göran Järvefelt. Stockholm. Santa Fe, NM. Lang.: Eng.   3824

1960-1985.   Institutions.
Attendance at Royal Swedish Opera: analysis, how to improve it. Stockholm. Lang.: Swe.   3730

1970-1987.   Performance/production.
Portrait of choreographer Efva Lilja. Stockholm. Lang.: Swe.   1470

Sweden — cont'd

Interview with playwright Cannie Möller. Järfälla. Lang.: Swe. 2735
1987. Theory/criticism.
Shift of August Strindberg from naturalism to expressionism. Lang.: Eng. 3061

Switzerland
1416-1879. Performance/production.
History of Bernese carnival. Berne. Lang.: Ger. 3298
1453-1616. Performance/production.
Role of the director in the Lucerne Passion play. Lucerne. Lang.: Eng. 2030
1834-1870. Relation to other fields.
Influence of Arthur Schopenhauer on Wagner's works. Lang.: Eng. 3945
1850-1855. Theory/criticism.
Gottfried Keller's theory of drama. Berlin. Lang.: Ger. 3062
1864-1918. Plays/librettos/scripts.
Biography of Swiss playwright Frank Wedekind. Lenzburg. Berlin. Paris. Lang.: Ger. 2746
1873-1928. Design/technology.
Designer Adolphe Appia's concepts and scenery for Wagner's operas. Germany. Lang.: Eng. 3694
1886-1986. Performance/production.
Work of composer Othmar Schoeck. Lang.: Ger. 3826
1889-1984. Plays/librettos/scripts.
Standard German and the German Swiss dialects on and off stage. Lang.: Ger. 2744
1900-1930. Relation to other fields.
Paper reproductions of 19th-century stage sets. Germany. Lang.: Ger. 1239
1902-1987. Performance/production.
Interview with Swiss tenor Hugues Cuénod. Vevey. Lang.: Eng. 3827
1911-1987. Plays/librettos/scripts.
Realism in the plays of Max Frisch. Lang.: Rus. 2742
1939-1947. Performance/production.
Music for Brecht's *Mutter Courage und ihre Kinder (Mother Courage and Her Children)*. Zürich. Finland. Lang.: Ger. 2027
1945-1986. Plays/librettos/scripts.
Analysis of plays of Friedrich Dürrenmatt, comparison with Bertolt Brecht. Germany, West. Lang.: Ger. 2745
1949. Performance/production.
Leonard Steckel's production of *Faust II* as a turning point of Swiss theatre. Zürich. Lang.: Ger. 2028
1950-1986. Performance/production.
Problems of dancers outside established companies. Lang.: Ger, Eng. 1411
1955-1987. Institutions.
History of ballet companies: their origins in opera companies, later autonomy. Lang.: Eng, Ger. 1430
1960-1985. Relation to other fields.
The sociopolitical role of the critic in theatrical criticism. Lang.: Ger. 1255
1967-1987. Performance/production.
Theatre activities in Baden. Baden. Lang.: Ger. 895
1968-1987. Relation to other fields.
Claque Theatre, a professional provincial ensemble. Baden. Lang.: Ger. 3001
1971-1982. Plays/librettos/scripts.
Analysis of Dürrenmatt's *Play Strindberg*, adaptation of Strindberg's *Dödsdansen (The Dance of Death)*. Lang.: Eng. 2743
1980-1987. Performance/production.
Twenty opera productions at Grand Théâtre. Geneva. Lang.: Fre. 3828
1982-1986. Institutions.
Failure of a Swiss project to promote playwrights. Lang.: Ger. 563
1984-1987. Performance/production.
Comprehensive survey of Romansh theatre. Lang.: Ger. 894
1985-1986. Relation to other fields.
The functions and aims of FiT (Women in Theatre). Lang.: Ger, Fre. 1254
1986. Performance spaces.
Telecast of Donizetti's *Lucia di Lammermoor* into a large performing area. Basel. Lang.: Fre, Ger. 3737
1986-1987. Reference materials.
Theatre demographics in German-speaking Europe. Germany, West. Austria. Lang.: Ger. 1203

1986-1987. Relation to other fields.
Analysis of the role of political drama in Europe. Basel. Mönchengladbach. Lang.: Ger. 3002
1986-1988. Performance/production.
Children's theatrical productions outside of theatres. Includes playtexts. Lang.: Ger. 2026
1987. Administration.
Questions about the role of private sponsorship in publicly funded theatre. Lang.: Ger. 43
Attempts by private sponsors to influence artistic decisions. Lang.: Ger. 44
1987. Audience.
Function of the audience in theatre. Lang.: Ger. 289
1987. Performance/production.
Yearly productions of Calderón's *El gran teatro del mundo (The Great Stage of the World)*. Einsiedeln. Lang.: Ger. 893
Open-air theatre and festivals. Lang.: Ger. 896
Benno Besson directs Molière's *Dom Juan*. Geneva. Lang.: Fre. 2029
Mime Samy Molcho: his new work as lecturer and author. Lang.: Ger. 3235
1987. Plays/librettos/scripts.
Chance in the plays of P.G. du Plessis and Friedrich Dürrenmatt. South Africa, Republic of. Lang.: Afr. 1153
Comparison of Dürrenmatt's *The Physicists (Die Physiker)*, *Macbeth* and *Doctor Faustus*. Lang.: Heb. 2747
1987. Reference materials.
Content and intent of an exhibition on all European theatre history since the ancient Greek. Berne. Lang.: Fre, Ger. 1211
Bibliography of texts, reviews, and criticism of German-speaking Swiss theatrical activity. Lang.: Ger. 1212
1987. Relation to other fields.
Discussion by theatre women on management, social security. Lang.: Ger. 1253
Government funding of official theatre and opera companies. Lang.: Ger. 1256
The role of ballet and ballet dancers in Swiss theatres. Lang.: Ger. 1456
1987. Training.
Circus productions by performers' children. Lang.: Ger. 3307
Review of circus acts by children. Lang.: Ger. 3308
1987-1988. Performance/production.
Yearbook of Swiss theatrical activity, with bibliography. Lang.: Fre, Ger, Ita. 892

Taiwan
1986. Basic theatrical documents.
Text of *Yu-wang-cheng-gue (A City of Desire)* by Li Hui-min, based on Shakespeare's *Macbeth*. Lang.: Chi. 3443
1986. Performance/production.
Beijing opera *Yu-wang-cheng-gue (A City of Desire)*, based on Shakespeare's *Macbeth*. Taipei. Lang.: Chi. 3541
1987. Performance/production.
The life of Chinese puppeteer Shiu Fu-Neng. Lang.: Chi. 3540
A review of *Yian de-yi yuan (A Marriage of Good Fortune)*. Taipei. Lang.: Chi. 3542
1987. Reference materials.
Source materials on development of Chinese opera. Lang.: Chi. 3580

Turkey
1900-1987. Performance/production.
Role of festivals in Turkish theatre. Lang.: Ger. 897

Uganda
1962-1974. Plays/librettos/scripts.
Analysis of the plays of E.N. Ziramu. Buganda. Lang.: Eng. 2748
1987. Performance/production.
Role of theatre in the face of political turmoil. Managua. Lang.: Eng. 864

Ukraine
1800-1987. Performance/production.
Materials on traditional Ukrainian folk puppet theatre. Lang.: Ukr. 3984
1830-1889. Plays/librettos/scripts.
Ukrainian Romantic drama. Lang.: Rus. 2833
1917-1987. Performance/production.
Overview of Soviet Ukrainian theatre. Lang.: Ukr. 924
Soviet dramaturgy on the Ukrainian stage. Lang.: Rus. 2310

UK-England — cont'd

Collection of newspaper reviews by London theatre critics.
London. Lang.: Eng.   2067

Collection of newspaper reviews by London theatre critics.
London. Lang.: Eng.   2068

Collection of newspaper reviews by London theatre critics.
London. Lang.: Eng.   2069

Collection of newspaper reviews by London theatre critics.
London. Lang.: Eng.   2070

Collection of newspaper reviews by London theatre critics.
London. Lang.: Eng.   2071

Collection of newspaper reviews by London theatre critics.
London. Lang.: Eng.   2072

Collection of newspaper reviews by London theatre critics.
London. Lang.: Eng.   2075

Collection of newspaper reviews by London theatre critics.
London. Lang.: Eng.   2076

Collection of newspaper reviews by London theatre critics.
London. Lang.: Eng.   2077

Collection of newspaper reviews by London theatre critics.
London. Lang.: Eng.   2078

Collection of newspaper reviews by London theatre critics.
London. Lang.: Eng.   2079

Collection of newspaper reviews by London theatre critics.
London. Lang.: Eng.   2080

Collection of newspaper reviews by London theatre critics.
London. Lang.: Eng.   2081

Collection of newspaper reviews by London theatre critics.
London. Lang.: Eng.   2082

Collection of newspaper reviews by London theatre critics.
London. Lang.: Eng.   2083

Collection of newspaper reviews by London theatre critics.
London. Lang.: Eng.   2084

Collection of newspaper reviews by London theatre critics.
London. Lang.: Eng.   2085

Collection of newspaper reviews by London theatre critics.
London. Lang.: Eng.   2086

Collection of newspaper reviews by London theatre critics.
London. Lang.: Eng.   2087

Collection of newspaper reviews by London theatre critics.
London. Lang.: Eng.   2088

Collection of newspaper reviews by London theatre critics.
London. Lang.: Eng.   2089

Collection of newspaper reviews by London theatre critics.
London. Lang.: Eng.   2090

Collection of newspaper reviews by London theatre critics.
London. Lang.: Eng.   2091

Collection of newspaper reviews by London theatre critics.
London. Lang.: Eng.   2092

Collection of newspaper reviews by London theatre critics.
London. Lang.: Eng.   2093

Collection of newspaper reviews by London theatre critics.
London. Lang.: Eng.   2094

Collection of newspaper reviews by London theatre critics.
London. Lang.: Eng.   2095

Collection of newspaper reviews by London theatre critics.
London. Lang.: Eng.   2096

Collection of newspaper reviews by London theatre critics.
London. Lang.: Eng.   2097

Collection of newspaper reviews by London theatre critics.
London. Lang.: Eng.   2098

Collection of newspaper reviews by London theatre critics.
London. Lang.: Eng.   2099

Collection of newspaper reviews by London theatre critics.
London. Lang.: Eng.   2100

Collection of newspaper reviews by London theatre critics.
London. Lang.: Eng.   2101

Collection of newspaper reviews by London theatre critics.
London. Lang.: Eng.   2102

Collection of newspaper reviews by London theatre critics.
London. Lang.: Eng.   2103

Collection of newspaper reviews by London theatre critics.
London. Lang.: Eng.   2104

Collection of newspaper reviews by London theatre critics.
London. Lang.: Eng.   2105

Collection of newspaper reviews by London theatre critics.
London. Lang.: Eng.   2106

Collection of newspaper reviews by London theatre critics.
London. Lang.: Eng.   2107

Collection of newspaper reviews by London theatre critics.
London. Lang.: Eng.   2108

Collection of newspaper reviews by London theatre critics.
London. Lang.: Eng.   2109

Collection of newspaper reviews by London theatre critics.
London. Lang.: Eng.   2110

Collection of newspaper reviews by London theatre critics.
London. Lang.: Eng.   2111

Collection of newspaper reviews by London theatre critics.
London. Lang.: Eng.   2112

Collection of newspaper reviews by London theatre critics.
London. Lang.: Eng.   2113

Collection of newspaper reviews by London theatre critics.
London. Lang.: Eng.   2114

Collection of newspaper reviews by London theatre critics.
London. Lang.: Eng.   2115

Collection of newspaper reviews by London theatre critics.
London. Lang.: Eng.   2116

Collection of newspaper reviews by London theatre critics.
London. Lang.: Eng.   2117

Collection of newspaper reviews by London theatre critics.
London. Lang.: Eng.   2118

Collection of newspaper reviews by London theatre critics.
London. Lang.: Eng.   2119

Collection of newspaper reviews by London theatre critics.
London. Lang.: Eng.   2120

Collection of newspaper reviews by London theatre critics.
London. Lang.: Eng.   2121

Collection of newspaper reviews by London theatre critics.
London. Lang.: Eng.   2122

Collection of newspaper reviews by London theatre critics.
London. Lang.: Eng.   2123

Collection of newspaper reviews by London theatre critics.
London. Lang.: Eng.   2124

Collection of newspaper reviews by London theatre critics.
London. Lang.: Eng.   2125

Collection of newspaper reviews by London theatre critics.
London. Lang.: Eng.   2126

Collection of newspaper reviews by London theatre critics.
London. Lang.: Eng.   2127

Collection of newspaper reviews by London theatre critics.
London. Lang.: Eng.   2128

Collection of newspaper reviews by London theatre critics.
London. Lang.: Eng.   2129

Collection of newspaper reviews by London theatre critics.
London. Lang.: Eng.   2130

Collection of newspaper reviews by London theatre critics.
London. Lang.: Eng.   2131

Collection of newspaper reviews by London theatre critics.
London. Lang.: Eng.   2132

Collection of newspaper reviews by London theatre critics.
London. Lang.: Eng.   2133

Collection of newspaper reviews by London theatre critics.
London. Lang.: Eng.   2134

Collection of newspaper reviews by London theatre critics.
London. Lang.: Eng.   2135

Collection of newspaper reviews by London theatre critics.
London. Lang.: Eng.   2136

Collection of newspaper reviews by London theatre critics.
London. Lang.: Eng.   2137

Collection of newspaper reviews by London theatre critics.
London. Lang.: Eng.   2138

Collection of newspaper reviews by London theatre critics.
London. Lang.: Eng.   2139

Collection of newspaper reviews by London theatre critics.
London. Lang.: Eng.   2140

UK-England — cont'd

Puppets used in community development workshops. London. Lang.: Eng.   3997

Puppetry in education of hearing-impaired. London. Lang.: Eng.   4011

UK-Ireland

1860-1925.   **Plays/librettos/scripts.**
Shaw's use of Irish stereotypes in *John Bull's Other Ireland*. UK-England. Lang.: Eng.   2787

1875-1938.   **Relation to other fields.**
Literary figures of the Irish Literary Renaissance. Ireland. Lang.: Eng.   2995

1891-1983.   **Research/historiography.**
Overview of Canadian research on twentieth-century Irish drama. Ireland. Canada. Lang.: Eng.   3011

1900-1982.   **Plays/librettos/scripts.**
Ulster drama before Sam Thompson. Lang.: Eng.   2829

1916-1987.   **Plays/librettos/scripts.**
Yeats's dance plays: effect of the elements of performance on text. Lang.: Eng.   2832

1930-1985.   **Plays/librettos/scripts.**
Interview with playwright John Boyd: influences and plays. Belfast. Lang.: Eng.   2828

1965-1984.   **Institutions.**
Difficulty in obtaining funding for theatre building repair. Dublin. Cork. Belfast. Lang.: Eng.   545

1970-1987.   **Relation to other fields.**
Interview with founders of the Charabanc Theatre Company. Lang.: Eng.   1260

1974-1987.   **Institutions.**
The touring company Irish Theatre Company. Lang.: Eng.   569

1975.   **Plays/librettos/scripts.**
Metaphor of archaeology in Friel's *Volunteers*, poems of Heaney. Dublin. Lang.: Eng.   2651

1975-1987.   **Theory/criticism.**
Performance artists Declan McGonagle and Alistair MacLennan. Belfast. Lang.: Eng.   3374

1979-1987.   **Plays/librettos/scripts.**
Avoidance of political themes in drama of Northern Ireland. Lang.: Eng.   2830

1979-1987.   **Training.**
Genesis and development of various youth theatre groups. Lang.: Eng.   1388

1983-1987.   **Plays/librettos/scripts.**
Christina Reid's *Tea in a China Cup*: a woman's view of Belfast. Belfast. Lang.: Eng.   2831

1984.   **Theory/criticism.**
Stewart Parker's *Northern Star*. Lang.: Eng.   3065

1986-1987.   **Performance/production.**
Productions and political philosophy of Field Day Theatre Company. Londonderry. Lang.: Eng.   2309

1987.   **Theory/criticism.**
Assessment of the series *Lost Beginning*, its relation to Stewart Parker's *Pentecost*. Lang.: Eng.   3218

1987.   **Training.**
Interview with Michael Poyner, director of Ulster Youth Theatre. Lang.: Eng.   1386

Current state of Northern Ireland's young theatre community. Lang.: Eng.   1387

UK-Scotland

1970-1987.   **Theory/criticism.**
Richard Demarco on performance art. Edinburgh. Lang.: Eng.   3376

1982.   **Administration.**
Methods of funding the Edinburgh Festival. Edinburgh. Lang.: Eng.   57

1987.   **Design/technology.**
Problems associated with setting up a training course in design. Glasgow. Lang.: Eng.   380

1987.   **Institutions.**
Edinburgh Festival's productions less competitive. Edinburgh. Lang.: Eng.   3392

1987.   **Performance/production.**
Review of Scottish theatre for the first 6 months of 1987. Edinburgh. Lang.: Eng.   921

Classical theatre is diminishing in the provinces due to financial cutbacks. London. Liverpool. Edinburgh. Lang.: Eng.   2301

Review of the 1987 Edinburgh Fringe Festival. Edinburgh. Lang.: Eng.   3271

1987.   **Theory/criticism.**
Influences on work of performance artist Richard Demarco. Edinburgh. Lang.: Eng.   3375

UK-Wales

1901-1987.   **Design/technology.**
Restoration of the stage machinery at the Grand Theatre. Llandudno. Lang.: Eng.   381

1960-1987.   **Performance/production.**
Theatre groups existing in small countries and communities. South America. Lang.: Eng.   884

1983-1987.   **Institutions.**
Brian McMaster's direction of the Vancouver Opera. Vancouver, BC. Lang.: Eng.   3721

1986.   **Institutions.**
First festival of women's work in experimental theatre. Cardiff. Lang.: Eng.   1649

1986.   **Performance/production.**
Overview of the 'Magdalena 86' festival. Cardiff. Lang.: Eng.   3360

1986-1987.   **Performance/production.**
An experimental women's theatre workshop. Cardiff. Lang.: Eng.   922

1987.   **Performance/production.**
Radio 4's Welsh Drama Week 1987 reviewed. UK-England. Lang.: Eng.   3111

USA

Performance/production.
Relations between acting, theatre photography. Lang.: Eng.   942

Interview with playwright/actor Robert Perring. Lang.: Eng.   2354

Work of film director Andrei Konchalovsky. Moscow. Lang.: Eng.   3166

Origins of jazz, its evolution in vaudeville. New Orleans, LA. New York, NY. Chicago, IL. Lang.: Eng.   3650

Mezzo soprano Risë Stevens. New York, NY. Lang.: Eng.   3856

Plays/librettos/scripts.
Roadside Theatre's production of *Leaving Egypt*. Whitesburg, KY. Lang.: Eng.   1170

Adaptation of Alan Bowne's *Forty Deuce* as stage play and film. New York, NY. Lang.: Eng.   2891

Legal and ethical rights of playwrights regarding interpretations of their works. Lang.: Eng.   2904

500 B.C.-1987 A.D.   **Theory/criticism.**
Perceptions of tragedy and new perspective on its analysis. UK-England. Greece. Lang.: Eng.   3066

400 B.C.-1987 A.D.   **Performance/production.**
Orientalism in Peter Brook's production of *The Mahabharata*. India. New York, NY. Lang.: Eng.   1932

400 B.C.-1987 A.D.   **Theory/criticism.**
Comic space from the ancient Greeks to the present. Europe. Greece. Lang.: Eng.   3032

1500-1987.   **Performance/production.**
Standardization of musical pitch. Europe. Lang.: Eng.   3399

1564-1616.   **Plays/librettos/scripts.**
Recent studies of the life of William Shakespeare. UK-England. Lang.: Eng.   2857

1586-1987.   **Performance/production.**
Black theatre in South Africa: influence of traditional forms. South Africa, Republic of. London. New York, NY. Lang.: Eng.   2005

1590-1987.   **Theory/criticism.**
Gesture and sign in Shakespearean performance. England. Lang.: Eng.   1326

1598-1965.   **Performance/production.**
Retrospective of two centuries of Hispanic theatre. Lang.: Eng.   2345

1598-1983.   **Plays/librettos/scripts.**
Influences of Spanish-language theatre on Chicano theatre. Lang.: Eng.   2874

1600-1987.   **Design/technology.**
Instruction in scene painting. Lang.: Eng.   434

1600-1987.   **Performance/production.**
The influence of African music on America. Lang.: Eng.   943

Designing and using puppets in classical works. Lang.: Eng.   3985

1901-1987. **Design/technology.**
Controversy over 1901 cylinder recording of *Les Huguenots.*
Lang.: Eng. 3699
1902-1987. **Performance/production.**
Soprano Bidú Sayão. New York, NY. Brazil. Lang.: Eng.
3861
1903-1979. **Performance/production.**
Biographical account of Beatriz Escalona, La Chata Noloesca.
San Antonio, TX. Lang.: Spa. 2369
1903-1987. **Theory/criticism.**
Representation of women by Hollywood film industry. Los
Angeles, CA. Lang.: Eng. 3188
1904-1987. **Performance/production.**
Early phonograph records of opera singers. Italy. Germany.
Lang.: Eng. 3113
Interview with tenor Martial Singher. France. Santa Barbara,
CA. Lang.: Eng. 3771
1909-1987. **Performance/production.**
The career of dancer/choreographer Katherine Dunham. New
York, NY. Chicago, IL. Las Vegas, NV. Lang.: Eng. 1412
1910-1940. **Institutions.**
Impact of German expressionist theatre. UK-England.
Germany. Lang.: Eng. 1648
1912-1913. **Performance/production.**
History of the first Passing Show. New York, NY. Lang.:
Eng. 3645
1913. **Plays/librettos/scripts.**
Family relationships in Eugene O'Neill's early plays. Lang.:
Eng. 2926
1913-1987. **Performance/production.**
Millicent Hodson speaks about how she managed to
reconstruct Nižinskij's *Le sacre du printemps.* Los Angeles,
CA. Lang.: Swe. 1473
1914-1924. **Administration.**
Lee Shubert's role in the formation of the American film
industry. New York, NY. Lang.: Eng. 3123
1914-1958. **Plays/librettos/scripts.**
History of the World Film Corporation, division of the
Shubert Organization and its adaptations of stage plays into
films. Lang.: Eng. 3179
1915-1923. **Institutions.**
Development of El Teatro Carmen. Tucson, AZ. Lang.: Spa.
606
1915-1985. **Design/technology.**
Index of Broadway costume designs and designers. New
York, NY. Lang.: Eng. 444
1915-1986. **Plays/librettos/scripts.**
Distorted race relations in Western films. Lang.: Eng. 3181
1915-1987. **Institutions.**
Black theatre as an art and industry. New York, NY. Lang.:
Eng. 600
1915-1987. **Performance spaces.**
History of the Garden Theatre designed by Thomas H. Scott.
Pittsburgh, PA. Lang.: Eng. 3144
1916-1983. **Plays/librettos/scripts.**
Successful film versions of Shakespeare's *King Lear.* UK-
England. USSR. Lang.: Eng. 3099
1917-1985. **Theory/criticism.**
The language of theatrical criticism. New York, NY. Lang.:
Eng. 1367
1917-1987. **Performance/production.**
Influence of Pirandello on modern theatre. Italy. Lang.: Eng.
2338
1919. **Administration.**
Ziegfeld Follies strike. New York, NY. Lang.: Eng. 167
1920. **Plays/librettos/scripts.**
Women's roles in Broadway plays at the time of women's
suffrage. New York, NY. Lang.: Eng. 2850
Family and male-female relationships in O'Neill's *Desire
Under the Elms.* Lang.: Eng. 2885
1920-1922. **Plays/librettos/scripts.**
Symbolism in *The Hairy Ape* by Eugene O'Neill. Lang.:
Eng. 2929
1920-1930. **Performance/production.**
Interview with actress Barbara Barondess MacLean. New
York, NY. Lang.: Eng. 3652
1920-1962. **Plays/librettos/scripts.**
Eugene O'Neill's influence on William Faulkner. New York,
NY. Lang.: Eng. 2858
1920-1982. **Administration.**
History of Astoria Studios. New York, NY. Lang.: Eng. 124

1920-1982. **Institutions.**
Astoria Studios' restoration to operating film studio. Queens,
NY. Lang.: Eng. 3140
1920-1982. **Plays/librettos/scripts.**
Comparison of themes and dramaturgical techniques in plays
of Eugene O'Neill and Peter Shaffer. Lang.: Eng. 2872
1920-1986. **Design/technology.**
Essays on historical costuming in Hollywood films.
Hollywood, CA. Lang.: Eng. 3133
1920-1987. **Performance/production.**
History of dance marathons. Lang.: Eng. 957
Career of actor Jack Gilford. New York, NY. Lang.: Eng.
3292
1921. **Plays/librettos/scripts.**
Parallels between O'Neill's *Anna Christie* and Homer's
Odyssey. Lang.: Eng. 2906
1921-1925. **Institutions.**
Actors' Equity strike against Producing Managers Association.
New York, NY. Lang.: Eng. 573
1921-1959. **Performance/production.**
Life and career of singer Mario Lanza. Lang.: Swe. 3171
1922-1947. **Plays/librettos/scripts.**
O'Neill's transcendence of melodrama in *A Touch of the
Poet* and *A Moon for the Misbegotten.* Lang.: Eng. 2886
1922-1987. **Performance/production.**
History of incorporating film into a theatrical performance.
New York, NY. Lang.: Eng. 3196
1923-1977. **Performance/production.**
Evaluation of soprano Maria Meneghini Callas. Greece. Italy.
Lang.: Eng. 3790
1923-1983. **Performance/production.**
Index of Broadway productions which ran for one night
only. New York, NY. Lang.: Eng. 951
1923-1987. **Performance/production.**
Method acting: its origins and development. New York, NY.
Moscow. Lang.: Eng. 2359
1924-1981. **Performance/production.**
Stephen Porter on directing Shaw. Lang.: Eng. 2353
1924-1983. **Performances spaces.**
History and renovations of City Center. New York, NY.
Lang.: Eng. 1094
1924-1987. **Plays/librettos/scripts.**
Career of Broadway musical author Michael Short. New
York, NY. UK-England. Lang.: Eng. 3673
1925-1979. **Design/technology.**
Career of Broadway set designer Boris Aronson. Lang.: Eng.
449
1925-1981. **Relation to other fields.**
Interview with caricaturist Al Hirschfeld. New York, NY.
Lang.: Eng. 1272
1926-1962. **Performance/production.**
Hungarian translation of Norman Mailer's biography of
Marilyn Monroe. Lang.: Hun. 3169
1926-1970. **Theory/criticism.**
Reception theory, performance and American influence in
Korea. Korea. Lang.: Kor. 1370
1926-1986. **Institutions.**
Overview of Martha Graham Dance Company. Lang.: Ger.
1467
1926-1986. **Performance/production.**
Listing of films made from books or plays and their
production information. UK-England. Lang.: Eng. 3162
1926-1987. **Performance spaces.**
Many uses of the Uptown Theatre. Kansas City, MO. Lang.:
Eng. 3143
1926-1987. **Performance/production.**
Interview with tenor James McCracken. Gary, IN. Europe.
Lang.: Eng. 3855
1926-1987. **Theory/criticism.**
Portrayals of African-Americans in media and literature.
Lang.: Eng. 3104
Portrayal of African-American artists in literature. Lang.:
Eng. 3105
1927. **Performance/production.**
Interview with Mary Arbenz on the original production of
Mourning Becomes Electra. New York, NY. Lang.: Eng.
2355
1927. **Plays/librettos/scripts.**
Influence of Herman Melville on Eugene O'Neill. Lang.:
Eng. 2888

Revival of *Love Life* by Kurt Weill and Alan Jay Lerner.
New York, NY. Ann Arbor, MI. Lang.: Eng.   3653

1945-1987.   Performance/production.
Career of conductor/educator Max Rudolf. Italy. New York,
NY. Lang.: Eng.   3803

1946-1947.   Institutions.
The beginnings and failure of the United States Opera
Company. Chicago, IL. Lang.: Eng.   3731

1946-1987.   Theory/criticism.
Balanchine ballerinas: female domination in the ballet. Lang.:
Eng.   1457

The work and writings of theatre critics Eric Bentley and
Gordon Rogoff. Lang.: Eng.   3071

1947.   Design/technology.
Mapleson cylinders: controversy over *Les Huguenots*. New
York, NY. Lang.: Eng.   3700

1947-1987.   Performance spaces.
Architecture of La Jolla Playhouse and challenges it presents
for designers. La Jolla, CA. Lang.: Eng.   694

1947-1987.   Plays/librettos/scripts.
Characterizations of stage spaces: examples from Brecht,
Pinter, Douglas Turner Ward. UK-England. Lang.: Eng. 2798

1948-1971.   Plays/librettos/scripts.
Polanski, Welles and Kurosawa's versions of Shakespeare's
Macbeth. Japan. UK-England. Lang.: Eng.   3183

1948-1987.   Performance/production.
Swedish opera director, Göran Järvefelt. Stockholm. Santa
Fe, NM. Lang.: Eng.   3824

1949-1962.   Plays/librettos/scripts.
Eugene O'Neill's influence on Edward Albee. Lang.: Eng.
          2841

1950-1951.   Performance/production.
Personal anecdotes and photographs from the making of *The
African Queen*. Hollywood, CA. Lang.: Eng.   3168

1950-1955.   Plays/librettos/scripts.
Elia Kazan's influence on playwright Ray Lawler. Australia.
Lang.: Eng.   2445

1950-1972.   Administration.
Career of Sir Rudolph Bing, challenges of managing the
Metropolitan Opera. New York, NY. Lang.: Eng.   3682

1950-1980.   Plays/librettos/scripts.
Space and audience-performer relationship—examples from
Ellen Sebastian and Maria Irene Fornes. Lang.: Eng.   2838

1950-1985.   Plays/librettos/scripts.
The German radio play *Hörspiel* and its history. Cologne.
Lang.: Eng.   3117

1950-1987.   Administration.
Enforcing restrictions on blacked-out sports events. Lang.:
Eng.   3090

1950-1987.   Design/technology.
Czech scenographers Josef Svoboda and Ladislav Vychodil.
Prague. Lang.: Eng.   309

1950-1987.   Performance/production.
Theatre career of photo-journalist Bert Andrews. New York,
NY. Lang.: Eng.   2367

How film industry has shaped racist attitudes toward Blacks.
Lang.: Eng.   3095

Interview with actress Margaret Avery. San Diego, CA.
Hollywood, CA. Lang.: Eng.   3167

Analysis of art of television and comparison to live theatre.
Lang.: Eng.   3194

Profile of soprano Jeannine Altmeyer. New York, NY.
Lang.: Eng.   3853

1950-1987.   Plays/librettos/scripts.
Interview with cartoonist-playwright Jules Feiffer. Lang.: Eng.
          1168

Dramatic treatment of material about the Holocaust.
Germany, West. Lang.: Eng.   2917

Roles of Black males in American TV. Lang.: Eng.   3215

1950-1987.   Relation to other fields.
Analysis of past and current perceptions of the human body,
how they affect the human experience and the arts. Lang.:
Eng.   1266

1950-1987.   Theory/criticism.
Brechtian influence on contemporary art. Europe. Lang.: Eng.
          1353

1951-1983.   Institutions.
Profile of Ecotheatre and its artistic director Maryat Lee.
Hinton, WV. Lang.: Eng.   1651

1952.   Plays/librettos/scripts.
Orson Welles's adaptation of *Othello*: cinematic technique
and time. Lang.: Eng.   3180

1952-1981.   Performance/production.
Careers of three female opera stars: Mary McCormic, Maria
Jeritza, Bidú Sayão. Lang.: Eng.   3835

1952-1983.   Institutions.
Opera theatre program at the University of Louisville.
Louisville, KY. Lang.: Eng.   3732

1952-1986.   Theory/criticism.
Eric Bentley's critical essays on theatre. Lang.: Eng.   1350

1953-1987.   Performance/production.
Interview with actor James Earl Jones. New York, NY.
Lang.: Eng.   2340

1954-1982.   Administration.
Laws governing music and performance piracy. New York,
NY. Lang.: Eng.   162

1954-1987.   Plays/librettos/scripts.
Life of playwright John O. Killens. New York, NY. Lang.:
Eng.   2836

1955-1985.   Performance/production.
Organizational and production history of the American
Shakespeare Festival. Stratford, CT. Lang.: Eng.   934

1955-1987.   Performance/production.
Soprano Susan Dunn. New York, NY. Lang.: Eng.   3854

1956-1984.   Performance/production.
Broadway musical's shift from song and dance to aria and
recitative. New York, NY. Lang.: Eng.   3655

1957-1983.   Institutions.
Profile of Dell'Arte Players and their productions. Blue Lake,
CA. Lang.: Eng.   3310

1957-1985.   Performance/production.
Interview with actress Georgia Brown. New York, NY.
London. Lang.: Eng.   3651

1957-1987.   Performance/production.
Interview with actor and playwright Joe Seneca. New York,
NY. Cleveland, OH. Lang.: Eng.   2364

Martin Charnin's work in musical theatre. New York, NY.
Lang.: Eng.   3658

1957-1987.   Plays/librettos/scripts.
Adaptations of fairy tales and fantasies for children's plays.
Lang.: Eng.   1165

1958-1966.   Performance/production.
History of musical version, *Breakfast at Tiffany's*. New
York, NY. Philadelphia, PA. Boston, MA. Lang.: Eng. 3644

1958-1982.   Administration.
Negative effects of injunctions. Lang.: Eng.   201

1958-1985.   Relation to other fields.
Artaud's philosophy of theatre mediating between dream and
history. Lang.: Eng.   1265

1959-1986.   Plays/librettos/scripts.
The career of playwright Wole Soyinka. New York, NY.
Nigeria. Lang.: Eng.   2865

1959-1987.   Institutions.
Second City improvisational comedy troupe. Chicago, IL.
Toronto, ON. Lang.: Eng.   605

1959-1987.   Plays/librettos/scripts.
Playwright Fernando Arrabal and productions of his work.
Paris. Lang.: Eng.   1175

Interview with playwright Charles Fuller. Philadelphia, PA.
New York, NY. Korea, South. Lang.: Eng.   2921

1960-1969.   Plays/librettos/scripts.
Albee, racism, politics in American theatre of the sixties.
Lang.: Rus.   2901

1960-1975.   Performance spaces.
The streets of New York as experimental performance space.
New York, NY. Lang.: Eng.   688

1960-1979.   Performance/production.
Protest theatre, its social and artistic aspects. Lang.: Rus. 933

1960-1980.   Performance/production.
Decentralization of American theatre. Lang.: Eng.   958

1960-1983.   Institutions.
New York State Council on the Arts' Presenting
Organizations Program. New York. Lang.: Eng.   601

1960-1985.   Institutions.
History of New York's Little Players puppet theatre. New
York, NY. Lang.: Eng.   3967

1960-1986.   Performance spaces.
Rebuilding theatres constructed in the 1960s. Lang.: Eng. 702

1960-1986.   Theory/criticism.
Essays and reviews by Gordon Rogoff. Lang.: Eng.   1366

1982-1987. **Performance/production.**
Script and staging of Shaliko's *The Yellow House*. Baltimore, MD. Lang.: Eng.   1487

1983. **Administration.**
Illness of star rule arbitrated *re*: Richard Harris in *Camelot*. New York, NY. Lang.: Eng.   115

Circle Repertory Theatre's plan to increase roles for minority actors. New York, NY. Lang.: Eng.   116

Advisory Committee on Chorus Affairs and Equity devise procedures for chorus calls. New York, NY. Lang.: Eng.   117

Broadway producer Dorothy Olim on commercial theatre. New York, NY. Lang.: Eng.   189

Charles Ziff on marketing research. New York, NY. Lang.: Eng.   210

Services and operations of Independent Booking Office. New York, NY. Lang.: Eng.   211

Aspects of paying for works in the public domain. New York, NY. Lang.: Eng.   213

Technical information for the new computer user. Lang.: Eng.   228

1983. **Performance/produciton.**
Johanna Boyce's *With Longings to Realize* presented by the Performance Group. New York, NY. Lang.: Eng.   1478

1983. **Performance/production.**
Director Anne Bogart's production of *Women and Men: A Big Dance*. New York, NY. Lang.: Eng.   1418

Career of American Ballet Theatre dancer Hilda Morales. New York, NY. Lang.: Eng.   1443

Production of *Spring* by Simone Forti presented at the Danspace at St. Mark's Church. New York, NY. Lang.: Eng.   2337

Director Matthew Maguire's production of *The American Mysteries* presented by Creation at La Mama. New York, NY. Lang.: Eng.   2361

1983-1984. **Administration.**
Evaluation of computer support systems in arts organizations. Lang.: Eng.   241

Current computer vendor developments in information systems. Lang.: Eng.   249

1983-1986. **Administration.**
Analysis of how American Theatre Association ceased to exist. Lang.: Eng.   163

1983-1987. **Administration.**
Advantages to volunteer programs in corporations. Lang.: Eng.   119

1983-1987. **Design/technology.**
Different casting and design approaches to *Brighton Beach Memoirs*. Lang.: Eng.   427

1983-1987. **Performance spaces.**
History of the Alice Arts Center, new home of the Oakland Ensemble Theatre. Oakland, CA. Lang.: Eng.   696

Renovation of the Seattle Center Playhouse into the new home of the Intiman Theatre. Seattle, WA. Lang.: Eng.   705

1983-1987. **Performance/production.**
Transformation of *La Cage aux Folles* from movie to a Broadway musical. New York, NY. Lang.: Eng.   940

A Green Party that mixes politics, experimental theatre. New Haven, CT. Lang.: Eng.   973

Role of feminist in cultural critique. India. Lang.: Eng.   1496

Birgit Nilsson's master voice class at Manhattan School of Music. New York, NY. Lang.: Eng.   3859

1983-1987. **Plays/librettos/scripts.**
Male and female responses to Marsha Norman's *'Night, Mother*. Lang.: Eng.   2918

1984. **Administration.**
Meeting between Actors' Equity and British Equity. Washington, DC. UK-England. Lang.: Eng.   76

Meeting of LORT member organizations to create stronger liaisons. New York, NY. Chicago, IL. Lang.: Eng.   85

Economic analyses of arts organizations. Lang.: Eng.   140

Results of market research survey for a small arts center. Lang.: Eng.   171

Historical look at the Copyright Act. Lang.: Eng.   206

Ford Foundation's support for the field of dance. Lang.: Eng.   1428

1984. **Design/technology.**
Gershwin Theatre's accommodation of RSC touring productions. New York, NY. Lang.: Eng.   420

1984. **Institutions.**
Profile of Brooklyn Academy of Music's Next Wave Festival. New York, NY. Lang.: Eng.   590

1984. **Performance spaces.**
Architect Roger Morgan discusses plans for restoring seven Broadway theatres. New York, NY. Lang.: Eng.   683

Commitment of Shubert Organization to cleaning up Broadway theatre district. New York, NY. Lang.: Eng.   691

Proposal for renovations of Broadway theatres. New York, NY. Lang.: Eng.   713

1984. **Performance/production.**
The 1984 season of the Next Wave at BAM. New York, NY. Lang.: Eng.   967

Critique of the 1984 Broadway production of *Death of a Salesman*. New York, NY. Lang.: Eng.   2330

1984. **Relation to other fields.**
Roundtable discussion on the state of arts education. Lang.: Eng.   1281

1984-1985. **Performance/production.**
Outdoor summer series of dance and performance art. New York, NY. Lang.: Eng.   1413

Musical Theatre Project explores Broadway musical material available in Shubert Archive. New York, NY. Lang.: Eng.   3666

1984-1985. **Plays/librettos/scripts.**
Theme of René-Daniel Dubois's *Being at Home with Claude*. Quebec, PQ. New York, NY. Lang.: Eng.   2473

1984-1986. **Administration.**
Exploitation of artists' work in the marketplace. Lang.: Eng.   169

1984-1987. **Administration.**
Influence of TV ads on success of Broadway plays. New York, NY. Lang.: Eng.   179

Impact of new laws on nonprofit theatre funding. Lang.: Eng.   234

Bequest program for Wisconsin Public Broadcasting. Madison, WI. Lang.: Eng.   3108

1984-1987. **Design/technology.**
Sound designer Guy Sherman's innovations. New York, NY. Lang.: Eng.   392

1984-1987. **Performance spaces.**
Major expansion of the facilities at the Omaha Community Playhouse. Omaha, NE. Lang.: Eng.   699

1984-1987. **Performance/production.**
Irondale Ensemble's production of *Ubu roi (King Ubu)* by Alfred Jarry. New York, NY. Lang.: Eng.   2370

Russian director Jurij Liubimov and his productions in the USSR and USA. Moscow. Washington, DC. Lang.: Eng.   2400

Interview with director Paula Kalustian. New York, NY. Lang.: Eng.   3662

1984-1987. **Relation to other fields.**
John Malpede's performance workshop for the homeless. Los Angeles, CA. Lang.: Eng.   1267

1985. **Administration.**
Potential for League of Resident Theatres strike. New York, NY. Lang.: Eng.   62

National Actors' Equity conference. New York, NY. Lang.: Eng.   63

Playwrights' opinion on showcase 'Letter of Agreement and Tiered Code'. New York, NY. Lang.: Eng.   64

Revisions in eligibility, insurance coverage rules, Equity League Welfare Fund. Lang.: Eng.   65

Equity ratifies League of Resident Theatres pact: gains for members. New York, NY. Lang.: Eng.   66

Changes in Equity welfare benefits. New York, NY. Lang.: Eng.   67

Actor exchange: discussions of Equity, Royal Shakespeare Company. UK-England. Lang.: Eng.   74

Results of audit on the Equity Welfare plan. Lang.: Eng.   81

Contract between Actors' Equity and the American Dinner Theatre Institute. New York, NY. Lang.: Eng.   83

Current trends and future of summer stock companies. Lang.: Eng.   121

Interview with male performer Ethyl Eichelberger. New York, NY. Lang.: Eng. 2314

Collection of newspaper reviews by New York theatre critics. New York, NY. Lang.: Eng. 2315

Collection of newspaper reviews by New York theatre critics. New York, NY. Lang.: Eng. 2316

Collection of newspaper reviews by New York theatre critics. New York, NY. Lang.: Eng. 2317

Collection of newspaper reviews by New York theatre critics. New York, NY. Lang.: Eng. 2318

Collection of newspaper reviews by New York theatre critics. New York, NY. Lang.: Eng. 2319

Collection of newspaper reviews by New York theatre critics. New York, NY. Lang.: Eng. 2320

Collection of newspaper reviews by New York theatre critics. New York, NY. Lang.: Eng. 2321

Collection of newspaper reviews by New York theatre critics. New York, NY. Lang.: Eng. 2322

Collection of newspaper reviews by New York theatre critics. New York, NY. Lang.: Eng. 2323

Collection of newspaper reviews by New York critics. New York, NY. Lang.: Eng. 2324

Collection of newspaper reviews by New York theatre critics. New York, NY. Lang.: Eng. 2325

Collection of newspaper reviews by New York theatre critics. New York, NY. Lang.: Eng. 2326

Career of director Ron Lagomarsino, his style and technique. Lang.: Eng. 2327

Functions, influence of dramaturgs and literary managers. Lang.: Eng. 2332

Differentiation between camp and burlesque styles. Lang.: Eng. 2333

Profile of character actor Matthew Locricchio. New York, NY. Lang.: Eng. 2334

Philip Bosco's portrayals of characters in the plays of George Bernard Shaw. Lang.: Eng. 2335

Three actors discuss their approaches to the characters of Samuel Beckett. Lang.: Eng. 2343

Sanford Meisner's method of teaching acting. New York, NY. Lang.: Eng. 2349

Interviews with teachers of acting. New York, NY. Los Angeles, CA. Lang.: Eng. 2350

Peter Sellars' American National Theatre on European tour. Netherlands. Lang.: Dut. 2351

New production of *Macbeth* set in 1927 Chicago. New York, NY. Lang.: Eng. 2357

Hedda Gabler at American Ibsen Theatre. Pittsburgh, PA. Lang.: Eng. 2358

Interview with actor/director Austin Pendleton. Lang.: Eng. 2360

The African actor in Africa, Italy and the United States. Brooklyn, NY. Freetown. Rome. Lang.: Eng. 2362

George C. Wolfe and L. Kenneth Richardson discuss *The Colored Museum*. New York, NY. New Brunswick, NJ. Lang.: Eng. 2363

Metropolitan/Deutsche Grammophon recording, Wagner's *Ring*, conducted by James Levine. New York, NY. Lang.: Eng. 3114

Conventions of film adaptation of stage classics. Hollywood, CA. Lang.: Eng. 3165

Review of ABC videocast of Pinter's *The Dumb Waiter*. Lang.: Eng. 3209

Ritual and theatrical nature of TV evangelism. Lang.: Eng. 3210

Theatrical nature of televised wrestling. Lang.: Eng. 3211

History that formed the mimes of the 1980s. Lang.: Eng. 3230

Use of actors to simulate symptoms at medical conferences. Lang.: Eng. 3275

The Polish cabaret performance group Piwnica. Cracow. New York, NY. Lang.: Eng. 3287

The cabaret-style musical revue *Oil City Symphony*. New York, NY. Lang.: Eng. 3289

Ethyl Eichelberger and Lily Savage: their approaches to acting. UK-England. Lang.: Eng. 3290

Introduction to articles on art of theatrical clowning. Lang.: Eng. 3304

Celebration of Chinese Lunar New Year: Lion dancing and its martial arts background. New York, NY. Lang.: Eng. 3334

Theatrical elements of gay rights parade. New York, NY. Lang.: Eng. 3335

Techniques of the image theatre and effects on actor and audience. Canada. Europe. Lang.: Eng. 3345

Collaboration of Robert Wilson and Heiner Müller on *Hamlet Machine (Hamletmaschine)*. New York, NY. Hamburg. Lang.: Eng. 3361

Performance artists and their work in New Orleans. New Orleans, LA. New York, NY. Lang.: Eng. 3362

Richard Foreman's production of *Film is Evil: Radio is Good*. New York, NY. Lang.: Eng. 3365

Performance artists Ishmael Houston-Jones, John Kelly, Karen Finley, Richard Elovich. Lang.: Eng. 3366

The performance art piece, *Living Room Project*, of Danny Mydlack. Boston, MA. Lang.: Eng. 3367

The theatre techniques of performance artist Richard Foreman. New York, NY. Lang.: Eng. 3368

Development of Michael Smith from painter to performance artist. Lang.: Eng. 3369

Golden Fleece, Ltd. bridges classical music, opera and musical theatre. New York, NY. Lang.: Eng. 3412

Successful London revival of *Follies* by Stephen Sondheim. London. New York, NY. Lang.: Eng. 3638

Plot synopsis of musical *Mademoiselle Colombe* based on Anouilh's *Colombe*. New York, NY. Lang.: Eng. 3647

Interview with musical conductor Paul Gemignani. New York, NY. Lang.: Eng. 3649

Interview with actor Giancarlo Esposito. New York, NY. Lang.: Eng. 3654

Trend of gospel musicals on and off Broadway. New York, NY. Lang.: Eng. 3656

Career of Broadway actress Connie Day. New York, NY. Lang.: Eng. 3657

Career of composer Charles DeForest. New York, NY. Lang.: Eng. 3659

Career of actor William McCauley. Lang.: Eng. 3660

Career of actor Lee Roy Reams. New York, NY. Lang.: Eng. 3661

Interview with composer Jack Eric Williams, focus on his musical *Mrs. Farmer's Daughter*. New York, NY. Lang.: Eng. 3663

Quality of and access to opera training in North America. Canada. Lang.: Eng. 3753

Background on Lyric Opera radio broadcast performances. Chicago, IL. Lang.: Eng. 3832

Background on San Francisco opera radio broadcasts. San Francisco, CA. Lang.: Eng. 3833

Background on Opera Company of Philadelphia telecast, *Un Ballo in Maschera*. Philadelphia, PA. Lang.: Eng. 3834

Soprano Renata Scotto directs Metropolitan Opera production of *Madama Butterfly*. New York, NY. Lang.: Eng. 3836

Background on Metropolitan radio broadcast performances. New York, NY. Lang.: Eng. 3837

Background on Metropolitan radio broadcast performances. New York, NY. Lang.: Eng. 3838

Background on Metropolitan telecast performances. New York, NY. Lang.: Eng. 3839

Repertoire and artistic achievement of the Opera Theatre of St. Louis. St. Louis, MO. Lang.: Eng. 3840

Premiere of the docu-opera, *Nixon in China*, Houston Grand Opera. Houston, TX. Lang.: Eng. 3843

Vasile Moldoveanu's views on the current state of opera. Lang.: Eng. 3844

Vietnam
900-1985.   **Performance/production.**
Vietnamese water puppets. Lang.: Eng.   3990
980-1986.   **Performance/production.**
Development of Vietnamese theatre through the centuries.
Lang.: Eng.   2402
Wales
SEE
UK-Wales.
West Indies
                 Performance/production.
Growth of West Indian carnival traditions. Lang.: Eng.   3277
Yugoslavia
1900-1987.   **Performance/production.**
Yugoslav theatre festivals. Lang.: Ger.   1093
1923-1941.   **Performance/production.**
Belgrade folk ballet. Belgrade. Lang.: Rus.   1453
1947-1986.   **Performance/production.**
Interview with National Theatre director Ljubiša Ristić.
Subotica. Lang.: Hun.   2408
1986.   **Performance/production.**
Survey of the international theatre festival BITEF-88.
Belgrade. Lang.: Rus.   1090
Director Ljubiša Ristić and 'Shakespeare Fest '86'. Subotica.
Palić. Lang.: Hun.   2403
Ljubiša Ristić adapts and directs Imre Madách's *Az ember
tragédiája (The Tragedy of a Man)*. Subotica. Lang.: Hun.
                 2404

Review of *Hamlet, Julius Caesar* and *Titus Andronicus* at
'Shakespeare Fest '86'. Palić. Lang.: Hun.   2405
'Shakespeare Fest '86' reviews. Palić. Lang.: Hun.   2407
1987.   **Performance/production.**
Overview of the YU Fest. Dubrovnik. Belgrade. Kotor.
Budva. Subotica. Lang.: Eng.   1091
Review of three interludes by Cervantes. Lang.: Fre.   1092
Tóték (The Tót Family) by István Örkény at Hungarian
Theatre, guest director Gábor Székely. Novi Sad. Lang.:
Hun.   2406
Zaire
1987.   **Basic theatrical documents.**
English translations of contemporary African plays. Senegal.
Lang.: Eng.   1566
Zambia
1951-1985.   **Relation to other fields.**
Evolution of ritual and ritual dances in the Nolembu tribe.
Lang.: Eng.   1466
1966-1987.   **Plays/librettos/scripts.**
Theme of aggression between fathers and sons: Zambian
National Theatre Arts Association festival. Lang.: Eng.   2972
Zimbabwe
1987.   **Relation to other fields.**
Teachers discuss creative drama's role in adult education.
Jamaica. Bangladesh. Lang.: Swe.   2996

DOCUMENT AUTHORS INDEX

A, Jia. 3472, 3473, 3474
Abah, O.S. 3248
Abkowicz, Jerzy. 2492
Ablonczy, László. 802, 1791, 1792, 1793, 1794
Abramson, Jan. 2000
Abramson, Kjell. 1674, 1675
Abrash, Victoria. 118
Abud, Ronald. 1464
Abukova, F.A. 3865
Accolas, Claude. 3192
Achmadullin, A.G. 2936
Achmedžanova, T. 997
Acker, Iris. 587
Acker, Kathy. 1576
Adamovič, I.I. 766
Agapova, L.A. 2742
Agapova, T. 1525
Agarkov-Miklashevsky, Tamar, transl. 2376
Aggarbati, Fabrizio. 649
Aguilar, Sigfrido. 3225
Ahn, Min-Soo. 3047
Ahu, Mim-Soo. 31
Ajchenval'd, Ju. A. 998
Akalaitis, JoAnne. 1577
Akimova, B. 999
Alberg, Ian. 371
Alberti, Carmelo. 548, 1129, 3316
Albini, Umberto. 2618
Albiro, Hartwig. 1778
Albright, Ann Cooper. 1416
Albuquerque, Severino João. 2456
Alcàntara Penya, Pere d'. 1567
Alekseev, A. 2937
Alemany Ferrer, Rafael. 2732
Alexander, David. 1669
Alexander, Robert I. 296
Allanzarov, T. 2938
Allegri, Luigi, ed. 3322
Allen, Bonnie. 1412
Allen, Deborah. 864
Allen, Kenn. 119
Allen, Richard. 505, 3713, 3954
Allen, Woody. 3129
Almási, Miklós. 1795, 1796, 1797, 1798, 3630
Alonge, Roberto. 1245
Altaev, A. 259
Amiard-Chevrel, Claudine, ed. 2987
Amico, Nino. 4001
Amministrazione Provinciale di Pavia. 819
An, Chi. 3015
Anarina, N. 487
Anderson, Wayne. 1650
Andō, Tsunejirō. 1506
Andreoli, Annamaria. 2661

Angove, Colleen. 1419
Anikst, A. 898, 2373
Anikst, A., ed. 2939
Anselmo, Stefano. 346
Anthoine, Robert. 120
Antonucci, Giovanni, ed. 547
Apakidze, Ju. 3866
Aponte, Barbara Bockus. 2694
Apothéloz, Anne-Lise. 1254
Apothéloz, Anne-Lise, comp. 892
Archer, Lynn. 121, 122
Ardoin, John. 3680, 3682, 3800, 3835
Arian, Max. 3814
Armitage, Daniel. 2497
Arnau, Carme. 2730
Arnold, Peter. 3001
Arnold, Peter, comp. 2026
Arnold, Stephanie K. 2838
Aronson, Arnold. 305, 385, 680
Aronson, Lisa. 449
Asahi shimbun, ed. 1482
Ashcroft, Peggy. 899, 2278
Ashwell, Ariel. 3225
Asplund, Carin. 40
Astington, John H. 316, 3321
Aszyk, Urszula. 1156
Atkinson, Roslyn. 1512
Attisani, Antonio. 650
Aufiero, Raffaele. 1345
Augustsson, Tinn. 362
Ault, C. Thomas. 347
Ault, Thomas C. 651
Auslander, Philip. 3007
Austin, Bruce A. 3120
Austin, Gayle. 2839
Avila, Norma. 1463
Aviñoa, Xosé. 1410
Ayers, P.K. 2498
Ayling, Ronald. 3011
Babajan, I.K. 2940
Babel, Tara. 3349
Bablet, Denis. 633
Badejo, Diedre L. 2704
Badiou, Maryse, ed., intro. 2010
Bagdasarjan, N., ed. 1000
Bagley, Mary. 3143
Baird, Lorrayne Y. 2499
Bakanidze, D. 2374
Bakanova, E.R. 2751
Baker, Candida. 2433, 2434
Baker, Denys. 123
Baker, Stuart E. 3066
Baker, Susan. 2500
Balašova, N. 1001
Baldo, Jonathan. 3184

Baldry, H.C. 2619
Baldwin, Olive. 3895
Balk, H. Wesley. 3683
Balk, Steven. 386
Ballantine, Frank. 124, 3140
Ballard, Frank. 3985
Baló, Júlia. 803, 1437, 1799, 1800, 1801, 3127, 3151, 3156
Bán, Magda. 1802, 3172
Baniewicz, Elżbieta. 871, 1987, 1988, 1989
Banu, Georges. 784, 1331, 1751, 1752
Bar-Shovit, Shlomo. 1620, 1621
Barba, Eugenio. 1728
Barber, David. 3741, 3894
Barbour, David. 2327, 3289, 3640
Barbour, Sheena, ed. 1213
Barcikowska, Małgorzata. 1208
Barclay, Ian A. 3243
Barlett, Robin. 125
Barna, Márta. 3152
Barnes, Noreen C. 2328
Barnes, Peter. 2501
Barnet, David. 3024
Barr, Richard. 3061
Bart, István, transl. 3169
Bartalotta, Gianfranco. 1130, 2569
Bartha, Andrea. 331
Barthol, Bruce. 864
Bartlett, Neil. 3290, 3339, 3829
Bartomeus, Antoni. 558, 1634
Barton, Ann. 2752
Bartow, Arthur. 1274, 2329
Bartra, Agustí. 1571
Bassnett, Susan. 922, 1649, 1729, 1941
Bassnett, Susan, transl. 1752, 1947
Batchelder, Norma Woodward. 2979
Bate, Jonathan. 3003
Bates, Brian. 900
Bathrick, David. 2992
Battaglia, Carl. 3801, 3802, 3836, 3952
Bauer, Oswald G. 797
Baugh, Christopher. 317
Bauschard, Jane. 681
Bazzoni, Jana O'Keefe. 2662
Beacham, Richard C. 3694
Bean, Robert. 3383
Beck, András. 2628
Beck, Kirsten. 126
Becker, Maria. 289
Becker, Peter von, ed. 1203
Beckers, Anne-Marie. 3023
Bécsy, Tamás. 1803, 1804, 1805, 1806, 1807, 1808, 2629, 2630, 2734
Begunov, V. 260
Beik, Janet. 865

FINDING LIST OF PERIODICAL TITLES WITH ACRONYMS

Canadian Drama/Art Dramatique Canadien ..CDr
Canadian Literature/Littérature Canadienne.CanL
Canadian Theatre Review (Toronto).............CTR
Canadian Theatre Checklist....................CTCheck
Canadian Theatre Review Yearbook (Downsview)..CTRY
Caratula..Caratula
Castelets...Castelets
Celcit...Celcit
Central Opera Service Bulletin......................COS
Ceskoslovenski Loutkar..............................CeskL
Chhaya Nat...Chhaya
Children's Theatre Review..........................ChTR
Chinese Literature......................................ChinL
Chronico...Chronico
Cineschedario: Letture Drammatiche.........CineLD
Circus-Parade...CircusP
Circuszeitung, Die...Cz
Cirque dans l'Univers, Le..............................CU
Città Aperta...CittaA
City Arts Monthly......................................CAM
City Limits...CityL
Claudel Studies..ClaudelS
CLSU Journal of the Arts........................CLSUJ
Coleçao Teatro..ColecaoT
College English..CE
College Language Association Journal..........CLAJ
Columbia-VLA Journal of Law & the Arts...ColJL&A
Comédie de l'Ouest..CO
Comédie-Française..CF
Comedy...Comedy
Communications from the International Brecht Society..ComIBS
Comparative Drama.................................CompD
Confessio...Confes
Confluent..Cfl
Conjunto: Revista de Teatro Latinamericano...Cjo
Connoisseur...Con
Contact Quarterly.................................ContactQ
Contemporary French Civilization.................CFT
Contenido..Contenido
CORD Dance Research Annual.................CORD
Corps écrit...CorpsE
Costume Society of America......................CSAN
Costume: The Journal of the Costume Society..Costume
Courrier Dramatique de l'Ouest...................CDO
Courrier du Centre international d'études poétiques..CCIEP
Creative Drama..CreD
Crépuscule, Le.......................................Crepuscl
Crisis...Crisis
Critical Arts..CrAr
Critical Digest..CritD
Critical Quarterly.......................................CritQ
Critique...CritNY
Cuadernos El Publico..............................Cuaderno
Cue New York...CueNY
Cue, The...CueM
Cue: Technical Theatre Review......................Cue
Cultural Post...CuPo
Culture et Communication...........................CetC
Culture...Culture
C'wan t'ong Xiju Yishu/Art of Traditional Opera..CTXY
Dalnij Vostok: (Far East)....................DalVostok
Dance and Dancers......................................D&D
Dance Australia..DA
Dance Chronicle..DnC
Dance in Canada/Danse au Canada..............DC
Dance Magazine...Dm
Dance Research..DRs
Dance Research Journal................................DRJ
Dance Theatre Journal..................................DTJ
Dancing Times..DTi
Dekorativnojè Iskusstvo SSR.................DekorIsk
Detskaja Literatura.....................................DetLit
Deutsche Bühne, Die......................................DB
Deutsche Zeitschrift für Philosophie.............DZP
Deutsches Bühnenjahrbuch.............................DBj
Deutsches Institut für Puppenspiel Forschung und Lehre..DIPFL
Devlet Tijatrolari (State Theatres).............Devlet
Dewan Budaya..Dewan
Dialog: Miesiecznik Poswiecony Dramaturgii Wspolczesnej......................................DialogW
Dialog...DialogA
Dialogue: Canadian Philosophical Review..Dialogue
Dialogue (Tunisia).................................DialogTu
Dioniso...Dioniso
Directors Notes.......................................DirNotes
Diskurs...Diskurs
Diskurs..DRostock
Divadelni Noviny..DiN
Divadelní revue..DivR
Divadlo: (Theatre)..DTh
Dix-Huitième Siècle.......................................DHS
Dix-Septième Siècle......................................DSS
Dockteatereko...Dockt
Documentation Théâtrale............................DocTh
Documents del Centre Dramatic...................DCD
DOE..DOE
Dokumenti Slovenskega Gledaliskega Muzeja...DSGM
Don Saturio: Boletin Informativo de Teatro Gallego...DSat
Dong-Guk Dramatic Art......................DongukDA
Drama and the School...........................DSchool
Drama and Theater.......................................D&T
Drama and Theatre Newsletter....................DTN
Drama Review, The......................................TDR
Drama Review...DrRev
Drama: Nordisk dramapedagogisk Tidskrift..DNDT
Drama: The Quarterly Theatre Review.......Drama
Drama..DramaY
Dramatherapy: SEE: Journal of Dramatherapy (JDt)..Dtherapy
Dramatics...DMC
Dramatists Guild Quarterly...........................DGQ
Dramatists Sourcebook..................................DSo
Dramaturgi: Tedri Og Praksis....................DTOP
Dramma...DrammaR
Dramma: Il Mensile dello Spettacolo....DrammaT
Dress...Dress
Družba..Druzba
Družba Narodov....................................DruzNar
Ebony...Ebony
Echanges...Echanges
Economic Efficiency and the Performing Arts...EE&PA
Economic History Review...........................EHR
Economist Financial Report.........................Econ
EDAM Newsletter.....................................EDAM
Editorial Nuevo Grupo................................ENG
Educational Theatre News............................ETN
Eire-Ireland..Eire
Elet és Irodalom: irodalmi es politkai hetilap..EII
Eletunk...Elet
Elizabethan Theatre.......................................ETh
Empirical Research in Theatre......................ERT
Enact: monthly theatre magazine................Enact
Encore (Australia).................................EncoreA
Encore (Georgia).....................................Encore
Engekikai: Theatre World..............................Egk
English Academy Review, The....................EAR
English Literary Renaissance Journal............ELR
English Studies in Africa..............................ESA
Entertainment and Arts Manager...............E&AM
Entré...Entre
Envers du Décor, L'..ED
Epic Theatre...EpicT
Equity Journal...EquityJ
Equity News...EN
Escena: Informativo Teatral..........................EIT
Escena..Escena
Espill, L'...Espill
Esprit Créateur, L'..ECR
Esprit...Esprit
Essays in Theatre..ET
Essence...Essence
Estafeta Literaria: La Revista...................EstLit
Estreno: Journal on the Contemporary Spanish Theater..Estreno
Estudis Escenics..EECIT
Etoile de la Foire..Etoile
Eugene O'Neill Newsletter, The...................EON
Europe: Revue Littéraire Mensuelle..........Europe
Evento Teatrale..Evento
Exchange...Exchange
Ežegodnik MChAT..................................MChAT
Farsa, La...Farsa
Federal One..FO
Feminist Review...FemR
Fight Master, The..FMa
Figurentheater...Ftr
Film a Divadlo...FDi
Film, Szinház, Muzsika................................FSM
Filologičeskije Nauki.......................................FN
Filológiai Közlöny..FiloK
FIRT/SIBMAS Bulletin d'information...FIRTSIB
Footnotes...Fnotes
Forrás...Forras
France Théâtre..FranceT
Freedomways: A Quarterly Review of the Freedom Movement...Fds
Fremantle Gazette..FG
French Forum..FrF
French Review, The..FR
French Studies...FS
Fundarte..Fundarte
Fundraising Management..........................FundM
Gambit..Gambit
Gap, The...Gap
Garcin: Libro de Cultura..........................Garcin
Gazette des Beaux Arts..............................GdBA
Gazette du Français.......................................GdF
Gazette Officielle du Spectacle....................GOS
Gazit..Gazit
George Spelvin's Theatre Book..................GSTB
Georgia Review...GaR
German Life and Letters............................GL&L
German Quarterly..GQ
German Studies Review............................GerSR
Gestos: Teoria y practica del teatro hispanico...Gestos
Gestus: A Quarterly Journal of Brechtian Studies..Gestus
Gilbert and Sullivan Journal..........................GSJ
Giornale dello Spettacolo..............................GdS
Gosteri: Performance................................Gosteri
Grande République...................................GrandR
Grupo Teatral Antifaz: Revista..................GTAR
Guida dello Spettacolo..............................Guida
Guidateatro: Estera..GtE
Guidateatro: Italiana.......................................GtI
Hamlet Studies...HSt
Harlekijn...Harlekijn
Hecate: Women's Interdisciplinary Journal Hecate
Helikon: Vilagirodalmi................................Helik
Hermes: Zeitschrift...................................Hermes
Higeki Kigeki: Tragedy and Comedy............HgK
High Performance..HP
Hispanic Arts...HispArts
Historical Journal of Film, TV, Radio.....HJFTR
Historical Studies.......................................HisSt
History Workshop..HW
Horisont...Horis
Hungarian Theatre/Hungarian Drama.......HTHD
Ibsen News & Comments..............................INC
Ibsenårboken/Ibsen Yearbook..........................IA
Impressum...Impressum

676 International Bibliography of Theatre: 1987

STILB ....STILB
Stratford-upon-Avon Studies ....SuAS
Strindbergiana ....Strind
Studenčeskij Meridian ....StudM
Studia i Materialy do Dziejow Teatru
  Polskiego ....StudiaP
Studies in American Drama, 1945-Present ....SAD
Studies in Philology ....StPh
Studies in Popular Culture ....SPC
Studii si Cercetari de Istoria Artei ....StudiiR
STYolainen ....STYol
Suffloren ....Suffloren
Suid-Afrikaan, Die ....SuidAfr
Svét a divadlo ....Svet
Swedish Theater/Théâtre Suédois ....SwTS
Szene Schweiz/Scène-Suisse/Scena
  Svizzera ....SSSS
Szene: Fachzeitschrift der DDR ....SzeneAT
Szene ....Szene
Szinház (Theatre) ....Sz
Szinháztechnikai Fórum ....SFo
Szinháztudomanyi Szemle ....SzSz
Tablas: Cuban Theatre ....Tablas
Tabs ....Tabs
Talent Management ....Talent
TamKang Review ....TkR
Tampereen Tyovaen Teatteri ....Tampereen
Tanecni Listy ....Tanecni
Tantsovo Izkustvo ....TantI
Tanz und Gymnastik ....TanzG
TCG National Working Conference
  Proceedings ....TCGNWCP
Teat'r žurnal dramaturgii i teatra ....TeatrM
Teatarski Glasnik ....TGlasnik
Teater Film & TV ....TF&TV
Teater i Danmark: Theatre in Denmark ..TeaterD
Teater Jaarboek voor Vlaanderen ....TJV
Teater, Musika, Kyno ....TMK
Teaterårsboken ....TArsb
Teaterforum (Sweden) ....Teaterf
Teaterforum (South Africa) ....TF
Teatern ....Teatern
Teatervetenskap ....Tv
Teatervidenskabelige Studier ....TSt
Teatoro ....Teatoro
Teatr Lalek ....TeatL
Teatr ....TeatrW
Teatralnaja Zizn ....TeatZ
Teatraluri Moambe ....TeatM
Teatras ....Teatras
Teatro Archivio ....TArch
Teatro Clásico: Boletin ....TCB
Teatro Contemporaneo ....TeatrC
Teatro del Siglo de Oro: Ediciones Críticas ..TSO
Teatro del Siglo de Oro: Estudios de
  Literatura ....TSOL
Teatro e Cinema ....TeC
Teatro e Storia ....TeatroS
Teatro en España ....TeatrE
Teatron ....TeatY
Teatron ....Teatron
TeatroSM ....TeatroSM
Teatrul ....Teatrul
Teatteri ....Teat
Teatur ....TeaturS
Technical Brief ....TechB
Tenaz Talks Teatro ....TTT
Tennessee Williams Review ....TWNew
Textual ....Textual
Textuel ....Textuel

Théâtre de l'Est Parisien ....TEP
Théâtre en Europe ....ThE
Théâtre Enfance et Jeunesse ....TEJ
Théâtre et Animation ....TAnim
Théâtre et université ....TU
Théâtre International ....TI
Théâtre National de Strasbourg: Actualité .....TNS
Théâtre Ouvert/Ecritures ....TOE
Théâtre Professionnel ....TProf
Théâtre ....Th
Théâtre Public ....ThPu
Theater Across America ....TAAm
Theater Computer Users Group Notes ....TCUG
Theater der Zeit ....TZ
Theater Heute ....THeute
Theater in Graz ....TGraz
Theater Magazine ....ThM
Theater Rundschau ....TR
Theaterarbeit in der DDR ....TDDR
Theaterbuch ....Tbuch
Theaterpaedagogische Bibliothek ....TpaedB
TheaterWeek ....TheaterW
Theaterwissenschaftlicher Informationsdienst ...TWI
Theaterwork ....Tk
Theaterzeitschrift ....Tzs
Theatre Annual ....TA
Theatre Australia ....TAus
Theatre Chicago ....TChicago
Theatre Communications ....TCom
Theatre Crafts ....ThCr
Theatre Design and Technology ....TD&T
Theatre History in Canada/Histoire du
  Théâtre ....THC
Theatre History Studies ....THSt
Theatre in Poland/Théâtre en Pologne ....TP
Theatre in the GDR ....TGDR
Theatre Insight ....TInsight
Theatre Ireland ....ThIr
Theatre Journal ....TJ
Theatre Movement Journal ....TMJ
Theatre News ....ThNe
Theatre Notebook ....TN
Theatre Notes ....TNotes
Theatre Papers ....ThPa
Theatre Quarterly ....TQ
Theatre Research International ....ThR
Theatre SA: Quarterly for South African
  Theater ....TSA
Theatre Southwest ....ThSw
Theatre Studies ....TheatreS
Theatre Survey ....ThS
Theatre Three ....TheatreT
Theatre Times ....TT
Theatre Today ....ThToday
Theatre Year ....ThYear
Theatre: Ex ....TheatreEx
Theatre: News from the Finnish Theatre ....NFT
Theatrecraft ....TCraft
Theatrephile ....ThPh
Theatrika ....Tka
Theatro ....Theatro
Theatron ....Theatron
Theatrum: A Theatre Journal ....Theatrum
Themes in Drama ....TID
Theoria ....Theoria
Thespis ....Thespis
Tijatro Arastirmalari Dergisi (Theatre Research
  Magazine) ....TAD
Tijatro ....Tijatro
Tijdschrift voor Theaterwetenschap ....TvT

Tiszatáj ....Tisz
Toneel Teatraal ....Toneel
Tournées de Spectacles ....Tournees
Tréteaux ....Treteaux
Traces ....Traces
Tramoya: Cuaderno de teatro ....Tramoya
Travail Théâtral ....TTh
Trujaman ....Trujaman
Tvorchestvo ....TVOR
Tydskrif vir Letterkunde ....TvL
Tydskrif vir Volkskunde en Volkstaal ....TvVV
Ufahamu ....Ufa
Uj Irás ....UjIras
Ukrainskij Teat'r ....UTeatr
UNIMA France ....UNIMA
Unisa English Studies ....UES
Universidad de Murcia Catedra de Teatro
  Cuadernos ....UMurcia
Universitas Tarraconensis ....UTarra
University of Dar es Salaam ....UDSalaam
Unterhaltungskunst ....UZ
Upstart Crow, The ....UCrow
Usbu Al-Masrah ....Usbu
USITT Newsletter ....USITT
Uusi-Laulu ....Uusi
V sověckom teatře ....VSov
Valóság ....Valo
Valiverho ....Valivero
Vantage Point: Issues in American Arts ....VantageP
Vestnik MGU: Series 9-Filologia ....VMGUf
Victorian Studies ....VS
Vigilia ....Vig
Világszinház ....Vilag
Voprosy filosofii ....VFil
Voprosy Literatury ....VLit
Voprosy Teatra ....Voprosy
Vyakat ....Vyakat
Waiguo Xiju ....Waiguo
Washington International Arts ....WIAL
Weimarer Beiträge ....WB
West Coast Plays ....WCP
Western Journal of Black Studies ....WJBS
White Tops ....WTops
Wiener Forschungen zur Theater und
  Medienwissenschaft ....WFTM
Wiener Gesellschaft für Theaterforschung
  Jahrbuch ....WGTJ
WIJ, Poppenspelers ....WijP
Women & Performance ....WPerf
Women's Review ....WomenR
World Literature Today ....WLT
World of Opera ....WOpera
World Premieres Listing ....WPList
Xiju Luncong: Selected Essays of Theatre .XLunc
Xiju Xuexi: Theatre ....XXuexi
Xiju Yishu: Theatre Arts ....XYishu
Xiqu Yanjiu ....XYanj
Yorick: Revista e Teatro ....Yorick
Young Cinema & Theatre/Jeune Cinéma et
  Théâtre ....YCT
Youth Theatre Journal ....YTJ
Zahranicni Divadlo: (Theatre Abroad) ....ZDi
Zeitschrift für Anglistik und Amerikanistik ....ZAA
Zeitschrift für Kulturaustausch ....ZfK
Zeitschrift für Germanistik ....ZG
Zeitschrift für Slawistik ....ZS
Znamya ....Znamya
Zpravy ....Zpravy
Zreliščnyjë Iskusstva (Performing Arts) .....ZreIssk
Zvezda ....Zvezda

LIST OF PERIODICALS

The following list is an attempt to provide an updated and comprehensive listing of periodical literature, current and recent past, devoted to theatre and related subjects.

This Bibliography provides full coverage of materials published in periodicals marked "Full" and selected coverage of those marked "Scan".

We have not dropped periodicals that are no longer published for the sake of researchers for whom that information can be valuable. We also note and list title changes.

A&A   *Art & Artists*. Freq: 12; Cov: Scan; Lang: Eng; Subj: Related. ISSN: 0004-3001 ▪Artist Publishing Co.; 102 High St.; TN30 6HT Tenderden, Kent; UK.

A&B   *Architect & Builder*. Freq: 12; Began: 1951; Cov: Scan; Lang: Eng; Subj: Related.   ISSN: 0003-8407 ▪Laurie Wale (Pty) Ltd.; Box 4591; Cape Town; SOUTH AFRICA.

A&AR   *Art and Artists*. Formerly: *Art Workers News; Art Workers Newsletter*. Freq: 10; Began: 1971; Lang: Eng; Subj: Related.   ISSN: 0740-5723 ▪Foundation for the Community of Artists; 280 Broadway, Ste 412; New York, NY 10007; USA.

A&L   *Art and the Law*: Columbia Journal of Art and the Law. Freq: 4; Began: 1974; Ceased: 1985; Cov: Full; Lang: Eng; Subj: Related.   ISSN: 0743-5266 ▪Volunteer Lawyers for the Arts; 435 West 116th St.; New York, NY 10027; USA.

AAinNYLH   *Afro-Americans in New York Life and History*. Freq: 2; Began: 1977; Cov: Scan; Lang: Eng; Subj: Related. ISSN: 0364-2437 ▪Afro-American Historical Assoc. of the, Niagara Frontier; Box 1663, Hertel Station; Buffalo, NY 14216; USA.

AATTN   *AATT News*. Freq: 11; Began: 1976; Lang: Eng; Subj: Theatre. ▪Australian Assoc. for Theatre Tech.; 40 Wave Avenue Mountain; 3149 Waverly; AUSTRALIA.

Abel   *Abel Value News*. Formerly: 1: Panem et Circenses/Bread and Circuses. Freq: 12; Began: 1969; Lang: Eng; Subj: Theatre.   ISSN: 0001-3153 ▪Abel News Agencies; 403 1st Ave.; Estherville, IA 51334-2223; USA.

AbhC   *Abhinaya*. Freq: 12; Lang: Ben; Subj: Theatre. ▪121 Harish Mukherjee Road; Calcutta; INDIA.

AbhD   *Abhinaya*. Freq: 25; Lang: Hin; Subj: Theatre. ▪Yuvamanch; 4526 Amirchand Marg; Delhi; INDIA.

AbqN   *Arabesque*: A magazine of international dance. Freq: 6; Began: 1975; Cov: Scan; Lang: Eng; Subj: Related. ISSN: 0148-5865

▪Ibrahim Farrah Inc.; One Sherman Square, Suite 22F; New York, NY 10023; USA.

ACH   *Australian Cultural History*. Freq: 1; Began: 1982; Cov: Scan; Lang: Eng; Subj: Related.   ISSN: 0728-8433 ▪University of New South Wales; School of History; P.O. Box 1; Kensington 2033; AUSTRALIA.

ACCTV   *Almanacco della Canzone e del Cinema e della TV*. Lang: Ita; Subj: Theatre. ▪Viale del Vignola 105; Rome; ITALY.

ACom   *Art Com*: Contemporary Art Communication. Formerly: *Mamelle Magazine: Art Contemporary*. Freq: 4; Began: 1975; Cov: Scan; Lang: Eng; Subj: Related.   ISSN: 0732-2852 ▪Contemporary Arts Press; Box 3123; San Francisco, CA 94119; USA.

Act   *Act*: Theatre in New Zealand. Formerly: *Theatre*. Freq: 6; Began: 1976; Lang: Eng; Subj: Theatre. ISSN: 0010-0106 ▪Playmarket Inc.; Box 9767; Wellington; NEW ZEALAND.

ACTA   *Acta Classica (Proceedings of the Classical Association of South Africa)*. Freq: 1; Began: 1958; Cov: Scan; Lang: Eng.; Subj: Related.   ISSN: 0065-1141 ▪Classical Association of South Africa; P.O. Box 392; Pretoria 0001; SOUTH AFRICA.

Acteurs   *Acteurs/Auteurs*. Formerly: *Acteurs*. Freq: 10; Began: 1982; Cov: Scan; Lang: Fre; Subj: Theatre. ▪28, rue Sevin-Vincent; 92210 Saint-Cloud; FRANCE.

ActS   *Actualité de la Scénographie*. Freq: 6; Began: 1977; Lang: Fre; Subj: Theatre. ▪Assoc. Belgique des Scenographes et Techniciens de Théâtre; Avenue Herbert Hoover 5; 1320 Genval; BELGIUM.

ActT   *Action Théâtre*. Lang: Fre; Subj: Theatre. ▪Action Culturelle de Sud-Est; 4 rue du Théâtre Français; 13001 Marseille; FRANCE.

Actualites   *Actualités*. Lang: Fre; Subj: Theatre. ▪Actualités Spectacles; 1 rue Marietta Martin; 75016 Paris; FRANCE.

AD   *After Dark*. Freq: 12; Began: 1968; Lang: Eng; Subj: Theatre.   ISSN: 0002-0702 ▪After Dark Magazine, Inc.; 175 Fifth Avenue; New York, NY 10010; USA.

ADoc   *Arts Documentation Monthly*. Freq: 12; Began: 1979; Lang: Eng; Subj: Theatre.   ISSN: 0140-6965 ▪The Arts Council of Great Britain Library, Information and Research Section; 105 Piccadilly; W1V OAU London; UK.

AdP   *Atti dello Psicodramma*. Freq: 1; Began: 1975; Lang: Ita; Subj: Related. ▪Astrolabio-Ubaldini, Via Lungara 3, 00165 Rome; ITALY.

ADS   *Australasian Drama Studies*. Freq: 2; Began: 1982; Lang: Eng; Subj: Theatre.   ISSN: 0810-4123 ▪Australasia Drama Studies, English Dept., University of Queensland; Q 4067 St. Lucia; AUSTRALIA.

AdSpect   *Annuaire du Spectacle*. Freq: 1; Began: 1956; Lang: Fre; Subj: Theatre.   ISSN: 0066-3026 ▪Editions Raoult; 220 F. Editions Raoult; Tour CIT 3 rue de l'Arrivee 75015 Paris; FRANCE.

AdT   *Art du Théâtre, L'*. Freq: 3; Began: 1985; Cov: Full; Lang: Fre; Subj: Theatre. ▪Théâtre National de Chaillot; 1 Place du Tracadero; 75116 Paris; FRANCE.

AdTI   *Annuario del Teatro Italiano*. Freq: 1; Began: 1934; Lang: Ita; Subj: Theatre. ▪S.I.A.E. - I.D.I.; Viale della Letteratura 30; 00100 Rome; ITALY.

AETR   *AET Revista*. Lang: Spa; Subj: Theatre. ▪Associacion de Estudiantes de Teatro; Viamonte 1443; Buenos Aires; ARGENTINA.

AfAmArt   *African American Art*. Formerly: *Black American Quarterly*. Freq: 4; Cov: Scan; Lang: Eng; Subj: Related. ISSN: 0145-8116 ▪Los Angeles, CA; USA.

Afr   *Afrasia*. Lang: Eng; Subj: Theatre. ▪42 Commercial Buildings; Shahrah-e-Quaid-e-Azam; Lahore; PAKISTAN.

AfrA   *African Arts*. Freq: 4; Began: 1967; Cov: Scan; Lang: Eng; Subj: Related.
ISSN: 0001-9933
■African Studies Center, Univ. of California, Los Angeles; 405 Hilgard Avenue; Los Angeles, CA 90024; USA.

AfricaP   *Africa Perspective*. Freq: 2; Began: 1976; Cov: Scan; Lang: Eng; Subj: Related.   ISSN: 0145-5311
■Students' African Studies Society, Univ. of Witwatersrand; 1 Jan Smuts Ave; 2001 Johannesburg; SOUTH AFRICA.

AfTR   *African Theatre Review*. Freq: IRR; Began: 1985; Lang: Eng; Subj: Theatre.
■Dept. of African Literature, Fac. of Letters & Social Science; University Yaoumde, PO Box 755; Yaounde; CAMEROON.

AG   *An Gael*: Irish Traditional Culture Alive in America Today. Freq: 4; Began: 1975; Lang: Eng; Subj: Related.
■An Claidheamh Soluis, The Irish Arts Center; 553 W. 51st Street; New York, NY 10019; USA.

AHA   *Aha! Hispanic Arts News*. Freq: 10; Began: 1976; Lang: Eng/Spa; Subj: Related.
■Association of Hispanic Arts; 200 E. 87 St.; New York, NY 10038; USA.

AHAT   *Al-Hayat At-T'aqafiyya*. Lang: Ara; Subj: Theatre.
■Ministère des Affaires Culturelles; La Kasbah; Tunis; TUNISIA.

AInf   *Artist and Influence*. Freq: 1; Began: 1981; Cov: Scan; Lang: Eng; Subj: Related.
■Hatch-Billops Collection, Inc.; 691 Broadway; New York, NY; USA.

AIT   *Annuaire International du Théâtre*: SEE: Miedzynarodowny Rocznik Teatralny (Acro: MRT). Freq: 1; Began: 1977; Lang: Fre/Eng; Subj: Theatre.
■Warsaw; POLAND.

AIWAT   *Al-Idaa Wa At-Talfaza*. Lang: Ara; Subj: Theatre.
■R.T.T.; 71 Avenue de la Liberté; Tunis; TUNISIA.

AJCS   *Australian Journal of Cultural Studies*. Freq: 2; Began: 1983; Ceased: 1987; Cov: Scan; Lang: Eng; Subj: Related. ISSN: 0810-9648
■School of English; Western Australian Institute of Technology; Bentley, Western Australia 6102; AUSTRALIA.

AKT   *AKT*: Aktuelles Theater. Freq: 12; Began: 1969; Lang: Ger; Subj: Theatre.
■Frankfurter Bund für Volksbildung GmbH; Eschersheimer Landstrasse 2; 6000 Frankfurt/1, W; WEST GERMANY.

AL   *American Literature*. Freq: 4; Began: 1929; Cov: Scan; Lang: Eng; Subj: Related.   ISSN: 0002-9831
■Duke Univ. Press, Box 6697; College Station; Durham, NC 27708; USA.

Alfold   *Alföld*. Freq: 12; Began: 1954; Cov: Scan; Lang: Hun; Subj: Related.
ISSN: 0401-3174
■Hajdu Megyei Lapkiado Vallalat; Vörös Hadsereg útja 26/A I. em.; 4024 Debrecen; HUNGARY.

Alif   *Alif*. Lang: Fre; Subj: Theatre.
■24 rue Gamel Abdel-Nasser; Tunis; TUNISIA.

Alive   *Alive*: The New Performance Magazine. Freq: 24; Began: 1982; Lang: Eng; Subj: Theatre.
■New York, NY; USA.

Almanach   *Almanach Sceny Polskiej*. Freq: 1; Began: 1961; Lang: Pol; Subj: Theatre.
■Wydawnicta Artystyczne i Filmowe; Pulawska 61; 02 595 Warsaw; POLAND.

ALS   *Australian Literary Studies*. Freq: 2; Began: 1963; Cov: Scan; Lang: Eng; Subj: Related.
■Univ. of Queensland, Dept. of English; Box 88; St. Lucia; Queensland 4067; AUSTRALIA.

AltT   *Alternatives Théâtrales*. Freq: 4; Began: 1979; Cov: Scan; Lang: Fre; Subj: Theatre.
■13 rue des Poissonniers, bte 15-1000 Brussels; BELGIUM.

AmatS   *Amateur Stage*. Freq: 11; Began: 1946; Lang: Eng; Subj: Theatre.   ISSN: 0002-6867
■Stacey Publications; 1 Hawthorndene Rd.; Hayes, Bromley Kent; UK.

AmatT   *Amateur Theatre Yearbook*. Freq: 1; Began: 1988; Lang: Eng; Subj: Theatre.
■Platform Publications; 30 Culver Road; St. Albans, Herts, AL1 4ED; UK.

AMN   *Arts Management Newsletter*. Freq: 5; Began: 1962; Lang: Eng; Subj: Related.   ISSN: 0004-4067
■Radius Group, Inc.; 408 W. 57th Street; New York, NY 10019; USA.

AmS   *Amatérská Scéna*: Ochotnicke divadlo. Freq: 12; Began: 1964; Lang: Cze; Subj: Theatre.   ISSN: 0002-6786
■Panorama; Halkova 1; 120 72 Prague 2; CZECHOSLOVAKIA.

AmTh   *American Theatre*. Formerly: Theatre Communications. Freq: 11; Began: 1984; Cov: Full; Lang: Eng; Subj: Theatre. ISSN: 0275-5971
■Theatre Communications Group; 355 Lexington Avenue; New York, NY 10017; USA.

Amyri   *Amyri*. Freq: 4; Lang: Fin; Subj: Theatre.
■Suomen Nayttelijaliitto r.y.; Arkadiankatu 12 A 18; 00100 Helsinki 10/52; FINLAND.

Anim   *Animations*: Review of Puppets and Related Theatre. Freq: 6; Began: 1977; Cov: Scan; Lang: Eng; Subj: Theatre. ISSN: 0140-7740
■Puppet Centre Trust, Battersea Arts Centre; Lavender Hill; SW11 5TJ London; UK.

Annuel   *Annuel de Théâtre*. Freq: 1; Lang: Fre; Subj: Theatre.
■Association Loi de 1901; 30, rue de la Belgique; 92190 Meudon; FRANCE.

AnSt   *Another Standard*. Freq: 6; Ceased: 1986; Cov: Scan; Lang: Eng; Subj: Related.
■PO Box 900; B70 6JP West Bromwich; UK.

AnT   *Annuaire Théâtral, L'*. Freq: 1; Lang: Fre; Subj: Theatre.
■Montreal, PQ; CANADA.

Apollo   *Apollo*: The international magazine of art and antiques. Freq: 12; Began: 1925; Cov: Scan; Lang: Eng; Subj: Related.
ISSN: 0003-6536
■Apollo Magazine Ltd.; 22 Davies Street; W1 London; UK.

Apuntes   *Apuntes*. Freq: 2; Began: 1960; Lang: Spa; Subj: Theatre.
■Universidad Católica de Chile, Escuela de Artes de la Comunicacion; Diagonal Oriente 3300, Casilla 114D; Santiago; CHILE.

AQ   *American Quarterly*. Freq: 24; Began: 1949; Cov: Scan; Lang: Eng; Subj: Related.   ISSN: 0003-0678
■Univ. of Philadelphia; 307 College Hall; Philadelphia, PA 19104 6303; USA.

Araldo   *Araldo dello Spettacolo, L'*. Lang: Ita; Subj: Theatre.
■Via Aureliana 63; Rome; ITALY.

Archivio   *Archivio del Teatro Italiano*. Freq: IRR; Began: 1968; Lang: Ita; Subj: Theatre.
ISSN: 0066-6661
■Edizioni Il Polifilo; Via Borgonuovo2; 20121 Milan; ITALY.

Arco   *Arcoscenico*. Freq: 12; Began: 1945; Lang: Ita; Subj: Theatre.
■Via Ormisda 10; Rome; ITALY.

AReview   *Arts Review*. Freq: 4; Began: 1983; Ceased: 1988; Lang: Eng; Subj: Related.
■National Endowment for the Arts; 1100 Pennsylvania Avenue NW; Washington, DC 20506; USA.

Ariel   *Ariel*. Freq: 3; Began: 1986; Cov: Full; Lang: Ita; Subj: Theatre.
■Instituto di Studi Pirandelliani; Bulzoni Editore; Via dei Liburni n. 14; 00185 Rome; ITALY.

Ark   *Arkkitehti*: The Finnish Architectural Review. Freq: 8; Began: 1903; Cov: Scan; Lang: Fin; Subj: Related.
■Association of Finnish Architects; Etelaesplanacli 22A; 00130 Helsinki 13; FINLAND.

ArNy   *Arte Nyt*. Lang: Dut; Subj: Related.
■Hvidkildevej 64; 2400 Copenhagen; DENMARK.

Arrel   *Arrel*. Freq: 4; Cov: Scan; Lang: Spa; Subj: Theatre.
■Disputacio de Barcelona; Placa de Sant Juame 1; 08002 Barcelona; SPAIN.

ArsU   *Ars-Uomo*. Freq: 12; Began: 1975; Lang: Ita; Subj: Theatre.
■Bulzoni Editore; Via F. Cocco Ortu 120; 00139 Rome; ITALY.

ArtP   *Art-Press (International)*. Freq: 12; Cov: Scan; Lang: Fre; Subj: Related.
■Paris; FRANCE.

ArtsAd   *Arts Advocate*. Freq: 3; Began: 1988; Lang: Eng; Formerly: In the Arts; Subj: Theatre.
■Ohio State University College of the Arts; Office of Communications; 403 Mershon Auditorium; 30 West 15th Ave. Columbus, OH 43210-1305; USA.

ArtsAtl   *Arts Atlantic*: Atlantic Canada's Journal of the Arts. Freq: 4; Began: 1977; Cov: Scan; Lang: Eng; Subj: Related. ISSN: 0704-7916

■Confederation Centre, Art Gallery and Museum; P.O.Box 848; Charlottetown, PE C1A 7L9; CANADA.

ArtsRS *Arts Reporting Service, The*. Freq: 24; Began: 1970; Lang: Eng; Subj: Theatre.
■Charles Christopher Mark; PO Box 39008; Washington, DC 20016; USA.

ASabah *As-Sabah*. Lang: Ara; Subj: Theatre.
■4 rue Ali Bach Hamba; Tunis; TUNISIA.

ASamvad *Abhnaya Samvad*. Freq: 12; Lang: Hin; Subj: Theatre.
■20 Muktaram Babu Street; Calcutta; INDIA.

ASBelg *Arts du Spectacle en Belgique*. Formerly: *Centre d'Etudes Theatrales, Louvain: Annuaire*. Freq: IRR; Began: 1968; Lang: Fre; Subj: Theatre. ISSN: 0069-1860
■Université Catholique de Louvain, Centre d'Etudes Théâtrales; 1, place de l'Université; 1348 Louvain-la-Neuve; BELGIUM.

AScene *Autre Scène, L'*. Lang: Fre; Subj: Theatre.
■Editions Albatros; 14 rue de l'Amérique; 75015 Paris; FRANCE.

ASCFB *Annuaire du Spectacle de la Communauté Française de Belgique*. Freq: 1; Began: 1981; Lang: Fre; Subj: Theatre.
■Archives et Musée de la Littérature, ASBL; 4 Bd de l'Empereur; 1000 Brussels; BELGIUM.

ASInt *American Studies International*. Freq: 4; Cov: Scan; Lang: Eng; Subj: Related. ISSN: 0003-1321
■American Studies Program, George Washington University; Washington, DC 20052; USA.

ASO *Avant Scène Opéra, L'*. Freq: 6; Began: 1976; Lang: Fre; Subj: Theatre.
■27 rue St. André des Arts; 75006 Paris; FRANCE.

ASSAPHc *ASSAPH*: Section C. Freq: 1; Began: 1984; Cov: Full; Lang: Eng; Subj: Theatre. ISSN: 0334-5963
■Dept. of Theatre Arts, Tel Aviv University; 69978 Ramat Aviv Tel Aviv; ISRAEL.

AST *Avant Scène Théâtre, L'*. Freq: 20; Began: 1949; Lang: Fre; Subj: Theatre. ISSN: 0045-1169
■Editions de l'Avant Scène; 16 rue des Quatre Vents; 75006 Paris; FRANCE.

AStage *American Stage*. Freq: 10; Began: 1979; Lang: Eng; Subj: Theatre.
■American Stage Publishing Company; 217 East 28th Street; New York, NY 10016; USA.

ASTRN *ASTR Newsletter*. Freq: 2; Began: 1972; Cov: Scan; Lang: Eng; Subj: Theatre. ISSN: 0044-7927
■American Society for Theatre Research, C.W. Post College; Department of English; Brookvale, NY 11548; USA.

ATAC *Aujourd'hui Tendances Art Culture*. Formerly: *Partenaires*. Lang: Fre; Subj: Related.
■FRANCE.

ATArg *Annuario del Teatro Argentino*. Freq: 1; Lang: Spa; Subj: Theatre.
■F.N.A.; Calle Alsina 673; Buenos Aires; ARGENTINA.

ATB *Annuario do Teatro Brasileiro*. Freq: 1; Began: 1976; Lang: Por; Subj: Theatre.

■Ministerio da Educacao e Cultura; Service Nacional de Teatro; Rio de Janeiro; BRAZIL.

AThR *Australian Theatre Review*. Lang: Eng; Subj: Theatre. ISSN: 0310-6381
■Australian Centre of the ITI, c/o School of Drama; University of NSW; NSW 2066 Kensington; AUSTRALIA.

ATJ *Asian Theatre Journal*. Formerly: *Asian Theatre Reports*. Freq: 2; Began: 1984; Cov: Full; Lang: Eng; Subj: Theatre. ISSN: 0742-5457
■Univ. of Hawaii Press; 2840 Kolowalu Street; Honolulu, HI 96822; USA.

ATR *Australian Theatre Record*. Freq: 12; Began: 1987; Lang: Eng; Subj: Theatre. ISSN: 0819-1182
■Australian Studies Theatre Centre of ITI, University of New South Wales; POBox 1; NSW 2033 Kensington; AUSTRALIA.

ATT *Amers Theatrical Times*. Freq: 12; Began: 1976; Lang: Eng; Subj: Related.
■William Amer (Pty) Ltd.; 15 Montgomery Avenue; NSW 2142 South Granville; AUSTRALIA.

Audiences *Audiences Magazine*. Freq: 12; Lang: Fre; Subj: Theatre.
■55 avenue Jean Jaures; 75019 Paris; FRANCE.

AULLA *Journal of the Australian Universities Language & Literature Association*. Freq: 2; Began: 1953; Cov: Scan; Lang: Eng; Subj: Related. ISSN: 0001-2793
■Australasian Universities Language & Literature Association; Monash University; Clayton, Victoria 3168; AUSTRALIA.

Autores *Autores*. Freq: 4; Lang: Por; Subj: Theatre.
■Sociedade Portuguesa de Autores; Av. Duque de Loule, 31; 1098 Lisbon Codex; PORTUGAL.

Avrora *Avrora*. Freq: 12; Began: 1969; Cov: Scan; Lang: Rus; Subj: Related.
■Leningrad; USSR.

Baal *Baal Rangmanch*. Freq: 12; Lang: Hin; Subj: Theatre.
■325 Shradanand Nagar (Bashirat Gunj); Lucknow; INDIA.

Bahub *Bahubacana*. Began: 1978; Lang: Ben; Subj: Theatre.
■Bahubacana Natyagoshthi; 11/2 Jaynag Road, Bakshi Bazar; Dacca 1; BANGLADESH.

BaI *Ballett International*: Aktuelle Monatszeitung für Ballett und Tanztheater. Formerly: *Ballett Info*. Freq: 12; Began: 1978; Lang: Ger/Eng; Subj: Related. ISSN: 0722-6268
■Ballett International Verlags GmbH, P.O. Box 270 443; Richard-Wagner Strasse 33; D5000 Cologne 1; WEST GERMANY.

BALF *Black American Literature Forum*. Formerly: *Negro American Literature*. Freq: 4; Began: 1967; Cov: Scan; Lang: Eng; Subj: Related. ISSN: 0148-6179
■Parsons Hall 237, Indiana State Univ.; Terre Haute, IN 47809; USA.

Bamah *Bamah*: Educational Theatre Review. Freq: 4; Began: 1959; Cov: Full; Lang: Heb; Subj: Theatre. ISSN: 0045-138X

■Bamah Association; PO Box 7098; 910 70 Jerusalem; ISRAEL.

BAMu *Buenos Aires Musical*. Lang: Spa; Subj: Theatre.
■Calle Alsina 912; Buenos Aires; ARGENTINA.

Band *Bandwagon*. Freq: 6; Began: 1939; Cov: Scan; Lang: Eng; Subj: Theatre. ISSN: 0005-4968
■Circus Historical Society; 2515 Dorset Road; Columbus, OH 43221; USA.

BaNe *Ballet News*. Freq: 12; Began: 1979; Lang: Eng; Subj: Related. ISSN: 0191-2690
■Metropolitan Opera Guild, Inc.; 1865 Broadway; New York, NY 10023; USA.

BASSITEJ *Bulletin ASSITEJ*. Formerly: *Bulletin d'Information ASSITEJ*. Freq: 3; Began: 1966; Lang: Fre/Eng/Rus; Subj: Theatre.
■ASSITEJ; Celetna 17; 110 01 Prague 1; CZECHOSLOVAKIA.

BCl *Beckett Circle/Cercle de Beckett*. Freq: 2; Began: 1978; Lang: Eng/Fre; Subj: Theatre.
■Samuel Beckett Society; University of California at Los Angeles; Los Angeles, CA 90024; USA.

BCom *Bulletin of the Commediantes*. Freq: 2; Began: 1949; Lang: Eng; Subj: Theatre.
■James A. Parr, Dept. of Spa. & Portuguese; University of California; Los Angeles, CA 90007; USA.

BelgITI *Bulletin*: Van het Belgisch Centrum ITI. Lang: Fre; Subj: Theatre.
■Belgisch Centrum van het ITI, c/o Mark Hermans; Rudolfstraat 33; B 2000 Antwerp; BELGIUM.

Bergens *Bergens Theatermuseum Skrifter*. Began: 1970; Lang: Nor; Subj: Theatre.
■Bergens Theatermuseum, Kolstadgt 1; Box 2959 Toeyen; 6 Oslo; NORWAY.

Bericht *Bericht*. Lang: Ger; Subj: Theatre. ISSN: 0067-6047
■UMLOsterreichischer Bundestheaterverband; Goethegasse 1; A 1010 Vienna; AUSTRIA.

BFant *Botteghe della Fantasia, Le*. Lang: Ita; Subj: Theatre.
■Via S. Manlio 13; Milan; ITALY.

BGs *Bühnengenossenschaft*. Freq: 10; Began: 1949; Lang: Ger; Subj: Theatre. ISSN: 0007-3083
■Bühnenschriften-Vertriebs-Gesellschaft; Feldsbrunnenstrasse 74; 2000 Hamburg 13; WEST GERMANY.

BGTA *Bibliographic Guide to Theatre Arts*. Freq: 1; Lang: Eng; Subj: Theatre. ISSN: 0360-2788
■G. K. Hall & Co.; 70 Lincoln Street; Boston, MA 02111; USA.

BIINET *Boletin Informativo del Instituto Nacional de Estudios de Teatro*. Freq: 10; Began: 1978; Lang: Spa; Subj: Theatre.
■1055 Avenida Cordoba; 1199 Buenos Aires; ARGENTINA.

Biladi *Biladi*. Lang: Ara; Subj: Theatre.
■Parti Socialiste Desourien, Maison du Parti, BP 1033; Blvd. du 9 Avril, La Kasbah; Tunis; TUNISIA.

BiT   *Biblioteca Teatrale*. Freq: 4; Began: 1986; Cov: Full; Lang: Ita; Subj: Theatre.   ISSN: 0045-1959
■Bulzoni Editore; 14 Via dei Liburni; 00185 Rome; ITALY.

BITIJ   *Boletin Iberoamericano de Teatro para la Infancia y la Juventud*. Lang: Spa; Subj: Theatre.
■Associacion Espanola de Teatro para la Infancia y la Juventud; Claudio Coello 141; 6 Madrid; SPAIN.

BK   *Bauten der Kultur*. Freq: 4; Began: 1976; Lang: Ger; Subj: Related.   ISSN: 0323-5696
■Institut für Kulturbauten; Clara-Zetkin-Strasse 105; 1080 Berlin; WEST GERMANY.

BlackM   *Black Masks*. Freq: 12; Began: 1984; Cov: Scan; Lang: Eng; Subj: Related.
■New York, NY, USA.

BlC   *Black Collegian, The*: The National Magazine of Black College Students. Formerly: *Expressions*. Freq: IRR; Began: 1970; Cov: Scan; Lang: Eng; Subj: Related.   ISSN: 0192-3757
■Black Collegiate Services, Inc.; 1240 South Broad Street; New Orleans, LA 70125; USA.

BM   *Burlington Magazine*. Freq: 12; Began: 1903; Cov: Scan; Lang: Eng; Subj: Related.   ISSN: 0007-6287
■Burlington Magazine Publications, Elm House; 10-16 Elm Street; WC1X 0BP London; UK.

BMT   *Biuletyn Mlodego Teatru*. Began: 1978; Lang: Pol; Subj: Theatre.
■Gwido Zlatkes; Bednarska 24 m; 00 321 Warsaw; POLAND.

BNJMtd   *Biblioteca Nacional José Marti*: Informacion y Documentacion de la Cultura. Serie Teatro y Danza. Freq: 12; Lang: Spa; Subj: Theatre.
■Biblioteca Nacional José Marti, Dept. Info. y Doc. de Cultura; Plaza de la Revolución; Havana; CUBA.

BNS   *Builder N.S.* Formerly: *Builder N.S.W.*. Freq: 12; Began: 1907; Cov: Scan; Lang: Eng; Subj: Related.
■Master Builders Asso. of New South Wales; Private Bag 9; Broadway; N.S.W. 2007; AUSTRALIA. Tel: 660-7188

BooksC   *Books in Canada*. Freq: 9; Began: 1971; Cov: Scan; Lang: Eng/Fre; Subj: Related.   ISSN: 0045-2564
■Canadian Review of Books; 366 Adelaide Street East, Suite 432; Toronto, ON M5A 3X9; CANADA.

Bouff   *Bouffonneries*. Lang: Fre; Subj: Theatre.
■Domaine de Lestanière; 11000 Cazilhac; FRANCE.

BPAN   *British Performing Arts Newsletter*. Ceased: 1980; Lang: Eng; Subj: Related.
■London; UK.

BPM   *Black Perspective in Music*. Freq: 2; Began: 1973; Ceased: 1990; Cov: Scan; Lang: Eng; Subj: Related.   ISSN: 0090-7790
■Foundation for Research in the Afro-American Creative Arts; P.O. Drawer One; Cambria Heights, NY 11411; USA.

BPTV   *Bühne und Parkett*: Theater Journal Volksbühnen-Spiegel. Formerly: *Volksbuhnen-Spiegel*. Freq: 3; Began: 1955; Lang: Ger; Subj: Theatre.   ISSN: 0172-1321
■Verband der deutschen Volksbühne e.v.; Bismarckstrasse 17; 1000 Berlin 12; WEST GERMANY.

BR   *Ballet Review*. Freq: 4; Began: 1965; Lang: Eng; Subj: Related.   ISSN: 0522-0653
■Dance Research Foundation, Inc.; 46 Morton Street; New York, NY 10014; USA.

BrechtJ   *Brecht Jahrbuch*. Freq: 1; Began: 1971; Ceased: 1987; Lang: Ger/Eng/Fre; Subj: Theatre.
■Wayne State University; 5959 Woodward Ave.; Detroit, MI 48202; USA.

Brs   *Broadside*. Freq: 4; Began: 1940; Lang: Eng; Subj: Theatre.   ISSN: 0068-2748
■Theatre Library Assoc.; 111 Amsterdam Avenue; New York, NY 10023; USA.

BSOAS   *Bulletin of the School of Oriental & African Studies*. Lang: Eng; Subj: Related.
■London; UK.

BSPC   *Bulletin de la Société Paul Claudel*. Freq: 4; Cov: Scan; Lang: Fre; Subj: Related.
■13, rue du Pont Louis-Philippe; 75004 Paris; FRANCE.

BSSJ   *Bernard Shaw Newsletter*. Formerly: *Newsletter & Journal of the Shaw Society of London*. Freq: 1; Began: 1976; Lang: Eng; Subj: Related.
■Bernard Shaw Centre, High Orchard; 125 Markyate Road; EM8 2LB Dagenahm, Essex; UK.

BTA   *Børneteateravisen*. Freq: 4; Began: 1972; Lang: Dan; Subj: Theatre.
■Samarbejdsudvalget; Frederiksborggade 20; 1360 Copenhagen; DENMARK.

BTlog   *British Theatrelog*. Freq: 4; Began: 1978; Ceased: 1980; Lang: Eng; Subj: Theatre.   ISSN: 0141-9056
■Associate British Centre of the ITI; 15 Hanover Sq.; WIR 9AJ London; UK.

BtR   *Bühnentechnische Rundschau*: Zeitschrift für Theatertechnik, Bühnenbau und Bühnengestaltung. Freq: 6; Began: 1907; Lang: Ger; Subj: Theatre.
■Orell Fuessli & Friedrich Verlag; Dietzingerstrasse 3; CH8036 Zurich; SWITZERLAND.

Buhne   *Bühne, Die*. Freq: 12; Began: 1958; Cov: Full; Lang: Ger; Subj: Theatre.   ISSN: 0007-3075
■Geyer Gesellschaft mb H; Arbeitergasse 1-7; A1051 Vienna; AUSTRIA.

CahiersC   *Cahiers Césairiens*. Freq: 2; Began: 1974; Lang: Eng/Fre; Subj: Theatre.
■Pennsylvania State University, Dept. of French; University Park, PA 16802; USA.

CahiersCC   *Cahiers CERT/CIRCE*. Lang: Fre; Subj: Theatre.
■Centre Etudes Recherches Théâtrale, Université de Bordeaux III; Esplanade des Antilles; 33405 Talence; FRANCE.

Callaloo   *Callaloo*: A Black South Journal of Arts and Letters. Freq: 3; Began: 1976; Cov: Scan; Lang: Eng; Subj: Related.   ISSN: 0161-2492
■Johns Hopkins U. Press, 701 W. 40th St. #275; Baltimore, MD 21211; USA.

CallB   *Call Boy, The*: Journal of the British Music Hall Society. Freq: 4; Began: 1963; Lang: Eng; Subj: Theatre.
■British Music Hall Society; 32 Hazelbourne Road; SW12 London; UK.

Callboard   *Callboard*. Freq: 4; Began: 1951; Lang: Eng; Subj: Theatre.   ISSN: 0045-4044
■Nova Scotia Drama League; 5516 Spring Garden Road, Suite 305; Halifax, NS B3J 1G6; CANADA.

Calliope   *Calliope*. Freq: 12; Began: 1968; Lang: Eng; Subj: Theatre.
■Clowns of America Inc.; 1052 Foxwood Ln.; Baltimore, MD 21221; USA.

CAM   *City Arts Monthly*. Freq: 12; Lang: Eng; Subj: Related.
■640 Natoma St.; San Francisco, CA 94103; USA.

CanL   *Canadian Literature / Littérature Canadienne*: A Quarterly of Criticism and Review. Freq: 4; Began: 1959; Cov: Scan; Lang: Eng/Fre; Subj: Related.   ISSN: 0008-4360
■University of British Columbia; 223-2029 West Mall; Vancouver, BC V6T 1W5; CANADA.

Caratula   *Caratula*. Freq: 12; Lang: Spa; Subj: Theatre.
■Sanchez Pacheco 83; 2 Madrid; SPAIN.

Castelets   *Castelets*. Lang: Fre; Subj: Theatre.
■Centre Belge de l'UNIMA, Section francophone; 66 rue de Lot; 1650 Beersel; BELGIUM.

CaTheatre   *Cahiers Théâtre*. Freq: 1; Began: 1968; Lang: Fre; Subj: Theatre.   ISSN: 0068-5232
■Université Catholique de Louvain, Centre d'Etudes Théâtrales; 1 Place de l'Université; 1348 Louvain-la-Neuve; BELGIUM.

CB   *Call Board*. Formerly: *Monthly Theatre Magazine of TCCBA*. Freq: IRR; Began: 1931; Lang: Eng; Subj: Theatre.   ISSN: 0008-1701
■Theatre Communications Center of the Bay Area; 2940 16th St., Suite 102; San Francisco, CA 94116; USA.

CBGB   *Cahiers de la Bibliothèque Gaston Baty*. Lang: Fre; Subj: Related.
■Paris; FRANCE.

CCIEP   *Courrier du Centre international d'études poétiques*. Freq: 6; Cov: Scan; Lang: Fre; Subj: Theatre.
■Centre d'études poétiques; Bibliothèque royale; Boulevard de l'empereur, 4; 1000 Bruxelles; BELGIUM.

CDO   *Courrier Dramatique de l'Ouest*. Freq: 4; Began: 1973; Lang: Fre; Subj: Theatre.
■Théâtre du Bout du Monde, Ctre Dramatique Natl de l'Ouest; 9B Avenue Janvier; 35100 Rennes; FRANCE.

CDr   *Canadian Drama / Art Dramatique Canadien*. Freq: 2; Began: 1975; Cov: Full; Lang: Eng/Fre; Subj: Theatre.   ISSN: 0317-9044
■Dept. of English, University of Waterloo; Waterloo, ON N2L 3G1; CANADA.

CdRideau *Cahiers du Rideau*. Freq: 3; Began: 1976; Lang: Fre; Subj: Theatre. ■Rideau de Bruxelles; 23 rue Ravenstein; B 1000 Bruxelles; BELGIUM.

CE *College English*. Freq: 8; Began: 1937; Cov: Scan; Lang: Eng; Subj: Related. ISSN: 0010-0994 ■National Council of Teachers of English; 1111 Kenyon Road; Urbana, IL 61801; USA.

Celcit *Celcit*. Lang: Spa; Subj: Theatre. ■Apartado 662; 105 Caracas; VENEZUELA.

CeskL *Ceskoslovenskí Loutkář*. Began: 1951; Lang: Cze; Subj: Theatre. ■Panorama; Mrstikova 23; 10 000 Prague 10; CZECHOSLOVAKIA.

CetC *Culture et Communication*. Freq: 10; Lang: Fre; Subj: Theatre. ■Min. de la Culture et de la Documentation; 3 rue de Valois; 75001 Paris; FRANCE.

CF *Comédie-Française*. Freq: 10; Began: 1971; Cov: Full; Lang: Fre; Subj: Theatre. ■1 Place Colette; 75001 Paris; FRANCE.

Cfl *Confluent*. Freq: 9; Began: 1974; Lang: Fre; Subj: Related. ISSN: 0150-2441 ■Maison de la Culture de Rennes; 1, rue St. Helier; 35008 Rennes; FRANCE.

CFT *Contemporary French Civilization*. Freq: 3; Began: 1976; Cov: Scan; Lang: Fre/Eng; Subj: Related. ISSN: 0147-9156 ■Dept. of Modern Languages, Montana State University; Bozeman, MT 59717; USA.

Chhaya *Chhaya Nat*. Freq: 4; Lang: Hin; Subj: Theatre. ■U.P. Sangeet Natak Akademi; Lucknow; INDIA.

ChinL *Chinese Literature*. Freq: 4; Began: 1951; Cov: Scan; Lang: Eng; Subj: Related. ISSN: 0009-4617 ■Bai Wan Zhuang; Peking 37; CHINA.

Chronico *Chronico*. Lang: Gre; Subj: Theatre. ■ Horo'; Xenofontos 7; Athens; GREECE.

ChTR *Children's Theatre Review*. Freq: 4; Began: 1952; Cov: Full; Ceased: 1985; Lang: Eng; Subj: Theatre. ISSN: 0009-4196 ■c/o Milton W. Hamlin, Shoreline High School; 18560 1st Avenue N.E.; Seattle, WA 98155; USA.

CineLD *Cineschedario*: Letture Drammatiche. Freq: 12; Began: 1964; Lang: Ita; Subj: Related. ISSN: 0024-1458 ■Centro Salesiano dello Spettacolo; Via M. Ausiliatrice 32; Turin 10121; ITALY.

CIQ *Callahan's Irish Quarterly*. Freq: 4; Ceased: 1983; Cov: Scan; Lang: Eng; Subj: Related. ■P.O. Box 5935; Berkeley, CA 94705; USA.

CircusP *Circus-Parade*. Freq: 12; Began: 1976; Lang: Ger; Subj: Theatre. ■Circus-Club International; Klosterhof 10; 2308 Preetz; WEST GERMANY.

CircusR *Circus Report*. Freq: IRR; Began: 1972; Lang: Eng; Subj: Theatre; ISSN: 0889-5996 ■525 Oak St.; El Cerrito, CA 94530-3699; USA.

CittaA *Città Aperta*. Freq: 1; Began: 1981; Lang: Ita; Subj: Theatre. ■Associazione Piccolo Teatro; Via Cesalpino 20; 52100 Arezzo; ITALY.

CityL *City Limits*. Freq: 10; Began: 1976; Cov: Scan; Lang: Eng; Subj: Related. ISSN: 0199-0330 ■City Limits, Community Information Services; 424 W. 33rd Street; New York, NY 10001; USA.

CJC *Cahiers Jean Cocteau*. Freq: 1; Began: 1969; Lang: Fre; Subj: Theatre. ISSN: 0068-5178 ■6 rue Bonaparte; 75006 Paris; FRANCE.

CJG *Cahiers Jean Giraudoux*. Freq: 1; Began: 1972; Lang: Fre; Subj: Theatre. ■Editions Bernard Grasset; 61, rue des Saints-Pères; 75006 Paris; FRANCE.

Cjo *Conjunto*: Revista de Teatro Latinamericano. Freq: 4; Began: 1964; Cov: Full; Lang: Spa; Subj: Theatre. ISSN: 0010-5937 ■Departamento de Teatro Latino Americano, Casa de las Americas; Ediciones Cubanes, Obispo No. 527; Aptdo. 605, Havana; CUBA.

CLAJ *College Language Association Journal*. Freq: 4; Began: 1957; Lang: Eng; Subj: Related. ISSN: 0007-8549 ■College Language Assoc., c/o Cason Hill; Morehouse College; Atlanta, GA 30314; USA.

ClaudelS *Claudel Studies*. Freq: 2; Began: 1972; Cov: Scan; Lang: Eng; Subj: Related. ISSN: 0090-1237 ■University of Dallas, Dept. of French; PO Box 464; Irving, TX 75061; USA.

Clip *Clipper Studies in the American Theater*. Freq: IRR; Began 1985; Lang: Eng; Subj: Theatre. ISSN: 0748-237X ■Borgo Press; Box 2845; San Bernardino, CA 92406; USA.

CLSUJ *CLSU Journal of the Arts*. Freq: 1; Began: 1981; Lang: Eng/Phi; Subj: Theatre. ■Central Luzon State University, Publications House; Munoz; Nueva Ecija; PHILIPPINES.

CMJV *Cahiers de la Maison Jean Vilar*. Lang: Fre; Subj: Theatre. ■Avignon; FRANCE.

CNCT *Cahiers de la NCT*. Freq: 3; Began: 1965; Cov: Scan; Lang: Fre; Subj: Theatre. ■Nouvelle Compagnie Théâtrale; 4353 rue Ste. Catherine est.; Montreal, PQ H1V 1F2; CANADA.

CO *Comédie de l'Ouest*. Lang: Fre; Subj: Theatre. ■Rennes; FRANCE.

ColecaoT *Coleçao Teatro*. Freq: IRR; Began: 1974; Lang: Por; Subj: Theatre. ■Universidade Federal do Rio Grande do Sul; Porto Alegre; BRAZIL.

ColJL&A *Columbia-VLA Journal of Law & the Arts*. Formerly: *Art & the Law*. Freq: 4; Began: 1985; Cov: Full; Lang: Eng; Subj: Related. ISSN: 0743-5226 ■Columbia University School of Law &, Volunteer Lawyers for the Arts; 435 West 116 Street; New York, NY 10027; USA.

Comedy *Comedy*. Freq: 4; Began: 1980; Lang: Eng; Subj: Theatre. ISSN: 0272-7404 ■Trite Explanations Ltd.; Box 505, Canal Street Station; New York, NY 10013; USA.

ComIBS *Communications from the International Brecht Society*: The Global Brecht. Freq: 2; Began: 1970; Cov: Scan; Lang: Eng; Subj: Theatre. ISSN: 0740-8943 ■Editor of the Communications from the IBS, Dep. Foreign Langs & Literatures; Valparaiso University; Valparaiso, IN 46383; USA.

CompD *Comparative Drama*. Freq: 4; Began: 1967; Cov: Full; Lang: Eng; Subj: Theatre. ISSN: 0010-4078 ■Department of English, Western Michigan University; Kalamazoo, MI 49008; USA.

Con *Connoisseur*. Freq: 12; Began: 1901; Cov: Scan; Lang: Eng; Subj: Related. ISSN: 0010-6275 ■Hearst Magazines, Connoisseur; 250 W. 55th St.; New York, NY 10019; USA.

Confes *Confessio*. Freq: 4; Began: 1976; Cov: Scan; Lang: Hun; Subj: Related. ■Bulletin of the Hungarian Reformed Church; XIV. Abonyi u. 21.; 1146 Budapest; HUNGARY.

ContactQ *Contact Quarterly*. Freq: 3; Began: 1975; Lang: Eng; Subj: Theatre. ISSN: 0198-9634 ■Contact Collaborations Inc.; Box 603; Northampton, MA 01061; USA.

Contenido *Contenido*. Lang: Spa; Subj: Theatre. ■Centro Venezolano del ITI; Apartado 51-456; 105 Caracas; VENEZUELA.

CORD *CORD Dance Research Annual*. Lang: Eng; Subj: Related. ■CORD Editorial Board, NYU Dance and Dance Educ. Dept.; 35 W. 4th St., Room 675; New York, NY 10003; USA.

CorpsE *Corps écrit*. Freq: 4; Cov: Scan; Lang: Fre; Subj: Theatre. ■Presses Universitaires de France; 12, rue Jean de Beauvais; 75005 Paris; FRANCE.

COS *Central Opera Service Bulletin*. Freq: 4; Began: 1954; Lang: Eng; Subj: Theatre. ISSN: 0008-9508 ■Metropolitan Opera Nat'l Council, Central Opera Service; Lincoln Center; New York, NY 10023; USA.

Costume *Costume*: The Journal of the Costume Society. Freq: 1; Began: 1967; Cov: Full; Lang: Eng; Subj: Related. ISSN: 0590-8876 ■c/o Miss Anne Brogden; 63 Salisbury Road; LI9 0PH Liverpool; UK.

CrAr *Critical Arts*. Freq: IRR; Began: 1980; Cov: Scan; Lang: Eng; Subj: Related. ■Crital Arts Study Group, c/o Dept. of Journalism & Media; Rhodes University; 6140 Grahamstown; SOUTH AFRICA.

CRB *Cahiers Renaud Barrault*. Freq: 4; Began: 1953; Cov: Scan; Lang: Fre; Subj: Theatre. ISSN: 0008-0470 ■Editions Gallimard; 5 rue Sebastien-Bottin; 75007 Paris; FRANCE.

CreD *Creative Drama*. Freq: 1; Began: 1949; Lang: Eng; Subj: Theatre. ISSN: 0011-0892 ■Educational Drama Association, c/o Stacey

Publications; 1 Hawthorndene Road; BR2 7DZ Kent; UK.

Crepuscl *Crépuscule, Le*. Ceased: 1979; Lang: Fre; Subj: Theatre.
■Théâtre du Crepuscule; rue Scailquin 30; Brussels 3; BELGIUM.

Crisis *Crisis*. Freq: 6; Began: 1910; Cov: Scan; Lang: Eng; Subj: Related. ISSN: 0011-1422
■Crisis Publishing Co.; 186 Remsen St.; Brooklyn, NY 11201; USA.

CritD *Critical Digest*. Freq: 24; Began: 1948; Ceased: 1985; Lang: Eng; Subj: Theatre.
■225 West 34th Street, Room 918; New York, NY 10001; USA.

CritNY *Critique*. Freq: 4; Began: 1976; Lang: Eng; Subj: Theatre
■417 Convent Avenue; New York, NY 10031; USA.

CritQ *Critical Quarterly*. Freq: 4; Began: 1959; Lang: Eng; Subj: Related. ISSN: 0011-1562
■Manchester University Press; Oxford Road; M13 9PL Manchester; UK.

CRT *Cabra, La*: Revista de Teatro. Lang: Spa; Subj: Theatre.
■Mexico City; MEXICO.

CS *Canada on Stage*. Freq: 1; Began: 1975; Lang: Eng; Subj: Theatre. ISSN: 0380-9455
■Drama Department, University of Guelph; Guelph, ON N1G 2W1; CANADA.

CSAN *Costume Society of America Newsletter*. Began: 1975; Lang: Eng; Subj: Related.
■The Costume Society of America; 55 Edgewater Drive; P.O. Box 73 Earleville, MD 21919; USA.

CShav *Californian Shavian*. Freq: 6; Began: 1958; Ceased: 1966; Lang: Eng; Subj: Theatre. ISSN: 0008-154X
■Shaw Society of California; 1933 S. Broadway; Los Angeles, CA 90007; USA.

CTA *California Theatre Annual*. Ceased: 1986; Freq: 1; Lang: Eng; Subj: Theatre. ISSN: 0733-5806
■Performing Arts Network; 9025 Wilshire Blvd.; Beverly Hills, CA 90211; USA.

CTCheck *Canadian Theatre Checklist*. Formerly: *Checklist of Canadian Theatres*. Freq: 1; Began: 1979; Ceased: 1983; Lang: Eng; Subj: Theatre. ISSN: 0226-5125
■University of Toronto Press; 63A St. George Street; Toronto, ON M5S 1A6; CANADA.

CTL *Cahiers Théâtre Louvain*. Freq: 4; Began: 1968; Cov: Full; Lang: Fre; Subj: Theatre. ISSN: 0771-4653
■q. 1450 Fr. Ferme de Blocry, Place de l' Hocaille; B-1348 Louvain-La-Neuve; BELGIUM.

CTPA *Cahiers du Théâtre Populaire d'Amiens*. Began: 1984; Lang: Fre; Subj: Theatre.
■Amiens; FRANCE.

CTR *Canadian Theatre Review*. Freq: 4; Began: 1974; Ceased: 1989; Cov: Full; Lang: Eng; Subj: Theatre. ISSN: 0315-0836

■University of Toronto Press, 63A St. George St.; Toronto, ON M55 1A6; CANADA.

CTRY *Canadian Theatre Review Yearbook*. Freq: 1; Began: 1974; Lang: Eng; Subj: Theatre. ISSN: 0380-9455
■Canadian Theatre Review Publications, 222 Admin. Studies; York University; Downsview, ON M3J 1P3; CANADA.

CTXY *C'wan t'ong Xiju Yishu/Art of Traditional Opera*. Freq: 4; Began: 1979; Lang: Chi; Subj: Theatre.
■Institute of Traditional Chinese Opera; Peking; CHINA.

CU *Cirque dans l'Univers, Le*. Freq: 4; Began: 1950; Cov: Scan; Lang: Fre; Subj: Theatre. ISSN: 0009-7373
■Club du Cirque; 11, rue Ch-Silvestri; 94300 Vincennes; FRANCE.

Cuaderno *Cuadernos El Publico*. Began: 1985; Lang: Spa/Cat; Subj: Theatre. ISSN: 8602-3573
■Centro de Documentacion Teatral, Organismo Autonomo Teatros Ncnl; c/ Capitan Haya 44; 28020 Madrid; SPAIN.

Cue *Cue International*. Freq: 6; Began: 1979; Cov: Full; Lang: Eng; Subj: Theatre. ISSN: 0144-6088
■Cue Publishing Ltd.; Kangley Bridge Rd., Sydenham, London SE26 SAQ; UK.

CueM *Cue, The*. Freq: 2; Began: 1928; Cov: Scan; Lang: Eng; Subj: Theatre. ISSN: 0011-2666
■Theta Alpha Phi Fraternity, Dept. of Speech/ Theatre; Montclair State College; Upper Montclair, NJ 07043; USA.

CueNY *Cue New York*. Freq: 26; Began: 1932; Lang: Eng; Subj: Theatre.2 ISSN: 0011-2658
■North American Publishing Company; 545 Madison Avenue; New York, NY 10022; USA.

Culture *Culture*. Freq: 12; Lang: Fre; Subj: Theatre.
■Maison de la Culture de La Rochelle; 11 rue Chef-de-Ville; 17000 La Rochelle; FRANCE.

CuPo *Cultural Post*. Lang: Eng; Subj: Related.
■National Endowment for the Arts; 1100 Pennsylvania Avenue N.W.; Washington, DC 20506; USA.

Cz *Circuszeitung, Die*. Freq: 12; Began: 1955; Lang: Ger; Subj: Theatre.
■Gesellschaft für Circusfreunde; Klosterhof 10; 2308 Preetz; WEST GERMANY.

D&D *Dance and Dancers*. Freq: 12; Began: 1950; Lang: Eng; Subj: Related. ISSN: 0011-5983
■Brevet Publishing Ltd.; 43B Gloucester Rd.; CR0 2DH Croydon, Surrey; UK.

D&T *Drama and Theater*. Freq: 3; Began: 1968; Ceased: 1980; Lang: Eng; Subj: Theatre.
■Dept. of English, State University; Fredonia, NY 14063; USA.

DA *Dance Australia*. Freq: 4; Began: 1980; Cov: Scan; Lang: Eng; Subj: Related. ISSN: 0159-6330
■Dance Australia Publications; 2 Yaralla Court; 3173 Keysborough; AUSTRALIA.

DalVostok *Dalnij Vostok*: (Far East). Freq: 12; Began: 1933; Cov: Scan; Lang: Rus; Subj: Related. ISSN: 0130-3023
■Khabarovsk; USSR.

DB *Deutsche Bühne, Die*. Freq: 12; Began: 1909; Cov: Scan; Lang: Ger; Subj: Theatre. ISSN: 0011-975X
■Deutscher Buehnenverein, Quatermarkt 5; D-5000 Cologne; WEST GERMANY.

DBj *Deutsches Bühnenjahrbuch*. Freq: 1; Lang: Ger; Subj: Theatre.
■Buhnenschriften-Vetrieb-Gesellschaft; Feldbrunnenstrasse 74; 2000 Hamburg 13; WEST GERMANY.

DC *Dance in Canada/Danse au Canada*. Freq: 4; Began: 1973; Lang: Eng/Fre; Subj: Theatre. ISSN: 0317-9737
■Dance in Canada Association; 4700 Keele St.; Downsview, ON M3J 1P3; CANADA.

DCD *Documents del Centre Dramatic*. Freq: 4; Cov: Scan; Lang: Spa; Subj: Theatre.
■c/o Hospital, 51, 1er; Barcelona 08001; SPAIN.

DekorIsk *Dekorativnoje Iskusstvo SSR*. Freq: 12; Began: 1957; Cov: Scan; Lang: Rus; Subj: Related. ISSN: 0418-5153
■Soveckij Chudožnik; Moscow; USSR.

DetLit *Detskaja Literatura*. Freq: 12; Began: 1932; Cov: Scan; Lang: Rus; Subj: Related. ISSN: 0130-3104
■Moscow; USSR.

Devlet *Devlet Tijatrolari (State Theatres)*. Freq: 4; Lang: Tur; Subj: Theatre.
■Genel Mudurugu; Ankara; TURKEY.

Dewan *Dewan Budaya*. Freq: 12; Began: 1979; Lang: Mal; Subj: Theatre. ISSN: 0126-8473
■Peti Surat 803; Kuala Lumpur; MALAYSIA.

DGQ *Dramatists Guild Quarterly*. Freq: 4; Began: 1964; Cov: Scan; Lang: Eng; Subj: Theatre. ISSN: 0012-6004
■The Dramatists Guild, Inc.; 234 W. 44th St.; New York, NY 10036; USA.

DHS *Dix-Huitième Siècle*. Freq: 1; Began: 1969; Cov: Scan; Lang: Fre; Subj: Related. ISSN: 0070-6760
■Soc. Française d'Etude du 18e Siecle; 23 Quai de Grenelle; 75015 Paris; FRANCE.

DialogA *Dialog*. Freq: 10; Began: 1973; Lang: Ger; Subj: Theatre. ISSN: 0378-6935
■Verlag Sauerländer; Laurenzenvorstadt 89; CH 5001 Aarau; SWITZERLAND.

DialogTu *Dialogue*. Lang: Fre; Subj: Theatre.
■Parti Socialiste Desourien, Maison du Parti, BP 1033; Blvd. du 9 Avril, La Kasbah; Tunis; TUNISIA.

Dialogue *Dialogue*: Canadian Philosophical Review/Revue Canadienne de Philosophie. Freq: 4; Began: 1962; Lang: Eng; Subj: Related. ISSN: 0012-2173
■Montreal, PQ; CANADA.

DialogW *Dialog*: Miesiecznik Poswiecony Dramaturgii Wspolczesnej. Freq: 12; Began: 1956; Cov: Full; Lang: Pol; Subj: Theatre. ISSN: 0012-2041
■Wydawnictwo Wspolczesne, RSW Prasa-Ksiazka-Ruch; Ul. Wiejska 12; 00-420 Warsaw; POLAND.

DiN *Divadelni Noviny.* Freq: 26; Began: 1970; Lang: Cze; Subj: Theatre.
ISSN: 0012-4141
■Svaz Ceskoslovenskych Divadelnich a Rozhlasovych Umelcu; Valdstejnske nam. 3; Prague 1; CZECHOSLOVAKIA.

Dioniso *Dioniso.* Freq: 1; Began: 1929; Lang: Ita/Eng/Fre/Spa; Subj: Theatre.
■Instituto Nazionale del Dramma Antico; Corso Matteoti 29; Siracusa; ITALY.

DIPFL *Deutsches Institut für Puppenspiel Forschung und Lehre.* Freq: IRR; Began: 1964; Lang: Ger; Subj: Theatre. ISSN: 0070-4490
■Deutsches Institut für Puppenspiel; Bergstrasse 115; 4630 Bochum; WEST GERMANY.

DirNotes *Directors Notes.* Lang: Eng; Subj: Theatre.
■American Directors Institute; 248 W. 74th St., Suite 10; New York, NY 10023; USA.

Diskurs *Diskurs.* Freq: 4; Lang: Ger; Subj: Theatre.
■Schauble Verlag; Waldgurtel 5; 506 Bensberg; WEST GERMANY.

DivR *Divadelni revue.* Freq: 4; Began: 1990; Lang: Cze; Subj: Theatre. ISSN: 0862-5409
■Academia; Vodickova 40; Prague 1; CZECHOSLOVAKIA.

Dm *Dance Magazine.* Freq: 12; Began: 1926; Lang: Eng; Subj: Related.
ISSN: 0011-6009
■Dance Magazine, Inc.; 33 W. 60th St.; New York, NY 10023; USA.

DMC *Dramatics.* Freq: 9; Began: 1929; Lang: Eng; Subj: Theatre. ISSN: 0012-5989
■International Thespian Society; 3368 Central Parkway; Cincinnati, OH 45225; USA.

DnC *Dance Chronicle: Studies in Dance & the Related Arts.* Freq: 2; Began: 1978; Cov: Scan; Lang: Eng; Subj: Theatre. ISSN: 0147-2526
■Marcel Dekker Journals; 270 Madison Avenue; New York, NY 10016; USA.

DNDT *Drama:* Nordisk dramapedagogisk Tidskrift. Freq: 4; Began: 1963; Lang: Nor/Swe/Dan; Subj: Theatre.
■Landslaget Drama i skolen, Jerikoveien 97A; Furuset; 10 Oslo; NORWAY.

Dockt *Dockteatereko.* Freq: 4; Began: 1971; Lang: Swe; Subj: Theatre. ISSN: 0349-9944
■Dockteaterforeningen; Sandavagen 10; 14032 Grodinge; SWEDEN.

DocTh *Documentation Théâtrale.* Began: 1974; Lang: Fre; Subj: Theatre.
■Centre d'Etudes Théâtrales, Université Paris X; 200 Avenue de la République; 92001 Nanterre Cedex; FRANCE.

DOE *DOE.* Formerly: *Speel.* Freq: 24; Began: 1951; Lang: Dut; Subj: Theatre.
ISSN: 0038-7258
■Stichting Ons Leekenspel'; Gudelalaan 2; Bussum; NETHERLANDS.

DongukDA *Dong-Guk Dramatic Art.* Freq: 1; Began: 1970; Cov: Full; Lang: Kor; Subj: Theatre.
■Department of Drama & Cinema, Dong-guk University; Seoul; KOREA.

Drama *Drama: The Quarterly Theatre Review:* Third Series. Formerly: *Drama.* Freq: 4; Began: 1919; Ceased: 1989; Cov: Scan; Lang: Eng; Subj: Theatre. ISSN: 0012-5946
■British Theatre Association, Regent's College Inner Circle; Regent's Park; London NW1 4NW; UK.

DramaY *Drama.* Lang: Slo; Subj: Theatre.
■Erjavceva; Ljubljana; YUGOSLAVIA.

DrammaR *Dramma.* Freq: 12; Began: 1925; Cov: Scan; Lang: Ita; Subj: Theatre. ISSN: 0012-6004
■Romana Teatri s.r.l.; Via Torino 29; 00184 Rome; ITALY.

DrammaT *Dramma:* Il Mensile dello Spettacolo. Freq: 12; Lang: Ita; Subj: Theatre.
■I.L.T.E.; Corso Bramante 20; Turin; ITALY.

Dress *Dress.* Freq: 1; Lang: Eng; Subj: Related.
■Costume Society of America; 15 Little John Road, PO Box 761; Englishtown, NJ 07726; USA.

DRJ *Dance Research Journal.* Freq: 2; Began: 1967; Lang: Eng; Subj: Related.
ISSN: 0149-7677
■Congress on Research in Dance, NYU Dept. Dance Education 675D; 35 W. 4th St.; New York, NY 10003; USA.

DRostock *Diskurs.* Freq: 3; Began: 1973; Lang: Ger; Subj: Theatre.
■Volkstheater Rostock; Patriotischer Weg 33; 25 Rostock; EAST GERMANY.

DrRev *Drama Review.* Freq: 2; Began: 1970; Lang: Kor; Subj: Theatre.
■Yonguk-pyongron-sa; 131-51 Nokbun-dong, Eunpyong-ku; 122 Seoul; SOUTH KOREA.

DRs *Dance Research.* Freq: 2; Lang: Eng; Subj: Related.
■17 Dules's Road; WC 1H 9AB London; UK.

Druzba *Družba.* Freq: 6; Began: 1977; Cov: Scan; Lang: Rus/Bul; Subj: Related.
ISSN: 0320-1021
■Moscow;.

DruzNar *Družba Narodov.* Freq: 12; Began: 1939; Cov: Scan; Lang: Rus; Subj: Related.
ISSN: 0012-6756
■Moscow; USSR.

DSat *Don Saturio: Boletin Informativo de Teatro Gallego.* Lang: Spa; Subj: Theatre.
■Coruna 70-30; Esda; SPAIN.

DSchool *Drama and the School.* Freq: 2; Began: 1948; Lang: Eng; Subj: Theatre.
■Whitehall Productions; 63 Elizabeth Bay Road; NSW 2011 Elizabeth Bay; AUSTRALIA.

DSGM *Dokumenti Slovenskega Gledaliskega Muzeja.* Freq: 2; Began: 1964; Lang: Slo; Subj: Theatre.
■Slovenski Gledaliski in Filski muzej; Cankarjeva 11; Ljubljana; YUGOSLAVIA.

DSo *Dramatists Sourcebook.* Formerly: *Information for Playwrights.* Freq: 1; Began: 1981; Cov: Scan; Lang: Eng; Subj: Theatre.
ISSN: 0733-1606
■Theatre Comm. Group, Inc; 355 Lexington Ave.; New York, NY 10017; USA.

DSS *Dix-Septième Siècle.* Freq: 4; Began: 1949; Cov: Scan; Lang: Fre; Subj: Related. ISSN: 0012-4273

■Commission des Publications, c/o Collège de France; 11 Place M. Berthelot; 75005 Paris; FRANCE.

DTh *Divadlo:* (Theatre). Freq: 2; Lang: Slo; Subj: Theatre.
■Prague; CZECHOSLOVAKIA.

Dtherapy *Dramatherapy:* SEE: Journal of Dramatherapy (JDt). Lang: Eng; Subj: Theatre.
■The Old Mill, Tolpuddle; Dorchester; Dorset DT2 7EX; UK.

DTi *Dancing Times.* Freq: 12; Began: 1910; Lang: Eng; Subj: Theatre. ISSN: 0011-605X
■Dancing Times Ltd., Clerkenwell House; 45-47 Clerkenwell Green; EC1R 0BE London; UK.

DTJ *Dance Theatre Journal.* Freq: 4; Began: 1983; Cov: Scan; Lang: Eng; Subj: Theatre.
■Laban Centre for Movement & Dance, Goldsmiths' College; SE15 6NW London; UK.

DTN *Drama and Theatre Newsletter.* Freq: 4; Began: 1975; Ceased: 1982; Lang: Eng; Subj: Theatre.
■British Theatre Institute; 30 Clareville Street; SW7 5AW London; UK.

DTOP *Dramaturgi: Tedri Og Praksis.* Lang: Dan; Subj: Theatre.
■Akademisk Forlag; St. Kannikestraede 8; 1169 Copenhagen; DENMARK.

DZP *Deutsche Zeitschrift für Philosophie.* Freq: 12; Began: 1953; Cov: Scan; Lang: Ger; Subj: Related. ISSN: 0012-1045
■VEB Deutscher Verlag der Wissenschaften; Johannes-Dieckmann-Str. 10, Postfach 1216; 1080 Berlin; EAST GERMANY.

E&AM *Entertainment and Arts Manager.* Formerly: *Entertainment and Arts Management.* Freq: 4; Began: 1973; Ceased: 1989; Cov: Scan; Lang: Eng; Subj: Theatre. ISSN: 0143-8980
■Assoc. of Entertainment & Arts Mangement, T.G. Scott and Son Ltd.; 30-32 Southampton St., Covent Garden; WC2E 7HR London; UK.

EAR *English Academy Review, The.* Began: 1983; Cov: Scan; Lang: Eng; Subj: Related.
■English Academy of Southern Africa, Bollater House; 35 Melle St., Braamfontein; 2001 Johannesburg; SOUTH AFRICA.

Ebony *Ebony.* Freq: 12; Began: 1945; Cov: Scan; Lang: Eng; Subj: Related. ISSN: 0012-9011
■Johnson Publishing Co., Inc.; 820 S. Michigan; Chicago, IL 60605; USA.

Echanges *Echanges.* Freq: 12; Lang: Fre; Subj: Theatre.
■Théâtre Romain-Rolland; rue Eugène Varlin; 94 Villejuif; FRANCE.

Econ *Economist Financial Report.* Freq: 48; Began: 1976; Lang: Eng; Subj: Related.
ISSN: 0013-0613
■Economist Newspaper Ltd.; 25 St. James St.; SW1A 1HG London; UK.

ECr *Esprit Créateur, L'.* Freq: 4; Began: 1961; Lang: Fre; Subj: Theatre.
ISSN: 0014-0767
■John D. Erickson; Box 222; Lawrence, KS 66044; USA.

ECrit   *Essays in Criticism*. Freq: 4; Began: 1951; Lang: Eng; Subj: Related.
ISSN: 0014-0856
■6A Rawlinson Rd.; Oxford OX2 6UE; UK.

ED   *Envers du Décor, L'*. Freq: 6; Began: 1973; Lang: Fre; Subj: Theatre.
ISSN: 0319-8650
■Théâtre du Nouveau Monde; 84 Ouest, Rue Ste-Catharine; Montreal, PQ H2X 1Z6; CANADA.

EDAM   *EDAM Newsletter*. Freq: 2; Began: 1978; Cov: Scan; Lang: Eng; Subj: Theatre.
ISSN: 0196-5816
■Medieval Institute Publications; Western Michigan University; Kalamazoo, MI 49008; USA.

EE&PA   *Economic Efficiency and the Performing Arts*. Lang: Eng; Subj: Theatre.
■Association for Cultural Economics, University of Akron; Akron, OH 44235; USA.

EECIT   *Estudis Escenics*. Freq: 2; Began: 1979; Cov: Full; Lang: Cat; Subj: Theatre.
ISSN: 0212-3819
■Inst. del Theatre de Barcelona, c/o Nou de la Rambla; 08001 Barcelona 3; SPAIN.

Egk   *Engekikai*: Theatre World. Freq: 12; Began: 1940; Lang: Jap; Subj: Theatre.
■Engeki Shuppan-sha, Chiyoda-ku; 2-11 Kanda-Jinpo-cho; Tokyo 101; JAPAN.

EHR   *Economic History Review*. Freq: 4; Began: 1927; Lang: Eng; Subj: Related.
ISSN: 0013-0117
■Economic History Society, University of Birmingham; Faculty of Commerce & Social Science; Birmingham; UK.

Eire   *Eire-Ireland*. Freq: 4; Began: 1966; Cov: Scan; Lang: Eng; Subj: Related.
ISSN: 0013-2683
■Irish American Cultural Institute; 683 Osceola Ave.; St. Paul, MN 55105; USA.

EIT   *Escena*: Informativo Teatral. Freq: 4; Began: 1979; Lang: Spa; Subj: Theatre.
■Universidad de Costa Rica, Teatro Universitario, Apt. 92; San Pedro de Montes de Oca; San José; COSTA RICA.

Elet   *Eletünk*. Freq: 04; Began: 1963; Cov: Scan; Lang: Hun; Subj: Related.
ISSN: 0133-4751
■Vas Megyei Lapkiado Vallalat; P.O.B. 168; 9701 Szombathely; HUNGARY.

ElI   *Elet és Irodalom*: irodalmi es politkai hetilap. Freq: 52; Began: 1957; Lang: Hun; Subj: Related. ISSN: 0424-8848
■Ft. Lapkiado Vallalat; Széchenyi rkp. 1; 1054 Budapest V; HUNGARY.

ElM   *Marges, El*. Freq: 3; Cov: Scan; Lang: Cat; Subj: Related.
■Curial Edicions Catalanes del Bruc; 144 Baixos; 08037 Barcelona; SPAIN.

ElPu   *Publico, El*: Periodico mensual de teatro. Freq: 12; Began: 1983; Cov: Scan; Lang: Spa; Subj: Theatre. ISSN: 0213-4926
■Centro de Documentación Teatral; c/ Capitán Haya, 44; 28020 Madrid; SPAIN.

ELR   *English Literary Renaissance Journal*. Cov: Scan; Lang: Eng; Subj: Related.
■University of Massachusetts; Boston, MA 02125; USA.

EN   *Equity News*. Freq: 12; Began: 1915; Cov: Scan; Lang: Eng; Subj: Theatre.
ISSN: 0013-9890
■Actors Equity Association; 165 W. 46 St.; New York, NY 10036; USA.

Enact   *Enact*: monthly theatre magazine. Freq: 12; Began: 1967; Cov: Scan; Lang: Eng; Subj: Theatre. ISSN: 0013-6980
■Paul's Press, E44-11; Okhla Industrial Area, Phase II; 110020 New Delhi; INDIA.

Encore   *Encore*. Lang: Eng; Subj: Theatre.
■Fort Valley State College; Fort Valley, GA 31030; USA.

EncoreA   *Encore*. Freq: 12; Began: 1976; Lang: Eng; Subj: Theatre.
■PO Box 247; NSW 2154 Castle Hill; AUSTRALIA.

ENG   *Editorial Nuevo Grupo*. Lang: Spa; Subj: Theatre.
■Avenida La Colina, Prolongación Los Manolos; La Florida; 105 Caracas; VENEZUELA.

Entre   *Entré*. Freq: 6; Began: 1974; Cov: Full; Lang: Swe; Subj: Theatre. ISSN: 0345-2581
■Svenska Riksteatern, Swedish National Theatre Centre; S-145 83 ; Norsborg; SWEDEN.

EON   *Eugene O'Neill Review*. Freq: 3; Began: 1977; Cov: Full; Lang: Eng; Subj: Theatre. Formerly: Eugene O'Neill Newsletter, The   ISSN: 0733-0456
■Suffolk University, Department of English; Boston, MA 02114; USA.

EpicT   *Epic Theatre*. Freq: 4; Lang: Ben; Subj: Theatre.
■140/24 Netaji Subhashchandra Bose Road; Calcutta; INDIA.

EquityJ   *Equity Journal*. Freq: 4; Began: 1931; Lang: Eng; Subj: Theatre. ISSN: 0141-3147
■British Actor's Equity Association; 8 Harley St.; London W1N 2AB; UK.

ERT   *Empirical Research in Theatre*. Freq: 1; Began: 1971; Ceased: 1984; Cov: Full; Lang: Eng; Subj: Theatre. ISSN: 0361-2767
■Center for Communications Research; Bowling Green State University; Bowling Green, OH 43403; USA.

ESA   *English Studies in Africa: A Journal of the Humanities*. Freq: 2; Began: 1958; Cov: Scan; Lang: Eng; Subj: Related. ISSN: 0013-8398
■Witwatersrand Univ. Press; Jan Smuts Ave.; Johannesburg 2001; SOUTH AFRICA.

Escena   *Escena*. Lang: Spa; Subj: Theatre.
■Departamento de Publicaciones, Consejo Nacional de la Cultura; Calle Paris, Edificio Macanao 3er. Piso; 106 Caracas; VENEZUELA.

Espill   *Espill, L'*. Freq: 4; Cov: Scan; Lang: Cat; Subj: Related.
■Editorial 3 i 4, c/o Moratin 15; Porta 3; 46002 Valencia; SPAIN.

Esprit   *Esprit*. Freq: 12; Began: 1932; Lang: Fre; Subj: Related. ISSN: 0014-0759
■19, rue Jacob; 75006 Paris; FRANCE.

Essence   *Essence*. Freq: 12; Began: 1970; Cov: Scan; Lang: Eng; Subj: Related. ISSN: 0014-0880

■Essence Comm., Inc.; P.O. Box 53400 Boulder, CO 80322-3400; USA.

EstLit   *Estafeta Literaria*: La Revista Quincenal de Libros, Artes y Espetáculos. Freq: 24; Began: 1958; Lang: Spa; Subj: Theatre. ISSN: 0014-1186
■Avda. de José Antonio, 62; 13 Madrid; SPAIN.

Estreno   *Estreno*: Journal on the Contemporary Spanish Theater. Freq: 2; Began: 1975; Cov: Full; Lang: Eng/Spa; Subj: Theatre.
ISSN: 0097-8663
■University of Cincinnati, Dept. of Romance Languages & Lit; Cincinnati, OH 45221; USA.

ET   *Essays in Theatre*. Freq: 2; Began: 1982; Cov: Full; Lang: Eng; Subj: Theatre.
ISSN: 0821-4425
■University of Guelph, Department of Drama; Guelph, ON N1G 2W1; CANADA.

ETh   *Elizabethan Theatre*. Began: 1968; Lang: Eng; Subj: Theatre. ISSN: 0071-0032
■Archon Books; 995 Sherman Avenue; Hamden, CT 06514; USA.

ETN   *Educational Theatre News*. Freq: 6; Began: 1953; Lang: Eng; Subj: Theatre.
ISSN: 0013-1997
■Southern California Education Theatre Association; 9811 Pounds Avenue; Whittier, CA 90603; USA.

Etoile   *Etoile de la Foire*. Freq: 12; Began: 1945; Lang: Fle/Fre; Subj: Theatre.
ISSN: 0014-1895
■15 rue Vanderlinden; Brussels 3; BELGIUM.

Europe   *Europe*: Revue Littéraire Mensuelle. Freq: 8; Began: 1923; Cov: Scan; Lang: Fre; Subj: Related. ISSN: 0014-2751
■146, rue du Fg. Poisonnière; 75010 Paris; FRANCE.

Evento   *Evento Teatrale*. Freq: 3; Began: 1975; Lang: Ita; Subj: Theatre.
■A.BE.TE.spa; Via Presentina 683; 00155 Rome; ITALY.

Exchange   *Exchange*. Freq: 3; Began: 1977; Lang: Eng; Subj: Theatre.
■University of Missouri: Columbia, Dept. of Speech/Drama; 129 Fine Arts Centre; Columbia, MS 65211; USA.

Farsa   *Farsa, La*. Freq: 20; Lang: Spa; Subj: Theatre.
■Pza. de los Mostenses 11; 9 Madrid; SPAIN.

FDi   *Film a Divadlo*. Freq: 26; Lang: Cze; Subj: Related.
■Theatre Intitute in Bratislava; Obzor, Ceskoslovenskej Armady 35; Bratislava 815 85; CZECHOSLOVAKIA.

Fds   *Freedomways*: A Quarterly Review of the Freedom Movement. Freq: 4; Began: 1961; Cov: Scan; Lang: Eng; Subj: Related. ISSN: 0016-061X
■Freedomways Assoc., Inc.; 799 Broadway; New York, NY 10003 6849; USA.

FemR   *Feminist Review*. Freq: 3; Began: 1979; Lang: Eng; Subj: Related. ISSN: 0141-7789
■11 Carleton Gardens, Brecknock Rd.; London N19 5AQ; UK.

FG   *Fremantle Gazette*. Freq: 24; Began: 1977; Cov: Scan; Lang: Eng; Subj: Related.

■Community Newspapers; 7 High Street; Fremantle WA 6160; AUSTRALIA.

Fikr   *Al Fikr*. Lang: Ara; Subj: Theatre.
■Rue Dar Eg-gild; Tunis; TUNISIA.

FiloK   *Filológiai Közlöny*: Philological Review. Freq: 4; Began: 1955; Cov: Scan; Lang: Hun; Subj: Related. ISSN: 0015-1785
■Akademiai Kiado, Hungarian Academy of Sciences; Pesti Barnabás u. 1. IV. em 5-6; 1052 Budapest V; HUNGARY.

FIRTSIB   *FIRT/SIBMAS Bulletin d'information*. Freq: 4; Began: 1977; Lang: Fre/Eng; Subj: Theatre. Federation International pour la Recherch Theatrale; c/o van Eeghenstraat 11311, 1071 EZ Amsterdam; NETHERLANDS.

FMa   *Fight Master, The*. Freq: 4; Lang: Eng; Subj: Theatre.
■Society of American Fight Directors; 1834 Camp Avenue; Rockford, IL 61103; USA.

FN   *Filologičeskije Nauki*. Freq: 6; Began: 1958; Cov: Scan; Lang: Rus; Subj: Related. ISSN: 0470-4649
■Izdatelstvo VysšajaŠkola; Prospekt Marksa 18; 103009 Moscow K-9; USSR.

Fnotes   *Footnotes*. Freq: 1; Began: 1975; Lang: Eng; Subj: Theatre.
■Stagestep; Box 328; Philadelphia, PA 19105; USA.

FO   *Federal One*. Freq: IRR; Began: 1975; Cov: Scan; Lang: Eng; Subj: Related.
■George Mason University; 4400 University Dr.; Fairfax, VA 22030; USA.

Forras   *Forrás*. Freq: 10; Began: 1969; Cov: Scan; Lang: Hun; Subj: Related.
■Bacs Kiskun Megyei, Lapkiado Vallalat; Szabadság tér l/a; 6001 Kecskemét; HUNGARY.

FR   *French Review, The*. Freq: 6; Began: 1927; Lang: Fre/Eng; Subj: Related. ISSN: 0016-111X
■American Association of Teachers of French; 57 E. Armory Ave.; Champaign, IL 61820; USA.

FranceT   *France Théâtre*. Freq: 24; Began: 1957; Lang: Fre; Subj: Theatre. ISSN: 0015-9433
■Syndicat National des Agences; 16 Avenue l'Opéra; 75001 Paris; FRANCE.

FrF   *French Forum*. Freq: 3; Began: 1976; Lang: Fre/Eng; Subj: Related. ISSN: 0098-9355
■French Forum Publishers, Inc.; Box 5108; Lexington, KY 40505; USA.

FS   *French Studies*: A quarterly review. Freq: 4; Began: 1947; Lang: Eng; Subj: Related.2 ISSN: 0016-1128
■Society for French Studies, c/o M.J. Tilby; Selwyn College; CB3 9DQ Cambridge; UK.

FSM   *Film, Szinház, Muzsika*. Freq: 52; Began: 1957; Cov: Scan; Lang: Hun; Subj: Theatre. ISSN: 0015-1416
■Lapkiado Vallalat; Lenin korut 9-11; 1073 Budapest VII; HUNGARY.

Ftr   *Figurentheater*. Freq: IRR; Began: 1923; Lang: Ger; Subj: Theatre. ISSN: 0430-3873

■Deutsches Institut für Puppenspiel; Hattingerstr. 467; D-4630 Bochum; WEST GERMANY.

Fundarte   *Fundarte*. Lang: Spa; Subj: Theatre.
■Edificio Tajamar, P.H., Parque Central; Avenida Lecuna; 105 Caracas; VENEZUELA.

FundM   *Fundraising Management*. Freq: 12; Began: 1972; Cov: Scan; Lang: Eng; Subj: Related.
■Hoke Communications Inc.; 224 7th Street; Garden City, NY 11530-5771 USA.

Funoun   *Al Funoun*: The Arts. Freq: 12; Lang: Ara; Subj: Theatre.
■Ministry of Information, Dept. of Culture and Arts; PO Box 6140; Amman; JORDAN.

Gambit   *Gambit*. Freq: IRR; Began: 1963; Ceased: 1986; Cov: Scan; Lang: Eng; Subj: Theatre. ISSN: 0016-4283
■John Calder, Ltd.; 9-15 Neal Street; WC2H 9TU London; UK.

Gap   *Gap, The*. Cov: Scan; Lang: Eng; Subj: Related.
■Washington, DC; USA.

GaR   *Georgia Review*. Freq: 4; Began: 1947; Lang: Eng; Subj: Related. ISSN: 0016-8386
■University of Georgia; Athens, GA 30602; USA.

Garcin   *Garcin: Libro de Cultura*. Freq: 12; Began: 1981; Lang: Spa; Subj: Related.
■Acali Editoria; Ituzaingo 1495; Montevideo; URUGUAY.

Gazit   *Gazit*. Lang: Heb; Subj: Theatre.
■8 Brook Street; Tel Aviv; ISRAEL.

GdBA   *Gazette des Beaux Arts*. Freq: 10; Began: 1859; Cov: Scan; Lang: Fre; Subj: Related. ISSN: 0016-5530
■Imprimerie Louis Jean, B.P. 87; Gap Cedex 05002; SWITZERLAND.

GdF   *Gazette du Français*. Lang: Fre; Subj: Related.
■Paris; FRANCE.

GdS   *Giornale dello Spettacolo*. Freq: 52; Lang: Ita; Subj: Theatre. ISSN: 0017-0232
■Associazione Generale Italiana dello Spettacolo; Via di Villa Patrizi 10; 00161 Rome; ITALY.

GerSR   *German Studies Review*. Freq: 3; Began: 1978; Cov: Scan; Lang: Ger; Subj: Related. ISSN: 0149-7952
■German Studies Association, c/o Prof. Gerald R. Kleinfeld; Arizona State University; Tempe, AZ 85287; USA.

Gestos   *Gestos*: teoria y practica del teatro hispanico. Began: 1984; Cov: Scan; Lang:Eng /Spa; Subj: Theatre. ISSN: 1040-483X
■University of California, Irvine, School of Humanities; Dept. of Spanish and Portugese; Irvine, CA 92717; USA.

Gestus   *Gestus*: A Quarterly Journal of Brechtian Studies. Freq: 4; Began: 1985; Cov: Full; Lang: Eng/Ger/Fre/Ita/Spa; Subj: Theatre. ISSN: 0749-7644
■Brecht Society of America; 59 S. New St.; Dover, DE 19901; USA.

GL&L   *German Life and Letters*. Freq: 4; Began: 1936; Cov: Scan; Lang: Eng; Subj: Related. ISSN: 0016-8777
■Basil Blackwell Publisher, Ltd.; 108 Cowley Road; 0X4 1JF Oxford; UK.

GOS   *Gazette Officielle du Spectacle*. Freq: 36; Began: 1969; Lang: Fre; Subj: Theatre.
■Office des Nouvelles Internationales; 12 rue de Miromesnil; 75008 Paris; FRANCE.

Gosteri   *Gosteri*: Performance. Freq: 12; Lang: Tur; Subj: Theatre.
■Uluslararasi Sanat Gosterileri A.S.; Narlpbahce Sok. 15; Cagaloglu-Istanbul; TURKEY.

GQ   *German Quarterly*. Freq: 4; Began: 1928; Cov: Scan; Lang: Ger; Subj: Related. ISSN: 0016-8831
■American Assoc. of Teachers of German; 523 Building, Suite 201, Rt. 38; Cherry Hill, NJ 08034; USA.

GrandR   *Grande République*. Formerly: *Pratiques Théâtrales*. Freq: 3; Began: 1978; Ceased: 1981; Lang: Fre; Subj: Theatre. ISSN: 0714-8178
■University of Québec; 200 Rue Sherbrooke Ouest; Montreal, PQ H2X 3P2; CANADA.

GSJ   *Gilbert and Sullivan Journal*. Freq: 3; Began: 1925; Ceased: 1986; Lang: Eng; Subj: Theatre. ISSN: 0016-9951
■Gilbert and Sullivan Society; 23 Burnside, Sawbridgeworth; CM21 OEP Hertfordshire; UK.

GSTB   *George Spelvin's Theatre Book*. Freq: 3; Began: 1978; Cov: Scan; Lang: Eng; Subj: Theatre. ISSN: 0730-6431
■Proscenium Press; Box 361; Newark, NJ 19711; USA.

GTAR   *Grupo Teatral Antifaz: Revista*. Freq: 12; Lang: Spa; Subj: Theatre.
■San Addres 146; 16 Barcelona; SPAIN.

GtE   *Guidateatro: Estera*. Freq: 1; Began: 1967; Lang: Ita; Subj: Theatre.
■Edizione Teatron; Via Fabiola 1; 00152 Rome; ITALY.

GtI   *Guidateatro: Italiana*. Freq: 1; Began: 1967; Lang: Ita; Subj: Theatre.
■Edizione Teatron; Via Fabiola 1; 00152 Rome; ITALY.

Guida   *Guida dello Spettacolo*. Lang: Ita; Subj: Theatre.
■Via Palombini 6; Rome; ITALY.

Harlekijn   *Harlekijn*. Freq: 4; Began: 1970; Lang: Dut; Subj: Theatre.
■Kerkdijk 11; 3615 BA Westbroek; NETHERLANDS.

Hecate   *Hecate: Women's Interdisciplinary Journal*. Freq: 2; Began: 1975; Cov: Scan; Lang: Eng; Subj: Related. ISSN: 0311-4198
■Hecate Press; English Dept., University of Queensland; P.O. Box 99 St. Lucia, Qld. 4067; AUSTRALIA.

Helik   *Helikon*: Vilagirodalmi Figyelo. Freq: 4; Began: 1955; Lang: Hun; Subj: Related. ISSN: 0017-999X
■Akademiai Kiado,; Ménesi u. 11-13; 1118 Budapest; HUNGARY.

Hermes   *Hermes: Zeitschrift für Klassische Philologie*. Freq: 4; Began: 1866; Cov: Scan; Lang: Ger; Subj: Related. ISSN: 0018-0777

■Franz Steiner Verlag Wiesbaden GmbH; Birkenwaldstr. 44; Postfach 347; D-7000; Stuttgart 1; WEST GERMANY.

HgK   *Higeki Kigeki*: Tragedy and Comedy. Freq: 12; Began: 1948; Lang: Jap; Subj: Theatre.
■Hayakawa-Shobo, Chiyoda-ku; 2-2 Kanda-Tacho; 101 Tokyo; JAPAN.

HispArts   *Hispanic Arts*. Freq: 5; Began: 1976; Lang: Spa/Eng; Subj: Theatre.
■Association of Hispanic Arts Inc.; 200 East 87th Street; New York, NY 10028; USA.

HisSt   *Historical Studies*. Formerly: *Historical Studies: Australia and New Zealand*. Freq: 2; Began: 1940; Lang: Eng; Subj: Related.   ISSN: 0018-2559
■University of Melbourne, Dept. of History; Parkville 3052; AUSTRALIA.

HJFTR   *Historical Journal of Film, TV, Radio*. Freq: 2; Began: 1980; Lang: Eng; Subj: Related.   ISSN: 0143-9685
■Carfax Pulbishing Co.; Box 25; OX14 3UE Abingdon; UK.

Horis   *Horisont*. Freq: 6; Began: 1954; Cov: Scan; Lang: Swe; Subj: Related. ISSN: 0439-5530
■Svenska Oesterbottens Litteratur.; Fasanvagen 4; S 775 00 Krylbo; SWEDEN.

HP   *High Performance*. Freq: 4; Began: 1978; Lang: Eng; Subj: Related.   ISSN: 0160-9769
■Astro Artz; 240 S. Broadway, 5th Floor; Los Angeles, CA 90012; USA.

HSt   *Hamlet Studies*. Freq: 2; Began: 1978; Lang: Eng; Subj: Related.   ISSN: 0256-2480
■Rangoon Villa; 1/10 West Patel Nagar; 110 008 New Delhi; INDIA.

HTHD   *Hungarian Theatre/Hungarian Drama*. Freq: 1; Began: 1981; Lang: Eng; Subj: Theatre.   ISSN: 0230-1237
■Hungarian Theatre Institute; Kriszina krt. 57; 1016 Budapest; HUNGARY.

HW   *History Workshop*. Freq: 2; Began: 1976; Lang: Eng; Subj: Related.   ISSN: 0309-2984
■Routledge & Kegan Paul Ltd., Broadway House; Newton Rd.; RG9 1EN Henley-on-Thames; UK.

IA   *Ibsenårboken/Ibsen Yearbook*: Contemporary Approaches to Ibsen. Freq: 1; Began: 1952; Cov: Full; Lang: Nor/Eng; Subj: Theatre.   ISSN: 0073-4365
■Universitetssorleget; Box 2959; 0608 Oslo 6; NORWAY.

IAS   *Interscena/Acta Scaenographica*. Freq: 2; Lang: Eng/Fre/Ger; Subj: Theatre.
■Divadelni Ustav; Celetna 17; Prague 1; CZECHOSLOVAKIA.

IdS   *Information du Spectacle, L'*. Freq: 11; Lang: Fre; Subj: Theatre.
■7 rue du Helder; 75009 Paris; FRANCE.

IDSelect   *Irish Drama Selections*. Freq: IRR; Began: 1982; Lang: Eng; Subj: Theatre.   ISSN: 0260-7964
■Colin Smythe Ltd., Box 6; Gerrards Cross; SL9 8XA Buckinghamshire; UK.

IHoL   *Irodalomtörténet*. Freq: 4; Began: 1912; Cov: Scan; Lang: Hun; Subj: Related.   ISSN: 0021-1478
■Akademiai Kiado, Pub. Hse. of Hung. Acad. Science; Pesti Barnabás u.1; 1052 Budapest V; HUNGARY.

IHS   *Irish Historical Studies*. Freq: 2; Began: 1938; Lang: Eng; Subj: Related.   ISSN: 0021-1214
■Irish Historical Society, Dept. of Modern Irish History; Arts-Commerce Bldg, University College; Dublin 4; IRELAND.

IITBI   *Instituto Internacional del Teatro, Centro Espanol*: Boletin Informativo. Freq: 4; Lang: Spa; Subj: Theatre.
■Paseo de Recoletos 18-60; 1 Madrid; SPAIN.

IK   *Irodalomtudományi Közlemények*. Freq: 24; Began: 1891; Cov: Scan; Lang: Hun; Subj: Related.   ISSN: 0021-1486
■Akademiai Kiado, Hungarian Academy of Sciences; Ménesi u. 11-13; 1118 Budapest XI; HUNGARY.

Impressum   *Impressum*. Freq: 4; Lang: Ger; Subj: Related.
■Henschelverlag Kunst und Gesellschaft; Oranienburger Strasse 67/68; 1040 Berlin; EAST GERMANY.

InArts   *In the Arts*: Search, Research, and Discovery. Began: 1978; Ceased: 1988; Lang: Eng; Subj: Related.
■Ohio State University, College of the Arts; Columbus, OH 43210; USA.

INC   *Ibsen News & Comments*. Freq: 1; Began: 1980; Cov: Scan; Lang: Eng; Subj: Theatre.
■Ibsen Society in America, Mellon Programs, Dekalb Hall 3; Pratt Institute; Brooklyn, NY 11205; USA.

Indonesia   *Indonesia*. Freq: 2; Began: 1966; Cov: Scan; Lang: Eng; Subj: Related. ISSN: 0019-7289
■Cornell University, Southeast Asia Program; 120 Uris Hall; Ithaca, NY 14853; USA.

IndSh   *Independent Shavian*. Freq: 3; Began: 1962; Lang: Eng; Subj: Theatre.   ISSN: 0019-3763
■The Bernard Shaw Society; Box 1373, Grand Central Station; New York, NY 10163; USA.

Info   *Information*, Lang: Eng; Subj: Theatre.   ISSN: 0133-2902
■Hungarian Centre of the ITI; Hevesi Sandor ter. 2; 1077 Budapest VII; HUNGARY.

InoLit   *Inostrannaja Literatura*: (Foreign Literature). Freq: 12; Began: 1955; Cov: Scan; Lang: Rus; Subj: Related. ISSN: 0130-6545
■Moscow; USSR.

ISK   *Iskusstvo Kino*. Freq: 12; Cov: Scan; Lang: Rus; Subj: Related.   ISSN: 0021-1788

Iskusstvo   *Iskusstvo*. Freq: 12; Began: 1918; Cov: Scan; Lang: Rus; Subj: Related. ISSN: 0131-2278
■Tsvetnoi Bulvar 25; K 51 Moscow; USSR.

ISPTC   *Istituto di Studi Pirandelliani e sul Teatro Contemporaneo*. Freq: 1; Began: 1967; Lang: Ita; Subj: Theatre.   ISSN: 0075-1480
■Casa Editrice Felice le Monnier; Via Scipione Ammirato 100; 50136 Florence; ITALY.

ISST   *In Sachen Spiel und Theater*. Freq: 6; Began: 1949; Lang: Ger; Subj: Theatre.
■Höfling Verlag, Dr. V. Mayer; Str. 18-22; 6940 Weinheim; WEST GERMANY.

ITY   *International Theatre Yearbook*: SEE: Miedzynarodowny Rocznik Teatralny (Acro: MRT). Lang: Pol; Subj: Theatre.
■Warsaw; POLAND.

IUR   *Irish University Review*. Freq: 2; Began: 1970; Cov: Scan; Lang: Eng; Subj: Related.   ISSN: 0021-1427
■Wolfhound Press, University College; Room J210, Belfield; Dublin 4; IRELAND.

IW   *Ireland of the Welcomes*. Freq: 24; Began: 1952; Cov: Scan; Lang: Eng; Subj: Related.   ISSN: 0021-0943
■Bord Failte - Irish Tourist Board; Baggot St. Bridge; Dublin 2; IRELAND.

JAC   *Journal of American Culture*. Freq: 4; Began: 1978; Cov: Scan; Lang: Eng; Subj: Related.   ISSN: 0191-1813
■American Culture Association, Bowling Green State University; Popular Culture Center; Bowling Green, OH 43403; USA.

JADT   *Journal of American Drama and Theatre, The*. Freq: 3; Began: 1989; Lang: Eng; Subj: Theatre.
■CASTA, Grad. School and Univ. Centre, City University of New York; 33 West 42nd Street; New York, NY 10036; USA.

JAfS   *Journal of African Studies*. Freq: 4; Began: 1974; Cov: Scan; Lang: Eng; Subj: Related.   ISSN: 0095-4993
■Heldref Publications; 4000 Albemarle St, N.W.; Wasington, DC 20016; USA.

JAML   *Journal of Arts Management and Law*. Freq: 4; Began: 1969; Cov: Full; Lang: Eng; Subj: Related.   ISSN: 0733-5113
■Heldref Publications; 400 Albemarle St., N.W.; Washington, DC 20016; USA.

JAP&M   *Journal of Arts Policy and Mangement*. Freq: 3; Began: 1984; Ceased: 1989; Cov: Full; Lang: Eng; Subj: Theatre. ISSN: 0265-0924
■City University, Dept. of Arts Policy and Management; Level 12, Frobisher Crescent; Barbican, Silk Street; EC2Y 8HB London; UK.

JASt   *Journal of Asian Studies*. Freq: 4; Began: 1941; Cov: Scan; Lang: Eng; Subj: Related.   ISSN: 0021-9118
■Association for Asian Studies, Inc., University of Michigan; One Lane Hall; Ann Arbor, MI 48109; USA.

Javisko   *Javisko*. Freq: 12; Lang: Cze; Subj: Related.
■Cultural Institute in Bratislava; Obzor, Ceskoslovenskij Armady 35; 815 85 Bratislava; CZECHOSLOVAKIA.

JBeckS   *Journal of Beckett Studies*. Freq: 2; Began: 1976; Cov: Full; Lang: Eng; Subj: Theatre.   ISSN: 0309-5207
■John Calder Ltd.; 9-15 Neal Street; WC2H 9TU London; UK.

JCNREC   *Journal of Canadian Studies/Revue d'études canadiennes*. Freq: 4; Began: 1966; Cov: Scan; Lang: Eng/Fre; Subj: Related.   ISSN: 0021-9495
■Trent Uiversity; Peterborough, ON K9J 7B8; CANADA.

JCSt *Journal of Caribbean Studies.* Freq: 2; Began: 1970; Cov: Scan; Lang: Eng/Fre/Spa; Subj: Related. ISSN: 0190-2008 ■Association of Caribbean Studies; Box 248231; Coral Gables, FL 33124; USA.

JCT *Jeu*: Cahiers de Théâtre. Freq: 4; Began: 1976; Cov: Full; Lang: Fre; Subj: Theatre. ISSN: 0382-0335 ■Cahiers de Theatre Jeu Inc.; 426 rue Sherbrooke Est.; Bur 102 Montreal, PQ H2L IJ6; CANADA.

JdCh *Journal de Chaillot.* Freq: 8; Began: 1974; Cov: Scan; Lang: Fre; Subj: Related. ■Chaillot Théâtre National; Place du Tracadero; 75116 Paris; FRANCE.

JDS *Jacobean Drama Studies.* Freq: IRR; Began: 1972; Ceased: 1987; Lang: Eng; Subj: Theatre. ■Universität Salzburg, Institut für Englische Sprach; Akademiestr. 24; A 5020 Salzburg; AUSTRIA.

JDSh *Jahrbuch der Deutsche Shakespeare-Gesellschaft.* Cov: Scan; Lang: Ger; Subj: Theatre. ■Deutsche Shakespeare-Gesellschaft West; Rathaus; D 4630 Bochum; WEST GERMANY.

JDt *Journal of Dramatherapy.* Formerly: *Dramatherapy.* Freq: 2; Began: 1977; Cov: Scan; Lang: Eng; Subj: Related. ISSN: 0263-0672 ■David Powley, British Association for Dramatherapy; PO Box 98; YD6 6EX Kirkbymoorside; UK.

JDTC *Journal of Dramatic Theory and Criticism.* Freq: 2; Began: 1986; Cov: Full; Lang: Eng; Subj: Theatre. ■University of Kansas, Dept. of Theatre and Media Arts; Murphy Hall; Lawrence, KS 66045; USA.

JEBT *JEB Théâtre.* Lang: Fre; Ceased: 1982; Subj: Theatre. ■Documentation Générale de la jeunes, des Loisirs; Galerie Ravenstein 78; 1000 Brussels; BELGIUM.

Jelenkor *Jelenkor.* Freq: 12; Began: 1958; Cov: Scan; Lang: Hun; Subj: Related. ISSN: 0447-6425 ■Ft. Baranya Megyei, Lapkiado Vallalat; Széchenyi tér 17.I.; 7621 Pécs; HUNGARY.

JENS *Journal of the Eighteen Nineties Society.* Freq: 1; Began: 1970; Lang: Eng; Subj: Related. ISSN: 0144-008X ■28 Carlingford Rd., Hampstead; NW3 1RQ London; UK.

JGG *Jahrbuch der Grillparzer-Gesellschaft.* Lang: Ger; Cov: Scan; Subj: Related. ■Grillparzer-Gesellschaft; Gumpendorfer Strasse 15/1; A 1060 Vienna; AUSTRIA.

JGT *Journal du Grenier de Toulouse.* Freq: 12; Lang: Fre; Subj: Theatre. ■Grenier de Toulouse; 3, rue de la Digue; 31300 Toulouse; FRANCE.

JITT *JITT.* Lang: Jap; Subj: Theatre. ■Japanese Institute for Theatre Technology; 4-437 Ikebukuro, Toshima-ku; Tokyo; JAPAN.

JJS *Journal of Japanese Studies.* Freq: 2; Began: 1974; Lang: Eng; Subj: Related. ISSN: 0095-6848 ■Society for Japanese Studies, University of Washington; Thomson Hall DR-05; Seattle, WA 98195; USA.

JLS/TLW *Journal of Literary Studies/Tydskrif vir Literatuurwetenskap.* Freq: 4; Began: 1985; Cov: Scan; Lang: Eng/Afr; Subj: Related. ■South African Society for, General Literary Studies; Pretoria; SOUTH AFRICA.

JMH *Journal of Magic History.* Lang: Eng; Subj: Related. ■Toledo, OH; USA.

JNZL *Journal of New Zealand Literature.* Lang: Eng; Subj: Related. ■Wellington; NEW ZEALAND.

JPC *Journal of Popular Culture.* Freq: 4; Began: 1967; Cov: Scan; Lang: Eng; Subj: Related. ISSN: 0022-3840 ■Popular Culture Association, Bowling Green State University; 100 University Hall; Bowling Green, OH 43402; USA.

JRASM *Journal of the Royal Asiatic Society of Malaysia.* Lang: Eng; Subj: Related. ■Kuala Lumpur; MALAYSIA.

JSH *Journal of Social History.* Freq: 4; Began: 1967; Cov: Scan; Lang: Eng; Subj: Related. ISSN: 0022-4529 ■Carnegie-Mellon University Press; Schenley Park; Pittsburgh, PA 15213; USA.

JSSB *Journal of the Siam Society.* Cov: Scan; Lang: Tha; Subj: Related. ■131 Soi Asoki; Sukhumvit Rd.; Bangkok; THAILAND.

JT *Jeune Théâtre.* Began: 1970; Ceased: 1982; Lang: Fre; Subj: Theatre. ISSN: 0315-0402 ■Assoc. Québecoise du, Jeune Théâtre; 952 rue Cherrier; Montreal, PQ H2L 1H7; CANADA.

JTPR *Journal du Théâtre Populaire Romand.* Freq: 8; Began: 1962; Lang: Fre; Subj: Theatre. ■Case Postale 80; 2301 La Chaux-de-Fonds; SWITZERLAND.

JTV *Journal du Théâtre de la Ville.* Freq: 4; Began: 1968; Lang: Fre; Subj: Theatre. ■Theatre de la Ville; 16 quai de Gesvres; Paris; FRANCE.

Juben *Juben*: (Playtexts). Freq: 12; Began: 1956; Lang: Chi; Subj: Theatre. ■52 Dongai Batiao; Beijing; CHINA.

JugoIgre *Jugoslovenske*: Pozorišne Igre. Began: 1962; Lang: Ser; Subj: Theatre. ■Sterijino Pozorje; Zmaj Jovina 22; Novi Sad; YUGOSLAVIA.

Junkanoo *Junkanoo.* Freq: 12; Lang: Eng; Subj: Theatre. ■Junkanoo Publications; Box N 4923; Nassau; BAHAMAS.

JWCI *Journal of the Warburg & Courtauld Institutes.* Freq: 1; Began: 1937; Cov: Scan; Lang: Eng; Subj: Related. ■Woburn Square; WC1H OAB London; UK.

JWGT *Jahrbuch der Wiener Gesellschaft für Theaterforschung.* Freq: 1; Lang: Ger; Subj: Related. ■Vienna; AUSTRIA.

Kabuki *Kabuki.* Lang: Jap; Subj: Theatre. ■4-12-15 Ginza; 104 Chuo-ku, Tokyo; JAPAN.

Kalak *Kalakalpam.* Freq: 2; Began: 1966; Lang: Eng; Subj: Theatre. ■Karyalaya Matya Kala Institute; 30-A Paddapukur Road; 20 Calcutta; INDIA.

Kanava *Kanava.* Formerly: *Aika.* Freq: 9; Began: 1932; Cov: Scan; Lang: Fin; Subj: Related. ISSN: 0355-0303 ■Yhtyneet Kuvalehdet Oy; Hietalahdenranta 13; 00180 Helsinki 18; FINLAND.

KAPM *Kassette*: Almanach für Bühne, Podium und Manege. Freq: 1; Lang: Ger; Subj: Theatre. ■Berlin; EAST GERMANY.

Kathakali *Kathakali.* Freq: 4; Began: 1969; Lang: Eng/Hin; Subj: Theatre. ISSN: 0022-9326 ■International Centre for Kathakali; 1-84 Rajandra Nagar; New Delhi; INDIA.

Kazal *Kazaliste.* Freq: 26; Began: 1965; Lang: Yug; Subj: Theatre. ■Prolaz Radoslava Bacica 1; Osijek; YUGOSLAVIA.

KB *Kunst Bulletin.* Freq: 12; Cov: Scan; Subj: Related. ■Fr. Hallwag AG; Nording 4; 4001 Bern; SWITZERLAND.

Keshet *Keshet.* Lang: Heb; Subj: Theatre. ■9 Bialik Street; Tel Aviv; ISRAEL.

KesK *Kultura és Közösség.* Freq: 6; Began: 1974; Cov: Scan; Lang: Hun; Subj: Related. ■Corvin tér 8; 1011 Budapest I; HUNGARY.

KingP *King Pole Circus Magazine.* Freq: 4; Began: 1934; Cov: Scan; Lang: Eng; Subj: Theatre. ■Circus Fans' Assoc. of UK, c/o John Exton; 43 Waterloo Lane; Skellingthorpe, Lincoln LN6 5SJ; UK.

KJAZU *Kronika*: Zavoda za kniževnost i teatrologiju. Began: 1976; Lang: Slo; Subj: Theatre. ■Jugosl. Akad. Znanosti i Umjetnosti; Opatička 18; Zagreb; YUGOSLAVIA.

Klub *Klub i Chudožestvennaja Samodejetelnost.* Freq: 26; Lang: Rus; Subj: Theatre. ■Profizdat; Ulitza Korova 13; Moscow; USSR.

KMFB *KMFB.* Freq: 11; Began: 1945; Lang: Ger; Subj: Theatre. ■UMLOsterreichischer Gewerkschaftsbund, Gewrkshft. Kunst, Medien, Berufe; Maria-Theresienstrasse 11; A 1090 Vienna; AUSTRIA.

KoJ *Korea Journal.* Freq: 12; Began: 1961; Cov: Scan; Lang: Kor; Subj: Related. ISSN: 0023-3900 ■Korean Natl. Comm. for UNESCO; Box Central 64; Seoul; SOUTH KOREA.

Kommunist *Kommunist.* Began: 1924; Cov: Scan; Lang: Rus; Subj: Related. ISSN: 0131-1212 ■Moscow; USSR.

KoreanD   *Korean Drama*. Lang: Kor; Subj: Theatre.
■National Drama Association of Korea, Insadong, Jongno-gu; Fed. of Arts & Cult. Org. Building; 110 Seoul; SOUTH KOREA.

Kortars   *Kortárs*. Freq: 12; Began: 1957; Cov: Scan; Lang: Hun; Subj: Related.
           ISSN: 0023-415X
■Lapkiado Vallalat; Széchényi rkp. 1; 1054 Budapest V; HUNGARY.

KPR   *Kulturno-Prosvetitelnaja Rabota*. Freq: 12; Lang: Rus; Subj: Related.
■Sovĕckaja Rossija; Bersenevskaja Naberežnaja 22; Moscow; USSR.

Krit   *Kritika*. Freq: 12; Began: 1963; Cov: Scan; Lang: Hun; Subj: Related.
           ISSN: 0023-4818
■Lapkiado Lenin; Korut 9-11; 1073 Budapest 7; HUNGARY.

KSF   *Korean Studies Forum*. Freq: 2; Began: 1976; Lang: Kor; Subj: Related.
           ISSN: 0147-6335
■Korean-American Educ. Commission, Garden Towers; No. 1803, 98-78 Wooni-Dong, Chongro-Ku; Seoul 110; SOUTH KOREA.

KSGT   *Kleine Schriften der Gesellschaft für Theatergeschichte*. Lang: Ger; Subj: Theatre.
■Gesellschaft für Theatergeschichte; 1 Berlin; WEST GERMANY.

KTR   *Korean Theatre Review*. Freq: 12; Lang: Kor; Cov: Scan; Subj: Theatre.
■National Theatre Association of Korea;; Yechong Bldg; 1-117 Dongsoon-dong; Chongnoku Seoul 110; KOREA.

Kulis   *Kulis*. Freq: 12; Began: 1946; Lang: Arm; Subj: Theatre.
■H. Ayvaz; PK 83; 10 A Cagaloglu Yokusu; TURKEY.

Kvihkot   *Kultuurivihkot*. Freq: 8; Began: 1973; Lang: Fin/Swe; Subj: Theatre.
■Kultuurityontekijain Liitto; Korkeavuorenkatu 4 C 15; 00130 Helsinki; FINLAND.

KWN   *Kurt Weill Newsletter*. Freq: 2; Began: 1983; Cov: Scan; Lang: Eng; Subj: Related.   ISSN: 0899-6407
■Weill Foundation for Music; 7 East 20th Street; New York, NY 10003-1106; USA.

KZ   *Kultura i Zizn*. (Culture and Life). Freq: 12; Began: 1957; Cov: Scan; Lang: Rus/Eng/Ger/Fre/Spa; Subj: Related.   ISSN: 0023-5199
■Sovĕckaja Rossija; Projĕzd Sapunova 13-15; Moscow K-12; USSR.

L&DA   *Lighting Design & Application*. Freq: 12; Began: 1906; Cov: Scan; Lang: Eng; Subj: Theatre.   ISSN: 0360-6325
■Illuminating Engineering Society; 345 E. 47th St.; New York, NY 10017; USA.

L&H   *Literature & History*. Freq: 2; Began: 1975; Lang: Eng; Subj: Related.
           ISSN: 0306-1973
■Ohio State University, Dept. of English; 421 Denney Hall; 164 W. 17th Ave. OH 43210; USA.

Laien   *Laientheater*. Freq: 12; Began: 1972; Lang: Ger; Subj: Theatre.
■Schweizerischen Volkstheater; 30 Bern; SWITZERLAND.

LAQ   *Livres et Auteurs Québecois*. Freq: 1; Began: 1969; Lang: Fre; Subj: Related.
           ISSN: 0316-2621
■Presses de l'Université Laval, Cité Universitaire; Québec, PQ G1K 7R4; CANADA.

LATR   *Latin American Theatre Review*. Freq: 2; Began: 1967; Cov: Full; Lang: Eng/Spa/Por; Subj: Theatre.   ISSN: 0023-8813
■University of Kansas, Center of Latin American Studies; 107 Lippincott Hall; Lawrence, KS 66044; USA.

LDim   *Lighting Dimensions*: For the Entertainment Lighting Industry. Freq: 6; Began: 1977; Cov: Full; Lang: Eng; Subj: Theatre.
■Lighting Dimensions Publishing; 1590 S. Coast Highway, Suite 8; Laguna, CA 92651; USA.

LetQu   *Lettres Québecoises*. Freq: 4; Began: 1976; Lang: Fre; Subj: Related.
           ISSN: 0382-084X
■Editions Jumonville; Box 1840, Succarsale B; Montreal, PQ H3B 3L4; CANADA.

Letture   *Letture*: Libro e spettacolo, mensile di studi e rassegne. Freq: 10; Began: 1946; Lang: Ita; Subj: Related.   ISSN: 0024-144X
■Edizioni Letture; Piazza San Fedele 4; 20121 Milan; ITALY.

LFQ   *Literature / Film Quarterly*. Freq: 4; Began: 1973; Lang: Eng; Subj: Related.
           ISSN: 0090-4260
■Salisbury State College; Salisbury, MD 21801; USA.

Light   *Light*. Freq: 24; Began: 1921; Lang: Eng; Subj: Theatre.
■Ahmadiyya Building; Brandreth Road; Lahore; PAKISTAN.

LiNQ   *Literature in North Queensland*. Freq: 3; Began: 1971; Cov: Scan; Lang: Eng; Subj: Related.
■Dept. of English; James Cook University of North Queensland; Townsville, 4811; AUSTRALIA.

LinzerT   *Linzer Theaterzeitung*. Freq: 10; Began: 1955; Lang: Ger; Subj: Theatre.
           ISSN: 0024-4139
■Landestheater Linz; Promenade 39; A 4010 Linz; AUSTRIA.

Lipika   *Lipika*. Freq: 4; Began: 1972; Lang: Eng; Subj: Theatre.
■F-20 Nizzamudin West; 10013 New Delhi; INDIA.

Literatura   *Literatura*. Freq: 4; Began: 1974; Lang: Hun; Subj: Related. ISSN: 0133-2368
■Akademiai Kiado, Hungarian Academy of Sciences; Ménesi u. 11-13; 1118 Budapest XI; HUNGARY.

LitGruzia   *Literaturnaja Gruzia*. Freq: 12; Began: 1957; Cov: Scan; Lang: Rus; Subj: Related.   ISSN: 0130-3600
■Tbilisi, Georg. SSR; USSR.

Live   *Live*. Freq: 4; Lang: Eng; Subj: Related.
■New York, NY; USA.

LLJ   *La Trobe Library Journal*. Freq: 2; Began: 1968; Cov: Scan; Lang: Eng; Subj: Related.   ISSN: 0041-3151
■Friends of the State Library of Victoria; State Library of Victoria; Swanston Street; Melbourne, 3000; AUSTRALIA.

LO   *Literaturnoje Obozrenijë*. Freq: 12; Began: 1973; Cov: Scan; Lang: Rus; Subj: Related.   ISSN: 0321-2904
■Sojuz Pisatelej SSSR; 9/10 ul. Dobroliubova; 127254 Moscow I-254; USSR.

Loisir   *Loisir*. Freq: 4; Began: 1962; Lang: Fre; Subj: Theatre.
■Comédie de Caen; 120 rue St. Pierre; 1400 Caen; FRANCE.

LokK   *Lok Kala*. Freq: 2; Lang: Hin; Subj: Theatre.
■Bharatiya Lok Kala Mandal; Udaipur; INDIA.

Lowdown   *Lowdown*. Freq: 6; Began: 1979; Lang: Eng; Subj: Theatre.
■Australian Youth Performing Arts Assoc., c/o Theatre Workshop; University of Sydney; NSW 2006 Sydney; AUSTRALIA.

LPer   *Literature in Performance*. Freq: 2; Began: 1980; Lang: Eng; Subj: Theatre.
           ISSN: 0734-0796
■Inter. Div.,Speech Comm. Assoc., Dept. of Speech Communication; U. of NC, 115 Bingham Hall; Chapel Hall, NC 27514; USA.

LTR   *London Theatre Record*. Freq: 26; Began: 1981; Cov: Full; Lang: Eng; Subj: Theatre.   ISSN: 0261-5282
■4 Cross Deep Gardens; TW1 4QU Twickenham, Midlsex; UK.

Ludus   *Ludus*: List Udruženja Dramskih Umetnika Srbije. Freq: 6; Began: 1983; Lang: Ser; Subj: Theatre.
■Udruženja Dramskih Umetnika Srbije; Terazije 26; Belgrade; YUGOSLAVIA.

Lutka   *Lutka*: Revija za lutkovno kulturo. Freq: 3; Began: 1966; Lang: Slo; Subj: Theatre.   ISSN: 0350-9303
■Zveza kulturnih organizacij Slovenije; Kidričeva 5; Ljubljana; YUGOSLAVIA.

M&T   *Musik & Teater*. Freq: 6; Began: 1979; Lang: Dan; Subj: Theatre.
■Bagsvard Horedgade 9914E; 2800 Bagsvard; DENMARK.

Maksla   *Maksla*. Lang: Lat; Subj: Related.
■Riga, Latvian SSR; USSR.

MAL   *Modern Austrian Literature*. Freq: 4; Began: 1961; Lang: Eng/Ger; Subj: Related.   ISSN: 0026-7503
■Intl A. Schnitzler Research Assoc., c/o Donald G. Daviau, Ed.; Dept. of Lit. & Langs, Univ. of CA; Riverside, CA 92521; USA.

Mamulengo   *Mamulengo*. Lang: Por; Subj: Theatre.
■Assoc. Brasileira de Teatro de Bonecos; Rua Barata Ribeiro; 60 C 01 Guanabara; BRAZIL.

Manip   *Manipulation*. Lang: Eng; Subj: Theatre.
■Mrs. Maeve Vella; 28 Macarthur Place; 3053 Carlton, Victoria; AUSTRALIA.

MarqJTHS   *Marquee*: The Journal of the Theatre Historical Society. Freq: 4; Began: 1969; Cov: Scan; Lang: Eng; Subj: Theatre. ISSN: 0025-3928
■624 Wynne Rd; Springfield, PA 19064; USA.

Marquee   *Marquee*. Freq: 8; Began: 1976; Lang: Eng; Subj: Related. ISSN: 0700-5008
■Marquee Communications Inc.; 277 Richmond St. W.; Toronto, ON M5V 1X1; CANADA.

Mask *Mask*. Freq: 6; Began: 1967; Lang: Eng; Subj: Theatre. ISSN: 0726-9072 ■Simon Pryor, Executive Officer, VADIE; 117 Bouverie Street; 3053 Carlton; AUSTRALIA.

Maske *Maske*. Began: 1985; Lang: Slo; Subj: Theatre. ISSN: 0352-7913 ■Zveza kulturnih organizacij Slovenije; Ljubljana; YUGOSLAVIA.

Masque *Masque*. Freq: 24; Began: 1967; Lang: Eng; Subj: Theatre. ISSN: 0025-469X ■Masque Publications; 22 Steam Mill St.; 2000 Sydney NSW; AUSTRALIA.

Mast *Masterstvo*. Freq: 6; Lang: Ukr; Subj: Theatre. ■Pouchkineskaia Street 5; Kiev; USSR.

Matya *Matya Prasanga*. Freq: 12; Lang: Ben; Subj: Theatre. ■54/1 B Patuatola Lane; Emherst Street; Calcutta; INDIA.

MAvilia *Monte Avilia*. Freq: 12; Began: 1980; Lang: Spa; Subj: Theatre. ■Apartado 70-712; 107 Caracas; VENEZUELA.

MBB *Mala Biblioteka Baletowa*. Began: 1957; Lang: Pol; Subj: Theatre. ■Polskie Wydawnictwo Muzyczne; Al. Krasiskiego 11; Cracow; POLAND.

MC&S *Media, Culture and Society*. Freq: 4; Began: 1979; Lang: Eng; Subj: Related. ISSN: 0163-4437 ■Academic Press Ltd.; 24-28 Oval Road; NW1 7DX London; UK.

MChAT *Ežegodnik MChAT*. Freq: 1; Lang: Rus; Subj: Theatre. ■Association of Soviet Writers; Hertsen 49; Moscow; USSR.

MD *Modern Drama*. Freq: 4; Began: 1958; Cov: Full; Lang: Eng; Subj: Theatre. ISSN: 0026-7694 ■Univ. of Toronto Press; 5201 Dufferin Street; Downsview, ON M3H 5T8; CANADA.

MdVO *Mitteilungen der Vereinigung Österreichischer Bibliotheken*. Lang: Ger; Subj: Related. ■Vienna; AUSTRIA.

Meanjin *Meanjin*. Formerly: *Meanjin Quarterly* Freq: 3; Began: 1940; Cov: Scan; Lang: Eng; Subj: Theatre. ISSN: 0025-6293 ■Meanjin Co. Ltd.; 211 Grattan Street; Parkville, Victoria 3052; AUSTRALIA.

MeisterP *Meister des Puppenspiels*. Freq: IRR; Began: 1959; Lang: Ger; Subj: Theatre. ISSN: 0076-6216 ■Deutsches Institut für Puppenspiel; Hattingerstr. 467; 4630 Bochum; WEST GERMANY.

Merker *Merker, Der*. Lang: Ger; Subj: Theatre. ■Kurt Grisold; Karlplusgasse 1-39/Stg. 10; A 1100 Vienna; AUSTRIA.

MET *Medieval English Theatre*. Freq: 2; Began: 1979; Cov: Full; Lang: Eng; Subj: Theatre. ISSN: 0143-3784 ■c/o M. Twycross, Dept. of English, Language and Medieval Literature; University of Lancaster; LA1 4YT Lancaster; UK.

MGL *Mestno Gledalisce Ljubljansko*. Began: 1959; Lang: Yug; Subj: Theatre. ■Ljubljana; 14 Copova; YUGOSLAVIA.

MHall *Music Hall*. Freq: 6; Began: 1978; Lang: Eng; Subj: Theatre. ■Tony Barker; 50 Reperton Road; SW6 London; UK.

MID *Modern International Drama*: Magazine for Contemporary International Drama in Translation. Freq: 2; Began: 1967; Cov: Full; Lang: Eng; Subj: Theatre. ISSN: 0026-4385 ■State University of NY; Max Reinhardt Archive; Binghamton, NY 13901; USA.

Mim *Mim: Revija za glumu i glumište*: Glasilo Udruženja dramskih umjetnika Hrvatske. Freq: 12; Began: 1984; Lang: Cro; Subj: Theatre. ■Udruž. Dramskih Umjetnika Hrvatske; Ilica 42; Zagreb; YUGOSLAVIA.

MimeJ *Mime Journal*. Freq: 1; Began: 1974; Cov: Full; Lang: Eng; Subj: Theatre. ISSN: 0145-787X ■Pamona College Theater Department, Claremont Colleges; Claremont, CA 91711; USA.

MimeN *Mime News*. Freq: 5; Began: 1983; Cov: Scan; Lang: Eng; Subj: Theatre. ■National Mime Association; Box 148277; Chicago, IL 60614; USA.

Mimos *Mimos*. Freq: 4; Began: 1949; Cov: Scan; Lang: Ger; Subj: Theatre. ISSN: 0026-4385 ■Swiss Assoc. for Theatre Research, c/o Louis Naef; Postfach 180; CH-6130 Willisau; SWITZERLAND.

MK *Molodoi Kommunist*. Freq: 12; Began: 1918; Cov: Scan; Lang: Rus; Subj: Related. ISSN: 0026-9077 ■Izdatel'stvo Molodaya Gvardiya, Ul.; Sushevskaya, 21; Moscow A-55; Russian S.F.S.R.; U.S.S.R.

MLet *Music & Letters*. Freq: 4; Began: 1920; Cov: Scan; Lang: Eng; Subj: Related. ISSN: 0027-4224 ■Oxford University Press; Walton Street; OX2 6DP Oxford; UK.

MLR *Modern Language Review*. Freq: 4; Began: 1905; Cov: Scan; Lang: Eng; Subj: Related. ISSN: 0026-7937 ■Modern Humanities Research Assoc.; King's College; WC2 R 2LS London; UK.

MMDN *Medieval Music-Drama News*. Freq: 2; Lang: Eng; Subj: Related. ■Staunton, VA; USA.

MMDTA *Monographs on Music, Dance and Theater in Asia*. Freq: 1; Began: 1971; Lang: Eng; Subj: Theatre. ■The Asia Society, Performing Arts Program; 133 East 58th Street; New York, NY 10022; USA.

MN *Monumenta Nipponica*: Studies in Japanese Culture. Freq: 4; Began: 1938; Cov: Scan; Lang: Eng; Subj: Related. ISSN: 0027-0741 ■Sophia University, 7-1 Kioi-cho; Chiyoda-ku; 102 Tokyo; JAPAN.

Mobile *Mobile*. Freq: 12; Lang: Fre; Subj: Theatre. ■Maison de la Culture d'Amiens; Place Léon Gontier; 80000 Amiens; FRANCE.

MoD *Monthly Diary*. Lang: Eng; Subj: Theatre. ■Sydney; AUSTRALIA.

MolGvar *Molodaja Gvardija*. Freq: 12; Began: 1922; Cov: Scan; Lang: Rus; Subj: Related. ISSN: 0131-1225 ■Moscow; USSR.

Monsalvat *Monsalvat*. Freq: 11; Began: 1973; Lang: Spa; Subj: Theatre. ■Ediciones de Nuevo Arte; Plaza Gala Placidia 1; 6 Barcelona; SPAIN.

Mosk *Moskva*. Freq: 12; Began: 1957; Cov: Scan; Lang: Rus; Subj: Related. ISSN: 0027-1411 ■24 Rub. Soyuz Pisatelei Rossiiskoi S.F.S.R.; Moscow Russia S.F.S.R.; U.S.S.R.

Mozgo *Mozgó Világ*. Freq: 12; Began: 1971; Cov: Scan; Lang: Hun; Subj: Related. ■Münnich F. u. 26; 1051 Budapest V; HUNGARY.

MP *Modern Philology*: Research in Medieval and Modern Literature. Freq: 4; Began: 1903; Cov: Scan; Lang: Eng; Subj: Related. ISSN: 0026-8232 ■University of Chicago Press; 5801 S. Ellis Avenue; Chicago, IL 60637; USA.

MPI *Manadens Premiarer och Information*. Lang: Swe; Subj: Related. ■Stockholm; SWEDEN.

MPSKD *Mitteilungen der Puppentheatersammlung der Staatlicher Kunstsammlungen Dresde*. Freq: 4; Began: 1958; Lang: Ger; Subj: Theatre. ■Rolf Maser; Barkengasse 6; 8122 Radebeul; EAST GERMANY.

MRenD *Medieval and Renaissance Drama*. Lang: Eng; Began: 1984; Cov: Full; Subj: Theatre. ■AMS Press; 56 E. 13th Street; New York, NY 10003; USA.

MRT *Miedzynarodowny Rocznik Teatralny*: Annuaire Intl. du Théâtre/Intl. Theatre Yearbook. Freq: 1; Began: 1977; Lang: Pol/Fre/Eng; Subj: Theatre. ■International Association of Theatre Critics; ul. Moliera 1; 00 076 Warsaw; POLAND.

MSD *Milliyet Sanat Dergisi*. Freq: 26; Lang: Tur; Subj: Theatre. ■Aydin Dogan; Nurosmaniye Cad. 65/67; Cagaloglu-Istanbul; TURKEY.

MT *Material zum Theater*. Freq: 12; Began: 1970; Lang: Ger; Subj: Theatre. ■Verband der Theaterschaffended der DDR; Hermann-Matern-Strasse 18; 1040 Berlin; EAST GERMANY.

MuD *MusikDramatik*. Freq: 4; Cov: Full; Lang: Swe; Subj: Theatre. ■Stockholm; SWEDEN.

Muhely *Mühely*. Freq: 12; Began: 1978; Lang: Hun; Cov: Scan; Subj: Related. ■Tanácsköztársaság útja 51.II10; 9022 Gyór; HUNGARY.

MuK *Maske und Kothurn*: Internationale Beiträge zur Theaterwissenschaft. Freq: 4; Began: 1955; Cov: Full; Lang: Ger/Eng/Fre; Subj: Theatre. ISSN: 0025-4606 ■Hermann Boehlaus Nachf., c/o Dr. Karl Lueger Ring 12; Postfach 581, A 1010 Vienna; AUSTRIA.

MuQ *Musical Quarterly*. Freq: 4; Began: 1915; Cov: Scan; Lang: Eng; Subj: Related. ISSN: 0027-4631

■G. Schirmer, Inc.; 866 Third Avenue; New York, NY 10022; USA.

MusGes *Musik und Gesellschaft*. Freq: 12; Began: 1951; Cov: Scan; Lang: Ger; Subj: Related. ISSN: 0027-4755 ■Henschelverlag Kunst und Gesellschaft; Oranienburger Str. 67/68; 1040 Berlin; EAST GERMANY.

MuT *Musik und Theater*. Die aktuelle schweizerische Kulturzeitschrift. Freq: 12; Began: 1980; Cov: Scan; Lang: Ger; Subj: Theatre. ■Postfach 926; 9001 St. Gallen; SWITZERLAND.

MuZizn *Muzykalnaja Žizn*: (Musical Life). Freq: 24; Began: 1957; Cov: Scan; Lang: Rus; Subj: Related. ISSN: 0131-2303 ■Moscow; USSR.

Muzsika *Muzsika*. Freq: 12; Began: 1958; Cov: Scan; Lang: Hun; Subj: Related. ISSN: 0027-5336 ■Lapkiado Vallalat; Lenin korut 9-11; 1073 Budapest VII; HUNGARY.

Muzyka *Muzyka*. Freq: 12; Began: 1973; Cov: Full; Lang: Rus; Subj: Related. ISSN: 0208-3086 ■Gos. Biblioteka SSSR im. Lenina, NIO Informkultura; Prospekt Kalinina; 101000 Moscow; USSR.

MV *Minority Voices*: An Interdisciplinary Journal of Literature & Arts. Freq: 2; Began: 1977; Ceased: 1989; Lang: Eng; Subj: Theatre. ■Paul Robeson Cultural Center, 114 Walnut Bldg.; Pennsylvania State Univ.; University Park, PA 16802; USA.

Mykenae *Mykenae*. Freq: 36; Began: 1950; Lang: Ger; Subj: Theatre. ■Mykenae Verlag; Ahastrasse 9; 6100 Darmstadt; WEST GERMANY.

Napj *Napjaink*. Freq: 12; Began: 1962; Cov: Scan; Lang: Hun; Subj: Related. ISSN: 0027-7819 ■Borsod Megyei Lapkiado Vallalat; Korvin Ottó u. 1; 3530 Miskolc; HUNGARY.

NasSovr *Naš Sovremennik*. Freq: 12; Began: 1933; Cov: Scan; Lang: Rus; Subj: Related. ISSN: 0027-8238 ■Moscow; USSR.

Natrang *Natrang*. Freq: 4; Lang: Hin; Subj: Theatre. ■I-47 Jangoura Extension; New Delhi; INDIA.

Natya *Natya*. Freq: 4; Began: 1969; Lang: Eng; Subj: Theatre. ISSN: 0028-1115 ■Bharatiya Natya Sangh; 34 New Central Market; New Delhi; INDIA.

Nayt *Naytelmauutiset*. Lang: Fin; Subj: Theatre. ■Tyovaen Nayttamoiden; Vuoritaku 6 A 7; Liitti; FINLAND.

NBT *Neue Blätter des Theaters in Der Josefstadt*. Freq: 6; Began: 1953; Lang: Ger/Eng/Fre; Subj: Theatre. ISSN: 0028-3096 ■Theater in der Josefstadt, Direktion; Josefstaedterstrasse 26; A 1082 Vienna; AUSTRIA.

NCBSBV *Netherlands Centraal Bureau Voor de Statistiek*: Bezoek aan Vermakelukheidsinstellingen. Freq: 1; Began: 1940; Lang: Dut/Eng; Subj: Related. ISSN: 0077-6688

■Centraal Bureau voor de Statistiek; Prinses Beatrixlaan 428; Voorburg; NETHERLANDS.

NCBSMT *Netherlands Centraal Bureau voor de Statistiek*: Muziek en Theater. Formerly: *Statistiek van het Gesubsidieerde Toneel*. Lang: Dut; Subj: Theatre. ■Centraal Bureau voor de Statistiek; Prinses Beatrixlaan 428; Voorburg; NETHERLANDS.

NCM *Nineteenth Century Music*. Cov: Scan; Lang: Eng; Subj: Related. ■University of California; Berkeley, CA; USA.

NConL *Notes on Contemporary Literature*. Freq: 4; Began: 1971; Lang: Eng; Subj: Related. ISSN: 0029-4047 ■English Department, West Georgia College; Carollton, GA 30118; USA.

NCPA *National Center for the Performing Arts*: Quarterly Journal. Freq: 4; Began: 1972; Lang: Eng; Subj: Related. ■Natl Cter for the Performing Arts; Nariman Point; 400021 Bombay; INDIA.

NCT *Nineteenth Century Theatre*. Formerly: *Nineteenth Century Theatre Research*. Freq: 2; Began: 1987; Lang: Eng; Subj: Theatre. ISSN: 0893-3766 ■Amherst, MA 01003; USA.

NCTR *Nineteenth Century Theatre Research*. Freq: 2; Began: 1973; Ceased: 1986; Cov: Full; Lang: Eng; Subj: Theatre. ISSN: 0316-5329 ■Department of English, University of Arizona; Tuscon, AZ 85721; USA.

Neva *Neva*. Freq: 12; Began: 1955; Cov: Scan; Lang: Rus; Subj: Related. ISSN: 0130-741X ■Leningrad; USSR.

NewPerf *New Performance*. Freq: 4; Began: 1977; Lang: Eng; Subj: Theatre. ISSN: 0277-514X ■One 14th Street; San Francisco, CA 94103; USA.

NFT *Theatre*: News from the Finnish Theatre. Formerly: *News from the Finnish Theatre*. Freq: IRR; Began: 1958; Cov: Scan; Lang: Eng/Fre; Subj: Theatre. ISSN: 0358-3627 ■Finnish Center of the ITI; Vuorikatu 6 A3; 00100 Helsinki 10; FINLAND.

NihonU *Nihon-Unima*. Lang: Jap; Subj: Theatre. ■Taoko Kawajiri, Puppet Theatre PUK; 2-12 Yoyogi, Shibuya; 151 Tokyo; JAPAN.

NIMBZ *Notate*: Informations-und-Mitteilungsblatt des Brecht-Zentrums der DDR. Lang: Ger; Subj: Theatre. ■Brecht Zentrum der DDR; Chausseestrasse 125; 1040 Berlin; EAST GERMANY.

NiR *Nauka i Religija*: (Science and Religion). Freq: 12; Began: 1959; Cov: Scan; Lang: Rus; Subj: Related. ISSN: 0130-7045 ■Moscow; USSR.

Nk *Näköpiiri*. Ceased: 1983; Lang: Fin; Subj: Theatre. ■Osuuskunta Näköpiiri; Annakatu 13 B; 00120 Helsinki 12; FINLAND.

NKala *Natya Kala*. Freq: 12; Lang: Tel; Subj: Theatre. ■Kala Bhawan; Saifabad; Hyderabad; INDIA.

NNews *Natya News*. Freq: 4; Lang: Eng; Subj: Theatre. ■F. 34 New Central Market; New Delhi; INDIA.

NO *New Observations*. Freq: 10; Lang: Eng; Subj: Related. ■144 Greene Street; New York, NY 10012; USA.

Noh *Noh*. Freq: 12; Lang: Jap; Subj: Theatre. ■Ginza-Nohgakudo Building; 6-5-15 Ginza, Chuo-Ku; 104 Tokyo; JAPAN.

NoK *Nōgaku-kenkyū*. Freq: Irreg. exchange basis; Began: 1916; Cov: Scan; Lang: Jap; Subj: Related. ISSN: 0029-0874 ■Okayama Univ.; Ohara Institute fuer Landwirtschaftliche Biologie-Ohara Institute for Agricultural Biology; 2-20-1 Chuo; Kurashiki 710; JAPAN.

NovyjMir *Novyj Mir*. Freq: 12; Began: 1925; Cov: Scan; Lang: Rus; Subj: Related. ISSN: 0130-7673 ■Moscow; USSR.

Ns *Nestroyana*: Blätter der Internationalen Nestroy-Gesellschaft. Freq: 4; Began: 1979; Cov: Scan; Lang: Ger; Subj: Theatre. ■Internationale Nestroy-Gesellschaft, Volkstheater; Neustiftgasse 1; A 1070 Vienna; AUSTRIA.

NT *Nya Teatertidningen*. Freq: 4; Began: 1977; Cov: Full; Lang: Swe; Subj: Theatre. ISSN: 0348-0119 ■Teatercentrum, Bjorkhagens Skola; Karlskrondvagen 10; 121 52 Johanneshov; SWEDEN.

NTE *Narodna Tvorcist' ta Ethnohrafija*. Freq: 6; Began: 1925; Lang: Ukr; Subj: Related. ISSN: 0130-6936 ■Naukova Dumka; Repina 3; Kiev, Ukrainian SSR; USSR.

NTimes *Nohgaku Times*. Freq: 12; Began: 1953; Lang: Jap; Subj: Theatre. ■Nohgaku Shorin Ltd.; 3-6 Kanda-Jinpo-cho, Chiyoda-ku; 101 Tokyo; JAPAN.

NTQ *New Theatre Quarterly*. Freq: 4; Began: 1985; Cov: Full; Lang: Eng; Subj: Theatre. ISSN: 0266-464X ■Cambridge University Press, Edinburgh Bldg.; Shaftesbury Rd.; CB2 2RU Cambridge; UK.

NTS *Nordic Theatre Studies*: Yearbook for Theatre Research in Scandinavia. Freq: 1; Began: 1988; Lang: Eng; Subj: Theatre. ■Munksgaard; Postbox 2148; 1016 Copenhagen K; DENMARK.

NTTJ *Nederlands Theatre-en-Televisie Jaarboek*. Freq: 1; Lang: Dut; Subj: Theatre. ■Amsterdam; NETHERLANDS.

Numero *Numero*. Freq: 12; Lang: Spa; Subj: Related. ■Apt. Post. 75570; El Marques; Caracas; VENEZUELA.

NVarta *Natya Varta*. Freq: 12; Lang: Hin; Subj: Theatre. ■Anakima; 4 Bishop Lefroy Road; Calcutta; INDIA.

Nvilag *Nagyvilág*. Freq: 12; Began: 1956; Cov: Scan; Lang: Hun; Subj: Related. ISSN: 1613-1547

■Széchenyi rkp. 1; 1054 Budapest V; HUNGARY.

NWR *NeWest Review*: A Journal of Culture and Current Events in the West. Freq: 12; Began: 1975; Lang: Eng; Subj: Theatre.
ISSN: 0380-2817
■NeWest Publishers Ltd.; Box 394, Sub Post Office 6; Saskatoon, SK S7N 0W0; CANADA.

NYO *New York Onstage*. Freq: 12; Lang: Eng; Subj: Theatre.
■New York, NY; USA.

NYTCR *New York Theatre Critics Review*. Freq: 30; Began: 1940; Cov: Full; Lang: Eng; Subj: Theatre. ISSN: 0028-7784
■Critics Theatre Review; 4 Park Avenue, Suite 21-D; New York, NY 10016; USA.

NYTR *New York Theatre Reviews*. Began: 1977; Ceased: 1980; Lang: Eng; Subj: Theatre.
■Ira J. Bilowit; 55 West 42nd Street; New York, NY 10036; USA.

Obliques *Obliques*. Lang: Fre; Subj: Related.
■Roger Borderie; BP1, Les Pilles; 26110 Lyons; FRANCE.

OC *Opera Canada*. Freq: 4; Began: 1960; Cov: Scan; Lang: Eng; Subj: Theatre.
ISSN: 0030-3577
■Foundation for Coast to Coast, Opera Publication; 366 Adelaide Street E., Suite 433; Toronto, ON M5A 3X9; CANADA.

OCA *O'Casey Annual*. Freq: 1; Began: 1982; Cov: Scan; Lang: Eng; Subj: Theatre.
■MacMillan Publishers Ltd.; 4 Little Essex Street; WC2R 3LF London; UK.

ODG *Österreichische Dramatiker der Gegenwart*. Lang: Ger; Subj: Theatre.
■Inst. für Österreichische Dramaturgie; Singerstrasse 26; A 1010 Vienna; AUSTRIA.

OI *Opéra International*. Freq: 12; Began: 1963; Lang: Fre; Subj: Theatre.
■10 Galerie Vero-Dodat; 75001 Paris; FRANCE.

OJ *Opera Journal*. Freq: 4; Began: 1968; Cov: Scan; Lang: Eng; Subj: Theatre.
ISSN: 0030-3585
■National Opera Association, Inc., University of Mississippi; Division of Continuing Ed. and Extension; University, MS 38677; USA.

OK *Oper und Konzert*. Freq: 12; Began: 1963; Lang: Ger; Subj: Theatre.
ISSN: 0030-3518
■A. Hanuschik; Ungererstrasse 19/VI (Fuchsbau); 8000 Munich 40; WEST GERMANY.

Oktiabr *Oktiabr*. Freq: 12; Began: 1924; Cov: Scan; Lang: Rus; Subj: Related. ISSN: 0132-0637
■Moscow; USSR.

Opal *Opal*. Freq: 6; Began: 1962; Lang: Eng; Subj: Theatre. ISSN: 0030-3062
■Ontario Puppetry Association; 171 Avondale Avenue; Willowdale, ON M2N 2V4; CANADA.

Oper *Oper*. Freq: 1; Lang: Ger; Subj: Theatre.
■Zurich; SWITZERLAND.

Opera *Opera*. Freq: 12; Began: 1950; Cov: Scan; Lang: Eng; Subj: Theatre. ISSN: 0030-3542

■Seymour Press Ltd.; 336 Woodland Rise; N10 3UH London; UK.

OperaA *Opera Australia*. Freq: 12; Began: 1978; Lang: Eng; Subj: Theatre. ISSN: 0155-4980
■PO Box R361; NSW 2000 Royal Exchange; AUSTRALIA.

OperaCT *Opera*. Freq: 4; Began: 1974; Lang: Eng/Afr; Subj: Theatre.
■Cape Performing Arts Board; POB 4107; 8000 Cape Town; SOUTH AFRICA.

OperaR *Opera*. Freq: 4; Began: 1965; Lang: Ita/Eng/Fre/Ger/Spa; Subj: Theatre.
ISSN: 0030-3542
■Editoriale Fenarete; Via Beruto 7; Milan; ITALY.

OperH *Oper Heute*. Lang: Ger; Subj: Theatre.
■East Berlin; EAST GERMANY.

OpN *Opera News*. Freq: 12; Began: 1936; Cov: Full; Lang: Eng; Subj: Theatre. ISSN: 0030-3607
■Metropolitan Opera Guild, Inc.; 1865 Broadway; New York, NY 10023; USA.

Opuscula *Opuscula*. Freq: 3; Began: 1976; Lang: Dan; Subj: Theatre.
■Det Teatervidenskabelige Institot; Fredericingade 18; 1310 Copenhagen; DENMARK.

Opw *Opernwelt*: Die deutsche Opernzeitschrift. Freq: 12; Began: 1963; Cov: Scan; Lang: Ger; Subj: Theatre. ISSN: 0030-3690
■Orell Fuessli & Friedrich Verlag; Dietzingerstrasse 3; CH 8036 Zurich; SWITZERLAND.

OQ *Opera Quarterly*. Freq: 4; Began: 1983; Cov: Full; Lang: Eng; Subj: Theatre.
ISSN: 0736-0053
■University of North Carolina Press; Box 2288; Chapel Hill, NC 27514; USA.

Organon *Organon*. Freq: 1; Began: 1975; Lang: Fre; Subj: Theatre.
■Ctre de Recherches Théâtrales, Univ. Lyon II; Ensemble Univ., Ave. de l'Universite; 69500 Bron; FRANCE.

OSS *On-Stage Studies*. Formerly: *Colorado Shakespeare Festival Annual*. Freq: 1; Began: 1976; Cov: Scan; Lang: Eng; Subj: Theatre. ISSN: 0749-1549
■Colorado Shakespeare Festival, Campus Box 261; University of Colorado; Boulder, CO 80309 0261; USA.

OvA *Overture*. Freq: 12; Began: 1919; Cov: Scan; Lang: Eng; Subj: Theatre. ISSN: 0030-7556
■American Federation of Musicians, Local 47, AFL-CIO; 817 N. Vine Street; Los Angeles, CA 90038; USA.

P&L *Philosophy and Literature*. Freq: 2; Began: 1976; Lang: Eng; Subj: Related.
ISSN: 0190-0013
■University of Michigan; Dearborn, MI 48128; USA.

PA *Présence Africaine*. Freq: 4; Began: 1947; Lang: Fre/Eng; Subj: Related.
ISSN: 0032-7638
■Nouvelle Société Presence Africaine; 25 bis rue des Ecoles; Paris 75005; FRANCE.

Pa&Pr *Past and Present*: A Journal of Historical Studies. Freq: 4; Began: 1952; Lang: Eng; Subj: Related. ISSN: 0031-2746
■Past and Present Society; Corpus Christi College; Oxford; UK.

PAA *Performing Arts Annual*. Freq: 1; Began: 1986; Cov: Full; Lang: Eng; Subj: Theatre. ISSN: 0887-8234
■Library of Congress, Performing Arts Library Resources; Dist. by G.O.P.; Washington, DC 20540; USA.

PAC *Performing Arts in Canada*. Freq: 4; Began: 1961; Cov: Full; Lang: Eng; Subj: Theatre. ISSN: 0031-5230
■Canadian Stage & Arts Publ.; 263 Adelaide St. W.; Toronto, ON M5H 1Y2; CANADA.

Pamir *Pamir*. Freq: 12; Began: 1949; Cov: Scan; Lang: Rus; Subj: Related. ISSN: 0131-2650
■Dushanbe; USSR.

Pantallas *Pantallas y Escenarios*. Freq: 5; Lang: Spa; Subj: Theatre.
■Maria Lostal 24; 8 Zaragoza; SPAIN.

PAR *Performing Arts Resources*. Freq: 1; Began: 1974; Cov: Scan; Lang: Eng; Subj: Theatre. ISSN: 0360-3814
■111 Amsterdam Avenue New York, NY 10023; USA.

Parnass *Parnass*: Die Österreichische Kunst- und Kulturzeitschrift. Freq: 6; Began: 1981; Cov: Scan; Lang: Ger; Subj: Theatre.
■C & E Grosser, Druckerei Verlag; Wiener Strasse 290; A 4020 Linz; AUSTRIA.

Parnasso *Parnasso*. Freq: 8; Began: 1951; Lang: Fin; Subj: Theatre. ISSN: 0031-2320
■Yhtyneet Kuvalehdet Oy; Maistraatinportti 1; 00240 Helsinki; FINLAND.

PArts *Performing Arts*: The Music and Theatre Monthly. Freq: 12; Began: 1967; Lang: Eng; Subj: Theatre. ISSN: 0031-5222
■Performing Arts Network; 3539 Motor Ave.; Los Angeles, CA 90034-4800; USA.

PArtsSF *Performing Arts Magazine*: San Francisco Music & Theatre Monthly. Freq: 12; Began: 1967; Ceased: 1987; Lang: Eng; Subj: Theatre. ISSN: 0480-0257
■Theatre Publications, Inc.; 2999 Overland Ave., Ste. 201; Los Angeles, CA 90064; USA.

PasShowA *Passing Show*. Freq: IRR; Began: 1981; Lang: Eng; Subj: Theatre. ISSN: 0706-1897
■Performing Arts Museum, Victorian Arts Centre; 1 City Rd; 3205 S. Melbourne, Victoria; AUSTRALIA

PasShow *Passing Show*: Newsletter of the Shubert Archive. Freq: 3; Began: 1983; Lang: Eng; Subj: Theatre.
■Shubert Archive, Lyceum Theatre; 149 West 45th Street; New York, NY 10026; USA.

PaT *Pamiętnik Teatralny*: Poswiecony historii i krytyce teatru. Freq: 4; Began: 1952; Cov: Full; Lang: Pol; Subj: Theatre. ISSN: 0031-0522
■Ossolineum, Polish Academy of Sciences; Rynek 9; Wroclaw; POLAND.

PaV *Paraules al Vent*. Freq: 12; Cov: Scan; Lang: Spa; Subj: Related.
■Associació de Joves 'Paraules al Vent'; Casal de Sant Jordi; Sant Jordi Desvalls; SPAIN.

PAYBA   *Performing Arts Year Book of Australia*. Freq: 1; Began: 1977; Lang: Eng; Subj: Theatre.
■Showcast Publications Ltd; Box 141; 2088 Spit Junction N.S.W; AUSTRALIA.

Pb   *Playbill*: A National Magazine of the Theatre. Freq: 12; Began: 1982; Lang: Eng; Subj: Theatre.   ISSN: 0032-146X
■Playbill Incorporated; 71 Vanderbilt Avenue; New York, NY 10169; USA.

PCD   *Premiery Ceskoslovenskych Divadel*. Freq: 12; Lang: Cze; Subj: Theatre.
■Valdstejnske 3; Prague 1; CZECHOSLOVAKIA.

PdO   *Pantuflas del Obispo*. Began: 1966; Lang: Spa; Subj: Theatre.
■Semanario Sabado; Vargas 219; Quito; ECUADOR.

Pe   *Performance*. Freq: 6; Began: 1981; Lang: Eng; Subj: Related.
■Brevet Publishing Ltd.; 445 Brighton Road; CR2 6EU South Croydon; UK.

PeM   *Pesti Müsor*. Freq: 52; Began: 1957; Lang: Hun; Subj: Theatre.
■Garay u.5; 1076 Budapest VII; HUNGARY.

PerAJ   *Performing Arts Journal*. Freq: 3; Began: 1976; Cov: Full; Lang: Eng; Subj: Theatre.   ISSN: 0735-8393
■Performing Arts Journal, Inc.; 131 Varick Street, Room 902; New York, NY 10013; USA.

PerfNZ   *Performance: A Handbook of the Performing Arts in New Zealand*. Freq: 5; Began: 1980; Cov: Full; Lang: Eng; Subj: Theatre.   ISSN: 0112-0654
■Association of Community Theatres; P.O. 68-257; Newton, Aukland; NEW ZEALAND.

Perlicko   *Perlicko-Perlacko*. Began: 1950; Lang: Ger; Subj: Theatre.
■Dr. Hans R. Purschke; Postfach 550135; 6000 Frankfurt; WEST GERMANY.

Pf   *Platform*. Freq: 2; Began: 1979; Ceased: 1983; Cov: Scan; Lang: Eng; Subj: Theatre.
■Dept of Literature, University of Essex; Wivenhoe Park; Colchester; UK.

PFr   *Présence Francophone*. Freq: 2; Began: 1970; Ceased: 1970; Cov: Scan; Lang: Fre; Subj: Related. ISSN: 0048-5195
■Université de Sherbrooke; Sherbrooke, PQ J1K 2R1; CANADA.

PI   *Plays International*. Formerly: *Plays/Plays International*. Freq: 12; Began: 1985; Cov: Scan; Lang: Eng; Subj: Theatre.
■Chancery Publications Ltd.; 55 Hatton Garden; ECIN 8HP London; UK.

PInfo   *Puppenspiel-Information*. Began: 1967; Lang: Ger; Subj: Theatre.
■Hans Scheu; Stahlsberg 46; 5600 Wuppertal 2; WEST GERMANY.

PintR   *Pinter Review*. Began: 1987; Lang: Eng; Subj: Theatre.   ISSN: 0895-9706
■Harold Pinter Society; University of Tampa; Box 11F Tampa, FL 33606; USA.

PiP   *Plays in Process*. Lang: Eng; Subj: Theatre.
■Theatre Communications Group 355 Lexington Avenue; New York, NY 10017; USA.

Pja   *Pipirijaina*. Freq: 6; Began: 1979; Lang: Spa; Subj: Theatre.
■c/o San Enrique 16; 20 Madrid; SPAIN.

Plateaux   *Plateaux*. Formerly: *Bulletin de l'Union des Artistes*. Freq: 6; Began: 1925; Lang: Fre; Subj: Theatre.
■Syndicat Français des Artistes et Interpretes; 21 bis, rue Victor-Masse; 75009 Paris; FRANCE.

Play   *Play*. Freq: 12; Began: 1974; Lang: Eng; Subj: Theatre. ISSN: 0311-4031
■Main Street; PO Box 67; 5245 Hahndorf; SOUTH AFRICA.

PlayM   *Players Magazine*. Freq: 22; Began: 1924; Lang: Eng; Subj: Theatre.   ISSN: 0032-1486
■National Collegiate Players, Northern Illinois University; University Theatre; Dekalb, IL 60115; USA.

Plays   *Plays*: (In 1985 became part of *Plays and Players*). Formerly: *Plays/Plays International*. Freq: 12; Began: 1983; Ceased: 1985; Cov: Scan; Lang: Eng; Subj: Theatre.
■Ocean Publications; 34 Buckingham Palace Road; SW1 London; UK.

PlPl   *Plays and Players*. Freq: 12; Began: 1953; Cov: Scan; Lang: Eng; Subj: Theatre.   ISSN: 0032-1540
■Brevet Publishing Ltd.; 43B Gloucester Rd.; CR0 2DH Croyden, Surrey; UK.

PLUG   *PLUG*: Maandelijks informatie-blad van het Cultureel Jongeren Paspoort. Freq: 12; Began: 1967; Lang: Dut; Subj: Theatre.   ISSN: 0032-1621
■Cultureel Jongeren Paspoort; Kleine Gartmanplts. 10; 1017 RR Amsterdam; NETHERLANDS.

PM   *Performance Magazine, The*. Freq: 6; Began: 1979; Cov: Scan; Lang: Eng; Subj: Theatre.   ISSN: 0144-5901
■Performance Magazine Ltd.; 14 Peto Place; NW1 London; UK.

PMLA   *PMLA*: Publications of the Modern Language Assoc. of America. Freq: 6; Began: 1929; Cov: Scan; Lang: Eng; Subj: Related.   ISSN: 0030-8129
■Modern Language Assoc. of America; 62 5th Avenue; New York, NY 10011; USA.

Pnpa   *Peuples noirs, peuples africains*. Freq: 4; Began: 1977; Cov: Scan; Lang: Fre; Subj: Related.
■82, avenue de la Porte-des-Champs; 76000 Rouen; FRANCE.

Podium   *Podium*. Lang: Dut; Subj: Theatre.
■Rijswijk; NETHERLANDS.

PodiumB   *Podium*: Zeitschrift für Bühnenbildner und Theatertechnik. Freq: 4; Lang: Ger; Subj: Theatre.
■Abteilung Berufsbildung; Munzstrasse 21; 1020 Berlin; EAST GERMANY.

Poppen   *Poppenspelbereichten*. Freq: 4; Lang: Dut; Subj: Theatre.
■Mechelen; BELGIUM.

PozL   *Pozoriste*: List Srpskog narodnog pozorišta. Freq: 10; Began: 1871; Lang: Ser; Subj: Theatre.   ISSN: 0032-616X
■1959 narodno pozoriste; Tuzla; YUGOSLAVIA.

Pozoriste   *Pozorište*: Časopis za pozorišnu umjetnost. Freq: 8; Began: 1959; Lang: Cro; Subj: Theatre.   ISSN: 0032-616X
■Narodno Pozorište; Matija Gupca 6; 75000 Tuzla; YUGOSLAVIA.

PQ   *Philological Quarterly*: Investigation of Classical & Modern Langs. and Lit.. Freq: 4; Began: 1922; Cov: Scan; Lang: Eng; Subj: Related.   ISSN: 0031-7977
■Editor, Philological Quarterly; University of Iowa; Iowa City, IA 52242; USA.

PQCS   *Philippine Quarterly of Culture and Society*. Freq: 4; Began: 1973; Lang: Eng; Subj: Related.   ISSN: 0115-0243
■San Carlos Publications; 6401 Cebu City; PHILIPPINES.

PrAc   *Primer Acto*. Freq: 5; Began: 1957; Lang: Spa; Subj: Theatre.
■Pza. de los Mostenses 11; 8 Madrid; SPAIN.

Preface   *Préface*. Freq: 12; Lang: Fre; Subj: Theatre.
■Centre National Nice-Côte d'Azur; Esplanade des Victoires; 06300 Nice; FRANCE.

Premijera   *Premijera*: List Narodnog Pozorista Sombor. Lang: Ser; Subj: Theatre.
■Koste Trifkovica 2; Sombor; YUGOSLAVIA.

Prof   *Profile*: The Newsletter of the New Zealand Assoc. of Theatre Technicians. Freq: 4; Lang: Eng; Subj: Related.
■Ponsonby, Auckland; NEW ZEALAND.

Program   *Program*. Began: 1925; Lang: Cze; Subj: Theatre.
■Zemske divadlo; Dvorakova 11; Brno; CZECHOSLOVAKIA.

Programa   *Programa*. Began: 1978; Lang: Por; Subj: Theatre.
■Grupo de Teatro de Campolide; 43, 20 D. Cde. Antas; Lisbon; PORTUGAL.

Prolog   *Prolog*: Revija za dramsku umjetnost. In 1986 became Novi Prolog. Freq: 2; Began: 1968; Lang: Cro; Subj: Theatre.
■Centar za kulturnu djelatnost; Mihanoviceva 28/1; 41000 Zagreb; YUGOSLAVIA.

PrologTX   *Prolog*. Freq: 4; Began: 1973; Lang: Eng; Subj: Theatre.   ISSN: 0271-7743
■Theatre Sources Inc., c/o Michael Firth; 104 North St. Mary; Dallas, TX 75214; USA.

Prologue   *Prologue*. Freq: 4; Began: 1944; Lang: Eng; Subj: Theatre.   ISSN: 0033-1007
■Arena Theater; Tufts University; Medford, MA 02155; USA.

Prompts   *Prompts*. Freq: IRR; Began: 1981; Lang: Eng; Subj: Theatre.
■Irish Theatre Archive, Archives Division; City Hall; 2 Dublin; IRELAND.

ProScen   *ProScen*. Freq: 4; Began: 1986; Cov: Full; Lang: Swe; Subj: Theatre.
■Svensk Teaterteknisk Sörening, Section of OISTT; P.O. Box 45003; 10430 Stockholm 45; SWEDEN.

PrTh   *Pratiques Théâtrales*: In 1978 became Grande République. Freq: 3; Ceased: 1978; Lang: Fre; Subj: Theatre.
■200 Ouest rue Sherbrooke; Montreal, PQ H2Y 3P2; CANADA.

Ptk   *Publiekstheaterkrant*. Freq: 5; Began: 1978; Lang: Dut; Subj: Theatre.
■Publiekstheater; Marnixstraat 427; 1017 PK Amsterdam; NETHERLANDS.

PuJ *Puppetry Journal*. Freq: 4; Began: 1949; Cov: Full; Lang: Eng; Subj: Theatre. ISSN: 0033-443X ■Puppeteers of America; 8005 Swallow Dr.; Macedonia, OH 44056; USA.

PupM *Puppet Master*. Began: 1946; Lang: Eng; Subj: Theatre. ■British Puppet and Model Theatre Guild, c/o Gordon Shapley (Hon. Sec.); 18 Maple Road, Yeading, Nr Hayes; Middlesex; UK.

Pusp *Puppenspiel und Puppenspieler*. Freq: 2; Began: 1960; Lang: Ger/Fre; Subj: Theatre. ISSN: 0033-4405 ■Schweiz. Vereinigung Puppenspiel, c/o Gustav Gysin, Ed.; Roggenstr. 1; Riehen CH-4125; SWITZERLAND.

Pz *Proszenium*. Lang: Ger; Subj: Theatre. ■Zurich; SWITZERLAND.

QT *Quaderni di Teatro*: Rivista Trimestrale del Teatro Regionale Toscano. Freq: 4; Began: 1978; Ceased: 1987; Cov: Full; Lang: Ita; Subj: Theatre. ■Casa Editrice Vallecchi; Viale Milton 7; 50129 Florence; ITALY.

QTST *Quaderni del Teatro Stabile di Torino*. Freq: IRR; Lang: Ita; Subj: Theatre. ■Teatro Stabile di Torino; Turin; ITALY.

Quarta *Quarta Parete*. Freq: 4; Lang: Ita; Subj: Theatre. ■Via Sant'Ottavio 15; Turin; ITALY.

QuellenT *Quellen zur Theatergeschichte*. Freq: IRR; Began: 1981; Lang: Ger; Subj: Theatre. ISSN: 0259-0786 ■Verband der Wissenschaftlichen, Gesellschaften Oesterreichs; Lindengasse 37; A1070 Vienna; AUSTRIA.

Raduga *Raduga*. Freq: 12; Began: 1986; Cov: Scan; Lang: Rus; Subj: Related. ISSN: 0234-8179 ■Talin, Eston. SSR; USSR.

Raja *Rajatabla*. Lang: Spa; Subj: Theatre. ■Apartado 662; 105 Caracas; VENEZUELA.

RAL *Research in African Literature*. Freq: 4; Began: 1970; Cov: Scan; Lang: Eng; Subj: Related. ISSN: 0034-5210 ■Indiana Univ. Press; 10th and Morton Sts.; Bloomington, IN 47405; USA.

Rampel *Rampelyset*. Freq: 6; Began: 1948; Lang: Dan; Subj: Theatre. ■Danske Amatør Teater Samvirke; Box 70; DK 6300 Grasten; DENMARK.

Randa *Randa*. Freq: 2; Cov: Scan; Lang: Spa; Subj: Related. ■Curial Edicions Catalanes, c/o Bruc; 144 Baixos; 08037 Barcelona; SPAIN.

Rangarupa *Rangarupa*. Began: 1976; Lang: Ben; Subj: Theatre. ■Rangarup Natya Academy; 27/76 Central Rd.; Dhanmondi, Dacca; BANGLADESH.

Rangayan *Rangayan*. Freq: 12; Lang: Hin; Subj: Theatre. ■Bharatiya Lok Kala Mandal; Udaipur; INDIA.

Rangyog *Rangyog*. Freq: 4; Lang: Hin; Subj: Theatre. ■Rajasthan Sangeet Natak Adademi; Paota; Jodhpur; INDIA.

Raritan *Raritan*. Freq: 4; Began: 1981; Lang: Eng; Subj: Related. ISSN: 0275-1607 ■Rutgers University; 165 College Ave.; New Brunswick, NJ 08903; USA.

Rbharati *Rangbharati*. Freq: 12; Lang: Hin; Subj: Theatre. ■Bharatendu Rangmanch; Chowk; Lucknow; INDIA.

RdA *Revue de l'Art*. Freq: 4; Began: 1968; Cov: Scan; Lang: Fre; Subj: Related. ISSN: 0035-1326 ■Editions du CNRS; 15 quai Anatole France; 75700 Paris; FRANCE.

RdArt *Revista d'Art*. Freq: 1; Cov: Scan; Lang: Spa; Subj: Related. ■c/o Baldiri Reixac, Departament d'Historia de l'Art; Facultat de Geografia i Historia; 08028 Barcelona; SPAIN.

RdD *Rassegna di Diritto Cinematografico, Teatrale e della Televisione*. Lang: Ita; Subj: Theatre. ■Via Ennio Quirino Visconti 99; Rome; ITALY.

RdS *Rassegna dello Spettacolo*. Began: 1953; Lang: Ita; Subj: Theatre. ISSN: 0033-9474 ■Assoc. Gen. Italiana dello Spettacolo; Via di Villa Patrizi 10; 00161 Rome; ITALY.

RE *Revue d'esthétique*. Freq 4; Cov: Scan; Lang: Fre; Subj: Theatre. ■Privat et Cie; 14, rue des Arts; 31068 Toulouse CEDEX; FRANCE.

Recorder *Recorder, The: A Journal of the American Irish Historical Society*. Freq: 2; Began: 1985; Cov: Scan; Lang: Eng; Subj: Related. ■American Irish Historical Society; 991 Fifth Avenue; New York, NY 10028; USA.

REEDN *Records of Early English Drama Newsletter*. Freq: 2; Began: 1976; Cov: Full; Lang: Eng; Subj: Theatre. ISSN: 0070-9283 ■University of Toronto, Erindale College, English Section; Mississauga, ON L5L 1C6; CANADA.

RenD *Renaissance Drama*. Freq: 1; Began: 1964; Cov: Full; Lang: Eng; Subj: Theatre. ISSN: 0486-3739 ■English Dept.; Northwestern University; 625 Colfax; Evanston, IL 60201; USA.

Renmin *Renmin Xiju*: People's Theatre. Freq: 12; Began: 1950; Lang: Chi; Subj: Theatre. ■52 Dongai Batiao; Peking; CHINA.

Repliikki *Repliikki*. Freq: 4; Began: 1970; Lang: Fin; Subj: Theatre. ■Suomen Harrastajateatteriliitto; r.y. Museokatu 7B12; 00100 Helsinki 10; FINLAND.

REsT *Revista de Estudios de Teatro*: Boletin. Freq: 3; Began: 1964; Lang: Spa; Subj: Theatre. ISSN: 0034-8171 ■Instituto Nacional de Estudios de Teatro; Cordoba 1199; Buenos Aires; ARGENTINA.

Restor *Restoration and Eighteenth Century Theatre Research*. Freq: 2; Began: 1962; Cov: Full; Lang: Eng; Subj: Theatre. ISSN: 0034-5822 ■Loyola University of Chicago, Dept. of English; 6525 North Sheridan Road; Chicago, IL 60626; USA.

Revue *Revue*. Freq: 6; Lang: Fre; Subj: Theatre. ■Theatre de la Commune, BP 157; 2 rue Edouard Poisson; 93304 Aubervilliers; FRANCE.

RHSTMC *Revue Roumaine d'Histoire de l'Art*: Série Théâtre, Musique, Cinéma. Freq: 4; Began: 1980; Lang: Fre; Subj: Related. ■Ed. Academiei Rep. Soc. Romania; Calea Victoriei 125; 79717 Bucharest; ROMANIA.

RHT *Revue d'Histoire du Théâtre*. Freq: 4; Began: 1948; Cov: Full; Lang: Fre; Subj: Theatre. ISSN: 0035-2373 ■Société d'Histoire du Théâtre; 98 Boulevard Kellermann; 75013 Paris; FRANCE.

RIDr *Rivista Italiana di Drammaturgia*. Freq: 4; Began: 1976; Lang: Ita; Subj: Theatre. ■Istituto del Dramma Italiano; Via Monte della Farina 42; Rome; ITALY.

RLC *Revue de Littérature Comparée*. Freq: 4; Began: 1921; Cov: Scan; Lang: Fre/Eng/Ger; Subj: Related. ISSN: 0035-1466 ■F. Didier Erudition; 6 rue de la Sorbonne; 75005 Paris; FRANCE.

RLit *Russkaja Literatura: Istoriko-Literaturnyj Žurnal*: (Russian Literature: Historical Literary Journal). Freq: 4; Began: 1958; Cov: Scan; Lang: Rus; Subj: Related. ISSN: 0557-5362 ■Inst. Russkoj Lit. Akademii Nauk SSSR, Puškinskij Dom; Nab. Makarova 4; 199164 Leningrad; USSR.

RLtrs *Red Letters*. Freq: 3; Began: 1976; Lang: Eng; Subj: Related. ISSN: 0308-6852 ■A Journal of Cultural Politics; 16 St. John Street; EC1M 4AY London; UK.

RMelo *Rassegna Melodrammatica*. Lang: Ita; Subj: Theatre. ■Corso di Porta Romana 80; Milan; ITALY.

RN *Rouge et Noir*. Freq: 9; Began: 1968; Lang: Fre; Subj: Related. ■Maison de la Culture de Grenoble; BP 70-40; 38020 Grenoble; FRANCE.

Roda *Roda Lyktan*. Freq: 1; Began: 1976; Lang: Swe; Subj: Theatre. ISSN: 0040-0750 ■Skanska Teatern; Osterg 31; 26134 Landskrona; SWEDEN.

RORD *Research Opportunities in Renaissance Drama*. Freq: 1/2 yrs; Began: 1956; Cov: Full; Lang: Eng; Subj: Theatre. ■Department of English; University of Kansas; Lawrence, KS 66045; USA.

RRMT *Ridotto*: Rassegna Mensile di Teatro. Freq: 12; Began: 1951; Cov: Scan; Lang: Ita; Subj: Theatre. ISSN: 0035-5186 ■Società Italiana Autori Drammatici; Via Po 10; 00198 Rome; ITALY.

RSP *Rivista di Studi Pirandelliani*. Freq: 3; Began: 1978; Cov: Scan; Lang: Ita; Subj: Theatre. ■Centro Nazionale di Studi Pirandelliani; Agrigento; ITALY.

SAADYT *SAADYT Journal*. Formerly: *SAADYT Newsletter*. Began: 1979; Cov: Scan; Lang: Eng/Afr; Subj: Theatre. ■South African Assoc. for Drama and, Youth Theatre; Private Bag X41; Pretoria; SOUTH AFRICA.

SAD *Studies in American Drama, 1945-Present.* Freq: 1; Began: 1986; Cov: Full; Lang: Eng; Subj: Theatre. ISSN: 0886-7097 ■Ohio State University Press; 1070 Carmack Road; Columbus, OH 43210; USA.

Sage *Sage*: A Scholarly Journal on Black Women. Freq: 2; Began: 1984; Cov: Scan; Lang: Eng; Subj: Related. ISSN: 0741-8369 ■Sage Women's Educational Press, Inc.; Box 42741; Atlanta, GA 30311 0741; USA.

Sahne *Sahne (The Stage).* Freq: 12; Began: 1981; Lang: Tur; Subj: Theatre. ■Nes'e Altiner; Cagaloglu Yokusu 2; Istanbul; TURKEY.

SAITT *SAITT Focus.* Freq: IRR; Began: 1969; Lang: Eng/Afr; Subj: Theatre. ■S. African Inst. for Theatre Technology; Pretoria; SOUTH AFRICA.

SAJAL *South African Journal of African Languages.* Freq: 4; Began: 1981; Lang: Eng & Afrikaans; Subj: Related. ISSN: 0257-2117 ■African Languages Asso. of Southern Africa; Bureau for Scientific Publications; Box 1758; Pretoria 0001; SOUTH AFRICA.

SanatO *Sanat Olayi (Art Event).* Freq: 12; Lang: Tur; Subj: Theatre. ■Karacan Yayinlari; Basin Sarayi; Cagaloglu-Istanbul; TURKEY.

SATJ *South African Theatre Journal.* Freq: 2; Began: 1987; Lang: Eng; Subj: Theatre. ■Drama Department; University of Witwatersrand; WITS 2050; SOUTH AFRICA.

SCagdas *Sanajans Cagdas.* Freq: 12; Lang: Tur; Subj: Theatre. ■Istiklal Caddesi Botter Han; 475/479 Kat. 3; Istanbul; TURKEY.

ScCh *Scene Changes.* Freq: 9; Began: 1973; Ceased: 1981; Cov: Scan; Lang: Eng; Subj: Theatre. ISSN: 0381-8098 ■Theatre Ontario; 8 York Street, 7th floor; Toronto, ON M5R 1J2; CANADA.

Scena *Scena*: Časopis za pozorišnu umetnost. Freq: 6; Began: 1965; Lang: Ser; Subj: Theatre. ISSN: 0036-5734 ■Sterijino Pozorje; Zmaj Jovina 22; 21000 Novi Sad; YUGOSLAVIA.

ScenaB *Scena.* Freq: 4; Began: 1962; Lang: Ger; Subj: Theatre. ISSN: 0036-5726 ■Institut für Technologie Kultureller Einrichtung; Clara Zetkin-Str. 1205; 108 Berlin; EAST GERMANY.

ScenaE *Scena*: Theatre Arts Review. Freq: 1; Began: 1978; Lang: Eng; Subj: Theatre. ■Sterijino Pozorje; Novi Sad; YUGOSLAVIA.

ScenaM *Scena.* Freq: 12; Began: 1976; Lang: Ita; Subj: Theatre. ■Morrison Hotel; Via Modena 16; 20129 Milan; ITALY.

ScenaP *Scéna.* Freq: 26; Began: 1976; Cov: Scan; Lang: Cze; Subj: Theatre. ISSN: 0139-5386 ■Scena; Valdstejnske nam. 3; Prague 1; CZECHOSLOVAKIA.

Scenaria *Scenaria.* Freq: 24; Began: 1977; Cov: Scan; Lang: Eng; Subj: Theatre. ISSN: 0256-002X

■Triad Publishers Ltd.; Box 72161, Parkview 2122; Johannesburg; SOUTH AFRICA.

Scenarium *Scenarium.* Freq: 10; Began: 1879; Lang: Dut; Subj: Theatre. ■De Walburg Pres; P. O. Box 222; 7200 AE Zutphen; NETHERLANDS.

ScenaW *Scena.* Formerly: *Poradnik Teatrow, Lirnik Wioskowy.* Freq: 48; Began: 1908; Lang: Pol; Subj: Theatre. ■Wydawnictwo Prasa ZSL; ul. Reja 9; 02 053 Warsaw; POLAND.

Scene *Scene, De.* Freq: 10; Began: 1959; Lang: Dut; Subj: Theatre. ■Theatercentrum; Jan van Rijswijcklaan 28; B 2000 Antwerpen; BELGIUM.

Scenograf *Scenografie.* Freq: 4; Began: 1963; Lang: Cze; Subj: Theatre. ISSN: 0036-5815 ■Divadelni Ustav; Valdstejnske 3; Prague 1; CZECHOSLOVAKIA.

ScenoS *Scen och Salong.* Freq: 12; Began: 1915; Lang: Swe; Subj: Theatre. ISSN: 0036-5718 ■Folkparkernas Centralorganisation; Svedenborgsgatan 1; S 116 48 Stockholm; SWEDEN.

Schaus *Schauspielfuehrer*: Der Inhalt der wichtigsten Theaterstuecke aus aller Welt. Freq: IRR; Began: 1953; Lang: Ger; Subj: Theatre. ISSN: 0342-4553 ■Anton Hiersemann Verlag, Rosenbergstr 113; Postfach 723; 7000 Stuttgart 1; WEST GERMANY.

SchwT *Schweizer Theaterjahrbuch.* Freq: 1; Lang: Ger; Subj: Related. ■Swiss Association for Theatre Research; c/o Louis Naef; Postfach 180, CH-6130 Willisau; SWITZERLAND.

ScIDI *Scena IDI, La.* Freq: 4; Began: 1971; Lang: Ita; Subj: Theatre. ■Bulzoni Editore; Via Liburni 14; 00185 Rome; ITALY.

Screen *Screen.* Freq: 24; Began: 1959; Cov: Scan; Lang: Eng; Subj: Related. ISSN: 0036-9543 ■Society for Educ. in Film & TV; 29 Old Compton St.; W1V 5PL London; UK.

SCYPT *SCYPT Journal.* Freq: 2; Began: 1977; Ceased: 1986; Cov: Scan; Lang: Eng; Subj: Theatre. ■Standing Conf. on Young People's Theatre, c/o Cockpit Theatre; Gateforth Street; NW8 London; UK.

SDi *Slovenské Divadlo.* Freq: 4; Began: 1952; Cov: Full; Lang: Slo; Subj: Theatre. ISSN: 0037-699X ■Slovanian Acad. of Sciences; Klemensova 19; 814 30 Bratislava; CZECHOSLOVAKIA.

SdO *Serra d'Or.* Freq: 12; Began: 1959; Cov: Scan; Lang: Spa; Subj: Related. ISSN: 0037-2501 ■Publicacions de l'Abadia de Montser, Ausias March 92-98; Apdo. 244; 13 Barcelona; SPAIN.

SEEA *Slavic & East European Arts.* Freq: 2; Began: 1982; Cov: Full; Lang: Eng; Subj: Related. ■State Univ. of NY, Stonybrook, Dept. of Germanic & Slavic Lang.; Slavic & East European Arts; Stonybrook, NY 11794; USA.

SEEDTF *Soviet and East-European Drama, Theatre and Film.* Formerly: *Newsnotes on Soviet & East European Drama &Theatre.* Freq: 3; Began: 1981; Cov: Scan; Lang: Eng; Subj: Theatre. ■Inst. for Contemporary East European and Soviet Drama and Theatre; Graduate Ctre, CUNY, 33 West 42nd St., Room 1206A; New York, NY 10036; USA.

Segmundo *Segismundo.* Freq: 6; Began: 1965; Lang: Spa; Subj: Theatre. ■Consejo Superior de Investigaciones Cientificas; Vitruvio 8, Apartado 14.458; Madrid 6; SPAIN.

Sehir *Sehir Tijatrolari (City Theatre).* Freq: 12; Began: 1930; Lang: Tur; Subj: Theatre. ■Sunusi Tekiner; Basin ve Halka Iliskiler Danismanligi; Harbiye-Istanbul; TURKEY.

Sembianza *Sembianza.* Freq: 6; Began: 1981; Lang: Ita; Subj: Theatre. ■Via Manzoni 14; 20121 Milan; ITALY.

SFN *Shakespeare on Film Newsletter.* Freq: 2; Began: 1977; Cov: Scan; Lang: Eng; Subj: Related. ■Dept. of English; Nassau Community College; Garden City, NY 11530; USA.

SFo *Szinháztechnikai Fórum.* Freq: 4; Began: 1977; Cov: Full; Lang: Hun; Subj: Theatre. ISSN: 0139-1542 ■OPAKFI; Anker köz. 1; 1061 Budapest VII; HUNGARY.

Sg *Shingeki.* Freq: 12; Began: 1954; Lang: Jap; Subj: Theatre. ■Hakusui-sha, Chiyoda-ku; 3-24 Kanda-Ogawamachi; 101 Tokyo; JAPAN.

SGIP *Sovetskoe Gosudarstvo i Pravo.* Freq: 12; Began: 1927; Cov: Scan; Lang: Rus; Subj: Related. ISSN: 0038-5204 ■Akad. Nauk S.S.S.R.; Inst. Gosudarstva i Prava; Izdatel'stvo Nauka; Podsosenskii Per., 21; Moscow K-62; Russian S.F.S.R.; U.S.S.R.

SGT *Schriften der Gesellschaft für Theatergeschichte.* Lang: Ger; Subj: Theatre. ■Berlin; WEST GERMANY.

SGTJ *Schweizerische Gesellschaft für Theaterkultur Jahrbücher.* Freq: IRR; Began: 1928; Lang: Ger; Subj: Theatre. ■Swiss Association for Theatre Research, c/o Louis Naef; Postfach 180; CH-6130 Willisau; SWITZERLAND.

SGTS *Schweizerische Gesellschaft für Theaterkultur Schriften.* Freq: IRR; Began: 1928; Ceased: 1982; Lang: Ger; Subj: Theatre. ■Swiss Association for Theatre Research, c/o Louis Naef; Postfach 180; CH-6130 Willisau; SWITZERLAND.

Shahaab *Shahaab.* Lang: Ara; Subj: Theatre. ■Hayassat Building; Cooper Road; Rawlpindi; PAKISTAN.

ShakS *Shakespeare Studies.* Freq: 1; Lang: Eng; Subj: Theatre. ■New York, NY; USA.

ShakSN *Shakespeare Studies.* Lang: Eng; Subj: Theatre. ■Nashville, TN; USA.

Shavian   *Shavian*. Freq: 1; Began: 1946; Lang: Eng; Subj: Theatre. ISSN: 0037-3346 ▪High Orchard Press, High Orchard; 125 Markyate Rd.; RM8 2LB Dgenham, Essex; UK.

ShawR   *Shaw*: The Annual of Bernard Shaw Studies. Formerly: *Shaw Review (ISSN: 0037-3354)*. Freq: 1; Began: 1981; Cov: Scan; Lang: Eng; Subj: Theatre. ISSN: 0741-5842 ▪Pennsylvania State Univ. Press; S234 Burrowes Bldg South; University Park, PA 16802; USA.

ShN   *Shakespeare Newsletter*. Freq: 4; Began: 1951; Lang: Eng; Subj: Theatre. ISSN: 0037-3214 ▪Louis Marder, Ed. & Pub.; 1217 Ashland Ave.; Evanston, IL 60202; USA.

Show   *Show*. Lang: Eng; Subj: Theatre. ▪9/2 Nazimabad; Karachi; PAKISTAN.

ShS   *Shakespeare Survey*. Freq: 1; Began: 1948; Cov: Full; Lang: Eng; Subj: Theatre. ISSN: 0080-9152 ▪Cambridge University Press, The Edinburgh Building; Shaftesbury Road; CB2 2RU Cambridge; UK.

Silex   *Silex*. Lang: Fre; Subj: Theatre. ▪BP 554 RP; 38013 Grenoble; FRANCE.

Sin   *Sightline*: The Journal of Theatre Technology and Design. Freq: 2; Began: 1974; Cov: Scan; Lang: Eng; Subj: Theatre. ISSN: 0265-9808 ▪Assoc. of British Theatre Technicians; 4 Gt. Pulteney Street; W1R 3DF London; UK.

Sipario   *Sipario*. Freq: 12; Began: 1946; Lang: Ita; Subj: Theatre. ▪Sipario Editrice S.R.L.; Via Flaminia 167; 00196 Rome; ITALY.

Sis   *Sightlines*. Freq: 4; Began: 1965; Cov: Scan; Lang: Eng; Subj: Related. ISSN: 0565-6311 ▪USITT; 330 West 42nd St., Ste. 1702; New York, NY 10036; USA.

SiSo   *Sight and Sound*. Freq: 4; Began: 1932; Lang: Eng; Subj: Related. ISSN: 0037-4806 ▪British Film Institute; 127 Charing Cross Rd.; WC2H 0EA London; UK.

SjV   *Sirp ja Vasar*. Freq: 52; Began: 1940; Lang: Est; Subj: Theatre. ▪Postkast 388, Pikk t. 40; 200 001 Talin, Estonian SSR; USSR.

SJW   *Shakespeare Jahrbuch*. Freq: 1; Began: 1865; Cov: Scan; Lang: Ger; Subj: Theatre. ISSN: 0080-9128 ▪Deutsche Shakespeare Gesellschaft, Hermann Bohlaus Nachfolger; Meyerstrasse 50a; 53 Weimar; EAST GERMANY.

Skript   *Skript*. Freq: 10; Lang: Dut; Subj: Theatre. ▪N.C.A.; Postbus 64; 3600 AB Maarssen; NETHERLANDS.

SM   *Spectacles Magazine*. Freq: 12; Lang: Fre; Subj: Theatre. ▪42 Blvd. du Temple; 75011 Paris; FRANCE.

Smena   *Smena*. Freq: 12; Began: 1924; Cov: Scan; Lang: Rus; Subj: Related. ISSN: 0131-6656 ▪Moscow; USSR.

SMR   *SourceMonthly*: The Resource for Mimes, Clowns, Jugglers, and Puppeteers. Freq: 12; Cov: Scan; Lang: Eng; Subj: Theatre. ▪Mimesource Inc.; 125 Sherman Str.; Brooklyn, NY 11218; USA.

SNJPA   *Sangeet Natak*: Journal of the Performing Arts. Freq: 4; Began: 1965; Cov: Scan; Lang: Eng; Subj: Theatre. ISSN: 0036-4339 ▪Sangeet Natak Akademi, Rabindra Bhavan; Ferozeshah Rd.; 110001 New Delhi; INDIA.

SobCh   *Sobcota Chelovneta*. Lang: Geo; Subj: Theatre. ▪Tbilisi, Georg. SSR; USSR.

Sobesednik   *Sobesednik*. Freq: 12; Began: 1949; Cov: Scan; Lang: Rus; Subj: Related. ISSN: 0202-3180 ▪Moscow; USSE.

SObzor   *Scenograficky Obzor*. Freq: 6; Lang: Cze; Subj: Theatre. ▪Vinohradska 2; Prague 1; CZECHO-SLOVAKIA.

SocH   *Social History*. Freq: 3; Began: 1976; Lang: Eng; Subj: Related. ISSN: 0307-1022 ▪Methuen and Co. Ltd.; 11 New Fetter Lane; EC4P 4EE London; UK.

SoM   *Speaking of Mime*. Freq: IRR; Began: 1976; Lang: Eng; Subj: Theatre. ▪Canadian Mime Council; Niagara, ON L0S 1J0; CANADA.

Somo   *Somogy*. Freq: 6; Began: 1970; Cov: Scan; Lang: Hun; Subj: Related. ▪Május 1. u. 10; 7400 Kaposvár; HUNGARY.

SON   *Scottish Opera News*. Freq: 12; Lang: Eng; Subj: Theatre. ISSN: 0309-7323 ▪Scottish Opera Club; Elmbank Crescent; G2 4PT Glasgow; UK.

SoQ   *Southern Quarterly, The*: A Journal of the Arts in the South. Freq: 4; Began: 1962; Lang: Eng; Subj: Related. ISSN: 0038-4496 ▪PO Box 5078 Southern Station; Hattiesburg, MS 39401; USA.

SORev   *Sean O'Casey Review, The*. Freq: 2; Began: 1974; Lang: Eng; Subj: Theatre. ISSN: 0365-2245 ▪O'Casey Studies; PO Box 333; Holbrook, NY 11741; USA.

SoSaw   *Southern Sawdust*. Freq: 4; Began: 1954; Lang: Eng; Subj: Theatre. ISSN: 0038-4542 ▪L. Wilson Poarch Jr.; 2965 Freeman Avenue; Sarasota, FL 33580; USA.

SoTh   *Southern Theatre*. Began: 1964; Cov: Scan; Lang: Eng; Subj: Theatre. ISSN: 0584-4738 ▪Southeastern Theatre Conference; University of Carolina; 506 Stirling St. Greensboro, NC 27412; USA.

SOUTHERLY   *Southerly: A Review of Australian Literature*. Freq: 4; Began: 1939; Cov: Scan; Lang: Eng; Subj: Related. ISSN: 0038-3732 ▪Dept. of English; Univ. of Sydney; Sydney N.S.W. 2006; AUSTRALIA.

SovAr   *Sovetskie Arkhivy*. Freq: 6; Began: 1966; Cov: Scan; Lang: Rus; Subj: Related. ISSN: 0038-5166

▪Glavnoe Arkhivnoe Upravlenie; Pirogovskaya 17; Moscow G-435; Russian S.F.S.R.; U.S.S.R.

SovBal   *Sovĕckij Balet*. Cov: Scan; Lang: Rus; Subj: Theatre. ▪Moscow; USSR.

SovD   *Sovremĕnnaja Dramaturgija*. Freq: 4; Began: 1982; Cov: Scan; Lang: Rus; Subj: Theatre. ISSN: 6207-7698 ▪Moscow; USSR.

SovEC   *Sovĕckaja Estrada i Cirk*. Freq: 12; Cov: Scan; Lang: Rus; Subj: Theatre. ▪Moscow; USSR.

SovEt   *Sovĕckaja Ethnografia*. Freq: 6; Began: 1926; Cov: Scan; Lang: Rus; Subj: Related. ISSN: 0038-5050 ▪Ulica D. Uljanova 19; B 36 Moscow; USSR.

SovKult   *Sovĕckaja Kultura*. Cov: Scan; Lang: Rus; Subj: Related. ▪Novoslobodskaja ul. 73; K 55 Moscow; USSR.

SovMuzyka   *Sovĕckaja Muzyka*: (Soviet Music). Freq: 12; Began: 1933; Cov: Scan; Lang: Rus; Subj: Related. ISSN: 0131-6818 ▪Moscow; USSR.

SovSlav   *Sovĕckojĕ Slavjanovĕdĕnjĕ*: (Soviet Slavonic Studies). Freq: 6; Began: 1965; Cov: Scan; Lang: Rus; Subj: Related. ISSN: 0584-5394 ▪Izdatel'stvo Nauka; Podsosenskii Per. 21; K 62 Moscow; USSR.

SovT   *Sovĕckij Teat'r/Soviet Theatre*. Freq: 4; Began: 1976; Cov: Scan; Lang: Rus/Ger/Eng/Fre/Spa; Subj: Theatre. ▪Copyright Agency of the USSR; 6a Bolshaya Bronnaya St.; K 104 Moscow 103670; USSR.

Spa   *Shilpakala*. Lang: Ben; Subj: Related. ▪Dacca; BANGLADESH.

SPC   *Studies in Popular Culture*. Freq: 2; Began: 1977; Lang: Eng; Subj: Related. ▪Popular Culture Association in the South, Florida State Univ., English Dp.; Tallahassee, FL 32306; USA.

Speak   *Speak*. Began: 1977; Lang: Eng; Subj: Theatre. ▪PO Box 126, Newlands; 7725 Cape Town; SOUTH AFRICA.

Spettacolo   *Spettacolo, Lo*. Freq: 4; Began: 1951; Lang: Ita; Subj: Theatre. ISSN: 0038-738X ▪S.I.A.E.; Viale della Letteratura 30; 00100 Rome; ITALY.

Spirale   *Spirale: Art, letters, spectacles, sciences humaines*. Freq: 12; Began: 1979; Lang: Fre; Subj: Theatre. ISSN: 0225-9004 ▪C.P. 98, Succ. E; Montreal, PQ; CANADA.

SpIt   *Spettacolo in Italia, Lo*. Freq: 1; Began: 1951; Lang: Ita; Subj: Theatre. ISSN: 0038-738X ▪S.I.A.E.; Viale della Letteratura 30; 00100 Rome; ITALY.

Spl   *Spielplan, Der*. Freq: 12; Began: 1954; Lang: Ger; Subj: Theatre. ISSN: 0038-7517 ▪P.-A. Schmueking; Kastanienallee 2a; 3300 Braunschweig; WEST GERMANY.

SpViag *Spettacolo Viaggiante*. Began: 1948; Lang: Ita; Subj: Theatre.
■Assoc. Naz. Eserc. Spet. Viaggianti; Via di Villa Patrizi 10; 00161 Rome; ITALY.

SQ *Shakespeare Quarterly*. Freq: 4; Began: 1950; Cov: Scan; Lang: Eng; Subj: Related. ISSN: 0037-3222
■Folger Shakespeare Library; 201 E. Capitol St. S.E.; Washington, DC 20003; USA.

SSSS *Szene Schweiz/Scène Suisse/ Scena Svizzera*. Freq: 1; Began: 1973; Cov: Scan; Lang: Ger/Fre/Ita; Subj: Theatre.
■Swiss Association for Theatre Research; c/o Louis Naef; Postfach 180; CH-6130 Willisau; SWITZERLAND.

SSTJ *Secondary School Theater Journal*. Freq: 3; Began: 1962; Lang: Eng; Subj: Theatre.
■American Theatre Association, Secondary School Theatre Assoc.; 1010 Wisconsin Ave., N.W., Suite 630; Washington, DC 20007; USA.

Staff *Staffrider*. Freq: 4; Began: 1978; Lang: Eng; Subj: Related.
■Ravan Press Ltd.; Box 31134; 2017 Braamfontein; SOUTH AFRICA.

StageZ *Stage*. Freq: IRR; Began: 1956; Lang: Eng; Subj: Theatre.
■Lusaka Theatre Club Ltd; Box 30615; Lusaka; ZAMBIA.

Standpunte *Standpunte*. Freq: 6; Began: 1945; Cov: Scan; Lang: Afr; Subj: Related. ISSN: 0038-9730
■Tafelberg Publishers; c/o J.C. Kannemeyer, Ed.; P.O. Box 91073; Auckland Park 2006; SOUTH AFRICA.

Sterijino *Sterijino Pozorje*: Informativno Glasilo. Freq: IRR; Began: 1982; Lang: Ser; Subj: Theatre.
■Sterijino Pozorje; Zmaj Jovina 22; Novi Sad; YUGOSLAVIA.

Stikord *Stikord*. Freq: 4; Began: 1981; Lang: Dan; Subj: Theatre. ISSN: 0107-6582
■Foreningen Hidovre Teater; Hidovre Strandvej 70A; 2650 Hidovre; DENMARK.

STILB *STILB*. Freq: 5; Began: 1981; Lang: Ita; Subj: Theatre.
■Via della Fosse di Castello 6; 00193 Rome; ITALY.

STN *Scottish Theater News*. Freq: 12; Began: 1981; Ceased: 1986; Cov: Scan; Lang: Eng; Subj: Theatre. ISSN: 0261-4057
■Scottish Society of Playwrights; 346 Sauchiehall St.; G2 3JD Glasgow; UK.

StPh *Studies in Philology*. Freq: 3; Began: 1906; Cov: Scan; Lang: Eng; Subj: Related. ISSN: 0039-3738
■University of North Carolina Press; Box 2288; Chapel Hill, NC 27514; USA.

Strind *Strindbergiana*: Meddelanden från Strindbergssällskapet. Formerly: *Meddelanden från Strindbergssällskapet*. Freq: 1; Began: 1985; Cov: Full; Lang: Swe; Subj: Theatre.
■Strindbergssällskapet, c/o C. R. Smedmark; Drottninggatan 85; 111 60 Stockholm; SWEDEN.

STT *Sceničeskaja Technika i Technologija*. Freq: 6; Began: 1963; Cov: Full; Lang: Rus; Subj: Theatre. ISSN: 0131-9248

■Serebriančeskij Per. 2/5; 109028 Moscow; USSR.

StudiaP *Studia i Materialy do Dziejow Teatru Polskiego*. Formerly: *Studia i Materialy z Dziejow Teatru Polskiego*. Freq: IRR; Began: 1957; Lang: Pol; Subj: Theatre. ISSN: 0208-404X
■Polish Academy of Sciences; Rynek 9; Wroclaw; POLAND.

StudiiR *Studii si Cercetari de Istoria Artei*: Seria Teatru-Muzica-Cinematografie. Freq: 1; Began: 1954; Lang: Rom; Subj: Theatre. ISSN: 0039-3991
■Academia Rep. Soc. Romania; Calea Victoriei 125; 79717 Bucharest; ROMANIA.

StudM *Studenčeskij Meridian*. Freq: 1?; Began: 1924; Cov: Scan, Lang: Rus; Subj: Related. ISSN: 0321-3803
■Moscow; USSR.

STYol *STYolainen*. Freq: 6; Began: 1975; Lang: Fin; Subj: Theatre.
■Suomen Teatterityontekijain, Yhteisjarjesto; Maneesikatu 4c; 00170 Helsinki 17; FINLAND.

SuAS *Stratford-upon-Avon Studies*. Freq: IRR; Began: 1961; Lang: Eng; Subj: Theatre.
■Edward Arnold Ltd; 41 Bedford Square; WC1B 3DQ London; UK.

SuF *Sinn und Form: Beiträge zur Literatur*. Freq: 6; Began: 1949; Cov: Scan; Lang: Ger; Subj: Related. ISSN: 0037-5756
■Verlag Rütten & Loening; Französische Str. 32; 1080 Berlin; EAST GERMANY.

Suffloren *Suffløren*. Lang: Dan; Subj: Theatre.
■Medlemsblad for Dansk Dukketeaterforening; Vestergrade 3; 1456 Copenhagen; DENMARK.

SuidAfr *Suid-Afrikaan, Die*. Began: 1985; Cov: Scan; Lang: Afr; Subj: Related.
■Die Suid-Afrikaan; P.O. Box 7010; 7610 Dalsig Stellembosch; SOUTH AFRICA.

Svet *Svět a divadlo*. Began: 1990; Cov: Scan; Lang: Cze;; Subj: Theatre. ISSN: 0862-7258
■Divadelni obec; Valdstejnske nam. 3; Prague 1; CZECHOSLOVAKIA.

SWR *Southwest Review*. Freq: 4; Began: 1924; Lang: Eng; Subj: Related. ISSN: 0038-4712
■Southern Methodist University; Dallas, TX 75275; USA.

SwTS *Swedish Theater/Théâtre Suédois*. Lang: Eng/Fre; Subj: Theatre.
■Stockholm; SWEDEN.

Sz *Szinház*: (Theatre). Freq: 12; Began: 1968; Cov: Full; Lang: Hun; Subj: Theatre. ISSN: 0039-8136
■Lapkiado Vallalat; Lenin Korut 9-11; 1073 Budapest 7; HUNGARY.

Szene *Szene*. Lang: Ger; Subj: Theatre.
■UMLOsterreichischer Bundestheaterverband; Goethegasse 1; A 1010 Vienna; AUSTRIA.

SzeneAT *Szene: Fachzeitschrift der DDR Amateur-theater, -kabarett, -puppenspiel und -ntomime*. Freq: 4; Began: 1966; Cov: Scan; Lang: Ger; Subj: Theatre. ISSN: 0039-811X
■Zentralhaus für Kulturarbeit, Dittrichring 4;

Postfach 1051; 7010 Leipzig; EAST GERMANY.

SzSz *Szinháztudomanyi Szemle*. Freq: 3; Began: 1977; Cov: Full; Lang: Hun; Subj: Theatre.
■Hungarian Theatre Institute; Krisztina Krt. 57; 1016 Budapest I; HUNGARY.

TA *Theatre Annual*. Freq: 1; Began: 1942; Cov: Full; Lang: Eng; Subj: Theatre. ISSN: 0082-3821
■Dept. of Music, Theatre, and Dance, University of Akron; Akron, OH 44325-1005; USA.

TAAm *Theater Across America*. Freq: 5; Began: 1975; Lang: Eng; Subj: Theatre.
■Theatre Sources Inc.; 104 North St. Mary; Dallas, TX 75214; USA.

Tablas *Tablas*: Cuban Theatre. Freq: 4; Began: 1982; Lang: Spa; Subj: Theatre.
■Unidad Presupuestada de Teatro y Danza, Ed. Cubanas Publc. y Promocion; Obispo No 461, Apartado 605; Habana; CUBA.

Tabs *Tabs*. Freq: 2; Began: 1937; Ceased: 1986; Cov: Scan; Lang: Eng; Subj: Theatre. ISSN: 0306-9389
■Rank Strand Ltd., P.O. Box 51, Great West Road; Brentford; TW8 9HR Middlesex; UK.

TAD *Tijatro Arastirmalari Dergisi (Theatre Research Magazine)*. Freq: 1; Began: 1970; Lang: Tur/Eng/Fre; Subj: Theatre.
■Tijatro Arastirmalari Enstitusu, Ankara Universitesi D.T.C.; Fakultesi; Shhiye; Ankara; TURKEY.

Talent *Talent Management*. Freq: 12; Began: 1981; Lang: Eng; Subj: Related.
■T M Publishing; 1501 Broadway; New York, NY 10036; USA.

Tampereen *Tampereen Tyovaen Teatteri*. Lang: Fin; Subj: Theatre.
■Hallituskatu 19; 33003 Tampere 300; FINLAND.

Tanecni *Tanecni Listy*. Freq: 10; Began: 1963; Lang: Cze; Subj: Theatre. ISSN: 0039-937X
■Panorama; Halkova 1; 120 72 Prague 2; CZECHOSLOVAKIA.

TAnim *Théâtre et Animation*. Freq: 4; Began: 1976; Lang: Fre; Subj: Theatre. ISSN: 0398-0049
■Fédération National du Théâtre et d'Animation; 12 Chaussée d'Antin; 75441 Paris Cedex 09; FRANCE.

TantI *Tantsovo Izkustvo*. Freq: 12; Began: 1954; Lang: Bul; Subj: Theatre.
■Izdatelstvo Nauka i Izkustvo; 6 Rouski Blvd; Sofia; BULGARIA.

TanzG *Tanz und Gymnastik*. Freq: 4; Began: 1944; Cov: Scan; Lang: Ger; Subj: Theatre.
■Schweizerischer Berufsverband für Tanz und Gymnastik; Riedbergstrasse 1; 4059 Basel; SWITZERLAND.

TArch *Teatro Archivio*. Formerly: *Bolletino del Museo Biblioteca dell'attore*. Freq: IRR; Began: 1979; Cov: Full; Lang: Ita; Subj: Theatre.
■Bulzoni Editore; Via dei Liburni n 14; 00185 Rome; ITALY.

TArsb   *Teaterårsboken*. Freq: 1; Began: 1982; Cov: Scan; Lang: Swe; Subj: Theatre. ∎Svenska Riksteatern; Råsundavägen 150; S 171 30 Solna; SWEDEN.

TAus   *Theatre Australia*. Freq: 12; Began: 1976; Lang: Eng; Subj: Theatre. ∎Theatre Publications Ltd.; 80 Elizabeth Street; NSW 2304 Mayfield; AUSTRALIA.

Tbuch   *Theaterbuch*. Freq: 1; Lang: Ger; Subj: Theatre. ∎Munich; WEST GERMANY.

TCB   *Teatro Clásico: Boletin*. Freq: 1; Lang: Spa; Subj: Theatre. ∎Teatro Clásico de Mexico; Apartado 61-077; MEXICO.

TCGNWCP   *TCG National Working Conference Proceedings*. Freq: IRR; Began: 1976; Lang: Eng; Subj: Theatre. ∎Theatre Communications Group; 355 Lexington Ave; New York, NY 10017; USA.

TChicago   *Theatre Chicago*. Freq: 12; Began: 1986; Lang: Eng; Subj: Theatre. ∎22 W Monroe, Suite 801; 60603 Chicago;.

TCom   *Theatre Communications*. Freq: 12; Began: 1979; Ceased: 1983; Lang: Eng; Subj: Theatre.   ISSN: 0275-5971 ∎Theatre Communications Group Inc; 355 Lexington Avenue; New York, NY 10017; USA.

TCraft   *Theatrecraft*. Freq: 12; Began: 1964; Lang: Eng; Subj: Theatre. ∎G. Hilton, Victoria Drama League, First Floor; 256 Flindera Street; Melbourne, Victoria; AUSTRALIA.

TCUG   *Theater Computer Users Group Notes*. Began: 1978; Lang: Eng; Subj: Theatre. ∎Theatre Sources Inc.; 104 N Saint Mary; Dallas, TX 76214; USA.

TD&T   *Theatre Design and Technology*. Freq: 4; Began: 1965; Cov: Full; Lang: Eng; Subj: Theatre.   ISSN: 0040-5477 ∎US Inst. for Theatre Technology; 330 W. 42nd St. Suite 1702; New York, NY 10036; USA.

TDDR   *Theaterarbeit in der DDR*. Freq: 3; Began: 1979; Lang: Ger; Subj: Theatre. ∎Verband der Theaterschaffended der DDR; Hermann-Matern-Strasse 18; 1040 Berlin; EAST GERMANY.

TDR   *Drama Review, The*. Freq: 4; Began: 1955; Cov: Full; Lang: Eng; Subj: Theatre.   ISSN: 0012-5962 ∎MIT Press; 55 Haywood St.; Cambridge, MA 02142; USA.

Teat   *Teatteri*. Freq: 12; Began: 1945; Cov: Full; Lang: Fin; Subj: Theatre. ∎Kustannus Oy Teatteri; Vuorikatu 6 A 8; 00100 Helsinki 10; FINLAND.

TeaterD   *Teater i Danmark*: Theatre in Denmark. Freq: 1; Began: 1980; Lang: Dan; Subj: Theatre.   ISSN: 0106-7672 ∎Bibliotekscentralen; Telegrafvej 5; DK 2750 Ballerup; DENMARK.

Teaterf   *Teaterforum*. Freq: 6; Began: 1968; Cov: Full; Lang: Swe; Subj: Theatre. ∎Swedish Society for Amateur Theatres; Von Rosens Väg 1A; 77300 Fagersta; SWEDEN.

Teatern   *Teatern*. Freq: 4; Began: 1934; Lang: Swe; Subj: Theatre. ISSN: 0040-0750 ∎Riksteatern; Swedish National Theatre; S-145 83 Norsburg; SWEDEN.

TeatL   *Teatr Lalek*. Lang: Pol; Subj: Theatre. ∎Warsaw; POLAND.

TeatM   *Teatraluri Moambe*. Lang: Geo; Subj: Theatre. ∎Tbilisi, Georgian S; USSR.

Teatoro   *Teatoro*. Freq: 12; Began: 1944; Lang: Jap; Subj: Theatre. ∎c/o Hagiwara Building, 2-3-1 Sarugaku-cho; Chiyoda-ku; 101 Tokyo; JAPAN.

Teatras   *Teatras*. Lang: Lit; Subj: Theatre. ∎Vilnius, Lithuanian, SSR; USSR.

TeatrC   *Teatro Contemporaneo*. Freq: 3; Began: 1982; Cov: Full; Lang: Ita; Subj: Theatre. ∎Via Trionfale 8406; 00135 Rome; ITALY.

TeatrE   *Teatro en España*. Lang: Spa; Subj: Theatre. ∎Madrid; SPAIN.

TeatrM   *Teat'r*. žurnal dramaturgii i teatra. Freq: 12; Began: 1937; Cov: Full; Lang: Rus; Subj: Theatre.   ISSN: 0040-0777 ∎Izdatel'stvo Iskusstvo; Tsvetnoi bulvar 25; Moscow K-51; USSR.

Teatron   *Teatron*. Began: 1962; Lang: Heb; Subj: Theatre. ∎Municipal Theatre; 20 Pevsner Street; Haifa; ISRAEL.

TeatroS   *Teatro e Storia*. Began: 1986; Cov: Scan; Lang: Ita; Subj: Theatre. ∎Centro per la Sperimentazione e la Ricerca Teatrale di Pontedera; Societa Editrice Il Mulino, Strada Maggiore 37 40125 Bologna; ITALY.

TeatroSM   *TeatroSM*. Began: 1980; Lang: Spa; Subj: Theatre. ∎Teatro Municipal General San Martin; Ave. Corrientes 1530, 50 piso; 1042 Buenos Aires; ARGENTINA.

Teatrul   *Teatrul*. Freq: 12; Began: 1956; Lang: Rom; Subj: Theatre. ISSN: 0040-0815 ∎Consiliul Culturii si Educatiei Socialiste; Calea Victoriei 174; Bucharest; ROMANIA.

TeatrW   *Teatr*. Freq: 26; Began: 1946; Cov: Scan; Lang: Pol; Subj: Theatre. ISSN: 0040-0769 ∎Wydawnictwo Wspolczesne, RSW Prasa-Ksiazka; Ul. Wiejska 12; 00-420 Warsaw; POLAND.

TeaturS   *Teatur*. Freq: 12; Began: 1946; Cov: Full; Lang: Bul; Subj: Theatre. ISSN: 0204-6253 ∎Komitet za Izkustvo i Kultura; 7 Levsky St.; 1000 Sofia; BULGARIA.

TeatY   *Teatron*: Časopis za pozirišnu istoriju i teatrologiju. Began: 1974; Lang: Ser; Subj: Theatre. ∎Muzej Pozorišne umetnosti SR Srbije; Gospodar Jevremova 19; 11000 Belgrade; YUGOSLAVIA.

TeatZ   *Teatralnaja Žizn*. Freq: 24; Began: 1958; Cov: Scan; Lang: Rus; Subj: Theatre.   ISSN: 0040-0785 ∎Vserossij. Teatr. Obščestvo; Moscow; USSR.

TeC   *Teatro e Cinema*. Freq: 4; Began: 1968; Lang: Ita; Subj: Theatre. ISSN: 0040-0807 ∎Silva Editore; Viale Salita Salvatore 1; 28 16128 Genoa; ITALY.

TechB   *Technical Brief*. Freq: 3; Began: 1982; Cov: Full; Lang: Eng; Subj: Theatre. ∎TD&P Dept., Yale School of Drama; 222 York St.; New Haven, CT 06520; USA.

TEJ   *Théâtre Enfance et Jeunesse*. Freq: 2; Began: 1963; Lang: Fre/Eng; Subj: Theatre.   ISSN: 0049-3597 ∎Assoc. du Théâtre pour l'Enfance, et la Jeunesse; 98 Blvd. Kellermann; 75013 Paris; FRANCE.

TEP   *Théâtre de l'Est Parisien*: TEP Actualité. Lang: Fre; Subj: Theatre. ∎Paris; FRANCE.

Textual   *Textual*. Lang: Spa; Subj: Theatre. ∎I.N.C.; Ancash; 390 Idma; PERU.

Textuel   *Textuel*. Freq: 2; Cov: Scan; Lang: Fre; Subj: Theatre. ∎Université de Paris VII; 2, place Jussieu; 75221 Paris CEDEX 05; FRANCE.

TF   *Teaterforum*. Freq: 2; Began: 1980; Cov: Scan; Lang: Eng/Afr; Subj: Theatre. ∎University of Potchefstroom, Departement Spraakler en Drama; Potchefstroom; SOUTH AFRICA.

TF&TV   *Teater Film & TV*. Freq: 8; Began: 1974; Lang: Dan; Subj: Theatre. ∎Faellesforbundet for Teater Film & TV; Ny Oestergade 12; DK 1101 Copenhagen; DENMARK.

TGDR   *Theatre in the GDR*. Lang: Ger; Subj: Theatre. ∎Berlin; EAST GERMANY.

TGlasnik   *Teatarski Glasnik*: Spisanie na teatrite vo SR Makedonija. Freq: 2; Began: 1977; Lang: Slo; Subj: Theatre. ∎Dramski Teatar Skopje;Sekspirova 15; 91000 Skopje; YUGOSLAVIA.

TGraz   *Theater in Graz*. Freq: 4; Began: 1952; Lang: Ger; Subj: Theatre. ∎Vereinigte Bühnen Graz; Burggasse 16; A 8010 Graz; AUSTRIA.

Th   *Théâtre*. Formerly: *Théâtre du Trident*. Lang: Fre; Subj: Theatre. ∎Théâtre du Trident, Edifice Palais Montcalm; 975 Place d'Youville; Quebec, PQ; CANADA.

THC   *Theatre History in Canada/ Histoire du Théâtre*. Freq: 2; Began: 1980; Cov: Full; Lang: Eng/Fre; Subj: Theatre.   ISSN: 0226-5761 ∎Graduate Centre for the Study of Drama, University of Toronto; 214 College Street; Toronto, ON M5T 2Z9; CANADA.

ThCr   *Theatre Crafts*. Freq: 9; Began: 1967; Cov: Full; Lang: Eng; Subj: Theatre.   ISSN: 0040-5469 ∎Theatre Crafts Associates; 135 Fifth Avenue; New York, NY 10010; USA.

ThE   *Théâtre en Europe*. Freq: 4; Began: 1984; Cov: Scan; Lang: Fre; Subj: Theatre. ∎Theatre de l'Europe, 1; Place Paul Claudel; 75006 Paris; FRANCE.

TheaterW *TheaterWeek*. Freq: 52; Began: 1987; Lang: Eng; Subj: Theatre. ISSN: 0896-1956
■That New Magazine; 28 West 25th St., 4th Floor; New York, NY 10010; USA.

TheatreEx *Theatre: Ex*. Freq: 3; Began: 1985; Lang: Eng; Subj: Theatre.
■104 E. 4th Street; New York, NY 10003; USA.

TheatreS *Theatre Studies*. Freq: 1; Began: 1954; Cov: Full; Lang: Eng; Subj: Theatre. ISSN: 0362-0964
■Ohio State Univ., Lawrence and Lee, Theatre Research Institute; 1430 Lincoln Tower, 1800 Cannon Drive; Columbus, OH 43210 1234; USA.

TheatreT *Theatre Three*. Began: 1986; Ceased: 1991; Lang: Eng; Subj: Theatre.
■Carnegie Mellon, Department of Drama; Pittsburgh, PA 15213; USA.

Theatro *Theatro*. Lang: Gre; Subj: Theatre.
■Kosta Nitsos; Christou Lada 5-7; Athens; GREECE.

Theatron *Theatron*: Rivista quindicinale di cultura, documentazione ed informazione teatrale. Freq: 26; Began: 1961; Lang: Ita/Eng/Ger; Subj: Theatre. ISSN: 0040-5604
■Centro Teatrale Intl. di Documentazione e Collaborazione tra Teatri di Ricerca e Univ.; Via Fabiola 1; 00152 Rome; ITALY.

Theatrum *Theatrum: A Theatre Journal*. Freq: 3; Began: 1985; Cov: Full; Lang: Eng; Subj: Theatre.
■Theatrum; P.O. Box 688, Station C; Toronto, ON M6J 3S1; CANADA.

Theoria *Theoria*: A Journal of Studies in the Arts, Humanities and Social Studies. Freq: 2; Began: 1947; Cov: Scan; Lang: Eng; Subj: Related. ISSN: 0040-5817
■University of Natal Press; Box 375; Pietermaritzburg; SOUTH AFRICA.

Thespis *Thespis*. Lang: Gre; Subj: Theatre.
■Greek Centre of the ITI; Anthinou Gazi 9; Athens; GREECE.

THeute *Theater Heute*. Freq: 12; Began: 1960; Cov: Scan; Lang: Ger; Subj: Theatre. ISSN: 0040-5507
■Orell Fuessli & Friedrich Verlag; Dietzingerstr. 3; CH 8036 Zurich; SWITZERLAND.

ThIr *Theatre Ireland*. Freq: 3; Began: 1982; Cov: Scan; Lang: Eng; Subj: Theatre. ISSN: 0263-6344
■Theatre Ireland, Ltd; 16b Adelaide Park; BT9 6FX Belfast; IRELAND.

ThM *Theater Magazine*. Freq: 3; Began: 1968; Cov: Full; Lang: Eng; Subj: Theatre. ISSN: 0160-0775
■Yale University, School of Theater; 222 York Street Yale Station; New Haven, CT 06520; USA.

ThNe *Theatre News*. Freq: 6; Began: 1968; Ceased: 1985; Cov: Scan; Lang: Eng; Subj: Theatre. ISSN: 0563-4040
■American Theatre Association; 1010 Wisconsin Ave., NW, Suite 620; Washington, DC 20007; USA.

ThPa *Theatre Papers*. Freq: IRR; Began: 1978; Cov: Full; Lang: Eng; Subj: Theatre. ISSN: 0309-8036

■Documentation Unit, Dartington College of Arts; Totnes; TQ9 6EJ Devon; UK.

ThPh *Theatrephile*. Freq: 4; Began: 1983; Ceased: 1985; Cov: Full; Lang: Eng; Subj: Theatre. ISSN: 0265-2609
■D. Cheshire & S. McCarthy Eds. & Publ.; 5 Dryden Street, Covent Garden; WC2E 9NW London; UK.

ThPu *Théâtre Public*. Freq: 6; Began: 1974; Cov: Scan; Lang: Fre; Subj: Theatre. ISSN: 0335-2927
■Théâtre de Gennevilliers; 41, avenue des Gresillons; 92230 Gennevilliers; FRANCE.

ThR *Theatre Research International*. Freq: 3; Began: 1958; Cov: Full; Lang: Eng; Subj: Theatre. ISSN: 0307-8833
■Oxford University Press; Pinkhill House; Southfield Road, OX8 1JJ Eynsham, Oxford; UK.

ThS *Theatre Survey*. Freq: 2; Began: 1960; Cov: Full; Lang: Eng; Subj: Theatre. ISSN: 0040-5574
■ASTR; Department of Theatre; Indiana University; Bloomington, IN 47405; USA.

THSt *Theatre History Studies*. Freq: 1; Began: 1981; Cov: Full; Lang: Eng; Subj: Theatre. ISSN: 0733-2033
■Dept. of Theatre Arts; Univ. of North Dakota; Grand Forks, ND 58202; USA.

ThSw *Theatre Southwest*. Freq: 3; Began: 1974; Cov: Full; Lang: Eng; Subj: Theatre.
■Oklahoma State University; 102 Seretean Center; Stillwater, OK 74078; USA.

ThToday *Theatre Today*. Lang: Eng; Subj: Theatre.
■Advanced Institute for Development, American Repertory Theatre; 245 West 52nd Street; New York, NY 10019; USA.

ThYear *Theatre Year*. Freq: 1; Began: 1980; Ceased: 1983; Cov: Scan; Lang: Eng; Subj: Theatre. ISSN: 0261-2348
■In (Parenthesis) Ltd.; 21 Wellington Street; WC2E 7DN London; UK.

TI *Théâtre International*. Freq: 4; Began: 1981; Ceased: 1984; Lang: Eng/Fre; Subj: Theatre.
■British Centre of the ITI; 31 Shelton Street; WC2H 9HT London; UK.

TID *Themes in Drama*. Freq: 1; Began: 1979; Cov: Full; Lang: Eng; Subj: Theatre. ISSN: 0263-676X
■Cambridge Univ. Press; Edinburgh Bldg., Shaftesbury Road, CB2 2RU Cambridge; UK.

Tijatro *Tijatro*. Freq: 12; Began: 1970; Lang: Tur; Subj: Theatre.
■PK 58; Besiktas-Istanbul; TURKEY.

TInsight *Theatre Insight*: A Journal of Contemporary Performance Thought. Freq: 3; Began: 1988; Lang: Eng; Subj: Theatre.
■Program in Theatre History and Criticism, Univ. of Texas; Winshop Building; Austin, TX 78712; USA.

Tisz *Tiszatáj*. Freq: 12; Began: 1947; Cov: Scan; Lang: Hun; Subj: Theatre.
■Csongrad Megyei Lapkidiado Vallalat; Tanácsköztarsaság útja 10; 6720 Szeged; HUNGARY.

TJ *Theatre Journal*. Formerly: *Educational Theatre Journal*. Freq: 4; Began: 1949; Cov: Full; Lang: Eng; Subj: Theatre. ISSN: 0192-2282
■Univ./College Theatre Assoc., The Johns Hopkins Univ. Press; 701 West 40th St. Suite 275; Baltimore, MD 21211; USA.

TJV *Teater Jaarboek voor Vlaanderen*. Lang: Dut; Subj: Theatre.
■Antwerp; BELGIUM.

Tk *Theaterwork*. Freq: 6; Began: 1980; Ceased: 1983; Cov: Full; Lang: Eng; Subj: Theatre. ISSN: 0735-1895
■Theaterwork; Box 8150; Sante Fe, NM 87504-8150; USA.

Tka *Theatriku*. Freq: 52; Lang: Eng; Subj: Theatre.
■Athens; GREECE.

TkR *TamKang Review*: Comparative Studies Between Chinese & Foreign Literature. Freq: 4; Began: 1970; Lang: Eng; Subj: Related.
■Tamkang University, Grad. Inst. of West. Langs & Lit.; Tamsui; Taipei Hsien 251; TAIWAN.

TMJ *Theatre Movement Journal*. Lang: Eng; Subj: Theatre.
■Ohio State University, Dept. of Theatre; 1849 Cannon Drive; Columbus, OH 43210; USA.

TMK *Teater, Musika, Kyno*. Lang: Est; Subj: Theatre.
■Talin, Estonian SSR; USSR.

TN *Theatre Notebook*: Journal of the History and Technique of the British Theatre. Freq: 3; Began: 1946; Cov: Full; Lang: Eng; Subj: Theatre. ISSN: 0040-5523
■The Society for Theatre Research; c/o The Theatre Museum 1E Tavistock St.; WC2E 7PA London; UK.

TNotes *Theatre Notes*. Freq: 10; Began: 1970; Lang: Eng; Subj: Theatre.
■US Centre of the ITI; 1860 Broadway, Suite 1510; New York, NY 10023; USA.

TNS *Théâtre National de Strasbourg*: Actualité. Lang: Fre; Subj: Theatre.
■Théâtre National; Strasbourg; FRANCE.

TOE *Théâtre Ouvert/Ecritures*. Freq: 4; Began: 1978; Lang: Fre; Subj: Theatre. ISSN: 0181-5393
■21 rue Cassette; 75006 Paris; FRANCE.

Toneel *Toneel Teatraal*. Formerly: *Mickery Mouth and Toneel Teatraal*. Freq: 10; Began: 1879; Lang: Dut; Subj: Theatre. ISSN: 0040-9170
■Nederlands Theaterinstituut; Herengracht 166-168; 1016 BP Amsterdam; NETHERLANDS.

Tournees *Tournées de Spectacles*. Freq: 12; Began: 1975; Cov: Scan; Lang: Fre; Subj: Theatre. ISSN: 0317-5979
■Conseil des Arts du Canada; Office des Tournées; Ottawa, ON; CANADA.

TP *Theatre in Poland/Théâtre en Pologne*. Freq: 12; Began: 1958; Cov: Full; Lang: Eng/Fre; Subj: Theatre. ISSN: 0040-5493
■ITI, Polish Center; Ul. Moliera 1; 00 072 Warsaw; POLAND.

TpaedB   *Theaterpaedagogische Bibliothek*. Freq: IRR; Began: 1983; Lang: Ger; Subj: Theatre.
■Heinrichshofen Buecher; Valoisstrasse 11; 2940 Wilhelmshaven; WEST GERMANY.

TProf   *Théâtre Professionnel*. Lang: Fre; Subj: Theatre.
■14 rue de la Promenade; Asnieres; FRANCE.

TQ   *Theatre Quarterly*: Since 1985 published as New Theatre Quarterly (NTQ). Freq: 4; Began: 1971; Ceased: 1981; Lang: Eng; Subj: Theatre.   ISSN: 0049-3600
■TQ Publications, Ltd.; 44 Earlham Street; WC2 9LA London; UK.

TR   *Theater Rundschau*. Freq: 12; Began: 1955; Lang: Ger; Subj: Theatre.   ISSN: 0040-5442
■Bund der Theatergemeinden e.V. Bonn, Theater Rundschau Verlagsgesell.; Bonner Talweg 10; 5300 Bonn; WEST GERMANY.

Traces   *Traces*. Freq: 6; Lang: Fre; Subj: Theatre.
■Comédie de Rennes; Théâtre de la Parcheminerie; 35100 Rennes; FRANCE.

Tramoya   *Tramoya*: Cuaderno de teatro. Freq: 4; Lang: Spa; Subj: Theatre.
■Universidad Veracruzana; Clavijero 10; Xalapa; MEXICO.

Treteaux   *Tréteaux*. Freq: 2; Lang: Eng; Subj: Theatre.   ISSN: 0161-4479
■University of Maine at Orono Press; University of Maine; Farmington, ME 04938; USA.

Trujaman   *Trujaman*. Lang: Spa; Subj: Theatre.
■Casilla de Correos 3234; Buenos Aires; ARGENTINA.

TSA   *Theatre SA*: Quarterly for South African Theater. Freq: 4; Began: 1968; Lang: Eng; Subj: Theatre.
■PO Box 2153; Cape Town; SOUTH AFRICA.

TSO   *Teatro del Siglo de Oro: Ediciones Críticas*. Freq: 2; Began: 1982; Lang: Eng/ Spa/Fre; Subj: Theatre.   ISSN: 7188-4400
■Edition Reichenberger; Pfannkuchstr. 4; D 3500 Kassel; WEST GERMANY.

TSOL   *Teatro del Siglo de Oro: Estudios de Literatura*. Freq: IRR; Began: 1984; Lang: Spa/Eng; Subj: Theatre.   ISSN: 7200-9300
■Edition Reichenberger; Pfannkuchstr. 4; D 3500 Kassel; WEST GERMANY.

TSt   *Teatervidenskabelige Studier*. Freq: 1; Began: 1974; Lang: Dan; Subj: Theatre.
■Akademisk Forlag; St. Kannikestraede 8; 1169 Copenhagen; DENMARK.

TT   *Theatre Times*. Formerly: *OOBA Newsletter (OOBA Guidebook to Theatre)*. Freq: 6; Began: 1982; Cov: Scan; Lang: Eng; Subj: Theatre.   ISSN: 0732-300X
■Alliance of Resident Theatres; 131 Varick Street, Suite 904; New York, NY 10013-1410; USA.

TTh   *Travail Théâtral*. Freq: 4; Began: 1970; Lang: Fre; Subj: Theatre.   ISSN: 0049-4534
■Editions l'Age d'Homme-la Cite; Case Postale 263; 1000 Lausanne 9; SWITZERLAND.

TTT   *Tenaz Talks Teatro*. Freq: 4; Began: 1977; Lang: Eng/Spa; Subj: Theatre.
■University of California-La Jolla, Chicano Studies Program, D-009; La Jolla, CA 92093; USA.

TU   *Théâtre et université*. Lang: Fre; Subj: Theatre.
■Centre Universitaire International, Form. & Recherche Dramatique; Nancy; FRANCE.

Tv   *Teatervetenskap*. Freq: 2; Began: 1968; Lang: Swe/Eng; Subj: Theatre.
■Inst. for Teater & Filmvetenskap; Box 27026; S 102 Stockholm 27; SWEDEN.

TvL   *Tydskrif vir Letterkunde*. Freq: 4; Began: 1951; Cov: Scan; Lang: Eng & Afrikaans; Subj: Related.   ISSN: 0041-476X
■Elize Botha; Posbus 1758; Pretoria; SOUTH AFRICA.

TVOR   *Tvorchestvo*. Freq: 12; Began: 1957; Cov: Scan; Lang: Rus; Subj: Related.   ISSN: 0041-4565
■Izdatel'stvo Sovetskii Khudozhnik; Ul. Chernyakhovskogo; 4A; Moscow; U.S.S.R.

TvT   *Tijdschrift voor Theaterwetenschap*. Freq: 4; Lang: Dut; Subj: Theatre.
■Instituut voor Wetenschap, Nw.; Doelenstraat 16; 1012 CP Amsterdam; NETHERLANDS.

TvVV   *Tydskrif vir Volkskunde en Volkstaal*. Freq: 3; Began: 1944; Cov: Scan; Lang: Eng. & Afrikaans; Subj: Related.   ISSN: 0049-4933
■Genootskap vir Afrikaanse Volkskunde; Box 4585; Johannesburg 2000; SOUTH AFRICA.

TWI   *Theaterwissenschaftlicher Informationsdienst*. Lang: Ger; Subj: Theatre.
■Theaterhochschule Hans Otto'; Sec. für Theaterwissenschaftliche Dok.; Leipzig; EAST GERMANY.

TWNew   *Tennessee Williams Review*. Formerly: *Tennessee Williams Newsletter*. Freq: 2; Began: 1980; Ceased: 1983; Lang: Eng; Subj: Theatre.   ISSN: 0276-993X
■Northeastern University, Division of the Arts; 360 Huntington Ave. Boston, MA 02115; USA.

TZ   *Theater der Zeit*. Freq: 12; Began: 1946; Cov: Full; Lang: Ger; Subj: Theatre.   ISSN: 0040-5418
■Henschelverlag Kunst und Gesellschaft; Orienburger Strasse 67/68; 1040 Berlin; EAST GERMANY.

Tzs   *Theaterzeitschrift*: Beiträge zu Theater, Medien, Kulturpolitik. Cov: Scan; Lang: Ger; Subj: Theatre.
■Verein zur Erforschung theatraler Verkehrsformen; Tzs-Wochenschau Verlag; Adolf-Damaschke Str. 103 6231 Schawlbach; WEST GERMANY.

UCrow   *Upstart Crow, The*. Freq: 1; Began: 1978; Lang: Eng; Subj: Theatre.
■P.O. Box 740; Martin, TN 38237; USA.

UDSalaam   *University of Dar es Salaam: Theatre Arts Department*: Annual Report. Freq: 1; Lang: Eng; Subj: Theatre.
■University of Dar es Salaam, Theatre Arts Department; Box 35091; Dar es Salaam; TANZANIA.

UES   *Unisa English Studies: Journal of the Department of English*. Freq: 2; Began: 1963; Cov: Scan; Lang: Eng & Afr; Subj: Related.   ISSN: 0041-5359

■S.G. Kossick, Ed.; Dept. of English; Univ. of South Africa; P.O. Box 392; 0001 Pretoria; SOUTH AFRICA.

Ufa   *Ufahamu*: Journal of the African Activist Association. Freq: 3; Began: 1970; Cov: Scan; Lang: Eng; Subj: Related. ISSN: 0041-5715
■University of California, African Studies Center; 405 Hilgard Ave.; Los Angeles, CA 90024; USA.

UjIras   *Uj Irás*. Freq: 12; Began: 1961; Cov: Scan; Lang: Hun; Subj: Related.   ISSN: 0041-5952
■Lapkiado Vallalat; Lenin krt. 9-11; 1073 Budapest VII; HUNGARY.

UMurcia   *Universidad de Murcia Catedra de Teatro Cuadernos*. Freq: IRR; Began: 1978; Lang: Spa; Subj: Theatre.
■Universidad de Murcia, Secretariado de Publicaciones y Intercambio Cientifico; Santo Cristo 1; Murcia; SPAIN.

UNIMA   *UNIMA France*. Freq: 4; Began: 1962; Lang: Fre; Subj: Theatre.
■Union Internationale de la Marionette, Section Française; 7 Rue du Helder; 75009 Paris; FRANCE.

Usbu   *Usbu Al-Masrah*. Lang: Ara; Subj: Theatre.
■Ministère des Affaires Culturelles; La Kasbah; Tunis; TUNISIA.

USITT   *USITT Newsletter*. Freq: 4; Began: 1965; Cov: Scan; Lang: Eng; Subj: Theatre.   ISSN: 0565-6311
■US Inst. for Theatre Technology; 330 W. 42nd St., Suite 1702; New York, NY 10036; USA.

UTarra   *Universitas Tarraconensis*. Freq: 1; Cov: Scan; Lang: Spa; Subj: Related.
■División de Filologia; Placa Imperial Tarraco, 1; 43005 Tarragona; SPAIN.

UTeatr   *Ukrainskij Teat'r*. Lang: Ukr; Subj: Related.
■Kiev, Ukrainian SSR; USSR.

Uusi   *Uusi-Laulu*. Lang: Fin; Subj: Theatre.
■Uusi-Laulu-yhdistys; Eerikinkatu 14 A 9; 00100 Helsinki 10; FINLAND.

UZ   *Unterhaltungskunst*: Zeitschrift für Bühne, Podium und Manege. Freq: 12; Began: 1969; Lang: Ger; Subj: Related.   ISSN: 0042-0565
■Henschelverlag Kunst und, Gesellschaft; Oranienburger Strasse 67/68; 104 Berlin; EAST GERMANY.

Valivero   *Valiverho*. Freq: 3; Lang: Fin; Subj: Theatre.
■Helsinki; FINLAND.

Valo   *Valóság*. Freq: 12; Began: 1964; Cov: Scan; Lang: Hun; Subj: Related.
■Kirlapkiado; Lenin krt. 5; 1073 Budapest VII; HUNGARY.

VantageP   *Vantage Point*: Issues in American Arts. Formerly: *American Arts*. Freq: 6; Began: 1984; Cov: Scan; Lang: Eng; Subj: Related.   ISSN: 0194-1305
■American Council for the Arts; 1285 Ave. of the Americas, 3rd Floor; New York, NY 10019; USA.

VFil *Voprosy filosofii.* Freq: 12; Began: 1947; Lang: Eng/Rus; Subj: Related. ISSN: 0042-8744
■Akademiya Nauk S.S.S.R., Institut Filosofii; Izdatel'stvo Pravda, Ul. Pravdy, 24; Moscow 125047; USSR.

Vig *Vigília.* Freq: 12; Began: 1935; Cov: Scan; Lang: Hun; Subj: Related.
■Actio Catholica; Kossuth L. u. 1; 1053 Budapest V; HUNGARY.

Vilag *Világszínház:* A magyar színházi intézet havi folyóirata. Formerly: *Dramaturgical News 1965-1982.* Freq: 12; Began: 1982; Cov: Full; Lang: Hun; Subj: Theatre. ISSN: 0231-4541
■Hungarian Theatre Institute; Krisztina krt. 57; 1016 Budapest I; HUNGARY.

VLit *Voprosy Literatury.* Freq: 12; Began: 1957; Cov: Scan; Lang: Rus; Subj: Related.
ISSN: 0042-8795
■Sojuz Pisatelej SSSR, Inst. Mirovoj Literatury; Bolšoj Gnezdnikovskij per 10; 103009 Moscow; USSR.

VMGUf *Vestnik MGU:* Series 9-Filologia. Freq: 6; Began: 1946; Cov: Scan; Lang: Rus; Subj: Related. ISSN: 0579-9449
■Moscow State University; Ul. Gercena 5/7; 103009 Moscow; USSR.

Voprosy *Voprosy Teatra.* Freq: 1; Lang: Rus; Subj: Theatre. ISSN: 0507-3952
■Vserossiskoe Teatral'noe Obshchestvo; Ul. Gorkogo; 16, Moscow; USSR.

VS *Victorian Studies:* A Journal of the Humanities, Arts and Sciences. Freq: 4; Began: 1957; Cov: Scan; Lang: Eng; Subj: Related. ISSN: 0042-5222
■Program for Victorian Studies, Indiana University; Ballantine Hall; Bloomington, IN 47405; USA.

VSov *V sovéckom teatré.* Cov: Scan; Lang: Rus; Subj: Theatre.
■Moscow; USSR.

Vyakat *Vyakat.* Freq: 4; Lang: Eng; Subj: Theatre.
■A-28 Nizamuddin West; New Delhi; INDIA.

Waiguo *Waiguo Xiju.* Freq: 4; Began: 1962; Lang: Chi; Subj: Theatre.
■52 Dongai Ba tiao; Beijing; CHINA.

WB *Weimarer Beiträge:* Zeitschrift für Literaturwissenschaft, Aesthetik und Kultur. Freq: 12; Began: 1955; Cov: Scan; Lang: Ger; Subj: Related. ISSN: 0043-2199
■Aufbau-Verlag Berlin und Weimar; Französische Strasse 32; 1080 Berlin; EAST GERMANY.

WCP *West Coast Plays.* Freq: 2; Began: 1977; Ceased: 1988; Lang: Eng; Subj: Theatre. ISSN: 0147-4502
■California Theatre Council; 135 N. Grand Ave.; Los Angeles, CA 90014; USA.

WFTM *Wiener Forschungen zur Theater und Medienwissenschaft.* Freq: IRR; Began: 1972; Lang: Ger; Subj: Theatre.
■Universitäts-Verlagsbuchhandlung Gmb; Servitengasse 5; A1092 Vienna; AUSTRIA.

WGTJ *Wiener Gesellschaft für Theaterforschung Jahrbuch.* Freq: IRR; Began: 1944; Ceased: 1986; Lang: Ger; Subj: Theatre.
■Verband der Wissenshaftlichen, Gesellschaften Oesterreichs; Lindengasse 37; A1070 Vienna; AUSTRIA.

WIAL *Washington International Arts Letter.* Freq: 10; Began: 1962; Lang: Eng; Subj: Related. ISSN: 0043-0609
■Box 9005; Washington, DC 20003; USA.

WijP *WIJ, Poppenspelers.* Lang: Dut; Subj: Theatre.
■M. Ruth van der Steenhoven; Westeinde 252; 3351 AS Papendrecht; NETHERLANDS.

WJBS *Western Journal of Black Studies.* Freq: 4; Began: 1977; Cov: Scan; Lang: Eng; Subj: Related. ISSN: 0197-4327
■Washington State Univ. Press; Pullman, WA 99164 5910; USA.

WLT *World Literature Today:* a literary quarterly of the University of Oklahoma. Formerly: *Books Abroad.* Freq: 4; Began: 1927; Lang: Eng; Subj: Related.
■University of Oklahoma Press; 110 Monnet Hall; Norman, OK 73019; USA.

WomenR *Women's Review.* Freq: 12; Began: 1985; Ceased: 1986; Cov: Scan; Lang: Eng; Subj: Related. ISSN: 0267-5080
■1-4 Christina St.; EC2A 4PA London; UK.

WOpera *World of Opera.* Freq: 6; Lang: Eng; Subj: Theatre. ISSN: 0160-8673
■Marcel Dekker Inc.; 270 Madison Avenue; New York, NY 10016; USA.

WPerf *Women & Performance:* A Journal of Feminist Theory. Freq: 2; Began: 1983; Cov: Full; Lang: Eng; Subj: Theatre. ISSN: 0740-770X
■NYU Tisch School of the Arts, Women and Performance Project; 721 Broadway, 6th Floor; New York, NY 10003; USA.

WPList *World Premieres Listing.* Began: 1981; Lang: Eng; Subj: Theatre.
■Hungarian Centre of the ITI; Hevesi Sandor Ter. 2; 1077 Budapest VII; HUNGARY.

WTops *White Tops.* Freq: 6; Began: 1927; Lang: Eng; Subj: Theatre. ISSN: 0043-499X
■Circus Fans Assoc. of America; Rt. 1, Box 6735; White Stone, VA 22578; USA.

XLunc *Xiju Luncong:* Selected Essays of Theatre. Freq: 4; Began: 1957; Cov: Full; Lang: Chi; Subj: Theatre.
■52 Dongai Ba tiao; Beijing; CHINA.

XXuexi *Xiju Xuexi:* Theatre. Freq: 4; Began: 1957; Lang: Chi; Subj: Theatre.
■Central Institute for Modern Theatre; Jiaonan Qitiao; Beijing; CHINA.

XYanj *Xiqu Yanjiu.* Freq: 4; Began: 1980; Cov: Full; Lang: Chi; Subj: Theatre.
■Cultural and Artistic Publishing; 17 Qianhai Xijie; Beijing; CHINA.

XYishu *Xiju Yishu:* Theatre Arts. Freq: 4; Began: 1978; Cov: Full; Lang: Chi; Subj: Theatre. ISSN: 0257-943X

■630 Huashan Road; 4 274 Shanghai; CHINA.

YCT *Young Cinema & Theatre/Jeune Cinéma et Théâtre:* Cultural Magazine of the IUS. Freq: 4; Began: 1964; Lang: Eng/Fre/Spa; Subj: Theatre.
■International Union of Students; 17th November Street; 110 01 Prague 1; CZECHOSLOVAKIA.

Yorick *Yorick:* Revista de Teatro. Lang: Spa; Subj: Theatre.
■Via Layetana 30; 3 Barcelona; SPAIN.

YTJ *Youth Theatre Journal.* Freq: 4; Began: 1986; Lang: Eng; Formerly: *Children's Theatre Review;* Subj: Theatre.
ISSN: 0009-4196
■American Alliance for Theatre and Education; Theatre Department; Arizona State University; Tempe, AZ 85287-2002; USA.

ZAA *Zeitschrift für Anglistik und Amerikanistik.* Freq: 4; Began: 1953; Cov: Scan; Lang: Ger/Eng; Subj: Related. ISSN: 0044-2305
■Verlag Enzyklopädie; Gerichtsweg 26; 7010 Leipzig; EAST GERMANY.

ZDi *Zahranicni Divadlo:* (Theatre Abroad). Lang: Cze; Subj: Theatre.
■Prague; CZECHOSLOVAKIA.

ZfK *Zeitschrift für Kulturaustausch.* Freq: 4; Lang: Ger; Subj: Theatre. ISSN: 0044-2976
■Horst Erdmann Verlag für, Internationalen-Kulturaustausch; Hartmeyerstrasse 117; 7400 Tübingen 1; WEST GERMANY.

ZG *Zeitschrift für Germanistik.* Freq: 6; Began: 1980; Cov: Scan; Lang: Ger; Subj: Related. ISSN: 0323-7982
■Verlag Enzyklopädie; Gerichtsweg 26; 7010 Leipzig; EAST GERMANY.

Znamya *Znamya.* Freq: 12; Began: 1931; Lang: Rus; Subj: Related. ISSN: 0044-4898
■Soyuz Pisatelei S.S.S.R.; Moscow; USSR.

Zpravy *Zpravy.* Freq: 3; Lang: Cze/Eng; Subj: Theatre.
■Dilia Theatrical and Literary Agency; Vysehradska 28; 128 24 Prague 2; CZECHOSLOVAKIA.

ZreIssk *Zreliščnyjé Iskusstva* (Performing Arts). Freq: 12; Began: 1983; Cov: Full; Lang: Rus; Subj: Theatre. ISSN: 0207-9739
■Gos. Biblioteka SSSR im. Lenina, NIO Informkultura; Prospekt Kalinina 3; 101000 Moscow; USSR.

ZS *Zeitschrift für Slawistik.* Freq: 6; Began: 1956; Cov: Scan; Lang: Ger/Rus; Subj: Related. ISSN: 0044-3506
■Akademie der Wissenschaften der DDR, Inst. für Literaturgeschichte; Akademie-Verlag, Leipziger Str. 3-4; 1086 Berlin; EAST GERMANY.

Zvezda *Zvezda.* Freq: 12; Began: 1924; Cov: Scan; Lang: Rus; Subj: Related. ISSN: 0039-7105
■Izdatel. Chudožestvennaja Literatura; Mochovaja 20; 192028 Leningrad; USSR.

Photocomposition and printing services for this volume
of the *International Bibliography of Theatre* were
provided by Volt Information Sciences Inc.,

Cover Design by Irving M. Brown

International Bibliography of Theatre: 1987